PREFACE

Monser's Topical Index and Digest of the Bible is the result of an effort to bring the topical analyses found in the *Monser's Cross-Reference Bible* within the reach of the masses. The Cross-Reference Bible is recognized by all to be the greatest edition of the Bible ever published, being the only edition of the Bible in which the footnotes are the work of a large corps of America's best Bible scholars. *Monser's Topical Index and Digest of the Bible* contains all the topical analyses or footnotes of the Cross-Reference Bible. These have been carefully revised by at least seven associate editors of the Cross-Reference Bible and Drs. Jacobs and Weidner of the Lutheran Church and are therefore strictly undenominational in character. To these have been added an alphabetical index of the verbs of the Bible and a complete list of persons and places.

While all of these topical analyses have been carefully revised by many editors, yet as each topic represents the composite work of many men, the editor-in-chief assumes the final responsibility for what appears in this volume. The Outline Studies in the Books contain the Introductory Studies in the Books of the Bible found in the Cross-Reference Bible, but very extensive additions have been made in the Old Testament. Dr. A. T. Robertson is the author of the Outline Studies in the Books of the New Testament, Dr. Zenos of the Outline Studies in "Job," "Psalms," and "Daniel," Dr. John R. Sampey of those in Ecclesiastes, "Song of Songs," "Isaiah," "Jeremiah," and "Ezekiel." The Outline Studies in the other Books of the Old Testament were prepared by the editor-in-chief. All the work in this volume is original work and great care has been taken to make it both accurate and helpful. With the earnest desire that this volume may render material service in opening up the treasuries of God's Holy Word it is sent forth on its mission.

INDEX TO OUTLINE STUDIES IN THE BOOKS

THE OLD TESTAMENT.

This volume presents a "Digest" or Analysis of the English Bible of today with the "Books" arranged in the order of the English Bible. It is an attempt to make the Bible its own interpreter, and its value will depend on the ability of its editors to do this without injecting their own personal opinions. Therefore, it is not concerned with either "Higher" or Textual Criticism. It must be admitted that many modern scholars accept the theory of the composite authorship of the Pentateuch—that textual criticism of the Pentateuch shows traces of many authors, who lived in different periods covering a span of many centuries reaching even beyond the exile. Scholars do not seem to agree on any definite theory, and if we accept any one of these modern theories we grope in blindness through a maze of material without definite plan or purpose.

In the interpretation and division of the Old Testament much depends on the place and chronology of the Pentateuch in its relation to the other Books of the Bible and the history of Israel. If we say that Moses wrote or supervised the writing of most of the Pentateuch, using such records, tablets and traditions as were in existence in his time, then the Old Testament presents a definite plan. (See PENTATEUCH.) We may then see in the Old Testament the ever widening purpose of God flowing down through the ages, being turned aside frequently by man's sin, and ever beating against the rocks of Israel's idolatry.

Genesis holds the key to the whole Bible.—G. Campbell Morgan divides Genesis into three great divisions— Generation, Degeneration and Regeneration. This is the history of Israel. Beginning with Abraham, passing under the rod in Egypt, wandering through the wilderness, establishing a home in Canaan, coming to splendor under David, this mighty nation begins to degenerate under Solomon, sinks lower and lower in the degradation of idolatry with its accompanying lusts, until it is torn by dissension, in captivity, and clothed with the sackcloth of mourning. Then Isaiah, Jeremiah, and other prophets sing a song of a coming Messiah, a new kingdom, and foretell the regeneration in Jesus Christ, who is to come to fulfill all of God's wonderful purpose.

We may also see in the Old Testament three successive couplets of periods— negative and positive: (1) The Patriarchal period presents the longing for the land of promise as foretold to Abraham. This longing finds its satisfaction in the "Pentateuch" and "Joshua" as the children of Israel take possession of the land of Canaan. (2) Then because Israel turned away from Jehovah, He seemed to turn away from them. Strife and disorder arose and there came need of a closer organization, which would enable Israel to stand against its powerful enemies. This need was supplied in David, and Solomon, and the poetical Books which were used in the splendid worship in the temple. (3) In captivity, wanderers from home, humiliated and persecuted, Israel once more turns to the Living God and longs for one who can lead her children back to Jerusalem. In the fulness of time, when Judaism had been weighed in the balance and found wanting, Jesus the Messiah came to set at liberty the captive, to heal the broken hearted. When the fulness of time came God sent his Son, born of a woman, born under the law, that He might redeem them that were under the Law, that we might receive the adoption of sons. (Gal. 4:4, 5.) God promised Abraham that in him and his seed should all the families of the earth be blessed. (Gen. 12:3; 22: 18.) Peter quotes this promise and shows that in Jesus Christ it was fulfilled (Acts 3:25, 26). Paul asks the question—"What then is the law? It was added because of transgressions, till the seed should come to whom the promise hath been made. (Gal. 3:19.) Now to Abraham were the promises spoken, and to his seed. He saith not, and to seeds as of many, but as of one, and to thy seed, which is Christ." (Gal. 3:16.)

God also promised Abraham and his seed all the land of Canaan for an everlasting possession. (Gen. 17:1–8.) Yet Abraham's seed, the Jews, did not keep that land. Why? Because the continued possession of this land depended upon Israel obeying God's commandments and walking in His Statutes (See COVENANTS in this volume). Moses the servant of God warned the Israelites that they would be driven into captivity and would suffer drouth, and famine, and perish in a foreign land if they bowed down to strange gods.

The prophecies of Isaiah, Jeremiah, Ezekiel, and Minor Prophets throb with new meaning when read in the light of this covenant with Abraham and the Book of Deuteronomy.

Just as the drama and novel present the hero and the villain as studies in character, so God in the Old Testament presented to all future generations the Drama of the Ages, to teach the old, old lesson—"Whatsoever a man soweth that shall he also reap." Adam, Saul, Samson, Solomon, Jeroboam, Ahab, and Jezebel, present pictures of those who tried to live without God in the world. Enoch, Noah, Abraham, Joseph, Moses, Aaron, Joshua, Job, David, Isaiah, Jeremiah, Daniel, and others walked with God in paths of peace even when these paths led into strange lands or into the fiery furnace of affliction.

Progressive Revelation.—In reading the Old Testament we must remember that God is dealing with Israel as a father deals with a child. Just as the father gradually reveals his will and

mind to the child, as its capacity will permit him to enter into sympathy with the father's purposes, so God gradually unveils Himself to Israel.

The little boy says, "My father can whip your father." His father is his hero, a strong man. After a while it begins to dawn on him that his father is too big; too moral to fight. At last he says, "My father is a good man—a gentle man."

In the Pentateuch we see many anthropomorphic conceptions. The Lord is a strong and mighty warrior. But David says, "The Lord is my shepherd." Even David has not the conception of the Fatherhood of God, as taught in the New Testament. God is a Father, but he is the Father of a nation, and the individual is lost in the mass of the nation. In Isaiah we begin to see the importance of the individual as distinct from the nation. He stands alone though the nation falls. Isaiah has a foregleam of the possibilities and worth of the individual, but it remained for Jesus to say "There is joy in the presence of the angels of God over one sinner that repenteth."

"Old Testament religion in Old Testament Theology is *genetic*. This means not only that Old Testament in *genesi*, that is, in the condition of actually arising or originating, but that its progress was, so to speak, organic. It grew, and that not by mere accretion or the external addition of truth to truth. The succeeding truth rose out of the former truth. This was due to the fact that the kingdom of God was planted into the life of a people, and thus its progress was inseparably connected with the progress and destiny of the nation of Israel. We cannot get a religious progress without a religious subject in whose mind we observe the progress. Now, the religious subject in the Old Testament was the people of Israel—and the progress can be studied in the mind of this subject as influenced by its history. Revelation of truth was not, so to speak, communicated from without; but the organs of revelation rose within the people in the persons of its highest representatives, men in whom its life beat fullest and its aspirations were most perfectly embodied. Thus the truths concerning the kingdom of God which they were enabled, stage after stage, to reach, had a connection with one another parallel to the connection between the stages of the life of the people. The truths regarding the kingdom of God appearing in the Old Testament are all given in terms, so to speak, of the history, institutions, and the life of the people of Israel. It is customary to regard the institutions of Israel, its offices and ordinances, as all prearranged parallels to the things of the Christian Church, shadows and adumbrations or types, as they are called, of the realities of the New Testament kingdom. Now, of course, it must be maintained that the perfect form of the kingdom of God, the form which it was to have in the New Testament, was contemplated from the beginning. There was a determinism impressed on the Old Testament kingdom toward its perfect form; it was a growth, an organism of which we see the complete stature only in the New Testament kingdom. But we must not regard those institutions in Israel as only having this use of foreshadowing the future.

They were real institutions and offices there, and their reference to the future was probably, in many instances, not understood or even surmised. The way they bore reference to the future in the minds of the people was rather this: The highest thinkers among the people, such as the prophets, perceived the idea lying in the offices and institutions, and expressed their longing and certainty that the idea would be yet realized.

The Old Testament contains the same truths as the New Testament, but in a less developed form, and we must avoid two errors which are not uncommon. The one is the mistake of separating the Old Testament from the New in such a way as leaves us with no authoritative truth in the Old. The other is to confuse the New and the Old so that

we shall find the Old equally advanced with the New. The difference between the New and the Old is not that the same truths are not found in both, but that in the one the truths are found in a less degree of development than in the other. The Old Testament is as good authority for a truth as the New; only we must not go beyond the degree which the truth has yet reached in the Old Testament.

This fact, however, that the progress of the kingdom was organic and at last culminated, suggests that the Old Testament should be read by us always in the light of the end, and that in forming an Old Testament Theology we should have the New Testament completion of it in our view.''—''Theology of the Old Testament,'' Davidson.

Thus we see that the New Testament lies folded like a leaf away back in the Pentateuch or, that the Old Testament unfolds in all its mighty purpose and promise in the New Testament.

If the reader will study the O. T. prophecies concerning Jesus as found in this volume, under the subject JESUS, he will see that from Genesis to Revelation there ever runs the scarlet thread of the blood of Jesus and the meaning of Exodus is found in Calvary. The Paschal Lamb was slain for Israel, and no bones were to be broken because Jesus was to be the Paschal Lamb slain for the sins of the world. Thus Genesis, Exodus, and Leviticus, point forward to the tragedy of the Cross. One of the elders before the throne of God said to John, ''These are they that come out of the great tribulation, and they washed their robes, and made them white in the Blood of the Lamb'' (Rev. 7:14). On the Cross of Calvary, Jesus said, ''It is finished.'' The Old Testament had been fulfilled. So the law of ordinances was nailed to the Cross, and done away and the New Testament was sealed by His blood. See COVENANTS.

DIVISION OF THE OLD TESTAMENT.

Jesus divides the Old Testament into "The law of Moses, and the prophets, and the Psalms."—(Lu. 24:44.)

The Hebrew Scriptures are divided into—The Law (*Torah*), the Prophets (*Nebhim*), the Writings (*Kethubhim*) or *Hagiographa* (sacred writings). These are grouped as follows:

THE LAW or PENTATEUCH.—Genesis, Exodus, Leviticus, Numbers, Deuteronomy.

THE PROPHETS—Former.—Joshua, Judges, Samuel, Kings.

Latter.—Isaiah, Jeremiah, Ezekiel, The Twelve or Minor Prophets.

WRITINGS.—Heb. *Kethubhim*, Gr. *Hagiographa:*

Poetical Books: Psalms, Proverbs, Job.

Megilloth or Five Rolls: Song of Songs, Ruth, Lamentations, Ecclesiastes, Esther.

Non-prophetical Historical Books: Daniel, Ezra and Nehemiah, Chronicles.

"The five *Megilloth* are so called because each was written on a roll for reading at Jewish festivals, the Song of Songs at the Passover, Ruth at the Feast of Weeks or Pentecost, Ecclesiastes at the Feast of Tabernacles, Esther at the Feast of Purim, while Lamentations was recited on the anniversary of the destruction of Jerusalem."—"Handbook of the Bible," Angus-Green.

Josephus, born A.D. 37, says: "We have not tens of thousands of books, discordant and conflicting, but only twenty-two containing the record of all time, which have been justly believed to be divine. And of these five are the books of Moses, which embrace the laws and the tradition from the creation of man until his death.—From the death of Moses, to the reign of Artaxerxes, the successor of Xerxes, king of Persia, the prophets who suc-

ceeded Moses wrote what was done in thirteen books. The remaining four books embrace hymns to God and counsels for men for the conduct of life. From Artaxerxes until our time everything has been recorded but has not been deemed worthy of like credit with what preceded, because the exact succession of the prophets ceased. But what faith we have placed in our own writings is evident by our conduct: for though so long a time has now passed, no one has dared either to add anything to them, or to take anything from them, or to alter anything in them. But it is instinctive in all Jews at once from their very birth to regard them as commands of God, and to abide by them and, if need be, willingly to die for them."

·In this catalogue of Books, Ruth is counted with Judges, Lamentations with Jeremiah, I and II Samuel, I and II Kings, I and II Chronicles are not divided into two Books each, but the six Books are considered as three—Ezra and Nehemiah as one Book and The Twelve or Minor Prophets as one. The thirteen Books succeeding the Law would then be: Joshua, Judges (with Ruth), Samuel, Kings, Chronicles, Ezra and Nehemiah, Esther, Job, Isaiah, Jeremiah (with Lamentations), Ezekiel, Daniel, The Minor Prophets.

The Septuagint Version of the Old Testament was a Greek translation made in Alexandria between 250 and 150 B. C. The Books of this Version were arranged thus:

1. **The Law:** Genesis, Exodus, Leviticus, Numbers, Deuteronomy.

2. **The Historical Books:** Joshua, Judges, Ruth, I and II Samuel, I and II Kings, I and II Chronicles, Ezra, Nehemiah, Esther.

3. **The Poetical Books:** Job, Psalms, Proverbs, Ecclesiastes, Song of Solomon.

4

4. **The Prophetical Books:** Isaiah, Jeremiah, Lamentations, Ezekiel, Daniel, and The Twelve Minor Prophets.

So we see that Jesus and His apostles had substantially the same Old Testament we have, and referred to the same collection of Books in referring to, or quoting from the Scriptures.

Old Testament History may be divided as follows: Creation to Call of Abraham; I Theocracy (1). Patriarchal Age, (2). Forming of the Nation; II The monarchy (1). One kingdom under Saul, David, Solomon (2). The divided kingdom; III The Captivity; IV The Restoration.

	THEOCRACY		MONARCHY		
Period	Call of Abraham to anointing of Saul (B.C. 2000–1039)		Anointing of Saul to Captivity (B.C. 1039–586)	Captivity B.C. 586–538	Restoration to Christ

Beginnings .... Creation to call of Abraham—B.C. 2000

Division	Book & Reference	Content	Period
LAW PENT.	Gen. 1–11	Beginnings	
	Gen. 12–60. Abr. Is. Ja. Jos.	Israel	Patriarchal Age
	Ex. Way out of Egypt	in Egypt	
	Lev. Law of priesthood	To Canaan	
	Num. Wilderness		
APPEAL TO CONSCIENCE	Deut. 2nd giving of law		
PROPHETS *(History)*	Joshua	Conquest of Canaan	Forming of Nation
	Judges; Ruth	Conquest to Saul; Deb.	
	I Samuel	Samson; Gideon; Ruth; Eli; Sam.	
	I and II Sam; I Ki. 1–11	Monarchy under Saul; David; Solomon	
	I Chron.; II Chron. 1–9	Jerusalem taken; temple built	
	I Ki. 12–22; II Ki.	Elijah; Obadiah; Elisha; Ahab	Kingdom divided
APPEAL TO	II Chron. 10–36	Reh.; Jer.; Asa; Joash; Hez.; Jos.	
EXPERIENCE *(Prophecy)*	Jonah; Amos	Israel: 19 kings, 9 dynasties	
	Hosea; Micah	Samaria capital fell B.C. 722	
	Joel; Isaiah; Nahum	Judah: 20 kings, 1 dynasty	
	Zeph.; Jer.; Lam.; Hab.	Jerusalem cap. fell B.C. 588	
	Jeremiah; Obadiah; Daniel;	Ezra	
	Hag.; Zech.; Mal.	Rebuilding of temple; restoration	
PSALMS	Hist. Ezra; Esther; Neh.	Jerusalem; Zer.; Ezra; Neh.	
APPEAL TO HEART	Job; Proverbs; Ecclesiastes—*Wisdom literature.*		
	Psalms; Song of Solomon—*Poetry.*		

THE PENTATEUCH.

NAME.—Because they are mostly legislative in character, the first five Books of the Old Testament—Genesis, Exodus, Leviticus, Numbers, and Deuteronomy—are called: The Law (*Torah*) —Josh. 1:7; 8:34. The book of the law —Josh. 1:8; 8:34. The law of Moses— I Ki. 2:3; II Ki. 23:25; II Chr. 23:18; Ezra 3:2; 7:6; Dan. 9:11, 13; Lu. 24: 44; Acts 28:23. The book of the law of Moses—Josh. 8:31; 23:6; II Ki. 14:6; Neh. 8:1. The book of the law of God —Josh. 24:26; Neh. 8:18. The book of the law of Jehovah—II Chr. 17:9. Book of Moses—II Chr. 25:4; 36:12; Ezra 6:18; Neh. 13:1; Mk. 12:26.

Author.—Wide difference of opinion as to authorship. See article on OLD TESTAMENT. While the Bible nowhere states that Moses was the author of the entire Pentateuch as it appears in its present form, yet he is frequently referred to as the author of "The Law," and quotations are made from the various Books of the Pentateuch as from Moses. It is admitted that Moses probably used records in existence during his time or depended upon oral tradition for part of his material. He probably did both. There were also probably some editorial additions—*e. g.*, the account of his death (Deut. ch. 34).

Testimony of the Bible.—Moses is referred to as the author in the Pentateuch—Ex. 17:14; 24:3-7; Lev. 26:46; 27:34; Num. 33:2; Deut. 31:9. Joshua, who was a contemporary of Moses, refers to Moses as author—Josh. 1:7, 8; 8:30-35; 23:6. David quotes Moses as author—I Ki. 2:3 (See Deut. 17:18-20). Solomon mentions Moses as author—I Ki. 8:53-56. Pentateuch quoted in "Kings" and "Chronicles" as the work of Moses—II Ki. 14:6 (Deut. 24: 16); 21:8; 23:24, 25 (Deut. 18:10-12); II Chr. 23:18; 25:4 (Deut. 24:16); 33: 8; 34:14; 35:6, 12. Ezra and Nehemiah

refer to Moses frequently as the author of "The Law"—Ezra 3:2; 6:18 (Num. 3:6; 8:9); Neh. 1:7-9; 8:1-8, 14, 18; 9:14; 13:1. Daniel refers to Leviticus and Deuteronomy as "the law of Moses"—Dan. 9:11, 13 (Lev. 26:14-45; Deut. 28:15-68).

New Testament References.—Jesus states that Moses gave the law—John 7:19-23. Quotes one of the ten commandments as recorded in Ex. 20:12; 21:17; Lev. 20:9; Deut. 5:16 as written by Moses—Mk. 7:10. Refers to Lev. 13:49; 14:2-10 as written by Moses— Mt. 8:4; Mk. 1:44; Lu. 5:14. Refers to Ex. 3:6 as being in the book of Moses —Mk. 12:26; Lu. 20:37. Refers to Deut. 24:1-3 as Moses' commandment—Mt. 19:8; Mk. 10:3-5. Hinges salvation of the brethren of the "Rich Man" on their hearing Moses and the prophets— Lu. 16:29, 31. He said He came to fulfil the things written by Moses and the prophets—Lu. 24:27, 44; John 5:45-47. Pharisees and Sadducees in time of Jesus recognized Moses as author of the Law—Mt. 19:7; Mk. 10:5; 12:18, 19; Lu. 20:28; John 9:28, 29; Acts 15: 1, 5. The apostle John said, "The Law was given by Moses"—John 1:17. Philip the apostle sees in Jesus the fulfilment of Mosaic prophecy—John 1:45. Peter and Stephen refer to a prophecy concerning Jesus (Deut. 18:15) as given by Moses—Acts 3:22; 7:37. James said: "Moses from generations of old hath in every city them that preach him, being read in the synagogues every Sabbath"—Acts 15:21.

Church in Jerusalem was still zealous for the law of Moses—Acts 15:1, 5, 21; 21:21. Paul refers to the law as written by Moses—Acts 13:39; Rom. 10:15, 19 (Lev. 18:5; Deut. 32:21); I Cor. 9:9 (Deut. 25:4); II Cor. 3:13-15. In his address before Agrippa, Paul appeals to the prophecies of Moses to prove the divinity of Jesus—Acts 26: 22. Reasoned a whole day from the law of Moses and the prophets to prove divinity of Jesus—Acts 28:23. Writer of Hebrew letter calls the law Moses' law and quotes Deut. 32:35; Heb. 10: 28–30. Song of Moses and the Lamb sung in heaven, probably referring to Ex. ch. 15—Rev. 15:2, 3.

Internal evidence.—''An exact correspondence between the narrative and the institutions, showing that both had one author. The laws are not given in the form of statutes, but are mixed with narrative, and are inserted as the exigencies requiring them arose. They are often briefly sketched, and afterwards repeated at greater length, with such modifications as were demanded by altered circumstances.'' No less remarkable is the agreement between the style of the different books and the circumstances of Moses, as depicted. In the earlier narrative of Exodus and Numbers, the style is broken and abrupt, as that of a journal kept from time to time, with frequent interruptions. In Deuteronomy it is continuous and hortatory. The Five Books, at the same time, exhibit the unity of design which bespeaks a single author.

Written by a Hebrew or Hebrew speaking the language and cherishing the sentiments of Israel. Written by a Hebrew acquainted with Egypt and Arabia, their customs and learning. The parts of the Pentateuch referring to Egypt show many evidences of familiarity with that country difficult to obtain centuries later. ''Egyptian learning was carefully concealed from foreigners. The priest alone, and the royal family, who were reckoned as priests, had access to it (see Herodotus, ii. 3, 164, 168, &c.). To this class, therefore, the writer must have belonged.'' This familiarity is seen in the use of: Names, *e. g.*, Pote-phera—Gen. 41:45; 46:20. Potephar—Gen. 37:36; 39:1. Name given to Joseph—Zaphenath-paneah—Gen. 41:45; name of Joseph's wife—Asenath—Gen. 41:45. Priest of On—Gen. 41:45. Rameses—Gen. 47:11; Ex. 1:11; 12:37; Num. 33:3, 5. Pithom—Ex. 1:11. Customs—Linen garments given to Joseph—Ex. 28:39; 39:27–29. Separation of Joseph's brethren at table—Gen. 43:32. Embalming of bodies—Gen. 50:2, 3, 26, etc.

CONTENTS—The Political Constitution of Israel. The Moral Code. The Ceremonial for Worship (Ritual). The History of Israel with a Sketch of the World before Abraham.

Division—Historical.—Gen. ch. 1–Ex. 19.

Legal.—Ex. 20–Deut. ch. 34. Genesis—Beginnings. Exodus—Way out of Egypt, Redemption through Blood. Leviticus—Priestly Law, Separation and Sacrifice. Numbers—Wandering in wilderness. Deuteronomy—Second giving of law, Obedience.

Resume of Events of the Pentateuch. —Acts 7:1–45.

GENESIS.

NAME.—First Book of Moses—
"Genesis" from the Septuagint, meaning "Beginnings."

"**In the beginning.**" Genesis is a history of beginnings—of generations. —Heavens and earth, life, man, marriage, animals, fish and birds, sin, redemption, prophecy, God's purpose looking toward Christ, Israel.

Author.—See PENTATEUCH.

Keyword.—Beginnings.

Principal characters.—Adam, Noah, Abraham, Isaac, Jacob, Joseph.

Plan.—"It is evident from the first glance that the book is designed to be the first book in the collection. It goes back to the earliest possible commencement, 'the beginning,' when God created the heavens and the earth; and it indicates at its close that it is the opening of a long history which is to follow. And as the whole Old Testament is the national religious literature of the people of Israel, this first Book is obviously intended to trace the history from its source. All the nations of the world that have become historical have asked themselves whence they came, and have given various answers to the question as to the origin of all things. The Book of Genesis, looked at by itself, may be regarded as the Scripture answer to such questions. The main purpose is to trace the history of Israel from its source; and to do·this the narrative begins with the source of all things."

Ten Books of Generations.—(1) The heavens and the earth—Gen. 1:1-31; 2:1. (2) Seth and his posterity—5:1-32. (3) Noah—6:9, 10. (4) Sons of Noah, Origin of nations—ch. 10. After this chapter all descendants of Noah disappear except line of Shem. (5) Shem—First step in the selection of a people—11:10-26. (6) Terah—Second step. Birth of Abraham—11:27. (7) Ishmael (Arabs)—The rejected line—25:12.

After this Ishmael disappears except incidentally. (8) Isaac—Chosen offspring —25:19. (9) Esau (Edomites)—Second rejection—36:1, 9. (10) Jacob—Gen. 37:2.

"But the literary form is not so striking as the *inner* plan, which evidently is to exhibit the election and preparation of a special people for a great purpose. In pursuance of this plan the writer goes back to the very beginning of things, and as he comes down the course of history we see how he singles out the righteous in their generation, and contracts his regard from time to time, till he confines himself entirely to the sons of Jacob. Adam, Noah, Abraham, Isaac, and Jacob mark the five great stages of progress; and the dropping of other names, as soon as they fall out of the line of the onward march, is as remarkable as the increasing clearness of the purpose that is to be served by the family that comes to the front. The first part of the book is essentially and purposely introductory to the second; there is an internal unity in the whole.

G. Campbell Morgan divides Genesis into

Three great divisions.—Generation— Chs. 1, 2. Degeneration from the garden of Eden to Abraham—chs. 3-11. Regeneration through Abraham and his seed—Isaac, Jacob, Joseph.

Another division.—(1) History of Beginnings—chs. 1-11. (2) Patriarchal History—chs. 12-50.

History of Beginnings. World before Abraham.

"In the beginning the earth was without form and void." This does not mean that the earth had never been inhabited before. It might have been previously inhabited and have been reduced to a chaotic condition for some reason. A very large number of conservative Bible scholars regard the word "beginning" as used relatively.

Outline.—Beginning of material universe in relation to man. History of creation in outline—Ch. 1. Beginning of man in his relation to God. History of creation in detail—Ch. 2. Word "create" used three times in first chapter: Beginning of material things—1:1; beginning of life—1:21; creation of man—1:27. The fall and punishment of Adam—Ch. 3. Adam driven from Garden of Eden "lest he take, also of the tree of life, and eat, and live forever"—Gen. 3:22-24. See Rev. 2:7; 22:2, 14. First prophecy concerning Jesus —3:15 (Rom. 16:20). Eve tempted by the serpent — Gen. 3:1-14-16. Paul states his faith in this incident—II Cor. 11:3. Satan is identified as the serpent —Rev. 12:9; 20:2. See Serpents. Serpent worship almost universal in ancient times in all parts of the world. Cain and Abel—Gen. 4:1, 2. First sacrifice mentioned—Gen. 4:3-5. Cain murders Abel—Gen. 4:6-8. His punishment and descendants—4:9-24. See Mt. 23:35; Lu. 11:51; Heb. 12:24; I John 3:12. Development of arts—Gen. 4:17-22. Seth and his descendants—4:25; 5:1-32. Adam begat sons and daughters—5:4. This verse is overlooked when the question is asked "Where did Cain get his wife?" We do not know even the names of Seth's brothers and sisters. This shows that the Bible does not give us a history of the world but only a few striking events in the lives of a few persons belonging to the line from which should come the Messiah, or where others are mentioned they are only spoken of in their association or relation to those selected individuals. The Corruption of mankind—6:1-8. Noah instructed to make an ark—6:9-7:12.

The flood—7:13-24. Clean and unclean animals recognized by Noah—7:2. Noah offers clean animals—8:20. Subsidence of the waters—8:1-22. Blessing of Noah: Covenant of the Rainbow—9:1-20. From the Flood to Abraham—Chs. 10, 11. The Posterity of Noah—10:1-32. The Tower of Babel (Confusion of tongues)—11:1-9. Genealogy of Abraham—11:10-32.

Abraham to Joseph.—The Hebrews one tribe—Abraham—Chs. 12-25:11. Covenant made with Abraham—Gen. 12:1-3; 17:1-14. This covenant is the key to the whole Bible and gives meaning to the Old Testament. See THE OLD TESTAMENT and COVENANTS. Altar built by Abraham—12:7, 8. Destruction of Sodom and Gomorrah—Chs. 18, 19. Isaac—Gen. 25:12-27:46. Esau sells his birthright—25:27-34. Jacob—28:1-35:25. Esau—36:1-43. Joseph—37:1-50:26. For details of this period see ABRAHAM, LOT, ISHMAEL, ISAAC, JACOB, ESAU, and JOSEPH in DIGEST OF THE BIBLE.

New Testament references.—Events and persons of Genesis. For the very frequent references to the incidents and persons of the first chapters of Genesis see INCIDENTS IN THE OLD TESTAMENT REFERRED TO IN THE NEW TESTAMENT in this volume.

Chronology.—The chief difficulty in Genesis is found in the period from Adam to Abraham based on the genealogies of Chs. 5 and 11. These chapters show that Adam lived about 4000 years before Jesus. But we know that there was a high state of civilization in Egypt and Babylon probably before that date.

The only satisfactory explanation is that these genealogies may not be complete but mention only a few of the principal names.

EXODUS.

Name.—Second Book of Moses; Exodus—Taken from the Septuagint Version and meaning "going out."

Author.—See THE PENTATEUCH.

Keyword.—Blood.

Principal characters.—Moses, Aaron, Miriam, Joshua, and Pharaoh. (Probably Rameses II and his son Merenptah. See PHARAOH.)

Contents.—Exodus is a continuation of Genesis, "and continues the story of the chosen people. The theme of the book is the deliverance of Israel from the oppression of Egypt, and their separation to God."

I. **The Story of the Deliverance.**—Chs. 1–19. The oppression in Egypt—1:1–22. Appearance of Moses the deliverer—2:1–25. Moses about forty years of age when he slew the Egyptian and fled to Midian—Acts 7:23. He dwelt in Midian as a shepherd for about 40 years—Acts 7:30. So he was about 80 years of age when God called him to deliver Egypt—Ex. 7:7. He was the leader of Israel forty years—Deut. 34:7. God calls Moses to deliver Israel—3:1–22. Because of the timidity of Moses and his slowness of speech, Aaron is made Moses' spokesman—Ex. 4:10–16. Moses returns to Egypt—4:18–31. Burdens of Israel increase—5:1–22. Jehovah declares Himself, revealing His majesty and power—6:1–9. Note the frequent use of the pronoun "I" in this remarkable passage. Genealogy of Moses and Aaron—6:14-27. God sends Moses and Aaron to Pharaoh—7:1–13. Ten plagues—7:20–12:36.

"The Ten Plagues, which attested the Divine commission of Moses and Aaron, though in part connected with ordinary phenomena of Egyptian life, were specially significant as proving the power of God, and rebuking idolatry. 1. The Nile-blood; an object of worship turned into an object of abhorrence. 2. The sacred frog itself their plague. 3. Lice, which the Egyptians deemed so polluting that to enter a temple with them was a profanation, cover the country like dust. 4. The gadfly (Zebub), an object of Egyptian reverence, becomes their torture. 5. The cattle, which were objects of Egyptian worship, fall dead before their worshipers. 6. The ashes, which the priests scattered as signs of blessing, become boils. 7. Isis and Osiris, the deities of water and fire, are unable to protect Egypt, even at a season when storms and rain were unknown, from the fire and hail of God. 8. Isis and Serapis were supposed to protect the country from locusts. West winds might bring these enemies; but an east wind the Egyptian never feared, for the Red Sea defended him. But now Isis fails; and the very east wind he reverenced becomes his destruction. 9. The heavenly hosts, the objects of worship, are themselves shown to be under Divine control. 10. The last plague explains the whole. God's firstborn Egypt had oppressed; and now the firstborn of Egypt are all destroyed. The first two plagues, it will be noticed, were foretold by Moses, and imitated by the Egyptians. The rest they failed to copy, and confessed that they were wrought by the finger of God."—"Handbook of the Bible," Angus-Green.

The ten plagues—7:20–12:36. For a detailed description and explanation see PLAGUES in DIGEST OF THE BIBLE. Flight from Egypt—12:37-51. The passover—12:41-51; 13:1-10. See PASSOVER. Consecration of the First born—13:11-16. See FIRST-BORN. Crossing the Red Sea—14. Song of Moses and Miriam—15:1-21. March from the Red Sea to the wilderness of Sin—15:22-16:3. Complaints: Quails and manna given in answer—16:4-36. Water from the rock at Rephidim—17:1-7. War with Amalek

—17:8–16. Organization by Jethro, father-in-law of Moses—18:1–17. Arrival at Sinai—19:1–25.

II. Legislation for the delivered people given at Sinai.—Chs. 20–40.

1. "The Book of the Covenant"—Chs. 20–24. The Ten Commandments—20:1–17. Laws based on the Decalogue—20:18–23:33. The Covenant—24:1–18.

2. Ceremonial Laws—Chs. 25–40. The ark, the table of shewbread, the candlestick, the curtains of the tabernacle—25:1–40. The tabernacle—26:1–37. The altar of burnt-offering—27:1–21. The priestly robes—28:1–43. The consecration of priests—29:1–46. The altar of incense—30:1–10. Atonement money; the anointing oil—30:11–38.

Bezalel and Oholiab—31:1–11. Observance of Sabbaths—12–18.

3. Historical Episode of the Golden Calf—32:1–35:23;—See Acts 7:41; I Cor. 10:7. Renewal of the covenant—34:1–35.

4. Construction of the Sanctuary—35:1–40:38.

New Testament References to events and persons.—See INCIDENTS IN THE OLD TESTAMENT REFERRED TO IN THE NEW TESTAMENT in this volume.

For further details and the relation of the tabernacle to New Testament institutions see MOSES, AARON, ISRAEL, COMMANDMENTS, PASSOVER, PLAGUES, FEASTS, TABERNACLE, in DIGEST OF THE BIBLE in this volume.

LEVITICUS.

1. **Name.**—The Third Book of Moses; Leviticus (The Levitical [Law]).

2. **Author.**—See THE PENTATEUCH.

3. **Principal characters.**—Moses, Aaron and his sons.

4. **Keywords.**—Sin, Holiness, Separation, Atonement, Redemption.

5. **Subject.**—The Law of the Ceremonial.

Contents.—Exodus closes with the completion of the Tabernacle. Leviticus begins with regulations for the offerings and ritual of the Tabernacle. "We have in Leviticus, not the Lawgiver speaking in awful tones or writing on tablets of stone, but the Portion of Israel, dwelling in the midst of His people and teaching them how they might draw near to His presence and abide in communion with Him"—Donald Fraser. (SYNOPTICAL LECTURES, Vol. 1, p. 29.) The Book of Hebrews should be read carefully in connection with Leviticus.

I. Sacrifices—Chs. 1–5. The burnt-offering—1:1–17. The meal-offering—2:1–16. The peace-offering—3:1–17. The sin-offering—4:1–35. The trespass-offering—5:1–19.

II. The priesthood—Chs. 6–10. The priest's function in sacrifice—6:1–7:38. The consecration of the priest—8:1–36.

Sacrifices of Aaron—9:1–24. Nadab and Abihu: Temperance of priests—10:1–20.

III. Clean and unclean—Chs. 11–15. Purification of women—12:1–8. Leprosy, its kinds, its tests and purification—13:1–14:57. Ceremonial uncleanness—15:1–33.

IV. The Ritual of the Day of Atonement—16:1–34.

V. The law of holiness—Chs. 17–22. The Israelites' sacrifice: Abstinence from blood—17:1–16. Prohibition of incest and impurity—18:1–30. Laws against idolatry, unchastity and uncleanness—19:1–20:27. The priests' character and mode of life—21:1–22:33.

VI. Feasts—23–25.

VII. Blessings and penalties—26:1–46.

VIII. Law of vows and tithes.

New Testament references — 7:12 (Heb. 13:15); 11:44 (I Pet. 1:16); 12:3 (John 7:22); 12:6 (Lu. 2:22–24); 13:49; 14:2–32 (Mt. 8:4; Lu. 17:14); 16:18, 27 (Heb. 9:12, 13; 10:4; 13:11–13); 16:29–34 (Heb. 9:7); 19:12 (I Pet. 1:16); 19:18 (Mt. 19:19; 22:39; Mk. 12:31; Lu. 10:27; Rom. 13:9; Gal. 5:14; Jas. 2:8); 20:7 (I Pet. 1:16); 20:10 (John 8:5); 24:5, 9 (Mt. 12:3, 4).

For details see OFFERINGS, SACRIFICE, PRIESTS, CEREMONIAL CLEANSING, PURIFICATION, PRIESTS.

NUMBERS.

1. **Name.**—The Fourth Book of Moses; Numbers (from the census recorded in Chs. 1–4, 26).

2. **Author.**—See THE PENTATEUCH.

3. **Keyword.**—Pilgrimage.

4. **Principal characters.**—Moses, Aaron, Joshua, Caleb, Balaam, and Balak.

5. **Subject.**—Story of the Israelites' journey from Sinai to the Plains of Moab.

6. **Connection.**—Exodus, Chs. 1–19.

7. **Contents:**

I. Enumeration of men of war, priests, and Levites—Chs. 1–4.

II. Legislation—Concerning jealousy with test of adultery (ch. 5), and concerning the Nazarite vow—Ch. 6.

III. Oblations of the princes—Ch. 7.

IV. Legislation—C o n c e r n i n g the seven lamps of the sanctuary, the purification of the Levites and the keeping of the passover—Chs. 8, 9. The silver trumpets—Ch. 10:1–10.

V. The march from Sinai to Taberah —10:11–11:3. Murmurings: appointment of seventy elders, Eldad and Medad, quails and plague, arrival at Hazeroth—11:4–35. Miriam's rebellion and leprosy—12:1–15. From Hazeroth to the wilderness of Paran—12:16. The spies: their discouraging reports; the people's distrust and condemnation to forty years' wandering—Chs. 13, 14.

VI. Legislation—Concerning offerings —Ch. 15.

VII. Rebellion of Korah—Confirmation of Aaron's priesthood—Chs. 18, 19.

VIII. Legislation—Concerning priesthood, tithes, purification with the ashes of a red heifer—Chs. 18, 19.

IX. Sin of Moses and Aaron at Meribah—20:1–13. Because of this sin Moses and Aaron were not permitted to enter the promised land—20:12, 24; 27:12–15. Journey to Mt. Hor; refusal of Edom to allow Israel to pass; death of Aaron— Ch. 20. Fiery serpents, brazen serpent— Ch. 21. See John 3:14.

X. Balaam and Balak—Chs. 22–24. Sojourn in Moab; sin of people; zeal of Phinehas—Ch. 25. New census—Ch. 26. Zelophehad's daughters—Ch. 27.

XI. Legislation—Concerning offerings at the festivals—Chs. 28, 29. Vows—Ch. 30.

XII. Conquest of Midianites—Ch. 31. Settlement of two and one-half tribes east of Jordan—Ch. 32.

XIII. List of encampments from Egypt to plains of Moab—Ch. 33.

XIV. Division of Canaan—Chs. 34–36. Directions concerning conquest and partition of Canaan, Levitical cities and cities' of refuge—Chs. 34, 35:28. Concerning murder—35:29–34. Heiresses— 36:1–13.

New Testament references. — 12:7 (Heb. 3:5, 6); 14:16 (I Cor. 10:5; Heb. 3:17); 14:32 (Jude 5); 14:33 (Acts 7:36, 42; Heb. 3:9); 16:15 (II Tim. 2: 19); 16:32, 33 (Jude 11); 17:2, 4, 10 (Heb. 9:4); 19:1–9 (Heb. 9:13); 21:6 (I Cor. 10:9); 21:8 (John 3:14); Ch. 22 (II Pet. 2:15; Jude 11); 25:1–9 (I Cor. 10:1–10).

For details. — See ISRAEL, MOSES, AARON, JOSHUA, PRIESTS, PRINCES.

DEUTERONOMY.

1. Name.—The fifth Book of Moses; Deuteronomy ([Book of] Second Law).

2. Author.—See PENTATEUCH. Deuteronomy is a book of speeches of Moses and covers a very brief period of history. The Jews had a tradition that Joshua wrote the account of the death of Moses. As he was Moses' prime minister and secretary, it is quite possible that he also recorded these speeches. The book would still be the Book of Moses because it is practically only a record of his speeches.

3. Subject. — Popular summary of Moses' leadership.

4. Presupposes.—Exodus, Leviticus and Numbers.

5. Keyword.—Obedience.

6. Contents.—A review of forty years' wandering in the wilderness. Moses' first speech begins at the end of the forty years' wandering and one month and seven days before crossing the Jordan. A new generation had grown up which had not heard the law at Sinai.

7. Division of Book.—İ. Discourses of Moses—1–30. II. Delivery of the law to the priests—31:1–29. III. Song of Moses —32:1–43. Moses goes up to Mt. Nebo—32:48–52. IV. Blessing of Moses—33. V. Death of Moses.

8. Outline.

I. Historical review by Moses—Chs. 1–4.

II. Recapitulation of the law—Chs. 5–26.

Moral provisions—Chs. 5–11.

The Ten Commandments—5:1–33. Exhortation to faithfulness—6:1–25. Warning against apostasy—7:1–11. Promise of blessing and help—12–26. Rehearsal of history—8:1–10:22. Reasons for obedience: study of the law—11:1–32.

Ceremonial provisions—Chs. 12–26.

Unity of worship—12:1–32. Prohibition of idolatry—13:1–18. Of idolatrous practices—14:1–29. Provision of year of release for debt and of bond-servants—15:1–23. Feasts: passover, pentecost, and tabernacles—16:1–17. Administration of justice—16:18–17:13. The law of the king—17:14–20. The portion of the Levites — 18:1–8. Promise of true prophets—9–22. Cities of refuge—19:1–10. Laws concerning landmarks and testimony—11–21. Laws concerning warfare—20:1–20. Expiation of murder whose perpetrator is unknown—21:1–11. Marriage of captive women; the treatment of sons—12–23. Laws of property and chastity—22:1–30. Laws concerning the assembly, clemency in war, vows, divorce, loans, payment of wages, unjust judgments—23:1–25:4. The "Levirate" law—25:5–10 (concerning marriage). Fairness in conflict and commerce—25:11–16. Destruction of Amalek—17–19. First-fruits—26:1–19.

III. Sanctions of the law—Chs. 27–30.

Curses upon violators (to be pronounced at Ebal)—27:1–26. Blessings upon the obedient (to be pronounced at Gerizim)—28:1–14. Additional warnings of evils of disobedience—15–68. The covenant at Moab—29:1–30:20.

IV. Last days of Moses—Chs. 31–34.

Delivery of the law to the priests—31:1–29. The Song of Moses—31:30–32:47. The ascent of Nebo: the blessing of Moses — 32:48–33:29. The death of Moses—34:1–12.

New Testament references and quotations.—Jesus quoted from Deuteronomy when He was tempted by Satan—Mt. 4:7, 10 (Deut. 8:3; 6:16; 6:13). He refers to Deut. 24:1–4 as given by Moses and explains why Moses so commanded—Mt. 5:31; 19:7; Mk. 10:3–5. Moses considered himself a prophet and prophesied that Jehovah would raise up a prophet like unto himself—18:15, 17, 18. Philip, Peter, and Stephen all testified that this prophecy was fulfilled in Jesus and refer to the prophecy as that of Moses—John 1:45; Acts 3:22, 23; 7:37. See THE PEN-TATEUCH. See also—1:31 (Acts 13:18); 4:35 (Mk. 12:32, 33); 6:4 (Mk. 12:29, 32, 33); 6:5 (Mt. 22:37; Mk. 12:30; John 4:21); 9:19 (Heb. 12:21); 19:15 (Mt. 18:16; John 8:17; II Cor. 13:1; I Tim. 5:19); 21:23 (Gal. 3:13); 23: 21 (Mt. 5:33); 24:14, 15 (I Tim. 5: 18); 25:4 (I Cor. 9:9; I Tim. 5:18); 25:5 (Mt. 22:24; Mk. 12:19; Lu. 20:38); 27:26 (Gal. 3:10); 30:12–14 (Rom. 10:6–8); 31:6 (Heb. 13:5); 32:21 (Rom. 10:19; I Cor. 10:22); 32:35 (Rom. 12:19; Heb. 10: 30); 32:43 (Rom. 15:10).

For details.—See ISRAEL, LAW, MOSES, JOSHUA.

JOSHUA, BOOK OF.

1. **Name.**—Derived from the chief character in the book.

2. **Author.**—Not known.

3. **Subject.**—The conquest and partition of Canaan.

4. **Presupposes.**—The Pentateuch.

5. **Keywords.**—Courage, conquest.

6. Principal c h a r a c t e r s—Joshua, Caleb.

7. **Contents**—This book covers a period of about 25 years; from the crossing of the Jordan to the division of the land.

I. The conquest—Chs. 1–12. The commission of Joshua—1:1–18. The sending of spies to Jericho—2:1–24. The crossing of Jordan—3:1–17. The memorial of the crossing—4:1–24. Preparations for conquest—5:1–15. Siege and capture of Jericho—6:1–27. Defeat at Ai: the sin of Achan—7:1–26. Renewed attack and capture of Ai—8:1–29. Reading of the law at Ebal—30–35. Stratagem of Gibeon—9:1–27. War with the five kings—10:1–43. Completion of the campaign—11:1–12:24.

II. The partition—Chs. 13–22. The portion of Reuben, Gad and half of Manasseh—13:1–32. Provision for Levi; the portion of Caleb—14:1–15. The portion of Judah—15:1–63. The portion of Ephraim—16:1–10. The portion of Manasseh—17:1–18. The portion of Benjamin—18:1–28. The portions of Simeon, Zebulun, Issachar, Asher, Naphtali and Dan—19:1–51. The cities of refuge—20: 1–9. The Levitical cities—21:1–45. The relations of the transjordanic tribes to the rest defined—22:1–34.

III. The retirement of Joshua—Chs. 23, 24. Joshua's farewell—23:1–16. Renewal of the covenant—24:1–28. Death and burial of Joshua and of Eleazar—29–33.

New Testament references and quotations.—1:5 (Heb. 13:5); 2:16 (Heb. 11: 31; Jas. 2:25); 6:12–20 (Heb. 11:30); 6:23 (Heb. 11:31); 14:2 (Acts 13:19); 18:1 (Acts 7:45); 24:32 (Heb. 11:22).

For details.—See CANAAN, ISRAEL, JOSHUA.

JUDGES, BOOK OF.

1. **Name.**—Derived from that of the leaders of Israel immediately after the settlement in Canaan.

2. **Author.**—Unknown, though Jewish tradition ascribes to Samuel. Modern scholarship is opposed to this view.

3. **Subject.**—History of Israel between Joshua and the monarchy.

4. **Presupposes.**—The Book of Joshua.

5. **Keyword.**—"Deliverance." Man's weakness and strength in dependence on Jehovah.

6. **Principal characters**—Othniel, Deborah, Barak, Gideon, Jephthah, Samson.

7. **Contents.**—History of period between the conquest and Samuel during the forming of the nation. (See Acts 13: 20.) It was a period of apostasy, of immorality. "In those days there was no king in Israel; every man did that which was right in his own eyes"—Judges 17:6. Thirteen judges are named (See JUDGES.) They were not merely judges in the modern sense, but were political and military leaders, raised up for the deliverance of the people. "The author's purpose is not merely to interpret the history, and explain upon religious principles why such evils befell Israel in the days of the judges, but to impress upon his readers the lesson that unfaithfulness to Yahweh is always punished; that whenever Israel falls away from him, he withdraws his protection and leaves it defenseless before its foes. By historical examples he would warn his contemporaries against a like apostasy. His motive and aim are thus not historical, but religious. In a different, but not less effective way, he inculcates the same truth which all the prophets preached; Yahweh is Israel's God, and the religion of Israel is to keep itself to him alone."—G. F. Moore, "International Critical Commentary." Chapters 3-16 record seven failures through sin, God's punishment because of sin and his deliverance of his people afterwards. The "Song of Deborah," and the stories of Gideon, Jephthah and Samson are among the most familiar and thrilling passages in the Old Testament.

Outline:

I. Condition of affairs after Joshua's death—Chs. 1:1-3:6. The subjugation of Canaanite clans—1:1-36.. Demoralization in Israel: Unconquered clans—2:1-3:6.

II. The Judges—Chs. 3:7-16:31. Othniel—3:7-11. Ehud—3:12-30. Shamgar—3:31. Barak and Deborah—4:1-24. The Song of Deborah—5:1-31. Gideon—6:1-8:35. Abimelech's attempt at monarchy—9:1-57. Tola—10:1-2. Jair—3-5. Apostasy and repentance — 10:6-18. Jephtha—11:1-40. Civil war—12:1-7. Ibzah—12:8-10. Elon—11-12. Abdon—13-15. Samson—13:1-16:31.

III. Lawlessness of the period—Chs. 17-21. A case of idolatry: Micah—17:1-13. Violence of the Danites—18:1-31. The outrage at Gibeah—19:1-30. Decimation of Benjamin—20:1-48. Scheme for the restoration of the tribe—21:1-25.

Chronology.—This is a very difficult problem. See COMMENTARY ON JUDGES, by George F. Moore.

New Testament references. — The principal references are the reference to the period of the Judges in Acts 13:20, and the reference to Gideon, Barak, Samson and Jephthah in Heb. 11:32.

16

RUTH.

1. **Name.**—Derived from the heroine of the story.

2. **Author.**—Unknown.

3. **Subject.**—The experience of a Moabite ancestress of David (and of the Messiah).

4. **Supplement.**—To the Book of Judges (especially Chs. 17–21), illustrating the happier side of life. Instructive on social conditions and legal practice.

5. **Design.**—To trace descent of David showing that a foreigner was in the ancestral line. Boaz, the husband of Ruth, was a descendant of Rahab—Mt. 1:5. This book was one of the Megilloth or Festal Rolls, and was read at the Feast of Pentecost.

6. **"Lessons.**—This book is remarkably rich in examples of faith, patience, industry, and kindness, nor less so in intimations of the special care which God takes of our concerns; 'still out of seeming ill educing good.' Elimelech's misfortunes; his son's marriage to a Moabitess; Ruth's loss of her husband—all end in her own conversion, and in the honor of her adopted family. What changes ten years have produced! They have turned Naomi ('pleasantness') into Mara ('bitter'). She who went out full has come home again empty. Her fortitude and faith, however, sustain her; and in her trouble she shows equal wisdom and tenderness. When her daughters are told what they must expect if they accompany her to Canaan, Orpah weeps, but returns to her idols; Ruth cleaves to her, indicating thereby depth of affection and religious decision (1–16; 2–12). Her reward she received 'of Jehovah, the God of Israel, under whose wings she came to trust.' Incidentally, the book contains some of the loveliest pictures of Israelitish rural life to be found in Scripture. Boaz, the genial landowner, his willing laborers, the gleaners in the harvest-field, the purity and simplicity of the family affections displayed—all form a beautiful contrast to the ruder scenes of conflict and passion which marked the era, and seem to single out Bethlehem from the rest of the unquiet land."—"Handbook of the Bible," Angus-Green.

7. **Contents:**

Famine in Judah; removal of Elimelech to Moab; death of Elimelech; return of Naomi and Ruth to Judah—1: 1–22. The lowly life of Ruth; gleaning in the fields of Boaz—2:1–23. Ruth's request to Boaz to take the kinsman's part —3:1–18. Redemption of Elimelech's inheritance by Boaz—4:1–12. Marriage of Ruth to Boaz; posterity up to David— 4:13–22. See RUTH, BOAZ.

SAMUEL, FIRST BOOK OF.

1. Name.—Derived from the prophetic judge of Israel, who established the kingdom. In Greek version: First Book of Kingdoms.

2. Subject.—The last judge and the first king of Israel.

3. Embodies.—Experiences of three great personalities—Samuel, Saul and David.

4. Presupposes.—The Book of Judges.

5. Principal characters.—Eli, Samuel, Saul, David, Jonathan.

6. Contents.—In the Hebrew Scriptures I and II Samuel are considered as one book. The First Book of Samuel describes a transition period, from the period of the judges to the monarchy and the choice of the first king of Israel. Samuel was a prophet—I Sam. 3:20. He was classed in the Old Testament with Moses and Aaron—Ps. 99:6; Jer. 15:1.

"The period covered by these books may be estimated at about a hundred years. It was evidently one of the most important centuries in the life of Israel, for in it was effected the transition from the tribal form of government (if government it may be called) to the settled monarchy of David. At the opening of the period the prominent figures (Eli, Samuel) are classed by the author with the heroes of the Book of Judges. Saul is the first who attempts to cement the people together by the monarchy. Although his experiment ended in disaster, there is no reason to doubt that his failure paved the way for David's success. In the long struggle against the Philistine oppressor the nation realized its own unity, learned its own strength, and prepared to play its part in the history of the world. What light we have upon this time of storm and stress, of heroic struggle and high achievement, comes from the Books of Samuel."— H. P. Smith, "International Critical Commentary."

"**The prophets.**—We see in First Samuel, side by side with the constitution of the monarchy, the beginning of prophecy as a settled constituent of the religious life. 'All the people knew that Samuel was established to be a prophet of the Lord' (I Sam. 3:20). The function is spoken of as a well-known thing, for Moses was regarded as the typical prophet who receives revelations of God's will, 'not in dark speeches,' but plainly (Num. 12:8), and authoritatively communicates it to the people. But it is in the time of Samuel that we first see prophecy as a continuous and even organized institution; and so he is in the New Testament spoken of as the first of the long line of prophets who foretold the days of the gospel (Acts 3:24). His weighty words to Saul, 'To obey is better than sacrifice' (I Sam. 15:22), are the substance of all prophetic teaching, and the part he took in the setting up of the throne of David associates prophecy in its early phases with the promise to be fulfilled at the end of the dispensation in David's Son and Lord.

Prophetic historians.—The names of some of the prophetic men of this period, Nathan, Gad, and Samuel himself, are given in the first book of the Chronicles as writers of history (I Chr. 29:29, R.V.), and the second Book mentions historical works written by other prophetic men in later reigns. What the works referred to may have been, or whether they are incorporated with the existing historical books, it is hard to say. But there is nothing at all improbable in the supposition that these men thus early occupied themselves with the writing of the nation's history. The prophets were men looking at the past and at the future, seeking to make the experience of the one a lesson for the other; and as they singly and collectively endeavored to rouse the national spirit and maintain it at a due level, it is most reasonable to suppose that in their societies, and in the addresses they gave to the people who resorted to them, the facts of the nation's history would be the text of their exhortations. The historical books are all more or less imbued with the prophetic spirit, and written from a prophetic point of view; and this is the reason for the name the Jews gave to these books—"the former prophets.

'The literary features of the Books of Samuel show that this was an independent composition, from a different hand than that which wrote the books of Kings. The Law is not once quoted, and only once referred to (I. Sam. 10:25), whereas the books of Kings continually treat it as the standard by which the actions of the rulers were to be tested. In the Books of Samuel also there is no distinct reference to authorities for the facts recorded, whereas the author of Kings refers to writings in which fuller details are to be found. Since there is no mention of the Captivity in the Books of Samuel, nor even any hint of the decline of the kingdom of the ten tribes, it has been concluded that the books were written before the deportation of the inhabitants of the northern kingdom by the Assyrians; but the writer of the books of Kings has before him the downfall of both kingdoms.

The appearance of the books suggests that, though the writer makes no mention of *written* sources from which he drew his materials, he freely incorporated in his narrative pieces found in writing, or handed down orally. The song of Hannah, for example (I Sam. 2:1–10), David's elegies over Saul and Jonathan and over Abner, and the poetical pieces at the close of the second book, one of which (II Sam. 22) is found in the book of Psalms (Ps. 18), are evidently not given as the compositions of the historian himself. The lists of heroes, and statistical and antiquarian tables which occur in the second book, may have been drawn from state records, for among the officials at the court there appear a "recorder" (or, perhaps, chronicler), and a "scribe" or secretary (see II Sam. 8:16, 17, and *cf.* 20:24, 25).' "—Nelson's "Bible Treasury."

Outline:

I. The decline of the judgeship as a form of government—Chs. 1–8. The birth of Samuel—Ch. 1:1–28. Hannah's song of thanksgiving—2:1–11. Corruption in Israel—12–36. Samuel's prophetic call—3:1–21. Defeat of Israel by the Philistines: downfall of the house of Eli—4:1–22. The ark in the temple of Dagon: its return—5:1–6:20. Samuel's judgeship: victory over Philistines—7:1–17. Demand of the people for a King: Protest and consent of Samuel—8:1–22.

II. The reign of Saul—Chs. 9:15. Saul's providential guidance to Samuel—9:1–27. Saul's designation as king—10:1–27. Saul's championship of Israel against the Ammonites—11:1–14. Samuel's farewell as prophet-judge—12:1–25. Beginnings of Saul's reign—13:1–23. The campaign of Michmash: Jonathan's bravery and peril—14:1–52. War with Amalek: Saul's failure and rejection—15:1–35.

III. Selection and training of David—Chs. 16–27. Samuel's visit to Jesse: Anointing of David; invitation to the court—16:1–23. David's feat of slaying Goliath—17:1–58. Saul's jealousy of David—18:1–30. David's flight from court—19:1–24. Jonathan's friendship for David—20:1–42. David's life as exile and fugitive—21:1–27:12.

IV. Last campaign and death of Saul.—Chs. 28–31. Saul's consultation with witch of En-dor—28:1–25. Philistine encampment at Aphek; their distrust of David—29:1–11. David's attack on Amalekites—30:1–31. Battle of Gilboa; death of Saul and his son—31:1–13.

New Testament references and quotations.—3:20 (Acts 13:20); 8:5 (Acts 13:21); 10:21, 24 (Acts 13:21, 22); 13:14 (Acts 13:22); 21:1 (Mt. 12:3, 4); 21:6 (Mt. 12:3, 4).

For details see ISRAEL, SAMUEL, SAUL, DAVID.

SAMUEL, SECOND BOOK OF.

1. **Name.**—Probably given because it is a continuation of I Samuel. In Greek Version: Second Book of Kingdoms.

2. **Subject:** Reign of David. His sin and punishment.

3. **Presupposes:** I Samuel.

4. **Principal Characters.**—David, Nathan, Absalom.

5. **Contents:**

I. David king over Judah—Chs. 1–4. Announcement of Saul's death—1:1–16. David's lament over Saul—1:17–27. David's assumption of sovereignty at Hebron—2:1–7. Ishbosheth set over Israel; Civil war—2:8–3:1. Defection of Abner from Ishbosheth to David; Assassination of Ishbosheth—4:1–12.

II. David king over all Israel—Chs. 5–24. (a) Period of prosperity—Chs. 5–12. Assumption of rule; Capture of Zion; Conquest of Philistines—5:1–25. Removal of ark to Jerusalem—6:1–23. Plan to build a temple; Postponement; Prayer of thanksgiving—7:1–29. Victories over Philistines and Edom—8:1–18. David's kindness to Mephibosheth —9:1–13. Conquest of Ammon and Syria—10:1–19. Sin against Uriah; Marriage with Bathsheba; Birth of Solomon—11:1–12:31. (b) Period of trials and rebellions—Chs. 12–20. Ammon's abuse of Tamar avenged by Absalom— 13:1–39. Flight and recall of Absalom— 14:1–33. Conspiracy and rebellion of Absalom—15:1–12. Flight of David; Deception of Tiba; Curse of Shimei— 16:13. Civil war; Counsels—16:15–17: 26. End of war; Absalom's defeat and death—17:27–18:33. Return of David to Jerusalem—18:1–43. Sheba's rebellion —20:1–26. (c) David's latter days—Chs. 21–24. The avenging of the Gibeonites; Heroism of Rizpah—21:1–11. Reëntombment of Saul and Jonathan—21: 1–14. War with Philistines—15:22. David's Psalm of praise—22:1–51. Last song—23:1–7. David's mighty men—23: 8–39. Census; Pestilence; Purchase of Araunah's threshing-floor—24:1–25.

For details see ISRAEL, DAVID, ABSALOM, PHILISTINES.

KINGS, FIRST BOOK OF.

Name.—Derived from the contents. In Greek Version, Third Book of Kingdoms.

Author.—Unknown. "The compiler of Kings, though not probably (as has sometimes been supposed), Jeremiah himself, was nevertheless a man like-minded with Jeremiah and almost certainly a contemporary who lived and wrote under the same influences. Deuteronomy is the standard by which the compiler judges both men and actions; and the history from the beginning of Solomon's reign, is presented not in purely objective form, but from the point of view of the . Deuteronomic code."—Driver.

Subject: History of Solomon and his successors to Jehoshaphat and Ahab.

Principal Characters.—David, Solomon, Rehoboam, Jeroboam, Ahab, Jezebel, Elijah.

Division.—David's death and Solomon's reign. Period of Israel's greatest splendor—Chs. 4–11. Revolt of Jeroboam and division of kingdom—Chs. 12–22.

Connection.—I and II Kings are considered as one Book in the Hebrew Scriptures. "These books are intimately related to the two books of Samuel with which they are numbered in the Septuagint. They take up the royal and prophetic history where Samuel laid it down and carry it forward in the same spirit. The books of Kings trace the history of the united kingdom from Solomon's accession and of the divided kingdom until its two parts were conquered by Assyria and Babylon. This period is over four centuries and its *terminus ad quem* is the release of Jehoiachim by Evil-Merodach in 561 B. C. These are the only books recording the entire political history of Israel, for Chronicles not only gives no record of the Northern Kingdom, but seems to avoid reference to it."—Driver.

I and II Kings gives the history of Israel from the prophetic standpoint. I and II Chronicles from the priestly.

Contents: This Book records the old age and death of David, reign of Solomon, building of the temple, the division of the kingdom under Rehoboam, and the conflict between Elijah and Ahab and Jezebel. David was not allowed to build the temple because he was a man of war and had shed blood—I Chr. 28: 3, 4. Solomon was chosen to build the temple—II Sam. 7:12, 13; I Chr. 28:6. God appears to Solomon in a dream and tells him to "Ask what I shall give thee"— 3:5. Solomon asks for an understanding heart and the choice pleases Jehovah, who promises him riches and honor—3:10–13. But this promise is based on one condition—3:14. His heart went out after foreign women, contrary to God's commandment and they led him into idolatry—Ch. 11. Because of this his kingdom was divided under Rehoboam—Chs. 12–16. After Solomon there is demoralization and degradation. The last part of the Book records the conflict between Elijah the prophet and Ahab and his foreign wife Jezebel, who is known as the most wicked woman of the Bible—Chs. 17–22.

"**The point of view** from which the books of Kings are written is made pretty plain by the writer himself. Whatever materials he may have had access to, and may have employed, he has a controlling plan in the presentation of them. His whole aim is not to furnish the greatest possible amount of information; for he passes lightly over many things that he must have known minutely, and employs a scale of proportion, in the treatment of different subjects, out of all keeping with the degree in which they bulked in the history of the kings. His fixed principle is that faithfulness to God and observance of His statutes and ordinances ensure prosperity, and that unfaithfulness entails disaster. Writing from a point of time at which the truth of this principle had been fully confirmed by the ruin of the nation, he can estimate all the successive reigns by its standard, and pronounce judgment on the whole course of the history.

This is in fact the prophetic standpoint; and if we were to remove from the books of Kings all that may be included under the prophetic element, the residue would be but a chronicle of bare and not very interesting facts. Not only are the doings of Elijah and Elisha narrated at length and with evident predilection, but at many points of the history we find prophets appearing at critical times and intervening with authority in public affairs. Nathan plays a more prominent part than either David or Solomon at the accession of the latter to the throne; Ahijah of Shiloh tells Jeroboam the fate that would befall him (I Kings 11:29-39), and Shemaiah similarly warns Rehoboam (I Kings 12:22-24). And so it is all down the history. We know from other sources how Isaiah, who is mentioned in Kings, and Jeremiah who is not, were involved in the momentous events of their time, though their connection with them is not recorded in these books. In like manner there may have been other prophets who were actively engaged in these events, although their names are not mentioned in the historical narrative. It is not to be lost sight of that whereas the author of the books of Kings refers in somewhat general terms to the written sources of his work, the author of the Chronicles speaks with greater minuteness of the same or similar sources by the names of their authors. Among these are Gad, Nathan, and other prophetic men who, as they appear in the history, probably occupied themselves in writing down the events.

'Literary features.—The literary form of the books of Kings is quite different from that of the books of Samuel. There is an almost stereotyped framework, resembling that of the book of Judges, within which the events of the successive reigns are placed. When the name of a new king is introduced, it is stated how old he was when he came to the throne, how many years he reigned, and, in regard to the kings of Judah, what was his mother's name. Then a general character is pronounced upon his reign, the events are recorded at greater or less length, and at the close a reference is usually given to another authority for fuller details. When the divided monarchy is to be treated, the usual proceeding is to give the record of the northern kingdom first, and then the corresponding record for the southern, the history thus falling into periods longer or shorter. And this course is followed so closely that sometimes the same event is twice related if it concerns the two kingdoms.

These features make it probable that the book is composed from other written materials, or at least largely based upon them. And the frequent references to books of Chronicles of the kings of Judah or of Israel favor the inference that state records of the respective kingdoms, containing lists of officials, statistical matters, and memoranda of events in the different reigns, were available for the purpose. There were also, in all probability, narratives of the doings of Elijah, Elisha, and other prophets, preserved in the prophetic circles, which would furnish information of another kind. A work extending over so long a period could not be the expression of the direct personal knowledge of any one writer and could only be composed in the way indicated.' "
—Nelson's "Bible Treasury."

Outline:

I. Israel united under Solomon—Chs. 1-11. Accession of Solomon (David's last days; Plot to make Adonijah his successor; Bath-sheba's counterplot; its success)—1:1-53. Charge of David to Solomon; First acts as king—2:1-46. Solomon's marriage; his wisdom—3:1-28. Solomon's officers, power, and wisdom—4:1-34. League with Hiram of Tyre regarding building the temple—5:1-18. Building the temple—6:1-38. Solomon's palace—7:1–12.; the architect Hiram's work in the temple and its furniture—13–51. Dedication of the temple—8:1–66. Jehovah's covenant with Solomon; Transactions with Hiram; Administration; Navy—9:1–28. Visit of the Queen of Sheba; Solomon's glory—10:1–29. Sins and adversaries of Solomon; his death—11:1–43.

II. The disruption to the appearance of Elijah—Chs. 12–16. Rehoboam's policy; the disruption—12:1–33. The disobedient prophet (an episode)—13:1–34. Reigns of Jeroboam in Israel and Reho-boam in Judah—14:1–31. Abijam and Asa; Nadab and Baasha—15:1–16:7. Elah, Zimri, Omri, and Ahab in Israel—16:8–34.

III. The Prophet Elijah—Chs. 17–21. Elijah's prediction of drought; raising the widow's son—17:1–24. The contest on Mt. Carmel; End of drought—18:1–46. Elijah's flight to Horeb—19:1–21. Ahab's victory over Ben-hadad—20:1–43. Ahab's seizure of Naboth's vineyard—21:1–29.

IV. War of Ahab and Jehoshaphat against Syria; Death of Ahab—Ch. 22.

KINGS, SECOND BOOK OF.

1. **Name.**—Derived from contents. In Greek Version, Fourth Book of Kingdoms.

2. **Subject.**—History of Israel and Judah from the alliance between Ahab and Jehoshaphat to the capture of Jerusalem by Nebuchadrezzar (586 B.C.).

3. **Continuation and conclusion of I Kings.**

4. **Principal characters.**—Elijah, Elisha, Hezekiah, Josiah. **Connection.**—See Books of ISAIAH, JEREMIAH, JONAH, AMOS and HOSEA.

5. **Division.**—Story of Elisha—1–9. Corruption of Israel and Judah—10–17. Hezekiah and Josiah—18–23:30. Captivity—23:31–25.

6. **Contents:**

In the First Book of Kings we see Israel in its greatest splendor. Prosperity too often breeds decay. Because Solomon tried to serve two masters and bowed down to strange gods his kingdom was divided after his death and Israel and Judah resulted. Israel had 19 kings and nine dynasties—Jeroboam, Nadab, Baasha, Elah, Zimri, Omri, Ahab, Ahaziah, Jehoram, Jehu, Jehoahaz, Jeroboam II, Zechariah, Shallum, Menahem, Pekahiah, Pekah, and Hoshea.

Judah had 20 kings and only one dynasty—Rehoboam, Abijah, Asa, Jehoshaphat, Jehoram, Ahaziah, Queen Athaliah, Jehoash, Amaziah, Uzziah (Azariah), Jotham, Ahaz, Hezekiah, Manasseh, Amon, Josiah, Jehoahaz, Jehoiachim, Jehoiachin (Coniah) and Zedekiah. Judah had only one dynasty, because out of Judah was to come the Messiah and we see the kingly line unbroken. This Book records a period of corruption and breaking down. There are short periods of turning back to Jehovah, but too late. God had warned Israel through Moses and the prophets who followed him that he would drive her into captivity if she went after strange gods. Read the 28th chapter of Deuteronomy, the prophecies of Isaiah, Jeremiah, Amos and Hosea. Then read this Book again and see how the statements in Deuteronomy were verified. The Book closes with both Israel and Judah in captivity, Israel to finally disappear and only a remnant of Judah to be preserved. While this was a period of corruption and humiliation, it was also a period of important prophets—Jonah, Amos, and Hosea were prophets in Israel. Joel, Isaiah, who began his work as a prophet in the days of Uzziah (Azariah), and Nahum succeeded in rescuing Judah from Assyria. Micah lived during the reigns of Jotham, Ahaz and Hezekiah, Zephaniah during reign of Josiah, Habbakuk probably during the reign of Jehoiakim. The great prophet Jeremiah was probably born toward the close of Jehoiakim's reign and lived to witness the capture of Jerusalem and his beloved people carried away in captivity to Babylon.

"Jehoshaphat's son and successor, Jehoram, who married Athaliah, the daughter of Jezebel, was succeeded by his son, Ahaziah, who was involved in the ruin of the house of Ahab. For Joram of Israel, while sick of wounds he had received in battle, was suddenly attacked by his general Jehu. Jezebel also was put to death, and Ahaziah, the king of Judah, who had come to Jezreel to visit his kinsman, shared their fate. Jehu, acting as the executioner of the divine sentence, roots out the Baal worship, kills all the members of the royal family on whom he can lay hands, and becomes the first of a new dynasty, (9, 10). Hearing the news at Jerusalem, Athaliah, the queen-mother, puts to death all the seed-royal and seizes the throne. One child only escapes her fury, the infant Joash, who is kept hidden in the chambers of the Temple for six years, at the end of which time he is publicly exhibited to the people by Jehoiada the priest, and set upon the throne, Athaliah being put to death (11).

Culmination of the northern kingdom.—With the disappearance of the house of Omri, the alliance of the two kingdoms falls to pieces. Joash introduces reforms in Jerusalem, but has to buy off an invasion of Hazael of Damascus (12). The house of Jehu waxes stronger (13:1–13, 22–25), inflicting humiliation also upon the kingdom of Judah (14:1–16); and the northern kingdom may be said to have reached its culmination in the time of Jeroboam II., who reigned for forty-one years, and extended the kingdom to its ancient boundaries (14:23–29). At the same time also, under Uzziah, who had a reign of fifty-two years in Jerusalem, the southern kingdom enjoyed unwonted prosperity.

Decay and downfall of the northern kingdom.—From its climax of greatness the northern kingdom very swiftly declined to ruin after the powerful hand of Jeroboam was relaxed. His son Zechariah was the last of the dynasty of Jehu, after whom there is a rapid succession of usurpers; and meanwhile the colossal power of Assyria is gradually making itself felt till Tiglath-pileser falls upon Israel, takes a great part of the territory and carries away many of the inhabitants. Assyria, in fact, makes profit of the rivalries of the kingdoms of Damascus, Israel, and Judah, coming to the help of one or another, and gaining at each move an advantage for itself. Thus Jotham, the successor of Uzziah in Judah, suffers from a hostile combination of Pekah of Israel and Rezin of Damascus (15:32–38); and his successor Ahaz is so hard pressed that he makes offers of submission to Tiglath-pileser on condition of receiving help (16:1–8). So the king of Assyria comes against Rezin of Damascus and kills him; Hoshea the king of Israel becomes tributary to save his throne; but later on, Shalmaneser IV., finding 'conspiracy in him,' sends an army against him, which after a siege of three years

takes Samaria, and puts an end to the northern kingdom, many of the people being carried away and foreigners settled in the land (16:9 to 17:41).

The surviving kingdom of Judah.—Thus the kingdom of the ten tribes comes to an end, and the rest of the book is concerned with the remaining kingdom of Judah. Hezekiah was in the sixth year of his reign when Samaria was taken, and his reign is remarkable for the friendship between him and the prophet Isaiah, and the reforms that he endeavored to carry out. His deliverance from the army of Sennacherib is memorable, and his restoration from a dangerous illness, when he made a display of his wealth to ambassadors from Babylon, gave occasion to a warning of the doom from that quarter that was to overtake his kingdom (18–20).

Manasseh and Amon were degenerate successors of Hezekiah, whose impiety accelerated the national doom (21). There was a brief bright space in the reign of Josiah, who sought the Lord in his youth, in whose reign the Lawbook was discovered in the Temple, and a more thorough reformation of religion was set on foot. But Josiah fell fighting at Megiddo, in an attempt to intercept the march of an Egyptian army to fight with Assyria (22:1 to 23:30); and his successors are mere puppets or vassals of either the Egyptian or the great eastern empire. Jehoiakim is set on the throne by the Egyptians in preference to another son of Josiah, who had by the will of the people reigned three months. But when the Babylonian supremacy supervened he had to own allegiance to a new master; and his successor Jehoiachin was so hard pressed that he surrendered to Nebuchadrezzar (or Nebuchadnezzar), and was led away with 10,000 of the inhabitants, his uncle Zedekiah being set on the throne.

Fall of Jerusalem.—This was the last king of the house of David. Nebuchadrezzar, finding him unfaithful, marched an army into Judah, and, after a siege of about three years, took and destroyed Jerusalem, carrying captive or killing large numbers of the inhabitants, and appointing Gedaliah governor. The people, however, rose against him and killed him, and then fearing the vengeance of the king of Babylon took refuge in Egypt. Thus was the land wasted of its inhabitants, the independence of Israel was gone; and the book closes when thirty-seven years of the Captivity had passed, Jehoiachin being a state prisoner in Babylon (23:31 to 25:30).

Jeremiah was probably born toward the close of Jehoiakim's reign and lived to witness the capture of Jerusalem and his beloved people carried away in captivity to Babylon."—Nelson's "Bible Treasury."

I. **Outline.**—Israel and Judah to the end of the northern kingdom—Chs. 1–17. Elijah and Ahaziah—1:1–18. Ascension of Elijah; Elisha his successor—2:1–25. Rebellion and defeat of Mesha, king of Moab—3:1–27. The Miracles of Elisha (increase of the widow's oil; raising of the Shunammite's son; healing the poisonous pottage; multiplication of loaves)—4:1–44. Healing of the leprosy of Naaman—5:1–27. The miracles of Elisha (floating of the axe-head; blinding of Syrian warriors); Siege of Samaria; Famine—6:1–33. Prediction of the end of famine and its fulfillment—7:1–20. Elisha's influence (restoration of widow's land; Change of dynasty in Syria, in Israel), 8:1–29. Jehu made king of Israel; death of Jezebel—9:1–37. Annihilation of the house of Ahab—10:1–17. Overthrow of Baal-worship—18–36. Athaliah's usurpation in Judah —11:1–21. Joash: Reforms; Buying off attack by Hazael—12:1–21. Jehoahaz, Joash, Jeroboam II in Israel; Death of Elisha—13:1–25. Amaziah of Judah; War between Israel and Judah—14:1–29. Azariah in Judah; Zechariah, Shallum, Menahen, Pekahiah, and Pekah in Israel—15:1–38. Assyrian invasion; Jotham and Ahaz in Judah; Syro-Ephraimite war—16:1–20. Hoshea; Fall of Samaria; Deportation of ten tribes—17:1–41.

II. History of Judah from Hezekiah to the exile—Chs. 18–25. Reign of Hezekiah: Invasion of Sennacherib—18:1–37. Appeal to Isaiah and prayer to Jehovah; Failure of Sennacherib—19:1–37. Hezekiah's sickness and recovery; his indiscretion and death—20:1–21. Reigns of Manasseh and Amon—21:1–26. Reign of Josiah; Discovery of the Book of the Law—22:1–20. Reformation of Josiah —23:1–27; Invasion of Pharaoh-Necoh; Death of Josiah; Jehoahaz, Jehoiakim —28:37. Invasion of Nebuchadrezzar; Death of Jehoiakim; Capture of Jerusalem; Accession of Zedekiah—24:1–20. Rebellion of Zedekiah; Second invasion of Judah; Capture of Jerusalem and deportation to Babylon—25:1–30.

See ISRAEL, JUDAH, ASSYRIA, BABYLON, PROPHECY.

CHRONICLES, FIRST BOOK OF.

1. Name.—From apparent summary of the historical facts.

2. Subject.—The Hebrews to the planning of the temple by David.

3. Contents.—While the two Books of Chronicles seem to cover a great deal of the same ground as that covered by I and II Kings, yet I and II Chronicles center about Judah, Jerusalem, the temple and its worship. "Through all the preceding books we have the record of God's ways with His chosen people, the seed of Abraham. The record is carried forward through the second Book of Kings, when it is broken off, no less in sorrow than in anger. With Chronicles the sacred writer goes back to the beginning and starts again with Adam, Seth, etc., and dwells with great minuteness on the tribe of Judah, and the house of David. With Chronicles, therefore, begins the second great division of the Bible. Up to this point failure has marked the whole history. A fresh start is now made; and David's Divine Son, in whom all will be made good, comes more and more into prominence. The Books of Chronicles are related to the new order of things, not to the old. They are not linked with Samuel and Kings, but with Ezra and Nehemiah, with Zechariah and Malachi. They do not look back, but forward. The antediluvian economy failed through man's sin; the patriarchal likewise; the Jewish next, in its national capacity. But here begins a new epoch. A remnant according to the election of grace returns from captivity to the land of promise; and the Spirit of God turns their faces toward Him who is promised, who will not fail.

A second purpose is, to secure the genealogy of Christ, as the Son of David. Hence the lineage of David's house, and indeed of the whole tribe of Judah, is very fully given. Evidently, Matthew and Luke availed themselves of Chron-icles in tracing the human descent of our Lord."—Moorehead, "Outline Studies in the Books of the Old Testament."—Copyright 1893 by Fleming H. Revell Company.

"**The place** of these books in the Hebrew Bible is to be noted. In our version they are placed after Kings, so as to keep the historical books together; but their original position is in the third division, among the Hagiographa. An obvious explanation of this fact is that the books are of much later date than the antecedent historical books. For evidence of this, there is the mention of Cyrus (II Chr. 36:22); and again, the descendants of David are traced to the sixth generation after Zerubbabel (I Chr. 3:19 ff.), which would bring the date of composition down to the close of the Persian period, or the early part of the Greek period, say about 330 B.C. In the Hebrew Bible the Chronicles stand last in the whole collection, though this is not to be taken as a proof that they were the last written.

The point of view of the writer of the Chronicles is mainly explained by the date at which he wrote. Though national independence had departed from the Jewish people, two things remained: the temple and its worship subsisted, and the seed of David still survived. Prophecy was silent, but round these two things centered the hopes of the people for a better future; these two things knit them to the better days of the past. Looking back to those days, we need not wonder if a halo of glory surrounded all that was dearest in memory, and so the author dwells with predilection on those things of which a memorial, though faded, still remained. The book is in one aspect the result of the work that had been done by Ezra in consolidating the people around the temple and its worship; in another aspect it shows influences at work that tended to the exclusive separation of the chosen people, and even exhibits the dangers of such separation in the direction of a pride and satisfaction in formal worship.

The sources of information which were accessible to the writer of these books are partly mentioned by himself, and may be partly inferred from the nature of the details. The registers and genealogies have the appearance of having been carefully preserved. Moreover, the 'book of the kings of Judah and Israel,' whatever it was, to which he refers so often (II Chr. 16:11; 25, 26, etc.), was evidently some well-known compilation, similar to or partly identical with the existing books of Kings; and other works with similar names are also mentioned. It is most probable that by that time many works of a historical character were in existence. It was a time when all known documents of the past would be carefully treasured, and when even forgotten writings, which had not attracted the attention of former historians, would be sought out, and their materials preserved in the pages of newer compositions. Books were beginning to be multiplied, and the author of the Chronicles seems anxious to assure his readers that he had done his best to verify his facts."—Nelson's "Bible Treasury."

Outline:

I. Genealogical lists to the age of David—Chs. 1–9. From Adam to Jacob (Israel)—1:1–54. Descendants of Judah (Jerahmeel and Caleb)—2:1–55. Descendants of David to Zerubbabel—3:1–24. Descendants of Simeon—4:1–43.

Descendants of Reuben, Gad, and (part of those) of Manasseh—5:1–26. Descendants of Levi (singers, priests, cities of the levites)—6:1–81. Descendants of Issachar, Benjamin, Naphtali (part of), Manasseh, and Ephraim—7:1–40. Descendants of Asher and Benjamin—8:1–40. Supplementary lists of preëxilic inhabitants of Jerusalem and temple servants—9:1–44.

II. David and the temple—Chs. 10–29. Battle of Gilboa and death of Saul—10:1–14. Accession of David; His mighty men—11:1–47. David's friends and helpers—12:1–40. Transfer of the ark to the house of Ober-edom—13:1–14. David's family; his victory over the Philistines—14:1–17. Removal of the ark to Jerusalem—15:1–29. Celebration; Psalm of thanksgiving—16:1–43. David's desire to build a temple; God's message to him and his prayer—17:1–27. David's conquest of Philistia, Moab, and Edom—18:1–17. David's conquest of Ammon and Syria—19:1–19. David's capture of Rabbah and defeat of the Philistines—20:1–8. David's census of Israel; Pestilence—21:1–22:1. David's charge to Solomon to build the temple—22:1–16. David's prescription of Levitical offices—22:17–23:32. Priestly courses; Aaronic and levitical—24:1–29. Courses of singers—25:1–31. Courses of doorkeepers—26:1–19; Keepers of the treasures of the temple; Overseers of business—20–28. Captains of the host; Captains of the tribes; Overseers of the king's possessions—27:1–34. David's final address and charge concerning the temple—28:1–29:5. Contributions; David's prayer—29:6–19. Sacrifices; Coronation of Solomon; David's death—20–30 .

CHRONICLES, SECOND BOOK OF.

1. Name.—From apparent summary of the historical facts.

2. Subject.—From the building of the temple to the rebuilding of the same by decree of Cyrus.

"The contents of the second book, which is simply a continuation of the first, reveal the same plan and purpose —viz., to exhibit prominently all that related to the observances of religion; and the author's pre-occupation with the house of David and the kingdom of Judah goes so far that he only mentions the kingdom of Israel when its affairs touched closely those of the southern kingdom. There are nine chapters devoted to the reign of Solomon, six of them being given to the building and service of the temple (2–7), and two chapters sufficing (8, 9) for the general arrangements in the administration of the kingdom.

In narrating the history of the kings, the chronological order is followed; but it is to be noted that the author dwells at greater length on reigns in which religion was better observed, and also that he gives prominence to the prophets who appear from time to time to remind the kings and the people of their duty. The reigns that are thus dwelt upon are those of Asa (14, 15), whose 'heart was perfect all his days;' of Jehoshaphat (17:1 to 21:1), in whose time provision was made for the instruction of the people in the Law by itinerating priests and Levites (17:7–9); of Hezekiah (29–32), which furnishes the congenial topics of the cleansing of the temple, the observance of a great Passover, and sundry ordinances for the support of the priests and Levites; and of Josiah (34, 35), with the finding of the Law-book, the observance of the Passover, and the general reformation of religion that took place.

The priestly tone of the books of Chronicles may be recognized in the carefully preserved genealogies of the Levitical families, in the manifest interest the author takes in all that relates to the service of the temple, and in his minute acquaintance with its details. This was to be expected of one writing at the time and in the circumstances in which he was placed, when the observance of the ritual was the greatest remaining symbol of the nation's glory. But it should not make us overlook the fact that he is careful to emphasize the activity of prophetic men in the pre-Exilian period when prophecy was an operative factor in the national life. Ahijah the Shilonite (10:15) and Shemaiah 'the man of God' (11:2; 12:5), Azariah the son of Oded (15:1), and Hanani 'the seer' (16:7), and the martyr prophet Zechariah (24:21), are piously commemorated; and the writer, in referring to the works from which he drew materials for his book, cites them by the names of the prophetic men who composed them.''—Nelson's "Bible Treasury.''

3. Outline.—I. Erection of the temple—Chs. 1–7. Solomon's prayer for wisdom; his wealth—1:1–17. Solomon's plan to build the temple; Huram's aid—2:1–18. Description of the temple—3:1–17. The furniture of the temple—4:1–22. Removal of the ark into it—5:1–14. Solomon's address and prayer of dedication—6:1–42. Ceremony and feast of dedication—7:1–22.

II. From Solomon to Jehoshaphat—Chs. 8–20. Solomon's building enterprises; his religious services; his commerce—8:1–18. Visit of the Queen of Sheba; Solomon's glory; his death—9:1–31. Accession of Rehoboam; Evil counsel followed by him; Disruption—10:1–19. Segregation of levites to Judah; Rehoboam's family—11:1–23. In-

29

vasion of Judah by Shishak; Despoiling of the temple; Death of Rehoboam—12:1-15. Reign of Abijah; War with Jeroboam—13:1-22. Reign of Asa; Victory over Zerah the Ethiopian—14:1-15. Reformation under Asa—15:1-19. War with Baasha; Alliance with Ben-hadad (condemned by Haman the seer)—16:1-14. Accession of Jehoshaphat; his greatness—17:1-19. Alliance with Ahab; War with Syria; Consultation of prophets; Michaiah's warning and punishment; Ahab's death—18:1-34. Reformation under Jehoshaphat—19:1-11. War with Ammon and Moab; Victory; Alliance with Ahaziah of Israel—20:1-37.

III. From Jehoram to Hezekiah—Chs. 21-28. Reign of Jehoram: Rebellion of Edom; Elijah's letter; Death of Jehoram—21:1-20. Reign of Ahaziah; Murder by Jehu; Usurpation of Athaliah—22:1-12. Conspiracy of Jehoiada; Deposition and death of Athaliah; Accession of Joash—23:1-21. Reign of Joash: Repairs on the temple; Apostasy and con-

demnation of people by Zechariah—24:1-27. Reign of Amaziah: Wars with Edom and Israel; Defeat—25:1-27. Reign of Uzziah: his leprosy—26:1-23. Reign of Jotham—27:1-9. Reign of Ahaz: Syro-Ephraimite war; Idolatry of Ahaz—28:1-27.

IV. From Hezekiah to the exile and restoration—Chs. 29-36. Accession of Hezekiah: Cleansing of the temple; Sacrifices offered—29:1-36. Observance of the passover—30:1-27. Reformation under Hezekiah—31:1-21. Invasion of Sennacherib; Prosperity of Hezekiah—32:1-32. Reign of Manasseh: Apostasy, punishment, and conversion—33:1-20; Reign of Amon—21-25. Reign of Josiah: Discovery of the Book of the Law; Reformation—34:1-33. Observance of passover under Josiah; Invasion of Neco; Death of Josiah—35:1-27. Reigns of Jehoiakim, Jehoiachin, and Zedekiah; the exile; Decree of Cyrus permitting the rebuilding of the temple—36:1-23.

See JUDAH, ISRAEL, JEREMIAH, ISAIAH, THE MINOR PROPHETS.

EZRA, BOOK OF.

"**The name of Ezra** has been given to the book which introduces into the history of post-Exilian Judaism the scribe who exercised a most powerful influence on its future development. But the book neither professes to have been written by him, nor does it contain all that we know of his activity. Certain portions of it, which are written in the first person—viz., chs. 7:27 to 9:15, are no doubt from his hand; but this very circumstance seems to indicate that the rest, in which he is spoken of in the third person, are not. And it will be found that an account of the most important part of his work is contained in the book of Nehemiah. These two Books, in fact, go together as one whole, and in the Jewish Canon they are reckoned as one book. So, in the Talmud and by Josephus, the two are sometimes spoken of collectively as the book of Ezra, and sometimes its two parts are called first and second Ezra.

Its place in the Hebrew Bible is immediately after the book of Daniel, among the Hagiographa. In this way its account of the Restoration continues the history of the time of the Exile, which is the standpoint of Daniel, and along with Nehemiah it carries on that history as far as the sacred books have carried it; the books of Chronicles closing the Canon with a comprehensive survey of the whole. In our version, on the other hand, the books of Chronicles, which bring down the history to the eve of the Return (though the genealogies extend further), stand immediately after the books of Kings, and then Ezra and Nehemiah follow. And it will be observed that the books of Chronicles break off at a sentence which is found completed in the opening of the book of Ezra.

The time covered by the two books of Ezra and Nehemiah together is about a century; for the narrative of Ezra begins in the first year of the reign of Cyrus, 538 B. C., and that of Nehemiah stops soon after the thirty-second years of Artaxerxes, 432 B. C. A great part of this space, however, is left without record, as we shall see presently; and we may distinguish three periods: 1. The period that elapsed from the first return of exiles to the completion of the temple; 2. The time of Ezra's activity as leader of the second colony of returned exiles; and 3. The period when Ezra and Nehemiah are seen together in the work of reformation at Jerusalem. The first two periods are embraced in the book of Ezra; the last, in the book of Nehemiah.

The contents of the book of Ezra thus fall into two sections, ch. 1–6 giving an account of what happened before he arrived at Jerusalem, and ch. 7–10 narrating Ezra's own journey and the planting of the colony that accompanied him.

1. Cyrus having issued a decree permitting the return of exiled Jews to their own land, a colony under Zerubbabel, or Sheshbazzar, accompanied by Joshua the high-priest, took advantage of the edict, and, arriving at Jerusalem, set up an altar for burnt offering and celebrated the Feast of Tabernacles (1 to 3:6). In the second year the foundations of the temple were laid (3:8–13); but the work of building was impeded by the Samaritans, whose offers of assistance had been refused, till the reign of Darius (4). In the second year of that king's reign the work was resumed under the earnest instigation of the prophets Haggai and Zechariah, though the adversaries did their utmost to hinder it (5); and finally, in the sixth year of Darius—*i. e.*, the year 515 B.C. —the temple was finished, the dedication was celebrated in a joyous feast,

31

and the Passover was observed in the same month (6).

2. A period of fifty-seven years now elapses, till the seventh year of Artaxerxes I., called Longimanus—*i. e.*, 458 B.C. In that year Ezra obtained leave to bring a second colony to the holy city, receiving orders to the local governors, and offerings for the holy house. The journey occupied four months (8:1-32, *cf.* 7:8-10); and Ezra, delivering his credentials and presents to the proper authorities (8:33-36), set about inquiring into the condition of the inhabitants (*cf.* 7:14). When he found that the people, and even the Levites, had contracted mixed marriages and adopted heathen customs, he 'sat down astonied till the evening sacrifice' (9:1-4); and then, in the hearing of the people, made public confession of the national sin (9:5-15). This so moved the people that a public assembly was convened, at which it was agreed that all cases of trespass should be searched out. In two months this work was completed (10: 1-17); and the book closes abruptly with a list of those who had offended, and who pledged themselves to put away their strange wives (10:18-44).'' Nelson's ''Bible Treasury.''

1. **A history of the rebuilding of the second temple (520-458 B.C.) and the restoration of Judah from a priestly standpoint.**

2. **Presuppositions: Historical—The Exile. Literary—Book of Chronicles.**

3. **Language:** Hebrew, ch. 1:1-4:6; 6:19-7:11; 7:28-10:44; Aramaic, 4:7-6: 18; 7:12-28.

4. **Outline:**

I. The restoration—Chs. 1-6. (Time, 520 B.C.). Edict of Cyrus, permitting Jews to return and build the temple in Jerusalem—1:1-10. A list of the returned—2:1-70. Restoration of altar and laying of foundations of temple—3:1-13. Arrest of the work of building at the instigation of adversaries—4:1-24. Resumption of building under encouragement by the prophets Haggai and Zechariah—5:1-5. The letter written by Tattenai to Darius—5:6-17. Edict of Darius in response—6:1-12. Completion of the work; dedication. Observance of passover—6:13-22.

II. The work of Ezra—Chs. 7-10. (Time, 458 B.C.) Appointment by Artaxerxes to beautify the temple—7: 1-10. Letter (commission) given to Ezra by the king—7:11-28. List of Ezra's companions—8:1-14; Halt at the river Ahava—15-30; Arrival at Jerusalem—31-36. Information of mixed marriages: Ezra stupefied—9:1-4; his prayer, 5-15. Reformation under Ezra —10:1-16; List of the offenders—17-44. See JUDAH.

NEHEMIAH, BOOK OF.

"**The name of this book** is given to it from the principal personage who appears in its pages, in the same way as Ezra's name is given to the book which is a companion to this. Certain parts are here also, as in the book of Ezra, written in the first person—viz., ch. 1–7; 12:27–43; 13:4–31, and these we may accept as the work of Nehemiah himself. This book and the book of Ezra properly form one whole, as has been explained under 'the book of Ezra.'

The contents form the sequel to the narrative of the book of Ezra. Ezra arrived in Jerusalem in the seventh year of Artaxerxes, and after the events that are related of him immediately on his arrival we hear nothing more of him till the arrival of Nehemiah, thirteen years later. In the twentieth year of Artaxerxes, Nehemiah, who was cupbearer to the king, being sad at the reports he had received of the condition of Judah, (1) obtained leave of absence, and was sent to Jerusalem as governor of the city. The favor shown to the Jews, and the dignity conferred on a Jewish governor, gave offence to the Samaritans (2:9, 10); but Nehemiah at once took measures for the repairing of the city wall, the local authorities giving him vigorous aid (2:11 to 3:32). He had to keep his workmen under arms to repel threatened attacks of Ammonites and Arabians (4). At the same time, he did not neglect the relief of the poor in the city (5). In fifty-two days the walls were completed. Meantime he had to exercise great prudence in eluding the machinations of his enemies (6); but the work was completed, and faithful men were put in charge over the city and the gates (7:1–4).

About a week after this, Ezra again comes on the scene. There is a great assembly, at which he publicly reads the Law, supported by priests and Levites, who explain what is read, the service being continued from early morn till noon (8:1–12). Then came a celebration of the Feast of Tabernacles, during which there was another public reading of the Law (8:13–18). After this 'the seed of Israel separated themselves from all strangers' (9:1–3), and entered into a solemn covenant to observe the ordinances of the Law (9:4 to 10:39). The population of the city was increased by bringing within the walls a number of inhabitants from the surrounding country (11), and there was a formal service of dedication of the walls (12). Nehemiah was recalled to Persia in the thirty-second year of Artaxerxes (13:6); and when he returned to Jerusalem (at some undefined time), he found that the high-priest, who was related to the Samaritan governor, had actually assigned a chamber in the temple to Tobiah, the governor's associate. Nehemiah cast forth the furniture of Tobiah, and cleansed the chamber, being still engaged in similar work for the protection of the purity of the worship, when the book abruptly closes (13).

The period embraced in the narrative of the book of Nehemiah is only about twelve years, unless Nehemiah's absence at the court of Persia was prolonged. It was, however, a momentous period in the history of the Jews. After the precarious position of the struggling community at the time of Ezra's arrival, the time of the joint activity of Ezra and Nehemiah looked quite prosperous. The building of the wall and the orderly arrangement of the city under a governor of their own race, with all the prestige of the Persian empire, gave the Jews an advantage which the Samaritans might well envy. Above all, we observe now the high regard paid to the Law, and the reading of it as a regular institution, which, more than all walls, more than all imperial favors, tended to foster community of interest, to preserve the national separation of the Jews, and to fit them for the task they had yet to perform in the divine purpose of redemption. From this time onwards there was given special attention to the preservation of the sacred Scriptures, and under a soil that seemed far from fertile lay the seed that was betimes to germinate into a new life.''—Nelson's ''Bible Treasury.''

1. **Supplement to Ezra.**

2. **Subject:** History of the rebuilding of the walls of Jerusalem.

3. **Contents:**

ESTHER, BOOK OF

1. The subject.—Story of preservation of Jews from annihilation.

2. Interest.—Origin of Feast of Purim. Read at this feast.

3. Scene of action.—Court of Persia. Time: Reign of Ahasuerus (Xerxes). More precisely, 483-479 B.C.

"The name of the Hebrew maiden who at the court of Ahasuerus, king of Persia, was the means of saving her people at a crisis in their history, has been given to the little book recording the incidents; and the 'roll of.Esther,' or '*the* roll,' as it is usually called, *par excellence,* is to the Jews one of the most highly valued of the Old Testament writings.

Its place in the English Bible has been determined by the desire to bring together the whole of the historical books. But even thus, it is not in its strict chronological order; and, moreover, in the Hebrew Bible it stands in the third division of the Canon, or Hagiographa, and is reckoned one of the five rolls.

The contents are familiar. Ahasuerus, believed to be Xerxes I., the successor of Darius, having repudiated his queen Vashti, Esther is selected from among the fairest maidens of the empire to take her place. She is a Jewess, brought up by her kinsman Mordecai, who sits at the king's gate; but she conceals her lineage. Haman, a court favorite, takes offence at the want of respect shown to him by Mordecai, and contrives a plot for the massacre of the Jews and the confiscation of their property. Casting lots for an auspicious day on which to present his request to the king, he obtains the desired decree. Mordecai makes known the plot to Esther, and entreats her to intercede with the king for her nation, which she determines to do. In furtherance of her plan, she invites the king and Haman to a banquet. Haman, taking this as a token of royal favor, flatters himself with the success of his scheme, and prepares a gallows for Mordecai. The king, in a sleepless night, has the state records read to him, and learns that Mordecai had once discovered a plot against him, for which he had not been rewarded. When he meets Haman next day he asks him, 'What shall be done to the man whom the king delighteth to honour?' and Haman, thinking only of himself, suggests a state pageant and a proclamation, and is ordered to carry out the suggestion in honor of Mordecai. Esther reveals the plot of Haman, who is hanged on the gallows he had prepared for his enemy; and orders are issued to the Jews in all the provinces to defend themselves against the attack which Haman's proclamation had authorized. In memory of their deliverance, and with reference to Haman's casting of lots, the feast of Purim (*i. e.,* 'lots') is instituted. The feast continues to be observed to the present day.

The historical value of the book can scarcely be called in question. The reference to the feast of Purim at an early date (II Macc.) as 'the feast of Mordecai,' and the continued celebration of it to the present time, can have no other explanation. All that is known of Xerxes also agrees with the part he plays in the book. He was fickle, capricious, ruled by court favorites, extravagant in his habits. The third year of his reign, at which the book opens, which would be about 482 B.C., would answer to the time at which his army was collected for the disastrous war with the Greeks, and between that and the seventh year, when Esther was made queen, would fall his defeats at Thermopylæ and Salamis, 480 B. C.''—Nelson's "Bible Treasury."

4. Contents:

I. The danger of the Jews—Chs. 1-5.

JOB.

Poem (poetical book) in which the problem of the righteous man suffering is dramatically discussed.

1. **The principal persons:**

Job: a wealthy and upright man in the land of Uz.

Satan: Accuser, who raises charge of selfishness as the motive of Job's goodness.

Job's friends: Eliphaz, the Temanite; Bildad, the Shuhite; Zophar, the Naamathite. Advocates of the current view: that suffering is the punishment of sin.

Elihu, the Buzite: Defender of God's righteousness in inflicting suffering.

Jehovah: Challenger of Job in his own behalf.

2. **The plan:**

I. PROLOGUE.—Narrative introduction:

Picturing Job and recounting:

(1) The occasion and circumstances of Job's loss of his children and property—1:1-22.

(2) The infliction of disease on his person—2:1-10.

(3) The arrival of his friends— 2:11-13.

The Theme.—Job's criticism of providence; the problem of suffering— 3:1-26.

II. THE DISCUSSION BETWEEN JOB AND HIS FRIENDS:

A. *First cycle of speeches*—Chs. 4-14.

Eliphaz's first speech: God is just; man is insignificant—4: 1-21.

The wicked are insecure—5:1-7. God helps the needy—5:8-16. Chastisement is beneficial—5:17-27.

Job's answer: (a) He is in wretchedness. His friends are deceitful—6:1-13. His life is wearisome—6:14-23; 6:24-30.

(b) He appeals to God—7:1-21.

Bildad's first speech: God favors the righteous and destroys the sinner—8:1-22.

Job's answer: (a) God is indeed powerful—9:1-24; but He is arbitrary—9:25-35. (b) He protests to God against his treatment—10:1-22.

Zophar's first speech: Job's impiety—11:1-6. Ignorance—11: 7-12. He must put away iniquity—11:13-20.

Job's answer: (a) Scorns his accusers—12:1-6; and affirms God's power—12:7-25; and his own integrity—13:1-19. (b) Prays to be delivered—13:20-28; and plead's man frailty— 14:1-22.

B. *Second cycle of speeches*—Chs. 15-21.

Eliphaz's second speech: Job is presumptuous—15:1-16. Sinners shall be speedily cut off— 15:17-35.

Job's answer: (a) Reproaches his friends—16:1-5; and complains of God's treatment—16:6-17. (b) Appeals to God to testify for him—16:18-17:5; and laments his condition—17:6-16.

Bildad's second speech: Job claims too much—18:1-4. The lot of sinners is awful—18:5-21.

Job's answer: God is his advocate ("Redeemer")—19:1-29.

Zophar's second speech: Vengeance comes swift upon sinners—20:1-29.

Job's answer: The wicked prosper—21:1-16. Sinners are not always punished—21:17-34.

C. *Third cycle of speeches*—Chs. 22-31.

Eliphaz's third speech: Job is guilty of great iniquity—22:1-

37

20. He must return to God—22:21-30.

Job's answer: He longs for access to God—23:1-9. Declares his innocence—23:10-17. God is indifferent to moral issues—24:1-25.

Bildad's third speech: Man's nothingness before God—25:1-6.

Job's answer: God is indeed supreme—26:1-14.

(Zophar fails to make a third speech.)

Job's supplementary discourses:

First discourse.—He is right as against his friends—27:1-12. Vanity of the hope of the godless—27:13-23. The difficult search for wisdom—28:1-28.

Second discourse.—Job's past happiness—29:1-25. His present wretchedness—30:1-31. The integrity of his life—31:1-40.

III. JUDGMENT OF ELIHU.—Son of Barachel, the Buzite: Dissatisfied with the views expressed—32:1-6.

(1) His impatience, desire to speak and qualifications for so doing—Vs. 7-31. His reproof of Job for self-justification—33:1-12. God does reveal himself in dreams—Vs. 13-18. In sickness—Vs. 19-22. By angels—Vs. 23-33.

(2) Vindicates God's justice. States Job's case—34:1-9. God is just—Vs. 10-15. He is supreme—Vs. 16-20. He governs all—Vs. 21-30. Job has sinned—Vs. 31-37.

(3) God is above being hurt by the wickedness of man or benefited by his righteousness—35:1-8. He is the source of all good; gives but does not receive—35:9-16.

(4) God in his sovereignty uses affliction for the good of men—36:1-16. Job ought to submit to chastisement—Vs. 17-23; and magnify God for his unsearchable greatness in nature—Vs. 24-33 (rainstorm) 37:1-13. His inscrutable ways in nature—Vs. 13-24.

IV. JEHOVAH'S SELF-VINDICATION.

(1) First challenge Job's ignorance and impotence as to:

The origin of the world—38:1-7.
The boundaries and restraints—Vs. 8-11.
The day and the night—Vs. 12-15.
The sea and land—Vs. 16-18.
Light, snow and hail, rain and ice—Vs. 19-30.
The stars—Vs. 31-33.
Thunder, lightning and flood—Vs. 34-38.
Wild beasts—Vs. 39:4-12.
Birds—Vs. 13-18.
The war-horse—Vs. 19-25.
The hawk and the eagle—Vs. 26-30.

Summary: Challenge—40:1, 2. Job's first surrender—Vs. 3:5.

(2) Jehovah's second challenge—40:6-41:34. Job's powerlessness—40:7-14.

Description of behemoth—40:15-24.

Description of leviathan—41:1-34.

Job's complete surrender—42:1-6.

V. THE EPILOGUE: Job's restored prosperity—42:7-17.

PSALMS.

Poetic expressions of religious feeling and thought.—I Chr. 16:7, 9; Ps. 95:2, 105:2; Eph. 5:19; Col. 3:16; Jas. 5:13.

Book of Psalms (*Psalter*): Alluded to in N. T.—Lu. 20:42; 24:44; Acts 1:20.

Subdivision into five books: I. Ps. 1–41. II. Ps. 42–72. III. Ps. 73–89. IV. Ps. 90–106. V. Ps. 107–150.

A. Classification according to titles:

ASCRIBED TO: David, in title—Ps. 3–32, 34–41, 51–65, 68–70, 72, 86, 101, 103, 108–110, 122, 124, 131, 133, 138–145. David elsewhere—Ps. 2, in Acts 4:25; Ps. 95, in Heb. 4:7. Asaph—Ps. 50, 73–83. Korah, the sons of—Ps. 42, 44–49, 84, 85, 87, 88 (also Heman). Solomon—Ps. 72, 127. Moses—Ps. 90. Ethan—Ps. 89. Heman—Ps. 88. (Also to "Sons of Korah.")

ANONYMOUS: (1) With merely descriptive titles—Ps. 66, 67, 92, 98, 100, 102, 120, 121, 123, 125, 126, 128–130, 132, 134, 135. (2) Without titles of any kind ("orphaned" Psalms)—Ps. 1, 2, 10, 33, 43, 71, 91, 93–97, 99, 104–107, 111–119, 136, 137, 146–150. Psalms with historic occasions—Ps. 3, 7, 18, 34, 51, 52, 54, 56, 57, 59, 60, 63, 102, 142.

B. Classification according to subject-matter and design:

I. DIDACTIC: The ideal man—Ps. 1, 15, 112, 128. The wicked man—Ps. 10, 14, 36, 37, 52, 53, 73, 75, 82. God a helper—Ps. 12. Power and majesty of God—Ps. 76, 77. Works and word of God—Ps. 19, 119. Omniscience of God—Ps. 139. Jehovah the true God—Ps. 115. Vanity of human life—Ps. 39, 49, 90. Zion's glory—Ps. 48, 122. Citizenship in Zion—Ps. 87. Fraternal unity—Ps. 133.

II. DEVOTIONAL: *Adoration*—Of the Creator of man—Ps. 8. Of the Lord of the storm—Ps. 29. Of the King of the earth—Ps. 47, 67, 93, 95. Of the Judge—Ps. 50. Exhortation to worship—Ps. 134. Consecration—Ps. 116.

Thanksgiving—Ps. 30, 40, 66, 92, 104, 138, 145.

Praise: General—Ps. 22, 28, 31, 103, 111, 113, 117, 138, 149, 150. For deliverance—Ps. 21, 107, 124, 126. For mercy in providence and nature—Ps. 33, 34, 65, 66, 92, 104, 136, 148. For mercy and judgment—Ps. 101. For power and mercy—Ps. 147. For righteousness—Ps. 98. For fidelity to Israel—Ps. 97, 100, 108. For forgiveness—Ps. 32. For victory—Ps. 18, 68. Praise and trust—Ps. 146.

Penitence—Ps. 6, 32, 38, 51, 102, 130, 143.

Petition: For help—Ps. 13, 28, 40, 70. For protection—Ps. 17. For victory over enemies—Ps. 20. For guidance and pardon—Ps. 25. For rescue from enemies—Ps. 35, 57. For deliverance from trouble—Ps. 43, 44, 56, 59, 64, 71, 140, 144. For defence against enemies—Ps. 54. For the punishment of the wicked—Ps. 55, 58. For mercy—Ps. 86, 123. Against death—Ps. 88. For divine favor—Ps. 143. For guidance—Ps. 141. Comfort in prayer—Ps. 142.

Imprecation—Ps. 35, 58, 69, 83, 109, 129.

Complaint—Ps. 31, 41, 74, 120.

Lament—Ps. 60, 79, 102, 137.

Longing—Ps. 84.

Comfort—Ps. 77.

Trust—Ps. 3, 4, 7, 11, 16, 23, 27, 37, 42, 46, 61, 62, 91, 118, 121, 125, 127, 130.

Humility—Ps. 131.

III. HISTORICAL—Ps. 78, 81, 89, 105, 106, 114, 132.

IV. PROCESSIONAL—Ps. 24.

V. MESSIANIC—Ps. 2, 22, 40, 45, 72, 97, 110, 118 (mostly indirect).

C. Classification according to literary form and original design:

Temple songs—Ps. 4, 11, 15, 19, 23, 26, 27, 30, 33, 44–47, 49, 50, 65, 67, 74, 76, 79, 81, 82, 92, 95, 100.

Historical poems—Ps. 78, 81, 89, 104–107, 114, 132. *The captivity*— Ps. 40, 42, 43, 70, 102. *The return* —Ps. 78, 124, 126, 129.

Elegies—Ps. 39, 90.

Hymns—Ps. 62, 91, 93, 96, 97, 103, 139. *The Hallel*—Ps. 113, 115– 117. *Hallelujah*—Ps. 146–150.

Pilgrim Psalms—Ps. 121–123, 125, 127, 128, 130, 131, 133, 134.

Acrostics—Ps. 37, 111, 145, 9, 10, 25, 119.

Royal Psalms—Ps. 20, 21, 61, 101, 24, 8, 19, 29.

The Temple: Laying the foundations—Ps. 85, 132, 136. The building—Ps. 118.

Messianic: The suffering Messiah— Ps. 22, 35, 69. The triumphant Messiah—Ps. 2, 72, 110.

Confessional—Ps. 6, 13, 38.

LITURGICAL AND MUSICAL TERMS:—*Liturgical: Psalm,* prefixed to 57 Psalm (generally Davidic). *Song,* prefixed to 30 Psalms. *Prayer,* prefixed to Pss. 17, 86, 90, 102, 142. *Praise,* prefixed to Ps. 145. *Maschil* (meditation)—Pss. 32, 42, 44, 45, 52–55, 74, 78, 88, 89, 142. *Michtam* (Golden piece, gem, Select song)—Pss. 16, 56–60. *Shiggaion* (Obscure term, may be musical)—Ps. 7.

MUSICAL.—*General*: *To the Chief musician* (R. *For the Chief musician*), prefixed to 55 Psalms, all Davidic but 66 and 67. *Selah* (used 71 times, in some Psalms more than once).

MUSICAL INSTRUMENTS: *On Neginoth* (R. *On stringed instruments*)— Pss. 4, 6, 54, 55, 67, 76. Upon *Neginah* (R. *On a stringed instrument*)—Ps. 61. *Upon Nehiloth* (R. *With the Nehiloth,* mg. *Wind instruments*)—Ps. 5.

MELODIES OR TUNES: *Upon Alamoth* (R. *Set to Alamoth, in the manner of maidens,* or *for maidens' voices:* Soprano)—Ps. 46. *Upon Sheminith* (R. *Set to the Sheminith,* or *Eighth*: Tenor or Bass)—Pss. 6, 12. *Upon Gittith* (R. *Set to the Gittith,* or *Gittite melody*)—Pss. 8, 81, 84. *To Jeduthun* (R. *After the manner of Jeduthun,* probably melody named after a chief musician)—Pss. 62, 77. *Set to Muthlabben*—Ps. 9. *Set to Aijeleth Hash-Shahar,* mg. *The hind of the morning*—Ps. 22. *Set to Shoshannim* (mg. *Lilies*)—Pss. 45. 69. *Set to Shoshannim-eduth* (mg. *Lilies, a testimony*)—Ps. 80. *Set to Shushan-eduth* (mg. *The Lily of testimony*)—Ps. 60. *Set to Jonath elem rehokim* (mg. *"The silent dove of them that are afar off," "the dove of the distant terebinths"*)—Ps. 56. *Set to Altashheth* (mg. *"destroy not"*)—Pss. 57, 58, 59, 75. *Set to Mahalath*— Ps. 53. *Set to Mahalath Leannoth* (mg. *"for singing"*)—Ps. 88.

METHOD OF PERFORMANCE: *A Song of degrees* (R. *A Song of ascents*), either processional up to the temple, or from the place of recitation, or from the nature of the music accompanying the words— Pss. 120–134. See POETRY.

FORMS OF WISDOM LITERATURE.*

Wisdom.—The Biblical term corresponding to our philosophy and science.

Unit Proverb.

Popular proverbs, quoted in I *Samuel* x. 12, xxiv. 13; *Ezekiel* xvi. 44. **Riddles** (*Song of Songs* viii. 8–9; *Judges* xv. 16). (**Cycle**, or Game of riddles —*Judges* xiv.)

Sayings or sentences of the wise: Unit of thought in unit of form.

Doctrine and supplement, such as *Proverbs* x. 1; xvi. 32; xi. 31, etc.

Doctrine distributed, such as *Proverbs* xx. 14; xv. 16; xxiv. 26.

Here may be mentioned the **Fable** (*Judges* ix. 8–15; II *Kings* xiv. 9) and the **Parable** (in the Gospels; or II *Samuel* xii. 1–6, xiv. 4–9). These, however, never attain distinctness as a separate literary form; the nearest approach to this is the **Dramatized Parable** of the *Book of Job*, in which Wisdom literature, Epic, Drama, and Rhetoric are amalgamated.

Wisdom literature tending prosewards.

Maxims: in the form of texts with comments.—*Ecclesiasticus* i. 22–24, 25–27, 28–30; ii. 1–6; v. 4–8; vi. 2–4; vii. 4–6; xi. 7–8, 10; xviii. 30–1; xviii. 32–xix. 1(a); xix. 1(b)–3; xx. 14–15, 24–26; xxi. 2, 22–24; xxii. 7, 8, 13; xxv. 3–6; xxvi. 29–xxvii. 2; xxvii. 16–21, 22–4; xxxii. 18; xxxiv. 9–12; xl. 28–30. *St. James* i. ·2–4, 5–8, 9–11; iv. 11–12; v. 19–20. *Ecclesiastes* iv. 9–12, 13–16; v. 1–7, 8–9; vii. 1–6, 8–10, 11–12, 13–14, 15–18, 20–22; x. 2–3, 5–7, 12–14; xi. 6. The Maxims enlarge into the **discourses:** *St. James* iv. 1–10; iv. 13–v. 18.

Proverb cluster: Aggregation of unit proverbs (with epigrams and max-

ims) on a common theme.—*Proverbs* xxv. 2–7—The king; xxvi. 3–12— On fools; xxvi. 13–16—On sluggards; xxvi. 17–26—On social pests. *Ecclesiasticus* v. 9–vi. 1—Government of the tongue; xi. 7–10—Meddlesomeness; xviii. 15–18 — Graciousness; xxi. 1–10—Sin and its judgment; 11–26—Wise men and fools; xxi. 27–xxii. 5—Hatefulness of evil; xxii. 6–15—Commerce with fools intolerable; xxv. 16–xxvi. 18 —Women bad and good; xxvii. 11– 15—Discourse of fools.

The Essay: *Ecclesiasticus* iii. 1–16— Honor to parents; iii. 17–28—Meekness; iv. 1–10—Considerateness for high and low; iv. 11–19—Wisdom's way with her children; iv. 20:8— True and false shame; vi. 5–17— Friendship; vi. 18:37—Pursuit of wisdom; vii. 19–36—Household precepts; viii.–ix. 16—Adaptation of behaviour to various sorts of men; ix. 17–x. 5—Wisdom and government; x. 6–xi. 6—Pride and true greatness; xi. 11–28—Prosperity and adversity from the Lord; xi. 29–xiii. 24—Choice of company; xiv. 3–19—Niggardliness; xiv. 20– xv. 10—The pursuer of wisdom and his reward; xv. 11–20—Free will; xvi. 1–23—No safety for sinners in numbers; xvi. 24–xviii. 14—God's work of creation and restoration; xviii. 19–27—On taking heed in time; xix. 4–17— Against gossip; xix. 20–xx. 13— Wisdom and its counterfeits; xxii. 16:26—The steadfast friend and the uncertain; xxiii. 7–15—The discipline of the mouth; xxiii. 16–27— The horror of adultery; xxv. 16– xxvi. 4—Women bad and good; xxvii. 25–xxviii. 11—Retribution

---

and vengeance; xxviii. 12–26—On the tongue; xxix. 1–20—On the lending and suretyship; xxix. 21–28 —The blessing of a house of one's own; xxx. 1–13—Chastisement of children; xxx. 14–25—On health; xxxi. 1–11—On riches; xxxi. 12–xxxii. 13—On feasting; xxxiii. 7–15—An analogy; xxxiii. 19–23—On giving and bequeathing; xxxiii. 24–31—On servants; xxxiv. 1–8—On dreams; xxxiv. 18–xxxv—Sacrifices, evil and acceptable; xxxvi. 21–26 —On wives; xxxvii. 1–6—False Friends; xxxvii. 7–26—On counsel and counsellors; xxxvii. 27–xxxviii. 15—Disease and physicians; xxxviii. 16–23—On mourning for the dead; xxxviii. 24–xxxix. 11—There is one wisdom for the busy and one for the man of leisure; xl. 1–10—The burden of life; xli. 5–13—The posterity of sinners; xli. 14–xlii. 8—Things to be ashamed of; xlii. 9–14 —Women as a source of trouble. St. James i. 12–27—On the sources of the evil and the good in us; ii. 1–13—On respect of persons; ii. 14–26 —On faith and works; iii. 1–12— On the responsibility of speech; iii. 13–18—The earthly wisdom and the wisdom from above. *Ecclesiastes* i. 12–ii.—Solomon's search for wisdom; iii.–iv. 8—The philosophy of times and seasons (including a sonnet); v. 10–vi. 12—The vanity of desire; vii. 23–ix. 16—The search for wisdom, with notes by the way; xi. 7–xii. 7—Life as a joy shadowed by the judgment (latter part in sonnet form).

The (Rhetoric) Encomium: *Ecclesiasticus* xxxix. 16–31—On God's works (inwoven into preface to Book IV); xlii. 15–xliii—On the works of the Lord; xliv. 1–24—On famous men.

Wisdom literature tending versewards.

Epigram: a unit proverb organically enlarged.—*Proverbs* xxiii. 1–3—Awe before appetite; xxiii. 4–5—The transitoriness of riches; xxiii. 6–8—Hospitality of the evil eye; xxiii. 19–21—Gluttony; xxiii. 26–28 —The pit of whoredom; xxiv. 11–12

—The duty of rescue; xxiv. 13–14—Wisdom and honey; xxiv. 23–25—Respect of persons; xxx. 32–33—The restraining of wrath; xxxi. 4–9 —Kings and wine. *Ecclesiasticus* vii. 1–3—Sowing sin and reaping; xxv. 13–15—The wrath of an enemy; xxvii. 5–7—Reasoning the test of men. Other epigrams are: *Proverbs* i. 8–9; ix. 7–9, 10–12; xxii. 22–23, 24–25, 26–27; xxiii. 10–11, 13–14, 15–16, 17–18, 24–25; xxiv. 1–2, 3–4, 5–6, 15–16, 17–18, 19–20, 21–22, 24–25, 28–29; xxv. 6–7, 9–10, 21–22; xxvi. 24–26; xxvii. 10, 15–16; xxx. 5–6, 17, 20. *Ecclesiasticus* v. 2–3, 14, 15; xiv. 1–2; xx. 16–17, 30–31; xxi. 11–12, 13–14, 15, 16–17, 19–21; xxii. 1–2; xxvii. 4–7; xxxii. 16–17, 20–22; xxxvi. 18–19; l. 28–29. *Ecclesiastes* x. 16–17, 20; xi. 3.

Fixed or number sonnet: *Proverbs* vi. 16–19—The sower of discord; xxx. 7–9—The golden mean; xxx. 15–16 —Things never satisfied; xxx. 18–19—Things not to be known; xxx. 21–23—Things not to be borne; xxx. 24–28—Little and wise; xxx. 29–31—Things stately in their going. *Ecclesiasticus* xxiii. 16–18 (part of an essay); xxv. 1–2—What wisdom hates and loves; xxv. 7–11—The love of the Lord; xxvi. 5–6—Women bad and good; xxvi. 28—The backslider; l. 25–26—The hated nations.

Free sonnet: *Proverbs* i. 10–19—The company of sinners; ii.—Wisdom the preservative from evil; iii. 1–10—The commandment and its reward; iii. 11–20—Wisdom the prize in view; iii. 21–26—Wisdom and security; iii. 27–35—Wisdom and perversity; iv. 1–9—The tradition of wisdom; iv. 10–19—The two paths; iv. 20–27—Wisdom and health; v.—The strange woman; vi. 1–5—Suretyship; vi. 6–11—The sluggard; vi. 12–19 (a pair of sonnets)—The sower of discord; vi. 20–35—The folly of adultery; ix. (sonnet of sonnets)—The house of wisdom and the house of folly; xxiii. 29–35—Woes of wine; xxiv. 30–34—The field of the slothful;

xxvii. 23–27—Folk song of good husbandry; xxx. 1–4—The unsearchableness of God; xxx. 11–14—An evil generation; xxxi. 10–31 (acrostic)—The virtuous woman. *Ecclesiasticus* i. 1–20—Wisdom and the fear of the Lord; ii. 7–18—True and false fear; xxii. 11–12—Fools and the dead; xxii. 27–xxiii. 6—Watchfulness of lips and heart; xxvi. 7–18—Women bad and good; xxxiv. 13–17—The fearers of the Lord; xl. 11–27 (a pair of sonnets)—A garden of blessings; xli. 1–4—On death.

Ecclesiastes iii. 1–8 (part of an essay)—Times and seasons; xii. 1–7 (part of an essay)—The coming of the evil days.

Dramatic monologue: *Proverbs* i. 20–33—Wisdom's cry of warning; vii.–viii.—Wisdom and the strange woman. *Ecclesiasticus* xxiv. 3–22—Wisdom's praise of herself. Compare *Ecclesiastes* i. 12–ii.—Solomon's search for wisdom. *Wisdom of Solomon* ii. 1–20 and v. 3–13—The wicked before and after death; vi.–ix.—Solomon on wisdom.

THE PROVERBS.*

A miscellany of wisdom in five books.

i. 1–6. *Title to the whole collection*
7. *Motto to the whole collection.*

BOOK I.

Sonnets on wisdom.

i–ix.

i. 8–9. Epigram.
10–19. Sonnet: The company of sinners.
20–33. Dramatic monologue: Wisdom's cry of warning.
ii. Sonnet: Wisdom the deliverer from evil.
iii. 1–10. Sonnet: The commandment and the reward.
11–20. Sonnet: The creator has made wisdom the supreme prize.
21–6. Sonnet: Wisdom and security.
27–35. Sonnet: Wisdom and perversity.
iv. 1–9. Sonnet: The tradition of wisdom.
10–19. Sonnet: The two paths.
20–7. Sonnet: Wisdom and health.
v. Sonnet: The strange woman.
vi. 1–5. Sonnet: Suretyship.
6–11. Sonnet: The sluggard.
12–19. A pair of sonnets: The sower of discord.
20–35. Sonnet: Adultery the supreme folly.
vii.–viii. Monologue—Wisdom: Wisdom and the strange woman.
ix. Sonnet of sonnets: The house of wisdom and the house of folly [1–6 (sonnet) is strophe to which 13–18 is antistrophe; 7–9 (epigram) is strophe to which 10–12 is antistrophe].

BOOK II.

The Proverbs of Solomon.

x–xxii:16.

x.–xxii. 16. *Collection of isolated unit proverbs; no appearance of arrangement.*

BOOK III.

A Wisdom Epistle.

xxii:17–xxiv.

xxii. 17–21. *Superscription to the epistle.*
22–9. *Disconnected sayings [Short epigrams and unit Proverbs].*
xxiii. 1–3. Epigram: Awe before appetite.
4–5. Epigram: Transitoriness of riches.
6–8. Epigram: Hospitality of the evil eye.
9–18. *Disconnected sayings.*
19–21. Epigram: Gluttony.
22–5. *Disconnected sayings.*
26–8. Epigram: The pit of whoredom.
29–35. Sonnet: Wine and woe.
xxiv. 1–10. *Disconnected sayings.*
11–12. Epigram: The duty of rescue.
13–14. Epigram: Wisdom and honey.
15–22. *Disconnected sayings.*
Postscript.
xxiv. 23–5. Epigram: Respect of persons.
26–9. *Disconnected sayings.*
30–4. Sonnet: The field of the slothful.

* Taken from the "Literary Study of the Bible," by Richard G. Moulton. Copyright, 1895 and 1899. Used by permission.

ECCLESIASTES.

Text.—The preacher takes for his text the pessimistic words, "Vanity of vanities, all is vanity." He sticks to his text throughout. Hence we do not have a book of good cheer and hopefulness, but a catalogue of things that disappointed the preacher. He gives himself up to a study of all that is painful and unsatisfying in human experience. He pours forth his complaints as boldly as did Job, and he seems not to have had any such deep experience of grace as that of the great patriarch. He was a man of reflection, a sage sorely disturbed by the evils all about him in human life. He gives such full and frank expression to his scepticism and his pessimism that he is counted by many modern critics as a confirmed doubter, the expressions of his faith in a general judgment and a future life being regarded as interpolations or additions to his manuscript. While frankly recognizing the many sceptical and gloomy paragraphs as coming from the inspired author, we must protest against the notion that he rested permanently on the lower levels reached in his search for the evils of human life. He has described fearlessly all that he could find fault with in man's experience. He sets out to paint the vanity of human life, and he sticks to his text. The result is not atheism nor materialism nor confirmed pessimism, but a doctrine of man's littleness and helplessness apart from faith. There can be no doubt about the author's belief in God and the judgment. He calls his readers to a prudent enjoyment of life's pleasures, reminding them of the inevitable sorrows and disappointments of life. He is made sad by the oppressions and miseries around him, and his note nowhere becomes jubilant. Moderation, prudence, contentment, and resignation in the face of life's sorrows and evils are the goal to which he would conduct his readers.

Contents.

Title.—Eccl. 1:1. The monotonous repetitions in nature and in man lead to no goal. Man's labor brings him no permanent profit—1:2-11. Even wisdom fails to satisfy man's soul or to enable him to set things right—1:12-18. Pleasure also fails to satisfy, even when one is able to provide for himself all that men seek as an aid to enjoyment—2:1-11. Though wisdom is superior to folly, the wise man dies even as the fool, and often a wise man leaves the fruits of his toil to a fool—2:12-23. The best course open to the wise man is the enjoyment in moderation of what God gives him—2:24-26. Men are powerless in the grip of the Almighty, who foreordains all things. Although God has set eternity in man's heart, yet he cannot find out God's work. The best thing possible is the quiet enjoyment of what God gives him—3:1-15. The preacher has tried to get satisfaction in the thought of a judgment by God hereafter; but man resembles the beasts in his subjection to death—3:16-22. Man's misery may be seen in the oppression of man by his fellow and in foolish rivalries—4:1-6. A solitary man is at a great disadvantage as compared with a man who has a companion—4:7-12. The vanity of popular enthusiasm for a new king—4:13-16. Ignorance and hypocrisy mar man's religious life—5:1-7. Oppression and violence mar man's social life—5:8, 9. Riches only bring greater burdens on the owner, and an evil chance often sweeps them away—5:10-17. Hence it is wise for a man to enjoy the fruits of his labor while he can—5:18-20. God often gives a man riches with no power to enjoy them, and even if a man has good digestion, hunger keeps on his track—6:1-9. Man is helpless and short-sighted—6:10-12. Sad things are to be preferred. Wisdom is better than prop-

46

erty—7:1–14. Seek "the golden mean" between extremes—7:15–18. Wisdom is valuable, but one must not know everything, lest he hear his servant curse him —7:19–22. Man is hardly to be trusted, and woman not at all—7:23–29. Wisdom is valuable in a time of oppression, for the wise man will be patient and prudent; but he cannot read the future nor vanquish death—8:1–8. The wicked are often honored, and even when they are punished, there is often great delay before the sentence is executed—8:9–13. The wicked and the righteous do not receive their just deserts. When the preacher tried to understand this problem he failed altogether—8:14–9:1. It is an evil that death comes alike to the wise man and to the fool, and after death men are forgotten—9:2–6. Hence man ought to enjoy himself as best he can, and do with his might whatever he finds to do—9:7–10. Man cannot control circumstances nor foresee the day of his death—9:11, 12. The wise man often loses the reward due him—9:13–16. A group of proverbs contrasting wisdom and folly—9:17–10:20. The wisdom of a beneficent and industrious life. There will be sad days enough—11:1–8. Enjoy life in youth, not unmindful of the Creator, nor forgetting the weakness and helplessness of old age—11:9–12:8. Concluding proverbs—12:9–12. The end of the matter is to fear God and keep His commandments, for God will finally bring every work into judgment— 12:13, 14.

It is fitting that the Bible should contain a book in which the ills of human life should be portrayed in all their nakedness. The preacher was tempted to renounce God, but he didn't. We have much greater light than he, and would be without excuse, if we should fall into pessimism in the gospel dispensation.

THE SONG OF SONGS.

Character of the book.—Many of the best commentators of the last century have treated the song as a unity. They speak of it as belonging to the realm of dramatic poetry, though none imagine that it was to be acted before an audience. Many recent students prefer to regard it as a collection of love songs with no well-defined plot. The early Jewish and Christian interpreters regarded it as an allegory, the bridegroom representing Jehovah, or Christ, and the bride being his people or the soul of the believer. Modern opinion leans toward a literal interpretation rather than the allegorical. According to the literal interpretation, the Song is a collection of short poems in which the mutual love of man and woman finds fervid and chaste expression. Marriage, we are told, is ordained of God's Word. A few combine the literal and the allegorical views into a typical interpretation, the lovers being in the first instance Solomon and a Shulammite maiden, but typical of Christ and the church. The Song of Songs was written primarily for Orientals, and, judged by their standards, is eminently chaste.

Outline.—No two commentators make precisely the same analysis of the poem. We may be able to help the English reader by distinguishing the male and the female addresses throughout the poem. The poem opens with an address to the bride—1:2–7. The first response is perhaps made by the daughters of Jerusalem—1:8. Then the bridegroom speaks to the bride—1:9–11. The bride replies to her lover—1:12–14. The bridegroom then praises the bride—1:15, and the bride replies—1:16–2:1. The lover again praises the bride—2:2, and she reciprocates—2:3–6. The following verse should be rendered: "I adjure you, O daughters of Jerusalem, by the roes or by the hinds of the fields, that ye stir not up, nor awake love, until it please" —2:7. The bride continues her address —2:8–14. The following verse should be translated like 2:7, as above. The speaker in the remainder of chapter 3 is not fully revealed, though it may well be the bride—4:1–15. The bride makes a brief response—4:16. The bridegroom then speaks again—5:1. The bride relates a distressing experience—perhaps a dream—5:2–8. The daughters of Jerusalem reply to the bride's closing words —5:9. The bride sings the praises of her lover to the daughters of Jerusalem— 5:10–16. Response of the daughters of Jerusalem—6:1. The bride replies—6:2, 3. The bridegroom again addresses the bride—6:4–9. The speakers in the remainder of chapter 6 are not so clearly revealed; but verse 10 and the first half of verse 13 are probably by the daughters of Jerusalem, and verses 11, 12, and the latter half of 13 by the bride. The bridegroom again describes the physical charms of the bride—7:1–9a. The bride responds—7:9b–8:3. Translate 8:4 as 2:7. In each case it seems to close an address by the bride. Perhaps the daughters of Jerusalem ask the question in the first part of 8:5. Then the bride speaks—8:5b–7. We do not know who the speakers are in 8:8, 9; possibly the brother of the Shulammite. The bride resumes—8:10–12. The closing words of the bridegroom follow—8:13, and the bride's words are the last in the Song— 8:14.

We may be permitted to say in closing that this poem seems more chaste and beautiful after twenty years of careful study than it did at first.

ISAIAH.

Meaning of the name.—Isaiah in Hebrew means *"The Salvation of Jehovah."* **The son of Amoz.**—Is. 1:1; 2:1; 13:1; 20:2; 37:2, etc. We know nothing additional concerning Amoz, but he must not be confounded with Amos the prophet, whose name is spelled quite differently in Hebrew.

Home.—Isaiah lived in Jerusalem—Is. 7:3; 8:1, 2; 37:1-7, 33-35; 38:1-8; 39:1-8. Isaiah was probably born and educated in Jerusalem, and his devotion to his native city has never been surpassed by any of the world's greatest patriots. His message was to Judah and Jerusalem.

Wife and sons.—His wife he calls "the prophetess," which probably means that she, too, received messages from God like Deborah and Huldah—Is. 8:3. There were born to them two sons, whose names were signs of coming events: Shear-jashub, meaning "a remnant shall return," while Maher-shalal-hash-baz meant "speed-spoil-hurry-prey"—Is. 7:3; 8:3, 18.

Date.—Isaiah began to prophesy in the year that King Uzziah died—Is. 6:1. Ussher's date for this event is 758 B.C., but recent scholars, following the lead of the students of Assyrian history, prefer a date from 740 to 736 B.C. Isaiah prophesied throughout the reigns of Jotham, Ahaz and Hezekiah—Is. 1:1. His ministry must have continued to the close of the eighth century B.C., and probably came to an end in the first decade of the seventh century B.C. He was contemporary with Hosea and Micah.

Relation to kings of Judah.—Began to prophesy in the year that King Uzziah died—Is. 6:1. Wrote a history of Uzziah's reign—II Chr. 26:22. Prophesied during the prosperous reign of Jotham—Is. 1:1. Sought to induce Ahaz to lean on Jehovah, rather than Pul, for aid—Is. 7:1-17. Predicted disasters that would come upon Judah through the foolish policy of Ahaz in inviting the Assyrians to attack his foes, Syria and Israel—Is. 7:18-25. Predicted the recovery of Hezekiah from a mortal illness—Is. 20:1-7. Foretold the downfall of Egypt and Ethiopia before the Assyrians—Is. 20:1-6. Rebuked Hezekiah for the reception he tendered the ambassadors of Merodach Baladan of Babylon, and foretold the Babylonian captivity—Is. 39:1-8. Thundered against the Egyptian alliance advocated by Hezekiah's political advisers—Is. 30:1-7; 31:1-3. Encouraged Hezekiah when Sennacherib threatened to storm Jerusalem and carry the people into exile—Is. 37:1-7, 21-35.

Symbolical actions.—Gave names to his sons that were significant: Shear-jashub, indicating the preservation of a remnant from the destruction of exile, and Maher-shalal-hash-baz, pointing to the speedy overthrow of the allied Kings of Damascus and Samaria—Is. 7:3; 8:3, 4. Used display tablet to arrest attention—Is. 8:1. Walked three years without mantle and sandals as a sign of the downfall of Egypt before the Assyrians—Is. 20:1-4.

Miracles.—Offers to Ahaz a miraculous sign from his God—Is. 7:10-16. Encourages Hezekiah by the sign of the returning shadow on the steps of the dial of Ahaz—Is. 38:7, 8.

Outbursts of the Prophet's emotions.—Fear in the presence of Jehovah in the heavenly temple—Is. 6:5. Disappointment in view of the difficult and discouraging task assigned him—Is. 6:11. Indignant prayer against the corrupt nation—Is. 2:9. Pity for suffering Moab—Is. 15:5; 16:11. Grief over the downfall of Babylon—Is. 21:1-10. Sorrow at the cowardice of Judah's rulers—Is. 22:3, 4.

Isaiah as a moral reformer.—Pleads for justice and kindness—Is. 1:16, 17.

Rebukes murder, theft, bribery and cruel indifference—Is. 1:21–23. Attacks luxury, militarism and haughtiness—Is. 2: 7, 11. Rebukes the ruling classes for grinding the face of the poor—Is. 2:14, 15. Rebukes the women of Jerusalem for wantonness and love of finery—Is. 3:16–4:1. Delivers a broadside against social abuses such as monopoly, intemperance, defiant unbelief, perversion of moral distinctions, conceit and injustice—Is. 5:8–23. Emphasizes justice as one of the chief characteristics of the messianic reign—Is. 11:1–5. Condemns Moab for pride and boasting—Is. 15:6. Rebukes epicureanism in a time of disaster—Is. 22:12–14. Rebukes the pride of Tyre's merchant princes—Is. 23:8, 9. Exposes the evils of drunkenness—Is. 28:1–13. Preaches a vigorous, aggressive type of morality—Is. 33:13–16. Pleads for cessation of all oppression and injustice—Is. 58:1–12; 59:1–18.

Isaiah an inspired statesman.—Urges Ahaz to trust in Jehovah and be quiet when Syria and Israel were in alliance to dethrone Ahaz. He estimated the allies at their real strength as only smoking stumps of firebrands, ready to go out —Is. 7:1–9. Predicts the disasters that will come upon Judah through the shortsighted policy of Ahaz in inviting the Assyrians to come to his aid against Pekah and Rezin—Is. 7:17–25. Foretold the speedy collapse of the alliance against Judah—Is. 8:1–4. Foresaw the dangers that the coming of the Assyrians would bring in, and announced the failure of Assyrian aggression in Jehovah's land —Is. 8:5–10. Took the measure of the Assyrian and boldly proclaimed him to be a rod with which to chastise rebellious Judah—Is. 10:5, 6. Foretold the overthrow of the proud Assyrian in the land of Judah—Is. 10:7–19, 24–27, 33, 34; 14:24–27; 17:12–14; 29:5–8; 30:27–33; 31:8,9; 33:1–12,17–24; 37:5–7,21–38. Took the measure of Egypt and Ethiopia and opposed the policy of leaning upon Egypt for help against Assyria— Is. 30:1–7; 31:1–3; 20:1–6. Announced to Hezekiah the folly of showing Judah's treasures to ambassadors from Babylon, for Judah would one day be taken captive to Babylon—Is. 39:1–7.

Predicted the fall of Babylon before the Medes—Is. 13:17–19. From his prophetic watchtower, Isaiah studied the history and character of the nations of the world in his day and foretold their fate—Is. chs. 13–23. Predicted the victorious career of Cyrus—Is. 41:25–27; 44:24; 45:7.

Isaiah as a teacher of religion: (1) Teaching as to God. Isaiah's favorite name for God is ''The Holy One of Israel''—Is. 1:4; 5:19, 24; 10:20; 12:6; 17:7; 29:19; 30:11, 12, 15; 31:1; 37:23; 41:14, 16, 20; 43:3, 14; 45:11; 47:4, 48: 17; 49:7; 54:5; 55:5; 60:9, 14. The same idea found in—Is. 6:3; 10:17; 29:23; 40:25; 43:15; 49:7. If separation was the original meaning of the Hebrew word for holiness, it presently came to represent the moral perfection of Jehovah. In Is. 6:1–5 the holiness ascribed to Jehovah by the Seraphim includes moral purity as well as transcendent glory. In striking contrast with Jehovah's holiness is the uncleanness of the prophet's lips.

God is over all (transcendence)—Is. 6:1; 2:11, 17, 19–21; 3:13–15; 5:16; 24:1; 31:4, 5; 40:12–31; 44:24–28.

Jehovah presides over all nations and includes all in his providential rule—Is. 5:26–30; 7:18–20; 10:5, 6, 12–19; 13:2–5; 14:1, 2, 24–27; 18:4–7; 19:1–4, 19–25; 23:8, 9; 41:1–4; 44:24; 45:7; 48:12–15.

Jehovah is just, and will mete out justice to offenders—Is. 1:5–7; 24–31; 2:10, 11, 19; 3:13; 4:1; 5:5, 6, 8–10, 13–17, 24–30; 6:9–13; 7:17–25; 8:5–8; 9:8; 10:4; 10:22–27, 33, 34; 13:2–11; 16:6, 7; 24: 21, 22; 26:8–10; 28:14–22; 30:12–17, 27–33; 33:3–5; 34:1–17; 37:29, 36; 42:24, 25; 49:24–26; 50:1, 11; 59:17–19; 63:1–7; 65:6, 7, 11–16; 66:6, 15–17, 24.

Jehovah is gracious and merciful—Is. 1:18; 12:1; 14:1; 19:19–22; 25:6–8; 27: 5; 30:18–21;38:1–8;40:1, 2,11, 27–31; 41: 17–20; 42:1–7; 43:1–7, 25; 44:1–5, 21–23; 45:20–25; 49:1–23; 51:12–16; 52:13–55:13; 60:1–62:12; 63:7–9; 65:17–25; 66: 10–14.

Jehovah in special relations with Israel: Has nourished them as His own children—Is. 1:2. Chastises as a faithful father—Is. 1:5, 6. Does not exterminate sinful Israel—Is. 1:9. Cleanses and restores Jerusalem—Is. 1:25–27. Will make Zion the religious capital of the world—Is. 2:2–4. Jehovah must enter into judgment with Israel—Is. 2:5–4:1; 5:1–30. After Jerusalem is purged the glory of Jehovah again returns and abides over the city—Is. 4:2–6. Brings the Assyrian as a scourge upon unbelieving Judah—Is. 7:10–25; 8:5–8; 10:5, 6. But He will save Judah from annihilation—Is. 8:9, 10; 9:1–7; 10:24–27; 11:1–16; 14:32; 26:1, 2; 29:1–8; 30:18–26; 31:5; 33:17–24; 37:33–35. Jehovah will deliver His people from the Babylonian exile—Is. 43:14–21; 44:24–28; 48:20, 21; 49:22–26; 52:1–12. He will make Zion beautiful and glorious—Is. 4:2–6; 25:6–8; 33:20–22; 35:10; 44:26; 52:1, 2; 54:1–17; 60:1–22; 62:1–12; 66:10–14.

(2) Teaching as to the Messiah: (a) The Messiah and His kingdom—Is. 7:14; 9:1–7; 11:1–10; 16:5; 32:1–5. (b) The suffering servant and his redemption—Is. 42:1–12; 49:1–13; 50:4–11; 52:13–53:12; 61:1–11. (c) Future growth of Jehovah's kingdom—Is. 2:2–4; 19:24, 25. (d) Future prosperity of Zion—Is. 4:2–6; 12:1–6; 25:6–8; 28:16; 49:14–26; 54:1–17; 60:1–22; 62:1–12; 65:17–25; 66:10–14.

(3) Teachings as to the Holy Spirit—Is. 11:2; 32:15; 44:3; 59:21.

(4) Teachings as to the salvation of sinners—Is. 1:18–20; 53:4–6; 55:6–9.

JEREMIAH.

Name and descent.—Jeremiah means either "Jehovah hurls" or "Jehovah founds." The prophet was the son of Hilkiah, of a priestly family residing in Anathoth, a town a little over three miles northeast of Jerusalem in the land of Benjamin—Jer. 1:1, 2. He probably belonged to the line of Ithamar—I Ki. 2:26.

Life and times of Jeremiah.—He was probably born toward the close of the long and wicked reign of Manasseh (698–643 B.C.), and began to prophesy in the thirteenth year of Josiah's reign (628 B.C.)—Jer. 1:2; 25:3. He was already known as a fearless prophet when the Book of the Law was found by Hilkiah in the eighteenth year of Josiah (623 B.C.) and the great reformation was inaugurated by Josiah. He was perhaps unpopular because of his severe denunciation of Judah's sins, so that the officers of King Josiah consulted the prophetess Huldah rather than Jeremiah as to the possibility of escape from the curses found in Deuteronomy against apostasy—II Ki. 22:14–20. He seems to have estimated at its real value the iconoclastic reformation inaugurated by Josiah, neither condemning the movement, which sprang solely from the zeal of the reforming king, nor permitting himself to expect too much from a superficial reformation. He knew that the hearts of the people were not really weaned from idolatry and its attendant evils. We perhaps have little from Jeremiah during the period between 623 B.C. and the death of Josiah (610 B.C.). Some scholars think that he preached in Jerusalem and the cities of Judah in advocacy of the covenant made by Josiah to observe the Mosaic law—Jer. 1:1–8. It is by no means certain that this tour of Judah was made during the reign of Josiah. Jeremiah was greatly grieved at the tragic death of good king Josiah, and composed a lamentation over his death—II Chr. 35:25.

Jeremiah predicted that Jehoahaz (Shallum), who was dethroned by Pharaoh-necoh after a reign of only three months, would never return from Egypt, whither he had been carried captive—Jer. 22:10–12.

Under Jehoiakim (609–598 B.C.) Jeremiah's trials multiplied. In the beginning of Jehoiakim's reign he was arrested for his fearless preaching in the court of the temple and put on trial for his life—Jer. 26:1–15. But for the fairness of the princes, the priests and false prophets would have put him to death—Jer. 26:16–19. His colleague Uriah was put to death by King Jehoiakim—Jer. 26:20–24. Much of Jer. 7–20 belongs to the early part of Jehoiakim's reign, especially 7:1–20. The prophet's grief over the incurable stubbornness of his rebellious people was intense—Jer. 8:18–9:6. Jeremiah's life was threatened by the men of Anathoth, his native town—Jer. 11:18–23. Even his own family joined those who were plotting to destroy him —Jer. 12:5, 6. His tender appeal to his people was unheeded—Jer. 13:15–17. He was cursed by all—Jer. 15:10. In his loneliness and isolation he was forbidden to marry—Jer. 16:2. The prophet is finally arrested by the chief officer of the temple and put in the stocks—Jer. 20:1, 2. Smarting under the sense of injustice and failure, Jeremiah curses the day of his birth—Jer. 20:14–18. In the fourth year of Jehoiakim (605 B.C.) the Egyptians and the Bablyonians fought at Carchemish a battle that decided the fate of Syria and Palestine. Jeremiah foretold the defeat of the Egyptians— Jer. 46:1–12. From this fateful year to the close of his life Jeremiah preached submission to Nebuchadrezzar of Baby- lon—Jer. 25:1–11; 27:1–22; 28:12–14; 29:1–9; 21:1–14; 34:1–7; 37:3–10, 16–20;

38:1–3, 14–23. Jeremiah witnessed the sad departure of young Jehoiachin for Babylon in 598 B.C.

Under Zedekiah Jeremiah suffered less from royal opposition, but the patriotic party in Jerusalem came to regard him as a traitor, and he was arrested and imprisoned as he sought to escape from Jerusalem during the absence of the besieging army, when the Babylonians broke up the siege in order to repel the army of Pharoah-hophra—Jer. 37:11–15. His confinement was mitigated by the favor of the king, though he was still held as a prisoner—Jer. 37:16–21. For advising men to surrender to the Chaldeans Jeremiah was cast into a pit to die, but was delivered through the kindness of an Ethiopian—Jer. 38:1–13. He remained a prisoner until the capture of the city by the Babylonians—Jer. 38:14–39:10.

At the capture of Jerusalem, Jeremiah was first taken in chains to Ramah, but he was released by the Babylonians and sent back to support Gedaliah, the governor appointed by the Babylonians —Jer. 40:1–6. After the assassination of Gedaliah Jeremiah was carried by force into Egypt—Jer. 42:1–43:7. He sought in vain to wean his people from the worship of idols—Jer. 44. According to a Jewish tradition he was put to death by his own countrymen.

The ministry of Jeremiah, though long and faithful, was apparently a complete failure. An intense patriot, he was accounted a traitor; longing to turn his people from sin and captivity, he must constantly announce the certainty of exile; a lover of peace, he spent his life battling against idolatry.

The Book of Jeremiah.—Interesting light upon the composition of the book may be found in statements contained in the roll of his prophecies. During the first twenty-three years of his ministry he seems to have put forth no book, but depended rather upon the spoken word. In 605 B.C., the year of Nebuchadrezzar's invasion of Syria and Palestine, Jeremiah was commanded to put in writing the substance of his messages for the previous twenty-three years—Jer. 36:1–8. The following year this roll of

Jeremiah's prophecies was read by Baruch in the court of the temple—Jer. 36:9, 10. It was then read in the hearing of the princes, and when they reported to the king the importance of the messages it contained, the roll was brought before Jehoiakim, who cut it to pieces and threw it into the fire—Jer. 36:11–26. The prophet was then commissioned to reproduce the roll, and many like words were added to the prophecies—Jer. 36:27–32. Possibly this second edition contained the first twenty chapters of our present book. It is impossible to trace the growth of the roll with accuracy, but the genuineness of practically all the present book cannot be successfully challenged. The Septuagint text differs widely from the Hebrew; but the Hebrew edition of Jeremiah's prophecies is in general to be preferred, though in some passages the Greek translation may have preserved the true text.

Characteristic teachings.—(1) Folly, ingratitude and vileness of idolatry— Jer. 1:16; 2:9–3:22; 5:7–9, 19; 7:29–34; 9:12–16; 11:9–13; 16:10–13; 17:1, 2; 18:13–17; 19:4–9; 25:4–7; 32:26–35; 44:1–30.

(2) Freedom of Jehovah to change His attitude to meet the changed attitude of men—Jer. 18:1–12. God's warnings and promises are usually conditional, even when the condition is not expressly stated.

(3) The infinite superiority of obedience to burnt-offerings and sacrifices— Jer. 7:21–26.

(4) Intercessory prayer not always availing—Jer. 7:16–20; 11:14; 15:1–4. Men may go so far in transgression that prayer on their behalf cannot be answered.

(5) Jehovah's patience with His impatient messenger—Jer. 1:17–19; 4:10; 12:1–6; 14:13–15; 15:10; 17:14–18; 18:18–23; 20:7–18; 32:24–26, 42–44.

(6) Individual responsibility—Jer. 31:29, 30. Ezekiel develops and enforces this doctrine—Ez. 18.

(7) The new covenant—Jer. 31:31–34. This doctrine is the fitting climax to Jeremiah's ministry. Living in a period when the kingdom of God seemed

about to be swallowed up by the heathen world-power, Jeremiah taught that Jehovah would make a new covenant and write His law in men's hearts. No longer would He deal with the nation as a whole and with commandments on tables of stone, but with individuals in whose hearts He would write His law. See Heb. 8:6–13 for the rich significance of this prophecy of a new covenant.

LAMENTATIONS.

Its place in the Bible.—Our English version follows the Septuagint in placing Lamentations directly after Jeremiah. In the mode of counting which reduces the number of the Old Testament books to twenty-two, Lamentations is counted as part of Jeremiah. In the Hebrew Bible, however, it is transferred to the Hagiographa, where it is placed between Ruth and Ecclesiastes.

Structure.—It consists of five separate poems, all on the same subject. The first four are acrostic in structure—that is to say, the first verse begins with the first letter of the Hebrew alphabet, the second with the second letter, and so on throughout the twenty-two letters. There is a variation in the third chapter, where the first three verses begin each with the first letter, the second three each with the second letter, and so on. There are certain variations in the order of the letters, interesting to students of the alphabet. On the whole, it is surprising how little this artificial arrangement seems to cramp the flow of feeling in the poems.

Subject.—They are songs of mourning over Jerusalem, after she had been desolated by Nebuchadrezzar. There is no strong insistence upon ethical or spiritual lessons, though of necessity such lessons are taught, but rather an outpouring of indignant but heartbroken sorrow and grief.

Authorship.—Tradition attributes it to Jeremiah. The tradition is of great antiquity. It appears in the Septuagint as a heading to the book. There is always an element of weakness in anonymous tradition, but in this case the tradition is in itself probable. It is confirmed by the fresh and graphic character of the lamentations themselves, an indication that they were composed while the calamity was still fresh in the memory of those who suffered. There are some linguistic differences between these threnodies and the prophecies of Jeremiah, but not more than is found in the works of other versatile men, when they engage in different kinds of literary composition.

EZEKIEL.

Name.—Ezekiel means "God strengthens."

Personal history.—Ezekiel was a priest by birth and training, called in the fifth year of King Jehoiachin's captivity (593 B.C.) to be a prophet among the exiles by the river Chebar in Babylonia—Ez. 1:1–3. It is thought by many that he was thirty years of age at the time of his call to the prophetic office—Ez. 1:1. He was inducted into the prophetic ministry by a vision of Jehovah seated on a throne which was borne up by four living creatures—Ez. 1:4–28. He was profoundly moved by the visions that God gave him—Ez. 1:28–2:2; 3:12–15; 8:1–4; 11:13, 22–25. He was frequently consulted by the elders of Israel—Ez. 8:1; 14:1; 20:1. He seems to have been an eloquent and popular speaker—Ez. 33:30–33. The scene of his ministry was Tel-abib, on the canal Chebar in lower Babylonia—Ez. 3:15. He lived in his own house among the exiles—Ez. 8:1; 12:1–7. He was married, but his wife died during the siege of Jerusalem about 588 B.C.—Ez. 24:15–24. He exercised his ministry from 593 B.C. to 571 B.C.—Ez. 1:1–3; 29:17. Like Jeremiah, Ezekiel was made strong and bold for his difficult ministry—Ez. 3:4–9.

Style of Ezekiel.—He is fond of symbolical actions performed as object lessons—Ez. 4:1–5:4; 6:11; 12:3–7, 17; 21: 6, 12, 14; 24:15–18. He also employs riddles—Ez. 17:1–24. He is fond of parables—Ez. 20:49; 24:3–14. He paints pictures, not with a few bold strokes like Isaiah, but with attention to the minutest details—Ez. 1:4–28; 10:1–22; 27:1–36; 37:1–10; 39:1–20; 40:1–48:35. He traces analogies with great fulness of detail—Ez. 16:1–63; 23:1–49; 31:1–18; 34:1–31.

Nature of Ezekiel's ministry.—He was called to be a watchman—Ez. 3:17–21; 33:1–9. He was to speak Jehovah's message to Israel as a whole—Ez. 3:1–11. In Ezekiel's time the nation was crumbling to pieces, and he was inspired to develop and emphasize Jeremiah's teaching concerning individual responsibility. Ezekiel was therefore much like a modern pastor, watching over individual souls.

From 593 B.C. to 587 B. C. his message was largely one of rebuke and warning. Like his contemporary and teacher, Jeremiah, he punctured the false hopes of his people—Ez. 4–24. After the fall of Jerusalem in 587 B.C. he was inspired to encourage the dispirited exiles with promises of restoration to the land of Israel and a renewal of the divine blessing—Ez. 33–48. The transition between rebuke and consolation is made in the prophecies against the enemies of Israel—Ez. 25–32.

In Ezekiel's experience the trance or ecstasy plays a larger part than in the experience of earlier prophets—Ez. 8–11; 40–48. Daniel and Zechariah follow Ezekiel in this particular.

Ezekiel's message to men of all ages.—The early prophets have more that is of a permanent value in the realm of civic righteousness, for they addressed a nation in its own land charged with the responsibility of national life. The exile scattered the members of the Jewish people far and wide over the earth, and they no longer had native kings and could have little corporate unity in matters of civil government. Hence the message of Ezekiel is largely a message to the individual concerning his religious duties. The following are some of the doctrines most impressively taught by Ezekiel:

(1) *Jehovah's care for His name among the nations of mankind.* Israel had profaned His name by its sins, but Jehovah will jealously guard His name in the interest of all mankind, that the

glory of God be not obscured through Israel's faithlessness—Ez. 20:9, 14, 22, 44; 36:20–36; 39:7.

(2) *Individual freedom and responsibility.* Chapters 18 and 33 are classic passages for this important doctrine. Ezekiel teaches that no one is necessarily under the dominion of his father's righteousness or wickedness: he may break away from either, and will be judged accordingly—Ez. 18:1–20. Furthermore, no man is necessarily under the dominion of his own past life, whether righteous or wicked: he may break away from it, and will be judged accordingly—Ez. 18:21–32; 33:10–16. No man can presume upon his father's goodness or his own righteous past, and no man need despair because of his father's wickedness or his own wicked past.

(3) *Jehovah longs for the salvation of all men*—Ez. 18:23, 32; 33:11. He takes an oath by Himself that He has no pleasure in the death of the wicked.

(4) *Jehovah's promise of spiritual renewing*—Ez. 11:19; 36:24–28. Here again Ezekiel develops the teaching of Jeremiah concerning the new covenant—Jer. 31:31–34; 32:37–40.

(5) *The messianic teaching*—(a) The new heart—Ez. 11:16–20; 36:25–36. (b) The wonderful cedar spring—Ez. 17:22–24. (c) False rulers give way to Him whose right it is to reign—Ez. 21:26, 27. (d) Unfaithful shepherds removed before the true Shepherd, the Second David—Ez. 34:11–31. (e) The resurrection of dead Israel to be followed by the reunion of divided Israel—Ez. 37. (f) Overthrow of all enemies of Jehovah's kingdom—Ez. Chs. 38 and 39. (g) The stream that gives life—Ez. 47:1–12. The Dead Sea is transformed into a picture of life and prosperity by the stream that took its rise on the temple hill. Ezekiel's message is one of boundless hope for the moral and spiritual transformation of **mankind.**

DANIEL, BOOK OF.

Form.—Prophetic vision.

Characteristic. — Symbolic presentation of world-powers in their conflict with the kingdom of God.

Source of Symbolism.—Largely derived from Babylonian and Persian lore.

Design.—To comfort the oppressed people of God by holding before them the victory of their Divine King over the world-powers.

Language.—Hebrew, ch. 1, 2:4; chs. 8:12; Aramaic 2:4–7:28.

Allusion in the N. T.—Mt. 24:15.

Outline of contents:

Historical Introduction—Daniel and his three friends. Ch. 1.

Their deportation and settlement at the court of Nebuchadrezzar—1–7. Loyalty to the law; refusal to eat dainties; test; prosperity, 8–21.

I. Daniel the sage.—Chs. 2–6.

1. Interprets Nebuchadrezzar's dream of the metallic image, Ch. 2:

   The king dreams and forgets the dream—his Chaldeans fail to restore and interpret it, 1–13. Daniel requests an opportunity to recover and interpret it and secures it, 14–30. He succeeds. The Dream: Gigantic figure, 31–35; its interpretation, 36–45; Daniel's reward, 46–49.

2. Daniel's three friends' refusal to worship the king's image, Ch. 3.

   Nebuchadrezzar sets up an image of gold in the plain of Dura, 1–7. The three Hebrews charged with disobeying the order to worship it, 8–12. They are cast into the fiery furnace, but remain unharmed, 13–23. Nebuchadrezzar releases them and praises their God, 24–30.

3. Daniel interprets Nebuchadrezzar's dream of the tree, Ch. 4.

   Nebuchadrezzar's proclamation, 1–3. Tells of his dream, 4–18. Daniel's interpretation, 19–27. Its fulfilment: the king afflicted with temporary loss of reason, 28–33. Restored to normal life, 34–37.

4. Daniel interprets the handwriting on the wall, Ch. 5.

   Belshazzar's feast, 1–4. The writing on the wall, 5–9. The queen remembers Daniel, 10–12. Daniel is summoned, 13–16. He interprets the writing, 17–28. Daniel is rewarded, 29. Babylon captured, 30, 31.

5. Daniel in the lions' den, Ch. 6.

   Daniel promoted under Darius, 1–3. Decree forbidding all worship but that of the king for thirty days, 4–9. Daniel's refusal to obey, 10–15. Daniel cast into the lions' den and spared by the lions, 16–28. The king's conversion and decree to worship Daniel's God, 24–28.

II. Daniel the seer.—Chs. 7–12.

1. The dream of the four beasts, Ch. 7.

   a. The four great beasts, 1–8. The ancient of days on his throne, 9–12. The Son of Man given authority, 13–14.

   b. The interpretation, 15–28.

2. The vision of the ram, the he-goat, and the little horn, Ch. 8.

   Time and place of the vision, 1, 2. The ram, 3, 4. The he-goat, 5–8. The little horn, 9–14. The interpretation by Gabriel, 15–27.

3. The seventy weeks, Ch. 9.

   The time and occasion, 1, 2. Daniel's prayer, 3–19. **The an-**

swer brought by Gabriel, 20–23.
The seventy weeks decreed until the anointed prince, 24–27.
4. Vision of the man with the prediction, Chs. 10, 11, 12.
  The occasion, time, and place,
  1–4. The appearance of the man,
  5–9. Daniel's fear and strengthening, 10–17. Announcement
  of the subject, 10:18–11:1. The
  prediction; the kings of Persia;
  their defeat by king of Greece;
  the breaking of his kingdom,
  2–4. The kings of the south
  and of the north: their conflicts, 5:19; the "raiser of
  taxes," 20; the "vile person,"
  21–30. His desecration of the
  temple and persecution of the
  saints, 31–36. His insane self-
  exaltation and self-deification,
  37–39. His final campaign, 40–
  45. Deliverance of God's people by Michael, 12:1–4. Conclusion and application of the
  lesson of the vision, 5–13.

BRANCHES: Natural. Of trees.—
Job 14:7; Is. 17:6. Palm—Lev. 23:40;
Song of Sol. 7:8; Is. 9:14; 19:15; John
12:13. Olive—Neh. 8:15; Jer. 11:16;
Zech. 4:12. Myrtle—Neh. 8:15. Thick
trees—Neh. 8:15. Cedar—Ps. 80:11; Ez.
17:23; 31:3.

Figurative.—Joel 1:7.

Of vines.—Ez. 15:2; 17:6, 8; Nah. 2:2.
Destroyed—Is. 16:8.

Of grapes.—Num. 13:23.

Uses of.—For booths—Neh. 8:15.
Shelter for birds—Ps. 104:12; Ez. 17:
23; 31:6, 13; Dan. 4:21; Mt. 13:32; Mk.
4:32; Lu. 13:19. Shelter for animals—
Ez. 31:6, 13. Food for cattle—Is. 27:10.
As a design for candlestick—Ex. 25:32–
36; 37:18, 19, 21, 22. Triumphal entry—
Mk. 11:8; John 12:13.

Illustrative.—Prosperity—Gen. 49:22.
Wickedness—Job 15:32; Is. 14:19. Idolatrous worship—Ez. 8:17. Righteousness — Is. 60:21; Jer. 23:5; 33:15.
Strength—Ps. 80:15.

Figurative.—Wicked destroyed—Job
15:30; 18:16; Is. 18:5; Mal. 4:1. Of Job
—Job 29:19. Jehovah—Is. 4:2. Jesse—
Is. 11:1. Israel—Ez. 19:10, 11, 14; 36:8;
Hos. 14:6.

Messianic.—Assyrian—Ez. 31:3, 5–9,
12, 13.

Servant.—Zech. 3:8. The branch—
Jer. 23:5; Zech. 6:12.

Followers of Christ.—John 15:2, 5, 6;
Rom. 11:16–21, 24.

Apocalyptic (symbolical).—Of tree—
Dan. 4:14, 21. Of vine—Gen. 40:10, 12.
Of candlestick—Zech. 4:12.

Called of God.—Pr. 1:24–33; Is. 45:
22; 65:12; 66:4; Jer. 7:13; Mt. 20:16;
22:3, 8, 9, 14; Acts 2:39; Rom. 4:17–25;
8:30; 9:10–13; I Thess. 5:24; Heb. 9:15;
II Pet. 1:2–11; Rev. 17:14. According
to His purpose—Rom. 8:28; 9:23, 24; II
Tim. 1:9. To fellowship with Jesus—
I Cor. 1:9. To holiness—I Thess. 4:7;
II Pet. 1:15, 16. To be saints—Rom.
1:6, 7; I Cor. 1:2. To peace—II Cor.
7:15. To eternal glory—Rom. 8:30; II
Thess. 2:14; I Pet. 5:10. To eternal life
—I Tim. 6:12. To liberty—I Cor. 7:20–
24; Gal. 5:13. The high—Phil. 3:14. A
holy—II Tim. 1:9. A heavenly—Heb.
3:1. The hope of your—Eph. 1:18; 4:4.
Walking worthily of—Eph. 4:1; II Thess.
1:11. Blessedness of receiving the call
—Rev. 19:9.

How called?—In the Old Testament.—
By the works of God—Ps. 19:2, 3; Rom.
1:18–23. By the prophets—II Chr. 36:
15–17; Jer. 7:21–28; 25:4–8; 29:15–19;
35:15; Zech. 7:7; Mal. 2:7.

In the New Testament.—By Christ—
Mt. 6:33; 9:13; 11:28; 23:37; Mk. 2:17;
Lu. 5:32; 19:41; John 5:40; 6:37; 7:37;
I Pet. 5:10. By the Spirit—Rev. 22:17.
By the bride—Rev. 22:17. By the
preaching of the gospel—II Cor. 3:6;
5:18–21; Eph. 6:20. By the gospel—
Mt. 7:24–28; Lu. 6:47–49; John 12:48;
Rom. 9:23–33; I Cor. 1:18–28; II Cor.
5:18–21; Gal. 1:6–14; Eph. 1:17–19; I
Thess. 1:4–10; 2:12–14; II Thess. 2:13–
15; II Tim. 1:9–11.

HOSEA, BOOK OF.

The prophet.—Family unknown, except name of father, Beeri—Hos.1:1. Time of Uzziah to Hezekiah (790-690) and Jeroboam II (784-745)—Hos. 1:1. Wife, Gomer, daughter of Diblaim, family unknown—1:3.

First child, a son, named Jezreel, after Jehu's royal city—1:4. Name accompanied by prediction of fall of Jehu's dynasty—1:4.

Second child, a daughter, named Loruhamah (unpitied)—1:6. Name associated with oracle of withdrawal of Divine mercy from Israel—1:6.

Third child, a son, named Lo-ammi (not my people)—1:8, 9. This name memorialized divine rejection of Israel—1:9. Names followed by prediction of hope for Israel, the greatness of Jezreel and reacceptance of the people—1:10-2:1.

Gomer became a faithless wife—1:2; 2:5. She was counted an emblem of Israel unfaithful to Jehovah—1:2; 2:2-20; 3:1. Her lovers symbolized the false gods in Israel—2:7, 13, 17; 3:1. Israel rebuked as faithless like Gomer—2:2-20; 3:4, 5.

Gomer, enslaved to a paramour, is bought back by the prophet—3:2. She for a season is denied honors of a wife to any man—3:3. During same time Hosea is husband to no woman—3:3. So Israel for a time shall be denied king and God—3:4. Later Israel will return to Jehovah—3:5.

Book: "Historical setting.—Hosea is the last of the great prophets of the northern kingdom. To understand his place in history and prophecy, we must note the twofold division of his writings. Chs. 1-3 were written about 748 B.C., and chs. 4-14 about 734 B.C. At the former date the house of Jehu (1:4) was still upon the throne. Jeroboam, its most powerful representative, was then in his latest years. Israel was felt to be nearing its doom; and Hosea (3:4) predicts the coming captivity with more definiteness than had been done by Amos. The domestic political situation is nearly the same as under Amos. In the second part, the inner condition of Israel is materially affected for the worse. Pekah, the last independent king of Samaria, is now upon the throne. In the interval has occurred a series of revolutions and usurpations such as those which marked the early history of the northern kingdom. The brief reign of Zechariah, the last of the line of Jehu, was followed by the briefer term of the usurper Shallum. Then came another *coup d'état* under Menahem. His son, Pekahiah (737, 736), was in his turn dethroned by Pekah, whose reign was signalized by the alliance with Damascus against Assyria and Judah, its defeat by Tiglath-pileser, and the annexation to Assyria of most of Israel east and west of Jordan. Hosea's prophecies were uttered before this last event. But the crisis was manifestly approaching. The situation was complicated by the policy of an alliance with Egypt. Hosea had always perceived that this must end in the absolute ruin of Israel, and at the very beginning of the new reign he warns his people against it. The moral condition of the community is shown, by the allusions of the prophet, to have kept pace in its degeneration with the decay and dissolution of the nation. It is apparently even worse than the state of things depicted by Amos. Isa. 28 and Mic. 1, which follow close in time upon Hosea, may serve as a supplement to his description of the public and private morals of Samaria in the days of its decline.

The prophet's message.—I. Chs. 1-3 have to do with the painful and pathetic personal history of Hosea. They symbolized Jehovah's separation from His people, the deprivation they thereby endured, and their restoration to the privileges of His worship and favor.

II. Chs. 4–14—It is impossible to give even a brief analysis of this longer division. To summarize it, one would need to give the contents of a large number of short sections. But the division into chapters enables us to form larger groups, each of them having a characteristic tone and drift. 1. In chs. 4–6 we find mainly charges of gross *iniquity*, ch. 4 being directed against the people at large, ch. 5 specially against the priests and princes as their leaders in wrongdoing, and ch. 6 against Israel in general, as still obdurate in spite of an earnest call to repentance. 2. In chs. 7–10 'the predominating thought is impending *punishment*, culminating in exile (9:3, 6; 10:5, 6), as the consequence of unfaithfulness and transgression. 3. Chs. 11–13 show more of a relenting mind; there is more in them of hopeful *remonstrance* and tender expostulation. These are present in the earlier sections, but here they seem to overflow in tears which almost blot out the threatenings and accusations. 4. Ch. 14 consists exclusively of *entreaty* and rich promises of blessing as the result of inward and heartfelt repentance.'' —Nelson's ''Bible Treasury.''

Outline.—Part first relates account of prophet's household and application to Israel—Chaps. 1–3.

Part second contains rebukes, threats and promises for Israel—Chaps. 4–14. Judah is mentioned, but incidentally— 1:1, 11; 4:15; 5:5, 13; 6:4; 12:2.

Chief theme is Israel's sins—4:1, 2, 8–18; 5:3–5; 6:7–10; 7:3–7; 9:9, 10, 15; 10:9, 10, 13; 12:7; 13:2, 12.

Chief punishments shall be: Devastation of the country—4:3; 5:7, 9; 10:7, 8; 10:14. Burning of cities—8:14. Cap-tivity—9:6, 17; 11:11. Bereavement— 9:12, 16. Cruel death—13:14, 16.

Chief promises are prosperity—1:10, 11; 2:21, 22; 14:5–7. Acceptance with God—1:10; 2:1, 23; 14:4. Return from captivity—11:10, 11.

''**Character and style.**—The difficulty of analyzing the main portion of the prophecy is partly due to the fact that we have in it an *abstract* of numerous discourses, extending over many years, each of the utterances being condensed to an extreme degree. But it is also largely due to the prevailing mood of the prophet and his habit of mind. He is the most *subjective* and individual of the prophets. His own feelings are intense, easily aroused, and readily swayed from the extreme of despondency to high expectation. In mental disposition Hosea is a perfect contrast to Amos, who is one of the most objective of all writers, his message carrying weight by its inherent force alone. Hosea had the temperament of the lyric poet, and many of his passages are odes or dirges pure and simple. In 'tragic pathos' he is unexcelled. There is great variety of thought and of emotional coloring in his book. His images are not, as a rule, elaborated, but are struck off in a word or two. His style in general is ejaculatory, as if he were eager to relieve his soul of its strain and burden. Withal he is so rich in sympathy and moral insight that his discourses are full of pregnant observations on life and manners, as well as of moral reflections, and these are all the more easily remembered on account of the epigrammatic mode of expression.''—Nelson's ''Bible Treasury.''

Quotations in New Testament.—1:10 (Rom. 9:26); 2:23 (Rom. 9:25); 6:6 (Mt. 9:13); 9:7 (Lu. 21:22); 10:8 (Lu. 23: 30); 11:1 (Mt. 2:15); 13:14 (I Cor. 15: 55).

JOEL, BOOK OF.

The prophet.—Son of Pethuel; family unknown—Joel 1:1. A prophet for Judah and Jerusalem—2:1, 15, 22, 31; 3:1, 15–19. A prophet of religious and moral reform—1:14; 2:12–17. A prophet of hopefulness—2:18–31; 3:15–19. Ministry undated, but at a time of plagues and drought—1:4–12, 17–20; 2:1–10. A prophet of poetic thought—1:2; 2:17; almost all poetry. Style descriptive and scenic, almost dramatic—1:2–13; 2:3–11; 3:9–16.

Book: "Historical setting.—The date of Joel is difficult to fix with certainty; but most probably it was about 770 B.C., a few years before Amos and Hosea. Coincidences with Amos are marked (cf. chs. 3:16 with Amos 1:2, chs. 3:18 with Amos 9:13). Many nations are cited as hostile, but Syria is not referred to, perhaps because Judah had not greatly suffered like Israel from Damascus. The Assyrians are not mentioned, but at that date they were inactive and innocuous. It was a time of many and grave natural calamities in Western Asia, and Joel deals with them particularly.

The prophet's message.—I. Chs. 1 to 2:17.—There is to be a 'day of Jehovah'—i. e., a day of his power and judgment—for Judah and Jerusalem, symbolized by a plague of locusts, whose devastation is described. To meet the calamity, Joel calls for prayer and fasting (ch. 1). A still more vivid and figurative description of the same plague is again given, and a more earnest entreaty made for penitence and mourning (2:1–17).

II. Chs. 2:18 to 3:21.—Jehovah Himself gives His answer to the prayer for help: a promise of relief from famine, of abundance of rain and rich harvests to make up for the spoiling of the locusts (2:18–27). A new spirit is to come from God upon all the people, so that, when days of fiery trial come, they shall remember to call upon Him and be saved (28–32). Jehovah's restoration of His people, who have been sold into slavery by the Phœnicians and Philistines, is to be accompanied by a judgment upon their foes, who in their turn are to be sold by the Jews into bondage and exile (3:1–8). The nations are summoned to muster themselves to meet God in judgment (9–14). In the terrors of that day Jerusalem shall find refuge in its Lord. Instead of destruction, prosperity shall be the portion of God's people, while the persecuting nations shall be desolate (15–21).''—Nelson's "Bible Treasury.''

Outline.—Part first presents calamities and a call to fasting, prayer and repentance—1:1–2:17.

Part second, material and spiritual blessings following reformation—2:18–3:21.

The calamities are: The palmer-worm, locust, canker-worm, caterpillar and drought—1:4, 10–12, 17–20; 2:4–10, 23, 24.

The blessings are: Rains, fruits, outpourings of the Holy Spirit and overthrow of cruel enemies—2:20–25, 28, 29; 3:1–8, 14, 18–21.

Special themes of the Book are: "The Day of Jehovah'' as a day of terrible judgments—1:15; 2:1, 2, 11, 31. Fasting and self-denial, in the face of calamity—1:8, 14; 2:12, 15, 17. As assembly for prayer—1:14; 2:15, 16. The merciful character of Jehovah—2:12–14, 18–27. The just punishment of nations hostile to Judah—3:1–13, 19.

Chief doctrines: Judah's calamities are a call to penitence and service to Jehovah—1:14; 2:12–17. And Jehovah will turn with blessings to those who turn to Him—2:12–14, 18–28.

"Character and style.—For the understanding of Joel an appreciation of Oriental symbolism is necessary, as well

61

as a knowledge of the relation of Judah to its closest neighbors. We must continually translate metaphor into fact, and reduce poetic hyperbole to the measure of historic reality. The aim of the prophet was to both warn and encourage his people in view of great national calamities. They should be saved, while their malicious foes should be grievously afflicted. But the relief depends upon repentance and amendment. The style of Joel is smooth and flowing, as of one who had himself (unlike Hosea and Jeremiah) no inward doubts and struggles, whatever might be the national or the individual outlook."—Nelson's "Bible Treasury."

Peculiar expressions.—"The day of Jehovah"—1:15; 2:1, 11, 31; 3:14. See Zech. 14:7. The harvest—3:13. See Mt. 13:37–42; Rev. 14:18–20.

Quotations in New Testament.—The most familiar one is Peter's quotation concerning the outpouring of the Holy Spirit on the Day of Pentecost—2:28–32 (Acts 2:16–21). See also 2:30, 31 (Lu. 21:25, 26); 2:32 (Rom. 10:13); 4:16 (Mt. 24:29).

AMOS, BOOK OF.

The prophet.—Probably a man of Judah, as his home was Tekoa—Amos 1:1. A herdsman—1:1; 7:14. A cultivator of sycamore trees—7:14; and not of a prophetic family—7:14, 15. Call direct from God—7:15. Felt constrained to prophesy—3:8. Prophesied mainly for Israel—1:1, 2; 2:6; 3:13; 4:1, 5, 12; 5:1, 4; 7:8, 9; 8:2; 9:7. Incidentally of Judah—2:4, 5; 3:1; 9:11.

Time.—"Two years before the earthquake," in days of Uzziah and Jeroboam II—1:1; Zech. 14:5; *cf.* Jos. Ant. ix:x:4.

Accused of treason and ordered away by the priest Amaziah—7:10-13.

Amos related his commission and pronounced a judgment on Amaziah—7:14-17.

Book: "Historical setting.—Amos was a shepherd, and a cultivator of sycamore trees, living at Tekoa, nine miles south of Jerusalem. He was thus a Judaite, though his prophecy has to do directly with the northern kingdom. He appeared at Bethel, the chief seat of the semi-idolatrous worship of Israel, about 765 B.C., moved to speak on behalf of Jehovah and righteousness among unsympathetic and even hostile surroundings. He was not a professional prophet—that is to say, he did not belong to one of the prophetic guilds or schools, membership in which was, as a rule, hereditary (7:14 ff.). Nor had he pursued his vocation under the auspices of the court in Jerusalem. He was simply moved to prophesy by the force of the Spirit of God within him (3:8). His public life fell on a critical time for his own country, and especially for the kindred nations. Both Judah and Israel had had a time of unprecedented prosperity, including an increase of territory, of commercial advantages, and of material wealth. But in this very self-aggrandizement there lay the seeds of

political and religious dissolution for both nationalities. Northern Israel was in the greatest danger for reasons which the prophecy unfolds. Hence the stern and solemn warning of Amos. Yet the kingdom was outwardly at peace. It was the middle of the reign of Jeroboam II., while Uzziah was king in Judah. The force of the long oppression by the Syrians of Damascus, east and west of Jordan, had been broken by the repeated onslaughts of the Assyrians, and Israel could breathe freely. Assyria itself was now harmless—torn by internal dissensions and depressed by national disasters. Amos treats freely of the surrounding peoples. He foresees the rise of Assyria to greater power than ever, and her dominion over Israel as a punishment for the sins and follies which he is sent to rebuke, and against which throughout his prophecy he protests in vain.

The prophet's message.—The essence of the message of Amos is—(1) That Israel, as the professed people of Jehovah, is bound to follow after *righteousness*; and (2) that immorality and irreligion, which are essentially sins against Jehovah's nature and claims, necessarily bring *punishment* from Jehovah. These ideas are enforced in different ways in each of the three divisions of the book.

I. Chs. 1 and 2 illustrate, by means of a historical survey, the results of evil conduct upon a national scale. A brief introduction (1:1, 2) declares that Jehovah is coming in His might for judgment upon the land. Then the people of Damascus are cited as examples of His vengeance (1:3-5). In the style proper to Hebrew prophecy, a single feature of the Syrian national policy is chosen as characteristic of the whole—namely, the merciless repression of Israel east of the Jordan. For its dealings with Israel, therefore, Damascus is to lose its independence; it is to be taken by storm, and its people are to be carried away to their original home in Kir (*cf.* 9:7). Similarly each of the surrounding nations is arraigned for some typical act of cruelty. Thus condemnation and judgment are uttered against the Philistian cities (1:6–8), Tyre (1:9, 10), Edom (1:11, 12), Ammon (1:13–15), and Moab (2:1–3). Judah is next threatened for direct rejection of the commands of Jehovah (2:4, 5). Thus the way is prepared for the special application of the law of righteousness and judgment to Israel (2:6–16), for greed, dishonesty, licentiousness, and profanity.

II. Chs. 3–6.—This division is an expansion and exposition of the preceding summary indictment of Israel. Its three parts (chs. 3, 4, 5 and 6) are each marked by the introductory challenge, 'Hear ye this word.' 1. Ch. 3. Israel is Jehovah's own people, therefore in faithfulness He must chastise it for its sins, and that according to just laws of retribution: (a) Evil that happens to God's chosen people comes from His superintendence. Its announcement by the prophets is really the utterance of His voice (ver. 1–8). (b) The very heathen are called to witness the enormities that are committed in Samaria (ver. 9, 10. (c) An 'adversary' is to be raised up against Samaria—the terrible Assyrian—who shall make an end of the prosperity and pride of its nobles and people, its monuments of luxury, and its religious vanities (ver. 11–15). 2. Ch. 4. (a) The voluptuousness and careless cruelty of the women of the upper classes in Samaria shall bring its just reward (ver. 1–3). (b) An ironical suggestion is offered to the transgressors to resort to their sacred places and sacrifices for relief (ver. 4, 5). (c) They are reminded of their manifold chastisement: famine, drought, blasted and withered crops, death by plague and battle and earthquake; and now, since these have failed of their due effect, they must prepare to meet their final doom (ver. 6–13). 3. Chs. 5 6. (a) A lamentation is uttered over

the impending ruin of Israel (5:1–3). (b) Repeated adjurations are made to 'seek· Jehovah and live' (ver. 4–9). (c) Charges of various sorts of injustice are renewed, with a prediction of the sad time that is coming to those who refuse to 'seek good and not evil' (ver. 10–17). (d) The absurdity of their desiring the intervention of Jehovah is set forth (ver. 18–20). (e) Their religious gatherings, so mixed with idolatry, their sacrifice and worship, are loathsome to Jehovah; they and their idols alike shall go into exile (ver. 21–27). (f) With all the prestige, self-confidence, luxury, and selfishness of the nobles of Samaria, they shall be the first to go into captivity (6:1–7). (g) Pestilence, with all its domestic horrors, makes another prelude to the loss of home and country through the dreaded Assyrian (ver. 8–14).

III. Chs. 7–9.—The framework of this section is a series of visions setting forth in striking images the threatened judgments. 1. Visions of locusts, of fire, and of a plumbline testing the houses and sanctuaries of Israel (7:1–9). 2. These are followed by the only narrative contained in the prophecy: the attempt of the priest of Bethel to silence Amos and secure his expulsion from the kingdom of Jeroboam, with the announcement by the prophet of his awful fate (ver. 10–17). 3. The vision of a basket of summer fruit so speedily devoured, with its application to the people who have earned swift and lamentable destruction by their dishonesty and rapacity (ch. 8). 4. A vision of the temple smitten and shattered, and falling upon the devoted heads of the congregation of Israel so that none shall escape (9:1–6). 5. Yet in a brighter future a remnant, the true Israel, shall be saved, while the 'sinners' shall perish. The redeemed shall return to the old land, shall rebuild and replant it, and shall flourish under the blessing of the God of the covenant (ver. 7–15).''—Nelson's ''Bible Treasury.''

Outline.—Introduction, Sins of other nations, then of Israel—Chaps. 1-2. Addresses—Chaps. 3-6. Visions—7:1-9:10.

Conclusion, a messianic prophecy—9: 11-15.

Style.—Bold, vivid, direct, authoritative, especially chs. 3–6. Sometimes poetic—2:13–16; 5:2; and parts of chs. 1 and 4 are poetic in the original, sometimes broken by sudden changes—3:3, 9; 4:4; 8:4; 9:5; and parentheses—5:10, 13, 15; 7:10–17; 9:5, 6.

Historical allusions.—To cruelties of Damascus, Gaza, Tyre, Edom, Moab, Israel—1:3, 6, 9, 13; 2:16, 17; 3:9–11. To defections of Judah—2:4. To famines, blights, plagues and pestilences in Israel—4:6–13. To corrupting of prophets and nazirites—2:11, 12. To Exodus from Egypt—3:1; 9:7. And migrations of Philistines and Syrians—9:7. To the wandering in the wilderness and conquest of Amorites—2:10. And to the sin of idolatry at Bethel and Gilgal—3:14; 4:4; 5:5.

Leading ideas.—Persistent transgression will bring swift punishment—1:3; 3:1; 3:13–15; 4:1–13. Israel as well as other nations will be judged for sin—1:3; 3:1; 3:9–12, 14, 15; 5:7, 11: 6:3–7. The worship of Jehovah through idols will not avail—4:4; 5:22–27; cf. I Ki. 12:28–33; 13:33, 34. Jehovah is the God of nature and able for any task—4:7, 9, 13; 5:8; 7:4; 8:9; 9:5, 6. Yet God is gracious—5:4, 15; 7:3, 6; and will ultimately establish Israel in their land—9:11–15.

"**Character and style.**—Next to Isaiah and Jeremiah, Amos is the greatest of the prophets. Both in matter and form his prophecy stands quite in the highest rank of Biblical compositions. He was the pioneer prophet in giving systematic expression to the faith of the true Israel. He was the founder of that great school of which Isaiah and Micah were the leading later representatives, and whose cardinal doctrines were that private and social morality are a necessary outcome of the religion of Jehovah, and that they are also essential to the well-being of the state. Apart from his significance as a reformer and teacher of his own age and nation, he is one of the great prophets of all time. His book is a manual of the principles of social reform. None have ever shown better than he the evil consequences in personal and in political life of love of gain, of dishonesty, of indifference to the claims of the weak and helpless, of the practical infidelity which ignores God in the business of life, and in ordinary human relationships. The style of Amos is incomparably apt and forcible, corresponding to his insight and to his energy of character. While not so ornate as that of Isaiah, its homely directness makes it equally effective. His imagination, which is very lively, is of the practical kind. Yet his knowledge is wide, and he brings home to his hearers with equal ease and power the lessons of history, of the processes of nature, and of the commonest actions in the life of the trader and the husbandman.''—Nelson's "Bible Treasury."

New Testament quotations.—5:25–27 (Acts 7:42, 43); 9:11, 12 (Acts 15:16, 17).

OBADIAH, BOOK OF.

The prophet.—Although this name occurs several times in the Old Testament (I Ki. 18:3; I Chr. 9:16; 3:25; 8:38; 27:19; *et al.*), this prophet is not elsewhere mentioned—V. 1. Probably lived in Judah—V. 11. His time uncertain, perhaps when Jerusalem was taken by Nebuchadrezzar (586 B.C.)—V. 11.

Book.—It is a doom prophecy against Edom—Vs. 6, 8, 19, 21. Occasion, the cruelty of Edomites against Judah at a time of helplessness—Vs. 10–14; Ps. 137:7.

Punishment: To suffer like cruelty from other nations—Vs. 7, 15, 16; *cf.* Jer. 50:29; Ez. 35:11–15. Destruction of the wise and strong that all may perish —Vs. 8, 9. None of the Edomites shall remain—V. 18. Edom shall be judged by people of Zion—V. 21. Israel and Judah shall repossess the lands they —Vs. 17–21.

Other prophecies against Edom.- 137:7; Is. 34:5–15; 63:1–6; Jer. 4 22; Ez. 25:12–14; Amos 1:11, 12.

''**Character and style.**—The single of purpose in the prophecy reminds of Nahum. Its explanation is the cient enmity between Judah and Ed and here we are told how the long count is to be closed. The brevity of prophecy gives little scope for the e cise of lofty powers. Its strength, h ever, lies in its severe plainness energy of expression (*cf.* Ps. 137:7

Poetic (vs. 1–7 are poetry) and m tory—Vs. 8–16, 18, 19. The poetical tion is almost identical with Jer.— 14–16.''—Nelson's ''Bible Treasury.''

JONAH, BOOK OF.

The prophet.—He was the son of Amittai; family otherwise unknown—Jonah 1:1; II Ki. 14:25. From the town of Gath-hepher in tribe of Zebulun—II Ki. 14:25; cf. Josh. 19:10, 13.

Prophesied for Israel under Jeroboam II—II Ki. 14:24, 25. Here against Nineveh—Jonah 1:2; 3:2-4.

An unwilling missionary to Nineveh —1:2, 3; and displeased that the city was spared on repentance—3:10; 4:11. Nineveh under Shalmaneser II had defeated Ahab and forced Jehu to pay tribute (see SHAL. INSCRIPTIONS), and hence was Israel's enemy.

Jonah tried to flee from Jehovah to Tarshish in Spain—1:3. Caught in a storm, was thrown into the sea—1:4-15. Taken up by a fish, he was carried ashore —1:17; 2:10; Mt. 12:39, 40. He went and preached in Nineveh and the people, repenting, were saved—3:1-10. By the value of a gourd God taught him the value of human beings—4:6-11.

In disposition, Jonah seems to have been hasty, petulant and clannish—1:3; 4:1-3, 8, 9.

Book: "Historical setting.—The narrative portion of the book relates to the earlier years of Jeroboam II. All that we know of Jonah, beyond what is here told, we learn from II Kings 14, 25, which tells how he predicted to Jeroboam his victories over the Syrians. In the present instance he appears as a prophet with an altogether unique mission—viz., that of preaching repentance to the great city of Nineveh. The Assyrians were in his time much reduced in power, and were playing no great part in the affairs of the world. They had had much calamity, and were therefore perhaps the less unwilling to hear a messenger of evil. The result of his mission was that they took to heart his message, and the predicted ruin of their city was postponed for over a century and a half."—Nelson's "Bible Treasury."

Outline.—Has one theme: Jonah's mission to Nineveh—1:1; 3:2-4. Has one strong contrast: between Jonah's thought and God's thought—1:2-4; 3:10; 4:1-11. Has one great lesson: the value of all men—4:10, 11.

In composition, the book is a story with one inserted poem—2:2-9. It is marked with vividness and brief, detailed scenes—1:4-16; 2:1-10; 3:4-10; 4:1-11.

Lessons to Jonah.—The universality of divine love. The presence of Jehovah cannot be escaped—1:3-17. The servant of Jehovah must obey—1:12; 3:1-3. Anger with God is vanity—4:1-11. There is worth even among the heathen —3:5-10; 4:11.

Lessons to sailors.—Jehovah is God of the sea—1:9-16.

Lessons to heathen.—Jehovah condemns sin in all nations—3:4-8; but he is merciful to the penitent—3:9, 10.

Character and form.—The motive of the story is plain—to rebuke the exclusive spirit of Israel, and its rejoicing over the calamities of outside nations. The lesson is the more telling from the fact that Assyria had been, and was again to be, the most powerful and dangerous foe of Palestine. In *form* the book is not a prophecy in the ordinary sense at all, and the only justification for its place among the Prophets is its educative character.

New Testament references.—Jesus refers to Jonah in the whale's belly in speaking of His own death and resurrection—Mt. 12:40; 16:4 (Jonah 1:17). Mentions his mission to Nineveh—Lu. 11:30 (Jonah 3:4).

67

MICAH, BOOK OF.

The prophet.—A resident of Moresheth-gath in Judah—1:14. Family and history unknown, but called Morashtite —1:1; Jer. 26:18.

Time.—During reign of Jotham, Ahaz, Hezekiah (740-700 B.C.)—1:1; Jer. 26:18.

Prophesied against Israel and Judah —1:1, 5; Jer. 26:18.

Book: ''Historical setting.—Micah was a resident of Western Judah. The little town of Moresheth, his home, had been a dependency of the famous Philistian city of Gath, but since the conquests of Uzziah (II Chr. 26) the whole adjacent territory, including Gath, had been confirmed in the possession of Judah. His residence in the country gave him an interest in the fortunes of Judah outside of the capital, which makes his prophecy a welcome supplement to that of his great contemporary, Isaiah of Jerusalem. As he lived by the great international highway, he was led to cultivate a large view of political movements in Western Asia, and their effects upon his own people. Micah's main public work was performed during the reign of Hezekiah (cf. 3:12, and Jer. 26:18). His first prophecy was given before the fall of Samaria (722 B.C.), and ch. 6 is thought to belong to the reign of Manasseh. Hence we must suppose that his prophetic career lasted about thirty years. Ch. 1:1 is still more comprehensive in its limits of time. Micah was thus contemporary with the critical events in the history of Israel—which turned upon the relations with Assyria —the end of the northern kingdom, and the invasions of Palestine by Sargon and Sennacherib. He was also a witness of the corruption in morals and religion which were partly reformed by Hezekiah, and of the deeper degeneration under Manasseh.

The prophet's message.—The book of Micah consists of four discourses: Chs. 1, 2; 3, 4; 5; 6, 7. The mark of individuality in the divisions is that in each of them reproof and threatening are followed by encouragement and hopeful promise. A general similarity characterizes the first three sections as distinguished from the fourth. The first five chapters, which may be regarded as forming a larger group by themselves, deal mostly with the sins of the ruling classes—judges, priests, and prophets. In the last two the people as a whole are charged with guilt. For this reason, and on account of a marked difference in style, many have supposed that chs. 5 and 6 were written by another and later prophet than Micah; while a few maintain that a still later writer composed 7:7-20. Neither of these assumptions can be considered as proved.

A brief analysis of the book is as follows:—1. (a) Ch. 1. The prophet describes Jehovah as coming to destroy Samaria for its incurable corruption (ver. 1-8). He then declares that Judah deserves the same condemnation, illustrating, particularly by playing on the names of places in his own neighborhood, the character of the chastisement to be inflicted upon his home and country (ver. 9-16). (b) Ch. 2. The magnates, as representatives of the people, are accused of grasping dishonesty towards the poor. When they protest, Micah avers that the threatened punishment comes from a just and reasonable God, and is earned by their injustice and cruelty. The popular prophets favor self-indulgence, but are false both in their counsel and in their promises (ver. 1-11). Then an abrupt turn of the discourse pictures the return from banishment of the people expelled from the land for their sins (ver. 12, 13).—II. (a) Ch. 3 is a stronger and more detailed assertion of the cruelty and rapacity of the leaders of the people, and the official misdeeds of judges, priests, and prophets. It closes with the announcement that for such iniquity Jerusalem should be made desolate. (b) Ch. 4 is a bright picture of Israel restored and become the spiritual center of the world, with renewed domestic peace, after having triumphed over her assembled foes. —III. Ch. 5 begins by telling of the near approach of the Assyrian invader (ver. 1), and then dwells upon the image of a great deliverer who should in due time arise out of Bethlehem, who should carry the war into Assyria itself, and restore in numbers and power the remnant of Israel (ver. 2–9). Then all forms of false worship should cease, as well as reliance on any defence but Jehovah Himself (ver. 10–15).—IV. Chs. 6 and 7 shift the scene to the reign of Manasseh, and the whole people, not merely the rich men and officials, come under the prophet's criticism. (a) Ch. 6:1–8 is a splendid dramatic representa‑ tion (cf. Ps. 50) of God appearing in controversy with Israel. He asks why He has been slighted and ignored? The people defend themselves by inquiring how they could have gone beyond what they have done in propitiatory sacrifice. He replies that what He requires is justice, kindness, and humility towards God. (b) In ver. 9–16 the dishonesty and greed that prevail in the capital are denounced, and the results are shown by Jehovah Himself to be certain deprivation and desolation. (c) The prophet pierces to the center of the moral evils of Israel by revealing the dishonor and treachery that are rampant not only in official but in family and domestic life (7:1–6). (d) On behalf of his people, now humbly turning to righteousness, he declares his confidence in God under the taunts of his enemies (ver. 7–10). (e) Jerusalem shall be rebuilt and strengthened; but in the meantime many nations shall come against her, and the land shall be desolate (ver. 11–13). (f) A lyrical conclusion predicts the restoration of Israel and the subjection of the nations, and celebrates the pardoning love and faithfulness of Jehovah (ver. 14–20)." —Nelson's "Bible Treasury."

Outline.—Part first: Coming of Jehovah for judgment against sins of Jacob —Chaps. 1, 2. Part second: Rulers and false prophets condemned, but later shall be peace—Chaps. 3–5. Part third: Exhortations and warnings—Chaps. 6–7.

Chief sins were: Idolatry—1:7; 5:13, 14. Seizure of property—2:2, 8. False prophecy—2:11; 3:5–7; 5:12. Cruelties —3:1–3, 10; 7:2; 6:12. Injustice—3:9– 11; 7:3. Dishonor to parents—7:6. Chief punishments: Overthrow and desolation—1:6; 2:4, 5; 5:10, 11; 7:15. Captains and captivity—1:16, 17; 2:10, 12, 13; 4:10; 5:1, 3. Jehovah's refusal to help—3:4, 6, 7. Chief promises: Return from captivity—2:12, 13; 4:10. Reign of Jehovah in Zion—4:1–8; cf. Is. 2:2–4; 7:12. A ruler to be raised up from Bethlehem— 5:2–5. Success against enemies—4:13; 5:6–9; 7:16, 17. Pardon from Jehovah —7:18–20. Chief advices: Justice, kindness, humility before God—6:8.

"Character and style.—Micah is distinguished, like all the prophets of his period, by intense sympathy with the poor and the helpless, and indignation against their deceivers and oppressors. Their wrongs, as well as the general moral corruptions of society, form the ground on which the ruin of the state is determined and justified. Micah presents this issue in a greater variety of aspects than any of his predecessors. He is also alive to the true conditions of reformation, and joins Isaiah in the prophecy of a king of David's line, who shall save his people, not only from their foes, but from their sins (ch. 5). He discerns and formulates with unequalled clearness and power the essence of religious service (6:6–8). Thus he has had, next to Isaiah, the greatest influence upon the future. He employs many styles with success. In the later chapters his writing is smooth and artistic. The following passages are poetic—1:8–16; 2:4, 12, 13. The following half dramatic—6:1–8; 6:10; 7:17. Rebukes and threats—1:5–7; 2:2–5, 8– 13; Chaps. 3:5; 6:9–16. Hopes and promises—4:1–8, 12, 13; 5:2–9; 7:15, 18–20. Marked with earnestness, fervor, plays on words, sudden changes of thought."—Nelson's "Bible Treasury."

New Testament quotations.—5:2 (Mt. 2:6); 6:15 (John 4:37); 7:6 (Mt. 10:35, 36; Mk. 13:12; Lu. 12:53); 7:20 (Lu. 2: 73).

NAHUM, BOOK OF.

The prophet.—Unknown, except by Book of Nahum. Residence, Elkosh; Location uncertain—Nah. 1:1. Prophecies as if a Judæan—1:15.

Time.—After fall of No-amon (Thebes, 663 B.C.)—3:8-10; before fall of Nineveh (606 B.C.)—2:1, 8-13; 3: 1-17.

Book: "Historical setting.—Nahum follows Zephaniah by but a few years. The destruction of Nineveh (606 B.C.), which was to the latter an event of general anticipation, is regarded by the former as impending. The enemy is now at hand, and about to strike. The date is not far from 610 B.C. The catastrophe is so tremendous that the fate of no other nation claims the prophet's attention. Nothing is known of the person of the prophet.

The prophet's message.—The fall of Nineveh is dwelt upon as Jehovah's punishment for manifold iniquity, and as a means for securing the release of His people.

I. Ch. 1 begins with a sublime vision, like that of Habakkuk, or Micah, or Ps. 18, or Ps. 50, depicting God's coming for judgment (ver. 1-6). To those who trust Him, God is good (ver. 7). But His enemies, represented by the Assyrians, are doomed to utter destruction; while Israel, relieved from the tyrant, shall welcome the tidings of his fall (ver. 8-15).

II. Ch. 2 describes the actual taking of Nineveh by terrible unnamed foes (the Medes and Chaldæans), the desperate defence, capture, and spoiling. The description begins (ver. 2) by announcing this as a token of the restoration of Israel, and ends by declaring the destruction to be the work of Jehovah.

III. Ch. 3 is an expansion of the theme of ch. 2. New details are given, new figures employed, and the fall of

Thebes in Egypt (about 668 B.C.) is cited as an example of what was to happen to Assyria, its conqueror (ver. 8 ff.), in spite of its defences, its wealth, and its military discipline.

Leading thought.—Nineveh will be destroyed—1:1, 8, 12; 2:7-13; 3:7, 18, 19. Doctrine of God: Jehovah, though slow to wrath, takes vengeance on enemies—1:2, 3, 8, 12. He is mighty in nature—1:4-6. He is good to them that trust Him—1:7, 15. He will destroy Nineveh—1:9-13; 5:5, 6; 2:13.

Accusation against Nineveh.—Drunkenness—1:10; 3:11. King counsels against Jehovah—1:9, 11. Idolatry—1:14. Rapacity—2:11-13; 3:1, 16, 17. Harlotry and witchcraft—3:4. Military weakness at last—1:10; 2:5, 6; 3:11-17.

Fate of the city.—Siege and poor defence—2:1, 5, 8; 3:1-3, 14. Gates broken open—2:6; 3:13. Spoil taken—2:9, 10. Burning with fire—2:6, 13; 3:13, 15. Fear and mourning of people—2:7, 8, 10. Hopeless waste—1:12, 15; 2:10; 3: 17-19.

Character and style.—A distinguishing feature of the prophecy is its unity of design and subject. More remarkable still is the fact that it contains no homilies, nor even a hint of the errors of Israel and their punishment. Its view of providence is wide and general. To this largeness of conception the style admirably corresponds. It is very powerful and effective, both in its literal and in its prevailing figurative dress. The poetic structure is regular throughout, and the lofty tone of the introduction is maintained with dignity and solemnity to the end. Nervous: Threatening to the enemy; Hopeful to Judah—1:9-15; 3:1-7. Poetical—Chaps. 2, 3. Plaintive—3:18, 19. Graphic—1:4-8; 2:3-13; 3:1-7. Argumentative—3:8-17."
—Nelson's "Bible Treasury."

HABAKKUK, BOOK OF.

The prophet.—Family unknown—Hab. 1:1; 2:1–3; 3:1. A poet—Chap. 3 is poetry.

Book: "Historical setting.—Habakkuk prophesied about 604 B.C., in the reign of Jehoiakim (608-597 B.C.), in the middle period of the career of Jeremiah. He follows Nahum closely, who busies himself with the impending fall of Nineveh. With Habakkuk the Assyrians are past and gone, and it is with the Chaldæans that Israel has to deal. Of the prophet's person we know nothing, but his character is marked in his unconscious self-revelation.

The prophet's message.—The book falls into two distinct portions—the first (chs. 1 and 2) written in ordinary prophetic style, the second (ch. 3) being a psalm or hymn.

I. Chs. 1 and 2 are concerned with the work and fate of the Chaldæans. Chs. 1 to 2:4 is in the form of a colloquy between the prophet and Jehovah. A cry of bewilderment and amazement is uttered over the evils that run riot in Israel (1:1–4). Jehovah explains the delay of judgment by declaring that it is coming in the form of an onslaught by the Chaldæans, that terrible, relentless, and resistless nation (ver. 5–11). But, again urges the prophet, are the Chaldæans to destroy the good and the bad indiscriminately, and are the righteous to perish? (ver. 12 to 2:1.) Jehovah answers that though the Chaldæans would have it so, yet a remnant shall be preserved, and that by their fidelity to and trust in Jehovah (2:2–4). Finally, the prophet, after describing the Chaldæans as inflamed with lust of power and conquest (ver. 5), utters a series of denunciations on them, which are put into the mouths of the nations exulting in the fall of the oppressor. In these five 'woes' of the Chaldæans (each occupying three verses) they are condemned on account of their greed (ver. 6–8); their self-destructive ambition (ver. 9–11); the cruelty and godlessness of their conquests (ver. 12–14); their shameless treatment of the nations,

making them helpless like drunken men (ver. 15–17); their idolatry in the face of Jehovah in His temple (ver. 18–20). II. Ch. 3 puts in lyric form, with ample detail, the thought of the vision of Jehovah with which the prophecy opens (ver. 1–15), and its effect upon the prophet's own spirit. Speaking for his people, he exults that no privation or suffering can rob him of his trust and joy in God (ver. 16–19)."—Nelson's "Bible Treasury."

Vital theme.—Iniquity ought to be punished—1:2-4.

Vital doctrines.—Jehovah will punish any wicked people—1:13; 2:16; 3:13. The righteous shall live by faith—2:4.

Sins of Judah.—Violence, strife, injustice and greed—1:2-4, 13–17.

Sins of Chaldæans.—Vanity, rapacity, bloodshed, debauchery and idolatry—2:4-19.

Punishments.—Chaldæans shall overrun Judah—1:5-10. Woe, plunder, and shame shall overtake the Chaldæans—2:6-16.

Teaching of the poem.—Jehovah's glory and power—3:3-11. Jehovah's mercy and justice—3:2, 12-15. Jehovah saves and sustains His people—3:13, 18, 19.

"**Character and style.**—The prophecy is distinguished as much for moral and spiritual insight and fervor as it is for rich and varied beauty of form and expression. The problem of the outcome of the work of the Chaldæans is only solved by tracing its profound results, and especially its inward effects, upon the hearts and consciences of those who are tried by its inflictions. For majesty and splendor of diction, as well as for liveliness and depth of imagination, Habakkuk stands among the first of the sacred authors. He is perhaps the most essentially poetic of the prophets. Conversational—1:2, 5, 12; 2:2. Descriptive—1:3, 4, 6–11; 2:4, 5; 3:3–15. Indignant—1:3, 4, 16, 17; 2:4-19. Appreciative of Jehovah—1:12, 13; 2:20; 3:1–19."—Nelson's "Bible Treasury."

71

ZEPHANIAH, BOOK OF.

The prophet.—Son of Cushi, descendant of Hezekiah—Zeph. 1:1. If this be king Hezekiah, the prophet was also a prince—*cf.* II Ki. 18:1 ff. Prophesies against royal family freely—1:8.

Book: "Historical setting.—Zephaniah's brief but pregnant prophecy was delivered just after the time of the first appearance of Jeremiah (626 B.C.)—*i. e.*, in the first half of the reign of Josiah. The next preceding prophet was Micah, who died in the early part of the reign of Manasseh. In the intervening period there had been political quiet in Palestine, which was only interrupted by the brief revolt of Manasseh. But the condition of the whole of Western Asia, including Palestine, portended a speedy upheaval. Above all, Ninevah was beginning its memorable decline after the death of its king, Assur-banipal (668-626 B.C.). Morally and religiously the Jewish nation had improved but little since the degeneracy that had followed the death of Hezekiah, and Josiah's reform (621 B.C.) had not yet begun, if we may judge from the invectives of the prophet against idolatrous practices. Zephaniah was apparently a descendant of king Hezekiah.

The prophet's message.—Zephaniah spoke and wrote primarily for the correction and warning of Judah and Jerusalem, though he draws illustrations from the sins and fates of other peoples. The culmination of these is found in the iniquities, the pride, and the speedy fall of Nineveh. A division into four parts is as follows:

I. The threatening: ch. 1.—1. The whole world—that is, the Semitic world —is to undergo exemplary punishment, particularly Jerusalem and its apostates from Jehovah (ver. 1-6). 2. The classes of people that are to be thus visited—the royal house, the nobles, the wealthy traders, the careless and defiant generally—are characterized, and their chastisement set forth in language largely figurative (ver. 7-18).

II. The lesson from the nations: ch. 2.—God's own people are warned to repent in time (ver. 1-3), and so avoid the doom that is about to fall upon the Philistines (ver. 4-7), Moab (ver. 8-11), Egypt, under the name of Ethiopia (ver. 12), and finally Assyria and Ninevah (ver. 13-15).

III. The remonstrance: ch. 3:1-7.— Rebellious and obstinate Jerusalem is urged to repent by the righteous and reasonable God, in view of coming woes; for the lesson of the fate of other nations has so far been unheeded.

IV. The promised redemption: ch. 3: 8-20.—1. The faithful remnant is bidden to wait and trust. It shall survive the ruin of the nations, be joined by exiled brethren from far and near, and rest in quiet content (ver. 8-13). 2. Joyous thanksgiving is now in place, for Jehovah is in the midst of Jerusalem, to comfort and bless His people. Their reproach is taken away; dispersion and captivity are at an end (ver. 14-20)."— Nelson's "Bible Treasury."

Central thought.—Jehovah's terror to idolatry and determination that all nations shall serve Him—2:11.

The "day of Jehovah" is described as a day of Wrath—1:7, 14-16; 2:3; *cf.* Joel 1:15-18 (poetry in both books).

The promises.—A people free from haughtiness, falsehood and deceit—3: 9-13. Expulsion of enemies—3:15. Jehovah dwelling among His people—3: 15-17. Return from captivity—3:19, 20.

Character and style.—The lessons of the time are skilfully drawn, and are enforced with the earnestness of conviction and lofty motive. There is no great originality of thought or expression, but the style is forcible and pointed, and rises towards the close to lyrical grace and sweetness. Chiefly that of doom prophecy—1:2-18; 2:4-14. Yet brightened by promise—3:9-20. Inset with poetry—1:7, 14-16; 2:1-3, 15; 3:1-3, 14-17. Name "Jehovah" used thirty-four times in three chapters.

HAGGAI, BOOK OF.

The prophet.—No personal history in title of the Book—Hag. 1:1.

Book: "Historical setting.—None of the minor prophets belongs to the long period of the Exile. For an account of it we must have recourse to Ezekiel and the second part of Isaiah. Haggai was the earliest of the prophets of the restoration. After the return (536 B.C.), many years elapsed before the people began seriously to rebuild the temple. In 520 B.C., Haggai urged them to undertake the work. Four months later he was joined by Zechariah. In four years the temple was completed. We know nothing further of Haggai personally.

The prophet's message.—The four sections of the prophecy are the following:

I. Ch. 1.—The people are reminded of the desolation of the temple, while they are living in comfortable homes. Such neglect has already brought upon them failure of crops and general scarcity. The result of the appeal is that all, from the highest to the lowest, set themselves to the work of restoration.

II. Ch. 2:1–9 is uttered to cheer the workers. The glory of this latter house, they are assured, will be greater than that of the former.

III. Ch. 2:10–19 is a further reminder of the connection between neglect of duty towards God and national prosperity. Hitherto the people have been as though they were 'unclean' in God's sight, and therefore had been excluded from His favor. Henceforth they are to be blessed.

IV. Ch. 2:20–23 is a promise to the leader Zerubbabel, that he will be honored and shielded by Jehovah when the nations shall be in commotion and terror at His approaching judgment."— Nelson's "Bible Treasury."

Outline: Divisions.—Four messages are formally introduced by dates—Chs. 1; 2:1–9; 2:10–19; 2:20–23.

Purposes.—To promote the building of the temple at Jerusalem—1:2–8; 2:9, 15–19; and to encourage the governor and high priest—1:12–15; 2:2–5, 23.

Leading messages.—It is time to build the temple—1:2–6. Prosperity can be expected only after building—1:6–11; 2:15–19. God will bless the governor and high priest—2:4, 5, 20–23. Nations shall give aid, not hindrance, to Judah—2:6–9, 21, 22.

"Character and style.—The prophecy is partly historical, explanations and connections being duly made in the progress of the discourse. Especially noticeable is the exact dating of the several sections, and the methodical character of the whole narrative. Poetical form is not neglected, but in general the style is plain and unadorned. Argumentative—1:4–6, 9–11; 2:11–14. Hortatory—1:7, 8, 13; 2:4, 5. Optimistic—2:6–9, 19, 21–23. Historical and oracular (history mingled with Divine messages)—1:1–5, and throughout.

ZECHARIAH, BOOK OF.

The prophet.—Family: Son of Berechiah, son of Iddo—Zech. 1:1. Of priestly descent—Neh. 12:12, 16.

Prophetic work.—To encourage righteousness and loyalty to God—1:4–6; 6:9–14; 8:15–23. To inspire hope in Judah—1:14–17, 21; 2:4–13; 8:2–8, 11–15. To promote the building of the temple—4:7–10; 6:11, 15; 8:9–11. To foretell the branch—3:8; 6:12, 13; cf. Is. 11:1; Jer. 33:15.

Book: "Historical setting.—According to Ezra 5:1; 6:14, Zechariah was a coadjutor of Haggai in promoting the rebuilding of the temple, and according to his own statement he prophesied in 520 and 518 B.C. (1:1, 7; 7:1). The issues with which he deals are the same as those which confronted Haggai—the maintenance of the national worship, and the correction of national vices.

The prophet's message.—But the mode of approaching these problems is quite different from that adopted by Haggai. The greater portion of the prophecy consists of *visions* intended to present motives for confidence and effort. Outside opposition should come to naught, and the Jewish leaders had the might of Jehovah on their side. An introduction (1:1–6) contains a general exhortation to repentance, and a warning to the people not to imitate their fathers, who did not listen to the prophetic word. Thereafter we have two large sections:

I. Chs. 1:7 to 6:15 contains nine symbols, mostly visions, accompanied by their interpretations:

1. Ch. 1:8–17, a vision of the horses of Jehovah, which, as His messengers, report to Him; along with His reply.

2. Ch. 1:18–21, four horns, representing the opponents of Israel, are broken.

3. Ch. 2, a man with a measuring-line lays out the restored Jerusalem.

4. Ch. 3, Joshua the high-priest is, accused by Satan, and acquitted, and is honored with commissions and revelations from Jehovah.

5. Ch. 4, the beautiful symbol of the golden candlestick and two olive trees, with the practical application of encouragement to Zerubbabel.

6. Ch. 5:1–4, a flying roll recording a curse upon immoral actions.

7. Ch. 5:5–11, an ephah measure containing a woman is seen carried away to Babylon.

8. Ch. 6:1–8, four chariots, each having horses of a particular color, are the four heavenly spirits charged to carry out God's purposes in the earth.

9. Ch. 6:9–15, the symbolical action of crowns of silver and gold being made and placed upon the head of Joshua the high-priest, who thus represents the Messiah-priest upon His throne.

II. In ch. 7, the prophet, in answer to a question as to observance of a certain fast, replies that the true fast is justice, mercy, and piety, which had been so much neglected in earlier generations. This suggests, in ch. 8, the coming Messianic time, when the city shall be populous and happy under the renewed protection of Jehovah, and the fasts shall be joyful feasts, attended by multitudes of strangers seeking His favor.

There is so much that is matter of dispute in chs. 9–14, as regards their date and immediate application, that we shall have to content ourselves with a summary and a few general remarks. The contents are largely symbolic and figurative.

Chs. 9–11 form a division by themselves, perhaps written by the Zechariah of Isa. 8:2. It has an entirely different historical setting from that of chs. 1–8. Here we are transported back to the eighth century B.C. Ch. 9:1–8 refers to conquests made by Tiglath-pileser III. (745-727 B.C.). Northern Israel is still in existence, and Assyria is still in its 'pride' (10:10 ff.). These allusions form part of the very texture of the prophecy, and are assumed by some to be old fragments embedded in a post-Exilic work.—Ch. 9:1–8.—Syria, Phœnicia, and Philistia are to be brought low. Yet a remnant of the Philistines shall be united with Judah, and both shall be under the protection of Jehovah.

Ch. 9:9–17.—The Messiah shall come as the Prince of Peace to restore the dispersed of Israel, and save them from their enemies.

Ch. 10.—The people are entreated to turn to Jehovah in their troubles, and not to diviners and images. Jehovah will be the defender alike of Judah and Israel, restoring and strengthening them, and bringing low their oppressors.

Ch. 11 announces the shock of war which appals the rulers of Judah (ver. 1–3). The rest of the chapter is allegorical. It represents Jehovah as rejected by His people, they being in turn rejected by Him, their true Shepherd. By an expressive figure, the brotherhood of Judah and Israel is declared to be broken.

Chs. 12:1 to 13:6.—The nations come against Jerusalem; but Jehovah defends and saves it. The conflict is shown to be spiritual, for a spirit of grace and supplication is to be poured upon Judah and Jerusalem. Also a fountain is to be opened for the cleansing of guilt, and the idols and false prophets are to be banished.

Ch. 14.—Again Jerusalem is besieged, and this time it is taken, half the people going into exile; but the residue are saved. After various figurative illustrations of the processes and results of the Messianic reign, it is declared that the survivors among the nations shall go up to worship in Jerusalem, which shall be wholly consecrated to Jehovah.

Character and style.—Zechariah illustrates well in what divers manners God spoke by the prophets, also how different methods of revealing God's will were adapted to different ages and to changed conditions of His ancient people. The symbolic vision or action, though not unknown earlier, does not predominate in any prophetic book till the time of the Exile. And yet two of the post-Exilic prophets, Haggai and Malachi, have none of it. This apocalyptic style had great advantage in impressiveness, and led to the production, in imitation of it, of a vast body of uncanonical literature. In the hands of Zechariah it is as instructive as it is powerful. Hortatory—1:2–6; 8:9–23. Illustrative (by visions)—1:8–11; 18:21; 2:1–5; 3:1–5; 4:2–6; 5:1, 2, 5–11; 6:1–8. Hopeful—1:14–17, 21; 2:4–13; 3:4, 5, 10; 4:7–10; 6:12–15; 8:2–8.''—Nelson's ''Bible Treasury.''

MALACHI, BOOK OF.

Malachi.—Malachi means, "My messenger," and may be the title of the book—Mal. 1:1; 3:1. Author is wholly unknown.

"Historical setting. — Malachi, the latest of the literary prophets, wrote about 450 B.C., and was thus contemporary with Ezra and Nehemiah. The great task of the reformers of that era was to maintain the integrity of the nation, and the purity and regularity of the worship of Jehovah. The one depended on the other; for unless the services should be kept up at the central sanctuary, the influences of the heathen around them would soon divide and scatter them. But the temple services were being marred by the indifference and neglect of both worshippers and priests. Another element of great danger was intermarriage with the surrounding peoples—a danger with which Nehemiah had to contend. We see, then, that as Haggai and Zechariah commemorated the rebuilding of the temple, so Malachi gave voice to the movement for reform in worship and morals.

The prophet's message.—I. An introduction (1:2–5) proves, by the way in which Edom is treated as compared with Israel, that Jehovah still loves and favors His own nation.

II. Chs. 1:6 to 2:9 condemns the neglect and moral degeneracy of the priests: 1. They despise and are ungrateful to God, the true Father and Master of His people, by their mean and worthless sacrifices. Such service is profanation and contempt (1:6–14). 2. Such conduct, unrepented of, will bring a curse (2:1–3). 3. The true priest recognizes his covenant obligation to God, and his life and service are in keeping with it. But they have betrayed their own trust and the people committed to them, whose contempt they have rightly earned (2:4–9).

III. Chs. 2:10 to 3:18 deals with the shortcomings of the people. 1. Intermarriages with heathen women, and the divorce of rightful wives, are stigmatized as abomination and treachery (2:10–16). 2. The coming of God's messenger is announced. He is to be followed by Jehovah Himself, appearing in judgment against all unworthy temple worship, and all evil conduct (2:17 to 3:6). 3. Temporal prosperity is made to depend upon a reformation in worship (3:7–12). 4. God's discipline has developed a twofold spirit: some, vexed by misfortune, are filled with mistrust of God, and with envy and bitterness; others, by God's fear and mutual helpfulness, are kept in remembrance against the testing day (3:13–18).

IV. Ch. 4.—The day of Jehovah is near, for the destruction of the wicked and the vindication and triumph of the righteous. To prepare for that time the law of Moses must be the guide, and the prophet Elijah shall return to show the people of Israel how they may become one united whole again by common faith in God, and so escape the impending sentence of doom."—Nelson's "Bible Treasury."

Outline:

Time.—When offerings not acceptable —1:7, 10. Tithes were not brought—3:7–10; *cf.* Neh. 13:10–12. And marriage laws were violated—2:10–16; *cf.* Ezra 9:2; 10:3, 17, 18. Perhaps in time of Ezra and Nehemiah, about 444 B.C., or a little later.

Leading sins.—Sacrilege—1:6–14. Violation of marriage laws—2:10–16. Falsehood and oppression—3:5. Refusal of tithes—3:7–10. Disregard of God—2:17; 3:13–15.

Leading promises.—To send the messenger of the covenant—3:1–3; 4:5, 6. To accept offerings—3:4. To grant material blessings—3:10–12. To give victory over enemies—4:2, 3. To hold the faithful as God's own possession—3: 16–18.

"**Character and style.**—The book of Malachi is essentially an argumentative composition. It represents the practical matter-of-fact temper and spirit of the later Jewish age. With the exception of a few obscure passages, it is plain and convincing. Its chief characteristic is the prophet's art of exciting attention by introducing objections to the truths stated by him, and then replying to them, with emphatic additions to his original statement. This form of treatment serves to bring out very clearly the points at issue; and there is perhaps no prophecy which gives in equal space so full a presentation of contemporary moral and religious life. Poetic form is not much observed, but in its place comes the more purely rhetorical style, with reasoning as the principal motive. Teaching by question and answer—1: 2–4, 6–9; 2:10, 11, 14–17; 3:2, 7–9, 13– 15. By accusation—1:7, 8, 12–14; 2:8, 11, 13, 17; 3:8, 9, 13–15. By exhortation to reform—1:9; 2:15; 3:10, 18. By threatening—1:14; 2:2, 3; 12, 4:1.''— Nelson's "Bible Treasury."

INCIDENTS IN THE OLD TESTAMENT REFERRED TO IN THE NEW TESTAMENT.*

Gen.	1	Creation	Acts 14:15; Heb. 11:3
"	1:3	Creation of Light	II Cor. 4:6
"	1:11, 12	Earth produces Herbs	Heb. 6:7
"	1:26	Man Likeness of God	Jas. 3:9
"	1:27	God's Image Man and Woman	Mt. 19:4; I Cor. 11:7-12
"	1:28; 9:2	Man's Dominion	Heb. 2:8
"	2:2, 3	God rested	Mk. 2:27, 28; Heb. 4:4
"	2:7	Man a Living Soul	I Cor. 15:45-47
"	2:9	Tree of Life	Rev. 2:7; 22:2
"	2:21-23	First Man then Woman	I Cor. 11:9; I Tim. 2:13
"	2:21	Woman from Man	I Cor. 11:8
"	2:24	Marriage	Mt. 19:4-6
"	3:1-5	Serpent	II Cor. 11:3; Rev. 12:9
"	3:6	Eve first sinned	I Tim. 2:14
"	3:6-8	Sin's results	Rom. 5:12-19
"	3:15	Conflict between Good and Evil	I John 3:8-10
"	3:15	Victory for Good	Rom. 16:20; Heb. 2:14, 15
"	3:17-19	Creation is in Pain	Rom. 8:22
"	4:4	Abel's Acceptance	Heb. 11:4
"	4:8	Cain's Murder of Abel	I John 3:12; Jude 11
"	4:10	Blood of Abel	Lu. 11:51; Heb. 12:24
"	5:21-24	Enoch's Life	Heb. 11:5; Jude 14, 15
"	6:14-16	The Ark	Heb. 11:7; I Pet. 3:20
"	7:1-8, 12	The Deluge	Lu. 17:26, 27; II Pet. 3:6
"	8:15-17	Noah's Family Saved	I Pet. 3:20; II Pet. 2:5
"	9:6	Murderer to be slain	Rev. 13:10
"	11:31	Abraham in Haran	Acts 7:4
"	12:1	Call of Abraham	Heb. 11:8
"	12:2, 3	Promised Blessing	Acts 3:25; Gal. 3:8
"	12:5-8	Sojourn in Canaan	Acts 7:4; Heb. 11:9
"	13:15	Canaan promised	Acts 7:5
"	14:18-20	Melchizedek	Heb. 7:1-4
"	15:1-5	Abraham's Seed	Heb. 11:12
"	15:6	Abraham's Faith	Rom. 4:3; Gal. 3:6
"	15:13, 14	Bondage of Seed	Acts 7:6, 7
"	16:7-16	Hagar and Ishmael	Gal. 4:23-25

* By Professor Ira M. Price, Ph.D. Copyright, 1903, by Thomas Nelson & Sons. Used by permission, and revised by author for the Cross-Reference Bible.

Gen.	17:5	Father of Nations	Rom. 4:17
"	17:7	Abraham foresees	John 8:56
"	17:10	Circumcision	Acts 7:8; Rom. 4:11, 12
"	18:2-5; 19:1	Angels to Abraham	Heb. 13:2
"	18:11, 12, 18	Sarah's Faith	Heb. 11:11
"	18:12	Sarah says, ''My Lord''	I Pet. 3:6
"	18:18	Abraham a Blessing	Gal. 3:8
"	Ch. 19	Sodom and Gomorrah	Mt. 11:24; Rom. 9:29
"	19:26	Lot's Wife	Lu. 17:32
"	21:1-3	Isaac's Birth	Gal. 4:23, 28
"	21:4	Isaac circumcised	Acts 7:8
"	21:9	Ishmael mocking	Gal. 4:29
"	21:14	Hagar sent away	Gal. 4:30
"	22:10	Isaac offered up	Heb. 11:17-19
"	25:23-28	Jacob and Esau	Rom. 9:7-13
"	25:33	Esau's Sale	Heb. 12:16
"	27:27-39	Isaac's Blessing	Heb. 11:20
"	27:34	Esau's Sorrow	Heb. 12:17
"	28:10-15	Jacob's Dream	John 1:51
"	33:19	Burial at Shechem	Acts 7:16
"	37:1	Jacob in Canaan	Acts 7:8; Heb. 11:9
"	37:28	Joseph sold into Egypt	Acts 7:9
"	39:2, 4, 21	Joseph favored	Acts 7:10
"	41:37-39	Joseph's Gift	Acts 7:10
"	41:40	Joseph Ruler in Egypt	Acts 7:10
"	41:54	Famine in Land	Acts 7:11
"	42:2-3	Buy Corn in Egypt	Acts 7:12
"	42:13	Twelve Brothers	Acts 7:8
"	45:1	Joseph made known	Acts 7:13
"	45:9; 46:5, 6	Descent to Egypt	Acts 7:14, 15
"	47:31	Jacob's Frailty	Heb. 11:21
"	48:9-22	Jacob, Joseph's Son	Heb. 11:21
"	49:33	Jacob's Death	Acts 7:15
"	50:25	Joseph's Bones	Heb. 11:22
Ex.	1:7	Israel increased	Acts 7:17
"	1:8	A New King	Acts 7:18
"	1:10	Cunning Pharaoh	Acts 7:19
"	1:22	Destroying Children	Acts 7:19
"	2:2	Moses concealed	Acts 7:20
"	2:3-10	Moses adopted	Acts 7:21
"	2:11	Moses to his People	Heb. 11:25
"	2:11-14	Slays Egyptian	Acts 7:24-28
"	2:15	Moses' Flight	Acts 7:29; Heb. 11:27
"	3:2	Burning Bush	Luke 20:37; Acts 7:30
"	3:15-18	Moses' Mission	Acts 7:35
"	4:7-12	Signs in Egypt	Acts 7:36
"	7:20	Water became Blood	Rev. 16:3, 4
"	12:21-29	Passover in Egypt	Heb. 11:28
"	12:41; 14:1-22	Exodus	Acts 7:36; Heb. 11:29
"	13:21	Pillar of Cloud	I Cor. 10:1
"	14:23-31	Egyptians drowned	Heb. 11:29
"	Ch. 15	Song of Moses	Rev. 15:3
"	15:23-25	Signs in Wilderness	Acts 7:36

Ex.	16:15	Manna to eat	John 6:31, 32, 49, **58**; I Cor. 10:3
"	16:18	Gathering Manna	II Cor. 8:15
"	16:33, 34	Pot of Manna	Heb. 9:4
"	17:5, 6	Rock smitten	I Cor. 10:4
"	19:12	Touch not the Mount	Heb. 12:20
"	Ch. 20	Law from Sinai	Acts 7:38; Gal. 3:19
"	24:8	Blood sprinkled	Heb. 9:19, 20
"	25:10-16	Ark, Mercy Seat	Heb. 9:4, 5
"	25:26	Tabernacle, Furniture	Heb. 9:2, 3
"	26:31-37	Most Holy Place	Heb. 9:7, 8, 10, 19
"	29:38	Daily Sacrifice	Heb. 10:11
"	32:4-6	Golden Calf	Acts 7:40, 41; I Cor. 10:7
"	32:15, 16	Tables of Stone	Heb. 9:4
"	34:33	Moses' Veil	II Cor. 3:13
Lev.	12:3	Circumcision	John 7:22
"	12:6	Purification	Lu. 2:22-24
"	14:2-32	Law for Leprosy	Mt. 8:4; Lu. 17:14
"	16:29-34	Day of Atonement	Heb. 9:7
"	20:10	Penalty for Adultery	John 8:5
"	24:5, 9	Priests' Allowance	Mt. 12:3, 4
Num.	14:32	Death of Unbelievers	Jude 5
"	14:33	Forty Years	Acts 7:36, 42; Heb. 3:9
"	16:32, 33	Korah's Rebellion	Jude 11
"	17:2, 4, 10	Aaron's Rod	Heb. 9:4
"	21:6	Fiery Serpents	I Cor. 10:9
"	21:8	Serpents of Brass	John 3:14
"	Ch. 22	Balaam's Reward	II Pet. 2:15; Jude 11
"	25:1-9	Rebellions of Israel	I Cor. 10:1-10
Deut.	7:1	Canaanites expelled	Acts 13:19
"	34:5, 6	Body of Moses	Jude 9
Josh.	2:16	Rahab and Spies	Heb. 11:31; Jas. 2:25
"	6:12-20	Walls of Jericho	Heb. 11:30
"	6:23	Rahab spared	Heb. 11:31
"	14:2	Canaan by Lot	Acts 13:19
"	18:1	Tabernacle at Shiloh	Acts 7:45
"	24:32	Joseph's Bones	Heb. 11:22
Judges	2:16	Judges' Rule	Acts 13:20
"	Ch. 4	Barak	Heb. 11:32
"	Chs. 6-8	Gideon	Heb. 11:32
"	Ch. 11	Jephthah	Heb. 11:32
"	14:16	Samson	Heb. 11:32
I Sam.	3:20	Samuel, Judge, Prophet	Acts 13:20
"	8:5	Israel desires a King	Acts 13:21
"	10:21, 24	Reign of Saul	Acts 13:21, 22
"	13:14	David to be King	Acts 13:22
"	21:1	David at Nob	Mt. 12:3, 4
"	21:6	David, Shewbread	Mt. 12:3, 4
II Sam.	7:2, 3	David and a Temple	Acts 7:46
"	7:12	David's Seed	Acts 13:23
I Ki.	6:1	Solomon's House	Acts 7:47
"	10:1	Queen of Sheba	Mt. 12:42; Lu. 11:31
"	16:31-33	Jezebel	Rev. 2:20

I Ki.	17:1	Elijah and Drought	Lu. 4:25; Jas. 5:17
"	17:9	Widow of Zarephath	Lu. 4:26
"	17:23	Raising her Son	Heb. 11:35
"	19:14	Elijah's Intercession	Rom. 11:3
"	19:18	Seven Thousand Faithful	Rom. 11:4
II Ki.	4:34	Shunammite's Son	Heb. 11:35
"	5:14	Healing Naaman	Lu. 4:27
"	17:16	Worship Heavens	Acts 7:42
"	24:15	Exile at Babylon	Acts 7:43
I Chr.	10:14	Saul and David	Acts 13:22
II Chr.	24:20-22	Murder of Zachariah	Mt. 23:35
"	24:20, 21	Murder of Abel and Zachariah	Lu. 11:51
Ezra	3:2	Zerubbabel	Mt. 1:12
Job	1:21, 22	Patience of Job	Jas. 5:11
Ps.	95:10, 11	Forty Years	Acts 7:36
Dan.	3:27	Fiery Furnace	Heb. 11:34
"	6:22	Daniel, Lions' Den	Heb. 11:33
"	6:22	Daniel the Prophet	Mt. 24:15
Jonah	1:17	In the Fish	Mt. 12:40; 16:4
"	3:4	Mission to Ninevites	Lu. 11:30

PASSAGES QUOTED OR PARAPHRASED IN THE NEW TESTAMENT FROM THE OLD TESTAMENT.

Mt.	1:23	Immanuel	Is. 7:14
"	2:6	Bethlehem	Mic. 5:2
"	2:15	Out of Egypt	Hos. 11:1
"	2:18	In Ramah	Jer. 31:15
"	3:3	Voice crying	Is. 40:3
"	4:4	Bread alone	Deut. 8:3
"	4:6	Angels Charge	Ps. 91:11, 12
"	4:7	Tempt not	Deut. 6:16
"	4:10	Worship Lord	Ex. 20:3
"	4:15, 16	Land of Shadow	Is. 9:1, 2
"	*5:5	Meek inherit	Ps. 37:11
"	*5:8	Pure in Heart	Ps. 24:3-5
"	5:21	Kill not	Ex. 20:13
"	5:27	No Adultery	Ex. 20:14
"	5:31	Divorcement	Deut. 24:1
"	5:33	Perjury	Deut. 23:21
"	5:34	God's Throne	Is. 66:1
"	5:35	King's City	Ps. 48:2
"	5:38	Eye for Eye	Lev. 24:20
"	5:43	Love Neighbor	Lev. 19:18
"	5:48	Be perfect	Deut. 18:13
"	*6:6	Enter thy Chamber	Is. 26:20
"	*7:22	Prophesy	Jer. 14:14
"	7:23	Work Iniquity	Ps. 6:8
"	8:17	Took Infirmities	Is. 53:4
"	9:13	Desire Mercy	Hos. 6:6
"	*9:36	Sheep astray	Num. 27:17
"	*10:35, 36	Man's Foes, of his Own House	Mic. 7:6
"	11:5	Blind, Poor	Is. 29:18, 19; 61:1
"	11:10	My Messenger	Mal. 3:1
"	12:18-21	My Servant	Is. 42:1-4
"	13:14, 15	Understand not	Is. 6:9, 10
"	13:35	In Parables	Ps. 78:2
"	*13:43	Righteous shine	Dan. 12:3
"	15:4	Honor Parents	Ex. 20:12
"	15:8, 9	Lips, Doctrines	Is. 29:13
"	17:10	Elijah come	Mal. 4:5
"	18:16	Witnesses	Deut. 19:15
"	19:4	Male and Female	Gen. 1:27
"	19:5	Two One	Gen. 2:24
"	19:7	Divorcement	Deut. 24:1
"	19:18	Shalt not kill	Ex. 20:13-16
"	19:19	Honor Parents	Ex. 20:12
"	19:19	Love Neighbor	Lev. 19:18

* Designates passages used in free adaptation from Old Testament.

Mt.	*19:26	God can do it	Gen. 18:14
"	21:5	Behold thy King	Is. 62:11
"	21:9	Hosanna	Ps. 118:26
"	21:13	House of Prayer	Is. 56:7
"	21:16	Mouth of Babes	Ps. 8:2
"	21:33	Vineyard Parable	Is. 5:1, 2
"	21:42	Rejected Stone	Ps. 118:22, 23
"	*21:44	Stumbling Stone	Is. 8:14
"	22:24	Levirate Law	Deut. 25:5
"	22:32	God of Abraham	Ex. 3:6
"	22:37	Love the Lord	Deut. 6:5
"	22:39	Love Neighbor	Lev. 19:18
"	22:44	The Lord unto my Lord	Ps. 110:1
"	*23:38	Desolate House	Ps. 69:25
"	23:39	Hosanna	Ps. 118:26
"	24:15	Abomination	Dan. 9:27; 12:11
"	24:21	Tribulation	Dan. 12:1
"	24:29	Darkness of Judgment	Joel 4:16
"	24:30	Son of Man	Dan. 7:13
"	*24:35	Enduring for ever	Is. 51:6
"	*25:31	With Angels	Zech. 14:5
"	26:28	Covenant Blood	Ex. 24:8
"	26:31	Shepherd smitten	Zech. 13:7
"	26:64	Son with Power	Dan. 7:13, 14
"	27:9, 10	Thirty Pieces	Zech. 11:13
"	*27:34	Vinegar Drink	Ps. 69:21
"	27:35	Garments parted	Ps. 22:18
"	*27:39	Railed on Him	Ps. 22:7
"	*27:43	Trusteth on God	Ps. 22:8
"	27:46	My God, My God	Ps. 22:1
Mark	1:2	My Messenger	Mal. 3:1
"	1:3	Voice crying	Is. 40:3
"	4:12	Perceive not	Is. 6:9, 10
"	4:32	Marvellous Growth	Dan. 4:9
"	7:6, 7	Lip Honor	Is. 29:13
"	7:10	Honor Parents	Ex. 20:12
"	7:10	Curses Parents	Ex. 21:17
"	8:18	Useless Organs	Is. 6:9, 10
"	*9:48	Worm dieth not	Is. 66:24
"	10:4	Divorcement	Deut. 24:1
"	10:6	Male and Female	Gen. 1:27
"	10:7, 8	Two One	Gen. 2:24
"	10:19	No Adultery	Ex. 20:13-16
"	10:19	Kill not	Ex. 20:13
"	10:27	God can do it	Gen. 18:14
"	11:17	House of Prayer	Is. 56:7
"	11:17	Den of Robbers	Jer. 7:11
"	12:2	Vineyard Parable	Is. 5:1, 2
"	12:10, 11	Rejected Stone	Ps. 118:22, 23
"	12:19	Levirate Law	Deut. 25:5
"	12:26	God of Abraham	Ex. 3:6
"	12:29	One Lord	Deut. 6:4
"	12:30	Love the Lord	Deut. 6:5
"	12:31	Love Neighbor	Lev. 19:18

* Designates passages used in free adaptation from Old Testament.

Mark	*12:32, 33	One God	Deut. 4:35; 6:4
"	12:36	To my Lord	Ps. 110:1
"	13:12	Family Quarrels	Mic. 7:6
"	13:14	Abomination	Dan. 9:27
"	13:19	Tribulation	Dan. 12:1
"	*13:22	False Prophets	Deut. 13:1-5
"	13:26	Son of Man	Dan. 7:13
"	14:7	Poor with you	Deut. 15:11
"	14:18	Mine Enemy	Ps. 41:9
"	14:24	Covenant Blood	Zech. 9:11; Ex. 24:8
"	14:27	Shepherd smitten	Zech. 13:7
"	*14:34	Soul sorrowful	Ps. 42:5
"	14:62	Son with Power	Dan. 7:13, 14
"	15:24	Garments parted	Ps. 22:18
"	15:29	Railed on him	Ps. 22:7
"	15:34	My God, my God	Ps. 22:1
"	15:36	Vinegar Drink	Ps. 69:21
Luke	1:15	Nazirite Law	Num. 6:3
"	1:17	Turn Hearts	Mal. 3:1; 4:6
"	1:32	David's Throne	Is. 9:7
"	1:33	Endless Reign	Dan. 4:3
"	1:37	God powerful	Gen. 18:14
"	1:46	Hannah's Song	I Sam. 2:1
"	1:48	Gospel Anticipation	I Sam. 1:11
"	1:50	Lovingkindness everlasting	Ps. 103-17
"	1:68	Blessedness of God	Ps. 106:48
"	1:73	Holy Covenant	Gen. 12:3; 22:16-18
"	1:76	Messenger	Mal. 3:1
"	2:22-24	Purification	Ex. 13:2; Lev. 12:2-4, 6
"	3:4, 6	Voice crying	Is. 40:3-5
"	4:4	Bread alone	Deut. 8:3
"	4:8	Worship God	Deut. 6:13
"	4:10, 11	Angels Charge	Ps. 91:11, 12
"	4:12	Tempt not	Deut. 6:16
"	4:18, 19	Gospel for Poor	Is. 61:1, 2
"	6:21	Blessed	Is. 61:2
"	7:27	My Messenger	Mal. 3:1
"	8:10	Understand not	Is. 6:9, 10
"	10:27	Love God	Deut. 6:5
"	10:28	Do and Live	Lev. 18:5
"	*11:49	Prophets slain	II Chr. 24:18-22
"	12:53	Family Quarrels	Mic. 7:6
"	13:19	Marvellous Growth	Dan. 4:9
"	13:35	House Desolate	Ps. 118:26; Jer. 22:5
"	18:20	Do not	Ex. 20:12-17
"	19:38	Hosanna	Ps. 118:26
"	19:46	House of Prayer	Is. 56:7
"	19:46	Den of Robbers	Jer. 7:11
"	20:17	Rejected Stone	Ps. 118:22, 23
"	20:38	Levirate Law	Deut. 25:5
"	20:37	Moses' Bush	Ex. 3:6
"	20:42, 43	To my Lord	Ps. 110:1
"	21:20	Destruction	Dan. 9:27

* Designates passages used in free adaptation from Old Testament.

Luke	*21:22	Vengeance Days	Hos. 9:7
"	21:25, 26	Final Judgment	Joel 2:30, 31
"	*21:27	Son of Man seated	Dan. 7:13
"	22:37	Transgressor	Is. 53:12
"	22:69	Son of Man seated	Dan. 7:13
"	23:30	Fall on us	Hos. 10:8
"	23:34	Garments parted	Ps. 22:18
"	23:35	Scoffed at him	Ps. 22:7
"	23:46	Submission	Ps. 31:5
John	1:23	Voice crying	Is. 40:3
"	1:29, 36	Lamb of God	Is. 53:7
"	2:17	Consuming Zeal	Ps. 69:9
"	4:37	Sowing, Reaping	Mic. 6:15
"	6:31	Bread of Heaven	Ex. 16:4, 15; Ps. 78:24
"	6:45	Taught of God	Is. 54:13
"	*7:37	Come thirsty	Is. 55:1
"	7:38	Man's Words	Pr. 18:4
"	7:42	Seed of David	Is. 11:1
"	8:17	Witnesses	Deut. 19:15
"	9:39	Effect of Gospel	Is. 6:9, 10
"	10:34	Ye are Gods	Ps. 82:6
"	12:13	Hosanna	Ps. 118:25, 26
"	12:14, 15	King cometh	Zech. 9:9
"	*12:34	Christ for ever	Is. 9:7
"	12:38	Who believeth?	Is. 53:1
"	12:40	Blind Eyes	Is. 6:9, 10
"	*12:49	Words to speak	Deut. 18:18
"	13:18	Betrayer	Ps. 41:9
"	15:25	Causeless Hate	Ps. 69:4
"	19:24	Garments parted	Ps. 22:18
"	*19:28-30	I thirst	Ps. 69:21
"	19:36	No Bone broken	Ex. 12:46
"	19:37	Pierced One	Zech. 12:10
"	*20:9	Rise again	Ps. 16:10
Acts	1:20	Habitation desolate	Ps. 69:25
"	2:17-21	Spirit's Anointing	Joel 2:28-32
"	2:25-28	Beheld the Lord	Ps. 16:8-11
"	*2:30	God's Oath	Ps. 132:11
"	2:31	He was not left	Ps. 16:10
"	2:34, 35	To my Lord	Ps. 110:1
"	2:39	Those afar off	Is. 59:19
"	3:13	Moses (Bush)	Ex. 3:6
"	3:22, 23	Prophet like me	Deut. 18:15
"	3:25	Earth blessed	Gen. 12:3; 22:18
"	4:11	Rejected Stone	Ps. 118:22
"	4:25, 26	Gentiles rage	Ps. 2:1, 2
"	*5:30	Hanged on a tree	Deut. 21:22, 23
"	7:3	Migrate	Gen. 12:1
"	7:6	Strange Land	Gen. 15:13, 14
"	7:7	In Bondage	Ex. 3:12
"	7:8	Circumcision	Gen. 17:10
"	7:9	Act of Jealousy	Gen. 37:11
"	7:9	God with him	Gen. 39:2, 21

* Designates passages used in free adaptation from Old Testament.

Acts	7:10	Favor his	Gen. 39:21
"	7:11	Famine in Land	Gen. 41:54, 55
"	7:12	Jacob heard	Gen. 42:2
"	7:13	Joseph unmasked	Gen. 45:1
"	7:14	Souls migrated	Deut. 10:22
"	7:15	Jacob died	Gen. 49:33
"	7:16	Abraham's Sepulchre	Josh. 24:32
"	7:16	Unto Shechem	Gen. 50:13
"	7:17-19	People multiplied	Ex. 1:7-18
"	7:27, 28	Ruler over us?	Ex. 2:13, 14
"	7:29	Moses fled	Ex. 2:15-22
"	7:31-34	Message to Moses	Ex. 3:3-10, 15
"	7:35	Ruler and Deliverer	Ex. 2:14
"	7:36	Wonders and Signs	Ex. 7:3
"	7:37	Prophet to rise	Deut. 18:15, 18
"	7:40	Make us Gods	Ex. 32:1, 23
"	7:42, 43	Bloody Offerings	Amos 5:25-27
"	7:46, 47	Built him a House	I Ki. 8:17-20
"	7:48-50	God's Throne	Is. 66:1, 2
"	7:51	Uncircumcised	Ex. 33:3, 5
"	8:32, 33	Sheep to Slaughter	Is. 53:7, 8
"	13:18	Israel in Wilderness	Deut. 1:31
"	13:22	David, son of Jesse	Ps. 89:18-36
"	13:33	My Son	Ps. 2:7
"	13:34	Sure Blessings	Is. 55:3
"	13:35	Holy One	Ps. 16:10
"	13:41	Wonder and perish	Hab. 1:5
"	13:47	Light for Gentiles	Is. 49:6
"	*14:15	Maker of All	Ex. 20:11
"	15:16, 17	Tabernacle rebuilt	Amos 9:11, 12
"	*17:24	God Creator	Ex. 20:11
"	21:26	Purification	Num. 6:13
"	23:5	Speak not Evil	Ex. 22:28
"	*26:18	Open Blind Eyes	Is. 42:7
"	28:26, 27	Understand not	Is. 6:9, 10
Rom.	1:17	Live by Faith	Hab. 2:4
"	2:6	Just Deserts	Deut. 7:10; Ps. 62:12
"	2:24	God blasphemed	Is. 52:5
"	3:4	God justified	Ps. 51:4
"	3:10-12	None righteous	Ps. 14:1-3
"	3:13	Putrid Throat	Ps. 5:9
"	3:14	Cursing Mouth	Ps. 10:7
"	3:15	Eager Murderers	Is. 59:7, 8
"	3:16, 17	Road to Perdition	Is. 59:7, 8
"	3:18	God unfeared	Ps. 36:1
"	*3:20	None justified	Ps. 143:2
"	4:3, 9	Imputed Righteousness	Gen. 15:6
"	4:7, 8	Forgiveness blessed	Ps. 32:1, 2
"	4:17	Father of Nations	Gen. 17:5
"	4:18	So thy Seed	Gen. 15:5
"	4:25	For our Trespasses	Is. 53:12
"	7:7	Covet not	Ex. 20:17
"	8:33	Who condemns	Is. 50:8, 9
"	8:34	At Right Hand	Ps. 110:1

* Designates passages used in free adaptation from Old Testament.

Rom.	8:36	Continually killed	Ps. 44:22
"	9:7	In Isaac	Gen. 21:12
"	9:9	Sarah's Son	Gen. 18:10
"	9:12	Elder a Servant	Gen. 25:23
"	9:13	Jacob and Esau	Mal. 1:2, 3
"	9:15	Mercy granted	Ex. 33:19
"	9:17	God's purpose	Ex. 9:16
"	9:20-22	Potter's Power	Is. 29:16; Jer. 18:3-6
"	9:25	My People	Hos. 2:23
"	9:26	Not my People	Hos. 1:10
"	9:27, 28	Remnant saved	Is. 10:22, 23
"	9:29	Seed left us	Is. 1:9
"	9:33	Stumbling Stone	Is. 28:16
"	10:5	Do and live	Lev. 18:5
"	10:6-8	Who to Heaven?	Deut. 30:12-14
"	10:11	Belief, no Shame	Is. 28:16
"	10:13	Whosoever calls	Joel 2:32
"	10:15	Welcome Gospel	Is. 52:7
"	10:16	Our Report	Is. 53:1
"	10:18	In All the Earth	Ps. 19:4
"	10:19	Jealousy provoked	Deut. 32:21
"	10:20	Found unsought	Is. 65:1
"	10:21	Exhortation	Is. 65:2
"	11:3	Prophets killed	I Ki. 19:10, 14
"	11:4	Reserves	I Ki. 19:18
"	11:8	Spirit of Stupor	Is. 29:10
"	11:9, 10	Table a Snare	Ps. 69:22, 23
"	11:26	Sion's Deliverance	Is. 59:20, 21
"	11:27	My Covenant	Is. 27:9
"	11:34	Mind of Lord	Is. 40:13
"	*11:35	Who first gave?	Job 41:11
"	12:16	Be not wise	Pr. 3:7
"	12:17	Provide Things honorable	Pr. 3:4
"	12:19	Vengeance is God's	Deut. 32:35
"	12:20	Feed thine Enemy	Pr. 25:21, 22
"	13:9	Love thy Neighbor	Lev. 19:18
"	14:11	Predicted Homage	Is. 45:23
"	15:3	Reproaches on me	Ps. 69:9
"	15:9	Open Confession	Ps. 18:49
"	15:10	Rejoice, Gentiles	Deut. 32:43
"	15:11	Praise the Lord	Ps. 117:1
"	15:12	Root of Jesse	Is. 11:10
"	15:21	Marvellous Sight	Is. 52:15
I Cor.	1:19	Destroy Wisdom	Is. 29:14
"	1:31	Glory in God	Is. 41:16; 45:25
"	2:9	Eye saw not	Is. 64:4
"	2:16	God's Mind Unknown	Is. 40:13
"	3:19	Trap for Wise	Job 5:13
"	3:20	Lord knoweth	Ps. 94:11
"	*5:7	Our Passover	Ex. 12:21
"	5:13	Put away Wickedness	Josh. 7:13
"	6:16	Twain One	Gen. 2:24
"	9:9	Just Allowance	Deut. 25:4
"	10:7	Careless Ease	Ex. 32:6

* Designates passages used in free adaptation from Old Testament.

I Cor.*10:20	Sacrifice not to Demons	Deut. 32:17
" 10:22	Jealousy	Deut. 32:2
" 10:26	Earth is Lord's	Ps. 24:1
" 14:21	Strange Tongues	Is. 28:11
" 15:25-27	Subjection to him	Ps. 8:6; 110:1
" *15:32	Make merry	Is. 22:13
" 15:45, 47	Adam, Living Soul	Gen. 2:7
" 15:54	Victory in Death	Is. 25:8
" 15:55	Death's Sting?	Hos. 13:14
II Cor. 3:3	Written in Hearts	Jer. 31:33
" 3:13	Moses' Veil	Ex. 34:33
" 4:6	Let there be Light	Gen. 1:3
" 4:13	Conviction's Words	Ps. 116:10
" 6:2	Accepted Time	Is. 49:8
" 6:16	God's Indwelling	Lev. 26:11, 12
" 6:17	Come out	Is. 52:11
" 6:18	My Children	Is. 43:6; Jer. 3:19
" 8:15	No Surplus	Ex. 16:18
" *9:7	Bountiful Eye	Pr. 22:9
" 9:9	Scattered	Ps. 112:9
" 10:17	Glory in God	Jer. 9:23, 24
" 13:1	Witnesses	Deut. 19:15
Gal. 3:6	Imputed Righteousness	Gen. 15:6
" 3:8	Nations blessed	Gen. 12:3
" 3:10	Curses	Deut. 27:26
" 3:11	Live by Faith	Hab. 2:4
" 3:12	Do and Live	Lev. 18:5
" 3:13	Hanged cursed	Deut. 21:23
" 3:16	To thy Seed	Gen. 12:7; 22:18
" 4:27	Rejoice, thou Barren	Is. 54:1
" 4:30	Eject Aliens	Gen. 21:10
" 5:14	Love Neighbor	Lev. 19:18
Eph. 1:22	Subjection to him	Ps. 8:6
" 4:8	Captivity Captive	Ps. 68:18
" 4:25	Neighborly Conduct	Zech. 8:16
" 4:26	Be angry, sin not	Ps. 4:4
" 5:14	Awake, Sleeper	Is. 26:19; 60:1
" 5:31	Forsake Parents	Gen. 2:24
" 6:2, 3	Honor Parents	Ex. 20:12
Phil. 2:10, 11	Predicted Homage	Is. 45:23
Col. 3:1	On Right Hand	Ps. 110:1
" 3:20	Obey Parents	Ex. 20:12
I Thess. *2:4	God tries Hearts	Pr. 17:3
" *4:8	Spirit to you	Ez. 36:27
I Tim. 5:18	Muzzle no Ox	Deut. 25:4
" 5:18	Worthy of Hire	Deut. 24:14, 15
" 5:19	Witnesses	Deut. 19:15
II Tim. 2:19	Lord knoweth	Num. 16:5
" 2:19	Naming Christ	Is. 26:13
" *4:17	From Lion's Mouth	Ps. 22:21
Heb. 1:3	On Right Hand	Ps. 110:1
" 1:5	My Son	Ps. 2:7
" 1:5	To him a Father	II Sam. 7:14
" 1:6	Angels worship	Ps. 97:7

* Designates passages used in free adaptation from Old Testament.

Heb.	1:7 ·	Angels Wings	Ps. 104:4
"	1:8, 9	Everlasting Throne	Ps. 45:6, 7
"	1:10-12	Lord the Founder	Ps. 102:25-27
"	1:13	On Right Hand	Ps. 110:1
"	2:6-8	What is Man?	Ps. 8:4-6
"	2:12	Declare thy Name	Ps. 22:22
"	2:13	Trust in Him	Is. 12:2
"	2:13	My Family	Is. 8:18
"	3:7-11, 15	Harden not	Ps. 95:7-11
"	4:3-5	God's Oath	Ps. 95:11
"	4:4	God rested	Gen. 2:2
"	4:7	Harden not	Ps. 95:7-11
"	5:5	My Son	Ps. 2:7
"	5:6, 10	Everlasting Priest	Ps. 110:4
"	6:14, 17, 18	Will bless thee	Gen. 22:16, 17
"	6:20	After Melchizedek	Ps. 110:4
"	7:1-3	Melchizedek met	Gen. 14:17-20
"	7:11, 15, 17, 21, 24, 28	Priest, perfect for ever	Ps. 110:4
"	8:5	Given Pattern	Ex. 25:9, 40
"	8:8-12	Days come	Jer. 31:31-34
"	9:19, 20	Covenant Blood	Ex. 24:5-8
"	10:5-7	Not Sacrifices	Ps. 40:6-8
"	10:12, 13	Sat down	Ps. 110:1
"	10:16, 17	Law in Hearts	Jer. 31:33, 34
"	10:30	Lord is Avenger	Deut. 32:35, 36
"	10:37, 38	He will come	Hab. 2:3, 4
"	*11:4	Abel's Sacrifice	Gen. 4:4
"	11:5	Enoch translated	Gen. 5:24
"	11:18	In Isaac	Gen. 21:12
"	*11:23	Moses hid	Ex. 2:2
"	*11:26	Reproach of Christ	Ps. 89:50, 51
"	12:5, 6	Lord's Chastening	Pr. 3:11, 12
"	12:12	Lift the Hands	Is. 35:3
"	*12:14	Seek Peace	Ps. 34:14
"	12:20	Touch not	Ex. 19:12
"	12:21	Fear and quake	Deut. 9:19
"	12:26	Universe quaking	Hag. 2:6
"	13:5	Never forsaken	Deut. 31:6
"	13:6	Lord my Helper	Ps. 118:6
"	13:15	Praise Sacrifices	Ps. 50:14, 23
Jas.	1:10, 11	Flower fadeth	Is. 40:6, 7
"	2:8	Love thy Neighbor	Lev. 19:18
"	2:11	No Adultery	Ex. 20:13, 14
"	2:23	Imputed Righteousness	Gen. 15:6
"	*3:9	Likeness of God	Gen. 1:26
"	4:6	Proud resisted	Pr. 3:34
"	5:11	Lord Pitiful	Ps. 103:8
I Pet.	1:16	Be ye holy	Lev. 11:44; 19:2
"	1:24, 25	Flesh is Grass	Is. 40:6, 8
"	2:3	Lord gracious	Ps. 34:8
"	2:6, 8	Foundation Stone	Is. 28:16
"	2:7	Rejected Stone	Ps. 118:22
"	2:8	Stumbling Stone	Is. 8:14

* Designates passages used in free adaptation from Old Testament.

I Pet.	2:17	Fear God	Pr. 24:21
"	2:24	Bare our Sins	Is. 53:4, 5
"	3:10-12	Restrain thyself	Ps. 34:12-16
"	4:8	Covereth Sins	Pr. 10:12
"	5:5	Proud resisted	Pr. 3:34
II Pet.	2:22	Dog to his Vomit	Pr. 26:11
"	3:8	Thousand Years, One Day	Ps. 90:4
"	*3:12	Heaven dissolve	Is. 34:4
"	3:13	New Universe	Is. 65:17; 66:22
John	4:21	Love Brother also	Deut. 6:5; Lev. 19:18
Jude	9	Michael	Dan. 12:1
"	9	Lord rebuke	Zech. 3:2
"	14	Lord cometh	Deut. 33:2

The Book of Revelation is saturated with the Old Testament from beginning to end, there being nearly four hundred references to thoughts and events mentioned in the Law, the Prophets, and the Writings. Too numerous to tabulate in the space at command, the student will find ample marginal references to fasten each such incident in its proper Old-Testament locality.

* Designates passages used in free adaptation from Old Testament.

INTRODUCTION TO THE NEW TESTAMENT.

By Professor M. B. Riddle, D.D., LL.D.

"**Unity.**—The New Testament is a collection of twenty-seven distinct writings, from eight (or nine) different hands. Of these writers, four were apostles—St. Matthew, St. John, St. Paul, and St. Peter; two were companions of the apostles—St. Mark and St. Luke; two were our Lord's brothers, probably not apostles—St. James and St. Jude. The books are usually classed as Historical (five), Didactic (twenty-one), Prophetical (one); though the writings of the first class include much more than one-half of the entire matter. The unity of the whole is remarkable: all the books find their center in Jesus Christ our Lord. The four Gospels narrate His life on earth; the fifth historical book tells how the new life, that came from Him through the Holy Spirit, passed from Jerusalem to Rome. The epistles, written by men of varied personal character and temperament, set forth the significance of the Gospel facts, as revealed to them, according to our Lord's promise (John 16:12, 13). The single prophetical book, however it is to be interpreted, shows the Lamb as King, to become Victor on earth, where His church is preparing through conflict to share His triumph.

Order.—In our English Bible the order is not chronological. In ancient manuscripts there was much variation in position; the seven General Epistles were usually placed immediately after Acts, the Gospels coming first, though not always in the order now universal. The Pauline Epistles seem to have been arranged according to length, so that the earliest and the latest stand together (I and II Thess., with I and II Tim. and Titus).

Progress of doctrine.—There is evident in these writings an advance of Christian thought toward maturity; but the progress is not along divergent lines, nor can all the books be classified according to assumed types of doctrine.

Biblical Theology properly discusses the theology of the several writings; but the theology of the New Testament is one, whatever progress is discernible. Moreover, the advance in St. Paul's teaching, as indicated by a comparison of Thessalonians with Ephesians, is almost as marked as that between the General Epistles of St. James and St. John, which are regarded as presenting the respective extremes in the progress of doctrine. The Gospels cannot be classified by any such principle; for while St. John, from its purpose, presents the most mature statements, there is no appreciable advance in doctrine from St. Matthew to St. Luke. The same Lord Jesus Christ was apprehended by all the writers in substantially the same way.

THE GOSPELS.

The four Gospels were written primarily for different circles of readers; each has its peculiar design, and each evangelist has his distinctive method. Only by a comparison of all four can a complete view be obtained of the history of our Lord's life on earth, and thus of His person and work. One fact should be noted: the four Gospels place the emphasis on the closing events. More than one-half of all the narratives describes the events of the last year—one of conflict; more than one-third is devoted to the few weeks which closed with the death and resurrection of our Lord. From early times the 'symbols' of Rev. 4:7 have been assigned to the four Evangelists, but in different ways. That of Jerome is usually accepted: Matthew, the man; Mark, the lion; Luke, the calf; John, the eagle. But this does not suggest very clearly their distinctive peculiarities. A comparison of the methods employed by the evangelists confirms the view of Godet: St. Matthew gives long discourses—he writes as a preacher; St. Mark depicts events as they occurred, one after the other—he is a chronicler; St. Luke arranges the incidents with reference to their relations—he is a historian; while St. John selects such facts and discourses as prove a given truth—he is a theologian. The Gospel of St. John, evidently written last, is properly distinguished from the others, which resemble each other more closely.

SYNOPTIC GOSPELS.

The Gospels of St. Matthew, St. Mark and St. Luke have been termed 'Synoptic,' and the writers 'Synoptists,' because a common outline is pursued. Much of the matter throughout is common to all three; but there are many points of difference. The arrangement is rarely the same in all three, even when the events of the same period are narrated, except in the accounts of Passion Week. In language the differences are remarkable. When the same incident is given by all, they rarely agree exactly for ten consecutive words (in the Greek). So that, whatever be the source of the common matter, there is *literary independence*.

How are these agreements and differences to be accounted for? The safest view is: that the common matter represents in general the story of Jesus Christ as it was at first preached by the apostles and others; that when written Gospels were needed, these three writers, independently of each other, each with added material, wrote the accounts we now have. St. Matthew had his own knowledge of the events; St. Mark learned from St. Peter; St. Luke gathered material when in Palestine (58-60 A.D.), while eye-witnesses were living, probably using, for the parts peculiar to his narrative (especially chs. 1, 2), some written documents or memoranda. But many hold that there was a common document or documents on which all three Gospels were based.

By many the 'double source' theory is now accepted. This assumes that there were two original documents referred to by Papias (died 163 A. D.); one, by St. Matthew, containing the Oracles (Logia) in the Hebrew dialect;

the other, by St. Mark, derived from St. Peter. The one consisted mainly of discourses; the other, of narratives. But there is no agreement as to the extent of these assumed documents. The one, it is asserted by some, contained only discourses; according to others, it also included narratives. The other is held by some to be a briefer form of Mark's Gospel; by others, to be that Gospel as we now have it. St. Luke's Gospel is regarded as the last composite result of the combinations. But none of these theories accounts satisfactorily for the obvious literary independence of the Synoptic Gospels.

The faithful use of a common document or documents would have led to greater similarity both in order and in language. If the writers purposely deviated from the common source or sources, valid reasons must be discovered for the modifications. The reasons assigned often assume that these writers had the literary habits of modern authors or reporters; too often they imply, though in smoother phrase, that the changes were purposed corruptions. That the reasons are not valid is rendered highly probable by the fact that two critics of equal ability, both holding the 'double source' theory, frequently reach conclusions diametrically opposed to each other, in applying the theory to most of the sections containing common matter. The problem is an interesting one; but prolonged discussion has not as yet yielded any positive result. At least, there is no prospect of obtaining in this way a more faithful portrayal of our Lord's person and of His work than that derived from the canonical Gospels, which, from the days preceding Justin Martyr, have been read in Christian assemblies, cited by Christian authors, and cherished by Christian hearts.

The independence of the Synoptic Gospels involves the probability that they were written within a few years of each other, and that the testimony they present is that of three distinct witnesses to the main facts respecting our Lord's life on earth.''—Nelson's ''Bible Treasury.''

NEW TESTAMENT.

CONVINCE — GOSPELS

	AUTHOR		FOR WHOM WRITTEN	Christ
Outward Acts / Synoptic — Missionary / Galilean	Matthew	Publican	Jews	Messiah
	Mark	Servant	Romans	Servant
	Luke	Physician	Greeks	Son of Man
Judaean / Spiritual	John	Loved Apostle	Church	Son of God

CONVERT

ACTS......1–12—Building the Church. 13–28—Paul's Missionary Journeys.

CONFIRM — EPISTLES

Paul's — To Churches:

Romans—Need and plan of redemption; sin and grace
I Corinthians—Divine authority of Gospel; factions; discipline
II Corinthians—Self-defence. Galatians—Gospel gives spiritual freedom
Ephesians—The Church; unity in Christ
Philippians—Christ Gospel theme; pattern; object; strength
Colossians—Headship of Christ. I and II Thessalonians—Second coming
To individuals: Philemon. Pastoral. I and II Timothy. Titus

GENERAL:

Hebrews—Old and new covenants
James—Faith resulting in works
I and II Peter—Faith looks forward in hope
I, II and III John—Faith resulting in love. Jude—Contend for faith

COMPLETE — REVELATION

MATTHEW.

Names.—Matthew—Mt. 9:9; 10:3; Mk. 3:18; Lu. 6:15; Acts 1:13. Levi— Mk. 2:14; Lu. 5:27, 29. Son of Alpheus —Mk. 2:14.
Home.—Capernaum—Mk. 2:1, 13 ff. **Business.**—Publican—Mt. 10:3; Lu. 5:27. Hence not a Pharisee nor a disciple of John the Baptist. Called to follow Jesus while at the custom-house— Mt. 9:9; Mk. 2:14; Lu. 5:27. Gave up office and wealth for Jesus—Lu. 5:28. **Gave Jesus a great feast in gratitude.** —Mt. 9:10; Mk. 2:15; Lu. 5:29. Invited many of his old friends ("publicans and sinners") to the feast—Mt. 9:10, etc. Other disciples of Jesus there also —Mt. 9:10. Many of the publicans and sinners led to follow Jesus—Mk. 2:15. Pharisees and their scribes uninvited— Mt. 9:11; Mk. 2:16; Lu. 5:30. Many complain to Christ's disciples about this social fellowship of Jesus with publicans and sinners—Mt. 9:11; Mk. 2:16; Lu. 5:30. Jesus justifies it, and thus his call of Matthew the publican—Mt. 9:12 f; Mk. 2:17; Lu. 5:31 f. **Chosen as one of the twelve apostles.** —Mt. 10:3; Mk. 3:18; Lu. 6:15; Acts 1:13. **Always linked in the Gospel lists with Thomas (twin).**—Either as his twin brother or as more probably his friend —Mt. 10:3 (after Thomas). In Mk. 3:18 and Lu. 6:15 (before Thomas). But in Acts 1:13 Bartholomew and Matthew (and in this order) are joined together. **Traditions.**—Eusebius (H. E. III. 24) mentions that he preached to Hebrews in Judæa, and before leaving wrote the Gospel—Heb. (Aramaic) that bears his name (Greek). Other traditions connect his name with Ethiopia, Macedonia, Persia. **Date of Gospel of Matthew not known.**—Probably between Mark and Luke, and may be as early as A. D. 60. Exact relation of the Aramaic Matthew and Greek Matthew not known. Probably a book of logia or sayings of Jesus preceded the present Matthew.

CHARACTERISTICS OF THE GOSPEL OF MATTHEW.

Evidently written by a Jew.—This is plain from the absence of explanation of Jewish customs. Cf. Mk. 7:2-5. Lu. 2:4-13 explains topography of Judæa, but not so Matthew—John 4:4, 10, likewise explains enmity between Jews and Samaritans. Author is much interested also in Jewish origin and aspect of Christianity, though willing to tell the fate of the Jewish people—Mt. 21:43. **Tone anti-Pharisaic.**—This appears throughout and in particular in Chap. 23, which he alone reports. Here Jesus is represented as denouncing the Pharisees and Scribes with much vehemence. Cf. also the debate in the temple in Mt., Chaps. 21 and 22. As we know, publicans and Pharisees were very antagonistic. **Conceals his identity.**—The name of Matthew occurs in the Gospel only twice—Mt. 9:9; 10:3. Does not hesitate to call himself a hated publican in Mt. 10:3. **Style impersonal.**—As a methodical business man, tax collector and perhaps bookkeeper, one would expect little that is distinctive in his style. Some verbal peculiarities will be noted later. **Familiarity with money.**—Mentioned more frequently than in Mk. and Lu. Cf. Luckock's "Characteristics of the Gospels," page 33. Three kinds of money—Mt. 10:9. Gives two parables of talents not elsewhere found—Mt. 18:23-35; 25:14-30. Cf. Parable of pounds—Lu. 19:11-27. **For Jews.**—This is plain from the number of points of view. His use of O. T. quotations, to show that Jesus was the promised Messiah of the O. T., the Abrahamic genealogy of Jesus, the giving of the "Sermon on the Mount" where the teaching of Christ is related to that of the O. T., these and other points prove it. The readers are supposed to be familiar with Jewish customs—Mt. 15:1 f; 27:62. This is assumed, as in Mt. 15:2. Has Jewish estimate of value of dreams—1:20; 2:13. He has "Father in Heaven" 15 times, while Mk. has it only twice, and Lu. none. He calls Jerusalem the "Holy City" twice—4:5; 27:53. Not an objective narrative: The book is written with a purpose and selects material to prove that purpose. He combines the words and the deeds of Jesus. Sometimes he alternates:—Thus, Deeds—Chap. 4; Words—Chap. 5–7; Deeds—Chaps. 8 and 9; Words—Chaps. 10 and 11:18, etc. Probably the author used a book of sayings of Jesus and marks objective narratives with extra touches of his own from personal knowledge.

Genealogy of Jesus.—As a Jew, and for the Jews he begins (Mt. 1:1–17) his book with a genealogy. Thus he shows that Jesus was a descendant of David (legally through Joseph, his reputed father) as the Messiah must be (the Son of David)—Mt. 21:9. He began with Abraham, the father of the Jewish people. In an appeal to Jews this matter was important.

Conception of Jesus.—He is the Jewish Messiah—1:1–17. Begotten of the Holy Spirit—1:18. Born of the Virgin Mary—1:18, 25; 2:1. As a babe, worshipped by the Wise Men from the East —2:2, 11. Acknowledged as the Son of God, by the Father at his baptism— 3:17. His Sonship challenged by the devil—4:1, 6. The demons recognize his divine Sonship—8:29. He claims to be the Son of God in a special sense— 11:25–27. His favorite term for Himself is the Son of Man—Cf. 12:8, 32 etc. But this Son of Man has a supernatural aspect as Judge with glory and power— 16:28; 19:28; 24:30; 25:31; 26:64. He was indeed God with us—1:23. He definitely claimed to his disciples to be the Messiah—16:16–20. Yet He foretold His death at the hands of the Jewish rulers and rebuked Peter for not understanding—16:21–23. The Father identified Him as His Son on the "Mount of Transfiguration"—17:5. He foresaw His death on the cross as a ransom for many—20:19, 28. He formally announced Himself as the King Messiah by the triumphal entry—21:1–9. They hailed Him as prophet—21:11. He was thus, prophet, priest and king as the Son of David, yet David called Him Lord (humanity and deity)—22:42–45. Claimed to be Judge over Jerusalem and the whole world—24 and 25. Shed His blood for the remission of sins as symbolized by the Cup in the Lord's Supper —26:28. Claimed to be the Christ, the Son of God, on oath before Caiaphas— 26:63 f. Claimed power of Supreme Judge over Caiaphas and the sanhedrin —26:64. Rose from the dead in proof of His claim to be the Son of God, the Messiah—28:9 f. Appeared to the disciples and commanded them to take the world for Him away from the devil—28:16–20. This in brief is a sketch of Matthew's picture of Jesus the Christ.

Kingdom of Heaven.—This is Matthew's favorite expression, occurring 32 times and nowhere else in the Gospel— 3:2; 4:17; 5:3, 10, 19, 20; 7:21; 8:11; 10:7; 11:11, 12; 13:11, 24, 31, 33, 44, 45, 47, 52; 16:19; 18:1, 3, 4, 23; 20:1; 22:2; 23:14; 25:1. The phrase kingdom of God appears in Mt. 4 times—12:28; 19:24; 21:31, 43. But Mark uses it 14 times, Luke 34 times (8 more in Acts), Paul 8, John 2 (Rev. one more). Cf. Hawkins' "Horæ Synopticæ," page 25. But this is not all, for Matthew also has the expression, "Kingdom of my Father" (28:29), "Thy kingdom" (6:10; 20:21), "His kingdom" (16:28, referring to Himself), "The kingdom of their father" (13:43), "His kingdom" (13:41, referring to the Father. Cf. 6:33), and just "The kingdom" (13:38, sons of the kingdom), "Gospel of the kingdom" (4:23; 9:35; 24:14), "The word of the kingdom" (13:19). The term kingdom itself has a Jewish connotation and varies in exact shading from kingdomship or sovereignty (16:28), territory (4:8), organization (12:25), subjects (19:14), reign (4:17).

It is regarded as already present (4:17; 10:7; 12:28; 13:38), but still to come in greater power and to have a future consummation (13:31, 41; 20:21; 25:34; 26:29). The phrase, "kingdom of heaven," was practically the same as "kingdom of God," and was probably used so much out of deference to Jewish sentiment concerning avoidance of the name of deity. It accented also the idea that it was not a temporal earthly kingdom, but an inward spiritual growth.

Old Testament quotations.—These are more frequent in Matthew than in the other Gospels; though, as a matter of fact, Mt. is the longest Gospel. There are about 65 in Mt. and 43 in Lu. In Mt. 43 are direct citations, while only 19 are so in Lu. Matthew, himself, apart from the discourses of Jesus, makes 10 quotations from the O. T. Mark, only one. These agree less closely with the Septuagint than the others in Mt. *Cf.* Hawkins' "Horæ Synopticæ," page 123. These are 1:23; 2:15, 18, 23; 4:15 f; 8:17; 12:18–21; 13:35; 21:5; 27:9 f. These in particular Mt. uses, the expression "that it might be fulfilled" (1:22); as "there was fulfilled" (2:17); to show how in the life of Jesus was fulfilled the Messianic hope of Israel. The other quotations in Mt. are 2:6 (by the Scribes); 3:3, 17; 4:4, 6, 7, 10; 5:4, 5, 6, 7, 8, 21, 27, 31, 33, 43; 9:13; 11:10, 23; 12:7; 13:32; 15:4, 8, 9; 16:27; 17:5; 18:16; 19:4, 5, 18, 19, 26; 21:9, 13, 16, 33, 42, 44; 22:24, 32, 37, 39, 44; 23:38; 24:15, 21, 29, 30; 26:31, 64; 27:35, 46. A number of these are not quoted in the other Gospels, especially those in the "Sermon on the Mount." **Sermon on the Mount:** This is one of the outstanding peculiarities of the Gospel of Mt. Chaps. 5–7. In Lu. 6:17–49 we find what is probably a briefer report of the same sermon. But a large section of the discourse (Mt. 5:13; 6:34) appears in Mt. alone, though certain phrases in Mt. 6:19–34 do reappear in Lu. 12:22–34. But the famous passage in Mt. 5:17–42, where the teachings of Jesus are set over against that of the O. T. and the current teaching, is not reported in Luke. Mt. alone gives this section which bore so vitally upon the Jewish problem—Lu. 6:27–36 does contain the passage about "love one's enemies" in even a fuller form than in Mt. 5:43–48.

Parables.—Mt. has two groups of parables, one—Mt. Chap. 13; the other in 24:32; 25:46. Ten of these occur only in Mt., viz.: The tares—13:24–30, 36–43. The hid treasure—13:44. The net—13:47–50. The pearl—13:45 f. The unmerciful servant—18:21–35. The laborers in the vineyard—20:1–16. The two sons—22:1–14. The ten virgins—25:1–13. The talents—25:14–30. The parables in Mt. deal with the kingdom.

Extended discourses of Jesus.—Besides the Sermon on the Mount and the extended parables, there are other addresses of Jesus in this Gospel not in the other Gospels. In particular may be noted the Gracious Invitation in 11:28–30, the prophecy of Simon Peter in 16:17–19; the exhortation about forgiveness in 18:15–20; the denunciation of the scribes and the pharisees in Chap. 23; the picture of the judgment in 25:31–46; the Great Commission in 28:16–20. *Cf.* Vincent's "Word Studies," Vol. I, p. 5. Hence in Mt. special emphasis is given to the teaching of Jesus.

Topical arrangement.—In Mk. and Lu. the narratives follow in general chronological order, as is also true of John's Gospel. But this is not always true of Mt. The "Sermon on the Mount" comes earlier than it probably was delivered as a specimen discourse. Then in Chaps. 8 and 9 we have a group of miracles, as in Chap. 13 we find a group of parables. The same system runs through the most of the Gospels.

Eschatology.—At many points in the Gospel we have accent put upon the eschatological aspects of the ministry of the Messiah. To some extent this is in harmony with the current Jewish apocalyptic teaching, but it is free from the merely temporal aspects. Particularly in Chaps. 24 and 25 do we have a Christian apocalypse (*cf.* the Book of Revelation), spoken by Jesus in view of His own death and of the destruction of Jerusalem, with the end of the world as the further background. Mt. gives this eschatological discourse at much greater length than Mk. and Lu., and Chap. 25 occurs nowhere else.

World outlook.—While the Gospel is Jewish in point of view, it is yet distinctively Christian and cosmopolitan. The essential moral teaching of the O. T. is carried further by Jesus from the mere external to the very spirit and life (Chaps. 5 and 6). But Mt. is not blind to the larger outlook. He records the worship of the babe at Bethlehem by the Magi—2:11. Christ's praise of a Gentile's faith—8:10 f. Christ's visit to heathen territory—15:28. The threat of taking the kingdom away from the Jews—21:43. The commission to carry the Gospel to all the world—28:19.

Special phrases.—Some of these have already been discussed, such as "kingdom of heaven," "Father in heaven," references to money, etc. Other characteristic expressions may be noted, like the frequent use of "their," "our (your) Father," "fulfil" of scriptures, "The evil one appeared," "Son of David," "And behold," "To swear by," etc.

MARK.

Names.—John Mark—Acts 12:12, 25; 15:37. The Jewish name John alone—John 13:5, 13. The Roman name Mark alone—Acts 15:39; Col. 4:10; Philemon 24; I Pet. 5:13; II Tim. 4:11. *Cf.* Jewish and Roman names combined in Saint Paul.

Home.—Jerusalem and mother's name Mary—Acts 12:12, 25. This home the place where many disciples gathered for prayer—Acts 12:12 ff.

Cousin of Barnabas.—Col. 4:10, and so probably a native of Cyprus, and possibly also a Levite like Barnabas (if father a brother of Barnabas). *Cf.* Acts 3:36.

Uncertain whether personal follower of Jesus.—Some consider him the young man mentioned in Mk. 14:51 f. This is quite possible if the "upper room" was in his mother's house—Mk. 14:15. *Cf.* Acts 12:12. But certainly a Christian when name first mentioned in Acts.

Goes to Antioch with Barnabas and Saul.—Acts 12:25. Probably invited by Barnabas, the leader of the new work among the Greeks at Antioch. As a cousin of Barnabas, and probably a Hellenistic Jew, he would be interested in the new developments there.

Assistant to Barnabas and Saul.—Acts 13:5. Either subordinate or possibly "synagogue minister" (Chase, *Hastings' Bible Dictionary*).

Leaves Paul and Barnabas at Perga.—Acts 13:13. Returns to Jerusalem—Acts 13:13. Refused by Paul as companion for second missionary tour—Acts 15:37 f. Follows Barnabas to Cyprus—Acts 37:39. Fellow-worker of Paul in Rome—Philemon 24. Commended by Paul to the Colossians—Col. 4:10. With Peter in Babylon (Rome?) —I Pet. 5:13. Desired by Paul in last imprisonment along with Timothy—II Tim. 4:11.

Peter's interpreter.—So Papias as quoted in Eusebius (H. E. iii. 39). *Cf.* Swete on Mark, p. xviii. This old tradition in harmony with association with Peter (I Pet. 5:13) and Peter's expressed wish to help the readers of his second Epistle (II Pet. 1:15) to "be able to call these things to remembrance" after his decease. Character of the Gospel of Mark in harmony also with story of Papias that Mark, as Peter's interpreter, wrote down accurately what he remembered of the words and deeds of Jesus.

GOSPEL OF MARK.

Date of the Gospel of Mark.—The general opinion among modern students of the Synoptic problem is that the Gospel of Mark is a genuine work and the earliest of the four Gospels. Swete, p. xxxv, thinks that it cannot be later than A. D. 70. It may indeed quite possibly be between 55 and 60 A.D.

Place of writing.—This is not known,

but is usually supposed to be Rome. We have seen Mark in Rome with Paul (Philemon 24) and probably with Peter (I Pet. 5:13). But one cannot be positive when nothing is told.

Characteristics of the Gospel of Mark.—For Romans especially. This is the early tradition, and it is supported by the probable fact that it was written in Rome. There is also a distinct absence of peculiar Jewish features such as are seen in the Gospel of Matthew. No Jewish genealogy occurs here.

Humanity of Jesus accented.—This Gospel is not, therefore, a theological treatise after the order of Matthew, though the conception of Christ is the same. He is "Jesus Christ, the Son of God" (Mk. 1:1), whose Gospel is here narrated. He is divine as well as human.

Beginning of Christ's Gospel, not of His life.—Mk. 1:1. Mark does not narrate the birth and childhood of Jesus. He even skips the first year of His ministry after His baptism. Possibly a year (according to John's gospel) comes in between verse 13 and 14 in Chap. 1.

Mainly the Galilean Gospel.—1:14–9:50, counting the period of withdrawal into regions around Galilee.

Climax in Jerusalem during the last passover.—Chaps. 11–16. Galilee and Jerusalem, the two foci of Christ's ministry, according to Mark. This is precisely what Peter does in his sketch of Christ's work in His early apostolic preaching. The work and death of Christ (and resurrection) the main elements in the earliest preaching.

Deeds of Jesus rather than His words.—Hence the miracles are numerous in Mark. Same number (18) as that in Matthew and only 20 in Luke. But Mark has only 4 parables, while Matthew has 15. The sayings of Christ seem to have been first collected into a group of Logia. Mark represents the crisp record of His deeds.

Person of Christ in action.—Thus he teaches the truth about Jesus. There is rapid movement, power, results. Jesus is shown to be the Son of God, with divine power. The Greek adverb εὐθύς (straightway) occurs 41 times in Mark. There are 151 "historic presents" in Mark, while only 78 in Matthew, and not over 6 in Luke (list of Westcott and Hort). *Cf.* Hawkins, "Horæ Synopticæ," p. 114 ff. Energy is the word that best describes Mark's narratives. The ancients compared Mark's Gospel to the lion.

Vividness of detail.—There are constant changes of tense in Mark, due to vividness of conception. *Cf.* 5:15 ff.; 6:14 ff., &c. As the reporter of Peter's descriptions there are naturally marks of an eye-witness—7:17; 10:17; 12:41. These vivid details come out particularly in story of the demoniac in the rocks (Mk. 5:1–20) where many items are alone in Mark. This pictorial autoptic character of the Gospel is in harmony with notion of its early date and Petrine influence. Mark tells of the gestures of Jesus (9:36), looks of Jesus (5:32; 6:6, &c.), love for the young ruler and his look of despondency (10:21 f), &c. After Peter's denial these details are fewer. The matters that would tend to recall Peter are usually absent from the Gospel.

Emotions of Jesus.—Sternness (1:43), anger (3:5), wonder (6:6), indignation (10:14), amazement in the Garden of Gethsemane (14:33 f.).

Deity of Christ.—Yet withal no Gospel gives a stronger impression of the deity of Jesus, not even John's Gospel. This comes out in the claims of Jesus as Lord of the Sabbath (2:28), with power to forgive sins (2:5, 10), with power and glory (14:62), &c.

Pauline character.—Pfleiderer holds that this Gospel represents the Pauline Gospel of grace for all men, both Gentile and Jew. This is true, but it is also true of every book in the New Testament. They are all Pauline in that sense, that Paul rightly interpreted the mind of Christ on the point of Gentile freedom.

Independent matter in Mark.—There are only some eighty verses (Swete, Comm., p. lxviii.) in Mark not in the Synoptic Gospels. But in the matters reported by him, brief as his Gospel is, he is usually fuller than the other Gospels, another sign of Peter's descriptive powers as reported by Mark. Chief matters in Mark alone occur in 3:20 f.; 4:26–29; 7:31–37; 8:22–26; 14:51 ff.

Chronological order.—So almost uniformly in this Gospel as in Luke. But his Gospel is no more a history than the others are.

Explanation by Mark.—He gives the Aramaic a few times and then translates into Greek as in 5:41; 7:11, 34; &c. Sometimes he explains the conduct of Christ as in 5:30; 8:19. He uses rather more Latin words than the other Gospels, like denarius, legion, centurion, &c.

Quotations from the Old Testament. —There are 67 references in Mark to the Old Testament, 23 merely verbal allusions and only 7 peculiar to Mark. Mark's more formal quotations are found in 1:2, 3; 4:12, 32; 7:6, 7, 10, 8:18; 9:48; 10:4, 6, 7, 8, 19, 27; 11:9; 12:2, 10, 11, 19, 31, 36; 13:12, 14, 19, 24, 26; 14:27, 34, 62.

Special phrases.—Besides the vivid terms and adverbs in Mark already mentioned, a few others call for mention. Constant use of the first person as in 4:39; 5:8, 9, 12; 6:2, &c. He uses many diminutives. It is in the vernacular Greek of the time, and the conversational style is apparent all through the book. The vocabulary is not peculiar at all, though a few unusual words occur as in 9:47.

Gospel for children.—As the earliest and simplest Gospel, Mark is the favorite of the children, and is best adapted for them. Around this simple objective picture of Jesus at work among men, it is easy to group the other Gospels (Matthew, Luke and John).

Teaching of Mark.—It is only necessary to say that the picture of Jesus is at the bottom the same in Mark that we find elsewhere. He gave his life a ransom for men (10:45; 14:24). His power is compassionate and beneficial, not destructive. Jesus is not merely the Great Teacher, but the Great Worker. His miracles are acted parables and His deeds speak louder than any words.

LUKE.

Name.—Not the same as Lucius in Acts 13:1. Probably an abbreviated pet name from Lucanus, a common custom of the time with many names. The name occurs only three times in the New Testament. (Philemon 24, Col. 4:14; II Tim. 4:11.)

Birthplace.—Absolutely unknown. Antioch in Syria, Antioch in Pisidia, Philippi in Macedonia have all been suggested.

Home.—Luke lived in Philippi apparently, from Paul's first visit there (Acts 16:12; 17:1) till Paul's return by Philippi on his way to Jerusalem during the third tour (Acts 20: 5 f.). This is apparent from the use of ''we'' and ''they.'' It is possible indeed that Luke had come from Macedonia to Troas and that his visit led to Paul's vision recorded in Acts 16:10 ff. Luke shows unusual interest in Philippi,

manifesting local pride in its claim to ''first'' as opposed to Amphipolis (Acts 16:12).

Family.—Also unknown, unless Titus is his brother. Curiously, neither Luke nor Titus are mentioned in Acts. Luke is not mentioned because he wrote the book. Why not Titus? Cf. II Cor. 12:18. Paul mentions ''the brother'' in connection with Titus where he seems to mean ''his brother.'' A. Souter (Hastings' D. B.) considers this passage and II Cor. 8:18 proof that Luke is this brother (cf. Acts above). If so, we have this interesting detail.

Gentile.—Titus was a Greek (Gal. 2:3). If Luke was his brother, he would be, of course, Greek also. The failure to mention Luke in the list of Jewish brethren (Col. 4:10 f.), putting him apart with Greek names in Col. 4:14 f., indicates that he was not a Jew. Luke's

Greek style (Lu. 1:1–4), when uninfluenced by his Aramaic or Jewish sources, corroborates this idea.

Man of culture.—His two books (Gospel and Acts) show him to be a man of education. His introduction to his Gospel is worthy of any historian. He has the historian's skill in the use of his material.

Physician.—Expressly called by Paul (Col. 4:14) "Luke, the beloved physician." Many current medical terms in both Gospel and Acts. *Cf.* Hobart, "The Medical Language of Luke."

Companion of Paul.—He was with Paul at Troas and Philippi during second missionary tour—Acts 16:10–40. He joins Paul again at Philippi on his third tour *en route* to Jerusalem (Acts 20:7) and is with him at Jerusalem, Cæsarea, voyage to Rome (Acts 20–28). If II Cor. 8:18 and 12:18 refer to Luke, he was in Macedonia with Paul also when in Macedonia during the third tour on his way from Ephesus to Corinth *via* Macedonia. Luke was with Paul most of the first imprisonment in Rome—Phil. 24; Col. 1:14. He was with him again in the second imprisonment—II Tim. 4:11.

Not a personal disciple of Jesus.—Some have supposed that he was one of the "seventy" sent out by Jesus, others have thought him one of the two disciples to whom Jesus appeared on the way to Emmaus; others have thought that he was one of the Greeks who came to see Jesus (John 12:20). But there is no support for any of these ideas. Others think that he was led to Christ by Paul and that he was Paul's physician when he was taken sick in Galatia (Gal. 4:13). The implication in Lu. 1:1–4 is that Luke did not know Jesus personally.

Legend that he was a painter.—That is possible, but no real proof of it exists. He has great literary skill at any rate.

Harnack's admission about Luke.—It is now admitted by Harnack that Luke wrote both Gospel and Acts. This is a victory for solid interpretation. *Cf.* Harnack, "Luke the Physician;" Ramsay, "Luke the Physician."

Same Author for Gospel and Acts.—This is plain from Lu. 1:1–4 and Acts 1:1, as well as from the general style of both books. The vocabulary is largely the same.

Luke a reliable historian.—Sir W. M. Ramsay's various books on Luke and Paul have proven the great value of Luke as an historian. He has been shown by discoveries to be right on various items where once he seemed to stand alone—such as the proconsul of Cyprus, the politarchs of Thessalonica, the "First" man of Melita, &c.

Explanation of method of work.—In his introduction to his Gospel (1:1–4) he explains his use of his materials. He sought information from oral and written sources. He wished first-hand testimony (eye-witness) whenever he could get it. He tested it all himself, put it in order, and sought to be accurate.

Main known sources.—It seems clear that Luke had the Gospel of Mark among his written sources. He seems to have had a book of "Logia" or "Sayings of Jesus," and also the present Matthew. Then he apparently had another source different from both of them. The inference is from his own words that he had a rather large amount of material in hand.

Date of Luke's Gospel.—This matter is not perfectly clear, though scholars see more nearly together about it now. It must come after Mark and the Logia. It must come before the Acts. If Acts was written while Luke was in Rome during the first imprisonment, the conclusion would be easy. That is the most natural meaning of Luke's words in Acts 28:30. He closes Acts after two years in Rome because the events had gone no further. The other view makes Luke's close of Acts merely an artistic one. He had it in mind to bring Paul to Rome. If the first view is correct, the Gospel was written during the two years with Paul in Cæsarea. Luke then had leisure to make his researches (in Palestine) about the life of Jesus. He would also have Paul's help. In that case the Gospel would come before A.D. 60. Otherwise it may come as late as 80 A.D. The earlier date is on the whole the most probable.

Characteristics of Luke's Gospel.— Reason for writing given—1:1-4. It is the historical ground that many others had written about Jesus. He wishes to give Theophilus (*cf.* Acts also) the benefit of his researches into the life of Jesus. Theophilus is probably a real character, a man of some importance.

Editorial notes.—A. Wright (St. Luke's Gospel in Greek, Art. Luke—Hastings' D. B.) finds many editorial comments in Luke. This is natural in a true historian who is not a mere copyist in the use of his material. There is evidence of much reflection and theological interpretation in Luke as in Matthew and John.

Doctrinal tendency.—Luke's Gospel is not an objective realistic setting forth of the facts of the life of Christ as in Mark. The facts are there, but they are interpreted. This is in truth a higher form of history. There is no perversion of the facts to advance the cause of Paul against Peter as Baur charged.

Pauline influence.—The book does correspond in theological outlook with that of Paul, as seen in his Epistles. Luke was greatly indebted to Paul (*cf.* Mk. also). There is nothing hostile to Peter in the Gospel, and the Gospel has many stern judgments of the Jews; *cf.* Plummer, Comm. p. 26. The Gospel is not a theological polemic; 101 words occur only in Luke and Paul in the New Testament.

Historical allusions.—The Gospel (Acts more so) has reference to the general history of the times as one would expect from a man of the Greek world like Luke. *Cf.* Luke 3:1 ff., where he mentions the imperial and provincial, as well as the ecclesiastical, rulers of the time when John the Baptist began his work. *Cf.* 13:1 ff. for an incident of the rule of Pontius Pilate.

Universal outlook.—As a Greek Christian, familiar with Paul's work in the Roman Empire and his plans for the evangelization of the Roman world, Luke naturally shows sympathy with the wider aspects of the work of Christ. His Gospel is for the Gentiles as well as for the Jews. He traces the genealogy of Christ back to Adam. He seems to give the real lineage of Jesus through his mother Mary. He notes that Jesus is enrolled along with Joseph and Mary according to the regulations of the Roman emperor Augustus. He records the song of peace for men of good will at the birth of Jesus (Lu. 2:14).

Infancy of Jesus from Mary's point of view.—As Matthew gives the birth of Jesus from the standpoint of Joseph in harmony with the Jewish character of his Gospel, so Luke records the universal interest of humanity in the birth of Jesus as seen in the experience of Mary. The source of Luke's information was probably oral and must have come ultimately from Mary herself, but Luke probably obtained the story from a friend of Mary.

First Christian hymnologist.—Thus Farrar ("Messages of the Books") aptly describes Luke's "Hymns of the Nativity," "Songs of Elisabeth," "Mary," "Zacharias." They bear the stamp of genuineness in the strongly marked Semitic tone and style. Luke was himself a Greek, but he has preserved the Hebrew spirit of the original source. Chaps. 1 and 2 differ greatly in style from the introduction (1:1-4) and from the rest of the Gospel.

Arrangement chronological.—So in the main as he explained in 1:3, many of the incidents recorded have no special sequence, and Luke may not have known the real chronological order. *Cf.* Plummer, Comm. p. 37. This was Luke's method in the Acts and strengthens the opinion that he followed the same method in the Gospel.

Series of pictures.—In the development of his narrative Luke shows much artistic skill. Each incident has a setting more or less distinct. The circumstances, time and place are roughly sketched. Usually the time element is very vague; as about that time, at that very hour, &c. But each incident, miracle or parable is treated as a whole. Sometimes no connection in the series is indicated.

Luke's special contribution.—The largest part of the Gospel (9:51–19; 27, the last six months of the ministry of

Christ) belongs to the period where we have very little in the other Gospels. Matthew has two chapters (19 and 20), Mark one (10), while John has more (7–11), but matter pertaining to the Jerusalem ministry and different from Luke's account. A good deal of Luke's material is repetition in various details of sayings recorded by Matthew and Mark in the Galilean ministry; and some incidents are parallel. Some scholars think that Luke has here grouped together what really belongs to the Galilean period. It is difficult to think of Luke's doing that. Repetition is common for a teacher. Like teaching also has like results, as every popular preacher knows. Hence Luke has a source for this section different from Mark or the Logia.

Marcion's use of Luke.—Marcion built his heretical system partly upon Luke's Gospel. He began with Chap. 4 and omitted all portions that did not coincide with his dogmatic views. He was a dogmatic destructive critic of Luke.

Tolerant in tone.—Luke's breadth of sympathy is revealed in his recording Christ's rebuke of John for his narrowness of spirit (9:49 f.), in the rebuke of the bitterness of John and James toward the Samaritans (9:51–56), in the story of the "Good Samaritan" (10:30–37), in the gratitude of the Samaritan leper (17:11–19). Luke was truly catholic in spirit.

Gospel of sympathy.—This appears in a number of ways. The story of the "Rich Man and Lazarus" (16:19–31) has even led to the charge that Luke was hostile to men of wealth. But this is unjust and a false interpretation. The Pharisees were indignant at the story of the "Unjust Steward" (16:14), because they loved money greatly. But Luke does present Jesus as the friend of the poor, the sick and the sinful. Jesus here in immortal parables (ch. 15) justifies his work among publicans and sinners. He is not ashamed, according to Luke, to receive the worship of a sinful woman and to cleanse her (7:36–50), but she is not Mary Magdalene, nor Mary of Bethany. Luke (8:2) re-

cords the work of a group of noble women for Jesus. He mentions more miracles (20) than any other Gospel and more Sabbath cures also. Only six of his miracles are peculiar to Luke. As a physician this is natural, as is his frequent use of medical terms. The gentleness of Christ comes out well in Luke. *Cf.* II Cor. 10:1 f.

Praying of Jesus accented.—This done seven times in Luke when not recorded elsewhere. Thus at His baptism (3:21), collision with the rulers (5:16), choice of the apostles (6:12), foretelling His death (9:18), the transfiguration (19:29), before teaching the model prayer (11:1), on the cross (23:34, 46). He alone gives some of the parables about prayer, like the "Friend at Midnight" (11:5–13), "Unrighteous Judge" (18:1–6), "Pharisee and Publican" (18:11–13). *Cf.* Plummer. Comm. p. 45 f.

Parables.—Luke has several groups of parables not in Matthew. So the three about the feast (14), the three about publicans and pharisees (15), two about riches (16), two about prayer (18). In Matthew the parables are usually concerned with the growth, expansion and communication of the Messianic reign. In Luke the parables of Jesus deal chiefly with the personal aspects of religion. There are twenty-three parables in Luke and all but five are peculiar to him. See "Parables of Jesus."

Versatility.—Luke has the finest literary style and flavor of any of the Gospels, yet he shows most acquaintance with Aramaic sources and the Septuagint. He can be as free from Hebraisms as Plutarch. He has a rich and varied vocabulary, using some seven hundred words in the Gospel and Acts that do not occur elsewhere in the New Testament. Yet he reveals many times, in the Gospel in particular, his Aramaic or Hebrew sources by the idioms which his Greek contains.

Contrasts.—In Luke we have a wide range and many sharp contrasts. See the publicans and pharisees in 15, the "Rich Man and Lazarus" in 16, &c.

Old Testament quotations.—The chief quotations from the Old Testament are contained in 1:17, 37, 46 f., 48, 49, 50, 51, 52, 53, 54, 68, 69, 71, 76, 78, 79; 2: 23 f.; 3:4–6; 4:4, 8, 10 f., 12, 18 f.; 6:21; 7:27; 8:10; 10:25; 12:53; 18:20; 19:38, 46; 20:9, 17; 28, 42 f.; 21:20, 22, 25 f., 27; 22:37, 69; 23:46. It will be observed that nearly half of these quotations occur in Chapter 1, the songs of Mary and Zacharias. See p. 1747.

Special phrases.—Luke is fond of the expression "and it came to pass." So he often uses phrases like "at that very hour." The word "favor," "grace" or "gift" is frequent in Luke as are "Saviour" and "salvation." It is the longest of the Gospels and the richest in the human side of the life of Jesus. Yet chapter 24 in Luke reveals the deity of Jesus conclusively and beautifully.

Beauty of the book.—Renan as a critic of style called it the most beautiful book in the world.

Relation to Acts.—It is really Part I of Luke's account of the Origin of Christianity. Acts constitutes Part II (Acts 1:1). See Acts.

Teaching.—The doctrines of Luke have already been sufficiently indicated. He presents a universal Gospel of grace in full harmony with the exposition of Paul and indeed of Jesus as presented by Matthew and Mark.

JOHN THE EVANGELIST.

Life.—Son of Zebedee—Mt. 4:21. Mother, Salome—Mt. 17:56; Mk. 15:40. Home probably originally Bethsaida—John 1:44. In fishing business with father and brother James at Capernaum —Mt. 4:21. Home in Jerusalem also—John 19:27. Acquainted with family of Annas—John 18:13. Not very poor, had hired servants—Mk. 1:20. *Cf.* possible reference to his mother in Lu. 8:3. Possibly younger than brother James—Mt. 4:21; 10:2. Disciple of John the Baptist in all probability—John 1:40. Mentions name of Andrew and implies that the other disciple of John is himself. Probably this is one of the two disciples who first followed Jesus—John 1:35 f. Probably led brother James to Christ—John 1:41. This is not clearly stated, but probable. One of the four fishermen later called to personal service—Mt. 4:21 f. Belongs to the first of the three groups of the Apostles—Mt. 10:2 f.; Mk. 3: 16 f.; Lu. 6:14 f.; Acts 1:13 f. One of the minor circle of three present at the raising of Jaïrus's daughter (Mk. 5:37), the transfiguration (Lu. 9:28), the agony in Gethsemane (Mk. 14:33). Ambitious for position—Mt. 19:20. Willing for baptism of blood in ignorance of it—Mt. 20:22. Had no rabbinical education —Acts 4:13. Nicknamed "Boanerges" along with James (sons of thunder)—Mk. 3:17. Proof of vehemence of nature: Vindictive toward the Samaritans —Lu. 9:51. Shows spirit of narrowness toward other workers for Christ—Mk. 9:38. Possibly kin to the Bethany family—John chap. 11. Messenger with Peter to prepare for the last passover—Lu. 22:8. Had post of honor at the meal, reclining next to Christ—John 13:25. Favorite term for himself in the Gospel is "the disciple whom Jesus loved"—John 13:23; 19:26; 20:2; 21:7, 20. Asked Jesus who the betrayer was—John 13: 25. One of the three in search for Christ in Gethsemane—Mt. 26:37. Entered the court of the high priest at the trial of Jesus—John 18:15. Alone of the apostles; also stood by the cross—John 19: 26. Honored by Jesus with care of His Mother—John 19:27. Saw proof of the death of Jesus and of His real humanity —John 19:35. Visits tomb of Jesus with Peter—John 20:4. Recognizes Jesus by the Sea of Galilee—John 21:7. Peter misunderstands Christ's remark about John's living long—John 2:21. With Peter in worship in the Temple after the coming of the Holy Spirit—Acts 3:1. Shows boldness before the Sanhedrin—Acts 4:13. Receives Samaritan Christians as brethren (*cf.* wishing to call down fire before)—Acts 8:14. Escapes death when his brother James is slain—Acts 12:2. One of the chief figures in the Jerusalem conference, and gives

Paul the right hand of fellowship and approval in his work—Gal. 2:9. Lived to old age—I John 2:1, 18. Travels much —III John 10. Banished to Patmos— Rev. 1:9. Interest in the Seven Churches of Asia (Rev. 1:11) suggests previous residence in Ephesus in harmony with tradition. Much more known about John in the Gospels and Acts where the twelve as a whole are mentioned. Tradition adds much more. Irenæus says expressly that John lived till the time of Trajan, who reigned 98–117. John is a link between the first and third generations of Christians.

Character.—Marked by energy, love, elevation, and spiritual insight. Lived long and reflected profoundly on the great aspects of Christ and Christianity. Probably a celibate. Known as "John the Theologian," "John the Eagle."

GOSPEL OF JOHN.

Authorship.—The writer refers to himself as the disciple whom Jesus loved and never mentions his name. *Cf.* Luke's "we" sections in Acts. The writer was a Jew, lived in Jerusalem, was an eye-witness of most that he records, was one of the close disciples of Jesus. He was John, since Peter and James are ruled out.

Date.—After the Synoptic Gospels, and probably a good while after them. Somewhere about A.D. 90.

Place not known.—But assuming the Ephesian residence of John, Ephesus was probably the place. *Cf.* possible endorsement of Ephesian elders to the book ("we know"—John 21:24).

Occasion.—The spread of Gnosticism in Asia (*cf.* Paul's Epistles to the Colossians and Ephesians) made John anxious to correct the perverted views of the person of Christ.

Purpose.—Stated by the author himself in John 20:30 f. He offers proof from the miracles of Jesus that He is the Son of God.

Person of Christ.—Jesus. God (John 1:1) and man (1:14) both. He had real blood (19:34), and He is the only begotten Son (1:18).

Pre-existence of the Word.—Christ as God's Son existed before His human birth—1:1; 17:5.

Prologue.—John 1:1–18 is a remarkable theological interpretation, by the author, of the twofold nature of Christ, a forecast of the entire Gospel.

Argument.—21:19–20:31 the author discusses the proof of the incarnation of the God-Man.

Epilogue.—Chap. 21 is by way of addition after the argument was made.

Manifestation of the Messiah.—The body of the Book shows how Jesus progressively revealed Himself as the Messiah.

Development of hostility.—The hatred of Christ's enemies grows with His self-revelation.

Style.—John writes as an old man after long reflection and contemplation. He has much repetition and even monotony of manner, but the calm elevation of style suits his introspective insight.

Dialogues.—The book is remarkable for vivid dialogue, as in chaps. 1, 3, 4, 5, 6, 7–10, 11, 12, 13–17, 21. In 15 and 16 monologue appears. In 17 the wonderful prayer.

Narratives.—Beautiful narratives occur also in chaps. 1, 2, 4, 11, 21.

Historical value.—This Gospel has been fiercely attacked as of little historical worth because the style in the dialogues is practically the same as that of the narrative portions. Hence the whole is put by some on a lower plane than the Synoptic Gospels. But none of the Gospels give verbatim reports of the exact Aramaic speeches of Jesus. John gives the sense rather more freely, probably, but still he correctly interprets Jesus' miracles. Only eight miracles occur in this Gospel, but several of them are treated at some length and become the occasion of extended address to the people. *Cf.* John Chaps. 5, 6, 9, 21.

Resurrection of Lazarus.—This famous passage (ch. 11) is bitterly attacked by those who deny the deity of Jesus. Probably Lazarus was still alive when the Synoptic Gospels were written, and hence they did not refer to it.

They do give resurrections from the dead by Jesus.

Parables.—No parable occurs in John except brief proverbs or crisp sayings like that in John 2:19, and the allegory of the "Good Shepherd" in Chap. 10, and the "Vine and the Branches" in Chap. 15. These symbols (door, shepherd, vine, &c.) are essentially parables.

Demons.—No demoniacs are recorded as healed in this Gospel, though the word occurs, John 8:48.

The Jews.—The author, though a Jew, wrote after the destruction of Jerusalem and probably in Ephesus long after the line was sharply drawn between the Jews and the Christians. Hence he refers to the Jews as hostile to Jesus. *Cf.* Chaps. 7, 8, 9, &c.

The Samaritans.—A good deal about them. *Cf.* John the Baptist's ministry there (ch. 3:23). Woman at Well of Sychar (ch. 4), Jewish sneer at Samaritans (8:48).

Testimony of the Baptist.—In John Chap. 1. Much not elsewhere about the Baptist's testimony to Jesus.

Relation to Synoptics.—Entirely new matter, save feeding of the five thousand (ch. 6) and passover week (18–20).

Supplementary, not contradictory.—Evidently written in full view of the Synoptic Gospels and gives additional and confirmatory matter. **Picture of Jesus essentially the same.**—In the Synoptic Gospels (*cf.* Warfield's "*Lord of Glory*," Denney's "*Jesus and the Gospel*") Jesus is both divine and human. The human side of Jesus is prominent also in the Fourth Gospel (*cf.* ch. 4, 6, 12).

First year of ministry.—But for John's Gospel the entire first year of Christ's active work would be unknown.

Feasts and chronology.—John mentions three Passovers in the Lord's ministry (2:13; 6:4; 13:1). Hence the ministry was over two years in length. There was probably another Passover not mentioned (*cf.* 5:1). But for John's Gospel no more than one year would be known.

Jerusalem.—In the Synoptic Gospels Galilee is the centre of Christ's work. In John, Jerusalem is the centre. Luke (13:34) implies this Jerusalem ministry. John fills it out.

Striking character.—We are indebted to John's Gospel for pictures of a number of interesting persons like John the Baptist, Simon Peter, Nathaniel, Nicodemus, the woman at the well, the man born blind, Lazarus, Mary, Martha, Annas, Caiaphas, Pilate, Joseph of Arimathea, Philip and Thomas.

The Comforter.—This Gospel gives the fullest treatment (14–16) of the work and mission of the Holy Spirit.

Key words.—Truth, as in 1:17; 8:32; 16:13; 17:17. Life, as in 1:4; 6:33–56; 11:25. Light, as in 1:4 ff.; 1:9; 8:12; 9:5;12:35. Witness, as in 5:31; 15:27, &c. Believe, as in 1:12; 5:31; 6:30; 8:31, &c. Love, as in 13:34; 14:21; 15:2, &c. Judgment, as in 3:19; 5:22, 27; 9:39; &c. World, as in 1:10; 17:13 f. Darkness, 1:5, &c.

Quotations.—Much fewer than in the Synoptic Gospels. They are found in John 1:23, 29, 51; 2:17; 6:31; 7:38, 42; 8:17, 39; 10:34; 12:13, 14, 27, 38, 40; 13:18; 15:25; 19:24, 36, 37.

Relation to John's Epistles.—The same general style is manifest in the Epistles of John, and the same man wrote them. The Epistles assume the Gospel (Westcott). In the Gospel the deity of Jesus is proved on the assumption of His humanity. In the epistles the humanity is shown on the assumption of His deity (Westcott).

Relation to Apocalypse.—The differences between the Apocalypse and the Fourth Gospel are so many that some scholars refuse to credit both books to the same author. Some reject one, some the other. There are, however, many points of peculiar contrast and the variations have an explanation. The Apocalypse may be in John's own unedited Greek (Acts 4:13; Rev. 1:19), while the Gospel may have had revision by the elders of Ephesus (John 21:24).

ACTS OF THE APOSTLES.

Title.—Not in all the early manuscripts and, in truth, it is not an exact description of the book. Most of the twelve apostles are not referred to after chap. 2, and the bulk of the book recounts the work of other than the twelve, as Stephen and Philip (6–8), Barnabas (11), and Paul (9, 13–28). Besides, a number of speeches occur also by Peter, Stephen, Paul. But the title is not likely to be displaced by a better one, if such an one could be found.

Author.—He is the same as the author of the Gospel according to Luke (Acts 1:1), to which book he alludes. He is a companion of Paul (Acts 16:10) and a physician. It is now demonstrated that Luke is the author of both Gospel and Acts.

Theophilus.—He is called "most excellent" (Lu. 1:3), and probably was a man of some standing. "The Acts," as the "Gospel," was intended not merely for his personal but for general circulation, especially among the Gentile Christians. Luke had in mind the same circle of readers for both books.

Date.—It was written after the Gospel, though how long after is not known. Critics do not agree, but it is probable on the whole that Acts was written by Luke in Rome while with Paul during his first imprisonment. This would explain best the sudden close of Acts with Paul still prisoner (28:30 f.), after two years in Rome in his own hired house.

Two possible editions.—Lightfoot suggested that Luke made two editions of both Gospel and Acts. Blass holds that in the Acts he issued a rough first edition (text of D), and then revised it for Theophilus and sent it east (text of B). The revised he considers a briefer text. The point is still in dispute.

Relation to Luke's Gospel.—The Acts is a continuation of the Gospel. Indeed the same event, the ascension, closes one book and opens the other. Luke considers that it is the same story "concerning all that Jesus began, both to do and to teach" (Acts 1:1).

Relation to Paul's Epistles.—There is no mention of any of Paul's Epistles in the Acts. It is not certain that Luke had seen any of them when he wrote the book. If he wrote in Rome about A.D. 63, the pastoral epistles had not, of course, been written. The epistles of the first imprisonment had been sent on their mission. The other epistles were sent to Thessalonica, Corinth, Galatia, Rome. The one to Rome he could have seen. The one to Galatia he probably did not see. Thessalonica and Corinth were not far from Philippi. The account of the installation of the Lord's Supper in Lu. 22:17–20 is quite similar to that in I Cor. 11:23–26. Paul claims to have had a direct revelation from the Lord on the subject (I Cor. 11:23). Luke may indeed have seen Paul's narrative. But, however this may be, the Acts and the epistles supplement each other in a truly marvellous manner. Cf. Paley, "Horæ Paulinæ," and Knowling, "The Witness of the Epistles." The absence of references makes the supplementing all the more striking. There are difficulties as concerning Acts 15 and Gal. 2, but they are not insuperable.

Sources.—In the Gospel (1:1–4) Luke tells the character of the material used. As a competent historian we merely assume that he used the same care in writing Acts. He was himself a witness of part of the narrative and he there speaks in the first person—16:10–40; 20:6–28:31. We do not know his sources for the remainder of the book, but it is not difficult to guess it in part. For all of Paul's career sketched by Luke he had Paul himself with whom Luke was so long as in Cæsarea and Rome. Then, besides, John Mark was in Rome with Luke and could tell much about the early apostolic era. Luke saw also Mnason, an early disciple—21:16. He was the guest of Philip in Cæsarea (Acts 21:8), besides the long stay in Cæsarea. Luke saw James, the Lord's brother, in Jerusalem (21:18), who was present in Jerusalem continuously since the Great Day of Pentecost. *Cf.* Knowling, "Expositor's Greek Testament." It is plain that he had ample material.

Choice of material.—The principles that governed Luke in the use of the abundant material are not made plain to us in the book. One feels sure that accuracy and interest were two of them. He begins with Jerusalem, which, not Galilee, is now the centre of Christian life. Then he extends the circle to Samaria and Philistia. Then the Gentiles come in, and the whole Roman Empire is brought within the horizon. The book closes at Rome, the capital of the Empire.

Main personages.—The work expands through new agents. At Jerusalem the Holy Spirit falls upon the 120 and Peter is the leading spirit ably supported by John. Peter and John arouse the antagonism of the Sadducees by reason of the preaching of the resurrection of Jesus. But Stephen, not one of the twelve, stirs the Pharisees to activity by his accent on the spiritual nature of worship. Philip, another of the seven deacons, carries the Gospel to Samaria and Philistia. Peter and Barnabas (after the men of Cyprus and Cyrene) are the early instruments in starting the work among the Gentiles. But these all pale before Paul, the "Apostle to the Gentiles," whose activities occupy more than half of the Acts. Paul is Luke's hero in this volume. In the outward movement new leaders come to the front.

The first church history.—In a true sense of the term "The Acts" is the first book of church history. Luke has the grasp of the situation of the real historian. He is not a mere chronicler. He is interpreting for us the origin and early growth of Christianity. The cause of Christ has much to be grateful for in that the first historian of Christian origin was Luke.

A book of missions.—The dominant note of the book is the missionary cause. The disciples first had to understand the significance of the life and message of Jesus. They had won back faith and hope by the resurrection of Christ. With the outpouring of the Holy Spirit

on the Day of Pentecost they grasped the full meaning of the work of Christ in relation to the Old Testament and the present (see Peter's address in Acts chap. 2). They were charged with power to expound that story to others. The Acts is the wonderful unfolding of this growing apprehension how Hellenistic Jews could be saved by faith in Jesus, how Samaritans (half Jews) could be redeemed, how proselytes (*cf.* the Ethiopian eunuch) could be saved by Christ, how Romans (*cf.* Cornelius) and Greeks (Antioch and the missionary tours of Paul) could be redeemed without becoming Jews. This was a difficult process on the part of the twelve apostles themselves (*cf.* Peter at Joppa, Cæsarea, Jerusalem, Antioch), but it was accomplished. Some of the Jerusalem Christians never rose to this breadth of view. They fought Paul, who became the exponent of the free gospel of grace for the whole world. Acts recounts this battle for freedom and shows how Paul was finally caught in the meshes of Jewish hate. The book leaves Paul a prisoner in Rome because, probably, Luke wrote while in Rome with him.

Judaizing controversy.—The conflict with the Pharisaic wing of the Jerusalem Christians (Acts 15) gave a new conception of Christianity, one free from the shackles of Jewish ceremonialism. The Gospel took wings and flew all over the Roman world, a spiritual Gospel, the Pauline interpretation of the Gospel endorsed by Peter, John, and James, the Lord's brother.

Holy Spirit in Acts.—In a real sense the book is the record of how the Holy Spirit filled the early Christians and sent them out into the world as spiritual dynamos. The power of Peter, of Stephen, of Philip, of Paul, is the power of the Holy Spirit.

Power the keynote.—The dominant idea of the book is that of power, the power of the Holy Spirit.

Acts and the ministry of Jesus.—The writer of Acts is definitely aware of the work of Christ and refers to his own book on that subject (Acts 1:1). He conceives his second volume to be a continuation of the first volume and a continuation of the work of Jesus. In the Gospels we have the record of what "Jesus began both to do and to teach" (both works and teaching). In the Acts Jesus is still inspirer and director of the activities of the Christians. *Cf.* this conception of Luke (Acts 1:1), of the continuing activity of Jesus after his ascension with the last message of Jesus recorded in Mt. 28:20: "I am with you always, even unto the end of the world."

The Holy Spirit in Acts.—But Jesus works through the Holy Spirit in the apostolic period (and now). He had said that the Comforter would come to carry on His work "forever"—John 14:16. This great event is recorded as realized in Acts 2. The dispensation of the Holy Spirit is thus inaugurated. He was not simply to teach the disciples all truth (John 14:26), especially the comprehension of Christ Himself (John 16:14), but they would do greater works (in degree, not kind) than Jesus had done—John 14:12 f. This story of expansion is set forth in the Acts. The great Day of Pentecost itself shows more converts (three thousand) than all of the earthly ministry of Jesus did (above five hundred, I Cor. 15:6). The promise of the Father was realized on that day. The rest of the Book of Acts is a description of the disciples at work under the guidance of the Holy Spirit. It is, in a true sense, the Acts of the Holy Spirit. In Jerusalem, in Cæsarea, in Antioch, in Troas, the Holy Spirit moves and guides to the larger movements in the apostolic work.

Persecution.—Acts is full of persecution of the disciples by the Sadducees (4 and 5), by the Pharisees (6–9), by the state (Herod Agrippa, ch. 12), by pharisaic Christians (Acts 15:1 ff.), and from Acts 13 to the end of the book there is a succession of persecutions for Paul and his friends all over the world. But Paul is chief sufferer as he had once been chief persecutor.

Credibility of Acts.—It used to be the custom for some scholars to belittle the historical value of Acts. But Luke has been vindicated on so many points of detail that he is now in high favor as a reliable historian. See Chase, "*The Credibility of Acts*"; Ramsay, "*St. Paul the Traveller.*"

Speeches in Acts.—In particular the speeches in Acts are said to be made to order by Luke. But Luke heard Paul's speech at Miletus (ch. 20) and those in Jerusalem, Cæsarea, and Rome—chs. 21–28. The speeches of Paul at Antioch in Pisidia (ch. 13) and at Athens (ch. 17) may very well have been preserved by Paul in notes and suit marvellously the conditions. In like manner Luke may have gotten notes of Peter's addresses, and Paul heard Stephen's—Ch. 7. There is no real ground for disputing the accuracy of their addresses without insisting on a verbatim report.

Three parts of Acts.—The book falls naturally into three parts. One has Jerusalem for a centre (chs. 1–12); another has Antioch as a centre (chs. 13: 1–21:15); the other shows Paul battling with his enemies in Jerusalem, Cæsarea, Rome—chs. 21:15–28:31. These are thus shifting centres of Christian influence. The power of Christianity follows the line of missionary activity, not of mere verbal orthodoxy.

Picture of Jesus in Acts.—Jesus had said that the Holy Spirit would teach the disciples about Him. In "The Acts" we see the disciples expounding the work and words of Jesus. After the great Pentecost they are able to interpret Jesus to men with power. They use His resurrection in connection with His claims to prove His messiahship. They worship Him as Lord and Saviour. The Christology of the Acts is essentially the same as that of the Epistles and harmonizes with the claims of Jesus in the Gospels.

Conversion of Saul.—The two outstanding events in the Acts are the coming of the Holy Spirit at Pentecost and the conversion of Saul of Tarsus. These two events explain the story of the book and, indeed, largely explain the history of early Christianity.

Personality of Paul.—The figure of Paul dominates the book as he has largely dominated (and rightly so) Christian history since the first century.

Voyage to Rome.—Chapter 27 is a

notable contribution to the world's knowledge of ancient seafaring apart from one's interest in Paul, the most important source indeed for that knowledge.

Chronology of Acts.—Luke mentions several rulers like Herod Agrippa (death, ch. 12) and Felix and Festus. But it is not very easy to work out a consistent chronology of the events in Acts. As a working hypothesis we may assume that Paul was with Barnabas at Antioch about A.D. 44, and that Festus succeeded Felix A.D. 59 or 60.

Old Testament quotations.—They are found in Acts 1:20; 2:17–21, 25–28; 3: 22 f. (*cf.* 7:37), 25; 4:25, 26; 7:3, 5, 6 f., 9, 10, 11, 12, 13, 14, 15 f., 17–19, 20 f., 22, 23–29, 30, 31, 32, 33 f., 35, 37, 40, 44, 46 f., 49 f.; 8:32 f.; 13:17–21, 22, 25, 33, 34, 41, 47; 14:15 (17:24); 15:16 f.; 17:31; 23:5; 26:18, 22 f.; 28:26 f.

Acts and the Epistles of Paul.—It is clear that the Acts was written by Luke in complete independence of the Epistles of Paul. It is hardly probable that Luke while at Philippi saw the Thessalonian Epistles or the Corinthian group. It is reasonably clear that he had not seen Galatians when he wrote Acts 15. In Gal. chap. 2, Paul gives the private account of the Jerusalem conference to show his independence of the twelve, though showing his essential agreement with them. In Acts chap. 15, Luke gives the general recital of the public aspects of the meeting, but with hints of friction (Acts 15:4 f.). It is possible that Luke was the amanuensis of Paul during the first Roman captivity—Col. 4:14. If so, he would be familiar with the contents and style of these Epistles. It is just in these letters that we find most similarity between Acts and Paul's Epistles. But on the whole it may be said that the Epistles were written in independence of the Acts and the Acts in independence of the Epistles. The Epistles of the captivity do not touch the period covered by the Acts, save the two years in Rome—Acts 28:30.

Luke may have had the benefit of Paul's suggestions at many points for the latter part of Acts, as he may have received help from John Mark and Philip for the earlier portions, not to mention notes of the various addresses which Luke did not himself hear. But there is no apparent effort to harmonize Acts with the Epistles. Still they supplement each other in a marvellous manner. Wherever they touch they must be blended to get the full light. Paul is intent on the problems in hand when he writes his Epistles. Luke has in mind the movements of Christianity in its expanding progress and selects his material for his own purpose. Luke gives us a real history, though along a line of his own choosing.

ROMANS.

By Paul at Corinth.—We know where Paul was when he wrote to the Roman Christians. He is the guest of Gaius (Rom. 16:23), and Erastus the treasurer of the city *(ibid.)* sends salutation. He is about to leave these parts (15:23 f.) for Jerusalem, as he did later, *via* Macedonia (Acts 20:3 f.). Meanwhile he sends greeting to the Romans by Phœbe of Cenchrea (Rom. 16:1), the probable bearer of the letter.

Date.—The Epistle was written therefore just before Paul left Corinth for Jerusalem (Rom. 15:25 f.) with the collection. He arrived in Jerusalem with the collection at Pentecost—Acts 20:16; 21:26 f. The date of the Epistle is therefore early spring of A.D. 56 or 57.

Paul's plans.—He hopes to go on his way to Spain after his visit to Jerusalem —Acts 19:21; Rom. 15:24, 28.

Reason for visit to Rome.—He wishes fruit in Rome also (Rom. 1:13–15), and in particular wishes to develop the virgin soil of Spain in harmony with his profession for pioneer work—15:16–24.

Statesmanship of Paul.—He has the conception of a world-wide kingdom for Christ (*cf.* Mt. 28:19 ff.), that shall take in the east as well as the west—Rom.

1:15; 15:16 f. In a measure he has given his message to the east—15:23. He now yearns that the west may come to Christ.

No new purpose with Paul.—He had indeed often planned to go to Rome (1:13), but had been hindered till now —15:23.

Origin of the church in Rome.—No light is thrown on this subject save that Paul was not the founder. It is improbable that Peter was, else Paul would not have written as he did in Rom. 15: 19 f. about another man's foundation. The church in all probability was the indirect result of the conversion of some of the Jews and sojourners from Rome on the great Day of Pentecost—Acts 2:10.

Character of the church.—It was partly Jewish and partly Gentile; *cf.* Rom. 2:9 f.

Integrity of the Epistle.—Some critics argue that the original Epistle closed at the end of chapter 14, since in some MSS. the doxology of 16:25-27 comes at the close of that chapter. Others find a difficulty in the many names mentioned in chapter 16. But Rome was the center of the life of the world. Christians, like other people, drifted to Rome, and among them many of Paul's companions and friends from the east. The unity of the book is the most natural position in view of the facts.

Language.—Even in Rome Greek was the language in common use, especially among those who had drifted from the east. Latin was alone used in North Africa, but in Rome Greek was spoken by many who could not use Latin. Paul himself probably knew Latin, but Greek was the common means of communication in the Empire.

Gospel of Paul.—In a true sense this Epistle is Paul's Gospel—2:16. The very fact that he had not yet been to Rome led him to give a more extended discussion of the fundamental truths preached by him. It is thus more formal and less incidental than Galatians. It is a real letter, but partakes also of the nature of a treatise. It is not a book on systematic theology, but a vital ex-

position of the gospel message on broad lines properly related to Jewish ceremonialism and Greek speculative philosophy. Paul was the first true Christian philosopher.

Not polemical.—His purpose was not therefore primarily polemical, as was the case in Galatians. He aims rather to give an interpretation of the message of Christ to both Jew and Gentile. He expounds a universal Gospel. The Judaizing controversy is still in his mind as part of the historical background, but not as the main consideration or occasion of the Epistle.

Careful preface.—He has a more formal and extended preface (1:1-7) that really sketches the "Gospel of God" in broad outlines and Paul's relation to it and theirs also.

Apologetic statement of theme.—In 1:8-17 Paul explains why he writes and tells his message. He is to discuss "a righteousness of God" as revealed in the Gospel.

The Gentiles lost.—He first proves the need of the Gospel of God's righteousness since the Gentiles are lost without it—1:18-32.

The Jews lost.—He then shows that the Jews also are lost without this Gospel of grace—2:1-3:20. Hence all the world is lost in sin.

Brief exposition of Paul's Gospel.—In 3:21-31 in short compass Paul sets forth his Gospel, the atoning death of Christ as the basis, the personal trust of the believer in Jesus, the consequent justification of the believer by God.

Abraham and justification.—For the benefit of the Jewish Christians Paul shows how Abraham himself exercised faith and was justified (*cf.* ch. 4). The blessed peace of the Christian is set forth in 5:1-11.

Adam and Christ.—A parallel is run between the relation of Adam to the race and of Christ to the redeemed in Ch. 5:12-21.

Sanctification.—Justification does not mean approval of evil, but has for its ultimate object real goodness. God's righteousness begins with justification (imputed righteousness) and ends with sanctification—Chs. 6-8.

Failure of the Jews explained.—It was an unpleasant task, but Paul explains why the Gentiles have taken the place of the Jews in the spiritual Israel—Chs. 9–11.

Personal consecration.—With Paul election means the obligation to personal piety in practical relations with the church and the world—Chs. 12–13.

The weak brother.—In particular the strong brother was to help the weak in a matter like eating meats offered to idols—14:1–15:13.

The future for Paul.—He unbosoms his purpose to the Roman brethren—15:14–33.

Paul's influence in Rome.—It is already great, as is plain from his many friends there—Ch. 16. He has a host of fellow-workers all over the world.

I CORINTHIANS.

Universally admitted as Paul's. A very few eccentric critics indeed who doubt everything question this Epistle. But even Baur admitted the genuineness of I Corinthians.

Date.—We know the time of year, the spring, before Pentecost—I Cor. 16:8. The place of writing was Ephesus *(ibid.)*. It was written shortly before the close *(ibid.)* of his three years' stay in Ephesus—Acts 20:31. This year was probably either 56 or 57. It was during Paul's third missionary tour and a year before his final visit to Jerusalem.

Parties in Corinth.—Apparently four parties had sprung up in Corinth (I Cor. 1:12) since Paul's departure and Apollos' arrival. Appolos had left and would not return—I Cor. 12. The Pauline party and the Apollos party were drawn along lines of personal preference apparently. The Cephas party represented a doctrinal cleavage, the Judaizers, who made an improper use of the name of Peter. The Christ party probably was a reaction of a pious element against the spirit of faction that itself caused a new faction. But eventually (see chs. 10–13) there were only two parties—the Pauline party (the majority) and the Anti-Pauline Judaizers (the minority). The Apollos and Christ parties apparently took Paul's side in the controversy.

Paul's communications with the Corinthians.—Apollos himself could tell Paul much—I Cor. 16:8. The household of Chloe had told him the story of the divisions—1:11. Paul sent Timothy to them to restore order—4:17; 16:10. He purposed to come himself (4:19 ff.) and may possibly have made a short visit—II Cor. 2:2; 13:1. He had written them a letter now lost—I Cor. 5:9. The Corinthians had written Paul a letter concerning marriage (7:1), meats offered to idols (8:1), the spiritual gifts (12:1), and the resurrection—15:1. They had sent a special embassy (possibly with the letter) to see Paul—16:17. He replies with what we call "I Corinthians." Paul had finally sent Titus who was to report to him at Troas—II Cor. 2:12.

Complicated situation at Corinth.—It was a mixed condition of affairs that called forth this great Epistle. It was a great mission church in a commercial emporium open to all the breezes of error that blow, beset by every form of immorality, torn by strife, possessed of a large number of persons with high spiritual endowments; an excitable, inflammable church. The various problems are discussed separately.

The dissensions.—The first four chapters treat this vital question. There is much passion and even indignation in Paul's protest against the misuse made of his name in the matter. He takes occasion to make a formal exposition of his conception of the cross of Christ as the heart of the Gospel. He scouts their false, pretentious philosophy and urges the real wisdom of God.

Immoral practices.—In chapters 5 and 6 he condemns with much vehemence the church's lackadaisical passing by a case of incest and demands the man's expulsion from the church. He charges them with going to law with each other before the heathen and with the spirit of licentiousness.

Marriage.—Chapter 7 deals with marriage and its problems as existing in Corinth. There were two parties among them. One held that all should marry. The other held that none should marry. Both were wrong. The various aspects of the matter receive discussion.

Meats offered to idols.—Chapters 8–10 treat the grave problem (to them) of eating meat that had been presented as an offering in a heathen temple. It is a question of casuistry, and calls for a principle that applies to all casuistical problems.

Head dress of women in worship.—In 11:1–16 this matter receives earnest treatment.

Misconduct in observance of the

Lord's supper.—The excesses of the Corinthians went as far as this. Some of them actually got drunk at the Lord's table. Paul interprets the whole subject—11:17–34.

Spiritual gifts.—Chapters 12–14. Wrangling had come in the very use of the gifts of the Holy Spirit. Love (13) is the key to the matter.

The resurrection.—Chapter 15. The classic on the subject. He proves the fact of the resurrection of Jesus and explains the nature of the resurrection body.

Collection for the saints.—One of the great objects of Paul's second missionary tour was the collection for the poor saints at Jerusalem (16:1–4).

•Personal items.—16:5–24, as usual in Paul's Epistles he has many personal messages.

II CORINTHIANS.

Authenticity conceded by practically all competent scholars.

Integrity questioned.—A respectable number of scholars hold that our II Corinthians really combines two of Paul's Epistles (Chapters 1–9) being a fourth letter, Chapters 10–13 a third). An interesting idea, but not proven.

A lost letter possible.—It is, however, possible (cf. I Cor. 5:9) that Paul wrote another letter and sent it by Titus, one sharper in tone than I Corinthians and to which he alludes in II Cor. 2:4; 7:12.

Return of Titus.—At any rate the mission of Titus was more effective than that of Timothy. Paul met him, not at Troas as he had planned, but in Macedonia (II Cor. 2:12 f.), probably in Philippi.

Date of the Epistle.—He sends Titus and two other brethren back (probably Luke and Erastus, cf. II Cor. 8:18–9:5). They may have also been the bearers of the Epistle. But at any rate the date of writing is shortly after the arrival of Titus from Corinth, probably the latter part of A.D. 56 or 57.

Joy and sorrow.—Titus brought good news and bad news. Paul had been

grieving that he had written so sharply —2:1–4; 7:5–8. But now that the majority had acquiesced, he is happy over the result—2:5–3:6; 7:8–16. But a ''part'' (2:5) had not taken Paul's view of the situation. The letter therefore has a double character. The first part is mainly joyous, the second chiefly sad and indignant.

Paul's apology.—The Epistle is the most personal of all of Paul's letters and has been often called *Apologia pro Vita Sua*. He does make a formal defence of his work and gives a magnificent presentation of the grandeur of the New Testament ministry.

Style.—The passion of Paul's heart is reflected in the long and broken sentences which characterize the letter. It pulses with power and he is not careful to follow formal rhetoric.

Revelation of Paul's personality.— More of Paul's real self is manifest in this Epistle than is to be found anywhere else. The latest volcanic fires have burst forth. Timothy (1:1) sends greetings also, but it is Paul's experiences that are told.

Preacher's handbook.—It is a great

discussion of a true preacher's problems and so becomes a minister's *vade-mecum*.

Paul's narrow escape.—In 1:3–11. Paul tells of his recent nearness to death while at Ephesus due either to the mob or sickness or both.

Failure to go to Corinth.—He was charged with fickleness (1:12–2:4) because he had not come to them first before going into Macedonia as he had originally planned (1:15 f.), but had changed his mind—I Cor. 15:5.

Further personal explanations.—He is glad to set before his friends his real attitude towards the offender and the church, now that the majority has sustained Paul's view—2:5–7:16. He opens his heart and his mouth to them (6:11) and begs them to open their hearts to him—7:2. Throughout this discussion Paul maintains a position of great dignity with real sympathy.

The collection.—The formal discussion (Chaps. 8 and 9) of this important matter furnishes a powerful exposition of the whole question of beneficence. He wishes to bring to a successful conclusion the promises of the Achaian churches for this object, the great collection for the poor saints in Jerusalem from the four provinces of Asia, Galatia, Macedonia and Achaia. Achaia had been the first to promise, but is the last to pay.

Apostolic authority.—The tone of Chapters 10–13 is so very bitter in places that some explanation is needed. It is found in the stubborn resistance of the Cephas party of Judaizers to the authority of Paul in Corinth. The Apollos and Christ parties had apparently disappeared. The majority was with Paul. He had claimed his apostolic authority before—I Cor. 4:21; 5:3–5. The Judaizers resented this claim. They retorted that Paul was acting outside of his jurisdiction (II Cor. 10:14), that he was not a real apostle (not one of the twelve like Peter, 11:5; 12:11), that he was afraid to take pay because he was not a true apostle (11:7 ff.), that in reality he was indirectly after money for himself in this collection for the poor saints in Jerusalem (12:14–18), that he was afraid to come to Corinth anyhow (12:14; 13:1 ff.), and took it out in threatening letters—10:9 f.

The indignation of Paul is thoroughly aroused.—He answers the charges and makes counter ones. He calls the Judaizers false apostles and ministers of Satan (11:13 ff.). He has not been just "excusing" himself to them (12:19). He has remained away to spare them (1:23; 12:21). When he comes again, he will not spare (13:2), but will "deal sharply" if necessary (13:10).

Effect of the Epistle.—He waited awhile, went round about Illyricum (Rom. 15:19), and later spent three months peaceably at Corinth—Acts 20:3. To all appearances the Cephas party of Judaizers vanished. Peter had had no part in this strife and was in no way responsible for their use of his name. II Corinthians is a powerful document and evidently made a tremendous impression.

GALATIANS.

Authenticity.—Accepted by all critics save extreme Dutch school.

Readers—Very doubtful whether by Galatia (Gal. 1:2) and Galatians (3:1) Paul means the real Galatians (Celts) of North Galatia, the Lycaonian and Phrygian Christians alone (South Galatia, scene of Paul's first tour), or the Roman province as a whole. Each view has strong advocates, though the North Galatian view may still be accepted as a working hypothesis. That is the most natural way to take the language of Luke in Acts 16:6; 18:23. But it is even possible that Luke may use the term "region of Galatia" in the ethnographic sense like Phrygia, Lycaonia, and Pisidia, while Paul may have the Roman province in mind. If so, the matter becomes all the more difficult to decide. But this point of geography is not very material after all.

Date.—The date of the Epistle is involved in the character of the readers addressed. If they were the inhabitants of South Galatia, the first (''former'') time when he was with them would be the time of the first missionary tour. He may indeed have been there a second time, though not necessarily so. If true, this would be during the second tour. If, however, the true Galatians are in mind, the second tour would be the occasion of the first visit (Acts 16:6), and the third visit that of the second (Acts 18:23). In that case the date would be much later. The Epistle is therefore dated all the way from A.D. 50 to 57. In lieu of anything decisive, the doctrinal situation may be appealed to. It logically falls between II Corinthians and Romans. Tentatively the fall of A.D. 56 or 57 may be suggested and the place of composition Corinth.

Judaizers in Galatia.—After the Jerusalem Conference Paul distributed the decrees on his travels—Acts 16:4. The trouble in Galatia may have sprung up at once from Jews in the Galatian churches or may have been due, as is most likely true, to some active emissaries from the Jerusalem Judaizers—Gal. 3:1. The movement took on large proportions rapidly.

Appeal to Paul.—Some of those loyal to Paul, as at Corinth, evidently sent word to Paul concerning the situation. If it came to him after his return to Corinth in the fall of 56 or 57, he was in a proper frame of mind to apprehend the issue involved.

The issue at stake.—The very heart of the gospel was in the controversy. It was whether Christianity was sufficient in itself or must be supplemented by Judaism, whether Jewish ceremonialism was to be added to the spiritual gospel of liberty preached by Paul. He had faced this issue squarely at the Jerusalem Conference and had carried his point—Acts 15; Gal. 2:1-10. But it is necessary to make a fight over again. Paul conceives that the truth of the gospel is at stake—Gal. 2:5. He calls the doctrine of the Judaizers ''a differ-

ent gospel,'' really no Gospel—1:6 f. He pronounces anathema on these teachers—1:8 f.

Appeal to the Galatians.—He calls to them to come back (1:6; 3:1) and to be true to the gospel of liberty (5:1). He throws his very heart into this passionate plea—4:12-20.

Defence of his apostleship.—That had been challenged. He was called by the Judaizers not a true apostle. Hence Paul affirms his apostleship (1:1-5) and shows how he derived it from Christ and independently of the twelve (1:11-24), but he was their acknowledged equal as shown in the Jerusalem conference itself—2:1-10. He had indeed rebuked Peter to his face at Antioch—2:11-21.

The law and the gospel.—The law had its place, the ceremonial law, but it was that of the tutor or pedagogue before Christ came—3:1-22. It is not needed now that the Teacher Himself has come—3:23-4:7. Paul is afraid of them, these Gentile Christians observing Jewish ceremonies—4:8-11. He reminds them of the allegory of Sarah and Hagar—4:21-31.

Freedom, not license.—They must not misunderstand him. He does not wish them to be entangled again in a yoke of bondage (5:1-12) and so come from grace under law—5:4. Nor does he wish them to make freedom an occasion to the flesh to go into sin—5:13-26. The fruit of the Spirit and of the flesh are very different in quality.

Mutual help.—They must help, not hinder, each other—6:1-10.

The cross, not circumcision.—The cross of Christ is the main thing, not the ceremony of circumcision—6:11-18. This added summary is in Paul's own hand (6:11) and he pleads for loyalty on the ground of his sufferings for Christ—6:17.

Powerful apologetic.—This Epistle is vehement and passionate and presents the spiritual conception of Christianity over against Jewish ceremonialism. It met that issue grandly. It was also the battle cry of Luther in the reformation. To-day it is one of the bulwarks against the radical criticism of the New Testament.

EPHESIANS.

Genuineness.—This great Epistle has been attacked by a considerable number of German scholars, but on insufficient grounds. The difficulties vanish when the letter is properly understood.

Date.—Same date as Colossians (Col. 4:7 f.; Eph. 6:21 f.) and Philemon (10, 13). About A.D. 62 or 63.

Place.—From Rome—Acts 28:30 f.; Eph. 3:1.

Destination.—In the oldest MSS. in Eph. 1:1 the words "at Ephesus" are wanting. In Col. 4:16 Paul speaks of an Epistle sent to the church at Laodicea. Marcion calls the Epistle which we call "to the Ephesians" the one "to the Laodiceans." There are no personal items in the Ephesian letter, though Paul was three years in Ephesus—Acts 20:31. It seems clear therefore that the Ephesian letter was not addressed solely to the saints at Ephesus, though a copy went there. That copy is the one that came to be copied most because of the prominence of the church in Ephesus.

Circular letter.—It seems to be a general appeal addressed to the churches of Asia and sent to various churches. The Colossian letter, though designed specially for the Colossian church, was also to be sent to Laodicea—Col. 4:16. The apostle may have had the Ephesians chiefly in mind, but purposely wrote in general terms so as to suit the letter to its mission. *Cf.* the Letters to the Seven Churches (of Asia) in Rev. 2 and 3, where each letter is definite and particular in description.

Gnosticism.—The same doctrinal issue is under discussion here as in Colossians. See that Epistle for brief statement about Gnosticism. There is here less eagerness and passion perhaps, but more comprehensiveness and sobriety in the treatment.

Dignity of the church.—In Colossians the Headship of Christ is emphasized in contrast to the Gnostic notion of Æons. In Ephesians the dignity of the church as the body of Christ is set forth with great power.

General conception of the church.—The general conception of the body of Christ is natural in an Epistle designed for general circulation. In harmony with that idea Paul expounds the comprehensiveness of the body of Christ as including both Gentiles and Jews. Another figure for this idea is the Commonwealth of Israel"—Eph. 2:12. "One new man"—2:15. "One body" —2:16. "Household of God"—2:19. "A holy temple in the Lord"—2:21. "The church, which is His Body"—1:22 (*cf.* 5:23, &c.). Paul here grasps the kingdom of God as parallel in a sense with the world kingdom of Rome, but infinitely grander in scope and power.

Election includes both Jews and Gentiles.—This conception is not new with Paul (*cf.* Rom. 9:11), but is nowhere put with more force than in Eph. 1:3–14. The point of view here is that of thanksgiving to God for his elective grace.

True conception of Christ.—In opposition to the Gnostic degradation of Christ, he exalts Him to His true place —1:15–23. This is one of the two great prayers in the Epistle, a prayer for spiritual comprehension.

The spiritual revelation.—The tremendous change wrought by Christ in both Jews and Gentiles is discussed in Chapter 2.

Paul's mission to the Gentiles.—He expounds his knowledge of "the mystery of Christ" (3:4), how the Gentiles are included in the church 3:1–13.

Prayer for knowledge of Christ.—The Gnostic laid much stress on "knowledge." The highest knowledge is that of Christ. Paul here (3:14–21) makes a marvellous prayer.

Unity.—This passage (4:1–16) reminds one of Christ's prayer for unity in John—ch. 17.

Heathen vices.—Paul faithfully warns the Gentile Christians against lapsing into their former lax manner of life—4:17–5:20.

Domestic and social life.—As in Colossians so here (4:21-6:9) he discusses carefully and earnestly the duties of Christians in the various stations of life.

Final appeal.—In 6:10-20 Paul pleads powerfully for stedfastness in the midst of the Gnostic heresies.

Grandeur of the Epistle.—Nowhere has Paul, or anyone else, produced a greater treatment of the highest themes than in Eph. 1-3.

PHILIPPIANS.

Ties with Philippi.—Paul had presented the Gospel in Philippi and gathered there his first European church—Acts 16:11-40. There Lydia lived. There he had been in prison. It was the home of Luke, apparently, who had been so much with Paul. Timothy, now with Paul, was dear to them. He associates Timothy with him in the greeting —1:1. They had been very ready and liberal in the great collection (II Cor. 8:1-4; 9:1 f.; Phil. 1:6), as well as generous to Paul.

Fresh proof of the love of the Philippians for Paul.—They had several times sent relief for Paul's want when he was in Thessalonica—Phil. 4:16; indeed, when he departed from Macedonia, no other church had supplied his needs—4:15. He had later apparently received help from other churches also—II Cor. 11:8 f.; 12:13. He refused any help from the church at Corinth—I Cor. 9:18 ff.; II Cor. 11:7, 9; 12:13. They had now again remembered Paul in a most substantial way, and he appreciates it much —Phil. 4:14-18. He had not asked for the gift—4:17.

Paul's condition.—He is a prisoner, but has his own hired house in Rome—Phil. 1:13; Acts 28:30 f. He has apparently been in Rome some time—Acts 28:30 f. He is allowed to preach the Gospel unhindered—Acts 28:31; even in the Prætorian Guard (Phil. 1:13 f.) and to members of Cæsar's numerous household—4:22. He is permitted to see his friends (Acts 28:30) and so to keep in communication with the work in the east.

Paul's heart turns east again.—When he wrote Romans from Corinth, he was full of ambition to go to Rome and to Spain—Rom. 15:17-29. Now that he is at last in Rome, a prisoner, he longs to go back to the east. He hopes to get free and come to see the Philippians again—Phil. 1:25. The door to Spain for the present was closed and fresh troubles were brewing in the east. The care of all the churches was still on his heart.

Visit of Epaphroditus.—Among his other visitors was Epaphroditus from Philippi with bountiful tokens of the love of the church there—Phil. 4:18. He fell sick nigh unto death (2:27), and the Philippians heard of it—2:26. Epaphroditus learned of their anxiety about him and longed to go back on his recovery—2:26. Hence Paul sends this Epistle by him—2:25.

Genuineness.—Few scholars question the Pauline authorship of this letter. It has the stamp of reality in it.

Date.—It was written during the first Roman imprisonment, i. e., between A.D. 60 and 63. Some scholars would put the imprisonment A.D. 58-61. What is less clear is the precise period of this imprisonment. Most scholars put it at the close and after the writing of Philemon, Colossians, and Ephesians. That is possible, but by no means certain. He was expecting to be set free when he wrote Philippians (Phil. 1:25; 2:24) and Philemon (22). Luke seems not to be with him when he wrote Philippians (2:20), as he was when he wrote Philemon (23) and Colossians (4:14). But his absence may have been only temporary.

Doctrinal position.—The Epistle is not distinctly a doctrinal document, but in chapter 3 there is an echo of the Judaizing controversy (cf. the Corinthians Epistle, Galatians, and Romans). On the other hand in chapter 2 there is a forecast of the coming Christological controversy (*cf.* Colossians and Ephesians). It occupies therefore an intermediate position between these great Epistles and may also actually belong there in point of time.

Keynote.—The chief note of the Epistle is Joy—1:4, 18; 2:17; 3:1; 4:1, &c. One may compare the song at midnight in the Philippian jail—Acts 16:25.

Spiritual discernment.—This was a ground of thanksgiving about them, and Paul prays that they may have even more of it—1:1–11.

Good out of evil.—The bonds of Paul had been used for the furtherance of the Gospel in Rome—1:12–18. Paul is glad.

Life or death.—He has come to be anxious to depart and be with Christ, but he has work yet to do for Christ. Hence he is confident of freedom—1:19–26.

The example of Christ.—He is the supreme example of humility for all—1:27–2:11.

Working out salvation.—That is the problem of the Christian, to work out what God has wrought in—2:12–18.

Plans for communicating with the Philippians.—Timothy and himself soon, but now Epaphroditus—2:19–30.

Paul's passion for Christ.—He compares the barrenness of mere Jewish ceremonialism with the riches in Christ—3:1–16.

Warning against the Judaizers.—Echoes of the late controversy—3:17–21.

Peace of God.—Begin with each other and it will come—4:1–7.

Thinking and doing.—Value of high ideals—4:8 f.

Paul's lesson in contentment.—He had to learn it—4:10–20.

COLOSSIANS.

Date.—The date is the same as that of Philemon and Ephesians. Tychicus was the bearer of the Ephesian (Eph. 6:21 f.) letter and the Colossian (4:7 f.) letter. *Cf.* Philemon 10 and Col. 4:8. It belongs to the year A. D. 62 or 63.

Genuineness.—The school of Baur rejects it and considers it a late condensation of Ephesians. But the new knowledge of early Gnostic tendencies has removed the point of Baur's criticism. It is the work of Paul beyond a doubt.

Relation to Ephesians.—The manifest likeness to Ephesians in subject matter, general arrangement, style, and vocabulary is easily explained. The two Epistles were written about the same time and dispatched together. Probably Colossians was written first to meet a specific situation in Colossæ. Then the Ephesian letter was composed while the same theme was in Paul's mind at more length, more discursively, and with less passion. *Cf.* the relation between Galatians and Romans.

A church not founded by Paul.—They had not seen his face in the flesh (Col. 2:1), but had been taught by Epaphras (1:7) and probably also Archippus (4:17). This is the second church not founded by Paul to which he writes (*cf.* Rome).

Visit of Epaphras.—The coming of this brother to Rome stirred Paul's interest in the condition of things in Colossæ (1:8; 2:1). Paul's concern was not confined to the churches where he had labored.

The Colossian heresy.—Paul does not explain minutely the nature of the heresy in Colossæ. But his denunciation of the errors shows that it was a syncretistic philosophy. Lightfoot (see *Commentary on Colossians*) has shown that it was incipient Gnosticism which became rampant in the second century. These philosophers combined the speculation of the Greek Pythagoras with Persian mysticism and Essenic Judaism. They held matter to be essentially evil. Hence the origin of the world was a grave problem since God was good. They conceived a series of intermediate agents or æons to relieve God of the burden of the evil world. They at once had trouble with the person of Christ in their system when any of them accepted Christianity. They solved the matter by making Jesus one of the æons. In morals they had two extremes. One went to license, the other to asceticism.

Christological controversy.—At once therefore a new heresy arose and a fresh peril to the Gospel faced Paul in his imprisonment. He had feared some such trouble long ago—Acts 20:29 f. He throws himself into the matter heart and soul, as he did in the Judaizing controversy. Then he wrought out a clear view of spiritual religion. Now he grasps fully the deity of Jesus, and relates the person of Christ to the order of the Universe. We have to thank the Gnostic for being the occasion of this great contribution to the knowledge of Christ.

News of the Colossian Christians.—Paul is grateful for the knowledge which he has of them through Epaphras —1:3-8.

World relations of Christ.—Jesus was a man, but is more than a man or men. He in truth is the Son of God, partakes of the very nature of God, is the Creator and sustainer of the physical universe, is the head of the spiritual realm, the church general, the body of Christ— 1:9-23. The primacy of Christ over all other spiritual beings disposes of the Gnostic philosophy and asserts the real deity of Christ. He is head of both the physical and spiritual realms.

The mystery of Christ.—The Gnostics talked much about their "mysteries." No mystery is comparable to "the mystery of God, even Christ, in whom are all the treasures of wisdom and knowledge hidden."—1:24-2:7.

The philosophy of the cross.—The Gnostics had a false philosophy which beguiled many. The cross of Christ is the true philosophy of grace and of life (2:8-15). The Docetic Gnostics denied the reality of Christ's body. Paul affirmed the union of the Godhead with the body of Jesus—2:9. The Corinthian Gnostics separated Jesus from the Christ. Paul contended for their identity—2:6.

Supremacy of Christ.—The Gnostics worshipped angels and went off into idle speculation. The antidote for that idolatry is to maintain Jesus as head over all—2:16-19.

Ascetic rules.—One wing of the Gnostics, considering all matter to be evil, sought to live aloof from the world under the bondage of rules. Christianity put the spirit in control—2:20-23.

License.—The other wing of the Gnostics opened the flood gates of license and held that matter, though evil, could not harm the soul. Therefore the body had full license to indulge itself. Paul replied that the body must be put in subjection to the will of Christ—3:1-17.

Social aspects of Christianity.—Already it had become all-vital matter that the various classes in social life should fulfil their mission in accord with the mind of Christ. Paul sets forth this ideal—3:18-4:1.

Attic salt.—Wisdom in speech was needed by Paul and all teachers—4:2-6.

Personal matters.—This Epistle is peculiarly rich in those delightful personal details that Paul knew so well how to put in his letters. They give life and color to the Epistle—4:7-18.

I THESSALONIANS.

Genuineness.—Now accepted by nearly all critics of all schools as the work of Paul. Baur's attack on it has been overthrown.

Date.—A.D. 52. Earliest of Paul's Epistles and one of the earliest books of the New Testament. *Cf.* Epistle of James and Mark's Gospel. Date not long after Paul left Athens, while in Corinth, after Silas and Timothy came there from Thessalonica—Acts 18:1, 5; I Thess. 3:6. The date is fixed also by the coming of Gallio as Proconsul of Achaia—Acts 18:12. Paul had already been there a year and a half—18:11.

Recipients.—"The Church of the

Thessalonians''—I Thess. 1:1. This church was founded by Paul during his second missionary tour—Acts 17:1–9; I Thess. 1:9 f. It was in a great commercial city of Macedonia (Thessalonica the modern Salonica) and had already become ''an ensample to all that believe in Macedonia and in Achaia''—I Thess. 1:7. He associates Silas and Timothy (1:1) in the salutation because of their connection with them.

Occasion.—Silas and Timothy (Acts 18:5) had brought good news from Thessalonica—I Thess. 1:6. But needless misapprehension had arisen, since Paul's departure, concerning the second coming of Jesus. He had taught them the certainty of that coming, but the uncertainty of the time of the event—I Thess. 5:1–11. This misconception had led some to neglect their regular work, a thing against which he had expressly warned them—4:11. Hence it was necessary to write them. It is possible also that the Macedonians sent a letter to Paul by Silas and Timothy.

Purpose.—Paul had been long anxious to revisit Thessalonica, but had been hindered—2:18. The longing was material—3:6. He still prayed that he might come—3:11. Meanwhile he sends a message to cheer them as they had cheered him—2:17; 13:7. They do not need instruction about affliction (3:4) and love of the brethren (4:9), but he wishes them to abound yet more and more and to walk becomingly (4:10 ff.), as he charged them while with them— 4:1 f. He aims to confirm them in the Gospel which he had already preached to them that it might not be in vain— 2:1, 4, 8, 13; 3:9 f. He had sent Timothy unto them to avert this peril (3:5) as he now writes for the same purpose. He expects the Epistle to be read to all —5:27.

Contents.—The first chapter is an appreciation of the work of grace among the Thessalonians. The second chapter explains and defends Paul's preaching and conduct while with them. The third chapter shows his present concern about them. In the fourth chapter he exhorts them to be pure, to be mindful of their own business, to understand that those that are asleep will rise at the resurrection before those who are alive are changed. They will not be left in the graves. In the fifth chapter Paul repeats his teaching about the uncertainty of the time of the second coming of Christ and exhorts to orderly life.

Character.—The Epistle is informal and discursive, but perfectly natural and true to the historical situation. It is meant for the good of all (5:27) and so is a church letter. As the first of Paul's Epistles it is interesting as an exposition of his theology. It may be compared with the first extended report of an address of his—Acts 13:16–41. In this address the kernel of Paul's later theology (cf. Galatians and Romans) is found—(See ''Justification by Faith,'' Rom. 4:25)—Acts 13:38 f. So faith is emphasized in I Thessalonians, ''you that believe'' (2:13), ''your faith'' (3:6), ''your work of faith'' (1:3), &c. The development of Paul's teaching as traced in his Epistles is in harmony with his great experience of grace and the great message which he had for men. Cf. I Thess. 5:9 f.

Eschatology.—The second coming of Christ is discussed much in this Epistle because Paul had spoken especially about it while there. He had been misunderstood and so has to explain himself. This was a favorite topic in the early apostolic message (as in the later books also. ,Cf. II Peter, I John, Revelation). It will recur in Paul's later Epistles (I Cor. 7:31; II Cor. 5:1 ff.; I Tim. 5:14). The prominence of eschatological matters in I and II Thessalonians is due to the incident of his stress on that subject at Thessalonica, not to any essential change of view on the subject by Paul.

II THESSALONIANS.

Genuineness.—Rejected by some who accept I Thessalonians on the ground that it is an imitation of that Epistle and because of the apocalyptic passage in II Thess. 2:3 ff., about the man of sin. But the objection is not sustained. Paul came in vital touch with the worship of the Roman Emperor in Thessalonica. Naturally, according to the Jewish fashion of the time, he adopts the Apocalyptic imagery on that subject.

Date.—Not very long after the reception of First Thessalonians. Either later in A.D. 52 or more probably early in A.D. 53.

Occasion.—Paul evidently received further news after they had read his first letter. Some had refused his teaching on the subject of the second coming of Christ. They had misunderstood him at first and now preferred the misunderstanding to the explanation. Indeed, some went so far as to forge an "epistle as from" Paul to show that "the day of the Lord is just at hand" —II Thess. 2:3. He must try once more therefore. He gives a "token" by which his genuine Epistle may be recognized—3:17.

Tone.—This second Epistle is sharper in tone than the first. He does beseech them that they be not quickly shaken from their minds (2:1 f.) and expects them to "stand fast, and hold the traditions which ye were taught" (II Thess. 2:15), but he now "commands" (3:4, 6, 12) as he did while with them—3:10.

Authority of the Epistle.—Paul asserts the authority of his Epistle to those who had admitted his preaching as authoritative, "whether by word or by epistle of ours" (2:15), "our word by this epistle" (3:14). He makes obedience to his teaching a test of fellowship in the church, for he spoke "in the name of the Lord Jesus Christ" (3:6, 12, 14). He has confidence in their acquiescence—3:4.

Contents.—The first chapter gives his grounds of thanksgiving about them (and they are many and real) and his prayer for their further growth. The second chapter takes up at once the problem of the Second Coming, about which many of them are still in trouble and has a special thanksgiving because of their election and sanctification. The third chapter faces the practical issue with the recalcitrant who persist in error and idleness. They are to be disciplined.

The man of sin.—After Paul's disclaimer (2:1 f.) that he taught the immediate coming of Christ, he gives a further reason for the uncertainty of the time in the previous apostasy and manifestation of the man of sin—2:3 ff. The description of this one as "he that sitteth in the temple of God, setting himself forth as God" (2:5), seems to point to the worship of the Roman emperor. Paul reminds them of his teaching on this subject while with them— 2:5. The language, like all apocalyptic language (cf. Mt. chs. 24, 25 and Rev.), is obscure, but clearly Paul means to teach the certainty of Christ's coming and the uncertainty of the time.

Church discipline.—This is to be the last resort for the disorderly who refuse to work and are disturbers—3:6-15.

I TIMOTHY.

Timothy's connection with Paul.— Few of Paul's friends and helpers were more constantly with him than Timothy. He was converted during Paul's first tour while at Lystra, the home of Timothy—I Tim. 1:2; Acts 14.8; 16:1. He joins Paul during the second tour (Acts 16:1), having already won a good name. Though his father was a Greek, yet because his mother was a Jewess, he was circumcised to avoid friction. He is with Paul at Philippi (Acts 16:11 ff.), at Berœa (17:14), possibly Athens (17:15; I Thess. 3:2), at Thessalonica without Paul (I Thess. 3:6), at Corinth with Paul (Acts 18:5), at Ephesus in the third tour (I Cor. 4:17), sent to Corinth by Paul (*ibid.* 16:10), in Macedonia with Paul (II Cor. 1:1), in Rome with Paul (Phil. 1:1; 2:19), exhorted by Paul to remain at Ephesus (I Tim. 1:2), longed for by Paul in Rome before his death (II Tim. 4:9). He is with Paul when he writes to the Thessalonian Epistles (I Thess. 1:1; II Thess. 1:1), II Corinthians (1:1), Romans (16:21), Philippians (1:1), Philemon (1), Colossians (1:1). He himself receives two of Paul's Epistles.

Timothy and the work in Asia.—The church at Ephesus had great spiritual leadership—Aquila, Apollos, Paul, Timothy, John. Timothy was an evangelist (II Tim. 4:5) and was in some sense Paul's representative in the missionary work in Asia—I Tim. 1:3.

Four groups of Paul's Epistles.—1. First and Second Thessalonians A.D. 52 and 53. They deal largely with problems of eschatology. 2. First Corinthians, Second Corinthians, Galatians, Romans, A.D. 56–58. They discuss mainly great doctrinal questions, particularly justification by faith (over against the position of the Judaizers). 3. Philippians, Philemon, Colossians, Ephesians, A.D. 61-63. Christology, or the person of Christ comes to the front as opposed to the Gnostic heresy. 4. First Timothy, Titus, Second Timothy, A.D. 66–68. Pastoral and ecclesiastical problems concern Paul here.

Style of the fourth group.—There is a rather marked difference in style between this group and the others. Indeed each group has a style due to the topics discussed. Style is a function of the subject, a mark of the man, and varies with the man's age. *Cf.* Milton and Shakespeare. The style of the Pastoral Epistles is contemplative and discursive, as one would expect in an old man writing to young preachers.

Genuineness of this group.—With most scholars the Pastoral Epistles stand or fall together, though a few accept Titus and II Timothy and reject I Timothy. Some scholars admit Pauline fragments in those Epistles and claim that they were worked over by a later hand. Others reject them entirely as spurious. There are difficulties connected with this group of a special nature due in particular to the breaking off of the story in Acts. Some few scholars accept the Epistles and place this group during the period of the first imprisonment of Paul in Cæsarea and Rome. But most of those who accept the letters as genuine consider that Paul was set free in Rome before A.D. 64. They are the most doubtful of Paul's Epistles, but the arguments for their genuineness on the whole outweigh those against it. The genius of Paul the aged is manifest here. His spirit is softened, not broken, by age. He is still the masterful leader and the alert counsellor. Wisdom is the dominant note of Paul's teaching in this group.

Date.—Granting that Paul was set free before A.D. 64, the date of I Timothy belongs to the intervening time before his second imprisonment. The date of Paul's death is not absolutely certain. The most probable time is in A.D. 68, shortly before the death of Nero (June, A.D. 68). Some scholars contend that Paul was put to death in A.D. 64 in connection with the persecution growing out of the burning of Rome. Something can be said for that position, but it is not so probable as the one above. Somewhere between A.D. 64 and 68, therefore, I Timothy was written, probably in later summer or early fall of A.D. 67 (or 66).

Paul in Macedonia.—Paul appears to be in Macedonia at the time of the writing of the Epistle—I Tim. 1:3. He had probably come east on his release as he had planned (Philemon 22), and had then gone west to Spain. Now he is in the east again, and for the last time. He had touched at Miletus—II Tim. 4:20. Whether he actually went on to Ephesus or saw Timothy at Miletus is not certain. But he stopped also at Troas—II Tim. 4:13.

Heresies.—When Paul delivered his farewell discourse to the Ephesian elders at Miletus on his way to Jerusalem (Acts 20:29 f.), he had predicted the coming of "grievous wolves," and men should arise who would teach perverse things. The Epistle to the Colossians and Ephesians discussed the Gnostic heresy that had already come. The matter seems to be in a rather more developed state in I Timothy. Paul is particularly anxious that Timothy shall be able to withstand this dangerous form of error. The future of Christianity gives Paul grave concern.

Ecclesiology.—In I Timothy two well-defined sets of officers appear (*cf.* also Phil. 1:1). It has been objected by some that this sort of ecclesiastical growth did not come till the second century. But as already shown, the two sets of church officers (bishops and deacons) are found in Philippi. By the time of Ignatius, in the second century, three sets of officers are seen in this region (bishop, elder, deacon). But in the Pastoral Epistles bishop and elder are still one and the same—Acts 20:17, 28; Titus 1:5, 7; I Tim. 3:1; 5:17. The ecclesiastical situation in Ephesus is not beyond its probable development in A.D. 67.

"God our Saviour."—In the salutation (1:1 f.) occurs this expression, a common one in the Pastoral Epistles.

Purpose of the Epistle.—It is stated in—1:3–11. It is that Timothy may correct the false teaching now rife in Ephesus. It is a serious undertaking for a comparatively young man in so great a center of sin and error.

Paul's own career an example to Timothy.—Paul seemed a more unpromising agent for Christ than Timothy. If God used Paul, Timothy need not quail —1:12–17.

Prophecies about Timothy.—High hopes were wrapt up in Timothy. He had Hymenæus and Alexander to warn him—1:18–20.

Directions about public prayer.—He is not resentful against "kings."— 2:1–8.

Directions for the women in public worship.—In contrast to the conduct of some in Ephesus—2:9–15.

Qualifications of bishops—3:1–7.

Qualifications of deacons.—2:8–13. The reference to "women" in verse 11 is ambiguous, whether he means "women" simply, women or deaconesses, or wives of the deacons.

Conduct in the House of God.—One reason for his writing now to Timothy (3:14–16) is this.

The preacher and heresy.—4:1–11. Careful description of the ascetic and speculative tendencies of these Gnostics.

Timothy's self-improvement.—Devotion to study and progress—4:12–16.

Social problems in the church life.— Few things try a pastor more than these matters. The ages, the sexes, the officials, the servants, the sick, the poor, all test the mettle of the minister—5:1– 6:19. Many a preacher falls into one or the other of these pitfalls.

Appeal to Timothy.—Paul closes with a passionate appeal to Timothy to be faithful to his trust ("deposit")— 6:20 f.

II TIMOTHY.

Paul in Rome again.—Why he is in prison we do not know. No Luke has recorded this story. He may have been arrested at Nicopolis on the representation of some professional informer. It was now a crime to be a Christian, since Nero had charged the Christians with burning Rome. He has apparently been in Rome some time—II Tim. 1:15 ff.

First stage of the trial over.—At the first defence (II Tim. 4:16 f.) no one stood by him but the Lord Jesus. But he was delivered out of the mouth of the lion.

But death certain.—He cherishes no false illusions in the matter. He is going to the heavenly kingdom—4:18.

Paul's swan-song.—This is therefore Paul's last message. It has been often called his swan-song.

Date.—Probably in late spring of A.D. 68. An earlier date is advocated by some.

Bereft of friends.—It is not as it was when Paul was in Rome before. There he had many visitors. Now few are brave enough to risk a visit to his dungeon (no longer a hired house). Onesiphorus was loyal (II Tim. 1:16), but Demas forsook Paul (4:10); not to mention many from Asia—1:15. He was a doomed man and even his friends were afraid.

Faithfulness of Luke.—He alone was by his side (4:11), though he had other friends still in Rome—4:21.

Paul turns to Timothy for sympathy.—He had done much for Timothy (cf. I Timothy). Now the old preacher appeals to the young preacher. It was apparently not in vain (Heb. 13:23), for Timothy may have gotten into prison himself by coming to Paul's help.

Where was Timothy?—He may have been still in Ephesus, but the mission of Tychicus in II Tim. 4:12 rather implies that he was no longer there. He was still in the east.

Paul's interest in the work.—The great apostle keeps his hand upon his work to the end. He has sent messengers to different parts of the world (4:10, 12). Some one of his messengers probably bore this message to Timothy.

Paul's love for Timothy.—1:1 f.

Timothy's great inheritance.—His pious ancestry and training (1:3-5).

Timothy's gift.—1:6 f.

Not to be ashamed of Jesus nor of Paul.—Paul not ashamed of Christ. Some from Asia are ashamed of Paul—1:8-18.

Value of hardship for the minister.—2:1-13.

The skilled workman.—2:14-26. God is not ashamed of him.

Peril of impostors.—Real, but they cannot overturn truth of God—3:1-9.

Timothy to be loyal to Paul and the Scriptures.—He had had good teaching—3:10; 4:5.

Paul ready for his reward.—Cry of victory—4:6-8.

Men and books.—Paul wishes sympathy and the small comforts denied him in prison. He longs for his books—4:9-13.

The fight against Paul.—It is bitter and will be successful, but Jesus will guide him home—4:14-18.

Farewell.—His last farewell—4:19-22.

Paul's death.—It came apparently shortly after this Epistle was sent. We know for certain no details. He was possibly beheaded outside of Rome.

Paul and Nero.—These two names are forever united, for Nero had Paul put to death. It was only one of his many infamies. He little knew that he had been the cause of the death of the greatest man of his generation in the Roman Empire, one of the greatest of all time.

Paul's Epistles.—They constitute a large part of the New Testament and stand as the most important letters of history. They reveal Paul's own heart and picture the church life of the first century. But they do far more. They set forth the spirit of Christ by the greatest exponent of Christ that the world has ever seen.

9

TITUS.

Luke and Titus.—It is curious that Titus is not mentioned in the Acts of the Apostles, though he was such a trusted friend of Paul. Prof. A. Souter, of Oxford, has suggested that probably Titus is a brother of Luke and hence this silence. Some proof for this idea occurs in II Cor. 12:18. "I exhorted Titus, and I sent the brother with him." That in Greek naturally means Titus's brother. *Cf.* also II Cor. 8:18. Titus was a Greek and so was Luke. It is an entirely possible position.

Titus and Paul.—He first appears with Paul in Jerusalem at the conference (Gal. 2:1, 3) about A.D. 50. He is one of Paul's Greek converts (Titus 1:4) during the first tour and was not circumcised. The fight for Gentile freedom from the Jewish ceremonial law centered around him. Paul carried his point. Paul sent him to Corinth three times. Once he was sent when he began the collection there—II Cor. 8:6. A year later Paul sent Titus, possibly with a lost letter, but certainly with a vigorous message to the recalcitrant element in the church—II Cor. 2:12 f.; 7:6, 13; 12:17 f. Once more he, along with two other messengers (probably Luke and Erastus), goes to Corinth with a fresh message from Paul (probably II Corinthians) and with the burden of finishing the collection—II Cor. 8:16, 23. He is with Paul in Crete and is left as an evangelist in charge of the work—Titus 1:4. He is with Paul in Rome during his second imprisonment and is sent to Dalmatia—II Tim. 4:10.

Titus and Timothy.—They are naturally associated in our minds, because they received the Pastoral Epistles and were charged with similar work, that of the evangelist, the one in Crete, the other in Asia. They are both together with Paul in Macedonia—II Cor. 1:1; 7:13. They had both been to Corinth for Paul, but not at the same time. Timothy had apparently returned (I Cor. 4:17; II Cor. 1:1) before Titus went. Perhaps Timothy had not shown quite force enough to handle the difficult situation at Corinth—I Tim. 3:12. In Titus 2:15 "youth" is not used. Hence Titus was sent also. Timothy was less robust in health (I Tim. 5:23) than Titus. Both were Paul's children in the gospel and a joy to his old age. As he saw the end for his own work, he turned with hope to these young ministers (and others like them).

Work in Crete.—We do not know when it was established. Paul had not time to do gospel work in Crete when he touched there on his way to Rome.—Acts 27:7 ff. We do not know exactly when he was in Crete with Titus. It may have been on his return from Spain, assuming that he went there. It may have been on his way west.

Troubles in Crete.—The people themselves bore a bad reputation as liars and gluttons—Titus 1:12 f. The party of the circumcision (1:10), Pharisaic Christians (remnants of the Judaizers), are here as well as some of the newer heretics, the Gnostics—1:16. Altogether it was not a very hopeful outlook.

Genuineness.—The Pauline authorship of Titus stands or falls with the Epistles to Timothy. They are much of a piece in style and general character. Titus, though brief, is full of wisdom and gospel truth and can worthily be taken as Paul's own letter. Paul wrote all three.

Date.—It is not certain whether Titus is before or after I Timothy. Most probably it comes soon afterwards.

Paul in Macedonia.—He expects to winter in Nicopolis, a city of Epirus in Western Macedonia—Titus 3:12. He was in Macedonia also when he wrote I Timothy (1:3).

Purpose of the Epistle.—It is to give directions to Titus about setting things in order in Crete before Titus comes to Nicopolis to see Paul—1:5; 3:12.

Rather extended salutation.—For so brief a letter the greeting (1:1-4) is long. *Cf.* two verses only in I Timothy and II Timothy. Discusses Paul, the elect, the gospel, God, Christ, Titus.

Titus and the appointment of elders.—This important matter had apparently been overlooked when Paul was there—1:5-9.

Task before Titus and the elders in Crete.—A serious one, hence the need of care—1:10-16.

Social problems.—As in I Timothy, so here Paul gives pungent directions for the various classes in home and society—Ch. 2.

Practical Christian life.—The practical side of life is uppermost in Paul's mind in this Epistle—3:1-11.

Messengers of Paul.—Zenas the lawyer and Apollos are already in Crete, while Artemas or Tychicus will come—3:12 f.

Final exhortation to good works.—3:14.

With Christian friends.—3:15.

PHILEMON.

Date.—This Epistle was sent at the same time with Colossians and Ephesians—Philemon 10, 13; Col. 4:7-9; Eph. 6:21 f. Onesimus and Tychicus bear the Epistle to the Colossians (4:7-9), while Onesimus bears the one to Philemon (10) and Tychicus is the bearer of the Epistle to the Ephesians (6:21). Paul is still a prisoner in Rome (Philemon 1), and this group of letters was written while there, possibly just after the one to the Philippians and shortly before his release. *Cf.* Acts 28:30 f. The Epistle probably belongs to the year A.D. 62 or 63.

Personal character of the Epistle.—No great doctrinal matters are involved, nor is the letter addressed to a church. But it is a delightful picture of domestic life in Colossæ, one of the great cities in the Lycus Valley in the Province of Asia.

A family group.—Apphia seems to be the wife of Philemon and Archippus is their son—Philemon 1 f. It was a family of influence in the city and their home was used as a meeting place for the church in Colossæ—v. 2. The possession of slaves did not necessarily indicate great wealth, unless the number was considerable. It is possible that this family came under Paul's influence while he was in Ephesus—Acts 19:10.

Onesimus.—He had a good name, but he had not lived up to it—v. 10 f. He was not only a runaway slave, but had apparently stolen something as he left—v. 19. Rome was a favorite resort for runaway slaves, and Onesimus went there. He came under Paul's influence and was led to Christ by him—v. 10.

Christian slaves.—Slavery had its grip on the Roman empire. These slaves were not all degraded people by any means. Many of them were captives in war. Some of them were persons of real culture and distinction. But Roman law not only recognized slavery, but showed no sympathy with the slave. It was a delicate and dangerous situation. The conversion of the slaves to Christ often put master and slave in the same church. Nowhere does Paul show more consummate skill than in the handling of such a subject in this Epistle.

Sociological problems.—The modern problems in social life are old problems. They come into the horizon of this Epistle. The way that Christianity approaches such subjects is here finely illustrated.

Courtesy.—This is not essentially a Christian grace, but Christianity includes it. There is a fine flavor of courtesy in this Epistle. There is no railing at Philemon.

Delicacy.—So also Onesimus is not branded a mere runaway slave. Paul calls him his "child" (10); "a brother beloved" (16); "no longer a servant."

Compliment for Philemon.—It is not mere empty eulogy in 4-7, but sincere appreciation of his worth and work.

Return of Onesimus.—Paul acknowledges Philemon's legal claim on Onesimus, and so sends him back, but with a plea for his voluntary return—vs. 8–14.

Paul's pledge for Onesimus.—He guarantees him Christian character, pleads for his reception in that relation, and offers to repay what he may have taken when he left—vs. 15–20.

Suggestion of freedom.—In verse 21 Paul expresses the hope that he will set Onesimus free.

Gradual emancipation. — Evidently then Paul announces a spirit of love for Christian slaves as men and brethren which had in it the destruction of human slavery. This leaven of freedom has worked through the ages, and the Epistle to Philemon is a charter of freedom.

Group of friends.—Timothy is with Paul in Rome—1. Epaphras, who is from Colossæ (Col. 4:12), he calls his "fellow-prisoner" (Philemon 23), probably in a spiritual sense, though the point is not certain. John Mark is again with Paul (23), so that he has come back into Paul's favor. Luke, the faithful physician and friend, Aristarchus, and Demas are also Paul's "fellow-workers." He is not without sympathy and support in Rome.

HEBREWS.

Author.—Absolutely unknown. Origen said only God knew who wrote this wonderful book, one of the greatest in the New Testament. Paul, Barnabas, Apollos, Luke, Clement, Timothy, Silas, Priscilla, and others have advocates. Modern scholarship is on the whole against the Pauline authorship. But Pauline: In the sense that Paul's two great doctrines of a spiritual religion and one universal in scope run through the entire book. The writer may or may not have been a disciple of Paul, but he had Paul's conception of freedom from ceremony and the glory of the redemptive work of Christ: Heb. 2:9. Either Jew or Greek: The author's familiarity with the Levitical ritual and tabernacle service may indicate a Jewish mind; but, if so, it was one in touch with Hellenism and Greek philosophy—Heb. 1:2 f. The writer was in touch with both worlds of thought. Not a Hellenizer: But the author did not make a mere blend of Judaism and Hellenism after the manner of Philo and the other Jewish Alexandrian philosophers. The terms "effulgence," "image," "substance" (1:3) do show knowledge of Greek philosophical terms, but they are charged with a Christian content. Not a Judaizer: The prolonged discussion of the Jewish Ceremonial System made it impossible for the author to betray his sympathy with the position of the Judaizers (Acts 15:1, 5) if he had held it. On the contrary, he goes further than Paul (cf. Acts 21:22 ff.) and urges Jewish Christians to leave Mosaism—Heb. 13:13.

Readers.—Title may not be original; entire argument is meant for Jews. Probably Jewish Christians of Palestine, though not necessarily of one town like Jerusalem.

Place.—Author may be in Italy (Heb. 13:24), though the reference is ambiguous.

Date.—Probably just before destruction of the Temple in A.D. 70, since the mention of that fact would have greatly strengthened the argument about the vanishing of the Old Dispensation in 8:13. Timothy is released—Heb. 13:23. If he did go to Paul's relief (II Tim. 3:21) in A.D. 68 and was himself imprisoned, the date would be practically known as A.D. 69.

Temptation of readers.—Apostasy (Heb. 3:12, 14; 4:1, 11, 14, &c.) was the peril of these Hebrew Christians. Their Jewish neighbors had derided Christianity as not a true religion. They charged that it was a religion without a glorious past or origin, with no great heroes, with no priestly service, no Temple—the religion of a mere man, and a man of very humble estate and ignoble death. They had no prophets, no angels, no Moses, no Aaron, no Holy of Holies.

Contrast with peril of the Galatians. —The Galatians were urged by the Judaizers to add Judaism to Christianity in order to render it effective. The readers of the Epistle to the Hebrews are urged to give up Christianity entirely and return to Judaism, which was sufficient of itself.

Great Christian apologetic.—Judaism and Christianity are thus pitted against each other at the point where Judaism seemed strongest—the ritual and ceremonial. The author accepts the challenge and gives the Christian interpretation of the Jewish ceremonial and its bearing on Christianity. Jesus in the "Sermon on the Mount" contrasted His teaching of righteousness with that of the rabbis. Here the whole system of type and ceremony is shown to be meaningless apart from Christ, who was the reality to which all the types pointed.

Distinct type of Christian thought.— Priesthood of Christ. So here we have one great field of Christian thought hardly worked out at all elsewhere in the New Testament. It is indeed the very heart of the work of Christ, His atoning death, that is here presented in its priestly aspects. Jesus as priest is the burden of the book.

Argument by contrast.—The author uses the method of contrast to prove his great contention. He measures Jesus against every point of glory in the Old Testament dispensation.

Jesus the heart of the book.—He is the glory of Christianity. So the author does not shun the human name Jesus, but glories in it—2:9; 3:1. What the readers need is a true conception of Jesus.

Person of Christ.—Hence the book becomes the most extended discussion of Christology in the New Testament. Cf. Colossians, when Paul asserts the true idea of Christ's person as opposed to the Gnostic depreciation.

Son of God.—All through the book Jesus is presented as the Son of God— 1:2, 5–14; 4:14, &c.

Son of Man.—The Humanity of Jesus is not only admitted, but is shown to be His greatest glory and element of power in His priestly work—2:5–18. The purpose of the Incarnation is thus seen.

Nature of Jesus.—The terms used show His real humanity and real deity, avoiding both Sabellianism and Arianism—1:3 f. He is now in majesty by the Father's side.

Jesus superior to the Old Testament prophets.—1:1–3. Because He is God's Son. Hence His message demands more respect.

Jesus superior to angels.—1:4; 2:18. Because He is God's Son. Hence the new message calls for more earnest heed —2:1–4.

Jesus superior to Moses and Joshua. —3:1–4:13. Because He is God's Son. Hence the greater peril of disobeying Him.

Jesus superior to Aaron.—4:14; 7:28. Because He is a priest of a higher type, like Melchizedek. As God's Son He is able to do perfect and eternal service— 7:26–28.

Jesus works under a better covenant. —8:1–13. A covenant of grace which displaces the old—8:13.

Jesus serves in a better sanctuary.— 49:1–12. The one in Heaven, the true sanctuary.

Jesus presents a better sacrifice.— 9:13; 10:18. His own blood the only real sacrifice.

Jesus has better promises.—10:19; 12:3. In that they have come true in Him and are now clear to us—11:39 f.

The lesson of chastisement.—12:4. This their need.

The example of Esau.—12:14–17. A warning to them.

Contrast between Mount Sinai and Mount Zion.—12:18–29. One a symbol of the law, the other of grace (kingdom of God).

Loyalty to leaders.—Their real leaders, their own leaders (13:7, 17), instead of listening to outsiders and being led astray.

Loyalty to Jesus.—This the great exhortation all through the Epistle. Hold fast to Christ, hold on to the Confession. Cf. 2:1–4; 3:1, 6, 12, 14, 19; 4:1, 11–13, 14, 16, 5:11 f.; 6:1–8, 11; 10:19– 25, 28 f., 35, 39; 11:39 f., 12:1–3, 28 f.; 13:8, 10–14.

Separation from Judaism.—If necessary, let Jewish Christians renounce Judaism rather than Christianity. Follow Christ outside the gate (*cf.* Jerusalem, Judaism) and bear the reproach—13:12 f. Not that Judaism was wrong for Jews. It was useless—8:13. If Jews forced the issue, let reparation come.

Purpose of the author.—He aims to hold the wavering Hebrew Christians to Christianity. His powerful interpretation of Christianity in contrast to ceremonial Judaism has become the final word on that subject.

Tabernacle, not Temple.—Temple was still standing when the Epistle was written. But the tabernacle was the original from which the temple was fashioned. The tabernacle itself was patterned after the heavenly original. Hence the real contrast lay between these two.

Melchizedek.—The discussion about Melchizedek (ch. 7) is one of the most original parts of the book. The independence of Aaron removed Jesus entirely from the priestly line and mere ecclesiasticism.

Original language. — Most surely Greek, not Aramaic. The book shows no marks of being a translation.

Style.—The book has been said to begin like a treatise, proceed like a sermon, and close like a letter. The remark has justification. The argument is powerful, the passion is mighty and moving, the personal interest and appeal very real.

The real Judaism.—In a word, according to this book, Christianity is the real Judaism, the spiritual Israel (*cf.* Paul in Gal. 3:8; Rom. 2:28 f.). Judaism had no efficacy apart from Christ —9:18.

Testament or will.—Double sense in the Greek word for covenant or will is turned to good account in—9:15-20.

Relation of the Epistle to John the Baptist.—Teaching the sacrificial aspect of Christ's work appears in the mouth of the Baptist—John 1:29.

Relation to teaching of Jesus.—Jesus taught the sacrificial nature of His death.—Mt. 20:28; 26:28; Mk. 10:45; John 10:15, 17 f.

Relation to teaching of John the Evangelist.—*Cf.* I John 1:7; 2:1 f.; Rev. 1:18; 5:6, &c.

Relation to Paul's position.—*Cf.* II Cor. 5:14 ff.; Gal. 3:13; Rom. 5:8 f.

Relation to Peter's teaching.—*Cf.* I Pet. 1:19.

JAMES.

Brother of Jesus.—He was the oldest of four brothers (Mt. 13:55; Mk. 6:3), sons of Joseph and probably of Mary also—Mt. 1:25. For further account of brothers and sisters of Jesus, see Mt. 12:16-50; Mk. 3:31-35; Lu. 8:19-21; John 7:3-5.

Hostile attitude toward Jesus.—See Mt. 12:46; Mk. 3:31; Lu. 8:19; John 7:3 f.

Jesus appeared to him.—*Cf.* I Cor. 15:7. This event led to his conversion.

With the disciples at Pentecost.—*Cf.* Acts 1:14.

Visited by Paul on return from Damascus.—Gal. 1:19.

Soon the leader among the elders of Jerusalem.—Acts 12:17. So acknowledged by Peter.

Acknowledged as pillar by Paul.—Gal. 2:9. Along with Peter and John the Apostles.

Belongs to the Jewish phase of the work.—Gal. 2:8 f. Presides over the Jerusalem conference. This is the natural meaning of ''my judgment'' in Acts 15:19. His address (Acts 15:19-21) met the approval of the conference —15:22. He probably wrote the Epistle to the Christians of Antioch, Syria and Cilicia, which embodied his address and sustained Paul's contention of freedom for the Gentiles from the Mosaic ritual —Acts 15:23-29.

Name used by Judaizers.—They implied that James disapproved Peter's social freedom with the Gentile Christians—Gal. 2:12.

Not a Judaizer.—His address in Jerusalem (Acts 15:19–21) showed his sympathy with Paul's position. The Judaizers later claimed Peter, also because of his temporary desertion of Paul at Antioch—Gal. 2:11 ff. Both James and Peter continued in sympathy with Paul's contention.

Friendship for Paul.—This was shown at a critical time, when the Judaizers had grossly misrepresented Paul's position to the Jerusalem Christians—Acts 21:18–25.

Married Man.—See I Cor. 9:5.

Death.—Josephus (Ant., XX, IX, 1) tells the story of his death at the hands of the High Priest Ananus.

Called the Just.—In honor of his loyalty to Judaism, though a Christian.

He was not a Judaizer, but a true Jew, in love with his people and their customs.

EPISTLE OF JAMES.

Genuine.—Suits what we know of his theology and style from his address and the Letter in Acts 15.

Date.—Two views: one that it was written about A.D. 50 (probably correct), another that shortly before destruction of Jerusalem in A.D. 70.

Readers.—Twelve tribes of the Dispersion (Jewish Christians), probably before there were many Gentile Christians—James 1:1.

Does not claim kinship with Jesus.—Calls himself slave, or servant—Jas. 1:1.

Esteems Jesus as Lord.—Jas. 1:1. He is the subject and object of faith —2:1.

Familiar with teachings of Jesus.—Does not often mention the name of Christ, but is much like the "Sermon on the Mount" in subject-matter and imagery. *Cf.* 1:5–11, 25 f.; 2:6–26; 3:1–18.

Nearest Old Testament in point of view.—This is natural if, as is possible, it is one of the very earliest books of the New Testament. *Cf.* in particular James 4:7–10.

Worship still in synagogues.—James 2:2; 5:14.

Independent of (probably before) Paul's contention about Gentiles and the ceremonial law.—In 2:18 James has the point of view of John the Baptist and of Jesus. He asks for proof of faith as they did. He is not contradicting Paul, nor did Paul contradict James. Each is speaking of a different matter. Paul treats justification and trust as initial acts in the Christian life. James considers the life as a proof of one's profession. *Cf.* Paul's doctrine of sanctification in Rom., chaps. 6–8.

Practical ethics.—The Epistle is the "Gospel of Common Sense" (Deems) and a vital discussion of social problems (rich and poor, employer and employee, cure of the sick, question of teachers, &c).

Jewish Christian problems.—The vices condemned belong to an early type of church life and are not Gentile problems. *Cf.* oppression in 5:1–6; partiality in 2:1–7.

Beautiful images.—Varied and abundant pictures. *Cf.* 1:5–11; 3:1–12. Possibly used by other New Testament writers. Mayor considers that Epistles of John, of Hebrews, I Peter, Paul's Epistles to Galatians, Romans, and Timothy, all show traces of use of James. *Cf.* Mayor, "The Epistle of James."

Christian spirit of the Book.—Though Jewish in tone, the book is Christian in point of view, spirit and ideal. The outer life is demanded as an expression of the inner.

I PETER.

Author.—The writer calls himself "Peter, an Apostle of Jesus Christ" (1:1); the early writers (Papias, Polycarp, Irenæus, Clement of Alex., Origen, &c.) attribute the Epistle to Peter. It is acknowledged as genuine by the great majority of modern scholars. The internal character corresponds admirably with this claim. It is just the kind of a book that Peter would probably write, judging from the accounts of Peter in the Gospels and the Acts. For sketch of his life, see "Peter"—Mt. 4:18.

Companions in the salutation.—Mark is no longer with Barnabas (Acts 15:39), but is now with Peter—I Pet. 5:13. Peter travelled with his wife (I Cor. 9:5) and "she that is in Babylon elect" (I Pet. 5:13) may be his wife, or the reference may be to the church as is more probable.

Amanuensis and bearer.—It is probable that Silvanus (5:12) acted as both for Peter. If he was amanuensis, that fact may explain to some extent the style.

Place.—It is probable, though not certain, that Babylon in I Pet. 5:13 is used for Rome. The objection to that interpretation is that this is an Epistle, not an apocalypse. But the veiled image is probably used for precaution due to fear of the emperor. Still the provinces (1:1) are named from the standpoint of Babylon.

Date.—The time of Peter's death is not known. This was either about A.D. 64 or 68. The persecution as a Christian referred to in I Pet. 4:16 may be official or domestic. If official, it would be just after the Neronian persecution began (A.D. 64), which may very well have spread to the provinces of Asia where the emperor-worship had its chief home. The date would then be about 65. But the persecutions may have been mainly the scorn of neighbors and friends. If so, the date could be before 64.

Readers.—"The sojourners of the Dispersion in Pontus, Galatia, Cappadocia, Asia and Bithynia" (I Pet. 1:1) were probably both Jews and Gentiles, the spiritual Israel. The Roman provinces of Pamphylia and Cilicia are not mentioned. Paul had preached in these two and in Asia and Galatia. Who evangelized Pontus, Cappadocia and Bithynia we do not know. Peter himself may have done so, but he writes to two provinces where Paul had certainly wrought.

Relation to speeches in Acts.—There is undoubted similarity in doctrine, spirit, and languages between Peter's addresses in Acts and this Epistle. *Cf.* Acts 3:19–21 with I Pet. 3:20, for instance. See also Acts 1:22 and I Pet. 5:1; Acts 4:11 and I Pet. 2:4; Acts 10:34 and I Pet. 1:17. It is not probable that Luke had seen Peter's epistles or that Peter had seen Acts.

Knowledge of the Old Testament.—There are numerous marks of the Sept. in I Peter. His quotations are chiefly from Isaiah, Proverbs and the Psalms. *Cf.* I Pet. 1:18–20 and Is. 53; I Pet. 1:24 f. and Is. 40:6; I Pet. 2:17 and Prov. 24:21; I Pet. 4:8 and Prov. 10:12; I Pet. 3:10 f. and Ps. 34:12 f.

Knowledge of the life of Christ.—The Epistle shows no acquaintance with the Gospels, but does reflect real familiarity with the life and teachings of Jesus. In particular he uses some phrases and figures like those of Jesus in the Sermon on the Mount. *Cf.* I Pet. 2:12; 3:13–16; 3:14; 4:14; 5:6 and Mt. 5:10, 11, 16; 6:25, &c. The reference to the suffering and glory of Christ in I Pet. 5:1 may be an echo of the transfiguration. So in 1:8 the repetition of the fact that the readers had not seen Jesus accents the fact that Peter had seen Him in the flesh.

Relation to James.—There seems to be some connection between I Peter and the Epistle of James. James probably wrote first, and so Peter may have read his Epistle. *Cf.* Jas. 1:1 and I Pet. 1:1; Jas. 1:2 f. and I Pet. 1:6 f.; Jas. 1:11–22 and I Pet. 1:23–2:1.

Relation to Paul.—There are some vague general expressions in Ephesians and I Peter that correspond, which are easily explained, but the Epistle shows very remarkable kinship to the Epistle to the Romans. If Peter was in Rome when he wrote, he may very well have seen this great Pauline Epistle. *Cf.* I Pet. 1:14 and Rom. 12:2; I Pet. 1:21 and Rom. 4:24; I Pet. 2:5 and Rom. 12:1; I Pet. 2:6 f. and Rom. 9:33; I Pet. 3:8–12 and Rom. 12:14–19; I Pet. 3:22 and Rom. 8:34; I Pet. 4:1 and Rom. 6:7; I Pet. 5:1 and Rom. 8:18, &c.

Purpose.—The aim is distinctly practical, not doctrinal. *Cf.* also Peter's addresses in Acts where the hortatory element predominates. He sounds here a note of cheer and courage to meet the present trials. He makes appeal to the example of Christ and their own experience and expounds the Old Testament teaching. He urges trust and holy living as present duties.

Contents.—The introduction (1:1 f.) sets forth the doctrine of the Trinity and accents the atoning death of Jesus. The purposes of God are shown in the new birth of the believer and the eternal inheritance which is his—1:3–5. This blessed hope is ample cheer in present fiery trials for those who love the unseen Jesus—1:6–9. The prophets never saw what Christians now know by blessed experience in Christ—1:10–12. Sobriety and hope are the demands of the times—1:13–25. Steady growth will fulfil Christ's ideal for his people—2:1–10. He doubtless (2:5) has in mind Christ's promise—Mt. 16:18. All classes must exemplify the spirit of Christ and be a real brotherhood—2:11–3:12. No one can harm the Christian who has Christ supreme in his heart—3:13–22. They must, like Christ, set a good example for the Gentiles—4:1–11. If they have to suffer, let it be as innocent men —4:12–19. Peter can well exhort them to humility and steadfastness (5:1–11) in view of his own bitter experience.

Style.—The Epistle has a large number of words not found elsewhere in the New Testament, sixty-two in all. But the style, while dignified and elevated, is not florid. It is a bit oratorical, but not unduly so. It is possible that Silvanus, as Peter's amanuensis, was of some service in the use of the smooth vernacular Greek in which it is written.

Leading ideas.—Life of Jesus—This spotless life is stamped on the mind of Peter. *Cf.* 1:2, 3, 13, 18; 2:22 f.; 3:1, 18 f.; 4:14, &c. Election—1:1 f.; 20; 2:9. Last time—1:5 f. Salvation—1:5, 9 f. Prophecy—1:10 f. Blood of Christ —1:18 f.; 2:24. Obedience to the truth —1:22. Living stones—2:5. Spiritual house—2:5. Royal priesthood—2:9. Pilgrims—2:11. Duty to the state—2:13 f. Servants—2:18 f. Atoning death of Christ—2:24. Wives—3:1 ff. Husbands —3:7. Christ as Lord—3:15. Spirits in prison—3:18 ff. The ark and baptism—3:20 ff. Social virtues—4:7 ff. The Chief shepherd—5:4. The devil—5:8 f.

Grace.—Grace multiplied—I Pet. 1:2. The grace of life—I Pet. 3:7. Manifold grace of God—I Pet. 4:10. Grace to the humble—I Pet. 5:5. True grace—I Pet. 5:12.

Brother-love.—As a purpose of redemption—I Pet. 1:22. As a proof of submission—I Pet. 2:17. As an instance of reality—I Pet. 3:8. As an encouragement of faith—I Pet. 5:9.

Well-doing.—Bringing forth praise—I Pet. 2:14. Putting evil to silence—I Pet. 2:15. Involving suffering—I Pet. 2:20. Adopting good examples—I Pet. 3:6. Suffering because of—I Pet. 3:17. Obtaining protection—I Pet. 4:19.

Hope.—Its character—I Pet. 1:3. Its endurance—I Pet. 1:13. Its object—I Pet. 1:21; 3:5. Its possession—I Pet. 3:15.

Incorruptible things—The inheritance —1:4. Ransom—1:18. Seed—1:23. Character—3:4.

Suffering of Christ.—1:11; 2:23; 3:18; 4:1, 13; 5:1. Like Christ—2:21; 5:1, 9. For Christ—2:19–21; 3:14, 17; 4:15, 19; 5:10.

II PETER.

Author.—This is the most disputed book in the New Testament. Its genuineness is on the whole the most doubtful. Conservative scholars like Chase and Lechler consider it pseudonymous, while a radical critic like Spitta holds it genuine, as do conservative scholars like Bigg and Zahn. Probably its genuineness can never be fully and clearly determined to the satisfaction of all, for the arguments on both sides are strong. But on the whole the Epistle holds its own rightful place in the canon as the work of Simon Peter.

Author's claims.—The very frequency of these claims has been turned against the authenticity of the book. He calls himself Simon (Symeon in the Greek, the Aramaic form) Peter (1:1) rather than just Peter as in I Pet. 1:1. So in II Pet. 3:1. The writer definitely claims to have written another epistle. It is urged that "your apostles" (3:2) could not have been used by Peter, but that is not certain. The outspokenness of Peter is sufficient to explain all this.

Use of the Gospels.—No evidence is found of any use of the Gospel in II Peter, though the point of view in general is that of Mark, who was Peter's interpreter.

Knowledge of the life of Jesus.—Even more than in I Peter do we find reference to the work of Christ. It is done in the most natural way. Thus in 1:3 ("that called us") we may have allusion to the fact that Jesus called the apostles in person. In 1:14 the early death of Peter is mentioned as foretold by Jesus—John 21:18 f. The clear reference to the transfiguration (1:16 f.) is natural if Peter is the writer. His language here sounds like that of one who was present. Cf. also II Pet. 2:20; 3:4.

Synoptic eschatology.—The view of the second coming and of the end of the world is practically the same as this in the great eschatological discourse of Jesus on the Mount of Olives. There is the same confidence that Jesus will come, though the time is unknown. The doubt of some (ch. 3) shows that at least a generation had passed since the Ascension of Christ.

Relation to Peter's speeches.—As with I Peter, so here manifest similarities are are found with Peter's speeches in Acts. See Lumby.

Relation to I Peter.—The writer expressly refers to I Peter—3:1. And yet it is evident that the style of the two books differs very greatly. So much is this true that the language of II Peter has been called "Baboo Greek." Some have fancied a use of Josephus in II Peter, but it is not made out. The truth probably is that in I Peter Silvanus acted as Peter's amanuensis (I Pet. 5:12), while in II Peter there was another less accomplished amanuensis or, as is most probable, Peter had no amanuensis at all. He was called "unlearned and ignorant"—Acts 4:13. And here there is a certain uncouthness of style that may thus find its explanation. There is more reserve in I Peter, while the language of II Peter is full of unusual words. Some of them are due to the vernacular "Koinē" in which the New Testament is written (see the Papyri), but others are personal peculiarities. There are 231 words here not found in I Peter, but, on the other hand, the rest of the vocabulary is quite similar to that of I Peter. Cf. Bigg. Both Epistles are fond of repeating words and both use the plural of abstract nouns. Both (Marcus Dods in Standard B. D.) have the same mannerism of stating a thing both negatively and positively. The undercurrent of thought in both is the same. The variations of thought are here also. "In II Peter false teaching instead of persecution is a source of danger, knowledge takes the place of hope, and piety that of holiness." (Falcoms in Hastings' one vol. B. D.) Noah and the flood are mentioned in both.

Use of Jude.—It seems clear that either, as is probable, II Peter makes use of Jude (*cf*. ch. 2 with Jude) or that Jude is based on II Peter. Scholars are much divided. Jude is the more vivid and apparently the more original. This use of Jude does not discredit the book. *Cf*. the use of the O. T. words and phrases in the N. T.

Use of the O. T.—Express quotations are few, but the O. T. examples are used as in the case of Noah and Lot—Ch. 2. But *cf*. 3:7 and Is. 13:9–13; 3:8 and Ps. 90:4; 2:17 and Prov. 10:11. *Cf*. also the writer's theory of prophetic inspiration in the Old Testament—1:20 f.

Relation to Book of Enoch.—Some writers find a parallel between Enoch and Peter's mention of the fallen angels in 2:4, 11.

Mention of Paul's Epistles as Scripture.—Peter's praise of Paul in II Peter 3:15 is urged by some as proof that the book is not genuine, since Paul had rebuked Peter so sharply in Gal. 2:11 ff. But it was just like Peter to rebound in his affection as he had done toward Christ. It is argued also that the description of Paul's Epistles as Scripture in II Pet. 3:16 shows the book to be quite late, even in the second century. But Clement of Rome, before the end of the first century, shows that Paul's Epistles were already collected together. It is not to be forgotten also that Paul claimed authority for his Epistles—II Thess. 3:6, 14. It does not follow that Peter had read all of Paul's Epistles. But one need only to turn to II Cor., chs. 10–13, to see how Paul himself felt concerning his apostleship—Gal., chs. 1 and 2. It is by no means evident that the early Christians who were loyal to Paul did not consider Paul's Epistles as the Word of God, even on a par with the Old Testament.

External evidence.—It is only fair to say, however, that there is no certain mention of this Epistle in early Christian writers till the close of the second century. Clement of Alexandria knew and used it about 190 A.D. The early writers were divided on the genuineness of the book. Eusebius rejected it. It is at any rate a proof of some criticism on the part of the early Christians.

Date.—There is nothing decisive in this matter except that if it was written by Peter, it was before 68 A.D. If the book is not genuine, it may, of course, belong to the second century.

Place.—There is no hint as to the whereabouts of the writer at this time.

Readers.—He implies that they are the same as the readers of the First Epistle—II Pet. 3:1. They were probably chiefly Gentile Christians.

Aim.—The purpose is not precisely the same as I Peter. He has in mind not so much persecution as heresy. It is not clear where this incipient Gnosticism lies in the background, but certainly the readers are warned against a violent form of looseness in living. Perhaps some of the Gentile Christians in the east had turned Paul's principle of freedom to license—Gal. 5:1, 13. They were making the doctrines of grace a cover for the grossest immoralities (*cf*. Rom. 6:1 f.), like the Nicolaitans in Rev. 2:10–24. The keyword of this Epistle is knowledge. The readers must grow in the knowledge of Jesus so as to stem the tide of heresy around them. The writer is anxious to conserve for them his own knowledge of Christ (1:14 f.), a possible reference to the Gospel of Mark. Like I Peter the book is mainly exhortation.

Contents.—The introduction is very brief (1:1 f.), but sounds the key-note of the book in its accent on faith, righteousness and knowledge. Growth in the Christian virtues is urged in 1:3–11. He is now doing his part to help them on in this development in grace—1:12–21. They are warned against the current false teachers who are repetitions of those in the older days—Ch. 2. The second coming of Christ is sure, though delayed. God does not count time as men do—3:1–13. The practical duty of all is to be ready without spot and blameless when Jesus comes—3:14–18.

Leading ideas.—Deity of Jesus—1:1. "Our God and Saviour Jesus Christ." So margin, and correctly. Partakers of the divine nature—1:4. Diligence in acquiring Christian virtues—1:5–8. Election made sure—1:10 f. Body a tabernacle—1:13 f. Eyewitness of Christ's glory—1:16 f. Prophecy made more sure

—1:19. Holy Spirit the author of prophecy—1:20 f. False prophets and teachers—2:1 ff. Fallen angels—2:4, 11. Noah—2:5. Lot and Sodom and Gomorrah—2:6 ff. Balaam—2:15 f. Peril of relapse—2:20-22. Prophets and apostles—3:3. Scoffers of the second coming—3:4 ff. God's way of counting time —3:8 ff. End of the world—3:10, 11. New heaven and new earth—3:13. Praise of Paul—3:15 f. Warned against apostasy—3:17. Growth in grace—3:18.

FIRST EPISTLE OF JOHN.

Author.—John. No reference to the writer occurs, except that in the introduction. He claims to be a personal witness to the earthly life of Jesus—I John 1:1-4:

Style.—Almost identical with that of the Fourth Gospel, and obviously by the same author. We have here the same repetition, the same positive and negative statements, the same favorite ideas and words.

Literary form.—The book is less personal than II John and III John. It is like Hebrews, and rather more of a treatise than a personal Epistle. Yet the homiletical flavor is present in the frequent appeals and exhortations.

Date.—No means of determining for certain. No persecution appears in sight. John is an old man. Heresy is rife.

Place.—Probably from Ephesus.

Destination.—Probably to the same region as the Apocalypse, the churches of Asia (Roman province).

Occasion.—Laxity in views of the person of Christ and in practical morality. Spread of Gnostic views. Corrective of Gnostic views of Jesus—the Ebionites made Jesus a mere man. The Docetic Gnostics denied His real humanity. The Corinthian Gnostics combined both theories and made Jesus a mere man, but held that Christ was an Æon that came on Jesus at His baptism and left Him on the cross.

Asserts the truth about Christ.—Jesus Christ came in the flesh (I John 4:2) as against the Docetic Gnostics. Jesus is the same as Christ (I John 2:22) as opposed to Cerinthian Gnostics.

Purpose.—Polemical and for edification of native Christians.

Catholic Epistle.—General in destination and scope, not addressed to single church or person. There are no personal details.

Positive assertions rather than argument.—It is like the Gospel in setting forth in parallel form various aspects of a subject. Antithesis, repetition, parallelism, mark the Epistle.

Favorite words.—The Word of Life (I John 1:1) is like John 1:1. Life (eternal life) is a common word, as in I John 1:2. Note: the Father (1:2 f.). So: message (1:5), light (1:5), fellowship (1:6), darkness (1:5 f.), lie and truth (1:6), little children (2:1), advocate (2:1), sin (2:1 f), keep (2:3), know (2:5), hate (2:9), love (2:10), world (2:15), antichrist (2:18), righteous (3:7), prove (4:1), begotten (4:7), victory (5:4). These give a fair idea of the vocabulary of the Epistle. The ideas run in the same channel that we have in the Fourth Gospel, especially in the prologue.

II JOHN.

Same Obscurity.—Author same as in the case of First John. Date not necessarily the same, but probably the same general period. Place in similar obscurity. The elder—II John 1. This term does not mean that the author is not an apostle. *Cf.* I Pet. 5:1.

The elect lady.—II John 1. It is not certain whether the Epistle is addressed to an individual or a church. Kyria was used as a personal name. Probably on the whole we have a personal letter.

Not catholic.—At any rate it is not a general Epistle like First John. It is addressed to a single person or church. Christian hospitality not for extreme heretics—II John 10. Docetic Gnosticism condemned—II John 7. Teaching of Christ rule and standard of orthodoxy—II John 9.

Favorite words.—Love, truth, commandment, abide, teaching, confess.

Paper and ink mentioned.—II John 12. Probably papyrus (paper).

III JOHN.

Date.—Probably the same general period.

Personal, not catholic.—Letter addressed to Gaius by the Elder. Picture of missionary activity—III John 5 f. Inability to receive pay from the Gentiles—III John 7. "The Name" used of Christ as in Acts—III John 7. Diotrephes—III John 9–11. Bold sketch of ambitious man who refused to entertain John. Demetrius, the very opposite of Diotrephes—III John 12. Hospitality urged—III John 5 f.

Favorite words.—Love, truth, walk, know, witness, receive.

Picture of John.—These Epistles reveal John's own character—his real character. Man of love and of anger, of reserve and of passions, of mysticism and of practical wisdom, of tenderness and of vehement denunciation of wrong, of spiritual insight and great plainness of speech. The Epistles show many of the same traits manifest in the Apocalypse.

JUDE.

Common name.—From Judah, and so popular. Since the time of Judas Maccabeus this name was a favorite one with the loyal Jews. In the New Testament we have mentioned with this name an ancestor of Jesus (Lu. 3:30); Judas Iscariot (Mt. 10:4); Judas, not Iscariot, and probably same as Judas, the son of James, according to American Revision (Lu. 6:16; Acts 1:13); Judas of Damascus (Acts 9:11); Judas of Galilee (Acts 5:37); Judas Barsabas (Acts 15:22, 27, 32, 33); Jude the brother of James—Jude 1.

The Lord's brother.—Jesus had brothers (sons of Joseph and Mary and probably younger than Jesus), according to Mt. 13:55; Mk. 6:3; whose names were "James and Joseph and Simon and Judas." The brothers were hostile to Jesus (Mt. 12:46 ff.; Mk. 3:21; John 7:3 ff.) at first. But they were present as believers at the meeting preceding the great day of Pentecost (Acts 1:14). The appearance of Jesus after His resurrection (I Cor. 15:7) probably led to the conversion of all the brothers and sisters.

Does not claim kinship with Jesus.—Like James, his brother (Jude 1) and brother of the Lord Jesus (Gal. 1:19), he calls himself only "a servant of Jesus Christ"—Jude 1. A man claiming to be Jude, though not, would most probably have claimed to be a brother of Jesus. Eusebius (H. E. iii. 19, 20, 23) notes Hegesippus as saying that Domitian found the grandchildren of Jude, the Lord's brother according to the flesh, as men of humble station, but sturdy and honorable.

Under the shadow of James.—Jude appears not to have been so prominent nor active as his brother James, the leading elder in Jerusalem. Hence he calls himself the brother of James (Jude 1).

Not an apostle.—Jude was not one of the twelve apostles, nor was he an apostle in the sense that Paul was. His brother James is by implication called apostle in some sense by Paul in Gal. 1:19. But Jude is not apparently an apostle in that sense. He is "the servant of Jesus Christ."

Genuineness of the Epistle.—The Epistle by his name was not widely circulated, it appears at first. But modern scholars generally accept it as genuine. *Cf.* Biggs, Int. and Crit. Comm.

Date.—Most probably between A.D. 64 and 70.

Relation to II Peter.—Scholars are not a unit on this matter. Apparently Jude was acquainted with the second chapter of II Peter, or Peter was familiar with Jude. Not to argue the matter, one may assume that Jude is the earlier, on grounds of brevity and originality of style.

Use of non-scriptural books.—As Paul (Acts 17:28; Titus 1:12) quoted heathen writers, so Jude seems to quote the apocryphal book of Enoch—Jude 14. The word "prophesied" may be compared with Paul's use of "prophet" in Titus 1:12.

Language.—This short Epistle has a rather remarkable vocabulary. The writer is evidently familiar with the Septuagint, and uses the current language of the time, the *Koine*. He has the common tradition of Christian teaching. There is little that is distinctive in the general style outside of the full and rather sonorous vocabulary.

Many images.—The bold images in the Epistle may be compared with the figures in the Epistle of James (*cf.* also the Sermon on the Mount).

Readers of the Epistle.—The destination of the letter is not made clear, save that it is to the elect—Jude 1. Probably the same general readers are had in mind, as we find in I Peter (1:1) and II Peter (3:1). Some think that he has Corinth in mind.

Purpose.—The aim of the Epistle is to warn the elect against heresy and to exhort to earnest contention for the faith—Jude 3. The author shows much passion and zeal.

Theme.—The "common salvation" (Jude 3) is the general subject.

Type of heresy condemned.—Probably Gnosticism of the earlier form. *Cf.* Colossians, Ephesians, Timothy, Titus, II Timothy, Epistles of John. It is not necessarily the Gnosticism of the second century.

REVELATION.

Title.—Revelation is in Greek "Apocalypse," an unveiling—Rev. 1:1. It is the revealing of Jesus Christ.

Agents.—God gave the revelation to Jesus, who sent it to John, the writer, by an angel for the benefit of the servants of God—Rev. 1:1.

Author.—His name is John (1:1, 9), who is in exile in the isle of Patmos, because of persecution—1:9. Irenæus

identifies him with the Apostle John, and this view on the whole has the balance of evidence. Jesus has promised him the cup and baptism of woe—Mk. 10:38 ff.; Mt. 20:22 ff.

Date.—Two views exist about the date; one, and until recently the most popular among scholars, puts it just after Nero's death (A.D. 69), the other and the older view, and now again popular with scholars, locates it in the end of Domitian's reign (about A.D. 95) according to the testimony of Irenæus. The latter view is on the whole the more probable.

Destination.—The immediate servants of God who are readers (1:2, 3) are the members of the seven churches of Asia (1:11); Ephesus, Smyrna, Pergamum, Thyatira, Sardis, Philadelphia, Laodicea.

Why these churches?—Many other churches in the Province of Asia and in large cities. *Cf.* Colossæ and Hierapolis. But these seven make a circuit along important roads, and each the center of a district.

Real letters.—Each of the seven churches has a special message (Chaps. 2 and 3) adapted to the real situation and environment. *Cf.* Ramsay, "The Letters to the Seven Churches," for the historical and archæological details.

Varied types.—The seven churches with the letters to them present a fairly complete picture of church life in all the ages. Hence the perils and problems of modern city churches are here well outlined.

Whole book to each church.—But each church was to get the benefit of the messages to the other churches, and the entire Apocalypse was designed also for each church.

Unity of the book.—Many efforts have been made to disprove the unity of the Apocalypse. Hort, "The Apocalypse of St. John," p. 13, sums up thus: "They have done nothing whatever to shake the traditional unity of authorship."

Apocalyptic method.—This had come to be a favorite style of writing among the Jews and even among the Greeks and Romans (*cf.* Sybilline Oracles). Under the guise of symbols, past, present or future events were set forth in an oracular and vivid manner. To the initiated the method was very lucid, while to outsiders it was often mere cryptogram. One reason for its use was the safety thus secured for criticism of the ruling powers. Thus Peter (I Pet. 4:16) alludes to the Roman persecution of the Christians and seems to refer to Rome under the name Babylon—I Pet. 5:13.

Use of the Old Testament.—There are no express quotations from the Old Testament, but the book is a mosaic of Old Testament phrases, especially from the Apocalyptic portions, as certain passages of Isaiah, Zephaniah, Zechariah, Ezekiel and Daniel. Daniel is the typical Old Testament Apocalyptic book. As examples of this use of the Old Testament compare Rev. 1:13 ff. with Ez. 1:7; 43:2; Dan. 10:5; Rev. 4:1 with Ez. 1:26 f.; Rev. 4:6 ff. with Ez. 1:10; Is. 6:2; Rev. Ch. 5 with Ez. 2:2, 9; Zech. 5:1–3; Rev. 6:14 with Is. 34:4; Rev. 7:3 with Ez. 9:4; Rev. 10:5 f. with Dan. 12:7; Rev. 10:9–11 with Ez. 3:1–3; Rev. 11:1 with Zech. 2:1; Rev. 11:3 f. with Zech. 4:2, 11, 14; Rev. 12:7 with Dan. 7:2–8; Rev. 14:20 with Is. 63:3; Rev. 19:17 with Ez. 39:17–20; Rev. 20:8 with Ez. 38:2; 3:19; Rev. 20:12 with Dan. 7:10; 12:1; Rev. 21:1 with Is. 55:17-19; 66:22; Rev. 21:10 ff. with Ez. 48:30 ff.; Rev. 22:1 f. with Ez. 47:1, 12; Zech. 14:8. Chs. 17 and 18 are almost entirely from the Old Testament.

Current apocalypses.—The general plan of an Apocalypse may be well illustrated by such books as Enoch, Esdras, Baruch, Assumption of Moses, Sybilline Oracles, Shepherd of Hermas, Apocalypse of Peter. The Christians naturally employed the method so common to the writers of the time.

Apocalyptic method used by Jesus.—When this form of teaching was so common it is not surprising that Jesus made use of it. This He did on various occasions, especially in connection with the subject of the kingdom, as in—Mt. 16:27 f.; Mk. 9:1; Lu. 9:26 f.; 17:20–37. In particular, in the discourse on the Mount of Olives, during the last week, we find extensive use of Apocalyptic—*Cf.* Mt. 24 and 125; Mk. Ch. 13; Lu. Ch. 21.

Paul's use of apocalyptic.—*Cf.* II Thess. 2:1–12 (the man of sin).

Apocalyptic in I John.—See "Discussion of Antichrist" in I John 2:18–29. *Cf.* also Jude 12 ff., and II Pet. 3:5–13. The Apocalypse of John is the greatest of all the apocalyptic books.

Language.—The book has 871 distinct words besides names of persons and places, and 108 occur nowhere else in the New Testament. The peculiar subjects treated largely explain this number of individual words. The bulk of them occur in the common language of the time, as the papyri show. *Cf.* Swete, "The Apocalypse of St. John," p. 117. The grammar of the book is remarkable for the large number of variations from usual Greek usage in the matter of agreement in gender, number and case. These occur, as a rule, in opposition where the demand was not so insistent for such agreement. Some of them are due to design; others may be due to lack of revision or to excitement from the visions.

Parenthesis is frequent and anacoluthon.—These things occur in other Greek books, but more often in the Apocalypse. *Cf.* the statement in Acts 4:13 about John as an unlettered man.

Comparison with Gospel of John.— The style of the Apocalypse is both like and unlike the Gospel of John. Both the Gospel (John 21:24) and the Epistles may have had revision and supervision not true of the Apocalypse. Some of the favorite ideas of the Gospel are present, as power, witness, conquer, lead, know, keep, commandment, word, &c., while other common ideas of the Gospel do not appear. The two books are so different that it is difficult to make a just comparison. In the Gospel we see the contemplative, reflective side of the spiritual theologian. In the Apocalypse we have the Son of Thunder all ablaze with passion and power, though chastened by the love of Christ.

Leading ideas of the Apocalypse.— Some of the great teachings of the book are the glory and majesty of God, the deity of Jesus, the grandeur of the redemptive work of Jesus, the persecutions of the saints, the conflict with the Roman Empire, the fate of the wicked, the happiness of the redeemed.

Historical background.—The pictures in the book are drawn from the persecutions of Christians in the Roman Empire, probably in time of Domitian. Ramsay ("Letters to the Seven Churches") and Swete ("Apocalypse of St. John") both find in the imperial and provincial persecution the occasion for the intensity of the imagery. The emperor worship was the chief cult of the empire and was the form of idolatry that persecuted.

The two beasts.—According to this view the two beasts of Rev., Ch. 13, set forth the two aspects of the worship of the emperor (imperial and provincial).

Methods of interpretation.—In a general way these may be described as historical, spiritual, or a combination of the two. The purely spiritual. Many find no history in the symbols at all. The purely historical interpretation divides into preterite (all in the past), future (all in the future), continuous and synchronous (from the first century to the end). The continuous theory makes the series of seven successive, while the synchronous theory finds them more or less parallel. The combination of the historical and the spiritual considers the book as a portrayal of immediate conflict between Christianity and pagan Rome with the certainty of ultimate triumph, but without any attempt to set forth the course of Christian history. The struggle then on hand would, despite great carnage, result in victory for Christ, and heaven was sure and might be soon won.

Panorama.—The book is in reality, barring Chaps. 2 and 3 (Letters to the Seven Churches), a series of pictures. Each is complete in itself, and yet each prepares for the others. They are not necessarily successive nor necessarily parallel. But various aspects of the Titanic struggle between the kingdom of Christ and the kingdom of Satan are portrayed in turn. They one and all teach the same lesson of triumph.

Symbols inexplicable.—It is not possible to be sure about the meaning of all the various images used like the seals, the locusts, the bowls, the horses, the scorpions, &c. The grandeur of the imagery is impressive, and the main lessons of the book remain reasonably clear.

Spiritual and practical.—The book is written for the cheer of the saints in the churches of Asia. John is himself a "partaker with you in the tribulation and kingdom and patience which are in Jesus''—Rev. 1:9. He is finally overcome by the vision of victory and glory which he sees—Rev. 22:8 f. They only need courage and patience.

Final triumph of Jesus.—Jesus will win in the end. This is the supreme teaching of the Apocalypse—Rev. 11:15.

Picture of Jesus.—The whole book is in a sense the revelation of Jesus—Rev. 1:1. He is in heaven, the Redeemer, the Lamb that was slain, Lion of the Tribe of Judah, and He receives worship as the Father—Rev. Ch. 5. From heaven Jesus as the Captain of the Hosts directs the struggle on earth with Satan. Note the picture of Christ in Rev. 1: 13–20.

Second Coming of Christ.—The fact of the return of Christ is prominent throughout the book. This is the main note of Christ. The time of the Second Coming of Christ is said to be ''shortly'' (Rev. 1:1) and to be ''at hand'' (1:3) and ''I come quickly''—22:7, 20. John responds with a devout ''amen'' (22:20) to that promise. But one must recall the explanation of Peter, that God does not count time as we do. One thousand years and one day may be interchangeable as God looks at time—II Pet. 2:8 ff. The time is not made clear, but the fact is.

Millennium no stumbling-block.—No theory of the millennium (Rev. Ch. 20) should be allowed to obscure the main matter, the certainty of Christ's return. The term ''millennium,'' or ''thousand years,'' belongs to the symbolism of the book.

Doctrinal misuse of the book.—Robert South said that the Apocalypse either found one mad or left him so. That is the extreme reaction against the cock-sure ''keys'' (all different), which men have had for the interpretation of this wonderful Apocalypse. Chiliasm is the term applied to the literal interpretation of the images in the book, a grossly materialistic conception.

Antithesis.—The book is a book of contrasts, light and shadow, day and night, sorrow and joy; glimpses of hell and pictures of heaven alternate with each other. This method of contrast is similar to the style of the Gospel of John and the Epistles of John.

Picture of Hell.—The glimpses of the damned, the demons, and the final rout of the devil himself, present a fearfully vivid portrayal of the condition of the lost.

Picture of Heaven.—On the other hand the pictures of heaven are a comfort to the persecuted Christians.

Symbols.—Leading symbols in the book are Seven Spirits (1:4), for the Holy Spirit; Alpha and Omega (1:8); for God and for Jesus (22:13); Seven Candlesticks (1:20); for Churches; Seven Stars (1:20); for the Angels of the Churches; the Throne, the Rainbow, Sea of Glass, Four and Twenty Elders, the four living Creatures—Chap. 4. The Sealed Book, the Lamb that is the Lion—Chap 5. The Seven Seals and the Four Horses—Chaps. 6–7. The Seven Trumpets—Chaps. 8–10, with various other Images. (The peculiar Locusts of 9:3 ff. The Horses of 9:17 ff. The Bitter-Sweet Book of 10:9 ff.) The 1260 Days and the two Witnesses of Chap. 11. The Woman and the Man-child of 12:1–6. The various images of the Devil in 12:7 ff. The two Beasts of 13. The 144,000 of Chap. 14. The Seven Bowls of Chap. 16. The great Harlot Babylon in 17:1 and 18. The Marriage of the Lamb in 19:1–10. The Supper of God in 19:17 ff. The Thousand Years in 20. The Book of Death and the Book of Life in Chap. 20. The New Heaven and the New Earth of Chap. 21 and 22.

Purpose of the book.—Not primarily to teach doctrine, but to promote faith and courage. The book is full of doctrine, but that is incidental. It is a bugle-call to confidence and hope. ''In form it is an epistle, containing an Apocalyptic prophecy; in spirit and inner purpose, it is a pastoral.''—Swete, ''Apocalypse,'' p. 90.

Downfall of pagan Rome.—The exultant note of the Apocalypse (ch. 17 and 18) is the overthrow of Rome, mystically called Babylon. Rome had laid her heavy hand of oppression on the Christians. The end would be her own undoing. That came true in the sack of the city by the Goths and Vandals as well as in the downfall of the pagan power before Christianity.

Spirit of worship.—The numerous images of worship and glory in heaven inculcate the spirit of reverential worship.

Permanent value of the book.—Revelation, like all the books of the New Testament, met an immediate need on the part of those to whom it was addressed. But it is far more than a pamphlet for the times. The book is drawn on such grand lines that it furnished Christians with their highest conceptions of heaven, the noblest picture of the triumphant Christ, the glory of martyrdom for Christ, a mighty support in every hour of struggle.

DIGEST OF THE BIBLE

AARON, aâr'on. **Family history.**—Oldest son of Amram and Jochebed—Ex. 6:20; Num. 26:59. Brother of Moses and Miriam—Num. 25:59. Three years older than Moses—Ex. 7:7. Miriam his sister the oldest—Ex. 2:7. A Levite—Ex. 4:14; Num. 26:58, 59. Married Elishaba, daughter of Amminadab of Judah and sister of Nahshon—Ex. 6:23. Had four sons—Nadab and Abihu, who were slain for offering strange fire, and Eleazar and Ithamar—Ex. 6:23.

Made spokesman for Moses because of Moses' slowness of speech and lack of faith.—Ex. 4:10–16, 27–30; 6:12, 13, 28, 29; 7:1, 2; Heb. 5:4.

Appointed with Moses to lead Israel out of bondage.—Ex. 6:12, 13, 26, 27; Josh. 24:5; I Sam. 12:8; Ps. 77:20; 105:26; Mic. 6:40. Sent to meet Moses—Ex. 4:27, 28.

Works miracles with rod.—Ex. 7:8–13, 17–25, 8:5–7; 16–19.

Places pot of manna in ark.—Ex. 16:34.

With Hur holds up Moses' hands in Rephidim.—Ex. 17:8–12.

Aaron, his sons Nadab and Abihu, and seventy elders come to Mt. Sinai.—Ex. 19:24; 24:1, 9, 10.

Judges Israel in absence of Moses.—Ex. 24:14.

Makes golden calf.—Ex. 32:1–7, 25; Deut. 9:20, 21; Acts 7;39–42. Aaron's excuse—Ex. 32:21–24.

Consecrated to the priesthood.—Ex. chs. 28; 29; Lev. 8:1–9; Num. 18:1; Ps. 99:6; Heb. 5:4; 7:11. Offers sacrifice—Lev. ch. 9. Blesses Israel—Lev. 9: 22; Num. 6:23. Blossoming of rod confirms priesthood—Num. 17:1–10. Rod preserved in ark—Num. 17:10, 11; Heb. 9:4.

Israelites murmur against.—Ex. 5:20, 21; 16:2–10; Num. 14:24; 10; 16:3, 11, 41; 30:3; Ps. 106:16.

His sons Nadab and Abihu offer strange fire and are slain.—Lev. 10:1–5. Eleazar and Ithamar censured by Moses—Lev. 10:16–20.

Joins Miriam in murmuring against Moses, prompted by jealousy.—Num. 12: 1–3. Rebuked by God—Num. 12:4–9. Miriam becomes a leper—Num. 12:10–15. Aaron and Moses both plead for Miriam—Num. 12:11–13. Miriam restored after seven days. Num. 12:15.

Stops plague after rebellion of Korah.—Num. ch. 16.

Rebuked because of lack of faith "at the rock," which Moses smote, and forbidden to enter Canaan.—Num. 20: 10–13, 23–29.

Priest's office and garments given to his son Eleazar.—Num. 20:23–28.

Death and burial, aged 123 years.—Num. 20:28; 33; 39; Deut. 10:6; 32:50.

New Testament references.—Lu. 1:5; Acts 7:40; Heb. 5:4; 7:11; 9:4.

Descendants of.—I Chr. 6:3–15, 50–53; 12:27; 27:17; Lu. 1:5.

House of.—Priests who were descendants of Aaron—I Chr. 12:27; Ps. 115: 10, 12; 118:3; 135:19; see I Chr. 27:17; Heb. 7:11.

Sons of.—Priests who were descendants of Aaron.—I Chr. 6:50; 23:28, 32; 24: 19, 31; II Chr. 13:9, 10; 26:18; 39:19; 35:14; Neh. 10:38; 12:47. **Their dwelling places.**—Josh. 21:4–19; I Chr. 6:54–59. Called by David to bring the ark.—I Chr. 15:4. See ABIHU, ELEAZAR, ITHAMAR, NADAB, MOSES, PRIESTS.

AB: The fifth month of the Hebrew year (July-August) in which Aaron died.—Num. 33:38.

ABADDON, a-băd'don. Equivalent to "destruction" and so translated either in text or margin. Probably refers to lower abyss of Sheol—Job 26:6; Pr. 15:11. See margin of Job 28:22; 31: 12; Ps. 88:11. Name for Hades personified, Greek *Apollyon*—Rev. 9:11.

ABAGTHA, a-băg'thà. One of the seven chamberlains who served before Ahasuerus, king of Persia—Esther 1:10.

1

ABANAH, äb′a-nah. **A river of Damascus, mentioned by Naaman the leper,** now called Barada—II Ki. 5:12.

ABARIM, äb′a-rĭm. The range of mountains east of the Jordan. Israel encamped in—Num. 33:47, 48. Moses surveyed Canaan from the highest peak (Nebo, the top of Pisgah)—Num. 27:12; Deut. 3:27; 32:49. Moses died there—Deut. 34:1, 5. See Jer. 22:20.

ABASE. Job 40:11; Is. 31:4; Ez. 21:26; Dan. 4:37; Mt. 23:12 (A.V.); Lu. 14:11 (A.V.); 18:14 (A.V.). I know how to be abased—how to abound—Phil. 4:12. See II Cor. 11:7. See HUMILITY.

ABATED, i. e., decreased. Anger—Ju. 8:3. Fire—Num. 11:2. Natural forces—Deut. 34:7. Water—Gen. 8:8, 11.

ABATEMENT, i. e., reduction—Lev. 27:18.

ABBA, äb′bȧ. Emphatic form of Aramaic for "father"—Mk. 14:36; Rom. 8:15; Gal. 4:6.

ABDA, äb′dȧ. (1) **Father of Adoniram,** Solomon's overseer of "men subject to taskwork."—I Ki. 4:6.
(2) **Son of Shammua, a Levite in Jerusalem after the exile.**—Neh. 11:17.

ABDEEL, äb′de-el. **Father of Shelemiah,** who was ordered by Jehoiakim, King of Judah, "to take Baruch the scribe and Jeremiah the prophet."—Jer. 36:26.

ABDI, äb′dī. (1) **Grandfather of Ethan, father of Kish.**—I Chr. 6:44; II Chr. 29:12.
(2) **A descendant of Elam.**—Ezra 10:26.

ABDIEL, äb′di-el. **A Gadite dwelling in Gilead in Bashan.**—I Chr. 5:15.

ABDON, äb′don. (1) **One of the Judges of Israel, son of Hillel.**—Ju. 12:13, 15. See BEDAN.
(2) **A son of Shashak, a Benjamite dwelling in Jerusalem.**—I Chr. 8:23.
(3) **The first born son of Jeiel and Maacah, who dwelt in Gibeon of Benjamin.**
(4) **Son of Micah, sent by Josiah, king of Judah, to Huldah, the prophetess, to inquire of Jehovah concerning the "Book of the Law."**—II Chr. 34:20. Called Achbor in II Ki. 22:12.
(5) **A Levitical city in Asher.**—Josh.

21:30; I Chr. 6:74. Called Ebron in Josh. 19:28.

ABEDNEGO, a-bĕd′ne-gō′. **The name given to Azariah, one of the four young princes of Judah carried into captivity with Daniel by Nebuchadrezzar,** king of Babylon—Dan. 1:7; 2:49; 3:12–30.

ABEL, ā′bel. **Second son of Adam and Eve.**—Gen. 4:4. The offering accepted—Gen. 4:4. Cain converses with Abel—Gen. 4:8. Abel slain—Gen. 4:8. Cain's heartless question—Gen. 4:9.
New Testament references.—Righteous Abel—Mt. 23:35; I John 3:12. Blood of Abel—Lu. 11:51; Heb. 12:24. Faith of Abel—Heb. 11:4. God testifies of His gifts—Heb. 11:4.

ABEL-BETH-MAACAH, ā′bel-bĕth-mā′-a-cah. **A city of Naphtali, a stronghold of Sheba's rebellion.**—II Sam. 20:14–22. Besieged by Benhadad—I Ki. 15:20; by Tiglath-pileser—II Ki. 15:29.

ABEL-CHERAMIM, ā′bel-ke-rā′mim. **A locality in Ammon where Jepthah waged battle.**—Ju. 11:33.

ABEL-MAIM, ā′bel-mā′im. II Chr. 16:4. See ABEL-BETH-MAACAH.

ABEL-MEHOLAH, ā′bel-me-hō′lah. **Birthplace of Elisha, south of Bethshean.**—Ju. 7:22; I Ki. 4:12; 19:16–19.

ABEL-MIZRAIM, ā′bel-mĭz′ra-im. **Place where Joseph mourned seven days for Jacob.**—Gen. 50:11. See ATAD.

ABEL-SHITTIM, ā′bel-shĭt′tim. **A locality in the plains of Jordan where the Israelites made their last encampment before crossing the Jordan.**—Num. 33:49.

ABHOR. Affliction.—Ps. 22:24. Bloodthirsty and deceitful man—Ps. 5:6. Clothes shall abhor—Job 9:31. Covenant—Ps. 89:38. David—I Sam. 27:12. Edomite—Deut. 23:7. Egyptian—Deut. 23:7. Evil—Ps. 36:4; Rom. 12:9. Falsehood—Ps. 119:163. Flesh, an abhorring unto all—Is. 66:44. Food—Job. 33:20; Ps. 107:18. Friends abhor—Job. 19:19; 30:10. God abhors—Pr. 22:14. *Affliction*—Pr. 22:24. *Bloodthirsty and deceitful man*—Pr. 5:6. *Canaanites*—Lev. 20:23. I abhor myself—Job. 42:6. Idolatry—Deut. 7:26; Rom. 2:22. Israel—Ex. 5:21; Lev. 26:

11, 30, 44; Deut. 32:19; I Ki. 11:25; Ps. 78:59; 106:40; Jer. 14:21; Sam. 2:7; Amos 6:8. Justice—Mic. 3:9. Nations abhor—Pr. 24:24; Is. 49:7. Ordinances—Lev. 26:15, 43. Pharaoh, in the eyes of—Ex. 5:21. Rezon—I Ki. 11:25. Soul abhors—Lev. 26:11, 15, 30, 43; Ps. 107:18. Two kings—Is. 7: 16. Uprightly, Him that speaketh— Amos 5:10. See ABOMINATION, DESPISE, LOATHE, REJECT, RENOUNCE.

ABI, ABIJAH, ā′bī, a-bī′jah. **Wife of Ahaz, mother of Hezekiah and a daughter of Zechariah.**—II Ki. 18:2. See II Chr. 29:1.

ABI-ALBON, ā′bi-ăl′bon. **One of David's mighty men.**—II Sam. 23:31. See ABIEL in I Chr. 11:32.

ABIASAPH, a-bī′a-săph. **A Levite, son of Korah.**—Ex. 6:24. See EBIASAPH.

ABIATHAR, a-bī′a-thar. **Son of Abimelech, who escaped from Saul and followed David.**—I Sam. 22:20, 21. Carried an ephod—I Sam. 23:6, 9; 30:7. Priest under David—II Sam. 15:24, 29, 35; 20:25; I Ki. 4:4; I Chr. 18:16. Followed Adonijah—I Ki. 1:7. Deposed and sent to his home in Anathoth by Solomon—I Ki. 2:26, 27.

ABIB, or NISAN, ā′bib, or nī′san. **The first month of the old Hebrew year** (Mar. or April)—Ex. 12:2. The first passover—Ex. 12:1–28; 13:3–10; Lev. 23:6; Deut. 16:1. Departure from Egypt—Ex. 13:4. Setting up of the tabernacle—Ex. 40:2. Feast of unleavened bread—Ex. 23:15; Lev. 23:6–14. Children of Israel came unto the wilderness of Zin—Num. 20–1. They cross Jordan—Josh. 4:19. Time of the crucifixion of Jesus—Mt. 26:2; Mk. 14:1; Lu. 22:1.

ABIDA, a-bī′da. **Son of Midian and grandson of Abraham and Keturah.**— Gen. 25:4; I Chr. 1:33.

ABIDAN, ăb′i-dăn. **Son of Gideoni, of the tribe of Benjamin, one of those chosen to number Israel.**—Num. 1:11; 2:22, 7:60, 65; 10:24.

ABIDE. Anger of Jehovah, In—Nah. 1:6. Anointing—I John 2:20, 27. Apostles—Mt. 10:11; 17:22; 26:38; Mk. 6:10; Lu. 9:4; John 1:39; Acts— 1:13. Calling, In—I Cor. 7:20, 24. Christ, In—John 6:56; 15:4–9; I John

2:6, 27, 28; 3:6, 9, 24; II John 9. City, An abiding—Heb. 13:14. Darkness, In—John 12:46. Day of His coming —Mal. 3, 2. Death, In—John, 3:14. Earth abideth forever—Ps. 119:90; Eccl. 1:4. See Ps. 104:5. Eternal life —John 6:27; I John 3:15. Faith, Hope, Love—I Cor. 13:13. Flesh, In the—Phil. 1:24. Food—John 6:27. Fruit should—John 15:16. God—Ps. 102:12; I John 4:12, 13. *Love of God* —I John 3:17. *With God*—Ps. 91:1; I Cor. 7:24. See I Sam. 1:22. Holy Spirit—Hag. 2:5; John 1:32; 14:16, 17; I John 2:20, 27; 4:12, 13. Jesus Christ—John 8:35; 12:34; 14:25; II Tim. 2:13; Heb. 7:24. Light, In—I John 2:10. Love, In—John 15:10; I Cor. 13:13. Love of God—I John 3:17. Man—Ps. 49:12. Melchizedek—Heb. 7:3. Possession, An abiding—Heb. 10:34. Righteousness—Is. 32:16. Satisfied—Pr. 19:23. Servant—John 8:35. Shepherds—Lu. 2:8. Son—John 8:35. Unmarried—I Cor. 7:8, 40. See I Cor. 9:5. Wheat—John 12:24. Word of God—John 5:38; 15:7; I John 2:14, 24. Word, In—John 8:31. Work—I Cor. 3:14. Wrath—John 3:36. See Joel 2:11; Mal. 3:2. Zaccheus, With— Lu. 19:5. See CONTINUE, ENDURE, REMAIN.

ABIEL, ā′bi-el. (1) **Father of Kish and grandfather of Saul and Abner.**—I Sam. 9:1; 14:51.

(2) **One of the thirty heroes of David.**— I Chr. 11:32. See II Sam. 23:31.

ABIEZER, ā′bi-ē′zer. (1) **A member of the tribe of Manasseh**—Josh. 17:2; Ju. 6:11; 8:2, 32. See IEZER—Num. 26:30; Josh. 17:2; I Chr. 7:18.

(2) **One of David's 30 mighty men, an Anathothite of tribe of Benjamin.**— II Sam. 23:27; I Chr. 11:28; 27:12.

ABIGAIL, ăb′i-gāil. (1) **Probably sister of David, daughter of Jesse or of Nahash and mother of Amasa, who was made captain in place of Joab by Absalom.**—II Sam. 17:25; I Chr. 2:16, 17.

(2) **Wife of Nabal, who afterwards married David.**—I Sam. 25:3, 14, 42; 30:5; II Sam. 3:3.

ABIHAIL, ăb′i-hail. (1) **Father of Zuriel, a prince of the families of Merari,**

a Levite in the days of Moses.—Num. 3:35.

(2) **The wife of Abishur.**—I Chr. 2:29.

(3) **A member of the tribe of Gad.**—I Chr. 5:14.

(4) **Daughter of Eliab, niece of David** and mother-in-law of Rehoboam.—II Chr. 11:18.

(5) **Father of Esther.**—Esther 2:15; 9:29.

ABIHU, a-bī'hu. **Second son of Aaron.** Ex. 6:23; I Chr. 6:3; 24:1. Goes up to Mt. Sinai with Moses and Aaron— Ex. 24:9. Consecrated as a priest— Ex. 28:1. Offers strange fire and is slain—Lev. 10, 1, 2; Num. 3:4; 26:60, 61; I Chr. 6:3; 24:1, 2.

ABIHUD, a-bī'hud. **Son of Bela, grandson of Benjamin.**—I Chr. 8:3.

ABIJAH, a-bī'jah. (1) **King of Judah,** son of Rehoboam and Maachah, the daughter of Absalom. He was a wicked king—II Chr. 11:20, 22; 12:16; 13:1–22; 14:1. Spelled Abijam—I Ki. 14:31; 15:1–7.

(2) **Son of Samuel.**—I Sam. 8:2.

(3) **Son of Jeroboam, who died while a child** as foretold by Ahijah, the prophet.—I Ki. 14:1, 17.

(4) **A priest** (descendant of Aaron) **in the time of David,** to whom the eighth course fell by lot. Zechariah, the father of John the Baptist, belonged to this course—I Chr. 24:10; 26:20; Lu. 1:5.

(5) **A Benjamite, son of Becher.**—I Chr. 7:8.

(6) **Wife of Hezron.**—I Chr. 2:24.

(7) See ABI.

(8) **One of the priests who sealed the covenant** made by Nehemiah and the children of Israel.—Neh. 10:7.

(9) **A priest who returned from Babylon** with Zerubbabel. This is probably the same as (8)—Neh. 12:4–17.

ABIJAM, a-bī'jam. See ABIJAH.

ABILENE, ăb-i-lē'ne. **A tetrarchy in the north of Palestine** and east of the Jordan, ruled by Lysanias in the time of John the Baptist.—Lu. 3:1.

ABILITY. Give according to.—Lev. 5:7; 12:8; 14:22, 31, 32; 27:8; Deut. 16:10, 17; I Chr. 29:14, 11; Ezra 2:69; 46:5, 11; Acts 11:29; I Cor. 16:1, 2; II Cor. 8:13–15. See Neh. 5:8, GIVING, LIBERALITY.

Talents given according to.—Mt. 25:15.

To stand before kings.—Dan. 1:4. See ABLE, STRENGTH.

ABIMAEL, a-bĭm'a-el. **Descendant of Shem, son of Joktan.**—Gen. 10:28.

ABIMELECH, a-bĭm'e-lek. ''Father King''—Common title as ''Pharaoh,'' ''Caesar,'' etc. Hence Achish is called Abimelech (Ps. 34, title), which explains seeming discrepancy in I Sam. 21:11.

(1) **King of Gerar.** He takes Abraham's wife—Gen. 20. 20:8–14. Presents costly gifts and is healed in answer to Abraham's prayer—Gen. 20:14–18. Covenants with Abraham at Beersheba concerning a well which his servants had taken—Gen. 21:22–34. Rebukes Isaac for deceiving him about his wife—Gen. 26:16. Covenants with Isaac—Gen. 26:26–33.

(2) **King of Shechem, son of Gideon by a concubine.**—Ju. 8:30, 31. Slays all of his brethren but Jotham—Ju. 9: 1–5. Made king—Ju. 9:6, 16, 18. Jotham utters a fable on Mt. Gerizim— Ju. 9:7–21. Men of Shechem conspire against Abimelech and are slain—Ju. 9:22–49. He is slain—Ju. 9:50–57.

(3) **Son of Abiathar a priest in time of David.**—I Chr. 18:16.

(4) **A Philistine king.**—Ps. 34, *title.* See I Sam. 21:10.

ABINADAB, a-bĭn'a-dăb. (1) **A man of Kiriath-jearim** to whose house the ark was brought, where it remained 20 years.—I Sam. 7:1, 2. Ark taken to Jerusalem by David—II Sam. 6:3, 4; I Chr. 13:7.

(2) **Second son of Jesse and brother of David**—I Sam. 16:8; 17:13; I Chr. 2:13.

(3) **Son of Saul, slain with his brother Jonathan** by the Philistines at Gilboa —I Sam. 31:2; I Chr. 8:33; 9:39; 10:2.

(4) **Father of one of Solomon's twelve officers.**—I Ki. 4:11.

ABINOAM, a-bĭn'o-ăm. **Father of Barak,** who was called by Deborah, and who, with Deborah, defeated Sisera.— Ju. 4:6, 12; 5:1, 12.

ABIRAM, a-bī'ram. (1) **Son of Eliab,** who (with Dathan, Korah, and On) conspired against Moses and Aaron in the wilderness.—Num. 16:1-12, 49:27; 26:9; Deut. 11:6; Ps. 106:17.

(2) Son of Hiel, who began to rebuild the walls of Jericho—I Ki. 16:34. See Josh. 6:26.

ABISHAG, ăb′i-shăg. A beautiful Shunammite who was the nurse of David in his old age.—I Ki. 1:3, 4, 15. Adonijah requests Bathsheba to ask Solomon to give her to him as his wife, and is slain—I Ki. 2:13-25.

ABISHAI, a-bĭsh′a-ī. Son of Zeruiah, David's sister, brother of Joab.—I Sam. 26:6; II Sam. 16:9, 10; 18:2; 19: 21; I Chr. 2:16; 18:12.

One of David's warriors.—I Sam. 26: 7-9; II Sam. 2:18; 16:2, 11; 18:2, 5, 12; 20:6, 10; 23:18; I Chr. 2:16; 11:20, 21; 18:12; Pursues Abner—II Sam. 2:24. Fights the Ammonites—II Sam. 10:10-14; I Chr. 19:11-15. Abishai and Joab slay Abner—II Sam. 3:30. Slays Ishbi-beneb—II Sam. 21:15-17.

ABISHALOM, a-bĭsh′a-lom. II Ki. 15:2, 10. See ABSALOM.

ABISHUA, a-bĭsh′ū-a. (1) Son of Phinehas and grandson of Aaron.—I Chr. 6:4, 5, 50.

(2) Son of Bela and grandson of Benjamin.—I Chr. 8:4.

ABISHUR, a-bī′shur. Son of Shammai. —1 Chr. 2:28, 29.

ABITAL, ăb′i-tăl′. One of David's wives, mother of Shephatiah.—II Sam. 3:4; I Chr. 3:3.

ABITUB, ăb′i-tŭb. A Benjamite.—I Chr. 8:11.

ABIUD, a-bī′ud. A son of Zerubbabel.— Mt. 1:13.

ABLE to. Admonish—Rom. 15:14. Answer—Mt. 22:46. Bear—Num. 11:14; Deut. 1:9; Amos 7:10; Acts 15:10; I Cor. 3:2. Bridle—James 3:12. Build— II Chr. 2:6; Neh. 4:10; Lu. 14:29, 30; Acts 20:32. Call to remembrance—II Peter 1:15. Carry—Deut. 14:24. Come to knowledge—II Tim. 3:7. Comfort —II Cor. 1:4. Deliver—II Chr. 32:14, 15; Is. 36:14; Ez. 7:19; Dan. 3:17, 6:20; Zeph. 1:18. Destroy—I Ki. 9:21; Mt. 26:61; Jas. 4:12. Drink the cup— Mt. 20:22. Endure—Ex. 18:23; I Cor. 10:13. See BEAR, ENDURANCE. Enter—

Ex. 40:35; Lu. 15:14; Rev. 15:8. Escape —Jer. 11:11. Fight—Num. 22:11; I Sam. 17:9, 33; Lu. 14:31; Rev. 13:4. Find—Eccl. 8:17. Finish—Lu. 14:29, 30. Give. See ABILITY, GIVING, LIBERALITY, OFFER, OFFERING. Guard—Jude 24. Hear—Mk. 4:33. Hide—Jer. 49:10. Interpret—Dan. 2:26, 4:18. Jesus is—Mt. 9:28. Judge—I Ki. 3:9; I Cor. 6:5. Kill the soul—Mt. 10:28. Live—Ez. 33:12. Look up—Ps. 40:12. Make wise —II Tim. 3:15. Number—Gen. 15:5. Offer—Lev. 5:7-11; 12:8; 14:22, 31, 32, I Chr. 29:14. See GIVING, LIBERALITY, OFFERING. Open—Rev. 5:3. Overcome—Num. 13:30. Perform—Ex. 18: 18; Ps. 21:11. Profit—Is. 47:12. Promote—Num. 22:37. Put away—Is. 47: 12. Receive—Mt. 19:12. See HEAR. Redeem—Lev. 25:26-28. See REDEMPTION. Rise—Ps. 18:38; 36:12. Rule— Ex. 18:21, 25. Save—Heb. 5:7; 7:25; Jos. 1:21; 4:12. See SALVATION. See —Ex. 10:5. Separate—Rom. 8:39. Snatch—John 10:29. Speak—Lu. 1:20. Stand—I Sam. 6:20; Lam. 1:14; Eph. 6:11; Rev. 6:17. See ENDURANCE, WITHSTAND. Subject all things—Phil. 3:21. Succor—Heb. 2:18. Teach—Tit. 1:9; II Tim. 2:2. Tempted, Be—I Cor. 10:13. War—Rev. 13:4. See FIGHT. Withstand—Lu. 21:15; Eph. 6:13; Acts 6:10. See STAND. Work, For—I Chr. 9:13.

God is able to.—*Abase*—Dan. 4:37. *Bring*—Num. 14:16; Deut. 9:28. *Deliver*—Dan. 6:20. Do exceeding abundantly—Eph. 3:20. *Graft*—Rom. 11:23. *Guard*—II Tim. 1:12; Jude 24. Make him stand—Rom. 14:4. Make all grace abound—II Cor. 9:8. *Perform*—Rom. 4:21. *Raise up*—Mt. 3:9; Lu. 3:8; Heb. 11:19. See GOD IS ALMIGHTY. See ABILITY, POWER, STRENGTH.

ABLUTIONS. The ordinary bath.— Gen. 43:31; Ex. 2:5; 7:15; II Sam. 12:20; Ez. 16:4; 23:40; John 9:7, 11, 15; Acts 16:33.

Washing before and after meals.—Mt. 15:2; Mk. 7:2; Lu. 11:38. During fasts—Mt. 6:17.

Washing of hands.—Ex. 30:18-21; Deut. 21:6; Ps. 26:6; 73:13; Mt. 15:2; 27:4; Mk. 7:3, 4.

Washing of utensils, etc.—Ex. 19:10; Lev. 6:28; Mt. 23:25, 26; Mk. 7:4; Lu. 11:39.

Washing the dead.—Acts 9:37.

Metaphorical.—Heb. 10:22. See BAPTISM, CEREMONIAL CLEANSING, FOOTWASHING, PURIFICATION, WATER.

ABNER, ăb'ner. **Son of Ner and uncle of Saul.**—I Sam. 14:50; 51. Captain of the host—I Sam. 17:55; 26:5, 13–16; II Sam. 2:8; I Ki. 2:32. Brought David to Saul—I Sam. 17:55–57. His place at Saul's table—I Sam. 20:25. With Saul in wilderness of Ziph when David rebukes him for carelessness—I Sam. 26:14–16. Made Ish-bosheth king over Israel—II Sam. 2:8–10. Dedicated spoils of war to temple—I Chr. 26:28. Contest between Abner and Joab—II Sam. 2:10–31. Slays Asahel—II Sam. 2:18–23. Rebuked by Ish-bosheth because of conduct with Rizpah—II Sam. 3:6, 7. Being angry, revolts to David—II Sam. 3:8–21. Slain by Joab—II Sam. 3:20–30; 4:1; I Ki. 2:5. David mourns for—II Sam. 3:33–37. Head of Ish-bosheth buried in Abner's grave—II Sam. 4:12. Solomon avenges Abner's death in obedience to David's command—I Ki. 2:5, 6, 28–34. Jaasiel, son of Abner, made captain over Benjamin—I Chr. 27:21.

ABODE. Ps. 68:16; John 14:23. See ABIDE, DWELL, DWELLING, LODGED, CARRIED.

ABOLISH. Authority—I Cor. 15:24. Death—Cor. 15:26; II Tim. 1:10. Law—Eph. 2:15. See COVENANTS. Righteousness—Is. 51:6. Rule—I Cor. 15:24. Works—Ez. 6:6. See DESTROYED, DONE AWAY, PUT DOWN, PASSING AWAY.

ABOMINATION. Hateful thing—Gen. 43:32; 46:34; Deut. 25:16; Ps. 88:8; Lu. 16:15; Rev. 21:27.

Ceremonial impurity.—Lev. 11:10–13, 20, 23, 41, 42; Deut. 24:4; Is. 66:17; Jer. 2:7; Ez. 16:2–58.

Moral wrong.—In general—Pr. 15:9; 16:5, 12; Rev. 17:4, 5; 21:27. Impurity—Lev. 18:22; 20:13. Perversity—I Ki. 14:24; Pr. 3:32; 6:12–19; 11:20. Falsehood in speech—Pr. 8:7; 12:22. Dishonesty in trade—Pr. 11:1; 20:10,

23. Justifying the wicked or condemning the righteous—Pr. 17:15.

Religious offense.—From heathen point of view; to the Egyptians: Israelite's sacrifice—Ex. 8:26. From Christian point of view: A proud heart—Pr. 6:16; 16:15. Defective ritual—Deut. 17:1; Rev. 17:18. Ritual without ethical meaning—Is. 1:13. Offering—Lev. 7:18; Deut. 17:1; 23:18; Pr. 15:8; 21:27; Eccl. 5:1; Is. 1:11–15; Jer. 6: 20; Mic. 6:6–8. The prayer of the wicked—Pr. 15:8; 28:9 Their sacrifice—Pr. 15:8. Themselves—Is. 41:24.

Idols—In general—Deut. 7:25, 26; 27: 15; 29:17; Ez. 7:20. Milcom of the Ammonites—I Ki. 11:5. Ashtoreth of the Sidonians—II Ki. 23:13. Stock of tree—Is. 44:19.

Idolatrous practice.—Lev. 18:26; Deut. 17:4; 18:9, 12; II Ki. 11:5–8; 14:23, 24; II Ki. 21:2, 11; 23:13; II Chr. 28:3; 33:2; Ez. 8:6, 9, 13. Idols and idolatrous practices combined—Jer. 4:1; Ez. 5:9; 16:22; 18:12; 33:29. *Cf.* Hos. 9:10; Mal. 2:11.

Abomination of desolation (that desolates by its enormity).—Dan. 9:27; 11:31; 12:11; Mt. 24:15; Mk. 13:14.

ABOUND. I Cor. 14:12; Phil. 4:12, 18. Blessings—Pr. 28:20. Christian graces—II Cor. 8:7; II Pet. 1:8. See KNOWLEDGE, LOVE, THANKSGIVING. Comfort—II Cor. 1:5. Earnestness—II Cor. 8:7. Faith—II Cor. 8:7. Fountains with water—Pr. 8:24. Fruit—Phil. 4:17. Grace—Rom. 5:20; 6:1; II Cor. 9:8; Eph. 1:8; I Tim. 1:14. Hope, In—Rom. 15:13. Joy—II Cor. 8:2. Knowledge—I Cor. 8:7; Phil. 1:9. Love—II Cor. 8:7; Phil. 1:9; I Thess. 3:12; II Thess. 1:3. Poverty—II Cor. 8:2. Sufferings of Christ—II Cor. 1:5. Thanksgiving—II Cor. 4:15; 9:12; Col. 2:7. These things—II Pet. 1:8. Transgressions—Pr. 29:22. Trespass—Rom. 5: 20. Truth—Rom. 3:7; Work—I Cor. 15:58; II Cor. 9:8. See ABUNDANT, EXCEL, INCREASE.

ABOVE. All that we ask—Eph. 3:20. Disciple not above his master—Mt. 10:24; Lu. 6:40. Every name—Phil. 2:9. Heaven—Deut. 4:39; 5:8; Josh. 2:11; I Ki. 8:23; Job 31:28; Is. 7:11; 14:13; Jer. 4:28; 31:37; Acts 2:19;

Col. 3:12. From above—Josh. 3:13–16; II Sam. 22:17; Job 3:4; 31:2; Ps. 144:7; Is. 45:8. More than—Deut. 28:13; Lu. 13:2, 4; John 3:31; Col. 3:14. One day above another—Rom. 14:5. Tempted above—able—I Cor. 10:13.

ABRAHAM, ā′ bra - ham. Originally *"Abram." "Father of a multitude." "Exalted father"*—Gen. 17:5.

Son of Terah.—Gen. 11:26, 27. Marries Sarai—Gen. 11:29.

Residence.—Ur of Chaldees (in Mesopotamia in way to river Tigris or possibly Mugheir lying on right bank of Euphrates. Scholars differ. Last is favored).

Age of Abraham.—Seventy years when he left Ur, and seventy-five when he departed from Haran—Gen. 12:4; Acts 7:2–4.

Reason for leaving.—God's revelation came to him—Gen. 12:1. His renunciation of gods many made him a fit leader for Jehovah—Josh. 24:2, 3; Neh. 9:7, 8; Heb. 11:8–10.

Gift of Canaan first revealed at Shechem.—Gen. 12:6, 7. Abraham builds an altar at Shechem—Gen. 12:7.

Famine drove him down to Egypt.—Gen. 12:10. Abraham's error concerning his wife and Pharaoh and Abimelech—Gen. 12:11–20; 20:2–18.

His dispute and separation from Lot.—Gen. 13:7–12.

God confirms his promise to Abraham.—Gen. 13:14–17. Three points in promise: The land; the miracle son; The seed a blessing to all nations.

Abraham goes to the aid of Lot and his neighbors.—Gen. 14:1–16.

Melchizedek meets and blesses Abraham.—Gen. 14:18–20; Heb. 7:1–4.

God promises an heir to Abraham.—Gen. 15:3–5. God's way of proving himself —Gen. 15:9–18. Abraham's faith counted for righteousness—Gen. 15:6. Spiritual heirs—Rom. 4:11–12; Gal. 3:29.

Birth of Ishmael.—Gen. 16:1–15.

Covenant of circumcision.—Gen. 17:9–14, 23–27; Ex. 12:48. Privileges—Ex. 12:43–49. Obligation—Gal. 5:3. Abolished—Eph. 2:11–15. See CIRCUMCISION NOT NECESSARY.

Angels' visit.—Gen. 18:1–22; 19:1–3. Nefarious act of Sodomites—Gen. 19:4–11.

Sodom threatened, plead for, destroyed. —Gen. 18:17–21; 19:12–28; 23:33; Deut. 29:23; Mt. 10:15; 11:24; II Pet. 2:6.

Prepares for true heir by dismissing false heir.—Gen. 21:9–21; Gal. 4:22–31.

Birth of Isaac.—Gen. 21:1–8. Circumcised at eighth day—Gen. 21:4. Child of miracle—Rom. 4:18–21; Heb. 11:11, 12.

Ewald says, "Highest blessings bring highest trials." Note those of Abraham: Abandoning home in Ur—Gen. 11:31. Forsaking kindred at Haran—Gen. 12:1. Separation from Lot—Gen. 13.9. Homeless in Canaan—Acts 7:1–5. Hopes built on Ishmael—Gen. 17:18. Child of promise given—Gen. 21:2. Isaac's life demanded—Gen. 22:2. The father must slay the son—Gen. 22:2.

Abraham offers Isaac.—By miraculous birth God gave proof of power to restore Isaac—Gen. 17:17. Abraham must love nothing better than God—Mt. 10:34–38. Abraham's endurance of this test makes him the father of the faithful—Rom. 4:16–25. The way to escape trouble is through obedience —Gen. 22:12, 13. Abraham's act delightful to God—Gen. 22:12, 13.

Sarah dies and is buried.—Gen. 23:1, 20.

Sends for a wife for Isaac.—Gen. 24:1–67. Must not be of Canaanites—Gen. 24:3. His own country and kindred—Gen. 24:4.

Marries Keturah.—Gen. 25:1. Keturah called a concubine—I Chr. 1:32. Offspring by her—Gen. 25:2–4; I Chr. 1:32.

Invests Isaac with the inheritance.—Gen. 25:5.

Abraham's death.—Gen. 25:8. Buried in Machpelah—Gen. 25:9, 10.

Faith of Abraham distinguished from that of other ancestors in this: He obtains and holds the promise of salvation, not only for himself, but for his family—Gen. 22:16–17. Distinguished from Mosaic system by holding the promised blessing, "in the seed of Abraham," as a blessing for all people—Gen. 22:18; Mt. 28:19; Mk. 16:16; Lu. 24:45-48; Rom. 4: 13, 14.

Three great religious bodies—Jews, Christians, Mohammedans—unite in calling him father and friend of God. See NATIONS, LOT, ISAAC—Gen. 21:3. PROMISES—Jo. 14:2. See ISAAC, LOT, COVENANTS, NATIONS, SARAH.

ABROAD.—Noised—Lu. 1:65. Published Lu. 9:60; Rom. 9:17.

ABSALOM, ăb'sa-lom. **Son of David.** —II Sam. 3:3; 13:1; I Chr. 3:2; II Chr. 11:20, 21. Brother to Tamar— II Sam. 13:4. Tamar dwells with—II Sam. 13:20. Hatred for Amnon— II Sam. 13:22. Causes Amnon to be murdered—II Sam. 13:23-33. Flight of—II Sam. 13:34-39. David's sympathy for—II Sam. 14:1. David recalls Absalom; sends Joab for him—II Sam. 14:22-24. Beauty of—II Sam. 14:25, 26. Children of—II Sam. 14: 27. Dwelt in Jerusalem—II Sam. 14: 28. Anger against Joab—II Sam. 14: 29-32. Return to the king—II Sam. 14:33. Conspiracy against David—II Sam. 15:1-37. The kingdom delivered to—II Sam. 16:8, 15-23. Takes David's concubines—II Sam. 16:21-23.

War against David.—II Sam. 17:1-26. Battle in forest of Ephraim—II Sam. 18:5, 6, 8. David's flight from Absalom—I Ki. 2:7. Absalom hung by head on a tree—II Sam. 18:9, 10, 12.

Slain by Joab.—II Sam. 18:14, 15. Flight of Israelites—II Sam. 18:16.

Burial of.—II Sam. 18:17-32.

David's lament over.—II Sam. 18:33; 19:1, 4-10; Ps. 3. *Title, "A Psalm of David when he fled from Absalom."* See DAVID.

ABSENCE. Lu. 22:6; Phil. 2:12.

ABSENT. II Cor. 10:1; 11; 13:2, 10; Phil. 1:27. Body, In—I Cor. 5:3; Col. 2:5. From the—II Cor. 5:8, 9. Lord, From—II Cor. 5:6, 9. One from another—Gen. 31:49.

ABSTINENCE. Pr. 23:2-8; Lu. 21:34; Acts 27:21. Appearance of evil, From —I Thes. 5:22. Blood, from—Acts 15: 20, 29. See BLOOD. Fleshly lusts—I Pet. 2:11. See LUST. Fornication— Acts 15:20, 29. See FORNICATION.

Meats—Rom. 14:21, 23; I Cor. 8:13. See FOOD, UNCLEAN. Pollutions of idols—See ABOMINATIONS, IDOLATRY. Wine—Jer. 35:14; Dan. 1:8-16; Eph. 5:18. See DRUNKENNESS. See CHRISTIAN GRACES, SELF-CONTROL, CEREMONIAL CLEANSING.

ABUNDANCE. II Chr. 15:9; Eccl. 5: 10; Is. 15:7; Mt. 13:12; 25:29; II Cor. 8:14; 10:15. See Mk. 12:44; Lu. 21:4. Affection—II Cor. 7:15. All things— Deut. 28:47. Blossoms—Is. 35:2. Brass —I Chr. 22:3, 14. Cedars—I Ki. 10:27; I Chr. 22:4; II Chr. 1:15; 9:27. Complaint—I Sam. 1:16. Dead bodies—II Chr. 20:25. Do exceedingly abundant —Eph. 3:30. Enchantments—Is. 47:9. Entrance—II Pet. 1:11 (A.V.). Evident—Heb. 7:15. Food—Job 36:31. Fruit trees—Neh. 9:25. Glory—Is. 66: 11. Grace—Rom. 5:17; II Chr. 4:15. Grain—Ps. 72:16. Heart—Mt. 12:34; Lu. 6:45. Holy Spirit—Titus 3:6 (A.V.). Honor—II Chr. 17:5; 18:1; I Cor. 12: 23, 24. Horses—Ez. 26:10. Iron—I Chr. 22:3, 14. Joy—II Chr. 8:4. Labors—I Cor. 11:23; 15:10. See II Cor. 1:12. Life—John 10:10. *Consisteth not in*—Lu. 12:15. Loving-kindness—Ex. 34:6; Ps. 69:13; 103:8; Jonah 4:2. Milk—Is. 7:22. Oxen—See SHEEP AND OXEN. Pardon—Is. 55:7. Peace—Ps. 37:11; 72:7; Jer. 33:6. Poverty—II Cor. 8:2. Prisons—II Cor. 11:23. Rain —I Ki. 18:41; Job 36:28. Riches—II Chr. 17:5; 18:1; 20:25; 24:11; Ps. 37: 16; 52:7; Jer. 48:36; 51:13; Zech. 14: 14. See Eccl. 5:12; Ez. 16:49; Lu. 12: 15; WEALTH, TEACHING OF JESUS ON RICHES. Sacrifices—I Chr. 29:21; II Chr. 29:35; 31:5. Sea—Deut. 33:19; Is. 60:5. Sheep and oxen—I Ki. 10: 10; I Chr. 12:44; II Chr. 14:15; 18:2; 32:29. Shields—II Chr. 32:5. Spices— I Ki. 10:10; II Chr. 9:9. Stones—I Chr. 29:2. Timber—II Chr. 2:9. Truth —Ex. 34:6; Jer. 33:6. Vessels—II Chr. 4:18. Victuals—II Chr. 11:23. Waters—Num. 20:11; Job 32:11; 38:34. Wine—Esth. 1:7. Workmen—I Chr. 22:15. See ABOUND, BOUNTY, FULNESS, GOODS, PLENTEOUS, POSSESSIONS, SUPERFLUITY, WEALTH.

ABUSE. Levites' concubine—Ju. 19: 25. Saul—I Sam. 31:4; I Chr. 10:4.

Themselves—I Cor. 6:9; I Tim. 1:10. See DEFILE, USE TO FULL.

ABYSS. Name of Hades, the abode of the dead—Lu. 8:31; Rom. 10:7; Rev. 9:1; 20:1, 3. See DEEP, PIT.

ACACIA. A hard orange-red wood used in the tabernacle and its furniture. Ex. 25:5; 26:15; 36:20. See SHITTAH (A.V.), SHITTIM (A.V.). **Altar**—Ex. 27: 1, 6; 30:1; 37:25; 38:1–7. **Ark**—Ex. 25:10, 13; 37:1; Deut. 10:3. **Table**—Ex. 25:23; 37:10, 15.

ACCAD, ăk'kad. A very ancient city in the northern part of Babylon—Gen. 10:10.

ACCEPT. Acts 24:3; II Cor. 8:12 (A.V.). David accepted—I Sam. 8:5 (A.V.). *Accepts Abigail's offering*—I Sam. 25: 35. Deliverance—Heb. 11:35. Esau may accept—Gen. 32:20. Exhortation —II Cor. 8:17. God accepts—Gen. 19: 21. Offering—Lev. 1:4; 7:18; 10:19 (A.V.); 22:21; 23:11; I Sam. 26:19; Ps. 20:3; 119:108; Is. 56:7; 60:3; Jer. 14: 12; Hos. 8:13; Amos 5:22; Mal. 1:10, 13. Persons—Gen. 4:7; 11:3; Amos 24:23; Job 13:8, 10 (A.V.); 32:21 (A.V.); 34:19 (A.V.); 42:8, 9; Ps. 82:2 (A.V.); Jer. 14:10, 12; Ez. 20:40, 41; 43:27; Hos. 8:13; Mal. 1:8, 9; Acts 10:35 (A.V.); II Cor. 5:9 (A.V.); Gal. 2:6; Eph. 1:6 (A.V.). Work—Deut. 33:11; Eccl. 9:7. See Lu. 20:21. Mordecai—Esth. 10:3. See GOD ACCEPTS. Petition—Jer. 37:20 (A.V.); 42:2 (A.V.). Punishment—Lev. 26:41, 43. Saints—Rom. 15:31 (A.V.). Saying—I Tim. 1: 15; 4:9. Time—II Cor. 6:2 (A.V.). Words—Deut. 33:11; Eccl. 9:7. See RECEIVE, REGARD, RESPECT.

ACCEPTABLE. Pr. 10:32; II Cor. 8: 12; I Pet. 2:19. Brethren, To—Deut. 33:24. Counsel—Dan. 33:24. Day—Is. 58:5. God, To—I Tim. 2:3; 5:4; Heb. 12:28; I Pet. 2:20. Righteousness—Pr. 21:3; Acts 10:35; I Tim. 5:4. Sacrifices—See GOD, TO. Words of Mouth—Pr. 19:14. See ACCEPT, WELL-PLEASING, WILL.

ACCESS. Rom. 5:2; Eph. 2:18; 3:12. See GOD, ACCESS TO, RECONCILIATION, SALVATION.

ACCO, ăk'ko. A city on the coast of the Mediterranean Sea.—Ju. 1:31.

ACCOMPANY. Brethren accompany—Acts 10:23; 11:12; 20:4, 38. Salvation —Heb. 6:9. See BRING, BROUGHT.

ACCOMPLISH. Job 15:32; Ez. 4:6. Anger—See WRATH. Baptism—Lu. 12:50. See DEATH OF JESUS. Course—Acts 20:24. Day—Esth. 2:12; Job 14: 6; Jer. 25:34; Lu. 1:23 (A.V.); 2:6, 21, 22 (A. V.); Acts 21:6, 21:25 (A. V.). Death of Jesus—Lu. 9:31. See Lu. 12: 50; 22:37. Desire—I Ki. 5:9; Pr. 13: 19. Desolation of Jerusalem—Dan. 9:2. Indignation—See WRATH. Punishment Lam. 4:22. Scripture—John 19:28. See WORD. Search—Ps. 64:6. Services —Heb. 9:6. Seventy years—Jer. 25: 12; 29:10; Dan. 9:2. See Is. 33:11. Sufferings—I Pet. 5:9. Things, All—Mt. 5:18; 24:34; Mk. 13:4, 30; Lu. 2: 39; 18:31; 21:32; John 19:28 (A.V.). Vow—Lev. 22:21; 27:2; Jer. 44:25 (A.V.). Warfare—Is. 40:2. Words—II Chr. 36:22; Ezra 1:1; Rev. 17:17. Work—John 4:34; 5:36; 17:4. Wrath —Lam. 4:11; Ez. 5:13; 6:12; 7:8; 13: 15; 20:8, 21; Dan. 11:36. See Job 15: 32; Lam. 4:22. See ENDED, FINISH, FULFIL, PERFORM.

ACCORD. One.—Josh. 9:2; Jer. 5:5; Acts 1:14; 2:1 (A.V.); 2:46; 4:24; 5: 12; 7:57; 8:6; 2:20; 15:25; 8:12; 19: 29; Rom. 15:6; Phil. 2:2. See UNITY. **Own.**—Acts 12:10; II Cor. 8:17.

ACCOUNT. I Chr. 27:24; Eccl. 7:27; Phil. 4:17. **Give.**—Job 33:13; Dan. 6: 2; Mt. 12:36; Lu. 16:2; Acts 19:40; Rom. 14:12; Heb. 13:17. **Make.**—Ps. 144:3. **No.**—Is. 16:14; Acts 19:17; I Cor. 6:4; II Cor. 10:10. **Reckon, Think, Consider.**—Deut. 2:11, 20; I Ki. 10:21; II Chr. 9:20; Ps. 22:30 (A.V.); 44:22; Is. 2:22; Rom. 14:14; I Cor. 4:1; II Cor. 3:5; I Pet. 5:12; II Pet. 3:15. **Take.**—Mt. 18:23 (A.V.); John 11:50; I Cor. 13:5.

ACCURATELY. Lu. 1:3; Acts 18:25, 26.

ACCURSED. Persons.—Deut. 21:23; Josh. 6:18; 7:12; Is. 65:20; John 7:49; Rom. 9:3 (A.V.); I Cor. 12:3 (A.V.); Gal. 1:8, 9 (A.V.). **Things.**—Josh. 6:17, 18 (A.V.); 7:1, 11, 13, 15 (A.V.). See ABOMINATION, ANATHEMA, BAN, DEVOTED, IDOLATRY.

ACCUSATION. Against brethren.—Jas. 4:11; I Pet. 3:14, 16. Against an elder—I Tim. 5:19. **Jesus.**—Mt. 27: 37; Mk. 15:26; Lu. 6:17; John 18:29. **Jews.**—Ezra 4:6; Dan. 3:8. **Paul.**— Acts 24:19; 25:18.

False.—Ex. 23:1; Mt. 5:11; Lu. 3:14; 19:8 (A.V.); II Tim. 3:3 (A.V.); Titus 2:3 (A.V.); I Pet. 3:16 (A.V.). See WITNESS, FALSE.

Railing.—II Pet. 2:11 (A.V.); Jude 9 (A.V.). See JUDGMENT.

ACCUSE. John 5:45; Acts 19:38, 40; Rom 2:15; Titus 1:6. Daniel—Dan. 6:24. Jesus—Mt. 12:10; 27:12; Mk. 3:2; 15:3; Lu. 6:7; 11:54 (A.V.); 23: 2, 10, 14; John 8:6. Paul—Acts 22: 30; 23:28, 29, 35; 24:2, 8, 13; 25:5, 11, 16, 18; 26:2, 7. Satan—Rev. 12:10. Servant—Pr. 30:10 (A.V.). Steward— Lu. 16:1. Woman taken in adultery— John 8:10 (A.V.). See REBUKE, RE-PROACH.

ACCUSTOMED. Jer. 13:23.

ACHAIA, a-kā'ia. **A name used in N.T. for the whole of Greece. First fruits of.**—I Cor. 16:15.

Paul visits.—Acts 18:12, 27; 19:21; II Cor. 11:10.

Saints.—II Cor. 1:1. Contribute to the poor—Rom. 15:26; II Cor. 9:2.

ACHAN, ā'kan. **A member of the tribe of Judah.**—At the destruction of Jericho he stole a part of the spoil, contrary to commandment, and hid it. Because of this act, Israel was defeated at Ai and Achan, and his family were put to death—Josh. 7:1, 18–20, 24; 22: 20; I Chr. 2:7.

ACHBOR, ăk'bôr. (1) **Father of Baal-hanan, an Edomite king.**—Gen. 36:38, 39; I Chr. 1:49.

(2) **A messenger under Josiah and Jehoiakim,** sent to inquire of Huldah the prophetess concerning the words of the book found by Hilkiah—II Ki. 22:12, 14; Jer. 26:22; 36:12.

ACHIM, ā'kim. Ancestor of Joseph the husband of Mary.—Mt. 1:14.

ACHISH, ā'kish. (1) **A Philistine king of Gath who was David's friend.**—I Sam. 21:10–14; 27:2–12; 28:1, 2; 29: 2–9. (2) **Either the same king or a later king of Gath who reigned in the time of Solomon.**—I Ki. 2:39, 40.

ACHMETHA, ăk'me-thà. **A city in Media where the roll was found wherein** was the record of a decree of Cyrus permitting the return of the Jews.— Ezra 6:2.

ACHOR, ā'kor. **A valley near Jericho where Achan and his property were destroyed.**—Josh. 7:24, 26; 15:7; Is. 65:10; Hos. 2:15.

ACHSAH, ăk'sah. **Daughter of Caleb, wife of Othniel the judge.**—Josh. 15: 16, 17; Ju. 1:12, 13; I Chr. 2:49.

ACHSHAPH, ăk'shaph. **A city allotted to Asher.** The king of this city was allied with Jabin against Joshua— Josh. 11:1; 12:20; 19:24, 25.

ACHZIB, ăk'zib. (1) **A city of Asher on the coast south of Tyre.**—Josh. 19: 29; Ju. 1:31. (2) **A town of Judah.**— Josh. 15:44; Mic. 1:14.

ACKNOWLEDGE. Gen. 38:26; Is. 61: 9; 63:16; I Cor. 14:37 (A.V.); Col. 2:2; Philemon 6. Brethren—Deut. 33:9; I Cor. 16:18; II Cor. 1:13, 14. God—Pr. 3:6; Is. 33:13; Dan. 11:39. Sin—Ps. 32:5; 51:3 (A.V.); Jer. 3:13; 14:20. Truth—II Tim. 2:25 (A.V.); Tit. 1:1 (A.V.). See CONFESSION, KNOWLEDGE.

ACQUAINT. All my ways—Ps. 139:3. Grief, With—Is. 53:3. Thyself—Job 22:21. Wisdom—Eccl. 2:3 (A.V.).

ACQUAINTANCE. II Ki. 12:5, 7; Job 19:13; 42:11; Ps. 31:11; 55:13 (A.V.); 88:8, 18; Lu. 2:44; 23:49; Acts 24:23 (A.V.). See FRIENDSHIP.

ACQUIT. Job 10:14; Nah. 1:3 (A.V.).

ACRE. I Sam. 14:14; Is. 5:10. See LAND, MEASURES.

ACTS OF APOSTLES. See OUTLINE STUDIES IN THE BOOKS.

ADADAH, ăd-ā'dah. **A town in the southern part of Judah.**—Josh. 15: 21, 22.

ADAH, ā'dah. (1) **Wife of Lamech.**— Gen. 4:19–23. (2) **Wife of Esau.**— Gen. 36:2, 4, 10, 12, 16.

ADAIAH, a-dā'iah. (1) **Father of Jedidah,** the mother of Josiah.—II Ki. 22:1. (2) **A Levite of the sons of Kohath.**—I Chr. 6:41. (3) **A Benjamite, son of Shimei.**—I Chr. 8:21. (4) **A priest in Jerusalem.**—I Chr. 9:10–12. (5) Father of Maaseiah, a captain who aided Jehoiada in putting Josiah on the throne.—II Chr. 23:1. (6) **A son of Bani who took a foreign wife during the exile.**—Ezra 10:29. (7) **A son**

of a different family named Bani who was guilty of the same offense.—Ezra 10:34. (8) **A descendant of Perez dwelling in Jerusalem.**—Neh. 11:5. (9) **A priest, son of Jeroham, dwelling in Jerusalem after the exile** (probably same as 4).—Neh. 11:12.

ADALIA, ȧ-dā′li-ȧ. One of ten sons of Haman, hung with his father.—Esth. 9:8.

ADAM. Created in image of God.—Gen. 1:26–28; 2:7; 5:1; I Cor. 15:45; I Tim. 2:13. Placed in the Garden of Eden—Gen. 2:15–17. Names animals—Gen. 2:19, 20. Helpmeet created for—Gen. 2:20–23. His fall—Gen. 2:16, 17; 3:1–7; Job 31:33; Rom. 5:14; I Tim. 2:14. Jehovah rebukes—Gen. 3:8–19. Calls his wife Eve—Gen. 3:20. Expelled from Eden—Gen. 3:22–24. God clothes Adam and Eve—Gen. 3:21. Children of—Gen. 4:1, 2, 25; 5:3, 4. Age and death of—Gen. 5:5. Book of the generations of—Gen. 5:1–32; I Chr. 1:1–42.

N.T. References.—Lu. 3:38. Death came through—Rom. 5:14; I Cor. 15:22. Made a living soul—I Cor. 15:45.

ADAM, THE LAST. *I. e.,* Christ—I Cor. 15:45.

ADAM. A city or town east of the Jordan.—Josh. 3:16.

ADAMAH, ăd′a-mah. A city of Naphtali.—Josh. 19:36.

ADAMANT. A precious stone.—Ez. 3:9; Zech. 7:12.

ADAMI-NEKEB, ăd′ă-mī-nĕ′keb. A town of Naphtali.—Josh. 19:33.

ADAR, ā′dar. The twelfth month of the Jewish sacred year (March-April).— The Temple completed—Ezra 6:15. Decree against Jews—Esth. 3:7, 12, 13. Jews permitted to resist their enemies—Esth. 8:13. Feast of Purim—Esth. 9:1–21.

ADBEEL, ăd′be-el. Son of Ishmael, grandson of Abraham.—Gen. 25:13; I Chr. 1:29.

ADD. All these things shall be added—Mt. 6:33; Lu. 12:31. Church, To the—Acts 2:41, 47; 5:14; 11:24. Covenant, To—Gal. 3:15. Cubit to measure of life—Mt. 6:27; Lu. 12:25. Days, To—II Ki. 20:6; Pr. 3:2; Is. 38:5. Faith,

To—II Pet. 1:5. Law added because of transgression—Gal. 3:19. Sins, **To** —I Sam. 12:19; II Chr. 28:13; Job 34:37; Ps. 69:27; Is. 30:1; Lu. 3:20. Sorrow—Pr. 10:22; Jer. 45:3. Words, Shall not add to—Deut. 4:2; 12:32; Rev. 22:18. Yoke, To—I Ki. 12:11, 14; II Chr. 10:14.

ADDAN, ăd′dan. **The home of exiles who could not prove their genealogy.**— Ezra 2:59. Called *Adon* in Neh. 7:61.

ADDAR, ăd′dar. (1) **A Benjamite.**—I Chr. 8:3. (2) **A city in south Judah.**— Josh. 15:3. See HAZAR-AD-DAR (Num. 34:4).

ADDER. A poisonous serpent.—Gen. 49:17; Ps. 58:4; 91:13; 140:3; Is. 14:29. Biteth like an—Pr. 23:32. See SERPENT.

ADDI, ăd′dī. Ancestor of Joseph, husband of Mary.—Lu. 3:28.

ADDON, ăd′don. See ADDAN.

ADIEL, ā′di-el. (1) **A descendant of Simeon.**—I Chr. 4:36. (2) A priest—I Chr. 9:12. (3) **Father of Asmaveth, David's treasurer.**—I Chr. 27:25.

ADIN, ā′din. (1) **The ancestor of many who returned from Babylon with Zerubbabel.**—Ezra 2:15; 8:6; Neh. 7:20. (2) **The name of a family who assisted Nehemiah in sealing the covenant.**— Neh. 10:14–16.

ADINA, ăd′i-na. **One of David's captains, a chief of the Reubenites.**—I Chr. 11:42.

ADINO, ăd′i-no. One of David's thirty heroes.—II Sam. 23:8.

ADITHAIM, ăd-ĭ-thā′ĭm. A city of Judah.—Josh. 15:36.

ADJURE. Josh. 6:26 (A.V.); I Sam. 14:24; I Ki. 22:16; II Chr. 18:15; Pr. 29:24; Song of Sol. 2:7; Mt. 26:63; Mk. 5:7; Acts 19:13. See CHARGE, OATHS AND VOWS.

ADLAI, ăd′lāi. Father of Shaphat, David's overseer of the herds.—I Chr. 27:29.

ADMAH, ăd′mah. A town in the valley of Siddim destroyed with Sodom and Gomorrah.—Gen. 10:19; 14:8; Deut. 29:23; Hos. 11:8.

ADMATHA, ăd-mā′thȧ. One of the seven princes in court of Ahasuerus.—Esth. 1:14.

11

ADMINISTER. I Cor. 12:5 (A.V.); II Cor. 8:19, 20 (A.V.); 9:12 (A.V.). See MINISTER.

ADMIRE. II Thes. 1:10 (A.V.); Jude 16 (A.V.); Rev. 17:6 (A.V.). See MARVEL, RESPECT, WONDER.

ADMONISH. Eccl. 12:12; Jer. 42:19 (A.V.); Acts 20:31; 27:9; I Cor. 4:14; Col. 1:28; I Thes. 5:12. One another—Rom. 15:14; Col. 3:16; II Thes. 3:15. See EXHORTATION, TESTIFY, WARN.

ADMONITION. Eccl. 4:13; I Cor. 10: 11; Eph. 6:4; Tit. 3:10.

ADNA, ăd'na. (1) Son of Pahath-moab. —Ezra 10:30. (2) A priest in the days of Joiakim.—Neh. 12:15.

ADNAH, ăd'nah. (1) A member of the tribe of Manasseh who deserted Saul and followed David.—I Chr. 12:20. (2) A chief captain under Jehoshaphat. —II Chr. 17:14.

ADONIBEZEK, a-dō'ni-bē'zek. King of Bezek captured by Judah and Simeon and taken to Jerusalem.—Ju. 1:5–7.

ADONIJAH, ăd'on-ī'jah. (1) Fourth son of David.—II Sam. 3:4; I Ki. 1:5–51; 2:13–28; I Chr. 3:1, 2. (2) A Levite whom Jehoshaphat sent to teach the law.—II Chr. 17:8. (3) One of those who assisted Nehemiah in sealing the covenant.—Neh. 10:14–16.

ADONIKAM, a-dŏn'i-kăm. Ancestor of many who returned from Babylon.— Ezra 2:13; 8:13(?); Neh. 7:18.

ADONIRAM, ăd-o-nī'ram. Solomon's overseer of the "men subject to task-work."—I Ki. 4:6; 5:14.

ADONIZEDEK, a-dō'ni-zē'dek. King of Jerusalem, slain by Joshua.—Josh. 10:1.

ADOPTION (Gr. *Uiothesia*). The act of putting in a son's place.

Foreordained unto.—Acts 13:48; Rom. 8:29; Eph. 1:5, 11.

Of children of Israel.—Ex. 4:22; Num. 6:27; Deut. 26:18; 27:9; 28:10; Hos. 1:10; 11:1; Rom. 9:4.

Joy of.—Is. 60:1–5; 62:1–5; Lu. 15:7, 10, 21–24.

Pertaining unto.—Rom. 8:15; 9:4.

Waiting for.—Rom. 8:19, 23, 25; 7:24, 25; Gal. 5:5.

Receiving.—John 1:12, 13; Rom. 8:15; II Cor. 6:17, 18; Gal. 4:5; Eph. 2:18–20; 3:6; Phil. 2:15; II Pet. 1:4.

Spirit of.—Rom. 8:15.

See ELECTION, FOREORDINATION, GOSPEL, NEW BIRTH, SALVATION.

ADORAIM, ăd'o-rā'im. A city of S.W. Judah, built by Rehoboam.—II Chr. 11:5–9.

ADORAM, a-dō'ram. (1) David's overseer of "men subject to taskwork."— II Sam. 20:24. (2) An officer of Solomon and Rehoboam. I Ki. 12:18. See ADONIRAM.

ADORN. Jer. 31:4. Bride, As a—Is. 61:10; Rev. 21:2. Doctrine—Titus 2: 10. Temple—Lu. 21:5. Women—I Tim. 2:9; I Pet. 3:3, 5. See CLOTHING, WOMEN.

ADRAMMELECH, a-drăm'me-lěk'. (1) One of the gods of the Sepharvites in Assyria to which children were offered.—II Ki. 17:31. (2) One of the sons of Sennacharib, king of Assyria, who slew their father.—I Ki. 19:37; Is. 37:38.

ADRAMYTTIUM, ăd-ra-mÿt'ti-ŭm. A city of Mysia formerly located on the coast, but now six miles inland.—Acts 27:2.

ADRIA, ā'dri-a. Adriatic Sea.—Acts 27:27.

ADRIEL, ā'dri-el. Husband of Saul's daughter Merab, who had been promised to David.—I Sam. 18:19; II Sam. 21:8, marg.

ADULLAM, a-dŭl'lam. (1) A royal city Southwest of Jerusalem.—Josh. 12:15; 15:35; Neh. 11:25–30; Micah 1:15. Fortified by Rehoboam.—II Chr. 11: 5–7. (2) A cave near the city.—David found refuge in—I Sam. 22:1; II Sam. 23: 13; I Chr. 11:15.

ADULLAMITE. Gen. 38:1, 12, 20.

ADULTERY. Commandments concerning.—Ex. 20:14; Lev. 18:20; Num. 5: 12–31; Deut. 5:18; 22:22–27; 24:1–4; Jer. 3:1; 5:7–9; 29:21–23; Mt. 5:27–32; 19:3–9, 18; Mk. 10:19; Lu. 18:20; Jas. 2:11. Law of—Rom. 7:3.

Teaching of Jesus concerning.—Mt. 5: 27–32; 15:19; 19:9, 18; Mk. 7:21; 10: 11, 12, 19; Lu. 16:18; 18:20. See TEACHING OF JESUS.

Punished with death.—Lev. 18:20; 20: 10–12; Deut. 22:22–27; Pr. 9:18; Mt. 5:27–32; John 8:5; Gal. 5:19–21; Eph.

5:3–5; I Thes. 4:4–7; Heb. 13:4; Rev. 21:8; 22:15. By Jehovah—Jer. 7:9; Mal. 3:5.

Despoils life.—Deceives—Job 24:15; Ps. 50:18. Children of transgression—Pr. 6:26; 31:3; Is. 57:3.

Disgraces individual.—Path towards death—Pr. 2:18, 19. Woman deceives —Pr. 5:3, 4; 6:27–33; 22:14; 23:27, 28; 30:20; Eccl. 7:26.

Degrades a nation.—Lev. 19:29; Deut. 23:17; Job 31:9–12; Jer. 3:1; 7:9; Hos. 4:1–2, 11; Mt. 12:39; 16:4; Mk. 8:38; I Cor. 10:8; Jude 7; I Pet. 4:3; Rev. 2:22.

Debars fellowship.—Eph. 5:11, 12. With God—Jas. 4:4.

Dwarfs a soul.—Mk. 15:19; I Cor. 3:17; II Pet. 2:10, 14; Eph. 4:17, 19, 20; 5:3, 4.

Adulterers shall not inherit kingdom of God.—I Cor. 6:9; Gal. 5:19, 21; Eph. 5:5; Rev. 21:8; 22:5. God will judge— Jer. 7:9; 29:23; Ez. 22:9–11; Eph. 5:6; Col. 3:6; I Thess. 4:3–5; Heb. 13:4; Jude 7; Rev. 2:20, 22.

Judged by righteous men.—Ez. 23:45; Job. 31:11.

Examples of.—Shechem—Gen. 34:2. Reuben—Gen. 35:22. Judah—Gen. 38:1–24. Potiphar's wife—Gen. 39:7–12. Eli's sons—I Sam. 2:22. David—II Sam. 11:1–5. Absalom—II Sam. 16:22. Israelites—Jer. 5:7–9; 29:23; Ez. 22:9–11; 33:26. Herod—Mk. 6:17, 18. Samaritan woman—John 4:18. A woman —John 8:3–11. Corinthians—I Cor. 5:1. Gentiles—I Pet. 4:3.

Figurative.—Adulterous state of Zion— Jer. 9:2; 23:10; Hos. 2:2; 3:1; 7:4; Rom. 7:1–6.

SPIRITUAL ADULTERY—*i. e.*, **IDOLATRY. Fascinating.**—Parable—Num. 25:1–3; Ez. 16:30–34; Ch. 23; Hos. 4:18; 11:2.

Predicted.—Lev. 20:1–5; Deut. 31:16–18, 20, 29.

Prohibited.—Ex. 34:12–16.

Introduced by foreign wives.—I Ki. 11:1–8; II Ki. 9:22.

Practised by Israel and Judah.—Ju. 8:27, 33; I Chr. 5:25; Ps. 106:38, 39; Jer. 3:1, 2; Ez. 16:16, 17, 20–29; Hos. 1:2; 2:2–5; 4:12, 13; 5:3, 4, 6, 10; Mal. 2:

11. Nineveh—Nah. 3:4. Babylon— Rev. 17:1, 2.

Reproved.—Ju. 3:8–10; Gen. 13:27; Ez. 20:30–32, 39; Hos. 2:6–9; 4:14, 15.

Entreaty to return.—Jer. 3:14, 16; Ez. 43:7, 9.

Punished.—II Ki. 9:22; Ps. 73:27; Ez. 6:9; 16:35–43; Hos. 2:9–13; Rev. 17:16, 17; 18:2, 3, 5; 19:2.

See CHASTITY, COMMANDMENTS, FORMATION, IDOLATRY, LUST, MARRIAGE.

ADUMMIM, a-dŭm′mim. **A ridge of hills on road between Jerusalem and Jericho between Judah and Benjamin.** —Josh. 15:7; 18:17.

ADVANCE. I Sam. 12:6 (A.V.); Esth. 3:1; 5:11; 10:2; Lu. 2:52; Gal. 1:14.

ADVANTAGE. Job. 35:3; Eccl. 10:11; Lu. 9:25 (A.V.); I Cor. 15:32; II Cor. 2:11; Jude 16. Hath a Jew?—Rom. 3:1. Take advantage of—II Cor. 7:2; 12:17. See GAIN, PROFIT.

ADVENTURE. Deut. 28:56; Ju. 9:17; Eccl. 5:14; Acts 19:31.

ADVERSARY. I Cor. 16:9; Heb. 10:27. Agree with—Mt. 5:25; Lu. 12:58. Angel of the Lord an—Num. 22:22. Avenge me of mine—Lu. 18:3. Satan an adversary—I Tim. 5:14; I Pet. 5:8. See ENEMY, SATAN.

ADVERSITY. Adversities have a judicial aspect: Afflictions, an educatory. Both may be of God. The latter apply largely to His children and tend to their improvement—Babylon—Rev. 14:18–20. Bread of—Is. 30:20. Brother born for—Pr. 17:17. David in—II Sam. 4:9; Ps. 35:15; 89:38–45. Day of —Ps. 94:13; Pr. 24:10; Eccl. 7:14. Desolation of—Rev. 18:14. God sets adversity against prosperity—Ps. 10:6; Eccl. 7:14. Help not withheld in time of—Ps. 31:7, 8; 50:15; 107:9–14; Is. 41:17–20. Job put to proof by Satan —Job. 19:9–22. See OUTLINE STUDY OF JOB. Negligence, Sent because of— Jer. 48:11, 12. Punishment because of iniquity—II Chr. 15:6; Lam. 4:5, 6; Dan. 11:15, 16; Mic. 6:9–16. Saved out of—I Sam. 10:19 (A.V.). Sympathy for others—Heb. 13:3. Yield is weakness, To—Pr. 24:10. See AFFLICTION, CONSOLATION, GOD, PROVIDENCE OF; SORROW, SUFFERING.

ADVERTISE. Num. 24:14; Ruth 4:4 (A.V.).

ADVICE. Abigail, Of—I Sam. 25:33 (A.V.). Good—Pr. 20:18 (A.V.). Israel, Of—Ju. 20:7; II Sam. 19:43; II Chr. 10:14 (A.V.). Paul, Of—II Cor. 8:10 (A.V.). Prophet, Of a—II Chr. 25:17 (A.V.). See COUNSEL, WISDOM.

ADVISE. II Sam. 24:13; I Ki. 12:6 (A.V.); I Chr. 21:12 (A.V.); 12:19; Acts 27:12. See ADVICE.

ADVOCATE. I John 2:1. See JESUS, TITLES OF; HOLY SPIRIT.

AENEAS, ae'ne-as. **A paralytic healed by Peter.**—Acts 9:33, 34.

AENON, ae'non. **A place near Salim where John the Baptist was baptizing.**—John 3:23.

AFAR OFF. Acts 2:39; Eph. 2:17; Heb. 11:13. See ALIENS.

AFFAIRS. Ps. 112:5 (A.V.). King, Of the—I Chr. 26:32. Life, Of this—II Tim. 2:4. Paul's—Eph. 6:21, 22 (A.V.). Philippians'—Phil. 1:27. Provinces, Of—Dan. 2:49; 3:12. See CAUSE, STATE.

AFFECT. Gal. 4:17, 18 (A.V.). Evil—affected—Acts 14:2. Soul—Lam. 3:51.

AFFECTION. I Chr. 29:3; II Cor. 6:12; 7:15; I Thess. 2:8. Above, On things—Col. 3:1, 2 (A.V.). Flesh, Of the—Gal. 5:24. Natural, Without—Rom. 1:31; II Tim. 3:3. Tenderly affectioned—Rom. 12:10. Vile—Rom. 1:26 (A.V.); Col. 3:5 (A.V.). See HEART, LOVE, LUST, MIND, PASSION, SPIRIT.

AFFINITY. I Ki. 3:11; II Chr. 18:1; Ezra 9:14.

AFFIRM. Lu. 22:59; Acts 12:15; 25:19; Rom. 3:8; I Tim. 1:7; Titus 3:8.

AFFLICTION. Foretold.—Gen. 15:13; Num. 14:33, 34. To be expected—Job 5:6, 7; Eccl. 7:14; John 16:33.

Result of Sin.—II Sam. 12:14; Ps. 90:7, 8; Jer. 22:21, 22; Ez. Chap. 6.

Used for.—Chastening—Deut. 8:5; Job 5:17; Ps. 55:19; 94:12, 13; Pr. 3:12; Heb. 12:5-12. Endurance, Cultivating—II Sam. 22:19; Ps. 37:23, 24; 129:1, 2; Heb. 11:25, 26. Enlightenment—Job 36:8-10; Ps. 119:67, 71; Is. 26:9. Fruitful, Making—John 15:2; Heb. 12:10, 11. Gospel, Promoting—Phil. 1:12-14. Holding us fast to God—Job 34:31, 32; Is. 10:20; Ez. 14:10, 11. Pa-tience, Cultivating—Rom. 5:3; Jas. 1:3; I Pet. 2:20. Purification—Is. 48:10; Dan. 11:35; Rev. 7:14, 15. Repentance, Leading to—Deut. 4:30; 30:1-3; Neh. 1:8, 9; Ps. 78:34; Is. 10:20, 21; Hos. 2:6, 7. Righteousness, Teaching—Is. 26:9. Sin, Confessing—Ps. 119:67; Pr. 28:13, 14. Exposing—Job 36:8, 9; Lu. 15:16-20. Testing us—Job 23:10; Ps. 36:10-12; Pr. 17:3; Eccl. 8:14; II Cor. 4:17; Phil. 1:28-30. Works of God, Manifestation of—John 9:1-3; 11:3; 21:18, 19.

Divine Help in.—Companionship with God—Ps. 23:4; 34:19; 37:32, 33; Rom. 15:5; II Cor. 1:3; 7:6, 7; II Thess. 2:16-17. Consolation promised—Is. 66:13, 14; Ez. 14:22, 23; II Cor. 1:4; Phil. 4:19. Confirmed by oath—Heb. 6:16-20. Grounded in Christ—Is. 53:4-6; 61:1-3; Zech. 1:16-21; Lu. 14:18-21; John 14:18; II Cor. 1:5; I Thess. 5:9-11; Heb. 3:14, 15. Faith in Christ Removes—John 14:1-3. Fellowship with brethren—II Cor. 7:6, 7; I Thess. 5:9-11. Hope in—Job 19:25, 26; Ps. 71:13, 14; Rom. 15:3-6; II Cor. 4:8, 9. See CONSOLATION, HOPE, PROMISES. Through the Scriptures—Ps. 119:50, 76; Rom. 15:4.

Afflictions of wicked and unstable: National.—The flood—Gen. chaps. 6:7. Sodom and Gomorrah—Gen. 19:1-29. Plagues of Egypt—Ex. chaps. 7-11. Wanderings of Israel—Deut. 34-40. Exiles in Assyria and Babylon—II Ki. chaps. 16-17; Is. 39:5-7. Judgments visited on Jerusalem—II Ki. 23:26, 27; Is. chap. 29; Mt. chap. 24. See JERUSALEM; COMMANDMENTS, PUNISHMENT FOR VIOLATION OF.

Individual examples.—Adam and Eve—Gen. 3:1-24. Ahab and Jezebel—I Ki. chap. 22; II Ki. chap. 9. Ahaziah—II Ki. 1:1-4. Cain—Gen. 4:9-12. Gehazi—II Ki. 5:27. Jonah—Jonah chap. 2. Lot—Gen. chap. 19; Lu. 17:32; II Pet. 2:7, 8.

Come suddenly.—Num. 16:30-35; II Sam. 12:7-12; Pr. 6:15; Rev. 18:10. Sometimes harden—Neh. 9:28, 29; Jer. 5:3.

Sometimes without effect.—II Chr. 28:22; Is. 9:13; Jer. 2:30; Zeph. 3:2.

Duty of Christians toward the afflicted.
—Should comfort—Job. 4:3, 4; 16:5;
29:25; Is. 25:3, 4; II Cor. 1:4; I Thess.
4:18; Heb. 12:12. Kind towards, Be—
Job 6:14. See KINDNESS. Pray for—
Acts 12:5; II Cor. 1:11; Phil. 1:19;
Jas. 5:14, 15. Protect—Job 29:12; Ps.
82:3, 4; Pr. 22:22; 31:5. See OPPRES-
SION, JUSTICE. Relieve—Job 31:19–22;
Is. 58:7, 10; Ez. 18:7, 16; Mt. 25:34–
45; Phil. 4:14; I Tim. 5:10. See FRA-
TERNITY, LOVE, POOR. Sympathize with
—Rom. 12:15; 15:1; Gal. 6:2; Heb.
13:3. Visit—Mt. 25:36; Jas. 1:27;
5:14.

God's mercy makes an end.—Job 5:11;
11:16; Ps. 30:5; 112:4; Nah. 1:9, 12.
See ADVERSITY, BURDEN, CONSOLATION,
HOPE, JESUS, SUFFERINGS OF; JOB, PER-
SECUTION, PHARAOH, PROMISES, SOR-
ROW, SUFFERING.

AFFRIGHT. Rev. 11:13. Apostles—Mk.
16:5, 6; Horror, with—Is. 21:4. Israel
—Deut. 7:21; 20:3; Josh. 1:9; II Chr.
32:18. Men of war—Jer. 51:32. Peter
—Acts 10:4. Wicked—Job 18:20. See
AFRAID, FEAR, HORROR, TERROR.

AFORE. Prepared unto glory—Rom. 9:
23. Promised—Rom. 1:2.

AFORETIME. Deut. 2:20; Neh. 13:5;
Jer. 30:20; Dan. 6:10; John 9:13. Dis-
obedient—I Pet. 3:20. Sins done—
Rom. 3:25. Written—Rom. 15:4. See
TIME.

AFRAID. Mt. 9:8; Mk. 5:15; Lu. 2:9;
8:35; Gal. 4:11; Heb. 11:23; I Pet.
3:6, 14. See FEAR. Adam and Eve—
Gen. 3:10. Apostles—Mt. 14:27; 28:
10; Mk. 6:50; 16:8; Lu. 8:25; John
6:19, 20. Ask him, To—Mk. 9:32; Lu.
9:45. Evil tidings—Ps. 112:7. Heart—
John 14:27 (A.V.). Judgment of—
Rom. 13:3, 4. Moses—Ex. 3:6. Of
them that kill the body—Mt. 10:28.
Of whom shall I be—Ps. 27:1. Paul
—Acts 18:9. Paul, Of—Acts 9:26.
Pilate—John 19:8. Sorrows, Of all my
—Job. 9:28. See AFFRIGHTED, FEAR,
HORROR, TERROR.

AFRESH. Crucify.—Heb. 6:6.

AFTER. Flesh—II Pet. 2:10. Strange
Flesh—Jude 7. Jesus—Mt. 10:38; 16:
24; Mk. 1:17, 20; 8:34; Lu. 9:23; 14:
27; John 12:19. John the Baptist—
Mt. 3:11; Mk. 1:7; John 1:15, 27, 30.

Satan—I Tim. 5:15. Woman, The—
Rev. 12:15.

AGABUS, ăg'a-bus. A prophet of the
early Christian Church, who came to
Paul in Antioch and predicted a great
famine.—Acts 11:28; 21:10.

AGAG, ā'gag. A king of the Amalekites
spared by Saul contrary to God's command.—Num. 24:7; I Sam. 15, 8, 9, 20,
32, 33.

AGAGITE. A tribe of the Amalekites
of which Haman was a member.—
Esther 3:1, 10; 8:5; 9:24.

AGATE. A precious stone.—Is. 54:12
(A.V.); Ez. 27:16 (A.V.). Breastplate
of the priest, In the—Ex. 28:19; 39:12.

AGE. John 9:21, 23. Full.—Job. 5:26;
Heb. 5:14.

Old age a blessing.—Promised to Abraham—Gen. 15:15; Job 30:2; Ps. 91:16.
Bestowed—Gen. 25:8.

People of old age.—Called: Elders—Job
12:20. Gray-haired—Job 15:10. Aged
—Job 29:8.

Instances of.—Abraham and Sarah—
Gen. 18:11–13; 21:2, 7. Lot—Gen. 19:
31. Isaac—Gen. 27:2; Jacob—Gen. 37:
3; 44:20. Moses—Deut. 34:7. Joshua—
Josh. 13:1; 23:1, 2; Gideon—Ju. 8:32.
Man at Gibeah—Ju. 19:16, 17. Naomi
—Ruth 4:15. Eli—I Sam. 4:18. Samu-
el—I Sam. 12:2. Barzillai—II Sam.
19:32, 35. David—I Ki. 1:1, 15; I
Chr. 23:1; 29:28; Ps. 37:25. Solomon
—I Ki. 11:4. Prophet at Bethel—I Ki.
13:11, 25, 29. Ahijah—I Ki. 14:4. Asa
—I Ki. 15:23. Shunammite's husband
—II Ki. 4:14. Jehoiada—II Chr. 24:
15. Job—Job 32:6; 42:17. Elisabeth
—Lu. 1:7, 36. Zacharias—Lu. 1:7.
Anna—Lu. 2:36. Paul—Philemon 9.

Counsel with old men.—I Ki. 12:6, 8, 13;
II Chr. 10:6, 8, 13.

Proverbs concerning.—Pr. 17:6; 20:29;
22:6; 23:22.

Duties of the aged.—Titus 2:3.

Appeal to.—I John 2:13 f.

Prophecies concerning.—I Sam. 2:31;
Job. 5:26; Ps. 92:14; Is. 46:4; 65:20;
Jer. 6:11; 31:13; Joel 1:2; 2:28; Zech.
8:4; Acts 2:17.

Miscellaneous.—Men of Sodom—Gen.
19:4. No compassion on—II Chr. 36:
17. Jews—Esth. 3:13. Prayer of an
old man—Ps. 71:9, 18. King—Eccl.

4:13. Vanity of, unless filled with good—Eccl. 6:3; 12:1.

Figurative.—Lam. 2:21.

The title "elder" originally had reference to old age.—Ex. 3:16; Josh. 24: 31; I Ki. 20:8.

Attainment of old age a special blessing.—Job 5:26; Zech. 8:4.

Wisdom of the aged proverbial.—Job 12:12; 32:7.

Reverence to be shown the aged.—Lev. 19:32; Pr. 23:22.

Failure of reverence an evil.—Deut. 28: 50; I Ki. 12:8; Is. 47:6.

Past.—Heb. 11:11. See LIFE, WORLD, YEAR.

AGEE, ăg'e-ē. **Father of Shammah, one of David's mighty men.**—II Sam. 23:11.

AGES. All—Eph. 3:21 (A.V.). Come, To —Eph. 2:7. See Eccl. 1:10. End of— I Cor. 10:11; Heb. 9:26. Hid for— Eph. 3:9; Col. 1:26. Other—Eph. 3:5 (A.V.). See GENERATIONS, PROPHECY, WORLD.

AGONY. Jesus in agony in Gethsemane. —Lu. 22:44.

AGREE. Lu. 5:30; Rev. 17:17 (A.V.). Adversary, with thine—Mt. 5:25. Ananias and Sapphira—Acts 5:9. Gamaliel, with—Acts 5:40. Householder— Mt. 20:2, 13. Jews—John 9:22. One, In—I John 5:8. Two—Amos 3:3; Mt. 18:19. Witnesses—Mk. 14:56, 59. Words of the prophets—Acts 15:15. See ACCORD, FULFIL, MIND, OF ONE, ENMITY.

AGREEMENT. Dan. 11:6. Sheol, With —Is. 28:15, 18. Temple of God—II Cor. 6:16.

AGRICULTURE. Originated with God. —Gen. 2:15; 3:23. The first employment of man—Gen. 1:28; 4:2; 9:20. God stands voucher for the seasons— Gen. 8:22; Zech. 8:12; Ps. 107:36-38. Man must act discreetly—Deut. 22:9; Pr. 27:23-27; Eccl. 11:6; Is. 28:24-26; Gal. 6:7; II Cor. 9:6.

Fertility of soil depends upon obedience. —Lev. 25:18, 19; 26:3-10; Deut. 8:10; 11:10-15; Is. 30:21-24. Famine a result of disobedience—Is. 7:21-25; Jer. 5:24-26; Hos. 2:8; Joel 1:10-12.

Plowing.—Mixed team forbidden—Deut. 22:10. Oxen used—Job 1:14; I Ki. 19:

19. Should plow in hope—I Cor. 9:10. The sluggard shrinks—Pr. 20:4. Season for plowing limited—Is. 28:24-26.

Sowing.—Earliest mention—Gen. 26:12. Laws concerning—Ex. 23:10, 16; Lev. 19:19; 25:3, 4, 11, 20, 22; 26:5, 16; Deut. 11:10; 22:9; II Ki. 19:29. Destruction of—Ju. 6:3. In prophecy— Is. 19:7; 30:23; 40:24; 61:11; Jer. 2:2; 4:3; 35:7; 50:16; Ez. 36:10; Amos 9:13. Illustrative Use of—Eccl. 11:4, 6; Is. 32:20; 37:30; 55:10.

Planting.—Mixed seed forbidden—Deut. 23:24, 25. When to plant—Eccl. 11:6; Is. 28:24-26.

Harvesting.—Robbery forbidden—Deut. 23:24, 25. Reapers—Ruth 2:4-6. Joy in harvest—Is. 9:3; Hos. 6:11. Sorrowful harvest—Is. 18:4-11. Spiritual harvest—Mt. 13:8; Mk. 4:8; Lu. 8:8; 10:2; Rev. 14:15, 16.

Gleaning.—Lev. 19:9, 10; 23:22; Deut. 24:19-22; Ruth 2:2-23; Is. 17:6; 24: 13; Jer. 6:9; Mic. 7:1.

Threshing.—Is. 28:27, 28; 41:15, 16; Jer. 51:33; Ju. 6:11; II Sam. 24:18-22; I Chr. 21:20-23.

Tools.—I Sam. 13:19-21; II Sam. 12:31; Deut. 16:9; 23:25.

Protective laws.—Not to covet fields— Deut. 5:21. Not to trespass—Ex. 22:5; Deut. 23:25. Not to move landmarks —Deut. 19:14; Pr. 22:28. Not to injure produce—Ex. 22:6. Not to sow in sabbatical year—Ex. 23:10, 11. Produce given as rent—Mt. 21:33, 34.

Figurative.—Is. 28:24; Jer. 4:3; 12:13; Hos. 10:12, 13; Mt. 6:26; Chap. 13; 25:24, 26; Mk. 4:3-20; Lu. 8:5-15; 12: 24; 19:21, 22; John 4:35-38; I Cor. 3:6-9. See BARLEY, FIELD, GRAIN, SEED, HARVEST, LAND, WHEAT.

AGRIPPA, a-grĭp'pa. See HEROD.

AGROUND. Acts 27:41.

AGUR, ā'gur. **Son of Jakeh.**—Pr. 30:1.

AHAB. Son of Omri.—I Ki. 16:28. King of Israel—I Ki. 16:29. Married Jezebel, an idolatress, daughter of Ethbaal, king of the Sidonians—16:31. A weak and wicked king—I Ki. 16: 30-33; 21:26, 27. Famine brought upon Israel as a punishment—I Ki. 17: 1-24; 18:1-45. Troubled Israel—I Ki. 18:17, 18. Gathers all Israel unto Mt. Carmel, where choice is made between

Jehovah and Baal—I Ki. 18:19-40. Wars against Ben-hadad, king of Syria, and conquers him—I Ki. 20:1-34. Rebuked for his leniency—I Ki. 21:35-43. Covets Naboth's vineyard —I Ki. 21:1-16. Rebuked by Elijah —I Ki. 21:17-24. Ahab humbleth himself—I Ki. 21:27, 28. Prophecies concerning—I Ki. 22:8, 15-23; II Ki. 9:6-10. Victim of false prophets—I Ki. 22:5, 6, 19-23, 34-37. Death—I Ki. 22:29-37. Reigned 22 years—I Ki. 16:29. Left a bad name—I Ki. 22:51-53; II Chr. 21:6, 13; 22:3; Mic. 6:16.

AHARAH, a-här'ah. **Son of Benjamin.** —I Chr. 8:1.

AHARHEL, a-här'hel. **Son of Harum.—** I Chr. 4:8.

AHASAI, a-häs'a-ī. **A priest dwelling in Jerusalem after the exile.**—Neh. 11:13 (A.V.). See AHZAI.

AHASBAI, a-häs'ba-i. **Father of Eliphalet, one of David's mighty men.**— II Sam. 23:34.

AHASUERUS, a-hăs'u-ē'rus. (1) **King of Persia** (Cambyses)—Ezra 4:6.

(2) **Father of Darius the Mede.**—Dan. 9:1.

(3) **Xerxes, king of Persia, to whom Esther was married.**—Esth. 1:1-9; 2:1-21; 3:1-12; 6:2; 7:5; 8:1-12; 9:2, 20, 30; 10:1, 3.

AHAVA, a-hä'và. **A river in Media.**— Ezra 8:15, 21, 31.

AHAZ, ā'haz. **Son of Jotham.**—I Chr. 3:13; II Chr. 27:9. King of Judah— II Ki. 15:38; 16:1; 17:1. Attacked by Pekah and Rezin—II Ki. 16:5, 6; II Chr. 28:5-15; Is. 7:1. Refuses, and asks a sign of Isaiah—Is. 7:11, 12. Sends Presents to Tiglath-Pileser to ask for aid against Rezin and Pekah— II Ki. 16:7-9, 17, 18; II Chr. 28:16-21. Invasion of land by Edomites and Philistines—II Chr. 28:17-19. Idolatry of—II Ki. 16:2-4; 23:12; II Chr. 28:1-4; 29:3, 7, 19. Sun dial of—II Ki. 20:11; Is. 38:8. Prophets during his reign—Is. 1:1; Hos. 1:1; Mic. 1:1. Death of—Is. 14:28; II Ki. 16:20; II Chr. 28:27. Descendants of—II Ki. 18:1; I Chr. 3:13; 8:35, 36; I Chr. 9:41, 42.

AHAZIAH, ā'ha-zī'ah. **King of Judah.** Son and successor of Jehoram—II Ki.

8:25; I Chr. 3:11. Called Azariah—II Chr. 22:6. Jehoahaz—II Chr. 21:17; 25:23. Character of: Influenced by the evil counsel of his mother, Athaliah— II Ki. 8:26, 27; II Chr.22:2-5. Events: Dedicates treasures—II Ki. 12:18. Allied with Joram against Hazael, visits Joram at Jezreel and is slain by Jehu —II Ki. 8:28, 29; 9:16, 27; II Chr. 22:5-9. Burial of—II Ki. 9:28; II Chr. 22:9. Royal seed destroyed at his death—II Ki. 11:1. Descendants of— II Ki. 13:1; 14:13.

(2) **Son of Ahab.**—I Ki. 22:40, 49, 51. King of Israel—I Ki. 22:51. Character of: His wickedness and idolatry— I Ki. 22:52, 53; II Chr. 20:35. Events: Prophecy of his death—II Ki. 1:1-16. Joins Jehoshaphat in building ships for Tarshish, which were wrecked at Ezion-geber—I Ki. 22:49; II Chr. 20: 35-37. Death of—II Ki. 1:17. Record of his deeds—II Ki. 1:18.

AHBAN, äh'ban. **Son of Abishur and Abihail.**—I Chr. 2:29.

AHER, ā'her. **A Benjamite.**—I Chr. 7: 12. See AHIRAM.

AHI, a-hi. (1) **A Gadite.**—I Chr. 5:15.

(2) **A member of the tribe of Asher.**—I Chr. 7:34.

AHIAH, ā-hī'ah. See AHIJAH.

AHIAM, a-hī'am. **One of David's mighty men.**—II Sam. 23:33; I Chr. 11:35.

AHIAN, a-hī'an. **A member of the tribe of Manasseh.**—I Chr. 7:19.

AHIEZER, a-hī-ē'zer. (1) **A prince of Dan.**—Num. 1:12; 2:25; 7:66, 71; 10:25.

(2) **A chieftain of the tribe of Benjamin, who deserted Saul for David at Ziklag.**—I Chr. 12:3.

AHIHUD, a-hī'hud. (1) **A prince of the tribe of Asher.**—Num. 34:27.

(2) **A Benjamite.**—I Chr. 8:7.

AHIJAH, a-hī'jah. (1) **A prophet who warned Jeroboam of the revolt of the ten tribes.**—I Ki. 11:29, 30; 12:15; 14:4-6, 18:15-29; II Chr. 9:29; 10:15.

(2) **Father of Baasha, the king who conspired against Nadab, son of Jeroboam.**—I Ki. 15:27, 33; 21:22; II Ki. 9:9.

(3) **Son of Jerahmeel.**—I Chr. 2:25.

(4) One of David's mighty men.—I Chr. 11:36.

(5) A Levite, under David, who had charge of the sanctuary treasures.— I Chr. 26:20.

(6) A Levite who assisted Nehemiah in sealing the covenant.—Neh. 10:26.

(7) A Benjamite.—I Chr. 8:7.

(8) Son of Shisha.—I Ki. 4:3.

AHIKAM, a-hī′kam. One of the messengers sent by Josiah to consult Huldah, the prophetess.—II Ki. 22:12, 14; 25:22; II Chr. 34:20. A friend of Jeremiah—Jer. 26:24; 39:14; 40:5-16; 41: 1-16; 43:6.

AHILUD, a-hī′lud. Father of David's recorder.—II Sam. 8:16; 20:24; I Ki. 4:3, 12; I Chr. 18:15.

AHIMAAZ, a-hĭm′a-ăz. (1) Son of Zadok, the priest, who warned David concerning Absalom.—II Sam. 15:27, 36; 17:17; 20; 18:19-29; I Chr. 6:8; 9:53.

(2) Father of wife of Saul.—I Sam. 14:50.

(3) Son-in-law, and officer of Solomon. —I Ki. 4:15.

AHIMAN, a-hī′man. (1) One of three sons of Anak.—Num. 13:22; Josh. 15: 14; Ju. 1:10.

(2) A Levite porter in the temple, who returned from Babylon.—I Chr. 9:17.

AHIMELECH, a-hĭm′e-lek. (1) A priest at Nob, slain by Saul for assisting David.—I Sam. 21:1, 2, 8; 22:9-20; 23:6; 30:7; II Sam. 8:17; I Chr. 24:3, 6, 31.

(2) A Hittite officer under David.—I Sam. 26:6.

AHIMOTH, a-hī′moth. A Levite, son of Elkanah.—I Chr. 6:25.

AHINADAB, a-hĭn′a-dab. An officer under Solomon.—I Ki. 4:14.

AHINOAM, a-hĭn′ō-am. (1) Woman of Jezreel, wife of David and mother of Amnon.—I Sam. 25:43; 27:3; 30:5; II Sam. 2:2; 3:2; I Chr. 3:1.

AHIO, a-hī′o. (1) Son of Abinadab, in whose house the ark remained twenty years.—II Sam. 6:3, 4; I Chr. 13:7.

(2) A Benjamite.

(3) A Benjamite of Gibeon.—II Chr. 8: 31; 9:37.

AHIRA, a-hī′ra. A prince of Naphtali. —Num. 1:15; 2:29; 7:78, 83; 10:27.

AHIRAM, a-hī′ram. A Benjamite.— Num. 26:38. See EHI (Gen. 46:21) and AHER (I Chr. 7:12).

AHISAMACH, a-hĭs′a-măk. A Danite, father of Oholiab.—Ex. 31:6; 35:34; 38:23.

AHISHAHAR, a-hĭsh′a-här. A grandson of Benjamin.—I Chr. 7:10.

AHISHAR, a-hī′shar. Overseer of Solomon's household.—I Ki. 4:6.

AHITHOPHEL, a-hĭth′o-phĕl. Native of Giloh in Judah.—II Sam. 15:12. A counsellor of David, who conspires against him.—II Sam. 15:12, 31, 34; 16:15-23; 17:1-23; I Chr. 27:33, 34. Grandfather of Bath-sheba—II Sam. 11:3; 23:24. Commits suicide—II Sam. 17:23.

AHITUB, a-hī′tŭb. (1) Son of Phinehas, grandson of Eli, father of Ahimelech.—I Sam. 14:3; 22:9-12, 20.

(2) Father of David's high-priest, Zadok.—II Sam. 8:17; I Chr. 6:7, 8, 52; 18:16; Ezra 7:2.

(3) A priest descended from Zadok.—I Chr. 6:11, 12.

(4) A priest, ruler of the temple in the days of Nehemiah.—1 Chr. 9:11; Neh. 11:11.

AHLAB, äh′lăb. A city in Asher.—Ju. 1:3.

AHLAI, äh′lāi. (1) A child of Sheshan. —I Chr. 2:31.

(2) Father of Zabad, one of David's mighty men.—I Chr. 11:41.

AHOAH, a-hō′ah. A grandson of Benjamin.—I Chr. 8:4.

AHOHITE, ă-hō′hite. II Sam. 23:9, 28; I Chr. 11:12, 29; 27:4.

AHOLAH. See OHOLAH.

AHOLIAB. See OHOLIAB.

AHOLIBAH. See OHOLIBAH.

AHOLIBAMAH. See OHOLIBAMAH.

AHUMAI, a-hū′ma-ī. Son of Jahath, grandson of Shobal.—I Chr. 4:2.

AHUZZAM, a-hŭz′zam. Son of Ashur.— I Chr. 4:6.

AHUZZATH, a-hŭz′zath. Friend or counsellor of Abimelech, king of Gerar.—Gen. 26:26.

AI, ā′i. Ancient royal city of the Canaanites destroyed by Joshua.—Gen. 12:8; 13:3; Josh. 7:2-5; 8:1-29; 9:3; 10:1, 2; 12:9; Ezra 2:28; Neh. 7:32;

Jer. 49:3. See AIATH (Is. 10:28). AIGA (Neh. 11:31).

AIAH, a-i'ah. (1) **Son of Zibeon, and grandson of Seir, the Horite.**—Gen. 36:24; I Chr. 1:40.

(2) **Father of Rizpah, Saul's concubine.** —II Sam. 3:7; 21:8–11.

AIATH, ā'iăth. See AI.

AID. See HELP.

AIJA, āi'ja. See AI.

AIJALON, āi'ja-lon. (1) **A valley in Dan. N.W. of Jerusalem.**—Josh. 10:12.

(2) **A Levitical town in this valley.**— Josh. 19:42; 21:24; Ju. 1:35; I Sam. 14:31; I Chr. 8:13; II Chr. 11:10; 28:18.

(3) **A town in Zebulun.**—Ju. 12:12.

(4) **A Levitical city in Ephraim(?)**—I Chr. 6:69.

AILETH. Gen. 21:17; Ju. 18:23; I Sam. 11:5; II Sam. 14:5; II Ki. 6:28; Ps. 114:5; Is. 22:1. See DISEASE.

AIM. Arrows—Ps. 58:7; 64:3. Preach, So to—Rom. 15:20. Well pleasing, To be—II Cor. 5:9. See STRIVE.

AIN, a'in. (1) **A place in N.E. of Canaan, near Riblah**—Num. 34:11.

(2) **A Levitical city assigned to Simeon (?)**—Josh. 15:32; 19:7; 21:16; I Chr. 4:32.

AIR. Beateth the—II Cor. 9:26. Come between—Job 41:16. Darkened—Rev. 9:2. Fowls of—See BIRDS. Meet the Lord in—I Thess. 4:17. Pant for—Jer. 14:6. Poured his bowl into—Rev. 16:17. Prince of the powers of—Eph. 2:2. Speaking unto—I Cor. 14:9. See HEAVEN, METEOROLOGY, WIND.

AKAN, ā'kăn. Son of Ezer and grandson of Seir, the Horite—Gen. 36:27. See ZAAKAN (I Chr. 1:42).

AKELDAMA, ă-kel'da-ma. The name of the field purchased by Judas with the thirty pieces of money received for betraying Jesus—Acts 1:19.

AKKUB, ăk'kub. (1) **Son of Elioenai.**— I Chr. 3:24.

(2) **A porter in the second temple.**—I Chr. 9:17; Neh. 11:19; 12:25.

(3) **Hereditary porters in the temple after the exile.**—Ezra 2:42; Neh. 7:45.

(4) **A priest who expounded the law read by Ezra.**—Neh. 8:7.

AKRABBIM, ăk-răb'bim. "Ascent of the Scorpions" leading from the Dead

Sea to the highland of South Judah.— Num. 34:4; Josh. 15:3.

ALABASTER CRUSE. Used by the woman in anointing Jesus—Mt. 26:7; Mk. 14:3; Lu. 7:37.

ALAMOTH, ăl'a-mŏth. **A musical term.** —Soprano—I Chr. 15:20; Ps. 46, title.

ALARM. Trumpet, Of the—Num. 10:5, 6; Jer. 4:19; Jos. 2:1. War, Of—Jer. 49:2; Zeph. 1:16.

ALEMETH, ăl'e-mĕth. (1) **A Benjamite.**—I Chr. 7:8.

(2) **A descendant of Jonathan.**—I Chr. 8:36; 9:42.

ALEXANDER, ăl'ex-ăn'der. (1) **Son of Simon, the Cyrenian, who bore the cross of Jesus.**—Mk. 15:21.

(2) **Related to the high-priest when Peter was arrested.**—Acts 4:6.

(3) Acts 19:33.

(4) **The coppersmith.**—II Tim. 4:14.

(5) **An early disciple, who became an apostate.**—I Tim. 1:20.

ALEXANDRIA, ăl'ex-ăn'dri-a. **An ancient Egyptian city on the Nile,** founded by Alexander the Great, B.C. 332.—Here the Septuagint version of the O.T. was translated into Greek. It was famous for its museum and library—Acts 6:9; 18:24; 27:6; 28:11.

ALGUM TREES. II Chr. 2:8; 9:10; 11.

ALIENS. Heb. *Nok-ree*, "non-relative," "adulterous," "different," "alienate." Gr. *Apollotrio*, "To estrange away," "to render non-participant." (Distinct from the terms "foreigners" and "sojourners," since they once enjoyed holy associations.)

God alienated.—Num. 14:34 (margin); Ps. 78:59; 106:39, 40; Ez. 23:18; Amos 5:21.

Alienated from God.—Ps. 12:1–3; 78:58, 59; 106:39, 40; Jer. 6:8; Ez. 23:18; Mal. 3:14, 15; Rom. 5:10; Eph. 2:16 f. From the commonwealth of Israel— Eph. 2:12.

Nations alienated.—Lam. 5:6; Rom. 9:3–6; Eph. 2:12; Col. 1:21–23.

Strange woman alienated.—Pr. 2:16, 17; Ez. 32:22, 28.

First-fruits alienated.—Lev. 25:34; Ez. 44:30; 48:14.

Inheritance alienated.—Jer. 6:12; Lam. 5:2; Zeph. 1:13.

Deliverance from aliens.—Ps. 144:7, 8, 11. See SOJOURNERS.

ALIVE. I Thess. 4:15, 17; Rev. 1:18; 2:8. Dead, From the—Rom. 6:13. God, Unto—Rom. 6:11. Jesus alive after His resurrection—Mk. 16:11; Acts 1:3; 25:19. See JESUS, RESURRECTION OF. Lake of Fire, Into—Rev. 19:20. Law, Without—Rom. 7:9. Maketh—Deut. 32:39; I Sam. 2:6; I Cor. 15:22; Gal. 3:21; Eph. 2:1. See RESURRECTION, NEW BIRTH, PRESERVE—Jer. 49: 11. Sheol, Into—Num. 16:30. See LIFE, QUICK.

ALL. Done all, to. stand—Eph. 6:13. Father giveth me—John 6:37, 39. *Greater than all*—John 10:29. Flesh—Lu. 3:6; Acts 2:17; I Cor. 15:39; I Pet. 1:24. See FLESH. Forsook—Mt. 19:27; Lu. 5:11. See SELF-DENIAL. Heart, Soul, Mind—Mt. 22:37; Mk. 12:30, 33; 13:10; Lu. 10:27; Acts 8:37. See HEART, SOUL. Labor, All ye that—Mt. 11:28. See LABOR. Law—Mt. 5: 18; Mt. 22:40; Gal. 5:14. See COVENANTS, LAW. Scripture—II Tim. 3: 16, 17. See WORD OF GOD. Spent all—Mk. 5:26; Lu. 15:14. Subjected unto him—I Cor. 15:28; Rev. 2:8. Things are yours—I Cor. 3:22, 23. *Common*—Acts 4:32. Need of all these—Mt. 6: 33. World and preach—Mt. 24:14, 30; 28:19; Mk. 16:15, 16; Lu. 24:46, 47; Acts 1:8; Rom. 3:19; 10:18. See SALVATION FOR ALL MEN.

ALLAYETH. Eccl. 10:4.

ALLEGING. Acts 17:3.

ALLEGORY. Gal. 4:24. See PARABLES, SYMBOLS AND SIMILITUDES.

ALLIED. Neh. 13:4

ALLON, ăl'lon. Son of Jedarah—I Chr. 4:37.

ALLON-BACUTH, ăl'lon-băk'uth. Place where Deborah was buried, near Bethel.—Gen. 35:8.

ALLOT. Josh. 13:6; 23:4. See CASTING LOTS.

ALLOW. Rom. 7:15 (A.V.); 14:22 (A.V.). See ACCEPT, APPRAISE, CONSENT.

ALLOWANCE. II Ki. 25:30; Jer. 52:34.

ALLURE. Hos. 2:14. See ENTICE, TEMPTATION.

ALMIGHTY. See GOD IS ALMIGHTY.

ALMODAD, al-mō'dad. Son of Joktan. —Gen. 10:26; I Chr. 1:20.

ALMON, ăl'mon. A Levitical city in Benjamin.—Josh. 21:18.

ALMON-DIBLATHAIM, ăl'mon-dĭb-lä-thä'ĭm. One of Israel's encampments after leaving Egypt.—Num. 33:46, 47.

ALMOND. Gen. 43:11; Num. 17:8; Eccl. 12:5; Jer. 1:11. Imitated in the tabernacle—Ex. 25:33; 37:19, 20. See PLANTS, TREES AND FLOWERS.

ALMOST. All things purged by law—Heb. 9:22. Consumed me—Ps. 119:87. Evil, In all—Pr. 5:14. Feet almost gone—Ps. 73:2. Persuaded—Acts 26: 28, 29. Some almost dwelt in silence—Ps. 94:17.

ALMS: Giving of alms.—Pr. 31:20; Lu. 11:41; 12:33; Acts 10:2; 24:17.

Manner of giving.—Without ostentation Mt. 6:1–4. Generously—Deut. 15:11. With liberality—Rom. 12:8. With compassion—I John 3:17. With promptness—II Cor. 8:11, 12. With cheerfulness—II Cor. 9:7.

Asking of alms.—Lame man—Acts 3:3. The Blind man—John 9:8.

Reward of almsgiving.—Deut. 15:10; Job 29:11–13; Pr. 19:17; Mt. 19:21; Lu. 12:33; II Cor. 9:8–11.

Instances.—Dorcas—Acts 9:36. Cornelius—Acts 10:2. Paul—Acts 24:17. See FRATERNITY, GIVING, LIBERALITY, LOVE.

ALMUG-TREE. I Ki. 10:11, 12.

ALOES. Num. 24:6; Ps. 45:8; Pr. 7:17; So. of Sol. 4:14; John 19:39. See PLANTS, TREES and FLOWERS.

ALONE. Bread.—Mt. 4:4; Lu. 4:4. Elijah—I Ki. 19:14; Rom. 11:3. Faith—Jas. 2:17–26. High-priest—Heb. 9:7. Jesus—Mt. 14:23; Mk. 4:10; Lu. 9:18; 36; John 6:15; 8:9, 29; 16:32. Moses—Ex. 24:2; Num. 11:14; Deut. 1:9. Rejoicing in himself—Gal. 6:4. Sparrow, As a—Ps. 102:7.

ALOOF. Job. 30:10; Ps. 38:11.

ALOUD. See CRY.

ALPHA. First letter in the Greek alphabet. Title of Christ indicating His eternal character.—Rev. 1:8, 11; 21:6; 22:13.

ALPHEUS, ăl'phe-us. (1) **Father of James, who was one of the apostles**—Mt. 10:3; Mk. 3:18; Lu. 6:15; Acts 1:13. His wife was a sister to Mary, mother of Jesus—Mk. 15:40; John 19:2.

(2) **Father of Matthew, the apostle.**—Mk. 2:14.

ALTAR. From the root *Zabhah*, to slay. Place of sacrificial slaughter.

The most primitive altar consisted of a rock or a stone.—Ju. 13:19; I Sam. 14: 33–35. That of *Noah*—Gen. 8:20. Of *Abraham*, at Shechem—Gen. 12:7. At Bethel—Gen. 12:8. On Moriah—Gen. 22:9. Of *Isaac*, at Beer-sheba—Gen. 26:25. Of *Jacob*, at Bethel—Gen. 35:7. At Shechem—Gen. 33:18–20. Of *Moses*, at Rephidim—Ex. 17:15.

Jehovah, through Moses, gives instruction as to how and what.—Either earth or stone—Ex. 20:24–26; 27:1–7; Deut. 27:5–6; Josh. 8:30. Moses builds a sample altar after receiving the Law—Ex. 24:4.

In early times altars built on spots hallowed by presence of Jehovah.—Shechem—Gen. 12:7. Hebron—Gen. 13:18. Beer-sheba—Gen. 26:23–25. Bethel—Gen. 35:1.

Builders of idolatrous altars: Aaron—Ex. 32:5. Balaam builds seven altars, in three different places, at *Bamoth-Baal*—Num. 23:1–2. *Pisgah*—Num. 23: 14; *Peor*—Num. 23:29. Gideon's father—Ju. 6:25. Jeroboam—I Ki. 12:32–33. Ahab—I Ki. 16:32–33. Prophets of Baal—I Ki. 18:26. Ahaz—II Ki. 16: 10–16. Kings of Judah—II Ki. 23:12; II Chr. 33:3. Israel—Is. 27:9; 65:3. Ephraim—Hos. 8:11. Athenians—Acts 17:23.

Idolatrous altars built on tops of houses.—II Ki. 23:12; Jer. 19:13; 32:29.

Wooden symbols, called asherim, erected near altars.—Ex. 34:13; Deut. 7:5; 12:3; Ju. 3:7; 6:30; I Ki. 14:23; 16:32–33; 18:19; II Ki. 21:3; 23:14; II Chr. 14:3; 17:6; 33:3; 34:3; Is. 17:8; Jer. 17:2; Mic. 5:14.

Zealots for a pure altar: Moses—Ex. 32: 4–6, 19, 20. Gideon—Ju. 6:25–32. Samuel—I Sam. 7:17; 13:9–14. David—II Sam. 24:18–25. Elijah—I Ki. 18: 30–32. Isaiah—Is. 19:19–20; 27:9. Malachi—Mal. 1:10–13.

Distinction between the central and local altars.—Central, or national altar (Deut. 12:5) had horns at each

corner—Ex. 27:2; 38:1–2; Ps. 118:27. Sin represented as engraved on the horns—Jer. 17:1. Blood applied to horns with finger of priest—Ex. 29: 12; 30:10; Lev. 4:7, 18, 25, 30, 34. Moses applies blood—Lev. 8:15.

The horns of the altar resorted to for protection.—Ex. 21:14; I Ki. 1:50–51; 2:28–29.

Altars in the tabernacle: Of burnt offerings. *Its construction*—Ex. 27:1–8; 38: 1–7. *Its situation*—Ex. 40:6, 29. *Its use*—Lev. 1:1–17. *Its dedication*—Num. Chap. 7. *Continual fire*—Lev. 6: 13. Altar of incense (called the golden altar—Ex. 39:38): *Its construction*—Ex. 30:1–5; 37:25–29. In the temple, made of cedar-wood, overlaid with gold—I Ki. 6:20; 7:48; I Chr. 28:18. Covering—Num. 16:36–40. Its situation—Ex. 30:6; 40:5, 26, 27. Its use—Ex. 30:7–10; Lev. 4:7, 18. Blood of sin-offering put on its horns—Lev. 4:7, 18; 8:15; 9:9; 16:18. Things forbidden—Ex. 30:9. Sacred fire only to be used on—Lev. 10:1, 2; 16:12. Atonement thereon—Ex. 30:10; Lev. 16:18, 19. Anointed—Ex. 30:26–29; 40:10; Lev. 8:10, 11.

Atonement for the altar.—Ex. 29:36, 37.

Altars in Solomon's temple.—Of burnt offerings, made of bronze, and large—I Ki. 8:64; II Ki. 16:14; II Chr. 4:1. Asa renewed it, after neglect—II Chr. 15:3–8. Ahaz had it removed and another built—II Ki. 16:14–16. Cleansed by order of Hezekiah—II Chr. 29:18; 33:16. Repaired by Manasseh—II Chr. 33:16. Nothing polluted or defective to be offered on it—Lev. 22:21–22; Mal. 1:7–8.

Altar of incense.—I Chr. 28:18; II Chr. 4:19; I Ki. 7:48; 9:25; Is. 6:6.

Altar of second temple.—Ezra 3:2–6. Placed on spot as Solomon's (Josephus, *Ant.* ii:4, Sect. 1). Constructed of unhewn stones (I Macc. 4:47). Desecrated by Antiochus Epiphanes (I Macc. i:54).

Altar erected by Herod.—Size, 50 cubits broad and long; 15 high (Josephus 5, Sect. 6).

Visions of Ezekiel.—Ez. 8:16; 41:22; 43: 13–27.

New Testament references.—Mt. 5:23; 23:18, 35; Lu. 11:51; Acts 17:23; Rom. 11:3; I Cor. 9:13; 10:18; Heb. 7:13; 13:10; Rev. 6:9; 8:3; 9:13. See OFFER- INGS, SACRIFICE, TABERNACLE, TEMPLE.

ALWAYS. Abounding—I Cor. 15:58. Angels behold face of God—Mt. 18:10. Bearing about in body—II Cor. 4:10. See Phil. 1:20. Chide—Ps. 103:9. Con- science void of offence—Acts 24:16. Courage, Of good—II Cor. 5:6. Do al- ways things pleasing to Father—John 8:29. Fear Jehovah—Deut. 6:24; 14: 23. Father hearest me always—John 11:42. I am with you—Mt. 28:20. Lamp of tabernacle to burn—Ex. 27: 20. Leadeth us in triumph—II Cor. 2:14. Live—Job 7:16; Ps. 49:9. See LIFE, ETERNAL. Lord always before me —Ps. 16:8; Acts 2:25. See PRAYER.

Obey—Phil. 2:12. See John 8:29. See OBEDIENCE. Peace—II Thess. 3:16 (A.V.). Poor we have with us—Ps. 9:18; Mt. 26:11; Mk. 14:7; John 12:8. See POOR. Praying—Job 27:10; Lu. 18:1; 21:36; Acts 10:2; Rom. 1:9; I Cor. 1:4; Eph. 5:20; 6:18; Phil. 1:4; Col. 1:3; 4:12; I Thess. 1:2; II Thess. 1:3, 11; Philemon 4. See PRAYER. Ready to give an answer—I Pet. 3:15. Rejoicing—Pr. 8:30; II Cor.6:10; Phil. 4:4. See JOY. Remembrance, In—I Thess. 3:6; II Peter 1:12, 15. Resist the Holy Spirit—Acts 7:51. See HOLY SPIRIT, SIN AGAINST. Watch—Lu. 21: 36. Wroth—Is. 57:16. See ANGER. Zealously sought—Gal. 4:18 (A.V.). See CONTINUALLY, FOREVER, SEASONS AT ALL, TIMES AT ALL.

AMAD, ā'mad. **A town in Asher.**—Josh. 19:26.

AMAL, ā'mal. **A son of Helen, a de- scendant of Asher.**—I Chr. 7:35.

AMALEK, ăm'a-lek. **A grandson of Esau.**—Gen. 36:12, 16; I Cor. 1:36.

AMALEKITES, ăm'a-lek-ītes. Name of a people, supposed to have descended from Amalek. They dwelt South of Canaan in the desert region—Ps. 83:7.
Home of.—Gen. 14:5–7; Num. 13:29; 14: 25, 43; Deut. 2:11, 12.
First of the nations.—Num. 24:20.
Judgment against.—Ex. 17:14–16; Num. 24:20; Deut. 26:19.

Wars of.—Fight at Rephidim—Ex. 17: 8–13; Deut. 25:17–19. Invade Canaan —Ju. 3:13; 5:14; 6:3–33; 10:12. King Agag taken by Saul—I Sam. 14:48; 15:1–32; 28:18. Smitten by David—I Sam. 27:9; 30:13–20; II Sam. 1:1–16; 8:12; I Chr. 18:11. Remnant destroyed —I Chr. 4:43.

AMAM, ā-măm. **A city in Southern Judah (?).**—Josh. 15:26.

AMANA, ăm'a-na. **A ridge of moun- tains**—So. of Sol. 4:8.

AMARIAH, ăm'a-rī'ah. (1) **Grandfather of Zadok, David's high-priest.**—I Chr. 6:7, 52; Ezra 7:3.

(2) **A son of Azariah, a high-priest in Jerusalem.**—I Chr. 6:11.

(3) **A high-priest in time of Jehosha- phat, probably same as (2).**—I Chr. 19:11.

(4) **A Levite, descendant of Kohath.**—I Chr. 23:19; 24:23.

(5) **A Levite in time of Hezekiah, who assisted Kore the porter at the east gate of the temple to distribute the freewill offerings.**—II Chr. 31:15.

(6) **A member of the family of Bani who married a foreign woman during the exile.**—Ezra 10:42.

(7) **A priest, who with Nehemiah, sealed the covenant.**—Neh. 10:3; 12:2, 13.

(8) **A descendant of Perez, who dwelt in Jerusalem**—after the exile—Neh. 11:4.

(9) **An ancestor of Zephaniah.**—Zeph. 1:1.

AMASA, ăm'a-sa. Son of Jether—II Sam. 17:25; I Ki. 2:5; 2:32; I Chr. 2:17. Set over host—II Sam. 17:25. David's message to—II Sam. 19:13. Called men of Judah together—II Sam. 20:4, 5. Slain by Joab—II Sam. 20:8, 9, 10, 12; I Ki. 2:5, 32.

AMASAI, a-măs'a-ī. (1) **A Levite, son of Elkanah, a descendant of Kohath.** —I Chr. 6:25, 35; II Chr. 29:12.

(2) **A chief captain of David's.**—I Chr. 12:18.

(3) **A priest who blew a trumpet before the ark as it came to the house of Obed-Edom.**—I Chr. 15:24.

AMASHSAI, ă-măsh'să-ī. **A priest de- scended from Immer, who dwelt in Jerusalem.**—Neh. 11:13.

AMASIAH, ăm-a-sī′ah. **Son of Zichri, a captain in time of Jehoshaphat.**—II Chr. 17:16.

AMAZE. Job 32:15; Is. 13:8 (A.V.). Benjamin, Men of—Ju. 20:41 (A.V.). Disciples—Mt. 19:25 (A.V.); Mk. 6:51; 10:32; 16:5, 6; Lu. 4:36. Dukes of Edom—Ex. 15:15. Jesus—Mk. 14:33. Multitude—Ez. 32:10; Mt. 12:23; Mk. 1:27; 2:12; 5:42; 9:15; Lu. 2:47, 48; 9:43; Acts 2:7, 12; 9:21. Samaritans —Acts 8:9. See ASTONISH, DISMAY, MARVEL, WONDER.

AMAZEMENT. Mk. 5:42; Lu. 4:36; 5:26; Acts 3:10; I Pet. 3:6 (A.V.).

AMAZIAH, ăm′a-zī′ah. (1) **Son of Joash.**—II Ki. 12:21; 14:1; I Chr. 3:12; II Chr. 24:27. King of Judah—II Ki. 13:12; 14:1, 23. Slays his father's murderers—II Ki. 14:5, 6; II Chr. 25:3, 4. Conquers Edom—II Ki. 14:7; II Chr. 25:5–12. Defeated by Jehoash —II Ki. 14:8–17; II Chr. 25:17–26. Rebuked by prophet for idolatry—II Chr. 25:14–16. Conspiracy against—II Ki. 14:18, 21. Assassinated in Jerusalem—II Ki. 14:8–20; II Chr. 25:27, 28. His son made king—II Ki. 14:21; 15:1–3.

(2) **A descendant of Simeon.**—I Chr. 4:34. (3) **A Levite descended from Merari.**—I Chr. 6:45. (4) **A priest of Beth-el who sought to prevent Amos from prophesying by accusing him of conspiracy.**—Amos 7:10–14.

AMBASSADOR. Sent by Moses to Edom—Num. 20:14; Ju. 11:17. To Amorites—Ju. 21:21. To Heshbon—Deut. 2:26; Ju. 11:19. By Jephthah to Ammon—Ju. 11:12, 14. By Israel to Moab—Ju. 11:17. By Balak to Balaam —Num. 22:5. By Abner to David—II Sam. 3:12. By David to Ishbosheth—II Sam. 3:14. By Syria to Samaria—I Ki. 20:2, 5, 9. By Judah to Israel—II Ki. 14:8–10. By Judah to Assyria —II Ki. 16:7. By Israel to Egypt—II Ki. 17:4. By Rabshakah to Hezekiah—II Ki. 19:9, 14, 23; Is. 37:9. By Hiram to David—I Chr. 14:1. By David to Ammon—I Chr. 19:2. By Egypt to Israel—II Chr. 35:21. Ambassadors of Edom, Moab, Ammon, Tyre and Sidon in Jerusalem—Jer. 27:3, 4.

Sending of.—From the Gibeonites—Josh. 9:4. Of Babylon to Hezekiah—II Chr. 32:31. By Neco—II Chr. 35:21. Into Egypt—Ez. 17:15. From Egypt—Is. 30:4. From Ethiopia—Is. 18:2.

Kinds of.—Faithful—Pr. 13:17. Of peace—Is. 33:7.

Perilous to entertain.—II Ki. 20:12–18. To maltreat—II Sam. 10:2–14. To reject—II Chr. 35:20–24.

Fictitious.—Ehud—Ju. 3:20, 21.

Custom alluded to.—Lu. 14:32; 19:14.

Spiritual.—**Moses to Pharaoh.**—Ex. 3:10. Isaiah prepared—Is. 6:6, 8; Mal. 2:7 (Heb.). The apostles ministers, "ambassadors" for Christ—II Cor. 5:20; Eph. 6:20.

Figurative.—Jehovah sends an ambassador to the nations—Jer. 49:14; Ob. 1. Cf. Ju. 2:1. See RECONCILIATION, SALVATION.

AMBER. Ez. 1:4, 27 (A.V.); 8:2 (A.V.). See METALS.

AMBITION. Examples.—Absalom—II Sam. chs. 15-18. Adam and Eve—Gen. 3:4–6. Adonijah—I Ki. 1:1–53. Apostles—Mk. 9:33–35; Lu. 22:24–27. Babel—Gen. 11:1–9. Babylon—Is. 14:2–23; Jer. 51:53–58. Balaam—Num. 22:16–34. Belshazzar—Dan. 5:1–31. James and John, Mother of—Mt. 20:20–28. Korah, Dathan and Abiram—Num. 16:1–35. Miriam—Num. 12:1–15. Nebuchadrezzar—Dan. 5:20, 21. Pharaoh—Ez. 31:1–18. Sennacherib—II Ki. 19:20–37.

Condemned.—Job 20:5–11; Ps. 9:11–20; Pr. 11:2; 16:18; 17:19; 29:23; Is. 5:8–14; 14:12–23; Ez. 31:1–18; Da. 4:37; Mt. 18:1–4; 20:23–27; 23:10–12; Mk. 9:35; Lu. 22:26, 27; John 13:12–17; Rom. 12:16; II Thess. 2:3–8; I Pet. 5:5; III John 9, 10. See HUMILITY, PRIDE, SELF-DENIAL.

AMBUSH. Means of strategy in warfare.—Josh. 8:2–21; II Chr. 13:13; 20:22; Jer. 51:12. See LYING IN WAIT.

AMEN. Num. 5:22; Deut. 27:15, 26; Ps. 41:13; I Cor. 14:16; II Cor. 1:20; Rev. 1:6, 7; 3:14; 19:4.

AMEND. John 4:52. Your ways—Jer. 7:3.

AMENDS. Lev. 5:16. See RESTITUTION.

AMETHYST. A precious stone.—Ex. 28:19; 39:12; Rev. 21:20.

AMI, ā'mī. A servant of Solomon.—Ezra 2:57.

AMIABLE. Ps. 84:1.

AMISS. Lev. 5:16; Dan. 3:29; Lu. 23:41; Acts 28:6; Jas. 4:3. See ERROR, FAULT, PERVERSITY, SIN.

AMITTAI, a-mĭt'tāi. Father of Jonah the prophet.—II Ki. 14:25; Jonah 1:1.

AMMAH, ăm'mah. A hill east of Geah in wilderness of Gibeon where Abner was slain by Joab, captain of David's army.—II Sam. 2:24.

AMMI, ăm'mi. "My people." Symbolic name of Hosea's third child and used concerning Israel restored to divine favor.—Hos. 2:1.

AMMIEL, ăm'mi-el. (1) One of the spies sent into Canaan by Moses.—Num. 13:12. (2) Father of Machir, a member of the tribe of Manasseh in time of David.—II Sam. 9:4, 5; 17:27. (3) Father of Bathshua (Bathsheba, II Sam. 11:3; I Chr. 3:5). (4) A Levite, son of Abed-edom, a doorkeeper in the house of Jehovah.—I Chr. 26:5.

AMMIHUD, am-mī'hud. (1) Father of Elishama, prince of Ephraim.—Num. 1:10; 2:18; 7:48, 53; 10:22; I Chr. 7:26. (2) A descendant of Simeon.—Num. 34:20. (3) A member of the tribe of Naphtali.—Num. 34:28. (4) See AMMIHUR. (5) Son of Amri, descendant of Perez.—I Chr. 9:4.

AMMIHUR, ăm-mī'hŭr. Father of Talmai, King of Geshur to whom Absalom fled.—II Sam. 13:37.

AMMINADAB, am-mĭn'a-dăb. (1) Aaron's father-in-law.—Ex. 6:23. (2) A prince of Judah (possibly same as (1))—Num. 1:7; 2:3; 7:12, 17; 10:14; Ruth 4:19, 20; I Chr. 2:10; Mt. 1:4; Lu. 3:33. (3) Descendant of Kohath.—I Chr. 6:22. (4) A Levite who assisted in bringing the ark from the house of Obed-edom.—I Chr. 15:10, 11.

AMMINADIB, am-mĭn'a-dĭb. So. of Sol. 6:12 (A.V.).

AMMISHADDAI, am-mĭ-shăd'a-ī. Father of Ahiezer, prince of Dan.—Num. 1:12; 2:25; 7:66, 71; 10:25.

AMMIZABAD, am-mĭz'a-băd'. Son of Benaiah.—I Chr. 27:6.

AMMONITES, am-mon-ites. Descendants of Ben-ammi, son of Lot and his younger daughter. A people dwelling in the territory between the tribe of Gad and the Arabian desert.—Gen. 19:38. Called *Ammonites*—I Chr. 11:39; II Chr. 26:8; Neh. 2:10, 19; 4:3, 7. Called *Children of Ammon*—Gen. 19:38; Num. 21:24; Deut. 2:19, 20; 3:11, 16; Josh. 12:2; 13:10; Jer. 40:11.

Abomination of.—I Ki. 11:5; II Ki. 23:13; Ezra 9:1.

Idolaters.—Ju. 10:6; I Ki. 11:5, 7, 33; II Ki. 23:13.

Laws concerning.—Not to enter congregation of Israel.—Deut. 23:3; Neh. 13:1–3.

Possessions to remain inviolate.—Deut. 2:19, 37. See Josh. 13:25.

Women married to Jews.—I Ki. 11:1; Neh. 13:23. Naomah, wife of Solomon, mother of Rehoboam—I Ki. 14:21, 31; II Chr. 12:13. Shimeath—II Chr. 24:26.

Strifes of.—Ps. 83:7. Help Eglon, king of Moab to overthrow Israel—Ju. 3:13. Oppress Israel—Ju. 10:6–18. Jepthah conquers—Ju. 11:1–33; 12:1–3. Smitten by Saul—I Sam. 11:1–11; 14:47. David's servants abused—II Sam. 10:1–14, 19; I Chr. 19:4–15, 19. Destroyed by David—II Sam. 11:1; 12:26–31; See II Sam. 20:1–3. Royal city taken by Joab—II Sam. 12:26; I Chr. 20:1–3. Sent against Jehoiakim—II Ki. 24:1–4. Battle against Jehoshaphat—II Chr. 20:1–25. Fought with Jotham—II Chr. 27:5. Spoils dedicated unto Jehovah—II Sam. 8:12; I Chr. 18:11.

Prophecies concerning.—Is. 11:14; Jer. 9:26; 25:21; 27:2–11; 49:1, 2, 6; Ez. 21:20, 28; 25:1–10; Dan. 11:41; Amos 1:13; Zeph. 2:8, 9.

AMNON, ăm'non. (1) Eldest son of David and Ahinoam.—II Sam. 3:2; I Chr. 3:1. Abuses Tamar, his sister—II Sam. 13:1–19. Absalom avenges Tamar—II Sam. 13:20–32. David mourns Amnon—II Sam. 13:31–38.

(2) **Son of Shimon, a descendant of Judah.**—I Chr. 4:20.

AMOK, ā′mŏk. **A priest who went with Zerubbabel.**—Neh. 12:7, 20.

AMON, ā′mŏn. (1) King of Judah, father of Josiah and son of Manasseh—II Ki. 21:18–25; I Chr. 3:14; II Chr. 33:20–25; Jer. 1:2; 25:3; Zeph. 1:1.
(2) **Governor of Samaria in time of Ahab.**—I Ki. 22:26; II Chr. 18:25.
(3) **A servant of Solomon, ancestor of some of those who returned from Babylon.**—Neh. 7:59. (4) Son of Manasseh, ancestor of Jesus—Mt. 1:10.

AMORITES, ăm′o-rītes. Highlanders—Num. 13:29. Sons of Canaan—Gen. 10:15; I Chr. 1:14; Ez. 16:3, 45. Were giants—Amos 2:9. Were confederates with Abraham—Gen. Chap. 14. Boundaries of their land—Deut. 3:8–10; 4: 47–49; Ju. 11:22.

Land of the Amorite.—Gen. 14:7, 13; 15:21; Ex. 3:8, 17; 13:5; 23:23; Num. 13:29; 21:13, 31. Hill country of—Deut. 1:7, 19, 20, 44; Josh. 7:7; 12:8; 13:4; 24:8, 11, 15, 18; Ju. 1:36; Neh. 9:8.

Kings of.—Num. 21:21, 29, 34; 32:33; Deut. 1:4; 2:24; 3:2; 3:8, 9; 4:46, 47; 31:4; Josh. 2:10; 5:1; 9:1; 10:5, 6, 12; 11:3; 12:2; 24:12; Ju. 11:19; I Ki. 4: 19; Ps. 135:11; 136:19.

Jehovah uses them to punish Israel.—Deut. 1:44, 46. They refuse Israel passage through their land—Num. 21:21–23. Israel subdues them and takes possession—Num. 21:24–31; Deut. 2: 32–37; 31:4; Ju. 11:19–21. Joshua slays five of their kings—Josh. 10: 5–11. Amorites crowd back children of Dan, but are finally subdued—Ju. 1:34–36.

Miscellaneous.—Called Mount Hermon-Senir—Deut. 3:9. Were idolatrous—Ju. 6:10; 11:23, 24; I Ki. 21:26. Were wicked—Gen. 15:16; Ex. 23:23, 24; II Ki. 21:11; Ezra 9:1. Intermarry with God's people—Ezra 9:1, 2; 10: 18–44. Cities of—Num. 21:25; Josh. 13:10, 21. Delivered us into the hands of—Deut. 1:27. Portion out of the hand of—Gen. 48:22; Deut. 7:1; Josh. 3:10. Balak saw what Israel had done to—Num. 22:2. Israel shall destroy—Deut. 20:17; Ju. 11:21. Israel dwelt

among—Ju. 3:5; 6:10. Oppression of Israelites dwelling in land of Amorites by the Ammonites—Ju. 10:8. Israel possessed all the land of—Ju. 11:21, 22, 23; Amos 2:9, 10. Peace between Israel and the Amorites—I Sam. 7:14. Amorites dwelt in Heres—Ju. 1:35. Did I not save you from Amorites?—Ju. 10:11. Remnant of—II. Sam. 21:2; I Ki. 9:20; II Chr. 8:7. Manasseh more wicked than the Amorites—II Ki. 21:11.

AMOS, ā′mos. (1) See OUTLINE STUDIES IN THE BOOKS.
(2) **An ancestor of Joseph.**—Lu. 3:25.

AMOZ, ā-mŏz. **Father of Isaiah.**—II Ki. 19:2, 20; 20:1; II Chr. 26:22; 32: 20, 32; Is. 1:1; 2:1; 13:1; 20:2; 37:2, 21; 38:1.

AMPHIPOLIS, ăm-phĭp′o-lĭs. **A city of Macedonia through which Paul passed.** —Acts 17:1.

AMPLIATUS, ăm′pli-a-tus. **A Christian dwelling in Rome.**—Rom. 16:8.

AMRAM, ăm′răm. **Grandson of Levi and father of Moses, Aaron, and Miriam.**—Ex. 6:18, 20; Num. 3:19; 26: 58, 59; I Chr. 6:2, 3, 18; 23:12, 13; 24:20.
(2) **A son of Bani who had married a foreign wife.**—Ezra 10:34.

AMRAMITES, ăm′răm-ites. **Descendants of Amram.**—Num. 3:27; I Chr. 26:23.

AMRAPHEL, ăm′ra-phel. **King of Shinar in days of Abraham.**—Gen. 14: 1, 9.

AMULETS. Is. 3:20. See JEWELS.

AMUSEMENTS. Transitory.—Job 21: 11–13; Pr. 14:13; Eccl. 2:1–11; Is. 47:8.

Form a part of idolatrous worship.—Ex. 32:4–6, 19; Ju. 16:23–27; I Cor. 10: 1–7.

Lead to poverty.—Pr. 21:17.

Choke the Word of God.—Job 1:5; 21: 11–15; Is. 5:12, 13; Amos 6:1–6; Lu. 8:14; II Tim. 3:4.

Warnings against.—Eccl. 7:2–4; 11:9; Is. 5:11, 12; I Tim. 5:6; James 5:1–5; I Pet. 4:3–5; II Pet. 2:13–22.

Moses' wise choice.—Heb. 11:25. See CONFORMATION AND TRANSFORMATION, DANCING, LUST, PLEASURE, WORLDLINESS.

AMZI, ăm'zi. (1) A descendant of Merari and ancestor of Ethan.—I Chr. 6:46.

(2) An ancestor of Adaiah, a priest who dwelt in Jerusalem.—Neh. 11:12.

ANAB, ā'nab. A city in southern part of Canaan where the Anakim dwelt.—Josh. 11:21; 15:50.

ANAH, ā'nah. (1) A child of Zibeon.—Gen. 36:2, 14, 18, 25.

(2) Son of Seir the Horite.—Gen. 36:20, 29; I Chr. 1:38.

(3) Son of Zibeon and grandson of Seir the Horite.—Gen. 36:24; I Chr. 1:40, 41.

ANAHARATH, ăn'a-hā'rath. A city of Issachar.—Josh. 19:19.

ANAIAH, an-a-ī'ah. (1) One who stood beside Nehemiah when he read the law.—Neh. 8:4. (2) One of those who assisted Nehemiah in sealing the covenant.—Neh. 10:22.

ANAK, ā'nak. Son of Arba and ancestor of the giants of ''Anakim.''—Num. 13:22, 28, 33; Deut. 9:2; Josh. 15:13, 14; 21:11; Ju. 1:20.

ANAKIM, ăn'a-kĭm. Descendants of Anak, who were giants.—Deut. 1:28; 2:10, 11, 21; 9:2; Josh.11:21; 14:12, 15. See GIANTS.

ANAMIM, ăn'a-mĭm. Gen. 10:13; I Chr. 1:11.

ANAMMELECH, a-năm'me-lĕk. An idol worshiped by the Sepharvites. Worship of this idol was introduced among the Israelites by Shalmaneser.—II Ki. 17:31.

ANAN, ā'nan. One of those who assisted Nehemiah in sealing the covenant.—Neh. 10:26.

ANANI, ā-nā'nī. Son of Elioenai.—I Chr. 3:24.

ANANIAH, ăn'a-nī'ah. (1) Father of Maaseiah and grandfather of Azariah.—Neh. 3:23.

(2) A town in Benjamin.—Neh. 11:32.

ANANIAS, ăn-a-nī'as. (1) Husband of Sapphira, an early Christian who attempted to deceive Peter concerning the amount of his gift.—Acts 5:1–11.

(2) A disciple, living in Damascus, who baptized Paul.—Acts 5:10–18; 22:12–16.

(3) A high-priest in Jerusalem before whom Paul was brought.—Acts 23:2; 24:1.

ANATH, ā'nath. Father of Shamgar, a judge of Israel.—Ju. 3:31; 5:6.

ANATHEMA. A curse.—Rom. 9:3; I Cor. 12:3; Gal. 1:8, 9. See CURSES.

ANATHOTH, ăn'a-thŏth. (1) A Levitical city in Benjamin, home of Jeremiah.—Josh. 21:18; I Ki. 2:26; 1 Chr. 6:60; Ezra 2:23; Neh. 7:27; 11:32; Is. 10:30; Jer. 1:1; 11:21, 23; 29:27; 32:7–9.

(2) Son of Becher, a Benjamite.—I Chr. 7:8.

(3) One who assisted Nehemiah in sealing the covenant.—Neh. 10:19.

ANATHOTHITE. II Sam. 23:27; I Chr. 11:28; 12:3.

ANCHOR. Acts 27:29, 30, 40. Of the soul—Heb. 6:19.

ANCIENT. Landmark—Pr. 22:28. Paths—Jer. 18:15. See AGE, OLD, ELDERS OF ISRAEL.

ANCIENT OF DAYS. Dan. 7:9, 13, 22.

ANDREW, ăn'drew. See LIVES OF THE TWELVE APOSTLES.—Andrew—A fisherman of Bethsaida, and son of John—John 1:42. He was one of the first two who found the Messiah (John 1:41) and had been formerly a disciple of John the Baptist—John 1:35. He made for himself a good name by bringing his brother Simon; and was apparently broader in his feeling toward the Gentiles—John 12:2. But it is not clear that Andrew and Philip knew what to do with the problem of the Greeks.

ANDRONICUS, ăn-dro-nī'cus. A relative of Paul's at Rome.—Rom. 16:7.

ANEM, ā'nem. A city of Issachar.—I Chr. 6:73.

ANER, ā'ner. (1) A brother of Mamre, an ally of Abraham.—Gen. 14:13, 24.

(2) A city in Manasseh.—I Chr. 6:70.

ANGELS.—Heb. *Mal-akh.* Gr. *Angelos,* ''Messenger.''

Titles.—God's—Ps. 97:7; John 10:34. Holy ones—Deut. 33:2; Ps. 89:5; Dan. 4:13, 23; 8:13. Hosts—Ps. 103:21. Hosts of heaven—I Ki. 22:19. Men—Gen. 18:2, 16, 22; 19:5; 12:16; Mk. 16:5; Lu. 24:4; Acts 1:10. Ministers—Ps. 103:21; Heb. 1:7, 14. Principalities and powers—Eph. 3:10; Col. 1:16.

Winds—Ps. 104:4; Heb. 1:7. **Sons of God**—Gen. 6:2; Job 1:6; 2:1; 38:7. Sons of the mighty—Ps. 29:1; 89:6. Watches—Dan. 4:13, 17, 23.

Functions.—Adoration—Ps.103:20; 148: 2; Heb. 1:6; Rev. 5:11; 7:11. Execute God's will—Gen. 19:1–17; Num. 22: 31 (see below); Ju. 6:11–18; II Sam. 24:16. To fulfil God's word—Ps. 103: 20; Heb. 2:2.

Superior beings.—Angel of Jehovah—Gen. 22:11, 15; 31:11–13; Ex. 3:2; 14: 19; 23:23; 32:34; Num. 22:22; Ju. 6: 11; II Sam. 24:16, 17; II Ki. 1:3; Is. 63:9; Zech. 1:9–17. Angel of covenant—Dan. 11:22; Mal. 3:1 (marg.).

Distinction between Jehovah and angel not clear.—Gen. 16:7–13; 22:11, 15; Ex. 3:2–6; 23:20, 21; Ju. 6:11–24.

Limitations of other angels.—Charged with folly—Job 4:18. Lack knowledge—Mt. 24:36. Judged by men—I Cor. 6:3. Must not be worshipped—Col. 2:18; Rev. 19:10; 22:8, 9. Salvation of men unrevealed—I Pet. 1:12. Unmarried—Mt. 22:30. Subject to fall—II Pet. 2:4; Jude 6. Unredeemed—Heb. 2:16. The host of heaven—Ps. 68:17; Mt. 26:53; Lu. 2:13; Heb. 12: 22; I Pet. 3:22.

Visions of Angels.—By Jacob—Gen. 28: 12. At the birth of Jesus—Mt. 1:20; Lu. 1:26, 31; 2:8–15. At the restoration of Judah—Zech. Chaps. 1–6. Glory of Jesus—John 1:51. Resurrection of Jesus—Mt. 28:5; John 20:12; I Tim. 3:16. Adoration of Jesus—Phil. 2:10; Heb. 1:6; Rev. 5:8–14. Sealing of saints—Rev. 7:1–17. Consummation of worldly things—Rev. Chs. 8–10. Angels of wrath—Rev. Chaps. 14–18. Deliverance of saints—Rev. 19:20. Destruction of sin, death, and Hades—Rev. Chap. 20. Vision of Holy City—Rev. 21:9–27; 22:1–9.

Angels as witnesses.—Lu. 12:8, 9; I Cor. 4:9; I Tim. 3:16; 5:21; Heb. 12:22; Rev. 3:5.

Comparison with angels.—I Sam. 29:9; II Sam. 14:17, 20; Acts 6:15; Gal. 4: 14; Heb. 1:13, 14; 2:2, 3, 9; II Pet. 2:11.

Deception concerning angels.—I Ki. 13: 18; II Cor. 11:13–15; Gal. 1:8.

Testers of righteousness.—Abraham—

Gen. 22:11. Jacob—Gen. 32:24–30; Hos. 12:4. Jesus—Mt. 4:5–7.

Announcers of births.—Ishmael—Gen. 16:11. Isaac—Gen. 18:9–16. Samson—Ju. 13:3–5. John the Baptist—Lu. 1:11–13. Jesus—Mt. 1:20–21; Lu. 1: 30–33.

Attendants on Jesus.—To shepherds—Lu. 2:9–15. To Joseph—Mt. 2:13, 19. At temptation—Mt. 4:11; Mk. 1:13. In Gethsemane—Lu. 22:43. At sepulchre—Mt. 28:2–5; Mk. 16:5; Lu. 24: 23; John 20:12. At ascension—Acts 1:10, 11. As watchers—John 1:51.

Attendants on apostles, evangelists, etc. —To Peter and John—Acts 5:19. Philip—Acts 8:26. Cornelius—Acts 10:3, 7. Peter—Acts 12:7–11. Paul—Acts 27:23. John in Patmos. See VISIONS.

Messengers: Of deliverance — From Egypt—Num. 20:16. Midianites—Ju. 6:11–24. Assyrians—II Ki. 19:35; II Chr. 32:21; Is. 37:36, 37. Nebuchadrezzar—Dan. 3:28. Darius—Dan. 6:22. Herod—Mt. 2:13, 19. Jews—Acts 5: 19; 12:7–11.

Of joy.—To shepherds—Lu. 2:9, 10. Over returning ones—Lu. 15:7, 10.

Of judgment.—On Sodom—Gen. 19:15, 24. Israel—Ju. 2:1–5; II Sam. 24:16, 17; I Chr. 21:12–18. Meroz—Ju. 5:23. Assyrians—II Ki. 19:35; II Chr. 32: 21; Is. 37:36, 37. World—Mt. 13:39–41; 16:27; 24:31; Mk. 13:27; II Thess. 1:7, 8; Rev. 8:2–11; 14:8–15; 15:1; 16:3–17. Babylon—Rev. 17:1; 18:1–3, 21. Satan—Rev. 20:1–3.

Of mercy.—Elijah—I Ki. 19:5–7. Israel—Is. 63:9. Daniel—Dan. 9:20–23. Bethesda—John 5:3 (marg.).

Of protection.—Tree of life—Gen. 3:24. Hagar—Gen. 21:17–19. Isaac—Gen. 22:11, 12. Camp of Israel—Ex. 14:19, 20. Jesus—Ps. 91:11, 12; Mt. 4:6. Little ones—Mt. 18:10. Saints—Ps. 34:7. Lazarus—Lu. 16:22. To the prophets—I Ki. 1:15; Dan. 4:13–17; 8:15–17; 9:21–23; 10:5, 6; Zech. 1:9–17; Acts 8:26.

Of truth.—Ps. 103:20; Acts 7:53; Gal. 3:19; Heb. 1:13, 14; 2:2; Rev. 22:6.

Of warning.—To Lot—Gen. 19:12, 13, 15, 17. Balaam — Num. 22:22, 31, 35. Ahaziah—II Ki. 1:3, 4. Cornelius—Acts 10:22; 11:13. The churches—

Rev. Chs. 1–3. The world—Rev. 10: 5, 6. See MESSENGERS.

ANGER. God provoked to anger—I Ki. 21:22; Ezra 5:12; Neh. 4:5; Hos. 12: 14; Zech. 8:14. Because of idolatry— Deut. 9:7, 8, 18; 31:16, 17; 32:21; Ju. 2:12–15; I Ki. 14:9, 15; 16:2–4, 7, 13, 26, 33; II Ki. 17:9–18; 21:1–15; 22: 16, 17; 23:19, 26, 27; II Chron. 28:25; 33:1–11; 34:24, 25; Ps. 78:58; 106:28, 29; Is. 65:2–7; Jer. 7:18–20; 8:19; 11:17; 25:7–11; 32:26–35; 44:3, 7–30; Ez. 7:8.

His anger invoked.—Ps. 56:7; 59:13; 69: 24; 79:6, 7; 138:7; Jer. 18:23. Prophesied—Deut. 4:25, 26; 11:17; 13:17, 18; 29:18–28; 31:16, 17, 29; Josh. 23:16; 9:20.

Results of God's anger.—Num. 11:1; 12:9; 25:5, 9; 32:10–15; Deut. 32:22; Ju. 2:14, 20, 21; 3:8; 10:7; II Sam. 6:7; II Ki. 13:3; Job. 9:5; 21:17; Is. 42:24, 25; Ez. 16:26, 27.

Anger turned aside.—Prayer for: Judah to Joseph—Gen. 44:18. Aaron to Moses —Ex. 32:22. To God: By Moses—Ex. 32:12. Gideon—Ju. 6:39. Solomon—I Ki. 8:46; Ezra 9:14; Ps. 74:1; 80:4; 85:4, 5; 89:46, 47. Turned: Joseph— Gen. 45:4, 5, 7, 8. Gods—Ex. 32:14; Nah. 25:10; Josh. 7:26; Ezra 10:14; II Chr. 12:7, 12; Ps. 85:3; 106:23; Is. 12:1; Ez. 16:42; Hos. 14:4; Jonah 3:9, 10.

The wrath of the Lamb.—Ps. 2:5, 9, 12; Is. 63:3, 6; Mk. 3:5; Lu. 14:21; Rev. 6:16, 17.

Justifiable.—Jacob—Gen. 30:2; 31:36. Sons of Jacob—Gen. 34:7. Moses—Ex. 11:8; 32:19; Lev. 10:16; Num. 16:15. Ephraim—Ju. 8:3. Samson—Ju. 14: 19. Saul—I Sam. 11:6. Jonathan—I Sam. 20:34. David—II Sam. 12:5. Nehemiah—Neh. 5:6; 13:17, 25. Ahasuerus—Esth. 7:7, 10; Job. 18:4. Elihu— Job 32:2, 3, 5. Jeremiah—Jer. 15:17. Jesus—Mk. 3:5. Paul—Acts 17:16; 23:3. Corinthians—II Cor. 7:11.

Wicked anger.—Cain—Gen. 4:5, 6, 8. Esau—Gen. 27:41, 45. Potiphar—Gen. 39:19. Jacob's sons—Gen. 49:5–7. Moses—Num. 20:10, 11. Balaam—Num. 22:27. Balak—Num. 24:10. Zebul— Ju. 9:30. Eliab—I Sam. 17:28. Saul— I Sam. 20:30. Nabal—I Sam. 25:17. Army—II Chr. 25:10. Sanballat—

Neh. 4:1. King—Esth. 1:12; 2:1. Haman—Esth. 3:5; 5:9. Nebuchadrezzar —Dan. 2:12; Jonah 4:1, 4, 9. Ten Apostles—Mt. 20:24. Judas—Mk. 14: 4; John 12:4, 5. Nazarenes—Lu. 4:28. Ruler—Lu. 13:14. Elder brother— Lu. 15:28. Jews—John 7:27. Sadducees—Acts 5:17. Mob—Acts 7:54; 21: 35, 36. The Devil—Rev. 12:12, 17.

Laws against.—Provoking God to anger Deut. 6:14, 15; 7:1–4. Being angry— Num. 18:5; Ps. 37:8; Mt. 5:22; Rom. 12:19; Gal. 5:19; Eph. 4:26, 31; 6:4; Col. 3:8; Titus 1:7; Jas. 1:19, 20.

Proverbs concerning.—Pr. 11:4, 23; 14: 35; 15:1, 18; 16:14, 32; 19:19; 21:14, 19; 25:23; 27:4; Eccl. 7:9. See HATRED, MURDERER, WEALTH.

ANGLE. Cast angle.—Is. 19:8; Hab. 1:15. See FISH.

ANGUISH. Of spirit—Gen. 42:21; Ex. 6:9; Job 7:11; Rom. 2:9; II Cor. 2:4. Of Heshbon—Deut. 2:25. Of Saul—II Sam. 1:9. Of David—Ps. 119:143. Of king of Babylon—Jer. 50:43. Of woman—John 16:21. Of wicked—Job 15:24; Rom. 2:9. Result of fear—Pr. 1:27.

Figurative.—Is. 8:22; 30:6.

Illustrative.—Jer. 4:31; 6:24; 49:24; 50:43.

See DISTRESS, SORROW, SUFFERING.

ANIAM, a-ni'am. Son of Shemidah, a member of tribe of Manasseh.—I Chr. 7:19.

ANIM, ā'nim. A town of Judah.—Josh. 15:50.

ANIMALS: Creation of.—Gen. 1:20–25; 2:19; Jer. 27:5.

Man's dominion over.—Gen. 1:26, 28; 9: 2; Ps. 8:6–8; 49:14.

Man names them.—Gen. 2:19, 20.

Herbs for the food of.—Gen. 1:30.

God resolves to destroy all flesh.—Gen. 6:13, 17; 7:21–23.

Animals preserved in the ark for propagation.—Gen. 6:19, 20; 7:2, 3, 8, 9, 14– 16. Preserved for food.—Gen. 7:2, 3.

Blood not to be eaten.—Gen. 9:4; Lev. 7:26–27; 17:3; Deut. 12:15–25; Acts 15:20, 29. Life in the blood—Gen. 9: 4; Lev. 17:11–14. The penalty—Lev. 7:27; 17:10. Instance of transgression I Sam. 14:32–34.

Fat not to be eaten.—Lev. 3:17; 7:23–25.

Defilement of clean meats.—Lev. 11:39–40; 17:15; 22:8; Deut. 14:21.

Flesh torn of beasts—Ex. 22:31; Lev. 7:24; 17:15, 16; 22:8.

Various kinds of animals—Clean and unclean—Lev. 11:1–47; Deut. 14:4–20; Acts 10:12–15. Ezekiel's vision—1:5–14; 10:13–22. Daniel's vision—Dan. 7:3–24; 8:3–27. John's vision—Rev. 4:7, 8; 13:1–18. Antelope—Deut. 14:5; Is. 51:20. Ape—I Ki. 10:22; II Chr. 9:21. Bats—Lev. 11:18; Is. 2:20. Bear—II Sam. 17:8; Pr. 17:12; 28:15; Hos. 13:8. See BEAR. Cattle—Ex. 9:6, 7; 12:29; Job 42:12; Ps. 144:14. See CATTLE. *Used for sacrifice*—Gen. 8:20; Lev. 1:2–9; 9:2, 4, 8–11, 18–21; 16:3, 6, 11; 22:19; 23:18, 27, 28; Num. 15:24; 19:2–10; 28:27; 29:1–40. See OFFERINGS. Chameleon — Lev. 11:30. Chamois—Deut. 14:5. The coney—Lev. 11:5; Ps. 104:18; Pr. 30:26. Crocodile—Job. 41:1–34. See *marg.* Dogs Ju. 7:5; I Sam. 24:14; I Ki. 21:19; Ps. 59:6; Pr. 26:11; Eccl. 9:4; Is. 56:10, 11; Mt. 7:6; 15:27; Lu. 16:21. See DOG. Dromedary—Jer. 2:23. The fox—Ju. 15:4; Neh. 4:3; Ps. 63:10; Song of Sol. 2:15; Lam. 5:18; Ez. 13:4; Mt. 8:20; Lu. 9:58; 13:32. Gazelle—Deut. 12:15. Goats—Gen. 27:9, 16; 30:32, 33; 37:31; Ex. 12:5; 25:4; 26:7; 35:6, 26; 36:14; Lev. 1:10; 3:12; 4:23, 28; 5:6; 7:23; 9:3; 16:5; 17:3; 22:19, 27; 23:19; etc. See GOAT. OFFERINGS—Gen. 22:2. Hare—Lev. 11:6; Deut. 14:7. The hart—Deut. 12:15; Ps. 42:1; Is. 35:6. Hippopotamus—Job 40:15–24. See *marg.* Jackal—Is. 13:22; 34:13; Jer. 51:37; Lam. 4:3. The lion—Num. 23:24; Ju. 14:5–18; I Sam. 17:34–37; Job 4:10, 11; I Ki. 13:24–28; 20:36; II Ki. 17:25, 26; Ps. 10:9; 17:11, 12; Jer. 12:8; Dan. 6:7–27; Heb. 11:33. See LION. Leopard—Song of Sol. 4:8; Is. 11:6; Jer. 5:6; 13:23; Dan. 7:6; Hos. 13:7; Hab. 1:8; Rev. 13:2. Lizards—Lev. 11:29, 30. Moles—Is. 2:20. Mouse—Lev. 11:29; Is. 66:17. Night-monster—Is. 34:14. Pygarg—Deut. 14:5. Roebuck—Deut. 14:5. Sheep—Gen. 4:2; 12:16; 20:14; 21:27–31; 29:2, 3, 6–10; 30:32–35; 31:19; Ex. 12:5; 22:19, 27; Deut. 14:4; etc. See SHEEP. OFFERINGS—Gen. 22:2. Swine—Lev.

11:7; Deut. 14:8; Is. 65:4; Mt. 8:32; Lu. 15:15. See SWINE. Weasel—Lev. 11:29. The wolf—Is. 11:6; 65:25; Ez. 22:27; Mt. 10:16; John 10:12, 13.

Mercy to animals.—Ex. 23:19; 34:26; Lev. 22:28; Deut. 14:21; 22:4, 6, 7; 25:4; Pr. 12:10; Lu. 14:5; I Cor. 9:9; I Tim. 5:18.

God's care for.—Gen. 9:9, 10; Job 38:41; Ps. 36:6; 104:10–28; 145:15, 16; 147:9; Jonah 4:11; Mt. 6:26; 10:29; Lu. 12:6, 24; I Cor. 9:9.

The serpent under a curse.—Gen. 3:14. Used in the Plagues of Egypt—Ex. Chaps. 8, 9, 10; 11:5.

Man and animals compared.—Ps. 49:12; 104:21–23; Eccl. 3:19–21; 9:12.

Animals used for transportation.—Camels for riding—Gen. 24:61; 31:17, 18; I Sam. 30:17. Camels for burden bearing—Gen. 37:25; Ju. 6:5; 7:12; I Ki. 10:2; I Ki. 8:9. Asses for riding—Ex. 4:20; Num. 22:21; Ju. 10:4; 12:14; II Sam. 19:25, 26; I Ki. 13:23, 27; II Ki. 4:24. *White asses ridden by rulers*—Judges 5:10. *Ass ridden by Jesus*—Mt. 21:2–8. Asses for burdens—I Sam. 25:18; I Chr. 12:40. Horses for riding—Ex. 15:1, 19; Ps. 20:7; Esth. 6:8, 9; Is. 30:16; 31:1–3; Jer. 51:21; Amos 2:15. Horses for driving—II Ki. 9:20.

Kings forbidden to raise horses, lest the children of Israel should return to Egypt.—Deut. 17:16. Solomon's horses—I Ki. 4:26; 10:26–29. Horses as mail carriers—Esth. 8:10.

Hebrew law concerning damage by cattle.—Gen. 9:5; Ex. 21:28–36.

Figures drawn from animals.—Sheep—Ps. 44:11, 22; 74:1; 95:7; 100:3; Is. 53:6, 7; Jer. 12:3; 50:6; Ez. 34:2–22; Mt. 18:12–13; Lu. 15:4–7; John 1:29; 10:1–16; Acts 8:32, 33. Oxen—Deut. 25:4; Ps. 22:12, 13; Jer. 46:20; Amos 4:1; I Cor. 9:9. Wild ass—Jer. 2:23, 24. Horses—Job 39:19–25; Ps. 32:9; Rev. 9:16–19. Dogs—Ps. 59:6; Pr. 26:11; Is. 56:10, 11; II Pet. 2:22; Rev. 22:15. The bear—Pr. 17:12; 28:15; Is. 59:11. Fish—Mt. 4:19; 13:47–48. Birds—I Sam. 26:20; Ps. 124:7; Eccl. 9:12.

Man may learn wisdom from animals.—Job 12:7–8, 35:11; Pr. 6:6–8; 30:29–31.

Pre-natal influence shown.—Gen. 30: 31–41.

Instincts of animals.—Job 24:5; 39:1–30; 40:15–24; Ps. 124:7; Pr. 1:17; 6:5–8; 30:24–28; Is. 1:3; Jer. 2:24; 8:7; Lam. 4:3; Mt. 24:28; Lu. 17:37.

Abodes of animals.—Wild ass in the desert—Job 24:5; 39:5–8; Jer. 2:24. Wild goat in the rocks—I Sam. 24:2; Job 39:1; Ps. 104:18.

Wild beasts.—Job 37:8; Ps. 50:10; 104:20–22, 25; Song of Sol. 4:8; Is. 13:21, 22; 34:14, 15; 56:9; Jer. 50:39; 51:37; Mic. 5:8; Zeph. 2:14, 15; Mk. 1:13.

Services rendered of special sort.—The dove—Gen. 8:8–12. The raven—Gen. 8:7; I Ki. 17:4–6. Animals used in plagues of Egypt.—Ex. Chaps. 8, 9, 10. The goat—Lev. 16:10, 21, 22. The ass —Num. 22:28–30. The fish—Jonah 1: 17; 2:1–10.

Sacrificial animals.—Lev. 8:14–23; 9:2–4, 15–21; 12:6–8. See BEASTS, BIRDS, CREEPING THINGS, CATTLE, FISH, INSECTS (Pr. 30:25), OFFERINGS, REPTILES.

ANISE. Mt. 23:23.

ANKLE: As used in measurement.—To the ankles—Ez. 47:3.

Ornaments of the ankles.—Chains—Num. 31:50; Is. 3:20. Beauty of—Is. 3:18.

Bone of ankle.—Received strength—Acts 3:7.

ANNA, ăn′na. An aged prophetess at the time of the birth of Jesus.—Lu. 2:36.

ANNAS, ăn′nas. A Jewish high-priest before whom Jesus was brought.—Lu. 3:2; John 18:13, 24. Peter and John brought before—Acts 4:6.

ANNUL. Job 40:8; Is. 28:18. See ABOLISH, COVENANT, LAW.

ANOINTING: Antiquity of. — Jacob anoints stone—Gen. 28:18; 35:14.

Anointing of body.—Deut. 28:40; Ruth 3:3; Esth. 2:12; Ps. 92:10; 104:15; 141:5; Pr. 27:9; Eccl. 9:8; Song of Sol. 4:10; Is. 57:9; Amos 6:6; Mic. 6:15.

Anointing of things.—Tabernacle and furniture—Ex. 30:26, 27; 40:9; Lev. 8:10, 11; Num. 7:1. Brazen altar—Ex. 29:36; 40:10. Brazen laver—Ex. 40:11.

Anointing of persons.—Prophets—I Ki.

19:16; I Chr. 16:22; Is. 61:1; Ps. 105:15. Priests, high priests—Ex. 29:7, 29; 40:13; Lev. 4:3; 6:20; 8:12; 16:32; Num. 35:25; Ps. 133:2. Common priests Ex. 28:41; 30:30; 40:15; 8:30; Num. 3:3. Kings: Fable of the trees—Ju. 9:8, 15. Saul—I Sam. 9:16; 10:1; 15:1. David—I Sam. 16:3, 13; II Sam. 2:4; 5:3; 12:7; 19:21; I Chr. 11:3. Solomon—I Ki. 1:39; I Chr. 29:22. Jehu— I Ki. 19:6; II Ki. 9:1–3, 6, 12. Hazael —I Ki. 19:15. Cyrus—Is. 45:1. Guests —Lu. 7:46. Captives—II Chr. 28:15. The sick—Is. 1:6; Mk. 6:13; Lu. 10:34; Jas. 5:14; Rev. 3:18. The dead— Mt. 26:12; Mk. 14:8; 16:1; Lu. 23:56.

Material used.—Compound of spices— Ex. 30:22–25. Prepared by priests only —I Chr. 9:30. Rebuke for abusing—Ez. 23:41. Ointment used on Jesus—Lu. 7:37, 38; John 11:2; 12:3. Oil—Ps. 92:10; Lu. 7:46.

Oil of joy.—Is. 61:3.

Anointing of Holy Spirit.—Of Messiah foretold—Ps. 45:7; Is. 61:1; Dan. 9:24. Fulfilled—Lu. 4:18–21; Acts 4:27; 10:38; Heb. 1:9. Of saints—II Cor. 1:21; I John 2:20, 27. See PRIESTS, TABERNACLE.

ANSWER. Good conscience, Of.—I Pet. 3:21 (A.V.). Soft answer—Pr. 15:1. See DEFENSE, PRAYER, ANSWER TO.

ANSWERABLE. Ez. 40:18; 45:7.

ANT. Pr. 6:6; 30:25. See INSECTS.

ANTELOPE. Deut. 14:6; Is. 51:20. See ANIMALS.

ANTEDILUVIANS. Genealogies of.— Gen. 5:3–32; I Chr. 1:1–4. Were worshippers—Gen. 4:3, 4, 26. Tillers of the soil and shepherds—Gen. 2:15; 4:2. Longevity of—Gen. 5:3–32. Giants— Gen. 6:4. God sent out preachers among them.—I Pet. 3:19–20; II Pet. 2:5; Jude 14. They would not heed— Gen. 6:5; Mt. 24:37–39; Lu. 17:26–27; I Pet. 3:19, 20. The wicked destroyed —Gen. 6:13, 17. See FLOOD.

ANTHOTHIJAH, ăn′tho-thī′jah. A Benjamite. I Chr. 8:24.

ANTHROPOMORPHISM. See GOD.

ANTICHRIST. I John 2:18, 22; 4:3; II John 7. See Mt. 24:5, 24. See PROPHETS, FALSE.

ANTIOCH, ăn′ti-ŏk. (1) Capital of Syria, founded 300 B.C.—Acts 6:5. Gospel preached there—Acts 11:19, 20. Disciples called Christians in—Acts 11:26. Prophets from Jerusalem came to—Acts 11:22-28. Paul and Barnabas sent from—Acts 13:1-3. Return to—Acts 14:26-28; 15:1, 2. Deputation sent from Jerusalem to—Acts 15: 22-35; Gal. 2:11.

(2) **In Pisidia.**—Visited by Paul and his companions—Acts 13:13-51. Jews from Antioch stone Paul—Acts 14:19; II Tim. 3:11. Paul returns—Acts 14:21.

ANTIPAS, ăn'ti-păs. (1) See HEROD.
(2) **An early Christian martyr.**—Rev. 2:13.

ANTIPATRIS, ăn-tĭp'a-tris. A City built by Herod the Great, and named for his father Antipater.—Acts 23:31.

ANUB, a'nub. A descendant of Judah. —I Chr. 4:8.

ANVIL. Is. 41:7.

ANXIETY. Casting all your—I Pet. 5:7. For all the churches—II Cor. 11:28. See CARE, GOD, PROVIDENCE OF.

ANXIOUS. Be not anxious for your life —Mt. 6:25, 27, 28, 31, 34; Lu. 12:22. Martha—Lu. 10:41. Nothing, In— Phil. 4:6. See CAREFUL, THOUGHT, TAKE. Speak, How ye shall—Mt. 10: 19; Lu. 12:11, 12.

APE. I Ki. 10:22; II Chr. 9:21.

APELLES, ȧ-pĕl'les. A disciple of Rome, to whom Paul sent a greeting.—Rom. 16:10.

APHARSACHITES, ȧ-phär'săk-ītes. Ezra 5:6; 6:6.

APHARSITES, ȧ-phär'sītes. Ezra 4:9.

APHARSATHCITES, ȧ-phär'săth-kītes. Ezra 4:9.

APHEK, a'phek. (1) A city of the Canaanites taken by Joshua.—Josh. 12: 18; I Sam. 4:1; 29:1; I Ki. 20:26, 30 (?); II Ki. 13:17 (?).
(2) A city of Canaan never conquered. Josh. 19:30; Ju. 1:31. See APHIK.

APHEKAH, a-phē'kah. A city of Judah near Hebron.—Josh. 15:53.

APHIAH, a-phē'ah. One of King Saul's ancestors.—I Sam. 9:1.

APHIK, a'phik. See APHEK.

APHRAH, ăph'rah. A city in Benjamin. Mic. 1:10.

APOLLONIA, ăp'ol-lō'nĭ-a. A city of Macedonia about 28 miles west of Am-

phipolis and about 35 from Thessalonica.—I Acts 17:1.

APOLLOS, a-pŏl'los. An eloquent Jewish disciple of Alexandria, who came to Ephesus, and was there taught the way more perfectly by Aquila and Priscilla—Acts 18:24; 19:1. Corinthian church divided over him—I Cor. 1:12; 3:4-6, 22; 4:6. Paul esteemed him highly—I Cor. 16:12; Titus 3:13.

APOLLYON, a-pol-ly-on. See ABADDON.

APOSTASY, or BACKSLIDING. Political apostasy.—Ex. 1:10; I Sam. 14: 21; Jer. 37:13, 14; 39:9. People of Israel—I Cor. 10:1-13; Heb. 3:7, 8.

Religious apostasy.—Lu. 8:13; Heb. 6:6. A great apostasy foretold—II Thess. 2:1-10. Angels—Jude 6. Esau—Heb. 12:15-17. A smaller apostasy—I Tim. 4:1. Temporary: Peter—Mt. 26:31-35, 69-75. John Mark (merely deserted from work)—Acts 13:13; 15:38; II Tim. 4:11. Phygelus and Hermogenes —II Tim. 1:15. Demas—II Tim. 4:10.

A nation may backslide.—Jer. 18:9, 10. A nation can repent and return—Jer. 18:8; Jonah 3:5-10. The fall of the Jews—John 1:11; 5:40. Was the enriching of the Gentiles—Mt. 21:43; Rom. 11:11-15. The Galilæans left Jesus—John 6:60, 66. The Galilæans deserted Paul's gospel—Gal. 1:6; 5:4. The Gnostics made a return—I John 2:19. Occasions for apostasy: Tribulation or persecution—Mt. 13:20, 21. Cares, riches, and pleasures of this life —Lu. 8:14; I Tim. 3:6. Love of the world—II Tim. 4:10; I John 2:15-17. Fleshly lusts—I Pet. 2:11. Pride—Pr. 16:18; I Tim. 3:6. False teaching— Gal. 1:6; 5:4; II John 9-11.

God has no pleasure in such a one.—Heb. 10:38. It shows unfitness for Heaven —Lu. 9:62. Duty to turn again—I Ki. 8:33; II Chr. 6:24, 37, 38. God has promised to welcome the returning backslider—Neh. 1:8, 9; Is. 1:16-20; Ez. 18:30-32; Lu. 15:32; 19:8, 9. Rehoboam secured favor by humility— II Chr. 12:12. It may be final—Heb. 6:4-8; 10:26-29.

Not to fall, amid temptations, is victory and joy.—Jas. 1:2, 12. It is right to overcome error—Heb. 3:12-15; II Pet. 3:17. Christ can keep from falling—

Rom. 16:25; I Cor. 10:13; II Cor. 12:9; Jude 24. Many warnings against— Mt. 6:13; Mk. 13:9; 14:38; I Cor. 3:16, 17; II Thess. 2:3; Heb. 2:1–4; 3:1–4, 13; 6:1–8; 10:26–31; 12:15–29; 13:7–13; Jas. 1:13–15; Rev. 2:4, 6, 22–26.

Confidence in God's elective grace.— John 6:37, 39; 17:12; Rom. 8:26; 11:36; Eph. 1:3–14; I Thess. 1:4; Heb. 6:9–20; I Pet. 1:3–5; II Pet. 1:10, 11.

Proof of election is perseverance to the end.—Heb. 3:6–14. Paul opposed presumption of the believers—I Cor. 9:23; 10:22. The case of Judas is one who let the devil into his life—John 6:70; 13:2, 27. Jesus foresaw his destiny—John 6:64. And Judas went out to his own place—Acts 1:25.

Many difficulties in the subject of apostasy.—Is one aspect of human free agency. The true believer is confident of God's power and purpose to keep him to the end, but does not rashly rush into temptation. The test of real life is in the end of the day, as Jesus said in his sermon on the mount—Mt. 7:14–23.

APOSTLES. Gr. *Apostolos*, "To send on a mission."

Christ Himself was the Apostle of the Father.—John 17:18; Heb. 3:1, 2.

Paul uses the term in stating various commissions.—II Cor. 8:23; Phil. 2:25; Rom. 16:7.

But the ordinary application is to the twelve.—Matthias was added in the place of Judas Iscariot. The name was given to the twelve by Jesus—Lu. 6:13. A record of the group is found in —Mt. 10:2–4; Mk. 3:14–19; Lu. 6:13–16; Acts 1:13. The first appointment embraced twelve, corresponding to the twelve tribes of Israel—Rev. 21:12, 14. Afterwards 70 were sent forth (Lu. 10:1), indicating, perhaps prospectively, the broadening out of the commission, since the Jewish conception of mankind comprised 70 nations. But the term "apostles" was not applied to the 70 in the technical sense. The development was gradual. (1) Called to be companions and followers of Jesus—Mk. 1:16–20; John 1:35–50. (2) Organized into a band of twelve—Lu. 6:13–16. (3) Instructed in the

kingdom. The purpose threefold (1) That they might company with Him. (2) Witness His deeds, remember His words, and attest His resurrection as disciples. (3) That they might go into all the world as His commissioners (apostles)—Mk. 3:14; Mt. 28:19, 20. They wandered to and fro (Mt. 8:19, 20) and thus became detached from the world—John 17:16. The miracles were to prove to them the power of their leader—John 11:15. The parables were to utilize their knowledge of nature and of human nature—Mt. 13:51, 52. Half of them were in the training a trifle over 3 years. They were to become witnesses of Jesus, of His death and resurrection—Lu. 24:48; Acts 1:8. They were to preach the gospel to the world—Mt. 28:18–20; Mk. 16:15, 16; Lu. 24:45–47; Acts 2:41, 42. But they were to tarry in Jerusalem until they were endued with power from on high—Lu. 24:49. Paul was not a member of the body of twelve. He was an independent apostle on a par with them—Acts 14:4, 14. Barnabas and James, the Lord's brother, are sometimes called apostles, probably in the more general sense of the term.

Signs and qualifications of apostles.—II Cor. 12:12. Must have seen Jesus and be able to testify to what they had seen and heard—John 15:27; Acts 1:21, 22; 22:14, 15; I Cor. 9:1; 15:8. Must have been called—Mt. 10:2–4; Mk. 1:16–20; Lu. 6:13–16; Rom. 1:1; I Cor. 1:1; Gal. 1:1; I Tim. 2:7; II Tim. 1:11. Performed miracles—Mk. 16:17, 18, 20; Acts 2:43; Rom. 15:19; I Cor. 12:8–11; II Cor. 12:12. Had power to confer the gift of the holy spirit— Acts 6:6; 8:14–21; 19:6; I Tim. 4:14. See ANDREW, BARTHOLOMEW, JAMES, JOHN, JUDAS, MATTHEW, MATTHIAS, NATHANIEL, PETER, PHILIP, SIMON, THADDEUS, THOMAS.

APOSTLESHIP. Acts 1:25; Rom. 1:5; I Cor. 9:2; Gal. 2:8.

Apostolic authority, duty, faith, inspiration, knowledge, persecutions, witness. See JESUS, TEACHING OF.

APOTHECARY. See PERFUME.

APPAIM, ap-pa'im. Son of Nadab—I Chr. 2:30, 31.

APPAREL. White—Acts 1:10; Rev. 3: 18; 7:13. See CLOTHING, GARMENT.

APPEAL. Unto Cæsar—Acts 25:11, 12, 21, 25; 26:32; 28:19.

APPEAR. Approved—II Cor. 13:7. Before God—Ex. 23:17; 34:23, 24; Deut. 16:16; 31:11; I Sam. 1:22; Ps. 42:2; 84:7; Is. 1:12; II Cor. 5:10; Col. 3:4; Heb. 9:24; I Pet. 4:18. See JUDGMENT. Clever tongues—Acts 2:3. Countenance—Dan. 1:15. Dry land—Gen. 1:9. Evil from the north—Jer. 6:1 (A.V.). Fast, To—Mt. 6:16, 18. Flowers—So. of Sol. 2:12. Grace—Titus 2:11. Kindness and love of God—Titus 3:4. Leprosy—Lev. 13:14, 13, 57. Moses and Elijah—Mt. 17:3; Mk. 9:4. See Lu. 9:8. Shame—Jer. 13:26; Rev. 3:18 (A.V.). Sign of the Son of man—Mt. 24:30. Sin—Ez. 21:24; Rom. 9:8. Sun nor stars, Neither—Acts 27:20. Tares—Mt. 13:26. Things which do —Heb. 11:3. Ungodly and sinner— I Pet. 4:18. Vapor—Jas. 4:14. What we shall be—I John 3:2 (A.V.). Words —Lu. 24:11. Works—Ps. 90:16. See APPEARANCE, MANIFEST, MADE.

APPEARANCE. Angels. See ANGELS, APPEARANCES OF. Glory in—II Cor. 5:12. God—See GOD, APPEARANCES OF. Jesus—See JESUS, RESURRECTION OF. Judge not according to—John 7:24. Outward—I Sam. 16:7; II Cor. 10:7. See COUNTENANCE, DREAMS, FORM, REVEAL, REVELATION, VISION.

APPEASE. Ahasuerus — Esther 2:1 (A.V.). Esau—Gen. 32:20. God—Is. 57:6. Multitude—Acts 19:35 (A.V.). Strife—Pr. 15:18. See PACIFY, QUIET.

APPETITE. Man, Of—Pr. 23:2; Eccl. 6:7. Spiritual appetite—Is. 29:8. Young lions—Job 38:39. See HUNGER, LUST, THIRST.

APPHIA, ăp'phi-a. **A female disciple, one of those to whom Paul addressed the epistle of Philemon.**—Philemon 2.

APPIUS, ăp'pi-us. **Market of—A station 43 miles from Rome on the Appian way.**—Acts 28:15.

APPLE. So. of Sol. 2:3, 5; 7:8; 8:5; Joel 1:12. Gold, Of—Pr. 25:11.

APPLE OF THE EYE. Deut. 32:10; Ps. 17:8; Pr. 7:2; Lam. 2:18; Zech. 2:8.

APPLY. Heart unto instruction.—Pr. 23:12. Knowledge—Pr. 22:17. Understanding—Pr. 2:2. Wisdom—Ps. 90:12 (A.V.); Eccl. 7:25 (A.V.); 8:16. Work —Eccl. 8:9.

APPOINTED. Day—Pr. 7:20; Acts 17: 31; 28:23. Elders—Titus 1:5. See ELDERS. Flock for Sheol—Ps. 49:14. Heir of all things—Heb. 1:2. Kingdom—Lu. 22:29. Men once to die, Unto—Heb. 9:27. See Ps. 79:11. Minister—Acts 26:16. Portion with hypocrites—Mt. 24:51. Preacher—II Tim. 1:11. Seed—Gen. 4:25. Time—Job 7:3; 14:13; Jer. 8:7; Dan. 1:10; 11:27, 29; Heb. 3:2. See ELECTION, FOREORDAIN, ORDAIN, PREDESTINATION, SET APART.

APPORTIONED. II Cor. 10:13.

APPREHEND. John 1:5; Acts 12:4 (A.V.); II Cor. 11:32 (A.V.); Eph. 3:18; Phil. 3:12, 15 (A.V.). See LAY HOLD.

APPROVE. I Cor. 16:3. Disciples— Rom. 5:4; 14:18; 16:10; I Cor. 11:19; II Cor. 6:4 (A.V.); 7:11; 10:18; 13:7; Jas. 1:12. See God, Of. Excellent, Things that are—Rom. 2:18; Phil. 1: 10. See Rom. 14:22. God, Of—Acts 2:22; I Thess. 2:4; II Tim. 2:15. See ACCEPT, ACCEPTABLE, JUDGMENT. Sayings—Ps. 49:13. Subvert a man in his cause, God does not—Lam. 3:36.

APRON. Gen. 3:7; Acts 19:12.

APT. Teach, To—I Tim. 3:2; II Tim. 2:24. War, For—II Ki. 24:16.

AQUILA, ăq'ui-la. **A Jew of Pontus, who, with his wife, Priscilla, had been banished from Rome by Claudius, and whom Paul found in Corinth.**—Acts 18:2. Sails with Paul to Syria—Acts 18:18. Shows Apollos the more perfect way—Acts 18:24-26; 19:1-7. Paul salutes—Rom. 16:3; II Tim. 4:19. Send salutation—I Cor. 16:19.

AR, är. **A city of Moab, on the river Arnon.**—Num. 21:15, 28; Deut. 2:9, 18, 29; Is. 15:1.

ARA, ā'ra. **A member of the tribe of Asher.**—I Chr. 7:38.

ARAB, ā'rab. **A city of Judah.**—Josh. 15:48-52.

ARABAH, är'a-bah. **The name given to the whole depression from the sea of Galilee to the Gulf of Akabah, including the Dead Sea.**—Deut. 1:1; 2:8;

11:30; Josh. 11:2; Ez. 47:8. Brook of —Amos 6:14. Sea of (Dead Sea)— Deut. 4:49; Josh. 3:16; 12:3; II Ki. 14:25.

ARABIA, a-rā'bi-a. The oldest inhabitants were called Horites. Later it was inhabited by Ishmaelites, Edomites and Amalekites, afterwards inhabited by many other tribes.
Territory of.—Gen. 25:13–18; II Chr. 26:7.
Kings of.—I Ki. 10:15 (A.V.); II Chr. 9:14; Jer. 25:24.
Merchants of.—Ez. 27:21.
Prophecy concerning.—Is. 21:13–17.
Paul in.—Gal. 1:17.
ARABIANS.—Is. 13:20; Jer. 3:2. Jehoshaphat, brought presents to—II Chr. 17:11. War against Judah—II Chr. 21:16; 22:1; Neh. 2:19, 20; 4:7–15; 6:1–8.
ARAD, ä'rad. (1) **A town in the southern part of Judah.**—Josh. 12:14; Ju. 1:16. Its king attacked the Israelites —Num. 21:1; 33:40.
(2) **A Benjamite.** I Chr. 8:15.
ARAH, ä'rah. (1) **A member of tribe of Asher.**—I Chr. 7:39.
(2) The ancestor of some of those who returned from the exile.—Ezra 2:5; Neh. 7:10.
(3)Grandfather of the wife of Tobiah, who hindered Nehemiah in rebuilding Jerusalem.—Neh. 6:18.
ARAM, ä'ram. (1) **Son of Shem.**—Gen. 10:22, 23; I Chr. 1:17.
(2) **Son of Kemuel, the nephew of Abraham.**—Gen. 22:21.
(3)A name for Syria.—Num. 23:7. See I Chr. 2:23. See SYRIA.
(4) **Son of Shamer, an Asherite, an ancestor of Jesus.**—I Chr. 7:34; Mt. 1:3 marg.; Lu. 3:33 marg.
ARAMITESS. Concubine of Manasseh. —I Chr. 7:14.
ARAM-MAACAH, ä'ram-mā'a-kah. **Near Geshur.**—I Chr. 19:6. See Deut. 3:14; Josh. 13:13.
ARAM-NAHARAIM, ä'ram-nä'ha-rä'im. Mesopolamaia—Ps. 60 title. See MESOPOTAMIA.
ARAM-ZOBAH, ä'ram-zō'bah. **Land between the Orontes and the Euphrates.** —Ps. 60 title.

ARAN, ä'ran. **Son of Dishan.**—Gen. 36: 28; I Chr. 1:42.
ARARAT, är'a-rat. **A district in eastern Armenia,** altitude 6,000 to 7,000 feet above Mediterranean Sea.—Jer. 51:27. Ark rested in mountains of—Gen. 8:4. Sons of Sennacherib fled into—II Ki. 19:37; Is. 37:38.
ARAUNAH, a-rạu'nah. **A Jebusite,** whose threshing-floor David purchased on which to build an altar.— II Sam. 24:16–24; I Chr. 21:15–26.
ARBA, är'bȧ. **Ancestor of the Anakim and Nephilim.**—Gen. 35:27; Josh. 15: 13; 21:11. See ANAK, HEBRER.
ARBATHITE, är'bath-ite. **A citizen of Beth-arabah.**—II Sam. 23:31; I Chr. 11:32.
ARBITE, är'bīte. **A citizen of Arab.**—II Sam. 23:35.
ARCHANGEL. Michael—Jude 9. Voice of—I Thess. 4:16. See ANGELS.
ARCHELAUS, är'ke-lā'us. See HEROD.
ARCH. In the temple of Ezekiel—Ez. 40:21–36.
ARCHERY. Used in battle—Gen. 49: 23; I Sam. 31:3; Jer. 51:3; I Chr. 10: 13. Bound by archers—Is. 22:3. Compassed by—Job 16:3. Noise of—Ju. 5:11. Number of—Is. 21:17.
Archers.—Ishmael—Gen. 21:20. Sons of Ulam—I Chr. 8:40. Arrow shot—I Sam. 20:36, 37. Nor shoot an arrow— II Ki. 19:32; Is. 37:33. Will not make him flee—Job. 41:28; Ps. 91:5. Mark for—Ps. 45:5; Lam. 3:12. Upon them —Deut. 32:23; II. Chr. 26:15; Jer. 50:9, 14. Shot at mark—I Sam. 20:20. Shot forth and found—I Sam. 20:21, 22, 36, 38. Sent out—II Sam. 22:15. Shot forth—Jer. 51:11. Sent upon— Ez. 5:16; shaken, 21:21.
Arrow of deliverance.—II Ki. 13:17.
Wounded with.—Ps. 64:7.
Bow and arrow.—II Ki. 9:24; 13:15, 18; I Chr. 12:2; Ps. 7:13; 11:2; 76:3; Is. 5:28; 7:24; Ez. 39:3, 9.
Figurative.—With—Num. 24:8; Pr. 25: 18; 26:18; Jer. 9:8; Zech. 9:14; Deut. 32:42; Job 6:4; Ps. 18:14; 38:2; 57:4; 58:7; 64:3; 77:17; 120:4; 127:4; 144:6.
ARCHEVITES, är'ke-vites. Ezra 4:9.
ARCHIPPUS, ar-chip'us. **A disciple in the house of Philemon whom Paul exhorts**—Col. 4:17; Philemon 2.

ARCHITES, ar′chites—Josh. 16:2.
Hushai.—II Sam. 15:32; 16:16; 17:5, 14; I Chr. 27:33.

ARCTURUS, ärk′tū-rus. A constellation of stars known as "The Bear."—Job 9:9 (A.V.); 38:32 (A.V.).

ARCHIVES. See Rolls.

ARD, ärd. (1) Son of Benjamin.—Gen. 46:21.

(2) Son of Bela and grandson of Benjamin.—Num. 26:40.

ARDON, är′don. Son of Caleb, grandson of Hezron.—I Chr. 2:18.

ARELI, ā-rē′lī. Son of Gad.—Gen. 46: 16; Num. 26:17.

AREOPAGITE, ăr′e-ŏp′a-ġīte. Dionysius—Acts 17:34.

AREOPAGUS, ăr′e-ŏp′a-gus. A rock at the entrance to the Acropolis of Athens, where a court was held.—Acts 17:19.

ARETAS, är′e-tas. An ethnarch whose "governor" guarded Damascus to prevent Paul's escape.—II Cor. 11:32.

ARGOB, är′gŏb. (1) A district in Bashan.—Deut. 3:4, 13, 14; I Ki. 4:13.

(2) Name of man slain with Pekah in Samaria.—II Ki. 15:25.

ARGUE. Job 6:25 (A.V.); 23:4.

ARIDAI, a-rĭd′a-ī. Son of Haman, who was hung with his father—Esther 9:9.

ARIDATHA, a-rĭd′a-thà. Same as above—Esther 9:8.

ARIEH, a-ri′eh. Name of man slain with Pekah in Samaria.—II Ki. 15:25.

ARIEL, ā′ri-el. (1) A messenger of Ezra to Iddo.—Ezra 8:16.

(2) Symbolic name for Jerusalem.—Is. 29:1, 2, 7.

ARIGHT. Job 11:13; Ps. 50:23; 78:8; Pr. 15:2; 23:31 (A.V.); Is. 28:26; Jer. 8:6.

ARIMATHAEA, ăr′i-ma-thē′à. A name for Ramah, the home of Samuel. Home of Joseph, in whose tomb Jesus was buried.—Mt. 27:57; Mk. 15:43; Lu. 23:51; John 19:38.

ARIOCH, ā′ri-ŏch. (1) King of Ellasar in Assyria.—Gen. 14:1, 9.

(2) Captain of Nebuchadrezzar's guard, who had charge of Daniel and his companions.—Dan. 2:14, 15, 24, 25.

ARISAI, a-rĭs′a-ī. One of the sons of Haman, who was hung with him.—Esther 9:9.

ARISE, AROSE, ROSE.—Aeneas—Acts 9:34. Afflictions and persecutions—Mt. 13:21; Mk. 4:17. Apostles—John 14:31. Baptized, And be—Acts 22:16. Bed, And take up thy—Mt. 9:5-7; Mk. 2:9-12; Lu. 5:24. Bodies of the saints—Mt. 27:52. Damsel—Mt. 9:25; Mk. 5:41, 42; Lu. 8:54, 55. Dead, From the—Eph. 5:14. Epileptic boy—Mk. 9:27. False Christs—Mt. 24:24. Leper —Lu. 17:19. Peter—Acts 9:39; 10:20; 11:7; 12:7. Philip—Acts 8:26, 27. Prodigal son—Lu. 15:18, 20. Saul of Tarsus—Acts 9:6, 8, 11, 18; 22:10, 16. Simon's wife's mother—Mt. 8:15; Lu. 4:38, 39. Tabitha—Acts 9:40. Virgins, Ten—Mt. 25:7. Widow of Nain's son—Lu. 7:14. Withered hand, Man with—Lu. 6:8.

ARISTARCHUS, ăr′is-tär-kus. One of Paul's companions on his third missionary journey.—Acts 19:29; 20:4; 27:2; Col. 4:10; Philemon 24.

ARISTOBULUS, ăr′is-tō-bū′lus. A person in Rome to whose household Paul sent a salutation.—Rom. 16:10.

ARK, Noah's. Built by order of Jehovah.—Gen. 6:14; Heb. 11:7. Noah instructed how to build—Gen. 6:14, 16.
Dimensions of.—Gen. 16:15. The occupants.—Gen. 6:18; 7:7; Mt. 24:38; I Pet. 3:20.
Different classes of animals preserved in the ark.—Gen. 6:19, 20, 7:2, 3, 8, 9, 14-16; 8:17, 18.
Rested in the seventh month on the mountains of Ararat.—Gen. 8:4.
A raven sent from.—Gen. 8:7. A dove sent out.—Gen. 8:8-12.
Noah and family went forth in the second month of the next year.—Gen. 8:14-19.

ARK OF THE COVENANT. Material and construction.—Ex. 25:10-15; 37: 1-5.
Called.—Ark of God—I Sam. 3:3; II Sam. 15:25, 29. Ark of God's strength —II Chr. 6:41; Ps. 132:8. The Ark of the Covenant—Num. 10:33; 14:44; Deut. 10:8; 31:9, 25, 26; Josh. 3:6-17; 4:9; 6:6; Heb. 9:4. Ark of Jehovah— Josh. 4:5, 11; 6:6, 7; I Ki. 8:4. Ark of the Covenant of God—Ju. 20:27; I Sam. 4:4; II Sam. 15:24; I Chr. 16:6. Ark of Testimony—Ex. 25:22; 30:6;

Num. 7:89. Ark of the Covenant of Jehovah—Num. 10:33; Josh. 3:3, 5; 4:7, 18; 6:8, 11; 8:33; I Sam. 4:3, 5; I Ki. 3:15; 6:19; 8:1, 6; I Chr. 5:2, 7; Jer. 3:16.

Placed in Holy of Holies.—Ez. 26:33; 40:21; II Chr. 35:3; Heb. 9:3, 4.

Contained.—Tables of Testimony—Ex. 25:16, 21, 22; Deut. 10:1–5; I Ki. 8:9, 21; II Chr. 5:10; 6:11; Heb. 9:4. Pot of manna and Aaron's rod—Ex. 16:33, 34; Num. 17:10; Heb. 9:4. The Book of the Covenant—Deut. 31:24–26.

Anointing of.—Ex. 30:26.

Presence of ark made holy.—II Chr. 8:11.

Covered with veil before removal.—Num. 4:5, 6.

Profanation of punished.—Num. 1:51; 4:5, 15, 20; I Sam. 6:19; II Sam. 6:6–8; I Chr. 15:13.

Carried.—By priests or levites only—Num. 3:31; Deut. 10:8; Josh. 3:14; II Sam. 15:24; I Chr. 15:2. Before Israelites in journeying—Num. 10:33; Josh. 3:6. To the camp in time of war—I Sam. 4:4–7. Set up in Shiloh—Josh. 18:1. Served as director—Num. 14:44; Ju. 20:27, 28; I Sam. 4:3–7.

Symbol of God's presence.—Josh. 7:6; I Sam. 4:7. Prepared for conveyance—Num. 4:5–15.

History of.—Made at Sinai—Ex. 25:10–15; 37:1–9. Used to divide the Jordan—Josh. 3:14–17. Carried around Jericho—Josh. 6:6–20. Taken by Philistines—I Sam. 5:6–12. Restored to Israel—I Sam. 6:1–18. At Kiriath-jearim, 20 years—I Sam. 7:1, 2. Brought to house of Obed-edom—II Sam. 6:1–11. Brought to Jerusalem—II Sam. 6:12–15; I Chr. 15:2–28. Deposited in temple—I Ki. 8:1–16. John sees the ark in temple of God in heaven—Rev. 11:19. See PRIEST, TABERNACLE.

ARKITE, ärk′ite. Gen. 10:17; I Chr. 1:15.

ARM. Arm of flesh.—II Chr. 32:8; Jer. 17:5. Without strength—Job. 26:2. Of Job—Job. 31:22; Ps. 44:3. Of the mighty—Job 35:9; Ps. 44:3. Of wicked—Ps. 10:15. Used for toil—Is. 17:5. Broken—Job 38:15; Ps. 10:15; Jer. 48:25; Ez. 30:21.

Bracelets worn on.—II Sam. 1:10.

Symbolical.—Ez. 4:7; Dan. 10:6.

Prophecies concerning arm of the house of Eli.—I Sam. 2:31. Of Moab—Jer. 48:25. Eating of—Is. 9:20. Of south kingdom—Dan. 11:6. Of shepherds—Zech. 11:17.

Figurative.—Teareth the arm—Deut. 33:20. High arm broken—Job 38:15. Arm of Pharaoh—Ez. 30:21. See "Anthropomorphism" under GOD, HAND.

ARMLETS. Ex. 35:22; Num. 31:50.

ARMONI, ar-mō′nī. Daughter of Saul and Rizpah.—II Sam. 21:8–11.

ARMOR AND ARMS. Of Philistine—I Sam. 17:54. Every Man his—I Ki. 10:25. Moabites put on—II Ki. 3:21. Of Ahab—II Ki. 10:2. Of Hezekiah—II Ki. 20:13; Is. 39:2. Saul's armor taken—I Chr. 10:9, 10.

Armorbearer.—Of Jonathan—I Sam. 14:6, 7. David becomes Saul's—I Sam. 16:21. Of Saul—I Sam. 31:6. Of Goliath—I Sam. 17:7. Of Joab—II Sam. 18:15.

Buckler.—II Chr. 23:9; Job. 15:26. Song of Sol. 4:4; Jer. 46:3; Ez. 23:24; 38:4; 39:9.

Breastplate.—Ex. 25:7; 28:4, 22, 23, 24, 26, 28, 30; 29:5; 35:9; 39:8, 9, 15, 16, 17, 19–21; Lev. 8:8. Of judgment—Ex. 28:15, 29. Of righteousness—Is. 59:17; Eph. 6:14. Of faith and love—I Thess. 5:8. Of iron—Rev. 9:9.

Coat of mail.—I Sam. 17:38; II Chr. 26:14; Jer. 46:4.

Helmet.—Ez. 23:24; 27:10; 38:5. Of brass—I Sam. 17:5, 38. Of salvation—Is. 59:17; Jer. 46:4; Eph. 6:17. See SALVATION.

Battering rams.—Against the gate—Ez. 21:22.

Armor of Christian.—Of trust—Lu. 11:22. Of light—Rom. 13:12. Of righteousness—II Cor. 6:7. Of God—Eph. 6:11, 13. See SOLDIER, WAR.

ARMY. See BATTLEFIELDS, SOLDIERS, WAR.

ARNAN, är′nan. Descendants of David—I Chr. 3:21.

ARNI, ar′nī. See ARAM.

ARNON, är′non, *swift, roaring*. **A river east of Jordan.**

Boundary of.—Israel and Moab—Num. 21:13, 14, 15, 24, 26; 22:36; Deut. 2:24,

36; 3:8, 12, 16; 4:48; Josh. 12:1, 2; 13:9, 16; Ju. 11:18, 22, 26; II Ki. 10:33.

High places of.—Num. 21:28.

Fords of.—Is. 16:2.

Prophecy at.—Jer. 48:20.

AROD, ā'rod. **Son of Gad.**—Num. 26:17.

ARODI, är'o-dī. Gen. 46:16.

ARODITES. Num. 26:17.

AROER, är'o-er. (1) **A city near Rabbah of the Ammonites.**—Num. 32:34; Josh. 13:25; II Sam. 24:5; Is. 17:2.

(2) **A city on the river Arnon, assigned to the tribe of Reuben.**—Deut. 2:36; 3:12; 4:48; Josh. 12:2; 13:9, 16; Ju. 11:26, 33; II Ki. 10:33; I Chr. 5:8; Jer. 48:19.

(3) **A city in southern part of Judah.**— I Sam. 30:28.

AROERITE. I Chr. 11:44.

ARPAD, är'pad. **A city, once capital of an Aramean kingdom, and conquered by Assyria.**—II Ki. 18:34; 19:13; Is. 10:9; 36:19; 37:13; Jer. 49:23.

ARPACHSHAD, är-pǎks'hǎd. **Son of Shem, and a tribe east of the Tigris.**— Gen. 10:22, 24; 11:10–13; I Chr. 1:17, 18, 24; Lu. 3:36.

ARRAY. II Chr. 28:15; Esther 6:9, 11. Battle—Ju. 20:20, 22, 30, 33; I Sam. 4:2; 17:2, 8, 21; II Sam. 10:8–10, 17; I Chr. 12:33; 19:9–11, 17; II Chr. 13:3; 14:10; Jer. 6:23; 43:12; 50:9, 42; Acts 4:26. See ISRAEL, JUDAH, WAR. Garment sprinkled with blood, In—Rev. 19:13. Holy—Ps. 29:2; 96:6; 110:3. Honor and majesty, With—Job 40:10. Linen, In—Gen. 41:42; II Chr. 5:12; Rev. 19:8. Purple, In—John 19:2; Rev. 17:4. Royal apparel—Acts 12:21. Solomon not arrayed—Mt. 6:29; Lu. 12:27. Terrors of God—Job 6:4. White robes — Mk. 16:5; Rev. 7:13. See CLOTHING, RAIMENT.

ARRIVE. Lu. 8:26; Rom. 9:31.

ARROGANCE. I Sam. 2:3; Ps. 73:3; 75:4; 94:4; Pr. 8:13; 21:24; Is. 13:11; Jer. 16:6; 37:29; 48:29. See PRIDE.

ARROW. See ARCHERY.

ART. Ex. 30:25; II Chr. 16:14; Acts 17:29; 19:19.

TRADES AND ARTS. The Hebrews honored labor.—Saul and Aquila were tentmakers—Acts 18:3.

Armorer. See ARMS and ARMOUR—Ju. 15:14.

Artificer.—Ex. 31:4; Jer. 10:9.

Bakers. Usually women—Lev. 26:26. Wife—Gen. 18:6. Sister—II Sam. 13:8. Servant—I Sam. 8:13. Pharaoh had plenty—Gen. 40:2, 20, 22. A trade —Hos. 7:4–6. Bakers' street—Jer. 37: 21. See BREAD.

Barber.—Named but once—Ez. 5:1. See HAIR—II Sam. 14:26.

Brick makers.—Used brick for stone, bitumen for mortar—Gen. 11:3.ͦ Straw in bricks—Ex. 5:7, 16, 18. Hard work —Ex. 1:13, 14. Inferior to stone—Is. 9:10. Built cities, towers, altars— Gen. 10:4, 5; Ex. 1:11; Is. 65:3.

Brazier.—Gen. 4:22; Ex. 31:4. See BRASS—Josh. 22:8.

Butchers sold meat in shambles.—I Cor. 10:25.

Calker.—Ez. 27:9, 27.

Carpenters.—Ex. 37:1, 10, 25; 38:1; II Sam. 5:11; II Ki. 22:6; I Chr. 14:1; Is. 41:7; Mk. 6:3. See CARPENTER.

Cheese makers.—Cheese was curdled— Job 10:10. Made by a family—I Sam. 17:18. Given to David—II Sam. 17: 29. The Tyropoeon valley in Jerusalem is—*Lit.*—Valley of the cheese makers.

Cooks.—Men—Gen. 25:29; II Ki. 4:38. Women—Gen. 18:6. Princess—II Sam. 13:8.

Coppersmith.—Worker in bronze (called brass) in Old Testament; in New Testament, worker in copper—II Tim. 4: 14. Noted workers—Gen. 4:22. Bezalel —Ex. 31:4; 35:30, 32. Hiram—I Ki. 7:13, 14.

Dyer.—Ram's skins were dyed—Ex. 25:5; 26:14; 35:7, 23; 36:19. Colored yarns show that blue, purple and scarlet dyed garments were prized—Ju. 5:30.

Embroiderer.—Ex. 35:35; 38:23. Did fine work: Screen or veil—Ex. 26:36. High-priest's girdle—Ex. 28:39. Garments of a prince or princess—Ps. 45:13, 14; Ez. 26:16. Used dyed yarn and silver or gold thread—Ex. 26:36; 27:16; 35:35; 38:23.

Figurative.—The beauty of Israel—Ez. 16:10, 13, 18. Of Tyre—Ez. 27:7, 16, 24.

Engravers or carvers.—Sidonians excelled Hebrews—I Ki. 5:6. Bezalel inspired for—Ex. 31:5; 35:33. Solomon brought from Tyre—II Chr. 2:7, 13, 14. Carved signet rings—Gen. 38: 18; 41:42; Ex. 28:11, 21, 36; Jer. 22: 24. Ephod—Ex. 28:11, 12; 39:6, 14. Ten Commandments—Ex. 24:12; 31: 18; II Cor. 3:7. Sometimes on gold—Ex. 39:30. Or wood—I Ki. 6:18, 29, 32, 35. Aaron used a graving tool—Ex. 32:4. Diamond point—Jer. 17:1. Graven images (idols) prohibited—Ex. 20:4; Lev. 26:1; Deut. 4:16–18; 27:15; Is. 42:8; 44:9. (Yet) made—Ju. 17:3; 18:14–31; Is. 44:17.

Figurative.—Security of Israel—Is. 49:16.

Fishermen.—See FISHERMAN.

Founder.—Ju. 17:4.

Fuller.—Bleached undressed cloth—Mt. 9:16; Mk. 2:21; 9:3. Or cleaned soiled garments—Mal. 3:2. Used fuller's clay or soap out in a field—II Ki. 18: 17; Is. 7:3; 36:2.

Gardener.—Jer. 29:5; John 20:15. See GARDEN.

Goldsmith.—Ex. 31:4. Melted in a refining pot—Pr. 17:3. Tin—Is. 1:25. To purify—Pr. 25:4. Silver dross—Pr. 26:23. Brass, tin, iron, lead are dross of gold and silver—Ez. 22:18.

Kinds of work.—Casting—Num. 33:52; Hos. 13:2. Distinguished from graven work in—Nah. 1:14; II Chr. 34:3, 4. In tent of meeting—Ex. 25:12. Beating or hammering—Ex. 25:18, 31; 37: 7, 17, 22; Num. 8:4; I Ki. 10:16, 17; II Chr. 9:15, 16. Plating or overlaying—Ex. 25:11, 24; 26:29, 32; 30:3; 38:6; I Ki. 6:20 ff. Beaten into plates and cut into thread for embroidery—Ex. 39:3.

Goldsmiths made: Golden rings—Gen. 42:23, 30. Jewels—Gen. 24:53; Ex. 3:22; 11:2; 12:35. Chains—Gen. 41: 42. Rings—Gen. 41:42; Ex. 25:26. Cherubim—Ex. 25:18. Mercy-seat, candlestick, snuffdishes—Ex. 25:17, 25, 38. Idols—Is. 40:19; 40:7; 46:6. Put to shame—Jer. 10:14; 51:17. Skilful—Jer. 10:9. Worked by the side of the merchants in rebuilding the walls of Jerusalem—Neh. 3:8, 31, 32. See GOLD.

Husbandman.—Gen. 9:20; II Ki. 25:12; II Chr. 26:10; Jer. 31:24; 52:16; Mt. 21:33–41; Mk. 12:1–9; Lu. 20:9–16; John 15:1; II Tim. 2:6; Jas. 5:7.

Linen weaver.—See LINEN.

Mariners.—Calkers—Ez. 27:9, 27. Sailors—I Ki. 9:27; Is. 33:23; Ez. 27:9, 26, 29; John 1:5; Acts 27:27, 30; Rev. 18:17. Rowers—Ez. 27:8, 26, 29. Pilots—Ez. 27:8, 27–29; Jas. 3:4. Shipmaster—Jonah 1:6.

Mason.—II Sam. 5:11; II Ki. 12:12; 22:6; I Chr. 14:1; 22:2; II Chr. 24:12. Masons smoothed the stones and built —I Chr. 22:2, 15; Ezra 3:7.

Tools.—Plumb—II Ki. 21:13; Zech. 4: 10. Plumb line—Amos 7:7, 8. Large hammer for quarry—Jer. 23:29. Small hammer or pick—I Ki. 6:7. Measuring reed—Ez. 40:3. Hewed—I Ki. 5:17. Quarry—I Ki. 6:7. Squared—Ex. 20:25; II Ki. 12:12. Builders—Ps. 118:22. Had pattern or charts—Ex. 25:9; I Chr. 28:11. See STONE.

Musician.—See MUSIC.

Perfumer.—Ex. 30:25, 35. See PERFUMES.

Porter.—See PORTER.

Potters.—I Chr. 4:23. Tread clay with feet—Is. 41:25. Puts on wheels—Jer. 18:3. Firing—Ps. 22:15. See "Vessels" under FOOD.

Figurative.—God as a Potter forms: Man—Gen. 2:7. Animals—Gen. 2:19. Israel—Is. 43:1, 21; 44:21; 45:9, 11; 49:5. The Israelites—Is. 43:7. Prophet—Jer. 1:5. The eye—Ps. 94:9. Locust—Amos 7:1. Leviathan—Ps. 104: 26. The dry land—Ps. 95:5. The earth—Is. 45:18. Mountains—Amos 4:13. The universe—Jer. 10:16; 51: 19. Light—Is. 45:7. Summer and winter—Ps. 74:17. Spirit of man—Zech. 12:1. Hearts of men—Ps. 33: 15; Rom. 9:20, 21. Cf. Is. 29:16; 64:8. Clay exalted itself above the potter—Is. 29:16; 45:9; Lam. 4:2; Dan. 2:41; II Cor. 4:7; II Tim. 2:20. Of ruin—Jer. 19:1. Cf. Ps. 2:9.

Refiner.—Pr. 27:21; Mal. 3:3; Zech. 13:9.

Shipbuilders.—I Ki. 9:26. Boats made out of reeds—Is. 18:2. Large ships—Pr. 31:14; Ps. 107:23. Voyage to Tarshish—I Ki. 10:22, 48.

Figurative.—Built Tyre like a ship, planks, masts, oars, deck, awning and sails—Ez. 27:1-7. See SHIPS.

Silversmiths.—Work similar to goldsmiths: Craftsmen gathered together at Ephesus made silver idols of Diana —Acts 19:24-25.

Figurative.—Chastisement of God's people like refining process—Ps. 66:10; Pr. 17:3; 25:4; Is. 48:10; Jer. 6:28–30; Ez. 22:17–22; Zech. 13:9; Mal. 3:3.

Smelter.—Job 28:2.

Smiths.—I Sam. 13:19; Jer. 29:2.

Spinners.—Woman's work—Pr. 31:19. Used hand spindle—Ex. 35:25. Spun wool and flax—Pr. 31:13.

Figurative.—Lilies—Mt. 6:28; Lu. 12:27.

Tailor.—Ex. 28:3, 6; Eccl. 3:7. Patched —Mk. 2:21.

Tanner.—Skins used for clothing and other purposes—Gen. 3:21; Ex. 25:5; Lev. 13:48; Heb. 11:37. Only one tanner is named—Acts 9:43; 10:6, 32.

Tentmaker.—Acts 18:3. See TENT.

Vinedresser.—II Ki. 25:12; Is. 61:5; Jer. 52:16; Joel 1:11. See VINE, VINEYARD.

Weaver.—Ex. 26:17; 28:15; 35:35; Esth. 31:24; Pr. 31:21, 22; Is. 19:9.

Loom.—Ju. 16:14; I Sam. 17:7; II Sam. 21:19; I Chr. 11:23; 20:5.

Figurative.—Shuttle of swiftness of time—Job 7:6. Sudden death—Is. 38:12. See CLOTHING.

Wine-maker.—Is. 5:2; 63:2, 3; Neh. 13:15; Rev. 14:18-20. See WINE.

Workers in metal.—Founders: Melted metals and poured into molds—Ex. 32:24. Called molten—Ex. 24:4; Deut. 9:16. An alloy was used—Is. 1:25 *marg.* Clay for molds was in the Plain of Jordan—I Ki. 7:46. Solomon imported a founder—I Ki. 7:13, 14. (Black)smiths were not earliest, but became of greatest importance, being armorers and makers of weapons, hence forbidden in Israel under Philistine oppression—I Sam. 13:19. Two words in Hebrew (1) *Lit.*—A worker in iron—Is. 54:16. (2)—*Lit.*—a smith —II Ki. 24:14, 16. Nebuchadrezzar took all smiths away—Jer. 29:2. Made tools. See TOOLS. Vessels—Josh. 6:19, 24. War chariots—Josh. 7:16, 18; Ju. 1:19; 4:3, 13. Weapons—Num.

35:16, 24; I Sam. 13:19, 20; Job 20:24. Yokes—Deut. 28:48; Jer. 28:14.

Figurative.—Prayer unanswered; or drought—Lev. 26:19; Deut. 28:23, 24. Grief—Ps. 107:10. Despotism (rod of iron)—Ps. 2:9; Rev. 2:27; 12:5; 19:15. See IRON, METAL, GOLD, SILVER, BRASS.

Workers of the soil.—See AGRICULTURE (Is. 28:24), GARDEN, VINE, SHEEP, CATTLE.

Writer or Scribe.—Ezra 4:8–24; 7:11, 12; Neh. 8:1–8; Jer. 36:32. See SCRIBE.

ARTAXERXES, är'tax-ĕrx'es. (1) A Persian king called *Longimanus* (465–425 B.C.) in profane history.—Ezra 4:1–21; 8:1; Neh. 2:1; 5:14; 13:6.

(2) Probably Cambyses (54 B.C.).—Ezra 4:7, 8, 11, 23.

(3) Identity unknown.—Ezra 6:14.

ARTEMAS, är'te-mas. One of Paul's companions at Nicopolis.—Tit. 3:12.

ARTEMIS, är'te-mis. Greek for *Diana*. Acts 19:24 (margin).

ARTIFICER. See ARTS AND TRADES.

ARUBBOTH, ar-ŭb'both. One of Solomon's provision districts.—I Ki. 4:10.

ARUMAH, a-ru'mah. A city near Shechem.—Ju. 9:41.

ARVAD, är'vad. Gen. 10:18; I Chr. 1:16; Ez. 27:8, 11.

ARZA, är'zà. Overseer of Elah, king of Israel—I Ki. 16:9.

ASA, ä'sa. (1) Son of Abijah, grandson of Rehoboam.—I Chr. 3:10; II Chr. 14:1; Mt. 1:7. King of Judah—I Ki. 15:8–10, 25, 28; 16:8, 10, 23, 29; II Chr. 14:1; 21:12. A good king—I Ki. 15:11–15; II Chr. 14:2–7; 15:1–19. Removes Maacha—II Chr. 15:16. Wages war with Baasha, king of Israel—I Ki. 15:16–22, 32, 33; II Chr. 16:6; Jer. 41:9. Father of Jehoshaphat, king of Judah—I Ki. 15:24; 22:41-46; I Chr. 3:10; II Chr. 17:2; 20:31, 32; Mt. 1:8. Wages war with Zerah the Ethiopian and is victorious—II Chr. 14:8-15. Encouraged by Azariah—II Chr. 15:1-7. Rebuked by Hanani—II Chr. 16:7-10. Death of—I Ki. 15:23, 24; II Chr. 16:11-14.

(2) A Levite, son of Elkanah.—I Chr. 9:16.

ASAHEL, ā'sa-hĕl. (1) Son of Zeruiah, a sister of David—II Sam. 2:18-32; 3:27,30; 23:24; I Chr. 2:16; 11:26; 27:7.

(2) **A Levite sent by Jehoshaphat, king of Judah, to teach the law in all the cities of Judah.**—II Chr. 17:8.

(3) A Levite, an overseer under Hezekiah over the tithes and offerings.— II Chr. 31:13.

(4) Father of Jonathan, a census-taker appointed by Ezra.—Ezra 10:15.

ASAIAH, a-sā'iah. (1) **An officer of King Josiah sent to Huldah to enquire concerning the law.**—II Ki. 22:12,14; II. Chr. 34:20.

(2) **A descendant of Simeon.**—I Chr. 4:36.

(3) **A Shilonite.**—I Chr. 9:5.

(4) A Levite, ''son'' of Merari who assisted David in bringing up the ark to Jerusalem.—I Chr. 15:6,11. [Possibly same as (2).]

ASAPH. (1) Recorder to Hezekiah.— II Ki. 18:18, 37; Is. 36:3, 22. Son of— II Chr. 29:13.

(2) **Son of Berechiah.**—I Chr. 6:39; 15: 17. A singer—I Chr. 15:19; 16:5-7, 37; 25:1-9; II Chr. 5:12; 29:30; Neh. 7:44; 12:46. Sons of—II Chr. 20:14; 29:13; 35:15; Ezra 2:41; 3:10; Neh. 7:44; 11:17,22; 12:35. Psalms of— Ps. 50, 73, 74, 75, 76, 77, 78, 79, 80, 81, 82, 83.

(3) A Levite.—I Chr. 9:15.

(4) I Chr. 26:1.

(5) **Keeper of royal forests in Judah.**— Neh. 2:8.

ASAREL, ăs'ar-el. I Chr. 4:16.

ASCEND. Ps. 68:18; Ez. 38:9. Beast— Rev. 11:7 (A.V.); 17:8 (A.V.). Festus —Acts 25:1 (A.V.). Samuel—I Sam. 28:13,14. Smoke—Ex. 19:18; Josh. 8:20, 21; Ju. 20:40; Rev. 8:4; 14:11 (A.V.). Vapors—Ps. 135:7; Jer. 10: 13; 51:16.

Heaven, Into.—Angels—Gen. 28:12; Ju. 13:20; John 1:51; Rev. 7:2. See AN-GELS. Babylon—Is. 14:13,14. David —Ps. 139:8; Acts 2:34. Dead bodies— Rev. 11:12. Jesus—Lu. 24:51; John 3:13; 6:62; 7:33; 12:2,28; 16:5; 20: 17; Eph. 4:8-10. See JESUS, ASCEN-SION OF. Who shall?—Pr. 30:4; Rom. 10:6.

ASCENT. I Sam. 9:11; II Sam. 15:30-32; I Ki. 10:5; II Chr. 9:4. Adum-mim, Of—Josh. 15:7. Akrabbim, Of —Num. 34:4. Ziz, Of—II Chr. 20:16. See PSALMS.

ASCRIBE. David, Unto—I Sam. 18:8. Jehovah, Unto—Deut. 32:3; I Chr. 16:28; Job 36:3; Ps. 68:34.

ASENATH, ăs'e-năth. **Wife of Joseph and daughter of Poti-pherah, priest of On.**—Gen. 41:45,50; 46:20.

ASHAMED. Job 11:3; Pr. 12:4; II Thess. 3:14; Tit. 2:8. Adam and Eve —Gen. 2:25. Beg, To—Lu. 16:3. Christian, As a—I Pet. 4:16. God is not—Heb. 2:11; 11:16. Gospel, Of the—Rom. 1:16. Jesus, Before—I John 2:28. Of—Mk. 8:38; Lu. 9:26; Rom. 9:33; 10:11. Paul—Rom. 1:16; II Cor. 7:14; 9:4; 10:8; Phil. 1:20; II Tim. 1:12. Paul's chain, Of—II Tim. 1:16. Testimony of our Lord, Of the —II Tim. 1:8. Thief—Jer. 2:26. Workman need not be—II Tim. 2:15. See SHAME.

ASHAN, ā'shan. **A Levitical city in western Judah given to Simeon.**— Josh. 15:42; 19:7; I Chr. 4:32; 6:59.

ASHARELAH, ăsh'a-rē'lah. **A musician.**—I Chr. 25:2.

ASHBEA, ăsh'be-à. I Chr. 4:21.

ASHBEL, ăsh'bel. **Son of Benjamin.**— Gen. 46:21; Num. 26:38; I Chr. 8:1.

ASHDOD, ăsh'dod. **One of the five great cities of the Philistines.**—Josh. 11:22; 13:3; 15:46,47; I Sam. 6:17. Ark brought from Eben-ezer to—I Sam. 5:1. House of Dagon the idol in—I Sam. 5:1-7. Wall broken down by Uzziah—II Chr. 26:6. Conspires against Nehemiah—Neh. 4:7. King of Assyria sends Tartan to—Is. 20:1. See II Ki. 16:17. Women marry Jews contrary to Mosaic law—Neh. 13:23, 24. Prophecies concerning—Jer. 25: 20; Amos 1:8; 3:9; Zeph. 2:4; Zech. 9:6.

ASHDOTH-PISGAH. See PISGAH.

(1) **ASHER,** ''Happy.'' **Eighth son of Jacob, by Zilpah, Leah's handmaid.**— Gen. 3:13; 30:12,13; 35:26. Asher had four sons and one daughter.

(2) **Tribe of.**—Heads of families—Gen. 46:17; Num. 26:44-47; I Chr. 7:30-40. At the exodus the tribe numbered 41,-

500—Num. 1:40, 41. At the close of 40 years in the wilderness, 53,400—Num. 26:47. Encampment—Num. 2:25, 27; 10:25, 26. Allotment was the rich sea coast between Carmel and Lebanon—Josh. 19:24-31; Ju. 5:17. Did not drive out Canaanites—Ju. 1:31, 32. Princes of—Num. 1:13; 7:72-77; 34:27. Stood on Mt. Ebal—Deut. 27:13. 40,000 assisted David to become king over all Israel—I Chr. 12:36. Predictions concerning—Gen. 49:20; Deut. 33:24-25. Shrank from jeopardizing life against Sisera—Ju. 5:17. Assisted Gideon against Midianites—Ju. 6:35; 7:23. Aided in Hezekiah's reformation—II Chr. 30:11. See ISRAEL, JACOB.

(3) **A town in Shechem in Manasseh.**—Josh. 17:7.

ASHERAH (plural, **ASHERIM**).—As the stone pillar was the symbol of Baal, so the wooden post was the symbol of the Goddess Asherah. It passed through several stages until it took the form of an image spoken of in Is. 44:12 ff. According to Old Testament writers the word ''Asherah'' is used in three ways.
Canaanite Deity.—Ju. 3:7; I Ki. 18:19; II Ki. 21:7; 23:4.
Image of Asherah.—An idol much like others, consisting of wood decorated with gold, and woven hangings—II Chr. 15:16; II Ki. 23:7.
A Symbol.—The Asherah is often mentioned as an object associated with the altar of the Canaanite temples. It was wood (Ju. 6:26), could be planted in the ground (perhaps a relic of primitive tree-worship—Deut. 16: 21), and burned (Deut. 12:3). It was abolished—II Ki. 18:4; 23:3 ff. See IDOLATRY, IMAGES.

ASHES: Of furnace.—Ex. 9:8, 10. Valley of—Jer. 31:40. Sitting among—Job 2:8. Sodom and Gomorrah—II Pet. 2:6.
Connected with ceremonial.—Of altar of burnt-offerings—Ex. 27:3; Lev. 1:16. To be carried without the camp—Lev. 4:12; 6:11; Num. 4:13. Of the red heifer used for the water of purification—Num. 19:9, 10, 17; Heb. 9:13. Shall be poured out—I Ki. 13:3, 5.

Of vessels used in idolatry—II Ki. 23:4.
Worn in mourning.—II Sam. 13:19; Esth. 4:3; Is. 61:3; Jer. 6:26; 25:34. Sorrow for sin or repentance—Job 42:6; Is. 58:5; Dan. 9:3; Mt. 11:21; Lu. 10:13.
Figurative.—Job 13:12; 30:19; Ps. 147: 16; Mal. 4:3. I who am but dust and ashes—Gen. 18:27. Eaten—Ps. 102: 9; Is. 44:20.

ASHHUR, ăsh'hur. **Father of Tekoa.**—I Chr. 2:24; 4:5.
ASHIMA, ăsh'i-mà. **An idol worshipped by the men of Hamath.**—II Ki. 17:30.
ASHKELON, ăsh'ke-lŏn. City of the Philistines—Josh. 13:3; I Sam. 6:17. Captured by Judah—Ju. 1:18. Jehovah smote—Ju. 14:19. Golden tumor of—I Sam. 6:17. Streets of—II Sam. 1:20. Kings of—Jer. 25:20. Destruction prophesied—Jer. 47:5, 7. Judgment against—Amos 1:8; Zeph. 2:4; Zech. 9:5.
ASHKENAZ, ăsh'ke-năz. (1) **Son of Gomer, grandson of Japheth.**—Gen. 10:3; I Chr. 1:6.
(2) **A people who originally dwelt near Armenia.**—Jer. 51:27.
ASHNAH, ăsh'nah. (1) A town in Judah—Josh. 15:33.
(2) **A town in plains of Judah.**—Josh. 15:43.
ASHPENAZ, ăsh'pe-năz. **Master of eunuchs under Nebuchadrezzar.**—Dan. 1:3.
ASHTAROTH, ăsh'ta-rŏth (*or* Ashtaroth-Karnaim). A town of Bashan belonging to the Rephaim—Gen. 14: 5; Deut. 1:4; Josh. 9:10; 12:4. Given to Manasseh—Josh. 13:31. A Levitical city—I Chr. 6:71.
Ashtaroth, a goddess of the Sidonians.—I Ki. 11:33. Worshipped by the Israelites—Ju. 2:13; 10:6; I Sam. 7:3; 12:10. By the Philistines, who put Saul's armor in the temple of—I Sam. 31:10. By Solomon—I Ki. 11:5, 33. High places of, removed by Josiah—II Ki. 23:13.
ASHTERATHITE, ăsh'te-rath-īte. I Chr. 11:42.
ASHTEROTH-KARNAIM, ăsh'te-rŏth-kär'na-ĭm. See ASHTAROTH.

41

ASHUR, ăsh'ur. **Son of Hezron, grandson of Perez.**—I Chr. 2:24; 4:5.

ASHURITES. A tribe dwelling west of the Jordan.—II Sam. 2:9; Ezra 27:6.

ASHVATH, ăsh'văth. I Chr. 7:33.

ASIA, ā'si-à. **In the N.T. this meant the Roman Province of Asia, which included the western third of the peninsula which we call Asia Minor.**—Acts 2:9; 6:9; 27:2. Paul forbidden to preach in—Acts 16:6. Later on Paul preaches and wins many converts—Acts 19:10, 22, 26, 31; 20:4, 16, 18, 27; 24:18; II Cor. 1:8; II Tim. 1:1–5; I Pet. 1:1. Diana worshipped—Acts 19:23–28.

Churches of.—I Cor. 16:19; Rev. 1:4, 11.

ASIARCHS. Acts 19:31.

ASIEL, ā'si-el. I Chr. 4:35.

ASK. Alms—Acts 3:2. See ALMS, BEGGARS. Amiss—Jas. 4:2, 3. Before you ask him—Mt. 6:8. Do above all that ye—Eph. 3:20. Faith, In—Jas. 1:6. Give to him that—Mt. 5:42; Lu. 6:30. See FRATERNITY, GIVING, LIBERALITY. Know not what ye—Mt. 20:22; Mk. 10:38. One thing—Ps. 27:4. Signs, For—Mt. 16:1; I Cor. 1:22. Whatsoever ye ask—Mt. 7:7–11; 21:22; Mk. 11:24; Lu. 11:13; John 11:22; 14:13, 14; 15:7, 16, 23–26; I John 3:22; 5:14–16. See PRAYER.

ASLEEP. Apostles—Mt. 26:40, 43, 45; Mk. 14:37, 40, 41. Fallen asleep—Mt. 27:52; John 11:11; Acts 7:60; I Cor. 15:18, 20; I Thess. 4:13, 14; II Pet. 3:4. Jesus—Mt. 8:23, 24. See DEATH, SLEEP.

ASNAH, ăs'nah. Ezra 2:50.

ASP. A serpent.—Deut. 32:33; Job 20:14, 16; Is. 11:8; Rom. 3:13. See ADDER, SERPENT.

ASPATHA, ăs'pa-thà. **Son of Haman who was hung.**—Esth. 9:7.

ASPECT. Song of Sol. 5:15; Dan. 3:25. See COUNTENANCE, FACE, FORM.

ASRIEL, ăs'ri-el. (1) **Son of Gilead.**—Num. 26:31; Josh. 17:2.

(2) **Son of Manasseh.**—I Chr. 7:14.

ASSASSINS. Acts 21:38. See MURDERER.

ASSAULT. Esth. 8:11; Acts 17:5 (A.V.).

ASSAY. Deut. 4:34; I. Sam. 17:39; Job 4:2; Acts 9:26; 16:7; Heb. 11:29.

ASSEMBLE. Heb. 10:25. See CONGREGATION, GATHERED TOGETHER.

ASSES. Used for transportation.—Gen. 42:26; 44:3; 45:23; I Sam. 25:18; II Sam. 16:2; I Chr. 12:40; II Chr. 28:15; Neh. 13:15; Job 1:3; Is. 30:6.

Numbers of.—Num. 31:34, 39, 45; Ju. 19:3, 10; II Sam. 16:1; II Ki. 4:22; Ezra 2:67; Neh. 7:69; Job 42:12. A troop of—Is. 21:7.

A white ass—Ye that ride on—Ju. 5:10.

Jesus rode on.—John 12:14, 15. Ass's colt—Gen. 49:11. The king cometh, sitting upon ass's colt—Zech. 9:9; Mt. 21:5; John 12:15.

Wild asses.—Figurative—Job 24:5. Wild ass—Job 39:5; Ps. 104:11; Is. 32:14; Jer. 14:6.

Dumb ass.—II Pet. 2:16.

Laws concerning.—Ex. 13:13; 23:4, 5. Levy tribute—Num. 31:28, 30. Thou shalt not plow with an ox and ass together—Deut. 22:10.

Miscellaneous.—Abram owned—Gen. 12:16; 24:35; 30:43. Jacob owned—Gen. 32:5, 15; 34:28. Zibeon—Gen. 36:24. Benjamin—Gen. 43:18. Balaam and his ass—Num. Chap. 22. The murrain upon asses—Ex. 9:3. Joshua owned—Josh. 7:24. Asses smitten—I Sam. 22:19. Took away—I Sam. 27:9. Left—II Ki. 7:7. Saul seeks his father's—I Sam. 9:3; 10:14. Asses found—I Sam. 10:2, 16. Does not each loose his ass on Sabbath?—Lu. 13:15. Or having fallen in pit—Lu. 14:5.

Provender for.—Gen. 43:24; 47:17; Ju. 19:19, 21; Job 1:14; Is. 30:24.

ASSHUR, ăs'shur. (1) **The founder of Nineveh.**—Gen. 10:11.

(2) **Son of Shem.**—Gen. 10:22; I Chr. 1:17.

(3) **Used for Assyria.**—Num. 24:22, 24; Ez. 27:23; 32:22.

ASSHURIM, as-shu'rĭm. **Son of Dedan.**—Gen. 25:3.

ASSIGN. Josh. 20:2; II Sam. 11:16.

ASSIR, ăs'sir. (1) **Son of Korah, grandson of Kohath.**—Ex. 6:24; I Chr. 6:22.

(2) **A Levite, son of Ebiasoph.**—I Chr. 6:23, 37.

(3) **Son of Jeconiah, grandson of Jehoiakim.**—I Chr. 3:17.

ASSIST. Rom. 16:2. See HELP.

ASSOS, ăs'sŏs. A town in Mysia visited by Paul.—Acts 20:13, 14.

ASSUAGE. Gen. 8:1; Job 16:5; Nah. 3:19.

ASSURANCE.—Heb. *Aman*, "To go to the right hand," hence "Assurance"; Gr. *Plerophoria*, "Entire confidence," "To completely assure."

Of God's care.—Job. 13:15; Ps. 23:4; 46:1–3; 73:26; 118:5–6; Jer. 32:41; II Cor. 5:1; Eph. 3:12, 13; II Tim. 4:18.

Of acceptance with God.—Gen. 19:21; Is. 12:2; Acts 10:35; Rom. 5:1–2; I Thess. 1:4–5; II Pet. 1:10, 11; I John 3:19–22.

Of knowledge.—I Sam. 28:1; I Ki. 1: 13, 17, 30; Job 19:25; Acts 2:36; II Cor. 5:1; Phil. 4:12; Col. 2:2; II Tim. 1:12; 3:14, 15; I John 4:13.

Of life.—Ex. 20:12; Deut. 28:66; Job 24:22; Jer. 38:17; Mt. 10:39; Mk. 10: 17–21; John 5:24; 6:47, 51, 54; 10:10; II Cor. 12:8–10; Eph. 6:2, 3.

Of redemption.—Rom. 8:22, 23; I Cor. 6:14; 15:54–57; Eph. 1:7, 13, 14; 4:30; Rev. 5:9, 10; 14:1–5.

Of faith.—Rom. 5:1, 2; Eph. 3:12; Heb. 10:22 (margin); 11:1.

Of hope.—Job 14:14, 15; Ps. 42:11; Rom. 8:24, 25; II Cor. 4:8; Heb. 6:11, 19; I Pet. 1:3, 4.

Of love.—John 13:35; 15:13; Rom. 8:38, 39; Eph. 3:19; I John 3:18, 19; 4:7–13.

The effect of righteousness.—Lev. 27: 16–18; Is. 32:17, 18; John 13:17; Rev. 22:14.

Of righteous judgment.—Acts 17:30, 31; Rev. 22:10–12.

False assurance.—Ju. 9:15; 17:13 with 18:14–20; I Sam. 17:41, 42–44; II Ki. 8:12, 13; Pr. 25:19; Jer. 6:14; 8:11; 14:13–15; John 13:37, 38.

Assurance of punishment.—Ps. 9:17; Is. 57:20, 21; Jer. 8:12, 13; 49:12, 13; Ez. 7:25–27; Mt. 13:49, 50; 25:41–46; II Pet. 3:3–7; Rev. 20:14, 15. See Elec- tion, Faith.

ASSYRIA: Founded by Nimrod.—Gen. 10:11. Named from Asshur, Shem's son—Gen. 10:22. Its best known cap- ital was Nineveh, on the Tigris (or Hiddekel)—Gen. 2:14. Its length was about 500 miles, its breadth varied from 350 to 100 miles.—Gen. 10:11, 12; 25:18; Jonah 3:3; Is. 7:20.

Called.—The land of Nimrod.—Mic. 5:6. **War of kings against Jerusalem and Sa- maria.**—II Ki. Chs. 15–20; II Chr. Ch. 32. Tiglath-pileser takes Israel captive—II Ki. 15:29. Slaughter of Assyrians—II Ki. 19:35. Nineveh threatened because of intolerance— Nah. Ch. 3. Assyria used by Jeho- vah as a scourge—Is. 7:18, 19; 10:5, 6. Shalmaneser brought against Israel— II Ki. 17:2, 3; 18:9–12; Jer. 50:17.

Alliances sought.—II Ki. 16:7, 8; Hos. 5:13.

Prophesies concerning.—Is. 7:17; 8:4–8; 10:5–34; 14:24, 25; 19:23–25; 30:31– 33; 37:21–38; Jer. 1:15; Ez. Ch. 31; Jonah 3:1–4; Zech. 10:11. Attacked by Pharaoh-necoh—II Ki. 23:29.

ASTONISH, Astonishment. I Ki. 9:8; II Chr. 7:21; Job 18:20; 21:5; Ps. 60:3 (A.V.); Jer. 2:12. Babylon—Jer. 50: 13; 51:37. Belshazzar and his lords— Dan. 5:9 (A.V.). Daniel—Dan. 4:19 (A.V.); 8:27 (A.V.). Disciples—Mk. 7: 37; 10:24, 26; Lu. 24:22 (A.V.); Acts 10:45 (A.V.); 12:16 (A.V.). Edom—Jer. 49:17. Enemies—Lev. 26:32. Ezra— Ezra 9:3, 4 (A.V.). Ezekiel—Ez. 3:15 (A.V.). God—Jer. 14:9 (A.V.). Inhab- itants of the isles—Ez. 27:35. Israel —Deut. 28:28, 37; Jer. 18:16. Judah and Jerusalem—II Chr. 7:21; 29:8; Jer. 19:8; 25:9, 11, 18; 29:18; 42:18; 44:12, 22; Ez. 5:15; 23:33. Multitude —Mt. 7:28; 13:54; 22:33; Mk. 1:22; 6:2; 11:18; Lu. 4:32. Nebuchadrezzar —Dan. 3:24. Pillars of heaven—Job 26:11. Priests—Jer. 4:9. Princes of the sea—Ez. 26:16. Proconsul—Acts 13:12. Tyre—Ez. 27:35; 28:19. Up- right man—Job 17:8. See Amaze, Amazement, Dismay, Marvel, Sur- prise, Wonder.

ASTRAY. Animals.—Ex. 23:4; Mt. 18: 12, 13.

Persons.—Ps. 58:3; 119:176; Pr. 7:25; Is. 53:6; I Pet. 2:25; II Pet. 2:15.

Israel.—Jer. 50:6; Ez. 14:11; 44:10, 15; 48:11. See Idolatry, Sin.

ASTROLOGER. Is. 47:13; Dan. 1:20 (A.V.); 2:2, 10, 27 (A.V.); 4:7 (A.V.); 5: 7, 11, 15 (A.V.). See Astronomy, En- chanter, Magic.

ASTRONOMY. The sun, moon, and stars are frequently mentioned, but

the law of appearances governs the utterance. **The sun rises and sets—** Gen. 15:12, 17; 19:23; 28:11; 32:31; Ex. 22:3; Lev. 22:7. It and the moon become darkened—Is. 13:10; Ez. 32:7; Joel 2:10, 31; 3:15; Mt. 24:29; Mk. 13:24; Lu. 23:25; Acts 2:20. The stars are mentioned in clusters—Job. 9:9; 38:31, 32; Is. 13:10; Amos 5:8. But little more can be said, except as we deal with the miraculous. The sun (''Shemesh,'' ἥλιος) is the most splendid of God's works—Ps. 19:5–7. Its course is continuous, and includes a section under the earth traversed at night—Eccl. 1:5. It is the source of heat and light for the earth. Its darkening is the sign and expression of great calamities. Hence, ''the sun shall be darkened at mid-day,'' may describe the occurrence of an eclipse, always an occasion of superstitious dread among unscientific peoples—Is. 13:10; Joel 2:20; Amos 8:9; Mt. 24: 29; Mk. 13:24; Rev. 6:12. See SUN.

''**The Moon**'' (*Yārēăch*, poetical Lebhā-nāh, σελήνη) is the substitute of the sun for the night period—Gen. 1:16; Ps. 121:6; 136:9. Eclipses of the moon may be alluded to in the expression ''the moon turned into blood''—Joel 2:31; Rev. 6:12. See MOON.

''**Of the Stars**'' (Kōkhābhīm, ἀστερες), **as objects of interest in themselves, no account is made.**—In a small number of allusions, however, it is possible to detect current astronomical notions. The whole of the starry firmament, as a body, is called ''the host of heaven'' (Gen. 2:1), though that phrase does not always convey the same meaning—I Ki. 22:19; II Chr. 18:18. Of individual stars, including planets, Venus is mentioned under the name ''Day star'' (''Lucifer, son of the morning,'' A.V. Is. 14:12). Saturn appears under the name of Chiun (Amos 5:26) A. V. and E. R. V., but A. R. v. ''the shrine.'' See also Acts 7:43. ''Rephan,'' probably ''Saturn.''—A. C. Z. in *Standard Bible Dictionary.* See STARS.

The heavenly planets excited devotion. —Gen. 37:9; Deut. 4:19; II Ki. 23:5; Ps. 8:3–5; 19:1–4; 72:5; Eccl. 11:7, 8;

Jer. 19:13; Ez. 8:16; Rev. 21:23; 22:5. Invoked to praise God—Ps. 148:3.

The sun and moon appointed for seasons. —Gen. 1:14; Ps. 104:19; 136:8, 9; Jer. 10:2. For seasons of war—Josh. 10: 12; Ju. 5:20; Hab. 3:11. For feasts— I Sam. 20:5; Ps. 81:3, 4; I Chr. 23:31; II Chr. 8:13; Is. 1:13, 14; Ez. 45:17; Hos. 2:11. For end of time—Is. 13:10, 11; Mt. 24:29; Mk. 13:24; Lu. 21:25, 26.

Difference in sphere and glory.—Gen. 1:16; II Ki. 23:5; I Cor. 15:41; Rev. 12:1; 21:23.

Dissolution of planetary system.—Is. 13:13; 34:4; 51:6; Ez. 32:7, 8; Joel 2:30, 31.

ASUNDER. Lev. 1:17; II Ki. 2:11; Ps. 2:3; Mt. 19:6; Mk. 5:4; Lu. 12:46.

ASYNCRITUS, a-sўn′krĭ-tŭs. **A disciple to whom Paul sends a salutation.** —Rom. 16:14.

ATAD, ā′tăd. **The threshing floor where Joseph and his brethren mourned for Jacob.**—Gen. 50:10, 11.

ATARAH, ăt′a-rah. **Wife of Jerahmeel.** I Chr. 2:26.

ATAROTH, ăt′a-rŏth. (1) **A town east of the Jordan.**—Num. 32:3, 34.

(2) **A town in Ephraim.**—Josh. 16:5.

(3) Josh. 16:2, 7. (4) See ATROTH.

ATE. Lu. 17:27. Defiled hands, With— Mk. 7:2. Jesus ate after his resurrection—Lu. 24:43. Loaves—Mt. 14:20. See EAT, FOOD, MEALS.

ATER. a-ter. (1) **Ancestor of a family of exiles.**—Ezra 2:16; Neh. 7:21.

(2) **Ancestor of porters who came up with Zerubbabel.**—Ezra 2:42; Neh. 7:45.

(3) **One who sealed the covenant with Nehemiah.**—Neh. 10:17.

ATHACH, ā′thak. **A town in southern Judah.**—I Sam. 30:30.

ATHAIAH, a-tha-iah. **A Jew dwelling in Jerusalem in the time of Nehemiah.** —Neh. 11:4.

ATHALIAH. ăth′a-lī′ah. (1) **Daughter of the king of Israel.**—II Ki. 8:26; II Chr. 21:6. Wife of Jehoram—II Chr. 21:6. Evil influence over her husband and son—II Ki. 8:18; II Chr. 21:6, 13. Events: Murders all her grandchildren except Joash—II Ki. 11:1–3; II Chr. 22:10–12. Slain by order of Jehoiada—II Ki. 11:12–16, 20; II Chr. 23:12–15, 21. Descendants of —II Chr. 24:7.

(2) **Son of Jehoram.**—I Chr. 8:26.

(3) **Father of Josiah.**—Ezra 8:7.

AT HAND. Coming of the Lord—Jas. 5:8. See JESUS, SECOND COMING. Kingdom of heaven—Mt. 3:2; 4:17; 10:7; Mk. 1:15. See JESUS, KINGDOM OF. Passover—John 6:4. Time—Lu. 21:8. See HAND.

ATHARIM, ăth′a-rĭm. Num. 21:1.

ATHENS, ăth′ens. **Most famous city of Greece.** ·Paul preached there—Acts 17:15–22; 18:1; I Thess. 3:1.

ATHIRST. Ju. 15:18; Ruth 2:9; Mt. 25:37, 44; Rev. 21:5; 22:17. See THIRST.

ATHLAI, ăth′lāi. **One of those who married foreign wives.** Ezra 10:28.

ATONEMENT. *Kaphar,* to cover, to cancel; also to cleanse, to forgive.

The value of Scriptural atonement depends on one's conception of sin. Sin is lawlessness.—I John 3:4. Sin is yielding to lust—Gen. 3:6; I Pet. 4:3–4; I John 2:16. The result is separation from God—Deut. 31:17; Josh. 7:12; Ps. 78:59; Is. 59:2; 64:7; Ez. 23:18; Hos. 9:12; Mic. 3:4; Mt. 7:23; Lu. 13:27; Heb. 12:14.

The necessity of atonement grows out of two things: (1) Holiness of Jehovah—Ex. 3:5; 15:11; Lev. 19:2; Is. 6:3; (2) Disobedience of man—Gen. 3:17–19; Ex. 34:7; Acts 17:30–31; Rom. 3:9, 19; 5:12. Holding these two features in combination, we get a just conception of sin—Gen. 3:7–8; Ps. 46:10; Is. 55:8–9; Lev. 10:10.

Sacrifice the appointed means of approach to God.—Ex. 29:31–37; Lev. 4:1–35; 6:24–30; 23:26–31; Num. 29:1–11; Deut. 12:11–14.

Through whom atonement is made.— Must offer through the priest—Lev. 4:13–18, 22–26; 5:6, 8–10, 12–13; 6:6–7, 12–13; Mt. 8:4; Mk. 1:44; Lu. 5:14; Heb. 8:3; 9:6–7; 10:11. Great prophets sometimes offered sacrifices —·I Sam. 7:9, 10; I Ki. 18:30–39.

The principle of the atonement.—The life is in the blood—Lev. 17:11; Deut. 12:23. Life of no value in atonement unless offered up in death—See Lev.

Chs. 4, 5, 6, etc. Not possible for blood of animals to purge away sin—Heb. 10:1–4. These sacrifices foreshadow the death of Jesus—Heb. 9:11–14, 23–28; 10:11–14. "Except a grain of wheat fall into the earth and die, it abideth alone," etc.—John 12:24. "If I be lifted up from the earth, will draw," etc.—John 12:32–33. The atonement of Jesus effects our reconciliation with God—John 1:29; Rom. 5:8–11; II Cor. 5:14–19; Rom. 3:21–26. His obedience unto death, even the death of the cross, as related to the obedience of the race—Phil. 2:8; Rom. 5:19. We are instructed to die with Him in order to rise into the new life—Rom. 6:1–11; 8:10–13; II Cor. 5:14–17.

The attitude of the Old Testament prophets.—They favored sacrifice— Is. 56:6–7; 60:7; Jer. 17:26; 33:18. But opposed its abuse—Is. 66:3–4; Hos. 6:6; Mic. 6:6–8; Mal. 1:6–8. The servant of Jehovah takes upon himself an expiatory character—Is. 53:5, 6, 8, 10–12. (See also Zech. 12:10; 13:1; Dan. 9:24.) The moral character of the suffering servant set forth— Is. 52:13; 53:4, 7, 9. His life and death blend in the perfect sacrifice—Is. 11:1–5; 61:1–3; 63:1–3; Mic. 7:18–20; Zeph. 3:14–17.

The day of atonement.—On the tenth day of the seventh month (Tisri)— Ex. 30:10. Mode of observance—Lev. 16:3–10. Details—Lev. 16:11–34. Special victims—Num. 29:7–11. The action of the people—Lev. 23:26–32. To be kept as a Sabbath—Lev. 16:29–31; Num. Ch. 29. The day on which jubilee is to be proclaimed—Lev. 25:9. See also PRIESTS, OFFERINGS, SACRIFICES, BLOOD, BLOOD OF JESUS, DEATH OF JESUS.

ATROTH-BETH-JOAB, ăt′rŏth–bĕth–jō′ăb. I Chr. 2:54.

ATROTH-SHOPHAN, ăt′rŏth–shō′phan. Num. 32:35.

ATTAI, ăt′tāi. (1) **A descendant of Perez.**—I Chr. 2:35, 36.

(2) **A Gadite.**—I Chr. 12:11.

(3) **Son of Rehoboam.**—I Chr. 11:20.

ATTAIN. Gen. 47:9; II Sam. 23:19, 23; I Chr. 11:21, 25; Acts 27:12 (A.V.);

Phil. 3:12 (A.V.). Doctrine—1 Tim. 4:6 (A.V.). Innocency—Hos. 8:5. Knowledge—Ps. 139:6. See Pr. 1:5. Law of righteousness—Rom. 9:31. Paths of life—Pr. 2:19. Resurrection —Lu. 20:35; Phil. 3:11, 12. Righteousness—Rom. 9:30, 31; Phil. 3:16. See HOLD, OBTAIN, TAKE.

ATTALIA, ăt'ta-li'a. **A coast town of Pamphylia.**—Acts 14:25.

ATTEND. Job 32:12. Altar—Heb. 7:13. Cry (prayer)—Ps. 17:1; 55:2; 61:1; 66:19; 86:6 (A.V.); 142:6. Know understanding, To—Pr. 4:1. Lord, Upon the—I Cor. 7:35. Reading—I Tim. 4:13 (A.V.). Things—Acts 16:14 (A.V.); Rom. 13:6. Wisdom—Pr. 5:1. Words—Pr. 4:20; 7:24. See EARS, HEAR, OBEDIENCE.

ATTENTIVE. Job 37:2; Lu. 19:48. Ear —II Chr. 6:40; 7:15; Neh. 1:6, 11; Ps. 130:2.

ATTIRE. Lev. 16:4; II Ki. 9:30; Pr. 7:10; Jer. 2:32. See CLOTHING, GARMENT.

AUDIENCE. Gen. 23:10, 13, 16; Ex. 24:7; I Chr. 28:8; Neh. 13:1; Acts 22:22. See EAR, HEAR.

AUGHT. Mt. 5:23; 21:3; Mk. 7:12; Lu. 19:8; John 4:33; Acts 4:32; 28:19; Philemon 18.

AUGMENT. Num. 32:14; Pr. 28:8.

AUGUSTAN, au-gŭs'tan. Acts 27:1.

AUGUSTUS CÆSAR. Emperor of Rome succeeding Julius Cæsar.—Lu. 2:1; Acts 25:21, 25 (A.V.), 27:1 (A.V.). See CÆSAR.

AUNT. Lev. 18:14.

AUSTERE. Lu. 19:21, 22.

AUTHOR. Heb. 2:10; 5:9; 12:2.

AUTHORITY. Ju. 18:7. Mt. 20:25; Mk. 10:42; 13:34; Lu. 19:17; 22:25; I Pet. 3:22; Rev. 2:26. All—I Cor. 15:24; I Tim. 2:2 (A.V.); Titus 3:1. Apostles —Mt. 10:1; Lu. 9:1. Beast—Rev. 13:2. Centurion—Mt. 8:9; Lu. 7:8. Esther—Esth. 9:29. Eunuch—Acts 8:27. Governor—Lu. 20:20. Jesus—See JESUS, DIVINITY OF. Righteousness— Pr. 29:2 (A.V.). Saul, king of Israel— I Sam. 9:17. Saul of Tarsus—Acts 9:14; 26:10, 12; II Cor. 10:8; I Thess. 2:6. Titus—Titus 2:15. Woman—I Cor. 11:10; I Tim. 2:12 (A.V.). See GOD IS ALMIGHTY, JESUS, AUTHORITY OF, POWER.

AVAIL. Circumcision—Gal. 5:6; 6:15 (A.V.). Nothing—Esth. 5:13. Supplication of righteous man—Jas. 5:16. Sword—Job 41:26.

AVEN, ā'ven. **On, or Heliopolis. An Egyptian city.**—Gen. 41:45; 46:20; Ez. 30:17; Hos. 10:8; Amos 1:5.

AVENGE. Ps. 8:2; Lu. 18:3–8; Rom. 12:19; II Cor. 7:11; 10:6; I Thess. 4:6; Rev. 6:10; 19:2. See VENGEANCE.

AVERSE. Mic. 2:8.

AVIM, AVITES. See AVVIM, AVVITES.

AVITH, ā'vith. **Capital city of Hadad, an Edomite king.**—Gen. 26:35; I Chr. 1:46.

AVOID. II Cor. 8:20. David avoids Saul —I Sam. 18:11. Factions—Rom. 16:17 (A.V.). See QUESTIONINGS. Fornication —I Cor. 7:2 (A.V.). Path of the wicked —Pr. 4:15. Profane babblings—I Tim. 6:20 (A.V.). Questionings—II Tim. 2:23; Titus 3:9 (A.V.).

AVOUCHED. Deut. 26:17, 18.

AVVA, av-va. II Ki. 17:24. See IVVAH.

AVVIM, AVVITES, ăv'vim. (1) **A premosaic tribe.**—Deut. 2:23; Josh. 13:3. (2) **A city of Benjamin.**—Josh. 18:23. (3) II Ki. 17:31.

AWAIT. Acts 9:24 (A.V.).

AWAKE. Apostles—Lu. 9:32. Baal— I Ki. 18:27. David—Ps. 3:5; 17:15; 57:8; 139:18. Death, From—II Ki. 4:31; Job 14:12; Ps. 17:15; Dan. 12:2; John 11:11. See DEATH, RESURRECTION, SLEEP. Deborah—Ju. 5:12. Drunkard, The—Pr. 23:35; Joel 1:5. God—Job 8:6; Ps. 7:6; 35:23; 44:23; 59:4; 73:20; 78:65; Is. 51:9. Hungry man—Is. 29:8. Jeremiah—Jer. 31:26. Jerusalem—Is. 51:17; 52:1. See ZION. Jesus —Mt. 8:25; Mk. 4:38; Lu. 8:24. Judah —Is. 26:19. Judgment—Ez. 7:6; Hab. 2:7. Love, My—So. of Sol. 2:7; 3:5; 8:4. North wind—So. of Sol. 4:16. Peter—Acts 12:7. Psaltery and harp —Ps. 57:8; 108:2. Righteousness, To —I Cor. 15:34. Sleepest, Thou that— Rom. 13:11; Eph. 5:14. Sword—Zech. 13:7. Wood—Hab. 2:19. Zion—Is. 52:1.

AWARE. So. of Sol. 6:12; Jer. 50:24; Mt. 24:50 (A.V.); Lu. 11:44 (A.V.); 12:46 (A.V.); Acts 14:6.

AWAY. Carried—Heb. 13:9. Jesus, With—Lu. 23:18; John 19:15. Paul, With—Acts 21:36; 22:22. Putting away filthiness and wickedness—Jas. 1:21; I Pet. 2:1. Turning away—Num. 14:43; Job 11:14; Jer. 32:40; Zech. 7:11; Jas. 1:24.

AWE. I Sam. 18:15; Ps. 4:4; 22:23; 33:8; 119:161; Is. 29:23; Mal. 2:5; Heb. 12:28. See AMAZE, AMAZEMENT, ASTONISH, SURPRISE, WONDER.

AWNING. Ez. 27:7.

AXE. Cut trees with—Deut. 19:5; 20: 19; Ju. 9:48; Ps. 74:5; Is. 10:15; Jer. 10:3; 46:22. Sharpened—I Sam. 13: 20, 21. Of iron—II Sam. 12:31. Not used in building temple—I Ki. 6:7. People cut with—I Chr. 20:3. Made by smith—Is. 44:12. Lieth at root of tree—Mt. 3:10; Lu. 3:9.

AXLE. I Ki. 7:30.

AXLETREES. I Ki. 7:32, 33.

AZALIAH, ăz'a-lī'ah. Father of Shaphan the Scribe.—II Ki. 22:3; II Chr. 34:8.

AZANIAH, ăz'a-nī'ah. Father of one of those who sealed the covenant.—Neh. 10:9.

AZAREL, ăz'är-el. (1) A descendant of Korah, who came to David at Ziklag. I Chr. 12:6.

(2) A singer in the house of God under David.—I Chr. 25:18.

(3) A prince of Dan in time of David.— I Chr. 27:22.

(4) One of the family of Bani, who married a strange wife.—Ezra 10:41.

(5) Neh. 12:36. Possibly same as (1).

AZARIAH, ăz'a-rī'ah. (1) Son of Zadok, David's high-priest.—I Ki. 4:2.

(2) Son of Nathan, who was over Solomon's officers.—I Ki. 4:5.

(3) Son of Amaziah, made king of Judah.—II Ki. 14:21; 15:1-27; I Chr. 3:12. See UZZIAH.

(4) Son of Ethan and grandson of Zerah.—I Chr. 2:8.

(5) Grandson of Obed.—I Chr. 2:38.

(6) Son of Ahimaaz and grandson of Zadok.—I Chr. 6:9.

(7) Grandson of (6), a priest in Solomon's house.—I Chr. 6:10, 11.

(8) Son of Hilkiah the high-priest in time of Josiah.—I Chr. 6:13, 14; 9:11; Ezra 7:1.

(9) Son of Zephaniah, ancestor of Samuel.—I Chr. 6:36.

(10) A prophet sent to encourage Asa king of Judah.—II Chr. 15:1.

(11) Son of Jehoshaphat king of Judah. —II Chr. 21:2.

(12) Another son of Jehoshaphat.—II Chr. 21:2.

(13) Son of Jehoram king of Judah.— II Chr. 22:6.

(14) A captain who aided Jehoiada in seating Josiah as king.—II Chr. 23:1.

(15) Son of Obed, who also assisted Jehoiada.—II Chr. 23:1.

(16) A high-priest who sought to prevent Uzziah from burning incense.— II Chr. 26:17, 20.

(17) Son of Johanan, a head of a family of Ephraim.—II Chr. 28:12.

(18) A Levite under Hezekiah, a descendant of Kohath, who assisted in cleansing the temple.—II Chr. 29:12.

(19) A high-priest under Hezekiah.—II Chr. 31:10, 13.

(20) Grandfather of Ahitub, and great-grandfather of Zadok, the high-priest. —Ezra 7:3.

(21) One of those who assisted Nehemiah in repairing the wall of Jerusalem.—Neh. 3:23, 24.

(22) One of those who came up with Zerubbabel.—Neh. 7:7.

(23) A priest who interpreted the law while Ezra read.—Neh. 8:7. (Possibly same as 22.)

(24) A priest who assisted Nehemiah in sealing the covenant.—Neh. 10:2.

(25) A prince of Judah appointed by Nehemiah to march in procession.— Neh. 12:33.

(26) Son of Hoshaiah, who accused Jeremiah of speaking falsely.—Jer. 43:2.

(27) A Jewish youth carried captive into Babylon, and called Abed-nego. —Dan. 1:6-19; 2:17.

AZAZ, ā'zăz. Father of Bela, of the tribe of Reuben.—I Chr. 5:8.

AZAZEL, a-zā'zel. Lev. 16:8.

AZAZIAH, ăz'a-zī'ah. (1) A Levite musician, who accompanied the ark to Jerusalem.—I Chr. 15:21.

(2) Father of Hoshea, a prince of the tribe of Ephraim.—I Chr. 27:20.

(3) A Levite, ruler of the house of God under Hezekiah.—II Chr. 31:13.

13

AZBUK, ăz′buk. Neh. 3:16.

AZEKAH, a-zē′kah. **City of Judah.**— Josh. 15:35. Fortified by Rehoboam.— II Chr. 11:9.

Strifes of.—Besieged by Nebuchadrezzar—Jer. 34:7. Five kings slain near —Josh. 10:10, 11. Goliath slain near— I Sam. 17:51.

Rebuilt after the captivity.—Neh. 11:30.

AZEL, ā′zel. **A Benjamite.**—I Chr. 8:37, 38; 9:43, 44.

AZEM. See EZEM.

AZGAD, ăz′găd. (1) **Ancestor of some of those who returned with Zerubbabel.**—Ezra 2:12; Neh. 7:17.

(2) **One of those who returned from exile with Ezra.**—Ezra 8:12.

(3) **One of those who assisted Nehemiah in sealing the covenant.**—Neh. 10:15.

AZIEL, ā′zĭ-ĕl. **A singer who accompanied the ark to Jerusalem.**—I Chr. 15:20.

AZIZA, a-zī′za. **One of those who married foreign wives.**—Ezra 10:27.

AZMAVETH, ăz′ma-vĕth. (1) **One of David's thirty mighty men.**—II Sam. 23:31; I Chr. 11:33.

(2) **A descendant of Jonathan the son of Saul.**—I Chr. 8:36; 9:42.

(3) **Father of two men who came to David at Ziklag.**—I Chr. 12:3.

(4) **A village near Jerusalem.**—Ezra 2: 24; Neh. 12:29.

(5) **One of David's officers, who was over the king's treasures.**—I Chr. 27:25.

AZMON, ăz′mon. **A place near the torrent of Egypt.**—Num. 34:4, 5; Josh. 15:4.

AZNOTH-TABOR, ăz′noth-tā′bôr. Josh. 19:34.

AZOR, ā′zôr. **An ancestor of Jesus.**— Mt. 1:13, 14.

AZOTUS, a-zō′tus (Ashdod). **Place where Philip was found.**—Acts 8:40. See ASHDOD.

AZRIEL, ăz′ri-el. (1) **A member of half tribe of Manasseh.**—I Chr. 5:24.

(2) **Father of ruler of Naphtali under David.**—I Chr. 27:19.

(3) **Father of Seraiah who was sent to take Baruch.**—Jer. 36:26.

AZRIKAM, ăz′ri-kam. (1) I Chr. 3:23.

(2) I Chr. 8:38; 9:44.

(3) **A Levite, descended from Merari.**— I Chr. 9:14; Neh. 11:15.

(4) **Ruler of the house of Ahaz.**—II Chr. 28:7:

AZUBAH, a-zū′bah. (1) **Mother of Jehoshaphat king of Judah.**—I Ki. 22: 42; II Chr. 20:31.

(2) **Wife of Caleb son of Hezron.**—I Chr. 2:18, 19.

AZZAH, ăz′zah. **A city of the Philistines.**—Deut. 2:23; I Ki. 4:24; Jer. 25:20. See GAZA.

AZZAN, ăz′zan. **Father of Paltiel a prince of the tribe of Issachar.**—Num. 34:26.

AZZUR, ăz′zur. (1) **Father of a prince seen in a vision by Ezekiel.**—Ez. 11:1.

(2) **One of those who assisted Nehemiah in sealing the covenant.**—Neh. 10:17.

(3) **Father of Hananiah the prophet who prophesies falsely.**—Jer. 28:1.

BAAL, bā′al. (1) (The supreme male divinity of Phœnician and Canaanitish nations; supposed to correspond to the sun.) Worship of Baal prevailed in the time of Moses among the Moabites and Midianites (Num. 22: 41), and from them spread to the Israelites—Num. 25:3–18; Deut. 4:3. Became religion of court and people of ten tribes—I Ki. 16:31, 32; 13:19, 22. Seems never to have been abolished among them—I Ki. 16:32; 18:19, 26–28; II Ki. 10:22.

Worshipped by Israelites.—Num. 25:3– 18; Deut. 4:3; Ju. 2:11–13; I Sam. 7:4; II Ki. 17:16; Jer. 2:8, 23; 7:9; 9:14; 11:13, 17; 12:16; 19:5; 23:13, 27; 32: 29; Hos. 2:8, 13, 17; 13:1; Zeph. 1:4. By Ahab—I Ki. 16:31–33; 18:18; 19: 18; II Ki. 3:2. By Ahaziah—II Chr. 22:2–4; 24:7. By Ahaz—II Chr. 28:2. By Manasseh—II Ki. 21:3; II Chr. 33:3.

Idols and altars of.—Destroyed by Gideon—Ju. 6:25–32. By Jehu—II Ki. 10: 18–28. By Jehoiada—II Ki. 11:17, 18. By Josiah—II Ki. 23:4, 5.

Prophets of, maintained by Jezebel.— I Ki. 18:19.

Slain by Elijah.—I Ki. 18:40. By Jehu —II Ki. 10:18–25.

Have not bowed to Baal.—Rom. 11:4.

(2) **A city of the tribe of Simon.**—I Chr. 4:33.

(3) **A member of the tribe of Reuben.**— I Chr. 5:5.

(4) **A Benjamite.**—I Chr. 8:30.

BAALAH, bā′al-ah. (1) **A city of Judah.**—Josh. 15:9, 10; I Chr. 13:6.

(2) **A hill in southern Judah.**—Josh. 15:11.

(3) **A city in southern Judah.**—Josh. 15:29. See BALAH (Josh. 19:3), and BILHAH (I Chr. 4:29).

BAALATH, bā′al-ăth. **A town in Dan**— Josh. 19:44; I Ki. 9:18; II Chr. 8:6.

BAALATH-BEER, bā′al-ăth-bē′er. **A town in southern Judah.**—Josh. 19:8.

BAAL-BERITH, bā′al-bē′rith. **An idol worshipped by the Israelites.**—Ju. 8:33; 9:4. See EL-BERITH.

BAALE-JUDAH, bā′al-ē-ju′dah. II Sam. 6:2.

BAAL-GAD, bā′al-găd. **A place near Hermon.**—Josh. 11:17; 12:7; 13:5.

BAAL-HAMON, bā′al-hā′mon. **A place in Mt. Ephraim, where Solomon had a vineyard.**—So. of Sol. 8:11.

BAAL-HANAN, bā′al-hā′nan. (1) **An Edomite king.**—Gen. 36:38, 39; I Chr. 1:49, 50.

(2) **One of David's officers.**—I Chr. 27:28.

BAAL-HAZOR, bā′al-hā′zor. **A place near Ephraim, where Absalom slew his brother Amnon.**—II Sam. 1:23.

BAAL-HERMON, bā′al-hĕr′mon. Ju. 3:3; I Chr. 5:23.

BAALI, bā′al-ī′. **A title which God rejected as applied to Himself.**—Hos. 2:16.

BAALIS, bā′al-ĭs. **An Ammonite king.** —Jer. 40:14.

BAAL-MEON, bā′al-mē′on. **A town built by the tribe of Reuben.**—Num. 32:38; I Chr. 5:8; Ez. 25:9.

BAAL-PEOR, bā′al-pe-or. **Israel joined unto.**—Num. 25:3, 5; Ps. 106:28; Hos. 9:10. Followers destroyed—Num. 25:5; Deut. 4:3. See BAAL.

BAAL-PERAZIM, bā′al-pĕr′a-zĭm. **A place near valley of Rephaim where David conquered the Philistines.**—II Sam. 5:20; I Chr. 14:11.

BAAL-SHALISHAH, bā′al-shăl′i-shah. **A place in Ephraim.**—II Ki. 4:42.

BAAL-TAMAR, bā′al-tā′mar. **A place in Benjamin.**—Ju. 20:33.

BAAL-ZEBUB, bā′al-zē′bub. **The god of Ekron.** See BEELZEBUB.

BAANA, bā′an-à. (1) **One of Solomon's officers in Jezreel**—I Ki. 4:12.

(2) **Another of Solomon's officers in Asher.**—I Ki. 4:16.

(3) **Father of Zadok who returned with Zerubbabel and helped to repair the wall of Jerusalem.**—Neh. 3:4.

BAANAH, bā′a-nah. (1) **Father of one of David's thirty mighty men.**—II Sam. 23:29; I Chr. 11:30.

(2) **Captain in Ish-bosheth's army.**—II Sam. 4:2-9.

(3) **One who returned with Zerubbabel.** —Ezra 2:2; Neh. 7:7; 10:27.

BAARA, bā′a-rà. **Wife of Shaharaim.**— I Chr. 8:8.

BAASEIAH, bā′a-sē′iah. **An ancestor of Asaph, the musician.**—I Chr. 6:40.

BAASHA, bā′a-shà. **A member of the tribe of Issachar, son of Ahijah, who conspired against Nadab, and slew him, and became king of Israel in his stead.**—I Ki. 15:16-22, 27-33; II Chr. 16:1-6; Jer. 41:9. Jehu's prophecy concerning—I Ki. 16:1-4, 7, 12, 13. Dies—I Ki. 16:5, 6; 21:22. Succeeded by his son Elah—I Ki. 16:8. Zimri slays his family—I Ki. 16:8-13; 21:22.

BABBLER. Eccl. 10:11 (A.V.); Acts 17:18. See GOSSIP.

BABBLING. Pr. 23:29 (A.V.); I Tim. 6:20; II Tim. 2:16.

BABE, BABES. Ps. 17:14; Is. 3:4; Lu. 18:15. Christ, In—I Cor. 3:1; Heb. 5:13; I Pet. 2:2. Jesus—Lu. 1:41, 44; 2:12, 16. Moses—Ex. 2:6. Mouth, Out of the—Ps. 8:2; Mt. 21:16. Newborn, As—I Pet. 2:2. Revealed unto—Mt. 11:25; Lu. 10:21. Teacher of—Rom. 2:20. See CHILDREN.

BABEL, bā′bel. **A city in plain of Shinar, where the tower of Babel was built.**—Gen. 10:10; 11:1-9.

BABYLON, băb′y-lon. **Capital of the country of Shinar (Gen. 10:10), or Babylonia; later, Chaldea**—Dan. 4:30; Jer. 50:8-10. Nimrod was the founder (Gen. 10:10), and he named it Bab-il (*The Gate of the God*). Afterwards the name was explained as being derived from Balal, *to confound*. Babylon is the Greek form of *Babel*. Shinar was a vast alluvial plain to the northwest of the Persian Gulf, traversed in a later day by Abraham—Gen. 11:31. We get a glimpse of the power of Shinar when its king invaded Palestine and was overcome by Abraham—Gen. 14:9, 17.

Size of.—Herodotus gives circumference as 60 miles. Messengers had to go from post to post to obtain news—Jer. 51:31–32. Walls: Were 350 feet high and 87 broad—Jer. 51:58. They were pierced with 100 gates of brass, 25 on each side—Is. 45:1–2. Population: Said to be 1,200,000. Called the golden city—Is. 14:4.

Famous for manufactures.—Josh. 7:21. For merchandise—Ez. 17:4, 12.

Babylon, Empire of.—The later or second empire was founded by Nabopolassar. His son was Nebuchadrezzar, mentioned frequently in Scripture as attacking and depopulating Jerusalem—II Ki. 24:1–17; 25:1, 2; I Chr. 6:15; II Chr. 36:6, 7; Jer. 24:1; 29:1; 39:1; 52:28. This king boasted that he had built Babylon—Dan. 4:30. Kent says, ''Building was his master passion. In all his enterprises he succeeded.'' (for further particulars see BABYLONIAN PERIOD.).

Evil foretold.—Merodach, Nebuchadrezzar's son, succeeded to the throne, liberating the Judæan king from prison—II Ki. 25:27–30; Jer. 52:31–34.

Belshazzar has gained notoriety through the great feast during which he was slain—Dan. Ch. 5. Assault of the city—Jer. 51:30–32. Cyrus thus comes into power and provides for the return of the Jews—II Chr. 36:22; Ezra 1:1–4; 5:13–17. Darius and Artaxerxes aid in carrying out Jehovah's purpose—Ezra Chs. 6–7.

Prophecies concerning.—Judah's captivity—II Ki. 20:16–18; Jer. 21:1–10; 22:24–26; 25:7–11; Ez. 12:10–15; 17:11–16; 19:8, 9; Hab. 1:5–11. The destruction of Jerusalem—Jer. 32:26–35; 34:2–4; 38:17, 18; Ez. 21:19–23. Other nations subject to Babylon—Jer. 27:1–11; 28:12–14; 43:11–13; 46:13, 14, 25, 26; 49:28–33; Ez. 26:7–12; 29:17–20; 30:10–12; 32:11. The destruction of Babylon—Is. 13:1–22; 14:4–23; 21:1–10, 46:1, 2; 47:1–11; 48:14,

15; Jer. 25:12–14; 50:1–46; 51:1–64; Dan. 2:36–45; 5:22–31. The return of the Jews—Is. 14:1–4; 44:28; 48:20; Jer. 29:10–14; 50:4–8, 19; II Chr. 36:23; Ezra Ch. 1; 2:1–67.

Babylon represented figuratively by: A great eagle—Ez. 17:3. A head of gold—Dan. 2:32, 37, 38. A lion with eagle's wings—Dan. 7:4. It was a great naval power—Is. 43:14. A great military power—Jer. 5:16. It was arrogant—Is. 14:13–14. It was self-confident—Is. 47:7, 8. It was oppressive—Is. 14:4. An instrument of vengeance—Is. 47:6; Jer. 51:7.

BABYLONIA, băb′y-lō′ni-à. See CHALDEA.

BABYLONIANS. Ezra 4:9; Ez. 23:15–23. See BABYLON.

BABYLONISH. Josh. 7:21.

BACA, bā′kȧ, *weeping.* **A valley near Jerusalem(?).**—Ps. 84:6 (A.V.). Probably figurative.

BACK. Ex. 3:1; 26:12; Rev. 5:1. Body, Of the—Ez. 10:12; Dan. 7:6. Behind the—I Ki. 14:9; Neh. 9:26; Is. 38:17; Ez. 23:35. Bow down—Rom. 11:10. Gods—Ex. 33:21–23. Plowed upon—Ps. 129:3. Rod for the—Pr. 10:13; 19:29; 26:3. Smiters, Gave my back to the—Is. 50:6. Turn—Ex. 23:27; Josh. 7:8, 12; I Sam. 10:9; II Chr. 29:6; Ps. 21:12; Jer. 2:27; 18:17; 32:33; 48:39. Stand back—Gen. 19:9. Turn back—II Sam. 1:22; I Ki. 18:37; Ps. 9:3; 35:4; 44:10, 18; 56:9; Zeph. 1:6; Mt. 24:18; Mk. 13:16; Lu. 9:62; 17:31; John 6:66; 20:14. See APOSTASY or BACKSLIDING.

BACKBITING. Ps. 15:3; Pr. 25:23; Rom. 1:30; II Cor. 12:10. See GOSSIP.

BACKBONE. Lev. 3:9. See BODY.

BACKSLIDING. See APOSTASY.

BACKWARD. Fall—Gen. 49:17; I Sam. 4:18; Is. 28:13. Go—Gen. 9:23; Job 23:8; Is. 1:4; Jer. 7:24; John 18:6. Turned—II Ki. 20:10, 11; Ps. 40:14; 70:2; Is. 44:25; 50:5; 59:14; Lam. 1:8.

BAD. Figs.—Jer. 24:2.

Good and bad.—Lev. 27:10, 12, 14, 33. Discern—II Sam. 14:17. Do—Num. 24:13; II Cor. 5:10. Fish—Mt. 13:48. Guests—Mt. 22:10. Land—Num. 13:19. Speak—Gen. 24:50; 31:24, 29; II Sam. 13:22. See EVIL.

BADGER(?). Only in King James Version. Translation of this word doubtful. Translated *sealskins* in text of A. S. Version, and *porpoiseskins* in margin. **Used in the tabernacle.**—Ex. 25:5; 26: 14; 35:7; 35:23; 36:19; 39:34; Num. 4:6–14, 25; Ez. 16:10.

BADE. Gen. 27:19; Josh. 11:9; Mt. 16: 12; Lu. 14:16; Acts 11:12.

BADNESS. Gen. 41:19.

BAGS. Money—Pr. 7:20; Is. 46:6; Hag. 1:6; Lu. 12:33; John 12:6; 13:29. Shepherd's—I Sam. 17:40, 49. Transgression sealed up in a bag—Job 14:17. Weights—Deut. 25:13; Pr. 16:11; Mic. 6:11.

BAGGAGE. I Sam. 10:22; 17:22; 30: 24; Acts 21:15.

BAHURIM, ba-hū'rim. **A village on the road from the valley of the Jordan to Jerusalem.** II Sam. 3:16; 16:5. Home of Shimer—II Sam. 16:5; 19: 16; I Ki. 2:8. Place where Jonathan and Ahimaaz were concealed when acting as spies for David—II Sam. 17:18.

BAHARUMITE, ba-hā'rum-īte. II Sam. 23:31; I Chr. 11:33.

BAKBAKKAR, bak-băk'kar. A Levite who returned from exile.—I Chr. 9:15.

BAKBUK, băk'buk. Ancestor of some who returned from exile.—Ezra 2:51; Neh. 7:53.

BAKBUKIAH, băk'bu-kī'ah. A Levite who was leader of music in the temple worship of the exile.—Neh. 11:17; 12: 9, 25.

BAKE. Ex. 16:23; Gen. 40:17. Bread —Gen. 19:3; Ex. 12:39; Lev. 26:26; I Sam. 28:24; Is. 44:15, 19. See BREAD. Cakes—Lev. 24:5; Num. 11:8 (A.V.); II Sam. 13:8; I Ki. 19:6; Ez. 4:12. Manna — Num. 11:8 (A. V.). Meal-offering—Lev. 2:1–4; 6:17; 7:9; 23: 17; Ez. 46:20.

BAKER. See ARTS AND TRADES.

BALAAM, bā'laam. **Son of Beor.**— Num. 22:5. Moab sends messengers to—Num. 22:5, 7, 8; Josh. 24:9, 10; Mic. 6:5. God speaks to—Num. 22:9, 10, 12, 20. Refuses Moab's request— Num. 22:14. More messengers sent— Num. 22:16–18; Deut. 23:4, 5; Neh. 13:2. Goes with messengers—Num.

22:21, 35; II Pet. 2:15; Jude 11; Rev. 2:14. God's anger against—Num. 22: 22. Angel appears to—Num. 22:34. Balak receives—Num. 22:36–41. Offers sacrifice—Num. 23:2, 3. First prophecy—Num. 23:7–10. Second prophecy —Num. 23:16–25. Third prophecy— Num. 24:4–10. Fourth prophecy— Num. 24:15–25. Blesses Israelites— Num. 23:11, 12. Views of Israelites —Num. 24:10, 12. Slain by the Midianites—Num. 31:8; Josh. 13:22. **N. T. references.**—II Pet. 2:15; Jude 11; Rev. 2:14.

BALADAN, băl'a-dăn. **Father of Berodach-baladan, king of Babylon in time of Hezekiah.**—II Ki. 20:12; Is. 39:1.

BALAH, bā'lah. Josh. 19:3.

BALAK. **Son of Zipper, king of Moab, who employed Balaam to curse Israel.** —Num. 22:2–41; 23:1–30; 24:10–25; Josh. 24:9; Ju. 11:25; Mic. 6:5. See BALAAM.

BALANCES. Calamity laid in—Job 6:2. False—Pr. 11:1; 20:23; Hos. 12:7; Amos 8:5; Mic. 6:11. Just— Lev. 19:36; Pr. 11:1; 16:11; Ez. 45:10. Money weighed in—Job 31:6; Is. 46: 6; Jer. 32:10. Weighed in—Ps. 62:9; Is. 40:12, 15; Ez. 5:1; Dan. 5:27; Rev. 6:5.

BALDNESS. Elisha, At—II Ki. 2:23. Leprosy, In—Lev. 13:40–43. Mourning, In—Is. 3:24; 15:2; 22:12; Jer. 16:6; 47:5; 48:37; Ez. 7:18; 27:31; 29:18; Amos 8:10; Mic. 1:16. Forbidden to shave the head—Lev. 21:5; Deut. 14:1.

BALL. Is. 22:18.

BALM. Article of commerce.—Gen. 37: 25; 43:11; Ez. 27:17. In Gilead—Jer. 8:22; 46:11. **Used for healing wounds** —Jer. 8:22; 46:11; 51:8.

BAMAH, bā'mah. Name given to places where Israel offered sacrifices to idols. —Ez. 20:29.

BAMOTH, bā'moth. **A Moabite city on the river Arnon, taken by Sihon.**— Num. 21:19, 20.

BAMOTH-BAAL, bā-moth-bā'al. Probably same as BAMOTH.—Josh. 13:17.

BAN, THE. (Things devoted or cursed.) (1) **The war ban.** Vow of destruction if Jehovah gave the victory—Num. 21:2, 3. Three degrees: (a) Everything devoted. Penalty for idolatry—Deut. 20:16–18. Opposing Israel—I Sam. Ch. 15. Jericho—Josh. 6:17–19.

(b) Cattle and spoil saved—Deut. 2: 34, 35; 3:6, 7; 7:1–3; Josh. 8:27; 11:14.

(c) Some persons saved—Deut. 20: 10–15.

(2) **The religious ban.**—Confined to Israel, literal or spiritual. Complete devotion: An Israelite—Ex. 22:20; Lev. 27:29. Any city in Israel—Deut. 13: 12–18. Modified—Ezra 10:1–4, 7, 8. To be abolished—Zech. 14:11. The last word of the Old Testament—Mal. 4:6. Pronounced in New Testament—I Cor. 16:22; Gal. 1:8. No spiritual man says Jesus is cursed—I Cor. 12:3. Jewish—Lu. 6:22; John 9:22, 34; 12: 42; 16:2. Christian—Mt. 18:15–17; I Cor. 1:3–5. Restored—II Cor. 2:6–11; I Tim. 1:20; Titus 3:10; III John 9, 10. Modified form—II Thess. 3:14, 15; II John 10, 11.

(3) **Private ban.**—Lev. Ch. 27. Vowed or dedicated to religious use—Lev. 27:21; Num. 18:14. Belonged to the priest—Ez. 44:29. Personal vow: Jephthah—Ju. 11:30–39. King of Moab—II Ki. 3:27. By tradition, freed from the law—Mk. 7:9–13.

Miscellaneous references. — Things — Josh. 7:1. Gain—Mic. 4:13. Man—I Ki. 20:42. Chief of devoted things —I Sam. 15:21. Trespass against—I Chr. 2:7. Cursed—Deut. 7:26; 13:17. See CURSE, DEVOTED, VOWS.

BAND, Ephod, Of the.—Ex. 28:8, 27; 39:5.

l etters, or That which binds.—Acts 16: 26. Ass, Of the wild—Job 39:5. Body, Of the—Col. 2:19. See BODY. Demoniac, Of the—Lu. 8:29. Ezekiel, Of—Ez. 3:25; 4:8. Iron, Of—Dan. 4: 15, 23. Israel and Judah, Of—Ps. 2:3; 107:14; Is. 28:22; 52:2; Jer. 2:20. Love, Of—Hos. 11:4. Orion, Of—Job 38:31. Paul's—Acts 22:30 (A.V.). Rudder—Acts 27:40. Samson's—Ju. 15:14. Unicorn, Of the—Job 39:10 (A.V.). Wicked, Of the—Ps. 119:61 (A.V.); Is. 58:6. Wicked woman's hands, Of the—Eccl. 7:26. Yoke, Of the—Lev. 26:13 (A. V.); Ez. 34:27 (A.V.). See BAR, BIND, FETTERS, BONDS.

Locusts. Cf. Pr. 30:27.

Men and soldiers, Of.—Gen. 32:7, 10 (A.V.); I Sam. 10:26; II Sam. 4:2; I Ki. 11:24; II Ki. 5:2; 6:23; 13:20, 21; 24:2; I Chr. 7:4; 12:18, 21, 23; II Chr. 22:1; Job 1:17; Ez. 12:14; 17:21; 38: 6, 9, 33; 39:4; Mt. 27:27; Mk. 15:16; John 18:3, 12; Acts 10:1; 21:31; 23: 12; 27:1. See SOLDIERS, WAR.

Pangs. Ps. 73:4.

BANI, bā'ni. (1) **One of the tribe of Gad, and one of David's thirty mighty men.**—II Sam. 23:36.

(2) **One of the ''sons of Aaron'' descended from Merari.**—I Chr. 6:46.

(3) **A descendant of Perez.**—I Chr. 9:4.

(4) **Ancestor of some of those who returned with Zerubbabel.**—Ezra 2:10; 10:29. See BINNUI.

(5) **Ancestor of some who married foreign wives.**—Ezra 10:34.

(6) **A descendant of (5) who had married a foreign wife.**—Ezra 10:38.

(7) **A Levite whose son repaired part of the wall of Jerusalem.**—Neh. 3:17; 8:7; 9:4, 5.

(8) **A Levite who led the people in acknowledging God's goodness to Israel.**—Neh. 9:4; 10:13.

(9) **Father of Uzzi, who was overseer of the Levites in Jerusalem after the exile.**—Neh. 11:22.

BANISHED. II Sam. 14:13, 14. See CAPTIVITY.

BANISHMENT. Lam. 2:14. See CAPTIVITY.

BANK. A depository of money.—Mt. 25:27; Lu. 19:23. **Embankment or mound.**—II Sam. 20:15 (A.V.); II Ki. 19:32 (A.V.). Arnon, Of the—Deut. 4:48; Josh. 12:2; 13:9, 16. Jordan, Of —Josh. 3:15; 4:18; II Ki. 2:13; I Chr. 12:15. See BRINK.

BANNER. Song of Sol. 6:4; Is. 13:2 (A.V.). God's banner—Ps. 20:5; 60:4; Song of Sol. 2:4. See ENSIGN, SIGNAL, STANDARD.

BANQUET. Job 41:6.

Belshazzar's.—Dan. 5:10. **Esther's**—Esther 5:1–14; 6:14; 7:1, 2, 7, 8. See FEASTS, MEALS.

BANQUETING. Song of Sol. 2:4; I Pet. 4:3 (A.V.). See FEASTS, REVELLING.

(1) **B̄APTISM, JOHN'S—A PREPARATION: Where administered.**—Mt.

3:6, 13, 16; Mk. 1:5, 9, 10; John 1:28; 3:23.

Its Character.—Mt. 3:11; Mk. 1:4, 5; Lu. 3:3; John 1:31; Acts 13:24.

Its Reception.—Lu. 7:29, 30; Mt. 21: 24–26.

Jesus sets the example.—Mt. 3:13–17; Mk. 1:9–11; Lu. 3:21.

(2) BAPTISM—HOLY SPIRIT—POWER: To whom promised.—Mt. 3:11; Mk. 1:8; Lu. 3:16; Acts 1:5. In prophecy—Joel 2:28, 29.

How administered.—Acts 2:2, 3; 10:44; 11:15. See John 7:39. See HOLY SPIRIT.

Its Phenomena.—Acts 2:2–4, 33; 10:46.

(3) BAPTISM — WATER — IN THE NAME OF THE TRINITY: Commanded.—Mt. 28:19; Mk. 16:16; Acts 2:38; 10:48; 22:16. See John 3:3–5.

To whom administered.—Acts 11:41; 8:12, 36–38; 9:18; 16:15, 32, 33; 18:8; 19:5.

Its character.—Mk. 16:16; Acts 2:38; 16:30–34; 22:16; Rom. 6:4; Eph. 5:26; John 3:5; Acts 2:41; 8:39; Gal. 3:27; Rom. 6:5, 7, 17–18; II Cor. 12:13; Col. 2:12; Titus 3:5; II Pet. 3:21.

(4) BAPTISM — SUFFERING: Proof of patience.—Mt. 20:22, 23; Mk. 10: 39; Lu. 12:50.

(5) BAPTISM—FIRE: To whom promised.—Mt. 3:11, 12; Lu. 3:16, 17.

BAPTIST. See JOHN THE BAPTIST.

BAPTIZE. See BAPTISM.

BAR. Castle, Of the—Pr. 18:19. Earth —Jonah 2:6. Gates of cities fortified with—Deut. 3:5; Ju. 16:3; I Sam. 23: 7; I Ki. 4:13; II Chr. 8:5; 14:7; Neh. 3:3, 6, 13–15; 7:3; Ps. 147:13; Jer. 49: 31; 51:30; Lam. 2:9; Ez. 38:11; Amos 1:5; Nah. 3:13. Iron, Of—Job 40:18; Ps. 107:16; Is. 45:2. Sea, Of the—Job 38:10. Sheol, Of—Job 17:16. Tabernacle, Of the—Ex. 26:26–29; 35:11; 36:31–34; 39:33; 40:18; Num. 3:36; 4:10, 12, 31.

BARABBAS, bar-ăb′bas. Heb. *Son of Father.* A prisoner, leader of a band of robbers. Was released in place of Christ—Mt. 27:16, 26; Mk. 15:7–15; Lu. 23:18–25; John 18:40. Preferred to Christ—Mt. 27:17, 20, 21; Mk. 15: 7–15. Liberated to the mob, according to custom—Mt. 27:26; Mk. 15:15;

Lu. 23:18; John 18:40. A murderer— Mk. 15:7.

BARACHEL, băr′a-kel. Father of Elihu, who reasoned with Job.—Job 32: 2, 6.

BARACHIAH, băr′a-kī′ah. Father of the prophet Zechariah.—Zech. 1:1, 7; Mt. 23:35.

BARAK, bā′rak. Son of Abinoam who, with Deborah, defeated Sisera.—Ju. 4:6–22; 5:1, 12, 15; Heb. 11:32.

BARBARIAN. Acts 28:2, 4; I Cor. 14: 11. Debtor to—Rom. 1:14. Neither Greek nor barbarian—Col. 3:11. See ALIENS, SOJOURNER.

BARBED. Iron.—Job 41:7.

BARBER. Ez. 5:1.

BARE, *v.* Ark.—I Chr. 15:13. Cain and Abel—Gen. 4:1, 2. Diseases, Our—Mt. 8:17. Eagles' wings, On—Ex. 19:4. Foundation—Heb. 3:13. Foundation of the world—II Sam. 22:16; Ps. 18: 15. God's holy arm—Is. 52:10. Pull —Lam. 5:13. Secret parts lay bare— Is. 3:17. Sin of many—Is. 53:12. Witness—Sec. 4:22; Acts 13:22. False— Mk. 14:56, 57. See BARE, BEAR.

BARE, *adj.* Esau—Jer. 49:10. Fig-tree —Joel 1:7. Grain—I Cor. 15:37. Head —Lev. 13:45. See BALDNESS. Heights —Jer. 12:12. Leprosy—Lev. 13:55. Naked and—Is. 47:2, 3 (A.V.); Ez. 16: 7, 22, 39; 23:29.

BAREFOOT. II Sam. 15:30; Is. 20:2–4. See FOOT.

BARGAIN. Lev. 6:2.

BARHUMITE. See BAHARUMITE.

BARIAH, ba-rī′ah. **Son of Shecaniah.** —I Chr. 3:22.

BAR-JESUS, băr-jē′sus. **Son of Jesus** (Elymas).—**A false prophet who opposed Paul and Barnabas.**—Acts 13:6.

BAR-JONAH, băr-jō′nah. **Son of Jonah** —Surname of Simon Peter.—Mt. 16: 17.

BARK. Dogs—Is. 56:10. Fig-tree— Joel 1:7.

BARKOS, băr′kos. **Ancestor of some who returned with Zerubbabel.**—Ezra 2:53; Neh. 7:55.

BARLEY. An Egyptian grain—Ex. 9: 31. A product of Palestine—Deut. 8:8; I Chr. 11:13; Jer. 41:8. Inferior to wheat as an offering, the jealousy offering being of barley, the meal offering of wheat—Lev. 2:1; Num. 5: 15. Was also purchase price of Hosea's wife—Hos. 3:2. Measure of wheat equal in value to three of barley—Rev. 6:6. Sown during autumnal rains and harvested in May—II Sam. 21:9. Fed to horses—I Ki. 4:28. Used in people's offerings—Ez. 45:13. Gideon likened to a barley-cake—Ju. 7:13. Made into loaves—II Ki. 4:42; Ez. 4:9. Jesus feeds with five loaves—John 6:9–13. Priests place a value on —Lev. 27:16. Absalom burns Joab's field of—II Sam. 14:30.

BARN. Blessing in—Deut. 28:8. Broken down—Joel 1:17. Floor—II Ki. 6:27 (A.V.). Gather into—Job 39:12 (A.V.); Hag. 2:19; Mt. 6:26; 13:20. Ravens have no—Lu. 12:24. See STOREHOUSE, THRESHING-FLOOR.

BARNABAS, bär'na-bas. **A Levite of Cyprus who sold a field and brought its price to the apostles.**—Acts 4:36. A good man and full of the Holy Spirit—Acts 11:24. Brings Paul to the apostles—Acts 9:27. Sent as far as Antioch by the church in Jerusalem—Acts 11:22, 23. Goes to Tarsus to seek Paul, brings him to Antioch, and abides there with him for a year —Acts 11:25, 26. Carries relief to the brethren in Judaea—Acts 11:30. Returns from Jerusalem—Acts 12:25. Barnabas and Paul ordained and sent forth to preach by the church in Antioch—Acts 13:1–52; 14:1–28; I Cor. 9:6. Worshipped as Jupiter at Lystra —Acts 14:12–15. Sent with Paul unto the apostles and elders in Jerusalem concerning the reception of the Gentiles—Acts 15:1–29; Gal. 2:1–9. Returns to Antioch—Acts 15:30–35. Contends with Paul concerning Mark —Acts 15:36–39. Misled by Jewish Christians—Gal. 2:13.

BARREL. See JAR.

BARREN. Blessed are the—Lu. 23:29. Devoureth—Job 24:21. Disciples—II Pet. 1:8 (A.V.). Elisabeth—Lu. 1: 7, 36. Faith without works—Jas. 2: 20. Land—II Ki. 2:19, 21 (A.V.); Ps. 107:34 (A.V.); Joel 2:20. Manoah, mother of Samson—Ju. 13:2, 3. Night —Job 3:7. None—Ex. 23:26; Deut. 7:14; Song of Sol. 4:2 (A.V.); 6:6

(A.V.). Rachel—Gen. 29:31. Rebekah —Gen. 25:21. Rejoice—Gal. 4:27. Sarai—Gen. 11:30. Seven, born—I Sam. 2:5. Sing—Is. 54:1. Woman— Ps. 113:9. Womb—Pr. 30:16.

BARSABBAS, bär-sab'bas. (1) **Joseph called Barsabas, surnamed Justus, nominated with Matthew to succeed Judas.**—Acts 1:23. (2) **A disciple sent with Silas to accompany Paul and Barnabas from the church in Jerusalem to the brethren in Antioch, etc.**—Acts 15:22.

BARTHOLOMEW, bar-thŏl'o-mew. See APOSTLES.

BARTIMAEUS, bär'ti-mae'us. **A blind beggar in Jericho whom Jesus cured.** —Mk. 10:46.

BARUCH, bā'ruk. (1) **Son of Zabbai who helped to build the wall of Jerusalem.**—Neh. 3:20; 10:6. (2) **A descendant of Perez.**—Neh. 11:6. (3) **Jeremiah's secretary while he was in prison.**—Jer. 32:12–16; 36:4–32; 43:3, 6; 45:1, 2.

BARZILLAI, bär-zĭl'la-ī. (1) **A man of Gilead who befriended David in his flight.**—II Sam. 17:27; 19:31–39; I Ki. 2:7; Ezra 2:61; Neh. 7:63. (2) **Father-in-law of Michal, Saul's daughter.**—II Sam. 21:8. (3) **Ancestor of exiles whose genealogy was lost.**—Ezra 2:61; Neh. 7:63.

BASE. Zech. 5:11. **Brazen bases in the tabernacle.**—Ex. 30:18; 31:9; 35:16; 38:8; 39:39; 40:11; Lev. 4:7; 8:11. Candlestick, Of the—Ex. 25:31.

Brazen bases in the temple.—I Ki. 7:27–43; II Ki. 16:17; 25:13, 16; II Chr. 4:14; Jer. 27:19; 52:17, 20. See PEDESTAL.

Of low degree or character.—II Sam. 6:22; Job 30:8; Is. 3:5; Dan. 4:17 (A.V.); Mal. 2:9; II Cor. 10:1 (A.V.). Follow—II Sam. 16:7; Acts 17:5 (A.V.). See BELIAL.

Kingdom.—Ez. 17:14; 29:14, 15.

Things.—I Cor. 1:28.

Thought.—Deut. 15:9. See ABASE, HUMILITY.

BASEMATH, bǎs'e-mäth. (1) **Daughter of Solomon, wife of Ahimaaz.**—I Ki. 4:15. (2) **Wife of Esau, daughter of Elon the Hittite.**—Gen. 26:34.

(3) **Another wife of Esau, daughter of Ishmael.**—Gen. 36:3, 17.

BASHAN (bā'shan), *fruitful.* A large fertile region east of the Jordan, conquered—Num. 21:35.

Og, King of Bashan.—Josh. 12:4, 5; I Ki. 4:19; Ps. 135:11; 136:20.

Conquest of Bashan.—King smote— Deut. 1:4. Against Israel at Edrei— Deut. 3:1; 29:7; Josh. 13:12. Bashan is delivered unto Israel—Deut. 29:8. Smote by Hazael—II Ki. 10:33. Sons of Gad dwelt over against—I Chr. 5: 11, 12, 16. Bashan languisheth—Nah. 1:4; Is. 33:9.

Cities.—Taken and destroyed.—Deut. 3:4, 6. Golan, city of refuge, given to Manasseh—Deut. 4:43; Josh. 20:8; 21:27. Inhabitants destroyed—Deut. 3:6. King only remained—Deut. 3:11. Land of Bashan given to tribes—Num. 32:33; Deut. 3:13; Josh. 13:11, 30, 31; 17:1, 5; 21:6; 22:7; I Chr. 6:62, 71.

Israelites possess.—Neh. 9:22. He shall feed upon—Jer. 50:19. Let them feed in Bashan—Num. 7:14.

Mountain of God is mountain of Bashan. —Ps. 68:22.

Oaks of Bashan.—Is. 2:13; Ez. 27:6; Zech. 11:2.

Beasts of Bashan.—Rams of—Deut. 32: 14; Ez. 39:18. Lions—Deut. 33:22. Bulls of—Ps. 22:12. Kine of—Amos 4:1.

BASIN. Ex. 12:22; 24:6; II Sam. 17: 28; Neh. 7:70; John 13:5. **Tabernacle, Of the.**—Brazen—Ex. 27:3; 38:3; Num. 4:14.

Temple, Of the.—II Ki. 12:13; 25:15; Jer. 52:19. Brazen—I Ki. 7:40, 45. Gold—I Ki. 7:50; I Chr. 28:17; II Chr. 4:8, 11, 22. See BOWLS, VESSELS.

BASKET: Baskets for bread.—Gen. 40: 16, 18; Ex. 29:3, 23, 32; Lev. 8:2, 26, 31; Num. 6:15, 17, 19; Mt. 14:20; 16:9, 10; Mk. 6:43; 8:19, 20; Lu. 9:17; John 6:13.

Baskets for fruit.—Deut. 26:2, 4; Jer. 6: 9; 24:2; Amos 8:1, 2.

Baskets for meat.—Ju. 6:19; Mt. 15:37; Mk. 8:8.

Paul escapes in.—Acts 9:25: II Cor. 11:33.

Blessings and cursings on.—Deut. 28: 5, 17.

Heads put in.—II Ki. 10:7.

BASTARD. Deut. 23:2; Zech. 9:6; Heb. 12:8.

BAT. Lev. 11:19; Deut. 14:18; Is. 2:20.

BATH. A measure of about 8 gallons.— I Ki. 7:26, 38; II Chr. 2:10; 4:5; Ezra 7:22; Is. 5:10; Ez. 45:10–14.

BATHE. See ABLUTIONS, BAPTISM, CEREMONIAL CLEANSING, PURIFICATION, WASH, WATER.

BATHSHEBA, băth'shē-bà. **Daughter of Eliam or Ammiel, wife of David and mother of Solomon; called also** *Bathshua.*—II Sam. 11:3; 12:24; I Ki. 1:11–31; 2:13–19; Ps. 51 title.

BATHSHUA, băth-shu'à. (1) **Same as** *Bathsheba.*

(2) **Wife of Judah.**—Gen. 38:2, 12 (A.V.).

BATTER. II Sam. 20:15.

BATTERING-ENGINES. Ez. 26:9.

BATTERING-RAMS. Ez. 21:22.

BATTLE. I Cor. 14:8 (A.V.); Rev. 9:7, 9 (A.V.); 16:14 (A.V.); 20:8 (A.V.). See SOLDIERS, WAR, WEAPONS.

BATTLE-FIELDS. Abimelech.—Ju. 9: 27–44. Benjamin defeated—Ju. 20: 31–35. Philistines defeat Israel—I Sam. 4:2. Joab in field—II Sam. 11: 23. Field taken away—I Sam. 8:14. Army arrayed in—I Sam. 10:8. Encamped in—II Sam. 11:11. Strife in field—II Sam. 18:6. Against Israel— II Sam. 18:6. Punishment in fields— I Sam. 17:44. Syrians hide in—II Ki. 7:12. Joram cast in field of Naboth— II Ki. 9:25, 37. David hides in—I Sam. 20:5, 11, 24, 35. Ammon and Syria defeated—I Chr. 19:9; Ez. 7:17. Fields given—I Sam. 22:7. Of offerings—II Sam. 1:21. Death in—I Ki. 2:26; 11: 29; 14:11; 16:4; 21:24. Abel-beth-maachah—I Ki. 15:20. Adamah— Josh. 19:36. Admah—Gen. 10:19; 14:2, 8; Deut. 29:23; Hos. 1:8. Ai— Josh. 7:2–5; 8:1–28. Anneroth—I Ki. 15:20. Ashdod—Josh. 11:22; 13:3; 15:47; I Sam. 5:1–8; II Chr. 26:6; Neh. 4:7; 13:23, 24. Ashteroth Kainaim—Gen. 14:5. Baal-gad—Josh. 11:17; 12:7; 13:5. Baal-perazim—II Sam. 5:20; I Chr. 14:11. Bethel—Ju. 1:22; I Sam. 10:3; II Chr. 13:19. Beth-shean—Josh. 17:11 ff; Ju. 1:27; I Sam. 31:7. Beth-horon—Josh. 10:11. Bochin—Ju. 2:1. Carmel—I Sam. 15:12;

25:2; II Chr. 26:10. Chedor-laomer—Gen. 14:5. Dan—Ju. 1:34; I Ki. 15:20. Egypt—Deut. 28:68; II Ki. 23:29. Ekron—Josh. 13:3; I Sam. 5:10; 6:16; 7:14; 17:52. Eltekeh (Altaku)—Josh. 19:44; 21:33; Ju. 11:29. Elah—I Sam. 17:21. Field of Megiddo—Josh. 17:12, 13; Ju. 1:27, 28; I Ki. 9:15; II Ki. 9:27; 23:29, 30; II Chr. 35:22. Gath—II Sam. 24:5; II Ki. 12:17. Geba—I Sam. 14:5; II Sam. 5:25; Is. 10:28; Neh. 11:31; Ezra 2:26. Gezer—Ju. 1:29; I Chr. 20:4; I Ki. 9:15. Gibeon—Josh. 10:6; II Sam. 2:12-32; 20:9; Jer. 41:12. Gilboa—I Sam. 28:4, 5; II Sam. 5:17-25. Gilead—I Ki. 22:3; II Ki. 8:28; 9:1. Gilgal—Josh. 4:19; 10:6; Ju. 2:1. Gomorrah—Gen. 14:11. Hadadrimmon—Zech. 12:11. Ham—Gen. 14:5. Hamoth—II Ki. 23:29-35. Harosheth—Jer. 4:2, 13, 16. Hazazon-tamar—Gen. 14:7. Ijon—I Ki. 15:20. Jericho—Josh. 4:19; 6:20; II Sam. 10:5; II Ki. 25:5; Jer. 39:5; 52:8. Jerusalem—I Ki. 14:25; II Ki. 12:17; 16:5; 18:17; 25:1-4; II Chr. 12:1-4; Is. 7:1; Jer. 9:11; 26:18. Jezreel—Josh. 17:16; Ju. 6:33; Hos. 1:5. Jogbehah—Ju. 8:11. Judah—Zech. 12:2. Kedeshnaphtali—II Ki. 15:29. Kishon—Ju. 4:16; 5:19. Karkor—Ju. 8:10. Lachish—II Ki. 18:17; 19:8. Libnah—Josh. 10:29; II Ki. 18:17; 19:8. Megiddo—II Ki. 23:29; II Chr. 35:22; Zech. 12:11. Midian—Ju. 8:3. Mizpah—I Ki. 15:16-22. Nobah—Ju. 8:11. Ramoth-gilead—I Ki. 22:3, 15; II Ki. 8:28; 9:1. Rephaim—II Sam. 5:18. Samaria, besieged by Benhadad—I Ki. 20:1-12; II Ki. 6:24. *By Shalmaneser*—II Ki. 17:5, 6; 18:9, 10. Samaria delivered—II Ki. 7:6, 7. *Destruction of*—Is. 7:9; 28:1. Shaveh-kiriathaim—Gen. 14:1-8. Seir, Mt.—Gen. 14:6; 32:3. Shaaraim—I Sam. 17:52. Shechem—Josh. 24:1. Shiloh—Josh. 18:1; 22:12. Shunem—I Sam. 28:4. Sodom—Gen. 14:11. Tabor, Mt. —Ju. 4:6. See ISRAEL.

BATTLEMENTS. Deut. 22:8; II Chr. 26:15; Zeph. 3:6. See BULWARKS, FORTIFICATIONS.

BAVVAI, băv'va-ī. **A descendant of Henadad who helped rebuild the wall.** —Neh. 3:18.

BAY. Horse—Zech. 6:3, 7 (A.V.). Tree —Ps. 37:35 (A.V.). Water, Body of—Josh. 15:2, 5, 19; Acts 27:39.

BAYITH, bā'yith. Is. 15:2.

BAZLITH, băz'lith. **Ancestor of some who returned from exile.**—Ezra 2:52; Neh. 7:54.

BDELLIUM. A gum.—Gen. 2:12; Num. 11:7.

BEACH.—Acts 21:5; 27:39.

BEACON. Is. 30:17.

BEALIAH, bē'a-lī'ah. **A city in Judah near Salem.**—I Chr. 12:5.

BEALOTH, bē'a-lŏth'. **A city near Salem**—Josh. 15:24; I Ki. 4:16.

BEAM. Eye, Out of thine own—Mt. 7:3-5; Lu. 6:41-42. Gates, Of the—Neh. 3:3, 6. House, Of the—I Ki. 6:9, 36; 7:2, 3, 6, 12; II Chr. 3:7; Song of Sol. 1:17. See Ps. 104:3. Timber, Of —II Ki. 6.2, 5; Hab. 2:11. Weavers—Ju. 16:14; I Sam. 17:7; II Sam. 21:19; II Chr. 11:23; 20:5. See HOUSE, TOOLS AND IMPLEMENTS, WOOD.

BEANS. II Sam. 17:28; Ez. 4:9. See FOOD.

BEAR. Ps. 91:12; Rev. 2:2, 3. All things, Love beareth—I Cor. 13:7. Ark—Gen. 7:17; Ex. 25:14; 30:4; 37:5; Deut. 10:8. Blame—Gen. 43:9; 44:32. Branded in my body—Gal. 6:17. See II Cor. 4:10. Broken spirit—Pr. 18:14. Burden—I Ki. 5:15; Neh. 4:17; Ps. 68:19; Jer. 17:21, 27; Mt. 20:12; 23:4; Lu. 11:46; Gal. 6:2. Chastisement—Job 34:31. Cross—Mt. 27:32; Mk. 15:21; Lu. 14:27; 23:26; John 19:17. Ephah—Zech. 5:10. Favor—Ps. 106:4. Foolish, With the—II Cor. 11:19. Fruit—II Ki. 19:30; Is. 37:31; Ez. 17:8, 23; Hos. 9:15; Joel 2:22; Lu. 8:8; 13:9; John 15:2, 4, 8. Grief—Is. 53:4; Jer. 10:19. See INFIRMITIES. Ignorant and erring, With—Heb. 5:2. Image of earthly and heavenly—I Cor. 15:49. Infirmities—Mt. 8:17; Rom. 15:1; Heb. 5:2. See GRIEF. Insolently, Himself—Pr. 14:16. Judgment Ex. 28:30; Gal. 5:10. See SIN. Marks of Jesus—Gal. 6:17. Names—Ex. 28:12, 29; Acts 9:15. People, All this—Num. 11:14; Deut. 1:9, 12, 31; Neh. 9:30; Is. 1:14; 63:9; Jer. 44:22; Mt. 17:17. Punishment of Cain—Gen. 4:13. Reproach—Ps. 55:12; 69:7; 89:

50; Jer. 31:19; Ez. 36:15; Mic. 6:16; Heb. 13:13. Shame—Ez. 16:52-54, 58; 32:24, 25, 30; 34:29; 36:6, 7; 44:13. See REPROACH. Shoes, Not worthy to bear—Mt. 3:11. Sin—Ex. 28:38, 43; Lev. 5:1, 17; 7:18; 10:17; 16:22; 17: 16; 19:8; 20:17, 19, 20; 22:9, 16; 24: 15; Num. 5:31; 9:13; 14:33, 34; 18:1, 22, 23, 32; 30:15; Lam. 5:7; Ez. 4:4-5; 14:10; 16:52; 18:19, 20; 23:35, 49; 39: 26; 44:10, 12; Jas. 1:15. *Jesus bears our sins*—Is. 53:11, 12; II. Cor. 5:21; Heb. 9:28; I Pet. 2:24. See ATONE-MENT. Temptation—I Cor. 10:13. Thorns and thistles—Heb. 6:8. Witness—Job 16:8 (A.V.); John 1:15; Acts 10:43. See WITNESS. Word of exhortation—Heb. 13:22. Words—Amos 7:10; John 16:12. Yoke—Lam. 3:27. See Mt. 11:29, 30. See BARE, BRING, CARRY, ENDURE, FORBEAR, SUFFERING.

BEAR (animal). **Ferocity of.**—I Sam. 17:34; II Sam. 178; Pr. 17:12; 28:15; Hosea 13:8; Amos 5:19. Roar of—Is. 59:11. Killed by David—I Sam. 17: 34-37. Destroy 42 children in Bethel. —II Ki. 2:24.

Figurative.—Dan. 7:5; Rev. 13:2.

Prophecy concerning.—And the cow and bear shall feed—Is. 11:7. See ANIMALS.

BEARD. To be left natural—Lev. 19: 27. Priests not to shave corners—Lev. 21:5; Ps. 133:2. Neglected in grief—II Sam. 19:24. Symptom of leprosy in—Lev. 13:29-37. Clipped—Jer. 48:37. Shaven in sorrow for sin—Jer. 41:5. One half shaved in disgrace.—II Sam. 10:4, 5. Dribbling on, a sign of deranged mind—I Sam. 21:13. Taking hold of in friendship—II Sam. 20: 9. Plucked in anger—Ez. 9:3. Cut off in misfortune.—Is. 15:2. Egyptians wore none—Gen. 41:14.

Figurative.—Is. 7:20. See HAIR.

BEASTS: Literal.—All created by God —Gen. 1:24-30; 2:19, 20; 3:1. God a provider for—Gen. 1:30; 9:10; Ps. 36: 6; 104:11.

Dwelling places of.—Job. 12:7, 8; 37:8; 40:20. Ps. 104:20-25; Is. 13:21, 22; 34:14; Jer. 50:39; Mk. 1:13.

Given names by Adam.—Gen. 2:20.

Tamed by man—Jas. 3:7.

Solomon's wisdom concerning.—I Ki. 4:33.

Clean and unclean.—Lev. 7:21; 20:25; Deut. 14:4-19; Acts 10:14; 15:28 f.; Rom. 14:14; I Cor. 8:1-13.

Sacrifices.—Gen. 8:20. See ANIMALS, OFFERINGS.

In Judgment.—Lev. 26:22; Deut. 28:26; Ez. 5:17; 14:15; 32:4; Rev. 6:8.

Symbolical.—Is. 30:6; Dan. 7:5-7, 11, 19, 23; Acts 10:12; Rev. 11:7; 13:1-18; 14:9, 11; 15:2; 16:2, 10, 13; 17:3, 7, 8, 11, 12, 13, 16, 17; 19:19, 20; 20:4, 10. See ANIMALS.

BEAT, BEATEN. Abner—II Sam. 2:17. Altars of idols—II Ki. 23:12. Apostles —Acts 5:40; 16:22, 37; 21:32; 22:19. See PERSECUTION. Barley—Ruth 2:17. Ben-hadad—II Ki. 13:25 (A.V.). Cities —Ju. 9:45; II Ki. 3:25. Disciples—Mk. 13:9. See PERSECUTION. Door, At the—Ju. 19:22. Enemies—II Sam. 22: 43; Ps. 18:42; 89:23; Jer. 46:5. Drunkards—Pr. 23:35. Forty stripes, With —Deut. 25:2, 3. See II Cor. 11:24. Grain—Lev. 2:14. Graven images—II Chr. 34:7; Mic. 1:7. See Is. 27:9. House—Mt. 7:25, 27; Lu. 6:48, 49. Incense—Ex. 30:36. Israelites in Egypt—Ex. 5:14, 16. Manna—Num. 11:8. Olive oil—Ex. 27:20; 29:40; Lev. 24:2; Num. 28:5. Olive tree—Deut. 24:20. People—Josh. 8:15; Is. 3:15 (A.V.); Mic. 4:3. Plowshares into swords—Joel 3:10. Rods, With—Pr. 23:13, 14; II Cor. 11:25. Servants—Mt. 21:35; Mk. 12:3, 5; Lu. 12:45, 47, 48; 20:10, 11. Sosthenes—Acts 18:17. Stream—Lu. 6:48, 49. Sun—Jonah 4:8. Swords into plowshares—Is. 2:4; Mic. 4:3. Waves into boat—Mk. 4:37. Wicked man—Deut. 25:2. Winds against house—Mt. 7:25, 27.

BEATITUDES. Mt. 5:3-12. See Lu. 6: 20-23.

BEAUTY: Temporal.—Of ornaments—II Chr. 3:6; Is. 3:18; Ez. 7:20. House —Is. 64:11. Of riches—Ps. 49:14. Of Israel—Sam. 2:1. Of Egypt—Ez. 32: 19. Of Jerusalem—Ez. 16:14, 15, 25. Of Chaldean's pride—Is. 13:19. Of Tyre—Ez. 27:3, 4, 11. Of tree—Ez. 31:8; Hos. 14:6. Diadem of—Is. 28:5. Garments of—Ex. 28:2. Vain—Pr. 6:

25; 31:30. Of fading flowers—Is. 28:1. Gate—Acts 3:10.

Beauty of men.—Of old men—Pr. 20:29. Of man—Ps. 49:14. Of Absalom—II Sam. 14:25.

Beauty of women.—Of bride—Ps. 45:11. Of Vashti—Esth. 1:11. Fair women: Daughters—Gen. 6:2. Woman—Pr. 11:22; Song of Sol. 1:8; 5:9; 6:1; 6:10. Beautiful women—Deut. 21:11; II Sam. 11:2. Rachel—Gen. 29:17. Esther—Esth. 2:7. Fair character— Jer. 12:6; Acts 7:20; Rom. 16:18; Gal. 6:12; Dan. 1:15.

Spiritual.—Beauty of wisdom—Ez. 28:7, 12, 17. Of Jehovah—Ps. 27:4; Is. 53:2; Zech. 9:17. Of sanctuary—Ps. 96:6. Of Ephraim—Is. 28:4. Of king—Is. 33:17. Perfection—Ps. 50:2; II Sam. 2:15. Temple called beautiful—Acts 3:2.

Figurative.—Is. 4:2. Beautiful countenance—I Sam. 16:12; 25:3. Outwardly beautiful—Mt. 23:27. Feet—Song of Sol. 7:1; Is. 52:7; Rom. 10:15. Crown —Ez. 16:12; 23:42. Jerusalem—Ez. 16:13. Jehovah—Ps. 48:2. Everything —Eccl. 3:11. Flock—Jer. 13:20. Rod —Jer. 48:17. Garments—Is. 52:1.

Prophecies concerning.—Is. 3:24; Hos. 14:6; Zech. 11:7, 10. Beautify: House of Jehovah—Ezra 7:27. Meek—Ps. 149:4. Sanctuary—Is. 60:13.

BEBAI, bĕb′a-ī. (1) **Ancestor of some who returned with Zerubbabel.**—Ezra 2:11; Neh. 7:16.

(2) **Ancestor of some who returned with Ezra.**—Ezra 8:11; 10:28.

(3) **One who sealed the covenant with Nehemiah.**—Neh. 10:15.

BECHER, bē′ker. (1) **Son of Benjamin.** —Gen. 46:21; Num. 26:35; I Chr. 7:6, 8.

(2) **Son of Ephraim.**—Num. 26:35.

BECKON. Lu. 1:22 (A.V.); 5:7; John 13:24; Acts 12:17; 19:33; 21:40; 24:10.

BECOME. Worthily—Pr. 17:7; Mt. 3: 15; Rom. 16:2; Eph. 5:3; Phil. 1:27; I Thess. 4:12; I Tim. 2:10; Titus 2:1, 3; Heb. 2:10.

BECORATH, be-cō′rath. **Grandson of Becher.**—I Sam. 9:1.

BED. *Mittah, "A bed for sleeping or eating on." Mishkab, "A bed or couch." Cheder, "An inner chamber."* **The outer garment the bed of the poor.** —Taken as a pledge must be returned at sunset—Ex. 22:26–27; Deut. 24: 12–13.

A mat or mattress that could be rolled up.—Mt. 9:6–7; Mk. 2:4, 9–12; 6:55; Lu. 5:18–25; John 5:8–13; Acts 5:15.

The better class had beds and bedchambers.—Ex. 21:18; II Sam. 4:7; 13:5; II Ki. 1:4; 11:2; II Chr. 22:11; Song of Sol. 3:1. Bed-head—Gen. 47:31; I Sam. 19:13. Pillows—I Sam. 19:13- 16. Cushions—Amos 3:12. Other adornings—Pr. 7:16–17. Furniture of a bed chamber—II Ki. 4:10, 21.

Used as couches by day.—I Sam. 28:23; Job. 7:13; Esth. 1:5–6; 7:8; Ez. 23:40- 41; Amos 3:12.

Uses of beds.—Covered with frogs— Ex. 8:3. For meals—Amos 6:4. Taken for debt—Pr. 22:27. Furnished to David's followers—II Sam. 17:28. For solicitation—Pr. 7:17. For a king's burial—II Chr. 16:14. To devise iniquity on—Ps. 36:4; Eccl. 10:20; Mic. 2:1. To sing on—Ps. 149:5. To howl on—Hos. 7:14. To pout on—I Ki. 21:4. To hide light under—Mk. 4:21; Lu. 8:16. To cover the wicked—Is. 28:20.

Made of.—Iron (Og's)—Deut. 3:11. Of ivory—Amos 6:4. Of gold and silver —Esth. 1:6.

Unclean beds.—Issues of men—Lev. 15:4, 5, 24. Issues of women—Lev. 15: 21, 23, 26.

Polluting the bed.—Gen. 49:4; II Sam. 11:2, 4; 13:5, 14; I Chr. 5:1; Heb. 13:4; Rev. 2:21–22. By murder—II Sam. 4:7, 11.

Visions connected with Daniel upon.— Dan. 2:28, 29; 4:5, 10, 13; 7:1. See Couch.

BEDCHAMBER. Ex. 8:3; II Sam. 4:7; II Ki. 6:12; 11:2; II Chr. 22:11; Eccl. 10:20. See Chamber.

BEDAD, bē′dăd. **Father of Edomite king.**—Gen. 36:35; I Chr. 1:46.

BEDAN, bē′dan. (1) **A judge of Israel before Jephthah.**—I Sam. 12:11.

(2) **Descendant of Machir.**—I Chr. 7:17.

BEDEIAH, be-dē′iah. **One of the Bani family, who married a foreign wife.**— Ez. 10:35.

BEDSTEAD. Deut. 3:11.

BEE. Deut. 1:44; Ju. 14:8; Ps. 118:12; Is. 7:18. See HONEY, INSECTS.

BEELIADA, bē′e-lī′a-da. **A son of David.**—I Chr. 14:7. See ELIADA.

BEELZEBUB, bē-ĕl′ze-bŭb. A heathen deity, supposed by the Jews to be supreme among evil spirits—Mt. 10:25; 12:24, 27; Mk. 3:22; Lu. 11:15, 18, 19. See DEMONS, POSSESSION OF.

BEER, bē′er. Heb. Well. (1) **A station in the journey of Israel.**—Num. 21:16. (2) **A place west of Hebron to which Jotham ran to escape from his brother Abimelech.**—Ju. 9:21. See ABIMELECH.

BEERA, be-ē′ra. **An Asherite, son of Zophah.**—I Chr. 7:37.

BEERAH, be-ē′rah. **A prince of the tribe of Reuben, carried captive into Assyria by Tilgath-pilneser.**—I Chr. 5:6.

BEER-ELIM, bē′er-ēl′im. **A well in southern part of Moab**—Is. 15:8.

BEERI, bē-ē′ri. **A Hittite, father of Judith, wife of Esau.**—Gen. 26:34. (2) **Father of the prophet Hosea.**—Hos. 1:1.

BEER-LAHAI-ROI, bē′er-la-hāi′-roi. **Well between Kadesh and Bered.**— Gen. 16:14; 24:62; 25:11.

BEEROTH, be-ē′rŏth. (1) **A stopping place of Israel.**—Deut. 10:6. (2) **One of four Hivite cities which made a treaty of peace with Joshua.**— Josh. 9:17; 18:25; II Sam. 4:2; 3, 5, 9; 23:37; I Chr. 11:39; Ezra 2:25; Neh. 7:29.

BEER-SHEBA, bē′er-shē′ba, *Well of the oath.* Wilderness of—Gen. 21:14,31. City of—Gen. 26:33. Covenant of— Gen. 21:32. Tamarisk tree planted in —Gen. 21:33. Abraham dwelt there —Gen. 22:19. Isaac went to—Gen. 26: 23. Jacob went from—Gen. 28:10; 46:1, 5. Elijah goes to—I Ki. 19:3. Tribe of Judah inherits—Josh. 15:28; 19:2; Neh. 11:27, 30. Sons of Simeon dwelt in—I Chr. 4:28. From Dan even to Beer-sheba—Ju. 20:1; I Sam 3:20; II Sam. 3:10; 24:2; 24:15; I Ki. 4:24; II Ki. 23:8; I Chr. 21:2; II Chr. 30:5.

Judges in—I Sam. 8:2. South of Judah at—II Sam. 24:7. Jehoash's mother from Beer-sheba—II Ki. 12:1; II Chr. 24:4. Jehoshaphat among the people of—II Chr. 19:4. Pass not to Beer-sheba—Amos 5:5. As the way of Beer-sheba liveth—Amos 8:14.

BEESHTERAH, be-ĕsh′te-rah. **A city of the Levites in Manasseh, west of the Jordan.**—Josh. 21:27.

BEETLE. Lev. 11:22 (A.V.). See LOCUST.

BEFALL. Gen. 49:1; Lev. 10:19; I Sam. 20:26; Eccl. 3:19; Dan. 10:14; Mt. 8: 33; Mk. 5:16. All that—Gen. 42:29; Josh. 2:23; Ju. 6:13; Esth. 6:13. Evil —Deut. 31:29; II Sam. 19:7; Ps. 91: 10. Evils and troubles—Deut. 31:17, 21, 29. Hardening of heart—Rom. 11: 25. Harm—Gen. 42:4, 38; 44:29. Travail—Num. 20:14. Trials—Acts 20: 19, 22. Worse things—John 5:14.

BEFITTING. Eph. 5:4. See BEHOOVE, FITTING.

BEFORE. Abraham was, I am—John 8:58. Church, The—III John 6. Cock crow—Mt. 26:34, 75; Mk. 14:72; Lu. 22:61. Face—Ez. 14:3, 4, 7; Mt. 11: 10; Mk. 1:2; Lu. 1:17, 76; 7:27; 10:1; Acts 2:25; 7:45. Faith came—Gal. 3: 23. Foundation of the world—John 17:24; II Tim. 1:9; Titus 1:2; I Pet. 1:20. Gentiles—Acts 9:15. God—Gen. 6:11; 10:9; 13:10; 17:1, 18; 18:22; 19:27; Lam. 2:19; Dan. 6:26; Mt. 10: 32, 33; Lu. 1:6; 12:6–9; 24:19; Acts 7:46; 10:4, 33; Rom. 14:22; II Cor. 12: 19; Gal. 1:20; I Thess. 3:9, 13; I Tim. 5:3, 21; II Tim. 2:14; 4:1; Jas. 1:27; Rev. 3:2, 5; 8:4; 9:13; 11:4, 16; 12:10; 15:4; 20:12. Jesus—Mt. 25:32; Lu. 7:27; 21:36; I John 2:28; 3:19; Rev. 5:8. John the Baptist—John 1:15, 27, 30; 3:28. Judgment—II Cor. 5:10. Lamb before the shearers—Acts 8:32. Men—Mt. 5:16; 6:1; 10:32, 33; ·Mk. 1:2; Lu. 12:8, 9; 16:15; Acts 19:9, 19. Pontius Pilate—I Tim. 6:13.· Rulers— Mt. 10:18; Mk. 13:9; Acts 10:17; 23: 30; 24:19, 20; 25:9, 26; 26:2. See PERSECUTION. Throne of God—Rev. 4:5, 6, 10; 7:9, 11, 15; 8:3; 14:3, 5. See GOD. Two or three witnesses—I Tim. 5:19; 6:13. See WITNESS. Unrighteous —I Cor. 6:1. Worlds—I Cor. 2:7.

BEFOREHAND. Mt. 24:25.

BEGGARS. Mentioned: Bartimæus—Mk. 10:46. Lazarus—Lu. 16:20, 22. Blind man—Lu. 18:35; John 9:8. Lame man—Acts 3:2-5. Treatment of —I Sam. 2:8; Ps. 37:25. Shame of— Lu. 16:3. Beggary as punishment— Ps. 109:10; Pr. 20:4. See ALMS, FRA-TERNITY, POOR.

BEGGARLY RUDIMENTS. Gal. 4:9.

BEGINNINGS: Of creation.—Pr. 8:22-31; Is. 40:21; John 1:1-3; Mk. 13:19; Heb. 1:10; 11:3. Man created male and female—God ordained from the beginning that man should have but one wife—Gen. 1:27; 2:18, 21-24; 5:2; Mt. 19:4-6; Mk. 10:6-9; Eph. 5:31.

Beginning of sin.—Gen. 3:1-6; John 8: 44; Rom. 5:14-21; I John 3:8.

Of death.—Gen. 3:3, 22-24; 4:8; Rom. 5:14-18; I Cor. 15:22.

Of nations.—Gen. Ch. 10.

Of sacrifice.—Gen. 4:4.

Of the old covenant.—Gen. 12:1-3; 17: 1-14; Ex. 19:5; Gal. 4:24; Heb. 8:9. See COVENANTS.

Of the new covenant.—Mt. 26:28; Mk. 14:24; Lu. 22:20; I Cor. 11:25; Heb. 9:14-28.

Of bondage in Egypt.—Ex. 1:8-14.

Of the deliverance.—Ex. Chs. 3 and 4.

Of the departure from Egypt.—Ex. 12: 29-42.

Of the passover.—Ex. 12:1-28, 43-49; 13:1-10; 23:15; 34:18; Deut. 1:16.

Of keeping the sabbath day by man.— Ex. 16:22-30. See SABBATH.

Of the tabernacle and its furnishings.— Ex. Chs. 25, 26, 36-40.

Of the kingdom of Israel.—I Sam. 8:4-22; 9:15-27; 10:1-25; 11:15. See COM-MANDMENTS.

Of the temple.—I Ki. 5:1-18.

Of the division of the kingdom.—I Ki. 11:29-40; 12:1-33.

Of the captivity of Israel.—II Ki. 17:1-23.

Of the captivity of Judah.—II Ki. 24: 10-20; 25:1-12; II Chr. 36:11-21.

Of the restoration.—II Chr. 36:22, 23; Ezra, Chs. 1-3.

Jesus was in the beginning with God; He was God.—John 1:1-3; 8:58; Rom. 11:36; I Cor. 8:6; Col. 1:16-18; Heb. 1:2; I John 1:1; 2:13, 14.

Beginning of the ministry of Jesus.— Mt. 4:17; Mk. 1:14, 15; Lu. 1:2; 3:23; John 15:27; Acts 1:1, 21, 22. **Of the miracles of Jesus.**—John 2:11.

Jesus and His disciples began with Mo-ses and the prophets to prove the di-vinity of Jesus.—Lu. 24:27, 44; John 1:45; 3:14; 5:39, 45-47; Acts 2:22; 7:2-53; 8:35; 13:27; 28:23.

The beginning of the kingdom.—Among the Jews first—Dan. 2:44, 45; Mt. 16: 18, 19, 28; Lu. 24:47; Acts 1:4-8; 2:4; 11:15. Among the Gentiles—Acts 8: 4-40; 10:1-48; 11:1-23; 15:7-9.

The Gentiles chosen ''In the begin-ning.''—Eph. 1:4; I Thess. 2:13.

Beginning of wisdom is the fear of God. —Ps. 111:10; Pr. 1:7; 9:10.

Beginning of strife.—Pr. 17:14.

The beginning and the end; the Alpha and the Omega.—Rev. 1:8; 21:6; 22:13.

BEGOTTEN. Of God by the Holy Spirit.—John 1:13; 3:3-9; Titus 3:5; I John 2:29; 5:18.

Preaching of the Gospel, By—I Cor. 4: 15; Philemon 10; Jas. 1:18; I Pet. 1: 23. He that believeth that Jesus is the Son of God is begotten of God— John 1:14; I John 5:1-5. See NEW BIRTH.

Only begotten Son of God.—John 1:14, 18; 3:16, 18; Heb. 1:5; 11:17; I John 4:9; Rev. 1:5. See FIRST BORN.

BEGUILE. Gen. 29:25; Num. 25:18; Josh. 9:22. Serpent, By the—Gen. 3: 13; II Cor. 11:3; I Tim. 2:14. Sin, By —Rom. 7:11. See II Pet. 2:14. Speech, By smooth—Rom. 16:18; Col. 2:4 (A.V.). See DELUDE, TEMPTATION.

BEHALF. Children, Of—Ex. 27:21. Christ, Of—II Cor. 5:20, 21; Phil. 1: 29. God—Job 36:2. Our—II Cor. 1:11; 5:12, 21. Your—Rom. 16:19 (A.V.); II Cor. 9:3; Philemon 13.

BEHAVE. David—I Sam. 18:5; Ps. 35: 14; 101:2; 131:2. House of God, In the—I Tim. 3:15. Paul—II Cor. 1:12; I Thess. 2:10. Proudly—Job 15:25; 36:9; Is. 3:5. See PRIDE. Toward you —II Cor. 1:12; I Thess. 2:10. Un-blameably—I Thess. 2:10. Wicked, The—Job 15:25; 36:9. Wisely—Ps. 101:2. See JESUS, TEACHING ON CHAR-ACTER.

BEHAVIOR. Aged women—Titus 2:3–5 (A.V.). Bishops—I Tim. 3:2–6 (A.V.); Titus 1:7–9. Wives—I Pet. 3:1–2.

BEHEAD. Ish-bosheth—II Sam. 4:7. John the Baptist—Mt. 14:10; Mk. 6: 16, 27; Lu. 9:9. Souls of them beheaded—Rev. 20:4.

BEHELD. Jesus—I John 1:1. Ascending to heaven—Acts 1:9, 11. Before my face—Acts 2:25. See BEHOLD.

BEHEMOTH. Job 40:15 (A.V.). Supposed to be the hippopotamus.

BEHIND. Fill up that which is—Col. 1:24 (A.V.). Forgetting that which is —Phil. 3:13. Gift, In no—I Cor. 1:7. Jesus, A woman—Mt. 9:20; Mk. 5:27; Lu. 7:38; 8:44. Me, Satan—Mt. 16:23; Mk. 8:33; Lu. 4:8. Me, A voice—Rev. 1:10. See BACK.

BEHOLD, Chaste behavior—I Pet. 3:2. Face of my father—Mt. 18:10. Glory, His—John 1:14; 17:24; II Cor. 3:18. Goodness and severity of God—Rom. 11:22. Good works—I Pet. 2:12. Hands and feet, My—Lu. 24:39; John 20:27. I come quickly—Rev. 16:15; 22:7, 12. I make all things new—Rev. 21:5. Israel after the flesh—I Cor. 10:18. Lamb of God, The—John 1:29. Man, The—John 19:5. Me no more— Job 7:8; John 14:19. Mirror, As in a —II Cor. 3:18; Jas. 1:23, 24. See I Cor. 13:12. Mote in thy eye—Mt. 7:4; Lu. 6:41, 42. Satan as lightning—Lu. 10:18. Tabernacle of God is with men —Rev. 21:5. Upright, The—Ps. 37:37. What manner of love—I John 3:1.

BEHOOVED. Christ to suffer—Lu. 24: 26, 46; Acts 17:3; Heb. 2:17. See JESUS, SUFFERINGS OF.

BEING. Have our—Acts 17:28, 29.

BEKA, bē′kȧ. A measure—half shekel —Gen. 24:22 (marg.); Ex. 38:26. See MEASURES.

BEL, bĕl. **A heathen god, probably the Babylonian name for Baal.**—Is. 46:1; Jer. 50:2; 51:44. See BAAL, IDOLATRY.

BELA, bē′lȧ. (1) **A place near the valley of Siddim, called also** *Zoar*—Gen. 14:2, 8. See ZOAR.

(2) **King of Edom.**—Gen. 36:32, 33; I Chr. 1:43, 44.

(3) **Son of Benjamin.**—Gen. 46:21; Num. 26:38; I Chr. 7:6, 7; 8:1, 3.

(4) **A Reubenite, son of Azaz.**—I Chr. 5:8.

BELCH. Ps. 59:7. See Ps. 94:4; Pr. 15: 2, 28.

BELIAL, bē′li-al. Any worthless person —Base fellows—Deut. 13:13; Ju. 19: 22; 20:13 (A.V.); I Sam. 2:12 (A.V.); 10:27 (A.V.); 25:17, 25 (A.V.); 30:22 (A.V.); II Sam. 16:7 (A.V.); 20:1 (A.V.); 23:6 (A.V.); I Ki. 21:10–13 (A.V.); II Chr. 13:7 (A.V.). Daughter of—I Sam. 1:16. Satan—II Chr. 6:15.

BELIEF, BELIEVE. Mk. 9:23; 11:24; John 1:7.

God, In.—Gen. 15:6; Num. 14:11; II Ki. 17:14; Ps. 27:13; Acts 16:34; Rom. 4:3, 11, 18; Gal. 3:6; Jas. 2:23.

Gospel, The.—See GOSPEL MUST BE BELIEVED.

Jesus, On.—Mt. 8:13; 9:28; 27:42; Mk. 5:36; 16:16; Lu. 24:25; John 3:16, 36; 7:5; 11:25–27; 12:36, 44; 17:21; 20: 25; Acts 16:31; Rom. 10:9–11. See JESUS, DIVINITY OF.

Message, Our.—Is. 53:1.

Moses and the prophets.—John 5:45–47; Acts 26:27. See Lu. 24:44–47; Acts 28:23, 24.

Scriptures, The—John 2:22; 5:45–47. See FAITH.

BELIEVER. I Cor. 9:5; I Pet. 1:21. See DISCIPLES, FAITH.

BELL. Ex. 28:33, 34; 39:25, 26; Zech. 14:20.

BELLOW. Jer. 50:11 (A.V.).

BELLOWS. Jer. 6:29.

BELLY. Lev. 11:42; Ps. 17:14; Pr. 18: 20; Jer. 1:5; 51:34 (A.V.); Mt. 15:71; Mk. 7:19; John 7:38 (A.V.); Rom. 16: 18. Behemoth—Job 40:16. Cretans— Titus 1:12 (A.V.). Fish—Jonah 1:17; 2:1. See WHALE. Meats for—I Cor. 6:13. Nebuchadrezzar's image, which he saw in a vision, Of—Dan. 2:32. Pillars of the temple, Of the—I Ki. 7:20. Prodigal son—Lu. 15:16. Crawls on— Gen. 3:14. Sheol—Jonah 2:2. Whale —Mt. 12:40. See FISH. Whose God is —Phil. 3:19. Wicked, Of the—Job 20: 15, 20, 23; Pr. 13:25. See BODY, BREAST, BOWELS, INNERMOST PARTS, WOMB.

BELONG. Christ, To—Mk. 9:41 (A.V.). See I Cor. 3:23. God, To—I Cor. 6:19, 20; 7:32. Interpretations—Gen. 40:8.

Love—Ps. 62:12. Power—Ps. 62:11. Salvation—Ps. 3:8. Secret things—Deut. 29:29. Vengeance—Heb. 10:30.

BELOVED. Barnabas and Paul—Acts 15:25. City—Rev. 20:9. Elect—Rom. 1:7; 11:28; Col. 3:12; I Thess. 1:4; 2:13. Gentiles—Rom. 9:25. See GENTILES. Jesus—Mt. 12:18; Eph. 1:6. Beloved son—Mt. 3:17; Mk. 1:11; 9:7; 12:6; Lu. 3:22; 9:35; 20:12; II Pet. 1:17. Luke the physician—Col. 4:14. See BRETHREN, LOVE.

BELSHAZZAR, bel-shăz'zar. **Son of Nabonidus, and the last Chaldean king of Babylon.**—Dan. 5:1–30; 7:1; 8:1.

BELT. Job. 12:21.

BELTESHAZZAR, bel-te-shăz'zar. **Name given to Daniel by the prince of Eunuchs.**—Dan. 1:7; 2:26; 4:8, 9, 18, 19; 5:12; 10:1.

BEMOAN. Job. 42:11; Is. 51:19; Jer. 15:5; Nah. 3:7. See MOURNING, SORROW.

BEN, bĕn. (1) **A Levite, who had charge of the song-service under David.**—I Chr. 15:18.

(2) **Hebrew for** *Son.*

BEN-ABINADAB, bĕn-a-bĭn'a-dăb. I Ki. 4:11. See ABINADAB.

BENAIAH, be-nā'iah. (1) **Son of Jehoiada, one of David's officers.**— Priestly ancestry—I Chr. 27:5. Commander of David's bodyguard—II Sam. 8:18; 15:18; 20:23; 23:23; I Chr. 18:17. Counted among the heroes—II Sam. 23:22. Exploits—II Sam. 23:20, 21. Loyal to David in two rebellions —II Sam. 15:18; 20:23; I Ki. 1:24, 25, 32, 36–38. Loyal to Solomon, slew Adonijah—I Ki. 2:25. Joab—I Ki. 2:29, 34; Shimei—I Ki. 2:46. Became general of Solomon's army—I Ki. 1:35.

(2) **From Pirathon (Ephraim), one of the thirty heroes.**—II Sam. 23:30; I Chr. 11:31. A captain—I Chr. 27:14.

(3) **A prince of the tribe of Simeon.**—I Chr. 4:36.

(4) **A Levite of the second degree of singers.**—I Chr. 15:18–20; 16:5.

(5) **A priest and trumpeter.**—I Chr. 15:24; 16:6.

(6) **Ancestor of Jahaziel.**—II Chr. 20:14.

(7) **A Levite overseer of temple, in Hezekiah's reign.**—II Chr. 31:13.

(8) **Father of a wicked prince who fell dead.**—Ez. 11:1, 13.

(9–12) **Four Israelites who had married foreign women.**—Ezra 10:25, 30, 35, 43.

BEN-AMMI, bĕn'-ăm'mi. **Lot's son by his younger daughter.**—Gen. 19:38.

BENCH. Ez. 27:6.

BEND. Is. 60:14. Bow—See ARCHERY. Judah—Hos. 11:7; Zech. 9:13. Tongue —Jer. 9:3. See TONGUE. Vine—Ez. 17:7.

BEN-DEKER, bĕn-dē'ker. I Ki. 4:9.

BENEATH. Deep that coucheth—Deut. 33:13. Earth—Ex. 20:4; Deut. 4:18, 39; 5:8; Jer. 31:37; Acts 2:19. Israel not—Deut. 28:13. Sheol—Pr. 15:24. See SHEOL. Ye are from—John 8:23.

BENEBERAK, bĕn'e-bē'rak. **A city in Dan not far from Ashdod.**—Josh. 19:45.

BENEFACTORS. Lu. 22:25.

BENEFIT. II Chr. 32:25; Jer. 18:10; II Cor. 1:15; I Tim. 6:2. Forget not all his—Ps. 103:2. See Ps. 116:12.

BEN-JAAKAN, bĕn'jā'a-kăn. **A tribe whose name was given to several wells used by the Israelites on their journeys.**—Num. 33:31, 32.

BENEVOLENCE. I Cor. 7:3 (A.V.). See FRATERNITY.

BEN-GEBER, bĕn-gē'ber. I Ki. 4:13.

BEN-HADAD, bĕn-hā'dad. (1) **King of Syria, who made a treaty with Asa, king of Judah.**—I Ki. 15:18, 20; II Chr. 10:2, 4.

(2) **Son of (1), king of Syria, who reigned in time of Ahab.**—I Ki. 20:1–33; II Ki. 6:24; 8:7, 9.

(3) **Son of Hazael.**—II Ki. 13:3, 24, 25.

(4) **Title of kings of Damascus.**—Jer. 49:27.

BEN-HAIL, bĕn'-hā'il. **A prince of Judah under Jehoshaphat, king of Judah.** —II Chr. 17:7.

BEN-HANAN, bĕn-hā'nan. I Chr. 4:20.

BEN-HUR, bĕn'-hûr. I Ki. 4:8.

BENINU, bĕn'i-nu. **A Levite who assisted Nehemiah in sealing the covenant.**—Neh. 10:13.

BENJAMIN, bĕn'ja-min. (1) *Son of the right hand.* Named by Rachel *Benoni,* son of my sorrow—**Jacob's twelfth**

son, by Rachel, who died at his birth, only full brother of Joseph.—Gen. 35: 16–18, 24. Only son born in Palestine —Gen. 35:19. After Joseph went to Egypt, the father's favorite—Gen. 42:4, 36, 38; 44:30. Visits Joseph—Gen. Chs. 43–45. Predictions concerning— Gen. 49:27; Deut. 33:12.

(2) **Tribe.**—Descendants of—Gen. 46:21; Num. 26:38–41; I Chr. 7:6–12; 8:1–40. Strength of, when leaving Egypt, 35,- 400—Num. 1:36, 37. After 40 years in the wilderness, 45,600—Num. 26:38– 41. Stood on Mt. Gerizim—Deut. 27: 12. Cities and boundaries of inherit- ance—Josh. 18:11–28. Did not drive out the Canaanites—Ju. 1:21. Tribe of Benjamin defends men of Gibeah. They are finally defeated and their country ravaged—Ju. Chs. 19–20. Ben- jamites obtain wives at Jabesh-Gilead and at Shiloh—Ju. Ch. 21. Celebrated as bowmen and slingers—I Chr. 12:2. Many left-handed—Ju. 20:13–16; I Chr. 12:2. Armies of—I Chr. 12:2, 21; 27:12; II Chr. 11:1; 14:8; 17:17. En- campment—Num. 2:18, 22; 10:24. Princes—Num. 7:60–65; 34:21. As- sisted against Sisera—Ju. 5:14. Saul taken from tribe of Benjamin—I Sam. 9:1, 2, 15–17, 21; 10:20–24. Stood by the house of Saul—II Sam. Ch. 2; I Chr. 12:29. 1,000 came with Shimei to meet David on his return to Jerusa- lem—II Sam. 19:16, 17. 3,000 assist David to become king over all Israel —I Chr. 12:2, 16, 19. Ish-bosheth made king over Benjamites—II Sam. 2:9, 15. Rehoboam king over tribe of Benjamin—I Ki. 12:21. Saul of Tar- sus of this tribe—Rom. 11:1; Phil. 3:5. Other references—Ju. 3:15; 5:14· 10:9; 20:10; Ezra 1:5; Neh. 11:4. See ISRAEL.

(3) **Great grandson of Benjamin.**—I Chr. 7:10.

(4) **A descendant of Harim, who had married a foreign wife.**—Ezra 10:32.

(5) **One who helped to repair the wall of Jerusalem.**—Neh. 3:23.

(6) **One who took part in dedication of wall.**—Neh. 12:34.

(7) **One of the gates of Jerusalem.**—Jer. 20:2; 37:13; 38:7; Zech. 14:10.

BENO, bē'no. **A Levite, descended from Merari.**—I Chr. 24:26, 27.

BENONI, bĕn-ō'nī. **Name given to her second son by Rachel.**—Gen. 35:18.

BENZOHETH, bĕn'zō-heth. **A descend- ant of Judah.**—I Chr. 4:20.

BEON, bē'on. Num. 32:3. See BAAL- MEON.

BEOR, bē'or. (1) **Father of Bela, king of Edom.**—Gen. 36:32; I Chr. 1:43.

(2) **Father of Balaam.**—Num. 22:5; 24: 3, 15; 31:8; Deut. 23:4; Josh. 13:22; 24:9; Mic. 6:5.

BERA, bē-rá. **King of Sodom in the days of Abraham.**—Gen. 14:2.

BERACHAH, bĕr'a-kah. (1) **One of those who came to David at Ziklag.**— I Chr. 12:3.

(2) **A valley in southern part of Judah, near Tekoa, where Jehoshaphat and Judah blessed Jehovah.**—II Chr. 20:26.

BEREAVE. Gen. 27:45; 42:36; 43:14; Ps. 35:12; Eccl. 4:8 (A.V.); Ez. 5:17; 36:12–14; Hos. 9:12; 13:8. See AF- FLICTION, BARREN, MOURNING, SORROW.

BERECHIAH, bĕr'e-chī'ah. (1) **A de- scendant of Jehoiakim, king of Judah.** —I Chr. 3:20.

(2) **Father of Asaph, the singer.**—I Chr. 6:39; 15:17.

(3) **A Levite.**—I Chr. 9:16.

(4) **One of the Levites who was a door- keeper of the tabernacle.**—I Chr. 15:23.

(5) **An Ephraimite.**—II Chr. 28:12.

(6) **Father of Meshullam, who aided in repairing the wall.**—Neh. 3:4, 30; 6:18.

BERED, bē'red. (1) **A place in south- ern Canaan near which was the well La-hai-roi.**—Gen. 16:14.

(2) **An Ephraimite.**—I Chr. 7:20. See BECHER.

BERI, bē'rī. **Son of Zophah.**—I Chr. 7:36.

BERIAH, be-rī'ah. (1) **Son of Asher.**— Gen. 46:17; Num. 26:44, 45; I Chr. 7:30, 31.

(2) **Son of Ephraim.**—I Chr. 7:23.

(3) **A Benjamite.**—I Chr. 8:13, 16.

(4) **A Levite, descended from Gershom.** —I Chr. 23:10, 11.

BERIITES, be-rī'ītes. **A family of Asherites.**—Num. 26:44.

BERITES, bē′rites. **Descendants of Beri, whom Joab visited when he pursued Sheba.**—II Sam. 20:14.

BERNICE, ber-nī′ce. Acts 25:13, 23, 30. See HEROD.

BERODACH-BALADAN, be-rō′dak-bǎl′a-dän. **A king of Babylon, who sent a present to Hezekiah.**—II Ki. 20:12; Is. 39:1.

BEROEA, be-rœ′a. **A city in Macedonia where Paul and Silas taught.**—Acts 17:10; 20:4.

BEROTHAI, be-rō′thāī. **A city belonging to Hadadezer, king of Zobah.**—II Sam. 8:8.

BERRIES. Olive.—Is. 17:6.

BERYL. A precious stone.—So. of Sol. 5:14; Ez. 1:16; 10:9; 28:13; Dan. 10:6; Rev. 21:20. Breastplate, In the —Ex. 28:20; 39:13.

BESAI, bē-sāi. **One who returned with Zerubbabel.**—Ezra 2:49; Neh. 7:52.

BESEECH. Elijah—II Ki. 1:13. Esther 8:3. Fellow-servant—Mt. 18, 29. Festus—Acts 25:2. God—Ex. 32:11; Deut. 3:23; II Sam. 12:16; I Ki. 13:6; II Ki. 13:4; 20:3; II Chr. 33:12; Ezra 8:23; Neh. 1:5, 11; Ps. 116:4; 118:25; Is. 38:3; Jer. 26:19; Jonah 1:14; Mal. 1:9. See PRAYER. Jesus—Mt. 8:5, 31, 34; 14:36; 15:23; Mk. 1:40; 5:10, 12, 23; 6:56; 7:26, 32; 8:22; Lu. 4:38; 5:12; 7:3, 4; 8:31, 32, 37, 38, 41; 9:38, 40; 11:37; John 4:40, 47; 19:31, 38.

Paul **beseeches.**—Agrippa—Acts 26:3. Chief captain—Acts 21:39. Companions on way to Rome—Acts 27:33. Corinthians—I Cor. 1:10; 4:16; 16:15; II Cor. 2:8; 5:20; 6:1; 10:2, 8. Ephesians—Eph. 4:1. Galatians—Gal. 4:12. Rome, Church in—Rom. 12:1; 15:30; 16:17. Thessalonians—I Thess. 4:1, 10; 5:12; II Thess. 2:1. Timothy—I Tim. 1:3.

Paul **is besought by.**—Companions—Acts 21:12. Gentiles—Acts 13:42. Lydia—Acts 16:15. Magistrates—Acts 16:39. Strangers, As—I Pet. 2:11. See EXHORT, PRAYER.

BESET. Ps. 22:12; 139:5; Hos. 7:2. Sin which doth so easily—Heb. 12:1.

BESIDE. Desire beside thee—Ps. 73:25. No other God besides—Deut. 4:35; Is. 43:11; 45:21. Still waters—Ps. 23:2.

Themselves—Job 41:25; Mk. 3:21; Acts 26:24 (A.V.); II Cor. 5:13.

BESIEGE. See WAR.

BESODEIAH, běs-o-dē′iah. **One who helped to repair the old gate.**—Neh. 3:6.

BESOM. An old English word for broom—Is. 14:23.

BESOR, bē′sôr. **A brook where David pursued and slew the Amalekites.**—I Sam. 30:9, 10, 21.

BESOUGHT. See BESEECH.

BEST. Gifts—I Cor. 12:31. Robe—Lu. 15:22. Restitution from—Ex. 22:5. Sacrifice—Num. 18:12, 29, 30, 32. See FIRST-BORN, OFFERING.

BESTIR. II Sam. 5:24; Joel 3:12. See AWAKE.

BESTOW. Barns, In—Lu. 12:17, 18. Blessing—Ex. 32:9. See BLESSING. Cities, In—I Ki. 10:26; II Chr. 9:25. See CITIES, STORE. Dedicated things —II Chr. 24:7. Fruits—Lu. 12:17, 18. Goods—I Cor. 13:3. See FRATERNITY, LOVE. Grace—II Cor. 8:1 (A.V.). See GRACE. Honor, more abundant—I Cor. 12:23. Labor—John 4:38 (A.V.); Rom. 16:6; Gal. 4:11. See LABOR. Love— Is. 63:7; I John 3:1. See LOVE OF GOD. Majesty on Solomon—I Chr. 29:25. Money—Deut. 14:26; II Ki. 12:15 (A.V.). See GOODS, WEALTH.

BETAH, bē′tah. **One of Hadadezer's cities.**—I Sam. 8:8.

BETEN, bē′ten. **A city of Asher.**—Josh. 19:25.

BETHABARAH, běth-ăb′a-rah. **A place east of the Jordan.** See BETHANY.

BETHANATH, běth-ā′nath. **A city of Naphtali.**—Josh. 19:38; Ju. 1:33.

BETHANOTH, běth-ā′noth. **A city of Judah near Hebron.**—Josh. 15:59.

BETHANY, běth′a-ny. (1) **Village on Mount of Olives.**—Mk. 11:1; Lu. 19: 29. See John 11:18.

Jesus **frequently visited.**—Mt. 21:17; 26:6; Mk. 11:11, 12; 14:3.

Home of Lazarus, Mary, and Martha.— John 11:1; 12:1. Of Simon the Leper —Mk. 14:3.

Ascension of Jesus at.—Lu. 24:50.

(2) **Beyond Jordan.**—John 1:28.

BETHARABAH, běth-är′a-bah. **A city of Judah in the Arabah or valley of the Jordan.**—Josh. 15:6, 61; 18:22.

BETHARBEL, bĕth-är'bel. A city destroyed by the Assyrian king.—Hos. 10:14.

BETHAVEN, bĕth-ā'ven. A town in Benjamin.—Josh. 7:2; 18:12; I Sam. 13:5; 14:23; Hos. 4:15; 5:8; 10:5.

BETHAZMAVETH, bĕth-äz'ma-vĕth. A village of Judah or Benjamin.—Neh. 7:28. See AZMAVETH.

BETH-BAAL-MEON, bĕth-bā'al-mē'on. A town of Joab given to Reuben.—See BAAL-MEON.

BETHBARAH, bĕth-bā'rah. A place in Gad east of the Jordan.—Ju. 7:24.

BETH-BIRI, bĕth-bĭr'ī. A town of Simeon.—I Chr. 4:31.

BETH-CAR, bĕth-kär. A city of the Philistines near Mizpah.—I Sam. 7:11.

BETH-DAGON, bĕth-dā'gon. (1) A town of Judah.—Josh. 15:41.

(2) A town in Asher.—Josh. 19:27.

BETH-DIBLATHAIM, bĕth-dĭb-la-thā'-im. A town of Moab.—Jer. 48:22. See ALMON-DIBLATHAIM.

BETHEL, bĕth'ĕl. House of God. Ten miles north of Jerusalem. Formerly called Luz. Name changed by Jacob. —Gen. 28:19. Abraham first visited it, establishing an altar near by—Gen. 12:8; 13:3, 4. Bethel belonged by lot to Benjamin, but was taken by Ephraim through treachery—Josh. 18:13, 22; Ju. 1:22–25; Neh. 11:31. Jacob saw there, in vision, a ladder—Gen. 28:12; 31:13; Hos. 12:4. Dwells there and builds an altar—Gen. 35:1–15. Deborah, Rebekah's nurse, buried near—Gen. 35:8. Deborah the prophetess dwelt near—Ju. 4:5. Joshua and sons possess—I Chr. 7:28. Finally conquered by Joshua—Josh. 8:17; 12:7, 16. One of Samuel's courts for judging—I Sam. 7:16. Saul's men at—I Sam. 13:2. Resorted to for divine counsel—Ju. 20:18; 21:2–3. Feast of Shiloh near—Ju. 21:19. Three men going up to God to Bethel—I Sam. 10:3. David sends presents to friends in—I Sam. 30:27. Jeroboam establishes calf worship there—I Ki. 12: 28–29; 13:1–10. Old prophet foretells disaster—I Ki. 13:11–32. School of prophets at—II Ki. 2:3. Priests dwelt in—II Ki. 17:28; Amos 7:10,13. Young lads mock Elisha—II Ki. 2:23–24. Ashes

of Baal's vessels carried to—II Ki. 23:4, 15. Altar of Baal at—II Ki. 23: 17, 19; Amos 3:14. Bethel taken from Jeroboam—II Chr. 13:19. Men of Bethel return from Babylon—Ezra 2: 28; Neh. 7:32. House of Israel ashamed of—Jer. 48:13. Bethel destroys Israel because of wickedness—Hos. 10:15. Transgressions at—Amos 4:4; 5:6. Seek not—Amos 5:5. Was the king's sanctuary—Amos 7:13. Destruction prophesied—Amos 3:14–15.

BETHEMEK, bĕth-ē'mek. A town of Asher near the border.—Josh. 19:27.

BETHESDA, Be-thĕs'da. A pool in Jerusalem near the sheep gate, where Jesus performed a miracle of healing. —John 5:2.

BETH-EZEL, bĕth-ē'zel. A city in north Judah.—Mic. 1:11.

BETH-GADER, bĕth-gā'der. A descendant of Caleb.—I Chr. 2:51.

BETH-GAMUL, bĕth-gā'mul. A Moabite town.—Jer. 48:23.

BETH-GILGAL, bĕth-gĭl'găl. Neh. 12: 29. See GILGAL.

BETH-HACCHEREM, bĕth-hăk'ke-rĕm. A town of Judah between Jerusalem and Tekoa.—Neh. 3:14; Jer. 6:1.

BETH-HARAM, bĕth-hā'ram. A city in the valley of the Jordan.—Josh. 13:27.

BETH-HARAN, bĕth-hā'ran. A city of Gad near Gilead.—Num. 32:36.

BETH-HOGLAH, bĕth-hŏg'lah. A city of Benjamin 3 miles from Jericho.— Josh. 15:6; 18:19, 21.

BETH-HORON, bĕth-hō'ron. House of the Cave. Upper and Nether.—Two frontier towns of Benjamin and Ephraim, between which Joshua defeated the Ammonites.—Josh. 10:10, 11. Built by Sheerah—I Chr. 7:24. Upper—I Chr. 7:24. Nether—Josh. 18:13; I Chr. 7:24. Rebuilt by Solomon—I Ki. 9:17; II Chr. 8:5. Given as an inheritance to Ephraim.—Josh. 16:3, 5. Way to—I Sam. 13:18.

BETH-JESHIMOTH, bĕth-jĕsh'i-mŏth. A Moabite city near the mouth of the Jordan.—Num. 33:49; Josh. 12:3; 13: 20; Ez. 25:9.

BETH-LEBAOTH, bĕth-lĕb'a-ŏth. A town in Simeon.—Josh. 19:6.

BETHLEHEM, bĕth'le-hem. *House of Bread.* Is now a thriving Christian town of 5,000 inhabitants. The Church of the Nativity, with cave and manger, is found there. Bethlehem—Josh. 19:15. City of David—I Sam. 20:6; John 7:42. Built by Rehoboam—II Chr. 11:6. Of Bethlehem—Ibzan judged Israel—Ju. 12:8. Rachel was buried at Bethlehem—Gen. 35:19; 48:7. Ibzan was buried at—Ju. 12:10. Asahel buried at—II Sam. 2:32. Elhanan of—II Sam. 23:24; I Chr. 11:26. Children of—Ezra 2:21. Men of —Neh. 7:26. Came to—Ruth 1:19, 22; I Sam. 16:4. From—Ruth 2:4. Famous in—Ruth 4:11. Garrisons of Philistines—II Sam. 23:14; I Chr. 11:16. Ruth and Naomi at—Ruth 1:2–4. David feeds sheep at—I Sam. 17:15. By—Jer. 41:17. Well of—II Sam. 23:15, 16; I Chr. 11:17, 18. Prophecy concerning—Mic. 5:2. Anointing of David—I Sam. 16:13. Birthplace of our Lord—Mt. 2:1, 6; Lu. 2:4. Wise men sent to—Mt. 2:8. Shepherds go to—Lu. 2:15. Events connected with slaying of children at—Mt. 2:16.

BETH-MAACAH, bĕth–mā'a-kah. A city of Manasseh east of the Jordan and near Hermon.—II Sam. 20:14, 15, 18; II Ki. 15:29.

BETH-MARCABOTH, bĕth – mär'ka - bŏth. A city of Simeon in southern Judah.—Josh. 19:5; I Chr. 4:31.

BETH-MEON, bĕth–mē'on. A Moabite city.—Jer. 48:23. See BETH-BAAL-MEON.

BETH-NIMRAH, bĕth–nĭm'rah. A city of Gad.—Num. 32:36; Josh. 13:27. See NIMRAH.

BETH-PAZZEZ, bĕth'păz'zez. A town of Issachar.—Josh. 19:21.

BETH-PELET, bĕth–pē'let. Josh. 15:27; Neh. 11:26.

BETH-PEOR, bĕth–pē'or. A Moabite city east of the Jordan, near Mount Peor.—Deut. 3:29; 4:46; 34:6; Josh. 13:20.

BETHPHAGE, bĕth'pha-gē. A village near Bethany.—Mt. 21:1; Mk. 11:1; Lu. 19:29.

BETH-RAPHA, bĕth–rā'phȧ. I Chr. 4:12.

BETH-REHOB, bĕth–rē'hob. A place in northern Canaan.—Ju. 18:28; II Sam. 10:6.

BETH-SAIDA, bĕth–sā'i-da. (1) In Galilee, where Andrew, Peter, and Philip were born.—Mt. 11:21; Mk. 6:45; Lu. 10:13; John 1:44; 12:21.

(2) A town where the five thousand were fed.—Mk. 8:22; Lu. 9:10.

BETHSHEAN, bĕth'shē'an, *or* BETHSHAN (a town of Manasseh, west of the Jordan)—Josh. 17:11, 16; Ju. 1:27; I Ki. 4:12; I Chr. 7:29. Philistines fasten the bodies of Saul and his sons to the wall of—I Sam. 31:10, 12; II Sam. 21:12.

BETHSHEMESH, bĕth'shē'mesh. A frontier city of Judah—Josh. 15:10; I Ki. 4:9. City of: Priests—Josh. 21:16; I Chr. 6:59. Issachar—Josh. 19:22. Napthali—Josh. 19:38; Ju. 1:33.

Inhabitants of.—Became subject to task-work—Ju. 1:33.

Men of, smitten for looking into ark.—I Sam. 6:10–15, 19–21.

Battles at.—Between Joash and Amaziah—II Ki. 14:11–13; II Chr. 25:21–23. Taken by the Philistines in the reign of Ahaz—II Chr. 28:18.

Prophecy against.—Pillars to be broken, and houses of gods to be burnt.—Jer. 43:13.

BETH-SHITTAH, bĕth–shĭt'tah. Ju. 7:22.

BETH-TAPPUAH, bĕth–tăp'pu-ah. A city of Judah, near Hebron.—Josh. 15:53.

BETHUEL, be-thū'el. (1) Son of Nahor Abraham's brother, father of Rebekah.—Gen. 22:22, 23; 24:15, 24, 47, 50; 25:20; 28:2, 5.

(2) A town in Simeon.—I Chr. 4:30.

BETHUL, bē'thul. Same as *Bethuel* (I Chr. 4:30)—Josh. 19:4.

BETH-ZUR, bĕth–zûr. (1) A city in mountains of Judah, fortified by Rehoboam.—Josh. 15:58; II Chr. 11:7; Neh. 3:16.

(2) Son of Meon.—I Chr. 2:45.

BETIMES. Gen. 26:31; Pr. 13:24.

BETONIM, bĕt'o-nĭm. A town in Gad. —Josh. 13:26.

BETRAY. Brother—Mk. 13:12 (A.V.). Children by parents—Lu. 21:16 (A.V.). Fugitives—Is. 16:3. Jesus by Judas

Iscariot—Mt. 10:4; 26:25, 45–48; 27: 3, 4; Mk. 3:19; 14:10, 11, 41–44; Lu. 22:4, 6; John 6:64, 71; 18:2, 5; 21:20; I Cor. 11:23. Jesus prophesied—Mt. 17:22; 20:18; 26:2, 16, 21–24; Mk. 14: 18, 21; Lu. 22:21, 22, 48; John 13:2. One another—Mt. 24:10 (A.V.).

BETROTHAL. Espousal among the Hebrews was something more than a marriage engagement is with us. It was the beginning of marriage, was as legally binding as marriage itself, and could be broken off only by a bill of divorce. Hence we find that Joseph is called the husband of Mary—Mt. 1:18, 19. Parents chose the companion—Gen. 21:21; 34:4–6; 38:6; Deut. 22:16.

The marriage was not consummated for some time after the betrothal.—Ju. 14:7–8. Brothers were consulted—Gen. 24:58.

The betrothal was accompanied with gifts.—Gen. 24:53; 34:12. A dowry was given—I Sam. 18:25.

The bride remained at her home till taken by the bridegroom.—Deut. 20:7.

The friend of the bridegroom kept up communication between the two.—John 3:29. Compulsory betrothal—Ex. 22:16; Deut. 22:28–29. Violated betrothal—Lev. 19:20; Deut. 22:23. A blameless woman—Deut. 22:25. See MARRIAGE.

BETTER, Abana and Pharpar, than all the waters in Israel—II Ki. 5:12. Angels, Jesus better than—Heb. 1:4. Christ is far better, To be with—Phil. 1:23. Come up hither, than to be put lower in the presence of others—Lu. 14:7–11. See HUMILITY. Country—Heb. 11:8–10, 13–16. See POSSESSIONS, INHERITANCE. Covenant, New, than old —Heb. 7:22; 8:6; 12:24. Dead, than the living—Eccl. 4:3. Death, than day of birth, Day of—Eccl. 3:19–22; 4:3, 6; 7:1–9. See Jonah 4:3, 8. See EAT AND DRINK, MOURNING, SORROW. Die, than that any man make my glorying void—I Cor. 9:15. See II Cor. 11:10. Dinner of herbs, where love is, than a stalled ox with hatred —Ps. 15:17. See LITTLE, LOVE, POOR. Dry morsel with quietness, than a house full of feasting with strife—Pr.

17:1; Eccl. 4:6. Dwell in the corner of the housetop, than with a contentious woman in a wide house—Pr. 25: 24. Eat and drink, Nothing better—Eccl. 2:24; 3:22; 8:15. See Pr. 16:26; Eccl. 6:9. End, than beginning—Eccl. 7:8. See Ez. 36:11. Egypt, than to die in the wilderness—Ex. 14:12; Num. 14:3. Eye, than having two eyes to be cast into hell, Better have one—Mt. 18:9; Mk. 9:47, 48. See MAIMED AND HALT. Father, I am not better than my—I Ki. 19:4. Former days, than these—Eccl. 7:10. Good name, than precious oil—Eccl. 7:1. Handful with quietness, than two handfuls with labor and striving—Eccl. 4:6. House of mourning, than house of mirth—Eccl. 7:2. See Eccl. 2:16; 3:19–22. See DRY MORSEL, DWELL IN THE CORNER, SORROW THAN LAUGHTER. Jew, than Gentile—Rom. 3:1–31. See COVENANT. Law of God, than gold and silver—Ps. 119:72. Lightly esteemed and have a servant, than to honor himself and lack bread —Pr. 12:9. See HUMILITY, PRIDE. Little with fear of God, than great treasure with trouble—Pr. 15:16. Labor—See EAT AND DRINK. Little with righteousness, than revenues with injustice—Pr. 16:8. See DRY MORSEL, HANDFUL. Living dog, than dead lion —Eccl. 9:4. Love, than wine—Song of Sol. 1:2; 4:10. Loving favor, than silver and gold—Pr. 22:1. Lovingkindness of God, than life—Ps. 63:3. Maimed or halt, than to be cast into eternal fire—Mt. 18:8, 9; Mk. 9:43–45. Man, than birds—Mt. 6:26; Lu. 12:24. Marry, than burn—I Cor. 7:9; I Cor. 7:38. Millstone were hanged about his neck than to cause one of these little ones to stumble—Mt. 18:6; Mk. 9:42; Lu. 17:2. Name better than sons and daughters—Is. 56:5. See GOOD NAME, NAME. Neighbor near, than brother far off—Pr. 27:10. Old wine, than new—Lu. 5:39 marg. One eye—See EYE. Obey is better than sacrifice, To—I Sam. 15:22. Open rebuke, than love that is hidden—Pr. 27:5. See Ps. 141:5; Pr. 20:30. See REBUKE. Patience, than pride—Pr. 16:32; Eccl. 7:8, 9. See PATIENCE, PRIDE. Poor man, than a liar—Pr. 19:22. Poor and wise youth, than old and foolish king—Eccl. 4:13–16. Poor that walketh in integrity, than he that is perverse in lips and is a fool—Pr. 19:1; 28:6. See DRY MORSEL, HANDFUL, LITTLE, HUMILITY, JESUS' TEACHING ON CHARACTER. Possession—Heb. 10:34; 11:16. See HEAVEN, INHERITANCE. Quiet—See DRY MORSEL, HANDFUL, DWELL IN THE CORNER. Rebuke of the wise, than the song of fools—Eccl. 4:6; 9:17; 10:12–15. See Pr. 6:23; 13:18; 15:31, 32; 25:12. Labor, Nothing better than to—Eccl. 2:24; 3:22. See EAT AND DRINK. Resurrection—Heb. 11:35. Ruleth his spirit, than he that taketh a city—Pr. 16:32. See SELF-CONTROL. Sacrifice—Heb. 9:23–28. See OBEY. Sight of the eyes, than wandering of desire—Eccl. 6:9. Slain with sword, than slain with hunger—Lam. 4:9. Slow to anger, than the mighty—Pr. 16:32. See ANGER, PATIENCE, SELF-CONTROL. Sons, Seven—Ruth 4:15. Sons, Ten—I Sam. 1:8. Sorrow, than laughter—Eccl. 7:3. See Pr. 14:13; Eccl. 2:1, 2. Things—Heb. 6:9; 11:40; 12:24. Two, than one—Eccl. 4:8–12. Untimely birth, than wealth which cannot be enjoyed—Eccl. 6:1–3. Vow, than vow and not pay, Not—Eccl. 5:5. See VOWS. See Pr. 10:14; 18:7. Wisdom, than gold and silver—Pr. 3:14; 8:19. Ten rulers—Eccl. 9:17. Weapons of war—Eccl. 9:18. See BEST.

BETWEEN. Altar and sanctuary—Mt. 23:35; Lu. 11:51. Brethren—I Cor. 6:5. See Mt. 18:15–17; Lu. 17:3, 4; Gal. 6:1; II Thess. 3:15. Gulf between us and you—Lu. 16:26. No distinction between us and them—Acts 15:9. See Acts 10:28, 34; 11:12; Eph. 2:14. See SALVATION FOR ALL MEN. Thee and him alone—Mt. 18:15. Two opinions —I Ki. 18:21 (A.V.).

BETWIXT. Two—Phil. 1:23.

BEULAH, beū'lah. **A symbolic name for Israel.**—Is. 62:4.

BEWAIL. See MOURNING.

BEWARE. Acts 13:40. Alexander the coppersmith, Of—II Tim. 4:14, 15. Base thought, Of—Deut. 15:9. Concision, Of the—Phil. 3:2. See JUDAIZERS. Covetousness—Lu. 12:15 (A.V.). See

COVETOUSNESS. Dogs—Phil. 3:2. Evil workers—Phil. 3:2. Forget Jehovah, Lest ye—Deut. 6:12; 8:11. Hypocrisy—See HYPOCRISY, LEAVEN, PHARISEES, SCRIBES. Leaven of the Pharisees—Mt. 16:6, 11, 12; Mk. 8:15; Lu. 12:1. Scribes, Of the—Mk. 12:38–40; Lu. 20:45–47. Spoil you through philosophy and vain deceit—Col. 2:8.

BEWITCH. Acts 8:9, 11 (A.V.); Gal. 3:1. See MAGIC.

BEYOND. Measure, Will not glory—II Cor. 10:13. Things written—I Cor. 4:6. Word of Jehovah—Num. 22:18.

BEZAI, bē'zāi. (1) **Ancestor of some who returned from exile with Zerubbabel.**—Ez. 2:17; Neh. 7:23.

(2) **One who sealed the covenant.**—Neh. 10:18.

BEZALEL, bĕ-zăl'el. (1) **Son of Uri, grandson of Hur.** An artificer who had charge of making the works of art in the tabernacle—Ex. 31:2; 35:30; 36:1, 2; 37:1; 38:22; I Chr. 2:20; II Chr. 1:5.

(2) **One of those who married a foreign wife.**—Ezra 10:30.

BEZEK, bē'zek. (1) The home of Adonibezek in Judah—Ju. 1:4, 5.

(2) **Place where Saul numbered his forces.**—I Sam. 11:8.

BEZER, bē'zer. **A city of Reuben.**—Deut. 4:43; Josh. 20:8; 21:36; I Chr. 6:78.

(2) An Asherite—I Chr. 7:37.

BIBLE. See SCRIPTURES, OUTLINE STUDIES IN THE BOOKS, WORD OF GOD.

BICHRI, bĭk'rĭ. **Ancestor of Sheba, who fought with David.**—II Sam. 20:1–22.

BID, BIDDEN. Farewell—Lu. 9:61; Acts 18:21. Godspeed—II John 10, 11 (A.V.). Wedding supper—Mt. 22:3–9; Lu. 14:7–11.

BIDKAR, bĭd'kar. **One of Jehu's officers who executed Jehoram.**—II Ki. 9:25.

BIER. II Sam. 3:31; Lu. 7:14.

BIGTHA, bĭg'thà. **One of the chamberlains in the court of Ahasuerus.**—Esth. 1:10.

BIGTHAN, bĭg'than. **One of the chamberlains of the court of Ahasuerus who conspired against him.**—Esth. 2:21; 6:2.

BIGVAI, bĭg′va-ī. (1) **One who returned from exile with Zerubbabel.**—Ezra 2:2; Neh. 7:7.

(2) **Ancestor of some who returned with Zerubbabel.**—Ezra 2:14; Neh. 7:19.

(3) **Ancestor of some who returned with Ezra.**—Ezra 8:14.

(4) **Name of family who sealed covenant.**—Neh. 10:16.

BILDAD, bĭl′dăd. **One of Job's three friends, descended from Abraham's son by Keturah.**—Job 2:11; 8:1; 18:1; 25:1; 42:9.

BILEAM, bĭl-e-ăm. **A Levitical city in Manasseh.**—I Chr. 6:70.

BILGAH, bĭl′gah. (1) **A priest in the days of David.**—I Chr. 24:14.

(2) **A priest who returned with Zerubbabel.**—Neh. 12:5, 18.

BILGAI, bĭl′gāi. Neh. 10:8. See BIL-GAH (2).

BILHAH, bĭl′hah. (1) Laban gives to daughter Rachel—Gen. 29:29. Given by Rachel to Jacob—Gen. 30:3, 4, 5, 7. Defiled by Reuben—Gen. 35:22. Sons of—Gen. 35:25; 37:2; 46:25; I Chr. 7:13.

(2) **A town in Simeon.**—I Chr. 4:29.

BILHAN, bĭl′han. (1) **Son of Ezer, son of Seir the Horite.**—Gen. 36:27; I Chr. 1:42.

(2) **Grandson of Benjamin.**—I Chr. 7:10.

BILL. Lu. 16:6, 7. Divorcement, Of—Deut. 24:1–3; Is. 50:1; Jer. 3:8; Mk. 10:4. See WRITING.

BILLOW. Ps. 42:7; Jonah 2:3; Lu. 21:25. See WAVE.

BILSHAN, bĭl′shan. **A Jewish prince who returned with Zerubbabel.**—Ezra 2:2; Neh. 7:7.

BIMHAL, bĭm′hal. **An Asherite.**—I Chr. 7:33.

BIND. Arm of Pharaoh—Ez. 30:21. Breastplate—Ex. 28:28; 39:21. Broken heart—Is. 61:1. Burdens—Mt. 23:4. See Acts 15:10. Commandments on the hand—Deut. 6:8; 11:18. *Father and mother, Of*—Pr. 6:21; 7:3. Demoniac—Mk. 5:3, 4; Lu. 8:29. Disciples—Acts 9:2, 14, 21; 21:11. See PAUL, PERSECUTION, PETER, PRISON. Earth shall be bound in heaven, On—Mt. 16:19; 18:18. Faces—Job 40:13; John 11:44. Fetters, With—II Chr. 33:11; 36:6. *Brass, Of*—Ju. 16:21; II

Ki. 25:7. Floods—Job 28:11 (A.V.). See Pr. 30:4; STREAMS, WATERS. Hand and foot—Mt. 22:13; John 11:44; Acts 21:11. Head-tire—Ez. 24:17. Indictment, Job's—Job 31:36. Isaac—Gen. 22:9. Jehoiakim—II Chr. 36:6. Jesus—Mt. 27:2; Mk. 15:1; John 18:12, 24. Job—30:18. John the Baptist—Mt. 14:3; Mk. 6:17. Kindness and truth—Pr. 3:3. Leviathan—Job 41:5. Manasseh—II Chr. 33:11. Paul—Acts 20:22; 21:13, 33; 22:5, 29; 24:27. Peter—Acts 12:6. Pleiades—Job 38:31. Samson—Ju. 15:10–13; 16:5–21. Sandals—Acts 12:8. Satan hath bound—Lu. 13:16. See SATAN. Scarlet thread in window—Josh. 2:18, 21. Shadrach, Meshach, and Abednego—Dan. 3:20–24. Sheaves—Gen. 37:7; Ps. 129:7. Skirts, In—Ez. 5:3. Soul—Num. 30:2–13. See OATHS, VOWS. Stone in a sling—Pr. 26:8. Book, To the—Jer. 51:63. Strong man—Mt. 12:29; Mk. 3:27. Streams—Job 28:11. See FLOODS, WATERS. Tares—Mt. 13:30. Testimony—Is. 8:16. Vow, With a—Num. 30:1–15. See OATHS, VOWS. Wild-ox—Job 39:10. Woman with infirmity—Lu. 13:10–16. Wounds—Job 5:18; Ps. 147:3; Is. 30:26; Ez. 34:4, 16; Lu. 10:34. Zedikiah—II Ki. 25:7. See BOUND, FETTERS, OATH, VOW.

BINDING. Ex. 28:32. See CLOTHING.

BINEA, bĭn′e-a. **A descendant of Saul.**—I Chr. 8:37; 9:43.

BINNUI, bĭn-nū′i. (1) **A Levite who had charge of weighing the gold and silver vessels that Ezra brought from Babylon.**—Ezra 8:33.

(2) **One of those who had married foreign wives.**—Ezra 10:30.

(3) **One of the family of Bani who had married a foreign wife.**—Ezra 10:38.

(4) **Son of Benhadad who assisted in repairing the wall.**—Neh. 3:24; 10:9.

(5) **Ancestor of some of those who returned with Zerubbabel.**—Neh. 7:15. See BANI.

(6) **A Levite who returned with Zerubbabel.**—Neh. 12:8.

BIRDS AND FOWLS. Heb. *'oph*, "a flying thing," including even winged insects, though mostly used of birds. Ravenous birds are expressed by the Heb. *ait*, Gr. *aetos*, one that pounces on prey. Smaller birds, as the sparrow, are called in Heb. *tsippor*, the *tsip* imitating its note.

Part of God's primeval work.—Gen. 1: 20, 21, 26, 28.

Adam names them.—Gen. 2:20.

Admitted into ark.—Gen. 6:20; 7:3, 8, 14. Birds outside ark died—Gen. 7: 21–23. Birds sent out of ark—Gen. 8:7–12. Ark emptied—Gen. 8:17, 18.

Man again given control.—Gen. 9:2; Deut. 14:11; Ps. 8:5–8; Dan. 2:38; Jas. 3:7.

Food of Birds.—Herbs—Gen. 1:30. Grain Mt. 13:4; Mk. 4:4; Lu. 8:5.

God provides for birds.—Ps. 104:10–12; Mt. 6:26; 10:29; Mk. 4:32; Lu. 12:24; 13:19.

Nesting birds.—Job 39:27–30; Mt. 8:20.

Nesting in house of the Lord.—Ps. 84:3. In clefts of rocks—Num. 24:21; Jer. 48:28. In trees—Ps. 104:17; Ez. 31:6; Dan. 4:21. On the ground—Deut. 22:6.

Habitation of birds.—Mountains—Ps. 50:11. Deserts—Ps. 102:6; Is. 34: 11, 15. Housetop—Ps. 102:7. By the springs—Ps. 104:12. In branches of trees—Ps. 104:17; Ez. 31:6; Dan. 4:21; Mt. 13:32; Mk. 4:32.

Snaring of birds.—Ps. 91:3; 124:7; Pr. 1:17; Jer. 5:27; Hos. 9:8.

Migration of.—Deut. 4:17; Job 35:11; Jer. 8:7; Ez. 39:17; Hos. 11:11.

Birds in flight.—Gen. 8:7, 9-11; Ps. 11:1; Is. 31:5; Jer. 4:25; 9:10; Hos. 9:11; 11:11.

Care for young.—Deut. 32:11; Mt. 23: 37; Lu. 13:34.

Neglect of young.—Job 39:14–16.

Solomon speaks of them.—I Ki. 4:33.

Jehovah forbids likeness.—Deut. 4:17.

Worshipped by idolaters.—Rom. 1:23.

Used in sacrifice.—Gen. 15:9; Lev. 12:8; 14:4; Num. 6:10; Ez. 39:17; Lu. 2:24.

Clean birds.—Chickens—Mt. 23:37; 26: 34, 74; Mk. 14:30, 68, 72; Lu. 13:34; 22:34, 60, 61; John 13:38; 18:27. Crane —Is. 38:14; Jer. 8:7. Dove—Gen. 8:8. *Turtle-dove*—Lev. 14:22; Song of Sol. 2:12. Partridge—I Sam. 26:20; Jer. 17:11. Peacock(?)—I Ki. 10:22; II Chr. 9:21. Pigeon—Lev. 1:14; 12:6. Quail—Ex. 16:12, 13; Num. 11:31, 32; Ps. 105:40. Sparrow—Ps. 84:3; 102:7; Pr. 26:2; Mt. 10:29; Lu. 12:6. Swal-

low—Ps. 84:3; Is. 38:14; Jer. 8:7. Used for food—Deut. 14:11, 20. Used in sacrifice—Gen. 8:20; Lev. 1:14.

Unclean birds.—The bat—Lev. 11:19; Is. 2:20. Cormorant—Lev. 11:17. Dart-snake? (Great owl, A.V.)—Is. 34: 15. Eagle—Ex. 19:4; Lev. 11:13; II Sam. 1:23; Job 39:27; Ps. 103:5; Is. 40:31; Mt. 24:28; Rev. 8:13. See EAGLE. Falcon—Lev. 11:14; Job 28:7. Gier-eagle—Lev. 11:13; Deut. 14:12. Glede—Deut. 14:13. Hawk—Lev. 11: 16; Deut. 11:15; Job 39:26. *Nighthawk*—Lev. 11:16; Deut. 14:15. Heron —Lev. 11;19; Deut. 14:18. Hoopoe— Lev. 11:19; Deut. 14:18. Ibis—Lev. 11:19 *marg*. Kite—Lev. 11:14; Deut. 14:13. Ospray—Lev. 11:13; Deut. 14: 12. Ostrich—Lev. 11:16; Deut. 14:15; Job 30:29; 39:13; Is. 13:21; 34:13; 43:20; Jer. 50:39; Lam. 4:3; Mic. 1:8. Owl—Lev. 11:16. *Great owl*—Lev. 11: 17; Deut. 14:16. *Horned owl*—Lev. 11: 18; Deut. 14:16. *Little owl*—Lev. 11: 17; Deut. 14:16. Pelican—Lev. 11:18; Deut. 14:17; Ps. 102:6; Is. 34:11; Zeph. 2:14. Raven—Lev. 11:15; Deut. 14: 14. Porcupine? (Bittern, A.V.)—Is. 14:23; 34:11. See RAVEN. Sea-mew— Lev. 11:16; Deut. 14:15. Stork—Lev. 11:19; Deut. 14:18; Ps. 104:17; Jer. 8:7. Swan—Lev. 11:18 *marg*. Vulture —Lev. 11:13 *marg*.

Carnivorous birds.—Gen. 15:11; 40:19; Deut. 28:26; Dan. 4:33; Rev. 19:21.

Singing birds.—Ps. 104:12; Eccl. 12:4; Song of Sol. 2:12.

Suffer for man's sin.—Gen. 6:7; Jer. 12: 4; Ez. 38:20; Hos. 4:3.

"Birds" used figuratively.—Timid persons—Ez. 7:16; Hos. 7:11; 11:11. Wicked rich—Jer. 17:11. Cruel kings —Is. 46:11. Hostile nations—Jer. 12: 9. Wanderers—Pr. 27:8; Is. 16:2. Overshadowing nations—Ez. 31:6. Kingdom of heaven—Mt. 13:32. Silly youth—Eccl. 9:12. Designs of wicked—Ps. 124:7; Pr. 1:10–17; 7:23. Images of sorrow—Ps. 68:13; 102:6, 7.

BIRTH. Ex. 28:10; Eccl. 7:1; Is. 66:9; Ez. 16:3; 21:30; 29:14; Hos. 9:11; John 9:1.

Children, Of.—See CHILDREN.

Holy Spirit, Of.—See HOLY SPIRIT.

Jesus, Of.—See JESUS.

New.—See NEW BIRTH.

Untimely.—Job 3:16; Ps. 58:8; Eccl. 6:3.

BIRTHDAY. Gen. 40:20; Mt. 14:6; Mk. 6:21.

BIRTHRIGHT. See FIRST-BORN.

BIRTH-STOOL. Ex. 1:16.

BIRZAITH, bïr'zäith. **Grandson of Beriah, son of Asher.**—I Chr. 7:31.

BISHLAM, bïsh'lam. **An officer of Artaxerxes who wrote concerning the rebuilding of the temple.**—Ezra 4:7.

BISHOP. See MINISTERS.

BIT. Bridle—Ps. 32:9; Jas. 3:3 (A.V.).

BITE. People—Mic. 3:5; Gal. 5:15. See Is. 56:9–11. Serpents—Gen. 49:17; Num. 21:6, 9; Pr. 23:32; Eccl. 10:8, 11; Jer. 8:17; Amos 5:19. See SERPENT.

BITHIAH, bi-thï'ah. **Daughter of Pharaoh, wife of Mered, probably converted to Judaism.**—I Chr. 4:18.

BITHRON, bïth'ron. **A place in Gad in the Arabah or valley of the Jordan east of the Jordan.**—II Sam. 2:29.

BITHYNIA, bï-thÿn'i-à. **A province of Asia Minor, to whose inhabitants Peter addressed his first epistle.**—Acts 16:7; I Pet. 1:1.

BITTERNESS. II Sam. 2:26. Of people—Ex. 1:14. Esau—Gen. 27:34. Hannah—I Sam. 1:10. Mordecai—Esth. 4:1. Job—Job 9:18; 10:1; 13:26. Ezekiel—Ez. 3:14.

Of the soul.—I Sam. 1:10; Job 3:20; 7:11; 10:1; 21:25; Is. 38:15; Ez. 27:31. Of heart—Pr. 14:10.

Of Words.—Ps. 64:3; Rom. 3:14. Death —I Sam. 15:32. Water of—Num. 5:24.

Result of sin.—Pr. 5:4; 17:25; Eccl. 7:26; Is. 38:17; Jer. 2:19; 4:18; 6:26; 31:15; Lam. 1:4; 3:15; Ez. 21:6; 27:31; Zech. 12:10; Acts 8:23. Intemperance—Is. 24:9. Warning against—Eph. 4:31; Col. 3:19; Heb. 12:15; Jas. 3:14.

BIZIOTHIAH, biz-ï-o-thï'ah. **A town in southern part of Judah.**—Josh. 15:28.

BIZTHA, bïz'thà. **One of the seven chamberlains of Ahasuerus.**—Esth. 1:10.

BLACK. See COLORS.

BLACKNESS. See COLORS, DARKNESS.

BLADE. Grain, Of—Hos. 8:7; Mt. 13:26; Mk. 4:28. Shoulder—Job 31:22. Sword, Of a—Ju. 3:22.

BLAINS. A swelling—Ex. 9:9.

BLAME. Gen. 44:10; Josh. 2:7. Bear the—Gen. 43:9; 44:32. Peter—Gal. 2:11.

BLAMELESS. Bishop—I Tim. 3:2; Tit. 1:7. Deacon—I Tim. 3:10. Deaconess—I Tim. 5:7 (A.V.). Disciples—I Cor. 1:8 (A.V.); II Cor. 8:20; Eph. 1:4 (A.V.); Phil. 2:15; I Thess. 5:23; II Pet. 3:14. Paul—II Cor. 6:3; 8:20; Phil. 3:6. Priests—Mt. 12:5 (A.V.). Zacharias and Elizabeth, father and mother of John the Baptist—Lu. 1:6. See JESUS, TEACHING ON CHARACTER OF DISCIPLES, RIGHTEOUSNESS.

BLASPHEMY: False charges of.—I Ki. 21:10–13; Acts 6:11.

Blaspheming the name of God.—Lev. 24:11, 16; Ps. 74:10, 18; Is. 52:5; Rev. 13:6; 16:9.

Blaspheming God.—II Ki. 19:6, 22; Is. 37:6, 23; 65:7; Ez. 20:27; Rev. 13:6; 16:11, 21.

Blaspheming Jesus.—I Tim. 1:13; Jas. 2:7. Israel—Ps. 44:16. The word—Tit. 2:5. The goddess—Acts 19:37.

Jesus charged with.—Mt. 9:3; 26:65; Mk. 2:7; 14:64; Lu. 5:21; John 10:33, 36; I Tim. 1:13.

Blasphemy against Holy Spirit.—Mt. 12:31; Mk. 3:29; Lu. 12:10.

The act of blasphemy.—Acts 13:45; Rev. 2:9. Names of—Rev. 13:1; 17:3.

Tempting to blaspheme.—Acts 26:11. Causing bad deeds—II Sam. 12:14. Taught not to—I Tim. 1:20. Some forgiven—Mt. 12:31; Mk. 3:28.

BLAST. Blow or breath, To—II Ki. 19:7 (A.V.); Is. 25:4; 37:7 (A.V.). God's anger—Job 4:9; Is. 27:8; 30:30. God's nostrils—Ex. 15:8; II Sam. 22:16; Ps. 18:15. See BREATH.

BLIGHT. Gen. 41:6, 23, 27; Deut. 28:22; I Ki. 8:37; II Ki. 19:26; II Chr. 6:28; Is. 37:7 (A.V.); Amos—4:9. See DROUGHT, FAMINE.

BLASTUS, blās'tus. **A chamberlain of Herod Agrippa.**—Acts 12:30.

BLEATING. Of flocks—Ju. 5:16 (A.V.); I Sam. 15:14.

BLEMISH: Sacrifices to be without.—Ex. 12:5; 29:1; Lev. 1:3, 10; 3:1, 6; 4:3, 32, 5:15, 18; Lev. 6:6; 9:2, 3; 14:10; 22:19, 21; 23:12, 18; Num. 6:14; 19:2; 28:19, 31; 29:2, 36; Deut. 15:21;

17:1; Ez. 43:22, 25; 45:18, 23; 46:4, 13.

Priests must be without.—Lev. 21:17, 23.

Men without blemish.—II Sam. 14:25; Dan. 1:4; Heb. 9:14.

The Lord wants His children to be without.—Eph. 5:27; I Pet. 1:19.

Punishment for those who cause blemishes.—Lev. 24:19, 20; II Pet. 2:13.

BLESSINGS: Old Testament.—Blessings from God—Creatures of air and sea—Gen. 1:20-22. Adam and Eve—Gen. 1:28; 5:2. The sabbath—Gen. 2:3; Ex. 20:11. Noah and sons—Gen. 9:1.

Abrahamic blessing.—Gen. 12:2, 3; 18:18; 22:17, 18; Acts 3:25; Gal. 3:8, 9, 16. Sarah—Gen. 17:16. Isaac—Gen. 26:3, 4. Jacob—Gen. 28:14; 48:3, 4. Prophesied—Is. 51:1-3; 61:9; Ez. 34:25-31; Zech. 8:11-13; Mal. 3:10-12. Fulfilled in apostle's day—Acts 3:25; Gal. 3:8, 13. Jacob wrestles—Gen. 32:26-29; 35:9.

Children of Israel.—Ex. 20:24; Deut. 12:5, 12, 18; 14:26. Bless their bread and water—Ex. 23:25. Their crops—Lev. 25:18-22. Blessing through Balaam—Num. 22:12; 23:11, 12; Deut. 23:5. The work of their hands—Deut. 2:7; 12:7, 12. Because of liberality—II Chr. 31:10; Lu. 6:38. Being blessed, must bless others—Deut. 15:14; 16:10; I Pet. 3:9. Many blessings catalogued—Deut. 11:8-25; 28:1-14; 30:15-20. Samson—Ju. 13:24. Obed-edom protects ark—II Sam. 6:10-12; I Chr. 13:14; 26:5. David's prayer for blessing—I Chr. 17:26, 27. Job—Job 1:10; 42:12. Egypt blessed—Is. 19:25. Sacrifice to be blessed—I Sam. 9:13. Children a blessing—Gen. 5:29; Ps. 113:9; 127:3-5; Pr. 10:1; 15:20; 17:6; 23:24; 27:11; 29:3.

New Testament—The Beatitudes.—Mt. 5:3-12; Lu. 6:20-23. The seeing eye—Mt. 13:16-17; Lu. 10:23, 24. Blessing bread—Mt. 14:19; 15:36; 26:26; Mk. 6:41; 8:7; 14:22; Lu. 24:30; Acts 27:35; Rom. 14:6. Simon Bar-Jonah at Cæsarea Philippi—Mt. 16:17. Faithful servant—Mt. 24:45-47. Those on right hand—Mt. 25:34. Little children —Mk. 9:36, 37; 10:16. Hearers of word preferred—Lu. 11:27, 28. Watch-

ful servants—Lu. 12:37, 38. Those who feed the poor—Lu. 14:13, 14. Referring to John the Baptist—Mt. 11:6; Lu. 7:23. Jesus' departure—Lu. 24:50-51. Referring to Thomas—John 21:29. The forgiven—Rom. 4:7, 8. Saints blessed—Eph. 1:3. The earth—Heb. 6:6, 7. The tested man—Mt. 5:10; Lu. 6:22; Jas. 1:12; 5:11; I Pet. 3:14; 4:14. The obedient person—Lu. 11:28; John 13:17; Jas. 1:25. Called to inherit blessing—Gal. 3:14; Heb. 12:17; I Pet. 3:9. The Lamb worthy—Rev. 5:12, 13.

BLEW. Trumpets—Josh. 6:8, 9; Ju. 7:19, 20.

BLOOD: Israelites escaped death by use of.—Ex. 12:7, 13, 22, 23.

Water turned into.—Ex. 4:9; 7:19; Rev. 8:8; 11:16.

Punishment for shedding.—Gen. 4:10; 9:6; Num. 35:29-34; II Sam. 1:15-16; 4:11-12; I Ki. 21:19; Jer. 22:17-19; Lu. 11:50-51; Rom. 3:15. Blood forfeited, for cursing parents—Lev. 20:9. *For sexual crimes*—Lev. 20:10-27. Polluting blood—Ps. 106:38; Ez. 16:6; Hos. 6:8; Hab. 2:12; Mk. 5:25; Lu. 8:43. No punishment for killing a thief—Ex. 22:2-3.

Shedding innocent blood.—Deut. 19:10, 13; 21:6-9; 22:8; II Ki. 21:16; 24:4; Ps. 106:38; Pr. 6:17; Is. 59:7; Jer. 7:6; 19:4; 22:3, 17; Joel 3:19; Ez. 22:4; Mt. 27:4, 24.

The blood avenger.—Num. 35:19-33; Deut. 19:4-10; 32:41-43. An exceptional case—Deut. 17:8-9.

Forbidden to be eaten.—Deut. 12:16; 15:23; Lev. 3:17; 7:26; 19:26; I Sam. 14:34; Ez. 33:25; Acts 15:20, 29; 21:25. A definite reason given—Lev. 17:10-14; Deut. 12:16, 23. The law violated—I Sam. 14:33; Ez. 22:2-4. Must bring offering to the altar—Lev. 17:3-9.

Blood of atonement.—Ex. 30:10; Lev. 1:4-5; 4:1-7, 16-20, 25-35; 5:8-10; 6:25-30; 9:1-7; 16:14-27; II Chr. 29:21-24; Ps. 50:8-13; Heb. 9:7, 12-25; 10:19; 12:24; 13:20; Rev. 1:5; 5:9.

Blood of the Covenant.—Ex. 24:6-8; Zech. 9:11; Mt. 26:28; Mk. 14:24; Lu. 22:20; I Cor. 11:25; Heb. 9:19-20; 10:29.

Blood used in offerings.—Peace—Lev. 3:2, 8, 13, 17; 7:14, 26, 27, 33. Trespass—Lev. 7:2. Burnt—Lev. 9:9, 12, 18; Deut. 12:27. Sin—Lev. 10:18. Consecration of Aaron and sons—Lev. 8: 15–30. Of women—Lev. 12:1–8; 15: 19, 25. Of unclean—Num. 19:4–5. For leper—Lev. 14:6–28, 51–52. How to offer—Ex. 23:18; 29:12–21; 34:25.

Blood of Jesus.—Betrayed—Mt. 27:4. Assumed by enemies—Mt. 27:25. Shunned by enemies—Acts 5:28. Sweat as great drops of—Lu. 22:44. Drinketh my blood—John 6:54. My blood of New Covenant—Mk. 14:24. New Covenant in my blood—Lu. 22: 20. Came by water and blood—I John 5:6. Precious blood of—I Pet. 1:19. In blood of the lamb—Rev. 7:14. Purchased with His blood—Acts 20:28. Sanctified with His blood—Heb. 13: 12. Made peace through—Col. 1:20. See SALVATION.

Appertaining to discipleship.—Faith in His blood—Rom. 3:25. Must drink His blood—John 6:53–57. Made nigh by blood—Eph. 2:13. Flesh and blood cannot inherit heaven—I Cor. 15:50. Conferred not with—Gal. 1:16. Communion of blood—I Cor. 10:16. Guilty of—I Cor. 11:27. Wrestle not against —Eph. 6:12. Justified by His blood— Rom. 5:9. Redemption through blood —Eph. 1:7. See ATONEMENT, PRIESTS, OFFERINGS, SACRIFICES, JESUS, BLOOD OF, JESUS, DEATH OF.

BLOOD GUILTINESS. Ex. 22:3; Ps. 51:14.

BLOODTHIRSTY. Ps. 5:6; 55:23; 59:2; 139:19; Pr. 29:10.

BLOODY. City—Ez. 22:2 (A.V.); 24:6, 9; Nahum 3:1. Crimes—Ez. 7:23. See MURDERER. Flux—Acts 28:8 (A.V.). House—II Sam. 21:1. Husband—Ex. 4:25, 26 (A.V.). Man—II Sam. 16:8 (A.V.); Pr. 26:9 (A.V.). See BLOODTHIRSTY.

BLOOM. Ex. 9:31; Num. 17:8. See BLOSSOM.

BLOSSOM. Is. 5:24; 17:11; 27:6. Almond tree—Eccl. 12:5. Desert—Is. 35:1, 2. Rod—Ez. 7:10. Aaron's— Num. 17:5, 8. See Heb. 9:4. Vine— Gen. 40:10; So. of Sol. 2:13, 15; Is. 18:5.

BLOT. Job 31:7 (A.V.); Pr. 9:7. Bond written in ordinances—Col. 2:14. Books, of—Ex. 32:32, 33; Ps. 69:28; Rev. 3:5. Curses—Num. 5:23. Handwriting—See BOND. Name—Deut. 9: 14; 29:20; II Ki. 14:27; Ps. 109:13; Rev. 3:5. Remembrance—Deut. 25:19. Sin—Neh. 4:5; Ps. 109:14; Jer. 18:23; Acts 3:19. Transgressions—Ps. 51:1, 9; Is. 43:25; 44:22. See FORGIVENESS, TRIBE. Ju. 21:17.

BLOW, n. Ps. 39:10; Jer. 14:17 (A.V.); Mk. 14:65.

BLOW, v. Job 20:26; Is. 40:7, 24; Ez. 21:31; 22:20, 21; Hag. 1:9. Trumpets —See TRUMPET. Wind—Ex. 15:10; Ps. 78:26; 147:18; Song of Sol. 4:16; Lu. 12:55; John 3:8; 6:18; Acts 27:13; 28:13 (A.V.); Rev. 7:1. See BLAST, BREATH, WIND.

BLUE. See COLORS.

BLUNT. Eccl. 10:10.

BLUSH. Ezra 9:6; Jer. 6:15; 8:12.

BOANERGES, bō'a-nẽr'gēs. Surname of James and John, sons of Zebedee— Mk. 3:17.

BOAR. Wild—Ps. 80:13. See SWINE.

BOARD. Acts 27:44 (A.V.). Cedar, Of— I Ki. 6:9, 15, 16; So. of Sol. 8:9. Tabernacle, Of the—Ex. 26:15–29; 35:11; 36:20–34; 39:33; Num. 3:36; 4:31. See PLANK, WOOD.

BOASTING. Danger of.—I Ki. 20:11; II Chr. 25:19; Ps. 49:6–13; 52:1–7; 97:7; Pr. 20:14; 25:14; 27:1; Rom. 1:30; 11:18; Jas. 3:5; 4:16.

Folly of.—II Cor. 11:16–21; 12:1–5, 11.

Right of.—Rom. 5:2; II Cor. 1:14; Gal. 6:14. Of Paul—II Cor. 7:14; 8:24; 9:3; 11:10. In Christ—Rom. 2:17; II Cor. 10:8, 13, 15–17; 11:17; Heb. 3:6. In God—Ps. 44:8; Rom. 2:17. In law —Rom. 2:23.

Excluded.—Jer. 9:23; John 7:18; Rom. 3:27; 4:2; I Cor. 1:29; Eph. 2:9.

Of wicked.—Ps. 10:3; Ez. 35:13.

Examples of.—Goliath—I Sam. 17:44. Ben-hadad—I Ki. 20:10. Rabshakeh— II Ki. 18:17–37; Is. 36:1–22; 37:8–13. Haman—Esth. 5:11. Theudas—Acts 5:36.

Prophecies concerning.—Is. 61:6; II Tim. 3:2. See GLORYING, PRIDE.

BOATS. Ferry boat.—II Sam. 19:18.

Jesus and His disciples enter in.—John 6:22, 23.

Used in shipwreck.—Acts 27:16, 30, 32. See SHIPS.

BOAZ, Heb. *Quickness.* His genealogy—I Chr. 2:11–13; Mt. 1:5. Of family of Elimelech—Ruth 2:1. Wealthy and valorous—Ruth 2:1. Courteous to his servants—Ruth 2:4. Gives directions concerning Ruth—Ruth 2:5–9. Is won by her modesty—Ruth 3:9–11. Boaz inquires concerning Ruth's kinsman —Ruth 4:1–6. Boaz buys kinsman's right and marries Ruth—Ruth 4:10–13. Has a son by Ruth named Obed—Ruth 4:13, 17. Ancestor of Jesus—Lu. 3:32. See RUTH.

BOCHERU, bō-ke-ru. A Benjamite—I Chr. 8:38; 9:44.

BOCHIM, bō′chim. A place west of the Jordan—Ju. 2:1–5.

BODILY. Exercise—I Tim. 4:8. Godhead—Col. 2:9. Holy Spirit in bodily form—Lu. 3:22. Presence—II Cor. 10:10.

BODY. Absent in.—I Cor. 5:3; 6:16, 18, 19; II Cor. 5:6.

Anointed.—Mt. 26:12; Mk. 14:8.

Cherubim, Of.—Ez. 10:12.

Christ manifest in.—John 1:14; Phil. 1:20.

Christ's, Sacrifice of.—Rom. 4:19.

Church as.—Col. 1:18, 22. See CHURCH.

Dead.—Because of sin—Rom. 8:10. Destruction of—Pr. 5:11; Is. 10:18; Jer. 26:23; 36:30; Dan. 7:11; Mt. 10:28; Lu. 12:4; I Cor. 13:3. Fastened to the wall—I Sam. 31:10, 12. Found not—Lu. 24:3, 23; John 20:12. Jesus, Of—Mk. 15:43, 45; Lu. 23:52, 55; John 19:38, 40. Kings, Of—Ez. 43:7. Law through body of Jesus, To the—Rom. 7:4, 24. Making unclean—Lev. 21:11; Num. 6:6; Deut. 21:23; Hag. 2:13. Moses, Of—Jude 9. Resurrection of—Is. 26:19; Acts 9:40; I Cor. 15:35; Heb. 10:5, 10. Spirit, Without—Jas. 2:26. Took away—I Chr. 10:12. Took up—Mt. 14:12; 27:58, 59. Worms eat —Job. 19:26.

Deeds of.—Rom. 8:13; II Cor. 5:10.

Dew, Wet with.—Dan. 4:33; 5:21.

Fruits of.—Deut. 28:4, 11, 18, 53; 30:9; Ju. 8:30; Ps. 132:11; Mic. 6:7.

God gives.—I Cor. 15:38.

Healed.—Mk. 5:29; Acts 19:12.

Light of.—Mt. 6:22; Lu. 12:34, 36.

Members, Has many.—I Cor. 12:12, 16, 17, 24, 25; II Cor. 12:2, 3.

Needful to.—Jas. 2:16.

One in Christ.—Rom. 12:5; I Cor. 12:13–27; II Cor. 5:6, 8; Eph. 2:16; 3:6; 4:4, 12; 5:30; Col. 3:15.

Persecution of.—Gal. 6:17.

Power of.—I Cor. 7:4; 9:27.

Preservation of.—I Thess. 5:23.

Redemption of.—Rom. 8:23.

Savior of.—Eph. 5:23.

Sin of.—Rom. 6:6, 12; II Cor. 4:10; Phil. 3:21; Col. 2:11, 17, 23; I Pet. 2:24.

Spiritual.—Dan. 7:15; I Cor. 7:34; 15:37; II Cor. 5:1; I Cor. 15:44.

Thought of, No.—Mt. 6:25; Lu. 12:22, 23; 17:37.

Whole.—Mt. 5:29, 30; 6:23; Eph. 4:16; Jas. 3:3, 6.

Figurative.—Cometh out of—Job 20:25. Body like beryl—Dan. 10:6. Bread represents body of Christ—Mt. 26:26; Mk. 14:22; Lu. 22:19; I Cor. 10:16; 11:24, 27; Eph. 1:23. Body as a temple —John 2:21; I Cor. 6:19.

BOHAN, bō′hăn. A Reubenite.—Josh. 15:6; 18:17.

BOIL, *n.* **An ulcer.**—Ex. 9:9–11; Lev. 13:18–23; Deut. 28:35; II Ki. 20:7; Job 2:7; 7:5; 13:28; Is. 38:21.

BOIL, *v.* Deep—Job 41:31. Flesh—Ex. 29:31; Lev. 8:31; I Ki. 19:21; Ez. 24:5. Offering—Ez. 46:20, 24. Son—II Ki. 6:29. See FOOD, PREPARATION OF.

BOILING-HOUSES. Ez. 46:24.

BOILING PLACES. Ez. 46:23.

BOLDNESS: A Christian virtue.—Pr. 28:1; Jer. 30:21; II Cor. 11:21; Eph. 3:12; Phil. 1:20; I Tim. 3:13; Heb. 3:6; 4:16; 10:19, 35; I John 4:17.

Boldness in speech required of ministers of gospel.—Acts 4:13; 9:27, 29; 14:3; 18:26; 19:8; 28:31; II Cor. 3:12; Phil. 1:14; I Thess. 2:2.

Instances of.—Joseph—Mk. 15:43. Apollos—Acts 18:26. Isaiah—Rom. 10:20. See PAUL, JESUS, CHARACTER OF, COURAGE.

BOLSTER. See PILLOW.

BOLT. II Sam. 13:17, 18; So. of Sol. 5:5; Hab. 3:5. See TOOLS AND IMPLEMENTS.

BONDAGE. Of Israelites.—Ex. 2:23; 6:5–9; 13:3, 14; 20:2; Deut. 5:6; 6:12, 21; 8:14; 13:5; Josh. 24:17; Ju. 6:8; II Chr. 28:10; Ezra 9:8, 9; Neh. 9:17; Acts 7:6; Gal. 4:3; II Pet. 2:19; In hard service—Ex. 1:14; Is. 14:3. As punishment—Deut. 28:68. Brought out of bondage—Ex. 20:2; Lev. 26:13; Deut. 5:6; 6:12; 7:8; 8:14; 13:5; 15: 15; 16:12; 24:22; Josh. 24:17; Ju. 6:8; Jer. 34:13. Of Gibeonites—Josh. 9:23.
Spiritual bondage.—Rom. 8:15, 21; Gal. 2:4; 4:9; 5:1.
Illustrative.—Gal. 4:24, 25.
Bondservants mentioned.—Gen. 43:18; 44:9; Rev. 6:15. Of Joseph—Gen. 44: 33. Of Solomon—I Ki. 9:22. Jews as —Esth. 7:4. Handmaid—Gen. 21:10– 13; Gal. 4:23. Handmaid of Naaman's wife—II Ki. 5:2. See HANDMAID.
Laws concerning.—Redemption of servants—Lev. 25:39, 42, 44, 46. Maidservant—Lev. 19:20. Children of—Gal. 4:30, 31. Debtors as—II Ki. 4:1. Levy of bondservants—I Ki. 9:21. Usury a bondage—Neh. 5:5, 18.
Marriage a form of bondage.—I Cor. 7:15.
The new marriage bondage under Christ. —Rom. 7:1–6. Christians not to have two masters—Mt. 6:24. No longer bondservant of sin, but bondservant of righteousness—Rom. 6:16–23. Paul the bondservant of Christ—Eph. 3:1; 6:20; Phil. 1:1, 14; Philemon 1.
Duties of Christian slaves, or bondservants.—I Cor. 7:21–24; Eph. 6:5–8; Col. 3:11, 22–25; I Tim. 6:1, 2; Titus 2:9–14; Philemon 10–20; I Pet. 2:18– 25. See BOND, PERSECUTION, PRISON, SERVANT.
BONDMAN. See SERVANT.
BOND-SERVANT. See SERVANT.
BOND-WOMAN. See HAND-MAID, SERVANT.
BONES. Animal's.—Behemoth's like tubes of brass—Job 40:18. Break, Must not break paschal lamb's—Ex. 12:46; Num. 9:12; John 19:36.
Men's.—Num. 19:16, 18; Ez. 39:15. Aching—Job 30:17, 30; 33:19; Ps. 6:2; 22: 14; 38:3; 102:3; Jer. 20:9; Lam. 1:13. Ankle—Acts 3:7. Bone of my bone and flesh of my flesh—Gen. 2:23; 29: 14; Ju. 9:2; II Sam. 5:1; 19:12, 13; I

Chr. 11:1; Eph. 5:30. Boiled (fig.)— Ez. 24:4, 5. Break—Num. 24:8; Job 31:22; Ps. 34:20; 51:8; Pr. 25:15; Is. 38:13; Jer. 50:17; Dan. 6:24; Mic. 3:3. Bring—Jer. 8:1; Amos 6:10. Burial of—II Ki. 23:14, 16. *Elisha's* —II Ki. 13:21. *Joseph's*—Gen. 50:25; Ex. 13:19; Josh. 24:32; Heb. 11:22. *Prophet, Of the*—I Ki. 13:31; II Ki. 23: 17, 18. *Saul and his sons, Of*—I Sam. 31:13; II Sam. 21:12–14; I Chr. 10:12. Burn—I Ki. 13:2; II Ki. 23:20; II Chr. 34:5; Ps. 102:3; Jer. 20:9; Lam. 1:13; Ez. 24:10. Cleaveth to flesh— Job. 19:20; Ps. 102:5; Lam. 4:8. See STICK OUT. Count—Ps. 22:17. Dried— Ps. 22:17; Ez. 37:1–11. Fat—Pr. 15: 30. Flourish, Shall—Is. 66:14. Grow, How they—Eccl. 11:5. Health in—Ps. 38:3; Pr. 16:24. Iniquities are upon— Ez. 32:27. Knit together with—Job 10:11. Jesus—John 19:33–36. See PASCHAL LAMB. Marrow of—Job 21: 24; Pr. 3:8. Oil into—Ps. 109:18. Pierced—Job 30:17. See ACHING. Pluck flesh from—Mic. 3:2. Rottenness in—Pr. 12:4; 14:30; Hab. 3:16. Say—Ps. 35:10. Scatter—Ps. 53:5; 141:7; Jer. 8:1; Ez. 6:5. Shake—Job 4:14; Jer. 23:9. Spirit hath not—Lu. 24:39. Stick out—Ps. 22:17; Lam. 4:8. See CLEAVE. Strong in, As with a —Ps. 42:10. Touch—Job. 2:5. See ACHING. Wasted away—Ps. 32:3. Youth, Full of—Job. 20:11; 21:23, 24.
BONNETS. See CLOTHING, HEAD.
BOOKS. Lost books named.—Wars of Jehovah—Num. 21:14. Jashar—Josh. 10:13; II Sam. 1:18. Samuel, of the kingdom—I Sam. 10:25. Chronicles of David—I Chr. 27:24. Acts of Solomon —I Ki. 4:32; 11:41. Solomon's natural history—I Ki. 4:32, 33. History of the kings—I Ki. 9:1; II Chr. 20:34; 33:18. Samuel the seer—I Chr. 29:29. Nathan the seer—I Chr. 29:29; II Chr. 9:29. Shemaiah the seer—II Chr. 12: 15. Gad the seer—I Chr. 29:29. Saying of the seers—II Chr. 9:29. Ahijah the Shilonite—II Chr. 9:29. Visions of Iddo—II Chr. 9:29; 12:15. Jehu, the son of Hanani—II Chr. 20:34.
How written.—On tablets—Is. 8:1; Hab. 2:2; Lu. 1:63. Stone—Ex. 24:12; 34:1, 4; Deut. 4:13; Job 19:24. Papyrus

(roll)—Ezra 6:12; Is. 34:4; Jer. 36:2, 4, 6, 14, 20, 21, 23, 25, 27–29, 32; Ez. 2:9; 3:1, 2, 3; Zech. 5:1. Parchment— II Tim. 4:13. With iron pens and ink —Job 19:24; Jer. 17:1; 36:18; III John 13. Written on both sides—Ez. 2:10. Sealed—Is. 29:11; Dan. 12:4; Rev. 5:1, 2, 5, 9; 6:1, 3, 5, 7, 9, 12; 8:1. Dedicated—Lu. 1:1; Acts 1:1. Erasures possible—Ex. 32:33; Num. 5:23.

Numerous.—Eccl. 12:12; Acts 19:19.

History recorded.—See LOST BOOKS AND CHRONICLES.

Divine revelation and laws written.— Ex. 17:14; 24:4, 12; 34:1, 4, 28; Deut. 4:13; 9:10, 11; 17:18; 28:58, 61; 29:20, 21, 27; 30:10; 31:9.

Book of the Covenant.—Contained the law—Ex. 17:14; 24:7, 8; II Ki. 23:2, 3, 21, 24. Delivered to the priests and kept in the ark—Deut. 31:9–13, 24–26. To be read every seven years—Deut. 31:10, 11; Josh. 8:34, 35; II Ki. 23:2; II Chr. 34:18, 19; Neh. 8:8, 18; 9:3. Copies made—Deut. 17:18; Josh. 8:32. Lost and found—II Ki. 22:8; 23:21; II Chr. 34:14, 15, 30.

Book of the law.—Deut. 28:58, 61; 29: 20, 21; 30:10; 31:26; Josh. 1:8; 8:31, 34; 23:6; 24:26; II Ki. 14:6; 22:8, 11; 23:24; II Chr. 17:9; 25:4; 34:14, 15; Neh. 8:1–8, 18; 9:3.

Book of Moses.—II Chr. 35:12; Neh. 13:1.

Book of Chronicles.—I Ki. 14:19; 15:7, 23, 31; 16:5, 14, 20, 27; 22:39, 45; II Ki. 1:18; 8:23; 10:34; 12:19; 13:8, 12; 14:15, 18, 28; 15:6, 11, 15, 21, 26, 31, 36; 16:19; 20:20; 21:17, 25; 23:28; 24:5. Persian—Esth. 2:23; 6:1; 10:2.

Book of life.—Ps. 69:28; Dan. 7:10; 12:1; Phil. 4:3; Rev. 3:5; 13:8; 17:8; 20:12, 15; 21:27; 22:19.

Book of remembrance.—Ps. 139:16; Mal. 3:16.

BOOTHS: Uses of.—For dwellings— Lev. 23:42, 43; Neh. 8:14–17; Jonah 4:5. For cattle—Gen. 33:17. Illustrative—Job. 27:18; Is. 1:8.

BOOTY. See SPOILS.

BORDER. Altar, Of—Num. 35:26, 27.

Countries and places.—Ammonites— Num. 21:24; Josh. 12:2; 13:10; Amos 1:13. Amorites—Num. 21:13–21; Josh.

12:5; 13:4. Beth-horon—I Sam. 13:18. Bethshemesh—I Sam. 6:12. Canaanites—Gen. 10:19; Num. 34:1–12. Edom Num. 20:16–21; 34:3; Josh. 15:1, 21; Ob. 7. Egypt—Gen. 47:21; Ex. 8:2; I Ki. 4:21; II Chr. 9:26; Is. 19:19. Ekron—Josh. 13:3. Ethiopia—Ez. 29: 10. Gaza—II Ki. 18:8. Geshurites— Josh. 12:5; 13:11. Hamath—Zech. 9:2. Israel—Num. 34:1–15; Josh. 1:4; Jer. 31:17; Ez. 11:10, 11; 45:1, 7; 47: 13–20; Amos 6:2; Zeph. 2:8. Jericho— Josh. 4:19. Jerusalem—Ps. 147:14; Joel 3:6. See ZION. Jordan—Josh. 13: 23, 27; 18:20; 22:25. Judah—Jer. 15: 13; 17:3; Joel 3:6. Maacathites— Josh. 12:5; 13:11; Ju. 7:22. Moab— Num. 21:13–30; 22:36; 33:44; Ju. 11: 18; II Ki. 4:21; Is. 15:8. Og, king of Bashan—Josh. 13:11–31. Philistines— Josh. 13:2 (A.V.); Amos 6:2. Tribes of Israel—See TRIBES. Tyre—Ez. 27:4; Zech. 9:2; Mk. 7:24. See TYRE. Earth, Of the—Ps. 74:17. Enlarge—Ex. 34: 24; Amos 1:13. Garments—See CLOTHING. Peace in thy—Ps. 147:14. Precious stones, Of—Is. 54:12. Sanctuary—Ps. 78:54; Ez. 45:1–6; 48:8–14. Table of shewbread—Ex. 25:25, 27; 37:12, 14. Utmost—Jer. 50:26. Wickedness—Mal. 1:4. Widow, Of the—Pr. 15:25. Zion—Is. 54:12; 60:18; Mic. 5:6. See LEDGES, PANELS, PEDESTAL.

BORE. Ear, Through—Ex. 21:6. Jaw of Leviathan—Job 41:2 (A.V.). Lid of chest—II Ki. 12:9.

BORN. Again, Anew—See NEW BIRTH. Blind—John 9:2, 19, 20, 32, 34. See BLINDNESS. Blood, Not of—John 1:13. End was I born, To this—John 18:37. See JESUS, BIRTH OF. Flesh, Of—John 1:13; 3:6; Gal. 4:23, 29. Formation —John 8:41. God, Of—John 1:13. See BEGOTTEN, NEW BIRTH. Good if he had not been—Mt. 26:24. Holy Spirit— John 3:5–8. See HOLY SPIRIT, NEW BIRTH. Home-born—Ex. 12:49; Lev. 19:34; 23:42; 24:16; Num. 15:13, 29, 30; Josh. 8:33; Ez. 47:22. House, In the—Gen. 14:14; 15:3; 17:12, 13, 23, 27; Lev. 18:9; 22:11; Eccl. 2:7. King of the Jews—Mt. 2:2. See JESUS, DIVINITY OF. Land, In the—Ex. 12:19, 48; Num. 9:14. Man born into the world—John 16:21. Out of due time—

I Cor. 15:8. Sins, In—John 9:34. See SIN. Tongue, Wherein we were—Acts 2:8. Wilderness, In the—Josh. 5:5. Will of man, Of the—John 1:13. Woman, Of a—Job. 14:1; 15:14; 25:4; Mt. 11:11; Lu. 7:28; John 3:5–7. See BEGOTTEN, BIRTH, CHILDREN.

BORNE. See BARE, BEAR, SUFFERINGS.

BORROW. Axe-head—II Ki. 6:5. Egyptians, From—Ex. 3:22; 11:2; 12:35. Forbidden to—Deut. 15:6; 28:12. Land, Upon—Neh. 5:4. Neighbor, From—Ex. 22:14. Servant to lender, Borrower—Pr. 22:7. Turn not from borrower—Mt. 5:42. Vessels, Empty —II Ki. 4:3. Wicked borroweth and payeth not. See DEBT, FRATERNITY, USURY.

BOSOM. Abraham's—Lu. 16:22, 23. Anger in—Eccl. 7:9. Bribe out of—Pr. 17:23. Carry in—Num. 11:12; Is. 40: 11. Child in—Ruth 4:16; I Ki. 3:20; 17:19; Lam. 2:12. Father, Of the— John 1:18. Fire in—Pr. 6:27. Foreigner, Of the—Pr. 5:20. Give unto— Pr. 21:14; Lu. 6:38. Hand in—Ex. 4:6, 7; Pr. 19:24; 26:15. Husband of —Deut. 28:56. Jesus, Of—John 13:23. Lamb in—II Sam. 12:3; Is. 40:11. Pour their soul into—Lam. 2:12. Prayer returned into—Ps. 35:13. Present in—Pr. 21:14. Recompense into— Is. 65:6, 7; Jer. 32:18. Reproach in— Ps. 79:12; 89:50. Sheaves in—Ps. 129:7. Wife of—Deut. 13:6; 28:54; II Sam. 12:3, 8; Mic. 7:5. See Gen. 16:5; I Ki. 1:2.

BOSOR. See BEOR.

BOSS. Of his bucklers—Josh. 15:26.

BOTTLES: For holding water.—Gen. 21:14, 15, 19. For milk—Ju. 4:19. For wine—I Sam. 1:24; 10:3; 16:20; 25: 18; II Sam. 16:1; Jer. 13:12. Earthen —Jer. 19:1. Skin—Josh. 9:4. Wineskins—Lev. 8:17. Old and new—Mt. 9:17; Mk. 2:22; Lu. 5:37, 38. Broken —Jer. 19:10; 48:12.

Figurative.—Like wine-skin—Ps. 119: 83. Like new wine-skins—Job 32:19. Of heaven—Job 38:37. Of tears—Ps. 56:8. See VESSELS.

BOTTOM. So. of Sol. 3:10; Zech. 1:8. Altar, Of—Ez. 43:13, 14, 17. Den, Of —Dan. 6:24. Mountains, Of—Jonah 2:6. Sea, Of—Ex. 15:5 (A.V.); Job 36:30; Amos 9:3; Jonah 2:6. Veil of temple rent from top to—Mt. 27:51; Mk. 15:38. See BASE.

BOTTOMLESS. Pit—Rev. 9:1, 2, 11 (A.V.); 11:7 (A.V.); 17:8 (A.V.); 20:1, 3 (A.V.). See ABYSS, PIT, SHEOL.

BOUGH. Deut. 24:20; Ju. 9:48, 49; Job 14:9; Ps. 80:10, 11; Is. 10:33; Ez. 17: 23; 31:5, 8, 12. Absalom caught in— II Sam. 18:9. Feast of tabernacles, Used in—Lev. 23:40. See FEASTS. Forsaken—Is. 17:9 (A.V.). Fruitful—Gen. 49:22. Nests in—Ez. 31:6. Thick— Ez. 19:11; 31:3, 10, 14. Uppermost— Is. 17:6. See BRANCHES.

BOUGHT. Disciples—I Cor. 6:20. See REDEMPTION, SALVATION THROUGH BLOOD OF JESUS. Field—Lev. 27:22; Jer. 32: 43; Lu. 14:18. See LAND. Redeemed— Lev. 27:22. See REDEMPTION. Servants —Gen. 17:12, 13, 27; Ex. 12:44; Eccl. 2:7. See BONDAGE, HANDMAID, SERVANTS. Spices—Mk. 16:1. See JESUS, ANOINTING OF. Temple, In the—Mt. 21:12; Mk. 11:15. Tomb bought by Abraham—Acts 7:16. See BUY, COMMERCE, PURCHASE.

BOUND. Job 38:20; Is. 22:3. Affliction, In—Job 36:8; Ps. 107:10. Archers, By —Is. 22:3. Brethren, One of—Gen. 42: 19. Chains, With—Nah. 3:10; Lu. 8: 29; Acts 28:20. See Heb. 13:3. Chariots—Nah. 3:2. Covering bound on— Num. 19:15. Face—John 11:44. Fetters, With—Job 36:8. See CHAINS. Foolishness—Pr. 22:15. Great men— Nah. 3:10. Heart, In—Pr. 22:15. Infirmities—Heb. 5:1–3. Prison, In— Gen. 42:19; Ps. 68:6 (A.V.); Is. 49:9; 61:1. See Heb. 13:3. Rulers—Is. 22:3. Samson—Ju. 16:6, 10, 13. Shadrach, Meshach and Abed-nego—Dan. 3:21– 24. Soul—I Sam. 25:29. Spirit, In— Acts 20:22. Waters—Pr. 30:4. Wineskins—Josh. 9:4. Word of God not— II Tim. 2:9. See BIND, BONDAGE, PRISON.

Boundary of.—Everlasting hills—Gen. 49:26. Man—Job 13:27. Mount Sinai —Ex. 19:12, 23. People's—Ex. 19:12; 23:31 (A.V.); Deut. 32:8; Is. 10:13; Acts 17:26. Sea—Job 26:10; 38:10, 11; Ps. 104:9; Pr. 8:29; Jer. 5:22.

Ought to.—II Thess. 1:3; 2:13.

Wrapped up.—Iniquity of Ephraim—Hos. 13:12. Kneading-trough—Ex. 12:34. Life—Gen. 44:30. Wounds—Jer. 30:13.

BOUNTIFUL. Churl—Is. 32:5. Eye—Pr. 22:9. See ABUNDANCE.

BOUNTIFULLY. Deal—Ps. 13:16; 116:7; 119:17; 142:7. Sowing—II Cor. 9:6. See GIVING, FRATERNITY, LIBERALITY.

BOUNTY. Contribution to other disciples—I Cor. 16:3; II Cor. 8:20; 9:5. See ABUNDANCE, BOUNTIFULLY, FRATERNITY, LIBERALITY.

BOW, *n.* **Rainbow.**—Gen. 19:13–16; Ez. 1:28; Rev. 4:3; 10:1.

Weapon. See ARCHERY, WAR, WEAPONS.

BOW, *v.* Job 31:10; Ps. 145:14; 146:8; Eccl. 12:3; Is. 2:9, 11, 17; 10:4; 46:1, 2; 49:23; 60:14; 65:12. Angels, Before—Gen. 18:2; 19:1. Back, The—Rom. 11:10. See BACK. Ear, Down the—II Ki. 19:16 (A.V.); Ps. 17:6; 34:2, 86:1; Pr. 52:17 (A.V.). Everlasting hills—Hab. 3:6. Evil before good—Pr. 14:19. Faces—I Sam. 25:41; 28:14; Lu. 24:5. Head, The—See HEAD. Heavens—II Sam. 22:10; Ps. 18:9; 144:5. Knees—Gen. 41:43; Ju. 7:5, 6; I Ki. 19:18; Is. 45:23; Mt. 27:29; Mk. 15:19; Rom. 11:4; 14:11; Eph. 3:14; Phil. 2:10, 11. Mourning, In—Ps. 35:14; 38:6; 57:6. Shoulder—Gen. 49:15. Soul—Ps. 44:25; 57:6. Together—Lu. 13:11. Worship, In—Ex. 20:5; 23:24; Deut. 5:9; Josh. 23:7, 16; Ju. 2:12; II Ki. 5:18; 17:35; II Chr. 7:3; 20:18; 25:14; 29:29, 30; Ps. 22:29; 95:6; Mic. 6:6.

Persons, Before.—Abraham before—*Angels*—Gen. 18:12. *Children of Heth*—Gen. 23:7, 12. David before—*Jonathan* I Sam. 20:41. *Saul*—I Sam. 24:8. *Upon his bed*—I Ki. 1:47. Before David—*Abigail*—I Sam. 25:23. *Absalom*—II Sam. 14:33. *Araunah*—II Sam. 24:20; I Chr. 21:21. *Bathsheba*—I Ki. 1:16, 31. Joab—II Sam. 14:22 (A.V.). Elisha, Before—II Ki. 2:15; 4:37. Esau, Before—Gen. 33:3, 6, 7. Jacob—Gen. 33:3; 47:31. *Before Jacob*—Gen. 27:29. Joseph, Before—Gen. 37:10; 42:6; 43:26. Judah, Before—Gen. 49:8. Moses, Before—Ex. 11:8. Righteous king, Before—Ps. 72:9. Ruth before Boaz—Ruth 2:10. Samson—Ju. 16:30. Saul

before Samuel—I Sam. 28:14. Sisera in death—Ju. 5:27. Solomon—I Ki. 2:19. *Before Solomon—Adonijah*—II Ki. 1:53 (A.V.). See OBEISANCE, HEAD, PRAYER, WORSHIP.

BOWELS. Concerning heirs.—Gen. 15:4. Food for—Ez. 3:3; 7:19. Jehovah's prophecy to Rebekah—Gen. 25:23. To David—II Sam. 7:12. Descendants—II Sam. 16:11; II Chr. 32:21; 71:6; Is. 48:19; 49:1. Joab's death—II Sam. 20:10. Fate of Judas—Acts 1:18.

Disease of.—II Chr. 21:15, 18, 19.

Food in.—Job 20:14.

Inward parts.—Is. 16:11. See HEART.

BOWLS. Kinds of.—Gold, used in the tabernacle—Ex. 25:29; 37:16; Num. 4:7. Golden bowl full of incense—Rev. 5:8. In the temple—I Chr. 28:17; Jer. 52:19. Illustrative of—Eccl. 12:6. Of silver, In dedication of altar—Num. 7:84; Zech. 14:20; Jer. 52:19. For oblations of priests—Num. 7:13, 19, 25, 31, 37, 43, 49, 55, 61, 67, 73, 79. Of burnished brass, Of capitals—I Ki. 7:41, 42. Of candlesticks—Zech. 4:23.

Contents of.—Wine—Amos. 6:6. Filled like bowls—Zech. 9:15. Golden bowls full of—Rev. 5:8. With plagues—Rev. 21:9.

Figurative.—Filled with wrath of God—Rev. 16:1–10. With plagues—Rev. 21:9. See VESSELS.

BOWMEN. Jer. 4:29. See ARCHERY.

BOWSHOT. Gen. 21:16. See ARCHERY.

BOX. II Ki. 9:1, 3 (A.V.); Is. 3:20. Alabaster box—Mt. 26:7 (A.V.); Mk. 14:3 (A.V.); Lu. 7:37 (A.V.).

BOX-TREE. Is. 41:19; 60:13.

BOY. Gen. 25:27; I Sam. 20:22; Joel 3:3; Zech. 8:5; Lu. 2:43. See YOUNG MEN, YOUTHS.

BOZEZ, bō′zez. **A cliff or rock on one side of the Michmash ravine.**—I Sam. 14:4.

BOZKATH, bŏz′kath. **A town of Judah in the plain.**—Josh. 15:39; II Ki. 22:1.

BOZRAH, bŏz′rah. (1) **A city of Edom.**—Gen. 36:33; I Chr. 1:44; Is. 34:6; 63:1; Jer. 49:13, 22; Amos 1:12; Mic. 2:12.

(2) **A city in Moab.**—Jer. 48:24.

BRACELET. Gen. 24:22, 30, 47; 38:18, 25 (A.V.). Ex. 35:22 (A.V.); Num. 31:

50; II Sam. 1:10; Is. 3:19; Ez. 16:11; 23:42. See JEWELS.

BRAID. I Tim. 2:9.

BRAMBLE. Ju. 9:14, 15; Lu. 6:44. See THORNS.

BRANCH.
See BOUGH.

BRANCHES: Natural. Of trees.—Job 14:7; Is. 17:6. Palm—Lev. 23:40; Song of Sol. 7:8; Is. 9:14; 19:15; John 12:13. Olive—Neh. 8:15; Jer. 11:16; Zech. 4:12. Myrtle—Neh. 8:15. Thick trees—Neh. 8:15. Cedar—Ps. 80:11; Ez. 17:23; 31:3.

Figurative.—Joel 1:7.

Of vines.—Ez. 15:2; 17:6, 8; Nah. 2:2. Destroyed—Is. 16:8.

Of grapes.—Num. 13:23.

Uses of.—For booths—Neh. 8:15. Shelter for birds—Ps. 104:12; Ez. 17:23; 31:6, 13; Dan. 4:21; Mt. 13:32; Mk. 4:32; Lu. 13:19. Shelter for animals—Ez. 31:6, 13. Food for cattle—Is. 27:10. As a design for candlestick—Ex. 25:32-36; 37:18, 19, 21, 22. Triumphal entry—Mk. 11:8; John 12:13.

Illustrative. — Prosperity — Gen. 49:22. Wickedness—Job 15:32; Is. 14:19. Idolatrous worship—Ez. 8:17. Righteousness—Is. 60:21; Jer. 23:5; 33:15. Strength—Ps. 80:15.

Figurative. — Wicked destroyed — Job 15:30; 18:16; Is. 18:5; Mal. 4:1. Of Job—Job 29:19. Jehovah—Is. 4:2. Jesse—Is. 11:1. Israel—Ez. 19:10, 11, 14; 36:8; Hos. 14:6.

Messianic.—Assyrian—Ez. 31:3, 5–9, 12, 13.

Servant.—Zech. 3:8. The branch—Jer. 23:5; Zech. 6:12.

Followers of Christ.—John 15:2, 5, 6; Rom. 11:16–21, 24.

Apocalyptic (symbolical).—Of tree—Dan. 4:14, 21. Of vine—Gen. 40:10, 12. Of candlestick—Zech. 4:12.

BRAND. On fire—Ju. 15:5. Plucked from the burning—Amos 4:11; Zech. 3:2.

BRAND, v. In their own consciences—I Tim. 4:2. See Eph. 4:18, 19.

BRANDISH. Ez. 32:10.

BRASS. First mention—Tubal-cain—Gen. 4:22. Miscellaneous—Armor—I Sam. 17:5, 6, 38. See ARMS AND ARMOUR. Band of—I Ki. 4:13. Bones like—Job 40:18. Coat of mail—I Sam. 17:5. Cymbals—I Chr. 15:19. Earth as—Lev. 26:19. Ezekiel's vision—Ez. 1:7. See Ez. 40:17. Feet like—Rev. 1:15; 2:18. Fetters of—Ju. 16:21; II Ki. 25:7. Flesh of—Job 6:12. Furnace, In—Ez. 22:20. Gates—Ps. 107:16. Gold for—Is. 60:17. Greaves—I Sam. 17:6. Heavens like—Deut. 28:23. Helmet of—I Sam. 17:5, 38. Idols of—Dan. 5:4, 23; Rev. 9:20. Javelin of—I Sam. 17:6. Musical, Instruments—I Chr. 15:19; 16:5; Ps. 98:6; 150:5. Money—Mt. 10:9. See II Sam. 21:16. Nails (of body)—Dan. 2:32, 35, 39, 45. Purification of—Num. 31:22. Serpent—Num. 21:9; II Ki. 18:4. Shekels of—II Sam. 21:16. Shields of—I Ki. 14:27; II Chr. 12:10. Sounding—I Cor. 13:1. Spoils—Josh. 6:19, 24; II Sam. 8:8, 10; I Chr. 18:8, 10. Vessels—Lev. 6:28; Josh. 6:19, 24; II Sam. 8:10; Ez. 27:13; Mk. 7:4; Rev. 18:12. See TABERNACLE, TEMPLE, VESSELS. Walls of—Jer. 1:18; 15:20. Wood, As rotten—Is. 60:17. Wood for—Is. 60:17. Work of—Ex. 31:4; 35:32. Workers in—Gen. 4:22; I Ki. 7:14; II Chr. 2:7, 14; 24:12.

Tabernacle, In.—Altar—Ex. 38:29–31. Grating, Horns and vessels of—Ex. 27:2–6; 35:16; 38:2–6. Clasps—Ex. 30:18; 38:8. Mirrors—Ex. 38:8. Offering for—Ex. 25:3; 35:5, 24; 38:29; Josh. 6:19, 24. Pins—Ex. 27:19; 38:20, 23. Sockets of pillars—Ex. 26:37; 27:10, 11, 17, 18; 36:18; 38:10, 19, 30, 31.

Temple, Of the.—I Chr. 22:3, 14; 16:29; II Chr. 1:5, 6; 4:1; 7:7; Ez. 9:2. Bases—I Ki. 7:27–37. Bulls or oxen—I Ki. 7:29; II Ki. 16:17; Jer. 52:20. Dedicated to temple worship—II Sam. 8:8–11. Doors—II Chr. 4:9. Lovers—I Ki. 7:38. Pillars—I Ki. 7:15–22; II Ki. 25:13, 16, 17; I Chr. 18:8; Jer. 52:17, 21–23. Scaffold—II Chr. 6:13. Sea—I Ki. 7:23–26; II Ki. 25:13; I Chr. 18:8; Jer. 52:17. Instruments and vessels—I Ki. 7:40, 45, 47; II Ki. 25:14, 16; I Chr. 18:8; II Chr. 4:16, 18; Jer. 52:18.

Figurative use.—Lev. 26:19; Deut. 28:23; Job 6:12; Jer. 1:18; 6:28; 15:20; Ez. 22:18, 20; 24:11; Dan. 7:19.

BRAVERY. See COURAGE.

BRAWLER. Not a—I Tim. 3:3; Tit. 1:7; 3:2 (A.V.). Strong drink—Pr. 20: 1. Woman, Brawling—Pr. 21:9 (A.V.); 25:24 (A.V.). See CONTENTIONS, STRIFE.

BRAY. Job 6:5; 30:7; Pr. 27:22.

BRAZIER. Jer. 36:22. See BRASS, WORKER IN.

BREACH. Gen. 38:29; Lev. 24:20; Job 16:14; Ps. 106:23; Ez. 26:10; Amos 4:3; 6:11; 9:11. Heal—Ps. 60:2. House of Jehovah, In the—II Ki. 12: 5–8, 12; 22:5. Iniquity as—Is. 30:13. Jerusalem, In—I Ki. 11:27. Wall of, In—Neh. 4:7; 6:1. Promise, Of—Num. 14:34 (A.V.). Repairer of—Is. 58:12. Spirit, Of the—Pr. 15:4. Tribes of Israel, In—Ju. 21:15. Waters, Of—II Sam. 5:20. See BREAK, BURST.

BREAD. First mentioned in relation to penalty—Gen. 3:19; Ez. 4:15–17.

Kinds mentioned are leavened and unleavened, common and hallowed.—Leavened—Lev. 7:13; 23:17; Hos. 7:4; Amos 4:5; Mt. 13:33. Unleavened—Gen. 19:3; Ex. 29:2; Ju. 6:19; I Sam. 28:24. Common and hallowed—I Sam. 21:4–6.

Its influence on man.—To strengthen—Ps. 104:15. To gladden—Eccl. 9:7.

Staff of physical life.—Gen. 3:19; Ez. 4:16; Mt. 4:4; 6:11.

Made of wheat.—Ex. 29:2; Ps. 81:16. Of barley—Ju. 7:13; John 6:9. Of beans, millet—Ez. 4:9. Of manna—Num. 11:8.

How prepared.—With honey—Ex. 16:31. With oil—Ex. 29:2, 23. Kneaded—Gen. 18:6; Ex. 8:3; 12:34. Into loaves —I Sam. 10:3, 4; Mt. 14:17. Cakes—II Sam. 6:19; I Ki. 17:13. Wafers—Ex. 16:31; 29:23. Baked in ovens—Ex. 8:3; Lev. 2:4; 7:9; Hos. 7:4. On hearts—Gen. 18:6. On coals—I Ki. 19:6; Is. 44:19; John 21:9.

Principal food used by ancients.—Gen. 18:5; 21:14; 27:17; Ju. 19:5.

Kept in baskets.—Gen. 40:16; Ex. 29:32.

Made by women.—Lev. 26:26; I Sam. 8:13.

Scarcity of, sent as punishment.—Ps. 105:16; Is. 3:1; Ez. 5:16.

Offered to God as first fruits.—Num. 15: 19, 20; 28:2.

Other offerings.—I Sam. 1:36; II Ki. 23:9.

Typical.—Lev. 21:6, 8, 17, 21, 22.

Used in sacrifices.—Ex. 29:2, 23; Num. 28:2; Mk. 14:12; Lu. 22:7. By idolaters—Jer. 71:18; 44:19.

Shew bread.—Ex. 25:30; I Chr. 23:29; II Chr. 2:4; Heb. 9:2.

When scarce, sold by weight.—Lev. 26: 26; Ez. 4:16.

Refused to the unclean and blemished.—Lev. 21:21.

In New Testament Times: Multitudes fed.—Mt. 14:19–21; 15:34–37.

Jesus discourses on ''bread.''—John 6: 31–35; 48:51.

Used in communion.—Mt. 26:26; Acts 20:7; I Cor. 10:16–17; 11:23–29.

Used in social meals.—Acts 2:46.

Jesus warns through leavened bread.—Mt. 16:6–12; Mk. 8:15; Lu. 12:1.

Eating with defiled hands.—Mk. 7:2.

Not to be taken on journey.—Mk. 6:8.

David demands it to eat.—I Sam. 21: 3–6; Mt. 12:4; Mk. 2:26; Lu. 6:4.

Figurative.—I Ki. 22:27; II Chr. 18:26; Is. 30:20; 55:2; Hos. 9:4.

Paul uses it as a figure.—I Cor. 5:6–8. Used in connection with idleness—II Thess. 3:8–12.

BREADTH. Foot, Of—Deut. 2:5. Handbreadth—Ex. 25:25; 37:12; I Ki. 7: 26; II Chr. 4:5; Ps. 39:5; Ez. 40:5; 45:13. Land, Of—Gen. 13:17; Is. 8:8. Length, breadth, and height—Eph. 3: 18; Rev. 21:16. Waters, Of—Job 37: 10.

BREAK. Altars of idols—Ex. 34:15; Deut. 7:5; 12:3; II Ki. 11:18; 23:12, 15; II Chr. 23:17; 31:1; 34:4, 7. See HIGH PLACES, IMAGES, PILLARS. Arm—Job 22:9; 38:15; Ps. 10:15; 37:15; Ez. 30:21–25; Jer. 48:25. Arrows—Ps. 76: 3. Assyrian—Is. 14:25. Bars—Lev. 26:13; Jer. 51:30; Lam. 2:9; Ez. 34: 27; Amos 1:5. Beasts of Daniel's vision—Dan. 7:7, 19, 23. Bonds—Ps. 2: 3; Jer. 5:5; 30:8. Bones—Ex. 12:46; Num. 9:12; 24:8; Ps. 34:20; 51:8; Pr. 25:15; Is. 38:13; Lam. 3:4; Dan. 6:24; Mic. 3:3; John 19:36. Bottles—Jer. 19:11; 48:12. Bow—I Sam. 2:4; II Sam. 22:25; Ps. 18:34; 46:9; 76:3; 51:56; Jer. 49:35; Hos. 1:5; 2:18. Bread—Lev. 26:26; Lam. 4:4; Mt. 14:

19; 15:36; 26:26; Mk. 6:41; 8:6,19; 14:22; Lu. 9:16; 14:22; 24:30, 35; Acts 2:43, 46; 20:7, 11; 27:35; I Cor. 10:16. See LORD'S SUPPER. Brotherhood between Israel and Judah—Zech. 11:14. Bruised reed—Is. 42:3; Mt. 12:20. Carved work of temple—Ps. 74:6. Cedars—Ps. 29:5. Chariots—Jer. 51:21. Commandments—Num. 15:31; Ezra 9:14; Mt. 5:19; John 5: 18; Rom. 2:23, 25. See COVENANTS, TABLES. Covenant—Gen. 17:14; Lev. 26:15, 44; Deut. 31:16, 20; Ju. 2:1; Ps. 55:20 (A.V.); 89:34; Is. 24:5; Jer. 11: 10; 14:21; 31:32; 33:20, 21; Ez. 16:59; 17:15-19; 44:7; Zech. 11:10. Cruse—Mk. 14:3. Day, Of—Gen. 32:24, 26; II Sam. 2:32; Song of Sol. 2:17; 4:6; Acts 20:11. Door—Gen. 19:9. Eggs—Job 39:15 (A.V.). Elam, Bow of—Jer. 49:35. Enemies—I Chr. 14:11; Ps. 72: 4. Fetters—Mk. 5:14; Lu. 8:29. Gates of brass—Ps. 107:16; Is. 45:2. Heads —Ps. 74:13; Jer. 2:16. Heart—Ps. 69:20; Jer. 23:9; Acts 21:13. Hedges —Ps. 89:40. High places—II Ki. 23: 8, 15; II Chr. 31:1; 33:3; Ez. 16:39. Horns—Dan. 8:7, 8, 22. Horse and his rider—Jer. 51:21. House—Lev. 14:45. Baal, Of—II Ki. 10:27; 11:18. Sodomites, Of—II Ki. 23:7. Husbandman —Jer. 51:23. Images—II Ki. 11:18; II Chr. 23:17; 31:1; 34:4, 7; Is. 8:6; 21:6; Ez. 6:6. Iron—Ps. 2:9; Jer. 15:12; Dan. 2:40. Israel—Ps. 94:5; Is. 30:13, 14. Jaw—Job 29:7. Job—Job 9:17; 16:12, 14; 19:2. Judah, Into —II Chr. 21:7. Kingdom of Jesus will break other kingdoms—Dan. 2:35, 42-44; II:4. League—I Ki. 15:19; II Chr. 16:3. Legs—John 19:31-33. Loins—Ez. 21:6. Men and women—Job 34:24; Ps. 44:19; Jer. 51:22. Moab —Jer. 48:38. Nations—Ps. 2:9; Jer. 48:38; 51:20. Nebuchadrezzar's ''image''—Dan. 2:34, 35, 40, 45. Net—Lu. 5:6. Oppressor—Ps. 72:4. Perverse man—Pr. 6:15. Pillars: Of idols—Ex. 23:24; Deut. 7:5; II Ki. 10:27; 18:4; 23:14; II Chr. 14:3; 31:1; Is. 19:10; Jer. 43:13. Temple, Of—II Ki. 25:13; Jer. 52:17. Pitchers—Ju. 7:19. Plague, Break in—Ps. 106:29. Pride—Lev. 26:19; Is. 16:6-8. See PRIDE. Rahab —Ps. 89:10. Ranks—Joel 2:7. Rock

—II Ki. 19:11; Jer. 23:29. Sabbath— John 4:8. See COMMANDMENTS, COVENANT. Scriptures—John 10:35. See PROPHECY, FULFILMENT OF. Serpent, Brazen—II Ki. 18:4. Shepherd and his flock—Jer. 51:23. Ships—II Chr. 20:37; Ps. 48:7; Jonah 1:4; Acts 27: 41. Shoulder—Ez. 29:7. Skull—Ju. 9:53. Soul—Ps. 119:20. Staff, Of bread—Lev. 26:26; Ps. 105:16; Is. 3:1; Ez. 4:16; 5:16; 14:13. See BREAD. Wicked, Of the—Is. 14:5. Statutes— Ps. 89:31. Tables of commandments —Ex. 32:19; 34:1; Deut. 9:17; 10:2. Teeth—Job 4:10; Ps. 3:7; 58:6. Tower —Ju. 8:9. Tree—Ex. 29:7; Job 24:20; Ps. 105:33. Tyre—Ez. 27:26, 34. Vessels —Lev. 6:28; 11:33; 15:12; Ps. 31:12; Is. 30:14; Jer. 19:11; 22:28; Lam. 3:6; Rev. 2:17. See VESSELS. Wall—Eccl. 10: 8; Is. 30:13. Babylon, Of—Jer. 51:58. Gath, Of—II Chr. 26:6. Jerusalem—II Ki. 14:13; 25:10; II Chr. 25:23; 32:5; 36:19; Neh. 4:3; Ps. 80:12; Is. 22:5; Jer. 39:8; 52:14. Vineyard, Of—Is. 5:5. Withes—Ju. 16:9, 12. Word—Num. 30:2. Yoke—Gen. 27:40 (A.V.); Lev. 26:13; Is. 9:4; 58:6; Jer. 2:20; 5:5; 28:2, 4, 10-13; 30:8; 51:23; Ez. 30:18; Nah. 1:13. See Is. 14:25. See BREACH, DESTROY, PULL DOWN, RENT, FEAR.

BREAK AWAY. Servants—I Sam. 25: 10.

BREAK DOWN. Lev. 14:45; Ju. 8:9; Job 12:14; Ps. 74:16; Is. 16:8; Jer. 31: 28; 45:4; Ez. 16:39.

BREAK FORTH. Mic. 2:13. Children —Gen. 38:29; Hos. 13:13. Boil—Ex. 9:9, 10. See DISEASES. Cry, And— Gal. 4:27. Evil—Jer. 1:14. Jehovah —Ex. 19:22, 24; II Sam. 5:2 (A.V.). Joy, Into—Is. 52:9. Light—Is. 58:8. Perez—Gen. 38:29. Sea—Job 38:8. Singing, Into—Is. 14:7; 44:23; 49:13; 52:9; 54:1; 55:12.

BREAK IN. Oxen—Ps. 144:14.

BREAK OFF. Branches (fig.)—Rom. 11:17-20. Gold—Ex. 32:24. Ear-rings —Ex. 32:2, 3. Sins—Dan. 4:27.

BREAK OUT. Is. 59:5. Army of Chaldeans—Jer. 37:11. Fire—Ex. 22:6. *Like*—Amos 5:6. Leprosy—Lev. 13: 12, 20, 25; 14:43. Waters—Is. 35:6.

BREAK THROUGH. Edom, Unto king of—II Ki. 3:26. Jehovah, Unto—Ex.

19:21, 24. Philistines—II Sam. 23:16; I Chr. 11:18. Thieves break through —Mt. 6:19, 20; Lu. 12:39, 43.

BREAK UP. Ground—Is. 28:24 (A.V.); Jer. 4:3; Hos. 10:11, 21. House of Jehovah—II Chr. 24:7. Roof—Mk. 2:4. Synagogue—Acts 13:43.

BREAKER. Mic. 2:13; Rom. 1:31; 2: 25; II Tim. 3:3.

BREAST. Doves, Of—Nah. 2:7. Girded with golden girdles—Rev. 15:6. Jackals, Of—Lam. 4:3. Jesus, Of—John 13:25; 21:20. Nebuchadrezzar's "image," Of—Dan. 2:32. Publican, Of—Lu. 18:13. Smiting—Lu. 18:13; 23:14. Wave-offering, Used for—Lev. 7:30, 34; 8: 29; 9:20, 21; 10:14, 15; Num. 6:20; 18:18. *Ram, Of*—Ex. 29:26, 27. Belonged to Aaron and his sons—Lev. 7:30, 31, 34; Num. 18:18, 19. Woman's —Pr. 5:19; Song of Sol. 1:13; 4:5; 7:3, 7, 8; 8:8, 10; Hos. 9:14. *Blessings of*—Gen. 49:25. *Children at*—Job 3:12; Ps. 22:9; Song of Sol. 8:1; Is. 28:9. Joel 2:16.

Figurative.—Is. 66:11; Ez. 16:7; 23:3, 34. See BOSOM.

BREASTPLATE. Faith and love—I Thess. 5:8. Fire, hyacinth and brimstone—Rev. 9:17. Iron, Of—Rev. 9:9. Locusts, Of—Rev. 9:9. Priest, Of—Ex. 25:7; 28:4, 15, 22–30; 29:5; 39:9–21; Lev. 8:8. Righteousness, Of—Is. 59:17; Eph. 6:14. See ARMOR, CLOTHING, PRIESTS.

BREATH: Breath of God.—II Sam. 22: 16; Job 4:9; 33:4; 34:14; 37:10; 41: 21; Ps. 18:15; 33:6; Is. 30:28, 33; 42:5; Acts 17:25. Cause of destruction—Is. 11:4.

Breath of Christ.—John 20:22.

Breath of Man.—Breath of life—Gen. 2:7. Breath as life—Job 9:18; Is. 2: 22; Dan. 10:17. Given by God—Gen. 2:7; 7:22; Job 12:10; 19:17; Ps. 33:6; Is. 42:5. In God's hands—Dan. 5:23.

All of one breath from God.—Eccl. 3:19; Acts 17:25. Breath of all flesh—Gen. 6:17; 7:15, 22; Is. 33:11. Breath taken away—Deut. 20:16; I Ki. 15:29; Ps. 146:4.

Figurative.—Job 15:30; 17:1. No breath in false images—Jer. 10:14; 51:17. In wood—Hab. 2:19. Of Jeremiah—Lam.

3:56. Breath as a destroyer—Is. 33: 11. Vision of dry bones—Ez. 37:5–10. See BLAST.

BREECHES. See CLOTHING, PRIESTS.

BREED. Gen. 8:17; 16:20; Deut. 32:14. See REPRODUCTION.

BRETHREN. Neighbor better than brother far off—Pr. 27:10. Prophet of thy brethren—Deut. 18:15; Acts 7:37. Rule over, Ye shall not—Lev. 25:46; Deut. 24:14. Teach no more every man—Jer. 31:34; Heb. 8:11.

Disciples of Christ called brethren.—Establish—Lu. 22:31. Firstborn among —Rom. 8:29; I Cor. 15:20; Col. 1:18. Friend sticks closer than—Pr. 17:17; 18:24. Hating and loving—I John 1: 9–11; 3:10–12, 14, 15, 16. Heart lifted above—Deut. 17:18–20. Law with, Going to with—I Cor. 6:5–8. Least of, Inasmuch as—Rev. 22:9. Mother and—Mt. 12:49–50; Mk. 3:33. Reconciled with—Mt. 5:23, 24. Sinning—I John 5:16. Strife with, No—Gen. 13: 8; Ps. 133:1; Pr. 6:19; Acts 7:26; I Cor. 6:5–8; Jas. 4:11. Those who do will of God are my—Mt. 12:49–50; Mk. 3:33. Ye are my—Mt. 23:8–10. See BROTHER, FRATERNITY.

BRIBERY: Examples of.—Balaam and Balak—Num. Chs. 22–24. Samuel's sons—I Sam. 8:3. Haman—Esth. 3:9. Judas—Mt. 26:15. Roman soldiers—Mt. 28:12. Israel—Amos 5:12. Delilah—Ju. 16:5, 6.

Refused.—I Sam. 12:3; Is. 33:15; Pr. 15:27.

Given to judges.—Pr. 17:32; Amos 2:6.

Wicked received bribes.—Pr. 17:8, 23; Is. 5:23.

Taken for murder.—Deut. 27:25; Ez. 22: 12; Mic. 7:3.

Effects of.—Deut. 16:19; Eccl. 7:7; Is. 1:23.

Gifts taken as bribes.—Pr. 18:16; 21:14; 28:21; 29:4.

Given to appease wrath.—Gen. 32:20; I Sam. 25:27, 33.

Figurative.—Tents of—Job 15:34. Right hand full of—Ps. 26:10.

BRICK. The earliest mention of burned brick that of Babel—Gen. 11:3. Bitumen or slime used for mortar—Gen. 11:3. Babylonian brick resembled thick tiles—Ez. 4:1. Egyptians made lives of children of Israel bitter by severe task—Ex. 1:14; 5:7–19; Ps. 105:25; Acts 7:18–19. Substitution of altars of brick for those of stone—Is. 65:3. Stones hid in the brickwork as a symbol of conquest—Jer. 43:9. David compelled Ammonites to labor in brickyards—II Sam. 12:31. Samaria and Ephraim too proud in architecture— Is. 9:10.

BRIDE. See MARRIAGE.

BRIDE CHAMBER. Mt. 9:15; Mk. 2: 19; Lu. 5:34.

BRIDEGROOM. See MARRIAGE.

BRIDLE. Harness—II Sam. 8:1; II Ki. 19:28; Ps. 32:9; Pr. 26:3; Is. 37:29; Jas. 3:2, 3; Rev. 14:20. Tongue—Job 30:11; Ps. 39:1; Jas. 1:26; 3:3–10. See BIT.

BRIEFLY. I Pet. 5:12. See SUMMED UP.

BRIER. Emblem of wilderness—Ju. 8: 7, 16; Is. 5:6; 7:23, 24; 9:18; 10:17; 27:4; 32:13; 55:13; Ez. 2:6; 28:24; Mic. 7:4; Heb. 6:8. See BRAMBLE, THISTLE, THORN.

BRIGHT. Apparel—Acts 10:30. Arrows—Jer. 51:11 (A. V.); Ez. 21:21 (A.V.). Brass—I Ki. 7:45 (A.V.); II Chr. 4:16. Cloud—Job 37:11 (A.V.); Mt. 17:5. Fire—Ez. 1:13. Iron—Ez. 27:19. Ivory—Song of Sol. 5:14 (A.V.). Light—Job 37:21; Ez. 32:8. Spot a sign of leprosy—Lev. 13:2–39; 14:56. Star, Bright and morning—Rev. 22:16. Burnished, Light.—See SHINE.

BRIGHTNESS. I Sam. 22:13; Ps. 18: 12; 89:44; Is. 59:9; Ez. 1:4, 27, 28; Amos—5:20. Firmament, Of the— Dan. 12:3. Jehovah's glory—Ez. 10: 4; Hab. 3:4; Heb. 1:3 (A.V.). Moon, Of—Job 31:34; Is. 60:19. Nebuchadrezzar—Dan. 4:36. *His vision*—Dan. 2:31. Righteousness as—Is. 60:1. Sun, Of the—Acts 26:13. Tyre, Of the king of—Ez. 28:7, 17. Zion glorified —Is. 60:3; 62:1. See GLORY, LIGHT, SHINE.

BRIM. I Ki. 7:23–26; II Chr. 4:2, 5; John 2:6.

BRIMSTONE. A curse for disobedience —Deut. 29:23; Job 18:15; Ps. 11:6; Is. 30:33; 34:9; Ez. 39:22; Rev. 14:10. Horses in vision, Breastplates of— Rev. 9:17, 18. Mouth, Out of—Rev.

9:17, 18. Lake of—Rev. 14:10; 19:20; 20:10. Sodom and Gomorrah, Rained on—Gen. 19:24; Deut. 29:23; Lu. 17: 29. See FIRE, HELL.

BRING. Best robe—Lu. 15:22. Death —Jas. 1:15. Destructive heresies—II Pet. 2:1. Egypt, Out of—See DELIVERANCE FROM BONDAGE. Evil, Forth—Lu. 6:45. Firstlings, First - fruits — See FIRSTBORN, OFFERINGS, SACRIFICE. Fruit, Forth—Ps. 92:14; Mt. 3:8; 10:7, 17– 19; 13:8, 23, 26; 21:43; Mk. 4:18, 25; Lu. 3:8, 9; 6:43; John 12:24; 15:25; Jas. 5:18. See FRUIT, HARVEST, REAPING WHAT WE SOW. Good, Forth—Lu. 6:45. Good tidings—Acts 13:32. See GOSPEL. Home—Ex. 9:19; Ju. 11:9; Ruth 1:21; Job 39:12. Land, Into the —See CANAAN, ISRAEL. OFFERINGS— See OFFERINGS, SACRIFICE. Nothing into the world—I Tim. 6:7; Eccl. 5: 15. See Job 1:21. Rain—Pr. 25:23. Sin to remembrance—I Ki. 17:18; Ez. 21:23. See CONSCIENCE. Sin, Conviction of. Temptation, Bring us not into —Mt. 6:13. See TEMPTATION. Tithes —See LIBERALITY, TITHES. Treasure, Out of his—Mt. 13:52. Way, On our —Acts 15:3; 21:5; Rom. 15:24; I Cor. 16:6; II Cor. 1:16; Tit. 3:13. See ACCOMPANY, BARE, BEAR, BORNE, CARRY.

BRINGING IN. Better hope—Heb. 7: 19. Many sons unto glory—Heb. 2:10.

BRINK. Gen. 41:3, 17; Ex. 2:3; 7:3; 7:15; Deut. 2:36; Josh. 3:8. See BANK.

BROAD. Commandment exceeding— Ps. 119:96. Phylacteries—Mt. 23:5. Places—Job 36:16; Pr. 1:20; Jer. 5:1. Sea, Than the—Job 11:9. Wall of— Babylon—Jer. 51:58. Jerusalem—Neh. 3:8; 12:38. Way—Song of Sol. 3:2; Nah. 2:4; Mt. 7:13.

BROIDERED-WORK. Ex. 28:4 (A.V.); Ez. 16:10, 13, 18; 26:16; 27:7, 16, 24.

BROILED. Fish—Lu. 24:42; John 21:9.

BROKEN. Body—I Cor. 11:24. Boughs —Ez. 31:12. Bound the—Ez. 34:4. Bowl—Eccl. 12:6. Cisterns—Jer. 2: 13. Cord—Eccl. 12:6; Is. 33:20; Jer. 10:20. Earth—Is. 24:19. Ephraim— Is. 7:8. Hammer (fig.)—Jer. 50:23. Hearted—Ps. 34:18; 51:17; 109:11; 147:3; Is. 61:1; Jer. 23:9; Lu. 4:18. Jehovah—Ez. 6:9. Latchet of shoes—

Is. 5:27. Neck—I Sam. 4:18. Net—John 21:11. Offering—Lev. 22:22, 24. See OFFERING. Peoples—I Sam. 2:10; II Chr. 25:12; Is. 8:8, 9, 15; 28:13; Jer. 14:17; Ez. 26:2; 31:12; 32:28; Dan. 8:25; 11:22; Mt. 21:44; Lu. 20:18. Pieces—Mt. 15:37; Mk. 8:8. Pitcher—Eccl. 12:6. Rods (fig.)—Is. 14:29; Jer. 48:17; Ez. 19:12. Skin—Job 7:5. Snare—Ps. 124:7. Spirit—Ps. 51:17; Pr. 15:4, 13; 17:22. Staff—Jer. 48:17. Stones—Lev. 21:20. See BLEMISH. String—Ju. 16:9. See CORD. Unrighteousness—Job 24:20. See JUDGMENT, THE WICKED. Wheel—Eccl. 12:6. See BREACH, BREAK.

BROKEN DOWN. Babylon—Jer. 50:2 (A.V.). Barns—Joel 1:17. City—Pr. 25:28; Jer. 4:26. Everything—Lev. 11:35. Foundations—Ez. 30:4. Moab—Jer. 48:20, 39. Walls—Neh. 2:13; Pr. 24:31. Jerusalem, Of—Neh. 1:3. See BREACH, BREAK, BREAK DOWN, BROKEN.

BROKEN OFF. Boughs—Is. 27:11. Purposes—Job 17:11. See BREAK, BROKEN, BREAK OFF.

BROKEN THROUGH. House—Mt. 25:43; Lu. 12:39. See BREAK THROUGH.

BROKEN UP. City—See BREACH. Fountains of the deep—Gen. 7:11. See Pr. 3:20.

BROOCHES. Ex. 35:22. See JEWELS.

BROOD. Lu. 13:34.

BROOK. II Ki. 18:5; II Chr. 32:4; Neh. 2:15. Besor—I Sam. 30:9, 10, 21. Channel of—Job 6:15. Cherith—II Ki. 17:3-7. Deceitful as—Job 6:15. Doves beside—Song of Sol. 5:12. Dried up—Joel 1:20. Drink of—Ps. 110:7. Egypt, Of—Num. 34:5; I Ki. 8:65; Is. 27:12; Ez. 47:19. Flowing—Pr. 18:4. Gaash, Of—II Sam. 23:30; I Chr. 11:32. Honey of—Job 20:17 (A.V.). Kidron—II Sam. 15:23; I Ki. 2:37; 15:13; II Ki. 23:6, 12; II Chr. 15:16; 29:16; 30:14; Jer. 31:40. Keshon—I Ki. 18:40; Ps. 83:9. Land of brooks—Deut. 8:7. . Mount, · Out of—Deut. 9:21. Panteth after—Ps. 42:1. Stones of—I Sam. 17:40; Job 22:24. Willows of—Lev. 23:50; Job 40:22. See Is. 15:7. Zered—Deut. 2:13, 14. See RIVER, STREAM, WATER.

BROOM. Job 30:4. See BESOM.

BROTH. Ju. 6:19, 20; Is. 65:4.

BROTHER. Adversity, Born for—Pr. 17:17. Angry with—Mt. 5:22. See ANGER, HATRED. Beloved—Eph. 6:21; Col. 4:7, 9; Philemon 16:11; Pet. 3:15. See BELOVED, LOVE. Blood, Brother's —Gen. 4:10, 11. Defile for—Lev. 21:1-3; Ez. 44:25, 26. Destroyer, To—Pr. 18:9. Far off—Pr. 27:10. Forgive—Mt. 18:21, 22, 35; Lu. 17:3, 4. Friend closer than—Pr. 18:24. Grieved—Rom. 14:15; I Cor. 18:13. See OFFENDED. Hate—Lev. 19:17; I John 2:9-11, 15; 4:20. See ANGER, HATRED. Heel, Took his brother's—Gen. 25:26; Hos. 12:3. Help, Must—Lev. 25:25-43, 47, 48; Deut. 15:2-12; 22:1-4; 23:19, 20; Neh. 5:7; Is. 41:6; Jer. 34:9-18; Ez. 18:18; Ob. 10:12; Jas. 2:14-17; I John 3:17. See FRATERNITY, USURY. House, Brother's—Pr. 27:10. Inheritance, Divide with—Lu. 12:13. Jackals, To—Job 30:29. Jesus—Mt. 12:46; 13:55; Mk. 6:3; John 2:12; 7:3, 5, 10; Acts 1:14; I Cor. 9:5; Gal. 1:19. See Mt. 12:50; Mk. 3:35. Judge—Rom. 14:10; Jas. 4:11. Keeper, My brother's —Gen. 4:9. See FRATERNITY. Kiss—Song of Sol. 8:1. Law with, Going to—I Cor. 6:6. Loveth—I John 2:10; 3:10, 14-18; 4:20, 21. See LOVE. Mote in brother's eye—Mt. 7:3-5; Lu. 6:41, 42. Mourn for—Ps. 35:14; Jer. 22:14. Offended—Pr. 18:19; I Cor. 8:13. Oppress—Ez. 18:18. Reconciled to, Must be—Mt. 5:23, 24; 18:15-17. Redeem—Lev. 25:39-54. See HELP, KINSMAN, REDEMPTION. Slanderest—Ps. 50:20; Jas. 4:11. See Jer. 9:4. Slay every man his—Ex. 32:27, 29; Is. 3:6, 9, 12; 19:2; Ez. 38:21; Amos 1:11; Mic. 7:2; Hag. 2:22; Mt. 10:21; Mk. 13:12. Sticketh closer than—Pr. 18:14. Stumbleth—Rom. 14:15-21. See OFFENCES. Supplanteth—Jer. 9:4; Mal. 2:10. See JACOB. Teach—Jer. 31:34; Heb. 8:11. Tempted by—Deut. 13:6. Unclean for—Num. 6:7. See DEFILE. Usury—Lev. 25:36; Deut. 23:19, 20; Neh. 5:7; Job 22:6. See USURY. Violence onward—Ob. 10. Wife of—Gen. 38:8, 9; Lev. 18:16; 20:21; Deut. 25:5-10; Mt. 22:24, 25; Mk. 12:19; Lu. 20:28. See MARRIAGE, LEVIRATE. See BRETHREN, DISCIPLES, FRATERNITY.

BROTHERHOOD. Zech. 11:14; I Pet. 2:17.

BROTHER-IN-LAW. Ju. 4:11.

BROTHERLY. Covenant—Amos 1:9. Kindness—II Pet. 1:7. See KINDNESS. Love—II Pet. 1:7. See BRETHREN, FRATERNITY, LOVE.

BROUGHT. Back unto land—Ez. 38:8. Caesar, Before—Acts 27:24. Dishonor, To—Ps. 44:9. False brethren brought in—Gal. 2:4. Governors and rulers, Before—Mt. 10:18; Mk. 13:9; Acts 5: 21; 22:24; 25:6. Grace—I Pet. 1:13. Low—Ju. 6:6; Job 14:21; Eccl. 12:4; Is. 2:12; 25:5; Lu. 3:5. See BOW. Nothing, To—Acts 5:36 (A.V.). Presents—Is. 18:7. Together—Ez. 29:5. See BARE, BEAR, BORNE, BRING, CARRY.

BROUGHT DOWN. Ps. 20:8 (A.V.); Is. 5:15 (A.V.); 29:4; Ez. 31:18. Grave, To the—Job 21:32 (A.V.). Pride of Assyrian—Zech. 10:11. Sheol, To— Is. 14:11, 15.

BROUGHT FORTH. Jas. 1:18. Capernaum—Lu. 10:15. Mountains—Ps. 90: 2. Remnant—Ez. 14:22 (A.V.). Wicked—Job 21:30. Wisdom brought forth —Pr. 8:24, 25.

BROUGHT UP (*reared*). Esth. 2:20; Pr. 8:30; Lam. 4:5; Acts 13:1.

BROW. Is. 48:4; Lu. 4:29.

BRUISE, *n.* Is. 1:6. See HURT, WOUND.

BRUISE, BRUISED. Demoniac—Lu. 9: 39. Grain—Lev. 2:16. See GRAIN. Jesus—Is. 53:5, 10. See JESUS, SUFFERINGS OF. Lamech—Gen. 4:23. Offering, Must not offer—Lev. 22:24. See BLEMISH, OFFERING, SACRIFICE. Satan —Rom. 16:20. Serpent's head—Gen. 3:15. Set at liberty them that are— Lu. 4:18. See AFFLICTION, SUFFERING, WOUND.

BRUIT. See REPORT, RUMOR.

BRUTISH. Ps. 49:10; 92:6; 94:8; Pr. 12:1; 30:2; Is. 19:11; Jer. 10:8, 14, 21; 51:17; Ez. 21:31.

BUCKET. Num. 24:7; Is. 40:15.

BUCKLER. I Ki. 10:16; I Chr. 5:18; II Chr. 14:8; 23:9; Job 15:26; Ps. 35: 2; 91:4; Song of Sol. 4:4; Jer. 46:3; Ez. 23:24; 26:8; 38:4; 39:9. See ARMOR, SHIELD.

BUD, *n.* Is. 18:5 (A.V.); 61:1. Aaron's rod—Num. 17:8. See BLADE, BLOSSOM.

BUD, *v.* Is. 55:10; Aaron's rod—Num. 17:5, 10; Heb. 9:4. Earth—Is. 55:10. Horn—Ps. 132:17; Ez. 29:21. Israel— Is. 27:6. Pride—Ez. 7:10. Tree—Job 14:9. See PLANTS.

BUILD. See ALTAR, BUILDER, CITIES, FORTIFICATIONS, GATES, HIGH PLACES, HOUSE, SOLOMON, TABERNACLE, TEMPLE, TUMBLE, WALL.

BUILDER: Choice of foundation.—Wise choice—I Cor. 3:10, 11; Mt. 7:24, 25; Lu. 6:48; Col. 2:7. Foolish choice— Mt. 7:26, 27; Lu. 17:28; Ps. 118:22; Mt. 21:42; Mk. 12:10; Lu. 20:17; I Pet. 2:7, 8.

Style of structure.—Eph. 2:21, 22; 4: 11–16; Hab. 2:12; Col. 2:6, 7.

Permanence of.—Ps. 127:1; Is. 58:12; Ps. 102:16; I Cor. 3:12–15; II Cor. 10:8.

Man as a builder.—Cities—Gen. 11:4; Num. 32:24; Josh. 6:26; I Ki. 9:24; 16:34; II Chr. 14:7; Is. 45:13; Dan. 9: 25. Temple—I Chr. 28:2; II Chr. 2:1; 3:1; I Ki. Ch. 6; Zech. 6:12, 13. Tombs —Mt. 23:29; Lu. 11:47, 48. Barns— Lu. 12:18. Tower—Lu. 14:28–30. Building nations (fig.)—Jer. 1:10; Mal. 1:4.

God as a builder.—House of David—II Sam. 7:11, 12, 27–29; I Ki. 11:38; I Chr. 17:10; Acts 15:16. The cities of Judah—Ps. 69:35; 102:16; 147:2; Jer. 33:7. Israel as a nation—Jer. 24:6; 42:10; 18:6–10; 31:4. Abode of saints —II Cor. 5:1. Church on earth—Heb. 3:1–6. New Jerusalem—Heb. 11:10.

Christ as a builder.—The temple—Mt. 26:31; 27:40; Mk. 15:29; John 2:20. The church—Mt. 16:18. See CHURCH. The life—Eph. 4:11–16. See LIFE.

BUILDING. Mk. 13:1, 2; I Cor. 3:9, 16; II Cor. 5:1; Eph. 2:20–22; Col. 2:6, 7; II Pet. 2:5. See CHURCH.

BUKKI, bŭk'kī. (1) **Son of Abishua, a high-priest.**—I Chr. 6:5, 51; Ezra 7:4. (2) **A prince of Dan who was one of those chosen to divide the land among the tribes.**—Num. 34:22.

BUKKIAH, bŭk-kī'ah. **A Levite, descendant of Kohath, and a musician in the temple.**—I Chr. 25:4, 13.

BUL, bŭl. **Eighth month of the Jewish year** (Nov.–Dec.).—I Ki. 6:38.

BULL. Gen. 32:13–15; Job 21:10; Is. 34:7. Bashan, Of—Ps. 22:12. Blood of—Heb. 9:13; 10:4. Brazen—Jer. 52:20. See I Ki 7:20–25. See TEMPLE. Flesh of—Ps. 50:13. Multitude of—Ps. 68:30. See CATTLE, OFFERINGS, SACRIFICE.

BULLOCKS. Chastised as a—Jer. 31: 18 (A.V.). Fatted—Jer. 46:21 (A.V.). Slay—Jer. 50:27. See CALF, CATTLE, OFFERINGS, SACRIFICES, TEMPLE.

BULRUSH. Ark of—Ex. 2:3. Bow down head as—Is. 58:5. See PAPYRUS.

BULWARK. Deut. 20:20; Ps. 48:13; Eccl. 9:14; Is. 26:1; Jer. 50:15. See BATTLEMENTS, FORTIFICATIONS, WALL.

BUNAH, bū'nah. **A descendant of Perez.** —I Chr. 2:25.

BUNCH. Ex. 12:22.

BUNDLE of: Barley—Ruth 2:16. Life —I Sam. 25:29. Money—Gen. 42:35. Myrrh—Song of Sol. 1:13. Sticks—Acts 28:3. Tares—Mt. 13:30.

BUNNI, bŭn'nī. (1) **A Levite who assisted in teaching the law of Moses.**—Neh. 9:4.

(2) **An ancestor of Shemaiah.**—Neh. 11:15.

(3) **A family of Jews who sealed the covenant with Nehemiah.**—Neh. 10:15.

BURDEN: Bearing.—Ex. 18:22; Num. 4:24, 27; I Ki. 5:15; II Chr. 2:2, 18; 34:13; Neh. 4:10, 17. Every one his own—Gal. 6:5. One another's—Gal. 6:2.

Lying under.—Ex. 23:5.

Afflicted with.—Ex. 1:11; 5:4, 5; Neh. 13:15; Is. 58:6; Mt. 23:4; Lu. 11:46. Sent by Jehovah—II Ki. 9:25; II Chr. 24:27.

Released from.—II Chr. 35:3; Ps. 81:6; Is. 9:4; 10:27; 14:25, 28; 22:25; Rev. 2:24.

Spoken of, in parable.—Laborers in the vineyard—Mt. 20:12. Ships unlade—Acts 21:3.

Commandments concerning.—Ps. 55:22. No burdens on the Sabbath—Jer. 17: 21, 22, 24, 27; Neh. 13:19. Every man bear his own—Gal. 6:2. Bear ye one another's—Gal. 6:2.

Prophecies concerning.—Jer. 17:27; Ez. 12:10; Hos. 8:10; Hab. 1:1; Zeph. 3: 18. Jerusalem—Zech. 12:3.

Used figuratively.—Ps. 38:4.

Applied to prophecy.—II Ki. 9:25; Is. Chs. 13, 15, 17, 19, 21, 22, 23; Nah. 1:1.

Examples of.—Sons of Kohath—Num. 4:15, 19. Sons of Merari—Num. 4:31, 32, 47. Moses—Num. 11:11, 17; Deut. 1:12. David—II Sam. 15:33. Job—Job 7:20. Babylon—Is. 13:1. Egypt —Ex. 2:4; 6:6, 7; Is. 19:1. Wilderness —Is. 21:1. Dumah—Is. 21:11. Arabia —Is. 21:13. Valley—Is. 22:1. Tyre—Is. 23:1. Nineveh—Nah. 1:1. People at Antioch—Acts 15:28. Jehovah—II Sam. 19:35; Jer. 23:33, 34, 36, 38. Word of Jehovah—Zech. 9:1; 12:1; Mal. 1:1. Paul—II Cor. 12:16. Of the earth—II Ki. 5:17. Beasts—Is. 30:6; 46:1, 2. Camels—II Ki. 8:9. People of tabernacle—Num. 4:15; II Cor. 5:4. Of Jesus is light—Mt. 11: . 30. See TEACHING OF JESUS.

BURIAL. Cave of Machpelah mentioned earliest.—Gen. Ch. 23. Abraham and his posterity buried there—Gen. 25:9; 49:29–32.

Customs belonging to.—Embalming Jacob—Gen. 50:1–3. Joseph—Gen. 50: 26. Asa—II Chr. 16:14. Jesus—Mk. 16:1; Lu. 23:56. Mourning—Jer. 9:17. Jacob—Gen. 50:3, 4, 10, 11. Abner—II Sam. 3:31–34. Disobedient prophet —I Ki. 13:29–31. John the Baptist—Mt. 14:12. Widow's son—Lu. 7:13. Stephen—Acts 8:2. Body bound with linen—John 11:44; 19:40. Perfumes burned—II Chr. 16:14; Jer. 34:5. Bodies burned and bones buried: *Saul and sons*—I Sam. 31:12, 13. Bodies washed: *Dorcas*—Acts 9:37. Persons hanged, buried same day—Deut. 21: 23; John 19:31; Josh. 8:29.

Refusal of, a disgrace.—Israelites—Num. 14:29; Heb. 3:17. Jezebel—II Ki. 9:10. Citizens of Jerusalem—Ps. 79:2. Babylon—Is. 14:19–20. Children of Judah—Jer. 7:33; 22:19; 34:20.

Emblematic.—Of baptism—Rom. 6:4; Col. 2:12. See BURIAL PLACES, BURY, GRAVE, SEPULCHRE.

BURIAL PLACES. First account of.—Abraham purchases of children of Heth—Gen. 23:3–6.

The Cave of Machpelah was the burial place of Sarah, Abraham, Isaac, Rebekah, Leah, and Jacob.—Gen. 23:19; 25:9; 49:29–32; 50:13. Jacob buried Rachel near Bethlehem—Gen. 35:19. Burial place of Joseph was at Shechem

—Josh. 24:32. The cave of Machpelah and the field at Shechem were the only two permanent burial places and purchased possessions the patriarchs had in Canaan.

The burial place of kings was City of David.—David—I Ki. 2:10. Solomon —I Ki. 11:43. Ahaziah—II Ki. 9:28. Jehoram—II Chr. 21:20. Jehoiada— II Chr. 24:16. Saul an exception—II Sam. 21:12–14; I Chr. 10:11–12.

Bodies buried in.—Houses: *Samuel*—I Sam. 25:1. *Joab*—I Ki. 2:34. Natural caves: *Sarah*—Gen. 23:19. *Abraham, Isaac, Rebekah, Leah, Jacob. Lazarus*— John 11:38. Hewn caves—Is. 22:16. *Jesus*—Mt. 27:60. Gardens: *Manasseh* —II Ki. 21:18. *Amon*—II Ki. 21:26. Under trees: *Rebekah's nurse*—Gen. 35:8. *Saul and sons*—I Chr. 10:12. See BURY, GRAVE, SEPULCHRE.

BURN. Is. 1:31; II Cor. 11:29. Achan and his house—Josh. 7:1–25. Anger— Gen. 44:18; Deut. 32:22; Esther 1:12; Is. 30:27; 42:25; Jer. 7:20. See ANGER, WRATH. Asherim—Deut. 12:3; II Ki. 23:4–6. See ASHERIM, IDOLATRY. Bodies —Amos 6:10; I Cor. 13:3. See PERSECUTION. Books—Acts 19:19. Brass— Ez. 24:11; Rev. 1:15. Briers and thorns (fig.)—Is. 27:4. Bush—Ex. 3:2, 3; See Mt. 12:26; Lu. 20:37; Acts 7:30–35. Candlestick—II Chr. 4:20; 13:11. See CANDLESTICK, LAMP. Fir-tree—Is. 44:15. Chariots—II Ki. 23:11; Ps. 46:9; Nah. 2:3. See CHARIOTS. Children—Deut. 12:31; II Ki. 17:31; II Chr. 28:3; 33:6; Jer. 7:31; 19:5. Garments—Lev. 13:52–55. Harlot—Gen. 38:24; Lev. 21:32. High places—II Ki. 23:16. Images—Deut. 7:5, 25; 9:21; I Ki. 15: 13; II Ki. 10:26; II Chr. 15:16. See IDOLATRY. Incense—See INCENSE. Jacob (fig.)—Lam. 2:3. Jealousy—Ps. 79:5. Lamp—Ex. 27:20; Lev. 24:2; Is. 62:1; Lu. 12:35; John 5:35; Rev. 4:5. See CANDLESTICK, LAMP. Lebanon not sufficient—Is. 40:16. Lust, In— Rom. 1:27; I Cor. 7:9. Men's bones— Job 30:30; Ps. 102:3; I Ki. 13:2; II Ki. 15:20; II Chr. 34:5. Passover— See PASSOVER. Pitch—Is. 34:9. Roll— Jer. 36:25–32. Servants—Job. 1:15. Sheep—Job. 1:15. Sheol, Unto—Deut. 32:22. See SHEOL. Tares—Mt. 13:30,

40. Weapons—Ez. 39:9, 10. Wickedness—Is. 9:18. Wrath—Ps. 89:46; Jer. 4:4; 21:13. See ANGER, DESTRUCTION, FIRE, FLAME, FURNACE, OFFERING, PERSECUTION, SACRIFICE.

BURNING. Ex. 21:25; Lev. 10:6; Deut. 29:23; II Chr. 16:14; 21:19; Ps. 58:9; Is. 10:16; 33:14; Jer. 34:5; Rev. 18:9, 18. Coals of fire—Pr. 6:28; Ez. 1:13. Heat of famine—Lam. 5:10. Leprosy, Of—Lev. 13:23, 25–28. Lime—Is. 33: 12. Loins filled with—Ps. 38:1. Spirit of—Is. 4:4. Wind—Ps. 11:6; Jer. 4:11, 12. See BURN, DROUGHT, FIRE.

BURNISH. Brass—I Ki. 7:45; Dan. 10:6; Rev. 1:15. See BRIGHT.

BURST. Joel 2:8. Bonds—Jer. 2:20; 5:5; 30:8; Nah. 1:13. See BONDAGE, BREAK, CAPTIVITY, PRISON. Judas— Acts 1:18. Ready to—Job 32:19. Tempest—Jer. 23:19. Wine-skins—Mt. 9: 17; Mk. 2:22; Lu. 5:37.

BURY. See BURIAL, BURIAL PLACES, DEATH, GRAVE, SEPULCHRE.

BUSH. Bray among—Job 30:7. Burning—Ex. 3:2–4; Mk. 12:26; Lu. 20:37; Acts 7:30, 35. Mallows—Job 30:4 (A.V.). Salt-wort—Job 30:4. See BRAMBLE, BRIERS, PLANTS, THORNS.

BUSHEL. Lamp under a—Mt. 5:15; Mk. 4:21; Lu. 11:33.

BUSHY. Locks of hair—Song of Sol. 5:11.

BUSINESS. Josh. 2:14, 20; I Sam. 20: 19; Eccl. 8:16. Bridegroom not charged with—Deut. 24:5. Deacons, Of—Acts 6:3. Demetrius—Acts 19:24, 25. Diligent in—Pr. 22:29; Rom. 16: 11. Father's, My—Lu. 2:49. Haste, Requires—I Sam. 21:2, 8. Jehovah's —I Chr. 26:30; Neh. 11:16, 22; 13:13. See MINISTER. Kings—I Sam. 21:2, 8; Esth. 3:9; Dan. 8:27. Multitude of— Eccl. 5:5. Own—I Thess. 4:11. Seafaring—Ps. 107:23. See COMMERCE, DEALINGS, MATTER, WORKS.

BUSY. I Ki. 20:40.

BUSYBODY. Pr. 26:17; I Thess. 4:11; II Thess. 3:11; I Tim. 5:13; I Pet. 4: 15. See GOSSIP.

BUTLER. Gen. 40:1–23; 41:9.

BUTTER. Gen. 18:8; Deut. 32:14; Ju. 5:25; Pr. 30:33. Honey, And—II Sam.

17:29; Job 20:17; Is. 7:15, 22. Mouth smoother than—Ps. 55:21. Steps washed with—Job 29:6. See FOOD.

BUTTOCKS. II Sam. 10:4; I Chr. 19:4; Is. 20:4.

BUY. Lu. 17:28; I Cor. 7:30; Jas. 4:13; Rev. 13:17; 18:11. Bond-servants— Gen. 39:1; 47:19, 23; Ex. 21:2; Lev. 22:11; 25:44, 45, 50; Deut. 28:68. Disciples bought with blood of Jesus—I Cor. 6:20; 7:23; II Pet. 2:1. See REDEMPTION. Food—Gen. 42:7, 10; 43:2, 4, 20, 22; 44:25; Deut. 2:6; Is. 55:1; Mt. 14:15; Mk. 6:36, 37; Lu. 9:13; John 4:8; 6:5; 13:29. See FOOD. Gold —Rev. 3:18. Grain—Gen. 41:57; 42:2– 10; 47:14. Lamb—II Sam. 12:3. Land —Gen. 33:19; 47:19–23; 49:30; 50:13; Lev. 25:23–30; 27:24; Josh. 24:32; Ruth. 4:3–9; II Sam. 24:21–24; I Ki. 16:24; I Chr. 21:24; Neh. 5:16; Pr. 31:16; Lu. 14:18. Potters' field—Mt. 27:7. See LAND. Linen—Mk. 15:46. Neighbor, Of a—Lev. 25:14–17. Offerings material for—Ezra 7:17. See OFFERING. Oil—Mt. 25:9, 10. Oxen—Lu. 14:19. Pearl—Mt. 13:45, 46. Sabbath, Not to buy on—Neh. 10:31. Spies— Mk. 16:1. Stone, Hewn—II Ki. 12:12; 22:6; II Chr. 34:11. Sweet cane—Is. 43:24. Sword—Lu. 22:36. Temple, In the—Mt. 21:12; Mk. 11:17; Lu. 19:45. Timber—II Ki. 12:12; 22:6; II Chr. 34:11. Treasure-field—Mt. 13:44. Truth Pr. 23:23. Water—Deut. 2:6. Wife— Ruth 4:10; Hos. 3:2. See JACOB, MARRIAGE. Wine and milk—Is. 55:1. See BOUGHT, COMMERCE, PURCHASE, SELL.

BUYER. Pr. 20:14; Is. 24:2; Ez. 7:12.

BUZ, bŭz. (1) **Son of Nahor and Milcah. nephew of Abraham.**—Gen. 22:21.

(2) **A Gadite.**—I Chr. 5:14.

(3) **A region possibly in Arabia.**—Job 32:2, 6; Jer. 25:23.

BUZI, bū′zī. **Father of Ezekiel.**—Ez. 1:3.

BY PATHS. Jer. 18:15. See PATH.

BYWAYS. Ju. 5:6.

BYWORD. Deut. 28:37; I Ki. 9:7; I Chr. 7:20. Job. 17:6; 30:9; 44:14; Ez. 23:10. See REPROACH.

CABBON, kăb′bon. **A village in Judah.** —Josh. 15:40.

CABUL, kā′bul. (1) **A city in Asher.** —Josh. 19:27.

(2) **Name given to the twenty cities in Galilee, which Solomon gave to Hiram, king of Tyre.**—I Ki. 9:13.

CÆSAR, sē′sar. Tribute unto—Mk. 12:14, 16, 17; Lu. 20:22, 24, 25. Christ accused of being disloyal to—Lu. 23:2; John 19:12. Called king—John 19:15; Acts 17:7. Paul's loyalty to—Acts 25:8–12, 21; 27:24; 28:19.

Augustus.—Mt. 22:17–21; Lu. 2:1.

Claudius.—Acts 11:28.

Tiberius.—Lu. 3:1.

(Nero).—Acts 25:8; Phil. 4:22.

CAESAREA, cĕs′a-rē-a. **A city on the coast of the Mediterranean Sea.** Founded B.C. 10, and named in honor of Cæsar Augustus—Cornelius, Home of—Acts 10:1–48; 11:1–12. Disciples visit Jerusalem—Acts 21:16. Herod Agrippa I, Death of—Acts 12:19–23. Paul brought there from Damascus, sent thence to Tarsus. Sent to Felix— Acts 23:23, 33. Appears before Felix —Acts 24:1–27. Before Festus—Acts 25:1–13. Before Agrippa—Acts 25:13–27. Philip, the evangelist, came to —Acts 8:40.

CAESAREA PHILIPPI, sĕs-ă-rē′a phĭ-lĭp′pī. **A town in the northern part of Canaan—Place where Peter made the "Good Confession".**—Mt. 16:13; Mk. 8:27.

CAGE. Jer. 5:27; Rev. 18:2.

CAIAPHAS, kā′ia-phas. **The high priest before whom Jesus was brought.**—Mt. 26:3, 57; Lu. 3:2; John 11:49; 18:13–28; Acts 4:6.

CAIN, kāin. (1) **First son of Adam and Eve.**—*Cain* signifies "acquired." Eve supposed the birth of Cain was the fulfilment of the promise—"The seed of the woman," Gen. 3:15. "I have gotten a man," Gen. 4:1.

Cain a tiller of the ground.—Gen. 4:2. Brought fruit for offering—Gen. 4:3. God did not respect Cain's offering— Gen. 3:5. Cain murders Abel—Gen. 4:5–8. Jehovah questions—Gen. 4:9. Jehovah curses and banishes—Gen. 4:11, 12. Cain complains—Gen. 4:13, 14. Jehovah protects—Gen. 4:15. Cain dwells in Nod—Gen. 4:16. Cain marries, has a son, builds a city—Gen. 4:17. Lamech refers to Cain—Gen. 4:24. Eve appointed another seed—Gen.

4:25. Descendants of Cain—Gen. 4:17, 18.

New Testament references.—Heb. 11:4; I John 3:12; Jude 11.

(2) **A town in southern part of Judah.**—Josh. 15:57.

CAINAN, ka-ī'nan, or **KENAN.** (1) **Son of Enos, grandson of Seth.**—Gen. 5:9-14; I Chr. 1:2; Lu. 3:37.

(2) Son of Arphaxad, ancestor of Jesus.—Lu. 3:36.

CAKES. Gen. 18:6; II Sam. 13:6, 8, 10; I Ki. 19:6; Jer. 7:18; 44:19. Barley—Ju. 7:13; Ez. 4:12. Bread, Of—II Sam. 6:19; I Ki. 17:12, 13. *Leavened*—Lev. 7:13, 14. Figs, Of—I Sam. 25:18; 30:12; II Ki. 20:7; I Chr. 12:4; Is. 38:21. See FIGS. Manna—Num. 11:8. Raisins, Of—II Sam. 6:19. Shewbread—Lev. 24:5. See BREAD. Turned, Ephraim a cake not—Hos. 7:8. Unleavened—Ex. 12:39; Josh. 5:11; Ju. 6:19-21. Made of fine flour mixed with oil—Ex. 29:2, 23; Lev. 2:4; 7:12, 14; 8:26; Num. 6:15, 19.

CALAH, kā'lah. **A very ancient Assyrian city, residence of Sardanapolis.**—Gen. 10:11, 12.

CALAMITY. Balances, Laid in—Job 6:2. Comes suddenly—Pr. 6:15; 24:22; Jer. 48:16. Day of—Deut. 32:35; II Sam. 22:19; Ps. 18:18; Pr. 27:10; Jer. 18:17; 46:21; Ob. 13. Esau, Of—Jer. 49:8. Foolish son, A—Pr. 19:13. Glad at—Pr. 17:5. See Job 31:28, 29; Pr. 24:17; Ob. 12. Hazor, Of—Jer. 49:32. Joab, Of—Jer. 48:16. Over past—Ps. 57:1. Overthrown by—Pr. 24:16. Prayer in—Ps. 141:5 (A.V.). Ready at side of wicked—Job. 18:12. Saved out of—I Sam. 10:19. Set forward—Job 30:13. Unrighteous, To—Job 31:3. See ADVERSITY, AFFLICTION, CAPTIVITY, JUDGMENT, SIN, PUNISHMENT FOR, REAPING WHAT WE SOW.

CALAMUS. A reed.—Ex. 30:23; Song of Sol. 4:14; Ez. 27:19.

CALCOL, kăl'kŏl. **Son of Judah by his daughter-in-law, Tamar.**—I Chr. 2:6.

CALDRON. I Sam. 2:14; II Chr. 35:13; Job. 41:20 (A.V.); Jer. 52:18,19 (A.V.); Ez. 11:3, 7, 11; Mic. 3:3. See VESSELS.

CALEB, kā'leb. (1) **Son of Jephunneh.**—Num. 13:6; 32:12; Josh. 14:6.

Events of life.—Stilled people before Moses—Num. 13:30. Sent out as spy—Num. 14:6. His courage and reward—Num. 14:24, 30, 38; Deut. 1:36. Prince of Judah—Num. 34:19. His inheritance—Josh. 14:6-15; 15:13-16; Ju. 1:20; I Chr. 6:56. Gives daughter possessions—Ju. 1:14, 15.

Descendants.—I Sam. 25:3; 30:14; I Chr. 4:15.

(2) **Son of Hezron.**—I Chr. 2:18.

(3) **Son of Hur.**—I Chr. 2:50.

CALEB-EPHRATAH, kā'leb-ĕph'ra-tah. **A place near Bethlehem-Judah**—I Chr. 2:24.

CALF. Uses of.—For food—Gen. 18:7, 8; I Sam. 14:32; 28:24; Amos 6:4. Fatted calf—Lu. 15:23, 27, 30.

As victim in sacrifice.—Lev. 9:2, 3, 8; Num. 18:17; Mic. 6:6.

Especially to confirm a covenant.—Jer. 34:18, 19; Heb. 9:12, 19.

Idols made in the image of.—Ex. 32:4, 35; Deut. 9:16, 21; I Ki. 12:28, 32; II Ki. 10:29; 17:16; II Chr. 11:15; 13:8; Neh. 9:18; Ps. 68:30; 106:19; Hos. 8:5, 6; 10:5; 13:2; Acts 7:41.

Prophecies concerning.—Is. 11:6; 27:10.

Figurative.—Job 21:10.

Illustrative.—Ps. 29:6; Jer. 31:18; 46:21; Ez. 1:7; Hos. 14:2; Mal. 4:2; Rev. 4:7. See CATTLE, IDOLATRY.

CALKER. Ez. 27:9, 27.

CALLING. Gr. *Klesis.* **Invitation.**—"Not condition of life or occupation. Rather, the call of God into His kingdom. No dependence on human wisdom, power, or lineage."—VINCENT.

Into service.—Mt. 4:21; John 1:43; Rom. 1:7; 9:11, 12; II Tim. 1:9-11; Jude 1-3.

Unto salvation.—Lu. 19:5, 9; I Cor. 1:21-26; II Cor. 6:1, 2; I Pet. 2:9, 10.

To fellowship in Christ.—I Cor. 1:9; Eph. 1:18-20; 2:4-6; 3:6; I John 1:3.

From earth to heaven.—Rom. 11:29; Eph. 1:18; 4:4; Phil. 3:14; II Thess. 1:11; II Pet. 1:10, 11.

The caller faithful.—John 10:3-5; I Thess. 5:23, 24; Heb. 3:1-6; I Pet. 5:10.

The prize bound up with calling.—I Cor. 9:24; Phil. 3:13-16; Heb. 3:1, 2, 12-14.

Steadfastness in the calling.—I Cor. 7: 20–24; Eph. 4:1–6; Col. 3:15; II Pet. 1:10.

Growth necessary to increase its value. —Rom. 11:22; I Thess. 2:12; I Pet. 1:13–17; II Pet. 1:3–11.

The calling slighted.—Mt. 22:3–9; Lu. 14:16–24; 18:22–24; Heb. 2:1–4.

The calling perverted.—Gal. 1:6, 7; 5: 7–13; I Thess. 4:3–8. See ELECTION, SALVATION.

Called of God.—Pr. 1:24–33; Is. 45:22; 65:12; 66:4; Jer. 7:13; Mt. 20:16; 22:3, 8, 9, 14; Acts 2:39; Rom. 4:17–25; 8:30; 9:10–13; I Thess. 5:24; Heb. 9: 15; II Pet. 1:2–11; Rev. 17:14. According to His purpose—Rom. 8:28; 9:23, 24; II Tim. 1:9. To fellowship with Jesus—I Cor. 1:9. To holiness— I Thess. 4:7; II Pet. 1:15, 16. To be saints—Rom. 1:6, 7; I Cor. 1:2. To peace—I Cor. 7:15. To eternal glory —Rom. 8:30; II Thess. 2:14; I Pet. 5:10. To eternal life—I Tim. 6:12. To liberty—I Cor. 7:20–24; Gal. 5:13. The high—Phil. 3:14. A holy—II Tim. 1:9. A heavenly—Heb. 3:1. The hope of your—Eph. 1:18; 4:4. Walking worthily of—Eph. 4:1; II Thess. 1:11. Blessedness of receiving the call— Rev. 19:9.

How called?—In the Old Testament.— By the works of God—Ps. 19:2, 3; Rom. 1:18–23. By the prophets—II Chr. 36:15–17; Jer. 7:21–28; 25:4–8; 29:15–19; 35:15; Zech. 7:7; Mal. 2:7.

In the New Testament.—By Christ— Mt. 6:33; 9:13; 11:28; 23:37; Mk. 2: 17; Lu. 5:32; 19:41; John 5:40; 6:37; 7:37; I Pet. 5:10. By the Spirit—Rev. 22:17. By the bride—Rev. 22:17. By the preaching of the gospel—II Cor. 3:6; 5:18–21; Eph. 6:20. By the gospel—Mt. 7:24–28; Lu. 6:47–49; John 12:48; Rom. 9:23–33; I Cor. 1:18–28; II Cor. 5:18–21; Gal. 1:6–14; Eph. 1: 17–19; I Thess. 1:4–10; 2:12–14; II Thess. 2:13–15; II Tim. 1:9–11.

CALM. Ps. 107:29; Jonah 1:11, 12; Mt. 8:26; Mk. 4:39; Lu. 8:24.

CALNEH, kăl'neh. (1) One of the most ancient cities of Shinar.—Gen. 10:10. (2) An Assyrian city.—Amos 6:2.

CALNO, kal-no. Probably same as *Calneh* (?).

CALVARY (the skull). Place where Jesus was crucified.—Lu. 23:33 (A.V.). See GOLGOTHA, SKULL.

CAMEL. As property.—Of Abraham— Gen. 12:16; 24:10, 11, 19, 20, 31, 32, 35, 44, 46. Jacob—Gen. 30:43; 32:7, 15. Pharaoh—Ex. 9:3. Midianites— Ju. 6:5; 7:12. Babylonians—Ezra 2: 67; Neh. 7:69. Job—Job 1:3, 17; 42: 12. Adorned with chains—Ju. 8:21, 26. Overseer of—I Chr. 27:30.

Uses of.—As beast of burden—Gen. 37: 25; I Ki. 10:2; II Ki. 8:9; I Chr. 12: 40; II Chr. 9:1. Transportation—Gen. 24:61–64; 31:17, 34; I Sam. 30:17; Is. 30:6. Hair of for clothing—Mt. 3:4; Mk. 1:6.

Laws concerning eating of.—Lev. 11:4; Deut. 14:7.

Destruction of.—I Sam. 27:9. Taken in war—I Chr. 5:21; II Chr. 14:15.

Prophecies concerning.—Is. 21:7; 60:6; Jer. 49:29; Ez. 25:5; Zech. 14:15.

Illustrative.—Mt. 23:24. Pass through eye of a needle—Mt. 19:24; Mk. 10: 25; Lu. 18:25.

CAMP, ENCAMPMENT. Job 19:12; Ps. 53:5; Is. 29:3; Jer. 50:24; Ez. 4:2; Joel 2:11; Zech. 9:8. Abimelech—Ju. 9:5. Ammonites, Of the—Ju. 10:17; I Sam. 11:1. Amorites, Of the—Josh. 10:5. Angels of—Ps. 34:7. Assyrians, Of the—II Ki. 19:35; II Chr. 32:1, 2. Egyptians, Of the—Ex. 14:20. Host should encamp against me—Ps. 27:3.

Israelites.—Ex. 13:20; 14:2, 9; 15:27; 18:5; 19:2; Lev. 24:10–12; Num. 1:50, 52; 2:1–32; 3:38; 10:31; 11:26–30; 14: 44; 30:12–20; Josh. 4:19; 5:8–10; 6: 11–14; 9:6; 10:6, 15, 21, 31, 34, 43; Ju. 7:17–21; 10:17; 20:19; 21:8, 12; I Sam. 4:3–7; 17:17; 26:6; II Sam. 1:2, 3, 11; 12:28; I Ki. 16:15, 16; II Ki. 3:24; II Chr. 22:1; Ps. 106:16. Accursed— Josh. 6:18. Angel in—Ex. 14:19, 20; Is. 37:36. Fire devours—Num. 11:1. Golden calf in—Ex. 32:1–29. Journeyings of—Num. 10:2–36; 33:1–49. Nadab and Abihu carried out of—Lev. 10:5. Noise of war in—Ex. 32:17. Quails in—Ex. 16:13; Num. 11:31, 32; Ps. 78:28. Setting forward—Num. 4:5–15; 10:17–35. Sinai, At—Ex. 19:2, 16, 17. Sojourner in—Deut. 29:17.

Without.—Ex. 29:14; Lev. 16:20–26; 17:3; 24:14, 23; Num. 19:3, 7; 31:13; Heb. 13:13. Ashes—Lev. 6:11. Bullock burnt—Lev. 4:12, 21; 8:17; 9:11; 16:27, 28; Heb. 13:11, 13. Lepers—Lev. 13:46; 14:3–8; Num. 5:2; 12:9–15. Stoning—15:35, 36. Tent of meeting—Ex. 33:7, 11. See TABERNACLE. Unclean—Num. 5:3, 4; 31:19–24; Deut. 23:10–14. See ISRAEL, PURIFICATION.

CAMPHIRE. Song of Sol. 1:14 (A.V.); 4:13 (A.V.).

CANA, kā'na. **A village in Galilee where Jesus performed his first miracle.**—John 2:1–11; 4:46; 21:2.

CANAAN, kā'naan. (1) Heb. *Kana,* to depress—*"Lowland,""Land of Ham."*
Called.—Land of Canaan—Gen. 11:31; 17:8; 23:2; Acts 13:19. Land of the Hebrews—Gen. 40:15. Land of the Jews—Acts 10:39. Land of Israel—I Sam. 13:19. Land of promise—Heb. 11:9. Holy land—Zech. 2:12. Jehovah's land—Hos. 9:3. Immanuel's land—Is. 8:8. Beulah land—Is. 62:4.
Country fertile.—Ex. 3:8, 17; 13:5; Jer. 11:5.
Boundaries.—Gen. 10:19.
Different families residing there.—Gen. 10:15–18.
Seven distinct nations.—Deut. 7:1; Acts 13:19.
Language of.—Is. 19:18.
Characteristics of Canaanites.—Strong people—Num. 13:28; Deut. 7:1. Idolatrous—Deut. 29:17. Superstitious—Deut. 18:9–11. Wicked—Lev. 18:27; Deut. 9:5; 18:12.
Abraham called to dwell there.—Gen. 12:1–5. Promised it for inheritance—Gen. 13:14–17; 15:7, 18; 22:17; 24:7; 28:4; 35:12; Deut. 12:9–10; 34:4; Ps. 105:11; Ez. 47:13–14; Acts 7:5; Gal. 3:18. Renewed in Isaac—Gen. 26:2–3. In Jacob—Gen. 28:13; 35:12; Ps. 105:10–11. Given to Israelites—Ex. 3:8; 6:4; 15:17; Lev. 20:24; Deut. 3:28; 11:31; Josh. 1:3–4; Ps. 135:12; Ez. 36:28.
Inhabitants of Canaan terrified at approach of the Israelites—Ex. 15:15, 16; Jos. 2:9–11; 5:1.
Spies sent into Canaan.—Num. 13:1–33; 14:36, 37.

Murmurers forbidden to enter.—Num. 14:1–35.
Viewed by Moses.—Deut. 3:27; 34:1–4.
Israel commanded to make no alliance with.—Ex. 23:32; 34:12; Deut. 7:2; Ju. 2:2. Not to intermarry with—Gen. 24:3, 37; Ex. 34:14, 15; Deut. 7:3; Josh. 23:12, 13. Not to worship their idols—Ex. 23:23, 24; Deut. 7:5, 25. To destroy their idols and pillars—Ex. 23:24; Num. 33:52; Deut. 7:5; 12:3; II Ki. 18:4. Not to follow customs of —Lev. 18:26–29. To destroy them— Ex. 23:31; 34:11; Num. 33:52; Deut. 20:16. They were not wholly destroyed —Josh. 13:1, 13; 15:63; 16:10; 17:12; Ju. Chs. 1–3. Some descendants remained in the time of Jesus—Mt. 15:22; Mk. 7:26.
(2) **Son of Ham, grandson of Noah.**—Gen. 9:18–27; 10:6, 15; I Chr. 1:8, 13.
CANDACE, kän'da-sē. **Queen of Ethiopia, whose treasurer was the Ethiopian eunuch.**—Acts 8:27.
CANDLE. See LAMP.
CANDLESTICK. Used in tabernacle, made of pure gold.—Ex. 25:31; 37:17; 39:37; Lev. 24:4; Num. 8:4; Heb. 9:2. Beaten work—Ex. 25:31; 37:17; Num. 8:4. Six branches—Ex. 25:33, 35; 37:18, 19. Three branches on each side— Ex. 25:32; 37:18. Four cups in—Ex. 25:34; 37:20. Shall be placed against the table—Ex. 26:35; 40:24. Anointing of—Ex. 31:8. Used for light—Ex. 35:14; 40:4; 8:28. Levites take care of—Num. 3:31; 4:9; 8:2, 3.
Used in house of Jehovah.—I Ki. 7:49.
Candlestick in Elisha's chamber.—II Ki. 4:10.
David gives Solomon the pattern of candlesticks for temple.—I Chr. 28:15. Made of gold and for light—II Chr. 4:7, 20; 13:11. Carried to Babylon— Jer. 52:19.
Vision of.—Zech. 4:2, 11; Rev. 1:12, 13, 20; 2:1, 5; 11:4.
Handwriting on wall, near candlestick. —Dan. 5:5.
Called stand.—Mt. 5:15; Mk. 4:21; Lu. 8:16; 11:33.
CANE, SWEET. Is. 43:24; Jer. 6:20. See CALAMUS.
CANKER. II Tim. 2:17 (A.V.). See DISEASE, GANGRENE.

CANKERWORM. Joel 1:4; 2:25; Nah. 3:15, 16.

CANNEH, kăn'neh. **On the southern coast of Arabia.**—Ez. 27:23.

CAPERNAUM, ka-pẽr'na-um. **Location of.**—Mt. 4:13. Home of Jesus during Galilean ministry—Mt. 4:13; Mk. 1: 21; 2:1.

Dispute between disciples on way.—Mk. 9:33.

Jesus wrought miracles in.—Mt. 8:5–22; 9:1–26; 17:24–27; Mk. 1:21–45; 2; 3: 1–6; Lu. 7:1–10; John 4:46–53; 6:17–25, 59.

Chooses Levi the publican here.—Mt. 9: 9–13; Mk. 2:13–17; Lu. 5:27 ff.

Jesus walked on sea near.—John 6:17–21.

Miracle near.—Mt. 8:26, 27.

Prophecies against.—Mt. 11:23; Lu. 10: 15.

Jesus rejected by the people of.—John 6:22–71.

CAPHTOR, kăph'tor. **A seat of the Philistines.**—Gen. 10:14; Deut. 2:23; I Chr. 1:12; Jer. 47:4; Amos 9:7.

CAPITALS. Ex. 36:38; I Ki. 7:16–20; Amos 9:1; Zeph. 2:14. See TEMPLE.

CAPPADOCIA, kăp'pa-dō'si-a. **A plateau in the eastern part of Asia Minor.**—Acts 2:9; I Pet. 1:1.

CAPTAIN.—Applies to various bodies of men—Num. Ch. 2. Over all—Ex. 14:7. Of thousands—Num. 31:14, 48, 52, 54; Deut. 1:15; I Sam. 8:12; 22:7; II Sam. 5:2; 18:1; I Chr. 12:20; 13:1; 15:25; 26:26; 27:1; 28:1; 29:6; II Chr. 1:2; 17:14; 25:5. Of hundreds—Num. 31:14; Deut. 1:15; I Sam. 22:7; II Sam. 18:1; II Ki. 11:4, 9, 10, 15, 19; I Chr. 4:42; 13:1; II Chr. 23:1, 9, 14, 20. Of fifties—Deut. 1:15; I Sam. 8: 12; II Ki. 1:9, 14; Is. 3:3. Of tens—Deut. 1:15. Of the guard—Gen. 37:36; II Ki. 25:8. Sunk in the Red Sea—Ex. 15:4. Sisera, a captain of host—Ju. 4:2; I Sam. 12:9. Officers appoint captains of hosts—Deut. 20:9. Jephthah made chief or captain—Ju. 11:6. Captains sent to capture Elijah—II Ki. 1:9–15. Naaman a captain—II Ki. 5:1. Zadok's twenty captains—I Chr. 12:28. David's captains—II Sam. 19: 13; 23:8–39. Herod's captains—Mk. 6:21. Judas confers with captains—

Lu. 22:4. Chief captain seizes Jesus—John 18:12. Captains arrest apostles—Acts 5:24–26. Jesus called captain (or author)—Heb. 2:10. Captains of bands—II Sam. 4:2. Captains' charge concerning Absalom—II Sam. 18:5. Captain of hosts—Deut. 20:9; I Ki. 1:25; 2:5; II Ki. 9:5; I Chr. 12:14, 21; 25:1; 27:3. Solomon's captains—I Ki. 9:22. Captains of chariots—I Ki. 22:31–33; II Ki. 8:21; II Chr. 18:30, 32; 21:9. Captains of forces—II Ki. 25:23, 26; Jer. 40:7; 41:11; 42:1, 8; 43:4, 5. Naphtali a thousand captains—I Chr. 12:34. Rehoboam's captains—II Chr. 11:11. Captains of war—II Chr. 32:6, 21; 33:14; Neh. 2:9; Job 39:25. Agrippa and chief captain—Acts 25:23.

Figurative.—May eat the flesh of captains—Rev. 19:18. See PRINCE.

CAPTIVITY. Abram's brother—Gen. 14:14. Sons of Jacob take Shechem—Gen. 34:29.

Israel taken captive.—Num. 21:1; 24: 22; II Ki. 17:6, 23; I Chr. 5:26; Ezra 4:1; 9:4. Foretold—Is. 39:6; Jer. 13: 19; 20:4; 25:11. Fulfilled—II Ki. 18: 11; 24:15, 16; 25:11; II Chr. 36:6–10; Jer. Ch. 52. Return from—II Chr. 36: 23; Ezra 1:2; Neh. Ch. 2; Ps. 126. Mordecai a son of Israel—Esth. 2:6. Captives led away—Ps. 68:18; 137:3; Ezra 8:35; Jer. 29:4; Dan. 2:25; Eph. 4:8.

Led into captivity because of disobedience.—Deut. 28:47–52, 62–68; 29:25–28; 30:1–5; Ju. 3:7, 8; I Ki. 9:6–9; 14:1–16; II Ki. 17:18, 20, 23; 18:9–12; 23:27; 24:1–4; II Chr. 7:20; Neh. 1:8, 9; 9:26–30; Ps. 106:34–47; Jer. 21:3–14; 22:1–30; 24:1–10; 25:1–11; Ez. 39: 23, 24.

Proclaim liberty to.—Is. 61:1; Lu. 4:18.

Women taken captive.—Gen. 31:26; II Ki. 5:2; 24:15. See PRISON, TEN COMMANDMENTS.

CARAVANS. Is. 21:13; Ez. 27:25.

CARBUNCLE. A precious stone.—Ex. 28:17; 39:10; Is. 54:12; Ez. 28:13.

CARCAS, kär'kas. **One of the chamberlains of Ahasuerus.**—Esth. 1:10.

CARCASE. Mt. 24:28.

Animals, Of—Gen. 15:11. Lion, Of a—Ju. 14:8, 9. Unclean—Lev. 5:2; 11:8,

11, 24–28, 35, 40 (A.V.). Men, Of—Lev. 26:30 (A.V.); Is. 66:24 (A.V.); Ez. 6:5 (A.V.); Nah. 3:3 (A.V.). Ai, King of—Josh. 8:29. Birds, Food for—I Sam. 17:46 (A.V.); Jer. 7:33 (A.V.); 19:7 (A.V.). Dung, Fall as—Jer. 9:22 (A.V.); 16:4 (A.V.). Foot, Trodden under—Is. 14:19. Jezebel, Of—II Ki. 9:37 (A.V.). Kings—Josh. 8:29; Ez. 43:7, 9 (A.V.). Prophet, Of a—I Ki. 13:22–30 (A.V.). Refuse, As—Is. 5:25 (A.V.). Stench of—Is. 34:3 (A.V.). Wilderness, In the—Num. 14:29–33 (A.V.); Heb. 3:17 (A.V.). See BODY, DEATH.

CARCHEMISH, kär'ke-mish. A city on the Euphrates.—II Chr. 35:20; Is. 10: 5; Jer. 46:2.

CARE, n. Casting care on God—Ps. 9:9; 23:1; 62:1; I Pet. 5:7 (A.V.). Churches, For the—II Cor. 8:16; 11:28 (A.V.); Phil. 2:20; I Tim. 3:5. Disciples for each other—I Cor. 12:25. Earnest—II Cor. 7:11; Elisha, For—II Ki. 4:13. Free from—I Cor. 7:32. Life, Of this —Lu. 8:14; 21:34. See WORLD. Paul, For—II Cor. 7:12; Phil. 4:10. Without —Jer. 49:31. World, Of this—Mt. 13: 22; Mk. 4:19; Lu. 8:14; 12:22; John 6:27; I Cor. 7:32, 34; Phil. 4:6; I Tim. 6:8; Deut. 11:12. No man, For—Mt. 22:16; Mk. 12:14. Oxen, For—I Cor. 9:9. Perish, That we—Mk. 4:38. Poor, For the—John 12:6. Samaritan, Parable of the good—Lu. 10:20–27. Sheep, For the—John 10:13. Soul, My—Ps. 142:4. See ANXIETY, ANXIOUS, GOD, PROVIDENCE OF.

CAREFUL. Jer. 17:8. Elisha, For—II Ki. 4:13. Lord, For things of the—I Cor. 7:32, 34. Nothing, For—Phil. 4:6 (A.V.). Paul, For—Phil.4:10 (A.V.). Serving, About much—Lu. 10:41 (A.V.). Works, To maintain—Tit. 3:8. See ANXIOUS, THOUGHT.

CAREFULLY. Hearken—Deut. 15:5. Sent—Phil. 2:28 (A.V.). Walk—Eph. 5:15.

CAREFULNESS. Ez. 12:18, 19 (A.V.).

CARELESS. Ju. 18:7 (A.V.). Ethiopians—Ez. 30:9. Women—Is. 32:9–11. See THOUGHTLESS.

CARMEL, kär'mel. (1) Mount Carmel, in Palestine, noted for its fertility.—Josh. 12:22; 19:26; Is. 33:9; 35:2; Jer. 46:18; 50:19; Amos 1:2; 9:3; Mic. 7:4;

Nah. 1:4. Elijah and prophets of Baal, Contest between—I Ki. 18:17–46. Elisha goes to—II Ki. 2:25. Meets Shunammite woman—4:25–27. Head like—Song of Sol. 7:5. Husbandmen and vinedressers in—II Chr. 26:10 (A.V.).

(2) A town in Judah, famous as the home of Nabal, husband of Abigail, who afterwards married David.—Josh. 15:55; I Sam. 25:2–42; I·Sam. 27:3; 30:5. Saul goes to—I Sam. 15:12.

CARMI, kär'mi. (1) Father of Achan.—Josh. 7:1, 18; I Chr. 2:7; 4:1.

(2) A son of Reuben.—Gen. 46:9; Ex. 6:14; Num. 26:6; I Chr. 6:3.

CARMITES. Num. 26:6.

CARNAL. Rom. 7:14. Commandment—Heb. 7:16. Corinthian Church because of factions—I Cor. 3:1–4. Mind—Rom. 8:6, 7. Ordinances—Heb. 9:10. Things—Rom. 15:27; I Cor. 9:11. See FLESH, LUST.

CARNALLY. Lie—Lev. 18:20; 19:20. See FLESH, FORNICATION, LUST.

CAROUSINGS. I Pet. 4:3. See AMUSEMENTS, DRUNKENNESS, REVELLING.

CARPENTER. Encourages goldsmith—Is. 41:7. Work of—Is. 44:13. Jesus as a—Mt. 13:55; Mk. 6:3. Hiram sends carpenter to David—II Sam. 5:11; I Chr. 14:1. Wages of—II Ki. 12:11; 22:6; Ezra 3:7. Where hired to restore house of Jehovah—II Chr. 24:12. Called craftsmen in—Jer. 24:1; 29:2.

CARPETS. Ju. 5:10; I Pr. 7:16; 31:22.

CARPUS, kär'pus. A person at Troas, with whom Paul left a cloak.—II Tim. 4:13.

CARRIAGE. See BAGGAGE, CARRY.

CARRY, CARRIED. Ahaziah—II Ki. 9: 28. Angels, By—Lu. 16:22. Ark—I Sam. 5:8, 9; II Sam. 15:25; I Chr. 13:7; 15:2. Assyria, Into—II Ki. 15: 29; 16:2; 17:6, 23; 18:11; I Chr. 5:6, 26. Babylon, Into—II Ki. 20:17; 24: 10–16; 25:7, 11, 13, 21; I Chr. 6:15; 9:1; II Chr. 33:11; 36:6, 20; Ezra 2:1; 5:12; Neh. 7:6; Esth. 2:6; Is. 39:7; Jer. 20:4, 5; 27:22; 28:4; 29:1, 4, 7, 14; 39:7; 40:1, 7; 52:11, 17; Ezra 17: 4, 12; Mt. 1:17; Acts 7:43. See CAPTIVITY. Beast that—Rev. 17:7. Bosom, In—Num. 11:12; Is. 40:11. Bows—Ps. 78:9. Captivity, Into—See CAPTIV-

ITY. Daughters—Is. 49:22. Egypt, Into—II Chr. 36:4; Dan. 11:8; Hos. 12:1. Headlong—Job 5:13. Idols—Is. 46:7; Hos. 10:6. Jehovah carries— Num. 11:12; II Ki. 17:11; Is. 40:11; 46:4; 63:9. Job 10:9. Lame man— Acts 3:2. Oil into Egypt—Hos. 12:1. Peter—John 21:18. Purse—Lu. 10:4. Scarlet woman—Rev. 17:7. Shoes— Lu. 10:4. Sorrows, Our—Is. 53:4. Stephen—Acts 8:2. Vessels of the temple —II Chr. 36:7; Ezra—5:15; Joel 3:5. Babylon, Into—II Ki. 24:13; Jer. 27: 22; 28:3, 6; Dan. 1:2; 5:2. Voice carried by bird—Eccl. 10:20. Wallet— Lu. 10:4. See BEAR, BARE, BORNE, BRING, BROUGHT, LED, TAKE.

Carry about.—Ark—I Sam. 5:8, 9. Sick in beds—Mk. 6:55. Wind of doctrine, By every—Eph. 4:14.

CARRIED ALONG. Wind, By—Jude 12.

CARRIED AWAY. Is. 15:7. Assyria, Into—See CARRY. Babylon, Into—See CARRY. Barnabas—Gal. 2:13; 57:13. Camels—Job. 1:17 (A.V.). Captivity, Into—See CAPTIVITY. Chaff by storm —Job 21:18. Death, Unto—Pr. 24:11. Dwelling—Is. 38:12. Divers teachings, By—Heb. 13:9. Error, With—II Pet. 3:17. Flood, As with a—Ps. 90:5. Hand, In his—Eccl. 5:15. Heart carry thee—Job. 15:12. Idols, By—I Cor. 12:2. Jerusalem—II Ki. 24:14, 15. Jesus—Mk. 15:1. Jewels—II Chr. 20:25. See SPOILS. John—Rev. 17:3; 21:10. Nations—II Ki. 17:11. Nothing—Ps. 49:17. Prey—Is. 5:29. Spirit, In the —Rev. 17:3; 21:10. Spoils—I Sam. 30:18; II Chr. 12:9 (A.V.); 14:13, 15; 16:6; 20:24; 21:17. See SPOILS. Wind, By—Is. 41:16; 57:13 (A.V.); Dan. 2:35. See Eph. 4:14. See CARRY.

CARRY FORTH. Ashes—Lev. 6:11. Bullock without the camp—Lev. 4:21; 16:27. Burden on Sabbath day—Jer. 1:22. See SABBATH. Filthiness—II Chr. 29:5. House of Leper—Lev. 14: 45. See LEPROSY. Naboth—I Ki. 21: 10, 13. Paschal lamb—Ex. 12:46. See CARRY, PASSOVER.

CARRY OUT. Ez. 12:5, 12. Ahab—I Ki. 22:34. Ananias and Sapphira— Acts 5:6, 9, 10. Nothing—I Tim. 6:7; Deut. 28:38. Temple treasures—II

Ki. 24:13. Widow of Nain's son—Lu. 7:12. See CARRY.

CARRY OVER. Josh. 4:3, 8; Acts 7:16.

CARRY UP. Ex. 33:15. Jesus—Lu. 24: 51. See JESUS, ASCENSION OF. Joseph's bones—Gen. 50:25; Ex. 13:19.

CARSHENA, kär'she-nà. **One of the chamberlains of Ahasuerus.** — Esth. 1:4.

CART. Ark carried on—I Sam. 6:7-14; II Sam. 6:3; I Chr. 13:7. Rope—Is. 5:18. Sheaves, Full of—Amos 2:13. Wheel used for threshing—Is. 28:27, 28. See WAGON.

CARVE. Images—See GRAVEN IMAGES. Temple, In the—Ps. 74:6. Cedar—I Ki. 6:18. Doors—I Ki. 6:31-35. Walls —I Ki. 6:29. Wood—Ex. 31:5; 33:35. Work—Ps. 74:6.

CASE. Any, In—See SURELY. Mt. 19:10. Evil—Ex. 5:19; Jonah 4:6. Manslayer, Of—Deut. 19:4. No, In—Mt. 5:20. Paul's—Acts 25:14. Such a— Ps. 144:15.

CASIPHIA, ka-sĭph'ĭ-à. Ezra 8:17.

CASLUHIM, kăs'lu-hĭm. **A tribe descended from Ham.**—Gen. 10:14; I Chr. 1:12.

CASSIA. Ex. 30:24; Ps. 45:8; Ez. 27:19.

CAST, CASTING. Abyss, Into—Rev. 20:3. Altar, Beside—Lev. 1:16. *Brook, Into*—II Ki. 23:12; II Chr. 30:14. *Out of city*—II Chr. 33:15. Angle—Is. 19:8. Anxiety upon him—I Pet. 5:7. Back, Behind the—I Ki. 14:9; Neh. 9:29; Is. 38:17; Ez. 23:35. See Ps. 50: 17. Bodies, Dead—Lev. 26:30; Josh. 8:29; 10:27; II Sam. 18:17; I Ki. 13: 24, 25, 28; II Ki. 13:21; Jer. 26:23; 41:9. Book into Euphrates—Mk. 7:27. Waters, Upon—Eccl. 12:1. Burden upon Jehovah—Ps. 55:22. Care—See ANXIETY. Cave, Into—Josh. 10:27. Children — *Ishmael under shrubs* — Gen. 21:15. *River, Into*—Ex. 1:22. Crowns before the throne—Rev. 4:10. Daniel—Dan. 6:16. David—Ps. 22:10. Death—Rev. 20:14. Den of lions, Into —Dan. 6:7, 12, 16, 24. Devil—Rev. 20: 2, 3, 10. See CAST DOWN, DRAGON. Dogs, To—Ex. 22:31; Mt. 15:26; Mk. 7:27. Dungeons, Into—Jer. 38:6, 9. See PRISON. Dust—Air, Into—Acts 22: 23. *Altars, idols, and images, Of*—II Ki. 23:6, 12. See CAST UP. Earrings

—Ju. 8:25. Earth, Upon the—Mk. 4:
26; Rev. 14:19. See CAST DOWN.
Elisha—Mantle upon—I Ki. 19:19.
Mountain, Upon some—II Ki. 2:16.
Eyes—Gen. 39:7; Mt. 5:29; 18:9; Mk.
9:47. False prophet—Rev. 19:20; 20:
10. Feet, At his—Ex. 4:15. Foot—Mt.
18:8. Fierceness of anger—Job 20:
23; Ps. 78:49. See WRATH. Figs—
Rev. 6:13. Filth—Nah. 3:6. Fire,
Into—II Ki. 19:18; Ps. 140:10; Is.
37:19; Jer. 36:23; Ez. 5:4; 15:4; Mt.
3:10; 7:19; 13:42, 50; 18:8, 9; Mk. 9:
22; Lu. 3:9; John 15:6; Rev. 20:3, 14,
15. Upon the earth—Rev. 8:5, 7. See
FURNACE, HELL. Fitches, Abroad—
Is. 28:25. Fruit—Deut. 28:20; Mal.
3:11. Furnace, Into fiery—Dan. 3:6,
24; Mt. 13:42, 50. Garden, Into—Lu.
13:19. Garment, About—Acts 12:8.
See Mk. 14:51. Over—II Sam. 20:12;
Mk. 11:7; Lu. 19:35. Gifts into treas-
ury—Mk. 12:41–44; Lu. 21:1–4. Gods
into fire—II Ki. 19:18; Is. 37:19. See
IDOLS. Grass into oven—Mt. 6:30; Lu.
12:28. Ground, Thee to—Ez. 28:17.
Hades, Into—Rev. 20:14. See PIT,
SHEOL. Hair—Ez. 5:4. Hand from
thee—Mt. 5:30; 18:8. Hell, Into—
Mt. 5:29, 30; Mk. 9:45, 47; Lu. 12:5;
II Pet. 2:4. Hook—Mt. 17:27. Iniquity upon—Ps. 55:3. Ishmael under
shrubs—Gen. 21:15. Island, Upon an
—Acts 27:26. Jeremiah into dungeon
—Jer. 38:6, 9. Jezebel—Rev. 2:22.
Jonah—Jonah 2:3. See CAST FORTH.
Joseph—Gen. 37:22–24. Land, Into
another—Deut. 29:28; Jer. 22:28. See
Mic. 4:7. See CAST OUT, CAPTIVITY.
Law—Neh. 9:26. Mantle—I Ki. 19:19.
Meal—II Ki. 4:41. Mind, In her—Lu.
1:29. Mire, Into—Job 30:19. Mould-
ed—Ex. 25:12; 26:37; 32:24; 36:36;
37:3, 13; 38:5, 27; I Ki. 7:15, 24, 37,
46; II Chr. 4:3, 17; Is. 40:19. Mountain into sea—Mt. 21:21; Mk. 11:23;
Rev. 8:8. Upon a—II Ki. 19:19. Net
—Mt. 4:18; 13:47; Mk. 1:16; John 21:
6. Into a—Job 18:8. Oven, Into an—
Mt. 6:30; Lu. 12:28. Paul and his
companions—Acts 27:26. Pearls before swine—Mt. 7:6. Pit, Into—Gen.
37:20–24; II Sam. 18:17; Ps. 140:10;
Jer. 41:9. See HADES, SHEOL. Prison,
Into—Mt. 5:25; 18:30; Lu. 12:58; 23:

19, 25; John 3:24; Acts 16:23, 37; Rev.
2:10. Reproach upon Jesus—Mt. 27:
44. River, Into—Ex. 1:22; Jer. 51:63.
Roll into fire—Jer. 36:23. See BOOKS.
Salt—II Ki. 2:21; Ez. 43:21; Mt. 5:13;
Mk. 9:30; Lu. 14:35. Sea, Into—Mt.
18:6; Mk. 9:42; Lu. 17:2; Acts 27:43.
Locusts—Ex. 10:19. *Mountains*—Mt.
21:21; Mk. 11:23; Rev. 8:8. Net—
Mt. 13:47; John 21:6. *Peter*—John
21:7. *Pharaoh's hosts*—Ex. 15:4.
Sins—Mic. 7:19. *Stone*—Rev. 18:21.
Seed—Mk. 4:26; Lu. 13:19. Shadrach,
Meshach and Abednego—Dan. 3:20–
24. Shoe over Edom—Ps. 60:8; 108:9.
Sickle into the earth—Rev. 14:19.
Silver into street—Ez. 7:19. Thirty
pieces—Zech. 11:13. Sins behind the
back—Is. 38:17. *Into sea*—Mic. 7:19.
Sleep, Into—Ps. 19:15. Snare upon
you—I Cor. 7:35. Spear—I Sam. 18:
11; 20:33. Stars—Rev. 12:4. Stick
into Jordan—II Ki. 6:6. Stone—Num.
35:23; Ju. 9:53; II Sam. 11:21; 16:6;
II Ki. 3:25; Jer. 51:63; Lam. 3:53;
Lu. 22:41; John 8:7, 59; Rev. 18:21.
House of leper—Lev. 14:40. Stumbling-
block—Rev. 2:14. See STUMBLING.
Tax into chest—II Chr. 24:10. Tree
—Ex. 15:25; Mt. 3:10; 7:19; Lu. 3:9.
Unclean place, Into an—Lev. 14:40.
Vintage—Rev. 14:19. Waters, Into—
Ex. 15:25. Weight of lead—Zech. 5:8.
Wicked, The—Ps. 140:10; Mt. 13:42,
49, 50; Rev. 20:15. Wickedness—Zech.
5:8. See SINS. Winepress, Into—Rev.
14:19. Words of God—Ps. 78:49.
Young—Gen. 31:38; Ex. 23:26; Job
21:10. See BRING, THROW, THRUST.

CAST AWAY. Ps. 102:10; Eccl. 3:6;
Lu. 9:25; Rom. 11:15; I Cor. 9:27
(A.V.). Abominations — Ez: 20:7, 8.
Bad, The—Mt. 13:48. Boldness—Heb.
10:35. Cords—Ps. 2:3. Figtree—Joel
1:7. Garments—II Ki. 7:15; Mt. 10:
50. Idols—Is. 2:20; 31:7; Ez. 20:7, 8.
See IDOLATRY. Images—Is. 30:22. Is-
rael—Is. 41:9; Jer. 33:26; Hos. 9:17.
See ISRAEL. Jawbone—Jer. 15:17.
Perfect man—Job 8:20. Presence of
Jehovah, From—II Ki. 13:23; Ps. 51:
11. See CAST OFF. Stones—Eccl. 3:5.
Transgressions—Ez. 18:31. See CAST.

CAST DOWN. Angels—II Pet. 2:4;
Rev. 12:9. Beauty of Israel—Lam.

2:1. Comforting the—II Cor. 7:6
(A.V.). Destruction, To—Ps. 73:18.
Dragon—Rev. 12:9, 10, 13. Dust—II
Sam. 16:13. Earth, To—Is..28:2; Lam.
2:1; Rev. 12:4, 9, 10, 13. Ezra—Ezra
10:1. Hell, Into—II Pet. 2:4. See
CAST. Imaginations—II Cor. 10:5.
Jesus—Lu. 4:29. Cast thyself down—
Mt. 4:6; Lu. 4:9. Light of counte-
nance—Job 29:24. Men and women
—II Chr. 25:8, 12; Neh. 6:16; Job 22:
29; 41:9; Ps. 37:29; 62:4 (A.V.); Dan.
11:12; II Cor. 4:9 (A.V.). See WICKED.
Pit, Into—Ez. 32:18. See CAST, SHEOL.
Poor and needy—Ps. 37:14. Rod—Ex.
4:3; 7:9, 10, 12. Sanctuary, Place of
—Dan. 8:11. Satan—Rev. 12:9, 10, 13.
Sheol, Into—Ez. 31:16; 32:18. See
SHEOL. Silver, Thirty pieces of—Mt.
27:5. See Zech. 11:13. Slain men—
Ez. 6:4. Soul—Ps. 42:5, 6, 11; 43:5.
See DESPAIR. Stars to earth—Dan.
8:10; Rev. 12:4. Stones from heaven
—Josh. 10:11. Truth—Dan. 8:12.
Vine—Ez. 19:12. Wicked—Job 18:7;
Ps. 17:13; 36:12; 147:6 (A.V.); Jer.
6:15; Ez. 19:12. See MEN AND WOMEN.
Wounded by harlot—Pr. 7:26. See
BOW DOWN, CAST, CAST OFF, DESPAIR,
HUMILIATION.

CAST FORTH. Branch, As a—John
15:6. Dead bodies—Is. 26:19; Amos
8:13. Demon—Mk. 7:26. Darkness,
Into—Mt. 8:12. Grave, From the—
Is. 14:19. Ice—Ps. 147:17. Israel
cast forth roots—Jer. 16:13; Hos. 14:
5. Jehoiakim—Jer. 22:19. Jonah—
Jonah 1:12, 15; 2:4. Kingdom, Children of—Mt. 8:12. Lightning—Ps.
144:6. Pharaoh—Ez. 32:4. Roots—
Hos. 14:5. Tobiah and his household
stuff—Neh. 13:8. Wares—Jonah 1:5.
Waters—Jer. 6:7. Wickedness—Jer.
6:7. See CAST OUT.

CASTING LOTS: Method of.—Pr. 16:
33.

Examples of.—Saul and Jonathan—I
Sam. 14:42. Sons of Levites—I Chr.
24:31; Neh. 10:34. Priests—Neh. 10:
34. People—Neh. 10:34; 11:1. For
offices—I Chr. 24:31; 25:8; 26:13, 14;
Esth. 3:7; 9:24; Acts 1:26. To determine courses of priests—I Chr.
6:54–81; 24:5; 26:14. For inherit-

ances—Num. 26:55; Josh. 14:2; 15:1.
To find evil-doer—Jonah 1:7.

Lots mentioned.—Pur—Esth. 3:7; 9:24.
Scapegoat—Lev. 16:8. For vesture—
Ps. 22:18; Mt. 27:35; Mk. 15:24. Mat-
thias—Acts 1:26.

Figurative.—Is. 34:17.

CAST. MOULDING.—Ex. 25:12; 26:
37; 32:24; 36:36; 37:3, 13; 38:5, 27;
I Ki. 7:15; 24:37, 46; I Chr. 4:3, 17;
Is. 40:19.

CAST OFF. I Chr. 28:9; Ps. 43:2; 44:
9, 23; 60:1, 10; 71:9; 74:1; 77:7; 88:
14; 89:38; 94:14; 108:11; Jer. 33:24;
Lam. 3:31; Mic. 4:7; Zech. 10:6; Rom.
11:1–3. Altar—Lam. 2:7. Calf of Samaria—Hos. 8:5. Fear—Job 15:4
(A.V.). Flower—Job 15:33. Good, The
—Hos. 8:3. Israel, Seed of—Jer. 31:
37. Jerusalem—II Ki. 23:27. Levites
—II Chr. 11:14. Pity—Amos 1:11.
Pledge—I Tim. 5:12 (A.V.). Works of
darkness—Rom. 13:12.

CAST OUT. II Chr. 20:11; Neh. 1:9;
Jer. 22:28; 66:5; Mt. 5:13; John 6:37.
Anchors—Acts 27:29, 30. Baal, Wor-
shippers of—II Ki. 10:25. Babes—
Acts 7:19. Beam—Mt. 7:5; Lu. 6:42.
Blind man—John 9:34, 35. See HAND-
MAID. Church, Of—III John 10. Coniah—Jer. 22:26, 28. Demons—See
DEMONS, POSSESSION OF. Edom—Ez.
36:5. Enemies—Ps. 18:42; Zeph. 3:
15. Handmaid and her son—Gen. 21:
10; Gal. 4:30. Idols—II Chr. 33:15.
Israel—II Ki. 17:20; 24:20; Jer. 14:
16. Jehoiakim—Jer. 36:30. Jehovah
—Jer. 51:34. Jerusalem—Ez. 36:5.
Man without wedding garment—Mt.
22:13. Moses—Acts 7:21. Mote—Mt.
7:5; Lu. 6:42. Name as evil—Lu.
6:22. Nations—Ex. 34:24; Lev. 18:
24; 20:23; Deut. 7:1; I Ki. 21:26; II
Ki. 16:3; 17:8; 21:2; II Chr. 28:3;
33:2; Zech. 9:4 (A.V.). Pains—Job
39:13. Poor—Is. 58:7. Riches—Job
20:15. Scoffer—Pr. 22:10. Servants,
Unprofitable—Mt. 25:30. Slain—Is.
34:3. Son from vineyard—Mt. 21:39;
Mk. 12:8; Lu. 20:15. Stephen—Acts
7:58. Tables of Ten Commandments—
Ex. 32:19; Deut. 9:17. Tackling of
ship—Acts 27:19. Traders from temple—Mt. 21:12; Mk. 11:15; Lu. 19:45.
Waters out of mouth of serpent—Rev.

12:15, 16. Women—Mic. 2:9. See DRIVE OUT, THRUST OUT.

CAST UP. Mounds—II Sam. 20:15; II Ki. 19:32; Is. 37:33; Jer. 6:6; Ez. 4:2; 17:17; 21:22; 26:8; Dan. 11:15. See BANK, EMBANKMENT, FORTIFICATION.

CASTAWAY. I Cor. 9:27 (A.V.). See REJECT.

CASTLE. I Ki. 16:18; I Chr. 27:25; II Chr. 17:12; 27:4; Is. 13:22; Acts 23:16, 32. Bars of—Pr. 18:19. Paul brought into—Acts 21:34, 37; 22:24; 23:10. See ENCAMPMENT, FORTIFICATION, PALACES, STRONGHOLD.

CASTOR AND POLLUX. Name of ship in which Paul sailed to Rome.—Acts 28:11 (A.V.). Translated *twin brothers* in Revised Version.

CATCH, CAUGHT. Gen. 39:12; Ju. 1:6; 8:14; II Sam. 2:16; I Ki. 20:33; II Chr. 22:9; Ps. 109:11; Pr. 7:13. Absalom.by the hair—II Sam. 18:9. Beard, By the—I Sam. 17:35. Fire—Ex. 22: 6. See FIRE. Foxes, by Samson—Ju. 15:4. Horns of the altar—I Ki. 1:50; 2:28. Jesus—Mk. 12:24; II Cor. 12: 2, 4; Rev. 12:5. See JESUS, ASCENSION OF. Net, in—Ps. 35:8; Hab. 1:15. See NET. Philip—Acts 8:39. Poor—Ps. 10:9. Prey—Ez. 19:3, 6. Ship—Acts 27:15. Works—Lu. 11:54. See FIND, LAY HOLD, SEIZE, SNATCH, TAKE.

CATERPILLAR. I Ki. 8:37; II Chr. 6:28; Ps. 78:46; Is. 33:4; Joel 1:4; 2:25. See CANKER WORM.

CATTLE: In a general sense.—Created —Gen. 1:24, 25. Names given to— Gen. 2:20. Man has dominion over— Gen. 1:26.

The serpent "cursed above all cattle." —Gen. 3:14.

Cattle in relation to ark.—Entrance— Gen. 7:14. Destroyed by flood—Gen. 7:21, 23. Preserved—Gen. 8:1. Brought forth—Gen. 8:17. Covenant established with—Gen. 9:10.

Abram rich in.—Gen. 13:2. Isaac's possessions—Gen. 26:14. Jacob's—Gen. 31:9; 34:5; John 4:12.

Joseph's report of brethren's possessions to Pharaoh.—Gen. 46:32; 47:6. Egyptians surrender cattle for food—Gen. 47:17–18.

Jehovah's hand upon Egyptian cattle.— Ex. 9:3–7. Firstborn of cattle smitten—Ex. 12:29.

Miscellaneous.—Israel's cattle on the march—Ex. 12:38. Cattle to increase —Lev. 25:7. Levites' cattle taken— Num. 3:41–45. Edom refuses to allow cattle to pass—Num. 20:19–21. Gad and Reuben pasture cattle beyond the Jordan—Num. 32:1, 4, 16. Ai's cattle taken as spoil—Josh. 8:2, 27. Cattle on a thousand hills—Ps. 50:10. Grass to grow for—Ps. 104:14. Cattle praise him—Ps. 148:10.

Prophetic allusions.—Idols upon cattle— Is. 46:1. Hear not the voice of—Jer. 9:10. Calls for drought upon—Hag. 1:11. Jerusalem to be filled with— Zech. 2:4. Much cattle in Nineveh— Jonah 4:11.

CAUDA, kạu'dȧ. A small island south of Crete where the ship on which Paul was going to Rome was wrecked.— Acts 27:16. See CLAUDA—Acts 27:16 (A.V.).

CAUL. Law concerning offering: Of bullock—Ex. 29:13; Lev. 8:16. Of ram—Ex. 29:22; Lev. 8:25. In peaceoffering—Lev. 3:4, 10, 15. Sin-offering —Lev. 4:9; 8:16, 25; 9:10, 19. Trespassoffering—Lev. 7:4. Figurative: In prophecies—Is. 3:18; Hos. 13:8.

CAUSE, *n*. Jonah 1:7, 8; Eph. 3:1, 14; II Tim. 1:12; Heb. 2:11; II Pet. 1:5. Afflicted, Of—Ps. 140:12; Pr. 22:22, 23; 31:8. Commit unto God—Job 5:8. See PLEAD. Death, Of—Lu. 23:22; Acts 13:28; 28:18. Fatherless, Of—Ps. 23: 11; Jer. 5:28. Judge—Ex. 23:2, 3, 6; Jer. 5:28; 22:16; Lam. 3:59. Maintain—I Ki. 8:45, 49; II Chr. 6:35, 39; Ps. 9:4; 112:5; 140:12. Offender in— Is. 29:21. Plead—I Sam. 24:15; 25: 39; Ps. 43:1; 74:22; 119:154; Pr. 22: 33; 23:11; Jer. 30:13; 50:34; 51:36; Lam. 3:58; Mic. 7:9. Poor, Of the— Ex. 23:3, 6; Pr. 22:22, 23; 29:7; Jer. 22:16. Righteous, Is—Job 6:29. Widow, Of the—Is. 1:23. See WIDOW. Without—Ps. 25:3; 35:7; 69:4; 109:3; 119: 161; Pr. 1:11; 3:30.

CAUSEWAY. I Chr. 26:16, 18.

CAVES: Located in.—Field—Gen. 23:9, 11, 17. Rocks—Is. 2:19.

Used for.—Dwellings (Lot)—Gen. 19: 30; Ju. 6:2. Burial places—Gen. 23: 19, 20; 25:9; 49:29, 30, 32; 50:13; John 11:38. Hiding places—*Of five kings*—Josh. 10:16, 17, 18, 22, 23, 27. *Of David* —I Sam. 22:1; 24:3, 7, 8, 10; II Sam. 23:13; I Chr. 11:15. *Of prophets*—I Ki. 18:4, 13; 19:9. *Children of Israel*— I Sam. 13:6; Heb. 11:38.

Mentioned in title of.—Pss. 57, 142.

Prophecies concerning.—Ez. 33:27.

CEASE. Ju. 5:7; 15:7; 20:28; Ps. 12:1; Is. 30:11; Acts 21:14; Eph. 1:16. Anger —Ps. 37:8. Arrogancy—Is. 13:11. Contention—Pr. 18:18; 26:20. Egypt— Ez. 30:10, 18. Evil—Is. 1:16; 33:28. Gladness—Jer. 7:34; 16:9. Grinders —Eccl. 12:3. House of Israel—Jer. 31:36; Hos. 1:4. Idols—Ez. 6:6; 30: 13. Indignation—Ps. 85:4. Manna— Jas. 5:12. Mirth—Jer. 7:34; 16:9; Ez. 26:13; Hos. 2:11. Praying—I Sam. 7:8; 12:23; Lu. 11:1; Col. 1:9; I Thess. 5:17. Preach, Go—Acts 5:42; 20:31. Pride—Ez. 7:24. Reproach—Dan. 11: 18. Sacrifice—Dan. 9:27; Heb. 10:2. Sin—Ez. 16:41; 23:27, 48; I Pet. 4:1; II Pet. 2:14. Strife—Pr. 22:10. Teach —Acts 5:42. Thunder—Ex. 9:29, 33, 34. Tongues—I Cor. 13:8. Trouble— Job 3:17. Wars—Ps. 46:9. See DE-STROY, KEEP ALOOF, KILL.

CEDAR. Altar overlaid with—I Ki. 6: 20. Chest made of—Ez. 27:24. Lebanon celebrated for—Ju. 9:15; Ps. 92: 12. Leper, Used in purification of— Lev. 14:4–7; 49–52. Masts of ships, Used in—Ez. 27:5. Offering, Used in —Lev. 14:4, 6, 49, 51, 52; Num. 19:6. Palaces built of: *David's*—II Sam. 5: 11. *Solomon's*—I Ki. 7:2, 3, 7, 12. Palanquin or chariot made of—Song of Sol. 3:9. Temple, Used in—I Ki. 7:11. Water of separation—Num. 19:6.

Illustrative.—Num. 24:6; Ps. 92:12; Is. 10:33, 34; Ez. 17:22, 23; Amos 2:9.

CEDRON. See KIDRON.

CELEBRATE. Lev. 23:32, 41 (A. V.); Ju. 11:40; Is. 38:18.

CELESTIAL. Body—I Cor. 15:40. See ASTRONOMY.

CELLAR. Oil, Of—I Chr. 27:28. Wine, Of—I Chr. 27:27.

CENCHREAE, kĕn′kre·ae. **Eastern harbor of Corinth.**—Acts 18:18; Rom. 16:1.

CENSER. Incense burned in—Lev. 10: 5; 16:12; Num. 16:6, 17, 18, 46; II Chr. 26:19; Ez. 8:11; Rev. 8:3, 5. Tabernacle, In—Num. 9:4 (marg.). See FIREPANS, TABERNACLE.

CENTURION. Crucifixion, At—Mt. 27: 54; Mk. 15:39; Lu. 23:47. Cornelius— Acts 10:1–48. Jesus, Believes in—Lu. 7:2. Paul, *Arrests*—Acts 21:32; 22: 25, 26; 24:23. *Fears*—Acts 22:23, 26. *Saves*—Acts 27:43. Peter, Sends for— Acts 10:1, 22. Servant of—Lu. 7:1– 10. See SOLDIER.

CEPHAS, sē′phas. Simon Peter called —by Jesus—John 1:42. Followers of —I Cor. 1:12; 3:22. Jesus appears to—I Cor. 15:5. Paul visits—Gal. 1: 18. Gives hand of fellowship to Paul —Gal. 2:9. See PETER.

CEREMONIAL. See OFFERING, ORDINANCE, SACRIFICE.

CEREMONIAL CLEANSING. Typical of purification from sin. The Israelites underwent a severe training both for themselves and for us—Heb. 9: 8–10.

The priest.—The initiation—Ex. 29:4, 20; 40:12; Lev. 8:6. Daily ministrations—Ex. 30:19–21; 40:31–32; II Chr. 4:6. On Day of Atonement—Lev. 16: 4, 24, 26, 28. Purify the unclean— Num. 19:7–10. Cleansing the Levites —Num. 8:7.

The congregation.—Their garments— Ex. 19:10, 14; Lev. 11:25, 40. Themselves—Num. 31:24; II Chr. 30:17–18.

The individual.—Issues of men—Lev. 15:1–18; 22:4–7. Of women—Lev. 12: 6–8; Num. 5:16–28.

The leper.—Lev. Chs. 11, 13, 14. Miriam a leper—Num. 12:10–15.

Healed by Jesus.—Mt. 8:2–4; Mk. 1:40–44; Lu. 5:12–14.

The garments.—Of priests—Ex. 29:21; Lev. 6:27; Num. 19:7–10. Of people— Ex. 19:10, 14; Lev. 11:25, 40; 14:8, 47; 15:5–27.

The sacrifice.—Lev. 1:9, 13; 8:21; 9:14; II Chr. 4:6.

Altar, furniture, etc.—Ex. 29:20; 40:9– 11; Lev. 1:5, 11; 3:2, 8, 13; 7:2; 17:6;

Num. 18:17; Heb. 9:18–22. See PURI-
FICATION.

CERTAIN, CERTAINTY. I Sam. 23:
23; 26:4. Know—Josh. 23:13; I Ki.
2:37, 42; Jer. 26:15; Dan. 2:8; Lu.
1:4; Acts 21:34; 22:30.

CERTIFY. II Sam. 15:28; Ezra 4:14,
16; 5:10; 7:24. See WITNESS.

CHAFE. II Sam. 17:8.

CHAFF. Which the storm carrieth away
—Job 21:18. Which the wind driveth
away—Ps. 1:4; 35:5; Is. 17:13; Hos.
13:3. Burn up—Mt. 3:12; Lu. 3:17.

Figurative.—Is. 17:13; 29:5; 33:11; 41:
15; Dan. 2:35; Hos. 13:3; Zeph. 2:2.

CHAINS. Kinds of: Golden, worn as a
badge of office—Gen. 41:42; Dan. 5:7,
16, 29. Brass—Ju. 16:21. In the temple—I Ki. 7:17. Silver—For idols—
Is. 40:19. Of iron—Ps. 105:18.

Uses of.—As ornaments—Num. 31:50;
Song of Sol. 1:10; Is. 3:19, 20; Ez.
16:11. Put on high priest's breastplate—Ex. 28:14, 22, 24; 39:15, 17, 18.
In the temple—I Ki. 6:21. Worn on
camels' necks—Ju. 8:26. Bound with
—Jer. 40:1, 4; 52:1; Nah. 3:10; Lu.
8:29; Acts 12:6, 7; 21:33; 28:20. As
fetters—II Ki. 25:7; II Chr. 33:11;
36:6; Jer. 39:7; Mk. 5:4. Of brass—
Ju. 16:21. Of iron—Ps. 149:8. For
feet—II Sam. 3:34; Ps. 105:18.

Illustrative.—Ps. 73:6; Pr. 1:9; Lam.
3:7; Ez. 7:23–27; Rev. 20:1. See
BONDAGE, FETTERS.

CHALCEDONY. A precious stone—
Rev. 21:19.

CHALCOL. See CALCOL.

CHALDEA. Southern portion of Babylonia—Land of captivity—Ez. 11:24.

Inhabitants.—Babylonians — Ez. 23:15.
Temptation and unfaithfulness of—
Ez. 23:14–19. Prophecy against—Jer.
50:10; 51:24, 35.

CHALKSTONE. Is. 27:9.

CHAMBER. Bridegroom—Ps. 19:5;
Joel 2:16. Guard—I Ki. 14:28; II
Chr. 12:11. Temple, Of—I Ki. 6:5
(A.V.); I Chr. 9:33; II Chr. 31:11; Ezra
4:29; Neh. 10:37–39; 13:4, 7; Jer. 35:4.
Upper—Acts 1:13; 9:37, 39; 20:8. See
ROOM, STORY.

CHAMBERLAIN. II Ki. 23:11; Esth.
1:10, 12, 15; 2:3, 14, 15, 21; 4:4, 5; 6:

2, 14; 7:9; Jer. 51:59; Acts 12:20. See
TREASURER.

CHAMELEON. Lev. 11:30.

CHAMOIS. Deut. 14:5.

CHAMPION. I Sam. 17:4, 23, 51.

CHANCE. Deut. 22:6; II Sam. 1:6;
Eccl. 9:11; Lu. 10:31; I Cor. 15:37.

CHANCELLOR. Ezra 4:4, 9, 17.

CHANGE. Job 17:12; Pr. 24:21. Be-
havior—I Sam. 2:13; Ps. 34 title.
Body—Job 14:14 (A.V.); Jer. 13:23;
Dan. 3:2; I Cor. 15:51, 52; Phil. 3:21
(A.V.). Clothing—Gen. 35:2; 41:14;
45:22; Ju. 14:1, 13; II Sam. 12:20; II
Ki. 5:5, 22, 23; 25:29; Ps. 102:26; Ju.
53:33; Heb. 1:12. Countenance—Dan.
3:19; 5:6, 9, 10; 7:28. Customs of Mo-
ses—Acts 6:14. Glory—Ps. 106:20;
Jer. 2:11; Rom. 1:23. *Into shame*—
Hos. 4:7. God—Jer. 2:11. Gold—
Lam. 4:1. Heart—Ex. 14:5; Dan. 4:
16. Law—Dan. 6:8, 15; Heb. 7:12.
Mind—Heb. 1:11 (A.V.); Acts 28:6.
Money—John 2:14, 15. Money-chang-
ers—See TRADERS. Name—Num. 32:
38; II Ki. 24:17. People—Mic. 2:4.
Priesthood—Heb. 7:12. Seasons—Dan.
2:21. Wages—Gen. 31:7, 41. Word—
Dan. 3:28. See CLOTHING, EXCHANGE,
PASS, RELEASE, TRANSFORM.

CHANNEL. Job 6:15; 28:10; 38:25;
Ez. 31:4.

CHARACTER. See JESUS, CHARACTER
OF; JESUS' TEACHING ON CHARACTER;
BEHAVE, BEHAVIOR, CONDUCT, CHRIS-
TIAN GRACES, RIGHTEOUS, WICKED.

CHARGE. Mt. 9:30; Mk. 9:43; Lu. 9:
21. Accusers—Acts 23:30. Against,
Charges—Acts 25:27. Allotted charge
—I Pet. 5:3. David to Solomon—I
Ki. 2:1. Job sinned not nor charged
God—Job 1:22. Gospel without charge
—I Cor. 9:18. Grievous charge—Acts
25:7. Lay not—Acts 7:60. Love, end
of charge (*n.*)—I Tim. 1:5. Moses,
To—Ex. 6:13. Paul to Timothy—I
Tim. 5:21 (*v.*).

CHARGER. Head of John the Baptist
on—Mt. 4:8 (A.V.); Mk. 6:23, 28 (A.V.).
See PLATTER.

CHARIOT. **Used by.**—Absalom—II
Sam. 15:1. Adonijah prepares—I Ki.
1:5. Ahab—II Chr. 18:33, 34. Jehu—
II Ki. 10:2. Rehoboam—I Ki. 12:18.

Art, In.—Chariots of the sun—II Ki. 23:11. Cherubim-like—I Chr. 28:18. Merchandise of Babylon—Rev. 18:13. Wheels of, In brazen sea of temple—I Ki. 7:33.

God's providence, In.—Destruction of: *Israel*—Mic. 5:10. *Lachish*—Mic. 1:13. *Nineveh*—Nah. 3:2. *Philistines*—Jer. 47:3, 4. *Shebna*—Is. 22:18. Elijah ascended in—II Ki. 2:11, 12. Hosts of heaven use chariot of fire—II Ki. 6:17. Like noise of—Joel 2:5. Like a whirlwind—Is. 66:15; Jer. 4:13.

Peace, In.—Ethiopian journeys to worship—Acts 8:28, 29, 38. Joseph rides in—Gen. 41:43; 46:29; 50:9. Men ran before—Gen. 41:43; I Sam. 8:11. Naaman to find Elisha—II Ki. 5:9, 21, 26.

War, In.—Armed with swords—Jer. 50: 37. Captains—I Ki. 22:31-33; II Ki. 8:21. Chief captains—I Ki. 16:9. Construction of iron—Josh. 17:16, 18; Ju. 1:19; 4:3. Cost 600 shekels, imported from Egypt—I Ki. 10:29; II Chr. 1:17. Driver—I Ki. 22:34. Flash with steel —Nah. 2:3. Looked like torches, ran with lightning, raging in the streets—Nah. 2:3. Rushing—Jer. 47:3.

Battle, In.—David took 1,000—I Chr. 18:4. Hazael left only ten to Samaria—II Ki. 13:7. Israel not to fear —Deut. 20:1. Smote Syrian—I Ki. 20:1, 21, 25, 33. Not to trust on Egypt for—II Ki. 18:24. Battle-axe to destroy—Jer. 51:22. Jabin defeated—Josh. 11:4-6, 9. Nineveh's to be destroyed—Nah. 2:13. Pharaoh—Ex. 14:6, 7, 9, 17, 18, 23-28; Deut. 11:4; Josh. 24:6; Ps. 76:6. Philistines—I Sam. 13:5. Saul pursued by—II Sam. 1:6. Sennacherib against Jerusalem —II Ki. 19:23; Is. 37:24. Sisera—Ju. 4:7, 13, 15, 16. Syrians terrified by noise of—II Ki. 7:6. Trust in, Must not—Ps. 20:7.

Kings killed in.—Ahab—I Ki. 22:34, 35. Ahaziah—II Ki. 9:27-28. Joram—II Ki. 8:21; 9:21, 24.

Named in song and lament.—Deborah's —Ju. 5:28. Joash over Elisha—II Ki. 13:14. Mentioned in Moses' song—Ex. 15:14.

Number.—Ammonites hired 32,000—I Chr. 19:7. Egyptians had 1,200—II Chr. 12:3. Jabin had 900—Ju. 4:3.

Philistines claimed 30,000—I Sam. 13: 5. Solomon had 1,400—I Ki. 10:26; II Chr. 9:25. Syrians had 700—I Chr. 19:18. Zerah the Ethiopian had 300 —I Chr. 14:9.

Figurative. Comparison with Song of Solomon—1:9; 6:12. Israel to ride in, to make an oblation—Is. 66:20. Locusts wings sound like—Rev. 9:9.

Symbol of Omnipresence.—Ps. 68:17. Salvation—Hab. 3:8. Swiftness—Ps. 104:3. Vision of—Zech. 6:1, 2, 3, 6.

CHARITY. See LOVE.

CHARM. Ps. 58:5. See MAGIC.

CHARMER. Deut. 18:11; Ps. 58:5; Is. 19:3. See ENCHANTER, MAGIC.

CHASE. Enemies—Lev. 26:7. Hundred—Lev. 26:8. Mother—Pr. 19: 26. Nations shall be—Is. 17:13. Philistines—I Sam. 17:53. Roe—Is. 13: 14. Terrors—Job 18:11; 30:15 (A.V.). Thousand—Deut. 30:30; Josh. 23:10.

CHASTE, CHASTITY. Tit. 2:5; I Pet. 2:3; Eccl. 7:26. Enjoined—Pr. 21:3; Acts 15:20; Rom. 13:13; I Cor. 6:13-18; Col. 3:5; I Thess. 4:3; Tit. 2:5; Heb. 13:4; I Pet. 4:1-3. Heart, In—Pr. 6:24, 25. Look, In—Job 31:1; Mt. 5:28. Speech, In—Eph. 5:3. See TONGUE. Unchaste shall not enter heaven—Eph. 5:5, 6; Heb. 13:4; Rev. 22:14. Unchaste, Shun company of—Pr. 5:3-11; 7:10-27; 22:14; Eccl. 7: 26; I Cor. 5:11; I Pet. 3:1, 2. See HARLOT. Wicked are not—Eph. 4:19; II Pet. 2:14; Jude 8. See ABSTINENCE, ADULTERY, FORNICATION, LUST.

CHASTEN. Job 33:19; Heb. 12:11; Rev. 3:19. Children—Deut. 8:5; 21: 18; Pr. 13:24; 19:18. See CHILDREN, PUNISHMENT OF. God, By—Deut. 8:5; Job 5:17; Ps. 94:12; 118:18; Pr. 3:11; I Cor. 11:32; Eph. 6:4; Heb. 12:5, 7. Rod, With—II Sam. 7:14. See ROD. Self—Ps. 69:10; Dan.. 10:12 (A.V.). See PUNISHMENT, SELF-DENIAL.

CHASTISE. I Ki. 12:11, 14; II Chr. 10: 11, 14; Job 34:31; Jer. 31:18; Hos. 7: 12; 10:10; Heb. 12:8. Jehovah, By—Lev. 26:18, 28; Deut. 11:2; Ps. 94:10; Jer. 30:14. Jesus—Is. 53:5; Lu. 23: 16, 22. See AFFLICTION; JESUS, SUFFERINGS OF; PUNISHMENT.

CHATTER. Is. 38:14.

CHEBAR, ke'bar. A river mentioned by Ezekiel.—Ez. 1:1, 3; 3:15, 23; 10: 15, 20, 22; 43:3.

CHECK. I Sam. 24:7; Job 20:3 (A.V.).

CHECKERWORK. I Ki. 7:17.

CHEDORLAOMER, kĕd'or-lā'o-mer. King of Elam in days of Abraham— Gen. 14:1–17.

CHEEK. Smite—I Ki. 22:24; II Chr. 18:23; Job 16:10; Ps. 3:7; Is. 50:6; Lam. 3:30; Mic. 5:11; Mt. 5:39; Lu. 6:29. Turn other—Mt. 5:39; Lu. 6:29. See FACE.

CHEER. Eccl. 11:9; Job 9:27.

Good.—Mt. 9:2, 22; 14:27; Mk. 6:50; 10: 49; John 16:33; Acts 23:11; 27:22, 25, 36. Wife—Deut. 24:5.

CHEERFUL. I Sam. 15:32; Pr. 15:13– 15; 17:22; Zech. 8:19; Acts 24:14. Giver—II Cor. 9:7. See LIBERALITY.

CHEERFULNESS. Rom. 12:8.

CHEESE. I Sam. 17:18; II Sam. 17:29; Job 10:10.

CHELAL, ke'lal. One of the family of Pahath-moab who had married a foreign wife.—Ezra 10:30.

CHELUHI, kĕl'u-hī. One of the family of Bani who had married a foreign wife.—Ezra 10:35.

CHELUB, ke'lub. (1) Father of Mehir. —I Chr. 4:11.

(2) Father of Ezri.—I Chr. 27:26.

CHELUBAI, ke-lū'bāi. Son of Hezron. —I Chr. 2:9.

CHEMARIM, kĕm'a-rĭm. Zeph. 1:4.

CHEMOSH, ke-mŏsh. (The national idol of Moabites; Dibon was the chief seat of its worship.)—Num. 21:29, 30; I Ki. 11:33. Mentioned as god of the Ammonites—Ju. 11:24.

High place built for.—I Ki. 11:7; II Ki. 23:13.

Prophecy concerning.—Jer. 48:7, 13, 46.

CHENAANAH, ke-nā'a-nah. (1) Father of Zedekiah.—I Ki. 22:11, 24; II Chr. 18:10, 23.

(2) Son of Benjamin.—I Chr. 7:10.

CHENANI, kĕn'a-nī. A Levite who led worship after Ezra had finished reading the law.—Neh. 9:4.

CHEPHAR-AMMONI, ke'phar-ăm'mo-ni. A city of Benjamin.—Josh. 18:24.

CHEPHIRAH, ke-phī'rah. A village in Benjamin.—Josh. 9:17.

CHERAN, ke'ran. Son of Dishon.—Gen. 36:26; I Chr. 1:41.

CHERETHITES. (1) A Philistine tribe in southern part of Canaan.—I Sam. 30:14; Ez. 25:16; Zeph. 2:5.

(2) Officers of David.—II Sam. 8:18; 15:18; 20:7, 23; I Ki. 1:38, 44; I Chr. 18:17.

CHERISH. I Ki. 1:2, 4; Eph. 5:9; I Thess. 2:7. See NOURISH.

CHERITH. A brook near Jericho, where Elijah hid.—I Ki. 17:3, 5.

CHERUBIM. Placed at entrance of Eden—Gen. 3:24. Form and appearance of—Ez. 1:5–14. Working out purpose of God—I Sam. 4:4; Ez. 1:15– 21; 10:9–17. Display the glory of Jehovah—Is. 37:16; Ez. 9:3; 1:26–28; 10:4–5. Figures on walls of tabernacle—Ex. 26:1; 36:8; 37:7–9, On the veil—Ex. 26:31; 36:35. In the temple—I Ki. 6:23–29; II Chr. 3:10– 14. The ark was under wings of—I Ki. 8:6–7; I Chr. 5:7–8; 13:6; Ez. 28: 16. Figures of, on temple veil—II Chr. 3:14. On the walls—I Ki. 6:29– 35; II Chr. 3:7. On the lavers—I Ki. 7:29, 36. In Ezekiel's vision—Ez. 10: 20; 11:22; 41:18–25. Made of gold— Ex. 25:18–20; I Chr. 28:18. David refers to—Ps. 80:1; 18:10; II Sam. 22: 11. God manifested at place of—II Sam. 6:2; II Ki. 19:15; Ps. 99:1; Num. 7:89. Cherubim of glory, overshadowing mercy-seat—Heb. 9:5.

CHESALON, kĕs'a-lŏn. A village of Judah.—Josh. 15:10.

CHESED, ke'sed. Son of Nahor and nephew of Abraham.—Gen. 22:22.

CHESTNUT. Gen. 30:37 (A.V.); Ez. 31:8 (A.V.). See TREES.

CHEST. Clothing, Of—Ez. 27:24. Money —II Ki. 12:9, 10; II Chr. 20:6, 10, 11.

CHESULLOTH, ke-sŭl'loth. A town.— Josh. 19:18.

CHEZIB, ke'zeb. Birthplace of Shelah. —Gen. 38:5.

CHICKEN. See BIRDS AND FOWLS.

CHIDE. Gen. 31:36; 17:2, 7 (A.V.); Ju. 8:11; Ps. 103:9. See STRIVE.

CHIDON, kī'don. I Chr. 13:9.

CHIEF. See CAPTAIN, PRIEST, PRINCE, SEAT.

CHILDREN: The chosen type of the kingdom.—Mt. 18:2–5; 19:14; Mk. 10:

14, 15; Lu. 18:17; I Cor. 14:20; I Pet. 2:2.

Promised as an inducement to righteousness.—Gen. 15:5; 22:17; Ex. 32:13; Lev. 26:9; Deut. 7:12–14; 13:17; 30:5; Job 5:24, 25; Ps. 45:16, 17; 128:1–6; Is. 44:3, 4; 48:18, 19; Jer. 33:22; Rom. 4:18.

Come from God.—Gen. 4:1, 25; 17:20; 29:31–35; 30:2, 6, 17–20; 33:5; 48:9; Deut. 7:13; Ruth 4:13; I Sam. 1:19, 20; Ps. 107:41; 113:9; 127:3–5; 128:1–6.

Children a blessing.—Gen. 5:29; Ps. 113:9; 127:3–5; Pr. 10:1; 15:20; 17:6; 23:24; 27:11; 29:3.

Childlessness an affliction.—Gen. 15:2, 3; 30:1; I Sam. 1:6, 7; Jer. 20:30; 22:30; Lu. 1:25.

Given in answer to prayer.—Gen. 15:2–5; 25:21; I Sam. 1:10–20, 27; Lu. 1:13.

By special appointment.—Isaac—Gen. 15:2–6; 17:16; 21:1–3. Jacob and Esau—Gen. 15:21–26. Samuel—I Sam. 1:11, 19, 20. John the Baptist—Lu. 1:13–25, 57–80; Lu. 1:26–42. Jesus—Mt. 1:18–23; Lu. 1:26–38.

Children taken away in punishment.—Ex. 12:29, 30; Deut. 28:32, 41; II Sam. 12:14, 15; Job 27:14, 15; Ps. 21:10, 11; Hos. 9:12.

Covenant of circumcision.—Gen. 17:10–14; Lev. 12:3; Phil. 3:5.

Named.—Gen. 21:3; 30:6, 8, 10, 13, 18, 20, 21, 24; 41:51, 52; Ex. 2:22. Ruth 4:17; I Sam. 4:21. At circumcision—Lu. 1:59; 2:21. After relatives—Lu. 1:59, 61. From remarkable events—Gen. 21:3, 6; 18:13; Ex. 2:10; 18:3, 4. From circumstances connected with their birth—Gen. 25:25, 26; 35:18; I Chr. 4:9. Named by God—Is. 8:3; Hos. 1:4, 6, 9; Lu. 1:31.

Treatment at birth.—Ez. 16:4–6; Lu. 2:7, 12.

Brought early to the house of the Lord.—I Sam. 1:24.

Weaning of.—Gen. 21:8; I Sam. 1:22–24; I Ki. 11:20; Ps. 131:2; Is. 11:8; 28:9.

Nurses of.—Gen. 24:59; Ex. 2:7, 9; Ruth 4:16; II Sam. 4:4; II Ki. 11:2.

Adopted.—Gen. 48:5, 6; Ex. 2:10.

Education of.—Gen. 18:19; Ex. 10:2; 13:8–10; Deut. 4:9; 11:19; 31:12, 13;

Ps. 78:3–8; Pr. 4:1–22; 13:1, 24; 22:6, 15; Is. 28:9, 10; Lu. 2:46; II Tim. 3:14, 15.

Training of.—Pr. 22:6, 15; 29:17; Eph. 6:4.

Parental authority.—Gen. 9:24, 25; 18:19; 21:14; 38:24; Pr. 13:1, 24.

Parental indulgence.—Gen. 27:6–17, 42–45; 37:3, 4. Indulgence forbidden—Deut. 21:15–17.

Parental example.—Gen. 18:19; II Tim. 1:5.

Duties of children to parents.—Ex. 20:12; 21:15, 17; Lev. 19:3; 20:9; Deut. 5:16; 27:16; Pr. 1:8; 6:20; 15:5; 23:22; 24:21; Is. 45:10; Eph. 6:2, 3; Col. 3:20; I Tim. 5:4; I Pet. 5:5.

Penalty for disobedience.—Deut. 21:18–21; Pr. 30:17.

Prosperity of, greatly depended on obedience of parents.—Deut. 4:40; 12:25, 28; Ps. 128:1–3.

Amusements.—Job 21:11; Zech. 8:5; Mt. 11:16, 17; Lu. 7:31, 32.

Fellowship with parents.—Gen. 6:18; 13:15–16; Lev. 26:45.

Children sacrificed to idols.—Lev. 18:21; 20:2–5; Deut. 12:29–31; 18:10; II Ki. 17:31; II Chr. 28:3; 33:6; Ez. 16:20, 21.

Prayers for.—Gen. 17:18; I Chr. 29:19.

Discriminations: Male.—Redeemed as belonging to God—Ex. 13:13–15. Under care of tutors—II Ki. 10:1; Acts 22:3; Gal. 4:1, 2. Inherited possessions of their fathers—Deut. 21:16, 17; Lu. 12:13, 14. Received paternal blessing—Gen. 27:1–4; 48:15; 49:1–33.

Female.—Drawers of water—Gen. 24:13; Ex. 2:16. Inheritors of property in default of sons—Num. 27:1–8; Josh. 17:1–16. Were given in marriage by father, eldest preferred—Gen. 29:16–29. Being debarred from marriage a reproach—Jer. 11:37; Is. 4:1.

Illegitimate.—Disregarded by father—Heb. 12:8. Despised by brothers—Ju. 11:2. Excluded from congregation—Deut. 23:2. Exiled from family—Gen. 21:14; 25:6. Had no inheritance—Gen. 21:10–14; Gal. 4:30.

Good children.—Obey parents—Gen. 28:7; 47:29–31; Ex. 20:12; Pr. 10:1; 13:1; Col. 3:20. Observe the law of God—Ps. 119:9, 99; Pr. 28:7. Submit to discipline—Pr. 8:32-36; Heb. 12:9. Honor and care for parents—Gen. 45: 9-11; 46:29; 47:12; Pr. 10:1; 29:17. Respect the aged—Lev. 19:32.

Examples of.—Shem and Japheth—Gen. 9:23. Isaac—Gen. 22:6. Judah—Gen. 4:32. Joseph—Gen. 37:13; 46:29. Jacob's sons—Gen. 50:12. Jephthah's daughter—Ju. 11:36. Samuel—I Sam. 3:19; 22:6. David—I Sam. 17:20; Ps. 71:5. Solomon—II Ki. 2:19. Josiah—II Chr. 34:3. Esther—Esth. 2:20. The Rechabites—Jer. 35:5-10. Daniel—Dan. 1:6. Jesus—Lu. 2:51. Timothy—II Tim. 3:15.

Wicked children.—To their parents—Gen. 26:34, 35; Deut. 27:16; I Sam. 2:25; II Sam. 15:10-15; I Ki. 1:5-10; Pr. 15:5, 20; 19:26; 28:24; 29:15; 30: 11; Ez. 22:7. To their leaders—II Ki. 2:23, 24; Job 19:18. Not restrained by parents—I Sam. 3:11-14. Sons of Belial—I Sam. 2:12-17, 22-25; 8:1-3.

Punishment of.—Ex. 21:15; Deut. 21:18, 21; 27:16; II Ki. 2:23; Pr. 28:24; 30: 17; Mk. 7:10.

Fondness and care of mothers for.—Ex. 2:2-10; I Sam. 2:19; I Ki. 3:27; Is. 49: 15; I Thess. 2:7, 8.

Grief occasioned by loss of.—Gen. 37:35; 44:27-29; II Sam. 13:37; Jer. 6:26; 31:15.

Consequences of sin entailed on children in this world.—Ex. 20:5; 34:7; Lev. 26:39, 40; Num. 14:33; Deut. 5:9; I Ki. 14:9-10; Job 5:3-7; Ps. 21:10; 37: 28; Is. 1:4; 13:16; 14:20-22; Jer. 32: 18; Lam. 5:7; Mt. 23:32-36; John 9:2, 3, 34.

Children not punished for sins of parents.—Deut. 24:16; II Ki. 14:6; II Chr. 25:4; Jer. 31:29, 30; 32:18; Ez. 18:2-4, 20; Mt. 19:13, 14; Mk. 10:13-15; Lu. 18:15-17.

Children of God.—Heb. 12:5-9; I Pet. 1:14. See GOD, FATHERHOOD OF.

Children of light.—Lu. 16:8; John 12: 36; Eph. 5:8; I Thess. 5:5. See SON, DAUGHTER, BABE.

CHILEAB, kĭl'e-ăb. **Son of David.**—II Sam. 3:3. See I Chr. 3:1.

CHILION, kĭl'i-on. **Naomi's son.**—Ruth 1:2, 5; 4:9.

CHILMAD, kĭl-măd. **A merchant of Sheba.**—Ez. 27:23.

CHIMHAM, kĭm'hăm. **Son of Barzillai.**—II Sam. 19:37, 38, 40.

CHIMNEY. Hos. 13:3.

CHINNERETH, kĭn'ne-rĕth. **A district of Galilee.**—Num. 34:11; Deut. 3:17; Josh. 13:27; 19:35.

CHINNEROTH, kĭn'ne-roth. **Same as Chinnereth.**—Josh. 11:2; 12:3; I Ki. 15:20.

CHIOS, kī'os. **An island where Paul finds shelter.**—Acts 20:15.

CHIRP. Is. 8:19; 10:14.

CHISLEV, kĭs'lev. **Ninth month of the Hebrew year.**—Neh. 1:1.

CHISLON, kĭs'lon. **Father of Elidad.**—Num. 34:21.

CHISLOTH-TABOR, kĭs-loth-tā'bor. **Same as Chesulloth.**—Josh. 19:12.

CHLOE, klō'e. **A Christian woman in Corinth.**—I Cor. 1:11.

CHOICE. Man's endless future hangs on his choice.—Deut. 30:19; Mt. 7:13, 14, 24-27.

God chose.—Aaron—Num. 16:5, 7; 17:5, 8; Ps. 109:26. Abram—Gen. 12:1-3; Neh. 9:7. Apostles—Acts 10:41; Eph. 1:4. Christ—Mt. 12:18; Lu. 23:35. David—I Sam. 16:1, 10, 12; II Sam. 6:21; I Ki. 8:16; I Chr. 28:4; II Chr. 6:6; Ps. 78:70; 89:19; Jer. 33:21, 24. Delusions—Is. 66:4. Fathers of Israel—Acts 13:17. Foolish, weak and despised things—I Cor. 1:27, 28. Israel—Deut. 4:37; 7:6; 14:2; I Ki. 3:8; Ps. 33:12; 135:4; Is. 14:1; 41:8, 9; 43:10; 44:1, 2; 48:10; 49:7; Ez. 20:5. Jerusalem—I Ki. 8:44, 48; 11:13, 32, 36; 14: 21; II Ki. 21:7; 23:27; Neh. 6:6, 34, 38; 12:13; 33:7; Neh. 1:7; Zech. 1:17; 2:12. Judah—Ps. 78:68. Levites—Deut. 18:5; 21:5; I Sam. 2:28; I Chr. 15:2; II Chr. 29:11; Jer. 33:21, 24. Men—Ps. 65:4; Mt. 22:14; Mk. 13:20; Rom. 16:13; II Thess. 2:13; I Pet. 2:4, 9; Rev. 17:14. Our inheritance—Ps. 47: 4; I Pet. 1:4, 5. Peter—Acts 15:7. Saul as king—Deut. 17:15; I Sam. 10: 24. Solomon—I Chr. 22:9, 10; 28:5; 29:1. The poor—Jas. 2:5. The temple—II Chr. 7:12, 16. True fast—Is. 58:5, 6. Witnesses of resurrection—Lu. 24: 48; Acts 10:41. Zerubbabel—Hag. 2:23.

Christ chose.—Apostles—Twelve—Lu. 6:13; John 6:70; 13:18; 15:16, 19. Saul—Acts 9:15.

Men urged to choose.—Fear of God—Pr. 1:29; Mt. 10:28; Lu. 12:4, 5. Good name—Pr. 22:1. Jehovah—Jas. 24:14, 15. Life—Deut. 30:19; Is. 55:3; Lu. 10:28; John 6:27; I Tim. 6:19. Righteousness—Job 34:4; Ps. 25:12; Pr. 21:3. Wisdom—Pr. 8:10, 11, 19; 16:16.

Men chose.—Good—Is. 7:15, 16; Lu. 10:42; Heb. 11:25. Life—Acts 13:48. Truth—Ps. 119:30, 173. Will of God—Is. 56:4; 65:12. Worship—I Ki. 18:23, 25; Ps. 84:10. Plain of Sodom—Gen. 13:11. Iniquity—Job 15:5; 36:21; Is. 66:3, 4. Idolatry—Ju. 5:8; Is. 1:29; 40:20; 41:24. Death—Job 7:15; Jer. 8:3. Words—Job 9:14. Men: *Soldiers*—Ex. 17:9; Josh. 8:3; I Sam. 13:2; II Sam. 10:9; 17:1; I Chr. 19:10. *Deacons*—Acts 6:5. *Missionaries*—Acts 13:3; 14:26, 27; 15:40. *Delegate*—II Cor. 8:19. *Judges*—Ex. 18:25. *Chief seats*—Lu. 14:7.

David obliged to choose a punishment.—II Sam. 24:12; I Chr. 21:10.

CHOKE. Riches—Mt. 3:22; Mk. 4:19; Lu. 8:14. Thorns—Mt. 13:7.

CHOP. Mic. 3:3.

CHORAZIN, ko-rā'zin. **A doomed city on Sea of Tiberias near Capernaum.**—Mt. 11:21; Lu. 10:13.

CHOZEBA. See COZEBA.

CHRIST. See JESUS THE MESSIAH.

CHRISTIAN. Acts 11:26; 26:28; I Pet. 4:16. See BRETHREN, DISCIPLES, SAINTS.

CHRISTIAN GRACES. Faith.—Rom. 4:20; I Thess. 1:3; II Pet. 1:1; Jude 20, 21. Examples—Heb. Ch. 11. See FAITH.

Virtue.—Pr. 31:29; Phil. 4:8; II Pet. 1:3, 5. See FAITH.

Knowledge.—Rom. 15:14; I Cor. 1:5; II Cor. 4:6; Eph. 3:19; II Tim. 3:3; 4:13; Phil. 1:9; 3:8; Col. 1:9; 3:10. See KNOWLEDGE.

Self-control.—Pr. 23:1, 2; Acts 24:25; I Cor. 9:25; Gal. 5:23; Eph. 5:18; Tit. 1:8; 2:2; II Pet. 1:6.

Patience.—Lu. 8:15; Rom. 2:7; II Cor. 6:4; I Thess. 1:3; II Thess. 1:4; I Tim. 6:11; Tit. 2:2; Heb. 12:1; Jas. 1:4; 5:11; I Pet. 2:19–21; II Pet. 1:6; Rev. 2:2; 3:10. Examples—*Job*—Job 1:21.

Simeon—Lu. 2:25. *Paul*—II Tim. 3:10. *Abraham*—Heb. 6:15. *John*—Rev. 1:9.

Godliness.—I Tim. 2:2; 4:8; 6:6, 11; II Tim. 3:5; Tit. 1:1; II Pet. 1:3; 3:11. See RIGHTEOUSNESS.

Brotherly kindness.—I Sam. 15:6; II Sam. 9:3; Job 6:14; Pr. 3:3; 19:22; 31:26; Dan. 1:9; II Cor. 6:6; Gal. 5:22; Col. 3:12; II Pet. 1:7. Instances—Gen. 24:18–20; Ex. 2:17; Josh. 2:12; Ruth 2:8–16; I Sam. 20:8–16; II Sam. 9:1–7; Esth. 2:9; Acts 28:2; I Tim. 6:17–19; Heb. 13:16; Jas. 2:14–17; 3:13. See KINDNESS—Zech. 7:9. See FRATERNITY.

Love.—John 13:34; 15:12; Rom. 12:9, 10; I Cor. 13:1–13; Gal. 5:22; Col. 1:8; I Thess. 1:3; I John 4:7–12, 16–21. See LOVE.

Benevolence.—Rom. 12:13; 15:27; I Cor. 13:5–7; II Cor. 9:6–15; Gal. 2:10; Eph. 4:28; Phil. 4:14–16; Col. 3:12, 13; I Tim. 6:18, 19; Heb. 13:16. See LIBERALITY.

Mercy.—Mt. 5:7; 9:13; 18:21–35; Lu. 6:36; 7:40–43; Rom. 11:30, 31; 12:8; Phil. 2:1, 2; Col. 3:12–14. See MERCY.

Gentleness.—II Sam. 22:36; Ps. 18:35; II Tim. 2:24–26; Tit. 3:2; Jas. 3:17, 18.

Humility.—II Chr. 34:27; Pr. 16:19; 29:23; Is. 57:15; Mt. 18:3, 4; 23:12; Eph. 4:1, 2; Col. 3:12; Jas. 4:10; I Pet. 5:5, 6. See HUMILITY.

Meekness.—Num. 12:3; Ps. 22:26; 25:9; 37:11; 147:6; 149:4; Pr. 15:1; Is. 11:4; 29:19; 61:1; Mt. 5:5; 11:29; Gal. 5:23; Eph. 4:2; II Tim. 2:25; Tit. 3:2; Jas. 1:21; 3:13; I Pet. 3:4, 15.

Toleration.—Lu. 9:49, 50; 9:52–55; Rom. 14:1–21; I Cor. 6:1–8; 8:1–9; 10:23–33.

Peacefulness.—Job 22:21; Ps. 34:14; 122:6; Is. 32:17, 18; 48:22; 55:12; Jer. 6:14; 8:14, 15; Mt. 5:9; 10:13; Lu. 2:14; John 14:27; Acts 10:36; Rom. 5:1; 8:6; 12:18; 14:17–19; Gal. 5:22; Eph. 2:14, 15; 4:3; 6:15; Phil. 4:7; Col. 3:15; I Thess. 5:13; II Thess. 3:16; II Tim. 2:22; Jas. 3:17, 18. See PEACE.

Unselfishness.—Mt. 10:39; 16:25; 20:26–28; Mk. 8:35; 10:44, 45; Lu. 9:23; 12:15, 16–21; 16:19–26; Rom. 14:8; Gal. 5:13–15; Heb. 13:16; Jas. 2:14–17; 3:13. See SELF-DENIAL—Mt. 16:24.

Hospitality.—Mk. 9:41; Acts 16:15; Rom. 12:13; II Cor. 8:8–24; Phil. 4:9–18; II Tim. 1:16–18; I Pet. 4:9, 10; I John 3:17; III John 5–10. See Hospitality—Lu. 14:12.

Fellowship.—Acts 2:42; 4:32; Rom. 15:1–7; I Cor. 1:10; 10:16, 17; 12:13; Gal. 2:9; 6:2; Eph. 2:14–22; Phil. 1:3–5, 27; 2:1, 2; Heb. 10:24; I Pet. 3:8, 9; I John 1:3, 7. See Fellowship.

CHRONICLES. See Outline studies in the books.

CHRYSOLITE. Rev. 2:20.

CHRYSOPRASE. Rev. 21:20.

THE CHURCH. Gr. *Ecclesia.* Body of disciples of Christ.

Christ the founder.—Deut. 18:15–19; Is. 9:6, 7; Mic. 5:2; Mt. 2:5, 6; 16:18; Lu. 1:32, 33.

The foundation.—Ps. 118:22; Is. 28:16; I Cor. 3:10, 11; Eph. 2:19, 20; Col. 2:7.

The head.—Eph. 1:22; 4:15,16; 5:23; Col. 1:18; 2:19.

Time of establishment.—Jer. 31:31–33; 33:15, 16; Dan. 2:44; Mt. 16:28; Mk. 9:1; Lu. 9:27; 24:45–49; Acts 1:4–8; 2:1–4, 14–21, 30–36, 41–47; Heb. 1:1, 2; 2:2–4.

Place.—is. 2:2, 3; 9:7; 62:11, 12; Jer. 3:14–18; Ez. 17:22, 23; Mic. 4:2; Zech. 9:9; Mt. 21:4, 5; Lu. 24:46, 47; John 12:12–15; Acts 1:4–8.

Figurative representation of the Church.—Body—Rom. 12:4, 5; I Cor. 10:16, 17; 12:12–20; Eph. 2:14–16; 3:3–6; 4:4–16; 5:30–32; Col. 1:18; 2:17–19; 3: 15. Temple—I Cor. 3:9, 16, 17; II Cor. 2:6–16; Eph. 2:20, 22; Heb. 3:5, 6; I Pet. 2:4, 5; Rev. 3:12. God's husbandry—Mt. 13:19–23, 37–43; Mk. 4:14–20, 26–29; John 15:1–8; I Cor. 3:9. Light—Mt. 5:14–16; Lu. 16:8; John 12:36; Acts 26:18; Rom. 13:12; II Cor. 4:6; Eph. 5:8–14; Col. 1:12, 13; I Thess. 5:5–8; I Pet. 2:9. School—Is. 54:13; 7:28, 29; 28:20; John 6:45; Acts 2:42; 4:2; 13:1; 5:21, 42; 11:26; 18:25; 20:20; I Cor. 4:17; 12:28, 29; Gal. 1:12; 6:6; Eph. 4:20, 21; Col. 1: 28; 2:7; 3:16; II Thess. 2:15; I Tim. 1:3; Tit.1:9; 2:3–12; Heb. 5:12. House —Is. 2:2, 3; Mic. 4:1, 2; I Cor. 3:16; II Cor. 6:16; Eph. 2:21, 22; I Tim. 3:15; Heb. 3:6; 10:21; I Pet. 2:5. Household—Gal. 6:10; Eph. 2:19.

Flock—Is. 40:10, 11; 49:9, 10; Lu. 12: 32; John 10:1–16; 21:15–17; Acts 20: 28, 29; Heb. 13:20, 21; I Pet. 2:25; 5:4. City of God—Heb. 12:22; Rev. 21:2. Israel of God—Gal. 3:29; 6:16. General assembly of the first-born—Heb. 12:23. Church of God—I Cor. 11:16; II Cor. 1:1; I Tim. 3:15. See Congregation. Bride—II Cor. 11:2; Eph. 5:25–27; Rev. 19:7; 21:9. Church in God—I Thess. 1:1; II Thess. 1:1. Candlestick—Rev. 1:12; 2:5. Kingdom of God—Mt. 6:33; Mk. 1:14, 15; Lu. 10:9–11; 12:31; John 3:3–5; Acts 1:3; 8:12; 19:8; Rom. 14:17; I Cor. 4:20; Rev. 11:15; 12:10. Kingdom of heaven —Mt. 3:2; 4:17; 5:3–20; 10:7; 11:11; 13:11; 16:19; 18:1. God's dwelling or habitation—II Cor. 6:16; Eph. 2:22.

The mission of the Church.—To manifest God's wisdom—Gen. 3:15; 12:3; 18:18; 22:18; Acts 3:25, 26; Rom. 11: 32, 33; I Cor. 1:23, 24; 2:6–8; Gal. 3:8; Eph. 1:9–12; 3:10, 11; Col. 4:3–6; Jas. 1:5; 3:13–17. To glorify God—Ps. 86: 9–12; Is. 25:3; Mt. 5:16; Lu. 2:14; John 14:13; 15:8; Acts 4:21; 11:18; 13:48; 21:20; Rom. 11:36; 15:5–9; I Cor. 6:20; II Cor. 8:23; 9:12, 13; Gal. 1:5, 22–24; Eph. 1:5, 6; 3:20, 21; Phil. 1:10, 11; 4:20; II Thess. 1:10; 3:1; I Tim. 1:17; Heb. 13:21; I Pet. 2:12; 4:4–16; II Pet. 3:18; Jude 25; Rev. 15: 3, 4. To preach the gospel—Is. 2:3; 4; Mt. 24:14; 28:19, 20; Mk. 13:10; 16: 15, 16; Lu. 24:46–48; Acts 2:5–42; 5: 42; 6:3–10; 8:4–13; 8:25–40; 9:20; 10: 42; Rom. 10:8–15; I Cor. 1:23; 9:16; 15:11; Eph. 3:8, 9; II Tim. 4:2–5. See Missions. To overthrow sin—John 1: 29; 12:31; 16:8, 9; Acts 2:37–40; Rom. 3:19–26; 5:17–21; 6:10–23; 8:1–4; 12: 9–21; Heb. 9:24–28; I John 2:16, 17; 3:8; 5:4, 5; Rev. 18:1–10; 20:10–15. To establish righteousness—Ps. 97:2; Is. 26:9; 61:11; 62:1; Dan. 12:3; Mal. 4: 1–3; Mt. 6:33; 13:43; Acts 10:35; 24: 25; Rom. 1:16, 17; 5:19; 6:13–18; 10: 3–10; 14:17; I Cor. 15:34; II Cor. 5:21; Gal. 2:21; 5:5; Eph. 5:7–11; Phil. 2: 12, 13; I Tim. 6:10; II Tim. 4:7, 8; Heb. 1:8, 9; Jas. 1:19–22; I John 3:7–10. To conquer the world for Christ—Ps. 2:1–9; 110:1–6; Is. 6:7; 60:1–5; 61:1–9; Dan. 2:44; Mt. 12:18–21; 16:

18, 19; 28:18–20; Acts 2:34–36; Rom. 14:9–12; I Cor. 15:22–28; Eph. 1:19–23; Heb. 1:13; 10:12, 13; Rev. 11:15; 20:1–15. To provoke to love and good works—Mt. 13:33; Lu. 13:21; John 13:34, 35; 15:12–14; Acts 2:44–47; 6:1–4; Rom. 12:9–13; 14:13–17; I Cor. 8:8–13; Gal. 6:10; I Tim. 6:17–19; Heb. 10:23, 24; Jas. 1:27; I Pet. 3:8–11; II Pet. 1:5–14; I John 3:14–20; 4:7–17. To maintain the faith—Mt. 6:30; 8:26; 14:31; 17:20; Lu. 12:28; 18:8; John 20:30, 31; Acts 14:21, 22; 16:5; Rom. 1:17; 4:13, 14; I Cor. 13: 13; Gal. 5:22, 23; Eph. 4:4–6; 6:16; Phil. 1:25–27; I Thess. 5:8; I Tim. 1:19; 3:9; 4:1–2; II Tim. 3:10; 4:7; Heb. 10:22, 23; 11:6; 12:2; 13:7; II Pet. 1:1; I John 5:1–4; Jude 1, 3, 20; Rev. 2:13; 14:12. To hold fast to confession of our hope—Acts 23:6; 26:6; 28:20; Rom. 5:4, 5; 8:24; 15:13; I Cor. 13:13; II Cor. 3:12; Gal. 5:5; Eph. 1: 18; 4:4; Col. 1:23; I Thess. 1:3; 5:8; II Thess. 2:16, 17; Tit. 2:13; Heb. 3:6; 6:11–20; 7:19; 10:35; I Pet. 1:3–4; 3: 15; I John 3:2, 3. To preserve unity—Mt. 12:25; John 15:4, 5; 17:20, 21; Rom. 12:4–16; 15:5; I Cor. 1:10; 12: 12, 13, 25; II Cor. 13:11; Gal. 5:25, 26; Eph. 4:1–6, 16; Phil. 2:1–4; 3:15, 16; Col. 3:12–14; Jas. 3:13–18. To attain perfection—Mt. 5:48; 19:21; John 17: 22, 23; I Cor. 2:6; II Cor. 13:9–11; Eph. 4:11–16; 6:10–13; Phil. 3:12–14; Col. 1:28; 3:14; 4:12; I Thess. 5:23; I Tim. 6:13, 14; II Tim. 3:17; Heb. 6:1; 13:20, 21; Jas. 1:4; 2:10–12; I Pet. 5:10. To maintain purity—Ex. 20:14; Mt. 5:8, 28; Rom. 1:24–32; 6:19; 13: 14; I Cor. 3:17; 5:1–6; 10:6; II Cor. 6:6; 11:1–3; 12:21; Gal. 5:16–24; Eph. 1:4, 5; 2:3; 4:19–22; 5:3–5, 26, 27; Phil. 4:8; Col. 3:5–8; I Thess. 4:7; I Tim. 3:9; 5:22; 6:9; II Tim. 2:22; Tit. 1:15; 2:12; 3:3; Jas. 1:14, 15; 3:17; I Pet 2:11; II Pet. 1:4; 2:10–20; 3:1; I John 2:16; 3:3; Jude 7–19. To inculcate subjection to Christ—Dan. 7:13, 14; Mt. 7:24–29; 25:33–46; 28:18–20; Lu. 1:31–33; 6:46–49; John 3:35; 5:21, 23; 17:2; Acts 2:36; 5:31; 26:19; Rom. 12:1; 14:9; I Cor. 15:25–27; II Cor. 10:5, 6; Eph. 1:10–23; Phil. 2:9–11; Col. 1:18; II Thess. 1:7, 8; I Tim. 6:

14–16; Heb. 1:8; I Pet. 3:22; Rev. 1:5, 6; 17:14. To administer discipline—Mt. 18:17, 18; Rom. 14:1; 16:17; I Cor. 5:4; 6:2, 3; II Cor. 2:6, 8; 13:1, 2; Gal. 6:1; I Thess. 5:14, 15; II Thess. 3:6–14; I Tim. 3:4, 5; 5:17–20; Tit. 1:10, 11; Heb. 13:17. To promote companionship and helpfulness—Ps. 103; Mt. 5:23, 24; 6:12; 18:21, 22; 23:8; 25:33–46; Mk. 10:29, 30; Lu. 2:13, 14; 10:27–37; 14:12–14; John 15:15–17; Acts 4: 34, 35; 11:28, 29; Rom. 12:5–18; 14: 15–21; 15:1, 2, 26; I Cor. 16:1–3; II Cor. 8:1–4; 9:12–15; Gal. 6:1–10; Eph. 4:31, 32; Phil. 4:10–17; I Thess. 5:11–15, 26; I Tim. 6:18; Philemon 1–16; Heb. 12:12–15; 13:1–3; Jas. 4:4; I Pet. 1:22; 2:17; 3:8, 9; II Pet. 1:7; III John 14. To inspire to heroism—Mt. 5:10–12, 44; 10:28–33; 13:21; Mk. 4:7; Lu. 4:9; 12:22, 23; 18:29, 30; John 15: 18–24; Acts 5:40, 41; 8:1–4; 20:22–24; 21:11–14; Rom. 8:17, 18, 35–37; 12:14; I Cor. 4:10–13; 10:13; 11:32; II Cor. 1:3–6; 4:8–18; 6:4–10; 12:7–10; Gal. 5:11; 6:12–16; Eph. 3:13; Phil. 1:27–30; Col. 1:10, 11; I Thess. 3:2–5; II Thess. 1:4–7; I Tim. 1:18, 19; 4:10, 11; 6:11, 12; II Tim. 2:8–12; 3:10–12; 4: 6–8; Tit. 2:12–14; Heb. 11:33–38; 12: 1–11; Jas. 1:2–4; I Pet. 2:19–21; 3:13, 14; 4:12–19; II Pet. 3:14, 15; I John 5:4, 5; Rev. 3:19.

Ordinances of the church.—Baptism—Mt. 28:19; Mk. 16:16; John 3:5; 4:1, 2; Acts 2:38–41; 8:12, 13, 36–39; 9:18; 10:47, 48; 16:15, 33; 18:8, 25; 19:3–5; 22:16; Rom. 6:3–6; I Cor. 1:13–17; 12: 13; Gal. 3:27; Eph. 4:5; 5:25–27; Col. 2:12; 3:1; Tit. 3:5; Heb. 10:22; I Pet. 3:20, 21. The Lord's Supper—Mt. 26: 26–30; Mk. 14:22–26; Lu. 22:17–20; John 6:53–56; Acts 2:42; 20:7; I Cor. 10:15–21; 11:20–29.

Officers of the church.—Apostles—Mt. 10:1–7; 26:20; 28:16–20; Mk. 6:30; 14:17; 16:14–16; Lu. 6:13–16; 9:10; 17:5; 22:14, 15; 24:9, 10, 33–53; John 6:67–70; 14:15–27; 15:26, 27; 17:6–12; 20:19–26; Acts 1:15–26; 2:1–4, 14, 15, 32, 33, 43; 4:35–37; 5:17–29; 8:1; 15: 2–6, 22, 23; Rom. 1:1–5; 11:13; I Cor. 1:1; 4:9; 9:1, 2; 12:28; 15:5–9; II Cor. 1:1; 11:5; 12:11, 12; Gal. 1:1, 15–19; 2:7–9; Eph. 1:1; 3:5; 4:11, 12; Col.

1:1; I Thess. 2:6; I Tim. 1:1; II Tim. 1:1; Tit. 1:1; II Pet. 3:2; Jude 17, 18; Rev. 2:2; 18:20. Evangelists—Acts 21:8; Eph. 4:11; I Tim. 1:3, 4; 2:14, 15; 4:11–13; II Tim. 2:1, 2; 3:16, 17; 4:1–5; Tit. 1:5. Officers (ministry of the church)—Pastors, shepherds—John 21:15–17; Acts 20:28; Eph. 4:11; I Pet. 5:1–4. Elders, or, bishops—Acts 11:30; 14:23; 15:1–6, 22, 23; 16:4; 20: 17–28; Phil. 1:1–2; I Thess. 5:12, 13; I Tim. 3:1–7; 5:17–19; Tit. 1:5–9; Heb. 13:17; Jas. 5:14, 15; I Pet. 5:1–4. Deacons—Acts 6:1–6; Phil. 1:1; I Tim. 3:8–13. Deaconess—Rom. 16:1, 2; Phil. 4:2, 3. See MINISTER.

Membership of the church called.—(a) Believers—Acts 4:32; 5:11–14; I Tim. 4:12. (b) Brethren—Mt. 23:8; 25:40; John 21:23; Acts 11:29; 12:17; 14:2; 15:1–3, 22, 23; 17:10; 18:18; 21:7, 17; 28:15; Rom. 1:13; 8:29; 12:1; I Cor. 1:26; 8:12; II Cor. 13:11; Eph. 6:23; Phil. 1:14; Col. 1:2; I Thess. 4:1, 2; 5: 27; II Thess. 2:1, 2; I Tim. 4:6; Heb. 3:1; I Pet. 1:22; I John 3:14. (c) Christians—Acts 11:26; 26:28; Jas. 2:7; I Pet. 4:16. (d) Saints—Acts 9: 13, 32, 41; 26:10; Rom. 1:7; 8:27; I Cor. 1:2; 6:2; 14:33; II Cor. 1:1; Eph. 1:1; 2:19; 3:8; 4:12; Phil. 1:1; 4:22; Col. 1:2, 3, 12; II Thess. 1:10; Philemon 5, 7; Heb. 6:10; 13:24; Jude 3; Rev. 13:7; 14:12; 17:6; 20:9. (e) The elect of God—Mk. 13:27; Lu. 18:7; Rom. 8:33; Eph. 1:4; Col. 3:12; I Thess. 4:1, 2; II Thess. 2:13, 14; II Tim. 2:10; Tit. 1:1; Jas. 2:5; I Pet. 2:9; II Pet. 1:10. (f) Priests—Heb. 10:19–22; I Pet. 2:5–9; Rev. 1:6; 5:10. (g) First-born—Rom. 8:29; Heb. 12: 23. (h) Disciples—Mt. 10:42; 19:13; Mk. 10:13; Lu. 19:37; John 4:1; 8:31, 32; 15:8; 18:17; 21:24; Acts 9:1, 26; 11:26; 20:1, 30. (i) Members of Christ —Rom. 12:4, 5; I Cor. 6:15; 12:27; Eph. 5:30. See DISCIPLES, SAINTS, TEACHINGS OF PAUL ON THE CHURCH, JESUS, KINGDOM OF, UNITY.

CHURL. I Sam. 25:3; Is. 32:5, 7.

CHUZAS, kū săs. Herod's steward—Lu. 8:3.

CILICIA, sĭ-lĭ′si-a. **A province of Asia Minor.**—Church in—Acts 15:23. Home of Paul—Acts 21:39; 22:3; 23:34.

Paul visits—Acts 15:41; 27:5; Gal. 1:21. Stephen in—Acts 6:9.

CINNAMON. Ex. 20:23; Pr. 7:17; Song of Sol. 4:14. See SPICES.

CINNEROTH. See CHINNERETH.

CIRCLE. Earth, Of the—Is. 40:22.

CIRCUIT. Ends, Unto—Ps. 19:6. Made a—Acts 28:13. Wind returneth to—Eccl. 1:6. Year to year in—I Sam. 7:16.

CIRCUMSPECT. Ex. 23:13 (A.V.); Eph. 5:15 (A.V.).

CIRCUMCISION. Institution of.—Gen. 17:10; Rom. 4:11. Described—Gen. 17: 11. Appointed as the token of God's covenant—Gen. 17:11; Rom. 4:11. Performed on all home-born and bought males—Gen. 17:12, 13. Observed by Abraham—Gen. 17:24–26; 21:3, 4. Shechemites—Gen. 34:24. Zipporah—Ex. 4:25. Of strangers—in order to keep Passover—Ex. 12:48. Joshua at Gilgal—Josh. 5:1–9. By parents of John the Baptist—Luke 1:59. Of Christ —Luke 2:21. Of Paul—Phil. 3:5. Timothy—Acts 16:3. David circumcised slain bodies of Philistines—I Sam. 18: 25, 27; II Sam. 3:14. Omitted in the wilderness—Josh. 5:7. Painful rite— Gen. 34:25; Josh. 5:8. With knives of flint—Ex. 4:25; Josh. 5:2, 3. Done on eighth day—Gen. 17:12; Lu. 1:59; 2:21; Acts 7:8. Even if eighth day was the Sabbath—John 7:23.

Act in which child is named.—Gen. 21: 3, 4; Lu. 1:59; 2:21.

Enforced by law.—Lev. 12:3; John 7:22, 23.

The uncircumcised is cut off from his people.—Gen. 17:14.

Neglect causes punishment.—Ex. 4:24–26.

Jews called the circumcision.—Acts 10: 45; 11:2; Rom. 3:30; 4:9–12; Gal. 2:8, 9; Col. 4:11; Tit. 1:10.

Gentiles called uncircumcised.—I Sam. 14:6; Rom. 3:30; 4:9–12; Gal. 2:7; Eph. 2:11. Unlawful for Jews to intermarry with the uncircumcised— Gen. 34:14; Ju. 14:3. Wrong to associate with—Ez. 44:7; Acts 10:28; 11: 3; Gal. 2:12–14. Jews despised the uncircumcised—I Sam. 17:26, 36; Eph. 2:11.

Promises connected with.—Gen. 17:4-14; Rom. 3:1, 2; 4:11; 9:7-13.

Circumcision of heart.—Lev. 26:41; Deut. 10:16; 30:6; Jer. 4:4; Rom. 2:29; Phil. 3:3; Col. 2:11.

Circumcision abolished by Christ.—Eph. 2:13-15; Col. 3:11. Councils concerning—Acts 10:28-35; 11:1-18; 15:1-29. Paul denies its necessity—Gal. 2:3-5. Timothy circumcised as a matter of expediency—Acts 16:3. Paul is accused of opposing—Acts 21:21. Paul exposes Jewish sophistry—Rom. 2:25-27. Teaches the true circumcision to be of the heart—Rom. 2:28, 29; Phil. 3:3. Refers it to baptism—Col. 2:11, 12. False teaching concerning circumcision—Acts 15:24; Gal. 6:12; Tit. 1:10.

CISTERN. Drink from.—II Ki. 18:31; Pr. 5:15; Is. 36:16.

Cisterns hewed out.—Deut. 6:11; II Chr. 26:10; Neh. 9:25; Jer. 2:14.

Pitcher broken at the.—Eccl. 12:6.

Prophecies concerning.—Is. 30:14; Jer. 14:3.

CITIES. The modern conception not to be applied to ancient cities. Rather walled villages, or possibly mere hamlets. Later on were populous.

First mention of.—Gen. 4:17.

City of Shinar built to perpetuate a name.—Gen. 11:4.

Named.—After the family of the founder—Gen. 4:17; Ju. 18:29. The proprietor of the land—I Ki. 16:24. The country in which built—Dan. 4:29, 30.

For protection of families.—Num. 32:24-26.

Necessary habitations (cities and houses preceded tents).—For man—Gen. 10:10-12; Ps. 107:7, 36. For the Lord—Ps. 132:13.

Walled in.—Deut. 1:28; 3:5; II Chr. 8:4, 5.

Entered through gates.—Gen. 23:10, 18; 34:20, 24; Ruth 4:1, 11; Neh. 13:19. Solicitors sat at the gates—II Sam. 15:1-6; 19:8.

Fortified naturally.—Ps. 125:2; Is. 33:16.

Built for defence.—Deut. 1:28; II Chr. 11:5-10; 14:6, 7; Jer. 4:5.

Fortified and supplied.—II Chr. 11:11, 12; 33:14; Ps. 48:12, 13.

Arranged in streets and lanes.—Zech. 8:5; Lu. 14:21.

Result of slaughter.—Mic. 3:10; Hab. 2:12.

Result of iniquity.—Mic. 3:10; Hab. 2:12.

Built.—Num. 32:24-26. By Solomon—I Ki. 9:15-19; II Chr. 8:1-6. Near rivers—Babylon on Euphrates; Nineveh on Tigris; Rome on Tiber; Bethabara and Jericho on Jordan. Near Lake of Galilee—Capernaum, Bethsaida, Magdala, Dalmanutha, Tiberias. Near the Mediterranean—Cæsarea, Joppa. On hills—Mt. 5:14; Lu. 4:29. In plains—Gen. 11:2, 4; 13:12; 19:24, 25.

Early cities built of brick and slime.—Gen. 11:3. Of brick and mortar—Ex. 1:11-14.

Chariot.—II Chr. 1:14; 8:6; 9:25.

Levitical.—Lev. 25:32, 33; Num. 35:7, 8; Josh. 13:14; 21:1-42.

Merchant.—Is. 23:11 marg.; Ez. 17:4; 27:3.

Royal.—Num. 21:26; Josh. 10:2; II Sam. 12:26.

Store.—Ex. 1:11; I Ki. 9:19; II Chr. 8:4-6.

Dealing with cities of the enemy.—Deut. 20:10-20.

Water supply.—II Ki. 18:17; 20:20.

Ruled by captains of the army.—II Chr. 33:14. By governors—II Cor. 11:32.

Judges appointed.—Deut. 16:18; II Chr. 19:5.

Protected by watchmen.—Ps. 127:1; Is. 21:11.

Besieged.—Deut. 28:52; II Ki. 19:24, 25.

Captured.—Gen. 34:25-27; Ju. 8:17; II Sam. 12:26-29.

Wasted by pestilence and famine.—I Sam. 5:11; Jer. 52:6; Amos 4:6.

Depopulated.—Is. 17:9; Ez. 26:19.

Destroyed.—Num. 21:28; 31:10; Deut. 13:16; Ju. 1:8; 9:45, 48, 49; 20:48; Is. 25:2.

Jerusalem described.—City in which God's name was recorded—I Ki. 11:36. City of solemnities—Is. 33:20. City of God—46:4; 48:1, 8; City of the great king—Ps. 48:2. City of truth—Zech. 8:3.

The church symbolized.—Heb. 12:22. The Builder, God—Heb. 11:10. A city set on a hill—Mt. 5:14.

Christ and His disciples went first to cities.—Mt. 9:35; 11:1.

Paul preached in cities.—Athens—Acts 17:16–33. Corinth—Acts 18:1–11. Ephesus—Acts 19:1–10. Jerusalem—Acts 21:17–40; Chs. 22, 23. Philippi—Acts 16:11–40. Rome—Acts 28:16–31.

How to approach people of cities.—Mt. 10:11–14, 23.

CITIES OF REFUGE. Design of—Ex. 21:13; Num. 35:11; Josh. 20:3.

Names, etc., of.—Deut. 4:41–43; Josh. 20:7, 8.

Required to be easy of access.—Deut. 19:3; Is. 62:10. Open to all manslayers—Josh. 20:4.

Strangers might take advantage of.—Num. 35:15.

Those admitted were put on trial.—Num. 35:12, 24. Not protected outside of—Num. 35:26, 27. Obliged to remain in until the death of the high priest—Num. 35:25, 28.

Afforded no asylum to murderers.—Ex. 21:14; Num. 35:16–21.

Illustrative of Christ.—Ps. 91:2; Is. 25: 4. Of the hope of the gospel—Heb. 6:18. Of the way to Christ—Is. 35:8; John 14:6.

CITIZEN. Lu. 15:15; 19:14; Acts 21: 39; 22:28. **Heaven, Of.**—Phil. 3:20.

CLAD. I Sam. 17:5; 59:17. See CLOTHING.

CLAIM. Job 3:5.

CLAMOR. Acts 23:9; Eph. 4:31.

CLAMOROUS. Pr. 7:11; 9:13.

CLAP. Hands in derision or rebellion—Job 27:23; 34:37; Lam. 2:15; Ez. 25: 6; Nah. 3:19. Joy, To express—II Ki. 11:12; Ps. 47:1; 98:8; Is. 55:12.

CLAUDA. See CAUDA.

CLAUDIA. A female disciple in Rome.—II Tim. 4:21.

CLAUDIUS. Fourth Roman emperor, nephew of Tiberius and Mark Antony's grandson.—Acts 11:28; 18:2.

CLAUDIUS LYSIAS. A Roman captain in Jerusalem.—Acts 23:26.

CLAWS. Dan. 4:33.

CLAY. Miry—Ps. 40:2.

Uses of.—Vessels made of—I Ki. 7:46; II Chr. 4:17; Jer. 18:4. Houses made of—Job 4:19. In miracle—John 9:6, 11, 14, 15. As a seal—Job 38:14.

Working in.—Jer. 18:6; Rom. 9:21. Trod by potter—Is. 41:25; Nah. 3:14.

Man made of.—Job 10:9; 33:6; Is. 64:8.

Figurative.—Defense of—Job 13:12. Speech of—Is. 45:9. Vessels for honor and dishonor—Rom. 9:22 f. Treasure in—II Cor. 4:7.

Illustrative.—Raiment as—Job 27:16. Potter esteemed as—Is. 29:16.

Symbolical.—Dan. 2:33–35, 41–45.

CLEAN. Ps. 51:7. All—John 13:10, 11. All things—Lu. 11:41; Rom. 14:20. Blood, From—Acts 18:6. Cloth—Mt. 27:59. Crib—Pr. 14:4. Entirely, *i. e.*—Josh. 3:17; Ps. 77:8; Joel 1:7; Zech. 11:17. Eyes, In his own—Pr. 16:2. *In thine*—Job 11:4. Hands—II Sam. 22:21; Job 17:9; Ps. 18:20; 24:4. See RIGHTEOUS. Heart—Ps. 51:10; 73:1 (A.V.); Pr. 20:9. See HEART, PURE. Heavens not—Job 15:5. Made clean by Jesus—Mt. 8:2, 3; Mk. 1:41, 42; Lu. 5:13. Man—Job 15:14; 25:4. Meats—Mk. 7:19. See ANIMALS, FOOD, PURIFICATION. Mitre—Zech. 3:5. Outside—Mt. 23:26; Lu. 11:39. See HYPOCRISY. Faith—Amos 4:6. Transgression, Without—Job 33:9. See RIGHTEOUS, SIN. Unclean, Out of—Job 14:4. Wash and be—II Ki. 5: 10–14; Is. 1:16; John 13:10. Water—Ez. 36:25. Ways of a man—Pr. 16:2. White, And—Rev. 19:8, 14 (A.V.). Word, Because of—John 15:3. See ANIMALS, CEREMONIAL CLEANSING, FOOD, PURIFICATION.

CLEANSING. Blood of Christ, By—I John 1:7, 9. Conscience—Heb. 9:14. Defilement, From all—II Cor. 7:1. Forgotten—II Pet. 1:9. God hath, What—Acts 10:15; 11:9. Hands—Jas. 4:8. Heart—Ps. 73:13; Acts 15:9. Inside of the cup—Mt. 23:26. Leprosy, From—II Ki. 5:10–14; Mt. 8:3; 10:8; 11:5; Mk. 1:42; Lu. 17:17; 4:27; 7:22; Jehovah, By—Ez. 24:13. None—Lu. 4:27. Outside—Mt. 23:25. Threshing floor—Mt. 3:12. Unrighteousness—I John 1:9. See FORGIVENESS, REMISSION OF SINS. Washing of water—Eph. 5:26. Ways, His—Ps. 119:9. Yourselves—Is. 52:11. See

CLEAN, CEREMONIAL CLEANSING, PURIFICATION.

CLEAR, CLEARING, CLEARLY. Crystal—Rev. 22:1. Day—Amos 8:9. Guilty, From—Gen. 44:16; Ex. 34:7; Num. 14:18; II Cor. 7:11. Heat—Is. 18:4. I shall—Ps. 19:13. Judgest, When thou—Ps. 51:4. Life shall be—Job 11:17. Noonday, Than—Job 11:17. Oath, From—Gen. 24:8, 41. Ourselves—Gen. 44:16. Rain, After—II Sam. 23:4. See clearly—Mt. 7:5; Mk. 8:25; Rom. 1:20. Sky—II Sam. 23:4; Job 37:21. See Amos 8:9. Sun, As the—Song of Sol. 6:10. Waters—Ez. 34:18.

CLEAVE. Bone to skin—Job 19:20; Ps. 102:5; Lam. 4:8. Dust, Unto—Ps. 119:25. Earth—Hab. 3:9. Feet, Dust to—Lu. 10:11. Flames of fire—Ps. 29:7. Fountain, and flood—Ps. 74:15. Good, To that which is—Rom. 12:9. Inheritance, To—Num. 36:7. Jehovah, To—Deut. 4:4; 10:20; 11:22; 13:4; Josh. 23:8; II Ki. 18:6. Jesus, To—Acts 11:23. See BELIEVE, DISCIPLES, CHURCH, JESUS. Leprosy—II Ki. 5:27. Mouth, Tongue to—Job 29:10; Ps. 22:15; 137:6; Lam. 4:4. Mount of Olives—Zech. 14:4. Rock in wilderness—Ps. 78:15; Is. 48:21. Testimonies, To—Ps. 119:31. Tongues—See MOUTH. Wife, To—Gen. 2:24; Mt. 19:5; Mk. 10:5; Eph. 5:31. See CLING.

CLEFT. Rock—Ex. 33:22; Ju. 15:8; Song of Sol. 2:14; Is. 2:21; 51:5; Jer. 49:16; Ob. 3.

CLEMENCY. Acts 24:4.

CLEMENT, klĕm'ent. One of Paul's helpers.—Phil. 4:3.

CLEOPAS, klē'o-păs. An early disciple.—Lu. 24:18.

CLEOPHAS. See CLOPAS.

CLERK. Town—Acts 19:35.

CLIMB. I Sam. 14:13; Jer. 4:29; Joel 2:7, 9; Amos 9:2; Lu. 19:4; John 10:1.

CLIP. Jer. 48:37.

CLOAK. Mt. 5:40; Lu. 22:36; I Thess. 2:5; I Pet. 2:16. See CLOTHING, COAT.

CLOD. Job 7:5; 21:33; 38:38; Hos. 10:11; Joel 1:17.

CLOPAS, CLEOPHAS, ALPHEUS. Husband of Mary, who is considered by many to be the sister of the mother of Jesus.—Mt. 19:3; John 19:25.

CLOSET. Joel 2:16. See PRAYER, PRIVATE.

CLOSE, CLOSER. Book—Lu. 4:20. Breach—Amos 9:11. Earth—Num. 16:33; Jonah 2:6. Evil—Ju. 20:34. Eyes closed—Num. 24:3; Is. 29:10; Mt. 13:15; Acts 28:27. Place—II Sam. 22:46; Ps. 18:45. Sticketh closer than—Pr. 18:14. Windows—Ez. 40:16. Womb—Gen. 20:18. Words—Dan. 12:9.

CLOTH. Linen. Mt. 27:29; Lu. 24:12. New or undressed in old garment—Mt. 9:16; Mk. 2:21. Striped—Pr. 7:16.

CLOTHING: Originated with God.—Gen. 3:21.

Miraculously preserved.—Deut. 29:5.

Clothing as a mark of power.—Pr. 31:22–25; Mt. 11:8; Mk. 15:17; Lu. 16:19; Jas. 2:2–4. Figurative—Ps. 93:1; 132:9; 109:18; Pr. 23:21; Is. 61:10; 50:3; Mt. 6:30; Lu. 24:49.

Rending of.—Gen. 37:34; Num. 14:6; Ju. 11:35; II Sam. 15:32; Ezra 9:3, 5; Acts 14:14.

Washing of.—Ex. 19:10; Lev. 11:25, 40; 13:6; 14:8, 9, 47; 15:5, 8, 11, 22; 16:26, 28; Num. 8:7, 21; 19:10, 21; 31:20, 24; II Sam. 19:24.

Customs concerning clothes.—Pure white used—Esth. 8:15. Put off—Song of Sol. 5:3. Clothing of those slain with a sword not used—Is. 14:19. Rolled in blood—Is. 9:5. Washed in wine—Gen. 49:11. Garment as a pledge—Ex. 22:26; Deut. 24:12, 13.

Clothes called.—Clothes—II Chr. 28:15; Pr. 6:27; Ez. 16:10. Clothing—Job 22:6; 31:9. Vestments—II Ki. 10:22. Raiment—Gen. 28:20; 45:22; Deut. 8:4; Ju. 14:19; II Ki. 5:22. Garments—II Sam. 13:18; Acts 7:58; 22:23; Rev. 19:16. Vesture—Gen. 41:42; 49:11; Deut. 22:12. Apparel—Ju. 17:10; I Sam. 18:4; II Sam. 13:18; Esth. 5:1. Perfumed garments—Ps. 45:8; Song of Sol. 4:11. See PERFUME.

Clothing for special occasions.—Mourning: Sackcloth—Ez. 27:31; Jonah 3:5, 6. Apparel—Gen. 38:14; II Sam. 14:2. Wedding—Mt. 22:11.

Materials of.—Fig leaves—Gen. 3:7. Linen—I Chr. 15:27; II Chr. 5:12; Pr. 31:24. Fine linen—Ez. 16:10, 13. See LINEN. Priests' garments—Ex.

Chs. 28–39. Skins—Gen. 3:21; Heb. 11:37. Leather—II Ki. 1:8; Mt. 3:4. Woven work—Ex. 28:32; 29:5. Wool —Pr. 27:26; Ez. 34:3. Camel's hair— Mt. 3:4. Embroidered—Ex. 28:39; Ps. 45:14. Figurative—Ez. 16:10, 12; 27:24. Silk (fig.)—Ez. 16:10, 13. Rich —Ez. 27:24. Mixed materials—Lev. 19: 19; Deut. 22:11.

Colors of clothing.—Figurative: Dyed— Is. 63:1. Stained—Is. 63:3. Variegated: Joseph's coat—Gen. 27:3. Tamar—II Sam. 13:18, 19. Purple— Esth. 8:15; Jer. 10:9; Dan. 5:7, 16, 29; Lu. 16:19; John 19:2, 5. White—Eccl. 9:8; Esth. 8:15; Mt. 28:3; Rev. 3:18; 7:13. Blue—Esth. 8:15; Jer. 10:9; Ez. 23:6; 27:24. Figurative: Red— Is. 63:2. Scarlet—II Sam. 1:24; Mt. 27:28. Rich colored robes worn on special occasions called festal—Is. 3: 22.

Clothing used to distinguish social rank. —Rich: *Soft*—Mt. 11:8; Lu. 7:25. *Fine*—Jas. 2:2, 3. Royal: *Mordecai*— Esth. 8:15. *Herod*—Acts 12:21. Embroidered—Ps. 45:14. Perfumed— Ps. 45:8; Song of Sol. 4:11. Poor: *God giveth*—Deut. 10:18. *Vile*—Jas. 2:2. *Used as bedding*—Deut. 24:13. *As a pledge*—Deut. 24:12, 13. *Old*—Josh. 9:5. Figurative—Ps. 102:26. Israelites, lasted forty years—Deut. 8:4. Change of—Gen. 35:2; 41:14. Wicked —Job 27:16.

Worn by priests.—Sanctified garments— Ex. 28:3. Holy garments—Lev. 16:4. Breastplate — Ex. 28:4, 15, 22–28, 30; 29:5. Golden crown—Ex. 39:30. Coats —Ex. 28:40; 29:8. Ephods—Ex. 28:4, 6, 7, 12, 25, 28; 29:5. Skirt of robe of Ephod—Ex. 28:33, 34; 29:5; 39:24. Of blue—Ex. 39:22. Hole of—Ex. 39: 23. Ornaments—Ex. 39:24. Coat of checkerwork—Ex. 28:4, 40; 29:5. Coat of mail—Ex. 28:32. Linen coat—Lev. 16:4. Mitre—Ex. 28:4, 37; 29:6; 39: 28, 31; Lev. 16:4. Head tire—Ex. 28: 40; 29:9; 39:28. Girdle—Ex. 28:4, 8, 40; 29:5, 9; 39:5, 29; Lev. 8:7, 13; 16: 4. Lace—Ex. 28:28, 37; 39:31. Breeches —Ex. 28:42; 39:28; Lev. 16:4. Measurements of—Ex. 28:16. Woven work —Ex. 39:22. Bindings—Ex. 39:26. Colors: Blue, purple, scarlet—Ex. 39:

24. See Ex. Chs. 25–39. Law concerning—Lev. 6:10, 27; 13:47–59; 14: 55. .

Names of articles worn.—Coats: *Coats of skins*—Gen. 3:21. *Joseph's coat*— Gen. 37:3, 23, 31–33. *Embroidered coat for priest*—Ex. 28:4, 39, 40, 41; 29:5, 8; 39:27; 40:14; Lev. 8:7, 13; 16:4. *Nadab and Abihu carried out in*—Lev. 10: 5. *The coat of Goliath*—I Sam. 17:5. *Saul puts coat of mail on David*—I Sam. 17:38. *Hushai rends his coat*—II Sam. 15:32. *God binds Job as by collar of*— Job 30:18. New Testament References: *Take away coat*—Mt. 5:40. *Must not provide*—Mt. 10:10; Mk. 6:9; Lu. 9:3. *Instruction of John*—Lu. 3:11. *Nor withhold*—Lu. 6:29. *Parted the Saviour's coat*—John 19:23. *Peter puts on*—John 21:7. *Show coats Dorcas made*—Acts 9:39.

Robe (*an ornamental mantle worn over tunic*). *Robe exchanged for sackcloth* —Is. 3:24. *Festival*—Is. 3:22. *Put on Christ, Scarlet*—Mt. 27:28. *Purple*— Mk. 15:17. *Of kings*—Jonah 3:6; I Ki. 22:10, 30; I Chr. 15:27; 18:9, 29. *Of judge*—I Sam. 15:27; 24:11. *Eliakim clothed with*—Is. 22:21. *Ezra's*— Ezra 9:3, 5. *Gift to David*—I Sam. 18:4. *David's enemies*—Ps. 109:29. *Job's*—Job 1:20. *Rent*—Job 2:12. *Of king's daughters*—II Sam. 13:18. *Jesus'*—Mt. 27:28, 31; Lu. 23:11; John 19:2, 5. *For prodigal*—Lu. 15:22. *Scribes in long coats*—Lu. 20:46. *Symbolical*—Mic. 2:8. *Figurative*—Job 29: 14; Is. 61:10; Ez. 26:16; Rev. 6:11; 7:9, 13, 14.

Mantle. Song of Sol. 5:7. *Elijah*—I Ki. 19:13, 19; II Ki. 2:8, 13, 14. *Wanton women*—Is. 3:22. *Babylonish*—Josh. 7:21, 24. *Hebrew children bound in*— Dan. 3:21.

Trimmings used.—Fringe—Num. 15:38, 39; Deut. 22:12. Cord of blue—Num. 15:38. Borders—Mt. 23:5. Sashes— Is. 3:20. Mufflers—Is. 3:1.

Garments worn.—Tunic—Dan. 3:21. See Coats. Swaddling clothes, *Jesus wrapped in*—Lu. 2:7, 12. *Figurative, Swaddling bands*—Job 38:9, 14. Footwear: *Shoe; shod with spoils of war*— II Chr. 28:15. *Custom concerning*— Ruth 4:7, 8. *Removal of*—Ex. 3:5;

Josh. 5:15; Acts 7:33. *Loosed shoes*—Deut. 25:10. *Shoe-latchet*—Gen. 14:23; Is. 5:27; Mk. 1:7; Lu. 3:16. *Take no*—Mt. 10:10. *Figurative, Sealskin*—Ez. 16:10. Sandal; *a sole of leather*—Mk. 6:9; Acts 12:8. Head dress: *Crown.* See CROWN. *Head tire*—Lev. 8:13; Is. 3:20. Turban—Is. 3:23. Veil—Gen. 24:65; 38:14; Song of Sol. 6:7; Is. 3:23; I Cor. 11:3, 6, 7, 10. *Figurative*—Ez. 23:15. Cloak: *Used as a garment*—Mt. 24:18; Lu. 6:29. *For a covering by night. Used as a pledge of security*—Ex. 22:25; Deut. 24:12; Amos 2:8. *As a saddle*—Mt. 21:7. *As a rug*—II Ki. 9:13. *As a receptacle*—Ex. 12:34; Ju. 8:25; II Ki. 4:39; Hag. 2:12. *For decoration*—Ez. 16:16, 18. *Taken*—Mt. 5:40; Lu. 6:29. *Paul's cloak*—II Tim. 4:13. *Figurative*—I Pet. 2:16; I Thess. 2:5. Girdle—Ex. 28:39; Ps. 109:19; Is. 3:24; 22:21; Jer. 13:1–11. *Of linen*—Ez. 16:10. *Of sackcloth*—Is. 3:24; 20:2; 22:12; Ez. 27:31. *Aaron's Sons'*—Lev. 8:13. *Elijah's leather girdle*—II Ki. 1:8. *John the Baptist's leather*—Mt. 3:4; Mk. 1:6; Acts 21:11. *Gift of*—I Sam. 18:4; II Sam. 18:11. *Eliakim's*—Is. 22:21. *Delivers*—Pr. 31:24. *Of loins*—II Sam. 20:8; I Ki. 2:5; Job 12:18; Is. 5:27. *Of breast*—Rev. 1:13; 15:6. *Gird thyself*—Lu. 17:8; John 13:4. *Paul's*—Acts 21:11. *As a sword belt*—I Sam. 18:4; II Sam. 20:8. *Illustrative*—Joel 1:8, 13. *Figurative*—Job 12:18; Pr. 31:24; Is. 11:5; 22:21; Jer. 13:1–11; Ez. 23:15; Eph. 6:14; Rev. 15:6.

Women's special garments.—Eve's fig leaves—Gen. 3:7. Forbidden to wear men's—Deut. 22:5. Tamar's robe—II Sam. 13:18. Worn by men—Deut. 22:5; II Chr. 5:12. Breeches of Hebrew children—Dan. 3:21.

Uncovered or exposed.—Noah—Gen. 9:21–23. David in dancing—II Sam. 6:20. Joseph by Potiphar's wife—Gen. 39:12–18.

Clothed the naked.—II Chr. 28:15.

Dignity as clothing.—Pr. 31:25.

Figurative.—Remove clothing—Pr. 31:24; Is. 47:2; Jer. 14:22, 26; Nah. 3:5. Moth-eaten—Job 13:28. See JEWELS, WOMEN.

CLOUD. See METEOROLOGY.
CLOUD OF GLORY: Called.—The cloud—Ex. 34:5; 40:34–38. The pillar of cloud—Ex. 33:9, 10. The cloud of Jehovah—Num. 10:34. Pillar of cloud and pillar of fire—Ex. 13:22. Presence of Jehovah—Ex. 33:14, 15.

First appearance of.—Ex. 13:20, 21.

What designed for.—To decide the goings and stayings of Israel—Ex. 40:36–37; Num. 9:15–23. To guide them by day and by night—Ex. 13:21, 22; Neh. 9:12, 19; Ps. 78:14; 99:7; 105:39. To shield the ark and the people while journeying—Num. 10:33–36; Ps. 105:39; Is. 4:5–6. To protect Israel from foes—Ex. 14:19–20; Job 36:32; Ps. 105:38; I Cor. 10:2. To embody the glory of Jehovah at the tabernacle—Ex. 29:42–43; 33:9–10; 40:34–35; Lev. 16:2. *At Solomon's temple*—I Ki. 8:10–11; II Chr. 5:13–14. *Latter temple*—Ez. 10:3, 4, 18. *Over Jerusalem*—Ez. 11:22–23. *Paul speaks of this glory*—Rom. 9:4; I Cor. 10:2.

Clouds the medium through which Jehovah approached the people.—At Sinai—Ex. 16:10–12; 24:15–18; Deut. 5:22. On the journey—Ex. 33:10; Ps. 99:7. To produce faith in Moses—Ex. 19:9–16; 33:9; Num. 12:5–10. At transfiguration of Jesus—Mt. 17:5; Mk. 9:7; Lu. 9:34–35.

Nebulous haze typifies the hiding of Jehovah.—Job 22:14; 26:9; Ps. 97:2.
Cloud of fire symbolizes the purity of Jehovah.—Ex. 24:17; Dan. 7:9–10.
Return of cloud of glory foretold.—Is. 4:5; Ez. 43:2–4.
Ezekiel's further visions.—Ez. 1:4; 30:3.
Clouds in connection with Jesus.—Transfiguration—Mt. 17:5; Mk. 9:7. Ascension—Acts 1:9. Return to disciples—Mt. 24:30; Lu. 21:27. Crowned in the heavens—Rev. 14:14.
Clouds in connection with the saints.—I Thess. 4:17; Rev. 11:12. See GLORY.
CLUBS. Job 41:29.
CLOVEN. Foot—Lev. 11:3, 7, 26; Deut. 14:6–7. See ANIMALS, UNCLEAN. Tongues—Acts 2:3.
CLUSTER. Of grapes—Gen. 40:10; Num. 13:23, 24; Deut. 32:32; Song of Sol. 7:7; Is. 65:8; Mic. 7:1; Rev. 14:18. Henna flowers—Song of Sol. 1:14.

Pleiades—Job 38:31. Raisins—I Sam. 25:18; 30:12; II Sam. 16:1; I Chr. 12:40.

CNIDUS, knī'dus. **A seaport of Asia Minor which Paul passed on way to Rome.**—Acts 27:7.

COALS. II Sam. 14:7; Job 41:21; Is. 44:12; Lam. 4:8.

Fire, Of.—Lev. 16:12; II Sam. 22:9, 13; I Ki. 19:6; Ps. 18:8, 12, 13; 140:10; Is. 6:6; 44:19; 47:14; 54:16; Ez. 1:13; 10:2; 24:11; John 18:18; 21:9. Heap on head—Pr. 25:22; Rom. 12:20.

COAST. See BORDER, SEA.

COASTING. Acts 27:8.

COASTLAND. Is. 20:6.

COATS: Coats of skin.—Gen. 3:21. Joseph's coat—Gen. 37:3, 23, 31–33. Embroidered coat for priest—Ex. 28:4, 39, 40, 41; 29:5, 8; 39:27; 40:14; Lev. 8:7, 13; 16:4. Nadab and Abihu carried out in—Lev. 10:5. The coat of Goliath—I Sam. 17:5. Saul puts coat of mail on David—I Sam. 17:38. Hushai rends his coat—II Sam. 15:32. God binds Job as by a coat—Job 30:18.

New Testament references.—Take away coat—Mt. 5:40. Must not provide—Mt. 10:10; Mk. 6:9; Lu. 9:3. Instruction of John—Lu. 3:11. Nor withhold —Lu. 6:29. Parted the Savior's coat —John 19:23. Peter puts on—John 21:7. Show coats Dorcas made—Acts 9:39. See CLOTHING.

COCK. Crowing—Mk. 13:35. Peter denied Jesus before cock crew—Mt. 26:34, 74, 75; Mk. 14:30, 68, 72; Lu. 22:34, 60, 61; John 13:38; 18:27.

COCKATRICE. See ADDER.

COCKLE. Job 31:40.

COFFER. I Sam. 6:8, 11, 15.

COFFIN. Gen. 50:26.

COLD: Physical.—Gen. 8:22; Pr. 25:13; Acts 28:2; II Cor. 11:27. Cold water —Pr. 25:25; Mt. 10:42.

Spiritual.—Mt. 24:12; Rev. 3:15.

COLHOZEH, kol-hō'zeh. (1) **Father of Shallun.**—Neh. 3:15. (2) **Father of Baruch.**—Neh. 11:5.

COLLAR. Bindeth as—Job 30:18. Collection for the saints—I Cor. 16:1.

COLLEGE. II Ki. 22:14 (A.V.); II Chr. 34:22 (A.V.).

COLONY. Philippi a Roman.—Acts 16:12.

COLORS. In both Old and New Testaments. Only casual or primary distinctions are used.

Black.—Symbol of mourning or some disaster—Lev. 13:31, 37; Esth. 1:6; Job 30:28, 30; Lam. 4:8; 5:10; Jer. 14:2.

White.—Symbol of purity—Lev. 13:38, 39; Esth. 1:6; Ps. 51:7; Is. 1:18; Dan. 7:9; 12:10; Mt. 17:2; 28:3; Mark 9:3; 16:5; Lu. 9:29; John 20:12; Acts 1:10; Rev. 3:4, 5, 18; 4:4; 6:11; 7:9, 13, 14; 20:11. White denotes nobility and elegance—Esth. 8:15; Eccl. 9:8; Lam. 4:7. Whiteness of teeth, skin and hair —Gen. 49:12; Song of Sol. 5:10; Mt. 5:36; Rev. 1:14. Wool—Is. 1:18; Ez. 27:18; Rev. 1:14. Snow—Ex. 4:6; Num. 12:10; II Ki. 5:27; Lam. 4:7. Milk—Lam. 4:7. Marble—Esth. 1:6. Cloth—Esth. 1:6. Fields—John 4:35. Bread—Gen. 40:16. Sepulchres—Mt. 23:27.

Scarlet, purple, and red.—Badge of royalty.

Scarlet.—Gen. 38:28; Ex. 26:31, 36; 35:6, 23, 25; 36:8, 35; Lev. 14:4, 6; Num. 4:8; 19:6; Josh. 3:18, 21; II Sam. 1:24; Esth. 1:6; Pr. 31:21; Song of Sol. 4:3; Is. 1:18; Jer. 4:30; Lam. 4:5; Nah. 2:3; Mt. 27:28; Heb. 9:19; Rev. 17:3, 4; 18:12, 16.

Purple.—Ex. 26:31, 36; 36:6, 23, 25, 35; 36:8, 35; Num. 4:13; Ju. 8:26; II Chr. 2:7; 3:14; Esth. 1:6; 8:15; Song of Sol. 3:10; 7:5; Jer. 10:9; Ez. 27:7, 16; Dan. 5:7, 16, 29; Mk. 15:17, 20; Lu. 16:19; John 19:25; Acts 16:14; Rev. 17:4; 18:12, 16.

Other reds.—Gen. 25:25; Ex. 36:19; Lev. 13:19, 42, 43, 49; 14:37; II Chr. 2:7; 3:14; Esth. 1:6; Is. 1:18; Nah. 2:3. Skin—Gen. 25:25; I Sam. 16:12; 17:42; Song of Sol. 4:3; 5:10; Lam. 4:7. Animals—Num. 19:2; Zech. 1:8; Rev. 12:3. Wine—Pr. 23:31. Pottage— Gen. 25:30. Leather or cloth—Ex. 25:5; 26:14; 35:7; 36:19; 39:34; Is. 63:2. Wood—Jer. 22:14; Ez. 23:14; Nah. 2:3. Sky—Mt. 16:2-3. Eyes—Gen. 49:12; Pr. 23:29.

Blue.—Ex. 26:31, 36; 35:6, 23, 25, 35; 36:8; Num. 4:6, 12; 15:38; II Chr. 2:7,

14; 3:14; Esth. 1:6; 8:15; Jer. 10:9; Ez. 23:6; 27:7, 24.

Yellow.—Lev. 13:30, 32, 36; Esth. 1:6.

Green.—Lev. 13:49; 14:37; Esth. 1:6; Ps. 52:8; Jer. 17:8; Hos. 14:8; Rev. 9:4.

Materials in tabernacles and temple.—Ex. 26:31, 36; 35:6, 23, 25, 35; 36:8; Num. 4:6–13; 19:6; II Chr. 2:7; 3:14.

Test of leprosy.—Ex. 4:6; Lev. 13:17, 18, 20, 21, 24, 25, 30, 31, 38, 42, 43, 49, 55; 14:37; Num. 12:10; If Ki. 5:27.

Color meaning pretense.—Acts 27:30.

Various colors of animals.—Horses—Zech. 1:8; 6:3, 6; Rev. 19:14. Asses—Jer. 5:10. Sheep—Gen. 30:32–40. Beasts—Rev. 17:3.

Stones.—Esth. 1:6; Ps. 68:13; Is. 54:11; Rev. 2:17; 4:3. See PRECIOUS STONES.

Clothing of varied colors (may mean *pieces, ends*).—Gen. 37:3, 23, 32, 33; II Sam. 13:18, 19. Fig. Ez. 16:16.

Rainbow.—Rev. 4:3; 10:1.

COLOSSÆ, ko-lŏs'sæ. A famous city in Phrygia in Asia Minor in which was the church to which Paul wrote the Epistle to the Colossians. This was a great city in the days of Xerxes (481 B.C.).

COLOSSIANS. See OUTLINE STUDIES IN THE BOOKS.

COLT. Jesus rides in his triumphal entry—Mt. 21:2, 5, 7; Mk. 1:2, 7; Lu. 19:30, 33, 35; John 12:12–15. See Zech. 9:9. Man is born as—Job 11:12. Sons of judges each rides on—Ju. 10: 4; 12:14.

COME. After me, even he that—John 1:27. If any man would—Mt. 16:24. See DISCIPLE, SELF-DENIAL. All things alike to all—Eccl. 9:2. Call not the righteous, but sinners—Lu. 5:32. Christ in the flesh—II John 7. See JESUS, HUMANITY OF, SECOND COMING OF. Calamity—Pr. 6:15. See AFFLICTION, ADVERSITY, CALAMITY. Change, My—Job 14:14. Courts, Into His—Ps. 96: 8. Day of the Lord—Joel 2:1, 31. Days—Jer. 7:32; 9:25; 19:6. Death suddenly upon—Ps. 55:15. Departure, Time of my—II Tim. 4:6. Destruction—Job 5:21; Ps. 35:8; Pr. 1:27; Is. 13:6. Dispersions are fully—Jer. 25: 34. Elijah—Mt. 17:11; Mk. 15:36. Evil—Job 30:26. Fear—Pr. 1:27; 3:

25. Flesh, In the—II John 7. See JESUS, HUMANITY OF. Follow me, and —Mt. 19:21; Mk. 10:21; Lu. 18:22. Generation, Coming—Ps. 78:4, 6; 102: 18. Grave, To—Job 5:26. Heaven, From—*Holy City, Jerusalem*—Rev. 21: 10. *Jesus*—John 6:38; 8:42. See JESUS, DIVINITY OF. Wisdom—Jas. 3: 15. He that—Mt. 11:3. See JESUS. Help, My—Ps. 121:1. John the Baptist—Mt. 3:1. Judge, To—Ps. 96:13; 98:19. Kingdom of God—Lu. 11:2; 17:20. See JESUS, KINGDOM OF. Labor, All ye that—Mt. 11:28. Leper to Jesus—Mk. 1:40. Lord, Of the—Jas. 5:8. See JESUS, SECOND COMING OF. Master is come, The—John 11:28. Morning—Is. 21:12. Name of Jehovah, In—Ps. 118:26. Prayer—Ps. 88:2; 102:1; 119: 170. Presence, Before His—Ps. 100:2. Quickly, Behold, I come—Rev. 3:11; 22:7, 12, 20. Salvation and strength—Rev. 12:10. Satan came also—Job 1: 6, 7; 2:1, 2. See, And—John 1:39. Son of Man—Mt. 10:23; 16:27; Mk. 13:26; Lu. 21:27. See JESUS. Spirit upon Him—Mt. 3:16. See HOLY SPIRIT. Times to—Pr. 31:25; Eccl. 1:11; Is. 30:8. Together—see CONGREGATION. Tribulation, Out of—Rev. 7:14. Trouble—Deut. 31:17; Job 27:9. Victorious, Off—Rev. 15:2. Wisdom—Job 28: 20. World to—Lu. 18:30 (A.V.); Eph. 1:21. Worship and bow down—Ps. 95:6. Wrath—Mt. 3:7; I Thess. 2:16. Ye—Is. 56:12. *To the waters*—Is. 55: 1. Ye cannot—John 7:34.

COMELINESS. Abundant, more—I Cor. 12:23. Corruption, Was turned into—Dan. 10:8. Hath no form nor—Is. 53:2. Set forth thy—Ez. 27:10.

COMELY. Black, but—Song of Sol. 1:5. Cheeks—Song of Sol 1:10. Countenance is—Song of Sol. 2:14. Good and—Eccl. 5:18. Jerusalem, As—Song of Sol. 6:4. Person—I Sam. 16:18. Praise is—Ps. 33:1; 147:1.

COMFORT, COMFORTER. Bed shall—Job 7:13. Delight my soul—Ps. 94: 19. Faith, Concerning—I Thess. 3:2. Forgive and—II Cor. 2:7. Hearts—Eph. 6:22; Col. 4:8; II Thess. 2:17. Holy Spirit. See HOLY SPIRIT. Isaac was—Gen. 24:67. Judah was—Gen. 38:12. Looked for—Ps. 69:20. Men,

Neither shall—Jer. 16:7. Miserable, Are ye all—Job 16:2. Mother, As one who—Ps. 66:13. Women, They that—Mt. 5:4. Not—Is. 54:11. Oppressed and had no—Eccl. 4:1. Sorrow, Myself against—Jer. 8:18. Saul refused to be—Ps. 77:2. See CONSOLATION.

COMFORTABLY. Is. 40:2.

THE TEN COMMANDMENTS. Primarily the Decalogue, or Ten Words.—Ex. 20:3-17; Deut. 5:7-21. Given orally from Sinai—Ex. 20:1; 24:3; Deut. 5:4, 22-25; 9:10; 10:4. Written in Book of Covenant—Ex. 24:4. Written on tables of stone—Ex. 24:12; 34:1, 4; Deut. 4:13; 5:22; 9:9-11; II Cor. 3:3, 7. Moses broke the first tables of stone—Ex. 32:19; Deut. 9:17; 10:2. God gave a later copy—Ex. 31: 18; 34:1, 28; Deut. 10:1-5. God wrote —Ex. 24:12; 32:16; 34:1, 28; Deut. 4:13; 5:22; 9:19; 10:2, 4. Seem to fix number at ten—Ex. 34:28; Deut. 10:4. Put in the ark—Deut. 10:1-5; I Ki. 8:9; II Chr. 5:10; Heb. 9:4. Called covenant—Deut. 4:13. Words of the covenant—Ex. 34:28. Tables of the covenant—Deut. 9:9, 11; Heb. 9:4. Tables of testimony—Ex. 31:18; 32: 15, 16; 34:29. Ministration of death— Rom. 7:5; II Cor. 3:7, 9. Given to Moses for the children of Israel—Ex. 25:22; 34:3; Lev. 26:46; 27:34; Deut. 1:3.

Hints that the principles involved in these commandments had been taught before.—Gen. 26:5; I. Ex. 8:10; 9:14; II. Gen. 35:2; IV. Ex. 16:23-30; V. Gen. 9:20-27; VI. Gen. 4:9-11; 9:5, 6; VII. Gen. 20:2-7; 26:6-11; 39:7-9; VIII. Gen. 30:33; 31:19, 30, 32.

These commandments repeated prior to the death of Jesus:

I. Ex. 20:23; 22:20; 23:13, 24, 32; 34:14-16; Lev. 11:7; Deut. 4:35, 39; 5:7; 6:4, 14; 8:19, 20; 11:26-28; 13:1-11; 17: 2-7; 30:17, 18; Ju. 6:10; II Ki. 17:35-39; Is. 40:18-26; Jer. 2:11; 5:7, 12-17; 7:6; 25:6; 35:15; Hos. 13:4; Mk. 12: 29, 30; Lu. 10:27.

II. Ex. 20:23; 32:8, 19-35; 34:13-17; Lev. 19:4; 26:1; Deut. 4:16-23; 5:8-10; 16:21, 22; 27:15; 29:17-21; I Ki. 18:17-40; Jer. 16:20, 21.

III. Ex. 22:28; Lev. 18:21; 19:12; 20:3; 21:6; 22:32; 24:10-16, 23; Deut. 5:11; 6:13; 10:20; Mt. 5:33-37; 23:16-22.

IV. Ex, 23:12; 31:13-17; 34:21; 35:2, 3; Lev. 19:3, 30; 23:3; 26:2; Num. 15:32-36; Deut. 5:12-15; Neh. 13:15-21; Jer. 17:21-25; Ez. 20:12, 20; 44:24.

V. Ex. 21:15, 17; Lev. 19:3; 20:9; Deut. 5:16; 21:18-21; 27:16; Mt. 15:4; 19: 19; Mk. 7:10; 10:19; Lu. 18:20.

VI. Ex. 21:12, 14, 20, 21; Lev. 24:17, 21; Num. 35:16-21, 30-33; Deut. 5:17; 19: 10-13; Mt. 5:21-26; 19:18; 26:52; Mk. 10:19; Lu. 18:20.

VII. Lev. 18:20; Num. 5:12-31; 20:10; Deut. 5:18; 22:22-27; 24:1-4; Jer. 3:1; 5:7-9; 28:21-23; Mt. 5:27-32; 19:3-9, 18; Mk. 10:19; Lu. 18:20.

VIII. Ex. 21:16; 22:1-4, 7-15; Lev. 6:2-7; 19:11, 13, 35, 36; Deut. 5:19; 23:24, 25; 25:13-16; Amos. 8:4-11; Mic. 6: 10-15; Mt. 19:18; Mk. 10:19; Lu. 18: 20.

IX. Ex. 23:1, 7, 8; Lev. 19:11, 12; Deut. 5:20; 19:16-21; Mt. 19:18; Mk. 10:19; Lu. 18:20.

X. Deut. 5:21; Jer. 22:13-19; Amos 8:4-11; Mic. 2:1-3; Heb. 2:9; Lu. 12:15-21.

These commandments repeated after the death of Jesus:

I. Acts 17:23-31; Rom. 1:23-25; I Cor. 8:4-6.

II. Acts 14:11-17; 17:23-31; I Cor. 6:9, 10; 8:4-6; 10:7, 14, 19, 20; II Cor. 6: 16, 17; Gal. 5:19-21; Eph. 5:3-6; Col. 3:5; I John 5:21; Rev. 21:8; 22:15.

III. Jas. 5:12.

IV. The only commandment not repeated after the death of Jesus—Mk. 2:27. Not in force as a commandment after His death. See Mk. 2:27; Rom. 14:5, 16; Gal. 4:10, 11; Col. 2:16, 17; Heb. 8:5; 10:1, 9. See LORD'S DAY, Acts 20:7.

V. Eph. 6:1-3; Col. 3:20.

VI. Rom. 13:9; I John 3:15; Rev. 21:8; 22:15.

VII. Rom. 13:9; I Cor. 6:13-18; Gal. 5: 19-21; Eph. 5:3-6; Col. 3:5; I Thess. 4:4-7; Heb. 13:4; Rev. 22:15.

VIII. Rom. 13:9; I Cor 6:10, 11; Eph. 4:28.

IX. Rom. 13:9.

X. Rom. 7:7; 13:9; I Cor. 6:10; Eph. 5:5; Col. 3:5; I Tim. 6:9–11, 17; Heb. 13:5.

Bind on hand.—Ex. 13:9, 16; Deut. 6:8; 11:18. For frontlets—Ex. 13:9, 16; Deut. 6:8; 11:18. Written on doorposts and gates—Deut. 6:9; 11:20.

Keeping the commandments.—Lev. 18: 5; 22:31; Deut. 4:4, 6; 5:10, 29; 6:17; 8:6; 11:8, 22; 26:13, 18; 28:9; I Ki. 2:3; 3:14; 6:12; 8:58, 61; 9:4; II Ki. 23:1–24; I Chr. 29:19; Ps. 119:1–176; I Cor. 7:19; I John 5:2, 3; Rev. 12:17; 14:12.

Blessing pronounced on those who keep the commandments.—Lev. 18:5; Deut. 4:40; 5:10, 29; 7:9–11; 26:12–19; 28: 1–68; 29:10–28; 30:1–20; I Sam. 12: 14, 15; I Ki. 2:1–4; 3:14; 6:12, 13; 8: 56–61; 9:3–9; Ps. 78:5–72; 119:97–104; Is. 48:17–22; Mt. 19:17; Lu. 10: 28; Rom. 10:5; Gal. 3:12.

People taught to wear a fringe or border on their garments to remind the wearers of the commandments.—Num. 15: 37–41; Deut. 22:12.

Possession of the land dependent on the obedience of these commandments.—Deut. 4:40; 6:17–25; 7:17–26; 8:1–20; 11:7–15, 22–32; 29:22–28; 30:1–5; I Ki. 9:6–9; I Chr. 28:8; Neh. 9:13–25; Ez. 20:15–44. See Num. 13:30–33; 14: 1–38; Deut. 1:21–40; 9:23.

Violation of the commandments, instances of.—The children of Israel—Num. 15:30–36; Deut. 9:11–21; Ju. 2: 10–23; 3:1–8; II Ki. 17:1–17; Ps. 78: 8–78; Amos 2:1–16. Of Judah—I Ki. 14:22–25; II Ki. 17:19; II Chr. 12:1–12; Of Saul—I Sam. 13:14, 15; 15:3–28; Of David—II Sam. 12:7–15; Of Solomon—I Ki. 11:1–13; Of Jeroboam I Ki. 11:26–33; 13:1–5, 33, 34.

Led into captivity because of violation.—Deut. 28:47–52, 62–68; 29:25–28; 30: 1–5; Ju. 3:7, 8; I Ki. 9:6–9; 14:1–16; II Ki. 17:18, 20, 23; 18:9–12; 23:27; 24:1–4; II Chr. 7:20; Neh. 1:8, 9; 9: 26–30; Ps. 106:34–47; Jer. 21:3–14; 22:1–30; 24:1–10; 25:1–11; Ez. 39:23, 24.

The kingdom divided because of violation.—I Ki. 2:1–4; 9:7–9; 11:9–13, 26–39; 12:19, 20; 14:8; II Ki. 17:21; I

Chr. 28:6–9; II Chr. 7:17–22; Ps. 89: 29–33.

Making void through the traditions of men.—Mt. 15:1–9; Mk. 7:3–13.

Penalty for breaking the commandments.—Mt. 5:19; Jas. 2:10–13.

Death penalty for violation.—I. and II. Ex. 22:20; Lev. 17:7; Deut. 13:1–17; 17:2–7; 30:17, 18; Acts 17:23–31; I Cor. 6:9, 10; II Cor. 6:16, 17; Gal. 5: 19–21; Rev. 21:8; 22:15. III. Lev. 24: 10, 16, 23. IV, Ex. 31:13–17; Num. 15:32–36. V. Ex. 21:15, 17; Deut. 21: 18–21; Mt. 15:4–16; Mk. 7:10–13. VI. Ex. 21:12–14; Lev. 24:17, 21; Num. 35: 16–34; Deut. 19:1–13; Mt. 5:21, 22; 26:52; I John 3:15; Rev. 13:10; 21: 8; 22:15. VII. Lev. 18:20; 20:10–12; Deut. 22:22–27; Mt. 5:27–32; John 8: 5; Gal. 5:19–21; Eph. 5:3–5; I Thess. 4:4–7; Heb. 13:4; Rev. 21:8; 22:15. VIII. Ex. 21:16; 22:1–5, 7–12; Amos 8:4–11; Mic. 6:10–15; I Cor. 6:10. IX. Deut. 19:16–21; Rev. 21:8; 22:15. X. Josh. 7:20–26; I Cor. 6:10; Eph. 5:5; Col. 3:5, 6; I Tim. 6:9, 10; Jas. 5:1–6.

Knowledge of sin by the law.—Rom. 3: 20; 4:15; 5:13, 20; 7:7–13; I Cor. 15: 56; II Pet. 2:21.

As a law, commands are spiritual.—Mt. 5:17–40; Rom. 7:14.

The commandments summed up by Christ.—Mt. 22:35–40; Mk. 12:28–34; Lu. 10:25–37. See Lev. 19:18; Deut. 6:5; 10:12; 30:6, 16, 20; Mt. 5:43, 44; 7:12; 19:19; Lu. 6:31–35; Rom. 12:14, 20; 13:8–10; 15:1; Gal. 5:14, 15; 6:2; Jas. 2:8.

The new commandment.—John 13:34; 15:12, 17; I John 2:7–11; 3:10–16, 22–24; 4:20, 21; II John 5.

Keeping Jesus' commands.—John 14:15, 21, 23; 15:10–14; I Cor. 7:19; I John 2:3–5; 3:22–24; 5:2, 3; II John 6.

Commandments or precepts of men.—Mt. 15:9; Mk. 7:7; Col. 2:22; Tit. 1: 14. See COVENANTS, THE LORD'S DAY, SABBATH, LAW, STATUTES, OBEDIENCE.

COMMEND. Himself—II Cor. 10:18. Lord commendeth, The—II Cor. 10:18. Love of God—Rom. 5:8. Mirth—Eccl. 8:15. Ourselves—II Cor. 3:1; 6:4. Phoebe our sister—Rom. 16:1. Righteousness of God—Rom. 3:5. Spirit into thy hands—Ps. 31:3; Lu. 23:46.

Unrighteous steward—Lu. 16:8. Us to God—I Cor. 8:8. You to God—Acts 20:32.

COMMENTARY. II Chr. 24:27.

COMMISSION. Authority—Acts 26:12. Kings—Ezra 8:36.

The great commission.—Mt. 28:19, 20; Mk. 16:15, 16; Lu. 24:46, 47.

COMMIT. Antioch, from whence they have been.—Evil, Great—Jer. 26:19. Grace of God—Acts 14:26. Pits of darkness, To—II Pet. 2:4. Sin—John 8:34. See SIN. Souls—I Pet. 4:19. That, which I have carried unto him —II Tim. 1:12. Way unto Jehovah—Ps. 37:5. Works unto Jehovah—Pr. 16:3.

COMMODIOUS. Haven was not.—Acts 27:12.

COMMON. All things—Acts 2:44. Anything—Acts 10:14; 11:8. Bread under my hand—I Sam. 21:4. Call not—Acts 10:15; 11:9. Death—Num. 16:29. Faith—Tit. 1:4. Holy and—Lev. 10:10. Kindness—Acts 28:2. Men—Ez. 23:42. Nothing—Acts 11:8. People—Lev. 4:27; Jer. 26:23; John 12:9. Salvation—Jude 3. Temptation—I Cor. 10:13. Things—Acts 2:44. What God hath cleansed, Make not—Acts 10:15; 11:9.

COMMONWEALTH. Eph. 2:12.

COMMOTION. Jer. 10:22.

COMMUNE WITH. Abraham—Gen. 18:33. Chief priests—Jer. 22:4. David—I Sam. 18:22. Disciples on way to Emmaus—Lu. 24:15. Heart—Ps. 4:4; 77:6; Eccl. 1:16. Huldah—II Ki. 22:14. Jacob—Gen. 34:6. Job—Job 4:2. Moses—Ex. 25:22; 31:18. One another —Lu. 6:11. Paul—Acts 24:26. Saul—I Sam. 9:25; 19:3. Solomon—I Ki. 10:2; II Chr. 9:1. See SPEAK, TALK.

COMMUNICATE. Rom. 12:3; Gal. 6:6; Heb. 13:16.

COMMUNICATION. Lu. 24:17.

COMMUNION. See LORD'S SUPPER.

COMPACT. II Pet. 3:5.

COMPANY, COMPANIES. Gen. 32:7, 8, 21; 35:11; Num. 16:5, 6, 11, 40; 27:3; Ju. 18:23; Neh. 12:38; Job 16:7; 34:8; Ez. 27:27, 34; 32:3, 22, 23; Mk. 6:39; Lu. 2:44; 9:14; 24:22; Acts 4:23; 15:22; Rom. 15:24; Paul and his —Acts 13:13. Priest, Of—Hos. 6:9;

Acts 6:7. Prophets, Of—I Sam. 19:20. Warriors, Of—Gen. 50:9; Ju. 7:16, 20; 9:34, 43, 44; I Sam. 11:11; 13:17, 18; II Ki. 5:15; 9:17; I Chr. 20:12; 24:24; 28:1; Neh. 12:31, 38, 40; Job 6:19; Ps. 106:17, 18; Ez. 16:40; 17:17; 23:46, 47; 26:7; 38:4, 7, 13, 15. See BAND, CARAVAN, CONGREGATION, HOST, MULTITUDE, THRONG, TROOP.

COMPANION. Ezra 4:7, 9, 17, 23; 5:3, 6; 6:6, 13; Job. 30:29; 35:4; Ps. 119:63. Daniel, Of—Dan. 2:17. Evil—Ex. 32:27; Pr. 13:20; 29:7, 24; Is. 11:23. Joseph, Of—Ez. 37:16. Judah, Of—Ez. 37:16. Paul, Of—Acts 19:29. See FELLOW-WORKER, PARTAKER.

COMPARE. Lam. 2:4. Rom. 8:18. Bride with Pharaoh's horses—I Song of Sol. 1:9. God, To—Ps. 89:6; Is. 40:18; 46:5. Wisdom, To—Pr. 3:15; 8:11. See LIKENESS.

COMPASS. About—Ju. 16:2; I Sam. 23:26; II Sam. 18:15; I Ki. 7:15, 23, 35; II Ki. 11:8; II Chr. 8:2, 3; 23:7; Job 16:13; Ps. 7:7; 17:9; 22:12, 16; 118:10–12; 140:9; Lu. 19:43; 21:20; Heb. 11:30. Altar—Ps. 26:6. City—Josh. 6:3, 4, 7, 11, 14, 15; II Ki. 6:14. Death, With—II Sam. 22:5; Ps. 18:4; 116:3. Evil—Ps. 40:12. Favor, With —Ps. 5:12. Gall and travail, With—Lam. 3:5. Hatred, With—Ps. 109:3. Infirmity, With—Heb. 5:2. Iniquity, With—Ps. 49:5. Jehovah, By—Ps. 32:7, 10. Mark, With—Is. 44:13. Righteous, By—Ps. 142:7. Terror, With—Ps. 88:17. Wicked, By—Hab. 1:4. See CIRCUIT, LEDGE, TURN.

COMPASSION. Ex. 2:6; II Chr. 36:17; Is. 49:15; Dan. 1:9; Phil. 2:1; Col. 3:12; Heb. 10:34; I Pet. 3:8; I John 3:17. Father, Of—Lu. 15:20.

Jehovah, Of.—Deut. 13:17; 30:3; I Sam. 23:21; I Ki. 8:50; II Ki. 13:23; II Chr. 30:9; 36:15; Jer. 12:15; Lam. 3:22, 32; Hos. 11:8; Mic. 9:19; Rom. 9:15. Jesus, Of—Mt. 9:36; 14:14; 15:32; 18:27; 20:34; Mk. 1:41; 6:34; 8:2; 9:22; Lu. 7:13, 10:33. See LOVE, MERCY.

COMPEL. Esther 1:8; Mt. 5:41; Lu. 14:23 (A.V.); II Cor. 12:11; Gal. 2:3, 14; Mt. 27:32; Mk. 15:21. See MAKE, CONSTRAIN.

COMPENSATE. Esth. 7:4.

COMPLAINT. Of man.—Lam. 3:39. Job 10:1; 21:4; 23:2.

To God.—Of Job—Job 21:4. David—Ps. 55:2, 17; 64:1; 77:3; 142:2.

COMPLETE. Lev. 23:15; Ezra 5:16; Lu. 4:3, 13; 14:28; Acts 21:27; II Cor. 8:6; II Tim. 3:17. See ACCOMPLISH, FULFILL.

COMPOSITION. Ex. 30:32, 37.

COMPOUND. Ex. 30:25, 33.

COMPREHEND. Job 37:5; 38:18; Is. 40:12. See APPREHEND, LAY HOLD.

CONANIAH, kŏn'a-ni'ah. A Levite under Josiah—II Chr. 35:9. Ruler, Was a —II Chr. 31:12. Overseer under the hand of—II Chr. 31:13.

CONCEAL. Deut. 13:8; Job 27:11; Pr. 25:2. Blood, His—Gen. 37:26. Iniquity—Jer. 16:17. Knowledge—Pr. 12:23. Loving kindness, Thy—Ps. 40:10. Matter, A—Pr. 11:13. Saying was—Luke 9:45. Shame—Pr. 12:16. See DECEPTION, DENY, HIDE.

CONCEIT. Pr. 26:5, 12, 16; 28:11; Rom. 11:25; 12:16. Reproved—Job 11:12; Pr. 3:17; 14:12; 21:2; 30:1–5; Is. 5:21; 19:11; Jer. 8:8. See BOASTING, IMAGINATION, PRIDE.

CONCISION. Phil. 3:2. See CIRCUMCISION.

CONCLUDE. Acts 16:10. See RECKON.

CONCLUSION. See END.

CONCORD. II Cor. 6:15.

CONCOURSE. Pr. 1:21; Acts 19:40.

CONCUBINE. Hebrew concubinage grew out of a desire for offspring as associated with the hope of the promised Redeemer. The children were adopted as if the wife's own offspring —Gen. 30:1–24. Husband could take any of his own slaves as concubines, but could not take any of his wife's slaves without her consent—Gen. 16:2, 3; 30:3, 4, 9. Not illegal, but supplementary. Abraham sent Ishmael away to guard the rights of Isaac—Gen. 17:20, 21.

Laws concerning.—Ex. 21:7–11; Lev. 19:20–22; Deut. 21:9–14. Concubines called wives—Gen. 37:2; Ju. 19:1–4. Children, but not heirs—Gen. Ch. 49.

Incest with concubines.—Gen. 35:22; 49:4; I Chr. 5:1; II Sam. 16:21, 22.

Concubinage not right as we see it, but permitted for the time.—Acts 17:30; Mt. 19:3–12. Since Christ, fornication a sin against one's own body—I Cor. 6:15–20.

Examples in.—Abraham—Gen. 16:3; 25:6; I Chr. 1:32. Nahor—Gen. 22:24. Jacob—Gen. 30:4; 35:22; 49:4; I Chr. 5:1. Eliphaz—Gen. 36:12. Gideon—Ju. 8:31. Caleb—I Chr. 2:46. Manasseh—I Chr. 7:14. Saul—II Sam. 3:7; 21:11. David—II Sam. 5:13; 15:16; 19:5; 20:3; I Chr. 3:9. Solomon—I Ki. 11:3. Rehoboam—II Chr. 11:21. Belshazzar—Dan. 5:3.

CONCUPISCENCE. Rom. 7:8 (A.V.); Col. 3:5 (A.V.); I Thess. 4:5 (A.V.). See COVET, LUST, PASSION.

CONDEMN. Mt. 12:41, 42; Lu. 6:37; 31:32; John 8:11. Disbeliever—Mk. 16:16. Innocent—Ps. 94:21; Mt. 12:7; John 8:10. Jehovah, By—Job 10:2; Is. 54:17; I Cor. 11:32; Heb. 11:7. Jesus—Mt. 20:18; 27:3; Mk. 10:33; 14:64; Lu. 24:20; Acts 13:27, 34. Job —Job 32:3. Jesus, By—Rom. 8:34. Self—Job 9:20; 15:6; I John 3:20, 21; Rom. 2:1; Tit. 3:11. Sin—Rom. 8:3. Sodom and Gomorrah—II Pet. 2:6. Wicked—Ex. 22:9; Deut. 25:1; I Ki. 8:32; Pr. 12:2; Mt. 12:37. See FINE, JUDGE, JUDGMENT.

CONDEMNATION. Lu. 23:40; Rom. 5:16–18; 8:1; II Cor. 3:9; I Tim. 3:6; Jude 4. See JUDGMENT, LAW, OLD COVENANT.

CONDESCEND. Rom. 12:16. See HUMILITY.

CONDITIONS. Of peace—Lu. 14:32.

CONDUCT. II Sam. 19:31; Acts 17:15; II Tim. 3:10 (A.V.). See BEHAVE, BEHAVIOR, JESUS, TEACHING ON CHARACTER.

CONDUIT. II Ki. 20:20; 18:17; 7:3; Is. 36:2.

CONEY. See ANIMALS

CONFECTION, CONFECTIONERY. See PERFUME.

CONFEDERACY. Men of thy—Obah. 7.

CONFEDERATE. Abraham, With—Gen. 14:13. Syria with Ephraim—Is. 7:2.

CONFER. Among themselves—Acts 4:15. Festus with council—Acts 25:12.

Flesh and blood, Not with—Gal. 1:16.
Joab, With—I Ki. 1:7.
CONFESSION. Heb. *Yadah*, "to bemoan," "confess."
Confession of Jehovah's name.—I Ki.
8:33, 35; II Chr. 6:24, 26; Ezra 10:11;
Rom. 14:11, 12; 15:9. (See margin.)
Confession by deeds.—Mt. 27:3, 4; Lu.
15:18, 19; 23:40-42; Acts 19:19.
Confessions producing trouble.—Josh. 7:
20, 25; I Sam. 15:19, 24; John 9:33,
34; 12:42, 43.
Born of trouble.—Ps. 51:3, 4; Mt. 27:3,
4; 27:19.
Confession of sin.—Ex. 32:31, 32; Lev.
5:5; 26:40; Num. 5:7; Josh. 7:19; Ju.
10:15, 16; Ezra 10:1; Neh. 9:2, 3; Ps.
32:5; Pr. 28:13; Jer. 3:12, 13; Dan.
9:4, 20; Mt. 3:6; Mk. 1:5; Lu. 18:13,
14; I John 1:9.
Confession through priest.—Lev. 5:6;
16:21. Through Moses—Ex. 32:31;
Num. 14:19. Through Nehemiah—
Neh. 1:6. Through Jesus—I John 2:1.
Various confessions.—Of God's power
—Job 40:13, 14. Of thankfulness—II
Chr. 30:22. Of truths—John 1:20;
Acts 23:8. Of faults—Jas. 5:16.
Confessing Jesus.—Mt. 10:32; Lu. 12:8;
John 9:22; Acts 24:14; Rom. 10:9,
10; Phil. 2:11; I Tim. 6:13; I John
4:2, 3, 15; II John 7. Jesus confesses
us—Rev. 3:5. See DIVINITY OF JESUS.
CONFIDENT, CONFIDENCE. Access
in—Eph. 3:12. Art — Rom. 2:19.
Ashamed of Bethel their—Jer. 48:13.
Flesh, Have no confidence in—II Ki.
18:19, 20; Is. 30:1-5; Phil. 3:3. Friend,
In—Mic. 7:5. God, In—Ps. 40:4; 62:8;
Pr. 3:26; 16:20; Is. 26:3, 4; Jer. 17:7.
Gold, Thou art my—Job 31:24. Man,
In—Ps. 118:8. Minded, I was in this
matter—I Cor. 1:15. Obedience, In
thine—Philemon 21. Princes, In—Ps.
118:9. Rejected—Jer. 2:37. Strength, In
—Is. 30:15; 32:17. Strength shall be
in quietness—Is. 30:15. Thing, Of—
Phil. 1:6. Trusteth in—II Ki. 18:19;
Is. 36:4. See ASSURANCE, FAITH.
CONFIRM, CONFIRMATION. Brethren—Acts 15:32. Churches—Acts 15:
41. Christ, Testimony of—I Cor. 1:6.
Covenant—Gal. 3:15, 17; Heb. 6:17.
Esther—Esth. 9:32. Gospel—Phil. 1:7.
Inheritance—Ps. 68:9. Jacob to—I

Chr. 16:17. Kingdom—II Ki. 15:19.
Knees, Feeble—Is. 35:3. Love toward
him—II Cor. 2:8. Oath, For—Heb. 6:
16. Promises—Rom. 15:8. Souls of
disciples—I Cor. 1:8. Testimony of
Christ—I Cor. 1:6. Words—I Ki. 1:14.
See COVENANT, HOLY SPIRIT, LAW.
CONFISCATION. Goods, Of—Ezra 7:
26.
CONFLICT. Same—Which ye saw in
me—Phil. 1:30. See BATTLE, STRUGGLE,
TRIBULATION, WAR.
CONFORMATION AND TRANSFORMATION. Eph. 4:7; I Tim. 6:10; I
Pet. 4:3-6. In the world but not of it
—John 17:16, 17. Not conformed in
life and actions to—Rom. 12:2. A peculiar people—John 1:11-13; 15:19-
21; 17:14-16; Tit. 2:14; I Pet. 2:9, 10.
Temple of Holy Spirit—I Cor. 6:19.
Temple of God—I Cor. 3:16; II Cor.
6:16. Transformed by renewing—
Rom. 12:2. Into image of Christ—II
Cor. 3:18. Grace given for others—
Eph. 4:7; I John 4:6. Accomplished
by setting mind on and seeking chiefly
things that are above—Col. 3:1, 2.
Crucifying sin and its lusts—Rom. 6:
6-14; Col. 3:5-9.
CONFOUND. Hamath and Arpad—Jer.
49:23. Jews—Acts 9:22. Land—Jer.
51:47. Language—Gen. 11:7. Mother
—Jer. 50:12. Multitude—Acts 2:6.
We—Jer. 51:51. See ASHAMED, ASTONISH, SHAME.
CONFUSE, CONFUSION. City filled
with—Acts 19:29. Cover us—Jer. 3:
25. Face, Of—Ezra 9:7; Jer. 7:19;
Dan. 9:7. God is not—I Cor. 14:33.
Images are wind and—Is. 41:29. Jealousy and faction—Jas. 3:16. Line of
—Is. 34:11. See ASHAMED, ASTONISH,
SHAME.
CONGEAL. Deeps were—Ex. 15:8
(A.V.).
CONGRATULATE. See SALUTATION.
CONGREGATION (Assembly). **Of Israel.**—Ex. 12:3, 6, 19, 47; 16:1, 2, 3,
9, 10, 22; 17:1; 34:31; 35:1, 4, 20; 38:
25; Lev. 4:13, 21; 8:3, 5; 10:17; Num.
8:20; 10:7; 20:1, 22; 32:4; Deut. 23:8;
Josh. 18:1; 22:12; Ju. 20:1, 2; 21:5, 8,
10; I Ki. Ch. 8; I Chr. 13:2, 4; 28:8;
29:1, 10, 20; II Chr. 1:3, 5; 5:6; 6:3,
12, 13; 7:8; 23:3; 24:6; 28:14; 29:23,

28; 30:2, 4, 13; 7:8; 23:3; 24:6; 28:14; 29:23, 28; 30:2, 4, 13, 17, 23–25; Ezra 10:1, 12; Neh. 5:13. Of Judah and Jerusalem—II Chr. 20:5. Of people witnesses to David—I Sam. 17:47. Cut off from—Num. 19:20; Deut. 23:1, 2, 3. Sum of—Num. 1:2, 16, 18, 53; 26:2; 31:26, 27, 34; Ezra 2:64; Neh. 7:66. Charge of—Num. 3:7. Offices of—II Chr. 31:18. Princes—Num. 16:2; 27: 2; Josh. 9:15, 18, 19, 21; I Ki. 8:1; Ezra 10:14. Minister of—Num. 16:9. Priests—Num. 31:12, 13, 54; 32:2. Elders—Ju. 21:16; I Ki. 8:1. Joshua chosen as shepherd of—Num. 27:16–23. Joshua reads to—Josh. 8:35. Servants of—Josh. 9:27. Statute for—Num. 15:15. Praise of Jehovah in—Ps. 22:22; 26:12; 68:26; 107:32.

Offerings of.—Lev. 4:21; 16:5; Num. 19:9; II Chr. 29:31, 32. Atonement for—Num. 15:25, 26; 16:46, 47, 50.

Transgressors brought to.—Num. 15:23; 25:6, 7; 35:12, 24, 25; Josh. 20:6, 9; Pr. 26:26. Stoned by—Lev. 24:14, 16; Num. 14:10; 15:35, 36. Rebuke Transjordanic tribes—Josh. 22:16 ff. Go to battle—Ju. 21:10. Proclaim peace—Ju. 21:13. Spies return to—Num. 13: 25, 26; 14:1, 2, 5, 36.

Complain against Moses and Aaron.—Num. 16:42; 20:2, 3, 4; 26:9.

Jehovah speaks unto Moses concerning.—Num. 20:7–9, 12, 27. Jehovah speaks unto—Num. 16:19, 20, 22, 24; 16:42; II Chr. 20:14, 15. Moses speaks to—Num. 16:26; 20:10, 11; Deut. 31:30; Chs. 22, 23. Congregation mourns—Num. 20:29; 25:6. Ezra reads the law to—Neh. 8:2–6. Evil—Gen. 49:6; Num. 14:27, 35; 16:33; 27:14; Ps. 26:5; Jer. 9:2. Evil in—Pr. 5:14. Of the righteous—Ps. 1:5; 89:5; 111:1; 149:1. Of the people—Ps. 7:7; 107:32; Jer. 26: 17. Great assembly—Neh. 5:7; Ps. 22:25; 35:18; 40:9, 10. Of God—Neh. 13:1; Ps. 68:10; 74:2, 4; 82:1; Lam. 1:10; Mic. 2:5. Of the dead—Pr. 21: 16. Assembly of the captivity—Ezra 10:8; Neh. 8:17. Of them that make merry—Jer. 15:17. Solemn assembly —II Ki. 10:20; II Chr. 7:9. Church called general assembly—Acts 19:39; Heb. 12:23. In confusion—Acts 19:32.

Prophecies concerning.—Jer. 6:11, 18; 30:20; Hosea 7:12; Zeph. 3:18.

Illustrative.—Is. 14:13.

Miscellaneous.—Ask for help in—Job 30:28. No wrath on—Num. 1:53. To be sanctified—Joel 2:16. In confusion—Acts 19:32. Dismissed—Acts 19:41. See CHURCH, PLAGUES, TABERNACLE.

CONIAH, ko-ni'ah. **Name given to Jehoiachin, son of Jehoiakim.**—Jer. 22; 24. Vessel, Despised broken—Jer. 22: 28 (A.V.). See JEHOIACHIN.

CONQUER. Conquering and to—Rev. 6:2. More than—Rom. 8:37.

CONSCIENCE. Gr. *suneidesis*, ''Co-perception or moral consciousness.'' Term occurs thirty times in New Testament.

Sphere of.—Rom. 9:1, 2; 13:5; I Tim. 3:9; II Tim. 1:3; Heb. 10:22; I Pet. 3:21.

Heart the organ (*fig.*).—Mt. 10:37–39; Lu. 14:33–35; John 15:10–14; Acts 26:9.

Prophecy.—Is. 55:6–9; Jer. 23:16, 17; Amos 3:6–8; II Pet. 3:11–14.

Approving.—Job 27:6; Acts 23:1; Rom. 2:15; 9:1; II Cor. 1:12; I Tim. 1:5; Heb. 13:18; I Pet. 3:16.

Disapproving.—Rom. 2:15.

Active.—Gen. 31:36–42; 39:7–9; Job 31: 16–22; Dan. 1:8; Acts 4:19; 23:1; 24: 16; Rom. 2:15; I Pet. 2:19.

Conciliatory.—Rom. Ch. 13; 15:1, 2; I Cor. Ch. 8; 10:25–31; II Cor. 4:2.

Weak.—Lu. 14:33–35; I Cor. 8:7, 10, 12.

Accusing.—Ps. 32:3–5; 38:1–8; 51:3; Mt. 26:75; 27:3–5; Mk. 6:16–20; John 8:9; I Tim. 1:19.

Considerate.—I Cor. 10:25–29.

Seared.—Pr. 30:20; Jer. 6:15; Rom. 1: 21–25; I Tim. 4:2.

Defiled.—I Cor. 8:7; Tit. 1:15; Heb. 10: 22.

Conceit of.—Pr. 21:2; John 8:33; Acts 26:9.

Conscience acts according to the light possessed.—Rom. 2:10–16.

Consciences in conflict with each other. I Cor. 10:28 f.

Witness of the conscience.—Rom. 9:1 f. *Cf.* I John 5:10.

CONSECRATION. Aaron and his sons —Ex. 29:9. Anoint them and—Ex. 28: 41. Basket of—Lev. 8:31. Christians,

Of—I Pet. 2:9. Feasts were—Ezra 3:5. Flesh of—Ex. 29:34. Guests—Zeph. 1:7 (A.V.). Incense, to burn—II Chr. 26:18. Levite—Ju. 17:12. Micah, Son of—Ju. 17:5. Ram of—Ex. 29:22, 26, 27, 31. Way, Living—Heb. 10:20 (A.V.). Yourselves today—Ex. 32:29. See SANCTIFICATION.

CONSENT. Pr. 1:10; Acts 18:20. Consulted with one—Ps. 83:5. Council, To—Luke 23:5. Law, Unto the—Rom. 7:16. One—Lu. 14:18. See ACCORD, UNITY. Priests—II Ki. 12:8. Saul, unto his death—Acts 8:1. Season, For a—I Cor. 7:5. Serve him with, one—Zeph. 3:9. Words, Not to—I Tim. 6:3.

CONSIDER. Affliction—Ps. 119:153. Ant—Pr. 6:6. Beam—Mt. 7:3. Body good as dead—Rom. 4:19. Enemies, My—Ps. 25:19. Field—Pr. 31:16. God, Works of—Job 37:14. Hearts, In their —Hos. 7:2. Heavens—Ps. 8:3. Horns —Dan. 7:8. House of the wicked—Ps. 21:12. Jesus—Heb. 3:1. Job—Job 1:8; 2:3. Lilies—Mt. 6:28; Lu. 12: 27. Meditation, My—Ps. 5:1. Operation of his hand—Is. 5:12. People—Is. 1:3. Poor—Ps. 41:1. Ravens—Lu. 12:24. Testimonies—Ps. 119:95. Works —Ps. 53:15. Years of many—Deut. 23:7.

CONSIST. All things—Col. 1:17. Life of man—Lu. 12:15.

CONSOLATION. Lu. 2:25; Rom. 8:28. **Consolation from God.**—Job 5:15–26; 15:11; 16:19–21; 19:25–27; Ps. 9:9–10; 27:1–6; 34:6; 41:1–3; 46:1–5; 50:15; 51:17; 55:22; 69:33; 71:20, 21; 73:26; 94:17–19; 138:3–7; 140:12; 145:14; 147:3; Is. 12:1; 40:29–31; 41:10–20; 43:2–21; 49:13; 50:4–10; 51:3; 63:9; 66:13–14; Lam. 3:22–26; Acts 23:11; I Cor. 10:13; II Cor. 1:3–12; Heb. 13: 5, 6; I Pet. 5:7–10; II Pet. 2:9; Rev. 3:10.

Promised.—Is. 12:1; 40:1, 2; 49:13; 51: 3; Ez. 14:23; Hos. 2:14, 15; Zech. 1: 17; II Cor. 9:8; Phil. 4:19; Jas. 1:12.

Through hope of immortal life.—II Sam. 12:23; John 11:23–26; 14:1–3; I Cor. 15:19–58; II Cor. 5:1–8; II Tim. 2:12; Heb. 11:10, 13–16; Jas. 1:12; 2:5; I Pet. 1:1–21.

By promises of deliverance.—Ex. 3:7– 10; 6:6–8; 14:13–18; Ps. 37:32–33; Is. 30:19–20; Jer. 39:15–18; Hos. 2:14, 15; 6:1–3; Zeph. 3:18, 19; Zech. 1:16–21; Mt. 21:15–19.

In Jesus and His words.—Job 19:25; Is. 60:1–3; Lu. 2:25; 4:18, 19; 7:13; John 14:1–3, 18; 15:18–20; I Cor. 15: 12–28; II Cor. 1:5–7; 4:8–11; I Thess. 5:9–11; Heb. 4:15, 16.

Holy Spirit a comforter.—John 14:16, 17, 26; 15:26; 16:7, 8; Acts 9:31; Rom. 5:5; 8:26; 14:17.

Comfort to the tempted.—I Cor. 10:13; II Cor. 12:9, 10; Gal. 6:1, 2; Heb. 2: 18; 5:1, 2; Jas. 1:12–14; 4:7; II Pet. 2:9.

Comfort in the presence of death.—Job 19:25, 26; Ps. 23:4; John 14:1–4; 16: 20, 22; II Cor. 5:1–10; I Thess. 4:14; Heb. 4:9; 11:13–16; Rev. 14:13.

Comfort for persecuted.—John 15:18– 21; 16:33; Acts 14:22; II Cor. 12:9, 10; Rev. 7:14–17.

For those forsaken by friends.—Ps. 27: 10; 41:9–11; John 14:18; 15:18–21; II Cor. 4:7–15.

Comforting each other.—Job 16:5; 31: 19–22; Is. 40:1, 2; 50:4; 58:10; Acts 14:22; Rom. 12:15; II Cor. 1:3–6; Gal. 6:1, 2; Heb. 10:34; 13:3; Jas. 1:27.

His yoke is easy.—Mt. 11:28–30.

Through the promises in God's word.— Job 6:10; Ps. 119:50–54, 92; John 14: 1–3; Acts 15:30, 31; Rom. 4:22–25; 8: 28, 36–39; 15:4; I Cor. 10:10–13; II Cor. 4:8–18; II Tim. 2:12; Heb. 6:6– 20; 10:34; 11:10, 13–16; James 1:12; I Pet. 4:12, 13; Rev. 2:10; 3:10; 7:14– 17.

Chastisement or tribulation good for man.—Job 5:17, 18; Ps. 94:12, 13; Pr. 3:11, 12; Rom. 8:17, 18; II Cor. 1:4; 4:8–18; 12:7–10; II Tim. 2:12; Heb. 12:5–8; Jas. 1:12; 5:11; I Pet. 4:12–16; Rev. 2:10; 7:14–17.

Consolation and sympathy of men for others.—Job 31:19, 22; Is. 50:4; 58: 7–11; Acts 12:5; 14:21–22; 15:31; Rom. 12:13–15; I Cor. 14:3; II Cor. 1:4–8; 2:7; 7:6, 7; Gal. 6:2; Eph. 1: 13; I Thess. 5:11; II Tim. 1:16; Heb. 10:34; 13:3; Jas. 1:27; 2:14–17.

Consolation in riches.—Lu. 6:24.

Consolation of love.—Phil. 2:1.

See AFFLICTION, ADVERSITY, MOURNING, PROMISES.

CONSORT. Acts 17:4.

CONSPIRACY. Against Joseph—Gen. 37:18. Miriam and Aaron against Moses—Num. 12. Israelites against Moses' authority—Num. 14:1-10. Abimelech against Gideon's sons—Ju. 9: 1-6. Delilah against Samson—Ju. 16: 4-21. Ahimelech against Saul—I Sam. 22:11-19. Absalom against David— II Sam. 15:10-12. Baasha against Nadab—I Ki. 15:25-28. Zimri against Elah—I Ki. 16:8-10. Jezebel against Naboth—I Ki. 21:8-16. Jehu against Joram—II Ki. 9:14-26. Servants against Joash—II Ki. 12:20. Against Shadrach, etc.—Dan. 3:18-18. Against Daniel—Dan. 6:4-17. Against Jesus —Mt. 12:14; 21:38-41; 26:3-4; 27:1; Mk. 3:6; 14:1; Lu. 22:2; John 11:47-57; 13:18. Against Paul—Acts 18:12; 23:12-15.

Other conspiracies.—II Ki. 10:9; 14:19; 15:10, 25; 17:4; 21:23; II Chr. 24:21, 25; 25:27; 33:24; Neh. 4:8; Esth. 2: 21-23; Jer. 11:9; Ez. 22:25; Amos 7:10.

CONSTANT. I Chr. 28:7; Pr. 21:28; Rom. 16:3, 4. See CONTINUAL, FAITHFULNESS.

CONSTELLATION. Is. 13:10. See ASTRONOMY.

CONSTRAIN. Cæsar, To appeal unto —Acts 28:19. Christ, Love of—II Cor. 5:14. Disciples—Mt. 14:22; Mk. 6:45. Elisha—II Ki. 4:8. Spirit within me —Job 32:18.

CONSULT, CONSULTATION. Ps. 83: 5; Deut. 18:11. Chief priests held a— Mk. 15:1. David with captains—I Chr. 13:1. Hidden ones, Against—Ps. 83:3. Presidents have—Dan. 6:7 (A.V.). See COUNSEL.

CONSUME. Beard—Is. 7:20. Beasts are—Jer. 12:4. Burnt offering—Lev. 9:24. Bush was not—Ex. 3:2. Cloud is—Job 7:9. Eyes and tongue—Zech. 14:12. Famine, By—Gen. 41:30. Filthiness—Ez. 22:15. Fire, By—Deut. 5: 25. Flesh—Ju. 6:21. Generation doing evil—Num. 32:13. Glory of forest— Is. 10:18. God consuming fire—Heb. 12:29. Israel, Children of—II Chr. 8:8. Jacob, Sons of, are not—Mal. 3:6.

Man and beast—Zeph. 1:3. Oppressors are—Is. 16:4. People—Deut. 7:16. Prophets—Jer. 14:15. Remnant—Job 22:20. Roll—Jer. 36:23. See Deut. 28: 38. Sinners—Ps. 104:35. Syrians—I Ki. 22:11. Zeal, By—Ps. 119:139. See DESTRUCTION, FIRE.

CONSUMPTION. Deut. 28:22; Lev. 26: 16 (A.V.).

CONTAIN. I Cor. 7:9. Heavens cannot —I Ki. 8:27; II Chr. 2:6; 6:18. Law, In the—Rom. 2:14 (A.V.). Scripture, In—I Pet. 2:6. World itself would not—John 21:25.

CONTEMN. Counsel of most high.— Ps. 107:11. God—Ps. 10:13. Rod— Ez. 21:10 (A.V.). Utterly—Song of Sol. 8:7.

CONTEMPT. Wickedness accompanied by.—Pr. 18:3. **To be avoided.**—Ps. 119:22; 123:3, 4.

Contempt held.—Of proud—Ps. 123:4. For husbands—Esth. 1:17, 18. For princes—Job 12:21; Ps. 107:40. For families—Job 31:34. For righteous— Ps. 31:18. For honorable—Is. 23:9. For table of the Lord—Mal. 1:7. For God's food—Mal. 1:12.

Punishment to wicked.—Dan. 12:2; Mal. 2:9.

Act of despising as contempt.—Forbidden—I Cor. 16:11; I Tim. 4:12; 6:2. Toward God—Is. 60:14; Ez. 28:26. Of people—Neh. 4:4. Christ—Is. 53:3. Job —19:18. Poor man's wisdom—Eccl. 9:16.

Abhorrence as contempt.—Laws against Lev. 26:15, 16; Deut. 23:7.

Punishment for false prophets.—Pr. 24: 24. For abhorring God—Lev. 26:43.

Prophets abhorred.—Amos 5:10. Not to be abhorred—Jer. 14:21.

CONTEND. Deut. 2:9; Pr. 28:4. Almighty, With the—Job 40:2. Battle, In—Deut. 2:24. Devil, With—Jude 9. Forth, For the—Jude 3. Fire, By— Amos 7:4. God, For—Job 13:8. Horses, With—Jer. 12:5. Mountains, Before —Mic. 6:1. Nobles of Judah, With— Neh. 13:17. ·Rulers, With—Neh. 13: 11. See STRIFE, WAR.

CONTENTMENT: Proper attitude of mind.—With wages—Lu. 3:14. Food and raiment—I Tim. 6:8. With such things as ye have—Heb. 13:5. Godli-

ness with contentment is great gain—
I Tim. 6:6.
Examples of.—Moses—Ex. 2:21. Levite
—Ju. 17:11. Pilate gives to multi-
tude—Mk. 15:15. Paul—Phil. 4:11.
Lack of.—Pr. 6:35.
May be learned.—Phil. 4:11 f.
Found in Jesus.—Mt. 5:3-12; 11:28-30;
Lu. 6:20-23.
CONTENTION, CONTENTIOUS. Pr.
22:10. Bars of a castle, Are like—
Pr. 18:19. Cease, Cause to—Pr. 18:8.
Fool's lips enter into—Pr. 18:6. Man
of—Jer. 15:10. Man, So is a—Pr. 26:
21. Pride, by, cometh—Pr. 13:10.
Sharp—Acts 15:39. Who hath con-
tention?—Pr. 23:29. Woman, With a
—Pr. 21:19. See STRIFE.
CONTINUALLY, CONTINUE. Apostles teaching, In—Acts 2:42. Bread—
Num. 4:7; Neh. 10:33. Burnt offering—Ex. 29:42; Num. 28:3, 6, 10, 15,
23, 24, 31; 29:11, 16, 14, 22, 25, 28, 31,
34, 38. Covenant—Not in my—Heb.
8:9. Faith, In the—Acts 14:22. Col.
1:23. Fasting—Acts 27:33. Feast—
Pr. 15:15. Gates shall be open—Is.
60:11. Grace of God, In the—Acts
13:43. Hope, I will—Ps. 71:14. Jehovah will guide thee—Is. 5:8-11
(A.V.). Kingdom shall not—I Sam.
13:14. Lamp, To burn—Lev. 24:2.
Love, Let—Heb. 13:1. Loving-kindness
—Ps. 36:10. Memorial, For a—Ex.
28:29. Name, His—Ps. 72:17. Name
blasphemed—Is. 52:15. Not—Job
14:2. People provoke me—Is. 65:3.
Prayer, In—Acts 1:14; Col. 4:2; Rom.
12:12; I Tim. 5:5. Praise shall be—
Ps. 34:1. Priest, Abideth a—Heb. 7:3.
Sacrifice of praise—Heb. 13:15. Sorrow—Ps. 38:17. Teaching and preaching—Acts 15:35. Temptation, In—
Luke 22:28. Truth of Gospel—Gal.
2:5. Truth preserve me—Ps. 40:11.
Wait for thy God—Hosea 12:6. Watch-
tower, Upon the—Is. 21:8.
CONTRADICT. Paul, Things spoken
by—Acts 13:45.
CONTRARIWISE. II Col. 2:7; Gal.
2:7; I Pet. 3:9.
CONTRARY. Tit. 2:8; Gal. 5:17. De-
crees of Caesar, To the—Acts 17:7.
Doctrine, To—I Tim. 1:10; Acts 16:7.
Jesus of Nazareth, To name of—Acts

26:9. Nature, To—Rom. 11:24. Walk
—Lev. 26:21, 23, 24, 27, 28, 40, 41.
Wind—Matt. 14:24; Mk. 6:48; Acts
27:4. Worship God—Acts 18:13.
CONTRIBUTION. Poor, For the—Rom.
15:26; I Cor. 16:1, 2; II Cor. 8:1-4;
9:2-13. See GIVING, LIBERALITY.
CONTRITE. Heart—Ps. 51:17. Spirit
—Ps. 34:18; Is. 57:15; 66:2.
CONTROVERSY. Deut. 21:5. II Chr.
19:8. Gates, Within thy—Deut. 17:8.
Inhabitants, With—Ez. 44:24. Judah,
With—Mic. 6:2. Men, Between—Deut.
19:17; 25:1. Nations, With the—Jer.
25:31. Without—I Tim. 3:16. See
STRIFE.
CONVENIENT. Day—Mk. 6:21. De-
liver him—Mk. 14:11. Season—Acts
24:25. See BECOME, BEFITTING, FIT-
TING.
CONVERSATION. See BEHAVIOR, LIFE,
MANNER OF LIFE, WAY.
CONVERSION. Gr. *Epistrepho,* "to
turn about; revolution." In conver-
sion man is always active; in pardon
God alone is active. The two acts are
separate but complementary. The lat-
ter depends upon the former. To par-
don the impenitent would be the de-
struction of the kingdom of God—II
Chr. 6:26, 27; 7:14; 30:6-9; Neh. 1:9;
Lam. 3:40-42.
A perpetual divine call.—II Ki. 17:13,
14; Is. 31:6; Jer. 3:14; 18:8; 25:5, 6;
26:3; Ez. 3:19; 14:6; 18:21, 30; 33:9;
Joel 2:12, 13; Jonah 3:8-10; Zech. 1:3;
Acts 26:20.
Method of conversion.—Mt. 28:18-20;
Mk. 16:15, 16; Lu. 24:45-49; John 20:
30, 31; Acts 2:21; Rom. 10:6-17; II
Pet. 1:4-11.
How brought about.—Through Holy
Spirit—Lu. 24:46-49; Acts 2:1-4; 8:
29; 16:6-10. Through the Scriptures
—Ps. 19:7; 119:9, 93, 104, 105, 130;
Ez. 18:27; Acts 2:16-21; 8:32, 33.
Through preaching—Mk. 16:15; Lu.
24:47; Acts 8:35; Rom. 10:14; II Tim.
4:2-5. Through faithful associates—
I Cor. 7:14-16. Through distress—Ps.
78:34; Lu. 15:17-20. Through per-
sonal scrutiny—Ps. 119:59; Lam. 3:
39-41..
Conversion of the Jews.—Ps. 51:13; Is.
1:27; 2:2, 3; 6:10; 61:4-9; Jer. 31:31-

34; Mt. 13:15; 18:3; Mk. 4:12; John 12:40; Acts 2:37–42; 3:17–21; 4:4; 5:14; 6:7.

Conversion of Samaritans.—Acts 8:5–8, 12–13.

Conversion of Gentiles.—Is. 2:2, 3; 11: 10; 60:1–5; 66:12; Joel 2:28–32; Acts 8:34–39; 10:33–48; 15:3, 8–11; Rom. 11:11–13; Eph. 2:11.

Notable examples of.—Jews at Pentecost—Acts Ch. 2. The Ethiopian—Acts 8:26–40. Cornelius—Acts Ch. 10. Pro-consul Sergius Paulus—Acts 13: 7–13. Lydia—Acts 16:13–15. Philippian jailer—Acts 16:27–34. Judge Dionysius—Acts 17:34.

Special cases of.—Zacchaeus—Lu. 19: 8–10. Simon Peter—Lu. 22:32; John 21:5–17.

Ten new things for the new man.—Birth —John 3:3–6. Commandment—John 13:34. Covenant—Jer. 31:31–34; Heb. 8:7–13. Creature—II Cor. 5:17. Food —I Pet. 2:2, 3. Heart—Ez. 36:26; Lu. 8:15; Acts 4:32. Home—John 14: 2, 3; Rev. 21:5. Name—Acts 11:26; Rev. 2:17; 3:12. Song—Ps. 40:3; Acts 16:25; Rev. 5:9; 14:3. Way—Is. 25: 8, 9; Acts 9:2; 13:10.

Ten products of a converted life.—Faithfulness—Mt. 24:45–47; 25:21, 23; Lu. 16:10; 19:17; Gal. 3:9. Gentleness— II Cor. 10:1; I Thess. 2:7; II Tim. 2: 24; Tit. 3:2; Jas. 3:17. Kindness— Rom. 12:10; II Cor. 6:6; Col. 3:12; II Pet. 1:7. Longsuffering—II Cor. 6:6; Gal. 5:22; Col. 1:10–12; 3:12, 13; II Tim. 2:10–12; 3:10. Love—John 13: 34, 35; I Cor. 13; I John 2:10; 3:14; 4:7; 8:10–12. Meekness—Ps. 37:11; Is. 61:1; Mt. 5:5; Gal. 5:23; Eph. 4:2; Col. 3:12; I Tim. 6:11; Jas. 1:21. Obedience—Acts 6:7; 26:19; Rom. 6:17; 15:18; 16:19; II Cor. 2:9. Peacefulness—Mt. 5:9; Lu. 2:14; 24:36; John 14:27; Rom. 12:18; Col. 3:15; Jas. 3: 17, 18. Self-control—Acts 24:25; I Cor. 9:25; Gal. 5:23; Tit. 1:8; II Pet. 1:6. Self-denial—Mt. 10:39; 16:24; Mk. 8:34, 35; Lu. 9:23; 11:33; John 12:25.

CONVEY. John 5:13. See BRING.

CONVICT. John 8:46; 16:8; Tit. 1:9; Jas. 2:9; Jude 15. See SIN, CONVICTION OF.

CONVINCE. Job 32:12; John 8:46 (A.V.); Acts 18:28 (A.V.); I Cor. 14:24 (A.V.); Tit. 1:9 (A.V.); Jas. 2:9 (A.V.); Jude 15 (A.V.). See CONFUTE, CONVICT, REFUTE.

CONVOCATION. Holy—Ex. 12:16; Lev. 23:2–4, 7, 8, 21, 24, 27, 35–37;. Num. 28:18, 25, 26; 29:7, 12. See CONGREGATION, FEASTS.

COOK. I Sam. 8:13; 9:23, 24.

COOL. Pr. 17:27. Day—Gen. 3:8; Song of Sol. 2:17; 4:6. Tongue—Lu. 16:24.

COOS. See Cos.

COPING. I Ki. 7:9.

COPPER. Deut. 8:9. See BRASS.

COPPERSMITH, Alexander the—II Tim.

COPY. Ezra 4:11, 23; 5:6; 7:11; Pr. 25:1; Heb. 9:23. Law, Of the—Deut. 17:18; Josh. 8:32; Esth. 3:14; 4:8; 8:13.

COR. See MEASURES.

CORAL. Job 28:18; Ez. 27:16.

CORBAN. Mk. 7:11.

CORD. Josh. 2:15; Job 30:11; 36:8; 41:1; Ps. 2:3; 118:27; 140:5; Eccl. 4: 12; Is. 33:20; 54:2; Jer. 10:20; 38:6, 11–13; Ez. 27:24; John 2:15. Death, Of—Ps. 18:4. Decorations, Used as— Esth. 1:6. Falsehood, Of—Is. 5:18. Man, Of—Hos. 11:4. Silver—Eccl. 12:6. Sheol, Of—II Sam. 22:6; Ps. 18:5. Sin, Of—Pr. 5:40; Num. 3:26, 27; 4:26, 32. Wicked, Of the—Ps. 119:61; 129:4. See BAND, LINE, ROPE.

CORE. See KORAH.

CORIANDER. Ex. 16:31; Num. 11:7. See PLANTS.

CORINTH, kŏr'ĭnth. **A famous Grecian city, capital of Achaia Proper, situated on the isthmus. Famous for its wealth, learning, and wickedness**—Acts 19:1; II Cor. 1:23; II Tim. 4:20. **Church at** —I Cor. 1:2; II Cor. 1:1.

Inhabitants of.—Acts 18:8; II Cor. 6: 11.

Epistles to.—I Cor., II Cor.—*Paul.*

CORINTHIANS. See OUTLINE STUDIES IN THE BOOKS.

CORMORANT. An unclean bird—Lev. 11:17; Deut. 14:17.

CORN. See GRAIN, WHEAT.

CORNELIUS, kŏr-nē'lĭ-us. **A Roman centurion. First Gentile convert.**— Acts 10:3, 48.

CORNER. Ez. 41:22. Beard, Of—Lev. 19:27; 21:5. Earth, Of—Is. 11:12; 41:9; Rev. 7:1; 20:8. Four—Ex. 25: 26; 27:2, 4; 37:13; 38:2; I Ki. 30:34; Job 1:19; Is. 11:12; Ez. 7:2; 43:20; 45:19; 46:21, 22; Acts 10:11; 11:5; Rev. 7:1; 20:8. Hair, Of, cut off—Jer. 9:26; 25:23; 49:32. Head, Of—Mt. 21:42; Mk. 12:10; Lu. 20:17; Acts 4: 11. See JESUS. Housetops, Of—Pr. 21:9; 25:24. Street, Of—Pr. 7:8, 12; Mt. 6:5.

CORNER-STONE. See JESUS, STONES.

CORNET. I Chr. 15:28; II Chr. 15:14; Ps. 98:6; Dan. 3:5, 7, 10, 15; Hos. 5:8. See MUSICAL INSTRUMENTS.

CORPSE. See BODY.

CORRECT. Acts 24:2; II Tim. 2:25; 3:16. Child—Pr. 22:15; 23:13; 29:17. God, By—Job 5:17; 37:13; Ps. 39:11; 94:10; Pr. 3:1; Jer. 2:30; 5:3; 10:24; 30:11; 46:28; Hab. 1:12. Wickedness —Jer. 2:19. See CHASTEN, INSTRUCTION, REPROOF.

CORRUPT, CORRUPTION. Ps. 16:10; 49:9; Acts 2:27, 31; 13:34-37. Bondage, Of—Rom. 8:21. Covenant, Of— Mal. 2:8. Earth, Of—Gen. 6:11, 12; Ex. 8:24; II Pet. 1:4; Rev. 19:21. Fruit—See TREE. Images, With— Deut. 4:16, 25. Men, Of—Lev. 22:25; Neh. 1:7; Ps. 14:1; 49:9; 53:1; Pr. 25:25; Is. 1:4; Ez. 20:44; Eph. 4:22; I Tim. 6:5. Minds, Of—I Cor. 11:3; I Tim. 6:5; II Tim. 3:8. Morals, Of— I Cor. 15:33. Moth and dust, By—Mt. 6:19, 20 (A.V.). Lu. 12:33 (A.V.). Mount of—II Ki. 23:13. Reap—Gal. 6:8. Riches, By—Jas. 5:2. Self, Of— Ex. 32:7; Deut. 9:12; 31:29; Hos. 9:9. Speech, Of—Eph. 4:29. Tree, Of—Mt. 7:17; 12:33; Lu. 6:43. Water—Pr. 25:26. Wisdom, Of—Ez. 28:17. Word, Of—II Cor. 2:17. See CONSUME, DESTROY, REBUKE.

COSAM, kō′sam. **Ancestor of Jesus.—** Lu. 3:28.

COSMOLOGY. The world created by God, and consists of heavens, earth, and waters ("under the earth.")— Gen. 1:1; Ex. 20:4; Deut. 5:8.

The earth.—Wisdom of its structure— Pr. 3:19; Is. 40:12; Jer. 10:12; 51:15; Heb. 11:3. Construction: *Suspended over empty space*—Job 26:7. *Spread over waters*—Ps. 24:2. *Rests upon foundation (poetical) or "pillars"*—I Sam. 2:8; Job 38:4-6; Ps. 75:3; 102: 25; 104:5, 6; Pr. 8:29, 30; Is. 48:13; 51:13, 16. Form: *Flat*—Job 11:9; 38: 18; Rev. 4:1. *Square ("four corners" and "ends"*—Deut. 33:17; I Sam. 2: 10; Job 28:24; 37:3; 38:13; Ps. 19:6; 22:27; 48:10; 59:13; 65:5; 67:7; 98:3; 135:7; Pr. 17:24; 30:4; Is. 11:12; 40: 28; 41:5, 9; 43:6; 45:22; 52:10; Jer. 10:13; 16:19; 25:31; 51:16; Mic. 5:4; Zech. 9:10; Rom. 10:18; Rev. 7:1; 20:8. Use: *Habitation of man*—Ps. 115:16.

The heavens.—Wonderful in wisdom— Ps. 19:1; 33:6; 74:16; 102:25; 136:5; Pr. 3:19; Is. 40:12, 21-26; 44:24; 48:13; 51:13, 16; and beauty—Job 26:13; Ps. 19:1. In form of a vault, or tent, *stretched over the earth*—Is. 40:22; 48:13. *Planted like a tent*— Job 9:8; Is. 51:16. *Called also firmament (marg. "expanse")*—Gen. 1:6ff.; Ps. 19:1; Dan. 12:3. Conceived of as in successive stories—II Cor. 12:2. Serves as the residence of God—I Ki. 8:30; Ps. 2:4; 33:13; 115:3; 123:1; Eccl. 5:2; Amos 9:6. Also of angels— Is. 37:36; Mk. 12:25; Rev. 5:11.

Heavenly bodies.—Created by God— Gen. 1:14. Not to be worshipped— Deut. 4:19; Jer. 8:2; 19:13. Movements: *rising, setting*—Gen. 15:17; 19: 23; 28:11; 32:31; Ex. 22:3; Lev. 22:7; Num. 25:4; Deut. 23:11; 24:15; Josh. 1:4; Ju. 8:13; 9:33; 14:18; 19:14; II Sam. 3:35; Job 9:7; Ps. 104:22; Eccl. 1:5; Is. 60:20; Jer. 15:1-9; Amos 8:9; Jonah 4:8; Mic. 3:6; Nah. 3:17; Mt. 5:45; Mk. 1:32; Eph. 4:26.

The sun.—Source of light—Gen. 1:14-18; Ps. 136:7. Of heat—Ex. 16:21; Ps. 11:9, 11; Is. 49:10; Rev. 16:8. It endures—Ps. 72:5, 17; 89:36. But has limitations—Ps. 121:6; Ez. 32:7-8.

The moon.—Lesser light—Gen. 1:16. For the night—Gen. 1:16, 18; Ps. 106:9. Marks the seasons—Ps. 104:19.

The stars.—Their great number—Gen. 15:5; Ps. 147:4. Lesser lights for the night—Gen. 1:14; Ps. 136:9. Sources of influence—Job 28:31. And of power—Ju. 5:20. Personified—Ju. 5: 20; Job 38:7. Differ in splendor—I Cor. 15:41.

The waters.—Surround the earth and the heaven—Gen. 7:11. Kept within bounds—Gen. 1:6, 9, 10; Job 26:10; 28:25; 38:8–11; Ps. 104:7–9; Pr. 8:29. Seas, rivers, springs, issue from them —Job 28:4, 16. Their uses—Gen. 2:10; Deut. 8:7; Ps. 33:7; 72:6. Increase and diminish—I Ki. 18:5; Is. 19:5, 6; 50:2.

End (of the world).—Is. 51:6; 55:15–19; II Pet. 3:10.

COST. II Sam. 19:42; 24:24; I Chr. 21:25; Lu. 14:28.

COSTLINESS. Rev. 18:19.

COSTLY. Mk. 14:3; I Tim. 2:9. Redemption—Ps. 49:8. Stones—I Ki. 5:17; 7:9–11; I Cor. 3:12. See PRECIOUS STONES.

COTES. See FOLD.

COTTAGE. Zeph. 2:6. See BOOTH.

COUCH. Gen. 4:7; 49:25; Esth. 1:6; 7:8; Job 17:13; Ps. 6:6; 41:3; Amos 3:12; 6:4; Lu. 5:24; 22:66.

COULTER. I Sam. 13:20, 21.

COUNCIL. Gen. 49:6; Ps. 68:27; Matt. 12:14; 26:59; Mk. 14:55; 15:1; Lu. 22:66; John 11:47; Acts 25:12. Apostles before—Acts 4:15; 5:21, 27, 34, 41. Danger of—Matt. 5:22. Deliver to—Matt. 10:17; Mk. 13:9. Paul—Acts 22:30; 23:1, 6, 15, 20, 28; 24:20. Stephen before—Acts 6:12, 15. See SANHEDRIN.

COUNSEL. II Ki. 6:8; Ps. 33:10; Pr. 12:15; 15:22; 19:20; Eccl. 8:2; Is. 30:1; 47:13; Jer. 7:24; 18:18; Hos. 10:6; 11:6; Acts 27:39, 42. Ahab, Of —Mic. 6:16. Ahithophel, Of—II Sam. 15:31, 34; 16:20, 23; 17:7–23. Balaam, Of—Num. 31:16. Chief priests—Mt. 26:4; 27:1, 7; 28:12; Lu. 23:51; John 11:53; 12:10; 18:14. Daniel, Of—Dan. 2:14; 4:27. Egypt, Of—Is. 19:3, 11. Evildoers, Of—Ps. 64:2. False—I Chr. 20:13; II Chr. 22:5; Job 5:13; Acts 5:38. Friend, Of—Pr. 27:9. Jeremiah, Of—Jer. 38:15. Jerusalem, Of —Jer. 19:7. Judah, Of—Jer. 19:7. Kings—II Chr. 25:16. King, Of—I Ki. 12:28; II Chr. 25:16; Ps. 2:2. Moses, To—Ex. 18:19. Old men, Of— I Ki. 12:8, 13; II Chr. 10:6, 13. Peace, Of—Zech. 6:13. Pharisees, Of—Mt. 12:14; 22:15; Mk. 3:6. Princes, Of— Ezra 10:8. Prophets, Of—II Chr. 25:

16. Sound—Pr. 1:5. Spirit of—Is. 11:2. Sweet—Ps. 55:14. Together— Neh. 6:7; Ps. 31:13; 71:10; 83:3; Is. 8:10; 45:21; Acts 9:23. Young men, Of—I Ki. 12:9, 14; II Chr. 10:8. Wicked, Of—II Chr. 22:5; Job 22:18; Ps. 1:1; 5:10; Jer. 18:23; Ez. 11:2; Nah. 1:11.

God, Of.—Ju. 18:5; 20:18; I Sam. 14:37; Ezra 10:3; Ps. 16:7; 33:11; 73:24; 106:13; 107:11; Ps. 1:25, 30; 19:21; Is. 5:19; 25:1; 28:29; 46:10, 11; Jer. 23:18, 22; 32:19; 49:20; 50:45; Mic. 4:12; Lu. 7:30; Acts 2:23; 20:27; Eph. 1:11; Heb. 6:17; Rev. 3:18. See GUIDANCE, WISDOM.

COUNSELLOR. I Chr. 27:32; Ezra 4:5; Ps. 119:24; Pr. 11:14; 12:20; 15:22; 24:6; Is. 1:26; 3:3; 40:13; 41:28; Mic. 4:9; Rom. 11:34. David's—II Sam. 15:12; I Chr. 27:33. Discreet—I Chr. 26:14. King's—Ezra 7:14, 15, 28; 8:25. Nebuchadrezzar's—Dan. 3:2, 3, 24, 27; 4:36; 6:7. Pharaoh's—Is. 19:11. Wicked—II Chr. 22:3, 4.

Jesus called.—Is. 9:6.

Joseph of Arimathaea.—Mk. 15:43; Lu. 23:50.

COUNT. Apprehended — Phil. 3:13 (A.V.); Is. 33:18. Blood of covenant— Heb. 10:29. Cost—Lu. 14:28. Dust of Jacob—Num. 23:10. Enemy—As an—II Thess. 3:15. Faithful—I Tim. 1:12. Handmaid—I Sam. 1:16. Jehovah counteth—Ps. 87:6. Job—19:11, 15; 33:10. Faith—Rom. 4:5. Joy —Jas. 1:2. Laid hold, To have—Phil. 3:13. Levi and Benjamin—I Chr. 21:6. Life dear—Acts 20:24. Loss—Phil. 3:7, 8. Masters—I Tim. 6:1. Number of the beast—Rev. 13:8. Partner, A —Philemon 17. Pleasure—II Pet. 2:13. Price—Acts 19:19. Prophet, As a —Mt. 14:5; Mk. 11:32. Righteousness, For—Gen. 15:6; Rom. 4:3, 5. Sabbaths—Lev. 23:15. Slackness—II Pet. 3:9. Stranger, For—Job 19:15. Thoughts of God—Ps. 139:18. Uncircumcision—Rom. 2:26. Years—Lev. 25:27, 52. See CONSIDER, NUMBER, RECKON.

COUNTENANCE. Dan. 1:13; Gen. 4:5; Num. 6:26. Angel, Of an—Ju. 13:6. Angry—Pr. 25:23. Beautiful—I Sam. 16:12; 25:3. Changed—Dan. 5:10; 7:

28; 5:6, 9. Cheerful—Pr. 15:13. Comely—Song of Sol. 2:14. Fairer, Appeared—Dan. 1:15. Fallen—Gen. 4:6. Father's—Gen. 31:5. Fashion of—Lu. 9:29. Fierce of—Dan. 8:23. Friend, of—Pr. 27:17. Health, Of—Ps. 42:11; 43:5. Help of—Ps. 42:5. Laban, Of—Gen. 31:2. Light of—Job 29:24; Ps. 4:6; 44:3; 89:15. Look not on—I Sam. 16:7. Pride of—Ps. 10:4. Rebuke of—Ps. 80:16. Sad—Neh. 2:2, 3; I Sam. 1:18; Mt. 6:16. Sadness of—Eccl. 7:3. Show of—Is. 3:9. Sun shineth, As—Rev. 1:16. Troubled, Shall be—Ez. 27:35. Woman of fair—II Sam. 14:27. Youth of fair—I Sam. 17:42.

COUNTRY. All—II Chr. 34:33; Jer. 23:3, 8; 32:37; 40:11; Ez. 22:24. Far—I Ki. 8:41; II Ki. 20:14; II Chr. 6: 32; Pr. 25:25; Is. 8:9; 13:5; 46:11; Jer. 14:16; 6:20. Hill—See HILLS. Inhabitants of—Ju. 11:21; Josh. 9:11. Many—Ps. 110:6; Jer. 28:8. North—Zech. 6:8; Jer. 6:22; 10:22; 31:8; 46: 10; 50:9. Own—I Ki. 11:21, 22; Jer. 51:9; I Thess. 2:14; Mt. 13:54, 57; Mk. 6:1, 4; Lu. 4:24. South—Gen. 24: 62; Zech. 6:6. West—Zech. 8:7.

COUNTRYMEN. I Thess. 2:14; II Cor. 11:26.

COUPLE. Asses, Of—Ju. 19:3; II Sam. 16:1. Cakes, Of—II Sam. 13:6.

COUPLING. Curtains of tabernacle—Ex. 26:6, 9, 10, 11; 28:27; 36:10-20.

COURAGE. Be of good courage—Num. 13:20. Josh. 1:6; Pr. 28:1; Deut. 31: 6, 7, 23; Josh. 10:25; I Chr. 19:13; 22: 13; 28:20; II Sam. 10:12; Ezra 10:4;

Is. 41:6. Asa took courage and put away idolatry—II Chr. 15:8. Shall stir up, against king of the south—Dan. 11:25. He shall strengthen thy heart—Ps. 27:14. Let your heart take courage—Ps. 31:24. Courageous among mighty—Amos 2:16. Paul thanked God and took—Acts 28:15. Being always of good courage—II Cor. 5:6. Paul of good courage—II Cor. 10:1, 2. With good courage we say—Heb. 13:6.

Instances of.—Joshua and Caleb—Num. 13:30; 14:6-12. Deborah in leading the army of Israel—Ju. Ch. 4. David in slaying Goliath—I Sam. 17:32-50. In entering Saul's tent—I Sam. 26:7-12. Joab in reproving David—II Sam. 19:5-7. Esther in presenting herself to king in Jews' behalf—Esth. 4:8-16. The three Hebrews—Dan. 3:16-18. Daniel himself—Dan. 6:10. Nehemiah refusing shelter in the temple—Neh. 6:10-11. Joseph in caring for Jesus' body—Mk. 15:43. Peter and apostles—Acts 3:12-26; 4:9-13, 19, 20, 31; 5:29. Paul, when arrested—Acts 20:22-24; 24:14, 25. See PROPHETS.

COURSE. See PRIESTS.

COURT. Ps. 100:4; Ez. 40:14; Mk. 14: 66. Door of—Ez. 8:7. Guard, Of—Jer. 37:2. Guardeth his own—Lu. 11: 21. High priest, the—Mt. 26:3; Mk. 14:54; John 18:15. Midst of, In the—Lu. 22:55. Outer—Ez. 42:1. Sanctuary, Of—Is. 62:9. Solomon shall build—I Chr. 28:6. Tabernacle, Of—Ex. 27:9. Within the—Mk. 15: 16.

COURTEOUSLY. Acts 28:7. See KINDNESS.

COVENANTS.—Heb. *Berith.* Gr. *Diatheke.*—COVENANT, TESTAMENT, WILL.

BETWEEN GOD AND MEN.

THE OLD COVENANT.	THE NEW COVENANT.
Called:	**Called:**
Covenant of circumcision—Acts 7:8.	Better covenant—Heb. 7:22; 8:6.
Covenants of promise—Eph. 2:12.	Covenant of peace—Ez. 34:25; 37:26.
Everlasting covenant—Gen. 17:7, 13, 19; Ps. 105:10.	Everlasting covenant—Is. 55:3; 61:8; Jer. 32:40; 50:5; Ez. 37:26. *Eternal*—Heb. 13:20.
First covenant—Heb. 9:1, 15; 10:9.	Second covenant—Heb. 10:9.

Letter—Rom. 2:29; 7:6; II Cor. 3:6.

Ministration of condemnation—Rom. 3:20; II Cor. 3:9; Gal. 3:10–13. See Deut. 27:26; 29:31; Heb. 12:18–21; Jas. 2:10, 11, 13.

Ministration of death—II Cor. 3:7. See Gal. 3:21; PENALTY FOR VIOLATION OF COMMANDMENTS.

Old covenant—II Cor. 3:14; Heb. 9:13.

Yoke of bondage—Acts 15:10; Rom. 7:14–24; 8:15; Gal. 2:4; 3:10–13, 22; 4:1–3, 24, 30, 31; 5:1; Col. 2:14; Heb. 2:15; Jas. 2:12.

Spirit—Rom. 2:29; 7:6; II Cor. 3:6.

Ministration of righteousness—II Cor. 3:9. See Rom. 3:20, 21; Gal. 3:21.

Ministration of the spirit—II Cor. 3:8.

New covenant—Jer. 31:31; Lu. 22:20; I Cor. 11:25; II Cor. 3:6; Heb. 8:8, 13; 9:15; 12:24.

Law of liberty—Is. 54:1–8; Acts 15:10; Rom. 8:15; II Cor. 3:17; Gal. 2:4; 4:21–31; 5:1, 13; Jas. 2:12.

Heirs.

Abraham and his seed—Gen. 12:1–3; 15:4–21; 17:2–8; 18:18; 22:15–18; 26:3–5; 35:11, 12; Ex. 2:23, 24; 6:3–8; Lev. 26:42; Num. 32:11; Deut. 29:13; II Ki. 13:23; I Chr. 16:16; Neh. 9:7, 8; Ps. 105:7–9; Mic. 7:20; Lu. 1:72, 73; Acts 3:25.

Only by promise—Deut. 5:3 (Lu. 1:55); Rom. 4:13–25; Gal. 3:14–18; Heb. 6:13–18.

Born in house of Abraham—Gen. 17:13, 27.

Bought with his money—Gen. 17:13, 27; Ex. 12:44; Lev. 22:11.

Only male seed—Gen. 17:10–14; Ex. 12:48.

If circumcised—Gen. 17:10–14, 23–27; Ex. 12:48; Lev. 12:3; Lu. 1:59; 2:21; Rom. 4:11, 12; Phil. 3:5.

Males 8 days old, if circumcised, are heirs—Gen. 17:12; Lev. 12:3; Lu. 1:59; 2:21; Phil. 3:5.

In Isaac and his seed—Gen. 35:11, 12; 50:24; Ex. 2:23, 24; 6:3, 4, 8; Lev. 26:42; Num. 32:11; Deut. 29:13; II Ki. 13:23; I Chr. 16:16; Ps. 105:9–11.

Isaac the child of promise—Gen. 15:4; 17:15–21; Rom. 4:19, 21; 9:7–9; Gal. 4:23, 28; Heb. 11:18.

In Jacob and his seed—Gen. 25:21–26, 30–34; 27:1–37; 28:3, 4, 13–18; 35:11, 12; 50:24; Ex. 2:23, 24; 6:3, 4, 8; Lev. 26:42; Num. 32:11; Deut. 29:13; II Ki. 13:23; I Chr. 16:7; Ps. 105:9–11; Mic. 7:20.

Heirs.

The whole world—*The great commission*—Mt. 28:18–20; Mk. 16:15, 16; Lu. 24:46, 47. See Acts 1:8; SALVATION FOR ALL MEN.

If Christ's, then are ye Abraham's seed—Rom. 4:16–25; 9:6–33; Gal. 3:8, 14, 26–29.

Neither bond nor free—Gal. 3:28.

Neither male nor female—Gal. 3:28.

Circumcision not necessary—See SALVATION BY FAITH IN CHRIST WITHOUT THE WORKS OF THE LAW.

They shall be all taught of God—Is. 54:13; Jer. 31:34; John 6:45; Heb. 8:11.

Gentiles are children of promise—Rom. 4:9–25; 9:7; Gal. 3:29; 4:28.

Jacob typical of the Gentile—Is. 49:6, 7; Mal. 1:1–15; Rom. 9:9–33; 11:25–32.

Confirmed with an oath—Gen. 22:16; 26: 3; 50:24; Ex. 6:8; Num. 32:11; Deut. 4: 31; 7:8; 8:18; Ju. 2:1; I Chr. 16:16; Ps. 105:9–11; Mic. 7:20; Lu. 1:73; Rom. 9: 10–13; Gal. 3:15, 17; Heb. 6:13–18.

Israelites only—Gen. 17:7–14, 19; Ex. 2:23, 24; 6:4–8; 34:27–35; Lev. 24:8; 26:9–13, 45, 46; Num. 25:10–13; Deut. 4:13–20; 5:1–6; 8:11–20; 23:7, 8; 29: 1–28; I Ki. 8:9; II Ki. 17:34–38; I Chr. 16:17; Ps. 105:6–45; Jer. 11:1– 10; 31:32 (Heb. 8:9); 34:13; Mal. 4:4; Lu. 1:72–74; Rom. 2:13–16; 9:4–6; Eph. 2:12. See Mt. 10:6; 15:24; John 4:22.

Israelites a peculiar people—Ex. 19:5; 34:9–12; Deut. 7:6–24; 14:2; 26:18, 19.

WHAT WAS THE OLD COVENANT?
The Inheritance.

In thee and thy seed shall all nations be blessed.—Gen. 12:1–3; 18:18; 22:14– 18; Heb. 6:13, 14.

Repeated to David—II Sam. 23:5; I Ki. 11:13; II Chr. 21:7; Is. 55:3.

That his throne should be established forever—II Sam. 7:12–16; II Chr. 6:16; 7:18; Ps. 89:3, 4, 28–36.

Everlasting—II Chr. 21:7; Ps. 89:34–37; Is. 49:8–16; 54:4–10.

The land of Canaan.—Gen. 12:2; 13:15– 17; 15:7–21; 17:8, 26:2–4; 28:4; Ex. 6:4–8; 34:11–24; Lev. 26:1–13; Num. 32:11; Ju. 2:1–7; I Chr. 16:16–22; Neh. 9:7, 8; Ps. 105:9–13; Acts 7:5–8; Gal. 3:16–18.

An everlasting possession—Gen. 17:7, 8; Ps. 105:10, 11.

Possession conditional—*Upon obedience of commandments*—Ex. 19:5; Lev. 26: 1–46; Deut. 4:13, 14; 7:9–16; 8:11– 20; Josh. 7:2–25; Ju. 2:1–4; I Ki. 8: 23; II Ki. 17:13–23; Neh. 1:5; 9:7–37; Ps. 25:10, 14; 50:16–23; 78:31–64; 103: 17, 18; 132:12; Is. 56:4–8. *Must not be idolaters*—Ex. 23:20–33; 32:34, 35; 34: 12–28; Deut. 4:25–31; 7:16, 25, 26; 29: 14–28; Ju. 2:18–25; II Ki. 11:17–20. *Israelites punished for disobedience*— Ex. 32:34, 35; Num. 14:26–35; 32:11. **See** SIN.

Promises confirmed by the Holy Spirit— Acts 1:8; 19:11, 12; Rom. 15:18, 19; II Cor. 12:12; I Thess. 1:5; Heb. 2:1–4; II Pet. 1:16–21.

The middle wall of partition broken down—I Cor. 12:13; Eph. 2:11–19; Col. 3:11.

The promise to the Gentiles—See SALVATION.

Christians a peculiar people—John 1:11– 13; 15:19–21; 17:14–16; Tit. 2:14; I Pet. 2:9, 10.

WHAT IS THE NEW COVENANT?
The Inheritance.

Fulfilled in Christ.—Is. 49:6–10 (II Cor. 6:2); **54**:1–14 (Gal. 4:25–31); 55:1– 13; 59:20, 21; 61:1–11; Jer. 31:31–34; Lu. 1:46–55, 72–79; Acts 3:25, 26; 13: 22–40; Rom. 4:11–25; 11:25–28; Gal. 3:5–16, 19; Heb. 2:14–16; 6:14–20.

The kingdom of Christ established forever—Is. 11:1–10; Ez. 34:22–24, 26; Dan. 2:44; 7:13, 14, 18, 27; 9:7–24, 27; Amos 9:11–15 (Acts 15:12–18); Zech. 6:12, 13; Mt. 28:18; Lu. 1:32, 33; Acts 2:34–36; Rom. 1:1–14.

Everlasting—Is. 55:3–5; 61:8–11; Jer. 31:35–40; Dan. 2:44; Mt. 16:18, 19.

Christ given for a covenant.—Is. 42:6–9; 49:6–10; 59:20, 21. John the Baptist the messenger of the new covenant— Mal. 3:1 (Mt. 11:9–11; Mk. 1:2; Lu. 7:27, 28).

Eternal life called an inheritance.—Mt. 25:34; Mk. 10:17; Acts 20:32; 26:18; Rom. 8:17; Gal. 3:29; 4:7; Eph. 1:11, 14; 5:5; Phil. 3:11, 12; Col. 1:12; 3:24; I Thess. 2:12; II Tim. 2:12; Tit. 3:7; Heb. 1:14; 6:12–20; 9:15; 10:34; 11:13–16; 13:14; I Pet. 1:4; Rev. 21:7. See SALVATION CONDITIONAL.

What were the Conditions of the Old Covenant?

The Law.

The ten commandments—Deut. 4:12–14, 23; 5:1–22; 8:11–19; 17:2–5; 29:14–28; Josh. 7:11–25; 23:16; Jer. 2:19, 20.
Called covenant—Deut. 4:13; I Ki. 8:9, 21; II Chr. 6:11; Jer. 11:10, 13; 22:9.
Called words of the covenant—Ex. 34:28.
Tables of testimony—Ex. 31:18; 32:15, 16; 34:29.
Written on tables of stone and called "Tables of Stone"—Ex. 24:12; 31:18; 32:15, 16; 34:1–12; Deut. 4:13; 5:22; 9:9–11; II Cor. 3:3, 7, 8.
Put in the ark—Ex. 25:16, 21, 22; Deut. 10:1–5; I Ki. 8:9, 21; II Chr. 5:10; 6:11; Heb. 9:1–4. See ARK OF THE COVENANT, below.
Statutes and ordinances—Heb. 9:1. See Ex. 19:31; 34:1–33; 35:1–19. See Lev. 18:4, 5; 26:46; 27:34.
Book of the law called book of the covenant—Ex. 24:1–7; II Ki. 23:2, 3, 21; II Chr. 34:30.
Put in the side of the ark of the covenant—Deut. 31:9–13, 24–29.
Service of the tabernacle—Ex. 25:40; 38:21; 39:42, 43; Acts 7:44; Heb. 8:5; 9:1–28; 10:1–19.
Shadow of heavenly things—Col. 2:14–17; Heb. 8:5; 9:23; 10:1–9.
Priesthood—Lev. 1:1–17; 28:1–4; 8:1–36; Heb. 8:4; 9:6–10; 10:6–10.

After the order of Aaron—Ex. 29:9; 40:13–15; Lev. 8:1–39; Num. 18:1; 20:24–28; 25:10, 13; Heb. 7:11.
From the tribe of Levi—Ex. 38:21; Num. 3:5–10; 4:1–49; 8:6–22; 18:1–7; Deut. 10:8, 9; 18:1–8; Mal. 2:4–9; Heb. 7:5–11.
Priests offered blood of animals—Heb. 5:1–3; 8:3, 4; 9:6–10, 12, 13; 10:1–8, 11. See OFFERINGS.

Character of.

The law added because of transgression—Gal. 3:18, 19; I Tim. 1:8–10.

What were the Conditions of the New Covenant?

The Gospel.

Nine of the commandments repeated after the death of Jesus—See COMMANDMENTS, SABBATH.

Gentiles did not have the law—Rom. 2:11–16; 9:1–5; I Cor. 9:21; Gal. 3:2–14, 19.
Put in their minds and written on the tables of their hearts—John 6:45; II Cor. 3:3; Heb. 8:10.

The true tabernacle—Heb. 8:2; 9:11, 24.

To come—Heb. 10:1.

Priesthood changed—Heb. 7:12–28.

Christ our high priest—Heb. 2:17; 3:1; 4:14–16; 5:1–10; 6:20; 7:26–28; 8:1–3; 9:11–13.
After the order of Melchizedek—Heb. 5:6–10; 6:20; 7:11–17.

From the tribe of Judah—Mt. 2:6; Heb. 7:14; Rev. 5:5.

Christ offered his own blood—Heb. 2:17; 9:12, 14, 25–28; 10:10, 12, 14; I Pet. 2:24. See SALVATION.

Character of.

Till the seed should come—Gal. 3:16, 19; 4:1–5.

Could not make perfect—Heb. 7:11, 18, 19; 9:9, 10; 10:1, 2.

Could not justify—Acts 13:38, 39; Rom. 3:20, 27, 28; Gal. 2:16; 3:10–12; 5:4.

Righteousness could not come by the law—Rom. 3:21; 4:15; 5:13; 7:7; 9:30–32; Gal. 2:21; 3:21; Phil. 3:6.
Could not give peace of conscience— Heb. 9:9; 10:1, 2.
Could not give life—Rom. 4:15; 7:9–13; II Cor. 3:6–13; Gal. 2:19; 3:21.

No remission of sins—Heb. 9:9, 10; 10: 1–4, 11. See Lev. 4:1–35; 16:1–34.

High priest entered once every year into the Holiest of Holies—Lev. 16:11–17, 34; Heb. 9:7, 25; 10:1, 3.
A veil before the Holiest of Holies—Ex. 26:31–33; 36:35–38; Heb. 9:3.
Way into Holiest not made manifest while first tabernacle stood—Heb. 9: 7, 8.
Old covenant made at Mt. Sinai (called HOREB).—Ex. 19–32, 34; Lev. 26: 46; 27:34; Deut. 5:2; 29:25; 33:2; I Ki. 8:9; Jer. 11:4, 7; 31:32; Mal. 4:4; Gal. 4:24, 25.
About 430 years after promise made to Abraham—Gen. 15:13; Ex. 12:40, 41; Acts 7:6; Gal. 3:17.
Repeated in Moab.—Deut. Chs. 29, 30.
Moses the Mediator.—Ex. 19:5–25; 20: 18–21; Deut. 4:5; 5:1–5, 23–35; Ps 99:6; Mal. 4:4; John 1:17; 7:19; Gal. 3:19.
Sealed with blood of bulls and goats.— Ex. 24:6–8; Heb. 9:18–21.
Based on flesh.—John 3:6; Rom. 8:3, 4; II Cor. 11:18; Phil. 3:1–8; Gal. 4:21– 31; 6:12–14.
Blessings temporal.—Deut. 11:13–17; 28: 1–68; 29:1.

Israelites broke the covenant by dis- obedience.—Ex. 32:1–35; Lev. 26:14– 16; Deut. 9:9–29; 29:25, 26; I Ki. 17: 13–19, 40; 18:12; Ps. 78:10–58; Is. 24: 5; 33:8; Jer. 11:8, 10–17; Ez. 44:6, 7; Hos. 6:7; 8:1. See COMMANDMENTS.

Perfection the standard of New Testament—Mt. 5:48; John 17:23; I Cor. 1:8; II Cor. 13:7, 9–11; Gal. 3:3; Eph. 4:12; Phil. 3:12, 15; Col. 1:22, 28; Heb. 6:1; Jas. 1:4.
Justified by faith—Rom. 2:12–16; 3: 21–31; Gal. 2:16; 3:8–14; 5:4; Eph. 2:8–11; Tit. 3:3–7.
Righteousness which is of faith—Rom. 1:17; 3:21; 9:30; 10:6–10; I Cor. 1:30; Phil. 3:9; Heb. 11:7. See Rom. 4:9, 13.

He that hath the Son hath life— John 1:4; 3:15, 16, 36; 5:24; 6:33, 47, 50, 51; 10:10; 11:25, 26; 17:23; 20:30, 31.
Their sins and iniquities I will remember no more forever—Jer. 31:34; Heb. 8:12; 10:17, 18.
Holy place a type of heaven—Heb. 9:2.
Christ enters once for all—Heb. 7:27; 9:12, 26, 28; 10:10.
The veil of the temple rent in twain— Mt. 27:51; Mk. 15:38; Lu. 23:45.
Entrance into holy place through a new and living way—Heb. 6:19; 10:19, 20.

New covenant to begin at Jerusalem.— Is. 2:3; Mic. 4:2; Mt. 23:37; Lu. 13: 34; 24:47; Acts 1:8; 2:1–6.

Christ the mediator.—Rom. 8:34; Eph. 2:18; 3:11, 12; I Tim. 2:5, 6; Heb. 7: 24–27; 8:6; 9:15, 24; 12:24.

Sealed with blood of Christ.—Mt. 26:28; Mk. 14:24; Lu. 22:20; I Cor. 11:25.
Not based on flesh.—John 1:13; 3:5; Jas. 1:18; I Pet. 1:23.

Blessings eternal.—Mt. 6:19–34; 10:38, 39; 16:24–27; Mk. 8:34–38; Lu. 9:23– 26; 16:10–31; 17:33; John 12:25, 26.
See SALVATION.

Covenant not binding with God because broken by Israelites.—Num. 14:27-34; 26:64, 65; 32:6-15; I Cor. 10:5-12.

In force until all things were fulfilled.—Mt. 5:17-19; Lu. 16:17.

Glory of the old.—Ex. 34:29-35.

Finding fault with the first covenant.—Heb. 7:11, 18, 19; 8:7-12; 9:11-15.

He hath made the first old.—II Cor. 3: 14; Heb. 8:13; 9:13.

That which is old is ready to vanish away.—II Cor. 5:17; Heb. 8:13.

He taketh away the first.—Heb. 7:18, 19; 10:9.

We are become dead to the law.—Rom. 7:1-13.

The law our tutor to bring us to Christ.—Gal. 3:23-25; 4:1-5.

Bond written in ordinances taken out of the way; nailed to the cross.—Col. 2:14.

Cast out the handmaid and her child.—Gal. 4:21-31.

Old covenant in force until new properly sealed.—Heb. 9:11-22.

Fulfilled in the death of Jesus.—Mk. 1: 15; Lu. 24:44-47; Gal. 4:4; Eph. 1:9, 10.

Exceeded by the glory of the new.—II Cor. 3:7-11.

God promises a new covenant.—Jer. 31: 31-34; Heb. 8:6-12; 9:11-15.

In that he saith a new covenant.—Lu. 22:20; II Cor. 3:6; Heb. 7:22; 8:6, 13; 9:15; 12:24.

The new founded on better promises.—Heb. 7:22; 8:6; 9:15; 12:24.

That He may establish the second.—Heb. 7:18; 10:9.

By the body of Christ.—Rom. 7:4-6; I Pet. 2:24.

After the faith came, we were no longer under tutors.—Gal. 3:25; 4:2-5.

We are the children of the free woman.—Gal. 4:21-31. See NEW COVENANT SEALED WITH BLOOD.

Stephen stoned for changing customs.—Acts 6:9-15. See Acts 15:1-29; 21: 17-26.

Other covenants with men. — With Hezekiah—II Chr. 29:3-36. With Jehoiada—II Ki. 11:17-20. With Josiah II Chr. 34:29-33. With Noah—Gen. 6:18-21; 8:20-22; 9:9-17; Is. 54:9, 10.

Covenant of peace.—Num. 26:2; Is. 54: 10; Ez. 34:25; 37:26.

Covenant of priesthood.—Ex. 29:9; 40: 13-15; Num. 18:1-7; 25:13; Neh. 13: 29.

Made with the Levites—Num. 3:5-10; 8:6-22; 18:1-7; Deut. 10:8, 9; 18:1-8; Mal. 2:4-8.

Covenant of salt.—Num. 18:11-19; II Chr. 13:5.

Covenants ratified.—By an oath—See CONFIRMED WITH AN OATH, under *Heirs of Old Covenant.* By passing between the divided parts of a sacrifice—Gen. 15:9, 17; Jer. 34:18, 19. By giving the hand—II Ki. 10:15; Ezra 10:19; Lam 5:6; Pr. 11:21; 16:5; Lam. 5:6; Ez.

17:18. By striking hands—Job 17:3; Pr. 6:1; 17:18; 22:26. By loosing the shoe before witnesses—Ruth 4:7-11. By writing and sealing—Neh. 9:38; Jer. 32:10-12. By presents—Gen. 21: 27-30; I Sam. 18:3. By a heap of stones and a pillar—Gen. 31:45-52. With salt—Lev. 2:13; Num. 18:19; II Chr. 13:5.

Ark of the covenant. See ARK.

Blood of the covenant.—Of the old—Ex. 24:8; Zech. 9:11. Of the new—Matt. 26:28; Lu. 22:20; I Cor. 11:25; Heb. 10:29; 13:20.

Book of the covenant.—Law written in —Ex. 17:14; 24:7; II Ki. 23:3, 21, 24. Delivered to the priests—Deut. 31:9-13. Read to the Israelites—Deut. 31: 9-13; II Ki. 23:2, 3; II Chr. 34:30. Put in the ark—Deut. 31:24-26. Found by Hilkiah—II Ki. 22:8; 23:24; II Chr. 34:14, 15, 30.

BREAD OF THE COVENANT.—Lev. 24:5-9.
SALT OF THE COVENANT.—Lev. 2:13; Ez. 43:24.

COVER, COVERING. Altar—Mal. 2:
13. Anger, With—Lam. 3:43. Ark—
I Ki. 8:7; I Chr. 28:18; Num. 4:5.
Blood—Job 16:18. Candlestick—Num.
4:9. Cherubim—II Chr. 5:8. Cloud—
Ex. 24:15, 16; 40:34; Num. 9:15, 16.
Darkness—Job. 23:17. Dust—Lev.
17:13; Ez. 24:7. Earth, Face of—Ex.
10:5, 15; Num. 22:5, 11. Face—Gen.
38:15. Feet—Ju. 3:24. Floor—I Ki.
6:15. Glory—Hab. 3:3. Head—Ps.
140:7. Heaven—Ez. 32:7. House—
I Ki. 6:9. Horror shall—Ez. 7:18. In-
cense, Cloud of—Lev. 16:13. Land,
Frogs—Ex. 8:6. Lips—Ez. 24:17, 22;
Mic. 3:7. Love—Pr. 10:12; I Pet. 4:8
(A.V.). Mercy-seat—Ex. 25:20. Moun-
tains—Gen. 17:20. Name—Eccl. 6:4.
Pit—Ex. 21:33. Reproach—Ps. 71:13.
Sackcloth, With—II Ki. 19:2. Sea—Ex.
15:10. Silver, With—Ps. 68:13. Sin—
Ps. 32:1. Skin, Leprosy—Lev. 13:12, 13.
Sun—Ez. 32:7. Tent, For the—Ex.
26:14; 36:19. Transgression—Pr. 17:
9. Trees—Job 40:22. Valleys are—
Ps. 65:13. Violence—Pr. 10:6; Hab.
2:17. Waters—Is. 11:9; Ez. 26:19.
Windows were—Ez. 41:16. Worms—
Job 21:26; Is. 14:11.

COVERT. Abide in—Job 38:40. Destroyer, From—Is. 16:14. Mountain,
Of—I Sam. 25:20. Storm, From—Is.
4:6. Tempest, From—Is. 32:2. Wings,
Of—Ps. 61:4.

COVETOUSNESS.—Shut out from the
kingdom of God—I Cor. 6:9-10; 5:11;
Eph. 5:3-5; Col. 3:5-6. Riches make
entrance difficult—Mt. 19:23-24; Lu.
18:24-25.

Its Origin.—The heart—Ez. 33:31; Mk.
7:21-22; Mt. 6:19-21; II Pet. 2:14.

Its character.—A root of all kinds of
evil—I Tim. 6:10. Idolatry—Eph. 5:
5; Col. 3:5. Greedy—Pr. 21:26; Eccl.
4:8; 5:10; Is. 56:11; Lu. 12:15; Hab.
2:5-6.

What it leads to.—Punishment—Josh.
7:21, 25; Pr. 28:20; Mic. 2:2-3. Foolish and hurtful lusts—I Tim. 6:9. Infidelity—I Tim. 6:10. Sorrow—I Tim.
6:10. Domestic trouble—Pr. 15:27.

Murder—Pr. 1:18-19; Jas. 4:2. Oppression—Ez. 22:12.

Dangers multiply.—Robbing a brother—
Deut. 15:9. Shutting out the gospel—
Mt. 13:22. Choking the word—Mk.
4:19. Breeding unholy love—II Tim.
3:2; Heb. 13:5. Make merchandise
of you—II Pet. 2:3. Love the hire
of wrongdoing—II Pet. 2:15.

Punishment.—Job 20:15; 31:24, 25, 28;
Is. 57:17; Jer. 8:10; 22:17-19; Ez. 22:
12-16; Col. 3:5-6.

Examples: Eve—Gen. 3:6. Lot—Gen.
3:6. Laban—Gen. 24:30. Jacob obtaining Esau's birthright—Gen. 27:
36. Laban deceiving Jacob—Gen.
31:7. Balaam—Num. Ch. 22; II Pet.
2:15. Achan, at Jericho—Josh. 7:21.
Eli's sons—I Sam. 2:12-17. Samuel's
sons—I Sam. 8:3. Saul—I Sam. 15:
8, 9. Ahab, desiring Naboth's vineyard—I Ki. 21:2-26. David in his
act with Bathsheba and Uriah—II
Sam. Ch. 11. Gehazi—II Ki. 5:20-24.
Jews robbing their brethren—Neh. 5:
1-11. Tyrians—Ez. 28:19. Priests—
Mal. 1:10. Rich young ruler—Mt. 19:
16-22. Money-changers—Mt. 21:12,
13. The rich fool—Lu. 12:15-21.
Judas—Mt. 26:14-16. Mk. 14:10-11;
Lu. 22:3-6; John 12:4-6. Pharisees—
Lu. 16:14. Stewards—Lu. 16:1-8.
Men of Sodom—Lu. 17:28-30. Ana-
nias—Acts 5:1-10. Simon Magus—
Acts 8:18-23. Sorcerers—Acts 16:19.
Demetrius—Acts 19:24-27. Festus—
Acts 24:26. Demas—II Tim. 4:10.

COW. Num. 18:17; Job 21:10; Is. 7:21;
11:7; Ex. 4:15. See CATTLE.

COZBI, kŏz′bi. **A princess of Midian
slain by Phinehas.**—Num. 25:15-18.

COZEBA, ko̤-zē′ba. **A village in Judah.**
—I Chr. 4:22.

CRACKED. Ground—Jer. 14:4.

CRACKLING. Eccl. 7:6.

CRAFT. Is. 25:11. See CRAFTY.

CRAFTSMAN. II Ki. 24:14, 16; I Chr.
4:14; Neh. 11:35; Acts 19:24, 38; Rev.
18:22. Work of—Deut. 27:15; Hos.
13:2. See ARTS AND TRADES.

CRAFTY. Craft or deceit in state—
Dan. 8:25. In counsel—Ps. 83:3. Of
scribes against Jesus—Lu. 20:23. God
frustrates—Job 5:12, 13; I Cor. 3:19.

Prophecy concerning.—Rev. 18:22.

Saints not to walk in craftiness.—II Cor. 4:2; 12:16; Eph. 4:14.

CRANE. Is. 38:14; Jer. 8:7.

CRASHING. Zeph. 1:10.

CRAVE. Pr. 16:26; Mk. 15:43.

CREATE. See GOD THE CREATOR.

CREATION. All—Col. 1:15, 23. Beginning of—Mk. 10:6; 13:19; II Pet. 3:4; Rev. 3:14. Delivered from bondage of corruption—Rom. 8:21. Expectation of—Rom. 8:19. First-born of all —Col. 1:15. Invisible things since— Rom. 1:20. Subject to vanity—Rom. 8:20. This, Not of—Heb. 9:11. Whole —Mk. 16:15; Rom. 8:22. See GOD THE CREATOR.

CREATURE. Any other—Rom. 8:39. Every—Mk. 16:15 (A.V.); Col. 1:15, 23 (A.V.); I Tim. 4:4; Rev. 5:13. Firstfruits of—Jas. 1:18. Living—Gen. 1:20, 21, 24; 2:19; 9:10–16; Lev. 11: 46; Ez. 1:5, 13, 14, 15, 19–22; 3:13; 10: 15, 17, 20; Rev. 4:9; 6:3. Manifest, Not—Heb. 4:13. New—II Cor. 5:17; Gal. 6:15. Reason, Without—II Pet. 2:12; Jude 10. Third part of—Rev. 8:9. Worshipped—Rom. 1:25. See GOD THE CREATOR.

CREDITOR. Deut. 15:2; II Ki. 4:1; Is. 50:1. See DEBT.

CREEK. Acts 27:39 (A.V.).

CREEPING THINGS. General term for insects and reptiles—Gen. 1:26; Lev. 11:20–23, 29–31, 41–47; Ps. 104:20, 25; Rom. 1:23. Not to touch—Lev. 5:2; 11:20; Deut. 14:19. May eat of—Lev. 11:21–22. Uses of in false worship— Ez. 8:10. Overthrow of—Ez. 38:20. All manner of—Acts 10:12. Image of —Rom. 1:23. Every kind of—Jas. 3: 7. Creep into houses—II Tim. 3:6. Creep in privily—Jude 4.

CRESCENS, krĕs'cens. One of Paul's helpers—II Tim. 4:10.

CRESCENTS. Ju. 8:21.

CRETANS, krē'tans. Acts 2:11; Tit. 1:12.

CRETE, krēte. **A large island, now called Candra, visited by Paul.**—Acts 27:7, 12, 13, 21; Tit. 1:5.

CRIB. Abide by—Job 39:9. Clean— Pr. 14:4. Master's, His—Is. 1:3.

CRICKET. Lev. 11:22. See INSECTS.

CRIED. See CRY.

CRIME. Land full of—Ez. 7:23. See SIN.

CRIMSON. See COLORS.

CRIPPLE. From his mother's womb— Acts 14:8. See LAMENESS.

CRISPING PIN. Is. 3:22 (A.V.).

CRISPUS, krĭs'pus. **A ruler of the synagogue at Corinth, baptized by Paul.**—Acts 18:8; 1 Cor. 1:14.

CROOKED. Generation, Perverse and —Deut. 32:5. Paths, Made—Is. 59:8; Lam. 3:9. Serpent—Is. 27:1. *Straight, Cannot be made*—Eccl. 1:15. *Shall be made*—Lu. 3:5. *Which he made*—Eccl. 7:13. Things, I will make straight— Is. 45:2. Way, Such as turn aside unto—Ps. 125:5.

CROP. Lev. 1:16. Off—Ez. 17:4, 22.

CROSS. The gibbet upon which Christ died.

Christ crucified on.—Mt. 27:32–42; Mk. 15:16–39; Lu. 23:27–46; John 19:16– 30; Acts 2:23, 36; 4:10; 5:30; 10:39; 13:29; Gal. 3:1; Phil. 2:8; Heb. 12:2; I Pet. 2:24.

Title on.—Mt. 27:37; Mk. 15:26; Lu. 23: 38; John 19:19.

Carried by Simon.—Lu. 23:26.

Shame of.—Heb. 12:2.

Power of.—John 12:32; I Cor. 1:18.

Glory of.—Gal. 6:14.

Illustrative of self-denial.—Mt. 10:38; 16:24; Mk. 8:34; Lu. 9:23; 14:27. Of the gospel—I Cor. 1:17, 18; Gal. 5:11; 6:12, 14; Eph. 2:16; Phil. 3:18; Col. 1:20; 2:14. See "Teaching of Jesus" —Lu. 2:21.

CROSSWAY. Ob. 14.

CROUCH. Ps. 10:10. See BOW DOWN.

CROW. See COCK.

CROWN: Head.—Gen. 49:26; Deut. 33: 20; II Sam. 14:25; Job 2:7; Pr. 16:31; Is. 3:17; Jer. 2:16; 48:45.

Gold.—Ex. 25:11, 24, 25; 30:3, 4; 37:2, 11, 12, 26, 27; Esth. 8:15; Ps. 21:3; Zech. 6:11; Rev. 4:4; 9:7.

Silver.—Zech. 6:11.

Kings.—II Sam. 1:10; 12:30; II Ki. 11: 12; I Chr. 20:2; II Chr. 23:11; Esth 6:8; Ps. 132:18. Prophecy concerning —Ez. 21:26.

Queen.—Esth. 1:11; 2:17.

Holy crown.—Ex. 29:6; 39:30; Lev. 8:9

Anointing oil.—Lev. 21:12.

Crown profaned.—Ps. 89:39.

Thorns.—Mt. 27:29; Mk. 15:17; John 19:2, 5.

Prophecy concerning.—Rev. 4:10.

Figurative.—Job 31:36; Pr. 12:4. Crown of wise is their riches—Pr. 14:24; 17: 6; 27:24; Song of Sol. 3:11; Zech. 9: 16; Phil. 4:1. Independence and prosperity—Lam. 5:16. Of beauty—Pr. 4:9; Is. 62:3; Ez. 16:12; 23:42. Of glory taken—Job 19:9; Is. 28:5; Jer. 13:18; I Pet. 5:4. Crown of honor—Zech. 6:14. Of pride—Is. 28:3. Of righteousness—II Tim. 4:8. Of life—Jas. 1:12; Rev. 2:10; 3:11. Crown given—Rev. 6:2. Corruptible and incorruptible—I Cor. 9:25. Of rejoicing—I Thess. 2:19.

CRUCIFIXION. A Roman punishment. Mt. 20:19; John 18:31, 32.

Of the two robbers.—Mt. 27:38, 44; Mk. 15:27, 32; John 19:32. Of disciples—Mt. 23:34.

Of Christ.—Mention of—Mt. 20:19; 26: 2; 27:22, 23, 26, 31, 35; 28:5; Mk. 15: 13–15, 20, 24, 27; 16:6; Lu. 23:33; John 19:10; Acts 2:23–24; 4:10; I Cor. 1:13, 23; 2:2, 8; II Cor. 13:4; Phil. 2:8; Heb. 12:2; Rev. 11:8.

Term ''cursed.''—Gal. 3:13.

An offence.—Gal. 5:11.

Illustrative.—Rom. 6:6.

Figurative.—Gal. 2:20; 5:24; 6:14; Heb. 6:6. See JESUS.

CRUEL. Pr. 5:9; 11:17; Jer. 30:14. Bondage—Ex. 6:9. See BONDAGE. Daughter of my people—Lam. 4:3. Day of Jehovah—Is. 13:9. Grave, As the—Song of Sol. 8:6 (A.V.). Hatred—Ps. 25:19. Jealousy—Song of Sol. 8:6. Job, To—30:21. Lord, A—Is. 19:4. Man—Ps. 71:4. Messenger, A—Pr. 17:11. Oppressor—Ez. 18:18. See OPPRESSION. Venom of asps—Deut. 32: 33. Wicked—Pr. 12:10. Wrath—Gen. 49:7; Pr. 27:4.

CRUELTY. Rebuked—Gen. 49:7; Ex. 23:5; Ps. 27:12; Pr. 11:17; Ez. 18:18.

CRUMB. Dogs eat—Mt. 15:27; Mk. 7: 28. Rich man's table, From—Lu. 16: 21.

CRUSE. See VESSELS.

CRUSH. Lev. 22:24. Baalam's foot against the wall—Num. 22:25. Foot —Job 39:15. Gate, In the—Job 5:4. Moth, Before the—Job 4:19. Nebuch-adrezzar hath—Jer. 51:34. Needy—Amos 4:1. Oppressed and crushed alway—Deut. 28:33. Prisoners, Under his feet—Lam. 3:34. Young men, My —Lam. 1:15.

CRY. Unto Jehovah.—Deut. 15:9; I Sam. 7:8; Ps. 40:1; 57:2; 61:1; 86:3; 88:2. Of David—II Sam. 22:7; Ps. 89: 26. In affliction—II Chr. 20:9.

For help.—Ps. 28:1; 107:19, 28; 119:169; 141:1; 142:6. From Israel—Ps. 106: 44; Joel 1:14, 19, 20. From Nineveh—Jonah 3:8.

Cry of.—Supplication—Esau—Gen. 27: 34. *To God*—I Ki. 8:28; II Chr. 6:19; Job 19:7; Ps. 5:2; 17:1; 18:6; 27:7; 28:2; 39:12. Job—Job 30:20, 24; Heb. 5:7. *To king*—II Ki. 8:3. Israel at Red Sea—Neh. 9:9. Blind men—Mt. 9:27. Affliction—Zion—Ps. 102:1; Lam. 2: 19; 3:8, 56; Ez. 9:4; 21:12. Anguish—Ps. 22:2. Mordecai—Esth. 4:1. Blind beggar—Mk. 10:47. Children in the temple—Mt. 21:15. Complaints—I Sam. 8:18; 9:16; Neh. 5:1, 6; Job 16: 18. Demoniac—Mk. 5:5; Lu. 4:41. Egyptians—Ex. 11:6; 12:30. Widow and fatherless heard by Jehovah—Ex. 22:23. City—I Sam. 5:12. Fools—Eccl. 9:17. Grief—Heard by Eli—I Sam. 4: 14. Tamar—II Sam. 13:19. David—Ps. 69:3. Horonaim—Jer. 48:3. Joy —Is. 12:6; 54:1; Gal. 4:27. Leper—Lev. 13:45. Midnight, At—Mt. 25:6. Oppressed—Job 35:9, 12; Is. 5:7. Israel in bondage—Ex. 2:23; 3:7, 9; 5:8. Those overcome—Ex. 32:18. The perishing—Num. 16:3, 4. Pity—Is. 15:5. Poor—Job 34:28; Ps. 9:12; Pr. 21:13. Righteous—Ps. 34:15, 17. The elect—Lu. 18:7. Streets, In—Is. 24:11. Two daughters of the horseleach—Pr. 30: 15. Unclean—Acts 8:7. Warning—Is. 58:1; Jer. 2:2; 4:5; Jonah 1:2; Zech. 1:14, 17. By Paul and Barnabas—Acts 14:14. Wicked—Job 27:9. To idols—Ju. 10:14; I Ki. 18:17; Job 36:13; Is. 46:7. Sodom and Gomorrah—Gen. 18: 20, 21; 19:3. Wisdom—Pr. 8:1. Not heard of Jehovah—Ez. 8:18; Mic. 3:4; Hab. 1:2.

Voice of.—Is. 65:19.

To Jesus.—Defiance—Mt. 8:29. Faith—Mt. 9:27; Mk. 9:24. Fear—Mt. 14:26. Danger—Mt. 14:30. Intercession—Mt.

15:23. Importunity—Mt. 20:31. Children—Mt. 21:15. Hatred—Mt. 27:23. Unclean—Mk. 3:11. Subdued rage—Mk. 9:26. Testimony—John 1:15. Mob—John 19:15.

Cry of animals.—Ravens—Job 38:41; Ps. 147:9. Wolves—Is. 13:22. Goat—Is. 34:14. Lions—Amos 3:4.

Cry or words of peace.—Mic. 3:5. "Abba Father"—Rom. 8:15; Gal. 4:6.

Of Jews.—Acts 17:6; 21:28, 36; 25:24.

Servant shall not strive, nor cry aloud.—Mt. 12:19.

Prophecies concerning.—Child—Is. 8.4. Wolves—Is. 13:33. City—Is. 14:31. Heshbon—Is. 15:4, 8. Oppressed—Is. 19:20. For majesty—Is. 24:14. Jerusalem—Is. 30:19. Valiant—Is. 33:7. Goat—Is. 34:14. Servant—Is. 40:2. Jehovah—Is. 42:13, 14. People—Is. 58:9. Sorrow—Is. 65:14. To Jerusalem—Is. 40:2, 6. To Jehovah—Jer. 3:4. Judah—Jer. 11:11, 14; 14:12. Jerusalem—Jer. 18:22; 20:16. To Idols—Jer. 11:12. Shepherds—Jer. 25:34, 36. Babylon—Jer. 50:46; 51:54. Destruction—Jer. 48:4, 5, 20, 31, 34. Watchmen—Jer. 31:6. Heshbon—Jer. 49:3. Edom—Jer. 49:21. Kedar—Jer. 49:29. Egypt—Jer. 46:12, 17. Philistines—Jer. 47:2. Judah—Jer. 14:2. Zion—Jer. 8:19; Mic. 4:9. Command to—Jer. 7:16. Pilots of Tyre—Ez. 27:28, 30. Israel—Hos. 8:2. Nineveh—Nah. 2:8. From Fish-gate—Zeph. 1:10, 14. A voice in the wilderness—Mt. 3:3; Mk. 1:3; Lu. 3:4; John 1:23. Angel—Rev. 14:15. Crying to cease—Rev. 21:4.

Figurative. — Land — Job 31:38. To mountains—Is. 22:5. Stone cry to the wall—Hab. 2:11. Stones—Lu. 19:40.

CRYSTAL. Job 28:18. River, Bright as—Rev. 22:1. Sea of glass—Rev. 4:6. Terrible—Ez. 1:22.

CUB, cŭb. **Probably a Nubian.**—Ez. 30:5.

CUBIT, Lat. *Cubitus,* "The lower arm." The Hebrews used the forearm and hand as a standard of measure. But as arms and hands differed in size, so cubits varied. There is no certainty as respects the number of inches in a cubit. Some say 18, some 19, some 21 inches, and even 25.

"The cubit of a man."—Deut. 3:11. "The measure of a man"—Rev. 21:17.

The Egyptian cubit consisted of six handbreadths.—Jer. 52:21.

Early use of.—Noah's ark was 300 cubits long, 50 broad, and 30 high—Gen. 6:15.

Hebrews seem to have had two sizes of cubits.—Solomon's temple laid out on basis of a "cubit of first measure"—II Chr. 3:3. Ezekiel prophesies concerning a temple whose cubit measure is described as a cubit and a handbreadth—Ez. 40:5; 43:13. If so, this corresponds to Egyptian measurements, where there was a common and a royal cubit, the common being but six-sevenths of the other.

Ezekiel also speaks of great cubits.—Ez. 41:8.

Among the Hebrews the scale was as follows: The finger—Jer. 52:21. The handbreadth (I Ki. 7:26), which consisted of 4 fingers (Jer. 52:21); a span, which was 3 handbreadths (Ex. 28:16), and a cubit, which was 2 spans.

New Testament references.—Mt. 6:27; Lu. 12:25; John 21:8; Rev. 21:17.

CUCKOO. Lev. 11:16 (A.V.); Deut. 14:15 (A.V.).

CUCUMBER. Egypt, In—Num. 11:5. Garden of—Is. 1:8.

CUD. Lev. 11:3, 4; Deut. 14:6, 8. Camel—Lev. 11:4. Coney—Lev. 11:5. Hare—Lev. 11:6.

CUMBER. Deut. 1:12. Ground—Lu. 13:7. Martha—Lu. 10:40.

CUMI. Mk. 5:41.

CUMMIN. Is. 28:25, 27; Mk. 23:23.

CHUN. I Chr. 18:8. See BEROTHAI.

CUNNING. Job 5:12; II Pet. 1:16. See SKILFUL.

CUP. Cold water, Of—Mt. 10:42. Drink—Mt. 20:22, 23; Mk. 10:38; John 18:11; I Cor. 11:25–27. Lord's Supper, Used in—Mt. 26:27; Mk. 14:23; Lu. 22:17; I Cor. 11:25–28. Outside of—Mt. 23:25; Lu. 11:39. Pass, Let this—Mt. 26:39; Lu. 22:42. Portion of—Ps. 11:6. Runneth over—Ps. 23:5. Salvation, Of—Ps. 116:13. Sparkling in, Wine—Pr. 23:31. Washings of—Mk. 7:4. See VESSELS.

CURDLE. Cheese, Like—Job 10:10.

CURE. Jer. 33:6. Bethesda, At.—John 5:10. Boy—Mt. 17:18. Could not— Mt. 17:16. Diseases, Power to—Lu. 9:1. See HEALING.

CURIOUSLY. Wrought—Ps. 139:15.

CURRENT. Money with the merchant —Gen. 23:16.

CURSES. In Old Testament.—Upon the serpent—Gen. 3:14–15. Upon the ground—Gen. 3:17–19; 5:29; 6:7, 13. The curse removed—Gen. 8:21, 22. Upon Cain—Gen. 4:11. Upon Canaan —Gen. 9:25. Upon the disobedient— Lev. 26:14–39; Deut. 11:26–29; 27:13– 26; 28:15–46; 29:19–21; Josh. 8:34, 35; Pr. 3:23; Mal. 2:2. Upon Meroz— Ju. 5:23. Upon Shimei—II Sam. 16:5– 13. Upon Gehazi—II Ki. 5:27. Upon robbers of tithes—Mal. 3:9. Upon persecutors of the poor—Ps. 10:2; 109: 9–16. Cursing the name of Jehovah— Lev. 24:10–16, 23. Cursing father and mother forbidden—Ex. 21:17; Lev. 20:9; Ps. 109:17; Pr. 20:20; 30:11; Mt. 15:4; Mk. 7:10.

In New Testament.—Fig tree—Mk. 11: 21. Upon those ignorant of the law— John 7:49; Gal. 3:10. Upon those who preach another gospel—Gal. 1:8, 9. Upon those who love not Christ—I Cor. 16:22.

Curses uttered by men.—II Pet. 2:14. By Noah—Gen. 29:26. By Jotham— Ju. 9:20, 57. By Job—Job 3:1–10. By Jeremiah—Jer. 20:14. By Peter—Mt. 26:74; Mk. 14:71. From the tongue— Jas. 3:9, 10.

Infirmities considered by the Jews as curses from God.—John 9:2. **Bless them that curse you.**—Lu. 6:28; Rom. 12:14. **Christ redeems from the curse.** —Rom. 3:10; Gal. 3:10; Rev. 22:3.

CURTAINS. Curtains or hangings for rooms.—Curtains of tabernacle—Ex. 26:1–13; 36:8–17; Num. 4:25. Ark within curtains—II Sam. 7:2; I Chr. 17:1. Of palace—Esth. 1:6. Of Solomon—Song of Sol. 1:5. Hangings of court—Num. 3:26. Curtains of tents —Jer. 4:20; 10:20; 49:29. Curtains for idol—II Ki. 23:7.

Figurative.—Is. 54:2; Hab. 3:7.

Illustrative.—Is. 40:22; Ps. 104:2.

CUSH, kŭsh. (1) **Oldest son of Ham.**

(2) **A Benjamite, an enemy of David.**— Ps. (title).

(3) **A country.**—Gen. 2:13. See ETHIOPIA.

CUSHAN, kū'shăn. Hab. 3:9. See ETHIOPIA.

CUSHAN-RISHATHAIM, kū'shan–rĭsh-a-thā'im. **Defeated by Othniel.**

CUSHI, kū'shī. (1) **Father of Zephaniah.**—Zeph. 1:1.

(2) **Great-grandfather of Jehudi.**—Jer. 36:14.

CUSTODY. Hegai, king's chamberlain, Of—Esth. 2:3. Maidens, Of—Esth. 2:8, 14.

CUSTOM. Abominable—Lev. 18:30. Against—Acts 28:17. All—Acts 26:3. As his custom was—Lu. 4:16. Change —Acts 6:14. Feast, Of—Lu. 2:42. Have a—John 18:39. Impose—Ezra 7:24. Israel, In—Ju. 11:39. No such—I Col. 11:16. Law, Of—Lu. 2:27. Pay—Ezra 4:13. Priests, Of—I Sam. 2:13. Lu. 1:9. Render—Rom. 13:7. Sealed according to—Jer. 32:11. Vanity—Jer. 10:3 (A.V.). Walk after—Acts 21:21.

CUT, CUT OFF. Cords of the wicked— Ps. 129:4. Enemies, All thine—II Sam. 7:9. Everyone that stealeth, sweareth —Zech. 5:3. Evil does—Ps. 37:9. Heart, To the—Acts 7:54; 5:33. Hope shall not be—Pr. 24:14 (A.V.). If thy hand offend thee—Mk. 9:43. Israel— I Ki. 9:7. Judah, All—Jer. 44:11. Kindness—I Sam. 20:15. King is— Hos. 10:7. Life, My—Lam. 3:53. Lips, Flattering—Ps. 12:3. Nations cut off —Josh. 23:4. Posterity—Ps. 109:13. Pride of Philistines—Zech. 9:6. Prophets—I Ki. 18:4. Righteous—Ez. 21:3, 4. See, My—I Sam. 24:21. Shepherds, Three—Zech. 11:8. Soul—Num. 9:13; 15:30, 31; 19:13, 20. Stone out of mountain—Dan. 2:45. See STONE. Tribe of the families—Num. 4:18. Wicked—Ps. 101:8.

CUTHAH, kū'thah. **A Babylonian city.** —II Ki. 17:24.

CYMBALS. See MUSIC.

CYPRUS. An island in the Mediterranean.—Acts 21:3.

Men of Cyprus work at Antioch.—Acts 11:20.

Apostles' ministry in.—Acts 13:4; 15:39.
Residents of, mentioned.—Barnabas—
Acts 4:36. Mnason—Acts 21:16.
Cities of.—Salamis—Acts 13:5. Paphos
—Acts 13:6, 13.
CYRENE, sy-re'ne. A powerful Greek
city in North Africa—Acts 2:10. Lu-
cius of—Acts 13:1. Men of Cyprus
and—Acts 11:20. Simon of—Mt. 27:
32. Synagogue of—Acts 6:9.
CYRENIANS. Acts 6:9.
CYRENIUS. See QUIRINIUS.
CYRUS. The founder of the Persian em-
pire.—He conquered Babylon and assisted in the restoration of the Jews—
II Chr. 36:23; Ezra 1:1, 2, 7, 8;
3:7; 4:3, 5; 5:13–17; 6:3, 14; Is. 44:28;
45:1; Dan. 1:21; 6:28; 10:1.
DABAREH. See DABERATH.
DABBESHETH, dăb'be-shĕth. Josh. 19:
11.
DABERATH, dăb'e-rath. (1) Josh. 21:
28.
(2) A Levitical city.—Josh. 19:12.
DAGGER. See WEAPONS.
DAGON. A Philistine idol.—Fallen,
Was—I Sam. 5:3, 4. Hands and head
of—I Sam. 5:4. House of—I Sam.
5:2, 5. Priests of—I Sam. 5:5. Sacrifice unto—Ju. 16:23. Set up—I Sam.
5:4. Temple of—I Chr. 10:10.
DAILY. Bread—Mt. 6:11; Lu. 11:3.
Cross—Lu. 9:23. Offering—Num. 28:
24; Ezra 3:4; Ez. 45:23; 46:13; Heb.
7:27. Prayer—Ps. 88:9. Scriptures
read—Acts 17:11. Tasks—Ex. 5:13,
19. Teaching—Mt. 26:55; Mk. 14:49;
Lu. 19:47; 22:53; Acts 5:42; 17:17;
19:9. Worship—Ps. 61:8. See CONTIN-
UAL, DAY.
DAINTIES. Gen. 49:20; Ps. 141:4; Pr.
23:3. See FOOD.
DAINTY. Food. Job 33:20; Pr. 23:6;
Rev. 18:14.
DALAIAH. See DELAIAH.
DALE. II Sam. 18:18. See VALLEY.
DALMANUTHA, dăl'ma-nū'thȧ. A town
visited by Jesus.—Mk. 8:10.
DALMATIA, dăl-mā'ti-a. A country
east of the Adriatic.—Visited by Titus
—II Tim. 4:10.
DALPHON, dăl'phon. Son of Haman.—
Esth. 9:7.
DAM. Ex. 20:30; Lev. 22:27; Deut. 22:
6, 7.

DAMAGE. Ezra 4:22; Esth. 7:4; Pr. 26:
6; Dan. 6:2. See DESTRUCTION, LOSS.
DAMARIS, dăm'a-rĭs. A woman converted by Paul at Athens.—Acts 17:
34.
DAMASCENES. Inhabitants of Damascus.—II Cor. 11:32.
DAMASCUS. Chief city of North Syria.
—It lies in a plain east of the anti-
Lebanon chain of mountains, about 70
miles from the seacoast, and 133 miles,
in an air-line, from Jerusalem. It is
noted for its beauty and fertility, being watered by the Barada river (Abanah), which throws all its influence
over the 30-mile diameter of the Great
Plain. Coming down from the snowy
mountain sides, you approach the city
through miles of gardens, trailing
with briar roses and ablaze with pomegranate blossoms. On and on you
travel, expecting every minute to
feast your eyes with the city, only to
arrive at a new fig or apricot orchard
—to pass over a bridge, or through a
village. Finally the glittering minar-
ets burst into view.
Its importance.—It derives its importance from being in the highway between the Mesopotamian valley and
the Mediterranean coast, making it a
good center for the distribution of
wares. It has a modern importance because of the manufacture of furniture,
metal and textile work. It is essentially a commercial town, some 200
busy wealthy merchants being permanently connected with the city's
interests.
Its bazaars.—Damascus is noted for
these. They are long streets covered
with choice woodwork, and lined with
stalls, shops, magazines and cafés. The
magazines are stored with merchandise of all sorts, but particularly of
East Indian manufacture, brought by
caravans from Bagdad. In the midst
of the bazaars stands the finest Khan
in the Orient, with a cupola which recalls St. Peter's at Rome. Just a little way from there is the principal
mosque, formerly a church consecrated to St. John.
Its population.—In olden times it had a
large Jewish population, for Josephus

reports that, under Nero, over 10,000 Jews were slain in one massacre. The report of its present population varies largely. We put it at about 225,000.

Present conditions.—The interior does not correspond with the external beauty. ''In the Armenian quarter the houses are built with mud and pierced towards the street by a very few small grated windows.'' They are really huts, with flat, arched doors like those of stables. A filthy dunghill and a pool of stinking water are almost invariably before the doors. Then there is a fine wide street formed by the palaces of the Agas, who are the nobility of the land. It is said that the street ''straight,'' where Saul of Tarsus lodged, is still there.

Its Biblical history.—The first mention in Scripture is in connection with Abraham's pursuit of the five kings (Gen. 14:15). Abraham's steward, named Eliezer, is recorded as belonging to Damascus (Gen. 15:26). According to Josephus, Damascus was founded by Uz, the son of Aram, and grandson of Shem (Ant. 1:6). It touches the life of Israel, first of all, through its capture by David (II Sam. 8:3–7). In Solomon's day Rezon, a servant of Hadadezer, established himself as king of Damascus, and from this on, being the capital of Syria, it gave constant trouble to the people of Israel and Judah (I Ki. 11:3–25). It became noted through the story of Naaman (II Ki. Ch. 5).

The succession of kings.—After Rezon, Hezion occupied the throne. He was succeeded by his son Tabrimmon (I Ki. 15:18). Then began the reign of the Benhadads, of whom there were three. By this time Damascus became the head of a powerful empire, the king being able to muster 32 kings in his campaign against Samaria (I Ki. 20:1). The kings, in their order, according to Old Testament and Assyrian accounts, were: Benhadad I, Hazael I, Hadadezer II, Hazael II, Benhadad II (who became subject to Jeroboam for some years), Mari, Benhadad III, and Rezin, who was put to death by the Assyrians on the capture

of Damascus in 732 B.C. In spite of alliances with the princes of North Syria, Damascus fell before Tiglathpileser IV (II Ki. 16:9; Is. 7:8). Jeremiah speaks of the weakness of Damascus (Jer. 49:24, 27). It was attacked by Jonathan, brother of Judas Maccabeus, about 147 B.C. (I Macc. 11:62; 12:32); fell into the hands of Aretas; was conquered by Pompey in 65 B.C., and in the time of Paul another Aretas was king (Acts 9:2–25; 22:5–11; 26:12, 20; II Cor. 11:32).

The wars and acts of these kings may be found in summary in I Ki. Chs 11, 15, 19, 20; II Ki. 8:14, 16; I Chr. Ch. 18; II Chr. Chs. 16, 24, 28.

The deeds, good and evil, of Damascus. Is. Chs. 7, 8, 10, 17; Jer. Ch. 49; Ez. Chs. 27, 47, 48; Amos 1:3–5; Zech. Ch. 9.

New Testament history.—Saul of Tarsus was going thither to persecute the church—Acts 9:1–2. On his way he was stopped by the Christ—Acts 9:3–6. Being sent to Damascus, he was there found by Ananias—Acts 9:8–12, and embraced the faith—Acts 9:17–19, proclaiming Jesus to be the Son of God—Acts 9:19–22. See also Acts Chs. 22 and 26. Being threatened by the Jews, he was let down the wall of Damascus in a basket—Acts 9:23–25.

DAMNATION. See CONDEMNATION, JUDGMENT, PUNISHMENT.

DAMSEL. Ju. 5:30; 19:3–9. Abigail's —I Sam. 25:42. Abishag, the Shunammite—I Ki. 1:3, 4. Dead, Not—Mt. 9:24. Dinah—Gen. 34:3, 4, 12. Fair— I Ki. 1:3, 4. Head given to—Mt. 14:11; Mk. 6:28. King said to—Mk. 6:22. Moab, Of—Ruth 2:5, 6. Rebekah— Gen. 24:14–51. Rose and walked—Mk. 5:42. Virginity of—Deut. 22:15, 28.

DAN. (1) **Fifth son of Jacob by Bilhah,** Rachel's handmaid—Gen. 30:6; 35:25; 49:16, 17. Descendants—Gen. 46:23; Num. 1:38, 39; 26:24–43; Josh. 19:47; I Chr. 2:2.

(2) **Tribe of.**—Stood on Mt. Ebal—Deut. 27:13. Jacob prophesies that Dan shall judge his people as one of the tribes— Gen. 49:16. Judgeship in Samson possible fulfilment of this—Ju. 15:20. Samson of the tribe of Dan—Ju. 13:

1–24. Makes offering at dedication of altar—Num. 6:66–71. Blessed by Moses—Deut. 33:22. Forced by Amorites into hill-country—Ju. 1:34, 35. Borders of inheritance—Josh. 19:40–46; Ju. 18:1–26. Participated in conquests—Josh. 19:47–48; Ju. 18:27–29. Princes—Num. 13:12; 34:22. Encampment—Num. 2:25–31; 10:25. Armies of—I Chr. 12:35. Reproved for not aiding against Sisera—Ju. 5:17. Part of Jacob's prophecy concerning Dan being ''a serpent in the way that biteth the horse's heels'' fulfilled in the attack on Laish—Ju. Ch. 18. Strength of, when leaving Egypt, 62,700. Strength of, when entering Canaan, 34,400—Num. 26:43. See ISRAEL.

(3) **Most northern city in Canaan.**—Gen. 14:14; Deut. 34:1; Josh. 19:47. Calf of gold worshipped in—I Ki. 12:29, 30; II Ki. 10:29. See Amos 8:14. Beersheba, From Dan to—Ju. 20:1; I Sam. 3:20; II Sam. 3:10; 17:11; 24:2, 15; I Ki. 4:15; I Chr. 21:2. Benhadad smote—I Ki. 15:20; II Chr. 16:4. Snorting of horses from—Jer. 8:16. Voice from—Jer. 4:15. See ISRAEL, JACOB.

DANCING. Dancing about the golden calf.—Ex. 32:19.

Maidens dance together.—Miriam—Ex. 15:20; Ju. 21:21, 23; I Sam. 18:6; 21:11; 29:5; Jer. 31:13. Daughter of Herodias—Mt. 14:6; Mk. 6:22.

Timbrels used with dancing.—Ex. 15:20; Ju. 11:34; Ps. 150:4.

Men alone.—Jer. 31:13.

Drinking and dancing.—I Sam. 30:16.

Children dancing.—Job 21:11.

We piped, ye did not dance.—Mt. 11:17; Lu. 7:32.

David danced before Jehovah.—II Sam. 6:14; I Chr. 15:29.

Praise Jehovah with.—Ps. 149:3; 150:4.

Dancing as a sign of rejoicing.—Ex. 15:20. When prodigal son returned—Lu. 15:25.

Mourning turned into—Ps. 30:11.

Dancing turned to mourning.—Lam. 5:15.

Wild goats.—Is. 13:21.

A time to dance.—Eccl. 3:4.

Figurative.—Job 41:22; Ps. 87:7; Jer. 31:4.

DANDLE. Is. 66:12.

DANGER OF JUDGMENT. Mt. 5:21, 22. See HELL, JUDGMENT, PUNISHMENT.

DANIEL. See OUTLINE STUDIES IN THE BOOKS.

DANITES. Ju. 13:2. See DAN.

DAN-JAAN, dăn–jā'an. II Sam. 24:6.

DANNAH, dăn'nah. **A city in Judah.**—Josh. 15:49.

DARA, dā'ra. See DARDA—I Chr. 2:6.

DARDA, där'da. Son of Jahol—I Ki. 4:31.

DARE. Esth. 7:10; Mt. 22:46; Mk. 12:34; Lu. 20:40; John 21:12; Acts 7:32. Die, To—Rom. 5:7. Law, Go to—I Cor. 6:1. Speak, To—Rom. 15:18. See COURAGE.

DARICS. I Chr. 29:7. See MONEY.

DARIUS. (1) **The Mede mentioned in** ''**Daniel**'' **as succeeding Belshazzar.**—Dan. 5:31; 6:11, 25, 28; 11:1.

(2) **King of Persia.**—Ezra 4:5, 24. Letter sent to—Ezra 5:6. Decree made by—Ezra 6:1, 12. See Neh. 12:22.

DARKNESS. Natural; the absence of light—Gen. 1:2. Called night—Gen. 1:5. Light divided from—Gen. 1:18. God creates it—Job 38:9; Ps. 104:20; Is. 45:7. Dwells in it—Ex. 20:21; II Sam. 22:10, 12; I Ki. 8:12; Ps. 18:9, 11; 97:2. Causes stumbling—John 12:35. Occasion of prophetic vision—Gen. 15:12, 17. Adapted for beasts—Ps. 104:20.

Supernatural.—Passed over Egypt—Ex. 10:21. Produced by pillar of cloud—Ex. 14:20; Josh. 24:7. About Sinai—Ex. 19:16; 20:21; Heb. 12:18. At death of Jesus—Mt. 27:45; Mk. 15:33; Lu. 23:44. At destruction of Jerusalem—Mt. 24:29. Apocalyptic visions—Rev. 8:12; 9:2; 16:10. Destiny of the wicked—Pr. 4:19; 20:20; Is. 8:22; 60:2; Jer. 13:16; Ez. 32:7–9; Joel 2:1–2; Nah. 1:8; Mt. 8:12; 22:13; 25:30; II Pet. 2:4, 17; Jude 6.

Spiritual darkness.—Is. 9:2; 42:16; 50:10; Amos 5:20; Mic. 7:8; Mt. 4:16; 6:23; Lu. 1:79; John 1:5; 3:19; 8:12; Acts 26:18; Rom. 1:21; 2:19; 13:12; Eph. 4:18; 5:8–11; I Thess. 5:5; I Pet. 2:9.

Powers of.—Job 24:13–17; Lu. 22:53; Eph. 6:12; Col. 1:13.

Children of the wicked.—Sit in darkness—Ps. 107:10. Walk in darkness—Ps. 82:5. Sleep in darkness—I Thess. 5:6.

Emblematic of obscurity.—Job 23:15–17; 28:3; 37:19; Ps. 112:4; Eccl. 2:14; 5:17; Is. 60:2; John 1:5; 8:12.

DARKON, där'kon. **Ancestor of some of those who returned with Ezra**—Ezra 2:56.

DARLING. Ps. 22:20; 35:17; Jer. 31:20.

DASH. In pieces—Ex. 15:6; II Ki. 8: 12; Ps. 2:9; 137:9; Is. 13:16, 18; Jer. 13:14; Hos. 10:14; Nah. 3:10.

DATHAN, dā'than. **A Reubenite rebel, son of Eliab.**—Num. 26:9. Earth swallowed—Deut. 11:6; Ps. 106:7.

DAUB. Ex. 2:3; Ez. 13:10–14; 22:28.

DAUGHTERS OF. Babylon—Ps. 137:8; Is. 47:1; Jer. 50:42; 51:33; Zech. 2:7. Backsliding—Jer. 49:4. Canaanites—Gen. 24:3; 38:2. Chaldeans—Is. 47: 1, 5. Dibon—Jer. 48:18. Edom—Lam. 4:22. Egypt—Jer. 46:11, 19, 24. Foreign gods—Mal. 2:11. Gallim—Is. 10: 30. Herodias—Mt. 14:6; Mk. 6:22. Jephthah—Ju. 11:34–40. Jerusalem—Is. 22:4; 37:22; Jer. 4:11; 8:11, 19, 21, 22; 9:1, 7; 31:22; Lam. 2:11, 13, 15; 3:48; 4:3, 6, 10; Zeph. 3:10, 14; Zech. 9:9. Judah—Lam. 1:15; 2:2, 4, 5. Lebanon—II Ki. 14:9; II Chr. 25:18. Kings—Ps. 45:9, 13; Dan. 11:6. Pharaoh—Ex. 2:2–10; I Ki. 3:1; 7:8; 9:16, 24; 11:1; I Chr. 4:18; II Chr. 8:11; Acts 7:21; Heb. 11:24. Princes—Num. 25:18; Song of Sol. 7:1. Rabbah—Jer. 49:2, 3. Sidon—Is. 23:12. Tarshish—Is. 23:10. Troops—Mic. 5:1. Tyre—Ps. 45:12. Zion—II Ki. 19:21; Ps. 9: 14; Is. 10:32; 16:1; 37:22; 52:2; 62: 11; Jer. 4:31; 6:2, 23; Lam. 1:6; 2:1, 8, 10, 18; 4:21, 22; Mic. 1:13; 4:8, 10, 13; Zeph. 3:14; Zech. 2:10; 9:9; Mt. 21:5; John 12:15.

Hearken, O daughter.—Ps. 45:10.

Laws concerning.—Ex. 1:16, 22; 20:10; 21:7, 31; Lev. 18:9, 10, 11, 17; 19:29; 20:17; 21:2, 9; 22:12, 13; Deut. 5:14; 7:3; 12:18; 13:6; 16:11, 14; 18:10; 22: 16, 17; 27:22; 28:56. That no man might make his son or daughter to pass through fire to Molech—II Ki. 23:10; Ez. 44:25.

Purification of.—Lev. 12:6.

Inheritance determined.—Num. 27:6, 36.

Prophecies concerning.—Ez. 14:20; 16: 44, 45; 22:11. Shall give daughters of women—Dan. 11:17. And ye shall be to me—II Cor. 6:18.

Riseth against her mother.—Mic. 7:6; Mt. 10:35; Lu. 12:53.

Care of.—Mt. 9:18, 22; 15:22, 28; Mk. 5: 23, 34; 7:25, 26, 29; Lu. 8:42, 48.

He that loveth daughter more than me. —Mt. 10:37.

Figurative.—As a daughter—II Sam. 12:3.

DAUGHTER-IN-LAW. Gen. 38:16. Arose with—Ruth 1:6. Loveth—Ruth 4:15. Mother-in-law, Against—Mt. 10: 35; Lu. 12:53. Naomi said unto—Ruth 1:8. Ruth—Ruth 1:22; 2:22. Sarai—Gen. 11:31. Tamar—Gen. 38:11.

DAVID. Son of Jesse, childhood and youth.—Ruth 4:22; I Sam. 16:10, 11; I Chr. 2:13, 15; Mt. 1:6. Born in Bethlehem—I Sam. 17:12. Herded his father's sheep—I Sam. 16:11. A beautiful, ruddy youth—I Sam. 16:12. Chosen by Jehovah to succeed Saul as king—I Sam. 16:1. Anointed by Samuel—I Sam. 16:13.

At the court of Saul.—Is recommended to soothe Saul's distemper—I Sam. 16:16–20. Becomes Saul's armorbearer—I Sam. 16:21. Pacifies Saul with his harp—I Sam. 16:23. David subdues the Philistines by slaying Goliath—I Sam. 17:32–54. His valorous act won both Saul and Jonathan, Saul's son—I Sam. 18:1–4. Saul sets David over his men of war—I Sam. 18: 5. Jonathan consents to this appointment—I Sam. 18:4. The praise David won made Saul jealous—I Sam. 18:6–9. Saul becomes vicious towards David—I Sam. 18:10–13. Hoping to ensnare David, Saul gives his daughter Michal in marriage to him—I Sam. 18:17–21. But requires the foreskins of one hundred Philistines as a dowry —I Sam. 18:22–25. David obtains two hundred foreskins and secures his wife —I Sam. 18:27–28. Saul's enmity to David increases—I Sam. 18:29.

Flight from the court.—Saul pursues and persecutes David—I Sam. 19:10, 11, 19, 22; 21:10; 22:1–8. Jonathan's love for David—I Sam. 18:1; 19:1. He converses with his father concerning David's excellences—I Sam. 19:2-7. David makes a covenant with Jonathan —I Sam. 20:1-17. By a strategic act, Jonathan informs David of Saul's purpose toward him—I Sam. 20:18-42. Visit to priests of Nob—I Sam. 21: 1-10.

Outlaw life.—David, because of Saul's enmity, becomes an outlaw—I Sam. 21:10; 22:1-2. David with his small army begins fighting for Jehovah— I Sam. 23:1-5. He abides in the strongholds of the wilderness—I Sam. 23:14. Jonathan visits David, and they renew their covenant—I Sam. 23:15-18. Saul seeks to encompass David, but fails—I Sam. 23:24-29. Saul's life in David's hand, but he is spared—I Sam. 24:1-7. David seeks supplies from Nabal, but is refused—I Sam. 25:1-11. David's vengeance appeased by the wisdom of Nabal's wife—I Sam. 25:14-35. Nabal dies, and David takes Abigail to wife—I Sam. 25:38-42. He also takes Ahinoam of Jezreel to wife—I Sam. 25:43. David creeps up upon Saul and robs him of his spear —I Sam. 26:6-12. He holds a conversation with Saul, who relents—I Sam. 26:17-25.

Seeks refuge in Philistia.—I Sam. 27: 1-8. The Philistine princes resented this union, so David not permitted by Achish, the king, to go to battle with them—I Sam. Ch. 29. While David was absent from Ziklag, his wives were captured by the Amalekites—I Sam. 30:1-6. David pursues them with great slaughter and recaptures his wives—I Sam. 30:7-20. David divides the spoil, showing both mercy and justice—I Sam. 30:21-31. Saul and his sons fall in battle with the Philistines —I Sam. 31:1-13; I Chr. Ch. 10.

David becomes king over Judah.—II Sam. 2:1-11. Reigned at Hebron, over Judah, seven and one-half years—II Sam. 5:5; I Chr. 3:4.

Reigned in Jerusalem, over both Israel and Judah, 33 years.—II Sam. 5:5; I Chr. 3:4. Names of sons born to David in Hebron and Jerusalem—II Sam. 3:2-5; II Sam. 5:14-16; I Chr. 3:1-9.

Public acts as king.—Conquers Jerusalem—II Sam. 5:6-10; I Chr. 11:4-8. Builds a palace in Jerusalem—II Sam. 5:11; I Chr. 14:1. David attempts to bring the ark to Jerusalem—II Sam. 6:1-19; I Chr. 13:1-8. Uzzah struck dead for handling the ark—II Sam. 6:6-7; I Chr. 13:9-10. David displeased, left the ark at the house of Obed-edom—II Sam. 6:8-10; I Chr. 13:11-13. It remained there three months—II Sam. 6:11; I Chr. 13:14. David then brings ark to Jerusalem with joy and dancing—II Sam. 6:12-15; I Chr. 14:1-28. Michal, David's wife, sees the dancing and despises David—II Sam. 6:16; I Chr. 15:29. David and Michal quarrel—II Sam. 6:20-23. David appoints Levites to minister at the ark—I Chr. 16:4-6. He composes a thanksgiving song— I Chr. 16:7-36. He also plans to build a house for God, but is told this duty will devolve on his son—II Sam. 7:1-17; I Chr. 17:1-16. David addresses Jehovah concerning this purpose— II Sam. 7:18-29; I Chr. 17:16-27. David wins victories over the Philistines, Moab, Hadad-ezer, and the Syrians— II Sam. 8:1-14; I Chr. Ch. 18. He shows kindness to Saul's kin—II Sam. Ch. 9.

Domestic life and troubles.—The sad story of David's fall—He commits adultery with Bathsheba, Uriah's wife—II Sam. 11:2-5. Tries to cover his sin, but fails—II Sam. 11:6-13. Instructs Joab to put Uriah in the front of the battle—II Sam. 11:14-16. Uriah falls—II Sam. 11:17. David marries Bathsheba, but displeases Jehovah— II Sam. 11:26-27. Nathan the prophet sent to David by Jehovah—II Sam. 12:1-6. David is convicted and punished—II Sam. 12:7-23. Solomon, Bathsheba's son, is born—II Sam. 12: 24. Absalom, David's son, conspires against his father—II Sam. Chs. 15-17. His death and David's lament—II Sam. Ch. 18. Adonijah usurps the throne during David's last days—I Ki. 1:5-10. Nathan and Bathsheba induce David to declare for Solomon— I Ki. 1:11-40. Adonijah set aside—I Ki. 1:40-53. David sins in numbering the people—II Sam. 24:1–9; I Chr. 21: 1–17. Jehovah, through Gad, offers David three modes of punishment—II Sam. 24:11–14; I Chr. 21:9–13. David chooses pestilence—II Sam. 24:15; I Chr. 21:14.

Interest in public worship.—Divinely instructed, David purchases Araunah's threshing floor and rears an altar on it—II Sam. 24:18–25; I Chr. 21:18–27. This ground becomes the site of the temple—I Chr. 21:28–30; 22:1. David begins to gather material for the temple—I Chr. 22:2–5. David's charge to Solomon—I Ki. 2:1–9; I Chr. 22:6–19. He prescribes the offices and courses of the Levites—I Chr. Chs. 23–27. Calls together princes and instructs them for Solomon, giving his son the pattern for the temple—I Chr. Chs. 28–29. David dies—I Ki. 2:10; I Chr. 29:28.

David the musician.—He soothed Saul—I Sam. 16:16; 18:10; 19:9. Organized 24 bands—I Chr. Ch. 25. Played on all kinds of instruments—II Sam. 6:5; I Chr. 13:8.

David God's choice.—Ps. 18:50; 78:70–72; 89:3, 4, 19–37; II Sam. 7:8–12; I Ki. 2:33.

The ancestor of Jesus.—Ps. 2:6; Mt. 1:1; 9:27; Lu. 1:32; John 7:42; Acts 2:25; 13:22–23; Rom. 1:3; Rev. 5:5.

David's victories.—Jerusalem—II Sam. 5:6–7. Philistines—I Chr. 18:1. Moab —II Sam. 8:2; I Chr. 18:2. Hadadezer —I Chr. 18:3–4. Syrians—II Sam. 8: 3–14; I Chr. 18:5–6. Edom, Ammon, Amalek—I Chr. 18:11.

Justice shown by David—Weary soldiers—I Sam. 30:21–25. To his people —II Sam. 8:15; I Chr. 18:14.

Mercy shown by David.—Shimei—II Sam. 19:21–23. Compare I Ki. 2:8, 9. Mephibosheth—II Sam. 19:24–30. Barzillai—II Sam. 19:31–39.

Devotion of David.—To Saul—I Sam. 18:5, 14–16. To Jonathan—I Sam. 20: 41–42. To Toi, king of Hamath—II Sam. 8:9–13. To Jehovah—I Ki. 3:14; Acts 13:22–23. See ISRAEL, PSALMS, SOLOMON.

DAWN. Pr. 4:18; Is. 47:11. Day, of—Josh. 6:15; Ju. 19:26; Job 7:4; Ps. 119:147; Mt. 28:1; II Pet. 1:19.

DAY: Creative and time periods.—A period of time limited by context—Gen. 5:1, 2. Light called day—Gen. 1:5. Reckoned by Jews from evening to evening—Lev. 23:32. By Egyptians from morning to evening—Gen. 43:16. Six working days appointed—Ex. 20:9. Sixth, preparation day—Mk. 15:42; John 19:14, 31. Seventh, the Sabbath of the Jews—Gen. 2:2–3; Ex. 20:8–9; Deut. 5:12–13. First day of the week, the Lord's day—John 20:19, 26; Acts 20:7; Rev. 1:10. Day divided into 12 hours—Mt. 20:1–6; John 11:9. Governed by rise and set of sun—Gen. 32:24, 26.

Judicial periods.—Anger—Lam. 2:21. Wrath—Job 20:28; 21:30; Zeph. 1:15, 18; Rom. 2:5; Rev. 6:17. Visitation—Mic. 7:4. Destruction—Job 21:30. Darkness—Joel 2:2; Zeph. 1:15. Distress—Ps. 102:2–3. Calamity—Deut. 32:35; Jer. 18:17. Adversity—Pr. 24: 10. Vengeance—Pr. 6:34; Is. 34:8; 61:2. Slaughter—Is. 30:25; Jer. 12:3. Evil—Jer. 17:17; Amos 6:3; Eph. 6:13. Of Jehovah—Is. 2:12; 13:6; Zeph. 1:14.

Day of Judgment.—Job 21:30; Dan. 7:9; Mt. 7:22; 10:15; 11:22; 12:36; Lu. 10:12; John 12:48; Acts 17:31; Rom. 2:5, 16; I Cor. 3:13; I Tim. 4:1, 8; II Pet. 2:4, 9; 3:7, 10; I John 4:17; Jude 6; Rev. 6:17. See JUDGMENT.

Merciful periods.—Visitation—Jer. 27: 22; I Pet. 2:12. Of God's power—Ps. 110:3. Salvation—II Cor. 6:2. Redemption—Eph. 4:30.

Festive periods.—A good day—Esth. 8: 17. Day of good tidings—II Ki. 7:9. Day of gladness—Num. 10:10. Of solemn assembly—Hos. 9:5.

Special References: Old Testament.—God walked in cool of—Gen. 3:8. Gather a day's portion—Ex. 16:4. Sun stayed in midst of heaven—Josh. 10: 14. Choose you this—Josh. 24:15. Swifter than shuttle—Job 7:6. Few and full of trouble—Job 14:1. Meditate day and night—Ps. 1:2. Uttereth speech—Ps. 19:2. In thy courts—Ps. 84:10. Teach us to number—Ps. 90:12. As grass—Ps. 103:15. Length of, in right hand—Pr. 3:16. May bring forth—Pr. 27:1. Remember in days of youth—Eccl. 12:1. Kneeled 3 times a day—Dan. 6:10. Great and terrible—Joel 2:31. Despise day of small things—Zech. 4:10. Shall be mine in the day—Mal. 3:17.

New Testament.—Sufficient unto—Mt. 6:34. Third day be raised—Mt. 16:21. A shilling a day—Mt. 20:2. Make sure until the third—Mt. 27:64. Is far spent—Mk. 6:35; Lu. 24:29. After 3 days shall rise—Mk. 9:31. Born to you this—Lu. 2:11. More tolerable in that—Lu. 10:12. Rejoiced to see my. —John 8:56. Work while it is—John 9:4. Walk in the—John 11:9. Added day by day—Acts 2:47. Serving God night and—Acts 26:7. Esteemeth every day alike—Rom. 14:5. The day shall declare it—I Cor. 3:13. Day of the Lord at hand—II Thess. 2:2. Guard against that—II Tim. 1:12. This day have I begotten thee—Acts 13:33; Heb. 1:5; 5:5. See Ps. 2:7. See Good days—I Pet. 3:10. No rest day or night—Rev. 4:8. Serve him day and night—Rev. 7:15.

A day's journey, a measure of distance. —Ex. 3:18; I Ki. 19:4; Jonah 3:4. Sabbath-day journey—Acts 1:12.

DAYBREAK. Acts 5:21

DAY'S JOURNEY. Ex. 3:18; I Ki. 19:4; Jonah 3:4. Sabbath day's journey—Acts 1:12.

DAYSMAN. Job 9:33 (A.V.).

DAYSPRING. Job 38:12; Lu. 1:78. See Is. 60:1, 2; Mal. 4:2; Rev. 22:16.

DAYSTAR. Is. 14:12; II Pet. 1:19; Rev. 2:28; 22:16.

DAYTIME. Ps. 22:2; 42:8; 78:14; Is. 4:6; II Pet. 2:13.

DAZZLING. Lu. 9:29.

DEACON. Appointed — Acts 6:5, 6. Qualifications—I Tim. 3:8–15. Service—Acts 6:1–4.

DEACONESS. Rom. 16:1, 2. See I Tim. 3:11.

DEAD. See DEATH.

DEADLY. Arrow—Jer. 9:8 (A.V.). Enemies—Ps. 17:9. Pestilence—Ps. 91:3 (A.V.). Poison, Full of—Jas. 3:8. Thing—Mk. 16:18. Wicked one—Ez. 21:25 (A.V.).

DEAF: Made.—By Jehovah—Ex. 4:11. Cured by Jesus—Mt. 11:5; Mk. 7:32, 37; 9:25; Lu. 7:22.

Commandments concerning.—Lev. 19:14.
Prophecies concerning.—Is. 29:18; 35:5; Mic. 7:16.
Illustrative.—Is. 42:18, 19; 43:8.
Figurative.—Ps. 38:13. Adder—Ps. 58:4.

DEAL. Num. 11:15; II Chr. 2:3; Ez. 31:11. Arrogantly—Ps. 75:4. Bitterly—Ruth 1:20. Bountifully—Ps. 13: 6; 116:7; 119:17; 142:7. Corruptly—Neh. 1:7. Courageously—II Chr. 19: 11. Deceitfully—Ex. 8:29; 21:8; Job 6:15; Ps. 78:57. Evilly—I Sam. 2:23. Faithfully—II Ki. 12:15; 22:7. Falsely—Gen. 21:23; Lev. 19:11; Ps. 44: 17; Jer. 6:8; 8:10. Foolishly—Pr. 14: 12. Fury, In—Ez. 23:25. Gently—II Sam. 18:5. Graciously—Gen. 33:11. Hardly—Gen. 16:6. Hatred, In—Ez. 23:29. Kindly—Gen. 24:49; 47:29; Josh. 2:14; Ruth 1:8; I Sam. 20:8. Proudly—Ex. 18:11; Neh. 9:10, 16, 29; Ps. 31:23. Sharply—II Cor. 13:10. Sincerely—Ju. 9:19. Subtly—Ps. 105: 25. Treacherously—Ju. 9:25; Is. 21: 2; 24:16; 33:1; 48:8; Jer. 3:20; 5:11; 12:1, 6; Is. 21:2; 24:16; Lam. 1:2; Hos. 5:7; 6:7; Hab. 1:13; Mal. 2:10–16. Truly—Gen. 24:49; 47:29; Josh. 2:14; Ju. 9:19; Pr. 12:22; Ez. 18:9. Wickedly—II Chr. 6:37. Wisely—Ex. 1: 10; II Chr. 11:23; Is. 52:13; Jer. 23:5. Wrath, In—Ez. 8:18. Wrongfully—Is. 26:10.

DEAR. I Thess. 2:8. Life—Acts 20:24. Servant—Lu. 7:2. Son—Jer. 31:20. See LOVE.

DEARTH. II Ki. 4:38; Neh. 5:3. See DROUGHT, FAMINE.

DEATH.—Metaphorical equivalents of the term death: ''Returning to dust'' —Gen. 3:19; Ps. 104:29; Eccl. 3:20; 12:7. Going ''to the fathers''—Gen. 15:15. ''Gathered to his·people''— Gen. 25:8; 49:29. ''Giving up the ghost''—Gen. 25:8; 35:29. ''To sleep with thy fathers''—Deut. 31:16. ''Crushed like the moth''—Job 4:19. ''Tent cord pulled up''—Job 4:21. ''An exhaled breath''—Job 7:7. ''Not to be''—Job 7:8, 21; 27:19. ''Cut down like a flower''—Job 14:2. ''Not to be found''—Job 20:7, 9; cf. Gen. 5:24; Heb. 11:5. ''Brought to the king of terrors''—Job 18:14. Devoured by a divine fire—Job 20:26.

Lying down in the dust—Job 7:21; 21:26. The spirit going upward—Eccl. 3:21. The spirit returning to God—Eccl. 12:7. Going to his everlasting home—Eccl. 12:5. Sleeping in the dust of the earth—Dan. 12:2. A sleep—Mt. 9:24. Fallen asleep—John 11:11; Acts 7:60; 13:36; I Cor. 15:18, 51; I Thess. 4:14. Clothed with the house not made with hands—II Cor. 5:2. Swallowed up of life—II Cor. 5:4. Absence from the body—II Cor. 5:8. A journey—Phil. 1:23; II Tim. 4:6; II Pet. 1:15, marg. ''Putting off the tabernacle''—II Pet. 1:14; *cf.* John 1:14, marg.

Result of sin.—Pr. 2:18; 5:5; 7:27; 8:36; 11:19; 13:13, 14; 14:12; 15:10; 16:25; 21:6; 24:11; Ez. 18:32; 31:14; 33:11; John 5:14; Rom. 5:12–21; 6:16–23; 7: 5–8; 8:2–6; I Cor. 15:21; II Cor. 7:10; Jas. 1:15; I John 3:14.

Penalty for sin.—Gen. 2:17; Ex. 10:17; 11:5; Num. 14:35; 16:31–35; 35:30, 31; Deut. 30:15; I Ki. 1:52; II Chr. 24:24; Ezra 7:26; Pr. 10:21; Jer. 9: 21; 15:2; 21:8; 31:30; 43:11; Ez. 18:4; Amos 9:10; Mt. 15:4; Mk. 7:10; John 19:7; Rev. 18:8.

Mysterious and terrible.—II Sam. 22:5, 6; Job 3:5; 10:21; 12:22; 16:16; 18:4; 24:17; 28:3; 34:22; 38:17; Ps. 13:3; 23:4; 44:19; 55:4; 107:10–14; Is. 9:2; Jer. 2:6; 13:16; Amos 5:8; Mt. 4:16; Lu. 1:79; Heb. 2:15.

End of earthly things.—Ruth 1:17; Job 7:9, 10; 14:12; Ps. 6:5; Eccl. 9:5–10; 12:5–7; Is. 38:18; Rom. 7:2; I Cor. 7: 39; Gal. 2:19; Heb. 9:15–27.

Robs of our possessions.—Job 1:21; Ps. 49:17; Lu. 12:16–20.

To be braved in line of duty.—Ju. 5:18; Is. 53:12; Mt. 10:28, 39; 26:35; Mk. 14:31; Lu. 11:50, 51; 12:32, 33; 18:32, 33; 21:16; 22:33; Acts 20:24; 21:13; 25:11; Rom. 5:7; I Cor. 15:31; II Cor. 4:11, 12; 7:3; Phil. 2:8, 30; 3:10, 11; Heb. 2:9–15; 11:35–38; 12:2–4; I Pet. 2:24; Rev. 2:10; 12:11.

Figurative.—As a state of sin—John 5: 24, 40; 6:50; 8:21, 24; Rom. 7:9–11; Eph. 2:1, 5; Col. 2:13; I John 3:14; Rev. 3:1. It includes lack of knowledge of God and His Christ—John 17:3. Absence of faith—John 8:21,

24; Heb. 11:5, 6. Dwelling in darkness—Mt. 4:16; John 1:4, 9; 3:19, 20.

Alienation from God and Christ.—Ez. 18:4; John 15:5, 6; Rom. 8:6; Eph. 2:12, 13; 4:18.

Death is not annihilation.—Eccl. 12:5, 7; Mt. 17:3; 22:32; Mk. 9:4; Lu. 9:30, 31; 23:43; Acts 7:55, 56, 59; II Cor. 5:1–8; Phil. 1:20–26; II Tim. 1:10; 4: 6–8; II Pet. 1:13–15; Rev. 6:9, 10.

Christ saves by His death.—Is. 53:5, 6; Mt. 20:28; 26:26, 28; Mk. 10:45; 14: 22–24; Lu. 22:19, 20; 24:46, 47; John 3:14; 12:32; Acts 3:18; 4:12; Rom. 5:10; 6:3–5; I Cor. 1:22–24; Eph. 2: 16; Col. 1:20–22; I Tim. 2:6; Heb. 2: 9–15; I Pet. 2:24.

Jesus conquered death.—Mt. 9:23–25; 11:5; 28:1–10; Mk. 5:40–42; 16:1–7; Lu. 7:11–15; 8:49–55; 24:1–6; John 2:19; 10:18; 11:43, 44; 20:1–17; Acts 2:24; 9:36–40; 20:9, 10; Rom. 1:4; 6:23; 7:24, 25; 8:6–10; I Cor. 15:4, 20–22, 55–57; Eph. 4:8–10; Col. 2:12; 3:1; II Tim. 1:10; Heb. 2:14, 15.

Death of the wicked.—A judgment—Num. 16:29, 30; I Sam. 25:38; Is. 14: 9; Lu. 12:20; Heb. 9:27. Sudden—Job 21:13, 23; Pr. 10:25, 27; 29:1; Is. 17:14; Acts 5:3–10. Feared—Job 18: 11–15; 27:19–21. In sin—Ez. 3:19; John 8:21. Illustrated—Lu. 16:23–26.

Death of the righteous.—Release from toil and care—I Ki. 19:4; Job 3:21; 7:15; 14:13; I Cor. 9:15. From evil—II Ki. 22:20; Is. 57:1, 2. To a crown—II Tim. 4:8; Rev. 2:10. To rest—Job 3:13; II Thess. 1:7. To glory—Ps. 73:24–26. To Christ and gain—Phil. 1:21, 23. To new body—II Cor. 5:1, 2. Precious to God—Ps. 116:15; Rev. 14:13.

Entrance upon new state.—Pr. 14:32; Is. 25:8; Mt. 17:2, 3; 22:32; Mk. 12: 27; Lu. 16:19–31; 20:35–38; 23:43; John 5:28, 29; 12:24; I Cor. 3:22; II Cor. 5:6–8; Phil. 1:21–23; II Tim. 4:8; Heb. 9:27; Rev. 14:13.

Death chosen.—Num. 23:10; Jer. 8:3; Rev. 9:6.

For the believer.—Christ has abolished death—John 6:47, 50, 51; 8:51, 52; 11: 26; Heb. 2:9, 14; II Tim. 1:10.

Death is a separation from the source of life and joy.—(1) Physical: A branch

separated from the vine dies—John
15:6. A fish taken from water dies—
Is. 50:2. Man cut off from air dies—II
Ki. 8:15. (2) Spiritual: Fools die
from lack of wisdom—Pr. 10:21. Sin
kills—Rom. 7:10, 11, 24. Separates
from life and peace—Rom. 8:6. From
church and God—5:17, 18; Eph. 2:12;
I Tim. 5:6. (3) Eternal, or the second
death of the soul is banishment, under
a curse, from the kingdom, into the
eternal fire and company of wicked
angels—Mt. 25:41, 46; II Thess. 1:9.
Undying worm—Mk. 9:43-48. A lake
of fire—Rev. 2:11; 19:20; 20:6; 21:8.

Death penalty for crime.—Murder—Gen.
9:5, 6; Num. 35:16-21. Adultery—
Lev. 20:10; Deut. 22:24. Incest—Lev.
20:11, 12, 14. Sodomy—Lev. 18:22; 20:
13. Perjury—Zech. 5:4. Kidnapping
—Ex. 21:16. Witchcraft—Ex. 22:18.
Abusing parents—Ex. 21:15, 17. Blasphemy—Lev. 24:23. Sabbath-breaking—Ex. 35:2; Num. 15:32-36. False
teaching—Deut. 13:1-10. Sacrificing
to false gods—Ex. 22:20. See COM-
MANDMENTS.

**Death a penalty inflicted only on testi-
mony of two or more witnesses.**—Num.
35:30; Deut. 17:6.

Exemplified.—Korah. Num. 16:32. Absalom—II Sam. 18:9, 10.

DEATH-STROKE. Rev. 13:3, 12.

DEBASE. Is. 57:9. See BASE.

DEBATE. Pr. 25:9.

DEBIR, dē'bir. (1) **King of Eglon.**—
Josh. 10:3.

(2) **A city in Judah.**—Josh. 15:49; Ju.
1:11.

(3) **A place north of Judah.**—Josh. 15:7.

(4) **A district east of the Jordan.**—
Josh. 13:26.

DEBORAH, dĕb'o-rah. (1) **Rebekah's
nurse.**—Gen. 35:8.

(2) **One of the judges.**—Ju. 4:4. Song
of—Ju. Ch. 5.

DEBT: Leniency of Hebrew laws.—
Must not be as a creditor—Ex. 22:25;
Deut. 23:19-20; Ez. 18:18. No one
must take a mill for a pledge—Deut.
24:6. Must not take raiment—Ex.
22:25-27; Deut. 24:10-13; Job 22:6;
Amos 2:8. Must restore to debtor his
pledge—Ez. 18:7. Dealing to exact
payment on 7th year—Neh. 10:31.

What returning to the law involves.—
If circumcised, Debtor to the whole
law—Gal. 5:1-4. Doing works of law
is paying a debt—Rom. 4:4. Not debtors to a fleshly law—Rom. 8:12.

The severity of debt.—Children taken
for bond—II Ki. 4:1. A prophet's
intervention—II Ki. 4:1-7. Debtors
become outlaws—I Sam. 22:2. Warning against going security—Pr. 11:15;
22:26. The mortgaging of homes—
Neh. 5:1-13.

Christ's teaching respecting debt.—
Christians counselled not to contract
debt—Rom. 13:8. Jesus uses two parables to inculcate compassion—Mt.
18:23-35; Lu. 7:41-43. Parable of
the unrighteous steward—Lu. 16:1-8.
Our debt must obtain consideration—
Mt. 6:12; Lu. 11:4. Those who receive spiritual aid are debtors—Rom.
15:27. Paul a debtor to all men—
Rom. 1:14.

**To swear by the gold of the temple
makes one a debtor.**—Mt. 23:16-18.
See TEACHING OF JESUS concerning
DEBT and DEBTORS.

DECALOGUE. See COMMANDMENTS.

DECAPOLIS, de-căp'o-lis. Mt. 4:25.

DECAY. Outward—II Cor. 4:16. Strength
is—Neh. 4:10. See DEATH.

DECEASE, DECEASED. Is. 26:14. Accomplish—Lu. 9:31. After my—I Pet.
1:15. Married and—Mt. 22:25. See
DEATH.

DECENTLY. Done—I Cor. 14:40.

DECEPTION. Deceit is falsehood—Ps.
119:118; Pr. 14:25. Comes from the
heart—Mk. 7:22; Jer. 18:9. A continual habit with some—Ps. 38:12.
Hard to give up—Jer. 8:5. Unbecoming a saint—Job 27:4. God abhors—
Ps. 5:6. Warned against deceitful
testimony—Pr. 24:28. Devise against
peaceful people—Ps. 35:20. Such persons grow away from good—Ps. 36:3.
Cheat in wages—Pr. 11:18. Uncertain counsel—Pr. 12:5. Jeremiah has
a bad opinion of—Jer. 9:4-6. De-
ceived by pride of heart—Ob. 3. Wax
worse and worse—II Tim. 3:13. Not
to deceive ourselves—I Cor. 3:18. Nor
handle word of God deceitfully—II
Cor. 4:2. Nor mock God—Gal. 6:7.
Nor deny our sin—I John 1:8. Must

not blame sin on the wrong person— Jas. 1:13–16. False estimates—II Cor. 6:8. Deceivers who are antichrist. —II John 7.

Christ free from.—Is. 53:9; I Pet. 2:22. Saints free from—Job 31:5; Ps. 24:4; 111:7; 120:2–3; Eph. 4:14; 5:6; Col. 2:8; I Pet. 2:1; Rev. 14:5.

Satan a deceiver.—Gen. 3:4–5; I Ki. 22: 22; Lu. 22:3; John 8:44; 13:27; Acts 5:3; Rev. 12:9.

Exemplified.—Serpent and Eve—Gen. 3:1–5. Abraham and wife—Gen. 12: 18; 20:2. Isaac and wife—Gen. 26:7. Rebekah and Jacob deceive Isaac— Gen. 27:6–23. Laban substitutes Leah for Rachel—Gen. 29:23–25. Jacob's sons in entrapping the Shechemites— Gen. 34:13–29. Joseph's brethren deceive Jacob concerning Joseph—Gen. 37:31–35. Joseph in dealing with his brethren in Egypt—Gen. 42:7–17. Gibeonites, in misrepresenting place of residence—Josh. 9:3–15. Ehud deceives Eglon—Ju. 3:15–22. Jael and Sisera —Ju. 4:20. Delilah deceives Samson —Ju. 16:4–20. David feigns madness —I Sam. 21:13. Amnon deceives Tamar—II Sam. 13:6–11. The old prophet —I Ki. 13:18. Gehazi and Naaman— II Ki. 5:20–24. Herod concerning young child—Mt. 2:8. Pharisees seeking to entrap Jesus—Mt. 22:15–22. Also chief priests—Mk. 14:1. Ananias and Sapphira—Acts Ch. 5.

DECISION. Thyself hast—I Ki. 20:40. Valley of—Joel 3:14.

DECK. Bridegroom, As a—Is. 61:10. Earrings, Herself with—Hos. 2:13. Gold and precious stones—Rev. 17:4; 18:16; Ez. 16:13. Ornaments—Ez. 16:11; Jer. 4:30; Ez. 23:40.

DECLARE. Faithfulness—Ps. 40:10. Glory—Ps. 19:1; Is. 66:19; I Chr. 16: 24. Heavens—Ps. 19:1; Ps. 50:6. Iniquity—Ps. 38:18. Law—Deut. 1:5. Name—Ex. 9:16. Praise—Is. 42:12. Riddle—Ju. 14:15. Righteousness— Ps. 50:6; Is. 57:12; Ps. 97:6. Sin— Is. 3:9. Work of God—Ps. 64:9.

DECLINE. Heart, Let not thine—Pr. 7:25. Shadow, Like a—Ps. 102:11; 109:23. Steps, Neither have our—Ps. 44:18. Words, From the—Pr. 4:5.

DECREASE. Cattle, He suffereth not to—Ps. 107:38. I must—John 3:30. Waters—Gen. 8:5.

DECREE. Caesar Augustus, From—Lu. 2:1. Cyrus made a—Ezra 5:13. Established a—II Chr. 30:5. Given, Was —Esth. 2:8. King made a—Ezra 6:1, 3. Most High, Of the—Dan. 4:24. Removed, Shall be—Mic. 7:11. Unrighteous—Is. 10:1. Watchers, Of the— Dan. 4:17. Went forth—Dan. 2:13.

DEDAN, dē'dan. (1) **Great-grandson of Ham.**—Gen. 10:7; I Chr. 1:9.

(2) **Son of Abraham by Keturah.**—Gen. 25:3; I Chr. 1:22.

(3) **A district near Edom.**—Jer. 25:23; 49:8; Ez. 25:13; 27:15; 27:20; 38:13.

DEDANITES, de'dan-ites. Descendants of Dedan(?).

DEDICATE, DEDICATION. Altar, Of the—Num. 7:11, 84, 88; II Chr. 7:9. Captains of the host—I Chr. 26:26. Come to the—Dan. 3:2. David—II Sam. 8:11; II Chr. 18:11. Feast of the—John 10:22. God, House of— Ezra 6:16. Jerusalem, Wall of—Neh. 12:27. Joab—Neh. 26:28. Keep, To —Neh. 12:27. Kings of Judah had— II Ki. 12:18. Princes were gathered unto the—Dan. 3:3. Silver, unto—Ju. 17:3. Spoils won in battle—I Chr. 26:27. Things which father had—I Ki. 15:15; II Chr. 5:1; 15:18.

DEED. According to—Is. 59:18; Jer. 25:14. Evil, For our—Ezra 9:13. Good—Acts 4:9; Neh. 13:14. Lawless—II Pet. 2:8 (A.V.). Mighty in— Lu. 24:19. Obedience by word and— Rom. 15:18 (A.V.). Queen, Of the— Esth. 1:17, 18. Reward of—Lu. 23:41. What—Gen. 44:15. Whatsoever in word or—Col. 3:17.

DEEM. See CONSIDER, SURMISE.

DEEP THINGS OF GOD. Being of God—Job 11:7–9; Rom. 11:33, 34. Greatness—I Chr. 29:11; Ps. 145:3. Judgment—Ps. 36:6; Rom. 11:33. Knowledge—Ps. 139:4–6; Pr. 3:20; Rom. 11:33; Col. 2:2, 3. Lovingkindness—Ps. 108:4; John 3:16; Eph. 3: 14–19. Power—I Chr. 29:12; Eph. 1: 19, 20. Thoughts—Ps. 92:5; Is. 55:8, 9. Truth—Ps. 108:4. Understanding— Ps. 147:5. Universe—Ps. 8:3, 4; 139: 7–12. Ways—Is. 55:8, 9; Rom. 11:33.

Wisdom—Rom. 11:33; Eph. 3:8–11; Col. 2:2,3; I Cor. 2:6–16; Jas. 3:17. See MYSTERY—I Cor. 15:51.

Of man.—The heart—Ju. 5:15, 16; I Ki. 4:29; Ps. 10:6, 11, 13; Pr. 4:23; 14:10; 25:3; Eccl. 7:25; Jer. 17:9; Mt. 12:34, 35; 15:18, 19; I Cor. 2:11; Heb. 4:12; I Pet. 3:4. The lust of possession— Gen. 3:4–6; 13:10, 11; 25:29–34; 31:4–16; I Sam. 15:3, 9; II Sam. 15:1–10; I Ki. 21:1–16; Ps. 49:6–12, 16, 17; Eccl. 2:4–11; Mt. 19:22–29; 20:20, 21; 26: 14–16; I Tim. 6:6–11. Life—Mt. 6:25; 16:25, 26; Lu. 12:15, 22, 23; John 1:4; 4:13, 14; 10:10, 28; 14:6; Col. 3:3; I Tim. 4:8; I Tim. 1:10; Heb. 7:16; I John 5:11, 12. Sorrow—II Sam. 13: 30–36; Pr. 14:13; Mt. 26:38; Mk. 14: 34; John 11:32–35; II Cor. 7:10, 11; Heb. 12:16, 17; Rev. 18:5–8; 21:4. Death—Ps. 18:4, 5; 55:4, 5; 116:3, 4; Song of Sol. 8:6; Hab. 2:5; Lu. 16: 22–26; I Cor. 15:53–56.

DEFAME. I Cor. 4:13. See GOSSIP.

DEFEAT. Council of Ahithophel—II Sam. 15:34; 17:14.

DEFECT. I Cor. 6:7. See SIN.

DEFENSE. Cities for—II Chr. 11:5. City—II Ki. 19:34; 20:6; Is. 37:55. Hear ye—Acts 22:1. House of—Ps. 31:2. Jehovah of Hosts shall—Zech. 9:15 (A.V.). Place of—Is. 33:16. Wisdom is a—Eccl. 7:12.

DEFER. Dan. 9:19. Anger, Mine—Is. 48:9. Hope d. maketh the heart sick —Pr. 13:12. Man, The young—Gen. 34:19. Pay, Not to—Eccl. 5:4.

DEFILE. Body, The whole—Jas. 3:6. Brightness, Thy—Ez. 28:7. Camp, Not —Num. 5:3. Conscience—I Tim. 1:15. Feet, How shall I—Song of Sol. 5:3. Flesh, The—Jude 8. Garments—Rev. 3:4. Hands, With blood—Is. 59:3; Mk. 7:2. House—Ez. 9:7. Israel is— Hos. 5:3. Land, Not—Num. 35:34; Jer. 2:7. Mouth, Out of—Mt. 15:11. Name, My holy—Ez. 43:7, 8. Priesthood—Neh. 13:29. Sanctuary, My— Lev. 20:3; Num. 19:20; Ez. 5:11. Tabernacle—Lev. 15:31; Num. 19:13. Temple, Thy holy—Ps. 79:1. See PURIFICATION, SIN.

DEFINE. Heb. 4:7.

DEFRAUD. I Sam. 12:4; Mk. 10:19; I Cor. 6:7. Brethren—I Cor. 6:8. One

the other—I Cor. 7:5. Whom have I —I Sam. 12:3. See DECEPTION, FALSEHOOD.

DEFY. Num. 23:88. Armies—I Sam. 17:10, 26, 36. God—I Sam. 17:45. Israel—Num. 23:7; I Sam. 17:25; II Sam. 21:21. Philistines—II Sam. 23:9.

DEGENERATE. Branches—Jer. 2:21.

DEGREE. High, Man of—I Chr. 17:17. Law—Lu. 1:52; Jas. 1:9. Song of— See PSALMS. Shadow of—Is. 38:8.

DELAY. Command, Not to keep—Ps. 119:60. Coming—Matt. 24:48. Lu. 12:45. Moses—Ex. 32:1. Without— Acts 25:17.

DELICACY. Jer. 51:34 (A.V.).

DELICATE. Jer. 6:2. Feed—Lam. 4:5. Live—Lu. 7:25. Man—Deut. 28:54. No more—Is. 47:1. Woman—Deut. 28:56.

DELIGHT. Abominations—Is. 66:3. Almighty, In—Blessing, Not in—Ps. 109:17. Blood—Is. 1:11. Burnt offerings, In—I Sam. 15:22. Commandments—Ps. 112:1. Fatness—Is. 55:2. God, With—Job 34:9. Gold, Not— Is. 13:17. Goodness — Neh. 9:25. Honor, To—Esth. 6:6, 7, 9, 11. Law, In—Ps. 1:2 (A.V.); Ps. 119:70. Lies, In—Ps. 62:4. Lovingkindness—Mic. 7:18 (A.V.). Men, Sons of—Eccl. 2:8. Scoffing—Pr. 1:22 (A.V.); Son, In— Pr. 3:12. Soul, Unto—Pr. 29:17. Statutes, In—Ps. 119:16. Strength— Ps. 147:10. Truly, Deal—Pr. 12:22. Understanding, In—Pr. 18:2. Way, In his—Ps. 37:23. Weight is, A just— Pr. 11:1. Will, To do—Ps. 40:8.

DELIGHTSOME. Land—Mal. 3:12.

DELIVER, DELIVERANCE. Accepting—Heb. 11:35. Afflictions, Out of— Acts 7:10. Blood-guiltiness, From— Ps. 51:14. Book of Isaiah—Lu. 4:17. Chief priests had—Mk. 15:10. Commandment—II Pet. 2:21. Condemned, To be—Lu. 24:20. Councils, To—Mt. 15:17; Mk. 13:9. Creature—Rom. 8: 21. Crucified, To be—Matt. 27:26; John 19:16. Death, From—II Cor. 1:10. Envy, For—Matt. 27:18; Mk. 15:10. Evil, From—Matt. 6:13. Faith was—Jude 3. Fear, Them that—Ps. 34:7. Gentiles, To—Mk. 10:33; Lu. 18:32. Iniquity, Workers of—Ps. 59: 2. Jesus—Mk. 15:15; Lu. 23:25. Jews,

To—John 18:36. Judge, To the—Matt. 5:25. Kingdom—I Cor. 15:24. Mock, To—Matt. 20:19. Officer, To the—Matt. 5:25. Paul—Acts 27:1. People, From—Acts 26:17. Pilate, To—Matt. 27:2. Prisons, Into—Acts 22:4. Righteous, Seed of—Pr. 11:21. Satan, Unto—I Tim. 1:20.

DELIVERANCE OF THE CHILDREN OF ISRAEL. Were enslaved by Egyptians.—Ex. Chs. 1, 2, 5; Deut. 4:20; 7:18-36; Heb. 11:25. God heard complaint and called Moses to deliver them—Ex. Chs. 3, 4. Calls Aaron to assist—Ex. 4:10-17, 27-31. God visits plagues upon Egypt—Ex. Chs. 7-12. Israel exempt from plagues—Ex. 8:22, 23; 9:4, 6, 26; 10:23; 11:7; 12:13, 27, 28. Israel brought out of Egypt—Ex. 12:41-42. See ISRAEL IN EGYPT, MOSES. Israelites obtain jewels—Ex. 3:21, 22; 11:2, 3; 12:35, 36; Ps. 105:37. Institution of passover in memorial of the night of deliverance—Ex. 12:1-28, 43-49; 13:3-10; Heb. 11:28. See Deut. 5:15.

Children of Israel leave Egypt.—Ex. 12: 37-42, 51. Accompanied by a mixed multitude—Ex. 12:38. Their flocks and herds—Ex. 12:39; 34:3. Consecration of the first-born—Ex. 13:1-16. Led by the angel of the Lord—Ex. 14: 19; 23:20-23; 32:34; 33:2, 14; Deut. 1:33; Neh. 9:12, 19; Ps. 78:14. Defended by the pillar of cloud by night —Ex. 14:19, 20, 24; Ps. 105:39. See CLOUD OF GLORY.

Crossing the Red Sea, and destruction of Pharaoh.—Ex. 14:1-31; Deut. 11:4; Ps. 78:13; 106:7-11; 136:13-15. Song of Moses and Miriam—Ex. 15:1-24; Ps. 106:11, 12; Heb. 11:29; Rev. 15:3. See ISRAEL.

DELUDE. Col. 2:4; Jas. 1:22.

DELUSION. Is. 66:4. Strong—II Thess. 2:11. See DECEPTION.

DELVED. Num. 21:18.

DEMAND. Ex. 5:14; Neh. 5:18; Job 38:3; 40:7; Dan. 2:27. See ASK, INQUIRE.

DEMAS, dē′mas. One of Paul's companions and fellow workers.—II Tim. 4:10; Philemon 24.

DEMEANOR. Tit. 2:3. See BEHAVE, BEHAVIOR.

DEMETRIUS, de-mē′tri-us. (1) The silversmith.—Acts 19:24.

(2) An early disciple.—III John 12.

DEMOLISH. Num. 33:52. See DESTRUCTION.

POSSESSION BY DEMONS. Gr. *Daimonizomai*, ''to be *possessed* or *held* by a demon.'' In every New Testament passage it is ''demons,'' not ''devils.'' Still, there is an intimate relation between them. Jesus is represented as struggling with Satan in his casting out of demons—Mk. 3:27. Beelzebub the prince of the demons—Mk. 3:22. As reported in Mt. 8:29, the demons recognized their final abode, but whether they were demons who were to be cast into the lake of fire is questionable. The term is ''angelois'' —Mt. 25:41. The whole matter is involved in obscurity and it is best not to undertake to explain but to follow New Testament language.

''In such possession two features may generally be traced. It is allied with and yet distinct from physical disease, and there is almost always something abnormal with respect to the physical development or defect of the sufferer. It is given as the explanation in cases of dumbness—Mt. 9:32; Lu. 11:14. Of deafness and dumbness —Mk. 9:25. Of dumbness and blindness—Mt. 12:22. Of curvature of the spine—Lu. 13:11. And of epilepsy— Mk. 1:26. Elsewhere such complaints are referred to as merely disease, and no suggestion is made that they were caused or complicated by the action of an evil spirit—Mt. 15:30; Mk. 7: 32; Lu. 18:35. Sometimes possession and disease are even distinguished by different enumeration (Mt. 10:8; Mk. 1:32; Lu. 6:17-19; 7:21; 13:32), and once, at least, epileptics (or lunatics) and palsied occupy a different category from demoniacs''—Mt. 4:24.— HASTINGS, *Bible Dictionary*.

Instances of exorcism.—Syrian demoniacs—Mt. 4:24. At Capernaum—Mt. 8:16; Mk. 1:23-26, 32-34; Lu. 4:33-36. At Gadara—Mt. 8:28-33; Mk. 5:

15–19; Lu. 8:30–35. In Galilee—Mt.
9:32; 12:22. Near Mt. Hermon—Mt.
17:14–18; Mk. 9:17–29; Lu. 9:37–43.
Mary Magdalene—Mk. 16:9; Lu. 8:2.
In Samaria—Acts 8:7. At Philippi—
Acts 16:16–18. See JESUS' TEACHING
ON DEMONS.

DEMONSTRATION. Spirit, Of the—I
Cor. 2:4.

DEN. Ju. 6:2; Job 37:8; 38:40; Ps.
104:22; Is. 32:14. Adders—Is. 11:8.
Lion's—Song of Sol. 4:8; Dan. 6:7–
24; Amos 3:4; Nah. 2:11, 12. Robbers, Of—Jer. 7:11; Mt. 21:13; Mk.
11:17; Lu. 19:46. See CAVES, COVERT,
DWELLING-PLACE.

DENARIUS. Mt. 22:19; Mk. 12:15. See
MONEY.

DENIAL. Of Christ, by Peter, three
times—Mt. 26:70, 72, 74; Mk. 41:68,
69, 71. By the Jews—John 1:11; 18:
40; 19:15; Acts 3:13, 14; 4:18. By
apostles—Tit. 1:16; II Pet. 2:1; Jude
4. Of his wife by Abraham—Gen. 20:
1–5. By Isaac—Gen. 26:1–11. Denied
the faith—I Tim. 5:8; Rev. 2:13. See
DISBELIEVE, DOUBT, FAITH, LITTLE.

DENOUNCE. Job 17:5; Jer. 20:10.

DEPART. Bloodthirsty men—Ps. 139:
19. Evil, From—Job 28:28; Ps. 34:
14; 37:27; Ps. 3:7; 13:19; 14:16; 16:6,
17; Is. 59:15. Evildoers, From—Ps.
119:115; Mt. 25:41. God—Ez. 16:42;
Hos. 9:12. *From*—Job 21:14; 22:17;
Ps. 101:4; Jer. 17:13, 15; 32:40; Ez.
6:9. Sheol, From—Pr. 15:24. Snares
of death, From—Pr. 13:14; 14:27.
Statutes, From—II Sam. 22:23. Trained
child when old—Pr. 22:6. Unclean,
From—Lam. 4:15. Unrighteous, From
—II Tim. 2:19.

Workers of iniquity.—Ps. 6:8; Mt. 7:23;
Lu. 13:27. Words, From—Is. 59:21.
See ALIENATE, ISRAEL.

DEPOSE. II Chr. 36:3; Dan. 5:20; Acts
19:27.

DEPOSIT. Lev. 6:2. See COMMIT.

DEPRIVE. Job 39:17; Eccl. 4:8; Is.
38:10.

DEPTH. See DEEP THINGS.

DEPUTED. II Sam. 15:3.

DEPUTY. II Sam. 15:3; Jer. 51:23, 28;
Dan. 3:2, 3, 27; 6:7. King—I Ki. 22:
47. See PROCONSUL.

DERBE, dẽr'be. **A city of Lycaonia,
birthplace of Timothy.**—Acts 16:1.
Paul visits—Acts 14:6.

DERISION. Ex. 32:25; Job 30:1; Ps.
2:4; 44:13; 59:8; 79:4; 119:51; Jer.
20:8; 48:26, 27, 39; Lam. 3:14; Ez. 23:
32; 36:4; Hos. 7:16; Hab. 1:10. See
HANDS CLAPPED IN DERISION.

DESCEND. Ez. 26:20; 31:16; Mt. 7:
25, 27. Angels of God—Gen. 28:12;
Mt. 28:12; Mt. 28:2. Holy Spirit—
Mt. 3:16; Mk. 1:10; Lu. 3:22; John
1:32, 33, 51; Acts 10:11; 11:5. Jehovah—Ex. 19:18; 33:9–11; 34:5; I
Thess. 4:16. Jesus—John 3:13; Eph.
4:9, 10. Mount of Olives—Lu. 19:37.
See JESUS DESCENDED FROM HEAVEN.

DESCRIBE. Ju. 8:14. Land—Josh. 18:
4, 9; Job 26:10.

DESERT. A barren place.—Num. 21:
20; Job 21:5; Is. 40:3; Lu. 8:29.
Beasts of—Is. 13:21; 34:14; Jer. 50:
39. Fir tree in—Is. 41:19. Garden
of Jehovah, Like—Is. 51:3. Gaza—
Acts 8:26. Grieve him in—Ps. 78:40.
Health in—Jer. 17:6. Jesus in—Mk.
6:31; 8:4; Lu. 1:80; 4:42; 5:16. Led
through—Is. 48:21. Land—Deut. 32:
10; Jer. 2:6. Rejoice, Shall—Is. 35:1.
Ride through—Ps. 68:4. Rivers—Is.
43:19, 20. Sharon like—Is. 33:9.
Tempted God in—Ps. 68:4. Wandering in—Heb. 11:38. Way—Ps. 107:4.
See WASTE PLACES, WILDERNESS.

DESERT. Just dues, reward.—Ps. 94:2;
Ez. 7:27.

DESERTER. Jer. 38:19; 39:9; 52:15.

DESERVE. Ju. 9:16; Ezra 9:13; Job
11:6.

DESIRE. Ex. 10:11; Deut. 5:21; Job
13:3; 14:15; 31:16; 33:32; Is. 38:9;
132:13, 14; Pr. 19:22; 21:25; Eccl. 12:
5; Hab. 2:5; Lu. 23:20; I Cor. 14:1;
Gal. 4:9. Disciples, Of—Lu. 17:22.
Fulfilled—I Ki. 5:8, 9, 10; I Ki. 10:13;
II Chr. 9:12; Ps. 54:7; 59:10; 89:29;
92:11; 145:16, 19; Pr. 10:24; 13:99.
Glory—I Cor. 12:6. Gold—Deut. 7:
25; I Ki. 9:11. Hearts—Ps. 10:3, 17;
21:2; Rom. 10:1. Jehovah—II Sam.
23:5; Ps. 19:10; 73:25; Is. 26:8, 9;
Hos. 6:6; Mt. 27:43. Jesus—Lu. 7:36;
8:20; 23:8; John 16:19. Of—Lu. 22:
15. Knowledge—Job 21:14. Land—

Ex. 34:24. Prophets, Of—Mt. 13:17; 10:24. Righteous, Of—Pr. 10:24; Mt. 13:17. Solomon, Of—I Ki. 5:8, 9, 10; 9:1, 11, 19; II Chr. 8:6; 11:23. Soul, Of—I Sam. 23:20; I Ki. 11:37; Job 23:13; Is. 26:8, 9. Wicked, Of—Ps. 112:10; Pr. 12:12; 21:10. Wisdom— Pr. 3:15; 8:11. See COVET, DELIGHT.

DESOLATE, DESOLATION. Ps. 25: 16; 143:4; Is. 3:26; 10:3; 17:9; Jer. 2:12; Dan. 11:31; I Tim. 5:5. Altars —Ez. 6:4, 6. Children, Of—Is. 54:1. City become—Josh. 8:28; Job 15:2, 8; Is. 24:12; Jer. 48:9; 48:33; Ez. 6:6; 26:19; 35:4, 9; Zeph. 3:6; Mt. 12:25; Rev. 18:19. Babylon, Of—Jer. 51:43. Egypt, Of—Jer. 46:19; Ez. 30:7, 14. Judæa, Of—Lev. 26:31, 33; Is. 1:7; 64:10; Jer. 6:8; 9:11; 10:22; 25:18; 26:9; 33:10; 34:22; 44:2, 6; Ez. 12:19; Dan. 9:2, 18; Zeph. Restored—Is. 54: 3; 61:4; Ez. 36:35. Country—See LAND. Ephraim — Hos. 5:9; 12:1. House become—Is. 5:9; Jer. 22:5; Zeph. 1:3; Mt. ᴠ12:25; 23:38; Lu. 11: 17; 13:35. Idols—Mic. 1:7. Jerusalem become—Is. 64:10; Jer. 6:8; 25: 18; 33:10; 44:2, 6; Ez. 12:19; Dan. 9:2, 18; Mt. 23:38; Lu. 21:20. Land become—Is. 7:19; Jer. 12:10, 11; Ez. 6:14; 14:15, 16; 25:13; 35:3, 7, 9, 12, 14, 15; Joel 1:17, 18; Zeph. 2:4, 9, 13, 14; Lu. 11:17. *Babylon*—Is. 13:9; Jer. 25:12; 50:3, 13, 23; 51:26, 29, 43, 62. *Egypt*—Ez. 19:7; 23:33; 29:9–12; 30: 7; 32:15; Joel 3:19; Mic. 7:13. *Judaea* —Lev. 26:22, 31–33, 43; Is. 1:7; Jer. 4:7, 27; 25:11; 32:43; 44:22; Ez. 12: 19, 20; 15:8; 33:28, 29; Joel 2:3, 20. People become—II Ki. 22:19; II Chr. 30:7; Job 16:7; Ps. 40:15; 69:25; Is. 47:11; 51:9; Jer. 25:18; 49:2, 20; 50: 45; Lam. 1:16; 3:11; Ez. 7:27; 26:20; Mic. 6:13, 16; Zeph. 2:9; 3:6; Zech. 7: 14; Mt. 12:25; Acts 1:20. Places— Job 3:14; Ps. 109:10; Is. 49:19; Lam. 5:18. Sanctuary—Dan. 9:17; 11:31; 12:11; Amos 7:9. Waters—Is. 15:6; Jer. 48:34; Mt. 24:15; Mk. 23:14. Wicked, Of—Pr. 3:25. See ASTONISH-MENT, CONDEMN, RUIN, WASTE.

DESPAIR. I Sam. 27:1; Pr. 24:10; Is. 40:30; Jer. 51:46; Lu. 6:35; 18:1, 2; II Cor. 4:8; Gal. 6:9; Eph. 3:13. Heart to —Eccl. 2:20. Life, Of—II Cor. 1:8.

Instances of.—Is. 51:20. David—I Sam. 27:1; Ps. 27:7–13; 42:1–11. Jeremiah— Jer. 8:18; Lam. 1:22. Judas—Mt. 27: 12; Acts 1:18. Moses—Num. 11:10– 15. Paul—II Cor. 1:8; 4:8.

DESPERATE. Sorrow—Is. 17:11. Wind as—Job 6:26.

DESPISE. Mt. 6:24. Acts 13:41. Birth-right—Gen. 25:34. Chastening—Job 5:17; Pr. 3:11. Church of God—I Cor. 11:22. Cities—Is. 33:8. Dominion—I Pet. 2:10 (A.V.). Feasts—Amos 5:27. Heart—Ps. 51:17; Pr. 12:8. Holy things—Ez. 22:8. Jehovah—Num. 11: 20. Little ones—Mt. 18:10. Men, Of— Is. 53:3. Mother—Pr. 23:22. Name— Mal. 1:6. Neighbor—Pr. 14:21. Oath —Ez. 16:59. Obey, To—Pr. 30:17. Op-pressors, Gain of—Is. 33:15. People —Ju. 9:38. Prisoners, Not—Ps. 69:33. Prophesyings, Not—I Thess. 5:20. Re-proof—Pr. 1:30; 5:12. Riches of good-ness—Rom. 2:4. Shame—Heb. 12:2. Small things, Day of—Zech. 4:10. Temptation—Gal. 4:14. Wisdom—Pr. 1:7; 23:9. Word—Pr. 13:13; Num. 15: 31; Is. 30:12. Work—Job 10:3. Youth —I Tim. 4:12.

DESPITE. Soul, Of—Ez. 25:6, 15; 36:5. Unto spirit of grace—Heb. 10:29. See VENGEANCE.

DESPITEFUL. Rom. 1:30 (A.V.). See PERSECUTION.

DESPITEFULLY. Use you—Mt. 5:44 (A.V.); Lu. 6:28; Acts 14:5 (A.V.).

DESPOIL. Pr. 22:23; Col. 2:15. See SPOIL.

DESTINY. Is. 65:11.

DESTITUTE. Ps. 82:3; 102:17; 141:8; Heb. 11:37; Jas. 2:15 (A.V.).

DESTROY. See DESTRUCTION.

DESTRUCTION. The flood—Gen. 6:17; 7:11, 23; 8:1–3; Mt. 24:38, 39; Lu. 17: 27; II Pet. 2:5.

Destruction of nations.—Pharaoh and host—Ex. 14:27, 28. Amalekites—I Sam. 15:3, 20; I Chr. 4:43. Nameless nations—Deut. 8:20; II Ki. 21:19; Job 12:23.

Destruction of cities.—Ai—Josh. 8:19. Capernaum—Mt. 11:23; Lu. 10:15. Jericho—Josh. 6:24. Sodom and Go-morrah—Gen. 13:10; 19:29; Lu. 17:28, 29. Cities of Midianites—Num. 31:10. Of various nations—Deut. 20:16–18;

31:3; Josh. 11:19, 20. Destruction of Jerusalem—II Ki. 25:8, 9; Jer. 39:8; Dan. 9:2; Mt. 24:15–22; Lu. 21:20–24. See JERUSALEM.

Vandalism of temple.—Nebuchadrezzar—II Ki. 24:13; Ps. 74:5–8.

Destruction of persons.—Abel—Gen. 4:8. Achan—Josh. 7:25. Agag—I Sam. 15:33. Absalom—II Sam. 18:14. Baal's prophets—I Ki. 18:40; II Ki. 10:25, 28. Goliath—I Sam. 17:49. James—Acts 12:2. Jezebel—II Ki. 9:33. Job's children—Job 1:15–18. Judas—Mt. 27:5; Acts 1:18. Korah, etc.—Num. 16:31, 32. Nadab, etc.—Num. 3:4. Samson, etc.—Ju. 16:30. Stephen—Acts 7:59, 60. Uriah—II Sam. 11:14–17.

Destruction of armies.—Chedorlaomer, etc.—Gen. Ch. 14. Pharaoh and host—Ex. 14:27, 28. Army of Ai—Josh. 8:22. Sennacherib, etc.—II Ki. 19:35. Syrians—I Ki. 20:28, 29.

Destruction of altars and high places.—Ex. 34:13; Lev. 26:30; Deut. 7:5; Ju. 2:2; II Chr. 14:3; 23:17; 32:12; Hos. 10:2.

Calamities.—Egyptians—*Fish*—Ex. 7:21. *Cattle*—Ex. 9:6. *First-born children*—Ex. 12:29. Fall of the tower of Siloam—Lu. 13:4, 5. Fall of Aphek's wall—I Ki. 20:30. Pestilence—II Sam. 24:15–16. Poisonous serpents—Num. 21:8; John 3:14.

Destruction of wicked.—Is. 59:7; Mt. 10:28; 21:14; Mk. 12:9; Lu. 20:16; II Thess. 1:8–9; Rom. 9:22; I Tim. 6:9; I Cor. 10:10; II Pet. 3:16.

Destruction of sin.—I John 3:8; Rom. 6:6, 13; I Cor. 5:5; II Cor. 5:17.

Destruction of church's enemies.—II Thess. 2:8; Phil. 3:19; Heb. 2:14; II Pet. 2:1; Rev. 11:18; 20:9–10.

DETAIN. Ju. 13:15, 16; I Sam. 21:7.

DETERMINATE. Counsel of God.—Acts 2:23. See FOREORDINATION, JESUS FULFILLED SCRIPTURES.

DETERMINE. II Sam. 13:32; Dan. 11:36; Acts 15:2, 37; II Cor. 2:1. David to death, To—I Sam. 20:33. Days—Job 14:5. Death of Jesus—Lu. 22:22; Acts 2:23. Desolations—Dan. 9: 26, 27. Destroy, To—II Chr. 25:16; Is. 10:22, 23. Evil—I Sam. 20:7, 9; 25:17; Esth. 7:7. Heart, In his—I Cor. 7:37.

Judges, As—Ex. 21:22. Know anything, Not to—I Cor. 2:2. Paul's case—Acts 24:22. Release Jesus, To—Acts 3:13. Return, To—Acts 20:3. Sail, To—Acts 20:16; 27:1. Seasons—Acts 17:26. Send, To—Paul—Acts 25:25. Relief to brethren—Acts 11:29. Winter, To—Tit. 3:12. See DECISION, DECREE, FOREORDINATION, PURPOSE.

DETEST. Abomination—Deut. 7:26.

DETESTABLE. Things—Jer. 16:18; Ez. 5:11; 7:20; 11:18, 21; 37:23.

DEUEL. de-ū'el. **A Gadite.**—Num. 1:24. See REUEL.

DEUTERONOMY. See OUTLINE STUDIES IN THE BOOKS.

DEVASTATION. Lam. 3:47. See DESTRUCTION.

DEVICE. Abomination — Pr. 15:26 (A.V.). Crafty, Of—Job 5:12. Devised against Jews—Esth. 8:3. Filled with—Pr. 1:31. Heart, In a man's—Pr. 19:21. Ignorant of—II Cor. 2:11. Man, Of—Acts 17:29. Meek, To destroy—Is. 32:7. Perform, Not able to—Ps. 21:11. Sheol, In—Eccl. 9:10. Walk after—Jer. 18:12. Wicked—Ps. 37:7; Pr. 12:2; Is. 32:7.

DEVISE. II Sam. 21:5. Cunningly—II Pet. 1:16. Evil—Pr. 3:29; 14:22; Jer. 48:2. Tables—II Pet. 1:16. Good—Pr. 14:22. Heart, Of—I Ki. 12:33. Jews, Against—Esth. 8:3; 9:25. Iniquity—Mic. 2:1. Letters—Esth. 8:5. Life, To take—Ps. 31:13. Means—II Sam. 14:14. Purposes, Wicked—Pr. 6:18 (A.V.). Things—Is. 32:8 (A.V.). Works—Ex. 31:4; 35:32; 35:35.

DEVIL. See SATAN.

DEVILS. Possession of.—See DEMONS.

DEVILISH. Jas. 3:15.

DEVOTE. See BAN.

DEVOTION. Job 15:4. See WORSHIP.

DEVOUR, DEVOURING. I Pet. 5:8. Adversaries—Heb. 10:2. Beast hath—Gen. 37:20, 33; Ez. 34:28. Breath shall—Is. 33:11. Briars—Is. 9:18. Birds—Lu. 8:5 (A.V.). Child—Rev. 12:4. Curse—Is. 24:6. Deep—Amos 7:4. Famine shall—Ez. 7:15. Fire—See FIRE. Flesh—Deut. 32:42. Flies—Ps. 78:45. Fruit—Ez. 19:14. Israel—Is. 9:12. Jacob—Ps. 79:7. Judges—Hos. 7:7. King—Jer. 50:17; 51:34. Living—Lu. 15:30. Locusts—II Chr. 7:13.

Men—Ju. 9:20; Ez. 36:14. Moab—Jer. 48:45. Money—Gen. 31:15. Palaces—Jer. 17:27; Amos 1:4, 7, 10, 12, 14; 2:2, 5. Poor—Pr. 30:14. Souls—Ez. 22:25. Strength—Hos. 7:9. Sword shall—Deut. 32:42; II Sam. 2:26. Jer. 46:10, 14. Tree—Ez. 20:47. Widow's houses—Mk. 12:46. Words—Ps. 52:4. Worm—Amos 4:9.

DEVOUT. Ananias—Acts 22:12. Cornelius—Acts 10:2. Greeks—Acts 17:4. Men—Acts 2:5; 8:2. Persons—Acts 17:17. Proselytes—Acts 13:43. Simeon — Lu. 2:25. Soldiers — Acts 10:7. Women—Acts 13:50.

DEW. See METEOROLOGY.

DIADEM. Job 29:14. Beauty, Of—Is. 28:5. Many—Rev. 19:12. Royal—Is. 62:3. See CROWN.

DIAL. II Ki. 20:11; Is. 38:8.

DIAMOND. Ex. 28:8; 39:11; Jer. 17: 11; Ez. 28:13.

DIANA, dī-ā'nȧ. **An Ephesian goddess.** —Acts 19:24–35.

DIBLAH, dĭb'lah. Ez. 6:14. See RIBLAH.

DIBLAIM, dĭb'la-im. **Father-in-law of Hosea.**—Hos. 1:3.

DIBON, dī'bon. (1) **A town in Moab.**—Num. 21:30.

(2) **A village in Judah.**—Neh. 11:25.

DIBON-GAD, dī'bon–găd'. **A place of one of Israel's encampments.**—Num. 33:45, 46.

DIBRI, dĭb'ri. **A Danite, whose son was stoned for blasphemy.**—Lev. 24:11.

DIDYMUS, dĭd'y-mŭs. **Surname of Thomas.**—John 11:16; 20:24; 21:2.

DIE. Absalom, For—II Sam. 18:33. Adam all, In—I Cor. 15:22. See SIN. Better than to live—Jonah 4:3. Christ —See ATONEMENT, JESUS, DEATH OF. With—Rom. 6:8, 9; II Tim. 2:11. Common death—Num. 16:29. Death, The —Mt. 15:4. Desire to—Rev. 9:6. Eat and not—John 6:50. Faith, In—Heb. 11:13. Fool dieth, As a—II Sam. 3:33. See FOOLS. Foolish—Pr. 10:2. Gain, Is—Phil. 1:21. Himself, None to—Rom. 14:7. Live again, Shall he—Job 14:14. See LIFE. Live and not—II Ki. 18:32. Lord, In the—Rev. 14:13. See RIGHTEOUS. Nest, In—Job 29:18. Peace, In—Jer. 34:5. Renounce God and—Job 2:9. Reproof shall—He that hateth—Pr. 15:10. Rich man—Lu. 16:

22. Righteous, Death of—Num. 23:10. See RIGHTEOUS. Sin, In—II Chr. 25:4; Jer. 31:30; Ez. 18:4; 33:8, 14; John 8: 21. See SIN. To sin—Rom. 6:2, 10; I Pet. 2:24. See BAPTISM, NEW BIRTH. Surely—Gen. 2:17. Time to—Eccl. 3:2. *Before*—Eccl. 7:17. To-morrow—Is. 22:13. Ungodly, For the—Rom. 5:6. Wheat, Grain of—John 12:24; I Cor. 15:36. Why will ye—Jer. 27:13. Wicked men—Pr. 11:7. See SIN, WICKED. Wisdom, Without—Job. 4:21. *With you*—Job 12:2. See WISDOM. Wise men—Ps. 49:10; Eccl. 2:16. Worm —Is. 66:24. See WORM. Youth, In—Job 36:14. See DEATH, JUDGMENT, SIN.

DIFFER. Rom. 12:6; I Cor. 4:7; 15:41; Gal. 4:1.

DIFFERENCE. Ez. 44:23. See DISTINCTION.

DIFFERENT. Gospel—II Cor. 11:4; Gal. 1:6; I Tim. 1:3. Law—Rom. 7:23. Spirit—II Cor. 11:4.

DIFFICULT. Jer. 33:3; Acts 27:7, 8, 16. Pr. 26:27; Eccl. 10:8.

DIG. Is. 7:25; 51:1; Ez. 8:8; 12:5, 7, 12; Mt. 25:18; Lu. 6:48; 13:8; 16:3; Rom. 11:3. Grave—See GRAVE. Pit—See PIT. Soul, Pit for—Ps. 35:7; 57:6; 119:85; Jer. 18:20, 22. Well—See WELL. Wicked, Pit for—Ps. 94:13; Amos 9:2. Winepress—Mt. 21:33; Mk. 12:1.

DIGNITY. Heb. 1:7. Folly set in—Eccl. 10:6. Honor and—Esth. 6:3. Pre-eminence of—Gen. 49:3. Paul at—II Pet. 2:10; Jude 8. Strength and—Pr. 31: 25. Thrust from—Ps. 62:4.

DIKLAH, dĭk'lah. **Son of Joktan.**—Gen. 10:27; I Chr. 1:21.

DILEAN, dĭl'e-an. **A village in Judah.** —Josh. 15:38.

DILIGENCE, DILIGENT. Tit. 3:13. Ask—Deut. 13:14. Be—Pr. 27:23. Business, In—Pr. 22:29. Enquire—Deut. 17:4. Giving—Lu. 12:58; II Pet. 1:10. Jude 3. Hand of—Pr. 10:4; 12: 24. Hearken—Is. 21:7. Inquisition—Deut. 19:18. Keep thy heart with—Pr. 4:23. Man, Substance of—Pr. 12: 27. Observe—Deut. 24:8. Precepts—Ps. 119:4. Ruleth with—Rom. 12:8. Same—Heb. 6:11. Seek—Lu. 15:8; II

Tim. 1:17. Soul of—Pr. 13:4. Thoughts —Pr. 21:5.

DIM. Eyes—Gen. 27:1; 48:10; Deut. 34:7; I Sam. 3:2; 4:15; Job 17:7; Is. 32:3; Lam. 5:17.

DIMINISH. Ex. 5:8; Deut. 4:2. Ez. 29:15; Jer. 29:6. Food—Ez. 16:27. Marriage, Duty of—Ex. 21:10. Wealth —Pr. 13:11. Word—Jer. 26.2. Work— Ex. 5:11.

DIMNAH, dĭm′nah. Josh. 21:35. See RIMMON.

DIMON, dī′mon. Is. 15:9. See DIBON.

DINAH, dī′nah. **Jacob's daughter.**— Gen. 30:21.

DINAITES, dī′na-ītes. **A tribe in Samaria.**—Ezra 4:9.

DINE. Gen. 43:16. See MEALS.

DINHABAH, dĭn′ha-bah. Gen. 36:32.

DINNER. Pr. 15:17; Mt. 22:4; Lu. 11: 38. See MEALS.

DIONYSIUS, dī′o-nȳ-si-ŭs. **The Areopagite.**—Acts 17:24.

DIOTREPHES, dī-ŏt′re-phēs. III John 9.

DIP. Bird—Lev. 14:6, Blood, In—14: 51. Coat in blood—Gen. 37:31. Finger —Lev. 4:6, 17; 9:9. Food in oil— Deut. 33:24. Hand—Mt. 26:23. Honeycomb, In—I Sam. 14:27. Morsel in vinegar, One of twelve—Mk. 14:20. Naaman seven times—II Ki. 5:14. Sop —John 13:26. Water, In—Josh. 3:15.

DIRECT. Eccl. 10:10. Hearts—II Thess. 3:5. Lord Jesus—I Thess. 3:11. Paths —Pr. 3:6. Spirit—Is. 40:13. Steps— Pr. 16:9; Jer. 10:23. Way—Pr. 11:5. Words—Job 32:14.

DIRT. Waters cast up—Is. 57:20.

DISALLOW. Vows—Num. 30:5, 8, 11.

DISANNUL. Gal. 3:17; Heb. 7:18. See COVENANTS.

DISAPPOINT. Pr. 15:22.

DISASTER. Job 31:3; Ob. 12.

DISBELIEVE. Acts 28:24; I Pet. 2:7. See RESURRECTION—Mk. 16:11, 16; Lu. 24:41. See FAITH.

DISCERN. Gen. 27:23; 31:32; 38:25; Ruth 3:14; Ezra 3:13; Neh. 6:12; Job 4:16; 6:30; 38:20; Ps. 19:12; Pr. 1:2; 2:3; 7:7; 10:13; Dan. 9:13, 25; Jonah 4:11; Mal. 3:18; Mt. 16:3; I Cor. 1:19; 11:29, 31; 14:29; Phil. 1:9; Heb. 4:12. Good and evil—II Sam. 14:17; 19:35; I Ki. 3:9; Eccl. 8:5; Heb. 5:14. Justice—I Ki. 3:11; Job 6:30. Spirits—

I Cor. 12:10. Unclean—Ez. 22:26; 44: 23.

DISCHARGE. Eccl. 8:8; Rom. 7:2, 6.

DISCIPLES. Preached to.—Acts 1:15; 14:21; 20:7.

Characteristics of.—Hospitable—Acts 1:13; 2:1, 2; 14:28; 21:4, 6; 28:13, 14. Faithful—Acts 6:1, 2, 7; 9:1, 25; II Cor. 1:23. Courageous: Peter preached to Gentiles—Acts Ch. 10. Try to restrain Paul—Acts 15:10; 19:20; II Cor. 10:1. Prayerful—Rom. 15:30. Loyal—II Cor. 11:25-31. In love with their work—I Thess. 1:3.

Incidents.—Pluck corn on Sabbath—Mt. 12:1, 2; Mk. 2:23; Lu. 6:1. Disciples, His mother and brethren—Mt. 12:48. The twelve sent out—Mt. 10:1. Explains parables to—Mt. 13:10, 36; Mk 4:34; Lu. 8:9. Distributed loaves to five thousand—Mt. 14:15, 16; Mk. 6: 35, 41; Lu. 9:12, 14, 16; John 6:8, 11, 12. Distributed loaves to four thousand—Mt. 15:33, 36; Mk. 8:1, 4, 6. See TRANSFIGURATION—Mt. 17:6, 10, 13; Mk. 9:2; II Pet. 1:18; Lu. 9:28. Unable to cure epileptic—Mt. 17:16, 19. Ask about divorce—Mt. 19:10; Mk. 10:10. Ask who is greatest in kingdom—Mt. 18:1. Rebuked those bringing children—Mt. 19:13; Mk. 10:13; Lu. 18:15. Jesus eats passover with— Mt. 26:17, 18, 19, 26. The twelve (apostles)—Mt. 26:20; Lu. 6:13; 9:1. In Gethsemane—Mt. 26:35, 36, 40, 45, 56; Mk. 14:32; Lu. 22:39, 45; John 18: 1, 2. Jesus washes feet of—John 13:5. The eleven—Acts 2:14. Called Christians—Acts 11:26; 26:28; I Pet. 4:16. Known by love—John 13:35. Filled with Holy Spirit—Acts 13:52. Disciples of pharisees—Mt. 22:16; Mk. 2: 18; Lu. 5:33. Joseph of Arimathea, a disciple—Mt. 27:57; John 19:38. Resurrection told to—Mt. 28:7, 8, 13; Mk. 16:7.

Miscellaneous References.—Mt. 5:11; 8: 21 (8:25 Sinaitic MS.); 9:10, 19, 37; 14:26; 16:5, 21, 24; 19:23; 20:17; 21: 1; 23:1; 24:1, 3; 26:1, 26; 27:64; 28: 16; Mk. 2:16; 3:7; 5:31; 6:1, 45; 7:2, 5; 8:10, 34; 9:14, 18, 28; 10:23, 24, 46; 11:1; 12:43; 13:1; 14:12, 13, 16; Lu. 5:30; 6:17, 20, 40; 7:11; 8:22; 9:18, 40, 43, 54; 10:23; 11:1; 12:22; 16:1;

17:1, 22; 19:29, 37, 39; 20:45; 22:11; John 2:2, 22; 3:22; 4:1, 31; 6:3, 16, 22, 24, 60, 61, 66; 7:3; 8:31; 9:2, 28; 11:7, 54; 12:4, 16; 13:22, 23; 16:17, 29; 18: 15, 16, 19, 25; 19:26; 20:3, 4, 10, 18, 19, 25, 26; 21:1, 4, 24; Acts 9:1, 10, 19, 26, 38; 11:29; 14:20, 22, 28; 16:1; 18:23; 19:1; 20:1; 21:16; *mathetria*, Acts 9: 36.

Disciples of John.—Mt. 9:14; 11:2; 14: 12; Mk. 2:18; 6:28; Lu. 5:33; 7:18, 19; John 1:35, 37; 3:25; 4:1.

Disciples of Moses.—John 9:28.

Conditions of discipleship.—Must bear cross—Mt. 10:38; 16:24; Mk. 8:34; Lu. 9:23; 14:27. Must practise self-denial—Mt. 5:29; 10:39; 16:24–27; 16: 25; 18:18–30; 22:28–30; Mk. 8:34–38; 10:29, 30; Lu. 6:22, 23; 14:26, 33; John 12:25; I Cor. 9:24–27; Gal. 5:24; Col. 3: 5–7; II Tim. 2:12; Tit. 2:12. Must endure—Mt. 10:22; 24:13; Mk. 13:13; Rom. 11:22; I Cor. 9:24; 10:13; 15:2; Eph. 4:1; Col. 1:23; II Tim. 2:12; Heb. 3:6; 4:14; Jas. 5:7–11. Must not be conformed to this world—John 17:15; Rom. 12:2; Col. 3:2; I Pet. 4:3–6; I John 2: 15–17; 4:5. Must run a race—Heb. 12:1. Must put on the whole armor—Eph. 6: 11. Must suffer tribulation—John 15:18, 20; 16:33; Acts 9:16; 14:22; Rom. 5:3; 8:17; I Thess. 3:3; II Tim. 2:11; 3:12; Phil. 1:28, 29; I Pet. 1:6–9; 2:21; Rev. 2:9–11; 7:14. Must bear fruit—Mt. 7:16, 20; 12:31–35; Lu. 6:44; John 15: 5–8. Reward of—Rom. 2:1–8; II Tim. 2:11, 12, 13. See APOSTLES, JESUS' TEACHING ON CHARACTER, PAUL ON CHRISTIAN LIFE.

DISCIPLINE. II Tim. 1:7. See MINISTERS, PAUL, TEACHING OF.

DISCLOSE. Ruth 4:4; I Sam. 14:8–11; 20:2, 13; 22:8; Pr. 25:9; Is. 26:21.

DISCOMFIT. Ex. 17:13; Ju. 8:12; I Sam. 14:20; 22:5. Jehovah, By—Ex. 23:27; Deut. 7:23; Josh. 10:10; Ju. 4: 15; I Sam. 5:9; 7:10; II Sam. 22:15; Ps. 18:14.

DISCONTENT. I Sam. 22:2; Esth. 5: 13; Pr. 6:34, 35; Jonah 4:4–10.

DISCONTINUE. Jer. 17:4.

DISCORD. Rom. 1:29; II Cor. 12:20. Sower, Of—Pr. 6:14, 19; 26:20 (A.V.). See STRIFE.

DISCOURAGE. Is. 42:4; Col. 3:21. Israel—Num. 21:4; 32:7, 9.

DISCOURSE. Acts 20:7, 9.

Jesus, Of.—See JESUS.

DISCOVER. I Sam. 22:6. See UNCOVER.

DISCREET. Gen. 41:33, 39; I Chr. 26: 14; Mk. 12:34.

DISCRETION. I Sam. 25:33; I Chr. 22: 12; II Chr. 2:12; Ezra 8:18; Pr. 1:4; 2:11; 3:21; 5:2; 8:12; 11:22; 19:11.

DISDAIN. I Sam. 17:42; Job 30:1.

DISEASES. Kinds of.—Atrophy—Job 16:18; 19:20. Blains—Ex. 9:10. Blindness: *Disqualified for priesthood*—Lev. 21:18. *Of animals*—Lev. 22:22; Deut. 15:21; Mal. 1:18. Examples of blindness: *Isaac*—Gen. 27:1. *Jacob*—Gen. 48:10. *Eli*—I Sam. 4:15. *Ahijah*—I Ki. 14:4. *Inflicted on Sodomites*—Gen. 19: 11. *On Syrians*—II Ki. 6:18. *On Saul*—Acts 9:8. *On Elymas*—Acts 13:11. *Cured by Christ*—Mt. 9:27; 11:5; 12: 22; 20:30; Mk. 8:23; John 9:1. See BLINDNESS. Boils—Ex. 9:10; Deut. 28: 27; II Ki. 20:7; Job 2:7. Bruises—Ps. 38:5; Is. 1:6. Consumption—Lev. 21:18, 20; 26:26; Deut. 28:22, 27, 35. Deafness—Lev. 19:14; Ps. 38:13; Mt. 11:5; Mk. 7:32; 9:25. Demons—Mt. 4: 24. See DEMONS, POSSESSION OF. Dropsy—Lu. 14:2. Dumbness—Pr. 31: 8; Mt. 9:32; Lu. 1:20. See THE DEAF. Dysentery—II Chr. 21:12–19; Acts 28: 8. Epilepsy—Mt. 4:24; 17:15. Fever—Lev. 21:18, 20; 26:6; Deut. 28:22, 27; Mt. 8:14; Acts 28:8. Impediment in speech—Mk. 7:32. Infirmity—John 5:5. Inflammation—Deut. 28:22. Issue—Mt. 9:20. Itch—Deut. 28:27. See LEPROSY. Loss of appetite—Job 33: 20; Ps. 107:18. Lunacy—Mt. 4:24. See INSANITY. Madness — Deut. 28: 28; I Sam. 21:15; Pr. 26:18; Zech. 12:4. *Cured by Christ* — Mt. 4:24; 17:15. *Christ charged with*—John 10: 20. *Paul*—Acts 26:24. Palsy, *cured by Jesus*—Mt. 4:24; 8:6; 9:26; Mk. 2:3. *By Philip*—Acts 8:7. *By Peter*—Acts 9:33, 34. Pestilence, or plague—Deut. 28:21; II Sam. 34:15. See PLAGUE, SCURVY—Deut. 28:27. See LEPROSY. Sunstroke—II Ki. 4:19, 20; Is. 49:10. Tumor—I Sam. 5:6, 12. Ulcers—Lu. 16:20. Worms—Acts 12:23. **Wounds** —Ps. 38:5; Is. 1:6.

Spoken of as.—Evil—Ps. 41:8. Incurable—II Chr. 21:18; Jer. 14:19. Painful—Job 33:9.

Medicine used for curing.—Pr. 17:22; Is. 1:6.

God entreated to cure.—II Sam. 12:16; II Ki. 20:2, 3.

Over-excitement a cause of.—Dan. 8:27.

Inflicted by Jehovah.—Num. 12:10; Deut. 28:21; II Ki. 5:27; II Chr. 21:18; 26:21. As judgment—Ex. 15:26; Lev. 14:34; Ps. 38:2–4.

Intemperance a cause of.—Hos. 7:5.

Of Egypt.—Ex. 9:9; Deut. 7:15; 28:27, 60, 61.

Attributed to evil spirits.—I Sam. 16:14–16; Job 2:7; Mk. 9:17; Lu. 11:14; 13:16.

Physicians called.—Jer. 8:22; Mt. 9:12; Lu. 4:23. See PHYSICIANS, HEALING.

DISFIGURE. Job 30:18; Mt. 6:16. See Lev. 19:27, 28; Deut. 14:1; Jer. 9:26; 41:5; 48:37.

DISGRACE. Jer. 14:21.

DISGUISE. Self—I Sam. 28:8; I Ki. 14:2; 20:38; 22:30; II Chr. 18:29; 35:22; Job 24:15.

DISH. Ex. 25:29; 37:16; Num. 4:7; Ju. 5:25; II Ki. 21:13; Pr. 19:24; 26:15; Mt. 26:23; Mk. 14:20. See VESSELS.

DISHAN, dī'shăn. Son of Seir—Gen. 36:21, 28, 30; I Chr. 1:38, 42.

DISHON, dī'shŏn. Son of Seir—Gen. 36:21, 25, 26, 30; I Chr. 1:38, 41.

DISHONEST. Gain—Ez. 22:13, 27.

DISHONOR. Rom. 9:21; II Cor. 6:8; II Tim. 2:20. Bodies—Rom. 1:24. Clothed with—Ps. 35:26. Covered with—Ps. 71:13. Father—Mic. 7:6. Get, Shall—Pr. 6:33. Head—I Cor. 11:4, 5. God —Rom. 2:23. Kings—Ezra 4:14. Known—Ps. 69:19. Sown in—I Cor. 15:43.

DISINHERIT. Them—Num. 14:12.

DISMAY. Be—II Ki. 19:26; Is. 37:27; 10:2; 17:18; 50:36; Ob. 9; I Sam. 17:11. Be not—Deut. 31:8; Josh. 1:9; 8:1; 10:25; I Chr. 22:13; 28:20; II Chr. 20:15, 17; 32:7; Jer. 1:17; 30:10; 46:27; Ez. 2:6; 3:9; Is. 41:10. Cause to be—Jer. 49:37. See ASTONISH, SURPRISE, WONDER.

DISMISS. Assembly—Acts 19:41. Courses, Not—II Chr. 23:8. When they were—Acts 15:30.

DISOBEDIENCE, DISOBEDIENT. Lu. 1:17; Tit. 1:16; 3:3; Neh. 9:26; I Pet. 2:8. Avenge—II Cor. 10:6. Heavenly vision, Unto—Acts 26:19. Jehovah, Unto—I Ki. 13:21, 26. Man's—Rom. 5:19. Parents, To—Rom. 1:30; II Tim. 3:2. People, Unto—Rom. 10:21. Recompense, Received—Heb. 2:2. Sons of—Eph. 2:2; 5:6; Col. 3:6 (A.V.). Spirits—I Pet. 3:20. See REBELLION, SIN.

DISORDERLY. Behaved not—II Thess. 3:7. Walk—II Thess. 3:6, 11.

DISPATCH. Swords, With—Ez. 23:47.

DISPENSATION. Fullness of the times, Of—Eph. 1:10. God, Of—Col. 1:25. Grace of God, Of—Eph. 3:2. See COVENANT.

DISPERSE, DISPERSION. Ps. 112:9; Pr. 5:16. Come, Are—Jer. 25:34 (A.V.). Countries, Through—Ez. 20:23; 22:15; 29:12; 30:23, 26. Daughter of—Zeph. 3:10. Judah, Of—Is. 11:12. People, Among—I Sam. 14:34; Esth. 3:8. Wise, Lips of—Pr. 15:7. See ISRAEL, JUDAH.

DISPLAY. Ps. 60:4.

DISPLEASE, DISPLEASURE. Gen. 31:35; 48:17; I Sam. 8:6; 18:8; 29:7; II Sam. 6:8; I Ki. 20:43; 21:4; I Chr. 13:11; Dan. 6:14; Acts 12:20; Heb. 3:10, 17. Jehovah, Of—Num. 22:34; Deut. 9:19; II Sam. 11:27; I Chr. 21:7; Ps. 2:5; 6:1; 38:1; Pr. 24:18; Is. 59:15; Zech. 1:2, 15. See ANGER, INDIGNATION, WRATH.

DISPOSE, DISPOSITION. Job 34:13; Pr. 16:33; I Cor. 10:27.

DISPOSSESS. Num. 32:39; Deut. 7:17; 12:29; Ju. 11:23, 24; Zech. 9:4.

DISPUTATION. Mk. 9:34; Heb. 6:16; 7:7; II Tim. 2:8. Body of Moses, About —Jude 9. Jew, Against—Acts 9:29. Man, With—Acts 24:12. Stephen, With—Acts 6:9. Synagogue, In—Acts 17:17. Words—I Tim. 6:4. World, Of —I Cor. 1:20. See QUESTIONING, REASONING, WRANGLING.

DISQUIET. I Sam. 28:15; Ps. 38:8; 39:6; 42:5, 11; 43:5; 77:3; Gen. 4:19; 50:34.

DISSEMBLE. Josh. 7:11; Ps. 26:4; Pr. 26:24; Gal. 2:13. See DECEPTION, HYPOCRISY.

DISSENSION. Acts 15:2; 23:7, 10. See QUARREL, WRANGLING.

DISSIMULATION. Gal. 2:13. See HYPOCRISY.

DISSOLVE. Job 30:22. Doubts—Dan. 5:12, 16. Earth—Ps. 75:3. Elements—II Pet. 3:10. Heavens—II Pet. 3:12. Host of heaven—Is. 34:4. House, Earthly (body)—II Cor. 5:1. Palace—Nah. 2:6.

DISTAFF. Pr. 31:19.

DISTIL. Deut. 32:2; Job 36:27.

DISTINCTION. Ex. 9:4; Lev. 20:25; Acts 11:12; 15:9; Rom. 3:22; 10:12; I Cor. 14:7; Jas. 2:4. See DIFFERENCE.

DISTINCTLY. Neh. 8:8.

DISTINGUISHED. Dan. 6:3.

DISTRACT. Pr. 88:15.

DISTRESS. Gen. 42:21; Deut. 28:53; Ju. 11:7; I Sam. 22:2; II Chr. 15:4; 32:12; Ps. 4:1; 49:17; Lam. 1:20. In time of—Gen. 35:3; Ju. 10:14; II Chr. 15:4; Ob. 12. In distress and anguish—Job 15:24; Prov. 1:27. In distress and darkness—Ps. 107:12. Saved out of—Ps. 107:2.

DISTRICT. Neh. 3:14.

DISTRIBUTE, DISTRIBUTION. Brethren, Unto—Neh. 13:13. God hath, As—I Cor. 7:17. Inheritances—Josh. 13: 32; 14:1. Loaves and fishes—John 6: 11. Ablutions—II Chr. 31:14. Officers of the temple—II Chr. 23:18. Poor, Unto—Neh. 13:13; Lu. 18:22. Acts 4:35; Rom. 12:13; II Cor. 9:15; I Tim. 6:18. Sorrows—Job 21:17. See APPORTION, DIVIDE.

DITCH. Deep—Pr. 23:27. Fallen into—Ps. 7:15. Plunge me in—Job 9:31.

DIVERS. Colors—I Chr. 29:2; Ez. 17: 3. Manners—Heb. 1:1. Places, In—Mt. 24:7; Mk. 13:8; Lu. 21:11. Washings—Heb. 9:10.

DIVERSE. Beast—Dan. 7:3, 7, 19. Kind—Lev. 19:19. King—Dan. 7:24. Kingdom—Dan. 7:23. Laws—Esth. 3:8. Vessels—Esth. 1:7.

DIVERSITIES. Gifts, Of—I Cor. 12:4. Workings—I Cor. 12:6.

DIVIDE. Child—I Ki. 3:25, 26. Christ, Is—I Cor. 1:13. See UNITY. Church—See UNITY. City—Mt. 12:25. Concubine—Ju. 19:29. Day from night—Gen. 1:14. Death, Not in—II Sam. 1:23. Earth—Gen. 10:25; I Chr. 1:19.

Families—Gen. 10:32. Father against son—Lu. 12:53. Fields—Mic. 2:4. Fishes—Mk. 6:41. Flames—Ps. 29:7. Gifts—I Cor. 12:11. Hair—Ez. 5:1. Heart—Hos. 10:2. House—Mt. 12:25; Mk. 3:25; Lu. 11:17; 12:52. Hoof—Lev. 11:4-7, 26; Deut. 14:7, 8. Inheritance—Deut. 32:8; Ps. 78:55; Lu. 12: 13, 14; 22:17. See INHERITANCE, ISRAEL. Isles of Gentiles—Gen. 10:5. Kingdom—Dan. 2:41; 5:28; 11:4; Mt. 12:25; Mk. 3:24; Lu. 11:17. See ISRAEL. Land—II Sam. 19:29; Dan. 11: 39; Amos 7:17. See ISRAEL. Light from darkness—Gen. 1:4, 18. Multitude—Acts 14:4; 23:7. Offering—See OFFERING. Portion with the great—Is. 53:12. Prey—Num. 31:27. Satan—Mt. 12:25; Mk. 3:26; Lu. 11:18. Sea—Ex. 14:16; Neh. 9:11; Job 26:12; Ps. 74:13; 78:13; 136:13; Jer. 31:35. Shechem—Ps. 60:6; 108:7. Sheep—Mt. 25:32. Silver—Job 27:17. Simeon and Levi—Gen. 49:7. Soul and spirit—Heb. 4:12. Spoil—Gen. 49:27; Ex. 15: 9; Josh. 22:8; Ju. 5:30; Ps. 68:12; Pr. 16:19; Is. 9:3; 33:23; 53:12. Zech. 14:1; Lu. 11:22. Tongue—Ps. 55:9. See Acts 2:3. Veil—Ex. 26:33. Waters—Gen. 1:6, 7; Is. 63:12. Word of truth—II Tim. 2:15. See ALLOT, APPORTION, CASTING LOTS, DISTRIBUTE.

DIVINE. Nature—II Pet. 1:4. Power—II Pet. 1:3. Service—Heb. 9:1.

DIVINE, DIVINATION. See MAGIC.

DIVINITY. Rom. 1:20.

DIVISION. Disciples, Among—Rom. 16: 17; I Cor. 1:10; 3:3; 11:18. See FACTIONS, UNITY. Jesus came to bring—Lu. 12:51. Jews, Among—John 10:19. Land, Of—See ISRAEL. Multitude, In—John 7:43. Pharisees, Among—John 9:16. Priest, Of—See PRIESTS.

DIVORCE. Ex. 21:7-11; Deut. 21:14; 22:13-19, 28, 29; 24:1-4; 28:1-4; Mt. 5:31, 32; 19:3-9; Mk. 10:2-12; Lu. 16: 18; Rom. 7:2, 3; I Cor. 7:10-17. Moses allowed divorce because of the hardness of heart of the Jew—Mt. 19:8. Adultery breaks the marriage bond—Mt. 19:9.

DIZAHAB, di'za-häb. Deut. 1;1.

DOCTORS OF THE LAW. Were teachers of the law.—Lu. 2:46; 5:17; I Tim. 1:7. Lawyers—Mt. 22:35; Lu. 7:30;

11:46; 14:3; Tit. 3:13. See LAW, IN-STRUCTION.

DOCTRINE. In the gospels "teaching" is the word used to express what Jesus taught, not yet formulated into specific doctrines. See JESUS, TEACHING OF. The apostles had the living word and the following generation the inspired utterances of apostles and spirit-filled men. Doctrine in its usual sense occurs only in the later pastoral epistles—I Tim. 1:3; 1:10; 4:6, 13; 6:3; II Tim. 3:6; Tit. 1:9; 2:7, 10. Used in a disparaging sense—Mt. 15: 9; Mk. 7:7; Eph. 4:14; Col. 2:22. Meaning instruction—Deut. 32:2; Job 11:4; Prov. 4:2; Is. 29:24. First principles of—Heb. 6:1. False doctrine, called heresy—II Pet. 2:1.

False doctrine, to be avoided.—I Tim. 1:4; II Tim. 4:3; Rev. 2:14. Teachers of, described—Acts 20:29, II Cor. 11: 13; I Tim. 6:3, 4; II Tim. 3:8; Tit. 1: 11; II Pet. 2:3; Jude 4, 8.

DODAI, dō′dāi. I Chr. 27:4. See DODO.

DODANIM, dŏd′a-nim. Gen. 10:4.

DODAVAHU, dŏd-av′ă-hu. II Chr. 20:37.

DODO, dō′do. Grandfather of Tolah, a judge—Ju. 10:1; II Sam. 23:24.

DOEG, dō′eg. Chief of Saul's herdsmen —I Sam. 22:18.

DOER. Evil—Job 8:20; Ps. 26:5; II Tim. 2:9. See SIN, WICKED. Law, Of the—Rom. 2:13; Jas. 4:11. See OBEDIENCE. Wicked—Ps. 101:8; Pr. 17:4. See SIN, WICKED. Word, Of the—Jas. 1:20, 23. See OBEDIENCE. Worketh, That—Jas. 12:25.

DOG. Watchers of flocks.—Job 30:1. **Of houses.**—Is. 56:10.

Noted for noise.—Ps. 59:6, 14, 15. **For savageness.**—Ps. 22:16, 20.

Devours dead bodies.—Jezebel's—I Ki. 21:19, 23; II Ki. 9:10, 36. Jeroboam's posterity—I Ki. 14:11. Baasha's posterity—I Ki. 16:4. Ahab's posterity —I Ki. 21:24.

Things torn by beasts given to.—Ex. 22: 31; Lev. 7:24.

Fond of blood.—I Ki. 21:19; 22:38. Licks wounds—Lu. 16:21.

Used to belittle one.—I Sam. 17:43; 24: 14; II Sam. 3:8; 9:8; 16:9; II Ki. 8:13.

Despised by Israelites.—II Sam. 3:8. Price of, may not pay a vow (fig.)— Deut. 23:18. Unholy sacrifice—Is. 66:3.

Israel protected against.—Ex. 11:7. Judah threatened—Jer. 15:3.

Returns to its vomit.—Pr. 26:11; II Pet. 2:22.

Illustrative of.—Humble recipients of Jesus—Mt. 15:26-27; Mk. 7:27-28. Unwise interference—Pr. 26:17. Of Jehovah's watchmen—Is. 56:10-11. Of enemies—Phil. 3:2. Of castaways —Rev. 22:15. Drinking habit used to select warriors—Ju. 7:5-7.

DOING. According to—Hos. 12:2; Zech. 1:6; Ez. 24:14. Against, Are—Is. 3:8. Amend—Jer. 7:5; 26:13; 35:15. Beset —Hos. 7:2. Canaan, Of—Lev. 18:3. Consider of—Ps. 64:9. Corrupt—Ez. 20:44; Zeph. 3:7. Declare—Ps. 9:11; Is. 12:4. Egypt, Of—Lev. 18:3. Evil —I Sam. 25:3; Jer. 4:4; 21:12; 23:2, 22; 25:5; 44:22. Fruit of—Is. 3:10; Jer. 17:10; 21:14; 32:19. Mic. 7:13. Israel—II Chr. 17:4. Known by—Pr. 20:11. Remember—Ez. 36:31; 20:43. Requite—Hos. 4:9 (A.V.). See Ez. 14: 22, 23. Shame, Put to—Zeph. 3:1 (A.V.). Sins appear in—Ez. 21:24. Terrible in—Ps. 66:5. Well—Rom. 2:7; Gal. 6:9. Wickedness of—Hos. 9:15.

DOLEFUL. Creatures—Is. 13:21. Lamentation—Mic. 2:4.

DOMINION. Eph. 1:21. Col. 1:16. According to—Dan. 11:4. All—II Ki. 20: 13; Is. 39:2; Dan. 7:27. Death hath no —Rom. 6:9. Earth, To end of—Dan. 4: 22. Everlasting—Dan. 4:34; 7:14. Forever—I Pet. 4:11; 5:11; Jude 25; Rev. 1:6. Generation, From—Dan. 4:3. Given—Dan. 7:6, 14. Great—Dan. 11: 3, 5. Have—Gen. 1:26, 28; 37:8. Num. 24:19; I Ki. 4:24; Ps. 8:6; 49:14. Israel was his—Ps. 114:2. Kingdoms of —Jer. 34:1. Land of—I Ki. 9:19; II Chr. 8:6; Jer. 51:28. Places of—Ps. 103:22. Region, Over—I Ki. 4:24. Sea to sea, From—Zech. 9:10. Taken away —Dan. 7:12, 26.

DOOMED. I Cor. 4:9. See CONDEMNATION, SIN.

DOOR. Gen. 19:9; Ex. 12:23; Job 31: 34; Ps. 141:3; 26:14; Song of Sol. 5:4; 8:9; Ez. 8:8.

At the door.—Acts 5:9. Base men—Gen. 19:6, 9–11; Ju. 19:22, 26, 27. Beggar laid at door of the temple—Acts 3:2. Child dies—I Ki. 14:17. Colt tied—Mk. 11:4. Damsel stoned—Deut. 22:21. Ear punched—Deut. 15:17. Every man—Ex. 33:8, 10; Num. 11:10. Jeroboam, Wife of—I Ki. 14:6. Jesus—Mt. 24:33; Mk. 13:20; Jas. 5:9; Rev. 3:20. Joseph's door—Gen. 43:19. King's house—II Sam. 11:9. Multitude gathered—Mk. 1:33; 2:2. Naaman—II Ki. 5:9, 10. Neighbor's—Job 31:9. Peter—John 18:16, 17; Acts 12:13. Pillar of cloud—Ex. 33:9. Priests—Neh. 3:20, 21. Shunammite woman—II Ki. 4:15. Sin coucheth—Gen. 4:7. Tower, Of—Ju. 9:52. Wisdom—Pr. 9:14.

Entrance by.—John 10:1; Rev. 3:20.

Everlasting.—Ps. 24:7.

Jesus the door.—John 10:

Open.—II Ki. 9:3, 10; Acts 12:16; 14:27; 16:26; I Cor. 16:9; II Cor. 2:12; Col. 4:3; Rev. 3:8, 20; 4:1.

Shut.—Gen. 19:6, 10; II Sam. 13:17, 18; II Ki. 4:4, 5, 21, 33; 9:3, 10; Neh. 6:10; Mal. 1:10; Mt. 6:6; 25:10; Lu. 11:7; 13:25; John 20:19, 26; Acts 21:30.

DOOR OF: Ark.—Gen. 6:16.

Court.—Ez. 8:3, 7.

Gate.—Ju. 16:3; I Sam. 21:13; I Chr. 22:3; Ez. 8:3, 14; 11:1; Acts 12:13.

Hope.—Hos. 2:15.

House.—Lev. 14:38; Josh. 2:19; Ju. 19:27; I Sam. 3:15; II Ki. 5:9; II Chr. 28:24; 29:3; Neh. 3:20; Pr. 5:8; 9:14; Ez. 33:30; 47:1.

Sheepfold.—John 10:1, 2, 7, 9.

Tabernacle.—Ex. 40:6, 29.

Temple.—I Ki. 6:8, 34; Neh. 6:10; Ez. 8:14, 16; 40:13; 41:11, 16, 17, 20, 24, 25; 42:2, 11, 12; 46:3; Acts 3:2. Of gold—I Ki. 7:50; II Ki. 18:16.

Tent.—Ex. 33:8, 10; Num. 11:10; 16:27; Ju. 4:20. Jehovah appears at—Gen. 18:1, 2, 10; 26:25; Deut. 31:15. Of the Tent of Meeting—Ex. 26:36; 29:4, 10, 11, 32, 42; 33:9, 10; 35:15; 36:37; 38:8, 30; 39:38; 40:5, 6, 12, 28, 29; Lev. 1:3, 5; 3:2; 4:4, 7, 18; 8:3, 4, 31, 33, 35; 10:7; 12:6; 14:11, 23; 15:14, 29; 16:7; 17:4, 5, 6, 9; 19:21; Num. 3:25, 26; 4:25, 26; 6:10, 13, 18; 10:3; 12:5; 16:18, 19, 50; 20:6; 25:6; 27:2; Josh. 19:57; I Sam. 2:22; I Chr. 9:21.

Tomb.—Mt. 27:60; Mk. 15:46; 16:3.

Doorkeeper.—I Ki. 14:27, 28; I Chr. 15:18; Ps. 84:10; Acts 12:6. See PORTER.

Door-posts.—Ex. 21:6; Deut. 11:20; I Ki. 6:33.

DOPHKAH, dŏph'kah. Num. 33:12.

DOR, dôr. Josh. 11:2.

DORCAS, dôr-kas. **A female disciple who was charitable to the poor, restored to life by Peter.**—Acts 9:36–40.

DOTHAN. Town near Shechem—Gen. 37:17; II Ki. 6:13.

DOTING. Ez. 23:11; I Tim. 6:4.

DOUBLE. Breastplate—Ex. 39:9. Destruction—Gen. 17:18. Dream—Gen. 41:32. Heart—I Chr. 12:33; Ps. 12:2. Hire—Deut. 15:18. Honor—I Tim. 5:17. Minded—Ps. 119:113; Jas. 1:8; 4:8. See HYPOCRISY. Money—Gen. 43:12. Pay—Ex. 22:4. Portion—Deut. 21:17; II Ki. 2:9. Possession—Is. 61:7. Render—Zech. 9:12; Rev. 18:6. Restore—Ex. 22:4, 7, 9. Sins, For—Is. 40:2; Jer. 16:18. Tongued—I Tim. 3:8.

DOUBT. Gen. 37:33; Deut. 28:66; Dan. 5:12, 16; John 13:22; Acts 28:4; Rom. 14:23; Jas. 1:6; Jude 22. Christ—Mt. 14:31; 21:21; 28:17; Mk. 11:23; Lu. 12:29; Acts 10:20. See DISBELIEF, FAITH, PERPLEX.

DOUBTLESS. Job 38:1; Ps. 126:6; Lu. 4:23. See CERTAINLY, SURELY, VERIFY.

DOUGH. See BREAD.

DOVE: Dwells in rocks.—Song of Sol. 2:14; Jer. 48:28. **Frequents streams and rivers.**—Song of Sol. 5:12.

Emblem of peace.—Gen. 8:7–12.

Sent out of ark.—Gen. 8:8–12.

Clean and used as food.—Gen. 14:11.

Easily domesticated.—Is. 60:8.

Characteristics.—As harmless as doves—Mt. 10:16. Like a silly dove—Hos. 7:11. Gregarious—Is. 60:8. Timid—Ps. 74:19; Jer. 48:28; Hos. 11:11. Fleeing before danger—Ps. 11:1, 2.

Mourning like a dove.—Nah. 2:7; Ez. 7:16. Weariness—Ps. 55:6; Is. 38:14.

Used in sacrifices.—Gen. 15:9; Lev. 1:14; 5:7, 11; 12:6–8; Num. 6:10; Lu. 2:24.

Sold in temple for use in offerings.—Mt. 21:12; Mk. 11:15; John 2:14.

Holy Spirit descends in form of a dove.—Mt. 3:16; Lu. 3:22; John 1:32.

DOWN. Lain—Job 3:13. Ran—Mt. 8: 32; Mk. 5:13; Lu. 8:33. Stooped—John·8:6. Sun—II Sam. 3:35. Tossed up and—Ps. 109:23. Thread—Is. 18:7. See BREAK DOWN, CAST DOWN.

DOWNSITTING. Ps. 139:2.

DOWRY. Gen. 30:20. See MARRIAGE.

DRAG. Jer. 49:20; 50:45; Hab. 1:15, 16; John 21:8; Acts 8:3; 17:6; Lu. 12:58. Paul—Acts 14:19; 16:19; 21: 30. See DRAW.

DRAGON. Rev. 12:3, 4, 7, 9, 16, 17; 12: 9; 13:2; 20:2, 7. See SERPENTS.

DRAIN. Lev. 1:15; 5:9; Ps. 73:10; Is. 51:17; Ez. 23:34.

DRAM. See MONEY.

DRANK. Gen. 24:46; 27:25; 43:34; Num. 20:11; II Sam. 12:3; I Ki. 13: 19; 17:6; Lu. 17:27, 28; John 4:12. Disciples—Mk. 14:23. Rock, Of—I Cor. 10:4. Wine—Gen. 9:21; Deut. 32:38; Dan. 1:5, 8; 5:1–4. See DRINK, DRUNKENNESS.

DRAUGHT. II Ki. 10:27; Mt. 15:17. Fish, Of—Lu. 5:4, 9. See John 21:6.

DRAW. Back—Lam. 2:3. Bow—II Chr. 18:33; Is. 66:19. City, From—Ju. 20:32; Josh. 8:6. Cords, With—Hos. 11:4. Disciples—Acts 20:30. Evening, Toward—Ju. 19:9. Father, The—John 6:44. Hand, Back—Gen. 38:29; Josh. 8:26. Heaven, Into—Acts 11:10. Iniquity—Is. 5:18. Jeremiah—Jer. 38:13. Loving-kindness, With—Jer. 31:3. Men, All—John 12: 32. Net, Into—Ps. 10:9. John—21: 11. Stars—Rev. 12:4. Sword—See SWORD. Syrians—I Chr. 19:16. Water—Gen. 24:13, 19, 20, 43, 45; I Sam. 7:6; 9:11; II Sam. 23:16; I Chr. 11:18; Is. 12:3; John 4:7.

DRAW NIGH. Is. 41:5; Ex. 3:5; Ps. 119:150. Abraham—Gen. 18:23. Bethphage, Unto—Lu. 19:29. Counsel of Holy One—Is. 5:19. David, To meet —I Sam. 17:48. Day—Ez. 7:12; 22:4. Decree—Esth. 5:2. Feast of unleavened bread—Lu. 22:1. Fruit, Time of —Mt. 21:34. Gates of death—Ps. 107: 18. God, Unto—I Sam. 14:36; Ps. 73: 28; Jas. 4:8. Heart, With—Heb. 10: 22. Jerusalem, Unto—Mt. 21:1. Jesus, Unto—Lu. 22:47. Philistine—I Sam. 17:41. Pharaoh—Ex. 14:10. Promise, Time of—Acts 7:17. Pub-

licans—Lu. 15:1. Redemption—Lu. 21:28. Sheol, Unto—Ps. 88:3. Soul—Ps. 69:18. Time—Gen. 47:29. Years—Eccl. 12:1.

DRAW OUT. John 2:8; 4:11. Anger—Ps. 85:5. Counsel—Pr. 20:5. Joseph —Gen. 37:28. Lamb—Ex. 12:21. Soul —Is. 58:10. Spear—Ps. 35:3. Sword—See SWORD. Vessels—Hag. 2:16. Waters —II Sam. 22:17; Ps. 18:16.

DRAWERS. Waters, Of—Deut. 29:11; Josh. 9:21, 23, 27.

DRAWN. Jer. 22:19; Job 20:25; Deut. 30:17. Breasts, From—Is. 28:9. City, Away from—Josh. 8:16; Ju. 20:31. Lust, By—Jas. 1:14. Sword—Is. 21: 15; Ez. 21:28; Num. 22:23, 31; Josh. 5:13; I Chr. 21:16.

DREAD. Make afraid—Job 13:21. Beast, Upon—Job 13:11. Jehovah be your—Is. 8:13. Land, Upon—Deut. 11:25.

DREADFUL. God—Dan. 9:4. Place—Gen. 28:17. Rings—Ez. 1:18.

DREAMS. Sent from God to Abimelech —Gen. 20:3, 6. Jacob's ladder—Gen. 28:12. Jacob's dream of cattle—Gen. 31:10. God came to Laban in a dream —Gen. 31-24. Joseph's dream—Gen. 37:5–10. Of Pharaoh's baker and butler—Gen. 40:5–19. Of Pharaoh—Gen. Ch. 41. The Midianite—Ju. 7:13. Solomon—I Ki. 3:5–15. Nebuchadrezzar's dream of an image—Dan. Ch. 2. Of a great tree—Dan. 4:9–18. Daniel—Dan. Ch. 7. The Lord will speak in a dream —Num. 12:6; Job 33:14–16. Joseph—Mt. 1:20, 21; 2:13, 19, 22. Wise men —Mt. 2:12. Pilate's wife—Mt. 27:19. Vanity of dreams—Job 20:8; Ps. 73: 20; Eccl. 5:3; Is. 29:7, 8; Jer. 23:28; Zech. 10:2. And your men shall dream dreams—Joel 2:28; Acts 2:17.

Appearances.—Gen. 12:7; 17:1; 18:1; 26:2, 24; 32:24–30; 35:9, etc., are instances of miraculous appearances, made to persons in normal condition. Dreams and visions seem to be employed in Scripture often as synonymous, but strictly speaking a communication by dream is to one asleep; by vision, to one in a rapt or supernormal condition while awake. See APPEARANCES OF GOD, VISIONS.

DREGS. Ps. 75:8.

DRESS. Gen. 2:15; II Sam. 12:4; I Ki. 18:25. See CLOTHING, WOMEN.

DRESSER. Amos 7:14.

DRIED. Arm—Zech. 11:17. Bones— Ez. 37:11. Brooks—I Ki. 17:7; Joel 1:20. Earth—Gen. 8:14. Grapes— Num. 6:3. Hand—I Ki. 13:4. Pastures—Jer. 23:10. Rivers—Is. 19:5, 6. Root—Job 18:16; Hos. 9:16. Sea— Ps. 106:9; Is. 51:10. Soul—Num. 11: 6. Strength—Ps. 22:15. Throat—Ps. 69:3. Waters—Gen. 8:7, 8, 13; Jer. 18: 14; 30:38. Wine—Joel 1:10. Withes —Ju. 16:7, 8. See DROUGHT, DRY, FAMINE, PARCHED, WITHER.

DRIFT AWAY. Heb. 2:1.

DRINK. Apostles with Jesus.—Acts 10:41.

Bitter water.—Num. 5:24-27.

Blood.—Ps. 50:13; Ez. 39:17-19. Of Jesus—John 6:53-56. See SPIRITUAL.

Commanded to give.—Pr. 25:21; Mt. 25: 35-45; Rom. 12:20.

Did not.—Ex. 34:28; Deut. 9:9, 18; II Sam. 23:16, 17; I Ki. 13:8, 9, 16-18; I Chr. 11:18, 19; Ezra 10:6; Esth. 4:16. See THIRST. Days, Like—Ju. 7:5, 6.

Eat and drink.—Ex. 24:1; 32:6; Ju. 9: 27; II Sam. 11:13; I Ki. 1:25; 13:22; 18:41, 42; II Ki. 6:22; 7:8; 9:34; I Chr. 29:23; II Chr. 28:15; Acts 9:9; 23:12, 21; Rom. 14:17; I Cor. 15:32. Have no anxiety for—Mt. 6:25, 31; Lu. 12:29, 30. Right of—I Cor. 9:4. To the glory of God—I Cor. 10:31. Place of—I Cor. 11:22. Warning— Col. 2:16.

Fear and trembling, With.—Ez. 4:16; 12:18, 19. Gall, Water of—Jer. 8:14; 9:15; 23:15.

Golden calf, Ashes of.—Ex. 32:20.

Golden vessels, From.—Dan. 5:2.

Jesus, Given to.—Wine mingled with gall—Mt. 27:34. Vinegar—Mt. 27:48; Mk. 15:36. Wine mingled with myrrh —Mk. 15:23.

No water to drink.—Ex. 7:18, 21, 24; 15: 23, 24; 17:1, 2, 6; Num. 20:5, 8, 17; 33:14. See THIRST.

Offering.—See OFFERING.

Pleasure, Of water of.—Ps. 36:8.

Poisonous.—Mk. 16:18.

Publicans and sinners, With.—Lu. 5:30.

Samaritan woman, Jesus with.—John 4:7-9.

Rock, Of.—Ex. 17:6; Ps. 78:15; 105:41; 114:8; Is. 48:21; I Cor. 10:4. **Samaritan woman, Jesus with.**—John 4:7-9.

Strong drink.—Lu. 1:15; 12:45; 17:8; Rom. 14:21. See DRUNKENNESS, WINE.

Weary, To—Job 22:7.

Figurative.—Blood—John 6:53-56; **Rev.** 16:6. Cup that Jesus drank—Mt. 20: 22, 23; Mk. 10:38, 39; John 18:11. Sorrow—Ez. 23:32, 34. Sweet—Neh. 8: 10, 12. Tears—Ps. 80:5; 102:9. Wrath —Job 21:20; Jer. 25:15-17; 26:28; 49: 12; Rev. 14:8, 10.

Spiritual.—I Cor. 10:4, 21; 12:13. Living water—John 4:10-15; 7:37-38. The cup that Jesus drank—Mt. 20:22, 23; Mk. 10:38, 39; John 18:11. Promise to disciples—Lu. 22:30. Wine in the Lord's Supper—Mt. 26:27-29; Mk. 14:23-25; Lu. 22:18-20; I Cor. 11: 25-29.

Illustrative.—A cup of cold water—Mt. 10:42; Mk. 9:41. *Given to the thirsty*— Mt. 25:35, 37, 42. Jesus' sorrow—Mt. 26:42. Of worldly—I Cor. 10:7. Cup of demons—I Cor. 10:21. Drinking of wine—I Tim. 5:23.

DRIVE, DRIVEN. Acts 27:15, 17; Deut. 4:19. Angel, By—Ps. 35:5. Army, Northern—Joel 2:20. Away—Ez. 34: 4, 16. Cart—II Sam. 6:3; I Chr. 13:7. Chaff—Ps. 1:4; Hos. 13:13. Darkness, Into—Is. 8:22; Job 18:18. Eden, Out of—Gen. 3:23, 24. Demon, Of—Lu. 8: 29. Fields—Is. 19:7. Flocks—I Sam. 30:20; Jer. 23:2. Foolishness—Pr. 22:15. Israel and Judah by Jehovah —Deut. 30:1; II Ki. 17:21; Is. 59:19; Jer. 8:3; 16:15; 23:38; 24:9; 29:14, 15; 32:37; 46:15, 28; Ez. 4:13; Dan. 9:7. Jehu, Of—II Ki. 9:20. Jews—II Ki. 16:6. Jordan—Ps. 114:3, 5. Judgment seat, From—Acts 18:16. Leaves —Lev. 26:36. Men, From—Dan. 4:33. Nations—Ps. 80:8; Hab. 3:6. Nebuchadrezzar—Dan. 4:25, 32. Ship—Acts 27:39. Smoke—Ps. 68:2. Spirit, By— Mk. 1:12. Stubble—Is. 41:2. Temple, From—John 2:15. To and fro—Acts 27:27. Vapor—Pr. 21:6. Wicked, By —Ps. 36:11. Wind, By—Jas. 1:6; 3:4. Wisdom—Job 6:13. See THRUST.

DRIVE OUT. Josh 3:10; 14:12; Ju. 1: 32; Jer. 27:10, 15; 49:5. Amorite— Ex. 34:11. Asher—Ju. 1:31. Ashdod—Zeph. 2:4. Before you—Josh 24:12, 18. Canaanite—Ex. 33:2; Josh. 16:10; Ju. 1:29. Egypt, Of—Num. 22: 11. Enemies—Num. 32:21. Ephraim —Ju. 1:29. Ground, From face of— Gen. 4:14. Hastily—Ju. 2:23. Hivite —Ex. 23:28. Hornets—Josh. 24:12. House, Of—Hos. 9:15. Inhabitants— Num. 33:52, 55; Josh. 17:12; Ju. 1:19, 27. Jebusites—Ju. 1:21. Jehovah— Josh. 23:9, 13. Judah, Children of— Josh. 15:63. Land, Of—Ex. 6:1; Num. 22:6. Man—Gen. 3:24. Nations—Ju. 2:21; Ps. 808; I Chr. 17:21; Naphtali —Ju. 1:33. Pharaoh's presence, From —Ex. 10:11. Utterly—Josh. 17:13; Ju. 1:28. Wickedness, For—Ez. 31:11. Zebulun—Ju. 1:30.

DRIVER. I Ki. 22:34; II Chr. 18:33; Job 39:7.

DROMEDARY. Is. 60:6; Jer. 2:23. See CAMEL.

DROP. Ju. 5:14; Ps. 65:11, 12; Joel 3: 18; Amos 9:13. Blood, Of—Lu. 22:44. Bucket, Of a—Is. 40:15. Dew—Deut. 33:28; Job 38:28; Pr. 3:20. Doctrine —Deut. 32:2. Honey—I Sam. 14:26; Pr. 5:3; Song of Sol. 4:11. Myrrh— Song of Sol. 5:5, 13. Water, Of—Ju. 5:4; Job 36:27, 28; Ps. 68:8; Pr. 27:15. Word—Ez. 20:46; 21:2; Amos 7:16.

DROPSY. Lu. 14:2. See DISEASE.

DROSS. Pr. 25:4; Is. 1:22, 25. Wicked like—Ps. 119:119; Pr. 26:23; Ez. 22: 18, 19.

DROUGHT. Gen. 31:40; Job 24:19; Ps. 32:4; Jer. 2:6; 14:1; 17:8; 50:38; Hos. 13:5; Hab. 1:11. See DRY, FAMINE.

DROWN. Song of Sol. 8:7; I Tim. 6:9.

DROWSINESS. Pr. 23:21. See SLEEP.

DRUNKENNESS. Curse of.—Shall not enter heaven—Deut. 29:19, 20 (marg.); I Cor. 6:10; Gal. 5:21. Consumed— Nah. 1:10. Stoned to death—Deut. 21:20, 21. Trodden upon—Is. 28:3. Cut asunder—Mt. 24:49-51; Lu. 12:45, 46. Sorrows of—Pr. 23:29-35; Is. 5:11, 22; 28:1; Hos. 7:13, 14; Joel 1:5; Hab. 2:15, 17. Made sick by—Hos. 7:5.

Disgrace of.—Lawbreakers—Pr. 31:5; Is. 28:1. Loss of battle—I Ki. 20:16. Destroys judgment—Is. 28:1; Hos. 4:

11. Idolatrous revelry—Is. 56:12; Amos 2:8, 12; 6:6, 7; Mic. 2:11. Shall not be rich—Pr.21:17; 23:21. Neglects duty—Mt. 24:49, 50. Praise ye not— I Cor. 11:21. Mockery of drunkards —Ps. 69:12; Pr. 20:1; I Pet. 4:3-5. Sold a girl for wine—Joel 3:3. Who shall be given drink?—*They that are perishing*—Pr. 31:6. *They that are poor*—Pr. 31:7. Do not eat with—I Cor. 5:11. The priest and prophets err through—Is. 28:7. Take heed lest ye be overcome with—Lu. 21:34; Rom. 13:13; Eph. 5:18. Drunken in night— I Thess. 5:7, 8. Woe unto makers of —Hab. 2:15, 17.

Abstinence. — Nazirite vow against — Num. 6:3; Ju. 13:7-14. Rechabites— Jer. Ch. 35. Hebrew children—Dan. 1:5. Accused of—Acts 2:13-15. Princes eat not for—Eccl. 10:17. Wine a poison—Deut. 32:33. Princes and wise men made drunk—Jer. 51:57.

Examples of.—Noah—Gen. 9:21. Lot— Gen. 19:33. Nabal—I Sam. 25:36. Uriah—II Sam. 11:13. Elah—I Ki. 16: 9. Benhadad—I Ki. 20:16. Ahasuerus —Esth. 1:10, 11. Belshazzar—Dan. 5:1-6. Princes of Israel—Hos. 7:5. Corinthians—I Cor. 11:21.

Warnings against.—Pr. 20:1; Lu. 21:34; Rom. 13:13; Eph. 5:18; I Thess. 5:7, 8; Tit. 2:2, 3. Avoiding—Pr. 23:31. Change of character—I Sam. 25:3, 36. Cruelty—Mk. 6:2. Disarms—II Sam. 13:28, 29. Danger—Lev. 10:8, 9. Degrades—Esth. 1:10, 11. Forgetfulness —Pr. 31:4, 5. Poison of—Pr. 23:32. Shameless—Esth. 1:10, 11. Profanity —Dan. 5:1, 2.

Figurative.—Deut. 32:42; Is. 63:6; 51: 17; 24:20; Job 12:25.

DRUSILLA, dru-sĭl'lă. **Daughter of Agrippa.**—Acts 24:24. See HEROD.

DRY. Job 12:15; 13:25; 15:30; Is. 42: 15; 44:27; 50:2; Hos. 13:15; Zeph. 2: 13. Bones—Ez. 37:2, 4. Fleece—Ju. 6:37, 38, 40. Land—Gen. 1:9, 10; 7:22; 8:13; Ex. 4:9; 14:16, 21, 22, 29; 15: 19; Josh. 3:17; 4:18, 22; II Ki. 2:8; Neh. 9:10; Ps. 63:1; 66:6; 95:5; 105: 41; 107:35; Is. 25:5; 32:2; 41:18; 44: 3; Jer. 51:43; Hos. 2:3; Jonah 1:9; 2: 10; Haz. 2:6; Heb. 11:29. Provisions— Josh. 9:5, 12; Pr. 17:1. Rivers—Josh.

3:17; 4:18, 22; Is. 44:27; Ez. 30:12; Nah. 2:4; Zech. 10:11. Sea—Jer. 51: 43; Nah. 2:4. Tree—Is. 56:3; Ez. 17: 24; 20:47; Lu. 23:31. See DROUGHT.

DRYSHOD. Is. 11:15.

DUE. Pr. 3:27; Mt. 18:34; Lu. 23:41; Rom. 13:7; I Cor. 7:3. Glory—I Chr. 16:29; Ps. 29:2; 96:8. Priests—Deut. 18:3. Season—Num. 28:2; Ps. 104:27; 145:15; Pr. 15:23; Eccl. 10:17; Mt. 24: 45; Lu. 12:42; Rom. 5:6; Gal. 6:9; I Pet. 5:6.

DUKE. Gen. 36:15–43; Ex. 15:15; Josh. 13:41; I Chr. 1:51–54.

DULCIMER. See MUSIC.

DULL. Of hearing.—Mt. 13:15; Heb. 5:11. See EARS.

DUMAH, dū′mah. (1) **Son of Ishmael.** —Gen. 25:14; I Chr. 1:30.
(2) **A city of Judah.**—Josh. 15:52.
(3) Is. 21:11.

DUMB. Jehovah makes people dumb.— Ex. 4:11; Dan. 10:15.

Cured by Jesus.—Mt. 9:32, 33; 12:22; 15:30, 31; Mk. 7:37; 9:17, 25; Lu. 11: 14.

"Opened not his mouth."—Ps. 38:13; 39:2; Pr. 31:8; Is. 53:7.

Promises concerning the.—Is. 35:6; Ez. 24:27.

As punishment.—Ez. 3:26; 33:22; Lu. 1: 20.

Idols.—Hab. 2:18; I Cor. 12:2. Animals —Acts 8:32; II Pet. 2:16.

With silence.—Ps. 39:2.

Figurative.—Ps. 38:13. Dogs—Is. 56:10. Stone—Hab. 2:19.

DUNG. I Ki. 14:10; II Ki. 6:25; 9:37; 18:27; Job 20:7; Ps. 83:10; Jer. 8:2; 9:22; 16:4; 25:33; Ez. 4:12, 15; Zeph. 1:17; Mal. 2:3; Lu. 13:8. Offering, In —Ex. 29:14; Lev. 4:11; 8:17; 16:27. See REFUSE.

DUNG-GATE. Neh. 2:13; 3:13, 14; 12: 31.

DUNG-HILL. I Sam. 2:8; Ezra 6:11; Ps. 113:7; Is. 25:10; Lam. 4:5; Dan. 2:5; 3:29; Lu. 4:35.

DUNGEON. Brought out of—Gen. 4:14. Captive in—Ex. 12:29. Cut off life in—Lam. 3:53. Low—Lam. 3:55. Malchijah, Of—Jer. 38:6. Put into—Gen. 40:15; Jer. 38:9, 11. Jeremiah—Jer. 37:16; 38:7, 10, 13. See PRISON.

DURA, dū′rä. **Image set up at.**—Dan. 3:1.

DURABLE. Pr. 8:18; Is. 23:8.

DURST. Esth. 7:5; Mt. 22:46; John 21:12; Acts 5:13. See DARE.

DUST. Laws concerning.—Lev. 17:13; Num. 5:17.

Man made of.—Gen. 2:7; 3:19; Job. 10: 9; Ps. 103:14; Eccl. 3:20. Man to return to dust—Gen. 3:19; Job 17:16; 20:11; 21:26; 34:16; Ps. 104:29; Eccl. 12:7.

Symbolic of: Dust upon the head, grief —Josh. 7:6; Job 2:12; 5:6; Lam. 2:10; Ez. 27:30. Prostrating in dust, humility—Job 7:21; 16:15; 42:6; Ps. 44:25; Lam. 3:29; Mic. 1:10. Scorn—II Sam. 16:13; II Ki. 23:12; II Chr. 34:4; Mt. 10:14; Mk. 6:11; Lu. 9:5; 10:11; Acts 13:51; 22:23.

Prophecies concerning.—Brought down to dust as punishment—Is. 25:12; 26: 5, 19; 29:4, 5; 34:7, 9; 40:12, 15; 41:2; 47:1; 49:23; 52:2; Ez. 24:7; 26:4, 10; Mic. 7:17.

Figurative.—Gen. 13:16; 18:27; 28:14; Num. 28:10; Deut. 9:21; 28:24; I Sam. 2:8; II Sam. 22:43; I Ki. 16:2; II Ki. 13:7; II Chr. 1:9; Job 4:19; 7:5; 27: 16; 28:6; 30:19; Ps. 7:5; 18:42; 22:15, 29; 30:9; 72:9; 78:27; 102:14; 113:7; 119:25; Nah. 1:3; Hab. 1:10; Zeph. 1:17; Zech. 9:3. Wicked to hide in— Job 40:13; Is. 2:10.

Illustrative.—Is. 5:24.

Miscellaneous.—Dust burnt—I Ki. 18: 39. Dust of Samaria—I Ki. 20:10. Crawling things of—Deut. 32:24; Mic. 7:17. Serpent shall eat—Gen. 3:14; Is. 65:25. Treasures in dust—Job 22:24. Ostrich eggs warmed in—Job 39:14. Dust in a mass—Job 38:38. Used in plague—Ex. 9:9. Dust of earth—Ex. 8:16, 17; Job 14:19; Pr. 8:26; Dan. 12: 2; Amos 2:7.

DUTY. The whole duty of men.—Eccl. 12:13.

Duties domestic—To husbands.—To respect their faith—I Ki. 11:4. To give them honor—Esth. 1:20; Eph. 5:22, 33; Col. 3:18. To win them to Christ— I Pet. 3:1. To love them—Tit. 2:4. **To wives.**—To love them—Eph. 5:25. To render her benevolence—I Cor. 7:

3. To remain faithful to her—I Cor. 7:11, 14. To trust in her—Pr. 31:11.

To children.—To teach them God's truth—Deut. 4:9; 31:12, 13; Josh. 22: 21–25; Ps. 78:1–4, 6; Pr. 22:6; Eph. 6:4. To love them—Tit. 2:4. Not to provoke to wrath—Eph. 6:4. Of children to parents: To obey them—Eph. 6:1–3; Col. 3:20; Heb. 13:17. (For servants and masters, see WORLDLY DUTIES.)

Duties of disciples.—Not to forsake assembling—Heb. 10:25. To forgive one another—Mt. 6:14, 15; Lu. 6:37; Eph. 4:32; II Cor. 2:6–11; Gal. 6:1. To fill our own sphere—I Cor. 12:13–21; II Cor. 3:4–9. To work out our own salvation—Phil. 2:12. To bear each other's burdens—Gal. 6:2. To love one another—I John 3:11, 14, 23; 4:7, 11. To love Christ—John 14:21; I John 5:1; II Cor. 5:14, 15. To love God—Mt. 22:37–40; Mk. 12:29–31. To obey those who have rule over you—Heb. 13:17.

Worldly duties. — To neighbors — Lev. 19:13–18; Mt. 19:19; 22:39; Mk. 12: 31. To strangers—Ex. 20:10; 23:12; Lev. 19:33, 34; Deut. 1:16; 10:19; Job 31:32; Mt. 25:35. To enemies—Mt. 5: 44–48; Lu. 6:27–29. To the world itself—Mt. 28:19; Mk. 16:15. To servants: Must compensate—Jer. 22:13; Col. 4:1. Pay promptly—Lev. 19:13; Deut. 24:15; Jas. 5:4. Must not oppress—Lev. 25:43; Deut. 24:14; Job 31:13–14; Pr. 22:16. Should show kindness—Philemon 10–16. To masters: To be obedient—Mt. 8:9; Eph. 6:5–8; Col. 3:22–25; I Pet. 2:18. To be trustworthy—Tit. 2:9, 10. To honor —Mal. 1:6; I Tim. 6:1, 2. See FRATERNITY, CHRISTIAN GRACES, SERVANT.

DWARF. Lev. 21:20.

DWELL. Alone—Lev. 13:46; Num. 23: 9. Carelessly—Jer. 49:21; Ez. 39:6. Christ in heart—Eph. 3:17. Corner, In a—Pr. 21:9; 25:24. Earth, On the—Rev. 3:10; 6:10; 11:10; 12:12; 13:6, 12, 14; 14:6; 17:8. Entry of sea, At—Ez. 25:3. Father, The—John 14:10, 17. See GOD. Fulness—Col. 1:19; 2:9. God —Ex. 15:17; 25:8; 29:43–46; Lev. 26: 11, 12; Num. 5:3; 35:34; I Ki. 8:13; Ps. 132:14; Mic. 1:2; Hab. 2:20; Zech.

8:3; Mt. 23:21; John 14:10, 17, 21; Acts 7:48; II Cor. 6:16; I John 4:12, 15, 16; Rev. 21:3. Here will I—Ps. 132:14. High and holy place, In—Is. 57:15. Holy Spirit—Rom. 8:9, 11; I Cor. 3:16; II Tim. 1:14; Jas. 4:5. See HOLY SPIRIT. House, In—Is. 44:13; Acts 7:48. See HOUSE. House of Jehovah, In—Ps. 23:6. See TABERNACLE, TEMPLE. Land of shadow of death, In —Is. 9:2. Light—Job 38:19. See Dan. 2:22, LIGHT. Richly — Col. 3:16. Safety, In—Deut. 12:10; 33:12, 28; Ps. 4:8; 16:9; Pr. 1:33; Jer. 23:6; 33: 16; Ez. 34:25, 28; 38:8. Satan—Rev. 2:13. Secret place, In—Ps. 91:1. Sin —Rom. 7:17, 18. See SIN. Tents, In—See TENTS. Things which ye have seen, In—Col. 2:18. Unity, Together in—Ps. 133:1. See UNITY. Unrighteousness—Job 11:14. Wilderness, In —Pr. 21:19; Is. 23:13; 32:16; Jer. 9: 26. See WILDERNESS. Wisdom with prudence—Pr. 8:12. Wolf with lamb —Is. 11:6. See ABIDE, LIFE, SOJOURN.

DWELLING-PLACE. God is thy—Deut. 33:27. Hired—Acts 28:30. Jackals, Of —Jer. 9:11. Lord, Thou hast been our —Ps. 90:1. Pluck out of—Ps. 52:5. Prudence my—Pr. 8:12. Royal—Dan. 4:30. Soul hath long had her—Ps. 120:6. Wicked, Of the—Job 8:22. See WOMEN, DWELLING OF, TEMPLE.

DYE, DYED. Garments—Is. 63:1. Ram, skins—Ex. 25:5; 26:14; 35:7; 36:19; 39:34. See ARTS AND TRADES, COLORS.

DYING. Of Jesus—II Cor. 4:10. See JESUS, DEATH OF. Dying, and behold we live—II Cor. 6:9. See NEW BIRTH, SELF-DENIAL.

DYSENTERY. Acts 28:8.

EAGLE. Training its young.—Youthful Israel—Ex. 19:4; Deut. 32:11.

Transplanting and nourishing.—Ez. 17: 3–8; Deut. 32:9–12.

Renewing, by moulting.—Israel dropping decayed powers and taking on new—Ps. 103:5. By circling flight—Pr. 30:19; Is. 40:31.

Resemblances.—To Jehovah—Ez. 1:10; 10:4, 5, 14. To Nebuchadrezzar—Dan. 4:33. To redeemed man—Rev. 4:7. To the church—Rev. 12:14.

Swiftness.—Of the flight of days—Job 9:25–26. Of the flight of riches—Pr.

23:5. Of warriors—II Sam. 1:23; Jer. 4:13; Lam. 4:19.

Fierceness.—World-powers—Deut. 28: 49–50; Jer. 48:40; Hos. 8:1–3; Hab. 1:8; Ez. 17:3–4; Dan. 7:4.

Predaceous ways.—Deut. 28:49–51; Job 39:28–30; Jer. 49:22; Ez. 17:3–4; Pr. 30:17; Mt. 24:28; Lu. 17:37.

Setting its nest in high places to avoid interruption.—Job 39:27; Jer. 49:16; Ob. 4.

Baldness of.—Shaving head in mourning—Mic. 1:16; Is. 22:12.

Forbidden as food.—Lev. 11:13; Deut. 14:12.

EAR. Attentive.—Ex. 15:26; I Sam. 3: 3–10; 9:15. (*See margin.*) Is. 6:10; 50:4–5; Neh. 1:6; Pr. 20:12; Mt. 10: 27; 11:15; 13:23; Lu. 8:15; Acts 17: 11, 12, 34; Rev. 2:7.

Blood-tipped.—Ex. 29:20; Lev. 8:23; 14:14.

Clogged.—Ps. 40:6; 115:6; 135:17; Pr. 21:13; 28:9; Is. 6:9–10; 59:1; Jer. 5: 21; 6:10; Mt. 13:14–15, 22; Mk. 4:19; Lu. 8:14; John 7:36; 8:6; Acts 7:51; 28:27.

Deaf.—Is. 35:5; 43:8; Mic. 3:1–6; Mk. 7:33; Lu. 9:44–45. See GOD, ANTHROPOMORPHISM—Gen. 1:1; TEACHING OF JESUS CONCERNING EAR.

Eager.—Is. 48:8; Pr. 25:12; Acts 10:33; 17:11–12. Inclining—Ps. 45:10; 78:1; Pr. 22:17; Is. 55:3.

Fearful.—Ex. 15:14; 20:19; Deut. 5:25; 13:11; 17:13; 19:20; 31:13; John 6:60; 9:22–23; Acts 5:13.

Gracious.—Gen. 23:13–14; Deut. 1:16–17; I Ki. 8:28–30; Job 29:11; Lu. 10:39.

Indifferent.—Ps. 115:6; Neh. 9:30; Is. 42:20; 43:8; Mt. 7:26–27; 13:12; Mk. 4:15; 8:18; Lu. 8:12; Rom. 11:8; Jas. 1:23–24.

Mistaken.—Pr. 19:27; Eccl. 7:5, 21; Is. 30:9–10; Mt. 27:46, 47; John 12:29.

Perforated.—Ex. 21:6; Deut. 15:17.

Reasonable.—Job 12:11; 29:21; 32:11; 34:3; Ps. 94:9; Pr. 1:5; 15:31; John 6:45–46; 10:21.

Unprofitable.—Mt. 13:20; Mk. 4:16–17; 6:20; Lu. 8:13; Acts 17:19, 32; 24:24–25; 26:1, 24–29.

Vicious.—Is. 33:15; Ez. 12:2; Zech. 7: 11; Lu. 4:22–23; John 7:47–48; 8:43;

10:20; Acts 7:57–58; 13:45, 50; II Tim. 4:3, 4.

EAR-RING. Gen. 35:4; Ex. 32:2, 3; Num. 31:50; Ju. 8:24–26; Is. 3:21; Ez. 16:12; Hos. 2:13.

EAR (of Grain).—Gen. 41:5–27; Ex. 9: 31; Lev. 2:14; 23:14; Deut. 23:25; Ruth 2:2; II Ki. 4:42; Job 24:24; Is. 17:5; Mt. 12:1; Mk. 4:28; Lu. 6:1.

EARLY. John 18:28. Awake—Ps. 57:8; 108:2. Cometh—John 20:1. Destroy the wicked—Ps. 101:8. Dew—Hos. 6: 4; 13:3. He was risen—Mk. 16:9. Help —Ps. 46:5. Mary cometh—John 20:1. Morning, In—I Sam. 29:10; Gen. 19: 27; Dan. 6:19. Rain—Jas. 5:7. Rise —Ps. 127:2. Satisfy us—Ps. 90:14. Tomb, At—Lu. 24:22 (A.V.). Vineyards, To—Song of Sol. 7:12. Way, On your—Ju. 19:9.

EARN. Pr. 11:18; Hag. 1:6.

EARNEST, EARNESTLY. Inheritance, Of—Eph. 1:14. Look—Lu. 22:56. Prayed—Lu. 22:44. Spirit, Of—II Cor. 1:22; 5:5.

EARTH. The creation of God.—Gen. 1:1; Ex. 20:11; 31:17; II Ki. 19:15; II Chr. 2:12; Neh. 9:6; Job 38:4; Ps. 90:2; 102:25; 104:5; 115:15; 121:2; 124:8; 134:3; 146:6; Pr. 8:26; Is. 37: 16; 42:5; 45:12, 18; Jer. 10:12; 27:5; 32:17; 51:15, 16. John 1:1–3; Acts 14: 15; Heb. 1:10; 11:3; II Pet. 3:5; Rev. 10:6; 14:7.

The residence of man.—Gen. 1:27, 28; Ps. 8:6; 115:16; Is. 42:5; 45:18.

Separated from the waters.—Gen. 1:9; Job 38:4–11; Ps. 104:6–9; Pr. 8:26–29; Jer. 5:22; II Pet. 3:5.

Functions of the earth.—Gen. 1:11, 20, 24; 2:19. Of the waters—Gen. 1:20–22.

The earth comprehensively considered. —Embraces sea, sky, etc.—Gen. 1:1, 2. Early divisions—Gen. Chs. 10 and 11.

Suspended in space.—Job 26:7.

The ancients believed it to be flat.—Job 11:9; 38:18; Rev. 4:1. That it rested on pillars—I Sam. 2:8; Ps. 75:3. That it had four corners—Is. 11:12; Rev. 7:1; 20:8.

The earth God's footstool.—Is. 66:1; Mt. 5:35; Acts 7:49.

Man formed out of earth.—Gen. 2:7; 3:19; Job 4:19; 33:6; Ps.103:14; Eccl. 3:20; 12:7; I Cor. 15:42-49; II Cor. 4:7.

Man given dominion over the earth.— Gen. 1:26, 28; Ps. 8:6-8; 115:16.

Cursed of God.—Gen. 3:17-19; 5:29; 6:7, 13. The curse removed—Gen. 8: 21, 22.

Destruction foretold.—Ps. 102:25, 26; Is. 24:19, 20; 34:4; 51:6; Mt. 5:18; 24:35; Mk. 13:31; Lu. 21:33; II Pet. 3:7, 10; Rev. 6:14; 20:11; 21:1.

A new earth foretold.—Is. 65:17; 66:22; II Pet. 3:13; Rev. 21:1.

The saints shall inherit the earth.—Ps. 25:13; Mt. 5:5.

Satan goes to and fro on the earth.— Job 1:7; 2:2; I Pet. 5:8.

The earth shall be filled with the knowledge of God.—Ps. 2:8; 22:27; 98:2, 3; Is. 11:9; 45:6; 52:10; Hab. 2:14.

EARTHEN VESSELS. Pr. 26:23; Lam. 4:2; II Cor. 4:7.

EARTHLY. II Cor. 5:11; Phil. 3:19; Jas. 3:15.

EARTHQUAKE. Ex. 19:18; Num. 16: 31, 32; I Sam. 14:15; I Ki. 19:11; Amos 1:1; Zech. 14:5; Mt. 27:51; 28: 2; Acts 16:26.

Illustrative.—Is. 24:19, 20; 29:6; Jer. 4:24; Rev. 8:5.

Symbolical.—Rev. 6:12-14; 11:13, 19; 16:18, 20.

EARTHY. I Cor. 15:47-49.

EASE. Job 12:5; 16:12; 21:23; Ps. 123: 4; Jer. 46:27. Couch shall—Job 7:13. Dwell at—Ps. 25:13. Find no—Deut. 28:65. Moab hath been—Jer. 48:11. Multitude at—Ez. 23:42. Take thine —Lu. 12:19. Women at—Is. 32:9, 11.

EASIER. Ex. 18:22. Camel, For a—Mt. 19:24; Mk. 10:25; Lu. 18:25. Heaven to pass, For—Lu. 16:17. Say, To— Mt. 9:5; Mk. 2:9; Lu. 5:23.

EASILY. Sin beset—Heb. 12:1.

EAST. Angel from—Rev. 7:2. As far as east from west—Ps. 103:12. Children of—Ju. 6:33; 7:12; 8:10; I Ki. 4:30. Country—Gen. 25:6; Zech. 8:7. Faces toward—Ez. 8:16. Garden of Eden, Of—Gen. 3:24. Gate—Neh. 3: 26; Jer. 19:2; 31:40; Ez. 10:19; 11:1; 40:6, 22, 23, 44; 42:15; 43:1, 4; Rev. 21:13. Glory of God from—Ez. 43:2.

Horn waxed great towards—Dan. 8:9. Kings of—Rev. 16:12. Lifting up from—Ps. 75:6. Lightning from— Mt. 24:17. Many shall come from —Mt. 8:11. Men of—Job 1:3; Jer. 49:28; Ez. 25:4, 10. Place towards —Ez. 41:14. Raised up from—Is. 41:2. Ravenous bird, Calling—Is. 46: 11. Sea—Ez. 47:18; Joel 2:20. Seed from, Bring—Is. 43:5. Tidings out of —Zech. 14:4. West and east—Ps. 103: 12. Win—Gen. 41:6, 23, 27; Ex. 10: 13; 14:21; Job 15:2; 27:21; 38:24; Ps. 48:7; 78:26; Is. 27:8; Jer. 18:7; Ez. 17:10; 19:12; 27:26; Hos. 12:1; 13:14; Hab. 1:9. Wise men from—Mt. 2:1. Worship towards—Ez. 8:16.

EASY. Entreated, To be—Jas. 3:17. Knowledge—Pr. 14:6. Speech—I Cor. 14:9. Yoke, My—Mt. 11:30.

EAT. Mt. 11:18; 14:20; 15:37; Mk. 14: 18, 22; Lu. 5:33; 7:34; 10:8; Acts 27: 35; Rom. 14:3; II Thess. 3:10. Body— Mt. 26:26; Mk. 14:22; I Cor. 11:24. Bread—Mk. 7:2, 5; I Cor. 11:26, 27, 28; John 6:58; 13:18; Lu. 14:15; John 6:31; Acts 20:11. Common—Acts 10: 14. Crumbs, Dogs—Mt. 15:27; Mk. 7: 28. Ears—Mt. 12:1; Lu. 6:1. Enough —Acts 27:38. Five thousand—Mt. 14: 21. Flesh, My—John 6:52, 53, 54, 56; I Cor. 8:13. Four thousand—Mt. 15: 38; Mk. 8:9. Fruit—Mk. 11:14. Fruit of lies—Hos. 10:13. Give ye them to —Mk. 6:37; Lu. 9:13. Glory of God to —I Cor. 10:31. Herbs—Rom. 14:2. Him With—Acts 10:41. Home, At—I Cor. 11:34. Houses, In—I Cor. 11:22. Husks—Lu. 15:16. Jews—Mk. 7:3. Kill—Acts 10:13. Loaves, Of—Mk. 6:44. Locusts—Mk. 1:6. Lord, Unto —Rom. 14:6. Lord's Supper—I Cor. 11:20. Meat—John 4:32. Manna— John 6:31. Men, With—Acts 11:3. Milk, Of—I Cor. 9:7. Nothing—Mk. 8:1, 2; Lu. 4:2. Offense, With—Rom. 14:20. Passover—Mk. 14:12, 14; Lu. 22:8, 11; John 18:28. Publicans, With —Mk. 2:16; Lu. 5:30. Quietness, With —II Thess. 3:12. Sacrifices, Of—I Cor. 10:18, 28. Shewbread—Mt. 12:4; Mk. 2:26; Lu. 6:4. Sinners, With— Mt. 9:11; Lu. 15:2. Sour grapes— Jer. 31:29. Swine did—Lu. 15:16. Things offered to idols—I Cor. 8:4, 7,

10; Rev. 2:14, 20. Tree of life—Rev. 2:7. Wash hands when—Mt. 15:2. Word shall—II Tit. 2:17. Worms, Eater 'of—Acts 12:23. See DRINK, FOOD, HOSPITALITY, MEALS.

EATER. Ju. 14:14. Bread to the—Is. 55:10. Mouth of—Nah. 3:12.

EATING. Mt. 26:26. According to—Ex. 12:4; 16:16, 18, 21. Concerning the—I Cor. 8:4. In—I Cor. 11:21. While—Job 20:23.

EBAL, ē′bal. (1) **A mountain.**—Deut. 27:13; Josh. 8:30.

(2) **Son of Joktan.**—I Chr. 1:22.

(3) **Descendant of Seir, the Horite.**—Gen. 36:23.

EBED, ē′bĕd. **Father of Gaal.**—Ju. 9:26.

EBED-MELECH, ē′bed–mē′lek. **An Ethiopian eunuch under Zedekiah, who took pity on Jeremiah.**—Jer. 38:7.

EBENEZER, ĕb′en-ē-zer. **Name of stone set up by Samuel to commemorate victory over the Philistines.**—I Sam. 7:12.

EBER, ē′ber. (1) Gen. 10:21; Num. 24:24.

(2) I Chr. 5:13.

(3) **Son of Elpaal.**—I Chr. 8:12.

(4) **Son of Shashak.**—I Chr. 8:22.

(5) **A priest.**—Neh. 12:20.

EBEZ, ē′bĕz. **A town in Issachar.**—Josh. 19:20.

EBIASAPH, e-bī′a-săph. I Chr. 6:23. See ABIASAPH.

EBONY. Ez. 27:14.

EBRON, ē′bron. **A town in Asher.**—Josh. 19:28.

EBRONAH. See ABRONAH.

ECBATANA, ek-băt′a-na. Ezra 6:2 marg. See ACHMETHA.

ECCLESIASTES. See OUTLINE STUDIES IN THE BOOKS.

ED. An altar—Josh. 22:34.

EDEN, ē′den, signifies *delight.* (1) The *LXX* has "paradise." The word garden must not be taken as meaning a small place. Probably a rich champaign land lying between rivers. This is no theme for the insertion of modern ideas. In N. W. Mesopotamia an Eden is mentioned near the Tigris (II Ki. 12:12; Is. 37:12; Ez. 27:23). See Amos 1:5. Our Eden was somewhere in the locality where the Euphrates and Ti-

gris (Hiddekel) join, but we know nothing definite about location. God planted a garden in.—Gen. 2:8. River went out of to water.—Gen. 2:10. Adam appointed to cultivate it.—Gen. 2:15. Trees and fruit permitted for use.—Gen. 2:16. One tree forbidden with threat.—Gen. 2:17. Serpent introduces himself.—Gen. 3:1. Conversation with woman.—Gen. 3:2-5. Woman eats fruit and gives to husband.—Gen. 3:6. Shame seizes them.—Gen. 3:7-8. Jehovah arraigns them.—Gen. 3:9-20. Adam and Eve thrust out.—Gen. 3:23. Cherubim placed as guards at the east.—Gen. 3:24.

Cain settles east of Eden.—Gen. 4:16.

Allusions to Garden of Eden.—Reclaim wilderness.—Is. 51:3. Traffickers from Ez. 27:23. In the garden—Ez. 28:13. Trees of, envious—Ez. 31:9. Trees of, comforted—Ez. 31:16. Trees brought into humiliation.—Ez. 31:18. Desolate land like Eden—Ez. 36:35. Compared to Eden—Joel 2:3.

(2) **An Aramaean region.**—II Ki. 19:12; Is. 37:12; Ez. 27:23; Amos 1:5.

(3) **Son of Joah.**—II Chr. 29:12; 31:23.

(4) **A Levite in time of Hezekiah.**—II Chr. 31:15.

EDER, ē′der. (1) **A Levite.**—I Chr. 23:23.

(2) **Tower of.**—Gen. 35:21.

(3) **A town of Judah.**—Josh. 15:21; I Chr. 8:15. See ADER.

EDGE. Curtain, Of—Ex. 26:4, 10; 36:11, 17. Dagger had two—Ju. 3:16. Joined at—Ex. 39:4. Land, Of—Num. 33:37. Sword, Of—Gen. 34:26; Ex. 17:13; Num. 21:24; Deut. 13:15; 20:13; Josh. 6:21; 8:24; 10:28, 30, 32, 35, 37, 39; 11:11, 12, 14; 19:47; Ju. 1:8, 25; 4:15, 16; 18:27; 20:37, 48; 21:10; I Sam. 15:8; 22:19; II Sam. 15:14; II Ki. 10:25; Job 1:15; Jer. 21:7; Ps. 89:43; Lu. 21:24; Heb. 11:34. Teeth are set on —Jer. 31:29, 30; Ez. 18:2. Whet—Eccl. 10:10. Wilderness, Of—Ex. 13:20; Num. 33:6.

EDIFICATION. An essential to Christian life.—Rom. 15:2; II Cor. 12:19. **Love edifies.**—I Cor. 8:1. See LOVE—I Cor. 13:1.

Edification the perfection of saints.—Rom. 14:19; 15:2; I Cor. 14:26; Eph. 4:12–16, 29; I Thess. 5:11.

Instruments of.—Acts 20:32. Paul's teaching as—I Cor. 13:10.

Edification of the church.—Acts 9:31; I Cor. 14:3–5, 12, 26; II Cor. 10:8; 13:10.

All things do not edify.—Rom. 16:17, 18; I Cor. 10:23; 14:17. See CHRISTIAN GRACES.

EDOM. Land of Edomites.—Gen. 32:3.

Previously called Mt. Seir, a hilly region south of the Salt Sea and reaching to the Elanitic Gulf.

Border of Edom.—Josh. 15:1.

Cities of Judah toward coast of.—Josh. 15:21.

Mountains.—Halak—Josh. 12:7. Hor—Num. 20:22. Moab—Gen. 36:35.

Wilderness of Edom.—II Ki. 3:8.

Rulers.—Dukes of—Gen. 36:9–43; Ex. 15:15; I Chr. 1:51–54. Kings of—Gen. 36:31–39; Num. 20:14; I Chr. 1:43–50; Ez. 32:29; Amos 2:1. No king in Edom—I Ki. 22:47.

Inhabitants of. — Horites — Deut. 2:12. Esauites—Gen. 32:4. Edomites—Deut. 2:4.

Strifes of Edom.—Messengers sent unto king, and Edom refuses passage to Israel—Num. 20:14, 23; 21:4. Saul against Edom—I Sam. 14:47. Edom subdued by David—II Sam. 8:14. Solomon makes navy of ships in—I Ki. 9:26. Hadad an adversary to Solomon—I Ki. 11:14–16. Under a regent—I Ki. 22:47. Revolt against Joram and defeat—II Ki. 8:20–22. Jehoshaphat defeats them—II Chr. 20:22. Defeated by Amaziah—II Ki. 14:7, 10. Invade Judah—II Chr. 28:17. Devastation threatened—Ez. 25:12–14; Amos 1:9–11; Ob. 1:16. Edom shall be a possession—Num. 24:18.

Prophecies concerning Edom.—Pride of Edom humbled—Ob. 1–21. Burden of Dumah (Edom)—Is. 21:11. Subjection to Israel—Gen. 25:23; 27:29, 37, 40; Is. 11:14; Amos 9:12. Edom a possession of Israel—Num. 24:18; Ob. 17–19. Edom to suffer in the punishment of nations—Is. 63:1–7; Jer. 9:26; 25:15–27; Lam. 4:21; Ez. 32:29. Devastation of Edom—Is. 34:5–17; Jer. 27:3–6; 49:7–22; Ez. 25:12–14; 35:7–15; Ob. 18; Mal. 1:3–5. Edom punished for persecuting—Is. 34:5–8; 63:1–4; Lam. 4:21; Ez. 25:13, 14; Joel 3:19; Amos 1:11, 12; 2:1, 12; Ob. 10, 15.

EDREI, ĕd′rei. (1) **A residence of Og, king of Bashan.**—Josh. 12:4; Num. 21:33.

(2) **A city of Naphtali.**—Josh. 19:37.

EDUCATION. See INSTRUCTION.

EFFECT. Faithfulness of God none—Rom. 3:3. Promise of none—Rom. 4:14; Gal. 3:17. See ABOLISH, COVENANT, LAW. Prosperously—II Chr. 7:11.

EFFECTUAL. Door—I Cor. 16:9.

EFFULGENCE. Heb. 1:3. See BRIGHT, BRIGHTNESS.

EGG. Job 6:6; Is. 59:5; Lu. 11:12.

EGLAH, eg′lah. One of David's wives—II Sam. 3:5; I Chr. 3:3.

EGLAIM, ĕg′la-ĭm. **A Moabite town.**—Is. 15:8.

EGLATH-SHELISHIHAH, ĕg′lăth–shelish′ĭ-yäh. Is. 15:5; Jer. 48:34.

EGLON, ĕg′lon. (1) **King of Moab, who formed an alliance against Israel.**—Ju. 3:12–14.

(2) **A city of the Amorites.**—Josh. 10:3, 16–27.

EGYPT, ē′gўpt. Called *"house of bondage"*—Ex. 13:3, 14; Deut. 7:8. *"Land of Ham"*—Ps. 105:23; 106:22. *"Mizraim"*—Gen. 10:6; I Chr. 1:8. *Rahab*—Job 9:13; 26:12; Ps. 87:4; 89:10; Is. 30:7; 51:9.

Boundaries of.—Ez. 29:10.

Characteristics.—Ambitious—Jer. 46:8. Proud—Jer. 46:8; Ez. 29:3; 30:6, 18; 32:12. Strong—Is. 30:2, 3. Treacherous—Is. 36:6. Wise—I Ki. 4:30; Is. 19:11; Acts 7:22.

Commercial.—Gen. 41:57; Pr. 7:16; Is. 23:3; Ez. 27:7. Cloth made in—Pr. 7; 16; Is. 19:9. Solomon bought horses—I Ki. 10:28, 29. Store cities—Ex. 1:11.

Congregation of Jews.—Egyptians permitted to enter in the third generation because of hospitality—Deut. 23: 7, 8.

Drought.—Deut. 11:10, 11; Ez. 30:12.

Embalming.—Gen. 50:2, 3, 26.

Famines in.—Gen. 41:30, 54–57; 45:6; 47:13–21; Ez. 29:9; 30:7–12; Acts 7: 11.

Fertility due to being well watered.—Gen. 13:10; Deut. 11:10, 11. Watered by the Nile—Gen. 41:1–3; Ex. 1:22; Jer. 46:7, 8. By the river Shihor (probably the river Nile)—Josh. 13: 3; I Chr. 13:5; Is. 23:3; Jer. 2:18.

Inhabitants of.—Hospitable—Gen. 43: 32–34; 47:5, 6; I Ki. 11:18. Intermarry with foreigners—Gen. 21:21; I Ki. 3:1; 11:19; I Chr. 2:34, 35.

Inundations.—Jer. 46:7, 8; Amos 8:8; 9:5.

Land owned and controlled by Pharaoh.—Gen. 47:22–26.

Magic practised.—Gen. 41:8; Ex. 7:11, 22; 8:7; Is. 19:3.

Plagues.—Deut. 7:15; 28:27, 60. See Ex. 7:19–25; Chs. 8–12.

Refuge for strangers.—Abraham—Gen. 12:10. Joseph's kinsmen—Gen. 47:4. Hadad—I Ki. 11:17. Solomon—I Ki. 11:40. Judah—II Ki. 25:26; Jer. 43: 4–7. Joseph and Mary—Mt. 2:13.

Religion.—Idolatry—Ex. 12:12; 32:1–9; Num. 33:4; Is. 19:1; Ez. 20:8; Acts 7:39, 40. Eating with Hebrews an abomination—Gen. 43:32. Priests—Gen. 41:45, 50; 47:22. Sacrifice of oxen abhorred—Ex. 8:26. Shepherds an abomination—Gen. 46:34.

Ruled by kings who were called "Pharaoh"—Gen. 12:14–20; 40:1, 2; Ex. 1:8, 11, 19, 22; Chs. 7–14; I Ki. 3:1; 11:19. See PHARAOH. Had princes and counsellors—Gen. 12:15; Is. 19:11; 30: 4. Joseph made governor—Gen. 41: 37–44; 42:6; 44:18; 45:25, 26; Acts 7:10.

Armies of.—Ex. 14:7–9; II Chr. 12:3. Destroyed in the Red Sea—Ex. 14:23–31; 15:4–10; Josh. 24:6, 7. Captured and burned Gezer—I Ki. 9:16. Besieged and plundered Jerusalem when Rehoboam was king—I Ki. 14:25, 26; II Chr. 12:2–11. Invaded Assyria and killed Josiah, who was an ally of Assyria—II Ki. 23:29, 30; II Chr. 35: 20–24. Deposed Jehoahaz and made Judea tributary—II Ki. 23:31–35; II Chr. 36:3, 4. Assistance of, sought by Judah against the Chaldees—Jer. 37: 5, 10; Ez. 17:15. Civil war in Egypt—

Is. 19:2. Conquered by Nebuchadrezzar—II Ki. 24:7; Jer. 43:9–11; 46:1–26; Ez. 29:18–20; 30:2–19; 32:9–32.

Israel in Egypt.—Abraham and his descendants dwelt in Ur and Egypt 430 years—Gen. 15:13; Ex. 12:40, 41; Acts 7:6; Gal. 3:17. Abraham goes to Egypt—Gen. 12:10–20. Returns to Canaan—Gen. 13:1–4. Jehovah predicts Egyptian bondage—Gen. 15:13, 14; Acts 7:6, 7. Joseph taken into Egypt by Ishmaelites—Gen. 37:28; 59:1. Joseph and Potiphar's wife—Gen. 39:1–18. Joseph cast into prison—Gen. 39: 18–23. Interprets the dreams of the butler and baker—Gen. 40:1–23. Interprets Pharaoh's dream and counsels Pharaoh —Gen. 41:1–36. Made governor—Gen. 41:37–44. Provides against famine—Gen. 41:46–57. Jacob's sons sent to Egypt for food—Gen. 42:1–38; 43:1–25. Joseph feasts with his brethren—Gen. 43: 26–34; 44:1–34; 45:1–7. Jacob and sons come to Egypt—Gen. 45:9; 46:27. Israel dwells in land of Goshen—Gen. 45:10; 46:28–34; 47:11, 27. The famine and Joseph's provision against it —Gen. 47:13–26. Jacob blesses Joseph's sons—Gen. 48:1–22. Jacob's prophecy concerning his sons—Gen. 49:1–28. Jacob's death and burial—Gen. 49:29–33; 50:1–14. Israel oppressed in Egypt—Ex. 1:22; 5:1–23. Moses born and hidden—Ex. 2:1–4. Adopted and educated by Pharaoh's daughter—Ex. 2:5–10; Acts 7:21, 22. Moses slays an Egyptian—Ex. 2:11, 12. God calls Moses to deliver Israel —Ex. Chs. 3 and 4; 6:1–13; 7:1–13. The plagues—Ex. 7:14; 11:6; 12:29, 30. Passover—Ex. 12:1–28, 43–49. Departure from Egypt—Gen. 12:30–42; 13:17–22; Heb. 11:27. Pharaoh and his army pursue and are destroyed—Gen. 14:1–31. About 70 men went into Egypt with Jacob—Gen. 46:8–27; Ex. 1:1–5; Deut. 10:22; Acts 7:14. Six hundred thousand men, besides children, went out—Ex. 12:37, 38.

Prophecies concerning Egypt.—Folly of relying on Egypt—Is. 31:3. Israel's affliction foretold — Gen. 15:13–14. Egypt in fear—Is. 19:1, 16–17. Civil war in—Is. 19:2. Oppression of their king—Is. 19:4. Failure of resources—

Is. 19:5–10. Utter desolation for forty years—Ez. 29:8–12; 30:12–19. Ever to be a base kingdom—Ez. 29:15. Nebuchadrezzar overcomes Egypt—Jer. 46: 3–12; II Ki. 24:7; Ez. 32:11–16. Destruction of its power—Ez. 30:24–26. Destruction of its cities—Ez. 30:14–17. Destruction of its idols—Jer. 43: 12–13; 46:25. Captivity of people— Is. 20:4; Jer. 46:19–26; Ez. 30:4. Jews who practised its idolatries to share its punishment—Jer. 44:7–28; Hos. 8: 11–14. Egypt shall submit to Jehovah —Is. 19:18–22. Christ to be called out of—Hos. 11:1; Mt. 2:15. Jehovah threatens Egypt for violence to Judah —Joel 3:19–21. Ephraim to return— Zech. 10:7–12. Egypt used as symbol —Rev. 11:8.

EHI, ē'hī. Gen. 46:21. See AHIRAM.

EHUD, ē'hud. (1) **One of the judges who slew Eglon.**—Ju. 3:15.

(2) **Great grandson of Benjamin.**—I Chr. 7:10.

EITHER. Mt. 6:24; 12:33; John 19:18.

EKER, ē'ker. **Son of Ram.**—I Chr. 2:27. See ACHAR.

EKRON, ĕk'ron. **A Philistine city.**— Josh. 13:3; 15:45; Ju. 1:18; I Sam. 5:10; 6:16; II Ki. 1:2, 3, 6.

ELA, ē'la. **Father of Shimei.**—I Ki. 4:18.

ELAH. (1) **Valley of.**—I Sam. 17:2.

(2) **Son of Caleb.**—I Chr. 4:15.

(3) **Father of Hoshea, king of Israel.**— II Ki. 15:30.

(4) **Son of Baasha, king of Israel.**—I Ki. 16:6–14.

(5) **A duke of Edom.**—Gen. 36:41.

(6) **A Benjamite.**—I Chr. 9:8.

ELAM, ē'lam. (1) **Persia.**—Gen. 14:1, 9; Is. 11:11; 21:2; 22:6; Jer. 25:25; 49:34–39; Ez. 32:24; Dan. 8:2.

(2) **A Kohathite.**—I Chr. 26:3.

(3) **Son of Shashak.**—I Chr. 8:24.

(4) **Ancestor of a family who returned from exile.**—Ezra 2:7; Neh. 7:12.

(5) **Ancestor of another family returning from exile.**—Ezra 2:31; Neh. 7:34.

(6) **Son of Shem.**—Gen. 10:22; I Chr. 1: 17.

(7) **Ancestor of some who returned with Ezra.**—Ezra 8:7.

(8) **One who, with Nehemiah, sealed the covenant.**—Neh. 10:14.

(9) **Ancestor of Shechaniah.**—Ezra 10: 2, 26.

(10) **A priest.**—Neh. 12:42.

ELAMITES, ē'lam-ites. Ezra 4:9; Acts 2:9.

ELASAH, ĕl'a-sah. Ezra 10:22; Jer. 29:3.

ELATH, ē'lath. **A town on the Red Sea.** —Deut. 2:8.

EL-BERITH, ĕl–bē'rith. Ju. 9:46. See BAAL-BERITH.

EL-BETHEL. Gen. 35:7. See BETHEL.

ELDAAH, ĕl'da-ah. Gen. 25:4; I Chr. 1: 33.

ELDERS OF THE CHURCH. See MINISTERS.

ELDERS OF ISRAEL. Gather the elders of Israel—Ex. 3:16. Moses called for—Ex. 12:21. Elders came to eat— Ex. 18:12. Seventy elders go up to Sinai—Ex. 24:1. Come before the tent of meeting—Num. 11:16, 24. Lay hands on head of bullock—Lev. 4:15. Bring rebellious son before—Deut. 21:19–20. They command the people—Deut. 27: 1. Moses delivers the law to—Deut. 31:9, 28. Join Joshua in mourning Achan's sin—Josh. 7:6. Come to David at Hebron—II Sam. 5:3; II Chr. 5:4. Saul seeks honor before—I Sam. 15:30. Boaz takes elders to justify Ruth—Ruth 4:2. Eye of God on— Ezra 5:5. The tradition of the—Mt. 15:2; Mk. 7:3. Suffer things of—Mt. 16:21; 27:12. Sought false witness— Mt. 26:59. Persuaded the multitude— Mt. 27:20. Jesus must be rejected by —Mk. 8:31; Lu. 9:22. Hold consultation against Jesus—Mk. 15:1. Gathered together against Apostles—Acts 4:5, 23. Elders stirred up—Acts 6:12. See AGE, ISRAEL, JEWS.

ELEAD, ē'le-ăd. I Chr. 7:21.

ELEADAH, ē'le-ā'dah. I Chr. 7:20.

ELEALEH, ē'le-ā'leh. **A town of Moab.** —Num. 32:3.

ELEASAH, e-lē'a-sah. (1) **An officer under Zedekiah.**—Jer. 29:3.

(2) **A descendant of Judah.**—I Chr. 2: 39.

(3) **A descendant of Jonathan.**—I Chr. 8:37; 9:43.

(4) **A son of Pashhur.**—Ezra 10:22.

ELEAZAR, e-le-a'zar. (1) **Third son of Aaron.**—Ex. 6:23, 25; Num. 3:2, 4;

26:1; 26:60; I Chr. 6:3, 50; 24:1, 2, 3. Prince of princes—Num. 3:32. His charge—Num. 4:16. Numbered children of Israel—Num. 26:63. Divided the land—Num. 34:17; Josh. 19:51. Sons of—Num. 25:7–11; Num. 31:6; Josh. 22:13, 31, 32; Ju. 20:28; I Chr. 9:20; 24:4, 5, 6; Ezra 7:5. Succeeds Aaron—Num. 20:25–28; Deut. 10:6. Angers Moses—Lev. 10:16. Priest— Num. 16:37–39; 19:3, 4; 26:1, 3; 27:2; 27:19, 21, 22; 31:12–13, 21, 26, 29, 31, 41, 51, 54; 32:2, 28; 34:17; Josh. 14:1; 17:4; 21:1. Death and burial—Josh. 24:33.

(2) **Son of Abinadab.**—Keeper of ark— I Sam. 7:1.

(3) **Son of Eliud.**—Mt. 1:15. With David—I Chr. 11:12–14.

(4) **Son of Phinehas.**—Ezra 8:33; 10: 25; Neh. 12:42.

(5) **Son of Dosai.**—II Sam. 23:9.

(6) **Son of Mahli.**—I Chr. 23:21. Died without sons—I Chr. 23:22; 24:28.

ELECTION. Israel—Ex. 6:7; Lev. 20: 26; Deut. 4:20, 37; 7:6; 9:29; 10:15; 14:2; 26:18, 19; 28:9; 29:10–29; I Ki. 8:51–53; Ps. 33:12; 95:7; Is. 41:8; 43: 1; 45:4; Amos 3:2. A remnant of Israel—Rom. 11:5–12, 28. Abraham— Gen. 12:1–3; Neh. 9:7. Isaac—Gen. 21:12; Rom. 9:7, 8; Heb. 11:18. Jacob —Rom. 9:11–13. Zerubbabel—Hag. 2: 23. Jesus as the Messiah—Is. 42:1; I Pet. 2:6. Angels—I Tim. 5:21. The Church—I Pet. 5:13. The Apostles— Lu. 6:13; John 13:18; 15:16–19; 17:6; I Pet. 1:2. Paul—Acts 9:15; 13:2; 22: 14, 21; 26:17; Rom. 1:1; I Cor. 15:10; Gal. 1:15; I Tim. 2:7; II Tim. 1:11. The poor and weak things—I Cor. 1: 27; Jas. 2:5. Disciples chosen in Christ —Eph. 1:4, 11; 2:10. Unto salvation through sanctification of the Spirit— II Thess. 2:13; I Pet. 1:2–5. To be soldiers—II Tim. 2:4. According to the purpose of God—Rom. 9:11.

Conditional.—Eph. 1:13, 18–20; I Thess. 1:4–6; II Thess. 2:13, 14; I Pet. 1:2; II Pet. 1:10; 2:6–10. See CHOICE, FOREORDINATION, PAUL, PURPOSE.

EL-ELOHE-ISRAEL, ĕl-e-lō′he-ĭs′ra-el. Gen. 33:20.

ELEMENTS. II Pet. 3:10. See RUDIMENTS.

ELEPH, ē′leph. **A Benjamite town.**— Josh. 18:28.

ELEVATION. Ps. 48:2.

ELEVEN. Apostles, Numbered with— Acts 1:26. **Appeared unto the**—Mk. 16:14. Cubits—Ez. 40:49. Curtains— Ex. 26:7, 8; 36:14, 15. Found, gathered—Lu. 24:33. Hour—Mt. 20:6, 9. Peter, standing up with—Acts 2:14. Stars made obeisance—Gen. 37:9. Told these things to—Lu. 24:9.

ELHANAN, el′hā′nan. (1) **Son of Jair.** —II Sam. 21:19.

(2) II Sam. 23:24; I Chr. 11:26.

ELI, ē′li. A high priest—I Sam. 1:9. Judges Israel forty years—I Sam. 4: 18. Blesses Hannah the mother of Samuel—I Sam. 1:17. Trains Samuel —I Sam. 2:11. Sons are wicked—I Sam. 2:17; 3:13. House prophesied against—I Sam. 2:31. Sons slain—I Sam. 4:11. Death—I Sam. 4:18.

ELI. Part of the cry of Jesus on the cross—Mt. 27:46.

ELIAB, e-lī′ab. (1) **Son of Helon.**— Num. 1:9; 2:7.

(2) **Father of Dathan and Abiram.**— Num. 16:1, 12.

(3) **Brother of David, son of Jesse.**—I Sam. 16:6.

(4) **A man of God.**—I Chr. 12:9.

ELIADA, e-lī′a-dà. (1) **One of David's sons.**—II Sam. 5:16; I Chr. 3:8. See BEELIADA.

(2) **A captain under Jehoshaphat.**—II Chr. 17:17.

(3) **Father of Rezon.**—I Ki. 11:23.

ELIAHBA, e-lī′ah-bà. **One of David's warriors.**—II Sam. 23:32; I Chr. 11: 33.

ELIAKIM, e-lī′a-kim. (1) **Son of Hilkiah,** who was overseer of Hezekiah's household—II Ki. 18:18, 26, 37. Conference with Rabshakeh—II Ki. 18: 18–26; Is. 36:3, 11, 22. Sent to Isaiah —II Ki. 19:2; Is. 37:2.

(2) **Son of Josiah.**—II Ki. 23:34. His name changed to Jehoiakim. Made king over Judah and Jerusalem—II Ki. 23:34; II Chr. 36:4.

(3) **A priest that assisted at the dedication of the wall in the time of Nehemiah.**—Neh. 12:41.

(4) **Eldest son of Abiud, or Judah.**—Mt. 1:13.

(5) **Son of Melea.**—Lu. 3:30.

ELIAM, e-lī′am. (1) **Father of Bath-sheba.**—II Sam. 11:3. See AMMIEL.

(2) **Son of Ahithophel.**—II Sam. 23:34.

ELIAS. See ELIJAH.

ELIASAPH, e-lī′a-săph. (1) **A census taker.**—Num. 2:14.

(2) **A Levite**—Num. 3:24.

ELIASHIB, e-lī′a-shĭb. (1) I Chr. 24:12.

(2) **Son of Eleoenai.**—I Chr. 3:24.

(3) **A high priest in Nehemiah's time.** —Neh. 3:1, 20; 13:4, 7.

(4) **A Levite singer.**—Ezra 10:24.

(5) **One of those who had married a foreign wife.**—Ezra 10:27.

(6) **Father of Jehohanan.**—Ezra 10:6.

(7) **A member of the family of Bani who had married a foreign wife.**— Ezra 10:36.

ELIATHAH, e-lī′a-thah. I Chr. 25:4, 27.

ELIDAD, e-lī′dad. Num. 34:21.

ELIEHOENAI, ĕl′ie-ho-ē′na-ī. (1) **A descendant of David.**—I Chr. 3:23.

(2) **A Benjamite.**—I Chr. 7:8.

(3) **A member of tribe of Simeon.**—I Chr. 4:36.

(4) **Another Benjamite.**—I Chr. 8:20.

(5) **Son of Meshelemiah.**—I Chr. 26:3.

(6) **A priest.**—Ezra 10:22.

(7) **Leader of the sons of Pahath-moab.** —Ezra 8:4.

(8) **One of those who married foreign wives.**—Ezra 10:27.

ELIEL, ē′li-el. (1) **Chief of the half tribe of Manasseh.**—I Chr. 5:24.

(2) **A Benjamite.**—I Chr. 8:20.

(3) **A Kohathite.**—I Chr. 6:34.

(4) **Another Benjamite.**—I Chr. 8:22.

(5, 6, 7) **Three of David's thirty warriors.**—I Chr. 11:46; 12:11.

(8) **A Levite.**—I Chr. 15:9, 11.

(9) **A Levite in time of Hezekiah.**—II Chr. 31:13.

ELIENAI, ē′li-ē′na-i. See ELIEHOENAI.

ELIEZER, ē′li-ē′zer. (1) **Second son of Moses.**—Ex. 18:4; I Chr. 23:15.

(2) **Abraham's steward.**—Gen. 15:2.

(3) **Prophet in days of Jehoshaphat.**— II Chr. 20:37.

(4) **A Benjamite.**—I Chr. 7:8.

(5) **A priest who went with ark on way to Jerusalem.**—I Chr. 15:24.

(6) **One of Ezra's messengers.**—Ezra 8:16.

(7) **A Reubenite.**—I Chr. 27:16.

(8-10) **Men who had married foreign wives.**—Ezra 10:18, 23, 31.

(11) **Ancestor of Jesus.**—Lu. 3:29.

ELEHOREPH, ĕl′e-hō′reph. **One of Solomon's secretaries.**—I Ki. 4:3.

ELIHU, e-lī′hu. (1) **A captain of Manasseh who joined David at Ziklag.**— I Chr. 12:20.

(2) **Samuel's great-grandfather.**— I Sam. 1:1.

(3) **A doorkeeper.**—I Chr. 26:7.

(4) **Brother of David.**—I Chr. 27:18. See ELIAB.

(5) **One of Job's friends.**—Job. chs. 32–37.

ELIJAH, e-lī′jah. **The Tishbite.**—Sojourner of Gilead—I Ki. 17:1.

Sudden appearance, like Melchizedek and John.—A rugged character in a hairy mantle—II Ki. 1:8. He was God's scourge for Ahab—I Ki. 18:17; 21:20–22.

His startling message. — A 3½ - year drought—I Ki. 17:1; Jas. 5:17. He hides by the brook Cherith, and is fed by ravens—I Ki. 17:2–7. Goes to a widow in Zarephath—I Ki. 17:8–16. Death of her son and restoration by the prophet—I Ki. 17:17–24.

Shows himself to Ahab.—Meets Obadiah, who informs Ahab—I Ki. 18:1–15. Ahab charged with forsaking Jehovah's commandments—I Ki. 18:18. Proposition as to assembling of Israel and Baal's prophets on Mount Carmel agreed on—I Ki. 18:19, 20. A decision as to the true God determined on— I Ki. 18:21, 38, 39. Proposal as respects the two offerings—I Ki. 18:22–24. Baal's failure to respond—I Ki. 18:25–29.

Elijah assumes control.—Jehovah's altar built—I Ki. 18:32. Puts Jehovah's power to the severest test—I Ki. 18:32–35. Elijah's prayer and results—I Ki. 18:36–39. Baal's prophets slain by the brook Kishon—I Ki. 18:40. The rain beginning, Ahab was ordered to depart—I Ki. 18:41–46.

Ahab and Jezebel in the ascendant.— Upon receiving information from Ahab, Jezebel threatens Elijah—I Ki. 19:1, 2. He flees for his life—I Ki. 19:3. Dejection under a juniper tree—I Ki. 19:4, 5. The angelic visitation—I

Ki. 19:5–8. Communes with Jehovah — I Ki. 19:9–14.

Elijah acts under divine appointment.— He anoints Hazael and Jehu, to be kings of Syria and Israel—I Ki. 19:15, 16. He calls Elisha as his successor— I Ki. 19:19–21.

Elijah announces Ahab's punishment for killing Naboth.—I Ki. 21:17–24. Punishment postponed because Ahab humbled himself—I Ki. 21:27–29. Jehovah's threat realized—II Ki. chs. 9 and 10.

Elijah sent to Ahaziah, king of Israel, with a message of death.—II Ki. 1: 1–4. Ahaziah's messengers return at Elijah's bidding—II Ki. 1:5–8. The king sends captains and troops, which are destroyed by fire—II Ki. 1:9–12. On account of humility, one band is spared—II Ki. 1:13–15. Because of consulting Baal instead of Jehovah the king dies—II Ki. 1:16, 17.

Elijah makes his ascension—Smites the Jordan with his mantle and crosses over—II Ki. 2:8. Elisha persists in following—II Ki. 2:2–7. Elisha asks for a double portion of Spirit—II Ki. 2:9, 10. Elijah departs by a whirlwind into heaven—II Ki. 2:11–14.

Elijah in the New Testament.—Was expected—(Mal. 4:5); Mt. 11:14; 17: 10–12; Mk. 9:11–13; Lu. 1:17. Some thought Jesus was Elijah—Mt. 16:14; Mk. 6:15; 8:28; Lu. 9:19. Elijah appeared at transfiguration—Mt. 17:3; Mk. 9:4, 5; Lu. 9:30, 33. Allusion to famine in Samaria—Lu. 4:25, 26. Enquiry as to whether John is Elijah— John 1:21, 25. Paul's reference to Elijah—Rom. 11:2. James' allusion to—Jas. 5:17.

Character of Elijah.—Stern—I Ki. 21: 20; II Ki. 1:10. Of ordinary passions— Jas. 5:17. Kind to the needy—I Ki. 17:14, 20–24; Lu. 4:25. Restorer of righteousness—Mt. 17:11. Uniting the alienated—Mal. 4:6; Lu. 1:17. See ELISHA, ISRAEL, PROPHETS.

ELIKA, ĕl'i-kà. One of David's warriors.—II Sam. 23:23.

ELIM, ē'lim. Place of one of Israel's encampments.—Ex. 15:27; Num. 33:9.

ELIMELECH e-lim'e-lĕk. Husband of Naomi.—Ruth 1:2.

ELIOENAI, e-lī'o-ē-na-i. See ELIEHOE-NAI.

ELIPHAL, ĕl'i-phal. See ELIPHELET.

ELIPHAZ, ĕl'i-phaz. (1) Gen. 36:4, 10, 15; I Chr. 1:35.

(2) One of Job's friends.—Job 2:11.

ELIPHELEHU, e-līph'e-lĕh-u. A musician in the temple.—I Chr. 15:18, 21.

ELIPHELET, e-līph'e-lĕt. (1) Son of David.—II Sam. 5:16; I Chr. 3:6, 8; 14:5, 7.

(2) One of David's warriors.—II Sam. 23:34; I Chr. 11:35.

(3) A descendant of Saul.—I Chr. 8:39.

(4) One of those who returned with Ezra.—Ezra 8:13.

(5) One of those who married foreign wives.—Ezra 10:33.

ELISABETH, e-lĭs'a-bĕth. Mother of John the Baptist.—Lu. 1:57. Wife of Zacharias.—Lu. 1:5.

ELISHA, e-lī'shà. The son of Shaphat of Abel-meholah—I Ki. 19:16. Appointed at Horeb as successor to Elijah—I Ki. 19:16. The 7000 who had not bowed down to Baal (I Ki. 19:18), of whom were Shaphat and son, were no doubt stimulated by the victory at Carmel. All looked bright, so when the mantle was cast on Elisha's shoulder (I Ki. 19:19), he slew the oxen in the field and kissed father and mother good-bye, making a feast for the people—I Ki. 19:20, 21. He immediately became a servant to Elijah (II Ki. 3: 11), who was called his master (II Ki. 2:3), following him everywhere till the ascension—II Ki. 2:2, 4, 6, 10–12.

Elisha is accepted as the leader.—II Ki. 2:15. His ministry covered half a century, embracing the reigns of 4 kings, Jehoram, Jehu, Jehoahaz and Joash— II Ki. chs. 3–13. He seems to have done his best work during the first 12 years of his ministry—II Ki. chs. 3–9. While Elijah corrected the kings, Elisha directed them—II Ki. 9:1–10. He was looked upon as the best strength of the nation in the Syrian wars—II Ki. 13:14–19. Yet there is a smack of political intrigue in his management of affairs which both Elijah and Isaiah would have disdained—II Ki. 8: 10; 9:3, 11, 12. His reputation for diplomacy was such that even in Damascus his influence was felt, Benhadad sending to him during an illness—II Ki. 8:7-10. He prophesies evil of Hazael, who assassinates Benhadad—II Ki. 8:12-15. Elisha so controls the campaign against Samaria as to baffle and defeat Benhadad—II Ki. chs. 6-7. Joash credits Elisha with saving Israel—II Ki. 13:14-19.

Elisha as a worker of miracles.—His act of mercy at Jericho—II Ki. 2:19-22. His judgment upon his mockers—II Ki. 2:23-25. Supplies a widow's need—II Ki. 4:1-7. The Shunammite's son restored to life—II Ki. 4:8-37. Purifies pot of pottage—II Ki. 4:38-41. Miracle of the loaves and corn—II Ki. 4:42-44. Of the axehead—II Ki. 6:1-7.

The removal of Naaman's leprosy.—II Ki. 5:1-19. Who Naaman was—II Ki. 5:1. His leprosy—II Ki. 5:1. The maid's information—II Ki. 5:2-3. The king's plan—II Ki. 5:5, 6. How the king of Israel received it—II Ki. 5:7. Elisha takes the matter in hand—II Ki. 5:8. Naaman presents himself to Elisha, but is disappointed—II Ki. 5:10-12. His servants rebuke him—v. 13. Naaman obeys and is healed—II Ki. 5:14-19.

Naaman's five mistakes.—(1) Went to the healer with his own remedy. (2) Was angry when his remedy was rejected. (3) Anxious to be blessed with a cure, but unwilling to accept the terms. (4) All he thought of was being healed; Elisha determined to prove his worthiness. (5) Naaman forestalls measures by filling himself with his own thought.

Gehazi's greed for gain.—He solicits for himself part of Naaman's present—II Ki. 5:20-22. His lies known to Elisha—II Ki. 5:22, 25. He is rebuked and smitten with leprosy—II Ki. 5:26, 27.

Prophecies of Elisha.—Foretells birth of Shunammite's son—II Ki. 4:16. Prophesies plenty for the suffering of Samaria—II Ki. 7:1. Declares the death of an unbelieving captain—II Ki. 7:2, 19. Announces 7 years of famine—II Ki. 8:1. The death of Ben-hadad—II Ki. 8:7-10. The reign

of Hazael—II Ki. 8:13. Triumph of Jehoash over Syria—II Ki. 13:14-19.

Last days and death.—Elisha sickens unto death—II Ki. 13:14. Busy to the very last, symbolizing the victory of Joash—II Ki. 13:15-19. Dies and is buried—II Ki. 13:20. His bones serve to restore a life—II Ki. 3:21.

Characteristics of Elisha.—Influenced by music—II Ki. 3:15. Severe to the fraudulent—II Ki. 5:27. Firm before kings—II Ki. 3:13. Resentful—II Ki. 2:24. Artful—II Ki. 6:18-20. Merciful—II Ki. 6:21, 22. Diplomatic—II Ki. 6:23. Grateful—II Ki. 4:12-16. See ELIJAH, ISRAEL, PROPHETS.

ELISHAH, e-lī'shah. (1) **Son of Javan.** Gen. 10:4.

(2) **Islands.**—Ez. 27:7.

ELISHAMA, e-lĭsh'a-má. (1) **A chief of Ephraim.**—Num. 1:10.

(2) II Sam. 5:16; I Chr. 3:8; 14:7.

(3) **A man of Judah.**—I Chr. 2:4.

(4) **A priest in time of Jehoshaphat.**—II Chr. 17:8.

(5) **A scribe of Jehoiakim's.**—Jer. 36:12.

(6) **Grandfather of Ishmael.**—II Ki. 25:25; Jer. 41:1.

ELISHAPHAT, e-lĭsh'a-phăt. II Chr. 23:1.

ELISHEBA, e-lĭsh'e-bá. **Wife of Aaron.** Ex. 6:23.

ELISHUA, ĕl'i-shu-à. **Son of David.**—II Sam. 5:15; I Chr. 14:15.

ELIUD, e-lī'ud. **Ancestor of Joseph.**—Mt. 1:14.

ELIZAPHAN, e-lĭz'a-phăn. (1) **A prince of Zebulun.**—Num. 34:25.

(2) **A Levite.**—Num. 3:30; I Chr. 15:8; II Chr. 29:13.

ELIZUR, e-lī'zur. **A prince of Reuben.**—Num. 1:5.

ELKANAH, ĕl'ka-nah. (1) **A Levite.**—I Chr. 6:26, 35.

(2) **Son of Joel.**—I Chr. 6:36.

(3) **Son of Jehoram, father of Samuel.**—I Sam. 1:1; I Chr. 6:27, 34.

(4) **Grandson of Korah.**—Ex. 6:24; I Chr. 6:23.

(5) **A doorkeeper.**—I Chr. 15:23.

(6) **Grandfather of Berechiah.**—I Chr. 9:16.

(7) **One of David's warriors.**—I Chr. 12:6.

(8) **An officer under Ahaz.**—II Chr. 28:7.

ELKOSHITE, ĕl'kosh-ite. **An inhabitant of Elkosh.**—Nah.

ELLASAR, ĕl'la-sar. **The city Larsa.**— Gen. 14:1.

ELMADAM, el-mā'dam. **Ancestor of Jesus.**—Lu. 3:28. See ALMODAD.

ELNAAM, ĕl'na-ăm. **One of David's mighty men.**—I Chr. 11:46.

ELNATHAN, ĕl'na-than. (1) **Grandfather of Jehoiakim.**—II Ki. 24:8.

(2) **A prince of Judah in time of Jehoiakim.**—Jer. 26:22; 36:12, 25.

(3–5) **Three men sent on mission by Ezra.**—Ezra 8:16.

ELOI, ELOI, LAMA SABACHTHANI. **Words uttered by Jesus on the cross.** —Mk. 15:34.

ELON, ē'lon. (1) **A judge of Israel.**— Ju. 12:11.

(2) **Son of Zebulun.**—Gen. 46:14.

(3) **Father-in-law of Esau.**—Gen. 26:34; 36:2.

(4) **A town in Dan.**—Josh. 19:43.

ELON-BETH-HANAN, ē'lon-bĕth'-hā'-nan. I Ki. 4:9.

ELONITES, ē'lon-ites. Num. 26:26.

ELOQUENT. Ex. 4:10; Acts 18:24.

ELOTH, ē'loth. See ELATH.

ELPAAL, ĕl'pa-ăl. **A Benjamite.**—I Chr. 8:11, 18.

EL-PARAN, ĕl'–pā'ran. **A place in Edom.**—Gen. 14:6.

ELPELET, ĕl'pe-lĕt. See ELIPHELET.

ELTEKE, ĕl'te-kē'. **A city of Dan.**— Josh. 21:23.

ELTOLAD, ĕl-tō'lad. **A city in southern Judah.**—Josh. 15:30; 19:4. See TOLAD.

ELUL, ē'lul. **Sixth month of Jewish year.**—Neh. 6:15.

ELUZAI, e-lū'zai. **One of those who forsook Saul for David.**—I Chr. 12:5.

ELYMAS, ĕl'y-măs. **The sorcerer struck blind by Paul.**—Acts 13:11.

ELZABAD, ĕl'ză-băd. (1) **A man of God who followed David.**—I Chr. 12:12.

(2) **A doorkeeper in the temple.**—I Chr. 26:7.

ELZAPHAN, ĕl'za-phăn. (1) **Son of Uzziel.**—Ex. 6:22; Lev. 10:4; Num. 3:30.

(2) **A Levite.**—II Chr. 29:13.

EMBALM. **Joseph's body.**—Gen. 50: 2, 3. See BURIAL.

EMBARKING. Acts 27:22.

EMBERS. Pr. 26:21.

EMBOLDENED. **To eat**—I Cor. 8:10. See COURAGE.

EMBRACE. Gen. 29:13; 33:4; 48:10; Acts 20:10. A son, Thou shalt—II Ki. 4:16. A time to—Eccl. 3:5. Bosom— Pr. 5:20. Hand—Song of Sol. 2:6; 8:3. Rock, The—Job 24:8. When thou dost—Pr. 4:8.

EMBROIDERER. In blue and in purple—Ex. 35:35; 38:23. See ARTS AND TRADES.

EMEK-KEZEZ, ē'mek–kē'zĕz. **A valley in Benjamin.**—Josh. 18:21.

EMERALD. Ex. 28:18; Rev. 4:3. See PRECIOUS STONES.

EMIM, ē'mim. Gen. 14:5; Deut. 2:10. See REPHAIM.

EMMAUS, em-mā'us. **A village toward which Jesus' disciples were walking.** Lu. 24:13.

EMPTINESS. Ex. 23:15; 34:20; Deut. 15:13; 16:16; Ruth 3:17; I Sam. 6:3.

EMPTY. Ez. 24:11; Nah. 2:10. Appear before me—Ex. 23:15; 34:20. Chest—II Chr. 24:11. Clouds—Eccl. 11:3. David's place—I Sam. 20:25, 27. Ears—Gen. 41:27. Earth—Is. 24:1. Go not—Ruth 3:17. Golden oil—Zech. 4:12. House—Mt. 12:44. Land—Jer. 51:2. Net—Hab. 1:17. Pit—Gen. 37: 24. Pitcher—Ju. 7:16. Sack—Gen. 42: 35. Seat—I Sam. 20:18. Sent away— Gen. 31:42; I Sam. 6:3; Job 22:9. Soul—Is. 29:8; Is. 32:6. Space—Job 26:7 (A.V.). Vessel—II Ki. 4:3; Jer. 14:3; 51:34.

ENABLED. I Tim. 1:12. See ABLE, ABILITY.

ENACTED. Heb. 8:6. See COVENANT, LAW.

ENAM, ē'nam. **A town in Judah.**—Josh. 15:34.

ENAN, ē'nan. **Father of Ahira.**—Num. 1:15.

ENCAMPMENT. See CAMP.

ENCHANTER. Is. 3:3; Dan. 2:10. See MAGIC.

ENCHANTMENT. Lev. 19:26; Deut. 18:9; Is. 47:6. See MAGIC.

ENCOUNTER. Pr. 27:16; Lu. 14:31.

ENCOURAGE. Deut. 1:38; 3:28; II Sam. 11:25. Carpenter, the goldsmith

—Is. 41:7. Service, To the—II Chr. 35:2.

END. Blessing, Of—Gen. 27:30. Christ both died and lived again to this—Rom. 14:9. Communing, Of—Ex. 31: 18. Darkness, To—Job 28:3. Death, Ways of—Pr. 14:12; 16:25. Dividing, Of—Josh. 19:51. Earth, Of—Deut. 33: 17; I Sam. 2:10; Ps. 59:13; 67:7; 72:8; 98:3; Pr. 30:4; Is. 45:22; 52:10; Jer. 16:19; Mic. 5:4; Zech. 9:10. Endureth to the—Mt. 10:22; 24:13; Mk. 13:13. Faith, Of—I Pet. 1:9. Full—Jer. 4: 27; 5:10, 18; 30:11; 46:28; Ez. 11:13. Hand, Is at—I Pet. 4:7. Heaven, Of—Mt. 24:31. Hope in—Jer. 31:17. I am the beginning and the—Rev. 21:6; 22: 13. I am with you alway, Even unto the—Mt. 28:20. Iniquity shall have an—Ez. 21:25, 29; 35:5. Kingdom, Of his—Lu. 1:33. Labor, Of—Eccl. 4:8. Law, Of—Rom. 10:4. Life, Of—Heb. 7:3. Loved unto the—John 13:1. Men, Of all—Eccl. 7:2. Mirth, Of—Pr. 14: 13. Perfection, Of all—Ps. 119:96. Praying, Of—I Ki. 8:54. Prophesying, Of—I Sam. 10:13. Sins, Of—Dan. 9:24. Tithing, Of—Deut. 26:12. To this end was I born—John 18:37. Treasures, Of—Is. 2:7. Vain words shall—Job 16:3. War—Ps. 46:9; Dan. 9:26. Wicked, Of the—Ps. 37:38. Wits, At their—Ps. 107:27. World, Of —Mt. 13:39, 40, 49. World without—Is. 45:17. Writing, Of—Deut. 31:24.

ENDOR, ĕn'dôr. Witch of—I Sam. 28:7.

ENDOW. Gen. 30:20. See MARRIAGE.

ENDURANCE. He that endureth to the end shall be saved—Mt. 10:22; 24:13; Mt. 13:13. Continue in His goodness —Rom. 11:22. So run, that ye may attain—I Cor. 9:24. Enduring temptation—I Cor. 10:13; Jas. 1:12. Continue in the faith, grounded and steadfast—Col. 1:23. Hold fast unto the end—Heb. 3:6, 14; 4:14. We are not of them that hold back—Heb. 10:39. We call them blessed that endured—Jas. 5:11.

ENEGLAIM, ĕn-ĕg'la-ĭm. Ez. 47:10.

ENEMY. Personal.—Saul—I Sam. 18: 29; 19:17. Haman—Esth. 8:1. Job's —Job 16:9, 10. Opponent at law—Mt. 5:25; Lu. 12:58.

National enemies.—Of Sodom—Gen. 14: 8, 10, 11. Of Israel: *Absalom's revolt* —II Sam. 15:1, 12–14; 18:6. *Amalek*—Ex. 17:8, 13. *Amalekites*—I Sam. 15:2, 20; 30:3, 17. *Ammon*—II Sam. 1:9–14, 17, 19; 11:1. *Arad*—Num. 21:1–3. *Assyria*—II Ki. 15:29; 16:5, 7–9; 17:1–3, 5, 6; 18:9–13; 19:35. *Babylon*—II Ki. 24:1–4, 10, 12–16. *Bezek*—Ju. 1:5. *Canaan*—Num. 14:45; Josh. 6:20, 21; 7: 4; 8:3, 11, 24; 9:1, 2; 10:5, 10, 28–40; 11:5, 8, 10, 11. *Egypt*—Ex. 14:9, 10, 13, 14, 25, 28; 15:3, 4. *Hebron*—Ju. 1: 10. *Israel and Judah*—I Ki. 15:16. *Jerusalem*—Ju. 1:8. *Kiriath-sepher*—Ju. 1:13. *Moab*—II Sam. 8:2; II Ki. 3:24. *Midian*—Num. 31:3, 7. *Og*—Num. 21:33–35. *Philistines*—I Sam. 4: 1, 2, 10; 7:7, 10, 13, 14; 13:5; 14:20, 23; 17:1, 2, 51, 52; 31:1; II Sam. 5:17, 18, 20, 25; 8:1. *Sihon*—Num. 21:23–26. *Shishek*—I Ki. 14:25, 26. *Syria*—I Ki. 20:1, 21, 26, 29, 30; 22:29, 30; II Ki. 6:24; 7:6, 7; 10:32; 12:17, 18. *Zephath* —Ju. 1:77. *Zobah*—II Sam. 8:3.

National enemy used as a rod or a jail.—Natives left to prove Israel—Ju. 3:1. Apostasy and punishment—Ju. 3:7, 8. Under: Moab—Ju. 3:12–14. Jabin—Ju. 4:1–3. Philistines—Ju. 3:31; 13:1. Israel under Assyria—II Ki. 17:23. Judah under Babylon—II Ki. 24:15, 16.

Deliverance from oppression. — From Egypt—Ex. 14:13. Cushon—Ju. 3:10. Moab—Ju. 3:28, 29. Philistines—Ju. 3:31; 15:14, 15, 20. Jabin—Ju. 4:15. Midian—Ju. 7:19–23. Philistines and Ammonites—Ju. 11:32, 33. Babylon —II Chr. 36:22, 23; Ezra 1:1–4.

Prophecies concerning enemies.—Lev. 26:25; Deut. 28:25, 36, 37, 48–57, 68; 33:29; I Sam. 20:15, 16; 25:29; I Chr. 17:10; 22:9; Jer. 15:9, 14; 19:7–9; 20: 4, 5; 21:7; 34:20; 44:30; Mt. 24:15–22; Lu. 19:43, 44.

Spiritual enemies.—God's—II Sam. 12: 14; Ps. 8:2; 37:20; 68:1; 83:2; 89:10, 51; 92:9; 139:20, 22; Is. 42:13; 59:18; 66:6, 14; Rom. 5:10; Col. 1:21. Of Christ: *The devil*—Mt. 13:39. *The wicked*—Mt. 13:36; 21:46; 26:4; Mk. 11:18; 12:12; 14:1, 2, 10, 11, 55, 56, 64; 15:3, 10, 11, 29, 30; Lu. 19:47; 20:19, 43; 22:2–6, 52, 53; 23:2; John 5:16,

18; 7:1, 19, 25; 8:37, 40; 11:53; I Cor.
15:25, 26; Phil. 3:18; Heb. 1:13; 10:
13. Of Holy Spirit—Mt. 12:24, 31, 32;
Mk. 3:22, 28–30; Lu. 12:10. Of saints:
The accuser—Job 1:9–11; 2:3–4; I Pet.
5:8; Rev. 12:10. *The wicked*—Mt. 10:
16, 17, 25; Lu. 22:35–38; Acts 4:21,
26, 29; 5:17, 18, 33, 40; 6:9–14; 7:59;
8:1, 3; 12:1–3; 14:19; 21:30, 31; 23:14.
Own household—Mic. 7:6; Mt. 10:21,
35, 36.

Become enemy by speaking the truth.—
Gal. 4:16.

Treatment of personal enemies.—I Sam.
24:4–6, 11, 19; 26:8, 9; Pr. 24:17, 18;
25:21, 22; Mt. 5:25, 43, 44; Lu. 6:27,
35; 22:50, 51; 23:34; Acts 7:60; 9:3–6;
13:9–11; 16:28, 37. See Salvation
from enemies, Forgiveness—Pr. 25:
21.

EN-GANNIM, ĕn'-găn'nim. (1) **A city
of Issachar.**—Josh. 19:21; 21:29.
(2) **A city of Judah.**—Josh. 15:34.

ENGEDI, ĕn'gĕ'dī. **A region on the Dead
Sea.**—Josh. 15:62.

ENGINES. II Chr. 26:15; Ez. 26:9.

ENGRAVE. Ex. 35:35; 38:23.

ENGRAVING. Ex. 28:11, 21, 36; 32:4;
39:6; I Ki. 7:31, 36; II Chr. 3:7; Zech.
3:9. See Arts and trades.

EN-HADDAH, ĕn'-hăd'dah. **A place in
Issachar.**—Josh. 19:21.

EN-HAKKORE, ĕn'-hăk'ko-re. **Name
of a spring where Samson drank.**—Ju.
15:19.

EN-HAZOR, ĕn'-hā'zor. **A town in
Naphtali.**—Josh. 19:37.

ENJOIN. Esth. 9:21, 31; Job 36:23;
Philemon 8; Heb. 2:20.

ENJOY. Eccl. 2:1, 24, 25; 3:13; 5:18;
Is. 65:22; Ju. 31:5; I Tim. 6:17; Heb.
11:25. Peace—Acts 24:2. Sabbath—
Lev. 26:34, 43; II Chr. 36:21. See Joy,
Rejoice, Possess.

ENLARGE. Gen. 9:27; Deut. 33:20; I
Sam. 2:1; II Sam. 22:37; Ps. 18:36;
Is. 5:14; Mic. 1:16; Hab. 2:5. Heart—
Ps. 119:32; Is. 60:5; II Cor. 6:11, 13.
Land—Ex. 34:24; Deut. 12:20; 19:8;
I Chr. 4:10; Job 12:23; Is. 26:15; 54:
2; Amos 1:13; Mt. 23:5. Troubles—
Ps. 25:17. See Abound.

ENLIGHTEN. Job 33:30; Ps. 18:28;
97:4; Heb. 6:4; 10:32. Heart—Eph.
1:18. Eyes—I Sam. 14:27, 29; Ps. 19:

8; Eph. 1:18. See Gospel, Instruction.

ENMISHPAT, ĕn'mĭsh'pat. ˊ Gen. 14:7.
See Kadesh.

ENOCH, ē'noch. Heb. *''initiated.''* Son
of Jared—Gen. 5:18. Father of Methuselah—Gen. 5:21; I Chr. 1:2, 3.
Preached to his generation—Jude 14,
15. Lived 365 years—Gen. 5:23. Of
Noah and Enoch alone is it written,
''They walked with God.'' Others
walked ''before God''—Gen. 5:24;
17:1. Translated—Gen. 5:24; Heb. 11:
5. He pleased God—Heb. 1:5.

ENOSH, ē'nŏsh. **Son of Seth.**—Gen.
4:26.

ENOUGH. Gen. 33:9. Bread enough—
Lu. 15:17. Disciple, For the—Mt. 10:
25. Four that say—Pr. 30:15. It is—
Mk. 14:4. Room—Mal. 3:10.

ENQUIRE. See Inquire, Prayer.

ENRICH. I Sam. 17:25; Ps. 65:9; Ez.
27:33; I Cor. 1:5; II Cor. 9:11. See
Riches.

EN-RIMMON, ĕn'-rĭm'mon. **A town in
Judah.** See Ain, Rimmon.

EN-ROGEL, ĕn'-rō'gel. **A fountain near
Jerusalem.**—Josh. 15:7.

ENSAMPLE. II Pet. 2:6. Apostles, Of
—Phil. 3:17; II Thess. 3:9; I Tim. 1:
16. Christian, Of—I Thess. 1:7; I Tim.
4:12; Tit. 2:7. Elders, Of—I Pet. 5:3.
See Example.

EN-SHEMESH, ĕn'-shē'mesh. **A spring
between Judah and Benjamin.**—Josh.
15:7; 18:17.

ENSIGN. Is. 11:10, 12; 18:3; Ez. 27:7.
Armies, Of—Num. 2:2; Ps. 74:4; Is.
5:26; 13:2; 30:17; 31:9; 62:10. Jehovah, Of—Is. 49:22. See Banner,
Standard.

ENSLAVE. Tit. 2:3. See Drunkenness, Slavery.

ENSNARE. Deut. 12:30; Job 34:30. Jesus—Mt. 22:15.

ENTANGLE. Ex. 14:3; Nah. 1:10; Gal.
5:1; II Pet. 2:20. See Ensnare.

EN-TAPPUAH, ĕn-tăp'pū-äh. Town in
Samaria—Josh. 17:7.

ENTER. Jer. 2:7; Ez. 37:5; John 10:1,
2. Ark—Gen. 7:13; Mt. 24:38; Lu. 17:
27. Assembly of Jehovah—Deut. 23:
1–8. Canaan—Num. 20:24. Capernaum—Mt. 8:5; Mk. 1:21; 2:1; Lu.
7:1. Covenant, Into—Deut. 29:12; II

Sam. 15:12; Jer. 34:10; Ez. 16:8. Egypt—Gen. 12:11; Jer. 41:17; 42:15, 18. Gates with thanksgiving—Ps. 100: 4. Israel, Land of—Ez. 13:9; 20:38. Jerusalem—Lam. 4:12; Ob. 11–13; Mk. 11:11; Judah—II Chr. 32:1. Judgment, Into—Job 22:4; Ps. 143:2; Is. 3:14. Kingdom of God—Ps. 118:20; Is. 26:2; Mt. 5:20; 7:21; 18:3; 19:17, 23, 24; Mk. 9:47; 10:15, 23–25; Lu. 18:17, 24, 25; John 3:5; 10:9; Acts 14:22. Peace, Into—Is. 57.2. Rest— Ps. 95:11; Heb. 3:11, 18, 19; 4:3, 5, 6, 10, 11. Service of Jehovah—Num. 4:3, 23, 30, 35. Spirit—Ez. 2:22; 3:24. Synagogue—Mk. 1:21; 3:1; Lu. 4:38, 6:6. Tabernacle—Ex. 33:9; 40:35; II Chr. 7:2; 12:11; 23:19. Temple—II Chr. 27:2; 30:8; Lam. 1:10; Ez. 42:14; 44:2–21; 46:2, 8; Mt. 12:4; Acts 3:2, 8; 5:21; 21:26. Temptation—Pr. 4:14; Mt. 7:13; 21:12; 26:41; Mk. 14:38; Lu. 13:24; 22:40, 46. Tomb of Jesus —Mk. 16:5; Lu. 24:3.

ENTERPRISE. Job 5:12.

ENTERTAIN. Acts 28:7. Angels—Heb. 13:2. See HOSPITALITY.

ENTICE. Jer. 20:10; Jas. 1:14. Ahab— I Ki. 22:20; II Chr. 18:19–21. Heart— Job 31:9, 27. Neighbor—Pr. 16:29. Samson—Ju. 14:15; 16:5. Secretly— Deut. 13:6; Job 31:27. Sinners entice thee, If—Pr. 1:10. Virgin—Ex. 22:16. See PERSUADE, SEDUCTION, TEMPTATION.

ENTICING. Words—I Cor. 2:4; Col. 2:4.

ENTIRE. Jas. 1:4.

ENTRANCE. City, Into—Ju. 1:24, 25. Gate—Pr. 1:21; Ez. 40:15. Samaria, Of—I Ki. 22:10. Gedor—I Chr. 4:39. Jezreel—I Ki. 18:46. Ministered, Shall be—II Pet. 1:11 (A.V.). Paul, Of—I Thess. 4:1. Words, Of—Ps. 119:130.

ENTREAT. Acts 28:20. Corinthians— II Cor. 9:5; 10:1. Courteously—Acts 27:3 (A.V.). Evil—Ex. 5:22 (A.V.); Deut. 26:6; Job 24:21 (A.V.); Acts 7:6. Jehovah—I Ki. 13:6. Shamefully— Lu. 20:1 (A.V.); I Thess. 2:2 (A.V.). Spitefully—Mt. 22:6 (A.V.); Lu. 18:32 (A.V.). Two men—Acts 9:38. Well— Jer. 15:11. See DEAL, PRAYER, TREAT, USE.

ENTRY. See ENTER, DOOR, GATE, WAY.

ENVY, ENVIOUS. Christ of, Preach— Phil. 1:15. Edom, Against—Ez. 35:11. Evil men, Be not envious against—Pr. 24:1, 19. Foolish, Against—Ps. 73:3. Full of—Rom. 1:29. Love envieth not —I Cor. 13:4. Malice and—Tit. 3:3. Murder and—Gal. 5:21. Put away— I Pet. 2:21. Rottenness of bones, Is —Pr. 14:30. Slayeth silly ones—Job 5:2. Strife and—Rom. 13:13; I Cor. 3:3; II Cor. 12:20; Phil. 1:15; I Tim. 6:4; Jas. 3:14, 16. Unrighteous, Of— Ps. 37:1. Violence, Man of—Pr. 3:31. **Examples.**—Eccl. 31:9. Aaron and Miriam—Num. 12:2. Arrogant, Against —Ps. 73:3. Cain—Gen. 4:5. Ephraim —Is. 11:13. Jesus, Against—Mt. 27: 18; Mk. 15:10. Joseph's brethren— Gen. 37:11; Acts 7:9. Korah—Num. 16:3; Ps. 106:16. Moses, Against— Num. 12:2; 16:3; Ps. 106:16. Philistines—Gen. 26:14. Rachel—Gen. 30: 1. Saul—I Sam. 18:8. Sinners, Against —Pr. 23:17. Trees of Eden—Ez. 31:9. See JEALOUSY, HATRED.

EPAENETUS, e-pæn′e-tŭs. A disciple mentioned by Paul as the first fruit of Asia.—Rom. 16:5.

EPAPHRAS, ĕp′a-phrăs. One of Paul's fellow-workers.—Col. 1:7; 4:12; Philemon 23.

EPAPHRODITUS, ē-păph-rŏ-dī′tus. A fellow-worker with Paul, messenger of Philippian church.—Phil. 2:25–30; 4:18.

EPHAH, ē′phah. (1) Son of Jahdai.— I Chr. 2:27.

(2) Caleb's concubine.—I Chr. 2:46.

(3) Gen. 25:4.

(4) A measure.—See MEASURES.

EPHAI, ē′phā′i. Jer. 40:8.

EPHER, ē′pher. (1) A Midianite.—Gen. 25:4; I Chr. 1:33.

(2) A man of Judah.—I Chr. 4:17.

(3) A man of Manasseh.—I Chr. 5:24.

EPHESDAMMIM, ē′phes-dăm′mim. An encampment of the Philistines.—I Sam. 17:1. See CAMP.

EPHESIANS. See OUTLINE STUDIES IN THE BOOKS.

EPHESUS, ĕph′e-sŭs. A very ancient city; older than 1100 B.C. In the time of Christ it was the third largest city of the Christian world, with about

225,000 inhabitants. Paul visits—Acts 18:19. Diana the goddess of—Acts Ch. 19. Demetrius, the silversmith, raises an uproar—Acts 19:24. Paul addresses elders of—Acts 20:17. Paul fights wild beasts at—I Cor. 15:32. Paul addresses epistle to—Eph. 1:1. One of seven churches—Rev. 1:11. See OUTLINE STUDIES IN THE BOOKS, PAUL.

EPHLAL, ĕph′lal. I Chr. 2:37.

EPHOD. (1) See PRIESTS.

(2) Ju. 8:27; 17:5; 18:14; I Sam. 2:28; 14:3; 23:69; 30:7.

EPHPHATHA, ĕph′pha-thă. **Word spoken by Jesus.**—Mk. 7:34.

EPHRAIM, ē′phra-ĭm. (1) **Youngest son of Joseph.**—Gen. 41:52; 46:20; 48:1-5, 13-20; 50:23.

(2) **Half-tribe of.**—Ju. 5:14; Ps. 60:7; 78:67; 80:2; 108:8.

Inheritance.—Josh. 14:4;, 16:4-9; 17:8-18; 21:5, 20, 21; I Chr. 6:66; 7:28, 29. Did not drive out Canaanites—Ju. 1:29.

Number.—Num. 1:32, 33; 2:19, 24; I Chr. 12:30.

Battles.—With Midian—Ju. 7:24, 25. Quarrel with Gideon—Ju. 8:1-3. With Ammonites—Ju. 10:9. With Jephthah and Gilead—Ju. 12:1-6. Helped David become king—I Chr. 12:23, 30. Amaziah rejected—II Chr. 25:7, 10. Captives returned—II Chr. 28:8-15.

Camp.—Num. 2:18; 10:22.

Captains and princes.—Num. 1:10; 7:48; 10:22; 34:24; I Chr. 27:10, 14, 20; II Chr. 28:7, 12.

Genealogies.—Num. 26:35-37; I Chr. 7:20-27.

Miscellaneous references.—Abner king of—II Sam. 2:9. Idolatry of—II Chr. 31:1; 34:5-7. Letters sent to—II Chr. 30:1, 10. Passover kept without cleansing—II Chr. 30:1, 10, 18. Spy sent out—Num. 13:8. Temple, Gave money to repair—II Chr. 34:8, 9.

Country called "Hill-country," or Mt. Ephraim—II Chr. 19:4. Ben-Hur in—I Ki. 4:8. Bethlehem—Judah—Ju. 19:1, 18. Blew a trumpet in—Ju. 3:27. Buried him in—Josh. 24:30, 33; Ju. 2:9. Cities—II Chr. 15:8. Hid themselves in—I Sam. 14:22. Garrisons in —II Chr. 17:2. Micah, A man of—Ju.

17:1, 8; 18:12, 13. Palm tree of Deborah in—Ju. 4:5. Passed through—I Sam. 9:4. Pirathon in—Ju. 12:15. Publish evil from—Jer. 4:15. Ramathaimzophim of the—I Sam. 1:1. Shamar, In—Ju. 10:1. Sheba, A man of —II Sam. 20:21. Shechem, In—Josh. 20:7; I Ki. 12:25; I Chr. 6:7. Sojourners out of—II Chr. 15:9. Timnath-serah in—Josh. 19:50. Two young men from—II Ki. 5:22. Zemaraim Mount —II Chr. 13:4.

(3) **Used to denote the northern kingdom.**—Ps. 78:9; Is. 7:2-17; 9:9, 21; 11:13; 17:3; 28:1, 3; Jer. 4:15; 7:15; 31:6, 9, 18, 20; 50:19; Ez. 37:16, 19; 48:5, 6; Hos. 4:17; 5:3-14; 6:4, 10; 7:1, 8, 11; 9:3, 8, 11, 13, 16; 10:6, 11; 11:3, 8, 9, 12; 12:1, 8, 14; 13:1, 12; 14:8; Ob. 1:19; Zech. 9:10, 13; 10:7.

(4) **A city in Judea.**—John 11:54.

EPHRAIM. Forest of.—II Sam. 18:6.

EPHRAIM. Gate of temple.—II Sam. 14:13; II Chr. 25:3; Neh. 8:16; 12:39.

EPHRAIMITE. Josh. 16:10; Ju. 12:4-6.

EPHRAIN. See EPHRON.

EPHRATH, EPHRATHAH, ĕph′rath, ĕph′rath-ah. (1) **Wife of Caleb.**—I Chr. 2:19, 50; 4:4.

(2) **An ancient city of Judah.** Some of these references are to Bethlehem, but it is not certain that all are—Gen. 35:16, 19; 48:7; Ruth 4:11; Ps. 132:6; Mic. 5:2.

EPHRATHITE. Ruth 1:2; I Sam. 1:1; 17:12; I Ki. 11:26.

EPHRON, ē′phron. (1) **Name of the man from whom Abraham purchased a field in which to bury Sarah.**—Gen. 23:8-17; 25:9; 49:29, 30; 50:13.

(2) **A mountain.**—Josh. 15:9.

EPICUREAN, ĕp′i-cu-rē′an. **An Athenian philosopher.**—Acts 17:18.

EPILEPTIC. Mt. 4:24; 17:15. See DISEASE.

EPISTLE. See LETTERS, OUTLINE STUDIES IN THE BOOKS.

EQUAL. Ps. 55:13; Is. 46:5; Lam. 2:13; Mt. 20:12. Breadth and height are—Rev. 21:16. God, With—John 5:18. Gold cannot—Job 28:17. Topaz shall not—Job 28:19. Way is not—Ez. 18:25, 29; 33:17, 20.

EQUALITY. II Cor. 8:14.

EQUITY. Is. 11:4; Mal. 2:6. Establish —Ps. 99:4. Instruction in—Pr. 1:3. Judge with—Ps. 98:9. Pervert—Mic. 3:9. Understand—Pr. 2:9. See JUS-TICE.

ER, ẽr. (1) **Oldest son of Judah.**—Gen. 38:3, 6, 7; 46:12.

(2) **Son of Shelah.**—I Chr. 4:21.

(3) **Ancestor of Jesus.**—Lu. 3:28.

ERAN, ẽ'ran. **Grandson of Ephraim.**—Num. 26:36.

ERANITES, ẽ'ran-ites. **Descendants of Eran.**—Num. 26:36.

ERASTUS, ẽ-răs'tŭs. (1) **A Christian sent to Macedonia by Paul.**—Acts 19:22; II Ti. 4:20.

(2) **One of Paul's converts, possibly same as** (1).—Rom. 16:23.

ERECH, ẽ'rech. **A city of Babylon.**—Gen. 10:10.

ERI, ẽ'ri. **A man of God.**—Gen. 46:16; Num. 26:16.

ERITES, ẽ'rītes. **Descendants of Eri.**—Num. 26:16.

ERR, ERRED. Lev. 5:18; Num. 15:22; I Sam. 26:21; Job 6:24; 19:4; Ps. 119:118; Pr. 10:17; 14:22; Ez. 45:20; Mt. 22:29; Mk. 12:24, 27; I Tim. 6:21. Heart, In—Ps. 95:10; Heb. 3:10. Instruction causes—Pr. 19:27. Lies caused to—Amos 2:4. People—Is. 9:16; Jer. 23:32; Mic. 3:5. Spirit, In—Is. 29:24. Truth, From—II Tim. 2:18; Jas. 5:19. Vision, In—Is. 28:7. Wayfaring men shall not—Is. 35:8. Wine, Through—Is. 28:7. See SIN.

ERRAND. Have—II Ki. 9:5. Secret—Ju. 3:19. Told—Gen. 24:33.

ERROR. Job 19:4; Eccl. 5:6; 10:5; Dan. 6:4. Baalam, Of—Jude 11. Converteth a sinner from—Jas. 5:20. Last shall be worse—Mt. 27:64. Live in—II Pet. 2:18. People, Of—Heb. 9:7. Recompence of—Rom. 1:27. Smote for—II Sam. 6:7. Spirit of—I John 4:6. Utter—Is. 32:6. Way, Of his—Jas. 5:20. Wicked, Of—II Pet. 3:17. See SIN.

ESAIAS. See ISAIAH.

ESAR-HADDON, ẽ'sar-hăd'don. **An Assyrian king.**—II Ki. 19:37.

ESAU, ẽ'sạu. Twin brother of Jacob—Name signifies ''hairy''—Gen. 25:25. Birth—Gen. 25:19-26. Was a lover of nature, a hunter—Gen. 25:27. Won his father with his venison—Gen. 25:28. During a search for venison Jacob prepared pottage—Gen. 25:29. Esàu, being hungry, was tempted to sell birthright—Gen. 25:30-34: Rebekah, who loved Jacob, prepared for the robbery of the blessing—Gen. 27:1-26. Isaac confers Esau's blessing upon Jacob—Gen. 27:27-29. Esau, on returning from field, discovers treachery and weeps—Gen. 27:30-38. Isaac blesses Esau, who hates Jacob—Gen. 27:39-41. Fear of Esau's wrath drives Jacob to Haran—Gen. 27:43-45. Esau marries two Hittites, grieving his father—Gen. 2:34. Marries also an Ishmaelite—Gen. 28:9. Dwells in Mount Seir—Deut. 2:4-8. Enmity between Esau and Jacob, personally, ceased—Gen. 33:8-16. But enmity between descendants remained—Ob. 10-18. Caused by Edomites refusing Israel passage through their country—Num. 20:17-21. Esau's descendants divinely protected from hand of Israel—Deut. 2:4-7. Because of idolatry, God punished them—Mal. 1:2-5; Rom. 9:13; Heb. 11:20; 12:16. See JACOB.

ESCAPE. Absalom, From—II Sam. 15:14. Alone—Job 1:15, 16, 17, 19. Corruption—II Pet. 1:4. David—I Sam. 19:18; 22:1. Destruction—I Thess. 5:3. Egypt shall not—Dan. 11:42. See EGYPT, PROPHECIES. How shall we—Heb. 2:3. Iniquity, By—Ps. 56:7. Judgment of God—Rom. 2:3. Judgment of hell—Mt. 23:33 (A.V.). See SIN. Lies, He that speaketh—Pr. 19:5. Life, For thy—Gen. 19:17. Mountain, To—Gen. 19:17, 19. None—II Chr. 20:24. Safe—Acts 27:44. Salvation, If we neglect—Heb. 2:3. Soul is—Ps. 124:7. Skin of teeth, With—Job 19:20. Sword—Jer. 44:28; 51:50; Ez. 6:8; Heb. 11:34. Temptation, From—I Cor. 10:13. Way of, He will make—I Cor. 10:13. Wicked shall not—Job 11:20.

ESEK, ẽ'sek. **Name of Isaac's well**—Gen. 26:20.

ESHAN, ẽ'shan. **A city of Judah.**—Josh. 15:32.

ESHBAAL. See ISH-BOSHETH.

ESHBAN, ẽsh'ban. Gen. 36:26; I Chr. 1:4.

ESHCOL, ĕsh'kŏl. (1) **Brother of Mamre.**—Gen. 14:13, 24.

(2) **Valley noted for its grapes.**—Num. 13:23; 32:9; Deut. 1:24.

ESHEK, ē'shek. I Chr. 8:39.

ESHTAOL, ĕsh'ta-ŏl. **A town in Judah.** —Josh. 15:33; 19:41; Ju. 13:25; 16: 31; 18:2, 8, 11.

ESHTAOLITES. Inhabitants of Eshtaol.—I Chr. 2:23.

ESHTEMOA, ĕsh'te-mō-a. (1) **A Levitical town in Judah.**—Josh. 15:50; 21: 14; I Sam. 30:28; I Chr. 6:37.

(2) **A descendant of Ezra.**—I Chr. 4: 17, 19.

ESHTON, ĕsh'ton. **A man of Judah.**—I Chr. 4:11, 12.

ESLI, ĕs'lī. **Ancestor of Joseph.**—Lu. 3:25.

ESPECIALLY. Household of faith, Unto—Gal. 6:10. Labor in the word, Those who—I Tim. 5:17. Parchments II Tim. 4:13.

ESPOUSE. Ex. 21:8. See BETROTHAL.

ESPY. See SPIES.

ESTABLISH. God's covenant — Gen. 6:18. His word—I Ki. 2:4. The oath —Gen. 26:3. World is established—I Chr. 16:30. God's throne—I Chr. 17: 12; Ps. 103:19. My kings—Ps. 40:2. The work of our hands—Ps. 90:17. The heavens—Prov. 8:27. Truthful life shall be established—Prov. 12:19. Throne established by righteousness —Prov. 16:12. His ways—Prov. 21: 29. Establish your hearts—I Thess. 5:17. Comfort and establish your hearts—II Thess. 2:17. See COVENANT, THE CHURCH.

ESTATE. Know your—Col. 4:8. Man of high degree, Of—I Chr. 17:17.

ESTEEM. Day—Rom. 14:5. Field as a forest—Is. 29:17. Lightly—I Sam. 2: 30; 18:23. Love, In—I Thess. 5:13. Pitchers, As earthen—Lam. 4:2. Potter's clay, As—Is. 29:16.

ESTHER. See OUTLINE STUDIES IN THE BOOKS.

ESTIMATE. Lev. 5:15, 18; 6:6; 27:2–27; Num. 18:16.

ESTRANGE. Ps. 58:3; 78:30; Is. 1:4; Jer. 19:4. Friends—Job 19:13. Idols, Through—Ez. 14:5. See ALIEN.

ETAM, ē'tam. (1) **A district in Judah.** Ju. 15:8, 11.

(2) **A village in Simeon.**—I Chr. 4:32.

(3) **A town in Judea.**—II Chr. 11:6.

ETERNAL. Is. 60:15; II Cor. 4:18. Comfort—II Thess. 2:16. Destruction—II Thess. 1:9. Fire—Mt. 18:8; 25:41; Jude 7. Glory—II Cor. 4:11; II Tim. 2:10; I Pet. 5:10. God—Deut. 33:27; Rom. 16:26. Gospel—Rev. 14:6. Honor —I Tim. 6:16. Inheritance—Heb. 9: 14. Judgment—Heb. 6:2. King—I Tim. 1:17. Kingdom of God—II Pet. 1:11. Life—See LIFE. Mountains— Hab. 3:6. Power—I Tim. 6:16. Punishment—Mt. 25:46. Purpose—Eph. 3:11. Redemption—Heb. 9:2. Salvation—Heb. 5:9. Sin—Mk. 3:29. Spirit —Heb. 9:15. See EVERLASTING.

ETERNITY. Eccl. 3:11; Is. 57:15.

ETHAM, ē'tham. One of Israel's encampments—Ex. 13:20; Num. 33:20; 33:6–8.

ETHAN, ē'than. (1) **Ancestor of Asaph.** I Chr. 6:42.

(2) **Author of Ps. 89.**—I Ki. 4:31; Ps. 89 (title).

(3) I Chr. 6:44; 15:17, 19.

ETHANIM, ĕth'a-nĭm. **The seventh month of Jewish year.**—I Ki. 8:2.

ETHBAAL, ĕth'bā-al. **King of Sidon, father of Jezebel.**—I Ki. 16:31.

ETHER, ē'ther. **A town of Judah.**— Josh. 15:42.

ETHIOPIA, ē-thi-ō'pi-a. **Land of.**— Called Cush—Gen. 2:13; Jer. 46:9; Ez. 38:5. Inhabitants of—II Chr. 12:3. Given for ransom—Is. 43:3. Rulers of —II Ki. 19:9; Esth. 1:1; 8:9; Is. 37:9. Citizenship of—Ps. 87:4. Topaz found in—Job 28:19. Rivers of—Is. 18:1; Zeph. 3:10. Border of—Ez. 29:10; II Chr. 21:16. Eunuch—Jer. 38:7, 10, 12; 39:16; Acts 8:27. Strength—Nah. 3:9. Moses married a woman of—Num. 12: 1. Children of—Amos 9:7. Strife with —II Chr. 14:9, 12, 13; 16:8.

Prophecies concerning.—Ps. 68:31; Is. 20:3, 4, 5; Ez. 30:4, 5; 38:5; Dan. 11: 43; Zeph. 2:12. Merchandise of—Is. 45:14.

Illustrative.—Skin of—Jer. 13:23.

ETHKAZIN, ĕth'kā'zin. **A town in Zebulun.**—Josh. 19:13.

ETHNAN, ĕth'nan. I Chr. 4:7.

ETHNI, ĕth'ni. A Levite—I Chr. 6:41.

EUBULUS, eū'bū-lus. **A disciple in Rome to whom a salutation is sent.**—II Tim. 4:21.

EUNICE, eū-nī'se. **Mother of Timothy.** —Acts 16:1; II Tim. 1:5.

EUNUCH. In Jezreel.—Looked out to Jehu—II Ki. 9:32. In the palace of king of Babylon—II Ki. 20:18; Is. 39:7; Dan. 1:3, 7, 8, 9, 10, 11, 18. Departed from Jerusalem—Jer. 29:2. From Ethiopia—Jer. 38:7. Philip and the Eunuch, and his baptism—Acts 8:26-38. From Gibeon—Jer. 41:16.

Kinds of.—That keep the Sabbath—Is. 56:4. Born eunuchs, made eunuchs by men, and make of themselves eunuchs for the kingdom of heaven's sake—Mt. 19:12.

Prophecy concerning.—Jer. 34:19.

EUODIA, eū-ō'di-a. **A female disciple, fellow-worker with Paul.**—Phil. 4:2, 3.

EUPHRATES, eū-phrā'tēs. One of the Edenic rivers—Gen. 2:14. Known as "the river"—Ex. 23:31; Josh. 24:2; Neh. 2:7; Ps. 72:8. Appointed as eastern boundary for Israelites—Gen. 15:18; Ex. 23:31; Deut. 1:7; 11:24; Josh. 1:4; II Sam. 8:3; I Ki. 4:21; I Chr. 5:9; 18:3. Assyria bounded by—II Ki. 23:29; Is. 7:20. King of Assyria symbolized by—Is. 8:6-8. Pharaoh-nechoh conquered up to—II Ki. 24:7; Jer. 46:2-10. Babylon situated upon—Jer. 51:13, 36. Egyptian army destroyed at—Jer. 46:2-10. Captive Jews wept at—Ps. 137:1-3. Jeremiah hides girdle at—Jer. 13:1-9. Book as a sign thrown into—Jer. 51:63. Apocalyptic symbols—Rev. 9:14; 16:12.

EURAQUILO, eū-răq'ui-lo. **Name of wind beating against Paul's ship on way to Rome.**—Acts 27:13.

EUTYCHUS, eū'ty-kus. **A lad who fell from window while Paul was preaching.**—Acts 20:7-12.

EVANGELIST. Acts 21:8; Eph. 4:11; II Tim. 4:5. See MINISTERS.

EVE. "Life."

Her creation—Gen. 1:27; 2:21, 22; Mt. 19:4; I Cor. 11:8, 9; I Tim. 2:13. In image of God—Gen. 1:26, 27; 5:1, 2; I Cor. 11:7; Col. 3:10.

Accepted by Adam.—Gen. 2:23, 24. Named—Gen. 2:23; 3:20; 5:2.

Blessed by Jehovah.—Gen. 1:27, 28; 5:1, 2.

A typical wedlock.—Mt. 19:5, 6; Mk. 10:6, 9; Eph. 5:31.

Commanded to be fruitful.—Gen. 1:28; 9:1, 7; Ps. 127:3-5.

Her fall.—Tempted by the serpent—Gen. 3:1-6; John 8:44; II Cor. 11:3; I Tim. 2:14; Rev. 12:9. Recognizes her shame—Gen. 3:7, 8; Is. 47:3; Lam. 1:8. Curse pronounced—Gen. 3:16; I Cor. 14:34; I Tim. 2:14. Clothed by Jehovah—Gen. 3:21. Sent forth from garden—Gen. 3:32. Has sons and daughters—Gen. 4:2; 5:4.

Conditional promises.—I Tim. 2:15. Conquests of her seed predicted—Gen. 3:15.

EVENING. Evening and the morning —Gen. Ch. 1. Israel shall kill it in the —Ex. 12:6. Stood by Moses from morning till—Ex. 18:13. The Philistine drew near morning and—I Sam. 17:16. In the evening cut down—Ps. 90:6. Makest outgoings to rejoice— Ps. 65:8. Goeth to labor until—Ps. 104:23. Went to her house in the—Pr. 7:8, 9. In the evening withhold not thy hand—Eccl. 11:6. At evening time there shall be light—Zech. 14:7. Toward evening—Lu. 24:29. Jesus came at evening—John 20:19. Paul persuaded Jews from morning till evening—Acts 28:23. See MORNING.

EVENTIDE. Gen. 8:11; Is. 17:14.

EVER. Christ. See JESUS, DIVINITY OF. Confidence—Is. 32:17. Counsel of Jehovah—Is. 33:11. Desolate for—Ps. 9:6. Dwell in tabernacle—Ps. 61:4. God—See GOD IS EVERLASTING. House of Jehovah, In—Ps. 23:6. King for— Ps. 9:7; 29:10. Live for—Gen. 3:22; Deut. 32:40; Ps. 22:26. Prophecy—II Pet. 1:21. Riches not for—Pr. 27:24. Sin ever before me—Ps. 51:3. Statutes—Ps. 119:12. Time—Ps. 81:15. Trust—Ps. 52:8; Is. 26:4. Truth—Ps. 146:6. See ETERNAL, EVERLASTING.

EVERLASTING. Mic. 5:2; Hab. 1:12. Bonds—Jude 6. Burnings—Is. 33:14. Contempt—Dan. 12:2. Covenant— Gen. 9:16; 17:7, 13, 19; Lev. 24:8; II Sam. 23:5; I Chr. 16:17; Ps. 105:10; Is. 24:5; 55:3; 61:8; Jer. 32:40; Ez. 16:60; 37:26. Dishonor—Jer. 20:11.

Everlasting, To—I Chr. 16:36; Neh. 9:5; Ps. 41:13; 90:2; 103:17; 106:48. Father—Is. 9:6. God—Gen. 21:33; Ps. 93:2; Is. 40:28. See GOD. Jesus—See JESUS. Joy—Is. 35:10; 51:11; 61:7. King—Jer. 10:10. Kingdom—Ps. 145: 13; Dan. 4:3, 34; 7:14, 27. Light—Is. 60:19, 20. Love—Jer. 31:3. Loving kindness—Is. 54:8. Name—Is. 56:5; 63:12. Possession—Gen. 17:8; 48:4. Priesthood—Ex. 40:15; Num. 25:13. Redeemer—Is. 63:16. Remembrance —Ps. 112:6. Reproach—Jer. 23:40. Righteousness—Ps. 119:142; Pr. 10: 25; Dan. 9:24. Rock—Is. 26:4. Salvation—Is. 45:17. Sign—Is. 55:13. Statutes—Lev. 16:34. Way—Ps. 139:24. See ETERNAL, EVER, EVERMORE.

EVERMORE. Alive—Rev. 1:18. Dwell —Ps. 37:27. Give us bread—John 6: 34. Jehovah—See GOD IS EVERLASTING. Old, From of—Jer. 7:7. Perfected for —Heb. 7:28. Pleasures for—Ps. 16:11.

EVERY. Family—Eph. 3:15. Gift— Jas. 1:17. Good path—Pr. 2:9. Good work—II Tim. 2:21. Knee shall bow —Rom. 14:11. Imagination—Gen. 6:5. Living creature—Gen. 1:21. Name— Eph. 1:21. One—*Angry*—Mt. 5:22. *Asking*—Mt. 7:8. *Born*—John 3:8. *Godly*—Ps. 32:6. *Hath, That*—Lu. 19: 26. *Loveth, That*—I John 4:7. *Nameth, That*—II Tim. 2:19. Spirit—I John 4:1. Thought—II Cor. 10:11. Weight —Heb. 12:1. Word of God—Mt. 4:4.

EVIDENT. Heb. 7:14. No man is justified is—Gal. 3:11. Token of perdition —Phil. 1:28.

EVIL. Genesis.—Gen. 3:5, 22; Mk. 7: 20–23; I Tim. 6:10. Plea of evil—Gen. 3:1–6; Pr. 7:10–21.

Development.—Gen. 6:5; Deut. 31:29; Ju. 2:11–15; I Sam. 12:19; Mt. 12:45; II Tim. 3:3; Jude 12:15.

Consciousness.—Gen. 3:7, 8; Mt. 5:11; Lu. 18:13, 14; John 3:20; Rom. 3:20; 7:19.

Instruments.—Gen. 2:9; 3:1; Ex. 32:1– 6; II Ki. 18:4; Mt. 15:3–6; I John 5:19.

Transformation.—Gen. 3:5; Is. 5:20; Mt. 2:8; 5:39; 7:15, 16; Is. 5:20.

Constraint.—Gen. 3:12, 13; Jer. 23:9– 12; John 3:19; Rom. 7:15–19.

Limitation.—Ex. 32:14; Ps. 34:13, 14; Mt. 6:13; John 17:15; Acts 19:15, 16; I Cor. 13:5; Eph. 6:16; I Thess. 5:15; Tit. 3:2; I John 5:18; Rev. 20:1–3.

Punishment.—Ps. 34:21; Mt. 25:45, 46; John 5:29; Rev. 20:14, 15.

Overcoming.—Pr. 25:21, 22; Lu. 6:27– 38; John 16:8–10, 33; Rom. 12:9, 21; I Pet. 3:9–12; I John 5:4, 5; Rev. 2: 7; 5:5.

Old Testament references.—Shall we not receive evil—Job 2:10. Depart from evil and do good—Ps. 34:21; Is. 1:16, 17. I will fear no evil—Ps. 23:4. Evil shall slay the wicked—Ps. 34:21. They sleep not except they do evil— Pr. 4:16. Jehovah keepeth watch upon evil—Pr. 15:3. People committed two evils—Jer. 2:13. Turn from evil, I will repent—Jer. 18:8; 26:3, 13, 19; 42:10.

New Testament references.—Causeth his sun to rise upon the evil—Mt. 5: 45. Sufficient unto day is—Mt. 6:34. Why think ye evil in your hearts— Mt. 9:4. Good tree cannot bring forth —Mt. 7:18. Then cometh evil one— Mt. 13:9. What evil hath he done— Mt. 27:23; Mk. 15:14; Lu. 23:22. If I have spoken evil—John 18:23. Have heard how much evil he hath done— Acts 9:13. See WICKED, SIN.

EVIL-DOERS. Is. 9:17; I Pet. 2:12; 4: 15. Cut off, Shall be—Ps. 37:9. Depart from—Ps. 119:115. Fret not because of—Ps. 37:1. Hand of—Jer. 20: 13; 23:14. House of—Is. 31:2. Punishment of—I Pet. 2:14 (A.V.). Seed of—Is. 1:4; 14:20. See SIN.

EVIL DOING. Suffer for—I Pet. 3:17.

EWES. Cast young—Gen. 31:38. Lambs —Gen. 21:28, 29, 30; Lev. 14:10; Num. 6:14; II Sam. 12:3. See SHEEP.

EXACT. Enemy shall not—Ps. 89:22. Foreigner, Of—Deut. 15:3. God—Job 11:6. Labors—Is. 58:3. Money—II Ki. 15:20. Neighbor, Of—Deut. 15:2. Usury—Neh. 5:7. See OPPRESSION, USURY.

EXACTION. Debt, Of every—Neh. 10: 31. Take away—Ez. 45:9. See OPPRESSION, EXTORTION, USURY.

EXALT. Blessing, Above—Neh. 9:5. City is—Pr. 11:11. Degree, Them of low—Lu. 1:52. Enemy—Ps. 13:2.

God—Acts 2:33; 5:31; Phil. 2:9. Heaven, Unto—Matt. 11:23; Lu. 10: 15. Highways shall be—Is. 49:11. Hills, Above—Is. 2:2; Mic. 4:1. Honor, With—Ps. 112:9. Humbleth himself, He that—Matt. 23:12; Lu. 14:11. Jehovah our God—Ps. 99:5, 9. Kingdom, His—II Sam. 5:12; Num. 24:7. Let God of my salvation be —Ps. 18:46. Low—Ez. 17:24; 21:26. Measure, Above—II Cor. 12:7 (A.V.). Name, His—Ps. 34:3; Is. 12:4. Rebellious, The—Ps. 66:7. Righteousness, A nation—Pr. 14:34. Stature was—Ez. 19:11. Time, In due—I Pet. 5:6. Throne—Is. 14:13. Valley shall be—Is. 40:4. Voice, Thy—Is. 37:23.

EXAMINE. Himself—II Cor. 11:28. Jesus—Lu. 23:14. Keepers—Acts 12: 19. Matter, The—Ezra 10:16. We— Ps. 26:2. Paul—Acts 22:29; 24:8; 28: 18; I Chr. 9:3. Peter and John— Acts 4:9. Scriptures daily—Acts 17: 11. Yourselves—II Cor. 13:5. See SEARCH, TRY.

EXAMPLE: Christ an example.—John 13:15; Acts 20:35; I Pet. 2:21, 22; I John 2:6; 3:3.

Christians admonished to be.—Mt. 5: 48; II Cor. 4:10; Eph. 3:19; Phil. 2:5; 3:17; I Thess. 1:6, 7; II Thess. 3:9; Heb. 7:26; 12:3-5; I Pet. 1:15, 16; I John 2:6; 3:3. To youth—I Tim. 4:12. Paul as an example as far as he imitated Christ—I Cor. 11:1; I Tim. 1:16.

Like prophets.—Jas. 5:10.

Elders.—I Pet. 5:3.

Examples of disobedience.—I Cor. 10:6, 11; Heb. 4:11; II Pet. 2:6; Jude 7.

Miscellaneous.—Example to Moses— Heb. 8:5. Many may not be public example—Mt. 1:19. See ENSAMPLE.

EXCEED. David—I Sam. 20:41. Forty stripes—Deut. 25:3. Kings, All the— II Chr. 9:22. Righteousness—Mt. 5: 20; II Cor. 3:9. Solomon—I Ki. 10:7, 23; II Chr. 9:6. Transgressions—Job 36:9. See BEYOND.

EXCEEDING. Abounded—I Tim. 1:14. Abundantly—Eph. 3:20. Beautiful— Ez. 16:13. Better cry—Ez. 16:13. Broad—Ps. 119:96. Corrupt—Jer. 17: 9. Crooked—Pr. 21:18. Deep—Eccl. 7:24. Dreadful—Dan. 8:28. Endeavor —I Thess. 2:17. Fair—Acts 7:20.

Fierce—Mt. 7:19. Faith groweth—II Thess. 1:3. Fruitful—Gen. 17:6. Glad —Ps. 21:6; Dan. 6:23; Jonah 4:6; Mt. 5:12; Lu. 23:8. Glory—II Cor. 4:17. Good—Num. 14:7. Grace—II Cor. 9: 14. Great—II Chr. 16:12; Ez. 9:9; 37: 10; 47:10; Dan. 8:9; Jonah 3:3. Plague—Rev. 16:21. Great and precious promise—II Pet. 1:4. Hatred, Great—II Sam. 13:15. High mountain—Mt. 4:8. Highly—I Thess. 5:13. Hot—Dan. 3:22. Joy—Ps. 43:4; Mt. 2:10; I Pet. 4:13; Jude 24. Land— Ex. 19:16. Mad—Acts 26:11. Magnificent—I Chr. 22:5. Many—*Chariots and horsemen*—II Chr. 16:8. *Flocks* —II Sam. 12:2. *Riches*—II Chr. 32:27. *Vessels*—I Ki. 7:27. Mighty—Ex. 1:7. Much—*Brass*—II Sam. 8:6. *Spoil*—I Chr. 20:2. *Wisdom and understanding* —I Ki. 4:29. Proud—I Sam. 2:3; Jer. 48:29. Reward, Great—Gen. 15:1. Riches of grace—Eph. 2:17. Sinful— Rom. 7:13. Sorrowful—Mt. 17:23; 26:22, 38; Mk. 6:26; 14:34. Strong— II Chr. 11:12. White—Mk. 9:3. Wise —Pr. 30:24.

EXCEEDINGLY. Afraid—II Ki. 10:4; Jonah 1:10. Cried—Mk. 15:14. Displeased—Jonah 4:1. Err—I Sam. 26: 21. Filled—Ps. 123:3, 4. Great—II Chr. 17:12. Grieved—Esth. 4:4; Neh. 2:10. Hated—II Sam. 13:15. Love— Ps. 119:167. Lusted—Ps. 106:14. Mad Acts 26:11. Multiply—Gen. 17:2, 20; 47:27. Praying—I Thess. 3:10. Prevailed—Gen. 7:19. Solomon, Magnified—I Chr. 29:25. Strong—Dan. 7:7. Zealous—Gal. 1:14.

EXCEL. Pr. 31:29; Is. 10:10. Wisdom —I Ki. 4:30. Eccl. 2:13.

EXCELLENCY. Ex. 15:7; Job 40:10; Is. 35:2; 60:15. Israel, Of—Nah. 2:2. Jacob, Of—Amos 6:8; 8:7; Nah. 2:2. Jehovah, Of—Deut. 33:26, 29; Ps. 68: 34; I Pet. 2:9. Speech, Of—I Cor. 2:1. Wisdom, Of—Eccl. 7:12; Phil. 3:8.

EXCELLENT. Ps. 16:3. Rom. 2:18. Jehovah—Ps. 8:1; 76:4; 150:2. Ministry—Heb. 8:6. Name—Heb. 1:4. Power, In—Job 37:23. Sacrifice— Heb. 11:4. Speech—Pr. 17:7. Spirit —Dan. 5:12; 6:3. Wisdom—Dan. 5: 14.

EXCEPT. Gen. 32:26; John 4:48. Born anew, One be—John 3:3. God be with —Gen. 31:42; Ps. 127:1; John 3:2. I drink it—Mt. 26:42. Ye repent—Lu. 13:3. Sent, They be—Rom. 10:15.

EXCHANGE. Ez. 27:15. Cattle—Lev. 27:10. Horses—Gen. 47:17. Jewels— Job 28:17. Land—Ez. 48:14. Life, For—Mt. 16:26; Mk. 8:37. Soul—See LIFE.

EXCUSE. Lu. 14:18; John 15:22; Rom. 1:2.

EXECRATION. Jer. 42:18; 44:12. See CURSE.

EXECUTE. Judgment — Ex. 12:12; Num. 33:4; II Sam. 8:15; I Ki. 6:12; I Chr. 18:14; II Chr. 24:14; Ps. 9:16; 99:4; 103:6; 119:84; 146:7; 149:9; Is. 16:3; 66:12; Jer. 5:1; etc. See JUDG-MENT. Justice—Jer. 21:12. Right-eous acts—Ps. 103:6. Vengeance— Lev. 26:25. See VENGEANCE. Word— I Rom. 9:28. Wrath—I Sam. 28:18. See JUDGMENT, PUNISHMENT.

EXERCISE. Bodily—I Tim. 4:8. Cha-stening, By—Heb. 12:11. Loving-kindness—Jer. 9:24. Myself—Ps. 131:1; Acts 24:16. Thyself—I Tim. 4:7.

EXHORTATION: Christian exhorta-tions by.—Peter—Acts 2:40; I Pet. 5: 1, 12. Paul—Acts 13:15, 16; 14:22; 20:2; 27:22; I Cor. 14:3; I Tim. 2:1; Heb. 13:22. Barnabas—Acts 11:23; 14:22. Judas and Silas—Acts 15:32. John the Baptist—Lu. 3:18; Jude 3. Apostles—II Cor. 8:17; I Thess. 2:11; 4:1; 5:14; II Thess. 3:12.

Command to exhort.—I Tim. 4:13; II Tim. 4:2; Tit. 1:9; 2:6, 9, 15; Heb. 3: 13. Unheeded—Heb. 12:5. Given to— Rom. 12:8. See ADMONISH.

EXILE. Ezra 8:35; Is. 20:4; Ez. 12:4. See CAPTIVITY, ISRAEL, JUDAH.

EXODUS. See OUTLINE STUDIES IN THE BOOKS.

EXORCISTS. Acts 19:13. See MAGIC.

EXPECTATION. Is. 20:5, 6; Lam. 3: 18; Zech. 9:5; Rom. 8:19; Phil. 1:20; Heb. 10:13. God, Of—Ps. 62:5. Jesus, Of—Lu. 3:15. Jesus, Of—Acts 12:11. Judgment, Of—Heb. 10:27. Poor, Of —Ps. 9:18. Wicked, Of—Pr. 10:28; 11:7, 23. See HOPE.

EXPEDIENT. I Cor. 6:12; 10:23; II Cor. 8:10; 12:1. Jesus, Crucifixion of —John 11:50; 16:7; 18:14.

EXPERIENCE. Heb. 5:13.

EXPERT. Is. 3:3; Acts 26:3.

EXPIATION. Num. 35:33; I Sam. 3:14. See PUNISHMENT, SIN.

EXPLAIN. Mt. 13:36.

EXPLORE. Eccl. 9:1.

EXPOUND. Mk. 4:34; Acts 28:23. See GOSPEL, PREACH.

EXTEND. Ezra 7:28; Ps. 109:12; Is. 66:12.

EXTINCT. Ps. 76:5, 6; Is. 43:17.

EXTOL. Ps. 30:1; 66:17; 141:1. See PRAISE.

EXTORTION. Heb. *Oshek*, oppression; *Nashak*, to bite.

Extortions.—Gen. 25:31; 47:13–26; Neh. 5:1–13; Ez. 22:12; Mic. 3:1–3; Lu. 18:11; I Cor. 5:11.

Greed of the merchants of Israel.—Hos. 12:7, 8; Amos 2:6–8; 5:11–13; 8:4–8. Exaction—II Ki. 15:20; 23:35.

Blackmail levied by publicans.—Mt. 23: 25; Lu. 19:8.

Lying in wait for the needy.—Ps. 10: 8–10; 17:12; 109:11; Pr. 1:12, 13; Mic. 7:2, 3.

Forbidden to take usury from the poor. —Ex. 22:25; Lev. 25:35–37; Ps. 15:5; Ez. 18:12, 13.

Forbidden to make exactions or to cheat. —Lev. 19:35, 36; Deut. 25:13–15; Ps. 89:22; Ez. 45:9–12; Lu. 3:13, 14.

Judgment upon.—Job 20:15; Is. 16:4; 24:2; 49:26; 51:13; I Cor. 6:10. De-liverance from—Is. 9:4; 14:4; 54:14. See DEBT, OPPRESSION, USURY.

EXULT, EXULTING. Ps. 68:3, 4. Field —I Chr. 16:32. Glory, In—Ps. 149:5. Pain, In—Job 6:10. Proudly—Is. 13: 3; Zeph. 3:11. See REJOICE.

EYE: Old Testament references.—The serpent's deception—Gen. 3:5. Treat-ment of Hagar—Gen. 16:6. Isaac's dimness—Gen. 27:1. Leah's—Gen. 29:17. Judah's—Gen. 49:12. Hobab's guiding eye—Num. 10:31. Balaam's —Num. 24:3. Moses' on Pisgah— Deut. 3:27. Every man followed own eyes—Ju. 17:6. Saul eyed David—I Sam. 18:9. Eyes of Israel on king— I Ki. 1:20. Prayer for God's eye on temple—I Ki. 8:29. Disguise of proph-

et—I Ki. 20:38. Elisha desires servant's eyes to see heavenly chariots—
II Ki. 6:17, 18. Also to open eyes of
enemies—II Ki. 6:20. Eyes of Jehovah run to and fro—II Chr. 16:9; Job
7:8; Ps. 11:4; 34:15. Enlightening
the eyes—Ps. 19:8. No fear of God
before his—Ps. 36:1. Open thou my—
Ps. 119:18. I will not give sleep to—
Ps. 132:4. Eyes of all wait—Ps. 145:
15. Eyes of man never satisfied—Pr.
27:20. Eye that mocketh at—Pr. 30:
17. Wise man's eyes in head—Eccl.
2:14. Eyes not satisfied with riches—
Eccl. 4:8. Eyes shall see king in
beauty—Is. 33:17. To open blind—
Is. 42:7. See eye to eye—Is. 52:8.
Eyes a fountain of tears—Jer. 9:1;
14:17. Of purer eye than to behold
iniquity—Hab. 1:13.

New Testament references.—Eye causeth thee to stumble—Mt. 5:29; 18:9.
An eye for eye—Mt. 5:38. Lamp of
body is—Mt. 6:22. Having eyes, see
not—Gen. 5:21; Mk. 8:18. Were eye
witnesses—Lu. 1:2. Their eyes were
holden—Lu. 24:16. This man, who
opened—John 11:37. Fastening eyes
upon—Acts 3:12; 6:15; 10:4. Things
which eyes saw not—I Cor. 2:9. Plucked
out—Gal. 4:15. Eyes of your heart—
Eph. 1:18. Having eyes full of adultery—II Pet. 2:14. Lust of the—I
John 2:16. Every eye shall see—Rev.
1:7. Lamb having seven—Rev. 5:6.
Wipe away tears—Rev. 7:17; 21:4.

EYE-SERVICE. Eph. 6:6; Col. 3:22.
See HYPOCRISY.

EZBAI, ĕz′bāi. I Chr. 11:37.

EZBON, ĕz′bon. (1) **A man of God.**—
Gen. 46:16.

(2) **A Benjamite.**—I Chr. 7:7.

EZEKIEL. See OUTLINE STUDIES IN
THE BOOKS.

EZEL, ē′zel. I Sam. 20:19.

EZEM, ē′zem. **A town in Simeon.**—
Josh. 19:3; I Chr. 4:29.

EZER, ē′zer. (1) **A man of Judah.**—
I Chr. 4:4.

(2) **An Ephraimite.**—I Chr. 7:21.

(3) **A man of Gad who joined David at
Ziklag.**—I Chr. 12:9.

(4) **One of those who assisted in repairing the wall of Jerusalem.**—Neh. 3:19.

(5) **A musician who assisted at dedication of the wall.**—Neh. 12:42.

EZION-GEBER, ē′zi-on-gē′ber. **A place
on the Red Sea.**—Num. 33:35, 36;
Deut. 2:8; I Ki. 9:26; 22:48; II Chr.
8:17; 20:36.

EZNITE. See ADINO.

EZRA, ĕz′ra. (1) See OUTLINE STUDIES
IN THE BOOKS.

(2) **A priest who returned with Nehemiah.**—Neh. 10:2(?); 12:1.

(3) **Another priest.**—Neh. 12:33.

EZRAH, ĕz′rah. **A man of Judah.**—I
Chr. 4:17.

EZRAHITE, ĕz′ra-hite. **Name of Ethan
and Heman.**—I Ki. 4:31; Ps. 88 (title).

EZRI, ĕz′rī. **One of David's officers.**—
I Chr. 27:26.

FABLES. I Tim. 1:4.

FACE: Faces mentioned.—Face of Jehovah—Ex. 33:23; Ps. 17:15; 89:14;
Jer. 16:17; 21:10; 32:31; Lam. 2:19;
3:35; Ez. 7:22; 14:3, 4, 6, 7; 15:7. Hid
his face—Deut. 31:18; 32:20; Mic.
3:4; Lu. 1:76. Will not turn away his
face—II Chr. 30:9. Declare to—Job
21:31. Against—Ez. 14:8. Turned
away—Jer. 18:17. Set his face against
—Lev. 17:10; 20:3, 5, 6; 26:17. Fled
from the face of Jehovah—II Chr.
29:6.

Faces of: Abner—II Sam. 2:22. Ahab—
I Ki. 21:4. Angels—Lu. 24:5. Anointed
—Ps. 85:9; 132:10; Pr. 21:27. Benhadad's—II Ki. 8:15. Captain—II Ki.
18:24; Is. 36:9. Cephas—Gal. 2:11.
Children of Dan—Ju. 18:23. Child—
II Ki. 4:29, 31. Cherubim—Ex. 25:
20; 37:9; II Chr. 3:13. David—Acts
2:25. Eleazar—Num. 19:3. Elders
—Lam. 5:12. Eliphaz—Job 4:15.
Fathers—Acts 7:45. Flocks—Gen. 30:
40. Jacob—Gen. 32:22. Jehu—II Ki.
9:32. Joseph—Gen. 43:31; 44:23, 26;
46:28, 30; 48:11, 12. Judges—Job 9:
24. Job—Job 11:15; 16:8, 16; 22:26;
23:17. King—I Ki. 8:14; II Chr. 5:3;
42:1. Lazarus—John 11:44. Leviathan—Job 41:14. Zion—I Chr. 12:8.
Moses—II Cor. 3:7. Man (*not to be
feared*)—Deut. 1:17. People—I Ki. 2:
15; Mk. 1:2; Lu. 2:31. Poor—Is. 3:15.
Paul—Acts 20:25, 38; Gal. 1:22; Col.
2:1. Pharaoh—Ex. 2:15. Philistine—

I Sam. 17:49. Sarah—Gen. 16:6, 8. Stephen—Acts 6:15. Thessalonians—I Thess. 2:17; 3:10. Wicked—Job 40: 13; Ps. 21:12. Youth—Dan. 1:10.

Forbidden to see the face.—Absalom not to see face of king—II Sam. 14:24, 28. Judah not to see face of Joseph—Gen. 43:3, 5. Moses not to see the face of Pharaoh—Ex. 10:28, 29. David not to show his face to Abner—II Sam. 3:13.

Set toward.—Jerusalem—I Ki. 12:17; Ez. 21:2, 6; Lu. 9:53. City—Ez. 4: 3, 7. Zion—Jer. 50:5. East—Ez. 8: 16. South — Ez. 20:46, 47. Mount Gilead—Gen. 31:21. Wall—II Ki. 20: 2. Wilderness—Num. 24:1. Egypt—Jer. 42:15, 17. Mount of Israel—Ez. 6:2. Ammon—Ez. 25:2. Sidon—Ez. 28:21. Pharaoh—Ez. 29:2. Mount Seir—Ez. 35:2.

Obeisance to man.—Bowing with face to the ground: Abigail before David—I Sam. 25:23. Absalom before king—II Sam. 14:32, 33. Araunah before king—II Sam. 24:20. David before Jonathan—I Sam. 20:4. Joseph—Gen. 48:12; 50:18. Mephibosheth before David—II Sam. 9:6. Ornan before David—I Chr. 21:21. Saul before Samuel—I Sam. 28:14. Obadiah before Elijah—I Ki. 18:7. Ruth before Boaz—Ruth 2:10. Nebuchadrezzar to Daniel—Dan. 2:46.

Obeisance to God.—Abraham talked with God—Gen. 17:3, 17. Balaam—Num. 22:31. Jehoshaphat—II Cor. 20:18. Ezekiel fell on—Ez. 3:23; 1: 28; 9:8; 11:13; 43:3; 44:4. Daniel—Dan. 8:17, 18. Jesus prays—Mt. 26: 39. Dagon—I Sam. 5:3, 4. David and elders—I Chr. 21:16. Elijah—I Ki. 18:42. Joshua—Josh. 5:14; 7:6, 10. Lot—Gen. 19:1. Moses and Aaron—Num. 14:5; 16:4. Moses—Num. 16:4, 22, 45; 20:6. Manoah and wife—Ju. 13:20. People at Mount Carmel—I Ki. 18:39. People at burnt-offering—Lev. 9:24. Unbelievers—I Cor. 14:25. Turned face from Jehovah—II Chr. 35:22. Renounced to Jehovah's face —Job 1:11; 2:5.

Face to face.—Gen. 32:30; Ju. 6:22; II Ki. 14:8; II Chr. 25:17, 21; Ez. 20:35; Acts 25:16; I Cor. 13:12.

Seeking the face of the Lord.—I Chr. 16:11; II Chr. 7:14; Ps. 27:8; 105:4; Pr. 7:15; Hos. 5:15.

Hidden face.—Job 13:24; Ps. 44:24; 51:9; 88:14, 69; 102:2; 143:7; Ez. 39: 23, 24, 29. Of Jehovah—Job 34:29; Ps. 10:11; 13:1; 30:7; Is. 16:4; 64:7; Jer. 33:3. Moses hides face from God —Ex. 3:6.

Veiled face.—Moses—Ex. 34:33; II Cor. 3:13. Seraphim—Is. 6:2.

Covered.—II Sam. 19:4; Ez. 12:6, 12. Jesus' face was covered—Mk. 14:65. Elijah wrapped face in mantle—I Ki. 19:13. Tamar—Gen. 38:15. Haman—Esth. 7:8.

Obeisance to Jesus.—Man of leprosy—Lu. 5:12. Samaritan—Lu. 17:16.

Figurative.—Face of Israel—Ex. 14:25. Of earth—Gen. 1:2, 29; 2:6; 4:14; 6:1, 7; 7:3, 4, 18, 23; 8:8, 9, 13; 9:23; 11:4; 41:56; Ex. 10:5, 15; 32:12; 33:16; Num. 11:31; 12:3; 22:5, 11; Deut. 6: 15; 7:6; I Sam. 20:15; I Ki. 13:34; Job 37:12; Is. 14:21; 23:17; 27:6; Jer. 8:2; 28:16; Ez. 34:6; 38:20; Dan. 8:5; Amos 5:8; 9:6; Lu. 12:56; 17:26; 21: 35. Of the wilderness—Ex. 16:14. Of heaven—Mt. 16:3. Of field—II Ki. 9: 37; Is. 28:25. Of his throne—Job 25:9. Of the deep—Job 38:30; Pr. 8:27. Of vineyard—Pr. 24:31. Of covering—Is. 25:7, 8. Of ground—Jer. 16:4; 18:17; 32:33.

Illustrative of.—Ps. 5:8; Pr. 27:19; Is. 13:8; Jer. 5:3. Face in mirror—Jas. 1:23.

Kinds of.—Hard—Ez. 3:8. Pale—Joel 2:6; Nah. 2:10; Jer. 30:6. Impudent—Pr. 7:13. Degenerate—Is. 3:9; Mt. 6:16. Resolute, *Jesus*—Lu. 9:51. Transfigured, *Moses*—Ex. 34:29. *Jesus*—Mt. 17:2; Lu. 9:29.

Shame of.—II Chr. 32:21; Ezra 9:6, 7; Ps. 44:15; 83:16; Jer. 7:19; 13:26; 51:51; Ez. 7:18.

Spitting in the face.—Num. 12:14; Deut. 25:9; Job 30:10. In face of Jesus—Mt. 26:67.

Smitten on.—II Cor. 11:20.

Faces in vision.—Ez. 1:6, 8, 10, 11, 15; 10:14, 21, 22; Dan. 10:6, 9, 15; Rev. 4: 7; 6:16; 7:11; 9:7; 10:1; 11:16; 12:14; 22:4.

Prophecies.—Is. 49:23; 50:6, 7; 65:3; Jer. 30:6. Description of temple—Ez. 41:19, 21, 25. War—Ez. 13:17; Dan. 11:17, 18, 19. Priests—Mal. 2:3.

Miscellaneous.—Care of the face in fasting—Mt. 6:17. Oil used on the face—Ps. 144:15, 29, 30. Punishment before face of judge—Deut. 25:2. Jehovah will repay to their face—Deut. 7:10.

FACTION. Rom. 2:8; I Cor. 11:19; Gal. 5:19, 20; Phil. 1:17; Tit. 3:10; Jas. 3:16. See DIVIDE, DIVISION, UNITY.

FADE. Crown of glory—I Pet. 5:4. Earth—Is. 24:4. Flower—Is. 28:1, 4; 40:7, 8. Inheritance—I Pet. 1:4. Leaf —Is. 1:30; Jer. 8:13; Ez. 47:12. Rich man—Jas. 1:11.

FAIL. Deut. 28:32; 31:6, 8; Josh. 1:5; I Chr. 28:20; Is. 42:4; Lu. 22:32. Bread—Is. 51:14. Compassions—Lam. 3:22. Cruse of oil—I Ki. 17:14, 16. Drink—Is. 32:6. Eyes—Job 11:20; 17:5. Ps. 69:3; 119:82, 123; Is. 38:14; Jer. 14:6; Lam. 2:11; 4:17. Faithful —Ps. 12:1; 89:33. Flesh—Ps. 73:26; 109:24. Glory of Kedar—Is. 21:16. Grass—Is. 15:6. Heart—Gen. 42:28; I Sam. 17:32. King, To sit with—I Sam. 20:5. Kinsfolk—Job 19:14. Law, One tittle of—Lu. 16:17. Love never —I Cor. 13:8. Man—I Ki. 2:4; 8:25; 9:5; II Chr. 6:16; 7:18. Money—Gen. 47:10, 15, 16. Promise—Ps. 77:8. Prophecies—I Cor. 13:8 (A.V.). Refuge—Ps. 142:4. Soul—Song of Sol. 5:6. Spirit—Ps. 143:7. Strength— Ps. 31:10; 38:10; 71:9; Is. 44:12. Time —Heb. 11:32. Tongue—Is. 41:17. Treasure—Lu. 12:33. Vintage—Is. 32:10. Waters—Job 14:11; Is. 19:5; 58:11.

FAIN. Lu. 15:16.

FAINT. Job 4:5; Pr. 24:10; Lu. 18:1. Daniel—Dan. 8:27. David—II Sam. 21:15; Ps. 27:13; 38:8; 84:2; 119:81. Heart—Gen. 45:26; Lev. 26:36; Deut. 20:3, 8; Job 23:16; Is. 1:5; 7:4; Jer. 8:18; 51:46; Lam. 1:22; 5:17; Jonah 2:7. Jacob—Gen. 25:29, 30; 45: 26. Jehovah prevents—Is. 40:28-31. Jonah—Jonah 4:8. People, All—Gen. 47:13; Deut. 25:18; I Sam. 14:28, 31; II Sam. 16:2; Ps. 107:5; Is. 51:20; Lam. 2:19; Amos 18:13; Mt. 32:15; Mk. 8:3. Pray and faint not—Lu.

18:1. Soldiers—Ju. 8:4, 5; I Sam. 30: 10, 21. Spirit—Ez. 21:7.

Figurative.—II Cor. 4:1, 16; Gal. 6:9; Eph. 3:13; Heb. 12:3, 5.

FAIR. Colors—Is. 54:11. Countenances —Dan. 1:15. Daughters—Gen. 6:2. Judah—Jer. 4:30. Moses—Acts 7:20. Show—Gal. 6:12. Speech—Pr. 26:25; Rom. 16:18. Weather—Mt. 16:2. Women—Pr. 11:22; Song of Sol. 1:8; 2:10; 5:9; 6:1. Words—Jer. 12:6. See BEAUTY.

FAIR-HAVENS. A Cretan harbor.— Acts 27:8.

FAITH. *Pisteuo,* to believe. A union of assurance and conviction—Heb. 11:1. See Hab. 2:4; Mt. 6:25-34; Lu. 12:22-31; 18:8; Heb. 13:7.

Given by God.—Lu. 17:5, 6; Rom. 12:3; I Cor. 2:4, 5; 12:8, 9.

Comes by hearing the Word of God.— Acts 15:7; Rom. 10:13-17; I Cor. 1:21; Gal. 3:1, 2; I Thess. 2:13.

Distinction between Old Testament and New Testament faith. In Old Testament: In God.—II Chr. 20:20; Ps. 3: 3-6; 4:3, 8; 7:1, 10; 9:9, 10; 13:5; 23: 1-6; 32:10; 33:18-22; 36:7-9; 40:3, 4; 55:22; 56:3, 4; 62:8; 84:5, 12; 91:2; 115:9-18; 116:10; 118:8, 9; 125:1; 143: 8; Pr. 3:5, 6, 24-26; 16:20; 29:25; Eccl. 11:1; 12:2; Is. 26:3, 4; 41:10-14; 43: 1-5; 49:15; 50:10; 51:12, 13; Jer. 17: 7, 8.

In the New Testament: Faith is usually in Christ.—John 1:12; 3:14-18, 36; 6: 29, 40; 7:38; 8:12, 21-32; 9:35-38; 10: 25-28; 12:36, 46; 14:1; 20:31; Acts **2**: 36-41; 8:37 *marg.*; 10:43; 13:38, 39; 14:22; 15:11; 16:29-34; 18:8; 19:4, 5; 20:21; 26:18; Rom. 1:16, 17; 3:21-26; 5:1, 2; 10:1-10; I Cor. 1:21-24; 3:10, 11; Gal. 2:20; 3:22; Eph. 1:12-14; 2: 19-22; 3:11, 12; Phil. 1:27-29; 3:9-11; Col. 2:12; I Tim. 1:13, 14; II Tim. 1: 12; Philemon 5; I John 5:1, 10, 13; Heb. 12:1, 2; Jas. 2:1.

In God.—Lu. 1:38-55; Acts 27:25; Heb. 6:1; I Pet. 1:21; 4:19; I John 3:21.

Facts produce feeling.—Mt. 23:37-38; 27:3-5, 54; Lu. 15:4-10, 16-20; John 11:8, 16, 32-33; 21:15-17; Acts 2:22-24, 37; 5:27-28; 7:51-54; II Cor. 5: 14-15.

Testimony produces faith.—John 1:7; 3:11–12; Acts 2:40–42; 8:4–8; 10:39–43; 26:16–18; Rom. 10:13–17; I John 1:1–3; 5:8–10.

The assurance of faith.—John 1:12; 3:16; 5:24; 6:35, 47; 11:26; Rom. 8:1; Eph. 1:13; 2:6–8; Phil. 1:6; II Tim. 1:12; Heb. 6:12; I Pet. 1:8; I John 2:23–25; 5:5, 10.

Great faith.—Mt. 8:10, 13; 9:2, 22, 29; 15:28; Mk. 2:5; 5:34; 10:53; Lu. 5:20; 7:9, 50; 8:48; 17:19; 18:42; II Cor. 8:7.

Apostolic faith weak.—Mt. 6:26–34; 8:24–27; 14:23–33; 16:5–12, 21–23; 17:7; 19:23–29; Mk. 6:47–52; 8:14–21; Lu. 5:9–11; 12:22–34; 24:19–27; John 6:16–21; 14:7–13.

Faith an active principle.—Leads to utterance—II Cor. 4:13. Grows exceedingly—II Thess. 1:3. Obtains a fulness—Heb. 10:22. The work of God—John 6:9. Works through love—Gal. 5:6. Purifies the heart—Acts 15:9. Brings salvation—Acts 16:31. Assures life—John 3:14–16, 36; 5:24; 6:47; 11:25, 26; Rom. 1:17; Gal. 3:11; Heb. 10:38, 39. Enables us to stand—Rom. 11:20; I Cor. 16:13; II Cor. 1:24; Col. 1:23. Enables us to walk—II Cor. 5:7. To fight—II Cor. 4:7, 8; I Tim. 6:11–17. Helps to overcome—I John 2:14; 5:4. Is the means of justification—Rom. 3:25–28. Awards the sonship to us—Gal. 3:26. Makes us heirs and joint heirs—Rom. 8:17. Gives us access to God—Rom. 5:2; Eph. 3:12. Secures peace with God—Rom. 5:1. Enables us to please God—Heb. 11:6. Leads to sanctification—John 17:17; Acts 26:18; Col. 1:23, 24.

Objects of faith.—God—Num. 20:12; Deut. 1:32; 9:23; II Ki. 17:14; I Chr. 5:20; II Chr. 20:20; Ps. 78:22, 32; 118:8, 9; Is. 26:3; 43:10, 12; Dan. 3:17, 18; 6:23; Mt. 6:25–34. Christ—See IN NEW TESTAMENT: IN CHRIST. The prophets—II Chr. 20:20; Lu. 24:44–45; Acts 26:27. The word of God—Deut. 32:1–3; Ps. 119:15, 16, 24, 35, 40, 97, 98, 99, 105, 111. The Gospel—Mt. 13:18–23; Mk. 4:14; 16:15–16; Lu. 8:11–15; John 8:31–32; 20:31; Rom. 1:16–17; II Thess. 2:12; II Tim. 3:15; Heb. 4:2; I Pet. 1:22–23.

The power of faith.—Mt. 21:21; Mk. 9:23; 11:23; Lu. 17:5, 6; John 14:12. Curing the blind—Mt. 9:27–30. Child possessed with evil spirit—Mk. 9:17–29.

Unity of faith.—John 17:17–21; I Cor. 1:10–13; 12:13–20; Eph. 2:19–21; 4:1–6, 15, 16, 25.

Faith as a grain of mustard seed.—Mt. 17:19, 20; Lu. 17:5, 6. Faith of Abraham—Rom. 4:18–22. In quenching fiery darts—Eph. 6:16. The prayer of faith—Jas. 5:15. (See also Heb. Ch. 11.)

The aim of faith.—To grow in the knowledge of the truth—Ps. 119:97–105, 129–131; John 8:31–32; II Tim. 2:15; Heb. 6:4–6; I John 2:5, 14. To grow into the favor of God—Acts 2:46–47; Rom. 4:4–5; 5:2; I Cor. 15:10; Eph. 4:15; Heb. 4:16. To attain unto a perfect manhood—Eph. 2:20–22; 4:1–3, 11–13, 15–16. To be transformed into the image of Christ—Rom. 8:29; I Cor. 15:49; II Cor. 3:18; 4:3–6. To be kept in constant security—Rom. 6:12–14; .11:20; I Cor. 9:27; 15:1–2; Phil. 4:7; II Thess. 3:3; II Tim. 4:7–8; I Pet. 1:3–5; I John 1:9. To be joyful on earth—Rom. 5:2–5, 11; 15:13; Phil. 1:18–19; 2:17–18.

The obedience of faith.—Mt. 28:19–20; Acts 6:7; Rom. 6:8–14; 8:1–11; Phil. 2:1–16; 3:8–16. Not works of law—Rom. 3:27–28; 4:1–8. The work tells—Mt. 3:8; John 6:29; Rom. 6:16–18; 16:19; II Cor. 10:5–6; II Thess. 1:8; I Tim. 1:5; Heb. 5:8–9; Jas. 2:14–18, 26; 3:13; I Pet. 3:1–2.

Works of faith.—Gal. 5:6; I Thess. 1:3; 2:13; II Thess. 1:11; Jas. 1:3.

Righteousness of faith.—Rom. 1:17; 3:21–30; 4:3, 11; 9:31–33; 10:4–11; Gal. 2:16; Phil. 3:9; Heb. 11:7.

The testing of faith.—I Pet. 1:5–9, 21; 4:19; Abraham's offering—Gen. 22:15–18. Caleb's courage—Num. 13:30. Joshua's renunciation—Josh. 24:14–15. Job's patience—Job 19:25–27. Daniel's refusal—Dan. 1:8. Shadrach, etc.—Dan. 3:16–18. Martha's trustfulness—John 11:21–22. Jesus in Gethsemane—Mt. 26:36–46; Mk. 14:32–42; Lu. 22:40–46. Peter and John—Acts 4:19–20. Stephen—Acts Ch. 7.

Paul's afflictions—Rom. 8:28, 35-39; II Cor. 4:8-18; 6:3-10; 11:23-29; Phil. 1:21; I Tim. 1:15-17. Trials in life—Jas. 1:3; I Pet. 1:7.

The fruits of faith.—Remission of sins—Lu. 24:47; John 20:22-23; Acts 2:38-39; 3:19; 10:43. The indwelling of Christ—Eph. 3:17-19. The sealing of the spirit—Gal. 3:14. The father's love — John 16:27; Rom. 8:35-39. Heavenly mansions—John 14:2. The crown of life—Rev. 2:10. Eternal life—John 10:28; I Tim. 4:10; I Pet. 1:9. See FAITH AN ACTIVE PRINCIPLE.

Failing faith is fatal.—Mt. 14:30-31; Lu. 22:31-32; John 20:25-29; I Cor. 15:12-19; I Tim. 6:10-11; II Tim. 4: 3-4; Heb. 3:14-19; I Pet. 5:8-9; II Pet. 1:5-9.

What faith is proof of: Unworthiness—Mt. 8:8; Lu. 15:18-19. Teachableness—Mt. 13:23; Lu. 8:15; Jas. 1:21, 25. Adoption—John 1:12-13; Rom. 8:14-16; Gal. 3:26-27. Entrance into rest—Heb. 4:1-3.

Prayer without faith is vain.—Pr. 28:9; Mt. 21:22; Acts 10:31-33; Eph. 6:16-18; Heb. 10:21, 22; 11:6; Jas. 1:5-7; 5:15-18.

The denial of faith.—Josh. 24:27; Pr. 30:8-9; Mt. 10:33; 26:34; Mk. 14:30; 16:16; Lu. 12:9; I Cor. 15:12-14; I Tim. 5:8; II Tim. 3:5; II Pet. 2:1; I John 2:22-23; Jude 3; Rev. 2:13; 3:8.

Whatsoever is not of faith is sin.—Rom. 14:22, 23.

Unfeigned faith.—II Tim. 1:5.

Through the spirit by faith wait for the hope of righteousness.—Gal. 5:5-7.

Breastplate of faith.—I Thess. 5:8.

Shield of faith.—Eph. 6:16.

Examples in the Old Testament.—Abel—Heb. 11:4. Abraham—Gen. 12:1-7; 15:4-18; 22:1-10; 24:7, 40; John 8:56; Rom. 4:18-21; Heb. 11:8-19. Caleb—Num. 13:30; Josh. 14:6, 12. Daniel—Dan. 6:4-23. David—I Sam. 17:45-49; 30:6; I Chr. 27:23; Acts 2:25-31; Heb. 11:32. See THE PSALMS. Elijah—I Ki. 17:13-16; 18:21-39. Enoch—Heb. 11:5. Gideon—Ju. 6:14-18, 36-40; Heb. 11:32, 33, 39. Habakkuk—Hab. 2:4; 3:17-19. Hagar—Gen. 16:

13. Hezekiah—II Ki. 18:5, 19. Isaac—Heb. 11:20. Isaiah—II Ki. 19:6, 7; 20:8-11. Jacob—Gen. 48:8-21; 49:1-27; Heb. 11:21. Jahaziel—II Chr. 20: 15-17. Jehoshaphat—II Chr. 20:20. Job—Job 1:21, 22; 2:9, 10; 5:6-27; 13:15, 16; 14:14, 15; 16:19; 19:25-27; 23:6. Jonah—Jonah 2:2; 3:1-4. Joseph—Gen. 50:20, 24; Heb. 11:22. Joshua—Num. 14:6-9; Josh. 1:11-15; 10:25. Manoah, Wife of; Mother of Samson—Ju. 13:23. Micah—Mic. 7: 7-9, 18-20. Moses—Ex. 14:13-31; 15: 1-19; 17:15; Num. 16:28, 29; Deut. 1: 20, 21, 29-31; 3:2, 22; 7:1-24; 8:2; 20: 1; 31:8, 23; Heb. 11:24-29. *Lack of faith*—Ex. 3:11, 12; 4:10-16. Nehemiah—Neh. 4:20; 8:22. Ninevites—Jonah 3:5. Noah—Gen. 6:14-22; 7:1-24; Heb. 11:7. Rahab—Josh. 2:9-21; Heb. 11:31. Shadrach, Meshach and Abed-nego—Dan. 3:8-30. Widow of Zarephath with cruise of oil and a handful of meal—I Ki. 17:18-24.

In the New Testament: Anna the prophetess—Lu. 2:36-38. Antioch, People of—Acts 11:21-24. Barnabas—Acts 11:24. Blind men—Mt. 9:27-31; 20: 30-33; Mk. 10:46-52; Lu. 18:35-42; John 9:1-38. Canaanitish woman—Mt. 15:21-28. Colossians—Mk. 7:24-30; Col. 1:2-4. Cripple at Lystra—Acts 14:8-10. Crispus and Corinthians—Acts 18:8; I Cor. 1:14; 15:11. Disciples—John 2:11, 22; 16:30, 31; 17:7, 8, 20. Elisabeth—Lu. 1:25. Ephesians—Eph. 1:15. Ethiopian eunuch—Acts 8:26-39. Eunice, Lois and Timothy—Acts 16:1; II Tim. 1:5. Father of epileptic boy—Mt. 17:14-19; Mk. 9:17-24; Lu. 9:38-42. Five thousand—Acts 4:4. Gentiles—Acts 11:19-21; 13:48; 15:7. Jailer, Philippian—Acts 16:25-34. Jews at Jerusalem—John 2:23; 8:30; 11:45; 12:11. Jews at Rome—Acts 28:24. John—John 20:8. Joppa, People of—Acts 9:42. Joseph, Husband of Mary—Mt. 1:18-25; 2: 13, 14. Lepers, Ten—Lu. 17:11-19. Lydda and Sharon, People of—Acts 9:35. Lydia—Acts 16:14. Martha—John 11:27. Mary (Martha's sister)—Lu. 10:39, 42; John 11:32. Mary, Mother of Jesus—Lu. 1:38-55. Multitudes—Acts 5:14. Nathaniel—John

1:49. Nobleman—John 4:50–53. Paralytic, Friends of—Mk. 2:4, 5. Paul —Acts 9:29; 27:23–25; II Tim. 4:7. Peter—Mt. 16:15–20; Lu. 5:8; Acts 3:16. Philemon—Philemon 1, 5. Philip John 1:45, 46. Priests—Acts 6:7. Ruler—Mt. 9:18, 19, 23–25; Mk. 5: 22–24, 35–42; Lu. 8:41, 42, 49–56. Samaritans—John 4:39–42; Acts 8:12. Sergius Paulus—Acts 13:12. Sick of Gennesaret—Mt. 14:34–36; Mk. 6: 54–56. Simeon—Lu. 2:23–25. Simon the sorcerer—Acts 8:13. Stephen— Acts 6:8. Thessalonians—I Thess. 1: 6; 3:6–8; II Thess. 1:3, 4. Thomas— John 20:28. Three thousand at Pentecost—Acts 2:41. Timothy—I Tim. 6: 12. Unclean spirit, Man with—Mk. 1:24; Lu. 4:34. Woman with issue of blood—Mt. 9:20–22; Mk. 5:25–34; Lu. 8:43–48.

FAITHFULNESS. Consistency with expressed or known character.

God's faithfulness.—Deut. 7:9; Ps. 143: 1; 119:86, 138; Is. 49:7; Jer. 42:5; I Cor. 1:9; 10:13; I Pet. 4:19; Heb. 10: 23. Extent of—Ps. 36:5; 40:10; 88: 11; 119:75, 90. Exalted—Ps. 89:1, 2, 5, 8, 24, 33; 92:2; Is. 25:1; Lam. 3:23. See GOD, FAITHFULNESS OF.

God's promise to the faithful.—I Sam. 2:35; Ps. 31:23; 101:6; Pr. 28:20.

Of Christ.—Is. 11:5; I Thess. 5:24; II Thess. 3:3; II Tim. 2:13; Heb. 2:17; 3:2; 10:23; I John 1:9; Rev. 1:5; 19:11. See PROMISES—John 14:2.

Of followers of Christ.—Eph. 1:1; Col. 1:2, 7; Rev. 17:14. Required—I Cor. 4:2; Rev. 2:10. See DISCIPLESHIP— Mt. 20:17.

Of words.—I Tim. 4:9; II Tim. 2:11; Tit. 1:9; 3:8; Rev. 21:5; 22:6.

Of men.—Neh. 13:13; II Tim. 2:2. Special mention of: Moses—Num. 12:7; Heb. 3:5. Abraham—Neh. 9:8; Gal. 3:9. Hanani—Neh. 7:2. Hananiah— Neh. 7:2. Daniel—Dan. 6:4. Tychicus—Eph. 6:21; Col. 4:7. Onesimus— Col. 4:9. Paul—I Tim. 1:12. Silvanus—I Pet. 5:12. Timothy—I Cor. 4:17. Prophets—See PROPHETS, FAITHFULNESS OF.

Lack of faithfulness in enemies.—Ps. 5:9.

Of women.—II Sam. 20:19. Admonished —I Tim. 3:11. Examples of: Sarah— Heb. 11:11. Lydia—Acts 16:15.

Of people in service to God.—II Ki. 12: 15; 22:7; II Chr. 19:9; 31:12; 34:12; Hos. 11:12; III John 5. Witnesses— Ps. 89:37; Pr. 14:5; Is. 8:2.

Proverbs concerning.—Pr. 11:31; 13:17; 14:5; 20:6; 25:13; 27:6.

Figurative.—Hos. 2:20. City—Is. 1:21, 26.

FAITHLESS. Be not—John 20:27. Generation—Mt. 17:17; Mk. 9:19; Lu. 9: 41.

FALCON. Job 28:7.

FALL, *n.* Day of—Ez. 26:18; 32:10. Great was—Mt. 7:27. Haughty spirit before a—Pr. 16:18. Noise of—Jer. 49:21. Righteous—Pr. 29:16. Salvation come by their—Rom. 11:11. Set for—Lu. 2:34. Sound of—Ez. 26:15; 31:16.

FALL, *v.* Ps. 37:24; 145:14; Eccl. 4:10. Anger—Jer. 3:12. Arm—Job 31:22; Ez. 30:25. Arrows—Ez. 39:3. Asleep in Jesus—I Cor. 15:18. Away—Lu. 8: 13; Gal. 5:4; I Tim. 4:1; Hab. 6:6. See APOSTASY. Backward—Gen. 49:17; Is. 28:13. Before—Lev. 26:7, 8; II Chr. 25:8; Ps. 72:11. Blood—I Sam. 26:20. Bowels—II Chr. 21:15. Cause some to —Pr. 4:16. See STUMBLE. Condemnation, Into—I Tim. 3:6; Jas. 5:12. See CONDEMNATION, JUDGMENT. Crumbs— Mt. 15:27. Dew—II Sam. 17:12. Die —See DEATH, PUNISHMENT. Destruction, Into—Ps. 35:8. See DESTRUCTION. Ditch, Into—Mt. 15:14; Lu. 6:39. Down in worship—Is. 44:17, 19; 45: 14; 46:6; Dan. 3:5, 6, 10, 15; Mt. 4:9; Rev. 4:10. See IDOLATRY, WORSHIP. Dread—Ex. 15:16; Job 13:11. Earth —Is. 24:20. Flower—Jas. 1:11; I Pet. 1:24. Fire, Into—Mt. 17:15. Fool— Pr. 10:8, 10. Great man—II Sam. 3: 38. Hailstones—Ez. 13:11. See METEOROLOGY. Hair—I Sam. 14:45; II Sam. 14:1; I Ki. 1:52; Acts 27:34. Hand, Into the—Ju. 15:18; II Sam. 24:14; I Chr. 21:13; Heb. 10:31. Helpfulness—Ps. 10:10. Haughty spirit— Pr. 16:18. House—Mt. 7:27; 11:17. Land—Lev. 19:29; Ez. 47:14. Law— Lu. 16:18. See COVENANTS, LAW.

Lightning—Lu. 10:18. Matter, The—Ruth 3:18. Mischief, Into—Pr. 28:14; Is. 47:11. Mountains—Lu. 23:30; Rev. 6:16. Nail—Is. 22:15. Nations—Ez. 36:15. Net, Into—Ps. 141:10. See NET. Never—II Pet. 1:10. Out of the way—Gen. 45:24. See AWAY. Ox or an ass—Ex. 21:35; Deut. 22:4. Pit, Into—Ex. 21:35; Pr. 22:14; 26:27; 28:10; Eccl. 10:8; Is. 24:18; Mt. 12:11. Pleasant places, Into—Ps. 16:6. Portion of goods—Mt. 15:12. Quails —Num. 11:31; Ps. 78:28. Ready to— Ps. 38:17; Is. 30:13. Reproach, Into— I Tim. 3:7. See REPROACH. Righteous —Ps. 37:24. Satan—Lu. 10:8. Short —Hab. 1:15. Sleep, Into—Job 4:13; 35:15. Snare, Into—I Tim. 3:7. See SNARE, TEMPTATION. Sparrows—Mt. 10:29. Stars—Mt. 24:29; Mk. 13:25; Rev. 9:1. Steadfastness, From—II Pet. 3:17. See STEADFAST. Stone—Mt. 21:44; Lu. 20:18. See STUMBLE. Sword, By the—See SWORD, JUDGMENT, PUNISHMENT. Take heed lest ye—I Cor. 10:12. Temptation, Into— I Tim. 6:9; Heb. 4:11; Jas. 1:2. See TEMPTATION. Towers—Is. 30:25. Tree —Eccl. 11:3. Upon—See ATTACK, JUDGMENT, WAR. Wall—Ez. 38:20. See JERUSALEM, WALL OF. Wheat— John 12:24. Wicked—Ps. 141:10; Pr. 11:5, 28; 24:16; 28:18; 29:16. See JUDGMENT, WICKED. Words—I Sam. 3:19. Young men—Is. 40:30; Jer. 49:26.

FALLEN. Babylon—Is. 21:9; Jer. 51:8. Countenance—Gen. 4:6. Crown—Lam. 5:16. Dagon—I Sam. 5:3, 4. Ditch, Into—Ps. 7:15. Feet, Under—II Sam. 22:39. Fire of God—Job 1:16. Haman —Esth. 7:8. Inheritance—Num. 32:19. Iniquity, Workers of—Ps. 36:12. Jews—Jer. 38:19. Judah—Is. 3:8. Mighty—II Sam. 1:25, 27; Jer. 46:12. Men—II Sam. 3:38; Lam. 2:21. People—II Sam. 1:4. Reproach—Ps. 69:9. Saul—I Sam. 31:8; I Chr. 10:8. Sleep, Deep—I Sam. 26:12. Sword, By—II Sam. 1:12. Truth—Is. 59:14.

FALLING. Num. 24:4; Job 4:4. Feet from—Ps. 56:13; 116:8. Mountain— Job 14:18.

FALLOW. Ground—Jer. 4:3; Hos. 10:12.

FALSEHOOD. Father of.—Ps. 7:14; John 8:44.

Falsehood begets falsehood.—II Ki. 5: 21–27; Mk. 14:70–71.

Falsehood.—For grain—Acts 5:1–9. For concealment—Mt. 28:12–15. For conquest—I Ki. 22:20–22. For worship— Jer. 10:14; 51:17.

Dealing falsely.—Gen. 21:23; Ps. 119:118; 144:8, 11; Is. 28:15; 57:4; 59:13; Jer. 13:25.

False witness.—Ex. 20:16; 23:1; Deut. 5:20; 19:16–18; II Ki. 9:12; Ps. 27:12; 35:11; Pr. 6:19; 12:17; 14:5; 17:4; 19:5, 9; 21:28; 25:18; Mt. 15:19; 19:18; 26:59, 60; Mk. 10:19; 14:56–57; Lu. 18:20.

False persons and things.—Accusations —II Ki. 9:12; Jer. 40:16; Lu. 19:8; II Tim. 3:3; Tit. 2:3; I Pet. 3:16. Answers—Job 21:34. Apostles—II Cor. 11:13. Balances—Pr. 11:1; 20:23; Amos 8:5; Hos. 12:7. Brethren—II Cor. 11:26; Gal. 2:4. Christs—Mt. 24:24; Mk. 13:22. Anti-christs—I John 2:18, 22; 4:3; II John 7. Divinations —Ez. 21:23; Jer. 14:14. Dreams— Jer. 23:32; Zech. 10:2. Gifts—Pr. 25:14. Lips—Job 27:4; Pr. 17:4. Oaths— Zech. 8:17. Prophets—I Ki. 13:17–18; Is. 30:10; Jer. 5:31; 29:9; Acts 13:6; II Pet. 2:1; I John 4:1; Mt. 7:15; 24:11, 24; Mk. 13:22; Lu. 6:26; Rev. 16:13. Reports—Ex. 23:1; Jer. 37:14. Swearers—Lev. 6:3, 5; 19:12; Jer. 5:2; 7:9; Hos. 10:4; Zech. 5:4; Mal. 3:5. Teachers—II Pet. 2:1. Tongues —Job 27:4; Ps. 120:3; Rom. 3:13; Jas. 1:26; 3:5–9. Visions—Jer. 14:14; Lam. 2:14. See LYING, WITNESS, FALSE, DECEPTION, PERJURY.

FALSE TEACHER. See INSTRUCTION.

FAME, FAMOUS. Bethlehem, In—Ruth 4:11. David, Of—I Chr. 14:17. Heard —Num. 14:15; I Ki. 10:11; II Chr. 9:1; Is. 66:19. House of—I Chr. 22:5. Kings—Ps. 136:18. Men—I Chr. 5:24; 12:30. Mordecai, Of—Esth. 9:4. Nations—I Ki. 4:31; Ez. 32:18. Prosperity exceed—I Ki. 10:7. See JESUS, POPULARITY OF.

FAMILIAR. Friend—Job 19:14; Ps. 41:9; Jer. 20:10. Spirit—Lev. 19:31; 20:6, 27; Deut. 18:11; I Sam. 28:3, 7, 8, 9; II Ki. 21:6; 23:24; I Chr. 10:13;

II Chr. 33:6; Is. 8:19; 19:3; 29:4. See MAGIC.

FAMILY. Divinely established—Gen. 1:28; 2:18, 22.

Laws of.—Gen. 29:21; Lev. 18:18; Num. 36:12.

Promise to.—Gen. 12:3; 28:14; Ps. 68:6; Is. 59:21; 65:23; Jer. 31:1.

Prophecies concerning families of the north.—Jer. 1:15; 25:9. Of Israel—Jer. 2:4; 31:1.

Heads of.—Called chiefs, heads, Elders and householders—Gen. 36:40; 47:12; Ex. 6:14-25; 12:21; Num. 36:1.

Inheritance allotted according to.—Josh. Chs. 13–17.

Families as servants.—Ex. 21:2-5; Lev. 25:45.

Punished for worship of.—Molech—Lev. 20:5. Wood and stone—Ez. 20:32-34.

Warriors numbered.—Num. 1:2, 18-42; 2:34. Levites—Num. 3:15-39.

Numbering the people.—Num. 4:2, 18-46; 26:7, 12-58.

In year of jubilee every man returned to.—Lev. 25:10, 41.

A man may be redeemed by.—Lev. 25:49.

Punishment of.—Jer. 10:25; Zech. 14:18.

Families of the earth.—Amos 3:2.

Sells families through witchcrafts.—Nah. 3:4.

Contempt of families terrified.—Job 31:34.

Noah and his family saved.—Gen. 7:13, 23.

Terah and his family moved to the land of Canaan.—Gen. 11:31.

Figurative.—Like flocks—Ps. 107:41. Family of God—Eph. 3:14. See HOUSE, HOUSEHOLD, FATHER, MOTHER, PARENTS, BRETHREN, SISTERS, CHILDREN, HOME, HUSBAND, WIFE, HEAD.

FAMINE. Description of.—Deut. 28:53, 58; Is. 5:13; Jer. 5:17; 14:1-6; 48:33; Lam. 2:11-22; 4:4-10; Joel 1:17-20.

A judgment from God.—For disobedience—Lev. 26:19, 20; Deut. 28:23, 24, 38-42; I Ki. 17:1; II Ki. 8:1; I Chr. 21:12; Ps. 105:16; Is. 3:1-8; 51:19; Jer. 5:12; 11:22; 14:12; 34:17; Ez. 4:16, 17; 5:16, 17; 14:13, 21; Amos 4:6-9; 5:16, 17; Hag. 1:10, 11; Lu. 21:11; Rev. 6:5-8.

Promise of deliverance from.—Job 5:20; Ps. 33:19; Ps. 37:19; Jer. 14:13, 15; Ez. 12:16; 36:29, 30.

Prophecies concerning. — In Egypt — Gen. 41:27, 30; 41:31, 36, 50. All the world—Acts 11:28. In Philistia—Is. 14:30. Judah—Jer. 15:2; 16:4; 18:21; 21:7, 9; 24:10; 29:17, 18; 32:24, 36; 44:12, 13, 18. Jerusalem—Jer. 52:6; Ez. 5:12, 16, 17. Israel—Ez. 6:11, 12; 7:15; Amos 8:11; Lu. 4:25. Fall of Babylon—Rev. 18:8.

Examples of.—In Egypt—Gen. 12:10; 26:1; 47:20. In Canaan—Gen. 42:5, 19, 33; 43:1; 45:6, 11; 47:4, 13. In Israel—Ruth 1:1; II Sam. 21:1; 24:13; I Ki. 8:37; I Chr. 21:12. Samaria—I Ki. 18:2; II Ki. 6:25; 7:4. Jerusalem—II Ki. 25:3. Judah—II Chr. 20:9; 32:11. Prodigal's experience with—Lu. 15:14. Of captives—Lam. 5:10.

Figurative.—Famished soul—Lam. 1:11, 19. See HUNGER, DROUGHT.

FAMISH. Gen. 41:55; Pr. 10:3; Is. 5:13; Zeph. 2:11. See HUNGER, THIRST.

FAN. Mt. 3:12; Lu. 3:17.

FAR. Abroad—II Chr. 26:15. Away—Job 11:14; 22:23; Is. 6:12; 19:6; Ez. 44:10; Amos 6:3. Better—Phil. 1:23. Blessing—Ps. 109:17. Brethren—Job 19:13; Pr. 27:10. Come from—Is. 10:3; 13:5. Comforter—Lam. 1:16. Counsel of wicked—Job 22:18. Country—Josh. 9:6, 9; I Ki. 8:41; II Ki. 20:14; II Chr. 6:32, 36; Is. 8:9; 13:5; 39:3; 46:11; Jer. 4:16; 6:20; Lam. 3:17; Zech. 10:9; Mt. 21:33; 25:14; Mk. 12:1; Lu. 15:13; 19:12; 20:9. East from west—Ps. 103:12. Exalted above—Ps. 97:9. Exceeding, More—II Cor. 4:17. Foolishness—Pr. 22:15. Friends—Ps. 88:18; Pr. 19:7. Glory, From me to—Gal. 6:14. God, From—Gen. 18:25; I Sam. 2:30; Job 34:10; Ps. 22:11, 19; 27:9; 35:22; 38:21; 71:12; 73:27; Is. 29:13; Ez. 11:15. See Acts 17:27; ALIENS. Hand—Job 13:21. Heart from me—Mt. 15:8; Mk. 7:6. Heavens, Above—Eph. 4:10. Helping, From—Ps. 22:1. Hence—Acts 22:21. Iniquity—Acts 22:21; Job 22:23. Judgments—Ps. 16:5; Is. 59:9. Kingdom, From the—Mk. 12:34. Law, From—Ps. 119:150. Lord, From thee—Mt. 16:22. Nations—Is. 5:26. See COUNTRY.

Off—Deut. 13:7; 20:15; II Sam. 15:17; II Ki. 6:36; Ps. 55:7; Is. 17:13; 33:13, 17; 57:9, 19; Jer. 49:30; Ez. 6:12; 12: 27; Dan. 9:7; Joel 2:20; 3:8. Oppressor, From—Is. 54:14. See OPPRESSION. Perverse lips—Pr. 4:24. Principalities, Above—Eph. 1:21. Price above rubies —Pr. 31:10. Righteousness, From—Is. 46:12, 13. Safety, From—Job 5:4. Salvation, From—Ps. 119:155; Is. 59:11. See SALVATION. Sons—Is. 60:4, 9. Spent—Ju. 19:11; Mk. 6:35; Lu. 24: 29; Rom. 13:12; Eph. 2:13, 17. Strange woman—Pr. 5:8. See HARLOT. Thorns and snares—Pr. 22:5. Transgressions —Ps. 103:12. See SIN. Vanity, From —Pr. 30:8. Wicked, From—Pr. 5:8; 15:29. See SIN, WICKED.

FARE. Brethren, How—I Sam. 17:18. Paid the—Jon. 1:3. People—II Sam. 11:7. Sumptuously—Lu. 16:19.

FAREWELL. Acts 15:29. Bade—Acts 21:5. Bid—Lu. 9:61. Finally, Brethren—II Cor. 13:11. See SALUTATION.

FARING. See SEAFARING, WAYFARING.

FARM. Mt. 22:5. See AGRICULTURE.

FARTHER. See FURTHER.

FARTHING. Last, Paid the—Mt. 5:26. Two mites make a—Mk. 12:42.

FASHION. According to this world— Rom. 12:2. Anew—Phil. 3:21. Body —Phil. 3:21. Clay—Job 10:9; Is. 45:9. God, A—Is. 44:10. Hammers, With —Is. 44:12. Hands—Job 10:8; Ps. 119:73. Hearts—Ps. 33:15. Ministers —II Cor. 11:15. Satan—II Cor. 11:14. Tool, With—Ex. 32:4. Womb, In— Job 31:15. Yourselves—I Pet. 1:14. See CONFORMATION AND TRANSFORMATION.

FAST. Abide—Ruth 2:8. Asleep—Ju. 4:21 (A.V.); Jonah 1:5. Bind—Ju. 15: 13; 16:11. Cleave—Job 38:38; Ps. 41: 8. Closed—Gen. 20:18. Feet—Acts 16: 24. Hasteth—Jer. 48:16. Hold—II Ki. 6:32; Job 2:3, 9; 8:15; 27:5, 6; Pr. 4: 13; Jer. 8:5; 50:33; I Cor. 15:2; I Thess. 5:21; II Tim. 1:13. Keep— Ruth 2:21, 23; Tit. 1:9; Heb. 3:6; 4: 14; 10:23; Rev. 2:13, 25; 3:3, 11. Set —Ps. 65:6. Stand—Ps. 33:9; 89:28; 111:8; Jer. 46:18; I Cor. 16:31; Gal. 5:1; Phil. 1:7; 4:1; I Thess. 3:8; II Thess. 2:15. See STEADFAST. Stick— Ps. 38:2; Acts 27:4.

FASTEN. Body, Saul's—I Sam. 31:12. Cords, With—Esth. 1:6. Eyes—Lu. 4:20; Acts 3:4; 11:6. Foundations— Job 38:6. Head—I Chr. 10:10. Hooks —Ez. 40:43. Golden plate—Ex. 39:31. Nail—Eccl. 12:11; Is. 22:23, 25; 41:7; Jer. 10:4. Pin, With a—Ju. 16:14. Steps to throne—II Chr. 9:18. Sword —II Sam. 20:8. Viper in Paul's hand —Acts 28:3.

FASTING. Fast proclaimed.—Lev. 23: 27; II Chr. 20:3; Ezra 8:21; Neh. 9:1; Esth. 4:3, 16; Joel 2:12, 16; Jonah 3:5. Recommended—II Cor. 6:5.

Spirit of prayer.—Ez. 8:21-23; Dan. 9:3.

Confession.—I Sam. 7:6; Neh. 9:1, 2.

Mourning.—Joel 2:12. **Humiliation.**— Deut. 9:18; Neh. 9:1; Ps. 35:13; 69:10.

Manner of.—Esth. 9:31; Mt. 6:17.

Kinds of.—False—Is. 58:4; Jer. 14:12; Mt. 6:16; Lu. 18:12. True—I Sam. 31: 13; I Chr. 10:12; Neh. 1:4; Is. 58:6; Acts 13:2, 3; 14:23; 27:33.

Time.—Neh. 9:1; Jer. 36:6; Mk. 2:19. Length of—Forty days and forty nights: *Moses*—Ex. 34:28; Deut. 9:9, 18. Elijah—I Ki. 19:8. *Our Lord*— Mt. 4:2. Fourteen days—Acts 27:33. Effects of—Ps. 109:24; Mt. 15:32; Mk. 8:3. Promises connected with— Is. 58:8-12; Mt. 6:18.

How often.—Lu. 18:12; II Cor. 11:27.

Recommended.—II Cor. 6:5.

Examples of.—Moses—Ex. 24:18; 34: 28; Deut. 9:9, 18. David—II Sam. 1: 12; 3:35; 12:16. Elijah—I Ki. 19:8. Children of Israel—Ju. 20:26; I Sam. 7:6; 14:24-30; I Chr. 10:12. Men of Jabesh-Gilead—I Sam. 31:13. Ahab— I Ki. 21:27. Jehoshaphat—II Cor. 20: 3. Ninevites—Jonah 3:5-10. Darius —Dan. 6:18. People of Judah—Jer. 36:9. Daniel—Dan. 9:3; 10:1-3. Ezra —Ez. 11:6; 8:21-23. Nehemiah—Neh. 1:4. Disciples of John—Mt. 9:14; Mk. 2:19. Anna—Lu. 2:37. Pharisee—Lu. 18:12. Apostles—II Cor. 6:5. Christ— Mt. 4:2. Barnabas and Saul—Acts 14: 23. Saul—Acts 9:9. Paul—II Cor. 11: 27. Disciples of Christ—John 21:12, 15. **Christ defends his disciples for not.**— Mt. 9:14, 15; Mk. 2:19; Lu. 5:33-35.

FASTNESS. See FORTIFICATIONS.

FAT. Animals not to be eaten—See ANIMALS. Become—Neh. 9:25. Bones—

Pr. 15:30; Is. 58:11. Bread—Gen. 49:
20. Cattle—Gen. 41:4, 20. See Cattle.
Destroy—Ez. 34:16. Dust—Is. 34:7.
Eglon—Ju. 3:17, 22. Flock, Of—Gen.
4:4. Heart—Ps. 119:18. See Mt. 13:
15. Inclosed in—Ps. 17:10. Lambs, Of
—Deut. 32:14; Ps. 37:20. Land—
Num. 13:20; Neh. 9:25, 35. Land, Of
the—Gen. 45:18. Mighty, Of the—II
Sam. 1:22. Ones—Is. 5:17; 10:16. Pas-
ture—I Chr. 4:40; Ez. 34:14. Portion
—Hab. 1:16. Rams, Of—I Sam. 15:22.
Trust makes—Pr. 28:25. Waxed—
Deut. 31:20; 32:15; Jer. 5:28. See Mt.
13:15. See Offering.

FATHER (*Heb.* Ab; *Chald.* abba. Ancestor, source. Ab, when a prefix to a
name, signifies ''father of'').

As an ancestor.—Gen. 2:24; 9:18, 22;
10:21; 11:28, 29; 22:7, 21; 26:3, 15, 18,
24; 31:3; 47:3, 9, 30; 48:15; 49:29; Ex.
8:13; 10:6; 13:5; Deut. 1:8, 11; Josh.
24:6; Ju. 2:10; I Sam. 12:6, 8, 15; II
Sam. 7:12; I Ki. 11:12; 13:22; II Ki.
8:24; I Chr. 29:18; II Chr. 9:31; Ezra
7:27; Neh. 9:2, 9; Ps. 22:4; 49:19;
106:7; Jer. 7:7; 11:10; Ez. 18:2; Zech.
1:4; 23:10; Mk. 11:10; Lu. 1:32, 73;
6:23, 26; John 7:22; Acts 7:2.

As chief or ruler.—Priest—Ju. 17:10;
18:19; Acts 22:1. Prophet—II Ki. 2:
12; 6:21; 13:14. King—Josh. 15:13;
I Ki. 15:24. Apostle—I Cor. 4:15. Syrian general—II Ki. 5:13.

Father of nations or tribes.—Gen. 17:4,
5; 19:37, 38; 36:9, 43; 45:18; Num. 3:
30; Josh. 17:1; I Chr. Chs. 2, 4; 9:19.
(In Num. Ch. 17, *house* is used for
tribe.)

Father, as related to household.—Gen.
12:1; 20:13; 24:7, 23, 38, 40; 28:21;
31:14; 38:11; 41:51; 46:31; 50:8, 22;
Lev. 22:13; Num. 2:2; 18:1; Deut. 22:
21; Josh. 2:12; Ju. 6:15; 9:5, 18; 11:2,
7; I Sam. 2:31; 9:20; 18:2; 22:1, 11,
16, 22; II Sam. 3:29; 14:9; I Ki. 18:
18; I Chr. 7:2; II Chr. 21:13; Neh. 1:
6; Is. 7:17; 22:23, 24; Lu. 2:49; 16:27;
Acts 7:20.

Father as source or inventor of.—Gen.
4:21; Job 17:14; 38:28; John 8:44;
Rom. 4:11, 12; 9:5; I Cor. 4:15; II
Cor. 1:3.

As an object of respect.—II Ki. 2:12; 5:
13; 6:21; Jer. 2:27; Acts 7:2; 22:1.

**In earliest times his jurisdiction was su-
preme.**—Gen. 22:31, 32; 38:24; 42:37.

**In later times his jurisdiction was distrib-
uted.**—Court of judges determine—
Ex. 21:22, 15, 17; Lev. 20:9; Deut. 21:
18–21. Power to sacrifice children, still
his—II Ki. 16:3; Jer. 7:31; 19:5; Ez.
16:20; 20:26. Done in violation of law
—Lev. 18:21; 20:1–5; Deut. 12:31;
18:10.

**Children treated by fathers as slaves or
chattels.**—Arbitrary marriages—Gen.
38:6; Ju. 12:9; Ezra 9:2. Children
pledged or sold—II Ki. 4:1; Is. 50:1.
Harlotry of daughters forbidden—
Lev. 19:29. Bonds of daughters disal-
lowed—Num. 30:5. Wives divorced
at pleasure—Gen. 21:9–10.

Blessing of father.—Gen. 27:4–38; 48:9–
22; 49:1–28.

Malediction of father.—Gen. 9:25–27;
27:27–40; 48:17–19; 49:1–28. (In
which blessing and curse mingle.)

Qualities of a father: To command—
Gen. 18:19; 49:33; Deut. 32:46. To
provide—Ju. 1:14–15; Mt. 7:9–11; Lu.
11:11–13; 12:32; 15:12. To renounce
—Gen. 22:2–3; Hos. 11:8; Lu. 15:11–
12. To pity—Ps. 103:13. To grieve—
Gen. 21:11–12; 37:34–35; 42:38; 44:
29; II Sam. 18:33. To love—Gen. 25:
28; 37:3; II Sam. 2:32. To protect—
Job 29:16; Ps. 27:10; 68:5; Deut. 32:6.
To correct—Pr. 3:12; 23:13; 29:17;
Heb. 12:9.

Duties of children to fathers: To obey—
Gen. 27:8, 13, 43; Deut. 21:18–21; Jer.
35:14; Eph. 6:1; Col. 3:20. To honor
—Ex. 20:12; Lev. 19:3; Mt. 15:4; 19:
19. To love—Gen. 45:9–11; 46:29; 47:
12, 29–30. To gladden—Pr. 10:1; 17:
21; Phil. 2:22.

Influence of fathers upon posterity: Evil
influence—Ex. 20:5; 34:7; Lev. 26:39;
Num. 14:18; Deut. 5:9; 8:3; I Ki. 15:
12; II Ki. 17:14, 41; II Chr. 30:7, 8;
Neh. 9:2, 16; Ps. 78:57; 106:6; Is. 14:
21; 65:7; Jer. 2:5–9; 6:21; 7:26; 9:16;
13:14; 14:20; 16:12; 19:4; 44:9; Lam.
5:7; Ez. 20:30–32; Dan. 9:16. Amos
2:4; Zech. 1:4–6; Mal. 2:10; Mt. 23:
29–32; Lu. 11:47–48; Acts 7:51–53.
Good influence—Gen. 15:15; 47:9; I
Ki. 2:10; 15:11, 12, 23, 24; II Chr. 14:
2–6; 32:32–33; Heb. **12:9.**

Children not to suffer for sins of fathers.—Deut. 24:16; II Ki. 14:6; II Chr. 25:4; Jer. 31:29–30; Ez. Ch. 18.

Fatherless.—Abuse of—Ex. 22:22; Job 6:27; 22:9; 24:9; Ps. 94:6; 109:10–12; Is. 10:2; Jer. 7:6; 22:3; Ez. 22:7; Zech. 7:10. To be cared for—Deut. 14:29; 16:11, 14; II Sam. 9:3; II Ki. 11:1–2; Job 31:17–18; Ps. 68:5; 146:9; Jer. 49:11; Jas. 1:27.

Father-in-law.—Gen. 38:13; Ex. 2:18; 3:1; 18:1–27; Num. 10:29; Ju. 1:16; 4:11; 19:4, 7, 9; I Sam. 4:19, 21.

New Testament references.—Whose son asks for a loaf—Mt. 7:9–11. To bury my father—Mt. 8:21; Lu. 9:59. He that loveth father more—Mt. 10:37. Father give me the portion—Lu. 15:12. Devil is father of lies—John 8:34. Father of all that believe—Rom. 4:11, 17. As a child serveth father—Phil. 2:22. Father of our flesh—Heb. 12:9. Your father tried me—Heb. 3:9. See GOD, FATHERHOOD OF, PARENTS, CHILDREN.

FATHERLESS. See ORPHANS.

FATHOMS. Acts 27:28.

FATLINGS. II Sam. 6:13; I Ki. 1:9, 19, 25; Ps. 66:15; Is. 11:6; Mt. 22:4. See OFFERING.

FATNESS. Covered face with—Job 15:27. Earth, Of the—Gen. 27:28, 39. Eyes stand out with—Ps. 73:7. Flesh faileth—Ps. 109:4; Is. 17:4. Full of—Job 36:16. House, Of thy—Ps. 36:8. Made fat with—Is. 34:6, 7. Olive tree, Of—Ju. 9:9; Rom. 11:17. Paths drop—Ps. 65:11. Reason of, By—Is. 10:27. Satisfied with—Ps. 36:8; 63:5. Soul delight in—Is. 55:2; Jer. 31:14.

FATTED CALF. Lu. 15:23, 27, 30.

FATTEST. Ps. 78:31; Dan. 11:21.

FAULT. II Sam. 3:8; Mt. 18:15. Hidden—Ps. 19:12. No fault in—I Sam. 29:3; Dan. 6:4; Lu. 23:4, 14. Self, Of—Gen. 41:9; Ex. 5:16; Ps. 59:4. See BLEMISH, CRIME, DEFECT, SIN.

FAULTLESS. Heb. 8:7. See BLAMELESS.

FAVOR. Gen. 29:17; Ps. 5:12; Pr. 19:6; 21:10; 22:1; 28:23; Is. 26:10; Lam. 4:16. Cattle—Gen. 41:2–27. Egyptians, In sight of—Ex. 3:21; 11:3; 12:36; Acts 7:10. Esther finds—Esth. 2:15, 17; 5:2, 8; 7:3; 8:5. Jehovah, In sight of—Gen. 18:3; Num. 11:11, 15; I Sam. 2:26; II Sam. 15:25; Ps. 30:5, 7; 119:58; Pr. 3:4; 8:35; 12:2; 18:22; Is. 27:11; 60:10; Ju. 16:13; Lu. 1:2, 8, 30; 2:52; Acts 7:46; Kings—Pr. 14:35; 16:15; 19:12. Sight, In—Gen. 30:27; 39:21; Ruth 2:13; I Sam. 16:22; 20:29. See GRACE.

FAVORABLE. Job 33:26; Ps. 77:7; 85:1.

FAWNS. Song of Sol. 4:5; 7:3. See ANIMALS.

FEAR. From *faeren*, to frighten, to be afraid, to terrify. Scriptural fear is "the apprehension of incurring, or solicitude to avoid, God's wrath"—Ex. 15:16; Deut. 28:65–67; Job 9:34; 35; Ps. 90:11.

Guilty conscience leads to.—Adam and Eve—Gen. 3:12. Jacob—Gen. 31:31. Accusers of woman—John 8:9. Felix—Acts 24:25. Demons—Jas. 2:19.

Overwhelming odds.—Cain—Gen. 4:14. Aaron—Ex. 32:22–24. The ten spies—Num. 13:28, 29. Men of Israel meeting Goliath—I Sam. 17:24. David fleeing—II Sam. 15:13–17. Disciples at sea—Mt. 8:26; Mk. 4:38; Lu. 8:25. Peter's denial—Mt. 26:69–74; Mk. 14:66–72; Lu. 22:54–60. Pilate—John 19:8.

Rank cowardice.—Israelites—Num. 14:3. Gideon's army—Ju. 7:3. Midianites—Ju. 7:21, 22. Saul—I Sam. 28:5, 20. Parents of blind man—John 9:22.

Fear as a judgment.—Gen. 4:13, 14; Lev. 26:16, 17; Job 15:20–22; Is. 2:19; Jer. 49:5; Lu. 21:26; Acts 5:11; Heb. 10:26, 27; Rev. 6:15–17.

Reverential fear of God.—Deut. 4:10; 10:12; II Cor. 5:11; Heb. 10:31; Jude 23; Rev. 19:5. The beginning of wisdom—Job 28:28; Ps. 111:10; Pr. 1:7; 9:10; 15:33.

Instances: Abel—Gen. 4:4. Enoch—Gen. 5:24. Noah—Gen. 6:9; Heb. 11:7. Abraham—Gen. 22:12. Jacob—Gen. 28:16, 17. Joseph—Gen. 42:18; Job 1:8. David—Ps. 5:7. Cornelius—Acts 10:2.

Motives to fear God.—Obedience—Deut. 31:12, 13; Is. 8:12, 13; Jer. 42:6; Rom. 6:16, 17. Greatness of God—Lev. 19:14; Deut. 28:58; Josh. 4:24; Jer. 8:13;

10:7. Providence—Gen. 22:13, 14; Ps. 91:1-7; Jer. 1:8; Mt. 6:26-33. The judgment—Mt. 10:28; Lu. 12:5; Rom. 11:20-22; Heb. 10:30, 31; Rev. 14:7. Forgiveness — Ps. 103:2-18; 130:4; Mt. 28:18-20; Mk. 16:15, 16; Lu. 1: 77-79; 24:45-48. God's love—Ps. 103: 11; John 3:16, 17; 15:13; Rom. 8:35-39; II Cor. 5:14; I John 4:18.

Blessings resulting from fear of God.— Prosperity—Deut. 5:29; Eccl. 8:12; Mal. 4:2. Food provided—Ps. 111:5. Lives preserved—Ps. 33:18; Pr. 10: 27; 22:4; Lu. 1:50. Riches, honor and life—Pr. 22:4. Friendship of God— Ps. 25:14; 147:11. Mercy of God—Ps. 85:9; Lu. 1:50. Eternal life—Rev. 11:18.

FEARFUL. Rev. 21:8. Appearance— Heb. 10:21. Expectation of judgment —Heb. 10:27. Let it be—John 14:27. Thing—Heb. 10:31. Why are ye—Mt. 8:26; Mk. 4:40.

FEASTS. Human origin: Hospitality.—Abram—Gen. 18:3-8. Lot—Gen. 19:3. Nabal—I Sam. 25:36. Ahasuerus—Esth. 1:2. Vashti—Esth. 1:9. Esther's—Esth. 6:4, 6, 8; 7:1-8. Job's sons—Job 1:13. Matthew (Levi)— Lu. 5:29. Pharisee's dinner—Lu. 11: 37, 38. Martha's supper—John 12:2. Jesus—John 21:9-15.

Special occasions.—Weaning of Isaac— Gen. 21:8.

Feast unto Jehovah.—In Egypt—Ex. 5: 23; 10:9. In wilderness—Ex. 23:5, 6.

Idolatrous.—Aaron's golden calf—Ex. 32:6. Moabites—Num. 25:1, 9. Jeroboam—I Ki. 12:32. Belshazzar—Dan. 5:1, 31.

For reconciliation.—Jacob and brethren —Gen. 31:54. Isaac and Abimelech —Gen. 26:30. Joseph and brethren— Gen. 43:16-32.

Marriage.—Laban—Gen. 29:22. Sampson—Ju. 14:10. Esther—Esth. 2:18. Parable of—Mt. 22:2. Ten virgins— Mt. 25:1. Cana—John 2:1. The lamb —Rev. 19:7, 8, 9.

Birthday.—Pharaoh—Gen. 40:20. Herod Mk. 6:21.

Commemorative. — (1) Purim (Lots), celebrated on the 14th and 15th days of Adar (March), the time Jews were delivered from Haman. Joyous, Book

of Esther read—Esth. Ch. 9. (2) Dedication. Solomon instituted seven-days' feast—II Chr. 7:9. Judas Maccabæus re-established temple and altar worship in 165 B.C. See ''IV Macc. 59:2.'' Called ''Feast of lights.'' Occurred in winter—John 10:22.

FEASTS. Divine origin: Called ''set feasts''—Lev. 23:2, 4, 37, 44; Num. 29:39; II Chr. 8:13; Ez. 46:9. Renewed: *By David*—I Chr. 23:31. *By Hezekiah*—II Chr. 31:3. *By Solomon*— II Chr. 8:13. *By Ezra*—Ezra 3:5. To meet expense of—Neh. 10:32. Hatred of God—Is. 1:14; Amos 5:21. To cease—Hos. 2:11; Amos 8:10.

Seven days'.—Ex. 23:18; Deut. 16:13, 15; Ju. 14:12; Ez. 45:21, 25.

Seventh month.—Num. 29:1; I Ki. 8:2; II Chr. 5:3; Neh. 8:14; Ez. 45:25. Offering at: Burnt-, Meal-, Peace-, Sin-, Drink-, of oil, and a sacrifice—Lev. 23:37; Ez. 45:15, 17, 25; 46:2, 4.

Events at time of.—Lu. 2:41, 42; John 4:45; 5:1; 7:2-14; 11:56. Jesus teaches at—John 2:23; 7:37; 10:22. Jesus coming to—John 12:12. Greeks at— John 12:20. Buy for—John 13:29. Invite poor—Lu. 14:13, 14.

Three a year.—Ex. 23:14; Deut. 16:16; II Chr. 8:13.

(1) **The sabbath.**—Lev. 23:3, 38; I Chr. 23:31; II Chr. 8:13; 31:3; Neh. 10:33; Ez. 45:17; 46:1, 3.

The new moon.—I Chr. 23:31; II Chr. 8:13; 31:3; Ezra 3:5; Neh. 10:33; Ez. 45:17; 46:1, 3; Hos. 2:11.

Trumpets.—Lev. 25:9; Num. 29:1.

(2) **Passover** (followed by unleavened bread).—In the spring month (Abib or Nisan), 14th day—Lev. 23:5-8; Ezra 6:19, 21; Ez. 45:21. Who shall eat of—Ex. 12:43-49. Where eaten— Ex. 12:46. Anniversary of the exodus —Ex. 12:13, 27; Num. 9:1-14; Deut. 16:1; II Ki. 23:21-23. Kept on leaving Egypt—Ex. 12:28-50; Heb. 11:28. In the wilderness—Num. 9:3-5. On entering Canaan—Josh. 5:10, 11. Kept by: *Moses*—Ex. 12:21; Heb. 11:28. *Joshua*—Josh. 5:10, 11. *Hezekiah*—II Chr. Ch. 30. *Josiah*—II Ki. 23:21; II Chr. 35:1-19. *Ezra*—Ezra 6:19-22. *Christ*—Mt. 26:17, 19; Mk. 14:1, 12;

Lu. 22:1, 7, 8; John 13:1. Distinguished from feast of Unleavened Bread—Lev. 23:6; Num. 28:16-25. No distinction made in gospels—Mt. 26: 17, 19; Mk. 14:1, 12; Lu. 22:1, 7, 8. At time of crucifixion—Mt. 26:2, 17; Mk. 14:1, 12, 16; Lu. 22:1, 11, 15; John 19:14; 31:42. Paschal lamb eaten at—Ex. 12:3-15; Lu. 22:7. Where killed—Deut. 16:5-7. By Levites—II Chr. 30:17; 35:3-11; Ezra 6:20. Blood sprinkled—Ex. 12:7; II Chr. 30:16. No broken bones—Ex. 12:45; Num. 9:12 (see John 19:33, 36). Roasted whole—Ex. 12:8, 9; II Chr. 35:13. Eaten with: Wine—Mt. 26:27-29; Lu. 22:15-20. Bitter herbs—Ex. 12:8; Num. 9:11. Unleavened bread—Ex. 12:8, 15, 20; 13:3, 6; 7:23, 15; Lev. 23:6; Num. 9:11; Deut. 16:3, 4; Mk. 14:12. Figurative—I Cor. 5:8. Hastily—Ex. 12:11. Punishment for eating leavened bread—Ex. 12:15. A prisoner released at—Mt. 27:15; Lu. 23:18-20. Christ as: Lamb of God, our passover—I Cor. 5:7. Take away sin —John 1:29. Perfect sacrifice—Mt. 27:35-43; Mk. 15:22-32; Lu. 23:33-42. No bones broken—John 19:33, 36. The Lord's Supper a memorial of Him —Lu. 22:19; I Cor. 11:23-26.

Unleavened bread (following passover). —As a memorial—Ex. 12:14-21; 23: 15; 34:18, 25. On 15th day of month (Abib or Nisan)—Lev. 23:6; Num. 28:17. Commanded to attend—Deut. 16:8, 16. Assembled for—II Chr. 30: 13, 21; 35:17; Ezra 6:22; Ez. 45:15; Lu. 22:1, 7; Acts 12:3; 20:7. Kept idolatrously—I Ki. 12:32.

(3) **Pentecost** (or, **Weeks**, or, **Harvest**). —It was held fifty days after passover. Hence called "feast of weeks," *i. e.*, seven times seven weeks; the following day being fiftieth—Ex. 34:22; Lev. 23:17, 21; Num. 28:26; Deut. 16:9-12. Loaves called "first-fruits" Lev. 23:17. Holy Spirit given on— Acts 2:1-4. "First-fruits" of Spirit's work—Acts 2:38-41. The beginning—Acts 11:15. Christ the "first-fruits" of them that slept—I Cor. 15:20.

(4) **Tabernacles** (or, Ingatherings at end of the year).—Seventh month (Tishri)

Ex. 23:16; 34:22; Ez. 45:21. A remembrance of the time the Israelites dwelt in booths—Lev. 23:34-42; Neh. 8:14-16. Kept seven days—Lev. 23:34; Num. 29:12; Deut. 16:13, 15. Every seventh year at occurrence of this feast a sabbatical year began—Deut. 31:10-12; Neh. 8:18.

(5) **Sabbatical year.**—Lev. 25:48. Jubilee, joy in liberty, freedom of slaves —Lev. 25:8-12. Fixed price of land —Lev. 25:13, 16. Occurred every fifty years—Lev. 25:10, 11, 12.

FEATHER. Ez. 17:3, 7; Dan. 4:33. See BIRDS, PINIONS, WINGS.

FEEBLE. Job 4:4; Pr. 30:26; Is. 13:7; 35:3. Christians—I Cor. 12:22. Damascus—Jer. 49:24. Flocks—Gen. 30: 42. Hands—II Sam. 4:1; Jer. 6:24; 47:3; 50:43; Ez. 7:17; 21:7. Israelites—Deut. 25:18; II Chr. 28:15; Neh. 4:2; Ps. 105:37; Zech. 12:8. See FAINT, WEARY, WEAK.

FEED. Job 1:14; Ez. 34:23; Hos. 9:2; Jon. 3:7; Zeph. 2:7; Jude 12. Affliction, Bread of—I Ki. 22:27; II Chr. 18:26. See BREAD. Ashes, On—Is. 44: 20. Bashan, In—Mic. 7:14. Beasts— Ps. 80:13. Birds, of the heaven—Mt. 6:26; Lu. 12:24. Calf shall—Is. 27:10. Carmel, On—Jer. 50:19. Cow and bear shall—Is. 11:7. Delicately—Lam. 4:5. Enemies, Your—Rom. 12:20. Faithfulness, On—Ps. 37:3. Field, In—Ex. 22:5. Finest of wheat, With—Ps. 81: 16. Flock—Gen. 30:36; 37:12, 13, 16; Job 24:2; Song of Sol. 6:3; Is. 61:5; I Cor. 9:7. Folly, On—Pr. 15:14. Full, To the—Jer. 5:7. Grass, With—Dan. 5:21. Heritage of Jacob—Is. 58:14. Justice, In—Ez. 34:16. Lamb, As a— Hos. 4:16. Lambs—Is. 5:17; John 21: 15. Lilies, Among—Song of Sol. 2:16; 4:5. Lip of unrighteous—Pr. 10:21. Lord, When—Mt. 25:37. Meadow, In —Gen. 41:2, 18. Mountain, On—Ez. 34:13, 14. Needful food, With—Pr. 30:8. Pastures, In—Is. 30:23. People —Jer. 23:2. Place—Nah. 2:11. Prophets—I Ki. 18:4, 13. Ravens—I Ki. 17: 4. Sharon, In—I Chr. 27:29. Sheep— Gen. 29:7; I Sam. 17:15; Ez. 34:2, 3, 10, 15; John 21:16, 17. Shepherds— Ez. 34:8; Jude 12. Slaughter, Flocks of—Zech. 11:4, 7. Strength of Jehovah, In—Mic. 5:4. Swine, Herd of—Mt. 8:30; Mk. 5:11; Lu. 8:32; 15:15. Tears, Bread of—Ps. 80:5. Wind, On—Hos. 12:1. Wolf and lamb together—Is. 65:25. Wormwood, With—Jer. 9:15; 23:15.

FEEL. Gen. 27:12, 21, 22; Jer. 10:18; Acts 17:27. Body, In—Mk. 5:29. Not—Pr. 23:35. Pillars—Ju. 16:26.

FEELING. Infirmities, Of—Heb. 4:15. Past—Eph. 4:19. See SOUL.

FEET. (The word "feet" is used in Scripture in a great variety of ways to express action.)

Indicative of: Reverence—Ex. 3:5; Josh. 5:15; Eccl. 5:1; Lu. 7:38; Rev. 19:10. Of possession—Josh. 1:3; II Chr. 33:8; Acts 7:5. Of supporting others—Ju. 5:15; Job 29:15. Of agility—II Sam. 2:18; 22:34; Ps. 18:33, 36; Amos 2:15; Hab. 3:14. Of contempt—Job 12:5; Ez. 25:6-7; Heb. 10:29. Breadth of opportunity—Deut. 33:24; Ps. 31:8; 36:11; Is. 60:13. Of receptive attitude—Ez. 2:1; Lu. 8:35; Acts 26:16; Rev. 3:9. Of watchfulness—Ps. 119:101; Pr. 4:26-27. Of Divine guidance—Ps. 91:12; 94:18; 119:105; 121:3; Is. 41:2-3; Mt. 4:6; Lu. 4:11. Of evil tendencies—Pr. 1:16; 6:18; Is. 1:6; 59:7; Jer. 2:25; 12:10; 14:10; 38:22; Ez. 16:25; Rom. 3:15.

Habits of evil men and women.—Pr. 5:5; 6:28-29; 7:11, 12. Avoidance of evil tendencies—Job 31:5; Ps. 119:59, 101; Pr. 4:25-27; 6:27-28; 25:17; Jer. 13:16.

Protection from temptation.—Ps. 56:13; 66:9; 73:2; 116:8; Is. 58:13-14; Heb. 12:13. Ground of security—I Sam. 2:9; Ps. 26:12; 40:2; 122:2; Pr. 3:23, 26; Eph. 6:15. Divine interposition—Ps. 60:13.

Washing the feet.—Abraham and angels—Gen. 18:4. Lot and angels—Gen. 19:2. Isaac's servant with Laban—Gen. 24:32. Joseph's brethren—Gen. 43:24. Aaron and sons, as priests—Ex. 30:19; 40:31. Jesus sets a good example of humility—John 13:4-14. A good work—I Tim. 5:10. Act of cleanliness—II Sam. 19:24.

Modes of punishment. — Fetters — II Sam. 3:34; Job 13:27. Cutting off feet—II Sam. 4:12; Mt. 18:8; Mk. 9:45. Crushing out life—Ps. 68:23.

A type of disaster.—Ez. 24:17-24.

Destruction of nations.—Dan. 7:7.

Mode of: Ensnaring—Job 18:8; Ps. 9:15; Pr. 29:5; Jer. 18:22; Lam. 1:13. Journeying—Ju. 4:15; Mt. 14:13; Mk. 6:33; Acts 20:13. Submission—Ruth 3:8; Job 23:11; Acts 5:2, 9. Crucifixion—Ps. 22:16; Mt. 27:35; John 20:25. Humility—The demoniac—Lu. 8:35. The Magdalene—Lu. 7:37-38. Mary—John 11:2; 12:3. Humiliation—Is. 49:23.

Attitude of pupils.—Deut. 33:3; Lu. 10:39; Acts 22:3.

Preparation for ease and sleep.—Ju. 3:24; I Sam. 24:3.

Terror of conscience.—Job 18:11. Of apparitions—Rev. 1:17.

Persons recognized by sound of.—I Ki. 14:6; II Ki. 6:32.

An abnormal foot.—Citizen of Gath—I Sam. 21:20. Mephibosheth—II Sam. 4:4.

Feet dipped in Jordan.—Josh. 3:15. In Red Sea—Ps. 66:6.

Feet must co-operate with other parts of body.—I Cor. 12:14-21.

Jesus identified by.—Lu. 24:39-40. The activities of providence—Ez. 1:5-7.

Lame legs typical of unbalanced conduct.—Pr. 25:19; 26:6-7.

As expression of dying.—Gen. 49:33. Preparation for burial—John 11:44.

Foot, Sole of.—Dove—Gen. 8:9. Delicate woman—Deut. 28:56, 65. Gift of Canaan—Josh. 1:3. Absalom without blemish—II Sam. 14:25. Unsound throughout—Is. 1:6. Description of Ezekiel's creatures—Ez. 1:7.

Footstool.—For God—I Chr. 28:2. To worship at—Ps. 99:5; 132:7. Of one's enemies—Ps. 110:1; Mt. 22:44; Mk. 12:36; Lu. 20:43; Acts 2:35; Heb. 1:13; 10:13. Earth a footstool—Is. 66:1; Mt. 5:35; Acts 7:49. Under my footstool—Jas. 2:3.

Symbol of: Beauty—II Sam. 14:25; Song of Sol. 7:1; Is. 3:16-18; 52:7; Nah. 1:15; Rom. 10:15. Of subjection—Josh. 10:24; II Ki. 9:33; Ps. 110:1; Is. 14:25; 18:7; 20:3-5; 26:6; 60:14; Rom. 16:20; I Cor. 15:25, 27; Eph. 1:22; Heb. 2:8; Rev. 11:2. Of insecurity—

Gen. 8:9; Deut. 28:56, 65; 32:35; Job 39:15; Ps. 38:16. Of Christ's kingdom—Dan. 2:33, 34, 41, 44. Of warning—Ez. 6:11. Of desolation—Ez. 29:11; 32:13; Dan. 8:13-14. Of repudiation—Mt. 10:14; Mk. 6:11; Lu. 9:3; 10:11; Acts 13:51. Of captivity—Mt. 22:13; Acts 21:11. Of deliverance—Ps. 25:15. Of unfitness—Mt. 5:13.

FOOTWASHING.—A necessary act— Gen. 43:24; Song of Sol. 5:3.

An act of courtesy—Gen. 18:4; 24:32.

Ceremonial cleansing—Ex. 30:19-21; 40:30-31.

Good work—I Tim. 5:10.

Example—John 13:5-15.

Act of humility—I Sam. 25:41; **John 13:16.**

Act of gratitude—Lu. 7:38.

Symbol of vengeance—Ps. 58:10.

King's strategy—II Sam. 11:8.

FEIGN. Jer. 3:10. Another woman, To be—I Ki. 14:5, 6. David—I Sam. 21: 13. Lips—Ps. 17:1. Mourner, To be —II Sam. 14:2. Righteous, To be— Lu. 20:20. Words—II Pet. 2:3.

FELL. Countenance—Gen. 4:5. Asleep —Lu. 8:23; Acts 13:36; II Pet. 3:4. Away—Jer. 39:9; Heb. 6:6. Beam— II Ki. 18:38. Down—Rev. 5:8. Fire —I Ki. 18:38. Holy Spirit—Acts 10: 44. See HOLY SPIRIT. House—Lu. 6:49. Judas—Acts 1:25. Neck, On his—Lu. 15:20. Reproaches—Rom. 15:3. Trees—II Ki. 3:19, 25. Wall— Josh. 6:20. Wounded—Ju. 9:40. See FALL.

FELLOES. I Ki. 7:33.

FELLOWSHIP: With Christ (I Cor. 1: 9; I John 1:3).—Life—John 14:19; II Tim. 2:11. In sufferings—Rom. 8:17; Phil. 3:10; Col. 1:24. Death—Rom. 6:3 f., 10, 11; Col. 2:12; II Tim. 2:11. Resurrection—Rom. 6:5 f.; Col. 2:12; Eph. 2:6. Sonship—I John 3:2. Heirship—Rom. 8:17. Fruitfulness—John 15:1-5. Power—John 14:12; Phil. 4: 13. Authority—I Cor. 6:2, 3; II Tim. 2:12; Rev. 2:26, 27. Possession—John 16:15; I Cor. 3:21-23. Baptism—Rom. 6:1, 3-10; Col. 2:12.

Fellowship of Jesus with us.—II Cor. 8:9; Heb. 2:10-18.

With the saints.—Standing and responsibility—Rom. 11:17-21; I Cor. 14:20; Eph. 2:19-22; 4:17-24; Tit. 3:1, 2. Unity—Ps. 133:1-3; Eph. 4:1-6, 11-16; I John 1:7; Rev. 2:13. Coöperation—Neh. 4:6, 15; Acts 2:44, 45; 4: 32-35; Rom. 12:4-8; I Cor. 3:8, 9; 12: 4-11; II Cor. 8:4; Phil. 1:5; Heb. 10: 24, 25. Duties—Ex. 17:12, 13; Num. 32:6, 7; II Sam. 10:11, 12; I Ki. 22:4; Ezra 1:3, 4; Rom. 12:1; I Cor. 12:14-27; Gal. 6:2. Worship—Mt. 18:19, 20; Acts 1:14; 2:1, 42; Eph. 5:19, 20; Heb. 10:25. Sympathy—Acts 11:29; Rom. 12:15, 16; Gal. 2:9; 6:2; Eph. 4:31, 32; Phil. 2:1, 2. Study of Scriptures— Deut. 4:9, 10; Neh. 8:1, 2; John 5:39; Acts 17:11; I Cor. 10:11, 12. Liberality—II Cor. 8:1-4, 11-15. Love— John 13:34, 35; Eph. 5:1, 2; I John 4:7-13. Joy—I John 1:3, 4.

With friends.—Ruth 1:16, 17; I Sam. 20:16, 17; Lu. 15:6, 9; III John 14.

Dangerous fellowship. — Gen. 11:5, 6; Num. 14:4-10; Ezra 4:1, 2; Pr. 19:4; Acts 8:19-21; I Cor. 5:11; Eph. 5:11; I John 1:6.

Fellowship with God.—Ps. 94:20; Acts 8:19-21; 10:20; II Cor. 6:14-18.

Fellowship.—(Its nature)—As respects word of life—I John 1:3. Sinfulness —I John 1:5-10. Advocacy with Father—I John 2:1-2. Obedience—I John 2:3-11. Its fruit—Holiness—I John 3:1-10. Love of brethren—I John 3:11-24. Its law—Truth—I John 4: 1-6. Its life—Love—I John 4:7-21. Its root—Faith—I John 5:1-21.

Results of Fellowship.—Partakers of: Flesh and blood—Heb. 2:14. Divine nature—II Pet. 1:4. Holy Spirit—I Cor. 12:13; Heb. 6:4. Christ—Heb. 3:14. Holiness—Heb. 12:10. Promise—Eph. 3:6. Heavenly calling— Heb. 3:1. Sufferings—II Cor. 1:7; I Pet. 4:13. Chastisement—Heb. 12:8. Comfort—II Cor. 1:7. Unity—John 17:20, 21. Future inheritance—Rom. 8:38, 39; Col. 1:12; Heb. 12:22, 23. Future glory—Rom. 8:18; I Pet. 5:1.

FEMALE. See MALE AND FEMALE.

FEN. Job 40:21.

FENCE. To and fro among—Jer. 49:3. Tottering—Ps. 62:3.

FERRYBOAT. II Sam. 19:18.

FERVENT. Heat, With—II Pet. 3:10, 12. Lips—Pr. 26:23. Love—I Pet. 1:22. Prayed—Jas. 5:17. Spirit, I?—Acts 18:25; Rom. 12:11.

FESTIVALS. See FEASTS.

FESTUS. Roman successor of Felix.—Acts Ch. 25.

FETCH. Ark—Ex. 2:5; I Sam. 4:3; 6:21; 7:1. Bread—Gen. 18:5. Brother —Gen. 42:16. Calf—Gen. 18:7. Chariot—II Chr. 1:17. God will—Deut. 30:4. Hiram—I Ki. 7:13. Image—Ju. 18:18. Jephthah—Ju. 11:5. Knowledge—Job 36:3. Micaiiah—I Ki. 22: 9. Pledge—Deut. 24:10. Roll—Jer. ?6:21. Sheaf—Deut. 24:19. Simon Peter—Acts 10:5; 11:13. Spear—I Sam. 26:22. Stroke with the ax—Deut. 19:5. Victual for the people—Ju. 20:10. Water—Gen. 18:4; I Ki. 17:10. Wise woman—I Sam. 14:2. See BRING.

FEW. Num. 26:56; I Sam. 14:6. Days —Gen. 24:55; 29:20; 47:9; Num. 9:20; Job 14:1. Chosen—Mt. 22:14. Faithful over—Mt. 25:21. Find the way, That—Mt. 7:14. Fishes—Mt. 15:34; Mk. 8:7. Laborers—Mt. 9:37; Lu. 10:2. Men—I Chr. 16:19; Is. 21:17. Names—Rev. 3:4. Saved, That be—Lu. 13:23; I Pet. 3:20. Sick—Mk. 6:5. Sleep, That—I Cor. 11:30. Stripes—Lu. 12:48. Words—Eccl. 5:2.

FICKLENESS. II Cor. 1:17.

FIDELITY. Tit. 2:10. See FAITHFULNESS.

FIELD. No plant of the field—Gen. 2:5. Cain and Abel in—Gen. 4:8. Isaac meditates in—Gen. 24:63. Field and cave become Abraham's—Gen. 23:20; 25:9, 10, 27. Smell of Jacob as that of—Gen. 27:27. Jacob desired to be buried in Abraham's—Gen. 49:30; 50: 13. Hail smites all in field—Ex. 9: 19–25. No manna in, on Sabbath—Ex. 16:25. Blessed in field—Lev. 26: 4; Deut. 28:3. Cursed in—Deut. 28:16. Moses tries to pass through—Num. 20:17; 21:22. Six years shalt sow thy —Ex. 23:11, 16–24; Lev. 25:3. Go not to glean in another—Ruth 2:9, 22. Must buy field of Ruth—Ruth 4:5. Shunammite woman's field—II Ki. 8:6. Why set my field afire?—II Sam.

14:30–31. Rabshakeh stands in fuller's field—II Ki. 18:17; Is. 36:2. Woe to them who lay field to field—Is. 5:8. Wilderness becomes a fruitful—Is. 32:15. Good seed in his—Mt. 13:44. Field is world—Mt. 13:38. Like a treasure hid in—Mt. 13:44. Bought potter's—Mt. 27:7–8. Branches cut from, spread in way—Mk. 11:8. I have bought a—Lu. 14:18. Going through on Sabbath—Mk. 2:23. Lift up eyes and look on—John 4:35. Having a field, sold it—Acts 4:37. Shepherds abiding in—Lu. 2:8. Clothe grass in—Mt. 6:30; Lu. 12:28. Elder son in—Lu. 15:25. Consider lilies of —Mt. 6:28. Reap your—Jas. 5:4. Judas—Acts 1:18.

Beasts of.—Gen. 1:24; Ps. 50:11; 80:13; 104:11; Is. 43:20; 56:9; Jer. 27:6; 28: 14; Ez. 31:6; 32:4; 33:27; 34:5, 8; 38: 20; 39:4; Dan. 2:38; 4:12, 21, 25; Hos. 2:12, 18; 4:3; Joel 1:20; 2:22.

Grass of.—Ps. 103:15; Is. 40:6; Dan. 4: 15, 23; Zech. 10:1; Mt. 6:30; Lu. 12: 28.

Tares and mustard seed in.—Mt. 13:31, 36.

Two men in.—Mt. 24:40.

Sacrifice in open field.—Lev. 17:5.

Sundry laws concerning fields.—Trespass laws—Ex. 22:5–31; Lev. 19:9, 19; 23:22. Year of jubilee—Lev. 25:31, 34; 27:17–28; 19:16; Deut. 20:19; 21: 1; 22:25, 27; 28:38. Tithing—Deut. 14:22; II Chr. 31:5. Caleb's fields—Achsah's request for a field—Josh. 15:18; Ju. 1:14. Given to Caleb—Josh. 21:12; I Chr. 6:56.

FIERCE. II Tim. 3:3. Anger—Gen. 49:7; Deut. 13:17; II Chr. 29:10; 30:8; Job 20:23; Ps. 78:49; 85:3; Is. 42:25; Rev. 16:19; 19:15. See ANGER. Demons—Mt. 8:28. Fire—Heb. 10:27. See FIRE. Words—II Sam. 19:43.

FIERY. Darts—Eph. 6:6. Flames—Dan. 7:9. Furnace—Ps. 21:9; Dan. 3:6. Heat—Deut. 28:22. Serpents—Num. 21:6; Is. 14:29. Shafts—Ps. 7: 13. Trial—I Pet. 4:12. See FIRE.

FIFTIES. Mk. 6:40; Lu. 9:14. See JUBILEE, PENTECOST.

FIG-TREE. Teenah, common fig, or *Ficus carica.*

Leaves used for covering.—Gen. 3:7.

A prevalent tree in Palestine.—Deut. 8: 8; Ju. 9:10; I Ki. 4:25; Ps. 105:33; Jer. 5:17; Hos. 2:12; Amos 4:9; Hag. 2:19.

Putting forth an early indication of summer.—Song of Sol. 2:11–13; Mt. 24:32; Mk. 13:28; Lu. 21:29.

Fruit used for food.—Early fruit plucked from tree—II Ki. 18:31; Is. 28:4; 36: 16; Jer. 24:2; Hos. 9:10; Mic. 7:1. Made into cakes—I Sam. 25:18; 30: 12; I Chr. 12:40.

Failure of fruit a calamity.—Jer. 5:17; 8:13; Joel 1:7, 12; Hab. 3:17–18.

Used for shelter from heat.—I Ki. 4:25; Mic. 4:4; Zech. 3:10; John 1:48.

Used for medicinal purposes.—II Ki. 20:7; Is. 38:21.

Parables of.—Ju. 9:10–11; Lu. 13:6–9; 21:29–31. Parable referring to Jews —Mt. 21:18–21; Mk. 11:12–14.

Judgment visited upon, to punish or warn people.—Ps. 105:33; Jer. 5:17; Amos 4:9; Mt. 21:19; Mk. 11:12–14.

Figurative use.—Describing captive Judah—Jer. 24:1–10. Sign of prosperity —Deut. 8:8; I Ki. 4:25. Nation spared for worthier life—Lu. 13:6–9. Sign of calamity—Rev. 6:13. Fruit corresponds with tree—Mt. 7:16; Lu. 6:44.

FIGHT. Ex. 1:10; Num. 22:11; Deut. 3:22; I Sam. 25:28; II Chr. 18:31; Ps. 31:1; 144:1. Is. 37:9. Faith, Fight of—I Tim. 1:18; 6:12. Servants of Jesus—John 18:36. So fight I—I Cor. 9:26. See STRIFE, WAR.

FIGURE. Pr. 1:6. According to the— Acts 7:41. Carved—I Ki. 6:29. Him that was to come, Of—Rom. 5:14. Man, Of—Is. 44:13. Received back in a—Heb. 11:19. Stone—Lev. 26:1; Num. 33:52. Time, For the—Heb. 9:9. Worship, Made to—Acts 7:43.

FILE. I Sam. 13:21.

FILL. Amazement, With—Acts 3:10. Belly—Lu. 15:16. Bitterness, With— Job 9:18; Lam. 3:15. Comfort, With —II Cor. 7:4. Contempt, With—Ps. 123:3. Covetousness, With—Rom. 1: 28. Deceit, With—Rom. 1:28. Eat— Lev. 25:19; Deut. 23:24; 26:12; 31:20; Neh. 9:25; Mt. 4:20; 15:37; Mk. 6:42; 8:8; Lu. 9:17. Envy, With—Rom. 1: 28. Evil, With—Pr. 12:21; 14:14; Ps. 80:5; Is. 27:6. Glory of God, With—

Ex. 40:34, 35; Num. 14:21; I Ki. 8:10, 11; II Chr. 5:13, 14; 7:1, 2; Ps. 71:8; 72:19; Is. 6:14; Ez. 10:3, 4; 43:5; 44:4. Goodness, With—Ps. 107:9; Rom. 15: 14. Indignation, With—Jer. 15:17. Jealousy, With—Acts 5:17; 13:45. Joy, With—II Tim. 1:40. Justice, With—Is. 33:5. Laughter, With—Ps. 126:2. Maliciousness, With—Rom. 1:28. Malignity, With—Rom. 1:28. Murder, With—Rom. 1:28. Righteousness, With—Is. 33:5; Mt. 5:6; Phil. 1:11. Reproach, With—Lam. 3:30. Scorn, With—Ps. 123:4. Shame, With —Hab. 2:16. Spirit—See HOLY SPIRIT. Strife, With—Rom. 1:28. Unrighteousness, With—Rom. 1:28. Violence, With—Gen. 6:11, 13; Ez. 8:17; 28:16. Wickedness, With—Rom. 1:28. Wisdom, With—See WISDOM. Wonder, With—Acts 3:10.

FILTH. Flesh, Of—I Pet. 3:21. See FLESH. Washed away—Is. 4:4. World, Of—I Cor. 4:13. See LASCIVIOUSNESS, LUST, SIN, UNCLEANNESS.

FILTHINESS. Eph. 5:4. Carry out— II Chr. 29:5. Cleanse from—Ez. 36: 25; II Cor. 7:1. Consume—Ez. 22:15. Molten—Ez. 24:11. Nations, Of— Ezra 6:21. People, Of—Ezra 9:11. Poured out—Ez. 16:36. Purification from—Is. 4:4; Ez. 36:1; I Cor. 6:11. Putting away all—Jas. 1:21. Sin, Descriptive of—Ps. 14:3; Is. 1:6; Ez. 24:13. Skirts, In—Lam. 1:9. Tables are full of—Is. 28:8. Washed from— Pr. 30:12. See LASCIVIOUSNESS, LUST, SIN, UNCLEANNESS.

FILTHY. Become—Ps. 14:3; 53:3. Garments—Zech. 3:3, 4. Lucre—I Tim. 3:8; Tit. 1:7, 11; I Pet. 5:2. Still, Let him be—Rev. 22:11. See LASCIVIOUSNESS, LUST, SIN, UNCLEANNESS.

FIND. Acceptable words—Eccl. 12:10. Account—Eccl. 7:27. Accusation— Lu. 6:7. All precious substance—Pr. 1:13. Asleep—Mt. 26:40; Mk. 13:36; 14:37, 40; Lu. 22:43. Arrows—I Sam. 20:21, 36. Babe, The—Lu. 2:8, 12. Blameless—I Tim. 3:10. Book—II Ki. 22:13; 23:2, 24; II Chr. 34:14, 15, 21; Ezra 4:15; Neh. 7:5. Bread on waters—Eccl. 11:1. Comforters—69:20. Compassion—II Chr. 30:9. Damsel— Deut. 22:25, 28. Death—Rev. 9:6.

Evil—Acts 23:9. See FAULT. Enemies—I Ki. 21:20; Ps. 21:8; Is. 41:12. Evil—I Sam. 29:6; Acts 23:9. See EVIL, SIN. Faith—Mt. 8:10; Lu. 7:9, 10; 18:8. See FAITH. Faithful man —Pr. 20:6; I Cor. 15:2. See FAITHFULNESS. Fault—I Sam. 29:3; Dan. 6:4; Mk. 7:2; Lu. 23:4; John 18:38; 19:4, 6; Rom. 8:8; 9:19. See Acts 4:21. Favor—Gen. 6:8; 18:3; 19:19; 32:5; 33:8, 15; etc. Figs, No—Lu. 13:7. Fish—John 21:6. God—II Chr. 15:2, 4, 15; Job 11:7; 23:3; 37:23; Ps. 32:6; Is. 55:6; 65:1; Jer. 29:13; Acts 17:27. *Word of God*—Amos 8:12. *Work of God*—Eccl. 3:11; 8:17. God made man upright—Eccl. 7:28. Gold—II Ki. 14: 14; 16:18; I Chr. 20:2; Ezra 7:16. Good—Pr. 16:20; 17:20; 19:8; Rom. 17:18. Grace—Heb. 4:16. See GRACE. Grave—Job 3:22. Hand finds to— Eccl. 9:10. Heart in his—I Chr. 17: 25. Helpmeet—Gen. 2:20. Iniquity —Gen. 49:16; Jer. 2:5; 50:20; Ez. 28: 15; Hos. 2:6; Mal. 2:6. See SIN. Law —Rom. 7:10, 21. Life—Pr. 4:22; 8: 35; 21:21; Mt. 10:39; 16:25. Man— Jer. 5:1. Mercy—Hos. 14:3; II Tim. 1:18; Heb. 4:16. Messiah, The—John 1:41, 45. Money—II Ki. 12:10; II Chr. 34:17; Mt. 17:27; Lu. 15:8. See SILVER. Naked—II Cor. 5:3. Nathaniel—John 1:45. Nothing—Ps. 17:3; Eccl. 7:14; Mt. 21:19. Occasion—Job 33:10; Dan. 6:4, 5. Past finding out— Job 9:10. Pasture—I Chr. 4:40; John 10:9. Pasture, No—Lam. 1:6. Pearl —Mt. 13:44, 46. Philip—John 1:43. Pleasure—Is. 58:3, 13. Prodigal son— Lu. 15:24, 32. Quickening of soul— Is. 57:10. Rest—Gen. 8:9; Ruth 1:9; Is. 34:14; Jer. 6:16; 45:3; Mt. 11:39; 12:43; Lu. 11:24. See REST. Righteous men in Sodom—Gen. 18:26-32. Righteousness, In way of—Pr. 16:3. Saul—I Sam. 31:18; I Chr. 10:8. Seek and ye shall—II Chr. 15:2, 4; Mt. 7: 7, 8; Lu. 11:9, 10. Set time—Ps. 75:2. Sheep—Mt. 18:13; Lu. 15:4-6. Silver —II Ki. 16:8; 18:15; Ezra 7:16; Acts 19:19. Sin will find you out—Num. 32:33. See SIN. Spoil—Ps. 119:162. Stone rolled away—Lu. 24:2. Tabernacle—Acts 7:46. Thief—Ex. 22:2-8; Deut. 24:7; Jer. 2:26. See STEALING.

Trouble and sorrow—Ps. 116:3. Uncleanness—Deut. 24:1; II Chr. 29:16. Unprepared—II Cor. 9:4; 12:20. Vision, No—Lam. 2:9. Water—Gen. 26: 32; Ex. 15:22; II Chr. 32:4. Watching—Lu. 11:9. See WATCHFULNESS. Way, According to—Job 34:11. Past finding out—Job 34:24. That leadeth to life—Mt. 7:14. Wickedness—I Ki. 1:52; Ps. 10:15; 17:3; Jer. 5:26; 23:11. Wife—Pr. 18:22. Wisdom—Job 28: 12, 13; 32:13; Pr. 1:28; 3:4, 13; 4:22; 8:17, 35; 10:13; Eccl. 7:24; Dan. 5:11. See WISDOM. Wise man—Job 17:10. Witness — Mt. 26:60; Mk. 14:55. Woman—*Fair*—Job 42:15. *Virtuous*— Pr. 31:10. *Wicked*—Eccl. 7:26. See Pr. 7:7-23. Written—Rev. 20:15.

FINE, FINER, FINEST. Brass—See BRASS. Clothing—Jas. 2:2, 3. Dust— Deut. 9:21. Flour—See FLOUR. Gold —See GOLD. Hair—See HAIR. Linen— See LINEN. Meal—Gen. 18:6. Wheat —Ps. 81:16; 147:14.

FINGER: Of God.—Ex. 8:19. Written with—Ex. 31:18; Deut. 9:10. Work of—Ps. 8:3. Cast out devils—Lu. 11: 20. Heaven the work of—Ps. 8:3.

Of Jesus.—Wrote on ground—John 8:6. Into deaf man's ears—Mk. 7:33.

Miscellaneous.—Of iniquity—Is. 59:3. Of Moses—Ex. 29:12; Lev. 8:15. Idols made with—Is. 2:8; 17:8. Of Lazarus—Lu. 16:24. Of Thomas—Into print of nails—John 20:25, 27. Of priest—Shall dip in blood—Lev. 4:6, 17, 25, 30, 34; Lev. 14:16, 27. Eleazar shall take of her blood with—Num. 19:4. Of Aaron—Lev. 9:9; 16:14, 19. Of David—Fingers to fight—Ps. 144: 1. Little finger—I Ki. 12:10; II Chr. 10:10. Thickness measured by—Jer. 52:21. Putting forth of—Is. 58:9. Writing on the wall—Dan. 5:5. Of Goliath—Six on each hand—II Sam. 21:20; I Chr. 20:6. Signs with fingers —Pr. 6:13. Upon fingers bind commandments—Pr. 7:3.

Figurative.—Song of Sol. 5:5; Mt. 23:4; Lu. 11:46.

FINISH. Deut. 31:30; I Chr. 27:24; II Chr. 31:7; Dan. 12:7; John 19:28; Rev. 20:7. Commandment, According to— Ez. 6:14. Course, The—II Tim. 4:7. Cubit, To a—Gen. 6:16. Foundation

—Lu. 14:29. Heaven and earth—Gen. 2:1. Hands shall—Zech. 4:9. House—I Ki. 6:9, 14, 38; 7:1; 9:1; II Chr. 7:11; 8:16; Ezra 5:16; 6:15. It is, He said—John 19:30. Mystery of God—Rev. 10:7. Offering, Burnt—II Chr. 29:28. Parables—Mt. 13:53. Plagues—Rev. 15:8. Testimony—Rev. 11:7. Thousand years—Rev. 20:5. Transgression—Dan. 9:24. Voyage—Acts 21:7. Wall—Neh. 6:15. Words—Rom. 9:28; Mt. 19:1; 26:1. Work—Ex. 39:32; 40:33; I Chr. 28:20; II Chr. 5:1; Heb. 4:3. Wrath of God—Rev. 15:1.

FINISHER. Faith, Of our—Heb. 12:2 (A.V.).

FINS. See FISH.

FIRE: Used on altar.—Gen. 22:6, 7; Lev. 6:13; 9:24; 22:22; 23:8, 13, 18, 25, 27, 36, 37; 24:7, 9; Ju. 13:20; II Chr. 35:13.

Offerings made with fire.—Ex. 29:18, 25, 41; 30:20; Lev. 1:7, 8, 9, 13, 17; 2:2, 3, 9, 10, 11, 16; 3:3; 5, 9, 11, 14, 16; 6:17, 18; 7:5, 25; 8:21, 28; 10:12, 13; 16:12, 13; 21:6–21; 22:27; 23:8, 13, 18, 25, 27, 36, 37; 24:7; Num. 15:3, 10, 13, 14, 25; 18:17; 28:2, 3, 6, 8, 13, 19, 24; 29:6, 13; Deut. 18:1; Josh. 13:14; Ps. 148:8; etc.

Incense must only be burned on the altar fire.—Lev. 6:9, 10, 12, 13; 10:1; 16:12; Num. 16:46.

Used miraculously.—Ps. 18:12, 13. Abraham—Gen. 15:17. Aaron—Lev. 9:24. Gideon—Ju. 6:21. Manoah—Ju. 13:20. David—I Chr. 21:26. Solomon—II Chr. 7:1. Elijah—I Ki. 18:23–25, 38; 19:12; II Ki. 1:10, 12, 14; 2:11.

Coming down from heaven.—Gen. 19:24; Ex. 9:23, 24; I Ki. 18:24, 38; II Chr. 7:1, 3; Job 1:16; Ez. 38:22; Lu. 9:54; 17:29; Rev. 8:5, 7; 9:18; 13:13; 16:8; 20:9.

Used as a symbol of God's presence.—To Abraham—Gen. 15:17. To children of Israel—Ex. 19:18; Deut. 4:11, 12, 15, 33, 36; Is. 4:5. In burning bush—Ex. 3:2; Acts 7:30. At Sinai—Ex. 19:18; Lev. 10:2; Deut. 5:4, 5, 22, 24, 26; 9:10, 15; 10:4; Heb. 12:18. At Pentecost—Acts 2:3.

Used as a propitiation to Molech.—Lev. 18:21; I Ki. 11:7; II Ki. 16:3; 17:17; 23:10.

Child sacrifice forbidden.—Lev. 18:21; 20:2–5; Deut. 18:10.

Sons and daughters pass through fire.—II Ki. 17:17, 31; 21:6; 23:10, 11; II Chr. 28:3; 33:6; Jer. 7:31; 19:5; Ez. 16:21; 20:26, 31; 23:37.

Cooking with.—Ex. 12:8, 9; Lev. 10:12; John 21:9.

Burnt with fire.—Ps. 80:16. Remains of offering—Ex. 12:10; 29:14, 34; Lev. 4:12; 7:17, 19; 8:17, 32; 9:11; 16:27; 19:6. Chariots—Josh. 11:6, 9; II Ki. 23:11. Fir-trees—Is. 44:16, 19. Forest—Ps. 83:14; Jer. 21:14; 22:7; Ez. 15:1–8; 20:46–48; Joel 1:19, 20; Zech. 11:1. Golden calf—Ex. 32:20; Deut. 9:21. Grain—Ex. 22:6; Ju. 15:5; II Sam. 14:30, 31. Gods—Is. 37:19; Jer. 43:13. Graven images—Deut. 7:5, 25; II Ki. 19:18. Asherim—Deut. 12:3. Hair of Nazirite—Num. 6:18. Rings cast into fire—Ex. 32:24. Weapons—Ez. 39:9, 10. Hires—Mic. 1:7.

Consuming fire.—Job 31:12; Jer. 48:45. Cities and encampment—Num. 21:28; 31:10; Deut. 13:16; Josh. 6:24; 8:8; Ju. 1:8; 9:49, 52; II Ki. 8:12; Neh. 1:3; 2:3, 13, 17; Ps. 74:7; Is. 1:7; Jer. 21:10; 32:29; 34:2, 22; 37:8, 10; 38:17, 18, 23; 39:8; 49:2, 27; 50:32; 51:31, 32, 58; 52:13; Ez. 5:2; 15:1–8; 23:47; Hos. 8:14; Amos 1:4, 7, 10, 12, 14; 2:2, 5. Adversaries—Job 22:20; Ps. 97:3; Is. 26:11. Sheep and servants—Job 1:16. Tents of bribery—Job 15:34.

Punishment.—Josh. 7:15, 25; Job 31:11; Ps. 11:6; 21:9; 68:2; 89:46; 105:32; 140:10; Is. 9:5, 18, 19; 47:14. Upon Egypt—Ex. 9:23, 24; Ez. 30:8–16. Upon Sodom and Gomorrah—Gen. 19:24, 25; Lu. 17:29; Jude 7. Consumes Korah's followers—Lev. 21:9; Num. 16:35; Ps. 106:18. At Taberah—Num. 11:1–3. Elijah—II Ki. 1:9–12.

Used as a torture.—Lev. 21:9; Deut. 18:10; Jer. 29:22; Dan. 3:6.

Burning of garments for leprosy.—Lev. 13:52, 55, 57.

Fire of vengeance.—Deut. 32:22; Ju. 12:1; 14:15; 15:6; 18:27; 20:48; I Sam. 30:1, 3, 14; I Ki. 9:16; 16:18; II Ki. 25:9; I Chr. 14:12; II Chr. 36:19; Neh. 1:3; Ps. 78:21; Is. 50:11; 66:15, 16, 24; Jer. 4:4; 5:14; 15:14; 17:4, 27; Lam. 1:12, 13; Ez. 16:41; 21:31, 32; 23:25

24:8–12; 28:18; 39:6; Joel 1:19, 20; 2:3, 5; Amos 1:4, 7, 10, 12, 14; 2:2, 5; 5:6; Ob. 18; Mic. 1:4; Zeph. 1:18; 3:8; Zech. 9:4; Heb. 12:29; Jude 7, 23; Rev. 17:16; 18:8. See HELL.

Used as a war signal.—Ju. 20:38, 40; Jer. 6:1.

A refining process.—Num. 31:23; Ps. 12: 6; Is. 48:10; Zech. 13:9; Mal. 3:2; Mt. 3:10–12; Rev. 1:15; 3:18.

Forbidden.—Not to be kindled on the Sabbath—Ex. 35:3. Vain—Mal. 1:10.

Pillar of.—Ex. 13:21–22; 14:24; 40:38; Num. 9:15–16; 14:14; Deut. 1:33; Neh. 9:12, 19; Ps. 78:14; 105:39; Rev. 10:1.

The righteous endure it.—Is. 33:14–16; Dan. 3:24–27.

Strange.—Lev. 10:1; Num. 3:4; 26:61.

Eternal.—Mt. 18:8; 25:41.

Hell of fire.—Mt. 5:22; 13:40–42, 50; 18: 9; Mk. 9:43, 45–48; Jas. 3:6; II Pet. 3:7; Jude 7, 23; Rev. 14:10, 11. See VENGEANCE, HELL.

Unquenchable.—Mk. 9:43.

Lake of.—Rev. 19:20; 20:10, 14, 15; 21:8.

Salted with.—Mk. 9:49.

Baptism of (*fig.*).—Mt. 3:11–12; Lu. 3: 16–17; 12:49.

References.—Abraham carries fire in his hand—Gen. 22:6. Like as—Pr. 6:27; 26:20, 21; Is. 5:24. Chariots of—II Ki. 6:17. Of jealousy—Ps. 79:5; Song of Sol. 8:6; Ez. 36:5; Zeph. 1:18; 3:8. Heap coals of—Pr. 25:22; Rom. 12:20. Contend by—Amos 7:4. Unsatisfied— Pr. 30:16. Devouring—Ex. 24:17; Deut. 4:24; 9:3; 32:22; Ju. 9:15, 20; Job 20:26; Ps. 18:8; 21:9; 50:3; Is. 29:6; 30:30, 33. See Deut. 18:16; Is. 30:17. Reserved from—Num. 18:9. Stones of—Ez. 28:14, 16; Rev. 18:16. Burnt flax—Ju. 15:14; 16:9. Take fire from the hearth—Is. 30:14. Kindle a —Jer. 7:18; 11:16; 17:27; 21:14; 43: 12; 44:27; 50:32; Lam. 4:11; Ez. 20: 47; Amos 1:14; Acts 28:2. Flames of —Ps. 29:7; 104:4; Dan. 3:22; Hos. 7:6. Through fire and water—Ps. 66:12; Is. 43:2. In the brazier—Jer. 36:22, 23, 32. Underneath the earth—Job 28:5. Furnace of—Gen. 15:17; Ps. 21:9; Dan. 3:11, 15. Wall of—Zech. 2:5. Quench power of—Heb. 12:18. Brand from the—Zech. 3:2. Pan of—Zech. 12:6. See FIREPAN. Heavens on—II

Pet. 3:7, 12. Falling in—Mt. 17:15; Mk. 9:22. Branches and trees cut down and cast into—Mt. 3:10; 7:19; Lu. 3:9, 17; John 15:6; Rev. 14:18. Peter warming by—Mk. 14:54, 67; Lu. 22:55, 56; John 18:18. Shook off serpent into—Acts 28:2–5. Fuel for—Is. 9:5, 19; Ez. 15:4, 6; 21:32.

Figurative.—II Sam. 22:13; Job 41:19; Is. 10:16, 17; 65:5; Ez. 1:4, 13, 27; 5:2, 4; 8:2; 10:2, 6, 7; 19:12, 14; Dan. 7:9; 10;6; Hos. 7:6; Joel 2:30; Acts 2:19; Rev. 1:14; 2:18; 4:5; 8:8; 9:17; 11:5. Of Jehovah—II Sam. 22:9; Is. 31:9. Anger—Ps. 39:3; 57:4; 78:21; Is. 42: 25; Jer. 4:4; 20:9; 21:12; Lam. 2:3, 4; Ez. 21:31, 32; 22:20–22, 31; 38:19; Nah. 1:6. Thorns burnt in—II Sam. 23:6, 7; Ps. 58:9; 118:12; Is. 33:12. Breath as—Is. 33:11. Tares burnt— Mt. 13:40–43. Tongue on—Pr. 16:27; Jas. 3:6. Word of Jehovah as—Jer. 5:14; 23:29. Ministers a flame of— Heb. 1:7. Lips as scorching—Pr. 16: 27. Sea of glass mingled with—Rev. 15:2. Flesh as—Jas. 5:3. Tested by —I Cor. 3:13–15. See HELL, THE JUDGMENT, PUNISHMENT.

FIREBRAND. Burned as a—Ps. 102:3. Casteth—Pr. 26:18. Gird yourselves with—Is. 50:11. Midst, In the—Ju. 15:4. Smoking—Is. 7:4.

FIREPAN. See VESSELS.

FIR TREE. See CEDAR, TREES.

FIRKIN. See MEASURES.

FIRM. End, Unto—Heb. 3:14. Flesh —Job 41:23. Heart, As a stone—Job 41:24. Hope—Heb. 3:6. Millstone, As—Job 41:24. Skies, Made—Pr. 8: 28. Stood—Josh. 3:17; 4:3. Strength is—Ps. 73:4. Ways are—Ps. 10:5. See CONFIRM.

FIRMAMENT. Birds fly in—Gen. 1:20. Brightness of—Dan. 12:3. God made the—Gen. 1:7. Heaven, Called—Gen. 1:8. Let there be a—Gen. 1:6. Lights in—Gen. 1:14. Likeness of a—Ez. 1: 22. Power, Of his—Ps. 150:1. Showeth his handiwork—Ps. 19:1. Voice above—Ez. 1:25. See HEAVEN.

FIRST. Mk. 9:35; Lu. 12:1; I Cor. 15: 13; II Cor. 11:18. Annas, To—John 18:13. Apostles—I Cor. 12:28. Appeared to—Mk. 16:9. Baptizing— John 10:40. Bind the strong man—

Mt. 12:29; Mk. 3:27. Came by night —John 19:39. Cast out beam—Mt. 7:5; Lu. 6:42. Cast stone—John 8:7. Christians—Acts 11:26. Cleanse inside—Mt. 23:26. Commandment—Mt. 22:38; Mk. 12:28. Day—Ex. 12:15. Elijah must come—Mt. 7:10,11; Mk. 9:11,12. Falling away—II Thess. 2:3. Famine—Gen. 26:1. Gave selves —II Cor. 8:5. God, I thank—Rom. 1:8. God visited Gentiles, How—Acts 15:14. Gospel must be preached—Mk. 13:10. Grandmother, In—II Tim. 1:5. Heaven and earth are passed away—Rev. 21:1. I am the—Rev. 1:17. Jews, To—Rom. 1:16; 2:9,10. Last, Shall be—Mt. 19:30; 20:16; Mk. 10:31. Learn to show piety—I Tim. 5:4. Name of—Gen. 2:11. Natural—I Cor. 15:46. Pledge—I Tim. 5:12. Proclaim light—Acts. 26:23. Proved, Be —I Tim. 3:10. Pure—Jas. 3:17. Reconciled to brother, Be—Mt. 5:24. Resurrection, This is the—Rev. 20:5. Rise, Dead in Christ shall—I Thess. 4:16. Seek ye his kingdom—Mt. 6:33. Simon—Mt. 10:2. Sins, For own—Heb. 7:27. Suffer, Must—Lu. 17:25. Tables of stone—Deut. 10:1. Tares, Gather up—Mt. 13:30. Time—Gen. 43:18,20. Unleavened bread, Day of —Mt. 26:17; Mk. 14:12. Week, Day of—Mt. 28:1; Mk. 16:2,9; Lu. 24:1; John 20:1,19; Acts 20:7; I Cor. 16:2. Word of God spoken—Acts 13:46. Worse than—Mt. 12:45; 27:64; Lu. 11:26; II Pet. 2:20. Writing, According to—Deut. 10:4. See COVENANTS, FRUITS, FIRST.

FIRST-BORN: Birthright.—Gen. 25:31; 27:29,35–37; 43:33; 48:18; 49:3; Deut. 21:17; I Chr. 5:1; Ps. 89:27,

Set aside.—*Cain*—Gen. 4:4,5,9–16. *Ishmael*—Gen. 17:19–21. *Esau*—Gen. 25: 23,33,34; 27:30–37 (Heb. 12:16). *Manasseh*—Gen. 48:15–20. *Reuben*—Gen. 49:3,4; I Chr. 5:1,2. *David's brothers* —I Sam. 16:2–12. *Adonijah*—I Ki. 2:15. *Hosah's son*—I Chr. 26:10.

Of Egyptian slain.—Ex. 11:5; 12:12,29, 30; 13:15; Num. 3:13; 8:17; 33:4.

Consecration of first-born.—Of man and beast to God, to commemorate sparing of first-born of Israel in Egypt—Ex. 13:2,12–15; 22:29,30; Num. 3:13; 8:

17; Deut. 15:19,20; Neh. 10:36; Lu. 2:23.

Redemption.—Levites taken instead of —Num. 3:12,13,40–45; 8:16–18. Five shekels taken for each of the 273 more than the number of Levites—Num. 3: 40–50; 18:16. Price given to the priests—Num. 3:48–51.

Of kings to succeed to the throne.—II Ki. 3:27; II Chr. 21:3.

Sacrificed to idols.—II Ki. 3:27; Mic. 6:7.

Daughters married first.—Gen. 29:26.

Term of honor.—Ex. 4:22; Ps. 89:27; Jer. 31:9; Rom. 8:29; Col. 1:15; Heb. 12:23; Rev. 1:5.

First-born of animals: Of clean—Shall not labor nor be shorn—Deut. 15:19. Remains with dam for seven days—Ex. 22:30; Lev. 22:27. Offered in sacrifice—Gen. 4:4; Ex. 34:19; Lev. 18:17; 22:27; 27:26; Num. 18:17; Deut. 15:19–22; Neh. 10:36. Could not be a free-will offering—Lev. 27:26. Flesh to belong to priests—Num. 18:18,19. Of unclean: Redemption of—Lev. 27: 27; Num. 18:15,16. Firstling of the ass redeemed with a lamb or its neck to be broken—Ex. 13:13; 34:20. See OFFERINGS OF FIRST-FRUITS, INHERITANCE.

FISH. Heb. *dag,* implying increase or fecundity.

Created by God.—Gen. 1:20,21. **God destroys fish in Egypt.**—Ex. 7:21.

Man has dominion over.—Gen. 1:26; Ps. 8:8.

Found in seas.—Gen. 9:2; Num. 11:22; Ez. 47:10. In rivers—Ex. 7:18; Is. 19:8; Ez. 29:5; 47:9.

Appointed for food.—Clean and unclean —Lev. 11:9–12. Used as food by Egyptians—Ex. 7:18–21; Num. 11:5; Ps. 105:29; Is. 19:8. By Jews—Num. 11:5,22; Mt. 4:18; Mk. 1:16; Lu. 5:2. By mixed multitudes—Mt. 7:10; 14: 17; 15:34–38; Mk. 6:38–43; 8:7,8; Lu. 5:6–9; 9:13–16; John 6:9. By disciples —John 21:5–13. **Mode of cooking.**— Lu. 24:42; John 21:9. **Selling of fish at the fish gate.**—II Chr. 33:14; Neh. 3:3; 12:39; 13:16.

Catching of fish.—Net—Eccl. 9:12; Ez. 26:5; 47:10; Hab. 1:15; Mt. 4:18–22; 13:47,48; Mk. 1:19; Lu. 5:2,4; John

21:6. Hook—Job 41:1; Is. 19:8; Amos 4:2; Mt. 17:27. Spear—Job 41:7.

Flesh different from that of other animals.—I Cor. 15:39.

Likenesses of, forbidden.—Ex. 20:4; Deut. 4:18.

Worshipped as emblem of fecundity.— Dagon, half fish and half man—Ju. 16:23; I Sam. 5:1–5; I Chr. 10:10.

Miracles concerning: Slaying of Egyptian fish—Ex. 7:18, 21. Jonah—Jonah 2:1–10. Multiplying them—Mt. 14: 17–21; 15:34–38; Mk. 6:38–43; 8:7, 8; Lu. 9:13–16; John 6:9. Immense draughts—Lu. 5:6, 9; John 21:6–11. Procuring tribute money—Mt. 17:27.

Dressed on shore.—John 21:9.

Figurative, The Gospel net (prophetic). —Ez. 47:10. Fishers of men—Mt. 4: 19; Lu. 5:10. Separation of righteous and wicked—Mt. 13:48. Pharaoh— Ez. 29:3–5. Ignorance of future events—Eccl. 9:12. Ensnared by wicked—Hab. 1:14. See ANIMALS.

FISHERMEN. Sent by Jehovah—Jer. 16:16. Spiritual—Mt. 4:19–22; Mk. 1:16, 17; Lu. 5:10, 11. Disciples as— John 21:2–6. Prophecies concerning —Jer. 16:16; Ez. 47:10.

FIST. Ex. 21:18; Pr. 30:4; Is. 58:4.

FIT. Destruction, Unto—Rom. 9:22. Kingdom of God, For—Lu. 9:62. Land, For—Lu. 14:35. Live, For—Lu. 14:35. Live, To—Acts 22:22. Lord, In the— Col. 3:18.

FITCHES. See FOOD.

FITLY. Spoken—Pr. 11.

FITTING. Rom. 1:28; Col. 3:18.

FIVE. Brethren—Lu. 16:18. Cubits— See CUBITS. Curtains—See CURTAINS. Forty stripes, Five times—II Cor. 11: 24. House, Five in one—Lu. 12:52. Husbands—John 4:18. Loaves—Mt. 14: 17, 19; 16:9; Mk. 6:38, 41; 8:19; Lu. 9:13, 16; John 6:9, 13. Months—Rev. 9:5, 10. See MONTHS. Pillars—See PILLARS. Pounds—Lu. 19:18, 19. Sparrows—Lu. 12:6. Talents—Mt. 25:15, 16, 20. Virgins—Mt. 25:2. Words—I Cor. 14:19. Years—See YEARS. Years of famine—See FAMINE. Yoke of oxen —Lu. 14:19.

FIX. Great gulf—Lu. 16:26. Heart is —Ps. 57:7; 108:1; 112:7.

FLAG. Ex. 2:3, 5; Job 8:11; Is. 19:6.

FLAGONS. Is. 22:24.

FLAKES. Job 41:23.

FLAMES. See FIRE.

FLANK. See LOIN.

FLASK. Job 41:18; Nah. 2:3. Eyes— Job 15:12. Fire—Song of Sol. 8:6. Spear—Job 39:23. Sword—Nah. 3:3.

FLATTERY. Job 32:21, 22; I Thess. 2:5. Danger of—Ps. 26:28; 28:23; 29:5; Dan. 11:21, 52, 34. False—Ps. 5:9; 12:2, 3; Pr. 2:16; 6:24; 7:5, 21; Ez. 12:24. Self—Ps. 36:2.

FLAUNT. Pr. 13:16.

FLAX. See GRAIN.

FLAY. Mic. 3:3. Burnt offerings—Lu. 1:6; II Chr. 29:34. Passover lamb— II Chr. 35:11.

FLEA. I Sam. 24:14; 26:20.

FLEE. City of refuge—See CITIES. Death—Rev. 9:6. David—James 4:7. Disciples—Mt. 26:56; Mk. 14:50, 52. Egypt, To—Mt. 2:13. Fornication— I Cor. 6:18. Hireling—John 10:12, 13. Idolatry, From—I Cor. 10:14. Jehovah, From—Num. 10:35; Ps. 104:7; 139:7; Is. 24:18; Amos 2:16; 5:19; Jonah 1:3, 10; 4:2. To—Ps. 143:9. Mountain, To—Gen. 14:10; Ps. 11:1. Presence, From thy—Ps. 139:7; Jonah 1:10. Prisoners—Acts 16:27. Shadow, As a—Job 14:2. Shadows—Song of Sol. 2:17; 4:6. Sin, From—I Cor. 6: 18; I Tim. 6:11; II Tim. 2:22. Sorrow and sighing—Is. 51:11. Tent, To his —I Sam. 4:10. When none pursue— Lev. 26:17. Wicked—Pr. 28:1, 17. Wilderness, To—Josh. 8:15, 20; Ju. 20:45; Job 30:3; Rev. 12:6. Wrath to come, From—Mt. 3:7. Youthful lusts —II Tim. 2:2.

FLEECE. See SHEEP.

FLESH. Many kinds of flesh.—I Cor. 15:39. Human nature called flesh— Gen. 6:3; Ps. 78:39; John 1:13. Also mankind as a whole—Gen. 6:19; 7:15, 16, 21; 8:17; 9:11, 15, 16, 17; Num. 18:15, 18; Zech. 2:13. To God—Ps. 65:2; 136:25; Is. 40:5, 6; Eccl. 4:5; Jer. 17:5; 32:27.

One flesh.—Man and wife—Gen. 2:24; Mt. 19:5, 6; Mk. 10:8; I Cor. 6:16; Eph. 5:31; I Cor. 7:28.

Blood relatives called one's flesh.—Gen. 29:14; 37:27; Ju. 9:2; II Sam. 5:1; 19:

23

12, 13; I Chr. 11:1; Neh. 5:5; Rom. 4:1; 9:3; Heb. 12:9.

Body called flesh.—Gen. 6:12, 13, 17; Ex. 30:32; Ju. 8:7; Jer. 11:15; Col. 2:1, 5, 11, 13, 23; 3:22; Philemon 16; Heb. 2:14; 5:7; 10:20. To return to dust—Job 34:15. Spirit of—Num. 16: 22; 27:16; Joel 2:28. Of Daniel—Dan. 1:15; 10:3.

Law against cutting of.—Lev. 19:28; 21:5.

God's covenant with Abraham—Circumcision of flesh.—Gen. 17:11, 13, 14, 23, 24; Lev. 12:3; Ez. 44:7, 9; Rom. 2:28.

Life of flesh in blood.—Lev. 17:11, 14.

Eating human flesh threatened as worst possible penalty.—Lev. 26:29; Deut. 28:53, 55; Jer. 19:9; Mic. 3:3.

Destroyed by.—Birds—Gen. 40:19; I Sam. 17:44; Ps. 79:2. Sword—Deut. 32:42. Beasts—Ps. 79:2. Dogs—II Ki. 9:36. Through judgment—Is. 66:16, 17, 23, 24; Jer. 12:12; Jude 8, 23; Rev. 17:16; 19:18, 21.

Diseases of flesh.—Lev. 17:16; 22:16; Num. 8:7; 19:7, 8; Heb. 9:13.

Leprosy.—Lev. 13:2, 3, 4, 10, 11, 13–18, 24, 25, 26. Miracles of—*Hand of Moses changed*—Ex. 4:7. *Miriam*—Num. 12: 12. *Naaman cured*—II Ki. 5:10, 14. See LEPROSY, HEALING.

Consumed.—Ju. 6:19–21. Food brought to Elijah—I Ki. 17:6; 19:21. Child restored to life—II Ki. 4:34.

Proverbs concerning.—Pr. 5:11; 11:17; 14:30; 23:20. Much study weariness to—Eccl. 12:12. Flesh to sin—Eccl. 5:6; 11:10.

Clothing of the flesh.—Lev. 6:10; 16:4; I Ki. 21:27; II Ki. 6:30. See CLOTHING. With flesh—Job 10:11. Horror of—Job 21:6.

Prophecies concerning.—God judges all flesh—Jer. 25:31; 45:5. Eating of—Ez. 39:17, 18. Destroyed—Ez. 21:4, 5; 32:5; Zech. 14:12. Restored—Ez. 37: 6, 8. Obedience of food law—Ez. 4:14. All flesh destroyed—Is. 66:16, 17. Violence done to—Jer. 51:35; Mic. 3:2, 3.

Mentioned.—Lam. 3:4; Ez. 16:26; 20: 48; 23:20; 24:10; 36:26.

Figurative.—Job 2:5; 4:15; 6:12; 7:5; 10:4; 13:14; 14:22; 19:20, 22, 26; 21: 6; 33:21, 25; 41:23; Ps. 16:9; 27:2; 38:3, 7; 50:13; 56:4; 63:1; 84:2; 109:

24; 119:120; 145:21; Pr. 4:22. Eating of own flesh—Is. 9:20; 49:26. Fatness of—Is. 17:4. Folly of idols—Is. 44:16, 19. Hide from own flesh—Is. 58:7. Eating of flesh—Is. 22:13. Destroyed —Jas. 5:3. As grass—I Pet. 1:24. Fleshly in wisdom—II Cor. 1:12; Col. 2:18. In hearts—II Cor. 3:3. In lusts —I Pet. 2:11.

Illustrative.—Ez. 11:3, 7, 11, 19. Arm of flesh—II Chr. 32:8. As Dung—Zeph. 1:17.

Christianity versus flesh.—See TEACHINGS OF JESUS. Christ has authority over all flesh, *i. e.*, mankind—John 17: 2; II Pet. 2:10, 18; I John 2:16.

Teaching of Paul.—Flesh corrupts moral nature—Flesh and spirit contrasted—II Cor. 7:1, 5; Gal. 5:16–24; Rom. 7: 18, 23, 25; 8:5–13; 9:8; Col. 3:5–11; Eph. 4:17–32.

Warfare of flesh.—Rom. 8:12, 13; Eph. 6:12. Lusts of flesh—I Cor. 10:18; II Cor. 5:16; 10:2, 3; 11:18; Gal. 5:24; 6:8, 12, 13; Eph. 2:3, 11; Phil. 3:3, 4. Flesh to be overcome—II Cor. 1:17; 4:11; Gal. 3:3; 5:13, 16, 17, 19; Eph. 2:15; 5:29. No strength in flesh—Rom. 6:19; 7:5, 18, 25; 8:3–9, 12, 13; Phil. 1:22, 24.

Flesh not justified, and not to return to God.—Rom. 3:20; I Cor. 15:50; Gal. 1:16; 2:16, 20; 4:23, 29.

Spirit not flesh.—Lu. 24:39; Rom. 9:8; I Cor. 1:26, 29. Flesh to be destroyed—I Cor. 5:5.

Abstinence admonished.—Rom. 14:21; I Cor. 8:13.

Obedience admonished.—Eph. 6:5. Promises to—Lu. 3:6; Acts 2:17, 26.

Christ the word became flesh.—Rom. 1:3. Flesh not corrupted—Acts 2:31.

Flesh of Christ sacrificed.—Col. 1:22, 24; I Pet. 3:18, 21; 4:1, 2, 6.

Flesh of animals.—I Cor. 15:39. Horses —Is. 31:3. Swine—Is. 65:4. Sheep—Zech. 11:16. Uses of food laws concerning—Gen. 9:4; Ex. 12:46; 21:28; 22:31; 29:32, 34; Deut. 12:15, 20, 23; 14:8. At passover—Ex. 12:8. In wilderness—Ex. 16:8, 12; Num. 11:4, 13, 18, 21, 33; Ps. 78:20, 27. Command to eat—Jer. 7:21.

Offerings.—Ex. 29:14, 31, 32, 34; Lev. 4:11; 6:29; 7:15, 17, 19, 20; 8:17, 31,

32; 9:11; 16:27; Num. 19:5; Deut. 12:
27; 16:4; I Sam. 2:13, 15; Hos. 8:13.

Flesh of kings.—Rev. 19:18.

Problem of meat offered to idols.—Acts
15:29; Rom. 14:1–15; I Cor. 8:1–11, 15.

Flesh-hooks.—Ex. 27:3; 38:3; I Sam. 2:
13, 14; I Chr. 28:17; II Chr. 4:16.

Flesh-pots.—Ex. 16:3.

FLIES. See PLAGUE.

FLINT. Ex. 4:25; Deut. 32:13; Ps. 114:
8; Is. 5:28; 50:7; Ez. 3:9. Knives, Of
—Josh. 5:2. Water springs from—
Deut. 8:15; Ps. 114:8.

FLOCKS. Flocks of sheep.—Gen. 21:
28; 29:2, 3; Num. 32:26; I Sam. 17:34;
Song of Sol. 4:2; 6:6; Ez. 34:12; Joel
1:18; Micah 5:8.

Of goats.—Gen. 27:9; 38:17; Song of
Sol. 4:1; 6:5.

Gathered together.—Gen. 29:8. In folds
—II Chr. 32:28. Pipings for—Ju.
5:16.

Increase of.—Deut. 7:13; 8:13; 28:4, 18.

Division of.—Gen. 30:32; 32:7; Num.
31:30.

Shepherds of.—Gen. 4:4; 30:31, 36; 37:
2, 12–16; 46:32; I Chr. 27:30; Is. 63:
11; Amos 7:15; Lu. 2:8.

Laws concerning.—Ex. 34:3; Deut. 12:
17, 21; 14:23.

Uses of.—Food—Amos 6:4. See SHEEP,
CLOTHING.

As victims in sacrifice.—Lev. 1:2, 10;
3:6; 5:6, 15, 18; 6:6; Num. 15:3; Deut.
12:6; 15:14, 19; 16:2; Ezra 10:19;
Neh. 10:36; Ez. 43:23, 25. See SACRI-
FICE.

Tithe of.—Lev. 27:32.

Owners of.—Jacob—Gen. 30:37–43; 31:
4, 38; 32:5; 33:13; 45:10; 47:1; 50:8.
Isaac—Gen. 26:14; 27:9. Lot—Gen.
13:5. Laban—Gen. 29:10; 31:43.
Jethro—Ex. 2:16, 17, 19; 3:1. Moses—
Ex. 10:9, 24. Moses and Aaron—Ex.
12:31, 32. Multitude—Ex. 12:38. Jehoshaphat—II Chr. 17:11. Hezekiah
—II Chr. 32:29. Josiah—II Chr. 35:7.
Nabal—I Sam. 25:2. Uzziah—II Chr.
26:10.

Prophecies concerning.—Is. 60:7; 61:5;
65:10; Jer. 3:24; 5:17; 13:20; 23:2,
3; 25:34–36; 31:12; 33:12, 13; 49:20,
29; 50:8, 45; 51:23; Ez. 24:5; 25:5;
34:2–31; Hos. 5:6; Micah 7:14; Hab.
3:17; Zeph. 2:6.

Illustrative.—I Ki. 20:27; Job 21:11;
Ps. 77:20; 80:1; 107:41; Jer. 31:10;
Ez. 36:37, 38; Zech. 9:16; 10:2; 11:4,
7, 11, 17; I Cor. 9:7.

Figurative.—II Sam. 12:2, 4; Job 30:1;
Ps. 78:52; Pr. 27:23; Song of Sol. 1:7,
8; Mt. 26:31; Lu. 12:32; Acts 20:28,
29; I Pet. 5:2, 3.

Miscellaneous. — Slain — Num. 11:22.
Taken as spoil by David—I Sam. 30:
20. Bread in exchange for—Gen. 47:
17. See GOATS, SHEEP.

**THE FLOOD. Jehovah declares his pur-
pose.**—Gen. 6:17; 7:4.

Time of.—Gen. 7:6, 10, 11.

Described.—Gen. 7:10–12, 17–20.

Waters assuaged.—Gen. 8:1–19.

**Description of animals preserved in the
ark.**—Gen. 6:19, 20; 7:2–16.

Length of time the ark floated.—Gen.
7:24.

**Promise that the flood should not occur
again.**—Gen. 8:21; 9:8–17; Is. 54:9.

References to.—Job. 22:15, 16; Ps. 90:5;
Mt. 24:38, 39; Lu. 17:26, 27; Heb. 11:
7; I Pet. 3:20; II Pet. 2:5; 3:4–7.

"Flood" used in other senses.—House
of the foolish man destroyed—Mt. 7:
27; Lu. 6:48. In floods of great waters
the godly shall come nigh—Ps. 32:6.
David's prayer—Ps. 69:15. Destruction of city and sanctuary—Dan. 9:
26. Jehovah pursuing wicked—Nah.
1:8. The crossing of the Red Sea—
Ex. 15:8. World founded on—Ps. 24:
2. The might of Jehovah—Ps. 93:2–4;
98:7–9. Floods cannot drown love—
Song of Sol. 8:7. Floods compassing
Jonah—Jonah 2:3.

FLOOR. I Ki. 7:7. Atad, Of—Gen. 50:
11. Grain—Is. 21:10; Hos. 9:1; Joel
2:24. Purge—Mt. 3:12; Lu. 3:17. Tabernacle, Of—Num. 5:17. See TABER-
NACLE. Temple, Of—I Ki. 6:15, 16,
30; 7:7. See THRESHING-FLOOR.

FLOUR. Ephah of—Ex. 29:40; Num.
15:4, 6, 9; 28:5, 9, 12. Fine—Lev. 2:2;
6:15; Rev. 18:13. Kneaded—I Sam.
28:24; II Sam. 13:8. Meal offering of
—Num. 28:20, 28; 29:3, 9, 14. Unleavened cakes of—Ju. 6:19.

FLOURISH. Bones shall—Is. 66:14.
Courts of our God, In—Ps. 92:13.
Crown—Ps. 132:18. Dry tree to—Ez.
17:24. Flower of the field, As—Ps.

103:15. Grass, Like—Ps. 72:16. Green leaf, As—Pr. 11:28. Men, Young—Zech. 9:17. Morning, In the—Ps. 90:6. Palace, In—Dan. 4:4. Righteous—Ps. 72:7; 92:12; Pr. 11:28. Upright, Tent of—Pr. 14:11. Workers of iniquity—Ps. 92:7.

FLOW. Brook—II Chr. 32:4; Pr. 18:4. Goodness of Jehovah, Unto—Jer. 3:12. Goods shall—Job 20:28. Hills shall—Joel 3:18. Milk and honey, With—Ex. 3:8, 17; Lev. 20:24. Nations shall—Is. 2:2; Jer. 51:44. Peoples shall—Mic. 4:1. Spices—Song of Sol. 4:16. Stream, Overflowing—Is. 66:12. Valley—Jer. 49:4. Water—Num. 24:7; Ps. 147:18; Is. 48:21; Jer. 18:14; Lam. 3:54; John 7:38.

Flower. Ex. 25:31, 33, 34; 37:17, 19, 20; Num. 8:4; I Ki. 7:49. Age, Of—I Cor. 7:36; I Sam. 2:33. Appear—Song of Sol. 2:12. Cometh forth like a—Job 14:2. Fadeth—Is. 40:7. Fading—Is. 28:1. Falleth—I Pet. 1:24; Jas. 1:11. Field, Of—Ps. 103:15; Is. 40:6. Gold, Of—II Chr. 4:21. Grape, Becometh a ripening—Is. 18:5. Grass, Of—Jas. 1:10. Lebanon, Of—Nah. 1:4. Lily, Of —I Ki. 7:26; II Chr. 4:5. Open—I Ki. 6:18, 29, 32, 35. Pass away as—Jas. 1:10. Pomegranates are in—Song of Sol. 7:12. See PLANTS AND TREES.

FLUTE. Sound of—Dan. 3:5, 7, 10.

FLUTTER. Eagle over her young—Deut. 32:11. Heart—Is. 21:4.

FLY, *n.* Eccl. 10:1; Is. 7:18. See FLIES.

FLY, *v.* Gen. 1:20; Deut. 4:17; Ps. 148:10; Hos. 9:11. Angel—Rev. 14:6. Arrow—Ps. 91:5. Away—Ps. 55:6; 90:10. Bird that—Rev. 19:17. Cloud, As —Is. 60:8. Dream, As a—Job 20:8. Eagle, As an—Pr. 23:5; Deut. 28:49; Jer. 48:40; 49:22; Hab. 1:8; Rev. 4:7; 8:13. Heaven, Toward—Moab may—Jer. 48:9. Roll—Zech. 5:1, 2. Seraphim 6:6. Serpent—Is. 14:29; 30:6. Shoulder, Down upon—Is. 11:14. Souls, Make—Ez. 30:20. Spoil, Upon the—I Sam. 14:32; 15:19. Swiftly—Dan. 9:21. Wilderness, Into—Rev. 12:14. Wind, Upon wings of—Ps. 18:10; II Sam. 22:11. Swallow in her—Pr. 26:2.

FOAL. Gen. 32:15; 49:11; Zech. 9:9; Mt. 21:5.

FOAM. Hos. 10:7; Jude 13. Mouth, At —Mk. 9:18, 20; Lu. 9:39.

FODDER. Ju. 19:21; Job 6:5.

FOES. See ENEMY.

FOLD. I Ki. 6:34; Jer. 25:37. Hands—Pr. 6:10; 24:33; Eccl. 4:5. Sheep and goats—Num. 32:16, 24, 36; II Chr. 32:28; Job 5:24; Ps. 50:9; Is. 13:20; 65:10; Jer. 23:3; 25:30; Ez. 34:4; Hab. 3:17; Zeph. 2:6; John 10:1, 16.

FOLK. Gen. 33:15; Pr. 30:26; Mk. 6:5; Acts 5:16.

FOLLOW. Gen. 24:8; Deut. 11:6; Hos. 6:3; Mk. 5:37; 9:38; I Tim. 4:6; Lu. 17:23. Angel—Rev. 14:8, 9. Baal—I Ki. 18:18, 21. See II Ki. 13:2, 11. Baalam, Way of—II Pet. 2:15. See Num. Chs. 22-24. Baal-peor—Deut. 4:3. See Num. 25:1-9. Fables, Cunningly devised—II Pet. 1:16. Good, After—I Thess. 5:15. Good work, Every—I Tim. 5:10. Glories that should—I Pet. 1:11. Hades—Rev. 6:8. Hard after—Ju. 20:42, 45; Ps. 63:8. Heart, After own—Num. 15:39. Jehovah—I Ki. 18:21. Jews—John 11:31. Lamb—Rev. 14:4. Lascivious doings —II Pet. 2:2. Love, After—I Cor. 14:1. Paul—Acts 13:43; 16:17; II Thess. 3:7, 9. Peace, After—Rom. 14:19; Heb. 12:4. Peter, Afar off—Mt. 26:58; Mk. 14:54; Lu. 22:54. Rewards —Is. 1:23. Righteousness, After—Pr. 15:9; 21:21; Is. 51:1; Rom. 9:30, 31; II Tim. 2:22. Signs that—Mk. 16:17, 20. Sins—I Tim. 5:24. Soul followeth —Ps. 63:8. Spiritual rock—I Cor. 10:4. Steps of—I Pet. 2:21. Stranger, Will not follow—John 10:5. Vain persons—Pr. 28:29. Wickedness—Ps. 119:150. Works follow—Rev. 14:13. John 1:37. Andrew—John 1:40. Blind men —Mt. 9:27.

Jesus.—Acts 21:36. Cross, Take up and follow—Mt. 10:38; 16:24; Mk. 8:34; Lu. 9:23. Disciples—Mt. 8:23; Mk. 6:1; Lu. 22:39. Left all and—Mt. 19:27; 10:28; Lu. 5:11, 28. Left nets and —Mt. 4:20; Mk. 1:18. Loved, Disciple—John 21:20. Me—Mt. 8:22; 9:9; 19:21; Mk. 2:14; 10:21; Lu. 5:27; 9:59, 61; John 1:43; 12:26; 21:22. Multitudes—Mt. 4:25; 8:1; 19:2; 20:29; Mk. 3:7; John 6:2. Received sight and—Mt. 20:34; Mk. 10:52; Lu. 18:

43. Sheep—John 10:4, 27. Ship, Left and—Mt. 4:22. Simon—John 18:15; 20:6. Whithersoever thou goest—Mt. 8:19; Lu. 9:57. Women, Many—Mt. 27:55. Young man—Mk. 14:51.

FOLLY. Job 4:18; 24:12; 42:8; Ps. 49: 13; 85:8; Pr. 5:23; 14:29; 18:13; Eccl. 10:1, 6; Is. 9:17; II Tim. 3:9. Fool, Of —Pr. 13:16; 14:8, 18, 24; 15:21; 16: 22; 17:12; 26:4, 5, 11. Prophets, Of— Jer. 23:13. Recognize—II Sam. 13:12; Eccl. 1:17; 2:3, 12, 13; 7:25. Wrought —Gen. 34:7. Deut. 22:21; Josh. 7:15; Ju. 20:6, 10; II Sam. 13:12. See FOOL, FOOLISHNESS.

FOOD. A gift of God—Gen. 1:29, 30; 2:9; 6:21; 9:3; Ex. 16:32–34; Ruth 1:6; I Ki. 17:2–5.

Necessity of.—I Ki. 18:41; I Sam. 14: 29–31; 30:11–12; Mk. 8:1–4; Acts 9: 19; 27:33–26.

Articles of.—Bread—Gen. 18:5; I Sam. 16:20; 17:17; 25:18; 30:12; II Sam. 16:1; I Chr. 12:40; Mt. 4:3, 4; 14:20, 21; Mk. 8:5–9; John 6:7–13, 26. See BREAD. Butter—Gen. 18:8; Deut. 32: 14; II Sam. 17:29; Pr. 30:33; Is. 7:15. Cheese—I Sam. 17:18; II Sam. 17:29. Condiments—*Anise*—Mt. 23:23. *Cassia*—Ex. 30:24; Ps. 45:8; Ez. 27:19. *Cinnamon*—Ex. 30:23; Pr. 7:17; Rev. 18:13. *Coriander*—Ex. 16:31; Num. 11:17. *Cummin*—Is. 28:25, 27; Mt. 23: 23. *Black cummin*—Is. 28:25 marg. *Mint*—Mt. 23:23; Lu. 11:42. *Mustard*— Mt. 13:31; 17:20; Mk. 4:31; Lu. 13: 19; 17:6. *Salt*—Job 6:6; Is. 30:24; Mt. 5:13. See SALT. Eggs—Job 6:6; Is. 10:14; Lu. 11:12.

Flesh—Ex. 16:8, 12; Lev. 6:26; 7:31; 10:14; 11:2, 3, 9, 21, 22; Deut. 12:15; 14:4–6; II Sam. 6:19. See FLESH, *Of cattle*—Gen. 18:6; Deut. 14:4; I Sam. 14:32; I Ki. 19:21. See CATTLE. *Of fish*—Ex. 7:18–21; Lev. 11:9–12; Num. 11:5, 22; Ps. 105:29; Is. 19:8; Mt. 4: 18; 7:10; 14:17; 15:34–28; Mk. 1:16; 6:38–43; 8:7, 8; Lu. 5:2, 6–9; 9:13–16; John 6:9; 21:5–13. See FISH. *Fowl*— Deut. 14:20; I Ki. 4:23. See BIRD. *Gazelle and hart*—Deut. 12:15, 22; 14:5; I Ki. 4:23. *Of goats*—Gen. 27:9, 10, 14–25; Ex. 23:19; 34:26; Deut. 14:4; I Sam. 16:20; Lu. 15:29. See GOATS. *Insects*—See INSECTS. Lev. 11:20–22.

Mutton—Ex. 12:8; 29:32; Deut. 14:4; 32:14; I Sam. 7:9; 14:32; 25:18; II Sam. 17:29; I Ki. 4:23. *Quail*—Ex. 16:12, 13; Num. 11:31, 32. *Roebuck*— Deut. 14:5; I Ki. 4:23. *Venison*—Gen. 27:7, 25; Deut. 12:16.

Fruit—Gen. 3:2; Lev. 19:23–25; II Sam. 16:1. *Apple*—Song of Sol. 2:3, 5; 7:8; 8:5; Joel 1:12. (*This is probably not our apple.*) *Figs*—Num. 13:23; 20:5; I Sam. 25:18; II Ki. 18:32; I Chr. 12: 40; Neh. 13:15; Joel 1:12. See FIG-TREE. *Grapes.*—Gen. 40:11; Num. 6:3; 13:23; Deut. 23:24; 24:20; 32:14; Neh. 13:15. See GRAPE. *Mulberries*—II Sam. 5:23, 24; I Chr. 14:14, 15. *Olives*— Deut. 8:8; 24:20; II Ki. 18:32. *Pomegranates*—Num. 20:5; Deut. 8:8; Song of Sol. 8:2; Joel 1:12. *Raisins*—I Sam. 25:18; II Sam. 6:19; 16:1; I Chr. 16:3; 12:40; Song of Sol. 2:5; Hos. 3:1. *Summer fruits*—I Sam. 16:1. *Sycomore* (*resembling the fig*)—I Chr. 27:28; Amos 7:14.

Grain—Gen. 42:33; Lev. 23:14; II Ki. 4:42; 18:32; Mt. 12:1. *Parched grain* —Lev. 23:14; Josh. 5:11; Ruth 2:14; I Sam. 25:8; II Sam. 17:28. *Barley*—II Ki. 4:42; Ez. 4:9, 12; John 6:9, 13. See BARLEY. *Fitches*—Is. 28:25. *Millet*— Ez. 4:9. *Spelt*—Ex. 9:32; Is. 28:25; Ez. 4:9. *Wheat*—Deut. 32:14; Ps. 81: 16; 147:14; Ez. 4:9. See WHEAT.

Herbs—Gen. 3:18; 9:3; Ex. 12:8; Num. 9:11; II Ki. 4:39; Pr. 4:39; Rom. 14:2. Honey—Deut. 8:8; 32:13; Ju. 14:8, 9; I Sam. 14:25–29, 43; Ps. 81:16; Pr. 24: 13, 14; 25:16; Is. 7:15. Manna—Ex. 16:14–31. See MANNA. Meal—Gen. 18:6; II Sam. 17:28; I Ki. 17:12, 16; I Chr. 12:40; Is. 47:2; Mt. 13:33. Milk —Gen. 18:8; Ex. 23:19; 34:26; Num. 13:27; Deut. 32:14; Ju. 4:19; 5:25; Pr. 27:27; 30:33; Song of Sol. 5:1. See MILK. Nuts—Gen. 43:11; Song of Sol. 6:11; Lu. 15:16 marg. Oil—Lev. 2:4, 5; Num. 11:8; I Ki. 17:12–16; I Chr. 12:40; Pr. 21:17; Ez. 16:13. See OIL. Vegetables—*Beans*—II Sam. 17:28; Ez. 4:9. *Cucumbers*—Num. 11:5. *Garlic, leek and onions* (*usually eaten raw*) —Num. 11:5. *Lentils* (*sometimes ground and mixed with flour to make bread; usually made into a pottage*)—Gen. 25:34; II Sam. 17:28; 23:11; Ez. 4:9.

Melons—Num. 11:5. Pulse—II Sam. 17:28; Dan. 1:12, 16.

Vinegar—Num. 6:3; Ruth 2:14; Mt. 27: 48. Wine—Gen. 9:20; 14:18; 27:25; Num. 6:3; II Sam. 16:1; Neh. 13:15; I Chr. 12:40.

Forbidden food.—Gen. 2:17; 3:3; Lev. 19:23-25. Blood—Gen. 9:4; Lev. 7:26, 27; 17:10-14; 19:26; Deut. 12:15-25; 15:23; Acts 15:20, 29. See BLOOD. Fat —Lev. 3:17; 7:23-25. Flesh torn of beasts—Ex. 22:31; Lev. 7:24; 17:15, 16; 22:8. That which dieth of itself—Lev. 7:24; 17:15, 22:8; Deut. 14:21. Unclean meat—Lev. 7:15-19; 19:5-8. Unclean animals—Lev. 11:1-47; 17: 10-14; Deut. 14:3, 7, 8, 12-19. *Peter's vision*—Acts 10:10-16. *Food offered to idols*—Rom. 14:1-23; 8:4-13; 10:18-32. Forbidden to eat other food in connection with the Lord's Supper—I Cor. 11: 20-22. Custom founded in Jacob—Shrunk sinew—Gen. 32:32. Eating human flesh. Threatened—Lev. 26: 27-29; Deut. 28:53-57; Is. 9:20; 49: 26; Jer. 19:9. Symbolic—Mic. 3:2-3. Because of starvation—II Ki. 6:28-29. Leavened bread—Ex. 12:18-20; 23:18; 34:25.

Cooked food.—Gen. 25:29; Deut. 14:21; II Sam. 13:6-8. ''Savory meat''—Gen. 27:4, 9, 14, 17, 31.

Blessing before partaking.—Mk. 8:6; Acts 27:35.

Feasting.—I Sam. 9:22-24; Job 1:4, 13; I Ki. 3:15; 8:65-66; Pr. 23:1-8; Lu. 14:12; Jude 12. See FEASTS.

Gluttony.—Num. 11:4-13; Ps. 78:29-30; 106:14-15; Pr. 23:20; 25:16; John 6:26.

Fasting.—Gen. 24:33; Deut. 29:6; I Ki. 13:7-17; 21:4; Dan. 10:3; Lu. 5:33-35.

Famine.—Gen. 12:10; 26:1; 41:53-54; 45:6; 47:13-21; Deut. 28:33-40; II Sam. 21:1; I Ki. 18:2; II Ki. 8:1-2; Lam. 1:11; 2:11-12; Ez. 6:11-14. See MEAL, SERVING OF.

Figurative use.—Ez. 11:3, 7, 11; 24:6, 10, 11, 12; Hos. 7:3-8.

Preparation of food.—By the wife—Gen. 18:6; Pr. 31:15. Servant—Gen. 18:7; Lu. 12:42. Special servant or cook—I Sam. 8:13; 9:23, 24. Meat boiled—Ex. 23:19; 34:26; Deut. 14: 21; I Sam. 2:15; Ez. 24:3-11. Broil-

ing fish—Lu. 24:42; John 21:9. Roasting—Ex. 12:8, 9; Deut. 16:7; I Sam. 2:15; II Chr. 35:11; Is. 44:16, 19. Vegetables boiled in water or with milk or butter—Gen. 25:29; II Ki. 4:38.

FOOLS. Are: Corrupt and abominable —Ps. 14:1; Pr. 30:22; I Cor. 3:18. Self-sufficient—Pr. 12:15; Rom. 1:22. Slothful—Eccl. 4:5. Self-confident—Pr. 14:16. Self-deceivers—Pr. 14:8; 17:28. Angry—Eccl. 7:9; Pr. 7:7; 12: 16; 27:3; 29:11, 20. Mere professors of religion—Mt. 25:2-12. Conceited—Pr. 26:12. Full of words—Eccl. 5:3; 10:14. Given to meddling—Pr. 20:3. Slanderers—Pr. 10:18. Liars—Pr. 10: 18. Contentious—Pr. 18:6. A grief to parents—Pr. 17:21, 25; 19:13.

Come to shame.—Pr. 3:35. Death—II Sam. 3:33; 13:13.

Destroy themselves.—By their speech—Pr. 10:8, 10, 14; 26:45; Eccl. 4:5; 10: 12. By their ease—Pr. 1:32.

Exemplified.—Rehoboam—I Ki. 12:8. Israel—Jer. 4:22. Pharisees—Mt. 23:17, 19. Saul—I Sam. 26:21.

Company of: Is ruinous—Pr. 13:20; 26:6.

Folly of.—Pr. 14:8, 24; 15:2, 14; 26:4, 5, 11; 27:22.

Vanity of.—Eccl. 2:15, 16, 19; 7:6. Worship idols—Jer. 10:8; Rom. 1:22. Trust to their own heart—Pr. 28:26. Depend upon their wealth—Jer. 17:11; Lu. 12:20. Obey not the gospel—Mt. 7:26. Deny God—Ps. 14:1; 53:1. Blaspheme God—Ps. 74:18.

Mouth of.—Pours out folly—Pr. 7:5; 15:2; Eccl. 10:3. Feedeth on folly—Pr. 15:14. Parable in mouth of—Pr. 26:7.

Lips of.—Snare to the soul—Pr. 18:7; Eccl. 9:17.

Correction of is folly.—Pr. 16:22.

Punishment of.—Job 30:8; Ps. 49:10; 107:17; Pr. 7:22; 17:10; 19:29; 26: 3, 10.

Fools mentioned.—Delight not in understanding—Ps. 92:6; Pr. 17:16, 24; 18: 2; 24:7. Perverse man and a fool—Pr. 19:1. Sport themselves in mischief—Pr. 10:23. Has same advantage as wise man—Eccl. 6:8. Walk in darkness—Eccl. 2:14. Shall not call thy brother fool—Mt. 5:22. Hate to depart from evil—Pr. 13:19. Prophet called fool—Hos. 9:7. Sacrifice of, hateful to God—Eccl. 5:1. Delicate living unseemly for—Pr. 19:10. Flaunteth his folly—Pr. 13:16; 16:22. Excellent speech unbecoming for—Pr. 17:7. Honor is unbecoming for—Pr. 26:1, 8. Die for lack of understanding—Pr. 10:21. God has no pleasure in—Eccl. 5:4. God abases arrogant—Ps. 75:4. Avoid them—Pr. 14:7. Exhorted to seek wisdom—Ps. 94:8; Pr. 8:5. Despise instruction—Pr. 1:7; 23:9. Make a mock at—Pr. 14:9. Reproach God—Ps. 74:22. Princes of Zoan become—Is. 19:13. Hate knowledge—Pr. 1:22. Judges become—Job 12:17.

Prophecies concerning.—Is. 35:8. Shall not stand in the presence of God—Ps. 5:5. Shall be servants to the wise—Pr. 11:29.

Proverbs concerning.—Pr. 7:7; 12:23; Eccl. 10:2.

In teachings of Paul.—I Cor. 4:10.

FOOLISH. King—Eccl. 4:13. Labor of —Eccl. 10:15. Prophets—Ez. 13:3. Shepherd—Zech. 11:15. See FOOL, FOOLISHNESS.

FOOLISHNESS. II Sam. 15:31; Ps. 38: 5; 69:5; 19:3; 24:9; Eccl. 7:25; 10:13; Mk. 7:22; I Cor. 1:18, 23; 3:19. Child, Of—Pr. 22:15. Fool, Of—Pr. 12:23; 27:22. Preaching, Of—I Cor. 1:21, 25; 2:14.

FOOT. See FEET.

FOOTMEN. II Sam. 10:6; I Ki. 20:29; I Chr. 19:18; Jer. 12:5. Israel, Of—Num. 11:21; Ju. 20:2; I Sam. 4:10; 15:4; II Sam. 8:4; II Ki. 13:7; I Chr. 18:4. See SERVANT, SOLDIER.

FORBADE. See FORBID.

FORBEAR. Ex. 23:5; II Chr. 35:21; Job 16:6; Pr. 25:15; Jer. 40:4; 41:8; Zech. 11:12; II Cor. 12:6; I Thess. 3:1, 5. Children of Israel—Ez. 2:5, 7; 3:11, 27. Fight, To—I Sam. 23:13; I Ki. 22:6, 15; II Chr. 18:5, 14. One another —Eph. 4:2; 6:9; Col. 3:13. Prophet—II Chr. 25:16. Vow, To—Deut. 23:22. Weary, Of—Jer. 20:9. Working—I Cor. 9:6. See FORGIVENESS, LOVE.

FORBEARANCE. Mt. 18:33; Eph. 4:2; 6:9; Phil. 4:5; Col. 3:13; II Tim. 2:24. God, Of—Ps. 50:21; Is. 30:18; Rom. 3:25; I Pet. 3:20; II Pet. 3:9.

FORBID. Acts 24:23; 28:31; I Cor. 14: 39; III John 10. Children, Not—Mt. 19:14; Mk. 10:14; Lu. 18:16. Demons, To cast out—Mk. 9:38, 39; Lu. 9:49, 50. Holy Spirit, By—Acts 16:6. Gentiles, To speak to—I Thess. 2:16. God —Num. 11:28; Deut. 2:37; 4:23; I Sam. 24:6; 26:11; I Ki. 21:3; I Chr. 11:19; Lu. 20:16; Rom. 2:4, 6, 31; 6:2, 15; 7:7, 13; 9:14; 11:1, 11; I Cor. 6:15; Gal. 2:17; 3:21. Marriage—I Tim. 4:3. Tribute, To give—Lu. 23:2. Water—Acts 10:47.

FORCE. Job 40:16. By—*Cease, Made to* —Ezra 4:23. *Ruled*—Ez. 34:4. *Take*— I Sam. 2:16; Mt. 11:12; John 6:15; Acts 23:10. Dan, Children of—Ju. 1: 34. God's—Job 30:18. See GOD IS ALMIGHTY. Man, A—Pr. 7:21. Natural —Deut. 34:7. Strengthen—Amos 2:14. Testament if of—Heb. 9:17. Woman —Deut. 22:25; Ju. 19:24–30; 20:1–5; Esth. 7:8. See STRENGTH.

FORCES. II Ki. 25:23; II Chr. 17:2; Job 36:19; Jer. 40:7; 41:11; 42:1, 8; 43:4, 5; Dan. 11:10. See SOLDIERS, WAR.

FORCIBLE. Job. 6:25.

FORCING. Deut. 20:19; Pr. 30:13.

FORD. Gen. 32:22; Is. 16:2. Jordan, Of —Josh. 2:7; Ju. 3:28; 12:6.

FOREFATHER. II Tim. 1:3. Iniquities of—Ps. 79:8; Jer. 11:10. See FATHER.

FOREFRONT. Army, Of—II Chr. 20: 27. Battle, Of—II Sam. 11:15. Mitre, Of—Ex. 28:37. Tabernacle, Of—Ex. 26:9. Temple, Of—II Ki. 16:14; Ez. 40:19; 47:1.

FOREHEAD. See HEAD.

FOREIGNER. See ALIENS, SOJOURNER.

FOREKNOWLEDGE. See GOD, KNOWLEDGE.

FOREMOST. Gen. 32:17; 33:2; II Sam. 18:27.

FOREORDAINED. See FOREORDINATION.

FOREORDINATION. Gr. *Prognosis,* from *Proginosko,* "To foreknow." Pro(h)orizo, "To ordain beforehand." "Another name for the eternal plan, design, purpose, counsel of God, which executes itself in providence."—HASTINGS, *Bible Dictionary.*

Concerning man.—Control of the earth —Gen. 1:26; Ps. 8:6–8; Heb. 2:7, 8.

Results of sin—Gen. 2:17; 3:16–19.
Conquest of tempter—Gen. 3:15; John
12:31.
Concerning planets and seasons.—Gen.
1:14–18; Is. 13:10; Ez. 32:7, 8; Joel
2:30, 31; Mt. 24:29.
Concerning nations.—Jer. 18:7–10; 30:
11; Acts 10:35; 17:26, 27.
Concerning floods.—Gen. 9:11–15.
Concerning human life and action.—Joseph in Egypt—Gen. 45:5–8; Ps. 105:
17–24; Acts 7:9, 10. Pharaoh, the tyrant—Ex. 4:21, 22; 7:3–5; 9:12; Rom.
9:17. Call of Israel—Gen. 15:13, 14;
Ex. 3:16, 17; Hos. 11:1; Mt. 2:15. Call
of Jacob rather than Esau—Rom. 9:13.
Destruction of Canaanites—Josh. 11:
20. Rending of Solomon's kingdom—
I Ki. 11:11–13, 31–39. Bringing in of
Gentiles—Is. 55:4, 5; 60:2, 3; Rom.
9:30–32; Eph. 1:9–11; Col. 1:25–27. Cyrus God's shepherd—Is. 44:24–28; 45:
1–7. Judas Iscariot—Mk. 14:18–21;
Lu. 22:21, 22; John 13:18, 19, 27; Acts
1:18–20; 2:23. Herod, Pilate, etc—
Acts 4:27, 28.
Sufferings and glory of the Christ.—Ps.
2:2–6; Is. 53:10; Lu. 24:25–27; John
12:31, 32.
Triumph of the church.—Gen. 3:15; Mt.
16:18; Rom. 8:28–30, 35–39; Rev. 2:
17, 26–28; 3:5, 12, 21.
**God foreordains that all nations shall be
blessed through the seed of Abraham.**
—Gen. 12:3; 18:17, 18; 22:16–18; 26:
4; Is. 41:1–20; 45:9–15; 46:9–13; Acts
3:25; Rom. 4:1–25; 9:1–8; Gal. 3:6–9,
14, 16–29.
That in Isaac shall all nations be blessed.
—Gen. 21:12; Rom. 9:7–9; Gal. 4:22–
31; Heb. 11:17–18.
**That Esau should be rejected and Jacob
accepted.**—Gen. 25:23; Mal. 1:2–5;
Rom. 9:10–13.
**Esau and Jacob typical of the Jewish
and Gentile nations respectively; rejection of the Jews and acceptance of
Gentiles.**—Jer. 18:1–10; Rom. 9:4–33;
11:1–32.
**God foreordains that all nations shall be
saved through the death of Jesus.**—Is.
53:1–12; Mt. 26:24; Mk. 9:12; Lu. 22:
22; 24:26, 27, 44–47; Acts 2:23; 3:18;
4:27, 28; 17:2, 3; 26:22, 23; Rom. 8:

28–35; 16:25, 26; I Pet. 1:18–21; Rev.
13:8.
**God foreordains that Jesus shall be a
stone of stumbling to those who reject
Him.**—Ps. 118:22; Is. 8:14, 15; 28:16;
Mt. 21:42–45; Mk. 12:1–10; Lu. 2:34;
20:9, 18; Acts 4:10–12; Rom. 9:33;
I Pet. 2:6, 10.
**God foreordains that the Gentiles shall
be saved through Christ and the
preaching of the gospel.**—Hos. 1:10;
2:23; Acts 9:15; 17:26, 27; Rom. 4:1–
25; 9:17–33; Gal. 1:15, 16; 3:8–29;
Eph. 1:4–7, 11; 2:13, 14; I Thess. 1:4;
II Thess. 2:13, 14; I Pet. 2:10; 5:9.
**That those who are saved should be con-
formed to the image of Christ.**—Rom.
8:29–39; Phil. 3:10. See ELECTION,
PURPOSE, SALVATION.
FOREPART. Breastplate, Of—Ex. 28:
27. Ephod, Of—Ex. 39:20; Joel 2:20.
FORERUNNER. Heb. 6:20.
FORESEE. Acts 2:31; Gal. 3:8.
FORESHIP. Acts 27:30, 41. See SHIP.
FORESKIN. See CIRCUMCISION.
FOREST. Is. 22:8; 44:14, 23; Jer. 26:
18; Hos. 2:12; Mic. 3:12. Arabia, Of
—Is. 21:13. Breast, Of—Ps. 50:10;
104:20; Is. 56:9; Ju. 5:6; 12:8; Amos
3:4; Mic. 5:8. Destroy—Is. 10:18, 19,
34; 29:17; 32:15, 19; Jer. 46:23; Zech.
11:2. Fire in—Ps. 83:14; Is. 9:18; Ju.
21:14. Hereth, Of—I Sam. 22:5. Kings
—Neh. 2:8. Lebanon, Of—I Ki. 7:2; 10:
17, 21; II Ki. 19:23; II Chr. 9:16, 20;
Is. 10:34; 29:17; 37:24. South, Of the
—Ez. 20:46, 47. See WOOD.
FOREWARN. Gal. 5:21; I Thess. 4:6.
See WARNING.
FORFEIT. Deut. 22:9; Ezra 10:8. Soul
—Mt. 16:26; Mk. 8:36; Lu. 9:25.
FORGE. Lies—Job 13:4; Ps. 119:69.
FORGET, FORGETFUL, FORGOTTEN.
Affliction—Ps. 44:24. Amalekites—
Deut. 25:19. Behind, Those things
which are—Phil. 3:13. Bridal attire
—Jer. 2:32. Commandments—Deut.
4:9; 26:13; Ps. 119:176. Complaint—
Job 9:27. Covenant—Deut. 4:9, 23,
31; II Ki. 17:38; Pr. 2:17. Do good,
To—Heb. 13:2. Eat, To—Ps. 102:4.
Eggs, Ostrich—Job 39:15. Entertain,
To—Heb. 13:2. Exhortation—Heb.
12:5. Father's house—Ps. 45:10. God

—Deut. 6:12; 8:11, 14, 19; 9:7; 32:18; Ju. 3:7; I Sam. 12:9; Job 8:13; Ps. 9:17; 44:17, 20; 50:22; 59:11; 78:7, 11; 103:2; 106:13, 21; Is. 17:10; 51:13; 65:11; Jer. 2:32; 3:21; 13:25; 23:27; 50:6; Ez. 22:12; 23:35; Hos. 2:13. Gracious, To be—Ps. 77:9. Handmaid, Thy—I Sam. 1:11. Hearer, Forgetful —Jas. 1:25. Jerusalem—Ps. 137:5. Job—Job 19:14. Joseph—Gen. 40:23. Judah—Jer. 23:39; 30:14; Lam. 5:20. Law of God—Ps. 119:61, 83, 109, 141, 153; Pr. 3:1; 31:5; Hos. 4:6; 8:14; 13:6. Misery—Job 11:16; Pr. 31:7. Ornaments—Jer. 2:32. Poor, The—Ps. 9:12; 10:11, 12; 74:19. Poverty—Pr. 31:7. Prosperity—Lam. 3:17. Resting-place—Jer. 50:6. Sabbaths—Lam. 2:6. Sheaf in field—Deut. 24:19. Sinners—Job 24:20. Sparrows not forgotten—Lu. 12:6. Toil—Gen. 41:51. Understanding—Pr. 4:5. Voice of adversaries—Ps. 74:23. What manner of Man—Jas. 1:24. Wickedness—Jer. 44:9. See SIN. Word of God—Ps. 119:16, 139. Work, your—Heb. 6:10. See LABOR. Zion—Is. 49:14, 15.

FORKS. See FOOD.

FORM. Adam—I Tim. 2:13. All things —Jer. 10:16; 51:19. Beast, Every—Gen. 2:19. Bodily, In—Lu. 3:22. Cherubim—I Ki. 6:25. Christ—Rom. 9:20. Creeping things—Ez. 8:10. Earth—Gen. 1:2 (A.V.); 4:23 (A.V.); Ps. 90:2; 95:5; Is. 45:18. Evil, Of— I Thess. 5:22. Eye, The—Ps. 94:9. God, Of—Num. 12:8; Ps. 17:5; Is. 43:10; Phil. 2:6. Godliness, Of—II Tim. 3:5. Hand, Of a—Ez. 8:3. Holy Spirit, Of—Lu. 3:22. House, Of—Ez. 43:11. It—II Ki. 19:25; Is. 37:26; Jer. 33:2. Jeremiah—Jer. 1:5. Jesus, Of—Is. 52:14; 53:2; Mk. 16:12; Phil. 2:6, 7. Knowledge, Of—Rom. 2:20. Letter—Acts 23:25. Leviathan—Ps. 104:26. Locusts—Amos 7:1. Light, The—Is. 45:7. Man—Gen. 2:7, 8; Deut. 32:18; Job 33:6; Is. 27:10; 43:1, 7, 21; 44:2, 21, 24; 49:5. Mountains—Amos 4:13. Nebuchadrezzar—*Images*—Dan. 2:11. *Visage*—Dan. 3:19. People—Is. 43:21. Potter and clay—Is. 29:16. Samuel, Of—I Sam. 28:14. Saw no—Deut. 4:12. Servant, Of—Phil. 2:7. Sound words—II Tim. 1:13 (A.V.).

Spirit, Of—Job 4:16; Zech. 12:1. Teaching, Of—Rom. 6:17. Weapon—Is. 54:17. See CONFORM, CREATE, FASHION, PATTERN.

FORMER. Age—Job 8:8. Captains—II Ki. 1:14. Days—Eccl. 7:10; Zech. 8:11; Heb. 10:32. Desolations—Is. 61:4. Estate—Ez. 16:55. Generations —Eccl. 1:11. Glory—Hag. 2:9. Governors—Neh. 5:15. Husband—Deut. 24:4. Kings—Num. 21:16; Jer. 34:5. Loving-kindness—Ps. 89:49. Lusts— I Pet. 1:14. Manner—Gen. 40:13; I Sam. 17:30; II Ki. 17:34, 40; Eph. 4:22. Multitude—Dan. 11:13. Prophets —1:4; 7:7, 12. Rain—Deut. 11:14; Jer. 5:24; Hos. 6:3; Joel 2:23. Things —Is. 41:22; 42:9; 43:9, 18; 48:3; Rev. 21:4. Time—Ruth 4:7; Is. 9:1; Dan. 11:29. Treatise—Acts 1:1. Troubles —Is. 65:16. Words—Jer. 56:28. See ANCIENT, OLD.

FORNICATION. Forbidden—Ex. 22:16, 17. With bond-maiden—Lev. 19:20. Offering to be made on account of —Lev. 19:21–22. Midianitish woman —Num. 25:6, 8. Take a wife and hate her—Deut. 22:13–22. A betrothed virgin—Deut. 22:23, 29. No prostitutes in house of God—Deut. 23:17. Jerusalem's—Ez. 16:15, 29. Delivered from strange woman—Pr. 2:16; 5:3; 6:25, 26. Young men warned of—Pr. Ch. 7; 31:3. The foolish woman's entreaty—Pr. 9:13–18. Mouth of strange woman—Pr. 22:14; 23:27; 29:3. Out of the heart comes—Mt. 15:19; Mk. 7:21. Putting away wife save for—Mt. 5:32; 19:9. Were not born of fornication—John 8:41. Abstain from —Acts 15:20, 29; I Cor. 6:9; I Thess. 4:3. Have no company with fornication—I Cor. 5:9. Shall not inherit Kingdom of Heaven—I Cor. 6:9. The works—Gal. 5:19; Eph. 5:3. Put to death your members—Col. 3:5. Law made for—I Tim. 1:10. God will judge —Heb. 13:4. To commit—Rev. 2:14. Second death for—Rev. 21:8. Without are fornicators—Rev. 22:15. Gentiles abstain from—Acts 21:25. Among the Jews—I Cor. 5:1. Body not for— I Cor. 6:13, 18. Let every man have his own wife, To avoid—I Cor. 7:2. Repented not of—II Cor. 12:21.

Examples of: Lot—Gen. 19:31. Reuben —Gen. 35:22. Judah—Gen. 38:1–24. Samson—Ju. 16:1. Eli's sons—I Sam. 2:22. Amnon—II Sam. 13:1–20. Gentiles—Eph. 4:17–19; I Pet. 4:3. See ADULTERY, CHASTITY, INCEST, LUST.

Spiritual (Idolatry).—Ez. 16:22. Take thee a wife of—Hos. 1:2, 3. Err because of—Hos. 4:11. Cities given over to—Jude 7. Wrath of—Rev. 14: 8; 18:3. Kings of earth counted— Rev. 17:2, 4; 18:3. Repented not of— Rev. 9:21. Corrupted the earth with —Rev. 19:2. See IDOLATRY.

FORSAKE. Jer. 7:29; Gen. 24:27; Deut. 31:17; Josh. 1:5; I Chr. 28:20; Ps. 38:21; 71:9, 11, 18; Is. 49:14; 54:7; Lam. 5:20. All—Lu. 5:28. Cities— I Chr. 10:7; Is. 17:2; 62:12; Jer. 4:29; Ez. 36:4. Assembling together—Heb. 11:27. Commandments—Ezra 9:10. Counsel—I Ki. 12:8, 13; II Chr. 10:8, 13. Covenant—Deut. 29:25; I Ki. 19: 10, 14; Jer. 22:9; Dan. 11:30. Earth— Job 18:4. Eggs—Is. 10:14. Egypt— Heb. 11:27. Father and mother, When —Ps. 27:10. Fear of the Almighty— Job 6:14. Fountain of living waters —Jer. 2:13; 17:13. Friend—Pr. 2: 17; 27:10. Gaza—Zeph. 2:4. God— Deut. 28:20; 31:16; 32:15; Josh. 24: 16, 20; Ju. 2:12, 13; 10:6, 10, 13; I Sam. 8:8; 12:10; 15:11; I Ki. 18:18; II Ki. 17:7–18; 21:22; 22:17; II Chr. 7:19, 22; 12:1, 5; 13:10, 11; 15:2; 21:10; 24:20, 24; 28:6; 29:6; 34:25; Is. 1:4, 28; 65:11; Jer. 1:16; 2:17, 19; 5:7, 19; 16:11; 19:4; Ezra 8:22; Ez. 6:9; John 6:66; II Cor. 15:2; II Pet. 2:15. Habitations—Jer. 2:13; Is. 27:10. House of God—Neh. 10:39; 13:11; Jer. 12:7. Inheritance—Ps. 94:14. Israel—Jer. 51: 5. Jehovah will not—Deut. 31: 6, 8; I Sam. 12:22; I Ki. 6:13; 8:57; Neh. 9:17, 19; Ps. 9:10; 27:10; 37:28; Is. 41:17; 42:16. Kindness and truth, Let not—Pr. 3:3. Land—Is. 7:16; Jer. 9:13; Ez. 8:12; 9:9. Law—Ps. 89:30; 119:53; Pr. 4:2; 28:4; Jer. 9:13. Mercy—Jonah 2:8. Moses— Acts 21:21. Mother, Law of—Pr. 1:8; 6:20. Ordinance of God—Is. 58:2. Palace—Is. 32:14. Paths—Pr. 2:13. People, Thy—Is. 2:6. Places—Is. 6: 12; 17:9. Precepts—Ps. 119:87. Pun-

ishment of—II Ki. 22:16, 17; Is. 1:28; Jer. 1:16; 5:19. Pursued yet not—II Cor. 4:9. Reproof—Pr. 10:17. Righteous—Ps. 37:25. Sweetness—Ju. 9:11. Tabernacle—Ps. 78:60. Utterly—Ps. 119:8. Way—Pr. 15:10; Is. 55:7; II Pet. 2:15. Why hast thou, My God— Ps. 22:1; Mt. 27:46; Mk. 15:34. Work of thy hands—Ps. 138:8. Wrath—Ps. 37:8.

FORSWEAR. Mt. 5:33. See OATHS, VOWS.

FORTH. See BEAR, BREAK, BRING, CARRY, GO, TAKE, WENT.

FORTHWITH. Mk. 6:25; Acts 10:33; 23:30; Phil. 2:23.

FORTIFICATION. The earliest cities of Palestine were usually planted on the spur of a mountain, the builders thus availing themselves of the steep rock-faces as the first line of defence. ''The walls of brick or stone, supplied by art, and supplementing the work of nature, followed the course of the ridge, the rock itself being frequently cut away to form artificial scarps.''

Walls.—These fortifying walls were the distinguishing feature of the city, villages being without walls and having merely a watch-tower—Deut. 3:4, 5; II Sam. 20:15; I Ki. 3:1; 21:23; II Ki. 14:13; 17:19; 18:8; Is. 2:15; Ez. 38:11; Zeph. 1:16.

Use of towers in cities and strongholds. —Babylon—Gen. 11:4, 5. Shechem— Ju. 9:44–49. Thebez—Ju. 9:50–55. Jezreel—II Ki. 9:17. Jerusalem—II Chr. 26:9, 15; 32:5; Ps. 48:12, 13; Is. 32:14. Judah—II Chr. 11:5–12; 14:6, 7; 27:4. At the gates of Tyre—Ez. 26:8.

The metaphorical use of.—Ps. 18:2; 61: 3; 144:2; Jer. 6:27; Hab. 2:1.

FORTUNATE. Gen. 30:11.

FORTUNATUS, fôr-tu-nā'tus. **One of** Paul's companions.—I Cor. 16:17.

FORTUNE. Is. 65:11.

FORTY. Righteous men in Sodom— Gen. 18:29. Stripes—Deut. 25:3; II Cor. 11:24.

Days.—*Forty* as connected with *days* seems to have been used to cover an extraordinary period of time—one that would arrest the attention of the reader. The flood of rain—Gen. 7:4, 17. Raven sent out—Gen. 8:6. Embalming of Jacob's body—Gen. 50:3. Moses in the mount—Ex. 24:18; 34: 28; Deut. 9:9, 11, 18, 25; 10:10. Spies in Canaan—Num. 13:25; 14:34. Goliath before Israel's army—I Sam. 17:16. Ezekiel symbolizes judgment —Ez. 4:6. Jonah threatens Nineveh— Jonah 3:4. Jesus in the wilderness— Mt. 4:2; Mk. 1:13; Lu. 4:2. Jesus tarries after resurrection—Acts 1:3. Ninevites during preaching of Jonah —Jonah 3:5. Elijah going toward Horeb—I Ki. 19:8.

Years.—Egypt desolate—Ez. 29:11-13. Esau when he married Judith—Gen. 26:20. Isaac when he married Rebekah—Gen. 25:30. Joshua when sent to spy out Canaan—Josh. 14:7. Kings reigned: *Saul*—Acts 13:21. *David*— I Ki. 2:11; I Chr. 29:27. *Solomon*—I Ki. 11:42; II Chr. 9:30. *Joash*—II Ki. 12:1; II Chr. 24:1. Manna eaten— Ex. 16:35. Moses when he visited his brethren—Acts 7:23. *In Midian*— Acts 7:30. *Leads Israel*—Deut. 34:7. Wilderness, Israel in—Num. 14:33, 34; 32:13; Deut. 2:7; 8:2, 4; 29:5; Josh. 7:6; Ps. 95:10; Amos 2:10; 5:25; Acts 7:36; 13:18; Heb. 3:8, 9, 17.

FORWARD. Mt. 26:39. Backward and not—Jer. 7:24. Calamity, Set my— Job 30:13. Day, From that—Ez. 39: 22; I Sam. 16:13; 30:25. Go—I Sam. 10:3; Job 23:8. Israel—See ISRAEL. Kohathites set—See ISRAEL. Saul eyed David from that day—I Sam. 18:9. Standard—See ISRAEL. Straight —Ez. 10:22. Tabernacle setteth—See ISRAEL.

FOSTER-BROTHER. Acts 13:1.

FOUGHT. Beasts at Ephesus, With— I Cor. 15:32. Good fight—II Tim. 4:7. Stars in their courses—Ju. 5:20. See FIGHT, ISRAEL, STRIFE, WAR.

FOUL. Waters—Ex. 7:18; Ez. 34:18, 19. Weather—Mt. 16:3. See UNCLEAN.

FOUND. See FIND.

FOUND. To build, establish—Ex. 9:18. Chaldea, Land of—Is. 23:13. Earth— Ps. 24:2; 89:11; Pr. 3:19; Amos 9:6. See Ps. 104:8. Egypt—Ex. 9:18. Heavens—Ps. 89:11. House upon rock —Mt. 7:25; Lu. 6:48. Seas, Upon—

Ps. 24:2. Testimonies—Ps. 119:152. Zion—Is. 14:32.

FOUNDATION. Hab. 3:13. Another man's—Rom. 15:20; I Cor. 3:10, 11. Apostles, Of—Eph. 2:20. Babylon, Of —Jer. 50:15; 51:26. Christ—I Cor. 3:11. See CONFESSION. City which hath—Heb. 11:10. Destroyed—Ps. 11:3. Dust, In the—Job 4:19. Earth, Of the—Job 38:4, 6; Ps. 82:5; 102: 25; 104:5; Pr. 8:29; Is. 24:18; 40:21; 48:13; 51:13, 16; Jer. 31:37; Mic. 6:2; Zech. 12:1; Heb. 1:10. Egypt, Of— Ez. 30:4. Generations—Is. 58:12. God, Of—II Tim. 2:19. Gold, Silver, etc.— I Cor. 3:12. Good—I Tim. 6:19. Heaps, Of—II Chr. 31:7. Heaven, Of—II Sam. 22:8. House on rock and sand— Lu. 6:48, 49. Jerusalem, Of—Ps. 137: 7. Jericho, Of—Josh. 6:26; I Ki. 16: 34. Man, Of—Job 4:19. Mountain, In holy—Ps. 87:1. Mountains, Of— Deut. 32:22; Ps. 18:7. New Jerusalem —Rev. 21:14, 19. Other—I Cor. 3:11. Prison, Of—Acts 16:26. Repentance —Heb. 6:1. Righteous—Pr. 10:25. Samaria—Mic. 1:6. Stone—Is. 28:16, 18. Temple, Of—I Ki. 5:7; 6:37; 7:9, 11; II Chr. 8:16; 23:5; Ezra 3:6, 10- 12; 5:16; 6:3; Is. 44:28; Hag. 2:18; Zech. 4:9; 8:9. Throne of God—Ps. 89:14. Tower, Of—Lu. 14:29. Wall, Of—Ezra 4:12; Ez. 13:14. World, Of the—Ps. 18:15; Mt. 13:35; 25:34; Lu. 11:50; John 17:24; Eph. 1:4; Heb. 4:3; 9:26; I Pet. 1:20; Rev. 13:8; 17: 8. Zion—Is. 54:11.

FOUNTAIN. Created by God.—Ps. 74:15.

Kinds of.—Water—Gen. 16:7; Lev. 11: 36; Josh. 15:9; I Ki. 18:5; Ps. 114:8; Pr. 8:24; Joel 3:18; Jas. 3:11; Rev. 14:7; 16:4; 21:6. Living waters—Jer. 2:13; 17:13; Rev. 7:17; 8:10; 21:6. Of great deep—Gen. 7:11; 8:2; Pr. 8:28.

Where found.—In the way to Shur— Gen. 16:7. In Jezreel—I Sam. 29:1. In valleys and hills—Deut. 8:7; Is. 41:18.

Jacob's fountain.—Deut. 33:28. **Of Israel.**—Ps. 68:26.

Fountain gate.—Neh. 2:14; 3:15; 12:37.

Figurative.—Fountain of life—Ps. 36:9; Pr. 13:14; 14:27; Rev. 21:6. Troubled —Pr. 25:26. Sealed—Song of Sol. 4:

12. Of gardens—Song of Sol. 4:15.
Of tears—Jer. 9:1. Waters stopped
—II Chr. 32:3, 4.

Miscellaneous.—Lev. 20:18; Mk. 5:29.
Pitcher broken at—Eccl. 12:6.

Prophecies concerning.—Shall be dried
up—Hos. 13:15. Shall come forth—
Joel 3:18. Shall be opened—Zech.
13:1.

FOUR. Corners—See CORNERS. Fold, Restore—II Sam. 12:6; Lu. 19:8. Kingdoms—Dan. 2:36–43; 7:3–23. Living
creatures—Ez. 1:4–25; 10:10–22; Rev.
4:6; 5:14; 6:6, 7; 19:4. Months and
then harvest—John 4:35. Score years
—Gen. 16:16; 35:18; Ex. 7:7; Ju. 3:
30; II Sam. 19:32, 35; Ps. 90:10; Lu.
2:37; 16:7. Square—See ALTAR. Thousand fed—Mt. 15:38; 16:10; Mk. 8:9,
20. Twenty elders, And—See REVELA-
TION. Winds—See WINDS.

FOURTEEN. Generations—Mt. 1:17.
Jacob served fourteen years for Leah
and Rachel—Gen. 31:41. Paul—II
Cor. 12:2; Gal. 2:1.

FOURTEENTH. Day—Acts 27:33. See
DAY, PASSOVER.

FOURTH. Gen. 1:19; 2:14. Angel—
Rev. 8:12; 16:8. Beast—Rev. 4:7;
6:7. Row—See PRIESTS, GARMENTS.
Seal—Rev. 6:7. Watch—Mt. 14:25;
Mk. 6:48. See WATCH.

FOWLS. See BIRDS.

FOWLER. Ps. 91:3; 124:7; Pr. 5:5;
Jer. 5:26; Hos. 9:8. See SNARE.

FOX. Caught three hundred, Samson—
Ju. 15:4. Go and say to that—Lu. 13:
31. Have holes—Mt. 8:20; Lu. 9:58.
Little—Song of Sol. 2:15. Portion for
—Ps. 63:10. Prophets like—Ez. 13:4.
Stone wall, Shall break—Neh. 4:3.
Walk on mountain—Lam. 5:18.

FRAGRANCE. Give forth—Song of
Sol. 2:13; 7:13. Oils have a goodly—
Song of Sol. 1:3.

FRAIL. Ps. 39:4.

FRAME. Deut. 31:21. City, Of a—Ez.
40:2. Deceit, Tongue—Ps. 50:19. Evil—
Jer. 18:11. Fitly—Eph. 2:21. Goodly—
Job 4:12. Hands have—Job 10:8. He
knoweth our—Ps. 103:14. Hidden,
Was not—Ps. 139:15. Mischief—Ps.
94:20. Pronounce, To—Ju. 12:6.
Worlds have been—Heb. 11:3.

FRANKINCENSE. Ex. 30:34; Lev. 2:1,
15, 16; 5:11; 6:15; 24:7; Num. 5:15; I
Chr. 9:29; Neh. 13:5, 9; Rev. 18:13.
Hill of—Song of Sol. 4:6. Offered him
gold and—Mt. 2:11. Trees of—Song
of Sol. 4:14.

FRATERNITY. Every man is his brother's keeper—Gen. 4:9–12.

To preserve him from harm.—Lev. 19:
11–18; 24:19, 20; 35:39–54; Deut. 15:
1–4, 7–18; 22:1–4.

**Five of Ten Commandments given to
protect interests of fellow-men and
women:**

1. Thou shalt not kill—Gen. 4:9–12; Ex.
20:12; 21:12–14; Num. 35:16–31; Deut.
5:17; 19:4–13; Mt. 5:21, 22; 19:18;
26:52; Mk. 10:19; Rev. 21:8; 22:15.
See MURDERER, TEN COMMANDMENTS.

2. Thou shalt not commit adultery—Ex.
20:14; Lev. 18:20; 20:10; Num. 5:
12–31; Deut. 5:18; 22:22; 24:1–4; Jer.
3:1; 5:7–9; Mt. 5:27, 28. See ADUL-
TERY.

3. Thou shalt not steal—Ex. 20:15; 21:
16; 22:7; Lev. 6:2–7; 19:11–13; Deut.
5:19; Eph. 4:28. See STEALING.

4. Thou shalt not bear false witness—
Ex. 20:16; Lev. 19:16; Deut. 5:20;
19:15–21; Ps. 24:28. See FALSE WIT-
NESS.

5. Thou shalt not covet—Ex. 20:14, 17;
Deut. 5:21. See COVETOUSNESS.

Must not oppress the poor.—Ex. 22:25–
27; Lev. 6:2–5; 19:13; 25:13; 25:17;
Deut. 24:14–18; Is. 33:14–16; Jer. 22:
16–18; Ez. 18:7–9; 16–18; Amos 8:4–
8; Mic. 2:2–4; 6:10–15; Zech. 7:8–10;
Mal. 3:5. See JUSTICE, OPPRESSION.

Must care for widow and orphan.—Ex.
22:22–24; Deut. 10:18; 24:17; Job 22:
16–22; 29:12, 13. See WIDOW.

Must forgive debts.—Deut. 15:1–4, 12–
18. See PARABLE OF UNMERCIFUL SERV-
ANT—Mt. 18:23–37. The jubilee—Lev.
25:23–34; 26:10–17, 23, 31, 35. See
DEBT, JUBILEE.

Must lend money.—Deut. 15:17; Mt. 5:
42. See USURY, EXTORTION.

Must help the poor.—Gen. 42:18–25; 50:
19–21; Job 29:11–16; Ps. 31:20; Is.
58:6–9; Mt. 19:21; Mk. 10:21; Lu. 6:
30; 19:8; Rom. 15:25–27; I Cor. 12:12–
26; 16:1–3; Eph. 4:28; James 2:14–17;
5:1–4.

Fields must not be gleaned but left for the poor.—Ex. 23:11; Lev. 19:10; 23: 22; Ruth 2:1-20.

Must give food and raiment.—Deut. 15: 12-15; Job 22:5-7; 31:16-22; Is. 58:7; Ez. 18:7-9; Mt. 25:34-46; Mk. 9:41; Lu. 3:11; Rom. 12:13; Jas. 2:15, 16. See ALMSGIVING, LIBERALITY, HOSPITALITY, POOR.

Must bear one another's burdens.—Rom. 15:1, 2; Gal. 6:1, 2. See BURDEN.

Must not be stumbling-block.—Mt. 18: 6; Mk. 9:42; Lu. 17:1, 2; Rom. 14:13-19; I Cor. 8:8-13.

Must forgive.—Mt. 6:12-15; 18:21-35; Mk. 11:25; Lu. 11:4; 17:34; II Cor. 2:6-10; Gal. 6:1. See Lu. 15:1-32. See FORGIVENESS.

How to settle disputes.—Mt. 18:15-17.

Must not judge harshly.—Mt. 7:1-5; Lu. 6:37-42; Jas. 4:11, 12. See JUDGMENT.

Must love enemies.—Lev. 19:18; Mt. 19:21-26, 42-47; 22:39; Lu. 6:27-35.

The "golden rule."—Mt. 7:12.

Love thy neighbor as thyself.—Lev. 19: 18, 33, 34; Deut. 10:18, 19; Mt. 22:39; Mk. 12:31-34; Lu. 10:27; see I John 4:7-11, 20, 21. "The Parable of the Good Samaritan."

Proverbs.—Lend today—3:28, 29. Save with your mouth—11:9-11. Guide—12:26; 16:29. Pity—14:20, 21. Love—17:17, 18. Brothers' quarrels are bitter—18:19, 24. Bad men suspect others—21:10. Settle quickly—25:8, 9. False witness a maul—25:17, 18. He who deceives a neighbor is a madman—26:18, 19. A neighbor nearer than a brother—27:10. Avoid flattery—29:5.

Examples. — Abraham and Lot — Gen. 12:5; 13:1, 7, 8. Abraham and allies—Gen. 14:15, 24. Joseph and brothers—Gen. 45:1-7; 50:15-21. Ruth and Naomi—Ruth 1:16, 17. Ruth and Boaz—2:8, 15, 16. Jonathan and David—I Sam. 18:1-4; 19:1-7; 20:4, 35-42. Obadiah and prophets—I Ki. 18:13. Elijah and hostess—II Ki. Ch. 4. Rechabites—Jer. 35:2-5, 18. Mary and apostles—Lu. 8:1-3. Good Samaritan—Lu. 10:25-37. Jerusalem church—Acts 2:44, 45. Antioch and Jerusalem—Acts 11:27-30. Barbarians and Paul—Acts 28:8-10. Greece for Palestine—Rom. 15:25-27; I Cor. 16:1-3.

Philippians and Paul—Phil. 4:23. Gaius and ministers—III John 5-8.

Men who failed.—Cain—Gen. 4:8. Joseph's brothers—Gen. 37:3, 4, 18-20, 28; 42:21, 22. Shechemites—Ju. 9:1-6, 22-24, 49, 53. David—II Sam. 12: 1-10. Jehu—II Ki. 9:1, 22-24, 27. Judah—Jer. 9:2-5; Mal. 2:10, 11; Jer. 34:13-17. Esau—Gen. 27:41; Amos 1: 11; Ob. 10. Persecutors—Mt. 10:21; John 16:2. The merciless—Mt. 25:41-45. Corinthians—I Cor. 6:1-8. Rich farmers—Jas. 5:1-4. See BRETHREN, FRIENDSHIP, LOVE.

FRAUD. Jas. 5:4. See DECEPTION, FALSE.

FREEDOM. Lev. 19:20; Deut. 24:5; Job 39:5; Rom. 7:3; Eph. 6:8; Rev. 13:16; 19:18. Cares, From—I Cor. 7: 32. Christ set us—Rom. 8:2; Gal. 5:1. Go—Ex. 21:2, 5, 26, 27; Deut. 15:12, 13, 18; Ps. 105:20. Indeed—John 8: 36. House—I Sam. 17:25. Iniquity, From—Num. 5:31. Jerusalem is—Gal. 4:26. Law of sin and death, From—Rom. 8:2. Love of money, From—Heb. 13:5. Men, From all—I Cor. 9: 19. Neither bond nor—Gal. 31:28. Oppressed, Of—Is. 58:6. Servant from master—Job 3:19; Jer. 34:9, 10. Service, From—I Chr. 9:33. Sin, From—Rom. 6:18, 22. Son shall make you—John 8:36. Sons are—Mt. 17:26. Truth shall make you—John 8:32. Using, Not—I Pet. 2:16. Water of bitterness, From—Num. 5:19. Will—Ezra 7:13. See LIBERTY, SALVATION.

FREELY. Drink—John 2:10. Eat—Gen. 2:16. Give—Mt. 10:8; Rev. 21:6. Justified—Rom. 3:24. Love them—Hos. 14:4. Say—Acts 2:29. Speak—Acts 26:26. Take water of life—Rev. 22:17.

FREEMAN. I Cor. 7:22; Col. 3:11.

FREE WILL. See OFFERING.

FREE WOMAN. Gal. 4:22, 23, 30, 31.

FREIGHT. Acts 27:18.

FRESH. Flesh—Job 33:25. Glory—Job 29:20. Oil—Num. 11:8; Ps. 92:10. See NEW.

FRET. Hannah—I Sam. 1:6. Heart—Pr. 19:3. Leprosy, Of—Lev. 13:51, 52, 55; 14:44. Themselves—Is. 8:21. Thyself, Not—Ps. 37:1, 7, 8; Pr. 24: 19. Fretful woman—Pr. 21:19.

FRIENDSHIP. Affection growing out of mutual good will.—Pr. 27:17; I Sam. 20:41-42.

True friendship.—I Sam. 18:1-3; Ps. 35: 13, 14; Pr. 17:17; 18:24; Mt. 2:10-11; Lu. 10:33, 34.

Value of.—II Sam. 16:1, 2; Eccl. 4:9-12. Loyalty required—Pr. 27:10. Test of—John 15:13-15.

Responsive friendship.—Pr. 18:24; 27: 17-19. It wins—Pr. 17:9; 22:11. Accepts good counsel—Pr. 27:6, 9.

Friendship with a motive.—Job 17:5; Pr. 14:20; 19:6; 27:14.

Treacherous.—Ps. 41:9; Mt. 26:48-50; Mk. 14:44, 45; Lu. 22:47, 48.

Distrusted friendship.—Job 16:20; Mic. 7:5; Mk. 9:38-39. Cautious—John 7: 12, 13; 19:38. Feeble—Lu. 11:5-7.

Dangerous friendship.—Deut. 13:6-9; II Sam. 13:3-5; Job 32:2-3; 42:7; Pr. 22:24.

False friendship.—Ju. 14:20; II Sam. 16:16-23; 20:9, 10; Jas. 4:4.

Deserted friendship.—Job 19:14-19; Ps. 88:18.

Friends of God.—Abraham—Jas. 2:23. Moses—Heb. 3:2. Friends of Jesus—Lu. 12:4; John 11:1-3, 11; John 15: 14, 15.

FRIGHTEN. Deut. 28:26; Jer. 7:33. See Affright, Fear.

FRIGHTFUL. Job 30:6. See Affright, Fear, Terror.

FRINGES. Num. 15:38; Deut. 22:12. See Clothing, Commandments.

FROGS. Ex. 8:2-13; Ps. 78:45; 105:30; Rev. 16:13.

FRONT. Num. 19:4; Josh. 8:33.

FRONTIERS. Ez. 25:9.

FRONTLET. Ex. 13:16; Deut. 6:8; 11:18.

FROST. Gen. 31:40; Ex. 16:14; Job 38: 29; Ps. 78:47; Jer. 36:30. See Ice.

FROWARD. II Sam. 22:27; I Pet. 2:18. See Crooked, Perverse, Wayward.

FRUIT. General.—Ex. 10:15; Lev. 19: 24, 25; 25:3, 4, 16, 21, 22; 26:4, 20; Num. 13:26, 27; Deut. 33:14; Josh. 5: 12; Ju. 9:11; II Sam. 9:10; II Ki. 8:6; 19:29; Job 31:39; Neh. 9:36; 10:35, 37; Ps. 105:35; 107:37; Eccl. 2:5; Is. 10:12; 13:18; 27:6, 9; 37:30, 31; Jer. 2:7; 29:5, 28; 32:19; Lam. 4:9; Ez. 25:4; 34:27; 47:12; Hag. 1:10; Zech.

8:12; Mal. 3:11; Lu. 1:42; Acts 2:30; II Tim. 2:6; Jas. 5:7, 18; Jude 12.

Spiritual fruit.—Mt. 3:8; 7:16, 20; Lu. 3:8; Rom. 1:13; 6:21, 22; 7:4, 5; 15: 28; Gal. 5:22; Eph. 5:9; Phil. 1:22; 4:17; Col. 1:6, 10; Rev. 18:14. Fruit of the wicked. See Wicked, Sins, Righteousness—Is. 3:10; Amos 6:12; II Cor. 9:10; Phil. 1:11; Heb. 12:11; Jas. 3:18.

Adder, Of.—Is. 14:29.

Doings, Of.—Jer. 21:14; Mic. 7:13.

Hands, Of.—Pr. 31:16, 31.

Lips, Of.—Is. 57:19; Heb. 13:15.

Mouth, Of.—Pr. 12:14; 13:2; 18:20, 21.

Parable of.—Ez. 17:8, 9, 23; Mt. 21:34, 41, 43; Lu. 12:17, 18; 13:6, 7.

Names of: Apple—Song of Sol. 2:3, 5; 7:8; 8:5; Joel 1:12. Date-palm—Ex. 15:27. Figs—Num. 13:23; 20:5; Ju. 9:11; I Sam. 25:18; II Ki. 18:31; I Chr. 12:40; Neh. 13:15; Is. 28:4; Joel 1:12; 2:22; Mic. 7:1; Hab. 3:17. See Fig Tree. Grapes—Gen. 40:11; Num. 6:3; 13:23; Deut. 23:24; 24:21; 32:14; Neh. 13:15. Vineyards—Neh. 9:25; Song of Sol. 8:11, 12; Amos 9:14; Lu. 20:10; I Cor. 9:7. See Grape—I Ki. 21:16. Mulberries—II Sam. 5:23, 24; I Chr. 14:14, 15. Olives—Deut. 8:8; 24:20; II Ki. 18:32. Pomegranates—Num. 13:23, 24; 20:5; Deut. 8:8; Song of Sol. 4:13; 6:11; 8:2; Joel 1:12. Precious—Song of Sol. 4:16; 7:13. Raisins—I Sam. 25:18; II Sam. 6:19; 16: 1; I Chr. 16:3; 12:40; Song of Sol. 2:5; Hos. 3:1. Summer fruits—II Sam. 16:1, 2; Is. 16:9; Jer. 40:10, 12; 48:32; Amos 8:1, 2; Mic. 7:1. Sweet fruit—Song of Sol. 2:3; Ju. 9:11.

Figurative.—II Ki. 19:29, 30; Ps. 1:3; 21:10; 72:16; 132:11; Pr. 8:19; Is. 14: 29; 28:4; 57:19; Jer. 6:19; 11:19; 12: 2; 17:8, 10; 21:14; Lam. 2:20; Ez. 19: 12, 14; 36:8, 11; Dan. 4:12, 14, 21; Hos. 9:16; 10:13; 14:8; Joel 2:22; Amos 2:9; 8:1, 2; Mic. 6:7; Mal. 1:12. Known by fruits—Mt. 3:10; 7:17, 18, 19; 13:8, 23, 26. I shall not drink of the fruit of the vine—Mt. 26:29; Mk. 14:25; Lu. 22:18. Yielded no—Mk. 4:7, 8; 11:14; Lu. 3:9; 8:14; 13:6, 7, 9; John 15:2, 4. Yielded much—Mt. 13: 8, 23; Mk. 4:20, 28, 29; 12:2; Lu. 6:43; 8:8; John 12:24; 15:5, 8, 16; Rev.

22:2. Gathereth for eternal life—John 4:36. Bring fruit with patience—Lu. 8:15; Jas. 5:7, 18. Fruit of righteous a tree of life—Pr. 11:30. Fruit worthy of repentance—Mt. 3:8; Lu. 3:8. By fruit ye shall know them—Mt. 7:16, 20; Lu. 6:44. Make tree good, etc.— Mt. 12:33. Every branch, etc.—John 15:2. Fruit unto God—Rom. 7:4. Peaceable fruits—Heb. 12:11.

References.—Fruit-bearing trees—Gen. 1:11–12, 29. Forbidden—Gen. 3:2–3, 6; Lev. 19:10; 23:40; Eccl. 2:5. Jacob made gifts of fruits—Gen. 43:11. Mixed seed forfeits—Deut. 22:9. Fruit denied one as punishment—Deut. 28: 30. Fruit of the ground—Gen. 4:3; Is. 4:2; Jer. 7:20. Fruitful land into a salt desert—Ps. 107:34. Shall shake like Lebanon—Ps. 72:16. Fruit of body for sin of soul—Mic. 6:7. Let there be no fruit from thee—Mt. 21: 19. Season of fruit drew near—Mt. 21:34. Full of good—Jas. 3:17. Trees without—Jude 12. Twelve manner of —Rev. 22:2.

Fruit destroyed as punishment.—Jer. 7: 20; Joel 1:2; Deut. 28:38–39.

Word "fruit" meaning offspring.—Gen. 30:2; Deut. 7:13; Ps. 21:10; 132:11; Lu. 1:42.

First fruits.—See OFFERING.

FRUITFUL. Gen. 26:22; 28:3; 41:52; 26:9; Hos. 13:15. Bough—Gen. 49:22. Branches—Is. 17:6. Exceeding—Gen. 17:6. Field—Is. 10:18; 16:10; 29:17; 32:15, 16; Jer. 4:26; Ez. 17:5. Hill— Is. 5:1. Land—Ps. 107:34. Multiply, And—Gen. 1:22, 28; 8:17; 9:1, 7; 17: 20; 35:11; 48:4; Jer. 23:3. Seasons— Acts 14:17. Trees—Ps. 148:9. Vine— Ps. 128:3; Is. 32:12; Ez. 19:10. Work, In every—Col. 1:10. See CHRISTIAN GRACES.

FRUSTRATE. Ezra 4:5; Job 5:2; Is. 44:25. See VOID, MAKE.

FUEL. Is. 9:5, 19; Ez. 15:4, 6; 21:32. See FIRE, WOOD.

FUGITIVE. All—Ez. 17:21. Betray not —Cain—Gen. 4:12, 14; Is. 16:3. Ephraim, Of—Ju. 12:4. I shall be— Is. 21:14.

FULFIL. All—Mk. 13:4; Lu. 21:22. Counsel—Ps. 20:4. Course—Acts 13: 25. Days—Gen. 25:24; 29:21; Ex. 7:

25; Lev. 12:4, 6; Num. 6:5, 13; II Sam. 1:12; I Chr. 17:11; Ez. 5:2. See PURIFICATION. Forty years—Acts 7: 30. Joy—John 3:29. Law—Mt. 5:17; Rom. 8:4; 13:8, 10; Gal. 5:14. See COVENANTS. Ministry—II Tim. 4:5. Obedience—II Cor. 10:6. Promise— I Ki. 8:15, 24; II Chr. 6:4, 15; Jer. 44:25. Prophecies—See JESUS, PROPH-ECY. Righteousness—Mt. 3:15. Task —Ex. 5:14. Week—Gen. 29:28; Dan. 10:3. See JESUS FULFILLED THE SCRIP-TURES, PROPHECY, WORD OF GOD.

FULL. Abominations—Rev. 17:4. Adul-terers, Of—Is. 23:10. Adultery, Of— II Pet. 2:14. Armor—Ez. 38:4. Bas-kets—Mk. 8:19. Be—Deut. 6:11; 8: 10, 12; 11:15; Phil. 4:12. Birds, Of— Jer. 5:27. Blood, Of—Is. 1:15; 15:9; Ez. 9:9. Bones, Of—Ez. 37:1; Mt. 23: 27. Boys and girls, Of—Zech. 8:5. Bribes, Of—Ps. 26:10. Crimes, Of— Ez. 7:23. Cry, Of thy—Jer. 46:12. Cursing, Of—Ps. 10:7; Rom. 3:14. Days, Of—Gen. 35:29; I Chr. 29:28; Job 42:17; Jer. 6:11. Ears—Gen. 41:7, 22. Eat to the—Ex. 16:3; Lev. 26:5. Envy, Of—Rom. 1:29. Evil, Of—Eccl. 9:3. Extortion, Of—Mt. 23:25. Lu. 11:37. Faith, Of—Acts 6:5. Fatness —Job 36:16. Fury, Of—Dan. 3:19. Garners—Ps. 144:13. Good works, Of —Acts 9:36. Gladness, Of—Acts 2:28. Glory, Of—I Pet. 1:8. Goodness, Of— Rom. 15:14. Grace and truth—John 1:14. Holy Spirit, Of—Lu. 4:1; Acts 3:6; 7:55; 11:24. Hypocrisy and in-iquity, Of—Mt. 23:28. Indignation, Of—Is. 30:27. Joy—John 3:29; 17: 13; 15:11; 16:24; I John 1:4; II John 12. Knowledge, Of—Is. 11:9. Lies— Nah. 3:1. Light, Of—Mt. 6:22; Lu. 11:36. Loving kindness, Of—Ps. 119: 64. Made, Ye are—Col. 2:10. Men and women, Of—Ju. 16:27. Mercy, Of —Jas. 3:17. Not yet—Gen. 15:16. Pity, Of—Jas. 5:11. Poison, Of—Jas. 3:8. Power, Of—Mic. 3:8. Praise, Of —Hab. 3:3. Price—Gen. 23:9. Re-store it in—Lev. 6:5. Reward—II John 8. Riches, Of—I Chr. 29:28; Ps. 104:24. Righteousness, Of—Ps. 48:10. Sheaves, Of—Amos 2:13. Soul—Pr. 27:7. Strength—II Ki. 9:24; Job 21: 23. Trouble, Of—Job 14:1; Ps. 88:3.

Violence—Ps. 74:20; Mic. 6:12. Wickedness, Of—Lev. 19:29. Wisdom—Deut. 34:9; Ez. 28:12. Wrath, Of—Esth. 3:5; Acts 19:28; Rev. 15:7. Years, Of—Gen. 25:8; Lev. 25:30. Youth, Of—Job 20:11.

FULLER. Mk. 9:3. Field—II Ki. 18: 17; Is. 7:3; 36:2. Soap—Mal. 3:2.

FULLGROWN. Among them that are —I Cor. 2:6. Man, Unto a—Eph. 4:13. Men, Is for—Heb. 5:14. Sin, When it is—Jas. 1:15.

FULLY. Assured—Col. 4:12. Followed —Num. 14:24. Jehovah, After—I Ki. 11:6. Preached the gospel—Rom. 15: 19. Set to do evil—Eccl. 8:11. Showed me—Ruth 2:11.

FULNESS. Rom. 11:17. Blessing—Rom. 15:29. Bread, Of—Ez. 16:49. Christ, Of—Eph. 4:13. Dwell—Col. 1: 19; 2:9. Earth of—Deut. 33:16; Ps. 24:1; Is. 34:1; I Cor. 10:26. Faith, Of —Heb. 10:22. Gentiles, Of—Rom. 11: 25. God head, Of—Col. 2:9. Hope, Of —Heb. 6:11. Joy, Of—Ps. 16:11. Land, Of—Ez. 19:7. Received, We all—John 1:16. Sea, Of—I Chr. 16:32; Ps. 96: 11; 97:7. Sufficiency—Job 20:22. Time, Of—Gal. 4:4; Eph. 1:10. Wine press, Of—Num. 18:27. World, Of—Ps. 50:12; 89:11.

FURIOUS. II Ki. 9:20; Dan. 2:12. See ANGER, WRATH.

FURLONG. Lu. 24:13; John 6:19; 11: 18; Rev. 14:20; 21:16.

FURNACE. Three kinds.—Oven for baking bread—Gen. 15:27; Ex. 8:3; Lev. 2:4; 7:9; 11:35; 26:26; Neh. 3: 11; 12:38; Mt. 6:30; Lu. 12:28.
Smelting furnace.—Gen. 19:28; Ex. 9:8, 10; Dan. Ch. 3.
Crucible.—Ps. 12:6; Pr. 17:3; 27:21.
Figurative.—Egypt a furnace—Deut. 4: 20; I Ki. 8:51; Jer. 11:4. Sinai—Ex. 19:18. Affliction—Lam. 5:10. Refine —Is. 31:9; 48:10; Ez. 22:18, 20, 22; Mal. 3:2, 3. To destroy wicked—Mal. 4:1; Mt. 13:42, 50; 9:2; Hos. 7:4, 6, 7; Rev. 1:15.

FURNISH. Deut. 15:14; I Ki. 9:11; Jer. 46:19; II Tim. 3:17. Room—Mk. 14: 15; Lu. 22:12. Table—Pr. 9:2.

FURNITURE. Nah. 2:9. Tabernacle, Of—See TABERNACLE.

FURROW. I Sam. 14:14; Job 31:38; 39: 10; Ps. 65:10; 129:3; Hos. 10:4; 12:11.

FURY. See ANGER.

FUTURE PUNISHMENT. See HELL, JUDGMENT, PUNISHMENT, SIN.

GAAL, gā'al. **Son of Ebed.**—Ju. 9:26.

GAASH, gā'ash. **A hill near which Joshua was buried.**—Josh. 24:30; Ju. 2:9.

GABBAI, găb'bāi. **A Benjamite.**—Neh. 11:8.

GABBATHA, găb'ba-thà. John 19:23.

GABRIEL, gā'bri-el. **Appears to Daniel.** —Dan. 8:16. To Zacharias—Lu. 1:19. To Mary—Lu. 1:26.

GAD, găd. (1) **Son of Jacob.**—Gen. 30: 10, 11; 35:26; 49:19.
(2) **Tribe.** Inheritance was east of Jordan—Num. 32:33. They were to cross Jordan and help subdue the Canaanites, leaving their families on east side—Num. 32:1-27; Josh. 1:12-18; 4:12-14; 22:1-34. Bounds of inheritance—Deut. 22:9; Josh. 13:24, 28; 18: 7; 22:9. Number leaving Egypt, 45,-650—Num. 1:24, 25. Number after forty years in wilderness, 45,000—Num. 26:15-18. Cities built—Num. 32: 34-36. Descendants of—Num. 26:15-18; I Chr. Chs. 2-4; 5:11-17. Encampment—Num. 2:10-14; 10:18-20. Princes—Num. 7:42-47. Stood on Mt. Ebal—Deut. 27:13. Blessing of Moses —Deut. 33:20, 21. Their prowess described—I Chr. 12:8. Make war with, and subdue Hagarites—I Chr. 5:18-22. David appoints rulers over—I Chr. 26:32. Land of Gad battlefield, for long time between Syria and Israel—II Ki. 10:33. Barzillai, one of their loyal, noble men—II Sam. 17:27-29; 19:31-40. Elijah was also a Gileadite —I Ki. 17:1. Strength of, when entering Canaan—Num. 26:18. See ISRAEL.
(3) **A prophet.**—I Sam. 22:5; I Chr. 29: 29. Valley of—II Sam. 24:5.

GADARENES, găd'a-renes. Mt. 8:28.

GADDI, găd'di. **A spy.**—Num. 13:11.

GADDIEL, găd'di-el. **A spy.**—Num. 13:10.

GADI, gā'di. **Father of Menahem.**—II Ki. 15:14, 17.

GADITES, găd'ītes. **Descendants of Gad.**—Deut. 3:12.

GAHAM, gā'ham. Gen. 22:24.

GAHAR, gā'har. Ezra 2:47; Neh. 7:49.

GAI, gā'i. **A place in Philistia.**—I Sam. 17:32.

GAIN. Job 22:3; 27:8; Mic. 9:13; Jas. 4:13. All—Jer. 20:5. Brother, Thy—Mt. 18:15. Brought master's much—Acts 16:16, 19. Christ—Phil. 3:8. Die is, To—Phil. 1:21. Disciples for Christ—I Cor. 19:22. Dishonest—Ez. 22:13, 27. Favor—Acts 24:27. Godliness is way of—I Tim. 6:5, 6. Goeth after—Ez. 33:31. Good standing—I Tim. 3: 13. Greedy of—Pr. 15:27; Is. 56:11; Ez. 22:12. Lack of, No—Pr. 31:11. Life, His—Lu. 17:33. Oppression, Of—Is. 33:15. Pounds—Lu. 19:15. Silver—Pr. 3:14. Talents—Mt. 25:17, 20, 22. Understanding—Pr. 3:14. Unjust—Ex. 18:21. What things were—Phil. 3:7. Whole world—Mt. 16:26; Mk. 8:36; Lu. 9:25.

GAINSAY. Lu. 21:15. Came without—Acts 10:29. Cannot be—Acts 19:36. Convict—Tit. 1:9. Korah, Of—Jude 11. Not—Tit. 2:9. People—Rom. 10: 21.

GAIUS, gā'ius. (1) **One of Paul's companions.**—Acts 19:20.

(2) **One of the two in the Corinthian church whom Paul baptized.**—I Cor. 1:14.

(3) **Paul's host.**—Rom. 16:23. Possibly same as (2).

(4) **The man to whom III John is addressed.**—III John 1.

GALAL, gā'lal. **Two Levites.**—I Chr. 9:15, 16; Neh. 11:17.

GALATIA, ga-lā'tia. **Central region of Asia Minor.**—Acts 16:6; 18:23.

GALATIANS. See OUTLINE STUDIES IN THE BOOKS.

GALBANUM. Ex. 30:34.

GALEED, găl'e-ĕd. Gen. 31:47, 48.

GALILÆANS, găl-ĭ-lē'ans. **Inhabitants of Galilee.**—Acts 2:7.

GALILEE, găl'i-lee. **Country of**—Location.—In district of Naphtali—Josh. 20:7; 21:32; II Ki. 15:29. "Beyond the Jordan"—Is. 9:1; Mt. 4:15. Border of—Lu. 17:11.

Sea of Galilee.—Mt. 4:18; 15:29; Mk. 1:16; 7:31; John 6:1. Called: Lake of Gennesaret—Lu. 5:1. Sea of Chinner-

eth—Num. 34:11. Sea of Tiberias—John 6:1. See SEA.

Cities of.—I Ki. 9:11; I Chr. 6:76; Mt. 2:22; 21:11; Mk. 1:9; Lu. 1:26; John 2:1; 12:21; 21:2.

Country around.—Lu. 8:26.

Inhabitants called Galileans.—Mt. 26: 69; Acts 2:7. Men of—Mk. 6:21; Acts 1:11. Peter accused of being a Galilean—Mk. 14:70. Tetrarch of—Lu. 3:1. Inhabitants conquered by the Syrians—I Ki. 15:20. Cruelly treated by Pilate—Lu. 13:1. Judas of Galilee—Acts 5:37. Under rule of Herod Antipas—Lu. 3:1. Early life and family home of Jesus in Nazareth of Galilee—Lu. 4:16. Headquarters long in Capernaum—Mt. 4:13.

Jesus in Galilee.—Mt. 3:13; 4:12; 21:11; 26:32; 28:7; Mk. 14:28; 15:41; 16:7; John 4:3, 43-45, 54; 7:1, 9, 41, 52. Jesus taught in Galilee—Mt. 4:23, 25; 19:1, 27; Mk. 1:14, 28, 39; Lu. 4:14, 31, 44; 23:5; 24:6. Disciples' abode in Galilee—Mt. 17:22; 28:16.

Followers of Jesus from Galilee.—Mt. 27:55; Mk. 3:7; Lu. 5:17; 23:55; Acts 13:31. Galileans desert Jesus—John 6:52, 60, 66.

Jesus' brethren go to Galilee.—Mt. 28: 10.

Joseph went up from Galilee.—Lu. 2:4.

Jesus passes through Galilee.—Mk. 9:30.

Apostles chosen at.—John 1:43. Beginning of miracles in Galilee—John 2: 11; 4:46, 47.

Churches established in.—Acts 9:31. Preaching in—Acts 10:37.

●Jesus appeared to disciples in Galilee after resurrection.—Mk. 14:28; John 21:1-14; Mt. 28:16.

GALL. Derived from a root—Deut. 29: 18.

Uses of.—For food—Ps. 69:21. Drink—Jer. 8:14; 9:15; 23:15; Mt. 27:34. Punishment—Lam. 3:5, 19; Mt. 27:34.

Figurative.—Amos 6:12; Acts 8:23; Job—Job 16:13. Asps—Job 20:14. Of wicked—Job 20:25. Grapes of—Deut. 32:32.

GALLANT. Is. 33:21.

GALLEY. Is. 33:21.

GALLIM, găl'lim. **A place in Benjamin.**—I Sam. 25:44.

GALLIO, găl'li-o. **Roman proconsul.**—Acts 18:12.

GALLOWS. Esth. 5:14; 6:4; 7:9, 10; 9:13, 25.

GAMALIEL, ga-mā'li-el. (1) **A prince of Manasseh.**—Num. 1:10; 2:20. (2) **Paul's teacher.**—Acts 5:34; 22:3.

GAMBOL. Mal. 4:2. See PLAY.

GAMES. Contend in—II Tim. 2:5. Public—I Cor. 9:24; Phil. 3:14; I Tim. 6: 12; II Tim. 2:5; 4:7; Heb. 12:1. Striveth in the—I Cor. 9:25. See AMUSEMENT.

GAMUL, gā'mul. **A priest.**—I Chr. 24: 17.

GANGRENE. Eat as—II Tim. 2:17.

GAP. Gone up into—Ez. 13:5. Stand in —Ez. 22:30.

GAPE. Substance, For their—Job 5:5. Upon me—Ps. 22:13.

GARDEN. Made by river-side—Num. 24:6. God planted a garden eastward —Gen. 2:8. Plain of Jordan like—Gen. 13:10. Zion likened to—Is. 51:3.

Lodges erected in.—Is. 1:8.

Gardens used for. — Entertainment — Song of Sol. 5:1. Retirement—John 18:1. Burial places—II Ki. 21:18, 26; John 19:41. Idolatrous worship—Is. 1:29; 65:3. Jews ordered to plant in Babylon—Jer. 29:5, 28. Peter accused of being in—John 18:26.

Israel to be as well-watered garden.—Is. 58:11; Jer. 31:12.

Wicked likened to.—Is. 1:30. See EDEN.

GAREB, gā'rĕb. II Sam. 23:38.

GARLAND. Ashes, For—Is. 61:3. Brought—Acts 14:13. Decked with a —Is. 61:10.

GARLIC. See FOOD.

GARMENTS. See CLOTHING.

GARMITE. I Chr. 4:19.

GARNER. Ps. 114:13; Is. 62:9; Joel 1: 17; Mt. 3:12; Lu. 3:11. See STOREHOUSE.

GARNISH. House—II Chr. 3:6; Mt. 12:44; Lu. 11:25. Sepulchres—Mt. 23: 29. Spirit—Job 26:13. See ADORN.

GARRISON. David, Of—II Sam. 8:6, 14; I Chr. 18:6, 13; II Chr. 17:2. Philistines, Of—I Sam. 10:5; 13:3, 4, 23; 14:1–15; I Chr. 11:16. See FORTIFICATION.

GASHMU, găsh'mu. Neh. 6:6.

GASP. Is. 42:14; Jer. 4:31.

GATAM, gā'tam. **Descendant of Esau—Son of Eliphaz**—Gen. 36:11, 16; I Chr. 1:36.

GATES: Made of.—Brass—Ps. 107:16; Is. 45:2. Iron—Acts 12:10.

Fastened with bars of iron.—See above.

Belong to.—Cities—I Ki. 17:10; Neh. 1:3; 2:3. Houses—Lu. 16:20; Acts 12: 14. Palaces—Esth. 5:13. Prisons—Acts 12:10. Camps—Ex. 32:26. Rivers —Nah. 2:6.

Put to following uses: For assembling at—Gen. 34:20; Jer. 17:19; Pr. 1:21. For sitting or standing at—Gen. 19:1; 23:10; I Sam. 4:18; Ps. 69:12; Pr. 8:3; Jer. 17:19; Lam. 5:14. For court of justice—Deut. 16:18; 17:5; 21:19; 22: 15; Josh. 20:4; Ruth 4:1; II Sam. 15: 2; Pr. 22:22; Zech. 8:16. Selling produce at—II Ki. 7:1, 18. Also land—Gen. 23:10, 16. For religious services —Neh. 8; Acts 14:13. For assembling of kings—I Ki. 22:10; II Chr. 18:9; Jer. 38:7. Violators of law punished outside of—Heb. 13:12. Exposure of bodies at—II Ki. 10:8. Review of troops at—II Sam. 18:4.

Battering rams used to destroy.—Ez. 21:22.

Sin-offering burned without.—Lev. 4: 12; Heb. 13:11–13.

Gates of the temple called: Gates of Zion—Lam. 1:4. Of righteousness—Ps. 118:19. Of the Lord—Ps. 118:20.

Of Jerusalem.—Fish—II Chr. 33:14; Neh. 3:3. Sheep—Neh. 3:1; John 5:2. Valley—Neh. 2:13; 3:13. Water—Neh. 3:26. Horse—Neh. 3:28; II Chr. 23:15. Old—Neh. 3:6. Corner—II Chr. 26:9. Dung—Neh. 3:14; 12:31. Fountain—Neh. 3:15. Of Benjamin—Jer. 20:2; 37:13. Of Hammiphkad—Neh. 3:31. Of Ephraim—Neh. 12:39.

Special references.—Gates of Sheol—Is. 38:10. Gates of Hades—Mt. 16:18. Wide and narrow—Mt. 7:13–14. Of Heaven—Gen. 28:17. Of Zion—Ps. 24: 7; Is. 60:11. Of shadow of death—Job 38:17. Twelve gates of Holy City —Rev. 21:12–13. Of Zion called praise —Is. 60:18.

GATH, găth. **One of the five chief cities of the Philistines.**—Josh. 13:3; I Sam. 6:17; Amos 6:2; Mic. 1:10. King of, Achish—I Ki. 2:39. Shimei seeks his servants at—I Ki. 2:40, 41. Home of Goliath—I Sam. 17:4, 23; II Sam. 21: 20, 22; I Chr. 20:5-8. Anakim left in Gath—Josh. 11:22. Restored to Israel —I Sam. 7:14. Ark of covenant taken to—I Sam. 5:8.

Strifes.—Wounded Philistines fall by the way to—I Sam. 17:52. David takes refuge with king of Gath—I Sam. 21:10, 15; 27:2-7. A band of Gittites join David—II Sam. 15:18-22. Taken by Hazael—II Ki. 12:17. Recovered by Jehoash—II Ki. 13:25. Besieged by Uzziah—II Chr. 36:6. A Psalm of David when the Philistines took him in Gath—Ps. 56.

GATH-HEPHER, găth-hē'pher. City of Zebulun—Josh. 19:13.

Birthplace of Jonah.—II Ki. 14:25.

GATH-RIMMON, găth-rĭm'mon. **A Levitical city.**—Josh. 19:45; 21:24, 25.

GATHER. Apostles—Mk. 6:30; Lu. 24: 33; Acts 20:7. Bones—II Sam. 21:13. Fathers, To his—Ju. 2:10; II Chr. 34: 28; Job 27:19. Flocks—See FLOCKS. Fruit—See FRUIT. Grain—See HARVEST. Israel, Shall be—Jer. 23:3; 32: 37; Ez. 22:19; 28:25; 38:8, 12, 13; 39: 27, 28; Hos. 1:11; Mt. 23:37; Lu. 13: 34. Jerusalem, At—II Chr. 12:5; 15: 10; 3:3. Manna—See MANNA. Multitude—Mt. 13:2; Mk. 4:1; 5:21; Lu. 8:4; 11:29; Acts 15:30. People, To his —Gen. 25:8, 17; 35:29; 49:29, 33; Num. 20:24, 26; 27:13; 31:2; Deut. 32:50. Rebellion, In—Num. 14:35; 16: 3, 11; 19:42; 20:2; Job 16:10; Ps. 35: 15. Substance—Gen. 12:5. Two or three in my name—Mt. 18:20. Worship, For—Ex. 4:29; 32:1; 35:1; Lev. 8:4; Num. 10:3, 7; Josh. 24:1; Ju. 20: 1; II Chr. 23:2; 24:5; 29:4, 15; 30:3; 34:29; Ezra 3:1; Neh. 8:1, 13; 12:28; Ps. 102:22; Acts 12:12; 14:27; 20:7; I Cor. 5:4.

GAVE. See GIFT, GIVING, LIBERALITY, PRESENTS.

GAZA, gā'zȧ. Gen. 10:19; Josh. 10:41; Ju. 6:4. Anakim left in—Josh. 11:22. Inheritance of Judah—Josh. 15:47; Ju. 1:18. Sampson went to—Ju. 16:1, 21. Tumors for—I Sam. 6:17. Smote Philistines in—II Ki. 18:8. Pharaoh smote—Jer. 47:1. Baldness is come upon—Jer. 47:5. For three transgres-

sions of—Amos 1:6, 7. Gaza shall be sore pained—Zech. 9:5. Way toward —Acts 8:26.

GAZE. Ex. 19:21; Job 30:20.

GAZELLE. Deut. 12:15.

GAZEZ, gā'zez. **Son of Caleb.**—I Chr. 2:46.

GAZITES, gā'zites. **Inhabitants of Gaza.** Josh. 13:3; Ju. 16:2.

GAZZAM, găz'zam. Ezra 2:48; Neh. 7:51.

GEAR. Acts 27:17.

GEBA, gē'bȧ. City of Benjamin—Josh. 18:24; 21:17; I Chr. 6:60. Defiled high places of—II Ki. 23:8. Rebuilt by Asa —I Ki. 15:22. Inhabitants of—I Chr. 8:6; Ez. 2:26. Prophecy concerning— Zech. 14:10. See GIBEAH.

GEBAL, gē'bal. Ps. 83:7; Ez. 27:9.

GEBALITES. I Ki. 5:18.

GEBIM, gē'bim. Is. 10:31.

GECKO. Lev. 11:30.

GEDALIAH, gĕd-a-lī'ah. (1) **Son of Ahikam.**—II Ki. 25:22; Jer. 41:18.
(2) **Son of Hezekiah, grandfather of Zephaniah.**—Zeph. 1:1.
(3) **Son of Jeduthun.**—I Chr. 25:3, 9.
(4) **Son of Pashhur.**—Jer. 38:1.
(5) **A priest who married a foreign wife.** —Ezra 10:18.

GEDER, gē'der. Josh. 12:13.

GEDERAH, gē-dē'rah. **A town in Judah.**—Josh. 15:36; I Chr. 4:23.

GEDERATHITE, gĕd'e-rath-ite. **Inhabitant of Gederah.**—I Chr. 12:4.

GEDERITE, gē'der-ite. **Inhabitant of Geder.**—I Chr. 27:28.

GEDEROTH, gē-dē'rŏth. Josh. 15:41.

GEDEROTHAIM, gĕd'e-ro-thā'im. Josh. 15:36.

GEDOR, gē'dôr. (1) **A Benjamite.**—I Chr. 8:31; 9:37.
(2) I Chr. 4:4, 18.
(3) **The residence of Jehoram.**—I Chr. 12:7.
(4) **A town in Judah.**—Josh. 15:58.
(5) See GERAR.

GEHAZI, ge-hā'zī. **Elisha's servant.**— II Ki. 4:31; 8:4.

GELILOTH, gĕl'i-lŏth. Josh. 18:17.

GEMALLI, gē-măl'lī. One of the spies. —Num. 13:12.

GEMARIAH, gĕm'a-rī'ah. (1) **Son of Hilkiah.**—Gen. 29:3.

(2) **Son of Shaphan, father of Michaiah.**
—Jer. 36:10–12, 25.

GENDER. Lev. 15:19; Job 38:29. Frost
—Job 38:29. Stripes—II Tim. 2:23.

GENEALOGIES. The Hebrews were a covenant people whose religion and belongings led them to trace their descent from Abraham. To them belonged the Messianic hope—Gen. 12:3. A system of land tenure—Num. 36:7; I Ki. 21:3. Of priesthood and kingship bound up with family succession —Ex. 29:9; Ps. 89:3, 4. These begot a concern for genealogies, which shows itself by a recurring formula (''these are the generations'') running throughout Genesis—Gen. 2:4; 5:1; 6:9; 10:1; 11:10; 11:27; 25:12, 19; 36:1. The genealogy of kings was viewed as of the first importance; *e. g.*, David—I Chr. Ch. 24. Genealogy of priests— I Chr. 9:1; II Chr. 31:16–19; Neh. 12: 22, 23. Genealogies satisfied interest regarding the populating of the earth —Gen. Ch. 5; I Chr. 1:1. The repopulating after flood—Gen. Ch. 10; I Chr. Ch. 1. The twelve tribes—I Chr. Chs. 2–5. Genealogies are sometimes regressive—I Chr. 6:33–43; Ezra 7: 1–5. And sometimes progressive— Ruth—4:18–22; I Chr. Ch. 3. Females are named in them when something remarkable occurs, or a land title is involved—Gen. 11:29; 22:23; 35:23– 26; Ex. 6:23; Num. 26:33; I Chr. 2:4, 16.

GENEALOGIES OF JESUS.

1. The genealogy given in Matthew is the genealogy of Joseph, the reputed father of Jesus, his father in the eyes of the law. The genealogy given in Luke is the genealogy of Mary, the mother of Jesus, and is the human genealogy of Jesus Christ in actual fact. The Gospel of Matthew was written for Jews. All through it Joseph is prominent, Mary is scarcely mentioned. In Luke, on the other hand, Mary is the chief personage in the whole account of the Saviour's conception and birth. Joseph is brought in only incidentally and because he was Mary's husband. In all of this, of course, there is a deep significance.

2. In Matthew, Jesus appears as the Messiah. In Luke, He appears as ''the Son of Man,'' our Brother and Redeemer, who belongs to the whole race and claims kindred with all kinds and conditions of men. So in Matthew, the genealogy descends from Abraham to Joseph and Jesus, because all the predictions and promises touching the Messiah are fulfilled in Him. But in Luke the genealogy ascends from Jesus to Adam, because the genealogy is being traced back to the head of the whole race, and shows the relation of the Second Adam to the First.

3. Joseph's line is the strictly royal line from David to Joseph. In Luke, though the line of descent is from David, it is not the royal line. In this Jesus is descended from David through Nathan, David's son indeed, but not in the royal line, and the list follows a line quite distinct from the royal line.

4. The Messiah, according to prediction, was to be the actual son of David according to the flesh (II Sam. 7:12– 19; Ps. 89:3, 4, 34–37; 132:11; Acts 2: 30; 13:22, 23; Rom. 1:3; II Tim. 2:8). These prophecies are fulfilled by Jesus being the Son of Mary, who was a lineal descendant of David, though not in the royal line. Joseph, who was of the royal line, was not his father according to the flesh, but was his father in the eyes of the law.

5. Mary was a descendant of David through her father, Heli. It is true that Luke 2:23 says that Joseph was the son of Heli. The simple explanation of this is that, Mary being a woman, her name according to Jewish usage could not come into the genealogy, males alone forming the line, so Joseph's name is introduced in the place of Mary's; he being Mary's husband, Heli was his father-in-law, and so Joseph is called the son of Heli, and the line thus completed. While Joseph was son-in-law of Heli, according to the flesh he was in actual fact the son of Jacob (Mt. 1:16).

6. Two genealogies are absolutely necessary to trace the lineage of our Lord and Saviour Jesus Christ, the one the royal and legal, the other the natural and literal, and these two genealogies we find, the legal and royal in Matthew's gospel, the gospel of law and kingship; the natural and literal in Luke's, the gospel of humanity.

7. We are told in Jer. 22:30 any descendant of Jeconiah could not come to the throne of David, and Joseph was of this line, and while Joseph's genealogy furnishes the royal line for Jesus, his son before the·law, nevertheless Jeremiah's prediction is fulfilled to the very letter, for Jesus, strictly speaking, was not Joseph's descendant and therefore was not of the seed of Jeconiah. If Jesus had been the son of Joseph in reality He could not have come to the throne, but he is Mary's son through Nathan, and can come to the throne legally by her marrying Joseph and so clearing His way legally to it.

As we study these two genealogies of Jesus carefully and read them in the light of Old Testament prediction, we find that, so far from constituting a reason for doubting the accuracy of the Bible, they are rather a confirmation of the minutest accuracy of that book. It is amazing how one part of the Bible fits into another part when we study it thus minutely. We need no longer stumble over the fact of there being two genealogies, but discover and rejoice in the deep meaning in the fact that there are two genealogies.—From R. A. Torrey's "Difficulties in the Bible.'' [Copyright, 1907, by Fleming H. Revell Company. Used by permission.]

GENERATION. Ps. 24:6; 145:4. All, To—Ps. 10:6; 79:13. Blessed, Shall call me—Lu. 1:48. Clean, Shall be—Num. 9:10. Crooked—Deut. 32:5; Acts 2:40. Dwelling place in all—Ps. 90:1. From, To—Is. 34:10. Goeth, One—Eccl. 1:4. Other, In—Eph. 3:5. Perverse—Phil. 2:15. Pure—Pr. 30:12. Rebellious—Ps. 78:8. Remembered in all—Ps. 45:17. Righteous, Of—Ps.

14:5. Upright, Of—Ps. 112:2. See GENEALOGIES.

GENESIS. See OUTLINE STUDIES IN THE BOOKS.

GENNESARET, gĕn-nĕs'ă-rĕt. Mt. 14: 34; Mk. 6:53; Lu. 5:1. See GALILEE.

GENTILES: Nations foreign to the Jews.—Gen. 10:2-10. In part, offshoots of Abrahamic stock; Moabites and Ammonites—Gen. 14:36-38. Ishmaelites—Gen. 25:12-16; I Chr. 1:28-31. Midianites—Gen. 25:1-4. Edomites—Gen. 36:1-28; I Chr. 1:35-42.

Called.—Uncircumcised—I Sam. 14:6; Rom. 2:26, 27; 3:30; 4:9-12. Nations—Ps. 2:1; 9:20; Is. 9:1. Gentiles—Is. 49:6; Mal. 1:11; Mt. 5:47; 10:5; 12: 21; 18:17; Acts 9:15; 13:46; 14:27; 18:6; Rom. 11:11; II Cor. 11:26; Gal. 3:8; I Tim. 2:7. Peoples—Ps. 96: 3-7. Foreigners—Is. 56:3; 60:10.

Prophecies concerning.—Abrahamic promise—Gen. 12:3; 22:18; 26:4; 28: 14. Jacob's prophecy—Gen. 49:10. Messianic prophecy—Ps. 2:7, 8. Davidic—Ps. 22:27, 28; 46:10; 66:4; 86: 9; 102:15. Isaiah—Is. 2:2-4; 9:1, 2; 54:1, 3; 56:3-8; 60:1-14. Jeremiah—Jer. 3:17; 4:2; 16:19, 20. Daniel—Dan. 2:44; 7:14. Hosea—Hos. 2:23; Joel 2:28-32; Mic. 4:1-5; Zech. 2:11. See SALVATION.

New Testament prophecies.—Mt. 4:12-17; 8:11; 12:17-21; Lu. 13:29, 30; John 10:16; Acts 9:15. Taking away of middle wall—Eph. 2:11-22; Col. 1:18-23; 2:13-15; 3:9-11; Gal. 3:23-29.

Conversion of.—Acts 8:5-13, 26-40; 10: 44-48; 11:1-18; 13:46-49; 15:7-20; 16:26-34; 17:32-34; 18:5-8; 20:18-21; 26:16-18; 28:25-28; Rom. 9:22-26; 11: 12-20; 15:8-12; Gal. 1:15-17; Eph. 3: 1-11; I Tim. 3:16.

Gentiles described as: Ignorant of God—Rom. 1:21; I Thess. 4:5. Refusing to know God—Rom. 1:28. Without the law—Rom. 2:14. Idolatrous—Rom. 1:23-25; I Cor. 12:2. Superstitious—Deut. 18:14.

GENTLENESS. See CHRISTIAN GRACES.

GENUBATH, gĕ-nū'băth. **Son of Hadad the Edomite.**—I Ki. 11:20.

GERA, gē'rä. (1) **Son of Benjamin.**—Gen. 46:21. Descendants of: Ehud, son of Gera—Ju. 3:15. Shimei, son

of Gera—II Sam. 16:5; 19:16, 18; I
Ki. 2:8.

(2) **Son of Belah.**—I Chr. 8:3, 5, 7.

GERAR, gē'rär. **A city of Gaza.**—Gen.
10:19; 20:1, 2; 26:1, 6, 17, 20, 26; II
Chr. 14:13, 14.

GERASENES, gēr'ā-sēnes. Mk. 5:1. See
GADARENES.

GERIZIM, gēr'i-zim. Mount of Blessing—Deut. 11:29; 27:12; Josh. 8:33;
Ju. 9:7.

GERSHOM, GERSHON, gēr'shŏm. (1)
Son of Moses.—Ex. 2:22; 18:3; I Chr.
23:15, 16; 26:24.

(2) **Called Gershon also.**—**Son of Levi.**
—Gen. 46:11; Ex. 6:16, 17; Num. 3:
17-25; 4:22-38; 4:22, 28, 38; 7:7; 10:
17; 26:57; Josh. 21:6; I Chr. 6:1, 16,
17, 20, 43, 62, 71; 15:7; 23:6.

(3) **A descendant of Phinehas.**—Ezra
8:2.

(4) **Father of Jonathan.**—Ju. 18:30.

GERSHONITES, gēr'shon-ītes. **Descendants of the son of Levi.**—Num. 3:21-
24; 4:24, 27; 26:5-7; Josh. 21:33; I
Chr. 23:7; 26:21; 29:8; II Chr. 29:12.

GESHAN, gē'shan. **A man of Judah.**—
I Chr. 2:47.

GESHEM, gē'shem. **An Arabian who
opposed Nehemiah.**—Neh. 2:9.

GESHUR, gē'shur. **A kingdom in Bashan.**—II Sam. 3:3; 13:37, 38; 14:23,
32; 15:8; I Chr. 2:23; 3:2.

GESHURITES, gĕsh'ū-rītes. **Inhabitants of Geshur.**—Deut. 3:14; Josh. 12:
5; 13:2, 11, 13; I Sam. 27:8.

GET. Ps. 144:22; Pr. 4:7; Mt. 4:10;
Lu. 18:12. Back—Lev. 25:28. Be-
hind me, Satan—Mt. 16:23; Mk. 8:33.
Fruits of increase—Ps. 107:37. Gain
—Hab. 2:9; Ez. 22:27. Gold—Mt.
10:9. See GAIN. Grain—Neh. 5:3.
Heart of wisdom—Ps. 90:12. Honor
—Ex. 14:17, 18. Knowledge—Pr. 18:
15. See KNOWLEDGE. Name, David—
II Sam. 8:13. Renown—Dan. 9:15.
Riches—Jer. 17:11. See WEALTH.
Treasures, Of—Pr. 21:6. Understand-
ing—Pr. 3:13; 4:5; 15:32; 16:16. See
WISDOM. Wealth—Deut. 8:17, 18.
Wisdom—Pr. 4:5, 7; 16:16; 19:8; Eccl.
1:16.

GETHER, gē-ther. **A son of Aram.**—
Gen. 10:23; I Chr. 1:17.

GETHSEMANE, gĕth-sĕm'a-ne. **The
garden where Jesus was in agony.**—
Mt. 26:36; Mk. 14:32.

GEUEL, ge-ū'el. **A spy.**—Num. 13:15.

GEZER, gē'zer. **An ancient city of Canaan.**—Josh. 10:33; 12:12; 16:3, 10;
21:21; Ju. 1:29; I Ki. 9:15-17; I Chr.
6:67; 7:28; 20:4.

GHOST. Gave up—Gen. 25:8, 17; 35:
29; 49:33; Job 3:11; 10:18; 13:19;
14:10; Lam. 1:19; Mk. 15:37, 39; Lu.
23:46; Acts 5:5, 10; 12:23. It is a—
Mt. 14:26. See HOLY SPIRIT.

GIAH, gī'ah. **A place in Benjamin.**—
II Sam. 2:24.

GIANTS. Mentioned: Ishbi-benob—II
Sam. 21:16. One with six fingers on
each hand—II Sam. 21:20; I Chr. 20:6.
Sippai—I Chr. 20:4. Og, king of
Bashan—Deut. 3:11, 13; Josh. 12:4;
13:12. Sons of—II Sam. 21:22. David kills—I Chr. 20:8; I Sam. 17:49.
Goliath—I Sam. Ch. 17. Called—
Nephilim—Gen. 6:4; Num. 13:33. Rephaim—Gen. 14:5; 15:20; Deut. 2:11,
20; II Sam. 23:13; Josh. 15:8; 17:15;
18:16. Figurative—Job 16:14.

GIBBAR, gĭb'bar. **One of those who returned with Zerubbabel.**—Ezra 2:20.

GIBBETHON, gĭb'be-thŏn. **A town in
Dan.**—Josh. 19:14; 21:23; I Ki. 15:21;
16:15, 17.

GIBEA, gĭb'e-a. **A descendant of Ju-
dah(?).**—I Chr. 2:49.

GIBEAH, gĭb'e-ah. **A city in Judah.**—
Saul's residence at—I Sam. 10:26;
15:34; 22:1, 6. Saul's sons hanged at
—II Sam. 21:6. Garrison of Philistines at—I Sam. 13:3. Philistines
smitten at—I Sam. 14:1-52. Abinadab's house in, and ark in—I Sam.
7:1; II Sam. 21:6. Destroyed by Israelites—Ju. 19:12-30; 20:1-48; Hos.
9:9; 10:9.

GIBEATHITE, gĭb'e-ath-ite. **An inhabitant of Gibeon.**—I Chr. 12:3.

GIBEON, gĭb'e-on. **A city of the Hivites where Jehovah triumphed
through David.**—(Geba) II Sam. 5:
25; I Chr. 14:16. Residence of: Han-
niah—Jer. 28:1. Jeiel—I Chr. 8:29;
9:35. Valley of—Is. 28:21.
Inhabitants of.—Josh. 9:3; 11:19.
Joshua smote Amorite king—Josh.
10:10, 12, 42. Civil war after Saul's

228

death—II Sam. Ch. 2; 5:25; I Chr. 14: 16. Joab slew Amasa—II Sam. 20:8, 10. Saul's descendants put to death at —II Sam. 21:1–9. Was appointed a priestly city—Josh. 21:17. Solomon offered his first sacrifice—I Ki. 3:4; 9:2. Tabernacle erected at—I Chr. 16:39; 21:29; II Chr. 1:3, 13. Inhabitants helped to rebuild Jerusalem— Neh. 3:7. Cities of children of Israel —Josh. 9:17. Of Benjamin—Josh. 18: 25. Abner and Joab meet at pool of —II Sam. 2:12, 13. Abner slays Asahel—II Sam. 2:12–24; 3:30. Inhabitants of, made peace with Israel— Josh. 10:1. Ninety and five returned from Babylon—Neh. 7:25. Battlefield —Jer. 41:12, 16.

GIDDALTI, gid-dăl'ti. **A Kohathite.—** I Chr. 25:4, 29.

GIDDEL, gĭd'del. (1) **Ancestor of some who returned with Zerubbabel.**—Ezra 2:47; Neh. 7:49. **Ancestral head of some of Solomon's servants.**—Ezra 2:56; Neh. 7:58.

GIDEON, gĭd'e-on. Heb. *Cutter down.* Called also Jerubbaal—Ju. 6:32. The son of Joash—Ju. 6:11, 19. He early in life obeys Jehovah—Ju. 6:25–29. Is made the messenger of Jehovah— Ju. 6:14–24. Baal worshippers seek to kill Gideon—Ju. 6:28. Gideon obtains certainty through a fleece—Ju. 6:36– 40. Being thus assured of God, he summons an army—Ju. 7:1–2. Thirty-two thousand men reduced to 300—Ju. 7:3–8. The Midianites delivered into his hand—Ju. 7:15–25. Ephraim angry at being slighted—Ju. 8:1–3. Succoth refuses food to the army and is punished—Ju. 8:13–21. Refuses to be made a king—Ju. 8:22. Gideon's one mistake in the matter of the Ephod— Ju. 8:24–27. The land rested forty years in Gideon's time—(v. 28). Gideon had seventy sons—Ju. 8:30. Dies in a good old age—Ju. 8:32.

GIDEONI, gĭd-e-ō'nī. **Father of Abidan.** —Num. 1:11; 2:22; 7:60, 65; 10:24.

GIDOM, gī'dŏm. Ju. 20:45.

GIER-EAGLE. Lev. 11:18; Deut. 14:17.

GIFT. Best—I Cor. 12:31. Bestowed on us—II Cor. 1:11. Christ, Of— Eph. 4:7. Desire—Phil. 4:17. Diversities of—I Cor. 12:4. Tree—Rom. 5:

18; 6:23. God, Of—Eccl. 3:13; 5:19; John 4:10; Acts 8:20; Rom. 6:23; 11: 29; I Cor. 7:7; Eph. 2:8; II Tim. 1:6. Healing, Of—I Cor. 12:9, 28,30. Heavenly—Heb. 6:4. Men, Unto—Eph. 4:8. Neglect not—I Tim. 4:14. See TALENTS. Perfect, Every — Jas. 1:17. Prophecy, Of—I Cor. 13:2. See PROPHECY. Sacrifices, And—Heb. 5:1; 8:3, 4; 9:9. See OFFERINGS, SACRIFICE. Tongues, Of—See TONGUE. Unspeakable—II Cor. 9:15. See PRESENTS, GIVING, HOLY SPIRIT, LIBERALITY, JESUS TEACHING.

GIHON, gī'hōn. (1) **A river in the Garden of Eden.**—Gen. 2:13.

(2) **A place near Jerusalem.**—I Ki. 1:33, 38, 45; II Chr. 32:30; 33:14.

GILALAI, gĭl'a-lāi. **A priest.** — Neh. 12:36.

GILBOA, gil-bō'a. **A district of Manasseh, where Saul was slain.**—I Sam. 28: 4; II Sam. 21:2.

GILEAD, gĭl'e-ad. (1) **A hard, rocky region.**—For a description of its boundary, see Deut. 3:12–17. Although largely mountainous, it formed a broad tableland on which grew rich pasturage—Num. 32:1–5.

Its aromatic spices and balm were exported to Egypt.—Gen. 37:25; Jer. 8:22.

It was the retreat of David when pursued by Absalom.—II Sam. 17: 22–29.

Ish-bosheth was made king of Gilead by Abner.—II Sam. 2:8–9.

From this region, Elijah sprang.—I Ki. 17:1.

Being a border land, it was exposed to marauders.—Josh. 17:1, 5–7; I Ki. 22:3–6.

Jesus twice withdrew to this country.— Mt. 4:1; Mk. 1:12; Lu. 4:1–2; John 10:39–40. See RAMOTH-GILEAD.

(2) **Mount.**—Ju. 7:3.

(3) **Father of Jephthah.**—Ju. 11:1, 2.

(4) **A man of Gad.**—I Chr. 5:14.

(5) **A grandson of Manasseh.**—Num. 26: 29, 30; 27:1; 36:1; Josh. 17:1, 3; I Chr. 2:21, 23; 7:14, 17.

GILEADITE, gĭl'e-ad-ite. **Inhabitant of Gilead.**—Num. 26:29; Ju. 10:3; 11:1, 40; 12:5, 7; II Sam. 17:27; 19:31; I

Ki. 2:7; II Ki. 15:25; Ezra 2:61; Neh. 7:63.

GILGAL, gĭl′găl. (1) **A district and town west of the Jordan.**—Deut. 11: 30. So called—Josh. 5:9. First encampment of Israel — Josh. 4:19. Twelve stones set up in—Josh. 4:20. Passover kept—Josh. 5:10. Headquarters of Joshua—Josh. 9:6; 10:6, 43; 14:6. Angel of Jehovah came up from —Ju. 2:1. Events connected with: Samuel judge of—I Sam. 7:16. Saul goes to—I Sam. 10:8; 15:12. Is made king—I Sam. 11:14, 15. The loss of his kingdom predicted—I Sam. 13:4-15. Made sacrifice in—I Sam. 15:21. Samuel slays Agag—I Sam. 15:33. David received by Judah—II Sam. 19: 15, 40. Elijah goes with Elisha from —II Ki. 2:1. Elisha's miracle at— II Ki. 4:38. Idolatry at—Ju. 3:19; Hos. 4:15; 9:15; 12:11; Amos 4:4; 5:5; Mic. 6:5.

(2) **A city.**—Josh. 12:23.

(3) **A city near Joppa.**—Josh. 9:6; 10:6, 7, 9, 15, 43.

(4) **A place near Gerizim where Elijah and Elisha lived.**—II Ki. 2:1; 4:38.

GILOH, gī′loh. **A town in Judah.**—Josh. 15:21; II Sam. 15:12.

GILONITE. An inhabitant of Giloh.— II Sam. 15:12; 23:34.

GIMZO, gĭm′zo. **A city in northern Judah.**—II Chr. 28:18.

GIN. Job 18:9; Ps. 140:5; 141:9; Is. 8: 14. See SNARE.

GINATH, gī′nath. **Father of Tibni.**—I Ki. 16:21, 22.

GINNETHOI, gĭn′ne-thōi. **One who assisted Nehemiah in sealing the covenant.**—Neh. 10:6; 12:4, 16.

GIRD. Is. 45:5; Lu. 12:37; John 13:4, 5; 21:18; Acts 12:8. Gladness, With— Ps. 30:11. Gold, With—Dan. 10:5. Humanity, With—I Pet. 5:5. Ephod, With—I Sam. 2:18; II Sam. 6:14. Fine linen, With—Ez. 16:10. Joy, With—Ps. 65:12. Loins—Ex. 12:11; II Ki. 18:46; 4:29; 9:1; Job 38:3. Sackcloth, With—II Sam. 3:31; I Ki. 20:32; Is. 15:3; 32:11; Ju. 4:8; 6:26; 49:3; Lam. 2:10; Ez. 7:18; 27:31; Joel 1:8, 13. Strength, With—I Sam. 2:4; II Sam. 22:40; Ps. 18:39; 65:6; 93:1. Sword on—Ju. 3:16; I Sam. 17:39;

25:13; II Sam. 20:8; 21:16; Neh. 4:18; Ps. 45:3. Fruit, With—Eph. 6:14. Weapon—Deut. 1:41. See GIRDLE.

GIRDLE. Ex. 28:4; II Sam. 18:11; Job 12:18; Ps. 109:19. Blood on—I Ki. 2: 5. Delivereth to merchant—Pr. 31:24. Gave David—I Sam. 18:4. Gird with —Ex. 29:9; Lev. 8:7, 13; 16:4; Ps. 109:19. Golden—Rev. 1:13; 15:6. Leathern—II Ki. 1:8; Mt. 3:4; Mk. 1:6. Loins, Of—II Sam. 20:8; Is. 5: 27; 11:5; Ez. 23:15. Linen—Jer. 13:1. Make—Ex. 28:39. Paul's—Acts 2:11. Profitable for nothing—Jer. 13:10. Rope instead of a—Is. 3:24. Strengthen with—Is. 22:21. Take—Jer. 13:4, 67. Twined linen, Of—Ex. 39:29.

GIRGASHITE, gĭr′ga-shite. **A Canaanite tribe.**—Gen. 10:16; 15:21; Deut. 7:1; Josh. 3:10; 24:11; I Chr. 1:14; Neh. 9:8.

GIRL. Joel 3:3; Zech. 8:5. See CHILDREN, HANDMAID.

GIRZITES, gĭr′zites. I Sam. 27:12.

GISHPA, gĭsh′pa. **An overseer of the Nethinim.**—Neh. 11:21.

GITTAIM, gĭt′ta-im. (1) **A place of refuge.**—II Sam. 4:3.

(2) **A place near Gath.**—Neh. 11:33.

GITTITES, gĭt′tites. **Inhabitants of Gath.**—Josh. 13:3; II Sam. 6:10, 11; 15:18, 19, 22; 18:2; 21:19; I Chr. 13: 13; 20:5.

GITTITH, gĭt′tith. Ps. 8 title; 81 title; 84 title. See MUSIC.

GIVE. Account—Mt. 12:36. See ACCOUNT. Alms—See ALMSGIVING. Asketh, To him—Mt. 5:42; 6:30. See LIBERALITY, PRAYER. Authority—See AUTHORITY. Bread, Daily—Mt. 6:11; Lu. 11:3. See BREAD. Desires—Ps. 37:4. Dogs, To—Mt. 7:6. Eat, To—Mt. 25: 35, 42. See ALMSGIVING, EAT, FOOD. Exchange for his soul, In — Mt. 16:26; Mk. 8:37. Freely—Mt. 10: 8. See LIBERALITY. Gifts—See GIFTS, HOLY SPIRIT. Heart—Pr. 23:26. See HEART. Hire—Mt. 20:8. See SERVANTS. Holy Spirit—See HOLY SPIRIT. Keys of the kingdom—Mt. 16:19. Kiss, No —Lu. 7:45. Know, To—Mt. 13:11; Mk. 4:11; Lu. 1:77; 8:10. See KNOWLEDGE. Life—Mt. 20:28; Mk. 10:45. See JESUS, LIFE, SALVATION THROUGH JESUS. No man gave—Lu. 15:16. Poor,

To—Mt. 19:21; Mk. 10:21. See ALMS-GIVING, LIBERALITY, POOR. Recompense —Is. 28:12. See RECOMPENSE, REWARD. Rest—Is. 28:12; Mt. 11:28. See REST. Sign—See SIGNS and WONDERS. Son, Only begotten—See GOD, LOVE OF, JESUS, SALVATION THROUGH JESUS CHRIST. Thanks—See THANKSGIVING. Tribute —See TRIBUTE. Up—See DELIVER. Way —Pr. 25:26. Whosoever hath, to him shall be given—Mt. 13:12; 25:29; Mk. 4:25; Lu. 8:18. Wisdom—I Ki. 3:9; II Chr. 1:10; Ps. 119:34; Mk. 6:2. See ALMSGIVING, GIFTS, FRATERNITY, LIBERALITY, PRESENTS, SALVATION OF, JESUS, TEACHING OF.

GIZONITE, gī′zo-nite. I Chr. 11:34.

GLADNESS: Reasons for.—Resting in God—Ps. 45:7; 51:8, 12; 53:6; 63:5-11; 64:10; 96:11-13; Is. 35:5-10. Worship—Ps. 122:1.

The Messianic hope.—John 8:56. Marriage of the Lamb—Rev. 19:7. Obedience to Jesus—Acts 2:46; 13:48, 52. Leading others into the king's palace —Ps. 45:14, 15. Finding lost sheep— Lu. 15:3-7. Finding treasure—Mt. 13: 45, 46. Because names are written in heaven—Lu. 10:20. Sowing in tears —Ps. 126:5, 6; Lu. 16:25. Benevolent acts—Job 29:13. A righteous life— Ps. 64:10; 97:11, 12.

False gladness.—Job 20:4, 5; Pr. 14:12, 13. See JOY, PLEASURE—Ps. 30:5.

GLASS. Job 28:17. Pure—Rev. 21:18. Sea of—Rev. 4:6; 15:2. Transparent —Rev. 21:21.

GLEAN. Ruth 2:7. Barley harvest, Unto end of—Ruth 2:23. Ears of grain, Among—Ruth 2:2. Even, Until —Ruth 2:17. Field, In—Ruth 2:3, 8. Gleaning—Lev. 19:20; 23:22. Grapes —Ju. 8:2; Mic. 7:1. Israel, Remnant of—Jer. 6:9. Left—Lev. 19:9, 10; Is. 17:6. Saw what she had—Ruth—2:18. Vineyard—Lev. 19:10; Deut. 24:21. Where hast thou—Ruth 2:19.

GLISTER. Garments—Mk. 9:3. See BRIGHT.

GLITTERING. Hab. 3:11. See BRIGHT. SHINE.

GLOOM. Anguish, Of—Is. 8:22. Day of—Joel 2:2; Zeph. 1:15. Wasteness, Of—Job 30:3. See DARKNESS.

GLORIED. II Cor. 7:14. See BOASTING, PRIDE.

GLORIFYING GOD. Incidents of people.—Ps. 86:12; Mt. 15:31; Mk. 2:12; Lu. 5:26; 7:16; Acts 4:21; 11:18; 21: 20; II Cor. 9:13. Gentiles—I Pet. 2: 12. Christian—I Pet. 4:16. All nations—Rev. 15:4.

Special mention of.—Shepherds—Lu. 2: 20. Palsied man—Lu. 5:25. Woman healed—Lu. 13:13. Leper—Lu. 17:15. Blind man—Lu. 18:43. Multitude— Lu. 23:47. Multitude—Mt. 9:8. By sickness—John 11:4. Through Paul— Gal. 1:24. In His saints—II Thess. 1: 10, 12; 3:1. Through His followers— Rom. 15:6, 9.

Command to glorify God.—Mt. 5:16; I Cor. 6:20.

God glorified through Jesus.—Lu. 4:15; John 12:28; 13:32; 14:13; 17:1, 4, 5; 21:19; I Pet. 4:11.

GLORY. Temporal.—Mt. 4:8; Lu. 4:6. Passeth away—Is. 20:5; I Cor. 15:40; II Cor. 5:12; 11:12, 18; I Pet. 1:7, 24. Turned to shame—Hos. 4:7. Of tribulation—Eph. 3:13. Of riches—Esth. 5:11. Cherubim of—Heb. 9:5. Garments of—Ex. 28:2, 40.

Of men.—Jer. 9:23, 24; Mt. 6:2; I Cor. 2:7, 8; 3:21; 4:7; 11:7; Gal. 6:13; I Thess. 2:6; Heb. 2:7. Of Jacob—Gen. 31:1; Is. 17:4. Of Joseph—Gen. 45: 13. Of Job—Job 19:9; 29:20. Of David—Ps. 3:3; 4:2; 30:12; 57:8; 62:7; 108:1; Ez. 20:6, 15; 25:9; 26:20. Of young men—Pr. 20:29. Of king of Assyria—Is. 8:7. Of Nebuchadrezzar— Dan. 5:18, 20; 7:14. Of Paul—II Cor. 7:4; 11:30; 12:1, 5, 6, 9.

Of women.—I Cor. 11:15.

Of children.—Pr. 17:6.

Of nations.—Is. 13:19; 61:6; 66:12; Jer. 4:2; Dan. 11:20; Zech. 2:8; Rev. 21: 24, 26. Of Moab—Is. 16:14. Of Jerusalem—Is. 66:11; Zech. 2:5; 12:7. Of Kedar—Is. 21:16. Of Israel—Ps. 106: 20; Is. 17:3; Jer. 2:11; Mic. 1:15; Lu. 2:32. Of Lebanon—Is. 35:2; 60:11-13; Zech. 11:3. Of Judah—Hag. 2:3, 7, 9. Sleep in—Is. 14:18.

Warnings against.—Jer. 9:23; Hab. 2: 16; I Cor. 1:29; 9:16; Gal. 5:26; Jas. 3:14; I Pet. 2:20.

Glory used in prophecy.—Chariots of—Is. 22:18, 24. Pride of all—Is. 23:9.

In wisdom.—Jer. 9:23. Of wicked—Is. 5:14; Phil. 3:19. Of Moab—Is. 16:14. Of Babylon—Is. 13:19. Of Zion—Is. 61:6; 66:12.

Of God.—Ex. 24:10; 33:20; 40:34; Deut. 28:58; Num. 14:21; Job 35:5-7; Ps. 8:1, 9; 18:9-15; 19:1; 24:7-10; 29:2; 57:5; 72:19; 85:9; 102:15, 16, 21, 22; Is. 5:1, 3; 43:7; 52:10; 61:1, 2; 63:14; Hab. 2:14; Eph. 1:6, 12; 2:7; 3:21; Phil. 2:11; I Tim. 6:15, 16; Heb. 12: 18-21; Jude 25; Rev. 4:11; 15:8; 21: 10, 11, 23.

Of Jesus.—Mt. 17:2-8; Lu. 9:26, 32; John 1:14; 2:11; 7:39; 12:16, 23; 13: 31, 32; 16:14; 17:1-5; 22:24; Rom. 9: 5; II Pet. 1:16-18.

Second coming of Jesus in.—Mt. 16:27; 24:27; 30:31; 25:64; Mk. 8:38; 13:26, 27; 14:62; Lu. 21:27.

Teaching of Jesus concerning.—Lu. 14: 10; John 8:50; 17:5, 22. Of God—Mt. 16:27; Mk. 8:38; Lu. 9:26; John 7:18; 8:50; 11:4, 40; 17:5, 22. From men—Mt. 6:2, 5, 16; Lu. 6:24; John 5:41. Solomon in all his—Mt. 6:2; Lu. 12:27.

Of the Gospel.—II Cor. 3:9, 10. Joy of believers full of—I Pet. 1:8. Wisdom foreordained unto our—I Cor. 2:7.

Spiritual.—Eternal—Ps. 73:24; Pr. 3: 35; Is. 24:16; Dan. 11:39; Rom. 2:7, 10; 8:18; II Cor. 4:17; Eph. 1:18; 3: 16, 21; Col. 3:4; II Cor. 4:17; I Thess. 2:20; II Tim. 2:10; Heb. 2:10; I Pet. 5:10. God gives grace and—Ps. 84:11; 85:9.

Celestial.—I Cor. 15:40, 41. Glory in highest—Lu. 19:38. Joy of—Ez. 24: 25. Throne of—I Sam. 2:8; Jer. 14: 21; Mt. 19:28.

Called to.—II Thess. 2:14.

Raised in.—I Cor. 15:43; Phil. 3:21; Col. 3:4; I Tim. 3:16; Heb. 3:10.

Crown of.—Pr. 16:31; Is. 28:5; Jer. 13: 18; Heb. 2:9; I Pet. 5:4.

Of light.—Acts 22:11.

GLORYING. Rom. 3:27; I Cor. 5:6; 15: 31; II Cor. 5:12; 7:4; Gal. 6:4; Phil. 1:26; I Thess. 2:19. See BOASTING, PRIDE.

GLOWING. Metal—Ez. 1:4. Sand—Is. 35:7.

GNASH. Job 16:9; Ps. 112:10; Lam. 2: 16; Mt. 8:12; 22:13; 24:51; 25:30; Acts 7:54.

GNAT. Mt. 23:24.

GNAW. Dry ground—Job 30:3. Pains—Job 30:17. Tongues—Rev. 16:10.

GO. Into all the world and preach the gospel—Mt. 28:19; Mk. 16:15, 16; Lu. 24:46, 47; Acts 1:8. Into hell—Mt. 5: 30. Jews, Only to—Mt. 10:1-23; Mk. 6:7-13; Lu. 9:1-6. Jerusalem to prepare place for last supper, To—Mt. 26:18; Mk. 14:13; Lu. 22:8. Joy, With—Is. 55:12. Law, To—Mt. 5:40. To whom shall we—John 6:68. Whither thou—Ruth 1:16. Yonder and pray—Mt. 26:36.

GOAL. Press on toward—Phil. 3:14.

GOADS. I Sam. 13:21; Eccl. 12:11; Acts 26:14.

GOAH, gō′ah. Jer. 31:39. Goal—Phil. 3:14.

GOAT. Five sorts: Syrian, Egyptian, Angora, Wild, and Harmless. Highly valued in Palestine.—Gen. 30:33; 32: 14; I Sam. 25:2; Pr. 27:26-27.

Uses of.—For sacrifice—Gen. 15:9; Ex. 12:5; Lev. 3:12; 9:15; Ez. 43:25. (See also under HE-GOATS, SHE-GOATS, and KIDS.) Several Scriptures do not designate sex, mostly in Leviticus—Lev. 3:12; 4:24; 7:23, 25; 9:15; 10:16; 17:3; 22:27; Num. 18:17. The Levitical law ran as follows, touching goats: For a ruler, a he-goat—Lev. 4: 22-24. For the common people, a she-goat—Lev. 4:27-29. For a priest or Levite, a he-goat—Lev. 8:18. On the day of atonement, two he-goats, one to be slain and one to be sent into the wilderness—The Azazel—Lev. 16:7-10, 11-28.

For food.—Designated as a clean animal—Deut. 14:4. Goats supplied much of the milk used in Palestine—Pr. 27: 27. Kids were the favorite food for family and guests—Gen. 27:9; Deut. 14:4-5; Ju. 6:19; 13:15. Not seethed in mother's milk—Ex. 23:19; 34:26.

Uses of hair and skin.—The hair was converted into curtains for tabernacle—Ex. 25:4; 26:7; 35:6, 23, 26; 36:14. For pillows—I Sam. 19:13. For clothing—Num. 31:20; Heb. 11:37. Skins of goats were tanned and used to

carry water and milk—Gen. 21:14;
Josh. 9:4, 13; Ju. 4:19; I Sam. 10:3;
16:20; Ps. 119:83; Mt. 9:17; Mk. 2:22;
Lu. 5:37.

Though sheep and goats were led to pasture together, they were parted for milking, herding, and feeding.—Ez. 34:17–22; Mt. 25:32.

Bare hills the result of the tramp of.—Ez. 34:17.

He-goats.—Gen. 30:35; 32:14; Lev. 9:3; 16:5; 23:19; Num. 7:16–88; 28:22; 29:11; II Chr. 17:11; 29:21, 23; Ezra 6:17; 8:35; Ps. 50:9; Pr. 30:31; Is. 1:11; Jer. 50:8; 51:40; Ez. 34:17; Dan. 8:5, 8.

She-goats.—Gen. 15:9; 30:35; 31:38; 32:14; Lev. 5:6; Num. 15:27.

Kids.—Gen. 27:9; Ex. 23:19; 34:26; Deut. 14:4–5, 21; Lev. 5:6; 9:3; Num. 7:16–87; 28:15, 30; 29:5, 16, 19, 25; Ez. 43:22; 45:23.

Wild goat.—Deut. 14:5; I Sam. 24:2; Job 39:1; Ps. 104:18.

Daniel's vision of the.—Dan. 8.

Blood of, cannot remove sins.—Heb. 9:12, 13, 19; 10:4.

Figurative uses of.—Wantonness and lust—Jer. 50:8; Zech. 10:3; Mt. 25:32–33. Stately leadership—Pr. 30:31. Diminutive in value—Lu. 15:29. Pushing vigorously in conquest—Dan. Ch. 8. Indicative of desolation—Is. 13:21. Used as objects of worship—Lev. 17:7. To express the beauty of hair—Song of Sol. 4:1.

GOB, gŏb. II Sam. 21:19.

GOD: Is Almighty.—Gen. 17:1; 28:3; 35:11; Ex. 6:3; Job 42:2; Acts 26:8; Rev. 1:8; 7:12; 19:6; 21:22. Nothing too hard for Him—Gen. 18:14; Jer. 32:17, 27; Mt. 19:26; Mk. 10:27; Lu. 1:37; 18:27.

Creator.—Gen. 21:26–30; Job 38:4–10; Pr. 16:4; Is. 40:22–26; 45:7; 66:1, 2; Amos 4:13; Mk. 13:19; Acts 7:50; 17:24–26, 28; Heb. 2:10; 3:4; Rev. 4:11. Of the heavens—Gen. 1:1, 6–8; Ex. 20:11; 31:17; I Chr. 16:26; Neh. 9:6; Job 37:18; Ps. 8:3; 19:1–4; 96:5; 102:25; 104:2; Pr. 8:27; Is. 37:16; 40:21, 22; 42:5; 44:24; 45:12, 18; 48:13; 51:13; Jer. 10:12; 32:17; 51:15; Zech. 12:1; Acts 4:24; 14:15; Rev. 10:6; 14:7.

Of the sun and moon—Gen. 1:14–18; Ps. 8:3; 74:16. Of the stars—Gen. 1:16; Job 9:8, 9; Ps. 8:3; 136:9; Amos 5:8. Of the earth—Gen. 1:1; 9:10; 2:1–4; Ex. 20:11; 31:17; I Sam. 2:8; Neh. 9:6; 38:4–10; Ps. 24:1, 2; 90:2; 95:5; 102:25; 104:5–14; Pr. 8:22–29; Is. 42:5; 44:24; 45:12, 18; Jer. 10:12; 27:5; 32:17; 51:15; Zech. 12:1; Acts 4:24; 14:15; 17:24; Rev. 10:6; 14:7. Of the inhabitants of the sea—Gen. 1:21; Ex. 20:11; Neh. 9:6; Ps. 104:25–30; Rev. 10:6. Of the beasts of the earth and the fowls of the air—Gen. 1:24, 25; 2:19; Jer. 27:5. Of vegetation—Gen. 1:29, 30; Job 32:27; 104:14; 147:8. **Of man.**—Gen. 2:7; Ex. 4:11; Deut. 4:32; 32:15; Job 10:3, 8, 11, 12; 14:15; 31:15; 34:19; Ps. 100:3; 119:73; 130:8; 139:15, 16; Pr. 22:2; Is. 43:7; 44:2, 24; 45:12; Jer. 27:5; Mk. 10:6; I Cor. 12:18, 24; Eph. 2:10; I Pet. 4:19. *Man made in the image of God*—Gen. 1:26–27; 5:1, 2; 9:6. *Man created a spiritual being*—Gen. 2:7; Job 32:8; 33:4; Is. 42:5; 57:16; Zech. 12:1; Acts 17:28, 29; Heb. 12:9. *God the potter; man the clay*—Job 10:9; Is. 29:16; 45:9; 64:8; Rev. 9:20, 21. See GOD IS OUR FATHER.

From everlasting to everlasting.—Gen. 21:33; Ex. 3:15; Deut. 33:27; I Chr. 16:36; Neh. 9:5; Job 36:26; Ps. 90:1–4; 102:12, 24–27; 145:13; Is. 40:28; 43:10; 44:6; 57:15; 63:16; Lam. 5:19; Dan. 4:34; Rom. 1:20; I Tim. 1:17; 16:15, 16; II Pet. 3:8; Rev. 1:8; 4:8, 9; 10:6.

He knows all.—Job 23:24; Ps. 39:1–6; 149:4, 5; Pr. 5:21; 15:3; Is. 40:12, 14, 26–28; 46:9, 10; Jer. 23:24; Mt. 24:36; Rom. 11:33, 34; I John 1:5. The searcher of hearts—Gen. 20:6; Deut. 32:21; I Sam. 16:7; I Ki. 8:39; I Chr. 28:9; II Chr. 6:30; Job 11:11; Ps. 7:9; 44:21; 139:1–16; Pr. 15:11; 17:3; 21:2; 24:12; Jer. 11:20; 17:10; Amos 4:13; Mt. 6:4, 8, 18, 32; Lu. 16:15; Acts 1:24; 15:8; I Cor. 3:20; I Thess. 2:4; Heb. 4:13. He knows man's condition and needs—Ex. 3:7; Deut. 2:7; II Chr. 16:9; Job 34:21, 22, 25; Ps. 1:6; 11:4; 33:13–15; 66:7; 103:13, 14; Is. 29:15; 37:28; 66:18; Jer. 32:19; Amos 9:2–4; Mt. 10:29, 30; I Cor. 8:3.

Foreknowledge.—Gen. 41:25–32; I Sam. 23:10–12; Ps. 139:15, 16; Is. 41:26; 42:9; 44:7; 45:11, 21; 46:10; 48:3, 5; Jer. 1:5; Dan. 2:28–45; 10:14; Mt. 6: 8, 32; 24:36; 26:24; Lu. 22:22; 24:27, 44; Acts 2:23; 3:18; 4:28; 15:18; Rom. 8:29; 11:2; Gal. 1:15, 16; II Tim. 1:9; I Pet. 1:2, 20. See PROPHECIES CONCERNING JESUS, PROPHECIES AND THEIR FULFILMENT, ELECTION, SALVATION, GOD PLANS—Acts 2:40; FOREORDINATION.

He is immutable.—Num. 23:19, 20; I Sam. 15:29; Job 23:13; Ps. 33:11; 102: 27; Is. 40:28; Mal. 3:6; Rom. 11:29; Tit: 1:2; Heb. 6:17, 18; Jas. 1:17.

He is omnipresent.—Gen. 28:16; Deut. 4:35–39; I Ki. 8:27; II Chr. 2:6; Ps. 34:18; 139:7–10; Pr. 15:3; Is. 57:15; 66:1; Jonah 1:3, 4; Jer. 23:23, 24; Acts 7:48, 49; 17:24–28.

His appearances to men.—To Adam—Gen. 3:8–24. To Cain—Gen. 4:6, 7, 9–15. To Abraham—Gen. 12:7; 17:1; 18:1–33; Ex. 6:3. To Isaac—Ex. 6:3. To Jacob—Gen. 32:30; 35:7, 9–13; 48: 3; Ex. 6:3. To Moses—Ex. 3:4–22; 4:1–17; 19:19–24; 24:1–18; Deut. 34: 10. To Moses and Joshua—Deut. 31: 14, 15. To Solomon—I Ki. 3:5–14; 9: 2–9; 11:9; II Chr. 1:7–12; 7:12–22. To Job—Job 42:5, 6. To Isaiah—Is. 6:1–8. To Ezekiel—Ez. 1:24–28; 2:1–9; 3: 1–27; 8:1–4; 43:2, 3. To Daniel—Dan. 7:9, 10. To Amos—Amos 9:1. To John —Rev. 4:2, 3; 20:11.

He is invisible.—Ex. 33:20; Job 9:11: 23:8, 9; Is. 6:1–8; John 1:18; 5:37; 6: 46; Rom. 1:20; Col. 1:15; I Tim. 1:17; 6:16; Heb. 11:27; 1 John 4:12, 20. God concealed in darkness—Ex. 19:16–21; 20:21; Deut. 4:11, 12, 15; 5:22; I Ki. 8:12; II Chr. 6:1; Ps. 18:11; 97:2.

His perfection.—Deut. 32:4; II Sam. 22: 31; Job 36:4; 37:16; Ps. 18:30; Mt. 5:48; Rom. 12:2; Jas. 1:17; I John 1:5.

His holiness.—Ex. 15:11; Lev. 19:2; 20: 26; Josh. 24:19; I Sam. 2:2; 6:20; Job 6:10; 15:15; 25:5; Ps. 22:3; 47:8; 60: 6; 89:35; 99:3, 9; 105:3; 111:9; Is. 5: 16, 24; 6:3; 12:6; 29:19, 23; 41:14, 16; 43:14, 15; 47:4; 49:7; 57:15; Ez. 36: 21, 22; 39:7, 25; Hos. 11:9; Hab. 1:12, 13; Lu. 1:49; John 17:11; Rom. 1:23; Rev. 4:8; 6:10; 15:4.

His righteousness.—Gen. 18:25; Ex. 9: 27; Ju. 5:11; I Sam. 12:7; Ezra 9:15; Neh. 9:8; Job 36:3; 37:23; Ps. 5:8; 7:9, 11; 11:7; 19:9; 31:1; 36:6; 48:10; 50:6; 71:2, 15, 19; 72:1; 88:12; 89:14, 16; 96:13; 97:2; 116:5; 119:7, 40, 75, 137, 142; 129:4; 143:1, 11; 145:7, 17; Is. 5:16; 41:10; 45:19, 23, 24; 46:13; 56:1; 63:1; Jer. 4:2; 9:24; 11:20; 12: 1; 23:6; Lam. 1:18; Dan. 9:7, 14; Mic. 6:5; 7:9; John 17:25; II Tim. 4:8; I John 1:9. Revealed in the gospel—Rom. 1:17; 3:1–5, 21–26; 10:3, 4; Phil. 3:9; II Pet. 1:1.

Goodness.—Ex. 33:19; I Ki. 8:66; I Chr. 16:34; II Chr. 5:13; 7:3; Ps. 25:8; 31: 19; 65:11; 68:10; 86:5; 100:5; 106:1; 118:29; 119:68; 135:3; 136:1; 145:7–9; Is. 63:7; Jer. 33:11; Lam. 3:25; Nah. 1:7; Mt. 19:17; Mk. 10:18; Acts 14:17; Rom. 2:4; 11:22.

Justice.—Gen. 18:25; Deut. 32:4; Ps. 89:14; Is. 45:21; Jer. 11:20; 14:23; 18: 25, 29, 30; 33:1–20; Zeph. 3:5; Zech. 9:9; Acts 17:31; Rom. 2:2; I John 1: 9; Rev. 15:3. He is impartial—No respecter of persons—Deut. 10:17, 18; 16:19; II Chr. 19:7; Job 34:18, 19; Acts 10:34, 35; Rom. 2:11; Gal. 2:6; Eph. 6:8, 9; Col. 3:25; I Pet. 1:17. He despises none—Job 36:5; Ps. 22:24; 69:33; 102:17.

Faithful who promised.—Gen. 9:16; 21: 1; 28:15; Ex. 2:24; 6:4, 5; Lev. 26:44, 45; Josh. 22:4; 23:10–14; Ju. 2:1; I Sam. 12:22; II Sam. 7:28; 23:5; I Ki. 8:56; II Ki. 13:23; Neh. 9:7, 8; Ps. 18:30; 19:9; 25:10; 33:4; 40:10; 100: 5; 132:11; Rom. 3:3, 4; 11:2, 29; 15:8; I Cor. 1:9; II Cor. 1:20; I Thess. 5:24; II Tim. 2:13; Tit. 1:2; I Pet. 4:19; Rev. 6:10; 15:3.

Long-suffering.—Gen. 6:3; Ex. 34:6, 7; Num. 4:17–21; Ps. 86:15; 103:8–14; Is. 5:1–4; 30:18; Jer. 7:13, 23–25; 15: 15; Ez. 33:11; Joel 2:13; Mt. 21:33–41; Acts 14:16, 17; 17:30; Rom. 2:4; 3:25; 9:22–24; 15:5; I Pet. 3:20–22; II Pet. 3:9, 15; Rev. 2:21. **His long-suffering is sometimes abused.**—It was so with Pharaoh; when the curse was removed he hardened his heart. Others have acted in the same way—Neh. 9:28–31; Pr. 1:24–27; 29:1; Eccl.

8:11; Mt. 23:37, 38; 24:48–51; Lu. 13:6–9.

Love of.—Deut. 10:15, 18; 23:5; II Sam. 12:24; Ps. 103:13; 146:8; Jer. 31:3; Mal. 1:2; John 3:16; 14:21, 23; 16:27; 17:10, 23, 26; Rom. 5:8; 9:13; II Cor. 9:7; 13:11; Eph. 2:4; II Thess. 2:16; Heb. 12:6; I John 3:1; 4:8, 9, 10, 16, 19; Jude 21. Love manifested—Ex. 6:7; 19:4; Lev. 25:42; 26:12; Deut. 28:9; 32:9–12; Ps. 31:19, 21; 90:1; 114:2; Is. 49:16; 54:5, 6, 10; Mal. 3:16, 17; Mt. 18:11–14; Rom. 5:8; 8:31, 32, 39; Eph. 3:1–6; Heb. 11:16; Jas. 1:18. See SALVATION.

Mercy of God a further exemplification of His love.—Ex. 20:2, 6, 22; 22:27; II Chr. 30:9; Ezra 9:9; Neh. 1:10; 9: 17, 27–31; Is. 54:9; 57:11; 65:2; Jer. 2:9; 3:12; 4:27; Hos. 2:14, 23; Lu. 6: 36; Acts 26:16–18; Rom. 10:10–13. See SALVATION.

Sovereignty.—Ex. 15:18; I Chr. 29:11, 12; II Chr. 20:6; Job 9:2–12; 25:2; 33: 12, 13; Ps. 59:13; 82:1, 8; 89:11–14; 93:1, 2; 97:1–6, 9; 103:19; 105:7; 113: 3–5; 135:5–21; 145:11–13; Is. 40:12–31; 66:1; Lam. 3:27; 5:19; Dan. 6:26; Mic. 4:7, 13; Mt. 6:10; 11:25; Lu. 10: 21; John 10:29; 19:11; Acts 7:48–50; 17:24–31; Rom. 9:19–33; 11:33–36; Heb. 1:1–14; Rev. 4:11; 19:6.

One God alone—Ex. 8:10; 9:14; Deut. 4:35, 39; 6:4; 32:39; Neh. 9:6; Ps. 83: 18; 86:10; Is. 37:16; 43:11–15; 44:6, 8; 45:5–12, 21–25; Mk. 12:29, 32; John 5:44; 17:3; I Cor. 8:4, 6; Eph. 4:6; I Tim. 1:17; 6:15; Jas. 4:12; Jude 25.

Lord of heaven and earth—Ex. 8:22; 9: 28, 29; 19:5; Deut. 10:14–22; Josh. 2: 11; 3:11; Ps. 24:1–10; 50:10–12; Is. 54:5; Jer. 10:10–16; Hag. 2:8; I Cor. 10:26.

Lord of all living—Num. 16:22; 27:16; I Sam. 2:6; Job 12:9, 10, 16–25; Ps. 22:27–29; 145:15–20; Eccl. 9:1; Is. 42: 5; 45:20–25; 57:16; Jer. 10:23; 18:1–17; Ez. 18:4; Dan. 5:23; Acts 17:28; Rom. 14:11.

Sovereignty in human affairs—Gen. 15: 5; 22:17; Deut. 1:10; 4:32–40; 10:22; 26:5–9; I Sam. 15:1–35; 16:1–13; Job 12:17–25; Ps. 75:9–25; 135:8–13; Is. 26:7; 45:9–25; Jer. 10:23; 27:5–22; 32:26–44; Ez. 16:50; 17:1–24; Dan. 2:

20–47; 4:3, 17, 25, 29–37; 5:5–31; 6: 10–27. See COMMANDMENTS, FOREORDINATION, SALVATION, ELECTION, DELIVERANCE FROM BONDAGE, RULERS OF ISRAEL.

Glory of.—Ex. 24:10; 33:20–23; 40:34; Deut. 28:58; Num. 14:21; Job 35:5–7; Ps. 8:1, 9; 18:9–15; 19:1; 24:7–10; 29: 2; 57:5; 72:19; 102:15, 16, 21, 22; Is. 6:1, 3; 43:7; 52:10; 61:1, 2; 63:14; Hab. 2:14; Eph. 1:6, 12; 2:7; 3:21; Phil. 2:11; I Tim. 6:15, 16; Heb. 12: 18–21; Jude 25; Rev. 4:11; 15:8; 21: 10, 11, 23.

God is a jealous God.—Ex. 20:5; 34:14; Deut. 4:24; 5:9; 6:15; 29:20; 32:15–27; Josh. 24:19, 20; I Ki. 14:22; II Chr. 16:7–9; Ps. 78:58; Is. 30:1–3; Ez. 8:17, 18; 23:25; 36:5, 6; 38:19; 39:25; Joel 2:18; Nah. 1:2; Zeph. 1:18; 3:8; Zech. 1:14; 8:2; I Cor. 10:22.

Vengeance belongeth unto the Lord.—Gen. 4:15; Deut. 32:41, 43; Ju. 11:36; Ps. 94:11; Pr. 6:34; Is. 34:8; 35:4; 47: 3; 61:2; 63:4; Jer. 11:20; 29:12; 46: 10; 51:6, 11, 36; Ez. 24:8; 25:14; 33: 12–16; Lu. 21:22; Acts 13:8–12; Rom. 2:2–11; 12:19; II Thess. 1:7–9; 2:7–12; I Pet. 4:17, 18.

A Person.—Ex. 3:14; 20:3, 4; 34:14; Deut. 4:35, 39; 6:4; 32:12, 39; Ju. 13: 16; I Sam. 7:3; II Sam. 7:22; II Ki. 19:15; Ezra 1:3; Neh. 9:6; Is. 44:6, 8; 46:5, 9; Jer. 10:6, 7; 32:27; Hos. 13:4; Mal. 2:10; Mt. 4:10; 23:9; John 14:9; 17:3; I Cor. 8:4–6; II Cor. 4:4; Gal. 3: 20; I Thess. 1:9; I Tim. 2:5; Heb. 1:3. This is indicated in all the Scriptures which speak of the unity of God—I Ki. 8:60; 20:28; Is. 42:8; Mk. 12:29.

A spirit.—John 4:24. But that involves no contradiction. The angels are spirits too. Yet they are individual personal beings. See SPIRIT, ANGELS.

Anthropomorphisms.—Ez. 43:6, 7. God represented as local—Ex. 19:17–21; 20:21; 24:12; Num. 23:15; Deut. 4:37; 5:5; I Ki. 19:11; Is. 40:22.

Dwells with men—Ex. 15:17; 25:8; 29: 43–46; Lev. 26:11, 12; Num. 5:3; 35: 34; I Ki. 8:13; Ps. 132:14; Mic. 1:2; Hab. 2:20; Zech. 8:3; Mt. 23:21; John 14:23; II Cor. 6:16; Rev. 21:3.

Moves about—Gen. 3:8; 11:5–7; 17:22; 18:20, 21, 33; 28:13; 35:13; 46:4; Ex.

3:8; 19:9, 11, 18, 20; 34:5; Lev. 26:12; Deut. 23:14; 33:2; Ju. 5:4; I Sam. 4:7; I Ki. 19:11; Neh. 9:13; Ps. 47:5; 68:7, 8; Is. 26:21; Jer. 14:8; Mic. 1:3; Hab. 3:3; Zech. 8:3; II Cor. 6:16; Rev. 2:1. Uses vehicles—II Sam. 22:11; Ps. 18: 10; Hab. 3:8, 15. *Rides upon the clouds* —Deut. 33:26; Ps. 68:33; 104:3; Is. 19:1; Zech. 9:14. See Mt. 26:64; Rev. 1:7.

Rests—Ex. 20:11; 31:17; Ps. 132:8, 14; Heb. 4:4, 10.

Has a face—Gen. 32:30; Ex. 33:11, 20; Num. 6:25, 26; 14:14; Deut. 5:4; 31: 17; 34:10; Ps. 4:6; 27:9; 31:16; 34:16; 44:3; 67:1; 69:17; 80:3, 7, 19; 102:2; 119:135; 143:7; Is. 8:17; 54:8; 59:2; Jer. 21:10; 44:11; Dan. 9:17; I Pet. 3: 12; Rev. 20:11.

Has eyes—Deut. 11:12; II Chr. 16:9; Neh. 1:6; Job 36:7; Ps. 11:4; 32:8; 33: 18; 34:15; 94:9; Pr. 15:3; Is. 1:15; 3:8; Amos 9:4; Hab. 1:13; Zech. 4:10; Heb. 4:13; I Pet. 3:12.

Ears—II Sam. 22:7; Neh. 1:6; Ps. 17:6; 31:2; 34:15; 39:12; 71:2; 77:1; 80:1; 86:1; 88:2; 94:9; 102:2; Is. 59:1, 2; Lam. 3:56; Jas. 5:4; I Pet. 3:12.

Mouth—Num. 12:8; Deut. 8:3; II Sam. 22:9; Ps. 18:8; 33:6; Is. 30:27; Mt. 4:4.

Nostrils—Ex. 15:8; II Sam. 22:9, 16; Ps. 18:15.

Voice and uses human speech—Ex. 3: 4; 19:19; 20:1, 19, 22; Lev. 1:1; Num. 7:89; 12:4; 22:9; Deut. 4:12, 33, 36; 5: 24–26; I Ki. 19:12, 13; Neh. 9:13; Job 26:14; 37:4, 5; 40:9; Ps. 18:13; 29:4, 5; 46:6; 68:33; Is. 42:13; Jer. 25:30; Ez. 1:24; 10:5; 43:6, 7; Joel 2:11; 3: 16; Amos 1:2; Acts 7:31; Heb. 12:19, 26. *Heard at the baptism of Jesus*— Mt. 3:17; Mk. 1:11; Lu. 3:22. *Heard by the disciples*—John 12:28. *At the transfiguration*—Mt. 17:5; Mk. 9:7; Lu. 9:35; II Pet. 1:17, 18. *By John*— Rev. 1:10.

Back—Ex. 33:21–23.

Shoulders—Deut. 33:12.

Feet—Ps. 18:9; Acts 7:49. *The earth His footstool*—Is. 66:1; Mt. 5:35; Acts 7: 49. *The temple His footstool*—I Chr. 28:2; Ps. 99:5; 132:7.

Arm—Ex. 15:16; Ps. 44:3; 77:15; 98:1; Is. 40:10, 11; 51:5, 9; 52:10; 53:1; 59:

16; 63:5, 12; Acts 13:17. *Outstretched arm*—Ex. 6:6; Deut. 4:34; 5:15; 7:19; 9:29; I Ki. 8:42; Jer. 21:5; 27:5; 32: 17. *The arm of His strength*—Ps. 89: 10, 13, 21; Is. 62:8; Lu. 1:51.

Hand—Ex. 7:4, 5; 9:3; I Sam. 7:13; I Ki. 18:46; II Ki. 3:15; Ps. 21:8; 89: 21; Jer. 6:12; 21:5; Ez. 1:3; 3:22; 8:1; 33:22; 37:1; 40:1; Hab. 3:4; Lu. 1:66; Acts 11:21. *Hand not shortened*—Num. 11:23; Is. 50:2; 59:1. *Hand strong or mighty*—Ex. 3:19, 20; 6:1; 13:3, 9, 14; Deut. 4:34; 5:15; 7:19; Josh. 4:24; I Ki. 8:42; Ps. 89:13; Is. 8:11; 40:10; Ez. 3:14. *Hand heavy*—I Sam. 5:6, 7, 9, 11. *Right hand*—Ex. 15:6; Ps. 44:3; 74:11; 98:1; 118:16; Is. 62:8; Lam. 2: 3. Fists—Pr. 30:4.

Finger—Ex. 8:19; Ps. 8:3; Lu. 11:20. *He wrote the ten commandments with His finger*—Ex. 31:18; Deut. 9:10.

Represented as laughing—Ps. 2:4; 37: 13; 59:8. As sleeping—Ps. 7:6; 44: 23; 73:20; 78:65. As wondering—Is. 59:16; 63:5.

Represented as a warrior—Ex. 15:3. *He uses a sword*—Deut. 32:41, 42; I Chr. 21:12; Ps. 7:12; 17:13; Is. 34:5, 6; Jer. 12:12; 47:6; Ez. 21:3–5, 9–12, 28; 30: 11, 24, 25; Amos 9:4; Zeph. 2:12. *Uses a bow*—Ps. 7:12; Lam. 2:4; 3:12; Hab. 3:9. *An arrow*—Num. 24:8; Deut. 32: 23, 42; II Ki. 13:17; Job 6:4; Ps. 7: 12, 13; 18:14; 38:2; 45:5; 58:7; 64:7; 77:17; 144:6; Lam. 3:12, 13; Hab. 3: 11; Zech. 9:14. *A spear*—Hab. 3:11.

Our Guide.—Gen. 12:1; Ex. 13:21; 33: 13–15; Deut. 32:10, 12; Neh. 9:19, 20; Ps. 5:8; 23:2, 3; 25:5, 9; 27:11; 31:3; 32:8; 48:14; 73:24; Is. 40:11; 42:16; 55:4; Lu. 1:79; John 10:3, 4; 16:13. As He guided the wise men to Bethlehem by the finger of light, so He makes so plain the path of duty that the wayfaring man, though a fool, shall not err therein—Is. 35:8.

Providences.—Are for the race—Gen. 1:29, 30; 2:6; 8:2, 22; 9:1–3; 29:1–3; Job 5:8–11; Ps. 65:9–13; 104:1–35; 145:15, 16; Pr. 16:33; Eccl. 2:15–26; 5:18, 19; Jer. 5:24; 27:6; Jonah 4:6– 11; Zech. 10:1; Mt. 5:45; Jas. 4:15.

Special.—To Abraham—Gen. 22:14–18; Is. 51:2. To Isaac—Gen. 24:7, 40–50; 26:1–5, 24. To Jacob—Gen. 28:20, 21;

48:15, 16; 49:24, 25. To the nation of Israel—Ex. 23:22-25; 34:24; Lev. 25: 20-22; 26:4-6; Deut. 1:10; 2:7; 5:29; 7:13-15; 8:4, 7-20; 11:12-17; 15:4-6; Chs. 28 and 29; I Chr. 29:14-16; Neh. 9:24, 25; Ps. 136:10-26; Is. 43:15-21; 48:21; Ez. 36:28-38; Hos. 2:8-13; Joel 2:18-27; John 6:31. To the poor— Deut. 10:18; 15:4; Ruth 1:6; I Sam. 2:7, 8; Lu. 1:48, 50; Gal. 2:10.

Even good men have not always understood God's providences—Job 12:16; Ps. 10:5; 72:2, 3, 13-17; Eccl. 7:15; 9:2, 11; Jer. 12:1, 2; Rom. 11:25; I Cor. 10:11; Phil. 1:12.

God overrules in the affairs of men for the good of His people—Gen. 50:20; Ex. 14:4; Num. 23:7, 8, 23; Deut. 23:4, 5; I Sam. 2:6-9; II Sam. 17:14; Esth. 6:1-12; 7:10; 9:1, 25; Ps. 23:1-6; 33: 10; 34:7-10; 37:1-25; 75:7; 107:1-43; 127:1, 2; 144:12-15; 147:8, 9, 13, 14; Mt. 6:25-34; 10:29-31; Lu. 12:6, 7, 22-30; 22:35; Acts 14:17; Rom. 1:10; 8: 28; I Cor. 4:19; 16:7; II Cor. 9:10; Phil. 1:12; Philemon 15; Jas. 4:15; Rev. 17:1. See SALVATION FROM ENEMIES, COMMANDMENTS, RULERS, ISRAEL.

Our Saviour.—Job 33:24-30; Ps. 3:8; 18:30, 31; 19:13, 14; 25:5; 27:1; 68: 19, 20; 96:2; Is. 25:4, 9; 45:17, 22; 47: 4; 52:3, 9, 10; Jer. 3:23; Jonah 2:9; Lu. 1:68; John 3:16, 17; Rom. 1:16; 6:23; 8:32; I Cor. 1:18; II Cor. 5:18-21; I Thess. 5:9; II Tim. 1:9; I John 4:9, 10.

Called a Saviour—II Sam. 22:3; Ps. 106:21; Is. 43:3-21; 45:15, 21, 22; 60: 16; 63:8, 9; Jer. 14:8; Hos. 13:4; Lu. 1:47; I Tim. 1:1; 2:3, 4; 4:10; Tit. 1: 1-3; 2:10-14; 3:4, 5; Jude 25. See SALVATION, REDEMPTION.

FATHERHOOD OF: **Old Testament.**—Ex. 4:22; Deut. 1:31; 14:1; 32:5, 6; II Sam. 7:14; I Chr. 29:10; Ps. 2:7 (Acts 13:33); Is. 1:2; 63:16; 64:8; Jer. 3:4, 19; 31:9; Hos. 1:10; 11:1; Mal. 2:10. Of Solomon—I Chr. 22:10; 28:6. Of the fatherless—Ps. 68:5. Of Christ— Ps. 2:7; 89:26, 27; Is. 9:6.

New Testament.—Revealed by Jesus— John 1:12, 14, 18; 4:21, 23; 5:36, 37, 43; 6:27, 44-46; 8:27, 28, 41, 42; 10: 15-18, 32; 11:52; 12:49, 50; 16:3, 10, 23; Acts 1:4.

Father of Jesus.—John 2:16; 5:17-23; 6:32; 8:19, 38, 49; 10:29, 30, 36-38; 11:41; 12:26-28; 13:1, 3; 14:2, 6-13, 16, 20, 21, 23, 26, 31; 15:8-10, 16, 23, 24, 26; 16:15, 25-28; 17:1, 5, 11, 21, 24, 25; 20:17, 21.

Fatherhood of God taught in the Epistles.—Rom. 1:7; I Cor. 1:3; 8:6; 15: 24; II Cor. 1:3; Gal. 1:1-4; Eph. 1:2, 3, 17; 3:14; 4:6; 5:20; Phil. 1:2; 4:20; Col. 1:2, 3, 12; 3:17; I Thess. 1:1, 3; 3: 11, 13; II Thess. 1:1, 2; 2:16; I Tim. 1: 2; II Tim. 1:2; Tit. 1:4; Heb. 12:9; Jas. 1:17, 27; 3:9; I Pet. 1:2, 3, 17; I John 1:2; 2:1, 13, 15, 22-24; 4:14; II John 3, 4, 9; Jude 1. *God was the Father of Jesus*—Rom. 1:3, 4; 15:6; Heb. 1:5, 6; 5:5; Rev. 1:6; 5:5. *Father of adopted children*—Rom. 8:14-19; 9:8, 26; II Cor. 6:16-18; Gal. 4:4-7; Eph. 2:12-19; 3:26, 29; I John 3:1, 2, 10. See ADOPTION.

Access to God.—Very desirable—Deut. 4:7; Ps. 27:4; 43:2; 65:4; I John 2:1. We must be pure in heart—Ps. 1:1-6; 24:3, 4; 51:10-12; 145:18; Is. 55:3; Mt. 5:8. Only through Christ can we come to the Father—John 10:7, 9; 14: 6; Rom. 5:1; Col. 1:21, 22; Eph. 2:13, 18; 3:12; Heb. 2:17; 4:16; 7:19, 25; 9:15; 10:19, 22; I Pet. 3:18; I Tim. 2:4, 5, 6. He will welcome all—Mt. 11:28-30; Acts 2:21; Rom. 10:12, 13. See SALVATION. The Father draws men to Christ—John 6:44, 45. Calls them by the Gospel—Mk. 1:17; Rom. 9:11; I Cor. 1:17; 4:15; Gal. 1:6; I Thess. 2:12; 5:24; II Thess. 2:14; II Tim. 1:9; Jas. 1:18; I Pet. 1:15. See CALLING.

God not only gives life and breath and all things (Acts 17:25, 28), **but He gives Christ to redeem us** (John 3:16; 4:10; 6:32, 33). See SALVATION, GOD PLANS.

Gives grace and glory.—Ps. 84:11. **Wisdom.**—Pr. 2:6; Jas. 1:5. **The Comforter.**—John 14:26; 15:26. See HOLY SPIRIT. **God would be worshipped.**— John 4:23, 24. See WORSHIP. **Loved.** —Mt. 22:37-40. See LOVE. **Honored by obedience.**—Eccl. 12:13, 14; Mt. 12:50; Lu. 1:6; John 14:23, 24; Heb. 5:8, 9; I John 2:3, 4; 3:22. See OBE-

DIENCE, JESUS THE SON OF GOD, THE DIVINITY OF JESUS, HOLY SPIRIT.

Names of God.—*Heb.* El. Mighty one—Gen. 16:13; etc. *Chald.* Elahh—Ezra 4:24; etc. *Heb.* Eloahh—Deut. 32:15; etc. *Heb.* Elohim—Gen. 1:1; etc. *Heb.* Jah (marg.)—Ps. 77:11. *Heb.* Jehovah—Gen. 2:4; etc. *Heb.* Tsur—Hab. 1:12. *Gr.* Theos—Mt. 1:23; etc. *Gr.* Kurios—Acts 19:20.

Aramaic — Abba, Father — Mk. 14:36; Rom. 8:15. Almighty—Gen. 17:1; etc. Creator—Eccl. 12:1; Is. 40:28; etc. Father—Mt. 5:48; etc. God—Ex. 3:6; etc. God Almighty—Ex. 6:3; etc. Holy One of Israel—Ps. 89:18. I AM THAT I AM—Ex. 3:13-15. Judge—Gen. 18:25. King—Ps. 5:2; 89:18; etc. Eternal King—I Tim. 1:17. Lord—Gen. 18:27; Acts 4:24. Lord of Heaven—Dan. 5:23. Lord of Kings—Dan. 2:47. Lord of Lords—I Tim. 6:15. Maker—Is. 54:5. Redeemer—Is. 47:4.

God manifested as Father, Son, and Holy Spirit.—Mt. 3:16; 28:19; John 10:30; 17:11, 22; 20:28; Acts 5:3, 4, 9; Rom. 8:9; I Cor. 2:14; 3:16; 6:19; 12:3; II Cor. 13:14; Eph. 4:4-6; I John 5:7.

GODDESS. See IDOLATRY.

GODHEAD. Acts 17:29; Col. 2:9. See JESUS, DIVINITY OF.

GODLINESS. See CHRISTIAN GRACES, MYSTERY OF.

GODS. See IDOLATRY.

GOG, gŏg. (1) **A prince in ancient Scythia.**—Ez. 38:2, 3, 14, 16, 18; 39:1, 11; Rev. 20:8.

(2) **A Reubenite**—I Chr. 5:4.

GOIIM. Gen. 14:1.

GOING. Hab. 3:6. Astray like sheep—I Pet. 2:25. Branches—Ex. 25:35. City, About—Josh. 3:6. Down, Sun—Ps. 104:19; Dan. 6:14. Establish my—Ps. 40:2. Forth—Mic. 5:2. House of Jehovah, To—Ju. 19:18. House to house, From—I Tim. 5:13. Jerusalem, Up to—Mt. 20:17; Mk. 10:32; Lu. 19:28. Lamps are out—Mt. 25:8. Let us be—Mt. 26:46. Man—Ps. 37:23; Pr. 20:24; Mt. 25:14. Out—Num. 33:2; Josh. 17:9. Pit, Into—Job 33:24. To and fro in earth—Job 1:7.

GOLAN, gō'lan. **A city of refuge.**—Deut. 4:43; Josh. 20:8; 21:17.

GOLD: Found in.—Havilah—Gen. 2:11. Ophir—I Ki. 9:28; 10:11; 22:48; I Chr. 29:4; II Chr. 8:18; Job 22:24; Ps. 45:9. Sheba—I Ki. 10:10; II Chr. 9:9; Ps. 72:15; Is. 60:6. Parvaim—II Chr. 3:6. Uphaz—Jer. 10:9.

Belongs to God.—Ez. 16:17; Joel 3:5; Hag. 2:8.

Comes into possession of man.—By trade—I Ki. 9:28; 10:11, 14, 15. By gifts—I Ki. 10:2; 15:19; Mt. 2:11. By tribute—I Ki. 20:3, 5, 7; II Ki. 23:33-35. By capture in war—Josh. 6:19; II Sam. 8:10-11; I Ki. 15:18.

Refined by man.—Job 28:1; Pr. 17:3; 27:21; Zech. 13:9; I Pet. 1:7. See ARTS AND TRADES.

Fine gold.—Job 28:19; Ps. 19:10; 21:3; Pr. 3:14; 8:19; Mal. 3:3.

Uses of.—For money—Gen. 44:8; I Chr. 21:25; Ezra 8:25-28; Is. 13:17; 60:9; Ez. 7:19; 28:4; Mt. 10:9; Acts 3:6; 20:23; I Pet. 1:18. For ornament—Gen. 24:22; Ex. 3:22; 11:2; 28:11; Num. 31:50; Pr. 25:11; Song of Sol. 1:10-11; 5:14; Ez. 16:17; Jas. 2:2; I Pet. 3:3. For tapestry—Ex. 26:6; 35:22, 25, 26; 36:37, 38; 39:3. For overlaying: Ark of tabernacle—Ex. 25:11, 13; 37:2, 4. Table—Ex. 25:24. Boards of—Ex. 26:29; 36:34-36. Altar of incense—Ex. 30:3, 5. Whole temple overlaid with—I Ki. 6:20-22, 28, 30, 35. Solomon's shields and throne—I Ki. 10:16-18. For vestments and apparel—Ex. 28:4-6; 39:1-31; Ps. 45:9, 13.

Articles made of.—Bedsteads—Esth. 1:6. Vessels and furniture—II Sam. 8:10; I Ki. 10:21, 25; 14:26; I Chr. 18:11; 22:14, 16; 28:14-17; 29:2-7; II Ki. 25:15; Jer. 52:19; Ezra 8:25-30; Dan. 5:3.

Abuse of.—Idols—Ex. 20:23; 32:2-4; I Ki. 12:28; Ps. 135:15; Is. 30:22; Dan. 5:4; Rev. 9:20. Coveting—Josh. 7:21; II Chr. 12:9; Job 31:24.

Vanity of.—Eccl. 2:8; Lam. 4:1-2; Is. 2:7-9; Jas. 5:3. Not to multiply—Deut. 17:17; Is. 2:7; Ps. 49.

Used in figurative sense.—Eccl. 12:6; Jer. 51:7; Lam. 4:1, 2; I Cor. 3:12; II Tim. 2:20; Rev. 3:18; 14:14; 21:15, 18.

Symbolical.—Dan. 2:32-45; Rev. 21:21.

Special references.—More precious than
—Ps. 19:10. Apples of gold in—Pr.
25:11. Get you no gold nor silver—
Mt. 10:9. Silver and gold have I none
—Acts 3:5. Coveted no man's—Acts
20:33. I counsel thee to buy of me—
Rev. 3:18. Street of city was pure
gold—Rev. 21:21.

GOLDSMITH. See ARTS AND TRADES.

GOLGOTHA, gŏl-go-thà. **Calvary.**—Mt.
27:33.

GOLIATH, go-lī'ath. **The Philistine
giant slain by David.**—I Sam. 17:4,
23; 21:9; 22:10; II Sam. 21:19; I Chr.
20:5.

GOMER, gō'mer. (1) **Son of Japheth.**—
Gen. 10:2, 3; I Chr. 1:5, 6.

(2) **Descendant of (1)**—Ez. 38:6.

(3) **Wife of Hosea.**—Hos. 1:3.

GOMORRAH, go-mŏr'rah. Arabic, *Gha-
mara.* To overwhelm with water. One
of the five cities of the plain or "Vale
of Siddim"—Gen. 13:10; 14:1-3.
Second to Sodom in importance and
in wickedness—Gen. 19:24. Under its
king it joined battle with Chedorlaomer—Gen. 14:2-8. Was discomfited
until Abraham came as a relief—Gen.
14:11-16. Its enormities were such
that the city is used as a warning to
others—Deut. 29:23; Is. 13:19; Jer.
23:14; 50:40; Zeph. 2:9; Amos 4:11;
Mt. 10:15; II Pet. 2:6; Jude 4-7. See
SODOM.

GONE. Pr. 19:7. After him, World—
John 12:19. Aside—I Ki. 18:27; Ps.
14:3. Astray—Ps. 119:176; Is. 53:6.
Back—Ps. 38:4. Deceivers—John 7.
Faith—I Thess. 1:8. Gods, After
other—Jer. 13:10. Iniquities, over
my head—Ps. 38:4. Mirth is—Is. 24:
11. Rain is—Song of Sol. 2:11. Salvation is—Is. 51:5. Strange flesh,
After—Jude 7. Shadow, Like a—Ps.
109:23. Whither is my beloved—
Song of Sol. 6:1. Wind is—Ps. 103:16.

GOOD. Gen. 1:4; 16:6; I Sam. 18:5;
Job 5:27; 21:25; Ps. 16:2; 73:28; 107:
9; Is. 47:7. Accept—Hos. 14:2. Afflicted, That I have been—Ps. 119:71.
All things work together for—Rom.
2:28. And faithful servant—Mt. 25:
21, 23. Cleave to—Rom. 12:9. Confession—I Tim. 6:13. Conscience—I
Pet. 3:16. Destroyeth much—Eccl. 9:

18. Do—Gen. 26:29; 32:12; Num. 10:
29; Ps. 14:1; 53:1, 3; Pr. 11:17; Rom.
3:12; Acts 10:38; I Pet. 3:11; III John
11. Eat—Is. 1:19. Fight of faith—
I Tim. 6:12. Findeth no—Pr. 17:20.
Follow after—I Thess. 5:15. Fruit—
Mt. 7:17; Jas. 3:17. Gifts—Mt. 7:11;
Lu. 11:13; Jas. 1:17. Ground—Mk.
4:8. Hold fast—I Thess. 5:21. Judgment and knowledge—Ps. 119:66.
Land—Ex. 3:8. Mary hath chosen
the—Lu. 10:42. Measure—Lu. 6:38.
Men—Pr. 2:20; Lu. 6:45. Minister
for—Rom. 13:4; I Tim. 4:6. Morals—
I Cor. 15:33. Name—Pr. 22:1; Eccl.
7:1. People — See RIGHTEOUSNESS.
Pleasure—I Cor. 1:21. Plenteous for
—Deut. 28:11. Praises, To sing—Ps.
147:1. Report, Of—Acts 6:3. See,
May—Ps. 34:12. Seed—Mt. 13:24,
27, 37, 38. Shepherd—John 10:11, 14.
Speak—Jer. 18:20. Soldier—II Tim.
2:3. Speed—Gen. 24:12. Strengthen
for—Jer. 15:11. Success—Josh. 1:7.
Tidings—See TIDINGS. Thing—II Sam.
7:28; Ps. 92:1; Mt. 19:16; Rom. 7:18.
Treasure—Deut. 28:12. Way—I Sam.
12:23; Jer. 6:7; Gal. 4:17. Will of
God—Rom. 12:2. Works—Mt. 5:16;
Rom. 2:10; II Cor. 9:8; Eph. 2:10; Col.
1:10; II Thess. 2:17; I Tim. 6:18; Tit.
2:14; I Pet. 2:12. See RIGHTEOUS.

GOODLY. Babylonish mantle—Josh.
7:21. Child—Heb. 11:23. Frame—
Job 4:12. Furniture—Nah. 2:9. Garments—Gen. 27:15. Heritage—Ps.
16:6. Matter—Ps. 45:1. Pearls—Mt.
13:45. Stones—Lu. 21:5. Tents—
Num. 24:5. Things—Gen. 24:10. Vessels—II Chr. 32:27; Dan. 11:8.

GOODNESS. All—Eph. 5:9. Cloud, Is
as—Hos. 6:4. Full of—Rom. 15:14.
God—See GOD, GOODNESS OF. House,
Of thy—Ps. 65:4.

GOODS. Carried away those of Lot,
Sodom, etc.—Gen. 14:11, 12, 16, 21.
Jacob departs with—Gen. 31:17-18.
Law concerning stolen goods—Ex. 22:
7-9. Earth swallows Korah and goods
—Num. 16:31-33. Israel takes goods
of Midian—Num. 31:9-12. Aided
their priests in removal—Ju. 18:21.
Cyrus urges help for Israel—Ezra 1:
4-6. Spoiling the strong man—Mt.
12:29; Mk. 3:27; Lu. 11:21. Delivers

goods to servants—Mt. 25:14. Ask not for return of—Lu. 6:30. The rich man—Lu. 12:15–21. Prodigal son— Lu. 15:12–13. Unjust steward—Lu. 16:1. Leave goods where they are— Lu. 17:31. Zacchaeus—Half of my goods—Lu. 19:8. Sold their goods— Acts 2:45. If I bestow all my goods— I Cor. 13:3. Took joyfully the spoiling of—Heb. 10:34. Whoso hath this world's—I John 3:17. I have gotten riches—Rev. 3:17. See POSSESSIONS, WEALTH.

GORE. Ex. 21:29.

GOSHEN, gō'shen. (1) **A district in southern Canaan.**—Josh. 10:41; 11:16. (2) **Name given to part of Egypt.**— Gen. 45:10; 46:28, 29; 47:1, 4, 6, 27; 50:8; Ex. 8:22; 9:26. (3) **A town in Judah.**—Josh. 15:51.

GOSPEL: In prophecy.—Gen. 3:15; 12: 3; 22:18; 49:10; Deut. 18:15; Job 19: 25, 26; Ps. 2:7, 8; 16:8–10; 110:4; Is. 9:6, 7; 35:4–10; 41:27; 49:6; 52:7; 61: 1–3; Jer. 31:31–34; Dan. 2:44; Joel 2:28–32; Mic. 4:1, 2; 5:2; Zech. 6:12, 13; Mal. 3:1–3; Lu. 24:25–27.

In preparation.—Mt. 2:1–6; 3:13–15; Lu. 2:29–32, 40, 49; 3:15–17, 21, 22; 4:1, 2; 24:44–47; John 1:14–17, 29, 34; 17:7, 8; Acts 1:6–9; 2:22–33.

In purpose.—John 1:29; 3:16, 17; 14:12; Rom. 1:13–17; 8:18–23; 10:4–13; Eph. 3:8–11; Phil. 2:5–11; Col. 1:19.

In progress.—Geographical—Acts 1:8; 2:8–11; 8:5; 9:19, 20; 10:17–22; 13:2– 6, 13, 14; 14:1, 6, 7; 15:39–41; 16:1, 6, 10–12; 18:1, 18, 19, 22, 23; 28:16.

Doctrinal.—John 1:16, 17; Acts 19:1–7; Rom. 5:1–5; 7:22; 8:11, 30; 10:8–17; 12:1, 2; 14:17–19; I Cor. 9:19–27; 13: 1–8; I Pet. 2:1–5; II Pet. 1:5–7.

In fulfillment.—Mt. 11:4, 5; Lu. 7:22. With—Is. Ch. 35; John 17:4; Acts 2: 16–21; 10:34–44; I Cor. 15:51–57; Col. 1:3–6; Rev. 15:3, 4; 19:5–9; 21:1–4; 22:1–5, 10–14.

What is the gospel?—Before the death of Jesus.—The kingdom of heaven is at hand—Dan. 2:44; Mt. 3:2; 4:17, 23; 9:35; 10:5–7; 24:14; Mk. 1:14, 15; Lu. 4:43; 8:1; 10:9–11; 11:20; 16:16; 21:31. Jesus the Christ—Mk. 1:1; Lu. 9:26; John 1:14–17, 29, 36; 3:14–17; 5:24; 6:33–45; 17:3; 20:31. The words

or sayings of Jesus—Mt. 7:24–27; 13: 3–9, 18–23; Mk. 4:3–9, 14–20; 8:38; 13:31; Lu. 6:46–49; 8:21; 9:26; 11:28; 21:33; John 6:63, 68; 8:31, 32, 37, 51; 12:48–50; 14:23, 24; 17:6–8.

After the death of Christ.—The kingdom of Christ—Acts 1:3, 6; 8:12; 20: 25; 28:23, 31.

Christ the Son of God, crucified and risen for sinners—The promise of the free forgiveness of sins for Christ's sake— Acts 1:8; 2:22–36; 3:13–26; 8:5, 12, 25, 35; 9:15, 20; 10:36–43; 15:7; 16: 30–32; 17:2, 3, 17, 18; 22:12–15; 24: 24, 25; 26:16–18; 28:23, 31; Rom. 10: 8–12; I Cor. 1:17–24; 2:2; 15:1–8, 12– 17; II Cor. 4:1–5; 5:18–21; Gal. 1:15, 16; 3:8; Eph. 1:12–14; 2:13–20; 3: 6–8; Phil. 1:15–18; Col. 1:27, 28; I Thess. 1:5–10; I Tim. 1:15; II Tim. 1:8–14; 2:8; I Pet. 1:10–12; Rev. 1:2, 9; 6:9; 20:4.

The great commission—Mt. 28:19, 20; Mk. 16:15, 16; Lu. 24:26, 27, 44–48.

The conditions of salvation, or of entrance into Christ—Acts 2:37–42; 3: 19; 8:12, 13, 36, 39; 10:44–48; 16:14, 15, 33; 22:16; Rom. 10:8–11. See OLD AND NEW COVENANTS.

The gospel must be preached: By Jesus. —Mk. 1:38, 39; Lu. 20:1; John 15:3. *To the poor and afflicted*—Is. 61:1–3; Mt. 11:5; Lu. 4:18, 19. *The gospel of the kingdom*—Mt. 4:23; 9:35; Mk. 1: 14, 15; Lu. 4:43; 8:1; 16:16. *The words which He received from the Father*— John 5:34; 8:38; 12:48–50; 17:6–8, 14. By His disciples—Is. 52:7; Nah. 1:15; John 6:44, 45; Acts 9:6; 11:19–21; 15: 32–36; 22:10; Rom. 1:16; 10:8–18; I Cor. 1:18–24; II Cor. 5:18–21; Eph. 1:13; 2:13–20; Phil. 2:14–16; 4:3; Col. 1:5, 6; I Thess. 1:5–10; Heb. 2:2–4; 4:2; I Pet. 1:12, 23–25; 4:6. *To the whole world*—Mt. 24:14; 26:13; 28:19, 20; Mk. 13:10; 14:9; 16:15; Col. 1:23.

By the seventy—Lu. 10:1–20.

By the apostles—Acts 5:20; 6:4, 7; 8:25. *The apostles sent out*—Mt. 10:5–15; 28:19, 20; Mk. 6:7–13; 16:15; Lu. 9: 2–6; 24:47–49. *By Peter*—Acts 2:14– 40; 3:12–26; 4:1–4, 29–37; 10:22, 34– 48; 11:1, 14; 15:7. *By Paul*—Acts 17: 2–4; 18:11; 20:24; 22:14, 15; 24:24,

25; 26:15–23; 28:23; I Cor. 1:17; 2: 4–6, 13; 4:15; 9:16–23; 15:1–4; II Cor. 4:1–5; Gal. 1:6–16; Eph. 6:17–20; Phil. 1:12–18; Col. 1:23–29; II Thess. 3:1; I Tim. 1:11–16. *Paul an apostle to the Gentiles*—Acts 9:15; 13:5–49; 14:5–7, 21–28; 16:6–17, 31–33; 19:1–5, 8–10, 18; 28:28–31; Rom. 1:13–15; 15:15–21; II Cor. 10:14–16; Gal. 2:2–10; 4: 13–15; Eph. 3:6–8; I Thess. 2:2–16; II Thess. 2:14, 15. *By Stephen*—Acts 6: 8, 10, 14; 7:2–53. *By Philip*—Acts 8: 4–6, 12, 13, 14, 30–40. *By Timothy*— II Tim. 4:1–5. *The gospel preached to Abraham*—Gal. 3:8. See WORD OF GOD.

GOSSIP. Deut. 22:14.

Talebearer.—Law against—Lev. 19:16. Denunciation of—Pr. 10:18; 11:13; 12:17; 14:5; 20:19.

False witness.—II Ki. 9:17. Laws concerning—Ex. 20:16; 23:7; Deut. 5: 20; 19:15–18; Pr. 19:5, 9; 21:28; Mt. 19:18; Mk. 10:19; Lu. 18:20; Rom. 13:9. Against the psalmist—Ps. 27: 12; 35:11. Hatred of Jehovah—Pr. 6:19; 11:1; 20:23; Zech. 8:17. Against Jesus—Mt. 26:59, 60; Mk. 14:56, 57; Acts 6:13. Of God—I Cor. 15:15.

Whisperings.—II Cor. 12:20. Whispers —Rom. 1:29. Whisperer—Pr. 18:8; 26:20, 22; Ps. 41:7. Slander—Jer. 6: 28; 9:4.

Slanderers.—I Tim. 4:11; Tit. 2:3, Slandered—II Sam. 19:27. Slanderest— Ps. 50:20.

Wicked lips.—Pr. 17:4.

Source of.—Mt. 15:19.

Talkers.—Ez. 36:3; Tit. 1:10.

Punishment of.—Mal. 3:5; Lu. 6:26.

Defaming.—Ps. 31:13; Jer. 20:10. Defamed—I Cor. 4:13.

Tattlers.—I Tim. 5:13.

Tongue a sharp sword.—Ps. 57:4; 64:3, 8; 140:3.

Lying.—Ps. 109:2; Pr. 6:17.

Deceitful.—Ps. 120:2, 3. Of fire—Jas. 3:6, 8.

Strife of.—Ps. 31:20.

Backbiters.—Ps. 15:3; Rom. 1:30. Backbiting—Pr. 25:23; II Cor. 12:20.

GOT. John 6:4.

GOTTEN. Gen. 4:1; Job 20:18; Ps. 74: 2; Rev. 3:17.

GORGEOUS. Clothing—Ez. 23:12; Lu. 7:25; 23:11. See CLOTHING.

GOURD. II Ki. 4:39. Jonah's—Jonah 4:6–10.

GOVERNMENT: (1) **Given to Adam and Eve.**—Gen. 1:26–28; 3:16.

(2) **To patriarchs** (children and servants treated as chattels).—Gen. 18: 17–19; 35:2–4; 35:6, 7.

(3) **To Moses.**—Ex. 18:19, 20; Mt. 23:3; Mk. 10:3.

(4) **To Moses' assistants.**—Ex. 18:21, 22; Num. 11:16; 13:2. Authority of elders—Ex. 3:16; 4:29; 12:21; 17:5, 6; Lev. 9:1; Num. 16:25; Deut. 5:23. Seventy special elders chosen—Num. 11:16; Deut. 1:13; Josh. 23:2.

(5) **Elders aid people in asking for king.**—Ju. 8:22, 23; 9:7–21; I Sam. 8: 4, 5. Objections to kings—I Sam. 8: 7–9. God consents to a king, under protest—I Sam. 8:7–9. Saul appointed by Samuel—I Sam. 9:20–27; 10:1.

(6) **Judicial system of Israel.**—Must give righteous judgment—Lev. 19:15; II Sam. 23:2–4; II Chr. 19:6, 7. Raised up for extraordinary duties— Ju. 2:16. Upheld by Jehovah—Ju. 2: 18. Not permanent or hereditary— Ju. 8:23. Disregarded by people—Ju. 2:19.

(7) **Israel comes under Egyptian government.**—(A training school) Begins with bondage of Joseph—Gen. 39:1–2. Joseph exalted to power—Gen. 41:38–57. Brings his kinsmen to Egypt— Gen. 45:9–11.

Prediction concerning enslavement.— Gen. 15:13; Acts 7:6–19. Enslavement begins—Ex. 1:8–14. God remembers his covenant with Israel— Ex. 2:23–25; 3:7–9; Neh. 9:9; Acts 7:34. Liberation of Israel demanded —Ex. 5:1–3. Pharaoh's refusal—Ex. 5:2–9. The struggle—Ex. Chs. 7–11. The release—Ex. 12:34–51.

(8) **Bondage and persecution fail to correct.**—Josh. 5:6; Ps. 106:24–27; Ez. 20:13–23. After failure of other rulers, God offers Himself as their Ruler — Hos. 13:9–11. High priest to be God's vicegerent—Ex. 28:30; Num. 27:18.

(9) **Gives precepts against corruption by adjoining nations.**—Lev. 18:2, 3; 20:23; Deut. 18:9; Josh. 23:7.

(10) **Laws with regard to land.**—Lev. 25:23–34. See LAND.

(11) **Instructions concerning municipal government.** — Deut. 19:12; 21:2–8; 22:13:21; 25:7–9; Ju. 8:14–16; 11:5–11; Ruth 4:2–11; Ezra 10:7–14.

(12) **Instructions to priests.**—Ex. 28:3; 29:4, 9–19, 21; 30:30; 40:15; Lev. 6: 12, 13; 8:6, 13, 33–36; 21:17–23; 24: 5–9; Num. 3:10; 6:23; Ch. 28; Deut. 17:8–13; 33:8,10; 18:1,2. See PRIESTS.

(13) **Government through prophets.**— Authority supreme over kings—I Sam. 15:13–28; II Sam. Ch. 12; I Ki. 18:17–20; Jer. 29:16–19. See PROPHETS.

(14) **Government through kings.**—God approves good kings—I Ki. 3:11–14; 14:7, 8; Is. 32:1. Characteristics described—Deut. 17:14–20. Laws for their governing written down—I Sam. 10:25; II Ki. 11:12. Power to make war—I Sam. 11:5–7. Exercised arbitrary power—I Sam. 22:17; II Sam. 1:13–15; I Ki. 2:23–25.

(15) **Men must respect government.**— Mt. 22:17–21; Rom. 13:1–7; I Pet. 2: 13–17.

(16) **Government of the church.** — Through apostles—Acts 4:32–35; 5: 3–13; 6:1–7; 15:6–11. Through elders —Acts 14:23; 15:22; 20:28; I Tim. 3:1–5; 5:17; Tit. 1:5–11. Through deacons—Acts 6:1–6; I Tim. 3:8–13; Rom. 16:1. Officers in their order— I Cor. 12:28; Eph. 4:11. Gifts and work—I Cor. 12:4–12; Eph. 4:12–16. See CHURCH, MINISTERS.

Ministers must govern.—Preach the word—II Tim. 4:2. Speak sound doctrine—Tit. 2:7, 8; Eph. 4:14. Endure hardship—II Tim. 2:3–5; 4:5. Shun foolish questions—Tit. 3:9. Tend the flock of God faithfully—I Pet. 5:2, 3. Commend himself to conscience—II Cor. 4:2. Declare whole counsel of God—Acts 20:27. Workman needing not to be ashamed—II Tim. 2:15.

GOVERNORS. Of Egypt, Joseph is governor—Gen. 42:6. Of the people —II Chr. 23:20. Of the country—I Ki. 10:15. Brought gold and silver to Solomon—II Chr. 9:14. Beyond the river—Ezra 5:3; 6:6, 13. Receive king's commissions—Ezra 8:36. Receive letters from king—Neh. 2:7, 9.

That appertained to the governors beyond the river—Neh. 3:7. Over every province receive letters from the king —Esth. 3:12. In land of Judah—Neh. 5:14, 15; Hag. 1:1; 2:2, 21. Chief governor of Babylon—Dan. 2:48. Of Syria—Lu. 2:2. Of Judaea, Pontius Pilate—Lu. 3:1. Gathered together unto dedication of the image that Nebuchadrezzar set up—Dan. 3:3, 27. Consultation of—Dan. 6:7. See GOVERNMENT, RULERS.

GOZAN, gō′zan. **A region in Central Asia.**—II Ki. 17:6.

GRACE. Gr. *Charis,* "Graciousness," "Good-will," "Favor," "Joy-bringing."

Winsomeness of person or character.— Ps. 45:2; Pr. 1:9; 3:22; 4:9; 22:11; 31:30.

Kindness sought.—Gen. 32:5; 33:8; 34: 11; 47:25; 50:4; Ex. 34:9; Num. 32:5; Ju. 6:17; Ruth 2:2; I Sam. 1:18; 27:5; II Sam. 16:4; Acts 25:3.

Kindness bestowed.—Gen. 6:8; 19:19; 39:4; Ex. 33:12, 13, 16, 17; I Sam. 20: 3; II Sam. 14:22; Jer. 31:2.

Good-will.—Lu. 1:30; 2:52; Acts 2:47; 7:10; Rom. 1:73; 16:20; I Cor. 1:3; 16:23; II Cor. 1:2; Gal. 1:3; Eph. 1:2; 6:24; Phil. 1:2; 4:23. (All salutations.)

God's spiritual force working through truth.—John 1:16; Acts 11:23; Rom. 5:2; I Cor. 15:9, 10; II Cor. 6:1; 8:1; 9:14; 12:9; Eph. 2:4, 5; I Tim. 1:14; II Tim. 2:1; I Pet. 3:18.

Free gift of God's love in contrast to bondage of law.—John 1:16; Rom. 5:2; Gal. 1:3; Eph. 2:8–10.

Salvation by grace.—Acts 11:19–23; 18: 27; 20:24–32; Rom. 3:24, 25; 4:4; 5:1, 2; 6:1, 14; 11:5–8; I Cor. 10:30; 15:10; II Cor. 1:12; 6:1; Eph. 2:5, 7; Heb. 12:15; Tit. 2:11–14; I Pet. 4:10.

God shows His grace in his kindness toward man through Christ.—John 1: 17; Acts 15:11; Rom. 1:4–7; 3:24; 5: 1, 2, 15–21; II Cor. 4:14, 15; 8:9; 9:8; Gal. 2:21; Eph. 1:4–11; 2:4–7; II Tim. 1:9, 10; Tit. 2:11–14; 3:4–7; Heb. 2:9, 10; 10:29.

We have access by faith into this grace. —Rom. 3:25; 4:16; 5:2; II Cor. 6:1; Eph. 2:8; I Pet. 1:7–11.

GRACIOUS. God—See GRACE. Woman —Pr. 11:16. Words—Eccl. 10:12.

GRAFT. Tree—Rom. 11:17–24.

GRAIN. Grain in Pharaoh's dream— Gen. 41:5. All came to buy grain— Gen. 41:57; 42:1. Grain given for famine—Gen. 42:33; Acts 7:12. Law on burning grain—Ex. 22:6. Grain for offering—Lev. 16:6. Offering before eating—Lev. 23:14. Likeness to heave-offering—Num. 18:27. Used as a measure of time—Deut. 16:9. Must not muzzle ox—Deut. 25:4; I Cor. 9: 9; I Tim. 5:18. Grain eaten after passover—Josh. 5:11. Ruth gleans among—Ruth 2:2. Lies down at heap —Ruth 3:3. David takes to brethren —I Sam. 17:17. Abigail takes to David's men—I Sam. 25:18. Inhabitants likened to blasted grain—II Ki. 19: 2b, Is. 37:27. Nehemiah's builders seek grain—Neh. 5:2. Aged man like shock of—Job 5:26. Can a beast plan a harvest?—Job 39:12. God provides—Ps. 65:9, 13; 72:16; 78:24. Withholder is cursed—Pr. 11:26. Merely gleanings for wicked—Is. 17: 5–6. Wantonness like trampling heifer—Jer. 50:11. Idolatry punished —Hos. 8:7. Jehovah promises abundance—Joel 2:19, 24. Will sift Israel —Amos 9:9. Grain makes prosperous— Zech. 9:17.

New Testament uses parables.—Mt. 13: 1–8, 24–32; Mk. 4:1–32; Lu. 8:4–15. Also Mt. 17:20; Lu. 13:19; 17:6. Pull down my barns—Lu. 12:18. Except a grain of wheat die—John 12:24. Pluck ears of grain—Mt. 12:1; Mk. 2:23; Lu. 6:1. Argument for resurrection—I Cor. 15:37. See BARLEY, FOOD, WHEAT.

GRANDCHILDREN. I Tim. 5:4. See CHILDREN.

GRANDMOTHER. II Tim. 5:4.

GRANT. Apostles, To—Mk. 10:37. Deliverance—II Chr. 22:7; Lu. 1:74. Jehovah—Ruth 1:9; I Sam. 1:17; I Chr. 4:10; II Chr. 22:7; Job 6:8; Acts 14: 3; Rom. 15:5; Eph. 3:16. King—Ez. 7:6; Neh. 2:8. Knowledge—II Chr. 1:12. Life—Job 10:12. Loving-kindness—Job 10:12. Mercy—Neh. 1:11; II Tim. 1:16, 18. Petition—Esth. 5: 6; 7:2; 5:8; 8:11; 9:12, 13; Ps. 20:4.

Redemption of land—Lev. 25:24. Salvation—Ps. 85:7; Acts 11:18. Wisdom—II Chr. 1:12.

GRAPES: This vine was cultivated at an early period.—Gen. 9:20. A leading product of Palestine—Num. 13: 24; Ju. 9:27; I Ki. 21:1; Ps. 128:3; Song of Sol. 6:11; Jer. 31:5.

Grew to large size.—Grapes of Eshcol— Num. 13:23. Of Heshbon—Is. 15:8– 10. Of Sibmah—Jer. 48:32.

Finest grapes dried for raisins.—I Sam. 25:18; 30:12; II Sam. 16:1; I Chr. 12:40.

Time of ripening depends on location.— Along the coast of Palestine they ripen as early as July; in the highlands, about a month later; while those out of which wine is made are gleaned in September and October.

This was the time of the festivals of booths (Tisri).—Ju. 9:27; Is. 16:10; Jer. 25:30; 48:33.

Grapes made into wine.—The juice was pressed out, with the feet, in the winepress—Is. 63:2, 3. It passed from thence into a lower vat, usually hewn out of stone—Is. 5:2. Sometimes another vat was used to allow the "must" to settle and clarify—Hag. 2:16.

The wine was poured off into jars.— Sealed, and stowed away in cellars— I Chr. 27:27. Or, it was poured from bottle to bottle, to refine it—Is. 25:6; Zeph. 1:12 (marg.); Mt. 9:17.

New wine had to stand 40 days.—After that it was used for the drink-offering in the sanctuary (Mishna).

The use of wine was common among Hebrews.—There was an exception where a vow had been taken, such as the Nazirite—Num. 6:2–4. Even he had a time to drink it (Num. 6:20), and the Rechabite—Jer. 35:1–14.

Priests not permitted wine when entering Holy Place.—Lev. 10:9.

Hebrew wines were light, often diluted with water.—II Macc. 15:39.

The wine of Sharon often mixed with two parts of water.—Talmud.

As it was, the Hebrews recognized the danger.—Pr. 20:1; 23:29–32; Is. 5:11, 22; 28:1–8; Hos. 4:11; Nah. 1:10; Hab. 2:15.

Paul's principle a correct one.—I Cor. 8:8–13; Rom. 14:13–21. See VINE-YARD.

GRASPED. Phil. 2:6.

GRASS. Earth brings forth—Gen. 1:11. Israel licks up everything as an ox—Num. 22:4. Give grass for thy cattle —Deut. 11:15; Ps. 106:20. Ahab searches for grass to save horses—I Ki. 18:5. Offspring shall be as—Job 5:25. Behemoth eateth grass as an ox—Job 40:15. Nebuchadrezzar made to eat grass as oxen—Dan. 4:25, 32, 33; 5:21. Wicked spring as the —Ps. 37:2; 92:7; Pr. 9:12. Mown grass—Ps. 72:6. Dew on the—Pr. 19: 12; Dan. 4:15, 23. If God doth so clothe the—Mt. 6:30; Lu. 12:28. There was much—Mk. 6:39; John 6:10. Locusts should not hurt—Rev. 9:4. No grass grow—Deut. 29:23; II Sam. 23: 4; Jer. 14:5. Tender—Deut. 32:2; Pr. 27:25; Is. 15:6; Dan. 4:15, 23; Mk. 6:39. Flourish like—Ps. 72:16; 90:5; 104:14; 147:8; Is. 35:7; Zech. 10:1. Locusts eat—Amos 7:2. Made to sit down on—Mt. 14:19; Mk. 6:39; John 6:10. Among the—Is. 44:4. Withered—Ps. 102:4, 11; 129:6; Is. 15:6; 37:27; 40:6–8; 51:12; Mic. 5:7; Jas. 1:10. Burnt up—Rev. 8:7.

Brevity of life, compared to grass.—II Ki. 19:26; Ps. 90:5; 102:11; 103:15; 129:6; Is. 40:6, 7; I Pet. 1:24. See PLANTS.

GRASSHOPPERS. See INSECTS.

GRATING. Ex. 27:4; 35:16; 38:4, 5, 30; 39:39.

GRAVE, *adj.* I Tim. 3:8; Tit. 2:2. See SOBRIETY.

GRAVE, *n.* No graves in Egypt—Ex. 14:11. Of Rachel—Gen. 35:20. Of Jacob: In Canaan—Gen. 50:5. Of Abner—II Sam. 3:32. Of Barzillai—II Sam. 19:37. Man of God laid in prophet's grave—I Ki. 13:30. Of Asshur—Ez. 32:22, 23. Of Elam—Ez. 32:24, 25. Of Meshech—Ez. 32:26. Of common people—II Ki. 23:6; Jer. 26: 23. Shall come to—I Ki. 14:13; Job 5:26; 10:19. Thou shalt be gathered unto—II Ki. 22:20; II Chr. 34:28. Borne to—Job 21:32. Lie in—Ps. 88: 5. Declared in—Ps. 88:11. With wicked—Is. 53:9. Make—Nah. 1:14.

Find grave—Job 3:22. Strewed upon —II Chr. 34:4. Made ready—Job 17: 1. Among—Is. 65:4. Out of—Jer. 8: 1; Ez. 37:13.

Law of.—Num. 19:16, 18.

Prophecy concerning.—Ez. 37:12.

Figurative.—Jer. 20:17. See BURIAL PLACES, SEPULCHRE.

GRAVE, *v.* See ARTS AND TRADES, IMAGES.

GRAVEL. Pr. 20:17; Lam. 3:16.

GRAVEN IMAGES. See IMAGES, IDOLATRY.

GRAVITY. I Tim. 2:2. See GRAVE, SOBRIETY.

GRAY. See COLORS.

GRAY-HEADED. Job 15:10. See AGE, OLD, HAIR, HEAD.

GREAT. Abominations—Ez. 8:6. Commandment—Mt. 22:38. Cloud of witnesses, A—Heb. 12:1. Glory—Ps. 21: 5; II Cor. 7:4. God—Tit. 2:13. Iniquity—Ps. 25:11. Jehovah is—II Sam. 7:22; I Chr. 16:25; Ps. 48:1; 95:3; 145:3. See GOD. Mercy—I Pet. 1:3. Name—Mal. 1:11. Portion with the, A—Is. 53:12. Power—Ex. 32:11. Promises—II Pet. 1:4. Reward in heaven—Mt. 5:12. Salvation—Heb. 2:3. Seed—Job 5:25. Shepherd—Heb. 13:20. Strength—Ps. 33:16. Throne—Rev. 20:11. Wickedness—Gen. 6:5; I Sam. 12:17.

GREATER. Barns, Build—Lu. 12:18. Father than all—John 10:29. Gifts —I Cor. 12:13. God than—Job 33:12; I John 3:20. John the Baptist, Than —Mt. 11:11. Joy—III John 4. Solomon, Than—Mt. 12:42. Temple, Than —Mt. 12:6. Things, See—John 1:50. Waxed—II Sam. 5:10.

GREATEST. In the kingdom of heaven —Mt. 18:1. Love, Is—I Cor. 13:13. Man—Job 1:3. To a thousand—I Chr. 12:14.

GREATLY. Amazed—Mk. 14:33. Feared Jehovah—I Ki. 18:3. Heart rejoiceth —Ps. 28:7. Err—Mk. 12:27. Exalted —Ps. 47:9. Man beloved—Dan. 10: 11. Pain, Multiply—Gen. 3:16. Praised, To be—I Chr. 16:25; Ps. 48:1; 143:3. Rejoice—Ps. 21:1; 61:10; Zech. 9:9. Sinned—II Sam. 24:10.

GREATNESS. Dan. 5:18. Added, Was —Dan. 4:36. All—II Sam. 7:21.

Ascribe unto God—Deut. 32:3. Excellency, Of—Ex. 15:7. Increase of—Ps. 71:21. Jehovah, Thine is the—I Chr. 29:11. Lovingkindness, Of thy—Neh. 13:22. Power, Of—Ps. 66:3; II Cor. 4:7. Revelations, Of—II Cor. 12:7. Strength, Of—Is. 63:1. Unsearchable —Ps. 145:3.

GREAVES. I Sam. 17:6.

GREECE. Prophecies concerning.—Dan. 8:5–21; 10:20; 11:2. See JAVAN.

GREEKS. Mentioned.—John 7:35; 12: 20; Acts 11:20; 14:1; 17:4; 18:4; 19: 10; Rom. 1:16; Gal. 2:3.

Distinction between Jew and Greek broken down.—Rom. 1:14, 16; 3:22; 10:12; I Cor. 12:13; Gal. 3:23; Col. 3:11.

Timothy's father a Greek.—Acts 16:1, 3.

GRECIAN, or GREEK-SPEAKING JEWS. In Acts 6:1 a distinction is made between the Christian Jews who belonged to the Dispersion and spoke Greek (Hellenists), and the Christian Jews who were Palestinians and spoke Aramic (Hebrews). The term Hellenist occurs also in Acts 9:29 for Jews of the Dispersion now in Jerusalem; while in Acts 11:20 the Revised Version (American) correctly reads "Greeks also," not Jews at all. For Greek in the usual, non-Jewish sense, see Acts 16:1; 18:4; Rom. 1:14, 16; 10:12; John 12:20; Gal. 3:28.

GREEDY. Dogs—Is. 56:11. Lion, As a —Ps. 17:12. Men—Pr. 1:19; 15:27; 21:26; Eph. 4:19; I Tim. 3:8. See GLUTTONY, COVETOUSNESS.

GREEN. See COLORS.

GREETING. I Sam. 25:5; Acts 15:23; 23:26; Heb. 11:13; Jas. 1:1; II John 10:11. See SALUTATION.

GREW. See GROW.

GRIEF. Eccl. 1:18; 2:23; Lam. 3:32; Heb. 13:17; I Pet. 1:6; 2:19. Children cause—Gen. 26:35; Pr. 17:25. David, Of—Ps. 6:7; 31:9. See DAVID'S LAMENT OVER ABSALOM. Day of—Is. 17: 11. Jeremiah, Of—Jer. 10:19. See JEREMIAH, IN OUTLINE STUDIES. Jesus, Of—Is. 53:3, 4, 10. See JESUS, SUFFERINGS OF. Job—Job 2:13; 15:5, 6. See SORROW.

GRIEVING. Neh. 8:10; Ps. 119:158. Brother—Rom. 14:15. Eli—I Sam. 2:

33. Forty years—Ps. 95:10; Heb. 3:10, 11. God—Gen. 6:6; Ps. 78:40; 95:10; Heb. 3:10, 17. Hardening of heart, At—Mk. 3:3. Heart—I Sam. 1:8; Ps. 73:21; Ez. 13:22. Holy Spirit—Is. 63: 10; Eph. 4:30; Heb. 10:29. Peter— John 21:17. Samuel—I Sam. 15:11. Soul—Ju. 10:16; I Sam. 30:6; Ps. 73: 21. See GRIEF, SORROW.

GRIEVOUS. Burdens—Mt. 23:4. See BURDEN. Chastening — Heb. 12:11. Commandments—I John 5:3. Destruction—Mic. 2:10. Evil—Eccl. 5:13. Mourning—Gen. 50:11. Swarms of flies—Ex. 8:24. Times—II Tim. 3:1. Tormented—Mt. 8:6. Vexed—Mt. 15: 22. Wolves—Acts 20:29. Word—Pr. 15:1.

GRIEVOUSLY. Mt. 17:15; Mk. 9:20; Lu. 9:42.

GRIND. Cease—Eccl. 12:3. Face of the poor—Is. 3:15. Prison house, In— Ju. 16:21. Sound of—Eccl. 12:4. Teeth —Mk. 9:18.

GRIZZLED. Gen. 31:10.

GROAN. Beasts—Joel 1:18. Creation —Rom. 8:22. David—Ps. 6:6; 22:1; 32:3; 38:8. God heard—Ex. 2:24. Jesus—John 11:33. Job—Job 3:24. Men —Job 24:12. Weary with—Ps. 6:6; Jer. 45:3. We ourselves—Rom. 8:23. Wounded—Jer. 51:52. See AFFLICTION, ANGUISH, MOURNING, SORROW.

GROPE. Deut. 28:29; Job 12:25.

GROSS. Darkness—Is. 60:2. Heart— Mt. 13:15.

GROUND. Used in formation of man.— Gen. 2:6, 7, 19.

The occupation of man.—Gen. 2:5, 8, 15; 3:18–19, 23; 4:2, 3, 12; I Chr. 27:26.

Cursed for man's sake.—Gen. 3:17; 5: 29. Is dried—Gen. 8:8, 13. Not to be cursed again—Gen. 8:21, 22.

Cultivation of.—Job 14:8; Ps. 107:33; Is. 28:24; 30:23–25; Jer. 4:3; Hos. 10: 12; Mt. 13:8, 23; Mk. 4:5, 8; Lu. 8:8, 15; 13:7; John 12:24.

Piece of.—Josh. 24:32; II Ki. 9:26.

Fruits of.—Deut. 28:4, 11; I Sam. 8:12; II Sam. 23:11; I Chr. 11:13; Neh. 10: 35; Ps. 105:35; 107:35; Jer. 7:20; Zech. 8:12; Mal. 3:11; Lu. 12:16.

Out of.—Job 5:6.

Fell or cast upon.—Gen. 38:9; Ex. 4:3; I Sam. 3:19; 5:4; 14:25–26; II Sam. 14:4, 22; 17:12; Job 1:20; 38:27; Lam. 2:2; Ps. 89:39, 44; 143:3; 147:6; Is. 14:12; 21:9; 25:12; 26:5; Ez. 13:14; 19:12; 26:11; 38:20; Dan. 8:7, 10, 12; 10:9, 15; Amos 3:14; Ob. 3; Mt. 10:29; Mk. 9:20; 14:35; Lu. 22:44; John 18: 6; Acts 22:7.

Upon the.—Gen. 19:25; Ex. 8:21; 16:14; Deut. 9:21; 15:23; 28:56; Ju. 13:20; 20:21, 25; I Sam. 2:22; 14:23, 45; 20: 31; 26:7; II Sam. 8:2; 14:14; 18:11; 20:10; II Ki. 13:18; Job 16:13; Ps. 74:7; Is. 3:26; 47:1; Jer. 14:2; Lam. 2:10, 21; Ez. 24:7; 26:16; 41:16, 20; 44:3; 47:1; Hos. 2:18; Mt. 15:35; John 8:6, 8; 9:6.

Bowed to.—Gen. 33:3; Ju. 13:20; Ruth 2:10; I Sam. 20:41; 25:23; 28:14; II Sam. 14:33; I Ki. 1:23; II Ki. 2:15; 4:37; 21:21; II Chr. 7:3; Neh. 8:6; Is. 51:23; Lam. 2:10.

Trouble from.—Gen. 4:10; II Ki. 2:19; Job 5:16; 18:10; Jer. 14:4.

Holy.—Ex. 3:5; Ps. 99:9; Ez. 45:1; Acts 7:33.

Used for casting brass.—I Ki. 7:46; II Chr. 4:17.

Jerusalem brought low.—Is. 29:4; Lam. 2:9; Lu. 19:44.

Purchase or gift of.—Gen. 23:11–13; Lu. 14:18; John 4:4.

Ground as a basis.—I Chr. 21:21–22; Eph. 3:17; Col. 1:23; I Tim. 3:15.

Swallowed the wicked: Korah, etc.—Num. 16:30–33.

Sisera pinned to.—Ju. 4:21.

Gideon's test.—Ju. 6:36–40.

Thirsty or dry.—Is. 35:7; 44:3; 53:2.

On dry ground through sea.—Ex. 14:16, 22. **Through Jordan.**—Josh. 3:17.

Fire ran down.—Ex. 9:23.

Bird's nest upon.—Deut. 22:6. See EARTH, LAND.

GROUND, *v.* Is. 28:28.

GROUNDED. Eph. 3:17; Col. 1:23. See ESTABLISH, FOUND, FOUNDATION.

GROW. Ez. 31:4; Zech. 6:12; I Pet. 2:2. All things, Into—Eph. 4:15. Faith—II Cor. 10:15; II Thess. 1:3. Holy temple, Into—Eph. 2:21. Lilies of the field—Mt. 6:28. Grace, In—II Pet. 2:2. Jesus—Lu. 1:80; 2:40. Mustard

seed—Mt. 13:32; Mk. 4:32. Seed—Lu. 13:19. Thorns—Mt. 13:7; Mk. 4: 7; Lu. 8:7. Together until harvest—Mt. 13:30. Word of God—Mt. 13:30; Acts 12:24; 19:20; Lu. 8:6.

GROWLING. Is. 31:4.

GRUDGE. Bear—Lev. 19:18. Do not—II Cor. 9:7.

GUARD, *n.* Be a—Neh. 4:22; Ez. 38:7. Bare shields—I Ki. 14:28. Captain of —Gen. 37:36; 39:1; 40:3, 4; 41:10, 12; II Ki. 35:8, 10, 12, 15, 18; Jer. 39:9; 40:1, 2, 5; 41:10; 43:6; 52:12, 14, 15, 16, 19, 24, 26, 30; Dan. 2:14. Cast them out—II Ki. 10:25. Court of—Neh. 3:25; Jer. 32:2. Examined the—Acts 12:19. Followed—Neh. 4:23. Over his—II Sam. 23:23; I Chr. 11:25. Stood—I Sam. 22:17; II Ki. 11:11.

GUARD, *v.* Lu. 4:10; Acts 12:4; I Tim. 6:20; II Tim. 1:12. City—II Cor. 11: 32. Evil one, From—II Thess. 3:3. Faith, Through—I Pet. 1:5. Holy Spirit, Through—II Tim. 1:14. Idols, From—I John 5:21. Mouth, His—Pr. 13:3. Peace of God shall—Phil. 4:7. Soldier—Acts 28:16. See GOD, PROVIDENCE OF.

GUARDIANS. Gal. 4:2.

GUDGODAH, gŭd'go-dah. Deut. 10:7.

GUEST-CHAMBER. I Sam. 9:22. See CHAMBER, HOSPITALITY.

GUESTS. I Ki. 1:41. Wedding—Mt. 22: 10. See HOSPITALITY, MARRIAGE.

GUIDANCE. Job 37:12. Wise—Pr. 11: 14; 20:18; 24:6.

GUIDE. Canst thou guide the bear—Job 38:32. Blind—Mt. 15:14; 23:16, 24; Lu. 6:39. Death, Even unto—Ps. 48:14. Except some man should—Rom. 2:19; Acts 8:31. Eye, With mine—Ps. 32:8. Feet in way of peace—Lu. 1:79. Fountains, Unto—Rev. 7:17. God is our—See GOD. Heart, Thine—Pr. 23:19. Holy Spirit—See HOLY SPIRIT. Justice, In—Ps. 25:9. Paths, In—Ps. 23:3. Perfect—II Sam. 22:33. Righteous is a—Pr. 12:26. Truth, Into all—Ps. 25:5; John 16:13. See HOLY SPIRIT, TRUTH. Youth, Of my—Jer. 3:4.

GUILE. Ps. 54:11; Pr. 26:26; John 1: 47; Acts 13:10; I Thess. 2:3; Heb. 2: 26; I Pet. 2:1, 2. Answer with—Gen. 34:13. Brother, Of—Gen. 27:35. Catch

with—II Cor. 12:16. Slay with—Ex. 21:14. Speak with—Ps. 34:13; I Pet. 2:22; 3:10. Spirit, In—Ps. 32:2.
GUILT. Bear—Hos. 13:16. Cause of—I Chr. 21:3.
GUILTINESS. Gen. 26:10. Grown up, Is —Ezra 9:6. Still in his—Ps. 68:21.
GUILTLESS. Mt. 12:5. Be—Num. 32: 22; I Sam. 26:9. Condemned—Mt. 12: 7. Hold him not—I Ki. 2:9. Kingdom —II Sam. 3:28. King and his throne —II Sam. 14:9. Lord will not hold him—Ex. 20:7; Deut. 5:11. Oath, Of —Josh. 2:20. We shall be—Josh. 2:19.
GUILTY. All, Of—Jas. 2:10. Be—Lev. 4:13, 27; 5:2, 3, 4, 5, 17; 6:4; Num. 5:6; Ju. 21:22. Become—Ez. 22:4. Being—Ezra 10:19. Body and blood, Of —I Cor. 11:27. Clear, By no means—Ex. 34:7; Num. 14:18; Nah. 1:3. Come forth—Ps. 109:7. Exceedingly—Ezra 9:7. Found—Is. 24:6. Held—Jer. 2:3; Pr. 30:10. Jehovah, Towards—II Chr. 19:10. Murder, That is—Num. 35:31. Not—Zech. 11:4. One—II Sam. 14:13. Sin, Of an eternal—Mk. 3:29. We are verily—Gen. 42:21.
GULF. Fixed—Lu. 16:26.
GUNI, gū-ni. (1) A member of the tribe of Naphtali.—Gen. 46:24; Num. 26: 48; I Chr. 7:13.
(2) I Chr. 5:15.
GUNITES. Descendants of Guni.—(1) Num. 26:48.
GUR, gûr. Place where Ahaziah was wounded—II Ki. 9:27.
GUR-BAAL, gûr-bā'al. II Chr. 26:7.
HAAHASHTARI, hā'a-hāsh'ta-ri. A descendant of Judah.—I Chr. 4:6.
HABAKKUK, ha-bǎk'kuk. See OUTLINE STUDIES IN THE BOOKS.
HABAZZINIAH, hǎb'az-zi-nī'ah. A Rechabite.—Jer. 35:3.
HABITABLE. Pr. 8:31.
HABITATION. Angels left their—Jude 6. Birds had—Dan. 4:21. Builded together for a—Eph. 2:22. City of—Ps. 107:4, 7. Clothed upon with our—II Cor. 5:2. Deceit, In midst of—Jer. 9:6. Desolate—Acts 1:20. God, Of—Deut. 26:15; II Chr. 6:2; 30:27; Ps. 83:12. High—Ob. 3. Land of—Num. 15:2. Most high thy—Ps. 91:9. No—Ps. 49: 14. Peaceable—Is. 32:18. Place of—Ps. 33:14. Righteous, Of—Ps. 74:20.

Rock of—Ps. 71:3. Sun and moon in their—Hab. 3:11. Temple—II Chr. 6: 2; 30:27. Ps. 26:8. Violence, Of—Ps. 74:20. Waste, Laid—Ps. 79:7. See HOUSE, TEMPLE.
HABOR, hā'bôr. A river flowing into the Euphrates.—II Ki. 17:6; I Chr. 5:26.
HACALIAH, hǎk'a-lī'ah. Father of Nehemiah.—Neh. 1:1; 10:1.
HACHILAH, hǎk'i-lah. A hill.—I Sam. 23:19; 26:1.
HACHMONI, hǎk'mo-nī. One of David's mighty men.—I Chr. 27:32.
HACHMONITE. I Chr. 11:11.
HADAD, hā'dǎd. (1) A king of Edom. —Gen. 36:35; I Chr. 1:46.
(2) Another king of Edom.—I Chr. 1:50.
(3) An Edomite.—I Ki. 11:14. See HADAR.
HADADEZER, hǎd'ad-ē'zer. II Sam. 8: 3, 12; I Ki. 11:23. See HADAREZER.
HADADRIMMON, hā'dad-rǐm'mon. A city in Jezreel.—Zech. 12:11.
HADAREZER. II Sam. 10:16, 19. See HADADERER.
HADASHAH, hǎd'a-shah. A town in Judah.—Josh. 15:37.
HADASSAH. Another name for Esther. —Esth. 2:7.
HADES. *Heb.* Sheol. The underworld, abode of the dead, hence sometimes death. Brought down unto—Lu. 10: 15. Cast into lake of fire—Rev. 20:14. Church, Shall not prevail against—Mt. 16:18. Dead, Gave up—Rev. 20: 13. Death, Hades followed—Rev. 20: 14. Go down unto—Mt. 11:23. Keys of—Rev. 1:18. Rich man in—Lu. 16: 23. Soul, Will not leave my soul in—Acts 2:27, 31. See GRAVE, SHEOL.
HADID, hā'did. Ez. 2:33; Neh. 7:37.
HADLAI, hǎd'lai. Father of Amasa—II Chr. 28:12.
HADORAM, ha-dō'ram. Gen. 10:27; I Chr. 18:10; II Chr. 10:18.
HADRACH, hā'drach. Zech. 9:1.
HAFT. Ju. 3:22.
HAGAB, hā'gab. Ezra 2:46.
HAGABA. Neh. 7:48.
HAGAR, hā'gar. Handmaid of Sarai—Gen. 16:1. Taken as legal concubine at Sarai's suggestion—Gen. 16:2, 3. Hagar despises Sarai—Gen. 16:5. Causes trouble—Gen. 16:5, 6. Hagar flees into

wilderness, but is sent back by an angel—Gen. 16:7–9. Her seed to be multiplied—Gen. 16:10; 17:20; 21:18. Descendants—Gen. 16:12, 15, 25; 12–18; I Chr. 5:10, 19, 20; 27:31; Ps. 83:6. Descendants described—Gen. 16:12. Ishmael born—Gen. 16:11–16. Hagar recognizes Jehovah—Gen. 16:13. Hagar sent away—Gen. 21:9–16. God appears unto Hagar—Gen. 21:17–20.

Figurative.—Gal. 4:24–25. See SARAH, ISHMAEL.

HAGGAI, hăg'ga-i. See OUTLINE STUDIES IN THE BOOKS.

HAGGI, hăg'gi. **A Gadite.**—Gen. 49:16; Num. 26:15.

HAGGIAH, hăg'gī'ah. A Levite—I Chr. 6:30.

HAGGITES, hăg'gites. **Descendants of Haggi.**—Num. 26:15.

HAGGITH, hăg'gĭth. **Wife of David, mother of Adonijah.**—II Sam. 3:4; I Ki. 1:5.

HAGRI, hăg'ri. (1) I Chr. 11:38.

HAGRITES. Ps. 83:6; I Chr. 5:10; 27:30.

HAIL. See METEOROLOGY.

HAIL. An interjection.—Mt. 26:49; 27:29; Mk. 15:18; Lu. 1:28.

HAIR. Hair of man.—Gray hair—Gen. 42:38; 44:29. Hairs of my head—Ps. 40:12; 69:4. There shall not one hair fall to the ground—I Sam. 14:45; II Sam. 14:11; I Ki. 1:52. Shall not perish—Lu. 21:18; Acts 27:34. Long hair—I Cor. 11:14, 15. Braided, not with—I Tim. 2:9; I Pet. 3:3. Hair of Absalom—II Sam. 14:26. Samson—Ju. 16:22. Shadrach, Meshach and Abednego not singed—Dan. 5:27. Mary wiped His feet with her hair—John 11:2; 12:3. Plucked off—Ezra 9:3; Neh. 13:25; Is. 50:6. Thou shalt not swear by thy head—Mt. 5:36.

Laws concerning.—Num. 6:5, 18, 19. Works of goat's hair—Num. 31:20.

Test of leprosy.—In plague—Lev. 13:3, 4, 10, 20, 25, 26, 30, 37, 40, 41.

Shaven.—To be cleansed—Lev. 14:8, 9.

Hair of flesh.—Job 4:15.

Hair of goats.—Ex. 25:4; 26:7; 35:6, 23, 26; 36:14. Pillow of goat's hair—I Sam. 19:13, 16.

Camel's hair.—John was clothed with—Mt. 3:4; Mk. 1:6.

HAKKATAN, hăk'ka-tăn. **Father of Johanan.**—Ezra 8:12.

HAKKOZ, hăk'kŏz. (1) **A man of Judah.**—I Chr. 4:8.

(2) **A priest.**—I Chr. 24:10; Ezra 2:61; Neh. 3:4, 21; 7:63.

HAKUPHA, ha-kū-phà. Ezra 2:51; Neh. 7:53.

HALAH, hā'lah. **A district in Media.**—II Ki. 17:6.

HALAK, hā'lak. Josh. 11:17; 12:7.

HALF. Blood—Ex. 24:6. Cubit—See CUBIT. Days, Of their—Ps. 55:23. Goods, Of my—Lu. 19:8. Hour—Rev. 8:1. Kingdom, Of—Esth. 5:3, 6; 7:2; Mk. 6:23. Shekel—See SHEKEL. Time and a—Dan. 7:25.

HALHUL, hăl'hul. **A town in Judah.**—Josh. 15:58.

HALI, hā'li. **A town on border of Asher.**—Josh. 19:25.

HALLELUJAH. See PRAISE, PSALMS.

HALLOHESH, hal-lō'hesh. Neh. 3:12; 10:24.

HALLOW, HALLOWED. Altar—Lev. 16:19. Aaron shall be—Ex. 29:21. Be thy name—Mt. 6:9; Lu. 11:2. Court—I Ki. 8:64; II Chr. 7:7. First-born in Israel—Num. 3:13. Head—Num. 6:11. House, This—I Ki. 9:3, 7; II Chr. 7:16; 36:14. Jehovah—Lev. 22:32. Sabbath day—Ex. 20:11; Jer. 17:22, 24, 27; Ex. 20:20; 44:24. Tabernacle—Ex. 40:9. The fiftieth year—Lev. 25:10. Things—Lev. 12:4; 22:2, 3; Num. 5:10; II Ki. 12:18. See HOLINESS, SANCTIFICATION.

HALT. Mt. 18:8. See LAMENESS.

HAM. Signifies ''hot.'' (1) **Son of Noah.**—Gen. 5:32; 9:18; I Chr. 1:4.

Is indecent toward his father, for which he and his descendants are cursed.—Gen. 9:22–25.

His children.—Gen. 10:6–20; I Chr. 1:8–16.

Egyptians his descendants.—Ps. 78:51; 105:23. Ancestors of Cush (Ethiopia), Mizraim (Egypt), Phut (Libya), and Canaan.

First steps in arts and sciences seemingly due to Hamites. Descendants of Ham smitten by the Simeonites—I Chr. 4:40–42.

(2) See EGYPT.

HAMAN, hā′man. **Prime-minister of Ahasuerus.** See ESTHER, BOOK OF.

HAMATH, hā′math. **A Syrian town.**—Num. 34:8.

HAMATHITE. Gen. 10:18.

HAMATH-ZOBAH, hā′math–zō′bah. **A place in Syria.**—II Chr. 8:2.

HAMMATH, hăm′math. (1) I Chr. 2:55.

(2) **A town in Naphtali.**—Josh. 19:35.

HAMMEDATHA, ham-mĕd′a-thá. **Father of Haman.**—Esth. 3:1; 8:5.

HAMMELECH, hăm′me-lek. Jer. 36:26 marg.

HAMMER. Break down with—Ps. 74:6. Earth, Of whole—Jer. 50:23. Fashioneth it with—Is. 44:12. Fasten with—Jer. 10:4. Heard, Was not—I Ki. 6:7. Like a—Jer. 23:29. Smootheth it with —Is. 41:7. Took a—Ju. 4:21. Workmen's—Ju. 5:26.

HAMMOCK. Sway like a—Is. 24:20.

HAMMOLECHETH, ham-mŏl′e-keth. I Chr. 7:18.

HAMMON, hăm′mon. (1) **A town of Asher.**—Josh. 19:28.

(2) **A Levitical city.**—I Chr. 6:76.

HAMMOTH-DOR, hăm′moth–dôr. **A Levitical city in Naphtali.**—Josh. 21:32. See HAMMOTH and HAMMON.

HAMMUEL, hăm′mū-el. **A Simeonite.** —I Chr. 4:26.

HAMONAH, hăm′o-nah. Ez. 39:11, 15.

HAMON-GOG, hā′mon–gŏg. **A valley.** —Ez. 39:11, 15.

HAMOR, hā′mor. **Father of Shechem.**— Gen. 33:19.

HAMUL, hā′mul. Gen. 46:12; Num. 26:21.

HAMUTAL, ha-mū′tal. **Wife of Josiah, mother of Jehoahaz and Zedekiah.**— II Ki. 23:31.

HANAMEL, ha-năm′el. **A cousin of Jeremiah.**—Jer. 32:7.

HANAN, hā′nan. (1) **A descendant of Saul.**—I Chr. 8:34; 9:44.

(2) **A Benjamite.**—I Chr. 8:23.

(3) **One of David's warriors.**—I Chr. 11:43.

(4) **One of those who returned with Zerubbabel.**—Ezra 2:46; Neh. 7:49.

(5) **Son of Igdaliah.**—Jer. 35:4.

(6) **One who assisted Ezra in explaining the law.**—Neh. 8:7.

(7) **One who had charge of tithes.**—Neh. 13:13.

(8, 9) **Two who assisted in sealing the covenant.**—Neh. 10:22, 26.

HANANEL, ha-năn′el. Neh. 3:1.

HANANI, ha-nā′ni. (1) **A relative of Nehemiah.**—Neh. 1:2; 7:2.

(2) **Father of Jehu.**—I Ki. 16:1, 7; II Chr. 19:2; 20:34.

(3) **A musician who helped to dedicate the wall.**—Neh. 12:36.

(4) **A priest who married a foreign wife.** —Ezra 10:20.

(5) **A musician under David.**—I Chr. 25:4, 25.

HANANIAH, hăn′a-nī′ah. (1) **Father of Zedekiah.**—Jer. 36:12.

(2) **A prophet who opposed Jeremiah.**— Jer. Ch. 28.

(3) **An official under Uzziah.**—II Chr. 26:11.

(4) Jer. 37:13.

(5) **One of Daniel's companions.**—Dan. 1:6; 2:17. See DANIEL.

(6) **A musician.**—I Chr. 25:4, 23.

(7) **A descendant of David.**—I Chr. 3: 19, 21.

(8) **A Benjamite.**—I Chr. 8:24.

(9) **One of those who married foreign wives.**—Ezra 10:28.

(10) **A perfumer who helped to repair the wall.**—Neh. 3:8.

(11) **Another who helped to repair the wall.**—Neh. 3:30.

(12) **One who signed the covenant.**— Neh. 10:23.

(13) **One of Nehemiah's officers.**—Neh. 7:2.

(14) **A priest.**—Neh. 12:12, 41.

HAND. Necessary member of the body. —I Cor. 12:21.

Parts of hand.—Palm—Is. 49:16; Mt. 26:67. Fingers—See FINGER. Thumb —Ex. 29:20; Lev. 8:23, 24; 14:14, 17; Ju. 1:6, 7.

Right and left hand distinguished between: Right hand—Ex. 29:20; Lev. 8:23, 24; 14:14, 17; I Chr. 12:2; Acts 3:7. Left hand—Gen. 14:15; Ju. 3:15; 7:20; 20:16; I Chr. 12:2; Acts 21:3.

Anger, Hands smitten together in.— Num. 24:10; Ez. 6:11; 21:14, 17; 22:13.

Beard held by the hand when kissing.— II Sam. 20:9.

Bloody.—Is. 1:15; 59:3.

Clapping hands in derision or rebellion. —Job 27:23; 34:37; Lam. 2:15; Ez.

25:6; Nah. 3:19. To express joy—I Ki. 11:12; Ps. 47:1; 98:8; Is. 55:12.

Criminals bound by the hand.—Mt. 22: 13; Acts 21:11. Deprived of hands—Deut. 25:12; II Sam. 4:12. Hung by the hands—Lam. 5:12.

Dandling children.—Lam. 2:20, 22.

Derision, hands stretched out in.—Hos. 7:5; Zeph. 2:15.

Eating with.—Mt. 15:20; 26:23.

Fellowship, right hand of.—Gal. 2:9.

Handling (feeling).—Ps. 115:7; Lu. 24: 39; John 20:27; I John 1:1.

Holding.—Ex. 4:17; Num. 35:18; Ju. 7: 2; Pr. 31:19; Rev. 10:2; 17:4.

Innocence, washing hands symbol of. —Deut. 21:6, 7; Mt. 27:24.

Kissing an idolatrous worship.—Job 31:27.

Laying on of.—Heb. 6:2. Aaron and sons consecrated—Ex. 29:10, 15; Lev. 8:18, 22. Accused, on head of—Lev. 24:13; Deut. 13:9; 17:7. Blessing—*Jacob and Joseph's sons*—Gen. 48:14, 20. *Little children*—Mt. 19:13, 15; Mk. 10:16. Elders to lay hand on head of offering—Lev. 4:4. Gifts of the Holy Spirit imparting—Acts 8:17; 19:6. See Acts 9:17. Goat, laying hands on—Lev. 4:24; 16:21, 22. Healing—Mk. 5:23; 6:5; 7:32, 35; 8:23; Lu. 4:40; 13:13; Acts 9:17; 28:8. Ordination—I Tim. 4:14; 5:22; II Tim. 1:6. *Deacons*—Acts 6:6. *Paul and Barnabas*—Acts 13:3. Priests to lay hand on head of burnt-offering—Ex. 29:10, 15, 19; Lev. 1:4; 3:2, 8, 13; Num. 8:12. Sin-offering—Ex. 29:10, 15; Lev. 4:4, 24, 33; 8:14; Num. 8:12, 14. Setting apart —*Joshua*—Num. 28:18, 23; Deut. 34:9. *Levites*—Num. 8:10.

Leaning on.—II Ki. 5:8; 7:2, 7.

Left-handed.—Ju. 3:15; 20:16.

Lifted up.—Against—Job 31:21; II Sam. 20:21; see Gen. 16:12. In blessing—Lev. 9:22; Ps. 134:2; Lu. 24:50. In praise—Ps. 63:4; 134:2. In prayer —Ex. 9:29; Ezra 9:5; Job 11:13; Ps. 28:2; 63:4; 88:9; 134:2; 141:2; 143:6; Lam. 2:19; 3:41; I Tim. 2:8. In making an oath—Gen. 14:22; Rev. 10:5.

Measure, Used as.—Ex. 37:12; I Ki. 7: 26; Ps. 39:5.

Oath taken: With uplifted (right)—Gen. 14:22; 32:40; II Ki. 10:15; Pr.

11:21; Ez. 17:18. By placing hand under thigh of person with whom oath is made—Gen. 24:2, 3; 47:29, 31.

Poor, Hand stretched out to.—Pr. 3:27; 31:20; Acts 3:7.

Prayer. — Hands lifted in — Ps. 28:2; 134:2; 141:2; Lam. 2:19; 3:41; I Tim. 2:8. Spread out in—Ex. 9:29; Ezra 9:5; Job 11:13; Ps. 88:9; 143:6.

Strengthen.—Ju. 9:24; I Sam. 23:16; II Sam. 2:7; Neh. 2:18; Zech. 8:9; see II Sam. 4:1.

Striking with.—Mt. 26:67; John 18:22; 19:3.

Sureties given by striking.—Job 17:3; Pr. 6:1; 17:18; 22:26.

Treaties made by joining.—II Ki. 10: 15; Ezra 10:19; Pr. 11:21; 16:5; Lam. 5:6; Ez. 17:18.

Violent.—Ps. 58:2; Is. 58:4; 59:6.

Washing. — Before eating—Mt. 15:2; Mk. 7:3, 5; Lu. 11:38. After touching unclean person—Lev. 15:11. In token of innocency—Deut. 21:6, 7; Mt. 27: 24.

Wicked.—Mic. 7:3. Bloody—Is. 1:15; 59:3. Bribing—Ps. 26:10. Ensnaring —Ps. 9:16. Violent—Ps. 58:2; Is. 58: 4; 59:6.

Withered.—I Ki. 13:4, 6; Mt. 12:10; Mk. 3:1, 5; Lu. 6:6.

Work of.—Deut. 2:7; 30:9; Job 1:10; Ps. 9:16; 90:17. Righteous—Blessed in work of—Deut. 30:9; Job 1:10; 31: 25; Ps. 90:17; Pr. 12:14. Wicked to be recompensed according to works of—Ps. 28:4; Pr. 12:14; Is. 3:11.

Working with.—Pr. 31:19; Eph. 4:28; I Thess. 4:11. See Pr. 21:25.

Writing.—Is. 44:5; I Cor. 16:21; Gal. 6:11; Col. 4:18; II Thess. 3:17.

Right.—Embracing with—Song of Sol. 2:6; 8:3. Fellowship, Right hand of—Gal. 2:9. Right hand of leper touched with blood of sacrifice—Lev. 14:14, 17, 25. With oil—Lev. 14:28. Right hand of priests washed with blood of consecration—Ex. 29:20; Lev. 8:23, 24. Signet ring worn on—Jer. 22:24. Staff carried in—Ex. 12:11; II Ki. 4:29.

Right hand (*location*).—Accuser stood on the right hand of accused—Ps.

109:6; Zech. 3:1. Honor, Place of—
I Ki. 2:19; Ps. 45:9; 110:1. Power,
place of—Ps. 110:1; Mt. 26:64; Mk.
16:19; Lu. 22:69; Acts 7:55; Rom. 8:
34; Eph. 1:20; Col. 3:1; Heb. 1:3; 8:1;
10:12; I Pet. 3:22. Standing at right
hand (*protection*)—Ps. 16:8; 109:31;
110:5.

Figurative use.—At the hand of (from)
—Gen. 9:5; 33:10; II Ki. 9:7; Is. 1:12;
Rev. 19:2. By the hand of—Ex. 4:13.
Cutting off (self-denial)—Mt. 5:30;
18:8. Come to one's hand (to have)—
I Sam. 25:8. Held by the right hand
(for support)—Ps. 73:23; Is. 41:13;
42:6; 45:5. High hand—Ex. 14:8;
Num. 15:30; 33:3. Influence, Power—
Ju. 1:35; I Sam. 22:17. In hand (in
progress)—I Sam. 20:19. In one's
hand (possession—power)—Gen. 24:
10; 35:4; 39:3; Deut. 24:1; Josh. 9:
25; Ju. 8:24; I Sam. 17:22; I Chr. 29:
12; II Chr. 20:6; Job 12:10; Is. 44:20;
Jer. 26:14; 38:5. Into the hand (power
over)—Gen. 9:2. Lay hands upon (to
take)—Esth. 9:10, 15, 16. Mouth, to
lay hand on (silence)—Ju. 15:19; Job
21:5; 29:9; 40:4; Mic. 7:16. Of one's
hand (from)—Gen. 21:30; 31:29; 39:
1. Open the hand (to be liberal)—
Deut. 15:7, 8; Ps. 104:28; 145:16. Out
of hand (out of the power of)—Gen.
37:21. (At once)—Num. 11:15. Person—Gen. 4:11; 38:20; I Sam. 23:16;
Ps. 144:8, 11; Pr. 3:27; Is. 44:20. Put
one's hand with (go with, to take
part with)—Ex. 23:1. Put one's life
in one's hand (to risk it)—Ju. 12:3;
I Sam. 19:5; 28:21; Job 13:14; Ps.
119:109. Strength or power—Deut.
34:12; Ju. 9:24; I Sam. 23:16; II Sam.
2:7; 4:1; Ps. 76:5; 78:42. Under the
hands of (under the power of)—Ex.
21:20; Num. 4:28; Ju. 9:29; I Sam.
21:3. To be in captivity—Gen. 41:35;
II Ki. 13:5. At hand (to be near)—
Gen. 27:41; Deut. 15:9; 32:35; Is. 13:
6; Ez. 12:23; 36:8; Joel 1:15; Zeph.
1:7; Mt. 3:2; 4:17; 10:7; 26:45, 46;
Mk. 1:15; 14:42; John 2:13; 7:2; Rom.
13:12; Phil. 4:5; I Pet. 4:7. See Hand
in Anthropomorphisms, under GOD.

HANDED. Down—I Pet. 1:18.

HANDFUL. Gen. 41:47; Lev. 2:2; I Ki.
17:12; Eccl. 4:6.

HANDIWORKS. Ez. 27:16.

HANDLE. Ps. 115:7; Ez. 21:11; 23:3.
Bow—Amos 2:15. Hands have—I John
1:1. Harp—Gen. 4:21. Law—Jer. 2:8.
Me and see—Lu. 24:39. Not—Col. 2:
21. Oar—Ez. 27:29. Shamefully, Him
—Lu. 20:11. Sickle—Jer. 50:16. Spear
and shield—II Chr. 25:5. Staff, Mar-
shal's—Ju. 5:14. Sword—Song of
Sol. 3:8; Ez. 38:4. Word of God—II
Cor. 4:2; II Tim. 2:15.

HANDMAID. Word used broadly.—
Ruth 3:9; II Sam. 14:6.

Applied to bondservants.—Hagar—Gen.
16:1; Gal. 4:22. Maids of Leah and
Rachel—Gen. 29:24, 29.

Voluntary servitude.—Mary—Lu. 1:38.
Hannah—I Sam. 1:11.

Expressive of humility.—Bath-sheba—I
Ki. 1:11-31. Esther—Esth. 5:1-8. Ruth
—Ruth 3:9.

An unbearable heirship. — Pr. 30:23.
Sarah and Hagar—Gen. 21:10; Gal. 4:
30. See SERVANTS, CONCUBINE.

HANES, hā'nēs. An Egyptian city.—
Is. 30:4.

HANG. Gen. 40:22; 41:13; Num. 25:4;
Deut. 21:23; Josh. 10:26, 27; II Sam.
21:9; Esth. 7:9, 10; 9:14. John 19:31;
Gal. 3:13. Absalom in oak—II Sam.
18:10. Afar—Job 28:4. Chief baker
—Gen. 40:22. Creature—Acts 28:4.
Earth upon nothing—Job 26:7. Hands
—Heb. 12:12. Judas—Mt. 27:5. Law
and prophets—Mt. 22:40. Legs of the
lame—Pr. 26:7. Millstone about neck
—Mt. 18:6. Tree, On a—Gen. 40:19;
Acts 5:30; 10:39; Gal. 3:13. Work—I
Ki. 7:29.

HANNAH, hăn'nah. Mother of Samuel.
—I Sam. Chs. 1, 2.

HANNATHON, hăn'na-thŏn. Josh. 19:
14.

**HANNIEL, hăn'ni-el. (1) A man of
Manasseh.**—Num. 34:23.

(2) **A man of Asher.**—I Chr. 7:39.

**HANOCH, hā'noch. (1) A Midianite
chief.**—Gen. 24:4; I Chr. 1:33.

(2) **A Reubenite.**—Gen. 46:9; Num. 26:5.

**HANUN, hā'nun. (1) Son of Nahash,
the Ammonite king.**—II Sam. 10:1;
I Chr. 19:1.

(2, 3) **Two persons who assisted in repairing the wall.**—Neh. 3:13, 30.

HAPHARAIM,·hăph'ā-rā'im. **A town in Issachar.**—Josh. 19:19.

HAPLY. Lu. 4:29; Heb. 2:1. If he might find—Mt. 11:13. If the people —I Sam. 14:30. If they might feel—Acts 17:27. Lest thou dash thy foot—Mt. 4:6; Lu. 4:11. Lest ye be found fighting against God—Acts 5:39.

HAPPEN. II Pet. 2:22. Chance—I Sam. 1:6; 6:9. Eccl. 9:11. Declare what shall—Is. 41:22. Event—Eccl. 2:14. Evil—Jer. 44:23. Fool, To—Eccl. 2:15. Mischief, No—Pr. 12:21. Punishment, No—I Sam. 28:10. Things—Mk. 10:32; 24:14; I Cor. 10:11; I Pet. 4:14. Unto righteous men—Eccl. 8:14.

HAPPIZZEZ, hăp'piz-zĕz. I Chr. 24:15.

HAPPY. Am I—Gen. 30:13. Art thou, Oh Israel—Deut. 33:29. Call him, Shall—Ps. 27:17. End—Ps. 37:3. He that hath the God of Jacob, Is—Ps. 146:5. He that hath pity on the poor, Is—Pr. 14:21. He that keepeth the law, Is—Pr. 28:18. He that judgeth not, Is—Rom. 14:22. I think myself—Acts 26:2. Man that feareth—Pr. 28:14. Man that hath quiver full—Ps. 127:5. Man that findeth wisdom—Pr. 3:13. Man whom God correcteth—Job 5:17. People whose God is Jehovah—Ps. 144:15. Proud, We call the proud—Mal. 3:15. Servants—I Ki. 10:8. Who trusteth in Jehovah—Pr. 16:20.

HARA, hā'rà. I Chr. 5:26.

HARADAH, hăr'a-dah. **One of the encampments of Israel.**—Num. 33:24, 25.

HARAN, hā'ran. (1) **Brother of Abraham, father of Lot.**—Gen. 11:26, 31.
(2) **A Levite under David.**—I Chr. 23:9.
(3) **Son of Caleb.**—I Chr. 2:46.
(4) **The place to which Abraham went from Ur.**—Gen. 11:31, 32; 12:4, 5; 27:43; 28:10; 29:4; II Ki. 19:12; Is. 37:12; Ez. 27:23; Acts 7:34.

HARAHITE. II Sam. 23:11, 33; I Chr. 11:34, 35.

HARASS. Job 13:25.

HARBONAH, har-bō'nah. **A chamberlain under Ahasuerus.**—Esth. 1:10; 7:9.

HARD. Bondage—Deut. 26:6. Causes—Ex. 18:26. For a rich man—Mt. 19:23. Forehead—Ez. 3:7. Is anything too—Gen. 18:14; Jer. 32:17, 27. Language—Ez. 3:5, 6. Kick against the pricks, To—Acts 26:14. Man—Mt. 25:24. Not too—Deut. 30:11. Nothing too—Jer. 32:17. Questions—I Ki. 10:1; II Chr. 9:1. Saying—John 6:60. Service—Ex. 1:14; Is. 14:3. Things—II Ki. 2:10; Ps. 60:3; Jude 15. Understood, To be—II Pet. 3:16. Way of transgressor is—Pr. 13:15.

HARDEN. Face—Pr. 21:29. Heart—Ex. 4:21; 7:13; 14:17; Deut. 2:30; Josh. 11:20; I Sam. 6:6; Neh. 9:16, 17, 29; Ps. 95:8; Pr. 21:29; 28:14; 29:1; Is. 63:17; Dan. 5:20. Minds—II Cor. 3:14. Neck—Pr. 29:1; Neh. 9:16, 17, 29; Pr. 29:1. One of you be, Lest—Heb. 3:13. Some were—Acts 19:9. Spirit—Deut. 2:30; Dan. 5:20.

HARDER. Adamant than flint—Ez. 3:9. Faces, Than a rock—Jer. 5:3.

HARDLY. Deal—Gen. 16:6; Job 19:3. Departeth—Lu. 9:39. How shall they that have riches—Mk. 10:23; Lu. 18:24. Let us go—Ex. 13:15.

HARDNESS. Face, Of—Eccl. 8:1. Heart, Of—Lam. 3:65; Mt. 19:8; Mk. 10:5; 16:14; Rom. 2:5.

HARDSHIP. Gospel, For—II Tim. 1:8; 2:3, 9; 4:5. See ENDURANCE, SOLDIER.

HARE. Lev. 11:6; Deut. 14:7.

HAREPH, hā'reph. **Son of Caleb.**—I Chr. 2:51.

HARHAIAH, här-hā'iah. Neh. 3:8.

HARHAS, här'has. **Husband of Huldah, the prophetess.**—II Ki. 22:14.

HARHUR, här-hur. **One of the Nethinim who returned from exile.**—Ez. 2:51; Neh. 7:53.

HARIM, hā'rim. (1) Ezra 2:32; Neh. 7:53.
(2) **Ancestor of some who married foreign wives.**—Ezra 10:31.
(3) **A priest.**—I Chr. 24:8; Ezra 2:39; 10:21; Neh. 3:11.
(4) **One of those who assisted Nehemiah in sealing the covenant.**—Neh. 10:27.
(5) **Name of others who sealed the covenant.**—Neh. 10:27; 12:15.

HARIPH, hā'riph. (1) **Name of some who returned with Zerubbabel.**—Neh. 7:24.
(2) **Ancestor of some who sealed the covenant with Nehemiah.**—Neh. 10:19.

HARLOT. For hire.—Gen. 34:21; Num. 25:1, 6; Ju. 11:1; 16:1; 19:2, 25; I Ki. 3:16; Amos 2:7.

In heathen worship.—Gen. 38:21; Ex. 34:15, 16; Hos. 4:14.

Legislation against.—Common—Lev. 19: 29; Deut. 23:18. Religious—Ex. 34: 12–16; Lev. 21:7, 9, 14; Deut. 23:17; Hos. 1:2; 4:12; Ez. 16:26.

Warnings.—Pr. 6:26; 7:7–23; 23:27; 29: 3; Hos. 4:11–14.

Punishment.—Burned or stoned to death —Gen. 38:24; Lev. 20:10–12; Deut. 22:22–25; John 8:5.

The New Covenant demands purity of heart and life.—Mt. 5:8, 27, 28, 31, 32; Acts 15:20, 29; I Cor. 6:9, 10, 13–20; Eph. 5:3–5; Col. 3:5–8; Tit. 1:15; 2: 12; Jas. 4:4, 8. See FORNICATION, IDOLATRY, ADULTERY.

HARM. Gen. 31:52; 42:4; I Sam. 26: 21; II Ki. 4:41; I Chr. 16:22; Ps. 105: 15; Mk. 3:4; Acts 18:10; I Pet. 3:13. Harmless.—Mt. 10:16.

HARMLESS. Mt. 10:16.

HARNEPHER, här'ne-pher. **Son of Zophah.**—I Chr. 7:36.

HARNESS. Jer. 46:4. Trappings—Ps. 32:9. Pieces of harness mentioned: Bit—Ps. 32:9. Bridle—Ps. 32:9; Pr. 26:3; Jas. 3:3; Rev. 14:20.

Used figuratively.—II Ki. 19:28; Job 30:11; Ps. 39:1; Is. 30:28; 37:29. Saddle—Gen. 22:3; Lev. 15:9; Num. 22: 21; Ju. 19:10; II Sam. 16:1; 17:23; 19:26; I Ki. 2:40; 13:13, 23, 27; II Ki. 4:24.

HAROD, hā'rod. **A well or village.**— Ju. 7:1.

HARODITE, hā'ro-dite. **Inhabitant of Harod.**—II Sam. 23:25.

HAROSHETH, ha-rō'shĕth. **A city of Galilee, home of Sisera.**—Ju. 4:2, 13, 16.

HARP. ''Jubal—he was the father of all such as handle the harp and pipe'' —Gen. 4:21.

Used by prophets.—I Sam. 10:5; II Ki. 3:15; I Chr. 25:1–3; Ps. 49:4.

In festivities.—Gen. 31:27; Job 21:11– 12; Ps. 149:3; Is. 5:12; 24:8; Ez. 26: 13.

In rejoicing after victories.—II Chr. 20: 28, 29; Is. 30:32.

To remove melancholy.—I Sam. 16:16– 23; 18:10; 19:9.

In mourning.—Is. 16:9–11; Job 30:31. Not used—Ps. 137:2.

At dedications.—Neh. 12:27; I Chr. 16: 4, 5.

For service of song.—I Chr. 25:1–8; II Chr. 5:11–13.

For worship of Jehovah.—II Sam. 6:5; I Chr. 13:8; 15:16; II Chr. 29:25; Ps. 33:2; 43:4; 57:8, 9; 71:22; 81:1–4; 92: 1–4; 98:5; 108:1–4; 147:7, 8; 149:1–4; 150:3.

To promote idolatry.—Dan. 3:5, 7, 10, 15.

To glorify the Lamb.—Rev. 5:8; 14:2; 15:2.

Figurative.—Uncertain sounds valueless —I Cor. 14:7.

HARROW. II Sam. 12:31; I Chr. 20:3; Job 39:10.

HARSHA, här-shä. **Ancestor of Nethinim who returned with Zerubbabel.**— Ezra 2:52; Neh. 7:54.

HART. Deut. 12:15; Ps. 42:1; Is. 35:6.

HARUM, hā'rum. I Chr. 4:8.

HARUMAPH, ha-ru'maph. Neh. 3:10.

HARUPHITE, här-u-phite. **An inhabitant of Hariph.**—I Chr. 2:5.

HARUZ, hā'ruz. II Ki. 21:19.

HARVEST. Season—Josh. 3:15; Ruth 2:23; I Sam. 12:17; II Sam. 21:10; 23:13; Pr. 6:8; 10:5; 20:4; 25:13; 26: 1; Is. 9:3; 18:4, 5; Jer. 5:24; 8:20; Amos 4:7.

Laws concerning.—Gen. 8:22; Ex. 22: 29; 34:21; Lev. 19:9, 10; 23:10, 22; 25:5; Deut. 24:19; 25:4; Ruth 2:2–23; I Cor. 9:9; I Tim. 5:18.

Harvests mentioned.—Barley—Ruth 1: 22; 2:23; II Sam. 21:9. Wheat—Gen. 30:14; Ju. 15:1; Ruth 2:21; I Sam. 6:13; 12:16. Of the Nile—Is. 23:3.

Laborers called.—Binders—Gen. 37:7; Ps. 129:7. Harvest-men—Is. 17:5.

Reapers.—Ruth 2:3, 4, 7, 9, 14; II Ki. 4:18; Amos 9:13; Mt. 13:30, 39.

Harvesting.—Reaping—I Sam. 8:12; II Ki. 19:29. Binding—Gen. 37:7; Ex. 22:6; Lev. 23:10. Gleaning—Lev. 19: 9, 10; 23:22; Deut. 24:19–22; Ruth 2: 2–23; Is. 17:6; 24:13; Jer. 6:9; Mic. 7:1. Threshing—Ju. 5:11; II Sam. 24:18–22; I Chr. 21:20–23; Is. 28:27, 28; 41:15, 16; Jer. 51:33. Instruments used—II Sam. 24:22; Is. 28:27, 28.

Fork and shovel—Is. 30:24. Sickle—Deut. 16:9; Jer. 50:16. Threshing-floor—Ruth 3:6. Ingathering—Ex. 23:16; 34:22.

Winnow.—Boaz—Ruth 3:2. Winnowed provender—Is. 30:24.

Failure of.—Gen. 45:6; I Sam. 12:11, 18; Pr. 10:5; Is. 16:9; 17:10, 11; Joel 1:4, 11; Amos 4:7.

Feasts of harvests.—Ex. 23:16. Of ingathering — Ex. 23:16; 34:22. Of weeks—Ex. 34:22.

Prophecies concerning.—Gen. 45:6; Is. 16:9; 17:11; Jer. 5:17; Hos. 6:11; Joel 1:11; 3:13.

Illustrative.—Job 5:5; Is. 18:4; Jer. 8:20; Joel 3:13; Mt. 9:37, 38; 13:30; John 4:35.

Spiritual.—Mt. 9:37, 38; 13:30, 39; Mk. 4:29; John 4:35. Spiritual reaping—Eccl. 11:4; Jer. 12:13; Hos. 8:7; 10:12; Mic. 6:15. Used in prophecy—Is. 37:30; Hos. 8:7. Illustrative—Job 4:8; 24:6; Ps. 126:5; Pr. 22:8. See TEACHING OF JESUS, TEACHINGS OF PAUL; I Cor. 9:6, 11; Gal. 6:7–9.

HASADIAH, hăs'a-dī'ah. **Son of Zerubbabel.**—I Chr. 3:20.

HASHABIAH, hăsh'a-bī'ah. (1) **A Levite.**—I Chr. 9:4.

(2) **Another Levite.**—I Chr. 6:45.

(3) **Son of Jeduthun.**—I Chr. 25:3.

(4) **A descendant of Kohath.**—I Chr. 26:30.

(5) **Son of Kemuel.**—I Chr. 27:17.

(6) **A Levite.**—II Chr. 35:9.

(7) **A Levite who accompanied Ezra from Babylon.**—Ezra 8:19.

(8) **A priest.**—Ezra 8:24.

(9) **One of those who helped to repair the wall.**—Neh. 3:17.

(10) **One of those who helped to seal the covenant.**—Neh. 10:11.

(11, 12) **Two Levites.**—Neh. 10:11; 11:22.

(13) **A priest.**—Neh. 12:21.

(14) **Another Levite.**—Neh. 12:24.

HASHABNAH, ha-shăb'nah. **One of those who helped to seal the covenant.** —Neh. 10:25.

HASHABNEIAH, hăsh'ab-nei'ah. (1) Neh. 3:10.

(2) **A Levite.**—Neh. 9:5.

HASHEM, hă'shem. I Chr. 11:34.

HASHMONAH, hăsh'mō'nah. **An encampment of the Israelites.**—Num. 33:29.

HASHUBAH, ha-shu'bah. **Son of Zerubbabel.**—I Chr. 3:20.

HASHUM, hă'shum. (1) **Ancestor of some who returned with Zerubbabel.** —Ezra 2:19; 10:35; Neh. 7:22.

(2) **One who sealed the covenant.**—Neh. 10:18.

(3) **A priest who stood beside Ezra.**— Neh. 8:4.

HASRAH, hăs'rah. See HARHAS.

HASSENAAH, hăs'se-nā'ah. Neh. 3:3.

HASSENUAH, hăs'se-nū'ah. I Chr. 9:7.

HASSHUB, hăs'shub. (1) **Father of Shemaiah.**—I Chr. 9:14; Neh. 11:15.

(2) **Son of Pahath.**—Moab—Neh. 3:11.

(3) **One of those who sealed the covenant.**—Neh. 10:23.

(4) **One of those who helped to repair the wall.**—Neh. 3:23.

HASSOPHERETH, hăs-sōph'er-eth. Ezra 2:55.

HASTE. Gen. 19:22; 44:11; Eccl. 7:9; Acts 20:16; Jas. 1:19; I Tim. 5:22. Abraham—Gen. 18:6. Answer, To—Ps. 143:7. Brought him out—Gen. 41:14. Business required—I Sam. 21:8. Called for Moses and Aaron in—Ex. 10:16. Came out of Egypt in—Deut. 16:3. Cast away garments—II Ki. 7:15. Catch, To—I Ki. 20:33. Cattle—Ex. 9:19. David—I Sam. 17:48. Day of Jehovah—Zeph. 1:14. Deceit, To—Job 31:5. Devour, To—Hab. 1:8. Dress it, To—Gen. 18:7. Drive out—Ju. 2:23. Eat in—Ex. 12:11. Feet, With—Pr. 19:2. Go out in—Is. 52:12. Hanan, To bring—Esth. 6:14. Help, To—Ps. 22:191; 38:22. Inheritance may be gotten—Pr. 20:21. Jehovah will—Is. 60:22. Jerusalem, To—Ezra 4:23. King, Unto—Mk. 6:25. Lot, Angel—Gen. 19:15. Man—I Sam. 4:14. Nation—Hab. 1:6. Riches, After—Pr. 28:22. Rose—Dan. 3:24. Said in—Ps. 31:22; 116:11. Shed blood, To—Pr. 1:16; Is. 59:7. Shelter, To—Ps. 55:8. Spirit—Pr. 14:29; Eccl. 7:9. Stretch out, To—Ps. 63:31. Strive, To —Pr. 25:8. Utter, To—Eccl. 5:2. Wall, To the—Nah. 2:5. Want, To—Pr. 20:

5. Words, In—Pr. 29:20. Work—Is. 5:19.

HASUPHA, ha-su'phà. (1) **Family that returned with Ezra.**—Ez. 2:43.

(2) **Family that returned with Nehemiah.**—Neh. 7:46.

HATCH. Adders' eggs—Is. 59:5. Dart —Snake—Is. 34:15.

HATCHET. See Tools and implements.

HATHATH, hă'thăth. **Judge of Israel.** —I Chr. 4:13.

HATIPHA, hăt'i-phà. (1) **Family that returned with Ezra.**—Ez. 2:54.-

(2) **Family that returned with Nehemiah.**—Neh. 7:56.

HATITA, hăt'i-tà. **Gate-keeper in the temple.**—Ezra 2:42; Neh. 7:45.

HATRED. A virtue to hate.—Covetousness—Ex. 18:21; Pr. 28:16. Evil—Ps. 97:10; Amos 5:15; Rom. 7:15; 12:9. Falsehood—Ps. 119:104, 128, 163. Haters of God—II Chr. 19:2. Idolatry—Deut. 7:25, 26; Rom. 2:22. Lying—Ps. 119:163; Pr. 13:5. Spotted garment—Jude 23. Unfaithfulness—Ps. 101:3; 119:113.

What God hates.—Divorce—Mal. 2:16; Mt. 5:31, 32; 19:8. Evil—Ps. 45:7; Heb. 1:19. False oaths—Zech. 8:17. Four things—Pr. 8:13, 14. Idols—Deut. 16:22; Jer. 44:4, 5. Liars—Ps. 5: 4-6. Nations: Canaan—Lev. 20:23. Edom—Jer. 49:7-10; Ob. Ch. 1. Israel—Deut. 32:19; Ps. 78:59; 106:40; Jer. 12:7, 8; Hos. 9:15; Amos 6:8. Robbery—Is. 61:8. Sacrifice of children—Deut. 12:31. Seven things—Pr. 6:16-19. Vain worship—Is. 1:14; 66: 3, 4; Amos 5:21. Violent and wicked —Ps. 11:5. Workers of iniquity—Ps. 5:5.

A vice to hate.—A brother—Lev. 19:17; I John 2:9, 10; 3:15; 4:20. Apostles of Christ—Mt. 10:22; 24:9; Mk. 13: 13; Lu. 21:17; John 15:19; 17:14. Christians—I John 3:13. Enemy—Mt. 5:43, 44; Lu. 6:27, 28, 35. God or Christ—John 7:7; 15:18, 23, 24. Without a cause—John 7:25. Good—Mic. 3:2. Instruction—Pr. 5:12. Light—John 3:19, 20. One another—Tit. 3:3. Peace—Ps. 120:6. Poor—Pr. 14:20. True prophets—I Ki. 22:7, 8; Amos 5:10; Mt. 23:32-35; Lu. 11:47-51.

Wisdom—Pr. 1:22, 29; 8:36. Zion—Ps. 129:5.

Fruits.—Deceit and falsehood—Ps. 109: 1; Pr. 26:24-26. Evil for good—Ps. 109:5; John 7:7; 8:59; 10:31, 32; 15: 25. Murder—Num. 35:20, 21; Deut. 19:4, 11, 12; II Sam. 13:22, 28, 29. Selling into bondage—Gen. 37:4, 8, 12-21, 28. Strife—Pr. 10:12.

Examples.—Cain—Gen. 4:5, 8. Esau— Gen. 27:41. Sons of Jacob—Gen. 37: 4, 5. Saul—I Sam. 18:8, 9. Absalom— II Sam. 13:22, 28. Ahab—I Ki. 22:8, 34, 35. Haman—Esth. 5:9; 7:9, 10. Pharisees—Mt. 26:3, 4; Mk. 14:1; Lu. 22:2; John 15:18. Herodias—Mt. 14: 6-8; Mk. 6:17-19. Jews—Acts 22:27-31. Christian Jews—Gal. 1:6, 7; 4:29; 5:11, 12.

Recompense.—Deut. 32:41. Cursed—Deut. 30:17. Disease and evil—Deut. 7:15. Fall into a deep pit—Pr. 22:14. Punished—Ex. 20:5.

Shame will cover.—Job 8:22. Slain—Num. 35:20, 21; Deut. 4:42; 19:11, 12; Josh. 20:5.

Prayer and thanks for God's hate on enemies.—Deut. 3:11; Ps. 18:40; 44:7; 58:1; 137:7, 8. Jacob hated Leah, loved Rachel—Gen. 29:30, 31.

Hating father or life.—Mt. 10:37; Lu. 14:26; John 12:25. See Reject.

Hatred returned for love.—II Sam. 13: 15; Ps. 109:5; John 10:31, 32.

HATTIL, hăt'til. (1) **Family that returned with Ezra.**—Ezra 2:57.

(2) **Family that returned with Nehemiah.**—Neh. 7:59.

HATTUSH, hăt'tush. (1) **Descendant of David.**—Ezra 8:2; Neh. 3:10; 10:4.

(2) **Son of Shechaniah.**—I Chr. 3:22.

(3) **A priest who returned with Zerubbabel.**—Neh. 12:2.

HAUGHTY. I Sam. 23:22; Ps. 138:6; 21:24; Is. 2:12; 3:16; Ez. 16:50; Hab. 2:5; Zeph. 3:11; Rom. 1:30; II Tim. 3:2. Eyes—Ps. 18:27; Pr. 6:17. Heart —Ps. 131:1; Pr. 18:12. Spirit—Pr. 16:18. See Pride.

HAVE. God, To—Rom. 1:28. Let them —Ex. 12:36. Lordship—Lu. 22:25.

HAVEN. Gen. 49:13; Ps. 107:30; Acts 27:8, 12.

HAVILAH, hăv'i-lah. (1) **A district south of Egypt.**—Gen. 2:11.

(2) **A descendant of Ham.**—Gen. 10:7; I Chr. 1:9.

(3) **A district in Arabia.**—Gen. 25:18; I Sam. 15:7.

(4) **A descendant of Shem.**—Gen. 10:29; I Chr. 1:23.

HAVOC. Ps. 74:8; Acts 9:21; Gal. 1:13, 23. See DESTRUCTION.

HAVVOTH-JAIR, hăv'voth-jāir. **Village east of the Jordan.**—Num. 32:41; Deut. 3:14; Ju. 10:4.

HAWK. Lev. 11:16; Deut. 14:15; Job 39:26. See NIGHTHAWK, BIRDS.

HAY. Pr. 27:25; I Cor. 3:12.

HAZAEL, hăz'a-el. **King of Syria.**—Conspiracy against—II Ki. 9:14, 15; II Chr. 22:5, 6. Death of—II Ki. 13: 24, 25. House of—Amos 1:4. Jehoash sends presents to—II Ki. 12:18; 13:3. Jehovah orders anointment of—I Ki. 19:15, 17. Persecutes Jews—II Ki. 10:32; 12:17; 13:22. Sent to Elijah—II Ki. 8:8, 9, 12, 13. Usurps throne—II Ki. 8:15, 28, 29.

HAZAIAH, hă-zā'iah. **A descendant of Shelah.**—Neh. 11:5.

HAZAR-ADDAR, hā'zar-ăd'dar. **Village in promised land.**—Num. 34:4.

HAZARD. Acts 15:26.

HAZAR-ENAN, hā'zar-ē'nan. **Boundary point of promised land.**—Num. 34:9, 10; Ez. 47:17; 48:1.

HAZAR-GADDAH, hā'zar-găd'dah. **Village in south Judah.**—Josh. 15:27.

HAZARMAVETH, hā'zar-mā'veth. **A descendant of Shem.**—Gen. 10:26; I Chr. 1:20.

HAZAR-SHUAL, hā'zar-shu'al. **A village in south Judah.**—Josh. 15:28; 19: 3; I Chr. 4:28; Neh. 11:27.

HAZAR-SUSAH, hā'zar-sū-sah. **A village in Judah allotted to Simeon.**—Josh. 19:5.

HAZAR-SUSIM, hā'zar-sū'sim. **A village allotted to Simeon.**—I Chr. 4:31.

HAZAZON-TAMAR, hăz'a-zŏn-tā'mar. **Ancient name for Engedi.**—Gen. 14:7; II Chr. 20:2.

HAZER-HATTICON, hā'zer-hăt'ti-cŏn. **Boundary point of Hauron.**—Ez. 47: 16.

HAZEROTH, ha-zē'roth. **Stopping place of Israel in the desert.**—Num. 11:35; 12:16; 33:17, 18; Deut. 1:1.

HAZIEL, hā'zi-el. **A Levite at the time of David.**—I Chr. 23:9.

HAZO, hā'zo. **Son of Milcah.**—Gen. 22:22.

HAZOR, hā'zor. (1) **A city in south Judah.**—Josh. 15:23; I Ki. 9:15.

(2) **A district in Arabia.**—Jer. 49:28, 30, 33.

(3) **A fortified city of Naphtali.**—Josh. 11:1, 10, 11, 13; 12:19; 19:36; Ju. 4:2, 17; I Sam. 12:9; II Ki. 15:29.

(4) **A stopping place of the Benjamites on the return from captivity.**—Neh. 11:33.

(5) **Another town in south Judah.**—Josh. 15:25.

HAZOR-HADATTAH, hā'zor-ha-dăt'-tah. **A town in Judah.**—Josh. 15:25.

HAZZELELPONI, hā'ze-lĕl-pō'ni. **Ancestor of Judah.**—I Chr. 4:3.

HEAD. Head of the body.—Gen. 3:15; 24:26; 40:16, 17, 19; 49:26; Dan. 2:8. Vow concerning—I Sam. 1:11. Crowning—Ex. 29:6; Lev. 8:9; I Sam. 1:10. David crowned—II Sam. 12:30; I Chr. 20:2. Esther is crowned—Esth. 2:17. Jerusalem—Ez. 16:12. High priest, Joshua—Zech. 3:5. Hair of—Ju. 16: 13; I Sam. 14:45; II Sam. 14:26; Ez. 5:1; 8:3. Hair is shorn for vengeance —Ju. 16:19, 22. Hair is singed—Dan. 3:27. Jesus' feet wiped with hair—Lu. 7:38, 44.

Chief member of body.—Is. 1:6; II Ki. 6:31. Keeper of—I Sam. 28:2. Body is supported and supplied by—Eph. 4:16. Covered with helmet of brass—I Sam. 17:5, 38. Often anointed—Ex. 29:7; Lev. 8:12; 14:18, 20; 21:10; I Sam. 10:1; II Ki. 9:3, 6; Ps. 35:5; 133:2; 141:5; Eccl. 9:8; Mt. 6:17. Of Jesus—Mt. 26:7; Mk. 14:3; Lu. 7:46.

Parts of.—Skull—Ju. 9:53; II Ki. 9:35; Mt. 27:33. Crown—Gen. 49:26; Deut. 28:35; 33:16,20; II Sam. 14:25. *Broken* —Jer. 2:16. Forehead—I Sam. 17:49; Ez. 9:4. Temple—Ju. 4:21, 22; Song of Sol. 4:3. Face—Gen. 48:12; II Ki. 9:30. See FACE. Hair—Ju. 16:22; Ps. 40:12. See HAIR. Scalp—Ps. 68:21.

Of enemies.—Pierced with tent-pin—Ju. 5:26; I Chr. 10:9. Broken—Ju. 9:53. Cut off in war—I Sam. 17:51, 57; 31: 9; II Sam. 2:16. Thrown over wall—

II Sam. 20:21. Of Sheba, cut off—II Sam. 20:22.

When hoary with age.—To be respected —Lev. 19:32; I Ki. 2:6, 9; Pr. 16:31; 20:29. Defence of—Ps. 60:7; 108:8.

Men's heads mentioned.—Of Oreb and Zeeb—Ju. 7:25. Wise man—Eccl. 2: 14. Joab—II Sam. 3:29. Absalom caught in tree—II Sam. 18:9. Jonah, *Weeds wrapped around*—Jonah 2:5. *Shade over*—Jonah 4:6. Elisha—II Ki. 6:31, 32. High priest, Joshua—Zech. 6:11. John the Baptist—Mt. 14:8, 11; Mk. 6:24-28. Peter—John 13:9. Paul's shorn—Acts 18:18. Wounded servant —Mk. 12:4.

Shaken.—In derision—II Ki. 19:21; Job 16:4; Ps. 22:7; 44:14; 109:25; Is. 37: 22; Sam. 2:15; Mt. 27:39. In astonishment—Jer. 18:16.

Visions concerning.—Cake and water— I Ki. 19:6. Horns—Dan. 7:20; Zech. 1:21. Of cherubim—Ez. 10:1, 11; Dan. 4:5, 10, 13; 7:1, 15. Hair like wool— Dan. 7:9. Of gold—Dan. 2:32, 38.

Description of.—Song of Sol. 5:11; 7:5.

Bowed down in worship.—Gen. 24:26, 48; 43:28; Ex. 4:31; 12:27; 34:8; Num. 22:31; I Chr. 12:20; II Chr. 20: 18; 29:30; Neh. 8:16; Job 1:20. In respect—Gen. 43:28; 47:31; Job 10:15.

In grief.—Is covered—II Sam. 15:30; Esth. 6:12; Ez. 24:17. Shorn—Job 1: 20. Sprinkled with dust—Josh. 7:6; I Sam. 4:12; II Sam. 1:2; 15:32; Job 2:12; Amos 2:7. With ashes—II Sam. 13:19; Is. 58:5.

Wagged in mockery.—Ps. 22:7; Is. 22: 37; Jer. 18:16; Mt. 27:39.

Hands placed on.—Gen. 48:14, 17. In violence—Lev. 24:14; II Sam. 13:19; Jer. 2:37.

Diseases of head.—Leprosy—Lev. 13:12, 30, 42-45. Scab—Is. 3:17. Baldness— Lev. 13:40-44; 21:5; II Ki. 2:23; Is. 15:2; Jer. 48:37; Ez. 7:18; 29:18; Amos 8:10. Sunstroke—II Ki. 4:19. Wounds—Is. 1:5.

Commandments concerning. — Priests forbidden to shave—Lev. 21:5, 10; Ez. 44:20. Nazirites forbidden to shave —Num. 6:5, 7; Ju. 13:5; 16:17. Shalt not swear by—Mt. 5:36. Men—I Cor. 11:4, 7. Women—I Cor. 11:5, 20. Hair

loosed—Lev. 10:6. Corners of—Lev. 19:27.

Customs concerning. — Shaving — Lev. 14:9; Num. 6:9, 18. Woman's head— Deut. 21:12. Hair left loose—Num. 5:18. In war—I Ki. 20:3, 32. Covered —II Ki. 9:30. Covered in shame—Jer. 14:3, 4. Covered with kerchief—Ez. 13:18. Turbans and crowns upon—Ez. 23:15, 42. Swords upon—Ez. 32:27. Dust upon head in humiliation—Josh. 7:6; Job 2:12; Lam. 2:10; Ez. 27:30; Rev. 18:19.

Official heads.—House—Ex. 6:14, 25; Num. 1:4; 7:2; 17:3; 25:15; I Chr. 5: 24; 7:2, 11, 40; 8:6, 10, 13, 28; 9:13; Josh. 22:14, 21, 30. Inhabitants—Ju. 10:18; 11:8, 9, 11. People—Ex. 18:25; Num. 1:15; 10:4; 13:3; 25:4, 15; Deut. 28:13, 44; 33:5, 21; Josh. 23:2; 24:1; I Chr. 12:19, 32; Ez. 1:22, 25, 26. Chief men—Gen. 40:13, 20; Is. 9:14, 15. Kingdom—Josh. 11:10. Tribes—Num. 30:1; I Sam. 15:17; I Ki. 8:1; II Chr. 3:16; 5:2. Subdued—Ju. 8:28. Nations—II Sam. 22:44; Ps. 15:43; Is. 7:9; Hos. 1:11. Rulers—Jer. 52:31; I Sam. 15:17; II Ki. 25:27; Dan. 2:38.

Rivers.—Gen. 2:10.

Beasts.—Dan. 7:6; Rev. 17:3, 7, 9. Horses, like lions—Rev. 9:17. Dragons —Rev. 12:3. Sea monsters—Rev. 13: 1, 3. Leviathan—Job 41:7.

Promises concerning.—In teachings of Jesus—Mt. 10:30; Lu. 12:7; 21:18, 28. By Paul—Acts 27:34.

Punishment of.—Blood upon head— Josh. 2:19; Ju. 9:57; II Sam. 1:16; I Ki. 2:32, 37; Ez. 11:21; 22:31; 33:4; I Sam. 5:4, 17, 46; 25:39. Wicked—I Ki. 2:44; 8:32; II Chr. 6:23; Neh. 4:4; Esth. 9:25; Ps. 7:16; 68:21; Jer. 23: 19; Ez. 9:10; 17:19; Joel 3:4, 7; Ob. 1:15; Hab. 3:13, 14; Acts 18:6.

Prophecies concerning.—Is. 7:9; Dan. 1:10.

Headed.—See BEHEADED.

Headlong.—Counsel is carried—Job 5: 13. Jesus cast—Lu. 4:29. Falling— Acts 1:18.

Headtires.—Is. 3:20; Ez. 24:23; 44:18.

Headstrong.—II Tim. 3:4.

Beheaded.—Men: Ishbosheth—II Sam. 4:7. John—Mt. 14:10; Mk. 4:16, 27; Lu. 9:9. Martyrs—Rev. 20:4.

Grayheaded.—Aged men—I Sam. 12:2;
Job 15:10; Ps. 7:18; Pr. 20:29.

Spiritual heads.—Jehovah, head of all—
I Chr. 29:11; Mic. 2:13; I Cor. 11:3.
Of Jesus, Physical: Hath not where
to lay His head—Mt. 8:20; Lu. 9:58.
Crown of thorns upon—Mt. 27:29;
Mk. 15:17; John 19:2. Smitten—Mt.
27:30; Mk. 15:19. Inscription set over
—Mt. 27:37. Bowed and gave up the
spirit—John 19:30. Napkin upon—
John 20:7. Angel at tomb—John 20:
12. Of Jesus, Spiritual—Of church—
Eph. 1:22; 4:15; 5:22; Col. 1:18; 2:
10, 11.

Figurative.—Heavens of brass over—
Deut. 28:23. Concerning Elijah—II
Ki. 2:3, 5. Reached into clouds—Job
20:6. Light shined on—Job 29:3.
Lifted up, in exaltation—Ps. 3:3; 110:
7. In joy—Ps. 27:6; Is. 51:11. Iniquities upon—Ps. 38:4; 40:12. More enemies than hair on head—Ps. 69:4. Of
gates—Ps. 24:7, 9; 66:12. Dragons—
Ps. 74:13, 14. Shaken in reproach—
Ps. 109:25. Of many countries—Ps.
110:6. Everlasting joy upon—Is. 35:
10. Gold crowns upon—Rev. 4:4; 9:7.
Enemies lift up—Ps. 83:2. Helmet of
salvation upon—Is. 59:17. Head of
valley—Is. 28:1, 4. Of streets—Is. 51:
20. Of water—Jer. 9:1; Lam. 3:54. Of
every way—Ez. 16:25, 31, 43; 21:19,
21. Of wicked—Jer. 53:19; 30:23.
Head of corner—Ps. 118:22; Mt. 21:
42; Mk. 12:10; Lu. 20:17; Acts 4:11;
I Pet. 2:7. Hair white as wool—Rev.
1:14. Rainbow on—Rev. 10:1. Crown
of stars on—Rev. 12:1. Golden crown
on—Rev. 14:14. Many crowns on—
Rev. 19:12. Heap coals of fire upon—
Pr. 25:22; Rom. 12:20.

HEAD-BAND. See HEAD.

HEADLONG. Job 5:13; Jer. 8:6; Lu.
4:29; Acts 1:18.

HEADSTRONG. See HEAD.

HEADTIRES. See HEAD.

HEALING. Healing was considered by
the Hebrews as a token of forgiveness
—Ex. 15:26. The connection of priest
with physician was very close. Medical knowledge of their day was quite
defective. Such a thing as a science
of medicine was then unknown, but
there were physicians. From II Chr.
16:12 it would seem that the writer
considered it a sin to consult physicians. Priests had the supervision in
cases of leprosy—Lev. Chs. 13, 14;
and prophets, even, were applied to
for medical advice—I Ki. 14:2; II Ki.
4:22-25.

God the healer.—Deut. 32:39; Ps. 6:2;
30:2; 103:3. Abimelech and his family—Gen. 20:17, 18; Jer. 3:22; •17:14;
30:17; Hos. 14:4.

Prophets as healers.—Ahijah consulted
about Abijah's sickness—I Ki. 14:
1-13. Elisha raises child from dead—
II Ki. 4:18, 19, 32-35. Naaman healed
through Elisha—II Ki. 5:8-15. Benhadad consults Elisha—II Ki. 8:7-11.
Prophets prevented by Elisha from
being poisoned by wild gourds—II Ki.
4:39-41.

Jesus the great healer.—The multitudes
—Mt. 4:24; 8:16; 9:35; Mk. 1:32; 3:5,
6, 9, 10; Lu. 4:40. A leper—Mt. 8:2-4;
Mk. 1:40-45; Lu. 5:12-16. Man with
palsy—Mt. 9:2-8; Mk. 2:1-12; Lu. 5:
17-26. Man with a withered hand—
Mt. 12:9-13; Mk. 3:1-5; Lu. 6:6-10.
The nobleman's son—John 4:46-53.
The impotent man—John 5:2-9. Peter's mother-in-law—Mt. 8:14, 15;
Mk. 1:29-34; Lu. 4:38-41. Centurion's
servant—Mt. 8:5-13; Lu. 7:1-10.
Jairus's daughter—Mt. 9:22-26; Mk.
5:35-42; Lu. 8:49-56. Blind and dumb
—Mt. 9:27-33; 12:22; 20:30-34; Mk.
8:22-25; 10:46-52; Lu. 18:35-43.
Woman with issue of blood—Mt. 9:
20-22; Mk. 5:25-34; Lu. 8:43-48.
Daughter of Syrophœnician—Mt. 15:
22-28; Mk. 7:25-30. Woman with infirmity—Lu. 13:10-21. Ten lepers—
Lu. 17:12-14. Demoniacs—Mt. 8:28-
34; 12:22; 17:14-18; Mk. 1:21-28; 5:
1-20; 9:14-27; Lu. 4:31-37; 8:26-36;
9:38-42; 11:14. Aids the apostles—
Acts 4:30. See MIRACLES OF JESUS.

Apostles as healers.—Appointment given
—Mt. 10:1-8; Mk. 3:13-15; 16:18; Lu.
9:1-6. To the seventy—Lu. 10:9-17.
Lame man—Acts 3:2-10; 14:8-10.
Sick in Jerusalem—Acts 5:15, 16.
Æneas—Acts 9:33, 34. In Melita—
Acts 28:8, 9. Failure of—Mt. 17:16.
Gift of—I Cor. 12:9. Peter and John
—Acts 3:1-10. All the apostles—Acts

5:12. Shadow of Peter—Acts 5:15 f. Stephen—Acts 6:8. Philip—Acts 8:6 f. Peter at Lydda and Joppa—Acts 9:32–43. Paul at Lystra—Acts 14:8–10. In Galatia—Gal. 3:5. At Philippi—Acts 16:16–18. At Ephesus—Acts 19:11–16. Elders to pray for the sick—Jas. 5:13–18.

In answer to prayer.—Miriam—Num. 12:12–15. Jeroboam—I Ki. 13:4–6. Hezekiah—II Ki. 20:1–7.

Manners of healing.—Strange remedies —Num. 21:9; II Ki. 5:10; John 3:14; 9:6, 7.

Provision for.—Ex. 21:19. Gradual healing—Mk. 8:23–25. Failure in—Jer. 46: 11. Threefold healing—Mt. 12:22. Gratitude for—Lu. 4:38, 39. Physicians—II Chr. 16:12; Jer. 8:22; Mt. 9:12; Lu. 4:23; Col. 4:14.

Medical treatment.—II Chr. 16:12; II Ki. 8:29; Lu. 10:34.

Medicines.—A cheerful heart—Pr. 17: 22. Leaves for healing—Ez. 47:12; Rev. 22:2. No healing medicines at hand—Jer. 30:13; Ez. 30:21. Vain medicines—Jer. 46:11.

Remedies.—Balm (for pain)—Jer. 8:22; 46:11; 51:8. Caperberry (for desire) —Eccl. 12:5 (*marg.*). Mint, anise, cummin (for carminatives)—Mt. 23: 23; Lu. 11:42. Salt (to purify water) —II Ki. 2:20, 21. Oil (for wounds)— Is. 1:6; Lu. 10:34; (for sickness)— Jas. 5:14. Poultices of figs (for boils) —II Ki. 20:7; Is. 38:21. Wine (for exhaustion)—Lu. 10:34; (for infirmities)—I Tim. 5:23; (for narcotics) —Mt. 27:34; Mk. 15:23. (Figurative use for healing) applied to troubled soul—Ps. 6:2. To impure and wronged nations—Jer. 14:19. To those in captivity—Jer. 8:22; 30:17. The capturer needs it—Jer. 51:8, 9. False healing —Jer. 6:14; 8:11. See DISEASES.

HEALTH. Ps. 38:3; Pr. 13:17. Bones, To the—Pr. 16:24. Prosper and be in —III John 2. Restore—Jer. 8:22; 30: 17; 33:6. Spiritual—Ex. 15:26; II Chr. 30:20; Ps. 42:11; 103:3; Pr. 3:8; 4:22; 12:18; Is. 30:26; 58:8; Jer. 3:22; 8:22; 17:14; 30:17; 33:6; Hos. 6:1; 7:1; 11:3. See HEALING.

HEAP, *n.* Josh. 3:13, 16; Ps. 33:7; 78: 13. Babylon shall become—Ju. 51:37.

Become—Job 15:28. Behold this— Gen. 31:51. City, Of—Is. 25:2. Corpses, Of—Neh. 3:3. Floods stood upright as a—Ex. 15:8. Foundation of—II Chr. 31:7. Furrows in—12:11. Gathered together in—Ex. 8:14. Grain, Of—Ruth 3:7. Heaps, Upon—Ju. 15:16. I will not pass over this—Gen. 31:52. Jerusalem—Ps. 79:1; Jer. 9:11; Mic. 3:2. Laid them in two—II Ki. 10:8. Made a—Gen. 31:46. Ruinous—II Ki. 19: 25; Is. 37:26; 17:1. Samaria, As—Mic. 1:6. Saw the—II Chr. 31:8. Stones, Of—Josh. 7:26; 8:29; II Sam. 18:17. Twenty measures, Of—Hag. 2:16. Waters, Of mighty—Hab. 3:15. Wheat, Of—Song of Sol. 7:2. Witness, Is— Gen. 31:48.

HEAP, *v.* Coals of fire—Pr. 25:22; Rom. 12:20. Dust—Hab. 1:10. Evils—Deut. 32:23. Peoples, Unto him—Hab. 2:5. Riches—Ps. 39:6. Silver as dust—Job 27:16; Zech. 9:3. Teachers, To themselves—II Tim. 4:3. Wood—Ez. 24:10.

HEAR. Advice—Mt. 18:15–17. Deaf— Mt. 11:5; Mk. 7:37; Lu. 7:22. Father's instruction of—Pr. 1:5, 8; 4:1; 8:33; 19:20, 27; 22:17; 23:19. Gospel—See GOSPEL. Hearing they hear not—Mt. 13:13, 14; Mk. 8:18; Lu. 8:8. Jesus— Mt. 17:5; Mk. 7:14; Lu. 5:1, 15; 6:17; 10:24; 15:1; 19:48. Moses and the prophets—Lu. 16:29, 31. Prayer—See PRAYER. Preacher, Without—Rom. 10: 14. Who hath ears let him—Mt. 11: 15; 13:9, 43; Mk. 4:9, 23; 7:16; Lu. 14:35; Rom. 11:8; Rev. 2:7, 29; 3:6, 13, 22; 13:9. Word—See GOSPEL. Ye him—Mt. 17:5. See EAR.

HEARD. Disciples—See DISCIPLES. Gospel—See GOSPEL. Herod—See HEROD. Jesus—Mt. 8:10; 9:12; 14:13; Mk. 2: 17; Lu. 7:9; 8:50; 18:2, 23; John 9:35; 11:4. That John was in prison—Mt. 4:12. See JESUS. Law—See LAW. Miracles, Of—See MIRACLES. Pharisees —Mt. 12:24; 21:45; Mk. 11:18; John 4:1; 7:32, 40; 9:40. Prayer—See PRAYER. Word—See GOSPEL, EAR.

HEART. Heb. *Lebh.* Gr. *Kardia.* **Seat of affection and source of energy.**— Gen. 6:5; 8:21; Deut. 29:19; I Chr. 29:18; Lu. 24:38.

The center of desires.—Gen. 6:5; Ps. 37: 4; Mt. 12:34; Acts 5:3–4.

Resolutions originate therein.—Deut. 8: 5; Ju. 5:15, 16; I Ki. 12:33; I Chr. 17: 19; Mk. 2:6, 8; Acts 8:22; I Cor. 7:37.

Breeding ground of bad deeds.—Ps. 73: 7; 140:2; Pr. 6:18; Jer. 3:17; 7:24; 16: 12; Mt. 12:34; 15:18, 19; Mk. 7:20, 21.

Seed bed of character.—Mt. 13:19; Mk. 4:15; Lu. 8:12–15.

Workshop of spiritual activities.—Ex. 35:5, 21, 26, 29; Pr. 4:23; Mt. 6:21; 12:35.

Gives assurance of perfect service.—Ex. 35:34, 35; I Chr. 28:2, 9; II Chr. 19:3, 9; 31:21.

Seat of courage.—Josh. 5:1; I Sam. 17: 32; Ps. 27:14.

Different kinds. — Bitter — Pr. 14:10. Broken and contrite—Ps. 34:18; 51: 17; 69:20; 147:3. Cheerful—Pr. 15:13, 15; 17:22; Eph. 5:19. Clean—Ps. 51: 10; Pr. 20:9. Double—Ps. 12:2. Enlarged—Ps. 119:32; II Cor. 6:11. Erring—Ps. 95:10; Heb. 3:10. Fickle—I Ki. 11:2–4. Foolish—Pr. 22:15; Rom. 1:21. Hardened—Ex. 4:21; 7:3, 13, 14, 22; 8:15, 19, 32; 9:7, 12, 34, 35; 10:1, 20, 27; 11:10; 14:4, 8; Deut. 15: 7; Ps. 95:8; Pr. 28:14; Mt. 19:8; Mk. 3:5; 16:14; John 12:40; Rom. 2:5. Heavy—Pr. 25:20. Melting—II Sam. 17:10; Ps. 22:14; Nahum 2:10. New— Ez. 18:31; 36:26. Perfect—I Ki. 8:61; 15:14; II Ki. 20:3; I Chr. 12:38; 28:9; 29:9, 19; II Chr. 16:9; 19:9; Ps. 101:2. Perverse—Ps. 101:4; Pr. 11:20; 12:8; 17:20. Proud—Pr. 21:4; Ob. 3. Pure— Ps. 73:1; Pr. 22:11; Mt. 5:8; I Tim. 1:5; II Tim. 2:22; I Pet. 1:22. Secretive—Ps. 44:21; I Cor. 14:25. Sick— Pr. 13:12. Trembling—Deut. 28:65; I Sam. 4:13; 17:32; 28:5; Job 37:1. Troubled—John 14:1, 27; 16:6; Rom. 9:2. Understanding—I Ki. 3:9, 12; Ps. 49:3; Pr. 2:2; 8:5; 14:33. Upright— Ps. 36:10; 94:15; 119:7. Wicked— Deut. 15:9; Pr. 6:18; 10:20; 26:23. Willing—Ex. 35:5, 29; II Cor. 9:7; Eph. 6:6. Wise—Pr. 2:10; 10:8; 23: 15. Whole—Ps. 86:12; 119:10, 34, 58, 69, 145; 138:1.

Heart not always distinguished from intellect and will.—Sometimes the whole inner man. *Cf.* Rom. 10:5–10, where the ''heart'' is the source of faith. In general the psychological terms of the Bible are used rather freely, not always technically. See TEACHINGS OF JESUS, MAN, SALVATION.

HEARTH. Jer. 17:6; 48:6. See TEMPLE, HEARTH.

HEAT. Physical.—Of the elements— Gen. 8:22; 18:1; I Sam. 11:11; II Sam. 4:5; Is. 18:4; Jer. 17:8. Endured during labor—Mt. 20:12; Rev. 16:9. Caused by fire—Dan. 3:19; Hos. 7:4; Acts 28:3. Of man—I Ki. 1:1, 2; Eccl. 4:11; Jer. 51:39.

Mentioned.—In parable—Lu. 12:55. As punishment—Deut. 32:24; Jer. 36:30. To consume—Job 24:19; II Pet. 3: 10, 12.

Spiritual heat.—Of Jehovah—Deut. 29: 24; Ps. 19:6. Of Ezekiel—Ez. 3:14.

Prophecy concerning.—Is. 4:6; 49:10; Rev. 7:16.

Illustrative of God's power.—Is. 18:4; 25:4, 5.

Figurative.—Job 30:30.

HEATHEN. See GENTILES, IDOLATRY, NATIONS.

HEAVEN. Physical heavens.—Created by God—Gen. 1:1; Ex. 20:11; II Ki. 19:15; I Chr. 16:26; II Chr. 2:12; Neh. 9:6; Ps. 8:3; 33:6; 148:5–6; Pr. 8:27; Is. 37:16; 42:5; Jer. 10:12; 32:17; 51: 15; Acts 4:24; Heb. 1:10; Rev. 10:6; 14:7.

Their function.—To declare God's glory —Ps. 19:1. To declare His righteousness—Ps. 50:6; 97:6. To shew His wonders—Mt. 24:29; Acts 2:19. To contain the lights—Gen. 1:14–19.

Their destruction.—Ps. 102:26; Is. 34:4; 51:6; Mt. 24:35; Heb. 1:11–12; II Pet. 3:10; Rev. 6:12; 20:11.

The new heavens.—Is. 65:17; 66:22; II Pet. 3:13; Rev. 21:1. See COSMOLOGY.

Heaven, the dwelling-place of God.— Deut. 26:15; I Ki. 8:30, 39, 43, 49; II Chr. 6:21, 27, 30, 33, 35, 39; Neh. 9:37; Ps. 2:4; 11:4; 20:6; 33:13; 102:19; Is. 63:15; 66:1; Mt. 5:34; 6:9; 10:22; 12: 50; 16:17; 18:10; Mk. 11:25; Acts 7:48.

Of the Christ—Mt. 24:30; Mk. 14:62; John 3:13, 31; 6:38; 14:2–3; Acts 1: 11; I Cor. 15:47; I Thess. 1:10; 4:16; Heb. 1:3; Rev. 22:1.

Of the angels—Lu. 2:13–15; Rev. 1:4; 18:1; 20:1.

Of the righteous—Mt. 5:12; 25:34, 46; John 12:26; 14:2–3; 17:24; I Thess. 4:17; Phil. 3:20; Rev. 2:7; 3:21; 22:14.

God reigns in heaven.—Ps. 103:20; Mt. 6:10; Deut. 4:35–36; 33:26–27; I Sam. 12:12–15; Ps. 47:8; Jer. 23:23, 24. Over the devil—Job 1:12; 2:6; Lu. 10:18; II Pet. 2:4; Jude 6; Rev. 20:1–3.

Hears petitions in.—I Ki. 8:30, 32, 34, 36, 39, 54–56; I Chr. 21:26; II Chr. 7: 14; Neh. 9:27; Ps. 20:6; Mt. 6:9; 7: 7–11.

Sends His judgments from.—Gen. 19: 24; I Sam. 2:10; Dan. 4:13–17; Rom. 1:18.

Descriptions of.—The Father's house— John 14:2. A garner—Mt. 3:12. A city—Heb. 11:10, 16. A kingdom— Mt. 25:34; Lu. 12:32; Eph. 5:5. Paradise—II Cor. 12:4. The holy city— Rev. 21:1–3, 10–27; 22:1–5.

Characteristics of.—No marriages there —Mt. 22:30. No sorrow—Rev. 7:17; 21:4. No curse—Rev. 22:3. No pain— Rev. 7:16; 21:4. No night—Rev. 22:5. No death—Rev. 21:4. No flesh and blood—I Cor. 15:50. No corruption— I Cor. 15:42, 50. Joy there—Ps. 16: 11; Lu. 15:7, 10. Treasure in—Mt. 6: 20; 19:21. Righteousness in—II Pet. 3:13. Service in—Rev. 7:15.

Conditions of entrance.—Mt. 25:34–36, 46; Lu. 6:47–48; 13:24; John 3:5, 18, 21; 8:24; 11:25–26; 20:31; Rom. 8:17; 12:1–2; II Pet. 1:5–11; Rev. 2:7, 10– 11; 21:7; 22:14.

Conditions which bar entrance.—Mt. 5: 29–30; 7:26–27; 10:37–39; 13:41–42; Lu. 13:23–28; I Cor. 6:9–10; Gal. 5: 19–20; Eph. 5:5; Jude 14, 15; Rev. 21: 8; 22:11, 15.

Signs of the heavens.—Planets and bow originally for signs—Gen. 1:14; 9:13. Nations became dismayed because of them—Jer. 10:2. Astrologers vainly interpreted them—Is. 47:12–14. Pharisees seek signs from heaven—Mt. 12: 38; 16:1–3; Mk. 8:11; Lu. 11:16; 12: 54–56; I Cor. 1:22. Used as witness for spiritual truth—Ps. 89:36–37; 72: 5. Inability to read heavenly signs— Job 37:14–17, 21–22. The signs of the Son of Man—Mt. 24:29–31; Mk. 13: 24–27. Visions of John—Rev. 4:1; 7:

1–3; 10:1–6; 12:1–3; 15:1; 18:1; 20: 1–3; 21:1–2; 22:1–2. See JESUS' ASCENSION AND DIVINITY, LIFE, ETERNAL, RESURRECTION, IMMORTALITY.

HEAVENLY. I Cor. 15:48, 49. Bodies —See ASTRONOMY, COSMOLOGY. Calling —Heb. 3:1. Country—Heb. 11:16. Father—See GOD. Gift—Heb. 6:4. Jerusalem—Heb. 12:22. Kingdom—II Tim. 4:18. Places—Eph. 1:3, 20; 2:6; 3:10; 6:12. Things—John 3:12; Heb. 8:5; 9:23. Vision—Acts 26:19. See HEAVEN.

HEAVE. Offering—See OFFERING.

HEAVILY. Drove—Ex. 14:25. Laid yoke—Is. 47:6.

HEAVINESS. End of mirth is—Pr. 14: 13. Full of—Ps. 69:20. Hear, In— Pr. 12:25. Joy turned to—Jas. 4:9. Mother, Of—Pr. 10:1. My soul melteth for—Ps. 119:28. Spirit of—Is. 61:3.

HEAVY. Bondage—Neh. 5:18. Burden —Ps. 38:4; Mt. 23:4. Chain—Lam. 3:7. Ears—Is. 6:10; 59:1. Eyes—Mt. 26:43; Mk. 14:40. Fool's vexation— Pr. 27:3. God, Hand of—I Sam. 5:6, 11. Hair—II Sam. 14:26. Hands—Ex. 17:12; Ps. 32:4. Heart—Pr. 25:20. Judgment—Jas. 3:1. Laden—Mt. 11: 28. Men, Upon—Eccl. 6:1. Sand, Than —Job. 6:3. Sleep, With—Lu. 9:32. Stone—Pr. 27:3. Stroke—Job 23:2. Tidings—I Ki. 14:6. Too—Ex. 18:18; Num. 11:14. Transgression—Is. 24:20. Yoke—I Ki. 12:4, 10, 11, 14.

HEBER, hē′ber. (1) **A Gadite.**—I Chr. 5:13.

(2) **Son of Beriah, grandson of Asher.**— Gen. 46:17; Num. 26:45; I Chr. 7:51, 32; Lu. 3:35.

(3) **Son of Shashak.**—I Chr. 8:22.

(4) **Son of Joel, who slew Sisera — Ju.** 4:11, 17, 21; 5:24.

(5) **Son of Ezra.**—I Chr. 4:18.

(6) **A Benjamite, son of Elpaal.**—I Chr. 8:17.

HEBERITES. Descendants of Heber (2).—Num. 26:45.

HEBREW. (1) **People.**—Abraham the — Gen. 14:13. Being — Jer. 34:9. Brought in a—Gen. 39:14. Children, One of—Ex. 2:6. I am a—Jon. 1:9. Man or woman—Deut. 15:12. Midwives—Ex. 1:15. Servant—Gen. 39:

17; 41:12; Ex. 21:2. Smiting a—Ex. 2:11. Women—Ex. 1:16, 19; 2:7.

(2) **Tongue.** John 5:2; 19:13, 17, 20; Acts 21:40; 22:2; 26:14; Rev. 9:11; 16:16.

HEBREWS, BOOK OF. See OUTLINE STUDIES IN THE BOOKS.

HEBRON, hē′bron. (1) **A city of Judah south of Jerusalem, in plain of Mamre.** —Gen. 13:18; 23:2, 19; Num. 13:22; II Chr. 11:10. Abraham, Isaac and Jacob dwelt in—Gen. 35:27; 37:14. King of—Josh. 10:3, 5, 23; 12:10. Joshua fights with—Josh. 10:36–39; 11:21; Ju. 1:10. Given to Caleb for an inheritance—Josh. 14:13–15; 15:13, 54; Ju. 1:20. A city of refuge—Josh. 20:7. Given to the Levites—Josh. 21:11, 13; I Chr. 6:55, 57. Samson carries doors to—Ju. 16:3. David sent spoil to—I Sam. 30:3. David in—II Sam. 2:1–11; 3:2, 5, 19–27; 5:1–13; I Ki. 2:11; I Chr. 3:1, 4; 11:1, 3; 12:23, 38; 29:27. Joab at—II Sam. 2:32. Abner dead in—II Sam. 4:1. Head of Ish-bosheth brought to—II Sam. 4:8–12. Absalom made a vow in—Num. 3:19; II Sam. 15:7–10.

(2) I Chr. 2:42, 43; 15:9.

(3) **A Levite.**—Ex. 6:18; Num. 3:19; I Chr. 6:2, 18; 23:12, 19.

HEBRONITES. Num. 3:27; 26:58; I Chr. 26:23, 30, 31.

HEDGE. Is. 17:11. Encamp in—Nah. 3:17. Go out into highways and—Lu. 14:23. God hath—Job 3:23. Made—Job 1:10. Set about—Mt. 21:33; Mk. 12:1. Take away—Is. 5:5. Thorns, Of—Pr. 15:19. Way with thorns—Hos. 2:6.

HEED. Gave no—II Chr. 33:10. Give—Pr. 16:20; 29:19; I Tim. 4:13. Take—Gen. 31:24; Ex. 23:21; Deut. 2:4; 4:15; Josh. 23:11; Ps. 119:9; Col. 2:8. Word—Mk. 5:36.

HEEL. Biteth horse's—Gen. 49:17. Bruise his—Gen. 3:15. Esau's—Gen. 25:26. Gin shall take him by—Job 18:9. Iniquity at—Ps. 49:5. Lifted up against me—Ps. 41:9; John 13:18. Press upon their—Gen. 49:19. Suffer violence—Jer. 13:22. Took brother by—Hos. 12:3. See FOOT.

HEGAI, hē-gāi. **A chamberlain under the king of Persia.**—Esth. 2:3, 8, 5.

HE-GOAT. See GOAT.

HEIFER. Gen. 15:9; Num. 19:2; Deut. 21:3; I Sam. 16:2; Hos. 4:16; 10:11; Heb. 9:13. See CATTLE, OFFERING.

HEIGHT. Above—Is. 7:11. Farthest—Is. 37:24. Heart lifted up in—Ez. 31:10. Heaven, Of—Job 22:12. Israel—Ez. 17:23; 20:40. Length, breadth and—Eph. 3:18; Rev. 21:16. Mountains, Of—Ps. 95:4. Nor height, nor depth—Rom. 8:59. Praise in—Ps. 148:1; Jer. 31:12.

HEIR. According to hope—Tit. 3:7. Believers are—Rom. 4:13; 8:17; Gal. 3:29; Heb. 6:17; 11:7; Jas. 2:5. Christ the—Col. 1:15, 16; Heb. 1:2. Destroy—II Sam. 14:7. God, Of—Rom. 8:17. Hath he no—Jer. 49:1. Kingdom, Of—Jas. 2:5. One born in my house—Gen. 15:3. Righteousness, Of—Heb. 11:7. This is the—Mt. 21:38; Mk. 12:7; Lu. 20:14. World, Of—Rom. 4:13. See COVENANTS, INHERITANCE.

HELAH, hē′lah. **Wife of Asher.**—I Chr. 4:5, 7.

HELAM, hē′lam. **A place east of the Jordan.**—II Sam. 16:17.

HELBAH, hĕl′bah. **A town in Asher.**—Ju. 1:31.

HELBON, hĕl′bon. **A city celebrated for its wine.**—Ez. 27:18.

HEN. Gathereth her chickens, As—Mt. 23:37. Gathereth her own brood—Lu. 13:34.

Son of Zephaniah.—Zech. 6:14.

HEREAFTER. Gen. 30:33; Dan. 2:29, 45. Come yet two woes—Rev. 9:12. Declare things to come—Is. 41:23. Things come to pass—Rev. 1:19; 4:1. Understand—John 13:7.

HENA, hē′na. **A city of Mesopotamia.**—II Ki. 18:24; 19:13; Is. 37:13.

HENADAD, hĕn′a-dăd. **A Levite who aided in rebuilding the temple.**—Ezra 3:9; Neh. 3:18, 24; 10:9.

HENNA. See PLANTS.

HEPHER, hē′pher. (1) **Son of Ashur.**—I Chr. 4:6.

(2) **One of the thirty heroes of David's guard.**—I Chr. 11:36.

(3) **Head of the family of the Hepherites.**—Num. 26:32; 27:1; Josh. 17:2, 3.

(4) **Canaanite city west of the Jordan.**—Josh. 12:17; I Ki. 4:10.

HEPHERITES, hē′pher-ites. Num. 26: 32.

HEPHZI-BAH, hĕph′zĭ-bäh. (1) **Mother of Manasseh.**—II Ki. 21:1.

(2) **Future name for Jerusalem.**—Is. 62:4.

HERALD. Dan. 3:4.

HERBS. Herbs yielding seed—Gen. 1: 11. , Locusts ate every herb of the land—Ex. 10:15. Ate passover with bitter—Ex. 12:8; Num. 9:11. Land of Egypt as a garden of—Deut. 11:10. Wither as the green—Ps. 37:2. Herb for service of man—Ps. 104:14. Better a dinner of—Pr. 15:17. The dew is as dew of herb—Is. 26:19. Will dry up all their—Is. 42:15. Is greatest among—Mt. 13:32; Mk. 4:32. Ye tithe every—Lu. 11:42. He that is weak eateth—Rom. 14:2. Land bringeth forth—Heb. 6:7. See GRASS, PLANTS.

HERD. See CATTLE.

HERDSMEN. Gen. 13:7, 8; 26:20; I Sam. 21:7; Amos 1:1; 7:14.

HERES, hē′rĕs. Mount on border of Judah—Ju. 1:35; 8:13.

HERESH, hē′resh. **A Levite.**—I Chr. 9:15.

HERESY. Acts 24:14; Gal. 5:20; II Pet. 2:1.

HERETH, hē′reth. **A forest in the hills of Judah.**—I Sam. 22:5.

HERITAGE. Abomination—Jer. 2:7; Ex. 6:8. Afflict—Ps. 94:5. Almighty, From—Appointed by God—Job 20:29. Desolate—Is. 49:8; Job 31:2. Flock of—Mic. 7:14. Goodly—Ps. 16:6; Jer. 3:19; Is. 58:14. Jehovah, Of—Ps. 127:3. Land for a—Ps. 135:12. Oppressors, Of—Job 27:13. Remnant of—Mic. 7:18. Reproach, Give to—Joel 2:17. Servants of Jehovah, Of—Is. 54:17. Taken testimonies as—Ps. 119:111. Waste, Laid—Mal. 1:3. See INHERITANCE.

HERMAS, hēr′mas. **A Christian in Rome.**—Rom. 16:14.

HERMES, hēr′mēs. (Same as above.)

HERMOGENES, her-mŏg′e-nēs. **One who deserted Paul.**—II Tim. 1:15.

HERMON, *sacred mountain.* A mountain of the anti-Lebanon range. Called Sirion—Deut. 3:8, 9; Ps. 29:6. Sion —Deut. 4:48. Senir—Deut. 3:9; I

Chr. 5:23; Song of Sol. 4:8. Inhabitants of—Josh. 11:3, 17; 12:1, 5; 13:5, 11. Rejoice in thy name—Ps. 89:12.

HERODS: Eleven members of the family in the New Testament.—Herod the Great—Mt. 2:1; Archelaus—Mt. 2:22; Herod Antipas—Lu. 3:1; Mk. 6:14; Herodias—Mk. 6:17; her daughter Salome—Mk. 6:22; Philip, the first husband of Herodias—Mk. 6:17; Philip the Tetrarch. *Cf.* Trachonitis and Ituræa—Lu. 3:1; Herod Agrippa I— Acts 12:1; Herod Agrippa II—Acts 25:13; Drusilla—Acts 24:24; Bernice —Acts 25:13.

Name Herod applied to three.—Only three of the family have the term Herod in the New Testament: Herod the Great, who slew the male children in Bethlehem—Mt. 2:16; Herod Antipas, who beheaded John the Baptist —Mk. 6:14; Herod Agrippa I, who slew James, the brother of John— Acts 12:1.

Idumean dynasty.—Antipas the Idumean ingratiated himself into the good graces of John Hyrcanus II, made use of his fears and his weaknesses, became useful to Julius Cæsar, and finally his personal representative in the government.

Herod the Great.—Son of Antipater the Idumean. Born B.C. 74 and died B.C. 4, being about 70 years old (Josephus, Ant. XVII, VI, I). He was a vassal king of Rome and a Greek in sympathy. His marriage with Mariamne, daughter of John Hyrcanus II, gave his throne more legitimacy with the Jews. But he had ten wives in all. Josephus tells the story of his splendor, his cruelty to his own family (putting to death Mariamne and her mother Alexandra, Mariamne's two sons, besides Antipater and many others). He managed to keep the friendship of Augustus Cæsar, but lost the love of the Jews. He antagonized their customs and introduced many Hellenizing practices. The slaughter of the babes in Bethlehem (Mt. 2:13- 18) was in perfect harmony with his character in Josephus. He would brook no rival and no interference with his plans. Message of the wise men "troubled" Herod (Mt. 2:3) about the succession to the throne. Hence his inquiry of the chief priests and scribes about the birth-place of the promised Messiah (2:4). His duplicity with the wise men (2:7 f.) is in accord with his picture in Josephus.

Archelaus.—Elder son of Herod the Great by Malthace the Samaritan. He was the heir of Herod the Great by his last will. Was given only Judæa, Samaria, and Idumea, and obtained the title of ethnarch from Augustus with promise of king if he behaved properly. He was popularly called king. He was the very worst of the sons of Herod living after the death of Antipater. Hence the dread of Joseph in Egypt—Mt. 2:22. He ruled only ten years, till A.D. 6, when he was deposed by the emperor. His career is probably referred to by Jesus in the parable of the pounds—Lu. 19: 12 ff. When Jesus came to Jerusalem at twelve years of age (Lu. 2:42), He would probably hear talk of the recent downfall of Archelaus.

Herod Antipas.—Second son of Herod the Great by Malthace. He obtained, B.C. 4, Galilee and Peræa with the title of tetrarch. Ruled till banished to Lyons in Gaul in A.D. 39. The youth and most of the ministry of Jesus were spent in the territory of Herod Antipas. Yet he never saw Jesus till the trial of Jesus—Lu. 23:8. His court was at Tiberius, a city that Jesus avoided. Jesus knew that Herod would be hostile toward him, and warned his disciples against the leaven of Herod—Mk. 8:15. The Pharisees once reported that Herod was plotting to kill him, and Christ called him, "that fox"—Lu. 13:31 f. He feared the reports about Jesus, thinking that he was John the Baptist come to life again—Mt. 14:1 f.; Mk. 6:14; Lu. 9: 7-9. He had imprisoned John for denouncing his adulterous marriage with Herodias—Mt. 14:3 f.; Mk. 6:17. Josephus adds a political motive for the arrest of John—Ant. XVIII, V. 2. He had divorced his wife, a daughter of Aretas, in order to marry Herodias, the wife of Herod Philip of Rome.

Herodias was indeed the niece of this Philip (half-brother of Antipas). Both were close kin to Antipas. The shameful marriage outraged the Jews, and John's rebuke ultimately cost his head through the resentment of Herodias (Mk. 6:19), who used Herod Antipas's love for the dancing of her own daughter for that purpose—Mt. 14:6-12; Mk. 6:20-29. The jealousy of Herodias toward Agrippa I led to the banishment of Antipas and herself.

Philip of Rome.—Son of Herod the Great by Mariamne (daughter of Simon, not the Maccabee). He lived in Rome and comes into the New Testament merely as the first husband of Herodias—Mk. 6:17.

Herodias.—She was a Maccabean in part, daughter of Aristobulus, son of Mariamne (daughter of Hyrcanus II, and wife of Herod the Great). Her mother was Bernice, daughter of Salôme (Herod's sister). She is a sad specimen of the degenerate woman of the time. She probably deserted Philip for Antipas for ambition, and for ambition lost all at last. She never forgave John the Baptist (Mk. 6:19), and prostituted her own daughter to the public dance to get revenge on him— Mk. 6:24; Mt. 14:8.

Salome.—Daughter of Herodias by Herod Philip, her first husband. She is called Herodias also in some manuscripts in Mk. 6:22. She performed the disgraceful dance that won the head of John the Baptist on a platter—Mt. 14:8-11; Mk. 6:25-28. She married Philip tetrarch of Trachonitis, and later Aristobulus of Chalcis.

Philip of Trachonitis.—Son of Herod the Great by Cleopatra of Jerusalem. He obtained (B.C. 4) Trachonitis and Ituræa with the title of tetrarch (Lu. 3:1), which he ruled till his death (A.D. 34). He was the best of Herod the Great's sons who succeeded him, and was free from ambition, cruelty, and lust. He founded Cæsarea Philippi. Jesus made a journey into this region —Mt. 16:13; Mk. 8:27. Jesus withdrew to Bethsaida (Lu. 9:10); also on an earlier occasion, which was in

Philip's territory. He was here free from the jealousy of Herod Antipas.

Herod Agrippa I.—Son of Aristobulus, who was son of Mariamne the Maccabee and Herod the Great. His mother was Bernice, daughter of Salome (sister of Herod the Great). He was brought up in Rome as friend of Caligula, who when he became emperor made Agrippa king of the tetrarchies of Philip and Lyranias (A.D. 38). On the banishment of Herod Antipas, in A.D. 39, he has Galilee and Peræa added to his realm. In A.D. 42 Claudius gives him also Judæa and Samaria, so that for a brief period a Herod again is king of all Palestine. The death of James and imprisonment of Peter by Herod Agrippa belong to this period—Acts 12:1 ff. His shameful death at Cæsarea in A.D. 44 was a fitting close to a disgraceful career—Acts 12:19–23. *Cf.* Josephus, Ant. XIX, VIII, 2.

Herod Agrippa II.—Son of Herod Agrippa I and Cypros. Was only seventeen years old on death of his father in A.D. 44. Hence Claudius refused to give him his father's kingdom. Later made tetrarch of Chalcis with oversight of the temple in Jerusalem and then received instead of the tetrarchies of Philip and Lyranias. Reports had it that he lived unlawfully with his sister Bernice—Acts 25:13, 23; 26:30. He is called king in Acts 25:13, 26; 26:2, 30. He is on good terms with Festus, the Roman procurator of Judæa—Acts 25:13–27. Paul commends his knowledge of Jewish customs (Acts 25:3), though he was a lover of Hellenism, like all the Herods. He supported Rome during the Jewish war. His interest in Paul was at first indifferent (Acts 25:22); was never great (Acts 26:28), though he saw clearly that Paul was innocent of any crime—Acts 26:32. He died about A.D. 100, the last of the Herods.

Bernice.—Eldest daughter of Agrippa I. She had a varied career as wife of her uncle, Herod of Chalcis, and of Polemon, king of Cilicia; as paramour of her brother Agrippa and of Titus the Roman emperor. She only appears once in New Testament history, but is mentioned three times (Acts 25:13, 23; 26:30) in connection with her brother Agrippa. She attracted notice by her charms.

Drusilla.—Youngest of the daughters of Agrippa I. She married first Azizus, king of Emesa, but left him for Felix, who married her. She is with him while he is procurator of Judæa, and heard Paul preach (Acts 24:24), when Paul made him tremble. She probably perished in an eruption of Mt. Vesuvius, in the reign of Titus, together with her son, by Felix, named Agrippa.

HERODIANS, he-rō'di-ans. **Followers of Herod.**—Josephus (War, I, XVI, 6) uses a slightly different word for the party of Herod the Great. The Herodians in the New Testament may be the same party. If so, they are a political party, not a religious sect. This matter is not clear. But certainly they represent those under Roman rule who wished for a restoration of the rule of the Herods, probably under Herod Antipas. Hence in Galilee (Mk. 3:6) Jesus warned the disciples against the leaven of Herod Antipas (Mk. 8:15), but this need not have been either that of the Pharisees or of the Sadducees (Mt. 16:6). A distinction seems to be drawn between the Herodians and both Pharisees and Sadducees in Mt. 22:15 f., 23; Mk. 12:13, 18; Lu. 20:20, 27. As in Mk. 3:6, so here they join with the Pharisees in attacking Jesus about tribute to Cæsar. As advocates of the dynasty of Herod they opposed paying taxes to Rome.

HERODIAS, he-rō'di-as. See HEROD.

HERODION, he-rō'di-ŏn. **Roman kinsman of Paul.**—Rom. 16:11.

HERON. See BIRDS.

HESHBON, hĕsh'bon. Heb. *Reckoning.* —A Levitical city east of Jordan— Num. 21:25, 26, 27, 28, 30, 34; 32:3, 37; Josh. 21:39; I Chr. 6:81.

Sihon, King of.—Deut. 1:4; 2:24, 26, 30; 3:2, 6; 4:46; 29:7; Josh. 9:10; 12:2, 5; 13:21, 27; Ju. 11:19; Neh. 9:22.

Land of.—Ju. 11:26; Is. 15:4; 16:8; Jer. 48:2, 34. Pools of—Song of Sol. 7:4.

City of Reuben and Gad.—Josh. 13:17,
21, 26.
HESHMON, hĕsh'mon. Town in Judah.
—Josh. 15:27.
HETH, hĕth. Ancestor of Hittites.—
Gen. 10:5. Children of—23:3–20; 27:
46; 49:32; I Chr. 1:13.
HETH-LON, hĕth'–lŏn. Place in Prom-
ised Land.—Ez. 47:15; 48:1.
HEW. Is. 10:15; Hos. 6:5. Agag—I
Sam. 15:33. Cedars—Is. 44:14. Cis-
terns—Deut. 6:11; Jer. 2:13. Down—
Mt. 3:10; 7:19; Lu. 3:9. Graven im-
ages—Deut. 12:3. High of stature—
Is. 10:33. Palace, After fashion of—
Ps. 144:12. Pillars—Pr. 9:1. Rock,
In the—Mt. 27:60; Mk. 15:46. Stone
—Ex. 20:25; I Ki. 6:36; 7:9, 11, 12;
II Ki. 12:12; 22:6; I Chr. 22:2; II Chr.
34:11; Eccl. 10:9; Is. 9:10; Lam. 13:9;
Ez. 40:42; Amos 5:11; Lu. 23:53. Ta-
bles—Ex. 34:1, 4; Deut. 10:1, 3. Trees
—Jer. 6:6; Dan. 4:14, 23. Whence ye
were—Is. 51:1. Wood—Deut. 19:5.
HEWER. I Ki. 5:15; I Chr. 22:15; II
Chr. 2:2, 18. Of wood—Deut. 29:11;
Josh. 9:21, 23, 27; II Chr. 2:10; Jer.
46:22.
HEZEKIAH, hĕz-e-kī'ah. Son of Ahaz
—II Ki. 16:20; 18:1; I Chr. 3:13; II
Chr. 28:27. King of Judah—Pr. 25:1;
Is. 1:1; 36:22; 37:10; Jer. 15:4; 26:19;
Hos. 1:1; Mic. 1:1. Reign of, in
Judah—II Ki. 16:20; 18:1, 9, 10; II
Chr. 29:1. Encounter with Sennacherib—II Ki. 18:13–19, 22, 29–32, 37;
II Chr. 32:2–19; Is. 36:1, 2, 4, 7, 15, 16,
18, 22, 23. Cleansing of the temple—
II Chr. 29:18, 20, 27, 30, 31, 36. Godly
character of—II Ki. 19:1–5, 9, 10, 14,
15, 20; II Chr. 30:1, 18, 20, 22, 24; 31:2,
8, 9, 11, 13, 20; 32:8, 9, 11, 12; Is. 37:1,
3, 5, 9, 10, 15, 21; 38:22; 39:8. Recovery from illness—II Ki. 20:1–3, 5, 8,
10, 12, 13–16, 19, 20; II Chr. 32:24, 25,
26; Is. 38:1, 2, 3, 5, 9; 39:1, 2, 3. Song
of thanksgiving—Is. 38:10–21. Prosperity of—II Chr. 32:26, 27–31. Death
and burial—II Ki. 20:21; II Chr. 32:
33. Records—II Ki. 20:20; I Chr. 4:4,
41; II Chr. 32:32. Descendants—II
Ki. 21:3; II Chr. 33:3; Ezra 2:16;
Neh. 7:21.
HEZION, hē'zi-ŏn. Ancestor of a Syrian
king.—I Ki. 15:18.

HEZIR, hē'zir. (1) One who sealed the
covenant with Nehemiah.—Neh. 10:
20.
(2) A priest in the time of David.—I
Chr. 24:15.
HEZRO, hĕz'ro. One of the thirty
heroes with David.—II Sam. 23:35;
I Chr. 11:37.
HEZRON, hĕz'ron. (1) Ancestor of a
family of tribe of Reuben.—Gen. 46:
9; Ex. 6:14; Num. 26:6; I Chr. 5:3.
(2) A son of Perez, ancestor of family
of Judah.—Gen. 46:12; Num. 26:21;
Ruth 4:18, 19; I Chr. 2:5. See Mt.
1:3; Lu. 3:33.
(3) A place on south boundary of Judah,
west of Kadesh-barnea.—Josh. 15:3
(Hazzar-addar, Num. 34:4).
(4) A town in South Judea (Kerioth-
hezron [called HAZOR]).—Josh. 15:25.
Strifes of.—Only city burnt—Josh. 11:
13, 17.
Israelites sold to Jabin, who reigned in
Hazor.—Ju. 4:2; I Sam. 12:9.
Taken captive to Assyria.—II Ki. 15:29.
Peace is made between Jabin and the
house of Heber.—Ju. 4:17.
HEZRONITES, hĕz'ron-ites. Descend-
ants of Hezron—Num. 26:6.
HID. Found and—Mt. 13:43. Himself
—John 12:36. Sins are not—Ps. 69:5.
Themselves—Gen. 3:8. With Christ in
God—Col. 3:3.
HIDDAI, hĭd'dāi. One of David's thirty
heroes.—II Sam. 23:30.
HIDDEKEL, hĭd'de-kĕl. A river in
Paradise.—Gen. 2:14; Dan. 10:4.
HIDDEN. Lev. 5:2. Cave, In—Josh.
10:17. Faults—Ps. 19:12. Frome
was not—Ps. 139:15. Love—Pr. 27:5.
Place—Job 40:13. Rocks—Jude 12.
Snare—Ps. 142:3. Things—Eccl. 12:
14; Mt. 13:35; II Cor. 4:2. Treasures
—Deut. 33:19.
HIDE. Abraham, From—Gen. 18:17.
Commandments, Not — Ps. 119:19.
Counsel—Is. 29:15. Dust, In—Job
40:13; Is. 2:10. Face—Is. 53:3; Ez.
39:29. Heart, In—Job 10:13. No
longer, Could—Ex. 2:3. Place—Ps.
32:7; 119:114; Is. 32:2. Secret coun-
sel, From—Ps. 64:2. Shadow, Under
—Ps. 17:8. Sheol, In—Job 14:13.
Snow—Job 6:16. Themselves—Pr.

28:12. Things—Mt. 11:25. Where he—I Sam. 23:23.

HIEL, hi'el. **One who rebuilt Jericho.—** I Ki. 16:34.

HIERAPOLIS, hī'e-răp'o-lĭs. **A city of Phrygia.**—Col. 4:13.

HIGGAION, hig-gā'ion. Ps. 9:16.

HIGH. Calling of God—I Tim. 2:2. City, Not a—Deut. 2:36. Day—Gen. 29:7. Day spring from on—Lu. 1:78. Displeased—Acts 12:20. Exalted— Phil. 2:9. Favored—Lu. 1:28. Glory to God on—Lu. 2:14. Hand—Num. 15:30. Higher and—Deut. 28:43; Ez. 41:7. Higher than the—Eccl. 5:8. King—Num. 24:7; Ps. 89:27. Lifted on—Zech. 9:16. Most—Ps. 18:13; 87: 5; Lu. 1:32. My way—Is. 55:9. Mountain—Is. 57:7. Sent from—II Sam. 22:17. Setteth up on—Job 5:11.

HELDAI, hĕl'dāi. (1) I Chr. 27:15. (2) Zech. 6:10.

HELEB, hē'leb. **One of David's mighty men.**—II Sam. 23:29.

HELED, hē'led. I Chr. 11:30.

HELEK, hē'lek. **Son of Gilead.**—Num. 26:30; Josh. 17:2.

HELEKITES. **Descendants of Helek.** —Num. 26:30.

HELEM, hē'lem. (1) **A descendant of Asher.**—I Chr. 7:35. (2) Zech. 6:14.

HELEPH, hē'leph. **A town of Naphtali.**—Josh. 19:33.

HELEZ, hē'lez. (1) II Sam. 23:26; I Chr. 11:27; 27:10. (2) **A man of Judah.**—I Chr. 2:39.

HELI, hē'li. **Father of Joseph the husband of Mary.**—Lu. 3:23.

HELKAI, hĕl'kāi. **A priest.**—Neh. 12: 15.

HELKATH, hĕl'kath. **A town allotted to the Levites.**—Josh. 19:25; 21:31.

HELKATH-HAZZURIM, hĕl'kath–hăz-zu-rim. II Sam. 2:16.

HELL. Gr. *Gehenna,* "Valley of Hinnom." From Heb. *Gē,* "valley," and "Hinnom," name of the owner. (West of Jerusalem, where noxious things were burned up.) Used figuratively as name or place of everlasting punishment. Distinct from Hades. which is the place or state of all departed souls, and corresponds to Sheol in Old Testament. The expression

"lowest sheol" in Old Testament is indicative of Hell.

References in Old Testament where hell is probably meant.—Deut. 32:22; Ps. 86:13; Pr. 9:18; 15:24; 23:14; Is. 14: 15; 28:18, 19; 30:33; 33:14. Proselytes of—Mt. 23:15; II Pet. 2:10–12.

Danger of.—Mt. 5:22, 29, 30; 10:28; 18:8, 9; Mk. 9:43–48; Lu. 12:5.·

The judgment of.—Mt. 23:33; Lu. 16:23, 25, 26; II Pet. 2:4. (*Cf.* Mk. 14:64; II Cor. 1:9.)

Its destructive nature.—Mt. 3:12; 10: 28; Lu. 3:17; Jas. 3:6.

The abode of the wicked.—Mt. 13:41, 42; 25:41–46; Lu. 16:23; Rev. 19:20; 20:14, 15.

Not in O.T. of A.R.V. N.T. usage.

(1) "Hades" translated "hell" ten times in A.V. ("death" once) is translated "hades" in A.R.V. ten times ("death" once). Sometimes "hades" is used in context where it is clear that the abode of the wicked is meant. *Cf.* Lu. 16:23, "in hades," "in torments." Death and hades cast into the lake of fire—Rev. 20:14. English word "hell" is from Anglo-Saxon *helan,* to hide, conceal. Originally the other world, like "hades" the "unseen" world, then confined to the abode of the damned.

(2) "Tartarus" used but once, limited to evil angels, is retained in A.R.V. II Pet. 2:4.

(3) "Gehenna" used eleven times by Jesus, once by James and by no others, is translated hell uniformly. See FIRE, PUNISHMENT, SHEOL, JUDGMENT, DESTRUCTION, DEATH.

HELMET. Ez. 23:24; 38:7. Brass, Of —I Sam. 17:5, 38. Hanged shield and —Ez. 27:10. Hope of salvation, For a—I Thess. 5:8. Salvation, Of—Is. 59:17; Eph. 6:17. Stand forth with— Jer. 46:4. Ussiah prepared—II Chr. 26:14. See ARMOR.

HELON, hē'lon. **Chief of one of the tribes in the wilderness.**—Num. 1:9; 2:7; 7:24, 29; 10:16.

HELP: Spiritual.—Power of God—II Chr. 25:8.

Power of Spirit.—Rom. 8:26.

God a willing helper to mankind.—Gen. 49:25; Deut. 33:29; Ps. 27:9; 28:7;

30:10; 33:20; 37:40; 38:22; 40:13, 17; 42:5; 44:26; 46:1, 5; 54:4; 59:4; 63:7; 70:1, 5; 71:12; 79:9; 86:17; 94:17; 109: 26; 115:9; 118:7; 121:1, 2; 124:8; 146: 5; Is. 41:10, 13, 14; 50:7, 9; Heb. 4:16; 13:6.

To fatherless.—Ps. 10:14. To poor— Ps. 72:12.

In time of war.—Ex. 18:4; I Sam. 7:12; II Chr. 18:31; 20:4; 26:7, 15; 32:8.

Saints inspired by God's help.—Acts 26:22.

God called upon for help.—II Chr. 14: 11; 20:4; Ps. 12:1; 20:2; 22:19. Against Jehovah's adversaries — Deut. 33:7.

Curse for not coming to the help of Jehovah.—Ju. 5:23.

Nations help forward affliction.—Zech. 1:15.

Nations and warriors helped each other in war.—Josh. 10:4, 6, 33; II Sam. 10: 11, 19; I Chr. 5:20; 12:19, 21; 19:12, 19; II Chr. 20:23; 26:13; 28:16; Jer. 37:7.

Examples.—To David—I Chr. 12:1, 18; Ps. 3:2, 3. Of Rahab—Job 9:13. Help of Man—Job 26:2; Ps. 60:11; 108:12; 146:3; Dan. 10:13. To Adonijah—I Ki. 1:7. To Benhadad—I Ki. 20:16. To David—I Chr. 12:1, 17, 18, 22; Ps. 35:2; 89:19-21. Of fishermen—Lu. 5:7. To Jews—Esth. 9:3. Of Meshullam and Shabbethai—Ezra 10:15. Of men—Josh. 1:14. Of Moses—Ex. 2: 17. To priests—II Chr. 29:34. Of princes to Hezekiah—II Chr. 32:3. Of wicked—II Chr. 19:2. Sought from king—II Sam. 14:4; II Ki. 6:26. Help-meet of man—Gen. 2:18, 20. Help of Mary—Lu. 10:40.

Business help.—In building of the temples—I Chr. 22:17; Ezra 1:4; 5:2.

Help of idols.—Deut. 32:38; II Chr. 28: 23.

No help.—II Chr. 28:21; Job 6:13; Ps. 22:11; 107:12; Is. 63:5; Lam. 1:7.

For Israel.—II Ki. 14:26. For men— Job 30:13.

For women.—II Ki. 6:27.

Neighborly.—Deut. 22:4; Is. 41:6.

Of Christians.—Acts 18:27; I Cor. 16: 16; II Cor. 1:11, 24; Phil. 4:3. Heb. 4:16.

Asked of Jesus.—Mt. 15:25; Mk. 9:22, 24.

Help these women.—Phil. 4:3.

Prophecies concerning.—Is. 10:3; 20:6; 30:5; Ez. 12:14; 32:21; Dan. 11:34, 45; Hos. 13:9. Of Tyre and Sidon— Jer. 47:4. Of Egypt—Is. 31:3; Ez. 30: 8; Nah. 3:9. Future help from God— Is. 41:10, 13, 14; 44:2, 3; 50:7, 9. To Jews—Is. 94:8. Vain help—Is. 30:7; Lam. 4:17.

In Revelation—Earth to woman—Rev. 12:16.

Help, the name of a vaguely defined office or function in the early church. —I Cor. 12:28.

Figurative.—''Rideth upon heavens for thy help''—Deut. 33:26. Helps in undergirding the ship—Acts 27:17. Help in the gate—Job 31:21.

Jesus helps the tempted.—Heb. 2:18. See AID.

HELVE. Deut. 19:5. See AXE.

HEM. See BORDER.

HEMAN, hē'man. (1) **A grandson of Samuel who sang in the temple.**—I Chr. 6:33; 15:17, 19; 16:41; 25:1-6; II Chr. 5:12; 29:14; 35:15; Ps. 88 (*title*) (2) **A descendant of Jacob.**—I Ki. 4:31; I Chr. 2:6.

HEMDAN, hĕm'dan. **Son of Dishon.**— Gen. 36:26.

HEMLOCK. Hos. 10:4. See PLANTS AND TREES.

HIGH PLACES. Dead bodies of kings in.—Ez. 43:7.

Forbidden.—I Ki. 12:31, 32; 13:2; 14:23; Jer. 3:6-11.

The people sacrificed in high places.— I Ki. 3:2, 4; Ez. 6:3, 6; 16:16; 20: 29, 30.

Called lofty places.—Ex. 16:24, 31.

Called open places.—Neh. 4:13. See IDOLATRY.

HIGH PRIESTS. See PRIEST.

HIGHWAY. Mt. 22:10; Lu. 14:23. Cast up the—Is. 62:10. Egypt, Out of—Is. 19:23. Exalted—Is. 49:11. Fuller's field, Of—II Ki. 18:17; Is. 36:2. Gleaned in—Ju. 20:45. God, For—Is. 40:3. Heart, In the—Ps. 84:5. Lie waste—Is. 33:8. Parting of—Mt. 22: 9. Set thine heart toward—Jer. 31:21. Unoccupied—Ju. 5:6. Unto—Ju. 20:

32. Upright, Of the—Pr. 16:17. Went along the—I Sam. 6:12.

HILEN, hī'len. **City assigned to the Levites.**—I Chr. 6:58.

HILKIAH, hĭl-kī'ăh. (1) **Father of Eliakim.**—II Ki. 18:18, 26, 37; Is. 22: 20. Overseer of the house of Hezekiah —II Ki. 18:18, 37; Is. 36:3, 22. Prophecy concerning Eliakim—Is. 22:20.

(2) **High priest in the time of Josiah, king of Judah.**—II Ki. 22:4. Son of Shallum—I Chr. 6:13. Ruler of House of God—II Chr. 35:8. Assists Josiah in his reformations and in repairing the temple—II Ki. Chs. 22 and 23; II Chr. 34:9–12. Finds the Book of Law —II Chr. 6:13; 9:11; Ezra 7:1; Jer. 29:3.

(3) **A descendant of Merari, son of Levi.**—I Chr. 6:45.

(4) **Son of Hosah, a gate-keeper of the tabernacle in time of David.**—I Chr. 26:11.

(5) **Priest of Anathoth and father of Jeremiah.**—Jer. 1:1.

(6) **A priest.**—Neh. 8:4; 12:7, 21. Son of —Neh. 11:11.

HILL COUNTRY. See HILLS.

HILLEL, hĭl'lel. **A Pirathonite.**—Ju. 12: 13, 15.

HILLS. Number of.—Ps. 50:10.

Kinds of. — Everlasting — Gen. 49:26; Deut. 33:15; Hab. 3:6. High—I Ki. 14:23; II Ki. 17:10; Is. 30:25; Jer. 2: 20; 49:16; Ez. 6:13; 20:28. Little—Ps. 114:4, 6. Fruitful—Is. 5:1.

Hills mentioned.—Palestine, Land of —Deut. 11:11. Moreh—Ju. 7:1. Hill of God—I Sam. 10:5. Hills around Zion—Is. 31:4. Hachilah—I Sam. 23: 19; 26:1, 3. Of Ammah—II Sam. 2: 24. Samaria—I Ki. 16:24. Zion—Ps. 2:6; 3:4; Ps. 15:1 (fig.); Ps. 24:3; 43: 3; 99:9. Mizar—Ps. 42:6. Jerusalem —Is. 10:32. Gareb—Jer. 31:39.

From the hills.—Balaam beholds—Num. 23:9. Salvation is hoped for—Jer. 3:23.

Upon the hill.—Ex. 14:44; 17:9, 10; Ps. 50:10; Song of Sol. 2:8; Is. 2:14; Jer. 13:27. Stood—II Sam. 2:25. Offer sacrifice—Deut. 12:2; II Ki. 16:4; II Chr. 28:4; Jer. 17:2; Hos. 4:13. Israel scattered—I Ki. 22:17. Blasphemed— Is. 65:7.

God of.—I Ki. 20:23, 28.

Miscellaneous.—Born before—Job 15:7; Pr. 8:25. Fountains in—Deut. 8:7. House of Abinadab in—I Sam. 7:1. Elijah dwelt in—II Ki. 1:9; 4:27. Brass dug out of—Deut. 8:9. See Job 28:2.

Hill-side.—II Sam. 13:34. Brow of, Jesus brought to—Lu. 4:29.

Hill-country.—Josh. 9:1, 10; 16:40; 11: 2, 3, 16, 21; 12:8; 13:6; 15:48; 17:16, 18; 18:12; 20:7; Ju. 1:9, 19, 34; 3:27. Of Ephraim—Josh. 24:30, 33; Ju. 2:9. Of Amorites—Deut. 1:7. Beyond the Jordan—Josh. 9:1. Of Judah—Josh. 21:11; II Chr. 27:4. Of Judæa—Lu. 1: 65. Mary went into the hill-country— Lu. 1:39. Hill-country smitten—Josh. 10:40; 11:16.

In prophecy. — Jerusalem — Is. 7:25. Every hill shall be made low—Is. 40: 4, 12. Shall make the hills as chaff— Is. 41:15. Shall lay waste the—Is. 42: 15. May be removed—Is. 54:10. Shall break forth before you into singing (fig.)—Is. 55:12. Hills move (fig.)— Jer. 4:24. To be destroyed—Ez. 6:3; 35:8; Hos. 10:8; Zeph. 1:10. Shall flow with milk (fig.) — Joel 3:18. All the hills shall melt—Amos 9:13; Nah. 1:5. Ensign on—Is. 30:17. Are lifted up—Is. 2:14. Blessed by Jehovah—Ez. 36:4, 6. That shall be digged —Is. 7:25. The slain shall fall in— Ez. 35:8. Sheep have gone from mountains to hills (fig.)—Jer. 50:6; Ez. 34: 6. Exalted above—Is. 2:2; Mic. 4:1. Then shall they say to the hills, cover us—Lu. 23:30.

Figurative.—Ps. 65:12; 72:3; 98:8; 114: 4, 6; 148:9. Hill of frankincense— Song of Sol. 4:6. Hills in balance— Is. 40:12. Address to the—Mic. 6:1.

In teaching of Jesus.—A city set on a hill cannot be hid—Mt. 5:14.

HINDER, v. Gal. 5:7. Coming, From— Num. 22:16; Rom. 15:22. Continuing, From—Heb. 7:23. John would have— Mt. 3:14. Me not—Gen. 24:56. Prayers be no—I Pet. 3:7. Satan—I Thess. 2:18. Truth, The—Rom. 1:18. What doth—Acts 8:36. Who can—Job 9:12; 11:10; Is. 43:13.

HINDER, adj. II Sam. 2:23; I Ki. 7:25; II Chr. 4:4.

HINDRANCE. I Cor. 9:12.

HINGE. Door turneth on—Pr. 26:14. Gold, Of—I Ki. 7:50. See TOOLS AND IMPLEMENTS.

HINNOM, hĭn′nom. Valley of—Josh. 15:8; 18:16; II Ki. 23:10; Jer. 7:31, 32; 19:2, 6.

Incidents connected with. — Incense burnt in the valley of—II Chr. 28:3. Fire in valley of—II Chr. 33:6. Encampment in—Neh. 11:30. High places of Baal built in valley of—Jer. 32:35. Burning of children—Jer. 7:31. See HELL.

HIP. See BODY.

HIPPOPOTAMUS. See ANIMALS.

HIRAH, hī′rah. **A friend of Judah.**—Gen. 38:1, 12.

HIRAM, hī′ram (Huram). (1) King of Tyre—II Sam. 5:11; I Ki. 5:1; 9:11, 12; I Chr. 14:1; II Chr. 2:3, 11, 12, 13. Gave cities to Solomon—II Chr. 8:2, 18. Servants of—II Chr. 9:10, 21. Helped build Solomon's temple—I Ki. Ch. 5; 9:14, 27; 10:11, 22. Descendants of—I Chr. 8:5.

(2) A skilful worker in brass—I Ki. 7: 13, 40, 45; II Chr. 4:11, 16.

HIRE. Among nations—Hos. 8:10. Baalam—Deut. 23:4; Neh. 13:2. Bread, For—I Sam. 2:5. Burned, Shall be—Mic. 1:7. Chariots—I Chr. 19:6, 7. Counsellors—Ezra 4:5. Dwelling—Acts 28:30. Give—Gen. 30:18; Jer. 22:13; Ez. 16:34. God hath given—Gen. 30:18. Goldsmith—Is. 46:6. Hireling, Of—Deut. 15:18. Holiness to Jehovah shall be—Is. 23:18. Laborers—Mt. 20:1; Jas. 5:4. Lovers—Hos. 8:9. Man, For—Zech. 8:10. Masons and carpenters—II Chr. 24:12. Mighty men of valor—II Chr. 25:6. No man hath—Mt. 20:7. Pay—Mt. 20:8. Scornest—Ez. 16:31. Servants—I Ki. 5:6; Mk. 1:20; Lu. 15:17, 19. Thing—Ex. 22:15. Syrians—II Sam. 10:6. Upon grain floor—Hos. 9:1. Vain and light fellows—Ju. 9:4. Weighed for my—Zech. 11:12. Work for—Is. 19: 10. Worthy of—Lu. 10:7; I Tim. 5:18. Wrong-doing, Of—II Pet. 2:13, 15. See SERVANT, WAGES.

HIRELING. Job—14:6. Days of—Job 7:1. Fleeth—John 10:12, 13. Oppress —Mal. 3:5. Wages, Look for—Job

7:2. Years of—Is. 16:14; 21:16. See SERVANT, TEACHING OF JESUS.

HISS. Hissing at nations accompanies their downfall.—Jer. 18:16. Israel—I Ki. 9:8. Edom—Jer. 49:17. Judah —II Chr. 27:8; Jer. 25:9, 18; Lam. 2:15, 16; Jerusalem—Jer. 19:8. Babylon—Jer. 50:13; 51:37. Nineveh—Zeph. 2:15.

Hissing as a mockery to wicked men.—Job 27:23. King of Tyre—Ez. 27:36. People of Judah—Jer. 29:18; Mic. 6:16.

Jehovah's hiss, to assemble the people.—Is. 5:26; 7:18; Zech. 10:8.

HISTORY. I Chr. 29:29; II Chr. 33:19.

HITTITES, hĭt′tites. Descendants of Heth, 2d son of Canaan—Gen. 10:15; 23:10.

First important mention of them has to do with the sale of the burying ground to Abraham.—Gen. 23:3–18; 25:9–10.

They were immigrants, their original seat being in Cappadocia and the mountain region of the Taurus (Sayce).

In their earliest settlement not noted.—Gen. 12:6; 13:7.

Grew so strong as to give name to Palestine for the Assyrians (Sayce).

Settled in and about Hebron and Jebus (Jerusalem).—Gen. 23:19; Num. 13: 29; Josh. 12:8; Ez. 16:3, 45.

Were generous and commercial in their dealings.—Gen. 23:15–20. Solomon bought of them horses and chariots—I Ki. 10:29; II Chr. 1:17. A man builds a city—Ju. 1:26.

Were warriors.—Join with others to resist Israel—Josh. 9:1–2; 11:3–5; 24: 11. The Syrians feared them—II Ki. 7:6–7. Although subdued by Joshua (Josh. 11 and 12) and by Solomon (I Ki. 9:20–21) they were not destroyed. Permitted kings—I Ki. 10: 29; II Ki. 7:6; II Chr. 1:17.

Jehovah makes a covenant with Abraham to give his posterity their land.—Gen. 15:18–21; Neh. 9:7–8. Also to Moses—Ex. 3:8, 17; 13:5; Josh. 1:4.

To be driven out of their land.—Ex. 23: 23; Deut. 7:1; 20:17; Josh. 3:10.

Reason for driving Hittites out.—Wickedness—Deut. 9:5. To prevent inter marriage and idolatry—Deut. 7:1-5; 20:17-18; Josh. 23:4-13.

Must not be driven out at once.—Danger of wild beasts—Deut. 7:22. Needed as servants to aid in Jehovah's work—I Ki. 9:15-21; I Chr. 8:7-8.

Children of Israel dwell among them.—Ju. 3:5. Rebekah troubled because of daughters of Heth—Gen. 27:46. Isaac troubled also—Gen. 28:8. Solomon marries Hittite women—I Ki. 11:1-3.

Two Hittites attached to service of David.—Uriah (one of 37 of David's body-guard)—II Sam. 11:6-7; 23:39; I Chr. 11:41. Ahimelech—I Sam. 26:6.

Names of Hittites in Bible: Adah—Gen. 36:2. Ahimelech—I Sam. 26:6. Basemath—Gen. 26:34. Beeri—Gen. 26:34. Elon—Gen. 26:34. Ephron—Gen. 23:10-14; Judith—Gen. 26:34. Uriah—II Sam. 11:3; 23:39. Zohar—Gen. 23:8.

HIVITES, hiv'ites. **Tribe of Canaan.**—Gen. 10:17; 34:2; 36:2; Ex. 3:8; 13:58; 23:23, 28; 33:2; 34:11; Deut. 7:1; 20:17; Josh. 3:10; 9:1, 7; 11:3, 19; 12:8; 24:11; Ju. 3:3, 5; II Sam. 24:7; I Ki. 9:20; I Chr. 1:15; II Chr. 8:7.

HIZKIAH, hiz'ki-ah. **Ancestor of Zephaniah.**—Zeph. 1:1.

HOARY-HEADED. See HEAD.

HOBAB, ho'bab. **Kinsman of Moses.**—Num. 10:29; Ju. 4:11.

HOBAH, ho'bah. **A place north of Damascus.**—Gen. 14:15.

HOBAIAH, ho-ba'iah. **Ancestor of some who returned with Zerubbabel.**—Ezra 2:61; Neh. 7:63.

HOCK. Horse, Of—Josh. 11:6; II Sam. 8:4. Ox, Of—Gen. 49:6.

HOD, hod. **A descendant of Asher.**—I Chr. 7:37.

HODAVIAH, hod'a-vi'ah. (1) **A Levite.**—Ezra 2:40.
(2) **A chief of the tribe of Manasseh.**—I Chr. 5:24.
(3) **A Benjamite.**—I Chr. 9:7.

HODESH, ho'desh. **Wife of Shaharaim.**—I Chr. 8:9.

HODEVAH, ho-de'vah. **A Levite who returned with Zerubbabel.**—Neh. 7:43.

HODIAH, ho-di'ah. (1) **A chief under Nehemiah.**—Neh. 10:18.

(2) **A Levite.**—Neh. 8:7; 9:5; 10:10, 13.
(3) **Wife of Ezra.**—I Chr. 4:19.

HOE. Is. 5:6. See TOOLS AND IMPLEMENTS.

HOG. See SWINE.

HOGLAH, hog'lah. **Daughter of Zelophehad.**—Num. 26:33; 27:1; 36:11; Josh. 17:3.

HOHAM, ho'ham. **An Amorite king**—Josh. 10:3.

HOIST. Acts 27:40.

HOLD. Ps. 32:9; 71:6; Mt. 14:31. Confession, Fast—Heb. 10:23. Covenant—Is. 56:6. Fast—Job 2:3; 16:8; Jer. 50:33; Lu. 8:15. Feet, Of—Mt. 28:9. Guiltless—Ex. 20:7; Deut. 5:11. Hand—Gen. 21:18; Ps. 139:10; Is. 41:13. Lay—Ex. 4:4; Mt. 18:28; 21:46; Phil. 3:12. Life dear—Acts 20:24. Paul and Silas—Acts 16:19. Peace—Gen. 24:21; Num. 30:4, 7; II Ki. 7:9; Job 33:33; Lu. 8:15. Possession, For a—Lev. 25:46. Shields—Jer. 51:11. Stars—Rev. 2:1. That which is good, Fast—I Thess. 5:21. Tradition, Fast—Mk. 7:8; I Cor. 11:22. Unclean spirit, Of—Rev. 18:2. Water, No—Jer. 2:13.

HOLE. Asp, Of—Is. 11:8. Bag with—Hag. 1:6. Door, Of—Song of Sol. 5:4. Earth, Of—Heb. 11:38; Is. 2:19. Foxes have—Mt. 8:20; Lu. 9:58. Head, For the—Ex. 28:32. Lid, In—II Ki. 12:9. Out of—I Sam. 14:11. Pit, Of—Is. 51:1. Robe, Of—Ex. 39:23. Snared in—Is. 42:22. Wall, In—Ez. 8:7.

HOLINESS. From Heb. *Ka-dash*. "To be clean ceremonially or morally." Gr. *Hosiotes*. "Piety." "Holiness."
God's holy memorial name.—Ps. 30:4; 97:12.
Habitation of holiness.—Ps. 93:5; Is. 63:15; Jer. 31:23; Ob. 17; I Pet. 2:5. The way to—Is. 35:8.
Worship in the beauty of holiness.—I Chr. 16:29; II Chr. 20:21; Ps. 29:2; 96:9; 110:3.
Holiness of speech.—Ps. 108:7; Jer. 23:9; Amos 4:2; II Pet. 1:21; 3:2.
Sanctified in holiness.—II Chr. 31:18; Eph. 4:24; II Thess. 3:13; 4:7.
Holiness of service.—Lu. 1:75; Rom. 6:19; II Cor. 7:1; I Thess. 2:10; I Pet. 1:15, 16; Rev. 20:6. Partakers of—

Heb. 12:10. Profanation of—Mal. 2:11.

Spirit of holiness.—Rom. 1:4; II Pet. 3:11.

Holiness of Jesus.—Heb. 7:26.

Persons or things dedicated to.—Is. 23:18; Jer. 2:3; Zech. 14:20, 21. See CEREMONIAL CLEANSING, CONSECRATION, GOD, PURIFICATION, SANCTIFICATION.

HOLLOW. Jer. 52:21. Hand, Of—Is. 40:12. Place—Ju. 15:19. Planks, With—Ex. 27:8; 38:7. Streaks—Lev. 14:37. Thigh, Of—Gen. 32:25, 32.

HOLON, hō′lon. (1) **A Moabite town east of the Jordan.**—Jer. 48:21.
(2) **A city assigned to the Levites.**—Josh. 15:51; 21:15.

HOLY. See HOLY SPIRIT, HOLINESS, SANCTIFICATION, GOD, GROUND.

HOLY SPIRIT. The Spirit of God in the Old Testament: *Ruach*—Ps. 51:11, 12; 139:7; 143:10; Is. 40:7-13; 59:19, 21; Ez. 36:27; 37:14; Mic. 2:7; Hag. 2:5; Zech. 4:6; 7:12.

Directs the movements of the prophets.—I Ki. 16:12; II Ki. 2:16; Is. 48:16; 63:11-14; Ez. 3:12, 14, 24; 8:3; 11:1; 37:1; 43:5.

The Spirit creative.—Gen. 1:2; 2:7; Job 26:13; 33:4; Ps. 104:30.

Personality of the Holy Spirit.—John 14:17, 26; 15:26; 16:7-13; Rom. 8:26; I Cor. 2:10; 12:11.

By whom sent.—John 14:16, 26; 15:26; 16:7; Acts 2:33.

Will not come to dwell in the world until after the death of Jesus.—John 7:38, 39; 15:26; 16:7; Acts 1:4, 8; 2:33.

To whom promised.—Joel 2:28-32; Lu. 11:13. The apostles—John 14:17; 15:26; Acts 1:4, 8; 2:4, 33. Disciples—John 14:17; Acts 2:38; Rom. 8:4-17; I Cor. 3:16, 17; II Cor. 3:3; I Thess. 4:7, 8; I John 3:23, 24; 4:13. Sons of God—Lu. 11:13; Rom. 8:14-17; Gal. 4:6, 29. Believers—

John 7:39; Acts 10:44; 15:7-9; Eph. 1:13; Heb. 6:4. Those that obey—Acts 5:32.

Baptism in the Holy Spirit.—Is. 32:15; 44:3; Joel 2:28-32; Ez. 39:29; Mt. 3:11; Mk. 1:8; Lu. 3:16; John 1:33; Acts 1:5, 8; 2:4, 33; 4:8, 31; 10:45; 11:15; I Cor. 12:13.

Filled with the Holy Spirit.—Lu. 1:15; Acts 2:4; 4:8, 31; 6:3, 5; 7:55; 11:24; 13:9, 52; Eph. 5:18.

The Holy Spirit poured upon.—Is. 32:15; 44:3; Ez. 39:29; Joel 2:28, 29; Zech. 12:10; Acts 2:17, 33; 10:45; 11:15, 16.

The Holy Spirit conferred by the laying on of the apostles' hands.—Acts 6:6; 8:14-21; 19:6; I Tim. 4:14.

Gifts of the Spirit.—Acts 2:38; 10:46; 19:6; Rom. 12:6-8; I Cor. 2:4-6; 12:4-11; Eph. 4:7, 8; II Tim. 1:6; Heb. 2:4.

Conception of Jesus by the Holy Spirit.—Mt. 1:18-20; Lu. 1:35.

Jesus anointed and led by the Holy Spirit.—Is. 11:2; 42:1; 61:1; Mt. 3:16; 4:1; 12:28; Mk. 1:10, 12; Lu. 3:22; 4:1, 14, 18; John 1:32, 33; 3:34; Acts 1:2; 4:27; 5:32; 10:38; Heb. 1:9; 9:14.

How was the Holy Spirit given?—Without mediation—See "Baptism of the Holy Spirit" and "The Holy Spirit poured out." With mediation—Through laying on of hands of the apostles—Acts 8:17-19; 19:6. Given in answer to prayer—Lu. 11:13; Acts 8:15. Received by the hearing of faith—Gal. 3:2, 3, 14. Given to those who obey gospel commands—Acts 2:38; Eph. 1:13.

Christians are temples of the Holy Spirit.—John 14:17; Rom. 8:9-17; I Cor. 3:16, 17; 6:19; Eph. 2:21, 22; 3:16, 17; II Tim. 1:14.

Communion of the Holy Spirit.—II Cor. 3:6-18; 11:4; 12:18; 13:14; Phil. 2:1; Col. 1:8.

Inspires.—Num. 12:6, 8; II Ki. 17:13; Neh. 9:20-30; Is. 59:21; Zech. 7:12

Mt. 10:20; Mk. 13:11; Lu. 1:70; 12: 11, 12; Acts 3:18; 4:8; 11:28; 20: 23; 21:10, 11; Rom. 1:1, 2; 3:21; 16:26; I Cor. 2:4, 9–14; 7:40; 12:3; Eph. 3:5, 6; II Tim. 3:16; Heb. 1:1; 3:7, 8; 9:8; 10:15, 16; I Pet. 1:10–12; II Pet. 1:21; Rev. 2:7; 22:6.

Instances of inspiration: Noah—I Pet. 3:18–20. Joseph—Gen. 41:38. Bezalel —Ex. 31:3; 35:31. Seventy elders— Num. 11:16, 17, 25, 26–29. Joshua —Num. 27:18; Deut. 34:9. Balaam —Num. 24:2. The Judges: *Gideon*— Ju. 6:34. *Othniel*—Ju. 3:10. *Jephthah*—Num. 11:29. *Samson*—Ju. 13: 25; 14:6, 19; 15:14; 16:28. Saul— I Sam. 10:6, 13; 11:6; 16:13, 14; 19: 23, 24. Messengers of Saul—I Sam. 19:20, 21. David—II Sam. 23:2; I Chr. 28:11, 12; Mk. 12:36; Acts 1: 16. Amasai—I Chr. 12:18. Azariah—II Chr. 15:1; Ez. 2:1–4; 11: 5, 24. Elijah—II Ki. 1:9–15; 2:15. See Lu. 1:15–17. Elisha—II Ki. 1: 9–15; 2:15–22. Micaiah—I Ki. 22: 14, 23, 28; II Chr. 18:23, 27. Jahaziel—II Chr. 20:14. Zechariah— II Chr. 24:20. Micah—Mic. 3:8. Isaiah—Is. 59:21; Acts 28:25. Ezekiel—Ez. 2:2. Elizabeth—Lu. 1:41. John the Baptist—Lu. 1:15; Zacharias—Lu. 1:67. Simeon—Lu. 2:25– 27. Apostles—Mt. 10:20; Mk. 13: 11. John 20:22; Acts 2:4; 4:8; 9: 17; Rev. 1:10, 11. Agabus—Acts 11:28; 21:10, 11. Stephen — Acts 7:55. Disciples at Tyre—Acts 21:4. See PROPHETS, INSPIRATION OF.

Reveals.—Mk 12:36; Lu. 2:26; I Cor. 2:10, 11; Eph. 3:5; I Tim. 4:1; I Pet. 1:12; Rev. 2:7, 11, 29; 14:13.

Teaches or guides into all truth.— Neh. 9:20; Is. 40:13, 14; Mk. 12: 36; 13:11; Lu. 2:26, 27; 12:12; 24: 49; John 12:16; 14:26; 16:13, 14; Acts 13:2–4; 15:28; 16:6–10; Rom. 8:26; I Cor. 2:13; 12:8; Eph. 1: 16, 17; I John 2:20, 27.

Confirms the word.—Lu. 24:49; Acts 1:4, 8; 2:38; 19:11, 12; Rom. 15: 18, 19; I Cor. 2:4; II Cor. 6:6; 12: 12; I Thess. 1:5; Heb. 2:2. See "Gifts of the Spirit."

Comforts the Christian.—John 14:16, 17, 26; 15:26; 16:7, 8; Acts 9:31; Rom. 5:5; 8:26; 14.17.

Begotten or "born of" the Spirit.— Lu. 8:11; John 1:12, 13; 3:3–8; 6: 63; I Cor. 4:15; Gal. 4:19; Philemon 10; Jas. 1:18; I Pet. 1:23. See NEW BIRTH.

Convinces the world of sin.—Gen. 3:6; John 6:44, 45; 16:7–9; Acts 7:51, 52; Gal. 5:16–23; Eph. 6:17.

Commissions.—Acts 13:2–4; 20:28.

Baptism in the name of the Father, Son, and Holy Spirit.—Mt. 28:19.

Invites to salvation.—Rev. 22:17.

Makes intercession.—Rom. 8:26; Eph. 2:18; 6:18; Jude 20.

Sanctifies.—Rom. 15:16; I Cor. 6:11; II Thess. 2:13; I Pet. 1:2.

Bears witness.—John 15:26; 16:14; Acts 5:32; Rom. 8:15, 16; 9:1; I Cor. 12:3; II Cor. 6:6; Gal. 4:6; Heb. 10:15; I John 3:24; 4:13; 5: 6–8.

Earnest of the Spirit.—Rom. 8:23; II Cor. 1:22; 5:5; Eph. 1:14; 4:30; Rev. 2:7.

Sealed by the Spirit.—II Cor. 1:22; Eph. 1:13; 4:30.

Sin against the Holy Spirit.—Acts 8: 18–23; I John 5:16. Blasphemy— Mt. 12:31, 32; Mk. 3:29; Lu. 12:10. Resisting—Is. 63:10; Acts 5:1–3, 9; 7:51, 52. Grieving—Is. 63:10; Eph. 4:30; Heb. 10:29. Quenching—I Thess. 5:19.

Unity of the Spirit.—I Cor. 12:13; Eph. 4:3–6. See "Communion of the Spirit."

Fruits of the Spirit.—John 15:2; Rom. 8:23; Gal. 5:22, 23.

Walking in.—Rom. 8:4; II Cor. 12:18; Gal. 5:16.

The word the sword of the spirit.— Eph. 6:17.

HOMAM, hō'mam. I Chr. 1:39.

HOME. At home.—I Ki. 5:14; Lam. 1:20.

Going, coming, bringing home.—Gen. 39:16; 43:26; Ex. 9:19; Ju. 11:9; 19: 9; Ruth 1:21; I Sam. 18:2; 24:22; I Ki. 13:15; I Chr. 13:12; Jer. 39:14; John 19:27; 20:10.

Government of.—Gen. 3:16. Controlling children—Gen. 18:19; I Tim. 3:4. Giving honor to husbands—Esth. 1:20–22; I Pet. 3:1–6.

References.—Protected from invasion by creditors—Deut. 24:10–11. Preparing for a home—Deut. 21:10–14. Infelicity at—Pr. 14:1; 15:17. Blessing bestowed upon—I Sam. 2:20. Purifying home by sacrifices—Job 1:5. Good conduct at—Ps. 101:2. Jealousy among children caused by favoritism —Gen. 27;5–46. Must provide for—I Tim. 5:8. Jesus' compassion on those He dismisses—Mk. 8:3, 26. Home rejoicing for sheep finding—Lu. 15:6. John takes Jesus' mother to—John 19:27. Broke bread at home—Acts 2: 46. Taught at—Acts 5:42. Hungry disciples must not devour the Lord's Supper—I Cor. 11:34. At home in body, with the Lord—II Cor. 5:6. Workers at home—Tit. 2:5.

Unhappiness caused by plurality of women.—Gen. 16:5; 21:10–11; 29:30–34. By contemptuous conduct—II Sam. 6:16, 20–23. By riotous life—Esth. 1:10–22.

Home, as future abode.—Eccl. 12:5; II Cor. 5:8. See Job 17:13; 30:23. See FAMILY, HOUSE, HEAVEN.

HOMER. Bath, tenth part of—Ez. 45: 11, 14. Barley, Of—Hos. 3:2. See, Of —Lev. 27:16; Is. 5:10. Ten—Num. 11:32. Wheat, Of—Ez. 45:13.

HONEY. See FOOD.

HONOR. Belongs to God.—I Chr. 16: 27; 29:12; Ps. 71:8; 96:6; 104:1; 145: 5; Is. 43:20; 58:13; Dan. 4:37; Mal. 1:6; John 8:49; I Tim. 1:17; Rev. 4: 9–11; 7:11, 12.

Honoring.—The son—Mt. 3:16, 17; Mk. 1:9;11; Lu. 3:21, 22; John 1:32–34; 5:23; Heb. 2:9; 3:3; 5:4, 5; II Pet. 1: 17; Rev. 5:12, 13. Father and mother —Deut. 5:16; Ex. 20:12; Lev. 19:3;

Mt. 15:4–6; 19:19; Eph. 6:2. Husbands—Esth. 1:20; Eph. 5:22, 23. Wives—Eph. 5:25, 28; Col. 3:18; I Pet. 3:7. Widows—I Tim. 5:3. All men—I Pet. 2:17. Elders—I Tim. 5: 17. Masters—I Tim. 6:1. Holy City—Rev. 21:26.

Held in.—David—II Sam. 6:22; Ps. 21: 5. Hezekiah—II Chr. 32:33. Uncomely parts of body—I Cor. 12:23, 24. Honor begets—I Sam. 2:30; 15:30; Rom. 13:7.

Promotion to.—Balaam—Num. 22:17, 37; 24:11. Joshua—Num. 27:20. Israel—Deut. 26:19. Mordecai—Esth. 6:3–10. Man—Ps. 8:5. God's gift to Solomon—I Ki. 3:13; 10:23–25. No power to enjoy it—Eccl. 6:2.

Righteous are honored.—Ps. 91:15; 112: 9; 149:9; Pr. 21:21; Rom. 2:7–10; I Pet. 1:7. Apostles—Mt. 19:27, 28.

Honoring false objects.—Dan. 11:38. Fleeting—Ps. 49:12, 20; Is. 29:13. False judgments wanting in—Lev. 19: 15. Neglect of—Mt. 13:57; Mk. 6:4; John 4:44. Folly outweighs—Pr. 26: 8; Eccl. 10:1.

Positions of.—Joseph—Gen. 41:41–43. Olive-tree—Ju. 9:8, 9. Abishai—I Chr. 11:20, 21. Mordecai—Esth. 8:15. Apostles—Mt. 19:27, 38; Mk. 10: 37–40.

Seeking. — Haman — Esth. 5:11, 12. Korah, etc.—Num. 16-8-10. Mother of Zebedee's sons—Mt. 20:20, 21.

Vessels of.—Rom. 9:21; I Thess. 4:4; II Tim. 2:20, 21.

Wisdom possesses.—Pr. 3:16; 8:18. The gift of wisdom—Pr. 4:8.

Humility precedes.—Pr. 15:33; 18:12; 22:4; Mt. 18:2–4; III John 9, 10.

Acts of.—Avoiding strife—Pr. 20:3. Giving preference—Rom. 12:10. Devotion of wealth to Jehovah—Pr. 3:9.

HOOF. Ex. 10:26; Ps. 69:31; Ez. 32: 13; Mic. 4:13; Zech. 11:1 Divided —Lev. 11:3–7, 26; Deut. 14:6–8. Horses—Is. 5:28; Jer. 47:3; Ez. 26:11. See FOOT.

HOOK. Ex. 26:32; II Ki. 19:28; Job 41:2; Is. 37:29; Ez. 19:4; 29:4; 38:4; 40:43; Amos 4:2; Mt. 17:27.

HOPE: What is it? A union of desire and expectation.—Rom. 8:25.

A reasonable act.—I Pet. 3:15.

One of the three graces.—I Cor. 13:13.

A triumphant fact.—Rom. 8:38, 39.

Its basis.—Job 4:6; I Pet 1:3; Acts 26: 6–8.

Objects of.—Ps 39:7; 130:6; 131:3; Jer. 17:7, 13; Lam. 3:24; Joel 3:16; Rom. 15:13; I Pet. 1:21. The Christ—I Cor. 15:19; I Tim. 1:1 The promises—Acts 26:6, 7; Tit. 1:2. The word—Ps. 119: 81; 130:5. Righteousness—Gal. 5:5. Gladness—Pr. 10:28.

HOPHNI, hŏph'ni. Son of Eli.—I Sam. 1:3; 2:34; 4:4, 11, 17.

HOR, hôr. (1) The mountain on which Aaron died.—Num. 20:22–27; 21:4; Deut. 32:50.

(2) A hill in northern Israel.—Num. 34:7, 8.

HORAM, hō'ram. A king of Gezer.— Josh. 10:33.

HORDES. Ez. 39:4.

HOREB, hō'reb. A range of mountains. —Ex. 3:1, 17:6; 33:6; Deut. 1:2, 6, 19; 4:10, 15; 5:2; 9:8; 18:16; 29:1; I Ki. 8:9; 19:8; II Chr. 5:10; Ps. 106:19; Mal. 4:4. See SINAI.

HOREM, hō'rem. A place in Naphtali. Josh. 19:38.

HOR-HAGGIDGAD, hôr'–hag-gĭd'gad. An encampment of the Israelites.— Num. 38:32.

HORI, hō'ri. (1) Son of Lotan, grandson of Seir.—Gen. 36:22, 30. (2) A Simeonite.—Num. 13:5.

HORIM, HORITES, Inhabitants of Mt. Seir.—Gen. 14:6; 36:20; 21, 29; Deut. 2:12, 22.

HORMAH, hôr-mah. A town once belonging to the Canaanites, but afterwards to the tribe of Simeon.—Num. 14:45; 21:3; Deut. 1:44; Josh. 12:14;

15:30; 19:4; Ju. 1:11; I Sam. 30:30; I Chr. 4:3.

HORN: Of animals mentioned.—Bullock —Ps. 69:31. Goat—Dan. 8:5. Ram— Gen. 22:43. Wild ox—Deut. 33:17; Ps. 22:21.

Kinds of.—Ivory and ebony—Ez. 27:15. Iron—I Ki. 22:11; II Chr. 18:10.

Uses of.—As bottles—I Sam. 16:I; I Ki. 1:39.

Musical instruments.—Josh. 6:4, 6, 13.

On altar.—Ex. 27:2; 29:12; 30:2, 3, 10; 37:25, 26; 38:2; Lev. 4:7, 18, 25, 30, 34; 8:15; 9:9; 16:18; I Ki. 1:50, 51; 2:28.

Symbolical.—Of God—Ps. 18:2; Hab. 3:4. Power of Christ—Lu. 1:69; Rev. 5:6. Power of Ephraim—Deut. 33:17. Power of wicked—Ps. 22:21; 75:10; Amos 6:13; Rev. 13:1; 17:3, 7. Of righteous—Ps. 75:10. Of God's power —Rev. 5:6; 9:13; 12:3. Of arrogance —Ps. 75:4, 5. Of power—I Sam. 2:1, 10; Ps. 89:17, 24; 92:10; 112:9. When broken or lowered: Of degredation— Job 16:15; Ps. 75:10; Jer. 48:25; Lam. 2:3. Horn on altar—Ps. 118:27; Gen. 17:1; Amos 3:14. In vision of Daniel —Dan. 7:7, 8, 20, 24; 8:3; 6–7, 20. Seen by Zechariah—Zech. 1:18, 19, 21.

HORNET. See INSECTS.

HORONAIM, hŏr-o-nā'im. A Moabite town.—Is. 15:5; Jer. 48:3, 5, 34.

HORONITE, hŏr'o-nite. Inhabitant of Beth-horon.—Neh. 2:10, 19; 13:28.

HORRIBLE. Afraid—Jer. 2:12; Ez. 32: 10; 27:35. Pit—Ps. 40:2. Thing—Jer. 18:13; 23:14; Hos. 6:10.

HORROR. Gen. 15:12; Job. 21:6; Ps. 55:5; 119:53; Is. 21:4; Ez. 7:18. See TERROR.

HORSE. Deut. 20:1; I Ki. 20:25; 22:4; Job 39:19; Ez. 23:6. Absalom prepared—II Sam. 15:1. Barley and straw for—I Ki. 4:28. Be not as the—Ps. 32:9. Bells of—Zech. 14:20. Black— Zech. 6:2, 6; Rev. 6:5. Bridles—Jas. 3:3; Rev. 14:20. Brought out of Egypt —I Ki. 10:28. Eat flesh of—Rev. 19: 18. Escaped on—I Ki. 20:20. Exchange for the—Gen. 47:17. Fire, Of—

II Ki. 2:11. Gate—Neh. 3:28. Goodly —Zech. 10:3. Heels, Biteth—Gen. 49: 17. Hock—Josh. 11:6, 9. Left—II Ki. 7:7. Many—Josh. 11:4. Mountains full of—II Ki. 6:17. Multiply—Deut. 17:16. Neigh as—Jer. 50:11. Noise— of—II Ki. 7:6. Pale—Rev. 6:8. People, Of—Zech. 14:12. Prepared, Is— Pr. 21:31. Red—Zech. 1:8. Rider, And —Ex. 15:1, 21; Hag. 2:22. Rusheth headlong in battle—Jer. 8:6. Save— I Ki. 18:5. Scatter it—Is. 28:28. Smote—I Ki. 20:21. Stalls of—I Ki. 4:26. Strength of—Ps. 147:10. Swifter than eagles—Jer. 4:13. Swifter than leopards—Hab. 1:6. Vain thing, Is— Ps. 33:17. Whip for the—Pr. 26:3. White—Zech. 6:3; Rev. 6:2; 19:11, 14.

HOSEN. Dan. 3:27.

HOSHAIAH, ho-shā'iah. (1) Neh. 12:32. (2) **Father of Jezaniah, a famous man in time of Nebuchadrezzar.**—Jer. 42: 1; 43:2.

HOSHAMA, hŏsh'a-má. **Son of Jehoiachin.**—I Chr. 3:18.

HOSHEA, ho-shē'à. (1) **The original name of Joshua, the son of Nun.**— Deut. 32:44.
(2) **The ruler of the tribe of Ephraim in David's time.**—I Chr. 27:20.
(3) **The son of Elah.**—II Ki. 15:30; 17:1. King of Israel—II Ki. 17:1; 18:1. Character of—II Ki. 17:2. Strife with Assyria—II Ki. 17:4–6. Samaria taken—II Ki. 18:9, 10.
(4) **A Jew who sealed the covenant with Nehemiah.**—Neh. 10:23.

HOSPITALITY. Duties to strangers.— Heb. 13:2; III John 5–8. See Sojourners.

To the poor.—Is. 58:7.

Given to.—Rom. 12:13; I Tim. 3:2; 5: 10; Tit. 1:8. One to another—I Pet. 4:9.

Examples of.—Melchizedek—Gen. 14: 18. Abraham—Gen. 18:3–9. Lot— Gen. 19:1. Laban—Gen. 24:31. Jethro —Ex. 2:20. Manoah—Ju. 13:15. The old man of Gibeah—Ju. 19:16–21. Samuel—I Sam. 9:22. David—II Sam. 6:19. Widow of Zarephath—I Ki. 17: 10–16. The Shunammite woman—II Ki. 4:8. Elisha—II Ki. 6:22. Israelites—I Chr. 12:39. Nehemiah—Neh. 5:17. Mary and Martha and Lazarus

in Bethany—Lu. 10:38–42; John 12: 1–9. See Mt. 21:17; 26:6–13; Mk. 11: 11; 14:3–9. Zacchæus—Lu. 19:1–7. Goodman of the house entertains Jesus—Mt. 26:17–19; Mk. 14:12–16; Lu. 22:8–14. Mason—Acts 21:16. Melitans —Acts 28:2. Publius—Acts 28:7. Gaius—III John 5–8.

HOST. Ex. 6:26. All the—Gen. 2:1. Angels, Of—Heb. 12:22. Bands of— I Chr. 7:4. Bless Jehovah, All ye his —Ps. 103:21. Captain of—Gen. 26: 26. Great—Ps. 68:11. Heavenly—Lu. 2:13. Jehovah, Of—Ex. 12:41. Lord, Of—Gen. 32:2; Josh. 5:14. Overthrow —Pharaoh and—Ps. 136:15. War, For —I Chr. 7:11. With him—I Sam. 10: 26. See Soldiers, War.

HOSTAGES. II Ki. 14:14.

HOT. Anger—Ex. 11:8; 32:19, 22; Ju. 2:14; 3:8; 6:39; 10:7. Battle—II Sam. 11:15. Bread—Josh. 9:12; I Sam. 21:6. Coals—Pr. 6:28. Displeasure—Deut. 9:19; Ps. 6:1; 38:1. Furnace—Dan. 3:22. Heart—Deut. 19:6; Ps. 39:3. Iron—I Tim. 4:2. Neither cold nor— Rev. 3:15; 16:16. Oven, As—Hos. 7:7. Pursued—Gen. 31:36. Sun—Ex. 16: 21; I Sam. 11:9; Neh. 7:3. Thunderbolts—Ps. 78:48. Wind—Jer. 4:11. Wrath—Ex. 22:24; 32:10, 11; Jer. 31: 24. See Anger, Heat.

HOTHAM, hō'tham. (1) **Son of Heber.** —I Chr. 7:32.
(2) **An Aroerite.**—I Chr. 11:44.

HOTHIR, hō'thir. Son of Heman—I Chr. 25:4, 28.

HOUR. Ancients had no minutes, hence hour may mean ''a few minutes'' or ''immediately.'' (''The Hebrews had terms for the days in relation to one another 'the previous evening,' yesterday, to-morrow, the day before yesterday. But they did not divide the days into hours until late; in fact, the custom long persisted of counting by portions of the day. The term רגע (in derivation='moment,' movimentum) meant an 'instant,' or a longer, but still very brief, interval of time, the chief idea being suddenness or rapid passage. שָׁעָה 'hour' is Aramaic (Dan. 3:6) and is common in Syriac and in later Hebrew. Originally it denoted any small interval of time and was only gradually fixed to what we call an 'hour' (driver). The hours of the Mishna differed in duration, as they were reckoned as one-twelfth of the actual day. Earlier than the division of the day into hours was the division of the night into three watches, Lam. 2:19; Ju. 7:19; Ex. 14: 24; I Sam. 11:11. . . . The length of the hour varied, therefore, according to the length of the day. It was about 75 minutes long at midsummer, and hardly more than 45 at midwinter, while at the equinox it was exactly 60 minutes, like the hour in our modern custom. See Acts 19:34; 5:7; Lu. 22: 59; Mt. 20:12; 26:40; Mk. 14:37.''— Hastings' BIBLE DICTIONARY.)—Dan. 3:6, 15; 4:33; 5:5; Mt. 8:13; 9:22; 10: 19; 15:28; 17:18; 26:55; Mk. 13:11; Lu. 12:12; 20:19; 24:33; John 4:53; Acts 16:18, 33; 22:13.

Hour may mean ''opportunity'' or ''set time.''—Mt. 24:36, 44, 50; 25:13; 26: 45; Mk. 14:41; Lu. 7:21; 10:21; 12:39, 46; 22:14, 53; John 2:4; 4:21, 23; 5: 25, 28; 7:30; 8:20; 12:23; 13:1; 16:32; 17:1; 19:27; Acts 3:1; I Cor. 4:11; 15: 30; Rev. 3:3.

Duration of time. Half an hour.— Silence—Rev. 8:1. One hour: Surprise —Dan. 4:19. Watching—Mt. 26:40; Mk. 14:37; Lu. 22:59; Gal. 2:5. Two hours: Cried out—Acts 19:34. Three hours: Sapphira—Acts 5:7.

Jewish reckoning from 6 a.m.—Third hour (9 A.M.)—Mt. 20:3. Sixth and ninth (12 M., 3 P.M.)—Mt. 20:5. Eleventh (5 P.M.)—Mt. 20:6, 9, 12. Sixth to ninth (12 M. to 3 P.M.)—Mt. 27:45, 46. Third (9 A.M.)—Mk. 15:25. Sixth until ninth (12 M. till 3 P.M.)— Mk. 15:33, 34; Lu. 23:44. Third (9 A.M.)—Acts 2:15. Ninth (3 P.M.) —Acts 3:1; 10:3, 30. Sixth (12 M.)— Acts 10:9. Third of night (9 P.M.)— Acts 23:23.

Roman reckoning from midnight. — Tenth hour (10 A.M.)—John 1:39. Sixth (6 P.M.)—John 4:6. Seventh (7 P.M.)—John 4:52. Sixth (6 A.M.)— 19:14.

Figurative time or day.—I Cor. 8:7; Rev. 3:10; 11:13; 14:7. Allotted ex-

perience—Mk. 14:35; John 12:27; 16: 21. One hour—Rev. 9:15; 17:12.

HOUSE. None other than house of God —Gen. 28:17, 22. Must not covet neighbor's—Ex. 20:17.

Houses used for dwellings and for worship.—Gen. 43:16-17; Josh. 24:15; Neh. 13:11; Acts 12:12; Rom. 16:5; I Cor. 16:19; Col. 4:15.

House made of: Stone—Lev. 14:40-45; Amos 5:11. Clay—Job 4:19. Bricks— Ex. 1:11-14; Is. 9:10. Built on walls— Josh. 2:15; II Cor. 11:33.

Antiquity of.—Gen. 4:17; 12:1; 19:3.

Flat roofs used: For battlements—Deut. 22:8. For booths—II Sam. 16:22; Neh. 8:16; Pr. 21:9. For idolatrous altars—II Ki. 23:12; Jer. 19:13; Zeph. 1:5. For drying flax—Josh. 2:6. For exercise—II Sam. 11:2; Dan. 4:29. For devotion—Acts 10:9. For making proclamations—Lu. 12:3.

Construction of: Foundation—I Ki. 7:9; Ezra 6:3-4; Jer. 51:26. Porches—Ju. 3:23; I Ki. 7:6-7. Courts—Esth. 1:5. Summer houses—Ju. 3:20; Amos 3:15. Winter houses—Amos 3:15. Inner chamber—I Ki. 22:25. Chambers of— Gen. 43:30; II Sam. 18:33; I Ki. 17: 19; II Ki. 1:2; 4:10. Upper chamber —Acts 1:13; 9:37; 20:8. Pillars of— Ju. 16:29. Windows—Josh. 2:15; Ju. 5:28; Acts 20:9.

Figurative.—Of the body—Job 4:19; II Cor. 5:1. Of the grave—Job 30:23. Of the Church—Heb. 3:6; I Pet. 2:5. Of saints' inheritance—John Ch. 14; II Cor. 5:1. On sand—Mt. 7:26-27. On rock—Mt. 7:24-25; Lu. 6:48, 49. Of pilgrimage—Ps. 119:54. Of mourning and of feasting—Eccl. 7:2. My Father's—Lu. 2:49; John 14:1. Divided—Mt. 12:25. Is left unto you desolate—Mt. 23:38. See Jer. 22:5. See TABERNACLE, TEMPLE, HOME, HOUSEHOLD.

HOUSEHOLD. Abraham commands his —Gen. 18:19. Jacob—Gen. 31:37. *Commands his household to put away foreign gods*—Gen. 35:2. Jacob and household go to Egypt to avoid famine —Gen. 45:1-11. Are taken care of— Gen. 47:12. Companions on way to Egypt—Ex. 1:1, 4. Pharaoh's promise to Joseph's brethren—Gen. 45:18.

Judging between Jacob's and Laban's household stuff—Gen. 31:37. Job—Job 1:3. Isaac, Great household of—Gen. 26:14. David and household go to Jerusalem—II Sam. 15:16. Provisions for—II Sam. 16:2. Cross the Jordan —II Sam. 19:18, 41. Rahab and— Josh. 2:18. *Saved*—Josh. 6:25. Gideon fears his father's—Ju. 6:27. Of king—I Ki. 7:9, 11. Shunammite woman—II Ki. 8:1, 2. Tobiah—Neh. 13:8. Aristobulus—Rom. 16:11. Narcissus—Rom. 16:10. Chloe—I Chr. 1:11. Cæsar—Phil. 4:22. Worthless— I Sam. 25:17. Every man with his—I Sam. 27:3; II Sam. 2:3. Dathan and Abiram, Destruction of—Deut. 11:6.

Blessed by: Jehovah—Deut. 12:7; II Sam. 6:11. David—II Sam. 6:20. Promise to, by Jehovah—Deut. 14:26.

Chosen. — By Jehovah — Josh. 7:14. Achan's—Josh. 7:18.

Laws concerning.—Offerings—Ex. 12:4; Deut. 15:20. Annual atonement—Lev. 16:17. Food for—I Ki. 5:9, 11; Num. 18:3; Pr. 27:27; 31:15.

Warning to Micah's.—Ju. 18:25.

Baptism of.—Lydia and her—Ex. 16:15. Stephanus—I Chr. 1:16.

Figurative.—Pr. 31:21, 27. Of the faith —Gal. 6:10. Of Jehovah—Eph. 2:19.

Rule of.—I Tim. 5:14. Overseers—I Ki. 4:6; II Ki. 10:5. Of Solomon's—I Ki. 4:7. King's son—II Ki. 15:5. Eliakim—II Ki. 18:18; 19:2; Is. 36:3, 22; 37:2.

Servants of Cornelius's.—Acts 10:7.

Used figuratively in teachings of Jesus. —Wise servant—Mt. 24:45; Lu. 12: 42. See FAMILY, HOUSE.

HOUSETOP. Mt. 24:17; Mk. 13:15; Lu. 17:31. Alone upon—Ps. 101:7. Corner of—Pr. 21:9; 25:24. Gone up to— Is. 22:1. Grass on, As—II Ki. 19:26; Ps. 129:6; Is. 37:27. Pray, To—Acts 10:9. Moab, Of—Jer. 48:38. Proclaim upon—Mt. 10:27; Lu. 12:3. Went up to—Lu. 5:19. Worship upon —Zeph. 1:5.

HOWL. Weep and—Jas. 5:1. Wilderness—Deut. 32:10. See MOURNING, WAIL.

HOZAI, hō'zai. II Chr. 33:19.

HUKKOK, hŭk'kok. **A town in Naphtali.**—Josh. 19:24.

HUKOK, hū'kok. **A city in Asher.**—I Chr. 6:75.

HUL, hŭl. **Son of Aram, grandson of Shem.**—Gen. 10:23; I Chr. 1:17.

HULDAH, hŭl'dah. **A prophetess in the days of Josiah.**—II Ki. 22:14; II Chr. 34:22.

HUMAN AFFAIRS. God's providence in. See GOD, PROVIDENCE OF.

HUMAN AGENCY IN CONVERSION OR SALVATION. See SALVATION.

HUMANITY OF JESUS. See JESUS.

HUMILIATION. Ezra 9:5; Mic. 6:4; Acts 8:33; Phil. 3:2.

HUMILIATION OF JESUS. See JESUS.

HUMILITY—

HUMTAH, hŭm'tah. **A city in Judah.**— Josh. 15:54.

HUNDRED. Gen. 5:3. Fold—Mk. 4:8, 20; Lu. 8:8. Sheep—Mt. 18:12. Stripes —Pr. 17:10. Times—Eccl. 8:12.

HUNG. See HANG.

HUNGER. Physical, of Esau—Gen. 25: 30. Of David—I Sam. 21:3-6. Of Elijah—I Ki. 17:11-13. Of Jeremiah— Jer. 38:9. Of Peter—Acts 10:10. Of Paul—II Cor. 6:5. Of Jesus—Mt. 4: 2-3; 21:18; Mk. 11:12; Lu. 4:2-4; John 4:8. Of men—Pr. 16:26; 27:7; Mt. 12:1.

Wasted with.—Deut. 32:24; I Sam. 30: 11-12; Acts 27:33.

Drives to desperation.—Gen. 25:30-33; Ex. 16:3; I Sam. 14:31-32; II Ki. 6: 29; Lu. 15:16-18.

Hunger running riot.—Pr. 23:1-2; Num. 11:4-5, 19-20.

Necessary.—Mt. 14:14-21; 15:32-38; Mk. 6:31-44; Lu. 9:12-17.

As a punishment.—Deut. 28:48; Is. 8: 21; 9:20.

Divinely supplied.—Ex. 16:4-21; I Sam. 2:5; Neh. 9:15; Ps. 37:25; 104:15; Is. 55:10; Mt. 6:11; Lu. 11:3; 1:53; John 6:31-32.

Men to relieve one another.—II Sam. 17:28-29; Pr. 25:21; Is. 58:7; Jer. 37: 21; Ez. 18:7; Rom. 12:20.

Results in affliction of soul.—Lev. 16: 29-31; II Sam. 3:35; Is. 58:5; Acts 9:9.

Prevented by feeding on Christ.—Is. 55: 1-2; John 6:33-35, 48-58. On truth— Ex. 34:28; Deut. 8:3; Mt. 4:4; Lu. 4:4.

Hungering after righteousness.—Is. 55: 2; Mt. 5:6; Lu. 1:53; 6:21.

HUNTING. Nimrod—Gen. 10:8–12; Lev. 17:13. Of men by Evil—Ps. 140:11. By Jehovah—Job 10:16; Jer. 16:16. Soul hunting—Ez. 13:18. Israel in distress—Jer. 50:17. Saul hunting David—I Sam. 26:20. Hunting of animals—Job 38:39; Pr. 12:27. Ishmael—Gen. 21:20. Esau—Gen. 25: 27; 27:3–5, 30–33. Permitted by Moses —Lev. 17:13.

Symbolic passages.—Ps. 141:9, 10; Pr. 1:17; 6:5; Eccl. 9:12; Law 3:2; Amos 3:5.

HUPHAM, hū′pham. **Son of Benjamin.** —Num. 26:39.

HUPHAMITES. Descendants of Hupham.—Num. 26:39.

HUPPAH, hŭp′pah. **A priest in time of David.**—I Chr. 24:13.

HUPPIM, hŭp′pim. **A Benjamite.**—Gen. 46:21; I Chr. 7:12, 13.

HUR. (1) **A companion of Moses and Aaron.**—Ex. 17:10, 12; 24:14.

(2) **A king of Midian.**—Num. 31:8; Josh. 13:21.

(3) **Son of Caleb.**—Ex. 31:2; 35:30; 38: 22; I Chr. 2:19, 20; II Chr. 1:5.

(4) **Father of Caleb and son of Ephratah.**—I Chr. 2:50; 4:4.

(5) **One of Solomon's officers.**—I Ki. 4:8.

(6) **Son of Judah.**—I Chr. 4:1.

(7) **Ruler of half of Jerusalem.**—Neh. 3:9.

HURAI, hū′rāi. I Chr. 11:32.

HURAM, hū′ram. (1) King of Tyre— II Chr. 2:3, 12.

(2) **Son of Bela.**—I Chr. 8:5.

(3) II Chr. 4:11, 16. See HIRAM.

HURI, hŭ′rī. **Father of Abihail.**—I Chr. 5:14.

HURL. Num. 35:20; Job 27:21.

HURT, _n._ Jer. 10:19; 30:15; Eccl. 8:9. Assuaging of, No—Nah. 3:19. Bindeth up—Is. 30:26. Daughter, Of—Jer. 8: 21. Delight in my—Ps. 70:2. Demon —Lu. 4:35. Devise—Ps. 35:4; 41:7. Do—Gen. 26:29; 31:29; II Sam. 18:32; Dan. 6:22. Found upon him, No—Dan. 6:23. Have no—Dan. 3:25. Healed— Jer. 6:14; 8:11. Kings, Of—Ezra 4: 22. Meddle to thy—II Ki. 14:10; II Chr. 25:19. Provoke me to anger to your—Jer. 25:7. Rejoice at my—Ps. 35:26. Riches kept to his—Eccl. 5:13.

See—I Sam. 24:9; Esth. 9:2; Ps. 38: 12; 71:13, 24; Jer. 38:4. Sweareth to his—Ps. 15:4. Walk after other gods to your—Jer. 7:6.

HURT, _v._ Num. 16:15; Is. 11:9; Mk. 16:18. Aught of neighbor be—Gen. 22:14. Deadly thing shall not—Mk. 16:18. Desire to—Rev. 11:5. Earth, Not—Rev. 7:3. Feet with fetters— Ps. 105:18. God suffered him not to— Gen. 31:7. Grass, Not—Rev. 9:4. Heads, With—Rev. 9:19. I was not— Pr. 23:35. Lions have not—Dan. 6:22. Men—Rev. 9:10. Nothing shall—Lu. 10:19. One—Num. 16:15. Oil, Not— Rev. 6:6. Ox—Gen. 21:35. Second death—Rev. 2:11. Wickedness may— Job 35:8. Woman—Ex. 21:22.

HURTFUL. Kings, Unto—Ezra 4:13, 15. Lusts—I Tim. 6:9. Sword—Ps. 144:10.

HUSBAND: Laws concerning.—Ex. 21: 22; Lev. 19:20; 21:3, 7; Num. 30:6–16; Deut. 22:22, 23; 24:5; 25:11; 28:56; Ez. 44:25. Jealousy—Num. 5:13, 19, 29–31. Marriage of captive women— Deut. 21:13. Bishops—I Tim. 3:2. Elders—Tit. 1:6. Divorce—Deut. 24: 3, 4; Mt. 5:31, 32; 19:3–9; Mk. 10:12; Lu. 16:18; Rom. 7:2, 3.

Duties of.—Deut. 24:5; Pr. 5:18; I Cor. 7:2–4, 10, 16, 34, 39; Eph. 5:23–33; Col. 3:19; I Tim. 5:8; I Pet. 3:7.

Exhortation to.—Eccl. 9:9; Eph. 5:23– 33; Col. 3:19; I Tim. 5:8; I Pet. 3:7.

Making husbands contemptible.—Esth. 1:17.

Prophecy concerning.—Jer. 6:11.

Figurative.—Is. 54:5; Jer. 31:32; II Cor. 11:2; Gal. 4:27. Christ the husband of His people—Eph. 5:25–32; Rev. 19: 7 f.

Illustrative.—Jer. 3:1; Ez. 16:32, 45; Hos. 2:2, 7; Joel 1:8; Rev. 21:2.

Mention of.—Adam to Eve—Gen. 2:18, 23, 24; 3:6, 16. Abraham to Sarai— Gen. 16:3. Isaac to Rebekah—Gen. 24:67. Jacob to Leah—Gen. 29:32, 34; 30:15, 18, 20. Manoah—Ju. 13:6, 9, 10. Samson to Philistine woman— Ju. 14:15. Elimelech to Naomi—Ruth 1:3, 5, 12. Of Ruth—Ruth 1:9, 12; 2: 11. Of Orpah—Ruth 1:9, 12. Elkanah to Hannah—I Sam. 1:8, 22, 23; 2:19– 21. Phinehas as—I Sam. 4:19, 21. Nabal to Abigail—I Sam. 25:19. Paltiel to Michal—II Sam. 3:15, 16. Uriah to Bathsheba—II Sam. 11:26. To woman of Tekoa—II Sam. 14:5, 7. To the Shunammite woman—II Ki. 4:9, 14, 22, 26. Sons of prophets were—II Ki. 4:1. Of a worthy woman—Pr. 12:4; 31:11, 23, 28. To Samaritan—John 4: 16–18. Zacharias to Elizabeth—Lu. 1:5, 13, 39, 40. Joseph to Mary—Mt. 1:16, 19. To Anna— Lu. 2:36. Ananias to Sapphira—Acts 5:9, 10. Aquila to Priscilla—Acts 18:24–28; I Cor. 16:19.

Husband head of the house.—Esth. 1:22; Eph. 5:23; Col. 3:18.

HUSBANDMAN. Gen. 9:20; II Ki. 25: 12; II Chr. 26:10; Mt. 21:35, 38, 40; Mk. 12:7. Break in pieces—Jer. 51: 23. Destroy—Mk. 12:9; Lu. 20:16. My Father is—John 15:1. Laboreth, That—II Tim. 2:6. Let vineyard out to—Mt. 21:33; Mk. 12:1; Lu. 20:9. Reasoned—Lu. 20:14. Sent servants to—Mt. 21:34; Mk. 12:2; Lu. 20:10. Waiteth for fruit—Jas. 5:7.

HUSBANDRY. II Chr. 26:10; I Cor. 3:9.

HUSHAH, hū'shah. **A man of Judah.**— I Chr. 4:4.

HUSHAI, hū'shāi. **A friend of David.**— II Sam. 15:32, 37; 16:16–18; 17:5–15; I Ki. 4:16; I Chr. 27:33.

HUSHAM, hū'sham. **A king of Edom.** —Gen. 36:34, 35; I Chr. 1:45, 46.

HUSHATHITE. Inhabitants of Hushah.—II Chr. 21:18; 23:27; I Chr. 21:18; 23:27; 11:29; 20:4; 27:11.

HUSHED. Job 29:10.

HUSHIM, hū'shim. (1) **Son of Aher.**— I Chr. 7:12.

(2) **Son of Dan.**—Gen. 46:23.

(3) **A wife of Shaharaim.**—I Chr. 8:8, 11.

HUSK. Num. 6:4; II Ki. 4:42; Lu. 15:16.

HYACINTH. Rev. 7:19.

HYMENÆUS, hў'me-næ'us. **One who had gone off into heresy.**—I Tim. 1: 20; 2:17.

HYMN. Mt. 26:30; Mk. 14:26; Acts 16:25; Eph. 5:19. See MUSIC.

HYPOCRISY. Gr. *Hupokrisis*, ''acting under a feigned part.''

Profession rather than practice.—Ps. 5:9, 10; Jer. 9:8; Ez. 33:31, 32; Mic. 3:11; Zech. 7:5, 6; Mt. 23:3; Rom. 2: 17–23; II Tim. 3:5.

Governed by appearances.—Mt. 6:2, 5, 16; 23:5–7; II Cor. 5:12. Not to be emulated—Mt. 6:2.

Associated with minor and major duties.—Mt. 23:23; Lu. 11:42.

Fault-finding.—Mt. 7:4, 5; Lu. 6:42; 13: 15, 16.

Heartless.—Job 15:34, 35; Ps. 55:12–14; 78:36–37; Is. 32:6, 7; Mt. 7:4, 5, 6.

Concealed.—II Sam. 20:9, 10; Is. 29:15; Mt. 22:15–18; Mk. 3:6; 12:13–15; Lu. 11:44; 20:20.

Detection of.—Is. 29:15, 16; Lu. 12:56; Gal. 2:11–13; Rev. 2:2.

Denounced.—Ez. 13:1–7; Mt. 23:13, 15, 23, 25, 27, 29; Lu. 11:44; 12:1, 2; 13: 15–17; I Tim. 4:1–5.

Arch-hypocrites.—Jacob—Gen. Ch. 27. Delilah—Ju. 16:4–20. Herod—Mt. 2: 7, 8. Pharisees—Mt. 22:15–17. Judas —Mt. 26:47–50; Mk. 14:43–46; Lu. 22:47, 48; John 18:2–5.

Hypocrisy punished.—Remnant of Judah—Jer. 42:19–22. False prophets— Ez. 13:8–14. The steward—Mt. 24: 48–51. Pharisees—Mt. 23:32–36. Ananias and wife—Acts 5:1–11. Herod —Acts 12:23. See DECEPTION, FALSE.

HYSSOP. Ex. 12:22; Lev. 14:4, 6, 51, 52; Num. 19:6, 18; I Ki. 4:33; Ps. 51: 7; John 19:29; Heb. 9:19. See PLANTS AND TREES.

I. Abraham was, Before—I am—John 8:58. Alive for ever more, Am—Rev. 1:18. Alpha and Omega, I am—Rev. 1:18; 21:6; 22:13. AM THAT I AM —Ex. 3:14. Baptize you with water— Mt. 3:11. Decrease, He must increase, but I must—John 9:4. Father greater than I—John 14:28. Father's house, I must be in—Lu. 2:49. Glory, That I should—Gal. 6:14. Go to prepare a place for you—John 14:1–6. Life, I lay down my—John 10:15. Lifted up, If I be—John 12:32. Passover, I have desired to eat this—Lu. 22:15. Sent, Therefore was I—Lu. 4:43. Sheep, I have other—John 10:16. Silver and gold have I none—Acts 3:6. Way, the Truth, and the Life, I am—John

14:6. Whom say ye that I am?—Mt. 16:13-15; Mk. 8:27-29; Lu. 9:18-20. Work the works of Him that sent me, I must—John 9:4. See JESUS, DIVINITY OF.

IBHAR, ĭb′har. **Son of David.**—II Sam. 5:15; I Chr. 1:3; 14:5.

IBLEAM, ĭb′le-ăm. **A city of Manasseh.**—Josh. 17:11; Ju. 1:27; II Ki. 9:27.

IBNEIAH, ĭb-nē′iah. **Son of Jehoram.** —I Chr. 9:8.

IBNIJAH, ĭb-nī′jah. **A Benjamite.**—I Chr. 9:8.

IBRI, ĭb′ri. **A Merarite.**—I Chr. 24:27.

IBZAN, ĭb′zăn. **A judge of Israel.**—Ju. 12:8, 10.

ICE. See METEOROLOGY.

ICHABOD, ĭk′a-bod. **Son of Phinehas.** —I Sam. 4:21; 14:3.

ICONIUM, ī-kō′ni-um. **A district in Asia Minor Paul visits.**—Acts 13:51; 14: 1; 19:21; 16:2; II Tim. 3:11.

IDALAH, ĭd′a-lah. **A town of Zebulun.** —Josh. 19:15.

IDBASH, ĭd′băsh. I Chr. 4:3.

IDDO, ĭd′do. (1) **Son of Zechariah of Manasseh.**—I Chr. 27:21.

(2) **Father of Ahinadab.**—I Ki. 4:14.

(3) **A Levite.**—I Chr. 6:21.

(4) **A seer in the days of Jeroboam.**— II Chr. 9:29; 12:15; 13:22.

(5) **Ancestor of Zechariah the prophet.** —Ezra 5:1; 6:14; Zech. 1:1.

(6) **A priest who returned from Babylon.**—Neh. 12:4, 16.

(7) Ezra 8:17.

IDLENESS. Pr. 31:27. Children of Israel, Of—Ex. 5:8, 17. Christian should not be—Rom. 12:11; I Tim. 5:13; Heb. 6:12; II Pet. 1:8. Punished—Pr. 6:69; 10:4; 12:24; 13:4; 19:5; 20:4, 13; 21:25; 24:30, 31; Eccl. 10:18; I Thess. 4:11; II Thess. 3:10. Widows are—I Tim. 5:13. Word—Mt. 12:36; Lu. 24:11.

IDOLATRY: Idol worship forbidden.— Gen. 35:2; Ex. 20:3; 23:13, 24; Deut. 5:7; 7:26; 11:16; 12:30; Josh. 24:14; I Sam. 7:3; II Ki. 17:35; Ps. 81:9; Jer. 25:6; Ez. 20:7; I Cor. 10:7, 14; I John 5:21.

Idol-making forbidden.—Ex. 20:23; 34: 17; Lev. 19:4; 26:1; Deut. 4:16, 17, 18.

Intercourse with idolaters forbidden.— Ex. 34:15, 16; Deut. 7:3, 4; I Ki. 18: 21; II Cor. 6:15, 16.

Objects of idolatry.—Foreign gods— Gen. 31:19, 30; 35:2, 4; Josh. 24:20. New gods—Deut. 32:17; Ju. 5:8. Sun, moon, and stars—Deut. 4:19; II Ki. 17:16; 21:35; Job 31:26-28; Jer. 7: 17-20; Ez. 8:15, 16; Acts 7:42, 43. Golden calf—Ex. 32:4-31; Deut. 9: 12-16; Neh. 9:18; Acts 7:40-41. Dumb idols—Is. 46:1, 7; Hab. 2:18; I Cor. 12:2. Graven images—Deut. 7:5, 25; Ju. 18:18; II Ki. 19:18; Is. 44:17; 45: 20; Hos. 11:2. Pillars—Ex. 23:24; 34:13; Lev. 26:1; Deut. 7:5; II Ki. 3:2; 18:4; Jer. 43:13. Stones and stocks—Is. 44:16, 17; Hab. 2:19; Jer. 3:9; Hos. 4:12. Angels—Col. 2:18. Asherim—Ex. 34:13; Ju. 6:25, 26. Brazen serpent—II Ki. 18:4.

Child sacrifice to Molech.—Lev. 18:21; I Ki. 11:7; II Ki. 16:3; 17:17; 23:10.

Child sacrifice forbidden.—Lev. 18:21; 20:2-5; Deut. 18:10.

Sons and daughters pass through fire.— II Ki. 17:17, 31; 21:6; 23:10, 11; II Chr. 28:3; 33:6; Jer. 7:31; 19:5; Ez. 16:21; 20:26, 31; 23:37.

Folly of idolatry.—Ps. 115:8; Is. 41:28, 29; 44:9, 15, 16, 17, 19, 20; Jer. 10:8, 14, 15; 51:17, 18; Zech. 10:2; Acts 17:29; Rom. 1:21, 22, 23, 25. Helplessness of idolatry—Deut. 32:37, 38; Ju. 6:28-32; 10:14; I Ki. 18:29; II Ki. 18:33, 34, 35; 19:17; II Chr. 25:15; 32: 13; Jer. 2:28; Ps. 115:4-7; Is. 46:1-2.

What it consists in.—Offering human sacrifices—Lev. 18:21; 20:2-5; Deut. 12:31; 18:10; II Ki. 3:26; Ps. 106:37, 38; Is. 57:5; Jer. 7:31; Ez. 16:20. Worshipping angels—Col. 2:18. Worshipping devils—Mt. 4:9-10; Rev. 9:20. Worshipping host of heaven—Deut. 4:19; 17:3. Accompanied by licentiousness—Ex. 32:6; Num. 25:1-3; I Ki. 14:24; 15:12; II Ki. 17:30; 23:7; Amos 2:8; Mic. 1:7; Rom. 1:24-27; I Cor. 10:7; I Pet. 4:3-4; Rev. 2:14; 9:20, 21; 14:8; 17:1-6. Worshipping the dead—Ps. 106:28. Setting up idols in the heart—Ez. 14:3-4. Worshipping in groves—Deut. 16:21; Is. 17:8; Ez. 6:13; Mic. 5:14. Worshipping Baal—Num. 25:3; Ju. 8:33; I Ki. 16:

31; 18:17–26; II Ki. 10:18–22. Worshipping images—Ps. 106:38; Is. 44: 17; Dan. 3:5–15. Worshipping any other gods—Deut. 30:17; Ps. 81:9; Hos. 3:1; Acts 17:16–23; 19:23–37; I Cor. 12:2; Gal. 4:8; I Thess. 1:9. Swearing by—Jer. 12:16; Zeph. 1:5.

Results to worshipper.—Obscurity and impurity—Ex. 32:25; Num. 25:1–3. Ruin of Israel—II Chr. 28:22–23. Estrangement from God—Ez. 14:5; 44: 10. Hatred of God—II Chr. 19:2–3. Vanity of imagination—Rom. 1:21.

Results to God.—Pollute His temple—Ez. 5:11. Defile His name—Ez. 20:39. Forget God—Deut. 8:19; Jer. 18:15. Provoke God—Deut. 31:20; Is. 65:3; Jer. 25:6.

Styles of worship.—With burnt-offerings—Ex. 32:6; II Ki. 10:25; Acts 14:13. With libations—Is. 57:6; 65:11; Jer. 7:18. Of blood—Ps. 16:4; Zech. 9:7. Of wine—Deut. 32:38. With incense—Jer. 48:35. With singing and dancing—Ex. 32:18–19; I Ki. 18:26; I Cor. 10:7. With meal-offerings—Is. 57:6; Jer. 7:18; Ez. 16:19. With incense burned on altars—I Ki. 12:33; Is. 65: 3; Jer. 1:16; 11:12. Kissing—I Ki. 19:18; Hos. 13:2. Cutting the flesh—I Ki. 18:28; Jer. 41:5. Prophecies relating to—Ex. 12:12; Is. 2:18; 17: 7; 19:1; Jer. 10:11; Ez. 43:7; Zech. 13:2.

Idolatrous things destroyed.—II Ki. 23: 4–19; II Chr. 14:3; 17:6; 19:3; 30:14; Is. 36:7. Golden calf—Ex. 32:20; Deut. 9:21.

Threats against.—Ex. 12:12; Is. 2:18; 19:1; Jer. 46:25; 51:44–52; Ez. 30:13; Mic. 5:13; Zeph. 2:11.

Persistence of Jews.—Ju. 2:17–19; Is. 65:3; Jer. 44:17–18; Hos. 4:17; 9:10; Amos 5:26; Acts 7:43.

Penalties against.—Ex. 32:34–35; Lev. 26:30; Deut. 31:17–18; II Ki. 22:16–17; II Chr. 34:24; Jer. 1:16–17; 16:10–21; Ez. 5:11; Hos. 2:13.

National extermination.—Deut. 4:25–26; 6:14–15; 8:19–20; Josh. 23:16; Jer. 18:15–16; 22:8–9; 44:2–8. See PILLARS, HIGH PLACES, COMMANDMENTS.

IDUMEA. See EDOM.

IGAL, i'gal. (1) A spy—Num. 13:7.

(2) **A guard under David.**—II Sam. 23: 26.

(3) **Son of Shemaiah.**—II Chr. 3:22.

IGDALIAH, ig'da-lī'ah. Father of Hanan—Jer. 35:4.

IGNOMINY. Pr. 18:3. See CONTEMPT, SHAME.

IGNORANCE: Concerning God.—Job 18:21; John 7:28; 8:19; 8:55; 15:21; Acts 17:23; II Thess. 1:8.

Concerning the things of God.—Ps. 92: 5, 6; Eccl. 11:2–6; Is. 1:2, 3; Jer. 33:3; Mk. 4:27; John 15:15; Rom. 10:3; 11: 25; I Cor. 2:4–14; 8:2; 10:1–4.

Respecting the Christ.—Mt. 16:13, 14; Mk. 6:14–16; Lu. 9:7–9; John 1:26; 4:32; 8:19; 9:29; 11:49–52; 13:7; 14:5.

Spirit.—Mt. 12:24–28; Lu. 9:25 (margin); John 14:17; I Cor. 12:1–3; I John 4:1–3.

Coming of the Lord.—Mt. 24:42; 25:13; Mk. 13:32; Rev. 3:3.

Scriptures.—Mt. 22:29; Mk. 12:24; I Tim. 6:3–5.

Sinning.—Lev. 4:2, 13, 22, 27; 5:15, 18; Num. 15:24–29; Lu. 12:48; 23:34; Acts 3:17; 17:30, 31; Eph. 4:18; I Tim. 1:13; I Pet. 1:14.

Idolatry.—John 4:22; I Cor. 8:1–13.

Revelation.—I Cor. 13:9–12; 14:36–40.

Ignorance of the way.—John 12:35; 14: 5–7; Heb. 11:8; I John 2:11.

Of the future.—Eccl. 8:6–8; 9:1, 12; I Thess. 4:13, 14.

Wilful ignorance.—John 8:19, 42, 43; 9: 15–24; II Pet. 3:5.

Pretended ignorance.—Mt. 26:70–74; Mk. 14:68; Lu. 22:57–60; Tit. 1:16.

Ignorant asking.—Mt. 20:22; Mk. 10:38; Rom. 8:26.

Respecting riches.—Ps. 39:6; Pr. 23:4, 5; I Tim. 6:9, 17.

Respecting Satan.—Mt. 13:19; Mk. 4: 15; Lu. 8:12; II Cor. 2:10, 11; Rev. 2:24.

Punishment of ignorance is more ignorance.—I Cor. 14:38.

IIM, ī'im. (1) **A town in Judah.**—Josh. 15:29.

(2) **One of Israel's encampments.**—Num. 33:45.

IJON, ī'jon. **A town of Naphtali.**—I Ki. 15:20; II Ki. 15:29; II Chr. 16:4.

IKKESH, ĭk′kesh. **Father of one of David's mighty men.**—II Sam. 23:26; I Chr. 11:28; 27:9.

ILAI, i′lāi. **One of David's warriors.**—I Chr. 11:29.

ILL. Favor—Gen. 41:3, 4, 19, 20, 21, 27. Love worketh no—Rom. 13:10. Treatment—Heb. 11:25, 37; 13:3. With—Ps. 106:32; Is. 3:11. See DISEASE, EVIL.

ILLEGITIMATE CHILDREN. See CHILDREN.

ILLYRICUM, il-lўr′i-kŭm. **A district lying east of the Adriatic Sea.**—Rom. 15:19.

IMAGES: Man the image of God.—Gen. 1:26–27; 5:1; 9:6; I Cor. 11:7; Jas. 3:9; Job 4:17. **Of Christ.**—Rom. 8: 29; I Cor. 15:49; II Cor. 3:18.

Offspring, the image of parent.—Seth—Gen. 5:3; I Cor. 15:49.

Christ bears the image of His Father.—II Cor. 4:4; Col. 1:15; Heb. 1:3.

Man, by regeneration, takes divine image.—Col. 3:10; Rom. 8:29; I John 3:1–3. (See also above.)

Images in visions.—Job's—Job 4:15–16. Nebuchadrezzar's—Dan. 2:31–35; 3:1–7. Of the beast—Rev. 13:14–18; 15:2; 16:2; 19:20.

Images as idols.—Forbidden—Ex. 20:4; 32:7–8; Lev. 26:1; Deut. 16:21–22; 7: 5; Num. 33:52; I Ki. 14:9, 23; II Ki. 17:9; 17:23, 24; Ps. 73:20; Is. 17:8; 27:9; Jer. 50:2; Ez. 6:4; 7:20; 16:17; 30:13; Dan. 11:8; Hos. 13:2; Amos 5:26–27; Mic. 5:13. See IDOLATRY.

As symbols.—Cæsar's—Mt. 22:20; Mk. 12:16; Lu. 20:24. Jupiter's—Acts 19: 35. Brute beasts—Rom. 1:23.

IMAGINATION, IMAGINE. II Cor. 10:5. Evil—Gen. 6:5; 8:21; Deut. 31: 21. Jehovah understands—I Chr. 28: 9. Proud, Of—Lu. 1:51. Rich, Of—Pr. 18:11. Righteous—I Chr. 29:18. Vain things—Acts 4:25. See DEVISE, MEDITATE, MIND, SIN, THOUGHT.

IMITATE. Disciples—II Thess. 3:7, 9. Evil—III John 11. Faith—Heb. 13:7.

IMITATORS. Churches in Judea, Of—I Thess. 2:14. Disciples, Of—I Cor. 4:16; 11:1; Phil. 3:17; I Thess. 1:6. Faithful, Of—Heb. 6:12. God, Of—Eph. 5:1; I Thess. 1:6.

IMLA, ĭm′lä. **Father of Micaiah.**—I Ki. 22:8, 9; II Chr. 18:7, 8.

IMMANUEL, im-măn′u-el. **God is with us—A title given to Jesus.**—Is. 7:14; Mt. 1:23.

IMMEDIATE, IMMEDIATELY. Baptized, he and all his—Acts 16:33. End not—Lu. 21:8. Sent for Peter, Cornelius—Acts 10:33; 11:11. Tribulation of those days, After—Mt. 24:29. See STRAIGHTWAY.

IMMER, ĭm′mer. (1) **A priest in time of David.**—I Chr. 24:14.

(2) **A family of priests.**—I Chr. 9:12; Ezra 2:37; 10:20; Neh. 7:40; 11:13.

(3) **One of those who had lost their genealogies.**—Ezra 2:59; Neh. 7:61.

(4) **A priest in time of Jeremiah.**—Jer. 20:1.

(5) **Father of Zadok.**—Neh. 3:29.

IMMORTAL. God is—I Tim. 1:17. See ETERNAL LIFE.

IMMORTALITY. God has—I Tim. 6: 16. Jesus brings through gospel—II Tim. 1:10. Mortal put on—I Cor. 15: 53, 54. See ETERNAL LIFE.

IMMUTABLE. God is—Heb. 6:17, 19. See GOD.

IMNA, ĭm′na. **An Asherite.**—I Chr. 7:35.

IMNAH, ĭm′nah. (1) **Son of Asher.**—I Chr. 7:30.

(2) **A Levite.**—II Chr. 31:14.

IMPART. Gal. 2:6. Coat—Lu. 3:11. Gospel—I Thess. 2:8. Spiritual gift—Rom. 1:11. Understanding—Job 39: 17.

IMPATIENT. Job 21:4.

IMPEDIMENT. Speech, In—Mk. 7:32.

IMPENITENT. Heart—Rom. 2:5.

IMPLACABLE. II Tim. 3:23.

IMPLANT. Word—Jas. 1:21.

IMPORTUNE. Friend — Luke 11:8. Neighbor—Pr. 6:3. Prayer, Of—See PRAYER.

IMPOSE. Ordinances—Heb. 9:10. Tribute—Ezra 7:24.

IMPOSSIBLE. Mt. 17:20; Heb. 11:6. See GOD IS ALMIGHTY.

IMPOSTOR. II Tim. 3:13. See HYPOCRISY.

IMPOTENT. Man healed—Acts 4:9; 14:8. See HEALING, SICK.

IMPOVERISH. Ju. 14:15; Is. 40:20. See POVERTY.

IMPRISONMENT. Evildoers, Of — Ezra 7:26. Disciples, Of—Acts 22:19; II Cor. 6:5; Heb. 11:36. See PRISON.

IMPUDENT. Children—Ez. 2:4. Face, With—Pr. 7:13. Harlot—Ez. 16:30.

IMPULSE. Jas. 3:4.

IMPURITY. Lev. 12:2, 5; 15:19–24, 33; 20:21. See PURIFICATION, SIN, UNCLEAN.

IMPUTE. Iniquity—Ps. 32:2. Offering—Lev. 7:18; 17:4.

IMRAH, ĭm′rah. **An Asherite.**—I Chr. 7:36.

IMRI, ĭm′ri. (1) Neh. 3:2. (2) **A man of Judah.**—I Chr. 9:4.

INASMUCH. As ye did it unto these—Mt. 25:40.

INCENSE: Sweet incense.—Ex. 25:6. Its composition—Ex. 30:34–35. Altar to burn on—Ex. 30:1–8; 40:5, 27; II Chr. 2:4; 32:12. Aaron offers it—Lev. 16:12–13. Unlawfully offered by Nadab and Abihu—Lev. 10:1. By Korah and others—Num. 16:6. 250 men offer it—Num. 16:17–18. They are devoured—Num. 16:35. Example of rebellion—Num. 16:36–40. Bezalel made it—Ex. 37:29. Offered morning and evening—Ex. 30:7–8; II Chr. 13:11. Prayer goes forth as—Ps. 141:2. Indication of praise—Mal. 1:11. Of approved service—Eph. 5:2. Presented by wise men to Jesus—Mt. 2:11.

Offered in idolatry.—I Ki. 11:8; 12:33; II Ki. 17:11; II Chr. 25:14; 28:3; Jer. 19:13; Ez. 8:11. See OFFERINGS, ALTAR.

INCENSED. Song of Sol. 1:6.

INCEST. See FORNICATION.

IN CHRIST. All shall be made alive—I Cor. 15:22. Approved—Rom. 16:10. Babes—I Cor. 3:1. Before me—Rom. 16:7. Churches—Gal. 1:22. Dead—I Thess. 4:16. Done away—II Cor. 3:14. Establish us—II Cor. 1:21. Exhortation—Phil. 2:1. Faith—Col. 1:4. Fallen asleep—I Cor. 15:18. Fellowworker—Rom. 16:9. God was—II Cor. 5:19. Heavenly places—Eph. 1:3; 2:6. Hoped—I Cor. 15:19; Eph. 1:12. Man —II Cor. 12:2. Manifest, Bonds became—Phil. 1:13. New creature—I Cor. 5:17. One body—Rom. 12:5. Saints and faithful brethren—Col. 1:2. Sanctified—I Cor. 1:2. Sum up all things—Eph. 1:10. Triumph—II Cor. 2:14. Wrought—Eph. 1:20.

INCLINE. Ps. 40:1. **Ear.**—Ps. 17:6; 45:10; 49:4; 71:2; 78:1; 88:2; 102:2; 116:2; Pr. 2:2, 18; 4:20; 5:13; Is. 37: 17; 55:3; Jer. 7:24, 26; 11:8; 17:23; 25:4; 34:14; 35:15; 44:5; Dan. 9:18. **Heart.**—Josh. 24:23; Ju. 9:3; I Ki. 8: 58; Ps. 119:36, 112; 141:4.

INCLOSE. Benjamites — Ju. 20:43. Company of evildoers have—Ps. 22: 16. Face of throne—Job 26:9. Fat, In—Ps. 17:10. Gold, In setting of— Ex. 28:20; 39:6, 13. Multitude of fishes—Lu. 5:6.

INCONTINENCY. I Cor. 7:5; II Tim. 3:3. See CHASTITY, FORNICATION.

INCORRUPTIBLE. Apparel—I Pet. 3:4. Crown—I Cor. 9:25. Dead raised —I Cor. 15:52. Inheritance—I Pet. 1:4. Love—Eph. 6:24. See—I Pet. 1:23.

INCORRUPTION. Rom. 2:7; I Cor. 15: 42–54.

INCREASE, n. Body, Of—Eph. 4:16. Cattle, Of—Deut. 7:13; 28:18, 51. Destroyed—Ju. 6:4. Earth hath yielded —Ps. 67:6. Eat—Lev. 25:12; Deut. 32:13. First-fruits of—Pr. 3:9. Food, For—Lev. 25:7. Gather in—Ex. 23: 10; Lev. 25:20. God gave—I Cor. 3:6. God, Of—Col. 2:19. Government—Is. 9:7. Ground, Of—Is. 30:23. House, Of—I Sam. 2:33. Land shall yield— Lev. 26:4, 20. Seed, Of—Deut. 14:22. Sinful men, Of—Num. 32:14. Take no—Lev. 25:56. Take—Lev. 25:36; Ez. 18:13. Tithe of—Deut. 14:28; 26: 12. Threshing-floor, Of—Num. 18:30. Vineyards, Of—I Chr. 27:27. Wicked, Of—Pr. 10:16. Yield—Lev. 19:25.

INCREASE, v. Ps. 115:14. Army—Ju. 9:29. Beasts—Deut. 7:22. Faith— Lu. 17:5. Fruit—Phil. 4:17. Growing up and—Mk. 4:8. He must—John 3:30. Israel—I Chr. 27:23. Joy—Is. 9:3. Knowledge shall be—Eccl. 1:18; Dan. 12:4. Learning in—Pr. 1:5. Love, In—I Thess. 3:12. Mightily— Deut. 6:3. Nation—Is. 26:15. Number, In—Acts 16:5. Price—Lev. 25: 16. Riches—Ps. 62:10. Righteous are —Pr. 29:2. Righteousness, Fruits of— II Cor. 9:10. Saul—Acts 9:22. Strength —Is. 40:29. Waters—Gen. 7:17. Wicked are—Pr. 29:16. Word of God—Acts 6:7.

INCREDIBLE. Acts 26:8.

INCURABLE. Disease—II Chr. 21:18. Hurt—Jer. 30:12. Pain—Jer. 30:15. Wound—Job 34:6; Jer. 15:18; Mic. 1:9. See DISEASE.

INDIA, in'di-a. Esth. 1:1; 8:9.

INDICTMENT. Job 31:35.

INDIGNATION. See ANGER.

INDULGENCE. Acts 24:23.

INDUSTRIOUS. I Ki. 11:28. Exemplified—Gen. 29:9; 31:6; Ex. 2:16; Ruth 2:2, 3; I Sam. 16:11; Acts 9:39; 18:3; I Cor. 4:12. Referred to—Gen. 2:15; 3:17; Pr. 6:6, 12; 24:22, 29; Eph. 4:28; I Thess. 4:11; Tit. 3:14. Reward of—Pr. 10:4; 13:4, 11; 31:13. See LABOR.

INFAMY. Pr. 25:10. See SHAME.

INFANTS. I Sam. 15:3. Days, Of—Is. 65:20. Dashed in pieces—Is. 13:16; Hos. 13:16. See BABES, CHILDREN.

INFINITE. Strength—Nah. 3:9. Understanding—Ps. 147:5. See GOD.

INFIRMITY. Bear—Rom. 15:1. Compassed with—Heb. 5:2. Feeling of our—Heb. 4:15. Flesh, Of—Rom. 6:19; Gal. 4:13. Healed of—Lu. 5:15; 8:2. Helpeth our—Rom. 8:26. Loosed from—Lu. 13:12. Often—I Tim. 5:23. Priests—Heb. 7:28. Spirit of—Lu. 13:11. Sustain, Will—Pr. 18:14. Thirty and eight years in—John 5:5. This is my—Ps. 77:10. Took our—Mt. 8:17. Weak, Of the—Rom. 15:1. See AFFLICTION, DISEASE.

INFLAME. Strife—Pr. 26:21. Wine—Is. 5:11.

INFLICT. Punishment—II Cor. 2:6.

INFORM. Concerning thee—Acts 21:21, 24. Governor—Acts 24:1. Jews—Acts 25:15. Paul, Against—Acts 25:2.

INGATHERING. Gen. 47:24. Come, Shall not—Is. 32:10. Feast—Ex. 23:16; 34:22.

IN GOD. Hid with Christ—Col. 3:3. The Father—I Thess. 1:1. Wrought—John 3:21.

INGRATITUDE: Of those benefited.—Absalom—II Sam. 15:1-6. Hezekiah—II Chr. 32:25. Israel—Ps. 78:16, 17, 42. Nebuchadrezzar—Dan. 5:18-20. The nine lepers—Lu. 17:15-17.

Ingratitude acknowledged.—Saul to David—I Sam. 19:1-5; 24:16-19; 26:21. Ahasuerus concerning Mordecai—Esth. 6:1-3.

Ingratitude of Israel.—To Moses in wilderness—Ex. 16:3; Num. 20:5. Concerning water out of the rock—Ex. 17:1-3. To Gideon—Ju. 8:33-35. To Jeremiah—Jer. 18:19, 20.

The world's unthankfulness towards God.—Lu. 6:35; Rom. 1:21; II Tim. 3:2-5.

Rewarding evil for good.—Joseph's ruse concerning cup—Gen. 44:4-6. David's enemies—Ps. 35:12; 38:20. Anyone—Pr. 17:13.

Gratitude overlooked.—Pharaoh's butler—Gen. 41:9-12.

Gratitude abused.—Joash—II Chr. 24:22.

Ingratitude punished. — Israel — Deut. 28:47-57. King Baasha—I Ki. 16:1-4. Hezekiah—II Chr. 32:35.

Gratitude commanded by Jesus.—Lu. 17:17-19. Practised by Jesus—John 11:41, 42.

Exhorted by Paul.—Phil. 4:6.

Practised by Paul.—Phil. 1:3-7.

INHABIT. Is. 45:18; Ez. 36:11. Another—Is. 65:22. Eternally—Is. 57:15. Houses—Job 15:28; Is. 65:21; Zeph. 1:13. Jerusalem—Ju. 1:21; Is. 44:26; Zech. 7:7. Kedar doth—Ps. 42:11. Land—Num. 35:34. Parched places—Jer. 17:6. Praises—Ps. 22:3. Waste cities—Amos 9:14. Waste places—Ez. 33:24. Zephath—Ju. 1:17.

INHABITANT. Ps. 49:1. Cities, Of—Gen. 19:25. Drive—Num. 33:52, 53. See ISRAEL, CANAAN. Earth, Of—Dan. 4:35; Rev. 17:2. Land, Of—Gen. 34:30; 36:20. Land without—Jer. 44:22. Sela, Of—Is. 42:11. Sorrow shall take hold on—Ex. 15:14. Tyre, Of—Ps. 83:7. Without—Jer. 2:15; 4:7; 9:9; 11:26:9; 33:10.

INHERITANCE—Land taken in war called Caanan.—Num. 16:14; 26:53, 56; 32:18; 34:2, 18. East of Jordan—Num. 32:19, 32; 34:14, 15; Deut. 29:8; Josh. 13:15, 23, 24, 28, 29; 14:3, 9; 16:9. Hebron—Josh. 14:13, 14.

Land the principal inheritance.—Josh. 13:32, 33; Num. 34:17, 18; Josh. 19:51. Land belonged to the family, not to individual—Num. 27:4, 7; Num. 36: 2-9. Daughters allowed to receive— Num. 27:1-7; Job 42:15. But must marry within the tribe—Num. 36:6, 8. Law of—Num. 27:8-11. Conquered land divided by lot—Num. 33:53, 54; 34:13; Josh. 18:3-6.

Levites had tithes and cities, no land: God their inheritance.—Num. 18:20-24; Deut. 10:9; 12:12; 14:27-29; 18:1, 2; Josh. 13:14, 33; 21:3, 8, 41.

Division to tribes.—Josh. Chs. 13-21.

First-born received double of household goods, cattle, and slaves.—Deut. 21:15-17.

Ruth's.—Ruth 4:3-5, 10.

Naboth's—I Ki. 21:3, 4.

Prince could not take.—Ez. 46:16-18.

Israel was Jehovah's.—Ex. 34:9; Deut. 32:9; I Sam. 26:9; II Sam. 14:16; 20: 19; 21:3; Ps. 16:5; 28:9; 33:12; 74:2; 78:71; 94:14; 106:5; Is. 19:25; 63:17; Jer. 10:16; 51:19; Ez. 44:28. God angry with His—Ps. 78:62; 106:40; Is. 47:6.

The messianic king receives nations for. —Ps. 2:8. Jehovah receives nations for—Ps. 22:27, 28. Christ receives Christians for—Eph. 1:11, 18; Tit. 2:14.

God's children to receive.—Blessing—I Pet. 3:9. God chooses—Ps. 47:4. Among the sanctified—Acts 20:32; 26: 18; Eph. 1:18; Col. 3:24. Forever—Ps. 37:18. In light—Col. 1:12. Holy spirit is earnest of our inheritance—Eph. 1:14. The kingdom of God is—Eph. 5:5.

A good man leaves.—Pr. 13:22.

Wisdom is good as.—Eccl. 7:11.

God's promises are an.—Gal. 3:14, 18.

Israel was a minor: Did not receive.—Gal. 4:1, 7.

Christ inherited a name more excellent than angels.—Heb. 1:4.

Christ not the judge of earthly inheritance.—Lu. 12:13.

Hasty, soon lost.—Pr. 20:21.

INIQUITY. Ps. 51:5; Mt. 24:12; II Cor. 6:14. Amorites, Of—Acts 8:23. Bonds of—Acts 8:23. Cleansing of—Ez. 36: 33; Hos. 14:2. Correction of—Ps. 39: 11; Acts 3:26. Drink—Job 15:16. Fathers, Of—Ex. 20:5; 34:7; Ps. 79:8. Forgiveness, Of—Ps. 25:11; 32:5; 51:

2, 9; 79:8; 103:3; Is. 6:7; 40:2; Jer. 3:13; Hos. 14:2; Mic. 7:18; Rom. 4:7; Heb. 8:12. God has no—Deut. 32:4. Hate—Heb. 1:9. Israel, Of—Jer. 3: 13; 50:20. Jacob had no—Num. 23:21. Jesus crucified for—Is. 53:5, 6, 11. Man of—Pr. 6:12. Overcome by—Ps. 38:4. Prophet, Of—Ez. 14:10. Punishment of—Pr. 6:12; 11:6, 7; Is. 61:8, 9; Jer. 31:30; Ez. 33:8; Acts 1:18; Rev. 18:5. Redeem from—Tit. 2:14. Seek—Job 11:11. Tongue, Of—Ps. 10:7; Jas. 3:6. Workers of—Mt. 7:23; 13:41. Worry with—Is. 43:24. See Sin.

INJURIOUS. I Tim. 1:13. See Hurt, Wound.

INJURY. Acts 27:21; II Cor. 12:10.

INJUSTICE. By reason of—Pr. 13:23. Condemned—Pr. 18:5; 29:7; Eccl. 5:8. Forbidden—Lev. 19:15, 35; Deut. 16: 19. Instances of—Gen. 39:20; II Sam. 8:3; I Ki. 21:10, 15, 16; Is. 59:14; Mt. 27:4, 24-26; Acts 27:4. On my tongue —Job 6:30. Rebuked—Is. 1:23; 10:1; Lam. 3:34-36; Mic. 3:9; Zech. 7:9; Lu. 16:10. Results of—Pr. 11:7; Amos 5:11; Mic. 6:10; I Thess. 4:6; II Pet. 2:9. See Justice, Oppression.

INK. Jer. 36:18; II Cor. 3:3; II John 12; III John 13.

INKHORN. Writer's—Ez. 9:2, 3, 11.

INLAID. Work—I Chr. 29:2.

INN. Brought him to—Lu. 10:34. No room in—Lu. 2:7.

INNER. Chambers—I Chr. 28:11; Mt. 24:26. Court—I Ki. 6:26; 7:12; Esth. 4:11; 5:1; Ez. 8:3; 40:15, 19, 23, 27, 28, 32; 42:3; 43:5; 44:17, 21, 27; 45: 19; 46:1. Doors—II Chr. 4:22. Gate— Ez. 40:44. House—I Ki. 6:27; 7:50; Ez. 41:17. Prison—Acts 16:24. Temple—Ez. 41:15.

INNERMOST. Pr. 18:18; 26:22.

INNOCENCE. Who are innocent?— Adam and Eve—Gen. 2:25. Jesus—Is. 53:9; John 8:46; II Cor. 5:21; I Pet. 2:22; 3:18.

Little children.—Mt. 18:2, 3, 10; 19:14.

In some things.—Abimelech—Gen. 20:5. David and his kingdom—I Sam. 3: 28; Ps. 26:6. Job—Job 33:9. Asaph —Ps. 73:13. Jeremiah—Jer. 26:15. Daniel—Dan. 6:22. Nathaniel—John

1:47. Disciples as to sabbath-breaking—Mt. 12:7. Pilate claimed—Mt. 27:24.

Do the innocent perish?—No—Job 4:7. Yes—Job 9:22, 23, 28.

The wicked slay the innocent.—II Ki. 21:16; Ps. 10:8; 94:20, 21; 106:38; Pr. 1:10, 11; 6:17; Is. 59:7; Jer. 2:34; 7:6; 19:4; 22:17.

Taker of bribe to slay innocent is cursed.—Deut. 27:25.

Refuser of bribe against the innocent is blessed.—Ps. 15:5.

Innocent blood avenged.—Deut. 19:10–13; II Ki. 24:3, 4; Jer. 19:4; Jonah 1:14; Joel 3:19.

Israel to be careful.—Ex. 23:7.

Judges to determine.—Deut. 19:12, 18; 21:1–9.

Judas betrayed.—Mt. 27:4.

Innocent to inherit wealth.—Job 27:17.

Innocent are blessed.—Ps. 32:2; Rom. 4:8.

Keep lips innocent.—Ps. 34:13; I Pet. 3:10.

Keep heart innocent.—I Pet. 2:1.

Who are not innocent?—Israel—Ju. 2: 35. Profane—Ex. 20:7; Deut. 5:11.

No one absolutely innocent.—Job 9:30–33; 15:14–16; Ps. 14:2, 3; 53:1–3; Rom. 3:10–12.

INNUMERABLE. Before him—Job. 21: 33. Evils—Ps. 40:12. Forest—Jer. 46: 23. Hosts of angels—Heb. 12:12. Sand—Heb. 11:12. Things creeping—Ps. 104:25.

INQUIRE. Gen. 24:57; Mt. 2:4; Lu. 15: 26; John 21:12; Acts 4:7. Jehovah, Of—Is. 65:1; Jer. 10:21; Ez. 36:37. See ASK, PRAYER.

INQUIRY. Pr. 20:25; Acts 10:17. See ASK, PRAYER.

INQUISITION. Deut. 19:18; Ps. 9:12. See TRIAL.

INSCRIBE. Job 19:23; Is. 30:8. See WRITING.

INSCRIPTION. Acts 17:23. See WRITING.

INSERTED. II Chr. 20:34.

INSIDE. I Ki. 6:15. Cup, Of the—Mt. 23:26.

INSOLENT. Rom. 1:30. See IMPUDENT, HAUGHTY, PRIDE.

INSOLENTLY. Pr. 14:16; Mk. 1:45; Acts 1:19; II Cor. 8:6.

INSPIRATION. Job 32:8; II Tim. 3:16. Prophets, Of—See PROPHETS. Word, Of—See WORD OF GOD.

INSPIRED. II Tim. 3:16.

INSTANT. Is. 29:5; 30:13; Jer. 18:7, 9; Lu. 2:38; 22:23; Rom. 12:12; II Tim. 4:2. See PRAYER.

INSTANTLY. Lu. 7:4; Acts 26:7.

INSTEAD. Gen. 2:21; 30:2; Ps. 45:16; Is. 55:13.

INSTRUCTION, or, TEACHING, and TEACHERS: Importance.—Valued as one's life—Pr. 4:13; 6:23. Die without—Job 4:21; 36:12; Pr. 5:23. Gives freedom—John 8:32. Better than gold—Pr. 8:10; I Cor. 14:6. Wisdom is knowledge of God and the way of life—Ps. 34:11–14; Pr. 1:7; 8:32–35; 23: 15–18; John 7:17; 17:3; 20:31.

Who instruct?—God—Deut. 4:36; Job 35:11; 36:22; Ps. 71:17; 90:12; 94:10, 12. He taught Moses—Ex. 4:12, 15. Ordinances—Ps. 119:108. Statutes—Ps. 119:93, 102, 171. The good way—I Ki. 8:36; II Chr. 6:27; Ps. 25:8, 12; 27:11; 32:8; 86:11; Is. 2:3; 8:11; 48: 17; Mic. 4:2. War—II Sam. 22:35; Ps. 18:34; 144:1. How to live—Tit. 2:12.

The Holy Spirit.—Neh. 9:20; Is. 44:3, 4; Joel 2:28, 29; Zech. 12:10; Mt. 10: 19, 20; Lu. 12:12; John 14:26; 16:13; Acts 2:4, 11, 17, 18, 33, 36; 4:8; 6:10; 10:19, 20; I John 2:27.

Jesus called teacher.—Mt. 8:19; 9:11; 10:24, 25; 12:38; 17:24; 19:16; 22:16, 24, 36; 26:18; Mk. 4:38; 5:35; 9:17, 38; 10:17, 20, 35; 12:14, 19, 32; 13:1; 14:14; Lu. 3:12; 6:40; 7:40; 8:49; 9: 38; 10:25; 11:45; 12:13; 18:18; 19:39; 20:21, 28, 39; 21:7; 22:11; John 1:38; 3:2; 8:4; 11:28; 13:13, 14; 20:16. He taught with authority—Mt. 7:29; Mk. 1:38, 39; Lu. 4:32. Sitting down—Mt. 5:1; Lu. 5:3; John 4:6. Claims to teach God's words only—John 3:11–13; 5:19; 8:28. By apostles—Acts 4:2, 18; 5:21, 25, 28, 42; Eph. 4:20, 21; II John 9, 10. Still teaching—Acts 1:1.

Parents.—Abraham—Gen. 18:19. Jonadab—Jer. 35:6, 8, 18. The law—Ex. 12:26, 27; 13:8, 14, 15; Deut. 4:9, 10; 6:7, 20–25; 11:19; Pr. 1:8; 4:1–4, 11; 6:20; 13:1; 30:17; 31:1; Song of Sol. 8:2; Joel 1:3; II Tim. 3:14; Tit. 2:3.

Doctors called rabbis.—Mt. 23:7, 8; Lu. 2:46; 5:17; John 1:38, 49; 3:2, 26; 6:25.

Moses.—Ex. 18:20; 24:12; Deut. 4:1, 5, 14; 5:31.

Priests.—Lev. 10:11; Deut. 24:8; 33:10; II Chr. 35:3; Ezra 7:10,.25.

Princes.—II Chr. 17:7, 9.

Judges.—Deut. 17:10, 11; I Sam. 12:23.

Sages.—Job 4:3; Dan. 11:33.

Scribes.—Ezra 7:6, 10; Neh. 8:1–3; Mt. 7:29; 13:52; 23:22; Mk. 1:22; 9:11; 12:35.

Apostles.—Their commission.—Mt. 28: 20. Their practice—Acts 2:42; 4:2; 5: 21, 28, 42; 11:26; 15:35; 18:11; 20:20; I Cor. 4:17; Col. 1:28; 3:16.

Pharisees.—Jews—Mt. 16:6, 11, 12; 23: 2, 3; Mk. 8:15–21; Lu. 12:1.

Christians.—Acts 15:1, 5.

Evangelists.—I Tim. 4:11; 6:2; II Tim. 4:2.

Figurative.—Beasts—Job 12:7. Old age —Job 32:7. Former age—Job 8:8. Thy right hand—Ps. 45:4. Heart— Pr. 16:23. Earth—Job 12:8. Idols cannot teach—Jer. 10:8; Hab. 2:19.

False teaching.—Prophets—I Ki. 13:11– 18; 22:5, 6, 10–12, 19–23; Jer. 14:13– 16; 23:31, 32; 28:8, 9, 21–23; Zech. 10: 2. Idolaters taught abomination— Deut. 20:18. Teachers—I Tim. 1:7; II Tim. 2:7, 8; 4:3, 4; Tit. 1:9, 10. For money—Mic. 3:11; Tit. 1:11. Juda- izes—II Cor. 11:13–15; Gal. 1:6–9.

What was taught.—Arts—Gen. 4:21, 22; Ez. 17:17; Deut. 31:19, 22; II Sam. 1:18; I Chr. 25:7, 8; Dan. 1:4. Jeho- vah is the one God and is to be loved —Deut. 6:4–7; Ps. 25:4, 5, 9; 34:11. The law—Deut. 6:1; 31:9–13; Josh. 8: 32–35; II Ki. 23:2; Ezra 7:10; Neh. 8:1–3, 8, 9; Ps. 119:12, 26, 64, 68, 124, 135; I Tim. 1:7. Jesus Christ or the gospel—Acts 4:2; 5:20, 21, 28, 40–42; 14:21; 15:35; 18:11; 20:24; 28:23; I Cor. 4:17; I Tim. 1:10; 2:7; II Tim. 1:11; Tit. 1:9; 2:7, 12; Heb. 5:12; 8:11; I John 2:27; II John 9:10.

Who were taught?—All Israel—Ex. 4: 12; Lev. 10:11; Deut. 17:11; 24:8; 33: 10; I Ki. 8:36; II Chr. 6:27; Jer. 6:8; Ez. 44:23. Children—Ex. 12:26, 27; 13:8, 14; Deut. 4:10; Rom. 2:20. All nations—Is. 2:3, 4; 42:4; 60:3; Mic.

4:2; Zech. 2:10, 11; Mt. 28:19, 20. Christians—Lu. 1:3, 4; Acts 2:42; 18: 25, 26; I Cor. 14:26; Col. 1:28; 2:7; 3:16.

Methods of instruction.—Miracle. See MIRACLES. Parable. See PARABLE. Pre- cept—Neh. 9:14; Ps. 119:4, 15, 27, 40, 45, 56, 63, 69, 78, 87, 93, 94, 100, 104, 110, 128, 134, 141, 159, 168, 173; Is. 28: 10, 13; 29:13; Jer. 35:18; Dan. 9:5; Mk. 10:5; Heb. 9:19. Prophecy. See PROPHECY. Proverbs. See PROVERBS— Ez. 12:22. Revelation—Deut. 29:29; I Sam. 3:7, 19–21; Is. 22:14; Dan. 2:19, 22, 28, 29, 30, 47; Mt. 11:25, 27; 16: 17; Lu. 10:21, 22; I Cor. 2:10; 14:6, 26, 30; II Cor. 12:1, 7; Gal. 1:12; 2:2; 3:23; Eph. 1:17; 3:3, 5; I Pet 1:12; Rev. 1:1. Songs—See SONG. Scriptures. See WORD OF GOD.

INSTRUMENT. Death, Of—Ps. 7:13. Music, Of—See MUSICAL INSTRU- MENTS. Unrighteousness, Of—Rom. 6: 13. See TOOLS AND IMPLEMENTS.

INSURRECTION. Ezra 4:19; Lu. 23: 19; Acts 24:5. See REBELLION.

INTEGRITY. Job 4:6. Heart, Of— Gen. 20:5, 6; I Ki. 9:4; Ps. 78:72. Jude according to—Job 31:6; Ps. 7:8. Re- tain—Job 2:3, 9; 27:5; Ps. 25:21; 41: 12. Upright, Of—Pr. 11:3. Walk in— Ps. 26:1, 11; Pr. 2:7; 19:1; 20:7; 28:6. See HONOR, FAITHFULNESS.

INTELLECT. See MIND.

INTEND. Evil—Ps. 21:11; Acts 5:28. Leave, To—Acts 20:4, 13, 20.

INTERCESSION. Is. 53:12; 59:16; Jer. 27:18; Rom. 8:26, 34; Heb. 7:25. Christ, Of—See JESUS. Prayer—See PRAYER, SALVATION.

INTERDICT. Dan. 6:8–15.

INTEREST. Lev. 25:36; Mt. 25:27; Lu. 19:23. See USURY.

INTERMEDDLE. Stranger does—Pr. 14:10.

INTERMISSION. Lam. 3:49.

INTERPOSE. Heb. 6:17.

INTERPRETATION.

INTERROGATION. I Pet. 3:21.

IN THE LORD. I Cor. 7:39. Beloved and faithful child—I Cor. 4:17. Be strong—Eph. 6:10. Called—I Cor. 7: 22. Brother—Philemon 16. Die—Rev. 14:13. Fitting—Col. 3:18. Glory—I Cor. 1:31. Holy temple—Eph. 2:21.

Joy of thee—Philemon 20. Know them that are over you—I Thess. 5: 12. Mind, Of same—Phil. 4:2. Rejoice—Phil. 4:4.

INTREAT. Heb. 12:19; Jas. 3:17. Abraham, By—Gen. 23:21. Christian, By—I Cor. 4:13. Father, By—Lu. 15:28. Favor—Ps. 45:12; 119:58; Pr. 19:6. Jehovah—Gen. 25:21; Ex. 8:8, 9, 28–30; 9:28, 10; 17:8; Ju. 13:8; I Sam. 2:25; II Sam. 21:14; 24:25; I Ki. 13:6; I Chr. 5:20; II Chr. 33:13,19; Ezra 8: 23; Ps. 45:12; 119:58; Is. 19:20; I Cor. 4:13. See PRAYER. Land, For—II Sam. 21:14; 24:25. Moses, By—Ex. 8: 9, 28–30; 9:28; 10:17, 18. Peter—Acts 9:38. Pharaoh, For—Ex. 8:9, 28–30; 9:28; 10:17, 18. Ruth, By—Ruth 1:16. Sinner, For—I Sam. 2:25.

INTRUST. Rom. 3:2; I Cor. 9:17; I Thess.2:4; Tit.1:3. See COMMIT, TRUST.

INVENT. II Chr. 26:15; Amos 6:5; Rom. 1:30.

INVENTIONS. Ps. 99:8; 106:29, 39; Pr. 8:12; Eccl. 7:29.

INVENTOR. Rom. 1:30.

INVISIBLE. Rom. 1:20; Col. 1:15; I Tim. 1:17; Heb. 11:27. See GOD IS INVISIBLE.

INVITATIONS. Abide in Christ, To—John 15:4–10; I John 2:28. Ask, To—Ps. 2:8; Mt. 7:7; 21:22; Mk. 11:24; Lu. 11:9. Believe, To—John 14:1–11. Come, To—Mt. 11:28; 22:1–14; Lu. 14:15–24; 1:39; 6:35; 7:37; Rev. 22: 17. Follow, To—Mt. 8:22; 9:9; 19:21; Mk. 2:14; Lu. 9:59; John 1:43; 12:26; 21:19. See SALVATION.

INWARD. Curse—Ps. 62:4. Jew, who is one—Rom. 2:29. Man—Rom. 8:22; II Cor. 4:16; Eph. 3:16. Parts—Job 38: 36; Ps. 5:9; 51:6; Pr. 14:33; Is. 16:11; Jer. 31:33. Ravening wolves, Are—Mt. 7:15; Lu. 11:39. Thoughts—Ps. 49:11.

INWARDS. Ex. 12:9.

INWROUGHT. Ps. 45:13.

IPHDEIAH, iph-dē'iah. **Son of Shashak.**—I Chr. 8:25.

IR, ir. **A Benjamite.**—I Chr. 7:12.

IRA, i'ra. (1) **One of David's warriors.**—I Chr. 11:28; 27:9; II Chr. 23:58.

(2) **A priest under David.**—II Sam. 20: 26.

(3) **Another of David's guard.**—I Sam. 23:26; I Chr. 11:40.

IRAD, i'răd. **Son of Enoch, grandson of Cain.**—Gen. 4:18.

IRAM, i'ram. **A duke of Edom.**—Gen. 36:43.

IRI, i'ri. **Son of Bela, grandson of Benjamin.**—I Chr. 7:7.

IRIJAH, i-ri'jah. **A captain in Jerusalem.**—Jer. 37:13, 14.

IRKSOME. Phil. 3:1. See BURDEN.

IRNAHASH, ir'nā'hăsh. **A man of Judah.**—I Chr. 4:12.

IRON, i'ron. (1) **A city of Naphtali.**—Josh. 19:58.

(2) **A metal.**
Tubal-cain first forged iron.—Gen. 4:22.
Where found.—Deut. 8:9; Job 28:2.
Utilized in war.—Chariots—Josh. 17:16, 18; Ju. 1:19; 4:3. Harrows and axes—II Sam. 12:31. Spear—I Sam. 17:7; Job 20:24. Pan—Ez. 4:3. Horns—I Ki. 22:11. Breastplate—Rev. 9:9.
In domestic life.—Bedsteads—Deut. 3: 11. Axes—Is. 10:34. Threshing tools—Amos 1:3. Vessels of iron—Josh. 6:24. File—Pr. 27:17.
For use in the temple.—Nails and couplings—I Chr. 22:3. Various things—I Chr. 29:2.
Instruments of punishment.—Fetters—Ps. 105:18; 107:10; 149:8. Rods—Ps. 2:9; Rev. 2:27; 12:5; 19:15. Yokes—Deut. 28:48; Jer. 28:13, 14.
Images made of.—Dan. 2:33; 7:19.
Various purposes.—Gates—Acts 12:10. Pen—Job 19:24; Jer. 17:1. Fish-spear—Job 41:7. Murderer's weapon—Num. 35:16; II Sam. 23:7. To brand—I Tim. 4:2.

IRPEEL, ir-pe-el. **A city of Benjamin.**—Josh. 18:27.

IRSHMESH, ir-shē'mesh. **A city of Dan.**—Josh. 19:41.

IRU, i'ru. **Oldest son of Caleb.**—I Chr. 4:15.

ISAAC. Name signifies *"laughter"*—Gen. 17:17; 18:12.
Isaac a miracle son.—Abraham and Sarah respectively 100 and 90 years of age at Isaac's birth—Gen. 17:17; 18:9–15; 21:1–3. Isaac, a gift from God—Gen. 17:16; 18:14; 21:1–2; Josh. 24:3; John 1:13; Rom. 4:17–22; Gal. 4:23; Heb. 11:11–12.
Ishmael, a son of the flesh.—Gen. 16:2–4. Son of a bondwoman—Gen. 16:1, 2,

15; Gal. 4:23. Ishmael mocks Isaac—Gen. 21:8-9. Struggles for supremacy between flesh and spirit—Rom. 7:14-25.

Abraham's seed to be called in Isaac.—Gen. 17:18-19, 21. Ishmael obtains a limited blessing—Gen. 17:20. Isaac an unlimited blessing—Gen. 17:21; 22: 16-18; Rom. 9:6-9; Heb. 11:17-18.

Given to Sarah to decide between the two sons.—Gen. 21:10. Abraham, though grieved, consents—Gen. 21: 11-14. Jesus' Application—John 8: 34-35. Paul's—Rom. 4:19-20; Gal. 4: 21-31.

Abraham put to the final test.—Jehovah's demand on Abraham—Gen. 22: 1-2. Abraham obeys God—Gen. 22:3-5. Preparation for the sacrifice—Gen. 22:6-10. His hand stayed by the angel—Gen. 22:11-12. Jehovah provided a ram—Gen. 22:13. Abraham and Isaac abundantly blessed—Gen. 22:15-18; Heb. 11:17-19. Isaac's deliverance in harmony with covenant—Gen. 17:19.

Wife chosen for Isaac from Abraham's kindred.—Gen. 24:3-4. At 40 he marries his cousin, Rebekah—Gen. 24:67. At 60 two sons were born to him—Jacob and Esau—Gen. 25:24-26. Birth of these twins the beginning of two nations—Gen. 25:23.

Abraham gives Isaac an inheritance.—Gen. 25:5. Merely gives gifts to sons of concubines, separating them from Isaac—Gen. 25:6. Isaac and Ishmael bury their father—Gen. 25:9-10. God blesses Isaac—Gen. 25:11. Isaac dwells near Beer-lahai-roi—Gen. 25: 11.

A famine induces change of residence.—Gen. 26:1. Jehovah forbids going to Egypt—Gen. 26:2-6. Isaac dwells in Gerar—Gen. 26:1-6. Fearing to lose his life, he falsifies concerning Rebekah to the man—Gen. 26:7. Abimelech reproves Isaac and protects him—Gen. 26:8-11.

Isaac grows wealthy at Gerar.—Gen. 26:12-13. He accumulates flocks and herds—Gen. 26:14. The Philistines envy him and strive for his wells—Gen. 26:15-22. Is sent away by Abimelech—Gen. 26:16. His household

grows (Gen. 26:14) and he finds room in Beer-sheba—Gen. 26:23. He builds an altar there and Jehovah blesses him—Gen. 26:23-25. Abimelech and Isaac make a covenant of peace—Gen. 26:26-31.

Rebekah and Jacob practise deceit upon Isaac.—Gen. 27. By strategy, Jacob secures the blessing—Gen. 27:5-29. Esau, returning from the hunt, prepares venison for his father—Gen. 27: 30-31. The deception is revealed and Esau has been supplanted—Gen. 27: 32-37. Isaac blesses Esau—Gen. 27: 39-40. Esau hates Jacob—Gen. 27:41. Esau's marriage provokes Isaac—Gen. 26:35. Jacob sent to Paddan-aram to avoid Esau and obtain a wife—Gen. 27:42-45; 28:1-5. Jacob returns before Isaac's death—Gen. 35:27. Isaac dies at the age of 180—Gen. 35:28-29. Buried in cave of Machpelah—Gen. 49:30-31. The characteristics of Isaac: *Peaceful*—Gen. 25:14-31. *Submissive*—Gen. 22:9. *Devout*—Gen. 24: 63; 25:21; 26:25. *Easily entreated*—Gen. 27:22-27; 27:35-40.

Ancestor of Jesus Christ—Mt. 1:2; Lu. 3:34.

Prophecies concerning—Gen. 17:16-21; 21:12; Ex. 32:13-14.

ISAIAH. See Outline Studies in the Books.

ISCAH, is'cah. Lot's sister—Gen. 11:29.

ISCARIOT, is-căr'i-ot. See Judas.

ISHBAH, ish'bah. I Chr. 4:17.

ISHBAK, ish'băk. **Son of Abraham by Keturah.**—Gen. 25:2; I Chr. 32.

ISHBIBENOB, ish'bi-bē'nob. **A Philistine giant.**—II Sam. 21:16.

ISH-BOSHETH, ish-bō'sheth. Son of Saul—II Sam. 2:8, 12, 15; 3:14. Reign of Israel—II Sam. 2:10. Trouble between Ish-bosheth and Abner—II Sam. 3:7, 8. Messengers sent to, by David—II Sam. 3:14, 15. House of—II Sam. 4:5. Slain by sons of Rimmon—II Sam. 4:8. Head of, buried—II Sam. 4:12.

ISHHOD, ish'hŏd. I Chr. 7:18.

ISHI, ish'ī. (1) **Son of Appaim.**—I Chr. 2:31.

(2) **A descendant of Caleb, the spy**—I Chr. 4:20.

(3) **A Simeonite.**—I Chr. 4:42.

(4) **A man of Manasseh.**—I Chr. 5:24.

(5) **A symbolic name given to God.**—Hos. 2:16.

ISHMA, ĭsh'mȧ. **A descendant of Caleb.** —I Chr. 4:3.

ISHMAEL, *"God is hearing."* (1) **The son of Abraham by Hagar, the handmaid**—Gen. 16:11-16; I Chr. 1:28. Names of the sons of Ishmael—I Chr. 1:20-31. Abraham begs God to grant Ishmael as heir—Gen. 17:18. Ishmael circumcised at thirteenth year (this because covenant established then)—Gen. 17:23. His mocking Isaac caused his exile—Gen. 21:9-19; Gal. 4:29. Blessed of God—Gen. 21:18, 20. Dwells in the wilderness and becomes an archer—Gen. 21:20. His daughter marries Esau—Gen. 28:9; 36:2, 3. With Isaac he buries his father Abraham—Gen. 25:9. Died at 137 years of age—Gen. 25:17.

(2) **A Benjamite**—I Chr. 8:38; 9:44.

(3) **A descendant of Zebadiah.**—II Chr. 19:11.

(4) **A captain under Joash.**—II Chr. 23:1.

(5) **A priest who had married a foreign wife.**—Ezra 10:22.

(6) **Son of Nethaniah.**—Murders Gedaliah at the instigation of the king of Ammon—II Ki. 25:23-25; Jer.˙ 40:8-16. Defeated by Johanan—Jer. 41: 1-18.

ISHMAELITE. Descendants divided into twelve nations—Gen. 25:12-16; I Chr. 1:28-31. Ishmaelites called Hagrites—I Chr. 5:10; 27:30. Hagarenes —Ps. 83:6. Arabians—Is. 13:20. Midianites—Gen. 37:28, 36; Ju. 8:24, 26. Their boundaries—Gen. 25:18. Princes appointed over them—Gen. 25:16; Jer. 25:24. Were migratory—Is. 13: 20. Grazed cattle—I Chr. 5:21. Wore golden ear-rings—Ju. 8:24. Predatory and rapacious—Gen. 16:12; Jer. 3:2. Conquered by Gideon—Ju. 8:10-24. By tribes of Reuben, Gad, and half tribe of Manasseh—I Chr. 5:10, 18-20. By Uzziah—II Chr. 26:7. Fulfilled predictions—Gen. 13:18; 16:11, 12; 17:20. Under the divine threat—Jer. 25:23-25.

ISHMAIAH, ĭsh-mā'iah. **A prince in David's time.**—I Chr. 8:18.

ISHMERAI, ĭsh'me-rāi. **A Benjamite.**—I Chr. 8:18.

ISHPAH, ĭsh'pah. I Chr. 8:16.

ISHPAN, ĭsh'păn. **Son of Shashak.**—I Chr. 8:22.

ISHVAH, ĭsh'văh. I Chr. 7:30.

ISHVI, ĭsh'vī. (1) **Son of Asher.**—Gen. 46:17; Num. 26:44; I Chr. 7:30.

(2) **Son of Saul.**—I Sam. 14:49.

ISLANDS: Of the nations.—Gen. 10:5; Zeph. 2:11. Afar off—Is. 49:1; 66:19; Jer. 31:10. Inhabitants of—Is. 42:10; Ez. 27:35. Merchandise of—Ez. 27:3, 6, 7, 15. Multitude of—Ps. 97:1.

Islands mentioned.—Cauda—Acts 27:16. Chios—Acts 20:15. Cos—Acts 21:1. Crete—Acts 27:12; Tit. 1:5. Cyprus —Acts 11:19; 13:6. Elishah—Ez. 27: 7. Kittim—Jer. 2:10; Ez. 27:6. Melita —Acts 28:1, 7, 9. Patmos—Rev. 1:9. Rhodes—Acts 21:1. Samos—Acts 20: 15. Samothrace—Acts 16:11.

Of the sea.—Esth. 10:1; Is. 11:11. Beyond the sea—Jer. 25:22. A certain island—Acts 27:26.

Figurative.—Is. 41:1; 49:1.

Prophecies concerning.—Ps. 72:10; Is. 40:15; 41:5; 42:4, 10, 12, 15; 51:5; 59: 18; 60:9; Ez. 26:15, 18; 39:6; Dan. 11: 18; Rev. 6:14; 16:20.

ISMACHIAH, ĭs'ma-kī'ah. **An overseer in the temple in the time of Hezekiah.** —II Chr. 31:13.

ISRAEL. Heb. *God persists*, or *perseveres*, or, perhaps, *God is a warrior.*

Name given to Jacob for striving with God.—Gen. 32:28; 35:10; I Ki. 18:31; II Ki. 17:34.

Names given to descendants of Abraham, Isaac, and Jacob.—Hebrews—Gen. 14:13; 39:14, 17; 40:15; 41:12; 43:32; Ex. 1:15, 16, 19; 2:6, 7, 11, 13; 3:18; 7:16; 9:1, 13; 10:3; 21:2; Deut. 15:12; I Sam. 4:6, 9; 13:3, 7, 19; 14: 11, 21; 29:3; Jer. 34:9, 14; Jonah 1:9; Acts 6:1; II Cor. 11:22; Phil. 3:5. Israel—Ex. 3:16; Lev. 17:3, 8, 10; Deut. 5:1; Josh. 3:17; 8:24; 13:6; I Sam. 25:1; II Ki. 7:13; II Chr. 9:2, etc. Israelites—Ex. 9:7; Lev. 24:10, 11; Ju. 20:21; I Sam. 2:14; 13:20; 14:21; 29: 1; II Sam. 4:1; 17:25; II Ki. 3:24; John 1:47; Rom. 9:4; 11:1; II Cor. 11: 22. Children of Israel—Gen. 32:32; 36:31; 46:8; Ex. 1:9, 12, 13; 12:42;

Lev. 23:42-44; Deut. 1:3; 3:18; 10:6; Josh. 13:6, 13, etc. Children of Jacob —I Chr. 16:13; Ps. 105:6. Seed of Abraham—Ps. 105:6; Is. 41:8; Jer. 33:26. Seed of Isaac—Jer. 33:26. Seed of Jacob—Jer. 33:26.

Described as.—A peculiar people—Deut. 14:2. A holy nation—Ex. 19:6. A holy people—Deut. 7:6; 14:2, 21; 26:19. The possession of Jehovah—Ex. 19:5; Deut. 7:6; 26:18. Jehovah's portion—Deut. 32:9. A kingdom of priests—Ex. 19:6. A separate people—Ex. 33:16; Lev. 20:24, 26; I Ki. 8:53. God's inheritance—Ex. 34:9; Deut. 4:20; 9:26, 29; I Ki. 8:51, 53; II Sam. 21:3; Ps. 33:12; 68:9; Jer. 10:16.

Tribes took the name of Jacob's sons, as follows: Reuben, Simeon, Levi, Judah, Dan, Naphtali, Gad, Asher, Issachar, Zebulun, Joseph, Benjamin. (For full particulars of tribes see footnotes under each of these names.)

Half of the tribes—Simeon, Levi, Judah, Issachar, Joseph, and Benjamin—stood on Mt. Gerizim to pronounce the blessing.

Half—Reuben, Gad, Asher, Zebulun, Dan, and Naphtali—stood on Mt. Ebal "for the curse" (to say "amen" when curses were pronounced).—Deut. 27:12, 13; Josh. 8:32, 33.

Tribes divided into families, each having a chief.—Num. 26:5-61; 36:1; Josh. 7:14; I Chr. Chs. 4-8.

Land to be divided among the tribes and the inheritance of each tribe was to remain within that tribe.—Num. 26:52-56, 62; 27:1-11; 32:1-33; Chs. 34 and 35; 36:1-13; Josh. Chs. 13-22; I Ki. 21:3; I Chr. 23:22. Ephraim and Manasseh, the sons of Joseph, were adopted by Jacob, and inherited in place of Joseph—Gen. 48:5, 6; Num. 32:33; Josh. 14:2, 3. The Levites did not participate in the division of the land—Deut. 18:1-8; Josh. 13:14; 14:3.

Number of, at different periods.—Going down to Egypt: Seventy souls—Gen. 46:8-27; Ex. 1:5; Deut. 10:22; Acts 7:14. At the time of the exodus: 600,-000 men, besides children—Ex. 12:37, 38; 38:26; Num. 11:21. Numbered by tribes at Sinai: 603,550, over 20 years of age and able to go to war (this does not include the Levites)—Num. 1:1-50; 2:32, 33. After the plague at Shittim: 601,730 men over 20 years of age and able to go to war, besides 23,-000 Levites—Num. Ch. 26. When David numbered: 1,570,000 warriors—II Sam. 24:1-9; I Chr. 21:5, 6; 27:23, 24. Warriors in actual service in David's army: 288,000—I Chr. 27:1-15. After the Babylonian captivity: 42,360, besides servants and men and women singers—Ezra 2:64; Neh. 7:7-67. John's vision: 144,000—Rev. 7:1-8.

Settle in Goshen.—Gen. Chs. 46 and 47; Ex. 1:1-6; Acts 7:15.

Dwelt in Egypt 400 years.—Gen. 15:13; Acts 7:6. Four hundred and thirty years from the call of Abraham—Ex. 12:40-41; Gal. 3:17. (Possibly the years they were "strangers and sojourners" in Canaan are to be counted in this 430 years. Again, the limit may be between "the promise" and "the giving of the law.")

Were enslaved by Egyptians.—Ex. Chs. 1, 2, 5; Deut. 4:20; Acts 7:18-36; Heb. 11:25. God heard complaint and calls Moses to deliver them—Ex. Chs. 3, 4. Calls Aaron to assist—Ex. 4:10-17, 27-31. God visits plagues upon Egypt—Ex. Chs. 7-12. Israel exempt from plagues—Ex. 8:22, 23; 9:4, 6, 26; 10:23; 11:7; 12:13, 27, 28. Israel brought out of Egypt—Ex. 12:41-42. See EGYPT, MOSES. Israelites obtain jewels—Ex. 3:21, 22; 11:2, 3; 12:35, 36; Ps. 105:37. Institution of passover in memorial of the night of deliverance—Ex. 12:1-28, 43-49; 13:3-10; Heb. 11:28. See Deut. 5:15.

Children of Israel leave Egypt.—Ex. 12:37-42, 51. Accompanied by a mixed multitude—Ex. 12:38. Their flocks and herds—Ex. 12:38; 34:3. Consecration of the first-born—Ex. 13:1-16. Led by the angel of the Lord—Ex. 14:19; 23:20-23; 32:34; 33:2, 14; Deut. 4:37; Is. 63:11-14. By a pillar of cloud—Ex. 13:21, 22; 40:36-38; Num. 9:15-22; 10:11, 12, 33-36; 14:14; Deut. 1:33; Neh. 9:12, 19; Ps. 78:14. Defended by the pillar of cloud by night—Ex. 14:19, 20, 24; Ps. 105:39. See CLOUD OF GLORY.

Crossing the Red Sea and destruction of Pharaoh.—Ex. 14:1–31; Deut. 11:4; Ps. 78:13; 106:7–11; 136:13–15. Song of Moses and Miriam—Ex. 15:1–24; Ps. 106:11, 12; Heb. 11:29; Rev. 15:3.

Narration of journeys.—Num. 33:1–49. Children of Israel murmur at **Marah** —Waters made sweet—Ex. 15:22–27. Murmur for bread—Ex. 16:1–3. Manna and quails sent—Ex. 16:4–36. See Num. 11:1–35; Deut. 8:3; Neh. 9:15, 20; Ps. 78:23–25; 105:40; John 6:31, 32; I Cor. 10:3. Israelites fed on manna for 40 years—Ex. 16:35. Pot of manna laid up for a memorial—Ex. 16:33, 34; Heb. 9:4. See Rev. 2:17. People murmur at **Rephidim.** Water from the rock at **Massah** and **Meribah** —Ex. 17:1–7; Ps. 81:7. Amalek defeated by Joshua—Ex. 17:8–16; Deut. 25:17, 18. By advice of Jethro, Moses appoints assistant judges—Ex. 18:1–27; Deut. 1:9–17.

Israel encamps at Sinai in the third month. The giving of the law.—Ex. Chs. 19:1; 23:19; 24:1–12. See LAW, MOSES.

Instructions concerning the building of the tabernacle and its furniture.—Ex. Chs. 25–27.

The Aaronic priesthood, services, and ritual of the tabernacle.—Ex. Chs. 28–31. See LEVITICUS, TABERNACLE, PRIEST. The tables of stone given—Ex. 31:18. Worshipping the golden calf—Ex. 32: 1–14, 20–24. The tables of stone broken —Ex. 32:15–19. The Levites slay 3,000 men—Ex. 32:28. New tables of stone given, covenant renewed—Ex. 34: 1–35.

Tabernacle and the furniture constructed.—Ex. Chs. 35–40. Second passover observed—Num. 9:1–5. Nadab and Abihu offered strange fire and are slain—Lev. 10:1–5.

Numbering the Israelites.—Num. Chs. 1–4. Service of the Levites—Num. Ch. 4. Various ceremonies—Num. Chs. 5, 6. Oblations of the princes—Num. Ch. 7. Purification of the Levites— Num. Ch. 8.

The journey resumed.—Num. 9:15–23; 10:1–36. The silver trumpets—Num. 10:1–10. Hobab invited to accom-

pany the Israelites—Num. 10:29–32. The people murmur and many are consumed at **Taberah**—Num. 11:1–3. At **Kibrothhattaavah,** manna and quails sent. Plague follows—Num. 11:4–9, 18–23, 31–35. Seventy elders chosen —Num. 11:16, 17, 24, 25. At Hazeroth, Miriam and Aaron rebuke Moses for marrying a Cushite woman—Num. 12: 1–3. See Ex. 2:16–22. Miriam stricken with leprosy—Num. 12:9–15; Deut. 24:9.

In the Wilderness of Paran.—Spies sent out—Num. 13:1–33; 32:8–13; Deut. 1:19–36; Josh. 14:7. The people rebel and are compelled to wander 40 years, and all except Caleb and Joshua die in the wilderness—Num. 14:1–45; 26: 64, 65; 32:13; Deut. 2:7, 14; 8:2–4; 29:5; Josh. 5:6; Ps. 106:26; I Cor. 10:5. The ten spies die by a plague— Num. 14:36–38. See Num. 11:30–33. Korah, Dathan, and Abiram with 250 princes rebel and are swallowed up by the ground—Num. 16:1–35. Altar made from their censers—Num. 16: 36–46; Jude 11. People murmur and plague follows—Num. 16:41–50; Deut. 11:6; Ps. 106:16–18. Aaron's rod buds —Num. 17:1–13; Heb. 9:4.

Kadesh.—Miriam dies and is buried— Num. 20:1–3. Moses smites the rock at **Meribah.** Is told that he may not enter land of Canaan—Num. 20:2–13; Is. 48:21. **Passage through Edom refused.**—Num. 20:14–22; Ju. 11:17. **Mt. Hor.**—Death of Aaron, being 123 years of age. Appointment of Eleazar, his son, as high priest—Num. 20: 22–29; 33:38, 39; Deut. 10:6. Arad the Canaanite is conquered—Num. 21:1–3. **The Dead Sea.**—The fiery serpents and the brazen serpent—Num. 21:4–9. See II Ki. 18:4; John 3:14, 15. **From Oboth to Pisgah.**—Israelites conquer the Amorites and the king of Bashan —Num. 21:1–35; Deut. 2:24–37; 3: 1–17.

Israel encamped in the Plains of Moab, east of Jordan.—Balaam and Balak— Num. Chs. 22–24; II Pet. 2:15, 16; Jude 11. Idolatry in Moab—Num. 25: 1–5. Plague in consequence; 24,000 slain. Zeal of Phinehas—Num. 25:1– 18; 26:1; Ps. 106:28–31.

The numbering in Shittim.—Num. Ch. 26. Daughters of Zelophehad claim their inheritance—Num. 27:1–11. See Num. 26:33; 36:1–3; Josh. 17:3–6.

Moses warned of his death. Joshua appointed his successor.—Num. 27:15–23; Deut. 4:9; 32:23. Slaughter of the Midianites—Num. Ch. 31. **Reuben, Gad, and half-tribe of Manasseh settle in Gilead.**—Num. Ch. 32.

Division of Canaan and the names of those who were to make the division. —Num. Chs. 34 and 35; 36:1–13. See Num. 26:52–56, 62; 27:1–11; 32:1–33.

Moses delivers three parting addresses. He recounts the history of the wanderings of the Israelites.—Deut. Chs. 1–4. **Repeats the law.**—Deut. Chs. 5–11. **The book of the covenant.**—Deut. Chs. 12–26. The law to be recorded at Mt. Ebal. The blessings and curses—Deut. Chs. 27 and 28. Renewal of the covenant—Deut. Chs. 29, 30. The law delivered to the priests. Law put beside the ark—Deut. 31:9–26. Song of Moses—Deut. 31:30; 32:43. See Rev. 15:3. Blessing of Moses—Deut. Ch. 33. Death of Moses—Deut. 31:48–52; 34:1–8. **Joshua prepares to cross the Jordan into Caanan.**—Josh. Ch. 1. Spies sent to Jericho and saved by Rahab—Josh. Ch. 2; Heb. 11:31. **Israelites pass over Jordan on dry ground, and the ark going before.**—Josh. Chs. 3, 4. Memorials of this crossing set up—Josh. 4:1–9, 20–24. The people circumcised—Josh. 5:2–9. Israelites ate passover and manna ceased—Josh. 5:10–12. Joshua's vision and Jericho taken. Rahab saved—Josh. 5:13–15; 6:1–27. Israel defeated at Ai because of Achan—Josh. Ch. 7. Destruction of Ai—Josh. 8:1–29. The reading of the law on **Mts. Ebal and Gerizim.**— Deut. 27:1–26; Josh. 8:30–35. The Gibeonites make a league with Joshua. The long days of the battle. **Joshua's conquests.**—Josh. Chs. 9–12. See Josh. 10:41, 42.

Division of the land of Canaan among the tribes.—Josh. 13:1–33; 14:1–5; Chs. 15–19. Hebron assigned to Caleb —Josh. 14:6–15. **Three cities of refuge appointed.**—West of the Jordan: Kedesh-Naphtali, Shechem in Ephraim, Hebron in Judah. East of the Jordan: Bezer, in the wilderness of the tribe of Reuben, Ramoth in Gilead of the tribe of Gad, and Golan in Bashan of the tribe of Manasseh— Josh. Ch. 20. Cities assigned to the Levites—Jos. Ch. 21. The transjordanic tribes, Gad, Reuben and the half-tribe of Manasseh, return, build an altar which offends. Understanding reached—Josh. Ch. 22. Joshua's farewell address—Josh. Chs. 23 and 24. Covenant renewed at Shechem— Josh. 24:14–27. Death and burial of Joshua and Eleazar—Josh. 24:29–33; Ju. 2:6–9.

Settled in Canaan.—Num. 34:1–12; Josh. 14:1–5. Inhabitants not wholly expelled—Ju. 1:27–36; 3:1–7. Israel turns away to idolatry—Ju. 2:10–23. Under theocracy till Samuel's time— Ex. 19:4–6; I Sam. 8:7–9. Judges first suggested by Jethro—Ex. 18:13–27.

Government administered by judges for over 300 years.—Ju. 2:16–18; Acts 13: 20. Idolatry practiced—Ju. 3:7. **Subject to Mesopotamia.**—Being sold to king of Mesopotamia, they repent when delivered after 8 years by **Othniel the first judge.**—Ju. 3:8–11. **Subject to Moab.**—Return to idolatry and tribute is levied by Eglon, King of Moab 18 years—Ju. 3:12–14. **Ehud, of southern Canaan, the second judge,** delivers them by slaying Eglon, king of Moab —Ju. 3:15–30. Israel has rest for 80 years—Ju. 3:30. **Shamgar, of southern Canaan, the third judge,** slays 600 Philistines with an ox-goad—Ju. 3:31. **Subject to Jabin, king of Hazor** for 20 years—Ju. 4:1–3. Delivered by **Deborah of northern Canaan, the fourth judge.**—Ju. Ch. 4. Song of Deborah and Barak—Ju. Ch. 5. **Subject to Midian seven years,** but delivered by **Gideon, the fifth judge.**—Ju. Chs. 6 and 7; 8:1–28. Land rested 40 years— Ju. 8:28. **Abimelech, the sixth judge,** foments war—Ju. 9. Slays 70 of his brethren and usurps the judgeship around **Shechem. Tola** judges for 23 years—Ju. 10:1–2. **Jair, eighth judge,** judges for 22 years—Ju. 10:3–4. **Subject to Ammon for 18 years** and delivered by **Jephthah, the ninth judge.**

His vow. His daughter sacrificed—Ju. 10:6–11, 40. Inter-tribal war: 42,-000 Ephraimites slain at the fords of the Jordan. Jephthah judges Israel 6 years—Ju. 12:1–7. **Ibzan, tenth judge,** judges for 7 years; **Elon, eleventh judge,** for 10 years; **Abdon, the twelfth judge,** for 8 years—Ju. Ch. 12. **Eli, high priest and probably thirteenth judge.** Samuel born—I Sam. Ch. 1:4, 18. Sons of Eli profane tabernacle service—I Sam. 2:12–17, 22–25. Prophecy of death of Hophni and Phinehas in one day and forfeiture of the priesthood—I Sam. 2:27–36. **Israel in bondage to the Philistines** 40 years—Ju. 13:1; 14:4. Samson born—Ju. 13:2–24. **Samson, the fourteenth judge.**—Ju. 15:20. Judges Israel for 20 years—Ju. Ch. 15. Samson marries a Philistine woman; slays a lion—Ju. Ch. 14. Samson and the foxes. Samson bound with new ropes. Slays Philistines with the jawbone of an ass—Ju. 15:4–17. Death of Samson—Ju. Ch. 16. Story of Micah and the Levite—Ju. Chs. 17, 18. Abuse of the Levite's concubine in Gibeah—Ju. Ch. 19. War between the Benjamites and the other tribes in consequence—Ju. Chs. 20, 21. Samuel's vision and prophetic call in Shiloh—I Sam. Ch. 3. **Samuel, the fifteenth judge.**—I Sam. 7:6, 15. Philistines take the ark at Ebenezer and slay Hophni and Phinehas. Death of Eli and wife of Phinehas—I Sam. Ch. 4.

Ark set up in house of Dagon—I Sam. 5:1–5.

Philistines suffer seven months with plagues and restore the ark with presents—I Sam. Ch. 6. **Ruth and Boaz probably lived at this time.**—Ruth Chs. 1–4.

On account of Samuel's sons being unsatisfactory, a king is demanded.—I Sam. 8:4–22; Acts 13:21. Characteristics of king given by Samuel—I Sam. 8:10–18. Israelites refuse to listen, so king granted—I Sam. 8:22.

Israel under kings before separation into two kingdoms. Saul established as king.—I Sam. 9:15–27; 10:1; 11:15. Saul and his people gain victory over Ammonites—I Sam. 11:6–11. Makes

war with the Philistines—I Sam. Chs. **13 and 14.** Jonathan, Saul's son, sentenced to death—I Sam. 14:43–44. People rescue him—I Sam. 14:45–46. Saul's disobedience respecting Amalek—I Sam. 15:1–9. Jehovah arraigns him—I Sam. 15:10–23. Saul is rejected as king—I Sam. 15:23–28. Samuel hews Agag to pieces—I Sam. 15:33. No longer visits Saul—I Sam. 15:34, 39.

David is anointed as king.—I Sam. 16:13. God's spirit departs from Saul and an evil spirit takes possession—I Sam. 16:14–15. David chosen to dispel evil spirit—I Sam. 16:17–23. He becomes Saul's armor-bearer—I Sam. 16:17–23. Saul engages in war with Philistines—I Sam. 17:1–3. Goliath's challenges—vs. 4–11. David visits camp and hears challenge—I Sam. 17:12–30. David offers to meet Goliath, does so, and slays him—vs. 31–50. This produces panic among Philistines and defeats them—vs. 51–53.

David and Jonathan.—I Sam. 18:1–4; 20:1–42; 23:15–18. Saul jealous of David—I Sam. 18:6–16. Saul gives Michal to David as his wife—I Sam. 18:17–30. Saul seeks to kill David; David saved by Jonathan and Michal—I Sam. 19:1–19. Saul and his messengers prophesy—I Sam. 19:18–24. David is helped by Ahimelech the priest and eats showbread—I Sam. 21:1–9; Mt. 12:3, 4; Mk. 2:25, 26. Flees to Achish, king of Gath; feigns madness—I Sam. 21:10–15. Escapes to the cave of Adullam; 400 followers gathered together—I Sam. 22:1–5. Doeg slays the priests at Nob—I Sam. 22:6–23. David saves Keilah; is pursued by Saul—I Sam. 23:1–15, 19–29. David saves the life of Saul at En-gedi and Saul relents—I Sam. Ch. 24. Death of Samuel—I Sam. 25:1; 28:3. Nabal refuses David food; Abigail intercedes; Nabal dies; David marries Abigail and Ahinoam, Saul having given Michal to Palti—I Sam. Ch. 25. David spares Saul's life at Ziph—I Sam. Ch. 26. David makes an alliance with Achish king of the Philistines—I Sam. Chs. 27–30. Saul consults the witch at En-dor. He learns his fate—I Sam. Ch. 28.

Saul and his sons slain by Philistines—I Sam. Ch. 31. Buried at Jabesh-Gilead—I Sam. Ch. 31. David mourns for Saul and Jonathan. The song of the bow—II Sam. Ch. 1.

David made king over Judah. Israelites tenacious concerning Saul's succession and choose Ishbosheth as king of Israel.—II Sam. 2:8, 9. Strife begins between Judah and Israel—II Sam. 2:12–17; 3:1. Sons born to David—II Sam. 3:8–21. Joab suspects Abner and murders him. David mourns for him—II Sam. Ch. 4.

David becomes king over all Israel.—II Sam. 5:1–5; I Chr. 12:23–40.

He captures Jerusalem and makes it his capital.—II Sam. 5:7–9. Defeating the Philistines, he brings the ark up to Jerusalem—II Sam. Chs. 6 and 7. Death of Uzzah—II Sam. 6:6–11. David proposes to build God a house—II Sam. 7:1–3. Jehovah is gracious but chooses Solomon for that work—II Sam. 7:4–17. David is victorious over Philistia, Moab, Zobah, and Syria—II Sam. Ch. 8. His kindness to Mephibosheth, Jonathan's son—II Sam. Ch. 9. Wages war against the Ammonites and their Syrian allies—II Sam. Ch. 10. His sin with Bath-sheba, wife of Uriah. Death of Uriah—II Sam. Ch. 11. Nathan's parable. Death of Bathsheba's child. Solomon born—II Sam. Ch. 12. Amnon ravishes his sister Tamar—II Sam. 13:1–19. Murder of Amnon in revenge—II Sam. 13:23–38. Joab pleads for Absalom and he is recalled—II Sam. Ch. 14. **Absalom conspires against David.**—II Sam. Chs. 15–18. **Death of Absalom.**—David mourns for him—II Sam. 18:6–33; 19:1–8. Jealousy between Israel and Judah. Rebellion of Sheba—II Sam. Chs. 19 and 20. Three years of famine—II Sam. 21:1. Seven sons of Saul slain to avenge the death of the Gibeonites—II Sam. 21:1–11. Bones of Saul and Jonathan brought from Jabesh-Gilead and buried in the sepulchre of Kish—II Sam. 21:12–14. David's psalm of praise—II Sam. 22:1–51; 23:1–7. The people numbered. David buys the threshing-floor of Araunah and builds an altar—II Sam. Ch. 24.

Adonijah seeks to usurp the throne—I Ki. 1:5–10.

Solomon anointed as David's successor.—Adonijah spared—I Ki. 1:11–53; 2–12. David's charge to Solomon—I Ki. 2:1–9; I Chr. Chs. 28 and 29. Death of David—I Ki. 2:10–12; I Chr. 29:26–30. See DAVID. Solomon's vision—I Ki. 3:5–15. His wise judgment concerning the child—I Ki. 3:16–28. Solomon's great wealth. Visit of the queen of Sheba—I Ki. Chs. 4, 9, 10; Mt. 6:29; 12:42; Lu. 11:31; 12:27.

In league with Hiram, king of Tyre, Solomon builds the temple. The palace of Solomon. Dedication of temple.—I Ki. Chs. 5–9. Solomon corrupts his kingdom by foreign marriages.—I Ki. 3:1–3; 11:1–8. God is angry and threatens to rend the kingdom asunder—I Ki. 11:9–13, 29–44; 12:15, 16, 20; I Sam. 2:30.

The division of the kingdom.—The misconduct of Rehoboam causes revolt—I Ki. 12:1–19; II Chr. 10. **Jeroboam returns from exile and is accepted as king over ten tribes** (v. 20). Rehoboam is for going to battle, but is forbidden by Jehovah—I Ki. 12:21–24. Jehovah's threat to Solomon fulfilled (v. 24). See PHARAOH, PRIESTS, TABERNACLE, COMMANDMENTS.

The division of the kingdom—Israel.—The revolt of the ten tribes was according to the word of Jehovah to Solomon, on account of his going after strange gods—I Ki. 11:11–13. The "servant" spoken of was Jeroboam—I Ki. 11:26–28. Ahijah, the prophet, predicted that ten of the tribes should fall to Jeroboam—I Ki. 11:29–37; Ch. 12; II Chr. Ch. 10.

Jeroboam becomes king.—After Jeroboam became king, fearing the competition of Judah, he set up two calves of gold for the worship of Israel, in Bethel and Dan—I Ki. 12:26–29; II Ki. 10:29. He is warned of his sin by a prophet of Judah—I Ki. 13:1–10. He persists in his wickedness, making priests of any and every one—I Ki. 13:33, 34. He and Rehoboam, king of Judah, were continually at war with one another—I Ki. 14:30.

The king's residences.—Shechem was the first capital of the new kingdom—I Ki. 12:25. It was venerable for its traditions—Gen. 33:18; 37:12–14; Josh. 24:1. Penuel—I Ki. 12:25. After this Tirzah, noted for its loveliness (Song of Sol. 6:4), became the royal residence, if not the capital—I Ki. 14:17; 15:33; 16:8, 9, 17, 23. Samaria, having qualities of beauty and strength, was selected by Omri—I Ki. 16:24. Royal residence at Jezreel—I Ki. 18:46; 21:1.

The kings from Jeroboam to Ahab.—(As this article contains a complete schedule of the kings, reference will only be made to a few facts.) After Jeroboam, no one of importance reigns until Omri. The kingdom was at loose ends and the kings had difficulty in keeping control. Two of them, Nadab and Elah, were slain by conspirators—I Ki. 15:27; 16:9, 10. Omri exceeded any of them in actual ability. He was the real founder of the kingdom of Israel (I Ki. 16:27), selecting Samaria, a hill of natural defence, for his capital. "His policy won Judah over to permanent and almost unbroken friendship"—I Ki. 16:24. However, his was a record of evil—I Ki. 16:25.

Elijah the Tishbite makes his appearance.—Simultaneous with Elijah we get our introduction to Ahab. He was the son of Omri—I Ki. 16:29. He pursued the same policy as his father, forming alliances to check the aggression of the Aramæans in north Galilee. His greatest mistake was his marriage to Jezebel, daughter of the Sidonian king. She was permitted to raise shrines to her native deities, Melkart and Ashtarte of Tyre—I Ki. 16:32, 33. On account of this Baal-worship Elijah called down a famine upon Ahab's country—I Ki. Chs. 17 and 18. His expostulation with Ahab—I Ki. 18: 16–19. The issue on Mount Carmel—I Ki. 18:20–40. The drought, after continuing 3½ years (Jas. 5:17), comes to a close—I Ki. 18:41–46. Ahab and Jezebel seize Naboth's vineyard (I Ki. 21:1–16), which is the cause of their violent death—I Ki. 21:17–24.

Conflicts of Israel with Syria.—Benhadad makes war with Ahab and is defeated—I Ki. 20:26–30. Ahab and Jehoshaphat form an alliance against Syria—I Ki. 22:1–4, 29. Ahab killed in battle—I Ki. 22:34–37. King of Syria attempts war with Israel, but is diverted from this by Elisha—II Ki. 6:24–33; 7:1–7.

Ahaziah, son of Ahab, king over Israel for two years.—Worshipped Baal—I Ki. 22:51–53. Inquires of Baal and is rebuked by Elijah—II Ki. 1:1–4. Sends messengers to Elijah. Fire from heaven consumes messengers—II Ki. 1:9–16. Ahaziah dies—II Ki. 1:17.

Jehoram, son of Ahab, becomes king of Israel.—II Ki. 1:17. An evil king, but not as bad as Ahab—II Ki. 3:1–3. Mesha, king of Moab, rebels and is defeated—II Ki. 3:4–27. The widow's oil increased—II Ki. 4:1–7. Elisha and the Shunammite woman—II Ki. 4:8–17. Elisha raises the Shunammites dead son—II Ki. 4:17–37. Naaman healed—II Ki. 5:1–14. Gehazi, the servant of Elisha, punished—II Ki. 5:15–27. King of Syria attempts war with Israel. Elisha interferes. Syrians stricken with blindness—II Ki. 6:1–23. Samaria besieged by Benhadad. Flight of Syrians discovered by lepers—II Ki. 6:24–7:20.

Jehu anointed king over Israel.—II Ki. 9:1–13. Conspires against Joram, and slays him and Ahaziah, king of Judah—II Ki. 9:14–27. He slays Ahab's seventy sons, the brethren of Adaziah and worshippers of Baal—II Ki. 10: 1–28. An idolatrous king—II Ki. 10: 31. His death—II Ki. 10:35. Jehoahaz his son reigns in his stead—II Ki. 10: 35; 13:1. A wicked king. Oppressed by king of Syria—II Ki. 13:1–9.

Jehoash reigns over Israel.—Elisha's last sickness. His sign: the bow and arrows—II Ki. 13:14–19. Wars with Moab and Syria—II . Ki. 13:20–25. War between Amaziah, king of Judah, and Jehoash, king of Israel; Amaziah defeated—II Ki. 14:1–15.

Jeroboam II, son of Jehoash, becomes king over Israel.—Restores border of Israel—II Ki. 14:16, 23–29.

Zechariah, Shallum, Menahem, and Pekahiah rule over Israel.—Evil kings—II Ki. 15:1–23.

Pekah conspires against Pekahiah and slays him and reigns in his stead.—II Ki. 15:23–31.

Hoshea, son of Elah, conspires against Pekah, slays him and becomes king.— II Ki. 15:30; 17:1, 2.

Final punishment of Israel.—Conquered and carried to Assyria—II Ki. Ch. 17. Land repeopled by Assyrians—II Ki. 17:24. After captivity the remnant of Israel joined Judah—II Chr. 30:18–26; 35:18.

Prophecies involving punishment.—I Ki. 14:7–16; 16:1–4; 17:1; 19:15–18; 21: 17–26; 22:14–23; II Ki. 8:1; Is. 9:8–21; 17:3–11; 28:1–4; Hos. 2:1–13; also Chs. 4–14; Amos 2:6–16; 3:9; Jer. 32: 30–32. See PROPHECY.

Concerning restoration.—Jer. 30:1–24; 31:1–34; Hos. 2:16–20; 11:8–11; 13: 13, 14. See PROPHECY, JEWS, JUDAH, PROPHETS, KINGS.

According to the received chronology, the division began 975 B.C., Israel being carried into captivity 721 B.C. and Judah in the year 586 B.C. Recent students prefer 931 B.C. as the date for the division of the kingdom. Asa was contemporary with the first seven kings of Israel. Jehu and Athaliah began to reign in 884 (or, better, 842) B.C., and Samaria was captured by the Assyrians in 722 B.C., which was the sixth year of Hezekiah's reign in Judah. See next page.

ISSACHAR, is'sa-kar. (1) Son of Jacob by Leah.—Gen. 30:18; 35:23; 46: 13, 14; Ex. 1:3; I Chr. 2:1; 7:1.

(2) Tribe of.—Deut. 33:18; Lu. 10:1; I Ki. 4:17; 15:27; I Chr. 12:32, 40. Numbering and division of land—Num. 1: 8, 28–29; 34:26. Encampment of— Num. 2:5. Inheritance—Josh. 17:10, 11; 19:17–23; 21:6, 28; I Chr. 6:62, 72; Ez. 48:25, 26, 33. Prince of—Num. 7: 18–23; 10:15; 13:7; 34:26; I Chr. 27: 18. Stand on Mt. Gerizim—Deut. 27: 12. Assist Deborah against Sisera— Ju. 5:15. Insurgents join David—I Chr. 12:32, 33. Join with kingdom of Judah at passover—II Chr. 30:18. Strength when leaving Egypt, 54,000

—Num. 1:28, 29. Strength when entering Canaan, 64,300. Number given in "Chronicles," 87,000. Did not cleanse themselves—II Chr. 30:18.

(3) A porter of the tabernacle in time of David.—I Chr. 26:5.

ISSHIAH, is-shī'ah. I Chr. 7:3; 24:21.

ISSUE. Is. 22:24; 39:7; Ez. 23:20. Blood, Of—Mt. 9:20; Mk. 5:25; Lu. 8:43, 44. Cleansing of—Lev. 15:2–33; 22:4; Num. 5:2. Fiery stream—Dan. 7:10. Hezekiah, Of—II Ki. 20:18. Jacob, Of—Gen. 48:6. Leper, Of— Lev. 22:4; Num. 5:2; II Sam. 3:29. Life, Of—Pr. 4:23; Heb. 13:7. Water —Job 38:8; Ez. 47:1, 8, 12.

ITALIAN. Cornelius—Acts 10:1.

ITALY. Acts 18:2; 27:1, 6; Heb. 13:24.

ITCH. Deut. 28:27.

ITCHING. Ears—II Tim. 4:3.

ITHAI, ī'thāi. One of David's warriors.—I Chr. 11:31.

ITHAMAR, ĭth'a-mar. Youngest son of Aaron—Son of Aaron and Elisheba— Ex. 6:23; 28:1; 38:21; Num. 3:2; I Chr. 24:1. Descendants of—I Chr. 24: 1–19. Forbidden to mourn for Nadab and Abihu—Lev. 10:6. Moses' anger against—Lev. 10:16.

Offices of.—Ministered in the priest's office—Ex. 28:1; Num. 3:4. Chief of the Gershonites and Merarites—Num. 4:28, 33; 7:8. Treasurer of the offerings for tabernacle—Ex. 38:21.

ITHIEL, ĭth'i-el. (1) Pr. 30:1. A Benjamite.—Neh. 11:7.

ITHMAH, ĭth'mah. A Moabite.—I Chr. 11:46.

ITHNAN, ĭth'nan. A town in Judah.— Josh. 15:23.

ITHRA, ĭth'rà. Father of Amasa.—II Sam. 17:25.

ITHRAN, ĭth'ran. (1) Son of Zophah.— I Chr. 7:37.

(2) Son of Deshon.—Gen. 36:26; I Chr. 1:41.

ITHREAM, ĭth're-ăm. Son of David.— II Sam. 3:5; 1 Chr. 3:3.

ITHRITES. II Sam. 23:38; I Chr. 2:53; 11:40.

ITSELF. Bear fruit of—John 15:4. Creation—Rom. 8:21. Dieth of—Lev. 7:24; 17:15; 22:8; Deut. 14:21; Ez. 4:14; 44:31. Groweth of—Lev. 25: 11; Is. 37:30. Heart reveal—Pr. 18:2.

CONTEMPORARY KINGS AND PROPHETS OF ISRAEL AND JUDAH.

The figures in parentheses indicate number of years of reign.

Kings of Israel.	Prophets of Israel.	Kings of Judah.	Prophets of Judah.
Jeroboam (22), I Ki. 14: 20.	Ahijah.	Reboboam (17), I Ki. 14:21.	Shemaiah.
Nadab (2), I Ki. 15:25.		Abijah (3), I Ki. 15:2.	
Baasha (24), I Ki. 15:33.	Hanani.	Asa (41), I Ki. 15:10.	Azariah.
Elah (2), I Ki. 16:6, 8. Zimri (7 days), I Ki. 16: 15.			
Omri (12), I Ki. 16:23.			
Ahab (22), I Ki. 16:29.	Elijah. Jehu, son of Hanani.	Jehoshaphat (25), I Ki. 22:42.	
Ahaziah (2), I Ki. 22:40, 51.		Jehoram (8), II Ki. 8:17.	
Jehoram (12), II Ki. 1: 17; 3:1.	Elisha.	Ahaziah (1), II Ki. 8: 25, 26. Athaliah [usurper (6)], II Ki. 11:1-3.	
Jehu (28), II Ki. 9:13; 10:36.		Joash (40), II Ki. 12:1.	Joel, 830-810.
Jehoahaz (17), II Ki. 10: 35; 13:1.	Jonah, about 800.		
Jehoash (16), II Ki. 13: 10.		Amaziah (29), II Ki. 14:2.	
Jeroboam II (41), II Ki. 14:23.	Amos, about 760.		
		Uzziah (52), II Ki. 15:2.	
Zechariah (6 months), II Ki. 14:29; 15:8. Shallum (1 month), II Ki. 15:13, 17. Pekahiah (2), II Ki. 15: 23.	Hosea, about 750-725.		
Pekah (20), II Ki. 15:27; Is. 7:1.			
		Jotham (16), II Ki. 15: 32, 33.	Isaiah from the reign of Uzziah to reign of Manasseh, about 740-695.
Hoshea (9), II Ki. 15:30; 17:1.			
Menahem (10), II Ki. 15:14-17.		Ahaz (16), II Ki. 16:1-2.	
		Hezekiah (29), II Ki. 18: 1-8.	Micah, about 735-700. From the reign of Jotham to that of Hezekiah.
		Manasseh (55), II Ki. 21:1-9.	
		Amon (2), II Ki. 21:18-20.	Nahum [?], about 640-610.
		Josiah (31), II Ki. 22: 1-2.	Zephaniah. about 630.
		Jehoahaz (3 months), II Ki. 23:31. Jehoiakim (11), II Ki. 23:36. Jehoiachin (3 months), II Ki. 24:8. Zedekiah (11), II Ki. 24: 18.	Jeremiah, about 628-585. Habakkuk, during the reign of Jehoiakim, about 609-600.

299

Heaven—Heb. 9:24. Kingdom divided against—Mt. 12:25; Lu. 11:17. Lift up—Ez. 17:14; 29:15. Love—I Cor. 13:4, 5. Morrow, Be anxious for —Mt. 6:34. Nature—I Cor. 11:14. Showeth—Pr. 27:25. Truth—III John 12. World—John 21:25.

ITTAI, ĭt'tāi. (1) A Philistine in David's army.—II Sam. 15:19–22; 18:2, 5, 12.

(2) A Benjamite.—II Sam. 23:29. See ITHAI.

ITURÆA, it'u-ræ'a. Tetrarchy of Philip. —Lu. 3:1.

IVORY. Solomon's throne made of—I Ki. 10:18; II Chr. 9:17. House of— Amos 3:15. Ahab built house of—I Ki. 22:39. Importation of—I Ki. 10: 22; II Chr. 9:21; Ez. 27:15. Palaces of—Ps. 45:8. Type of beauty—Song of Sol. 5:14; 7:4. Benches of—Ez. 27:6. Beds of—Amos 6:4. Vessels of —Rev. 18:12.

IVVAH, ĭv'vah. A district in Babylonia.—II Ki. 18:34; 19:13; Is. 37:13.

IYIM, ĭ'yĭm. Num. 33:4.

IZHAR, ĭz'här. Son of Kolath.—Ex. 6: 18, 21; Num. 3:19; 16:1; I Chr. 6:2, 18, 38; 23:12, 18.

IZHARITES. Num. 3:27; I Chr. 24:22; 26:23, 29.

IZRAHIAH, ĭz'ra-hī'ah. Grandson of Tola the son of Issachar.—I Chr. 7:3.

IZRAHITE. II Chr. 27:8.

IZRI, ĭz'rī. A Levite.—I Chr. 25:11.

JAAKAN, jā'a-kăn. Deut. 10:6; I Chr. 1:42.

JAAKOBAH, jā'a-kō'bah. A prince of Simeon.—I Chr. 4:36.

JAALA, ja-ā'lä. One of Solomon's servants.—Neh. 7:58.

JAALAH, ja-ā'lah. Ezra 2:56.

JAARE-OREGIM, jā'a-re-ŏr'e-gim. Father of Elhanan.—II Sam. 21:19.

JAARESHIAH, jā'a-rē-shiäh. I Chr. 8: 27.

JAASIEL, jā'a-sī'el. (1) Son of Abner. —I Chr. 27:21.

(2) One of David's warriors.—I Chr. 11:47.

JAASU, jā'a-su. One of the family of Bani who married a foreign wife.— Ezra 10:37.

JAAZANIAH, ja-ăz'a-nī'ah. (1) A Maachathite captain.—II Ki. 25:23.

(2) A Rechabite.—Jer. 35:3.

(3) Ez. 8:11.

(4) Ez. 11:1.

JAAZIAH, jā'a-zī'ah. I Chr. 24:26.

JAAZIEL, ja-ā'zi-el. I Chr. 15:18.

JABAL, jā'bal. Son of Adah and Lamech.—Gen. 4:20.

JABBOK, jăb'bok. A brook flowing into the Jordan between the Dead Sea and the Sea of Tiberias.—Gen. 32:22; Num. 21:24; Deut. 2:37; 3:16; Josh. 12:2; Ju. 11:13, 22.

JABESH-GILEAD, jā'besh-gĭl'e-ad (a town of Manasseh, east of Jordan). Smitten by Israelites for not joining in war against Benjamin—Ju. 21:8– 12. Besieged by Nahash and relieved by Saul—I Sam. 11:1–11. Valiant men of, bury Saul—I Sam. 31:11–13; II Sam. 2:4–7; 21:14; I Chr. 10:12.

JABEZ, jā'bez. (1) A city of Judah.— I Chr. 2:55.

(2) A man of Judah.—I Chr. 4:9, 10.

JABIN, jā'bin. (1) A king of Hazor who oppressed Israel.—Ju. 4:2, 7, 17, 23, 24; Ps. 83:9.

(2) Another king of Hazor defeated by Joshua.—Josh. 11:1.

JABNEEL, jăb'ne-el. (1) A city of Judah.—Josh. 15:11.

(2) A city of Naphtali.—Josh. 19:33.

JABNEH, jăb'neh. A Philistine city.— II Chr. 26:6.

JACAN, ja-kan. A Gadite.—I Chr. 5:13.

JACHIN, jā-kin. (1) Son of Simeon.— Gen. 46:10; Ex. 6:15; Num. 26:12.

(2) A pillar in Solomon's temple.—I Ki. 7:21; II Chr. 3:17.

(3) A priest.—I Chr. 9:10; Neh. 11:10.

(4) A Levite. I Chr. 24:17.

JACHINITE. Num. 26:12.

JACINTH. Rev. 9:17; 21:20.

JACKAL. See ANIMALS.

JACOB, Heb. ''Supplanter.''—According to others, ''re-enforcement,'' ''straggler.''

Son of Isaac and Rebekah.—Gen. 25:26. Took Esau by heel—Gen. 25:26; Hos. 12:3. Given in answer to prayer— Gen. 25:21. A quiet man dwelling in tents—Gen. 25:27.

Tricked Esau out of birthright.—Gen. 25:29–34. At Rebekah's suggestion he obtained Esau's blessing—Gen. 27: 1–38. Fled from anger of Esau to

Paddan-aram—Gen. 27:41–46. Took Isaac's blessing with him—Gen. 28: 1–5. Jacob's vision by the way—Gen. 28:12–22; Hos. 12:4; John 1:51. **Coming to Haran, meets Rachel.**—Gen. 29:19. Laban employs him as a shepherd—Gen. 29:14–15. Jacob stipulates for Rachel as his wages—Gen. 29:18–21. Laban breaking contract, gives him Leah—Gen. 29:23. Jacob serves seven years more after marrying Rachel—Gen. 29:25–30. Children are born to Jacob by Leah, Rachel, Bilhah and Zilpah—Gen. 30:1–25. Angry at Rachel—Gen. 30:2. By craft, Jacob secures large flocks—Gen. 30:31–43. Laban becoming jealous, Jacob returns to Canaan—Gen. 31:1–21. Laban pursues—Gen. 31:22–35. Meets angels on the way—Gen. 32:1–2. Sends messengers to pacify Esau—Gen. 32:9–12. Sends present to Esau—Gen. 32:13–21. Wrestles with angel at Jabbok—Gen. 32:24–32; Hos. 12:3–4. **Name becomes Israel.**—Gen. 32:28. Wins Esau and they are reconciled—Gen. 33:1–16. Purchases ground at Shechem and rears altar—Gen. 33:18–20; Josh. 24:32. **Shechem defiles Dinah.**—Gen. 34:1–3. Jacob refers act to his sons—Gen. 34:5. Hamor, the father, asks Dinah for a wife—Gen. 34:6–12. Jacob's sons propose circumcision and slay entire family of males—Gen. 34:15–29. Reserve wives and stock—Gen. 34:28, 29. Jacob vainly protests—Gen. 34:30. **God orders Jacob to return to Bethel.**—Gen. 35:1. Puts away foreign gods and builds altar—Gen. 35:2–7. Erects pillar—Gen. 35:14. God renews covenant with Jacob there. Benjamin is born, but Rachel dies—Gen. 35:16–19. Pillar erected upon Rachel's grave—Gen. 35:20. Visits his father Isaac—Gen. 35:27. **Partiality for Joseph and the result.**—Gen. 37:1–24. Joseph sold and carried to Egypt—Gen. 37:25–36. **Famine drove Jacob to send to Egypt.**—Gen. 42:1, 2. Negotiations for food—Gen. Chs. 42 and 43. Jacob is sent for—Gen. 45:16–28; 46:1–7; Josh. 24: 4; I Sam. 12:8. Settles in Goshen—Gen. 45:28. List of sons and children going to Egypt—Gen. 46:8–27; Ex. 1: 1–5. Jacob blesses Pharaoh—Gen. 47: 1–10. Lives in Egypt seventeen years—Gen. 47:1–12, 28. Before passing away, Jacob blesses his children, prophesying—Gen. Ch. 49; Heb. 11: 21. Jacob lived to be 147 years of age—Gen. 47:28. Joseph and sons visit Jacob—Gen. 48:1–22. Jacob dies and is buried with his fathers—Gen. 49: 29–33; 50:1–13.

Sons of Jacob furnish basis of covenant relation destined to possess land of Canaan.—Gen. Chs. 48 and 49; Deut. 4:37; 7:8.

God makes covenant with Jacob.—Gen. 28:13–15; 35:9–12; 48:4; Ex. 2:24; 6: 8; 33:1; Lev. 26:42; Num. 32:11; Deut. 1:8; 6:10; 9:5; 29:13; 30:20; 34:4; II Ki. 13:23; Ps. 105:10.

Tribes of Israel took names of sons of Jacob.—Gen. 35:23–26; 46:8–27; 49:1–22; Ex. 6:14–25; I Ki. 18:31; I Chr. Ch. 2.

Israelites called Jacob.—Num. 23:7, 10; 24:5, 17, 19; 32:1; Deut. 32:9; 33:4, 10, 28; I Chr. 16:17; Ps. 14:7; 24:6; 44:4; 53:6; 78:5, 21, 71; 79:7; 99:4; 105:23; 135:4; 147:19; Nah. 2:2; Mal. 2:12. Children of Jacob—II Ki. 17:34; I Chr. 16:13; Ps. 105:6. Called house of Jacob—Ex. 19:3. Seed of Jacob—Ps. 20:1; 22:23. Sons of Jacob—Ps. 77: 15; Mal. 3:6. Tribes of the sons of Jacob—I Ki. 18:31.

God loved Jacob rather than Esau.—Mal. 1:2.

Jacob typical of the Gentiles.—Is. 49: 6, 7; Mal. 1:1–15; Rom. 9:9–33; 11: 25–32.

New Testament references.—Acts 7:8, 12, 15, 32, 46; Rom. 9:13; 11:26. Abraham, Isaac, and Jacob in the Kingdom of God—Mt. 8:11; Lu. 13:28. Jacob's well—John 4:5, 6, 12.

Father of Joseph, the husband of Mary.—Mt. 1:15, 16.

JADA, jā′dȧ. **Grandson of Jerahmeel.**—I Chr. 2:28, 32.

JADDUA, jad-dū′ȧ. (1) **A descendant of Jeshua the high priest.**—Neh. 12: 11, 22.

(2) **A Levite who helped to seal the covenant.**—Neh. 10:21.

JADON, jā′don. One who helped to repair the wall.—Neh. 3:7.

JAEL, jā′el. Wife of Heber, who slays Sisera.—Ju. 4:17–22; 5:6, 24.

JAGUR, jā′gur. A town in Judah.— Josh. 15:21.

JAHATH, jā′hăth. (1) A descendant of Gershom.—I Chr. 6:20, 43.

(2) A descendant of Shobal.—I Chr. 4:2.

(3) A Levite.—I Chr. 23:10, 11.

(4) Descendant of Kohath.—I Chr. 24: 22.

(5) A descendant of Merari.—II Chr. 34:12.

JAHAZ, jā′hăz. A town of Moab.— Josh. 13:18; 21:36; Is. 15:4. Scene of battle.—Num. 21:23; Deut. 2:32; Ju. 11:20. Prophecy.—Jer. 48:21, 34.

JAHAZIEL, ja-hā′zi-el. (1) A priest.— I Chr. 16:6.

(2) One of those who joined David at Ziklag.—I Chr. 12:4.

(3) Son of Hebron.—I Chr. 23:19; 24:23.

(4) A Levite.—II Chr. 20:14.

(5) Ezra 8:5.

JAHDAI, jäh′dāi. A descendant of Caleb the spy.—I Chr. 2:27.

JAHDIEL, jäh′di-el. A man of Manasseh.—I Chr. 5:24.

JAHDO, jäh′do. I Chr. 5:14.

JAHLEEL, jäh′le-el. Son of Zebulun.— Gen. 46:14; Num. 26:26.

JAHMAI, jäh′māi. A grandson of Issachar.—I Chr. 7:2.

JAHZAH, jäh′zah. A city of Reuben.— I Chr. 6:78.

JAHZEEL, jäh′ze-el. Son of Naphtali. —Gen. 46:24; Num. 26:48; I Chr. 7:13.

JAHZEIAH, jäh′ze-iäh. Ezra 10:15.

JAHZERAH, jäh′ze-rah. A priest.—I Chr. 9:12.

JAHZIEL, jäh′zi-el. I Chr. 7:13.

JAIL. See Prison.

JAILOR. Conversion of.—Acts 16:25–34.

JAIR, jā′ir. (1) Num. 32:41; Deut. 3: 14; I Ki. 4:13; I Chr. 2:22.

(2) A judge of Israel.—Ju. 10:3, 5.

(3) Havoth-jair.—Josh. 13:30; I Chr. 2: 23. See Havoth-jair.

(4) Father of Ethanan.—I Chr. 20:5.

(5) A Benjamite.—Esth. 2:5.

JAIRITE. Descendant of Jair.—II Sam. 20:26.

JAIRUS, ja-ī′rus. A ruler of a synagogue in Galilee whose daughter was healed.—Mk. 5:22; Lu. 8:4.

JAKEH, jā′keh. Father of Agur.—Pr. 30:1.

JAKIM, jā′kim. (1) I Chr. 24:12.

(2) A Benjamite.—I Chr. 8:19.

JALON, jā′lon. A descendant of Caleb the spy.—I Chr. 4:17.

JAMBRES, jăm′brēs. Probably an Egyptian magician.—II Tim. 3:8.

JAMES. (1) Son of Zebedee and probably of Salome. Brother of John the evangelist and probably a cousin of Jesus.—Mt. 4:21; 27:56; Mk. 15:40. A fisherman—Mt. 4:21; Mk. 1:19; Lu. 5:1–10. Called from his nets to follow Jesus—Mt. 4:21, 22; Mk. 1:19, 20. One of the twelve apostles—Mt. 10:2; Mk. 3: 19; Lu. 6:14; Acts 1:13. With Jesus, Peter and John: *At the transfiguration* —Mt. 17:1–8; Mk. 9:2–8; Lu. 9:28–36. *At the healing of Jairus's daughter*— Mk. 5:37; 8:51. *At Gethsemane*—Mt. 26:37; Mk. 14:33. *On Mount of Olives* —Mk. 13:3. Called ''Boanerges'' or ''Son of thunder'' by Jesus—Mk. 3: 17. With John, seeks a prominent place in the new kingdom—Mk. 10: 35–41. See Mt. 20:20–28. Asks Jesus to bring down fire from heaven to slay Samaritans—Lu. 9:51–54. Slain by Herod—Acts 12:2.

(2) The son of Alphæus (probably Clopas of John 19:25)—Lu. 6:16. His mother was Mary, one of the women who stood around the cross of Jesus. He is called ''the Less,'' or ''the Little''—Mk. 15:40. Brother of Joses —Mk. 15:40; 16:1; John 19:25.

(3) Father of Judas the apostle (not Iscariot)—Lu. 6:16. See Apostles.

(4) The brother of Jesus—See ''Epistle of James'' in Outline Studies in the Books.

JAMIN, jā′min. (1) Son of Simeon.— Gen. 46:10; Ex. 6:15; Num. 26:12; I Chr. 4:24.

(2) Descendant of Hezron.—I Chr. 2:27.

(3) A priest who assisted in explaining the law.—Neh. 8:7.

JAMINITES. Descendants of Jamin.— I Chr. 4:34.

JAMLECH, jăm′lek. I Chr. 4:34.

JANIM, jā′nim. A city.—Josh. 15:53.

JANNAI, jăn'na-i. An ancestor of Joseph, the husband of Mary.—Lu. 3:24.

JANNES, jăn'nēs. An Egyptian magician.—II Tim. 3:8.

JANOAH, ja-nō'ah. A town in Naphtali.—Josh. 16:6, 7; II Ki. 15:29.

JAPHETH, jā'pheth. From *pathah*, "to extend," enlargement.

One of Noah's three sons.—Gen. 10:1.

Descendants of Japheth.—Gen. 10:2-5; I Chr. 1:5-7. Gomer (Cymri or Celts); Magog (Scythians and Slavonians); Medai (Medes or Aryans); Javan (Ionians or Greeks); Tubal (the Tibareni); Meshech (the Moschi); Tirans (the Thracians or Teutons).

Divided the honor with Shem in filial treatment—Gen. 9:23. Blessed by Noah—Gen. 9:27.

JAPHIA, ja-phī'a. (1) A town near Carmel.—Josh. 19:12.

(2) King of Lachish.—Josh. 10:3.

(3) Son of David.—II Sam. 5:15; I Chr. 3:7; 14:6.

JAPHLET, jăph'let. Grandson of Beriah.—I Chr. 7:32, 33.

JAPHLETITES. Josh. 16:3.

JAR. See VESSELS.

JARAH, jā'rah. A Benjamite.—I Chr. 9:42.

JAREB, jā'reb. A name given to the king of Assyria.—Hos. 5:13; 10:6.

JARED, jā'red. (1) A descendant of Seth.—Gen. 5:15-20.

(2) An ancestor of Jesus.—Lu. 3:37.

JARHA, jär-hȧ. An Egyptian servant.—I Chr. 8:27.

JARIB, jā'rib. (1) Son of Simeon.—I Chr. 4:24.

(2) A priest who married a foreign wife.—Ezra 10:18.

(3) One who returned with Ezra.—Ezra 8:16.

JARMUTH, jär'muth. (1) A city in Judah.—Josh. 10:3, 5, 23; 12:11; 15:35; Neh. 11:29.

(2) A city in Issachar.—Josh. 21:29.

JAROAH, ja-rō'ah. A Gadite.—I Chr. 5:14.

JASHAR, jā'shär. Book of.—Josh. 10:13; II Sam. 1:18.

JASHEN, jā'shen. II Sam. 23:32.

JASHOBEAM, ja-shō'be-ăm. (1) One of David's captains.—I Chr. 11:11; 27:2.

(2) A descendant of Kohath.—I Chr. 12:6.

JASHUB, jā'shub. (1) Son of Issachar.—Num. 26:24; I Chr. 7:1.

(2) One of the family of Bani who married a foreign wife.—Ezra 10:29.

JASHUBI-LEHEM, jăsh'u-bī-lē'hem. A descendant of Shelah.—I Chr. 4:22.

JASHUBITES. Descendants of Jashub, son of Issachar.—Num. 26:24.

JASON, jā'son. (1) A disciple in Thessalonica.—Acts 17:5-9.

(2) A kinsman of Paul's whom Paul salutes.—Rom. 16:21.

JASPER. See PRECIOUS STONES.

JATHNIEL, jăth'ni-el. I Chr. 26:2.

JATTIR, jăt'tir. A Levitical city in Judah.—Josh. 15:48; 21:14; I Sam. 30:27; I Chr. 6:57.

JAVAN, jā'van. (1) Son of Japheth.—Gen. 10:2, 4; I Chr. 1:5, 7.

(2) Descendants of Japheth and land of.—Is. 66:19.

(3) A city in Arabia.—Ez. 27:13, 19.

JAVELIN. Josh. 8:18; I Sam. 17:6, 45; Job 41:29. See WEAPONS.

JAW. Ass, Samson slays Philistines with jawbone of—Ju. 15:15-17. Bridle in jaws of people—Is. 30:28. Hooks in—Ez. 29:4; 38:4. Leviathan, Of the —Job 41:2. Teeth as knives—Pr. 30:14. Tongue cleaveth to—Ps. 22:15. Unrighteous, Of the—Job 29:17. Yoke on—Hos. 11:4. See TEETH.

JAZER, jā'zer. Num. 32:1.

JAZIZ, jā'ziz. I Chr. 27:30.

JEALOUSY. Motherly.—Gen. 30:1.

National.—II Ki. 5:12; Lu. 9:52-53.

Implacable.—Pr. 6:34-35; Song of Sol. 8:6; I Sam. 18:28.

Fraternal.—Ju. 8:1-3; II Sam. 19:43; Mt. 20:23-24; Lu. 15:28; II Cor. 11:2.

Ordeal of.—Num. 5:11-31; Pr. 6:34.

Of Jehovah.—Ex. 20:5; 34:14; Deut. 4:24; 5:9; 6:15; 29:20; 32:16, 21; Josh. 24:19; Ez. 39:25; Joel 2:18; Nah. 1:2; I Ki. 14:22; Ps. 78:58; 79:5; Ez. 16:42; 23:25; 36:5-6; 38:19; 39:25; Joel 2:18; Nah. 1:2; Zeph. 1:18; 3:8.

For Jehovah.—I Ki. 19:10, 14; Num. 25:11.

For Jerusalem.—Zech. 1:14; 8:2; Ez. 8:3, 5.

Free from jealousy.—Moses—Num. 11:28. Paul—Phil. 1:15-18.

Provoked to.—Rom. 10:19; 11:11; Gal. 1:8–9; I Cor. 10:22.

Character of.—Song of Sol. 8:6; Ez. 16:38.

Condemned.—Rom. 13:14; I Cor. 3:3; II Cor. 12:20; Gal. 5:20; Jas. 3:14–16. See ENVY.

JEARIM, jē'a-rim. A hill.—Josh. 15:10.

JEATHERAI, je-ăth'e-rāi. A Levite.— I Chr. 6:21.

JEBERECHIAH, je-bĕr'e-kī'ah. Father of Zechariah.—Is. 8:2.

JEBUS, jē'bus. An early name of Jerusalem.—Josh. 18:16, 28; Ju. 19:10, 11; I Chr. 11:4, 5.

JEBUSITES. Descendants of Caanan, the son of Ham, who lived in and around Jebus.—Gen. 10:16; 15:21; Ex. 3:8; 13:5; 23:23; 33:2; 34:11; Num. 13:29; Deut. 7:1; 20:17; Josh. 3:10; 9:1; 11:3; 12:8; 15:8, 63; 24:11; Ju. 1:21; 3:5; 19:11; II Sam. 5:6, 8; 24:16, 18; I Ki. 9:20; I Chr. 1:14; 11:4, 6; 21:15, 18, 28; II Chr. 3:1; 8:7; Ezra 9:1; Neh. 9:8; Zech. 9:7. See JERUSALEM.

JECHILIAH, jĕk'i-lī'ah. Mother of Uzziah, king of Judah.—II Chr. 26:3.

JECHOLIAH, jĕk'o-lī'ah. Mother of Azariah, king of Judah.—II Ki. 15:2.

JECHONIAH, jĕk-o-nī'ah. Son of Josiah, king of Judah.—Mt. 1:11.

JECONIAH, jĕk'o-nī'ah. I Chr. 3:16. See JEHOIACHIN.

JEDAIAH, je-dā'iah. (1) A Simeonite. —I Chr. 4:37.

(2) One of those who helped to rebuild the wall.—Neh. 3:10.

(3) Ancestor of priests.—I Chr. 9:10; 24:7; Ezra 2:38; Neh. 7:39; 11:10; 12:6, 7, 19.

(4) Another priest.—Neh. 12:7, 21.

(5) One who returned from exile.—6:9, 14.

JEDIAEL, je-dī'a-el. (1) A Benjamite. —I Chr. 7:6.

(2) One of David's mighty men.—I Chr. 11:45; 12:20.

(3) A doorkeeper.—I Chr. 26:2.

JEDIDAH, je-dī'dah. Mother of Amon, king of Judah.—II Ki. 22:1.

JEDIDIAH, jĕd'i-dī'ah. God's name for Solomon.—II Sam. 12:25.

JEDUTHUN, je-dū'thun. A singer in the sanctuary in the time of David.—

I Chr. 9:16; 38; 25:1; II Chr. 5:12; 29:14; 35:15; Neh. 11:17.

JEGAR-SAHADUTHA, jĕ'gar–sā'ha-dū'tha. Gen. 31:47.

JEHALELEEL, je-hăl-el-ē'el. (1) A descendant of Caleb.—I Chr. 4:16.

(2) A Levite.—II Chr. 29:12.

JEHDEIAH, jeh-dē'iah. (1) An overseer under David.—I Chr. 27:50.

(2) A Levite.—I Chr. 24:20.

JEHEZKEL, je-hĕz'kĕl. I Chr. 24:16. See EZEKIEL.

JEHIAH, je-hī'ah. A doorkeeper.—I Chr. 15:24.

JEHIEL, je-hī'el. (1) Son of Jehoshaphat.—II Chr. 21:2.

(2) An officer under David.—I Chr. 27:32.

(3) A priest.—II Chr. 35:8.

(4) Ancestor of Levite family.—I Chr. 23:8; 26:21.

(5) Father of Obadiah.—Ezra 8:9.

(6) Ezra 10:2, 26.

(7, 8) Two Levites.—I Chr. 15:18, 20; 16:5; II Chr. 31:13.

(9) A priest.—Ezra 10:21.

JEHIELI, je-hī'e-li. I Chr. 26:21. See JEHIEL (4).

JEHIZKIAH, jĕ'hiz-kī'ah. A prince of Ephraim—II Chr. 28:12.

JEHOADDAH, jē'ho-ad-dah. I Chr. 8:36.

JEHOADDIN, jē'ho-ăd-din. Wife of king Jehoach.—II Ki. 14:2.

JEHOAHAZ, je-hō'a-hăz. (1) Son of Jehu.—King of Israel—II Ki. 10:35; 13:1. Delivered from the Syrians—II Ki. 13:3–7. Death—II Ki. 13:9. Record of his deeds—II Ki. 13:8. Descendants of—II Ki. 13:10; 14:1, 8, 17; II Chr. 25:17, 25.

(2) Son of Josiah.—King of Judah.—II Ki. 23:30, 31; II Chr. 36:1. Character of—II Ki. 23:32. Deposed by Pharaoh-necoh—II Ki. 23:33–34; II Chr. 36:3, 4.

(3) Son of Jehoram.—II Chr. 21:17. Father of Joash—II Chr. 25:23.

JEHOASH, je-hō'ash. (1) Called Joash —II Ki. 11:2; 12:1, 2, 4–7, 18; 13:1; II Chr. 22:11. Rescued—II Ki. 11:2, 3. King at seven—II Ki. 11:4–16, 21; II Chr. 23:1–11. Reformation—II Ki. 11:17. Not complete—II Ki. 12:3; II Chr. 24:18–22. Syrians executed judgment on him—II Chr. 24:23, 24. Slain by his servants—II Ki. 12:20; II Chr. 24:25, 26.

(2) **Son of Jehoahaz.**—King of Israel—II Ki. 13:9, 25; 14:9, 11, 13. Reigned in Samaria sixteen years—II Ki. 13:10. Called Joash—II Ki. 13:12-14. Visited Elisha on deathbed—II Ki. 13:14-19. Smote the Syrians—II Ki. 13:22-25. Defeated king of Judah and took Jerusalem—II Ki. 14:8-14. Record of his deeds—II Ki. 14:15. Burial of—II Ki. 14:16. Descendants of—II Ki. 14:17.

(3) **Son of Becher.**—I Chr. 7:8.

(4) **A keeper under David.**—I Chr. 27:28.

(5) **Father of Gideon.**—Ju. 6:11.

(6) **Son of Ahab.**—I Ki. 22:26.

(7) **One of David's warriors.**—I Chr. 12:3.

(8) **A man of Judah.**—I Chr. 4:22.

JEHOHANAN, jĕ'ho-hā'nan. (1) **A captain under Jehoshaphat.**—II Chr. 17:15.

(2) **A gatekeeper of the tabernacle under David.**—I Chr. 26:3.

(3) **One of those who married foreign wives.**—Ezra 10:28.

(4) **A priest in the days of Nehemiah.**—Neh. 12:42.

(5) **A priest under Jehoiakim.** — Neh. 12:13.

JEHOIACHIN, je-hoi'a-kĭn. Son of Jehoiakim—II Ki. 25:6. King of Judah—II Ki. 25:8, 12, 27; II Chr. 36:9. Captivity of—II Ki. 25:15, 27; Jer. 52:31; Ez. 1:2. Records of his deeds—II Chr. 36:8.

JEHOIADA, je-hoi'a-dȧ. **The father of Benaiah, one of David's officers.**—II Sam. 8:18; 20:23; 23:22; I Ki. 1:8, 26, 32, 36, 38, 44; 2:25, 29, 34, 35, 46; 4:4; I Chr. 11:22, 24; 18:17; 27:5.

(2) **High priest.**—Recovers the throne of Judah for Joash. Causes Athaliah to be put to death—II Ki. Ch. 11; II Chr. Ch. 23.

Assists Joash in repairing temple—II Ki. 12:4-16; II Chr. 24:4-14.

Descendants of—II Chr. 24:20, 25.

Good influence on Joash—II Ki. 12:2; I Chr. 24:2, 16, 22.

Delivered weapons to officers—II Chr. 23:9.

Preparations for crowning of Joash—II Chr. 23:11.

Death and burial—II Chr. 24:15, 16.

(3) **A leader of the Aaronites, who joined David at Hebron.**—I Chr. 12:27.

(4) **Son of Benaiah,** the third of David's counsellors—I Chr. 27:34.

(5) **One of the family of Paseah** (called Joida), who repaired a gate of Jerusalem—Neh. 3:6.

(6) **A priest of Jerusalem before the exile,** possibly displaced by Zephaniah—Jer. 29:26.

JEHOIAKIM, je-hoi'a-kĭm. **Son of Josiah.**—II Ki. 23:34, 35; II Chr. 3:15; Jer. 1:3. Name changed—II Ki. 23:34; II Chr. 36:4. King of Judah—II Ki. 23:36; II Chr. 36:5; Jer. 1:3; 22:18; 25:1; 26:1; 27:1; 35:1; 36:1; 45:1. Wickedness of—II Ki. 24:19; Jer. 52:2.

Events of reign.—Slays Uriah—Jer. 26:20-23. Jerusalem seized by Nebuchadrezzar—Dan. 1:1. Burns Jeremiah's roll—Jer. 36:9-32. Servant to Nebuchadrezzar—II Ki. 24:1; Dan. 1:2.

Prophecy concerning.—Jer. 22:18, 24; 24:1.

Records of.—II Ki. 24:5; II Chr. 36:8. Burial of—II Ki. 24:6.

Descendants of.—I Chr. 3:15; Jer. 22:24; 24:1; 27:20; 28:4; 37:1.

JEHOIARIB, je-hoi'a-rĭb. **Name of a course of priests.**—I Chr. 9:10; 24:7; Neh. 12:6.

JEHONADAB, je-hŏn'a-dăb. (1) **Son of Rechab.**—II Ki. 15:15.

(2) **David's nephew.**—II Sam. 13:3-6.

JEHONATHAN, je-hŏn'a-than. II Chr. 17:8; Neh. 12:18. See JONATHAN.

JEHORAM, je-hō'ram. (1) Son of Jehoshaphat—I Ki. 22:50; II Ki. 8:16. King of Judah—II Ki. 8:16; 12:18. Character of—II Chr. 21:6-13. Marries Athaliah, daughter of Ahab—II Ki. 8:18; II Chr. 21:6. Murders his brethren—II Chr. 21:4, 13. Death and burial of—II Chr. 21:18-20. Descendants of—II Ki. 8:25, 29; II Chr. 22:1, 6, 11.

(2) Son of Ahab—II Ki. 1:17; 3:1; II Chr. 22:5, 6. King of Israel—II Ki. 3:1; II Chr. 22:5. Events: League with Judah—II Ki. 3:6-10. War with Moabites—II Ki. 1:1; 3:7-27. War

with Syria—II Ki. 6:8–23. Receives letter from Ben-hadad—II Ki. 5:6. Threatens Elisha on account of famine —II Ki. 6:30, 31. Restores the Shunammite woman's land—II Ki. 8: 4–6. Wages war with Hazael and is wounded—II Ki. 8:28, 29; II Chr. 22: 5, 6. Slain by Jehu—II Ki. 9:14–24.

(3) A priest sent by Jehoshaphat with Elishama to teach Judah—II Chr. 17:8.

JEHOSHABEATH, jē'ho-shăb'e-ăth. **Daughter of King Jehoram and wife of Jehoiada, the priest.**—II Chr. 22: 11. See JEHOSHEBA.

JEHOSHAPHAT, je-hŏsh'a-phăt. (1) David's recorder, son of Ahilud—II Sam. 8:16; 20:24; I Ki. 4:3; I Chr. 18:15.

(2) **Officer of Solomon.**—Son of Paruah —I Ki. 4:17.

(3) **Son of Asa.**—I Ki. 15:24; 22:41; I Chr. 3:10; Mt. 1:8. King of Judah— I Ki. 15:24; 22:41; II Chr. 17:1; 19:2, 4, 8; 20:27, 30, 31. War against Ammonites—II Chr. 20:1–27. War against Syria—I Ki. 22:2–49. Records of—II Chr. 20:34. Fortifies his kingdom against Israel—II Chr. 17:2. Is paid tribute—II Chr. 17:5, 11. League with king of Israel against Moab—II Ki. 3:7–14; II Chr. 18:3, 4, 9, 28–31; 20: 35, 36, 37. Prosperity of—II Chr. 17: 12; 18:1. Loyalty to Jehovah—II Chr. 17:3; 18:6, 7, 17. Exempt from war— II Chr. 17:10. Death and burial—I Ki. 22:50; II Chr. 21:1. Descendants —I Ki. 22:51; II Ki. 1:17; II Chr. 21: 2, 12; 22:9.

(4) **Father of Jehu.**—II Ki. 9:14.

JEHOSHEBA, je-hŏsh'e-bȧ. **Sister of Ahaziah**—See JEHOSHEBEATH.

JEHOVAH. See GOD.

JEHOVAH-JIREH, je-hō'vah–jī'reh. **Jehovah seeth.**—Gen. 22:14.

JEHOVAH-NISSI, je-hō'vah–nĭs'sī. **Jehovah is my banner.**—Ex. 17:15.

JEHOVAH-SHALOM, je-hō'vah–shā'-lom. **Jehovah is peace.**—Ju. 6:24.

JEHOVAH-SHAMMAH, je-hō'vah–shăm'mah. **Jehovah is there.**—Ez. 48: 35 (*marg.*).

JEHOZABAD, jé-hŏz'a-băd. (1) **Son of Obed-edom.**—I Chr. 26:4.

(2) **One of those who slew Joash, king of Judah.**—II Ki. 12:21; 14:5, 6; II Chr. 24:26.

(3) **An officer under Jehoshaphat.**—II Chr. 17:18.

JEHOZADAK, je-hŏz'a-dăk. **A priest who returned with Zerubbabel.**—I Chr. 6:14; Ezra 3:2, 8; Hag. 1:1; Zech. 6:11.

JEHU, jē'hu. (1) **Son of Jehoshaphat.**—Anointed king of Israel—I Ki. 19:16, 17; II Ki. 9:2–13. Conspires against Joram—II Ki. 9:14–26. Wounds Ahaziah, king of Judah—II Ki. 9:16, 21–28. Directs the slaying of Jezebel—9: 30–37. Sends letters to elders of Jezreel—II Ki. 10:1–6. Slays Ahab's sons and followers and Ahaziah's brethren —II Ki. 10:7–17. Slays worshippers of Baal—II Ki. 10:18–28. His sin— II Ki. 10:29–31. His death—II Ki. 10:35.

(2) **Son of Hanani, who denounced Baasha, king of Israel.**—I Ki. 16:1, 7, 12.

(3) **Son of Obed.**—I Chr. 2:38.

(4) **One of David's warriors.**—I Chr. 12:3.

(5) **A Simeonite.**—I Chr. 4:35.

JEHUBBAH, je-hŭb'bah. **A man of Asher.**—I Chr. 7:34.

JEHUCAL, je-hū'cal. **One of Zedekiah's officers.**—Jer. 37:3.

JEHUD, jē'hud. **A city of Dan.**—Josh. 19:45.

JEHUDI, je-hū'di. **An officer under Jehoiakim.**—Jer. 36:14.

JEHUEL, jē'hū-ĕl. **A Levite.**—II Chr. 29:14.

JEIEL, je-ī'el. (1) **One of David's mighty men.**—I Chr. 11:44.

(2) **A Reubenite.**—I Chr. 5:7.

(3) **An ancestor of Saul.**—I Chr. 9:35.

(4) **A Levite.**—I Chr. 15:18, 21; 16:5; II Chr. 20:14.

(5) **Another Levite.**—II Chr. 35:9.

(6) **A scribe.**—II Chr. 26:11.

(7) Ezra 10:4, 3.

JEKABZEEL, je-kăb'ze-el. Neh. 11:25. See KABZEEL.

JEKAMEAM, jĕk'a-mē'am. **Head of a Levite family.**—I Chr. 23:19; 24:23.

JEKAMIAH, jĕk-a-mī'ah. (1) **A descendant of Jerahmeel.**—I Chr. 2:41.

(2) **A descendant of David.**—I Chr. 3:18.

JEKUTHIEL, je-kū'thi-el. **A descendant of Caleb.**—I Chr. 4:18.

JEMIMAH, je-mī'mah. **Job's daughter.** —Job 42:14.

JEMUEL, jĕm'u-el. Gen. 46:10.

JEOPARDY. II Sam. 23:17; Lu. 8:23; I Cor. 15:30.

JEPHTHAH, jĕph'thah. **A judge of Israel.**—Son of a harlot—Ju. 11:1, 2. Led a band of outlaws—Ju. 11:3. Elders of Gilead ask him to lead them against the Ammonites—Ju. 11:4–11. Message sent to Ammonite king—Ju. 11:12–28. Victory over the Ammonites —Ju. 11:29, 32, 33. His vow—Ju. 11: 30, 31, 34–40. Fights Ephraim—Ju. 12:1–6. Judge Israel seven years— Ju. 12:7. Death—Ju. 12:7.

JEPHUNNEH, je-phŭn'neh. (1) **Caleb's father.**—Num. 13:6.

(2) **An Asherite.**—I Chr. 7:38.

JERAH, jē'rah. Son of Joktan—Gen. 10:26; I Chr. 1:20.

JERAHMEEL, je-räh'me-el. (1) I Sam. 27:10; 30:29; I Chr. 2:9, 25, 27, 33, 42.

(2) **Son of Jehoiakim, king of Judah.**— Jer. 36:26.

(3) **A family of Levites.**—I Chr. 24:29.

JERED, jē'red. I Chr. 4:18.

JEREMAI, jĕr'e-mãi. Ezra 10:33.

JEREMIAH, jĕr'e-mī'ah. (1) See OUT-LINE STUDIES IN THE BOOKS.

(2) **Father-in-law of Josiah and grandfather of Jehoahaz and Zedekiah.**—II Ki. 23:31; 24:18.

(3) **A man of Manasseh.**—I Chr. 5:24.

(4) **A Benjamite who joined David at Ziklag.**—I Chr. 12:4.

(5, 6) **Two Gadites.**—I Chr. 12:10, 13.

(7) **A priest who returned with Zerubbabel.**—Neh. 10:2; 12:1, 34.

(8) **A Rechabite.**—Jer. 35:3.

JEREMOTH, jĕr'e-moth. (1) **A Benjamite.**—I Chr. 7:8.

(2) **Another Benjamite.**—I Chr. 8:14.

(3) **A man of Naphtali in the time of David.**—I Chr. 27:19.

(4) **A Levite.**—I Chr. 23:23; 24:30.

(5, 6) **Two who married foreign wives.** —Ezra 10:26, 27.

JERIAH, je-rī'ah. **Head of a course of Levites.**—I Chr. 23:19; 24:23.

JERIBAI, jĕr'i-bāi. **One of David's mighty men.**—I Chr. 11:46.

JERICHO, jĕr'i-kō. A Canaanite city of great antiquity situated in the valley of the Jordan about five miles from the north end of the Dead Sea and some thirteen miles northeast of Jerusalem. The name occurs twelve times between Num. 22:1 and Deut. 34:3 as that of a "city near the Jordan." It is frequently called "The City of Palm-trees"—Deut. 34:3; Ju. 1:16; 3:13; II Chr. 28:15.

Altitude and climate.—It was 820 feet below the Mediterranean Sea, with a sub-tropical climate and a soil rich enough to largely supply Jerusalem with fruits and food.

Defences.—Its natural defences were superior, but on account of the hot atmosphere, its inhabitants were enervated. Geo. A. Smith thinks little of its people as warriors, stating that the Biblical account, so far as the ease with which the city was taken, corresponds with later sieges and surrenders.—*Hist. Geog.,* 268.

Joshua sends spies to view the city.— Josh. 2:1. Cared for by Rahab, who dwelt there—Josh. Ch. 2. Israel crosses Jordan opposite Jericho—Josh. 3:14–16. Army gathers in Plain of—Josh. 4:12–14. God gives Jericho into hands of Joshua—Josh. 6:1, 2.

First city in Canaan attacked by Israel. —Josh. 6:1–16. Rahab spared for shielding the spies—Josh. 6:17, 22, 23. Israel defeated at Ai because of Achan's theft—Josh. 7:1–5. Achan stoned to death—Josh. 7:6–26.

Joshua pronounces a curse on him who rebuilds the city.—Josh. 6:26, 27. Hiel, the Beth-elite, rebuilds it in the days of Ahab, but lost his eldest and youngest son according to the terms of the curse—I Ki. 16:34.

Inhabited long before Hiel's day. (No effort to make a great city of it.) For instances of habitation see Ju. 1:16; 3:13; II Sam. 10:5; I Chr. 19:5. One of Benjamin's cities—Josh. 18:21. Sons of prophets dwell there—II Ki. 2:15. Elisha heals waters for them—II Ki. 2:19–22. King Zedekiah captured near there by Babylonians after his escape from Jerusalem—II Ki. 25:5; Jer. 39:5; 52:8.

It was re-inhabited after captivity.— Drawn upon by Nehemiah for help in building walls of Jerusalem—Ezra 2: 34; Neh. 3:2. Afterwards held by Greeks (I Macc. 9:50), about 160 B.C. Pompey passed through it in 63 B.C. It was then famous for palms, and balsam gardens were established which were eventually given to Cleopatra by Antony, about 32 B.C. The city which Herod rebuilt was not on the old site, at the springs, but closer to the mountains.

Jesus' association with Jericho.—The road to it furnished Him with the Parable of the Good Samaritan—Lu. 10: 30–37. On His last return to Jerusalem He passed through Jericho, healing Bartimæus—Mt. 20:29; Mk. 10: 46; Lu. 18:35. He also brought salvation to Zacchæus—Lu. 19:1–10.

Author of "Hebrews" refers to its fall. —Heb. 11:30.

JERIEL, jē′ri-el. **A man of Issachar.**— I Chr. 7:2.

JERIMOTH, jĕr′i-moth. (1) **A Benjamite.**—I Chr. 7:7.

(2) **One of David's mighty men.**—I Chr. 12:5.

(3) **A musician.**—I Chr. 25:4.

(4) **Son of David.**—II Chr. 11:18. See JEREMOTH.

JERIOTH, jē′ri-ŏth. I Chr. 2:18.

JEROBOAM, jĕr′o-bō′am. (1) **Son of Nebat, servant of Solomon.**—I Ki. 11:26.

Man of valor.—I Ki. 11:28.

Ahijah predicts his being king.—I Ki. 11:29–39.

Dwelt in.—Egypt—I Ki. 12:2; II Chr. 10:2. Ephraim—I Ki. 12:25.

Events in life.—Revolt against Solomon —I Ki. 11:26. Solomon seeks his life— I Ki. 11:40. Made king—I Ki. 12:20. Reign of—I Ki. 14:16; II Ki. 17:21, 22; II Chr. 10:12–15. Sets up calves as objects of worship at Dan and Bethel—I Ki. 12:26–33. Reproved and punished at Bethel—I Ki. Ch. 13. Death of his child, according to Ahijah's prophecy—I Ki. 14:1–18.

Strifes with Rehoboam.—I Ki. 14:30; 15:6; II Chr. 11:1–4; 12:15.

Defeated by Abijah.—II Chr. 13:3–20.

Death.—I Ki. 14:20; II Chr. 13:20.

(2) Thirteenth king of Israel; reigned forty-one years. Son of Jehoash—II Ki. 14:16, 23. Reign of—II Ki. 14:24. Recovers Hamath and Damascus—II Ki. 14:25–28. Death of—II Ki. 14:29.

Genealogies written in his reign.—I Chr. 5:17.

Prophecy concerning.—Amos 7:7–13.

JEROHAM, je-rō′ham. (1) **Grandfather of Samuel.**—I Sam. 1:1.

(2) I Chr. 12:7.

(3) **A Benjamite.**—I Chr. 8:27; 9:8.

(4) **A Danite.**—I Chr. 27:22.

(5) **A priest.**—I Chr. 9:12; Neh. 11:12.

(6) **Father of Azariah.**—II Chr. 23:1.

JERUBBAAL, je-rŭb-ba-ăl. Ju. 6:32. See GIDEON.

JERUBBESHETH, je-rŭb′be-shĕth. II Sam. 11:21. See GIDEON.

JERUEL, jĕr′u-el. **A part of wilderness of Judah.**—II Chr. 20:16.

JERUSALEM. Heb. *Yerushalaim;* Gr. *Ierousalem.*

The ancient Salem.—Gen. 14:18; Ps. 76:2.

Called: Jebus—Josh. 18:28; Ju. 19:10. Zion—I Ki. 8:1; Is. 60:14; Zech. 9:13. City of God—Ps. 46:4; 48:1; Is. 60:14. City of Judah—II Chr. 25:28. City of Great King—Ps. 48:2; Mt. 4:5. City of Solemnities—Is. 33:20. City of Righteousness—Is. 1:26. City of Truth —Zech. 8:3. City not forsaken—Is. 62: 12. Ariel—Is. 29:1. Faithful City— Is. 1:21, 26. Holy City—Neh. 11:1; Is. 48:2; Mt. 4:5. Throne of the Lord —Jer. 3:17. Perfection of Beauty— Lam. 2:15. Princess among Provinces —Lam. 1:1.

Situation.—Lies on a broad mountainridge, some thirty-five miles east from Joppa, and eighteen miles west of the north end of the Dead Sea. It is twenty-two miles west of the Jordan. It is 2,500 feet above the level of the ocean, and 3,812 feet higher than the Dead Sea, the latter being about 1,300 feet below the Mediterranean Sea.

Its defences. Surrounded by mountains —Ps. 125:2. By a wall—I Ki. 3:1; Neh. 4:1, 6; 6:1, 6, 15. Protected by forts and bulwarks—Ps. 48:12, 13. Entered by gates—Ps. 122:2; Jer. 17:19, 21.

Spoils of war kept there—I Sam. 17: 54; II Sam. 8:7.

Inhabitants and structure.—Jebusites formerly dwelt there, hence it was a Canaanitish city—Ju. 19:10, 11. Tribes of Judah and Benjamin could not dispossess them—Josh. 15:63; Ju. 1:21. Dispossessed by David—II Sam. 5:6-9; I Chr. 11:5-8. Chosen to place his name there, by Jehovah—I Ki. 5:3-5; II Chr. 6:4-6; 12:13. Chief Levites dwelt in—I Chr. 9:34. David's capital —I Ki. 15:4; II Ki. 19:34; II Chr. 6:6; 12:13. David brings up the ark from Baale-judah—II Sam. 6:1-15. Purchases Araunah's threshing-floor for altar site—II Sam. 24:18-25. Prepares to build temple—I Chr. 28:11-21. City brought into magnificent proportions by Solomon—I Ki. 3:1; II Chr. 7:11; 8:1, 6; 9:11, 27. (1) The temple which stood on the summit of the east hill, a little west of the rock which marks the site of the altar of burnt-offering. (2) The king's house. *This adjoined the temple*—I Ki. 6:36; 7:8, 12. (3) The house of Pharaoh's daughter. *Surrounded by a court*—I Ki. 7:8; 9:24. (4) The porch of judgment, served as the royal audience chamber and contained the throne of ivory and gold— I Ki. 7:7; 10:18-20. (5) The porch of pillars—I Ki. 7:6. (6) House of forest of Lebanon—I Ki. 10:17. For 200 years after Solomon's death there was no improvement of the city. The fortunes of Judah revived as the northern kingdom declined. Uzziah is the first king of whom large building work is recorded—II Chr. 26:9-15. Jotham, his son, continued this improvement— II Chr. 27:3-4. Hezekiah built pools and conduit to supply the inhabitants— II Ki. 20:20. He made other improvements—II Chr. 32:5; Is. 22:9-11. Manasseh enlarges the City of David, which at first was limited in size, and must be distinguished from Jerusalem —I Ki. 8:1; II Ki. 9:28; 14:20; Is. 22:9, 10. The fact is, as the City of David grew, the wall was extended by Solomon—I Ki. 3:1. By Hezekiah—II Chr. 32:5. By Manasseh—II Chr. 33: 14. The "City of David" being originally built out of a structure called

"millo," which protected the north end of the southeast hill—II Sam. 5:9; I Ki. 9:15, 24; 11:27; II Chr. 32:5. (We have a noted modern example in the old City of London, whose walls included a few important structures like Old Bailey, etc.) Nehemiah rebuilt on the old lines by order of Cyrus—Ezra 1:3, 4. Taking in what David, Solomon, Hezekiah, and Manasseh planned for—Neh. 2:2-18; 3:1-32. During the captivity of Judah the palace or castle was the residence of the Persian governor, and later of the Maccabean priest-kings. It was rebuilt by Herod the Great and named Antonia in honor of Mark Antony. It was garrisoned by Roman soldiers—Acts 21:30-32; 23:10, 16, 32. Seat of government— Mt. 27:2-19. Transferred to Cæsarea —Acts 23:23-24; 25:1-13.

The pools of Jerusalem.—(1) Bethesda— John 5:2. Perhaps to be identified with the Gihon, or Virgin's fountain. Fed by an intermittent spring. Near the sheep gate (Neh. 3:1). (2) Siloam. The names Shiloah, Shelah (Neh. 3: 15) identical with Siloam. It is fed by a tunnel cut through the rock from the Gihon. Hezekiah, in the days of Sennacherib, stopped the channel and changed the course of the Gihon—II Ki. 20:20; II Chr. 32:4. People bathed in these pools—John 5:7; 9:7.

The gates of Jerusalem.—Old gate, Fish gate, Sheep gate, Prison gate—Neh. 3:1, 3, 6, 32; 12:30. Gate of Ephraim— II Chr. 25:23; Neh. 12:39. Gate of Benjamin—Jer. 37:13; Zech. 14:10. Gate of Joshua—II Ki. 23:8. Corner gate—Zech. 14:10. Valley gate—Neh. 2:13; 3:13. Dung gate—Neh. 2:13; 3:13; 12:31. Gate of the fountain— Neh. 2:14; 3:15; 12:37. Water gate— Neh. 3:26; 8:1; 12:37. Horse gate— Neh. 3:28. King's gate—I Chr. 9:18; II Chr. 23:20. Gate of Shallecheth— I Chr. 26:16. East gate—Neh. 3:29. Gate of Hammiphkad—Neh. 3:31. Middle gate—Jer. 39:3. First gate— Zech. 14:10.

The valleys of Jerusalem.—(1) Of Kidron, lying east of city—II Sam. 15:23; I Ki. 2:37. (2) Of Hinnom, enclosing Jerusalem on the west and south—

Josh. 15:8. (3) Of Rephaim, lying west of Hinnom—Josh. 15:8; 18:16. (4) Of Shaveh, where Melchizedek met Abraham—Gen. 14:17. (5) The Tyropeon, dividing the upper from the lower city.

The hills of Jerusalem.—Acra (N.W.), Bezetha (N.E.), Zion (S.W.), Ophel (S.E.). This last is divided again into Ophel proper and Moriah.

Character of Jerusalem. — Populous — —Lam. 1:1. Full of business—Is. 22:3. Full of wealth—I Ki. 10:26, 27. Wicked —II Ki. 21:12–15; II Chr. 24:18; 28: 24; Jer. 5:1–5; Lam. 1:8. Wins the protection of Jehovah—II Sam. 24: 16; II Ki. 19:32; II Chr. 12:7; Is. 31:5.

Calamities of Jerusalem.—Taken and plundered by Shishak—I Ki. 14:25, 26; II Chr. 12:1–4. Taken and plundered by Jehoash—II Ki. 14:13, 14. Besieged by Rezin and Pekah—II Ki. 16:5; Is. 7:1. By Sennacherib—II Ki. 18:17; Ch. 19. Made tributary by Pharaoh-necoh—II Ki. 23:33–35. Besieged by Nebuchadrezzar—II Ki. 24: 10, 11. Taken and burned by Nebuchadrezzar—II Ki. Ch. 25; Jer. 39:1–8. Threatened by Sanballat—Neh. 4:7, 8.

Relation of Jews to.—Went up to feasts —Ps. 122:6; Deut. 16:16; Ez. 36:38; Lu. 2:42; John 4:20; 5:1; 7:1–14; 12: 20. Prayed towards—I Ki. 8:44; Dan. 6:10. Lamented affliction of—Neh. 1: 2–4. Prayed for prosperity—Ps. 51: 18; 122:4.

Prophecies concerning.—To be taken by king of Babylon—Jer. 20:5. To be made a heap of ruins—Jer. 9:11; 26: 18. Pestilence, famine, and war to overtake it—Is. 22:1–14; Jer. 34:2; Ez. 5:12. To become a wilderness—Is. 64:10. To be rebuilt by Cyrus—Is. 44: 26–28. To be a quiet habitation—Is. 33:20. To be a terror to its-enemies— Zech. 12:2, 3. The gospel to go forth from—Is. 2:3; 40:9. To be destroyed by Romans—Lu. 19:42–44. Its capture, with calamities—Mt. 24:21, 29; Lu. 21:23, 24. Signs preceding destruction —Mt. 24:6–15; Lu. 21:7–11, 25, 28. The restoration of Zion—Is. 54:1–8; Ez. 48:30–35.

The relation of Christ to.—Preached in —Lu. 21:37, 38; John 18:20. Did miracles in—John 4:45. Entered into as king—Mt. 21:9, 10. Lamented over— Mt. 23:37; Lu. 19:41. Put to death at —Lu. 9:31; Acts 13:27, 29. Gospel first preached at—Lu. 24:47; Acts 2: 14. Miraculous gift of Holy Spirit at —Acts 1:4; 2:1–5. Persecuted of church at—Acts 2:1; 8:1. First council held at—Acts 15:4, 6.

Illustrative of.—The church—Gal. 4:25, 26; Heb. 12:22. The church glorified —Rev. 3:12; 21:2, 10.

JERUSHA, je-ru'shà. **Mother of Jotham king of Judah.**—II Ki. 15:33; II Chr. 27:1.

JESHAIAH, jĕsh'a-iah. (1) **A descendant of Moses.**—I Chr. 26:25.

(2) **A descendant of David.**—I Chr. 3: 21.

(3) **A musician.**—I Chr. 25:3, 15.

(4) **A Levite.**—Ezra 8:19.

(5) **One of those who returned with Ezra.**—Ezra 8:7.

(6) **A Benjamite.**—Neh. 11:7.

JESHANAH, jĕsh'a-nah. **A town of Ephraim.**—II Chr. 13:19.

JESHARELAH, jĕsh'a-rē'lah. **A musician.**—I Chr. 25:14.

JESHEBEAB, je-shĕb'e-ăb. **A priest.**— I Chr. 24:13.

JESHER, jē'sher. **Son of Caleb.**—I Chr. 2:18.

JESHISHAI, je-shī'shāi. **A Gadite.**—I Chr. 5:14.

JESHOHAIAH, jĕsh'o-hā'iah. **A Simeonite.**—I Chr. 4:36.

JESHUA, jĕsh'u-à. Joshua. (1) **Son of Nun.**—Neh. 8:17.

(2) **A family of Pahath-moab.**—Ezra 2: 6; Neh. 7:11.

(3) **Name of a course of priests.**—I Chr. 24:11.

(4) **A Levite in charge of the tithes.**— II Chr. 31:15.

(5) **A high priest who returned from exile with Zerubbabel.**—Ezra 2:2; 3: 2, 8; 4:3; 5:2; 10:18; Neh. 7:7; 12:1, 7, 10, 26; Zech. 3:1.

(6) **A family of Levites.**—Ezra 2:40; 3:9; Neh. 3:19; 7:43; 8:7; 9:4, 5; 12: 8, 24.

(7) **A town in Judah after the exile.**— Neh. 11:26.

JESHURUN, jĕsh'u-rŭn. A poetical name for Israel—Deut. 32:15; 33:5, 26; Is. 44:2.

JESIMIEL, je-sĭm'i-el. **A Simeonite.**— I Chr. 4:36.

JESSE, jĕs'se. **Father of David.**—Birth and parentage—Ruth 4:17, 22; Mt. 1: 5. Sons of Jesse—I Sam. 16:8–13. Sends David to Saul—I Sam. 16:20. Sends David into camp—I Sam. 17: 17, 18. Dwells with king of Moab—I Sam. 22:4.

Descendants.—I Chr. 2:13–17; Is. 11:1.

JESUS. Greek form of *Joshua.* **(1) Son of Nun, the leader with Moses.**—Acts 7:45; Heb. 4:8.

(2) A Jewish convert.—Col. 4:11.

JESUS CHRIST: His life and deeds.— The genealogies—Mt. 1:1–17; Lu. 3: 23–38. He was born of a virgin—Is. 7:14; Mt. 1:18–23; Lu. 1:26–38; Gal. 4:4. His birth announced to Mary— Lu. 1:26–38. (*Nazareth.*) The visit of Mary to Elisabeth—Lu. 1:39–56. (*Jutta?*) Her song of praise—Lu. 1: 46–55. Her return to Nazareth—Lu. 1:56. (*Nazareth.*) Joseph's vision— Mt. 1:20–25. (*Nazareth.*)

The birth of Jesus.—At Bethlehem—Mt. 2:5, 6; Lu. 2:1–7 (Mic. 5:2). The angels and the shepherds. The shepherds announce him—Lu. 2:8–20. (*Near Bethlehem.*) His circumcision—Lu. 2:21. (*Jerusalem.*) Presentation and purification in the temple—Lu. 2:22–24. (*Jerusalem.*) Prophecies of Simeon and Anna—Lu. 2:25–39. (*Jerusalem.*) Visit of the wise men—Mt. 2:1–12. (*Jerusalem* and *Bethlehem.*) Because of Herod's cruelty the parents take the child into Egypt—Mt. 2:13–18. Return to Nazareth—Mt. 2:19–23; Lu. 2:39. Jesus' growth in Nazareth— Lu. 2:51–52. At twelve years old goes up to Jerusalem to the passover—Lu. 2:41–43. Found in the temple with the doctors—Lu. 2:43–50. (*Jerusalem.*)

John introduces Jesus into public life.— His announcement of the Christ—Mt. 3:1–12; Mk. 1:7–8; Lu. 3:15–18; John 1:26–30. (*Bethany* [*Bèthabarah, marg.*] *beyond the Jordan.*) Jesus is baptized —Mt. 3:13–17; Mk. 1:9–11; Lu. 3:21– 22; John 1:31–34. (*The Jordan.*) The temptation of Jesus—Mt. 4:1–11; Mk.

1:12–13; Lu. 4:1–13. (*Desert of Judæa.*)

"THE YEAR OF OBSCURITY."

Disciples of John the Baptist—Peter and Andrew—follow Jesus—John 1: 37–51. (*The Jordan. Galilee?*) Jesus returns to Galilee and finds disciples —John 1:43–51. His first miracle at a wedding in Cana—John 2:1–11. Visit to Capernaum—John 2:12.

The first passover during our Lord's ministry.—Jesus goes up to Jerusalem —John 2:13. He expels the traders from the temple—John 2:13–22. (*Jerusalem.*) His discourse with Nicodemus—John 3:1–21. (*Jerusalem.*) Departs into the country of Judæa and makes disciples—John 3:22. (*Judæa.*) John testifies of Jesus again—John 3: 26:30. (*Ænon.*) To avoid provoking jealousy, Jesus passes through Samaria—John 4:1–6. Converses with Samaritan woman at Jacob's well. The surprise of His disciples—John 4:7– 38. (*Sychar.*) Many Samaritans believe on Him—John 4:39–42. Jesus passes on into Galilee—John 4:43–45. Is received by those who met Him previously at Cana—John 4:45–46. He heals the nobleman's son lying ill in Capernaum (*Cana of Galilee*)—John 4: 46–54.

"THE YEAR OF POPULARITY.

Galilean ministry: Begins His public ministry in Galilee.—Mt. 4:17; Mk. 1: 14–15; Lu. 4:14–15; John 4:43–45. Rejected in Nazareth—Mt. 4:13–16; Lu. 4:16–31. He dwells in Capernaum— Mt. 4:13; Mk. 1:21; Lu. 4:31. Works the miracle of the fishes at Sea of Galilee and calls to Him disciples—Peter, Andrew, James and John—Mt. 4:18– 22; Mk. 1:16–20; Lu. 5:1–11. (*Near Capernaum.*) Heals a demoniac in synagogue of Capernaum—Mk. 1:21–28; Lu. 4:31–37. Heals Peter's mother-in-law and many others—Mt. 8:14–17; Mk. 1:29–34; Lu. 4:38–41. (*Capernaum.*)

Departs from Capernaum in His first preaching tour through Galilee.—Mt. 4:23–25; Mk. 1:35–39; Lu. 4:42–44.

311

Heals a leper—Mt. 8:2-4; Mk. 1:40-45; Lu. 5:12-16. His popularity drove Him into desert places—Mk. 1:45; Lu. 5:15-16. He returns to Capernaum and heals a paralytic—Mt. 9:2-8; Mk. 2:1-12; Lu. 5:17-26. Calls Matthew to the apostleship—Mt. 9:9; Mk. 2:13-14; Lu. 5:27-28. (Capernaum.)

The second passover during our Lord's ministry.—Goes from Capernaum to the passover at Jerusalem—John 5:1. Heals a man on the Sabbath at the pool of Bethesda—John 5:2-9. (Jerusalem.) Charged with breaking the Sabbath—John 5:10-16. Jesus defends Himself—John 5:17-47. (Jerusalem.) The Jews try to kill Him—John 5:18. (Jerusalem.) His disciples, plucking ears of grain on the Sabbath, give Jesus a chance for discussion—Mt. 12:1-8; Mk. 2:23-28; Lu. 6:1-5. (On way to Galilee?) Enters a Galilean synagogue and heals a man with withered hand—Mt. 12:9-14; Mk. 3:1-6; Lu. 6:6-11. Withdraws to Sea of Galilee and is followed by great multitude —Mt. 4:23-25; Mk. 3:7-12. Withdraws to a mountain to pray—Lu. 6:12. Chooses the twelve apostles—Mt. 10:2-4; Mk. 3:13-19; Lu. 6:12-19. (Near Capernaum.) Sitting on a mountain near Capernaum, He delivers His famous sermon—Mt. Chs. 5, 6, 7; Lu. 6:20-49. Heals centurion's servant—Mt. 8:5-13; Lu. 7:1-10. (Capernaum.) On His journey to Nain overtakes a funeral procession and brings to life a widow's son—Lu. 7:11-17. (Near Nain.) John the Baptist sends messenger to Jesus—Mt. 11:2-19; Lu. 7:18-35. Pronounces doom on unbelieving cities: Chorazin, Bethsaida, and Capernaum—Mt. 11:20-30; Lu. 10:12-16. Anointed by penitent woman in house of Simon the pharisee—Lu. 7:36-50.

With the twelve He makes His second preaching tour through Galilee.—Lu. 8:1-3. Returns to Capernaum and heals a blind and a dumb demoniac—Mt. 12:22. His power is ascribed to Beelzebub—Mt. 12:23-46; Mk. 3:22-30. His mother and brothers visit them —Mt. 12:46-50; Mk. 3:31-35; Lu. 8:19-21. Teaches the multitudes in par-

ables—Mt. 13:1-50; Mk. 4:1-34; Lu. 8:4-18. (Near Capernaum.) Jesus calms the storm on the lake—Mt. 8:23-27; Mk. 4:35-41; Lu. 8:22-25. (Sea of Galilee.) Crosses over to country of Gerasenes (Gergasenes or Gadarenes) and heals demoniacs. Sends demons into swine—Mt. 8:28-34; Mk. 5:1-20; Lu. 8:26-39. (Southeast coast of Galilee.) Returns to Capernaum—Mt. 9:1; Mk. 5:21. Feast at Matthew Levi's house—Mt. 9:10-13; Mk. 2:15-17; Lu. 5:29-39. (Capernaum.) Discourse concerning publicans and fasting—Mt. 9:12-17; Mk. 2:16-22; Lu. 5:30-39. Raised Jairus's daughter and heals woman with issue of blood—Mt. 9:18-26; Mk. 5:22-43; Lu. 8:41-56. Two blind men healed and a demon cast out—Mt. 9:27-34.

Jesus third tour through Galilee.—Mt. 9:35-38; 11:1; Mk. 6:6. Visits Nazareth and is again rejected—Mt. 13:53-58; Mk. 6:1-6. He sends forth the twelve apostles—Mt. Ch. 10; Mk. 6:7-13; Lu. 9:1-6. Herod supposes Jesus to be John the Baptist, whom he had beheaded. Death of John the Baptist —Mt. 14:1-12; Mk. 6:14-29; Lu. 9:7-9. The apostles return from their mission and go with Jesus into a desert place—Mt. 14:13; Mk. 6:30-32; Lu. 9:10; John 6:1. Multitudes follow and are miraculously fed—Mt. 14:13-21; Mk. 6:33-44; Lu. 9:11-17; John 6:5-13. (Northeast coast of the Sea of Galilee?) Jesus walks on the Sea of Galilee—Mt. 14:22-33; Mk. 6:45-51; John 6:16-21. (He goes to Gennesaret.)

The crisis at Capernaum.—The multitude follows Him to Capernaum, desiring to be fed—John 6:22-26. Jesus discourses to them and many disciples leave Him—John 6:26-66. Jesus appeals to the twelve and Peter confesses Him—John 6:67-71. (Capernaum.)

"THE YEAR OF OPPOSITION."

The third passover during our Lord's ministry.—Discourse on tradition of the elders, eating with unwashen hands (Capernaum)—Mt. 15:1-20; Mk. 7:1-23. Jesus goes northward to Tyre and Sidon—Mt. 15:21; Mk. 7:24. Heals the

Syrophœnician's daughter—Mt. 15:21–28; Mk. 7:25–30. Returns through Decapolis to the region near the Sea of Galilee—Mt. 15:29; Mk. 7:31. Multitudes gather about Him. He heals many—Mt. 15:30–31; Mk. 7:31–37. Feeds four thousand—Mt. 15:32–39; Mk. 8:1–9. Sends away multitudes and goes to Dalmanutha—Mt. 15:39; Mk. 8:9, 10. Pharisees and Sadducees demand a sign—Mt. 16:1–4; Mk. 8:11–21. Coming to Bethsaida, He heals a blind man—Mk. 8:22–26. At Cæsarea Philippi He asks, ''Who do men say I am?''—Mt. 16:13; Mk. 8:27; Lu. 9:18. Peter's great confession and the result—Mt. 16:14–20; Mk. 8:28–30; Lu. 9:19–21. Foretells His death and resurrection the third day —Mt. 16:21–28; Mk. 8:31–38; Lu. 9:22–27. See Mt. 12:40; Lu. 24:21; I Cor. 15:4. (*Region of Cæsarea Philippi.*) Is transfigured and acknowledged by His Father—Mt. 17:1–13; Mk. 9:2–13; Lu. 9:28–36. (*Region of Cæsarea Philippi.*) Finds a demoniac His apostles could not heal—Mt. 17:14–29; Lu. 9:37–43. (*Region of Cæsarea Philippi.*) Again He foretells His death and resurrection the third day —Mt. 17:22–23; Mk. 9:30–32; Lu. 9:44–45. He pays the tribute-money through a miracle—Mt. 17:24–27. The apostles' contention for the greatest places—Mt. 18:1–6; Mk. 9:33–37; Lu. 9:46–48. (*Capernaum.*) He discourses to them on humility—Mt. 18:3–20. Also rebukes their intolerance—Mk. 9:38–50; Lu. 9:49–50. (*Capernaum.*)

Going up to Jerusalem.—He is refused shelter in a Samaritan village—Lu. 9:51–56. He rebukes premature discipleship—Lu. 9:57–62. Seventy evangelists are sent out, two by two—Lu. 10:1–11. (*Samaria.*) Jesus at the feast of tabernacles—John 7:1–44. (*Jerusalem.*) Various opinions concerning Jesus at the feast—John 7:12, 25, 40–44. The rulers attempt to seize Him and fail—Jóhn 7:45–52. The woman taken in adultery—John 8:1–11. Discourse on ''The Light of the World'' —John 8:12–30. Discourse on ''spiritual freedom''—John 8:31–59. Asserts His pre-existence—John 8:58.

Reply to a lawyer's question. The Parable of the Good Samaritan—Lu. 10:25–37. Jesus visits Mary and Martha at Bethany—Lu. 10:38–42. He teaches His disciples to pray—Lu. 11:1–13. He heals a noted blind man who confesses Him—John Ch. 9. The Parable of the Good Shepherd—John 10:1–18. The seventy return from their mission—Lu. 10:17–20. Cautions His disciples against temptations— —Lu. Ch. 12. Jesus at the feast of dedication—John 10:22–42. Lazarus sick, dies, and is raised again—John Ch. 11. Parable of barren fig tree— Lu. 13:6–9. The chief priests plot to put Jesus to death—John 11:47–53. Jesus departs into the wilderness city of Ephraim—John 11:54.

PERÆAN MINISTRY.

Passing through Samaria, Galilee and Peræa, He approaches Jerusalem by way of Jericho, heals a woman, with infirmity, on the Sabbath—Mt. 19:1; Mk. 10:1; Lu. 13:10–21. (*Peræa.*) Ten lepers were healed, but only one was grateful—Lu. 17:12–19. Are there few that be saved?—Lu. 13:22–30. Reply to warning against Herod—Lu. 13:31–35. Jesus dines with a Pharisee and speaks the Parable of the Great Supper—Lu. 14:1–24. (*Peræa.*) He teaches the essentials of true discipleship—Lu. 14:25–35. (*Peræa.*) Pharisees murmur at the people flocking to Jesus. So He narrates the Parables of the Lost Sheep, the Lost Coin, and the Prodigal Son—Lu. Ch. 15. (*Peræa.*) The Parables of the Unjust Steward and the Rich Man and Lazarus—Lu. Ch. 16. (*Peræa.*) Jesus inculcates forgiveness and faith and humility—Lu. 17:1–10. Inquiry made about the coming of the kingdom of God—Lu. 17:20–37. Parables of ''The Importunate Widow'' and of ''The Pharisee and the Publican''—Lu. 18:1–14. Precepts concerning divorce given in Peræa— Mt. 19:3–12; Mk. 10:2–12. Jesus declares that to little children belongeth the kingdom of God—Mt. 19:13–15; Mk. 10:13–16; Lu. 18:15–17. The rich young ruler who did not obey Jesus—

Mt. 19:16–22; Mk. 10:17–22; Lu. 18:
18–25. Parables of the Laborers in
the Vineyard—Mt. 20:1–16. The third
time He foretells His sufferings, death
and resurrection—Mt. 20:17–19; Mk.
10:32–34; Lu. 18:31–34. Ambitious
request of James and John—Mt. 20:
20–28; Mk. 10:35–45. Two blind men
healed near Jericho—Mt. 20:29–34;
Mk. 10:46–52; Lu. 18:35–43. The conversion of Zacchæus—Lu. 19:2–10.
(*Jericho.*) Parable of the pounds used
to correct false impressions concerning the immediate coming of His kingdom—Lu. 19:11–28. (*Jericho.*) Jesus
goes to Bethany six days before the
passover—John 12:1. Is anointed by
Mary in Simon's house—Mt. 26:7; Mk.
14:3–9; John 12:1–8.

**The last passover week—Time, 7 days—
First day of the week.**—Triumphant
entry into Jerusalem—Mt. 21:1–11;
Mk. 11:1–11; Lu. 19:29–38; John 12:
12–19. Weeps over Jerusalem—Lu.
19:41. Returns to Bethany—Mt. 21:
17. He left Jerusalem each night and
returned in the morning—Mt. 21:18;
Mk. 11:11, 12; Lu. 21:37.

Second day of the week.—On His way
to the city He curses an unfruitful
fig tree—Mt. 21:18–22. Turns money-
changers, once more, out of temple—
Mt. 21:12–17; Mk. 11:15–17; Lu. 19:
45–46. Chief priests and scribes seek
to destroy Him—Mk. 11:18. Returns
to Bethany—Mk. 11:19.

Third day of the week.—Returns to
Jerusalem. Passes by the withered
fig tree. His authority being challenged, He speaks the Parables of the
Two Sons, the Vineyard, and the Wedding Feast—Mt. 21:23–43; 22:1–14;
Mk. 11:20–33; 12:1–12; Lu. 20:1–19.
Is questioned concerning paying tribute—Mt. 22:15–22; Mk. 12:13–17; Lu.
20:20–26. Questioned as to the greatest commandment—Mt. 22:34–40; Mk.
12:28–34. Jesus, in turn, questions
them as to sonship—Mt. 22:41–46; Mk.
12:35–37; Lu. 20:41–44. He warns
disciples and rebukes Jewish leaders—
Mt. Ch. 23; Mk. 12:38–40; Lu. 20:45–
47. Laments over Jerusalem—Mt. 23:
37–39. Comments on the widow's offering—Lu. 21:1–4. The Greeks de-

sire to see Jesus—John 12:20–50. He
leaves the city again, going to Bethany—Mt. 24:1. Discourses upon the
destruction of Jerusalem—Mt. 24:2–
51; Mk. 13:3–27; Lu. 21:5–36. Por-
trays the future through Parables of
the Ten Virgins and the Talents—Mt.
Ch. 25.

Fourth day of the week.—Enemies of
Jesus meet to plan His murder—Mt.
26:2–5; Mk. 14:1–2; Lu. 22:1–2. They
bargain with Judas Iscariot—Mt. 26:
14–16; Mk. 14:10–11; Lu. 22:3–6.

Fifth day of the week.—Jesus sends two
disciples to prepare the passover—Mt.
26:17–19; Mk. 14:12–16; Lu. 22:7–13.
Towards evening He follows them to
Jerusalem—Lu. 22:7–13.

**Sixth day of the week, beginning at sun-
set.**—He eats the passover with the
twelve—Mt. 26:20–30; Mk. 14:17–26;
Lu. 22:14–23. Jesus eats His Last
Supper and establishes it as an ordinance—Mt. 26:26–29; Mk. 14:22–25;
Lu. 22:14–20. Contention over who
should be greatest leads Jesus to
wash the disciples' feet—Lu. 22:24;
John 13:3–17. Satan tempts Judas
Iscariot to close his bargain—John
13:2. Jesus indicates His betrayer and
bids him go—Mt. 26:21–25; Mk. 14:
18–21; Lu. 22:21–23; John 13:18, 21–
30. Peter avows allegiance, which
Jesus disputes—Mt. 26:33–35; Mk. 14:
29–31; Lu. 22:31–34; John 13:36–38.
Valedictory discourses and intercessory prayer—John Chs. 14–17. About
midnight Jesus crosses the Kidron and
enters into Gethsemane (*Mount of
Olives*)—Mt. 26:36; Mk. 14:32; Lu.
22:39–40; John 18:1. He puts disciples on watch and agonizes in prayer
—Mt. 26:37–46; Mk. 14:33–42; Lu. 22:
40–46. Is betrayed and seized—Mt.
26:47–56; Mk. 14:43–52; Lu. 22:47–53;
John 18:2–12. Brought before Annas,
Caiaphas' father-in-law, during the
night—John 18:12–14, 19–24. Annas
sends Jesus to Caiaphas—Mt. 26:57–
75; Mk. 14:50–72; Lu. 22:54–62; John
18:28. Confesses His divinity—Mt.
26:63, 64; Lu. 22:67–71. Jesus passes
through a mock trial and is delivered
to Pilate—Mt. 27:1–2; Mk. 14:53–65;
15:1; Lu. 22:63–71; 23:1. Peter de-

nies Jesus three times—Mt. 26:69-75;
Mk. 14:54, 66-72; Lu. 22:54-62; John
18:25-27. Pilate pronounces Jesus innocent, sends Him to Herod, who returns Him—Lu. 23:6-12. Pilate seeks
to release Him, the Jews cry ''Crucify
Him,'' and demand the release of Barabbas. Jesus is scourged and sentenced to death—Mt. 27:11-26; Mk.
15:2-15; Lu. 23:13-25; John 18:33-40;
19:1-16. Judas repents and hangs himself—Mt. 27:3-10. Jesus is led away
to be crucified, being mocked by the
soldiers—Mt. 27:27-34; Mk. 15:16-22;
Lu. 23:26-32; John 19:17. The crucifixion—Mt. 27:35-44; Mk. 15:24-32;
Lu. 23:33-38; John 19:17-27. Two
thieves were hung with Jesus—Mt.
27:38-44; Mk. 15:27-32; Lu. 23:32-43.
Jesus dies on the cross with signs accompanying—Mt. 27:45-56; Mk. 15:
33-41; Lu. 23:44-49; John 19:28-30.
Jesus' body taken down, embalmed,
and buried—Mt. 27:57-61; Mk. 15:
42-47; Lu. 23:50-56; John 19:31-42.

Seventh day of the week.—Guard placed
at sepulchre—Mt. 27:62-66.

**The resurrection of our Lord—First day
of the week.**—Resurrection at dawn—
Mt. 28:2-4; Mk. 16:9; Lu. 24:1; John
20:1. Report of the guard—Mt. 28:
11-15. Mary finds Jesus in the garden, while Peter and John are visiting
the sepulchre—Lu. 24:12; John 20:3-
18. Jesus is seen by Peter and by
two near Emmaus—Mk. 16:12-13; Lu.
24:13-29; I Cor. 15:5. He also appears
to the apostles, Thomas being absent—
Mk. 16:14; Lu. 24:36-43; John 20:19-
23; I Cor. 15:5.

First day of second week.—Jesus appears
again when Thomas was present—John
20:24-29. The apostles having gone
to Galilee, Jesus shows Himself—Mt.
28:16; John 21:1-14. Jesus meets 500
disciples on a mountain in Galilee—I
Cor. 15:6. He is seen again by James,
and by all the apostles—I Cor. 15:7.
He commissions His apostles to preach
the gospel—Mt. 28:18-20; Mk. 16:15-
18.

**Ascension forty days after His resurrec-
tion.**—He ascends from Olivet—Mk.
16:19-20; Lu. 24:50-53; Acts 1:9-11.
Foretold—Ps. 68:18; Lu. 24:26; John

1:51; 6:62; 7:33; 14:2-4, 12, 28; 16:5,
7, 10, 16, 25, 28; 17:13; 20:17. See
Acts 2:33; 3:21; 5:31; 7:55, 56; Eph.
1:20; 4:8-10; Col. 3:1; I Tim. 3:16;
Heb. 1:3; 2:9; 4:14; 6:19, 20; 7:26;
8:1; 9:12, 24; 10:12, 13; 12:2; I Pet.
3:22; Rev. 1:5; 3:21.

Conclusion of John's gospel.—John 20:
30, 31; 21:25.

OLD TESTAMENT PROMISES CONCERNING
JESUS AND NEW TESTAMENT FULFIL-
MENT. The seed of the woman—Gen.
3:15 (Rom. 16:20; Gal. 4:4).

He should be of the seed of Abraham—
Gen. 12:3; 22:18; 26:4; 28:14 (Mt. 1:1;
Lu. 1:54, 55; Acts 3:25; Rom. 4:13;
Gal. 3:8).

He should be the seed of Isaac—Gen.
17:19; 26:2-5 (Rom. 9:6-8; Heb. 11:
18).

Judah should be in the line of descent—
Gen. 49:10; Ps. 60:7 (Mt. 1:2).

This promise was made to David—II
Sam. 7:11, 12, 27; Ps. 89:3, 4, 35-37;
Is. 9:6; 55:3, 4; Amos 9:11, 12 (Mt.
1:1; Lu. 1:32, 69; Acts 15:15-18); Ps.
16:8-10 (Acts 2:25-28; 13:34-37).

Christ was the prophet that was to come
—Deut. 18:15, 18, 19 (John 1:45; Acts
3:22, 23; 7:37).

He was to be born in Bethlehem in
Judæa—Mic. 5:2 (Mt. 2:6; John 7:42;
Heb. 7:14).

The time when He should come and the
time of His kingdom was told to Daniel
by the angel Gabriel—Dan. 9:22-27
(Mk. 1:15; Lu. 3:15).

He should be brought forth out of Egypt
—Hos. 11:1 (Mt. 2:14, 15).

A harbinger should precede Him in His
ministry and make ready a people prepared for Him and His kingdom—Is.
40:3-5 (John 1:19-25).

While John was not the person of Elijah
risen from the dead, he was the Elijah
that was to come—Mal. 3:1; 4:5, 6
(Mt. 11:14; 17:9-13; Mk. 9:13; Lu.
1:15-17, 76, 77; 7:37).

Death of the innocents—Jer. 31:15 (Mt.
2:16-18).

He was favored by God and men—Is.
40:5 (Lu. 2:40).

He was to lead the people as the faithful
shepherd—Is. 11:1-9; 42:1-4 (John
10:11-18).

He was to be the liberator of the race —Is. 61:1-3 (Lu. 4:16-22; Heb. 2:8-10).

He would live at Capernaum and give light to the land of Zebulun and Naphtali—Is. 9:1, 2 (Mt. 4:12-16).

He should be a healer of many—Is. 53:4 (Mt. 8:14-17; Acts 10:37-39).

The deaf should hear and the blind see— Is. 29:18, 19; 35:3-6; 42:5-8 (Mt. 11: 2-6; Lu. 7:22).

To be known and to save by His knowledge—Is. 53:11 (John 4:39-42).

He taught by the use of parables—Ps. 49:4; 78:2 (Mt. 13:1-53).

He did not lift up His voice in the streets—Is. 42:2.

His whole life attests the truth of the statement, ''He was the Prince of Peace''—Is. 9:6 (Eph. 2:14).

His zeal for the house of God greatly endangered Him—Ps. 69:9; 119:139; Is. 56:7; Jer. 7:11 (Mt. 21:13; Lu. 19: 46; John 2:17).

His triumphal entry into Jerusalem— Zech. 9:9 (John 12:12-16).

Taught the resurrection from the dead— Is. 26:19; Ez. 37:1-8; Dan. 12:1-4 (Mk. 12:18-27; John 5:28, 29).

In this way was His death foretold—Mt. 12:38-40; Mk. 8:31-33; 9:9, 10; 10:32-34; John 12:31-34; 20:6-10. See DIVINITY OF JESUS.

As a Shepherd of the flock He should be smitten, and the sheep should be scattered—Zech. 13:7 (Mt. 26:31).

He confounds His questioners—Is. 52: 13-15 (Mt. 22:34-40).

Herod and Pilate become friends to crucify Him—Ps. 2:1-5 (Acts 4:25-28).

He was betrayed for thirty pieces of silver—Ps. 41:9; 55:12-21; Zech. 11: 12, 13 (Mt. 26:14-16, 23, 48-50; 27:3-10; John 13:18-30).

The trials—Ps. 27:12; Is. 53:7 (Mk. 14: 53-64).

He was maltreated—Ps. 35:15; Is. 50:5, 6 (John 19:1-6).

They gave Him gall and vinegar—Ps. 69:21 (Mt. 27:34, 35, 48).

They crucified Him—Ps. 22:16; Zech. 12:10, 11 (Lu. 23:33; John 19:37).

He was put to death between thieves— Is. 53:8, 9, 12 (Lu. 22:37).

They cast lots for His vesture—Ps. 22: 17, 18 (Mt. 27:35).

The rabble railed on Him—Ps. 22:7, 8, 11; 35:16-22 (Mk. 15:29-32).

He suffered alone—Ps. 22:1; 53:3, 4; Is. 63:1-6 (Mt. 27:45-47).

His committal of His spirit—Ps. 31:5 (Lu. 23:46).

A bone of Him should not be broken— Ps. 34:20 (John 19:31-37).

He made intercession for the transgressors—Is. 53:12 (Lu. 23:34).

He was with the wicked and the rich in death and burial—Is. 53:9 (Mt. 27: 57-60; Mk. 15:42-47; Lu. 23:50-53; John 19:34-42).

He rose from the dead—Ps. 16:8-11 (John 20:1-10; Acts 2:25-32; 13:35-37; 17:2, 3; I Cor. 15:1-7).

He died that our sins might be forgiven . —Is. 53:4, 5, 6, 10, 11 (Mt. 20:28; 26: 28; Heb. 9:26-28; I Pet. 3:18).

He conquered death for us—Hos. 13:14 (I Cor. 15:20-23).

Christ ascended up into heaven—Ps. 24: 7-10; 68:18; Dan. 7:13, 14 (Eph. 4:9-11).

He was the stone that was rejected and yet made the head of the corner—Ps. 118:22; Is. 28:16 (Mt. 21:42; Mk. 12: 10, 11; Lu. 20:17; Acts 4:11).

He became priest and king upon His throne—Gen. 49:10; Ps. 2:6; 110:4; 132:11; Is. 2:4; 9:6, 7; 32:1; Zech. 6: 13 (Mt. 22:44, 45; Mk. 12:35-37; Lu. 20:40-43; Acts 2:30; Heb. 4:14, 15; 7:17; 9:24).

His kingdom is an everlasting kingdom —II Sam. 7:12, 13; Ps. 45:6, 7; 89:3, 4, 29-37; Dan. 2:44; Mic. 4:7 (Mk. 1:14, 15; Col. 1:13; Rev. 1:9).

Thus He swallowed up death in victory— Ps. 16:8-10; Is. 25:8; Hos. 13:14 (John 5:28, 29; 11:25, 26; Acts 2:24-28; Rom. 5:21; 6:9; I Cor. 15:21, 54, 55; Eph. 4: 8-10; Col. 2:15; Heb. 2:9, 14, 15; Rev. 1:18; 20:13, 14; 21:4).

Having ascended into heaven, He sent forth the Holy Spirit—Is. 32:15; Joel 2:28-32 (Lu. 24:49; John 14:16, 17, 25, 26; 16:7-14; Acts 1:4, 5; 2:1-4, 16-21).

This was the going forth of the new law of the kingdom—Is. 2:1-3; Jer. 31:31-34; Mic. 2:1, 2 (Acts 2:37-42; Heb. 8: 6-13).

The Son of God—Ps. 2:7 (Acts 13:33; Heb. 1:5; 5:5).

The Son of man—Ps. 8:4–6 (I Cor. 15:27, 28). Jesus calls Himself ''Son of Man'' in over fifty instances.)

His sinlessness—Is. 53:9 (John 8:46; I Pet. 2:22).

His innocence and meekness—Is. 53:7, 8 (Acts 8:32–35).

His sacrifice surpasses all others—Ps. 40:6–8 (Heb. 10:5–14).

THE MIRACLES OF JESUS. ''Miracle: Lit. *miraculum, i. e.,* a wonder-causing event, a marvel. Of the six Greek words used in the New Testament to describe the supernatural works of Christ on earth, the three most usual are applied also to those wrought by His apostles, *viz.,* (1) *teras,* A.V. wonder (*always*); (2) *semeion,* A.V. sign miracle (esp. in St. John), etc.; (3) *dunamis,* A.V. power, miracle (esp. in Acts and Epistles), etc.; (1) *Teras* (*i. e.,* 'wonder,' 'portent,' describes a miracle's startling effect, and is always accompanied by another of these words, esp. by *semeion,* to indicate the *moral intention,* the end and purpose of the wonder (*e. g.,* in A.V. 'wonders and signs,' Acts 2:22). (2) *Semeion, i. e.,* 'a sign' describes a miracle as ordained by God to be a mark whereby to identify the Messiah, an attestation of His teaching, an earnest of the blessings He brought, a specimen of God's methods for bringing these blessings home to man, as well as a type (or 'parable in action') of His spiritual gifts. (3) *Dunamis, i. e.,* 'power' (so rendered in A.V., also, generally in plural, 'mighty works'), describes a miracle as a 'new and higher force,' or *power of the world to come* (Heb. 6:5), entered upon and working in this world; an 'outcoming of the greatness' (*megaleia,* A.V. 'great things,' Lu. 1:49; Acts 2:1) of God's power and glory inherent in Christ, and lent to His witnesses and ambassadors.

''Miracles are also described at (4) *eudoxa,* A.V. 'glorious things,' Lu. 13:17, etc., *i. e.,* as manifestations of the glory of God, the Father, and Son; (5) *paradoxa* (A.V. 'strange things'; cp. 'new thing,' Num. 16:30), *i. e.,* as beyond human imagination, amazing (cp. Lu. 5:26), and as (6) *thaumasia,* A.V. 'wonderful' (Mt. 21:15; cp. Mt. 9:8), *i. e.,* astonishing, occurrences unprecedented in human experience (cp. Mt. 9:33), and (like *paradoxa*) ascribable to God only.''—TRENCH.

Peculiar to the Gospel of Matthew

Two blind men cured	Capernaum	9:27–31
Dumb spirit cast out	Capernaum	9:32, 33
Tribute money provided	Capernaum	17:24–27

Peculiar to the Gospel of Mark

Deaf and dumb man cured	L. of Galilee	7:31–37
Blind man cured	Bethsaida	8:22–26

Peculiar to the Gospel of Luke

Jesus passes unseen through the crowd	Nazareth	4:28–30
Draught of fishes	L. of Galilee	5:1–11
Widow's son raised	Nain	7:11–17
Woman's infirmity cured	Peræa	13:11–17
Man's dropsy cured	Peræa	14:1–6
Ten lepers cleansed	Samaria	17:11–19
Malchus' ear healed	Gethsemane	22:50–51

Peculiar to the Gospel of John

Water made wine	Cana	2:1–11
Fever of nobleman's son cured	Cana	4:46–54
Impotent man cured	Jerusalem	5:1–9

Peculiar to the Gospel of John

Jesus passes unseen through the crowd................In temple	8:59	
Man born blind cured................................Jerusalem	9:1–7	
Lazarus raised from dead............................Bethany	11:38–44	
Draught of 153 fishes...............................L. of Galilee	21:1–14	

Common to Matthew   *Mark*

Syrophœnician's daughter cured............District of Tyre	15:28	7:24
Four thousand fed........................L. of Galilee	15:32	8:1
Fig tree blasted.........................Mount of Olives	21:18	11:12

Common to Matthew Luke

Centurion's palsied servant cured...........Capernaum	8:5	7:1
Blind and dumb demoniac cured...........Galilee	12:22	11:14

Common to Mark   *Luke*

Demoniac in synagogue cured...............Capernaum	1:23	4:33

Common to Matt.   *Mark*   *Luke*

Peter's mother-in-law cured...........Capernaum	8:14	1:30	4:38
Tempest stilled.......................L. of Galilee	8:23	4:37	8:22
Demoniacs cured......................Gadara	8:28	5:1	8:26
Leper cured..........................Capernaum	8:2	1:40	5:12
Jairus' daughter raised...............Capernaum	9:23	5:23	8:41
Woman's issue of blood cured.........Capernaum	9:20	5:25	8:43
Paralytic cured......................Capernaum	9:2	2:3	5:18
Man's withered hand cured...........Galilee	12:10	3:1	6:6
Devil cast out of boy, near Cæsarea....Philippi (?Tabor)	17:14	9:14	9:37
Two blind men cured................Jericho	20:29	10:46	18:35

Common to Matt.   *Mark*   *John*

Christ walks on sea..................	14:25	6:48	6:15

Common to all Evangelists

5,000 fed...........................Lake of Galilee	Mt. 14:15	Lu. 9:10
	Mk. 6:30	John 6:1–14

Miracles an evidence of Christ's divinity —Mt. 11:20–23; Mk. 2:5–12; John 2: 11, 23; 3:2, 11; 4:48–53; 9:4; 10:37, 38; 11:45, 46; 14:11, 12; 20:30, 31; Acts 2:22. See MIRACLES.

Parable. "PARABLE is the Greek word *parabole,* which means *juxtaposition,* and so a comparison of objects, to show a certain likeness or similitude between them. The Jewish method of *teaching by parables* was apparently adopted by our Lord when the Jews had rejected His *direct* teaching (Mt. 13: 13); but also out of compassionate consideration for the infirmities of the listeners (cp. II Cor. 8:12). Proposed as a spiritual riddle to call the spiritual perceptions into exercise, the Parable—*either* attracted, interested, provoked inquiry, and thus sowed seed in the memory for future development by Christ Himself or by the Holy Ghost (cp. John 14:26); *or* left the self-righteous and obdurate self-condemned to spiritual blindness (John 9:30–41; 12:48). Thus the parable *sifted* the audience, and 'found out the willing hearers and led them on'; like the Shechinah (Ex. 14:20), it was light and guidance to God's children, but darkness and a hindrance to His opponents—Mk. 4:10–13, 33, 34; cp. John 3:19; 7:17; 8:43."

"CHRIST'S PARABLES illustrate the nature and principles of the Gospel dispensation (*the Mysteries, i. e.,* revealed secrets of *the Kingdom of Heaven*). They have been divided into three groups, according to the part of His Ministry in which they were delivered —*viz.*:

1. The earliest—Mt. 13; Mk. 4. Illustrations from common facts of nature.

2. Between the mission of the seventy and His last journey to Jerusalem. Illustrations of family and social life.

3. Immediately before and after His triumphal entry into Jerusalem. In answer to questions, cavils, etc.

Peculiar to the Gospel of Matthew

Tares (from a boat)	Lake of Galilee	13:1–24
Hidden treasure	Lake of Galilee	13:44
Pearl of great price	Lake of Galilee	13:45, 46
Drag-net	Lake of· Galilee	13:47
Unmerciful servant	Capernaum	18:23
Laborers in vineyard	In temple	20:1–17
Father and two sons	In temple	21:28–32
King's son's marriage	In temple	22:1–15
Ten virgins	Mt. of Olives	25:1–13
Talents	Mt. of Olives	25:14–30
Sheep and goats	Mt. of Olives	25:31–46

Peculiar to the Gospel of Mark

Growth of seed	Lake of Galilee	4:26–30
Household watching	Mt. of Olives	13:34, 35

Peculiar to the Gospel of Luke

Two debtors	Galilee	7:36–50
Good samaritan	In temple	10:25–37
Friend at midnight	Near Jerusalem	11:5–8
Rich fool	Galilee	12:16–21
Servants watching	Galilee	12:35–40
Steward on trial	Galilee	12:42–48
Barren fig-tree	Galilee	13:6–9
Great supper	Peræa	14:16–24
Tower and warring king	Peræa	14:28–33
Lost piece of money	Peræa	15:8–10
Prodigal son	Peræa	15:11–32
Dishonest steward	Peræa	16:1–13
Rich man and Lazarus	Peræa	16:19–31
Master and servant	Peræa	17:7–10
Importunate widow	Peræa	18:1–8
Pharisee and publican	Peræa	18:9–14
Pounds	Near Jerusalem	19:12–27

"*Parable*," John 10:6, A.V. is in Greek "proverb" (*paroimia*). See *marg.*

Common to the Gospels of Matt.		Luke
House on rock, sand	Near Capernaum 7:24–27	6:47–49
Leaven	Galilee 13:33	13:20, 21
Lost sheep	Peræa 18:12–14	15:3–7

Common to the Gospels of Mt.	*Mk.*	*Lu.*
Lamp under bushel—Lake of Galilee 5:15, 16	4:21	8:16; 11:33–36
New cloth, old garment — Lake of Galilee 9:16	2:21	5:36
New wine, old bottles—Lake of Galilee 9:17	2:22	5:37, 38

Common to the Gospels of Mt.	*Mk.*	*Lu.*
Sower—Lake of Galilee............ 13:1–8, 18–23	4:3–9, 13–20	8:5–9, 11–15
Mustard seed—Near Jerusalem..... 13:31, 32	4:30–32	13:18, 19
Vineyard and husbandmen—Near Jerusalem 21:33–42	12:1–12	20:9–19
Young leaves of fig-tree—Mt. of Olives 24:32–33	13:28–29	21:29–31

Atonement.—Jesus called the Lamb of God—John 1:29, 36; I Pet. 1:19; Rev. 7:10, 17; 12:10, 11; 14:4; 21:23, 27. See Ex. 12:5, 11, 14; I Cor. 5:7. See ATONEMENT.

Blood of Jesus, Man saved by.—See SALVATION.

Death of Jesus, Man saved by.—See SALVATION. Death foretold.

HIS DIVINITY: His testimony to His divinity.—John 7:29; 8:12–21, 25–47; 10:25–38; 14:1–24; 15:8–27; 17:1–8.

His pre-existence.—Mic. 5:2; I Cor. 10:4; II Cor. 8:9; Phil. 2:6–8; Heb. 11:26. In the beginning—John 1:12; 17:5, 24; Col. 1:17; I John 2:14.

Creator.—John 1:1–4, 10; I Cor. 8:6; Eph. 3:9; Col. 1:16; Heb. 1:2, 8–10; Rev. 3:14.

Descended from heaven.—John 3:13, 31–36; 6:38, 39, 62; 8:23. Came from the Father—John 1:18; 3:16, 17, 34; 5:36–38; 6:29, 38, 46, 57; 7:27–29; 8:42; 10:36; 13:3; 16:30; 17:5, 8, 18; I John 1:1–3. Was before Abraham—John 8:56–58.

Equality with God.—John 5:17, 18, 23; 10:30, 38; 12:44, 45; 14:6–11; 15:23; 17:10, 21–23; II Cor. 5:19; Phil. 2:5, 6; Col. 1:15; 2:9; Heb. 1:3–4, 10–12; 13:8.

Mutuality with God.—Mt. 11:27; John 5:17, 19, 23, 25–27, 37, 43; 12:44, 45; 14:23; 16:23, 24, 26–32; 17:9–12; II Thess. 1:2; I Tim. 1:2.

He is called God.—Is. 7:14 (Mt. 1:23); 9:6; Jer. 23:6; 33:16; Mt. 4:7; John 1:1–4; 10:33; 20:28; Acts 20:28; Rom. 9:5; Col. 1:15, 19; 2:9; I Tim. 3:16; Tit. 1:3; Heb. 1:8; I John 5:20.

The Son of God.—Mt. 2:15; 4:3; Mk. 1:1; John 5:26, 27; 20:30, 31; Rom. 1:1–4, 9; 5:10; 8:3, 29, 32; I Cor. 1:9; II Cor. 1:19; Gal. 1:16; 2:20; 4:4; 4:13; I Thess. 1:10; Heb. 1:2, 8; 3:5, 6; 4:14; 5:5–10; 6:6; 7:3, 28; 10:29; I John 1:3, 7, 22, 23; 3:23; 4:9, 10, 15; 5:5–12; II John 3.

Called ''Son'' by God.—At His baptism—Mt. 3:17; Mk. 1:11; Lu. 3:22. At the transfiguration—Mt. 17:5; Mk. 9:7; Lu. 9:35; II Pet. 1:17, 18. See Ps. 2:7 (Acts 13:33; Heb. 1:5–8; 5:5).

Christ calls Himself ''The Son of God.''—Mt. 11:27; 21:37–44; 26:63, 64; 27:43; Mk. 12:6–11; 14:61, 62; Lu. 20:13–18; John 3:16–18, 34–36; 5:19, 20, 25, 26; 6:40; 9:35–37; 10:36; 11:4; 19:7. See Lu. 10:22; I Tim. 6:13. *The Only Begotten Son*—John 3:16–18.

Confessed as the Son of God.—*By the Angel Gabriel*—Lu. 1:32, 35. *By John the Baptist*—John 1:29–34. *By Nathaniel*—John 1:49. *By the Gadarene demoniacs*—Mt. 8:29; Lu. 8:28. *By unclean spirits*—Mk. 3:11. *By disciples in boat*—Mt. 14:33. *By the eunuch*—Acts 8:37 (*marg.*). *By Martha*—John 11:27. *By Peter*—Mt. 16:16. See Acts 16:31, 34. *By Paul*—Acts 9:20.

He calls God His Father.—Mt. 15:13; 18:10, 19; 20:23; 26:53, 63, 64; Lu. 10:22; 22:29; John 5:19–21, 23, 26, 27, 30, 36, 37; 8:16, 19, 26–29, 38, 49, 54; 10:15, 17, 18, 29, 30, 36–38; 11:41; 12:49, 50; 13:3; 14:7, 9–11, 13, 16, 20, 21, 23, 24, 28, 31; 15:1, 8–10, 15, 23, 24; 16:15, 27, 28, 32; 17:1–26; 20:17, 21.

Only Begotten Son.—John 1:14, 18; 3:16, 18; I John 4:9.

Begotten by the Holy Spirit.—Mt. 1:18, 20; Lu. 1:35.

Lordship of.—He is called Lord—Ps. 110:1; Mt. 8:2, 6, 8, 21, 25; 14:28, 30; 15:22, 25, 27; 16:22; 17:4, 15; 18:21; 20:30, 31; 22:43–45; 24:42; 25:37, 44; 26:22; Mk. 7:28; 12:35–37; Lu. 1:43; 5:8, 12; 6:46; 7:6, 13; 9:54; 10:17, 40; 11:1; 12:41; 13:23; 18:41; 20:41–44; 22:33, 38, 49; John 6:34, 68; 8:11; 9:36, 38; 11:3, 12, 21, 27, 32, 34, 39; 13:6, 9, 13, 25, 36, 37; 14:5, 8, 22; 20:13; 21:

15, 16, 17, 20, 21; Acts 1:6; 2:36; 7:60; 9:5, 13; 22:8; 26:15; Rom. 10:9, 12; I Cor. 12:3, 5.

The Lord—Mt. 3:3; 4:7; 28:6; Mk. 1:3; 5:19; 11:3; Lu. 2:11; 3:4; 4:12; 10:1; 11:39; 12:42; 13:15; 17:5, 6; 18:6; 19: 31, 34; 22:61; 24:34; John 1:23; 4:1; 6:23; 11:2; 13:14; 20:2, 18, 20, 25; 21: 7, 12; Acts 2:20, 25; 5:14; 9:1, 5, 10, 11, 15, 17, 27, 29, 31, 35, 42; 11:21, 23, 24; 15:17; 18:8; Rom. 10:13; 16:2, 11, 12, 13, 22; I Cor. 1:31; 2:8; 4:5; 6:14, 17; 9:2, 5, 14; 10:21, 22; 11:23, 26, 27; 15:58; II Cor. 2:12; 4:5; Gal. 1:19; 5: 10; Phil. 2:11; I Thess. 1:6; 4:15–17; 5:2; II Thess. 3:16; II Tim. 1:8; Heb. 2:3; 7:14; Jas. 5:7, 8, 10; II Pet. 3:2.

The Lord Jesus—Mk. 16:19; Lu. 24:3; Acts 1:21; 4:33; 7:59; 8:16; 11:20; 15: 11; 16:31; 19:5, 13, 17; 20:24, 35; 21: 13; I Cor. 5:4, 5; 6:11; II Cor. 1:14; 4:14; Eph. 1:15; Phil. 2:19; Col. 3:17; I Thess. 2:15, 19; 3:11, 13; 4:1, 2; II Thess. 1:7, 8, 12; 2:8; Philemon 5.

The Lord Jesus Christ—Acts 11:17; 15: 26; 20:21; 28:31; Rom. 5:1, 11; 13:14; 15:6, 30; I Cor. 8:6; 15:57; II Cor. 8:9; Eph. 1:17; 5:20; Phil. 3:20; I Thess. 5:9; II Thess. 2:1, 14, 16; 3:6, 12; I Tim. 6:3, 14; Jas. 2:1; II Pet. 1:8, 11, 14, 16; 2:20; Jude 17. *Most of the Epistles have the expression ''The Lord Jesus Christ'' in beginning and closing* —Rom. 1:7; 16:20; I Cor. 1:2, 3, 7, 8, 10; 16:23; II Cor. 1:2, 3; 13:14; Gal. 1:3; 6:14, 18; Eph. 1:2, 3; 6:23, 24; Phil. 1:2; 4:23; Col. 1:3; I Thess. 1:1, 3; 5:23, 28; II Thess. 1:1; 3:18; Philemon 3, 25; Jas. 1:1; I Pet. 1:3; II Pet. 3:18; Jude 4, 25.

Jesus our Lord—I Cor. 9:1.

Jesus Christ our Lord—Rom. 1:4; 5:21; 6:23; 7:25; 8:39; I Cor. 1:9; 15:31; Eph. 3:11; Phil. 3:8; I Tim. 1:2, 12; II Tim. 1:2; Jude 25.

Lord Christ—Rom. 16:18; Col. 3:24.

Lord of all—Acts 10:36.

Lord of lords—Rev. 17:14; 19:16.

Lord of the sabbath—Mt. 12:8; Mk. 2: 28; Lu. 6:5.

His power.—Ps. 110:3; Is. 9:6; 63:1; Mt. 8:3, 16, 27; John 17:2; I Cor. 1:24, 30; Phil. 2:9, 10; II Thess. 1:9; Heb. 1:3; 7:25; II Pet. 1:16; Rev. 1:8, 13–18; 5:12. See CREATOR. Power to perform

miracles—Lu. 5:17; Acts 2:22. See MIRACLES OF JESUS.

He gave His disciples power to perform miracles—Mt. 10:1; Mk. 6:7; Lu. 11: 20–22. See HOLY SPIRIT.

Authority to forgive sins—Mt. 9:6; Mk. 2:5–12; Lu. 5:20–26; Heb. 1:3.

Power over life and death—Mt. 26:52–56; John 2:19–22; 5:21, 25–28; 10:17, 18, 28; I Cor. 15:24–28. Phil. 3:20, 21.

All authority given to him.—Mt. 28:18; John 3:35; 5:22, 23; Rom. 14:9; I Cor. 15:24–28; Eph. 1:20–23; Phil. 2:9–11; Col. 2:10; Heb. 7:26; I Pet. 3:22. See Mt. 11:27; John 5:27.

The judge of the world.—Ps. 96:12; Is. 2:4; Mt. 16:27; 25:31–46; John 5:22, 23, 27, 30; Acts 10:42; Rom. 2:16; I Cor. 4:5; II Cor. 5:10; II Tim. 4:1, 8; Rev. 22:12.

Kingship.—Mt. 27:42; I Cor. 15:24–28; Col. 1:13; Heb. 2:7, 8; Rev. 1:5, 9; 11: 15; 12:10; 14:14; 17:14; 19:11–16.

Prophecies concerning—Gen. 49:10; Ps. 2:6; 110:1–4; 132:11, 17, 18; Is. 2:4; 9:6, 7; 32:1; 52:7, 13; 55:3–5; Jer. 23:5; 30:9; 33:17; Ez. 34:23, 24; 37: 24, 25; Dan. 2:35, 44; 7:13, 14; 9:35; Hos. 3:5; Mic. 5:2; Zech. 6:12, 13; 9:9, 10; Mt. 2:2, 6; Lu. 1:32, 33; Acts 2: 29–36.

Anointed—Ps. 45:7; Is. 61:1; Dan. 9:24; Lu. 4:18–21; Acts 4:26, 27; 10:38. See Acts 2:29–36.

Crowned—Rev. 6:2; 14:14; 17:14.

Kingship acknowledged by Jesus Himself—Mt. 13:41; 16:27, 28; 25:31–46; 27:11; Lu. 22:29, 30; John 18:33–37. By the wise men—Mt. 2:2. By Nathaniel—John 1:49. By Pilate—John 18:39. By His disciples—John 6:15. *His triumphal entry*—Mt. 21:5; Lu. 19:38; John 12:13. By the thief on the cross—Lu. 23:42.

Written on the cross—Mt. 27:37; Lu. 23: 37, 38; John 19:19–21.

Seated on the throne of David.—Is. 9:7; Ez. 37:24, 25; Lu. 1:32, 33; Acts 2: 29–36.

Seated at the right hand of God.—Mt. 26:64; Mk. 16:19; Lu. 22:69; Acts 2: 33–36; 5:31; 7:55, 56; Rom. 8:34; Eph. 1:20–22; Col. 3:1; Heb. 1:3; 10:12, 13; 12:2; I Pet. 3:22; Rev. 1:5, 13–18; 3:21; 5:5–10; 7:9–12; 20:6.

King of Zion.—Ps. 2:6; 110:2; Is. 52:7, 13; Zech. 9:9; Mt. 21:5; John 12:13, 15.

HIS KINGDOM—"It is only when we take the fourfold narrative in its entirety that we begin to catch sight of the satisfying and convincing fulness of the idea of the kingdom of heaven. This idea underlies the whole Gospel of John. In the Synoptic Gospels we have the conditions of entrance into the kingdom, a childlike spirit, faith, repentance, and obedience—Mt. 18:3; 9:22; 5:20; Lu. 13:3. In John we have the spiritual birth by which alone those conditions are made possible—John 3:5. In the Synoptics we have the laws of the kingdom—Mt. 5–7. In John we have the new life in which alone those laws can be fulfilled—John 6:22–65. In the Synoptics we have the parables and pictures of the kingdom—Mt. 13, etc. In John we have the inmost sense of those parables, spoken directly to the soul, in words of which Christ Himself says 'they are spirit, and they are life.' In the Synoptics we have the new order of human society in the imitation by the disciples of Christ's obedience to the will of God—Mt. 12:50. In John we have the organizing principle of that new order in Christ's revelation of Himself to the disciples as the way, the truth, and the life—John 14:6. In the Synoptics we have the supremacy of Christ's example over men's hearts. In John we have the supremacy of Christ's teachings over men's minds."—HENRY VAN DYKE.

"Put together the Sermon on the Mount, the Charge to the Twelve Apostles, the Parables of the Kingdom, the Discourse in the Supper-room, and the institution of the two great Sacraments, and the plan of our Saviour is before you. And it is enunciated with an accent of calm, unfaltering conviction that it will be realized in human history."—HENRY P. LIDDON

Called: The Kingdom of God—Mt. 21: 31; Mk. 1:15; 4:11, 26, 30; 9:1, 47; 10:14, 15, 23–25; 12:34; 14:25; 15:43; Lu. 4:43; 6:20; 7:28; 8:1, 10; 9:2. 11.

27, 60, 62; 10:9, 11; 11:20; 13:20, 28, 29; 14:15; 16:16; 17:20, 21; 18:16, 17, 24, 25, 29; 19:11; 22:16; John 3:3, 5; Acts 1:3; 8:12; 14:22; 19:8; 28:23, 31; Rom. 14:17; I Cor. 6:9, 10; 15:50; Gal. 5:21; Col. 4:11; II Thess. 1:5; Rev. 12:10.

The Kingdom of Heaven—Mt. 3:2; 4:17, 5:19, 20; 7:21; 10:7; 11:11, 12; 13:11, 24, 31, 33, 44, 45, 47, 52; 18:1, 3, 4, 23; 19:12, 14, 23, 24; 20:1; 22:2; 23:13; 25:1.

The Kingdom of Christ and God—Eph. 5:5; Rev. 11:15.

His Kingdom—Mt. 6:33; 13:41; 16:28; 20:21; Lu. 1:33; 12:31; 22:29, 30; John 18:36; I Thess. 2:12; II Tim. 4:1, 18; Heb. 1:8.

Kingdom of their Father—Mt. 13:43.

My Father's Kingdom—Mt. 26:29.

The Kingdom of the Son of His Love—Col. 1:13.

Temporal kingdom, or, Kingdom of this world.—The disciples and Jews thought it was a—Mt. 20:21; Lu. 14:15; 19: 11–27; John 6:15; Acts 1:6.

Not of this world.—John 6:15; 18:36. See Mt. 26:52–56; Rom. 14:17; I Cor. 4:20.

Within you.—Lu. 17:20, 21.

Not established before death of Jesus. —Mt. 16:19, 28; Mk. 11:10; 15:43; Lu. 12:32; 17:20; 19:11; 21:31; 23: 42, 51; Acts 1:3, 6.

To be established "in the days of these kings."—Dan. 2:31–45. See Is. 9:6, 7.

At hand.—Mt. 3:2; 4:17; 10:7; Mk. 1: 15; Lu. 10:9, 11.

To come with power.—Mk. 9:1; Acts 1:4–8; 2:1–4.

During the lifetime of the disciples standing near Him.—Mt. 16:28; Mk. 9:1; Lu. 9:27; 21:31; 22:16, 18; Acts 1:6–8.

Prepared for you before the foundation of the world.—Mt. 25:34.

Jews natural heirs, but rejected.—Mt. 8:11–12; 21:43; 23:13.

Suffereth violence.—Mt. 11:12; Lu. 16: 16.

Kingdom in heaven.—Mt. 8:11, 12; 13: 37–42; 19:28; 25:31–46; Lu. 13:28, 29; 22:29, 30; I Cor. 15:50; Rev. 11:15.

Who may enter.—He that is but little, is greater than John the Baptist—Mt. 11:11; Lu. 7:28.

Seek first the kingdom—Mt. 6:33; Lu. 12:31.

Those who do the will of God—Mt. 5:19; 7:21–27.

Righteous—Mt. 5:20; I Cor. 6:9–11; Gal. 5:19–24; Eph. 5:3–6; II Thess. 1:5.

Repentance a condition—Mt. 3:2; 4:17.

Poor in spirit—Mt. 5:3; Lu. 6:20.

Publicans and harlots enter before the pharisees—Mt. 21:31; Lu. 7:29–50.

Hard for the rich to enter—Mt. 19:23, 24; Mk. 10:23–27; Lu. 18:24, 25, 29.

Those who do not look back—Lu. 9:62.

Must become as little children—Mt. 18: 1–4; 19:14; Mk. 10:14, 15; Lu. 18: 15–17.

Those who are born anew of water and the Spirit—John 3:3–5.

Those who endure tribulations—Mk. 9: 47; Lu. 18:29; Acts 14:22; II Thess. 1:5.

Everlasting kingdom.—II Sam. 7:12, 13; Ps. 45:6, 7 (Heb. 1:8, 9); 89:3, 4, 29–37; Dan. 2:44, 45; 7:14; Mic. 4:7; Lu. 1:33.

Righteous.—Ps. 45:6; Is. 9:7; 11:1–10; 62:1, 2; Jer. 23:5; 33:15; Zech. 9:9; Heb. 1:8, 9.

Universal.—Ps. 2:8; Is. 2:2–4; 11:9; 42: 4, 10–13; 62:1, 2; Jer. 31:34; Dan. 2: 44, 45; Zech. 14:9; Mt. 24:14; 28:18, 19; Mk. 16:15, 16; Lu. 24:46, 47; Acts 1:8; Rom. 10:18; Phil. 2:10; Col. 1:6, 23; Rev. 11:15.

Gospel of kingdom.—Mt. 4:23; 9:35; Lu. 4:43; 8:1; 9:2, 60; Acts 1:3. To be preached in the whole world—Mt. 24: 14; 28:18, 19; Mk. 16:15, 16; Lu. 24: 46, 47; Acts 1:8.

Word of the kingdom.—Mt. 13:19; Acts 8:12; 19:8; 20:25; 28:23–31.

Keys of.—Is. 22:22; Mt. 16:19; Rev. 3:7.

Mysteries of.—Mk. 4:11; Lu. 8:10.

Parables of.—The growth of the kingdom by addition from without: *The Sower*—Mt. 13:3–8, 18–23; Mk. 4:3–8, 13–20; Lu. 8:5–8, 11–15. *The Tares*—Mt. 13:24–30, 36–43; Mk. 4:26–29. *The Mustard Seed*—Mt. 13:31, 32; Mk. 4: 30–32; Lu. 13:18, 19. *The Net*—Mt. 13:47–50. Influence upon the world: *The Leaven*—Mt. 13:33; Lu: 13:20, 21.

Growth from within: *The Blade, the Ear, and the Full Grain in the Ear*—Mk. 4:26–29. *The Vine*—John 15:1–8.

Kingdom of God the supreme good: *The Hidden Treasure*—Mt. 13:44. *The Pearl*—Mt. 13:45, 46.

Rebuke to Phariseeism, Parables of grace: *The Lost Sheep*—Mt. 18:12, 13; Lu. 15: 4–6. *The Lost Piece of Silver*—Lu. 15: 8–10. *The Prodigal Son*—Lu. 15:11–32. *Pharisee and Publican*—Lu. 18: 9–14. *Two Debtors*—Lu. 7:36–50. *Strife for First Places at Feasts*—Lu. 14:7–11. *The Great Supper*—Mt. 22: 1–14; Lu. 14:16–24. *The Good Samaritan*—Lu. 10:30–37. *The Unjust Steward*—Lu. 16:1–12. *The Rich Man and Lazarus*—Lu. 16:19–31. The *Judgment—Children in the Marketplace*—Lu. 7:31–35. *The Barren Fig-tree*—Lu. 13:6–9. *The Wicked Husbandman*—Mt. 21:33–41; Mk. 12:1–9; Lu. 20: 9–17. *The Wedding Feast and the Wedding Robe*—Mt. 22:1–14. *The Unfaithful Servant*—Mt. 24:45–51. *The Ten Virgins*—Mt. 25:1–13. Service in the kingdom: *The Laborers*—Mt. 20:1–16. *The Hours, the Talents, and the Pounds*—Mt. 20:1–16; 25:14–30; Lu. 19:12–27.

The right use of wordly possessions: *The Unjust Steward*—Lu. 16:1–12. *The Rich Man and Lazarus*—Lu. 16:19–31. See CHURCH.

High priest, after the order of Melchizedek.—Ps. 110:4; Is. 53:12; Zech. 6:13; Rom. 8:34; Eph. 2:13, 18; I Tim. 2:5; Heb. 2:17, 18; 3:1; 4:14; 5:5–10; 6:20; 7:1–28; 8:1–6; 9:11–28; 10:1–21; I John 2:1.

Head of the Church.—Rom. 8:29; I Cor. 11:3; Eph. 1:10, 22, 23; 4:15; 5:23, 24; Col. 1:18; 2:10, 19; Heb. 3:3, 6; Rev. 3:7.

The head of the corner—Ps. 118:22; Is, 28:16; Mt. 21:42; Lu. 20:17; Acts 4: 11; Eph. 2:20; I Pet. 2:6, 7.

Eternity of.—Mt. 18:20; 28:20 (Acts 18: 10); John 1:1–4, 15; 6:62; 8:23, 58; 17:5; II Cor. 8:9; Eph. 4:10; Col. 1:17; Heb. 1:8–12; 6:20; 7:16, 24, 25; 13:8; Rev. 1:8, 17, 18; 21:6; 22:13. See "Pre-existence," under DIVINITY OF JESUS, above.

Exaltation.—Ps. 68:18; Mt. 28:18; Lu. 24:26; John 7:39; 12:23; 14:2, 3; Acts

1:2, 11; 3:13, 20, 21; Rom. 6:4; 8:17;
I Cor. 15:25–28; Eph. 4:8–10; Phil.
2:6–11; Heb. 2:9; 5:9; 9:12, 24; I Pet.
1:21; II Pet. 1:16.

Glory of.—Mt. 17:2–8; Lu. 9:26, 32; John
1:14; 2:11; 7:39; 12:16, 23; 13:31, 32;
16:14; 17:1–5, 22, 24; Rom. 9:5; II Pet.
1:16–18.

He came in fulfilment of the scriptures.
—Mt. 5:17; 26:52–56; Lu. 24:25–27,
44–47; John 5:39, 45, 46; Acts 8:32–
35; 13:27–40; 17:2, 3; 18:28; Gal. 4:4.
The prophet who was to come—Deut.
18:15 (John 1:21, 25; Acts 3:22; 7:37).
The Only Begotten Son—Ps. 2:7 (Acts
13:33; Heb. 1:5–8; 5:5). The Crowned
Son of David—Ps. 110:1 (Mt. 22:41–
46; Mk. 12:35–37; Lu. 20:41–44; Acts
2:34–36; Heb. 1:13; Rev. 8:5). The
stone which the builders rejected—
Ps. 118:22 (Mt. 21:42; Mk. 12:10, 11;
Lu. 20:17; Acts 4:11; Eph. 2:20; I Pet.
2:7, 8). Born of a virgin—Is. 7:14
(Mt. 1:23; Lu. 1:26–38). A light to
the Gentiles—Is. 9:1, 2 (Mt. 4:14–16).
The Spirit of the Lord upon Him—Is.
11:1, 2; 35:5; 42:1; 61:1, 2 (Mt. 11:5;
Lu. 2:28–32; Acts 2:2–4, 16–21, 33).
See PROPHECIES CONCERNING.

His miracles a proof of His divinity.—
Mt. 11:20–24; Mk. 2:5–12; John 2:11,
23; 3:2, 11; 4:48–53; 9:4; 10:37, 38;
11:45, 46; 14:11, 12; 15:24; 20:30, 31;
Acts 2:22.

**He foretold His own death, burial, and
resurrection on the third day.**—Mt.
12:40; 16:21; 17:9, 12, 22, 23; 20:17–
19; 21:33–45; 26:2, 12, 21–28, 32; 27:
63; Mk. 8:31; 9:9, 10; 10:33, 34; 14:
18–25, 28, 58; Lu. 9:22, 44; 18:32, 33;
22:15, 37; 24:7; John 2:19–21; 3:14;
8:28; 12:32, 33; 13:18–21; Chs. 14–17.

His resurrection a proof of His divinity.
—Acts 2:22–32; 3:15; 5:29–32; 10:39–
42; 13:30–37; 17:31; Rom. 10:9; I Cor.
15:1–19; I Pet. 1:21.

**He knew the thoughts and purposes of
men.**—Mt. 9:4; 12:25; Lu. 6:8; 7:39,
40; 9:47; John 1:42, 47–50; 2:24, 25;
6:61, 64; 13:11; 16:30.

His sinlessness.—John 8:46; II Cor. 5:
21; Heb. 4:15; 7:26–28; I Pet. 2:21–
23; I John 3:5.

He is the sufficer of all needs.—Mt. 11:
28–30; John 4:14; 6:35, 48–58; 8:31–
36, 51.

He will send the Holy Spirit.—John 14:
26; 15:26; Acts 2:33.

**He commanded to baptize in the name
of Father, Son, and Holy Spirit.**—Mt.
28:19.

Baptism was ''in His name.''—Acts 2:
38; 8:12, 16; 10:48; 19:5.

HUMANITY OF: The Word made flesh.
—Mt. 8:20; 11:19; Lu. 24:39; John 1:
14; 20:27; Acts 2:30; 13:23; Rom. 1:3;
8:3, 4, 29, 32; 9:5; II Cor. 5:16; 8:9;
Phil. 2:5–8; Col. 2:9; I Tim. 3:16; Heb.
2:9–18; 9:20; 10:5; I Pet. 1:20; I John
1:1–3; 3:5–8; 4:2; II John 7.

Made a little lower than the angels.—
Heb. 2:7–9.

Seed of Abraham.—Gen. 12:3; 22:18;
26:4; 28:14 (Mt. 1:1; Lu. 1:54, 55;
Acts 3:25; Rom. 4:13; Gal. 3:8).

Descendant of Isaac.—Gen. 17:19; 26:
2–5 (Rom. 9:6–8; Heb. 11:18). Judah
should be in the line of descent—Gen.
49:10; Ps. 60:7 (Mt. 1:2; Heb. 7:14).

The Son of David.—II Sam. 7:11, 12, 27;
Ps. 89:3, 4, 35–37; Is. 9:6; 11:1; 55:3,
4; Jer. 23:5; 35:15; Amos 9:11, 12
(Mt. 1:1; Lu. 1:32, 69; Acts 15:15–18;
Heb. 1:5); Ps. 16:8–10 (Acts 2:25–28;
13:34–37); Mt. 9:27; 12:23; 20:30, 31;
21:9; 22:42–45; Mk. 12:35–37; Lu. 18:
38; John 7:42; Rom. 1:3; Rev. 22:16.

Called the Son of Man.—Mt. 8:20; 9:6;
11:19; 12:8, 32, 40; 13:37, 41; 16:13,
27, 28; 17:9, 12, 22; 19:28; 20:18, 28;
24:27, 30; 26:2, 24, 45, 64; Mk. 2:28;
8:38; 9:9, 31; 14:21, 62; Lu. 6:22; 9:
44, 58; 11:30; 12:8, 10, 40; 17:22, 24,
30; 18:8, 31; 19:10; 21:36; 22:48; 24:
7; John 1:51; 3:13, 14; 5:27; 6:27;
12:34; 13:31; Acts 7:56; Rev. 1:13;
14:14. See Ez. 1:26; Dan. 7:13; 10:16.

Became poor for our sakes—Mt. 20:28;
II Cor. 8:9; Phil. 2:5–8. Had not
where to lay His head—Mt. 8:20; Lu.
9:58.

Tempted like as we are—Heb. 2:18;
4:15. See SUFFERINGS.

MISSION OF: Sent by the Father.—Is.
42:1–4; 49:6; 61:1–3; John 3:16, 17,
34; 4:34; 5:30, 36, 38; 6:29, 38, 57; 7:
29; 8:42; 10:36; 11:42; 17:3, 8, 18, 21,
23, 25; 20:21; I John 4:9, 10, 14. He

came in His Father's name—John 5: 43.

Bind up the broken-hearted, To—Is. 57: 15; 61:1. See Ps. 147:3.

Church, To establish His—Mt. 16:18. See CHURCH.

Comfort those that mourn, To—Is. 61:2; Mt. 5:4.

Condemn sin, To—Rom. 8:3, 4.

Example in His life, To set—Mt. 3:15; 11:29; John 13:12–16, 34; 17:14, 18, 21, 22; Rom. 8:29; 13:14; 15:2–5; II Cor. 3:18; 4:10; Gal. 4:19; Eph. 4:13, 15; 5:2; Phil. 2:5; Col. 3:10, 11; Heb. 12: 2–4; I Pet. 1:15, 16; 2:21–24; I John 2:6; 3:1–3, 7, 16; 4:17; Rev. 14:4.

Fatherhood of God, To reveal—John 1: 12, 14, 18; 4:21, 23; 5:36, 37, 43; 6:27, 44–46; 8:27, 28, 41, 42; 10:15–18, 32; 11:52; 12:49, 50; 14:1–13, 20–24, 28–31; 16:3, 10, 23–30.

Fulfil all righteousness, To—Mt. 3:15.

Fulfil the scriptures, To—See "He came in fulfilment of the scriptures," under DIVINITY.

Glorify the Father—John 13:31; 14:13; 17:4; I Pet. 4:11.

Judgment, For—Lu. 2:34; John 5:22, 23, 27; 9:39; Acts 10:42; 17:31. See John 12:47.

Kingdom, To establish—See KINGDOM.

Life, To give—John 1:4; 3:15, 36; 5:40; 6:33, 51; 10:10–28; 11:25; 14:6; Gal. 2:20; Col. 3:3, 4; I John 5:12, 20.

Light to the Gentiles, To bring—Is. 9: 1, 2; 42:6; 49:6; Mt. 4:13–16; Lu. 1: 78, 79; 2:30–32; Acts 26:23.

Light of the world, The—John 1:4, 5; 3:19; 8:12; 9:5; 12:35, 36, 46.

Lord of living and dead, To become— Rom. 14:9; 15:8–12; II Cor. 5:15.

Mediator, To be—See MEDIATOR.

Minister, To—Mt. 20:28; Mk. 10:45.

Peace, To give—Lu. 1:79; John 14:27; 16:33; 20:19; Col. 3:15.

Preach, To—Mk. 1:38. *Good tidings unto the poor*—Is. 61:1 (Lu. 4:17, 18). *The kingdom of God*—Mt. 4:23; 10:7; Lu. 4:43; 8:1; 16:16. *Remission of sins*— Lu. 1:77; 24:47. *To proclaim the year of Jehovah's favor*—Is. 49:8–13 (II Cor. 6:2); 61:2 (Lu. 4:19).

Propitiation for sins, To be a—John 1:29; Rom. 3:25; 4:25; 5:5–8; 8:3; I

Cor. 15:3; II Cor. 5:21; Gal. 1:4; 3:13; Heb. 9:26, 28.

Reconcile the world to God, To—Dan. 9:24; Rom. 5:9–11; II Cor. 5:17–21; Eph. 2:13–23; Col. 1:20–22; 2:14; Heb. 10:19–22.

Redeem mankind, To—Is. 53:4–12; I Cor. 5:7; 6:20; 7:23; Gal. 4:4, 5; I Thess. 1:10; I Pet. 1:18–21; II Pet. 2:1; I John 2:2; 3:16; 4:10; Rev. 5:9; 13:8. See SACRIFICES.

The life of Christ a ransom—Mt. 20:28; Mk. 10:45; I Tim. 2:6.

Christ gave His life for mankind—John 6:51; 10:11, 15; 11:49–53; 15:13; Rom. 4:25; 5:6–9; 8:3, 32; 14:15; II Cor. 5:14–21; Gal. 3:1, 8, 13, 14; Eph. 5:2, 25; I Thess. 5:9, 10; Tit. 2:13, 14; Heb. 2:9–18; 7:24–27; 9:11–17, 25–26; I Pet. 2:21–24; 3:18.

Redemption through His blood—Rom. 3: 24, 25; Eph. 1:7; Heb. 9:12–15; I Pet. 1:18–20.

Christ purchased with His blood—Acts 20:28; I Cor. 6:20; 7:23; II Pet. 2:1; Rev. 5:9.

Remission of sins, To give—Lu. 1:77; 24:47; Acts 10:43.

Christ's death for remission of sins—Dan. 9:24; Lu. 24:44–47; Acts 5:30, 31; Rom. 4:25; 5:6–8; 6:3–11; I Cor. 15: 1–3; Gal. 1:4; Heb. 1:3; 7:27; 9:14, 26–28; 10:12; I Pet. 2:24; 3:18.

Christ's blood shed for the remission of sins—Mt. 26:28; Mk. 14:24; Rom. 3: 25; Eph. 1:7; Col. 1:14; Heb. 9:11–14; 13:12; I John 1:7; Rev. 1:5; 7:14, 15.

Repentance, To call sinners to—Mt. 9: 13; Lu. 5:31, 32; 24:45–47; Acts 3:26; 5:31.

Save, To—See SALVATION.

Set at liberty them that are bruised, To —Is. 61:1 (Lu. 4:18). See Heb. 2:15.

Temptation, To deliver from—Heb. 2: 18; 4:15, 16.

Will of God, To do—John 4:34; 5:30; 6:38, 40.

Witness, To bear—John 7:29; 8:12–21, 25–47; 10:25–38; 14:1–24; 15:8–27; 17:1–8.

Works of the devil, To destroy—John 12:31; Heb. 2:14; I John 3:8; 4:4; 5:19.

MESSIAH. *Gr.* Christ, Anointed—Ps. 2:2 (Acts 4:26, 27; Heb. 1:8, 9); Dan. 9:24. See KINGSHIP, ANOINTED.

The Jews were looking for a Messiah.— Dan. 9:24-27; Mt. 11:3; 22:42-45; Mk. 12:35-37; Lu. 3:15; 20:41; John 1:20, 25, 41, 42; 4:25, 26, 29; Acts 3:18, 20, 24; 26:6, 7, 22, 23; I Pet. 1:11.

Prophecies concerning.—Born of a woman: the child of a virgin—Is. 7:14 (Mt. 1:18-23; Lu. 1:27-35).

Born in Bethlehem—Mic. 5:2 (Mt. 2:5, 6). The seed of Abraham: of the tribe of Judah—Gen. 49:10 (Heb. 7:14).

The Son of David—See THE WORD MADE FLESH, above.

Offices: Commander—Is. 55:4; cornerstone—See ''Head of the corner,'' under HEAD OF THE CHURCH, above. Counsellor—Is. 9:6. Ensign—Is. 11: 10, 12; 49:22; 62:10. See John 3:14, 15; 12:32.

Judge—Ps. 72:2-4; 110:6. See JUDGE, above.

King—See KINGSHIP, above.

Mediator—Is. 49:8. See MEDIATOR, below.

Priest—See PRIESTHOOD, above.

The Prophet—Deut. 18:15 (Mt. 21:11; John 1:21, 25; 6:14; 7:40; Acts 3:22; 7:37). A Prophet—Lu. 7:16, 39; 13: 33; 24:19; John 4:19; 9:17.

Servant—Is. 42:1; 49:3, 6; 52:13; 53:11; Mt. 20:28; Acts 3:13, 26; 4:27, 30; Phil. 2:7.

John the Baptist to be His messenger— Mal. 3:1; 4:5 (Mt. 11:10, 14; Mk. 1:2; Lu. 7:27).

His character. See CHARACTER OF JESUS, below. For prophecies concerning the Messiah, see Gen. 3:15.

Jesus is called Messiah.—By Andrew— John 1:41.

Called the Christ.—Mt. 1:16; 27:17. By the angel to the shepherds—Lu. 2:11. By Andrew—John 1:41. By John the Baptist—John 3:28. By Martha— John 11:27. By John—John 1:17; I John 5:6-9. By Peter—Mt. 16:16; Mk. 8:29; Lu. 9:20; Acts 3:18, 20; II Pet. 1:16-18; see I Pet. 1:10, 11. By Peter and John—Acts 4:26, 27 *marg.* By Paul—Acts 9:22; 17:3; 26:23; Rom. 1:1, 3; I Cor. 15:3, 12, 15-23, 31, 57. See ''Epistles have the expression

'Lord Jesus Christ' in beginning and closing,'' under LORDSHIP.

Jesus claims to be the Messiah.—John 4:25.

The Christ.—Mt. 16:16-20; 26:63, 64; Lu. 24:25-27; John 7:25, 26. See Mt. 11:1-6.

HUMILIATION OF JESUS. Acts 8:33. Acquainted with grief—Is. 53:3, 4; Mt. 26:38. Afflicted—Is. 53:4, 7; 63:9; Col. 1:24. Bore sin—Is. 53:5, 6, 11, 12; Rom. 4:25; 8:3; II Cor. 5:21; Heb. 9:28; I Pet. 2:24. Betrayed—Mt. 10: 4; 26:23-25; 27:4; Mk. 14:18-21, 41; Lu. 22:21, 22; John 6:71; 13:2, 21, 26. Bore griefs of men—Is. 53:4; Mt. 8: 17. Born of a woman—Mt. 1:18-25; Lu. 1:26-35; 2:1-11; Gal. 4:4; Phil. 2:7. Bound—Mt. 27:2. Bruised— Gen. 3:15; Is. 53:5, 10. Buffeted—Mt. 26:67. Buried—Is. 53:9; Mt. 27:57-60; Mk. 15:42-47; Lu. 23:50-56; John 19:38-42; Rom. 10:7; I Cor. 15:4. Cast forth—Lu. 4:29. Chastised—Is. 53:5; Lu. 23:16, 22; Heb. 5:8. Clothed with purple—Mk. 15:17. Condemned—Mt. 20:18; 27:3; Mk. 10:33; Lu. 24:20; Jas. 5:6. Crown of thorns, Wore a— See THORNS. Crucified—Mt. 26:2; 27: 35; 28:5; Lu. 23:33; John 19:20; Acts 2:23; I Cor. 2:2; Phil. 2:8; Heb. 6:6; 12:2. Cut off—Is. 53:8; Dan. 9:26. Curse, Became a—Gal. 3:13. Dead— John 19:31; I Thess. 4:14; 5:10. Delivered up—Mt. 20:18; 26:15; Lu. 22: 3, 6; 24:20; Acts 2:23; 3:13. Denied— Mt. 26:34, 69-75; Mk. 14:30, 68-72; Lu. 22:55-61; John 13:38; 18:25-27; Acts 3:14. Despised—Ps. 22:6, 7; 109: 25; Is. 53:3; Jer. 18:16 (Mt. 27:39; Mk. 15:29; Lu. 18:31-39). Endured the cross—Phil. 2:8; Heb. 12:2. Fasted—Mt. 4:2. Found in fashion as a man—Phil. 2:8. Gave Himself—John 6:51; Gal. 1:4; 2:20; Eph. 5:2, 25. Girded Himself—John 13:4. Groaned —John 11:33, 38. Hated without cause—John 7:7; 15:18, 24, 25. Homeless—Mt. 8:20; Lu. 9:58. Humbled— Rom. 15:3; II Cor. 8:9; Phil. 2:7, 8. Hungry—Mt. 4:2; 21:18; Mk. 11:12. Infirmity, Compassed with—Mt. 8:17; Heb. 5:2. Killed—Mt. 16:21; Mk. 9: 31; 10:34; Acts 2:23; 3:15. Laid down His life—John 10:11, 15, 17, 18; I

John 3:16. Laid in a manger—Lu. 2:7. Learned obedience—Mt. 3:15; 26:39; John 10:18; Rom. 5:19; Phil. 2:8; Heb. 5:8. Left alone—Mt. 26:56. See vs. 38-46. Lifted up—John 3:14; 8:28; 12:32, 34. Manifested in flesh—John 1:14; Rom. 1:3; 8:3; II Cor. 5:16; I Tim. 3:16; Heb. 10:5; I John 3:8. Marred—Is. 52:14. Mocked—Ps. 22: 8; Mt. 27:29, 31, 39-44; Mk. 10:34; 15: 20; Lu. 23:11. Numbered with transgressors—Is. 53:12; Lu. 22:37. Obedient unto death—Phil. 2:8. Offered—Eph. 5:2; Heb. 7:27; 9:14, 25-28; 10: 10, 12. Oppressed—Is. 53:7, 8. Persecuted—John 15:20. Pierced—Ps. 22: 16; Zech. 12:10; Mt. 27:35.

CHARACTER OF: Affectionate. — Lu. 13:34, 35; 19:41; John 11:1-44; 19: 25-27. Toward little children — Mt. 18:1-6; 19:13-15; Mk. 10:13-16; Lu. 18:15, 16. See LOVE and BENEVOLENT.

Benevolent.—Is. 35:5; 61:1-3; Mt. 4:23, 24; 8:16; 9:35; 11:4, 5; 14:14; 15:30, 31; 19:2; 21:14; Mk. 1:32-34; 3:9, 10; Lu. 4:18, 19, 40, 41; 7:21; John 10:32; Acts 10:38. See COMPASSIONATE and LOVING.

Compassionate.—Is. 40:11; 42:3 (Mt. 12: 20); 53:4 (Mt. 8:16, 17); Mt. 9:36; 14:14; 15:32; 20:34; Mk. 1:41; 6:34; 7:26-30; 8:2, 3; 10:13-21, 46-50; Lu. 7:13; 13:11-16; 14:12-14; 19:41-44; John 11:33-36; II Cor. 8:9; Heb. 4:15; 5:2. Parables of: The Good Samaritan—Lu. 10:30-37; The Lost Sheep—Mt. 18:12, 13; Lu. 15:4-7; The Prodigal Son—Lu. 15:11-32.

Courageous.—Lu. 4:21-29. Faces death bravely—Mt. 26:39-46; Mk. 10:32-34; Lu. 9:51; 13:31-33; John 11:7-10; 18: 4. Drives money-changers from temple—Mt. 21:12-16; Mk. 11:15-18; Lu. 19:45, 46; John 2:13-17.

Faithful.—Is. 11:5; 42:3; Lu. 2:44; John 17:4; II Thess. 3:3; II Tim. 2:13; Heb. 2:17; 3:2. To obey commandments—Lu. 4:43; John 4:34; 5:30; 6:38; 8:29; 9:4; 17:8. Faithful high priest—Heb. 2:17. Faithful witness—Rev. 1:5; 3:14.

Forgiving.—Mt. 5:43-46; 6:14, 15; 9:2, 6; 18:21-35; Mk. 2:5, 10; 11:25; Lu. 5:20, 24; 7:47-50; 17:3, 4; 22:50, 51;

23:34; John 8:1-11; Col. 3:13. See Eph. 4:32.

Gentle.—II Cor. 10:1; Heb. 5:2.

Guileless.—Is. 53:9; Heb. 7:26; I Pet. 2:22.

Hating iniquity.—Ps. 45:7; Heb. 1:9.

Holy.—Mk. 1:24; Lu. 1:35; 4:34; John 6:69; Acts 3:14; 4:27, 30; Eph. 1:4; Heb. 7:26; 9:14; I Pet. 1:19; Rev. 3:7. See SINLESS and RIGHTEOUS.

Humble.—Mk. 10:45; Lu. 22:27; John 13:5, 14; II Cor. 8:9; Phil. 2:8. He ate with publicans and sinners—Mt. 9:10-12; Mk. 2:15; Lu. 5:29-32.

Innocent.—Mt. 26:59, 60; 27:4, 23, 24; Mk. 15:14; Lu. 23:13-15, 41; John 18: 38; 19:16; Acts 13:28.

Just.—Is. 9:7; 11:4; 42:3, 4; Zech. 9:9. See RIGHTEOUS.

Kind.—Mt. 14:25-32; Lu. 19:5.

Long-suffering.—I Tim. 1:16.

Love of.—Passeth knowledge—Eph. 3: 17-19. Constraining—II Cor. 5:14. To the Father—John 14:31. For the lost —Is. 40:11; Mt. 23:37; Lu. 19:10; Mk. 3:5; 10:21. For His Church—Eph. 5: 2, 25, 29. For John the apostle—John 13:23; 19:26; 20:2; 21:7, 20. For His disciples—John 14:21; 15:9-15; Rom. 8:35-39; Gal. 2:20; II Thess. 2:13; I John 4:19; Rev. 1:5; 3:9, 19. Lazarus, Mary, and Martha—John 11:5, 33-36. See COMPASSIONATE and BENEVOLENT.

Lowly.—Zech. 9:9; Mt. 11:29.

Meek.—Ps. 45:4; Is. 42:1-3; 53:7; Mt. 11:29; 12:19, 20; 21:5; 27:12, 14; Mk. 14:60, 61; 15:3-5; Acts 8:32; II Cor. 10:1; I Pet. 2:21-23. See HUMILITY.

Merciful.—Heb. 2:17; 4:15; 5:2; Jas. 5:11.

Moderate (self-poised).—Mt. 8:19, 20; Mk. 12:14-17; Lu. 5:29-35; John 2:1-11; 6:15, 26-65.

Obedient.—Mt. 3:15; 26:39; John 4:34; 5:30; 6:38; 10:18; 17:4; Rom. 5:19; Phil. 2:8; Heb. 5:8.

Patient.—Is. 53:7; II Thess. 3:5; Rev. 1:9; 3:10.

Perfect.—Lu. 13:32; Heb. 5:9; 7:28. Through suffering—Heb. 2:10.

Pitiful (full of pity).—Jas. 5:11.

Pure.—I John 3:3. See SINLESSNESS, SPOTLESS, HOLY.

Righteous.—Is. 9:7; 11:4, 5; 63:1; Jer. 23:5; Mt. 27:19; Lu. 23:47; John 5:30; 7:18; Acts 3:14; 7:52; I Pet. 3:18; I John 2:1, 29.

Sanctified.—John 17:19.

Sincere.—Mt. 6:1–18; 10:16–39; 22:17–22; Mk. 12:38–40; Lu. 11:29–54; John 6:15, 26–71.

Sinless.—Is. 53:9; John 8:46; II Cor. 5:21; Eph. 1:4; Heb. 4:15; 7:26; I Pet. 2:22; I John 3:5.

Spotless.—I Pet. 1:19.

True.—John 1:14, 17; 7:18; 8:32; 14:6; 18:37.

Undefiled.—Heb. 7:26.

Unselfish.—Mt. 8:20; Lu. 9:58; II Cor. 8:9.

Zealous.—Ps. 69:9 (John 2:17); Mt. 4:23; Lu. 2:49; 9:51; 12:50; 13:34; John 4:34, 35; 8:29; 9:4.

POPULARITY: In Galilee.—Mt. 8:1; 9:26, 31; 13:2; 14:35, 36; Mk. 1:28, 32, 33; 2:2; 6:53–56; Lu. 4:14, 15, 37, 42; 5:1, 15; 9:11; John 6:15.

Multitudes from cities follow on foot—Mt. 14:13–15; Mk. 1:45; 6:32, 33.

Multitudes from Judæa and other regions follow Him—Mt. 4:23–25; Mk. 3:7, 8, 19–21; Lu. 5:17.

In Judæa.—Mt. 19:1, 2; Lu. 7:17; John 12:19.

His triumphal entry into Jerusalem—Mt. 21:1–11; Mk. 11:1–10; Lu. 19:29–38; John 12:12–18.

PRAYERS OF JESUS. Mt. 19:13; Lu. 3:21; 11:1; John 12:27, 28; Heb. 5:7.

Of thanksgiving.—Mt. 11:25, 26; 14:19; 15:36; 26:27; Mk. 6:41; 14:22; Lu. 22:17; John 11:41, 42; I Cor. 11:24.

In a mountain.—Mt. 14:23; Mk. 6:46; Lu. 6:12; 9:18, 28, 29.

All night in prayer.—Lu. 6:12.

In the upper room.—John 17:1–26.

For Peter.—Lu. 22:32.

In Gethsemane.—Mt. 26:36–42; Mk. 14:32–39; Lu. 22:41–45.

On the cross.—Mt. 27:46; Lu. 23:34, 46.

PROPHET. Deut. 18:15 (Mt. 21:11; John 1:21, 25; 6:14; 7:40; Acts 3:22; 7:37).

A prophet.—Lu. 7:16, 39; 13:33; 24:19; John 4:19; 9:17.

His predictions.—Mt. 8:11, 12; 11:23; 13:30–50; 19:28; Chs. 24, 25; 26:64; Mk. 10:30, 31; 14:62; 16:17; Lu.

10:15; 12:40–53; 13:24–35; 17:22–37; 18:29, 30; John 20:17.

The coming of the kingdom—Mt. 10:23, 24; 16:18, 19, 28; Mk. 9:1; Lu. 9:27; 17:20, 21; Acts 1:8.

Rejection of Christ and the gospel preached to the Gentiles—Mt. 21:33–45; Mk. 12:1–12; Lu. 20:9–19.

Raising of Lazarus—John 11:4, 11, 23, 40.

Destruction of Jerusalem—Mt. 23:29–38. See Mt. Ch. 24; Mk. Ch. 13; Lu. 19:42–44; 21:1–38; 23:28–31.

The colt—Mt. 21:1–5; Mk. 11:1–6; Lu. 19:29–35.

The fig-tree—Mt. 21:19; Mk. 11:14, 20.

Choice of the upper room—Mk. 14:12–16; Lu. 22:8–13.

Indicates His betrayer—Mt. 26:21–25, 46; Mk. 14:18–21, 42; Lu. 22:21, 22; John 13:11, 18, 21, 26–30.

Peter's denial—Mt. 26:34, 69–75; Mk. 14:30; Lu. 22:31–34, 54–61; John 13:38; 18:25–27.

Concerning death of Peter and John—John 21:18–23.

The baptism of the Holy Spirit—Lu. 24:49; John 7:39; 14:16, 17, 26; 15:26; 16:7; Acts 1:4–8.

Foretells His sufferings.—Mt. 16:21; 17:12; Mk. 9:12; Lu. 9:22; 17:25. That He would be condemned—Mt. 20:18; Mk. 10:33. Crucified—Mt. 20:19; John 3:14. Delivered up—Mt. 17:22; Mk. 9:31. *To the Gentiles*—Mt. 20:18, 19; Mk. 10:33; Lu. 18:32. Killed—Mt. 16:21; 17:23; Mk. 9:31; 10:34. Mocked—Mt. 20:19; Mk. 10:34; Lu. 18:32. Rejected—Mk. 8:31; Lu. 9:22; 17:25; 20:17, 18. Scourged—Mt. 20:19; Mk. 10:34; Lu. 18:33. Spit upon—Mk. 10:34.

Foretells His own death and resurrection the third day.—Mt. 12:40; 16:21; 17:9, 12, 22, 23; 20:17–19; 21:33–45; 26:2, 12, 21–28; Mk. 8:31; 10:33; 14:18–25; Lu. 9:22, 44; 22:15, 37; 24:7; John 2:19–21; 3:14; 8:28; 12:28; 12:32, 33; 13:18–21; Chs. 14–17.

RESURRECTION OF JESUS. Prophecies concerning.—Ps. 2:7 (Acts 13:33, 34); Ps. 16:9, 10 (Acts 2:25–35; 13:35–37).

Jesus foretold His death and resurrection on the third day.—Mt. 12:40; 16:

21; 17:9, 12, 22, 23; 20:17–19; 21:33–45; 26:2, 12, 21–28, 32; 27:63; Mk. 8: 31; 9:9, 10; 10:33; 14:18–25, 58; Lu. 9: 22, 44; 18:32, 33; 22:15, 37; 24:7; John 2:19–21; 3:14; 8:28; 12:32, 33; 13:18–21; Chs. 14–17.

Apostles testified concerning the resurrection.—Lu. 24:45–48; Acts 1:8, 22; 2:24–32; 3:15, 26; 4:10, 33; 5:30–32; 10:39–42; 13:30, 31–37; 17:3, 31; 26: 22, 23; Rom. 1:3, 4; 4:24; 6:3–10; 8:. 11; 10:9; I Cor. 6:14; 15:1–21; II Cor. 4:13, 14; Gal. 1:1; Eph. 1:20; Col. 2: 12; 3:1–4; I Thess. 1:10; 4:13–17; Heb. 13:20; I Pet. 1:21.

The foundation of Christianity.—John 11:25, 26; Rom. 1:3, 4; 6:3–11; 8:11; 10:9; I Cor. 3:10, 11; 15:1–20; Eph. 2:4–7; Col. 2:12; 3:1.

Only signs Jesus gave: Jonah—Mt. 12: 39, 40. The temple—Mk. 14:58; John 2:18–22.

Appearances.—Mary Magdalene—Mk. 16:9; John 20:18. The women—Mt. 28:9. Peter—Lu. 24:34. Two disciples—Lu. 24:13–31. Apostles, except Thomas—John 20:19, 24. Apostles with Thomas—John 20:26. Apostles at Sea of Galilee—John 21:1. Apostles in Galilee—Mt. 28:16, 17. Above 500 brethren—I Cor. 15:6. James—I Cor. 15:7. All the apostles—Lu. 24:36–51; Acts 1:4–9; I Cor. 15:7. Paul—I Cor. 15:8.

Raised by the power of God.—John 10: 18; Rom. 8:11; I Cor. 6:14; 15:43; II Cor. 5:1; 13:4; Eph. 1:19–21; Phil. 3:9–11; II Tim. 1:8–10.

Jesus' resurrection the earnest of ours. —Rom. 8:19–25, 32–34; I Cor. 15:54–57; Phil. 3:10–14; II Tim. 2:11, 12.

Baptism a symbol of the resurrection.— Rom. 6:3–11; Col. 2:11–13.

The resurrection commemorated by the first day of the week.—John 20:19–23, 26; Acts 20:7; Rev. 1:10.

SAVIOUR, THE. See ''Blessings through the Seed of Abraham'' and ''Man is saved through Jesus Christ,'' under SALVATION.

Second coming. Mt. 16:27; 24:36–39; 25:1–46; Mk. 8:38; 13:32–37; Lu. 9: 26; 18:7–8; 19:11–27; John 14:1–3, 28; 21:22, 23; Acts 1:9–11; 2:34, 35; 3:20, 21; Rom. 2:16; I Cor. 1:7, 8; 4:5; 11:

26; 15:23–25; Phil. 3:20; Col. 3:4; I Thess 4:16, 17; 5:1–3, 23; II Thess. 1:7–10; 2:1–4; II Tim. 4:1–8; Tit. 2: 13; Heb. 9:28; Jas. 5:7–9; I Pet. 5:4; II Pet. 3:7–11; I John 2:28; Jude 14-15; Rev. 1:7; 11:15; 22:10–12.

Time known only to God—Mt. 24:36–39; Mk. 13:32.

Long deferred—Mt. 25:19; Mk. 13:35, 36; Lu. 18:7, 8; 19:11–15; John 21:22, 23; Acts 2:34, 35; 3:21; I Cor. 15:23–25; II Thess. 2:1–4; II Pet. 3:3–11; Rev. 11:15.

Disciples looked for immediate—Lu. 19: 11; II Thess. 2:1, 2; Jas. 5:7, 8; I John 2:28.

·In glory—Mt. 16:27; 24:36–39; 25:31, 32; Mk. 8:38; Lu. 9:26; Col. 3:4; I Thess. 4:16, 17; II Thess. 1:10; Tit. 2:13; I Pet. 5:4.

With power—Acts 2:34, 35; Phil. 3:20; I Thess. 4:16, 17; II Thess. 1:7, 8; Jude 14–15; Rev. 1:7.

Without warning—Mt. 24:36–39; 25:1–13; Mk. 13:32–37; I Thess. 5:1–3; II Pet. 3:10.

To judge the world—Mt. 16:27; 25:31–46; Lu. 19:11–27; Rom. 2:16; I Cor. 1:7, 8; 4:5; II Thess. 1:7–10; II Tim. 4:1–8; Rev. 22:10–12.

Son of God.—See DIVINITY.

Son of Man.—See HUMANITY.

Sufferings of Jesus. Mt. 16:21; 17:12; Mk. 9:12; Lu. 9:22; 12:50; 17:25; 24: 26, 46; Acts 3:18; 17:3; II Cor. 1:5; Phil. 3:10; Heb. 2:9, 10; 5:7, 8; 12:2, 3; I Pet. 1:11; 2:22–23; 3:18; 4:1, 13.

Afflicted—Is. 53:4, 7; 63:9 (Col. 1:24).

Agonized—Lu. 22:44; Heb. 5:7, 8.

Bore griefs of men—Is. 53:4 (Mt. 8:17).

Bound—Mt. 27:2.

Bruised—Gen. 3:15; Is. 53:5, 10.

Buffeted—Mt. 26:67.

Cast forth—Lu. 4:29.

Chastised—Is. 53:5 (Lu. 23:16, 22; Heb. 5:8).

Clothed with purple—Mk. 15:17. See Lu. 23:11.

Clothed with scarlet—Mt. 27:28.

Condemned—Mt. 20:18; 27:3; Mk. 10: 33; Lu. 24:20; Jas. 5:6.

Crowned with thorns—Mt. 27:29; Mk. 15:17; John 19:2.

Crucified—Mt. 20:19; 26:2; 27:35; 28:5; Lu. 23:33; John 19:20; Acts 2:23; I

Cor. 2:2, 8; II Cor. 13:4; Phil. 2:8; Heb. 6:6; 12:2.

Curse, Became a—Gal. 3:13.

Cut off—Is. 53:8; Dan. 9:26.

Delivered up—Mt. 17:22; 20:18, 19; 26: 15; Mk. 9:31; 10:33; Lu. 22:3, 6; 24: 20; Acts 2:23; 3:13.

Despised.—Ps. 22:6, 7; 109:25; Is. 53:3; Jer. 18:16 (Mt. 27:39; Mk. 15:29; Lu. 18:31–33).

Forsaken—Ps. 22:1, 2 (Mt. 27:46; Mk. 15:34).

Garments parted by lot—Ps. 22:18 (Mt. 27:35; Lu. 23:34; John 19:24).

Groaned—John 11:33, 38.

Homeless—Mt. 8:20; Lu. 9:58.

Hungry—Mt. 4:2; 21:18; Mk. 11:12.

Infirmity, Compassed with—Mt. 8:17; Heb. 5:2.

Killed—Mt. 16:21; 17:23; Mk. 9:31; 10: 34; Acts 2:23; 3:15.

Left alone—Mt. 26:38–46, 56.

Marred visage—Is. 52:13, 14.

Mocked—Ps. 22:6–8 (Mt. 20:19; 27:29, 31, 39–44; Mk. 10:34; 15:20; Lu. 18: 32; 23:11, 36–38; I Pet. 2:23).

Numbered with transgressors—Is. 53: 12; Lu. 22:37.

Oppressed—Is. 53:7, 8.

Persecuted—John 5:16; 15:20.

Pierced—Ps. 22:16; Zech. 12:10 (Mt. 27: 35; Lu. 24:39, 40; John 19:34, 37; 20: 20, 25, 27; Rev. 1:7).

Poured out His soul unto death—Is. 53: 12 (Mt. 26:38–42).

Railed against—Mt. 27:39; Mk. 15:29.

Rejected—Ps. 118:22 (Mt. 21:42; Mk. 12:10, 11; Lu. 20:17; I Pet. 2:7).

Reproached—Ps. 22:6; 109:25 (Mt. 27: 41–44; Mk. 15:32; Rom. 15:3; Heb. 11:26; 13:13).

Sacrificed—I Cor. 5:7; I Pet. 1:19.

Scoffed at—Lu. 16:14; 23:35.

Scourged—Is. 53:5; Mt. 20:19; 27:26; Mk. 10:34; 15:15; John 19:1.

Sighed—Mk. 7:34; 8:12.

Smitten—Is. 50:6; 53:4; Mic. 5:1; Zech. 13:7; Mt. 26:67; 27:30; Mk. 15:19; Lu. 22:63; John 18:23.

Sorrowful—Is. 53:4; Mt. 26:38; Mk. 14:34.

Spit upon—Mt. 26:27; 27:30; Mk. 10:34; 14:65; 15:19.

Stricken—Is. 53:4.

Stripped—Mt. 27:28.

Struck—Mt. 26:68; John 18:22; 19:3.

Tempted—Mt. 4:1–11; 16:1; Mk. 1:13; Lu. 4:1–13; Heb. 2:18; 4:15; 5:2.

Thirsted—Ps. 69:21 (Mt. 27:34, 48; Mk. 15:23; Lu. 23:36; John 4:7; 19:28).

Travailed in soul—Is. 53:11.

Trodden under foot (*fig.*)—Heb. 10:29.

Troubled—John 11:33; 12:27; 13:21.

Wearied—John 4:9.

Wept—Lu. 19:41; John 11:33, 35. See Lu. 13:34, 35.

Wounded—Is. 53:5; Zech. 13:6.

Names and Titles: Adam, the last—I Cor. 15:45.

Advocate—I John 2:1.

Alpha and Omega—Rev. 1:8; 21:6; 22:13.

Amen—Rev. 3:14.

Anointed—Ps. 2:2; Is. 45:1; John 1:41 (*marg.*); Acts 4:26.

Anointed one, The prince—Dan. 9:25.

Apostle—Heb. 3:1.

Author and perfecter of faith—Heb. 12:2.

Author of salvation—Heb. 2:10 (*marg.*).

Beginning and the end—Rev. 21:6; 22:13.

Beloved—Eph. 1:6.

Bishop—I Pet. 2:25.

Branch—Is. 11:1, 2; Jer. 23:5; Zech. 3:8; 6:12.

Bread of life—John 6:48–50, 58.

Bridegroom—Mt. 9:15; John 3:29.

Bright and morning star—Rev. 22:16.

Carpenter—Mk. 6:3.

Carpenter's Son—Mt. 13:55.

Chosen—Is. 42:1; Lu. 23:35.

Christ—See CHRIST THE MESSIAH.

Commander—Is. 55:4.

Corner stone—Is. 28:16; Eph. 2:20; I Pet. 2:6.

Counsellor—Is. 9:6.

David—Jer. 30:9; Ez. 34:23; 37:24, 25; Hos. 3:5.

Dayspring from on high—Lu. 1:78.

Day star—II Pet. 1:19.

Deliverer—Rom. 11:26.

Door of the sheep—John 10:1, 7, 9.

Ensign—Is. 11:10, 12; 49:22.

Everlasting Father—Is. 9:6.

Elect—I Pet. 2:4.

Eternal life—I John 5:20.

Faithful and true—Rev. 19:11.

Faithful and true witness—Rev. 1:5; 3:14.

Firstborn—Ps. 89:27; Heb. 1:6.

Firstborn from the dead—Col. 1:18.

Forerunner—Heb. 6:20.

Foundation—Is. 28:16.

Fountain—Zech. 13:1.

Friend of publicans and sinners—Mt. 11:19.

Gift of God—John 4:10.

God with us—Mt. 1:23.

Good teacher—Mk. 10:17.

God—John 1:1; Heb. 1:8.

God blessed forever—Rom. 9:5.

Governor—Mic. 5:2; Mt. 2:6.

Great shepherd of the sheep — Heb. 13:20.

Head of the corner—Ps. 118:22; Mt. 21:42.

Head of every man—I Cor. 11:3.

Head of the church—Eph. 1:22; 5:23; Col. 1:18.

High priest—Heb. 2:17; 3:1; 4:14; 9:11; 10:21.

Holy one—Ps. 16:10; Is. 41:14; Mk. 1: 24; Acts 2:27; 3:14.

Holy servant Jesus—Acts 4:27, 30.

Holy thing—Lu. 1:35.

Hope of glory—Col. 1:27.

Horn of salvation—Ps. 89:17; Ez. 29:21; Lu. 1:69.

I am—John 8:58.

Image of God—II Cor. 4:4; Col. 1:15. See Phil. 2:6; Heb. 1:3.

Immanuel—Is. 7:14; Mt. 1:23.

Jehovah—Is. 40:3 (Mt. 3:3).

Jehovah our righteousness—Jer. 23:6; 33:16.

Jesus—Mt. 1:21, 25; Lu. 1:31; 2:21.

Jesus Christ—Mt. 1:1; John 1:17; 17:3; Acts 2:38, etc. See ''Called Christ,'' under MESSIAH.

Jesus Christ our Lord—Rom. 1:4; 5:21; 6:23; 7:25; 8:39; I Cor. 1:9; 15:31; Eph. 3:11; Phil. 3:8; I Tim. 1:2, 12; II Tim. 1:2; Jude 25.

Jesus Christ our Saviour—Tit. 3:6.

Jesus of Nazareth, the King of the Jews —Mt. 27:37; John 19:19.

Jesus the Son of Joseph—John 6:42.

Jesus the Son of God—Heb. 4:14.

Joseph's son—Lu. 4:22.

Judge—Acts 10:42. See ''Judge of the World,'' under DIVINITY.

King—Ps. 2:6; Zech. 9:9; Mt. 21:5; John 12:15. See ''Kingship,'' under DIVINITY.

King of Israel—Mt. 27:42; John 1:49; 12:13.

King of the Jews—Mt. 2:2; 27:37; Lu. 23:37, 38.

King of kings—Rev. 17:14; 19:16.

Lamb—Rev. 5:6, 8, 12, 13; 6:1, 16; 7:9, 10, 14, 17; 12:11; 13:8; 14:1, 4, 10; 15:3; 17:14; 19:7, 9; 21:9, 14, 22, 23, 27; 22:1, 3. See I Pet. 1:19.

Lamb of God—John 1:29, 36; I Pet. 1: 19; Rev. 7:10, 17; 12:10, 11; 14:4; 21: 23, 27.

Leader and Commander—Is. 55:4.

Life—John 11:25; 14:6; Col. 3:4. See I John 5:20.

Light—Is. 60:1, 3; Mt. 4:16; John 1:4, 9; 12:35, 36, 46.

Light of the Gentiles—Is. 42:6; 49:6; Lu. 2:32; Acts 13:47.

Light of the world—John 8:12; 9:5.

Lion of the tribe of Judah—Rev. 5:5.

Lord—See ''Lordship,'' under DIVINITY.

Lord, The—See ''Lordship,'' under DIVINITY.

Lord Jesus, The — See ''Lordship,'' under DIVINITY.

Lord Jesus Christ, The—See ''Lordship,'' under DIVINITY.

Lord, Jesus our Lord—See ''Lordship,'' under DIVINITY.

Lord Jesus Christ, Our—See ''Lordship,'' under DIVINITY.

Lord Christ—Rom. 16:18; Col. 3:24.

Lord of all—Acts 10:36.

Lord of lords—Rev. 17:14; 19:16.

Lord of the sabbath—Mt. 12:8; Mk. 2: 28; Lu. 6:5.

Man, The—John 19:5; I Tim. 2:5.

Man of sorrows—Is. 53:3.

Mediator—Gal. 3:19, 20; I Tim. 2:5; Heb. 8:6; 9:15; 12:24.

Messiah—See DIVINITY OF JESUS.

Mighty God—Is. 9:6.

Mighty one of Jacob—Is. 49:26.

Mighty to save—Is. 63:1.

Morning star—Rev. 2:28; 22:16.

Most holy—Dan. 9:24.

Nazarene—Mt. 2:23; Mk. 1:24; Lu. 24:19.

Offspring of David—Rev. 22:16.

Only Begotten of the Father—John 1: 14.

Only Begotten Son—John 1:14, 18; 3:16, 18; I John 4:9.

Our peace—Eph. 2:14.

Passover—I Cor. 5:7.

Peace, Our—Eph. 2:14.

Plantation for renown—Ez. 34:29.

Power of God—I Cor. 1:24.

Precious cornerstone—Is. 28:16.

Priest—Heb. 5:6; 7:17, 21. See HIGH
PRIEST.

Prince—Acts 5:31.

Prince of life—Acts 3:15.

Prince of peace—Is. 9:6.

Prophet, A—Lu. 7:16, 39; 13:33; 24:19;
John 4:19; 9:17.

Prophet, The—Deut. 18:15 (Mt. 21:11;
John 1:21, 25; 6:14; 7:40; Acts 3:22;
7:37).

Purifier—Mal. 3:3 (Tit. 2:14).

Rabbi—Mt. 26:25, 49; Mk. 9:5; 11:21;
14:45; John 1:38, 49; 3:2, 26; 4:31;
6:25; 11:8.

Rabboni—Mk. 10:51; John 20:16.

Ransom—I Tim. 2:6. See Mt. 20:28;
Mk. 10:45.

Redeemer—Is. 59:20.

Redemption—I Cor. 1:30.

Resurrection—John 11:25.

Righteous branch—Jer. 23:5.

Righteous judge—II Tim. 4:8.

Righteous man—Mt. 27:19, 24.

Righteousness—I Cor. 1:30.

Righteous one—Acts 3:14; 7:52; 22:14.

Rock—I Cor. 10:4.

Rock of offense—Is. 8:14; I Pet. 2:8.

Root of David—Rev. 5:5; 22:16.

Root of Jesse—Is. 11:10; Rom. 15:12.

Ruler of the kings of the earth—Rev.
1:5.

Saviour—Is. 19:20; Lu. 2:11; Acts 5:31;
13:23; Phil. 3:20; II Tim. 1:10; Tit.
1:4; 2:13; 3:6; II Pet. 1:1, 11; 2:20;
3:2, 18.

Saviour, God our—I Tim. 2:3-7.

Saviour of the body—Eph. 5:23.

Saviour of the world—John 4:42; I John
4:14.

Sceptre out of Israel—Gen. 49:10; Num.
24:17; Heb. 1:8.

Seed of the woman—Gen. 3:15; Gal.
3:16.

Servant—Is. 42:1; 49:3, 6; 52:13; 53:11;
Acts 3:13, 26; 4:27, 30; Phil. 2:7.

Shepherd—Is. 40:11; Zech. 13:7; Mk. 14:
27; John 10:11, 14; Heb. 13:20; I Pet.
5:4; Rev. 7:17.

Shepherd and bishop of your souls—I
Pet. 2:25.

Shiloh—Gen. 49:10.

Shoot—Is. 11:1.

Son of David—Mt. 9:27; 12:23; 15:22;
20:30; 21:9; Mk. 10:47, 48; Lu. 18:38.

Son of the blessed—Mk. 14:61.

Son of the Father—II John 3.

Son of Mary—Mk. 6:3.

Son of the most high—Lu. 1:32.

Son of God—See DIVINITY.

Son of man—See HUMANITY.

Son of God, The—Dan. 3:25.

Star—Num. 24:17; Rev. 22:16.

Stone, Tried, precious, corner—Ps. 118:
22; Is. 28:16; Mt. 21:42; Mk. 12:10,
11; Lu. 20:17; Acts 4:11; Rom. 9:32,
33; Eph. 2:20; I Pet. 2:6, 7.

Sun of righteousness—Mal. 4:2.

Teacher—Mt. 26:18; Mk. 14:14; Lu. 22:
11; John 3:2; 11:28.

True light—John 1:9; I John 2:8.

True vine—John 15:1.

Truth—John 14:6.

Vine—John 15:1, 5.

Way—John 14:6. See Is. 35:8; Heb.
10:20.

Witness—Rev. 1:5; 3:14.

Wonderful—Is. 9:6.

Word—John 1:1, 14.

Word of God—Rev. 19:13.

Word of life—I John 1:1.

Types of:

Abel—Gen. 4:8 (Heb. 12:24).

Adam—I Cor. 15:22, 45-47.

Branch—Is. 11:1; Jer. 23:5; 33:15; Zech.
6:12, 13.

Brazen serpent—Num. 21:9; John 3:14,
15.

David—Ez. 37:24; Rev. 5:5.

Jonah—Jonah 1:17; Mt. 12:40, 41.

Lamb—Ex. 29:38-42; John 1:29, 36;
Acts 8:32; I Pet. 1:19. See ''Called
a Lamb,'' under NAMES AND TITLES.

Melchizedek—Gen. 14:18-20; Heb. 5:5-
10; 6:20; 7:1-17.

Moses—Deut. 18:15 (John 1:21, 25; Acts
3:22; 7:37).

Offerings—Eph. 2:13; Col. 1:20; Heb.
10:8-10; I John 4:10, etc.

Passover—I Cor. 5:7.

Priesthood—See MELCHIZEDEK, above.

Rock in the wilderness—Ex. 17:6; I Cor.
10:4.

Sacrifices—I Cor. 5:7; Heb. 9:13, 14.
Tabernacle—Heb. 9:7-15; 10:1-10.
Temple—I Ki. 6:1-38; 8:12-21; Mk. 14: 58; John 2:19-21.

TEACHING OF JESUS. Principal discourses (chronologically arranged).— To Nicodemus—John 3:1-21; To the woman of Samaria—John 4:4-26; At Nazareth—Lu. 4:17-27; To the Jews in Jerusalem—John 5:17-47; Sermon on the Mount—Mt. 5, 6, and 7; Concerning John the Baptist—Mt. 11:7-19; Lu. 7:24-35; Upbraids Chorazin, Bethsaida, and Capernaum; invites the heavy laden—Mt. 11:20-30; In the house of Simon the Pharisee—Lu. 7:40-47; Warnings to scribes and pharisees because of blasphemous charge of alliance with satan—Mt. 12:22-37; Mk. 3:22-29; Lu. 11:14-26; Rebukes scribes and pharisees for asking for a sign—Mt. 12:38-50; Lu. 11:29-36; Parables by the sea—Mt. 13:1-53; Mk. 4:1-34; Lu. 4:4-18; Sends forth the twelve apostles—Mt. 10:5-42; Mk. 6:10-11; Lu. 9:3-5; On the bread of life—John 6:26-58; On eating with unwashen hands—Mt. 15: 1-20; Mk. 7:1-23; Replies to the Pharisees and Sadducees who demand a sign from heaven—Mt. 16:1-12; Responds to Peter's confession and foretells His death and resurrection—Mt. 16:13-28; Mk. 8:27-38; Lu. 9:18-27; Foretells His death and resurrection, the second time—Mt. 17:22, 23; Mk. 9:30-32; Lu. 9:44, 45; On humility, self-denial and forgiveness—Mt. 18:1-35; Mk. 9:35-50; Lu. 9:46-50; The Light of the world—John 8:12-29; Spiritual freedom—John 8:31-58; To the seventy—Lu. 10:1-24; Parable of *The Good Samaritan*—Lu. 10:25-37; *The Good Shepherd*—John 10:1-21; At the Feast of Dedication—John 10:25-38; On prayer—Lu. 11:2-13; Rebukes Pharisees for hypocrisy—Lu. 11:37-52; Warnings against phariseeisms—Lu. 12:1-59; On repentance—Lu. 13: 1-9; The few that be saved—Lu. 13: 20-30; Lament over Jerusalem—Lu. 13:31-35; Discourse in the Pharisee's house on "*Excuses*"—Lu. 14:1-24; On self-denial—Mk. 8:34-38; Lu. 14: 25-35.

Parables of *The Lost Sheep, The Lost Piece of Money,* and *The Prodigal Son* —Lu. 15:4-32; *The Unjust Steward*— Lu. 16:1-13; *The Rich Man and Lazarus*—Lu. 16:19-31; Stumbling-block's and faith—Lu. 17:1-10; Concerning the kingdom—Lu. 17:20-37; *The Unjust Judge*—Lu. 18:1-8; *The Pharisee and The Publican*—Lu. 18:9-14; Marriage and divorce—Mt. 19:3-12; The rich young ruler—Mt. 19:16-30; Mk. 10:17-31; Lu. 18:18-30; *The Labourers in the Vineyard*—Mt. 20:1-16; Foretells His crucifixion; the third time— Mt. 20:17-19; Mk. 10:32-39; Lu. 18: 31-34; *The Pounds*—Lu. 19:11-27; Destruction of Jerusalem—Lu. 19:41-44; *The Two Sons, The Husbandmen,* and *The Marriage Supper*—Mt. 21:28-31; 22:1-14; Mk. 12:12; Lu. 20:9-18; About tribute money, The resurrection, and "Which is the greatest commandment?"—Mt. 22:41-46; Mk. 12: 35-37; Lu. 20:45-47; Denunciation of the scribes and pharisees—Mt. 23:1-39; Mk. 12:38-40; Lu. 20:45-47; Discourse when the Greeks seek Jesus and the rejection by the Jews—John 12: 20-50; Destruction of Jerusalem and the end of the world—Mt. 24:1-51; 25:31-46; Mk. 13:1-37; Lu. 21:5-36. *The Ten Virgins* and *The Talents*—Mt. 24:4-51; 25:1-46; Mk. 13:5-37; Lu. 21:5-38; Christ's farewell discourses —Mt. 26:31-35; Mk. 14:27-31; Lu. 22:31-38; John 13:31; 16:33; The intercessory prayer—John, Ch. 17.

Teaching of Jesus concerning:

Access to God.—John 6:44-46.
Must be pure in heart—Mt. 5:8.
Through Christ—John 1:12; 10:1, 7-9; 12:32-34; 14:6; 15:6.
Through prayer—Mt. 6:6-15.
Accusation, False.—Mt. 5:11.
Adultery.—Mt. 5:27-32; 15:19; 19:9, 18; Mk. 7:21; 10:11, 12, 19; Lu. 16:18; 18:20.
Affection.—Mt. 6:21; Lu. 12:33, 34; 16: 27, 28.
Thou shalt love the Lord thy God with all thy heart, etc.—Mt. 22:37-40; Mk. 12:30, 32, 33; Lu. 10:27.
Thou shalt love thy neighbor as thyself —Mt. 5:43; 19:19; 22:37-40; Mk. 12:

TEACHINGS OF JESUS

31; Lu. 10:27, 28. *The Good Samaritan*
—Lu. 10:30–37.

Christ first—Mt. 10:37–39; Lu. 14:26;
John 15:9, 10; 21:15–17.

Love your enemies—Mt. 5:44–47; Lu.
6:27–32, 35.

Love, One for another—John 13:34, 35;
15:12, 17; 21:15–17.

Love waxing cold—Mt. 13:20, 21; 24:12;
Mk. 4:16, 17; Lu. 8:13. See LOVE.

Affliction.—John 9:1–3; 11:4; 14:1, 18;
21:19.

Benefit of—Lu. 15:17, 18; John 15:2.

Comfort in—Mt. 5:4, 10–12; 10:19–23;
11:28–30; 24:8–13; Lu. 6:21–23; 7:13;
21:16–19; John 14:1–3, 16, 18, 27, 28;
15:18–20; 16:20–24, 33.

Alms.—Mt. 5:42; 6:1–4; 19:21; Lu. 6:
34–38; 11:41; 12:33, 34; 18:22; 19:8.

Ambition.—Mt. 16:26; 19:1–3; 20:20–
28; 23:1–12; Mk. 9:33–37; 10:35–45;
12:38–39; Lu. 9:25, 46–48; 11:43; 14:
7–14; 18:10–14; 20:46; 22:24–30; John
5:41, 44; 13:5–16.

Amusements.—Mt. 11:16, 17; Lu. 15:
23–25.

Choke the word—Lu. 8:14.

Angels.—Mt. 13:39–41; Lu. 16:22; 18:
10; 24:31; 9:26; 15:10.

Anger.—Mt. 5:21–24, 38–39, 43–46.

Antichrist.—Mt. 24:5, 23–27.

Apostolic authority.—Mt. 10:1, 40; 16:
18, 19; 18:18, 19; 28:19, 20; Mk. 3:14,
15; 6:7; Lu. 9:1, 2; 22:28–30; John
20:23.

Apostolic duties.—Cast out demons—Mt.
10:1, 8; Mk. 3:14, 15; 6:7, 13.

Fishers of men—Mt. 4:18–22.

Heal all manner of diseases, To—Mt.
10:1, 8; Lu. 9:2, 6; 10:9.

Preach, To—Mt. 10:1–7; 28:19, 20; Mk.
3:14; 6:7–12; 16:15; Lu. 9:1–6; 24:47.

Apostolic faith, weak.—Mt. 6:26–34; 8:
24–27; 14:23–33; 16:5–12, 21–23; 17:7;
19:23–29; Mk. 6:47–52; 8:14–21; Lu.
5:9–11; 12:22–34; 24:19–27; John 6:
16–21; 14:7–13.

Apostolic inspiration.—Mt. 10:19, 20;
Lu. 21:14, 15.

By the Holy Spirit—Mk. 13:11; Lu. 12:
11, 12; 24:49; John 7:39; 14:26; 15:
26; 16:7, 13–15; Acts 1:4–8.

Apostolic knowledge limited.—Mt. 11:
25–27; 15:22–24; 19:23–29; Mk. 4:10–
13; 8:14–21; 9:9–13, 28–32; 10:13–16;

Lu. 9:44, 45; 18:34; 24:19–27; John
2:19–22; 4:31–38; 10:1–6; 11:12, 13;
12:12–16; 13:5–11; 14:4–12; 16:6, 7,
17, 18, 32; 20:9; Acts 1:6, 7.

Apostolic persecutions.—Mt. 5:10–12;
10:16–39; 13:21; 23:34; Mk. 4:17; 13:
9–13; Lu. 6:20–26; 12:11, 12, 49–53;
21:16–19; John 15:18–21; 16:2; 21:
18, 19.

Apostolic witness.—Lu. 24:44–48; John
15:27; 21:24; Acts 1:8. See APOSTOLIC
DUTIES.

Ascension into heaven.—John 3:13.

Ascension of Christ.—John 1:51; 6:62;
7:33; 14:2–4, 12, 28; 16:5, 7, 10, 16, 28;
17:13; 20:17.

Attraction.—Lu. 15:1–7; John 12:32–36.
See John 6:44, 45.

Authority.—Mt. 9:6, 8; 10:1; 16:18, 19;
18:18, 19; 21:23–27; Lu. 19:17, 19,
22–27; John 5:25–27. See Mt. 7:28,
29; Mk. 1:21, 22; Lu. 4:6, 31–32, 36.

All authority given to Jesus—Mt. 11:27;
28:18; John 17:2.

Babes.—Suffer little children, etc.—Mt.
19:13–15; Mk. 10:13–16; Lu. 18:15–17.

Revelation to babes—Mt. 11:25–27;
21:15–17; Lu. 10:21–24.

Backsliding.—Mt. 5:13; 11:6; 24:10–12;
26:31; Mk. 9:50; Lu. 9:62; John 6:67;
15:1–8; 16:32.

Parable of the sower—Mt. 13:5–7, 20–
22; Mk. 4:5–7, 16–19; Lu. 8:6, 7, 13, 14.

The unclean spirit—Mt. 12:43–45; Lu.
11:24–26.

Peter's denial—Mt. 26:34, 35, 69–75;
Mk. 14:27–31, 66–72; Lu. 22:31–33,
54–62.

Remember Lot's wife—Lu. 17:32.

Baptism of the Holy Spirit.—Lu. 24:49;
John 7:38, 39; Acts 1:4–8. See John
14:16, 17, 26; 15:26; 16:7.

Baptism of water.—Mt. 28:19; Mk. 16:
16; John 3:3–5, 22, 26; 4:1, 2.

John's baptism—Mt. 3:13–15; 21:25–27;
Mk. 11:30–33; Lu. 20:4–8; Acts 1:5.

Baptism of suffering.—Mt. 20:22, 23;
Mk. 10:38, 39; Lu. 12:50.

Beatitudes.—Mt. 5:1–12; Lu. 6:20–23.

Belief.—See FAITH.

Believers.—See FAITH.

Birds.—Mt. 8:20; 13:4, 32; Mk. 4:4, 32;
Lu. 8:5; 13:19.

God's care for—Mt. 6:26; 10:29; Lu. 12:6, 24. Raven—Lu. 12:24. Sparrows —Mt. 10:29–31; Lu. 12:6, 7.

Blasphemy.—Mt. 12:31; 15:19; Mk. 3: 28, 29; Lu. 12:10.

Blessing.—Mt. 5:2–12; 11:6; 13:16; 16: 17; 23:39; 24:46; 25:34; Lu. 1:45; 6: 22, 28; 7:23; 10:23, 24; 11:28; 12:37; 13:35; 14:14; 23:29; 24:50; John 13: 17.

Blindness, Spiritual.—Mt. 6:23; 13:14– 17; 15:14; 23:16–24; Mk. 4:11, 12; Lu. 6:39; 8:10; 10:23, 24; 19:42; John 1: 5; 3:19, 20; 8:12; 9:39; 12:40.

Blood.—Flesh and blood—Mt. 16:17. His blood—John 6:54–56. Of the New Testament—Mt. 26:28; Mk. 14:24; Lu. 22:20. Of the righteous—Mt. 23:33–36.

Bondage of sin.—John 8:34, 35. Deliverance from—Lu. 4:18; John 8: 32–35.

Bread.—Mt. 6:11; Mk. 6:8. Men shall not live by bread alone—Mt. 4:4. Miracles of multitudes fed—Mt. 14:19– 21; 15:34–38; 16:9, 10; Mk. 6:35–44; 8:1–9; John 6:5–14.

Bread, Leavened—Mt. 16:6–12; Mk. 8: 14–21; Lu. 12:1. Used to represent His body in the Lord's supper—Mt. 26:26; Mk. 14:22; Lu. 22:19. Bread of life—John 6:26, 27, 32, 35, 48–58.

Brethren.—Lu. 12:13–15; John 11:21–23. Anger toward—Mt. 5:22. Brother against brother—Mt. 10:21; Mk. 13: 12, 13. Mote in brother's eye—Mt. 7: 3–5; Lu. 6:41, 42. We must be reconciled to—Mt. 5:23, 24; 18:15–17. Forgive, we must—Mt. 18:21, 22; Lu. 17: 3, 4. *Prodigal son*—Lu. 15:11–32. Those who do His will are His brethren—Mt. 12:46–50; Mk. 3:31–35; Lu. 8:19–21. Disciples of Christ called brethren— Mt. 23:8–10; 25:40; Lu. 22:31.

Burdens.—Mt. 11:28–30; 20:12; 23:4; Lu. 11:46.

Care.—Apostles to have no care about money—Mt. 10:9–15; Mk. 6:8–11; Lu. 9:3–5; Lu. 10:3–12. This command repealed—Lu. 22:35, 36. Be not over anxious—Mt. 6:24–34; Lu. 12:11–34; John 6:26, 27. *Martha*—Lu. 10:39–42.

Character of His disciples.—Abiding in Christ—John 14:23; 15:1–7; 17:26. Believing—Mt. 16:13–17; Mk. 11:23, 24; 16:16; John 3:15–18, 36; 6:40; 11: 25–27; 14:12. See FAITH. Charitable —Mt. 10:42; 25:31–40; Mk. 9:41; Lu. 10:25–37. Cross-bearers—Mt. 10:38; 16:24; Mk. 8:34; Lu. 9:23; 14:27. Faithful—Mt. 24:45; 25:20–23; Lu. 16:10–12. Followers of Christ—Mt. 10:38; 16:24; Mk. 8:34; Lu. 9:23–26; 14:27; John 8:12; 15:1–8. Forgiving —Mt. 5:44; 6:12, 14, 15; 18:21–35; Mk. 11:25; Lu. 6:27–29; 11:4; 17:3, 4. Fruitful—Mt. 7:16–18; John 15:1–8. Harmless as doves—Mt. 10:16. Hearing the Saviour's words—Mt. 7:24, 25; Mk. 4:23, 24; Lu. 6:47; John 10:4, 27, 28. Humble—Mt. 5:3; 18:1–4; 20: 26–28; 23:5–12; Mk. 9:35–37; 10:15, 43; Lu. 14:11; 18:14, 17; John 13:4– 15. Hunger after righteousness—Mt. 5:4. See Lu. 6:24. Light-bearers—Mt. 5:14–16; Lu. 8:16; 11:33–36. Lovers of light—John 3:21. Loving—Mt. 5: 44; 22:39; Mk. 12:31–33; Lu. 6:31–35; 10:25–37; John 13:34, 35. See LOVE. Lowly—Mt. 11:29. Meek—Mt. 5:5; 11:29. Merciful—Mt. 5:7; 9:13; Lu. 6:36. Obedient—Mt. 5:19; 7:24, 25; 12:46–50; Mk. 3:31–35; Lu. 6:46–48; 8:19–21. See OBEDIENCE. Peace-makers—Mt. 5:9. Prayerful—Mt. 5:44; 6: 5–15; 7:7–11; 21:22; Mk. 11:24, 25; Lu. 11:9–13; John 14:13. See PRAYER. Pure in heart—Mt. 5:8. Righteous— Mt. 5:19; 10:41; 13:43; 25:37, 46. Separate from the world—Mt. 10:22; 24: 9; Lu. 6:22; John 15:18–21; 17:14–16. Sincere—Mt. 6:1–8, 16–18; 23:5, 6. Sons of God—Mt. 5:9, 45; Lu. 6:35. Sons of Light—Lu. 16:8; John 12:36. Watchful—Mt. 24:42–47; 25:13; Lu. 12:37–40. Wise—Mt. 7:24, 25; 25:1– 10. *Wise as serpents*—Mt. 10:16.

Character of the wicked.—Adulterous— Mt. 12:39; 15:19; 16:4; Mk. 7:21. Blind—Mt. 6:23; 13:13–15; 15:14; 23: 16, 24, 26; Mk. 4:12; Lu. 8:10; John 12:40. Children of the devil—Mt. 13: 38; John 8:41, 48. Corrupt—Mt. 7:16, 18, 20; Lu. 6:43. Defiled—Mt. 15:18; Mk. 7:20–23. Disobedient—Mt. 5:19; 7:26, 27; Mk. 7:8; Lu. 6:49; John 14: 24. Enemies of God—Lu. 19:14, 27;

Evil—Mt. 12:39; 16:4; Mk. 7:21-23; Lu. 6:35; 11:29. Evil-doers—Mt. 7:23; John 3:19, 20; 5:29; 7:7. Foolish —Mt. 7:26, 27; 23:17; 25:1-10; Mk. 7:22; Lu. 11:40; 12:16-21. Fornicators—Mt. 15:19; Mk. 7:21; Lu. 15:30. Hard-hearted—Mt. 11:20-24; 12:41, 42; 13:15, 19; 19:8; 23:37, 38; Mk. 10:5; Lu. 8:12; 13:34. Hating the light—John 3:20. Hypocrites—Mt. 6:2; 21:23-32; 23:5, 15-35; 24:51; Mk. 7:6-13; 12:13-17, 38-44; Lu. 6:42; 11:37-52; 20:3-7; John 8:6-9. Iniquity, Workers of—Mt. 7:23; 13:41; John 3:19; 7:7. Lascivious—Mk. 7:22. Liars —Mt. 15:19; Mk. 7:22. Lovers of darkness—John 3:19, 20. Lustful—Mt. 15:19; Mk. 7:21-23; Lu. 15:13; John 8:44. Murderers—Mt. 15:19; 23:29-35; Mk. 7:21; Lu. 11:49-51; John 8:37, 40; 16:2. Offspring of vipers—Mt. 12:34; 23:33. Oppressors—Mt. 23:4; Mk. 12:40; Lu. 11:46; 20:47. Persecutors—Mt. 10:23, 28; 23:34; Mk. 13:11-13; Lu. 11:49; John 15:19-22; 16:2. Perverse—Mt. 17:17. Proud —Mt. 23:5-12; Mk. 7:21; 9:35; 12:38-40; Lu. 11:43; 14:7-11; 20:46. Railers —Mt. 15:19; Mk. 7:21. Self-righteous —Mt. 7:22, 23; 21:31, 32; 23:29-31; Lu. 7:39-47; 10:29; 15:2, 29; 16:15; John 8:33, 41; 9:39-41. *The Pharisee and the Publican*—Lu. 18:10-14. *The Rich Young Ruler*—Mt. 19:16-22; Mk. 10:17-22; Lu. 18:18-25. Serpents—Mt. 23:33. Servants of sin—John 8:32-34. Slothful—Mt. 25:26. Sons of hell —Mt. 23:15. Unbelieving—Mt. 17:17; Mk. 16:16; Lu. 16:31; 22:67; John 3:11-19, 32, 36; 4:48; 5:38-47; 6:36, 64; 8:24, 45-47; 10:25, 26; 12:37, 47, 48; 14:17; 15:21-23; 16:9. Uncharitable—Mt. 25:42-45. Unclean—Mt. 23:27. Unfaithful—Lu. 16:12. Unprofitable servants—Mt. 25:30. Unrighteous—Mt. 5:20; Lu. 10:30-37. Unthankful—Lu. 6:35. Wasteful—Lu. 15:13. Whited sepulchres, Like—Mt. 23:27. Workers of iniquity—See SIN, WICKED.

Children.—Mt. 7:11; 18:14; Lu. 11:13. Have guardian angels—Mt. 18:10. Suffer little children—Mt. 19:13-15; Mk. 10:13, 14, 16; Lu. 18:15, 16. Receiving little children—Mk. 9:36, 37.

Receiving the kingdom as a child—Mt. 18:1-6; Mk. 10:15; Lu. 18:17. Children shall rise against parents—Mt. 10:21; Mk. 13:12. Children's bread—Mt. 15:26; Mk. 7:27, 28. Forsaking children—Mt. 19:29; Mk. 10:29. Revealed unto babes—Mt. 11:25; 21:16; Lu. 10:21.

Christ.—See JESUS.

Church.—Mt. 16:18; 18:17.

Comfort.—Mt. 5:4, 10-12; 11:28-30; Lu. 6:21-23; 7:13; 16:25; John 11:23-26; 14:1-4, 18, 26-29; 15:13, 20; 16:20-22, 33.

Comforter.—See HOLY SPIRIT, KINGDOM.

Commandments.—Of Moses—Mt. 19:7-9; Mk. 10:3-12. *Ten commandments*—Mt. 5:21-37; 15:4-6; 19:17-19; 23:16-22; Mk. 1:44; 7:8-13; 10:19, 20; 12:29, 30; Lu. 10:27; 18:20, 21. Making void through traditions of men—Mt. 15:1-6; Mk. 7:8-13. Jesus came to fulfil —Matthew 5:17-19. Commandments summed up by Christ—Mt. 5:43-48; 7:12; 22:35-40; Mk. 12:28-34; Lu. 6:31-38; 10:25-37. He commanded—Mt. 11:1; 14:19; 15:35; Mk. 6:39; Lu. 9:21; John 15:14, 17. A new commandment—John 13:34; 15:12, 17. Keeping commandments—Mt. 5:19; John 14:15, 21, 23; 15:10-14.

Compassion.—Mt. 9:36; 15:32; 18:10-14; Mk. 6:34-44; 8:2, 3; Lu. 7:13; 19:41-44.

Confession.—Mt. 16:13-18. Whosoever confesseth Me before men—Mt. 10:32; Lu. 12:8. Christ's confession—Mt. 26:63, 64; Mk. 14:61, 62; Lu. 22:67-70. See I Tim. 6:13.

Conviction of sin.—John 8:7-11, 46; 16:8-11.

Covetousness.—Mt. 6:19-24; 13:22; 19:23-24; Mk. 7:22; 10:24; Lu. 6:24; 12:15-21; 14:18; 16:10-15; 18:24, 25; John 6:27.

Cross-bearing.—Mt. 10:38; 16:24; Mk. 8:34; Lu. 9:23; 14:27.

Death.—Mt. 10:28; Lu. 12:20; John 6:49; 8:21, 24; 9:4; 11:4, 11-44; 21:19-23. Sorrowful even unto death—Mt. 26:38; Mk. 14:34. Brother shall deliver brother up to death—Mt. 10:21; Mk. 13:12. Taste of death—Mt. 16:28; Mk. 9:1; Lu. 9:27. He that believeth on Me shall never die—John 3:16;

6:47–51; 8:51; 11:25, 26. Conscious existence: *The Rich Man and Lazarus* —Lu. 16:19–31. *Neither marry nor given in marriage*—Mt. 22:23–30; Mk. 12:18–25; Lu. 20:27–36. Spiritual death eternal—Mt. 23:33; 25:30, 41, 46; John 5:29. See HELL. He foretold His own death, and resurrection the third day—Mt. 12:40; 16:21; 17: 9, 12, 22, 23; 20:17–19; 21:33–45; 26:2, 12, 21–28, 32; 27:63; Mk. 8:31; 9:9, 10; 10:33, 34; 14:18–25, 28, 58; Lu. 9: 22, 24; 18:32, 33; 22:15, 37; 24:7; John 2:19–21; 3:14; 8:28; 12:32, 33; 13:18–21; Chs. 14–17. See RESURRECTION.

Debt.—Mt. 18:23–25; 22:21; Mk. 12:17; Lu. 20:25. Figurative—Mt. 6:12.

Debtor.—Mt. 6:12; 23:16, 18; Lu. 7:41–43; 16:1–8.

Deceit.—Mk. 7:22. See LYING and FALSEHOOD.

Defilement.—Mt. 15:10, 20; Mk. 7:14–23.

Demons.—Mt. 10:38; Mk. 3:11, 12; Lu. 4:41. Jesus accused of casting out demons by Beelzebub—Mt. 9:34; 10: 25; 12:24–29; Mk. 3:22. His answer —Mt. 12:25–29; Mk. 3:23–27. Accused of having a demon—Mk. 3:28–30; John 7:20; 8:48, 52; 10:20. He casts out demons—Mt. 4:24; 8:16; 9: 32–34; 12:22; 15:22–28; 17:14–18; Mk. 1:23–27, 32; 9:20–29. *Mary Magdalene* —Lu. 8:2. Driven into swine—Mt. 8:28–33; Mk. 5:1–14; Lu. 8:26–39. Some only cast out with prayer—Mk. 9:20–29. The apostles given power to cast out demons—Mt. 10:8; Mk. 16:17; Lu. 9:1; 10:17–20. *One they could not cast out*—Mt. 17:14–20. The unclean spirit and seven others—Mt. 12:43–45.

Denial of Christ.—Mt. 10:33; 16:24, 25; Mk. 8:34, 38; Lu. 9:23–26; 12:9. Peter's denial—Mt. 26:34, 75; Mk. 14: 30, 72; Lu. 22:31–34, 61.

Destroy, To.—Lu. 6:9; John 10:10. Destroy both body and soul in hell—Mt. 10:28. Did not come to destroy the law or the prophets—Mt. 5:17.

Destruction.—The way that leads to—Mt. 7:13.

Destruction of Jerusalem.—Mt. 24:6–15, 21–29; Lu. 17:22–27; 19:42–44; 21:7–11, 25, 28.

Destruction of the temple.—Mt. 26:61; 27:40; Mk. 14:57, 58; 15:29; John 2: 19–22.

Devil.—Mt. 4:1–11; 5:37; 6:13; 12:24–27; 13:19, 38, 39; Mk. 3:23–26; 4:15; Lu. 4:1–13; 8:12; 11:17–19; 13:16; 22: 3, 31; John 8:44; 13:2, 27; 17:15. Satan falling from heaven—Lu. 10:18. See Mt. 16:23; Mk. 8:33; John 6:70. See SATAN.

Dipping into the dish a sign of "who should betray Him."—Mt. 26:23; Mk. 14:20; John 13:26. Dipping the tip of finger in water—Lu. 16:24.

Discipleship.—Mt. 10:12; Mk. 14:26, 27; Lu. 19:37–40; John 7:6–26; 8:31; 13: 5–20; 15:1–27. Disciple not above his Master—Mt. 10:24, 25; Lu. 6:40; John 13:16; 15:20. Concerning His disciples not fasting—Mt. 9:14, 15. See APOSTOLIC AUTHORITY, APOSTOLIC DUTIES, APOSTOLIC FAITH, WEAK, APOSTOLIC INSPIRATION, APOSTOLIC KNOWLEDGE LIMITED, APOSTOLIC PERSECUTIONS, APOSTOLIC WITNESS, CHARACTER OF HIS DISCIPLES.

Divinity of Jesus.—See JESUS.

Division.—Mt. 10:35, 36; Lu. 12:14, 51–53; 15:12. House divided against itself—Mt. 12:25–30; Mk. 3:24–27; Lu. 11:17–23.

Divorce.—Mt. 5:31, 32; 19:3–9; Mk. 10: 2–12; Lu. 16:18. Moses allowed divorce because of the hardness of heart of the Jews—Mt. 19:8; Mk. 10:5. Adultery breaks the marriage bond—Mt. 19:9.

Dog.—Mt. 7:6; 15:26, 27; Lu. 16:21.

Door.—Mt. 24:33; 25:10. Jesus the door —John 10:1, 10. Door shut—Mt. 6:6; 25:10–12; Lu. 13:24–30.

Draw.—Lu. 12:33; 14:5; John 4:11, 15.

Drink.—Mt. 10:42; 11:18, 19; 20:22; 25: 35–37; Mk. 16:18; Lu. 13:26; John 4: 9–14; 6:54–56; 7:37. Drinking the cup of the Lord's Supper—Mt. 26: 27–29; Mk. 14:23–25; Lu. 22:20. The cup of sorrow—Mt. 20:22; 26:39–42; John 18:11.

Drunkenness.—Mt. 24:49–51; Lu. 12:45, 46; 21:34.

Dust.—Mt. 21:44. Shake off the dust from your feet—Mt. 10:14; Mk. 6:11; Lu. 9:5; 10:11.

Ear, an organ.—Mt. 10:27; 11:15; 13:9, 15, 16, 43; Mk. 4:9, 23; Lu. 8:8; 9:44; 14:35.

Ears of grain.—Mt. 12:1–8; Mk. 4:28.

Earth.—Mt. 6:10, 19; 10:34; 13:5; 23:9; 25:18; Mk. 4:28, 31; Lu. 12:49; 18:8; John 3:31; 12:24, 31, 32; 17:4. Agree on earth—Mt. 18:19. Authority on earth, His—Mt. 9:6. Binding on earth—Mt. 16:19. Heart of the earth, In—Mt. 12:40. Inherit the earth—Mt. 5:5. Salt of the earth—Mt. 5:13. Swearing by—Mt. 5:34, 35.

East.—Mt. 8:11; Lu. 13:29. Lightning coming from the east—Mt. 24:27.

Eating.—Mt. 6:25; 15:26, 27; 25:35; Lu. 12:16–21; 13:26; 15:16, 23; 16:19–21; 22:27–30; John 4:30–34; 6:26, 27; 21:5–13. Miracles of feeding—Mt. 14:13–21; Mk. 6:35–44; John 6:9–13. Eating with washen hands—Mk. 7:4. Eating with unwashen hands—Mt. 15:2; Mk. 7:5; Lu. 11:38. Eating with publicans and sinners—Mt. 9:11; 11:19; Mk. 2:15–17; Lu. 5:30; 15:2. Eating the Living Bread—John 6:48–59. Eating ''The Lord's Supper''—Mt. 26:26–29; Mk. 14:12, 22–25; Lu. 22:17–20; John 13:1–4. Eating the passover—Mt. 26:2–5, 20–26; Mk. 14:1, 17–22; Lu. 22:1, 14–16; John 13:1–4.

Elect.—Mt. 22:14; 24:22–24, 31; Lu. 18:7, 8.

End.—Mt. 10:22; 12:42; Mk. 13:7; Lu. 11:31; John 18:37. End of the world—Mt. 13:39, 40, 49; 24:3; 28:20.

Endurance.—Mt. 13:21; Mk. 4:17. Endureth to the end—Mt. 10:22; 24:13.

Entrance.—Into closet to pray—Mt. 6:6. Into the kingdom—Lu. 16:16; John 3:5. Entrance into life—Mt. 19:17; 25:21; John 10:1–5. By the narrow gate—Mt. 7:13; Lu. 13:24.

Enemy.—Lu. 19:43, 44. Love your enemies—Mt. 5:43–48; Lu. 6:27–29, 35. Pray for—Mt. 5:44.

Escape.—Mt. 23:33; Lu. 21:36.

Evil.—Mt. 5:39, 45; 6:34; 12:39, 45; 15:19; 16:4; Mk. 7:21–23; Lu. 6:35; 11:29. Evil doing—Mt. 7:23; John 3:19, 20; 5:29; 7:7. Evil fruit—Mt. 7:18. Evil one—See DEVIL.

Exaltation.—Mt. 11:23; Lu. 16:15. Whosoever exalteth himself shall be abased—Mt. 23:12; Lu. 14:11; 18:14.

Exaltation of Christ.—See JESUS.

Eye.—Mt. 5:29, 38; 13:13–15; 18:9; Mk. 18:18; 9:47; John 11:37. The lamp of the body—Mt. 6:22, 23; Lu. 11:33–36.

Face.—Mt. 11:10; Lu. 7:27, 28.

Failure.—Lu. 12:33; 16:9; 22:32; John 2:3. Failure to reach men with the gospel—Mt. 23:37; Lu. 13:34. Parable of the Sower—Mt. 13:4–8, 13–22; Mk. 4:3–8, 11–19; Lu. 8:5–7, 11–14.

Fainting.—Mt. 15:32; Lu. 18:1; 21:26.

Faith.—Mt. 6:25, 32, 33; 10:29–31; 23:23; Mk. 4:40; 9:23; 11:22, 23; Lu. 8:25; 12:6, 7, 32; 18:8; John 6:29, 45. As a mustard seed—Mt. 17:19, 20; Lu. 17:5, 6. Great faith—Mt. 8:10, 13; 9:2, 22, 29; 15:28; Mk. 2:5; 5:34; 10:52; Lu. 5:20; 7:9, 50; 8:48; 17:19; 18:42. Man must believe—Lu. 8:12, 13. He that disbelieveth is condemned—Mk. 16:16. He that believeth hath eternal life—Mk. 16:16; John 5:24; 6:47; 11:25, 26. *On, or in Jesus*—John 3:14–18, 36; 6:29, 40. See APOSTOLIC FAITH, WEAK.

Faithful.—Mt. 24:45; 25:20–23; Lu. 12:42–46; 16:10–12.

Falling.—Mt. 7:27; 21:42–44; Lu. 8:13; 16:17; 20:17, 18. Into a pit—Mt. 15:14; Lu. 6:39. Satan falling out of heaven—Lu. 10:18. Sparrows—Mt. 10:29. Stars falling—Mk. 13:25.

False accusation.—Mt. 5:11.

False Christs.—Mt. 24:5, 24; Mk. 13:22.

False confidence.—Mt. 25:5; Mk. 10:24; Lu. 11:35; 12:16–21, 45, 46; 17:28–30; John 5:45.

Falsehood.—Mk. 7:22; John 8:44.

False teachers.—Mt. 5:19; 7:15, 22, 23; 15:9, 13, 14; 23:3, 4, 13; 24:4, 5, 24; Mk. 13:22; Lu. 11:35, 52; John 5:43; 10:1–12.

False witness.—Mt. 15:19.

Famine.—Mt. 24:7; Mk. 13:8; Lu. 15:14; 21:11.

Far.—Mk. 6:35. Be it far from thee—Mt. 16:22. Not far from the kingdom—Mk. 12:34.

Fasting.—Mt. 6:16–18; 15:32; 17:21 *marg.* His disciples did not fast—Mt. 9:14, 15; Mk. 2:18–20; Lu. 5:33–35.

Father.—Mt. 7:9–11; 10:21, 37; Lu. 15:11–32; John 8:44. Let me go and bury my father—Mt. 8:21; Lu. 9:59.

Fatherhood of God.—See GOD.

Fear.—Mt. 8:26; 14:27; 17:7; 28:10; Mk. 4:40, 41; 5:36; 6:50; Lv 5:10; 12:32; John 6:20; 14:27.

Fear of man.—Mt. 10:28; 21:26, 46; Mk. 10:32; 11:32; Lu. 12:4; 20:19. Fear of God—Mt. 10:28; Lu. 12:5.

Feasts.—Mt. 23:6; Mk. 12:39; Lu. 14: 7–24; John 7:1–8; 12:2. Parables of the Marriage Supper — Mt. 22:1–14; 25:1–13. See Lu. 14:16–24.

Few.—That be saved—Mt. 7:14; 22:14; Lu. 13:23–30. Few fishes, small—Mt. 15:34; Mk. 8:7. Few laborers—Mt. 9:37; Lu. 10:2. Few stripes—Lu. 12: 48. Few things, faithful over a—Mt. 25:21.

Field.—Mt. 13:38, 44; 24:40; Mk. 11:8; Lu. 14:18; John 4:35.

Fig.—Mt. 7:16; Mk. 11:13, 14.

Fig tree.—Mt. 24:32, 33; Mk. 13:28, 29; Lu. 21:29–32; John 1:48. Barren fig tree—Lu. 13:6–9.

Find.—Mt. 7:8, 14; 11:29; Lu. 18:8; John 10:9. He that findeth life shall lose it—Mt. 10:39; 16:25. Found sleeping—Mt. 26:40, 43; Mk. 13:36; 14:37, 40. Finding the lost piece of money—Lu. 15:8–10. Finding lost sheep—Lu. 15:4–7.

Finger.—Mt. 23:4; Lu. 16:24; John 8: 6–8. Finger of God—Lu. 11:20.

Fire.—Lu. 12:49. Hell of fire—Mt. 5: 22; 13:40–42; 18:9; 25:41; Mk. 9:43–49.

First.—Mt. 12:29, 45; 13:30; 23:26; Mk. 13:10; Lu. 17:25. Seek first His kingdom—Mt. 6:33. See Mt. 19:28–30; Mk. 10:28–31; Lu. 18:29, 30. First commandment—Mt. 22:38; Mk. 12:28, 29. He that would be first—Mt. 20: 27; Mk. 9:35; 10:44. First shall be last—Mt. 19:30; 20:16; Mk. 10:31; Lu. 13:30.

Fish.—Mt. 7:10; 12:40; Lu. 11:11. Miracles with fish—Mt. 14:17–19; 15:36; 17:27; Lu. 5:1–9; John 21:6–11.

Fishers of men.—Mt. 4:19–22; Lu. 5: 10, 11.

Flax, Smoking.—Mt. 12:20.

Flesh.—Mt. 24:22; 26:41; Mk. 13:20; 14:38; John 3:6; 6:63; 17:2. Eating His flesh—John 6:52–58. Flesh and blood—Mt. 16:17. Spirit hath not flesh—Lu. 24:39.

Flock.—Lu. 12:32; John 10:1–16; 21:15–17.

Following Him.—Mt. 10:38; 16:24; Mk. 8:34; Lu. 9:23–26, 57–62; 14:27; John 8:12; 15:1–8.

Food.—Mt. 6:25, 26; 10:10; 14:15; 24: 45; Lu. 9:13; 12:24; John 4:8. See BREAD, EATING, FASTING, FEAST.

Foolish.—Mt. 7:26, 27; 23:17; 25:1–10; Mk. 7:22; Lu. 11:40; 12:16–21; 24:25.

Forbid.—Mk. 9:39; 10:14; Lu. 9:50; 18:16.

Forethought.—Lu. 12:25, 26; 14:28–33. See WATCHFULNESS.

Forgiveness.—Mt. 9:2–6; 12:31, 32; Mk. 2:5–10; 3:28; 11:25; Lu. 7:36–48; 23: 34; 24:47; John 20:23. Forgive as we expect to be forgiven—Mt. 6:12–15; Lu. 11:4. Love your enemies—Mt. 5:39–48; Lu. 6:27–29, 35–37. Seven times seven—Mt. 18:21–35; Lu. 17: 3, 4. Unpardonable sin—Mt. 12:31, 32; Mk. 3:28–30.

Foundation.—Lu. 6:48.

Foxes.—Have holes—Mt. 8:20; Lu. 9:58. Calls Herod a fox—Lu. 13:32.

Fraternity.—See BRETHREN, GIVING, FRATERNITY, FRIENDSHIP, LOVE.

Free.—Mt. 10:8; John 8:32, 36.

Friendship.—Mt. 20:13; 22:12; 26:50; Mk. 5:19; Lu. 12:4; 14:10, 12; 15:6, 9; John 3:29; 11:3, 11. Greater love hath no man—John 15:13. Friend aroused at midnight—Lu. 11:5–8. Friend of publicans and sinners—Mt. 11:19. Not servants but friends—John 15:13–15.

Fruit.—Mt. 21:19, 41; Lu. 13:6–9. Fruit of the vine—Mt. 26:29; Mk. 14:25; Lu. 22:18. Figurative—Mt. 6:16–23; 12:33; 13:8, 22, 23; Mk. 4:7, 8, 19, 20; Lu. 6:43–45; 8:8, 14, 15; John 4:36; 15:1–8.

Fulfil.—All righteousness—Mt. 3:15. The law and the prophets—Mt. 4:14–16; 5:17–20; 11:5; 21:42; 22:41–46; 26: 54; Mk. 12:10, 11, 35–37; Lu. 20:17, 41–44; 22:37; 24:25–27, 44–47; John 5:39, 45–47. Time not fulfilled—John 7:6, 8.

Gain.—His life shall lose it—Mt. 10:39; Mk. 8:35; Lu. 9:24; 17:33; John 12:25. The whole world but lose his soul—Mt. 16:26–28; Mk. 8:36–38; Lu. 9: 24–26.

Garments.—New cloth in old—Mt. 9:16. Soft raiment—Mt. 11:8; Lu. 7:25. Wedding garment—Mt. 22:11.

Gate.—Narrow and wide—Mt. 7:13, 14. See Lu. 13:24–30. Of Hades—Mt. 16:18.

Giving.—Lu. 6:1–4, 38; 10:8; 11:9–13, 41. Giving all; receiving more—Mt. 19:28–30; Mk. 10:28–31; Lu. 18:29, 30. To him that asketh—Mt. 5:42; Lu. 6:34–38. Poor, To the—Mt. 10:42; 19:21–26; 25:34–46; Mk. 9:41; 10:21–25; Lu. 12:33, 34; 18:18–27. *Parable of Rich Man and Lazarus*—Lu. 16:19–31. See Lu. 16:9.

Glory.—Lu. 14:10; John 8:50; 17:5, 22. Glory of God—Mt. 16:27; Mk. 8:38; Lu. 9:26; John 11:4, 40; 17:5, 22. From men—Mt. 6:2, 5, 16; Lu. 6:24; John 5:41. Second coming of Jesus in glory—Mt. 16:27; 24:27, 30, 31; 25:31; 26:64; Mk. 8:38; 13:26, 27; 14:62; Lu. 21:27. Jesus shall sit on His throne in glory—John 8:54. Solomon in all his glory—Mt. 6:29; Lu. 12:27.

Glorify.—John 7:39; 8:54; 13:31, 32; 17:1.

Glorifying God.—Mt. 5:16; John 11:4; 12:28; 13:31, 32; 14:13; 15:8; 21:19.

Go.—Only to the Jews—Mt. 10:1–23; Mk. 6:7–13; Lu. 9:1–6. Into all the world, and preach the gospel—Mt. 28:19; Mk. 16:15, 16; Lu. 24:46, 47; Acts 1:8. Going into hell—Mt. 5:30. To Jerusalem to prepare place for last supper—Mt. 26:18; Mk. 14:13; Lu. 22:8. Going to law—Mt. 5:40. To whom shall we go?—John 6:68.

Goat.—Mt. 25:32, 33.

God.—Access to God—Mt. 5:8; John 10:1–10; 14:6. Almighty—Mt. 19:26; Mk. 10:27; Lu. 18:27. Creator—Mt. 19:4–6; Mk. 10:6–9; 13:19. Dwells with men—Mt. 23:21; John 14:23. Fatherhood—John 1:12, 18; 2:16; 4:21, 23; 5:17–23, 37, 43; 6:27, 32, 44–46; 8:19, 27, 28, 39, 41, 42, 49; 10:15–18, 29, 30, 32, 36–38; 11:41, 52; 12:26–28, 49, 50; 14:2, 6–13, 16, 20, 21, 23, 26; 15:8–10, 16, 23, 24, 26; 16:3, 10, 15, 23, 25–28; 17:1, 5, 11, 21, 24, 25; 20:17, 21. Father, Son, and Holy Spirit—Mt. 28:19; John 10:30; 17:11, 22. See JESUS, DIVINITY OF. Foreknowledge of God—Mt. 6:8, 32; 24:36; 26:24; Lu.

22:22; 24:27, 47. His holiness—Mt. 19:17; Mk. 10:18; John 17:11, 25. His perfection—Mt. 5:48. Holy Spirit, God sends—John 14:16, 26; 15:26. Knows all—Mt. 6:4, 8, 18, 32; 10:29, 30; 24:36; Lu. 16:15. Love of God—Mt. 5:45; 18:11–14; John 3:16, 17; 14:21, 23; 16:27; 17:10, 23, 26. Personality of—Mt. 4:10; 23:9; John 14:9; 17:3. Providence of—Mt. 5:45; 6:25–34; 10:29–31; Lu. 12:6, 7; 22:30; 22:35. Spirit, God is—John 4:24. Sovereignty—Mt. 5:45; 6:10; 11:25; Mk. 12:29, 30; Lu. 10:21; John 5:44; 10:29; 17:3; 19:11. Worshipped, God would be—John 4:23, 24.

Gold.—Mt. 10:9; 23:16, 17.

Good.—Mt. 5:44, 45; 12:12; 19:17; 20:15; 22:10; Mk. 3:4; 10:18; Lu. 5:39; 6:9, 27, 33, 35, 45; 18:19; John 5:29. Cheer—Mt. 9:2, 22; 14:27; Mk. 6:50; 10:49; John 16:33. Fish—Mt. 13:48. For nothing—Mt. 5:13. Fruit—Mt. 7:17–19; 12:33; Lu. 6:43. Gifts—Mt. 7:11; Lu. 11:13. Ground—Mt. 13:8, 23; Mk. 4:8, 20; Lu. 8:8, 15. Heart—Lu. 8:15. Man—Mt. 12:35. Measure—Lu. 6:38. Part—Lu. 10:42. Pleasure—Lu. 12:32. Salt—Lu. 14:34. Seed—Mt. 13:24, 27, 37, 38. Servant—Mt. 25:21, 23; Lu. 19:17. Shepherd—John 10:11, 14. Thing—Mt. 12:34, 35; Lu. 16:25. Tidings—Mt. 11:5; Lu. 4:18, 19, 43. Treasure—Mt. 12:35; Lu. 6:45. Tree—Mt. 7:17, 18; 12:33; Lu. 6:43. Wine—John 2:10.

Goods.—Mt. 12:29; 25:14; Mk. 3:27; Lu. 6:30; 11:21; 12:18, 19; 16:1; 17:31; 19:8.

Gospel, What is the?—The kingdom of heaven—Mt. 4:17, 23; 9:35; 10:5–7; 24:14; Lu. 4:43; 8:1; 10:9–11; 11:20; 16:16; 21:31; Acts 1:3. The words *or* sayings of Jesus—Mt. 7:24–27; 13:3–9, 18–23; Mk. 4:3–9, 14–20; 8:38; 13:31; Lu. 6:46–49; 8:21; 9:26; 11:28; 21:33; John 6:63; 8:31, 32, 37, 51; 12:48–50; 14:23, 24; 17:6–8. Jesus is the Christ, the Son of God—Mt. 10:33; Mk. 8:38; Lu. 9:26; 12:9; John 3:14–17; 5:24; 6:33–45; 17:3; Acts 1:8.

Revealed to the apostles—Mt. 11:25; 13:11; 16:17; 19:11. By the Holy Spirit—Mt. 10:19, 20; Mk. 13:11; Lu.

12:12; 21:15; 24:49; John 14:26; 16:
13.

Man saved by the gospel—Mt. 4:4; 10:
32, 33; Lu. 9:26; 12:9; John 5:34;
6:33-45, 63; 8:31, 32, 51; 12:48-50;
15:3; 17:6-8, 14, 17, 20.

Parable of the sower—Mt. 13:3-9, 18-
23; Mk. 4:3-9, 14-20; Lu. 8:5-15.

Must be preached—Lu. 16:16. Preached
to the poor—Mt. 11:5; Lu. 4:18, 19.
To the whole world—Mt. 24:14; 26:
13; 28:19, 20; Mk. 13:10; 14:9; 16:15,
16; Lu. 24:46, 47; Acts 1:8. Apostles
sent out—Mt. 10:1-15; 28:19, 20; Mk.
6:7-13; 16:15, 16; Lu. 9:1-6; 24:47-49.
Seventy sent out—Lu. 10:1-20.

Must be heard—Mt. 7:24, 25; 10:14; 13:
13-23; Mk. 4:12; Lu. 6:47; 8:21; 10:
16; 11:28; John 5:24, 25; 6:45; 8:43,
47; 9:27; 14:23, 24.

Must be believed—Mk. 16:16; Lu. 8:12,
13; John 3:14-16, 36; 5:24; 6:29, 40,
47; 8:24; 11:25, 26; 17:20.

Must be obeyed—Mt. 7:16-27; 12:50;
28:19, 20; Mk. 16:15, 16; Lu. 6:46-49;
8:21; 24:46, 47.

Great.—Mt. 20:25; Mk. 10:42, 43; Lu.
9:48. Branches—Mk. 4:32. Buildings—Mk. 13:2. Commandment—Mt.
22:38; Mk. 12:31. Darkness—Mt. 6:
23. Distress—Lu. 21:23. Earthquakes
—Lu. 21:11. Faith—Mt. 8:10; 15:28;
Lu. 7:9. Fall—Mt. 7:27. Glory—Mt.
24:30; Mk. 13:26; Lu. 21:27. Gulf—
Lu. 16:26. Harvest—Lu. 10:2. King
—Mt. 5:35. Kingdom, In the—Mt.
5:19. Light—Mt. 4:16. Power—Mk.
13:26. Price—Mt. 13:46. Reward—
Mt. 5:12; Lu. 6:23, 35. Signs and
wonders—Mt. 24:24; Lu. 21:11. Sound
of trumpets—Mt. 24:31. Supper—Lu.
14:16. Things—Mk. 5:19; Lu. 8:39.
Tribulation—Mt. 24:21. Way off—
Lu. 14:32.

Greater.—Mt. 13:32; Mk. 4:32; Lu. 12:
18; 22:26. Than John the Baptist—
Mt. 11:11; Lu. 7:28. God greater than
all—John 10:29; 14:28. Jesus greater
than Jonah—Mt. 12:41; Lu. 11:32.
Than Solomon—Mt. 12:42; Lu. 11:31.
Than the temple—Mt. 12:6. Servant
not greater than his lord—John 13:
16; 15:20. Condemnation—Mk. 12:
40; Lu. 20:47. Gift or altar?—Mt. 23:
19. Gold or temple?—Mt. 23:17. Love

—John 15:13. Sin—John 19:11. Witness—John 5:36. Works—John 5:20;
14:12.

Greatest.—Mt. 18:1-4; 23:11; Mk. 9:34;
Lu. 9:46; 22:24, 26; John 10:29.

Ground.—Mt. 10:29; 13:8, 23; 15:35;
Mk. 4:5, 8, 20; 8:6; Lu. 8:8, 15; 12:16;
13:7; 19:44.

Guide.—Mt. 15:14; Lu. 6:39; John 16:
13. Blind guides—Mt. 15:14; 23:16,
24.

Hades.—Consciousness in—Lu. 16:19-
28. Gates of Hades shall not prevail
against the Church—Mt. 16:18. Go
down into—Mt. 11:23; Lu. 10:15.
Rich man in—Lu. 16:19-31. Torment,
Place of—Lu. 16:19-28.

Hair.—Mt. 5:36; 10:30; Lu. 7:38, 44;
12:7; 21:18.

Harmless as doves.—Mt. 10:16.
See THE GOSPEL MUST BE HEARD.

Heart.—Doubt in the heart—Mk. 11:23.
Earth, Of the—Mt. 12:40. Forgive
from the—Mt. 18:35. God knows the
heart—Lu. 16:15. Good and honest
heart—Lu. 8:15. Hardness of heart—
Mt. 13:4, 19; 15:8; 19:8; Mk. 3:5;
6:52; 7:6; 8:17; 10:5; 16:14; John
12:40. Love the Lord with all thy
heart—Mt. 22:37; Mk. 12:30; Lu. 10:
27. Meek and lowly—Mt. 11:29. Over-
charged with surfeiting—Lu. 21:34.
Pure in heart—Mt. 5:8. Say in the
heart—Lu. 12:45. Settle it in your
hearts—Lu. 21:14. Slow of heart—
Lu. 24:25. Sorrow, Heart filled with
—John 16:6. Source of evil—Mt. 5:
28; 12:34-37; 15:18, 19; Mk. 7:19-23;
Lu. 6:45. Sown in the heart, Word—
Mt. 13:19; Lu. 8:12. Thoughts of the
heart—Mt. 9:4; Mk. 2:6-8; Lu. 9:47;
24:38. Treasure is where thy—Mt.
6:21; Lu. 12:34. Troubled—John 14:
1, 27. Understand with—Mt. 13:15.
Waxed gross—Mt. 13:15.

Heaven.—Angels in—Mt. 18:10; 22:30,
24:36; Mk. 13:32; John 1:51. See Mt.
16:27; Mk. 8:38. Ascending and
descending—John 1:51; 2:13. See
DWELLING PLACE OF JESUS. Baptism
of John the Baptist—From heaven or
men?—Mt. 21:25-27; Mk. 30-33; Lu.
20:4-7. Birds of the—Mt. 8:20. Bound
in—Mt. 18:18. Bread out of—John
6:32, 33, 50, 51, 58. Clouds of—Mt.

24:30; 26:64; Mk. 13:26; 14:62. Dwelling place of God—Mt. 5:16, 45; 6:9; 7:11; 10:32, 33; 11:25; 12:50; 16:17; 18:10, 14, 19; 23:9; Mk. 11:25; Lu. 10: 21. *God is Lord of*—Mt. 6:10; 11:25; Lu. 10:21. *Throne of God*—Mt. 5:34; 23:22. *Called Father's house*—John 14:1–3. Dwelling place of Jesus—John 12:26; 14:3; 17:5, 24. *Descended from*—John 3:13, 31–36; 6:38, 39, 62; 8:23. *Came from the Father*—John 3:16; 6:46; 8:42; 13:3; 16:28–30; 17: 5, 8, 18. *Ascending into*—Lu. 24:26; John 1:51; 6:62; 7:33; 14:2, 3, 12, 28; 16:5, 7, 10, 28; 17:13; 20:17. *Seated on right hand of God*—Mt. 26:64; Mk. 14:62; Lu. 22:69. *Shall come again from*—Mt. 24:30; Mk. 14:62; Lu. 21: 7; John 14:3, 18, 28. Dwelling place of the righteous—Mt. 5:12; 25:34; Lu. 6:23; John 14:1–3; 17:24. End, From one to another—Mt. 24:31; Mk. 13:27; Lu. 17:24. Exalted unto—Mt. 11:23; Lu. 10:15. Face of, Interpret—Lu. 12:56. See HEAVEN, Fire and brimstone from—Lu. 17:29. Joy in—Mt. 13:43; Lu. 15:7, 10. Lightning out of—Lu. 17:24. Marriage in heaven, No—Mt. 22:30–33; Mk. 12:18–27. Names written in—Lu. 10:20. Opened—John 1:51. Passing away, Heaven and earth—Mt. 5:18; 24:35; Mk. 13: 31; Lu. 16:17; 21:33; 24:35. Powers of heaven shaken—Mt. 24:29; Lu. 21: 26. Red—Mt. 16:2, 3. Reward in—Mt. 5:12; 25:34; Lu. 6:23. Satan falling from—Lu. 10:18. Sign of the Son of Man—Mt. 24:30. Sinned against—Lu. 15:21. Stars falling from—Mt. 24:29; Mk. 13:25. Swearing by—Mt. 5:34; 23:22. Terrors and signs from—Lu. 21:11. Throne of God—Mt. 5:34; 23:22. Treasures in—Mt. 6:20; 19:21; Mk. 10:21. Will done on earth as in heaven—Mt. 6:10. See LIFE, ETERNAL.

Kingdom of heaven.—Mt. 13:52. At hand—Mt. 4:17; Lu. 10:9, 11. Belongs to children—Mt. 19:14; Mk. 10: 15. Belongs to the poor—Mt. 5:3. Entrance into—Mt. 5:20; 7:21; 8:11; 18:3, 4; 19:14, 23; 25:34–46. Great in the kingdom of heaven—Mt. 5:19; 11: 11. Keys of—Mt. 16:19. Least in—Mt. 5:19; 11:11. Mysteries of—Mt.

13:11. Parables of—See HIS KINGDOM. Sake of, For the—Mt. 19:21. Shut by pharisees—Mt. 23:13. See Lu. 11:52.

Hell.—Cast into—Mt. 18:9; Mk. 9:43, 45, 47; Lu. 12:5. Body cast into—Mt. 5:29. Body and soul destroyed in—Mt. 10:28. Fire, Of—Mt. 5:22; 13: 40, 42, 50; 18:9. *Eternal fire*—Mt. 18: 8; 25:41. *Unquenchable fire*—Mk. 9: 43, 48. Judgment of—Mt. 23:33. Son of—Mt. 23:15. See Mt. 7:13, 14; 22: 13; 25:46.

Heir.—Mt. 21:38; Mk. 12:7; Lu. 20:14.

Hire.—Mt. 20:1, 7; Lu. 10:7; 15:19.

Hireling.—John 10:10–13.

Holiness.—Mt. 5:8; Lu. 6:45; John 1:47; 5:14; 13:10; 15:13, 19; 17:16, 17, 23.

Holy.—Mt. 7:6. Angels—Mk. 8:38; Lu. 9:26. Father—John 17:11. Place—Mt. 24:15.

Holy Spirit.—John 20:22. Anointing of Jesus—Lu. 4:18–21. Baptism in the name of the Father, Son, and Holy Spirit—Mt. 28:19. Baptism of the Holy Spirit—Lu. 24:49; Acts 1:5, 8. Born of the Spirit—John 3:5–8. Gifts of the Spirit—Mk. 16:17, 18. Given by God to disciples—John 3:34; 14: 16, 17. *Not given until Jesus was glorified*—John 7:38, 39; 16:7. *Sent in name of Jesus*—John 14:26. *Sent by Jesus from the Father*—John 15:26; 16:7. Inspiration of—Mt. 10:20; Mk. 12:36; 13:11; Lu. 12:11, 12; John 14:26; 16: 13. Sin against—Mt. 12:32. *Blasphemy*—Mk. 3:39; Lu. 12:10. Work of—John 16:8–14.

Honor.—God honors—Lu. 12:37; John 12:26. Father and mother, Honor—Mt. 15:4–6; 19:19; Mk. 7:10–13; 10: 19; Lu. 18:20. God, Honoring—John 5:23; 8:49. Jesus, Honoring—John 5:23. See Lu. 10:16. *Lips, With*—Mt. 15:8; Mk. 7:6. Prophet not without honor, save in his own country—Mt. 13:57; Mk. 6:4; Lu. 4:24; John 4:44.

Hospitality.—Mt. 10:9–15, 42; 25:31, 46; Mk. 6:7–11; 9:41; Lu. 9:1–5; 14: 12–14. Marriage Supper—Mt. 22:1–14; Lu. 14:8–10. Parable of the Good Samaritan—Lu. 10:30–37.

Hour.—Mt. 10:19; 26:45; Mk. 13:11; 14:35; Lu. 12:12; 22:53; John 4:21, 23; 11:9; 12:27. At hand—Mt. 26:45; Mk. 14:41; John 12:23; 17:1. See

John 16:21, 22. Cometh—John 4:21; 5:25, 28; 16:2, 25, 32. Not yet come—John 2:4. See John 7:6, 8, 30; 8:20. Coming of the Son of Man—Mt. 24: 36, 44, 50; 25:13; Mk. 13:32; Lu. 12: 39, 40, 46. Parable of the Hours—Mt. 20:3–16.

House.—Mt. 26:18; Lu. 18:14; John 8: 35. Abiding in—Mt. 10:11; Mk. 6:10; Lu. 9:4; 10:7. Broken into—Mt. 24: 43; Lu. 12:39. Desolate—Mt. 23:38; Lu. 13:35. Divided—Mt. 12:25; Mk. 3:25; Lu. 11:17; 12:52. Entering—Mk. 6:10; Lu. 7:44; Lu. 9:4. Entering, Salute—Mt. 10:12; Lu. 10:5. Father's house—John 14:2. God, Of—Mk. 2:26; Lu. 6:4. Israel, House of—Mt. 10:6; 15:24. Left houses—Mk. 10:29; Lu. 18:29. Leaving unworthy—Shake dust from your feet—Mt. 10: 14; Mk. 6:10, 11. Master of—Mt. 10: 25; 24:43; Mk. 13:35; 14:14; Lu. 12: 39; 13:25; 14:21, 22. Prayer, of—Mt. 21:13. Rock, On the—Mt. 7:24, 25; Lu. 6:48. Room in: *Guest chamber* —Mk. 14:14; Lu. 22:11. Salvation come to—Lu. 19:9. Sand, On the—Mt. 7:26, 27; Lu. 6:49. Spoiled—Mt. 12:29; Mk. 3:27. Things in—Mt. 24: 17; Mk. 13:15. Worthy—Mt. 10:13.

Household. — Mt. 24:45; Lu. 12:42. Household of Beelzebub—Mt. 10:25. Foes of one's own household—Mt. 10: 36.

Householder.—Mt. 13:27, 52; 20:1. Who had a vineyard—Mt. 20:1, 11; 21:33.

Hunger.—Mt. 25:35–45; Lu. 6:21, 25; 15:17; John 6:35. David eats showbread—Mt. 12:3, 4; Mk. 2:25, 26; Lu. 6:3, 4. Hungering after righteousness —Mt. 5:6; John 6:35.

Husband.—Mk. 10:12; Lu. 16:18; John 4:16–18. See Lu. 19:3–9; Mk. 10:6–12.

Husbandman.—John 15:1. Parable of—Mt. 21:33–41; Mk. 12:1–9; Lu. 20: 9–16.

Humility.—Mt. 11:29. Babes, Revelation to—Lu. 10:21. Becoming as a little child—Mt. 18:2–4; Mk. 9:34–37; Lu. 9:46–48. Humbleth himself shall be exalted, Whosoever—Mt. 23:12; Lu. 14:11; 18:14. Pharisee and publican, Parable of—Lu. 18:9–14. Poor in spirit—Mt. 5:8; Lu. 6:20. Lowest room—Lu. 14:10, 11. Minister, Who-

soever will be great, let him—Mt. 20: 25–28; Mk. 10:43, 44; Lu. 22:24–27. Washing disciples' feet—John 13:4–10. See MEEKNESS.

Hypocrites.—Mt. 15:11–20; 23:5; Lu. 6: 46; 11:42; 12:56; 13:15; 16:15. Beam and mote—Mt. 7:3–5; Lu. 6:41, 42. Blind—Mt. 23:17, 19, 26. Blind guides —Mt. 15:14; 23:16, 24. Called *Fools*—Mt. 23:17. *Foolish ones*—Lu. 11:40. *Whited sepulchres*—Mt. 23:27, 28. See Lu. 11:44. Chief seats, Love—Mt. 23:6; Mk. 12:39; Lu. 20:46. Cleanse the outside of cups and platters, inward parts full of extortion and wickedness—Mt. 23:25, 26; Lu. 11:39. Elders in the case of the woman taken in adultery—John 8:1–10. Leaven of the pharisees—Lu. 12:1. Lips, Honoring with—Mt. 15:8; Mk. 7:6. Making void the commandments by the traditions of men—Mt. 15:1–9; Mk. 7:7, 8. Oppressors—Mt. 23:3, 4; Mk. 12:40; Lu. 20:47. Punished—Mt. 24:51. Seen of men, Love to be—Mt. 6:2, 5, 16; 23: 5–7; Mk. 12:38; Lu. 20:46. Shut the kingdom of heaven—Mt. 23:13; Lu. 11:52. Signs of times, cannot discern —Mt. 16:3; Lu. 12:54–56. Strain at a gnat and swallow a camel—Mt. 23:24. Tribute money—Mt. 22:15–27; Mk. 12:13–17. See HYPOCRISY.

Image and superscription.—Mt. 22:20; Mk. 12:16; Lu. 20:24.

Importunity in prayer.—Lu. 11:5–8; 18: 1, 8.

Inheritance.—See LIFE ETERNAL.

Iniquity.—Mt. 7:23; 13:41; 24:12.

Israel.—Apostles sent only to house of Israel—Mt. 10:6; 15:24. Faith in Israel, Have not seen such—Mt. 8:10; Lu. 7:9. Judging twelve tribes of Israel—Mt. 19:28; Lu. 22:30. Many lepers in Israel in days of Elijah—Lu. 4:27. Many widows in Israel in the days of Elijah—Lu. 4:25. See JERUSALEM.

James the Apostle.—Called to be a disciple—Mt. 4:21; Mk. 1:19, 20. Fisher of men—Lu. 5:10. James and John called Boanerges—''Sons of thunder'' —Mk. 3:17. James and John rebuked for ambition—Mk. 10:35–41. See Mt. 20:20–24.

Jerusalem.—John 4:21. Baptism of Holy Spirit in—Lu. 24:49; Acts 1:4. City of the great king—Mt. 5:35. Destruction, Foretells of—Mt. 23:38; 24: 1–28; Mk. 13:1–37; Lu. 21:5–36; 23: 28–31. Foretells His sufferings in—Mt. 16:21; 20:18; Mk. 10:33, 34; Lu. 18:31. Lament over—Mt. 23:37; Lu. 13:34. Gospel preached among all nations beginning at Jerusalem—Lu. 24: 47; Acts 1:8.˙

JESUS. Teaching concerning Himself—Ascension.—See HEAVEN, THE DWELLING PLACE OF JESUS.

Blood of Jesus.—Shed for remission of sins—Mt. 26:28; Mk. 14:24.

Death of Jesus, Man saved by.—Lu. 24: 25–27; John 3:14–17, 18; 12:31–34. Christ gave His life for mankind—Mt. 20:28; Mk. 10:45; John 6:51; 10: 11; 11:49–53; 15:13. Jesus predicts His death and resurrection—See JESUS A PROPHET.

Divinity of.—John 17:2. Authority to forgive sins—Mt. 9:6–8; Mk. 2:5–12; Lu. 5:20–26. Power over life and death—Mt. 26:52–56; John 2:19–22; 5:21, 25–28; 10:17, 18, 28. All authority given to Him—Mt. 11:27; 28:18; John 3:35; 5:22, 23, 27. Judge of the world—Mt. 16:27; 25:31–46; John 5: 22, 23, 27, 30. Kingship—Mt. 13:41; 16:27, 28; 25:31–46; 27:11; 27:42; Lu. 22:29, 30; John 18:33–37. Anointed—Lu. 4:18–21. Seated on right hand of God—Mt. 26:64; Mk. 16:19; Lu. 22:69. Kingdom, His—Mt. 6:33; 13:19, 41; 16:28; 24:34; 26:29; Mk. 11:10; Lu. 12:31, 32; 22:29, 30; John 18:36. Called "The Kingdom of God"—Mt. 12:28; 19:24; 21:31; Mk. 1:15; 4:11, 26, 30; 9:1, 47; 10:14, 15, 23–25; 12:34; 14: 25; 15:43; Lu. 4:43; 6:20; 7:28; 8:1, 10; 9:2, 11, 27, 60, 62; 10:9, 11; 11:20; 13:18, 20, 28, 29; 14:15; 16:16; 17:20, 21; 18:16, 17, 24, 25, 29; 19:11; 22:16; John 3:3, 5; Acts 1:3. Kingdom of heaven—Mt. 4:17; 5:19, 20; 7:21; 10: 7; 11:11, 12; 13:11, 24, 31, 33, 44, 45, 47, 52; 16:19; 18:1, 3, 4, 23; 19:12, 14, 23; 20:1; 22:2; 23:13; 25:1. Not of this world—Mt. 26:52–56; John 6:15; 18:36. Within you—Lu. 17:20, 21. Not established before the death of Jesus—

Mt. 16:19, 28; Lu. 12:32; 21:31. At hand—Mt. 4:17; 10:7; Lu. 10:9, 11. To come with power—Mk. 9:1; Acts 1:4–8. Prepared for you from the foundation of the world—Mt. 25:34. Jews natural heirs but rejected—Mt. 8:11, 12; 21: 42–44. See Mt. 23:13. Suffereth violence—Mt. 11:12; Lu. 12:31. Who may enter?—He that is but little is greater than John the Baptist—Mt. 11:11; Lu. 7:28. Seek first the kingdom—Mt. 6: 33; Lu. 12:31. Those who do the will of God—Mt. 5:19, 20; 7:21–27. Repentance a condition—Mt. 4:17. Poor in spirit—Mt. 5:3; Lu. 6:20. Publicans and harlots enter before the pharisees—Mt. 21:31; Lu. 7:29–50. Hard for rich to enter—Mt. 19:23, 24; Mk. 10:23–27; Lu. 18:24, 25, 29. Those who do not look back—Lu. 9:42. Must become as little children—Mt. 18:1–4; 19:14; Mk. 10:14, 15; Lu. 18:15–17. Those who are born anew of water and spirit—John 3: 3–5. Those who endure tribulations—Mt. 19:29, 30; Mk. 10:29; Lu. 18:29. Universal kingdom—Mt. 24:14; 28:18, 19; Mk. 16:15, 16; Lu. 24:46, 47; Acts 1:8. Gospel of the kingdom—Mt. 4:23; 9:35; 24:14; Lu. 4:13; 8:1; 9:2, 60; 10:9, 11; Acts 1:8. Keys of the—Mt. 16:19. Mysteries of the kingdom—Mk. 4:11; Lu. 8:10. Parables of—See "Parables of the kingdom," under HIS KINGDOM. Glory of—Lu. 9:26; John 12:23; 13:31, 32; 16:14; 17:1–5, 22, 24. Fulfilment of Scriptures, His—Mt. 5:17; 26:52–56; Lu. 24:25–27, 44–47; John 5:39, 45, 46. The prophecy of David—Mt. 22:41–46; Mk. 12:35–37; Lu. 20: 41–44 (Ps. 110:1). The stone which the builders rejected—Mt. 21:42; Mk. 12: 10, 11; Lu. 20:17 (Ps. 118:22). The Spirit of the Lord upon Him—Mt. 11: 5; Lu. 2:28–32 (Is. 11:1, 2; 35:5; 42:1; 61:1, 2). His miracles a proof of His divinity—Mt. 11:20–24; Mk. 2:5–12; John 10:37, 38; 14:11, 12; 15:24. He foretells His own death, burial, and resurrection on the third day. See DIVINITY OF JESUS. Sinlessness, His—John 8:46. Sufficer of all needs—Mt. 11:28–30; John 4:14; 6:35, 48–58; 8: 31–36, 51. He will send the Holy Spirit—John 14:26; 15:26. He commanded to baptize in the name of the

Father, Son, and Holy Spirit—Mt. 28:19.

Christ calls Himself "The Son of God." —Mt. 11:27; 21:37–44; 26:63, 64; 27: 43; Mk. 12:6–11; 14:61, 62; Lu. 20:13– 18; John 3:16–18, 34–36; 5:19, 20, 25, 26; 6:40; 9:35–37; 10:36; 11:4; 19:7. See Lu. 10:22; I Tim. 6:13–15. The only begotten Son—John 3:16–18.

He calls God His Father.—Mt. 15:13; 18:10, 19; 20:23; 26:53, 63, 64; Lu. 10: 22; 22:29; John 5:19–21, 23, 26, 27, 30, 36, 37; 8:16, 19, 26–29, 38, 49, 54; 10: 15, 17, 18, 29, 30, 36–38; 11:41; 12:49, 50; 13:3; 14:7, 9–11, 13, 16, 20, 21, 23, 24, 28, 31; 15:1, 8–10, 15, 23, 24; 16: 15, 27, 28, 32; 17:1–26; 20:17, 21.

Lordship of.—Mt. 22:41–46; 24:42; 25: 37–44; Mk. 12:35–37; Lu. 20:41–47; John 13:13, 14. Lord of the Sabbath —Mt. 12:8; Mk. 2:28; Lu. 6:5.

Messiah.—Mt. 16:16–20; 22:42–45; 26: 63, 64; Mk. 12:35–37; Lu. 20:41–44; 24:25–27; John 4:25, 26. See Mt. 11: 1–6.

Humanity of.—Word made flesh—Mt. 11:19; Lu. 24:39; John 20:27. He calls Himself "The Son of Man." See DIVINITY OF JESUS. Became poor for our sakes—Mt. 8:20; 20:28; Lu. 9:58.

Character of.—Benevolent—Lu. 4:18, 19; John 10:32. Compassionate—Mt. 15:22; 8:2, 3. Faithful—John 4:34; 5:30; 6:38; 8:29; 9:4; 17:8. Forgiving —Mt. 9:2–6; Mk. 2:5, 10; Lu. 5:20–25; 7:47–50. Humble—Mk. 10:45; Lu. 22: 27. Living—John 14:21, 31; 15:9–15. Meek and lowly—Mt. 11:29. Obedient —Mt. 3:15; John 4:34; 5:50; 6:38; 17:4. Perfect—Lu. 13:32. Righteous —John 5:30; 7:18. Sanctified—John 17:19. Sinless—John 8:46. True— John 7:18; 8:32; 14:6; 18:37.

Humiliation.—Acquainted with grief— Mt. 26:38. Betrayed—Mt. 26:23–25; Mk. 14:18–21, 41; Lu. 22:21, 22; John 6:64, 71; 13:2, 21, 26. Condemned— Mt. 20:18; Mk. 10:33. Delivered up— Mt. 17:22; 20:18; Mk. 9:31; Lu. 18:32. Denied—Mt. 26:34, 69–75; Mk. 14:30, 68–72; Lu. 22:55–61; John 13:38; 18: 25–27. Despised—Lu. 18:32. Gave Himself—John 6:51. Hated without cause—John 7:7; 15:18, 24, 25. Home-

less—Mt. 8:20; Lu. 9:58. Killed—Mt. 16:21; 17:23; Mk. 9:31; 10:34. Laid down His life—John 10:11, 15, 17, 18. Lifted up—John 3:14–16; 8:28; 12:32, 34. Mocked—Mk. 10:34. Numbered with transgressors—Lu. 22:37. Perse- cuted—John 15:20.

Mission of.—John 3:16, 17, 34; 4:34; 5:30, 36, 38; 6:29, 38, 57; 7:29; 8:42; 10:36; 11:42; 17:3, 8, 21, 23, 25. He came in His Father's name—John 5: 43. To establish His church—Mt. 16: 18. To set example in His life—Mt. 3: 15; 11:29; John 13:12–16, 34; 17:14, 18, 21, 22. To reveal the fatherhood of God—John 6:44–46; 8:27, 28, 41, 42; 10:15–18, 32; 11:52; 12:49, 50; 14:1– 13, 20–24, 28–31; 16:3, 10, 23–30. Ful- fil the Scriptures, To. See HE CAME IN FULFILMENT OF THE SCRIPTURES. Glorify the Father, To—John 13:31; 14:13; 17:4. For judgment—John 5: 22, 23, 27; 9:39. Life, To give—John 3:15, 36; 5:40; 6:33, 51; 10:10–28; 11: 25; 14:6. Light of the world—John 3:19; 8:12; 9:5; 12:35, 36, 46. Minis- ter, To—Mt. 20:28; Mk. 10:45. Peace, To give—John 14:27; 16:33. Preach, To—Lu. 4:16–18, 43; 16:16; 24:47. To give His life a ransom for mankind— John 6:51; 10:11, 15; 15:13. Save, To —See "Man saved through Jesus Christ," under SALVATION—Acts 2:40. To set at liberty them that are bruised —Lu. 4:18. To do the will of God— John 4:34; 5:30; 6:38, 40. To bear witness—John 7:29; 8:12–21, 25–47; 10:25–38; 14:1–24; 15:8–27; 17:1–8.

Resurrection.—Foretells His resurrec- tion—See "Jesus foretold His death and resurrection on the third day," under RESURRECTION OF JESUS. Foun- dation of Christianity—John 11:25, 26. Only signs Jesus gave: Jonah— Mt. 12:39, 40. The temple—Mk. 14: 58; John 2:18, 22; 10:18.

Saviour.—Lu. 4:16–21; 24:44–47; John 3:14–17; 5:34–40; 12:47; 14:19. He came to save sinners—Mt. 9:13; Mk. 2:17; Lu. 5:30–32; 19:10. Jesus calls Himself: *The Bread of Life*—John 6: 33–56. *The Door or Way*—John 10:1, 7, 9. *The Life*—John 11:25, 26; 14:6. *The Light*—John 8:12; 9:5; 12:35, 36, 46. *The Resurrection*—John 11:25.

Second coming.—Mt. 16:27; 24:36-39; 25:1-46; Mk. 8:38; 13:32-37; Lu. 9: 26; 18:7, 8; 19:11-27; John 14:1-3, 28; 21:22, 23. Time known only to God— Mt. 24:36-39; Mk. 13:32. Long deferred—Mt. 25:19; Mk. 13:35, 36; Lu. 18:7, 8; 19:11-15; John 21:22, 23. Disciples looked for immediate coming—Lu. 19:11. In glory—Mt. 16:27; 24:36-39; 25:31, 32; Mk. 8:38; Lu. 9: 26. Without warning—Mt. 24:36-39; 25:1-13; Mk. 13:32-37. To judge the world—Mt. 16:27; 25:31-46; Lu. 19: 11-27.

Sufferings of Jesus.—Mt. 16:21; 17:12; Mk. 9:12; Lu. 9:22; 12:50; 17:25; 24: 26, 46. Condemned—Mt. 20:18; Mk. 10:33. Crucified—Mt. 20:19; 26:2; Lu. 23:33. Delivered up—Mt. 17:22; 20: 18; Mk. 9:31; Lu. 18:32. Homeless— Mt. 8:20; Lu. 9:58. Killed—Mt. 16:21; 17:23; Mk. 9:31; 10:34. Mocked— Mk. 10:34. Numbered with transgressors—Lu. 22:37. Persecuted—John 15: 20. Rejected—Mt. 21:42; Mk. 12:10, 11; Lu. 20:17. Scourged—Mt. 20:19; Mk. 10:34. Spit upon—Mk. 10:34. Troubled—John 12:27.

Names and titles used by Jesus: Bread of Life—John 6:48-50, 58. Bridegroom —Mk. 9:15; John 3:29. Christ—See MESSIAH. Door—John 10:1, 7, 9. King —Mt. 21:5; 25:40; John 12:15. The Life—John 11:25, 26; 14:6. The Light —John 8:12; 9:5; 12:35, 36, 46. Lord —Mt. 12:8; 24:42; Mk. 2:28; Lu. 6:5. Only Begotten Son—John 3:16, 18. Resurrection—John 11:25. Shepherd —Mk. 14:27; John 10:11, 14. Son of God—See DIVINITY OF JESUS. Stone that the builders rejected—Mt. 21:42; Mk. 12:10, 11; Lu. 20:17, 18. Teacher —Mt. 26:18; Mk. 14:14; Lu. 22:11. Truth—John 14:6. Vine—John 15:1, 5. Way—John 14:6.

John the Baptist.—Mt. 11:2-18; 21:32; Lu. 7:18-35. Neither eating nor drinking—Mt. 11:18; Lu. 7:33. All the prophets and the law until—Mt. 11: 12, 13; Lu. 16:16. Elijah that was to come—Mt. 11:13, 14; 17:10-13; Mk. 9:11-13. Baptism of John, whence was it?—Mt. 21:25-27; Mk. 11:30-33; Lu. 20:4-8. Witness to the truth— John 5:32-36.

John the apostle.—Call—Mt. 4:21; Mk. 1:19, 20. His last word concerning John—John 21:21-23. Fisher of Men —Lu. 5:10. James and John called Boanerges, "Sons of thunder"—Mk. 3:17. Jesus' mother committed to care of John—John 19:26, 27.

Joy.—Mt. 13:44; Lu. 6:23; 24:32, 52. Enter into the joy of your Lord—Mt. 25:21, 23. Receiving word with joy— Mt. 13:20; Lu. 8:13. Joy in heaven over sinners who repent—Lu. 15:7, 10. Joy made full—John 3:29; 15:11; 16: 24; 17:13. No one taketh away—John 16:22. Sorrow turned into joy—John 16:20-22. See Lu. 10:20.

Judæa.—Mt. 24:16; Mk. 13:14; Lu. 21: 21; John 11:7.

Judas Iscariot.—Calls Judas a devil— John 6:70. See John 13:2. The son of perdition—John 17:12. Predicts that Judas will betray Him—Mt. 26: 21-25; Mk. 14:18-21; Lu. 22:21-23; John 13:26-30. Says that this is in fulfilment of Scripture—John 17:12.

Judge.—Lu. 7:43; 11:19; 12:14; John 3:18; 5:22, 30; 7:24; 8:16. Judge not that ye be not judged—Mt. 7:1-5; Lu. 6:37-42. God sent Christ not to judge, but to save—John 3:17; 18:15, 16; 12: 47, 48. Christ will come to judge the world—Mt. 16:27; 25:31-46; Lu. 19: 11-27. Deliver thee to the judge—Mt. 5:25; Lu. 12:58. Parable of the unrighteous judge—Lu. 18:2-7.

Judgment.—Mt. 16:27; Mk. 8:38; Lu. 12:36; John 3:19; 5:29; 12:31; 16:8, 11. With what judgment ye judge— Mt. 7:1-5; Lu. 6:37-42. All judgment given to the son—John 5:22, 27, 30; 9:39. Righteous—John 5:30; 7:24; 8: 16. In danger of the—Mt. 5:21, 22. Day of—Mt. 10:15; 11:22, 24; 12:36, 41, 42; 13:30, 40-43; 22:11-13; 24:29-35; 25:31-46; Lu. 10:14; 11:31, 32. See Mt. 7:22, 23. Cometh not unto— John 5:24. See Lu. 12:47, 48, and "Parables of judgment," under HIS KINGDOM.

Justice.—Mt. 23:33; Lu. 11:42.

Justified.—Lu. 18:14. Desiring to justify himself—Lu. 10:29; 16:15. Justifying God—Lu. 7:29. By thy works— Mt. 12:37. Wisdom justified by her works—Mt. 11:19; Lu. 7:35.

Keep.—Pound kept—Lu. 19:20. Commandments—Mt. 19:20; Mk. 7:9; John 14:15, 21. Traditions—Mk. 7:9. Thee in on every side—Lu. 19:43. Them in thy name—John 17:11, 12. Passover —Mt. 26:18. The word—Lu. 11:28; John 8:51, 52, 55; 14:23, 24; 15:10, 20; 17:6. From covetousness—Lu. 12:15. Good wine to the last—John 2:10. Ointment against the day of His burying—John 12:7. From the evil one— John 17:15. One's life—John 12:25.

Kill.—Mk. 3:4; John 7:19; 8:37, 40; 10: 10; 16:2. Thou shalt not—Mt. 5:21; 19:18; Mk. 10:19; Lu. 18:20. Body, but not the soul—Mt. 10:28; Lu. 12:4, 5. Prophets—Mt. 23:34, 37; Lu. 11: 46–51; 13:34. He foretells that He will be killed—Mt. 16:21; 17:23; Mk. 8:31; 9:31; 10:34; Lu. 9:22. See THE PARABLE OF THE HUSBANDMEN—Mt. 21: 33–45; Mk. 12:1–12; Lu. 20:9–18. Oxen and fatlings—Mt. 22:4; Lu. 15: 23, 27, 30.

King.—Mt. 10:18; 11:8; 17:25; 18:23; Lu. 21:12; 22:25. The king who made marriage feast—Mt. 22:1–14. He calls Himself King—Mt. 21:5; 25:34, 40; John 18:37; 19:12, 21.

Kingdom.—Mt. 12:25, 26; 24:7; Mk. 6: 23; 13:8; Lu. 11:2, 17, 18; 22:29. See HIS KINGDOM.

Knowledge.—Mt. 6:3; 7:11; 10:26; 20: 25; Mk. 10:42; Lu. 11:13; 12:56; John 3:11; 8:14; 10:14; 17:25. Know that Jesus has authority to forgive sins— Mt. 9:6; Mk. 2:10; Lu. 5:24. Know by the fruit—Mt. 7:16, 20; 12:33. God's knowledge — Mt. 6:8; Lu. 16:15. Knowledge of God is eternal life— John 17:3. Knowledge of mysteries— Mt. 13:11; Mk. 4:11, 12; Lu. 8:10. Know that summer is nigh—Mt. 24: 32; Mk. 13:28. Know that He is nigh —Mt. 24:33; Mk. 13:29. Sheep know the voice of the shepherd—John 10:4, 5, 14. Lack of—Mt. 20:22; 25:12; Mk. 4:13; 10:38; 12:24; Lu. 11:44; John 8:14. He desired that He should not be known—Mt. 9:30; Mk. 5:43; 7:24; 9:30. No one knows the time of His coming—Mt. 24:42, 43; 25:13; Mk. 13:33, 35; Lu. 12:37–40.

Labor: Physical labor.—Jesus a carpenter—Mk. 6:3. Prepared a meal—John 21:9, 12, 13. Directed servants—John 2:7, 8. Parents—Mk. 5:43. Fishermen —Lu. 5:4. Wages small—Mt. 20:2, 9, 10. Should be paid—Mt. 10:10; Lu. 10:7. Hours long—Mt. 20:1, 2, 6, 8. Lands rented—Mt. 21:33, 34; Mk. 12: 1, 2; Lu. 20:9, 10. Hired servants— Mt. 20:1, 7; Mk. 1:20; Lu. 13:7. Sons worked with servants—Mt. 21:28, 29; Mk. 1:20; Lu. 15:25. God gives every man his work—Mt. 25:14, 15; Mk. 13: 34; Lu. 19:13, 14. Wicked servants: Lazy, drunken, tyrannical, unprofitable (Mt. 24:48; 25:26, 30), suddenly perished—Mt. 24:50, 51. Good servants: Faithful, wise (Mt. 26:45, 46), are blessed—Lu. 12:37, 43.

Spiritual labor.—God has a field, the world—Mt. 9:38; 13:38. Jesus sent on other business—Lu. 2:49. Laborers few—Mt. 9:37. Prayer for, Commanded—Mt. 9:38; Lu. 10:2. One sows, another reaps—John 4:37, 38. God's laborers plow—Lu. 9:62. Sow seed—Mt. 13:19, 20, 22, 37, 38; Mk. 4:14–20, 26, 27; Ju. 8:11–15. Reap— Mt. 9:37; Lu. 10:2; John 4:35, 36, 38. Trade—Lu. 19:15. Dress vines—Mt. 20:1. Build—Mt. 7:24; 16:18; Lu. 6: 48; 14:27–30.

Workers of the truth come to the light —John 3:21. Their work is in God— Mk. 16:20; John 3:21. Abides—John 15:7, 16. Greater work than Jesus did —John 14:12.

Satan has work and workers—Mt. 13:38, 39; Mk. 4:15; Lu. 8:12; John 8:38, 39, 41, 48. Works are evil—John 7:7. Iniquity—Mt. 7:23; Lu. 13:27. Hate the light—John 3:20. Words good, Works bad—Mt. 7:20, 21; 15:8, 9; 23: 3–5. Hear but do not heed—Mt. 7:24, 26; Lu. 6:49.

The day's labor decides destiny—Mt. 25:15, 19–28; Mk. 13:35–37; Lu. 12:47, 48; 19:15, 17, 24.

Motives for working evil: Praise of men—Mt. 6:1, 2, 5; 23:5; John 12:42, 43. Not hear truth—John 8:43, 45–47; 18:37. Habit—John 8:34, 38. For working good: The golden rule—Mt. 7:12. Duty—Mt. 23:23. Gratitude— Lu. 8:38, 39. Love—John 15:8–10; 14:15.

Laborer.—Mt. 9:37, 38; 20:1, 2; Lu. 10:7.

Lack.—Mt. 19:20; Mk. 10:21.

Lamb.—Lu. 10:3; John 21:15.

Lamp.—Mt. 5:15; 6:22; 25:1–8; Mk. 4: 21; Lu. 12:35; John 5:35.

Last.—Mt. 5:26; Mk. 12:6; Lu. 12:59. Last shall be first and first shall be last—Mt. 19:30; 20:8, 12, 14, 16; Mk. 9:35; 10:31; 13:30.

Last day—John 6:39, 40, 44, 54.

Last state—Mt. 12:45; Lu. 11:26.

Law.—Mt. 12:5; 23:23; Lu. 10:26; John 7:19, 23; 8:17; 10:34; 15:25. Go to law—Mt. 5:40. He came to fulfil—Mt. 5:17, 18; Lu. 16:17; 24:27. Law and the prophets—Mt. 5:17, 18; 7:12; 11: 13; 22:40; Lu. 16:16; 24:44.

Lay.—Mt. 23:4. Lay hands on—Mk. 16: 18; Lu. 21:12. Lay His head—Mt. 8: 20; Lu. 9:58. Lay down life—John 10:15, 17, 18; 13:37, 38; 15:13. Laying up treasure—Mt. 6:19–21.

Lead.—Mt. 24:4; Mk. 13:11, 22.

Learn.—Mt. 9:13; 11:29; Mk. 13:28; John 6:45.

Leaven.—Mt. 13:33; 16:6–12; Mk. 8:15–21; Lu. 12:1; 13:20, 21.

Left.—Mt. 24:41; Mk. 13:2; Lu. 17:34, 35; 21:6; John 8:29. Left houses, land, etc.—Mt. 19:29; Mk. 10:29; 13:34; Lu. 18:29, 30. Left desolate—Mt. 23:38; Lu. 13:35. Left hand—Mt. 6:3; 20: 23; 25:33, 41.

Lend.—Mt. 5:42; Lu. 6:34, 35; 11:5–8.

Life, Temporal.—Lu. 6:9; 8:14; 21:34; John 13:38. Value of life—Mt. 16:25, 26; 18:8, 9; Mk. 8:36, 37; Lu. 12:22, 23. Life consisteth not in the abundance of the things which a man hath —Mt. 6:25–34; Mk. 8:35–38; Lu. 12: 15–21. He that findeth his life shall lose it—Mt. 10:37–39; Mk. 8:35–38; Lu. 9:24–26; 14:25–27; 17:33; John 12:25. Lifetime—Lu. 16:25. Living or subsistence—Mk. 12:44; Lu. 8:43; 15:12, 30; 21:4.

Life, Spiritual.—John 5:21, 40; 6:33, 51, 53–57. We must be born again—John 3:3–5. We must be begotten through the gospel—Mt. 13:19, 23; Lu. 8:11, 12. We must become as little children —Mt. 18:3; 19:14; Mk. 10:15; Lu. 18: 17; John 13:33.

Life, Eternal.—Mt. 25:46; John 4:14, 36; 5:29, 39; 6:27, 35, 48, 54, 63, 68; 8:12; 10:28; 12:50. This is life eternal —To know God—John 17:2, 3. Jesus the resurrection and the life—John 5:26; 11:25; 14:6. Jesus lays down His life for the sheep—Mt. 20:28; Mk. 10:45; John 10:15, 17, 18; 15:13. See "Man saved through the death of Jesus," under SALVATION. Eternal life conditioned on faith—John 3:15, 16, 36; 5:24; 6:40, 47. Life more abundantly—John 10:10. Those who have left houses and lands shall inherit eternal life—Mt. 19:29; Mk. 10:29, 30; Lu. 18:29, 30. The narrow gate— Mt. 7:14. See Mt. 18:8, 9; Mk. 9:43, 45. The rich young ruler—Mt. 19:16–22; Mk. 10:17–22; Lu. 18:24.

Love.—Love of God for man—Mt. 5:45; 10:29–31; 18:1–14; Lu. 6:35; 12:6, 7; John 14:21, 23; 16:27; 17:23, 26. *God manifests His love for man by sending His son*—John 3:14–17; 14:21, 23; 15: 13; 17:26. Love of Christ—John 14: 21; 15:9–15. *For the Father*—John 14: 31. Love for Christ—John 3:35; 5: 20; 10:17; 15:9; 17:23, 24, 26. Love of man for God—Lu. 11:42; John 5:42. *With all the heart*—Mt. 22:37; Mk. 12: 30; Lu. 10:27. For Christ—John 8:42; 14:15, 21–24; 16:27; 21:15–17. Loving relatives more than Christ—Mt. 10: 37–39. One for another—John 13:34, 35; 15:12, 13, 17. For neighbors—Mt. 19:19; 22:39; Mk. 12:31; Lu. 10:27–37. For enemies—Mt. 5:43, 44, 46; Lu. 6:27, 32, 35. For his fellow-men—Mt. 25:34–40; Mk. 9:41; Lu. 6:31–35. Of mammon—Lu. 6:24; 16:13. Of life— Mt. 10:39, 16:25, 26; Mk. 8:35, 36; Lu. 9:24, 25; John 12:25, 26. Of children —Lu. 15:11–32. Fulfilling of the law —Mt. 22:40. Loving to stand praying —Mt. 6:5. Loving darkness rather than light—John 3:19. Waxing cold —Mt. 24:12. Loving chief seats—Mt. 23:6; Lu. 11:43; 20:46.

Lord.—Mt. 18:25–34; 20:8; 21:40; 24: 45, 50; 25:18–26; Mk. 12:9; Lu. 12: 36, 42–46; 14:23; 16:3, 5, 8; 19:16, 18, 20, 25; 20:13, 15; John 15:15. Servant not above his Lord—Mt. 10:24, 25; John 13:16; 15:20. See "Lordship of Jesus," under JESUS.

Lowly.—Mt. 11:29.

Mammon.—Mt. 6:24; Lu. 16:9, 11, 13.

Man.—Mt. 5:19; 7:9; 12:36; 17:22; 18:7, 12; 22:16; Lu. 7:14; 12:14; 14:24; John 6:10, 50; 7:22, 23, 51; 8:17, 40, 51; 11:10; 14:23; 15:6, 13. Abundance of things which he hath, Man's life consisteth not in—Lu. 12:15. Asunder, Let no man put—Mt. 19:6; Mk. 10:9. Austere—Lu. 19:22. Baptism of John —From God or men?—Mt. 21:25-27; Mk. 11:30-33; Lu. 20:4-8. Before men —Mt. 5:16; 6:1; Lu. 12:8, 9. Born, Good for that man if he had not been —Mk. 14:21. Bread alone, Man cannot live by—Mt. 4:4; Lu. 4:4. Built a house, Who—Mt. 7:27-29; Lu. 6:48, 49. Clothed in soft raiment—Mt. 11: 8; Lu. 7:25. Darkness rather than light, Loving—John 3:19. Defileth, That which proceedeth out of a—Mt. 15:11, 18, 20; Mk. 7:15-23. Evil man out of the evil treasure—Mt. 12:35; Lu. 6:45. Exchange for his soul—Mt. 16:25-28; Mk. 8:36, 37; Lu. 9:25. Fainting for fear—Lu. 21:36. Father and mother, Leaving—Mt. 19:5; Mk. 10:7. Fishers of men—Mt. 4:19; Mk. 1:17; Lu. 5:10. Foolish—Mt. 7:26. Forgive men—Mt. 6:14, 15; 12:3. Gavest me, Whom thou—John 17:6. Generation, Men of this—Lu. 7:31; 11:31. Glory not from—John 5:41. Gluttonous—Mt. 11:19; Lu. 7:34. Good man out of the good treasure—Mt. 12:35; Lu. 6:45. Impossible with men—Mt. 19:26; Mk. 10:23-27; Lu. 18:27. Nineveh, Men of—Mt. 12:41; Lu. 11:32. Pitcher, Man bearing a—Mk. 14:13; Lu. 22:10. Precepts of—Mt. 15:9; Mk. 7:7. Regarding not—Lu. 18:2, 4. Rich —Lu. 12:16-21; 16:1-8. Rich man and Lazarus—Lu. 16:19-31. Seen of men, To be—Mt. 6:2, 5, 16, 18; 23:5-7, 28. Sheep, Man more valuable than a— Mt. 12:11, 12. Sons of men—Mk. 3:28. Strong—Mt. 12:29; Mk. 3:27; Lu. 11: 21. Things of men—Mt. 16:33; Mk. 8:33. Traditions of men—Mk. 7:8. Unclean spirits coming out of—Mt. 12:43-45; Mk. 5:8; Lu. 11:24-26. Whatsoever ye would that men should do to you—Mt. 7:12; Lu. 6:31. Witness not from men—John 5:34. See "Son of man," under HUMANITY OF

JESUS, and "Parables," under LIFE OF JESUS.

Manner.—Mt. 5:11; 6:9.

Marriage.—Mt. 19:4-9; 24:38; Mk. 10: 5-12; Lu. 14:20; 17:27. No marriage in heaven—Mt. 22:30; Mk. 12:25; Lu. 20:34, 35. Marriage feast—Mt. 22:1-14; 25:1-10; Lu. 12:36; 14:8. Committing adultery—Mt. 5:32; 19:9; Mk. 10:11; Lu. 16:18.

Master.—Mt. 6:24; 23:10; Lu. 14:21; 16:13.

Measure.—Mt. 13:33; 23:32; Lu. 6:38; 13:21; 16:6; John 3:34. Measure of life—Mt. 6:27. With what measure ye measure—Mt. 7:2; Mk. 4:24.

Meekness.—Mt. 5:5; 11:29.

Mercy.—Mt. 5:7, 9:13; 12:7; 18:33; 23: 23; Mk. 5:19; Lu. 6:36; 18:13.

Messenger.—Mt. 11:10; Mk. 1:2; Lu. 7: 24-28.

Midnight.—Mt. 25:6; Mk. 13:35; Lu. 11:5.

Millstone.—Mt. 18:6; Mk. 9:42; Lu. 17:2.

Mind.—Mt. 16:23; 22:37; Mk. 12:30; Lu. 10:27; 12:29.

Money.—Mt. 17:24-27; 22:19; 25:18, 27; Mk. 6:8; Lu. 9:3; John 2:14, 15. Parable of the talents and pounds—Mt. 25:14-30; Lu. 19:12-27. Farthing— Mt. 5:26; 10:29; Lu. 12:6. Mites—Lu. 12:59. Shekels—Mt. 17:27. Piece of silver—Lu. 15:8.

Moses.—Mt. 19:8; 23:2; Mk. 1:44; 10:3, 4; 12:26; Lu. 5:14; 16:29-31; 24:44; John 3:14; 5:45-47; 6:32; 7:19-23.

Mote.—Mt. 7:3-5; Lu. 6:41-42.

Mourn.—Mt. 5:4; 9:15; 11:17; 24:30; Lu. 6:25.

Murder.—Mt. 15:19; 22:7; Mk. 7:21. See KILL.

Mustard Seed.—Mt. 13:19, 31-32; 17:20; Mk. 4:31, 32; Lu. 17:6; 13:18, 19.

Naked.—Mt. 25:36, 38, 43, 44.

Name.—Mt. 10:41, 42; Mk. 5:9; Lu. 6: 22; 8:30; 10:20; John 10:3. Of God— John 5:43; 10:25; 12:28; 17:6, 11, 12, 26. *Hallowed be Thy name*—Mt. 6:9; Lu. 11:2. Of Jesus—Mt. 7:22; 18:5, 20; 24:5; Mk. 9:37, 38, 41; 13:6; 16: 17; Lu. 9:48; 13:35; 21:8; John 3:18; 14:13, 26; 15:16; 16:23, 24, 26. *Suffering for His name's sake*—Mt. 10:22; 19:29; 24:9; Lu. 6:22; 21:12, 17. Baptizing in the name of Father, Son, and Holy Spirit—Mt. 28:19.

Need.—Mt. 6:8, 32; 14:16; Mk. 2:17.

Neighbor.—Mt. 5:43; 19:19; 22:39, 40; Lu. 10:27-37; 14:12; 15:6, 9.

Nest.—Mt. 8:20; Lu. 9:58.

Net.—Mt. 13:47; Lu. 5:4; John 21:6.

New.—Birth—John 3:3-8. Commandment—John 13:34. Covenant—Lu. 22:20. Drink the fruit of the vine new in the Father's kingdom—Mt. 26:28, 29; Mk. 14:24, 25. Cloth in old garments—Mt. 9:16; Mk. 2:21; Lu. 5:36. Wine in old wine-skins—Mt. 9:17; Mk. 2:22; Lu. 5:37-39. Things new and old—Mt. 13:52. Tongues, New—Mk. 16:17.

Nothing.—Mt. 23:16, 18; Mk. 1:44; 9:29; John 5:19, 30; 6:63. Apart from me ye can do—John 15:5. Asked nothing in name of Christ—John 16:24. Covered, Nothing—Mt. 10:26; Lu. 8:17; 12:2. Does nothing of Himself—John 5:19, 30. Eat, Nothing to—Mt. 15:32; Mk. 8:2; Lu. 11:6. Flesh profiteth—John 6:63. Glory, If I glorify myself—John 8:54. Good for—Mt. 5:13. Hurt, Nothing shall—Lu. 10:19. Impossible, Nothing—Mt. 17:20. Prince of this world hath nothing in Him—John 14:30. Spake nothing in secret—John 18:20. Take nothing for their journey—Mt. 10:9, 10; Mk. 6:8, 9; Lu. 9:3.. Without that goeth into a man, Nothing from—Mk. 7:15.

Oaths.—Mt. 5:33-37; 23:16-22.

Obedience.—Mt. 7:24-27; Lu. 6:46-49. See ''Keeping commandments,'' under COMMANDMENTS.

Observe.—Mt. 19:20; 23:3-5; 28:20.

Offer.—Mt. 5:23, 24; John 16:2.

Offspring of vipers.—Mt. 12:24; 23:33.

One.—Good—Mt. 19:17. One thing needful—John 10:42. See John 6:27. One thing thou lackest—Mt. 19:21; Mk. 10:21. One as God and Jesus are one —John 17:11, 21-26.

Ought to have done and not left the other undone—Mt. 23:23.

Own.—Mine—Mt. 20:15; John 10:14. His own—John 10:4; 13:1. Thine own —Mt. 25:25.

Parable.—Jesus teaches in parables—Mt. 13:10-18; Mk. 4:11-13, 30; Lu. 4:23; 8:10. See PARABLES OF JESUS.

Pass.—Lu. 11:42. Till heaven and earth pass away—Mt. 5:18; 24:35; Mk. 13:31, 32; Lu. 21:33. See Lu. 16:17. This generation shall not pass away till all things be accomplished—Mt. 24:34; Mk. 13:30; Lu. 21:32. He prays that the cup may pass away—Mt. 26:39; Mk. 14:36.

Passover.—Mt. 26:2, 18; Mk. 14:12-16; Lu. 22:8-13.

Pasture.—John 10:9.

Patience.—Mt. 18:26; Lu. 8:15.

Pay.—Mt. 18:26; 20:8-14; 5:26. See HIRE and PROFIT.

Peace.—Mk. 1:25; 5:34; 9:50; Lu. 7:50; 8:48; 11:21; 14:32; 19:40, 42. He came not to send peace—Mt. 10:34; Lu. 12:51-53. See HOUSE DIVIDED. Peace I leave with you—John 14:27; 16:33. Salutation—Mt. 10:13; Lu. 10:5, 6; 24:36; John 20:19, 20, 26.

Pearl.—Mt. 7:6; 13:46.

Perceive.—See and not perceive—Mt. 13:14-16; Mk. 4:12. Jesus perceives—Lu. 8:46. How is it that you do not perceive?—Mt. 15:17; 16:9, 11; Mk. 7:18.

Perfection.—Mt. 5:48; 19:21; Lu. 6:40; 8:14; 13:32.

Perish.—Mt. 5:29, 30; 9:17; Lu. 5:37; 13:33; 15:17; 21:18; John 6:27; 10:28; 11:50; 17:12. Except ye repent, ye shall perish—Lu. 13:3, 5. Whosoever believeth on Him should not perish—John 3:15, 16. They that take the sword shall perish by the sword—Mt. 26:52.

Persecution.—Mt. 5:10-12, 20, 44; 10:16, 22, 23; 23:34; Mk. 13:11; Lu. 21:12; John 15:18-25.

Pharisees.—Mt. 23:2. Condemns them—Mt. 23:1-39; Lu. 11:39-52. Leaven of —Mt. 16:6-12; Mk. 8:15-17; Lu. 12:1. See HYPOCRITES.

Pipe.—Mt. 11:17; Lu. 14:15.

Pit.—Mt. 15:14; Mk. 12:1. An ass or an ox falling into—Lu. 14:5. Sheep falling into a—Mt. 12:11.

Plants.—''Consider the lilies of the field''—Mt. 6:28. ''Every plant which my heavenly Father planted not shall be rooted up''—Mt. 15:13. The kingdom of heaven is like unto a grain of mustard seed—Mt. 13:31; Mk. 4:31; Lu. 13:19. ''As the branch cannot bear fruit of itself except it abide in the vine''—John 15:4. Parable of fig tree—Mt. 24:32; Lu. 13:6; 21:29. Of mustard seed—Mt. 13:31, 32; Mk. 4:30, 32; Lu. 13:18. ''If ye had faith as a grain of mustard seed'' —Mt. 17:20; Lu. 17:6.

Pleasing.—John 8:29. See John 4:34.

Pleasure.—Lu. 8:14; 12:32.

Plow.—Lu. 9:62; 17:7.

Poor.—Mt. 26:11; Mk. 14:7; John 12:8. Give to the poor—Mt. 19:21; 26:9; Mk. 10:21; 18:22. Gospel preached to them—Mt. 11:5; Lu. 4:18-21. In spirit —Mt. 5:3; Lu. 6:20. Poor widow— Mk. 12:42, 43; Lu. 21:2, 3.

Portion.—Mt. 24:51; Lu. 12:42, 46; 15: 12.

Power.—Mt. 9:6, 8; 24:29; Mk. 9:1; 13: 25; Lu. 9:1; 10:19; Lu. 12:5, 11; 21:26, 27; 22:53; John 19:11. Power of God —Mt. 22:29; 26:64; Mk. 12:24; 13:26; 14:62; Lu. 22:69. Power of Christ— Mt. 24:30; 28:18; Lu. 21:27; John 10: 18. Power of the Spirit—Lu. 4:14; 24:49.

Prayer.—Jesus set example: *Praying before or during baptism*—Lu. Ch. 3. *On preaching tour*—Mk. 1:35; Lu. 5:16. *Choosing apostles*—Lu. 6:12. *Feeding five thousand*—Mt. 14:19, 23; Mk. 6:41, 46; Lu. 9:16; John 6:11, 23. *Feeding four thousand*—Mt. 15:36; Mk. 8:6. *Revelation of Messiahship*—Lu. 9:18-21. *Transfiguration*—Lu. 9:28, 29. *Report of the seventy*—Mt. 11:25, 26; Lu. 10:21. *Teaching Lord's prayer*—Lu. 11:1. *Raising Lazarus*—John 11:41, 42. *Blessing children*—Mt. 19:13; Mk. 10:16. *Sending the Holy Spirit*—John 14:16. *Last Supper*—Mt. 26:26, 27; Mk. 14:22, 23; Lu. 22:17, 19, 32; I Cor. 11:23-25. *Betrayal*—John Ch. 17. *Gethsemane*—Mt. 26:36, 39, 42, 44; Mk. 14:32, 35, 36, 39; Lu. 22:41-44. *On the cross*—Mt. 27:46; Mk. 15:34; Lu. 23: 34, 46. *For Simon Peter*—Lu. 22:32. *For disciples*—John 17:9, 11, 15, 17, 20, 21. *All night*—Lu. 6:12. *He commends the man who prays*—Lu. 12:37; Acts 9:11. *Men need to be taught*—Lu. 11: 1, 2.

Teaches how to pray: *Not as the hypocrites*—Mt. 6:5. *Not with vain repetitions*—Mt. 6:7; Mk. 12:40; Lu. 20:47.

In thy chamber—Mt. 6:6. *In temple*— Lu. 18:10. *Kneeling or standing*—Mk. 11:25; Lu. 22:41.

God's relation to: *As a Father*—Mt. 6:9, 14, 15; 7:11; Lu. 11:13; John 14:16; 16:23. *Knowing before*—Mt. 6:8. *Able and willing to give*—Mt. 6:26, 30, 33; 7:11. *Seeking true worshippers*—John 4:23. *Duty to pray*—Mt. 7:7; 9:38; 26:41; Mk. 14:38.

How: (a) *Faith in God*—Mt. 17:20; 11: 21, 22; Mk. 11:22, 23, 24. *In Christ, pray in His name*—John 14:13, 14; 15: 16; 16:23, 24, 26. (b) *Abiding in Christ* —John 15:7, 16. (c) *Words of Christ abiding in us*—John 15:7. (d) *Heartfelt*—Mt. 15:8, 9; Lu. 11:5-10; John 4:23, 24. (e) *Forgiving enemies*—Mt. 6:14, 15; 18:21, 22, 35; Mk. 11:25. (f) *According to will of God*—Mt. 6:10; 26:39; Lu. 22:32. *Unselfish*—18:19, 20. *For others*—Mt. 6:12, 14, 15; 9:38. *Humble*—Lu. 18:13, 14. (g) *Like the Lord's prayer*—Mt. 6:9; Lu. 11:2.

What to pray for: *Persecutors*—Mt. 5:44. *Ministers*—Mt. 9:38; Lu. 10:2. *Deliverance from misfortune*—Mt. 24:20; Lu. 21:36. *To avoid temptation*—Mt. 6:13; Lu. 22:40. *Hallowing God's name*—Mt. 6:9; Lu. 11:2. *Triumph of kingdom*—Mt. 6:10; Lu. 11:2. *Will of God over the earth*—Mt. 6:10. *Food and raiment*—Mt. 6:11, 33; Lu. 11:3. *Forgiveness*—Mt. 6:14. *Mercy*—Lu. 18:13.

What blessings follow: *Good things*—Mt. 7:11. *What we need*—Mt. 6:8, 32, 33. *The Holy Spirit*—Lu. 11:13. *Power over evil*—Mk. 9:29. *Forgiveness*—Mt. 6:12, 14; Lu. 18:14. *Deliverance*—Mk. 13:18. *Recompense*—Mt. 6:6. *Justice* —Lu. 18:7, 8. *What asked for*—Mt. 18:19; John 14:13, 14; 15:7; 16:23.

Jesus prayed: *Not for world*—John 17:9. *For apostles*—John 17:9, 11, 15, 17, 24. *Believers*—John 17:20, 21.

Preach.—Mt. 10:5-20; 11:5; 24:14; 26: 13; Mk. 6:7-12; 13:10; 16:15; Lu. 4: 43; 9:2-6, 60; 16:16; 21:10-19; 24:47.

Presence.—Lu. 13:26; 14:10; 15:10.

Prevail.—Mt. 16:18; Lu. 21:36.

Pride.—An evil—Mt. 23:11, 12; Lu. 14: 11; 18:9-14. See HUMILITY.

Jesus taught by His example as well as by words, therefore on this subject the facts of His life are direct testimony. By His example He rebukes pride:

Men boast of: *Ability*—John 5:19, 30; 8:28. *Birth*—Lu. 2:7, 16, 24; John 1: 46. *Bigotry* or *exclusiveness*—Mk. 9: 38; Lu. 9:49, 50, 54, 55. *Dignity*—Mt. 5:3, 5; 26:38, 50. *He was from above*— John 3:31; 8:23. *Yet He humbled Himself*—Mk. 14:34, 65; 15:16–20; Lu. 22: 63–65; 23:11; John 19:1–3. *Genius and originality*—John 5:43; 7:18; 8: 28, 29, 54; 10:37, 38; 12:49, 50. *Independence*—Mt. 26:39, 42; Mk. 14:36, 39; Lu. 22:42; John 6:38. *Knowledge and learning*—John 7:14–17; 8:26–28; 14:24. *Personal appearance*—See Is. 53:2, 3. *Reputation*—Mt. 9:3; 10:25; 11:19; Mk. 3:21, 22; 6:3, 4; Lu. 5:21, 30; 15:2; 16:14; John 7:20; 8:48, 52; 10:20. *Resentment*—Mt. 26:50, 68; 27: 26–31, 39–44; Mk. 14:63–65; 15:3–5, 16–20, 29–32; Lu. 23:8–11, 33, 34, 39–41; John 19:1–9. *Social standing:* He was a carpenter—Mk. 6:3. *Of Nazareth*—John 5:46. *Called a Samaritan*— John 8:48. *Called insane*—John 10:20. *Crucified between thieves*—Lu. 23:32, 33. *Success*—Lu. 4:28, 29; 9:22–24; 18:31–33; John 1:11; 7:5; 19:17, 18. *Superiority:* He was meek and lowly— Mt. 11:29. *Servant*—Mt. 20:27, 28. *Subjected Himself*—Lu. 2:51. *Seeks and dies for lost sheep*—Lu. 15:3; John 10:11. *Washes feet*—John 13:4–10. *He that humbleth himself is exalted*— Mt. 23:12; Lu. 14:11; 18:9–14; 22:24–27.

His wealth: *Cradle*—Lu. 2:7, 16. *Carpenter's shop*—Mt. 13:55. *No money*— Mt. 17:24, 27; 22:19; 27:35. *No home* —Mt. 8:20; Lu. 9:58. *Women ministered to Him*—Lu. 8:2, 3.

He reversed the world's judgment as to pride: *The poor and needy*—Lu. 6:20, 21. *Mourner*—Mt. 5:4; Lu. 6:21. *Persecuted*—Mt. 5:10–12; Lu. 6:22, 23. *Rich*—Mt. 6:19–21, 24; Lu. 6:24; 16: 14, 15, 25. *Self-satisfied*—Mt. 7:21–23; Lu. 6:25, 26, 32; 13:25–28; 14:8–11; John 12:24–26.

He rebuked the pride of: *Fame seekers*— Mt. 9:30; 10:25; 17:9; Lu. 5:14; 9:23–26. *King, Born to be*—John 18:37. *Never seeks the glory*—Mt. 5:3; 20:28;

28:18–20. *Sent*—John 8:42. *Pharisees* —Mt. 23:5–7; Lu. 11:39, 43. *Warriors* —Mt. 5:5, 9, 44; John 10:11, 15.

Priest.—Mt. 8:4; Mk. 1:44; Lu. 5:14; 17:14.

Prince.—Of this world—John 12:31; 14: 30; 16:11.

Prison.—Mt. 5:25; 18:30; 25:36, 43.

Profit.—Mt. 16:26–28; Lu. 9:25, 26; John 6:63.

Promises.—Of the Father's care—Mt. 6:4, 6, 30–33; 7:7; Mk. 11:24; Lu. 12: 28–31. Kingdom—Mt. 5:3, 10; 25:34; Lu. 12:32; 22–29. Holy Spirit—Lu. 24:49; John 7:39; 14:16, 26; 15:26; 16:7–15; 20:22. Power—Mt. 17:20; 19:28; 21:21; Mk. 11:23; 16:17, 18; Lu. 17:6. Rest—Mt. 11:28. Guidance—Mt. 18:20; 28:20. Eternal life —Mt. 19:29; John 14:1–6. See LIFE.

Prophecy.—Mt. 11:10–13; 13:14; 15:7; Mk. 7:6. See FULFILMENT, HE CAME IN, and PROPHETS.

Prophet.—Mt. 10:41; 11:9; 13:57; Lu. 7:26. Not without honor, save in his country—Mt. 13:57; Mk. 6:4; Lu. 4: 24; John 4:44. False prophets—Mt. 7:15–23. Persecution of—Mt. 5:12; 23:29–37; Lu. 6:23; 11:47–50; 13:33, 34. Prophet cannot perish out of Jerusalem—Lu. 13:33. "Written by the prophets"—Mt. 7:12; 24:15; Lu. 18: 31; 24:25, 27, 44. Fulfilment of the law and prophets—Mt. 5:17; 26:24, 56. Law and the prophets till John—Mt. 11:12–14; Lu. 16:16. See FULFILMENT OF PROPHECY.

Punishment.—Mt. 5:22–30; 7:21–27; 10: 28; 18:7–9; Chs. 23–25; Mk. 9:42–49; Lu. 6:46–49; 12:5. Cities condemned —Mt. 11:20–24; Lu. 10:12–16. Rich man and Lazarus—Lu. 16:19–31. See HELL and JUDGMENT.

Purity.—Mt. 5:8; 15:11–20; Mk. 7:15–23; John 13:10; 15:3. See INNOCENCE.

Question.—Mt. 21:24–27; Mk. 9:16; Lu. 20:3–8.

Quickly.—Mt. 5:25; Mk. 9:39; Lu. 14: 21; John 13:27.

Raiment.—Mt. 6:25; Lu. 12:23. Soft raiment—Mt. 11:8; Lu. 7:25.

Rain.—Mt. 5:45; 7:24–27.

Raise.—Raise the dead—Mt. 10:8; John 5:21; 6:39, 40, 44, 54. Raise up the temple (His body)—John 2:19.

Reap.—Birds do not—Mt. 6:26; Lu. 12:
24. Reaping and not sowing—Mt. 25:
24, 26; Lu. 19:21, 22. Reaping harvest
unto life eternal—Mt. 13:30; John 4:
34, 35, 36.

Reason.—Mt. 16:8; Mk. 2:8; 8:17; Lu.
12:17.

Receive.—Mt. 10:8; 11:14; 19:12; 20:
10; 21:34; 25:27; Mk. 12:2; Lu. 6:24,
34; 16:4, 9, 25; John 3:27, 32, 33; 4:
36; 5:34, 41, 44; 7:23, 39. Receiving a
child—Mt. 18:5; Mk. 9:37; Lu. 9:48.
Receiving Christ—Mt. 18:5; Mk. 9:
37; John 5:43; 13:20. Greater condemnation—Mk. 12:40; Lu. 20:47. Receive a hundredfold—Mt. 19:29; Mk.
10:30. See Lu. 18:30. Receiving a
prophet—Mt. 10:41. Receiving a
righteous man—Mt. 10:41. Receiving
what we ask in prayer—Mt. 7:8; 21:
22; Mk. 11:24; Lu. 11:10; John 16:24.
Receiving the word—Mt. 13:20; 19:
11; Mk. 4:16, 20; Lu. 8:13; John 12:
48; 17:8. Whosoever shall receive you
—Mt. 10:40; Lu. 10:8; John 13:20.
Whosoever shall not receive you—Mt.
10:14, 15; Mk. 6:11; Lu. 9:5; 10:10.

Reckon.—Mt. 18:23, 24; 25:19; Lu. 22:
37.

Recompense.—Mt. 6:4; Lu. 14:12, 14.

Reed.—Mt. 11:7; Lu. 7:24.

Refuse.—Mt. 18:17. See Excuses and
Receive.

Regard.—Lu. 18:2, 4.

Reign.—Lu. 19:14, 27.

Rejection.—Lu. 7:30; 10:16. Of Christ
—Mt. 13:57, 58; 23:37, 38; Mk. 6:4, 5;
8:31; Lu. 10:16; 13:34, 35; 17:25;
John 5:36–47; 8:37–59; 12:48. The
stone that the builders rejected—Mt.
21:42; Mk. 12:10, 11; Lu. 20:17, 18.
Jews, Of the—Mt. 21:43, 44.

Rejoice.—John 4:36; 5:35; 8:56; 14:28;
16:20, 22. Because of reward in heav-
en—Mt. 5:12; Lu. 6:23; 10:20. Because the sheep was found—Mt. 18:
13; Lu. 15:6. Because piece of silver
was found—Lu. 15:9.

Remain.—Fragments—Mt. 14:20; Mk.
8:8; John 6:13.

Remember.—Mt. 16:9; Mk. 8:18; Lu. 16:
25; John 16:21. Remember Lot's wife
—Lu. 17:32. Remembering the words
of Jesus—John 15:20; 16:4. Remem-

berest that thy brother hath aught
against thee—Mt. 5:23.

Remission of sins.—Mt. 26:28; Mk. 14:
24; Lu. 24:47. See Salvation.

Remove.—Mt. 17:20; Lu. 22:42.

Rend.—Mt. 7:6.

Render.—Mt. 21:41; 22:21; Mk. 12:17;
Lu. 20:25.

Repentance.—Mt. 4:17; 21:28–32; Mk.
1:15; Lu. 13:3–5; 15:4–32; 16:30; 17:
3, 4; 24:47. Calls sinners to repentance—Lu. 5:30–32. Compares ancient
cities with the cities of His day, and
condemns those of His time—Mt. 11:
20–24; 12:41; Lu. 10:11–15; 11:29–32.

Reproach.—Mt. 5:11; Lu. 6:22.

Resist.—Mt. 5:39–44. See Lu. 21:15.

Rest.—Mt. 26:45; Mk. 6:31; 14:41; Lu.
10:6.

Restore.—Mt. 17:11; Mk. 9:12.

Resurrection.—Mt. 22:23–33; 25:31–46;
Mk. 12:18–27; Lu. 14:14; 20:27–38;
John 5:26–29; 11:23–26, 39–44. See
Life, Eternal, Rise, and He predicts
His own death, burial, and resurrec-
tion.

Reveal.—To whom the Son will reveal—
Mt. 11:27; Lu. 10:22. Flesh and blood
hath not revealed—Mt. 16:17. Revealed unto babes—Mt. 11:25; Lu. 10:
21. Nothing covered that shall not be
revealed—Mt. 10:26; Mk. 4:22; Lu.
8:17; 12:2. The day the Son of man
is revealed—Lu. 17:30.

Reward.—Mt. 5:12, 46; 6:1, 2, 5, 6; 10:
41, 42; Mk. 9:41; Lu. 6:23, 24, 35.

Riches.—Lu. 8:14; 14:12; 16:1–31. Deceitfulness of—Mt. 13:22; Mk. 4:19.
Hard for a rich man to enter the kingdom of heaven—Mt. 19:16–24; Mk.
10:17–25; Lu. 6:24; 12:15–34; 16:11–
13, 19–31; 18:24.

Righteous.—Mt. 10:41; 13:17, 43, 49;
23:28, 29, 35; 25:37, 46; Lu. 18:9; John
17:25. He came not to call the righteous—Mt. 9:13; Mk. 2:17; Lu. 5:32.
Judgment, Righteous—John 5:30; 7:
24.

Righteousness.—Mt. 5:6, 10, 20; 6:1, 33;
21:32. See John 16:8–10.

Ring.—Lu. 15:22.

Rise.—Mt. 5:45; 24:11; Mk. 4:27; 13:22;
Lu. 5:23, 24; 6:8; 11:8; 22:46; John
5:8. Rise up against—Mt. 10:21; 12:
41, 42; 24:7; Mk. 3:26; 13:8, 12; Lu.

11:8; 21:10. Risen from the dead—Mt. 17:9; 27:63; Mk. 8:31; 10:34; 12:25; Lu. 24:46; John 11:23. See Mt. 16:21; 20:19. See RESURRECTION.

Robber.—Mt. 21:13; 26:55; Lu. 10:30; John 10:18.

Robe.—Return of the prodigal—Lu. 15:22. Wedding garment—Mt. 22:11, 12.

Rock.—Church built on—Mt. 16:18. House built on—Mt. 7:24, 25; Lu. 6:48. Seed sown on—Mt. 13:5, 20; Mk. 4:5, 16; Lu. 8:6, 13.

Ruler.—Faithful servants made rulers—Mt. 24:45, 47; 25:21, 23; Lu. 12:42, 44.

Sabbath.—Mt. 12:1–13; Mk. 2:23–27; Lu. 6:1–11; 13:10–17; 14:1–6; John 7:22, 23.

Sacrifice.—Mt. 9:13; 12:7; Mk. 12:33.

Sadducees.—Mt. 16:1–6, 11, 12.

Sake.—For the sake of Christ—Mt. 5:11; 10:18, 39. Elect's—Mt. 24:22. Disciples'—John 11:15. Works—John 14:11.

Salt.—Mt. 5:13; Mk. 9:49, 50; Lu. 14:34, 35.

Salvation.—Prior to the death of Jesus—Mt. 9:12; 18:12–14; Mk. 2:17; Lu. 5:30–32; 7:36–50; 8:12; 15:1–32; 18:42; 19:9, 10; John 3:14–17; 4:22; 5:34; 12:47. For all men—Mt. 18:12–14; John 3:16, 17; 4:14; 7:37; 10:16; 12:47. The gospel to be preached to all men—Mt. 28:19, 20; Mk. 16:15, 16; Lu. 24:47; Acts 1:8. To the Jew first—Mt. 10:5, 6; 15:24; John 4:22. Beginning at Jerusalem—Mt. 23:37; Lu. 13:34; 24:47; Acts 1:8. Salvation rejected by the Jews—Mt. 11:20–24; 13:57; 23:37; Mk. 6:3, 4; Lu. 13:34; 19:14; John 5:36–47; 8:37–59. The stone that the builders rejected—Mt. 21:42; Mk. 12:10, 11; Lu. 20:17, 18. Parables concerning the rejection of Jesus by the Jews: *The Vineyard*—Mt. 21:33–46; Mk. 12:1–10; Lu. 20:9–19. *The Marriage Supper*—Mt. 22:1–10; Lu. 14:16–24. *The Prodigal Son*—Lu. 15:11–32. *The Rich Man and Lazarus*—Lu. 16:19–31. Salvation conditional before the death of Jesus—Mt. 7:13, 14; 13:23–30; 18:3; 23:37; 25:31–46; John 5:40; 7:34; 8:12; 10:9. Man must hear, believe, repent, and obey—Mt. 10:32–39; 13:15; Lu. 6:46–49; 8:12; John 3:3–19; 6:28, 29, 40, 44, 45.

Must practise self-denial, be unselfish, bear the cross—Mt. 10:22; 16:24–28; 19:23–30; 25:31–46; Mk. 8:34–38; 10:23–31; Lu. 9:23–26; 14:26, 27; 16:10–17; 18:24–30. *The Rich Young Ruler* Mt. 19:16–22; Mk. 10:17–25; Lu. 18:17–24. See RICHES. Instances of: *The Paralytic*—Mt. 9:1–7; Mk. 2:1–12. *The sinful woman in the pharisee's house*—Lu. 7:36–50. *Zacchæus the publican*—Lu. 19:1–10. *The woman taken in adultery*—John 8:1–11. Parables concerning conditional salvation: *The Sower*—Mt. 13:1–23; Mk. 4:1–20; Lu. 8:14–15. *The Tares*—Mt. 13:24–30; 36–43. *The Net*—Mt. 13:47–50. *The Laborers in the Vineyard*—Mt. 20:1–16. *The Two Sons*—Mt. 21:28–32. *The Wedding Supper*—Mt. 22:1–14. *The Lost Sheep, the Lost Coin, and the Lost Boy*—Lu. 15:1–31. *The Rich Man and Lazarus*—Lu. 16:19–31. *The Pharisee and the Publican*—Lu. 18:9–14. *The Pounds*—Lu. 19:12–27. *Ten Virgins*—Mt. 25:1–13. *The Talents*—Mt. 25:14–30. *The Judgment*—See JUDGMENT.

God the Author of salvation—Mt. 10:28; John 3:14–17, 27–36; 4:34; 5:30; 6:38, 44, 45, 63–65; 10:18; 14:28–31; 17:4; 18:11. *God loves men*—Mt. 5:43–45; Lu. 6:35; 12:6, 7; John 3:16, 17. *God plans man's salvation*—Mt. 21:33–42. *Prepares a place for His children*—Mt. 20:23; 25:34; Mk. 10:40.

Man is saved through Jesus Christ—See JESUS A SAVIOUR.

Salvation through the gospel—See GOSPEL.

Man must believe—See FAITH.

Commandments of the gospel must be obeyed—See COMMANDMENTS and OBEDIENCE. See REPENTANCE, BAPTISM, and LIFE, ETERNAL.

Sanctify.—Mt. 23:17, 19; John 10:36; 17:17, 19.

Sand.—Mt. 7:26.

Satan.—See DEVIL.

Save.—Save life—Mk. 3:4. Save me from this hour—John 12:27. Save—viz.—''Except''—Mt. 16:25; Mk. 9:8; Lu. 9:24; 17:18; 18:19; John 6:46; 13:10. See SALVATION.

Scribe.—Mt. 16:21; 20:18; 23:34; Mk. 8:31. Condemned by Christ—Mt. 5:

20; 15:1–9; 23:2–29; Mk. 12:38–40; Lu. 20:46, 47.

Scripture.—Mt. 21:42–44; Mk. 12:10; Lu. 4:21; John 5:39–47; 7:38, 42; 10: 35; 13:18; 15:25; 17:12. See FULFIL-MENT OF SCRIPTURES, MOSES, LAW, PROPHETS.

Sea.—Mt. 17:27; 21:21; 23:15; Mk. 12: 23; Lu. 17:6; 21:25. Net cast into the sea—Mt. 13:47. Cast into the depths of the sea—Mt. 18:6; Mk. 9:42; Lu. 17:2. Sea obeys His will—Mk. 4:39–41.

Search.—John 7:52. The Scriptures—John 5:39. Search out the worthy—Mt. 10:11.

Season.—Mt. 21:41; 24:32; Lu. 21:36; John 5:35. Season—Mk. 9:50; Lu. 14:34.

Secret.—Mt. 6:4; Mk. 4:22; Lu. 8:17.

See.—Mt. 11:4, 7–9; 22:11; 24:2, 15; Mk. 6:38; 12:15; 13:14; Lu. 7:24–26; 8:16; 12:54, 55; 21:20, 30, 31; 24:39; John 1:50, 51; 3:36; 4:48. Blind see—Mt. 15:31; Mk. 8:23; Lu. 7:22. See clearly—Mt. 7:5; Lu. 6:42. See Lu. 11:33–36. May not see—Mt. 13:13–17; Mk. 4:12; 8:17, 18; Lu. 8:10; 10:23, 24; 11:33; John 9:39–41; 12:40. See God —Mt. 5:8; John 14:9. Glory of—John 11:40. The kingdom of God—Lu. 9:27; John 3:3. See "The Son of Man"—Mt. 23:39; 28:10; Lu. 17:22; John 6:62; 16:16–22. *Coming in His kingdom*—Mt. 16:28. *On clouds of heaven*—Mt. 24:30; 26:64; Mk. 13:26; 14:62; Lu. 21:27. Seen of men—See HYPOCRISY. See your good works—Mt. 5:16. See or take heed—Mt. 8:4; 9:30; 24:6.

Seed.—Mk. 4:26. Parable of the Sower —Mt. 13:2–9, 18–23; Mk. 4:2–9, 14–20; Lu. 8. Parable of Tares—Mt. 13:24, 36, 43. Seed, Mustard—See MUSTARD SEED.

Seek.—Gentiles seek—Mt. 6:33. Nations seek—Lu. 12:30. Seek till she finds it—Lu. 15:8. Seek first the kingdom —Mt. 6:33. Many will seek to enter —Lu. 13:24. Jesus commands to seek —Mt. 6:33; 7:7; Lu. 11:9; 12:29, 31. Seeking a sign—Mk. 8:12. Seek to save life—Lu. 17:33. Seek that which was lost—Lu. 19:10. Gone astray—

Mt. 18:12. Seek and ye shall find—Mt. 7:7. Seeking rest—Mt. 12:43.

Self-denial.—Christ as an example—Mt. 4:8, 10; 8:20. Of apostles—Mt. 19:27–29; Mk. 1:16–20. Woman in Simon's house—Lu. 7:40–48. Poor widow—Lu. 21:3, 4.

Send.—Laborers—Mt. 9:38; Lu. 10:2; John 4:38. Peace—Mt. 10:34. See "God the author of salvation," under SALVATION, and DIVINITY OF JESUS.

Serpent.—Mt. 7:10; 23:33; Mk. 16:18; Lu. 10:19; John 3:14.

Servant.—Mt. 13:27–30; 14:2; 22:3–13; Mk. 9:35; 13:34; Lu. 15:17, 19, 22, 26; 19:13, 15. Friends, Not servants, but —John 15:15. Greater than his lord, Not—Mt. 10:24. Masters, No servant can serve two—Mt. 6:24; 16:13. Parable of the husbandmen—Mt. 21:33–41; Mk. 12:1–12; Lu. 20:9–19. Parable of the Pounds—Lu. 19:13–27. Parable of the Talents—Mt. 18:23–35. Unprofitable—Lu. 17:10. Watching—Mk. 13:34; Lu. 12:37, 38.

Serve.—Lu. 12:37; 17:8; 22:26; John 12:26. Only God—Mt. 4:10; Lu. 4:8. Cumbered with much serving—Lu. 10: 40–42. Two masters, No man can serve—Mt. 6:24; Lu. 16:13.

Set.—City set on a hill—Mt. 5:14. Hedge around vineyard—Mk. 12:1. Jesus set bruised ones at liberty—Lu. 4:18. Good Samaritan—Lu. 10:34. Set at variance—Mt. 10:35.

Shamefully.—Mt. 22:6; Mk. 12:4; Lu. 20:11.

Sheep.—Mt. 10:16; 12:11, 12; 26:31; Mk. 14:27; Lu. 17:7; John 10:2, 3. Lost sheep—Mt. 18:12–14; Lu. 15:4–7. Lost sheep of the house of Israel—Mt. 10: 6; 15:24. Sheep's clothing—Mt. 7:15. Without a shepherd—Mt. 9:36; Mk. 6:34. Sheep and goats—Mt. 25:32, 33.

Shepherd.—Mt. 9:36. Shepherd and the sheep—Mt. 26:31; Mk. 14:27; John 10:1–16, 26, 27; 21:15–17.

Shine.—Mt. 5:15, 16; 13:43; John 5:35. See LIGHT.

Sick.—Mt. 25:36, 43. Heal the sick—Mt. 10:8; Mk. 16:18; Lu. 10:9. They that are sick need a physician—Mt. 9:12, 13; Mk. 2:17; Lu. 5:31, 32.

Signs.—Mk. 13:4–8, 22; 16:17–18; Lu. 21:11; John 4:48. Seeking a sign—

Mt. 12:36–45; 16:2–4; Mk. 8:11,12; Lu. 11:29–32. Sign of the Son of Man —Mt. 24:29–30; Lu. 21:25–28. No sign but that of Jonah—Mt. 12:39, 40. Signs of the heavens—Mt. 16:2, 3; Lu. 12:54–56.

Sin.—John 9:3. Brother sin, If thy— Mt. 18:5–17. Conviction of—John 16:8–13. Die in—John 8:21, 24. Forgiveness of—Mt. 9:5, 6; 12:31; Mk. 2:5–12; 3:28; Lu. 5:20–25; 7:47–50; 17:3, 4; John 5:14; 8:1–11; 20:23. Knowledge, Through—John 9:41; 15: 22, 24. Servant of—John 8:34. Unpardonable—Mt. 12:31, 32; Mk. 3:28, 29; Lu. 12:10. Without sin, Jesus— John 8:46. See REMISSION OF SINS.

Sit.—In the kingdom of heaven—Mt. 8: 11; 20:23; Mk. 10:40; Lu. 13:29. Sit in lowest place—Lu. 14:8–11. Jesus sat in the temple—Mt. 26:55; Mk. 14: 49. Sit like children—Mt. 11:16; Lu. 7:32. Sit on right hand—Mt. 22:41– 45; Mk. 12:35–37; Lu. 20:41–44. Sat down—Mt. 13:48. Son of Man shall sit on throne—Mt. 19:28; 25:31. Sit on throne of glory—Mt. 25:31. Sit down to count cost—Lu. 14:28.

Smite.—John 18:23. On one cheek—Mt. 5:39; Lu. 6:29. The Shepherd and the sheep—Mt. 26:31; Mk. 14:27.

Sold.—Mt. 13:46; 18:25; Lu. 17:28. Two sparrows sold for a penny—Mt. 10:29; Lu. 12:6.

Solomon.—Mt. 6:29; Lu. 12:27. A greater than Solomon—Mt. 12:42; Lu. 11: 31.

Son.—Mt. 9:2; 17:25, 26; 21:37–39; 22: 2; Mk. 2:5, 19; 3:28; 12:6–8; Lu. 9:41; 11:11–13, 19; 12:53; John 19:26. Loving son more than Jesus—Mt. 10:37. Son of hell—Mt. 23:15. Sons of peace —Lu. 10:6. The prodigal son—Lu. 15: 11–31. The Son (Jesus)—Mt. 11:27. Whose Son is He?—Mt. 22:41–45; Mk. 12:35–37; Lu. 20:41–44. See ''The Son of God'' and ''The Son of Man,'' under JESUS.

Sorrow.—Mt. 24:8, 9; Mk. 13:8; John 14:6, 27; 16:6, 20–22. In Gethsemane —Mt. 26:28; Mk. 14:34; John 12:27.

Soul.—Mk. 14:34; Lu. 12:19, 20; 21:19; John 12:27. With thy heart and soul and mind—Mt. 22:37; Mk. 12:30; Lu. 10:27. Both body and soul destroyed in hell—Mt. 10:28. Rest for the soul —Mt. 11:29. See SPIRIT.

Sowing.—Mt. 25:24, 26; Lu. 19:21, 22; John 4:36–38. Birds of the heaven neither sow nor reap—Mt. 6:26; Lu. 12:24. Parable of the Mustard Seed— Mt. 13:31, 32; Mk. 4:31, 32. Parable of the Sower—Mt. 13:3–9, 18–23; Mk. 4:3–9, 14–20; Lu. 8:5–8; 11:15. Parable of the Tares—Mt. 13:24–30, 36– 43.

Speak.—Mt. 10:27; Lu. 6:26; 12:3; John 3:11; 4:26; 8:44; 9:37; 14:30. Abundance of the heart the mouth speaketh, Out of—Mt. 12:34, 35. Against the Son of Man—Mt. 12:31; Lu. 12:10. Against the Holy Spirit—Mt. 12:32. See Mk. 3:29; Lu. 12:10. Anxious how or what ye shall speak, Be not— Mt. 10:19, 20; Mk. 13:11; Lu. 12:11, 12. Bread, Spake not concerning—Mt. 16:11. Evil—Mt. 12:35; 15:4; Lu. 6: 45. Good things—Mt. 12:34, 35; Lu. 6:45. Judged by the words we speak —Mt. 12:36, 37. Parables, Speaking —Mk. 12:12. Tongue, With new— Mk. 16:17. Words which I have spoken—John 6:63; 8:26; 15:3. Word of God—John 3:34; 7:17, 18; 8:26–28, 38; 12:49, 50; 14:10; 16:13.

Spirit.—Lu. 23:46; 24:39; 26:41; John 3:3–8; 4:23; 6:63. God is a Spirit— John 4:24. Unclean spirit—Mk. 5:8; 9:25. See HOLY SPIRIT and SOUL.

Staff.—Mt. 10:10; 26:55; Mk. 6:8; 14: 48; Lu. 9:3; 22:52.

Stand.—Mt. 20:3, 6; Mk. 3:3; 13:14; Lu. 6:8; 13:25; 21:36; John 8:44. Stand and pray in synagogues and in corners—Mt. 6:5; Mk. 11:25; Lu. 18:11, 13. House divided shall not stand— Mt. 12:25, 26; Mk. 3:24, 26; Lu. 11:17, 18. Some standing here who shall not taste of death till the kingdom come —Mt. 16:28; Mk. 9:1; Lu. 9:27. Standing in the holy place—Mt. 24:15.

Stone.—Mt. 24:2; John 8:7; 10:32; 11: 39. Cry out, Would—Lu. 19:40. Not one stone left on another—Mk. 13:2; Lu. 21:5, 6. Stoning the prophets— Mt. 23:37; Lu. 13:34. Who will give his son a stone for a loaf?—Mt. 7:9; Lu. 11:11. Stone the builders rejected—Mt. 21:42–44; Mk. 12:10; Lu. 20: 17, 18. See ROCKS.

Stranger.—Mt. 25:35, 43; Lu. 17:18; John 10:5.

Strong.—Mt. 12:29; Mk. 3:27; Lu. 11:21.

Stumble.—Mt. 5:29; 13:41; 18:7, 9; John 6:61. Satan as a stumbling-block— Mt. 16:23.

Sun.—Mt. 5:45; 13:6, 43; 24:29; Mk. 4: 6; 13:24; Lu. 21:25.

Supper.—Lu. 14:12, 13, 16–24.

Swear.—Mt. 5:33–37; 23:16–22.

Sword.—Mt. 26:55; Mk. 14:48; Lu. 22: 52; John 18:11. I came not to send peace, but a sword—Mt. 10:34. They that take the sword shall perish with the sword—Mt. 26:52.

Synagogue.—Mt. 6:2, 5; Lu. 12:11; 21: 12; John 16:2; 18:20. Chief seats in— Mt. 23:6; Mk. 12:39; Lu. 11:43; 20:46. Scourging in—Mt. 10:17; 23:34; Mk. 13:9.

Table.—Lu. 22:21, 30.

Take.—Mt. 20:14; 21:38; 24:39; Lu. 19: 21–24; 22:17, 36; John 2:16; 16:15, 22. Away from, Taken—Mt. 9:15; 13:12; 21:43; 25:29; Lu. 2:20; 4:25; 5:35; 6:30; 10:42; 11:22; 16:3; John 16:22. Baskets, How many took ye up—Mt. 16:9, 10; Mk. 8:19, 20. Bed, Take up —Mt. 9:6; Mk. 2:9, 11; Lu. 5:24; John 5:8. Bond—Lu. 16:6, 7. Branch, Taketh away—John 15:2, 6. World, From —John 17:15. Bread, Took and blessed —Mt. 26:26; Mk. 14:22; Lu. 22:17. Children's bread, To take—Mt. 15:26; Mk. 7:27. Cloak, Taking—Mt. 24:18; Mk. 13:16; Lu. 6:29; 17:31. See Mt. 5:40. Cross, Take up—Mt. 10:38; 16: 24; Mk. 8:34; Lu. 9:23. Yoke upon you, Take my—Mt. 11:29. Force, Take it by—Mt. 11:12. Garment, Taketh from—Mt. 9:16; Mk. 2:21. Heed, Take—Mt. 6:1; 24:4; Mk. 8:15; 13:5, 9, 23, 33; Lu. 8:18; 12:15; 17:3; 21:8, 34. Key of knowledge, Took away— Lu. 11:52. Lamps, Took their—Mt. 25:1, 3. Life, Taking—John 10:11, 18. Lowest place, Take—Lu. 14:9. Let not the man on the housetop come down to take things away—Mt. 24:17; Mk. 13:15; Lu. 17:31. Took Me not— Mt. 26:35, 43, 55; Mk. 14:49. One is taken, the other left—Mt. 24:40, 41; Lu. 17:34, 35. Serpents, Take up— Mk. 16:18. Servants, Took—Mt. 21: 35. Stone, Take away—John 11:39.

Sword shall perish with the sword, They that take—Mt. 26:52. Talent, Take away the—Mt. 25:18. See Mt. 10:9, 10; Lu. 10:4. Witnesses, Take one or two—Mt. 18:16. Word, Taketh away the—Mk. 4:15; Lu. 8:12. See Mt. 13:19.

Talents.—Mt. 18:24. Parable of—Mt. 25:15–28.

Tares.—Mt. 13:24–30, 36–43.

Tarry.—Mt. 24:48; Lu. 24:49; John 21: 22. See Acts 1:4.

Teach.—Mt. 5:19; 28:20; Lu. 13:26; John 6:44, 45; 8:28. In the temple— Mt. 26:55; Mk. 14:49; John 18:20. Holy Spirit shall teach—Lu. 12:12; John 14:26; 16:13.

Teachers, False.—Mt. 24:5, 24; Mk. 13: 23.

Tell.—Fault—Mt. 18:15. Told their lord—Mt. 18:31. I have told you before—Mt. 24:25. Tell how great— Mk. 5:19.

Temple.—Destroy the temple—Mt. 26: 61; Mk. 14:58; John 2:19. See Mk. 15:29. One greater than the temple— Mt. 12:6. Swearing by—Mt. 23:16, 17, 21. Teaching in—Mk. 14:49; John 18:20. See Mt. 23:35.

Temptation.—Mt. 6:13; 13:21, 22; 26: 41; Mk. 14:38; Lu. 8:13, 14; 11:4; 22: 28, 31–34, 40, 46.

Testimony.—Mt. 10:18; 24:14; Mk. 6: 11; 13:9; Lu. 5:14; 9:5; 21:13.

Thief.—Mt. 6:19, 20; Lu. 12:33; John 10:8–10. Temple a den of robbers— Mt. 21:13; Mk. 11:17; Lu. 19:46. As a thief in the night—Mt. 24:43. On the way to Jericho—Lu. 10:30, 36.

Think.—Think not—Mt. 1:20; 3:9; 9:4. Think they shall be heard—Mt. 6:7. What think—Mt. 17:25; 21:28; 26:66. How think—Mt. 18:12; John 11:56. When ye think not—Mt. 24:44; Lu. 12:40. Which think—Lu. 10:36. Do not think—John 5:45. Think he hath —Lu. 8:18.

Thirst.—Mt. 5:6; John 4:13–15; 6:35; 7:37; 19:28.

Thorns.—Mt. 7:16; 13:7, 22; Mk. 4:7, 18; Lu. 6:44; 8:7, 14.

Three days.—Mt. 15:32; Mk. 8:2. Sign of Jonah—Mt. 12:40. Resurrection on the third day—Mt. 26:61; 27:63; **Mk.** 8:31; 14:58, 59; John 2:19.

Tidings.—Poor have tidings preached—Mt. 11:5; Lu. 4:18; 7:22.

Time.—Mk. 10:30; 13:33; Lu. 7:45; 12:56; 18:30; John 5:37; 21:16, 17. See John 16:4. At hand, My time is—Mt. 26:18; Lu. 21:8. See John 7:6, 8. Elisha, In the time of—Lu. 4:27. Harvest time—Mt. 13:30. John the Baptist, The time of—Lu. 16:16. Long—Mt. 25:19; Mk. 9:21; Lu. 20:9; John 14:9. Old, Of—Mt. 5:21, 23. Signs of the times—Mt. 16:3. Supper—Lu. 14:17. Temptation, In time of—Lu. 8:13. Time is past—Mt. 14:15. Visitation, Time of—Lu. 19:44.

To-day.—Mt. 14:30; Lu. 19:9; 23:43.

Toil.—Mt. 6:28; Lu. 12:27. See LABOR.

Touch.—Mk. 5:30, 31; Lu. 8:44–47; 11:46; John 20:17.

Tradition.—Mt. 15:1–9; Mk. 7:1–13.

Treasure.—Mt. 13:52; Lu. 12:16–21. Good man out of the good treasure of his heart—Mt. 12:35; Lu. 6:45. Evil man out of evil treasure—Mt. 12:35; Lu. 6:45. Hidden in a field—Mt. 13:44. Lay not up treasure on earth—Mt. 6:19, 20. Treasure in heaven—Mt. 6:20; 19:21; Lu. 12:33. Where thy treasure is, there will thy heart be also—Mt. 6:21; Lu. 12:34.

Tree.—Mt. 13:32. Known by its fruit—Mt: 7:16–20; 12:33; Lu. 6:43, 44. Fig tree—Mt. 21:19–21; Mk. 11:13, 14, 20–22; Mk. 13:28; Lu. 21:29, 30; John 1:48–50. Sycamine tree—Lu. 17:6.

Tribulation.—When tribulation arises—Mt. 13:21. Signs of coming—Mt. 24:21, 29; Mk. 13:24. Tribulation in world—John 16:33. Delivered unto tribulation—Mt. 24:9. See AFFLICTION.

Tribute.—Mt. 17:25; 22:17–21; Mk. 12:13–17; Lu. 20:20–26.

True.—God is true—John 3:33. Bread—John 6:32–35. Riches—Lu. 16:11. Vine—John 15:1. Witness—John 5:30–34.

Trust.—In riches—Mk. 10:24. In armor—Lu. 11:22.

Truth.—John 5:33; 16:7; 17:17. Jesus the Truth—John 14:6. The truth shall make you free—John 8:32. Spirit of truth—John 14:17; 15:26; 16:13.

Turn.—Mt. 13:15; 18:3; Mk. 4:12; Lu. 22:32; John 12:40. Other cheek—Mt. 5:39; Lu. 6:29.

Twelve.—John 6:70.

Two.—Mt. 5:41. Two shall become one flesh—Mt. 19:5; Mk. 10:8. Two men in one bed—Lu. 17:34. Two men in the field—Mt. 24:40. Two women grinding—Mt. 24:41; Lu. 17:35. Two mites—Mk. 12:42.

Understand.—Mt. 13:13–15; 15:10; 24:15; Mk. 13:14; John 3:10; 8:43; 10:38; 13:7. See PERCEIVE.

Unrighteous.—Lu. 16:10. Judge—Lu. 18:1–8. Mammon—Mt. 6:24; Lu. 16:11–13. Steward—Lu. 16:1–10.

Unrighteousness.—Lu. 16:9; John 7:18. See SIN and CHARACTER OF THE WICKED.

Vessels.—Mt. 13:48; 25:4; Lu. 8:16.

Vine.—John 15:1–8. Fruit of the vine—Mt. 26:29; Mk. 14:25; Lu. 22:18.

Vineyard.—Mt. 21:28; Lu. 13:6. Parable of—Mt. 20:1–14. Parable of the Husbandmen—Mt. 21:33–41; Mk. 12:1–9; Lu. 20:9–16.

Violence.—Mt. 11:12; Lu. 16:16.

Virgins, Parable of Ten.—Mt. 25:1–13.

Vision.—Mt. 17:9.

Visit.—Mt. 25:36, 43; Lu. 19:44.

Voice.—John 3:8; 12:30; 18:37. Sheep hear his voice—John 10:3–5, 16, 27.

Walk.—Mt. 9:5; Lu. 5:23; 11:44; 20:46; 24:17; John 21:18. Lame walk—Mt. 11:5; Mk. 2:9; Lu. 7:22; John 5:8. Walking in darkness—John 8:12; 11:9, 10; 12:35. See John 11:9, 10.

Want.—Mk. 12:44; Lu. 15:14; 21:4. See POOR.

Warn.—Lu. 12:5. See TAKE HEED.

Wash.—John 9:7. Thy face—Mt. 6:17. Washing feet—Lu. 7:44; John 13:4–10. Rebukes the Pharisees—Mt. 15:1–9; Lu. 11:38–41.

Waste.—Lu. 15:13. See John 6:12.

Watch.—Mt. 24:42–44; 25:1–13; Mk. 13:37; Lu. 12:37–40; 21:36. In Gethsemane—Mt. 26:38–46; Mk. 14:34–42. Watch and pray—Mt. 26:40; Mk. 13:33–35. See PRAYER, TAKE HEED.

Water.—Lu. 13:15; John 2:7; 13:5–10. Cup of water given—Mt. 10:42; Mk. 9:41. Bearing pitcher of water—Mk. 14:13; Lu. 22:10. Living water—John 4:10; 7:37, 38. Water for feet—Lu. 7:44; John 13:5–10.

Way.—Mt. 5:25; 15:32; Mk. 8:3; 9:33; Lu. 10:4; 12:58; 14:32. Jesus the way—John 14:4–9. Broad way—Mt. 7:13.

Straitened way—Mt. 7:14; Lu. 13:24. Way of the Gentiles—Mt. 10:5. Way of righteousness—Mt. 21:32. Way side —Mt. 13:4, 19; Mk. 4:4, 15; Lu. 8:5, 12.

Wax cold.—Mt. 24:12.

Weep.—Mk. 5:39; Lu. 6:21; 23:28; John 20:15. Weeping and gnashing of teeth at the judgment—Mt. 8:12; 13:42, 50; 22:13; 24:51; 25:30; Lu. 13:28. See MOURN.

Wheat.—Mt. 13:25, 29, 30; Lu. 16:7; 22:31; John 12:24.

White.—Mt. 5:36; 23:27; John 4:35.

Whole.—Mt. 9:12; Mk. 2:17. Made thee whole—Mt. 9:21, 22; 5:34; 10:52; Lu. 8:48; 17:19; John 5:6, 14; 7:23. Body —Mt. 5:29, 30; 6:22, 23; Lu. 11:34, 36. Law—Mt. 22:40. World—Mt. 16:26; 26:13; Mk. 8:36; 14:9; Lu. 9:25.

Wicked.—Mt. 18:32; 25:26; Lu. 11:39; 19:22. Parable of the tares—Mt. 13: 24–30, 36–43. See CHARACTER OF THE WICKED, EVIL.

Widow.—Mk. 12:42–44; Lu. 4:26; 18:3, 5; 21:2, 3. See MARRIAGE.

Wife.—Mt. 19:5–10; Mk. 10:7–12; Lu. 14:20, 26; 16:18; 18:29. Lot's wife— Lu. 17:32. See MARRIAGE.

Will.—Mt. 13:28; 15:28; 20:14, 15, 32; Mk. 10:51; 14:7; Lu. 18:41; John 8: 44; 15:7. Will of God—Mt. 18:14; 26:39; Mk. 3:35; 14:36; Lu. 22:42; John 4:34. Will of Jesus—Mt. 8:3, 4; 11:27; 26:39; Mk. 1:41; 14:36; Lu. 5: 13; 10:22; 22:42; John 5:21; 21:22, 23.

Willing.—Mt. 11:14; 26:41; Mk. 14:38; John 5:35.

Wind.—Mt. 11:7; Lu. 7:24; John 3:8.

Wine.—Mt. 9:17; Mk. 2:22; Lu. 5:37, 38; 7:33; 10:34; John 2:1–10. See VINE, FRUIT OF. Winebibber—Mt. 11: 19; Lu. 7:34. Wine-press—Mt. 21:33; Mk. 12:1. Wine-skins—Mt. 9:17; Mk. 2:22; Lu. 5:37, 38.

Wisdom.—Mt. 11:19; 21:15. Wisdom of Solomon—Mt. 12:42; Lu. 11:31.

Wise.—Mt. 5:20; 23:34. Hidden from wise and understanding—Mt. 11:25; Lu. 10:21. Wise man who built his house on the rock—Mt. 7:24, 25. Wise as serpents—Mt. 10:16. Wise servant —Mt. 24:45; Lu. 12:42; 16:8. Wise virgins—Mt. 25:2, 4, 8–10.

Witness.—John 3:11, 32–34; 5:34–47; 8: 13–18. See TESTIMONY.

Woman.—Mt. 5:28; 26:10; Lu. 7:44–50; John 8:1–10. See MARRIAGE, WIFE.

Word.—Mt. 13:19–23; Mk. 4:14–20; 8: 38; Lu. 8:11–15; 9:26; John 8:51, 55; 14:23, 24; 15:20; 17:6, 8, 17. Idle word—Mt. 12:36. Judged by words— Mt. 12:36, 37. See GOSPEL, KINGDOM.

Work.—Mt. 21:28; Mk. 13:34; Lu. 13: 14; John 5:17; 9:4. Work iniquity— Mt. 7:23.

Works.—Mt. 7:22; 23:3, 5; 26:10; Mk. 14:6; John 14:11, 12; 15:24. Abraham, Of—John 8:39. Evil—John 3:19; 7:7. Good works—Mt. 5:16. Mighty works —Mt. 11:21, 23. Greater works—John 5:20; 14:12. The work of God, Jesus sent to accomplish—John 4:34; 5:17, 36; 9:3, 4; 10:25, 32, 37, 38; 14:10; 17:4; 19:28, 30. Of Jesus—Mt. 7:21; John 5:17; 10:25, 38; 14:11, 12; 15:24. Of Pharisees—Mt. 23:3. Of their fathers—Lu. 11:48; John 8:41.

World.—John 7:4; 8:26; 14:31; 17:11, 13, 15, 25. Beholdeth—John 14:19. Believe, That the world may—John 17:21. Beginning of—Mt. 24:21. Care of—Mt. 13:22; Mk. 4:19. To come, The world—Mt. 12:32; Mk. 10:30; 18: 30; Lu. 20:35. End of—Mt. 13:39, 40, 49; 24:3. Field is the—Mt. 13:38. Foundation of—Mt. 13:35; 25:34; Lu. 11:50. Gain the whole—Mt. 16:26; Mk. 8:36; Lu. 9:25. Giveth, Not as the—John 14:27. Hateth, The world —John 7:7; 15:18, 19. Judgment of this—John 12:31, 47. Life of—John 6:51. Light of—Mt. 5:14; John 8:12; 9:5; 11:9; 12:46. Loves, God—John 3:16. Manifests to the—John 7:4; 14:22. Nations of—Lu. 12:30. Not of the—John 15:18, 19; 17:16. Prays not for, Christ—John 17:9. Preached in the whole—Mt. 24:14; 26:13; Mk. 14:9; 16:15. Prince of—John 12:31; 14:30; 16:11. Receive, The world cannot—John 14:17. Save the, To—John 12:47. Sent into the—John 3:17; 10: 36; 17:18. Sons of this—Lu. 16:8; 20: 34. This—Mt. 12:32; Lu. 16:8; 20:34; John 9:39; 12:25, 31. Whole—Mt. 16: 26; 24:14; 26:13; Mk. 8:36; 14:9; Lu. 9:25. Woe unto the—Mt. 18:7.

Worship.—Lu. 14:10; John 4:22–24. Thou shalt worship the Lord thy God —Mt. 4:10; Lu. 4:8. In vain—Mt. 15:9; Mk. 7:7.

Worthy.—Mt. 10:11, 13; 22:8; Lu. 20: 35. Laborer worthy of his food—Mt. 10:10; Lu. 10:7. Not worthy of me— Mt. 10:37, 38. Not worthy to be called thy son—Lu. 15:19, 21. Worthy of stripes—Lu. 12:48.

Write.—Mt. 5:31; Mk. 10:4; Lu. 16:6, 7. Moses wrote—Mk. 10:5; John 5:46, 47.

Written.—All things which are written —Lu. 21:22. See Lu. 22:37. It is written—Mt. 4:4, 7, 10; 11:10; 21:13; 26: 24, 31; Mk. 7:6; 9:12, 13; 11:17; 14: 21, 27; Lu. 4:4, 8; 7:27; 19:46; 20:17; 24:46; John 6:31, 45. Names written in heaven—Lu. 10:20. Written in the law—Lu. 10:26; 24:44; John 8:17; 10: 34; 15:25. Written through the prophets—Lu. 18:31; 24:44.

Wrong.—Mt. 20:13. See SIN, UNRIGHTEOUSNESS, WICKED.

Wrought.—Mt. 26:10; Mk. 6:2; 14:6; John 3:21.

Yoke.—Mt. 11:29, 30.

JETHER, jē'ther. (1) **Son of Gideon.**— Ju. 8:20.

(2) **Husband of Abigail and father of Amasa.**—I Ki. 2:5; I Chr. 7:38,

(3, 4) **Two men of Judah.**—I Chr. 2:32; 4:17.

JETHETH, jē'theth. **A duke of Edom.** —Gen. 36:40; I Chr. 1:51.

JETHRO, jē'thro. Moses' father-in-law, father of Zipporah—Ex. 3:1; 18:2. Called also, Raguel and Reuel. Moses became his herdsman—Ex. 3:1. Jethro's son accompanies Moses—Num. 10:29. Jethro advises the appointment of judges to relieve Moses—Ex. 18: 13–26. He visits Moses in the wilderness, bringing Moses' family to him— Ex. 18:1–7. After consultation, Jethro blessed Jehovah and made a burnt-offering—Ex. 18:8–12. See MOSES.

JETUR, jē'tur. **Son of Ishmael.**—Gen. 25:15.

JEUEL, jē'u-el. (1) **A Levite.**—II Chr. 29:13.

(2) **A man of Judah.**—I Chr. 9:6.

(3) **One who returned with Ezra.**—Ezra 8:13. See JEIEL.

JEUSH, jē'ush. (1) **Son of Esau.**—Gen. 36:5, 14, 18; I Chr. 1:35.

(2) **A Levitical family.**—I Chr. 23:10, 11.

(3) **A Benjamite.**—I Chr. 7:10.

(4) **Son of Rehoboam.**—II Chr. 11:19.

(5) **A Benjamite who was a member of Saul's family.**—I Chr. 8:39.

JEUZ, jē'uz. **A Benjamite.**—I Chr. 8:10.

JEWELS. Offering unto Jehovah.—Ex. 35:22. Ankle chains, bracelets, signet rings, ear rings, and armlets— Num. 31:50; Is. 3:18–24.

Fair jewels.—Ez. 16:17, 39; 23:26.

For Ephod.—Ex. 35:9; 39:6.

Breastplate.—Ex. 39:15, 16, 19, 21. Chains—Ex. 39:18. Engraved plate —Ex. 39:30.

Of silver or gold.—Gen. 24:53; Ex. 3: 22; 11:2; 12:35; 35:22; Num. 31:50, 51; I Sam. 6:8; 6:15; Pr. 11:22.

Wisdom not exchanged for.—Job 28:17, 19.

Signet as a seal.—Dan. 6:17; Hag. 2:23.

Taken from dead.—II Chr. 20:25.

Worn by women.—By vain women—Is. 3:18–24; I Tim. 2:9. Ear rings—Gen. 24:47; 35:4, 22; Ez. 16:12. Nose rings —Ex. 24:47; Is. 3:21. Bracelets— Gen. 24:22, 30, 47; 35:22; Is. 3:18; Ez. 16:11. Armlets—Is. 3:18. Golden ring —Gen. 24:22, 30. Signet rings—Ex. 35:22. Anklets—Is. 3:18. Armlets— Is. 3:20.

Jewels worn by men.—Ear rings—Gen. 35:4; Ex. 32:2, 3; 35:22; Ju. 8:24, 25, 26. Brooches—Gen. 35:22; Ex. 35:22. Signet rings—Gen. 38:18; Ex. 28:11; 35:22; Jer. 22:24; Lu. 15:22. Pharaoh —Gen. 41:42. King's ring—Esth. 3: 10; 8:2, 8, 10. Armlets—Gen. 35:22; Ex. 35:22. Ring of gold—Job 42:11.

JEWS. Although the children of Judah were called Jews while in Babylon, the Jewish community really begins with the restoration of Jerusalem. The two conspicuous characters in this restoration are Ezra and Nehemiah. Ezra was a Jewish priest and scribe (Ezra 7:11; Neh. 12:26), and the organizer of the post-exilic community. Supported by Artaxerxes, he led a band of 1,800 male Israelites from Persia to Palestine in 458 B.C. to strengthen Zerubbabel's colony. Nehemiah coöperated with Ezra, taking a colony to Jerusalem in 445 B.C., and was appointed governor of Judæa, building the walls of Jerusalem, despite the opposition of the Samaritans —Neh. Chs. 3–6. He also organized the service of God, returning to Persia in 433 B.C.

Jehovah arouses Cyrus, king of Persia, in behalf of the captive Jews.—II Chr. 36:22; Ezra 1:2–4. He makes a proclamation of release—II Chr. 36: 23. Artaxerxes also makes a proclamation to the same effect—Ezra 7:11–13. The silver and gold vessels taken from Jerusalem are returned—Ezra 1:7–11; 6:5; 7:14–23; 8:24–30. Lists of Jews returning from Babylon—Ezra Chs. 2 and 8; Neh. Chs. 7 and 12. They begin to build the temple—Ezra 3:8–13. Are opposed by the Samaritans because the Jews would not enter into partnership with them—Ezra 4:1–3. The Samaritans hire counsellors and write to the king, warning him against the builders—Ezra 4:4–16. The work on temple stops because of the royal decree—Ezra 4:17–24. Work is resumed by Zerubbabel and others, but questioned by the Persian authorities—Ezra 5:1–5. Darius consulted, and search made for the original decree of Cyrus. The decree found and the governor of Judæa ordered to let the builders alone, and to aid them—Ezra 6:1–15. The temple built and dedicated—Ezra 6:14, 15, 16. The passover is kept—Ezra 6:19–22. Ezra hears of mixed marriages with Canaanites and others and institutes reform—Ezra Chs. 9–10. Later on the walls of Jerusalem are being built by Nehemiah under the proclamation of Artaxerxes—Neh. Chs. 2–6. The builders are opposed by Samaritans, but by the help of armed guards the walls are built—Neh. Ch. 4. The Jews complain of hard treatment from their leaders —Neh. 5:1–5. Nehemiah abolishes usury—Neh. 5:6–13. Ezra reads the law to his people—Neh. 8:2. The Feast of Tabernacles restored—Neh. 8:14–18. Confession made of national sin —Neh. Ch. 9. The people covenant to maintain the temple worship—Neh.

Ch. 10. Foreigners excluded from the assembly—Neh. Ch. 13. Payment of tithes enjoined—Neh. 13:10–14. Sabbath-breaking condemned—Neh. 13: 15–22. Mixed marriages abolished—Neh. 13:23–31.

Interval prior to Jesus.—I. Persian period (537–330 B.C.). Generally speaking, the Jews, despite the heavy tribute, remained loyal to their rulers. Many Jews, however, were removed to Babylon for revolting about 350 B.C. To the last century of Persian rule belongs the final breach between the Jews and Samaritans.

II. The Greek period (330–167 B.C.). Alexander the Great grants peculiar privileges to the Jews, especially to those who settle in Alexandria. Here Judaism entered into its most intimate relations with the Greek world of literature. Judah an Egyptian province—301 B.C. Judah a Syrian province—198 B.C. The Septuagint Version was prepared in Alexandria about 150 B.C.

III. Maccabean period (167–63 B.C.). The outrages upon the national religion stung the Maccabees into revolt and aroused the Jews to the value of their faith. Wars began for the liberation from the yoke of Syria. The people were enthusiastic for liberty. The temple was restored, and re-dedicated (165 B.C.), and the rival temple and capital of Samaria razed to the ground.

IV. Roman period. Here the Herodians begin the reign. Antipater dies 43 B.C., and in 37 B.C. his son Herod (The Great) becomes, by Rome's aid, king of Judæa. His death in 4 B.C. makes way for the Tetrachies—Philip commanding east of Jordan; Antipas, Galilee and Peræa; Archelaus, Judæa and Samaria. After 6 A.D. Archelaus's kingdom passes under the direct rule of Rome, Pontius Pilate being procurator from 26 to 36 A.D.

The Jews during the time of Jesus and His apostles.—When John the Baptist and Jesus came into power, the Jews were divided into two strong parties —the Pharisees and the Sadducees. The Pharisees developed as a party after the victory of the Maccabees, devoting themselves to the most scrupulous fulfilment of the law. They were strictly a sect (Acts 15:5; 26:5), operating mostly in the synagogues—Mt. 23:2–7. While they upheld the righteousness of God, their faith ran largely to ritualism. They were censorious and hypocritical as a class—Lu. 11:39–44; 12:1. The Sadducees were in power at the temple. They were an exclusive caste, being attached to the aristocracy among the priests. They acknowledged the law to be binding, but rejected the tradítions of the scribes. They denied the messianic hope, the resurrection, and the existence of angels and spirits—Mk. 12:18–27; Lu. 20:27; Acts 4:1–7; 5:17; 23:7, 8.

Jesus' mission to the Jews.—Not to Gentiles nor to Samaritans, but to the lost sheep of the house of Israel—Mt. 10:5, 6; 15:24; Mk. 7:26, 27. To declare that the kingdom of heaven was approaching—Mt. 12:24, 38–42; 13:58; 15:1–14; 21:33–46; 22:1–45; Mk. 6:1–6; 8:11–13; 11:27–33; 12:1–27; Lu. 11:14–54; 13:31–35; 16:14–31; 18:9–14; 20:1–47; John 5:38–43; 6:36; 8:13–59; 9:13–41; 10:1–39.

The Jews plot to put Jesus to death.—Mt. 26:1, 2; Mk. 14:10, 11; Lu. 22:1, 2; John 11:47–53. Judas bargains with the Jews—Mt. 26:14–16; Mk. 14:10–11; Lu. 22:3–6; John 13:26–30. The betrayal and seizure—Mt. 26:47, 50; Mk. 14:43–46; Lu. 22:47–54; John 18:1–12. They try Him before the Sanhedrin—Mt. 26:57–68; Mk. 14:53–65; Lu. 22:66–71; John 18:12–14. The Jews take Him to Pilate for trial—Mt. 27:2; Mk. 15:1–3; Lu. 23:1–5; John 18:28–32. The Jews crucify Jesus—Mt. 27:22–26; Mk. 15:12–39; John 19:12–30. During Jesus' life some Jews believed on Him—Mt. 4:18–25; 7:28, 29; 14:8, 23; 15:30, 31; Lu. 5:26; John 4:1–3; 6:14, 15; 7:40–46; 8:31–32; 9:35–38; 11:45; 12:9–19.

The Jews' course towards the apostles and the church.—Devout Jews marvel during pentecost at the action of the apostles—Acts 2:5–12. The opinion of mockers—Acts 2:13. The apostles are imprisoned by the authorities—

Acts 4:1–23; 5:17–41. A great company of the priests obey the gospel—Acts 6:7. Stephen arouses enmity, is taken before high priest, and condemned to death—Acts 6:8–15; 7:54–60. Persecution at Jerusalem scatters the church—Acts 8:1–4. Saul of Tarsus seeks to destroy the church—Acts 9:1–3. After Saul's conversion the Jews plot to kill him—Acts 9:23. Many Jews follow Paul and Barnabas—Acts 13:43; 14:1. The jealousy of the Jews continues—Acts 13:45; 14:1, 19. The Jews try to force circumcision on the disciples—Acts 15:1–5; Rom. 2:24–29; Gal. 5:1–12. The Jews stir up evil against Paul—Acts 21:27, 28; 24:1–9. Paul calls together the chief of the Jews, pleading his own case—Acts 28:17. Some believed and some disbelieved—Acts 28:24. The Jews continued their opposition to christianity until Titus began the siege of Jerusalem in 70 A.D.—Mt. 24:16–27.

Promises concerning the Jews.—Pouring out of the Spirit upon them—Ez. 39:29; Joel 2:28, 29; Zech. 12:10. Removal of their blindness—Rom. 11:25; II Cor. 3:14–16. Their return and seeking of God—Hos. 3:5. Pardon of sin—Is. 44:22; Rom. 11:27. Salvation—Is. 59:20; Rom. 11:26–27. Sanctification—Jer. 33:8; Ez. 36:25. Joy at conversion of—Is. 44:23; 49:13; 52:8, 9; 66:10. Blessing to Gentiles through Jews—Is. 2:1–5; 60:5; 66:19; Rom. 11:12, 15. Reunion of—Jer. 3:18; Ez. 37:16–22; Hos. 1:11; Mic. 2:12. Restoration to their own land—Is. 11:15–16; 14:1–3; 27:12–13; Jer. 16:14, 15; Ez. 36:24; 37:21, 25; 39:25–28; Lu. 21:28. Gentiles to assist in their restoration—Is. 49:22–23; 60:10–14; 61:4–6. Future glory of—Is. 60:19; 62:3–4; Zeph. 3:19–20; Zech. 2:5. Future prosperity of—Is. 60:6–17; 61:4–6; Hos. 14:5, 6. A redeemer to come to them—Is. 59:20. To reign over them—Ez. 34:23, 24; 37:24, 25.

Punishment for: Idolatry—Ps. 78:58–64; Is. 65:3–7. Unbelief—Rom. 11:20. Covenant breaking—Is. 24:5. Jer. 11:10. Transgressing the law—Is. 1:4–7; 24:5–6. Changing the ordinances—Is. 24:5. Killing the prophets—Mt.

23:37, 38. Calling upon themselves the blood of Jesus—Mt. 27:25.

Kinds of Punishment.—Scattered among the nations—Deut. 28:64; Ez. 6:8; 36:19. Despised by the nations—Ez. 36:3. Their country trodden under foot by the Gentiles—Deut. 28:49-52; Lu. 21:24. Their house left desolate—Mt. 24:38. Their temple sacked and polluted—Mt. 24:2, 15. Deprived of civil and religious privileges—Hos. 3:4. See Israel, Judah, Judaizers, Salvation.

JEZANIAH, jĕz′a-nī′ah. Jer. 40:8.

JEZEBEL, jĕz′e-bel. **Born and reared an idolater.**—I Ki. 16:31.

Married Ahab, king of Israel.—I Ki. 16:31. Strongminded—I Ki. 19:1, 2; 21:7. Induced Ahab to build a temple and altar to Baal—I Ki. 16:32; 21:25, 26. Wicked—II Ki. 9:22. Zealous in idolatry—I Ki. 18:4, 13, 19; 19:1, 2. Caused murder of Naboth—I Ki. 21:5-16. Her death foretold—I Ki. 21:23; II Ki. 9:10. Fulfilled—II Ki. 9:30-37. Her name a synonym for seduction to idolatry—Rev. 2:20.

JEZER, jē′zer. Gen. 46:24.

JEZERITES. Descendants of Jezer.—Num. 26:49.

JEZIEL, jē′zi-el. **A soldier under David.**—I Chr. 12:3.

JEZRAHIAH, jĕz′ra-hī′ah. Neh. 12:42.

JEZREEL, jĕz′re-el. (1) **A place in Judah.**—Josh. 15:56; I Sam. 25:43. David's wife probably came from this place—I Sam. 27:3; 30:5; II Sam. 2:2. Attacked by Gideon—Ju. 7:1. A royal residence—I Ki. 18:45; 21:1. Jezebel and her son Jehoram were slain here —II Ki. 8:29; 9:10; 10:11.

(2) **A town in Issachar.**—Josh. 19:18.

(3) **A descendant of Judah.**—I Chr. 4:3.

(4) **Son of Hosea.**—Hos. 1:4.

JEZREELITE. I Ki. 21:6.

JIDLAPH, jĭd′laph. Gen. 22:22.

JOAB, jō′ab. (1) **Son of David's sister Zeruiah**—II Sam. 14:1; I Chr. 2:16; 11:39. Had two warlike brothers—II Sam. 23:18, 24. General of David's army—II Sam. 8:16; 20:23; I Chr. 18:15; 27:34.

Victories over: Abner—II Sam. 2:17. Syrians—II Sam. 10:9-14. Ammonites —II Sam. 11:1. Edomites—I Ki. 11:15, 16. Rabbah—II Sam. 12:26, 27; I Chr.

20:1. Absalom—II Sam. 18:6, 7, 14. Sheba—II Sam. 20:10, 15, 22.

Too headstrong for David.—II Sam. 3:24, 25, 34, 39. Brought Absalom back —II Sam. 14:1-24. Murdered Abner —II Sam. 3:27. Amasa—II Sam. 20:9, 10; I Ki. 2:5, 32. Uriah—II Sam. 11:14-17. Took a wise woman's advice— II Sam. 20:16-21. Reproved David— II Sam. 19:5-7; 24:3; I Chr. 4:3; 21:3. Took a census of Israel—II Sam. 24:4-9; I Chr. 21:4, 5. Joined Adonijah's rebellion—I Ki. 1:7, 41; 2:28. Repaired Jerusalem—I Chr. 11:8. Slain at the altar of Jehovah—I Ki. 2:29, 34.

(2) **A descendant of Caleb**—I Chr. 2:54.

(3) **Son of Seraiah**—I Chr. 4:14.

(4) **Founder of a clan**—Ez. 2:6; 8:9; Neh. 7:11.

JOAH, jō′ah. (1) **A Levite.**—I Chr. 6:21; II Chr. 29:12.

(2) **An officer under Hezekiah.**—II Ki. 18:18, 26; Is. 36:3.

(3) **An officer under Josiah.**—II Chr. 34:8.

(4) **A doorkeeper.**—I Chr. 26:4.

JOAHAZ, jō′a-hăz. II Chr. 3:48.

JOANAN, jo-ăn′an. **An ancestor of Jesus.**—Lu. 3:27.

JOANNA, jo-ăn′na. **A female disciple, wife of Ahuza, an officer under Herod.** One of the women who went to Jesus's tomb—Lu. 8:3; 24:10.

JOASH, jō′ash. (1) **Father of Gideon.**— Ju. 6:11. Protected Gideon—Ju. 6:29-31. Had a holy tree and altar of Baal —Ju. 6:25. Changed Gideon's name— Ju. 6:32.

(2) **Son of King Ahab.**—I Ki. 22:26; II Chr. 18:25. Jailer or regent for Ahab —I Ki. 22:27.

(3) **A descendant of Judah.**—I Chr. 4:22.

(4) **A Benjamite, one of David's followers.**—I Chr. 12:3.

(5) **A Benjamite, son of Becher.**—I Chr. 7:8.

(6) **Superintendent of David's oil cellars.**—I Chr. 27:28.

(7, 8) **Kings in Israel and Judah.**—See Jehoash.

JOB. See Outline Studies in the Books.

JOBAB, jō′băb. (1) **A son of Joktan.**— Gen. 10:29; I Chr. 1:23.

(2) **King of Madon.**—Josh. 11:1.

(3) **A king of Edom.**—Gen. 36:33.

(4, 5) **Two Benjamites.**—I Chr. 8:9, 18.

JOCHEBED, jŏk′e-bed. **Wife of Amram, mother of Moses and Aaron.**—Ex. 6:20; 26:59.

JODA, jō′dà. **An ancestor of Jesus.**—Lu. 3:26.

JOEL, jō′el. (1) **Son of Samuel.**—I Sam. 8:2; I Chr. 6:33.

(2) **An ancestor of Samuel.**—I Chr. 6:36.

(3) **A Reubenite.**—I Chr. 5:4, 8.

(4) **A Levite.**—I Chr. 15:7, 11, 17.

(5) **The prophet.**—See OUTLINE STUDIES IN THE BOOKS.

JOELAH, jo-ē′lah. **A soldier under David.**—I Chr. 12:7.

JOEZER, jo-ē′zer. **One of David's mighty men.**—I Chr. 12:6.

JOGBEHAH, jŏg′be-häh. **A city in Gad.**—Num. 32:35; Ju. 8:11.

JOGLI, jŏg′li. **A Danite.**—Num. 34:22.

JOHA, jō′hà. (1) **A Benjamite.**—I Chr. 8:16.

(2) **A soldier under David.**—I Chr. 11:45.

JOHANAN, jo-hā′nan. (1) **Son of Josiah, king of Judah.**—I Chr. 3:15.

(2) **A captain who led the remnant into Egypt.**—I Ki. 25:23; Jer. 40:8; 43:5.

(3) **A Levite.**—I Chr. 6:9.

(4) **A descendant of David.**—I Chr. 3:24.

(5) **An Ephraimite.**—II Chr. 28:12.

(6, 7) **Two soldiers.**—I Chr. 12:4, 12.

(8) **A high-priest.**—Neh. 12:22.

(9) **One who returned with Ezra.**—Ezra 8:12.

JOHN. (1) **A member of the Jewish Sanhedrin.**—Acts 4:6.

(2) **Father of Simon Peter.**—John 1:42; 21:15.

The apostle.—See OUTLINE STUDIES IN THE BOOKS.

(4) **John the Baptist: Career.**—Announcement of birth—Lu. 1:5–25. Time in days of Herod the Great B.C. 6 —Lu. 1:5. Piety and old age of Zacharias and Elisabeth—Lu. 1:6 f. Barrenness of Elisabeth—Lu. 1:7. Zacharias a priest in service when the angel Gabriel appears to him—Lu. 1:8–13. The name of the child (John) given by the angel—Lu. 1:13. Fore-

cast of the child's career made by the angel—Lu. 1:15–17. (Greatness, abstinence from strong drink, filled with the Holy Ghost from his birth, successful preacher of repentance, spirit and power of Elijah, reconciliation, righteousness among the people, preparing a people for the Lord.) Doubt of Zacharias—Lu. 1:18. Punishment of Zacharias—Lu. 1:19–23. The conception by Elisabeth—Lu. 1:24 f. Meeting of Elisabeth and Mary—Mary told about Elisabeth—Lu. 1:26 f. Mary's visit to Elisabeth—Lu. 1:40. The leaping of the babe—Lu. 1:41. Inspiration of Elisabeth and her song to Mary—Lu. 1:41–45. Birth of John—B.C. 5 (or 6). Place: The hill-country of Judæa—Lu. 1:39, 57. Elisabeth congratulated by her friends—Lu. 1:58. Naming the child—Lu. 1:59–79. Circumcised the eighth day—Lu. 1:59. Effort of friends to name him Zacharias—Lu. 1:59. Protest of Elisabeth—Lu. 1:60. Appeal to Zacharias and his written reply—Lu. 1:61–63. Tongue of Zacharias loosed—Lu. 1:64–66. His inspired song—Lu. 1:67–79. (Two parts, gratitude to God for fulfilling his prophecy of redemption, 67–75; sketch in prophetic plan of the career of the child, 76–79; as prophet, forerunner, preacher of remission of sins, bringing knowledge of the dayspring from on high for those in darkness.) The boy in the desert—Lu. 1:80.

Date of beginning of John's ministry.—Lu. 3:1 f. Fixed by names of imperial, provincial and ecclesiastical rulers (Tiberius, Pilate, Herod, Antipas, Philip, Lysanias, Annas, and Caiaphas). Probably A.D. 25 or 26. Sphere of his first ministry the wilderness of Judæa around the Jordan—Mt. 3:1; Lu. 3:2 f.; Mk. 1:4.

Wins a new name (The Baptist).—Mt. 3:1; Lu. 3:2 (*cf. merely* John in Mk. 1:4).

Message of John.—Word of God came to him—Lu. 3:2. Repentance and the advent of the kingdom—Mt. 3:2; Mk. 1:4; Lu. 3:3.

Fulfills the prophecy of Isaiah and Malachi about the forerunner of the Mes-

siah.—Mt. 3:3; Mk. 1:2 f.; Lu. 3:4–6; Is. 40:3 ff.; Mal. 3:1.

His new ordinance.—Baptism of repentance unto remissions of sins—Mk. 1: 4; Lu. 3:3.

His personal appearance.—Mt. 3:4; Mk. 1:6. His raiment and his food.

First results of his ministry.—Great crowds from Judæa and Jerusalem—Mt. 3:5; Mk. 1:5. Confession of sin and baptism in the Jordan—Mt. 3:6; Mk. 1:5. Even crowds of Pharisees and Sadducees came—Mt. 3:7; Lu. 3:7. So came also publicans—Lu. 3: 12. Soldiers also—Lu. 3:14.

Shows relation between himself and the Messiah.—This when considered to be the Messiah himself by many—Lu. 3: 15. Shows superiority of the Messiah by the baptism of the Holy Spirit and of fire and the separation of the wheat from the chaff—Mt. 3:11 f.; Mk. 1: 7 f.; Lu. 3:16 f.

Baptizes Jesus as the Messiah.—Came for that purpose—Mt. 3:13; Mk. 1:9. John shrinks from doing it, recognizing the Messiah before the sign—Mt. 3:14; John 1:33. John submits after Christ's insistence—Mt. 3:15. The baptism in the Jordan, exact place unknown—Mk. 1:9.

Receives embassy from the Sanhedrin. —At Bethany beyond Jordan—John 1:28. Sent by the Pharisees—John 1: 25. Composed of Sadducees (priests and Levites)—John 1:19. Their object to learn who he really is, whether the Messiah or not—John 1:19–22. Disclaimers of John to be either the Messiah, Elijah (in person), or the prophet (held by some to be distinct from the Messiah)—John 1:20–22. His description of himself as a voice crying in the wilderness—John 1:23 f. The embassy inquire therefore the reason for the new ordinance of baptism—John 1:25. The unknown Christ —John 1:26.

Identifies Jesus as the Messiah.—John 1:29–37. Testifies the first day that Jesus is the Lamb of God, the sin bearer for all the world—John 1:29. Repeats the superiority of Jesus to himself—John 1:30. Explains his baptizing as a Messianic manifestation—

John 1:31. Confirms his judgment of Jesus by the coming of the Holy Spirit upon him—John 1:32. This was the pre-arranged sign of God for John's recognition of the Messiah—John 1: 33. He·has seen the sign and testifies therefore that Jesus is the Son of God (as the Father said at the baptism)— John 1:34. Renewed testimony on the second day—John 1:35 f. Effect on two disciples of John—John 1:37.

Effort of John's disciples to make him jealous of Jesus.—John 3:23–30.

New scene of John's ministry, Aenon, near to Salim (Samaria)—John 3:23. Why here! (still free and much water here)—John 3:23 f. Dispute of John's disciples with a Jew about purifying (difference between John's baptism and Jewish ablutions)—John 3:25. They tell John about the success of Jesus— John 3:26. The joy of John as the friend of the bridegroom—John 3:27– 30. Cf. also John 4:1 f.

Teaches his disciples to pray.—Lu. 11:1.

Rebukes Herod Antipas and Herodias for their unlawful marriage.—Lu. 3: 13; Mt. 14:4; Mk. 6:18. Thrown into prison by Herod Antipas—Mt. 4:12; 14:3; Mk. 1:14; 6:17; Lu. 3:20. Place Machaerus—Josephus, Ant., 18, 5, 2.

Despondency of John in prison.—Hears the fame of Jesus as worker of miracles—Lu. 7:17 f., Mt. 11:2. Doubt about the Messiahship of Jesus—Mt. 11:3; Lu. 7:19.

Response of Jesus.—Heals many for the benefit of the embassy—Lu. 7:21. Bids them report what they have seen and heard—Lu. 7:22; Mt. 11:4 f. Warns John against doubt about Jesus—Mt. 11:6; Lu. 7:23.

Death of John.—Mt. 14:5–12; Mk. 6:19– 29; Lu. 9:9. Languished in prison a year or more. (Cf. Broadus on Mt. 11:2; 14:3). Hostility of Herodias to John—Mk. 6:19. Why John was not killed at once—Mk. 6:20; Mt. 14:5. Occasion of his death a promise to Salome, the daughter of Herodias, whose dancing pleased him—Mt. 14: 6 f.; Mk. 6:21–23. Put up to her demand of John's head by her mother— Mt. 14:8; Mk. 6:24 f. Regretful acquiescence of Herod—Mt. 14:9–11;

Mk. 6:26–28. Burial of John's body by his disciples—Mt. 14:12; Mk. 6:29. Report his death to Jesus—Mt. 14:12.

Estimates of John.—People as a whole: *Wonder if he is the Messiah*—Lu. 3:15. *Hold him as a prophet*—Mt. 11:9; 14:5; 21:26; Mk. 11:32; Lu. 7:26; 20:6. *Some think he came to life in Jesus*—Mt. 16:14; Mk. 8:28; Lu. 9:7, 19. Publicans: *Accepted his baptism and endorsed the view of Jesus*—Lu. 7:29. Sanhedrin: *Once interested in him*—John 1:19–27; 5:23. *Rejoiced for a season*—John 5:35. *Fear his reputation with the people*—Mt. 21:26; Mk. 11:32; Lu. 20:6 f. Pharisees and lawyers: *Reject his baptism and message*—Lu. 7:30. *Accused of having a demon*—Mt. 11:18; Lu. 7:33. Herod Antipas: *Fears that Jesus is John the Baptist come to life again*—Mt. 14:2; Mk. 6:14. Jesus: *John bore witness to the truth*—John 5:33. *A bright lamp*—John 5:35. *Testimony less than that of the Father*—John 5:36. *Not a reed in the wind*—Mt. 11:7; Lu. 7:24. *Not clothed in soft raiment*—Mt. 11:8; Lu. 7:25. *More than a prophet*—Mt. 11:9; Lu. 7:26. *Forerunner of Jesus*—Mt. 11:10; Lu. 7:27. *Paradox of his greatness*—Mt. 11:11; Lu. 7:28. *Epoch marking man, end of time of the law and the prophets*—Mt. 11:13; Lu. 16:16. *Was the promised Elijah in spirit*—Mt. 11:14; 17:10–13; Mk. 9:11–13. *His conduct justified by Jesus*—Mt. 11:19; Lu. 7:35. *Considers by implication that the baptism of John is from heaven*—Mt. 21:25; Mk. 11:30; Lu. 20:4. *For that reason he had received baptism from John over his protest*—Mt. 3:14 f. *John came in way of righteousness*—Mt. 21:32. *Promises baptism of the Holy Spirit in contrast to John's baptism of water*—Acts 1:5. Peter: *Mentions the baptism of Jesus by John beginning of Christ's ministry*—Acts 1:22; 10:37. Paul: *Preached before Christ began His ministry*—Acts 13:24. *Baptism of repentance*—Acts 13:24. *Felt his inferiority to Jesus*—Acts 13:25. John the Evangelist: *General estimate*—John 1:6–15. *Sent from God*—John 1:6. *Came to witness about Jesus*—John 1:7. *Not the*

Light himself—John 1:8. *Identifie[s] Jesus as the Messiah and as superior t[o] himself*—John 1:15. *Worked no mira[-] cles*—John 10:41.

Left disciples.—*Argue about purifying while John is alive*—John 3:25. *Kep[t] up the Jewish fasts*—Mt. 9:14; Mk. 2:18. *Complain to Jesus that His dis[-] ciples do not fast*—Mt. 9:14. *Visi[t] John in prison and serve him*—Mt. 11:2; Lu. 7:19. *Care for his body whe[n] dead*—Mt. 14:12. *Survive to the apostolic period*—Acts 18:25; 19:3. *Som[e] of them misunderstand John's teaching*—Acts 19:3–5.

Josephus.—*In his Ant. 18, 5, 2, gives [a] sketch of John from the political poin[t] of view, but he considers him a "goo[d] man" who "commanded the Jews t[o] exercise virtue, both as to righteous[-] ness towards one another, and piet[y] towards God, and so to come to bap[-] tism; for that the washing would b[e] acceptable to Him, if they made use o[f] it, not in order to the putting awa[y] of some sins, but for the purificatio[n] of the body; supposing still that th[e] soul was thoroughly purified before[-] hand by righteousness."*

Teaching.—Repentance: *Enjoined on al[l]* —Mt. 3:2. *Requisite for his baptism*— Mk. 1:4; Lu. 3:3. *With reference to Remission of sins*—Mk. 1:4; Lu. 3:3. *Confession of sin required*—Mt. 3:6; Mk. 1:5. *Proof of repentance de[-] manded in the life*—Mt. 3:8; Lu. 3:8. Kingdom of heaven: *Announced a[s] near*—Mt. 3:2. *A reason for repentanc[e]* —Mt. 3:2. Indictment of Pharisais[m] and Sadduceeism: *Calling offspring o[f] vipers*—Mt. 3:7; Lu. 3:7 (to the multi[-] tude under the domination of the Phari[-] sees and Sadducees). *Self-complacen[t] attitude as descendants of Abraham de[-] nounced*—Mt. 3:9; Lu. 3:8. *Judgmen[t] already at hand*—Mt. 3:10; Lu. 3:9. Liberality: *Enjoined on the multitude* —Lu. 3:10 f. Extortions: *Denounce[d] on the part of the publicans*—Lu. 3:12 f. Violence and discontent: *Con[-] demned on the part of the soldiers*— Lu. 3:14.

Estimate of self.—*Proper conception o[f] himself in relation to Christ*—Mt. 3[:]

11; Mk. 1:7; Lu. 3:13 f.; John 1:15 f., 19–26, 30; 3:27–30.

Doctrine of the Messiah.—The long-promised Messiah is at hand—Mt. 3: 3; Mk. 1:2 f.; Lu. 3:4–6. Comes for judgment—Mt. 3:10–12; Mk. 1:8; Lu. 3:9, 16 f. A double baptism of the Holy Spirit and of fire—Mt. 3:11; Lu. 3:16. The Passover Lamb bearing the sin of the world—John 1:29, 36. The Son of God—John 1:34. Jesus the true Messiah—Mt. 3:14; John 1:33; 3:28. The Bridegroom—John 3:29. His star to increase while John's fades —John 3:29. Already among the Jews, but not recognized by them—John 1:26.

The Holy Spirit.—Taught that the Messiah would baptize with the Holy Spirit—Mt. 3:11; Mk. 1:8; Lu. 3:16; John 1:33. Saw the Holy Spirit descend upon Jesus as a dove out of heaven—John 1:32 f.

(5) **John Mark.**—See OUTLINE STUDIES IN THE BOOKS.

John, Epistles of.—See OUTLINE STUDIES IN THE BOOKS.

JOIADA, joi'a-dà. (1) **A high priest.**— Neh. 12:10, 22; 13:28.

(2) **One of those who helped to repair the wall.**—Neh. 3:6.

JOIAKIM, joi'a-kim. Neh. 12:12. See JEHOIAKIM.

JOIARIB, joi'a-rib. (1) **One of Ezra's assistants.**—Ezra 8:16.

(2) **A priest.**—Neh. 11:10; 12:6, 19.

(3) **A descendant of Perez.**—Neh. 11:5.

JOIN. Acts 5:13; Rom. 7:3. Battle—I Sam. 4:2. Charge, In the—Acts 24:9. Citizen, To—Lu. 15:15. Enemies, To —Ex. 1:10. Ephraim, To idols—Hos. 4:17. Hand, in hand—Pr. 16:5. House to house—Is. 5:8. Living, With—Eccl. 9:4. Lord, Unto the—I Cor. 6:17. One to another—Ex. 26:17; 36:22. Together—Gen. 14:3. What God hath—Mt. 19:6; Mk. 10:9. Words—Job 16:4.

JOINT. Heb. 4:12. Bones are out of— Ps. 22:14. Foot out of—Pr. 25:19. Heirs of grace—Pet. 3:7. Heirs with Christ—Rom. 8:17. Knit together through—Col. 2:19. Loosed—Dan. 5: 6. Supplieth—Eph. 4:16.

JOKDEAM, jŏk'de-ăm. **A city of Judah.** —Josh. 15:56.

JOKIM, jō'kim. **A descendant of Judah.**—I Chr. 4:22.

JOKMEAM, jŏk'me-ăm. **A Levitical city of Ephraim.**—I Ki. 4:12; I Chr. 6:68.

JOKNEAM, jŏk'ne-ăm. **A Levitical city of Zebulun.**—Josh. 12:22; 19:11; 21: 34.

JOKSHAN, jŏk'shan. **Son of Abraham by Keturah.**—Gen. 25:2, 3; I Chr. 1:32.

JOKTAN, jŏk'tan. **Son of Eber.**—Gen. 10:25, 26, 29; I Chr. 1:19, 20, 23.

JOKTHEEL, jŏk'the-el. (1) **A city in Judah.**—Josh. 15:38.

(2) **A city in Edom.**—II Ki. 14:7.

JONADAB, jŏn'a-dab. (1) **One of David's nephews.**—II Sam. 13:3, 5, 32, 35.

(2) **Son of Rechab.**—Jer. 35:6–19.

JONAH, jō'nah. See OUTLINE STUDIES IN THE BOOKS.

JONAM, jō'nam. **Ancestor of Jesus.**— Lu. 3:30.

JONAS. (1) See JONAH.

(2) **Father of Peter.** See JOHN.

JONATH-ELEM-REHOKIM. Ps. 56 (title). See MUSIC, PSALMS.

JONATHAN, jŏn'a-than. **Son of Saul.** —I Sam. 14:1; 13:16; I Chr. 8:33; 9:39.

Officer in his father's army.—I Sam. 13: 3, 22. Victory at Michmash—I Sam. Ch. 14.

Friendship between David and Jonathan.—I Sam. Chs. 18–20; II Sam. 1: 17–27; 9:1, 7; 21:7.

Death.—I Sam. 31:2; II Sam. 1:4; I Chr. 10:2. Burial of—II Sam. 21:12–14. David's dirge over Saul and Jonathan —II Sam. 1:17–27.

Descendants of.—II Sam. 4:4; 9:3, 6; I Chr. 8:34; 9:40.

(2) **Son of Gershom.**—Ju. 18:30.

(3) **Son of Abiathar.**—II Sam. 15:27.

(4) **Son of Shimei.**—II Sam. 21:21. Nephew of David—I Chr. 27:32.

(5) **One of David's heroes.**—II Sam. 23:32; I Chr. 11:34.

(6) **Son of Uzziah.**—One of David's treasurers—I Chr. 27:25.

(7) **Son of Jada.**—I Chr. 2:32.

(8) **Father of Ebed.**—Ezra 8:6.

(9) **Son of Asahel.**—Ezra 10:15.

(10) **A Levite.**—II Chr. 17:8.

(11) **Son of Joiada.**—Neh. 12:11.

(12) **A priest.**—Neh. 12:14.

(13) **Son of Shemaiah.**—Neh. 12:18, 35.

(14) **A scribe in whose house Jeremiah was imprisoned.**—Jer. 37:15.

(15) **A son of Kareah.**—Jer. 40:8.

JOPPA, jŏp'pà, *or* **JAPHO: A seaport of Palestine.**—Josh. 19:46; II Chr. 2:16; Ezra 3:7; Jonah 1:3.

Work of Simon Peter in.—Acts 9:36–43. Vision of Peter on the housetop—Acts 10:1–23.

Home of Dorcas.—Acts 9:36. Lydda—Acts 9:38.

Simon the tanner.—Acts 9:43.

Disciples called to Cæsarea from.—Acts 10:5, 8, 23; 11:13.

Followers of Jesus from.—Acts 9:42.

JORAH, jō'rah. Ancestor of some who returned with Zerubbabel—Ezra 2:18.

JORAI, jō'rāi. **A Gadite.**—I Chr. 5:13.

JORAM, jō'ram. See JEHORAM.

JORDAN, jŏr'dan. *"The Descender."*—A river in Palestine which empties into the Dead Sea. From Sea of Galilee to Dead Sea is 65 miles, falling from 682 to 1,292 feet below sea level. Average width, 30 yards. Depth varies from 3 to 10 feet. Fords of the Jordan—Ju. 7:24. Crossed by Jacob—Gen. 32:10. Israel—Josh. 3:4; 5:1; II Ki. 2:6–8; Ps. 114:3. The spies—Josh. 2:7. Gideon—Ju. 8:4. Ammonites—Ju. 10:9. Abner and his men—II Sam. 2:9. Absalom—II Sam. 17:22; 19:15, 18, 31; I Chr. 19:17. Elisha—II Ki. 2:14. Israelites hold against the Moabites—Ju. 3:28. Ephraimites slain at, pronunciation of shibboleth a sign—Ju. 12:5, 6. Rising of, in the spring—I Chr. 12:15. At harvest—Josh. 3:15; Jer. 12:5. Waters divided by miracles—Josh. 3:4; 5:1; II Ki. 2:6–8, 14; Ps. 114:3. Naaman washes in—II Ki. 5:10–14. John the Baptist baptizes in—Mt. 3:6, 13; Mk. 1:5, 9; Lu. 3:3; John 1:28. Jesus baptized in—Mt. 3:13; Mk. 1:9. Beyond Jordan—Mt. 4:15, 25; 19:1; Mk. 3:8; 10:1; John 3:26; 10:40. Jesus returned from—Lu. 4:1.

JORIM, jō'rim. **Ancestor of Jesus.**—Lu. 3:29.

JORKEAM, jŏr'ke-am. **A descendant of Caleb.**—I Chr. 2:44.

JOSECH, jō'sek. **Ancestor of Jesus.**—Lu. 3:26.

JOSEPH, *"added to."* (1) Jacob's son by Rachel.—Gen. 30:24, 27. Fed the flock when seventeen—Gen. 37:2. Favoritism of Jacob produced jealousy—Gen. 37:3–4; Acts 7:9. Reciting of dreams to brothers angered them—Gen. 37:5–11. Visits them and is conspired against—Gen. 37:18. Reuben pleads for Joseph's life—Gen. 27:21–22. Sold to Ishmaelites and bought by Potiphar—Gen. 37:28; 39:1. Potiphar's wife entices him, but he consents not—Gen. 39:7–15. By falsifying she has him cast into prison—Gen. 39:17–20. Meanwhile, sons' lies cause Jacob to grieve—Gen. 37:31–35. Joseph interprets dreams of baker and butler—Gen. 40:5–23. Pharaoh has dreams no magician can solve—Gen. 41:9–13. The released butler recommends Joseph—Gen. 41:9–13. Joseph being sent for, interprets dreams — Gen. 41:14–45. Joseph is chosen as manager—Gen. 41:37–44.

At thirty, Joseph is made second only to king.—Gen. 41:46. Marries the daughter of a priest—Gen. 41:45. Gathers up all the food and stores it—Gen. 41:48–49. Buys everything of Egyptians, even themselves—Gen. 47:19–20. He spares priests, but exacts one-fifth—Gen. 47:22–24.

Jacob sends down to Egypt to buy food.—Gen. 42:1–3. Joseph recognizes brothers and calls them spies—Gen. 42:7–14. Holds Simeon, demands Benjamin, and grants food—Gen. 42:18–26. They find their money in sacks and are alarmed—Gen. 42:35. Jacob yields Benjamin under pressure of famine—Gen. 43:11–15. Joseph reveals himself and sends for Jacob—Gen. Chs. 45, 46, 47. Provides land of Goshen for family—Gen. 47. Mourns his father's death—Gen. 50:1–3. Buries him—Gen. 50:4–14. Joseph shows that hand of God is in all these things—Gen. 50:20; Ex. 1:5, 6, 8. Insists that his bones be taken to Canaan—Gen. 50:25; Ex. 13:19; Josh. 24:32. Joseph dies, being 110 years old—Gen. 50:26; Ex. 1:6.

References: Moses' Blessing—Deut. 33: 13–17. David's Song—Ps. 105:17–22.

Joseph's faith in God's promise.—Heb. 11:22.

Descendants of.—Num. 1:10, 32; 13:11; 26:28, 32; 27:1; 32:33; 36:12; Josh. 14:4; 16:1, 4; 17:1, 2, 14, 16, 17; 18:5, 11; Ju. 1:22, 23, 35; I Ki. 11:28; I Chr. 5:2; Rev. 7:8.

Redeemed by God.—Ps. 77:15.

Led by God.—Ps. 80:1; 81:5.

Tent of Joseph refused by God.—Ps. 78:67.

House of Joseph.—Amos 5:6, 15; Ob. 18; Zech. 10:6.

Affliction of Joseph.—Amos 6:6.

(2) **A man of Issachar.**—Num. 13:7.

(3) **Son of Bani.**—Ezra 10:42.

(4) **Head of the house of Shebaniah.**—Neh. 12:14.

(5) **Name found in genealogy of Jesus.**—Lu. 3:24.

(6) **Name found in genealogy of Jesus.**—Lu. 3:30.

(7) **Son of Heli and husband of Mary**—Mt. 1:16–19, 24; Lu. 3:24. A righteous man—Mt. 1:19. Of David's lineage—Mt. 1:20; Lu. 1:27; 2:4; John 1:45. Dwelt at Nazareth—Lu. 1:26; John 1:45. Showed his faith by his works—Mt. 1:19–25. Went to Bethlehem to enroll for taxes—Lu. 2:4. Joseph in company with Mary and the babe Jesus—Lu. 2:16. He marvelled at the words of Simeon—Lu. 2:33. Ordered to take the child into Egypt—Mt. 2:13–15. Commanded to return—Mt. 2:19–23. Went with Mary and Jesus to Jerusalem—Lu. 2:41–42. Spent three days searching for Jesus—Lu. 2:43–46.

8) **A brother of Jesus.**—Mt. 13:55; Mk. 6:3.

9) **Of Arimathea, member of Sanhedrin.**—Mk. 15:43. Waited for kingdom of God—Lu. 23:51. He feared the Jews—John 19:38. Was bold before Pilate—Mk. 15:43–45; Lu. 23:50, 52. Helped embalm body of Jesus—John 19:38, 40. The body laid in Joseph's new tomb—Lu. 23:53; John 19:41–42.

10) **Called Barsabus.**—One of the two chosen to fill the place of Judas—Acts 1:23.

11) **Son of Asaph.**—I Chr. 25:2, 9.

OSES. See JOSEPH.

OSHAH, jō'shah. **A descendant of Simeon.**—I Chr. 4:34.

JOSHAPHAT, jŏsh'a-phat. **One of David's mighty men.**—I Chr. 11:43; 15:24.

JOSHAVIAH, jŏsh'a-vī'ah. **One of David's mighty men.**—I Chr. 11:46.

JOSHBEKASHAH, jŏsh'be-kā'shah. **Son of Haman.**—I Chr. 25:4, 24.

JOSHUA, jŏsh'u-a. (1) Son of Nun.

JOSHUA, *"Deliverer."*— Called also HOSHEA, son of Nun.—Num. 13:8, 16; I Chr. 7:27.

Moses' minister and successor as a military leader.—Ex. 24:13; 32:17; 33:11; Deut. 31:14, 23; Josh. 1:1–3. Chosen by Moses to fight Amalek—Ex. 17:8–13. Spies out Canaan—Num. 13:16. Sends out spies—Josh. 2:1. Addresses his officers before passing over Jordan—Josh. 1:10. Crosses Jordan—Josh. Ch. 3. Erect memorial pillars at Jordan—Josh. Ch. 4. Re-enacts circumcision—Josh. 5:2–9. Besieges and captures Jericho—Josh. 6:1–21. Condemns Achan for appropriations—Josh. 7:19–26. Because of this sin, defeated at Ai—Josh. 7:2–5. Afterwards conquers Ai—Josh. Ch. 8. Kings of nations combine against him—Josh. 9:1–2. They are slain—Josh. 10:1–27. Other victories—Josh. Ch. 11. Commands sun to stand still—Josh. 10:12–14. List of kings overcome—Josh. Ch. 12. Gives portions of land to 12 tribes—Josh. Chs. 13–21. Gives charge to Reubenites—Ch. 22. Sets up tabernacle in Shiloh—Josh. 18:1. Exhorts people to obedience—Josh. Ch. 23. Appoints cities of refuge—Josh. Ch. 20. Assigns 48 cities to Levites—Josh. Ch. 21. Death and burial—Josh. 24:29–30; Ju. 2:8–9. See MOSES.

(2) **A Beth-shemite.**—I Sam. 6:14, 18.

(3) **Governor of Jerusalem under Josiah.**—II Ki. 23:8.

(4) **A high priest at the rebuilding of the temple.**—Hag. 1:1, 12, 14; 2:2, 4; 3:1, 3, 6–9; 6:11.

JOSIAH, jō-sī'ah. (1) **King of Judah.**—Prophesied—I Ki. 13:2. Ancestry—I Chr. 3:10, 13; Mt. 1:10. Crowned when eight years old by the people—II Ki. 21:24; 22:1; II Chr. 33:25; 34:1. Thirty-one years of righteous reign—II Ki. 22:1, 2; II Chr. 34:1. Tender-

hearted, humble, and loyal—II Ki. 22:
19; 23:4, 5; II Chr. 34:3, 27. Listened
to Book of the Law found by Hilkiah
—II Ki. 22:8, 10, 11; 23:2; II Chr. 34:
14, 16, 18, 19–21. Made a covenant
with Jehovah to obey the law—II Ki.
23:3; II Chr. 34:31. Repaired the
temple—II Ki. 22:4–6; II Chr. 34:8,
10, 11. Purged the land and temple of
idolatry—II Ki. 23:4–16, 24; II Chr.
34:3–7, 33; 35:3–5. Renewed the passover—II Ki. 23:21–23; II Chr. 35:1,
6–19. The exceptional king—II Ki.
23:25.

Prophets during his reign.—Jer. 1:1, 2;
25:3. Misunderstood the will of God
—II Chr. 35:20–22. Killed in battle—
II Chr. 35:23, 24. Buried and lament-
ed—II Ki. 23:30; II Chr. 35:24, 25.
Succeeded by unworthy son, Jehoahaz
—II Ki. 23:31, 32; II Chr. 36:1.

(2) **Son of Zephaniah.**—Zech. 6:10.

JOSIBIAH, jŏs'i-bī'ah. I Chr. 4:35.

JOSIPHIAH, jŏs'i-phī'ah. Ezra 8:10.

JOT. A small point from the smallest
—Hebrew letter *yod*.—Mt. 5:18.

JOTBAH, jŏt'bah. A place in Judah.—
II Ki. 21:19.

JOTBATHAH, jŏt'bath-ah. An encampment of Israel.—Num. 33:33, 34; Deut.
10:7. See CAMP.

JOTHAM, jō'tham. (1) **King of Judah.**
Son of Azariah.—II Ki. 15:1–7, 32–36;
16:1; I Chr. 3:12, 17; II Chr. 26:21, 23;
27:1, 6, 7. Death of—II Ki. 15:36–38;
II Chr. 27:9.

(2) **Son of Gideon.**—Ju. 9:5, 7, 21, 57.

(3) **Son of Jahdai.**—I Chr. 2:47.

JOURNEY: Three days' journey.—Distance between Laban's and Jacob's
herds—Gen. 30:36. Israel into wilderness—Num. 10:33; 33:8. Through the
streets of Nineveh—Jonah 3:3.

Sabbath day journey.—(About 2,000
cubits or 1,000 yards.) Probably based
on Ex. 16:29. The length was so short
that the Saviour advised the disciples
to pray that their flight might not be
on the sabbath—Mt. 24:20; Acts 1:12.

Prosperous journeys.—Abraham's from
Ur to Canaan—Gen. 12:1–2. Abraham's servant for Rebekah—Gen. 24:
21–27. Jacob's into Egypt—Gen. 46:
1–7. Entrance into Canaan—Deut.
1:6–8. Paul's—Rom. 1:10.

Missionary journeys.—Acts Ch. 13, 15,
16, and 18. Cornelius' servants—Acts
10:9–23. See PAUL.

**Journeys revealing power and presence
of Jehovah.**—Israel crossing the Red
Sea—Ex. 14:15–16. Under divine
shelter—Ex. 14:19–20; 40:34–38; Ps.
105; 106. Ahab's and Obadiah's—I
Ki. 18:5, 6, 41–45. The three kings
search for water—II Ki. 3:9–20.

Israel's arrested journeys.—By Edom—
Num. 20:17, 18. By Amorites—Num.
21:22–23. By Og—Num. 21:33–35.
By Moabites—Num. 22:5, 6.

**Custom of Israel in announcing jour-
neys.**—By trumpets—Num. 10:1–9.
Description of Israel's journeyings—
Num. Ch. 33. Return from Babylon
to Jerusalem—Ezra Chs. 1, 2, 7, 8, etc.

Forced journeys.—Adam and Eve—Gen.
3:22–24. Cain's—Gen. 4:14–16. Jacob's—Gen. 27:42, 43. Joseph's—
Gen. 37:28. Absalom's—II Sam. 13:
37, 38. Joseph and Mary's into Egypt
—Mt. 2:13, 14.

Journeys accompanied by surprises.—
Balaam's—Num. 22:21–31. Saul seeking asses—I Sam. Chs. 8, 9. Magi
noting Herod's ignorance—Mt. 2:1–
12. Mary misses Jesus—Lu. 2:41–48.
Jesus passing through Jericho—Lu.
19:1–9. On his way to Emmaus—Lu.
24:13–35. Saul on way to Damascus—
Acts 9:3–8.

Perilous journeys.—Jacob meeting Esau
—Gen. 32:6–11. Gibeonites treachery
—Josh. 9:3–21. Israelites near sea—
Ex. 14:2–12. Peter on the lake—Mt.
14:28–31. Paul's shipwreck—Acts 27.
His various journeyings—II Cor. 11:
26.

Joyful journeyings.—Departure from
Egypt—Ex. 12:37–42; 13:17–22; Ps.
114; 136. Return of captives from
Babylon—Ezra 8:15–36. Conveying
good news—Is. 52:7–8; Mt. 28:19; Mk.
16:15. Return of ransomed—Is. 35:
8–10.

Sad journeyings.—Abraham to Moriah—
Gen. 22:3. Israel on the way to Assyria—II Ki. 17:22, 23. Judah carried
into Babylon—II Ki. 25:11. Joseph
and Mary searching for Jesus—Lu.
2:41–48. Jesus on the way to Geth-

semane—Mk. 14:26-35. Prodigal son —Lu. 15:13-24.

Journeys preventing performance of duty.—Circumcision—Josh. 5:2-9. Paul, as to visiting Rome—Rom. 1:13-15.

Rendering assistance in journeyings.— I Cor. 16:6; III John 6.

Loyal journeys.—Abraham's—Heb. 11: 8. Moses'—Heb. 11:27. Ruth's— Ruth 1:15-18. Withdrawal of Mark —Acts 15:35-38.

Wearisome journeys. — Israel's — Deut. 1:19. Elijah's—I Ki. 19:4-8. Jesus' —John 4:6. Paul's—II Cor. 11:25-26.

JOY AND REJOICING: Wicked find joy in folly.—Pr. 15:21. In unrighteousness—II Thess. 2:12. In death— I Tim. 5:6. In carnal pleasures— Eccl. 2:10, 26. Deceptive—Eccl. 7:6; Is. 22:13. Faces the judgment day— Eccl. 11:9. Momentary—Job 8:19; 20:5. Fool gives none—Pr. 17:21.

Duty of righteous to rejoice.—It is strength—Ezra 6:22; Neh. 8:10; Ps. 42:4; Col. 1:11; 2:5. Commanded— Deut. 12:18; Ps. 43:4; Rom. 12:12; Phil. 3:1; 4:4; I Thess. 5:16; I Pet. 4:13.

Reasons for rejoicing.—Grace—Lu. 1: 47; Acts 2:28. Indwelling in Christ— John 15:10, 11. Answer to prayer— John 16:24. Fellowship of saints— II Tim. 1:4; I John 1:3, 5; II John 12. Care—Ps. 5:11; 16:89; 105:43. By faith—Ps. 89:16; 149:2; Heb. 3:8; Rom. 5:11. In hope—Rom. 5:2; Heb. 3:6. In the truth—II Cor. 2:3. In the Lord—Phil. 4:10. Even in persecutions, sorrow, trials, or calamities— Mt. 5:11, 12; Lu. 6:23; Heb. 10:34; II Chr. 6:10; Jas. 1:2; I Pet. 1:6; Heb. 3:17, 18; Rom. 8:28. Unspeakably great—Ps. 21:6; 32:11; 68:3; Zech. 9:9; Lu. 6:23; Acts 8:8; I Cor. 8:2. Abides forever—John 15:11; I Thess. 5:16. Joy follows affliction—Job 29: 13; Ps. 30:5; 126:5; Is. 35:10; John 16:20, 33; I Pet. 4:13. Presence of Christ gives—John 3:29; 17:13.

Gratitude for food and raiment.—Deut. 28:47; Ps. 65:13; Eccl. 5:19, 20; Mt. 6:11, 31-33; 7:11; Lu. 11:3; Acts 14: 17. For goodness—II Chr. 7:10; Ps. 67:4. For promises—Ps. 132:16; Is. 35:10; 55:12; 56:7; Jer. 31:13; 33:

9-11; Zech. 8:19; Heb. 6:18; I Pet. 1:4. For good preaching—Neh. 8:12; Jer. 15:16; Lu. 8:13; Acts 8:8; 13:48. For Zion—Ezra 6:16; Neh. 12:43; Ps. 48:2; Lam. 2:15; Gal. 4:26, 27; Heb. 12:22.

Joy of the gospel.—The very name, good tidings of great joy—Lu. 2:10. Abraham saw—John 8:56; Gal. 3:4. Prophets and angels desire to know—Mt. 13:17; I Pet. 1:10-12. Salvation—I Sam. 2:1; Ps. 9:14; 13:5; 20:5; 21:1; 35:9; 51:12; Is. 12:3; 25:9; 61:10; II Cor. 1:6. Better than lands—Ps. 4:7; Mt. 10:42; Lu. 12:15, 21. Future joy—Ps. 16:11; Mt. 25:21, 23; I Pet. 4:13; Jude 24.

Joy is to.—The just and upright—Ps. 32:11; 97:11; Pr. 21:15. Peacemakers —Pr. 12:20; Mt. 5:9. The meek—Is. 29:19; Mt. 5:5. The wise—Pr. 15:23. Parents of the good—Pr. 23:24; Ps. 113:9. Believers—Lu. 24:52; Acts 2: 46; 8:8, 39; 13:52; 15:3.

Ministers count converts as.—II Cor. 7:4; Phil. 2:2; 4:1; I Thess. 2:20; 3:9; Philemon 20; II John 4. Help—II Cor. 1:24; Phil. 1:25. Pray for—Rom. 15:13. Live in—Ps. 100:2; Rom. 15: 32. Die in—Acts 20:24. Render account in—Phil. 2:16; Heb. 13:17.

God rejoices over His people.—Zeph. 3: 17; Ps. 149:4. For fidelity: Enoch— Heb. 11:5. Fear—Ps. 147:11. Prayer —Pr. 15:8. Uprightness—I Chr. 29: 17; Pr. 11:20. Repentance—Lu. 15:7, 10. Obedience—II Chr. 30:26. To do them good—Num. 14:8; Deut. 30:9, 10; Jer. 32:41; II Sam. 22:20; II Chr. 20:27; Is. 49:13; 51:3, 11; 52:9; 60:15; 65:19.

Christ anointed to preach.—Is. 61:1, 3; Lu. 4:18. Holy Spirit's fruit is—Gal. 5:22. Kingdom of heaven is—Rom. 14:17. Shout for—Ezra 3:11-13.

Figurative.—Stars rejoice—Job 38:7. Trees—Ps. 96:12.

Results of.—Strength—Neh. 8:10; Phil. 4:10, 13. Sacrifice—Ps. 27:6. Liberality—I Chr. 29:9, 17; II Cor. 8:2.

JOZABAD, jŏz'a-băd. (1) **Two men of Manasseh who joined David at Ziklag.** —I Chr. 12:20.

(2) **A man of Judah.**—I Chr. 12:4.

(3) **An overseer under Hezekiah.**—II Chr. 31:13.

(4) **A Levite in days of Josiah.**—II Chr. 35:9.

(5) Ezra 8:33.

(6) **A priest who married a foreign wife.** —Ezra 10:23.

(7) **A Levite interpreter.**—Neh. 8:7.

(8) **A Levite in Jerusalem after the exile.**—Neh. 11:16.

JOZACAR, jŏz′a-kar. II Ki. 12:21.

JOZADAK, jŏz′a-dăk. **A priest, father of Jeshua.**—Ezra 3:2, 8; 5:2; 10:18; Neh. 12:26.

JUBAL, jū′bal. **Son of Lamech—Inventor of harp and pipe.**—Gen. 4:21.

JUBILEE. The year of jubilee was ushered in by the sound of trumpets throughout the land, every 50th year, on the 10th day of the seventh month —the great day of atonement—Lev. 25:9-10.

It was a sabbatical year of rest for the soil.—Lev. 25:11.

Two rest years for the soil came together every 50 years, the sabbatical year and the jubilee year.—Lev. 25:20-22; II Ki. 19:29; Is. 37:30.

Provision made for food during the rest years.—Lev. 25:14-17, 20-22.

The jubilee year to keep sacred the ownership of land as first allotted to the tribes and families.—Num. 36:2-4.

It kept a few wealthy ones from robbing the poor.—Lev. 25:25-28.

It preserved the title in Jehovah whose was the land.—Lev. 25:23.

All transfers of land were made with reference to jubilee year.—Lev. 27: 22-25; Num. 36:2-4.

Law for redeeming the land.—Lev. 27: 18-19. Also houses in villages—Lev. 25:29-34.

Land not redeemed went back to Jehovah.—Lev. 27:20-21.

Bondmen must be redeemed or freed in jubilee year.—Ex. 21:6; Lev. 25:39-55. See DEBT, FRATERNITY, POOR.

JUCAL, jū′cal. **A prince of Judah, an enemy of Jeremiah.**—Jer. 38:1.

JUDÆA, jū-dæ′a. **Borders of.**—Mt. 19: 1; Mk. 10:1.

Called.—"The Land of Judah"—Dan. 5:13; Mt. 2:6; John 7:1.

Description of.—Hill country—Lu. 1: 39, 65. Wilderness—Mt. 3:1. Desert —Acts 8:26. Region—Mk. 1:5; Lu. 7:17; John 4:2, 3; 7:1.

Towns of.—Arimathea—Mt. 27:57; John 19:38. Azotus, or Ashdod—Acts 8:40. Bethlehem—Mt. 2:1, 6, 16. Bethphage —Mt. 21:1. Emmaus—Lu. 24:13. Ephraim—John 11:54. Gaza—Acts 8:28. Jericho—Lu. 10:30; 19:1. Joppa —Acts 9:36; 10:5, 8. Lydda—Acts 9:32, 35, 38.

Rulers of.—Archelaus—Mt. 2:22. King of—Lu. 1:5.

Incidents connected with.—Joseph goes to—Lu. 2:4. John the Baptist in— Mt. 3:1-7. Followers of, in—Mt. 3:5; Mk. 1:5. Christ born in—Mt. 2:1, 5, 6. Tempted in the wilderness of—Mt. 4:1. Jesus taught in—Lu. 23:5; John 3:22; 4:1-3, 47, 54; 7:3; 11:7. Apostles in—Acts 11:1, 29. Peter—Acts 2:9, 14; 12:19. Paul—Acts 26:20; II Cor. 1:16. Complaint against church members—Rom. 15:31. Followers of Christ in—Mk. 3:7; Lu. 5:17, 6:17. Spreading the gospel in—Acts 10:37. Witness of Christ in—Acts 1:8. Churches in—Acts 8:1; 9:31; Gal. 1: 22; I Thess. 2:14. False preacher from—Acts 15:1. Prophet Agabus from—Acts 21:10.

Prophecy concerning.—Mt. 24:16; Mk. 13:14; Lu. 21:21.

JUDAH, jū′dah. (1) **Son of Jacob.** Jacob's fourth son by Leah.—Gen. 29: 35; 35:23. Saved Joseph from death by intercession—Gen. 37:26-27. Offers to be surety for Benjamin—Gen. 43:3-10. Stands for Benjamin also, respecting the cup found in sack— Gen. 44:1-10. Judah shows the way into land of Goshen—Gen. 46:28. Takes two wives—Gen. 28:1-6. Dwells at Chezib—Gen. 38:5. His incest with his daughter-in-law—Gen. 38:12-26. Jacob's prophecy concerning him— Gen. 49:8-12. Ancestor of Jesus— Gen. 49:10; Mt. 1:2-3; Heb. 7:14; Rev. 5:5.

(2) **Tribe of.**—The tribe first and most vigorous in driving out Canaanites— Ju. 1:3-19. Furnished the first judge —Ju. 3:9. Descendants—Gen. 46:12; Num. 26:19-22; I Chr. Ch. 2. Princes

—Num. 7:12–17; 13:6; 34:19. Moses blesses—Deut. 33:7. Inheritance—Josh. 15:1–12; 19:9. Bezalel of tribe of Judah—Ex. 31:2; 35:30. Achan—Josh. 7:16–26. Boaz—Ruth 2:1. Rehoboam made king over—I Ki. 12:21. Encampment—Num. 2:3, 9; 10:14. Tribe of Judah leads the war against the Benjamites—Ju. 20:18. Aided Saul in his wars—I Sam. 7:4–17. Reigned over by David, seven and one-half years—II Sam. 2:4, 11; 5:5. Other tribes jealous of, because of David—II Sam. 19:41–43; 20:11. Number who left Egypt, 74,600—Num. 1:26, 27; 2:4. Strength when entering Canaan, 76,500—Num. 26:22. See ISRAEL.

(3) **Levite who married a foreign wife.** —Ezra 10:23.

(4) **Ancestor of Kadmiel.**—Ezra 3:9.

(5) **A Benjamite.**—Neh. 11:9.

(6) **A prince of Judah.**—Neh. 12:34.

(7) **A Levite who returned with Zerubbabel.**—Neh. 12:8.

(8) **A priest and musician.**—Neh. 12:36.

(9) **Kingdom of.**—Consisted of the tribes of Judah and Benjamin. Division brought about by Rehoboam's folly—I Ki. 12:6–23. Also a fulfilment of Jehovah's threat—I Ki. 11:9–13. Jehovah's name to be enshrined at Jerusalem rather than at Samaria—I Ki. 14:21. People become idolatrous under Rehoboam and are punished by Shishak—I Ki. 14:22–26. Rehoboam dies—I Ki. 14:31.

Advantages of kingdom of Judah over that of Israel.—"A frontier less exposed to powerful enemies, a soil less fertile, a population hardier and more united, a fixed and venerated center of administration and religion, a hereditary aristocracy in the sacerdotal caste, an army always subordinate, a succession of kings which no revolution interrupted."—*Smith's Dictionary.*

Judah had three different lines of policy. —(1) War with Israel. (2) Alliance with Israel. (3) Deference, if not vassalage, to Assyria, Egypt, and the Neo-Babylonian empire.

War with Israel: The first three kings of Judah hoped to subdue Israel. Even the rapacity of Shishak, of Egypt, in robbing the temple of its treasures, seemed to make no headway in stopping the hostility of Judah—I Ki. 14: 25–28, 30; 15:7, 16; II Chr. 12:2–9, 15; 13:2, 13, 15; 16:1.

Alliance with Israel: Jehoshaphat and Ahab get together against the king of Syria—I Ki. 22:2–4. They go up together against Ramoth-Gilead, where Ahab is killed—I Ki. 22:34; II Chr. Ch. 18. Jehoram and Jehoshaphat unite their forces against Moab—II Ki. Ch. 3. Mesha, king of Moab, is defeated—II Ki. 3:21–27.

Important events in the history of Judah.—Edom revolts from under the hand of Judah—II Ki. 8:20; II Chr. 21:8. Libnah revolts also—II Ki. 8: 22; II Chr. 21:10. Jehu kills Ahaziah, king of Judah—II Ki. 9:27, 28. Jehu also slays Ahaziah's brethren—II Ki. 10:13, 14. Jehoash, king of Judah, levies a tax and repairs the temple—II Ki. 12:4–15; II Chr. Ch. 24. Amaziah, king of Judah, becomes bold and challenges the king of Israel, who defeats him, sacking the temple—II Ki. 14:8–14; II Chr. 25:17–24.

Assyria obtains a grasp of Judah.—II Ki. 16:5–18; 17:3–6. Sennacherib, king of Assyria, prepares to besiege Jerusalem; is overcome and slain—II Ki. Ch. 19; II Chr. Ch. 32; Is. Chs. 36, 37. Josiah, king of Judah, repairs the temple—II Ki. 22:1–7. Hilkiah finds the law, which is read in public, producing a reformation—II Ki. Chs. 22 and 23. Josiah was afterwards slain at Megiddo, in a battle with Pharaoh-Necoh—II Ki. 23:29. He was buried at Jerusalem—(v. 30).

From Jehoahaz to Zedekiah.—Egypt subdues Judah and reduces it to vassalage—II Ki. 23:31–33. Eliakim, son of Josiah, placed on the throne by Pharaoh - Necoh—II Ki. 23:34, 35. Babylon overcoming Egypt, Judah passed under the control of Nebuchadrezzar—II Ki. 24:1. Prompted by Egypt, Jehoiakim rebelled—II Ki. 24: 1. Jehovah sent bands of Chaldeans, Syrians, Moabites, and Ammon against Judah because of the sins of Manasseh—II Ki. 24:2–4. The children of

Judah carried away into Babylon, after the siege of Jerusalem—II Ki. 24:10-19; 25:1-21. Gedaliah appointed governor over those remaining behind—II Ki. 25:22-26.

The captivity and its results.—Number of Jews carried into Babylon—Jer. 52:28-30. They dwell by the river Chebar—Ez. 1:1. The sacking of the temple and conveyance of its vessels, etc., to Babylon—Jer. 52:17-23. Nebuchadrezzar trains young Jews for service—Dan. 1:1-7. Daniel refuses to eat the king's meat—Dan. 1:8-16. The king has dreams which his wise men cannot interpret—Dan. 2:1-13. Daniel repeats the dream and interprets it—Dan. 2:31-45. Being promoted, he recommends Shadrach, Meshach, and Abed-nego to take charge of affairs—Dan. 2:48, 49. The king makes an image, requiring all to bow before it—Dan. 3:1-7. The above three refuse and are cast into the furnace—Dan. 3:8-23. The king sees a man in the furnace, which leads him to bow before Jehovah—Dan. 3:24-30.

Darius king of Babylon.—Dan. 5:30, 31; 6:1-3. Darius promotes Daniel—Dan. 6:1-3. Being falsely accused, he is cast into a den of lions—Dan. 6:16-18. Comes out unhurt, while his enemies are destroyed—Dan. 6:19-24.

Cyrus issues a proclamation for return of Jews.—Ezra 1:1-4; II Chr. 36:22, 23.

Esther chosen queen instead of Vashti.—Esth. Chs. 1 and 2. Mordecai, Esther's foster-father, provokes the jealousy of Haman—Esth. 3:1-6. Haman plans the destruction of the Jews—Esth. 3:8-15. Plan frustrated and Haman hanged—Esth. 9:1-25.

The part played by the prophets.—As Elijah and Elisha were active in the northern kingdom, so Isaiah, Jeremiah, Ezekiel, and most of the lesser prophets found a fertile field in the checkered life of Judah—I Ki. Chs. 17-22; II Ki. Chs. 1-13; Amos 2:4, 5; Hab. 1:1-6; Zeph. 1:14-18. These were busy in upholding and purifying the conception of Jehovah—Is. 1:24; Jer. 14:7-12. The Assyrians were the rod used to chastise Judah for its sins

—Is. 10:5-11. So determined is Jehovah to uphold justice that he will eventually raise up a prince of righteousness and peace—Is. 9:6, 7. Isaiah has a vision of a kingdom where justice prevails—Is. 11:1-5. Jeremiah enlarges and develops spiritual religion—Jer. 4:1-4. Men must be held responsible for their own acts—Jer. 31:29, 30. The living God greater than all idols—Is. 40:13-26; 42:8-17; 44:9-28; 45:15-25; 46:1-7; 48:1-14; Jer. 10:8-10. Ezekiel insists upon human individuality—Ez. Ch. 18. He places great value upon a human soul—Ez. 14:3-8. Isaiah has the clearest conception of Jehovah as Ruler of earth—Is. 51:1-8; 65:17-25; 66:1-14. He contributes most largely to the Messianic idea—Is. Chs. 52 and 53. (For list of kings, see ISRAEL.) See JEWS, PROPHECY, ISRAEL.

JUDAIZERS.—The term does not itself occur in the New Testament, though the verb ("live as Jews") appears in Gal. 2:14.

"They of the circumcision."—This phrase used of Christian Jews as opposed to Gentiles (Acts 10:45; cf. Gal. 2:7, 8, 12; Col. 4:11) and also of Christian Jews of the stricter type who felt that all Christians ought to be Jews (Acts 11:2) who contended with Peter and reluctantly acquiesced in the conversion of Cornelius and his household—Acts 11:18. Cf. Tit. 1:10.

Pharisaic sect of Christians.—In Acts 15:5 this wing of the Church in Jerusalem is called "certain of the sect of the Pharisees."

Paul still a Pharisee.—In Acts 23:6 Paul called himself "a Pharisee, son of Pharisees," but touching "the hope and resurrection of the dead." On the points of difference between Pharisees and Sadducees he was a Pharisee after becoming a Christian. But Paul was not a Judaizer.

Contention of the Judaizers.—They held that Judaism was essential to the salvation of Gentiles—Acts 15:1, 5.

Resistance of Paul.—Paul fought for the freedom of the Gentile Christians. He won at Antioch—Acts 15:2.

Jerusalem conference on subject.—The first great Christian conference was on this important issue and resulted in victory for Paul's position—Acts 15:4–29; Gal. 2:1–10. The other apostles and James took Paul's view of the matter.

Strife renewed at Antioch.—The Judaizers reopen the conflict on social relations with Gentile Christians. Even Peter and Barnabas temporarily desert Paul—Gal. 2:11–21.

Paul loyal to the agreement.—Acts 16:4.

Judaizers create strife in Corinth.—*Cf.* I Cor. 1:10–17; Chs. 3 and 4; II Cor. Chs. 10–13. Threaten Galatian churches—Gal. 1:6; 5:5–15; 6:11–17. Endanger unity of Christendom— Rom. 16:30–33; Acts 20:22–24; 21:4, 11–14. Slander Paul at Jerusalem— Acts 21:20–26. Disturb him in Rome— Phil. 1:15 ff.; 3:2 f. See COVENANTS, CIRCUMCISION.

JUDAS, JUDE, jū'das. (1) **Judas Iscariot.**—The man of Kerioth, a town in the south of Judæa. He was the only one of the twelve who was not a Galilean. He was treasurer of the apostolic band. The temptation of the money-holder overcame him, and he sold his Lord for thirty pieces of silver—Mt. 26:14–16. (See Ex. 21:33.) Betrayal (kiss the sign of)—Mt. 26: 23, 25, 47–50; Mk. 3:19; 14:10, 11, 18, 20, 42–46; Lu. 22:3–6, 21, 47, 48; John 12:4–6; 13:21, 26, 27; 18:2, 3, 5. Prophecies concerning—Ps. 41:9; 55:12–21; Zech. 11:12, 13. After accepting the "hire" he became remorseful and went to his own place, by suicide—Mt. 27:3–5; Acts 1:16–19.

(2, 3, 4, 5, 6, 7)—See JUDE in OUTLINE STUDIES IN THE BOOKS.

JUDGES: In primitive times the head of the patriarchal family judged his dependents.—Gen. 38:24; Ex. 2:14.

The popular element of judicature.— (1) Princes—Num. 7:2, 10; 16:2; 17: 6; 34:18; Josh. 22:14; Ju. 8:14; II Sam. 15:3–4; Ezra 10:8; Job 29:7–9; Jer. 26:10. (2) Elders or rulers—Ex. 24:1, 9, 14; Num. 11:16, 17, 24, 25, 30; Deut. 19:12; 21:2; Josh. 24:1; Ju. 8: 14; I Ki. 21:8, 11; II Ki. 10:1; Ezra 10:8.

Originally judges were not priests.—Ju. 2:16–19; 3:9, 15 (Eli an exception— I Sam. 1:9; 4:18). Priests resorted to, for conference—Deut. 17:8–13.

Qualifications of judges.—Ex. 18:21; Lev. 19:15; Deut. 1:17; 16:18–20; II Chr. 19:6, 7.

Jurisdiction of.—To judge at all seasons —Ex. 18:22. Judge for Jehovah not for man—II Chr. 19:5–10. Difference between sinning against God and against man—I Sam. 2:25. Judge according to God's ordinances—Ez. 44: 24. Judge righteous judgment—John 7: 24. No respect of persons—Pr. 24: 23. As respects false witnesses—Deut. 19:16–19. Wicked to be punished— Deut. 25:1–3.

Seat of judgment.—The gate—Job 29: 7–9; Ps. 69:12; Pr. 8:15. Absalom sat in—II Sam. 15:3–4.

Kings act as.—Saul—I Sam. 11:13; 14: 44, 45. David—II Sam. 1:15; 15:6. Solomon—I Ki. 3:9; Ps. 72:1, 4. Burden, as in Moses' case, gets too heavy—I Chr. 23:4; 26:29.

Moses as a.—Ex. 18:13, 16. Father-in-law advises appointment of—Ex. 18: 17–22. Moses appoints—Ex. 18:24–26; Deut. 1:12–17. Jehovah confirms it— Deut. 16:18.

Period of the judges.—They were heroes and saviors of Israel, springing up in times of exigency—(1) Othniel—Ju. 3:9–11. (2) Ehud—Ju. 3:15–30. (3) Shamgar—Ju. 3:31. (4) Deborah and Barak—Ju. 4:4–9. (5) Gideon—Ju. 6: 11–40. (6) Abimelech—Ju. 9:1–54. (7) Tola—Ju. 10:1, 2. (8) Jair—Ju. 10: 3–5. (9) Jephthah—Ju. 12:7. (10) Ibzan—Ju. 12:8–10. (11) Elon—Ju. 12:11, 12. (12) Abdon—Ju. 12:13, 14. (13) Samson—Ju. 15:20. (14) Eli— I Sam. 4:18. (15) Samuel—I Sam. 7: 15. (16, 17) Samuel's two sons—I Sam. 8:1–3. See ISRAEL.

Priests as.—Deut. 17:9; I Chr. 23:4; II Chr. 19:8–11; Ez. 44:24; Mt. 26:57–66; Mk. 14:53–64; John 18:19–24; Acts 23:2–3.

Miscellaneous.—Pilate—Mt. 27:24; Mk. 15:15; Lu. 23:24; John 18:29–40. Herod—Lu. 23:7. Felix—Acts 24:22. Festus—Acts 25:6. The godless judge —Lu. 18:2.

Corrupt.—Is. 1:17, 21; 5:7; 10:2; 28:7; 56:1; 59:4; Jer. 2:8; 5:1; 7:5; 21:12; Ez. 22:27; 45:8, 9; Hos. 5:10; 7:5, 7; Amos 5:7, 15, 24; 6:12; Hab. 1:4.

Jehovah as a.—Of Egypt—Gen. 15:14. As to Abraham and Sarah—Gen. 16:5. Of Moses and Aaron—Ex. 5:21. Of his people—Deut. 32:36; II Chr. 6:23; Ps. 7:8; 50:4; 135:14; Is. 3:13–14; 33: 22; Heb. 10:30. Of nations—Ju. 11: 27. Of the ends of the earth—I Sam. 2:10. Of Saul and David—I Sam. 24: 12, 15. Of the wicked—I Ki. 8:32. Of the earth—I Chr. 16:33; Ps. 82:8; 94: 2; 96:13; 98:9. Of Ammon and Moab —II Chr. 20:12. Of Job—Job 9:15; 22:13; 23:7. Of the fatherless and oppressed—Ps. 10:18; Is. 1:17, 23. Of David—Ps. 26:1; 35:24; 54.1. Of the widows—Ps. 68:5. Of the poor—Ps. 72:4. Of the nations—Ps. 110:6; Is. 2:4; Joel 3:12. By his arms—Is. 51:5. Of Jeremiah—Lam. 3:59. According to his ways—Ez. 7:3, 8; 18:30; 33:20. According to desert—Ez. 7:27. In the border of Israel—Ez. 11:11. As women who break wedlock—Ez. 16:38. In the land of birth—Ez. 21:30. Between sheep and sheep—Ez. 34:17, 20–22. Of the world—Acts 17:31; Heb. 12:33. The secrets of men—Rom. 2:16; 3:6. Adulterers—Heb. 13:4. Is a righteous judge—Gen. 18:25; Ps. 9:8; 67:4; 72: 2; 75:7; 96:10, 13; 98:9; Pr. 31:9; Eccl. 3:17.

Jesus Christ as.—The Judge of the world —Ps. 96:13; Is. 2:4; Mt. 16:27; 25:31– 46; John 5:22, 23, 27, 30; Acts 10:42; Rom. 2:16; I Cor. 4:5; II Cor. 5:10; II Tim. 4:1, 8; Rev. 22:12. No judge of inheritance—Lu. 12:14; 19:22. Judges as He hears—John 5:30. True judgment—John 8:15, 16, 26. Judged by his work—John 12:47–48. Judge of living and dead—Acts 10:42; II Tim. 4:1, 8; I Pet. 4:5. Judges in righteousness—Rev. 19:11.

Disciples as.—Mt. 7:1, 2; Lu. 6:37; Rom. 14:3, 10, 13; I Cor. 5:12; 6:2, 3, 4, 5; 10:15; 11:13, 31; 14:29; II Cor. 5:14; Col. 2:16; Jas. 4:11, 12. See ISRAEL, JUDGMENT.

JUDGES, BOOK OF. See OUTLINE STUDIES IN THE BOOKS.

JUDGMENT: The Judge, God.—Gen. 16:5; Ju. 11:27; I Sam. 2:10; 24:12, 15; I Chr. 16:33; Job 21:22; Ps. 26:1, 2; 35:24; 50:4, 6; 58:11; 75:7; 76:8, 9; 82:8; 96:13; 135:14; Pr. 29:26; Eccl. 3:17; 11:9; 12:14; Is. 2:4; 3:13; 28:17; 30:18; 33:22; Dan. 7:10; Mal. 3:5; Acts 17:31; I Cor. 5:13; Heb. 10:30; 12:23; Rev. 11:17, 18; 16:5; 18:8.

Christ.—Mt. 16:27; 25:31–46; John 5:22, 23, 27, 30; Acts 10:42; Rom. 2:16; I Cor. 4:5; II Cor. 5:10; II Tim. 4:1, 8; Rev. 22:12.

The saints.—Mt. 19:28; I Cor. 6:2.

Sentence rendered according to righteousness.—Gen. 4:7; 18:25; I Sam. 26: 23; Job 34:11, 12; Ps. 62:12; Acts 10: 34, 25; Mt. 16:23; 23:13; Mk. 10:21; John 1:47; 6:70; Acts 10:34, 35.

According to one's deeds.—Pr. 12:14; 24:12; Is. 3:10, 11; 59:18; Jer. 17:10; 32:19; Ez. 7:3; 18:4, 9, 19–32; 33:8– 20; Hos. 4:9; 12:2; Zech. 1:6; Lu. 12: 47, 48; 19:12–24; John 3:20, 21.

Final judgment.—Mt. 13:30; 25:31–46; Acts 17:31; Heb. 9:27; II Pet. 3:7, 10, 12; Rev. 20:11–13. See ''Judgment,'' under SALVATION.

Judgment as criticism.—Mt. 7:3–5; Lu. 6:41, 42; Rom. 2:1; I Cor. 5:12.

Unfair judgment forbidden.—Mt. 7:1; Rom. 14:10, 13; Jas. 4:11.

Must not judge by appearances.—John 7:24; 8:15.

Must not usurp judgment.—Rom. 14:10; I Cor. 4:5. See JUDGES, PUNISHMENT, HELL, JUSTICE.

JUDITH, jū′dith. **Wife of Esau.**—Gen. 26:34.

JUICE. Song of Sol. 8:2.

JULIA, jū′li-à. **A female disciple in Rome.**—Rom. 16:15.

JULIUS, jū′li-us. **A centurion who had Paul in charge.**—Acts 27:1, 3.

JUNIAS, jū′ni-as. **Jewish Christian in Rome.**—Rom. 16:7.

JUNIPER-TREE. I Ki. 19:4, 5; Job 30: 4; Ps. 120:4.

JUPITER. A deity of the Greeks and Romans.—Acts 14:12, 13; 19:35.

JURISDICTION. Lu. 23:7.

JUSHAB-HESED, jū′shăb′-hē′sed. **A son of Zerubbabel.**—I Chr. 3:20.

JUSTICE: God's ways are just.—Gen. 18:25; Deut. 32:3, 4; Neh. 9:32, 33;

Job 4:17; 8:3; Ps. 9:8; 19:9; 67:4; 72:2; 89:14; Is. 45:21; 58:2; Mt. 5:45; Acts 10:34; Rom. 3:8, 26; Rev. 15:3.

Justice of the Messianic King.—Is. 9:7; 11:1–5.

Of Jesus.—Mt. 27:19; John 5:30; 8:3–11, 46; Acts 10:42; 17:31; II Tim. 4:8.

Impartial justice.—Charge to judges—Deut. 1:16, 17. An ideal judge—II Sam. 23:3, 4. A joy—Pr. 21:15. Priestly judges—Ez. 44:23, 24. Righteous judgment—John 7:24; Ps. 75:7.

Justice commanded.—Ex. 20:3–17; Ps. 82:3; Is. 56:1. Commended—Pr. 29:27; Is. 26:7; 33:14–16; Mic. 6:8; Acts 10:22; Phil. 4:8.

Appeals for.—David's—Ps. 58:1. Laborers in vineyard—Mt. 20:11–14. Division of inheritance—Lu. 12:13. The importunate widow—Lu. 18:3. Paul—Acts 21:39; 22:25–29; 25:10–12.

Executors of.—Samuel—I Sam. 12:3–5. The judges—II Chr. 19:5, 6. David—II Sam. 8:15; I Chr. 18:14; Ps. 119:121. Solomon—I Ki. 3:23–28. Righteous branch—Jer. 23:5. Princes of Israel—Ez. 45:9.

Exaction of, under Mosaic law.—Ex. 21:24; Lev. 24:19, 20; Deut. 19:21; Mt. 5:38.

No exaction under gospel.—Mt. 5:38–41; Lu. 6:29; Rom. 12:19–21; 14:13–17; I Cor. 6:7.

Rendering.—To Cæsar and God — Mt. 22:21; Mk. 12:17; Lu. 20:25. To owner of vineyard—Mt. 21:41.

In justice avenged.—Abimelech—Ju. 9:52–56. Adonibezek—Ju. 1:5–7. Dinah and Shechem—Gen. 34:1–31. Saul's sons—II Sam. 21:5, 6. Naboth and Ahab—II Ki. 9:25, 26. The widow—Lu. 18:1–5. Souls under altar—Rev. 6:10.

Overtaken by.—Agag—I Sam. 15:32, 33. Ahab—I Ki. 22:34–38. Jezebel—II Ki. 9:30–37. Herod—Acts 12:23. Haman—Esth. 7:9, 10.

Justice ignored.—Job 12:3, 4; Is. 29:21. Laban—Gen. 31:38–42.

Justice in weights, etc.—Lev. 19:36; Deut. 25:13–15; Pr. 11:1; 16:11; Ez. 45:10; Amos 8:5; Mic. 6:10, 11.

Wresting.—Ex. 23:2–7; Deut. 16:18–20; 27:19; Ps. 82:2.

Bribery prevents.—Ex. 23:8; Deut. 16:19; I Sam. 8:3; 12:3–5; II Chr. 19:7; Is. 26:10; Amos 5:12.

Travesty of.—Trial of Jesus—Mt. 27:11–26; Mk. 15:1–15; Lu. 23:13–25; John 19:1–16. Trial of Naboth—I Ki. 21:11–14.

Reward of.—II Sam. 23:3, 4; Is. 33:14–16; Ez. 18:5–9; Heb. 12:22, 23. See JUDGMENT.

JUSTIFICATION. Gr. *Dikaiosis*. I. As respects redemption.—The act of God—Is. 45:25; 50:8; Rom. 3:26; 8:33.

God cannot justify the wicked.—Ex. 23:7; Pr. 17:15; Is. 5:23.

Not by law.—Law requires perfect obedience—Rom. 10:5; Gal. 3:11, 12; Jas. 2:8–10.

Man cannot attain to it.—A trial permitted—Lev. 18:5. Must do as well as hear or teach—Rom. 2:13, 17–23. Task too great—Rom. 3:9–12, 19, 20, 23.

Not by works of law.—Rom. 3:20, 28; 4:1–5; Gal. 2:16.

Fate of those who return to law.—Gal. 4:21–23, 30; Gal. 5:1–4.

Is obtained only through Christ.—Acts 13:38, 39; Rom. 3:21–26; 5:1, 2, 16–18; I Cor. 6:11; II Cor. 1:19–22; Gal. 2:16, 17; Col. 1:12–14.

Freely by grace.—Rom. 3:24. By faith—Rom. 3:26; 5:1; Gal. 2:16; 3:24; 5:4 f.

Christians manifest it by their works.—Mt. 5:16; Rom. Chs. 6–8; Eph. 2:10; Phil. 2:12, 13; Jas. 2:14–26.

II. Other aspects of justification.—God's decisions justifiable—Gen. 18:25; Ps. 51:4; Rom. 3:4; 8:30–34.

Wrong to justify oneself.—Job 9:20; 11:2, 3; 32:2; Lu. 10:29; 16:15.

Wrong conceptions of.—Job. 11:2; 33:32, 33; Rom. 3:27–30.

One justified rather than the other.—Deut. 25:1; I Ki. 8:32; II Chr. 6:23; Job 32:2; Jer. 3:11–13; Ez. 16:51, 52; Lu. 18:14.

Consciousness of right.—Job 13:18; 27:5; I Cor. 4:4.

Words and works justify one.—Mt. 12:37; Lu. 7:31–35; Jas. 2:25.

III. Word studies.—Five aspects of. (1) Spring of—Grace—Rom. 3:24. (2) Principle of—Faith—Rom. 5:1; Gal. 3:24–26. (3) Ground of—Blood—

Rom. 5:9. (4) Acknowledgment of—Resurrection of Jesus—Rom. 4:25; I Pet. 1:3, 5. (5) Assurance of—Works —Mt. 11:19; Jas. 2:21, 24; Rom. Ch. 6–8.

Involved in four questions.—Who? Believer in Jesus—Acts 13:39; Rom. 3:26. Why? Because God loves us—John 3:16, 17; Rom. 5:8. Where? In the death of Jesus—Rom. 5:8, 9. What? On believing in Christ as personal saviour—Rom. 4:3 f.; 6:17 f.; 10:3–10.

JUSTUS, jŭs'tus. (1) **Surname of Barsabas.**—Acts 1:23.

(2) **A disciple in Corinth.**—Acts 18:7.

(3) **A disciple in Rome.**—Col. 4:11.

JUTAH, jū'tah. **A Levitical city in Judah.**—Josh. 15:55; 21:16.

KABZEEL, kăb'ze-el. **A city in Judah.** —Josh. 15:21; II Sam. 23:20; I Chr. 11:22.

KADESH, kā'desh. **Known as Kadesh-Barnea.**—It lay on the south boundary of the Amorite highlands, in the outermost border of Edom—Num. 34:3–4; Deut. 1:19; Josh. 15:1–3. It lies about sixty miles south of Hebron, almost midway between Dead Sea and Mediterranean coast (Geikie). Was noted as a watering place—Gen. 16:14; Ez. 47:19; 48:28.

A place of note in Abraham's day.— Gen. 14:7; 16:14. He dwelt near there by the fountains of water—Gen. 20:1. Thither Hagar went when cast out— Gen. 16:7, 14.

Israel encamped there preparatory to entering Canaan.—Num. 20:2. The fountain they sought had dried up, so they murmured—Num. 20:2–5. Moses smote the rock and obtained water, but Israel was turned back to the wilderness—Num. 20:22–24. See Moses.

Israel refused passage through Edom. —Num. 20:14–21; 21:21–31; Ju. 11:16–17; Ps. 29:8.

Moses sends spies by way of hill-country.—Num. 13:17–26; Deut. 1:24–25.

Kadesh a camping place frequently resorted to.—Num. 12:16; 13:26; 20:1; 33:36; Deut. 1:46; 2:14.

Miriam died there.—Num. 20:1.

Afterwards it was a battle center for Joshua.—Josh. 10:41.

Caleb calls for the fulfilment of Moses' promise while at Kadesh.—Deut. 1:36; Josh. 14:6–12. See Israel.

KADMIEL, kăd'mi-el. (1) **A Levite.**— Ezra 2:40; Neh. 7:43.

(2) **A man of Judah.**—Ezra 3:9.

(3) **Another Levite.**—Neh. 9:4, 5; 10:9; 12:8, 24.

KADMONITES, kăd'mon-ites. **A Phœnician tribe.**—Gen. 15:19.

KAIN, kā'in. Num. 24:22.

KALLAI, kăl'lai. **A priest.**—Neh. 12:20.

KANAH, kā'nah. (1) **A brook.**—Josh. 16:18; 17:9.

(2) **A city in Asher.**—Josh. 19:28.

KAREAH, ka-rē'ah. **Father of Johanan.** —II Ki. 25:23; Jer. 40:8, 13, 15, 16; 41:11, 13–16; 42:1, 8; 43:2–5.

KARKA, kär-kà. **A town of Judah.**— Josh. 15:3.

KARKOR, kär-kôr. **A city in Gad.**—J u. 8:10.

KARTAH, kär-tah. **A town in Zebulun.** —Josh. 21:34.

KARTAN, kär-tan. **A town in Naphtali.** —Josh. 21:32.

KATTATH, kăt'tath. **A city in Zebulun.** —Josh. 19:15.

KEDAR, kē'dar. (1) **Son of Ishmael.**— Gen. 25:13; I Chr. 1:29.

(2) **A tribe which descended from him.** —Ps. 120:5; Song of Sol. 1:5; Is. 21:16, 17; 42:11; 60:7; Jer. 2:10; 49:28; Ez. 27:21.

KEDEMAH, kĕd'e-mah. **Son of Ishmael.** —Gen. 25:15; I Chr. 1:31.

KEDEMOTH, kĕd'e-mŏth. (1) **A city of Reuben.**—Josh. 13:18; 21:37; I Chr. 6:79.

(2) **Wilderness in Reuben.**—Deut. 2:26.

KEDESH, kē'desh. (1) **A city of Naphtali.**—A city of refuge—Josh. 20:7; 21:32. Army assembled at—Ju. 4:6–9. Heber lived there—Ju. 4:11. Taken by Tiglath-pileser—II Ki. 15:29.

(2) **A city of the Canaanites.**—Josh. 12:22; 19:37.

(3) **A city in Issachar.**—I Chr. 6:72.

(4) **A city of Judah.**—Josh. 15:23.

KEEP. Gen. 2:15; 28:15; Ex. 23:20; Lev. 23:41; Num. 6:24; Ps. 17:8; 91:11; 121:3; John 12:25, 47; Rev. 1:3; 3:3. Apple of eye, As—Deut. 32:10. Anger—Ps. 103:9; Jer. 3:12. Bonds, In—Jude 6. City—Ps. 127:1. Close—

Is. 49:2. Commandments—I Ki. 6:12;
Pr. 3:1; 4:4; Eccl. 12:13; John 14:15.
Company—I Cor. 5:11. Covenant—Ps.
25:10. Covetousness, From—Lu. 12:
15. Evil one, From—John 17:15. Faith
—II Tim. 4:7. Feet of holy ones—I
Sam. 2:9. Feast—I Cor. 5:8. Flock—
Ex. 3:1. Holy—Ex. 20:8. Hour, From
—Rev. 3:10. Hour of prayer—Acts
10:30. Justice—Ps. 106:3. Kindness
—Hos. 12:6. Knowledge—Mal. 2:7.
Law—Jas. 2:10. Lovingkindness—Ex.
34:7. Nothing back—Jer. 42:4. Pass-
over—II Ki. 23:22; Heb. 11:28. Paths
—Pr. 2:20. Pure, Thyself—I Tim. 5:
22. Sabbath—Lev. 23:32. Safe—Mk.
6:20. Saying in mind—Gen. 37:11. Se-
cretly—Ps. 27:5; 31:20. Silence—
Lam. 2:10; I Cor. 14:30. Sheep—Lu.
17:7. Soul—Ps. 25:20; 121:7; Pr. 22:5.
Statutes—Ps. 105:45. See OBEDIENCE.
Strife, From—Pr. 20:3. Testimonies
—Ps. 119:2. Time to—Eccl. 3:6.
Tongue from evil—Ps. 34:13. Tradi-
tion—7:9. Understanding—Pr. 19:8.
Unity of spirit—Eph. 4:3. Ward, In—
Gal. 3:23. Unrighteous—II Pet. 2:9.
Unspotted — Jas. 1:27. Watch — II
Sam. 11:16; Job 21:32; Lu. 2:8. Way
—Gen. 3:24; 18:19. Wisdom—Pr. 3:
21. Word of God—Lu. 11:28; John
8:51; 14:23; Rev. 22:9. Works—Rev.
2:26.

KEEPER. Cattle, Of—Gen. 46:32, 34.
House, Of—Eccl. 12:3. Jehovah is thy
—Ps. 121:5. Sheep, Of—Gen. 4:2.

KEHELATHAH, ke-hĕl′a-thah. An encampment of Israel.—Num. 33:22, 23.
See CAMP, ISRAEL.

KEILAH, kēi′lah. (1) A city of Judah.
—Josh. 15:44; I Sam. 23:1–13; Neh.
3:17, 18.

(2) A descendant of Caleb.—I Chr.
4:19.

KELAIAH, ke-lā′iah. A Levite who
married a foreign wife.—Ezra 10:23.

KELITA, kĕl′i-ta. (1) A priest who explained the law.—Neh. 8:7.

(2) A Levite who helped to seal the covenant.—Neh. 10:10.

KEMUEL, kĕm′u-el. (1) Son of Nahor,
nephew of Abraham.—Gen. 22:21.

(2) A prince of Ephraim.—Num. 34:24.

(3) A Levite.—I Chr. 27:17.

KENAN, kē′nan. Son of Enosh.—I Chr.
1:2.

KENATH, kē′nath. A city in Bashan.—
Num. 32:42; I Chr. 2:23.

KENAZ, kē′naz. (1) Grandson of Esau.
—Gen. 36:11, 15; I Chr. 1:36.

(2) A duke of Edom.—Gen. 36:42; I
Chr. 1:53.

(3) Brother of Caleb, the son of Jephuneh, and father of Othniel, the judge.
—Josh. 15:17; Ju. 1:13; 3:9, 11; I Chr.
4:14.

(4) Grandson of Caleb.—I Chr. 4:15.

KENITES, kē′nītes. One of the tribes
of Palestine in the time of Abraham.
—Gen. 15:19; Num. 24:21, 24; Ju. 1:
16; I Sam. 15:6; 27:10; 3:29; I Chr.
2:55. Heber was a—Ju. 4:11, 17; 5:24.

KENIZZITES, kĕn′iz-zites. Another
tribe of Palestine.—Gen. 15:19.

KEPT. See KEEP.

KERCHIEFS. Ez. 13:18, 21.

KEREN-HAPPUCH, kĕr′en–hăp′puk.
Job's daughter.—Job 42:14.

KERIOTH, kē′ri-ŏth. (1) A city in Judah.—Josh. 15:25.

(2) A Moabite city.—Jer. 48:24, 41;
Amos 2:2.

KERNEL. Amos 9:9.

KEROS, kē′ros. One of the Nethinim
whose descendants returned with Zerubbabel.—Ezra 2:44; Neh. 7:47.

KETURAH, ke-tu-rah. Wife of Abraham.—Gen. 25:1, 4; I Chr. 1:32, 33.

KEY. Ju. 3:25. Uses of—Symbolic of
authority—Is. 22:22; Mt. 16:19 (fig.).
Figurative—Key of abyss—Rev. 9:1;
20:1. Of David—Rev. 3:7. Of death
—Rev. 1:18. Of kingdom of heaven—
Mt. 16:19. In teachings of Jesus—
Key of knowledge—Mt. 16:19.

KEZIAH, ke-zī′ah. A daughter of Job.
—Job 42:14.

KIBROTH-HATTAAVAH, kĭb′roth–
hat-tā′a-vah. An encampment of Israel.—Num. 11:34, 35. See CAMP, IS-
RAEL.

KIBZAIM, kĭb′za-ĭm. A Levitical city
in Ephraim.—Josh. 21:22.

KICK. Deut. 32:15; I Sam. 2:29; Acts
26:14.

KID. See GOATS.

KIDNEYS: Of animals.—Laws concerning the offerings—Lev. 3:4, 10, 15;
7:4. Bullock—Ex. 29:13; Lev. 4:9;

8:16, 25. Ram—Ex. 29:22; Lev. 9:19. Calf—Lev. 9:10. Ox—Lev. 9:19.

Figurative.—Of rams—Is. 34:6.

KIDRON, kĭd'ron. **The brook Kidron.** —II Sam. 15:23; I Ki. 2:37; 15:13; II Ki. 23:6, 12; II Chr. 15:16; 30:14; Jer. 31:40.

Fields of the Kidron.—II Ki. 23:4.

KILL. I Ki. 21:19; Pr. 9:2. And eat— Acts 11:7. Apostles—Lu. 11:49; John 16:2; Acts 9:29. Body—Mt. 10:28. Jehovah, By—Deut. 32:39; II Ki. 5:7; Ps. 44:22; Lu. 12:5. Jesus—Mk. 14:1; Lu. 9:22; 18:33; John 7:19; Acts 3: 15; I Thess. 2:15. Letter of law—II Cor. 3:6. Sabbath, On—Mk. 3:4; Jas. 5:6. Self—Acts 16:27. Soul—Mt. 10: 28. Thou shalt not—Ex. 20:13; Mt. 5:21. See COMMANDMENTS, MURDERER, OFFERING.

KIN. See KINSMAN.

KINAH, kī'nah. **A city in Judah.**—Josh. 15:22.

KIND. After its, his, their—Gen. 1:11, 12, 21, 24, 25; 6:20; 7:14; 8:19; Lev. 11:14, 15, 16, 19, 22, 29; Deut. 14:13– 18; Ez. 47:10. All kinds—Dan. 3:5, 7, 10, 15. Demon, Of—Mt. 17:21; Mk. 9: 29. Divers—II Chr. 16:14. Every king —Mt. 13:47; Jas. 3:7. Fish, Of—Mt. 13:47. Four—Jer. 15:3. Tongues, Of —I Cor. 12:10. Voices, Of—I Cor. 14: 10. See KINDNESS.

KINDLE. Anger—See ANGER. Coals— II Sam. 22:9, 13; Pr. 18:8. Fire—See FIRE.

Strife.—See STRIFE. Wrath—See ANGER.

KINDNESS. To the poor—Deut. 29:19; Job 29:12, 13; Pr. 19:17; Acts 10:2. Pharaoh's butler—Gen. 40:12–14. Rahab to spies—Josh. 2:12. Israel to Kenites—I Sam. 15:6. David to Saul's friends—I Sam. 24:11; II Sam. 9:7; 10:2–5. Barbarians to Paul, etc.— Acts 28:2.

To those in distress.—Death of Sarah— Gen. 23:5, 6. David's army—II Sam. 17:28, 29. Esther's people—Esth. 5:1– 8. Ruth—Ruth 2:5–13.

To brethren.—Rom. 12:10; Gal. 6:1, 2; I Thess. 4:9; II Pet. 1:7; Heb. 13:1; I John 3:17. To erring brethren—Mt. 18:21–22; Jas. 5:19, 20.

To enemies.—Esau's forgiveness—Gen. 33:8, 9. Shimei—II Sam. 16:11–14.

The wounded—Lu. 10:33–35. Anyone —Pr. 25:21; Rom. 12:20.

To prisoners.—Judah—II Chr. 28:15. Syrian army—II Ki. 6:21, 22. Jehoiachin—II Ki. 25:27–30; Jer. 52:31–34. Jeremiah—Jer. 38:12, 13. Christians —Heb. 10:34.

To servants.—Abraham's—Gen. 24:12– 18. Centurion's—Lu. 7:2, 3. Servant in parable—Mt. 18:27. Onesimus— Philemon 10:17. Servants and masters—Eph. 6:5–9.

To animals.—Gen. 24:19, 20; Ex. 23:5; Num. 32:16; Mt. 9:36; 18:12–14; Lu. 15:4, 5; John 10:11–15.

Mutual kindness.—David and Jonathan —I Sam. 19:1–7; 20:1–42. Naomi and Ruth—Ruth 1:8–18. **Remembered kindness:** Of Israel to God—Jer. 2:2, 3. David to Barzillai—II Sam. 19:33. **Unremembered kindness:** Joash—II Chr. 24:22. Nine lepers—Lu. 17:12–18.

Prayers beseeching.—Ps. 17:7; 40:10, 11; 51:1; 69:16–18.

Kindness of Jesus.—To little children— Mt. 19:14; Mk. 10:14; Lu. 18:16. To lepers—Mk. 1:41. To the blind at Jerusalem—John Ch. 9. Near Jericho Lu. 18:35–43. To the palsied—Mt. 9:2. To those of any disease—Mt. 11:4–6; Mk. 5:19. To the bereaved—John 11: 1–44; Lu. 7:13–15. To the disciples— John 15:13–16. To the multitudes— Mt. 9:36; 14:14; 15:32; Mk. 6:34; 8:2.

Lovingkindness of God.—Neh. 9:17; Ps. 26:3; 36:7–10; 42:8; 63:3–8; 103:4, 5; 107:43; 119:149; Is. 63:7–9; Jer. 9:24; 31:3–6. See GENTLENESS.

KINDRED. See KINSMAN.

KINE. Amos 4:1. Dray ark—I Sam. 6:7–14. Dream concerning—Gen. 41: 2–27. See CATTLE.

KINGDOM. Against kingdom—Mk. 13: 8; Lu. 21:10. Divided against itself— Mt. 12:25; Lu. 11:17. Division of— See ISRAEL. Everlasting—Ps. 145:13; Dan. 4:3. God, Of—See JESUS, KINGDOM OF. Half of—Mk. 6:23. Heathen, Of—II Chr. 20:6; Neh. 9:22; Is. 10:10; Jer. 10:7. Heaven, Of—See JESUS, KINGDOM OF. Israel—See ISRAEL, KINGDOM OF. Judah—See JUDAH, KINGDOM OF. Worth, Of the—Jer. 1:15. Prophecy concerning—Dan. 2:37–44; 4:3, 36; 5:7–31; 7:14–27. World, Of—Jer.

25:26; Mt. 4:8; Lu. 4:5; Rev. 11:15. Earth—II Chr. 36:23; Is. 37:16, 20; Jer. 15:4; 25:9; 29:18; 34:1, 17.

KINGS: King of kings.—Ezra 7:12; Ez. 26:7; Dan. 2:37. Jesus the true King— Mt. 2:1–3; John 18:36–37; Rev. 17:14. See Jesus, Kingship of—Lu. 2ª21.

Earliest.—Pharaoh—Gen. 12:15. Four kings war with kings of Sodom, Gomorrah, etc.—Gen. 14:1–10. The two Abimelechs—Gen. Chs. 20 and 26.

God the chooser.—Deut. 17:14–15; I Sam. 9:17; 16:12; II Sam. 7:8; I Ki. 11:34–35; 19:15.

Israel desires a.—I Sam. 8:5, 19, 20. To be as other nations—I Sam. 8:5, 20; 12:12; I Chr. 28:5, 6; Dan. 2:21; 4:17.

Israel is warned.—I Sam. 8:9. A rejection of Jehovah—I Sam. 8:7. Pronounced a sin—I Sam. 12:11–18.

Evil methods of a king described.—I Sam. 8:11–18; 22:17–18; II Sam. 1:15; 4:9–12; I Ki. 2:23, 25, 31.

Restrictions required in a.—Shall not multiply horses—Deut. 17:16. Shall not multiply wives—Deut. 17:17. Shall copy this law into a book—Deut. 17: 18–20. Not foreigners—Deut. 17:15.

Nature of appointment.—By anointing —Ju. 9:8–15; I Sam. 9:16; 10:1; 15:1; 16:3, 12, 13; II Sam. 2:4; 5:3; 12:7; 19:21; I Ki. 1:39; 19:16; 23:30; II Ki. 9:1–12; 11:12; I Chr. 11:3; 29:22; II Chr. 23:11; Is. 45:1. By proclamation —II Sam. 15:10; I Ki. 1:33–34; II Ki. 9:13; 11:12. By oath—II Ki. 11:4. By selection of the people—I Chr. 1: 43–51. By lot—I Sam. 10:20, 21. By succession—II Sam. 7:12–16; I Ki. 1: 28–30; II Chr. 21:34; Ps. 89:35–37.

Duties.—To be righteous—Pr. 16:12. To render true judgment—Pr. 16, 10, 13. To search out matters—Pr. 25:2. To establish the land in justice—Pr. 29:4, 14. To be temperate—Pr. 31:4–5. To succor their people—Is. 49:23. To prevent robbery—Jer. 21:12. To exercise clemency—I Sam. 11:13; II Sam. 16: 10–12.

Ceremonies at inauguration.—Crowning —II Ki. 11:12; II Chr. 23:11; Ps. 21:3. Proclaiming with trumpets—II Sam. 15:10; I Ki. 1:34; II Ki. 9:13; 11:14. Enthroning—I Ki. 1:35, 46; II Ki. 11:

19. Girding on sword—Ps. 45:3. See Anointing.

Chief officers of.—Grouped in—II Sam. 8:16–18, 20, 23–25. Also I Ki. 4:1–19; II Ki. 22:14; I Chr. 27:25; II Chr. 34:22.

Compensation of the king.—Voluntary contributions—I Sam. 10:27; 16:20; I Chr. 12:39, 40. Spoils—II Sam. 12: 30. Tribute from foreign nations—I Ki. 4:21–25; II Chr. 8:8; 17:11. Tithing of the land—I Ki. 4:7–19. Tax on foreign merchandise—I Ki. 10:15; II Sam. 8:2; 20:24. Their own flocks and herds—II Chr. 32:29. Poll tax—Mt. 17:24–27.

Obeisance paid to.—I Sam. 25:41; II Sam. 9:6, 8; I Ki. 1:16, 23; Mt. 27:29; Dan. 2:4; 6:6, 21.

Decrees unchangeable.—Esth. 8:8; Dan. 6:8, 9, 12–15.

Prayer for required.—I Tim. 2:1, 2. See Israel, Judah.

KINSFOLK. Lu. 1:58; 2:44; 21:16.

KINSMAN. "*Goel*": To support, redeem, avenge.

Duties of kinsman.—Must buy back property—Lev. 25:23–27. Must redeem him who sold himself—Lev. 25: 47–49. Must marry widow and raise up seed—Gen. 38:8; Deut. 25:5–10; Mt. 22:25; Lu. 20:28. Must avenge his blood—Ex. 21:12–14; Num. 35:9–34; Deut. 19:1–13; Job 19:25. Whole clan helps—II Sam. 14:7. Make restitution to kin for guilt—Num. 5:5–8.

Kinsfolk.—Zimri's slaughter—I Ki. 16: 11. Seeking Jesus among—Lu. 2:44. Elizabeth's—Lu. 1:58.

Kin.—Uncover nakedness—Lev. 18:6; 20:19. May defile for—Lev. 21:2. May redeem him—Lev. 25:49. Kin to king —II Sam. 19:42. Jesus among—Mk. 6:4.

Kinswoman.—Uncovering nakedness— Lev. 18:12–13, 17. Name for understanding—Pr. 7:4. Kinswoman of Mary—Lu. 1:36.

Naomi's kinsman.—Ruth 2:1, 20. Hebrew custom indicating willingness to marry—Ruth 3:9. Boaz pledges himself—Ruth 3:12–13. Meets a near kinsman—Ruth 4:1–8.

Kinsman fails in his duty.—Job 19:14; Ps. 38:11; Lu. 21:16. Not to be invited to feast—Lu. 14:12.

Paul's sympathy for.—Rom. 9:3. His own kinsmen—Rom. 16:7, 11, 21.

Miscellaneous.—Servant of high priest—John 18:26. Belonging to Cornelius' family—Acts 10:24.

KIR, kir. An Assyrian district.—I Ki. 16:9; Is. 22:6; Amos 1:5; 9:7.

KIR OF MOAB. Is. 15:1.

KIR-HARESETH, kir–hăr'e-seth. A city of Moab.—II Ki. 3:25; Is. 16:7.

KIR-HERES, kir–hē'res. Same as Kirharesheth.—Is. 16:11; 48:31.

KIRIATH, kir'i-ăth. Josh. 18:28.

KIRIATHAIM, kir'i-a-thā'im. (1) A city of Reuben.—Num. 32:37; Josh. 13:19; Jer. 48:1, 23; Ez. 25:9.

(2) **A city of Naphtali.**—I Chr. 6:76.

KIRIATH-ARBA, kir'i-ăth-är'ba. A city in Judæa.—Gen. 23:2; Josh. 14:15; 15:54; 20:7; Ju. 1:10; Neh. 11:25. See ARBA.

KIRIATHARIM, kir'i-ăth-ā'rim. Ezra 2:25. See KEREATH-JEARIM.

KIRIATH-BAAL, kir'i-ăth-bā'al. Josh. 15:60. See KIRIATH-JEARIM, BAAL.

KIRIATH-HUZOTH, kir'i-ăth-hū'zoth. Residence of Balak.—Num. 22:39. See GOD, JESUS, ISRAEL, JUDAH.

KIRIATH-JEARIM, kir'i-ath-jē'a-rĭm. (1) **A city of Judah.**—Josh. 9:17; 15:9, 60; 18:14, 15; Ju. 18:12; I Sam. 6:21; 7:1, 2; I Chr. 13:5, 6; II Chr. 1:4; Neh. 7:29; Jer. 26:20.

(2) I Chr. 2:50–53.

KIRIATH-SANNAH, kir'i-ath-săn'nah. A city in hill-country of Judah.—Josh. 15:49.

KIRIATH-SEPHER, kir'i-ăth-sē'pher. Same as Kiriathsannah—Josh. 15:15, 16; Ju. 1:11, 12.

KISH, kĭsh. (1) **Father of Saul.**—I Sam. 9:1, 3; 10:11, 21; 14:51; II Sam. 21:14; I Chr. 8:33; 9:39; 12:1; 26:28.

(2) **Another Benjamite.**—I Chr. 8:30; 9:36.

(3) **A Levite.**—I Chr. 23:21, 22; 24:29.

(4) **Another Levite.**—II Chr. 29:12.

(5) **Ancestor of Mordecai.**—Esth. 2:5.

KISHI, kĭsh'-i. A Levite.—I Chr. 6:44.

KISHION, kĭsh'i-ŏn. A city in Issachar.—Josh. 19:20; 21:28.

KISHON, kī'shon. A river.—Ju. 4:7, 13, 21; I Ki. 15:40; Ps. 83:9.

KISS: Of a kinsman. — Men: Jacob kisses Isaac—Gen. 27:26, 27. Laban kisses Jacob—Gen. 29:13. Esau kisses Jacob—Gen. 33:4. Jacob kisses Joseph's sons—Gen. 48:16. Joseph kisses Jacob—Gen. 50:1. Aaron kisses Moses—Ex. 4:27. Moses kisses father-in-law—Ex. 18:7. David kisses Absalom—II Sam. 14:33. Sons and daughters—Gen. 31:28, 55. Joseph kisses brethren—Gen. 45:15.

Men.—Samuel kisses Saul—I Sam. 10:1. David kisses Jonathan—I Sam. 20:41. Absalom kissed every Israelite—II Sam. 15:5. David kissed Barzillai—II Sam. 19:39. Joab kissed Amasa—II Sam. 20:9. Elisha asks permission to kiss his father—I Ki. 19:20.

Women.—Naomi kisses daughter-in-law—Ruth 1:9. Orpah kisses Naomi—Ruth 1:14.

Men and women.—Jacob kissed Rachel—Gen. 29:11.

Of seducer.—Pr. 7:13.

Of an enemy.—Pr. 27:6.

As a greeting, a holy kiss.—Rom. 16:16; I Cor. 16:20; II Cor. 13:12; I Thess. 5:26.

As a manifestation of love.—Song of Sol. 1:2; 8:1; Lu. 7:38, 45; 15:20; Acts 20:37; I Pet. 5:14.

In betrayal.—Mt. 26:48, 49; Mk. 14:44, 45; 15:20; Lu. 22:47, 48.

Kissing of idols.—Baal—I Ki. 19:18. Calves—Hos. 13:2. Kissed my hands—Job 31:27.

Figurative.—Righteousness and peace kiss—Ps. 85:10. Kisseth the lips—Pr. 24:26. Kiss son—Ps. 2:12.

KITE. A bird—Lev. 11:14; Deut. 14:13; Is. 34:15.

KITRON, kĭt'ron. A city of Zebulun.—Ju. 1:30.

KITTIM, kĭt'tim. Grandson of Japheth.—Gen. 10:4; I Chr. 1:7.

KNEAD. Gen. 18:6. Dough—Hos. 7:4.

KNEADING-TROUGH. Ex. 8:3; 12:34; Deut. 28:5, 17.

KNEEL. Mt. 17:14. Camels—Gen. 24:11. Down—Mt. 27:29; Mk. 1:40; 10:17; Acts 21:5. Jehovah, Before—Ps. 95:6. Prayer, In—See PRAYER, BOW, WORSHIP.

KNEW. Gen. 3:7; 28:16. Face to face—Deut. 34:10. Gift of God—John 4:10. I never—Mt. 7:23. Language, Not—Ps. 81:5. Me—John 8:19. Men—Mt. 14:35. Not that Jehovah—Ju. 16:20. Skin of face shone, Not—Ex. 34:29. Truth, Of a—John 17:8. What it was —Ex. 16:15. Whence they were—Josh. 2:4, 1. Ye not that I must be—Lu. 2: 49. See KNOWLEDGE.

KNIFE. Cut themselves with—I Ki. 18: 28. Flint, Of—Josh. 5:2. Jaw teeth as —Pr. 30:14. Put to throat—Pr. 23:2. Took—Gen. 22:10; Ju. 19:29. See TOOLS AND IMPLEMENTS.

KNIT. Bones and sinews, Together with —Job 10:11. Heart shall—I Chr. 12: 17. Love, Together in—Col. 2:2. Man, As one—Ju. 20:11. Soul, With—I Sam. 18:1. Together—Eph. 4:16; Col. 2:19.

KNOCK. And it shall be opened—Mt. 7:7, 8; Lu. 11:9, 10. Cometh and—Lu. 12:36. Door, At—Lu. 13:25. I stand at the door and—Rev. 3:20. Peter continued—Acts 12:16. Voice of my beloved—Song of Sol. 5:2.

KNOP. Ex. 25:33.

KNOWLEDGE, Divine: Practical application.—To prophesy—Deut. 29:29; 30:1-3; Dan. 2:19, 20, 27, 28, 45, 47. To prayer: Daily needs—Mt. 6:8. Special—II Ki. 11:14-20; Is. 37:14-23. Forgiveness—Ps. 44:21; 69:5; Mt. 18: 35. God's knowledge of man's needs —Ps. 94:11; 103:14; 139:1-6.

Human.—The Bible reveals God and duty, the highest and wisest subjects of thought; hence, human ignorance of nature is described—Job Chs. 38 and 39.

One subject at issue between God and man in each age. Adamic.—The sovereignty of God—Gen. 3:5, 9; 11:5; 18:20, 21; Heb. Ch. 11.

Mosaic.—Is Jehovah the God?—Ex. 7: 16, 17; 16:12; 31:13; Deut. 6:4.

Gospel.—Is Jesus the Christ, God's Son? —Mt. 16:16, 17, 20; Mk. 14:61-64; Lu. 2:11; John 1:1-3, 14; 11:27; 20:30; Acts 2:36; 4:12. Christ alone can reveal God—Mt. 11:27; Lu. 10:22. Lack of this knowledge is darkness and death—Hos. 4:6; Mt. 4:16. This knowledge is eternal life—John 1:4;

17:3. Not to be merely intellectual, but with the heart—Deut. 6:5, 6; Mt. 22:37; Mk. 12:30; Lu. 10:27; Rom. 10:9, 10; I Cor. 8:1-3; 13:1-3; Eph. 6: 24. With the life—Deut. 8:6; 11:26-28; 30:15-20; Mt. 7:24, 25; Lu. 6:47, 48; John 7:17; 8:31, 32; 15:1, 2; Rom. 1:21; 2:19-21; Heb. 6:4-6; 10:38, 39; Rev. 22:14.

Gift of God.—I Ki. 3:12; Dan. 1:17-20; 2:21; 9:22; Jer. 11:18; I Cor. 12:8; Eph. 12:8.

Fear of God the beginning of knowledge. —Ps. 111:10; Pr. 1:7; 9:10; 15:33; Is. 11:2.

Sin destroys man's knowledge of God.— I Sam. 2:12; Jer. 2:8; 9:3-6; 11:10; John 3:19, 20; Rom. 1:25, 28; Eph. 2:1, 11, 12.

It is power.—Neh. 10:28, 29; Pr. 24:5; Rom. 15:14; Eph. 3:18, 19.

Who possess it?—The wise—Pr. 5:2; 10: 14; 14:6; 15:2; 18:15; 21:11; Eccl. 12:9. The prudent—Pr. 13:16; 18:15.

Knowledge of the truth.—Lu. 1:77; John 8:32; I Tim. 2:4; II Tim. 3:7; Heb. 10:26; II Cor. 4:6; Phil. 3:8; Col. 1:9.

Value of.—Ps. 119:98-100; Pr. 8:10; Mal. 2:7; II Pet. 2:20. Is transient— I Cor. 13:8, 9. To increase—Is. 11:9; Dan. 12:4.

Knowledge of good and evil.—Tree of— Gen. 2:9, 17; 3:5. Discerning between —I Ki. 3:9. Children void of—Deut. 1:39.

Knowledge of sin.—John 9:41; 15:22, 24; Rom. 3:20; 7:7-12.

Holding to the form of.—Rom. 2:20-24; 6:17; II Tim. 1:13.

Wicked have no desire for.—Job 21:14; Pr. 1:22, 29; Hos. 4:6; Rom. 1:28.

What false knowledge does.—Puffs up— I Cor. 8:1; I Tim. 6:3-5. Destroys—I Cor. 8:11.

Desire for truth.—Ps. 119:66; Pr. 2:10; 15:14. Prayer for—I Ki. 3:9; II Chr. 1:10-12; John 17:3, 8, 23.

Fruitless knowledge.—Job 15:2-3; 35: 16; 38:2; 42:3; Is. 44:25; Rom. 10:2; I Cor. 1:19-21; 2:6; 3:19, 20.

Hindrance of.—Lu. 11:52; Rom. 1:18.

Responsibility for.—Deut. 17:12; I Sam. 2:3; Mal. 2:7; Lu. 12:47; John 9:41; Rom. 1:19-21; 2:17-21; Jas. 4:17. See GOD, KNOWLEDGE OF, WISDOM.

KOA, kō′à. Ez. 23:23.

KOHATH, kō′hath. **Son of Levi.**—Gen. 46:11; Ex. 6:16–18; Num. 3:17–29; 4:4, 15; 7:9; 16:1; 26:57, 58; Josh. 21: 5; 26:26; I Chr. 6:1, 2, 16, 22, 38, 61, 66, 70; 15:5; 23:6, 12. See LEVITES, PRIESTS.

KOHATHITES. Descendants of Kohath. —Num. 3:27, 30; 4:18, 34, 37; 10:21; 26:57; Josh. 21:4, 10; I Chr. 6:33, 54; 9:32; II Chr. 20:19; 29:12; 34:12. See LEVITES, PRIESTS.

KOLAIAH, ko-lā′iah. (1) **Father of Ahab.**—Jer. 29:21.

(2) **A Benjamite.**—Neh. 11:7.

KORAH, kō′rah. (1) **Son of Esau.**— Gen. 36:5, 14, 18; I Chr. 1:35.

(2) **A grandson of Esau.**—Gen. 36:16.

(3) **Great-grandson of Levi who conspired against Moses and Aaron.**—Ex. 6:21, 24; Num. 16:1–49; 26:9–11; 27: 3; I Chr. 6:37; 9:19.

(4) **Son of Hebron.**—I Chr. 2:43.

(5) **Grandson of Kohath.**—I Chr. 6:22; Ps. 42, 44, 45, 46–49, 84, 85, 87, 88 (titles).

KORAHITES. Ex. 6:24; Num. 26:58; I Chr. 9:19, 31; 12:6.

KORE, kō′re. (1) **A descendant of Korah.**—I Chr. 9:19; 26:1, 19.

(2) **A Levite.**—II Chr. 31:14.

KUSHAIAH, ku-shā′iah. I Chr. 15:17.

LAADAH, lā′a-dah. **Grandson of Judah.**—I Chr. 4:21.

LABAN, lā′ban. (1) **Father of Rachel and Leah, Jacob's wives.**—Gen. 24: 29, 30; 25:20; 27:43; 28:2, 5; 29:5, 10– 29; 30:25–42; 31:1–55; 32:4; 46:18, 25.

(2) **An encampment of Israel.**—Deut. 1:1. See CAMP, ISRAEL.

LABOR. Josh. 7:3; Neh. 4:22; 5:13; Job 20:18; 39:11; Ps. 90:10; 107:12; Pr. 5:10; 16:26; Is. 47:12, 15; 58:3; Jer. 20:18; Dan. 6:14; Hos. 12:8; Jonah 4:10; Hab. 2:13; 3:17; Mt. 11:28; Lu. 5:5; Rev. 14:13.

Is as old as man.—Gen. 1:28; 2:5, 15; 3:17–19.

Appointed of God in the law.—Ex. 20:9; 23:12; 34:21; Deut. 5:13; Lu. 13:14.

In Egypt.—Ex. 5:9; Deut. 26:7.

Approved by man.—Ps. 104:23; Eccl. 5:12; Acts 20:35; I Cor. 4:12; Eph. 4:28.

Benefits of.—Ps. 128:2; Pr. 10:16; 13:11; 14:23; Eccl. 5:12.

Labor of fools.—Eccl. 10:15.

Labor of hands.—Gen. 5:29; 31:42; Ps. 128:2; Pr. 21:25; Eccl. 2:11; 9:9, 10; Hag. 1:11; 2:17; I Cor. 4:12; Eph. 4: 28; I Thess. 4:11.

Of harvest.—Ex. 23:16; Deut. 28:33; John 4:36–38; Jas. 5:4.

Fruits of labor.—Eccl. 2:24; 3:13; 4:9; 5:18, 19; Ez. 29:20; I Cor. 3:8, 9; Phil. 1:22.

Labor not for that which satisfieth not. —Is. 55:2; John 6:27.

Labor in vain.—Deut. 6:10, 11; Josh. 24: 13; Job 9:29; 39:16; Ps. 78:46; Ps. 105:44; 109:11; 127:1; Eccl. 1:3; 2:10, 11, 18–24; 4:8; 5:15, 16; 6:7; 8:15–17; Is. 49:4; Jer. 3:24; 51:58; Ez. 23:29. See Is. 65:23; I Cor. 15:58; Gal. 4:11; Phil. 2:16; I Thess. 3:5.

Lilies toil not.—Mt. 6:28; Lu. 12:27.

Paul sets example.—Acts 18:3; 20:33– 35; I Cor. 4:12; 9:17–19; II Cor. 6:5; 11:23; Phil. 4:11–13; I Thess. 2:9; 4: 11, 12; II Thess. 3:7–13; I Tim. 4:10.

Labor in gospel.—Rom. 16:6, 12; I Cor. 3:5–15; 15:10, 58; II Cor. 10:15; Gal. 4:11; Phil. 1:22; 2:16; 4:3; Col. 1:29; I Thess. 1:3; 2:9; 3:5; 5:12; I Tim. 4:10; 5:17; Heb. 6:10; Rev. 2:2, 3.

Labor of love.—I Thess. 1:3; Heb. 6:10.

Labor in childbirth.—Gen. 35:16, 17; Mic. 4:10. See JESUS' TEACHING ON LABOR, WORK, WORKER, WORKS OF GOD.

LABORER. Deut. 25:4; Mt. 20:1, 2, 8. Worthy of his hire—Lu. 10:7; I Cor. 9:9; I Tim. 5:18; Jas. 5:4. Few—Mt. 9:37; Lu. 10:2. Send forth—Mt. 9:38; Lu. 10:2.

LACE. Blue—Ex. 28:28, 37; 39:21, 31.

LACHISH, lā′kish. A town of Judah— Josh. 15:39. Taken by Joshua—Josh. 10:31.

Strifes of.—Fortified by Rehoboam—II Chr. 11:9. Besieged by Sennacherib —II Ki. 18:13–17; 19:8; II Chr. 32:9. By Nebuchadrezzar—Jer. 34:7. Amaziah slain at—II Ki. 14:19.

Prophecy concerning.—Mic. 1:13.

LACK. I Ki. 11:22; II Sam. 2:30; I Cor. 16:17. Afflictions, Of—Col. 1:24. Any that—Acts 4:34. Anything— Deut. 8:9; Lu. 22:35. Bread—II Sam. 3:29; Pr. 12:9. Daily food, Of—Jas.

2:15. Faith, In—I Thess. 3:10. Five —Gen. 18:28. Flocks—Jer. 23:4. Gain, Of—Pr. 31:11. Had no—Ex. 16:18. He shall not—Pr. 28:27. Instruction, Of—Pr. 5:23. Knowledge, Of—Hos. 4:6. Madmen, Do I—I Sam. 21:15. Not one—II Sam. 17:22. Nothing— Deut. 2:7; I Sam. 30:19; I Ki. 4:27. Oil—Eccl. 9:8. One thing thou—Mk. 10:21; Lu. 18:22. Parts, In—Lev. 22: 23. Prey, Of—Job 4:11. Salt—Lev. 2:13. Service, In—Phil. 2:30. Tribe —Ju. 21:3. Truth is—Is. 59:15. Understanding, Of—Pr. 10:21. What lack I yet?—Mt. 19:20. Wisdom— Jas. 1:5. Young lions do—Ps. 34:10.

LAD. Gen. 22:5; 37:2; II Ki. 2:24. Because of the—Gen. 21:12-20. Bless the—Gen. 48:16. Brought alive—Acts 20:12. Cannot leave father—Gen. 44: 22-34. Held him by hand—Ju. 16:26. Here, There is a—John 6:9. Lay not hand on—Gen. 22:12. Saw them—II Sam. 17:18. Send the—Gen. 43:8; I Sam. 20:21-41.

LADAN, lā'dan. (1) **An Ephraimite.**— I Chr. 7:26.

(2) **A Levite.**—I Chr. 23:7-9; 26:21.

LADDER. Jacob's—Gen. 28:12.

LADEN. Neh. 4:17; Rev. 21:9. Asses— Gen. 44:13; Neh. 13:15. Beasts—Gen. 45:17. Blood, With—Pr. 28:17. Good things—Gen. 45:23. Grain, With— Gen. 42:26. Guilt, With—Pr. 21:8. Heavy—Mt. 11:28. Iniquity, With— Is. 1:4. Pledges, With—Hab. 2:6. Silver, With—Zeph. 1:11. Sins, With —II Tim. 3:6. See BURDEN. Well—Ps. 144:14. Yoke, With—I Ki. 12:11.

LADY. Ju. 5:29; II John 1. See WOMEN.

LAEL, lā'el. **A Levite.**—Num. 3:24.

LAHAD, lā'had. **A man of Judah.**—I Chr. 4:2.

LAHMAN, läh'man. **A city of Judah.** —Josh. 15:40.

LAHMI, läh'mi. **A brother of Goliath the giant.**—I Chr. 20:5.

LAID. Job 15:20; 24:1. Charge—Rom. 3:9. Crown, Up—II Tim. 4:8. Down —Ps. 3:5. Food, up—Gen. 41:48, 49. Foundation—I Cor. 3:10. Hand on— Lam. 4:6. Horn in dust—Job 16:15. Life, down—I John 3:16. Plot against —Acts 20:3. Shoulders, Upon—Gen.

9:23. Treasure, Up—Job 20:26; **Jas.** 5:3. Yoke, Upon—Lam. 3:28.

LAIN. Gen. 26:10; Lu. 23:53; John 20:12.

LAISH, lā'ish. (1) **A Sidonian city.**— Ju. 18:7, 14, 27, 29; Is. 10:30.

(2) **A Benjamite.**—I Sam. 25:44; II Sam. 3:15.

LAISHAH, lā'ish-ah. Is. 10:30.

LAKE. Gennesaret.—Lu. 5:1.

Fire, Of.—Rev. 14:15; 19:20; 20:10; 21: 8. See HELL.

LAKKUM, läk'kum. **A city in Naphtali.**—Josh. 19:33.

LAMB. Described as: Gentle—Jer. 11: 19. Playful—Ps. 114:4, 6. Patient— Is. 53:7; Jer. 11:19.

Used for: Clothing—Pr. 27:26. Food— Deut. 32:14; Amos 6:4.

Traffic in.—Ez. 39:18.

Offered in sacrifice.—Gen. 22:7, 8; Ex. 12:3, 4, 5, 21; 29:39, 41; Lev. 3:7; 4:32, 35; 5:6, 7; 9:3; 12:6, 8; 14:10, 13, 21, 24, 25; 17:3; 22:32; 23:12; Num. 6:12, 14; 7:15-81; 15:5, 11; 28:4, 7, 8, 13, 14, 21, 29; 29:4, 10, 15-37; I Sam. 7:9; Is. 34:6; 66:3; Ez. 45:15; 46:4, 5, 6, 7, 11, 15.

Slain by wild beasts.—I Sam. 17:34.

Disciples sent among wolves.—Lu. 10:3.

Covenant between Abimelech and Abraham.—Gen. 21:28-30.

Parable of.—II Sam. 12:3, 4, 6.

Figurative use.—Ps. 37:20; 144:4, 6; Is. 5:17; 11:6; 16:1; 40:11; 65:25; Hos. 4:16; Lu. 10:3; John 21:15.

Christ called.—Is. 53:7; John 1:29, 36; Acts 8:32; I Pet. 1:19; Rev. 5:6, 8, 12, 13; 6:1, 16; 7:9, 10, 14, 17; 12:11; 13:8, 11; 14:1, 4, 10; 15:3; 17:14; 19:7, 9; 21:14, 22, 23; 22:1, 3.

LAMECH, lā'měk. Heb. *"A strong young man."*—**Son of Methusael.**— Gen. 4:18; 5:25. Marries Adah and Zillah—Gen. 4:19. Father of Noah— Gen. 5:28, 29; Lu. 3:36; Jabal—Gen. 4:20; Jubal—Gen. 4:21; Tubal-cain and Naamah—Gen. 4:22. Refers to Cain and the murder of Abel and prophesies concerning his own curse —Gen. 4:23.

LAMENESS.—Disqualified for priesthood—Lev. 21:18. Lame not to be offered in sacrifice—Deut. 15:21; Mal. 1:8. Lame thrust in way of David's army—II Sam. 5:8. Cast off nation described as—Mic. 4:6. Feet to the lame—Job 29:15. Lame man leap as a hart—Is. 35:6. Bring in lame—Lu. 14:21. Tell John the lame walk—Mt. 11:5. Legs of, not equal—Pr. 26:7. Lame healed by Christ—Mt. 11:5; 21:14; Lu. 7:22. By apostles—Acts Ch. 3; 8:7. Figurative use—Heb. 12:13.

LAMENTATION. Abner, For—II Sam. 3:31. Babylon, For—Rev. 18:10. Christ, For—Lu. 23:27. Husband, For—II Sam. 11:26; Job 27:15. Jacob, For—Gen. 50:10. Nations, For—Is. 14:31; 49:3–5. Josiah, For—II Chr. 35:25. Saul, For—II Sam. 1:17. Stephen, For—Acts 8:2. Tyrus, For—Ez. 26: 17. See MOURNING.

LAMP. Nerah, To glisten (*Lappid*, a torch):

Used in tabernacle.—Ex. 25:37; 27:20; 35:14; 39:37; 40:4; Lev. 24:2, 4; Num. 4:9; 8:2, 3.

In temple.—I Sam. 3:3; I Ki. 7:49; I Chr. 28:15; II Chr. 4:20, 21; 13:11; 29:7.

Used in marriage ceremonies.—Mt. 25:1, 3, 7, 8. In sacrifices—Gen. 15:17. To light houses—Mt. 5:15.

Used figuratively.—Taken away from Judah—Jer. 25:10. To search Jerusalem—Zeph. 1:12. David to have a—I Ki. 11:36; II Ki. 8:19. Of wicked put out—Job 18:6; Pr. 13:9; 20:20. To light the way—II Sam. 22:29; Job 29:3; Ps. 119:105; 132:17; Pr. 6:23; II Pet. 1:19. Emblem of salvation—Is. 62:1; Zech. 4:2. Seven lamps before throne—Rev. 4:5. Description of John—John 5:35. Light of lamp not needed—Rev. 22:5. The lamp of the body is the eye—Mt. 6:22. Lamp thereof is the Lamb—Rev. 21:23. His God gave him a lamp in Jerusalem—I Ki. 15:4.

Lamps or torches.—Gideon—Ju. 7:16–20. War chariots—Nah. 2:4. Behemoth—Job 41:19. Samson's—Ju. 15: 4, 5. Hope for Judah—Zech. 12:6. Daniel's vision of a man—Dan. 10:6. Ezekiel's living creatures—Ez. 1:13. Star falls from heaven—Rev. 8:10. Pursuers of Jesus—John 18:3.

LAND. Creation of.—Gen. 1:9, 10; Ps. 95:5. Appeared on third day—Gen.

1:9. Deluged because of wickedness —Gen. 7:19–22. Noah's posterity settled in Land of Shinar—Gen. 11:2. From thence scattered everywhere—Gen. 11:9.

Jehovah covenants with Abraham concerning land for posterity.—Gen. 12: 1–7; 13:14–15; 15:18–20; 17:8; 24:7; Num. 32:11. Land rich and fertile—Num. 13:23–27; Deut. 11:9–15; 26:10, 15; Josh. 5:12. Unclean because of inhabitants—Deut. 9:4–5; Ezra 9:11–12.

Israel's relation to Land of Egypt.—Joseph sold into—Gen. 39:1; 40:15. He is set over the land—Gen. 41:41–45. Provides against famine—Gen. 41:46–57. His brethren visit Egypt to buy food—Gen. Chs. 42–44. Jacob and family move there—Gen. 45:16–28; 46:1–7; 47:1–6. They dwell in the Land of Goshen—Gen. 47:5, 27.

Gift of the Land of Canaan.—Promised: *To Abraham*—Gen. 12:1–7; 13:14–18; 15:7; 17:8; 28:4, 13; Neh. 9:8; Acts 7:3–6. *To Isaac*—Gen. 26:3. *To Jacob* —Gen. 35:12; 48:4. *To descendants of Abraham, Isaac, and Jacob*—Gen. 50:24; Ex. 6:4, 8; 12:25; 33:1; Lev. 23:10; 25:2, 38; Deut. 1:25; 8:7–10; 12:10; 17:14; 19:1, 8; 26:1, 2, 15; 28:8; Josh. 2:9, 14; Ps. 105:11; Jer. 11:5; Ez. 11:17.

Land given—Josh. 2:24; I Ki. 8:34; Neh. 9:35; Ps. 135:12; 136:12; Jer. 7:7; 32:22; Ez. 11:15; 33:24; 36:28; 37:25.

Gift conditional—Lev. 20:22; Num. 27: 12, 13; Deut. 1:34–36; 5:16; 6:23, 24; 9:6, 23; 11:31, 32; 15:4, 5; 16:20; 18:9; 25:19; 30:20; 32:49, 52; 34:4; Jer. 35: 15.

Israelites must conquer inhabitants and take possession—Num. 32:22; 33:53–56; Deut. 3:18–20; 4:37, 38; Josh. 1: 1–9; 9:24; Ju. 6:9.

Conquest of the.—Num. 32:22, 29; 33: 52–53; Deut. 1:8; 3:12, 20; 4:1, 22, 47; 6:1, 18; 8:1; 9:4, 5, 23; 10:11; 11:8, 11, 31; 12:29; 16:20; Josh. 1:11; 2:24; 9:24; 11:16, 23; 12:1–24; 23:5; 24:8; Ju. 2:4; 11:21–22; Ps. 44:3. Conquered little by little for fear of beasts—Lev. 26:6; Deut. 7:22. Land still to be conquered—Num. 33:52–56; Josh. 13: 1–6.

Division of.—Three men sent out from each tribe to describe and lay off—Josh. 18:1–10. Land allotted for inheritance—Num. 26:52–55; 32:22; 33: 54; 34:2–28; Josh. 13:8–33; Chs. 14–21; Ez. Ch. 48. Priests to have no inheritance in—Num. 18:20, 24. Land devoted to priests and Levites for residence—Ez. 48:10–14. Rechabites have no inheritance—Jer. 35:7. Jesus refuses to judge in division of—Lu. 12:13–14.

Boundary of. — Eden — Gen. 2:10–14. Nimrod's territory—Gen. 10:10–12. Children of Israel—Gen. 15:18–19; Ex. 23:31; Num. 34:2–12; Deut. 1:7–8; 11: 24; Josh. 1:2–4; Ez. 47:13–18.

Purchase, sale, and redemption of.—Abraham buys—Gen. 23:15–18. Jacob buys—Gen. 33:19. Joseph buys—Gen. 47:20, 26. Naomi sells—Ruth 4:3. Ananias sells—Acts 4:37. Land cannot be sold permanently—Lev. 25:10, 13, 23, 24; Num. 36:4; Jer. 32:7–15. Land of Egyptian priests not for sale —Gen. 47:22. Land bought and dedicated to Jehovah—Lev. 27:16–21. Dearth compels mortgage of—Neh. 5:1–5. Land not to pass out of family possession—Lev. 25:23–28; 27:22–24; II Ki. 8:1–6. Land returned in year of jubilee—Lev. 25:10–17; 27:22–25. Conveyance of title—Gen. 23:3–20; Num. 27:8–11; Ruth 4:3–8, 11; Jer. 32: 6–15. Land confiscated—II Ki. 8:1–6; Ezra 10:8. Land leased—Mt. 21:33–41; Mk. 12:1–9; Lu. 20:9–16. Land to rest every seven years—Ex. 23:11; 25:3–7; Lev. 26:34–35. See JUBILEE.

Famine in.—Canaan—Gen. 12:10; 26:1; 42:5; 43:5; 47:4, 13; Ruth 1:1; II Sam. 21:1; 24:13; I Ki. 8:37; 18:2; II Ki. 6:25; 7:4; 8:1; 25:3; I Chr. 21:12; II Chr. 20:9; 32:11; Ps. 105:16; Is. 14:30; Jer. 5:12; 11:22; 14:12–18; 15:2; 16:4; 18:21; 21:7–9; 24:10; 27:8, 13; 29:17–18; 32:24, 36; Ez. 5:12–17; 6:11–12; 7:15; Amos 8:11; Lu. 4:25; 15:14. In Egypt—Gen. 41:27–57; 47:13.

Miscellaneous.—Abraham and Lot—Gen. 13:1–12; Acts 7:2–7; Heb. 11:9. Abimelech and Abraham—Gen. 20:15. Jacob returning from Laban—Gen.

31:3; 32:3; 33:18–19. Esau removes from Canaan to Mt. Seir—Gen. 36: 6–8. Inhabitants and kings of Edom —Gen. Ch. 36. Rachel's death—Gen. 48:7. Land of Egypt filled with children of Israel—Ex. 1:7. Moses born there—Ex. 2:2. Dwelt in Land of Midian—Ex. 2:15. Brought brethren into Land of Canaan, etc.—Ex. 3:17. Through Land of Sin and Sinai—Ex. 17:1; 19:1–2. Spies sent to report on the—Num. 13:1–29. The mass die in the Land of the Wilderness—Num. 14:28–37; 26:65; Josh. 5:4–6. Fame went throughout—Mt. 9:26. More tolerable for—Mt. 10:15–24. Darkness over—Mt. 27:45; Mk. 15:33. See EARTH, FIELDS, GROUND, CANAAN.

LANDMARK. Deut. 19:14; 27:17; Job 24:2; Prov. 22:28; 23:10; Hos. 5:10.

LANGUAGES: The whole earth of one. —Gen. 11:1–6.

Of nations.—Is. 66:18; Zech. 8:23.

Wherein we were born.—Acts 2:8.

Gift of.—By Holy Spirit—Acts 2:7, 8; 10:46; 19:6; I Cor. 12:10.

Confounded.—Gen. 10:5; 11:7, 9; Acts 2:3; 19:6; I Cor. 12:10; 13:1; Rev. 7:9.

Kinds.—Strange—Ps. 81:5; 114:1. Unknown—Jer. 5:15. Pure—Zeph. 3:9. Latin—John 19:20. Of Canaanites—Is. 19:18. Jewish—II Ki. 18:26, 28; Esth. 8:9; Neh. 13:24. Lycaonian—Acts 14:11. Hebrew—Gen. 14:13; John 19:20. Of Ashdod—Neh. 13:24. Chaldean—Dan. 1:4. Greek—John 19:20. Syrian—II Ki. 18:26; Ezra 4:7; Dan. 2:4. Medes and Persians—Esth. 1:22; 3:12.

Figurative.—Heavens have no language —Ps. 19:3. A hard language—Ez. 3: 5, 6. Languages trembled—Dan. 5:19. See TONGUE.

LANGUISH. Bed of—Ps. 41:3. Earth —Is. 33:9. Fields—Is. 16:8. Fig-tree —Joel 1:12. Flower—Nah. 1:4. Gates —Jer. 14:2. Oil—Joel 1:10. People—Is. 19:8; 24:4; Jer. 15:9; Hos. 4:3. Vine—Is. 24:7. Wall—Lam. 2:8. World—Is. 24:4.

LAODICEA, la-ŏd'i-se'a. City of Phrygia forty miles from Ephesus.—Col. 2:1; 4:13–16; Rev. 1:11.

LAODICEANS. Paul's epistle to—Col. 4:16.

LAP. Full of gourds—II Ki. 4:39. Men —Ju. 7:6, 7. Shook out—Neh. 5:13. The lot is cast into—Pr. 16:33. Water —Ju. 7:5.

LAPPIDOTH, lăp′pi-dŏth. **Deborah's husband.**—Ju. 4:4.

LARGE. City—Neh. 7:4. Country— Is. 22:18. Cup—Ez. 23:32. Enough— Gen. 34:21. Heart—I Ki. 4:29. Land —Ex. 3:8; Ju. 18:10; Neh. 9:35. Letters—Gal. 6:11. Measure—Ps. 80:5. Pastures—Is. 30:23. Place—II Sam. 22:20; Ps. 18:19; 31:8; 118:5; Hos. 4:16. Tophet—Is. 30:33. Upper room —Mk. 14:15; Lu. 22:12. Work—Neh. 4:19.

LASCIVIOUSNESS. Mk. 7:22. Committed—II Cor. 12:21. Doings—II Pet. 2:2. Gave themselves up to— Eph. 4:19. Life—II Pet. 2:7. Turning grace of God into—Jude 4. Walked in—I Pet. 4:3. Works of the flesh— Gal. 5:19. See LUST, SIN.

LASEA, la-sē′a. **A city in Crete.**—Acts 27:8.

LASHA, lā′shȧ. **A place in southern Canaan.**—Gen. 10:19.

LASHARON, lă-shā′ron. Josh. 12:18.

LAST. See JESUS, TEACHING OF.

LAST DAYS. See DAYS, LATTER.

LATCHET. See SHOE.

LATE. Came up of—Deut. 32:17. Into the night—Is. 5:11. Sabbath, On the —Mt. 28:1. Take rest—Ps. 127:2.

LATTER. Days—Gen. 49:1; Num. 24: 14; Deut. 4:30; 31:39; Jer. 23:20; 30:24; 48:47; 49:39. End—Ruth 3: 10; II Sam. 2:26; Ps. 73:17; Pr. 19:20; Lam. 1:9. Glory—Hag. 2:9. Rain— Deut. 11:14; Job 29:23; Pr. 1:15; Jer. 3:3; 5:24; Hos. 6:3; Joel 2:23; Zech. 10:1; Jas. 5:7. Sign—Ex. 4:8.

LATTICE. Cried through—Ju. 5:28. Fell down through— II Ki. 1:2. Glanceth through—Song of Sol. 2:9. Looked through—Pr. 7:6.

LAUD. Him, all ye peoples—Ps. 117:1. Works—Ps. 145:4. See PRAISE.

LAUGHTER: With.—Fill thy mouth— Job 8:21. Our mouth filled—Ps. 126:2. The heart is sorrowful in—Pr. 14:13. Sorrow is better than—Eccl. 7:3. Of fool—Eccl. 7:6. Is mad—Eccl. 2:2. A feast is made for—Eccl. 10:19. Turned to mourning—Jas. 4:9. Abra-

ham fell upon his face and laughed— Gen. 17:17. Sarah laughed—Gen. 18: 12. Jehovah asks Sarah why she laughed—Gen. 18:13. Denial of—Gen. 18:15. Sarah says, ''God hath made me to laugh''—Gen. 21:6.

Laughed to scorn.—Daughter of Zion hath—II Ki. 19:21. Upright man is— Job 12:4; Is. 37:22. Innocent—Job 22:19. Us to—Neh. 2:19. Them to— II Chr. 30:10. Thou shalt be—Ez. 23:32. Me to—Ps. 22:7. Jesus is—Mt. 9:24; Mk. 5:40; Lu. 8:53. See GOD, ANTHROPOMORPHISMS, JOY, MIRTH, PLEASURE.

LAUNCH. Lu. 8:22.

LAVER. See TEMPLE.

LAW: Adamic.—Broad permission with but one prohibition—Gen. 2:16, 17; 3:2, 3.

The law given to Noah.—To abstain from eating blood, from murder, to multiply and replenish the earth— Gen. 9:4–7.

The Law of Moses.—Was added because of transgression—Rom. 5:20, 21; Gal. 3:19; I Tim. 1:8–10. Given by Jehovah, through Moses, at Sinai—Ex. 19: 11, 20; 20:1–17; Deut. 5:1–5, 27, 28; John 1:17; 7:19. See COMMANDMENTS.

The law of ordinances given.—Ex. Chs. 21–23. See LEVITICUS.

Given through the ministration of angels.—Acts 7:53; Gal. 3:19; Heb. 2:2.

Called.—Law of Moses—Ezra 7:6; Neh. 8:1; Heb. 10:28. Fiery law—Deut. 33:2. Letter—Rom. 2:29; II Cor. 3:6. Word spoken by angels—Heb. 2:2. Ministration of death—II Cor. 3:7. Ministration of condemnation—II Cor. 3:9; Gal. 3:10–13. See Deut. 27:26; 29:21; Heb. 12:18–21; Jas. 2:10–13. Living oracles—Acts 7:38; Rom. 3:2. Royal law—Jas. 2:8. Book of the law —Deut. 29:21; 30:10; 31:26; Josh. 1:8; 8:34; II Ki. 22:8; II Chr. 34:14, 15. Book of Moses—II Chr. 25:4; 35:12. Book of the covenant—Ex. 24:7; II Chr. 34:30.

The law given to the children of Israel. —Lev. 26:46; 27:34; Deut. 4:5; 29:1.

Gentiles did not have the decalogue.— Rom. 2:11–16; 9:1–5; I Cor. 9:21; Gal. 3:2–14, 19.

References to the law.—Moses cites the law—Deut. 5:1-21. He relates the circumstances connected with the giving of the law—Deut. 10:1-5; 33:1-4. Moses wrote the law in the book of the covenant and delivered it to the priests—Deut. 31:9-13, 24-29. He orders that it be put by the side of the ark—Deut. 31:26-29. Tables of the law put into the ark—Ex. 25:16, 21, 22; Deut. 10:5; I Ki. 8:9, 21; II Chr. 5:10; 6:11; Heb. 9:1-4. Written on stones—Deut. 27:2, 3. Upon gates and door-posts—Deut. 6:9; 11:20. Carried in frontlets between the eyes and bound on the hands—Ex. 13:9; Deut. 6:8. Read every seven years—Deut. 31: 9-10. By Joshua—Josh. 8:34.

Children of Israel required.—To know the law—Ex. 18:16. To keep the law —Deut. 4:5-9. Not to add to or diminish—Deut. 4:2. To teach it to their children—Deut. 4:9-10; 6:6; 11: 18-19. Lay it up in their hearts— Deut. 6:6; 11:18. To obey it—Deut. 4:40; 5:32-33; 6:17; 7:11; 10:12-13; 27:1; 30:10-14; Josh. 1:7; I Ki. 2:3-4.

The law rightly used.—Is a royal law— Lev. 19:18; Jas. 2:8. Is a revealer of sin—Rom. 3:20; 4:15; 7:7-8. It is holy and good—Rom. 7:12, 16. Is magnified and made honorable—Is. 42:21. Is a tutor to bring us to Christ—Gal. 3:24. A shadow of good things to come—Col. 2:14, 17; Heb. 8:5; 9:23; 10:1-9. See COVENANT.

The law violated.—Is a fiery law—Deut. 33:2; Heb. 12:18-20. Is a ministration of condemnation and death—II Cor. 3:7-9; Gal. 3:10-13. See Deut. 27:26; 29:21; Heb. 12:18-21; Jas. 2: 10-13. Is an administration of guilt and judgment—John 5:45; Rom. 2:12; 3:19, 20.

The law interpreted by.—Priests and Levites—Lev. 10:11; Deut. 33:10; II Chr. 35:2-3; Neh. 8:7; Mal. 2:7. Scribes—Ezra 7:10; Mt. 7:29; 13:52; Ch. 23. Apostles—Acts 13:15-16; 17: 1-3; 18:4. Jesus—Mt. 5:17-48; 22: 35-40; Mk. 12:28-34; Lu. 10:25-37.

Facts concerning.—Read responsively at Ebal and Gerizim—Deut. 27:12-26; Josh. 8:33-35. Discovered by Hilkiah in the temple—II Ki. 22:8; 23:2.

Read before Josiah the king with effect—II Ki. 22:10-20. Reformation instituted—II Ki. Ch. 23. Read by Ezra on the return from Babylon— Neh. Ch. 8. Read in the synagogues every sabbath—Acts 13:14-15; 15:21; II Cor. 3:14. Following after the law the Jews rejected Christ—Rom. 9:31-33. Christ accused of breaking it— John 19:7 (Lev. 24:16).

Inherent defects of the law as respects salvation.—Could not make perfect— Heb. 7:11, 18, 19; 9:9, 10; 10:1, 2. Could not justify—Acts 13:38, 39; Rom. 3:20, 27, 28; Gal. 2:16; 3:10-12; 5:4. Could not give peace of conscience—Heb. 9:9; 10:1, 2. Righteousness could not come by the law—Rom. 3:21; 4:15; 5:13; 7:7; 9:30-32; Gal. 2:21; 3:21; Phil. 3:6. Has no grace for man—John 1:17. Could not give life—Rom. 4:15; 7:9-13; II Cor. 3:6-13; Gal. 2:19; 3:21. See COVENANTS.

Christ fulfils.—Mt. 5:17; Mk. 1:15; Lu. 24:44-47; Acts 17:3; Rom. 10:4; Gal. 4:4-6; Eph. 1:9, 10.

Christ sums up.—Mt. 22:35-40; Mk. 12: 28-34; Lu. 10:25-37. See Lev. 19:18; Deut. 6:5; 10:12; 30:6, 16, 20; Mt. 5: 43, 44; 7:12; 19:19; Lu. 6:31-35; Rom. 12:14, 20; 13:8, 10; 15:1; Gal. 5:14, 15; 6:2; Jas. 2:8.

Temporary character of.—Rom. 7:1-6; II Cor. 3:7-14; Col. 2:14; Gal. 3:23-25; 4:1-5.

References.—Ps. 19:7; 119:70, 97, 109; Is. 8:20; Lu. 16:16, 17; John 7:51; I Cor. 6:1; I Tim. 1:7. See COMMANDMENTS, COVENANTS, STATUTES, IDOLATRY, SABBATH, BLASPHEMY, PERJURY, PARENTS and CHILDREN, CITIES OF REFUGE, MARRIAGE, CONCUBINAGE, WOMEN, ADULTERY, SEDUCTION, RAPE, SERVANTS, LAND, KINGS, RULERS OF ISRAEL, GOVERNMENT, PUNISHMENT, JUDGES, STEALING, LYING, FALSE WITNESS, POOR, DEBT, CAPTIVITY, ANIMALS, CLEAN AND UNCLEAN, FOOD, CLEAN AND UNCLEAN, CIRCUMCISION, TEMPLE, TABERNACLE, PRIESTS, OFFERINGS, CEREMONIAL CLEANSING, TITHES, FEASTS, JUBILEE.

LAWFUL. Ez. 18:5, 19, 21, 27; 33:14, 16. All things are—I Cor. 6:12. Captives—Is. 49:24. Do well on sabbath —Mt. 12:2, 5, 10, 12; Mk. 3:4; Lu. 6:9.

Eat, Not—Mt. 12:4; Mk. 2:26; Lu. 6:4. For thee to have her—Mt. 14:4; Mk. 6:18. Give tribute to Cæsar, To—Mt. 22:17; Mk. 12:14; Lu. 20:22. Heal on sabbath, To—Mt. 12:10; Lu. 14:3. Impose toll, To—Ezra 7:24. Scourge a man, To—Acts 22:25. Take up bed, To—John 5:10. Utter, To—II Cor. 12:4. Wife, To put away—Mt. 19:3; Mk. 10:2.

LAWGIVER. God the—Is. 33:22. Referred to—Gen. 49:10; Num. 21:18; Deut. 33:21; Ps. 60:7; 108:8. See GOD.

LAWLESS. Deeds—II Pet. 2:8. Law is made for the—I Tim. 1:9. One—II Thess. 2:8.

LAWLESSNESS. Mystery of—II Thess. 2:7. Sin is—I John 3:4.

LAWSUITS. Christian, censured—I Cor. 6:1. Jewish—Deut. 17:8; 25:1; II Sam. 15:2; Ez. 44:24. One with another—I Cor. 6:7.

LAWYER. See DOCTOR OF LAWS.

LAY. II Cor. 12:14. Anger—Job 36: 13. Anything—Rom. 8:33. Aside every weight—Heb. 12:1. Aside garments—John 13:4. Burden upon—Acts 15:28. Charge upon—Job 37:15. Commandments, Up—Pr. 2:1. Cornerstone—Job 38:6; I Pet. 2:6. Down life—John 10:11, 15; 15:13; I John 3: 16. Foundation—Ps. 104:5; Is. 28:16; I Cor. 3:10, 11. Head, Not where to—Mt. 8:20; Lu. 9:58. Heart, To—Deut. 4:39; Eccl. 7:2; Mal. 2:2. Hold—Job 18:9; Mk. 14:51; I Tim. 6:12, 19; Heb. 6:18. Knowledge, Up—Pr. 10:14. Me down and sleep—Ps. 4:8. Not up—Mt. 6:19. On him the iniquity—Is. 53:6. Plot—Acts 25:3. Sin to their charge—Acts 7:60. Snare—Ps. 119: 110. Stumbling-blocks—Jer. 6:21; Ez. 3:20. Treasures, Up—Mt. 6:20. Wait —Pr. 1:11. Waste—Jer. 25:36. Wickedness, Away—Pet. 2:1. Zion, In—Rom. 9:33.

LAZARUS, lăz′a-rus. (1) **The beggar.** —Lu. 16:20.

(2) **Brother of Mary, who was raised from the dead.**—John 11:1–43; 12: 1–17.

LEAD, *n.* Num. 31:22. Consumed, Is— Jer. 6:29. Gather—Ez. 22:20. Graven with—Job 19:24. In midst of furnace

—Ez. 22:18. Sank as—Ex. 15:10. Talent of—Zech. 5:7. Traded, With— Ez. 27:12. Weight of—Zech. 5:8. See METALS.

LEAD, *v.* Gen. 24:27; Ex. 13:17; I Chr. 15:21; Ps. 5:8; 43:3; 137:3; Is. 49:10. As a sheep to slaughter—Acts 8:32. Astray—Mt. 24:4, 24; Mk. 13:22; John 7:12; I John 2:26; 3:7. Away—I Cor. 12:2; II Tim. 3:6. Captives—Ps. 68: 18. Child shall—Is. 11:6. City, Into —Acts 12:10. Cloud—Ex. 13:21; Ps. 78:14. Crucify, To—Mk. 15:20. Edom, Into—Ps. 60:9. Forth—Is. 55:12; Acts 7:40. Gently—Gen. 33:14; Is. 40:11. Hand—Ps. 139:10. House of God, To—Ps. 42:4. Jehovah shall— Deut. 4:27. Joseph—Ps. 80:1. Life, Tranquil—I Tim. 2:2. Paths of uprightness, In—Pr. 4:11. People—II Chr. 25:11; Is. 9:16; 63:14. Repentance, To—Rom. 2:4. Rock, To—Ps. 61:2. Seed of house of Israel—Jer. 23:8. Singing of praise—II Chr. 23: 13. Spirit, Of—Mt. 4:1; Rom. 8:14; Gal. 5:18. Supplications, With—Jer. 31:9. Trained men—Gen. 14:14. Triumph, In—II Cor. 2:14. See LED.

LEAF: Kinds of plant.—Fig—Gen. 3:7; Is. 34:4; Mt. 21:19; Mk. 11:13. Olive —Gen. 8:11. Oak—Is. 1:30. Of vine— Is. 34:4.

Uses of.—Garments—Gen. 3:7.

Manuscript.—Jer. 36:23.

Prophecies concerning.—Jer. 8:13; Ez. 47:12.

Illustrative.—Of fear—Lev. 26:36. Righteous—Ps. 1:3. Transgressors—Is. 1: 30; 34:4; 64:6.

In parable.—Ez. 17:9; Mt. 21:19; Mk. 11:13. See TEACHING OF JESUS.

Figurative.—Driven leaf—Job 13:25. Of tree in vision—Dan. 4:12, 14, 21. Of tree of life—Rev. 22:2. Part of a door—I Ki. 6:34; Ez. 41:24. See PLANTS.

LEAGUE. I Sam. 22:18; Job 5:23; Is. 30:1; Ez. 30:5. See MEASURES.

LEAH, lē′ah. **Rachel's sister, and daughter of Laban.**—Gen. 29:16. Tender-eyed—Gen. 29:17. Married to Jacob —Gen. 29:23–26. Laban gives Zilpah to—Gen. 29:24. Children of—Gen. 29:31–35; 30:9–13, 17–21; 35:26. Reuben brings mandrakes to—Gen. 30:

14, 16. In field—Gen. 31:4. Asks father for portion—Gen. 31:14. Flees with Jacob—Gen. 31:19-21; 32:1, 22-23; 33:1-18. Daughter defiled—Gen. 34:1. Death of—Gen. 35:19; 49:31. Leah and Rachel referred to by Boaz as builders of house of Israel—Ruth 4:11. See JACOB.

LEAKETH. Eccl. 10:8.

LEAN. Gen. 41:20; Num. 13:20; Ju. 16:29; Ez. 29:7. Back—John 13:25; 21:20. Beloved, Upon—Song of Sol. 8:5. Day to day, From—II Sam. 13:4. Fleshed—Gen. 41:3, 4. Hand, On—II Ki. 5:18; 7:2, 17. House, Upon—Job 8:15. Jehovah, Upon—Mic. 3:11. Jesus' breast, On—John 13:25. Kine —Gen. 41:27. Not upon thine own understanding—Pr. 3:5. Pillars, On—Ju. 16:26. Sheep—Ez. 34:20. Spear, Upon—II Sam. 1:6. Staff, On—II Sam. 3:29. Top, Upon—Heb. 11:21.

LEANNESS. Job 16:8; Ps. 106:15; Is. 10:16. See FAMINE.

LEAP. Acts 3:8. About the altar—I Ki. 18:26. Babe—Lu. 1:41, 44. David —II Sam. 6:16. Earth, Upon—Lev. 11:21. Hart, As—Is. 35:6. Joy, For —Lu. 6:23. Made him—Job 39:20. Mountains, Upon—Song of Sol. 2:8. Punish those that—Zeph. 1:9. Sparks of fire—Job 41:19. Wall, Over—II Sam. 22:30; Ps. 18:29.

LEARN. Doctrines—Is. 29:24; Rom. 16:13; I Cor. 4:6. Industrious, To be—I Tim. 5:13. Jesus, Of—Mt. 9:13; 11:29; John 6:45; Eph. 4:20. Obedience —Heb. 5:8. Parable—Mt. 24:32; Mk. 13:28. Prudence—Pr. 19:25. Righteousness—Ps. 119:7; Is. 1:17; 26:9, 10; Jer. 12:16; Tit. 3:14. Statutes— Ps. 119:71, 73. War—Is. 2:4; Mic. 4:3. Wisdom—Pr. 30:3. See INSTRUCTION, JESUS, TEACHING OF, WISDOM.

LEAST. Mt. 25:40. Among you—Lu. 9:48. Apostles, Of—I Cor. 15:9. Commandment—Mt. 5:19. Greatest, Unto —Jer. 6:13; 8:10; 31:34; 42:1, 8; 44:12; Acts 8:10; Heb. 8:11. Kingdom of heaven, Of—Mt. 5:19. Mercies, Of— Gen. 32:10. Saints, Of—Eph. 3:8.

LEATHER. Girdle of—II Ki. 1:8; Mt. 3:4.

LEAVE. Blessing—Joel 2:14. Comfortless, Not—John 14:18. Command-

ment—Mk. 7:8. Contention—Pr. 17:14. Elijah—II Ki. 2:2, 4, 6; 4:30. Father and mother—Gen. 2:24; Mt. 19:5; Mk. 10:7; Eph. 5:31. Give— Ex. 3:19; Acts 21:40. Jehovah will not—Gen. 28:15; Ps. 37:33; Heb. 13:5. Intreat me not to—Ruth 1:16. Ninety and nine—Mt. 18:12. Nor forsake— I Ki. 8:57. Peace with you—John 14:27. Soul—Ps. 16:10; 141:8; Acts 2:27. Sweetness—Ju. 9:11. Undone— Lu. 11:42. World—John 16:28. See LEFT.

LEAVEN. Bread—See BREAD. Kingdom of heaven like—Mt. 13:33. Malice, Of—I Cor. 5:8. Pharisees, Of— Mt. 16:6, 11; Mk. 18:15; Lu. 12:1.

LEAVES. See LEAF.

LEBANA, lĕb'a-nà. Ancestor of some who returned with Zerubbabel.—Ezra 2:45; Neh. 7:48.

LEBANON, lĕb'a-non. North boundary of Palestine—Deut. 1:7; 3:25; 11:24; Josh. 1:4; 9:1.

Valley of.—Josh. 11:17; 12:7.

Streams of.—Song of Sol. 4:15.

Inhabitants of.—Josh. 13:5, 6; Ju. 3:3.

Trees of.—Cedars of—Ju. 9:15; I Ki. 4:33; 5:6, 9; II Ki. 14:9; 19:23; II Chr. 2:8, 16; Ezra 3:7; Ps. 29:5; 104:16; Is. 2:13; 10:34; 14:8; Ez. 27:5; 31:3. Fir—II Ki. 19:23.

Forests of.—I Ki. 7:2; 10:17, 21; II Chr. 9:20.

Wood of.—Song of Sol. 3:9.

Flower of.—Thistle—II Chr. 25:18; Nah. 1:4.

Workmen sent to.—I Ki. 5:14.

Illustrative.—Ps. 29:6; 72:16; 92:12; Song of Sol. 4:8, 11; 5:15; 7:4; Jer. 22:6, 23; Hos. 14:5, 6, 8; Zech. 11:1.

Prophecies concerning.—Is. 10:34; 29:17; 33:9; 35:2; 37:24; 40:16; 60:13; Jer. 18:14, 20; 22:20; Ez. 17:3; 31:15, 16. Flower of Lebanon—Nah. 1:4.

Violence done to Lebanon.—Hab. 2:17. Land of Lebanon—Zech. 10:10.

LEBAOTH, lĕb'a-ŏth. A city of Simeon. —Josh. 15:32.

LEBBEUS, lĕb'be-us. An apostle whose surname was Thaddeus, supposed to be Jude, brother of James.—Mt. 10:3.

LEBONAH, le-bō'nah. A city of Ephraim.—Ju. 21:19.

LECAH, lē'kah. **Son of Er, grandson of Shelah.**—I Chr. 4:21.

LED. Astray—John 7:47. Away—II Tim. 3:6; II Pet. 3:17. See APOSTASY, SIN. Captive. See CAPTIVITY. Forth —Is. 55:12; Acts 7:40. Jesus led by the Spirit—Mt. 4:1. Sheep to the slaughter, As—Acts 8:32. Spirit, By the—Mt. 4:1; Rom. 8:14; Gal. 5:18.

LEDGE. Ex. 27:5; 38:4; I Ki. 7:28, 29; Ez. 43:14.

LEEKS. Num. 11:5. See FOOD.

LEES. Is. 25:6; Jer. 48:11; Zeph. 1:12; Acts 27:4; 7:16.

LEFT. All—Mt. 19:27. Boat—Mt. 4:22. Desolate—Pr. 31:8. Hand—Gen. 13:9; Pr. 3:16. See HAND. Jesus—Mt. 26:56; John 8:9. Kindness, Not—Ruth 2:20. Nets—Mt. 4:20. Noah only was —Gen. 7:23. Nothing—Is. 39:6. Promise—Heb. 4:1. Remnant—Neh. 1:3; Is. 37:4; Jer. 40:11. Twin to right hand or—Gen. 24:49; Num. 20:17; 22:26; II Sam. 14:19. Undone—Mt. 23:23.

LEG. Laws concerning sacrifices.—Of lamb—Ex. 12:9. Of ram—Ex. 29:17; Lev. 8:21. Of bullock—Lev. 1:9, 13; 4:11. Of calf—Lev. 9:14.

Of image.—Dan. 2:33.

Above feet.—Lev. 11:21.

Punishment of.—Deut. 28:35.

Greaves of brass upon.—I Sam. 17:6.

Of man.—Ps. 147:10.

Of lame.—Pr. 26:7.

Figurative.—Song of Sol. 5:15; Is. 47:2. Used in prophecy—Amos 3:12.

The breaking of legs at crucifixion.— John 19:31–33.

LEGION. Mk. 5:15. Angels, Of—Mt. 26:53. Name is—Mk. 5:9; Lu. 8:30.

LEHABIM, lē'ha-bĭm. Libyans—Gen. 10:13; I Chr. 1:11.

LEHI, lē'hi. Samson's victory at—Ju. 15:9.

LEISURE. Mk. 6:31.

LEMUEL, lĕm'u-el. A king; probably Solomon—Pr. 31:1, 4.

LEND. Food—Lev. 25:37. Jehovah, Unto—Pr. 19:17. Nations, Unto—Deut. 15:6; 28:12. Loaves—Lu. 11:5. See FRATERNITY, DEBT, TEACHINGS OF JESUS, USURY.

LENGTH. Ark, Of—Gen. 61:5. Branches, Of his—Ez. 31:7. Breadth, And—Eph.

3:18; Rev. 21:16. Days, Of—Job 12:12; Ps. 21:4; Pr. 3:2, 16. Days, Of thy—Deut. 25:15; 30:20; I Ki. 3:14. Land, Of—Gen. 13:17. Tabernacle, Of —See TABERNACLE. Tranquility, Of thy —Dan. 4:27.

LENTILS. Gen. 25:34; II Sam. 17:28; 23:11; Ez. 4:9. See FOOD.

LEOPARD. Jer. 5:6; Hos. 13:6; Hab. 1:8. Change spots—Jer. 13:23. Kid, Lie down with—Is. 11:6. Mountains of the—Song of Sol. 4:8. Visions concerning—Dan. 7:6; Rev. 13:2. See ANIMALS.

LEPROSY. Disease possessing special ceremonial significance.

In the human body.—Lev. 13 ff.; Num. 5:2; Deut. 24:8.

False leprosy (plague of leprosy). Seven varieties: "Scab"—Lev. 13:6. "Quick, raw flesh"—Lev. 13:16. "Scar or boil"—Lev. 13:23; "Scall"—Lev. 13:37. "Tetter"—Lev. 13:39. "Baldness"—Lev. 13:41.

Treatment of genuine leprosy.—Lev. 13:45, 46; Deut. 24:8. Isolation of victims—Num. 5:2. Purification after cure—Lev. 14:1–32. Cured by Jesus— Mt. 8:2, 3; 11:5; Mk. 1:40–42; Lu. 5:12, 13; 7:22; 17:12. To be healed by the disciples—Mt. 10:8. In clothing— Lev. 13:47 ff. Purification in a house—Lev. 14:33. Purification—Lev. 14:43 ff.

Notable cases of leprosy.—In the hand of Moses as a sign—Ex. 4:6. Threatened on family of Joab—II Sam. 3:29. Visited as punishment on Miriam— Num. 12:10; Deut. 24:9. On Gehazi— II Ki. 5:27. Cured in Naaman—II Ki. 5:1, 11; Lu. 4:27. Attack of King Uzziah (Azariah)—II Ki. 15:5; II Chr. 26:19 ff. The four lepers of Samaria— II Ki. 7:3, 8. The ten lepers healed by Jesus—Lu. 17:12–19. Simon the leper —Mt. 26:6; Mk. 14:3.

LESHEM, lē'shem. **A city west of Mt. Hermon.**—Josh. 19:47.

LESS. How much—I Ki. 8:27; II Chr. 6:18; Job 4:19; 9:14; 25:6. James the —See JAMES. Least of all, Than the —Eph. 3:8. Nothing, Than—Is. 40:17; 32:15.

LESSER. Cattle—Is. 7:25. See CATTLE. Light—Gen. 1:16. Settle—Ez. 43:14.

LEST. Angry, He be—Ps. 2:12. Consumed, You be—Gen. 19:15, 17; Ex. 33:3; Num. 16:26. Die ye—Gen. 3:3; Lev. 10:7, 9; Num. 4:15, 20. Find you, He—Mk. 13:36. Enter into temptation, Ye—Lu. 22:46; Gal. 6:1; I Thess. 3:5. Put forth his hand—Gen. 3:22. Wrath be upon you—Josh. 9:20.

LET. Both grow together—Mt. 13:30. Children be filled—Mk. 7:27. Dead bury dead—Mt. 8:22; Lu. 9:60,, 61. Light, There be, etc.—Gen. 1:3-26. See CREATION. None remain—Josh. 8: 22; 10:28, 30. Cast mote out of eye—Mt. 7:4; Lu. 6:42. Let alone—Ex. 14: 12; 32:10; Deut. 9:14; Ju. 11:37; II Sam. 16:11; II Ki. 4:27; Job 7:16; 10: 10; Mt. 15:14; Mk. 1:24; 14:6; 15:36; Lu. 4:34; 13:8; John 11:48; 12:7. Bones—II Ki. 23:18. Ephraim—Hos. 4:17.

LET DOWN. Boat—Acts 27:30. David —I Sam. 19:12. Jeremiah—Jer. 38:6. Net—Lu. 5:4, 5. Palsied man—Mk. 2:4; Lu. 5:19. Paul—Acts 9:25; II Cor. 11:33. Pitcher—Gen. 24:14, 18, 46. Sheet—Acts 10:11; 11:5. Spies—Josh. 2:15, 18. Windows—Ez. 1:24, 25.

LET GO. Israelites—Ex. 3:20; 4:21, 23; 5:1, 2; 6:1, 11; 7:14, 16; 8:1-32; 9:1-35; 10:3-27; 11:1, 10; 13:15, 17; 14:5. Jonathan—I Sam. 20:29. Righteousness—Job 27:6. Wisdom—Pr. 4:13. See DELIVERANCE, FREEDOM.

LET OUT. Pr. 17:14; Song of Sol. 8:11; Mt. 21:33, 41; Mk. 12:1.

LETTER: LETTERS. Written by David to Joab—II Sam. 11:14. Sent to Artaxerxes—Ezra 4:7, 8, 11. Reply of Artaxerxes—Ezra 4:23. Written to Darius—Ezra 5:6-8. Reply of—Ezra 5:5. Written to Ezra, the priest—Ezra 7:11. Hezekiah's letters concerning passover—II Chr. 30:1. Sent to the governors for aid in rebuilding the wall—Neh. 2:7-9. Sent by Sanballat—Neh. 6:5. Of Ahasuerus—Esth. 1:22. Sent by posts to destroy the Jews—Esth. 3:13. Written by Mordecai to the Jews—Esth. 9:20-26. Letter of Purim—Esth. 9:29, 30. Jezebel forges letter—I Ki. 21:8-11. Letter from king of Syria to king of Israel—II Ki. 5:5, 7. Written by Jehu—II Ki. 10:1-7. Sennacherib's letters against Jehovah—II Ki. 19:14-16; II Chr. 32:17. King of Babylon's letters unto Hezekiah—II Ki. 20:12; Is. 39:1. Letter sent by Jeremiah to people of the captivity—Jer. 29:1. Shemaiah's letters to people at Jerusalem—Jer. 29:25, 29. Letters (of commission) granted from the high priests and the Sanhedrin to Saul—Acts 9:2. Claudius's letter to Felix—Acts 23:25-33. Letter from Judæa—Acts 28:21.

Letter in the sense of law.—Rom. 2:27, 29; 7:6; II Cor. 3:6.

Letter in the sense of knowledge.—John 7:15.

Letters, *i. e.*, Epistles.—Epistles of commendation—II Cor. 3:6. Paul's epistles—Thirteen epistles of Paul (besides Hebrews) in four groups: Eschatological—I and II Thessalonians. Doctrinal—I and II Corinthians; Galatians; Romans. Christological—Philippians; Philemon; Colossians; Ephesians. Pastoral—I Timothy; Titus; II Timothy; I Cor. 5:9.

Lost epistles.—Paul probably alluded to an epistle of the Corinthians. Another lost epistle of Paul's may also be referred to in II Cor. 2:3, 4; 7:8, 12, though the reference may be to I Corinthians. The epistles of Paul were at once imitated by pretenders—II Thess. 2:2. Paul usually used amanuenses, as Tertius in Romans—Rom. 16:22. But he signed the closing salutation in his own hand—I Cor. 16:21; Col. 14:18; II Thess. 3:17. In Gal. 6: 11-18 he seems to have written the whole paragraph (his large handwriting). He probably wrote the little Epistle of Philemon himself—Philemon 19. He considered his Epistles authoritative and binding on disciples —I Cor. 5:9; 7:40; 14:37; II Cor. 10: 10, 11; 13:10; Col. 4:16; I Thess. 5:27; II Thess. 2:15; 3:12, 13, 17; Philemon 21. Paul wrote business letters on church business—I Cor. 16:3. Some of his epistles passed from church to church—Col. 4:16. Peter puts them on a par with Old Testament scriptures—II Pet. 3:16. One may distinguish between a purely personal letter, like Philemon, full of the Christian spirit, however, and doctrinal or ecclesiastical discussions, like Galatians and Ephesians. The most of them partake of both features, and all are in the informal style of letters. The first part is usually doctrinal and the second part practical and personal. *Cf.* I Corinthians, Colossians, and the Epistles to Timothy and Titus. The Epistle to the Hebrews, while addressed to the Hebrews (of unknown authorship), is more of a treatise (ancient homily or sermon), though some personal items come at the close. The book is a great argument with strong exhortations.

The seven Catholic, or General Epistles (James, I Peter, Jude, II Peter, I, II, III John) are not all general. II John is addressed either to a church or a lady, while III John is sent to Gaius. The letters to the seven churches (Rev. 1:11) are real epistles to the circle of seven important cities in the Roman province of Asia. A copy of the Book of Revelation was probably sent to each church. Twenty-one of the twenty-seven New Testament books are thus Letters, and one of the other six (Revelation) has seven letters in the body of the Book (Chs. 2 and 3).

LETUSHIM, le-tū′shim. **Son of Dedan.** —Gen. 25:3.

LEUMMIM, le-ŭm′mim. **Another son of Dedan.**—Gen. 25:3.

LEVEL. Paths—Pr. 4:26; 5:21; Is. 40: 3. Place—Lu. 6:17.

LEVI, lē′vi, *"Joined."* (1) **Jacob's third son by Leah;** name expressive of trust.—Gen. 29:34. Levi joined Simeon in avenging Dinah—Gen. 34: 25–30. Jacob feels the sting of the brothers' act—Gen. 34:30. Prophecies concerning Levi—Gen. 49:5–7. Lived 137 years—Ex. 6:16.

(2) **A tribe descended from.**—Gen. 35: 23; 46:11–15; Ex. 6:16–27; Num. 3: 15–34; I Chr. 6:1–53; 24:20–31. Cities of the Levites—I Chr. 6:54–81. Princes of—Num. 3:35. Stood on Mt. Gerizim —Deut. 27:12. Moses a Levite—Ex. 2:1–10; Num. 26:59. Levites punish idolaters—Ex. 32:25–29. Made priests —Num. 3:5–13; Deut. 10:8, 9; 21:5; 31:9; 33:8. Had a tithe for an inherit-

ance—Num. 18:21–30; Deut. 10:8, 9; 18:1–8; Josh. 13:14, 33; Neh. 10:37– 39; Heb. 7:5, 9. See ISRAEL, PRIESTS.

LEVITES: Belonging to tribe of Levi. —Consisted of three families—Ex. 6: 16, 22; Num. 3:17–20. Not numbered with other tribes—Num. 1:47; 3: 14–16.

Duties of Levites stated.—Num. 1:48– 54; 3:5–10; I Chr. 23:28–32. Taken instead of first-born—Ex. 13:2; Num. 3:11–13, 41–45; 8:14–19. Age for service—Num. 4:3, 30, 47; 8:23–26; I Chr. 23:3, 27. Selected for courage—Ex. 32:25–28. Bore ark of covenant—Deut. 10:8; I Chr. 15:2, 26, 27. Had care of tithes and offerings—I Chr. 9:26–27; 26:20–26; 29:8; II Chr. 24:5, 11; 31: 11–19; 34:9. Had charge of tabernacle—Num. 1:50–53; 3:6–9, 21–37. Also, of temple—Ezra 8:24–34. See PRIEST, TABERNACLE, TEMPLE.

(3) See ''Matthew'' in OUTLINE STUDIES IN THE BOOKS.

(4) **An ancestor of Jesus.**—Lu. 3:24.

(5) **Another ancestor of Jesus.**—Lu. 3:29.

LEVIATHAN. Job 41:1; Ps. 74:14; 104:26; Is. 27:1.

LEVITICAL. Heb. 7:11. See LEVI, LEVITICUS, LAW.

LEVY. Men, Of—I Ki. 5:13, 14. Tribute, Of—Num. 31:28; I Ki. 9:21. See BONDAGE, TRIBUTE.

LEWDNESS. Ashamed of—Ez. 16:27. Committed—Ju. 20:6; Jer. 11:15; 13: 27; Ez. 16:43, 58; 22:9, 11; Hos. 6:9. Punishment of—Ez. 23:21–49; Hos. 2:10. See SIN.

LIAR. See LYING.

LIBERALITY (Christian virtue of loving consideration and succor of others): **Enjoined.**—Ex. 22:29, 30; 23: 15; 34:20; Lev. 23:22, 25:35–43; Pr. 3:9, 10, 27, 28; Eccl. 11:1, 2; Mt. 5:42; 19:21, 22; Mk. 10:21–26; Lu. 3:11; 6:38; 11:41; 12:33; 18:22–26; Acts 20: 35; Rom. 12:8; 15:27; II Cor. 8:7, 11– 15; I Tim. 6:18; Heb. 13:16.

Ministering to necessity.—Lev. 25:35– 41; Deut. 15:7–11; 24:19–22; Job 29: 11–16; Ps. 41:1–3; Pr. 25:21, 22; Is. 58:6, 7; Mt. 19:21, 22; Mk. 9:41; 10: 21, 22; Lu. 3:10, 11; 12:33, 34; Rom. 12:13; 15:26, 27; Gal. 2:10; Eph. 4:28;

Phil. 4:9–18; I Tim. 5:16; 6:17–19; Jas. 2:15, 16; I John 3:17.

According to ability.—Ex. 35:21–29; 36: 3–7; 38:8; Deut. 16:10, 17; I Cor. 16: 1, 2; II Cor. 8:13–15.

Willingly.—Ex. 25:2; I Chr. 29:3–9; Pr. 21:26; I Cor. 13:3; II Cor. 8:11, 12; 9: 5–15; Philemon 14.

The reward of.—Ps. 112:5, 9; Pr. 3:9, 10; 11:24–26; 19:17; 22:9; 28:27; Eccl. 11:1; Is. 32:7, 8; 58:10, 11; Ez. 18:7–17; Mt. 25:34–40; Lu. 6:30–35; 12:33, 34; Heb. 6:10.

Instances: In Old Testament.—Pharaoh to Jacob—Gen. 45:18–20. Israelites— Ez. 36:5. David—II Sam. 8:11; I Ki. 7:51; 8:17, 18; I Chr. 16:3; 21:24, 25. Barzillai and others to David—II Sam. 17:27–29; 24:22, 23.

In New Testament.—Joanna and others —Lu. 8:3. Zacchæus—Lu. 19:8. Centurion—Lu. 7:4, 5. The Samaritan— Lu. 10:33, 35. Poor widow—Lu. 21: 2–4; Mk. 12:41–44. Jerusalem Christians—Acts 2:45. Barnabas—Acts 4: 36, 37. Dorcas—Acts 9:36. Cornelius —Acts 10:2. Church at Antioch—Acts 11:29, 30. Lydia—Acts 16:15. Paul— Acts 20:34; 24:17. Churches of Macedonia—Rom. 15:26; II Cor. 8:1–5. Churches of Galatia—I Cor. 16:1. Churches of Corinth—Rom. 15:26; I Cor. 16:1; II Cor. 8:1–9, 15. Church in Philippi—Phil. 1:5; 4:15. Other Macedonian churches—II Cor. 11:7–10; 12:13. See CHRISTIAN GRACES, TEACHING OF JESUS on GIVING.

LIBERTINES: Jewish captives at Rome who had been freed and had returned to Jerusalem.—Acts 6:9.

LIBERTY. Of the gospel.—II Cor. 3: 17; Gal. 5:1. Law of liberty—Gal. 6:2; Jas. 1:25; 2:12. False teachers of —Gal. 2:4; II Pet. 2:19; Jude 4; Rev. 2:2. Not to be abused—I Cor. 8:9; Gal. 5:13; I Pet. 2:16; II Pet. 2:19. See CAPTIVITY, DELIVERANCE, JUBILEE, REDEMPTION, FREEDOM.

LIBNAH, lĭb'nah. (1) An encampment of Israel.—Num. 33:20, 21. See CAMP, ISRAEL.

(2) A Levitical city in Judah.—Josh. 10:29–39; 12:15; 15:42; II Ki. 8:22; 19:8; 23:31; 24:18; I Chr. 6:57; II Chr. 21:10; Is. 37:8; Jer. 52:1.

LIBNI, lĭb'ni. (1) Grandson of Merari. —I Chr. 6:29.

(2) Grandson of Levi.—Ex. 6:37; Num. 3:18; I Chr. 6:17, 20.

LIBNITES, lĭb'nītes. (1) Descendants of Libni. (2) Num. 3:21; 26:58.

LIBYA, lĭb'yȧ. A district in Africa.— Ez. 30:5; 38:5; Acts 2:10.

LIBYANS. Inhabitants of Libya.—Jer. 46:9; Dan. 11:43.

LICE. Ex. 8:16–19; Ps. 105:31.

LICK. Num. 22:4. Blood—I Ki. 21:19; 22:38. Dust—Ps. 72:9; Is. 49:23; Mic. 7:17. Sores—Lu. 16:21. Water—I Ki. 18:38.

LID. II Ki. 12:9. See COVER.

LIE. See LYING.

LIERS-IN-WAIT. II Chr. 20:22; Ezra 8:31. See AMBUSH.

LIFE, TEMPORAL OR PHYSICAL: What is it? It is given by the breath or Spirit of God.—Gen. 1:11–27: 2:7; Num. 16:22; Job. 27:3; 33:4; Ps. 36:9; Eccl. 12:7; Is. 38:16; 42:5; Zech. 12:1; Acts 17:25, 28; Heb. 12:9; Jas. 2:26.

Nephesh, Psyche (sometimes), Pneuma, Ruahh: Vitality — being animate. — Gen. 1:30; Lev. 17:11; Ju. 15:19; Lu. 8:55; John 10:11.

Hhayyim: Nearly the same as above.— Gen. 2:7; 7:22; Ps. 103:4; Pr. 14:30.

Hhayyim: Condition of vitality and the time during which vitality continues. —Life as a state of animation opposed to death—Gen. 27:46; Ex. 1:14; II Sam. 1:23; Job 3:20; 10:1; Ps. 17:14; 63:3; 66:9; Pr. 18:21; Jer. 8:3. The period during which one lives—Gen. 23:1; Ex. 6:16; Deut. 4:9; Josh. 1:5; II Sam. 18:18; I Ki. 11:34; Ps. 23:6; 128:5; Jer. 52:34.

Zoe: Opposed to death.—Acts 17:25; Rom. 8:38; I Cor. 3:22; II Cor. 4:12; Jas. 4:14.

Duration of life.—Lu. 1:75; 16:25; I Cor. 15:19.

Bios: The means of living or subsistence.—Mk. 12:44; Lu. 8:43; 15:12, 30; 21:4; I John 3:17.

Condition, mode or course of life.—Lu. 8:14; I Tim. 2:2; II Tim. 2:4; I Pet. 4:3; I John 2:16.

Long life.—Gen. 6:3; Ps. 91:16. Promised to the wise—Pr. 3:16; 9:11. To those who are obedient—Deut. 4:40; Pr. 3:1,

2; 10:27. To those who honor their parents—Ex. 20:12; Deut. 5:16; Eph. 6:1-3. To the pure in heart—Ps. 34: 13, 16; 91:1-10; Eccl. 3:12, 13; I Pet. 3:10, 12. To those who fear God and walk in the light and love of His truth—Pr. 10:27; Is. 65:18-21; 38: 2-5; Jas. 5:15. As they are protected of God—Job 2:6; Acts 18:9, 19; 27: 42, 43; Lu. 21:17-19; Mt. 28:20; I Pet. 3:13, 14.

The value of life.—Job 2:4; Mt. 16:25, 26; Mk. 8:36, 37.

Men should take proper care of their lives—Pr. 6:9-11; 12:14; 13:2-4; Acts 14:4-6; 27:34; I Tim. 5:23.

Yet this life should be given up if right and truth demand it—Dan. 3:17, 18; Mt. 10:37-39; Lu. 14:25-27; Acts 20: 22-24; 21:13-14; Rom. 8:35-38; II Cor. 12:9, 10; Phil. 2:17; I John 3:16.

From sorrow and pain some have come to wish for life to be taken away— Job 3:11; 6:11; 7:7, 15; 9:21; 10:1; 13:14.

The brevity of life.—It is compared to a pilgrimage—Gen. 47:9; a hand breadth—Ps. 39:5; a dream—Ps. 73: 20; a weaver's shuttle—Job 7:6; a sleep—Ps. 90:5; a vapor—Jas. 4:14; a shadow—I Chr. 29:15; Job 14:2; Eccl. 6:12; a flower—Job 14:2; Ps. 103:15; Is. 40:6; Jas. 1:10; grass—Ps. 37:2; 90:5, 6; 103:15; Is. 40:6-8; Jas. 1:10, 11; I Pet. 1:24; water spilt on the ground—II Sam. 14:14; waters drying up—Job 14:10-12.

Time itself is only duration which intervenes between two eternities—I Cor. 7:29-31.

Man should number his days—Ps. 90:12. Our life should be spent in the fear of God—Ps. 25:14; 33:18; 34:7, 9; 103: 11, 13; I Pet. 1:17; In His service— Mt. 4:10; Lu. 1:75; Acts 20:19; Rom. 12:11; Heb. 12:28.

Life consisteth not in the abundance of things which a man hath.—Job 1:13-19; Mt. 6:25-34; Mk. 8:35; Lu. 12:15, 16-21.

The life that we may now live in Christ Jesus—Spiritual life: The gift of God through Christ.—John 1:12, 13; 5:21, 40; 6:33, 51, 54-57; Rom. 6:23; I John 5:11-12.

We must be born again.—John 1:13; 3: 3-5; I Cor. 4:15; 6:11; II Cor. 5:17; Col. 3:10; Tit. 3:5; Heb. 10:22; Jas. 1:18.

Begotten through the gospel—Mt. 13: 19, 23; Lu. 8:11, 12; Rom. 10:8, 9, 17; I Cor. 4:15; Gal. 3:25-29; Jas. 1:18; I Pet. 1:23.

Is newness of life—Rom. 6:1-11.

The old man must die out and be buried and raised up into this new life. We should seek the things above—Rom. 6:3, 4; Col. 2:12; 3:1-4.

This life a growth.—Babes—I Cor. 3:1; Heb. 5:13; I Pet. 2:2. Little children —Mt. 18:3; 19:14; Mk. 10:15; Lu. 18: 17; John 13:33; Gal. 4:19; I John 2:1, 12, 28; 3:7, 18; 4:4; 5:21. Young men —I John 2:13, 14. Full grown men— I Cor. 14:20; Eph. 2:13; Heb. 5:14. Fathers—I John 2:14.

The presence of the spirit needed—John 14:17; 15:26; Rom. 5:5; 8:2, 6, 9-11; I Cor. 3:16, 17; 6:19, 20; Gal. 4:6.

Must open our minds and hearts to receive the things of God—Mt. 13:15; I Cor. 2:16.

The mind must be renewed and be like the mind of Christ—Eph. 2:1, 5; Phil. 2:2, 5; Col. 2:13; Heb. 5:8, 9; I Pet. 4:1; I John 3:14.

This new life will be seen in the imitation of the life of Christ—Acts 10:38; Rom. 14:19; I Cor. 14:1; Gal. 6:1-5; I Tim. 6:11; II Tim. 2:22.

This life hidden with Christ—Col. 3:3. See CHRISTIAN GRACES—II Pet. 1:5. Man should show mercy—Mt. 5:7; 23: 23; Lu. 10:25-37; Rom. 12:8; Eph. 2: 10; Jas. 2:13; 3:17; I John 3:16, 18.

Accomplishing good becomes a habit— Mt. 5:44, 45; Gal. 6:10; I Thess. 4:10, 11; I Tim. 4:4-6; Tit. 2:7; 3:8, 14; Heb. 6:9, 10; 10:34; 13:16; Jas. 3:13; I Pet. 2:12; I John 3:17, 18; III John 11.

Must bear much fruit—Mt. 3:8; 7:17-20; John 15:2-8; Rom. 6:22; 7:4; Gal. 5:22; Eph. 5:9; Phil. 1:11; Heb. 13: 15; Jas. 3:17, 18. See Col. 1:1, 10.

This growth springs out of love for God and men.—Ex. 20:6; Lev. 19:18; Deut. 5:10; 6:5; 10:19; 11:22; Ps. 97:10; Jer. 31:3; Amos 5:15; Mic. 6:8; Mt. 5:43, 44; John 8:42; 13:34; 14:15, 21;

15:9, 12, 17; Rom. 5:5; II Cor. 5:14; Eph. 5:2; Phil. 1:9; I Thess. 4:9; I Pet. 1:22; I John 2:10; 4:8–12; 5:1, 2. See Rom. 12:10; Heb. 13:1.

This character makes them saints, or holy ones.—I Sam. 2:9; Ps. 31:23; 85:8; 116:15; 132:16; 148:14; Dan. 7: 18–27; Zech. 14:5; Mt. 27:52; Acts 9:13, 32, 41; 26:10; Rom. 1:7; 8:27; 12:13; 15:25; 16:2; I Cor. 1:2; 6:1; 14:23; 16:1, 15; II Cor. 1:1; 8:4; Eph. 1:1; 2:19; 3:18; 4:12; 6:18; Phil. 1:1; Col. 1:2, 12; I Thess. 3:1, 13; II Thess. 1:10; I Tim. 5:10; Heb. 6:10; Jude 3; Rev. 5:8; 13:7; 16:6; 20:9.

Eternal life.—Mt. 19:16–21; Mk. 10:17–21, 29–30; Lu. 18:18–22, 29–30; John 3:15, 16, 36; 5:24; 6:27, 47, 54; 10:28; 17:2–3; Rom. 2:7; 6:23; I John 1:2; 2:25; 5:11, 20; Rev. 2:7; 21:6.

Eternal life, a present possession.—John 3:15, 36; 10:28; 11:25, 26; Rom. 6:11, 23; Eph. 2:6; I Tim. 6:12, 19; I John 5:11, 13.

There is a sin which is unto death, for which there is never forgiveness.—Mk. 3:29; I Cor. 9:27; I John 5:16; Jude 5, 6, 24.

God has ordained to eternal life those who believe and follow Christ.—John 6:54, 68; 10:28; 12:50; 17:2, 3; Acts 13:48; Rom. 2:7; 5:17, 21; 6:22; Gal. 6:7, 8; I Tim. 6:12, 19.

They must endure to the end.—Mt. 10: 22; 24:13; Heb. 2:1–4; 3:6–10; 4:1, 2, 14–16; 5:8, 9; 6:4–6; 10:23–31; 12:7, 14, 15, 25; Jas. 1:12; 2:5; Rev. 2:25, 26; 3:10–12.

The fountain of life.—Ps. 36:9; Jer. 2: 13; Ez. 47:1–12; Zech. 13:1; Rev. 7: 17; 21:6.

The issues of life, Source of.—Ps. 16:11; Pr. 4:23; 8:34–35; Mt. 15:18–20; Mk. 7:20–23.

The tree of life.—Gen. 2:9; 3:22; Pr. 3:18; 11:30; 13:12; 15:4; Rev. 2:7; 22:2, 14, 19.

LIFE BLOOD. Is. 63:3. See LIFE.

LIFE GIVING. I Cor. 15:45. See LIFE.

LIFE TIME. Divining—II Sam. 18:18; Lu. 16:25; Heb. 2:15. For a—Ps. 30:5.

LIFT. Countenance—Num. 6:26. Egypt shall not be—Ez. 29:15. Eyes—Ps. 121:1; 123:1; Lu. 16:23. Follow—Eccl.

4:10. See FRATERNITY. Gates—Ps. 24:7. Hands—Ps. 28:2; Is. 26:11; Heb. 12:12. See HANDS LIFTED UP. Head—Ps. 82:2; Lu. 21:28. See HEAD. Heart —II Chr. 17:6; Lam. 3:41. Jesus—John 3:14; 8:28; 12:32. Light—Ps. 4:6. Prayer—Is. 37:4. See PRAYER. Rage of adversaries—Ps. 7:6. Serpent—John 3:14. Soul—Ps. 25:1. Up —Gen. 4:7; I Sam. 2:7; Ps. 24:9; Is. 33:10; 52:13; John 3:14; 8:28; 12:32. Voice—Pr. 2:3; Is. 13:2; 42:2; Jer. 11:14. See CRY, VOICE.

LIGHT: Natural.—Gen. 1:3, 14–18; Ps. 74:16; Is. 45:7; Jer. 31:35; II Cor. 4:6.

Miraculous.—Gen. 15:17; Ex. 13:21; Deut. 1:33; Mt. 17:2; Mk. 9:3; Lu. 9: 29; Acts 9:3; 12:7; 26:13.

Artificial. — Ex. 25:37; 35:14; 40:25; Lev. 24:2; Jer. 25:10; Mt. 5:15; 25:1; Acts 16:29.

Figurative.—Of Jehovah—Ps. 27:1; 36: 9; Is. 60:12, 20; Jas. 1:17; I John 1:5, 7. Of His word—Ps. 19:8; 119:105, 130; Pr. 6:23. Of the Christ—Is. 49:6; Mal. 4:2; Mt. 4:16; Lu. 2:32; John 1:4–9; 3:19; 12:35, 36; I Tim. 6:16; II Tim. 1:10; Rev. 21:23, 24. Of the righteous—Ps. 56:13; 97:11; Lu. 16:8; Eph. 5:8, 14; Phil. 2:15; Col. 1:12; I Thess. 5:5. Of righteousness—Ps. 37: 6; 97:11; Pr. 4:18; Mt. 5:16; Acts 26:18; I Pet. 2:9. Of the wicked—Job 18:5; 24:13–17; 38:15; Ps. 49:16–19; Is. 5:20; Lu. 11:34–36; John 3:19–21; 11:10; Rom. 2:19; II Cor. 4:4; I John 1:6–7; 2:9–11.

Old Testament references.—Thou wilt light my lamp—Ps. 18:28. Arise, shine, for thy light is come—Is. 60: 1–3. Lift up the light of thy countenance—Ps. 4:6. Who coverest thyself with light—Ps. 104:2. If I say surely the darkness—Ps. 139:11, 12.

New Testament references.—John was a burning—John 5:35. Put on armor of light—Rom. 13:12. Bring to light hidden things—I Cor. 4:5. Until day dawn and day star arise—II Pet. 1:19. Were once darkness but now light—Eph. 5:9.

LIGHTNING. Job 28:26; 37:3; Ps. 77: 18; 135:7; Zech. 9:14. Appearance of —Dan. 10:6; Mt. 28:23. Caused—Job 37:15; Ps. 144:6; Zech. 10:1. Cloud of—Job 37:11. Cometh from east—Mt. 24:27. Protects David—II Sam. 22:15; Ps. 18:14. Satan falls as—Lu. 10:18. Thunder and—Ex. 19:16.

LIKE. Manner—Mt. 21:36; Lu. 22:20.

LIKEMINDED. Phil. 2:20; I Pet. 3:8. Be ye all—I Pet. 3:8.

LIKEN. Lu. 13:8.

LIKENESS TO CHRIST. Believers in God—I Pet. 1:21. Children of God—Phil. 2:15. Conformed to His image—Rom. 8:29. Doing God's will—John 5:30; 6:38; 8:28; 9:4. Glorifying God—John 17:4. Holy, Be—I Pet. 1:15. Humble as—Lu. 22:27; John 13:15, 16. Imitators of—I Cor. 11:1. Love not life—Rev. 12:11. Longsuffering—I Tim. 1:16; I Pet. 2:21; 3:17, 18. Meek and lowly as—Mt. 11:29. Walk as he walked—I John 2:6. Walk in love—Eph. 5:2. See EXAMPLE, IMAGE, JESUS, CHARACTER OF.

LIKHI, lĭk'hī. I Chr. 7:19.

LILY. Among—Song of Sol. 2:16. Blossom as—Hos. 14:5. Consider—Mt. 6:28; Lu. 12:27. Feed among—Song of Sol. 4:5. Flower of—I Ki. 7:26. Gather—Song of Sol. 6:2. Lips are as—Song of Sol. 5:13. Set about with—Song of Sol. 7:2. Thorns, Among—Song of Sol. 2:2. Valley, Of—Song of Sol. 2:1. Work—I Ki. 7:19. See PLANTS.

LIMB. Bars of iron, Like—Job 4:18. Divided her—Ju. 19:29.

LIME. Is. 33:12; Amos 2:1. See PLASTER.

LIMIT. Whole—Ez. 43:12. Wisdom—Job 15:8.

LIMPED. Between the two sides—I Ki. 18:21. Upon his thigh—Gen. 32:31. See LAMENESS.

LINE. Carpenter stretcheth—Is. 44:13. Fallen unto me—Ps. 16:6. Gone through all earth—Ps. 19:4. Line upon line—Is. 28:10, 13. Scarlet, Of—Josh. 2:18.

LINEN: Manufacture of.—I Chr. 4:21. By women—Pr. 31:24.

Kinds of: Fine—Gen. 41:42; Ex. 28:5, 8, 39; II Chr. 2:14; 3:14; 5:12; Esth. 1:6; 8:15; Is. 3:23; Ez. 16:10, 13; 27:7, 16; Lu. 16:19; Rev. 18:12, 16; 18:8, 14. Fine trimmed—Ex. 26:1; 27:9; 28:6, 8, 15. Clean—Mt. 27:59.

Uses of: For garments of women—Is. 3:23. For girdles—I Sam. 2:18; Jer. 13:1; Mk. 14:51, 53. For Ephod—I Sam. 22:18. For veils—II Chr. 3:14. For cords—Esth. 1:6. For tires—Ez. 44:18. Christ's body wrapped in—Mt. 27:59; Mk. 15:46; Lu. 23:53; John 19:40. Linen clothes laid by themselves—Lu. 24:12; John 20:5, 6, 7. Curtains for tabernacle—Ex. 2:1; 27:9. For garments of priests—Ex. 28:5-8, 15, 39-42; Lev. 6:10; 16:4, 23, 32; Ez. 44:17. For garments of men—Gen. 41:42; I Chr. 15:27; Esth. 8:15; Mk. 14:51, 52; Lu. 16:19.

Symbolical.—Ez. 9:2, 3, 11; 10:2, 6, 7; Dan. 10:5; 12:6, 7; Rev. 19:8, 14.

Figurative.—Ez. 16:10, 13.

LINGER. Gen. 19:16; 43:10; II Pet. 2:3.

LINUS, lī'nŭs. **A disciple in Rome.**—II Tim. 4:21.

LINTEL. Ex. 12:7. See DOOR.

LION. Gen. 49:9; Deut. 33:20; II Ki. 17:25, 26; Job 4:10, 11; Is. 30:6.

Strong.—Ps. 30:30; Is. 38:13; Jer. 14:19; Mic. 5:8.

Active.—Deut. 33:20.

Courageous.—II Sam. 17:10; Pr. 30:30; Is. 31:4; Nah. 2:11.

Fierce.—Job 4:10; 10:16; 28:8; Ps. 7:2; 17:12; 22:13; Jer. 2:15; 4:7; Hos. 13:8; Mic. 5:8; Nah. 2:12.

Cunning.—Ps. 10:9; 17:12; Lam. 3:10.

Roaring of.—Job 4:10; Ps. 22:13; 104:21; Pr. 20:2; Is. 31:4; Jer. 2:15; Amos 3:4, 8; I Pet. 5:8.

Teeth of.—Job 4:10; Ps. 58:6; Joel 1:6.

Old lion starving for lack of prey.—Job 4:11.

Haunts of.—Job 38:39, 40; Ps. 104:22; Song of Sol. 4:8; Jer. 4:7; 5:6; 25:38; 49:19; 50:44; Mic. 5:8; Nah. 2:11.

Restrained by God.—Prophet not torn—I Ki. 13:28. Daniel and the lion's den—Dan. 6:22, 27.

God provides for.—Job 38:39, 40; Ps. 104:21.

Attacks sheepfolds.—I Sam. 17:34; Jer. 50:17; Amos 3:12; Mic. 5:8.

Attacks and slays men.—I Ki. 13:24; 20:36.

Slain by: Samson—Ju. 14:5-8. David—I Sam. 17:34, 36. Benaiah—II Sam. 23:20.

Honey found in carcass of lion by Samson.—Ju. 14:8. Samson's riddle—Ju. 14:14, 18.

Parable.—Ez. 19:1–9.

Proverb concerning: A living dog and a dead lion—Eccl. 9:4.

Images of lions in the structure of the temple.—I Ki. 7:29, 36; 10:19, 20.

Illustrative.—II Sam. 17:10; Is. 11:7; 35:9; 65:25. Of Christ—Rev. 5:5. Of God—Is. 31:4; 38:13; Lam. 3:10; Hos. 5:14; 13:8. Of the devil—I Pet. 5:8. Of Israel—Num. 24:9. Of king of Israel—Ez. 19:2. Of tribe of Judah—Gen. 49:9. Of the tribe of Gad—Deut. 33:20. Of the righteous—Pr. 28:1. Of enemies—Ps. 57:4; 58:6; Is. 5:29; 15:9; Jer. 2:15; 4:7; 5:6; 49:19; 50:17; 51:38. Of imaginary dangers feared by the sluggard—Pr. 22:13; 26:13. Of a king's wrath—Pr. 19:12; 20:2. Of persecutors—Ps. 22:13; II Tim. 4:17. Of Saul and Jonathan—II Sam. 1:23.

Symbolical.—Ez. 1:10; 10:14; Dan. 7:4; Rev. 4:7; 9:8, 17; 13:2.

LIPS. God's are opened—Job 11:5. Give commandment—Job 23:12. Full of indignation—Is. 30:27. Utter unalterable words—Ps. 89:34. Keep the righteous from folly—Ps. 17:4.

Prophet's.—Touched by live coal—Is. 6:7. Touched by angel—Dan. 10:16. Quivered at voice of God—Ps. 119:13.

Men responsible for.—Ps. 12:4; Hos. 14:2; Heb. 13:15.

Of the righteous.—Kept shut sometimes—Pr. 17:28. Used in silent prayer—I Sam. 1:13. Do not name idols—Ps. 16:4. Make and fulfill vows—Ps. 66:13, 14. Proclaim righteousness—Ps. 40:9. Utter praise—Ps. 63:3; 119:171; Heb. 13:15. Utter truth—Pr. 8:7. Wickedness is an abomination to—Pr. 8:7. Have wisdom and knowledge—Pr. 10:13; 15:2. Refrain from much speaking—Pr. 10:19. Speak right things—Pr. 23:16. Let others praise them—Pr. 27:2. Know what is acceptable—Pr. 10:32. Delight kings—Pr. 16:13. Turn many from iniquity—Mal. 2:6. Disperse knowledge—Pr. 15:7. Comfort the sorrowing—Job 16:5. Inspired by the heart—Pr. 16:23. Speak sincerely—Job 33:3. Are joyful—Ps. 63:5. Are sweet—Pr. 16:21.

Reward for righteous use of.—God answers requests of—Ps. 21:2. Food promised—Pr. 18:20. The king will be his friend—Pr. 16:13; 22:11. Others rejoice—Pr. 23:16. Many are fed—Pr. 10:21. Are preserved—Pr. 14:3. Shall shout in joy—Job 8:21; Ps. 63:5; 71:23.

Of the wicked.—Lying—Ps. 31:18; 120:2; Pr. 10:18; 12:22; 17:7; Is. 59:3. Perverse—Pr. 4:24; 19:1. Feigned—Ps. 71:1. Flattering—Ps. 12:2, 3; Pr. 7:21. Speak guile—Ps. 34:13; I Pet. 3:10. Unclean—Is. 6:5. Speak honeyed words for deceit—Pr. 5:3. Scorch as fire—Pr. 16:27. Talk too much—Pr. 17:28. Contend—Pr. 18:6, 7. Swear with—Lev. 5:4. Sin with—Job 2:10; 27:4; 33:3. Honor God with lips, not with heart—Is. 29:13; Mt. 15:8; Mk. 7:6. Shoot out to ridicule the righteous—Ps. 22:7. Like earthen vessel covered with silver—Pr. 26:23. Full of mischief—Ps. 140:9. Transgress—Pr. 12:13. Deceive—Pr. 24:28; 26:24. Contain poison of adder—Ps. 140:3; Rom. 3:13. Sharp as swords—Ps. 59:7. Compressed bring evil—Pr. 16:30.

Punishment of wicked.—Taken in their pride and consumed—Ps. 59:12, 13. Slain—Is. 11:4. Bridle in—Is. 37:29. God hears judges—Lam. 3:61, 62. Condemn themselves—Eccl. 10:12.

Figurative.—Cover lips in grief or shame—Lev. 13:45; Ez. 24:17, 22; Mic. 3:7. A right answer is like kissing—Pr. 24:26. Uncircumcised—Ex. 6:12, 30; Is. 28:11; I Cor. 14:21. Divine sentences in lips of kings—Pr. 16:10.

Miscellaneous.—Rash vows—Num. 30:6, 8; Deut. 23:23. Bridle and hook in captives'—II Ki. 19:28. Moses spoke unadvisedly—Ps. 106:33.

LISTENING. Lu. 19:48. Prisoners were—Acts 16:25. See EAR.

LITTER. Song of Sol. 3:7. See Num. 7:3; Is. 66:20.

LITTLE. Gen. 30:30; Lu. 16:10; 19:17. Better is a—Pr. 6:10. Children—Mk. 10:13. Faith—Mt. 8:26; 14:31. Flock—Lu. 12:32. Forgiven—Lu. 7:47. Gathered—Ex. 16:18; II Cor. 8:15. Glory a—II Cor. 11:16. Here a—Is.

28:10. Kingdom, In—Mt. 11:11; Lu. 7:28. Leaven—Gal. 5:9. Little by—Ex. 23:30. Lower—Ps. 8:5. One—Is. 60:22. Persuasion—Acts 26:28. Profitable for a—I Tim. 4:8. Sleep—Pr. 6:10. Stature, Of—Lu. 19:3. Things which are—Pr. 30:24. While—Heb. 10:37.

LIVE. I Pet. 4:6. As God—Job 27:2. Bread only, By—Deut. 8:3. Faith, By —Gal. 3:11; Heb. 10:38. Forever—Gen. 3:22. God, Unto—Rom. 6:10. Honorably—Heb. 13:18. My Redeemer—Job 19:25. Righteousness, Unto—I Pet. 2:24. Shall also—John 14:19. Soberly—Tit. 2:12. Soul—Gen. 12:13; Ps. 119:175; Is. 55:3; Jer. 38:20. Spirit, By—Gal. 5:25. To live is Christ —Phil. 1:21. With him—II Tim. 2:11. Yet shall he—John 11:25. See LIFE.

LIVING. Bread—John 6:51. Creatures —Gen. 1:20; Ez. 1:4-28; Rev. 4:6-9; 5:6, 14; 6:1; 7:11; 14:3; 15:7; 19:4. Father—John 6:57. God—Ps. 42:2; II Cor. 3:3; I Thess. 1:9. Hope—I Pet. 1:3. Judge of—Acts 10:42. Land of —Ps. 27:13; Jer. 11:19. Light of—Ps. 56:13. Sacrifice—Rom. 12:1. Soul —Gen. 2:7; I Cor. 15:45. Waters—Jer. 2:13; Zech. 14:8; John 4:10; 7:38. Way—Heb. 10:20. Word of God—Heb. 4:12. See LIFE.

LIZARD. See ANIMALS.

LO. Mt. 19:27; Lu. 17:23.

LOAF. II Sam. 16:1; I Chr. 16:3. Ask —Mt. 7:9. Barley, Of—II Ki. 4:42. Bread, Of—Ex. 29:23; Ju. 8:5; Jer. 37:21. Miracles of—Mt. 14:17; 15:32; Mk. 6:35; 8:6; Lu. 9:12; John 6:5.

LO-AMMI, lō′-ăm-mǐ. Hos. 1:9.

LOATHE. Bread—Num. 21:5. Egyptians shall—Ex. 7:18. Honeycomb—Pr. 7:7. Life—Job 7:16. Husband—Ez. 16:45. Me, Soul—Zech. 11:8. Themselves—Ez. 6:9. Yourselves—Ez. 20:43; 36:31. Zion—Jer. 14:19.

LOATHSOME. Num. 11:20. Food—Job 6:7. Wicked man is—Pr. 13:5.

LOCK. Song of Sol. 4:1. Bushy and black—Song of Sol. 5:11. Doors were —Ju. 3:24. Filled with drops of night —Song of Sol. 5:2. Grow long, To—Ez. 44:20. Hair, Of—Num. 6:5. Head, Of—Ju. 16:13, 19. See HAIR.

LOCUST. Ju. 6:5; 7:12; Nah. 3:15, 17. Bring—Ex. 10:4. Came—Ps. 105:34. Consume it—Deut. 28:38. Devour land, To—II Chr. 7:13. Food was—Mt. 3:4; Mk. 1:6. Have no king—Pr. 30:27. Horses, Like—Rev. 9:7. Leap as—Job 39:20. Left, Hath—Joel 1:4. More than—Jer. 46:23. No such—Ex. 10:14. Running to and fro of—Is. 33:4. Tossed up and down as—Ps. 109:23.

LOD, lŏd. **A town in Benjamin.**—I Chr. 8:12; Ezra 2:33; Neh. 7:37; 11:35.

LO-DEBAR, lō′-dē′bạr. **A place east of the Jordan.**—II Sam. 17:27.

LODGE. Acts 28:23. Branches, In—Mt. 13:32. Every—Ez. 40:17. Farthest—II Ki. 19:23. Gone in to—Lu. 19:7. House to—Ju. 19:15. In—Gen. 42:27. Mount, In—Lu. 21:37. On way at—Ex. 4:24. Prepare me a—Philemon 22. Wilderness, In—Ps. 55:7. See HOSPITALITY.

LOFTINESS. Man, Of—Is. 2:17.

LOFTY. Brought low, Shall be—Is. 10:33. City—Is. 26:5. Eyes—Ps. 131:1; Pr. 30:13. High and—Is. 57:15. Humbled, Are—Is. 5:15. Looks—Is. 2:11. Mountain—Is. 30:25; 57:7. People—Is. 24:4. Place—Ez. 16:31. Speak—Ps. 73:8. Tower—Is. 2:15.

LOG. See MEASURES.

LOINS: Customs of people.—During mourning, *Sackcloth upon*—Gen. 37:34; I Ki. 20:31, 32. During war, *Sword fastened upon*—II Sam. 20:8. Priests' garments—Ex. 28:42; Ez. 44:18.

Used in measurement.—Water to the loins—Ez. 47:4.

Strength in.—Job 40:16.

Suffering of.—Ps. 38:7. Filled with anguish—Is. 21:3; Jer. 30:6; Nah. 2:10.

Fruits of.—Gen. 46:26; Ex. 1:5; Acts 2:30; Heb. 7:5, 10.

Illustrative of close union.—Cleaveth to —Jer. 13:11.

Girding of loins.—With girdle—Job 12:18; Ez. 23:15. Elijah girded—I Ki. 18:46. With leather—I Ki. 1:8; Mt. 3:4; Mk. 1:6. Like a man—Job 38:3; 40:7. With strength—Pr. 31:17. With sackcloth—Is. 32:11. With linen—Jer. 13:1, 4. With pure gold—Dan. 10:5.

Blood of war upon.—In time of peace—I Ki. 2:5.

Size of.—Little finger is thicker than—I Ki. 12:10; II Chr. 10:10.

Protest of Job.—Job 31:20.

Punishment, Continual shaking of.—Ps. 69:23.

Warning in regard to.—Women of Jerusalem—Is. 32:11. Moab—Jer. 48:37. Israel—Amos 8:10. Nineveh—Nah. 2:1.

Vision of.—Ez. 1:27; 8:2. Daniel—Dan. 10:5.

Laws concerning.—Passover—Ex. 12:11.

Prophecies concerning. — Kings — Gen. 35:11. Solomon—Of Jehovah to David—I Ki. 8:19; II Chr. 6:9. Nations —Is. 5:27. Cyprus—Is. 45:1. Jeremiah—Jer. 30:16. Land of Israel—Ez. 21:6. Against Egypt—Ez. 29:7. Concerning Israel and Judah—Jer. 30:6.

Commands concerning.—Moses, to children of Israel—Deut. 33:11. Elisha, son of prophet—II Ki. 9:1. Jehovah —Job 38:3; 40:7. To Isaiah—Is. 20:2. To Jeremiah—Jer. 1:17; 13:1. Gehazi —II Ki. 4:29. Son of prophet—II Ki. 9:1.

LOIS, lō'is. **Grandmother of Timothy.** —II Tim. 1:5.

LONG. Gal. 2:20; Philemon 16. After —Gen. 31:30; Phil. 2:26. Ago—Lu. 10:13. Envying, Unto—Jas. 4:5. For thee—Ps. 63:1. For the spiritual milk —I Pet. 2:2. Precepts, After—Ps. 119:40. Return, To—Jer. 22:27. Soul —Ps. 84:2. Suffereth—I Cor. 13:4. To see thee—II Tim. 1:4. Told—II Cor. 7:7.

LONGSUFFERING. Lu. 18:7; Rom. 9: 2; Gal. 5:22; Eph. 4:2; I Thess. 5:14; I Pet. 3:20; II Pet. 3:15. See MERCY OF GOD, CHARACTER OF JESUS, CHRISTIAN GRACES.

LOOK. Lu. 1:48. Anger, In—Jer. 3:12. Away—Job 7:19; 14:6. Back—Lu. 9:62. Behind—Gen. 19:17; II Ki. 2: 24. Blessed hope, For—Tit. 2:13. Carefully—Eph. 5:15. Coming of day of God, For—II Pet. 3:12. Death, Upon—Gen. 21:16. Eyes—Ps. 17:2; 123:2. Face, In the—II Ki. 14:8. Forth—Hab. 2:1. Heaven, To—Mt. 14:19; Mk. 7:34; Lu. 9:16; Acts 1:11. Heavens, Unto—Job 35:5. Help, For —Jer. 3:23. Jehovah—Ps. 33:13. Jesus—Mt. 19:26; Mk. 10:21. Jesus, Unto—Heb. 12:2. Light, For—Is. 59:9. Lord, For—Lu. 12:36. One on another—John 13:22. Sheol, For—Job 17:13. Steadfastly—Mk. 8:25; Acts 23:1. Thyself, To—Gal. 6:1. Unto me—Is. 45:22. Unto the rock— Is. 51:1.

LOOKING GLASS. See MIRROR.

LOOM. Is. 38:12.

LOOSE. Bands—Job 38:31. Belt—Job 12:21. Be not—Ex. 28:28. Bonds— Ps. 116:16. Let—Gen. 49:21. People —Ex. 5:4. On earth, in heaven—Mt. 16:19. Sackcloth—Ps. 30:11. Seals —Rev. 5:2.

LORD. Charge, Over—I Pet. 5:3. Gentiles—Mk. 10:42. High places, Of— Num. 21:28. House, Of the—Mk. 13: 35. Kept watch over your—I Sam. 26: 16. Many—I Cor. 8:5. My—Gen. 43: 20. Own—Rom. 14:4. Philistines, Of—Josh. 13:3; Ju. 3:3. Sabbath, Of —Lu. 6:5. Signet of—Dan. 6:17. Supper made to—Mk. 6:21. Words of—Dan. 5:10. See GOD, JESUS.

LORDSHIP. Faith, Over—II Cor. 1:24. See JESUS, DIVINITY OF.

LORD'S SUPPER (Gr. *Eucharist*).—I Cor. 11:20. Called "Communion of blood of Christ"—I Cor. 10:16. Called "The breaking of bread"—Acts 2: 42, 20:7.

Instances of.—Appointed by Christ— Mt. 26:26-30; Mk. 14:12-17; Lu. 22: 15-18. *Cf.* Lu. 22:15-18 and Lu. 22:19, 20. Enjoined by apostles—Acts 2:42. Observed by disciples—Acts 2:42; 20: 7; I Cor. 11:20-26.

Its purpose.—To proclaim the Lord's death—I Cor. 11:26. To commemorate Jesus—Lu. 2:19; I Cor. 11:24, 25. For a communion of brethren—I Cor. 10:16, 17. For spiritual sustenance— Mt. 26:26-28; Mk. 14:22-24; Lu. 22: 19, 20; John 6:52-57.

Paul's teaching respecting it.—Was direct from Christ—I Cor. 11:23. The reason for assembling—I Cor. 11:20. Must eat worthily—I Cor. 11:27. Was abused in Corinth—I Cor. 11:21 ff. Must prove himself—I Cor. 11:28-31.

Must partake jointly—I Cor. 10:17; 11:33. No communion with demons—I Cor. 10:20, 21. See CHURCH, ORDINANCES.

LOSE. Mt. 10:39. Life—Ju. 18:25. Not—II John 8. Reward—Mt. 10:42.

LOSS. Bare—Gen. 31:39. Counted, for Christ—Phil. 3:7. Much—Acts 27:10. Suffer—I Cor. 3:15; II Cor. 7:9; Phil. 3:8.

LOST. Army—I Ki. 20:25. Nothing be—John 6:12. Not one—John 18:9. Save that which was—Mt. 8:11; Lu. 15:4, 6, 9, 24, 32. Savor—Mt. 5:13. Sheep—Ps. 119:176. Thing—Ex. 22:9.

LOT. Son of Haran and nephew of Abraham—Gen. 11:27. Terah takes Lot to Haran to dwell there—Gen. 11:31. Abraham and Lot go to Canaan—Gen. 11:31; 12:4. Lot had flocks, herds, and tents—Gen. 13:5. A strife between herdsmen causes separation—Gen. 13:7. Lot selects plain of the Jordan—Gen. 13:7, 8. Dwells in cities of plain—Sodom—Gen. 13:9–12. Taken captive by four kings—Gen. 14:12. Rescued by Abraham—Gen. 14:13–16. Rescued from destruction by angels—Gen. 19:1–17. Proposes a change of place of refuge—Gen. 19:17–20. Lot's wife disobeys command and perishes—Gen. 19:16, 17, 26; Lu. 17:31, 32. Lot dwells in the mountain—Gen. 19:30. His daughters cause him to sin—Gen. 19:31–38. Peter justifies Lot—II Pet. 2:7, 8. Possession of children of Lot—Gen. 19:36, 37; Deut. 2:19. See ABRAHAM.

LOTS, CASTING. See CAST.

LOTAN, lō'tan. Son of Seir.—Gen. 36:20–29; I Chr. 1:38, 39.

LOUD. Cry—Esth. 4:1. Cymbals—Ps. 150:5. Exceeding—Ex. 19:16. Instruments—II Chr. 30:21. Noise—Ps. 33:3. Shout—Ezra 3:13. Trumpet—Lev. 25:9. Voice—Gen. 39:14; Deut. 27:14; Mt. 27:46, 50; Mk. 1:26; 5:7; 15:34.

LOVE. Song of Sol. 8:6, 7; Lu. 7:42, 47; I Cor. 8:1; 13:1–13; 16:14; Eph. 5:2; Phil. 1:9; Col. 3:12–14; I Thess. 5:8; I Tim. 1:5.

Source is in God.—I John 4:16.

Love of God.—For men—Ex. 20:6; Deut. 5:10; 7:9; 10:18; II Sam. 12:

24; Job 7:17; Ps. 91:14; 103:13, 14; Pr. 8:17; Mt. 5:43–45; 10:29–31; 18:1–14; Lu. 6:35; 12:6, 7; John 14:21, 23; 16:27; 17:23, 26; II Cor. 9:7; 13:19; II Thess. 2:16; I Tim. 2:3, 4; II Pet. 3:9, 15; I John 3:1; Jude 21.

He manifests His love for man—Ps. 31:19, 21; 90:1; Pr. 3:12; Is. 38:17; 56:6, 7; Jer. 32:18; Mal. 3:16–18; Mt. 5:45; I Cor. 2:9; Heb. 11:16; 12:6.

By sending His Son—John 3:16; 14:21, 23; 15:13; 17:26; Rom. 5:6–8; 8:31, 32, 38, 39; II Cor. 5:14–19; Gal. 2:20; Eph. 1:3–14; 2:4–7; 3:1–6; Col. 1:19, 20; Tit. 3:4–6; I John 4:7–19. For Israel—Ex. 6:7, 8; Deut. 4:37; 7:7, 8, 12, 13; 13:17; 23:5; Is. 43:3, 4; 63:9; Zeph. 3:17; Mal. 1:1–5; Rom. 11:28, 29.

His love manifested—Ex. 6:7, 8; 19:4; Lev. 25:42; 26:12; Deut. 28:9; 32:9–14; Is. 5:1–4; 49:14–23; 54:5–17; Jer. 31:1–14; Hos. 11:4.

For Christ—Mt. 3:17; 12:18; 17:5; Mk. 9:7; Lu. 9:35; John 3:35; 5:20; 15:9; 17:23, 24, 26.

Love for God.—Deut. 7:9; 10:12; 11:1, 22; 19:9; 30:6, 16, 20; Josh. 23:11; Ju. 5:31; Ps. 5:11; 18:1; 31:23; 37:4; 63:5, 6; 69:36; 73:25, 26; 97:10; Pr. 23:26; Lu. 11:42; 8:28; I Cor. 8:3; I Thess. 3:5; I John 5:2–5.

With all the heart—Deut. 6:5; 11:13; 13:3; 30:6; Josh. 22:5; Mt. 22:37; Mk. 12:30; Lu. 10:27.

Love of Christ.—Passeth knowledge—Eph. 3:17–19. Constraining—II Cor. 5:14. To the Father—John 14:31. For the lost—Is. 40:11; Mt. 23:37; Mk. 3:5; 10:21; Lu. 19:10. For His church—Eph. 5:2, 25, 29. For John the apostle—John 13:23; 19:26; 20:2; 21:7, 20. For Peter—Lu. 22:31–32.

For His disciples—John 14:21; 15:9–15; Rom. 8:35–39; Gal. 2:20; II Thess. 2:13; I John 4:19; Rev. 1:5; 3:9, 10. For Lazarus, Mary, and Martha—John 11:5, 33–36.

Love for Christ.—Mt. 10:37–39; 26:35; Mk. 16:10; Lu. 7:37–50; 23:27, 55, 56; 24:1–10; John 8:42; 10:17; 11:16; 13:37; 14:21–24; 19:38–42; 20:1–18; 21:15–17; II Cor. 8:8, 9; Jas. 1:12; I Pet. 1:8.

For brethren.—Ps. 33:1-3; Mal. 2:10; John 13:14, 15, 34, 35; 15:12, 13, 17; Acts 21:13; 28:15; Rom. 12:14-16; 13:8; 14:19, 21; 15:1-7; I Cor. 10:24; 16:22; Gal. 5:13-15; 6:1, 2, 10; Eph. 4:2, 32; Phil. 2:2; I Thess. 3:12; 4:9, 10, 18; Col. 2:2; Philemon 6; Heb. 13:1; I Pet. 1:22; 2:17; 3:8; 4:8; 3:10-19, 23; 4:7-11, 20, 21; 5:2.

For neighbors.—Ex. 20:17; Job 31:16-22; 42:11; Pr. 17:9; Mt. 7:12.

As thyself—Lev. 19:18; Mt. 19:19; 22:39, 40; Mk. 12:31, 33; Lu. 10:25-37; Rom. 13:8-10; Gal. 5:14, 15; Jas. 2:8.

For friends.—Ex. 32:31, 32; I Sam. 16:21; 18:1, 16; 20:16, 17; II Sam. 1:26; I Ki. 5:1; 18:4; Neh. 5:17-19; Pr. 17:17; 18:24; 27:10, 17; Lu. 7:2-10; John 11:11; 15:13-15.

Love for enemies.—Ex. 23:4, 5; Pr. 24:17; Mt. 5:43, 44, 46; Lu. 6:27, 32, 35; Acts 7:60; 26:29; Rom. 12:20; I Cor. 13:5.

For sojourners.—Ex. 22:21; Lev. 19:34; 25:35; Deut. 10:18, 19; II Ki. 6:21-23; Jer. 2:25.

Love for children.—Gen. 22:2; 30:1; 44:20; II Sam. 1:23; 18:33; Ps. 127:3-5; Is. 2:17-18; Mk. 10:13-16; Lu. 18:15-17; Tit. 2:4.

Man's love for his fellow-man.—Ps. 133:1-3; Mt. 25:34-40; Mk. 9:41; Lu. 6:31-35; I Cor. 10:24; Gal. 6:1, 2, 10; Eph. 4:2, 32; Phil. 2:2; I Thess. 5:8, 13, 14; Jas. 1:12. See FRATERNITY.

Love of man and woman.—Gen. 24:67; 29:18-20, 30, 32; 34:3, 12; Ju. 16:4; Ruth Chs. 2-4; I Sam. 1:5; II Sam. 13:1; I Ki. 11:1; II Chr. 11:21; Esth. 2:17; Song of Sol. 1:4, 7; 2:4-8; 3:2; 4:1, 7-10; 5:1, 9, 16; Hos. 3:1; John 11:5, 36; Eph. 5:25, 28-31; Col. 3:19; Tit. 2:4. See MARRIAGE.

Love for God cannot exist with: Love of the world—I John 2:15; Jas. 4:4. Love of mammon—Mt. 6:24; Lu. 16:13. Love of self—Mt. 10:39; 16:25-26; Mk. 8:35-36; Lu. 9:24-25; John 12:25-26. See SELF-DENIAL. Love of Satan—Ps. 97:10; Mt. 4:10; Lu. 4:8; John 12:31; 14:30. Sinful fear—II Tim. 1:7; I John 4:18. Hatred of a brother—Mt. 5:22; I John 3:10-16; 4:20-21. Love's antagonism with sin —Gen. 18:23-33; Ex. 20:5; Deut. 7:10-11; 10:17-18; Ps. 27:5; 97:10; Is. 63:1-4; Hos. 3:1; Mt. 23:37-39; 26:48-50; 27:3-5; Lu. 15:11-32; John 13:21-27; I Cor. 4:21; Heb. 12:6; Rev. 2:2-6; 2:9-10; 2:13-16; 2:19-28; 3:1-5; 3:8-12; 3:15-21.

Love as an active principle.—John 14:15; Gal. 2:19-20; Heb. 13:1-2; Jude 21; I John 2:5; 3:17; 4:8; II John 6.

An evidence of the new life.—John 13:35; 14:23-24; Gal. 2:19-20; Col. 1:4-8; I Thess. 1:3; II Tim. 1:7; I John 3:14-17; 4:12-13.

Love is the fulfilling of the law.—Mt. 22:40; Mk. 12:23; Lu. 10:28; Rom. 13:10; I Cor. 13:1-7; I Tim. 1:5.

Love is the fruit of the Spirit.—Mt. 7:16-20; Rom. 5:3-5; 6:21-22; I Cor. 13:4-7; Gal. 5:22; Eph. 5:8-11; Col. 3:12-14.

True love is without hypocrisy.—Mt. 7:3-5; 22:16-22; Rom. 12:9; Eph. 6:24; I Pet. 1:22; II Pet. 2:15.

The measure of love.—Mk. 12:33; John 3:16; 13:34; 15:13; Rom. 8:35-39; I Cor. 2:2; II Tim. 4:8; I John 4:10-11.

Love constrains to unselfish service.—I Cor. 4:9-13; 9:16-23; II Cor. 4:8-12; 5:14; Gal. 4:15; Phil. 4:12-13; Heb. 10:24; I Pet. 3:10.

Love at its topmost height.—Mt. 26:6-13; John 13:34-35; 15:12; I Cor. 16:14; Gal. 2:20; 6:14; Phil. 2:12-18; II Tim. 4:6-8.

The characteristics of love.—Precious—Pr. 15:17. Unquenchable—Pr. 17:17; Song of Sol. 8:7. Covereth sins—Pr. 10:12; I Pet. 4:8. Strong as death—Song of Sol. 8:6. Worketh no ill—Rom. 13:10. Casteth out fear—I John 4:18.

Is without hypocrisy.—Rom. 12:9. Is tenderly affectionate—Rom. 12:10.

In honor prefers another.—Rom. 2:10. Accords with others—Phil. 2:2. (See I Cor. Ch. 13.)

The Christian "in love," in twelve particulars: Before God in love—Eph. 1:4. Rooted and grounded in love—Eph. 3:17. Forbears one another in love—Eph. 4:2. Speaks the truth in love—Eph. 4:15. Edifies body in love —Eph. 4:16. Walks in love—Eph. 5:2. Knit together in love—Col. 2:2. Does all his acts in love—I Cor. 16:14.

Is unfeigned in love—II Cor. 6:6. Is truthful in love—I John 3:18. Keeps himself in love with God—Jude 21. Increases in love—I Thess. 3:12.

Forsaken love.—Mt. 26:14–16; John 5: 42; 6:66–67; Gal. 3:1–3; II Tim. 4:10; Rev. 2:4; 3:1–2.

Loving chief seats.—Mt. 23:6; Lu. 11: 43; 20:46.

Loving darkness rather than light.— John 3:19.

Love to stand praying.—Mt. 6:5.

LOVINGKINDNESS. See KINDNESS, LOVE, CHRISTIAN GRACES.

LOW. Angels, Than — Heb. 2:7, 9. Brought—Ju. 6:6; Is. 2:9, 11. Come down—Deut. 28:43. Degree—Jas. 1: 9. Estate—Ps. 136:23. God, Than— Ps. 8:5. Laid—Job 14:10; Is. 32:19. Nations—Is. 14:12. Pavement—Ez. 40:18. Place—Ps. 88:6; Lu. 14:9, 10. Pool—Is. 22:9. Sheol—Ps. 86:13.

LOWERED. Boat—Acts 27:30. Gear —Acts 27:17.

LOWLINESS. Eph. 4:2; Col. 3:12. Comforteth the—II Cor. 7:6. Heart, In—Mt. 11:29. I am—II Cor. 10:1. Mind, Of—Acts 20:19; Phil. 2:3. Respect unto the—Ps. 138:6. Spirit— Pr. 16:19. Things—Rom. 12:16. See HUMILITY.

LUBIM, lū′bim. **Inhabitants of North Africa.**—II Chr. 12:3; 16:8; Nah. 3:9.

LUCAS. See LUKE.

LUCIFER. Is. 14:12 (A.V.).

LUCIUS, lū′si-us. (1) **A disciple teacher in Antioch.**—Acts 13:1.

(2) **One of Paul's kinsmen.**—Rom. 16: 21.

LUCRE. Greedy of—I Tim. 3:8; Tit. 1:7. See COVETOUSNESS. Filthy—I Pet. 5:2. Sake of, For—Tit. 1:11. Turned aside after—I Sam. 8:3. See WEALTH, JESUS TEACHING ON RICHES.

LUD, lŭd. (1) **Son of Shem.**—Gen. 10: 22; I Chr. 1:17.

(2) **Descendants in Africa, Asia Minor, and Assyria.**—Is. 66:19; Ez. 27:10.

LUDIM, lū′dim. **Son of Mizraim.**— Gen. 10:13; I Chr. 1:11.

LUHITH, lū′hith. **A Moabite city.**— Is. 15:5; Jer. 48:5.

LUKE, lūke. See OUTLINE STUDIES IN THE BOOKS.

LUKEWARM. Rev. 3:16.

LUMP. See CAKE.

LURK. Ps. 10:9; 17:12; Pr. 1:11, 18.

LURKING-PLACES. I Sam. 23:23; Ps. 10:9.

LUST: Worldly.—II Pet. 1:4; I John 2:16, 17. Of appetite—Num. 11:4, 34; Ps. 78:18, 30; 106:14. Of flesh— Ju. 3:29; Is. 59:10; Rom. 1:24, 27; 6: 12; 13:14; I Cor. 10:6; Gal. 5:16, 17, 24; Eph. 2:3; I Thess. 4:5; II Tim. 3:6; 4:3; Tit. 3:3; Jas. 1:14; 4:2, 3; I Pet. 4:2, 3; II Pet. 2:10, 18; I John 2:16. Of the eyes—I John 2:16. Of deceit—Eph. 4:22.

Warnings against.—Pr. 6:25; I Tim. 6: 9; II Tim. 2:22; Tit. 2:12; I Pet. 1:14; 2:11; 4:2, 3; II Pet. 3:3; Jude 16, 18.

Punishment for.—Jas. 1:15; Rev. 18:14.

Is of the world, and passes away.—I John 2:16 f. See JESUS, TEACHING OF, FORNICATION, SIN.

LYING: As respects God.—Gen. 3:1–5; Num. 23:19; I Sam. 15:29; Rom. 3:4; Tit. 1:2; Heb. 6:18; I John 1:10; 5:10.

Forging lies.—Job 13:4; Ps. 119:69; Is. 44:20; Rev. 3:9; 21:27; 22:15.

Divining lies.—Ez. 21:29; 22:28; John 8:44.

Changing truth into.—Rom. 1:25; 3:7; Jas. 3:14; I John 1:6; 2:21, 27

Trusting in.—Jonah 2:8; Jer. 28:15; 7: 4, 8; II Thess. 2:11.

Lies as a refuge.—Ps. 89:35; Is. 28:15, 17; 59:4; Hos. 7:3.

Prophesying lies.—Is. 9:15; Jer. 14:14; 23:14–32; 27:10–16; 29:21; Ez. 13:1– 23; Mic. 3:11.

Speaking lies.—Ps. 109:2; Jer. 29:23; Zeph. 3:13; Zech. 13:3; John 8:44; Eph. 4:25; I Tim. 4:2.

Lying spirits.—I Ki. 22:22, 23; II Chr. 18:21, 22.

Lying tongues.—Pr. 17:4, 7; 21:6; 26: 28; Col. 3:9.

False witnesses.—Pr. 6:19; 14:5, 25.

Men as liars.—Job 11:3, 25; Ps. 58:3; 62:4; 116:11; Pr. 17:4; 19:22; 30:6; Tit. 1:12; I John 2:4, 22; 4:20; Rev. 2:2; 21:8.

Danger of.—Pr. 19:5, 9; 29:12; Is. 32:7; Hos. 10:13; Amos 2:4, 5.

Not guilty of.—Rom. 9:1; II Cor. 11:31; Gal. 1:20; I Tim. 2:7.

Hatred of lies.—Ps. 31:18; 59:12; 119:29, 163; 120:2; Pr. 6:17; 12:22. See FALSEHOOD, DECEPTION.

Barabbas, Bound—Mk. 15:7. Down—Ps. 139:3. Jesus saw him—John 5:6. Linen cloths—John 20:6. Mother, Sick—Mt. 8:14.

LYING IN WAIT. Abiding in upper chamber—Ju. 16:9. Heard of—Acts 23:16. See AMBUSH.

MAACAH, mā′a-cah. (1) **Wife of David and mother of Absalom.**—II Sam. 3:3; I Chr. 3:2.

(2) **Son of Nahor and nephew of Absalom.**—Gen. 22:24.

(3) **A district and city in Manasseh east of the Jordan.**—II Sam. 10:8; I Chr. 19:6, 7.

(4) **King of Maacah.**—II Sam. 10:6.

(5) **Wife of Rehoboam and mother of Abijah kings of Judah.**—I Ki. 15:2; II Chr. 11:20–22.

(6) **Father of Achish king of Gath.**—I Ki. 2:39.

(7) **Wife of Machir son of Manasseh.**—I Chr. 7:15, 16.

(8) **Concubine of Caleb son of Hezron.**—I Chr. 2:48.

(9) **Father of Hanum, one of David's mighty men.**—I Chr. 11:43.

(10) **Wife of Jehiel, who founded Gibeon.**—I Chr. 8:29; 9:35.

(11) **Father of Shephatiah.**—I Chr. 27:16.

MAACATHITES, ma-ăk′a-thītes. **Inhabitants of Maacah near Mt. Hermon.**—Deut. 3:14; Josh. 12:5; 13:11, 13; II Sam. 23:34; II Ki. 25:23; I Chr. 4:19; Jer. 40:8.

MAADAI, ma-ăd′āi. **One of those who married foreign wives.**—Ezra 10:34.

MAADIAH, mā′a-dī′ah. **A priest who returned with Zerubbabel.**—Neh. 12:5.

MAAI, ma-ā′i. **A priest after the exile.**—Neh. 12:26.

MAARATH, mā′a-răth. **A city of Judah.**—Josh. 15:59.

MAASEIAH, mā′a-sē′iah. (1) **A captain under Josiah.**—II Chr. 23:1.

(2) **A Levite.**—I Chr. 15:18, 20.

(3) **An officer under king Uzziah.**—II Chr. 26:11.

(4) **Son of Ahaz king of Judah.**—II Chr. 28:7.

(5) **Governor of Jerusalem under Josiah.**—II Chr. 34:8.

(6, 7, 8, 9) **Priests who married foreign wives.**—Ezra 10:8, 21, 22, 30.

(10) **A priest who explained the law for Ezra.**—Neh. 8:7.

(11) **A priest who assisted Ezra when he read the law.**—Neh. 8:4.

(12) **Father of Azariah who repaired the wall.**—Neh. 3:23.

(13) **One who assisted Nehemiah in sealing the covenant.**—Neh. 10:25.

(14) **Ancestor of some who dwelt in Jerusalem after the captivity.**—Neh. 11:7.

(15) **One who dwelt in Jerusalem after the captivity.**—Neh. 11:5.

(16, 17) **Two priests who assisted in purification of wall.**—Neh. 11:5, 7.

(18) **A priest, father of one sent by Zedekiah to inquire of Jehovah.**—Jer. 21:1; 29:25; 37:3.

(19) **An officer in the temple under Jehoiakim.**—Jer. 35:4.

(20) **Father of a false prophet during the captivity.**—Jer. 29:21.

(21) **Grandfather of Baruch, Jeremiah's secretary and messenger.**—Jer. 32:12; 51:59

MAATH, mā′ath. **Ancestor of Jesus.**—Lu. 3:26.

MAAZ, mā′ăz. **Son of Ram.**—1 Chr. 2:27.

MAAZIAH, mā′a-zī′ah. (1) **A priest under David.**—1 Chr. 24:18.

(2) **A priest who assisted Nehemiah in sealing the covenant.**—Neh. 10:8.

MACEDONIA, măs′e-dō′ni-a. **Important country in Europe.**—Paul's call and ministry in—Acts 16:9–12; 20:1, 3; I Cor. 16:5; II Cor. 1:16; 2:13; 7:5; Phil. 4:15; I Tim. 1:3. Silas and Timothy—Acts 18:5. Timothy and Erastus—Gaius and Aristarchus—Acts 19:22, 29. Timothy—Phil. 1:1; 2:19–23. Luke—Acts 16:10–16; 20:5–7. Spread the gospel in—II Cor. 8:1; 9:2, 4; I Thess. 1:7, 8; 4:10. Charity of—Rom. 15:26; II Cor. 11:9; Phil. 4:15

Cities of.—Philippi—Acts 16:12; 20:6; Phil. 1:1; I Thess. 2:2. Thessalonica—Acts 17:1; 27:2; Phil. 4:16; II Tim. 4:10. Amphipolis—Acts 17:1. Apollonia—Acts 17:1. Berœa—Acts 17:10, 13; 20:4. Neapolis—Acts 16:11.

Inhabitants called Macedonians.—Acts 27:2.

First convert in Macedonia was Lydia.—Acts 16:14.

Remarkable conversion of the philippian jailor.—Acts 16:23–33.

MACHBANNAI, măk'ban-nāi. A Gadite soldier who joined David at Ziklag.—I Chr. 12:13.

MACHBENA, măk'be-nà.—I Chr. 2:49.

MACHI, mā'ki. Father of one of the spies.—Num. 13:15.

MACHIR, mā'kir. (1) Son of Manasseh.—Gen. 50:23; Num. 26:29; 27:1; 32: 39, 40; 36:1; Deut. 3:15; Josh. 13:31; 17:1, 3; Ju. 5:14; I Chr. 2:21, 23; 7: 14–17.

(2) A man of Manasseh.—II Sam. 9:4, 5; 17:27.

MACHIRITES—Decendants of Machir.—Num. 26:29.

MACHNADEBAI, măk'na-dē'bāi. One of the sons of Bani who married a foreign wife.—Ezra 10:40.

MACHPELAH, măk-pē'lah. A field containing a cave which Abraham purchased for a burial place.—Abraham, Sarah, Isaac, Rebekah, Leah and Jacob buried there.—Gen. 23:9, 17:19; 25:9; 49:30; 50:13.

MAD.—Acts 26:24, 25. See INSANITY, MADNESS.

MADAI, măd'a-i. Son of Japheth from whom the Medes were descended.—Gen. 10:2; I Chr. 1:5.

MADE.—Alive in the spirit.—Eph. 2:5; I Pet. 3:18. Bondman—Zech. 13:5. See BONDAGE. Truthful—Gen. 41:52. Head of the corner—Mt. 21:42. See STONE. Him but little lower—Ps. 8:5. See MAN. Intercession — Is. 53:12. See PRAYER. Manifest—II Cor. 3:3. See MANIFEST. Ready — Rev. 21:2. See CREATE, CREATOR, GOD.

MADMANNAH, mad-măn'nah. (1) A city of Judah.—Josh. 15:31. (2) Son of Caleb son of Jephuneh.—I Chr. 2: 49.

MADMEN, măd-men. A Moabite town.—Jer. 48:2.

MADMENAH, mad-mē'nah. A Benjamite town.—Is. 10:31.

MADNESS.—John 10:20; I Cor. 14:23; Eccl. 2:12. Feigned—I Sam. 21:13. Filled with—Lu. 6:11. Foolishness is

—Eccl. 7:25. Mischievous—Eccl. 10: 13. Prophet, Of the—II Pet. 2:16. Smite with—Deut. 28:28; Zech. 12:4. See INSANITY.

MADON, mā'don. A Canaanite city.—Josh. 11:1.

MAGADAN, măg'a-dan. A town of Galilee.—Mt. 15:39.

MAGBISH, măg'bish.—Ezra 2:30.

MAGDALENE.—A woman of Magadan. See MARY.

MAGDIEL, măg'di-el. A duke of Edom.—Gen. 36:43; I Chr. 1:54.

MAGIC.—All the methods treated below have a relation to some belief in superhuman powers. They are usually found in any low form of civilization, and are utilized (1) to obtain a knowledge of the future; (2) to obtain some assistance in the affairs of life; (3) to produce or counteract evil influence.

Augury.—(This word, like enchantment, signifies by means of omens.) Lev. 19:26; Deut. 18:10; II Ki. 21:6; II Chr. 33:6.

Enchanters.—Deut. 18:10; II Ki. 21:6; Dan. 1:20; 2:2, 27; 4:7; 5:7, 11.

Enchantments.—II Chr. 33:6; Is. 47:9, 12. Familiar spirits (necromancy)—Lev. 19:31; 20:6, 27; Deut. 18:11; I Sam. 28:3, 7–9; II Ki. 21:6; 23:24; I Chr. 10:13; II Chr. 33:6; Is. 8:19; 19: 3; 29:4.

Magicians.—(Used to interpret dreams and to counteract evil influences.) Egyptian—Gen. 41:8, 24; Ex. 7:11, 22; 8:7, 18, 19; 9:11. Babylonian—Dan. 1:20; 2:2, 10, 27; 4:7, 9; 5:11.

Soothsayers.—(Makers of predictions.) Balaam—Josh. 13:22. Copyists from Philistines—Is. 2:6. Judah's false prophets — Jer. 27:9. Babylonian — Dan. 2:27; 4:7; 5:7, 11; Mic. 5:12. Soothsaying—Acts 16:16.

Diviners.—(Same as soothsayers.) Deut. 18:14; I Sam. 6:2; 28:8; Is. 44:25; Jer. 27:9; 29:8; Ez. 13:9, 23; 21:29; Mic. 3:6, 7, 11; Zech. 10:2.

Divination.—Num. 22:7; 23:23; Deut. 18:10; II Ki. 17:17; Jer. 14:14; Ez. 12:24; 13:6, 7; 21:21, 22, 23; Acts 16: 16.

Sorcerers.—(Mixers of ingredients for magical ends.) Ex. 7:11; Deut. 18:10;

Jer. 2:9; Dan. 2:2; Mal. 3:5; Acts 8:9–10; 13:6–8; 19:19; Rev. 21:8; 22:15. Sorceresses—Ex. 22:18; Is. 57:3. Sorcery—II Chr. 33:6; Is. 47:9, 12; Acts 8:9, 11; Gal. 5:20; Rev. 9:21; 18:23. Witch.—Ex. 22:18; Deut. 18:11; II Chr. 33:6. Witchcraft (to injure by magical arts)—I Sam. 15:23; 28:11–12; II Ki. 9:22; Nah. 3:4. Abolished—II Ki. 23:24; Mic. 5:12. Wizards. — (Originally wise men — Magi.) Lev. 19:31; 20:27; Deut. 18: 11; I Sam. 28:3, 9; II Ki. 21:6; 23:24; II Chr. 33:6; Is. 8:19; 19:3.

MAGISTRATE. Appoint — Ezra 7:25; Good, Examples of—Gen. 41:46; Ju. 8:35; I Sam. 12:3, 4; Neh. 3:16; Job. 8:35; Dan. 6:3. Rent garments—Acts 16:22. Wicked, Examples of—I Sam. 8:3; Mt. 27:24, 26; Acts 18:16, 17; Acts 24:26. See GOVERNMENT.

MAGNIFICENT. I Chr. 22:5; Acts 19: 27.

MAGNIFY. Begin to—Josh. 3:7. Christ shall be—Phil. 1:20. Himself—Dan. 8:4, 8. Jehovah — Ps. 34:3; 35:27. Lord Jesus was—Acts 19:17. Lovingkindness—Gen. 19:19. My soul doth —Lu. 1:46. We shall be—II Cor. 10: 15. See PRAISE.

MAGOG, mā'gŏg. (1) Son of Japheth.— Gen. 10:2; I Chr. 1:5.

(2) Descendants of Magog and their land.—Ez. 38:2; 39:6; Rev. 20:8.

MAGOR-MISSABIB, mā'gor-mĭs'sa-bĭb. —Jer. 20:3.

MAGPIASH, măg'pi-ăsh. Neh. 10:20.

MAHALALEEL, mā'hă-lā'le-el. (1) A grandson of Seth.—Gen. 5:12–17; I Chr. 1:2.

(2) Ancestor of some who dwelt in Jerusalem after the captivity.—Neh. 11:4.

MAHALATH, mā'ha-lath. (1) A daughter of Ishmael.—Gen. 28:9.

(2) Wife of Rehoboam, granddaughter of David.—II Chr. 11:18.

(3) Ps. 53, 88 titles. See MUSIC, PSALMS.

MAHALATH-LEANNOTH, mā'ha-lath-le-ăn'noth. Ps. 88 title. See LEANOTH.

MAHANAIM, mā'ha-nā'im. A place.— Josh. 13:26, 30. Jacob met angels here and named the place—Gen. 32:2. Assigned to the Levites—Josh. 21:38. Capital of Northern Israel under Ishbosheth—II Sam. 2:8, 12, 29. David

went there when Absalom revolted— II Sam. 17:24, 27; 19:33; I Ki. 2:8. Seat of one of Solomon's prefectures —I Ki. 4:14.

MAHANAIM. Dance of—Song of Sol. 6:13.

MAHANEH-DAN, mā'ha-neh-dăn. A place in Judah.—Ju. 18:12.

MAHARAI, ma-hăr'a-ī. One of David's soldiers.—II Sam. 23:28; I Chr. 11:30; 27:13.

MAHATH, mā'hath. (1) A descendant of Kohath.—I Chr. 6:35; II Chr. 29: 12.

(2) A Levite.—II Chr. 31:13.

MAHAVITE, mā'ha-vite. I Chr. 11:46.

MAHAZIOTH, ma-hā-zi-ŏth. Son of Heman.—I Chr. 25:4, 30.

MAHER-SHALAL-HASH-BAZ, mā'her-shăl'al–hăsh-băz. Symbolic name given to son of Isaiah.—Is. 8:1.

MAHLAH, mah'läh. Daughter of Zelophehad.—Num. 26:33; 27:1; 36:11; Josh. 17:3.

MAHLI, mäh-li. (1) Son of Merari.— Ex. 6:19; I Chr. 6:19, 29; 23:21; 24:26, 28; Ezra 8:18.

(2) Grandson of Merari.—I Chr. 6:47; 23:23; 24:30.

MAHLITES. Descendants of Mahli.— Num. 3:3; 26:58.

MAHLON. mäh-lon. Son of Naomi, first husband of Ruth.—Ruth 1:2, 5; 4:9, 10.

MAHOL, mā'hŏl. I Ki. 4:3.

MAID. Ps. 123:2; Mt. 26:69; Acts 12: 13; 16:16. See HANDMAID.

MAIDEN. Ex. 2:5; Ruth 2:8; II Ki. 5: 2; Esth. 2:7.

MAID-SERVANT. Ex. 20:10; II Sam. 17:17; Lu. 12:45. See HANDMAID, SERVANT.

MAIL. See ARMOR.

MAIM. Mt. 15:30, 31; Lu. 14:13, 21. Animal—Lev. 22:22. See LAMENESS.

MAINTAIN. Job 16:21; Ps. 9:4; 112: 5; Tit. 3:8.

MAINTENANCE. Pr. 27:27.

MAJESTIC. II Pet. 1:17.

MAJESTY. See GOD, JESUS.

MAKAZ, mā-kăz. A town—I Ki. 4:9.

MAKE. Abomination — Rev. 21:27. Known—II Cor. 8:1. Manifest—Heb. 11:14. Not thou common—Acts 10:15; 11:9. Path, Level—Pr. 4:26. Ready

—Mt. 26:17. Soul to pine away—Lev. 26:16. Storm calm—Ps. 107:29. Sure —I Sam. 23:22. Uproar—Is. 8:9. Way —Ps. 83:13. See CREATE, CREATOR, GOD.

MAKHELOTH, măk-hē′lŏth. One of Israel's encampments.—Num. 33:25, 26. See CAMP, ISRAEL.

MAKKEDAH, măk-kē′dăh. A city in Judah.—Josh. 10:10, 16-28; 12:16; 15:41.

MAKTESH, măk′těsh. A district in or near Jerusalem.—Zeph. 1:11.

MALACHI, măl′a-kī. See OUTLINE STUDIES IN THE BOOKS.

MALCHAM, măl′kam. (1) A Benjamite.—I Chr. 8:9.

(2) An idol of the Ammonites.—Zeph. 1:5.

MALCHIEL, măl′ki-el. Grandson of Asher.—Gen. 46:17; Num. 26:45; I Chr.•7:31.

MALCHIJAH, mal-kī′jah. (1) An Aaronite ancestor of some who dwelt in Jerusalem after the captivity.—I Chr. 9:12; Neh. 11:12.

(2) A Gershonite ancestor of Asaph.—I Chr. 6:40.

(3, 4, 5) Three who married foreign wives.—Ezra 10:25, 31.

(6) A priest.—I Chr. 24:9.

(7, 8, 9) Some who assisted in repairing the wall.—Neh. 3:11, 14, 31.

(10) One who stood beside Ezra when he read the law.—Neh. 8:4.

(11) A priest who assisted in purifying the wall.—Neh. 10:3; 12:42.

(12) Father of Pashur.—Jer. 21:1; 38:1.

MALCHIRAM, mal-kī′ram. I Chr. 3:18.

MALCHI-SHUA, măl′ki–shu′a. One of Saul's sons.—I Sam. 14:49; 31:2; I Chr. 8:33; 9:39; 10:2.

MALCHUS, măl′kus. A servant of the high-priest. Peter smote off his ear and Jesus healed him—Mt. 26:51; Lu. 22:51; John 18:10.

MALE AND FEMALE. Creation of male and female—Gen. 1:27; 5:2. See JESUS, TEACHING OF.

Laws concerning males.—Birth—Lev. 12:7; Lu. 2:23. Numbering of—Num. 1:2; 3:15, 22, 28, 39, 40; 26:62. Men of war—Num. 1:20; Deut. 20:13. Unclean—Num. 5:3; 31:17. Circumcision of—Gen. 17:10–27; 34:15, 22, 24;

Josh. 5:4. Laws of vows—Lev. 27:3–7. Tithes of—II Chr. 31:16, 19. Adultery of—Ju. 21:11. Males in priest's houses—Lev. 6:18, 29; 7:6; Num. 18:10; II Chr. 31:19.

Killed in war.—Gen. 34:25; Num. 31:7; I Ki. 11:15, 16.

List of males who went with Ezra.—Ezra 8:3–14.

Heirs of the covenants.—Deut. 7:14. See COVENANTS—Gen. 17:2.

Male children of Manasseh.—Josh. 17:2.

Female.—See WOMEN, DAUGHTER, VIRGIN.

Male and female children.—See CHILDREN.

Male and female gods.—Deut. 4:16.

Neither male nor female.—Gal. 3:28.

Animals.—Males and females in ark—Gen. 6:19; 7:2, 3, 9, 16. Used as offerings—Lev. 3:6. Of males: Sheep—Ex. 12:5; 34:19; Lev. 1:3, 10. Ox—Ex. 34:19. Bullock—Lev. 1:3, 10; 22:19. Goats—Lev. 3:6; 4:23. Herd—Mal. 1:14. Of females—Lev. 4:28, 32; 5:6.

Consecration of males.—Ex. 3:12, 15; 23:17; Deut. 15:19; 16:16. Circumcision and consecration of Jesus—Lu. 2:21–23.

MALEFACTOR. Lu. 23:39; II Tim. 2:9.

MALICE. See HATRED.

MALLOTHI, măl′lo-thi. A Levite, son of Heman.—I Chr. 25:4, 26.

MALLUCH, măl′luk. (1) A Merarite.—I Chr. 6:44.

(2, 3) Two who married foreign wives.—Ezra 10:29, 32.

(4) A priest who assisted in sealing the covenant.—Neh. 10:4; 12:2.

(5) One who assisted in sealing the covenant.—Neh. 10:27.

MAMMON. Ye cannot serve God and —Mt. 6:29; Lu. 16:13. Unrighteous —Lu. 16:9, 11. See WEALTH, JESUS' TEACHING ON RICHES.

MAMRE, măm′ṛe. (1) A place near where Abraham purchased a field containing a cave where he and his family were buried.—Gen. 13:18; 18:1; 23:17, 19; 35:27; 49:30; 50:13.

(2) An Amorite.—Gen. 14:13, 24.

MAN: Is created by God.—Gen. 2:7; Deut. 4:32; Job 4:17; 10:3, 8; 14:15;

31:15; 32:22; 33:4; 34:19; 35:10; 36: 3; Ps. 95:6; 100:3; 119:73; 138:8; 139:15, 16; Pr. 14:31; 22:2; Eccl. 7: 29; Is. 17:7; 45:12; Jer. 27:5; Hos. 8:14. See GOD THE CREATOR, THE FATHERHOOD OF GOD—Gen. 1:1.

Man made in the image of God.—Gen. 1:26, 27; 5:1, 2; 9:6; I Cor. 11:7; Jas. 3:9.

Man formed from the dust of the earth. —Gen. 2:7; 3:19; Job 4:19; 10:9; 33: 6; Is. 29:16; 45:9; 64:8; Jer. 18:6; Rom. 9:20, 21; II Cor. 4:7.

God gives to man the breath of life— The Father of his spirit—Gen. 2:7; Num. 16:22; 27:16; Job 12:10; 27:3; 33:4; 34:14; Is. 42:5; 57:16; Dan. 5: 23; Ez. 37:5, 6, 9, 10; Zech. 12:1; Acts 17:25; Heb. 12:9; Rev. 22:6.

Man consists of body (*Heb.* Basar. *Gr.* Soma).—**Soul** (*Heb.* Nephesh. *Gr.* Psuche). See SOUL. **Spirit** (*Heb.* Ruach, Neshama. *Gr.* Pneuma). See SPIRIT; Gen. 2:7; Job 32:8, 18; 34:14; Ps. 31:9; Is. 10:18; Mt. 10:28; II Cor. 5:6, 8; I Thess. 5:23; Heb. 4:12.

Man is the completion of creation.— Gen. 1:28; 2:4–7; Ps. 8:4–8; Heb. 2:6–8.

Made but a little lower than God.—Ps. 8:5. **Than angels.**—Heb. 2:7.

Granted dominion over the earth.—Gen. 1:26, 28; Ps. 8:6–8; 49:14; 72:8.

Wonderfully made.—Job 10:8–11; Ps. 149:14–16; Eccl. 11:5. A puzzled saint —Job 12:4–6; Rom. 7:15–24. Thwarted plans—Ps. 33:10–19.

Differs from everything else living.— I Cor. 15:39.

Male and female represented in.—Gen. 1:26–28; 5:2; Mt. 19:4; Mk. 10:6.

Endowed with intellect.—Job 13:3, 15; Is. 1:18; 41:1, 21; 43:26; Jer. 12:1; Mt. 11:25; 16:7.

Endowed with affections.—Gen. 3:16; Lev. 19:18; Deut. 18:6; I Chr. 29:3; Mt. 19:19; John 13:34; Rom. 12:10; 13:9, 10; Col. 3:12; I Thess. 4:9; Heb. 13:1; I Pet. 1:22; I John 3:14.

Man made to toil.—Gen. 1:28; 2:5, 15; 3:19; 31:42; Ex. 31:16; Ps. 104:23; Pr. 13:11; 14:23.

Full liberty granted with but one restriction.—Gen. 2:16, 17; 3:2, 3.

Fall of.—Gen. 3:1–8; Eccl. 7:27–29; Rom. 5:12–19; I Cor. 15:21, 22.

Enticed by the tempter.—Gen. 3:4, 5, 13; Pr. 1:10–19; 12:26; 16:29; John 8:44; II Cor. 11:3; I Tim. 2:14; I Thess. 3:5; I Tim. 2:14; Jas. 1:13–15; I John 2:16, 17; Rev. 12:9, 13.

Sinfulness of.—Gen. 6:5, 6, 12; 8:21; I Ki. 8:46; Job 15:14–16; Ps. 14:1–3; 51:5; Pr. 20:9; Eccl. 7:20; 9:3; Is. 53: 6; Jer. 17:9; Mk. 7:21–23; John 3:19; 7:7; Rom. 3:9–18; 7:18; Gal. 5:17; Jas. 1:13–15; I John 1:8. See SIN— Gen. 3:6.

Imperfection and weakness of.—Job 4: 17–21; Ps. 39:5–13; Is. 41:21–24; Mt. 6:27; Rom. 9:16; II Cor. 3:5; Gal. 6:3.

Man subject to suffering.—Gen. 3:17– 19; Job 5:7; 14:1, 2; Rom. 8:22, 23.

Man rebuked for perversity.—Is. 59:1– 15; John 8:21–24, 38–48.

Vanity of man's life.—Job 7:7–10, 16; Ps. 103:14–16; Eccl. Chs. 1; 2; 7:15; 12:1–8; I Pet. 1:24.

Equality of.—I Sam. 2:7; Job 21:23– 26; Ps. 49:6–14; Pr. 22:2; 29:13; Acts 10:34–35; Gal. 3:28; Eph. 6:5–9; Jas. 2:1–9.

The shortness of his life.—Job 14:1–22; Ps. 39:5; 49:6–14; 89:48; 90:5–10; Eccl. 1:4; 12:1–8; Heb. 9:27.

Man is great, though in ruins.—Lu. 15: 17–24; 19:7–10; Rom. 5:7–8.

Man honored in the assumption of humanity by Jesus.—I Cor. 15:45–49; Eph. 1:19–23; Phil. 2:5–9; Col. 1:12– 20; Heb. 2:5–18.

Man's salvation provided for from the beginning.—Gen. 3:15; 12:3; Is. 53: 1–12; Mt. 25:34; Rom. 16:25; Eph. 1:3–14; 3:1–11; II Thess. 2:13, 14; II Tim. 1:9, 10; Tit. 1:2, 3; II Pet. 1:10– 12, 18–20; Rev. 13:8. See GOD PLANS MAN'S SALVATION—Acts 2:40.

Man at his best when following Christ. —Mt. 4:19; 19:28, 29; II Cor. 3:18; 5:17; Eph. 2:4–7, 10; 4:11–13.

Man's individuality respected.—Lu. 12: 57; John 8:15; 12:47; 15:14–16; Rev. 3:20, 21.

Man obtains enlargement of life.—John 1:4; 5:21–26; 6:33–35; 10:10; 17:2, 3; 20:31; I John 3:1–3.

Endowed with will.—John 7:17; Rom. 7:18; I Cor. 9:17; Phil. 2:13; Rev. 22:17.

Value of.—Mt. 10:31; 12:12; 16:26; Mk. 2:27; John 3:16; I Cor. 11:7.

Whole duty of.—Deut. 10:12; Eccl. 12: 13; Mic. 6:8; I John 3:18-22.

Man proposes, but God disposes.—I Sam. 17:47; II Chr. 20:15; Eccl. 9: 11; Is. 10:11; 47:1-15; Jer. 9:23, 24; Amos 2:14-16; Lu. 12:16-21.

Obtains an advocate in time of trouble. —Rom. 8:34; I Tim. 2:5, 6; Heb. 7: 25; 9:24-28; I John 2:1, 2.

Man the partaker of the divine nature. —John 1:16; Eph. 3:19; 4:13, 24; Heb. 3:1, 14; 6:4; 12:10; II Pet. 1:4; I John 3:2.

He shall be recompensed according to his works.—Deut. Chs. 27; 28; Job 34:1, 12, 25; Ps. 62:12; Pr. 12:14; 24: 12; Is. 3:10, 11; Jer. 32:19; Mt. 7:15-27; 16:27; John 5:29; Rom. 2:5, 6; 6:20-23; 14:12; I Cor. 3:8; II Cor. 5: 10; Eph. 6:8; Col. 3:25; Rev. 2:23-27; 20:12, 13; 21:7, 8; 22:12.

MANAEN, măn'a-ĕn. **A teacher in Antioch.**—Acts 13:1.

MANAHATH, măn'a-hăth. (1) **Son of Shobal.**—Gen. 36:23; I Chr. 1:40.

(2) **A city in Benjamin.**—I Chr. 8:6.

MANAHATHITES. I Chr. 2:51.

MANASSEH, *One who makes to forget:*

(1) **First-born son of Joseph.**—Gen. 41: 51; Josh. 17:1. Adopted by Jacob— Gen. 48:5. His blessing—Gen. Ch. 48. The blessing of Moses—Deut. 33:17.

(2) **Tribe of.**—Passing over of Manasseh—Josh. 4:12. Pursue Midian—Ju. 7:23. Build an altar to Jehovah— Josh. 22:10, 15. Shall be against Judah—Is. 9:21. Incline to David's cause—I Chr. 12:19; II Chr. 15:9; 30:11. Summoned to keep passover— II Chr. 30:1. Manasseh is mine—Ps. 60:7; 108:8. His descendants—Num. 1:34; 26:29; Josh. 22:1; I Chr. 5:23; 7:14. Former inhabitants of Jerusalem—I Chr. 9:3. Inheritance—Num. 32:33; 34:14; Deut. 3:13, 14; 29:8; Josh. 13:7, 29, 31; 16:4; 17:1-17; 18: 7; 22:1-9.

(3) **King of Judah.**—II Ki. 20:21; 21:1; II Chr. 33:2. Evil reign—II Ki. 21: 2-9, 16, 17. Jehovah's wrath against

—II Ki. 23:26. Death of Manasseh— II Ki. 21:18; II Chr. 33:20.

(4) Ju. 18:30.

(5, 6) **Two who had married foreign wives.**—Ezra 10:30, 33.

MANDRAKES. Gen. 30:14-16; Song of Sol. 7:13.

MANEH. A weight—Ez. 45:12. See MEASURES.

MANGER. Jesus in—Lu. 2:7, 12, 16.

MANIFEST. Bonds became—Phil. 1: 13. Glory—John 2:11. God—Rom. 1: 19. In another form—Mk. 16:12. Life was—I John 1:2. Love of God—I John 4:9. Myself—John 14:21. Name —John 17:6. Not yet made—I John 3:2. Righteousness of God—Rom. 3: 21. Thyself to world—John 7:4. To all—Acts 4:16.

MANIFESTATION OF. Christ—Mt. 2: 11-13, 17; John 1:14; 2:11; I Tim. 3: 16; I John 1:2; 3:5, 8. Coming—II Thess. 2:8. God's righteousness— Rom. 3:21; II Thess. 1:5. His love— I John 4:9. Preaching of God's word —II Cor. 4:2; Tit. 1:3. Spirit—I Cor. 12:7.

MANIFOLD. Grace of God—I Pet. 4: 10. Lightnings—Ps. 18:14. Mercies —Neh. 9:19, 27, 31. More—Lu. 18: 30. Powers—Heb. 2:4. Temptations —Jas. 1:2. Transgressions—Amos 5: 12. Trials—I Pet. 1:6. Understanding, In—Job 11:6. Wisdom of God— Eph. 3:10. Works—Ps. 104:24.

MANKIND. Lev. 18:22; 20:13. Breath of—Job 12:10. Rest of—Rev. 9:20. Tamed by—Jas. 3:7.

MANNA: It is the bread which Jehovah hath given thee to eat.—Ex. 16: 15-31.

Description.—As coriander seed—Num. 11:7.

Given.—When Israel murmured for bread—Ex. 16:2, 3, 22, 26, 35; Deut. 8:3-16. In answer to Israel's prayer —Ps. 105:40.

Manna ceased.—When Israel entered Canaan—Josh. 5:12.

Names.—God's manna—Neh. 9:20. Food from heaven—Ps. 78:24.

Our fathers ate manna in the wilderness.—John 6:31, 49.

Bread of life.—John 6:58.

Put in ark of covenant.—Ex. 16:33; Heb. 9:4.

Promise of the hidden manna.—Rev. 2:17.

MANNER. Disease, Of—Mt. 9:35. Evil, Of—Mt. 5:11. Food, Of—Song of Sol. 4:10. Holy—I Pet. 1:15. Kingdom, Of—I Sam. 10:25. Life, Of—Gal. 1: 13; Eph. 4:22; I Tim. 4:12; Heb. 13: 7; I Pet. 1:15, 18; 3:16; II Pet. 3:11. See Jas. 3:13. Love, Of—I John 3:1. Man, Of—Mt. 8:27. Orderly—Ju. 6: 26. Works, Of—Ex. 12:16. See TEACHINGS OF JESUS.

MANNERS. Children of Israel, Of—Acts 13:18. See Deut. 9:7. Good—I Cor. 15:33.

MANOAH, ma-nō'ah. Father of Samson.—Ju. 13:2-22; 6:31.

MANSERVANTS. See SERVANTS.

MANSION. Many—John 14:2.

MANSLAYER. Num. 35:6, 11, 12; Deut. 19:6; I Tim. 1:9. See MURDERER.

MANSTEALER. I Tim. 1:10.

MANTELET. Nah. 2:5.

MANTLE. Song of Sol. 5:7; Heb. 1:12. Ruth's—Ruth 3:15. Elijah's—I Ki. 19:13, 19; II Ki. 2:8, 13, 14. Of wanton women—Is. 3:22.

MANY. Followed him—Mt. 12:15. Nations—Ps. 135:10. Ransom for—Mt. 20:28. Times proved—II Cor. 8:22. Waters—Jer. 51:55.

MAOCH, mā'ok. Father of Achish.—I Sam. 27:2.

MAON, mā'on. (1) A city and wilderness in Judah.—Josh. 15:55; I Sam. 25:2.

(2) A descendant of Caleb son of Hezron.—I Chr. 2:45.

MAONITES, mā'on-ites. Ju. 10:12.

MAR. Girdle—Jer. 13:7. Inheritance—Ruth 4:6. Land—I Sam. 6:5; II Ki. 3:19. Path—Job 30:13. Pride—Jer. 13:9. Vessel, So he made it again—Jer. 18:4. Visage—Lev. 19:27; Is. 52:14.

MARA, mā'rà. A name assumed by Naomi.—Ruth 1:20.

MARAH, mā'rah. First encampment of Israel.—Ex. 15:23; Num. 33:8, 9. See CAMP, ISRAEL.

MARALAH, mär'a-lah. A city of Zebulun.—Josh. 19:11.

MARANATHA, mär'ăn-ā'thà. I Cor. 16:22.

MARBLE. See STONE.

MARCH. Joel 2:7. Battle, Lo—Ex. 14: 10; Ju. 5:4; Is. 27:4; Ju. 46:22; Hab. 1:6; 3:12. Stately, In—Pr. 30:29; Is. 63:1. Wilderness, Through—Ps. 68:7.

MARESHAH, mă-rē'shäh. (1) A city of Judah.—Josh. 15:44; I Chr. 11:8; 14:9, 10; 20:37; Mic. 1:15.

(2) Father of Hebron.—I Chr. 2:42.

(3) Son of Laadah.—I Chr. 4:21.

MARINER. Ez. 27:9, 29; Jonah—1:5; Rev. 18:17.

MARK. See OUTLINE STUDIES IN THE BOOKS.

MARK. Foundations—Pr. 8:29. Identification, For—Ez. 9:4, 6; Rev. 13: 16, 17; 14:9, 11; 16:2; 19:20, 4. Land—See LAND. Out—Num. 34:7; Ruth 3:4. Paths—Job 13:27. Shout at—I Sam. 20:20; Lam. 3:12. See LANDMARK.

MARKET PLACE. Acts 16:19. Greeting in—Mt. 23:7; Mk. 12:38; Lu. 11: 43; 20:46. Rest in—Mt. 11:16; 20:3; Lu. 7:32. Sick in—Mk. 6:56.

MAROTH, mā'roth. A town in Judah.—Mic. 1:12.

MARRIAGE: Ordained of God.—Gen. 2:18, 24; Mt. 19:5, 6; Mk. 10:7, 8; I Cor. 6:16; 11:11, 12; Eph. 5:31; Heb. 13:4.

Expressed by.—Joining together—Mt. 19:6; Mk. 10:9. Making affinity—I Ki. 3:1; 7:8; 9:16; II Chr. 8:11. Taking to wife—Ex. 2:1; Ruth 4:13. Giving daughters to sons, and sons to daughters—Deut. 7:2; Ezra 9:12.

Commended.—Pr. 18:22; 31:10-12; Jer. 29:6; I Tim. 5:14, 15.

For this life only.—Mt. 22:30; Mk. 12: 23; Lu. 20:27-36.

Marriage of near relatives.—Abraham and Sarai were half brother and sister—Gen. 20:12. The mother of Moses and Aaron was the aunt of her husband—Ex. 6:20. Of cousins—Gen. 24: 50-67; 28:2; Num. 36:1-12.

Marriages contracted by parents.—Gen. 21:21; 24:1-67; 34:4-10; 38:6; Ex. 21:7; 22:17; Ju. 1:12; 14:2, 3; I Sam. 17:25; 18:17-27.

Father gave daughters in marriage.—Ex. 22:17; Deut. 7:3; Josh. 15:16, 17;

Ju. 14:20; 15:1-6; I Sam. 18:17-21; 25:44. Eldest daughter usually given first—Gen. 29:26. A dowry given to woman's parents before marriage—Gen. 24:53; 29:18; 34:12; Deut. 22: 29; I Sam. 18:25-28; Hos. 3:2.

Consent of parties necessary.—Gen. 24: 57, 58; I Sam. 18:20, 21; 25:40, 41.

Marriage contract made at gate of city. —Ruth 4:1-11.

Marriage laws of the Jews: Concerning near relatives.—Lev. 18:6-18, 24; 20: 11-21; Deut. 22:30; 27:20-23; Mk. 6:17-19. After seduction.—Deut. 22: 28, 29; Ex. 22:16.

Levirate marriage.—In case a man died without an heir—Brother or near kinsman to marry widow—Gen. 38: 8-11; Deut. 25:5-10; Ruth 2:1, 10-13; 3:2-18; 4:1-13; Mt. 22:24-28; Mk. 12:19-23; Lu. 20:28-33.

Marriages were to be between members of the same tribe.—Ex. 2:1; Num. 36:6-12.

Marriages of priests.—Lev. 21:7, 13, 14; Ez. 44:22.

Marriages with Gentiles forbidden because of idolatry.—Gen. 24:3-6; 27: 46; 28:1, 2, 6-9; 34:13, 14; Ex. 34:13-16; Deut. 7:3, 4; Num. 25:6-15; Josh. 23:12, 13; I Ki. 11:2; 16:31; Ezra 9: 11, 12; Neh. 10:30; 13:23-30.

Marriages made with Gentiles.—Jer. 14:1-5; I Ki. 11:1; Neh. 13:23-30.

Marriage of captives.—Deut. 21:10-14.

Married man exempted from going to war for one year after marriage.—Deut. 20:7; 24:5.

Infidelity of those contracted in marriage same as if married.—Deut. 22: 23, 24; Mt. 1:19. Tokens of virginity —Deut. 22:13-21.

Not to be married considered a calamity.—Ju. 11:37, 38; Ps. 78:63.

Weddings.—Celebrated with feasting—Gen. 29:22; Ju. 14:10-12; Esther 2: 18; Jer. 16:8, 9; 33:11; John 2:1-10. Feasting lasted seven days—Gen. 29: 27; Ju. 14:12. Garments provided for guests at the wedding—Mt. 22:12. Christ attends the wedding feast in Cana—John 2:1-10.

The bride.—The bath and anointing—Ruth 3:3. Receives presents—Gen. 24: 53. Given a handmaid—Gen. 24:59;

29:24, 29. Adorned—Ps. 45:13, 14; Is. 49:18; Jer. 2:32; Rev. 19:7, 8. With jewels—Is. 61:10. Attended by bridesmaids—Ps. 45:9. Stood on right hand of bridegroom—Ps. 45:9. Receives benediction—Gen. 24:60; Ruth 4:11, 12. Must forget father's house and people—Ruth 1:8-17; Ps. 45:10.

Bridegroom.—Specially clothed—Is. 61: 10. Attended by many friends—Ju. 14:11; John 3:29. Crowned with garlands—Song of Sol. 3:11; Is. 61:10. Rejoices over bride—Ps. 19:5; Is. 62: 5. Returns with bride to his house at night—Mt. 25:1-6.

Paul's teaching concerning—Advises marriage.—I Tim. 5:14, 15. For the sake of chastity—I Cor. 7:1-6, 9. Lawful in all—I Cor. 7:8-40; 9:5. Rebukes those who advise against marriage—I Tim. 4:3. Elders or bishops and deacons to be husbands of one wife—I Tim. 3:2, 12.

Should be only in the Lord.—I Cor. 7: 39. Honorable in all.—Heb. 13:4.

Seems to think that to remain unmarried and virtuous is better, because of persecution of that time.—I Cor. 7:8, 17, 25-40.

Be not unequally yoked with unbelievers.—II Cor. 6:14, 17.

Marriage of widows.—Rom. 7:1-3; I Cor. 7:39, 40.

Monogamy taught in the Bible.—Wife singular number—Mt. 19:5. God gave Adam one wife—Gen. 2:18-24. Each man had one wife in the ark—Gen. 7: 13. See Gen. 2:24; Mal. 2:15; Mt. 19: 5, 6; Mk. 10:7, 8; I Cor. 11:11, 12; Eph. 5:31; I Tim. 3:2, 12.

Polygamy and concubinage practised.—Lamech the first polygamist—Gen. 4: 19. Abraham—Gen. 12:5; 16:1-6; 25: 1, 6. Jacob—Gen. 29:25-30. Esau—Gen. 36:2, 3. Gideon the judge—Ju. 8:30, 31. Elkanah the father of Samuel—I Sam. 1:2. Saul—II Sam. 3:7. David—I Sam. 27:3; II Sam. 5:13; I Chr. 14:3. Solomon—I Ki. 11:1-3; Song of Sol. 6:8. Rehoboam—II Chr. 11:21.

Marriage figurative.—Symbolizes: Idolatry—Mal. 2:11. God's union with the Jews—Is. 54:5; Jer. 3:14; Hos. 2:19, 20. Christ's union with the church—Mt. 22:1-14; 25:1-10; Rom. 7:4; Eph. 5:23, 24, 32; Rev. 19:7.

MARROW. Job 21:24; Ps. 63:5; Pr. 3: 8; Heb. 4:12. Wine, Of—Is. 25:6.

MARSENA, mär'se-nà. **A Persian prince.**—Esth. 1:14.

MARSHALL. Jer. 51:27; Nah. 3:17. Staff, Of—Ju. 5:14.

MARSHES. Ez. 47:11.

MARS-HILL. A hill in Athens with an open court where the Areopagus, the supreme tribunal of justice, sat.—Acts 17:22.

MART. Ez. 27:15.

MARTHA. The oldest sister of Mary and Lazarus—Lu. 10; 38:41; John 11: 1, 5, 19-39; 12:2.

MARTYR. Rev. 17:6. See PERSECUTION, WITNESS.

MARVEL. Lu. 1:63. Disciples—Mt. 21: 20. At—Acts 2:7. Jesus—Mk. 6:6; 8: 10. Jesus, At—Mk. 5:20; 8:27; 9:33; 21:20; 22:22; 27:14; Mt. 12:17; 15:5, 44; Lu. 7:9; Lu. 8:25; 9:30; 11:14; 20:26; John 4:27; 5:20; 7:21; II Thess. 1:10. Jews—John 7:15. Not— Eccl. 5:8; John 3:7; 5:28; II Cor. 11: 14; I John 3:13. One at another— Gen. 43:33. Paul—Gal. 1:6. Peter and John, At—Acts 3:12; 4:13. Pharisees —Mt. 22:22; Lu. 11:38. Pilate—Mt. 15:5, 44. Zacharias, At—Lu. 1:21. See SIGNS AND WONDERS.

MARVELOUS. Rev. 15. Eyes, In— Zech. 8:6; Mt. 21:42; Mk. 12:11. Jehovah is—Job 10:16; 37:5; Ps. 118:23. Light—I Pet. 2:9. Lovingkindness of God—Ps. 17:7; 31:21. Things—Job 5: 9, 10; Ps. 78:12; 98:1; Dan. 11:36; Mic. 7:15. Wonders—Hab. 1:5. Works, Of God—Is. 29:14; I Chr. 16:9, 12, 24; Ps. 9:1; 103:2, 5; Rev. 15:3. See SIGNS AND WONDERS.

MARY. Heb. Mariam (1) **The virgin mother of Jesus.**—Mt. 1:18-21; Lu. 1:30-38; John 2:1; Acts 1:14.

Descendant of House of David.—Lu. 1: 27; Rom. 1:3. Sister to the wife of Clopas—John 19:25. Betrothed to Joseph—Mt. 1:18-22. Annunciation of Gabriel—Lu. 1:36-38. Conception of Jesus by the Holy Spirit—Mt. 1: 18-20. Mary honored by Joseph—Mt. 1:20, 25. Visits Elizabeth—Lu. 1:39, 40. Magnifies the Lord in wonderful

hymns—Lu. 1:46-55. Returned to Nazareth—Lu. 1:56. Journeys with Joseph to Bethlehem, because of the enrollment under Cyrenius—Lu. 2:1- 5. Gives birth to the Child Jesus in a manger—Lu. 2:7. Ponders eagerly the message of the shepherds—Lu. 2:19. Marvels at the words of Simeon—Lu. 2:33. Warned of her sorrows—Lu. 2: 34, 35. Gave Jesus careful training— Lu. 2:41. Taught Him the Scriptures —Lu. 2:40. Her sorrows begin—Lu. 2:43-49. Questions Jesus about His absence—Lu. 2:48. Still holds control —Lu. 2:51. Ponders the strange words of the Boy Jesus—Lu. 2:51. Addressed as woman—John 2:4; 19:26. Work of the Messiah not under her control —John 2:4. Her relation to Jesus changes: Doubt comes as to His sanity, due to His unexpected conduct— Mt. 12:46-50; Mk. 3:31-35; Lu. 8:19- 21. Committed to the care of the Apostle John—John 19:25-27. Attendant at the Cross—Mt. 27:56; Mk. 15:40; John 19:25-27. Was among earliest believers, after the resurrection of Jesus—Acts 1:14.

(2) **Mary Magdalene** (*Or*, of Magdala). —Seven demons cast out of her—Mk. 16:9; Lu. 8:2. Accompanied Jesus through Galilee—Lu. 8:1, 2. Ministered to Jesus' wants—Lu. 8:2. Also accompanied Jesus on last journey to Jerusalem—Mt. 27:55; Mk. 15:41; Lu. 23:55; 24:10. Lingered at the cross— Mt. 27:56; Lu. 23:33; John 19:25. Watched the tomb on Friday afternoon after the burial of Jesus—Mt. 27:61; Mk. 15:47. Visits the sepulchre, Saturday afternoon—Mt. 28:1. Brought spices after the sabbath was past—Mk. 16:1. Came early Sunday morning to anoint the body of Jesus —Mk. 16:2; John 20:1. Runs to tell Peter and John of the empty tomb— John 20:1-10. Weeps beside the tomb, and sees two angels—John 20:11-15. Recognizes Jesus after the resurrection—John 20:16, 17. Testifies to the resurrection of Jesus—John 20:18.

(3) **Mary of Bethany, the sister of Lazarus.**—Her family shared their home with Jesus—Mt. 21:17; 26:6; Mk. 11: 1; Lu. 19:29; John 12:1. Sat at Jesus'

feet as learner—Lu. 10:39. Implores Jesus concerning Lazarus—John 11: 31, 32. Anointed the head and feet of Jesus—Mt. 26:6-13; Mk. 14:3; Lu. 7: 36-38; John 12:3-7.

(4) **Mary, wife of Clopas.**—Sister of Jesus' mother—John 19:25. Followed Jesus in His journeys—Lu. 8:1-3. Watched at sepulchre of Jesus—Mt. 27:61; Mk. 15:47. Visited sepulchre, late on sabbath day—Mt. 28:1. Brought spices after the sabbath passed, about sunrise on Sunday to anoint the body of Jesus—Mk. 16:2.

(5) **Mary the mother of John Mark.**—Acts 12:12. Peter resorts thither on being released from prison—Acts 12: 12. Her house a house of prayer—Acts 12:12-17.

(6) **Mary the friend of Paul.**—Rom. 16: 6. (This enumeration of the Marys presents difficulties of identification and is not agreed to by all scholars.)

MASCHIL. See MUSIC, PSALMS.

MASH, măsh. Gen. 10:23. See MESHECH.

MASHAL, mā'shal. A town in Asher.—I Chr. 6:74.

MASON. See ARTS AND TRADES.

MASREKAH, măs're-kah. A city of Edom.—Gen. 36:36; I Chr. 1:47.

MASS. Job. 38:38.

MASSA, măs'sà. Son of Ishmael.—Gen. 25:14; I Chr. 1:30.

MASSACRE. Ju. 9:5; I Sam. 22:18, 19; I Ki. 18:4; II Ki. 10:7; Jer. 41:2, 3; Mt. 2:16.

MASSAH, măs'sah. A place in the wilderness where the people murmured for water.—Ex. 17:7; Deut. 6:16; 9: 22; 33:8. See MERIBAH.

MAST. Pr. 23:34; Is. 33:23; Ez. 27:5.

MASTER. Duty of—Lev. 19:13; 25:43; Deut. 24:14, 15; Job 31:13; Jer. 22; 13; Eph. 6:9; Col. 4:1; Jas. 5:4; Gen. 24:12, 35; 39:3. Examples of good—Abraham—Gen. 18:19. Centurion—Lu. 7:2, 3. Cornelius—Acts 10:2. Jacob—Gen. 35:2. Joshua—Josh. 24:15. Bad—Amalekite—I Sam. 30:13. Egyptians—Ex. 1:13, 14. Naval—I Sam. 25:17. God, Of—Jesus is. See JESUS, TITLES OF. No man can serve two—Mt. 6:24. Servant and—Gen. 24:35; 39:3; I Sam. 30:13; II Ki. 5:1;

Pr. 30:10. See BONDAGE, TEACHING OF JESUS.

MASTER BUILDER. I Cor. 3:10. See BUILDER.

MASTERY. Lions, Of—Dan. 6:24. Shout for—Ex. 32:18.

MATE. Is. 34:15, 16. See MARRIAGE.

MATRED, mā'tred. Mother-in-law of Hadar, last of the kings of Edom.—Gen. 36:39; I Chr. 1:50.

MATRITES, măt'rites. A Benjamite family.

MATTAN, măt'tan. (1) A priest of Baal.—II Ki. 11:18; II Chr. 23:17.

(2) Father of Shephatiah.—Jer. 38:1.

MATTANAH, măt'ta-nah. An encampment of Israel.—Num. 21:18, 19.

MATTANIAH, măt'ta-nī'ah. (1) A Levite descendant of Asaph.—I Chr. 9:15; II Chr. 20:14; Neh. 11:17; 12:8, 25, 35.

(2) Brother of Jehoiakim.—II Ki. 24: 17.

(3) Son of Heman the singer.—I Chr. 25:4, 16.

(4) A descendant of Asaph.—II Chr. 29:13.

(5, 6, 7, 8) Four who married foreign wives.—Ezra 10:26, 27, 30, 37.

(9) A Levite.—Neh. 13:13.

MATTATHA, măt'ta-thà. An ancestor of Jesus—Lu. 3:31.

MATTATHIAS, măt'ta-thī'as. Two ancestors of Jesus.—Lu. 3:25, 26.

MATTENAI, măt'te-nā'i. (1, 2) Two who married foreign wives.—Ezra 10: 33, 37.

(3) A priest.—Neh. 12:19.

MATTER. Defense concerning—Acts 25:16. Giving, Of—Phil. 4:15. Judge of—Acts 18:15. Meddling in another man's—I Pet. 4:15.

MATTHAN, măt'than. Ancestor of Jesus.—Mt. 1:15.

MATTHAT, măt'that. Two ancestors of Jesus.—Lu. 3:24, 29.

MATTHEW. See OUTLINE STUDIES IN THE BOOKS.

MATTHIAS, mat-thī'as. An apostle chosen by lot to succeed Judas Iscariot.—Acts 1:23, 26.

MATTITHIAH, măt'ti-thī'ah. (1) A descendant of Korah.—I Chr. 5:31.

(2) A Levite gatekeeper under David.—I Chr. 15:18, 21; 16:5.

(3) **One who married a foreign wife.**—Ezra 10:43.

(4) **Son of Jeduthun.**—I Chr. 25:5, 21.

(5) **One who stood beside Ezra when he read the law.**—Neh. 8:4.

MATTOCK. I Sam. 13:21. See TOOLS AND IMPLEMENTS.

MAUL. Pr. 25:18. See TOOLS AND IMPLEMENTS.

MAW. Deut. 18:3; Jer. 51:34. See STOMACH.

MAXIMS. See WISDOM, LITERATURE, PROVERBS.

MEADOW. Is. 19:7.

MEAL: Chief meals.—Dinner at noon—Gen. 43:16, 25; Ruth 2:14; I Ki. 13:7; Mt. 22:4. Supper in the evening—Ju. 19:16–21; Lu. 14:16–24; John 12:2. Meat served at supper—Ex. 16:12.

Preparation of people for meal.—Washing of hands—Mk. 7:3. Washing of feet before—Gen. 18:4; Ju. 19:21. After—John 13:5. At the meal—Lu. 7:44. Head anointed—Ps. 23:5; Amos 6:6; Lu. 7:46.

Position at the table.—Sat at table—Gen. 27:19; I Sam. 20:25; I Ki. 13:20. Prophecy concerning—Ez. 23:41; Amos 3:12; 6:4. Recline on couches—Lu. 7:38; John 13:23. Chief seat at table—Mt. 23:6. Contention because of—Lu. 22:24.

Prayer before meal.—I Sam. 9:13. Jesus brake bread and blessed it—Mt. 14:9; 15:36; 26:26, 27; Mk. 6:41; 8:6, 7; Lu. 9:16; 22:19; 24:30; John 6:11, 23; I Cor. 11:24. Paul gives thanks—Acts 27:35.

Giving thanks to God for food.—I Cor. 10:30; I Tim. 4:3, 5.

Meal served by women.—Mk. 1:31; Lu. 10:40. Servants.—I Ki. 10:5; John 2:5.

Breaking of Bread.—Mt. 15:36; Mk. 6: 41; 8:6, 7; Lu. 9:16; John 6:11–13. See LORD'S SUPPER.

Served in vessels. See FOOD, FEASTS.

MEAN. Pr. 22:29; Acts 21:39.

MEANS. By any—Ps. 49:7; I Cor. 9: 22; II Cor. 2:7; 9:4; Phil. 3:11. Mammon, Of the—Lu. 16:9. Redeem, By any—Ps. 49:7. Suffice not—Lev. 5:7.

MEARAH, me-ā'rah. **A place in Canaan.** —Josh. 13:4.

MEASURE. Astonished beyond—Mk. 7:37; 10:26. Correct in—Jer. 30:11; 46:28. Covetousness, Of—Jer. 51:13. Days, Of—Ps. 39:4. Faith, Of—Rom. 12:3. Fathers, Of—Mt. 23:32. Gift of Christ, Of—Eph. 4:7. Man, Of a—Rev. 21:17. Persecuted, Beyond—Gal. 1:23. Pressed down—Lu. 6:38. Rule, Of the—I Cor. 10:13. Spirit—John 3:24. Stature of the Fulness, Of—Eph. 4:13. Stripes above—II Cor. 11: 23.

MEASURES, TABLE OF. (Modern estimates vary so much we hardly feel justified in making one more attempt for accuracy, so we offer a table already prepared by good English scholars.)

MEASURES

LONG MEASURE

		Feet	Inches
A digit, or finger (Jer. 52:21)		—	0.912
4 digits	= 1 palm (Ex. 25:25)	—	3.648
3 palms	= 1 span (Ex. 28:16)	—	10.944
2 spans	= 1 cubit (Gen. 6:15)	1	9.888
4 cubits	= 1 fathom (Acts 27:28)	7	3.552
1.5 fathoms	= 1 reed (Ez. 40:3, 5)	10	11.328
13.3 reeds	= 1 line (Ez. 40:3)	145	11.04

LAND MEASURE

		Eng. Miles	Paces	Feet
A cubit		—	—	1.824
400 cubits	= 1 furlong (Lu. 24:13)	—	145	4.6
5 furlongs	= 1 sabbath day's journey (John 11:18; Acts 1:12)	—	727	3.0

LAND MEASURE—CONTINUED

			Eng.Miles	Paces	Feet
10 furlongs	= 1 mile (Mt. 5:41)		1	399	1.0
24 miles	= 1 day's journey		33	76	4.0

LIQUID MEASURE

			Gallons	Pints
A caph			—	0.625
1.3 caph	= 1 log (Lev. 14:10)		—	0.833
4 logs	= 1 cab		—	3.333
3 cabs	= 1 hin (Ex. 30:24)		1	2
2 hins	= 1 seah		2	4
3 seahs	= 1 bath, or ephah (I Ki. 7:26; John 2:6)		7	4.5
10 ephahs	= 1 kor, or homer (Is. 5:10; Ez. 45:14)		75	5.25

DRY MEASURE

			Pecks	Gallons	Pints
A gachal			—	—	0.1416
20 gachals	= 1 cab (II Ki. 6:25; Rev. 6:6)		—	—	2.8333
1.8 cab	= 1 omer (Ex. 16:36)		—	—	5.1
3.3 omers	= 1 seah (Mt. 13:33)		1	0	1
3 seahs	= 1 ephah (Ez. 45:11)		3	0	3
5 ephahs	= 1 letech (Hos. 3:2)		16	0	0
2 letechs	= 1 kor, or homer (Num. 11:32; Hos. 3:2)		32	0	0

N. B.—The above table will explain many texts in the Bible, especially those which are placed within brackets. Take, for instance, Is. 5:10: "Yea, ten acres of vineyard shall yield one bath, and the seed of an homer shall yield an ephah." This curse upon the covetous man was, that 10 acres of vines should produce only 7 gallons of wine, i. e., one acre should yield less than 3 quarts; and that 32 pecks of seed should only bring a crop of 3 pecks, or, in other words, that the harvest should produce a quantity equal to one-tenth only of the seed sown.

References.—Beyond our—II Cor. 10:15. Measure of my days—Ps. 39:4. Can add one cubit to the measure of his life—Mt. 6:27. With what measure ye mete—Mt. 7:2. Hid in 3 measures of meal—Mt. 13:33. Fill the measure of your father's—Mt. 23:32. Good measure pressed down—Lu. 6:38. A hundred measures of oil—Lu. 16:6. Giveth not the spirit by measure—John 3:34. In stripes above measure—II Cor. 11:23. Beyond measure I persecuted—Gal. 1:13. Measure of the stature—Eph. 4:13. According to the measure of a man—Rev. 21:17. To measure Jerusalem—Zech. 2:2; Rev. 11:1; 21:15-

17. Distances measured by reeds and lines—II Sam. 8:2; Jer. 31:39; Ez. 40:3, 5; Rev. 11:1; 21:15. Tears, In—Ps. 80:5. What measure ye mete—Mt. 7:2; Mk. 4:24; Lu. 6:38. Work—Is. 65:7.

MEAT. Causeth my brother to offend—I Cor. 8:13. My flesh is meat indeed—John 6:55. My meat is to do the will—John 4:34. See FLESH, FOOD, OFFERING, STUMBLING.

MEBUNNAI, me-bŭn'nāi. A hero in David's army—II Sam. 23:27. See I Chr. 11:29; 27:11.

MECHERATHITE, me-kē'rath-īte. A member of David's army.—I Chr. 11:36. See MAACATHITE.

MECONAH, me-kō'nah. A town in Judah.—Neh. 11:28.

MEDAD, mē'dăd. A prophetic elder of Israel.—Num. 11:26, 27.

MEDAN, mē'dan. Son of Abraham.—Gen. 25:2; I Chr. 1:32.

MEDDLE. I Pet. 4:15. To thy hurt—II Ki. 14:10, 11; II Chr. 25:19.

MEDEBA, mĕd-e-bà. A Moabite town conquered by Joshua.—Num. 21:30; Josh. 13:9, 16; I Chr. 19:7; Is. 15:2.

MEDES, mēdes. **Dwellers in Media.**—Acts 2:9. Cities of the—II Ki. 17:6; 18:11. Darius the—Dan. 11:1. Kingdoms given to—Dan. 5:28. Kings of the—Jer. 25:25; 51:11, 28. Laws of the—Esth. 1:19; Dan. 6:8, 15. Province, Of the—Ezra 6:2. Seed of the—Dan. 9:1. Stir up—Is. 13:17.

MEDIA. Power of—Esth. 1:3. Princes of—Esth. 1:14. Princesses of—Esth. 1:18. Kings of—Esth. 10:2; Jer. 25:25; Dan. 8:20. Seed of the Medes of—Dan. 9:1; 11:1. Prophecies—Is. 21:2; Dan. 8:20. Called Medes the inhabitants of—Acts 2:9. Cities of—II Ki. 17:6; 18:11. Province of—Ezra 6:2. Laws of—Esth. 1:19; Dan. 6:8, 12, 15. Strife of—Is. 13:17; Jer. 51:11, 28. Kingdom given to—Dan. 5:28.

MEDIATOR. Hand of—Gal. 3:19. One, Between God and men—I Tim. 2:5; Heb. 8:6; 9:15; 12:24. See JESUS, RECONCILIATION.

MEDICINE. Good—Pr. 17:22. Healing—Jer. 30:13. Many—Jer. 46:11.

MEDITATION. Ps. 104:34. All thy doings, On—Ps. 143:5. Beforehand—Lu. 21:14. Consider my—Ps. 5:1. Day and night—Josh. 1:8. Heart, Of—Ps. 19:14; 49:3. Isaac, Of—Gen. 24:63. Law, On—Ps. 1:2; 119:97. Night watches, In—Ps. 63:6. On God's word—Josh. 1:8; Ps. 1:2; 119:15, 23, 48, 97, 99, 148; 139:17, 18; 143:5; Pr. 4:20, 22. Peoples—Ps. 2:1. Precepts, On—Ps. 119:15. Testimonies are my—Ps. 119:99. Work, Upon—Ps. 77:12; 119:27.

MEEKNESS. See CHRISTIAN GRACES.

MEET. Help—Gen. 2:18. Rich and poor—Pr. 22:2. Solemn—Is. 1:13. Tent of—Ex. 40:34; Josh. 18:1. To make merry—Lu. 15:32. To take children's bread—Mt. 15:26.

MEGIDDO, me-gĭd'do. **Town of Manasseh, in Issachar.**—Josh. 17:11. Dwelt the children of Joseph, son of Israel—I Chr. 7:29.

Inhabitants of, not driven out.—Ju. 1:27.

Officers of.—I Ki. 4:12.

Strifes of.—At Taanach, by the waters of Megiddo.—Ju. 5:19. Fortified by Solomon—I Ki. 9:15. Ahaziah flees to, when wounded, and dies at—II Ki.

9:27. Josiah slain at—II Ki. 23:29, 30; II Chr. 35:22, 24.

Mourning of.—Zech. 12:11.

MEGIDDON, me-gĭd'don. See MEGIDDO.

MEHETABEL, me-hĕt'a-bel. (1) **Grandfather of one who tried to intimidate Nehemiah.**—Neh. 6:10.

(2) **Wife of Hadar.**—Gen. 36:39; I Chr. 1:50.

MEHIDA, me-hi'da. **Ancestor of some who returned with Zerubbabel.**—Ezra 2:52; Neh. 7:54.

MEHIR, mē'hir. **Son of Chelub.**—I Chr. 4:11.

MEHOLATHITE, me-hō'lath-īte. **A native of Abel-meholah.**—I Sam. 18:19; II Sam. 21:8.

MEHUJAEL, me-hū'ja-el. **A descendant of Cain and father of Methusael.**—Gen. 4:18.

MEHUMAN, me-hū'man. **One of Ahasuera's seven chamberlains.**—Esth. 1:10.

MEHUNIM, me-hū'nim. **Ancestor of some who returned with Zerubbabel.**—Ezra 2:50; Neh. 7:52.

ME-JARKON, mē'-jär'kon. **A city near Joppa in Dan.**—Josh. 19:46.

MELATIAH, mĕl'a-ti'ah. **One who helped repair the wall.**—Neh. 3:7.

MELCHI, mĕl'kī. (1) **Ancestor of Mary, mother of Jesus.**—Lu. 3:24.

(2) **Another ancestor of Jesus.**—Lu. 3:28.

MELCHIZEDEK, mĕl-chĭz'e-dĕk. Heb. "King of Righteousness."

King of Salem.—Gen. 14:18. Priest of God—Gen. 14:18-20. Met Abraham with bread and wine—Gen. 14:18. Blessed Abraham—Gen. 14:19. Abraham gave tithes to him—Gen. 14:20; Heb. 7:2. To distinguish the Messiah as eternal the Psalmist makes a type of—Ps. 110:4. Quoted in Hebrews—Heb. 5:6; 7:17, 21. Melchizedek, like Jesus, combines kingship and priesthood in one person—Gen. 14:18; Heb. 7:1. This priesthood has neither formal beginning nor succession—Heb. 7:3. In this feature contrasted with Levitical priesthood—Heb. 7:8-17. Superior to Levitical priesthood—Heb. 7:22-28. (Typological contrasts taken from Walter Scott.)

One priesthood was of Levi.
The former rested on genealogy.
The first was weak and unprofitable.
The one with succession.
First order had many priests.
First was for one nation.
Jewish for old covenant.
Levites offered for their own sins.
Their sacrifice cleansed not conscience.
Their annual sacrifices, though by thousands, availed not.

Other of Judah.
The latter on power.
The second most efficacious.
The other without succession.
The last but one.
The last of all nations.
The Christian for the new.
Christ had no sin.
Christ's did.
Christ's saves.

A synopsis of Heb. Ch. 7. See PRIEST.

MELEA, mē'le-à. Ancestor of Mary, mother of Jesus.—Lu. 3:31.

MELECH, mē'lek. A son of Micah.—I Chr. 8:35; 9:41.

MELITA, mĕl'i-ta. Ancient name for Malta.—Acts 28:1.

MELODY. Make, with your heart—Eph. 5:19. Sweet—Is. 23:16. Viols, Of—Amos 5:23. Voice of—Is. 51:3. See MUSIC.

MELON. Num. 11:5.

MELT. Away—Ex. 15:15; Josh. 2:9; Is. 14:31; Jer. 49:23. Earth—Ps. 46:6. Heart—Deut. 1:28; 20:8. Mountains—Mic. 1:4. Soul—Ps. 107:26; 119:28.

MEMBER. Christ, Of—I Cor. 6:15. Devour—Job 18:13. Law in—Rom. 7:23. Little—Jas. 3:5. Of one body—Rom. 12:4; I Cor. 12:12; Eph. 4:25. See BODY, UNITY.

MEMORIAL: Of God.—To all generations—Ex. 3:15.

Of woman.—Mt. 26:13; Mk. 14:9.

Name as.—Ps. 135:13; Hos. 12:5.

Alms as.—Acts 10:4.

Days of.—Ex. 12:14; Lev. 23:24; Esth. 9:28.

Ordinances observed in.—Passover—Ex. 13:9. Set up at Shechem—Josh. 24:19–29. Written in book—Ex. 17:14. The Lord's Supper—Mt. 26:27; Mk. 14:22–25; Lu. 22:4–20; I Cor. 11:23–25.

No memorial in Jerusalem.—Neh. 2:20.

Crowns of.—Zech. 6:14.

Stones of.—Ex. 28:12, 29; 39:7; Josh. 4:7.

Money as.—Ex. 30:16; Num. 31:54.

Offerings of.—Meal—Lev. 2:2, 9, 16; 5:12; 6:15; 24:7.

Law concerning jealousy.—Num. 5:15, 18, 26. Burnt—Num. 10:10; 16:40.

MEMORY. Goodness, Of—Ps. 145:7. Righteous, Of—Ps. 112:6; Pr. 10:7. Wicked, Of—Deut. 32:26; Job 18:17; Ps. 9:5; 34:16; Eccl. 8:10; 9:5; Is. 26:14.

MEMPHIS, mĕm'phis. Capital of northern Egypt.—Hos. 9:6.

MEMUCAN, me-mū'can. Prince of Medes and Persians.—Esth. 1:14, 16, 21.

MEN. See MAN.

MENAHEM, mĕn'a-hem. King of Israel.—II Ki. 15:14–23.

MENDING. Nets—Mk. 1:19.

MENE, mē'ne. To number—Dan. 5:25.

MENNA, mĕn'na. Ancestor of Jesus.—Lu. 3:31.

MEN-SINGERS. Eccl. 2:8.

MENTION. Is. 12:4; 19:17. Ark of God—I Sam. 4:18. Burden no more—Jer. 23:36. By name—I Chr. 4:38; Josh. 21:9. Coral or crystal—Job 28:18. Departure—Heb. 11:22. God of Israel—Is. 48:1. Jehovah—Jer. 20:9. Lovingkindness—Is. 63:7. Name—Ex. 23:13; Josh. 23:7; Is. 26:13; 49:1; Amos 6:10. Nations, To—Jer. 4:16. Prayer, In—Rom. 1:9, 16; Eph. 1:16; I Thess. 1:2; Philemon 4. Rahab—Ps. 87:4. Sodom—Ez. 16:56.

MEONENIM, me-ŏn'e-nĭm. A place near Shechem.—Ju. 9:37.

MEONOTHAI, me-ŏn'o-thāi. A descendant of Judah.—I Chr. 4:14

MEPHAATH, mĕph'a-ăth. A city in Reuben.—Josh. 13:18; 21:37; I Chr. 6:79; Jer. 48:21.

MEPHIBOSHETH, me-phĭb'o-shĕth. (1) Son of Jonathan.—II Sam. 4:4; 9:6,

13; 19:24. Made lame by a fall—II Sam. 4:4. Treated with kindness by David—II Sam. 9:6, 13. Land of Saul restored to—II Sam. 9:7. Dwelt with David—II Sam. 9:10, 11. Mica son of —II Sam. 9:12. Servants of—II Sam. 9:12. Met David—II Sam. 16:1, 4. Went to Jerusalem to meet David— II Sam. 19:25, 30. Spared by the king —II Sam. 21:7.

(2) **Son of Saul's concubine.**—II Sam. 21:8.

MERAB, mē′rab. **Daughter of Saul who was betrothed to David.**—I Sam. 14: 49; 18:17, 19.

MERAIAH, me-rā′iah. **A priest in the days of Joiakim.**—Neh. 12:12.

MERAIOTH, me-rā′ioth. (1) **An Aaronite priest.**—I Chr. 6:6, 7, 52; Ezra 7:3.

(2) **Another Aaronite priest.**—I Chr. 9: 11; Neh. 11:11.

(3) **Another priest.**—Neh. 12:15.

MERARI, me-rā′ri. **Son of Levi and founder of the family of Merarites.**— Gen. 46:11; Ex. 6:16; Num. 3:17; I Chr. 6:1, 6; 23:6. Families of—I Num. 3:33, 35. Sons of—Ex. 6:19; Num. 3:20, 36; 4:29, 33, 42, 45; 7:8; I Chr. 6:19, 29, 44, 47; 23:21; 24:26, 27.

MERARITES. Ex. 6:19; Num. 26:57; Josh. 21:7, 34, 40; I Chr. 9:14; 26:10, 27; II Chr. 29:12; 34:12; Ezra 8:19. Allotment to—I Chr. 6:63, 77. Bear tabernacle—Num. 10:17. David counsels with—I Chr. 15:6, 17. Doorkeepers of tabernacle—I Chr. 26:19. Service of—Num. 4:33.

MERATHAIM, mĕr′a-thā-im. **Name of Babylon**—Jer. 50:21.

MERCHANDISE. Ez. 27:13; Mt. 22:5. Buyeth—Rev. 18:11. Ethiopia, Of— Is. 45:14. Gold, Of—Rev. 18:12. House of—John 2:16. Profitable—Pr. 31:18. See COMMERCE.

MERCHANT. Ez. 27:12–30; Neh. 3:31, 32. Among—Job 41:6. Brought—II Chr. 9:14. City of—Ez. 17:4. Earth, Of—Rev. 18:3, 11. Girdles unto—Pr. 31:24. Kingdom of heaven is like— Mt. 13:45. Kings—I Ki. 10:28; II Chr. 1:16. Lodged without Jerusalem— Neh. 13:20. Money with—Gen. 26:16. Multiplied—Nah. 3:16. Peoples, Of— Ez. 27:3. Powers of—Song of Sol. 3:6. Princes—Is. 23:8; Rev. 18:23.

Ships—Pr. 31:14. Traffic of—I Ki. 10: 15. Merchantmen—Gen. 37:28. See COMMERCE.

MERCURY, mĕr′kū-ry. **A Roman god**— Acts 14:12.

MERCY: God's mercy.—Rom. 2:4. A merciful God—Neh. 9:27–31; Jas. 5: 11. God's great mercy—I Pet. 1:3–5. To Jerusalem—Jer. 4:27. To Israel— Hos. 2:14–23; Lu. 1:50. Saved by— Tit. 3:5. Obtained—II Cor. 4:1; I Pet. 2:10. Virgins have obtained mercy from Lord—I Cor. 7:25. Gentiles glorify God's mercy—Rom. 15:9. Is conditional—Ex. 20:6; 34:6, 7; Num. 14:18, 19; Deut. 5:10; 7:9, 12; II Chr. 30:9; Ps. 62:12; 106:17, 18; Is. 55:7; Joel 2:12, 13.

God is merciful.—Ex. 20:2, 6; 22:27; Deut. 4:31; II Chr. 30:1; Ezra 9:9; Ps. 98:3; 107:1; 111:4; 116:5; 130:7, 8; 136:4, 8, 26; 145:8, 9; Lam. 3:22, 23. Toward those who keep His commandments—Dan. 9:4. In spite of transgressions, God is merciful—Neh. 9:17–31; Ps. 78:38; 86:5, 15; 103:7– 16; 106:6–46; Jer. 3:12; Lu. 6:35–37; Acts 26:16–18; Rom. 10:10–13; 11:30– 32; I Tim. 13:16; Heb. 8:12.

Mercy to animals.—Ex. 23:19; 34:26; Lev. 22:28; Deut. 14:21; 22:4, 6, 7; 25:4; Pr. 12:10; Lu. 14:5; I Cor. 9:9; I Tim. 5:19.

Teaching of Jesus concerning.—Lu. 6: 36. Parables: Good Samaritan—Lu. 10:25–37. The two debtors—Lu. 7: 36–47.

MERED, mĕr′red. **A man of Judah.**— I Chr. 4:17, 18.

MEREMOTH, mĕr′e-mŏth. (1) **Son of Uriah the priest**—Ezra 8:33; Neh. 3:4, 21.

(2) **A priest who sealed the covenant.**— Neh. 10:5; 12:3.

(3) **One who married a foreign wife.**— Ezra 10:36.

MERES, mĕr′res. **One of the seven princes of Persia.**—Esth. 1:14.

MERIBAH, mĕr′i-bah. **A place in Rephidim, at Kadesh-barnea where Moses struck the rock.**—Ex. 17:7; Num. 20: 13, 24; 27:14; Deut. 32:51; 33:8; Ps. 81:7; 95:8; 106:32. See MASSAH, REPHIDIM.

MERIB-BAAL, mĕr'ĭb-bā'al. **Son of Jonathan, grandson of Saul.**—I Chr. 8:34; 9:40.

MERODACH, me-rō'dak. **A Babylonian idol.**—Jer. 50:2.

MERODACH-BALADAN, me-rō'dak-băl'a-dan. **King of Babylon in the days of Hezekiah.**—Is. 39:1.

MEROM, mē'rom. **A lake in Palestine near where Joshua won a great victory.**—Josh. 11:5, 7.

MERONOTHITE, me-rŏn'o-thite. I Chr. 27:30; Neh. 3:7.

MEROZ, mē'rŏz. **A place near Lake Merom.**—Ju. 5:23.

MERRY. Began to be—Lu. 15:24. Eat, drink, and be—Lu. 12:19. Heart—Ju. 16:25; 19:6, 9, 22; Ruth 3:7; I Sam. 25:36; II Sam. 13:28; I Ki. 21:7; Eccl. 9:7. Let us eat and make—Lu. 15:23. Make—Jer. 30:19; 31:4; Lu. 15:29, 32; Rev. 11:10. Were—Gen. 43:34. See JOY.

MESHA, mē'shà. (1) **A place in S. E. Arabia.**—Gen. 10:30.

(2) **A Benjamite.**—I Chr. 8:9.

MESHACH, mē'shak. **Name given to Mishael, one of Daniel's three companions.**—Dan. 1:7; 2:49; 3:12–30.

MESHECH, mē'shek. (1) **Son of Japheth.**—Gen. 10:2; I Chr. 1:5.

(2) **Son of Shem.**—I Chr. 1:17.

(3) **A tribe.**—Ps. 120:5.

(4) **Descendants of (1).**—Ez. 27:13; 32: 26; 38:2, 3.

MESHELEMIAH, me-shĕl'e-mī'ah. **A Kohathite.**—I Chr. 9:21; 26:1, 2, 9.

MESHEZABEL, me-shĕz'a-bel. (1) **Name of some who sealed the covenant.**—Neh. 10:21; 11:24.

(2) **Ancestor of Meshullam who helped repair the wall.**—Neh. 3:4.

MESHILLEMITH, me-shĭl'le-mĭth. **A priest**—I Chr. 9:12.

MESHILLEMOTH, me-shĭl'le-mŏth. (1) **A priest of the family of Immer.**—Neh. 11:13.

(2) **Father of Berechiah who opposed making slaves of Jewish captives.**—II Chr. 28:12.

MESHOBAB, me-shō'băb. **A Simeonite.**—I Chr. 4:34.

MESHULLAM, me-shŭl'lam. (1) **A descendant of Jehoiakim.**—I Chr. 3:19.

(2) **Grandfather of Shaphan, a scribe under Josiah.**—II Ki. 22:3.

(3) **A Gadite.**—I Chr. 5:13.

(4, 5, 6) **Three Benjamites.**—I Chr. 8: 17; 9:7, 8.

(7) **A member of the family of Zadok.**—I Chr. 9:11; Neh. 11:11.

(8) **A priest, ancestor of a family in Jerusalem.**—I Chr. 9:12.

(9) **One who returned with Ezra.**—Ezra 8:16.

(10) **A Kohathite.**—II Chr. 34:12.

(11, 12) **Two who married foreign wives.**—Ezra 10:15, 29.

(13, 14) **Two who helped to repair the wall.**—Neh. 3:4, 6, 30; 6:18.

(15) **A priest who sealed the covenant.**—Neh. 10:7.

(16) **One who stood beside Ezra when he read the law.**—Neh. 8:4.

(17) **One who sealed the covenant.**—Neh. 10:20.

(18) **A Benjamite. Ancestor of some who dwelt in Jerusalem.**—Neh. 11:7.

(19) **A priest who assisted in dedicating the wall.**—Neh. 12:13, 33.

(20) **A member of the family of Ginnethon.**—Neh. 12:16.

(21) **A Levite.**—Neh. 12:25.

MESHULLEMETH, me-shŭl'le-mĕth. **Wife of King Manasseh and mother of Amon.**—II Ki. 21:29.

MESOPOTAMIA, mĕs'o-po-ta-mi-a. *"Region between the Rivers."*—Country lying between the Tigris and the Euphrates Rivers. Its Hebrew name is Aram Naharaim, meaning the same, and giving us the term Aramaic.

This was the Plain of Shinar and seat of Babylon.—Gen. 11:2; 14:1. Abraham sent his servant thither—Gen. 24:10. The residence of Balaam—Deut. 23:4. Children of Israel sold to a Mesopotamian king—Ju. 3:8. Othniel delivered them and captured the king—Ju. 3:9–10. Ammon hires chariots and horsemen from Mesopotamia to defeat David—I Chr. 19:6–7.

Mesopotamians hear the gospel—Acts 2:9. Stephen refers to Abraham and this country in his sermon—Acts 7: 1–4. See SYRIA.

MESS. Benjamin's—Gen. 43:34. Food, Of—II Sam. 11:8. Meat, Of—Heb. 12:16. See Food.

MESSAGE. Believed—Is. 53:1. Have a—Ju. 3:20. Proclaimed—II Tim. 4: 17. Sent—Gen. 50:16. This is the—I John 1:5; 3:11. Understand—Is. 28: 9, 19. Word of—I Thess. 2:13. See Gospel, Word of God.

MESSENGERS: Of individuals. — Jacob—Gen. 32:3, 6. Moses—Num. 20: 14. Israel—Num. 21:2. Moab—Num. 22:5. Balak—Num. 24:12. Joshua—Josh. 7:22. Gideon—Ju. 7:24. Zebul —Ju. 9:31. Jephthah—Ju. 6:12, 13, 14, 17–21. Men of Beth-shemesh—I Sam. 6:21. Abner—II Sam. 3:12. Hiram—II Sam. 5:11; I Chr. 14:1. Joab—II Sam. 12:27. Jezebel—I Ki. 19:2. Ahaziah—II Ki. 1:2, 3, 5, 16. Elisha—II Ki. 5:10. Amaziah—II Ki. 14:8. Ahaz—II Ki. 16:7. Jehoshaphat—II Chr. 18:2. Oholibah—Ez. 23:16. Rahab—Jas. 2:25. John—Lu. 7:24.

Of prophets.—Elisha—II Ki. 5:10.

Of cities.—Josh. 6:17, 25. Nineveh—Nah. 2:13.

Of rulers.—II Ki. 10:8.

Of kings.—Saul—I Sam. 16:19; 19:11, 14–16, 20, 21; 23:27. David—I Sam. 25:14, 42; II Sam. 2:5; 3:14, 26; 11:4, 19–25; I Chr. 19:2. Of Syria—I Ki. 20:2, 5, 9. Of Samaria—II Ki. 6:32, 33; 7:15; 9:18. Of Assyria—II Ki. 17:4. Rabshakeh—II Ki. 19:8, 14. Hezekiah—II Ki. 19:23. Of Ethiopia —Is. 37:9, 14.

Of nations.—Is. 14:32. Syria—I Chr. 19:16. Judah—Jer. 27:3.

Of covenant.—Mal. 3:1.

Of Satan.—II Cor. 12:7.

Illustrative.—Wicked—Pr. 13:17. Of death—Pr. 16:14. Cruel—Pr. 17:11. Swift—Is. 18:2.

Of God.—Deut. 2:26; Ju. 6:35; I Ki. 22: 13; II Chr. 36:15, 16; Job 1:14; Is. 42:19; 44:26; Ez. 23:40; 30:9; Hag. 1:13; Mal. 2:7.

MESSIAH. See Jesus.

MET. Ju. 15:14.

METAL. Amber (?) — Ez. 1:4, 27 (*marg.*); 8:2 (*marg.*). Antimony (paint)—II Ki. 9:30; I Chr. 29:2 (*marg.*); Is. 54:11; Jer. 4:30; Ez. 23:

40. Brass — See Brass. Copper, *dug out of hills*—Deut. 8:9. *Coppersmith*—II Tim. 4:14. Gold—See Gold. Iron—See Iron—I Chr. 22:3. Lead—Num. 31:22. *Weight of*—Zech. 6:8. *Pen of* —Job 19:24. *Talent of*—Zech. 5:7. *In furnace*—Ez. 22:20. *Rich in*—Ez. 27: 12. *Consumed in fire*—Jer. 5:29. *Figurative*—Ex. 15:10; Ez. 22:18. Silver—See Silver—Job. 22:25. Steel, *Chariots flash with*—Nah. 2:3. Tin—Num. 31: 22. *In furnace*—Ez. 22:20. *Take away all thy*—Is. 1:25. *Rich in*—Ez. 27:12. *Purification of*—Num. 31:22.

METE. Job 28:25; Is. 18:2, 7; 40:12; Mt. 7:2. See Measure.

METEOROLOGY. Signs of the weather. —I Ki. 18:43–45; Job 37:21–22; Eccl. 11:4; Mt. 16:2–3; Lu. 12:54–57.

Clouds.—Deut. 4:11; Ju. 5:4; II Sam. 22:12; 23:4; I Ki. 18:45; Job. 20:6; 22:14; 26:8; 37:16; 38:34, 37; Ps. 18: 11, 12; 77:17; 97:2; 104:3; 147:8; Eccl. 11:3, 4; 12:2; Is. 5:6; 14:14; Jer. 4:13; Ez. 30:3; 34:12; Dan. 7:13; Joel 2:2; Nah. 1:3; Zeph. 1:15; Mt. 24:30; 26:64; Mk. 13:26; 14:62; I Thess. 4: 17; Rev. 1:7.

Mist.—Gen. 2:6; Acts 13:11; II Pet. 2: 17.

Rain.—Gen. 2:5; 7:4–24; Lev. 26:4; Deut. 11:11, 14, 17; 28:24; I Sam. 12: 17; II Sam. 1:21; I Ki. 8:35; 18:45; II Chr. 7:13; Job 5:10; 28:26; 37:6; 38:37, 38; Ps. 65:9, 10; 147:8; Pr. 27: 15; Is. 30:23; 55:10; Jer. 5:24; Ez. 22:24; 34:26; Joel 2:23; Amos 4:7; Zech. 10:1; 14:17; Acts 14:17; Jas. 5:17. See Rain.

Dew.—Gen. 27:28; Ex. 16:13, 14; Num. 11:9; Deut. 32:2; 33:13, 28; Ju. 6:37–40; II Sam. 1:21; 17:12; I Ki. 17:1; Job 29:19; 38:28; Ps. 110:3; 133:3; Pr. 3:20; Song of Sol. 5:2; Is. 18:4; 26:19; Dan. 4:15, 23, 25, 33; 5:21; Hos. 6:4; 13:3; 14:5; Mic. 5:7; Hag. 1:10; Zech. 8:12.

Snow.—II Sam. 23:20; II Chr. 11:22; Job 6:16; 9:30; 24:19; 37:6; 38:22; Ps. 51:7; 68:14; 147:16; 148:8; Is. 1: 18; 55:10; Jer. 18:14; Lam. 4:7; Dan. 7:9; Mt. 28:3; Rev. 1:14.

Hail.—Ex. 9:18–34; 10:5, 12, 15; Josh. 10:11; Job 38:22; Ps. 18:12, 13; 78:47, 48; 105:32; 148:8; Is. 28:2; 30:30; 32:

19; Ez. 13:11, 13; 38:22; Hag. 2:17; Rev. 8:7; 11:19; 16:21.

Ice.—Job 6:16; 37:10; 38:29; Ps. 147:17.

Frost.—Gen. 31:40; Ex. 16:14; Ps. 78:47.

Thunder.—Ex. 9:23; I Sam. 12:17; Job 28:26; Ps. 18:13.

Lightning.—Job 28:26; 36:32; 38:25, 35; Zech. 10:1.

Storm.—Is. 28:2; 29:6; II Pet. 2:17.

Wind.—Job 1:18, 19; 27:20, 21; 37:21; Ps. 77:18; 148:8; Is. 29:6; Ez. 13:13. See WIND.

METHUSAEL, me-thū′sa-el. A descendant of Cain.—Gen. 4:18.

METHUSELAH, mĕ-thū′sĕ-läh. Son of Enoch, grandfather of Noah, oldest man known.—Gen. 5:21-27.

MEUNIM, me-ū′nim. Neh. 7:52. See NEHUNIM.

ME-ZAHAB, me-zā′hab. Grandfather of Mehetabel wife of Hadar king of Edom.—Gen. 36:39; I Chr. 1:50.

MEZOBAITE, me-zō′bă-īte. I Chr. 11:47.

MIBHAR, mĭb′här. One of David's mighty men.—I Chr. 11:38.

MIBSAM, mĭb′sam. (1) Son of Ishmael.—Gen. 25:13; I Chr. 1:29.

(2) Son of Simeon.—I Chr. 4:25.

MIBZAR, mĭb′zär. A duke of Edom.—Gen. 36:42; I Chr. 1:53.

MICA, mī′ca (1) A Levite.—Neh. 11:17.

(2) Son of Jonathan.—II Sam. 9:12.

(3) A Levite who sealed the covenant.—Neh. 10:11.

MICAH, mī′cah. (1) A Reubenite.—I Chr. 5:5.

(2) An Ephraimite who employed a priest for his image.—Ju. 17:1–13; 18:2–31.

(3) A Kohathite.—I Chr. 23:20; 24:24, 25.

(4) Son of Merib-baal.—I Chr. 8:34, 35; 9:40, 41.

(5) Father of Abdon who enquired of the Lord when the Book of the Law was found.—II Chr. 34:20.

(7) The prophet.—See OUTLINE STUDIES IN THE BOOKS.

MICAIAH, mi-kā′iah. (1) A prophet who foretold the fall of Ahab.—I Ki. 22:8–28; II Chr. 18:7–27.

(2) Father of Achbor an officer under Josiah.—II Ki. 22:12.

(3) Daughter of Uriel, wife of Rehoboam.—II Chr. 13:2.

(4) A prince of Judah.—II Chr. 17:7.

(5) A priest of the family of Asaph.—Neh. 12:35, 41.

(6) A prince of Judah under Jehoiakim.—Jer. 36:11, 13.

MICHAEL, mī′ka-el. (1) The archangel.—Dan. 10:13, 21; 12:1; Jude 9; Rev. 12:7.

(2, 3) Two Gadites.—I Chr. 5:13, 14.

(4) An Asherite.—Num. 13:13.

(5) Great-grandfather of Asaph.—I Chr. 6:40.

(6) A man of Issachar.—I Chr. 7:3.

(7) A Benjamite.—I Chr. 8:16.

(8) A man of Manasseh.—I Chr. 12:20.

(9) Son of Jehoshaphat.—II Chr. 21:2.

(10) Father of Omri prince of Issachar.—I Chr. 27:18.

(11) Father of Zebadiah.—Ezra 8:8.

MICHAL, mī′kal. Daughter of Saul and wife of David.—I Sam. 14:49; 18:20, 27, 28; 19:11-17; 25:44; II Sam. 3:13, 14; 6:16-23; 21:8; I Chr. 15:29.

MICHMAS, mĭk′mas. A place.—Ezra 2:27; Neh. 7:31.

MICHMASH, mĭk-mash. A city in Benjamin.—I Sam. 13:2-23; 14:5, 31; Neh. 11:31; Is. 10:28.

MICHMETHATH, mĭk′me-thath. A city.—Josh. 16:6; 17:7.

MICHRI, mĭk′ri. A Benjamite.—I Chr. 9:8.

MICHTAM, mĭk′tam. See MUSIC, PSALMS.

MIDDAY. At—Acts 26:13. From morning until—Neh. 8:3. Past, Was—I Ki. 18:29.

MIDDIN, mĭd′din. A city in the desert.—Josh. 15:16.

MIDDLE. Night, Of—Pr. 7:9. Valley, Of—Josh. 12:2. Wall of partition—Eph. 2:14.

MIDNIGHT. About—Acts 27:27. Bridegroom cometh at—Mt. 25:6. Go unto him at—Lu. 11:5. Lord cometh at—Mk. 13:35. Prayer at—Ps. 119:62; Acts 16:25; 20:7. Smitten at—Ex. 12:29.

MIDIAN, MIDIANITES, mĭd′i-an. Descended from Midian, son of Abraham and Keturah—Gen. 25:1, 2, 4; I Chr. 1:32, 33. Called Ishmaelites—Gen. 37:25. Trade—Gen. 37:28. Territory—

Ex. 2:15; 3:1; I Ki. 11:18. Possessions of—Num. 31:32–40. Moses marries a daughter of Jethro, priest of Midian —Ex. 2:16, 21; 3:1; 4:19; 18:1; Num. 10:29. Join Moab in calling Balaam —Num. 22:4. Seduce Israel to idolatry —Num. 25:2. Commanded to be destroyed—Num. 25:17; 31:2, 3, 7. Cities destroyed by Moses—Num. 31:10; Josh. 13:21. Five kings destroyed— Num. 31:8; Josh. 13:21. Princes destroyed—Ju. 7:25; Ps. 83:11. Subdued by Gideon—Ju. 6:8; Ps. 83:9; Is. 9:4; 10:26. Prophecies of—Is. 60: 6; Hab. 3:7.

MIDNIGHT. Ex. 11:4; 12:29; Ju. 16:3; Job 10:22; Ps. 119:62; Mt. 25:6; Mk. 13:35; Lu. 11:5; Acts 16:25; 20:7. See NIGHT.

MIDST. Gen. 23:10; Ps. 46:5; Ez. 24:5. Danced in—Mt. 14:6. Sea, Of—Pr. 30:19. Set him in—Mt. 18:2. Teachers, Of—Lu. 2:46. Waters, Of—Gen. 1:6.

MIDWIVES. Gen. 35:17; 38:28; Ex. 1: 15–21. See CHILDREN.

MIGDAL-EL, mĭg-dal-el. **A city in Naphtali.**—Josh. 19:38.

MIGDAL-GAD, mĭg'dal-găd. **A city in Judah.**—Josh. 15:57.

MIGDOL, mĭg'dol. (1) **A city in Egypt.** —Jer. 44:1; 46:14.

(2) **A place west of Red Sea.**—Ex. 14: 2; Num. 33:7.

MIGHT. Acknowledge my—Is. 33:13. Acts of—Esth. 10:2. Ashamed of— Ez. 32:29, 30. Do it with thy—Eccl. 9:10. Failed—Jer. 51:30. Fulfilled— Mk. 14:49. Full of—Mic. 3:8. Guided with—Ps. 65:6. Given me—Dan. 2:23. Glory, Of—Col. 1:11. God, Of—See GOD IS ALMIGHTY. Knowledge increaseth—Pr. 24:5. Mighty glory in —Jer. 9:23. Love Jehovah with all thy—Deut. 6:5. Not by—Zech. 4:6. Reuben, My—Gen. 49:3. Ruleth by— Ps. 66:7. Strength of—Eph. 1:19; Col. 6:10. See GOD, POWER.

MIGHTIER. He that cometh after me is—Mt. 3:11. Nation—Num. 14:12; Deut. 4:38; 7:1; 9:1, 14. One cometh —Lu. 3:16. Than me—Gen. 26:16; Ex. 1:9. There cometh one—Mk. 1:7.

MIGHTILY. Do—I Sam. 26:25. Increase—Deut. 6:3.

MIGHTY. II Sam. 22:18. Angels—Ps. 103:20. Better than—Pr. 16:32. Breakers—Ps. 93:4. Acts—Deut. 3:24. City of—Pr. 21:22. Deed, In—Lu. 24:19. Deeds—II Sam. 23:20. Fallen, How are the—II Sam. 1:19. Famine—Lu. 15:14. Image—Dan. 2:31. Jehovah is —See GOD IS ALMIGHTY. Men—I Cor. 11:12, 24. One—Gen. 10:8; Ps. 89:8, 19; Is. 40:10. Power, In—Ps. 147:5. Rain—Job 37:6. War, In—Heb. 11: 34. Wind—Job 8:2; Acts 2:2. Word —Lu. 24:19. Works—Mt. 7:22; Acts 2:11, 22. Wrestlings—Gen. 30:8. See GOD IS ALMIGHTY.

MIGRON, mĭg'ron. **A city of Benjamin.** I Sam. 14:2; Is. 10:28.

MIJAMIN, mĭj'a-min. (1) **A priest under David.**—I Chr. 24:9.

(2) **A priest who sealed the covenant.**— Neh. 10:7.

MIKLOTH, mĭk'loth. (1) **A soldier under David.**—I Chr. 27:4.

(2) **A Benjamite in Jerusalem.**—I Chr. 8:32; 9:37, 38.

MIKNEIAH, mik-nē'iah. **A musician.** —I Chr. 15:18, 21.

MILALAI, mĭl'alā'i. **A priest who assisted in purifying the wall.**—Neh. 12:36.

MILCAH, mĭl'kah. (1) **Wife of Nahor, Abraham's brother.**—Gen. 11:29; 22: 20, 23; 24:15, 24, 47.

(2) **Daughter of Zelophehad.**—Num. 26: 33; 27:1; 36:11; Josh. 17:3.

MILCH. Gen. 32:15. See MILK.

MILCOM, mĭl'kom. **An idol of the Ammonites.**—I Ki. 11:5, 33; II Ki. 23:13. See MOLECH.

MILDEW. Deut. 28:22; I Ki. 8:37; II Chr. 6:26; Amos 4:9; Hag. 2:17.

MILE. Mt. 5:41. See MEASURES.

MILETUS, mi-lē'tus. Seaport and capital of Ionia—Paul addresses Ephesian elders at—Acts 20:5. Trophimus left at—II Tim. 4:20.

MILK, *Chalab,* Rich, Fat; *Matsat,* To suck.

From various animals.—Goats—Pr. 27: 27. Sheep—Deut. 32:14; Is. 7:21, 22. Camels—Gen. 32:15. Cows—Deut. 32:14; I Sam. 6:7, 10. Flock—I Cor. 9:7.

Food of children.—Is. 28:9; I Cor. 3:2; Heb. 5:12, 13; I Pet. 2:2.

Offered in hospitality.—Gen. 18:8; Ju. 4:19.

Prepared for drink.—Ju. 4:19; 5:25; Ez. 25:4. In bottles—Ju. 4:19.

A land flowing with.—Ex. 3:8, 17; 13:5; 33:3; Lev. 20:24; Num. 13:27; 14:8; 16:13, 14; Deut. 6:3; 11:9; 26:9, 15; 27:3; 31:20; Josh. 5:6; Jer. 11:5; 32: 22; Ez. 20:6, 15; Joel 3:18. Instances of prosperity—Job 21:24; 29:5, 6; Pr. 27:27. Of scarcity—Is. 7:22; Ez. 25:4.

Emblematic of gospel blessings.—Is. 55: 1; 60:16.

Law of Israel for avoiding heathen practice.—Ex. 23:19; 34:26; Deut. 14: 21. Milk converted into: Cheese—I Sam. 17:18; II Sam. 17:29. Butter—Job 29:5, 6; Ps. 55:21; Pr. 30:33.

Figurative use.—Is. 66:11. Judah's destiny—Gen. 49:12. Poured out like milk—Job 10:10. Craftiness—Is. 55: 1. Avoiding strife—Pr. 30:33. Bridal charms—Song of Sol. 4:11. Bridegroom's response—Song of Sol. 5:1, 12. Whiter than—Lam. 4:7.

MILL. Ex. 11:5; Num. 11:8; Deut. 24: 6; Mt. 24:41.

MILLET. Ez. 4:9. See GRAIN.

MILLO, mil'lo. (1) **A fortification near Jerusalem.**—II Sam. 5:9; I Ki. 9:15, 24; 11:27; II Ki. 12:20; I Chr. 11:8; II Chr. 32:5.

(2) **A fortification near Shechem.**—Ju. 9:6, 20.

MILLION. Gen. 24:60.

MILLSTONE. II Sam. 11:21; Job 41: 24; Rev. 18:21. Grind with—Is. 47:2. Hanged about—Ju. 9:53; Mt. 18:6; Mk. 9:42; Lu. 17:2. Nether or upper —Deut. 24:6. Sound of—Jer. 25:10; Rev. 18:22. See JESUS, TEACHING OF.

MINCING. Is. 3:16.

MIND: Image and likeness of God.—Gen. 1:26, 27; 5:1. Reference is to mind, not body, else animals would also be in image of God. Man is superior—Ps. 8:6-8. A little lower than God—Ps. 8:5. Or angels—Heb. 2:7. God without form—Deut. 4:15, 16. Mind speedily created—Gen. 2:7. In Christ there is a new creation, also in the image of God—Rom. 6:4; 7:6; II Cor. 5:17; Eph. 4:24; Col. 3:10. Man is responsible because he can reason and choose—Deut. 30:15-20; Josh.

24:15, 22; Ju. 10:14; I Ki. 18:21; Pr. 1:29-31; John 10:42; Acts 5:4; Phil. 1:22; Heb. 11:25. Mind as a field—Mt. 13:19-23; Mk. 4:14-20; John 4: 35; I Cor. 3:6-9.

A storehouse of thoughts and purposes. —Job 12:5; Ps. 10:4; 33:11; 92:5; 94: 11, 19; Pr. 12:5; 24:9; Is. 59:7; 65:2; 66:18; Jer. 4:14; Dan. 4:5, 36; Mic. 4:12; Mk. 12:30; Lu. 2:35, 47; 10:27; Acts 14:2; I Cor. 1:19; II Cor. 4:3; 10:5; Eph. 1:18; Heb. 8:10; 10:16; II Pet. 3:1; I John 5:20; Rev. 17:9.

The mind perceives.—Ez. 11:5; 20:32; Lu. 9:47; 24:38, 45; II Tim. 2:7; Rev. 13:18.

The mind remembers.—Deut. 30:1; Neh. 9:17; Ps. 8:4; 31:12; 111:5; 115:12; Is. 17:10; 46:8; 65:17; Jer. 3:16; 32: 35; 44:21; 51:50; Lam. 3:21; Mk. 14: 72; Tit. 3:1; Heb. 2:6.

The mind reasons.—Job 4:13; 13:6; 20: 2; Ps. 8:4; 31:12; 111:5; 115:12; 139: 23; Dan. 2:29, 30; 4:19; 5:6, 10; Amos 4:13; Mt. 9:4; 12:25; 15:17; 16:7-9, 11; 21:25; 24:15; Mk. 2:6-8; 8:16, 17; 11:31; 12:28; Lu. 3:15; 5:21, 22; 9: 46; 20:5, 14; 24:15, 45; John 12:40; Acts 8:22; Rom. 1:20; 2:15; 7:23, 25; I Cor. 3:20; 14:14; Eph. 3:4; I Tim. 1:7; Heb. 4:12; 11:3.

Feels.—Sorrow—Gen. 26:35; Deut. 28: 65; I Sam. 9:5. Worry—I Sam. 9:20; Mt. 6:25, 27, 28, 31, 34; 10:19; Mk. 13: 11; Lu. 12:11, 22, 25, 26. Anger—II Sam. 17:8. Hate—Col. 1:21. Love—Rom. 8:5; 12:16; Phil. 3:15, 19; Heb. 11:15.

Plans, forms a purpose.—Deut. 15:9; I Sam. 2:35; II Ki. 9:15; I Chr. 22:7; II Chr. 24:4; Job 17:11; 21:27; Ps. 40:5; 56:5; 146:4; Pr. 16:3; 21:5; Is. 55:7-9; Jer. 6:19; 19:5; 29:11; Ez. 24:25; 38:10; Mt. 1:19; John 5:15; Rom. 8:27; 15:5, 6; I Cor. 2:16; II Cor. 1:15, 17; 13:11; Gal. 5:10; Phil. 2:2, 5; 3:15; 4:2; II Thess. 2:2; I Pet. 3:8; 4:1; Rev. 17:13.

Desires.—Deut. 18:6; Neh. 4:6; Acts 13: 22; Eph. 2:3; I Pet. 4:3.

Decides.—I Chr. 28:9; Lu. 12:29; Acts 28:6; Rom. 7:23; Phil. 1:27; I Pet. 1:13.

Consents.—Gen. 23:8; Rom. 7:25; Phil. 1:14.

Can be persuaded.—Jer. 15:1; Acts 28: 23, 24.

Can be humble.—Acts 20:19; Phil. 2:3.

Imagines.—Gen. 6:5; I Chr. 28:9; 29:18.

Obeys or refuses.—Num. 16:28; 24:13; Rom. 6:12.

Should seek God.—Deut. 4:29; 10:12; Acts 17:27.

Can grow worse.—Ps. 119:113; Pr. 21: 27; Ez. 38:10; Rom. 1:28; 8:6, 7; II Cor. 3:14; 4:4; 11:3; Eph. 4:17, 18; Col. 2:18; I Tim. 6:5; II Tim. 3:8; Tit. 1:15; Heb. 12:3.

Can grow better.—Mk. 5:15; Lu. 8:35; Rom. 8:6; 12:2; Eph. 4:23, 24; Col. 1:9; 2:2, 3, 10.

See REASON, THOUGHT, SOUL, SPIRIT.

MINDFUL. Country, Of—Heb. 11:15. Covenant, Of—Ps. 111:5. Man, Of— Ps. 8:4; 115:12; Heb. 2:6. Rock, Of— Is. 17:10. Wonders, Of—Neh. 9:17.

MINE, n. Silver—Job 28:1.

MINE, v. Adversary—Lu. 18:3; 19:27. All things are—John 16:15. Behalf— II Cor. 12:5. Can of mine own self do nothing—John 5:30. Eyes—John 9: 15, 30. Glory, Mine own—John 8:50; II Cor. 12:5. Hand, Mine own—II Thess. 3:17; Philemon 19. Known of —John 10:14. Mine are thine—John 17:10. Name—Rev. 3:12. Profit, Mine own—I Cor. 10:33. Receive of—John 16:14. Self—Rom. 16:2. These sayings of—Mt. 7:24, 26. Will, Mine own— John 5:30; 6:38. Word not—John 14:24.

MINGLE. Cakes—See CAKES. Cloth— Lev. 19:19; Deut. 22:11. Drink—Ps. 102:9; Pr. 9:2, 5; Is. 5:22; Mt. 27:34; Mk. 15:23. Fire with glass with hail —Ex. 9:24; Rev. 8:7. Heathen, Among —Ps. 106:35. Offering—See OFFERING. People—Jer. 25:20, 24; 50:37; Ez. 30: 5. Sacrifices, With—Lu. 13:1. Seed— Ezra 9:2; Dan. 2:43. Spirit—Is. 19: 14.

MINIAMIN, mĭn'i-a-mĭn. (1) A priest who returned with Zerubbabel.—Neh. 12:17, 41.

(2) A Levite in the days of Hezekiah.— II Chr. 31:15.

MINISTERS. "But ye shall be named the priests of Jehovah; men shall call you the ministers of our God"—Is. 61:6. (Verses 1 and 2 are the ones

Jesus chose when reading in the synagogue at Nazareth.)

Broadly.—An officer in civil government. Joseph—Gen. 41:40–44. Joshua —Josh. 1:1. Ira—II Sam. 20:26. Ahithophel—I Chr. 27:33. Zebadiah —II Chr. 19:11. Elkanah—II Chr. 28:7. Haman—Esth. 3:1. Mordecai —Esth. 10:3. Daniel—Dan. 2:48; 6: 1–3.

A servant of God appointed to special work.—Prophets, ministers in public affairs—I Sam. 9:15, 16; 10:1; 12:6– 10; 16:1–3; II Ki. 4:13. Especially in warning kings—I Sam. 13:1–14; 15: 10–31; II Sam. 12:1–14; I Ki. 18:17. Priests, ministers—Ex. 28:1, 3, 4, 41; 29:1, 44; 30:30; 31:10; 35:19; 39:41; 40:13–15; Lev. 7:35; Num. 8:26; Deut. 10:8; 21:5; I Ki. 8:11; I Chr. 15:2; 23: 13; II Chr. 13:10; 31:2; Jer. 33:22.

Ministry of John.—Mt. 3:1, 2; Mk. 1: 2–5; Lu. 3:2–8; John 1:19–28.

Christ, Himself, a minister.—Mt. 20:28. Christ an example to others—Mt. 20: 25–27; Mk. 10:45; John 13:12–17.

A servant of Christ called to serve in the kingdom of God.—Apostles, ministers—Called by Christ as individuals —Mt. 4:18–22; Mk. 1:16–20; Lu. 5:2– 11; John 1:35–46. Apostolic corps formed and sent to Israel only—Mt. 10:1–7; Mk. 3:13–19; Lu. 9:1, 2. Seventy sent—Lu. 10:1, 17. Commissioned as ministers to the whole world— Mt. 28:18–20; Mk. 16:15, 16; Lu. 24: 46–48; John 20:21–23; II Cor. 5:18–20.

Duties of apostles when sent to. Israel only.—To preach the approach of the kingdom and to heal—Mt. 10:7, 8; Acts 1:6–8. Their outfit and course— Mt. 10:5–14; Mk. 6:7–13; Lu. 9:1–6.

Duties of apostles when sent to whole world.—To spread the kingdom—Mt. 16:18, 19; 25:31–34; Lu. 22:28–30. They thought that the kingdom was not yet established—Acts 1:6–8. (Kingdom established—Col. 1:13; Heb. 12: 28; II Pet. 1:11; Rev. 1:9.) To bear witness of Jesus' life, death, and resurrection—Lu. 24:28; John 15:27; Acts 1:21–26. To remit sins—Mt. 16:19; Lu. 24:47; John 20:23. To preach the gospel—Mt. 28:19; Mk. 16:15; I Cor. 1:17, 18; I Tim. 1:11. To work miracles and heal the sick—Mk. 16:17, 18. See MIRACLES. To teach disciples —Mt. 28:20; Acts 2:42. To produce fellowship among saints—Acts 2:42. To establish and confirm churches—Acts 2:47; 5:11; 14:23, 24; 15:3, 4, 22; 16:4, 5; I Cor. 4:17.

Varieties of ministry: Evangelists.—Duties of: Their ordination—I Tim. 4:14. Their preparation—I Tim. 4:12–16; Tit. 2:7, 8. To preach and teach—Acts 18:24–27. To reprove—I Tim. 5:20, 21; Tit. 1:13, 14; 2:15. The work of—II Tim. 4:5. To reject heretics—Tit. 3:10, 11. To supervise the congregation—I Tim. 1:3; 4:11–13; 5:19; II Tim. 4:2–5; Tit. 2:1–6, 9, 10. Ordain and appoint teachers and elders—I Tim. 5:22; II Tim. 2:2; Tit. 1:5. Such as Timothy and Titus under direction of apostles—I Cor. 4:17; I Thess. 3:1, 2; II Cor. 8:18, 19.

Duties of elders: Presbyters.—Appointed in every city—Acts 14:23. Qualifications—Acts 20:28–31; I Tim. 3:1–7; Tit. 1:6–8. Duties—Tit. 1:9–11; I Pet. 5:1–3. Their claim to respect and obedience—I Thess. 5:12, 13; I Tim. 5:17; Heb. 13:7, 17.

Duties of deacons.—Appointed—Acts 6: 5, 6. Qualifications—I Tim. 3:8–15. Service—Acts 6:1–4.

Deaconnesses.—Rom. 16:1, 2. *Cf.* I Tim. 3:11.

Functions of ministers: Preaching.—Preachers—Rom. 10:14; I Tim. 2:7; II Pet. 2:5. Sowers—Ps. 126:6; Mt. 13:3–8; Mk. 4:3–8; Lu. 8:5–8. Representing Christ (ambassadors)—II Cor. 5:20; Eph. 6:20. Overseeing—Acts 20:28. Caring for flock (pastors)—Jer. 3:15; Eph. 4:11. Shepherds—Jer. 23:4; John 21:16, 17. Evangelizing—Acts 21:8; Eph. 4:11; II Tim. 4:5. Serving the Church (angels)—Rev. 1:20; 2:1, 8, 12, 18; 3:1, 7, 14. Serving God (servants)—Tit. 1:1; Jas. 1:1. Fighting for Christ—II Tim. 2:3, 4. Administering affairs—I Cor. 4:11; Tit. 1:1. Carrying message of the Churches—II Cor. 8:23. Governing—Acts 20:28; Phil. 1:1; Tit. 1:7. Perhaps "angel" in Rev. Chs. 2 and 3 refers to the porter of the Church, but that is very doubtful.

Should preach.—The gospel—Acts 8:32–35; I Cor. 2:2; 15:1–4. According to oracles of God—I Pet. 4:11. Not with human wisdom—I Cor. 1:17; 2:1–4. With plainness of speech—II Cor. 3: 12. With boldness—Mt. 10:27, 28. In sincerity—II Cor. 2:17; 4:2; I Thess. 2:3–5. Approving themselves as ministers of God—II Cor. 6:4. Commending themselves to men's consciences—II Cor. 4:2. With right spirit—Phil. 1:15–17.

Their reward.—Mt. 24:45–47; I Cor. 3: 14; 8:17, 18; I Pet. 5:4. See MISSIONS, PROPHETS, PRIESTS, LEVITES.

MINISTRATION. II Cor. 9:13. Condemnation, Of—II Cor. 3:9. Dainty —Acts 6:1. Days of—Accomplished—Lu. 1:23; Acts 12:25. Death, Of—II Cor. 3:7. Diversities of—I Cor. 12:5. Righteousness—II Cor. 3:9. Spirit of —II Cor. 3:8. See COVENANTS, MINISTER.

MINNI, mĭn′ni. **A province in Armenia.** —Jer. 51:27.

MINNITH, mĭn′nith. **A city in Ammon.** —Ju. 11:33; Ez. 27:17.

MINSTREL. II Ki. 3:15; Ps. 68:25; Rev. 18:22.

MINT. Mt. 23:23; Lu. 11:42. See FOOD.

MIRACLES. From *mirari*, to wonder. Generally sign of divinity. *Dunamis*, Power.

Purpose of miracles.—To produce belief. —Ex. 4:5–9; John 2:23; 4:48; 11:42; 20:30, 31. To reveal God—Ex. 7:5; 16:12; I Ki. 18:23, 24. To show glory of God—Ex. 16:7; John 11:42. To show works of God—Num. 16:28–30; Josh. 3:10; John 9:3. To act as credentials—Ex. 4:1–5; Mt. 11:4, 5; Mk. 2:9–12; 16:20; Lu. 7:21, 22; John 2: 11; 4:48; 5:36; 11:4, 40–42; 14:11; 15: 24. To put difference between—Ex. 11:7; I Ki. 18:23, 24. To confirm the worker—Mk. 16:20; Heb. 2:3, 4. To produce fear toward God—I Sam. 12: 17, 18; Dan. 6:20–27; Jonah 1:14–16. To produce obedience—Ex. 16:4, 5; 19: 4, 5; Deut. 11:1–2; 29:2–9; Ps. 78:10–34. To aid in propagation of gospel—Acts 2:1–4; 3:6–16; 5:5, 12–14; 8:5–8; Rom. 15:18, 19. Miracles of Jesus wrought to confirm His claims about Himself—John 5:36; 10:25, 37 ff.; 14:

11; 15:24. Examples of the confession of Jesus—Mt. 9:36; 14:14; Mk. 3:10; Lu. 9:11; John 6:2.
To teach spiritual lessons.—Lu. 5:10.
Miracles foretold.—Birth of Isaac—Gen. 17:19; 18:10–14.· Smiting Egypt—Ex. 3:20; 7:17–19; 8:2–23; 9:2–5; 10:4–6. Driving out nations—Ex. 34:10–11. Downfall of Jeroboam—I Ki. 14:7–11. Virgin birth—Is. 7:14; Lu. 1:31. Birth of John—Lu. 1:13. Life and character of Jesus—Is. Ch. 53. Introduction of the gospel accompanied by miracles—Is. 61:1, 2; Joel 2:28–32; Acts 2:17.
Miracles of Old Testament.—Creation—Gen. 1:1–27. Translation of Enoch—Gen. 5:24. The flood—Gen. Ch. 6. Destruction of Sodom, etc.—Gen. 19:24. Lot's wife—Gen. 19:26. Burning bush —Ex. 3:3. Change of Moses' rod into serpent—Ex. 7:8–10. Ten plagues—Ex. Chs. 7–12. Crossing Red Sea—Ex. 14:21, 22. Bitter waters sweetened—Ex. 15:25. Manna—Ex. 16:13–36. Water from smitten rock—Ex. 17:5–8; Num. 20:7–13. Pillar of cloud and fire—Ex. 14:19, 24; 33:9. Moses' shining face—Ex. 34:29–35; II Cor. 3:7. Sacrificial fire from heaven—Gen. 15:17; Lev. 9:24; I Ki. 18:38; I Chr. 21:26; II Chr. 7:1. Strange fire and results—Lev. 10:1, 2. Miriam's leprosy—Num. 12:10–15. Earth swallows Korah et al.—Num. 16:31, 32. Budding of Aaron's rod—Num. 17:8. Brazen serpent—Num. 21:9; John 3: 14, 15. Speaking of Balaam's ass—Num. 22:28. Crossing Jordan by Israel—Josh. 3:14–17. Fall of walls of Jericho—Josh. 6:6–20. Stopping of sun and moon—Josh. 10:12–14. Dew on Gideon's fleece—Ju. 6:37–40. Dagon's fall before ark—I Sam. 5:1–12. Smiting of men of Bethshemesh—I Sam. 6:19. Uzzah's death—II Sam. 6:6, 7. Withering of Jeroboam's hand —I Ki. 13:4–6. Widow's cruse—I Ki. 17:12–16. Raising of her son—I Ki. 17:17–23. Answer to Elijah's prayers —I Ki. Chs. 17, 18. Feeding of Elijah by ravens—I Ki. 17:4–6. Destruction of captains by fire—II Ki. 1:9–12. Dividing Jordan by Elijah and Elisha —II Ki. 2:8–14. Elijah's ascension to heaven—II Ki. 2:11. Healing of

waters of Jericho—II Ki. 2:20–22. Destruction of young men by bears—II Ki. 2:24. Water for Jehoshaphat—II Ki. 3:16–20. Widow's oil—II Ki. 4:2–7. Shunammite's child—II Ki. 4: 16–37. Curing deadly pottage—II Ki. 4:38–41. Multiplication of bread—II Ki. 4:42–44. Cure of Naaman's leprosy—II Ki. 5:10–14. Gehazi's leprosy—II Ki. 5:26, 27. Floating of axehead—II Ki. 6:5–7. Foretelling Benhadad's plans—II Ki. 6:8–13. Smiting Syrian army—II Ki. 6:18–20. Revival of dead by touch with Elisha's bones—II Ki. 13:21. Destruction of Sennacherib's army—II Ki. 19:35. Uzziah's leprosy—II Chr. 26:16–21. Delivery of three children from fiery furnace—Dan. 3:19–27. Daniel in lions' den—Dan. 6:16–23. Preservation of Jonah—Jonah 2:1–10.
Miracles of New Testament.—See MIRACLES OF JESUS. Miracles of the tongues, Pentecost—Acts 2:3. Cornelius—Acts 10:46. John's disciples—Acts 19:6. Corinthians—I Cor. 12:10. Miracles of Peter: *At beautiful door*—Acts 3:6, 7. *Ananias and Sapphira*—Acts 5:5–10. *Peter's shadow*—Acts 5:15, 16. *Æneas*—Acts 9:34. *Tabitha* —Acts 9:40. Miracles of Stephen—Acts 6:8. Miracles of Philip: Acts 8:6, 7, 13. Miracles of Paul: *Blinding of Elymas*—Acts 13:11. *Healing of cripple*—Acts 14:10. *Casting out of demons and healing sick*—Acts Chs. 16, 19, 20. *Restoration of Eutychus*—Acts 20:10. *Viper on hand*—Acts 28:3. *Father of Publius*—Acts 28:8, 9. Disciples work miracles: *The seventy*—Lu. 10:17–20. One forbidden by apostles—Mk. 9:38. Corinthians—I Cor. 12:8–10.
Miracles were wrought: By power of God—Ex. 4:1–5; 8:19; John 3:2; Acts 14:3; 15:12; 19:11. By power of Christ Mt. 10:1; Mk. 3:13–15; 6:7. By power of Holy Spirit—Mt. 12:28; Acts 2:2–4; Rom. 15:18, 19; I Cor. 12:4–11. In the name of Christ—Mk. 9:38, 39; 16:17; Acts 3:16; 4:30. Through faith of the agent in God—Lack of faith is the reason for failure—But few instances—Mt. 17:20; 21:21; John 14:10–12.

Effect on spectators.—Old Testament: Children of Israel—Ex. 4:30, 31; 14: 31; Num. 17:1-13; Deut. 1:31-33; 10: 21; II Chr. 7:3; I Ki. 18:39; Ps. 78:42-56. Pharaoh—Ex. 10:16, 17; 12:31, 32. Servants of Pharaoh—Ex. 10:7. Egyptians—Ex. 12:33; I Sam. 6:6, 7. Rahab and Canaanites—Josh. 2:9-11; 5:1. Gideon—Ju. 6:17-22, 36-40. Philistines—I Sam. 4:8; 5:2-5. Naaman—II Ki. 5:14, 15. Nebuchadrezzar—Dan. 2:47; 3:28; 4:2, 3. Darius—Dan. 6:20-27.

New Testament disciples.—Fig-tree—Mt. 21:20. Jesus walks on sea—Mk. 6:45-51. Draft of fishes—Lu. 5:8, 9. Miracle of wine—John 2:9, 11. Destroying temple—John 2:19-22. The multitude—Mt. 15:31; Lu. 4:36; 5:26; 8:35-37; John 7:31; 11:45, 48; Acts 2:6-12; 3:10, 11; 8:6.

Pretended miracles.—Egyptian magicians—Ex. 7:11, 22; 8:7. False prophets and religion—Deut. 13:1-3. Witch of Endor—I Sam. 28:7-14. False prophets—Mt. 7:22; 24:24. False Christs—Mt. 24:24. Deceive the ungodly—II Thess. 2:9-12; Rev. 13:14; 16:14; 19:20. See TONGUES, SIGNS AND WONDERS.

MIRE: Literal.—Job 41:30. Miry places—Ps. 40:2; Ez. 47:11; Dan. 2:41, 43. Of the street—II Sam. 22:43; Is. 10: 6; Mic. 7:10; Zech. 9:3; 10:5. Rushes grow in—Job 8:11. Thrown in, for punishment—Jer. 38:6.

Prophecy concerning.—Ez. 47:11.

Figurative.—Job—Job 30:19.

Illustrative of.—Sin—Ps. 69:2, 14; Is. 57:20; Jer. 38:22; II Pet. 2:22.

MIRIAM, mĭr′ĭ-am. (1) Sister of Moses and Aaron—Ex. 15:20. Watches over Moses while in the ark—Ex. 2:4-8. Called "The prophetess"—Ex. 15:20. Ranks with Moses and Aaron—Mic. 6:4. Led the women in a song of deliverance—Ex. 15:20, 21. Stricken for being jealous of Moses—Num. Ch. 12; Deut. 24:9. Dies and is buried at Kadesh—Num. 20:1. See MOSES, AARON.

(2) **A daughter of Ezra.**—I Chr. 4:17.

MIRMAH, mĭr′mah. **A Benjamite.**—I Chr. 8:10.

MIRROR. Belongings of Zion's daughters—Is. 3:23. Used for laver of tabernacle—Ex. 38:8.

Description of sky.—Job 37:18. Of the glory of the Lord—II Cor. 3:18.

Partial vision.—I Cor. 13:12.

Superficial observation.—Jas. 1:23.

MIRTH. Cause to cease—Pr. 14:13; Hos. 2:11. Commended—Eccl. 8:15. Depart with—Gen. 31:27. Heaviness, Is—Pr. 14:13. House, Of—Eccl. 7:8. Land, Of—Is. 24:11. Mad, With—Eccl. 2:2. Make—Neh. 8:12; Ez. 21: 10. Prove, With—Eccl. 2:1. Require—Ps. 137:3. Voice of—Jer. 7:34; 16: 9; 25:10. See JOY.

MISCARRY. II Ki. 2:19.

MISCHIEF. Ps. 10:14. Befall—Is. 47: 11; Ez. 7:26. Devise—I Sam. 23:9; Neh. 6:2; Esth. 8:3; Job 15:35; Ps. 7:4; 28:3; 52:1; Ps. 94:30; Pr. 16:17; 24:2; Is. 59:4; Dan. 11:27; Hos. 7:15. Do—Ju. 15:3; I Ki. 11:25. Fall into—Pr. 28:14. Hearts, In—Ps. 28:3; 140: 2; Pr. 16:27; Dan. 11:27. Maker—Pr. 24:8. Midst, In the—Ps. 55:10. Punishment of—II Sam. 16:8; Ps. 2:16. Seek—I Ki. 20:7. Tongue, Of—Ps. 10:7; 140:9.

MISCHIEVOUS. Madness—Eccl. 10: 13. Things—Ps. 38:12. Tongue—Job 6:30.

MISERABLE. Rev. 3:17. Comforters—Job 16:2. Men—Mt. 21:41.

MISERY. Job 3:20; 11:16; 20:22; Pr. 31:7; Eccl. 8:6; Lam. 3:19. Jerusalem, Of—Lam. 1:7; Rom. 3:16. Israel, Of—Ju. 10:16. Rich, Of—Jas. 5:1.

MISFORTUNE. Job 12:5.

MISGAB, mĭs′găb. **A Moabite town** (?)—Jer. 48:1.

MISHAEL, mĭsh′a-el. (1) **One of Daniel's three companions.**—Dan. 1:6.

(2) **A Kohathite.**—Ex. 6:22; Lev. 10:4.

(3) **One of Ezra's assistants.**—Neh. 8:4.

MISHAL, mĭ′shal. **A town in Asher.**—Josh. 19:26; 21:30.

MISHAM, mĭ′sham. **A Benjamite.**—I Chr. 8:12.

MISHMA, mĭsh′ma. (1) **An Ishmaelite.**—Gen. 25:14; I Chr. 1:30.

(2) **A Simeonite.**—I Chr. 4:25.

MISHMANNAH, mĭsh-măn′nah. **A Gadite.**—I Chr. 12:10.

MISHRAITES. I Chr. 2:53.

MISPAR, mĭs'par. Ez. 2:2.

MISPERETH, mĭs'pe-reth. Neh. 7:7.

MISREPHOTH-MAIM, mĭs're-phŏth-mā'im. **A place near Sidon.**—Josh. 11:8; 13:6.

MISFORTUNE. Job 12:5.

MISS. I Sam. 20:18; 25:7, 15, 21; I Ki. 20:39; Job 5:24; Is. 34:16. David—I Sam. 20:6, 18. Mark—Ju. 20:16.

MIST. Gen. 2:6; Acts 13:11; II Pet. 2:17.

MISTRESS. II Ki. 5:3; Ps. 123:2; Pr. 30:23; Is. 24:2. Despise—Gen. 16:4. Flee from—Gen. 10:8. House, Of the —I Ki. 17:17. Kingdoms, Of—Is. 47:5. Return to—Gen. 16:9. Witchcrafts, Of—Nah. 3:4.

MITE. Lu. 12:59. Widow's—Mk. 12:42; Lu. 21:2.

MITHKAH, mĭth-kah. **An encampment of Israel.**—Num. 33:28. See CAMP, ISRAEL.

MITHNITE, mĭth'nite. **One of David's mighty men.**—I Chr. 11:43.

MITHREDATH, mĭth're-dăth. **A Persian treasurer.**—Ezra 1:8.

MITRE. High priests, Of—Ex. 28:4, 37, 39; 29:6; 39:28, 31; Lev. 8:9; 16:4; Ez. 21:26; Zech. 3:5.

MITYLENE, mĭt'y-lē'ne. **The principal city in the island of Lesbos.**—Paul spent a night at—Acts 20:14.

MIXED. Faith—Heb. 4:2. Iron—Dan. 2:41, 43. Multitude—Ex. 12:38; Num. 1:4; Neh. 13:3. People—Hos. 7:8. Spies —John 19:39. Wine—Ps. 75:8; Pr. 23:30; Is. 1:22.

MIZAR, mī'zar. A hill—Ps. 42:6.

MIZPAH, mĭz'pah, *Watch-tower.* Name —Gen. 31:49.

A city of Gilead.—Ju. 11:29; Hos. 5:1. Armies of Israel encamped in—Ju. 10:17; 11:11, 29; 20:1; 21:1, 5, 8; I Sam. 7:5; 6, 7; 10:17. Land of— Josh. 11:3, 8. City of Moab—I Sam. 22:3. Valley of—Josh. 11:8. Town in Judah—Josh. 15:38. Jeremiah dwells at—Jer. 40:6-15. City of Benjamin— Josh. 18:26; Ju. 20:1; Neh. 3:7, 15, 19. Built by Asa—I Ki. 15:22; II Chr. 16:6. Ishmael smites Gedaliah at— II Ki. 25:25; Jer. 41:1-16.

MIZRAIM, mĭz'ra-ĭm. (1) **Name of Egypt.**—I Chr. 1:8. See EGYPT.

(2) **Son of Ham.**—Gen. 10:6, 13.

MIZZAH, mĭz'zah. **An Edomite.**—Gen. 36:13, 17; I Chr. 1:37.

MNASON, mnā'son. **An early disciple.**— Acts 21:16.

MOAB, mō'ab. (1) **Lot's son.**—Gen. 19:37.

(2) **Name of a nation and country east of the Dead Sea.**—Plains of—Num. 22:1; 26:3, 63; 31:12; 33:48, 49, 50; 35:1; 36:13; Deut. 34:1, 5; Josh. 13:32. Land of—Deut. 1:5; 29:1; 32:49; 34: 5, 6, 8; Ju. 11:15, 18; Ruth 1:1-6, 22. Field of—Gen. 36:35; Num. 21:20; I Chr. 1:46; 8:8. Border of—Num. 33: 44; Deut. 2:18. Men of—Ex. 15:15. Wilderness before Moab—Num. 21:11, 13, 14, 15; Deut. 2:8. Corners of— Num. 24:17. Toward—Ju. 3:28. Tents of—Ps. 83:6. Dominion in—I Chr. 4: 22. Chemosh the abomination of—I Ki. 11:7. Children of Israel served the gods of—Ju. 10:6. Sons of Ariel slain in—II Sam. 23:20; I Chr. 11:22. Proverbs concerning—Num. 21:28, 29. Moab rebellious—II Ki. 1:1; 3:4, 5, 7, 10, 23, 24, 26. Kings of—Num. 21:26; 22:3; Josh. 24:9; Ju. 3:12, 14, 15, 17. Princes of—Num. 23:6, 17. Daughters of—Num. 25:1. Children of—II Chr. 20:1, 10, 22, 23; Jer. 9:26. Moabitish damsel—Ruth 2:6; 4:3. Saul fought against—I Sam. 14:47. David smote —II Sam. 8:2; I Chr. 18:2. David dedicates to Jehovah—II Sam. 8:12; I Chr. 18:11. Ephraim and Judah against—Is. 11:14. Jews married women of—Neh. 13:23.

MOADIAH, mō'a-dī'ah. Neh. 12:17. See MAADIAH.

MOAN. Ps. 55:2, 17; Ez. 24:23. See GROAN, MOURNING.

MOAT. Dan. 9:25.

MOCKING.—Kinds of: Profane—Ps. 35:16. Cruel (trial of)—Heb. 11:36. Accused of—Gen. 19:14; 39:14, 17. Samson is accused by Delilah—Ju. 16: 10, 13, 15. Animals: Ass—Num. 22: 29. Horse—Job 39:22. People—Elijah mocked the idolatrous people—I Ki. 18:27. Elisha is mocked by children—II Ki. 2:23. Posts were mocked by people—II Chr. 30:10. Messengers of God—II Chr. 36:16. Jews were mocked—Neh. 4:1. Job is—Job 17:2; 21:3. Fools—Pr. 14:9. Jeremiah—

Jer. 20:7. Zedekiah—Jer. 38:19. Jesus is mocked—Mt. 27:29, 31, 41; Mk. 15: 20, 31; Lu. 18:32; 22:63; 23:11, 36. Herod is mocked by wise men—Mt. 2:16. Is not mocked—Gal. 6:7. Apostles mocked—Acts 2:13. In prophecy, Wisdom will mock—Pr. 1:26. Jerusalem becomes a mocking—Ez. 22:4. There shall be mockers—Jude 8. Wine is a mocker—Pr. 20:1. See LAUGHTER, SCOFFING.

MOIST. Deut. 29:19. See METEOROLOGY.

MOISTEN. Ez. 46:14.

MOISTURE. Job 37:11; Ps. 32:4; 104: 16; Lu. 8:6.

MOLADAH, mŏl'a-dah. **A city in Judah.** —Josh. 15:26; 19:2; I Chr. 4:28.

MOLE. See ANIMALS.

MOLECH, mō'lĕk.

MOLECH, MOLOCH, or MILCOM (Heb. *Melekh,* "King").—God of the Ammonites—Acts 7:43.

Children "passed through the fire" to *i. e.,* were burned in sacrifice).—Lev. 18:21; 20:2–5; II Ki. 16:3; 21:6; 23: 10; II Chr. 28:3; Is. 57:5; Jer. 7:31; 19:5; 32:35; Ez. 16:20, 21; 20:31; 23: 37, 39; Mic. 6:7.

Solomon built a high place for.—I Ki. 11:7.

Destroyed by Josiah.—II Ki. 23:10.

Prophecies concerning.—Jer. 49:3; Amos 1:15. See IDOLATRY—Lev. 19:4.

MOLID, mō'lid. **A descendant of Jerahmeel.**—I Chr. 2:29.

MOLTEN. I Ki. 7:33. Brass—I Ki. 7:16. Image—Ju. 17:3, 4. Sea—I Ki. 7:23. Undersetters—I Ki. 7:30. See IMAGES.

MOMENT. For the—Ps. 30:5; II Cor. 4:17. Little—Ezra 9:8. Lying tongue is but for a—Pr. 12:19. One—Ex. 33:5. Time, Of—Lu. 4:5.

MONEY. Gold and silver used as—Gen. 13:2; Num. 22:18. Brass added by Romans—Mt. 10:9; 12:41. Silver used frequently—Gen. 17:12, 13, 23, 27; 20: 16 (upwards of 50 other instances in Old Testament). Gold referred to—Gen. 24:35; 34:8; I Chr. 21:25; Ezra 8:25–27; Is. 13:17; 46:6; 60:9; Ez. 7:19; 28:4. Usually taken by weight—Gen. 23:16; 43:21; Job 28: 15; Jer. 32:9–10; Zech. 11:12. Bag of—Pr. 7:20. Image on—Mt. 22:20–

21. Conscience money—Ju. 17:2; Mt. 27:3–5.

Values mentioned. — Old Testament: *Shekel* means weight, so used for spices —Ex. 30:23. Brass—Ex. 38:29. Uncoined bars till 500 B. C. Gold, *Shekel* — $9.96. *Mina (pound)* — $496.38. *Talent*—$29,728.96. Silver, *Shekel*— $0.67. *Mina (pound)*—$31.62. *Talent*— $1,995.26. Coined: Gold daric—I Chr. 29:7; Ezra 2:69; 8:27; Neh. 7:70–72. Value, $5.13.

New Testament: Gold alluded to once— Mt. 10:9. *Aureus,* value $4.98. Silver, *Denarius,* value, $0.198. *Drachma* or *Drachm,* same value, once only—Lu. 15; 8. *Didrachma* (2 *Drachma*)—Mt. 17: 24. Equal to holy shekel or temple tax. *Stater,* or *Tetadrachma* (4 *drachma*), Temple tax for two—Mt. 17:27. *Mina (pound)*—Lu. 19:13, 16, 18, 20, 24, 25. Value, $19.80. *Talent,* equivalent to 6000 denarii; value, $1,188.00. Copper or bronze: *Assarion* (penny)—Mt. 10: 29; Lu. 12:6. Value, $0.012. *Quadrans* (farthing)—Mt. 5:26; Mk. 12:42. Value, $0.003. *Lepton* (mite)—Mk. 12:42; Lu. 12:59; 21:2. Value, Three-twentieths of a cent.

Pieces of money.—Mt. 26:15 (probably the *stater*). Thirty pieces about 120 *denarii,* or $23.76. Acts 19:19—Books worth probably 50,000 *denarii,* equal to $9,900.00.

Money for ransom of souls.—Ex. 30:11– 16; Lev. 5:15–16.

Jewish money regulated by standard of Sanctuary.—Lev. 5:15; Num. 3:47.

Forbidden to take interest.—Ex. 22:25; Lev. 25:37; Deut. 23:19; Neh. 5:7, 10, 11, 13; Pr. 15:5.

Abraham used current money.—Gen. 23: 9, 13, 16.

Money-changing a trade. — Mt. 21:12; Mk. 11:15; John 2:15.

Given as offerings.—II Ki. 12:4–16; 22: 7, 9; II Chr. 24:5, 11, 14; 34:9, 14, 17; Ezra 2:68, 69; 7:17; Neh. 10:32; Mk 12:41; Acts 4:37. As alms—I Sam . 2:36; Acts 3:3–6. For tribute—II Ki 15:20; 23:33, 35; Neh. 5:4; Mt. 17:24 27; 22:17, 19.

Usefulness as a defence.—Eccl. 7:12.

Love of a root of evil.—Mic. 3:11; I Tim. 6:10.

Gifts.—Naaman to Gehazi—II Ki. 5:22, 26. To Job—Job 42:11. Queen of Sheba to Solomon—I Ki. 10:2; II Chr. 9: 9. Simon offers gift of Paul—Acts 8:18. Felix expects gift of Paul—Acts 24:26.

To purchase with.—Gen. 23:16; 39:19; I Ki. 9:14; 17:24; Ezra 3:7. Joseph puts his brother's money in sack—Gen. 42:25, 27, 28, 35; 43:12, 15, 18; 22:23; 47:14, 15, 16, 18. Food—Deut. 2:6, 28; 14:26. Fruit—Job 31:39. Pleasure—Eccl. 10:19. Slaves—Gen. 37:28; Ex. 12:44; 21:21; Lev. 22:11; 25:50, 51. Dowry of wives—Ex. 21:11; 22:17; Deut. 21:14. Vineyard—I Ki. 21:2, 6, 15.

Recompense money.—Ex. 21:11, 21, 30, 34, 35; 22:7. In year of jubilee—Lev. Ch. 27.

Redemption money.—Num. 3:48-51; 18: 16. Tithes, used in paying—Deut. 14:25.

Use in New Testament.—Silver—Mt. 25: 18, 27; 28:11, 15; Mk. 6:8; 14:11; Lu. 9:3; 19:15, 23; 22:5; Acts 7:16; 8:20. Gold—Mt. 2:11; 10:9; Acts 3:6; 20: 33; I Pet. 1:18.

MONSTER.—Is. 27:1; 51:9; 51:34; Ez. 32:2. See Sea-monster.

MONTHS: Sun and moon for signs and seasons.—Gen. 1:14.

Year divided into twelve.—I Ki. 4:7; I Chr. 27:1-15; Esth. 2:12.

Flood began in second.—Gen. 7:11.

Ark rested in seventh.—Gen. 8:4-5.

Time computed by.—Gen. 29:14. (Jephthah's daughter)—Ju. 11:37. (Ark in bondage)—I Sam. 6:1. (New moon began)—Ps. 81:3; Num. 10:10. Fruits came monthly—Rev. 22:2.

Names of Months.—I. **Abib or Nisan** (April).—Beginning of Jewish calendar—Ex. 12:2. The first passover—Ex. 12:1-28. Feast of unleavened bread. Departure from Egypt—Ex. 13:4. Setting up of tabernacle—Ex. 40:2. Arrive at Zin—Num. 20:1. Cross Jordan—Josh. 4:19. Crucifixion of Jesus—Mt. 26:2; Mk. 14:1; Lu. 22:1. II. **Zif** (May).—Building of the temple—I Ki. 6:1, 37. Rebuilding of temple—Ezra 3:8. III. **Sivan** (June).—Pentecost or Feast of Weeks—See Feasts. Jews warned by Mordecai—Esth. 8:9-14. Asa renews covenant—II Chr. 15:

10-15. IV. **Thammuz** (July).—A fast month—Zech. 8:19. Jerusalem taken by Nebuchadrezzar in—Jer. 39:2. V. **Ab** (August).—Aaron died in—Num. 33:38. Temple destroyed in—II Ki. 25:8-10. Captivity began in—Jer. 1:3. Ezra returns in—Ezra 7:8-9. VI. **Elul** (September).—Walls of Jerusalem finished—Neh. 6:15. VII. **Ethamin or Tizri** (October).—First month in Civil Year—I Ki. 8:2. Day of atonement in—Lev. 23:27. Feasts begin—Lev. 23:39-44. Beginning of Jubilee—Lev. 25:9-12. Altar renewed—Ezra 3:1-6. VIII. **Bul** (November).—Temple finished—I Ki. 6:38. Jeroboam's feast—I Ki. 12:32. IX. **Chisleu** (December).—Ezra accuses Jews of trespass in—Ezra 10:9-11. Feast of dedication—See Feasts. Fast proclaimed for sin—Jer. 36:9. X. **Tebeth** (January).—Esther chosen queen—Esth. 2: 16. Jerusalem besieged—II Ki. 25:1. XI. **Sebat** (February).—Jehovah speaks to Zechariah—Zech. 1:7. XII. **Adar** (March).—Decree against Jews—Esth. 3:12-13. House of Jehovah completed—Ezra 6:15. Feast of Purim—Esth. 9:1-26.

MONUMENT. Absalom's—II Sam. 18: 18. See II Ki. 23:17.

MOON.—Created by Jehovah—Gen. 1: 14; Ps. 8:3. To glorify God—148:3. To act as lesser light—Gen. 1:16. Has a glory of its own—I Cor. 15:41. Called queen of heaven—Jer. 7:18; 44:17, 19. Burned incense unto—Jer. 7:18; 44:17, 19. Warned against worship—Deut. 4:19; 17:3. Stands still—Josh. 10:12. Signs in, before destruction of Jerusalem—Lu. 21:25. Feast of—Num. 10:10; 28:11-15; I Sam. 20: 5; I Chr. 23:31; Ps. 81:3; Is. 1:13; Hos. 2:11.

Descriptive of: Glory in church—Is. 60: 19, 20. Of calamities—Is. 13:10; Joel 2:10; 3:15; Mt. 24:29. Of permanence of Israel's seed—Jer. 31:35-37. Of the woman—Rev. 12:1. See Cosmology.

MOORED. Mk. 6:53.

MORALS. I Cor. 15:33.

MORASHTITE, mō'rash-tīte. **Micah the prophet**—Jer. 26:18; Mic. 1:1.

MORDECAI, môr'de-kāi. A **Benjamite, son of Jair**—Esth. 2:5. Bowed not down to Haman—Esth. 3:5. Honored by king—Esth. 6-10. Informs king of plot—Esth. 2:21, 22. Put on sackcloth —Esth. 4:1.

MORE. John 14:30. Children, Are—Gal. 4:27. Diligence—II Pet. 1:10. Forty years, Than—Acts 4:22. Night no— Rev. 22:5. Part—Mk. 9:26. Servant, Than a—Philemon 16. Worketh—II Cor. 4:17.

MOREH, mō'reh. **Hill of.**—Ju. 7:1. Oak of—Gen. 12:6; Deut. 11:30.

MORIAH, mo-rī'ah. **A hill. Abraham takes Isaac to offer.**—Gen. 22:2. Solomon builds a temple on—II Chr. 3:1.

MORESHETH-GATH, mŏr'esh-eth-găth. **Birthplace of the prophet Micah.**— Mic. 1:14.

MORNING. And there was morning— Gen. 1:5, 8, 13, 19, 23, 31. Angels come to Lot in—Gen. 19:15. Gathered manna every—Ex. 16:21. Cloud taken up in—Num. 9:21. He shall be as the— II Sam. 23:4. Called on Baal from morning, etc.—I Ki. 18:26. Thou shalt seek me in the—Job 7:21. Hast thou commanded the—Job 38:12. Joy cometh in the—Ps. 30:5. I will sing of thy lovingkindness in the—Ps. 59:16. In the morning they are like grass—Ps. 90:5, 6. Oh, satisfy us in the—Ps. 90: 14. Ye say, in the morning it will be foul weather—Mt. 16:3. In the morning saw fig tree—Mk. 11:20. Early in morning came to sepulchre—Mt. 20:1; Mk. 16:2; Lu. 21:38. Entered temple early in—Acts 5:21.

MORROW. Against—Ex. 8:10. Anxious for the—Mt. 6:34. Boast not of—Pr. 27:1. From the—Lev. 23:15. On the —Lev. 19:6; 23:11; Num. 16:41; 17:8; 23:3; Josh. 5:11, 12. Till the—Zeph. 3:3. Unto the—Lev. 23:16; Acts 4:3. What shall be on—Jas. 4:14. See To-MORROW.

MORSEL. Bread, Of—Gen. 18:5; I Sam. 2:36; 28:22; I Ki. 17:11. Casteth forth ice like—Ps. 147:17. Dainty—Pr. 18: 8. Dip in vinegar—Ruth 2:14. Dry— Pr. 17:1. Eat—II Sam. 12:3; Job 31: 17; Pr. 32:8. Strengthen thy heart with—Ju. 19:5.

MORTAL. Body—Rom. 6:12; 8:11. Flesh—II Cor. 4:11. Man—Job 4:17.

Must put on immortality—I Cor. 15 53. Swallowed up of life—II Cor. 5:4

MORTALLY. Deut. 19:11.

MORTALITY. II Tim. 1:10.

MORTAR: Earliest mention of.—Slim (Bitumen, *marg.*) used for—Gen. 11: Used in hard service—Ex. 1:14. Man na beat in—Num. 11:8.

Law concerning.—Cleansing of infecte houses—Lev. 14:42, 45.

Illustrative use of.—Pr. 27:22; Is. 41 25; Ez. 13:10, 11, 14, 15; 22:28.

Prophecy.—Nah. 3:14.

MORTGAGES. Neh. 5:3. See DEBT.

MOSERAH, MOSEROTH, mo-sē'ra An encampment of Israel.—Num. 33 30; Deut. 10:6. See CAMP, ISRAEL.

MOSES, Heb. *"drawn out."*

Birth of.—Son of Amram and Jochebe —Ex. 6:20. A Levite—Ex. 6:16-2 Hidden three months at home becaus of Pharaoh's edict—Ex. 2:2; Acts 7 20; Heb. 11:23. Placed in an ark b the brink of the river—Ex. 2:3; Heb 11:23. Found and adopted by Pha raoh's daughter—Ex. 2:5-6. Miriam Moses' sister, proposes a nurse—E 2:7-10; Acts 7:21. Moses' mother appointed—Ex. 2:8-9.

Egyptian training.—The princess claim Moses as her son—Ex. 2:10; Acts 7 21. He was taught in all the wisdo of the Egyptians—Acts 7:22. (Trad tion says Moses studied at the temp of the sun in Heliopolis, and fough Pharaoh's battles.)

Moses' choice.—At 40 years of ag Moses visits his brethren—Ex. 2:1 Acts 7:23; Heb. 11:24-27. Is vexe at their burdens—Ex. 2:11. Smites a Egyptian—Ex. 2:11-12; Acts 7:2 Supposed his brethren ready for d liverance—Acts 7:25. Attempts part two quarrelsome Hebrews and repulsed—Ex. 2:13-14; Acts 7:26-2 Pharaoh, hearing, seeks to slay Mos —Ex. 2:15. Moses flees into the Lan of Midian—Ex. 2:15; Acts 7:29.

His training in Midian.—Defends Reuel daughters at the well—Ex. 2:16-1 Reuel makes a home for him, and giv him Zipporah as his wife—Ex. 2:2 21. Moses has two sons, Gershom an Eliezer—Ex. 2:22; 18:4. Fulfils for years herding for Jethro, and learning the land—Acts 7:30.

God appeared to Moses at the bush.— Ex. 3:2; Acts 7:30. Moses draws near —Ex. 3:3; Acts 7:31. Is commanded to remove his sandals—Ex. 3:5. God reveals Himself—Ex. 3:6; Acts 7:32. Declares in favor of Israel's deliverance—Ex. 3:7-10; Acts 7:34. Prophecies concerning deliverance—Gen. 15: 13-14; 46:4; 50:24-25. Moses hesitates, giving four reasons: (1) *Personal inability*—Ex. 3:11-12; (2) *Jehovah unknown*—Ex. 3:13-16; (3) *Needed confirmation*—Ex. 4:1-9; (4) *Lack of eloquence*—Ex. 4:10-17.

Moses and family start for Egypt.— Jethro sanctions it—Ex. 4:18-19. The start made—Ex. 4:20. Jehovah instructs—Ex. 4:21-23. Jehovah seeks to kill Moses for neglect of duty— Ex. 4:24. Zipporah circumcises Gershom—Ex. 4:25-26. She returns to her father—Ex. 18:1-7. Aaron meets Moses—Ex. 4:27. After conference, they gather together the elders of Israel—Ex. 4:29-31.

Moses and Aaron present themselves to Pharaoh.—Ex. 5:1. Pharaoh spurns them—Ex. 5:2. Pharaoh puts heavier burdens on Israel, for which Moses and Aaron get the blame—Ex. 5:4-21. The matter is referred to Jehovah and the Mosaic miracles begin—Ex. 5:22-23; 6:1-30; 7:1-9.

A contest between Moses and magicians —Ex. 7:10; 8:18. Moses wins—Ex. 18:19. The plagues of the flies, of boils, of hail, of locusts, of darkness, and of the death of the first-born succeed each other—Ex. 8:20; 12:30. See EXODUS in OUTLINE STUDIES IN THE BOOKS. Pharaoh relents—Ex. 12:31-33. Israel eats the passover, obeys respecting the blood, and girds itself for the exodus—Ex. 12:1-34. Laden with gifts, Israel departs—Ex. 12:35-41.

Moses as a leader.—From Rameses to Succoth—Ex. 12:37. Toward the Red Sea—Ex. 13:17-22. They encamp between Migdol and sea—Ex. 14:2. Pharaoh pursues Israel—Ex. 14:5-9. Israel becomes alarmed—Ex. 14:10-12. Moses interposes, but is ordered forward by Jehovah—Ex. 14:13-20. He

stretches out his hand over the sea and the crossing is made—Ex. 14:21-22; Ps. 78:13; 106:9-10; 136:13-14; Is. 63:11-13. Pharaoh's host follows and is drowned—Ex. 14:23-28; Ps. 106:11; 136:15. Moses writes a song of deliverance, which Israel sings— Ex. 15:1-21.

Moses' trials with his people.—Murmuring at Marah—Ex. 15:24. At sin— Ex. 16:2. At Rephidim—Ex. 17:2. Sweetens the waters at Marah—Ex. 15:25. Brings water from the rock— Ex. 17:5.

Moses as a ruler.—Had the care of three million people—Ex. 12:37; Deut. 1:9-10. Aaron and Miriam, his helpers, were hindrances—Ex. 32:1-6, 21-24. Aaron restrains not his sons—Lev. 10: 1-3. He did not restrain Moses—Num. 20:10-13. Aaron and Miriam rebelled —Num. 12:1-13. The burden heavy upon Moses—Ex. 18:13.

Moses as a judge.—Ex. 18:13. Advised by father-in-law to appoint judges— Ex. 18:14-23. Takes the advice, but difficult cases brought to Moses—Ex. 18:24-26; Deut. 1:9-18.

Moses' main dependencies. — Joshua, faithful from the first to last, won at Amalek—Ex. 17:8-13. Ascended mount with Moses, waiting for him 40 days— Ex. 24:13; 32:17. Attended Moses in his visits to the tabernacle—Ex. 33: 11. Brought true report from Canaan —Num. 14:6-10. With Moses when he sung his last song—Deut. 2:14. Moses' other dependant was Phinehas—Num. 25:6-8; Ps. 106:30; Num. 31:6-7.

Moses, the man of God.—Here was his greatest dependence—Josh. 14:6; Ezra 3:2; I Chr. 23:14; II Chr. 30:16; Deut. 33:1; 34:5; Num. 12:8; Josh. 1:1.

Moses, the lawgiver.—Chosen because of his aptitudes as a legislator—Ex. 18:19-20; 33:11; Deut. 34:10-12; Num. 11:16-17; 27:6-11. His ability to take in the divine plan—Ex. 14:15-30; Hos. 12:13. The law came from Jehovah's mouth but through the mind of Moses —Deut. 10:12-22; 11:1-8. Moses' individuality seen in his responsive actions—Ex. 19:14, 15, 25; Deut. 9:12-19; 20:21. Receives the law and enforces it upon the people—Ex. 20:23; Chs. 24–34.

Moses, the tabernacle builder. — His training in Egypt a preparation— Acts 7:22. Hating idolatry, he forsook Egypt—Heb. 11:27–28. He builds according to divine pattern—Ex. 25: 9, 40; 26:30; 27:8; Heb. 8:5; 9:23–24. The material Egyptian—Ex. 12:35, 36; 25:3–7; 35:5–9. Training for artistic work Egyptian—Gen. 15:13–14. (See Taylor's ''Moses'' and Rawlinson's ''Moses.'') Egyptian linen— Ex. 26:1, 31; 27:9; Ch. 28.

Further acts of Moses: Brings water from the rock, offending Jehovah— Num. 20:1–13. Makes a brazen serpent—Num. 21:8–9; John 3:14. Sends spies into Canaan—Num. 13:1–24. Views the promised land, but may not enter—Num. 20:12; 27:12. Appoints Joshua to succeed him—Num. 27:15. His death and burial—Deut. 34:5.

Moses as a prophet.—Surpassed all prophets in personal communion with Jehovah—Deut. 34:10; Ex. 17:4; 19: 20; 27:28; 33:11; Num. 8:4; 11:16–17; 12:7–8; 14:5; 27:5. Jehovah gave direct revelations to Moses—Ex. 3:6– 10; 14:15–18; Deut. 1:5–8, 34–40, 42– 45; 2:2–8, 9–13, 16–25. Welcomed other prophets—Num. 11:26–30.

Moses as a poet.—Had the historic imagination—Deut. 32:1–43; 33:1–29; Ps. 90.

Moses as an orator.—(1) Announcement of his deposition—Deut. 1:5–4, 39. (2) On the delivery of the covenant— Deut. 5:1; 11:30. (3) At the rehearsal of the blessings and cursings—Deut. 28:1–68. (4) The covenant in the Land of Moab—Deut. 29:2; 31:7. (See Moulton's Bible.)

Moses as an historian.—Accuracy—Gen. 1:1–31; 19:24–28; 26:2–5; Ex. 1:8–14; 6:1–8. Description—Gen. 3:1–21; 19: 1–22; 21:8–21; 24:10–49; 27:1–45; 42: 6–38. Comprehensiveness—Deut. 8: 1–20; 10:12–22.

Characteristics of Moses: Boldness before Jehovah—Ex. 3:10, 11, 13; 4:1, 10, 14; 5:22–23; 32:11–14; 33:12–13; Num. 16:15. Disparagement of speech —Ex. 3:11; 4:10; 6:30; 32:32; Num.

12:3. Intercession for others—Ex. 32: 30–35; Num. 12:11–13; 21:7–9. Hasty anger—Ex. 32:19–20; Num. 20:10–12.

Contrasts between Moses and Jesus.— The law came through Moses; grace and truth through Jesus Christ—John 1:17. Moses' covenant was a ministration of death (II Cor. 7); Jesus' covenant, the law of the spirit of life —Rom. 8:2. Moses was a faithful servant over God's house; Jesus built the house—Heb. 3:3–4. Moses pointed to the tables of stone (Ex. 34:32; Deut. 5:1–22); Jesus pointed to Himself—John 8:28, 58; 11:25; 14:6. Moses appeared at transfiguration and prophesies about Jesus' death (Lu. 9: 30–31); Jesus died for our sins—I Cor. 15:3. See COVENANT.

Jesus' references to Moses: Concerning marriage—Mk. 12:18–27; Lu. 20: 28. Concerning divorce—Mt. 19:3–9; Mk. 10:3. Scribes sitting on Moses' seat—Mt. 23:2. Not hearing Moses and the prophets—Lu. 16:29. That the dead are raised—Lu. 20:39–40. Gives interpretation of Moses and prophets—Lu. 24:27. As Moses lifted up the serpent—John 3:14. Moses the accuser—John 5:45–47. Moses gave them not bread—John 6:32. Moses gave circumcision—John 7:19–24.

Other New Testament references: Law given by Moses—John 1:17. Pharisees and blind man—John 9:28–29. Peter's sermon—Acts 3:22. False witness against Stephen—Acts 6:11. Stephen refers to Moses—Acts 7:20– 44. Not justified by law of Moses— Acts 13:39. Circumcision required according to Moses—Acts 15:1–5. Concerning the forsaking of law of Moses —Acts 21:21. Paul refers to Moses— Acts 26:22. Moses and veil—II Cor. 3:13–16. Jannes and Jambres withstand Moses—II Tim. 3:8. Moses faithful in all his house—Heb. 3:2–5 16. Moses sprinkles the book—Heb. 9:19. Cost of despising law of Moses —Heb. 10:28. Moses hid three months —Heb. 11:23. Moses fears and quakes —Heb. 12:21. Dispute about body of Moses—Jude 9. Sing the song of Moses—Rev. 15:3. (See also AARON, EGYPT, ISRAEL, LAW, EXODUS, TABER-

NACLE, PRIEST, PHARAOH, PLAGUES.)
See JESUS—Lu. 2:21.

MOST. I Cor. 10:5. At—I Cor. 14:27. Forgave—Lu. 7:43. Gladly—II Cor. 12:15. High—Mk. 5:7; Lu. 8:28; Acts 7:48; 16:17; Heb. 7:1. Love—Lu. 7: 42. Men—Pr. 20:6. Of all—Acts 20: 38. Pure gold—Lam. 4:1.. Works— Mt. 11:20.

MOST HOLY PLACE. Ex. 26:33, 34; I Ki. 6:16; 7:50; 8:6; I Chr. 6:49; Ez. 41:4.

Most holy house.—II Chr. 3:8, 10; 4:22; 5:7.

Holy of holies.—Way into not made known—Heb. 9:3.

MOTE. Beholdest thou the—Mt. 7:3; Lu. 6:41, 42. Cast out—Mt. 7:4, 5; Lu. 6:42.

MOTH. Hos. 5:12. And rust—Mt. 6:19. Buildeth as the—Job 27:18. Consume away like a—Ps. 39:11. Crushed before the—Job 4:19. Moth eaten—Job 13:28; Jas. 5:2. Shall eat them—Is. 50:9; 51:8.

MOTHER. Must honor her—Ex. 20:12; Deut. 5:16; Pr. 1:8; 23:22; Mt. 15:4; 19:19; Mk. 7:10; 10:19; Lu. 18:20; Eph. 6:2. Eve, the mother of all— Gen. 3:20. Love of mothers contrasted with God's—Is. 49:15. Sarah a mother of nations—Gen. 17:16. Punishment for maltreatment of—Ex. 21:15, 17; Lev. 18:7; 20:9; Pr. 30:11; 30:17. Foolish son heaviness of—Pr. 10:1. Despise not, when old—Pr. 23:22. He that loveth, more than Me—Mt. 10: 37. Mother of Lord come to Me—Lu. 1:43. Mother of Jesus was there— John 2:1. Peter's wife's mother—Mt. 8:14; Lu. 4:38. Who is my mother?— Mt. 12:48; Mk. 3:34. Mary, Mother of Jesus, steadfast—Acts 1:14. Can a man enter second time, etc.—John 3:4. Entreat elderly women as mothers—I Tim. 5:2.

MOTHER-IN-LAW. Not to be defiled— Lev. 18:17; 20:14; Deut. 27:23. Ruth's affection for—Ruth 1:14–17. Dwelt with—Ruth 2:23. Boaz provides for —Ruth 3:17. Rising up against—Mic. 7:6; Mt. 10:35; Lu. 12:53. Peter's mother-in-law healed by Jesus—Mk. 1:30–31.

MOULDY. Bread—Josh. 9:5, 12.

MOUND. Cast up against cities: Jerusalem—Jer. 6:6; 32:24; 33:4; Ez. 4:2; 21:22. Abel—II Sam. 20:15.

MOUNTAINS: Having Scriptural mention. Not named.—Gen. 12:8; 19:30; Ex. 15:17; 20:18; 32:12; Num. 14:40; 23:7; Deut. 33:19; Josh. 2:23; 18:16; II Ki. 2:16; Job 14:18; 24:8; Ps. 30:7; 65:6; 72:3; 78:54; 87:1; 90:2; 104:8, 13; 114:4, 6; 121:1; 148:9; Pr. 8:25; Song of Sol. 2:8; Is. 13:2; 22:5; 25: 10; 34:3; 40:4, 12; 41:15; 42:15; 49: 11; 52:7; 54:10; 65:9; Jer. 3:23; 4:24; 9:10; 13:16; 17:3; 26:18; 51:25; Ez. 11:23; 28:16; 31:12; 32:5, 6; 38:21; Dan. 2:35, 45; Amos 4:13; Jonah 2:6; Mic. 1:4; 7:12; Nah. 1:15; Hab. 3:10; Hag. 1:11; Zech. 4:7; 5:1.

Abode of: Birds—I Sam. 26:20; Ps. 50: 11; Is. 18:6; Ez. 17:23. Roes—I Chr. 12:8; Song of Sol. 2:17; 8:14. Leopards—Song of Sol. 4:8. Wolf, lamb, lion, ox—Is. 56:25. See Ps. 76:4. See ANIMALS.

Called: God's mountains—Ex. 4:27; Ps. 36:6; Is. 49:11. Ancient—Deut. 33:15. Eternal—Hab. 3:6. Holy mountain— Ps. 48:1; 87:1; Is. 11:9; 56:7; 65:11, 25; 66:20; Jer. 31:23; Ez. 20:40; 28: 14; Dan. 9:16, 20; 11:45; Joel 2:1; 3: 17; Ob. 16; Zeph. 3:11; Zech. 8:3. Mountain of Jehovah—Is. 30:29; Mic. 4:2. Pillars of heaven—Job 26:11.

Caves in.—Ju. 6:2; Heb. 11:38; Rev. 6: 15, 16.

Faith to remove.—Mt. 17:20; Mk. 11: 23; I Cor. 13:2.

Fire on.—Deut. 32:22; Ps. 83:14; Heb. 12:18, 20; Rev. 8:8. **Flee as a bird to.** —Ps. 11:1.

Flight into. — Gen. 14:10; 19:17, 19; Josh. 2:16, 22, 23; Song of Sol. 4:6; Lam. 4:19; Zech. 14:5; Mk. 13:14; Lu. 21:21. See Ju. 11:37, 38.

Horses and chariots of fire in.—II Ki. 6:17.

House of God.—Is. 2:2, 3, 14; Mic. 4: 1, 2.

Idol worship on.—Deut. 12:2; Is. 17:9; Ez. 6:13; 18:6, 11, 15; 22:9; Hos. 10:8.

Israel in.—I Sam. 17:3; II Chr. 18:16; 21:11; Is. 13:2–5; Jer. 3:6; 50:6; Ez. 6:2, 3; 19:19; 33:28; 34:6, 13, 14; 35:

12; 36:1, 4, 6, 8; 37:22; 38:8; 39:2, 4, 17.

Jerusalem, Around.—Ps. 125:2; John 4: 20, 21.

John carried to.—Rev. 21:10.

Laborers in.—Hewers—I Ki. 5:15; II Chr. 2:2, 18. Hunters in—Jer. 16:16. Vine dressers—II Chr. 26:10; Jer. 31:5.

Products.—II Sam. 1:21. Pasture—Job 39:8; 40:20. Grain—Ps. 72:16. Grass —Ps. 147:8; Pr. 27:25. Chaff—Is. 17: 13. Feast of fat things—Is. 25:6, 7. Herbs and trees—Ez. 17:23; Amos 9: 13; Hag. 1:8.

Quaked.—Ju. 5:5; I Ki. 19:11; Job 9:5, 6; Is. 64:1, 3; Nah. 1:5, 6; Rev. 6:14; 16:20. See Ps. 46:2, 3; Ez. 38:20.

Robbers in.—Ju. 9:25.

Shadow of.—Ju. 9:35.

Singing.—Is. 44:23; 49:13; 55:12.

Smoking.—Ex. 20:18; Ps. 144:5.

Top of.—Ju. 9:25, 36; Ps. 72:16; Song of Sol. 4:8; Is. 2:2, 3; 17:9; 18:3, 6; 30:17, 25; 40:9; 42:11; Ez. 7:7, 16; 17:22, 23; 43:12; Hos. 4:13; Joel 2:5; Mic. 4:1.

Use in war.—I Sam. 17:3; 24:26.

Water above.—Gen. 7:20; Ps. 104:6.

Names of:

Abarim, A chain including Nebo.—Num. 33:47, 48.

Ararat.—Ark rested on—Gen. 8:4.

Amalek, Hill country of Amalekites—Ju. 12:15.

Baalah.—Josh. 15:11.

Bashan, A mountain of God.—Ps. 68:15.

Bethel, A stronghold of Saul.—I Sam. 13:2.

Calvary, Place of crucifixion.—Lu. 23: 33.

Carmel, Where Elijah defeated Baal.— Josh. 19:26; I Ki. 18:19–42; Jer. 46:18.

Ebal, Curses pronounced there.—Deut. 11:29; 27:13.

Ephraim, Hill country of that tribe.— Josh. 17:15; Ju. 2:9. See EPHRAIM.

Ephron.—Josh. 15:9.

Gerizim, Blessing pronounced there.— Deut. 11:29; Ju. 9:7.

Gilboa, Where Saul was slain.—I Sam. 31:1–8; II Sam. 1:21.

Gilead, Where Laban overtook Jacob.— Gen. 31:23.

Hachilah, Hiding-place of David.—I Sam. 23:19.

Halak.—Josh. 11:17; 12:7.

Hermon, Supposed scene of transfiguration.—Josh. 13:11; Deut. 3:8–9; Josh. 11:17; Ps. 133:3; Song of Sol. 4:8; Mt. 17:1; Lu. 9:28. See HERMON.

Hor, Where Aaron died.—Num. 20:22; 34:7–8.

Horeb (Same as Sinai).—Place of giving of the law—Ex. 3:1; 19:1–11; Deut. 1:19; 4:10, 11; 5:2, 5, 22, 23.

Jearim (Chesalon).—Josh. 15:11.

Lebanon, Famous for cedars.—Deut. 3: 25; I Ki. 5:14; 7:2; Ps. 92:12; Is. 37:24.

Mizar, "The little mountain".—Ps. 42:6.

Moreh, Camping place of Gideon.—Ju. 7:1.

Moriah, Site of temple, Isaac offered.— Gen. 22:2; II Chr. 3:1.

Nebo, Where Moses was buried.—Num. 32:3; Deut. 32:49; 34:1.

Olives (or Olivet), Our Lord's ascension. David wept over Jerusalem—II Sam. 15:30; Zech. 14:4; Mt. 24:3; Acts 1:9–12.

Pisgah, Moses viewed Canaan.—Num. 21:20; Deut. 34:1.

Seir, Home of Esau.—Gen. 14:6; 36:8; Deut. 2:1, 3; Josh. 15:10; Song of Sol. 4:8; Ez. 35:7, 8. See Ob. 8, 9, 19, 21; Mal. 1:3. See SEIR.

Sinai (Same as Horeb).—Ex. 19:2–23; 31:18; Ju. 5:5; Gal. 4:24, 25. See SINAI.

Tabor.—Ju. 4:6; 12:14; Jer. 46:18.

Zalmon.—Ju. 9:48; Ps. 68:14.

Zion, Site of David's palace.—II Sam. 5:7; Ps. 48:2, 11, 12; 133:3; Lam. 5: 18; Ob. 17, 21; Mic. 4:7; Heb. 12:22.

Associated with Jesus.—Faith to remove—Mt. 17:20; Mk. 11:23. Tempted upon—Mt. 4:8. Preachers from—Mt. 5:1; 8:1; 15:29; 17:20; 18:12; 21:21; 24:16; Mk. 3:13. Goes up to pray—Mt. 17:1–8; Mk. 9:1–8; Lu. 9:28–36. Meets His disciples on, after resurrection—Mt. 28:16–17. See JESUS, ASCENSION OF.

MOURNING: Ancient customs in.—Wearing a special mourning-dress—Gen. 38:14; II Sam. 14:2; Jer. 6:26. See SACKCLOTH. Shaving—Ezra 9:3;

Jer. 7:29. Going about with uncovered head—Lev. 10:6; 13:45; 21:10; Num. 5:18. With face covered—II Sam. 15: 30; 19:4; Esth. 6:12. With upper lip covered—Lev. 13:45; Ez. 24:17, 22. Lying on the ground—II Sam. 12:16; 13:31. See ASHES. Rending of the garments—Gen. 37:29, 34; 44:13; Ju. 11:35; II Sam. 1:2, 11, 12; 3:31; 13: 19, 31; 15:32; II Ki. 2:12; 5:8; 6:30; 11:14; 19:1; 22:11, 19; Ezra 9:3, 5; Job 1:20; 2:12; Jer. 41:5; Mt. 26:65. Neglecting the personal appearance— II Sam. 14:2; 15:30; 19:24; Is. 20:2; Mic. 1:8, 11. Laying aside ornaments —Ex. 33:4, 6. Laying the hand on the head— II Sam. 13:19; Jer. 2:37. Fasting—I Sam. 31:13; II Sam. 1:12; 3: 35; Zech. 7:5. Uttering loud cries— Ex. 12:30; I Sam. 30:4; Jer. 22:18. See CRY. Cutting one's own flesh—Jer. 16:6; 41:5; 47:5; 48:37. (But this is forbidden to the Israelite as a pagan practice.) See FLESH. Days of—Job 2:13; Dan. 10:2.

Professional mourners.—II Chr. 35:25; Jer. 9:17; Amos 5:16; Mt. 9:23.

Dirges.—II Sam. 1:17–27; 3:33, 34; 18: 33; II Ki. 2:12; II Chr. 35:25.

House of.—Eccl. 7:2, 4; Jer. 16:5.

Laws concerning.—Cutting of flesh forbidden—Lev. 19:28; 21:5; Deut. 14:1. Defilement—Lev. 21:1–11. Mourning caused by oppression—Ps. 42:9; 43:2; Is. 22:12; Lam. 5:15.

Mourners comforted.—Esth. 9:22; Ps. 30:11; 57:18; 61:2, 3; 66:10; Jer. 16: 7; 31:13. See JESUS, TEACHINGS OF— Lu. 2:21.

Special cases of.—Abraham for Sarah— Gen. 23:2. Jacob—Gen. 37:24. For Jacob—Gen. 27:41; 50:3, 4, 10, 11. David—II Sam. 13:37; 19:1, 2; Ps. 35:14; 38:6; 88:9. Samuel for Saul— I Sam. 15:35; 16:1. Uriah's wife for her husband—II Sam. 11:26, 27. For Prophet—I Ki. 13:29, 30. For Abijah —I Ki. 14:13. Ephraim—I Chr. 7:22. Ezra—Ezra 10:6. Jews—Esth. 4:3. Job—Job 30:28. Israelites—Num. 14: 39; I Ki. 14:18. Hezekiah—Is. 38:14. The Prophet for Zion—Lam. 1:4. The wicked—Pr. 5:11; Jer. 2:37; 23:10; Ez. 31:15. Ezekiel—Ez. 24:17. Priests

—Joel 1:9. Rachel—Mt. 2:18. For Jesus—Mk. 16:10.

Mourning in judgment.—Is. 24:4; 33:9; 59:11; Jer. 12:11.

Spiritual mourning.—Joel 2:12; II Cor. 7:7; Jas. 4:9; Rev. 18:8.

Prophecies concerning.—Is. 16:7; 19:8; 51:11; 60:20; Jer. 4:28; 12:4; 48:31; Ez. 2:10; Hos. 4:3; 10:5; Joel 1:10; Amos 5:16; 8:8, 10; 9:5; Zech. 12:11; Mt. 24:30; Lu. 6:25; Rev. 18:8, 11.

Figurative.—Is. 3:26; Ez. 31:15; Amos 1:2; Mt. 11:17; Lu. 7:32; I Cor. 5:2; Jas. 4:9.

Illustrative.—Job 29:25; Jer. 6:26; Zech. 12:10, 12; Mt. 2:18; 9:15. See CONSOLATION, SORROW, GROAN, MOAN.

MOUSE. Lev. 11:29. Eating—Is. 66: 17. Golden—I Sam. 6:4, 11, 18. Images of—I Sam. 4:5.

MOUTH, as a means of communication. —Babes—Ps. 8:6; Mt. 21:16. Prophets —Ex. 4:16; Num. 23:5, 16; II Chr. 36:21; Jer. 36:18; Ez. 3:26, 27; Acts 1:16; 3:18, 21. False Prophets—I Ki. 2:13–23. Priests—Mal. 2:6–7. Wicked persons—Job. 20:13; Ps. 107:42; 109: 2; 144:8; Pr. 4:24; 5:3; 6:12; 19:28; 22:14; 26:28; Jer. 9:8; 51:44; Lu. 6: 45; Rom. 3:13, 14; Rev. 13:5. Righteous—Ex. 13:9; Deut. 23:23; Lu. 6:45.

The mouth of Jesus.—Mt. 5:2; Lu. 1:64; 4:22; 11:54; 22:71; John 19:29; I Pet. 2:22; Rev. 1:16; 19:15.

The mouth of God.—Deut. 8:3; II Sam. 22:9; Job 22:22; Is. 45:23; Lam. 3: 38; Mt. 4:4.

Mouths restrained.—Job 20:13; 29:9; 31:30; Ps. 38:13, 14; 39:1; 107:42; Pr. 13:3; Mt. 5:37; Eph. 4:29; Col. 3:8; Titus 1:11; Heb. 11:33; Jas. 3:3–12.

Mouths opened.— Earth — Gen. 4:11; Num. 16:30, 32; 26:10; Deut. 11:6; Rev. 12:16. Ass—Num. 22:28. Jephthah—Ju. 11:36. Hell (Sheol)—Is. 5: 14. Job—Job 3:1. Philip—Acts 8:32– 35. Paul—II Cor. 6:11.

Noble issues of.—Ps. 37:30; Pr. 4:23; 10:31; 31:26.

Confession made with.—Rom. 10:10; 15:6.

Mouth of fools.—Pr. 10:14; 14:3; 15:2, 14; 18:7; 26:7.

Source of defilement.—Job 31:30; Ps. 63:11; 144:8; Mt. 12:34, 35; 15:11;

Jas. 3:10; Rev. 13:5. **Sinning with.—** Job 31:30.

Mouth of: Cave.—Josh. 10:18, 22, 27. **Well.**—Gen. 29:3, 8, 10. **Sack.**—Gen. 42:27; 43:21; 44:1, 2, 8. **Pit.**—Ps. 69: 15. **Sheol.**—Ps. 141:7.

MOVE. II Chr. 18:2. Candlestick—Rev. 2:5. Jealousy, To—Deut. 32:16. In him we live and—Acts 17:28. Shall never be—Ps. 15:5. Shall not be—Ps. 16:8. Spirit of God—Gen. 1:2. Suffer righteous to be—Ps. 55:22. Tent— Gen. 13:12.

MOW. Fields—Jas. 5:4. Grass—Ps. 72: 6.

MOZA, mō′zä. (1) **A descendant of Saul.** I Chr. 8:36; 9:42.

(2) **Son of Caleb.**—I Chr. 2:46.

MOZAH, mō′zah. A Benjamite city.— Josh. 18:26.

MUCH. Lu. 18:13; Heb. 3:3. Beseecheth him—Mk. 5:23. Joy—Acts 8:8. Little or—Acts 26:29. Money—Mt. 28:12. Peace—Acts 24:2. Proof of affliction —II Cor. 8:2. Required—Lu. 12:48. Torn—Mk. 9:26. Wood is kindled— Jas. 3:5.

MUFFLERS. Is. 3:19.

MULBERRY TREES. II Sam. 5:23, 24; I Chr. 14:14, 15.

MULE: Used for riding.—II Sam. 13: 29; 18:9; Is. 66:20. Absalom rides— II Sam. 18:9. Solomon to ride upon David's mule—I Ki. 1:33; 38, 44.

For carrying burdens.—II Ki. 5:17; I Chr. 12:40. In war—Zech. 14:15. Brought in tribute—I Ki. 10:25. Number brought from Babylon—Ezra 2: 66; Neh. 7:68.

Trade in, by people of Tyre.—Ez. 27:14. Preparations for preservation—I Ki. 18:5. **Figurative.**—Ps. 32:9.

MULTIPLY. As they were—Hos. 4:7. Be fruitful and—Gen. 1:22; Jer. 23:3, etc. Church was—Acts 9:31. God, Word of—Acts 12:24. Grace—II Cor. 4:15; I Pet. 1:2; II Pet. 1:2. Iniquity shall be—Mt. 24:12. Nation—Is. 9:3. Number of disciples was—Acts 6:1, 7. Peace be—Dan. 4:1; 6:25; Jude 2. Seed—Gen. 16:10; 22:17. See COVENANTS. Sorrow shall be—Ps. 16:4. Transgressions—Job 35:6; Is. 59:12. Wonders—Ex. 11:9. Words—Job 35: 16; Eccl. 10:14.

MULTITUDE. Gen. 16:10. As stars in —Heb. 11:12. Devout Greeks, Of— Acts 17:4. Fishes, Of—Lu. 5:6. Great —Mk. 10:46. Heavenly host, Of— Lu. 2:13. Iniquities, Of—Ez. 28:18. Mercies, Of—Ps. 51:1; 69:16. Nations, Of—Gen. 17:4. Oppressions, Of—Job 35:9. People, Of—Pr. 14:28. Publicans, Of—Lu. 5:29. Riches, Of—Ez. 27:12, 33. Sins, Of—Jas. 5:20; I Pet. 4:8. Sorceries, Of—Is. 47:12. Words, Of— Pr. 10:19. See JESUS, POPULARITY OF.

MUNITIONS. Is. 33:16. See WEAPONS, WAR.

MUPPIM, mŭp′pim. Son of Benjamin. —Gen. 46:21.

MURDERER. Condemned—Ex. 20:13; Deut. 5:17. Why?—Gen. 9:6. Needs restraining—I Tim. 1:9. God's abhorrence of—Ps. 5:6; Pr. 6:16–17.

Modes of.—Beheading—Ju. 7:25; Mt. 14:10; Mk. 6:27. Drowning—Ex. 1: 22. Crucifixion—Mt. 27:35, 38. Shooting—II Sam. 18:14; II Ki. 9:24. Smiting with club—Num. 35:18. With fist —Gen. 4:8; Ex. 2:12; 21:8. With iron —Num. 35:16. With rod—Ex. 21:20. With stone—Num. 35:17. Spearing— II Sam. 23:21; I Chr. 11:23. Stabbing —II Sam. 3:27; I Ki. 2:5. Suffocation —II Ki. 8:15. Sword thrust—Gen. 34: 35; Ju. 8:20, 21; II Chr. 21:4; 23:21; Mt. 2:16; Acts 12:2. Sword of the enemy—II Sam. 12:9. Throwing from a window—II Ki. 9:33. Throwing a millstone on head—Ju. 9:53.

Motives.—Ambition—Ju. 9:5; I Ki. 16: 10; II Ki. 8:15. Anger—Gen. 4:8. Covetousness—I Ki. 21:7, 15; Pr. 1: 11, 13. Diplomacy—Ex. 1:9, 10, 16, 22; Mt. 2:16. Enmity—Num. 35:21; Ex. 21:14. Hiding crime—II Sam. 12:9. Jealousy—Gen. 37:20, 21. Patriotism —Ex. 2:12; II Ki. 9:33; II Sam. 18:14. Punishment of slave—Ex. 21:20. Revenge—Gen. 4:23; 34:26, 27; II Sam. 3:27, 30; Mt. 14:8, 10; Mk. 6:19, 24, 27.

Characteristics of.—Cowardly—Gen. 4: 14. Wanderers and fugitives fear presence of God—Gen. 4:16. Unprotected in refuge cities—Deut. 19:11– 12. No protection at altar—Ex. 21:14; I Ki. 2:28–34. Not to be sympathized with—Deut. 19:13.

Washing hands in token of innocency.—Deut. 21:1–9.

Punishment for.—Lev. 24:17; Deut. 19: 11–13; Ps. 55:23. Divine curse—Gen. 4:11. Death—Gen. 9:5, 6; Ex. 21:12; Num. 35:16; I Ki. 21:19–24; Ez. 35:6. No ransom for—Num. 35:22. Inflicted by nearest kin—Num. 35:19–21. Everlasting punishment—Rev. 21:8; 22:15.

New Testament conception of.—Mt. 5: 21–22; 15:19–20; Mk. 7:21–22; Rom. 13:9–10; I Tim. 1:9; James 2:11–13; I Pet. 4:14–19; I John 3:11–12, 15.

Noted instances in Old Testament.—Cain—Gen. 4:8. Lamech—Gen. 4:23–24. Sons of Jacob—Gen. 34:25–29. Pharaoh—Ex. 1:22. Abimelech—Ju. 9:5. Joab—II Sam. 3:27. The Amalekite—II Sam. 1:14–16. David—II Sam. 12:9. Absalom—II Sam. 13:29. Zimri—I Ki. 16:10. Jezebel—I Ki. 21:10, 19. Hazael—II Ki. 8:15. Jehu—II Ki. 9:24. Athaliah—II Ki. 11:1. Joash—II Ki. 12:20, 21. Menahem—II Ki. 15:16. Adrammelech—II Ki. 19:37. Manasseh—II Ki. 21:16.

New Testament instances.—Herod—Mt. 2:16; 14:10;. Mk. 6:27. Judas and Priests—Mt. 27:4. Barabbas—Mk. 15: 7; Acts 3:14. Herod Agrippi I—Acts 12:1–2. See COMMANDMENTS, HATRED.

MURMURING: Against Christ.—Lu. 5:30; 19:7; John 6:41.

Rebuked.—Pr. 19:3; Lam. 3:39; John 6:43; I Cor. 10:10; Phil. 2:14; Jude 16.

Instances.—Gen. 4:13, 14; Ex. 5:22, 23; 14:11; 15:24; 16:2; 17:2, 3; Num. 11: 1–9; 12:1, 2, 8; 21:5; I Ki. 19:4; Job 3:1; Jer. 20:14–18; Jonah 4:8, 9; Mk. 14:4, 5; Lu. 15:2; 19:7; John 6:41–43, 61; Acts 6:1.

MURRAIN. Ex. 9:3.

MUSE. I Ki. 18:27; Ps. 39:3. Doings, On—Ps. 77:12. Terror, On—Is. 33:18. Work, On—Ps. 143:5.

MUSHI, mū′shi. **Son of Merari.**—Ex. 6:19.

MUSHITES. Descendants of Mushi.—Num. 3:33.

MUSIC: Bible music, generally parallel to secular music.

Primitive stage.—Expression in a series of rhythmical intonations.

Later development.—Varied and artistic to a high degree.

First mention.—Gen. 4:20.

Motive.—Often religious; Songs part of divine worship—Amos 5:23; 6:5; Is. 5:12. Often associated with important incidents and occasions, i. e., Entertainments, Festivals, Funerals, Patriotic celebration, Battles, Victories.

Mode.—VOCAL: (1) Chant by one person accompanied by beating of time or shout at rhythmical intervals on the part of the multitude—Jer. 5:1–30. (2) Antiphonal singing (responsive: by chorus divided into parts)—Neh. 12:31; Is. 6:3. (3) Singing in unison, most common. Qualities regarded as excellencies: *Clearness, volume and enthusiasm*—II Chr. 5:13; Ps. 33:3.

INSTRUMENTAL: David regarded as its true founder in its constant form.

Musical instruments.—Invented by Jubal—Gen. 4:21. Made by David—I Chr. 23:5; II Chr. 7:6; 29:26; Neh. 12: 36. By Solomon—I Ki. 10:12; II Chr. 9:11. By Tyrians—Ez. 28:13.

Allusions to musical instruments in general.—I Sam. 18:6; I Chr. 15:16; 16: 42; 23:5; II Chr. 5:13; 7:6; 23:13; 30: 21; Eccl. 2:8; Ez. 23:32; Dan. 6:18; Amos 6:5. Made of Fir-wood—II Sam. 6:5.

I. PERCUSSIVE INSTRUMENTS (most primitive): (1) Hand-drum (*toph*), "a ring of wood or metal covered by a tightly-drawn skin, with small pieces of metal hung around the rim (of which the Toph was the Prototype), held by one hand and struck with the other." *Women chief players of*—I Sam. 10:5. Timbrel or tabret, a variety of hand-drum—Ex. 15:20; Ju. 11:34; I Sam. 18:6; II Sam. 6:5; I Chr. 13:8; Job 21:12; Ps. 68:25; 81:2; 149: 3; 150:4. Tabret in particular—Gen. 31:27; Is. 5:12; 24:8; 30:32; Jer. 31:4; Ez. 28:13.

(2) Cymbals (*mesillayim*), two flat plates (Castanets), played by being clashed together. Used in the temple to mark time—I Chr. 13:8; 15:16, 19, 28; 16:5, 42; 25:16; II Chr. 5:12, 13; 29:25; Ezra 3:10; Neh. 12:27; Ps. 150:5.

(3) Castanets (R.), Cornets (A.V.) (*Mene'ani'im*). Probably like Greek

sistrum: an oval frame with iron rods lying loosely in holes in the side. Rings were suspended from the ends of these rods and a handle supported the whole. Castanets used in the bringing up of the Ark—II Sam. 6:5.

(4) Triangle (*salisim*), somewhat like the modern article of that name, hung with rings and shaken instead of being struck—I Sam. 18:6.

II. WIND INSTRUMENTS: Pipe and reed (*Chalil*). See PIPE.

Flute—Dan. 3:5, 7, 10, 15.

Organ (*'ugab*); known as "Pan's pipes." "Had a wind chest containing 10 holes each, communicating with 10 pipes. These were brought under the control of the player by means of a keyboard."

Cornet (*shophar*), with varieties: Curved trumpet (*qeren*) and straight (metallic) trumpet (*chatsotserah*); Horn, either ram's or imitation in ivory and metal. *Used on great and solemn occasions*—I Chr. 15:28; II Chr. 15:14; Dan. 3:5, 7, 10, 15. (For the use of trumpet in religious services, see TRUMPETS.)

III. STRINGED INSTRUMENTS—Ps. 150:4.

Harp (*kinnor*), a kind of harp held in the hand while playing. See HARP.

Psaltery (*nebel*), made of fir-wood. An elaborate harp of sweet, rich tones with 12 strings—I Sam. 10:5; II Sam. 6:5. *Praise with*—I Chr. 13:8; 15:16, 28; 16:5; 25:16; II Chr. 5:12; 9:11; 29:25; Neh. 12:27; Ps. 33:2; 57:8; 71:22; 81:2; 92:3; 108:2; 144:9; 150:3. *Made by the king*—I Ki. 10:12. *Used in the worship of idols.*

Lute—Is. 5:12.

Viol—Amos 5:23; 6:5; Is. 14:11.

Lyre—I Cor. 14:7; Rev. 1:8; 14:2; 15: 12; 18:22.

Instrument of ten strings (*azor*)—Ps. 92:3.

Sackbut (*sabbokha*), a many-stringed harp of a high pitch—Dan. 3:5, 7, 10, 16.

Dulcimer (*psanterin*), a kind of harp made of a flat piece of wood, generally four-sided, with strings attached to fixed pins on one side and to movable pins on the other—Dan. 3:5, 10, 15.

Music in common life.—Occasions for: *Sacred processions*—Ex. 15:1, 20, 21; II Sam. 6:5, 14–16; I Chr. 13:8; 15: 16–29. *Sacrifices and feasts*—II Chr. 15:14; 23:18; 29:25–28; Is. 30:29; Mt. 26:30; Mk. 14:26. *At harvest*—Is. 16: 10. *Divine worship*—I Chr. 9:33; 23: 30; 25:6–8; II Chr. 30:21; Neh. 12:45; Acts 16:25; I Cor. 14:15, 26; Eph. 5: 19; Col. 3:16; Jas. 5:13. *Idol worship* —I Ki. 1:40; II Ki. 9:13; 11:14; II Chr. 23:13; Dan. 3:5–15. *Dedication*— Neh. 12:35–41. *Battles and victories*— Ju. 11:34; I Sam. 18:6; II Chr. 20:19– 28; Ez. 15:1, 20, 21. *Funerals*—II Chr. 35:25; Mt. 9:23.

Musicians as a class.—Singers—I Ki. 10:12; I Chr. 6:31–33; 9:33; 15:16; 25:7; II Chr. 9:11; 20:21; 23:13; 29: 26, 28; 35:15; Neh. 7:44; 11:22, 23; 12:27–29, 42, 45, 46, 47; 13:5, 10; Ps. 68:25; Ez. 2:40; 7:24; 40:44. *Men singers*—II Sam. 19:25; Neh. 7:67; Eccl. 3:8; Ez. 2:65. *Women singers*— I Sam. 18:7; II Sam. 19:35; Neh. 7:67; Ez. 2:65. *Men and women singing together*—II Sam. 19:35; II Chr. 35:25; Neh. 7:67; Eccl. 2:8.

Minstrels—Ps. 68:25; Rev. 18:21.

Levites—I Chr. 6:31, 33; 15:16, 19, 22, 27; II Chr. 5:12, 13; 29:25, 26, 30.

Priests—II Chr. 29:26.

Harpers—Rev. 18:21.

Flute Players (Professional mourners) —Mt. 9:23; Rev. 18:21.

Trumpeters—Lev. 25:9; Num. 10:2, 10; II Ki. 6:13; 11:14; I Chr. 16:42; Neh. 12:35, 41; Rev. 18:21.

Accompaniment of music.—Frequently dancing—I Sam. 18:6; I Chr. 15:29; Lu. 15:25.

Special features in New Testament.— Hymns—Mt. 26:30; Mk. 14:26; Eph. 5:19; Col. 3:16.

Spiritual songs.—Eph. 5:19; Col. 3:16.

Psalms.—Lu. 1:46–65; 68:79; 11:14, 28– 32.

Instances of singing.—Mt. 26:30; Mk. 14:26; Acts 16:25; I Cor. 14:15, 26; Jas. 5:13. See POETRY, LYRIC.

MUSTARD SEED. Became a tree—Lu. 13:19. Less than all seeds—Mt. 13: 31, 32; Mk. 4:31.

MUTH-LABBEN, mŭth'-lăb-ben. Ps. 9 (*title*).

MUTTER. Is. 8:19.

MUZZLE. Ox—Deut. 25:4; I Cor. 9:9; I Tim. 5:18.

MYRA, my̆'rȧ. **A town in Lycia.**—Acts 27:5.

MYRRH: As perfume.—Ex. 30:23; Song of Sol. 1:12, 13; 4:14; Mt. 2:11. Liquid myrrh—Song of Sol. 3:5, 13. As spice—Esth. 2:12; Ps. 45:8; Pr. 7:17; Song of Sol. 3:6; Mt. 2:11; Mk. 15:23. Used in embalming—John 19:39. Wise men offered gifts of—Mt. 2:11. Wine mingled with—Mk. 15:23. *Cf.* Mt. 27:34.

MYRTLE. Neh. 8:15; Is. 41:19; 55:13.

MYSIA, my̆'si-ȧ. **A province in Asia Minor.**—Acts 16:7.

MYSTERY. Gr. *Musterion*. From *Muo*, "To shut the Mouth." Hidden knowledge communicated to privileged persons. Babylon—Rev. 17:5. Christ (as respects Gentiles)—Eph. 1:9, 10; 3:3, 4, 9; 5:32; Col. 1:26, 27; 2:2, 3; 4:3. The faith—I Tim. 3:9. Of God—I Cor. 2:1 (*marg.* I Cor. 2:7; 4:1); Col. 2:2; Rev. 10:7. The gospel —Rom. 16:25, 26; I Cor. 2:7; Eph. 6:19. Godliness—I Tim. 3:16. Israel's stubbornness—Rom. 11:25. Lawlessness—II Thess. 2:7. The resurrection —I Cor. 15:21. Seven stars—Rev. 1:20. The woman—Rev. 17:7. See MAGIC, MIRACLES, DEEP THINGS.

MYSTERY OF GODLINESS OR OF GOD'S PLAN. That the Gentiles should hear the gospel and be saved. —Rom. 11:1-36; Eph. 1:3-11; Col. 1:25-29; 4:3, 4; I Tim. 3:16.

This mystery hidden from men before the advent of Jesus.—Is. 60:2, 3; Mt. 11:25; 13:34, 35; Lu. 8:16-18; 10:24; 12:2, 3; John 8:56; 15:21; Rom. 11:1-36; 16:25, 26; I Cor. 1:18-21; 2:7-9; II Cor. 3:13-16; 4:3-5; Eph. 3:4-9; Col. 1:26, 27; Heb. 9:8; 11:13, 39, 40; I Pet. 1:10-12.

Having eyes that see not and ears that hear not.—Is. 6:9, 10; Jer. 5:21; Ez. 12:2; Mt. 13:14-17; Mk. 4:11, 12; Lu. 8:10; John 12:37-41; Acts 28:23-28.

This mystery revealed to the apostles. —Mt. 10:26; 11:25; 13:11, 16; 16:16, 17; Mk. 4:11, 12, 22-25; Lu. 8:10, 16-18; 12:2, 3; I Cor. 4:1; II Cor. 4:5-7; Eph. 1:9, 10.

Revealed by the Spirit.—John 14:26; 16:13; I Cor. 2:9-16; Eph. 3:2-11.

This mystery made manifest through the death of Christ and the preaching of the gospel.—Lu. 12:2, 3; Rom. 11:1-36; 16:25, 26; I Cor. 1:18-28; 2:4-16; II Cor. 3:12-18; Eph. 6:19; Col. 1:25-29; 2:2, 3; 4:3, 4; I Tim. 3:9, 16; II Tim. 1:9-11; Heb. 9:8; I Pet. 1:12; I John 2:20, 27. See MAGIC.

NAAM, nā'am. **Son of Caleb.**—I Chr. 4:15.

NAAMAH, nā'a-mah. (1) **Wife of Solomon and mother of Rehoboam.**—I Ki. 14:21, 31; II Chr. 12:13.

(2) **Daughter of Lamech and sister of Tubal-cain.**—Gen. 4:22.

(3) **A town in Judah.**—Josh. 15:41.

NAAMAN, nā'a-măn. (1) **A Syrian officer cured of leprosy.** See ELISHA.

(2) **A grandson of Benjamin.**—Gen. 46:21; Num. 46:40.

(3) **Son of Ehud.**—I Chr. 8:7.

NAAMATHITES, nā'a-ma-thites. **Inhabitants of Naamah.**—Job 2:11; 11:1; 20:1; 42:9.

NAAMITES, nā'a-mites. **Family of Naaman.**—Num. 26:40.

NAARAH, nā'a-rah. (1) **A woman.**—I Chr. 4:5.

(2) **A town in Ephraim.**—Josh. 16:7.

NAARAI, nā'a-rāi. **One of David's mighty men.**—I Chr. 11:37.

NAARAN, nā'a-răn. I Chr. 7:28. See NAARAH (?).

NABAL, nā'bal. I Sam. 25:2-39; 30:5; II Sam. 2:2; 3:3.

NABOTH, nā'both. **A Jezeelite whose vineyard was coveted by Ahab.**—I Ki. 21:1-24.

NACON, nā'kon. **A Benjamite, owner of threshing-floor, where Uzzah was stricken for touching the ark.**—II Sam. 6:6.

NADAB, nā'dăb. (1) **Eldest son of Aaron.**—Ex. 6:23; Num. 3:2; 26:60. Goes up to the mount—Ex. 24:1, 9. Priest's office—Ex. 28:1. His trespass and death—Lev. 10:1, 2; Num. 3:4; 26:61. Reign—I Ki. 14:20; 15:25. Smote—I Ki. 15:27. Rest of his acts —I Ki. 15:31.

(2) **Son of Jeroboam I king of Israel.**
—I Ki. 14:20; 15:25-31.

(3) **A Benjamite.**—I Chr. 8:30; 9:36.

(4) **Great grandson of Jerahmeel.**—I Chr. 2:28, 30.

NAGGAI, năg′ga-i. **Ancestor of Jesus.** —Lu. 3:25.

NAHALAL, na-hăl′ăl. **A city in Zebulun.**—Josh. 19:15; 21:35; Ju. 1:30.

NAHALIEL, na-hā′li-el. **One of the encampments of Israel.**—Num. 21:19. See CAMP, ISRAEL.

NAHAM, nā′ham. **A man of Judah.**—I Chr. 4:19.

NAHAMANI, na-hăm′a-ni. **One who returned from captivity with Zerubbabel.**—Neh. 7:7.

NAHARAI, nā′ha-rāi. **One of David's mighty men.**—II. Sam. 23:37; I Chr. 11:39.

NAHASH, nā′hăsh. (1) **An Ammonite king.**—II Sam. 10:2; 17:27; I Chr. 19:1, 2.

(2) **Another Ammonite king.**—I Sam. 11:1, 2; 12:12.

(3) **Mother of Abigail, grandmother of Amasa, Absalom's general.**—II Sam. 17:25.

NAHATH, nā′hăth. (1) **Grandson of Esau.**—Gen. 36:13, 17; I Chr. 1:37.

(2) **A Levite.**—II Chr. 31:13.

(3) **A Kohathite.**—I Chr. 6:26.

NAHBI, năh′bi. **A prince of Naphtali, one of the spies.**—Num. 13:14.

NAHOR, nā′hôr. (1) **Grandfather of Abraham.**—Gen. 11:22-25; I Chr. 1:26.

(2) **Son of Terah, brother of Abraham.** —Gen. 11:26-29; 22:20, 23; 24:10, 15, 24, 47; 29:5; 31:53; Josh. 24:2.

NAHSHON, năh′shon. **Son of Aminadab, prince of Judah.**—Num. 1:7; 2:3; 7:12, 17; 10:14; Ruth 4:20; I Chr. 2:10, 11.

NAHUM, nā′hum. (1) **An ancestor of Jesus.**—Lu. 3:25.

(2) **One of the minor prophets.**—See OUTLINE STUDIES IN THE BOOKS.

NAIL. See TOOLS AND IMPLEMENTS.

NAIN, nā′in. **A city in Galilee where Jesus restored the widow's son to life** —Lu. 7:11.

NAIOTH, nā′ioth. **Home of Samuel, in Ramah.**—I Sam. 19:18-22; 20:1.

NAKEDNESS. Sin discloses nakedness —Gen. 3:7; John 21:7; Rev. 3:18.

Shame of.—Noah's—Gen. 9:21-27. Of kin—Lev. 20:17-21. Jonathan's—I Sam. 20:30. Nineveh's—Nah. 3:5. Drunkard's—Hab. 2:15, 16. Children of Israel—Hos. 2:9, 10. The church —Rev. 3:17, 18; 16:15.

Laws concerning.—Lev. 20:10-23.

Spiritual nakedness.—Babylon—Is. 47: 3. Jerusalem—Lam. 1:8-9; Ez. Ch. 16.

Inflicted as a punishment.—Against Israel and Judah—Hos. 2:3; Mic. 1:7-9. The harlot of the church—Rev. 17:16.

Clothing the naked a proof of righteousness.—Job 22:5-7; 31:19-22; Mt. 25: 35-40; Jas. 2:15.

Not able to separate from God.—Rom. 8:35; II Cor. 11:27.

References.—Job 1:21; Mk. 14:51, 52; II Cor. 5:3.

NAMAAH, nā′ma-ah. (1) **A town in Judah.**—Josh. 15:41.

(2) **Daughter of Lamech and sister of Tubal-cain.**—Gen. 4:22. See NAAMAH.

NAME: Import of names.—Gen. 2:19, 20; 4:25; 17:5; 32:28; Dan. 1:7; Mt. 1:21; Lu. 1:13, 59-63. Saul's name changed—Acts 13:9. Simon's name changed—Mt. 16:18; John 1:42.

Name as reputation and standing.—I Sam. 18:30; Ju. 13:17, 18; Pr. 22:1; Eccl. 7:1; Eph. 1:20, 21. What is due to God's—Ps. 29:2; 86:9, 12; 103:1.

Symbol of power.—Gen. 11:4; 12:2; Ex. 15:3; Num. 6:27; II Sam. 8:13; I Chr. 17:8, 21; Ps. 52:9; 54:1; 63:4; Jas. 5:14.

Symbol of authority.—Ex. 9:16; 23:21; Mt. 7:22; 18:20; 21:9; 23:39; 24:5; Mk. 9:37; Lu. 9:49; 10:17; Acts 4:7, 10, 12; Phil. 2:10.

Rallying force.—Gen. 48:16; Deut. 12:5, 11, 21; 14:23, 24; 16:2, 6, 11; II Sam. 7:13; Neh. 1:9; Is. 26:8; Mt. 12:21.

The superior thing.—Deut. 26:19; Ps. 111:9; Lu. 10:20; Heb. 1:4.

Used for base ends.—Jer. 14:14; 23:25; 27:15; 29:9, 21, 23; Zech. 13:3.

Received in the name of a prophet or righteous man.—Mt. 10:41. Of disciple—Mt. 10:42.

Cost of endorsing a good name.—Mt. 10:22; 24:9; Mk. 13:13; Lu. 21:12; John 15:21; Acts 9:16. Benefit derived from—Mt. 19:29; I Pet. 4:14; I John 2:12; Rev. 3:5, 8, 9.

The new name.—Is. 56:5; 62:2; Acts 11:26; Rev. 2:17; 3:12.

Security of good names.—Ps. 72:17; Lu. 10:20; Phil. 4:3.

The name of God.—Symbol of Himself —Gen. 13:4; 21:33; 26:25; Ps. 80:18; 99:6; 105:1; 116:4; Is. 12:4; Acts 2: 21; 22:16. See GOD.

Taken in vain.—Ex. 20:7; Lev. 18:21; 19:12; 22:2, 32; Deut. 5:11.

Name of God holy.—Lev. 20:3; Ps. 111: 9; I Chr. 16:10; Is. 57:15. Not to profane God's holy name—Lev. 22:2, 32; Ez. 39:7. Name of God terrible—Ps. 99:3. Absent from book of Esther—considered too holy to be called.

Asking in the name.—John 14:13, 14; 15:16; 16:23-26.

Believing in the.—John 1:12; 2:23; 3: 18; Acts 3:16; 8:12; I John 3:23; 5:13.

Baptized in the.—Acts 8:16; 10:48; 19: 5; I Cor. 1:13-15.

Suffering for the.—Acts 5:41.

Used in derision.—Acts 4:17, 18.

NAOMI, na-ō'mi. Mother-in-law of Ruth—Ruth 1:6-18; 3:1, 16, 17. Wife of Elimelech—Ruth 1:2. Husband dies—Ruth 1:3. Women in Bethlehem did not know Naomi—Ruth 1:20, 21. Came to Bethlehem in barley harvest —Ruth 1:22. Her kinsman—Ruth 2:1, 20, 22; 4:3. Buying Naomi's field—Ruth 4:5, 9. The women said to Naomi, "Blessed be Jehovah"—Ruth 4:14.

NAPHISH, nā'phish. (1) **Son of Ishmael.**—Gen. 25:15; I Chr. 1:31.

(2) **His descendants.**—I Chr. 5:19.

NAPHTALI, năph'ta-li. (1) **Jacob's sixth son, second by Bilhah, Rachel's maid.**—Gen. 30:8; 35:25. Had four sons when he went into Egypt—Gen. 46:24. Predictions respecting—Gen. 49:21; Deut. 33:23. (2) **Tribe of.**—Census of, for war, 53,400—Num. 1: 42-43. After 40 years in wilderness, 45,400—Num. 26:48-50. Bounds of inheritance—Josh. 19:32-39. Failed to drive out Canaanites—Ju. 1:33. Made them tributary—Ju. 1:33. Princes—Num. 2:29; 7:78; 34:28; Ps. 68:27. Descendants—I Chr. 7:13. Stood on Mt. Ebal—Deut. 27:13. Inheritance—

Josh. 21:6, 32; I Chr. 6:62, 76. Hill country—Josh. 20:7; Ju. 5:18. Hiram of Tyre was of the tribe of Naphtali —I Ki. 7:13, 14. Helped David to become king of all Israel—I Chr. 12:34. Cities destroyed—II Chr. 16:4; 34:6. Chosen to go against Sisera—Ju. 4:6-10. Land ravaged by Ben-hadad—I Ki. 15:20. Land purged of idols by Josiah—II Chr. 34:5-7. Taken captive by Tiglath-pileser—II Ki. 15:29. Land prominent in Jesus' ministry—Is. 9:1-2; Mt. 4:13-15. See ISRAEL.

NAPHTUHIM, năph'tu-him. **Inhabitants of Central Egypt.**—Gen. 10:13; I Chr. 1:11.

NAPKIN. Pound laid up in—Lu. 19:20. Lazarus' face found in—John 11:44. About Jesus' head—John 20:7.

NARCISSUS, nar-sĭs'sus. **A disciple in Rome to whose household Paul sends salutation.**—Rom. 16:11.

NARD. Mk. 14:3; John 12:3.

NARRATIVE. Lu. 1:1.

NARROW. Ju. 17:15. Covering—Is. 28: 20. Gate—Mt. 7:13. Pit—Pr. 23:27. Place—Num. 22:26. Way—Mt. 7:14.

NATHAN, nā'than, *he gave.* (1) A prophet in David's reign—II Sam. 7:2, 3; I Ki. 1:8, 10; I Chr. 29:29; II Chr. 9:29. Representative of family of prophets—Zech. 12:12. Spoken to, by Jehovah—II Sam. 7:4. Forbids building of temple by David—II Sam. 7:1-17; I Chr. 17:1-15. His parable and rebuke of David—II Sam. 12:1-15; Ps. 51. Tells David and Bathsheba about Adonijah's usurpation—I Ki. 1:10-14, 22-27. Names Solomon "Jedidiah"—II Sam. 12:25. Anoints Solomon king—I Ki. 1:32-45. Regulation of the service in temple—II Chr. 29:25. Honor of his children—I Ki. 4:5.

(2) **Son of David.**—II Sam. 5:14; I Chr. 3:5; 14:4.

NATHANAEL, na-thăn'a-el. **A native of Cana in Galilee. Supposed to be Bartholomew the apostle.**—John 1: 45-49; 2:2.

NATHAN-MELECH, nā'than-mē'lek. **An officer under King Josiah.**—II Ki. 23:11.

NATIONS: Origin of.—Gen. 9:18 to 10:32.

Unity of race destroyed.—Gen. 11:1–9.

Ham the founder of Babylon and Egypt. —Gen. 10:6–20.

Shem the founder of Assyria.—Nimrod —Gen. 10:11, 12 (*marg.*), 21–31.

Japheth the founder of European nations.—Gen. 10:2–5; I Chr. 1:5–7.

God the Governor and Judge.—Ps. 22: 28; 47:7–9; 67:4; Jer. 10:7; Is. 2:4.

God gave nations to Israel.—Neh. 9:22.

God's marvelous works among.—I Chr. 16:24–26.

Abraham the father of many.—Gen. 17: 4–6.

Abraham the founder of Israelitish.— Gen. 12:2.

Offshoots of Abrahamic stock.—Gen. 19: 36–38; 25:12–16; 25:1–4; 36:6–8.

All the nations and families blessed in Abraham.—Gen. 12:3; 22:18; Acts 3: 25; Gal. 3:8.

God's principle in governing.—I Sam. 12:14–15; Jer. 12:14–17; 18:7–10.

God, the builder and controller.—Job 12:23; Is. 9:3; 26:15; Dan. 4:35.

Israel enters into possession not because of righteousness.—Deut. 7:7–9; 9:4–5.

Reasons for destroying.—Deut. 7:1–6, 10, 16, 18; II Ki. 24:1–4; Ps. 9:17; Is. 3:8–9; 14:12–27; 19:1–10.

Mercy blended with judgment.—Jer. 30: 5–17; Hos. 2:14–20.

Encouragement to obedient.—Lev. 26: 3–12; Is. 2:4; 14:3–8; 60:10–22.

God hath made of one blood all.—Acts 17:26.

Gospel of kingdom preached to all.—Mt. 28:19; Mk. 13:10; Lu. 24:27; Rom. 16: 26. See SALVATION FOR ALL MEN.

Before Christ shall be gathered all.— Mt. 25:32.

Suffered to walk in their own ways.— Acts 14:16.

Disciples must not follow.—Lu. 12:29–30.

All nations come and worship God.— Rev. 15:4.

Devout men from every nation hear apostles.—Acts 2:5.

In every nation the God-fearing respected.—Acts 10:34–35.

Saints redeemed out of every.—Rev. 5:9.

Angel to bear good tidings to every.— Rev. 14:6.

Leaves of tree for healing of.—Rev. 22:2.

See CITIES, ARABIA, ASSYRIA, CANAAN, CHALDEA, EDOM, EGYPT, ETHIOPIA, GREECE, ISRAEL, JUDAH, MEDIA, MOAB, PADDANARAM (MESOPOTAMIA), PERSIA, ROME, SAMARIA, SYRIA, BABYLON, MACEDONIA.

NATIVE. County—Jer. 22:10. Soul— Ps. 37:35.

NATIVITY. Land of—Gen. 11:28; 24: 7; 31:13; Ruth 2:11; Jer. 46:16; Ez. 16:3, 4; 23:15. See BIRTH.

NATURAL. I Cor. 15:46; Jude 10. Affection—Rom. 1:31; II Tim. 3:3. Body —I Cor. 15:44. Branches—Rom. 11: 21, 24. Face—Jas. 1:23. Force—Deut. 34:7. Man—I Cor. 2:14. Use—Rom. 1:26, 27.

NATURE. Rom. 2:14, 27; Gal. 4:8; Jas. 3:6. Children of wrath, By—Eph. 2:3. Contrary to—Rom. 1:26; 11:24. Divine—II Pet. 1:4. Jesus by—Gal. 2: 15. Wild by—Rom. 11:24.

NAUGHTINESS. I Sam. 17:28.

NAVEL. Pr. 3:8; Ez. 16:4.

NAVY. Hiram, Of—I Ki. 9:27; 10:11, 22. Jehoshaphat, Of—I Ki. 22:48. Solomon, Of—I Ki. 9:26; II Chr. 8:17. Tharshish, Of—I Ki. 10:22.

NAZARENE. A native of Nazareth.— Mk. 16:6; Acts 24:5.

NAZARETH, năz′a-reth. **A city of Galilee.**—Mt. 2:23; 21:11; Mk. 1:9; Lu. 1:26. Built on a hill—Lu. 4:29.

Wicked and despised city.—John 1:46. Their unbelief—Mt. 13:54–58.

Home of Joseph and Mary.—Lu. 1:26–30; 2:51.

Home of Christ.—Mt. 2:23; 4:13; 13:54; 21:11; 26:71; Mk. 1:9, 24; 6:1; 10:47; 14:67; 16:6; Lu. 2:51; 4:34; 18:37; 24:19; John 1:45, 46; 19:19; Acts 2: 22; 3:6; 4:10; 6:14; 10:38; 22:8; 26:9. Christ rejected at—Mk. 6:1–6; Lu. 4:29.

NAZIRITE, năz′i-rīte. Vow of—Num. 6:2.

Children raised to be.—Ju. 13:5, 7; Amos 2:11, 12.

Laws concerning.—Num. 6:13, 18, 19, 20, 21; Ju. 16:17; Amos 2:12.

Examples of: *Samson*—Ju. 16:17. *John the Baptist*—Amos 2:11, 12; Mt. 11:

18; Lu. 1:15. *Possibly Paul*—Acts 18: 18; 21:23–26.

NEAH, nē′ah. A town of Zebulun— Josh. 19:13.

NEAPOLIS, ne-ăp′o-lĭs. **A seaport of Macedonia.**—Acts 16:11.

NEAR. City is—Gen. 19:20. Darkness —Job 17:12. Day of Jehovah is— Zeph. 1:14. Kinsman—Ruth 2:20. Neighbor that is—Pr. 27:10. Seeing only what is—II Pet. 1:9. Time drew —Gen. 47:29. Trouble is—Ps. 22:11. While he is—Is. 55:6.

NEARER. Kinsman—Ruth 3:12. Salvation—Rom. 13:11.

NEARIAH, nē′a-rī′ah. (1) **A Simeonite captain.**—I Chr. 4:42.

(2) I Chr. 3:22, 23.

NEBAIOTH, ne-bā′ioth. (1) **Son of Ishmael.**—Gen. 25:13; 28:9; 36:3; I Chr. 1:29.

(2) **His descendants.**—Is. 60:7.

NEBALLAT, ne-băl′lat. **A city.**—Neh. 11:34.

NEBAT, nē′băt. **Father of Jeroboam king of Israel.**—I Ki. 11:26; 12:2, 15, etc. See JEROBOAM.

NEBO, nē′bo. (1) **A city in Reuben.**— ·Num. 32:3, 38; 33:47; I Chr. 5:8; Is. 15:2; Jer. 48:1, 22.

(2) **A city in Judah.**—Ezra 2:29; Neh. 7:33.

(3) **A mountain where Moses died.**— Deut. 32:49; 34:1.

(4) **Ancestor of some who married foreign wives.**—Ezra 10:43.

(5) **A Chaldean idol.**—Is. 46:1.

NEBUCHADNEZZAR, nĕb-u-kad-nĕz′zar. Invades Judah; makes Jehoiakim tributary—II Ki. 24:1. Carries Jehoiakim to Babylon—II Chr. 36:5–7; Dan. 1:1, 2. Takes Jerusalem and spoils—II Ki. 24:10–16; I Chr. 6:15; II Chr. 36:6, 7, 10; Jer. 39:1, 11; 52: 4, 12, 28, 29, 30; Ezra 1:7; 2:1; 5:12, 14. Makes Zedekiah king—II Ki. 24: 17; II Chr. 36:10. Takes Jews captive —II Ki. Ch. 25; Jer. Ch. 39; I Chr. 6: 15; Ezra 1:7; 2:1; 5:12; Mt. 1:11, 17. Conquers Pharaoh—II Ki. 24:7; Jer. 46:2. Kind treatment of Jeremiah— Jer. 39:11–14. Invades Tyre—Ez. 29: 18. Invades Egypt—Jer. 46:13, 26. Descendants of—Ez. 29:18. Great power —Is. 14:4–14; Jer. 27:6; 37:1; 39:5;

50:23; 51:34; Ez. Ch. 26; Dan. 1:18; 5:18, 19. Dreams interpreted by Daniel—Dan. Chs. 2 and 4. Makes golden image—Dan. Ch. 3. Insane, restored to throne and acknowledges God—Dan. Ch. 4. Takes Kedar and Hazor—Jer.· 49:28, 30. Makes war against Israel—Jer. 21:2. Defeated by Israel—Jer. 57:2; Neh. 7:6; Esth. 2:6.

Prophecies concerning.—Jer. 21:2–7; 22:25; 24:1; 25:1, 9; 27:6, 8, 20; 28:3, 11, 14; 29:1, 3, 21; 32:1, 28; 34:1; 35: 11; 43:10, 11.

NEBUSHAZBAN, nĕb′u-shăz′ban. **One of Nebuchadrezzar's princes.**—Jer. 39:13.

NEBUZARADAN, neb′u-zar′a-dan′. **Captain of the guard whom Nebuchadrezzar left in Jerusalem.**—II Ki. 25:8, 11, 20; Jer. 39:9–13; 40:1; 41:10; 43:6; 52:12, 15, 16, 26, 30.

NECESSARY. Job 23:12; Tit. 3:14; Heb. 8:3.

NECESSITY. Rom. 12:13; II Cor. 6:4.

NECK: Of people.—Jacob's neck smooth—Gen. 27:16. Thine enemies— Gen. 49:8. Kings'—Josh. 10:24. Eli —I Sam. 4:18. Prodigal—Lu. 15:20. Paul—Acts 20:37. Wicked—Ez. 21: 29.

Of animals.—Camel's—Ju. 8:21, 26. Dog —Is. 66:3. Horse—Job 39:19.

Kinds of.—Stiff—Deut. 31:27; II Chr. 36:13; Job 15:26; Ps. 75:5; Jer. 7:26; 17:23; 19:15. Hardened—II Ki. 17:14; Neh. 9:16, 17, 29; Pr. 29:1. Broken— Neck of Eli—I Sam. 4:18.

Strength of.—Job 41:22; Is. 48:4.

Ornaments of.—Gold chain about Joseph's—Gen. 41:42. Shall have chain of gold—Dan. 5:7, 16, 29 (*Fig.*). Strings of jewels—Song of Sol. 1:10. Chain for—Ex. 4:9; Ez. 16:11. Camel's—Ju. 8:26.

Incidents concerning.—Fell on his—Gen. 33:4; 45:14; 46:29; Lu. 15:20; Acts 20:37.

Laws concerning.—Neck of beasts—Ex. 13:13; 34:20; Deut. 21:4. Trespass-offering—Lev. 5:8.

Figurative.—Yokes upon—Lam.. 1:14; Pr. 3:3; 6:21; Jer. 27:2. As punishment—28:48; Jer. 28:14. Pursuers upon—Lam. 5:5. Loosen from bonds

of—Is. 52:2. Yoke upon disciples—
Acts 15:10.

Miscellaneous.—Bar taken from Jeremiah's—Jer. 28:10, 12. Taken by—
Job 16:12. Put not their necks to the
work—Neh. 3:5. Thy neck is like
tower of David—Song of Sol. 4:4.
Like tower of ivory—Song of Sol. 7:4.

Prophecies concerning.—Is. 8:8; 30:28;
Hab. 3:13. That will not put their
neck under yoke—Jer. 27:8. They
shall bring their neck under yoke—
Jer. 27:11. Will break yoke—Jer. 30:
8. Shall not remove—Mic. 2:3.

Teachings of Jesus concerning.—That a
millstone should be hanged about his
—Mt. 18:6; Mk. 9:42; Lu. 17:2. Laid
down for my sake—Rom. 16:4.

NECO, nē′co. **An Egyptian king.**—Jer.
46:2.

NECOH, nē′coh. II Ki. 23:29.

NEDABIAH, nĕd′a-bī′ah. **Grandson of
Jehoiakim.**—I Chr. 3:18.

NEED. Lu. 11:8; Eph. 4:29. Answer,
No need to—Dan. 3:16. Any man had
—Acts 2:45. As we—Acts 28:10. Go
away, No need to—Mt. 14:16. Brother
in—I John 3:17. God shall supply
every—Phil. 4:19. Minister to my—
Phil. 2:25. Must—Gen. 17:13; II Cor.
12:1. Not—John 2:25. Nothing, Of—
I Thess. 4:12. Physician, Of—Mk. 2:
17. Sufficient for—Deut. 15:18. Sun,
No—Rev. 21:23. Time of—Heb. 4:16.
What things ye have—Mt. 6:8. Ye
have no—I Thess. 4:9.

NEEDFUL. Circumcise, To—Acts 15:5.
Body, To—Jas. 2:16. House of God—
Ezra 7:20. More—Phil. 1:24. One
thing is—Lu. 10:42. That scripture
should be fulfilled—Acts 1:16. See
POOR, NECESSARY.

NEEDLE. Eye—Mt. 19:24; Mk. 10:25;
Lu. 18:25.

NEEDS. Be in subjection—Rom. 13:5.
Come to pass—Mk. 13:7. Go and see
it—Lu. 14:18. Go out of the worlds
—I Cor. 5:10. Glory—II Cor. 11:30.

NEEDY. Deut. 15:11; Is. 14:30. Cast
down—Ps. 37:14. Crush—Amos 4:1.
Deliver the—Ps. 35:10; 72:12. Devour
—Pr. 30:14. Father to the—Job 29:
16. Forgotten, Not—Ps. 9:18. For
shoes—Amos 2:6; 8:6. I am—Ps. 40:
17; 109:22. Jude—Jer. 5:28; 22:16.

Justice to the—Pr. 31:9. Kill—Job
24:14. Lifteth up the—I Sam. 2:8.
Persecuted—Ps. 109:16. 'Praise thy
name—Ps. 74:21. Rescue—Ps. 82:4.
Robbeth—Ps. 35:10. Souls of—Ps.
72:13. Swallow—Amos 8:4. Turn out
—Job 24:4. See POOR.

NEGLECT. Not the gift.—I Tim. 4:14.
Salvation, So great—Heb. 2:3.
Widows—Acts 6:1.

NEGLIGENT. II Pet. 1:12. Be not—
II Chr. 29:11.

NEHELAMITE, ne-hĕl′a-mite. **A presumptuous person who was rebuked by
Jeremiah.**—Jer. 29:24–32.

NEHEMIAH, nē-he-mī′ah. (1) See OUTLINE STUDIES IN THE BOOKS.

(2) **One who returned from captivity.**—
Ezra 2:2; Neh. 7:7.

(3) **One who helped to repair the wall.**
—Neh. 3:16.

NEHILOTH, nē′hi-lŏth. Ps. 5 title. See
MUSIC, PSALMS.

NEHUM, nē′hum. **One who returned
from exile.**—Neh. 7:7.

NEHUSHTA, nē′hush-tà. **Wife of Jehoiakim and mother of Jehoiachin.**—
II Ki. 24:8.

NEHUSHTAN, nē′hush-tan. **Name given
to brazen serpent by Hezekiah
when the people began to worship it.**
—II Ki. 18:4.

NEIEL, ne-ī′ĕl. **A city in Asher.**—Josh.
19:27.

NEICH. Jer. 8:6.

NEIGHBORS: Laws concerning treatment of.—Ex. 20:16, 17; 21:14; 22:7–
14, 26; Lev. 6:2; 18:20; 19:13–18; 24:
19; 25:14, 15; Deut. 5:20, 21; 15:2;
19:11, 14; 22:24, 26; 23:24, 25; 27:17,
24; Ruth 4:7; I Ki. 8:31; II Chr. 6:22;
Ps. 15:3; 101:5; Rom. 13:9, 10; 15:2;
Gal. 5:14; Eph. 4:25; Jas. 2:8.

Murder of.—Deut. 4:42; 19:4, 5; Josh.
20:5.

Neighbor's offering.—Ex. 12:4.

Proverbs concerning.—Pr. 3:28, 29; 6:
29; 11:9, 12; 12:26; 14:20, 21; 16:29;
18:17; 21:10; 24:28; 25:8, 9, 17, 18;
26:19; 27:10; Mt. 5:43; 19:19; 22:39;
Mk. 12:31, 33; Lu. 10:27.

Relations with.—Borrowing from—Ex.
3:22; 11:2; II Ki. 4:3. Teaching
mourning to—Jer. 9:20. False speech

with—Ps. 12:2. Envious of neighbor's work—Eccl. 4:4.

Special mention of.—Israel—Josh. 9:16. Assyrians—Ez. 23:5, 12. Naomi—Ruth 4:17. Saul—I Sam. 15:28. David—I Sam. 28:17; II Sam. 12:11; Ps. 31:11; 44:13; 79:4, 12; 80:6; 89:41. Elisabeth—Lu. 1:58. Beggar—John 9:8. Egyptian—Acts 7:27. Reward for kind treatment of—Ps. 15:3.

Prophecies concerning.—Oppression by —Is. 3:5; Jer. 6:21. Strife of—Is. 19:2. Help of—Is. 41:6. Justice between man and his—Jer. 7:5. Slanderous—Jer. 9:4, 5, 8. Destruction of—Jer. 49:10, 18; 50:40; Ez. 16:26. Speech with—Jer. 22:8; 23:27, 30, 35; 31:34; 34:15, 17.

Punishment for ill treatment of.—Jer. 22:13; 29:23; Ez. 18:6, 11, 15; 22:11, 12; 33:26; Hab. 2:15.

Neighbors in golden age.—Zech. 3:10; 8:10, 16, 17; 11:6; 14:13; Heb. 8:11; Jas. 2:8. Evil neighbors—Jer. 12:14.

Figurative.—Jer. 5:8.

Illustrative.—Job 12:4; 16:21; 31:9; Ps. 28:3. See JESUS, TEACHING OF. Parable of the true neighbor—Lu. 10:25-27.

Love for neighbor one of the great commandments.—Mt. 22:39, 40. Love for neighbor the debt that can never be paid—Rom. 13:8, 9. See FRATERNITY —Ps. 133:1.

NEKODA, ne-kō'dà. (1) **Ancestor of some who returned from exile.**—Ezra 2:48; Neh. 7:50.

(2) **Ancestor of some who returned but who had lost their genealogies.**—Ezra 2:60; 7:62.

NEMUEL, něm'u-el. (1) **A Reubenite.** —Num. 26:9.

(2) **Son of Simeon.**—Num. 26:12; I Chr. 4:24.

NEPHEG, ně'pheg. (1) **Grandson of Kohath.**—Ex. 6:21.

(2) **Son of David.**—II Sam. 5:15; I Chr. 3:7; 14:6.

NEPHILIM. Gen. 6:4; Num. 13:33. See ANAK, GIANTS.

NEPHISIM, ne-phī'sĭm. **A family of the Nethinim who returned from exile.**—Ezra 2:50.

NEPHTOAH, něph'to-ah. A small stream—Josh. 15:9; 18:15.

NEPHUSHESIM, ne-phŭsh'e-sĭm. Neh. 7:52. See NEPHISIM.

NER, nĕr. **Grandfather of Saul and father of Abner his captain.**—I Sam. 14:50, 51; 26:5, 14; II Sam. 2:8, 12; 3:23-28, 37; I Ki. 2:5, 32; I Chr. 8:33; 9:36, 39; 26:28.

NEREUS, nē're-ūs. **A Christian in Rome.** —Rom. 16:15.

NERGAL, nĕr-gal. **An Assyrian idol.**— II Ki. 17:30.

NERGAL-SHAREZER, nĕr-gal-sha-rē'-zer. **Two princes of Nebuchadrezzar.** —Jer. 39:3, 13.

NERI, nē'rĭ. **Ancestor of Jesus.**—Lu. 3:27.

NERIAH, ne-rī'ah. **Father of Baruch the secretary of Jeremiah.**—Jer. 32:12, 16; 36:4, 8, 14, 32; 43:3, 6; 45:1; 51:59.

NEST. Birds have—Mt. 8:20; Lu. 9:58. Die in my—Job 29:18. Riches, As—Is. 10:14. Set in the rock—Num. 24:21. Swallow hath found—Ps. 84:3.

NET: For fish.—Eccl. 9:12; Ez. 26:5; Hab. 1:15-17; Mt. 4:18-21; 13:47; Mk. 1:16-19; Lu. 5:2-6; John 21:6-11.

For birds.—Pr. 1:17; 7:23; Amos 3:5. For beasts—Is. 51:20.

For men.—Job 18:8; 19:6; Ps. 9:16; 25:15; 31:4; 35:7, 8; 57:6; 66:11; 140:5, 10; Pr. 12:12; 29:5; Eccl. 7:26; Lam. 1:13; Ez. 12:13; 17:20; 19:8; 32:3; Hos. 5:1; 7:12; Mic. 7:2; Jer. 18:22.

NETAIM. I Chr. 4:23.

NETHANEL, ne-thăn'el. (1) **A prince of Issachar sent out as a spy.**—Num. 1:8; 2:5; 7:18, 23; 10:15.

(2) **A priest who helped to bring the ark from the house of Obed-edom.**— I Chr. 15:24.

(3) **Brother of David.**—I Chr. 2:14.

(4) **A Levite.**—I Chr. 24:6.

(5) **A Levite in days of Josiah.**—II Chr. 35:9.

(6) **Son of Obed-edom.**—I Chr. 26:4.

(7) **A prince of Judah whom Jehoshaphat appointed to teach the people.**— II Chr. 17:7.

(8) **One who married a foreign wife.**— Ezra 10:22.

(9) **A priest.**—Neh. 12:21.

(10 **A musician who assisted in the purification.**—Neh. 12:36.

NETHANIAH, nĕth′a-nī′ah. **Father of Ishmael who slew Gedaliah.**—II Ki. 23:25; Jer. 40:8, 14, 15; 41:1, 2, 6–18.
(2) **A Levite whom Jehoshaphat appointed to teach.**—II Chr. 17:8.
(3) **A singer under David.**—I Chr. 25: 2, 12.
(4) **Father of Jehudi.**—Jer. 36:14.

NETHER. Josh. 16:3; 18:13; I Ki. 9: 17; I Chr. 7:24; II Chr. 8:5. Millstone —Job 41:24. Part—Ex. 19:17; Ez. 31:14, 16, 18; 32:18, 24. Springs— Josh. 15:19; Ju. 1:15. Story—I Ki. 6:6.

NETHINIM, nĕth′i-nĭm. **Servants or assistants to the Levites.**—I Chr. 9:2; Ezra 2:43, 58, 70; 7:7, 24; 8:17, 20; Neh. 3:26, 31; 7:46, 60, 73; 10:28; 11:3, 21.

NETOPHAH, ne-tō′phah. **A town in Judah.**—Ezra 2:22; Neh. 7:26.

NETOPHATHITES, ne-tŏph′a-thites. II Sam. 23:28, 29; II Ki. 25:23; I Chr. 2:54; 9:16; 11:30; 27:13, 15; Neh. 12: 28; Jer. 40:8.

NETTLE. Hos. 9:6. A possession of— Zeph. 2:9. Cover with—Pr. 24:31. Shall come up—Is. 34:13. Brass, Of —Ex. 27:4; 38:4. Cover bowls, To— I Ki. 7:41. Pomegranates for—I Ki. 7:42.

NEVER. Gen. 41:19; Mk. 2:12; Lu. 15: 29. Be offended—Mt. 26:33. Be put to shame—Ps. 31:1. Break my covenant—Ju. 2:1. Despairing—Lu. 6:35. Forget—Ps. 119:93. Knew you—Mt. 7:23. Love, faileth—I Cor. 13:8. Man so spake—John 7:46. Stumble—II Pet. 1:10. Satisfied—Pr. 27:20. See death—John 8:21. Stumble—II Pet. 1:10. Thirst—John 4:14. Transgressed—Lu. 15:29.

NEW. Mt. 13:52. All things shall become—Rev. 21:5. Commandment— John 13:34. Covenant—Heb. 8:8; 12: 24. See COVENANTS. Creature—II Cor. 5:17; Gal. 6:15; II Pet. 1:4. Heaven and earth—II Pet. 3:13; Rev. 21:1. Man—Eph. 2:15; 4:24; Col. 3:10. Mercies—Lam. 3:23. Name written— Rev. 2:17. Song—Rev. 5:9; 19:1–3. Spirit—I John 2:8. Teaching—Mk. 1:27. Tongue—Mk. 16:17; Acts 2:4; 10:46; I Cor. 12:10. Way—Heb. 10: 10.

NEW BIRTH: Initial step in a radical change from spiritual apathy to life.
—Christians begin as babes—I Cor. 3:1; Gal. 6:15; Heb. 5:13; I Pet. 2:2.
Begotten of God by the Spirit.—John 1:13; 3:3–9; Titus 3:5; I John 2:29; 5:18.
Begotten by preaching of the gospel.—I Cor. 4:15; Philemon 10; Jas. 1:18; I Pet. 1:23.
He that believeth that Jesus is the Son of God is begotten of God.—John 1: 12; 5:1–5.
Constitutes men children of God.—Mt. 13:38; Lu. 20:34–36; John 11:52; Rom. 8:16–21; 9:26; Gal. 3:26; 4:5–6, 28; Eph. 1:5; 5:1–8; Phil. 2:15; I Thess. 5:5; Heb. 2:10; 12:7, 8; I Pet. 1:14–17; I John 3:1–10; 4:4; 5:2.
Constitutes men heirs of God.—Rom. 8: 16, 17; Gal. 3:26–29; 4:6, 7; Eph. 3:6; Titus 3:7; Heb. 6:17; 11:14; Jas. 2:5; I Pet. 3:7. See ADOPTION, CONVERSION, SALVATION.

NEWLY. Ju. 7:19.

NEWNESS. Of life—Rom. 6:4; 12:2; Eph. 4:21–24; Col. 3:9, 10. Of the spirit—Rom. 7:6.

NEWS. Good—Pr. 25:25.

NEXT. Generation—Ps. 71:18. Kinsman—Lev. 25:25. Sabbath—Acts 13: 42. Year—Gen. 17:21.

NEZIAH, ne-zī′ah. **Ancestor of some who returned with Zerubbabel.**—Ez. 2:54; 7:56.

NEZIB, nĕ′zib. **A city in Judah.**—Josh. 15:43.

NIBHAZ, nĭb′hăz. **An idol of the Avvites.**—II Ki. 17:31.

NIBSHAN, nĭb′shan. **A city of Judah.** —Josh. 15:62.

NICANOR, nĭ-cā′nor. **A deacon in the early church.**—Acts 6:5.

NICODEMUS, nĭk′o-dē′mus. **Member of the Jewish Sanhedrin.**—John 3:1. Interviews Jesus by night—John 7: 50. Brings spies to Jesus' burial— John 19:39.

NICOLAITANS, nĭk-o-lā′i-tans. **A heretical sect.**—Rev. 2:6, 15.

NICOLAUS, nĭk-ŏ-lā′us. **A proselyte of Antioch and one of the seven first deacons.**—Acts 6:5.

NICOPOLIS, ni-cŏp′o-lĭs. **A city of Thrace.**—Tit. 3:12.

NIGER, nī′ger. **Surname of Simeon one of the prophets and teachers in Antioch.**—Acts 13:1.

NIGH. Num. 24:17; Mt. 24:33. Bethany was—John 11:18. Death, Unto—Phil. 2:27, 30. Draw—Eccl. 1:5; Lu. 19:41. See DRAW NIGH. Jehovah is—Ps. 34: 18. Kin, Of—Lev. 25:49. Kingdom of God—Lu. 10:9; 21:31. Made—Eph. 2: 13. Preached peace to them that were —Eph. 2:17. Salvation is—Ps. 85:9. Thou art—Ps. 119:151. Unto vanishing away—Heb. 8:13. Word is—Deut. 30:14; Rom. 10:8.

NIGHT: Darkness first called night.— Gen. 1:5. Moon and stars to rule the —Gen. 1:16–18; Jer. 31:35. Established by covenant—Gen. 8:22. Divided into watches by Jews—Ex. 14: 24; Ju. 7:19; Ps. 63:6; 119:148; Lam. 2:19. By Romans—Mt. 14:25; Mk. 13:35; Lu. 12:38. Divided into hours —Acts 23:23. Unsuitable for labor— John 9:4. Designed for rest—Ps. 104: 23. Favorable to purposes of wicked —Gen. 31:39; Job 24:14–15; Ob. 5:1; Thess. 5:2–7. Must not hold wages over—Ex. 22:26, 27; Lev. 19:13. Bodies must not hang at—Deut. 21:23. Shepherd watch over flocks during— Gen. 31:40; Lu. 2:8. Fishermen continue during—Lu. 5:5; John 21:3. God revealed his will in—Gen. 31:24; 46:2; Num. 22:20; Dan. 7:2. God executed his judgments in—Ex. 12:12; II Ki. 19:35; Job 27:20; Dan. 5:30.

Special references.— Old Testament: When shall night be gone?—Job 7:4. Night unto night showeth knowledge —Ps. 19:2. Weeping may tarry for a —Ps. 30:5. Watchman, what of—Is. 21:11.

New Testament: This night before cock crows—Mt. 26:34. Continued all night in prayer—Lu. 6:12. Night is far spent—Rom. 13:12. We are not of the —I Thess. 5:5. No night there—Rev. 21:25. See DAY.

NILE. See RIVERS.

NIMRAH, nĭm′rah. **A city in Gad.**— Num. 32:3.

NIMRIM, nĭm′rim. **Waters on borders of Gad and Moab.**—Is. 15:6; Jer. 48: 34.

NIMROD, nĭm′rŏd. (1) **Grandson of Ham. A great hunter.**—Gen. 10:8, 9; I Chr. 1:10. (2) **Babylonia.**—Mic. 5:6.

NIMSHI, nĭm′shī. **Either father or grandfather of Jehu.**—I Ki. 19:16; II Ki. 9:2, 20; II Chr. 22:7.

NINE. Ninety and nine—Mt. 18:12, 13; Lu. 15:4, 7.

NINETY. And nine—Mt. 18:12, 13; Lu. 15:4, 7.

NINEVEH, nĭn′e-veh. **The capital of Assyria and founded by Nimrod.**— Gen. 10:11. Situated on the Tigris river—Nah. 2:6, 8. Made famous by the career of Sennacherib—II Ki. 19: 20–36; Is. 37:37. The death of Sennacherib—II Ki. 19:36, 37; Is. 37:37, 38. Had a large population—Jonah 4:11. Jonah sent to proclaim its destruction—Jonah 1:2; 3:1–4. Destruction averted by repentance—Jonah 3:10. Repentance noted by Jesus—Mt. 12:41; Lu. 11:32. Nineveh a great city—Jonah 1:2; 3:3. A rich city— Nah. 2:9. A wicked city—Jonah 1:2.

Predictions concerning.— Assyria an instrument in Jehovah's hand—Is. 7: 18–20; 36:2; II Ki. 18:17. Babylon assaults Nineveh—Nah. 2:1–4; 3:2. Her people destroyed—Nah. 1:12; 3:3. Their idols destroyed—Nah. 1:14; 2:7. Degradation and desolation—Zeph. 2:13–15.

NINTH. Mt. 20:5; Acts 10:3. About the ninth hour Jesus cried—Mt. 27: 46; Mk. 15:34. Darkness until the— Mt. 27:45; Mk. 15:33. Hour of prayer —Acts 3:1; 10:30.

NISAN, nī′san. **First month in Jewish year.**—See MONTHS.

NISROCH, nĭs′rŏk. **An Assyrian idol.**— II Ki. 19:37; Is. 37:38.

NITRE, Pr. 25:20 (A.V.); Jer. 2:22 (A.V.). See SODA.

NO. A city on the Nile, called Thebes and Diospolis.—Capital of Upper Egypt —Jer. 46:25; Ez. 30:14–16; Nah. 3:8. Account, Of—I Cor. 6:4. Counsel— Pr. 15:22. Distinction—Acts 11:12. Moisture—Lu. 8:6. Occasion of stumbling—Ps. 119:165. Truth—Acts 21: 24. Wise fail thee, In—Heb. 13:5.

NOADIAH, nō′a-dī′ah. (1) **A Levite.**— Ezra 8:33. (2) **A female follower of**

Sanballat and Tobiah, called a prophetess.—Neh. 6:14.

NOAH, nō'ah. Heb. *"Nahem,"* to comfort. (1) **Son of Lamech and tenth from Adam in Seth's line.**—Gen. Ch. 5.

Lamech's prophecy concerning Noah.—Gen. 5:29.

Noah's three sons.—Gen. 5:23.

God decides to destroy man because of wickedness.—Gen. 6:5–13.

Orders Noah to build an ark.—Gen. 6: 14. Describes the fashion of it—Gen. 6:14–16.

Noah and family find grace with Jehovah.—Gen. 6:18; 7:1; Heb. 11:7; II Pet. 2:5.

The antediluvians reckless, though forewarned.—Mt. 24:37–39; Lu. 17:26, 27; I Pet. 3:19, 20.

Noah and family enter ark.—Gen. 7:7. After 150 days, the waters decreased and the ark was emptied—Gen. 7:24; 8:3, 13–19. Every other living thing except inhabitants of the waters was destroyed—Gen. 7:21–23.

Noah builds an altar and makes an offering.—Gen. 8:20.

Jehovah covenants with him concerning future.—Gen. 8:21, 22; 9:11. Uses rainbow as a pledge of protection—Gen. 9:12–17. Must replenish the earth—Gen. 9:1. Everything good for food to be his—Gen. 9:3. Forbidden to use blood—Gen. 9:4, 5.

Noah plants a vineyard.—Gen. 9:20.

Is overcome with wine.—Gen. 9:21. Ham acts shamefully and is cursed by Noah —Gen. 9:24–27. Noah blesses Shem and Japheth—Gen. 9:26, 27. Lives 950 years—Gen. 9:29. Is matched with Daniel and Job for righteousness —Ez. 14:14, 20.

(2) **Daughter of Zelophehad.**—Num. 26: 33; 27:1; 36:11; Josh. 17:3.

NOB, nŏb. **A Benjamite city where 85 priests and their families were slain by Doeg.**—I Sam. 21:1; 22:9, 11, 19; Neh. 11:32; Is. 10:32.

NOBAH, nō'bah. **A man of Manasseh.** —Num. 32:42; Ju. 8:11.

NOBLE, NOBLEMAN. Lu. 19:12; John 4:46, 49. At rest—Nah. 3:18. Bind, with fetters—Ps. 149:8. Called—I Cor. 1:26. Children of Israel, Of—Ex. 24:11. Cleave to—Neh. 10:29. Flee—

Is. 15:5. Gather together—Neh. 7:5. Judah, Of—Neh. 6:17. Provinces, Of —Esth. 1:3. Put not necks to the work—Neh. 3:5. Smite, for uprightness—Pr. 17:26. Voice of—Job 29:10.

NOBLE, *adj.* Called—Is. 32:5. More— Acts 17:11. Princes—Esth. 6:9. Things —Is. 32:8. Vine—Jer. 2:21.

NOD, nŏd. **Land east of Eden.**—Gen. 4:16.

NODAB, nō'dăb. **A tribe east of the Jordan.**—I Chr. 5:19.

NOGAH, nō'gah. **Son of David.**—I Chr. 3:7; 14:6.

NOHAH, nō'hah. **Son of Benjamin.**— I Chr. 8:2.

NOISE, *n.* Chariots, Of—II Ki. 7:6. Fall, Of—Jer. 49:21. Great—Mic. 2:12; Is. 29:6; II Pet. 3:10. Horsemen, Of— Ez. 26:10. Joyful—Ps. 66:1; 81:1; 95: 1, 2; 98:4; Is. 16:10. Loud—Ps. 33:3. Pharaoh is but a—Jer. 46:17. Stamping, Of—Jer. 47:3. Trumpet, Of— Ex. 20:18. Tumult, Of—I Sam. 4:14. War—Ex. 32:17. Waters, Of—Ez. 1: 24. Weeping, Of—Ezra 3:13. Wheels, Of—Ez. 3:13. Whip, Of—Nah. 3:2.

NOISE, *v.* Mk. 2:1; Lu. 1:65.

NOISOME. Rev. 16:2.

NONE. Escaped—Joel 2:3. Good—Mk. 10:18; Lu. 18:19; Rom. 3:12. Knoweth—I Cor. 2:11. Of those men shall taste—Lu. 14:24. Other commandment greater—Mk. 12:31. Righteous —Rom. 3:10. Seeketh after God— Rom. 3:11.

NOON. About—Acts 22:6. At—I Ki. 18:27; 20:16. Dine with me at—Gen. 43:16. From morning until—I Ki. 18: 26. Rest at—Song of Sol. 1:7. Stumble at—Is. 59:10. Sun go down at—Amos 8:9.

NOONDAY. A destroyer at—Jer. 15:8. Clearer than—Job 11:17. Grope at— Deut. 28:29; Job 5:14. Justice as the —Ps. 37:6. Night in midst of—Is. 16:3. Wasteth at—Ps. 91:6.

NOONTIDE. Is. 38:10.

NOOSE. Job 18:10.

NOPHAH, nō'phăh. **A Moabite city.**— Num. 21:30.

NORTH. Country—Jer. 23:8; 31:8; 50: 9. Destruction out of—Jer. 46:20. Evil shall break forth, Out of—Jer. 1:14. Nation come out of—Jer. 50:3. People of—Jer. 46:24. Raised up one from—Is. 14:31. Wind—Ps. 25:23; Song of Sol. 4:16.

NOT. Fire go out—Lev. 6:13. Hope waver—Heb. 10:23. So—John 7:12. Where to lay his head—Mt. 8:20; Lu. 9:58. Wherewith to pay—Pr. 22:27.

NOTABLE. Day of the Lord—Acts 2: 20. Horn—Dan. 8:5, 8. Men—Amos 6:1. Miracle—Acts 8:16. Prisoner called Barabbas—Mt. 27:16.

NOTHING. III John 7. Against the truth—II Cor. 13:8. Apart from me ye can do—John 15:5. Carry away— Ps. 49:17. Changed—Dan. 6:17. Doubting—Jas. 1:6. Impossible—Mt. 17:20. Known—II Sam. 17:19. Lacked— Deut. 2:7. Leave—Zeph. 3:3. Rich yet hath—Pr. 13:7. Withholden—Gen. 11:6.

NOUGHT. Gen. 29:15; II Sam. 19:6. Bring to—Heb. 2:14. Brought to— Is. 16:4. Come to—Rom. 9:6. Counsel to—Ps. 33:10. Doth Job fear God for —Job 1:9. Eat for—Num. 11:50. God shall bring to—I Cor. 6:13. Gospel for —II Cor. 11:7. If Christ died for— Gal. 2:21. Sellest people for—Ps. 44: 12. Set at—Ps. 119:118; Lam. 1:15; Mk. 9:12; Lu. 18:9; Rom. 14:3; Heb. 10:28; Jude 8. Works are—Is. 41:29.

NOURISH. Gen. 45:11; Rev. 12:6. Children — Is. 1:2. Flesh — Eph. 5:29. Hearts—Jas. 5:5. In words of faith— I Tim. 4:6. Joseph, his father—Gen. 47:12. Lamb—II Sam. 12:3. Moses— Acts 7:20, 21. Rain doth—Is. 44:14. Young men—Is. 23:4.

NOW. I Cor. 8:1; Rom. 15:13; Heb. 9: 26. All things are ready—Lu. 14:17. Cannot bear them—John 16:12. From beginning until—Mt. 24:21. I rejoice —Col. 1:24. In Christ Jesus—Eph. 2:13. Life which I live—Gal. 2:20. No condemnation—Rom. 8:1. Pentecost was come—Acts 2:1. The accepted time—Is. 1:18; 49:8; 55:6; Mt. 22:4; Lu. 4:17; II Cor. 6:2; Heb. 3:7. To appear—Heb. 1:24. We children of God—I John 3:2. Worketh even until—John 5:17.

NUMBER, *n.* Bricks, Of—Ex. 5:8. By —Is. 40:26. Churches increased in— Acts 16:5. Days, Of—Ez. 4:4, 5, 9. Disciples, Of—Acts 6:7. Few in—

Gen. 34:30; Jer. 44:28. Forgotten me days without—Jer. 2:32. Full—I Sam. 18:27. Great—Lu. 6:17; Acts 11:21. Increased in—Acts 16:5. Israel, Of— See ISRAEL. Men, Of—Acts 4:4; 5:36. More than sand in—Ps. 139:18. Sand of the sea, As—Rev. 20:8. Souls, Of— Ex. 12:4. Stars, Of—Ps. 147:4. Without—Gen. 41:49; Job 5:9. Years, Of —Dan. 9:2.

NUMBER, *v.* II Cor. 17:14; Acts 1:17. Days—Ps. 90:12. Dust—Gen. 13:16. Hairs are—Mt. 10:30; Lu. 12:7. Israel —See ISRAEL. Kingdom—Dan. 5:26. No man could—Rev. 7:9. People— Num. 1:19; 2:26; 3:15; 4:34; 26:57; II Sam. 1–17; I Chr. 21:1–17. Stars— Gen. 15:5. Steps—Job 31:4. Wanting cannot be—Eccl. 1:15.

NUN, nŭn, *Fish.* Father of Joshua— Ex. 33:11; Num. 11:28; 13:8, 16; 14:6, 30, 38; 26:65; 27:18; 32:12, 28; 34:17; Deut. 1:38; 31:23; 32:44; 34:9; Josh. 1:1; 2:1, 23; 14:1; 17:4; 19:49, 51; Ju. 2:8; I Ki. 16:34; I Chr. 7:27; Neh. 8:17.

NURSE. Gen. 24:59. Became—Ruth 4: 16. Cherisheth children—I Thess. 2:7. Child—Ex. 2:7, 9. Rebekah's—Gen. 35:8. Stole away—II Ki. 11:2; II Chr. 22:11. Took him up—II Sam. 4:4. See CHILDREN.

NURSING-FATHER. Acts 13:18.

NURTURE. Eph. 6:4. See INSTRUCTION.

NYMPHAS, nȳm′phas. **An early disciple.**—Col. 4:15.

OAK. Josh. 19:33. Absalom hung in boughs of—II Sam. 18:9, 10. Among the—II Sam. 18:14; Is. 57:5. Ashamed of—Is. 1:29. Bashan, Of—Is. 2:13; Ez. 27:6; Zech. 11:2. Idols hid under —Gen. 35:48. Leaf—Is. 1:30. Moreh, Of—Gen. 12:6; Deut. 11:30. Strong as the—Amos 2:9. Under the—Josh. 24:26; Ju. 6:11, 19; I Ki. 13:14; I Chr. 10:12; Ez. 6:13. Wood of—Is. 6:13; 44:14; Hos. 4:13. See IDOLATRY.

OAR. Bashan, Of—Ez. 27:6. Galley, Of —Is. 33:21. Handlers of—Ez. 27:29. See SHIPS.

OATH: Invocation of God to witness the truth of a statement.—Ex. 33:1; Num. 32:11; Deut. 1:35; Josh. 1:6; Heb. 6:16.

Accompanies promises.—Josh. 2:12 ff.

Confirms vows.—Num. 30:2, 10, 13.

Ratifies covenants.—Josh. 9:15; Neh. 10:29; Ez. 17:13 ff.

Sacred and binding.—Josh. 9:20; Ju. 21: 5–7; II Sam. 21:7; I Ki. 2:43; Ps. 15: 4; Eccl. 8:2; Zech. 8:17.

Violation of, to be expiated by sin-offering.—Lev. 5:4.

May be exacted on important occasions. —Gen. 24:3 ff.; 50:25; Neh. 5:5; I Sam. 14:24. Especially in the test of adultery—Num. 5:21.

Swearing by idols.—Jer. 12:16; Zeph. 1:5.

Jehovah's oath: given as a means of greater assurance to his people.— Deut. 7:8; I Chr. 16:16; Ps. 105:9; Is. 62:8. Is inviolable—Jer. 11:5; Hab. 3:9; Lu. 1:73; Acts 2:30; Heb. 6:17.

Characterizes the high priesthood of Christ.—Heb. 7:20, 28.

Common use of oath forbidden.—Mt. 5:34; Jas. 5:12. See VOW, COMMANDMENTS.

OBADIAH, ŏ′ba-dī′ah. (1) **The minor prophet.**—See OUTLINE STUDIES IN THE BOOKS.

(2) **Governor of Ahab's house.**—I Ki. 18:3–7, 16.

(3) **A descendant of David.** — I Chr. 3:21.

(4) **A descendant of Issachar.**—I Chr. 7:3.

(5) **A Benjamite.**—I Chr. 8:38; 9:44.

(6) **A Gadite.**—I Chr. 12:9.

(7) **Son of a Levite.**—I Chr. 9:16.

(8) **A Levite overseer of repairs of the temple under Josiah.**—II Chr. 34:12.

(9) **One who returned with Ezra.**—Ezra 8:9.

(10) **A prince of Judah appointed by Jehoshaphat to teach in cities of Judah.**—II Chr. 17:7.

(11) **A gatekeeper of the sanctuary.**— Neh. 12:25.

(12) **A priest who sealed the covenant.** —Neh. 10:5.

OBAL, ō′bal. **Son of Joktan.**—Gen. 10:28.

OBED, ō′bed. (1) **Son of Boaz and Ruth and grandfather of David.**— Ruth 4:17, 21, 22; I Chr. 2:12; Mt. 1:5; Lu. 3:32.

(2) **One of David's mighty men.**—I Chr. 11:47.

(3) **A descendant of Judah.**—I Chr. 2: 37, 38.

(4) **A Kohathite.**—I Chr. 26:7.

(5) **Father of Azariah the captain.**—II Chr. 23:1.

OBED-EDOM, ō′bed–ē′dom. (1) **A Levite in whose house the ark was left three months.**—II Sam. 6:10–12; I Chr. 13:13–25.

(2) **Another Levite.**—I Chr. 16:5, 38.

(3) **A gatekeeper of the tabernacle appointed to bring the ark.**—I Chr. 15: 18–24; 26:4, 8, 15.

(4) **An Aaronite.**—II Chr. 25:24.

(5) **Son of Jeduthun.**—I Chr. 16:38.

OBEDIENCE. A fundamental law.— Deut. 13:1–4; Rom. 5:19; 6:16; Phil. 2:12.

Life depends on obedience.—God's instructions to Adam—Gen. 2:16–17. To Israel through Moses—Lev. 18:5; Deut. 8:1–3. Through Joshua—Josh. 5:6; Rom. 5:18–19.

Faith is assured by obedience.—Acts 6:7; 5:31–32; Rom. 1:5; 5:19; 6:17–18; II Cor. 7:15; Heb. 5:8–9; 11:7–8; I Pet. 1:22.

Christ an example of.—Mt. 3:14–15; John 15:10; Phil. 2:5–11; Heb. 5:8.

Can obey but one God.—Deut. 4:1–4; I Ki. 18:21; Lu. 16:13; Acts 5:29; Gal. 1:6–9.

Knowing depends on obedience.—John 7:17; 13:34–35; II Cor. 9:12–13; II Thess. 1:8; I John 1:3–6; 3:23–24; 5:2–3.

Fulfilment of promises depends on obedience.—Old Testament—Deut. 11:8–9, 26–28; 32:46–47; 28: 1–14; Jer. 38:20; Zech. 3:7. New Testament—Mt. 19: 17; Lu. 11:28; John 10:27–28; 14:15–16, 23; Acts 2:38–39; 3:19–20; Jas. 1:25; Rev. 22:14.

Obedience must be from the heart.— Deut. 11:13; Mk. 12:33; Rom. 10:8–10; 6:17.

Obedience better than sacrifice.—I Sam. 15:22; Ps. 50:8–15; 69:31; Pr. 15:8; 28:9; Is. 1:12–17; Jer. 6:20; Hos. 6:6; Amos 5:22; Mt. 9:13; 21:19; Mk. 12: 33.

Obedience must be rendered to masters. —Eph. 6:5; Col. 3:22; Tit. 2:9.

By children to parents.—Eph. 6:1; Col. 3:20. By Disciples—Tit. 3:1–2.

General fruits of obedience.—Gen. 18: 19; Lev. 26:3–13; Num. 14:24; Deut. 7:9, 12–15; 15:4; 28:1–15; Josh. 1:8; 14:6–14; I Ki. 2:3–4; II Ki. 21:8; I Chr. 22:13; 28:7–8; II Chr. 26:5; 27:6; Job 36:11; Is. 1:19; Jer. 7:3–7; 11:1–5; 22:16; Mal. 3:10–12. New Testament—Mt. 5:19; 7:24; 12:50; 25:20–23; Mk. 3:35; Lu. 6:46–48; 8:21; 11: 28; 12:37–38; John 12:26; 13:17; 14: 23; 15:10, 14; Jas. 1:25; I John 2:17; 3:24; Rev. 22:7.

Examples of obedience: Noah—Gen. 6: 22. Abram—Gen. 12:1–4; 22:3, 12; Heb. 11:8. Jacob—Gen. 35:1–4. Moses and Aaron—Ex. 7:6; 40:16–33. Israelites—Ex. 12:28; 24:7; 39:42–43; Num. 9:20–23. Caleb and Joshua—Num. 14: 24; 32:12; Josh. 10:40; 11:15. Elijah —I Ki. 17:5. David—I Ki. 11:34. Hezekiah—II Ki. 18:6–7. Josiah—II Ki. 22:2. Jehoshaphat—II Chr. 17: 3–6. The three Hebrews—Dan. Ch. 3. Cornelius—Acts 10:33. Paul—Acts 26:16–20. Disciples—Rom. 6:17. See COMMANDMENTS, TEACHING OF JESUS CONCERNING OBEDIENCE, GOSPEL MUST BE OBEYED, RIGHTEOUS, WICKED.

OBEISANCE. Absalom, By—II Sam. 15:5. David, To—II Sam. 1:2; 14:4; 16:4; I Ki. 1:16. Father-in-law—Ex. 18:7. Joseph, To—Gen. 37:7, 9; 43:28. King, To—II Chr. 24:17. Saul, To—I Sam. 24:8. Sheaf of—Gen. 37:7. See Bow, WORSHIP.

OBEY. See OBEDIENCE.

OBIL, ō′bil. **An Ishmaelite camel driver.** —I Chr. 27:30.

OBJECT. Worship, Of—Acts 17:23.

OBLATION. See OFFERINGS AND OB-LATIONS.

OBOTH, ō′both. **An encampment of Israel.**—Num. 21:10. See CAMP.

OBSCURITY. Blind see out of—Is. 29: 18. See DARKNESS.

OBSERVANCES. Neh. 13:14.

OBSERVATION. Lu. 17:20.

OBSERVE. Coming—Jer. 8:7. Customs —Acts 16:21. Days—Ex. 12:14; Deut. 28:13; Gal. 4:10. Feast—See FEAST. From my youth up—Mk. 10:20. Idols —Acts 17:23. Jehovah does—Ps. 66: 7. Roman laws—Acts 16:21. Leprosy—Deut. 24:8. Night of deliverance—Ex. 12:42. Ordinance—See

OBEDIENCE. Precepts—Ps. 105:63, 134. Sabbath day—Ex. 31:16; Deut. 12:5. These things—Ps. 107:43; Mt. 19:20; 28:20; Mk. 10:20; I Tim. 5:21. Words of Jehovah—Ps. 119:57, 88, 101, 146.

OBSTINATE. Deut. 2:30; Is. 48:4.

OBTAIN. Faith—II Pet. 1:1. Favor—See FAVOR. Field—Acts 1:18. Gladness—Is. 35:10; 51:11. Glory—II Thess. 2:14. Honor—Pr. 29:23. Joy—Is. 35:10; 51:11. Mercy—Pr. 8:35; Mt. 5:7; Rom. 11:30, 31; II Cor. 4:1; 7:25; I Tim. 1:13; I Pet. 2:10. Ministry, Excellent—Heb. 8:6. Promise—Heb. 6:15; 11:33. Redemption—Heb. 9:12. Riches—Pr. 11:16.

OCCASION. Enemies, To—II Sam. 12: 14; I Tim. 5:14. Fall in brothers way, To—Rom. 14:13. Find—Ju. 9:33. Flesh, To the—Gal. 5:13. Glorying, Of —II Cor. 5:12. See GLORYING. Seek—Gen. 43:18; 46:33; Ju. 14:4; Dan. 6:4, 5. Sin finds—Rom. 7:8, 11. Stumbling, Of—I John 2:10.

OCCUPATION. Gen. 46:33; 47:3; Jonah 1:8; Acts 19:25 See ARTS AND TRADES, BUSINESS.

OCCUPY. Self—Heb. 13:9.

OCCURRENCE. I Ki. 5:4.

OCHRAN, ŏk′ran. **An Asherite who helped to number the people.**—Num. 1:13; 2:27; 7:72, 77; 10:26.

ODED, ō′ded. (1) **Father of the prophet Azariah.**—II Chr. 15:1, 8.
(2) **A prophet in Samaria.**—II Chr. 28:9.

ODIOUS. Gen. 34:30; Pr. 30:23. David, To—II Sam. 10:6; I Chr. 19:6.

ODOR. Evil—Eccl. 10:1. House filled with—John 12:3. Incense—Ez. 8:11. Ointment, Of—John 12:3. Sweet—Lev. 26:31; II Chr. 16:14; Esth. 2:12; Dan. 2:46; Phil. 4:18. See SMELLING.

OFF. Cut off—Gen. 17. Earth—Gen. 7:4; 8:3, 7, 8, 11, 13. See BREAK OFF, CARRY OFF, CAST OFF.

OFFEND. Job 34:31. Brother—Pr. 18: 19. Jesus, At—Mt. 13:57; 15:12; Mk. 6:3. Because of—Mt. 26:31, 33; Mk. 14:27, 29. Pharisees are—Mt. 15:12. See STUMBLING.

OFFENDER. I Ki. 1:21; Is. 29:21; Lu. 13:4.

OFFENSE. Aaron, Of—Ex. 32:2–6. Conscience void of—Acts 24:16. Cross, Of the—Mt. 11:6; Lu. 7:23; Rom. 9:

33; I Cor. 1:23; Gal. 5:11. Gentleness allayeth—Eccl. 10:4. Gideon, Of—Ju. 8:27. Heart—I Sam. 25:31. Jeroboam, Of—I Ki. 12:26–30. Not to be given —Lu. 17:1, 2; Rom. 14:21; I Cor. 8: 13; 10:32; II Cor. 6:3; Phil. 1:10. Peter, Of—Mt. 16:23. Priests, Of— Mal. 2:8. Remedy for—Eccl. 10:4; Mt. 5:29; Mk. 9:43; Rom. 16:17. See STUMBLE, SIN. Rock of—Is. 8:14. Sons of Eli, Of—I Sam. 2:12–17. Woe be-cause of—Mt. 18:7. See STUMBLING.

OFFERINGS AND OBLATIONS: Gifts brought to God as a religious duty and privilege; Sacrificial, i. e., Brought to the altar, and Non-sacrificial, i. e., Sa-cred dues, votive and freewill-offerings.

For obligations brought to the altar, see SACRIFICE (Burnt-offering, Sin-offering, Peace-offering, Tresspass-offering, Meal-offering, Drink-offering, etc.).

Non-sacrificial offerings: In token of, Recognition of and Gratitude to God. —Gen. 4:3, 4.

First fruits: The earliest portion of the crop to be gathered in, consecrated to God.

Law of, Earliest form—Ex. 23:16, 19; 34:22, 26. Second form—Deut. 18:4. Third form—Lev. 23:10–14; Num. 18: 12–28.

Materials: Corn, wine, oil, and honey— II Chr. 31:5. All the increase—Pr. 3:9; Jer. 2:3; Ez. 20:40; 44:30; 48:14.

Allusions in history—Deut. 26:10; II Ki. 4:42; Neh. 10:35, 37; 12:44; 13:31.

Figurative: First fruits of the Spirit— Rom. 8:23; Jas. 1:18; Rev. 14:4. First converts to Christ—Rom. 16:5; I Cor. 16:15. Christ as subject to death and resurrection—I Cor. 15:20, 23.

Firstlings: First born of domestic animals, brought to God—Gen. 4:4; Ex. 13:12; Lev. 27:26. At the sanctuary —Deut. 12:6, 7; 14:23. Unclean, to be redeemed—Ex. 13:13; 34:20; Lev. 27:27; Num. 18:15. Not to be made source of gain—Deut. 15:19.

First-born sons under the same law. Tribe of Levi redeems them—Num. 3:41.

Allusions in history—Neh. 10:36.

Tithes: One-tenth of gain bestowed to the ministry of religion.

Pre-mosaic practice: Abraham's tithe to Melchizedek—Gen. 14:20; Heb. 7: 6–10. Jacob's promise to God—Gen. 28:22.

Mosaic law of tithes: Earliest form: Tenth of land crop brought to the sanctuary, and there consumed by offerer and priest—Deut. 14:22–29. Second form: Tenth of land crop, means of support of Levites—Num. 18:24–28. Third form: Tenth of crop and of increase of herds or flocks— Lev. 27:32–33; II Chr. 31:5–12.

Allusions in history—Neh. 10:37, 38; 12:44; 13:5. By prophets—Amos 4:4; Mal. 3:8, 10.

Pharisees' punctiliousness about tithes —Mt. 23:23; Lu. 11:42; 18:12. See TITHES.

Showbread.—Twelve loaves of unleav-ened bread presented at the sanctuary —Lev. 24:5 f.; Ex. 25:30; 35:13; 39: 36; II Chr. 2:4. ''Continual bread'' —Num. 4:7. On a special table— Num. 4:7; I Ki. 7:48; II Chr. 4:19; Heb. 9:2. Renewed each week—Lev. 24:8. To represent the twelve tribes of Israel—Lev. 24:8.

To be eaten by the priests only—I Sam. 21:2 f.; Mt. 12:4.

Maintained by special tax—Neh. 10:32.

Wood-offering.—Neh. 10:34; 13:31. See SACRIFICE.

OFFICE. Another take—Acts 1:20. Bishop, Of—I Tim. 3:1. Cast lots for —I Chr. 25:8. Like their brethren— I Chr. 26:12. Priests—Ex. 28:1, 3, 41; 29:1; 30:30; 31:10; 35:19; 39:41; 40: 13, 15; Lev. 7:35; 16:32; Num. 3:3, 4; Deut. 10:6; I Chr. 6:10; 24:2; II Chr. 11:14; Lu. 1:8. Restore thee unto— Gen. 40:13.

OFFICER. II Chr. 26:11. Chief—Jer. 20:1; 39:13. Took an—Jer. 52:25.

OFFSPRING. Acts 17:28. As grass— Job 5:25. David, Of—Rev. 22:16. Vipers, Of—Mt. 3:7; 12:34; 23:33.

OFT. II Ki. 4:8; II Chr. 12:11; Ps. 78:4.

OFTEN. Is. 28:19; Jer. 20:8. As ye eat this bread—I Cor. 11:26. See LORD'S SUPPER. Reproved—Pr. 29:1. See REPROOF. Would I have gathered you—Mt. 23:37.

OFT-TIMES. Mt. 17:15.

OG, ŏg. **King of Bashan.**—Num. 32:33; Ps. 135:11; 136:20. Smitten by Moses —Deut. 1:4; 29:7; 31:4. Delivered unto Israelites—Deut. 3:1, 3, 4, 10, 11, 13; 4:47. Utterly destroyed—Josh. 2:10; 9:10. Kingdom of—Deut. 1:4, 10, 13; 4:47; Josh. 12:4; 13:12, 30, 31; I Ki. 4:19; Neh. 9:22.

OHAD, ō'hăd. **Son of Simeon.**—Gen. 46:10; Ex. 6:15.

OHEL, ō'hel. **Son of Zerubbabel.**—I Chr. 3:20.

OHOLAH, o-hō'lah. **Symbolic name for Samaria and the ten tribes.**—Ez. 23:4, 5, 36, 44.

OHOLIAB, o-hō'li-ab. **A Danite in time of Moses.**—Ex. 31:6; 35:34; 36:1, 2, 23.

OHOLIBAMAH, o-hŏl'i-ba-mah. (1) **Wife of Esau, grand-daughter of Gideon.**—Gen. 36:2, 5, 14, 18, 25. (2) **A duke of Edom.**—Gen. 36:41; I Chr. 1:52.

OILS: Kinds of.—Olive, beaten and used for light—Ex. 27:20; 30:24; 35: 8, 14, 28; 39:37; Lev. 24:2; Num. 4: 16; Mt. 25:3, 4, 8. Fresh—Num. 11:8; Ps. 92:10. Myrrh—Esth. 2:12.

Made.—Job 24:11.

Out of flinty rock.—Deut. 32:13.

Measurements. — Hin of — Ex. 30:24. Fourth part of—Num. 15:4; 28:5. Third part of—Num. 15:6. Half of— Num. 15:9. Log—Lev. 14:10, 12, 15, 21, 24.

Kept in vessels.—Num. 4:9. Horn—I Sam. 16:1, 13; I Ki. 1:39. Cruse—I Ki. 17:12, 14, 16. Pot—II Ki. 4:2. Vial —II Ki. 9:3.

Abundance of.—Deut. 7:13; 11:14; I Chr. 12:40; 27:28; II Chr. 2:10, 15; 11:11; 32:28; Ezra 7:22; Jer. 41:8; Mic. 6:7.

Given to.—Best of, to Aaron—Num. 18: 12. People of Tyre and Sidon—Ezra 3:7. Jews—Ezra 6:9. Jehovah's wife = Israel—Hos. 2:5, 8.

Use of.—Holy anointing oil—Ex. 30:25, 31; 31:11; 35:8, 15, 28; Lev. 8:2, 12, 30. Of Jehovah—Lev. 10:7. Anointed with: *Aaron*—Ex. 29:7, 21. *Tabernacle* —Ex. 40:9; Lev. 8:10. *High priest*— Num. 35:25. *Saul*—I Sam. 10:1. *David* —I Sam. 16:13; Ps. 89:20. *Solomon*— I Ki. 1:39. *Jehu*—II Ki. 9:6. *David*— Ps. 23:5; 89:20. *With fresh oil*—Ps.

92:10. Sick—Mk. 6:13; Jas. 5:14. Not anointed with—Deut. 28:40; II Sam. 1:21; 14:2; Lu. 7:46. Used in offerings: Meal-offerings, Unleavened cakes and head, mingled and anointed with —Ex. 29:2. Upon flour—Lev. 2:1, 2, 4–7, 15, 16; 6:15. Made with—Lev. 6: 21. Mingled with—Lev. 7:10, 12; 9:4; Num. 6:15; 7:13, 19, 25, 31, 37, 43, 49, 55, 61, 67, 73, 79; 8:8; 28:9, 13, 20, 28; Ez. 45:14, 24, 25; 46:5, 7, 11, 14, 15. Not used in sin-offering—Lev. 5:11. Poured—Jacob poured oil on the stone he used for a pillow—Gen. 28:18. On man's wounds—Lu. 10:34. Dip in— Deut. 32:24.

Merchandise of.—Rev. 18:13. Sold to pay debt—II Ki. 4:7. Traded—Ez. 27:17. Carried into Egypt—Hos. 12:1. Owed a hundred measures of—Lu. 16:6.

Laws concerning.—Tithes of—Deut. 12: 17; 14:23. First fruits of, given to Jehovah—Deut. 18:4; II Chr. 31:5; Neh. 10:37, 39. For priests—Neh. 13: 5, 12. Touching of—Hag. 2:12. Consequence of disobedience: None to be left for them—Deut. 28:51. Oil languisheth—Joel 1:10. Shall not anoint with—Mic. 6:15. Drought upon—Hag. 1:11.

Prophecies concerning.—He that loveth wine and oil—Pr. 21:17. Oil-tree in wilderness—Is. 41:19. Shall flow to the oil—Jer. 31:12. The earth shall answer—Hos. 2:22. Promise of—Joel 2:19, 24. Hurt thou not—Rev. 6:6.

Figurative.—Job 29:6; Ps. 55:21; 109: 18; Pr. 5:3; Ez. 16:9, 13, 18, 19; 32:14. Gladness—Ps. 45:7; Heb. 1:9. Of joy —Is. 61:3. Golden—Zech. 4:12.

OINTMENT. *Anointed the Lord with —John 11:2. Cruse of—Mk. 14:3; Lu. 7:37. Name is as—Song of Sol. 1:3. Pot of—Job 41:31. Pound of—John 12:3. Precious—Mt. 26:7. Why not sold—John 12:5. See OIL, ANOINT.

OLD AGE. See AGE.

OLD COVENANT. See COVENANTS.

OLD TESTAMENT. See OUTLINE STUDIES IN THE BOOKS, INCIDENTS AND QUOTATIONS FROM OLD TESTAMENT, WORD OF GOD.

OLIVE. Native of Syria.

Grows wild.—Ju. 9:8–9; Neh. 8:15; Rom. 11:17–24.

Prolific in Canaan.—Deut. 6:11; 8:8; 28:40; Josh. 24:13; II Ki. 18:32; Neh. 9:25.

Olive-yards.—Ju. 15:5; I Sam. 8:14; I Chr. 27:28; II Ki. 5:26.

Cultivation of.—By kings—I Sam. 8:14; I Chr. 27:28. To lie fallow the seventh year—Ex. 23:11.

Used for furniture of temple.—Cherubim—I Ki. 6:23. Doors—I Ki. 6:23, 31, 32. Posts—I Ki. 6:33.

Other uses.—Oil of, in sanctuary—Ex. 27:20; 30:24; Lev. 24:2. For booths at feasts—Neh. 8:15. As exchange for labor—II Chr. 2:10. For sojourner and poor—Ex. 23:11; Deut. 24:20. As an allegory—Ju. 9:8–9.

Injuries to.—By wind—Job 15:33. By locusts—Amos 4:9. By Samson's raid —Ju. 15:5.

Emblematical of.—Prosperity—Ps. 52: 8; 128:3; Jer. 11:16; Hos. 14:6. Peace —Gen. 8:11. Children—Ps. 128:3. Punishment—Job 15:33; Hab. 3:17; Mic. 6:15; Hag. 2:19. Of word of Jehovah—Zech. 4:3–6. Of forlorn Damascus—Is. 17:6. Of sinful nations— Is. 24:13. Of consistency—Jas. 2:11. Of the witnesses—Rev. 11:3–4. Of Jewish delinquency—Rom. 11:17–24.

OLYMPAS, o-lўm'pas. **A disciple in Rome.**—Rom. 16:15.

OMAR, ō'mar. **Grandson of Esau.**— Gen. 36:11, 15; I Chr. 1:36.

OMEGA, o-mē'ga. **A title given to Jesus.**—Rev. 1:8; 21:6; 22:13.

OMER. See MEASURES.

OMRI, ŏm'ri. (1) **Father of Ahab.**—I Ki. 16:16–30; II Ki. 8:26; II Chr. 22: 2; Mic. 6:16.

(2) **A descendant of Judah.**—I Chr. 9:4.

(3) **A grandson of Benjamin.**—I Chr. 7:8.

(4) **A ruler of Issachar under David.**— I Chr. 27:18.

ON. (1) **Capital of Lower Egypt. Potiphera, priest of**—Gen. 41:45; 46:20.

(2) **A Reubenite, son of Peleth.**—Num. 16:1. See AVEN—Ez. 30:17; BETH-SHEMESH—Jer. 43:13.

ONAM, ō'nam. (1) **Son of Jerahmeel.** —I Chr. 2:26, 28.

(2) **Son of Shobal.**—Gen. 36:23; I Chr. 1:40.

ONAN, ō'nan. **Son of Judah.**—Gen. 38: 4, 8, 9; 46:12.

ONE. Mk. 2:7. Be born anew—John 3:3. Flesh—Gen. 2:24. Lord, faith, baptism—Eph. 4:5. Mighty of Jacob —Gen. 49:24; Ps. 132:2. That asketh —Lu. 6:30. That feared God—Job 1:1. There is, who is good—Mt. 19:17. Thing I know—John 9:25. Thing is needful—Lu. 10:42. Thing thou lackest—Mk. 10:21.

ONESIMUS, o-nĕs'i-mus. **A slave**—Col. 4:9; Philemon 10.

ONION. Num. 11:5.

ONLY. Be ye doers of the word and not hearers—Jas. 1:22. Begotten Son— Heb. 11:17. Believe me—Lu. 8:50. Cup of cold water—Mt. 10:42. Evil— Gen. 6:5. He is left—Gen. 42:38. He is my rock—Ps. 62:2. Hoped in Christ —I Cor. 15:19. Jesus—Mt. 17:8; Mk. 9:8. Leaves—Mt. 21:19. Man doth not live by bread—Deut. 8:3. Not by faith—Jas. 2:24. Not my feet—John 13:9. Not to me—II Tim. 4:8. Serve God—Mt. 4:10; Lu. 4:8. Take now thy son—Gen. 22:2.

ONO, ō'no. (1) **A city in Benjamin.**— I Chr. 8:12; Ezra 2:23; Neh. 7:37; 11:35.

(2) **A plain or valley.**—Neh. 6:2.

ONSET. Acts 14:5.

ONWARD. Is. 8:8; 18:7; II John 9.

ONYX. Probably the same as *onycha*, an ingredient of the sacred perfume used as incense—Ex. 30:34. Resembled agate.

Found in Arabia (Havilah). Gen. 2:12. A jewel—Job 28:16; Ez. 28:13.

Among the offerings.—Ex. 25:7; 35:5, 9. Chosen for memorial—Ex. 28:9, 10, 12; 39:6, 7. One of the jewels chosen for the breastplate and Ephod—Ex. 25:7; 35:9; 39:13.

Used in Solomon's temple.—I Chr. 29:2.

The fifth foundation of the New Jerusalem (sardonyx).—Rev. 21:20.

OPEN. Blind eyes—Is. 42:7. Blossom —Song of Sol. 7:12. Continually—Is. 28:24; 60:11. Door is—I Cor. 16:9. Eyes—Ps. 119:18. Firmament—Gen. 1:20. Gate, Of—Ez. 40:11. Hand— Ps. 104:28. Heavens—Acts 7:56. Knock

and it shall be—Mt. 7:7; Lu. 11:9.
Lips—Ps. 51:15; Pr. 20:19. Lord,
Open to us—Mt. 25:11. Mind—Lu.
24:45. Mouth—Acts 8:32. Prison
doors—Acts 5:19. Rebuke—Pr. 27:5.
Scriptures—Lu. 24:32. Treasures—
Mt. 2:11. Womb, The—See FIRST-
BORN. Words, Of—Ps. 119:130.

OPENLY. Enter city—Mk. 1:45. Known
—John 7:4. Saw in a vision—Acts
10:3. Set forth—Gal. 3:1. Showed—
Ps. 98:2. Spake—Mk. 8:32; John 7:
13; 18:20. Speaketh—John 7:26.
Walked among Jews—John 11:54.

OPERATION. Of hands—Ps. 28:5; Is.
5:12. See HANDS, WORK OF.

OPHEL, ō′phel. **Part of Jerusalem.—**
II Chr. 27:3; 33:14; Neh. 3:26, 27; 11:
21.

OPHIR, ō′phir. **A place in Arabia.—**
I Ki. 9:28; 10:11; 22:48; I Chr. 29:4;
II Chr. 8:18; 9:10; Job 22:24; 28:16;
Ps. 45:9; Is. 13:12.

OPHNI, ŏph′nī. **A place in Benjamin.—**
Josh. 18:24.

OPHRAH, ŏph′rah. (1) **A city in Manasseh.—**Ju. 6:11, 24; 8:27, 32; 9:5.
(2) **A city in Benjamin.—**Josh. 18:23;
I Sam. 13:17.

OPINION. Job 32:6.

OPPORTUNITY. Have—I Cor. 16:12;
Gal. 6:1; Heb. 11:15. Lacked—Phil.
4:10. To deliver—Mt. 26:16; Lu. 22:
6. To make defence—Acts 25:16.

OPPOSITION. Acts 18:6. Correcting
—II Tim. 2:25. Knowledge, Of—I
Tim. 6:20.

OPPOSITE. Ex. 26:5; 36:12.

OPPRESSION. Job 6:23; 35:9; Ps. 9:9,
10; 10:18; Is. 5:7; 30:12; 59:13; Mic.
2:2.

Oppression forbidden.—Sojourner—Ex.
22:21; Lev. 19:33, 39; Deut. 1:16; 27:
19; Ez. 22:7; Jer. 7:6; Zech. 7:10; Mal.
3:5. The widow and the fatherless—
Deut. 27:19; Job 24:9; Is. 10:2; Jer.
7:6; Mal. 3:5; Ez. 22:7; Zech. 7:10.
See WIDOW. Orphan—Lam. 5:3. The
poor—Job 24:9; Ps. 12:5; Pr. 14:31;
17:5; 22:16, 22; 30:14; Eccl. 5:8; Is.
3:14, 15; 10:1, 2; Ez. 18:12; Amos 8:
4; Jas. 2:6. See POOR. Servants—
Deut. 23:16; Mal. 3:5; Mt. 18:23-35;
Jas. 5:4. See SERVANTS, USURY.

Oppression punished.—Ps. 72:14; Pr.
22:16; Mal. 3:5.

Examples.—Pharaoh—Ex. 5:7. See PHA-
RAOH. Israel—Deut. 4:1. Nebuchadrezzar—Dan. 2:5. The unmerciful
servant—Mt. 18:28.

ORACLE. Of God—II Sam. 16:23; Ps.
28:2; Rom. 3:2; Heb. 5:12; I Pet. 4:11.
A part of the temple—I Ki. 6:5, 16,
19-23, 31; 7:49; 8:6, 8; II Chr. 3:16;
4:20; 5:7, 9. Living oracles—Acts 7:
38. See WORD OF GOD.

ORATION. Acts 12:21. See JESUS′
TEACHING, PAUL′S SPEECHES.

ORATOR. Acts 24:1.

ORCHARD. Song of Sol. 4:13.

ORDAIN. Angels, By—Acts 7:53. Eter-
nal life, To—Acts 13:48. God, Of—
Acts 10:42; 17:31; Rom. 13:1. Mount
Sinai, In—Num. 28:6. Peace—Is. 26:
12. To give thanks—I Chr. 16:7. See
ELECTION, FOREORDINATION, PURPOSE.

ORDER, *n.* After the—Ezra 3:10. Decently and in—I Cor. 14:40. In—Ps.
119:38; II Cor. 11:32. Laid in—Gen.
22:9. Set in—Job 37:19; Ps. 40:5; Tit.
1:5.

ORDER, *v.* I Chr. 24:19. Prayer—Ps.
5:3. Way aright—Ps. 50:23.

ORDERLY. Acts 21:24; I Tim. 3:2.

ORDINANCES (authoritative and established rites).

Ordinances of Israel.—Ex. 15:25; Num.
15:15, 16; Ps. 122:4. The passover—
Ex. 12:14, 24, 43; 13:8-10; Num. 9:14;
II Chr. 35:13. Trumpet blowing—Lev.
23:24; Num. 10:1-10; Ps. 81:3-5. Concerning building a house for Jehovah
—II Chr. 2:4. Ordinance of mourning
—II Chr. 35:25. Putting away false
gods—Josh. 24:23-25. Jehovah′s ordinances are compulsory—Lev. 18:4-5;
II Chr. 33:8.

The first covenant had ordinances.—
Num. 9:3, 14; Lev. 18:4-5; Heb. 9:
1-5.

These ordinances imposed for a time.—
Jer. 31:31-34; Heb. 9:10.

Ordinances blotted out.—Eph. 2:14-16;
Col. 2:14-15. Unduly depended upon
—Is. 1:10-14; Mic. 6:6-8.

**Folly of turning back to Jewish ordi-
nances.—**Gal. 5:1-14; 6:12-15; Eph. 2:
14-22; Col. 2:20-23; 3:1-4; Heb. 7:
11-19.

Ordinances of David.—Concerning the courses of priests and Levites—II Chr. 8:14. Concerning going to battle —I Sam. 30:22–25.

Teaching on ordinances.—Ps. 19:9; 119:13, 30, 39, 43, 62, 91, 102, 106, 149, 156, 160, 164, 175.

Ordinances of the Jews.—Concerning the altar—Ez. 43:18; 46:14. Failure to keep ordinances—Ez. 11:9–12; Mal. 3:13–15.

Walketh faithfully in the ordinances.— Neh. 12:28–33; Is. 58:2; Lu. 1:6.

Christian ordinances.—Baptism—Mt. 3: 15; 28:19–20; Mk. 16:16; Acts 2:38–39; Rom. 6:3–6. The Lord's Supper— Mt. 26:26–29; Mk. 14:22–25; Lu. 22: 14–20; I Cor. 11:23–26.

Civil ordinances.—Must submit—Rom. 13:2; I Pet. 2:13.

Ordinances of the heavens.—Job 38:33; Ps. 8:3–4; 19:1–4; Jer. 31:35–36; 33: 25. See STATUTES, LAW, COVENANTS.

ORDINARY. Ez. 16:27.

ORDINATION. Acts 6:6; 14:23; I Tim. 2:7; 3:1–13; 4:14; 5:22; II Tim. 2:2; Tit. 1:6–9. See FOREORDINATION, MINISTERS.

OREB, ō'reb. (1) **A prince of Midian slain by the Ephraimites at the Jordan.**—Ju. 7:25; 8:3; Ps. 83:11.

(2) **Rock where (1) was slain.**—Ju. 7: 25; Is. 10:26.

OREN, ō'ren. **Son of Jerahmeel.**—I Chr. 2:25.

ORGAN. See MUSIC.

ORION, o-rī'on. Job 9:9.

ORNAMENTS. See JEWELS, WOMEN.

ORNAN, ôr'nan. I Chr. 21:15–25; II Chr. 3:1. See ARAUNAH.

ORPHANS: The fatherless.—The wicked rob—Is. 10:2. Cast lots upon—Job 6:27. Vex—Ez. 22:7. Oppress—Job 22:9; 24:3. Murder—Ps. 94:6. Judge not for—Is. 1:17, 23; Jer. 5:28. A curse on those who oppress—Deut. 27:19. Promises with respect to— Jer. 49:11. Shall rejoice—Deut. 16: 11, 14.

God will be a Father of.—Ps. 68:5. Be a helper of—Deut. 26:12, 13; Ps. 10: 14, 18; 146:9; Is. 9:17. Hear the cry of—Ex. 22:23, 24. Execute the judgment of—Deut. 10:18; Ps. 10:18. Punish those who oppress—Ex. 22:24; Is.

10:1–3; Mal. 3:5. Punish those who judge not for—Jer. 5:28.

Disciples not left as orphans by Jesus.— John 14:18.

Orphans and fatherless.—Lam. 5:3.

Exemplified. — Lot — Gen. 11:27, 28. Daughter of Zelophehad—Num. 27: 1–5. Jotham—Ju. 9:16–21. Mephibosheth—II Sam. 9:3. Joash—II Ki. 11:1–12. Esther—Esth. 2:7.

Miscellaneous.—Visit in affliction—Jas. 1:27. Judge—Ps. 82:3. Let them share in our blessings—Deut. 14:29. Defend—Is. 1:17. Wrong not in judgment—Deut. 24:17, 19. Defraud not—Pr. 23:10. Afflict not—Ex. 22: 22. Oppress not—Zech. 7:10. Do no violence to—Jer. 22:3. Blessedness of taking care of—Deut. 14:29; Job 29: 12, 13; Jer. 7:6, 7. See FRATERNITY, LOVE.

OSTENTATION. See PRIDE.

OSTRICH. Lev. 11:16; Deut. 14:15; Is. 43:20. A court for—Is. 34:13. Companion to—Job 30:29. Dwell there— Is. 13:29; Jer. 50:39. Like—Mic. 1:8. Wilderness, In—Lam. 4:3. Wings of —Job 39:13.

OTHER. Cheek—Mt. 5:39; Lu. 6:29. Climbeth up some other way—John 10:1. Fell into good ground—Mk. 4:8; Lu. 8:8. Forgiving each—Eph. 4:32. Friends with each—Lu. 23:12. Gospel— II Cor. 11:4; Gal.. 1:7, 8; Rev. 22:18, 19. Hate the one and love the—Mt. 6:24. He saved—Mt. 27:42; Mk. 15: 31; Lu. 23:35. Passed by on—Lu. 16: 31, 32. Sheep—John 10:16. Teach— II Tim. 2:2. See FRATERNITY.

OTHNI, ŏth'ni. **Son of Shemaiah.**—I Chr. 26:7.

OTHNIEL, ŏth'ni-el. Judge for forty years. Brother of Caleb—Josh. 15:17; Ju. 1:73; 3:9, 11; I Chr. 4:13; 27:15.

OUGHT TO. I Chr. 12:32; Mt. 23:33. Lay down lives—I John 3:16. Love one another—I John 4:11. Pray—Lu. 18:1; Rom. 8:26. Walk—I John 2:6. Worship — John 4:20. See BOUND, DUTY.

OUT-CAST. See CAST OUT.

OUT-CRY. See CRY.

OUTER. Court—Ex. 40:17; 42:1; Ez. 10:5. Darkness—Mt. 8:12; 22:13; 25:

30. See DARKNESS. Garment — Job 41:13.

OUTERMOST. Camp, Part of—Ju. 7: 17, 19.

OUTGOING—Morning and evening, Of —Ps. 65:8.

OUTLIVE. Joshua—Josh. 24:31; Ju. 2: 7. See LIFE.

OUTRAN. Peter—John 20:4.

OUTSIDE. I Ki. 7:9. Cup, Of—Mt. 23: 25; Lu. 11:39. House, Of—Ez. 40:5.

OUTSTRETCHED. Arm—Deut. 26:8; Jer. 27:5. Hand—Jer. 21:5. See HAND, LIBERALITY.

OUTWARD. Adorning—I Pet. 3:3. Appearance—I Sam. 16:7. Court—Esth. 6:4. Man—II Cor. 4:16.

OUTWARDLY. Appear beautiful—Mt. 23:27. A Jew—Rom. 2:28.

OUTWEIGH. Eccl. 10:1.

OVEN. Ex. 8:3; Lev. 11:25. Baken in —Lev. 2:4; 7:9; 26:26. Black like— Lam. 5:10. Cast into—Mt. 6:30; Lu. 12:28. Heated by the baker—Hos. 7: 4. Hot as an—Hos. 7:7. Like—Hos. 7:6. See FURNACE.

OVERBOARD. Acts 27:43.

OVERCHARGE. Hearts—Lu. 21:34.

OVERCOME. Evil, Of — Rom. 12:21. Evil one—I John 2:13, 14. He that— Rev. 2:11, 26; 3:5; 21:7. Lamb shall —Rev. 17:14. To him that—Rev. 2:7, 17. Victory that hath—I John 5:4. Wine hath—Jer. 23:9. World—John 16:33; I John 5:4, 5.

OVERFLOW. Deut. 11:4; Is. 43:2. Anger, Of—Job 40:11. Banks—Josh. 3: 15; 1 Chr. 12:15. Joy, With—II Cor. 7:4. Righteousness, With—Is. 10:22. River—Job 40:23. Scourge — Is. 28: 15, 18. Stream—Ps. 78:20; Is. 66:12. Vats shall—Pr. 3:10. Waters—Ps. 32: 6; Is. 28:2. Wickedness, Of—Jas. 1: 21. Wine, With—Joel. 2:24.

OVERLOOK. Acts 17:30. See GOD, MERCY OF.

OVERSEER. Number of—II Chr. 2:18. Joseph—Gen. 39:4, 5. Uzzi—Neh. 11: 22. Jezrahiah—Neh. 12:42. Apostles —Acts 20:28.

Works of.—II Chr. 34:12, 13, 17.

Without.—Pr. 6:7.

OVERSHADOW. Cloud—Mt. 17:5; Mk. 9:7; Lu. 9:34. Mercy-seat—Heb. 9:5.

Peter's shadow might — Acts 5:15. Power—Lu. 1:35. See SHADOW.

OVERSIGHT. Gen. 42:12. Exercising —I Pet. 5:2. Gates, Of—I Chr. 9:23. Having—Ez. 44:11. House of Jehovah, Of—II Ki. 12:11; 22:5, 9; II Chr. 34:10. Work, Of—Ez. 3:8.

OVERTAKE. Gen. 44:4. Archers—I Sam. 31:3. Darkness — John 12:35. Enemies—Ps. 18:37. Evil—Amos 9:10. Fathers, Your—Zech. 1:6. Iniquities —Ps. 40:12. Plowman, The reaper— Amos 9:13. Righteousness—Is. 59:9. Terrors—Job 27:20. Thief, As a — I Thess. 5:4. Trespass, In a—Gal. 6:1. See SIN, TEMPTATION.

OVERTHROW. Gen. 19:21; Jer. 1:10; Hos. 4:14; Acts 5:38, 39. Anger, In— Deut. 29:35. Cities—Gen. 19:25, 29. Egyptians—Ex. 14:27. Houses—Tit. 1:11. Kings and people—Ezra 6:12. Mighty—Job 12:19. Nineveh shall be —Jonah 3:4. Palaces—Is. 23:13. Sinner—Pr. 13:6. Sodom and Gomorrah —Is. 13:19; Jer. 50:40; Amos 4:11. Tables of money-changers—Mt. 21:12; Mk. 11:15; John 2:15. Wicked are— Pr. 21:12; 24:16. Work—Rom. 14:20. Wrongfully—Ps. 119:78.

OVERTURN. Anger, In—Job 9:5. Earth —Job 12:15. I will—Ez. 21:27. Night, In the—Job 34:25.

OVERWHELM. Dan. 11:22. Anger is— Pr. 27:4. Darkness shall—Ps. 139:11. Enemies—Ps. 78:53. Heart is—Ps. 61: 2. Horror hath—Ps. 55:5. Spirit is— Ps. 77:3; 142:3; 143:4. Waterflood— Ps. 65:15.

OWE. Lu. 7:41. How much—Lu. 16:5, 7. No man anything—Rom. 13:8. Pay what thou—Mt. 18:28. Ten thousand talents—Mt. 18:24. Thine own self— Philemon 19. See DEBT.

OWL. Dwell therein—Is. 34:11. Horned —Lev. 11:18. Little and great—Lev. 11:17; Deut. 14:16. Waste places, Of —Ps. 102:6.

OWN. I Chr. 29:14; Mt. 20:15; John 10:4. Bitterness—Pr. 14:10. Came unto his—John 1:11. Destruction — II Pet. 3:16. Gift from God—I Cor. 7:7. I know mine—John 10:14. God, Our —Ps. 67:6. Hand—Lev. 14:26. Image —Gen. 1:27. Land not his—Heb. 11: 9. Language—Acts 2:6. Lips—Ps. 12:

4. Loved his—John 13:1. Possession —Ex. 19:5; Ps. 135:4. Sheep are not —John 10:12. Thou hast thine—Mt. 25:25. Times—I Tim. 2:6. Ye are not your—I Cor. 6:19.

OWNER. Lu. 19:33. Advantage of— Eccl. 5:11. Ox, Of—Ex. 21:28. Taketh life of—Pr. 1:19.

OXEN. See CATTLE.

OZEM, ō'zem. (1) **Brother David.**—I Chr. 2:15.

(2) **Son of Jerahmeel.**—I Chr. 2:25.

OZNI, ŏz'ni. **Son of Gad.**—Num. 26:16.

PAARAI, pā'a-rāi. **One of David's mighty men.**—II Sam. 23:35.

PACE. Gen. 33:14; II Sam. 6:13.

PACIFY. Esth. 2:1; 7:10; Pr. 16:14; 21:14.

PADDAN, pād'dan. Gen. 48:7. See PAD-DAN-ARAM.

PADDAN-ARAM, pād'dan-ā'ram. **Plains of Mesopotamia.**—Gen. 25:20; 28:5–7; 31:18; 33:18; 35:9, 26; 46:15. See MESOPOTAMIA.

PADON, pā'don. **Ancestor of some who returned with Zerubbabel.** — Ezra 2: 44; Neh. 7:47.

PAGIEL, pā'gi-el. **An Asherite chosen to number the people.**—Num. 1:13; 2:27; 7:72, 77; 10:26.

PAHATH-MOAB, pā-hăth-mō'ab. (1) **Ancestor of some who returned with Zerubbabel.**—Ezra 2:6; 10:30; Neh. 3:11; 7:11.

(2) **Ancestor of some who returned with Ezra.**—Ezra 8:4.

(3) **Name of a family.**—Neh. 10:14.

PAI, pā'i. **A city in Edom**—I Chr. 1:50.

PAID. See PAY, REDEMPTION, VOWS.

PAIN: Physical. — Of women—Gen. 3: 16; I Sam. 4:19; Is. 21:3; 26:17, 18; 66:7; Jer. 22:23; Rev. 12:2. Job—Job 6:10 14:22. See TRAVAIL.

Mental.—Of David—Ps. 73:16. Jeremi-ah—Jer. 4:19. Caused by a report—Is. 23:5.

Spiritual.—Is. 21:3; Jer. 12:13; 30:15; 45:3. David—Ps. 55:4; 73:15. Paul— Rom. 9:2. Babylon—Is. 13:8; Jer. 51: 8. Zion—Mic. 4:10. Creation—Rom. 8:22. Incurable — Jer. 15:18; 30:15. Wicked — Job 15:20; Ps. 48:6; Rev. 16:11. Sheol—Ps. 116:3.

Chastened with.—Job 33:19.

No pain in heaven.—Rev. 21:4.

PAINTING. Faces and eyes, Of—II Ki. 9:30; Jer. 4:30; Ez. 23:40. See WOM-EN. Rooms, Of—Jer. 22:14.

PAIR. Shoes, Of—Amos 2:6; 8:6. Tur-tledoves, Of—Lu. 2:24. See MALE AND FEMALE.

PALACES: Mentioned. — Of kings — I Ki. 16:18; II Ki. 15:25; Ezra 4:14; Ps. 45:15; Dan. 1:4; 5:5; 6:18; Pr. 30:28. Of Ahab—I Ki. 21:1. Nebu-chadrezzar—Dan. 4:4. Of Zion — Ps. 48:3, 13; Lam. 2:5, 7; Mic. 5:5. Of Solomon—I Ki. 7:1–12. Of Jacob— Amos 6:8. Of Babylon—II Ki. 20:18; Dan. 4:29; 5:5; 6:18; Is. 39:7. At Shushan—Neh. 1:1; Esth. 1:2, 5; 7:7; 8:14; 9:6, 11, 12; Dan. 8:2. Of stran-gers—Is. 25:2. In Media—Ez. 6:2. Of Israel—Ez. 19:7; Hos. 8:14. Of Jeru-salem — Ps. 122:7; Jer. 6:5; 17:27; Amos 2:5. For Jehovah—I Chr. 29:1, 19; II Chr. 9:11. Of the Chaldeans— Is. 23:13. Of Edom—Is. 34:13. Of. Ben-hadad—Jer. 49:27; Amos. 1:4. Of Gaza—Amos 1:7. Of Tyre—Amos 1: 10. Of Bozrah—Amos 1:12. Of Rab-bah—Amos 1:14. Of Kerioth—Amos 2:2. Of Ashdod—Amos 3:1.

Kinds of.—Of ivory—I Ki. 22:39; Ps. 45:8; Amos 3:15. Garden-house—II Ki. 9:27. Summer-house—Amos 3:15. Winter-house — Amos 3:15. Castle— Neh. 2:8; 7:2. Pleasant—Is. 13:22.

Contents of.—I Ki. 15:18; Ez. 6:2.

Divisions of.—Courts—Mt. 26:3, 58, 69; Mk. 14:54, 66; John 18:15.

Prætorians guard.—Phil. 1:13.

Prophecies concerning.—Shall be inhab-ited—Jer. 30:18. Tents of—Dan. 11: 45. Palace dissolved—Nah. 2:6. Shall be forsaken—Is. 32:14. Thorns and thistles shall come up in—Is. 34:13. Destruction of—II Chr. 36:19; Jer. 6: 5; 9:21; 17:27; 49:27; Lam. 2:5, 7; Amos 1:4, 10, 12, 14; 2:2, 5; 3:9, 10, 11.

PALAL, pā'lal. **One who helped to re-pair the wall.**—Neh. 3:25.

PALANQUIN. Song of Sol. 3:9.

PALATE. Job 12:11; 34:3.

PALE. Become—Is. 29:22; Jer. 30:6; Joel 2:6; Nah. 2:10.

PALLU, păl'lu. **Son of Reuben.**—Gen. 46:9; Ex. 6:14; Num. 26:5, 8; I Chr. 5:3.

PALM. II Ki. 9:35; Is. 49:16; Dan. 10: 10. Cut—I Sam. 5:4. Left hand, Of— Lu. 14:15. Smote with — Mt. 26:67. See HAND.

PALM BRANCH. Lev. 23:40; Neh. 8: 15; Is. 9:14; 19:15; John 12:13; Rev. 7:9. See BRANCHES.

PALMER WORM. Joel 1:4; 2:25; Amos 4:9.

PALM TREE. Ex. 15:27; Num. 33:9. Carved in temple—I Ki. 6:29–35; 7: 36; II Chr. 3:5; Ez. 40:16, 22, 26, 31, 34, 37; 41:18–26. City of—Deut. 34:3; Ju. 1:16; 3:13; II Chr. 28:15. Deborah, Of—Ju. 4:5. Righteous flourish like —Ps. 92:12. Stature like—Song of Sol. 7:7, 8; Jer. 10:5. Withered—Joel 1:12. See TREES.

PALSY. See DISEASE.

PALTI, păl′ti. **A Benjamite.** — Num. 13:9.

PALTIEL, păl′ti-el. (1) **Prince of Issachar.**—Num. 34:26. '

(2) **A Benjamite to whom Michal David's wife was given.**—II Sam. 3:15.

PALTITE, păl′tīte. **One of David's mighty men.**—II Sam. 23:26.

PAMPHYLIA, pam-phȳl′ia. **A province in Asia Minor.** Perga was one of its cities—Acts 2:10; 13:13; 14:24; 15: 38; 27:5.

PAN. II Sam. 13:9. Boiling—II Chr. 35:13. Baken—Lev. 2:5; 6:21; 7:9; I Chr. 9:31; 23:29. Fire, Of—Zech. 12:6. Frying—Lev. 7:9. Iron—Ez. 4:3. Offering, Used in—Lev. 2:5; 6:21; 7:9; 1 Sam. 2:14; I Chr. 9:31; 23:29; II Chr. 35:13. See FIREPANS, VESSELS.

PANEL. II Ki. 16:17.

PANGS. Ex. 15:14; Jer. 6:24. Cry out in—Is. 26:17. Death, Of—Acts 2:24. Take hold of—Is. 13:8; 21:3; Ju. 22: 23. Woman, Of—Jer. 48:41; 49:22;· 50:43; Mic. 4:9. See PAIN, SORROW.

PANT. Ps. 119:131; Is. 42:14; Jer. 14:6. Dust of the earth, After—Amos 2:7. Hart—Ps. 41:1. Heart—Is. 21:4. Soul —Ps. 42:1. See HUNGER, LONG, THIRST.

PAPER. II John 12.

PAPYRUS. Vessels of—Is. 18:2.

PARABLES IN THE OLD TESTAMENT. Trees choosing a king—Ju. 9:7–15. Ewe lamb—II Sam. 12:1–6. Woman of Tekoa—II Sam. 14:6–11. An escaped prisoner—I Ki. 20:35–40.

Vision of Micaiah—I Ki. 22:19, 23. Thistle and cedar—II Ki. 14:9. Vineyard and wild grapes — Is. 5:1–7. Plowman's methods — Is. 28:23–29. Great eagles and vine—Ez. 17:3–10. Lion's whelps—Ez. 19:2–9. Two harlots—Ez. Chap. 23. Boiling pot—Ez. 24:3–5. Cedar in Lebanon—Ez. Chap. 31. Dry bones in the valley—Ez. Ch. .37. Living waters—Ez. Ch. 47.

Parabolical narratives in the Old Testament.—Isaiah's action — Is. 20:2–4. Jeremiah dealing out wrath—Jer. 20: 2–4. The prophet dumb—Ez. 3:24–26. Siege of the city—Ez. 4:1–8. Distress during the siege—Ez. 4:9–17. Jonah's action. See *Book of Jonah* in OUTLINE STUDIES. (By Ira M. Price, Ph.D. Copyright 1900 by Thomas Nelson and Sons. Revised by Author for the Cross Reference Bible.)

PARABLES OF NEW TESTAMENT. See JESUS.

PARADISE. Caught into—II Cor. 12:4. Dwell in—Lu. 23:43. Midst of, In— Rev. 2:7. See HADES; HEAVEN, SHEOL.

PARAH, pā′rah. **A Benjamite city.—** Josh. 18:23.

PARAMOUR. Ez. 23:20.

PARAN, pā′ran. *dug out;* or, *cave district.*—Site of the Israelite encampment—Gen. 21:21; Num. 10:12; 12:16; 13:26; Deut. 33:2. David goes to Paran—I Sam. 25:1. And they came to Paran—I Ki. 11:18. And the Holy One from Mt. Paran—Hab. 3:3.

PARBAR, pär′bar. **A place west of the temple.**—I Chr. 26:18. Land, Of— Gen. 33:19; Josh. 24:32; Ruth 4:3; John 4:5.

PARCH. Lev. 2:14; Ps. 68:6; Is. 5:13. Corn—Lev. 23:14; Josh. 5:11; Ruth 2:14; I Sam. 17:17; 25:18; II Sam. 17:28. Places—Jer. 17:6. Pulse—II Sam. 17:28. See DRY, DROUGHT.

PARCHMENT. II Tim. 4:13.

PARDON. Jehovah, By—Ex. 23:21; 34: 9; Num. 14:19, 20; I Sam. 15:25; II Ki. 5:18; 24:4; Neh. 9:17; Job 7:21; Is. 40:2; 55:7; Jer. 5:1; 33:8; 50:20; Lam. 3:42; Mic. 7:18. See FORGIVENESS.

PARE.—Deut. 21:12.

PARENTS: The father.—Father was the priest of the family group—Gen.

31:53; 32:9; I Sam. 20:6. As such, Reverence due him—Ex. 21:15, 17; Mt. 15:4-6; Mk. 7:10-13.

House.—Fathers constituted elders of Hebrew communities—Ex. 3:16, 18; 4:29; 12:21; 17:5; 18:12; 24:1, 9. Ruled the household—Gen. 18:19; Pr. 3:12; 13:24; I Tim. 3:4, 5, 12; Tit. 1: 6; Heb. 12:7. Decided on marriages of children—Gen. 24:4; 28:2; Ju. 14:2. Sold daughters to bridegrooms—Ex. 21:7; Neh. 5:5.

Wives and mothers.—Wives were bought and paid for; thus legally property of husband—Gen. 29:18-30; 31:41; Ex. 20:17. Wife not a mere chattel. See SARAH, REBEKAH, ABIGAIL. Wife largely the provider—Pr. 31:10-29. Superior to concubine in that her children were preferred—Gen. 17:18-21. Law sympathetic to wife—Ex. 21:2, 12; Deut. 21:14.

Mother.—To be childless a disgrace—Gen. 30:1; I Sam. 1:5-7; Is. 4:1. To possess children a great joy—Gen. Ch. 30. Mother to be honored—Ex. 20:12; 21:15; Lev. 19:3; Mt. 15:4; 19:19; Eph. 6:2. Beloved by children —Pr. 31:28. Comforts her children—Is. 66:13.

Parents: Responsibilities of.—To maintain children—Pr. 19:14; II Cor. 12: 14. To educate—Gen. 18:19; Ex. 12: 26, 27; 13:8; Deut. 6:6, 7; Eph. 6:4. Sons depend on fathers after passing from mother's control—Pr. 1:8; 3:12; 4:1; 13:1.

Further duties of parents.—To love—Tit. 2:4. To train children up for God —Deut. 4:9; 11:19; Pr. 22:6; Is. 38: 19; Eph. 6:4. To command obedience to God—Deut. 32:46; I Chr. 28:9. To teach them God's power—Ex. 10:2; Ps. 78:4. His judgments—Joel 1:3, 4. To pity them—Ps. 103:13. To bless them—Gen. 48:15; Heb. 11:20. To provide for them—Job 42:15; II Cor. 12:14; I Tim. 5:8. To correct them—Pr. 13:24; 19:18; 23:13; 29:17; Heb. 12:7. Not to provoke them—Eph. 6: 4; Col. 3:21. Not to make unholy connections for them—Gen. 24:1-4; 28:1-2. To impress divine deeds and commands upon them—Deut. 4:9; 6:6; 11:19; 32:46; Ps. 44:2; 78:3-6.

PARK. Eccl. 2:5.

PARMASHTA, par-măsh'tà. **Son of Haman.**—Esth. 9:9.

PARMENAS, pär me-năs. **One of the first seven deacons.**—Acts 6:5.

PARNACH, pär'nak. **A man of Zebulun.**—Num. 34:25.

PAROSH, pā'rŏsh. (1) **One whose descendants returned with Ezra.**—Ezra 8:3.

(2) **One whose descendants returned with Zerubbabel.**—Ezra 2:3; Neh. 7:8.

(3) **Ancestor of some who married foreign wives.**—Ezra 10:25.

(4) **Father of Pedarah who helped to repair the wall.**—Neh. 3:25.

(5) **A family who sealed the covenant.** —Neh. 10:14.

PARSHANDATHA, par-shăn'da-thà. **Oldest son of Haman.**—Esth. 9:7.

PART, n. All parts—Acts 9:32. Chose good—Lu. 10:42. City—II Ki. 20:4. Beyond—II Cor. 10:16. Body of the —I Cor. 12:23. Inheritance, Of—Josh. 17:14. Inward—Ps. 5:9; 109: 18. Land, Of—Gen. 41:34. Multitude, Of—Mt. 21:8. Questioning on part of—John 3:25. Take—II Tim. 4:16. Wickedness. In—Rs. 5:9.

PART, v. Lev. 2:6. Asunder—Acts 15: 39. Death—Ruth 1:17. From them—Lu. 22:41; 24:51; 21:1. Garments—Ps. 22:18; Lu. 23:34. Hoof—Lev. 11: 4. See ANIMALS, UNCLEAN. Tongues—Acts 2:3. See DIVIDE, DIVISION.

PARTAKE. I Cor. 9:10; 10:21; Heb. 5:13. See FELLOWSHIP.

PARTAKER. Ps. 50:18; Heb. 10:33. Blood, In the—Mt. 23:30. Christ's sufferings, Of—I Pet. 4:13. Divine nature, Of—II Pet. 1:4. Heavenly calling—Heb. 3:1. Tribulation, In—Rev. 1:9. See FELLOWSHIP.

PARTIALITY. Job 13:8, 10; Jude 16. Condemned—Pr. 28:21; I Tim. 5:21; Jas. 2:1-9. Judgment, In—Ex. 23:3, 6; Lev. 19:15; Deut. 1:17; 16:19; Pr. 18:5; Is. 1:23; Mal. 2:9. See BRIBERY, GOD NO RESPECTER OF PERSONS, RESPECT, JUDGMENT.

PARTHIANS, pär'thi-ans. **Inhabitants of Parthia.**—Acts 2:9.

PARTING. Gift—Mic. 1:14. Way, Of the—Ez. 21:21.

PARTITION. Wall of—Eph. 2:14. See ALIENS, COVENANTS, LAW.

PARTNER. Beckoned to—Lu. 5:7. Countest me a—Philemon 17. Simon, With—Lu. 5:10. Thief, With a—Pr. 29:24. Titus is my—II Cor. 8:23.

PARTOOK. Heb. 2:14. See PARTAKE, FELLOWSHIP.

PARTRIDGE. Hunt a—I Sam. 26:20. Sitteth on eggs—Jer. 17:11.

PARUAH, pa-ru'ah. Father of one of Solomon's officers.—I Ki. 4:17.

PARVAIM, par-vā'ĭm. An unknown gold region.—II Chr. 3:6.

PASACH, pā'sak. A man of Asher.— I Chr. 7:33.

PAS-DAMMIN, păs'-dăm-min. A place in Judah—I Chr. 11:33.

PASEAH, pa-sē'ah. (1) Ancestor of some Nethinim.—Ezra 2:49; Neh. 7: 51.

(2) A descendant of Caleb son of Hur. —I Chr. 4:12.

(3) Father of Jehoiada who helped to repair the wall.—Neh. 3:6.

PASHHUR, păsh'hur. (1) A priest who helped to seal the covenant.—Neh. 10:3.

(2) Head of a family of priests in Jerusalem.—I Chr. 9:12; Ezra 2:38; 10:22; Neh. 7:41; 11:12.

(3) Governor of the house of the Lord in the time of Jeremiah.—Jer. 20: 1-6; 38:1.

(4) A prince of Judah.—Jer. 21:1; 38:1.

PASS, n. I Sam. 14:4; Is. 10:29.

PASS, v. Away—Eccl. 3:15; Is. 2:18; I Cor. 7:31; II Cor. 3:11, 13. Beauty, In—Ez. 32:19. By—Pr. 9:15; 26:10. Jericho, Through—Lu. 19:1. Jesus of Nazareth—Lu. 18:37. Knowledge— Eph. 3:19. Let this cup—Mt. 26:29. On—Gen. 18:5. Over the sea—Is. 16: 8. Through—Ex. 26:28; 36:33; Is. 8:8; Ez. 39:11; Mt. 12:43; Lu. 4:30. Understanding—Phil. 4:7.

PASSION. Col. 3:5. Flesh, Of—Gal. 5:24. Lust, Of—I Thess. 4:5. Men of like—Acts 14:15; Jas. 5:17. Sinful— Rom. 7:5. Vile—Rom. 1:26. See JESUS, SUFFERINGS OF.

PASSOVER: Institution of.—Ex. 12: 3-49; Heb. 11:28.

Placed in the law.—Ex. 23:15-18; 34: 18; Lev. 23:4-8; Num. 9:2-5; 5:13,

14; 28:16-25; Deut. 16:1-8, 16; Ps. 81:3, 5. Design of—Ex. 12:21-28.

Provision for those unclean.—Num. 9: 6-12; II Chr. 30:2-4.

For strangers.—Ex. 12:48, 49; Num. 9: 14; cf. Ez. 6:19-22.

To be observed at place designated by God.—Deut. 16:5-7. And as directed by Him—Ex. 12:8, 15-20; 13:3, 6; 23: 15; Lev. 23:6; Num. 9:11; 28:17; Deut. 16:3, 4; Mk. 14:12; Lu. 22:7; Acts 12:3; I Cor. 5:7, 8.

Observed by Joshua.—Josh. 5:10, 11. By Hezekiah—II Chr. 30:1-27. By Josiah—II Ki. 23:22, 23; II Chr. 35: 1, 18.

To be observed after returning from captivity.—Ezra 6:20; Ez. 45:21-24.

Observed by Christ.—Mt. 26:19-30; Lu. 22:15; John 2:13, 23. Christ crucified at the time of the passover—Mt. 26: 2; Mk. 14:1-2; John 18:28.

The lamb a type of Christ.—I Cor. 5:7. Pilate released a prisoner at the time of the passover—Mt. 27:15-18; Mk. 15:6; Lu. 23:16, 17; John 18:39, 40. Peter imprisoned at the time of the passover—Acts 12:3. Paul at Philippi —Acts 20:6.

Lamb a symbol of innocence.—Gen. 21: 28-30; Is. 11:6; 53:7; Acts 8:32; Lu. 10:3; I Pet. 1:19. A sin-offering— Lev. 4:32; 14:12-21, 24, 25; Num. 6: 12; 7:15, 21; 28:3-8.

Christ the lamb of God.—Is. 53:7; John 1:29, 36; I Pet. 1:19; Rev. 5:6, 12; 7: 9, 10, 14; 12:11; 14:4, 10; 15:3; 17:14; 19:7, 9; 21:9, 27; 22:3. See FEASTS.

PAST. Days of weeping—Gen. 50:4. Finding out—Job 9:10. Harvest is— Jer. 8:20. Resurrection is—II Tim. 2:18. Time—Mt. 14:15; Gal. 1:13; Col. 1:21. Tracing out—Rom. 11:33. Winter is—Song of Sol. 2:11. Wrath be—Job 14:13. Year—II Cor. 9:2. Yesterday when—Ps. 90:4.

PASTORS. And teachers—Eph. 4:11. See MINISTERS.

PASTURE. For flocks—Gen. 47:4; I Ki. 4:23; I Chr. 4:39-41; Ps. 65:13; Is. 32:14; Jer. 25:36; Joel 1:18. Of Israel—Ez. 45:15. Of the wilderness —Ps. 65:12; Joel 1:19, 20; 2:22.

Figurative.—Of Jehovah—Job 39:8. Sheep of—Ps. 74:1; 79:13; 95:7; 100:3; Jer. 23:1; Green pastures—Ps. 23:2.

Illustrative.—Lam. 1:6; Ez. 34:14, 18; Hos. 13:6.

Prophecies concerning.—Is. 30:23; 49:9. **In parable.**—John 10:9. See GRASS.

PATARA, păt′a-ra. **A city in Asia Minor.**—Acts 21:1.

PATCHED. Shoes—Josh. 9:5.

PATH: Of God.—Job 41:32; Ps. 17:5; 25:4, 10; 65:11; 77:19; 119:35; Is. 2:3; Mic. 4:2. Made paths in waters—Is. 43:16.

Of righteousness.—Ps. 23:3; Pr. 2:13, 20; 4:11, 18; 8:20; Is. 3:12; 30:11. Restored—Is. 58:12. Called: Light—Job 24:13. Good—Pr. 2:9. Life—Pr. 16:11; Pr. 2:19; 5:6. Plain—Ps. 27:11. Justice—Pr. 2:8; Is. 26:7; 40:14. Peace—Pr. 3:17. Old—Jer. 6:16; 18:15. Straight—Heb. 12:13.

Of wicked.—Job 8:13; Pr. 1:15; 2:15, 18; 4:14; 7:25; Is. 59:7; Hos. 2:6. Called crooked—Is. 59:8; Lam. 3:9.

Obstacles in.—Adder—Gen. 49:17. Darkness—Job 19:8. Marketh—Job 13:27; 30:13; 33:11.

Of men.—Ps. 119:105; 139:3; 142:3; Pr. 3:6; 4:26.

Of people in prophecy.—Joel 2:8.

Miscellaneous.—To house—Job 38:20. Unknown—Job 28:7; Is. 42:16. Meeting of—Pr. 8:2. Pathway—Pr. 12:28. Of sea—Ps. 8:8.

PATHROS, păth′ros. **Upper Egypt**—Is. 11:11; Jer. 44:1, 15; Ez. 29:14; 30:14.

PATHRUSIM, path-ru′sim. **A descendant of Ham.**—Gen. 10:14; I Chr. 1:12.

PATIENCE. See CHRISTIAN GRACES.

PATMOS, păt′mos. **An island.**—Rev. 1:9. See OUTLINE STUDIES IN THE BOOKS.

PATRIARCHS. Abraham—Heb. 7:4. David—Acts 2:29. Genealogy of—Gen. 5; I Chr. 1:1–4. Twelve—Acts 7:8, 9. See GENESIS IN OUTLINE STUDIES.

PATROBAS, păt′ro-bas. **A disciple in Rome.**—Rom. 16:14.

PATTERN. David gave—I Chr. 28:11. Hold the—II Tim. 1:13. Jehovah had showed Moses—Num. 8:4. Like to the true in—Heb. 9:24. Measure—Ez. 43:

10. Tabernacle, Of—Ex. 25:9, 40; Heb. 8:5. See EXAMPLE.

PAU, pā′u. **City of Hadar king of Edom.**—Gen. 36:39.

PAUL, Formerly Saul.—Called Saul sixteen times between Acts 7:58 and 13:7.

First mention of name Paul.—Acts 13:9.

Born in Tarsus of Cilicia.—Acts 9:11; 21:39; 22:3.

Roman citizen.—Acts 16:37; 22:25–28.

Of the tribe of Benjamin.—Rom. 11:1; Phil. 3:5.

A Pharisee.—Acts 23:6; 26:5; Phil. 3:5. **A Hebrew of the Hebrews**—II Cor. 11:22; Phil. 3:5.

Early life and education.—Acts 26:4–5. At the feet of Gamaliel—Acts 22:3.

Persecution of the church.—Acts 8:1–4; 9:1–3, 14–14, 21; 22:4–6, 8, 19–20; 26:9–11; I Cor. 15:9; Gal. 1:13; I Tim. 1:13. His part in death of Stephen—Acts 7:58; 8:1–3; 22:20.

His conversion.—Acts 9:3–19; 22:6–16; 26:11–18. His baptism—Acts 9:18; 22:16.

Call to apostleship.—Acts 9:4–6, 15–16; 22:14–16; 26:16–18; Rom. 1:1; I Cor. 1:1; 9:1; 15:8–9; Gal. 1:1, 15–17; Eph. 1:1; Col. 1:1; I Tim. 1:1; 2:7; II Tim. 1:1, 11; Tit. 1:1–3. The apostleship —I Cor. 15:10–11; II Cor. 10:7–16; 11:5–6; 12:11–12; Gal. 1:17–22; I Tim. 2:6–7.

Goes to Arabia.—Gal. 1:17.

Returns to Damascus and preaches.—Acts 9:20. Jews try to kill him—Acts 9:23. Aided by Aretas, the keeper of the garrison—II Cor. 11:32.

Paul escapes in a basket.—Acts 9:25; II Cor. 11:31–33.

Goes to Jerusalem.—Disciples afraid of him—Acts 9:26. Barnabas endorses him—Acts 9:27–28. He is accepted by other apostles and by the church—Acts 9:28–29; Gal. 1:17–20; 2:7–9.

Is brought down to Cæsarea and goes thence to Tarsus.—Acts 9:30.

Paul and Barnabas preach to the Greeks at Antioch.—Acts 11:26. Remain there a year—Acts 11:26. First Gentile church organized. Disciples called Christians first there—Acts 11:26. Carry contribution of church at Antioch to Jerusalem and return to Antioch—Acts 11:29, 30; 12:25.

Paul's first missionary tour (46–47 A.D.). —Barnabas accompanies him—Acts 13:2–3.

Go to **Seleucia, Salamis, Cyprus, and Paphos.**—Begin preaching at **Salamis** in the synagogues, having John Mark as their attendant—Acts 13:5. Find a certain sorcerer at **Paphos,** named Bar-Jesus, who tries to prevent Paul's influence over Sergius Paulus—Acts 13:6–8. Paul, by a miracle, inflicts blindness upon him—Acts 13:9–12. They pass on to **Perga,** John Mark deserting them—Acts 13:13. Thence to **Antioch,** where they remain over the sabbath day and Paul preaches in the synagogue—Acts 13:14–49. The Jews stirred up a persecution and cast them out of their borders—Acts 13:50. They come to **Iconium,** where they are again persecuted—Acts 14:1–5. They flee to **Lycaonia, Lystra,** and **Derbe**—Acts 14:6; II Tim. 3:11. The curing of a lame man leads the people to worship the apostles—Acts 14:11–13. The apostles protest—Acts 14:14–17. The Jews from Antioch and Iconium induce the multitude to stone Paul, and he is left for dead—Acts 14:19; II Cor. 11:25; II Tim. 3:11. Paul recovers and the apostles journey to **Derbe,** where they preach—Acts 14:20–21.

The apostles return to **Antioch,** passing through **Pisidia, Pamphylia, Perga,** and **Attalia,** confirming the disciples —Acts 14:21–26. Thus ends the first tour.

The consultation at Jerusalem.—Shortly after the return of Paul and Barnabas to **Antioch,** a difficulty arose concerning the admittance of the Gentiles into the church without observing circumcision—Acts 15:1. Paul and Barnabas, with others, sent to Jerusalem to inquire concerning this question—Acts 15:1–6. Peter declares that God makes no distinction, cleansing men's hearts through faith—Acts 15:7–11. It is decided not to trouble the Gentile converts further than with two or three precautions—Acts 15:22–29; Gal. 2:1–9. Men chosen to go with

Paul and Barnabas to announce the decision—Acts 15:22, 30–33. The apostles remain in **Antioch** teaching and preaching—Acts 15:35.

THE SECOND MISSIONARY TOUR (52–54 A.D.)—**They begin tour by returning to cities already visited,** Paul and Barnabas separating because of a dispute over John Mark—Acts 15:37–39. See Gal. 2:11–16; II Pet. 3:15. Paul takes Silas and passes through **Syria** and **Cilicia,** confirming the churches—Acts 15:40–41. In each church they stated the decision of the apostles and elders at Jerusalem concerning the Gentile observances—Acts 15:28–29; 16:4–5.

At **Lystra,** Paul comes across Timothy whom Paul took with him, circumcising him, as his father was a Greek, to conciliate the Jews—Acts 16:1–3. Forbidden by the Spirit to preach in **Asia** and **Bithynia,** they went through the **Region of Phrygia** and **Galatia** and by **Mysia**—Acts 16:6, 7. Coming to **Troas** a vision appears to Paul— "A man of **Macedonia,**" etc.—Acts 16:9.

CHRISTIANITY IN MACEDONIA. Accepting this as a token from God, they sail for Samothracia, go the next day to Neapolis, thence to **Philippi**—Acts 16:10–12; II Cor. 2:12, 13; I Thess. 2:2.

The meeting of **Paul** and **Lydia**—Acts 16:14. She and her household baptized—verse 15. Paul and Silas get into trouble over the casting out of an evil spirit—Acts 16:16–22. They are thrown into prison—vs. 23, 24. At midnight they sing, when, lo, an earthquake shakes the prison doors open— vs. 25–26. **The Jailer,** alarmed, believes on the Lord Jesus and is baptized—vs. 29–33. The magistrates order the release of Paul and Silas— Acts 16:35.

CHRISTIANITY IN THESSALONICA AND BERŒA. Paul and Silas passing through **Amphipolis** and **Apollonia,** come to **Thessalonica,** where Paul reasons with citizens on the sabbath day—Acts 17:1–3. Many disciples were made—Acts 17:4; Phil. 4:15, 16. A rabble forms about Jason's house—

vs. 5–9. Paul and Silas sent to Berœa —v. 10. The Berœans more noble than the Thessalonians—v. 11. The Jews follow Paul, making trouble again— v. 13. Paul being sent away, arrives at Athens—Acts 17:15.

CHRISTIANITY PENETRATING ATHENS. Paul sends Timothy to Thessalonica—I Thess. 3:1–5. The spell of Athens and how Paul is affected by it—Acts 17:16. He reasons in synagogue with the Jews and in the marketplace with the Greeks—v. 17. He encounters the philosophers, who bring him to the Areopagus to explain himself—Acts 17:18–21. Paul addresses them—vs. 22–31. Some mocked, some dodged and some believed—vs. 32–34.

PAUL AT CORINTH. Arriving at Corinth, he finds there Aquila and Priscilla, with whom he abides—Acts 18:1–3. He works at tent-making during the week and reasons with the Jews each sabbath day—vs. 3–4. Silas and Timothy join him—Acts 18:5. Driven out of the synagogue by the Jews, he enters the house of Justus, near the synagogue—v. 7. Many confessions were taken, notably that of Crispus and household—v. 8. He remains in Corinth a year and a half, thus instructed in a vision—v. 11. See I Cor. 1:1–17.

Writes I and II Thessalonian letters.— Paul is brought before Gallio's judgment-seat without results—Acts 18: 12–17.

THIRD MISSIONARY TOUR (55–59 A. D.): **PAUL AT EPHESUS.** Paul, accompanied by Aquila and Priscilla, sails for Ephesus—Acts 18:18. There he leaves his companions, departing for Cæsarea and Antioch, where he spends some time—vs. 22–23. After passing through the upper country he returns to Ephesus, where he finds some disciples of John the Baptist, whom he baptizes in the name of the Lord Jesus—Acts 19:1–7. Spends 3 months reasoning in the synagogue, after which, on account of opposition, he enters into the school of Tyrannus, where he remained two years—Acts 19:8–10. See I Cor. 15:32, 9. All Asia

thus heard the Word—Acts 19:8–10. Special miracles wrought through Paul—vs. 11–12. Seven sons of Sceva, a Jew, adjured evil spirits in the name of Jesus, and were discomfited—Acts 19:13–16. The name of the Lord Jesus being thus magnified, fear fell on all, and books of magical arts were burned—vs. 17–20.

Purposes to visit Macedonia and Corinth, before going to Jerusalem at Pentecost; afterwards Rome and Spain—Acts 19:21; 20:16; Rom. 1:10–15; 15:22–29.

Directs collection to be made for the brethren at Jerusalem—I Cor. 16:1–4.

Remaining in Asia, he sends Timothy and Erastus into Macedonia, Timothy to visit Corinth also—Acts 19:21, 22; I Cor. 16:10–12.

Writes First Epistle to the Corinthians.

Diana of the Ephesians defended.— Demetrius and the silversmiths, finding their trade injured by Paul's preaching, raise a mob. Paul's companions are seized—Acts 19:29. Town-clerk quiets the mob—Acts 20:1.

Paul possibly makes a second visit to Corinth.—II Cor. 2:1; 12:14; 13:1, 2.

During his stay of three years in Ephesus Paul probably organized churches of Roman Asia—Acts 20:18–35; Rom. 15:20. Leaves Timothy in Ephesus—I Tim. 1:3.

Starts for Macedonia—Acts 20:1.

Waits for Titus from Corinth—II Cor. 2:13.

Comes to Philippi and Macedonia.

At Philippi Paul meets Titus, who brings cheering news from Corinth— II Cor. 7:4–13.

Paul sends Titus back to Corinth to continue collection for saints at Jerusalem—II Cor. 8:6–24; Ch. 9.

Sends Second Epistle to the Corinthians by Titus and two others.

Paul writes Epistle to the Galatians.

Paul at Illyricum.—Rom. 15:19, 20.

Spends three months in Corinth.—Acts 20:2–6; I Cor. 16:6, 7.

Writes Epistle to the Romans, which he sends by Phœbe of Cenchreæ—Rom. 16:1.

Paul arrives at Philippi and next at Troas—Acts 20:6. On the Lord's Day he breaks bread with the disciples at **Troas** and discourses—v. 7. Eutychus, falling from an upper window, is restored by Paul—vs. 8–12. Paul meets companions at Assos, making a rapid journey through **Mitylene, Chios, Samos** and **Miletus**—Acts 20:13–15. Paul calls for elders of church at Ephesus and bids them adieu—vs. 17–38.

Departure from Ephesus.—The company makes a rapid run through **Cos, Rhodes** and **Patara** to **Tyre**—Acts 21: 1–3. Remain there 7 days, when Paul is advised to stay away from Jerusalem—v. 4. Pass on through **Ptolemais** to **Cæsarea,** where they find Philip the Evangelist, one of the seven—v. 8. Agabus, a prophet, comes down from Judæa to persuade Paul to stay away from Jerusalem—vs. 10–11.

Paul determines to go to Jerusalem.— Paul being incorrigible, the company depart for Jerusalem—Acts 21:15–17. Paul, with others, reports his success to the elders of the church, who rejoice—Acts 21:18–20.

Paul is advised to take a vow and so appease the Jewish wrath, which he does.—Acts 21:20–26. After the completion of the vow, being seen in the temple, he is misunderstood and seized by an infuriated mob—Acts 21:27–29.

They seek to kill him, but he is rescued by the soldiers.—vs. 30–36. Paul obtains leave to speak and addresses the multitude—Acts 21:37–40; 22:1–22. The impatient mob stops the speech and the chief captain orders Paul to be examined by scourging.—vs. 22–24.

Paul asserts his citizenship.—He declares himself a Roman—Acts 22:25–28. Paul was then unbound and permitted to defend himself—v. 30. He addresses the Jewish Council, but is interrupted by the high priest, Ananias—Acts 23:1–5. Paul, perceiving the assembly to consist of pharisees and sadducees, throws them into dissension by claiming protection from the former—vs. 6–9. The chief captain comes to the rescue, bringing Paul into the castle—v. 10.

The Jews again band themselves together to kill Paul, but are defeated by Paul's nephew—Acts 23:12–22. The chief captain hurries Paul away to Cæsarea, where he is brought before Felix—vs. 22–25.

Paul before Felix.—Speech of Tertullus Acts 24:1–9. Paul's defence—vs. 10–21. Felix defers the trial until Lysias, the chief captain, arrives—vs. 22–23. After some days Felix and Drusilla, his wife, send for Paul—v. 24. Paul addresses them upon righteousness, etc.—vs. 24–27. Two years were spent by Paul in prison.

Paul before Festus.—The chief priests informing against Paul, Festus went to Cæsarea and ordered Paul before him—Acts 25:1–6. The Jews unable to prove their charges, Paul appeals unto Cæsar. The appeal is granted by Festus—vs. 7–12. Meanwhile Agrippa comes to Cæsarea and desires an interview with Paul—Acts 25:13–22.

Paul before Agrippa.—Festus introduces Paul, declaring he had done nothing worthy of death—Acts 25:24–27. Agrippa allows Paul to speak for himself—Acts 26:1. Paul's address—vs. 2–23. Paul's doctrine sounds queer to Festus and he is charged with madness—v. 24. Paul's retort and appeal to Agrippa's conscience—vs. 25–29. Agrippa exonerates Paul—vs. 30–31. Paul sails for Rome—Acts 27:1–8.

Paul predicts a shipwreck.—His advice rejected—v. 11. A tempestuous wind arises, continuing many days, while the vessel was driven hither and thither—Acts 27:13–29. The sailors, alarmed, seek to flee from the ship, but are prevented by Paul—vs. 30–31. Paul predicts safety and practically takes charge—vs. 33–36. All finally escape to land—vs. 43–44.

Paul at Melita.—Association with the barbarians—Acts 28:1–2. A viper fastens on Paul's hand—v. 3. The barbarian's idea of justice avenging crime—v. 4. After Paul shakes off the viper, they declare he is a god—vs. 5–6.

Paul at Rome.—Taken to Rome, he abode two whole years in his **own**

hired dwelling, preaching the kingdom of God—Acts 28:11-31.

Writes the Epistle to Colossians, the Epistle to the Ephesians and the Epistle to the Philippians.—He writes Timothy he is ready to be offered up and the time of his departure is at hand—II Tim. 4:6. This is the last word of Scripture concerning Paul.

PAUL'S MOTIVES FOR ACTION.

He had a thorough conviction of Messianic salvation.—Acts 26:22-23, 29; I Cor. 15:10-11.

Worked with faith in an inworking God. —Acts 15:12; II Cor. 5:18-20.

He was constrained by love.—II Cor. 5:13-17; Phil. 2:3; 3:7-11.

He had a love for souls.—Rom. 9:1-3; 10:1.

Was a bond-slave of Christ's.—Rom. 1:1; I Cor. 3:23; 6:19, 20; II Cor. 10:7; Gal. 1:11; Phil. 1:1; 2:7; I Thess. 5:10; II Tim. 2:24; Titus 1:1.

He had the example of the Christ.— II Cor. 8:9; 10:1; Phil. 2:5. The terror of the Lord—II Cor. 5:11; II Thess. 1:7-9.

Distinguished temporal from eternal.— I Cor. 7:29; II Cor. 4:16-18.

Had hope in a future.—I Cor. 15:51; II Cor. 5:1-4; Phil. 3:20; Titus 2:13; II Tim. 4:8.

PAUL'S AIMS: To turn men to God.— Acts 26:16-19. **To give new life to the world.**—II Cor. 5:17. **To preach Christ.**—I Cor. 2:1-5. **To please Christ.** —I Cor. 7:32; Gal. 1:10.

Paul magnifies his office.—Rom. 1:5, 13-15; II Cor. 3:6; Eph. 3:1, 2, 7, 8; Col. 1:25-27; II Tim. 1:11.

HIS CITIZENSHIP. Acts 16:37; 17:22-29; 23:27; 25:12; Eph. 2:19; Phil. 3:20.

HIS DEPENDENCE UPON HIS TRADE. Acts 18:3; 20:33-35; I Cor. 9:17-19; Phil. 4:11-13; I Thess. 4:11-12.

HIS LANGUAGE. Acts 7:58; 8:1-3; 21:39-40; 22:2.

PAUL'S METHOD WITH MEN AND WOMEN. Tolerant—Rom. 14:1-13; I Cor. 8:1-13; 10:23-33; II Cor. 13:9; Gal. 2:7-10; Phil. 1:15-18. Firm— Gal. 2:14-21; I Cor. 5:1-7; 6:1-10.

Reasonable—I Cor. 7:20-31; 14:6-12; 15:12-19; Phil. 4:8-9. Adaptability— I Cor. 9:19-23; 11:3-15. Tenderness— I Thess. 2:7, 8, 11, 17, 18-20; 3:1-10. Love for his fellow-countrymen— Rom. 7:12. Desirous of attending their feasts—Acts 18:21; 20:16. Watched for the hope of Israel—Acts 23:6. Sought to win souls—I Thess. 2:19-20. Prayed for his fellow-men— I Tim. 2:1-4; II Thess. 1:11-12; 2:13, 16-17; 3:5, 16. His genius for friendship—Phil. 1:3-11; Gal. 4:12-20; II Tim. 1:1-5.

PAUL AS A WORKER.—He knew he was created for that purpose—Gal. 1:15-16; Eph. 2:10. He held God as a co-partner—I Cor. 3:9; II Cor. 6:1; 9:8; Eph. 3:7; Phil. 2:12; Col. 1:27-29. He had prepared himself for God's work —II Tim. 2:21; 3:16-17; Tit. 3:1-8. As leading in bringing the Gentiles unto Christ, he glorified his ministry —Rom. 11:13-14; Gal. 1:15-20; Eph. 3:8-12. He was an incessant personal worker—Acts 9:28-29; 20:18-21; 28:28-31. Nothing that presented itself daunted him—Rom. 1:14-15; I Cor. 15:10, 58. He was deliberate in judgment, but alert in action—Rom. 15:18-21; II Cor. 10:14-18. He knew how to enlist his co-workers—Acts 16:1-3; 20:4; Eph. 6:21-22; II Tim. 2:2; Tit. 1:5. He required nothing of them but what he submitted to—II Cor. 11:22-31. He always emphasized Christian work—Eph. 4:14-16; Col. 1:10; I Tim. 2:10; 5:9-10; 6:18; II Tim. 2:15, 21; 3:16; Tit. 2:14. He foresaw the triumph of Christ and induced others to work for it—Rom. 8:19-25; I Cor. 15:25-28, 56-58.

PAUL'S PRAYERS.—Rom. 1:9; 10:1; I Cor. 1:3; II Cor. 13:7; Gal. 6:16-18; Eph. 1:16-19; 3:14-19; Phil. 1:3-10; Col. 1:3, 9; I Thess. 1:2; 3:10-13; 5:23; II Thess. 1:11; 2:16, 17; 3:5, 16; II Tim. 1:3, 18; 2:7; 4:16; Philemon 4-6; Heb. 13:20, 21.

PAUL'S LETTERS.—They divide into four groups:

(1) The two to the Thessalonians written in winter of 53-54 A.D. (2) The two Corinthian letters, the Galatian and Roman, 58-59 A.D. (3) Colossians,

Philemon, Ephesians, and Philippians, 63 A.D. (4) The two Timothys and Titus, his last letters, 66 A.D.

The style of Paul's letters.—(1) **Variety:** Logical—Rom. 4:12–21. Legal —Rom. 2:11–29; 13:1–10. Didactic— I Cor. 10:21; II Cor. 9:6–14. Laconic —Rom. 12:9–18; 14:5–9; Eph. 4:26– 32. Elastic—I Cor. 9:19–23. Corrective—I Cor. 4:18–21; II Cor. 10:1–11; 13:1–10. Persuasive—I Cor. 4:14–17; Phil. 2:1–16. Imaginative—Rom. 8: 18–39. (2) **Intensity.**—I Cor. 15:54– 58; II Cor. 11:16–29; Gal. 4:12–20. (3) **Hopefulness.**—Rom. 8:20–25; 16:20; II Cor. 4:16–18; Phil. 1:19–26; II Tim. 4:18; I Thess. 4:13–18. (4) **Tact.**— The letter to Philemon—II Cor. 8:9– 10. (5) **Compactness.**—II Cor. 6:3–10; Eph. 1:3–14; 4:11–16; Col. 1:9–23; I Thess. 5:4–18. (6) **Strength.**—I Cor. 4:7–13; I Tim. 6:3–10; II Tim. 4:1–8. (7) **Comparison.**—Rom. 7:9–23; I Cor. 10:6–12.

TEACHING OF PAUL.

The Christian life.—Adoption—Rom. 8: 15, 23; 9:4; Gal. 4:5; Eph. 1:5. Adultery—Rom. 2:22; 13:9. Anger—Eph. 4:31; Col. 3:8. Apostasy—I Cor. 10: 12; I Tim. 3:6, 7; 4:1; 6:9. Assurance —Col. 2:2; I Thess. 1:5. Children— Eph. 2:3; 6:1; Col. 3:20; I Thess. 2: 11; I Tim. 3:4; 3:12; Tit. 2:4. Circumcision—Rom. 2:25–29; 3:1, 30; 4:9– 12; 15:8; I Cor. 7:19; Gal. 2:7, etc. Confidence—Eph. 3:12; Phil. 1:25; Heb. 3:14. Conscience—Rom. 2:15; 9:1; 13:5; I Cor. 8:7, 10, 12; 10:25, 27– 29; II Cor. 1:12; 4:2; 5:11; I Tim. 1:5, 19; 3:9; 4:2; II Tim. 1:3; Tit. 1:15. Contentment—Phil. 4:11; I Tim. 6:6, 8. Covetousness—Rom. 1:29; II Cor. 9:5; Eph. 4:19; 5:3; Col. 8:5; I Thess. 2:5. Drunkenness—Rom. 13:13; Eph. 5:18, etc. Fathers—Eph. 4:6; Col. 3: 21. Flesh—Rom. 1:3; 2:28; 3:20; 4:1; 6:19; 7:5, 18, 25; 8:3, 4, etc. Forgiveness—Rom. 4:7; Eph. 1:7; Col. 1:14; 2:13. Fornication—I Cor. 5:1; 6:13, 18; 7:2; 12:21; Gal. 5:19; Eph. 5:3; Col. 3:5; I Thess. 4:3. Gentiles—Rom. 1:13; 2:14, 24; 3:29; 9:24, 30; 11:11– 13, 25; 15:9, 10, etc. Gnosticism an-

nounced in the later epistles by right knowledge of Christ—Eph. 1:17; 3: 19; 4:13; Phil. 3:8; Col. 1:9, 10; 2:3; 3:10; I Tim. 2:4; 6:20; II Tim. 2:25; 3:7; Tit. 1:1. Gospel—Rom. 1:1, 9, 15 f.; 10:15 f.; 11:28; 15:16, etc. Grace —Rom. 1:5, 7; 3:24; 4:4, 16; 5:2, 15, 17, 20, 21; 6:1, 14, etc. Husbands— I Cor. 7:2, 4, 10, 11, 13, 14, 16, 34, 39; Eph. 5:22–25, 28, 33; Col. 3:19; I Tim. 3:2, 12; Tit. 1:6. Jews—Rom. 1:16; 2:9, 10, 17, 28, 29; 3:9, 10, 12, 24; 10: 12, etc. Justification—Rom. 2:13; 3:4, 20, 24, 28; 4:2, 25; 5:1, 9, 16, 18, etc. Law—Rom. 2:12–15, 17, 18, etc. Love —Rom. 5:5, 8; 8:35, 39; 12:9, 10; 13: 10; 14:15; 15:30; I Cor. 4:21; 8:1; 13:1, 2, 3, etc. Man of sin—II Thess. 2:3 ff. Masters—Eph. 6:9; Col. 4:1. Mothers—Eph. 6:2; I Tim. 5:2; II Tim. 1:5. Murder—Rom. 1:29; I Tim. 1:9. Parents—Rom. 1:30; II Cor. 12: 14; Eph. 6:1; Col. 3:20; I Tim. 5:4. Pharisees—Acts 26:5; Phil. 3:6. Praise —Eph. 1:6, 12, 14; Phil. 1:11; 4:8. Prayer—Rom. 12:12; I Cor. 7:5; Eph. 6:18; Phil. 4:6; Col. 4:2; I Tim. 4:5, etc. Reconciliation—Rom. 5:10, 11; 11:15; II Cor. 5:18–20; Eph. 2:16; Col. 1:20 f. Redemption—Rom. 3:24; 8:23; I Cor. 1:30; Eph. 1:14; Col. 1:14. Regeneration—Tit. 3:5. Relation between the weak and the strong—I Cor. 8:10; Rom. 14:1; 15:13. Repentance—Rom. 2:4; 11:29; II Cor. 7:9, 10; 12:21; II Tim. 2:25. Resurrection —Rom. 1:4; 6:5; I Cor. 15:12, 13, 21, 42; Phil. 3:10, 11; II Tim. 2:18; Heb. 6:2; 11:35. Rich—I Tim. 6:9, 17 ff. Righteousness—Rom. 1:17; 3:5, 21, 22, 25, 26; 4:3, 5, 6, 9, 11, 13, 22; 5:16, etc. Sect of the circumcision or Judaizing Christians—Gal. 2:12; Tit. 1:10. Salvation—Rom. 1:16; 10:10, 11; 13:11; II Cor. 6:2; 7:10; Eph. 1:13; 6:17; Phil. 1:19, 28; 2:12; I Thess. 5:8, 9; II Thess. 2:13; II Tim. 2:10; 3:15; Tit. 2:11. Sanctification—Rom. 6:19, 22; I Cor. 1:30; I Thess. 4:3, 4, 7; I Tim. 2:15. Servants—Eph. 6:5; Col. 3:22; I Tim. 6:1 f.; Tit. 2:9; I Pet. 2:18. Sins—Rom. 3:9; 4:8; 5:12, 13, 20, 21; 6:1, 2, 6, etc. Spiritual Israel—Rom. 2:28; 9:6; 11:26; Phil. 3:3; Eph. 2:12. Widows—I Cor. 7:8; I Tim. 5:3, **4, 5,**

9, 11, 14, 16. Wine—Rom. 14:21; Eph. 5:18; I Tim. 3:3; 5:23; Tit. 2:3. Wives —I Cor. 7:2-4, 10, 12, 14, 27, 33, 34, 39; Eph. 5:22, 24, 25, 28, 33; Col. 3:18. Works—Rom. 2:6; 3:20, 27, 28; 4:2, 6; 9:11; 11:6; 13:12; Gal. 2:16; 3:2, etc.

Christian, Christ's relation to.—Is the head of every man—I Cor. 11:3. Approves those who possess His mind—I Cor. 2:16. Dwells in the heart of the Christian—Rom. 8:9-11; II Cor. 13:5; Eph. 2:22; 3:17. Produces in us an inseparable love—Rom. 8:35. Is our life—Rom. 6:23; Phil. 1:21. Our passover—I Cor. 5:7. Makes us heirs of God—Rom. 8:17; Gal. 3:29; 4:4-7; Eph. 3:6; Tit. 3:7. Is the unifying power of all disciples—Rom. 12:5; I Cor. 12:12, 20, 27; Gal: 3:28, 29; Eph. 2:12-22. Unites us to Him by baptism—Rom. 6:3-5; Col. 2:14-15. Enables us to abound in comfort—II Cor. 1:5. Justifies through faith in Him—Rom. 4:25; 5:16-21; Gal. 2:17. Equips us for every good work—Phil. 4:12, 13. Is the medium of our hope—I Thess. 1:3; Heb. 6:13-20. Enables us to have joy in God—Rom. 5:11. Is the guarantee of our riches in glory—Phil. 4:19.

Church government.—Apostles and congregation coöperate—Acts 11:29-30; 13:3; I Cor. 12:28; Eph. 4:11-12. Paul concurs with Peter—Acts 1:15-26; 14:23 (where Greek word *cheirotonein* means voting by stretching out hand); 20:28. Choosing officers—I Tim. 3:1-13; Tit. 1:5-9; Eph. 4:11-13. Relation of officers to congregation—Rom. 12:4-8; I Cor. 16:15-16; II Cor. 1:11; I Thess. 5:12-15; I Tim. 3:4, 5, 12; 5:17-20. Support of the ministry—I Cor. 9:3-14; II Cor. 11:7-9; Gal. 6:6; Phil. 4:10-18; I Tim. 5:17-18. What the church should get out of its officiary—Acts 20:28; Rom. 12:6-11; I Cor. 12:26-28; 14:1-3; Eph. 4:11-13; Phil. 4:8-9; I Tim. 1:3-8; II Tim. 4:1-5; Tit. 1:7-9; 2:1-10. Bishop—Phil. 1:1; I Tim. 3:1, 2; Tit. 1:7. Elder—I Tim. 5:1, 19. Pastor—Eph. 4:11. Ministers —Rom. 13:6; I Cor. 3:5; 4:1; II Cor. 3:6; 6:4; 11:15, 23. Apostles—Rom. 1:1; 11:13; 16:7; I Cor. 4:9; 9:1, 2, 5; 15:9; 12:28, 29; 15:7, 9; II Cor. 1:12,

etc. Prophets—I Cor. 12:28 f.; Eph. 2:20; 3:5; 4:11; I Thess. 2:15; I Cor. 14:32. Teachers—I Cor. 12:28 f.; Eph. 4:11; I Tim. 1:7; II Tim. 4:3; Tit. 2:3. Evangelists—Eph. 4:11; II Tim. 4:5; Col. 2:12. Lord's Supper—I Cor. 10: 16 ff.; 11:20 ff.

Civil and national life.—The governing power comes from God—Rom. 13:1, 4; Tit. 3:1, 2. To be subject for conscience' sake—Rom. 13:5. Except when the command violates law—Acts 23:1-3. All honest dues must be met—Rom. 13:6-8. Nothing could prevent him from doing God's bidding —Acts 20:22-24; 21:10-14.

Covenants, Christ's relation to the two: To the old.—Christ the fulfilment of the promise to Abraham—"In thee and thy seed shall all the nations of the earth be blessed"—Rom. 4:11-25; 11:25-28; Gal. 3:5-16, 19; 4:21-31. The law added because of transgression till the seed should come—Rom. 5:20, 21; Gal. 3:16, 19; 4:1-5; I Tim. 1:8-10. Shadow of heavenly things to come imposed till coming of Christ—Col. 2:14-17. We are become dead to the law by the body of Christ—Rom. 7:4-6; 8:1-4; Gal. 4:1-5. Christ took away the bond written in ordinances —Col. 2:14. Veil done away in Christ —II Cor. 3:14.

To the new.—Christ is called a covenant —Is. 42:6-9; 49:6-10; 59:20, 21. Sealed new covenant with His blood—I Cor. 11:25. Christ the mediator of new covenant—Rom. 8:34; Eph. 2:18; 3:11, 12; I Tim. 2:5, 6.

Death.—Caused by sin—Rom. 5:12. Symbolized by baptism—Rom. 6:4. Wages of sin—Rom. 6:23. Overcome by thirst —I Cor. 15:26; 54. Sin the sting of—I Cor. 15:56. Does not separate us from Christ—Rom. 8:38, 39.

Demons (Devil).—Gentiles sacrifice to —I Cor. 10:20. Disciples not to have fellowship with—I Cor. 10:20. Avoid cup of—I Cor. 10:21. Avoid teachings of—I Tim. 4:1. Satan—To be resisted—Eph. 4:27; 6:11. Avoided by man of God—I Tim. 3:7; II Tim. 2:26. Some fall into condemnation of—I Tim. 3:6. God will praise—Rom. 16:20. Gets power over some—I Tim. 5:5.

Tempts—I Cor. 7:5. Gets advantage of some—II Cor. 2:11. Sent to Paul as messenger—II Cor. 12:7. Some have followed—I Tim. 1:29; 5:15. Hindered Paul—I Thess. 2:18. Transformed into angels of light—II Cor. 11:17.

Paul's views of discipline.—Not yet perfect himself—Phil. 3:12-14. Carries God's treasure in an earthen vessel—II Cor. 4:7. Keeps his body under lest he becomes a castaway—I Cor. 9:27. Each must enter kingdom through tribulation—Acts 14:22. He himself given a "thorn in the flesh"—II Cor. 12:7. Has his own disputes—Acts 15:36-39; 23:3-5. Some vessels to honor, some to dishonor—II Tim. 2:20. Church under constant cleansing—Eph. 5:25-27; II Cor. 7:1; Tit. 3:8-11. Spiritual diseases must be taken hold of in time—Rom. 16:17; I Cor. 5:1-13; II Cor. 6:14-18; Eph. 5:3-14; II Thess. 3:6-15; II Tim. 2:19-26.

Paul's view of election.—God chooses, but it is for service.—*Pharaoh*—Rom. 9:17. *Jacob and Esau*—Rom. 9:12-13. Seven thousand prophets—Rom. 11:14 (see also *Cyrus*—Is. 4:5; *Balaam*—Num. 22:20). God predetermines that Jesus shall be the Savior of men—Acts 17:30-31; Rom. 3:21-26; Eph. 1:9-10; Col. 1:17-20 (see also Gen. 3:15; 12:3 with Rom. 4:13 and 10:6-10; Is. 9:6-7). All who conform themselves to the image of Christ come within the scope of election—Rom. 6:3-7, 17-18; 8:29; I Cor. 15:21-25; Eph. 1:11-14; Col. 1:14. Those are rejected who go about to establish their own righteousness—Rom. 10:3-4, 16-21. See ELECTION.

Faith.—Given by God—Rom. 12:3; I Cor. 2:4, 5; 12:8, 9. Comes by hearing the Word of God—Rom. 10:13-17; I Cor. 1:21; Gal. 3:1, 2; I Thess. 2:13. In Christ—Acts 16:29-34; 18:8; 19:4, 5; 20:21; 26:18; Rom. 1:16, 17; 3:21-26; 5:1, 2; 10:1-10; I Cor. 1:21-24; 3:10, 11; Gal. 2:20; 3:22; Eph. 1:12-14; 2:19-22; 3:11, 12; Phil. 1:27-29; 3:9; Col. 2:12; I Tim. 1:14; II Tim. 1:12; Philemon 5. Assurance of—Rom. 8:1; Eph. 1:13; 2:6-8; Phil. 1:6; II

Tim. 1:12. An active principle; leads to utterance—II Cor. 4:13. Grows exceedingly—II Thess. 1:3. Works through love—Gal. 5:6. Brings salvation—Acts 16:31. Assures life—Rom. 1:17; Gal. 3:11. Enables us to stand—Rom. 11:20; I Cor. 16:13; II Cor. 1:24; Col. 1:23. Enables us to walk—II Cor. 5:7. Enables us to fight—II Cor. 4:7, 8; I Cor. 6:11-17. Is the means of justification—Rom. 3:25-28. Awards the sonship to us—Gal. 3:26. Makes us heirs and joint heirs—Rom. 8:17. Gives us access to God—Rom. 5:2; Eph. 3:12. Secures peace with God—Rom. 5:1. Leads to sanctification—Acts 26:18; Col. 1:23, 24.

Aim of faith—To grow in knowledge of truth—II Tim. 2:15. To grow into the favor of God—Rom. 4:4, 5; 5:2; I Cor. 15:10; Eph. 4:15. To attain unto a perfect manhood—Eph. 2:20-22; 4:1-3, 11-13, 15, 16. To be transformed into the image of Christ—Rom. 8:29; I Cor. 15:49; II Cor. 3:18; 4:3-6. To be kept in constant security—Rom. 6:12-14; 11:20; I Cor. 9:29; 15:1, 2; 4:7; II Thess. 3:3; II Tim. 4:7, 8. To be joyful on earth—Rom. 5:2-5, 11; 15:13; Phil. 1:18, 19; 2:17, 18. Breastplate of—I Thess. 5:8. Denial of—I Cor. 15:12-14; I Tim. 5:8; II Tim. 3:5; II Pet. 2:1. Of Abraham—Rom. 4:18-22.

Fruits of—Indwelling of Christ—Eph. 3:17-19. Sealing of Spirit—Gal. 3:14. The Father's Spirit—Rom. 8:35-39. Failing faith is fatal—I Cor. 15:12-19; I Tim. 6:10, 11; II Tim. 4:3, 4. Obedience of faith—Rom. 6:8-14; 8:1-11; Phil. 2:1-16; 3:8-16. Not works of law—Rom. 3:27, 28; 4:1-8. The works tell—Rom. 6:16-18; 16:19; I Cor. 10:5, 6; II Thess. 1:8; I Tim. 1:5. Prayer and—Eph. 6:16-18. A proof of adoption—Rom. 8:14-16; Gal. 3:26, 27. Righteousness of—Rom. 1:17; 3:21-30; 4:3, 11; 9:31-33; 10:4-11; Gal. 2:16; 3:6; Phil. 3:9. Unfeigned—II Tim. 1:5. Unity of—I Cor. 1:10-13; 12:13-20; 2:19-21; 4:1-6, 15, 16, 25. Whatsoever is not of, is sin—Rom. 14:22, 23. Works of—Gal. 5:6; I Thess. 1:3; 2:13; II Thess. 1:11.

God: Access—*Only through Christ can we come to the Father*—Rom. 5:1; Col. 1:21; Eph. 2:13, 18; 3:12. *He will welcome all*—Rom. 10:12, 13. *Calls them by His gospel*—Rom. 9:11; I Cor. 1:17; 4:15; Gal. 1:6; I Thess. 2:12; 5:24; II Thess. 2:14. Adoption—Rom. 8:14–19; 9:8, 26; II Cor. 6:16–18; Gal. 4:4–7; Eph. 2:12–19. All in all—I Cor. 3:23; 12:6; 15:28. Dwells with men—II Cor. 6:16. Eternity—Rom. 1:20; 16:26; I Tim. 1:17. Faithfulness—Rom. 3:3, 4; 11:2; 15:8; I Cor. 1:9; II Cor. 1:20; I Thess. 5:24; II Tim. 2:13; Tit. 1:2. Fatherhood of God—Rom. 1:7; I Cor. 1:3; 8:6; 15:24; II Cor. 1:3; Gal. 1:1–4; Eph. 1:2, 3, 17; 3:14; 4:6; 5:20; Phil. 1:2; 4:20; Col. 1:2, 3, 12; 3:17; I Thess. 1:1, 3; 3:11, 13; II Thess. 1:1, 2; 2:16; I Tim. 1:2; II. Tim. 1:2, 4. *God was the Father of Jesus*—Rom. 1:3, 4; 15:6. *God revealed as Father, Son, and Holy Spirit*—Rom. 8:9; I Cor. 2:14; 3:16; 6:19; Eph. 4:4–6. Glory—Eph. 1:6, 12; 3:21; Phil. 2:11; I Tim. 6:15, 16. Goodness—Acts 17:31; Rom. 2:4; 11:22. Immutability—Rom. 11:29; II Tim. 2:13; Tit. 1:2. Invisibility—Col. 1:15; I Tim. 1:17; 6:16. Jealousy—I Cor. 10:22. Judge—Rom. 2:16; 3:6. Justice—Acts 17:31; Rom. 2:2, 11; 3:26; Gal. 2:6; Eph. 6:8, 9; Col. 3:25. King—I Tim. 1:17. Knowledge—Rom. 11:33, 34; 16:27; I Cor. 3:20; Gal. 1:15, 16; II Tim. 1:9. *Foreknowledge*—Rom. 8:29; 11:2; Gal. 1:15, 16; II Tim. 1:9. Living God—Rom. 9:26. Longsuffering—Acts 14:16, 17; 17:30; Rom. 3:25; 4:2; 9:22–24. Lord of the earth—I Cor. 10:26. Lord of all living—Acts 17:28; Rom. 14:11. Love—Rom. 5:8; 9:13; II Cor. 9:7; 13:11; Eph. 2:4; II Thess. 2:16. Mercy—Acts 26:16–18; Rom. 10:10–13. Names of God—Aramaic, *Abba*, Father—Rom. 8:15. *Blessed and Only Potentate*—I Tim. 6:15. *Eternal King*—I Tim. 1:17. *Lord of Lords*—I Tim. 6:15. One God alone—I Cor. 8:4, 6; Gal. 3:20; Eph. 4:5, 6; I Tim. 1:17. Patience—Rom. 15:5. Personality—I Cor. 8:4–6; II Cor. 4:4; Gal. 3:20; I Thess. 1:9; I Tim. 2:5. Providence—*God overrules in the affairs of men for the good of His people*

—Acts 14:17; Rom. 1:10; 8:28; I Cor. 4:19; 16:7; II Cor. 9:10; Phil. 1:12; Philemon 15. Righteousness—Rom. 1:17; 3:1-5, 21–26; 10:3; Phil. 3:9. Saviour—Rom. 1:16; 6:23; 8:32; I Cor. 1:18; II Cor. 5:18–21; I Thess. 5:8, 9; II Tim. 1:9. *Called a Saviour*—Tit. 1:1–3; 2:10–14; 3:4–6; Jude 25. Sovereignty—Acts 17:24–31; Rom. 9:19–33; 11:33–36.

Heaven.—*Abode of the redeemed*—II Cor. 5:1; Eph. 3:15. *Where Jesus has gone*—Col. 3:1–3; Eph. 6:9. *Hope of the believer*—Col. 1:5. *Jesus will come back from heaven*—I Thess. 1:10; 4:16; II Thess. 1:7. *Culmination of the kingdom of God*—II Tim. 4:18. *Rich blessings of*—Eph. 1:3, 20.

Holy Spirit.—Access to the Father by—Eph. 2:18. Baptism in the—I Cor. 12:13. Baptized by one Spirit—Gal. 4:29. Bears witness—Rom. 8:15, 16; 9:1; I Cor. 12:3; Gal. 4:6. Christians are temples of—Rom. 8:9–17; I Cor. 3:16, 17; 6:19; Eph. 2:21, 22; 3:16–17; II Tim. 1:14. Communion—II Cor. 3:6–18; 11:4; 13:14; Phil. 2:1; Col. 1:8. Comforts the Christian—Rom. 5:5; 8:26; 14:17. Convinces the world of sin—Gal. 5:16–23; Eph. 6:17. Deity of—II Cor. 3:17; Eph. 1:13; 2:18; 4:30. Earnest of—II Cor. 1:22; 5:5; Eph. 1:14; 4:30. Fruits of—Rom. 8:23; Gal. 5:22, 23. Flesh lusts against—Gal. 5:17. God dwells in us through—Eph. 2:22. Inspires—Rom. 1:1–4; 3:21; I Cor. 2:4, 9–14; 7:40; 12:3; Eph. 3:5, 6; II Tim. 3:16. Helps our infirmities—Rom. 8:26. Helps us to pray—Rom. 8:26. Makes intercession—Rom. 8:26; Eph. 2:18; 6:18. Of God—Rom. 8:9; I Cor. 2:10, 12, etc. Of Christ—Rom. 8:9; II Cor. 3:17; Gal. 4:6. Personality of—Rom. 8:26; I Cor. 12:11; II Cor. 3:17. Relation of, to Jesus—Rom. 1:4. Presence of, the test of new life—Rom. 8:9. Present in the life—I Cor. 12:13; Gal. 5:16, 18, 22; 6:8; II Thess. 2:13. Principle of the new life—Rom. 8:2, 5. Quench not—I Thess. 5:19. Sealed in—II Cor. 1:22; Eph. 1:13; 4:30. Searches the heart—I Cor. 2:10. Unity of—I Cor. 12:13; Eph. 4:3–16. Uses of the Word as a sword—Eph. 6:17. Walking in—Rom.

8:4; II Cor. 12:18; Gal. 5:16-25. Relation between Christ and Adam—Rom. 5:14; I Cor. 15:22, 30, 45.

Jesus.—Not to be known after the flesh —II Cor. 5:16.

Has no concord with Belial—I Cor. 10: 20-22; II Cor. 6:15.

Is magnified in Paul's body—Phil. 1:20.

May be preached because of contention —Phil. 1:16.

Paul's glory only in cross of Christ— Rom. 15:17; I Cor. 1:17-24; II Cor. 2:2; Gal. 6:14; Phil. 3:3.

Atonement.—See SALVATION.

Character.—Faithful—II Thess. 3:3; II Tim. 2:13; Heb. 2:17; 3:2. Gentle— II Cor. 10:1. Guileless—Heb. 7:26. Hating iniquity—Heb. 1:9. Holy—II Cor. 5:21; Eph. 1:4; Heb. 7:26. Humble—Rom. 15:3; II Cor. 8:9; Phil. 2:8. Longsuffering—I Tim. 1:16. Love of—Rom. 8:23, 35-39; II Cor. 5:14; Gal. 5:20; Eph. 3:19; 5:2. Merciful—Heb. 2:17; 4:15; 5:2. Obedient —Rom. 5:19; 15:3; Phil. 2:8; Heb. 5:8. Patient—II Thess. 3:5. Perfect —Heb. 5:9; 7:28. *Through suffering* —Heb. 2:10. Pleased not Himself— Rom. 15:3; II Cor. 8:9. Sinless—II Cor. 5:21; Eph. 1:4. Undefiled—Heb. 7:26.

Cross of Christ—I Cor. 1:17, 18; Gal. 5:11; 6:12, 14; Eph. 2:16; Phil. 2:8; 3:18; Col. 1:20; 2:14.

Death for remission of sins—Rom. 3: 25; 4:25; 5:6-10; 6:3-11; I Cor. 15:1-3; Gal. 1:4; Eph. 1:7; Col. 1:14.

Divinity of Jesus—His pre-existence— I Cor. 10:4; I Cor. 8:9; Phil. 2:6-8; Col. 1:17. Equality with God—II Cor. 5:19; Phil. 2:5, 6; Col. 1:15; 2:9; II Thess. 1:2; I Tim. 1:2. Paul calls Jesus "God"—Rom. 9:5; Col. 2:9; I Tim. 3:16; Titus 1:3. See Col. 1:15, 19. Paul calls Jesus "The Son of God"—Acts 9:20; Rom. 1:1-4, 9; 5: 10; 8:3, 29, 32; II Cor. 1:19; Gal. 1: 16; 2:20; 4:4; Eph. 4:13; I Thess. 1:10. Lordship of Jesus—See DIVINITY OF JESUS. Power of Jesus—I Cor. 1:24, 30; Phil. 2:9, 10; II Thess. 1:9. *Power over life and death*—Rom. 14:9; I Cor. 3:20, 21; 15:24-28; I Thess. 5:10. *All authority given to Him*—Eph. 1:20-23; Phil. 2:9-11; Col. 2:10. The Judge of

the world—Rom. 2:16; I Cor. 4:5; II Cor. 5:10; II Tim. 4:1, 8. Kingship of Jesus—I Cor. 15:24-28; Col. 1:13. *Seated on the right hand of God*—Rom. 8:34; Eph. 1:20-22; Col. 3:1. Kingdom of Jesus—*Called "The Kingdom of God"*—Rom. 14:17; I Cor. 6:9, 10; 15:50; Gal. 5:21; Col. 4:11; II Thess. 1:5. *The kingdom of Christ and God*— Eph. 5:5. *His kingdom*—I Thess. 2:12; II Tim. 4:1, 18. *The kingdom of the Son of His love*—Col. 1:13. Not of this world—Rom. 14:17; I Cor. 4:20. Universal kingdom—Rom. 10:18; Phil. 2:10; Col. 1:6, 23. Who may enter?— *The righteous*—I Cor. 6:9-11; Gal. 5: 19-24; Eph. 5:3-6; II Thess. 1:5-10. His church.—*Is the body of Christ*— Rom. 12:5; I Cor. 12:12-27; Eph. 1:23; 4:12,16; 5:30; Col. 1:18, 24; 2:19. *Christ the Head*—Rom. 8:29; I Cor. 11:3; Eph. 1:22, 23; 4:15; 5:23, 24; Col. 1:18; 2:10, 19. *The foundation*— I Cor. 3:10-15; Eph. 2:20. *He cleansed it*—Eph. 5:26. *Loved it*—Eph. 5:2, 25, 29. *Nourisheth and cherisheth*—Eph. 5:29. *Presented it to Himself*—Eph. 5: 27. *Sanctified it*—I Cor. 1:2; Eph. 5: 26. *Is the cause of glory in the church* —Eph. 3:21. Christ a High Priest after the order of Melchizedek—Rom. 8:34; Eph. 2:13, 14; I Tim. 2:5. Eternity of Jesus—II Cor. 8:9; Eph. 4:10; Col. 1:17. Exaltation—Rom. 6:4; 8:17; I Cor. 15:25-28; Eph. 4:8-10; Phil. 2:6-11. Glory of—Rom. 9:5. Resurrection of Jesus a proof of His divinity and of our resurrection. Paul rests the whole question of our salvation upon death and resurrection of Jesus—Rom. 8:1-4, 32-34; 10:1-10; I Cor. 1:23, 24; 15:1-28, 57. Sinlessness of Jesus —II Cor. 5:21.

Headship of Christ.—*Over the outward universe*—Col. 1:15-17. *Over the spiritual realm or the church general*—Col. 1:18 ff. *Over the local church*—I Cor. 12:27. *Head of the individual*—I Cor. 11:3.

Humanity of Jesus.—According to the flesh—Rom. 1:3; 8:3, 4, 29, 32; 9:5; II Cor. 5:16, 21; 8:9; Phil. 2:5-8; Col. 2:9; I Tim. 3:16. Seed of Abraham— Rom. 4:13; Gal. 3:8. Descendant of Isaac—Rom. 9:6-8. Son of David—

Rom. 1:3; 9:5. Became poor for our sakes—II Cor. 8:9; Phil. 2:5-8.

Humiliation of Jesus.—Afflicted—Col. 1:24. Bore sin—Rom. 4:25; 8:3; II Cor. 5:21. Born of woman—Rom. 1:3; Gal. 4:4. Crucified—I Cor. 2:2; Phil. 2:8. Curse, Became a—Gal. 3:13. Died —I Thess. 4:14; 5:10. Gave Himself —Gal. 1:4; 2:20; Eph. 5:2, 25. Humbled—Rom. 15:3; II Cor. 8:9; Phil. 2:7, 8. Learned obedience—Rom. 5:19; Phil. 2:8. Manifested in the flesh—Rom. 1:3; 8:3; II Cor. 5:16; I Tim. 3:16. Offered—I Cor. 5:7; Eph. 5:2.

Incarnation of Christ—I Cor. 1:17, 18; Gal. 4:4; Rom. 1:3; Phil. 2:6-8.

Kingdom of Jesus: Called.—The Kingdom of God—Rom. 14:17; I Cor. 6:9, 10; 15:50; 5:21; Col. 4:11; II Thess. 1:5. The Kingdom of Christ and God —Eph. 5:5. His Kingdom—I Thess. 2:12; II Tim. 4:1. His heavenly Kingdom—II Tim. 4:18. Kingdom of the Son of his love—Col. 1:13. Not meat —Rom. 14:17. Not in mere word— I Cor. 4:20. Who may enter: Not flesh and blood—I Cor. 15:50. The righteous—I Cor. 6:9-11; Gal. 5:19-24; Eph. 5:3-6; II Thess. 1:5. Those who endure tribulation—Acts 14:22; II Thess. 1:5. Universal—Rom. 10:18; Phil. 2:10; Col. 1:6, 23. Delivered up to the Father—I Cor. 15:24.

His mission.—To condemn sin—Rom. 8: 3, 4. See II Cor. 5:21. Set an example in His life, To—Rom. 8:29; 13:14; 15:2-5; II Cor. 3:18; 4:10; Gal. 4:19; Eph. 4:13, 15; 5:2; Phil. 2:5; Col. 3: 10, 11; Heb. 12:2-4. Life, Jesus came to give—Rom. 5:17; 6:23; Gal. 2:20; Phil. 1:21; Col. 3:3, 4. Light, To give —Eph. 5:14. Propitiation for sin, To be a—Rom. 3:25; 4:25; 5:5-8; 8:3; I Cor. 15:3; II Cor. 5:21; Gal. 1:4; 3: 13; Heb. 9:26, 28. Reconcile the world to God, To—Rom. 5:9-11; II Cor. 5: 17-21; Eph. 2:13-23; Col. 1:20-22; 2:14; Heb. 10:11-22. Redeem mankind, To—Rom. 3:23-26; I Cor. 5:7; 6:20; 7:23; Gal. 4:4; I Thess. 1:10; I Tim. 2:6. *Christ gave His life for mankind*—Rom. 3:24, 25; 4:25; 5:6-9; 8:3, 32; 14:15; II Cor. 5:14-21; Gal. 3:1, 8, 13, 14; Eph. 5:2, 25; I Thess.

5:9, 10; Tit. 2:13, 14; Heb. 2:9-18; 7:24-27; 9:11-26. *Redemption through His blood*—Rom. 3:24, 25; I Cor. 6:20; 7:23; Eph. 1:7; Heb. 9:12-15.

Mystery of Christ—Rom. 16:25; I Cor. 5:14; Eph. 1:9; 3:3, 4, 9; 5:32; 6:19; Col. 2:2; I Tim. 3:9, 16.

Names of Jesus.—*Christ*—I Thess. 2:6. *Jesus Christ (especially in earlier Epistles)*—I Thess. 1:1. *Christ Jesus (especially in later Epistles)*—I Tim. 1:1. *Son of God*—II Cor. 1:19; Gal. 2:20; Rom. 1:4; Eph. 4:13. *Judge*—II Tim. 4:8. *Lord Jesus Christ*—I Tim. 6:14. *Blessed and only Potentate, the King of kings and Lord of lords*—I Tim. 6:15. *Saviour*—Phil. 3:20; Eph. 5:23; Tit. 1:4; 2:13; 3:4, 6. *Mediator* —I Tim. 2:5. See DIVINITY OF JESUS.

Resurrection of Jesus—The foundation of Christianity—Rom. 1:3, 4; 6:3-11; 8:11; 10:9; I Cor. 3:10, 11; 15:1-20; Eph. 2:4-7; Col. 2:12; 3:1.

Resurrection of Jesus the earnest of ours —Rom. 8:19-25, 32-34; I Cor. 15:18-26, 54-57; Phil. 3:10-14; II Tim. 2:11, 12.

Baptism a symbol of the resurrection— Rom. 6:3-11; Col. 2:11-13.

Riches of Christ—Eph. 3:8; Col. 1:27.

Saviour, Jesus the.—See SALVATION.

Second coming of Jesus—I Cor. 11:26; 15:23. The disciples looked for the immediate coming of Jesus.—I Cor. 1:7, 8; 4:5; Phil. 3:20, 21; 4:5; Col. 3:4; I Thess. 1:10; 2:19; 3:13; 4:15-17; 5:2, 3, 23; II Thess. 2:1-8; 3:5; I Tim. 6:14, 15; Tit. 2:13; Heb. 9:28. *In glory*—Col. 3:4; I Thess. 4:16. *With Power* — II Thess. 1:5-10. *Without Warning*—I Thess. 5:2, 3. *To judge the world*—Rom. 2:16; I Cor. 1:7, 8; 4:5; II Thess. 1:7-10; II Tim. 4:1.

Sufferings of Jesus—Rom. 15:3; I Cor. 2:2, 8; 5:7; II Cor. 1:5; Gal. 3:13; Phil. 2:8; 3:10; Heb. 2:9, 10; 5:2, 7, 8; 6:6; 11:26; 12:2, 3; 13:3.

Law, Christ's relation to the.—Law added because of transgression till the seed should come—Rom. 5:20, 21; Gal. 3:19; 4:1-5; I Tim. 1:8-10. Was a tutor to bring us unto Christ—Gal. 3:24, 25. Christ the end of the law unto righteousness—Rom. 7:1-4; 10: 4; Gal. 3:24; 4:4, 5. Christ died in

vain if righteousness could come by
the law—Gal. 2:21; 3:21. Christ
profits nothing if we are dependent
on circumcision—Gal. 5:1-6, 11. We
are made free from the law by the
body of Christ—Rom. 7:1-7; 8:1-4;
Gal. 4:1-5. Christ took away the bond
written in ordinances—Col. 2:14. Veil
done away in Christ—II Cor. 3:14.
Shadow of heavenly things to come—
Only in force till Christ came—Col.
2:14-17; Heb. 8:5; 9:6-11; 10:1.

Liberality.—Acts 24:17; Rom. 15:25-32;
I Cor. 16:1-4; II Cor. 8:1-15, 19-21;
9:1-15; Gal. 2:10; 6:6-10.

Love.—I Cor. 13:1-13; Col. 3:12-14; I
Tim. 1:5. Abounding—Phil. 1:9. An
active principle—Gal. 2:19, 20. An-
tagonism of, with sin—I Cor. 4:21.
Breastplate of faith and love—I
Thess. 5:8. Brethren—Rom. 12:14-16;
14:21; 15:1-7; Gal. 5:13-15; 6:1, 2;
Eph. 4:2, 32; Phil. 2:2; Col. 2:2; I
Thess. 3:12; 4:9, 10, 18; Philemon 16.
Characteristics of—*Worketh no ill*—
Rom. 13:10. *Children, For*—Tit. 2:4.
*Christian, in twelve particulars: Before
God in*—Eph. 1:4. *Does all in*—I Cor.
16:14. *Edifies the body in*—Eph. 4:16.
Forbears one another in—Eph. 4:2. *In-
creases in*—I Thess. 3:12. *Is truthful
in*—I John 3:18. *Is unfeigned in*—II
Cor. 6:6. *Keeps himself in*—Jude 21.
Knit together in—Col. 2:2. *Rooted and
grounded in*—Eph. 3:17. *Speaks truth
in*—Eph. 4:15. *Walks in*—Eph. 5:2.
Christ, Of—Rom. 8:35-39; II Cor. 5:
14; 8:8, 9; Gal. 2:20; Eph. 3:17-19;
5:2, 25, 29. Christ, For—I Cor. 16:22.
Edifieth—I Cor. 8:1. Enemies, For—
Acts 26:29; Rom. 12:20; I Cor. 13:5.
Evidence of a new life—Gal. 2:19, 20;
Col. 1:4-8; I Thess. 1:3; II Tim. 1:7.
Fellow-men, For—I Cor. 10:24; Gal.
6:1, 2, 10; Eph. 4:2, 32; Phil. 2:2; I
Thess. 5:8, 13, 14. Forsaken—Gal. 3:
1-3; II Tim. 4:10. Fulfilling of the
law—Rom. 13:10; I Cor. 13:1-7; I
Tim. 1:5. Fruit of the Spirit—Rom.
5:3-5; 6-21, 22; I Cor. 13:4-7; Gal.
5:22; Eph. 5:8-11; Col. 3:12-14. God,
For—I Cor. 8:3; II Thess. 3:5. God,
Of—Rom. 11:28, 29; II Cor. 9:7; II
Thess. 2:16. Manifests His love by
sending His Son—Rom. 5:6-8; 8:31,

32, 38, 39; II Cor. 5:14-19; Eph. 1:3-
14; 2:4-7; Col. 1:19, 20; Tit. 3:4-6.
Hypocrisy, Without—Rom. 12:9; Eph.
6:24. Man and woman—Eph. 5:25,
28-31; Col. 3:19; Tit. 2:4. Measure
of—Rom. 8:35-39; I Cor. 2:2; II Tim.
4:8. Preferring one another in—Rom.
12:10; Phil. 2:2. Thyself, As—Rom.
13:8-10; Gal. 5:14.

Marriage and celibacy.—The denial of
the conjugal life condemned—I Tim.
4:1-5. Marriage is right—I Cor. 7:2,
9-17, 27-28, 36; 9:5; I Tim. 3:2; 4:5,
12; Tit. 1:6. Celibacy recommended
in special cases—I Cor. 7:7-8, 32, 34,
37, 38, 40.

Servants.—Christianity proposes no
change in outward relations—I Cor.
7:17. Advice to servants—Eph. 6:5-
8. To Masters—Eph. 6:9. In Christ
all distinctions abolished—I Cor. 7:
20-24; Gal. 3:28; Philemon 10-20.
Getting Christ into you makes all
things new—II Cor. 5:17; Eph. 4:20-
24.

Sin.—Avoid appearance of—I Thess. 5:
22. Cleansing from—Eph. 1:7; 5:26.
Christ died for—I Cor. 15:4; 5:18-21;
Gal. 1:4; Tit. 2:14. Characterized as
bondage—Rom. 3:9; 6:6, 12, 15; 7:23,
24; 8:2, 21. Confession of, by Paul—
I Cor. 15:9; I Tim. 1:15. Conviction
of Paul's—Acts 22:10; I Cor. 15:9;
I Tim. 1:15. Forgiveness of, through
Christ—Eph. 1:17; Col. 1:14. Of the
Gentiles—Rom. 1:24-32. Lust of flesh
is—Rom. 7:13-25; 8:3, 5-7; Gal. 5:16-
21; Eph. 2:3. Is progressive—II Tim.
3:13. Protection from, by conscience,
to be put away—Eph. 4:22; Col. 3:9;
II Tim. 2:19. Reacts—Gal. 6:7, 8. Repugnant to the righteous—Rom. 7:15,
19, 23, 24. Saints dead to—Rom. 6:2,
11; Col. 3:3. Save that sins shall die
—Rom. 7:13; Eph. 2:1. Specifications
of: *Deceitful*—II Cor. 11:3; Eph. 4:22.
Not of faith—Rom. 14:23. *Open and
manifest*—I Tim. 5:24. *Secret*—Eph.
5:12. *Works of darkness*—Eph. 5:11.
Transgression, Sin as—Rom. 2:12-24;
8:7. Types of: *Uncleanness*—II Cor.
5:2-5; 6:17; Eph. 5:5; I Thess. 2:3;
4:7. .Universality of—Rom. 3:10-20,
23; 5:12; Gal. 3:22. What sin leads
to: Death—Rom. 6:21, 23; I Cor. 15:

56. Exclusion from heaven—I Cor. 6:9–10; Gal. 5:19–21; Eph. 5:5. Hardening of the heart—Rom. 1:32; Eph. 4:18, 19; I Tim. 4:2; Tit. 1:15. Hopelessness—Eph. 2:12; I Thess. 4:13. Shame—Rom. 6:21. Whence it comes: *From the devil*—Eph. 2:2. *Through heredity*—Rom. 5:12–19; Eph. 2:3, 5. *Through knowledge of the law*—Rom. 1:21, 32; 3:20; 4:15; 5:13, 20; I Cor. 15:56.

Spiritual gifts.—Diversities—I.Cor. 6:7; 12:4–6. Why given—I Cor. 12:7. The gifts enumerated—I Cor. 12:8–10. When gifts are profitless—I Cor. 13:1–2. Gifts must be coöperative—Rom. 12:4–7; I Cor. 12:13–27; Eph. 4:11–16. How gifts were communicated—Acts 19:6; I Tim. 4:14. Gifts to be desired—I Cor. 14:1–15. Gifts to pass away—I Cor. 13:8–9.

Women.—I Cor. 11:5–15; Eph. 5:22–24; Col. 3:18; I Tim. 3:11; 5:2–16; Tit. 2:3–5. Concerning public speaking—I Cor. 14:34–35; Gal. 3:28; I Tim. 2:12, 13. See CALLING, FOREORDINATION, FORGIVENESS, GENTILES, GOSPEL, HOPE, JUSTIFICATION, LIFE, MAN, MISSIONS, RECONCILIATION, REDEMPTION, RESURRECTION, SALVATION.

PAY. As judges determine—Ex. 21:22. Debt—See DEBTS. Double—Ex. 27:7, 9. Dowry—Ex. 22:17. Forfeit—I Ki. 20:39; Esth. 3:9; 4:7. Jehovah, Will—Pr. 19:17. Ox for ox—Ex. 21:1, 36. Surety for—Pr. 22:26, 27. Time, For loss of—Ex. 21:19. Tithes—See TITHES. Tribute—See TRIBUTE. Vows—See Vows.

PEACE: God the author of.—Job. 25:2; Ps. 147:14; Is. 45:7; Rom. 15:33; 16:20; I Cor. 14:33; II Cor. 13:11; Phil. 4:9.

Jesus the peacemaker.—John 16:33; Eph. 2:14; Col. 1:20; II Thess. 3:16. By way of the sword—Mt. 10:34; Lu. 12:51.

Peacemakers.—Pr. 12:20; Is. 27:5; Mt. 5:9; Jas. 3:18.

A gift.—John 14:27; Ps. 29:11; 72:7; Is. 57:19.

A command.—Mk. 1:25; 4:39; 10:48; Rom. 12:18; II Cor. 13:11.

Necessary for enjoyments.—Ps. 34:12–14; Phil. 4:7; I Pet. 3:10, 11.

Offering for.—Deut. 27:7; Ju. 20:26; I Sam. 5:12; 6:4; 10:8; 11:15; II Chr. 30:22.

Covenant of.—Gen. 9:14, 15; Num. 25:12; Josh. 9:15; I 'Sam. 20:42; I Ki. 5:12; Is. 54:10; Ez. 34:25; 37:26; Mal. 2:5.

Conditional.—Ps. 85:8; Pr. 3:2; 16:7; Is. 26:3; 48:18, 22; 57:21; Ez. 7:25; Mt. 10:13; Lu. 14:32; Rom. 5:1; 8:6.

Uncertain.—I Ki. 22:27, 28; II Ki. 9:17–22; Jer. 6:14; 8:11, 15; Ez. 13:10; Mt. 10:34.

Enforced.—Deut. 20:10–12; Job. 13:5, 13; Mk. 1:25; 4:39; Lu. 4:35; 19:38–40.

Worth the struggle.—Ps. 34:14; Pr. 17:1, 28; Ecc. 4:6; Lu. 19:42; Rom. 12:18; 14:19; II Cor. 13:11; Heb. 12:14.

Disposition for.—Gen. 13:8, 9; Esth. 10:3; II Sam. 2:26, 27; Lu. 14:31, 32; Acts 12:20.

National.—I Ki. 4:25; 5:4, 5; II Ki. 15:19; I Chr. 4:40; II Chr. 14:1, 2; Ps. 147:14. Universal—Is. 2:4; 9:7.

Preached to the world.—Is. 52:7; 62:6; Acts 10:36; 18:9; Rom. 10:15; Eph. 2:17.

Salutations.—John 20:26; I Cor. 1:3; II Cor. 1:2; Gal. 1:3; Eph. 1:2; Phil. 1:2; Col. 1:2; I Thess. 1:1; II Thess. 1:2; I Tim. 1:2; II Tim. 1:2; Tit. 1:4; Philemon 3; I Pet. 1:2; II Pet. 1:2; II John 3; Rev. 1:4.

Benedictions.—Ps. 125:5; Lu. 24:36; John 14:27; 20:19, 21, 26; Rom. 15:13; III John 14.

Bond of Unity.—Ju. 4:17; Is. 32:16–18; Zech. 8:19–23; Mk. 9:50; Eph. 2:15–17; 4:3; I Thess. 5:13.

Prayer for.—Ps. 122:6–9; Jer. 29:7; I Tim. 2:2.

Under chastisement.—Job 5:17–24; Is. 53:5; Heb. 12:11.

Happy ending of.—Gen. 15:15; Ex. 18:23; Ps. 37:37; Is. 55:12; Lu. 2:29; Rom. 8:6; 14:17; II Pet. 3:14.

Haters of.—Ps. 120:6, 7; 28:3; 35:20.

Opposers of peace.—Josh. 10:1–5; 11:19; Is. 59:8. False visions—Ez. 13:16.

Peace despised.—II Ki. 9:17, 18; Rom. 3:16, 17. See CONTENTMENT, HOLY SPIRIT, FRUITS OF, SALVATION, SPIRIT, FRUITS OF.

PEACE-OFFERINGS. See OFFERINGS.

PEACOCK. I Ki. 10:22; II Chr. 9:21.

PEARL. I Tim. 2:9; Rev. 17:4; 18:12, 16. Gate of New Jerusalem—Rev. 21:21. Price, Of great—Mt. 13:45, 46. Swine, Cast not before—Mt. 7:6.

PEDAHEL, pĕd'a-hĕl. **A prince of Naphtali.**—Num. 34:28.

PEDAHZUR, pe-däh'zur. **Father of Gamaliel a prince of Manasseh.**—Num. 1:10; 2:20.

PEDAIAH, pe-dā'iah. (1) **Son of Jehoiachin.**—I Chr. 3:18–19.

(2) **Great-grandfather of Jehoiakim.**—II Ki. 23:36.

(3) **One who helped to repair the wall.**—Neh. 3:25.

(4) **Father of a ruler under David.**—I Chr. 27:20.

(5) **One who stood by Ezra at the reading of the law.**—Neh. 8:4.

(6) **A Benjamite.**—Neh. 11:7.

(7) **A Levite.**—Neh. 13:13.

PEDESTAL. I Ki. 7:29. See TEMPLE.

PEDIGREE. Num. 1:18. See GENEALOGIES.

PEEL. Gen. 30:38.

PEKAH, pē'kah. **King of Israel.**—II Ki. 15:25–37; 16:1, 5; II Chr. 28:6; Is. 7:1.

PEKAHIAH, pĕk'a-hī'ah. **Son of Menahim, King of Israel.**—II Ki. 15:22–26. See ISRAEL.

PEKOD, pē'kŏd. **A Chaldean portion of the Babylonian army.**—Jer. 50:21; Ez. 23:23.

PELAIAH, pe-lā'iah. (1) **One of Ezra's assistants.**—Neh. 8:7.

(2) **A descendant of David.**—I Chr. 3: 24. (3) **A Levite.**—Neh. 10:10.

PELALIAH, pĕl'a-lī'ah. **A priest**—Neh. 11:12.

PELATIAH, pĕl'a-tī'ah. (1) **A prince of Judah**—Ez. 11:1, 13.

(2) **A Simeonite.**—I Chr. 4:42.

(3) **Grandson of Zerubbabel.**—I Chr. 3:21.

(4) **Name of a family who returned from exile.**—Neh. 10:22.

PELEG, pē'leg. **Son of Eber, ancestor of Jesus.**—Gen. 10:25; Lu. 3:35.

PELET, pē'let. (1) **A descendant of Caleb.**—I Chr. 2:47.

(2) **A Benjamite who followed David.**—I Chr. 12:2.

PELETH, pē'leth. (1) **A Reubenite.**—Num. 16:1.

(2) **A descendant of Jerahmeel.**—I Chr. 2:33.

PELETHITES. II Sam. 8:18.

PELICAN. Lev. 11:8; Ps. 102:6; Is. 34:11; Zeph. 2:14. See BIRDS.

PELONITE, pĕl'o-nite. I Chr. 11:27, 36.

PEN. False—Jer. 8:8. Man, Of a—Is. 8:1. Iron—Job 19:24; Jer. 17:1. My tongue is my—Ps. 45:1. With ink and —III John 13.

PENALTY. Bear—Pr. 19:19.

PENCE. Lu. 12:6.

PENIEL, pe-nī'el. Gen. 32:30. See PENUEL.

PENINNAH, pe-nĭn'nah. **Wife of Elkanah.**—I Sam. 1:2.

PENDANTS. Ju. 8:26; Is. 3:19.

PENKNIFE. See KNIFE.

PENNY. Mt. 10:29. See MONEY.

PENTECOST. Acts 2:1; 20:16; I Cor. 16:8. See FEASTS.

PENUEL, pe-nū'el. (1) **A place where Jacob crossed the river Jabbok.**—Gen. 32:30.

(2) I Chr. 4:4.

(3) **A Benjamite.**—I Chr. 8:25.

PENURY. Pr. 14:23.

PEOPLE. Ex. 6:7; Rev. 5:9, 10; 21:3. A joy—Is. 65:18. All the—Lu. 8:37. Ants not strong—Pr. 30:25. Blessed above all—Deut. 7:14. Committed evils—Jer. 2:13. Give—Is. 43:4. God, Of—Heb. 4:9. God's chosen—See CHOICE, ISRAEL. Happy—Ps. 144:15. Gods of—Ps. 96:5. Hearkened not—Ps. 81:11. One—Gen. 11:6. Known among—Ps. 105:1. Labor of—Ps. 105:44. Laden with iniquity—Is. 1:4. My—Rom. 9:25; II Cor. 6:16. Pleasure in—Ps. 149:4. Possession, For own—Tit. 2:14. Prepared—Lu. 1:17. Princely—Song of Sol. 6:12. Redemption for—Lu. 1:68. Save from sin—Mt. 1:21. Saved by Jehovah—Deut. 33:29. Sons of God, Called—Rom. 9: 26. Understanding, Of no—Is. 27:11. Whole—Amos 1:6, 9. Whom I have not known—II Sam. 22:44.

PEOR, pē'or. (1) **A mountain of Moab.**—Num. 23:28. A Moabite idol—Num. 25:18. See BAAL-PEOR.

PERADVENTURE. Fifty righteous—Gen. 18:24. For good man—Rom. 5:7.

God give repentance—II Tim. 2:25. Harm befall him—Gen. 42:4. He sleepeth—I Ki. 18:27. It will please God—Num. 23:27. It was an oversight—Gen. 43:12. Not enough—Mt. 25:9. People repent—Ex. 13:17.

PERAZIM, pĕr'a-zim. **A mountain.—** Is. 28:21.

PERCEIVE. Craftiness—Lu. 20:23. Ear, By—Is. 6:9. Eyes, With—Mt. 13:15. Grace—Gal. 2:9. Jesus—Mt. 26:10. Not—Is. 6:9; Mt. 15:17; John 8:27. Power—Lu. 8:46. That God is no respecter—See GOD. That thou art a prophet—John 4:19. Understanding —Eph. 3:4. Wickedness—Mt. 22:18.

PERDITION. I Tim. 6:9. End is— Phil. 3:19. Go into—Rev. 17:8, 11. Shrink back unto—Heb. 10:39. Son of—John 17:12; II Thess. 2:3. Token of—Phil. 1:28. See DESTRUCTION, HELL, JUDGMENT.

PERES, pē'rēs. **Part of the writing on the wall at the Feast of Belshazzar.—** Dan. 5:28.

PERESH, pē'resh. **Son of Machir.—I** Chr. 7:16.

PEREZ, pē'rez. **One of the twin sons of Judah and Tamar.—**Gen. 38:29; 46: 12; Num. 26:20, 21; Ruth 4:12, 18; I Chr. 2:4, 5; 4:1; 9:4; Neh. 11:4. Ancestor of Jesus—Lu. 3:33. See PHAREZ.

PEREZITES. Num. 26:20.

PEREZ-UZZAH, pē'rez-ŭz'za. **Name given to the place where Uzzah was slain for touching the ark.—**II Sam. 6:8; I Chr. 13:11.

PERFECTION. Heb. *Tamm,* ''Complete,'' ''Perfect,'' ''Upright.'' Gr. *Teleiótes,* ''Completion,'' ''Perfection.''

In Ideal.—Ps. 119:80; Mt. 5:48; Eph. 4:12, 13; Phil. 3:12–15; Jas. 3:2.

How to attain unto.—Gen. 17:1; Mt. 19:21; Lu. 6:40; II Cor. 13:9, 11; Col. 1:28, 29; 4:12, 13; Heb. 6:1; Jas. 1:4; 2:22; I John 2:5; 4:17, 18.

Help from God.—Ps. 18:32; 138:8; II Cor. 12:9; Heb. 13:20, 21; Jas. 1:17.

God delighted with.—Pr. 11:20. Commanded—Gen. 17:1; Deut. 18:13.

Perfection of heart.—I Ki. 8:61; 11:4; 15:3, 14; II Ki. 20:3; I Chr. 12:38;

28:9; 29:9, 19; II Chr. 15:17; 16:9; 19:9; 25:2; Ps. 101:2, 6.

Reward of.—II Sam. 22:26; Ps. 18:23, 24; 101:6; 119:1; Pr. 2:21; 28:10; 37: 37; Is. 26:2; Heb. 12:23.

Unity of.—John 17:23; I Cor. 13:10; Heb. 11:40.

Through suffering.—Heb. 2:10; I Pet. 5:10. Through obedience—Heb. 5:8, 9.

Prayed for.—Col. 4:12; I Thess. 3:10.

Of beauty.—Ps. 50:2; Lam. 2:15; Ez. 16:14; 27:4, 11; 28:12, 15.

No perfection under Moses.—Law—Gal. 2:3; Heb. 7:19; 10:1. Priesthood— Heb. 7:11. Sacrifices—Heb. 9:9, 10.

Perfection of law.—Ps. 19:7; 119:72, 142; Jas. 1:25.

Perfection provokes jealousy.—Ps. 64:4; Pr. 29:10. Productive of peace—Is. 26:3. Love the bond—Col. 3:14.

No instances of absolutely perfect men. —Noah—Gen. 6:9; Job—Job 1:1, 8; 2:3. David—I Ki. 11:4. Asa—I Ki. 15:14. Hezekiah—Is. 38:3. Paul— Phil. 3:12. Zacharias and Elisabeth— Lu. 1:5. See GOD, PERFECTION OF; JESUS, CHARACTER OF; SANCTIFICATION. The term perfect applied to men without necessarily committing the writer to their sinlessness.

PERFORM. Able to—Rom. 4:21. Commandments—I Sam. 15:11, 13. Intents of heart—Jer. 23:20; 30:24. Part of kinsman—Ruth 3:13. Promise—Neh. 5:13. Request—II Sam. 14:22. Vow —Ps. 65:1. Work—Is. 10:12. Zeal of Jehovah shall—II Ki. 19:31; Is. 9:7.

PERFUME: Kinds of.—Spices used as: Aloes—Ps. 45:8; Pr. 7:17; Song of Sol. 4:14. Calamus—Ex. 30:23; Song of Sol. 4:14. Cassia—Ex. 30:24; Ps. 45:8. Cinnamon—Ex. 30:23; Song of Sol. 4:14. Frankincense—Ex. 30:24; Song of Sol. 3:6; 4:14; John 19:39. Liquid myrrh—Song of Sol. 5:5, 13. Myrrh—Ex. 30:23; Song of Sol. 1:12, 13; 4:14; Mt. 2:11. Spikenard—Song of Sol. 1:2.

Use.—In holy anointing oil—Ex. 3:24. Purification of women—Esth. 2:12. Garments made fragrant with—Ps. 45:8. Of bride—Song of Sol. 3:6. Bed scented with—Pr. 7:17. Used as gifts:

To kings—Is. 57:9. *To Christ*—Mt. 2:
11. To embalm—John 19:39.

Perfumers.—Art of—Ex. 30:24, 35; 37:
29; Neh. 3:8; Eccl. 10:1.

Perfume boxes.—Carried by women—
Is. 3:20.

Effect of.—Pr. 27:9.

PERGA, pẽr'gȧ. **A city in Pamphylia**
visited by Paul—Acts 13:14; 14:25.

PERGAMUM, pẽr'ga-mum. **A city in**
Mysia.—Rev. 1:11.

PERHAPS. If perhaps the thought—
Acts 8:22.

PERIDA, pe-rī'dȧ. Neh. 7:57. See
PERUDA.

PERIL. Rom. 8:35. Lives, Of—Lam.
5:9. Rivers and robbers, Of—II Cor.
11:26. See DANGER.

PERISH. I Cor. 1:18. Carest thou not
that we—Mk. 4:38. Except ye repent
—Lu. 13:3, 5. Fallen asleep in Christ
—I Cor. 15:18. Flesh shall—Job 34:
15. Food which—John 6:27. Gold—I
Pet. 1:7. Hunger, With—Lu. 15:17.
Little ones, One of—Mt. 18:14. Members—Mt. 5:29. Not a hair—Lu. 21:
18; Acts 27:34. Save, Lord, we—Mt.
8:25. Silver—Acts 8:20. Way of
wicked—Ps. 1:6. Weak brother—I
Cor. 8:11. Wicked—Pr. 11:10. Wine
—Mk. 2:22. See DEATH.

PERIZZITE, pẽr'iz-zite. **A Canaanite**
race or tribe.—Gen. 13:7; 15:20; Ex.
3:8, 17; 23:23; 33:2; 34:11; Deut. 7:1;
20:17; Josh. 3:10; 9:1; 11:3; 12:8;
24:11; Ju. 3:5; Neh. 9:8.

PERJURY. Forswear thyself.—Ex. 20:
7; Lev. 19:12; Zech. 5:4; Mt. 23:16-
22; Jas. 5:12.

False witness.—Ex. 20:16; 23:1, 7; Lev.
6:3; 19:11; Deut. 5:20; Mal. 3:5; Mt.
19:18; I Tim. 1:10.

Breaking of covenant.—Ez. 16:59; 17:
16; Hos. 4:2, 3. See FALSE, FALSE-
HOOD.

PERPLEXED. About you—Gal. 4:20.
Being—Acts 25:20. City of Shushan
was—Esth. 3:15. Lords were—Dan.
5:9. Much—Mk. 6:20; Lu. 9:7; Acts
5:24; 10:17. Not unto despair—II Cor.
4:8.

PERPLEXITY. Mic. 7:4. Day of—Is.
22:5. Nations in—Lu. 21:25.

PERSECUTION: Causes of.—Ignorance
of a righteous purpose—Acts 3:17;

John 16:3. Prejudice—Mt. 11:18-19.
Jealousy—Acts 13:45-50. Mistaken
zeal—Acts 26:9-11. Hatred—John 15:
18-23. Opposition to good works—
John 5:36-38; 10:32-38; 15:24. In-
road against wickedness—John 7:7;
Acts 16:19-21. Envy—Acts 17:5-13.
Pride—Esth. 3:5-6; Ps. 10:2-11. False
accusations—Ps. 27:12; 35:11-16; Jer.
5:26; 18:20; Mt. 12:24; Mk. 3:22;
Lu. 11:15; Acts 6:9-15. Upright lives
—Gen. 39:7-19; Job 1:8-12; 2:3; Dan.
3:12-23; Mt. 11:18-19.

Persecution foretold. — Obadiah fears
Ahab—I Ki. 18:7-10. Elisha's retort
—II Ki. 6:31-33; 7:1-2. Concerning
servant of Jehovah—Is. 53:4-9. Imaginary persecutors—Lam. 3:5-18. Persecution of apostles and disciples—
Mt. 10:16-18, 21, 34-36; Mk. 13:9-13;
Lu. 10:3; 11:49-51; 21:12-19; John
15:20-21; 16:2-3; Acts 14:22; 20:22-
23; I Cor. 4:9; I Thess. 3:3-4; II Tim.
3:12.

Persecution of Jesus by Jews.—Mt. 2:
13-18; 12:14; 26:3 Mk. 3:6; 11:18;
Lu. 6:11; 13:31; 19:47; 23:21-23; John
5:16; 7:1, 20, 30-32; 8:37; 11:57. By
Roman soldiers—Mt. 27:25-30; Mk.
15:15-20; John 19:2-3.

Persecution of disciples.—Reproaches—
Acts 22:22, 23; II Cor. 6:8; Heb. 10:
33. Bitter hate—Acts 4:1-2; 5:17;
7:54; 9:1; 26:11. Silencing the word
—Acts 4:5-18; 5:27-40; I Thess. 2:
16. Conspiracy—John 12:10; Acts 5:
33; 14:2; 17:5-13; 23:12-22; 26:21.
Imprisonment—Acts 4:3; 5:18; 8:3;
9:2, 14; 12:3-4; 16:24; Heb. 10:34.
Banishment—Acts 8:1; 13:50; Rev.
1:9. Corporal punishment—Mk. 13:9;
Acts 16:22, 23; 22:19, 24; II Cor. 11:
23-25. Death—Acts 7:57, 58; 12:1-2;
22:4, 5; 26:10; Rom. 8:36; II Cor. 4:
10-12.

Persecution of Old Testament worthies.
—Lot—Gen. 19:9. Children of Israel
—Ex. 1:8-14. Moses—Ex. 17:4. David—I Sam. 26:18-25. Elijah—I Ki.
19:2. Jeremiah—Jer. 38:4-6. Elisha
—II Ki. 2:23. Zechariah—II Chr. 24:
21. The prophets—II Chr. 36:16. Micaiah—I Ki. 22:26; II Chr. 18:23.
Hanani—II Chr. 16:10. Uriah—Jer.
26:23.

Citations from Job.—Job 3:25–26; 16: 6–10; 30:12, 19–30.

Citations from Psalms.—Ps. 3:1–2; 27: 12; 35:11–16; 38:12, 20; 41:7; 54:3; 55:5–14; 56:1–6; 57:4, 6; 64:3–5; 69: 4, 8; 71:10, 11.

Conduct under persecution.—Joseph— Gen. 39:20–23. David—Ps. 119:87, 157, 161. Elijah—I Ki. 19:1–4. Jeremiah—Jer. 26:16–24. Daniel—Dan. 6:4–11. Israel—Is. 50:6–9. Jesus— Acts 4:25–26; Mt. 26:42; Lu. 9:51–56; 22:35; 23:34, 42, 43. John the Baptist—Mt. 11:3–6; Lu. 7:19–23. Apostles—Acts 4:1–13; 5:17–42; 6:9–15; 7:54–60; 12:1–11; 13:50–52; 14:2–7, 19–22; 16:19–28, 37–40; 17:5–10; 18: 12–17; 19:23–41; 20:22–27; 21:11–14, 27–39; 22:22–29; 23:9–24; I Cor. 4:9– 13; Rev. 1:9.

How saints of God should act.—Pray for deliverance—Ps. 7:11; 119:86. Pray for enemies—Mt. 5:44. Commit themselves to God—I Pet. 4:19. Rejoice—I Pet. 1:6; 4:14; Phil. 2:17–18; Col. 1:24. Glorifying in it—Rom. 5:3– 4; Eph. 3:13; II Thess. 1:4–5; I Pet. 4:16. Be emboldened—Phil. 1:12–14; II Tim. 1:8. Bless the persecutor— Rom. 12:14.

Punishment of persecutors.—Deut. 30:7; I Ki. 21:17–24; II Ki. 9:7; II Chr. 36: 16–17; Neh. 9:27; Ps. 27:2; 37:12–13; Pr. 14:11; Is. 51:7–8; Jer. 20:3, 4, 11; 26:14, 15; 31:16; Zeph. 2:8–10; Mt. 23:35; Lu. 11:50–51; II Thess. 1:6–8; Rev. 16:5–6.

Divine deliverance.—I Sam. 2:9; Ps. 8:2; 27:5; 31:4; 34:17; 102:18–21; 105:13–22; 125:3; 143:7; Rom. 8:35– 39; II Cor. 1:9–10; 12:7–9; II Tim. 3:10, 11; Rev. 3:10; 6:9–11; 7:13–17; 12:10, 11; 20:4.

PERSEVERANCE. Eph. 6:18. Referred to—Mk. 13:13; Lu. 9:62; Acts 1:14; 13:43; Rom. 12:12; I Cor. 15:58; Col. 1:23; 4:2; II Thess. 3:13; I Tim. 6:14; Heb. 3:6, 14; 6:11; II Pet. 3:17; Rev. 2:10, 25. See ENDURANCE.

PERMIT. If God—Heb. 6:3. If the Lord—I Cor. 16:7. Speak, To—Acts 26:1; I Cor. 14:34. Teach, To—I Tim. 2:12.

PERPETUAL. Backsliding—Jer. 8:5. Covenant—Ex. 31:16. Desolation—

Zeph. 2:9. Enmity—Ez. 35:5. Generations—Gen. 9:12. Pain—Jer. 15:18. Shame—Jer. 23:40.

PERPETUALLY. I Ki. 9:3; II Chr. 7:16. Anger did tear—Amos 1:11.

PERPETUITY. Lev. 25:23.

PERSIA, pĕr′si-à. Ez. 27:10; 38:5. Called Elam.—Is. 21:2; Jer. 25:25; 49: 34–39; Ez. 32:24; Dan. 8:2. **Kings of.**—Ezra 9:9; Esth. 10:2; Dan. 8:20; 10:13; 11:2. Princes of—Esth. 1:14; Dan. 10:20. Princesses of—Esth. 1:18. Power of—Esth. 1:3. ''King of Persia''—Ezra 1:1, 2, 7, 8; 3:7; Dan. 10:1. ''The Persian''—Dan. 6: 28. ''King of Babylon''—Ezra 5:13. Darius I—Ezra 5:5; 6:12, 13, 14; Hag. 1:1; 2:10; Zech. 1:1, 7. ''King of Persia''—Ezra 4:5. ''The Persian'' —Neh. 12:22. ''The King''—Ezra 5: 6, 7; 6:1, 15. Xerxes (''Ahasuerus'') —Esth. 1:1, 2. Artaxerxes I—Ezra 4:7. King of Persia—Ezra 6:14; 7:1. ''King of Babylon''—Neh. 13:6. ''The King''—Ezra 4:8, 11, 23; 7:7, 11, 21; 8:1; Neh. 2:1; 5:14. ''King of Kings''—Ezra 7:12.

Persians.—Dan. 5:28. Law of—Dan. 6: 12, 15.

Provinces of.—Esth. 1:1; Dan. 6:1; 8:2.

Laws of.—Dan. 6:8, 12; Esth. 8:8.

System of government.—Dan. 6:2–11.

Prophecies of.—Expedition of, against Babylon—Jer. 51:11–64; Ez. 32:24, 25; Dan. 2:21–39. Results of conquests of—Dan. 5:28; Chs. 7 and 8. Division of, as a kingdom—Dan. 11:1–4.

PERSIS, pĕr′sis. **A female disciple in Rome.**—Rom. 16:12.

PERSIST. Eccl. 8:3.

PERSONS. Christ no respecter of—Mt. 22:16; Mk. 12:14. Feeble—Ps. 105:37. Give me the—Gen. 14:21. God no respecter of—See GOD. Multitude of— Acts 1:15. Own—Philemon 12. Regardest not—Mt. 22:16. See SOUL, SPIRIT.

PERSUADE. Jer. 20:7, 10; Mt. 28:14; Lu. 16:31. Acts 17:4; Heb. 13:18. Almost thou—Acts 26:28 (A.V.). I am— Acts 26:26; Rom. 8:38; 14:14; 15:14; II Tim. 1:5, 12. Jews and Greeks— Acts 18:4. Multitude—Mt. 27:20; Acts 14:19. People, Paul—Acts 19:26.

PERSUASION. Gal. 5:8. With little—Acts 26:28.

PERUDA, pe-ru′dȧ. Ezra 2:55. See PERIDA.

PERVERSE. Num. 23:21; II Sam. 22:27; 24:17; II Chr. 6:37; Ps. 18:26; Pr. 3:32; 15:4; 16:28; Is. 10:1; Hab. 1:3, 13. Generation—Deut. 32:5, 20; Mt. 17:17. Heart—Pr. 11:20; 12:8; 23:33. Lips—Pr. 4:24. Things—Pr. 2:12. Tongue—Pr. 10:31.

Pervert.—Ex. 23:8; Job 8:3; Jer. 23:36; Dan. 11:32; Gal. 1:7; Tit. 3:11.

PESTILENCE. Ex. 5:3. Deliverer from —Ps. 91:3, 6; Jer. 21:7. Gave life over to—Ps. 78:50. Sent as punishment—Ex. 9:15; Lev. 26:25; Num. 11:33; 14:12; 25:9; Deut. 28:21; II Sam. 24:13, 15; I Chr. 21:12, 14; Ps. 78:50; Jer. 14:12; 29:17, 18; Ez. 5:12, 17; 6:11; 7:15; 28:23; Amos 4:10; Mt. 27:7; Lu. 21:11. See PLAGUE.

PETER. Names: Simon Barjona (Mt. 16:17); Simeon (Acts 15:14); Cephas (I Cor. 1:12).

Vocation.—Fisherman (Mt. 4:18); Made fisher of men—(Mt. 4:19).

Brought to Jesus by brother.—John 1:40–42.

Home.—Bethsaida—John 1:44.

Selected to lead in the apostleship.—Mt. 16:19; Acts 1:15–22; 15:7.

His sagacity and decision won his position.—Mt. 16:13–18; Mk. 8:29; Lu. 9:20.

Often too venturesome.—Walking on water—Mt. 14:28–31. Rebuking the Lord—Mt. 16:22–23. Ready to go to death—Lu. 22:31–34; John 13:36–38. Refuses foot washing—John 13:6–10. Declines to eat what God provided—Acts 10:14. Wants to know about John—John 21:21, 22.

Quick to detect falseness.—Ananias and Sapphira—Acts 5:1–11. Simon the sorcerer—Acts 8:18.

False himself when pressed.—Mt. 26:69–74; Mk. 14:66–71; Lu. 22:54–60; John 18:16–17.

Quick to see his sin and repent.—Mt. 26:75; Mk. 14:72; Lu. 22:62.

Satan sifting him.—Lu. 22:31.

Jesus befriends him and tests him.—Lu. 22:32; John 21:15–17.

Jesus predicts his death.—John 21:18–19; II Pet. 1:14.

Peter the leader in introducing gospel. —To the Jews—Acts 2:14–40; To Gentiles—Acts 10:5–18; 11:1–48; 15:7–9.

Defends the gospel against Annas and Caiaphas.—Acts 4:8–12.

Works miracles.—Man at beautiful gate —Acts 3:6–8; Aeneas, the palsied man —Acts 9:32–34. Restores Dorcas to life—Acts 9:36–42.

Rebuked by Paul for dissembling.—Gal. 2:11–14.

One of favored three apostles.—At the transfiguration—Mt. 17:1–8; Mk. 9:2–9; Lu. 9:28–36. Healing Jairus's daughter—Mk. 5:37–42; Lu. 8:51–56. In the Garden of Gethsemane—Mt. 26:37–46; Mk. 14:33–42.

Mostly active in Jerusalem.—In settling difficulties—Acts 15:1–11.

Endorses Paul's writings.—II Pet. 3:15–16.

Comforts brethren through Epistles.— I Pet. 1:3–9; II Pet. 1:1–11.

CHARACTER GROUPINGS: **Peter's Past.**— (1) Impulse; (2) Independence—John 21:18.

Peter's present.—(1) Relationship; (2) Loyalty—John 21:19.

Peter's future.—(1) Surrender; (2) Suffering; (3) Glory—John 21:18.

Peter's three sleeps.—The sleep of inexperience—Lu. 9:32. The sleep of weariness—Mk. 14:37. The sleep of trustfulness—Acts 12:6.

Peter's early character.—Hot tempered —John 18:10. A bargainer—Mt. 19:27. Boastful—Mk. 14:29. Blended courage and cowardice—Gal. 2:12. Self-confident—Lu. 22:33; John 13:37.

Peter's lesson on the water.—Faith produced by personal revelation—Mt. 14:27. Faith expressed by appeal—Mt. 14:28. Faith exercised in response to call—Mt. 14:29. Faith flags by fear of physical things—Mt. 14:30. Faith renewed by the master's interposition —Mt. 14:31. Faith instructed by a loving rebuke—Mt. 14:31. Faith made strong by a New Revelation of Jesus —Mt. 14:33.

Characteristics of personal ministry.— Devoted activity—Acts 9:32. Touched by human need—Acts 9:33. Prompt response to the call of sorrow—Acts 9:39. Dependence on the power of God for success—Acts 9:40. Tender ministrations—Acts 9:41.

THE INDUCTION OF THE GENTILES.—Acts Chs. 10–11:18.

The apostles' preparation.—The occasion—Acts 10:9–10. The vision—Acts 10:11–12. The command—Acts 10:13–14. The lesson—Acts 10:15.

The apostles' attitude.—Genuineness—Acts 10:26. Frankness—10:28. Fearlessness—Acts 10:28–29. Definiteness—Acts 10:29.

The apostles' testimony.—Conviction concerning God's character—Acts 10:34–35. Declaration of God's purpose—Acts 10:36–37. Revelation of God's love—Acts 10:38–41. Proclamation of the gospel—Acts 10:42–43.

The apostles' justification.—The Spirit witnessed to the truth—Acts 10:44. The Spirit bestowed power—Acts 10:45–46. The Spirit was the warrant for discipleship—Acts 10:47. The Spirit induced fellowship—Acts 10:48.

The apostles' defence.—Objection made—Acts 11:2–3. Explanation given—Acts 11:4–16. Challenge offered—Acts 11:17. Acknowledgment made—Acts 11:18.

What the apostle learned.—The significance of God's purpose—Acts 10:34–35. The simplicity of God's plan—Acts 10:47–48. The sufficiency of God's power—Acts 10:44–45. See EPISTLES OF PETER, APOSTLES.

PETER, EPISTLES OF. See OUTLINE STUDIES IN THE BOOKS.

PETHAHIAH, pĕth'a-hī'ah. (1) A Levite who married a foreign wife.—Ezra 10:23.

(2) A priest.—I Chr. 24:16.

(3) A Levite who assisted Ezra.—Neh. 9:5.

(4) Deputy governor of district of Jerusalem.—Neh. 11:24.

PETHOR, pē'thôr. Home of Balaam.—Num. 22:5; Deut. 23:4.

PETHUEL, pe-thū'el. Father of Joel the prophet.—Joel 1:1.

PETITION. Ask—I Sam. 2:20; I Ki. 2:20; I John 5:15. Grant—I Sam. 1:17. Jehovah fulfill all thy—Ps.

20:5. Make—Dan. 6:13. What is thy?—Esth. 5:6. See PRAYER.

PHILOSOPHERS. Acts 17:18.

PHILOSOPHY. Col. 2:8.

PEUELLETHAI, pē'ŭl-lē'thāi. A Korahite.—I Chr. 26:5.

PHANUEL, pha-nū'el. Father of Anna.—Lu. 2:36.

PHARAOH, phā'raŏh. An official title applied to the kings of Egypt, after 1000 B.C., and in the Bible to those who reigned before that date by accommodation.

(1) Unidentified Pharaoh of the time of Abraham.—Gen. 12:15–20.

(2) Unidentified patron of Joseph.—Gen. 37:36; 39:1; 40:2 ff.; Ps. 105:17–22. Dreams a dream—Gen. 41:1–7; which baffles his official interpreters—vs. 8–13; but is interpreted by Joseph—vs. 14–36. He accepts Joseph's advice regarding the storage of grain—vs. 37–40; and appointes him viceroy—vs. 41–44. He invites Joseph's father and family to Egypt—Gen. 45:16–21; and settles them in the land of Goshen—Gen. 47:3–11. He reduces his people to serfs in return for supporting them through the famine—vs. 19–26. He permits the return of Jacob's clan to bury his body in Canaan—Gen. 50:4–7.

(3) The Pharaoh of the oppression (Rameses II?).—Ex. 1:8, 11, 19. Uses the Israelites as slave-laborers in building treasure cities (Pithom and Raamses)—v. 11. Orders male children destroyed—vs. 15–22. His daughter saves Moses—Ex. 2:7 ff.

(4) The Pharaoh of the exodus (Merenptah).—Visited by Moses with the demand from Jehovah for the freedom of Israel—Ex. 4:19–23; 5:1–3. Refuses and strengthens the oppression—Ex. 5:6–14. Promises to yield repeatedly under pressure of plagues, but recalls his promises—Ex. 8:8, 15, 25, 28, 32; 9:5, 27, 35; 10:16, 28. His first-born is smitten—12:29. He lets Israel go—12:30, 31. But repents and pursues them—Ex. 14:5–9. Is overwhelmed in the Red Sea—vs. 26–31; Neh. 9:10; Ps. 135:9; 136:15; Acts 7:10, 13, 21; Rom. 9:17; Heb. 11:29.

(5) **Father-in-law of Mered.**—I Chr. 4: 18.

(6) **Tanaite king who gave refuge to Hadad.**—I Ki. 11:14 ff.

(7) **Solomon's father-in-law.**—I Ki. 3:1; same as (6)?; I Ki. 7:8; 9:16, 24; II Chr. 8:11.

(8) **Contemporary of Hezekiah and Sennacherib** (Tirhakah).—II Ki. 18:21; Is. 19:11; 30:23; 36:6.

(9) **Pharaoh Necoh.**—II Ki. 23:29–35; 24:7; II Chr. 35:22; 36:4; Jer. 46:2; 32:2, 31, 32.

(10) **Pharaoh Hophra.**—Jer. 37:5, 7, 11; 44:30; Ez. 17:17; 29:1–20; 30:21, 26; 31:2, 18; 32:2, 31, 32. See EGYPT, MOSES.

PHARISEES: Name.—Separated people, from Heb. *Parash;* separated not merely from the Gentiles, but from the common mass of Jews.

Origin.—The exact date is not known. They undoubtedly succeed the *Chasidim,* or Pious Party, who supported Mattathias in his rebellion against Antiochus Epiphanes, who sought to Hellenize the Jews (B.C. 167). Josephus, (Antiquities xiii, v. 9) traces the Pharisees and Sadducees as distinct parties to the time of Jonathan Maccabeus. But he first calls their names in the reign of John Hyrcanus I (B.C. 135–105).

History.—They strive with the Sadducees for supremacy. John Hyrcanus leaves the Pharisees for the Sadducees. The strife between Alexander Jannæus and the Pharisees is bitter. Salome Alexandra restores the Pharisees to power. The Psalms of Solomon show the hopes of the Pharisees at this time. The Pharisees lose political power, though still represented in the Sanhedrin. They gain and hold popular favor. They survive the destruction of the temple and Jerusalem. They find power in the synagogue and the scribes. The Talmud is the expression of pharisaism, which is still powerful among the Jews. They are at the acme of spiritual power when Jesus comes.

Teachings.—In brief they held to the immortality of the soul, the future judgment, the existence of angels and spirits, the resurrection of the body, the coming of a temporal Messiah. There were many apocalyptic features in their Messianic kingdom. Hence they often challenge Jesus.

Hypocrisy.—This undue emphasis on the external naturally led to hypocrisy on a large scale. This fact explains the harsh language used about them by John the Baptist (Mt. 3:7) and Jesus—Mt. 5:20; 6:2 ff.; 12:31, 34; Mk. 12:40; Lu. 11:39, 44; 16:15; 20:47; Mt. 23:13–36.

Rejected John the Baptist.—Came to hear John preach, but called by him offspring of vipers—Mt. 3:7. Sent a committee to investigate John—John 1:25. For a season rejoiced in his light —John 5:35. But refused his baptism —Lu. 7:30. Once had fellowship with some disciples of John—Mt. 9:14; Mk. 2:18; Lu. 5:33. Fear the power of John over the people—Mt. 21:26; Mk. 11:32; Lu. 20:6.

Pharisaic atmosphere.—When Jesus began His work He was in a world dominated by pharisaic traditions. This was true of Galilee as well as Judæa.

Nobler types of Pharisees.—Not all Pharisees were of the worst kind. Many of their teachings were true and in harmony with the spirit of the Old Testament. Joseph and Mary, Simeon and Anna, probably reflected the better phase of pharisaic piety. Gamaliel was neither the worst nor the best.

Bitterness towards Jesus.—The hostility towards Jesus began very early; according to John, at the first visit to Jerusalem during the ministry of Christ —John 2:16 ff. But Nicodemus, a Pharisee, rose above the opposition enough to come to see Jesus by night— John 3:1. They early become jealous of the popularity of Jesus—John 4:1 f. They dislike His claim to power to forgive sins, and consider it blasphemy— Mt. 9:3; Mk. 2:6 f.; Lu. 5:21. They murmur at His social freedom with publicans and sinners—Mt. 9:11; Mk. 2:16; Lu. 5:30; 15:1. They complain that disciples of Jesus do not observe stated fasts—Mt. 9:14; Mk. 2:18; Lu. 5:33. They accuse Christ of working His miracles by the power of the prince of the demons—Mt. 9:34; 11:

19; 12:24 ff.; Mk. 3:22 ff.; Lu. 11:14 ff. They attack Him for violating their rules of sabbath observance—Mt. 12: 2, 10; Mk. 2:23; 3:2; Lu. 6:5, 7; 13: 14 ff.; John 5:10, 18; 9:13 ff. Join with Herodians to kill Him—Mk. 3:6. With the Sadducees to tempt Him—Mt. 15:1. With Herodians—Mt. 22:15; Mk. 12: 13. Sadducees—Mt. 22:23, 34; Mk. 12:18; Lu. 22:27. To entrap Him pharisees and sadducees plot His death —Mt. 27:62; John 18:3. They accuse Jesus of blasphemy in claiming equality with God—John 5:18; 10:33. And finally for calling Himself the Messiah, the Son of God—Mt. 26:63 f.; Mk. 14:61 f. They ridicule Jesus— John 7:48. They accuse Jesus of being a Samaritan and having a demon— John 8:4, 48. They try to entrap Him on many points like: *Eternal life*— Lu. 10:25 ff. *Divorce*—Mt. 19:3; Mk. 10:2. *The greatest commandment*— Mt. 22:34 ff.; Mk. 12:28 ff. *Tribute to Cæsar*—Mt. 22:15 ff.; Mk. 12:13 ff.; Lu. 22:19 ff. They often ask for a sign from heaven, as in Mt. 12:38; 16:1; Mk. 8:11; John 6:30. They challenge His authority—Mt. 21:23, 45; Mk. 12:27; Lu. 20:1. They mock at Christ on the cross—Mt. 27:41 f. They put a guard by the tomb of Christ —Mt. 27:62 ff. They agree to bribe the soldiers to conceal the fact of the resurrection of Christ—Mt. 28:13 f.

Denounced by Jesus.—As hypocrites— Mt. 6:2–16; 15:7; 23:13–29. As not in the kingdom of heaven—Mt. 4:20. As offspring of vipers—Mt. 12:34; 23:33. As inwardly wicked—Lu. 11:39–49. As an adulterous generation—Mt. 12: 39; 16:4. As blind guides—Mt. 15:14; 23:16, 19, 24, 26. As whited sepulchres Mt. 23:27. As more careless of the kingdom than publicans and harlots— Mt. 21:31 f. As unworthy of Moses' seat, which they held—Mt. 32:2 f. As loving praise—Mt. 23:6 ff. As making their proselytes worse than they were themselves—Mt. 23:15. As unworthy of the kingdom, which shall be taken away from them—Mt. 21:43 ff.

Attitude towards the apostles.—Indifferent toward them when they merely proclaimed the resurrection of Jesus, a doctrine held by the pharisees. So Gamaliel opposed the death of the apostles—Acts 5:34–40. Resentment towards Stephen — he accented, as Jesus, the spiritual character of worship independent of place or mere ceremony. Hence Pharisees (elders, scribes —Acts 6:12) arraigned Stephen before the Sanhedrin and compassed his death—Acts 6:10–7:60.

Hatred of Paul.—After his conversion and return to Jerusalem, the Pharisees sought to kill him as a renegade Pharisee—Acts 9:29. It is the pharisaic Jews who oppose Paul all over the world—See Acts Chs. 13–19. It is pharisaic Jews from Ephesus who raise the cry against Paul in Jerusalem— Acts 21:27. Before the Sanhedrin Paul claims to be a Pharisee, as he was, on the point of the resurrection from the dead, to divide the Sanhedrin—Acts 23:6 ff. They assert Paul's innocence for the moment—Acts 23:9. But later join in the effort to kill him—Acts 24:1.

Pharisaic pride.—Shared in by Paul once —Acts 22:3 f.; 26:5; Gal. 1:14; Phil. 3:5.

PHARPAR, phär'par. **A river of Damascus.**—II Ki. 5:12.

PHICOL, phi'kol. **A captain under Abimelech, king of Gerar.**—Gen. 21:22, 32; 26:26.

PHILADELPHIA, phĭl'a-dĕl'phi-à. **A city of Lydia, seat of one of the seven churches.**—Rev. 3:7.

PHILEMON. See OUTLINE STUDIES IN THE BOOKS.

PHILETUS, phi-lē'tus. **A heretic.**—II Tim. 2:17.

PHILIP, the apostle. (1) **Philip of Bethsaida,** "the city of Andrew and Peter"—John 1:44. He was the first man to whom Jesus said, "Follow me"—John 1:43. Christ found him, not he Christ. This may show that he had a retiring spirit. At any rate, in all four lists of the twelve he stands fifth in order. John records three incidents in which Philip took a leading part: (1) He is consulted about feeding the multitude—John 6:5. (2) He shares with Andrew the honor of introducing the Greeks to Jesus—John 12:22. (3)

He seeks for a vision of the Father—
John 14:8. His answer to Nathaniel's
question made him famous—John 1:46.

(2) **The deacon.**—An evangelist—Acts
6:5; 21:8. Labors in Samaria—Acts
8:5–13. Baptizes the Ethiopian eunuch
—Acts 8:27. At Azotus and Cæsarea—
Acts 8:40. Entertains Paul—Acts 21:
8. Philip's daughters prophetesses—
Acts 21:9.

(3) **The brother of Herod the Great.**—
Acts 14:3. See HEROD.

(4) **Tetrarch of Ituræa.**—Lu. 3:1. See
HEROD.

PHILIPPI. See PHILIPPIANS in OUTLINE
STUDIES IN THE BOOKS.

PHILIPPIANS. See OUTLINE STUDIES
IN THE BOOKS.

PHILISTIA, phĭ-lĭs'tĭ-a. **Land of the
Philistines.**—Ps. 60:8; 83:7; 108:9.
See PHILISTINES.

PHILOLOGUS, phĭ-lŏl'o-gus. **A Christian in Rome whom Paul salutes.**—
Rom. 16:15.

PHILOSOPHERS. Acts 17:18.

PHILOSOPHY. Col. 2:8.

PHINEHAS, phĭn'e-has (*high priest*).
(1) **The high priest—Son of Eleazar.**—
Ex. 6:25; I Chr. 6:4, 50. Slays Zimri
and Cozbi and is promised an everlasting priesthood — Num. 25:7–15;
Ps. 106:30. Ruler of the Korahites—
I Chr. 9:20. Carries trumpets to war
against Midian—Num. 31:6. Against
Reubenites—Josh. 22:13–32. Inquires
of the Lord—Ju. 20:28. Property of—
In Ephraim—Josh. 24:33.

(2) **Son of Eli.**—I Sam. 1:3. Sin and
death of—Carries the ark against Philistines and is slain—I Sam. 4:4, 11, 17.
Death of his wife—I Sam. 4:19–22.

PHLEGON, phlē'gon. **A Roman convert.**
—Rom. 16:14.

PHŒBE, phœ'be. **A deaconess of Cenchreæ.**—Rom. 16:1.

PHŒNICIA, phœ'nĭ-si-a. **Territory on
east coast of the Mediterranean Sea,
famous for its commerce.**—Acts 11:
19; 21:2.

PHŒNIX, phœ'nix. **A place on south
coast of Crete.**—Acts 27:12.

PHRYGIA, phrў́g-ĭ-à. **A province in
Asia Minor.**—Acts 2:10.

PHYGELUS, phў-gĕ'lus. **An early Christian who deserted Paul—II Tim. 1:15.

PHYLACTERIES. Mt. 23:5. Strips of
parchment—Ex. 13:9, 16; Num. 15:38;
Deut. 6:8.

PHYSICIAN. As embalmer—Gen. 50:2.
Asa chose—II Chr. 16:12. Luke a
physician—Col. 4:14. They who need
—Mt. 9:12; Mk. 2:17; Lu. 5:31. Suffered many things of—Mk. 5:26; Lu.
8:43. In parable—Lu. 4:23. Illustrative—Job 13:4; Jer. 8:22. See DIS-
EASE, HEALING.

PI-BESETH, pi'–bē'seth. **A city in Lower Egypt.**—Ez. 30:17.

PIECE. Break in—Ex. 23:34. Broken
—Is. 19:10; Mt. 14:20; Mk. 5:4; 6:43;
8:8, 19; Lu. 9:17; John 6:13. Cloth,
Of—Mt. 9:16. Money, Of—Josh. 24:
32. Silver, Of—Gen. 37:28; Ju. 17:10;
I Sam. 2:36; II Sam. 18:11; Ps. 68:30;
Zech. 11:12; Mt. 26:15; Lu. 15:8.
Twelve—I Ki. 11:30.

PIERCE. Hands — Ps. 22:16. Nose,
Through—Job 40:24. Serpent — Job
26:13. Soul—Lu. 2:35. Spear, With—
John 19:34. Sword—Pr. 12:18. Through
—Ju. 4:21; I Tim. 6:10.

PIETY. I Tim. 5:4. See CHRISTIAN
GRACES, RIGHTEOUSNESS.

PIGEONS. Gen. 15:9; Lev. 1:14; 5:7;
12:6, 8; 14:22, 30; 15:14, 29; Num. 6:
10; Lu. 2:24. See DOVE.

PILATE, pī'late. **Governor.**—Mt. 27:2,
21; Lu. 3:1. Offered insult to the law
by mingling blood with sacrifices—
Lu. 13:1.

Jesus before Pilate.—Mt. 27:2, 13, 17, 22,
24; Mk. 15:1, 2, 4, 5, 9, 12, 15; Lu. 23:1,
3, 4, 6, 11, 12, 13, 20, 24; John 18:29,
31, 33, 35, 37, 38; 19:4–22.

Mentioned.—Acts 3:13; 4:27; 13:28; I
Tim. 6:13. Gives up body of Jesus—
Mt. 27:58; Mk. 15:43, 44; Lu. 23:52;
John 19:38. Has tomb of Jesus guard-
ed—Mt. 27:62, 65. Issues orders con-
cerning the crucified—John 19:31.

PILDASH, pĭl'dăsh. **Son of Nahor.**—
Gen. 22:22.

PILE. Is. 30:33; Ez. 24:9.

PILGRIM. Heb. 11:13; I Pet. 2:11. See
JOURNEY.

PILGRIMAGE. Life likened unto —
Gen. 47:9; Ps. 56:8; 119:54; II Cor.
5:1–8; Heb. 11:13; I Pet. 2:11. See
JOURNEY.

PILHA, pĭl'hà. Neh. 10:24.

PILLARS.—Of tabernacle — Ex. 26:32, 37; 27:10–17; 35:11, 17; 36:36, 38; 39: 33, 40; 40:18; Num. 3:36, 37; 4:31, 32. In Solomon's house—I Ki. 7:2, 3, 6, 15, 22, 41, 42. Of Temple—I Ki. 7:41, 42; 10:12; II Ki. 18:16; 25:13, 16, 17; II Chr. 3:15, 16, 17; 4:12; Jer. 52:21, 22; Ez. 40:49. In palace of Shushan—Esth. 1:6. Of brass—Jer. 52:17. Of silver—Song of Sol. 3:10. Of iron—Jer. 1:18. Of Salt—Gen. 19:26. Of Jacob—Gen. 28:18, 22; 31:13, 45; 35:14. Of fire—Ex. 13:21, 22; 14:24; Rev. 10: 1. Of smoke—Ju. 20:40; Song of Sol. 3:6. Of cloud—Ex. 13:21, 22; 14:19, 24; 33:9, 10; Num. 12:5; 14:14; Deut. 31:15; Neh. 9:12, 19; Ps. 99:7. In Shechem—Ju. 9:6. King stood by—II Ki. 11:14; 23:3; II Chr. 23:13. Absalom's monument—II Sam. 18:18. Used as tombstone — Gen. 35:20. Samson pulls down pillars—Ju. 16:25, 26, 29. As witness between Laban and Jacob—Gen. 31:51, 52. Memorial stones—Josh. 4:7; Is. 19:19. See IDOLATRY.

Figurative. — Of heaven — Job 26:11; Rev. 3:12. Of earth—I Sam. 2:8; Job 9:6; Ps. 75:3. Of marble—Song of Sol. 5:15. Of wisdom—Pr. 9:1. Of truth—Tim. 3:15. James and John as—Gal. 2:9.

PILLOW. I Sam. 19:13, 16; Ez. 13:18, 20.

PILTAI, pĭl′tāi. Neh. 12:17.

PIN. See TOOLS AND IMPLEMENTS.

PINE. Away—Lev. 26:16, 39; Lam. 4:9; Is. 24:16; Ez. 4:17; 24:23; 33:10; Mk. 9:18. Soul—Lev. 26:16; Deut. 28:65. See LONG.

PINE TREE. Is. 41:19; 60:13. See TREES.

PINION. Deut. 32:11; Ps. 91:4; Ez. 17:3.

PINNACLE. Is. 54:12; Mt. 4:5; Lu. 4:9.

PINON, pī′non. **A duke of Edom.**—Gen. 36:41.

PIPE. A musical instrument of earliest times—Gen. 4:21. Used by prophets—I Sam. 10:5. Used at coronation of kings—I Ki. 1:40. Wicked rejoice with—Job 21:12. Used in praises to Jehovah—Ps. 150:4. Prevalent at wine-feasts—Is. 5:11–12. Expresses gladness—Is. 30:29; Jer. 48:36. Recalling the prosperity of Tyre—Ez.

28:13. We piped and you did not dance—Mt. 11:17; Lu. 7:32. Must be distinct in sound—I Cor. 14:7. See MUSIC.

PIPINGS. Ju. 5:16.

PIRAM, pī′ram. **King of Jarmath put to death by Joshua.**—Josh. 10:3, 16–27.

PIRATHON, pĭr′a-thon. **Home of Abdon, one of the Judges**—Ju. 12:15.

PIRATHONITES. Ju. 12:13, 15; II Sam. 23:30; 1 Chr. 11:31; 27:14.

PISGAH, pĭs′gah. Heb. *Cleft.*—A hill in Moab. A ridge of mountains of Abarim in which Nebo is the highest point. Balak offers sacrifices at—Num. 21:20; 23:14. Moses views Canaan from—Deut. 3:27; Num. 27:12. Moses went up to top of—Deut. 34:1 The slope of—Deut. 3:17. Under the spring of—Deut. 4:49.

PISHON, pī′shon. **A river in Eden.**—Gen. 2:11.

PISIDIA, pi-sĭd′i-a. **A district in Asia Minor.**—Acts 13:14; 14:24.

PISPA, pĭs′pa. **A man of Asher.**—I Chr. 7:38.

PIT. Joseph cast into—Gen. 37:20, 22, 24, 28, 29. Ishmael cast dead bodies into—Jer. 41:7, 9. David hidden in—II Sam. 17:9. Absalom cast into—II Sam. 18:17. Israel taken in pit of enemies—Ez. 19:4. Proverb of—Pr. 26: 27. Slew a lion in the midst of—II Sam. 23:20; I Chr. 11:22. Land of—Jer. 2:6. Blind guides fall into—Mt. 15:14. Sheep in—Mt. 12:11. At a shearing place—II Ki. 10:14.

Pit used for: Winepress—Mk. 12:1. For water—Lev. 11:36. for hiding places—I Sam 13:6. As a prison—Is. 24:22; Zech. 9:11.

Figurative. Soul draweth near to—Job 33:22; Ps. 94:13; Is. 51:1. Tyre cast in—Ez. 28:8; 26:20. Nations sunk in—Ps. 9:15; Ez. 32:18–30. Digged—Ps. 119:85; Eccl. 10:8. Enemies digged—Ps. 35:7; 57:6; Jer. 18:20, 22; Lam. 3:47. Brought up from—Jonah 2:6. Go down into—Pr. 1:12; 28:17; Ez. 31:14, 16. Mouth of strange women like a—Pr. 22:14. Pit of abyss—Rev. 9:1, 2.

Chastisement. Ps. 28:1; 30:3; 40:2; 88: 4, 6; 140:10; 143:7; Pr. 28:10; Is. 24:17, 18; Jer. 48:43, 44.

Meaning Sheol. Job 33:18, 24, 28; Ps. 28:1; 30:3, 9; 69:15; 88:4; 143:7; Pr. 1:12; Is. 14:15, 19; 38:17, 18; 51:14; Lam. 4:20; Ez. 26:20; 32:18, 24, 29.

PITCH. Burning. Is. 34:9. Tabernacle —See TABERNACLE. Tents—See TENTS. Turned into — Is. 34:9. Within and without—Gen. 6:14; Ex. 2:3.

PITCHER. See VESSELS.

PITIABLE. I Cor. 15:19.

PITIFUL. Women—Lam. 4:10.

PITY: Pity of Jehovah.—Ps. 106:46. For Jerusalem—Joel 2:18. For Israel —Jer. 21:7; Zech. 1:5, 6. For Zion— Ps. 102:13, 14. The Lord is full of pity — Jas. 5:11. Has no pity for transgressors—Deut. 25:11. For Jerusalem—Jer. 5:11; 13:14; 15:5; Ez. 7: 4, 9; 8:18; 9:5, 10. For Zion—Lam. 2:2, 17, 21; 3:43.

Pitiful women of Zion.—Lam. 4:10.

Pity for the poor.—II Sam. 2:6; Ps. 72: 13; Pr. 14:21; 19:19; 28:8.

Pity on fatherless children.—Ps. 109: 12.

Pity expected.—Ps. 69:20.

Job's petition for.—Job 19:21.

Redeemed through pity.—Is. 63:9.

Laws concerning.—Deut. 25:11. No pity for idolaters—Deut. 7:16; 13:8. For murderers—Deut. 19:13, 21.

Used in prophecy.—Ez. 24:21. Edom cast off pity—Amos 1:11. No eye pitied Jerusalem—Ez. 16:5. No pity for Babylon—Is. 13:18.

Illustrative of.—As a father pitieth his children, so Jehovah pitieth them that fear Him—Ps. 103:13.

Teachings of Paul concerning.—Of all men most pitiable—I Cor. 15:19.

PLACE. Chief—Mt. 23:6. Dwelling— See DWELLING PLACE. Gather in one— Gen. 1:9; Acts 2:1. Give place unto wrath—Rom. 12:19. High—See HIGH PLACES. Holy—See MOST HOLY PLACE. Level—Lu. 6:17. Made with hands— Heb. 9:24. Prayer, Of—See PRAYER. Preach in all—I Chr. 17:6. Refuge, Of —See REFUGE. Rest, Of—See REST. Rocky—Mk. 4:16. Whereon the sole of your foot shall tread—Deut. 11:24; Josh. 1:3. Where the lord lay—Mt.

28:6. Where thy glory dwelleth—Ps. 26:8.

PLAGUES. Ex. Chs. 7–12.

A judgment:—Ps. 105:26–38; 135:8, 9; Acts 7:36. Ten in number, signifying completeness. Full flood of God's wrath upon the opposing world-Power —Ex. 8:22. (1) River turned into blood—Ex. 7:14–25. (2) Frogs infest homes—Ex. 8:1–15. (3) Lice on man and beast—Ex. 8:16–19. (4) Flies— Ex. 8:20. (5) Murrain among animals —Ex. 9:1–7. (6) Boils and blains— Ex. 9:8–12. (7) Hail and fire mingled—Ex. 9:22–34. (8) Locusts—Ex. 10:1–20. (9) Darkness for three days —Ex. 10:21–23. (10) Death of firstborn—Ex. 11:4–7; 12:29–30.

Plagues on Israel: For making golden calf—Ex. 32:35. For despising manna —Num. 11:33. For making evil report about Canaan—Num. 14:37. For murmuring at destruction of Korah— Num. 16:41–50. For loathing God's provisions—Num. 21:5–6. For idolatry with Baal-Peor—Num. 25:1–9; Josh. 22:17. For David's numbering the people—II Sam. 24:10–25. Israel spared from plagues—Ex. 8:22–23; Ex. 9:6– 7; 9:26; Ex. 10:23; 11:7; 12:27–28.

New Testament references. — Plaguestricken press upon Jesus—Mk. 3:10; Lu. 7:21. Woman healed of—Mk. 5:29. The plagues of revelation—9:20; 11: 6; 16:9, 21; 18:4; 22:18. See EGYPT and PHARAOH. See EXODUS in OUTLINE STUDIES IN THE BOOKS.

PLAIN. Josh. 20:8; II Sam. 18:23; Ps. 40:4; Ez. 3:22, 23; 8:4; Zech. 4:7; 14: 10. Cities of the—Gen. 13:12; 19:25, 29; Deut. 3:10. Country—Deut. 4:43; Neh. 12:28; Jer. 48:21. Destroyed— Jer. 48:8. Dura, Of—See DURA. Fight on—I Ki. 20:23, 25. Jericho, Of—See JERICHO. Jordan, Of — See JORDAN. Land of the—Gen. 19:28. Medeba, Of —See MEDEBA. Men, Of the—Neh. 3: 32. Moab, Of—See MOAB. Ono, Of— See ONO. Rock of the—Jer. 21:13. Shinar, Of—See BABYLON.

PLAIN, *adj.* Make—Pr. 8:9; Is. 28:25; Hab. 2:2. Man—Gen. 25:27. Path— Ps. 27:11. Speak—Mk. 7:35.

PLAINLY. Read — Ezra 4:18. See— Gen. 26:28. Show—John 16:25. Speak

—Ex. 21:5; Deut. 27:8; I Sam. 10:16;
Is. 32:4; John 10:24: 11:14; 16:29.

PLAITS. Song of Sol. 1:11—See HAIR.

PLAN OF SALVATION. See SALVATION.

PLANE. Is. 44:13. See TOOLS AND IMPLEMENTS.

PLANE TREE. Gen. 30:37.

PLANETS. II Ki. 23:5. See ASTRONOMY, COSMOLOGY.

PLANK. Ex. 27:8; Ez. 27:5; Acts 27:
44. See BOARD.

PLANS. Heart of—Pr. 16:1.

PLANTS: NATURAL HISTORY OF.—Origin:
Created by God—Gen. 1:11; 2:5. Law
of reproduction—Gen. 1:11; Gal. 6:7;
Jas. 3:12. Design: For man's use—
Gen. 2:16; 25:34. To be cultivated by
man—Ex. 15:17; Deut. 28:30, 39; Ps.
107:37.

KINDS OF.—**Trees, Shrubs, and Vines;
Grasses and Herbs.**

I. TREES.

Almond.—White blossom on barren
branches, emblem of hoary locks of
old age—Eccl. 12:5. Beauty of flower
furnishes shape of bowl of golden
candlestick—Ex. 25:33–35. Valuable
as a gift—Gen. 4:11. Emblem of swift
(early) judgment—Jer. 1:11, 12.

Algum.—Used in the construction of
the temple—II Chr. 2:8; 9:10, 11.

Almug.—Used in the construction of
the temple—I Ki. 10:11, 12; also in
palace and in construction of psalteries and harps—Ib.

Aloes.—Perfume plant used with myrrh
and cassia—Ps. 45:8; Song of Sol.
4:14; Pr. 7:17; John 19:39.

Apple.—More probably apricot—Song of
Sol. 2:3; 8:5. Named as shade tree—
Joel 1:12; also for fruit—Pr. 25:11.

Ash.—Is. 44:14; but R, "fir-tree."

Bay-tree.—Named for sturdy, vigorous
life—Ps. 37:35. (May be the laurel.)

Box-tree.—Associated with the fir and
pine—Is. 41:19; 60:13 (R adds Ez.
27:6).

Carob tree.—R; Lu. 15:16.—Tree whose
pods are called "husks."

Cedar.—Named for stateliness—I Ki. 4:
33; II Ki. 19:23; Ps. 92:12. Used in
building the temple—I Ki. 5:6; 6:9,

etc. Emblem of strength—I Ki. 10:
27; Ps. 29:5; Song of Sol. 5:15.

Chestnut (R, "plane").—Gen. 30:37;
Ez. 31:8.

Cypress ("holm-tree," Is. 44:14).—
From its trunks idols were made.

Ebony.—Imported and used as luxury—
Ez. 27:14.

Elm.—For "oak"—Hos. 4:13.

Fig.—Very common. Staple fruit tree—
Deut. 8:8; Pr. 27:18; Jer. 5:17; Amos
4:9; Lu. 13:6; Jas. 3:12. Leaves used
as garments—Gen. 3:7. Fruit, Staple
food—I Sam. 25:18; I Chr. 12:40; Neh.
13:15. Possession of a fig-tree sign of
independence—I Ki. 4:25; II Ki. 18:
31; Is. 36:16; Jer. 5:17; Hos. 2:12;
Mic. 4:4; Hag. 2:19; Zech. 3:10. Used
in parable—Ju. 9:10, 11; Mk. 14:28.
The barren fig-tree—Mk. 11:13.

Fir.—Either "cypress" or "pine"—II
Ki. 19:23; Is. 14:8.

Husks.—Pods of Carob trees, fed to
swine—Lu. 15:16.

Lign-aloes.—Unknown tree, noted for
vigorous life, resembling the gum
aloes of India—Num. 24:6.

Mulberry.—("Balsam," R marg.) Mistranslation for **poplar**—II Sam. 5:23;
I Chr. 14:14.

Mustard.—Grows around the Dead Sea.
Used as an emblem of the kingdom of
God—Mt. 13:31–32. Mustard seed,
Type of faith—Mt. 17:20; Mk. 4:31;
Lu. 17:6.

Myrtle.—Tree with fragrant flower and
aromatic oil-producing leaves, used in
tabernacle—Neh. 8:15. Sign of divine
blessing—Is. 41:19; 55:13.

Oak.—(1) Oak proper. Emblem of sturdy
life—Is. 6:13; Amos 2:9. Variety in
Bashan famous—Ez. 27:6; Zech. 11:2.
Idols made of wood—Is. 44:14. Shrines
placed under the shadow of—Josh.
24:26; Hos. 4:13. (2) Terebinth (R
marg.). Noted for thick boughs—II
Sam. 18:9, 10, 14. Associated with
idolatrous worship—Gen. 35:4; Ju. 6:
11, 19; Ez. 6:13.

Oil tree.—The oleaster used like the
myrtle—Neh. 8:15; Is. 41:19.

Olive.—Staple (with vine and fig-tree)
—Deut. 8:8; 24:20; 28:40; I Chr. 27:
28. Prized for its fruit—Hab. 3:17;
and its wood. Used in the temple—I

Ki. 6:23, 31, 33. Emblem of vigorous life—Ps. 52:8; 128:3; Jer. 11:16. Wild olive, inferior—Rom. 11:17, 24.

Palm tree.—Abundant in the region of Jericho—Deut. 34:3; Ju. 1:16; 3:13. Branches used at the feast of tabernacles—Lev. 23:40; Neh. 8:15. Noted for vigorous life and stateliness—Song of Sol. 7:7; Jer. 10:5.

Pine tree.—Probably **Plane tree.**—Is. 41:19; 60:13 R.

Plane tree.—Same as chestnut (also Pine)—Gen. 30:37; Ez. 31:8.

Pomegranate.—Fruit tree prized in Egypt and Canaan—Deut. 8:8. Form of fruit used as model for decoration—Ex. 28: 33, 34; I Ki. 7:18.

Poplar.—Probably the Styrax tree, a resinous shrub of 10 to 20 feet in height —Gen. 30:37; Hos. 4:13 R marg.

Shittah tree.—Shittim wood; Species of acacia tree, a sign of prosperity. Used in construction of tabernacle—Ex. 25:5, 10, etc.; 26:15; 27:1; 30:1; 35: 7; 36:20; 37:1; 38:1.

Sycamine.—The mulberry. Named for stability—Lu. 17:6.

Sycamore.—A species of fig-tree—Amos 7:14; Ps. 78:67. Contrasted with the cedar—II Chr. 1:15; 9:27.

Tamarisk.—R; Rendering for A. V., "grove"—Gen. 21:33; I Sam. 22:6.

Terebinth.—R marg. Cf. Oak (2).

Walnut.—Probably intended in "garden of nuts"—Song of Sol. 6:11.

Willow.—Perhaps the weeping willow— Lev. 23:40; Job 40:22; Ps. 137:2; Ez. 17:5.

II. BUSHES, SHRUBS, AND VINES.

Bramble.—Symbol of inferior value and quality—Ju. 9:14, 15; Is. 34:13; Lu. 6:44.

Brier.—A thorny bush, emblem of the wilderness—Ju. 8:7; Is. 5:6; 55:13; Ez. 28:24; Heb. 6:8.

Broom.—R; for **Juniper,** A.V.—Job 30:4. Also I Ki. 19:4; Ps. 120:4, R marg.

Bulrush.—The Egyptian papyrus, used in building light boats—Ex. 2:3; Is. 18:2. Found on river banks—Job 8:11.

Camphire.—(Camphor) mentioned for beautiful clusters of berries—R, Henna, Song of Sol. 1:14; 4:13.

Cane (Sweet).—Calamus, R marg. Is. 43:24; Jer. 6:20.

Caperberry.—Emblem of persistence— Eccl. 12:5.

Cockle ("noisome weed," R marg.).— Job 31:40, a weed contrasted with barley.

Copher.—(R marg. for "Camphire," "Henna") Song of Sol. 1:14.

Coriander.—Aromatic seed to which manna is compared—Ex. 16:31; Num. 11:7.

Gourd.—Designation of two distinct vegetables: (1) Wild vine with poisonous fruit—II Ki. 4:38–41. (2) Rapid-growing vine ("bottle gourd") common in Palestine—Jonah 4:6–11.

Henna.—Cf. **Camphire.**

Hyssop.—Bush whose branches were used in the Levitical ceremonial—Ex. 12:22; Lev. 14:4; Num. 19:6; Ps. 51:7. Used at the crucifixion—John 19:29.

Juniper.—A broom almost leafless, growing to a considerable height in the wilderness in the Jordan valley, with pinkish flower, convenient for shelter —I Ki. 19:4, 5. Rootstalk made into charcoal.

Papyrus. See BULRUSH.

Sodom vine.—Probably a wild gourd, Emblem of delusive hope—Deut. 32: 32.

Vine.—("Grape-vine") Staple with olive. Held in esteem for grapes, wine, and shadow—Gen. 40:9; Deut. 8:8; Ps. 78: 47; I Ki. 4:25. Figurative: Israel, a vine—Is. 5:1 ff.; Ps. 80:8; Hos. 10:1. Emblem of fruitfulness—Ps. 128:3. Jesus symbolized by—John 15:1. See GRAPES.

Wild vine.—II Ki. 4:39.

III. GRASSES, HERBS, GARDEN VEGETABLES.

Anise.—The common dill (R marg., Mt. 23:23).

Barley.—Used as breadstuff—II Chr. 2:10; John 6:9. Cultivated in Palestine—Ex. 9:31; Lev. 27:16; Deut. 8:8. Straw of, fed to horses—I Ki. 4:28.

Bean.—Used both as vegetable and ground for flour—II Sam. 17:28; Ez. 4:9.

Corn ("Grain").—Staple of life with wine—Gen. 27:28; Deut. 7:13; 11:14; 12:17; Joel 1:10; and oil—Hos. 2:3.

Cucumber.—Produced in Egypt—Num. 11:5. Garden of—Is. 1:8.

Cummin.—Valued for aromatic small fruit. Method of production—Is. 28:25, 27. Tithing of—Mt. 23:23.

Darnell.—(R marg. for "tares") Mt. 13:25.

Fitches.—Cf. Vetches.

Flag.—Weeds—Ex. 2:3. Miscellaneous herbage on river bank—Gen. 41:2; Job 8:11.

Flax.—Staple for manufacture of linen; hence valuable crop—Ex. 9:31; Pr. 31:13; Hos. 2:5, 9; Is. 19:9.

Gall.—Bitter, poisonous herb, probably same as gourd—II Ki. 4:39.

Garlic.—Garden vegetable grown in Egypt—Num. 11:5.

Grass.—Name for small vegetation (including weeds), which grows uncultivated—Gen. 1:11; Is. 15:6; 40:6; Mt. 6:30; Jas. 1:10.

Hay ("Grass," R marg.).—Pr. 27:25. Generally dry grass—Is. 15:6; I Cor. 3:12.

Heath (R marg. "Tamarisks").—Jer. 17:6; 48:6.

Hemlock.—(1) Poisonous herb growing in grain fields—Hos. 10:4. (2) **Wormwood.**—R. Amos 6:12.

Herb.—(1) Cultivated vegetation as opposed to grass—Gen. 1:12; Pr. 15:17. (2) Special kinds (perhaps from shape of blossom). "Sunshine"—II Ki. 4:30. (3) Collectively "bitter herbs"—Ex. 12:8 (including lettuce, endive, chicory, and nettle).

Leeks.—Garden vegetable grouped with onion and garlic—Num. 11:5.

Lentils.—Variety of vetch with lense-shaped seed, used for food—Gen. 25:30.

Lily.—Either scarlet martagon or scarlet anemone—Mt. 6:28.

Love-apple.—Cf. **Mandrake.**

Mallow.—Species of spinach growing in the salt marshes of the desert (R, "Saltwort"); used for food by the very poor—Job 30:4.

Mandrake.—Stemless plant with extensive branching root, dark green leaves, and yellow prune-sized fruit supposed to have power as love philter—Gen. 30:14; Song of Sol. 7:13.

Melon.—Cultivated in Egypt—Num. 11:15.

Millet.—Comprehensive name for several cereals; used in making bread—Ez. 4:9.

Mint.—Garden vegetable used as condiment—Lu. 11:42.

Nettles.—(1) Unknown weed—R, "Wild vetches"—Job 30:7; Pr. 24:31; Zeph. 2:9. (2) Common nettle—Is. 34:13.

Nigella Sativa.—Scientific name for fitch or vetch—R marg., Is. 28:25.

Onion.—Garden vegetable common in Egypt—Num. 11:5.

Pannag.—Probably millet (Egyptian variety)—Ez. 27:17.

Pulse (Heb. "Seeds").—In general, grain, but specially leguminous plants, such as peas or beans (latter favored by Greek version)—II Sam. 17:28; Deut. 1:12.

Purslain.—(R marg.) Job 6:6. Insipid pot herb.

Rye, Rie.—A.v. marg. "Spelt"—Ex. 9:32; Is. 28:25.

Rose.—R, "Crocus"—Is. 35:1; Song of Sol. 2:1. Bulbous plant. True rose unknown.

Rue.—Aromatic plant cultivated in gardens—Lu. 11:42.

Saffron.—Species of crocus used in making perfumes—Song of Sol. 4:14.

Saltwort.—See **Mallow.**

Spelt.—See **Rye, Rie.**

Tares.—"Bearded darnell," R marg. Harmful weed resembling poor wheat before seeding; Disease-producing if eaten—Mt. 13:25–27.

Vetches.—Species of buttercup with black seeds having a pungent taste; used in sprinkling over bread and for the flavoring of cakes—Is. 28:25; Ez. 4:9.

Wheat.—More commonly corn—Gen. 31:14, etc.

Wormwood.—Plant with strong odor and bitter taste; alluded to in proverbial sayings or illustrations—Deut. 29:18; Jer. 9:15; 23:15; Amos 5:7; Pr. 5:4; Lam. 3:15; Rev. 8:11.

IV. Plant Products.

Balm.—Odoriferous resin of balsamodendron (variety in Gilead especially valued). Used as gift—Gen. 37:25; 43:11. Also for medicinal purposes—Jer. 8:22; 46:11; 51:8.

Calamus.—Ingredient of unction oil—Ex. 30:23. Imported from Tyre—Ez. 27:19.

Cassia.—Ingredient of unction oil—Ex. 30:24; Ps. 45:8. Common in Syrian commerce.

Cinnamon.—Ingredient of unction oil—Ex. 30:23. Used to perfume beds—Pr. 7:17.

Cotton.—(R *marg.*, Esth. 1:6) Material was probably commonly used, but plant is never named.

Frankincense.—Odoriferous gum, ingredient of the holy oil—Ex. 30:34.

Galbanum.—Ingredient of holy oil—Ex. 30:34.

Ladanum.—(R *marg.* Gen. 37:25) Fragrant gum of the cistus.

Malobathron.—(R *marg.* Song of Sol. 2: 17) A spice leaf, but probably cinnamon.

Manna.—Food provided for Israel in wilderness—Ex. 16:15.

Myrrh.—Gum of an Arabian tree; ingredient of unction oil—Ex. 30:33. Used as perfume—Pr. 7:17. Also in purification—Esth. 2:12. And burial —Jer. 19:39.

Nuts.—(1) Pistachio nut—Gen. 43:11. (2) Walnut—Song of Sol. 6:11.

Onycha.—Ingredient of holy oil—Ex. 30:34.

Opobalsam.—Ingredient of holy oil.

Pistachio.—Cf. **Nuts.**

Pistic nard.—Cf. **Spikenard.**

Spicery.—(R, ''Gum Tragacanth'') Gen. 37:25; 43:11.

Spikenard (*Pistic nard*).—R *marg.* Mk. 14:3. Perfume made from roots of a Hindu plant—Lu. 7:37; John 12:3.

Stacte.—Droplike gum, resin of storax tree, ingredient of holy oil—Ex. 30: 34.

Thyine wood.—Tissue of a cypress from North Africa; Reddish brown; Hard and fragrant; used for expensive furniture—Rev. 18:12.

PLANT, *v.* Mt. 15:13. Gardens—Gen. 2:8; 29:5, 28. Good soil, In—Ez. 17:5, 8, 10. Grain—Ps. 94:9. Groves—Gen. 21:33; Lev. 19:23; Num. 24:6; Deut. 16:21; Ps. 104:16; Eccl. 2:5; Is. 44:14. Jehovah hath power to—Gen. 2:8; Jer. 1:10; 11:17; 17:8; 34:6; 31:28; 42:10; 45:4. Kingdom—Jer. 18:19; 32:41. Oliveyard—Deut. 6:11; Josh. 24:13. Sea, In the—Lu. 17:6. Time to—Eccl. 3:2. Vineyard—Gen. 9:20; Deut. 20: 6; 28:30, 39; II Ki. 19:29; Ps. 107:37; Pr. 31:16; Eccl. 2:40; Is. 5:2; 37:30; 65:21, 22; Jer. 31:5; Ez. 28:26; Amos 5:11; 9:14, 15; Zeph. 1:13; Mt. 21:33; Mk. 12:1; Lu. 13:6; 30:9; I Cor. 9:7. See VINEYARD. Wilderness, In—Is. 47: 19; Ez. 10:13.

Figurative.—Gen. 2:8; II Sam. 7:10; I Chr. 17:9; Ps. 1:3; 80:15; 92:3; 128:3; 144:12; Is. 5:7; 40:24; 51:16; 53:2; Jer. 2:21; 11:17; 12:2; 24:6; Ez. 39: 29; Dan. 11:45; Hos. 9:13; Mt. 15:13; I Cor. 3:6–8.

PLANTATION.—Ez. 17:7; 34:29.

PLASTER. Lev. 14:42, 43, 48; Deut. 27: 2, 4; Is. 38:21; Dan. 5:5.

PLAT. II Ki. 9:26.

PLATE. Altar, Covering for—Num. 16: 38; I Ki. 7:36. Gold, Of—Ex. 28:36; 39:3; Lev. 8:9. Holy crown, Of—Ex. 39:30. Silver, Of—Jer. 10:9.

PLATING. Is. 30:22.

PLATTER. See VESSELS.

PLAY. Ex. 32:6; II Sam. 10:12; **Job** 40:20; 41:5; Is. 11:8; Zech. 8:5; I Cor. 10:7. Fool, The—I Sam. 21:15; 26:21. Harlot, The—Gen. 38:24; Lev. 21:9; Deut. 22:21; Ju. 19:2; Jer. 2:20; 3:1, 6, 8; Ez. 16:28, 40; 23:5, 19; Hos. 2:5; 3:3; 4:15. Harp, On—I Sam. 16:16, 17, 23; 18:10; 19:9; II Sam. 2:14; II Ki. 3:15; I Chr. 15:29. Jehovah, Before— II Sam. 6:5, 21; I Chr. 13:8; I Sam. 16:18. See HARP. Musical instrument, On—Ps. 33:3; 68:25; Ez. 33:32. See CHILDREN.

PLEAD. I Sam. 12:7; 24:15; Jer. 5:28; Rom. 11:2. Baal, For—Ju. 6:31, 32. Cause—See CAUSE. Israel, With—Mic. 6:2. Mother, With—Hos. 2:2. Truth, In—Is. 59:4. Widow, For—Is. 1:17. See CAUSE, PRAYER.

PLEASANT. I Sam. 1:26; I Ki. 20:6; Ps. 133:1; 135:3. Child—Jer. 31:20.

City—II Ki. 2:19; 147:1; Pr. 5:19; 9:17. Houses—Ez. 26:12; Mic. 2:9. Knowledge—Pr. 2:10. Land—Ps. 106: 24; Jer. 3:19; Zech. 7:14. Lives—II Sam. 1:23. Places—Ps. 16:6; Hos. 9: 6, 13. Things—Pr. 22:18; Is. 64:11; Lam. 1:7, 10, 11; Dan. 11:38; Joel 3:5. Tree—Gen. 2:9. Vessels—Hos. 13:15. Voice—Ez. 33:32. Words—Pr. 15:26; 16:24.

PLEASANTNESS. Pr. 3:17.

PLEASE. Deut. 23:16; Job 6:28; John 8:29; I Cor. 10:33; Gal. 1:10; Eph. 6: 6; Col. 3:20. Herod—Mt. 14:6; Mk. 6:22. Jehovah—Ps. 69:31; 135:6; Pr. 16:7; Is. 53:10; Jer. 6:20; Mic. 6:7; Mt. 3:17; 12:18; 17:5; Mk. 1:11; Lu. 2:14; 3:22; Rom. 8:8; I Thess. 2:15; 4:1; I John 3:22. Jesus, By—Mt. 3: 17; Lu. 2:14; Rom. 15:3. Speech, With —I Ki. 3:10.

PLEASURE: Worldly.—Gen. 18:12; Deut. 23:24; Esth. 1:8; Job 36:11; Is. 47:8; Ez. 16:37; II Tim. 3:4; Tit. 3:3; Heb. 11:25; Jas. 5:5; II Pet. 2:13. Warnings against—Pr. 21:17; Eccl. 2:1; Is. 58:3, 13; I Tim. 5:6. No pleasure in—Eccl. 12:1. In sacrifices—Heb. 10:6, 8. In parable —Lu. 8:14.

Mental gratification, or will.—Of kings —Ezra 5:17; Neh. 9:37; Ps. 105:22. Of chosen one—Is. 48:14. Of freedom —Jer. 34:16.

Spiritual.—In uprightness—I Chr. 29:17. Of saint—Ps. 102:14; 111:2. Of God— Job 22:3; Ps. 5:4; 35:27; 51:18; 149: 4; Is. 44:28; 46:10; 53:10; Hag. 1:8; Lu. 12:32; Phil. 2:13; Heb. 10:38. Commended—Ezra 10:11; Ps. 103:21; Phil. 2:13. God has "no pleasure"— Ps. 147:10: In fools—Eccl. 5:4; In death of wicked—Ez. 18:23, 32; 33:11; In wicked—Mal. 1:10. Will of Christ —Eph. 1:5, 9.

PLEDGE: Demanded.—II Ki. 18:23; Is. 36:8.

Laws concerning.—Ex. 22:26; Deut. 24: 6, 10–13, 17.

Not to be taken.—Millstone—Deut. 24: 6. Widow's raiment—Deut. 24:17.

Not to be kept.—Neighbor's garment— Ex. 22:26.

Miscellaneous.—Job 22:6; 24:3, 9; Pr. 20:16; 28:13; Amos 2:8.

PLENTEOUS. Is. 30:23. Harvest—Mt. 9:37; Lu. 10:2. Jehovah make—Deut. 28:11; 30:9. Meat—Hab. 1:16. Mercy, In—Ps. 86:5, 15; 103:8. Redemption, In—Ps. 130:7. Righteousness—Job 37:23. Years—Gen. 41:34, 47. See FULL.

PLENTEOUSNESS. Pr. 21:5.

PLENTIFUL. Job 26:3; Lu. 12:26. Country—Jer. 2:7. Rain—Ps. 68:9. Reward—Ps. 31:23.

PLENTY. Bread, Of—Pr. 12:11; 28:19. Corn, Of—Gen. 27:28; Pr. 3:10. Food, Of—Jer. 44:17; Joel 2:26. Jehovah sends—Gen. 27:28; Deut. 16:10; 28: 11; 30:9; Ps. 65:8–13; 104:10–15; 144: 13; Jer. 5:24; Joel 2:26; Amos 9:14; Acts 14:17; I Cor. 16:2. Life—II Chr. 31:10. Seven years of—Gen. 41:29–31, 53. Trees, Of—I Ki. 10:11. Wine, Of —Gen. 27:28.

PLOT. Became known—Acts 9:24. Ground, Of—II Sam. 23:11; I Chr. 11:13. In midst of—II Sam. 23:12. Laying a—Acts 25:3. Man, Of—Ps. 31:20. Wicked against just—Ps. 37: 12.

PLOW. Gen. 45:6; Deut. 22:10; Ps. 141:7. Back, Upon—Ps. 129:3. Continually—Is. 28:24. Elisha was—I Ki. 19:19. Ground—I Sam. 8:12. Hope, In —I Cor. 9:10. Iniquity—Job 4:8. Man —Amos 9:13. Open were—Job 1:14. Servant—Lu. 17:7. Sluggard will not —Pr. 20:4. Wickedness—Hos. 10:13.

PLOWSHARES. Into swords—Joel 3: 10. Swords into—Is. 2:4; Mic. 4:3.

PLUCK. Ps. 80:12.. Brand—Amos 4:11. By roots—Jude 12. Ears—Mt. 12:1. Eyes, Out—Gal. 4:15. Fatherless— Job 24:9. Hair—Ezra 9:3; Neh. 13: 25. Net, Out of—Ps. 25:15; 31:4. Olive leaf—Gen. 8:11. Spear—II Sam. 23:21; I Chr. 11:23. Up—Eccl. 3:2; Jer. 1:10. Wool—Hos. 2:9.

PLUMB-LINE. II Ki. 21:13; Is. 28:17; Amos 7:7, 8.

PLUMMET. Is. 34:11; Zech. 4:10.

PLUNDER. Gen. 34:27; Jer. 50:11. See SPOIL.

POCHERETH - HAZZEBAIM, pŏk'e-reth-hăz'ze-bā'im. Ezra 2:57.

POETRY, BIBLICAL. Writing characterized by imaginative conception and versified form of expression.

Poetical books: Job, Psalms, Proverbs, Song of Solomon, Lamentations.

Prophetic literature, largely poetic in substance if not in form.

Poems in prose, in the Old Testament: Song of Lamech—Gen. 4:23, 24. Curse of Noah—Gen. 9:25–27. Oracle of Jacob and Esau—Gen. 25:23. Blessing of Isaac—Gen. 27:27–29, 39, 40. Blessing of Jacob—Gen. 49:2–27. Song of Miriam—Ex. 15:1–18. From the "Wars of Jehovah"—Num. 21:14, 15. The Song of the Well—Num. 21:17, 18. From the "Sayings of those who speak in proverbs"—Num. 21:37, 30. The Oracles of Balaam—Num. 23:7–10; 18:24; 24:3–9; 15:24. The Song of Moses—Deut. 32:1–43. The Blessing of Moses—Deut. 33:2–29. From the "Book of Jashar"—Josh. 10:12, 13. The Song of Deborah—Ju. 5:2–31. Samson's riddle and its answer—Ju. 14:14, 18. Samson's boast—Ju. 15:16. The Song of Hannah—I Sam. 2:1–10. The Praise of David—I Sam. 18:7; 21:11; 29:5. David's Lament over Saul and Jonathan—II Sam. 1:19–27. David's Lament over Abner—II Sam. 3:33, 34. David's Psalm of Praise—II Sam. 22:2–51. David's Last Words II Sam. 23:1–7. David's thanksgiving —I Chr. 16:8–36 (cf. Ps. 105:1–15). Hezekiah's thanksgiving—Is. 38:9–20. Jonah's prayer — Jonah 2:2–9. The prayer of Habakkuk—Hab. 3:2–19.

In the New Testament: The Magnificat —Lu. 1:46–55. The Benedictus—Lu. 1:68–79. The angel's Song (Gloria in Excelsis)—Lu. 2:14. The Nunc Dimittis — Lu. 2:29–32. From Cleanthes' Hymn—Acts 17:28. Spiritual Sight— I Cor. 2:9. Early liturgical fragment —I Tim. 3:16.

Kinds of Poetry in the Bible: Lyric, The Psalms. Elegiac, The Lament (Dirge) — II Sam. 1:19–27; 3:33, 34. Gnomic (Didactic), Proverbs. Special Type, The Riddle—Pr. 30:15, 16; Ju. 14:14, 18. Dramatic: In strict sense absent. Quasi-dramatic: Job, Song of Songs.

Versification: Chief feature parallelism, i. e., the expression of a thought in re-peated similar or contrasted forms. (1) Synonymous: Repetition in varied expression. Duplicate — Ps. 21:1, 2; Job 8:5. Triplicate—Num. 6:24–26; cf. Mt. 7:7, 8. (2) Antithetical, Contrasted expressions—Ps. 1:6; Pr. 1:7; 22:29; 27:10; Mt. 8:20. (3) Progressive—Ps. 23:1; Pr. 25:8. (4) Chiastic (Introverted) — Pr. 23:15, 16. (5) Synthetic—Ps. 25:12. (6) Climactic —Ps. 121:3, 4. (7) Comparative—Ps. 42:1; Pr. 15:16.

Rhythm: Made by accent rather than length of syllable.

Metre: Unit, the accented syllable; Prevalent measures, 3–3 Accents, 4–4 Accents, 2–2 Accents.

Strophes.—Marked by refrain—Ps. 42 and 43; 107.

Acrostics: Poems with artistic arrangement of initials.

Alphabetic poems—Ps. 25, 24; Lam. Chs. 1, 2, 3, 4. Poem of 22 stanzas, each stanza consisting of 8 verses with the same initials—Ps. 119.

Artificial acrostic, incorporating name of author in initials of lines (Pedaiah in the Heb. text)—Ps. 25.

FORMS OF LYRIC POETRY IN THE BIBLE.*

"Songs:

Folk Songs quoted.—Song of the Sword (Genesis iv. 23–4)—Of the Well (Numbers xxi. 17–18) — Husbandry Song (Proverbs xxvii. 23–7)—War Ballad (Joshua x. 12–13) —Fragments of others in Numbers xxi.

Odes—not a determinate form. As illustrations:

Triumphal Odes (the word suggests dance movements): such as Deborah's Song (Judges v)—Song of Moses and Miriam (Exodus xv)— with such a Link as the **Processional Ode** (Psalms lxviii) passes into Ritual Poetry.

National Anthems: Psalms cxxxvi, cv, lxxviii, cvi.—**Elegiac Ode** on the Covenant (Psalm lxxxix).

Odes on Themes: Of the Redeemed (Psalm cvii)—Of the World within

---

* From "The Literary Study of the Bible," by Richard G. Moulton. Copyright 1895 and 1899. Used by permission.

and the World without (Psalms ciii-iv).

Songs—the essential lyric form:

Occasional: Song of D e b o r a h (Judges v)—of Moses and Miriam (Exodus xv)—Psalms of Sennacherib's Overthrow (xlvi, xlviii, lxxvi).

Of Deliverance: P s a l m s xviii, cxxxviii, cxlii—in the Songs of Ascents: Psalms cxxiv, cxxvi.

Of Nature and Providence: Song of Moses (Deuteronomy xxxii)—Psalms xxix, cvii, ciii-civ.

Of Judgment: Psalms lii, lviii, lxxv, lxxxiii (national), xciv.

Of Trust: Psalms xi, lxii—and Consecration: Psalm xvi.

On Themes: Psalms ii, cx, lxxii, lxxxiv, lxxxvii, xciii.—In the Songs of Ascents: cxxv, cxxvii, cxxviii, cxxxiii.

The Songs of Ascents: A Psalter within a Psalter; Psalms cxx-cxxxiv.

Songs scattered through Works of Prophecy: e. g., Songs of Zion in the Rhapsody of Zion Redeemed.

Elegies resting on the Professional Wall:

National: Psalms xliv, lxxiv, lxxix, lxxx, lxxxix, cxxxvii.—Especially: Acrostic Suite of Elegies: The Book of Lamentations.

Personal: David's Lament over Saul and Jonathan (II Samuel i)—Psalm lxxxviii.

Meditations on Themes:

The Consecrated Life: Psalm xv— The Quiet Soul: Psalm cxxxi— The Protection of Jehovah: Psalms xxiii, cxxi. The Prosperity of the Wicked: Psalms xxxvii (acrostic), xlix, lxxiii. The Law of the Lord: Psalms i, cxix (acrostic). Man the Viceroy of God: Psalm viii—The Heavens Above and the Law Within: Psalm xix— Evil Unbounded and Infinite Good: Psalm xxxvi. Thoughts from the Song of Moses: Psalms xc, xci.

Monologues:

Monodies of Experience: Psalms xxxii, xxxix, xli, xlii-iii, lxxvii.

Prayers and **Litanies:**

Prayers: Psalms iv, v, xiii, xvii, xxvi, xxxviii, li, cxliii—In the Songs of Ascents: cxx, cxxiii, cxxx.

Litanies: Psalms· xxxv, lv, lxx, ·cix, cxl—In the Songs of Ascents: cxxix.

Dramatic Lyrics and **Anthems:**

Lyrics: Psalms iii, vi, xii, xxii, xxviii, liv, lvi, lvii, lxix, lxxi, cxxxix—Peculiar: xxxi.

Anthems: Psalms ix-x (acrostic), xxvii, lxxxv, cviii, cxliv.

Visions, dramatic, but not wholly monologue:

Psalms vii, l, xiv (=liii), lxxxii— compare in Prophecy Habakkuk's Vision (chapter iii).

Ritual Psalms:

Occasional Anthems: Inauguration of Jerusalem: Psalms xxiv, xxx, ci, cxxxii.

Festal Hymns and Anthems:

Hymns: Psalms xxxiii, xlv, xlvii, lxxxi—in the Songs of Ascents: Psalms cxxi, cxxii, cxxxiv.

Anthems: Psalms lxvii (a Festal Response), lxviii, xcv-c, cxxxv, cxlv-cl (cxlv is an acrostic preface).

War Ballads and Anthems:

War Ballad: Psalm lix.

War Anthems: Psalms xx-i, lx, and cviii (dramatic).

Votive Hymns and Anthems:

Hymns: Psalms xxxiv (acrostic), lxvi, xcii.

Anthems: Psalms cxi-cxxviii (the first two an acrostic preface).

National Anthems: Psalms cxxxvi, cv, lxxviii, cvi.

Liturgies: Psalms xxv (acrostic), xl, lxv, lxxxvi.

Doom Songs.—Utterances against Particular Nations or Cities: partly corresponding to Satires and Philippics of other literatures. **Prototype.** —The Curse (Genesis ix. 25).

Nineveh: *Nahum*, Assyria: *Isaiah* xiv. 24-7.

Babylon: *Isaiah* xiii-xiv. 23; *Jeremiah* l-li.

Egypt: *Isaiah* xix; *Jeremiah* xlvi.

3–12 and 14–28; *Ezekiel* xxix-xxxii (Sevenfold).

Tyre and Zidon: *Isaiah* xxiii; *Ezekiel* xxvi-xxviii (Threefold).

Philistia: *Isaiah* xiv. 28–32; *Jeremiah* xlvii; *Ezekiel* xxv. 15–17.

Damascus: *Isaiah* xvii. I–II; *Jeremiah* xlix. 23–27.

Moab: *Isaiah* xv-xvi; *Jeremiah* xlviii; *Ezekiel* xxv. 8–11.

Edom: *Jeremiah* xlix. 7:22; *Ezekiel* xxv. 12–14; *Obadiah* 8.

Ammon: *Jeremiah* xlix. 1–6; *Ezekiel* xxv. 1–7.

Others: *Isaiah* xvii. 12–14; xviii; xx; especially, The Prophetic Watchman xxi-xxii. 14; *Jeremiah* xlix. 28–39.

Books of Dooms: *Jeremiah* xlvi-li; *Ezekiel* xxv-xxxii.

Cycle of Dooms: *Isaiah* xiii-xxvii; *Ezekiel* xxv; *Amos* i-ii.

Prophetic Lyrics (396): Triumph Song over Babylon (*Isaiah* xlvii. 1–5)—Ezekiel's Doom on Egypt (xxxii. 17–32)—Isaiah's Sevenfold Denunciation (v. 8–30)—his Doom of the North (ix. 8–x. 4).

Prototype: Blessings and Last Words (of Jacob, *Genesis* xlix. 2–27; Of Moses, *Deuteronomy* xxxiii. 2–29; Of David, II *Samuel* xxiii. 1–7)."

Other Songs.—Blessing of Jacob—Gen. 49:1–27. David's Lament over Saul and Jonathan—II Sam. 1:19–27. Lament on death of Abner—II Sam. 3: 33, 38. Swan song—II Sam. 23:1–7. Song of Saul and David—I Sam. 18:7, 8. Taunt song—Job 30:9; Lam. 3:14, 63; Job 30:9; Ps. 69:12. Forgotten courtesan—Is. 23:16. Drinking song—Ps. 69:12; Amos 6:5, 6. Hannah—I Sam. 2:1–10. David's Psalm of praise—II Sam. 22:1–51; 23:1–7. Mary—Lu. 1:46–55. Zacharias—Lu. 1:67–79. Angels—Lu. 2:13, 14. Simeon—Lu. 2: 29. Redeemed—Rev. 5:9. See Rev. Ch. 19.

Singing men and women.—Ex. 32:18; II Sam. 19:35; I Chr. 15:16; II Chr. 5:15.

Hymns and spiritual songs.—Mt. 26:30; Mk. 14:26; Eph. 5:19; Col. 3:16. See MUSIC, PRAISE.

POINT. Job 20:25; Eccl. 5:16. Chief—Heb. 8:1. Diamond, Of—Jer. 17:1. Death, Of—Mk. 5:23; Lu. 7:2. Spirit of Christ did—I Pet. 1:11. Stumble in one—Jas. 2:10. Sword—Ez. 21:15. Tempted in all—Heb. 4:15.

POISON: Of crawling things.—Deut. 32:24, 33. Of asps—Job 20:16; Rom. 3:13. Vipers—Job 20:16. Of serpents—Ps. 58:4. See SERPENTS. Of adders—Ps. 140:3.

Of plants.—II Ki. 4:40.

Figurative.—Job 6:4; Jas. 3:8. See INSTRUCTION (False Teachings)—Is. 54: 13.

POLL. Num. 1:2, 18, 20; 3:47; I Chr. 23:3, 24.

POLLUTION. Ex. 20:25. Earth is—Is. 24:5. Garment—Is. 64:6. Land—Jer. 16:18. Legal—Lev. 5; 11; 13; 15; 21; 22; Num. 5; 9:6; Ez. 22. Of God's altar, etc.—Ex. 20:25; II Chr. 33:7; II Ki. 23:6; Ez. 44:7; Dan. 8:11; Mal. 1:7; Acts 21:28. Of God's name—Ez. 20:39; 39:7. Of heathen—Lev. 18:24; 20:3; Acts 15:20. Of sabbath—Neh. 13:15; Is. 56:2, 6; Ez. 20:13, 16, 21. See CORRUPTION, IDOLATRY, PURIFICATION, SIN, UNCLEANNESS.

POMEGRANATES. Ex. 28:33, 34; 39: 24; II Ki. 25:17; II Chr. 3:16; Song of Sol. 4:3, 13; 6:7, 11; 7:12.

POMP. Brought down to Sheol—Is. 14: 11. Come with great—Acts 25:23. Descend—Is. 5:14.

PONDER. Eccl. 12:9. Mary—Lu. 2:19.

PONDS. Ex. 7:19. See POOLS.

PONTIUS, pŏn′ti-us. See PILATE.

PONTUS, pŏn′tus. **Province of Asia Minor.**—Acts 2:9.

POOLS: Natural pools.—Of Egypt—Ex. 7:19; 8:5. Artificial pools—II Ki. 20:20; Neh. 3:16; Eccl. 2:6. (Swimming pond—John 5:2 ff.)

Pools mentioned.—Of Gibeon—II Sam. 2:13. In Hebron—II Sam. 4:12. Of Samaria—I Ki. 22:38. Conduit of the Upper pool, or King's pool—II Ki. 18:17; Neh. 2:14; Is. 7:3; 36:2. Lower pool, or Old pool—Is. 22:9, 11. Pool of Egypt—Ex. 7:19. Of Bethesda—John 5:2, 7. Of Shelah or Siloam—Neh. 3:15; John 9:7, 11. Of Heshbon—Song of Sol. 7:4.

Prophecies concerning.—Is. 14:23; 35:7; 41:18; 42:15.

Illustrative.—Song of Sol. 7:4; Nah. 2:8.

POOR: Pleading with Jehovah.—Job 31:16–22; Ps. 69:29, 33; 70:5; 74:19–21; 109:21–22.

Care of Jehovah.—Deut. 15:4–6; I Sam. 2:7–8; Job 5:15–16; Ps. 14:6; 34:6; 35:10; 40:17; 68:10; 107:41; Is. 14:30; 29:19; 66:2; Jer. 20:13.

Laws concerning. — Lending money — Ex. 22:25–27; Deut. 24:12; Job 24:9. If he sell himself—Lev. 25:39. To redeem him—Lev. 25:47. To redeem possessions—Lev. 25:25. Land to lie fallow — Ex. 23:11. Gleaning vineyards—Lev. 19:10. Reaping harvests —Lev. 23:22; Ruth 2:14–16.

Treatment of.—Kindness—Deut. 15:7–11; Esth. 9:22; Job 29:11–16; 31:16–22; Ps. 41:1; 132:15; Pr. 14:21; Is. 25:4. Benevolence—Job 29:16; Pr. 22:9; 31:20; Mt. 19:21; 26:9; Mk. 10:21; Lu. 19:8; Acts 9:36; 11:29–30; Rom. 15:25, 26. Must not neglect—Pr. 28:27; 29:7; 29:14; Gal. 2:10; Jas. 2:2–6. Deal justly—Ex. 23:3, 6; Lev. 19:15; Job 34:17–20; Ps. 9:18; 72:2, 12, 13; 82:3; Pr. 13:23; 31:9; Is. 10:2; 11:4. Employment—II Ki. 25:12; Pr. 10:4; 21:17. Harshness—Job 24:3–4; Ps. 10:2, 9; 37:14; Pr. 17:5; 18:23; 21:13; 28:15; Amos 8:4–6. Hypocrisy—Mk. 14:5; John 12:5–8. Hatred—Pr. 14:20; 19:7; Jer. 2:34. Preach gospel to them—Mt. 11:5; Lu. 4:18; 7:22. Call to feast—Lu. 14:13, 21. Equal before God—Pr. 22:2.

Oppression of.—Deut. 24:14–15; Job 20:19; Ps. 12:5; 109:15–16; Pr. 14:31; 22:16, 22; 28:3; Eccl. 5:8; Is. 3:14–15; Jer. 52:15; Amos 4:1. See OPPRESSION.

Duties of.—To pay offerings—Ex. 30:15; Lev. 14:21; Mk. 12:42–43. To listen to truth—Pr. 13:8; Is. 61:1; Lu. 4:18.

Characteristics of.—Integrity—Pr. 19:1; 28:6. Understanding—Pr. 28:11. Wisdom—Eccl. 4:13–14; 6:8; 9:15, 16. Patience—Lu. 16:20–21.

The true religion.—Is. 58:5–7; Dan. 4:27; Mt. 5:3; I Cor. 13:3.

False religion.—Rev. 13:16. Known and marked—Rev. 13:16.

What poverty does. — Separates — Pr. 19:4. Produces servitude—Pr. 22:7. Comes as a robber—Pr. 6:11; 24:34.

What brings poverty.—Famine—Gen. 45:11. Gluttony—Pr. 23:21. Indolence—Pr. 28:19; II Thess. 3:10–12. Dangers of—Pr. 30:8–9.

Benefits of.—Mt. 5:3; Lu. 6:20; 7:22.

Parables.—The Little Ewe Lamb—II Sam. 12:1–6. The Great Supper.—Lu. 14:16–24. See FRATERNITY.

POPLAR. Gen. 30:37; Hos. 4:13.

POPULARITY OF JESUS. See JESUS.

POPULOUS. Deut. 26:5.

PORATHA, pŏr′a-thä. **Son of Haman.** —Esth. 9:8.

PORCH. Ehud went forth into the—Ju. 3:23. David gave Solomon pattern of temple porch—I Chr. 28:11; I Ki. 7:6. Wicked Jews shut up doors of—II Chr. 29:7. Sunworshippers near porch of temple—Ez. 8:16. Priests ordered to weep there—Joel 2:17. Peter went into—Mt. 26:71; Mk. 14:68. Jesus walked in Solomon's—John 10:23. Together in Solomon's—Acts 3:11. With one accord in Solomon's—Acts 5:12. Bethesda having five porches—John 5:2.

PORCIUS FESTUS. Acts 24:27. See TESTUS.

PORCUPINE. Is. 14:23; 34:11.

PORTER. Doorkeepers, guards of palaces and of the temple.

Of the temple.—I Chr. 9:17–32; II Chr. 34:13; 35:15. Called keepers of the threshold—II Ki. 22:4; 23:4; 25:18; II Chr. 34:9; Jer. 35:4; 52:24. Gathered money for the temple—II Ki. 22:4; II Chr. 34:9.

Porters of the ark.—I Chr. 15:23, 24; 16:38.

Of palaces.—Called chamberlains—Esth. 2:21; 6:2.

Doorkeepers in the house of God.—Ps. 84:10.

Porter of the sheepfold.—John 10:3. See SERVANT.

PORTION. Gen. 14:24; 48:22; Ex. 29:26, 28; Lev. 10:13; Num. 18:8. Days —Ex. 16:4. Double—II Ki. 2:9. Food, Of—Lu. 12:42. Give a—Eccl. 11:2. Great, With the—Is. 53:12. Hypocrites—Mt. 24:51. Jehovah is—Ps. 16:5; 119:57; Lam. 3:24. Jehovah's—

Deut. 32:9. King's dainties, Of—Dan. 1:5. Labor, From—Eccl. 2:10. Pleasant—Jer. 12:10. Receive—Jer. 37:12. Rejoice in their—Is. 61:7. Seven—Josh. 18:5. Substance, Of—Lu. 15:12. Take his—Eccl. 5:19. Unfaithful, With—Lu. 12:46. Wicked man, Of—Job 20:29.

POSSESSIONS: Instances of such as had.—Abraham—(see COVENANT). Referred to—Acts 7:5. *Burying-place*—Gen. 23:4, 9, 18, 20; 49:30; 50:13. Canaan—To heirs of Abraham—Gen. 17:8; Lev. 14:34. *Children of Lot*—Deut. 2:9, 19. *Of Esau*—Deut. 2:5, 12. *Isaac*—Gen. 26:14. *Jacob*—Gen. 34:10; 47:11, 27; 48:4; Ob. 17. Edom—Gen. 36:43. Children of Israel—Lev. 25:10, 13, 18, 24, 41, 45; Deut. 32:49; Josh. 12:7; 21:41; I Chr. 9:2; II Chr. 20:11; 31:1; Neh. 11:3; Ps. 69:35; Ez. 11:15. Nabal—I Sam. 25:2. Ephraim—I Chr. 7:28. Hezekiah—II Chr. 32:29. Transjordanic tribes—*i. e.*, Reuben and Gad and the half-tribe of Manasseh—Num. 32:5, 22, 29, 30, 32; Deut. 3:20; Josh. 1:15; 12:6; 13:29; 22:4, 7, 9. Zelophehad's daughters—Num. 27:4, 7. Caleb—Josh. 21:12. Naboth—I Ki. 21:15, 16, 19. David—I Chr. 28:1. Preacher—Eccl. 2:7. Jehovah—Ps. 2:8. Ananias and Sapphira—Acts 5:1. Nations—Acts 7:45. Of Publius—Acts 28:7. Given to the poor—Acts 2:45.

Destruction of.—Deut. 11:6.

Laws concerning.—Redemption of—Lev. 25:25, 27, 28, 32–35. Inheritance—Lev. 25:46. Vows—Lev. 27:16, 21, 22, 24, 28. Division of inheritance—Num. 26:56. Division of Canaan—Num. 35:2, 8. Unclean possessions—Josh. 22:19. Of Levites—Lev. 25:32, 33, 34; II Chr. 11:14; Ez. 48:22.

Prophecies concerning.—Edom and Seir—Num. 24:18. Babylon—Is. 14:23. Ammon and Moab—Ez. 25:4, 10, 11. High places—Ez. 36:2. Israel—Ez. 36:3, 4, 5. Of priests—Ez. 44:28; 45:5. Of Israel—Ez. 45:6, 7. Princes—Ez. 45:8; 46:16, 18. Jerusalem—Ez. 48:20, 21.

Sacrifice of possessions in Christian life.—Mt. 19:22; Mk. 10:22; Acts 2:45; Eph. 1:14.

Christian has an eternal possession.—

Heb. 10:34. Reward in forsaking—Mk. 10:29 ff.

Voluntary surrender of, for the good of others in need.—Acts 2:45; 4:36 f.

Hypocrisy and punishment of Ananias and Sapphira.—Acts 5:1-11. See GOODS, WEALTH.

POSSIBLE. All things are—Mt. 19:26. Be at peace with all men, If—Rom. 12:18. Father, if it be—Mt. 26:39; Mk. 14:35. God, With—Lu. 18:27. Lead astray, If—Mt. 24:24. To him that believeth—Mk. 9:23.

POSTS (Couriers).—Of Hezekiah—II Chr. 30:6, 10. Of Ahasuerus—Esth. 3:13. Rode on swift steeds—Esth. 8:10, 14.

Prophecy concerning.—Jer. 51:31.

Figurative.—Job 9:25.

POT. See VESSELS.

POTENTATE. I Tim. 6:15.

POTIPHAR, pŏt′i-phar. **Pharaoh's captain.**—Gen. 37:36; 39:1.

POTI-PHERA, pŏt′i-phē′ra. **Joseph's father-in-law.**—Gen. 41:45.

POTSHERD. Job 2:8; 41:30; Is. 45:9.

POTTAGE. II Ki. 4:39. Eating of—II Ki. 4:40. Gave Esau bread and—Gen. 25:34. Jacob boiled—Gen. 25:29. Sons of prophets, For—II Ki. 4:38. Touch—Hag. 2:12.

POTTER. See TRADES AND ARTS.

POUND. Five thousand of silver—Ezra 2:69. Hundred—John 19:39. Ointment, Of—John 12:3. Ten—Lu. 19:13. Three, of gold—I Ki. 10:17. Two thousand, of silver—Neh. 7:71, 72. See MEASURES, MONEY.

POUR OUT. Blessing—Mal. 3:10. Blood, My—Mt. 26:28. Bottles of heaven—Job 38:37. Changer's money—John 2:15. Evil—Pr. 15:28. Foundation was—Job 22:16. God's wrath, Of—Ps. 79:6; Jer. 10:25; Ez. 7:8; Hos. 5:10. Grace is—Ps. 45:2. Heart—Ps. 62:8. Prayer—Is. 26:16. Soul—Job 30:16; Is. 53:12. Spirit, Of—Pr. 1:23; Is. 32:15; 44:3; Ez. 39:29; Zech. 2:10; Acts 2:10, 45. Upon us richly—Tit. 3:6.

POVERTY. Pr. 10:15; 13:18; Rev. 2:9. Become rich, Through—II Cor. 8:9. Come as robber—Pr. 6:11. Come to—Gen. 45:11; Pr. 20:13. Forget his—Pr. 31:7. Neither—Pr. 30:8. See POOR.

POWDER. Beat images into—II Chr. 34:7. Ground it to—Ex. 32:20. Make the rain—Deut. 28:24. Merchant, Of —Song of Sol. 3:6.

POWER. Zech. 4:6; John 10:8; Acts 25:5; Eph. 1:21; II Tim. 1:7. Anger, Of—Ps. 90:11. Bodies, Over our— Neh. 9:37. Clothed with—Lu. 24:49. Crucify, To—John 19:10. Death, Of— Heb. 2:14. Eat, To—Eccl. 5:19. Endless life, Of—Heb. 17:16. Everlasting —Rom. 1:20. Faint, To the—Is. 40: 29. Fire, Of—Heb. 11:34. Full of— Mic. 3:8. Giveth—Ps. 68:35. God, Of —See GOD IS ALMIGHTY. God, With— Hos. 12:3. Had gone forth—Lu. 8:46. Hand, Of—Pr. 3:27. Jesus, Of—I Cor. 5:4; II Cor. 12:9. Little—Rev. 3:8. Manifold—Heb. 2:4. Over day of death—Eccl. 8:8. Perfect—II Cor. 12: 9. Proceeding from him—Mk. 5:30. Raised in—I Cor. 15:43. Receive, Ye shall—Acts 1:8. Resurrection, Of— Phil. 3:10. Sheol, Of—Ps. 89:48. Signs, Of—Rom. 15:19. Sin, Of—I Cor. 15: 56. Spirit, Of—Lu. 4:14. Strengthened with—Eph. 3:16; Col. 1:11. See HOLY SPIRIT. Sword, Of the—Jer. 18: 21; Ez. 35:5. Tongue, Of—Pr. 18:21. Work in him—Mt. 14:2. Working of —Eph. 3:7. Void of—Lu. 1:37.

POWERFUL. II Cor. 13:3. Beast— Dan. 7:7. Voice of Jehovah—Ps. 29:4.

POWERFULLY. Acts 18:28.

PRACTICE. Rom. 1:32; 2:1; 7:19. Augury—Lev. 19:26; Deut. 18:10. Evil— Ps. 141:4; Mic. 2:1. Hypocrisy—Is. 32:6. Magical arts—Acts 19:19.

PRÆTORIAN. Guard—Phil. 1:13.

PRÆTORIUM. Mt. 27:27; Mk. 15:16; John 18:28; 19:9.

PRAISE: Is due to God for His lovingkindness.—II Chr. 20:21; Ps. 138:1-2. For all His benefits—Ps. 103:2-18; 145:2-9; 107:8-14; 108:3-4; Is. 63: 7-9. For His holiness—Ps. 99:3; Is. 6:3.

How offered: With the understanding— Ps. 47:6-7; I Cor. 14:15-16. With the whole heart—Ps. 9:1-2; 111:1-2. With uprightness of heart—Ps. 119:7. With the lips—Ps. 63:3-5; 119:171-172. With gladness—II Chr. 29:30; Jer. 33: 11; Ps. 98:4-9; Acts 2:46-47.

Why offered: For the gift of Christ— Rom. 15:8-13; John 12:12-13; Heb. 13:12-15; Rev. 5:12. For being planted in Christ—Is. 61:2-3; Eph. 1:3-6; Phil. 4:8; I Pet. 1:3-5; 2:9-10.

Old Testament: Instances of.—Melchizedek—Gen. 14:19-20. Moses—Ex. 15: 1-21. Jethro—Ex. 18:10-11. Deborah —Ju. 5:1-11. Asaph and his brethren —I Chr. 16:8-36. Hannah—I Sam. 2:1-10. David—I Chr. 29:10-13; Ps. 119:164; II Sam. Ch. 22. At laying foundation of temple—Ezra 3:10-11. Placing ark in temple—II Chr. 5:13-14. Hezekiah—Is. 38:19-20. Daniel— Dan. 2:20-23.

New Testament instances.—Mary—Lu. 1:46-55. Shepherds—Lu. 2:20. Zacharias—Lu. 1:68-69. Anna—Lu. 2:36-38. Disciples—Lu. 19:37-38. The people—Lu. 18:43. The apostles—Lu. 24: 53. Those first obedient to the faith —Acts 2:47. Lame man—Acts 3:8. Paul and Silas—Acts 16:25.

References from Old Testament.—Enter His courts with—Ps. 100:4. Praise is good—Ps. 147:1. Thou shalt call thy gates—Is. 60:18. The garment of praise for spirit of heaviness—Is. 61: 3. Bringing sacrifices of thanksgiving —Jer. 17:26. Earth full of His—Hab. 3:3.

From New Testament.—Out of mouth of babes Thou hast perfected—Mt. 21:6. Give God the praise—John 9: 24. Whose praise is not of men—Rom. 2:29. Do that which is good and thou shalt have—Rom. 13:3. Brother whose praise is in gospel—II Cor. 8:18. In this I praise you not—I Cor. 11:17. See SONGS, PSALMS, PRAYER.

PRATE. Ps. 94:4; Pr. 10:8, 10; III John 10.

PRAYER. What is prayer? It is the soul's desire for God—Ps. 42:1, 2; 63: 1-3; 84:2; 143:6-9.

It is as universal as man—Ps. 65:2; 86: 9; Is. 66:23. Began with Seth—Gen. 4:23.

It is a cry—a supplication—Ex. 22:23, 27; Job 23:3, 4; Ps. 34:15, 17; 86:3; 88:1, 2, 9, 13; Is. 19:20; 30:19; 58:9.

It is an instinct that must have utterance—Ps. 51:1-3; Is. 44:17; 45:20; Mt. 27:46; Mk. 15:34; Lu. 18:7, 13.

It is an appeal from the child to the father—Hos. 14:3; Mt. 6:6-13; Lu. 11:2-4.

It is a necessity—Hos. 14:1-3; Amos 5:6; Heb. 4:16.

Enjoined.—I Chr. 16:11, 35; 28:9; II Chr. 7:14, 15; Ps. 35:6; 62:8; 105:3, 4; Is. 55:6; 58:9; 65:24; Jer. 29:12, 13; 33:3; Lam. 2:10; 3:41; Ez. 36:37; Hos. 14:2; Zeph. 2:3; Zech. 10:1, 6; Mt. 7:7; 24:20; 26:41; Mk. 13:33; 14: 38; Lu. 11:5-13; 18:1; 21:36; John 16:24-27; Acts 8:22; Rom. 12:12; Eph. 6:17, 18; Phil. 4:6; Col. 4:2; I Thess. 5:17; I Tim. 2:1, 8; Heb. 4:16; Jas. 1:5-7; 5:13; I Pet. 4:7.

Confession.—Duty of—Lev. 5:5; Num. 5:6, 7; Jer. 3:13; Mt. 10:32; Lu. 12: 18; 15:21; John 9:22; Rom. 10:9; 14: 11; Phil. 2:11; Jas. 5:16. Blessedness of—Lev. 26:40-42; Job 33:27, 28; Pr. 28:13; I John 1:9. Individual—Gen. 32:9, 10; II Sam. 24:17; I Chr. 21:8; Job 40:4, 5; Ps. 32:5; 38:4; 40:11, 12; 41:4; 51:3, 4; 69:5; 119:176; 130:3; Is. 6:5; Dan. 9:20; Lu. 18:13.

National—Num. 14:40; Ju. 10:10, 15; I Sam. 7:6; 12:10; Neh. 9:2, 33-35; Ps. 106:6, 7; Jer. 3:25; 14:7, 20; Lam. 5:16; Dan. 9:5-15. *Moses* for Israel— Ex. 32:31, 32; 34:9; Num. 14:19. *Ezra* for Israel—Ezra 9:5-15; 10:1. *Nehemiah* for Judah—Neh. 1:4-11. *Isaiah* for Judah—Is. 64:6, 7. *Daniel* for Israel—Dan. 9:7-23. *Daniel* for Judah —Dan. 9:3-19.

Intercession.—Gen. 20:7; Jer. 27:18; 29:7; II Cor. 9:14; Eph. 6:18; I Tim. 2:1; II Tim. 4:16; Heb. 13:18-21; Jas. 5:14-16; I John 5:16. Priestly—Ex. 28:9-12, 29, 30, 38.

Instances of—Old Testament: *Abraham* for Abimelech—Gen. 20:7, 17, 18. For Ishmael—Gen. 17:18. For Sodom and Gomorrah—Gen. 18:23-32. *Boaz* for Ruth—Ruth 2:12. *Daniel* for Israel and Judah—Dan. 9:3-23. *David* for the Child of Bathsheba—II Sam. 12: 16. For Israel—II Sam. 24:17; I Chr. 29:10-19; Ps. 25:22; 28:9. For the righteous—Ps. 7:9; 36:10. For Solomon—I Chr. 29:19. *Eli* for Hannah— I Sam. 1:17. *Elisha* for the Shunammite's son—II Ki. 4:33. *Ezekiel* for Israel—Ez. 9:8. *Ezra* for Israel—Ezra

8:21-23; 9:5-15. *Hezekiah* for Judah— II Ki. 19:14-20. For those who had cleansed themselves for the passover —II Chr. 30:18-20. *Isaiah*—Is. 37:4; 63:16-19; 64:1-12. *Job* in behalf of his friends—Job 42:8-10. *Joshua* for Israel—Josh. 7:6-9. *Moses* for Israel— Ex. 32:11-14, 31, 32; 34:9; Num. 11:1, 2; 14:13-24; 21:7; Deut. 1:11; 9:18-20, 25-29; 10:10; Ps. 106:23. God's model for Moses—Num. 6:22-27. *Moses* for Aaron—Deut. 9:20. For Miriam—Num. 12:13. For Pharaoh— Ex. 8:12, 30, 31; 9:33, 34; 10:18, 19. *Naomi* for Ruth—Ruth 1:8, 9. *Nehemiah* for Judah—Neh. 1:4-11. *Samuel* for Israel—I Sam. 7:5-8; 12:19-23. *Solomon* for Israel—I Ki. 8:22-54; II Chr. 6:12-42. New Testament: *Jesus*: For Peter—Lu. 22:32. For His disciples—John 17:9-24. For those who crucified Him—Lu. 23:34 *Epaphras* for the Colossians—Col. 4:12. *Paul* for Israel—Rom. 10:1. For Christians of Rome—Rom. 1:9. For Ephesians—Eph. 1:16-21; 3:14-21. For Philippians—Phil. 1:3-7, 9. For Colossians—Col. 1:3, 9. For Thessalonians—I Thess. 1:2; 3:10-13; 5:23; II Thess. 1:11, 12; 2:16, 17; 3:5, 16. For Onesiphorus—II Tim. 1:16, 18. For Philemon—Philemon 4-6. *Philemon* for Paul—Philemon 22. *The Church in Jerusalem* for Peter—Acts 12:5. For the Sick—Jas. 5:14, 15. Paul asks for prayers of disciples—Rom. 15:30; II Cor. 1:11; Eph. 6:19; Col. 4:3; I Thess. 5:25; II Thess. 3:1; Heb. 13:18. See Phil. 1:19, 20. Forbidden to pray for—Jer. 7:13-16; 14:10-12.

Imprecation.—(Note that every instance belongs to Old Testament except three)—Commands to curse—Deut. 11:29-30; 26:11-13; Josh. 8:33; II Sam. 16:11-12. Commands not to curse—Num. 22:12; 23:25. Curses requested—Num. 22:6-11; 23:7-8; 24: 10; Josh. 24:9-10. *Upon one's self*— II Sam. 24:17; I Chr. 21:17; Job 3:1-10; Ps. 7:3-5. *Upon persecutors of poor* —Ps. 10:2; 109:9-16. *Upon enemies and transgressors*—Num. 16:15; Deut. 33:11; Ju. 16:28; I Sam. 26:19; Neh. 4:4-5; 5:13; Job 27:7; Ps. 5:10; 6:10; 9:20; 10:15; 28:4; 31:17-18; 35:4, 8,

9, 26; 40:14–15; 55:9, 15; 58:7; 59:5–15; 68:1, 2; 69:23–28; 70:2–3; 79:10–12; 83:13–17; 109:17–29; 119:78, 84; 129:5; 140:9, 10; 145:12; 144:6; Jer. 11:20; 12:3; 15:15; 17:18; 18:21–23; 20:12; Lam. 3:64–66.

New Testament: Upon preachers of another gospel—Gal. 1:8–9. Upon Alexander the.coppersmith—II Tim. 4:14. Upon those who love not Christ —I Cor. 16:22.

Praise.—Ps. 30:4; 59:16; 63:3; 92:1–2; 95:2; 106:1; 107:8, 21, 31; 147:7; Is. 12:5; 63:7; Jer. 20:13; Dan. 2:23; Lu. 1:64; 2:13, 28; 18:43; 19:37; Acts 2:47; 3:8; 16:25; Heb. 13:15; Rev. 4:9–11; 5:12.

Supplication.—Ex. 33:12–16, 18; I Ki. 8:22–53; II Ki. 20:3; II Chr. 6:12–42; Ezra 8:21–23; Job 8:5; Ps. 6:9; 22:19, 21; 28:2; 40:11–17; 69:1, 2, 13–18, 29; 70:5; 88:1–18; Jer. 36:7; Dan. 6:11; Jonah 1:14; Rom. 10:1; II Cor. 1:11; 9:14; Eph. 6:18; Phil. 1:4, 19; 4:6; I Tim. 5:5; II Tim. 1:3.

Thanksgiving.—Gen. 24:27; Ex. 18:10; I Sam. 2:1; I Ki. 8:15, 56; I Chr. 16:8; II Chr. 20:21–28; Neh. 12:31–40; Ps. 18:17–49; 75:1; 118:1–4; 140:13; Dan. 2:19, 23; Rom. 1:8; I Cor. 15:57; II Cor. 2:14, 15; 9:15; Eph. 1:3; Phil. 1:3–7; Col. 1:3, 12, 13; I Thess. 1:2; I Pet. 1:3.

HOW SHALL WE PRAY? Should be offered to God.—Deut. 6:13; Ps. 5:2. **As to a Father.**—Mt. 6:9–13; Lu. 11:2–4. **To Jesus.**—Acts 7:59.

In the name of Jesus.—Mt. 18:19–20; 28:18–20; John 14:13, 14; 15:16; 16:23–26; Eph. 2:18; 5:20; Col. 3:17; I Pet. 2:5. See Lu. 23:42.

Continually—Ps. 55:17; 88:1; Rom. 12:12; I Thess. 5:17. Faith, In—Ps. 56:9; 86:7; Mt. 21:21, 22; Mk. 11:24; Heb. 10:22; Jas. 1:6; I John 5:14. Fasting, With—Neh. 1:4; Dan. 9:3; Acts 13:3. Forgiving spirit, With—Mt. 6:11–15; 18:21–35; Mk. 11:25. Hasty, Not—Eccl. 5:2. Heart, With the—Lam. 3:41. Heart, With the whole—II Chr. 22:9; Ps. 119:58, 145; Jer. 24:7; 29:12, 13. Heart, With preparation of—Job 11:13; Heb. 10:22. Humility—II Chr. 7:14; 33:12. Importunity—Gen. 32:26–28; Mt. 7:

7–11; Lu. 11:8; 18:1–7. Model—Mt. 6:9–13; Lu. 11:2–4. Repetitions, Avoid vain—Mt. 6:7. Righteous, must be—Ps. 34:15, 17, 18; John 15:7, 16. Secret, In—Mt. 6:6. Sincerity—Mt. 6:5; Heb. 10:22. Spirit and understanding, With—John 4:22–24; I Cor. 14:14–19. Truth, In—Ps. 145:18; John 4:24. Unfeigned lips, With—Ps. 17:1. Watch and pray—Neh. 4:9; Ps. 5:3; Mt. 26:41; Lu. 21:36; Eph. 6:18; Col. 4:2, 3; I Pet. 4:7. Will of God, According to—I John 5:14–16. *Jesus in Gethsemane*—Mt. 26:39; Lu. 22:32.

Described as: Beseeching the Lord—Ex. 32:11. Calling on the Lord—Acts 7:59; Rom. 10:12–14; II Tim. 2:22. Calling on the name of the Lord—Gen. 4:26; 12:8; Ps. 116:4; Acts 22:16; I Cor. 1:2. Crying unto God. See "What is Prayer?" Drawing near to God—Ps. 73:28; Heb. 10:22. Lifting up the heart—Lam. 3:41. Lifting up the soul—Ps. 25:1. Pouring out the heart—Ps. 62:8. Pouring out the soul —I Sam. 1:15. Seeking the face of the Lord—Ps. 27:8. Seeking unto God —Job 8:5.

Postures in prayer.—Bowing down—Gen. 24:52; Ps. 95:6. Bowing the knees—Is. 45:23; Rom. 14:11; Eph. 3:14; Phil. 2:10. Bowing the head—Gen. 24:26, 48; Ex. 4:31; 12:27; II Chr. 20:18. Falling on face—Num. 16:22, 45; 20:6; Josh. 5:14; 7:6; I Chr. 21:16; II Chr. 20:18; Ez. 9:8; Mt. 26:39; Mk. 14:35. Kneeling—I Ki. 8:54; II Chr. 6:13; Ezra 9:5; Ps. 95:6; Dan. 6:10; Lu. 22:41; Acts 7:60; 9:40; 20:36; 21:5. Looking up—Ps. 5:3. Standing—I Sam. 1:26; I Ki. 8:14, 22, 55; II Chr. 20:9; Mk. 11:25; Lu. 18:11–13. Toward the temple in Jerusalem—I Ki. 8:35, 48, 49; II Chr. 6:38; Ps. 5:7; Dan. 6:10; Jonah 2:4. Lifting up the hands—Neh. 8:6; Ps. 28:2; 134:2; 141:2; Lam. 2:19; 3:41; I Tim. 2:8. Spreading out the hands —Ex. 9:29; I Ki. 8:22, 38, 54; Ezra 9:5; Job 11:13; Ps. 28:2; 63:4; 88:9; 143:6; Is. 1:15; Lam. 1:17.

Answers to prayer.—Ex. 22:23, 27; II Chr. 7:14; Job 12:4; 33:26; 34:28; Ps. 21:2, 4; 34:15, 17; 38:15; 55:16, 17; 56:9; 65:2, 5; 69:33; 86:5; 91:15;

99:6; 102:17, 18; 118:5; 138:3; 145: 18, 19; Pr. 15:8, 29; Is. 19:20; 30:19; 55:6, 7; 58:9; 65:24; Jer. 29:12, 13; Lam. 3:57; Ez. 36:37; Dan. 9:20–23; 10:12; Joel 2:32; Jonah 2:2; Zech. 13: 9; Mt. 6:6; 18:19; Lu. 11:13; 18:7; John 15:7; 16:23–27; Acts 4:31; II Cor. 12:8; Jas. 5:16–18; I John 3:22; 5:14, 15. Christ received answer— John 11:42; Heb. 5:7. Christ answers —John 14:13, 14.

Examples: Abraham—Gen. 15:1–20; 17: 20. Lot—Gen. 19:19–21. Abraham's servant—Gen. 24:12–21. Isaac—Gen. 25:21. Jacob—Gen. 32:24–30. Israelites—Ex. 2:23, 24; 14:10; Ju. 3:9, 15; 4:3, 23; 6:7–14; 10:10, 15, 16; I Sam. 12:10, 11; II Chr. 15:4, 15; Neh. 9:27; Ps. 106:15. Gideon—Ju. 6:36–40. Manoah—Ju. 13:8, 9. Samson—Ju. 15:18, 19; 16:28–30. Hannah—I Sam. 1:10–17, 27. Samuel—I Sam. 7:9. David—I Sam. 23:10–12; Ps. 18:6. Solomon—I Ki. 3:1–13; 9:2, 3. Man of God—I Ki. 13:6. Elijah—I Ki. 18:36– 39; Jas. 5:17, 18. Elisha—II Ki. 4:33– 35; 6:18, 19. Jehoahaz—II Ki. 13:4. Hezekiah and Isaiah—II Ki. 19:14– 20; 20:1–6, 10, 11; II Chr. 32:20, 21, 24. Jabez—I Chr. 4:10. Abijah's army—II Chr. 13:14–18. Asa—II Chr. 14:11–15; 15:16. Jehoshaphat—II Chr. 18:31; 20:6–27. Levites—II Chr. 30: 27. Manasseh—II Chr. 33:13, 19. Ezra —Ezra 8:21–23. Nehemiah—Neh. 4:9, 15. Job—Job 42:10. Jeremiah—Lam. 3:55, 56. Daniel—Dan. 9:20–23. Jonah —Jonah 2:2, 10. Reubenites—I Chr. 5:20. Jews—Ezra 8:21, 23; Zech. 7:1– 4. Zacharias—Lu. 1:13. Apostles— Acts 4:29–31. Ananias—Acts 10:4. Cornelius—Acts 10:4, 21. Disciples— Acts 12:5, 7. Paul—Acts 28:8. Paul and Silas—Acts 16:25, 26.

Prayer of wicked not answered.—Deut. 1:45; II Sam. 22:42; Job 35:12, 13; Ps. 18:41; 34:16; 66:18; Pr. 1:24–28; 15:8, 29; 21:13, 27; 28:9; Is. 1:15; 59: 2; Jer. 11:11; 14:12; 15:1; 18:17; Ez. 8:18; 20:3, 31; Hos. 5:6; Mic. 3:4; Zech. 7:12, 13; Mal. 2:11–13; Lu. 18: 11–14; John 9:31; Jas. 1:6–8; 4:3.

Christ as a mediator.—Rom. 8:34; Eph.

2:18; 3:12; I Tim. 2:5; Heb. 4:14–16; 13:15.

Aid of Holy Spirit.—Zech. 12:10; Rom. 8:26; Eph. 2:18; 6:18; Jude 20.

Assurances.—Ps. 37:4; 81:10; Is. 65:24; Jer. 33:3; Mt. 9:29; Mk. 11:24; John 14:14; 15:7, 16; Eph. 3:20; Jas. 5:16; I John 3:20.

Private prayer.—Job 22:27. Commanded —Mt. 6:6.

Examples of: Lot—Gen. 19:20. Abraham's servant—Gen. 24:12. Jacob— Gen. 32:9–12. Moses—Deut. 9:18–20. Gideon—Ju. 6:22, 36, 39. Hannah— I Sam. 1:9–15. David—II Sam. 7:18– 29. Hezekiah—II Ki. 20:2, 5. Isaiah— II Ki. 20:11. Manasseh—II Chr. 33: 12, 13. Ezra 9:5, 6. Nehemiah—Neh. 1:4; 2:4. Jeremiah—Jer. 32:16–25. Daniel—Dan. 9:3, 17–20. Daniel and companions—Dan. 2:17–23. Jonah— Jonah 2:1. Anna—Lu. 2:37.

Public prayer.—God hears—II Chr. 7: 14, 16. God accepts—Is. 56:7. Christ sanctions—Mt. 18:20. Form of prayer —Mt. 6:9–13; Lu. 11:2–4. Should be understood—I Cor. 14:14–16. Examples.—Joshua—Josh. 7:6–9. David —I Chr. 29:10–19. Solomon—II Chr. Ch. 6. Jehoshaphat—II Chr. 20:5– 13. Levites—Neh. Ch. 9. Jews—Lu. 1:10. Disciples—Acts 2:46; 4:24; 12: 5, 12; 13:3; 16:16.

*Prayers in Old Testament.—*Aaron and priests,* for blessing—*Num. 6:22–26. *Abraham, for a son—*Gen. 15:2. For Ishmael—Gen. 17:17, 18. For Sodom —Gen. 18:22–32. *Asa, for victory—*II Chr. 14:11. *Daniel, for Jerusalem—* Dan. 9:4–19. Toward Jerusalem— Dan. 6:10. *David, for his house—*II Sam. 7:18–29. For forgiveness and peace—Ps. 51. For Israel—II Sam. 24:17. At the end of his life—I Chr. 29:10–19. *Eliezer, for success—*Gen. 24:12–14, 27. *Elijah, for widow's son* —I Ki. 17:20. At Carmel—I Ki. 18: 36, 37. To die—I Ki. 19:4. *Elisha, for* opening inner eyes—II Ki. 6:17. For blinding the army—II Ki. 6:18. *Ezekiel, for people—*Ez. 9:8. *Ezra,* confession—Ezra 9:5–15. For protec-

* By Ira M. Price Ph. D. Copyright, 1903, by Thomas Nelson & Sons. Used by permission and revised for the Cross-Reference Bible by the author.

tion—Ezra 8:21–23. *Gideon*, colloquy with an angel—Ju. Ch. 6. *Habakkuk*, for a revival—Hab. 3:1–16. *Hannah*, for a son—I Sam. 1:11. In thanksgiving—I Sam. 2:1–10. *Hezekiah*, for his protection—II Ki. 19:15–19; 20:3; Is. 38:3. In the temple—Is. 37:16–20. For the uncleansed—II Chr. 30:18. *Isaiah*, a prayer, praise and thanksgiving—Is. 63:7; 64:12. *Israel*, for expiation—Deut. 21:6–8. Confession—Deut. 26:5–10. Tithing prayer—Deut. 26:13–15. *Jabez*, for blessing—I Chr. 4:10. *Jacob*, before Esau—Gen. 32:9–12. In a vow—Gen. 28:20. While wrestling with an angel—Gen. 32:24 (*cf.* Hos. 12:3, 4). *Jehoshaphat*, for deliverance—II Chr. 20:6–13. *Jeremiah*, in famine—Jer. 14:7–9. For comfort—Jer. 15:15–18. *Jonah*, for freedom—Jonah 2:2–9. At Nineveh—Jonah 4:2. *Joshua*, for mercy—Josh. 7:7–9. Against enemies—Josh. 10:12–14. *Levites*, confession—Neh. 9:5–38. *Manoah*, for guidance—Ju. 13:8, 9. *Men in general*—Gen. 4:26. *Moses*, in a colloquy with God—Ex. Chs. 3 and 4. Appeals to God—Ex. 5:22. Calls for relief for Pharaoh—Ex. 8:12, 29, 30; 9:33; 10:17, 18. For the people—Ex. 32:11–13. For guidance—Ex. 33:12–16. For God's presence—Num. 10:35, 36. For help—Num. 11:11–15. For Miriam—Num. 12:13. For murmurers—Num. 14:13–19. For a successor—Num. 27:15–17. To enter Canaan—Deut. 3:24. *Nehemiah*, for captives—Neh. 1:5–11. For protection—Neh. 4:4, 5. Levites' prayer—Neh. 9:5–38. *Psalmist*, in a large number of Psalms. *Samson*, for vengeance—Ju. 16:28. *Samuel*, for Israel—I Sam. 7:5–12. Regarding Israel's desire for a king—I Sam. Chs. 8 and 12. Attitude for Israel—I Sam. 12:23. *Solomon*, for wisdom—I Ki. 3:5–9. Temple dedication—I Ki. 8:23–61; II Chr. 6:14–42. Titles of Psalms—17; 86; 90; 102; 142.

Prayers of Jesus.—Mt. 19:13; Lu. 3:21; 11:1; John 12:27, 28; Heb. 5:7. Of thanksgiving—Mt. 11:25, 26; 14:19; 15:36; 26:27; Mk. 6:41; 14:22; Lu. 22:17; John 11:41, 42; I Cor. 11:24. In a mountain—Mt. 14:23; Mk. 6:46; Lu. 6:12. In the upper room—John 17:1–26. For Peter—Lu. 22:32. In Gethsemane—Mt. 26:36–42; Mk. 14:32–39; Lu. 22:41–45. On the cross—Mt. 27:46; Lu. 23:34, 46.

Paul's prayers.—Rom. 1:3; 10:1; I Cor. 1:3; II Cor. 13:7; Eph. 1:16–19; 3:14–19; Phil. 1:3–10; Col. 1:3, 9; I Thess. 1:2; 3:10–13; 5:23; II Thess. 1:11; 2:16, 17; 3:5, 16; II Tim. 1:3, 18; Philemon 4–6; Heb. 13:20, 21.

PREACH. Jonah 3:2; Mk. 13:10. Baptism—Mk. 1:4. Good tidings—Is. 61:1; Mt. 11:5; see GOSPEL, TIDINGS. Gospel—See GOSPEL MUST BE PREACHED. John the Baptist, By—Mt. 3:1. Jesus—See GOSPEL. Jesus, By—See JESUS. Prophets, By—Neh. 6:7. Word—See GOSPEL, WORD OF GOD.

PREACHER. Gospel, Of—See GOSPEL MUST BE PREACHED. How shall they hear without—Rom. 10:14. Ordained—I Tim. 2:7; II Tim. 1:11. Righteousness of—II Pet. 2:5. Words of—Eccl. 1:1, 2, 12; 7:27; 12:8, 9, 10. See GOSPEL, MINISTERS.

PRECEDE. I Thess. 4:15.

PRECEPT. Col. 2:22. Jehovah, Of—Ps. 19:8; 103:18; 119:4–173; Jer. 35:18; Dan. 9:5. Precept upon precept—Is. 28:10, 13. See COMMANDMENTS.

PRECINCTS. II Ki. 23:11.

PRECIOUS. Blood—Ps. 72:14; I Pet. 1:19. Clothes—Ez. 27:20. Faith—II Pet. 1:1. Fruits—Deut. 33:14–16; Jas. 5:7. Gold, As—Ezra 8:27. Jehovah, In sight of—II Ki. 1:13, 14; Ps. 116:15. Jesus is—I Pet. 2:4–7. Ointment—II Ki. 20:13; Ps. 133:2; Eccl. 7:1; Is. 39:2; Mt. 26:7. Life—Pr. 6:26. Promises—II Pet. 1:4. See PROMISES. Soul—I Sam. 26:21. Stones—See PRECIOUS STONES. Things—Gen. 24:53; Deut. 33:13, 14; II Ki. 20:13; II Chr. 21:3; Ezra 1:6; Job 28:10; Is. 39:2; Jer. 20:5; Ez. 22:25; Dan. 11:43. Thoughts—Ps. 139:17. Vessels—Dan. 11:8. Wood—Rev. 18:12. Word—I Sam. 3:1.

PRECIOUSNESS. I Pet. 2:7.

PRECIOUS STONES. The breastplate was set in stones in four rows, three stones in a row—Ex. 28:17; 39:9–13. Names of stones given to correspond to names of 12 tribes—Ex. 28:17–21; 39:10–14. (For names of tribes see

Gen. Ch. 49.) Precious stones set in kings' crowns—II Sam. 12:30. Queen of Sheba brought to Solomon—I Ki. 10:2, 10; II Chr. 9:2. Hiram's navy brought them from Ophir—I Ki. 10: 11. Voluntary offerings of Israelites for priests' garments—Ex. 35:27. David prepared for temple with—I Chr. 29:2. Ezekiel gives a list of, as belonging to the king of Tyre—Ez. 28: 13. David garnished temple with—II Chr. 3:6. Hezekiah built treasuries for —II Chr. 32:27. Tyre's traffic in—Ez. 27:22. Kings shall honor with—Dan. 11:38.

Used figuratively of establishing the church.—Is. 54:11-12; I Cor. 3:12; Rev. 21:19.

Kinds of.—Adamant—Ez. 3:9; Zech. 7: 12. Agate—Ex. 28:19; 39:12. Amethyst—Ex. 28:19; 39:12; Rev. 21:20. Beryl—Ex. 28:20; 39:13; Song of Sol. 5:14; Ez. 1:16; 10:9; Rev. 21:20. Carbuncle—Ex. 28:17; 39:10; Is. 54:12; Ez. 28:13. Chalcedony—Rev. 21:19. Chrysolite—Rev. 21:20. Chrysoprase —Rev. 21:20. Coral—Job 28:18; Ez. 27:16. Crystal—Job 28:18; Ez. 1:22; Rev. 4:6; 21:11; 22:1. Diamond—Ex. 28:18; Ez. 28:13; Jer. 17:1. Emerald —Ex. 28:18; Ez. 28:13. Jacinth—Ex. 28:19; Rev. 9:17; 21:20. Jasper—Ex. 28:20; 39:13; Ez. 28:13; Rev. 4:3; 21:11, 18, 19. Onyx—See Gen. 2:12; Job 28:16. See Jewels.

PREDESTINE. See Election, Foreordination, Purpose.

PREEMINENCE. Gen. 49:3, 4; Eccl. 3:19; Col. 1:18; III John 9.

PREFER. Ps. 137:6.

PREJUDICE. I Tim. 5:21. Examples of—Ephesians—Acts 19:34. Epicureans—Acts 17:18. Jesus' countrymen —Mt. 13:55. Naaman—II Ki. 5:12. Nathanael—John 1:46. Referred to— Pr. 24:23; John 7:24.

PREPARATION. Day of—Nah. 2:3; Mt. 27:62; Mk. 15:42; Lu. 23:54; John 19:42. Gospel, Of—Eph. 6:15. Heart, Of—Pr. 16:1. Make—I Chr. 22:5. Passover, For—John 19:14, 31.

PREPARE. Zech. 5:11; Lu. 12:20; II Cor. 9:2. Father, Of my—Mt. 20:23. Food—See Food, Preparation of. Earth—Ps. 65:9. Goodness, Of thy—

Ps. 68:10. Good work, For—II Tim. 2:21. Heart—I Chr. 29:18; Pr. 10:17. House—Gen. 24:31. Lovingkindness— Ps. 61:7. Lying—Dan. 2:9. Meet God, To—Amos 4:12; Lu. 12:20. Offering— See Offering. People—Lu. 1:17; 2:31. Place—John 14:2. Spies—Lu. 23:56. Table—Ps. 78:19; Is. 21:5; 65:11; Ez. 23:41. Temple—Heb. 9:6. Truth—Ps. 61:7. War, For—Jer. 6:4; Joel 3:9; Mic. 3:5. See War. Way—Is. 40:3; 57:14; 62:10; Mt. 11:10; Mk. 1:2. Wine—Rev. 14:10.

PRESBYTERY. I Tim. 4:14.

PRESCRIBE. Ezra 7:22.

PRESENCE. Angels, Of—Lu. 15:10. Corinthian church, Of—II Cor. 10:1. Enemies, Of—Ps. 23:5; Joel 2:6. Foolish man, Of—Pr. 14:7. Jesus, Of— Eat and drink in—Lu. 13:26. Paul's —Gal. 4:18, 20; Phil. 1:26; 2:12. Saints, Of—Ps. 52:9. **Jehovah, Of**— Angel of—Is. 63:9. *Angels and elders stand in*—Lu. 1:19; Rev. 5:8, 11; 7:11. *Awfulness of*—Ex. 19:10-12; 16:24; Deut. 33:2; Ju. 5:4; Ps. 18:7-16; Ju. 5:4; Ps. 18:6-15; 29:3-9; 114:7; Is. 64:1-3; Jer. 5:22; Ez. 38:20; Mic. 1:3, 4; Hab. 3:3-6. See God, Appearances of. *Cast from*—Ps. 51:11. *Fulness of joy in*—Ps. 16:11; 21:16. Glory of— Jude 24. Go from—Gen. 3:8; I Sam. 26:20; Job 1:12; Ps. 139:7; Jonah 1:3. *Go with*—Ex. 33:14, 15; Is. 63:9. *Hide —Cannot hide from*—Gen. 3:8-11; Ps. 139:7-12; Jer. 23:24; Amos 9:2; Jonah 1:3-10; 2:2, 7; Rev. 6:15-17. In covert of—Ps. 31:20. *Special places, In*—See God, Appearances of. *Terrified at*—Job 23:15; Ps. 14:7. *Upright shall dwell in*—Ps. 140:13. See Cloud of glory, Judgment.

PRESENT, *adj.* Bread, with the—Lev. 23:18. Evil is—Rom. 7:21. See Evil. Help—Ps. 46:1. See Help. Will is, To —Rom. 7:18. World—I Tim. 6:17. See World.

PRESENTS. A present for Esau—Gen. 32:13, 20, 21; 33:10, 11. Joseph's brethren bring—Gen. 43:15. Given to judges as bribes—Pr. 17:32; Amos 2:6. To king of Syria to gain help— I Ki. 15:18. Brought to Elisha and given to Gehabi—II Ki. 5:5-7, 20-27. To God—Ps. 68:29; 72:10; 76:11. Gift to Solomon—I Ki. 10:24, 25 (II Chr. 9:23, 24; Ps. 72:10).

Reasons for giving.—To appease angry feelings of others—Gen. 32:20; I Sam. 25:27, 28, 35. To confirm covenants—Gen. 21:28-30. To show respect—Ju. 6:18. To reward service—II Sam. 18:12; Dan. 2:6, 48. As a token of friendship—I Sam. 18:3, 4. As tribute—Ju. 3:15, 18; II Sam. 8:2; II Chr. 17:5.

When given.—On occasions of visits—II Ki. 8:8. Of public rejoicings—Neh. 8:12; Esth. 9:19. At marriages—Gen. 24:53; Ps. 45:12. On recovering from sickness—II Ki. 20:12. Parting gifts Gen. 45:22; Jer. 40:5; Mic. 1:14. On business matters—I Sam. 9:7. On restoration to prosperity—Job 42:10, 11.

Things given.—Ornaments—Gen. 24:22, 47; Job 42:11. Cattle—Gen. 32:14, 15, 18. Garments—Gen. 45:22; I Sam. 18:4. Money—Gen. 45:22; I Sam. 9:8; Job 42:11. Eatables—Gen. 43:11; I Sam. 25:18; I Ki. 14:3. Horses and mules—I Ki. 10:25. Gold and silver vessels—I Ki. 10:25. Precious stones —I Ki. 10:2. Weapons of war—I Sam. 18:4. Servants—Gen. 20:14; 29:24, 29.

Manner in which taken.—Conveyed on camels, etc.—I Sam. 25:18; II Ki. 8:9; II Chr. 9:1. Sometimes sent before the giver—Gen. 32:21. Presented in person—Gen. 43:15, 26; Ju. 3:17; I Sam. 25:27. With great ceremony—Gen. 43:25; Ju. 3:18; Mt. 2:11.

Not bringing, A mark of disrespect.—I Sam. 10:27. See GIFTS, GIVING, LIBERALITY.

PRESENT, v. Bodies living sacrifice—Rom. 12:1. Dorcas alive—Acts 9:41. Paul before Felix—Acts 23:33. Priest, Unto—Num. 5:9. See PURIFICATION. Supplication—Jer. 38:26. Thyself approved unto God—II Tim. 2:15. Your bodies sacrifice—Rom. 12:1. Yourselves unto God—Rom. 6:13.

PRESERVE. Josh. 24:17; I Sam. 30:23; Neh. 9:6; Ps. 121:7, 8; Is. 49:8; Jude 1. All them that love Jehovah—Ps. 145:20. Blame, Without—I Thess. 5:23. Charitable, The—Ps. 41:2. David—II Sam. 8:6; I Chr. 18:6, 13; Ps. 16:1; 25:21; 32:7; 40:11; 61:7; 64:1; 86:2; 140:1, 4. Death, Those appointed for—Ps. 79:11. Discretion—Pr. 5:2.

Eyes of Jehovah preserve—Ps. 22:12. Faithful—Ps. 31:23. Fatherless children—Jer. 49:11. Israel—Is. 49:6; Hos. 12:13. Jerusalem—Is. 31:5. Job —Job 10:12; 29:2. King, The—Ps. 61:7. Kindness and truth preserve—Pr. 20:28. Life—Gen. 32:30; 45:5; Deut. 6:24; Job 36:6; Ps. 64:1; Lu. 17:33. Man and beast—Ps. 36:6. Mighty, The—Ps. 24:22. Noah—II Pet. 2:5. Saints—Ps. 37:28; 97:10; Pr. 2:8. Sojourners—Ps. 146:9. Soul —Ps. 86:2; 97:10; 121:7; Pr. 16:17. Spirit—Job 10:12. Thessalonians—I Thess. 5:23. Wine and wine-skins—Mt. 9:17; Lu. 5:38. Wisdom—Pr. 4:6; 14:3.

PRESERVER. Job 7:20.

PRESIDENTS. Dan. 6:2-7.

PRESS, n. See CROWD, WINEPRESS.

PRESSURE. Job 33:7.

PRESUME. Num. 14:44; Esth. 7:5.

PRESUMPTUOUS. Deut. 1:43. Sins—Ps. 19:13. See BOASTING, PRIDE.

PRESUMPTUOUSLY. Ex. 21:17; Deut. 17:12, 13; 18:20, 22.

PRETENCE. Mk. 12:40; Lu. 20:47; Phil. 1:18. See HYPOCRISY.

PREVAIL. Lu. 21:36. Babylon—Is. 47:12. Balak—Num. 22:6. Blessings—Gen. 49:26. David—I Sam. 17:50; 26:25; Rev. 5:5. Distress and anguish—Job 15:24. Enemies—Ps. 13:4; 129:2; Jer. 1:19; 15:20; Lam. 1:16. Gates of Hades—Mt. 16:18. Goliath—I Sam. 17:9. God—Jer. 20:7; Rom. 3:4. Against God—II Chr. 14:11. Haman—Esth. 6:13. Iniquities—Ps. 65:3. Israel—Ex. 17:11; Ju. 4:24; Is. 7:1. Jacob—Gen. 32:25, 28. Jeremiah, Against—Jer. 20:10, 11. Man—I Sam. 2:9; II Sam. 11:23; Ps. 9:19; Eccl. 4:12. Moab —Is. 16:12. Pharisees—John 12:19. Philistines—Ju. 16:5. Pilate—Mt. 27:24. Spirit, A—I Ki. 22:22; II Chr. 18:21. Strength, Not by—I Sam. 2:9. Tongue, With—Ps. 12:4. Waters—Gen. 7:78-24. Word of God—Acts 19:20.

PREY. Gen. 49:9; Job 29:17; 38:41; Is. 10:2; Jer. 20:5; Ez. 34:22. See SPOIL.

PRICE. Pr. 17:16; Is. 45:13; I Pet. 3:4. Blood, Of—Mt. 27:6, 9. Books of magic—Acts 19:19. Bought with—I

Cor. 6:20; 7:23. Cave of Machpelah, Of—Gen. 23:9. Field—Ps. 27:26. Horses, Of—I Ki. 10:28; II Chr. 1:16. Judas, Of—Zech. 11:12, 13. Part of, Kept back—Acts 5:2, 3. Pearl of great—Mt. 13:46. People, Of—Ps. 44: 12. Redemption, Of—Lev. 25:16, 50–52. See REDEMPTION. Threshing-floor —II Sam. 24:24; I Chr. 21:22, 24. Virtuous woman, Of—Pr. 31:10. Water, Of—Num. 20:19. Wisdom, Of—Job 28:13, 15, 18. Without money and without—Is. 55:1. See Jer. 15:13.

PRIDE: Definition of.—Ps. 73:6.

Examples.—Of David—I Sam. 17:28. Of wicked—Job 35:12; Ps. 10:2, 4; Ez. 16:49; Mk. 7:22. Of power—Lev. 26: 19; Ez. 30:6. Of foolish—Pr. 14:3. Of Jehovah—Job 41:15, 34. Of heart —Is. 9:9; Ob. 3. Of Moab—Is. 16:6; Jer. 48:29. Of glory—Is. 23:9. Of Judah—Jer. 13:9. Of Jerusalem—Jer. 13:9. Of Sodom—Ez. 16:56.

Humbled.—II Chr. 32:26; Job 33:17; Ps. 59:12.

Warnings against.—Ps. 36:11; Pr. 8:13; 11:2; 13:10; 16:18; 29:23; Is. 25:11; 28:1, 3; Jer. 13:9, 17; Ez. 7:10.

Prophecies concerning.—Dan. 4:37; Hos. 5:5; 7:10; Zeph. 2:10; Zech. 9:6; 10: 11; 11:3. See JESUS, TEACHING OF, ON PRIDE.

PRIEST, Heb. *Cohen;* Gr. *Hiereus.*— There are four characteristics of the priest: (1) Chosen of God; (2) the property of God; (3) Holy to God; (4) Offers to, and receives gifts of God—Num. 16:5; Heb. 5:1–4.

First notice of persons acting at the altar, Cain and Abel.—Gen. 4:3–4. In patriarchal times, heads of families officiated—Gen. 8:20; 12:8; 13:4, 18; 35:7. Melchizedek was conspicuous as the priest who best typified Christ— Gen. 14:18–24; Heb. 5:5–6, 10; 6:20; 7:1–22. Jethro priest of Midian—Ex. 2:16. Priests before giving the law— Ex. 19:22, 24; 24:5.

Priests under Moses' administration.— Levites set apart for God—Num. 3:45. Aaron and his sons appointed—Ex. 28:1; 29:9, 44; Num. 3:10; 18:7; I Chr. 23:13. The priesthood to be for them and theirs for a permanent office—Ex. 27:21; 28:43; 29:9; 40:15. Garments made for Aaron and sons—Ex. Ch. 28. Their consecration—Ex. Ch. 29; 40: 12–16. Their ablutions—Ex. 40:30–32; Lev. 16:24. (See below.)

The Levites assigned to Aaron as assistants.—Num. 3:5–6; 16:9–10; Ez. 44:15–16. To keep his charge, the charge of congregation, to do service in the tabernacle, to bear the ark, etc.—Num. 3:7–9, 25–39; 16:9; Deut. 10:8; I Chr. 15:2. (See below, under "Services.")

Method of consecration.—Washing in water—Ex. 29:4; Lev. 8:6; 16:4. Clothed with holy garments—Ex. 29: 5–9; 40:14; Lev. 8:7–13; 16:4; Ez. 44:17–19. Anointed with oil—Ex. 29: 7; 30:30–33; 40:13–15. Sacrifices to be offered: The bullock—Ex. 29:10–14; Lev. 8:14–17. The two rams—Ex. 29:15–21; Lev. 8:18–24. The wave-offering—Ex. 29:22–28; Lev. 8:25–29. Aaron and sons eat portions of these sacrifices—Ex. 29:31–33; Lev. 8:31. The remainder to be burnt—Ex. 29: 34; Lev. 8:32. During seven days of consecration must remain in tabernacle—Ex. 29:35; Lev. 8:33–36. The altar also consecrated.—Ex. 29:36–37. No defective persons acceptable—Lev. 21:16–23. Later on, required to prove their genealogy—Ezra 2:62; Neh. 7: 64–65; Ez. 44:7.

Garments of.—Ex. 28:2–43; 29:29; 31: 10; 39:1; Lev. 6:10–11; 8:13; Ez. 44: 17. Specified thus: The breastplate— Ex. 28:15–30; 39:8–21. The ephod— Ex. 28:6–14; 39:2–7. The robe of the ephod—Ex. 28:31–35; 39:22–26. The coat or tunic—Ex. 28:39, 40; 39:27. The girdle—Ex. 28:39, 40; 39:29. The mitre—Ex. 28:39. The head-tires— Ex. 28:40; 39:28. The linen breeches —Ex. 28:42; 39:28. Sometimes provided by people—Ezra 2:69; Neh. 7: 70, 72. To be worn: *When consecrated* —Ex. 29:9; 40:15. *While serving in the tabernacle*—Ex. 28:43; 39:41. *While serving in temple*—Ez. 42:14; 44:17–19. *By high priest on day of atonement* —Lev. 16:4. To be purified by blood —Ex. 29:21.

The priest's service.—Must bathe in the laver before entering the sanctuary— Ex. 30:19–21; 40:31–32; Lev. 16:24.

Duties of especial kind confined to high priest, To designate Levites for certain services—Num. 4:19; I Sam. 2:34–36. To have charge of the treasury—II Ki. 12:10; 22:4; II Chr. 24:6; 34:9. To judge in cases of controversy —Deut. 17:8–13; Mt. 26:57; Mk. 14: 53. To officiate in the consecration of kings—I Ki. 1:34. To offer the animal as an atonement for his and the people's sins—Ex. 30:10; Lev. Ch. 16; Heb. 5:1–4; 9:7. Duties devolving on Aaron, his sons, his successors and appointees: *Keeping the charge of the tabernacle*—Num. 3:38; 18:1–7. *Lighting and trimming the lamps*—Ex. 27: 20–21; Lev. 24:3–4; II Chr. 13:10–11. *Preserving the sacred fire*—Lev. 6:12–13. *Covering sacred things on removal* —Num. 4:5–15. *Burning incense*—Ex. 30:7–8; Lu. 1:9. *To place and remove shewbread*—Lev. 24:5–9. *Offering sacrifices, general offerings*—Lev. 1:1–17; 5:6–10; 6:9–13; 17:8–9; 23:18; 23:26–37; Num. 15:24–25; 28:27; Ch. 29; I Chr. 16:40; II Chr. 29:31–35; 35:12–13; Heb. 10:11. *First-fruits*—Lev. 23: 10–11; Deut. 26:3–4. *For other sacrifices see under* OFFERINGS—Gen. 22:2. *Blessing the people*—Num. 6:23–27; Deut. 21:5; II Chr. 30:27. *Purifying the unclean*—Lev. 12:7; 15:15, 30, 31. *Deciding in cases of jealousy*—Num. 5:14, 15. *In cases of leprosy*—Lev. 13: 2–59; 14:34–57. *Instructing in the law* —Lev. 10:11; 24:8; Deut. 33:8–10. *Blowing the trumpets*—Num. 10:1–10; 31:6; Josh. 6:3–4. *Carrying the ark*— Josh. 3:6–17; 6:6–12. *Encouraging people in battle*—Deut. 20:1–4.

Means of support.—Cities with their suburbs—Num. 35:1–8; I Chr. 6:54–81; Josh. 21:3–42. (This includes cities of refuge and those of Levites. Aaron and sons had 13 cities.) Bought and possessed other lands—I Ki. 2:26; Jer. 32:8, 9. Lands devoted to the Lord— Lev. 27:21. Everything devoted— —Num. 5:10; 18:14. Tenth of tithes paid to Levites—Num. 18:26, 28; Neh. 10:34–39; Heb. 7:4–5. First-fruits— Lev. 23:20; 24:9; Num. 18:8–13; Deut. 18:3–4; Neh. 10:35–37. Redemption-money of first-born—Lev. 27:23; Num. 3:48–51; 18:15–16. First-born of animals—Ex. 13:12–13; Num. 18:17–19. Parts of animals and wool—Deut. 18: 3–4. Trespass money and offerings— Lev. 5:15–16; Num. 5:5–10; 18:9. Part of spoils of war—Num. 31:25–31. Showbread, after removal—Lev. 24:9; I Sam. 21:3–6; Mt. 12:4. A share in all offerings—Ex. 29:27–34; Lev. 2:2–10; 5:12–13; 6:15–18; 7:6–14, 31–34; 10:12–15; 14:12–13; Num. 6:19–20; 18:8–11; Deut. 18:3–5; I Sam. 2:13–14; Ez. 44:28–30; 45:1–4; I Cor. 9:13; 10:18.

Laws appertaining to priests.—Must not marry divorced or improper persons —Lev. 2:17, 13–14; Ezra 9:1–2; 10: 3–5. Must not defile himself for the dead, except for his kin—Lev. 21:1–6. Must not drink wine when serving— Lev. 10:9; Ez. 44:2. Must not eat what died of itself or was torn—Lev. 22:8. Must be clean when serving— Lev. 22:1, 2, 3–7; Num. 19:7. No sojourner or hired servant to eat of priest's portion—Lev. 22:10. Those bought or belonging to house may eat —Lev. 22:11. Children of, married to strangers, not to eat—Lev. 22:12. Restitution where one ignorantly eats— Lev. 22:14–16. Divided by David into 24 courses—I Chr. 24:1–19; II Chr. 8: 14; 35:4, 5. The four courses returning from Babylon were divided into 24 courses—Ez. 2:36–39. Each course had its president or chief—I Chr. 24:6, 31. Courses decided by lot—I Chr. 26: 12–19; Lu. 1:9. Punishment for invading the office of—Num. 16:1–35; 18:7; II Chr. 26:16–21.

Evil characteristics of.—Eli's sons—I Sam. 2:13–17, 22–24. Levites more upright than priests—II Chr. 29:34. Jeroboam takes people for priests—I Ki. 12:31. Priests sent back to Samaria— II Ki. 17:27–33. Priests who dealt falsely—Jer. 6:13. Drunken priests— Is. 28:7. Corrupters of the covenant— Mal. 2:7–8. Levitical priesthood imperfect—Heb. 7:11. Marriages with heathen nations—Ez. 9:1–2; 10:2–5. Taken captive to Babylon—Jer. 29:1. Restore the altar and offer sacrifice for sins—Ezra 3:1–7.

Priests in times of Jesus.—Enquire concerning Jesus—John 1:19. Zacharias serves in temple—Lu. 1:5. Leper ordered to show himself to priests—Mt. 8:4; Mk. 1:44; Lu. 5:15; 17:14. Priest passes by Samaritan—Lu. 10:31. Jesus refers to David, priests, and shewbread—Mt. 12:3-6; Mk. 2:25-26; Lu. 6:3-4. Priests arrest apostles—Acts 4:1-3; 5:17-41. Priests obedient to faith—Acts 6:7. Priest of Jupiter brought oxen—Acts 14:13. Priests conspire to take Jesus—Mt. 26:3-5, 15-16, 47; Mk. Ch. 14; Lu. 22:1-6, 50-71; John 11:47-57. Priests condemn Jesus—Mt. 26:57-68; 27:1-2; Mk. 14:53-65; Lu. 22:52-71; 23:13-23; John 18:15-32. Prefer Barabbas to Jesus—Mt. 27:20; Mk. 15:11; Lu. 23:18. Priests give authority to Saul of Tarsus—Acts 22:5. Try and condemn Stephen—Acts 6:12-15; 7:54-60; 8:1-2. Paul brought before priests —Acts 22:30; 23:1-5.

New Testament references.—Heb. 7:3, 11, 15, 20, 21, 23; 8:4, 10, 11; 9:6; Rev. 1:6; 5:10; 20:6. See TABERNACLE, TEMPLE, OFFERINGS, ISRAEL, ALTAR.

PRINCES: Appealed to.—Dan. 1:8.

Appointment made by.—Dan. 1:10, 11, 18.

Captured.—Ju. 7:25; 8:3, 6; Ez. 12:10, 12.

Characteristics of.—Ju. 8:14; I Chr. 7:40; Job 3:15; Pr. 17:7; 25:15; 31:4; Ps. 83:11; Eccl. 10:7, 16, 17.

Children of.—Song of Sol. 7:1.

David a prince.—Ez. 34:24; 37:25.

Destruction of.—Pr. 14:28; Is. 10:8; Lam. 1:6; 2:2, 9; 5:12; Ez. 26:16; Hab. 1:10. Grief over destruction of —Ez. 19:1; 21:12; 22:6.

Duties of.—Ez. 45:8; Is. 32:1.

Early mention of.—Gen. 12:15; 17:20; 23:6; 25:16; 34:2.

Evil princes rebuked.—Ez. 11:1; 17:12.

Gifts by.—II Chr. 35:8; Ez. 46:16, 17, 18; Dan. 1:7.

God is greater than.—Ps. 118:9; 146:3.

God turns against.—Job. 12:21; Ps. 76:12; 107:40; Is. 19:11, 13; Hos. 9:15.

God warns.—Is. 3:4, 14; Is. 23:8, 9; 30:4; 31:9; 34:12; 40:23; 41:25; 43:28; Jer. 1:18; 2:26; 4:9; 8:1; 17:25; 24:1, 8; 25:18, 19; 34:19, 21; 39:3, 13; 44:17, 21; 48:7; 49:3, 38; 50:35; 51:57;

52:10; Ez. 7:27; 32:29, 30; 39:18; Hos. 5:10; 8:10; Amos 1:15; 2:3.

Messiah called prince.—Dan. 9:25. Prince of Peace—Is. 9:6.

Jesus called prince.—Acts 5:31. Prince of Life—Acts 3:15.

Land given to.—Ez. 45:7; 48:21, 22.

Mercy shown by.—Dan. 1:9.

Miscellaneous.—Job 21:28; 31:37; Pr. 19:10; 25:7; Eccl. 10:7, 16, 17; Jer. 35:4; Ez. 23:15; 27:21; Hos. 13:10.

Moses called.—Ex. 2:14; Num. 16:13.

Mutiny against.—Pr. 14:28.

Offerings of prince for dedication of the altar.—Num. 7:11, 18, 24, 30, 36, 42, 48, 54, 60, 66, 72, 78.

Persecution by.—Ps. 119:23; Jer. 26:10, 11, 12; 37:14, 15; 38:4, 17, 18, 22, 25, 27.

Rule through God.—Pr. 8:15, 16.

Worship of God by princes.—Ez. 45:16, 17, 22; 46:2, 4, 8, 10, 12; Ps. 148:11; Is. 21:5; 49:7; Jer. 26:16, 21; 29:2; 34:10; Jer. 36:12, 14, 19, 21.

Princes.—Of Ammon—II Sam. 10:3; I Chr. 19:3; Amos 1:15. Of Balak or Moab—Num. 22:8, 13, 14, 15, 21, 35, 40; 23:6, 17; Amos 2:3. Of David—I Chr. 29:24. Of demons (or world)—Mt. 9:34; 12:24; Mk. 3:22; John 12:31; 14:30; 16:11; I Cor. 2:6, 8. Of Egypt—Gen. 12:15; Ez. 30:13; Ps. 68:31; 105:22. Of Gilead—Ju. 10:18. Of God—Gen. 23:6. Of Greece—Dan. 10:20. Of host—Dan. 8:11. Of Ishmael —Gen. 17:20; 25:16. Of Israel—Num. 1:16, 44; 7:2, 18, 24, 30, 36, 42, 48, 54, 60, 66, 72, 78, 84; 10:4; 16:2; 17:2, 6; 21:18; 25:14, 18; 27:2; 32:2; 34:13, 18, 22, 23, 24; 36:1; Josh. 9:15, 18, 19, 21; 17:4; 22:14, 30, 32; Ju. 5:3, 15; II Sam. 3:38; I Ki. 11:34; 16:2; I Chr. 5:6; 22:17; 23:2; 24:6; 28:1; 29:6; II Chr. 12:6; 21:4; Ez. 21:25; 45:8, 9; Hos. 3:4; Mic. 3:1, 9. Of Meshech and Tubal—Ez. 38:2, 3; 39:1. Of people —Ps. 47:9; 113:8. Of princes—Dan. 8:25. Of Persia—Dan. 10:13, 20; 11:18. Of the power of the air—Eph. 2:2. Of Shechem—Gen. 34:2. Of Sihon—Josh. 13:21. Of Solomon—I Ki. 4:2; 9:22; 20:14, 15, 17, 19. Of Tyre—Ez. 28:2. Michael, Prince of Judah—Dan. 10:20, 21; 12:1. Prince of this world—See OF DEMONS (OR WORLD).

PRINCESSES.—I Ki. 11:3; Lam. 1:1.

PRINCIPAL. Mic. 5:5; Lu. 19:47; Acts 25:13.

PRINCIPLES. Heb. 5:12; 6:1.

PRINT. Lev. 19:28; John 20:25. See MARK.

PRISCA, prĭs′ka. **An early female disciple.**—Acts 18:2; II Tim. 4:19.

PRISON. Is 24:22; 42:7, 22; 61:1; Mt. 5:25, 26; 25:26, 39, 43, 44; Lu. 12:58; 22:33.

First mentioned.—Gen. 39:20. Jehovah with Joseph in—Gen. 39:21-23. Joseph places brother in—Gen. 42:16-19. Samson confined in prison—Ju. 16: 21, 25. Jehoiachim in—II Ki. 25:27-29. Micaiah in—II Chr. 18:26. Jeremiah imprisoned—Jer. 32:2, 8, 12; 33: 1; 37:15-21; 38:6, 10, 28; 39:14, 15. John the Baptist in prison—Mt. 4:12; Mk. 1:14; 6:17-27; Lu. 3:19, 20. Paul and Silas—Acts 16:23-40. Peter—Acts 12:4-7, 17; John—Mt. 11:2; 14: 3; Mk. 6:17; John 3:24.

Use for confining.—Person accused of crime (Barabbas)—Lu. 23:19, 25. For blasphemy—Lev. 24:12. Accused of heresy (The apostles)—Acts 4:3; 5: 18-25. Condemned criminals till executed (Peter)—Acts 12:4-6. Enemies taken captive (Hoshea, king of Israel) —II Ki. 17:4. Zedekiah, king of Judah—Jer. 52:11. Debtors confined till they paid—Mt. 5:25-26, 18:30. Persecuting prophets—I Ki. 22:28; II Chr. 16:10. Prediction concerning apostles —Lu. 21:12. Saul imprisons disciples —Acts 8:3; 22:4; 26:10. Paul often in prison—II Cor. 11:23.

Spirits in prison.—I Pet. 3:19. See DUNGEON, PERSECUTION, PUNISHMENT.

PRIVILY. Bring in heresies—II Pet. 2:1. Brought in—Gal. 2:4. Called wise men—Mt. 2:7. Cast us out—Acts 16:37. Crept in—Jude 4. Cut skirt of Saul's robe—I Sam. 24:4. Put her away—Mt. 1:19. Slandereth his neighbor—Ps. 101:5.

PRIZE. Of the high calling—Phil. 3: 14. Receiveth—I Cor. 9:24. Rob of—Col. 2:18.

PROCEED. Evil thoughts—Mk. 7:21. Fire and smoke—Rev. 9:17. From the Father—John 15:26. Further in—II Tim. 2:16. From Jehovah—Gen. 24:50. Out of mouth—Deut. 8:3; Mt. 15:11, 18; Lu. 4:22; Eph. 4:29. Out of throne of God—Rev. 22:1. To do work—Is. 29:14.

PROCHORUS, prŏk′o-rus. A deacon— Acts 6:5.

PROCLAIM. Faith—Rom. 1:8. Foolishness—Pr. 12:23. Fully—II Tim. 4:17. Gospel—See GOSPEL MUST BE PREACHED. Housetops, Upon—Lu. 12:3. Jehovah's release—Deut. 15:2. Jesus—Acts 17:3. Liberty—Is. 61:1. Name—Ex. 33:19. Peace—Ju. 21:13. Righteousness—Ps. 40:9. Testimony of God —I Cor. 2:1. Year of Jehovah's favor —Is. 61:2. See PREACH, GOSPEL.

PROCLAMATION. Aaron made—Ex. 32:5. Cyrus made—II Chr. 36:22. Make—Lev. 23:21; Dan. 5:29. Throughout all Israel—II Chr. 30:5. Throughout all Judah—I Ki. 15:22; Ezra 10:7.

PROCONSUL. Acts 13:7, 8, 12; 18:12; 19:38.

PRODUCE *n.* Of field—Job 31:8.

PRODUCE *v.* Cause—Is. 41:21.

PROFANE. Ez. 28:16; I Tim. 1:9. Name of God—Lev. 18:21; 19:12; Amos 2:7; Ez. 22:26; 36:20, 21; Mal. 1:12. Offerings—Lev. 22:15. Prophets and priests—Jer. 23:11; Ez. 22:26. Sabbath—Neh. 13:17; Mt. 12:5. Temple —Acts 24:6. Woman—Lev. 21:7, 9. Babblings—I Tim. 6:20; II Tim. 2:16. Fables—I Tim. 4:7. Person—*Esau*— Heb. 12:16. Profaneness (hypocrisy) —Jer. 23:15.

PROFESS. I Tim. 6:21. Godliness—I Tim. 2:10. I never knew you—Mt. 7:23. They know God—Tit. 1:16. To be wise—Rom. 1:22. Unto Jehovah— Deut. 26:3. See CONFESSION.

PROFIT *n.* Heb. 12:10. Blood, In— Ps. 30:9. Circumcision, Of—Rom. 3:1. Earth, Of—Eccl. 5:9. Kings—Esth. 3:8. Labor, In—Pr. 14:23; Eccl. 1:3. No profit under the sun—Eccl. 2:11. Own, Not seeking—I Cor. 10:33. What —Gen. 25:32; Job 21:15; Mal. 3:14.

PROFIT, *v.* Cannot—I Sam. 12:21. Christ, Nothing—Gal. 5:2. Flesh, Nothing—John 6:63. Lying words, Cannot—Jer. 7:8. Not—Job 33:27; **Is.**

57:12. Riches, Not—Pr. 11:4. Righteousness may—Job 35:8. Teacheth
thee to—Is. 48:17. Treasures of wickedness, Nothing—Pr. 10:2. What doth
it—I Cor. 15:32. What is a man—Mt.
16:26; Lu. 9:25. Word did not—Heb.
4:2.

PROFITABLE. Mt. 5:29; 18:6. Any-
thing—Acts 20:20. Can a man be—
Job. 22:2. Godliness is—I Tim. 4:8.
Merchandise is—Pr. 31:18. Nothing,
For—Jer. 13:10. Teaching, For—II
Tim. 3:16. Wisdom is—Eccl. 10:10.

PROFUSE. Pr. 27:6.

PROGRESS. Phil. 1:12; I Tim. 4:15.

PROLONG. Days—Deut. 4:26; Pr. 10:
27. Speech—Acts 20:7.

PROMISES. *Promissum,* from *promittere,*
to send, or put forward. Commands
involved in promises—Ex. 19:5–8; 23:
20–33; II Cor. 7:1; Gal. 3:21, 22; Heb.
3:14–19.

Promises founded upon five pillars.—(1)
God's justice—Gen. 18:25; Job 8:3–
7; Is. 9:7. (2) God's goodness—Deut.
11:31–32; Is. 49:15, 16; Heb. 6:10. (3)
God's truth—Num. 23:19; Ps. 102:24–
28; Mal. 3:6; Heb. 1:10–12. (4) God's
power—II Chr. 20:6, 7; 25:7–9; Dan.
3:17; 6:20–22; Mt. 9:27–30; Acts 20:
32; Rom. 4:20, 22; 11:23; 14:4; I Cor.
10:13; II Cor. 9:8–11; Eph. 3:20; Phil.
3:20, 21; II Tim. 1:12; Heb. 2:18; 7:
25; Jude 24, 25. (5) God's oath—
Deut. 7:8; Ps. 89:3, 4; 105:9; Jer. 11:
6; Heb. 6:13–20.

**Promises dealing with Old Testament
covenants.**—From Creation to Israel:
Food—Gen. 1:27–29. Enmity of seeds
—Gen. 3:15. Cain—Gen. 4:11–15.
Flood—Gen. 6:17, 18. Noah's protection—Gen. 9:1–3. Bow in heavens—
Gen. 9:11–17. Abraham's departure—
Gen. 12:1–3. Separates from Lot—
Gen. 13:14–17. Vision of bondage—
Gen. 15:5–14. Name changed—Gen.
17:1–8. Concerning Sodom—Gen. 18:
26–33. Offering of Isaac—Gen. 22:15–
18. Covenant with Isaac—Gen. 26:3,
4. Covenant with Jacob—Gen. 28:13,
14. Covenant through Moses—Ex. 6:
2–8.

Promises to Israel. — Contents of
promise: The blessing—Deut. 28:1–

12. The fulfilment—Ex. 15:1–13; I
Ki. 8:55, 56; Ps. 77:8–15; 105:42–45.
In answer to Solomon's request—I
Ki. 8:22–26; 9:3–5; II Chr. 1:9–12.
While in captivity—Neh. 1:8–11; 2:4–
8; Jer. 32:42–44; 33:14–22. Messianic
—Gen. 3:15; 12:3; 22:18; 26:4; 28:
14; 49:10; Deut. 18:15; Ps. 2:6–8; 110:
1, 4; Is. 9:7; 42:1–4; 53:10, 11; 55:3–
5; 60:1–3; 61:1, 2; Dan. 2:44; 9:25 f.;
Mic. 5:2; Zech. 9:9; 13:1; Mal. 3:1–
3; John 1:41; 4:25. *Cf.* John 1:45.
Prophecy concerning Jesus—Gen. 3:
15. See JESUS, PROPHECIES CONCERN-
ING.

Promises confirmed in Christ.—Mt. 1:22,
23; 2:5, 6; Lu. 1:54, 55; 1:68–75;
Acts 3:22–26; Rom. 1:2–3; 15:8, 9;
Gal. 3:8–16.

Promises to Old Testament saints.—In
sorrow—Ps. 50:14, 15; 55:22; 91:1–7;
Is. 43:2. In affliction—II Ki. 14:26,
27; Job 33:29, 30; Ps. 9:9, 10; 12:5;
18:27; Is. 51:21–23; Mic. 4:6; Nah.
1:12, 13. To widows and orphans—
Ex. 22:22–24; Deut. 10:17, 18; Pr. 15:
25; Jer. 49:11. To worshippers—Ex.
20:24; Ps. 77:8–13; Is. 40:31. To the
liberal—Ps. 41:1–3; 112:9; Pr. 3:9, 10;
11:25; 22:9; 28:27; Eccl. 11:1; Is.
58:10–12; Mal. 3:10. To the meek—
Ps. 10:17; 22:26; 25:9; 37:11; 149:4;
Pr. 29:23; Is. 29:19. To the poor—
Ex. 22:27; Ps. 12:5; 35:10; 69:33;
72:2, 12–14; 109:31; Pr. 22:22, 23; Is.
41:17. To the penitent—Lev. 26:40–
42; Deut. 4:29–31; II Chr. 7:14; 30:9;
Ps. 34:18; Is. 1:18, 19; 55:7. To the
obedient—Ex. 15:26; 19:5, 6; Deut.
4:40; 12:28; Ps. 1:1–3; 25:10; 103–17,
18; Pr. 1:33; Is. 1:19; Ez. 18:19. To
seekers—Deut. 4:29; I Chr. 28:9; Ps.
34:10; 145:18; Is. 55:6, 7. To those
who fear God—Ps. 34:7; 103:11–14,
17; 112:1, 2; 115:12, 13; 128:1–4; 145:
19; Pr. 19:23; Eccl. 7:16–18; 8:12.

**Declarations dealing with the New Tes-
tament.**—Concerning new covenant—
Is. 55:3–5; Jer. 31:31–34; Gal. 4:24–
28; Heb. 8:8–12; 12:24; 13:20. Declarations of Christ—Mt. 5:3–12; 10:39–
42; 11:28–30; 16:18, 19; 16:27; 18:19;
21:21, 22; Lu. 6:35–38; 11:9–13; 12:8,
31; 18:22, 29, 30; 21;14, 15; John 6:
35–40, 51; 7:17; 10:9, 16, 28; 11:25,

26; 12:26, 32, 46; 14:3, 12, 21, 23;
15:7–10, 16; 16:22, 23.

Concerning the Holy Spirit.—Ez. 36:26–
28; Joel 2:28, 29; John 7:38, 39; 15:
26; 16:13; 20:22, 23; Acts 1:8, 16;
2:33, 38; 5:32; Gal. 4:6; 6:8.

Concerning the kingdom.—II Sam. 7:11–
17; Ps. 89:3–5, etc.; 145:11–13; Dan.
2:44; Ob. 21; Mt. 13:43; 16:18 f.; Lu.
1.32 f.; 22:29, 30; Acts 1:6–8; II Pet.
1:11.

Concerning the gospel.—Is. 61:1–3; 62:
1, 2; Mt. 4:23; 26:13; 28:19, 20; Mk.
16:13; Lu. 24:47.

Concerning sinners.—Mk. 16:16; Lu. 19:
10; 24:47; Acts 2:38, 39; 3:19, 20; 5:
31; 16:31.

Concerning the Church.—Mt. 16:18;
Eph. 3:6, 10; 5:26, 27; Heb. 2:12; Rev.
2:7, 10, 11, 17, 26–29; 3:5, 12, 20–22.

**Promises token of participation with
God.**—John 14:2, 3; I Cor. 15:48, 49;
II Cor. 4:14; Heb. 3:12–14; II Pet.
1:3–4; Rev. 21:7.

General promises.—Rom. 9:8; II Cor. 1:
20; 6:6–18; Gal. 3:22, 29; Eph. 3:6;
I Tim. 4:8; Titus 1:2; Heb. 10:23;
11:13, 33; Jas. 1:12; II Pet. 3:13; I
John 2:25. See COVENANTS, SALVATION,
GOD PLANS MAN'S, CONSOLATION.

PROOF. Affliction, Of—II Cor. 8:2.
Christ, Of—II Cor. 13:3. Faith, Of—
I Pet. 1:7. Love, Of—II Cor. 8:24.
Many—Acts 1:3. See WITNESS.

**PROPHECY: Nature of prophecy. It is
one person's speaking for another.**—
Illustrated by Aaron speaking for
Moses—Ex. 7:1, 2; *cf.* 4:16. Especially
it is man's speaking for God—Deut.
18:18; II Chr. 36:15, 16; Is. 45:21;
Jer. 20:7–9; 23:22; Ez. 3:17–19; Dan.
9:22; Amos 3:7, 8; Jonah 1:2; Hag.
1:13.

Source of prophecy.—Not the prophet's
private interpretation of the times,
but given of God—Num. 12:6; I Ki.
22:14; Jer. 19:14; Amos 3:8; 7:15;
Lu. 1:67; II Pet. 1:20, 21.

Delivery of prophecy.—To the masses—
Jer. 19:14; Ez. 33:31; Amos 5:1; 7:10;
Hag. 2:2–4. To individuals—I Ki.
20:13, 22, 39–42; Amos 7:14–17; Hag.
2:21–23. Committed to writing—Ex.
17:14; Is. 8:1, 2, 16; 30:8; Jer. 30:2;

36:1–4, 17, 18, 32; 45:1; 51:60; Dan.
12:4, 9; Rev. 1:11, 19; 21:5.

Material of prophecy.—Prediction—
Gen. 41:25; 49:1; Deut. 18:22; Num.
24:16, 17; I Ki. 11:29, 39; Is. 44:3;
Jer. 28:9; Dan. 2:45; Rev. 1:1, 19;
22:6. Warnings—Ex. 3:18; Deut. 18:
19; Is. 58:1; Jer. 1:16, 17; 26:2–6;
Ez. 33:7–9. Religious instruction—
Deut. 31:19, 21, 22; Is. 1:18; 2:3; Jer.
32:33. Moral exhortation—Is. 1:2–6,
16, 17; 3:10, 11; Jer. 25:4–6; Hos. 4:
1–14; 6:5. Political or practical advice—II Sam. 7:5; 2:25; I Ki. 1:11–
14; II Ki. 6:12, 21, 22; 14:25; Is. 7:3,
4; 37:21, 33; Jer. 27:1–15. Promotion
of an enterprise—Ez. 6:14; Hag. 1:2–
11. Interpretation of current events—
Joel 1:2; 2:27; Hag. 1:5, 6, 9–11; 2:
15–19. Revealing hidden things—
Gen. 40:8; II Ki. 6:12; 7:1, 2; Is. 48:
6; Dan. 2:19, 22, 23; 8:16–25; Mt. 26:
68. Blessings—Gen. 9:26, 27; 27:27–
29, 40; 49:3–27; Num. 23:9, 20–24;
24:7–9, 17–19; Lu. 2:29–32. Promises
—II Sam. 7:8–17; Is. 2:2–4; Jer. 2:1,
2, 4; Hos. 4:1; Joel 2:31, 32; 3:18–21;
Amos 3:1; Hag. 2:6–9; Zech. 13:1;
Mal. 3:1. Threats and judgment—I
Ki. 13:21, 22; II Sam. 12:10–12; Is.
1:20, 24–31. Doom of cities and nations: *Babylon*—Is. 13:1–22; 21:1–10;
Jer. 25:12–14. *Assyria*—Is. 14:24–27.
Damascus—Is. 17:1; Jer. 49:23–27;
Amos 1:3–5; Zech. 9:1. *Philistia*—Is.
14:29–31; Jer. 47:1–7. *Arabia*—Is. 21:
13–17. *Egypt*—Is. 19:1–22; 20:3, 4;
Jer. 46:13–26; Ex. 29:1–16, 19, 20;
30:4, 6; 32:32. *Moab*—Is. 15:1; 16:14;
Jer. 48:1–42. *Ammon*—Jer. 49:1–6;
Ez. 21:28–32; 25:2–11; Amos 1:13–15;
Zeph. 2:8, 9. *Edom*—Is. 21:11, 12; Jer.
49:7–22; Ez. 25:12–14; 35:1–15; Amos
1:11, 12; Ob. 1–21. *Tyre*—Is. 23:1–
18; Jer. 25:22; 47:4; Ez. 26:2; 28:24;
Amos 1:9, 10; Zech. 9:2–4. *Jerusalem*
—Is. 22:1–14; Jer. 26:18; 9:11; Mic.
3:12. *Judah*—Jer. 1:15–18; 4:16; 7:
30–34; 13:9–14, 19; 20:4, 5; 21:4–10;
Ez. 8:17, 18; Hos. 5:10; 6:4; Amos 2:
4–5.

Characteristics of prophecy.—Usually
fragmentary or limited in scope—I
Cor. 13:9; Heb. 1:1. Connected with
the times of utterance—*e. g.*, Gen. 3:

14–19; I Sam. 13:13, 14; Is. 7:10–17; and very often. Usually conditional, expressed—Is. 55:6, 7. Or unexpressed —*e. g.*, Jonah 3:5–10. For general principle, see Jer. 18:1–12. Conditions based on Jehovah's character—Joel 2:12–14; Jonah 4:2, 11. Some are unconditional, mostly messianic utterances—*e. g.*, II Sam. 7:14–16; Is. 55:3; Acts 13:34. Often for posterity—Deut. 18:18, 19; 31:19, 24–29; I Cor. 10:11; I Pet. 1:10–12. Rarely dates future events—*e. g.*, II Chr. 36:21; Jer. 25:11; 29:10; *cf.* Dan. 9:2. Exceeds other gifts in value—I Cor. 14:1–5.

Form of prophecy.—Public addresses—I Sam. 12:6–17; Is. 1:4–20; Jonah 3:4. Object lessons—I Ki. 18:38; Is. 8:1–4; Jer. 27:1–8; Ez. 37:15–23; Hos. 3:1–5. (See prophet's use of emblems). Historical illustrations—Ju. 6:7–10; Ez. 17:11–16; Hos. 11:1–4; Nah. 3:8; Hag. 2:5; Zech. 1:5, 6; Mt. 24:37, 38; II Pet. 2:5. Poetry (the following and many other prophecies have poetic form in the original language)—Gen. 9:25–27; 49:2–27; Ps. 2:7–9; 110:4–7; Is. 52:13–53:12; 61:1–9. Dramatic composition—*e. g.*, Ps. 24:7–10; 91:1–16; Is. 21:6–11; 63:1–6. Allegory or parable—*e. g.*, Is. 5:1–7; Ez. 17:1–24; 20:49; 24:3–14; Zech. 1:8–11, 18, 21; 2:1–5; 3:1–5; 4:2–14; Gal. 4:21–31.

Fulfilment of prophecy.—Many fulfilled in short time—Gen. 40:12–14, 18–22; 41:25–36, 47–56; Josh. 6:26; I Sam. 13:32; I Ki. 16:34; 20:13–21; II Ki. 2:10–14; 14:25; 15:12; 23:16; Acts 11:28; 21:11, 27–36. Many fulfilled in Christ. Some to be fulfilled after Christ's ascension—Acts 3:21. Others to be fulfilled at the end of the world —Dan. 12:2; Mt. 24:30, 31, 40, 41; 25:31–46; Jas. 5:28, 29; I Cor. 15:22–25; I Thess. 4:14–17; II Thess. 1:9, 10; II Pet. 3:10–13; Rev. 20:11. Fulfilments a confirmation of prophecy—I Sam. 2:34; *cf.* 4:11; I Ki. 13:3–6; 18:37–38; II Ki. 7:1–18; 19:32–37; Jer. 28:15–17.

Christ in prophecy.—As seed of the woman—Gen. 3:15. As Abraham's Seed—Gen. 22:17; Gal. 3:8, 16. As David's Seed—II Sam. 7:12–16; Ps. 89:35–37; Mt. 22:42–45. As King—I Chr. 17:12, 14; Ps. 2:6; 45:6; 110:1, 2; Is. 9:7; 16:5; 55:3, 4; Jer. 30:9; Ez. 37:24; Dan. 7:14. As Priest—Ps. 110:4; Ez. 21:26, 27; Zech. 3:5, 8; 6:12, 13. As Prophet—Deut. 18:15–19. As Shepherd—Is. 40:11; Ez. 24:23, 24; 37:24. As Judge—Is. 11:3, 4; 16:5; Ps. 110:6; Mic. 4:3. As Servant of Jehovah—Is. 52:13; 49:5, 6; 53:11. As a Sufferer—Is. 52:14, 15; 53:3–12; Zech. 13:7. As Son of God—II Sam. 7:14; Ps. 2:7. As a Redeemer—Job 19:25; Is. 59:20. As the Anointed—Ps. 2:2; Is. 61:1. As the Branch—Is. 11:1–5; Jer. 23:5; 33:15; Zech. 3:8; 6:12, 13. See JESUS, PROPHECIES CONCERNING.

Man in prophecy.—Gen. 1:26–30; Job 8:20; Ps. 8:4–8; 144:3, 4; Heb. 2:5–18.

Church in prophecy.—As Jehovah's people—Ps. 47:9; 87:5, 6; 110:3; Jer. 31:33, 34; Dan. 7:27; Hos. 2:23; Mic. 4:2–5; Zech. 13:9; 2:11. As a kingdom—Ps. 145:13; Is. 9:7; Dan. 2:45; 4:3; 7:27. As the redeemed—Ps. 107:2; Is. 35:9, 10; 62:12; 51:11.

World in prophecy.—Nations in unity under Jehovah—Ps. 22:27; 67:7; 82:8; Is. 19:23; 2:2–4; 56:6–8; Mic. 4:1–2. World's blessing—Gen. 22:18; Is. 11:9; Jer. 3:19; 4:21; Acts 3:25; Gal. 3:8, 16, 29. World's conquest—Ps. 2:8, 9; 65:2; 110:5, 6; Is. 66:18, 19; Jer. 3:17; 16:19. World judged—Ps. 58:11; 82:8; 110:6; Is. 66:23, 24; Jer. 25:31; Joel 3:2, 12–15; Mic. 4:3; Mt. 25:31, 32. World's salvation—Is. 45:22; 49:6; 52:10. New heavens and new earth —Is. 65:17; 66:22; Rom. 8:21, 22; II Pet. 3:13; Rev. 21:1, 2. See PROPHETS, REVELATION.

PROPHETS: Are God's messengers.—I Sam. 8:7–9; I Ki. 13:1, 3, 9; II Ki. 17:13, 23; 20:4, 5; II Chr. 36:15–21; Is. 6:8–11; 48:16; Jer. 7:13, 25; 11:7; 25:3, 4; 26:5; 32:33; Ez. 2:4; 3:4–11, 17–21, 27; Dan. 9:1, 6–10; Hos. 12:10; Amos 7:14, 15; Zech. 7:12; Heb. 1:1; Rev. 10:11.

Are inspired by Jehovah.—I Sam. 9:6; II Ki. 3:12; Is. 50:4, 5; Jer. 20:9; Amos 3:7, 8; Zech. 7:7; Lu. 1:70; Acts 3:18; Rom. 1:1, 2; Jas. 5:10; I Pet. 1:10, 11; II Pet. 1:21; Rev. 4:1; 10:7; 22:6.

Methods of Jehovah in communication to them: By voice.—To Moses—Ex. 6:13, 29; 7:2; 19:3–5; 25:22; 33:11; Lev. 1:1; Num. 1:1; 7:89; 9:8; 12:8; Deut. 5:5, 31; 18:18; 34:9, 10; Josh. 3:7. To Joshua—Josh. 3:7; 4:14. To Balaam—Num. 22:18–20, 38; 23:5–12, 16, 20, 26; 24:15, 16. To Samuel—I Sam. 3:4–14, 21; 9:15; 15:16, 19–21. To David—II Sam. 23:2. To Elijah—I Ki. 22:14, 28. To Isaiah—Is. 6:8, 9; 51:15, 16. To Jeremiah—II Chr. 36: 12, 15; Jer. 1:1–10; 13:1–3; 16:1; 18: 1; 24:4–10; 26:1, 2; 27:1, 2; 29:30; 33:1, 2; 34:1, 2; 42:4, 7; Dan. 9:2. To Ezekiel—Ez. 3:10, 11, 22, 27.

By dreams and visions—Gen. 41:15–40; Num. 12:6; I Chr. 17:15; II Chr. 26:5; Job 4:12–16; 33:14–17; Is. 6:1–9; Ez. Chs. 1–3, 8–10; Dan. 2:19; 7:13, 15; 8:1, 15–27; 10:7–9; Hos. 12:10; Joel 2:28.

By angels.—To Moses—Gal. 3:19; Heb. 2:2. See Heb. 3:2–5. To Balaam—Num. 22:35. To Gad—I Chr. 21:18, 20, 30. To Daniel—Dan. 7:13–28; 8:15–19. To John—Rev. 1:1; 17:1; 19:9, 10; 21:9; 22:1–9, 16.

By the Holy Spirit.—Neh. 9:20, 30; Joel 2:28; Zech. 7:12; Mt. 22:43; Acts 7:51, 52; Heb. 3:7–11; 10:15–17; I Pet. 1:10, 11; II Pet. 1:21; Rev. 1:10.

Instances of inspiration of the Holy Spirit.—Noah—I Pet. 3:18–20. Joseph—Gen. 41:38. Bezalel—Ex. 31:2, 3; 35:31. Seventy elders—Num. 11: 16, 17, 25, 26–29. Balaam—Num. 24:2. The judges: *Othniel*—Ju. 3:10. *Gideon*—Ju. 6:34. *Jephthah*—Ju. 11:29. *Samson*—Ju. 13:25; 14:6, 19; 15:14; 16:28. Saul—I Sam. 10:6, 13; 11:6; 16:13, 14; 19:23, 24. Messengers of Saul—I Sam. 19:20, 21. David—I Sam. 16:13; II Sam. 23:2; I Chr. 28:11, 12; Mk. 12: 36; Acts 1:16. Azariah—II Chr. 15:1. Ezekiel—Ez. 2:1–4; 11:5, 24. Micaiah—I Ki. 22:14, 23, 28; II Chr. 18: 23, 27. Jahaziel—II Chr. 20:14. Zechariah—II Chr. 24:20. Micah—Mic. 3: 8. Isaiah—Acts 28:25. Elisabeth—Lu. 1:41. John the Baptist—Lu. 1:15. Zacharias—Lu. 1:67. Simeon—Lu. 2: 25–27. Apostles—Mt. 10:20; Mk. 13: 11; John 20:22; Acts 2:4; 4:8; 9:17; Rev. 1:10, 11. Agabus—Acts 11:28;

21:10, 11. Stephen—Acts 7:55. Disciples at Tyre—Acts 21:4.

By the gift of knowledge and wisdom.—I Chr. 28:19; Job 32:8; Jer. 11:18; Dan. 1:17–20; 2:21, 23; 4:8, 9; 5:11–14; 9:22. See I Ki. 3:12, 28.

By permission of the divine name.—Ex. 3:13, 14; Deut. 18:18, 19; II Chr. 33: 18; Ez. 3:11; Jas. 5:10.

Christ came in fulfilment of prophecy.—II Sam. 7:12; Mic. 5:2 (Mt. 2:5; John 7:42); Lu. 1:70.

Christ appealed to Moses and the prophets as if they were inspired to show that He came to fulfil their predictions.—Lu. 24:27, 44, 45; John 1:45; 5:45, 46. See John 13:18; 17:12.

The apostles appealed to Moses and the prophets as if they were inspired.—Acts 1:16, 20; 2:25–35; 3:18, 22, 23; 7: 37 (Deut. 18:15); 8:28–35; 10:43; 13: 29, 33–41; 17:2, 3; 24:14, 15; 26:22, 23; 28:23–27; Rom. 1:1–4; 3:21; 15:8; 16: 25, 26. See JESUS, PROPHECIES CONCERNING.

Prophets worked miracles as their endorsement.—Moses—Ex. 4:1–9; 7:9; 8:16–19; Num. 16:28–33. Elijah—I Ki. 18:30–39. Elisha—II Ki. 5:3, 8, 14. Daniel—Dan. 3:19–28; 4:2.

They taught the people through emblems.—Is. 20:2–4; Jer. 19:1, 10, 11; 27:1–11; 43:8–10; 51:63; Ez. 4:1–13; 5:1–4; 7:23; 9:4–6; 12:3–7; 21:6, 7; 24:1–24; Hos. 1:2–9.

Wickedness destroys prophetic vision.—I Sam. 28:6; Lam. 2:9; Ez. 7:26–27.

Must deliver God's message faithfully.—Num. 22:8, 18, 19, 38; 23:5, 11, 12, 17, 26; 24:12, 13; I Sam. 3:16, 17; II Sam. 7:17; I Ki. 22:13–14; Is. 21:10; Jer. 6:27; 23:28; 26:2, 12; Ez. 3:10–21; 11:25; 13:10–14; Mic. 2:6, 7.

Jehovah supports His faithful prophets.—Ex. 4:10–12; Jer. 1:6–19; 15:19–21; Ez. 2:6; 3:8–9.

False prophets described and denounced.—Deut. 18:20; I Ki. 13:11–25; Is. 9: 15; Jer. 6:13–15; 14:13–16; 23:9–40; 27:14–18; 28:15–17; 29:8–9; Lam. 2: 14; Ez. 13:4–7, 22; 21:29; 22:25–28; Mic. 2:11; Mt. 24:11; Lu. 6:26; II Pet. 2:1; I John 4:1. Adulterous—Jer. 23:14; 29:21–23. Covetous—Mic. 3:11. Drunken—Is. 28:7.

The people are warned against them.—
Deut. 13:1-3; Jer. 23:16; 27:14-17;
29:8; Mt. 7:15; 24:5, 23-26; Mk. 13:6,
21-23; Lu. 21:8.

Punishment of false prophets.—Deut.
18:20; I Ki. 13:11-25; 18:22-40; 22:
24-25; Jer. 13:13-14; 14:15; 20:6; 23:
13, 15, 30-32; 28:15-17; 29:15-32; Ez.
13:2, 3, 8, 9; Mic. 3:5-7; Zech. 13:3-6.
Punishment of their followers—Jer.
14:16; Ez. 13:15-16; 14:10-11.

Maltreatment of God's prophets.—I Ki.
19:10; II Chr. 36:16; Neh. 9:26; Jer.
2:30; Mt. 5:12; 23:29-38; Lu. 11:47-
51; Rom. 11:3; I Thess. 2:14-16; Rev.
18:24. God avenges wrongs done to
His prophets—Deut. 32:43; II Ki. 9:7;
I Chr. 16:21, 22; Mt. 23:35-38; Lu.
11:47-51.

**List of prophets in their order according
to Old Testament.—**Enoch—Gen. 5:
21-24; Jude 14, 15. Noah—Gen. 9:25-
27; II Pet. 2:5 (see marginal note).
Jacob—Gen. 49:1. Moses—Deut. 18:
18; Acts 3:22; 7:37. Aaron—Ex. 7:1.
Balaam—Num. 22:20, 38; II Pet. 2:16.
The prophet sent to Israel—Ju. 6:8, 9.
The prophet sent to Eli—I Sam. 2:27.
Samuel—I Sam. 3:20-21; Acts 3:24;

13:20; Heb. 11:32-34. David—Ps. 22:
1, 16, 18; Acts 1:16; 2:25-31; 4:25, 26.
Nathan—II Sam. 7:2-3; 12:1-7. Gad
—II Sam. 24:11-14. Ahijah—I Ki. 11:
29-32. The prophet of Judah—I Ki.
13:1-10. Iddo—II Chr. 9:29. Shemaiah
—I Ki. 12:21-24; II Chr. 12:5. Azariah—II Chr. 15:2-7. Hanani—II Chr.
16:7-10. Jehu—I Ki. 16:1, 7, 12. Elijah—I Ki. 17:1; 18:1-2; 19:1-8; Rom.
11:2-4. Elisha—I Ki. 19:16, 19-21; II
Ki. 5:1-14; Lu. 4:27. Micaiah—I Ki.
22:7-9. Joel—Joel 1:1. Jonah—II Ki.
14:25; Mt. 12:39-41. Amos—Amos 1:
1; 7:14, 15. Hosea—Hos. 1:1. Isaiah—
II Ki. 19:2; Lu. 4:17. Micah—Mic.
1:1. Nahum—Nah. 1:1. Zephaniah—
Zeph. 1:1. Jeremiah—Jer. 1:1-2. Habakkuk—Hab. 1:1. Obadiah—Ob. 1, 2.
Ezekiel—Ez. 1:3. Daniel—Dan. 2:14-
16. Haggai—Ezra 5:1; Hag. 1:1. Zechariah—Ezra 5:1; Zech. 1:1. Malachi—
Mal. 1:1.

New Testament prophets.—Zacharias—
Lu. 1:67-79. John the Baptist—John
1:6, 29-31. Jesus—Mt. 6:14-21. (See
His prophecies throughout the gospels.)
Agabus—Acts 11:28; 21:10. Paul—I
Tim. 4:1. Peter—II Pet. 1:1-2; 3:3.
John—Rev. 1:1-3.

THE PROPHETS AND THEIR BOOKS IN THEIR ORDER.

Name.	Place of Ministry.	Date B.C.	Historical Connection.
Joel	Israel and Nineveh	About 830-810	In reign of Joash of Judah.
Jonah	Judah	About 800	In reign of Jehoahash of Israel.
Amos	Israel	About 760	In reign of Jeroboam II.
Hosea	Israel	About 750-725	From reign of Jeroboam II to that of Hezekiah.
Isaiah	Jerusalem	About 740-695	From death of Uzziah to reign of Manasseh.
Micah	Judah	About 735-700	From reign of Jotham to that of Hezekiah.
Nahum	Probably Judah	About 640-610	In reign of Assurbanipal or later.
Zephaniah	Judah	About 630	In reign of Josiah.
Jeremiah	Judah and Egypt	About 628-585	From reign of Josiah till after the commencement of Babylon exile.
Habakkuk	Judah	About 609-600	In reign of Jehoiakim.
Obadiah	Judah or Babylonia	About 585 (?)	Shortly after destruction of Jeru-salem.
Daniel	Babylon and Persia	About 602-534	During the exile.
Ezekiel	Chaldea	About 593-571	Among Jewish exiles.
Haggai	Judæa	About 520	In reign of Darius Hystaspes.
Zechariah	Judæa	About 520-480	During rebuilding of temple and afterwards.
Malachi	Judæa	About 433	Contemporary with Nehemiah.

Customs and habits.—Were anointed—
I Ki. 19:16. Attached to king's household—II Sam. 24:11; II Chr. 29:25;
35:15. Had servants—I Ki. 19:3; II
Ki. 3:11; 4:12. Presents offered—I
Sam. 9:7, 8; I Ki. 14:3; II Ki. 4:42.
Presents refused—Num. 22:18; II Ki.
5:5, 16. Frequently married men—II
Ki. 4:1; Ez. 24:18; Hos. 1:2, 3. Often
led a wandering life—I Ki. 18:10–12;
19:3, 8, 15; II Ki. 4:10. Wore coarse
mantle—Zech. 13:4; Mt. 3:4.

**Were sent to reprove and to call to
repentance.**—II Ki. 17:13; II Chr.
24:18, 19; Is. 62:6; Jer. 6:17; 7:3–7,
25; 11:7; 18:11; 25:4, 5; Ez. 3:17–21;
18:30–32; 33:7–9. To denounce the
weakness of kings: *Samuel to Saul*—
I Sam. 15:10–23. *Nathan to David*—
II Sam. 12:7–14. *Elijah to Ahab and
Jezebel*—I Ki. 18:17, 18; 21:17–29. To
predict the downfall of nations—Is.
Chs. 13–23; Jer. Chs. 46–51. To foretell the coming of the Messiah —
See JESUS, PROPHECIES CONCERNING,
PROPHECIES, PROMISES, OUTLINE STUDIES IN THE BOOKS.

PROPHETESSES.—Miriam—Ex. 15:20.
Deborah—Ju. 4:4. Huldah—II Ki.
22:14. Anna—Lu. 2:36. See Joel 2:
28; Acts 2:17–21.

SONS OF THE PROPHETS.—I Ki. 20:
35; II Ki. 2:3–7; 4:1, 38; 5:22; 9:1.

PROPITIATION. For sin—Lev. 16:15;
Rom. 3:25; Heb. 2:17; I John 2:2;
4:10. See JESUS, SALVATION, RECONCILIATION.

PROPORTION. Faith, Of—Rom. 12:6.

PROSELYTE. Devout — Acts 13:43.
Jews and—Acts 2:10. Make—Mt. 23:
15. Nicolaus a—Acts 6:5.

PROSPERITY. I Chr. 22:11; II Chr.
20:20; Ezra 5:8; Ps. 122:6; Pr. 17:8;
28:13; Ez. 16:13; 17:15; Rom. 1:10.
As he may—I Cor. 16:2. Chosen, Of
thy—Ps. 106:5 Dangers of—Deut. 6:
10–12; 28:47; 32:15; Neh. 9:25; Job
31:24, 25; Pr. 1:32; 30:8, 9; Hos. 13:
9; Lu. 6:24; I Tim. 6:9; Mt. 13:22;
Rev. 3:17; Jas. 5:1. Day of—Job 21:
13; 36:11; Eccl. 7:14. Ease—Ez. 16:
49. God will—Neh. 2:20. Habitation
of righteousness—Job 8:6. Jehovah
made all to—Gen. 39:3. Journey—
Gen. 24:21. In—Zech. 7:7. Liveth in

—I Sam. 25:6. Made to—II Chr. 26:5.
Not in hand—Job 26:16. Palaces,
Within—Ps. 122:7. Pleasure of Jehovah shall—Is. 53:10. Righteous, Of—
Ps. 36:8; 37:11, 17–19; 84:11; 112:2,
3; Pr. 3:2; 12:21; Eccl. 8:12; Mt. 5:5;
Mk. 10:30; I Tim. 4:8. Servant, Of—
Ps. 35:27. Soul—III John 2. Tents of
robbers—Job 12:6. Way—Gen. 24:
40; Josh. 1:8. Whatsoever he doeth
shall—Ps. 1:3. Wicked, Of—Job 12:
6; 21:7–12; Ps. 17:10; 37:1; 73:3–12;
92:7; Eccl. 9:2; Jer. 12:1, 2; Mal. 3:
15. See BLESSING.

PROTECT. Is. 31:5.

PROTEST. By glorying—I Cor. 15:31.
Solemnly—Gen. 43:3. Unto Joshua—
Zech. 3:6.

PROUD. See PRIDE.

PROUDLY. See PRIDE.

PROVE. Abraham—Gen. 22:1. Come
to—Ex. 20:20. Faith, Of—Jas. 1:3.
Fire shall—I Cor. 3:13. God may—
Eccl. 3:18. Heart—Ps. 17:3; I Thess.
2:4. Him—I Ki. 10:1; John 6:6. Israel—Ju. 2:22. Let a man—I Cor.
11:28. Me—Ps. 95:9. Servants—Dan.
1:12. Spirits—I John 4:1. This is
Christ—Acts 9:22. Them—Ex. 15:25;
Lu. 14:19. Us—Ps. 66:10. Ye shall be
—Gen. 42:15. Your own selves—II
Cor. 9:13. See WITNESS.

PROVENDER. Cut—Job 24:6. Eat
savory—Is. 30:24. Straw and—Gen.
24:25.

PROVERBS. Several words may be
translated "Proverb." "Taunting
proverb" against the Chaldean—
Hab. 2:6. "Dark speeches"—Num.
12:8. "Riddle"—Ju. 14:12–19; Ez.
17:2. "Hard questions"—I Ki. 10:1;
II Chr. 9:1. "Dark sayings"—Ps. 49:
4; 78:2; Pr. 1:6. "Dark sentences"
—Dan. 8:23. Translated "byword"
in Ps. 44:14; 69:11. Called "Parable"
when extended—Num. 23:7, 18; 24:3,
15, 20, 21, 23; Job 27:1; 29:1; Ps. 49:
4; 78:2; Pr. 26:7, 9; Ez. 17:2; 20:49;
24:3; Mic. 2:4; Hab. 2:6.

Samples of proverbs.—Num. 21:27–30.
Some proverbs prohibited—Ez. 12:23;
18:2, 3. A new proverb—Ez. 16:44.
Translated parable in—Ez. 17:2; 20:
49; 24:3.

Solomon spake 3,000.—I Ki. 4:32; Pr.

1:1, 6; 10:1; 25:1; Eccl. 12:9.

How a proverb arose.—I Sam. 10:12. Ancients used proverbs—I Sam. 24:13.

A reproach to be a proverb.—Deut. 28: 37; I Ki. 9:7; II Chr. 7:20.

Jesus used.—John 16:25, 29. Peter also —II Pet. 2:22.

PROVERBS, BOOK OF. See OUTLINE STUDIES IN THE BOOKS.

PROVIDE. Able men—Ex. 18:21. Beasts of burden—Acts 23:24. Cities—II Chr. 32:29. Food—Job 38:41; Ps. 65: 9; 78:20; Pr. 6:8; 30:25. God will— Gen. 22:8, 14; Heb. 11:40. King—I Sam. 16:1; II Sam. 19:32; I Ki. 4:7, 27. Own, For—Gen. 30:30; I Tim. 5:8.

PROVIDENCE. See GOD, PROVIDENCE OF.

PROVINCE. Babylon, Of—See BABYLON. Children, Of the—Ezra 2:1; Neh. 1:3; 7:6. Elam—See ELAM. Judea, Of—See JUDEA. Justice, In—Eccl. 5:8. Medes, Of—See MEDIA. Princes of the —I Ki. 20:14–19; Esth. 1:3. Young men of the—I Ki. 20:14, 15.

PROVOCATION. Job 17:2. Jehovah, Of—I Ki. 15:30; 21:22; II Ki. 23:26; Neh. 9:18, 26; Heb. 2:8, 15. Offering, Of—Ez. 20:28. See ANGER, IDOLATRY, SIN.

PROVOKE. See ANGER.

PRUDENCE. Heb. *Ormah*. ''Discretion,'' ''Subtlety,'' ''Wisdom.''

Among God's greatest gifts.—I Ki. 3: 5–9; II Chr. 2:12; Neh. 2:12–18; Pr. 19:14.

Jehovah exercised prudence in revealing His will.—Mt. 11:25; Lu. 10:21; I Cor. 1:19, 20; Eph. 1:8–9.

Wisdom dwells with.—Pr. 8:12; 16:21.

Promoted by reproof.—Pr. 15:5.

Must be fostered.—Jer. 49:7.

Relation to speech.—David—I Sam. 16: 18. The scribe—Mk. 12:32–34.

Rehoboam's counsellors.—I Ki. 12:6, 7.

Endowed with reserve.—Pr. 12:16, 23; 13:16; 14:15; Amos 5:13.

Promotes knowledge.—Pr. 14:8, 18; 18: 15; Hos. 14:9.

Foresees evil.—Pr. 22:3; 27:12.

Needed in intercourse with unbelievers. —Mt. 10:16; Eph. 5:15; Col. 4:5.

Self-estimation dangerous.—Is. 5:21; 29:14.

Prudence commended.—Unjust steward —Lu. 16:7, 8. Wise virgins—Mt. 25:

1–10. Building a tower—Lu. 14:28, 29. King making war—Lu. 14:31, 32.

Prudence exercised.—Jacob—Gen. 32:3-23. Joseph—Gen. 39:9, 10. Abigail— I Sam. 25:23–33. Gamaliel—Acts 5: 34–39. Paul—Acts 23:6, 7.

PRUNE. Vineyards—Lev. 25:3, 4; Is. 5:6; 18:5.

PRUNING HOOKS. Spears turned into —Is. 2:4; Joel 3:10; Mic. 4:3.

PSALMS. See OUTLINE STUDIES IN THE BOOKS.

PTOLEMAIS, ptŏl'e-mā'is. **A city in Galilee.**—Acts 21:7.

PUAH, pū'ah. **(1) Son of Issachar.**— Gen. 46:13; Num. 26:23.

(2) A midwife.—Ex. 1:15.

PUBLIC. Mt. 1:19.

PUBLICAN. Gr. *Tĕlōnēs*, a tax farmer. The Roman senate, as early as the II Punic war, began to farm the direct taxes and customs, including the duty on goods carried into and out of the cities, to capitalists who were to pay a given sum into the public treasury. These officers employed others to attend to the details of the work who were usually natives and frequently Jews. The word *Tĕlōnēs* referred to the latter class. The method for collection was as follows: The taxes were sold at auction. The auctioneer was censor, and the buyer became one of the company, so sharing the profits. They made the most they could out of the bargain, which gave rise to gross abuses. As the Jews stickled about paying taxes to Cæsar, the calling was considered dishonorable. They practised extortion, as charged by John the Baptist—Lu. 3:13. And confirmed by Zacchæus—Lu. 19:8.

They are exhorted to exact no more than their dues. — Lu. 3:13; 18:11; 19:8. Some publicans had doubtless come under John's influence—Mt. 21:31, 32; Lu. 3:12; 7:29; 18:13.

Chief publicans were rich.—Lu. 19:2.

Chosen by Jesus as types of character.— Mt. 5:46; 18:17; Lu. 7:29; 18:10–14. For an apostle—Mt. 9:9; 10:3; Mk. 3: 18; Lu. 6:14, 15.

Jesus partook of their hospitality.—Lu. 5:27–32; 19:5, 6. Jesus' association made Him enemies—Mt. 9:11; 11:19.

Held in contempt by Jews—Mt. 18:17; 21:31, 32; Lu. 15:2.

They respected Jesus.—Mk. 2:15; Lu. 15:1.

Responded to the message of Jesus more readily than the Pharisees.—Mt. 21:31.

PUBLICLY. John 7:10; Acts 16:37; Acts 18:28; 20:20.

PUBLIC OPINION. Men influenced by: Aaron—Ex. 32:1–6. Saul in the case of Jonathan—I Sam. 14:45. Saul in the case of Amalekites—I Sam. 15:24. Jehoshaphat—II Chr. 20:21. Hezekiah—II Chr. 30:2. Herod, concerning John—Mt. 14:5; Acts 12:3. Pilate at the trial of Jesus—Mt. 27:21–26; Mk. 15:8–15; Lu. 23:23; John 19:7–16. Views concerning—Mt. 16:13–15; Mk. 6:2–3. Concerning voice from heaven—John 12:28–30. Concerning source of Jesus' power—Mt. 12:23, 24; Mk. 3:21, 22. Concerning the value of the gospel—I Cor. 1:18–23; Gal. 1:6–12.

PUBLISH. Esth. 1:20; 3:14; 8:13; Jer. 4:15; Mt. 7:36; Lu. 9:60; Acts 10:37; Rom. 9:17. Decree—Jonah 3:7. Good tidings—Is. 52:7; Nah. 1:15. See GOSPEL MUST BE PREACHED.

PUBLIUS, pŭb'li-us. Entertains Paul in Malta—Acts 28:7.

PUDENS, pū'dens. A Chruban in Rome —II Tim. 4:21.

PUFF. Ps. 10:5; Hab. 2:4. Self up—I Cor. 4:6, 18, 19; 5:2; 8:1; 13:4; Col. 2:18; I Tim. 3:6; 6:14; II Tim. 3:4. See PRIDE.

PUL, pŭl. (1) **An Assyrian king.**—II Ki. 15:19.

(2) **An African country and people**— Is. 66:19.

PULL. Down—Ezra 6:11; Is. 22:19; Jer. 24:6; 42:10; Lu. 12:18. Like sheep to slaughter—Jer. 12:5. Pieces, In—Lam. 3:11; Zech. 7:11. Roots, Up by—Ez. 17:9.

PULPIT. Neh. 8:4.

PULSE. II Sam. 17:28; Dan. 1:12, 16.

PUNISHMENT. Gen. 3:13–24; 4:13, 14; Chs. 6 and 7; Lev. 24:10–23; 26:14–45; Num. 32:23; Deut. 11:26–29; 24:16; Chs. 27 and 28; 30:15–19; I Sam. 3:10–14; I Ki. 21:17–29; I Chr. 10:13, 14; Esth. 7:1–10; 9:14; Is. 26:21; Jer. 16:18; 30:14; 48:44; Lam. 3:

39; 4:22; Ez. Chs. 7–9, 21–35; Hos. Chs. 8–10; 13:16–21; Amos 1:3; Mic. Ch. 6; Nah. 1:12; Hab. 3:12; Zeph. 1:12; 3:8.

Discussed by Job and his friends.—Job. 4:7–9; 5:3–7; 8:20; 10:14; 11:20; 15:20–35; 18:1–21; 19:29; 20:1–29; 21:1–34; 27:13–23; 31:3.

Design of: To check crime—Gen. 9:5–6; Lev. 24:18–22; Deut. 24:7; 25:2–3; I Ki. 2:36–38. To correct the life—II Sam. 7:14–15; Job 5:17–20; 23:10; Ps. 94:12–13; Pr. 13:24; 19:18; 22:15; 23:13–14; Mal. 3:2–3; John 15:2; Eph. 6:4; Heb. 12:5–11; I Pet. 2:20. To warn others—Num. 16:1–21, 40; Deut. 13:11; 17:13; 19:20.

Kinds of capital punishment.—Burning —Gen. 38:24; Lev. 20:14; 21:9; Dan. 3:6. Hanging — Gen. 40:22; 41:13; Num. 25:4; Deut. 21:22–23; Josh. 8:29; II Sam. 21:9; Esth. 2:23; 7:9–10. Crucifixion — Mt. 20:19; 27:35; Mk. 15:24–25; Lu. 23:33. Beheading—Gen. 40:19; II Ki. 6:31; 10:7; Mt. 14:10; Mk. 6:16, 27. Stoning—Ex. 19:13; Lev. 20:2, 27; 24:14; Num. 15:35–36; Deut. 13:10; 17:5; 22:21–24; Josh. 7:25; I Ki. 21:10, 13; Ez. 16:40; John 8:5, 59; Acts 7:58–59; 14:19; II Cor. 11:25; Heb. 11:37. Slaying with sword —Ex. 32:27–28; I Sam. 15:8, 33; Acts 12:2. Cut in pieces—Dan 2:5. Exposing to wild beasts—Dan. 6:16, 24; I Cor. 15:32.

Punishment of lesser degree.—Imprisonment—Ezra 7:26; Mt. 5:25. Confinement in stocks—Jer. 20:2; Acts 16:24. In dungeon—Jer. 38:6; Zech. 9:11. See PRISON. Binding with fetters—Ps. 105:18. Restitution—Ex. 21:36; 21:1–4, 6, 11; Lev. 6:4–5; 24:18; Num. 5:6. Retaliation — Ex. 21:23–36; Lev. 24:17–22; Deut. 19:21. Scourging—Lev. 19:20; Deut. 25:1–3; Mt. 20:19; 23:34; 27:26; Mk. 10:34; Lu. 18:33; John 19:1; Acts 22:24, 25; II Cor. 11:24; Heb. 11:36. Beating with rods—Pr. 23:14; Acts 16:22. Selling the criminal—Mt. 18:25. Banishment — Ezra 7:26; Rev. 1:9. Confiscating property —Ezra 7:26.

Torturing.—By putting out eyes—Ju. 16:21; I Sam. 11:2. Cutting off nose and ears — Ez. 23:25. Hanging by hands—Lam. 5:12. Plucking out hair —Neh.–13:25; Is. 50:6. Fining—Ex. 21:22, 32; 22:1–4, 7–9, 16, 17; Deut. 22:18, 19, 28, 29.

General.—Mt. 18:34; 26:67; Acts 23:2.

Future punishment.—Mt. 3:10–12; 5:21, 22, 27–30; 7:18–23; 10:28; 18:5–9; 21: 41–44; Chs. 23–25; Mk. 9:43–48; Lu. 6:49; 12:5; 16:19–31; 19:27; 20:16–18; Acts 1:25; I Cor. 3:17; 6:9, 10; Eph. 5:3–6; Heb. 10:31; II Pet. 2:4–21; Rev. 21:27; 22:14, 15. See SIN, PUNISHMENT FOR, COMMANDMENTS, WICKED, JUDGMENT, HELL, SOWING AND REAPING, PRISON, TEACHING OF JESUS CONCERNING JUDGMENT AND HELL.

PUNITES, pū′nites. **Descendants of Pua.**—Num. 26:23.

PUNON, pū′non. An encampment of Israel—Num. 33:42. See CAMP, ISRAEL.

PUR, PURIM, pûr, pū′rim. Esth. 3:7; 9:26. See FEAST OF PURIM.

PURCHASE. Blood, With—Acts 20:28. Land, Of—See LAND. Wife—Ruth 4: 10. See BUY, REDEMPTION, RANSOM.

PURE. Blood, From—See BLOOD. Commandments — Ps. 19:8. Conscience— See CONSCIENCE. Doctrine—Job 11:4. See DOCTRINE. Gold—See GOLD. Heart —See HEART. Prayer—Job 16:17. See PRAYER. Religion—Jas. 1:27. See RELIGION. Wisdom—Jas. 3:17. See WISDOM. Words—Ps. 12:6; 119:140. See WORDS. See PURIFICATION, PURITY.

PURENESS. Pr. 22:11; II Cor. 6:6.

PURER. Lam. 4:7; Hab. 1:13.

PURGE. Ps. 51:7; 65:3; Ez. 20:38; I Cor. 5:7; II Tim. 2:21. Blood—Is. 4:4. Judah—II Chr. 34:7. Land—II Chr. 34:8. Sacrifice, With—I Sam. 3:14. Sins—Ps. 79:9; Pr. 16:6; Is. 1: 25; 6:7; 22:14; 27:9; Ez. 24:13. See PURIFICATION.

P U R I T Y, PURIFICATION (Clean, Cleansing). Correlative terms, Clean, Pure; Contrasted, Unclean, Impure.

Purification.—Removal of uncleanness; hence rendering clean (pure) what previously was unclean (defiled).

Clean and unclean (ceremonially). **(1) Of animals:** respectively fit and unfit for food—Gen. 7:2, 8; 8:20; Lev. 20: 25. Marks of distinction: Quadrupeds —Lev. 11:4, 5, 6, 7, 8; Deut. 14:7, 10. Birds—Lev. 11:13–19; Deut. 14:11–20.

Insects—Lev. 20:23. Reptiles—Lev. 11:29–31; Deut. 14:19. Fish—Lev. 11: 9–12. Unclean may not be offered on the altar—Lev. 22:25.

(2) Of persons, qualified or disqualified to appear in worship before God; hence also to mingle in society—Lev. 11:24, 39, 40, 47; 12:2, ′5; 13:3, 8 ff.; 15:2 ff.; Deut. 12:15, 22; 15:22.

The uncircumcised are unclean. — Is. 52:1.

Sources of personal defilement: Primary: Natural causes, issue out of one's flesh—Lev. 15:2, 3. Seed of copulation—Lev. 15:16. Sexual intercourse—v. 18. Issue from a woman in health—Lev. 15:9; in disease—v. 25 ff. Woman in childbirth—Lev. 12:1–5.

Contact with a corpse — Num. 19:11; Lev. 5:2; 21:1 ff.

Touching a carcass—Lev. 11:39.

Eating that which died of itself—Lev. 17:15; 22:8.

Transmission by heredity—Job 14:4.

Secondary: Accidental, touching an unclean person or thing—Lev. 15:4, 10; 22:5, 6. Sitting on anything that an unclean person has sat on—Lev. 15:4 ff.; or lying down on a bed occupied by an unclean person—Lev. 15:24.

Moral cause of uncleanness: Unnatural sins of unchastity (abominations)— Lev. 18:6–18; 19:23, 30; Job 36:14 marg. Incestuous relations—Lev. 20: 21, 25.

(3) Of places, respectively free or not free of ceremonially unclean objects. —Lev. 14:36, 40, 41. Leprous houses— Lev. 14:34–57 (see LEPROSY). Foreign lands—Amos 7:17. Any land defiled by sin—Lev. 18:25, 28; Num. 35:33; Josh. 22:19; Ez. 9:11; Lam. 4:15; Ez. 22:24.

Distinction between clean and unclean of vital importance.—Lev. 10:10; 20: 25; Deut. 23:14.

Regulations affecting the unclean.—Animals must be redeemed—Lev. 27:11, 27; Num. 18:15. Persons may not eat of holy things—Lev. 7:19–21; 22:4, 5. What they may eat—Deut. 12:15, 22. They may celebrate the passover at a special time—Num. 9:10. General disqualifications of—Is. 35:8. Priests especially must avoid defilement —

Num. 6:7; Is. 52:11. Also a Nazirite's mother—Ju. 13:4, 7, 14. Duty of teaching distinctions devolves on priests— Ez. 44:23. The temple to be guarded against uncleanness — II Chr. 23:19. Application of distinctions by Haggai —Hag. 2:13. Uncleanness a hardship —Hos. 9:3.

Confession of uncleanness. — Is. 6:5; 64:6.

Duration of uncleanness.—For secondary causes, "until even"—Lev. 11: 32, 39, 40; 15:5, 6, 8, 18, 21, 27; 17:15; 22:6; Num. 19:22. Priests in preparing water of purification—Num. 19:8, 21. In applying the same—Num. 19: 20.

For primary causes: Seven days—Woman after birth of a son—Lev. 12:2 (continued to forty days). Suspicion of leprosy—Lev. 13:4, 21, 26, 31, 50, 54. Contact with dead body—Num. 19:11, 14, 16. Two weeks—Woman after birth of a daughter—Lev. 12:5 (continued to 80 days). Indefinite, depending on length of impurity— Lev. 15:25 ff. Permanent. Leprosy pronounced incurable—Lev. 13:8, 15, 36, 44. In garments—Lev. 13:51, 55.

Modes of purification, Law of.—Num. 19:11–13. (1) Washing of one's clothes —Lev. 15:5, 6, 11, 13, 22. (2) Bathing the body with water—Lev. 15:5–7, 13. (3) Sacrifice of two turtle doves, one for a burnt-offering, the other for a sin-offering — Lev. 15:14, 15, 29, 30. Or a lamb in purification for childbirth, in case of wealthy mother— Lev. 12:6–8.

(4) **Special ceremonials.**—Water of purification made by mixture of ashes, of red heifer, cedar wood and hyssop —Num. 19:2 ff.; Heb. 9:13. (5) For leprosy — Lev. 14:21–32 (see also LEPROSY).

Applications of the law of purification. —Purging the altar—Lev. 8:15; Ez. 43:20, 25; II Chr. 34:5. The temple —II Chr. 29:18; Neh. 13:9; Dan. 8: 14. The Levites and priests—Num. 8:21; Ez. 6:20; Neh. 12:30. Bathsheba—II Sam. 11:4.

Purification according to Persian rite. —Esth. 2:3, 9, 12.

Moral purification.—Essential to normal relations with God—Ps. 24:4; 18:26; Job 4:17 marg.; 8:6; II Sam. 22:27; Pr. 20:9; 21:8; 30:12. Prayer for— Ps. 51:7; 79:9.

Purification in the N. T.—Ritual elaborate—Mt. 15:2 ff.; Mk. 7:3 ff.; Heb. 9:10, 22; John 11:65. Provisions made for—John 2:6.

Discussion about.—John 3:25.

Attitude of Jesus towards.—Lu. 11:38–41; Mt. 15:3–20; Mk. 7:6–23. Neglect by the disciples of Jesus—Mk. 7:1–5; Mt. 15:1, 2; but practised by Paul— Acts 21:26; and distinctions survive in Christian practice—Acts 10:10 ff.; 11:8. Transfer of distinction to that between idol worship and spiritual worship—Acts 15:29; but with abolition of inherent values—Rom. 14:14–20; I Cor. 6:13; Col. 2:16, 20–22; Tit. 1:15; Heb. 10:2; and symbolic use— Rev. 16:13; 18:2.

Distinction spiritualized.—II Cor. 6:17; Eph. 5:5; Heb. 9:23.

Spiritual purification through Jesus Christ.—I Pet. 1:22; II Pet. 1:9; Heb. 1:3; I John 3:3. See CEREMONIAL CLEANSING, FOOD.

PURIM. See FEASTS.

PURITY. See PURIFICATION.

PURPOSE: Divine purpose of Jehovah. —Is. 14:24, 26, 27; 19:12; 23:9; 46:11; Jer. 4:28; 26:3; 36:3; 49:20; 50:45; 51:29; Lam. 2:8; Rom. 9:11, 17. Christ —Eph. 1:9, 11; 3:11.

Special time for.—Eccl. 3:1, 17; 8:6.

Purpose (resolve).—I Ki. 5:5; II Chr. 20:10; 32:2; Pr. 20:18. Of saints— Acts 27:13, 43. Paul — Acts 19:21; Rom. 1:13; II Tim. 1:9; 3:10.

Purpose against evil.—Ps. 17:3; Dan. 1: 8. Reward for—Rom. 8:28.

Evil purposes.—Ps. 140:4; Jer. 49:30.

Purposes frustrated.—Ezra 4:5; Job 17: 11; 33:17; Pr. 15:22; Is. 30:7.

Purpose (Use).—Neh. 8:4.

Purpose (Cause).—Jer. 6:20; Mt. 26: 8; Acts 11:23; Eph. 6:22; Col. 4:8. See ELECTION, FOREORDINATION, SALVATION, GOD PLANS.

PURSE. Pr. 1:14: Mt. 6:8; 10:9; Lu. 10:4; 12:33; 22:35, 36.

PUT, pŭt. (1) **Son of Ham.**—Gen. 10:6. (2) **A land.**—Nah. 3:9.

PUT. Asunder—Mt. 19:6. Away—I Chr. 21:8; Mt. 5:32; Jas. 1:21; I Pet. 2:1. Forth—II Sam. 13:16. Grass, Forth—Gen. 1:11. Head, Upon—Lev. 14:18. Eyes, Out—I Sam. 11:2. Life in my hand—Ju. 12:3. Sea, To—Acts 27:4. Shame, Not to—Rom. 5:5. See SHAME.

PUTEOLI, pū-tē'ŏ-lī. A Roman seaport north of Naples. Paul at—Acts 28:13.

PUTHITES, pū'thites. I Chr. 2:53.

PUTIEL, pū'ti-el. Father-in-law of Eleazar, son of Aaron.—Ex. 6:25.

PUVAH, pū'vah. Num. 26:23. See PUAH.

QUAILS. Israel fed with—Ex. 16:12. Sent in anger—Num. 11:31; Ps. 78:27; 105:40.

QUAKE. Earth—Mt. 27:51. Fear and —Heb. 12:21. Foundations—Ps. 18:7. Mountains—Ex. 19:18; Ju. 5:5; Nah. 1:5. See FEAR.

QUARRELING. Pr. 17:14. See STRIFE.

QUARRY. By Gilgal—Ju. 3:19, 26. Stone made ready at—I Ki. 6:7.

QUARTER. Gen. 19:4; II Ki. 24:14; Jer. 51:31; Mk. 1:45.

QUARTERNION. Acts 12:4.

QUARTUS, quar-tus. A disciple to whom Paul sends salutation—Rom. 16:23.

QUEEN: Queen of Egypt.—Tahpenes —I Ki. 11:19. Queen of Sheba—I Ki. 10:1, 4, 10, 13; II Chr. 9:1, 3, 9, 12; Mt. 12:42; Lu. 11:31.

Queens of Persia.—(1) Vashti—Esth. 1:9, 11, 12, 15–17. (2) Esther—Esth. 2:17, 22; 4:4; 5:2, 3, 12; 7:1–8; 8:1, 7; 9:12, 29, 31. (3) Neh. 2:6.

Queen of the Chaldeans.—Dan. 5:10.

Queen of Ethiopia.—Acts 8:27.

Figurative.—Ps. 45:9; Rev. 18:7.

In Song.—Song of Sol. 6:8, 9.

Queen mother.—I Ki. 15:13; II Ki. 10:13; 11:3; II Chr. 15:16; Jer. 13:18; 29:2.

Queen of heaven.—Venus—Jer. 7:18; 44:17–19, 25.

QUENCH. All fiery darts—Eph. 6:16. Burning wick—Is. 42:3. Lamp—II Sam. 21:17. Love, Cannot—Song of Sol. 8:7. Not the Spirit—I Thess. 5:19. See HOLY SPIRIT. Power of fire— Heb. 11:34.

QUESTIONING. Heard them questioning together—Mk. 12:28. Had no small questioning with them—Acts 15:2, 7. Wherefore do questionings arise?—Lu. 24:38. Do all things without—Phil. 2:14. Fables which minister questionings—I Tim. 1:4. Doting about—I Tim. 6:4. Ignorant questionings refuse—II Tim. 2:23.

QUICKEN. I Cor. 15:36. Again—Ps. 71:20; 85:6. Lovingkindness, After —Ps. 119:88. Righteousness, In—Ps. 119:40. Spiritual—John 5:21; Rom. 4:17; I Cor. 15:45; II Cor. 3:6; Eph. 2:1; Col. 2:13; I Tim. 6:13; I Pet. 3:18. Strength, Of—Is. 57:10. Ways, In thy—Ps. 119:37. See NEW BIRTH.

QUICKLY. Agree with adversary—Mt. 5:25. Carry it—Num. 16:46. Destroy thee—Deut. 7:4. Evil, To speak—Mk. 9:39. Fetch—I Ki. 22:9. I come— Rev. 22:7, 12, 20. Make ready—Gen. 18:6. Removing—Gal. 1:6. Rose up— John 11:31. Send — II Sam. 17:16. Shaken—II Thess. 2:2. Turn aside— Ex. 32:8. What thou doest, do—John 13:27.

QUIET. All night—Ju. 16:2. Be—Is. 7:4. Habitation—Is. 33:20. Heard in —Eccl. 9:17. Life—I Tim. 2:2. Man— Gen. 25:27. Multitude—Acts 19:35. Myself—Is. 38:13. Sea — Jer. 49:23. Speak—II Sam. 3:27. Spirit—I Pet. 3:4. Soul—Ps. 131:2. Study to be —I Thess. 4:11. Wait—Lam. 3:26.

QUIETNESS. Better, a handful with— Eccl. 4:6. Effect of righteousness— Is. 32:17. God's gift of—Job 34:29; Pr. 1:33; Is. 30:15; 32:17, 18; 33:20; Jer. 30:10. Work with — II Thess. 3:12.

QUIT. Ex. 31:15. Like men—I Sam. 4:9.

QUIVER. See ARCHERY.

RAAMA, rā'a-mà. RAAMAH. (1) Son of Cush.—Gen. 10:7; I Chr. 1:9.

(2) A place in Arabia.—Ez. 27:22.

RAAMIAH, rā'a-mī'ah. One who returned with Zerubbabel.—Neh. 7:7.

RAAMSES, ra-ăm'sēs. A store-city in Egypt.—Ex. 1:11.

RABBAH, răb'bah. (1) Chief city of Ammon — Deut. 3:11; Josh. 13:25. Siege and capture of, by Joab—II Sam. 11:1; 12:26–31; I Chr. 20:1–3. Prophecies concerning Rabbah — Jer. 49:2, 3; Ez. 21:20; 25:5; Amos 1:14.

(2) **City of Judah.**—Josh. 15:60.

RABBI. Mt. 23:7; 26:49; John 1:38; 4:31; 9:2.

RABBITH, răb′bith. **A town in Issachar.**—Josh. 19:20.

RABBLE. Acts 17:5.

RAB-BONI, răb′bō-ni. John 20:16.

RAB-MAG, răb′-măg. **Title of Nergalsharezer.**—Jer. 39:3.

RAB-SARIS, răb′-sā′ris. II Ki. 18:17; Jer. 39:3.

RAB-SHAKEH, răb′-sha-kēh. II Ki. 18:17.

RACA, ră′cà. Mt. 5:22; II Sam. 6:20.

RACAL, ră′kăl. **A town in Judah**—I Sam. 30:29.

RACES OF PEOPLE. Mentioned in the Bible: Alexandrian—Acts 18:24. Chosen race—I Pet. 2:9. Cyprian—Acts 4:36. Joseph's race—Acts 7:13. Pontus—Acts 18:2. Syrophœnician—Mk. 7:26.

Races classified.— I. Aryans: *Greek*—Rom. 1:14. *Medes*—Acts 2:9. *Parthians*—Acts 2:9. *Persians*—Esther 1:19. *Romans* — John 11:48. II. Hamites: *Cushites* — Num. 12:1. *Egyptians*—Gen. 45:2. *Libyans* — Jer. 46:9. III. Semites: *Amalekites*—Gen. 14:7. *Ammonites*—Deut. 2:20. *Amorites*—Gen. 14:7. *Assyrians*—Is. 10:24. *Babylonians*—Ezra 4:9. *Canaanites*—Gen. 10:18. *Edomites* — Gen. 36:9. *Hivites*—Ex. 3:17. *Ishmaelites*—Ju. 8:24. *Israelites*—Ex. 9:7. See ISRAEL—Deut. 4:1. *Jebusites*—Gen. 15:21. *Midianites*—Num. 10:29. *Moabites*—Gen. 19:37. *Syrians*— Gen. 25:20. IV. Strange: *Elamites*—Ezra 4:9; Acts 2:9. *Hittites* (by many now considered Semitic)—Gen. 15:20. *Horites*—Gen. 36:29. *Meshech*—Gen. 10:2. *Philistines*—Ju. 3:31. *Tubal*—10:2. See NATIONS.

RACE, RUNNING: Scriptural usage purely figurative.—Christian life compared to a race. Swift in—Eccl. 9:11. Run with patience—Heb. 12:1. For prizes—I Cor. 9:24. Run well—Gal. 5:7. In vain—Gal. 2:2; Phil. 2:16.

Illustrative. — Ps. 19:5. Course—Acts 13:25; II Tim. 4:7.

RACHEL, ră′chel. Wife of Jacob and daughter of Laban—Gen. 29:6, 9, 10, 12, 16, 18, 29. Jacob serves 7 years for her—Gen. 29:20, 25. And yet 7 more—Gen. 29:30. Laban gives Bilhah· to—Gen. 29:29. Envies Leah—Gen. 30:1. Jacob angry with—Gen. 30:2. Blessed with sons—Gen. 30:6, 8, 24; 46:22, 25. Meets Jacob in field —Gen. 31:14. Asks father for portion —Gen. 31:14. Flees with Jacob—Gen. 30:25. Steals teraphim—Gen. 31:19, 32–35. Rachel and son follow company—Gen. 33:1, 2, 7. Rachel dies in travail—35:16, 19. Jacob mourns for Rachel—48:7. Leah and Rachel referred to by Boaz as builders of house of Israel—Ruth 4:11. See JACOB.

RADDAI, răd′dăi. **Son of Jesse.**—I Chr. 2:14.

RADIANT. Ps. 34:5; Is. 60:5.

RAGE. Ez. 16:43. Adversaries, Of—Ps. 7:6. Against wisdom—Pr. 18:1. Because of—II Ki. 19:28. In a—II Chr. 16:10; 28:9. Man, Of—Pr. 6:34. Nations—Ps. 2:1. Sea ceased from—Jon. 1:15. Strong drink is—Pr. 20:1 (A.V.). Tongue, Of—Hos. 7:16. Water, Of—Lu. 8:24. See ANGER.

RAGS. Clothe with—Pr. 23:21.

RAID. Made a—I Sam. 23:27; 30:14; 27:10; I Chr. 14:9, 13.

RAIMENT. Body is more than—Lu. 12:23. Camel's hair, Of—Mt. 3:4. Changes of—Ju. 14:12; II Ki. 5:22. Costly—I Tim. 2:9. Soft—Mt. 11:8. Waxed not old—Deut. 8:4. White—Dan. 7:9. See CLOTHING.

RAIN. *Matar,* Rain; *Geshem,* Violent Rain. **Divided into Early, Winter, and Latter.**—Early (in November, preparing for plowing)—Deut. 11:14; Is. 55:10; Jer. 5:24; Joel. 2:23. Winter (continuing through January and February). Song of Sol. 2:11. Latter (in March, before harvest)—Job 29:23; Pr. 16:15; Jer. 3:3; Hos. 6:3; Zech. 10:1; Jas. 5:7.

Showers. — Deut. 32:2; Job 36:27–28; Jer. 3:3; 14:22; Mic. 5:7; Ps. 65:10; 72:6. Continual dropping—Pr. 27:17.

Violent rains.—Job. 24:8; I Sam. 12:17–18; I Ki. 18:44–45; Pr. 28:3; Is. 4:6; Jer. 10:13; 51:16.

Where it comes from.—Job 36:27–28; I Ki. 18:43–44; Pr. 25:23; Lu. 12:54.

Average annual rain in Palestine.—From 20 to 22 inches.

Rain given or withheld, dependent on obedience.—Lev. 26:3, 4, 19; Deut. 11:13–15; 28:24; I Ki. 8:35–36; 17:1, 7, 14; II Ki. 3:17; Job 5:10–11; 37:11–13; Jer. 3:3; 5:24; 14:22; Jas. 5:17–18.

The blessings of.—Job 5:10–11; Ps. 68:9; 72:6; 78:24, 27; 84:6; 147:8; Is. 55:10–11; Hos. 10:12; Amos 4:7–8; Zech. 10:1; Mt. 5:45; Acts 14:17; Heb. 6:7; Jas. 5:7.

Ruinous.—Gen. 7:4, 12; 19:24; Ex. 9:23; I Sam. 12:17–18; Ps. 11:6; Pr. 26:1; 28:3; Mt. 7:26–27.

Want of—Not supplied by heathen gods—Jer. 14:22. Occasions famine—I Ki. 18:12. Dries up springs and fountains—I Ki. 17:7.

Removed by prayer.—I Ki. 8:35–36; Jas. 5:18.

Illustrative of.—Word of God — Deut. 32:1–3; Is. 55:10–11. Of a contentious woman—Pr. 27:17. Of righteousness—Hos. 10:12. Of God's judgments—Job 20:23; Ps. 11:6; Ez. 38:22. Of oppression—Pr. 28:3. See METEOROLOGY.

RAISIN-CAKES. Is. 16:7.

RAISINS. See FOOD.

RAKEM, rā'kem. **A man of Manasseh.**—I Chr. 7:16.

RAKKATH, răk'kath. **A city of Naphtali.**—Josh. 19:35.

RAKKON, răk'kon. **A city of Dan**—Josh. 19:46.

RAM, răm. (1) **An ancestor of David.**—Ruth 4:19; Mt. 1:3.

(2) **Brother of Jerahmeel.**—I Chr. 2:9.

(3) Job 32:2. See ARAM.

RAM. Num. 5:8; Dan. 8:20. Burnt-offerings of—Is. 1:11. Flock, Of the—Ez. 43:23. Head of—Ex. 29:15. Horns—Josh. 6:4. Incense of—Ps. 66:15. Skipped like—Ps. 114:4. Slay—Ex. 29:16. Three years old—Gen. 15:9. See GOATS, SHEEP.

RAMAH, rā'mah. **An eminence, a height, a high place.** Hence, many places are callad Ramah: (1) **The principal Ramah was a city of Benjamin.**—Josh. 18:25; Ju. 19:13; I Ki. 15:17; Ezra 2:26; Neh. 7:30; Jer. 31:15; 40:1; Hos. 5:8. Resettled by Benjaminites—Neh. 11:33. Rachel weeping for her children—Jer. 31:15; Mt. 2:18. Near it was the palm tree of Deborah—Ju. 4:5. And Rachel's grave—I Sam. 10:2. Levite lodges there on his fatal journey—Ju. 19:13. Ramah near Gibeah in Isaiah's picture of Assyrian advance—Is. 10:29. Yielded with Geba 621 men to the post-exilic census of Ezra—Ezra 2:26. Here Jeremiah was loosed from chains—Jer. 40:1. Home of Shimei (David's vine-dresser)—I Chr. 27:27.

(2) **A city in Mount Ephraim.**—Home of Elkanah; birthplace, home and burial-place of Samuel—I Sam. 1:1, 19; 2:11; 7:17; 8:4; 15:34; 16:13; 19:18–23; 20:1; 25:1; 28:3. Fortified by Baasha and destroyed by Asa—I Ki. 15:17–22; II Chr. 16:1–6.

(3) **City of Asher.**—Josh. 19:29.

(4) **City of Naphtali.**—Josh. 19:36.

(5) **City of Gilead.**—II Ki. 8:28, 29. See RAMOTH-GILEAD.

(6) **Town of Simeon, called Ramah of the South.**—Josh. 19:8; I Sam. 30:27. Ramoth Lehi (unknown), where Samson used jawbone as weapon—Ju. 15:17.

RAMATHAIM, rā'math-ā'im. **Birthplace of Samuel.**—I Sam. 1:1.

RAMATHITE. **An inhabitant of Ramah.**—I Chr. 27:27.

RAMATH-LEHI, rā'math-lē'hi. Ju. 15:17. See LEHI.

RAMATH-MIZPEH, rā'math-mĭz'peh. **A place in Gad.**—Josh. 13:16. See MIZPAH.

RAMESES, răm'e-sēs. **A city in Egypt.**—Jacob and his family at—Gen. 47:11. Israelites depart from—Ex. 12:37. See RAAMSES.

RAMIAH, ra-mī'ah. Ezra 10:25.

RAMOTH-GILEAD, rā'moth-gĭl'e-ad. **Called also** RAMAH.—II Ki. 8:29; II Chr. 22:6. Said to be the present Es-Salt. A great frontier fortress on the east of the Jordan commanding Argob and the Jair towns. It was the rallying place of the Trans-Jordanic tribes. It was also the central city of refuge on the eastern border for the tribe of Gad.—Deut. 4:43; Josh. 20:8; 21:38; I Chr. 6:80. It was constantly a point of contention between Syria and Israel—I Ki. 22:3. It was formerly the dividing line between Laban and Jacob—Gen. 31:48–52.

Ahab, king of Israel, lost his life trying to capture it.—I Ki. 22:29–37; II Chr. 18:33–34.

Joram recovered it from Syrians, but was wounded there.—II Ki. 8:28; 9: 14–15; II Chr. 22:5–6.

The constant question during the reigns of Ahab, Ahaziah, and Joram was, "Is it peace in Ramoth-Gilead?"—II Ki. 9:17–19.

Jehu was anointed there by a young prophet under direction of Elisha.— II Ki. 9:1–6. The fortress was occupied by Solomon's commissariat officer—I Ki. 4:13. See GILEAD.

RAMPART. Jezreel, Of—I Ki. 21:23. Stood against the—II Sam. 20:15.

RAN. Abraham—Gen. 18:7. And fell on his neck—Lu. 15:20. And took a sponge—Mt. 27:48. Down upon beard —Ps. 133:2. Fire—Ex. 9:23. Riotously—Jude 11. To bring word—Mt. 28:8. Together—Mk. 6:33. Unto tomb —Lu. 24:12. Vessel aground—Acts 27:41. See RACE.

RANK. Break not—Joel 2:7. Ears— Gen. 41:7. Good—Gen. 41:5. Sat down in—Mk. 6:40. Stalk—Gen. 41:5. Within the—II Ki. 11:8.

RANSOM. For all—I Tim. 2:6. For many—Mt. 2:28. Greatness of—Job 36:18. Jehovah, Of—Is. 51:11. Laid on him—Ex. 21:30. Life, For—Num. 35:31. Man's life, Of—Pr. 13:8. Me —Ps. 69:18. Righteous, For—Pr. 21: 18. Taken a—I Sam. 12:3. See REDEMPTION, SALVATION.

RAPHAH, rā′phah. **A Benjamite.**—I Chr. 8:2.

RAPHU, rā′phu. **Father of one of the spies.**—Num. 13:9.

RARE. More, than fine gold—Is. 13:12. Thing—Dan. 2:11.

RASE. Ps. 137:7.

RASH. Be not—Eccl. 5:2. Do nothing— Acts 19:36. Shall understand—Is. 32: 4. Words—Job 6:3.

RASHLY. Swear—Lev. 5:4.

RATED. II Ki. 12:4.

RATHER. Mt. 18:8. A good name is to be chosen—Pr. 22:1. Be a doorkeeper —Ps. 84:10. Be in subjection—Heb. 12:9. Darkness than light—John 3:19. Death -than bones—Job 7:15. Fear him—Mt. 10:28. God, Than—Job 32:

2. Men, Than—Acts 5:29. Release Barabbas—Mk. 5:11. Than a fool— Pr. 17:12. Understanding is, to be chosen—Pr. 16:16. See BETTER.

RAVAGE. Ps. 80:13.

RAVEN, *Oreb*, from a root, "*black.*"— Including the crow—Song of Sol. 5: 11. Called "the raven of the valley" —Pr. 30:17. Carnivorous—Pr. 30:17. Not to be used as food—Lev. 11:15; Deut. 14:14. Preserved by Noah in the ark—Gen. 8:7. Sent out, but never returned—Gen. 8:7. Solitary in disposition — Is. 34:11. Improvident — Lu. 12:24. Fed Elijah—I Ki. 17:4–6. Provided for—Job 38:41; Ps. 147:9; Luke 12:24.

RAVENETH. Wolf—Gen. 49:27.

RAVENING. Lion—Ps. 22:13. Prey— Ez. 22:25, 27. Wolves—Mt. 7:15.

RAVENOUS. Beast—Is. 35:9. Bird— Is. 46:11; Ez. 39:4.

RAW. Flesh—Ex. 12:9; Lev. 13:10, 14, 15, 16; I Sam. 2:15.

RAZOR. Barber's—Ez. 5:1. Cause to pass over—Num. 8:7. No razor shall come upon his head—Num. 6:5; Ju. 13:5. Sharp—Ps. 52:2.

REACH. After money—I Tim. 6:10. Hands—Pr. 31:20. Heaven, Unto— Gen. 11:4; Dan. 4:11, 20, 22; Rev. 18: 5. Hither thy finger—John 20:27. Innermost parts—Pr. 20:30. Phœnix— Acts 27:12. Shall not—Ps. 32:12.

READINESS. Is there, Of—II Cor. 8: 12. Know your—II Cor. 9:2. Man in —Lev. 16:21. Mind, Of—Acts 17:11. Our—II Cor. 8:19. To avenge disobedience—II Cor. 10:6. To will—II Cor. 8:11.

READING. I In.

READING: Of the law publicly.—By Moses—Ex. 24:7. By Joshua—Josh. 8:34. By Ezra—Ezra 9:3; 13:1; Neh. 8:1–8; 9:3. By Josiah—II Ki. 23:2. By Jehoiakim, who destroyed the roll —Jer. 36:21, 22.

Reading of the prophets.—Lu. 4:16–19. Acts 8:29–34; 9:32, 33; 13:15.

Of scripture commanded.—Deut. 17:19; Josh. 1:8; John 5:39.

Reading of Paul's Epistles.—Col. 4:16; I Thess. 5:27.

READY. II Pet. 1:12. Always—I Pet. 3:15. Armed—Num. 32:17; Josh. 4:

13. Be ye also—Mt. 24:44. Darkness is—Job 15:23. Die, To—Ps. 88:15; Rev. 3:2. Distribute, To—I Tim. 6:18. Forgive, To—Ps. 86:5. God, To pardon—Neh. 9:17. Grave is—Job 17:1. Go, To—Lu. 22:33. Jehovah, To save —Is. 38:20. Judge, To—I Pet. 4:5. Make it—Pr. 24:27. Perish, To—Pr. 31:6. Reward, For—Mic. 7:3. Room—Mk. 14:15. Rouse, To—Job 3:8. Speak, To—Is. 32:4. Wedding is—Mt.· 22:8. Writer—Ps. 45:1. See EAR, OBEDIENCE.

REALM. Ezra 7:13, 23; Dan. 1:20. Greece, Of—Dan. 11:2. King over—Dan. 9:1. Quiet—II Chr. 20:30. Set him over—Dan. 6:3.

REAP. See HARVEST, SOWING AND REAPING.

REASON, n. II Pet. 3:12. Affliction, Of —Ps. 88:9. Bondage, Of—Ex. 2:23. Concerning hope within you—I Pet. 3:15. Darkness, Of—Job 37:19. Disquietness, Of—Ps. 38:8. Glory, Of—II Cor. 3:10. Ice, Of—Job 6:16. Render a—Pr. 26:16. Shame, Of—Ps. 40: 15. Smoke, Of—Rev. 9:2. Strength, Of—Ps. 90:10. Things, Of—Eccl. 7: 25. Voice, Of—Ps. 102:5. Wine, Of—Ps. 78:65. Wind, Of—John 6:18. Without—II Pet. 2:12. See MIND, THOUGHT.

REASON, v. Acts 19:8. Among themselves—Mt. 16:7, 9. Cause—Jer. 12:1. God, With—Job 13:3. Hearts, In—Lu. 3:15. In the synagogue—Acts 17:17. Let us—Is. 1:18. Righteousness, Of—Acts 24:25. With him—Job 23:7. Within himself—Lu. 12:17. See MIND, THINK.

REBA, rē′bà. **A Midianite king.**—Num.· 31:8; Josh. 13:21.

REBEKAH, re-bĕk′ah. Arabic, "*A rope with a·noose.*"—Captivating. Bethuel's daughter, Laban's sister, Isaac's wife —Gen. 22:23; 24:15, 50–67. Passes as Isaac's sister—Gen. 26:6–11. Barren for 19 years, at last she had children, Esau and Jacob—Gen. 25:21–26; Rom. 9:10–12. Makes Jacob a favorite—Gen. 25:28. Partiality led her to deceive her husband—Gen. 27:6–29. Robs Esau of the blessing—Gen. 27:6–29. Saves Jacob from Esau's fury—Gen. 27:42–45. Buried in cave of Machpelah—Gen. 49:31. Paul refers to her —Rom. 9:10–13. See ISAAC, JACOB.

REBELLION OF: Meaning of.—I Sam. 15:23. The heart seat of—Jer. 5:23; Mt. 15:18, 19; Heb. 3:12.

Of nations.—Ez. 2:3. In cities—Ezra 4:19.

Mentioned.—Against house of David—I Ki. 12:19; II Chr. 10:19. Moab against Israel—II Ki. 3:5, 7. Hezekiah against king of Assyria—II Ki. 18:7. Jehoiakim against Nebuchadrezzar—II Ki. 24:1. Zedekiah against Nebuchadrezzar—II Chr. 36:13.

Of wicked.—Pr. 17:11. Against God—Num. 20:24; 27:14; Deut. 1:26; 9:7, 23, 24; 31:27; Neh. 9:17, 26; Job 34: 37; Ps. 5:10; 107:11; Is. 1:2; 30:9; 63:10; 65:2.

Not against God.—Ps. 105:28; Is. 50:5.

Law concerning rebellious sons.—Deut. 21:18–20. Warning against—Is. 30:1, 9; Ez. 17:12. Punishment for—Jer. 4:17; 28:16; 29:32. See REVOLT, SIN.

REBUKE. Pr. 27:5. Countenance, Of thy—Ps. 80:16. Devourer—Mal. 3:11. Fever—Lu. 4:39. Him—Mal. 16:22; Mk. 10:48; Lu. 17:3. Proud—Ps. 119: 21. Red Sea—Ps. 106:9. Seed—Mal. 2:3. Winds—Mt. 8:26. Wrathful—Ez. 25:17. See REPROOF.

RECEIVE. Abundance — Rom. 5:17. Adoption of sons—Gal. 4:5. Almighty, From—Job 27:13. Blessing—Ps. 24:5; Heb. 6:7. See BLESSING. Brother's blood—Gen. 4:11. See CAIN. Burntofferings—I Ki. 8:64; II Chr. 7:7. See OFFERING. Commandments—Pr. 10:8. Correction — Jer. 5:3. Corruptible crown—I Cor. 9:25. Crown of glory—I Pet. 5:4. Crown of life—Jas. 1:12. Edifying—I Cor. 14:5. See EDIFICATION. Good, Evil—Job 2:10. Grace—Rom. 1:5. Holy Spirit—Acts 2:38; 8:17, 19. See HOLY SPIRIT. Inheritance—Num. 34:14; Josh. 13:8; 18:7. Instruction—Pr. 1:3; 8:10. Interest—Ez. 18:17. Law—Gal. 22:12; Acts 7: 53. Me to glory—Ps. 73:21. Money—II Ki. 5:26. More blessed to give than —Acts 20:35. Plagues, Of—Rev. 18:4. Pledge — Gen. 38:20. Power — Acts 1:8. Prayer, My—Ps. 6:9. Prize—I Cor. 9:24. See PRAYER. Present—Gen. 33:10. Promise—Gal. 3:14; Heb. 11: 17. Recompence—Rom. 1:27; Col. 3: 24. Remission of sins—Acts 26:18.

Reward—II John 8; I Cor. 3:8. Sayings—Pr. 4:10. Shame—Hos. 10:6. Stripes—I Cor. 11:24. Testimony—Acts 2:18. Tithes—Heb. 7:8. Words, My—Pr. 2:1. Ye one another—Rom. 15:7. See JESUS, TEACHINGS OF.

RECAH, rē′kah. **A city in Judah.**—I Chr. 4:12.

RECHAB, rē′kăb. (1) **Son of Rimmon who slew Ishbosheth son of Saul.**—II Sam. 4:2–9.

(2) **Founder of a tribe who were taught to abstain from wine.**—I Ki. 10:15, 23; Jer. 35:2–19.

(3) **Father of Malchiah, who helped to repair the wall.**—Neh. 3:14.

(4) **A descendant of Hammath.**—I Chr. 2:55.

RECLINING. On Jesus' bosom.—John 13:23.

RECOMPENSE. Job 34:33; Rom. 11:9, 35; II Cor. 6:13. Affliction—II Thess. 1:6. Babylon—Jer. 50:29. Barzillai—II Sam. 19:36. Bosom, Into their—Is. 65:6. David—Ps. 18:20, 24. Day of—Hos. 9:7. Error, Of—Rom. 1:27. Evil—Pr. 20:22; Jer. 1:8–20; Rom. 12:17. God, Of—II Sam. 22:25; Is. 39:4; 40:10; 49:4; 32:18; 51:6; Lam. 3:14; Hos. 12:2; Joel 3:3, 4; Mt. 6:4; Rom. 12:19. Inheritance, Of—Col. 3:24. Lewdness—Ez. 23:49. Resurrection, In the—Lu. 14:14. Reward, Of—Heb. 2:2; 10:35; 11:26. Righteous—Pr. 11:31. Supper, For—Lu. 14:12. Truth, In—Is. 61:8. Vanity shall be—Job 15:31. Vengeance—Deut. 32:35, 40; Is. 59:18; Jer. 16:18; 51:6; Rom. 12:19; Heb. 10:30. Work, Thy—Ruth 2:12. Year of—Is. 34:8. See JUDGMENT, REWARD.

RECONCILIATION (Rendering friendly those who before were hostile).—Nature of the word (together with "reconcile") is retained in the R.V. Old Testament—I Sam. 29:4; Dan. 9:24. In the New Testament the verb occurs 14 times. Twice it is used of men who, mutually estranged, are to be reconciled—Mt. 5:24; I Cor. 7:11. In the former case the offender deals with his offence—I Sam. 29:4. Elsewhere, the reconciliation concerns the relations of God and man (compounds of *allassein* being used), and in all, except Rom. 11:15, Christ is directly

named as the "means of reconciliation."—*Standard Bible Dictionary.*

The establishment of a new relation to God.—Is. 53:10; 55:9–13; 59:16, 20, 21; 61:1–3; Eph. 2:11–13.

Reconciliation for iniquity predicted.—Is. 53:5; Dan. 9:24.

Angelic proclamation concerning.—Lu. 2:13, 14. A human echo of this—Lu. 19:38. Man alienated from God by sin—Col. 1:21; Rom. 5:20; Eph. 2:12. God the reconciler—II Cor. 5:18 f.; Col. 1:21; Rom. 5:20; Eph. 2:16.

Christ the means of reconciliation.—John 12:31, 32; Rom. 5:10; II Cor. 5:18–20; Eph. 2:13–18; Col. 1:19–23; Heb. 2:17; 10:19–22.

The death of Christ the basis of reconciliation.—Heb. 2:17; II Cor. 5:18; Eph. 2:16.

The gospel a ministry of reconciliation.—II Cor. 5:18–21.

The reconciliation of the nations (Gentiles).—Eph. 2:14–22.

The reconciliation of earthly and heavenly things.—Col. 1:19, 20. (To be distinguished from ATONEMENT and PURIFICATION.)

Reconciliation between husband and wife.—I Cor. 7:10, 11. See TEACHING OF JESUS, SALVATION.

RECORD. Ezra 6:2. Book of—Ezra 4:15; Esth. 6:1. Name—Ex. 20:24. See SCRIPTURES, WITNESS.

RECORDER: Recorders mentioned.—Jehovah as—Ex. 20:24. Jehoshaphat to David—II Sam. 8:16; 20:24; I Chr. 18:15. To Solomon—I Ki. 4:3. Joah, to Hezekiah—II Ki. 18:18, 37; Is. 36:3, 22. To Josiah—II Chr. 34:8.

RECOVER. Ju. 11:26; Mk. 16:18; John 11:12; II Tim. 2:26. All—I Sam. 30:8, 18. Health—Jer. 8:22. Leprosy, Of—II Ki. 5:3, 6, 7. Remnant of people—Is. 11:11. Sickness, Of—II Ki. 1:2; 8:8. Sight—Lu. 4:18. Spoil—I Sam. 30:22. Strength—Ps. 39:13.

RED. See COLORS.

REDEEM. See REDEMPTION, SALVATION.

REDEMPTION. Heb. *Padah*, "to release," "ransom," "rescue," "redeem." Used frequently (Deut. 7:8; 9:26; 13:5; 15:15; 21:8; 24:18) in relation to bondage. Another Heb. term is "Ga'al" from which Goel, "Redeemer,'' used of inheritances, tithes, etc. ''The goel is the kinsman who has the right to redeem.'' Used also as an avenger of blood (Num. 35:12) elsewhere, as in Job 19:25; Ps. 19:14. In Isaiah it denotes Jehovah as Vindicator, Deliverer, and Avenger—Is. 41: 14; 43:14. The New Testament employs two words; one, *Agorazo*, ''to buy or purchase''—I Cor. 6:20; 7: 23; II Pet. 2:1; Rev. 5:9; 14:3, 4. The other Greek word is *Lutroo*, from *Lutron*, ''a ransom.'' Paul's word for Redemption is *Apolutrosis* — Rom. 3: 24; 8:23; I Cor. 1:30; Eph. 1:7. In Rom. 11:26 ''Deliverer'' is used for the Old Testament ''Redeemer''— Is. 59:20.—HASTINGS, *Bible Dictionary*.

Various redemptions.—Of place: Jerusalem—Is. 52:9; Lu. 2:38; 21:38. Of time—Eph. 5:16; Col. 4:5. Of transgressions—Heb. 9:15. Of our body—Rom. 8:23. Of God's possession—Eph. 1:14. Of land—Lev. 25:24; 27:20–24; Jer. 32:7, 8. Of first-born—Num. 3: 44–51. Of bondmen—Lev. 25:47–54. Of soul—II Sam. 4:9; I Ki. 1:29; Ps. 71:23. Of persons: Israel or Judah—Deut. 21:8; 24:18; I Chr. 17:21; Neh. 1:10; 5:8; Ps. 77:15; 106:10; 107:2; 136:24; Is. 43:1; 44:22, 23; 48:20; 52:3, 9; 62:12; Jer. 31:11; Mic. 6:4; Zech. 10:8; Lu. 1:68; 24:21.

Redemption through Christ. — Rom. 3: 24; I Cor. 1:30; Gal. 3:13; Eph. 1:7; Col. 1:14; Heb. 9:12; I Pet. 1:18; Rev. 5:9; 14:3, 4. Christ spoke of His death for many as a ransom (*Lutron*)—Mt. 20:28; Mk. 10:45. So Paul also used ransom (*Antilutron*) concerning Christ's death for men—I Tim. 2:6. See SALVATION, JESUS.

REED. Beast of—Ps. 68:30. Bruised—II Ki. 18:21; Is. 36:6; 42:3; Mt. 12: 20. Burned—Jer. 51:32. Golden—Rev. 21:16; Measuring—Ez. 40:3, 5; 42:16. Put a sponge on—Mt. 27:48. Rod, Like a—Rev. 11:1. Shaken by wind —Mt. 11:7. Smote Christ with—Mt. 27:30. Wither, Shall—Is. 19:6.

REED-GRASS. Gen. 41:2.

REEL. To and fro—Ps. 107:27; Jer. 25: 16; With wine—Is. 28:7.

REELAIAH, rē'el-ā'iah. Ezra 2:2.

REFINE. Job 28:1; Dan. 11:35; 12:10.

Fire, By—Rev. 3:18. Furnace, In—Rev. 1:15. Gold—I Chr. 28:18. Pot—Pr. 17:3; 27:21. Silver—I Chr. 29:4; Zech. 13:9.

REFINER. Pr. 25:4; Mal. 3:3. Fire—Mal. 3:2.

REFORMATION. Time of—Heb. 9:10.

REFRAIN. Acts 5:38. Embracing, From—Eccl. 3:5. Feet—Ps. 119:101. Foot—Pr. 1:15. Haman—Esth. 5:10. Lips—Ps. 40:9; Pr. 10:19. Mouth—Job 7:11. Princes—Job 29:9. Talking, From—Job 29:9. Tongue—I Pet. 3:10. Weeping, From — Jer. 31:16. See ABSTINENCE.

REFRESHING. Thorough sabbatic rest —Ex. 23:12; 31:17. David refreshes Saul by music—I Sam. 16:23.

Refreshing after physical weariness.—David and People—II Sam. 16:14.

Captive Zion.—Lam. 1:11. The prophet refuses king's refreshment—I Ki. 13: 7–10.

Job finds relief in speech.—Job 32:20.

The refreshing of a messenger.—Pr. 25: 13.

God sends seasons of refreshing.—Acts 3:19.

Refreshed by brotherly acts.—I Cor. 16: 18; II Cor. 7:13; II Tim. 1:16. See FRATERNITY, REST.

REFUGE. Ps. 142:4; Is. 14:32. God is our refuge—Ruth 2:12; II Sam. 22:3; Ps. 2:12; 7:1; 11:1; 14:6; 17:8; 34:8; 36:7; 46:1, 7, 11; 48:3; 57:1; 62:7; 73:28; 91:2; Pr. 14:26; Is. 25:4; Jer. 17:17; Joel 3:16. Rock of refuge—Ps. 18:2; 71:7; 94:22; 104:18. See CITIES OF REFUGE.

Cities of. See CITIES.

REFUSE, *n.* Count them—Phil. 3:8. Made us—Lam. 3:45. Sell—Amos 8:7. Silver—Jer. 6:30.

REFUSE, *v.* Admonition — Tit. 3:10. Comforted, To be—Gen. 37:35. Commandments, To keep—Ex. 16:28. Correction—Pr. 13:18. Cup, To take—Jer. 25:28. Evil—Is. 7:15. Hear, To—Mt. 18:17. Humble thyself, To—Ex. 10:3. Let people go, To—Ex. 7:14. Not—Pr. 8:33. Profane fables—I Tim. 2:23. Touch, To—Job 6:7. Walk in law, To —Ps. 78:10. See REBELLION.

REGARD. Jas. 2:3. Captives—Jer. 24: 5. Christ, Of—Eph. 5:32. Folly, Not

—Job 24:12. Gourd, For—Jonah 4:10. Grace, Of—II Cor. 8:4. Have —Dan. 11:30. Iniquity, Not—Job 36: 21. Life—Pr. 12:10. Lightly, Not— Heb. 12:5. Lying words — Ex. 5:9. Man—Lu. 18:4. Oath, Of—Eccl. 8:2. Prayer—Ps. 102:17. Reproof—Pr. 15: 5: Rich — Job 34:19. Vanities—Ps. 31:6; Jonah 2:8. Word of Jehovah, Not—Ex. 9:21. Works—Ps. 28:5. See TAKE HEED, OBEY.

REGEM, rē′gem. **A descendant of Caleb.** —I Chr. 2:47.

REGEM-MELECH, rē′gem-mē′lek. **A person.** Zech. 7:2.

REGENERATION. Mt. 19:28; Tit. 3:5. See NEW BIRTH.

REGION. Achaia, Of—II Cor. 11:10. Argob, Of—Deut. 3:4, 13; I Ki. 4:13. Death, Of — Mt. 4:16. Fame went through—Lu. 4:14. Galatia, Of—Acts 16:6. Galilee, Of—Mk. 1:28. Jordan, About — Josh. 22:10; Mt. 3:5. Judæa, Of—Acts 8:1. Syria and Cilicia—Gal. 1:21. Whole—Mk. 6:55.

REHABIAH, rē′ha-bī′ah. **A family of Levites.**—I Chr. 23:17; 24:21; 26:25.

REHEARSE. All that God had done— Acts 14:27; 15:4. Before Saul—I Sam. 17:31. Ears, In—Ex. 17:14; I Sam. 8:21. Having—Acts 10:8. One by one—Acts 21:19. Righteous Acts— Ju. 5:11. Signs—Acts 15:12. Things —Lu. 24:35.

REHOB, rē′hŏb. (1) **A city in northern Israel.**—Num. 13:21; II Sam. 10:8.

(2) **A city in Asher.**—Josh. 19:28, 30; 21:31; Ju. 1:31; I Chr. 6:75.

(3) **Father of Hadadezer king of Zobah.** —II Sam. 8:3, 12.

(4) **A Levite.**—Neh. 10:11.

REHOBOAM, rē′ho-bō′am. **Son of Solomon, first king of Judah after division of the kingdom.**—I Ki. 11:43; 12:1-27; 14:21-31; 15:6; I Chr. 3:10; II Chr. 9:31; 10:1-18; 11:1-22; 12:1- 16; 13:7. See JUDAH, KINGDOM OF.

REHOBOTH, re-hō′both. (1) **A well dug by Isaac.**—Gen. 26:22.

(2) Gen. 36:37.

REHUM, rē′hum. (1) **A Persian officer who interfered with the work of rebuilding Jerusalem.**—Ezra 4:8-24.

(2) **One who returned with Zerubbabel.** —Ezra 2:2.

(3) **One who helped to seal the covenant.**—Neh. 10:25.

(4) **A Levite who helped to repair the wall.**—Neh. 3:17.

(5) **A priest who returned with Zerubbabel.**—Neh. 12:3.

REI, rē′ī. **An officer under David.**—I Ki. 1:8.

REIGN. Gen. 37:8. A thousand years— Rev. 20:6. Earth, Upon—Rev. 5:10. For ever—Rev. 22:5. Godless man— Job 34:30. Grace—Rom. 5:21. He must—I Cor. 15:25. Indeed—Gen. 37: 8. Jehovah—Ex. 15:18; Ps. 93:1. Kings—Pr. 8:15. Life, In—Rom. 5: 17. Nations, Over—Ps. 47:8. Over— Mt. 2:22. This man—Lu. 19:14. We also might—I Cor. 4:8. See KINGDOM.

REINS. Job 16:13; Rev. 2:23.

REJECT. Builders—Ps. 118:22; Mt. 21: 42; Lu. 20:17. Cast off and—Ps. 89: 38. Commandment—Mk. 7:9. Despised and—Is. 53:3. Elders, Of—Lu. 9:22. God hath—Ps. 53:5. I should be—I Cor. 9:27. Jehovah—Num. 11:20. Jesus, Of—See JESUS. Judah—Jer. 14: 19. Law—Amos 2:4. Man—I Thess. 4:8. Me—Jer. 15:6; Lu. 10:16. Ordinances—Ez. 5:6. Seed of Israel—II Ki. 17:20. Statutes—II Ki. 17:15. Stone—I Pet. 2:4, 7. This generation, Of—Lu. 17:25. Those in whom thou trustest. Us—Lam. 5:22.

REJOICE. See JOY.

REKEM, rē′kem. (1) **A king of Midian.** —Num. 31:8; Josh. 13:2.

(2) **A descendant of Caleb.**—I Chr. 2:43.

(3) **A town in Benjamin.**—Josh. 18:27.

RELEASE. Barabbas — Mt. 27:26. Brother—Gen. 43:14. Come—Job 14: 14. Jesus—Lu. 23:20, 22. Power to— John 19:10. Proclaim—Lu. 4:18. Provinces, To—Esth. 2:18. Sought to— John 19:12. Unto them—Mk. 15:6. Whom will ye that I—Mt. 27:17. Ye shall be—Lu. 6:37. Year of—Ex. 21:2; Deut. 15:1; 30:10; Jer. 34:14. See JUBILEE.

RELIEF. Arise—Esth. 4:14. Afflicted —I Tim. 5:10. Oppressed, Of—Is. 1: 17. Sent to brethren—Acts 11:29; 24: 17. See FRATERNITY, LIBERALITY.

RELIGION. Acts 25:19. Jew's—Gal. 1:13, 14. Man's—Jas. 1:26. Pure— Jas. 1:27. Sect of our—Acts 26:5.

RELIGIOUS. Thinketh himself—Jas. 1: 26. Very—Acts 17:22.

REMAIN. Cross over night, On—Deut. 21:23. Broken pieces—Mt. 14:20; 15: 37; Mk. 8:8; John 6:12. Canaan, Inhabitants of—Num. 33:55; Josh. 8:22; 10:27-30; 23:4-12. Captive woman—Deut. 21:13. Cross, Body on—Deut. 21:23; Josh. 8:29; 10:26; John 19:31. Dens, In—Job 37:8. Earth—Gen. 8: 22. Eating and drinking—Lu. 10:7. Elijah a prophet—I Ki. 18:22. Frogs—Ex. 8:9. Fruit—John 15:16. Joy—John 15:11. Land—Lev. 25:28. Leaven—Deut. 16:4. Offering—Ex. 12:10; 29:34; Lu. 19:6. Sabbath rest—Heb. 4:9. Sacrifice for sin, No more—Heb. 10:26. Seed—I John 3:6. Sodom—Mt. 11:23. Speechless—Lu. 1: 22. Strongholds, In—Jer. 51:30. Taste—Jer. 48:11. Things which—Rev. 3:2. Unmarried—I Cor. 7:11. Veil—II Cor. 3:14. Widow—Gen. 38:11. Years—Deut. 16:4. See REMNANT, RESIDUE, REST.

REMALIAH, rĕm'a-lī'ah. **Father of Pekah king of Israel.**—I Ki. 15:25; II Ki. 15:25, 27, 30, 32, 37; 16:1, 5; II Chr. 28:6; Is. 7:1, 4, 5, 9; 8:6.

REMEMBER. Job 10:9; 21:6; 24:20; Lam. 2:1. Covenant—Gen. 9:16; I Chr. 16:15. Creator, Thy—Eccl. 12:1. Days, Darkness, Of—Ex. 11:2. Old, Of—Deut. 32:7. Ends of the earth shall—Ps. 22:27. Faults—Gen. 41:9. Five waves—Mt. 16:2. Former things—Is. 43:18; 65:17. God—Neh. 4:14; Ps. 77:3; Eccl. 12:1; Is. 57:11. Holy word—Ps. 105:42. Iniquity—Jer. 14: 10; Hos. 8:13. Jeremiah—Jer. 15:15. Life is a breath—Job 7:7; Ps. 89:47. Lot's wife—Lu. 17:32. Mercy—Hab. 3:2; Lu. 1:54. Misery—Pr. 31:7. Nobles—Nah. 2:5. Poor—Gal. 2:10. Reproach—Lam. 5:1. Sabbath-day—Ex. 20:8. Sins, Not—Ps. 25:7; Jer. 31:34. Son remember—Lu. 16:25. Tears—II Tim. 1:4. Way—Deut. 8:2; Ez. 16: 61. Whence thou art—Rev. 2:5. Wickedness—Hos. 7:2. Works of God—I Chr. 16:12.

REMEMBRANCE. Gen. 40:14. Book of—Mal. 3:16. Call to—Ps. 77:6. Cut off—Ps. 34:16. Jehovah's—Is. 62:6. No remembrance for ever—Eccl. 2:16.

Perish—Job 18:17; Ps. 9:6. See MEMORIAL.

REMETH, rē'meth. Jósh. 19:21. See RAMAH.

REMINDED. II Tim. 1:5.

REMISSION OF SINS. See SIN, FORGIVENESS, TEACHING OF JESUS ON FORGIVENESS, REDEMPTION, SALVATION THROUGH THE BLOOD AND DEATH OF JESUS.

REMNANT. Zech. 8:11. According to election—Rom. 11:5. Flock, Of—Jer. 23:3. People, Of—Hag. 2:2. Preserve a—Gen. 45:7. Saved, Shall be—Rom. 9:27. Such a—Ezra 9:13. See JUDAH, REMAIN.

REMOVE. Blast, With—Is. 27:8. Cloud—Num. 12:10. Cup—Lu. 22:42. Defence—Num. 14:9. Far from me—Pr. 30:8. Falsehood, From—Pr. 30:8. Foot—Pr. 4:27. Heaven was—Rev. 6: 14. Hence—Mt. 17:20. Iniquity—Zech. 3:9. Landmarks—Job 24:2. Mountains—I Cor. 13:2. Righteous shall never be—Pr. 10:30. Sorrow—Eccl. 11:10. Stroke—Ps. 39:10. Stuff for—Ez. 12:7. Soul—Lam. 3:17. Way—Pr. 5:8.

REND. Caul of their heart—Hos. 13:8. New, The—Lu. 5:36. Not—John 19: 24. Pieces, In—Ps. 7:2. Shoulders—Ez. 29:7. Time to—Eccl. 3:7. Turn and—Mt. 7:6. Wind shall—Ez. 13:11.

RENDER. Cæsar, Unto—Mt. 22:21. Desert—Ps. 28:4; 94:2. Dues, To all—Rom. 13:7. Evil—Rom. 12:17; I Thess. 5:15; I Pet. 3:9. Fruits—Mt. 21:41. Lord will—II Tim. 4:14. Recompence—Is. 66:6; Jer. 51:6. Righteousness—I Sam. 26:23. Servants, Unto—Col. 4:1. To each man—Rev. 22:12. Vengeance—II Thess. 1:8. Rending of garments—See CLOTHING, JUDGMENT.

RENEW. Heb. 6:6. A right spirit within me—Ps. 51:10. Bow is—Job 29:20. Face of ground—Ps. 104:30. Inward man is—II Cor. 4:16. Kingdom—I Sam. 11:14. Strength—Is. 40:31. Witness against me—Job 10:17. Youth is—Ps. 103:5. See CONVERSION, NEW BIRTH.

RENOUNCE. God—Job 1:5. Hidden things—II Cor. 4:2. The covetous—Ps. 10:3. Thee to thy face—Job 1:11; 2:5. See SELF-DENIAL.

RENOWN. City—Ez. 26:17. Gotten—Dan. 9:15. Men of—Ez. 23:23. Raise a plantation for—Ez. 34:29.

RENT. Asunder—Mk. 5:4. Clothes—II Chr. 34:27. Cloud—Job 26:8. Earth—I Ki. 1:40; Is. 24:19. Garments—II Sam. 13:31. Heavens—Mk. 1:10. Kid, A—Ju. 14:6. Mountains—I Ki. 19:11. Should not be—Ex. 39:23. Veil of temple—Mt. 27:51. See REND.

REPAIR. Altar of Jehovah—I Ki. 18:30. Breaches—II Ki. 12:8. Foundations—Ezra 4:12. House—I Chr. 26:27; II Chr. 24:12. Ruins—Ezra 9:9. Waste cities—Is. 61:4.

REPENTANCE. Gr. *Metanoia*, Complete "Change of mind." A state of feeling—Gen. 6:6, 7; Ju. 2:18; 21:6, 15; I Sam. 15:11, 35; Job 42:6; Ps. 106:45; Jer. 8:6; 20:16; 31:19; Mt. 27:3; Rom. 2:4, 5; II Cor. 7:8–10; Heb. 6:1–6.

A change of purpose.—Ex. 13:17; 32:12–14; Num. 23:19; Deut. 32:36; I Sam. 15:29; II Sam. 24:16; I Ki. 8:47; I Chr. 21:15; Ps. 90:13; 110:4; 135:14; Jer. 4:28; 18:7–10; Ez. 24:14; Joel 2:12–14; Amos 7:3–6; Jonah 3:9, 10; 4:2; Mt. 3:1, 2; 9:13; 41:29–32; Mk. 1:4, 15; 6:12; Lu. 5:32; 16:30; 17:3, 4; Acts 2:38; 3:19; 13:24; 17:30; 19:4; 26:20; II Cor. 12:21; Rev. 2:5, 16; 3:3, 19–21; 16:9.

Essential to salvation.—I Ki. 8:47; Jer. 20:16; Mt. 11:20–22; 12:41; Mk. 1:4; Lu. 3:3; 5:37; 10:13, 14; 11:32; 13:3–5; 15:7–10; 24:47; Acts 2:38; 3:19; 8:22; 11:18; 17:30; II Cor. 7:10; II Tim. 2:25, 26; II Pet. 3:9.

Should lead to reformation of life.—Mt. 3:8–11; 21:29; Lu. 3:8; 5:32; 15:7; Acts 26:20. See Teachings of Jesus on REPENTANCE, SALVATION.

REPETITIONS. Mt. 6:7.

REPHAEL, rĕ′pha-el. **A doorkeeper in the second temple.**—I Chr. 26:7.

REPHAH, rĕ′phah. **An Ephraimite.**—I Chr. 7:25.

REPHAIAH, rĕph′a-iah. (1) **A Simeonite.**—I Chr. 4:42.

(2) **A descendant of David.**—I Chr. 3:21.

(3) **A man of Issachar.**—I Chr. 7:2.

(4) **A descendant of Saul.**—I Chr. 9:43.

(5) **One who helped to repair the wall.**—Neh. 3:9.

REPHAIM, rĕph′a-im. (1) **A race of people living south of Jerusalem.**—Gen. 14:15; 15:20.

(2) **A valley separating Judah and Benjamin.**—II Sam. 5:18, 22; 23:13; I Chr. 11:15; 14:9; Is. 17:5.

REPHIDIM, rĕph′i-dĭm. **An encampment of Israel where the people murmured for water and Moses struck the rods.**—Ex. 17:1–8; 19:2; Num. 33:14, 15. See MERIBAH.

REPLENISH. Gen. 1:28; Jer. 31:25; Ez. 26:2. See MULTIPLY.

REPLIEST. Rom. 9:20.

REPORT. Evil—Gen. 37:2; Num. 13:32; 14:36; II Cor. 6:8. False—Ex. 23:1. Gentiles, Concerning—Acts 11:22. Good, Of—Acts 6:3; 10:22; 22:12; II Cor. 6:8. Hear—Nah. 3:19; Hab. 3:2. Jesus, Concerning—Mt. 4:14; 14:1; Mk. 1:28; Lu. 5:15; 7:17. Words—Ex. 19:8; Acts 16:36. See REPROACH, TIDINGS.

REPROACH: A misfortune.—Job 19:5; 20:3; Lam. 3:30; Joel 2:17.

Blame.—Josh. 5:9; Ruth 2:15; Neh. 5:9; 6:13; Job 16:10; 19:3; 27:6; Ps. 15:3; 42:10; 57:3; 69:9, 20; 74:22; 89:50, 51; Pr. 14:3; 17:5; 18:3; Jer. 31:19; 51:51; Lam. 3:61; Ez. 21:28; 36:13–15; Dan. 9:16; Zeph. 2:8, 10; 3:18; Lu. 11:45; Rom. 15:3; I Tim. 3:7; Heb. 10:33; I Pet. 4:14.

Disgrace.—Gen. 34:14; I Sam. 11:2; Neh. 1:3; 4:4; Ps. 39:8; 44:13; 57:3; 69:7; 71:13; 78:66; 89:41; 119:22, 39; Pr. 6:33; Is. 54:4; Ju. 6:10; 20:8; 23:40; 24:9; 29:18; 42:18; 44:8, 12; 49:13; Lam. 5:1; Ez. 16:57; Mic. 6:16; Heb. 11:26; 13:13.

Curse.—Ps. 22:6; 31:11; 44:16; 55:12; 74:10, 18; 79:4, 12; 89:51; 102:8; 109:25, 28; Is. 30:5; 43:28; 51:7; Dan. 11:18; Hos. 12:14; Joel 2:19; Lu. 6:22.

How caused.—Barrenness—Gen. 30:23. Misfortune—Job 19:3. Desolation of Jerusalem—Neh. 1:3. A rebellious son—Pr. 19:26. Sin—Pr. 14:34. Idolatry and iniquity—Ez. 5:1–15; 22:4. Being rejected by Jehovah—Is. 43:28.

Removed by.—Bearing children—Gen. 30:23; Lu. 1:25. Rebuilding Jerusalem—Neh. 2:17. Obedience—Josh. 5:7, 9. Death of enemy—I Sam. 17:26; 25:39. By forgiveness on repentance

—Ez. 36:30, 31. Lovingkindness of
God—Ps. 119:42.

REPROBATE. II Cor. 13:5-7. Concern-
ing the faith—II Tim. 3:8. Despised
—Ps. 15:4. Unto every good work—
Tit. 1:16.

REPROOF: Laws concerning.—Lev. 19:
17; Pr. 9:8.

Examples of.—Abraham reproves Abimelech—Gen. 21:25. Rabshakeh reproves God—II Ki. 19:4; Is. 37:4. God
reproves kings—I Chr. 17:21; Ps. 105:
14. Reproved of God—Job 22:4; Ps.
50:8, 21; 141:5; Pr. 30:6. Herod's reproof—Lu. 3:18. Backsliding a—Jer.
2:19. Snare a—Is. 29:21. Warning a
—Hos. 4:4. Reproof from mouth—Ps.
38:14. Wisdom's—Pr. 1:23, 25, 30;
5:12; 6:23; 19:25; 25:12. Of deceitful
friends—Job 6:25, 26. Scoffer reproved—Pr. 15:12; 19:25. Reward of
—Pr. 10:17; 12:1; 13:18; 15:5, 10, 32;
29:15. Fear of—John 3:20.

Scripture for.—II Tim. 3:16.

Prophecy concerning.—Ez. 3:26. In
Teachings of Paul—Eph. 5:11, 13; II
Tim. 4:2. See REBUKE.

REPUTE. Gal. 2:2, 6. As nothing—Dan.
4:35.

REQUIRE. Ps. 10:4; 137:3. Blood—
Gen. 9:5; Lu. 11:50, 51. Duty of every
day—II Chr. 8:13. Jehovah—II Chr.
24:22. Much—Lu. 12:48. One thing—
II Sam. 3:13. Soul—Lu. 12:20.
Stewards, In—I Cor. 4:2. What doth
Jehovah—Deut. 10:12. See DEMAND,
ASK.

REQUITE. Evil—Gen. 50:15. God—
Ju. 1:7; 9:57. Hand, With thy—Ps.
10:14. Good—II Sam. 16:12. Jehovah
—Deut. 32:6. Kindness—II Sam. 2:6.
Parents—I Tim. 5:4. Surely—Jer. 51:
56. Wicked—II Chr. 6:23. See RE-
WARD, RECOMPENSE.

RESCUE. Ps. 22:8; 37:40; Acts 23:27.
Enemies, From—Ps. 18:48. Jonathan
—I Sam. 14:45. Me—Ps. 71:2; 144:7.
Poor, The—Ps. 82:4. Soul, My—Ps.
35:17. See SAVE.

RESEN, rē'sĕn. **A city near Nineveh.**—
Gen. 10:12.

RESERVE. I Sam. 9:24. Against the
time of trouble—Job 38:23. Blackness
of darkness—Jude 13. Blessing—Gen.
27:36. Darkness—II Pet. 2:17.

Heaven, In—I Pet. 1:4. Portion—
Deut. 33:21. To day of calamity—
Job 21:30.

RESERVOIR. Is. 22:11.

RESHEPH, rē'sheph. **An Ephraimite.**—
I Chr. 7:25.

RESIDUE. Amos 4:2. Brethren, Of—
Mic. 5:3. Foul the—Ez. 34:18. Israel,
Of—Ez. 9:8. Nations, Of—Ez. 36:4.
Shall fall—Ez. 23:25. Spirit, Of—
Mal. 2:15. Vessels, Of—Jer. 27:19.
Wrath, Of—Ps. 76:10. Years, Of—
Is. 38:10. See REMAIN, REMNANT,
REST.

RESIST. Blood, Unto—Heb. 12:4; Jas.
5:6. Devil, The—Jas. 4:7. Evil man
—Mt. 5:39. Face, To the—Gal. 2:11.
Holy Spirit—Acts 7:51. Power—Rom.
13:2. Proud, The—Jas. 4:6. See WITH-
STAND.

RESOLVE. Lu. 16:4.

RESORT. John 18:2. Continually—Ps.
71:3. Unto him—Mk. 2:13; Lu. 8:4.
See COME.

RESPECT. Covenant, Unto—Ps. 74:20.
Feast day, Of—Col. 2:16. Holy One,
To—Is. 17:7. Persons, Of—Job 32:21;
34:19; Pr. 24:23; 82:2; Mal. 2:9; Acts
10:34; Jas. 2:3; Jude 16. Prayer,
Unto—I Ki. 8:28. Proud, Not—Ps.
40:4. Wicked, Persons of—Ps. 82:2;
Pr. 18:5. See JUDGMENT.

RESPITE. Ex. 8:15; II Sam. 11:3.

REST; Physical.—Commanded by God
—Ex. 16:23; 23:12; 31:15; 34:21; 35:
2; Lev. 16:31; 23:3, 32; 25:4; Deut.
5:14. Day of rest—See SABBATH. Offered by Abraham to the strangers—
Gen. 18:4. Offered as a blessing—
Ruth 1:9. Christ offered, in desert
place—Mk. 6:31.

National.—From war—Josh. 14:15; Ju.
3:11, 30; 5:31; II Chr. 14:6, 7; Jer.
47:6. From enemies—Deut. 12:10; 25:
19; Josh. 21:44; 23:1; II Sam. 7:1,
11; Esth. 9:16; Ez. 38:11. From burdens—Ex. 5:5. No rest for people—
Deut. 28:65.

God gives.—Deut. 3:20; Josh. 1:13, 15;
22:4; Ps. 37:8; Jer. 6:16. To weary—
Is. 28:12. To Israel—I Ki. 8:56; I Chr.
22:18; 23:25; II Chr. 15:15; 20:30;
Is. 63:14; Jer. 31:2. To earth—Jer.
50:34.

Mental (Peace of mind).—Ruth—Ruth 3:1. Boaz—Ruth 3:18. Solomon—I Ki. 5:4; I Chr. 22:9. Job—Job 3:13, 26; 11:18; 14:6; 30:17. David—Ps. 116:7. Of Jeremiah—Jer. 45:3. Nebuchadrezzar—Dan. 4:4. Disciples—Mt. 26:45; Mk. 14:41.

Rest of soil.—Ex. 23:11; Lev. 25:5; 6: 34, 35.

Of animals.—Ex. 23:12.

Of flocks.—Song of Sol. 1:7.

Of birds.—Dove found no—Gen. 8:9. Night monster finds—Is. 34:14.

Spiritual.—Of Jehovah—Is. 62:1, 7; Zeph. 3:17. Of his wrath—Ez. 21:17; 24:13. Through gospel—II Thess. 1:7; Heb. 4:8. Rest through Christ—See TEACHING OF JESUS, ETERNAL LIFE.

Resting place.—Earthly—Gen. 49:15. Heavenly—Ps. 132:8, 14; Is. 11:10; 66:1; Mic. 2:10; Acts 7:49.

Prophecy of.—Zech. 9:1. See SABBATH.

RESTITUTION. Guilt, For—Num. 5:7, 8. Law of—Lev. 24:18–21; Pr. 6:31; Lu. 19:8. Make—Ex. 22:3; Lev. 5:16. Times of—Mt. 19:28; Acts 3:21. See RESTORE.

RESTLESS. Evil—Jas. 3:8. In complaint—Ps. 55:2.

RESTORE. Deut. 22:1, 2; Ps. 60:1; Heb. 13:19. All things—Mt. 17:11; Mk. 9: 12; Acts 3:21. Brother, A—Gal. 6:1. Fourfold—Lu. 19:8. Hand—Mk. 3:5. Judah—See JUDAH, KINGDOM OF. Kingdom—Acts 1:6. Life—See JESUS, MIRACLES OF. Pledge—Deut. 24:13. Righteousness—Job 33:26. Sight—Mk. 8:25. See BLINDNESS. Soul—Ps. 19:7; 23:3. See RESTITUTION.

RESTRAINT. Is. 23:10; II Thess. 2:6. Compassions are—Is. 63:15. No purpose can be—Job 42:2. One that—II Thess. 2:7. Rain was—Gen. 8:2. Spirit is without—Pr. 25:28. Wind—Pr. 27:16.

RESURRECTION. Anticipation in Old Testament.—Ps. 16:10; 110:1; Is. 26: 19; Dan. 12:2, 13; Hos. 13:14; Heb. 11:35.

Apostles testified concerning it.—Lu. 24:45–48; Acts 1:8, 22; 2:24–32; 4:10, 33; 5:31, 32; 10:39–42; 17:3, 31; 26: 22, 23; I Cor. 15:1–4; II Cor. 4:13, 14; Col. 3:1–4; I Thess. 4:13–17.

The foundation of Christianity.—John 11:25; Rom. 1:3, 4; 6:4–11; 8:11, 19–23; I Cor. 3:10, 11; 15:3, 4; Eph. 2:4–7; Col. 2:12; 3:1.

Jesus staked his claim upon his resurrection on the third day.—Mt. 16:21; 17: 22, 23; 20:18, 19; John 5:21, 25–29; 6:39, 40, 54; 11:23–27.

The sign Jesus gave of His Messiahship: Jonah—Mt. 12:39, 40. The Temple—John 2:18–22.

Scripture proofs of credibility.—Mt. 22: 29–32; Mk. 12:35, 36; Lu. 20:34–38; Acts 26:6–8; Rom. 8:28–34; I Cor. Ch. 15.

Paul's proof drawn from heaven.—Acts 9:3–5; 22:7, 8; 26:14–19; Gal. 1:15–17.

Appearances of Jesus: Mary Magdalene—Mk. 16:9; John 20:18. The women—Mt. 28:9. Peter—Lu. 24:34. Two Disciples—Lu. 24:13–31. Apostles and others, except Thomas—Mk. 16:14; Lu. 24:33–43; John 20:19–24. Apostles with Thomas—John 20:26. Apostles at sea of Galilee—John 21:1 ff. Apostles in Galilee ("Above 500 brethren in all")—Mt. 28:16, 17; I Cor. 15:6. James—I Cor. 15:7. All the apostles (Ascension)—Lu. 24:51; Acts 1:9; I Cor. 15:7. Stephen—Acts 7:55 f. Paul—I Cor. 15:8. John—Rev. 1:18.

Raised by the power of God.—Mt. 26:64; John 10:18; Rom. 1:4; 8:11; I Cor. 6:14; 15:43; II Cor. 5:1; 13:4; Eph. 1:19–21; Phil. 3:9–11; II Tim. 1:8–10.

The power of God produces hope.—Acts 23:6; Phil. 3:10, 11; I Pet. 1:3, 21; 3:21, 22.

Jesus' resurrection the earnest of ours.—Rom. 8:19–25, 32–34; I Cor. 15:54, 57; Phil. 3:10–14; II Tim. 2:11, 12.

The resurrection body.—Lu. 24:39; John 20:27; I Cor. 15:42–54; II Cor. 5:1–4; Phil. 3:21.

The order of the resurrection.—John 5: 29; Acts 24:15; I Cor. 15:20–23; I Thess. 4:15 ff.; Rev. 20:12, 13.

Form of baptism illustrates the resurrection.—Rom. 6:3–11; Col. 2:11–13.

Resurrection of Jesus commemorated on the first day of the week.—John 20: 19–23, 26; Acts 20:7; Rev. 1:10.

Typified by: Isaac—Gen. 22:13, with Heb. 11:19. Jonah 2:10, with Mt. 12:40.

Instances cited (but not resurrections strictly in the class with Jesus): The ruler's daughter—Mt. 9:18–26. Saints at crucifixion—Mt. 27:53. Son of widow at Nain—Lu. 7:14. Lazarus—John 11:44. Dorcas—Acts 9:40. Eutychus—Acts 20:9–12. Old Testament worthies—Heb. 11:35. The Shunammite's son—II Ki. 4:32–37. Man thrown into Elisha's sepulchre—II Ki. 13:20–21.

Resurrection of Jesus not understood by disciples at first.—Mt. 16:21, 22; Mk. 8:31–33; 9:9, 10; 16:14; Lu. 18:31–34; 24:36–43. Afterwards emboldened —Acts 2:14–32; 4:19, 20, 31–33; 26:8–19.

A stumbling block to the Greeks.—Acts 17:32; I Cor. 1:22, 23.

Resurrection of man.—Believed in by the Pharisees—Acts 23:5–8; 24:15; 26:6–8. By the Jews—John 11:24. Denied by the Sadducees—Mt. 22:23–28; Acts 23:6–8.

Errors concerning the resurrection.—I Cor. 15:12–19, 35–42; II Tim. 2:16–18. See JESUS, RESURRECTION OF.

RETAIN. Anger—Jer. 3:5; Mic. 7:18. Sins—John 20:23. Spirit—Eccl. 8:2. Strength, No—Dan. 10:8, 16. Wisdom —Pr. 3:18. Words—Pr. 4:4. See HOLD FAST.

RETURN. Abraham — Heb. 11:15. Ashamed—Ps. 74:21. Benjamin, Tribe of—Ju. 21:14. Children of men—Ps. 90:3. Clouds after rain—Eccl. 12:2. Corruption, To—Acts 13:34. See SIN. David's child—II Sam. 12:23. Days of youth, To—Job 33:25. Dog to his vomit—Pr. 26:11. Dove to the ark—Gen. 8:9, 12. Dust, Unto—Gen. 3:19; Job 10:9; Ps. 90:3; 104:29. See DEATH. Evil for good—I Sam. 25:21. See EVIL, VENGEANCE. Guiltless, And be—Num. 32:22. Israel—Jer. 3:22; 4:1; 15:7; 25:25; Ez. 14:6; Hos. 7:10; 14:2; Mal. 3:7. See JEWS, JUDAH, RESTORATION OF EZRA AND NEHEMIAH IN OUTLINE STUDIES IN THE BOOKS. Jerusalem, To—Neh. 7:6; Lu. 2:45; Acts 1:12; 8:25; 13:13. See JEWS. Jesus—Lu. 4:14. See JESUS. Naked—Job 1:21.

Not—II Sam. 12:23; Job 16:22; 39:4; Pr. 2:19; Mk. 13:16. Obey, And—Deut. 30:8. See REPENTANCE. Paul—Acts 15:36. Prayer—Ps. 35:13. See PRAYERS OF WICKED NOT ANSWERED. Pursuers—Josh. 2:16. Ransomed of Jehovah—Is. 35:10. See JEWS. Sea to its strength—Ex. 14:27. Seventy, The—Lu. 10:17. Shadow backward—II Ki. 20:10. Shepherd of your souls, To—I Pet. 2:25. Shepherds—Lu. 2:20. Spirit, Her—Lu. 8:55. See RESURRECTION. Sun ten steps—Is. 38:8. Vain, None in—Lu. 50:9. Vessels, With empty—Jer. 14:3. Wicked—Ez. 18:23. Word of God—Is. 55:11. See REPENTANCE.

REU, rē'u. **Son of Pelag.**—Gen. 11:18–21; I Chr. 1:25.

REUBEN, reu'ben. *"Behold a Son."* (1) Leah's son, and first born of Jacob—Gen. 29:32; 35:23. Gathered mandrakes for his mother—Gen. 30:15. By virtue of his birthright he was entitled to double portion and preeminence—Gen. 49:3. But because of incest (Gen. 35:22), he forfeits the birthright to sons of Joseph—Gen. 49:4; I Chr. 5:1. Seeks to save Joseph from murder by his brethren—Gen. 37:21–30; 42:22. Offers to stake his two sons' lives for safety of Benjamin—Gen. 42:37. Jacob pronounces benediction on him—Gen. 49:3–4. Reuben had four sons at migration into Egypt—Gen. 46:9. Had many cattle—Num. 32:1.

(2) **Tribe.** — Descendants — Gen. 46:9; Ex. 6:14; Num. 26:5–11; I Chr. 5:1–10. Princes—Num. 7:30; I Chr. 5:6. Encampment—Num. 2:10, 16; 10:18. Part of the tribe rebels against Moses and Aaron—Num. 16:1–3; Deut. 11:6. Stood on Mt. Ebal—Deut. 27:13. Moses blesses—Deut. 33:6. Armies of—Josh. 4:12; I Chr. 5:18–22; 12:37. Cities given to Levites—Josh. 21:7, 36. Builds an altar which gives offence to other tribes—Josh. 22:10–34. Taken captive—I Chr. 5:26. Reubenites had their inheritance East of Jordan, bordering on the Dead Sea—Num. Ch. 34; 34:14; Deut. 3:1–20; Josh. 12:6; 13:15–23; 18:7; 22:9, 10; I Chr. 6:63, 78, 79. Aided other tribes

in the conquest of region west of Jordan — Joshua 1:12-**18**; 22:1-6. Strength when leaving Egypt, 46,500 —Num. 1:20, 21. Strength, when receiving inheritance, 43,730—Num. 26: 7. See ISRAEL.

REUEL, reu'el. (1) **Son of Esau.**—Gen. 36:4, 10–17; I Chr. 1:35, 37.

(2) **A Gadite.**—Num. 2:14.

(3) **Father-in-law of Moses.**—Ex. 2:18. See JETHRO.

(4) **A Benjamite.**—I Chr. 9:8.

REUMAH, reu'mah. **Nahor's concubine.** —Gen. 22:24.

REVEAL. Deut. 29:29; I Sam. 2:27; Mt. 10:26; 11:27. Cause, My—Jer. 11: 20. Flesh and blood hath not—Mt. 16:17. Gates of death — Job 18:2. Glory—Rom. 8:18; I Pet. 4:13; 5:1. Heart—Pr. 18:2. Iniquity—Job 20: 27. Lawless one—II Thess. 2:8. Ready to be—I Pet. 1:5. Righteousness—Is. 56:1; Rom. 1:17. Secrets—Dan. 2:19, 22–29, 47. Thoughts—Lu. 2:35. Wrath, Of—Rom. 1:18. See REVELATION.

REVELATION: The disclosure of heavenly knowledge.—Ps. 119:19, 130; Eph. 1:17-20. Revelation is the self-manifestation of God as the God of a gracious purpose—Eph. 1:9, 10. Inspiration is that divine influence which imparts this manifestation to the human mind—John 16:13. Revelation has to do with the content— II Tim. 3:11–17. Inspiration with the mode of delivery—II Pet. 1:21.

Revelation of God in Christ.—Is. 7:14; Mt. 1:23; John 1:14; 3:16; 14:9, 10; I Cor. 1:24, 30; Eph. 1:9, 10; Rev. 1:1.

Revelation of Christ's glory.—John 17: 4, 5; Rom. 8:18; I Pet. 4:13, 14; 5:1.

Revelation of the Lord Jesus.—II Cor. 12:1-4; II Thess. 1:7. Of the Son of Man—Lu. 17:30.

How revelation came.—Through the prophets—Is. 9:6, 7; Rom. 16:25, 26; I Pet. 1:12. Through the Holy Spirit —Lu. 12:12; John 14:26; 15:26; 16: 13; I Cor. 2:10; Eph. 3:5. Through Jesus Christ—John 8:26; 17:8; Rom. 10:17; I Cor. 1:7, 24; 15:1-4; Gal. 3: 22-26. Through the apostles—Mt. 28: 19, 20; Mk. 16:15, 16; Lu. 12:11, 12; 24:45-49; John 15:27; I Cor. 2:6-16; 14:6; II Cor. 5:19, 20. Through the

gospel—Rom. 1:16, 17.

What revelation does.—Brings to nought human wisdom—I Cor. 1:20-29. Pierces the sinful heart—Acts 2:37. Giveth light—Ps. 119:130. Giveth knowledge of duty—Gal. 2:2. Reveals inheritance of God in Christ—Eph. 1:11-20. Brings truth to babes—Lu. 10:21; I Cor. 1:26-29.

Other revelations.—Of secrets—Deut. 29:29; Pr. 11:13; 20:19; Dan. 2:22, 28, 29, 47; Amos 3:7.

Of judgment.—John 3:18, 19; 8:21-24; 16:7-11; Rom. 2:5. Of wrath—Rom. 1:18; II Thess. 1:7-10.

Man of sin.—II Thess. 2:3-10. See DREAMS, VISIONS, PROPHETS, PROPHECY, REVELATION, BOOK OF, SEE OUTLINE STUDIES IN THE BOOKS.

REVELRY. Amos 6:7; Gal. 5:21; I Pet. 4:3. Day-time, In—II Pet. 2:13. Not in—Rom. 13:13.

REVENGE. See VENGEANCE.

REVENUE. Better than silver—Pr. 8: 19. Great—Pr. 16:8. Harvest was her —Is. 23:3. Wicked, Of—Pr. 15:6.

REVERENCE. Ps. 45:11; Heb. 12:9. Demeanor, In—Tit. 2:3. God—Ps. 111:9; Eccl. 5:2. Haman, To—Esth. 3:2, 5. House of God—Eccl. 5:1. My son—Mt. 21:37; Mk. 12:6; 20:13. Offer service with—Heb. 12:28. Sanctuary—Lev. 19:30; 26:2.

REVILE. Pr. 25:10; Lu. 22:65; I Cor. 4:12; I Tim. 5:14; I Pet. 2:23; 3:9, 6. See REPROACH.

REVIVE. Ju. 15:19; I Ki. 17:22; II Ki. 13:21. Grain, As—Hos. 14:7. Israel— Hos. 14:7. Sin—Rom. 7:9. See SIN. Spirit—Gen. 45:27; Is. 57:13. Stones —Neh. 4:2. Thought of Paul—Phil. 4:10. Work of Jehovah—Hab. 3:2. See LIFE, RESURRECTION.

REVOLT. II Ki. 8:20, 22; II Chr. 21:8, 10; Is. 1:5; 31:6; 59:13; Jer. 5:23; 6:28; Hos. 5:2. See REBELLION.

REWARD: Dispensing of.—God prepares it—Gen. 15:1; Mt. 25:34; I Cor. 2:9; Heb. 11:10, 16.

God and Christ give it.—Is. 40:10; 62: 11; Mt. 25:31-46; Lu. 12:32; Rev. 22: 12.

Ground of.—Dependent on character— Ez. Ch. 18; Mk. 16:16; Rev. 22:12. The righteous—II Sam. 22:21; Ps. 18:

20; 58:11; Mt. 25:34–36, 46; Lu. 6:22, 23, 35; Jas. 1:12; Rev. 2:10. The wicked—Gen. 2:17; 4:6, 7; II Sam. 3:39; Ps. 9:17; Mt. 6:1, 2, 5; 25:41–46; Rom. 2:8; Heb. 2:2, 3; 10:26; I Pet. 4:18; Rev. 22:15.

Reasons for reward.—Boldness—Heb. 10:35. Deeds—Ps. 31:23; Lu. 23:41. Desire for service—I Cor. 9:17, 18; Heb. 11:6. Faithfulness—I Cor. 4:1–4. Faith—Rom. 4:4, 5, 16; Heb. 11:6. Humility—Lu. 14:10, 11. Kindness—Lu. 6:35. Ministering to others—Mt. 25:34–36. Obedience—Ps. 19:11; Pr. 13:13. Patience—Rom. 2:7. Wisdom —Pr. 24:14.

Spiritual reward to be sought for.—Is. 55:6, 7; II John 8. Promise of—Joel 2:28, 29; Mt. 10:42; Mk. 9:41; Acts 2:17–21.

When spiritual rewards are given.—In present life—Mt. 5:4–7; 19:29; Mk. 10:30; Lu. 17:30; John 6:40; 17:2, 3; Rom. 6:23; Heb. 12:28; I John 5:11, 13; Rev. 2:26, 27. In the future life —Mt. 5:8; 16:27; 19:21; Lu. 12:33; 14:13, 14; 18:30; Rom. 2:7, 8; I Cor. 9:25; II Cor. 11:18; 5:1; Jas. 1:12; Rev. 2:7, 10, 17; 3:12, 21; 22:12.

Reward of the worker.—II Chr. 15:7; Jer. 31:16; Dan. 2:6; Rom. 4:4; I Cor. 3:8, 14. A prophet's—Mt. 10:40 f. A disciple's—Mt. 10:42.

No reward for iniquity.—Num. 14:20–23; Ps. 103:10; Pr. 24:20. For the dead—Eccl. 9:5.

Temporal.—To Abraham—Gen. 15:1. To Levites—Num. 18:31. Israel—Lev. 20:22–24. Caleb—Num. 14:24. Ruth —Ruth 2:12. Mordecai—Esth. 6:1–10. David—II Sam. 7:11, 12; Solomon— I Ki. 3:11–13. Disciples—Mt. 5:5.

Features of future.—Glory—Ps. 73:24; Rom. 8:17, 18; II Cor. 4:17; Phil. 3:21; Col. 3:4; I Pet. 5:4. Inheritance— Mt. 5:12; John 14:3; Acts 20:32; 26:18; Rom. 8:17; Col. 1:12; 3:24; Heb. 9:15; I Pet. 1:4; Rev. 21:7. Life— Dan. 12:2; Mt. 19:29; Mk. 10:30; Lu. 17:33; 18:30; John 6:40; I Cor. 15:51. Rest—Heb. 4:9, 10; Rev. 14:13. Eternal life gift of God—Rom. 6:23. See ETERNAL LIFE.

Rewards as bribes.—God declines them —Deut. 10:17. Men decline them—

Abraham—Gen. 14:22, 23. *Moses*— Heb. 11:26. *Samuel*—I Sam. 12:3. *Daniel*—Dan. 5:17. Some desire bribes —*Judas*—Mt. 26:14–16; Mk. 14:10, 11; Lu. 22:3–6; Acts 1:18. See also Ps. 15:5; 26:10; Is. 33:15; 45:13; Amos 5:12. Wages of sin—Rom. 6:23.

Rewards of men.—Just—II Sam. 19:36–38; Mt. 6:3, 5; Lu. 23:41. Evil for good—Gen. 44:4; II Chr. 20:11; Ps. 35:12; Pr. 17:13. Good for evil—I Sam. 24:19; Pr. 25:22; Rom. 12:20, 21. See JUDGMENT, REAPING WHAT WE SOW.

REZEPH, rē′zeph. **A city.**—II Ki. 19:12; Is. 37:12.

REZIN, rē′zin. (1) **King of Syria, slain by Tiglath-pileser.**—II Ki. 15:37; 16:5–9; Is. 7:1–8; 8:6; 9:11.

(2) **One of those who returned with Zerubbabel.**—Ezra 2:48; Neh. 7:50.

REZON, rē′zon. **Son of Eliadab.**—I Ki. 11:23, 24.

RHEGIUM, rhē′gi-um. **A town in Italy.** —Acts 28:13.

RHESA, rhē′sà. **An ancestor of Jesus.** —Lu. 3:27.

RHODA, rhō′dà. **A maiden in the home of Mary mother of Mark, who opened the door for Peter.**—Acts 12:13.

RHODES. An island in the Mediterranean Sea.—Acts 21:1.

RIBAI, rī′bāi. **A Benjamite.**—II Sam. 23:29; I Chr. 11:31.

RIBLAH, rĭb′lah. **A city.**—Num. 34:11; II Ki. 23:33; 25:6, 21; Jer. 39:5, 6; 52:9, 10, 26, 27.

RIBS. Gen. 2:21.

RICHES. See WEALTH, JESUS, TEACHING OF.

RICHLY. Christ dwell in you—Col. 3:16. Poured out upon us—Tit. 3:6. Supplied—II Pet. 1:11. See ABUNDANCE.

RID. Bondage, Out of—Ex. 6:6. Care, Of—Mt. 28:14.

RIDDLE. Ezekiel's—Ez. 17:2. Samson's—Ju. 14:12–19.

RIDE. Deut. 33:26; Job 30:22. Ass, Upon—Ju. 5:10; II Sam. 16:2; 19:26; Ez. 9:9; Mt. 21:5. Caused him to— Esth. 6:11. Chariot, In—II Ki. 10:16; Jer. 51:22. Cloud, Upon—Is. 19:1. Deserts, Through—Ps. 68:4. Heads, Over—Ps. 66:12. Heavens, Upon—

Deut. 33:26; Ps. 68:33. High places, On—Deut. 32:13. Horses, Upon—Jer. 6:23; 50:42. Mule, Upon—I Ki. 1:33, 38, 44. Prosperously—Ps. 45:4. Swift-steeds—Esth. 8:10.

RIDER. II Ki. 18:23. Break in pieces—Jer. 51:21. Come down—Hag. 2:22. Confounded—Zech. 10:5. Ephraim, On —Hos. 10:11. Falleth backward—Gen. 49:17. Horse and—Ex. 15:1, 21; Job 39:18. Smite with madness—Zech. 12:4. See HORSEMEN.

RIGHT. Gen. 20:16; Deut. 32:4; Job 35:2; Amos 5:12; Phil. 1:7. Answered —Lu. 10:28. Check—Mt. 5:39. Clay, Over—Rom. 9:21. Do—Gen. 18:25. Ear—Lu. 22:50; John 18:10. Eat, To —Heb. 13:10. Eye—Mt. 5:29. Giveth to afflicted—Job 36:6. Hand—See HAND. Heart—II Ki. 10:15; Ps. 78:37. In sight of God—Acts 4:19. Mind—Mk. 5:15; Lu. 8:35. Precepts of Jehovah are—Ps. 19:8. Seed—Jer. 2:21. Show—I Sam. 14:41; Job 33:23. Side of boat—John 21:6. Taken away—Job 27:2. Think it—II Pet. 1:13. To become children of God—John 1:12. To come to tree of life—Rev. 22:14. Way —Gen. 24:48; I Sam. 12:23; Pr. 12:15; Hos. 14:9; II Pet. 2:15. Whatsoever is—Mt. 20:4. Word of Jehovah is—Ps. 33:4. See RIGHTEOUS.

RIGHTEOUS. The righteous powerfully influence God—Gen. 18:23-33. God succors and supports—Pr. 2:7, 8. His secret is with them—Pr. 3:32. Their memory is blessed—Pr. 10:7. Likened to a fruitful tree—Ps. 1:3. Are led in pleasant paths—Ps. 23:3. Clothed with garments of salvation—Is. 61:10. Desire to be found in Christ—Phil. 3:9. Are willing to be judged in righteousness—Ps. 35:24. Witnesses testify to righteousness—Heb. 11:4. The Lord's eyes are upon them—I Pet. 2:12.

How to become.—Sow it—Hos. 10:12; Gal. 6:8. Seek it—Zeph. 2:3; Is. 55:6. Follow after it—Pr. 21:21; Heb. 12:14. Hunger for it—Mt. 5:6. Cease to do evil—Is. 1:16, 17. First of all, believe—Heb. 11:6. Believe and be baptized—Mk. 16:16. Change mind and turn—Acts 3:19. Confess the Lord Jesus—Rom. 10:9. Add the Christian graces—II Pet. 1:5-9. See SALVATION.

Evidences.—Dead to sin—Rom. 6:2-7. Freed from sin—Rom. 6:7, 18, 22. Fellow-citizens with saints—Eph. 2:19. Partakers of inheritance—Col. 1:12. New creatures—II Cor. 5:17; Eph. 2:15; 4:24. Imitators of Christ—Phil. 2:5; I John 2:6. Servants of Christ—Eph. 6:6. Servants of righteousness —Rom. 6:19. Sons of God—Rom. 8:14. Children of light—I Thess. 5:5. God's husbandry—I Cor. 3:9. God's building—I Cor. 3:9; II Cor. Ch. 6.

Traits of Character.—Holy and without blame—Eph. 1:4. Kind and tenderhearted—Eph. 4:32. Patient and longsuffering—Col. 1:11. Prayerful—I Tim. 2:1-4; Rev. 5:8. Forgiving—Eph. 4:32. Grounded in love—Eph. 3:17. Abhorring wickedness—Ps. 101:3, 4.

Compared to: Mount Zion—Ps. 125:1, 2. The sun—Ju. 5:31; Mt. 13:43. The stars—Dan. 12:3. To lights—Mt. 5:14; Phil. 2:15. Obedient children—I Pet. 1:14. Lively stones—I Pet. 2:5. Trees —Ps. 1:3; 92:12; 52:8; Jer. 17:8; Hos. 14:6. Salt—Mt. 5:13. A city on a hill —Mt. 5:14. Soldiers—II Tim. 2:3, 4. Sheep—Ps. 95:7; Is. 53:6; Zech. 13:7; Mt. 10:6; John 10:2-26; 21:16; Mt. 9:36; Mk. 6:34; 14:27; I Pet. 2:25. Runners in a race—I Cor. 9:24. Wrestlers—II Tim. 2:5. Members of a body —I Cor. 12:20, 27. Jewels—Mal. 3:17. Wheat—Mt. 3:12; 13:29. Gold—Job 23:10.

Promised.—To shine forth as sun—Mt. 13:43. Shall go into life eternal—Mt. 25:46. Shall be delivered from trouble —Job 5:19-24; 34:15; Pr. 3:25, 26; Is. 41:10-13. Be rescued from temptation—I Cor. 10:13. Given a crown of righteousness—II Tim. 4:8. Wipe away tears and sorrow—Is. 25:8; Rev. 21:4. Be divinely guided—Ps. 25:12; Heb. 13:5, 6. Shall dwell with Christ —John 14:1-5. Names to be written in heaven—Lu. 10:20. Shall inherit the earth—Mt. 5:5. Shall see God—Mt. 5:8. See CHARACTER OF DISCIPLES, under TEACHING OF JESUS, CHRISTIAN GRACES, DISCIPLES.

RIGHTLY. Song of Sol. 1:4. Dividing the word—II Pet. 2:15 (A.V.) Judged

—Lu. 7:43. Named — Gen. 27:36. Teachest—Lu. 20:21.

RIGOR. Ruled with—Lev. 25:46, 53; Ez. 34:4. Serve with—Ex. 1:13, 14; Lev. 25:43.

RIMMON, rĭm'mon. (1) **A rock in Benjamin.**—Ju. 20:45, 47; 21:13.

(2) **A city in Simeon.**—Josh. 15:32; Zech. 14:10.

(3) **A Syrian idol.**—Josh. 19:7; II Ki. 5:18.

(4) **A city.**—I Chr. 4:32.

(5) **A Benjamite.**—II Sam. 4:2–9.

(6) **A city in Zebulun.**—Josh. 19:13; I Chr. 6:77.

RIMMON-PEREZ, rĭm'mon–pē'rez. **An encampment of Israel.**—Num. 33:19, 20. See CAMP, ISRAEL.

RIMS. Ez. 1:18.

RING. See JEWELS.

RINGLEADER. Acts 24:5.

RINNAH, rĭn'nah. **A descendant of Caleb son of Jephuneh.**—I Chr. 4:20.

RIOT. Eph. 5:18; Tit. 1:6; I Pet. 4:4. See STRIFE, TURMOIL.

RIOTOUS. Living—Lu. 15:13.

RIOTOUSLY. Jude 11.

RIPE. Age—Job 30:2. Figs—Song of Sol. 2:13; Nah. 3:12. Grapes—Gen. 40:10; Is. 18:5. Harvest—Joel 3:13; Rev. 14:15. See HARVEST, JUDGMENT.

RIPENESS. Job 29:4.

RI-PHATH, rī'-phath. **Grandson of Japheth.**—Gen. 10:7; I Chr. 1:6.

RISE. Num. 23:24; Lam. 3:63; Lu. 16: 31; Acts 9:6. Against him—Deut. 33: 11; Job 20:27. Brightness of thy—Is. 60:3. Children—Mt. 10:21. Cloud—Lu. 12:54. Contention—Hab. 1:3. Dead, From—Mt. 9:10. Dead in Christ shall—I Thess. 4:16. False prophets—Mt. 24:11. Glean, To—Ruth 2:15. Glory of Jehovah is—Is. 60:1. God—Job 31:14. Israel, Out of—Num. 24: 17. Light, in darkness—Is. 58:10. Murderer—Job 24:14. Nation against nation—Mt. 24:7. No more—Jer. 25:27. Peter—Acts 10:13. Satan hath—Mk. 3:26. Sea—John 6:18. Son of man be —Mt. 17:9. Sun—Mt. 5:45; Mk. 16:2. The third day—Mt. 20:19; Lu. 18:33. Thy brother shall—John 11:23.

RISSAH, rĭs'sah. **An encampment of Israel.**—Num. 33:21, 22. See CAMP, ISRAEL.

RITHMAH, rĭth'mah. **Another encampment of Israel.**—Num. 13:18, 19. See CAMP, ISRAEL.

RIVERS: The four rivers of Eden.—Gen. 2:10–14.

The great river.—Euphrates—Gen. 2: 14; 15:18; Ex. 23:31; Deut. 1:7; 11: 24; Josh. 1:4; II Sam. 8:3; I Ki. 4:21; I Chr. 5:9; 18:3; Ps. 137:1. See EUPHRATES.

The river of Egypt.—The Nile—Gen. 15:18; 41:1, 17; Ex. 1:22; 2:5; 7:1–25; 8:1–11; Is. 11:15; 19:5–8; 23:3; Jer. 2:18; Ez. 29:3–10; Amos 8:8.

The rivers of Damascus.—Abanah and Pharpar—II Ki. 5:12.

The Jordan.—The descender—Gen. 13: 10; 32:10; Josh. 3:17; II Ki. 2:8, 14; 5:14; Jer. 12:5; 49:19; Ps. 114:13; Mt. 3:6; Mk. 1:9. See JORDAN.

The Kishon.—Winding—Ju. 4:7; I Ki. 18:40; Ps. 83:9.

Minor rivers classified.—Of Ahava—Ezra 8:15. Arnon—Deut. 2:36. See ARNON. Chebar—Ez. 1:1, 3; 10:15, 20. Of Ethiopia—Is. 18:1. Gozan—II Ki. 17:6; I Chr. 5:26. Jabbok—Deut. 2: 37; Josh. 12:2. See JABBOK. Of Jotbathah—Deut. 10:7. Of Judah—Joel 3:18. Kanah—Josh. 16:8. Of Philippi —Acts 16:13. Ulai—Dan. 8:16.

Ideal.—Ez. 47:1–12; Rev. 22:1.

Polluted.—Ex. 7:17–25; Rev. 8:10, 11.

Uses of.—For bathing—Ex. 2:5. For baptism—Mt. 3:5, 6, 13–16; Mk. 1: 4–9; Acts 8:36–38; 16:13–15. For cleansing—II Ki. 5:10–12. For commerce—Is. 23:3. For cultivation—Gen. 2:10; Num. 24:6. For drink—Ju. 7:5, 6; Ps. 36:8; Jer. 2:18. For fishing—Lev. 11:9, 10; Ez. 29:5.

Characteristics of.—Fruitful—Num. 24: 6; Ps. 1:3; 46:4; 65:9–11; Is. 32:2, 20; Jer. 17:8; Ez. 31:4–7. Boundary lines —Deut. 1:7; Josh. 22:25; I Ki. 4:24; II Ki. 24:7; I Chr. 5:9; Ps. 72:8; 80:11.

Figurative.—Job 20:17; 29:6; Ps. 36:8; 46:4; 119:136; Pr. 21:1; Is. 32:2; 43: 2; 48:18; Jer. 31:9; Lam. 2:18; 3:48; Ez. 32:2, 14; Mic. 6:7; John 7:38, 39; Rev. 8:10, 11; 22:1.

RIZPAH, rĭz'pah. **Saul's concubine.**—II Sam. 3:7; 21:8–11.

ROAR. Ps. 38:8. Adversaries—Ps. 74:4.

See ENEMIES. Bears, Like—Is. 59:11. Jehovah—Jer. 25:30. Lion—Ju. 14:5; Job 4:10; Ps. 22:13; 104:21; Is. 5:29; Jer. 2:15; 51:38; Ez. 22:25; Hos. 11: 10; Amos 3:4, 8; Zech. 11:3; I Pet. 5:8. Sea—I Chr. 16:32; Ps. 96:11; 98: 7; Is. 5:50; 17:12; 51:15; Jer. 5:22; 6:23; 31:35; 50:42; Lu. 21:25. Voice of enemy — Ps. 74:4; Jer. 50:42. Waters—Ps. 46:3; Jer. 51:55.

ROB. Ju. 9:25; Ps. 119:61; Is. 17:14; Ez. 39:10. Bear—II Sam. 17:8; Pr. 17:12. Children, Of—Lev. 26:22. Churches, Other—II Cor. 11:8. Father or mother—Pr. 28:24. God—Mal. 3: 8, 9. Neighbor—Lev. 19:13. Poor— Pr. 22:22; Is. 10:2. Prize, Of your —Col. 2:18. Temples — Rom. 2:22. Threshing-floors—I Sam. 23:1. Treasures—Is. 10:13. See STEALING, SPOIL.

ROBBER. Ez. 7:22; 18:10; Dan. 11:14; John 10:8. As against a—Mt. 26:25. Barabbas—John 18:40. Jesus crucified with two—Mt. 27:38. Den of— Jer. 7:11; Mt. 21:13. Entereth not by the door is—John 10:1. Fell among —Lu. 10:30.. Israel to—Is. 42:24. Perils of—II Cor. 11:26. Poverty as— Pr. 6:11. Wait as a, In—Pr. 23:28. See STEALING, SPOIL.

ROBBERY. Lev. 6:2, 4; Ps. 62:10; Ez. 22:29. God hates—Is. 61:8. See OPPRESSION. Thought it not—Phil. 2:6 (A.V.). See OPPRESSION, STEALING, SPOIL.

ROBE. Ps. 109:29. David's—I Chr. 15: 27. Festival—Is. 3:22. Instead of a— Is. 3:22. Jonathan's—I Sam. 18:4. King's daughters—II Sam. 13:18. Little—I Sam. 2:19. Saul's—I Sam. 24:4. Scarlet—Mt. 27:28. Skirt of—I Sam. 24:11. Walk in long—Mk. 12:38. Wash —Rev. 22:14. White—Mk. 16:5; Rev. 3:4, 5, 18; 4:4; 6:11; 7:9–14; 15:6; 19:8, 14. See CLOTHING.

ROCKS: Kinds of.—Flint—Job 28:9. Crags—I Sam. 14:4.

Uses of.—To dwell in—Ju. 6:2; 15:8, 13; Job 30:6; Pr. 30:26; Song of Sol. 2:14 (*fig.*). For birds and animals— Num. 24:21. For serpent—Pr. 30:19. To sacrifice upon—Ju. 13:19. Landmarks—Ju. 1:36; Is. 10:26. Cast from rock in punishment—II Chr. 25:12.

Tombs—Mt. 27:60; Mk. 15:46. Memorial—II Sam. 21:10.

Miracles of.—Water from—Ex. 17:6; Num. 20:8, 10, 11; Deut. 8:15; Neh. 9:15; Ps. 78:15, 16, 20; 105:41; 114:8; Is. 48:21. Honey out of—Deut. 32:13. Oil from—Deut. 32:13; Job 29:6. Fire from—Ju. 6:21.

Figurative.—God the Rock—Deut. 32:4, 15, 18, 31; I Sam. 2:2; II Sam. 22:47; Ps. 18:2, 31, 46; 19:14; 27:5; 28:1; 31: 2, 3; 40:2; 42:9; 61:2; 62:2, 6, 7; 71:3; 78:35; 89:26; 92:15; 94:22; 95:1; Hab. 1:12. Salvation—Deut. 32:15; II Sam. 22:47; Ps. 62:2, 7; 89:26; 95: 1; Is. 17:10. Refuge—Deut. 32:37; II Sam. 22:2, 3; Ps. 18:2, 30, 31; 71:2; 94:22. Of strength—Ps. 31:2. Rock of Israel—II Sam. 23:3; Is. 30:29. Everlasting—Is. 26:4. Christ the Rock —I Cor. 10:4. Other figurative uses— Job 14:18; 18:4; 19:24; 24:8; 28:10; Ps. 40:2; Ez. 24:7, 8. Of offense—Is. 8:14; Rom. 9:33; I Pet. 2:8. Of field —Jer. 18:14. *Cf.* Stone of stumbling —Mt. 21:42–46. Of plain—Jer. 21:13. Revelation—Refuge—Rev. 6:15, 16. Faith in Peter's confession called rock —Mt. 16:18. Peter himself called rock —John 1:42. In parable—Foundation of house—Mt. 7:24, 25. Grain on— Lu. 8:6, 13.

Prophecies concerning.—Is. 2:10, 19, 21; 7:19; 33:16; Jer. 4:29; 16:16; 48:28. Dwellers of—Ob. 3. As punishment— Ruin of Tyre—Ez. 26:4, 14. **Man as** the shade of rock—Is. 32:2.

Illustrative.—Power of God—Jer. 23: 29; 49:16; 51:25; Nah. 1:6. Punishment—Amos 6:12. Hardness of—Jer. 5:3.

Miscellaneous.—Moses stood on—Ex. 33: 21, 22. Rocky ground—Acts 27:29. Girdle hidden in—Jer. 13:4. Rocks rent—I Ki. 19:11; Mt. 27:51. See STONE.

ROD. Of Jacob—Gen. 30:37, 38, 39, 41. Of Moses—Ex. 4:2–4, 17, 20; 7:20; 14: 16; 17:9. Of Aaron.—Ex. 7:9–12; Num. 17:26–10; Heb. 9:4. Of God— Job 21:9. Thy rod—Ps. 23:4. Of strength—Ez. 19:11, 12. Rod of iron —Ps. 2:9. Strong rods—Ps. 110:2. Of iron—Rule nations with rod of iron—Rev. 12:5. For back of fools—

Pr. 10:13; 26:3. He that spareth—Pr. 13:24. Rod gives wisdom—Pr. 29:15. Cause to pass under—Ez. 20:37. Hear ye the rod—Mic. 6:9. Beaten with rods—II Cor. 11:25.

ROE. II Sam. 2:18; Song of Sol. 4:5; Is. 13:14. See ANIMALS.

ROEBUCK. Deut. 14:5.

ROGELIM, ro-gē'lim. **A city in Gilead.** —II Sam. 17:27; 19:31.

ROHGAH, rŏh'găh. **A man of Asher.**— I Chr. 7:34.

ROLL, *n.* Book, Of—Ezra 6:2; Ps. 40:7; Jer. 36:2, 4, 6, 14–32; Ez. 2:9; 3:1–3; Zech. 5:1, 2. See BOOKS. Prophecy, Of—Jer. 36:2; Ez. 2:9; Zech. 5:1.

ROLL, *v.* Heb. 1:12. Dust, In the—Mic. 1:10. Garments in blood—Is. 9:5. Reproach—Josh. 5:9. Stone—Gen. 29:3, 8; Josh. 10:18; Mt. 28:2; 15:46; 16:4; Lu. 24:2.

ROMAMTI-EZER, ro-măm'tĭ-ē'zer. **Son of Heman.**—I Chr. 25:4, 31.

ROME: Rule of.—Over the whole civilized world—Lu. 2:1; 3:1; Acts 23:24, 26; 25:1. Power of—John 11:48.

Soldiers of.—Mt. 8:8, 9; 28:11–14; Acts 21:31–36; 23:23, 24; II Tim. 2:4. Italian band (Roman soldiers)—Acts 10:1; 27:1. Criminals delivered to soldiers for execution—Mt. 27:26, 27. Garments given to—Mt. 27:35; John 19:23. Prisoners chained by—Acts 12:6; 21:32, 33; 28:16; II Tim. 1:16.

Rights of Roman citizenship.—Acts 16:21, 37, 38; 22:24, 25–29; 23:27; 25:16.

Games of.—Gladiatorial fights—I Cor. 15:32. Foot races—I Cor. 9:24. Wrestling—Eph. 6:12. Training of combatants—I Cor. 9:25, 27. Rules observed—II Tim. 2:5.

Emperors of. — Augustus — Lu. 2:1. Claudius—Acts 11:28. Nero—Phil. 4:22. Tiberius—Lu. 3:1. Emperor Highest Court of Appeal—Acts 25:11, 12; 26:32. See CAESAR.

Paul visits.—Acts 19:21; 23:11; 28:14. Paul a prisoner of—Acts 28:14–21. Letters written by Paul while in Rome to the Ephesians, Philippians, Colossians, Philemon.

Jews commanded to leave.—Acts 18:2.

Sojourners from.—Acts 2:10. See PAUL. ROMANS, EPISTLE TO—See OUTLINE STUDIES IN THE BOOKS.

ROOF. Josh 2:6, 8. Battlement for—Deut. 22:8. Burned—Jer. 19:13. Mouth, Of—Job 29:10; Ps. 137:6. King's house, Of—II Sam. 11:2. Shadow of—Gen. 19:8. Sinketh in—Eccl. 10:18. Tower, Of—Ju. 9:51. Uncovered—Mk. 2:4. Under my—Mt. 8:8. See HOUSE.

ROOM. Father's house, In—Gen. 24:23. Made—Gen. 26:22. No—Is. 5:8; Mk. 2:2; Lu. 2:7. Upper—Ju. 3:20; I Chr. 28:11; Mk. 14:15; Lu. 22:12; Acts 1:13. See CHAMBER.

ROOT. Job 5:3; 8:17; 28:9. Beareth—Deut. 29:18. Deep—Ps. 80:9. Dried up—Job 18:16. Evil, Of all—I Tim. 6:10. Grounded, And—Eph. 3:17. Had no—Mt. 13:6. Holy—Rom. 11:16. Jesse, Of—Is. 11:10. Out of a dry ground—Is. 53:2. Righteous, Of—Pr. 12:12. Serpent's—Is. 14:29. Shall be as rottenness—Is. 5:24. Trees, Of—Mt. 3:10. Up—Pr. 15:25; Lu. 17:6. Waxeth old—Job 14:8. Withered away from—Mk. 11:20.

ROPE. Ju. 15:13; 16:11; II Sam. 17:13; I Ki. 20:31, 32; Job 41:2; Is. 3:24; 5:18; Acts 27:32.

ROSE, *n.* Is. 35:1. Sharon, Of—Song of Sol. 2:1.

ROSE, *v.* Abraham—Gen. 22:3. Crag—I Sam. 14:5. Damsel—Mk. 5:42. Forsook all and—Lu. 5:28. Jews—Lu. 4:29; Acts 18:12. Matthew—Lu. 5:28. Prayer, From—Lu. 22:45. See RISE.

ROSH, rŏsh. **A son of Benjamin.**—Gen. 46:21.

ROTTENNESS. Is. 3:24; Hos. 5:12; Hab. 3:16. Bones, Of—Pr. 12:4; 14:30. Root shall be as—Is. 5:24. See CORRUPTION, DECAY.

ROUND ABOUT. Job 37:12; Ps. 18:5; Mk. 3:34. Archers compass me—Job 16:13. Chariots of fire—II Ki. 6:17. Dew lay—Ex. 16:13. Enemies—Deut. 12:10. Galilee—Mk. 1:28. Glory of Lord shone—Lu. 2:9. Jesus looked—Mk. 10:23. Jordan—Mt. 3:5. Throne —Rev. 5:11; 7:11.

ROUSE. Jailor, being—Acts 16:27. Sleep, Out of—Job 14:12. Who shall —Gen. 49:9; Num. 24:9.

ROYAL. Apparel.—Esth. 5:1; 6:8; 8:15; Acts 12:2. Cities—See CITIES.

Commandment—Esth. 1:19. Crown—
Esth. 2:17; 6:8. Diadem—Is. 62:3.
Dwelling-place—Dan. 4:30. Estate—
Jer. 10:7; Dan. 1:19. House—Esth.
1:9; 2:16, 51.

RUB. Lu. 6:1.

RUBBISH. Neh. 4:2, 10.

RUBIES. See PRECIOUS STONES.

RUDDER. Acts 27:40; Jas. 3:4.

RUDDY. I Sam. 16:12; 18:42; Song of
Sol. 5:10; Lam. 4:7. See COLORS.

RUDE. In speech—II Cor. 11:6.

RUDIMENTS. Gal. 4:3; Col. 2:8, 20;
Heb. 5:12.

RUE. Mint and—Lu. 11:42.

RUFUS, rū'fus. (1) **A disciple in Rome
whom Paul salutes.**—Rom. 16:13.

(2) **Son of Simon the Cyrenian who bore
Jesus' cross.**—Mk. 15:21.

RUG. Ju. 4:18.

RUHAMAH, ru-hā'mah. **A symbolic
name for Israel.**—Hos. 2:1.

RUIN. II Chr. 28:23; 34:6; Job 30:14;
Is. 3:6. Build again—Acts 15:16.
Flattering mouth worketh—Pr. 26:28.
House built on sand—Lu. 6:49.
Iniquity be your—Ez. 18:30. Per-
petual—Ps. 74:3. Repair—Ezra 9:9.
Strongholds to, Brought his—Ps. 89:
4. Wicked overthrown in—Pr. 21:12.
See DESTRUCTION.

**RULERS OF ISRAEL: God, the author
of power.**—II Chr. 20:6; Ps. 66:7;
89:34–37; Rom. 13:1.

Rulers dependent on God.—II Sam. 22:
30–37; I Ki. 3:7–9; 16:1–4.

Qualifications of.—Deut. 19:9–19; ·II
Sam. 23:3; Josh. 1:8; Pr. 20:8, 28;
28:2, 16; 31:4, 5; Eccl. 10:5–7, 16;
Ez. 45:8, 9; Rom. 12:8.

Required in a king.—Must be a native
—Deut. 17:15. Must not multiply
horses—Deut. 17:16. Nor allow return to Egypt—Deut. 17:16. Nor multiply wives—Deut. 17:17. Copy the
law and keep it—Deut. 17:18, 19. Fear
the Lord—Ps. 2:10, 11. Be faithful
in his office—Ps. 72:1–4; Mt. 25:21.
Rule over his own spirit—Pr. 16:32.
Righteous lips and thrones—Pr. 16:
10, 12, 13. Temperate in habit—Pr.
31:4, 5; Is. 5:22.

Rulers not a terror to good works.—Ex.
18:21; Deut. 16:18–20; II Chr. 19:6,
7; Rom. 13:3–5.

Good.—Joseph—Gen. 41:37–57. Pharaoh
—Gen. 47:5–10. Moses—See MOSES.
David—II Sam. 19:16–39; 21:1–4.
Hezekiah—II Ki. 18:3–6. Josiah—II
Ki. Ch. 22. Cyrus—Ezra Ch. 1. Ar-
taxerxes—Ezra Ch. 7. Nehemiah—
Neh. 2:1–8. Mentioned—Lu. 7:8.
Elders as—I Tim. 5:17. The typical
King—Is. 11:1–5; 33:14–17.

Wicked.—Shall be overthrown—Pr. 14:
11; Is. 24:2, 21. Wrath a death messenger—Pr. 16:14; 19:12. Opposing Jehovah—Ps. 2:2–4. Confiscate property—I Ki. Ch. 21. Enslave a people—
Ex. 1:8–14. Corrupted by intermarriage—I Ki. 11:4–8; 16:31. Encourage
idolatry—Ex. 32:2–6; I Ki. 18:18–40;
II Chr. 15:16. Brutal conduct to enemies—II Ki. 8:12, 13; Esth. Ch. 3;
Dan. 3:19–23; Mt. 2:16–18; 14:1–12;
26:59; Acts 23:2. Indulging in wickedness—I Sam. 15:8, 9; II Sam. 24:2–
10; I Ki. 11:1–4; II Ki. 17:1–12; Pr.
16:12; 25:28; Eccl. 2:1–11. Gifts are
dangerous—Pr. 29:4; Ez. 20:31.
Danger of hearkening to lies—Pr.
29:12; Mic. 2:11.

Corrupt pastors.—Jer. 10:21; 12:10–13;
23:1–4.

False prophets and priests.—I Ki. 18:19–
40; Jer. Ch. 23; 26:1–11; Mic. 3:11;
Mal. 2:1–9. Despise good counsel—
Zech. 7:9–14.

New Testament rulers and their duties.
—See CHURCH, GOVERNMENT, ISRAEL,
JUDAH, KINGS.

**RULERS OF SYNAGOGUE: Whose
duty was to superintend the external
order of public worship.**—Jaïrus—
Mk. 5:22, 35, 36, 38; Lu. 8:41. Ruler
of—Lu. 8:49; 13:14; Acts 13:15. Crispus—Acts 18:8. Sosthenes—Acts 18:
17. See SYNAGOGUE.

RUMAH, rū'mah. **A place**—II Ki. 23:
36.

RUMBLING. Of wheels—Jer. 47:3.

RUMOR. Concerning him—Lu. 4:37.
Shall be upon—Ez. 7:26. Wars, Of—
Mt. 24:6; Mk. 13:7. See GOSSIP,
NOISE, REPORT.

RUN. And not be weary—Is. 40:31.
Apace—Ps. 58:7. Chariots, Before—
II Sam. 8:11. Cup—Ps. 23:5. Down
with tears—Jer. 9:18; 13:17; 14:17.
Feet, to evil—Pr. 1:16. Not in vain—

Phil. 2:16. Over—Lu. 6:38. Race, In —I Cor. 9:24. Wall, Over—Gen. 49: 22. Water—Deut. 12:4. Well—Gal. 5: 7: Word may—II Thess. 3:1.

RUSH, *n.* Job 8:11; 41:20; Is. 9:14; 35: 7; 58:5.

RUSH, *v.* Ju. 9:44; Job 41:29; Is. 17: 12; Nah. 2:4; Acts 19:29. Swine rushed into the sea—Mt. 8:32; Mk. 5:13; Lu. 8:33.

RUSHING. Is. 17:12, 13; Acts 2:2.

RUST. Moth and—Mt. 6:19, 20. Not gone—Ez. 24:6. Gold and silver are —Jas. 5:3.

RUSTLING. Of wings—Is. 18:1.

RUTH, *Friend.* **Daughter-in-law of Naomi.**—Ruth 1:4, 6. Lived in Bethlehem—Ruth 1:19. Refused to leave Naomi—Ruth 1:14, 16–17. Gleans in Boaz's field—Ruth 2:2–3. Boaz recognizes her—Ruth 2:5–9. Presents for consideration a kinsman's duty—Ruth 3:1–9. Boaz submits and marries —Ruth 4:1–13. Obed, a son, is born, who in time begets Jesse, the father of David—Ruth 4:13, 17, 21, 22; Mt. 1:5–6. Ancestress of Jesus—Lu. 3:32. See BOAZ.

SABACHTHANI, sä-băk'thä'nī. **Part of one of Jesus' exclamations.**—Mt. 27: 46; Mk. 15:34.

SABAOTH, săb'a-oth. A title applied to the Lord as Ruler—Ròm. 9:29; Jas. 5:4.

SABBATH, *Shabbath,* to cease.

Called: Sabbath of the Lord—Ex. 20: 10; Lev. 23:3; Deut. 5:14. Sabbath of Rest—Ex. 31:15; 35:2; Lev. 16:31; 23:3, 32; 25:4. Rest of Holy Sabbath —Ex. 16:23. A Holy Day—Ex. 35:2; Neh. 9:14; Is. 58:13.

Four reasons for observance: (1) Day of rest—Gen. 2:2–3; Ex. 20:11. *No sort of work allowed*—Ex. 20:10; Lev. 23:3; Mk. 16:1; Lu. 23:54–56. *No burden to be carried*—Neh. 13:19; Jer. 17:21. *No purchases allowed*—Neh. 10: 31; 13:15–17. *Necessary demands allowed*—Mt. 12:1; Lu. 13:15; 14:1. (2) A deed of mercy: *Servants and stock must rest*—Ex. 20:10; Deut. 5:14. *Works of mercy lawful*—Mt. 12:12; Lu. 13:16; John 9:14. *Made to benefit man* —Mk. 2:27–28. (3) A memorial of the deliverance of the children of Israel

—Deut. 5:15; Jer. 17:21–22. (4) A holy day—Ex. 16:23; 20:8; 31:14–17; 35:2–3; Deut. 5:12–14; Neh. 9:14; Is. 58:13–14; Ez. 44:24. *Scriptures read on* —Acts 13:27; 15:21. *Word of God preached on*—Acts 13:14, 15, 44; 17:2; 18:4. *Religious instruction on*—Mk. 6:2; Lu. 4:16, 31; 6:6; 13:10; Acts 13:14, 42, 44; 15:21; 17:2; 18:4. *Religious works lawful*—Num. 28:9; Mt. 12:5; John 7:23. *Wrong observance of* —Is. 1:13; Ez. 20:13–24; 22:8, 26; 23:38.

Offerings prescribed for.—Lev. 24:8; Num. 28:9, 10; I Chr. 23:31; II Chr. 2:4; Ez. 46:4, 5. Morning and evening sacrifices doubled—Num. 28:9, 10. Shewbread set in order—Lev. 24:8.

As Children of Israel degenerated the sabbath became unpopular.—Amos 8: 5; Jer. 17:21–24.

The observance not approved by Jehovah.—Is. 1:13; Hos. 2:11. Punishment for violation—Ex. 35:2; Num. 15:32–36; Jer. 17:27.

The sabbath profaned.—Ez. 20:13, 16, 21, 24; 22:8, 26; 23:38.

After the captivity Nehemiah restored it.—Neh. 10:29–31. Shuts the gates of the city to prevent traffic on the sabbath—Neh. 13:15–22.

One thousand people massacred rather than profane sabbath.—I Macc. 2:32–41.

Jesus systematically set to work to break traditions.—He is Lord of—Mk. 2:28. His interpretation of—Mt. 12: 1–8; Lu. 6:1–10; 13:10–17; John 7:21–24; 9:14. Performed miracles on—Mt. 12:10–13; Mk. 3:1–5; Lu. 6:1–10; 13: 10–17; John 5:5–14; 7:21–24; 9:1–16. The sabbath was made for man—Mk. 2:27. Man greatest of all—Mt. 12:9–12.

With the establishment of Christianity the sabbath gradually passes away.— Col. 2:14. Paul counsels not to follow a shadow—Col. 2:16–17. See COVENANTS. Used as a symbol of future rest—Heb. 4:9–11.

The Lord's Day (Rev. 1:10), the Christian's holy day.—It was the day our Lord rose from the dead—Mt. 28: 1; Mk. 16:9; Lu. 24:1–3; John 20:1–2. He confirms this as the holy day by appearing upon it—Lu. 24:33-36; John 20:19, 26; 21:12-17. The disciples kept the ordinances on this day—Acts 20:7; I Cor. 11:18-26; 16:2. Justin Martyr (100-150 A.D.) says, ''On the Lord's Day come together and break bread and give thanks'' (Didache).

Other sabbaths.—First and seventh day of feast of the passover and unleavened bread—Lev. 23:7, 8. Day of first fruits—Lev. 23:21. Feast of trumpets—Lev. 23:24, 25. Day of atonement—Lev. 23:32. Feast of tabernacles, first and eighth day—Lev. 25:39. Every seventh year a sabbatical year—Lev. 23:1-4. Every fiftieth year a sabbatical year—Lev. 25:8-13. See LORD'S DAY, DAY, OLD AND NEW COVENANTS.

SABEANS, sa-bē'ans. (1) **Descendants of Seba.**—Is. 45:14; Ez. 23:42.

(2) **Descendants of Sheba the grandson of Abraham.**—Job 1:15; Joel 3:8.

SABTAH, săb'tah. **Son of Cush.**—Gen. 10:7; I Chr. 1:9.

SABTECA, săb'te-cà. **Son of Cush.**—Gen. 10:7; I Chr. 1:9.

SACAR, sā'kar. (1) **Father of one of David's mighty men.**—I Chr. 11:35.

(2) **A Kohathite.**—I Chr. 26:4.

SACK. Lev. 11:32. Benjamin's—Gen. 44:12. Mouth of—Gen. 42:27; 43:21. Opened—Gen. 44:11. Restore money in—Gen. 42:25, 28, 35.

SACKBUT. See MUSIC.

SACKCLOTH: Made of hair.—Rev. 6:12.

Worn in mourning.—By Jacob—Gen. 37:34. Joab and people—II Sam. 3:31. Servants of Benhadad—I Ki. 20:31, 32. Hezekiah, and elders and scribes—II Ki. 19:1, 2; Is. 37:1, 2. David and elders—I Chr. 21:16. Mordecai—Esth. 4:1, 2, 3, 4. Job—Job 16:15. The psalmist—Ps. 35:13. People of Jerusalem—Is. 22:12. People of Moab—Jer. 48:37. Of Zion—Lam. 2:10. Virgin—Joel 1:8. Rizpah put sackcloth upon the rock—II Sam. 21:10. See MOURNING.

Repent in.—Ahab—I Ki. 21:27. King of Israel—II Ki. 6:30. The psalmist—Ps. 69:11. Daniel—Dan. 9:3.

Pertaining to fasts.—Is. 58:5. People of Nineveh—Jonah 3:5, 6. By man and beast—Jonah 3:8. Priests—Joel 1:13. See FASTING.

Loosed sackcloth.—Ps. 30:11; Is. 20:2.

Prophecies concerning.—Is. 15:3. Women of Jerusalem to wear—Is. 3:24; 32:11. Heavens to be covered with—Is. 50:3. Daughter of God's people to wear—Jer. 6:26. Heshbon shall wear—Jer. 49:3. Punishment foretold—Jer. 4:8; Ez. 7:18; 27:31; Amos 8:10; Rev. 11:3.

Figurative.—Ps. 30:11; Is. 50:3; Rev. 6:12.

SACRED. Things—I Cor. 9:13. Writings—II Tim. 3:15. See HOLINESS, CONSECRATION.

SACRIFICE: Offering, designed to express, promote, or restore normal relations with God.—Hence embodies meanings of: (1) Communion, (2) Gift, (3) Propitiation. Communion—Gen. 4:3-5; Num. 22:40; 23:1-6, 14-17, 29-30.. Gift (tribute)—Gen. 8:20; as to a friend—Gen. 32:13-14; as an act of homage—I Sam. 10:27. Propitiation—Job 1:5; 42:7-9.

Sacrifice as old as mankind.—A sign of fellowship with God and self-dedication to Him—Gen. 4:3 ff.; 8:20; 12:7, 8; 13:18; 15:9; 26:25; 28:18; 33:20; 35:14; Num. 22:40; 23:1-6.

Offered by the heathens to their gods (idols).—Acts 7:41; I Cor. 8:4; 10:19 f., 28; Rev. 2:14, 20.

Practised by Abraham.—Gen. 15:9, 10. By Jacob—Gen. 31:54; 46:1. By the Israelites in Egypt—Ex. 12:27, 28.

Sacrifice of human victims.—First-born son (among the Phœnicians)—II Ki. 3:27; 17:31. (Among Israelites)—II Ki. 16:3; 21:6; 23:10; Is. 57:5; Jer. 7:31; 19:5; Ez. 16:20, 21; 23:37.

Mosaic legislation concerning it.—Forbids human sacrifice—Lev. 18:21; 20:2-5; Deut. 12:31; 18:10.

Distinguishes different kinds: Animal sacrifice. — (1) **The burnt-offering:** The universal sacrifice before Moses; adopted into Mosaic system—Ex. 20:24; 29:18, 25; Lev. Ch. 1; Num. 6:11, 14, 16: 7:15-81; Deut. 12:6-27. The daily sacrifice (continual)—Ex. 29:42; Num. 28:3-31; 29:11-38; Neh. 10:33. Doubled on weekly sabbath—

Num. 28:6–12; and on monthly sabbath (new moon), two bulls, one ram, seven lambs—Num. 28:11–15. Daily during passover week, two bulls, one ram, seven lambs—Num. 28:19–24. Daily during Feast of Tabernacles, beginning with thirteen bulls, two rams, fourteen lambs, on the first day; number lessening each day—Lev. 23:36, 37; Num. 29:13–40. With the sheaf of first fruits, a he-lamb—Lev. 23:12. On the Day of First Fruits, two young bulls, one ram, seven lambs—Num. 28:26–31. At Pentecost, one bull, two rams, seven lambs—Lev. 23:18. Or two bulls—Num. 28:27. On Day of Atonement, a ram for the high-priest—Lev. 16:5, 24; a ram for the congregation—Lev. 16:5, 24; and one bull, one ram, seven lambs—Num. 29:8. At consecration of priests, two rams—Ex. 29:15–25; Lev. 8:18–28; and one ram—Lev. 9:1–14. Consecration of Levites—Lev. 9:3, 4, 15–21. For sins of ignorance, one young bull —Num. 15:24, 25. Trespass-offering, for one who hears swearing (a turtledove or young pigeon)—Lev. 5:7–10. For purification of women, one lamb or pigeon—Lev. 12:6, 8. For lepers, one lamb or pigeon—Lev. 14:10, 21, 22, 31. For defilement, one pigeon—Lev. 15:15, 30. For Nazirite's defilement, one pigeon—Num. 6:11. On expiration of vow, one lamb—Num. 6:14, 16. At all festivals—I Chr. 23:31; II Chr. 2:4; 31:3.

Victim must be a male (a bullock, a ram, lamb, or a pair of turtle doves). —Lev. 9:2–14. Without blemish— Mal. 1:8. To be killed before Jehovah, the blood sprinkled upon the altar, and the body cut into pieces and burned completely (*holocaust*)—Lev. 1:3–17; 6:8–13; 9:2–24.

Instances in history.—Offered by Jethro —Ex. 18:12. By Aaron—I Chr. 6:49. Joshua—Josh. 8:31; 22:23–29. Vowed by Jephthah—Ju. 11:31. Offered by Manoah—Ju. 13:16, 23. By the people of Israel—Ju. 20:26; 21:4; I Sam. 6: 14, 15. By Samuel—I Sam. 7:9, 10; 10:8. Saul—I Sam. 13:9–12. David— II Sam. 6:17, 18; 24:24, 25; I Chr. 16: 2, 40; 21:26; 29:21. Solomon—I Ki.

3:4, 5; 8:64; 9:25; II Chr. 1:6; 2:4; 7:7, 8:12. Elijah—I Ki. 18:33, 38. Jehoiada—II Chr. 13:28; 24:14. Hezekiah—II Chr. 29:7–35; 30:15; 31:3. Ezra—3:2–6; 8:35; Job 1:5; 42:8.

(2) **The peace-offering.**—In general—Ex. 20:24; 24:5; 29:28; 32:6; Lev. 10:14; 17:5; 19:5; 22:21; 23:19; Num. 10:10; 15:8; 29:39; Deut. 27:7; Amos 5:22. Victim either male or female, but without blemish—Lev. 3:1; 4:10, 26, 31, 35; *cf.* Num. 6:14, 17, 18; 7:17–88. Of the herd or of the flock—Lev. 3:6. May be a **Thanksgiving-offering**— Lev. 7:11. Accompanied by meal-offering—vs. 12–14; to be eaten on prescribed conditions—v. 15. **Vow** or **Free-will-offering**—Lev. 7:16; to be eaten on prescribed conditions—vs. 17, 18. **Wave-offering**—Ex. 29:26; Lev. 7:30, 34; 8:27; 9:21; 10:14, 15; 14:12; 23:15, 20; Num. 6:20; 18:11, 18. **Heave-offering**—Ex. 29:27, 28; Lev. 7:14, 32; Num. 5:9; 15:19–21; 18: 8, 11, 19, 29; 31:29, 41; Deut. 12:6, 11, 17.

Instances in history: The Passover— Ex. 12:1–24. *Exceptional features:* Use of the blood—Ex. 12:7, 13, 22, 23; 34:25. Flesh eaten by all—Ex. 12:4, 8. Under Joshua—Josh. 8:31; 22:23, 27. During the period of Judges—Ju. 20: 26; 21:4. By Samuel—I Sam. 10:8, 11:15. By Saul—I Sam. 13:9. By David—II Sam. 6:17, 18; I Chr. 16:1, 2; II Sam. 24:25; I Chr. 21:26. By Solomon—I Ki. 3:15; 8:63, 64; II Chr. 7:7. By Ahaz—II Ki. 16:13. Under Hezekiah—II Chr. 29:35; 30:22; 31:2. By Manasseh—II Chr. 33:16. Foreshadowed by Ezekiel in the ideal temple—Ez. 43:27; 45:15, 17; 46:2, 12.

(3) **The sin-offering.**—To be offered for sins committed unwittingly—Lev. 4:2. Either (1) by the high priest—Lev. 4:2–12; (2) by the whole congregation—Ex. Ch. 29; Lev. 4:13–21; Num. 15:22–26; (3) by a ruler—Lev. 4:22– 26; or (4) by one of the common people—Lev. 4:27–35; Num. 15:27–29.

A special feature of the great Day of Atonement.—Ex. 30:10; Lev. 16:2–28.

Victims of.—For a ruler, a he-goat— Lev. 4:25. For an ordinary person, according to his means, a she-goat—Lev.

4:29; a ewe lamb—Lev. 4:32; a turtle-dove or young pigeon—Lev. 5:7 ff.; or a cereal offering—Lev. 5:11. For a priest or a Levite at their consecration, a bullock—Ex. 29:36; Lev. 4:3; Num. 8:8; for the whole congregation, a bullock and a he-goat—Num. 15:24. On the Day of Atonement, a bullock for the priest and two he-goats for the congregation—Lev. 16:3 ff.

Ritual.—Imposition of hands on the victim by the offerer—Lev. 4:4, 29, 33; by representatives when offered in behalf of the congregation—Lev. 4:15. Burning of the victim in part without the camp—Ex. 29:14; Lev. 4:8 ff.; Eating the remainder by the priests when not offered for themselves—Lev. 5:13; 10:16 ff. Regulations regarding the eating—Lev. 6:26, 30. Smearing of the blood on the horns of the altar and pouring of part at the base of the altar—Lev. 4:7, 34; 5:9.

Special occasions for sin-offering.—Lev. 12:6, 8. For cleansing of leper—Lev. 14:13, 19, 22, 31. For removal of ceremonial uncleanness—Lev. 15:15, 30. On the great Day of Atonement—Lev. 16:3-27. On Pentecost—Lev. 23:19. For redemption of vow—Num. 6:11-16. At the Feast of Tabernacles—Num. 29:11-38. At the beginning of the year—Num. 28:15. At the Passover—Num. 28:22.

Historic instances.—Upon the consecration of Aaron and his sons—Lev. 8:2, 14. By Aaron for the people—Lev. 9:2-22. By the princes of the tribes—Num. 7:16, 22, 28, 34, 40, 46, 52, 58, 64, 70, 76, 82, 87. Under Hezekiah—II Chr. 29:21, 24. Under Ezra—Ezra 8:35. Nehemiah 10:33. For the purification of the virgin Mary—Lu. 2:22-24. The law of, violated by Eleazar—Lev. 10:16-19.

(4) **The trespass-offering** ("Guilt-offering," *marg.*).—For guilt contracted through ceremonial uncleanness—Lev. 5:2, 3; Num. 6:12; or through rash swearing—v. 4.

Law of: Lev. 5:7, 15-18. To be offered by the priests—Num. 18:9.

Victim: A ram without blemish—Lev. 5:15; 6:6.

Ritual: Slaying of victim and disposition of the body—Lev. 7:2-10.

Special features: Compensation for damages, accompaniment—Num. 5:7, 8; I Sam. 6:17. Special trespass-offering for a leper when cleansed—Lev. 14:12-24. For a case of fornication—Lev. 19:21, 22.

Instances in history.—Called for with the ark from the Philistines—I Sam. 6:3-8. Provided for by Jehoiada—II Ki. 12:16. In the ideal temple of Ezekiel—Ez. 40:39; 42:13; 44:29. Foreshadowed by Ezekiel in the ideal temple service—Ez. 40:39; 42:13; 43:21-25; 44:27-29; 45:17-25; 46:20.

Vegetable sacrifices: The meal-offering: (a) of fine flour—Lev. 2:1-3; (b) of baked cakes—vs. 4-10; (c) of first fruits (grain in the ear)—vs. 14-16. Prohibition of leaven in—vs. 11-13; *cf.* Lev. 6:14-17. Not an independent sacrifice, but accompaniment of animal sacrifices. Hence, for historical instances, see "Burnt-offering," "Peace-offering," "Sin-offering," above.

Memorial offering.—Lev. 2:2, 9, 16; 5:12; 6:15; Num. 5:15, 18, 20.

Jealousy offering (oblation).—To be used upon the rise of suspicion, as a test of a woman's fidelity in the marriage relation—Num. 5:11-31.

First-fruits.—*Cf.* Offerings and Oblations.

Showbread, Not an altar-sacrifice. See OFFERINGS AND OBLATIONS.

Tithes, Not an altar sacrifice.—*Cf.* Offerings and Oblations, also TITHES.

Liquid sacrifices.—Drink-offerings (libations): Consisting of wine ("Fourth part of an hin for a lamb"), Accompaniment of every public burnt-offering, *i.e.* the daily (continual) burnt-offering—Ex. 29:40. The additional burnt-offering on the sabbath, the new moon and festival days—Lev. 23:13, 18, 37; Num. 28:9, 14; 29:18-38; *cf.* Num. 15:24. Offered in the holy place—Num. 28:7.

Consisting of water, accompaniment of the morning (burnt) offering during the week of the Feast of Tabernacles—Num. 29:12-38.

Odor sacrifices.—Savor-offering: Usually the odor of the burnt sacrifice—Gen. 8:21; Ex. 5:21; 29:18, 25, 41; Lev. 1:9, 13, 17; 2:2, 9, 12, etc.; possibly more generally of all sacrifice—Lev. 26:31; 37:29; 40:27. See SAVOR, SWEET.

Incense, The odor of burning—Ex. 37: 29; 40:27; Lev. 16:7, 17, 18, 35, 40, 46, 47. Offered on a special altar—Ex. 30:7; 31:8; 35:15; 37:25; 40:5; I Chr. 28:18. Accompanying the daily sacrifice—Num. 4:16; 7:14–80; II Chr. 13: 11; Lu. 1:10, 11. The offering of it a function of the priesthood—Ex. 30: 7; I Sam. 2:28; I Chr. 6:49; II Chr. 2:4; 13:11. A symbol of all worship —Rev. 8:3, 4; Ps. 66:15; 141:2; Is. 60:6. See INCENSE.

Offered unlawfully by Uzziah—II Chr. 26:16. By idolatrous worshippers in the temple in Ezekiel's day—Ez. 8:11; 23:41.

Omission to offer regarded as sin—II Chr. 29:7; Ez. 16:18.

Apart from pure heart unacceptable— Is. 1:13; Jer. 6:20.

Fire-offering.—Offered by fire. See BURNT-OFFERING.

Spiritual meaning of sacrifice.—Consecration of the heart—Deut. 33:19; Ps. 27:6; 51:17, 19; 107:22; 119:108; 141: 2; Eph. 5:2; Phil. 2:17; 4:18; Heb. 11:4; 13:15, 16; I Pet. 2:5; Hos. 15:2 (*Lit.* "Bullocks"); Rom. 12:1. Hence, right heart preferred to sacrifice—I Sam. 15:22; Ps. 40:6; 50:8–15; 69:31; Prov. 21:3, 27; Is. 1:12–17; Jer. 7:22, 23; Hos. 6:6; Amos 5:24–27; Mt. 9: 13; Mk. 12:33; Acts 7:42, 43.

Unacceptable.—Pr. 15:8; Is. 61:8; Jer. 6:20; Hos. 8:13; 9:4; Amos 5:21, 22; Mal. 1:10; 2:13.

Figurative.—Ez. 39:17; Zeph. 1:7; Ps. 51:17; Jer. 33:11; Rom. 12:1; Phil. 4:18; Heb. 13:15.

Remissness in.—Strange fire—Lev. 10:1, 2. Slow in presenting—Neh. 13:10–12. Defrauded Jehovah—Mal. 3:8. Gave their worst—Mal. 1:8, 13. Presented to idols—Ez. 20:28. Abhorred because of sin—I Sam. 3:14; Ps. 51:16; Mt. 5:23–24. Sons of Eli—I Sam. 2:12–17.

Sacrifice in the New Testament.—Offered by Zacharias—Lu. 1:9. Offered for the child Jesus—Lu. 2:22–24.

Allusions of Jesus to—Mt. 5:23; 8:4; 9: 13; 12:7; 23:18–20; Mk. 1:44; 12:33, 34; 14:12–15; Lu. 22:7–13, 37.

Jesus, the great sacrifice.—Foreshadowed in the O. T.—Is. Ch. 53; Acts 8:32; Rom. 4:25; Heb. 9:28; I Pet. 2:22–25. Needed none for Himself—Heb. 7:27. Offered Himself as a sacrifice—Heb. 9:14, 26. Once for all — Heb. 7:27; 9:25–26. Proposes thus to draw all men to Him—John 12:32. Superior to all other sacrifices —Heb. 9:13, 14, 23. Obtained thus eternal redemption—Heb. 9:12. Supersedes all others—Heb. 7:11, 15–19; 8: 1–13; Col. 2:14; Eph. 2:13–16.

Allusions by Paul—I Cor. 9:13; 10:18.

Pagan (idol sacrifice).—Golden calf— Acts 7:41. Other idolatrous sacrifices —I Cor. 8:4; 10:19, 20, 28; Rev. 2:14, 20.

Attempt to offer sacrifice to the apostles —Acts 14:13, 18. See PRIESTS, OFFERINGS, ALTAR.

SADDLE. See HARNESS.

SADDUCEES: Origin of name.—Very uncertain, though now generally derived from the proper name Zadok, followers of Zadok. Derivation from word meaning "righteous" now given up by most scholars.

Priestly extraction.—Not all priests were Sadducees, but all Sadducees were priests.

Aristocrats.—The Pharisees had more sympathy with the people, up to a certain extent. But the Sadducees were distinctly aristocratic. They belonged to the high priestly class (chief priests).

Connection with Sanhedrin.—In the time of Christ they formed a majority of the Sanhedrin and the high priests. Annas and Caiaphas were Sadducees. They held the power that remained to the Jews.

Sympathy with Hellenism.—They succeeded the priestly Hellenizing party of Jason and Menelaus and favored adoption of Greek customs in opposition to the Pharisees.

Origin.—Their first appearance was in connection with John Hyrcanus I (B. C. 135–105) whom they won away from the Pharisees because of their more liberal attitude. A bitter fight ensued between Pharisees and Sadducees for power. Now one side, now the other, was victorious. But finally the Romans robbed the Jews of political rule. Then Pharisees remained the chief ecclesiastical teachers (scribes), while the Sadducees held the reins of ecclesiastical power (priests).

Teachings.—They were more political than religious, cared nothing for the oral traditions of the Pharisees. They denied the resurrection of the body (Mt. 22:23; Mk. 12:18; Lu. 20:27; Acts 4:1, 2; 23:8). They did not believe in angels or spirits (Acts 23:8). They denied foreordination or fate (Josephus, Ant., xiii., v., 9; War, ii., viii., 14).

Denounced by John the Baptist.—(Cf. Mt. 3:7) as no better than the Pharisees. Joined with the Pharisees in embassy to John the Baptist (John 1:19).

Hated the Pharisees.—They sat with Pharisees in the Sanhedrin, but were ready for an explosion on occasion. Cf. Acts 5:34–39; 23:7–10.

Rejected and persecuted Jesus.—Mentioned by name in the Gospels on but three occasions, but really meant by chief priests (and Pharisees) as in John 7:32, 45; 11:47; Mt. 21:45. Sadducees aroused against Christ much later than the Pharisees and largely on political ground. They hate the Pharisees, but Jesus more. So they finally join with their old enemies against Jesus in tempting him with a demand for a sign from heaven—Mt. 16:1. They tried to arrest Jesus at the Feast of the Tabernacles—John 7:32, 45. The raising of Lazarus from the dead angered the Sadducees (chief priests) very much—John 11:47. Caiaphas (a Sadducee) offers a solution of the problem of Jesus, his death for personal and political reasons—John 11:48–50. They were enraged by the triumphal entry and entrance into the temple itself—Mt. 21:15. The cleansing of the temple angers them again so that they challenge the authority of Jesus—Mt. 21:

23; Mk. 11:27 f.; Lu. 20:1 f. They seek to catch Jesus in a tangle about the resurrection—Mt. 22:23; Mk. 12:18; Lu. 20:27. The Pharisees rejoice at the defeat of the Sadducees—Mt. 22:34. They take a leading part in the condemnation of Jesus by the Sanhedrin, being a majority of the body. Cf. Annas and his treatment of Jesus—John 18:13; 19:19. Caiaphas was chief prosecutor — Mt. 26:57, 63, 65. They are active in the charges before Pilate—Mt. 27:12; Mk. 15:3. They stir the multitude to ask for Barabbas instead of Jesus—Mt. 27:20; Mk. 15:11. They mock Jesus on the cross—Mt. 27:41; Mk. 15:31; Lu. 23:35. They join with the Pharisees in demanding a guard over the body of Jesus—Mt. 27:62. They use bribery on the Roman guard to conceal the fact of the resurrection of Jesus—Mt. 28:11.

Condemned by Jesus.—Along with the Pharisees (Mt. 15:6, 12), unworthy to have the kingdom of God—Mt. 21:43, 45. As in great error about the resurrection in the case of Jesus—Acts 4:1 f. Filled with jealousy at the success of the apostles — Acts 5:17. Wished to kill them after Peter's speech—Acts 5:33. Result apparently led to conversion of some Sadducees —Acts 6:7 (priests), though not all priests were Sadducees.

Oppose Paul.—Before the Sanhedrin Paul took the Pharisaic view of the resurrection and arrayed against him the Sadducees in the body—Acts 23:6 ff.

SADNESS. Gen. 40:6. Countenance—I Sam. 1:18; Neh. 2:2; Eccl. 7:3; Mt. 6:16. Look—Gen. 40:7; Lu. 24:17. Spirit—I Ki. 21:5. See SORROW.

SADOC, sā′dok. **An ancestor of Jesus.** —Mt. 1:14.

SAFE. See SALVATION, TEMPORAL.

SAFEGUARD. I Sam. 22:23.

SAFETY. Acts 27:34. Children far from —Job 5:4. Dwell in—I Sam. 12:11; Ps. 16:8. Horse vain thing for—Acts 27:34. Peace and—I Thess. 5:3. See SALVATION, TEMPORAL.

SAIL. Lu. 8:23; Acts 13:4; 18:21; 20:3; 21:1; 27:1; 28:10. See SHIPS.

SAILORS. Acts 27:27.

SAINTS. I Sam. 2:9. Holy ones—Job

5:1; 15:15; Ps. 16:3; 31:23; 34:9; 37:28; 50:5; 52:9; 79:2; 145:10; 148: 14; 149:9; Pr. 2:8; Dan. 7:21, 25; Hos. 11:12; Zech. 14:5.
Congregation or assembly of.—Ps. 89: 5, 7. Preserve or deliver—Ps. 97:10. Saints rejoice—II Chr. 6:41; Ps. 30:4; 132:9, 16; 149:1, 5. Death of—Ps. 116:15. To possess kingdom—Dan. 7: 18, 22, 27.
Christians.—Mt. 27:52; Acts 9:13, 32, 41; 26:10; Rom. 1:7; 16:2; I Cor. 1:2; II Cor. 1:1; Eph. 1:1, 15, 18; 2:19; 3: 8, 18; 5:3; Phil. 1:1; Col. 1:2, 4, 26; II Thess. 1:10; Philemon 5; Rev. 11:18; 13:7, 10; 14:12; 19:8; 20:9. Salute— Rom. 16:15; Heb. 13:24; II Cor. 13: 13; Phil. 4:22. Intercession for—Rom. 8:27; Eph. 6:18. Churches of—I Cor. 14:33. Ministering unto—Rom. 12: 13; 15:25, 26, 31; I Cor. 16:1, 15; II Cor. 8:4; 9:1, 12. Perfecting of—Eph. 4:12. Inheritance of—Col. 1:12. Christ coming with—I Thess. 3:13; Jude 14. Washed feet of—I Tim. 5:10. Faith delivered unto—Jude 3. Blood of— Rev. 16:6; 17:6; 18:24. Prayers of— Rev. 5:8; 8:3, 4. See DISCIPLES.
SAKE. Rom. 11:28. Became poor, For your—II Cor. 8:9. Blessed me for thy —Gen. 30:27. Bought for my—Mt. 10: 18. Brethren and companions'—Ps. 122:8. Cursed for thy—Gen. 3:17. Deal gently for my—II Sam. 18:5. Elect's—Mt. 24:22. Fools for Christ's —I Cor. 4:10. Forgiven, For your— II Cor. 2:10. Forty's, For—Gen. 18: 29. For whose, Christ died—I Cor. 8:11. Glad for your—John 11:15. Life, for my—Mt. 10:39. Loving-kindness, For — Ps. 6:4. Speak evil falsely for my—Mt. 5:11. Stomach's, For—I Tim. 5:23. Truth's, For—II John 2. Works, For very—John 14:11.
SALAMIS, săl′a-mis. **A city of Cyprus.** —Acts 13:5.
SALECAH, săl′e-kah (A.V. SALCAH). **A city in Gad.**—Deut. 3:10; Josh. 12:5; 13:11; I Chr. 5:11.
SALEM, sā′lem. **The city of Melchizedek.**—Gen. 14:18; Ps. 76:2; Heb. 7: 1, 2.
SALIM, sā′lim. **A city near Ænon where John the Baptist was baptizing.**—John 3:23.

SALLAI, săl′lāi. (1) **A Benjamite.**— Neh. 11:8.
(2) **A priest who returned with Zerubbabel.**—Neh. 12:20.
SALLU, săl′lu. (1) **'A priest who returned with Zerubbabel.**—Neh. 12:7.
(2) **A Benjamite.**—I Chr. 9:7; Neh. 11:7.
SALMA, săl′má. **Son of Caleb the son of Hur.**—I Chr. 2:51, 54.
SALMON, săl′mon. (1) **Father of Boaz, ancestor of Jesus.**—Ruth 4:20, 21; I Chr. 2:11; Mt. 1:4, 5; Lu. 3:32.
(2) **A mountain in Samaria.**—Ps. 68:14.
SALMONE, sal-mō′ne. **A promontory in Crete.**—Acts 27:7.
SALOME, sa-lō′me. (1) **Wife of Zebedee and mother of James and John**— Mt. 27:56. Desires chief places for her sons—Mt. 20:21. Witnesses the crucifixion—Mk. 15:40. Among first at the tomb—Mk. 16:1. See MARY.
SALT: A quality of value.—II Ki. 2:20, 21; Mt. 5:13; Mk. 9:50; Col. 4:6.
Covenant of.—Lev. 2:13; Num. 18:19; II Chr. 13:5.
Sacrifice of.—Lev. 2:13; Ezra 6:9; 7:22; Ez. 43:24; Mk. 9:49.
Tasteless salt.—Job 6:6; Mt. 5:13; Mk. 9:50; Lu. 14:34.
Deserted to salt.—Ez. 47:11; Zeph. 2:9.
City of.—Josh. 15:62; Ju. 9:45. Land of —Jer. 17:6.
Valley of.—II Sam. 8:13; II Ki. 14:7; I Chr. 18:12; II Chr. 25:11.
Pillar of (Lot's wife).—Gen. 19:26.
Sea of.—Gen. 14:3; Num. 34:3, 12; Deut. 3:17; Josh. 3:16; 12:3; 15:2, 5; 18:19.
SALUTATIONS: Customary in earliest ages.—Abraham—Gen. 18:2. Of Lot— Gen. 19:1.
Were given.—By brethren to each other —I Sam. 17:22; Acts 18:22; 21:7, 19. By Pharaoh to Jacob—Gen. 47:7, 8. By David to 200 men—I Sam. 30:21. By passers-by—I Sam. 10:3, 4; Ps. 129:8. On entering a house—Ju. 18: 15; Mt. 10:12; Lu. 1:40, 41, 44. Through messengers—I Sam. 25:5, 14; II Sam. 8:10. By letter—Rom. 16:5, 7, 9–16, 21–23; I Cor. 16:19, 21; II Cor. 13:13; Phil. 4:21, 22; Col. 4:10, 18; II Thess. 3:17; II Tim. 4:19; Tit. 3:15; Philemon 23; Heb. 13:24; I Pet. 5:13; III John 14.

Denied to persons of bad character.—
III John 10.

Urgent business excused one from giving.—II Ki. 4:29; Lu. 10:4.

In derision.—II Sam. 20:9; Mt. 26:49; 27:29.

Occasionally accompanied by.—Falling on the neck and kissing—Gen. 33:4; 45:14, 15; Lu. 15:20. Laying hold of the beard with the right hand—II Sam. 20:9. Jacob bowed seven times—Gen. 33:3. Embracing and kissing of the hem of the garment—Mt. 14:36. Falling prostrate on the ground—Esth. 8:3; Mt. 2:11; Lu. 8:41. Licking the dust—Ps. 72:9; Is. 49:23.

The Pharisees condemned for seeking salutation in public.—Mt. 23:7; Mk. 12:38.

The Jews were condemned for not saluting enemies.—Mt. 5:47.

Embracing and kissing the feet of Jesus.—Mt. 28:9; Lu. 7:38, 45.

Formulæ of salutations.—''Peace be unto thee''—Ju. 19:20. ''Peace be unto thee, and peace be to thy house, and peace be unto all that thou hast''—I Sam. 25:6. ''Jehovah be with you,'' ''Jehovah bless thee''—Ruth 2:4. ''Peace be to this house''—Lu. 10:5. ''The blessing of Jehovah be upon you, we bless you in the name of Jehovah''—Ps. 129:8. ''Blessed be thou of Jehovah''—I Sam. 15:13. ''God be gracious unto thee''—Gen. 43:29. ''Is it well with thee?''—II Sam. 20:9. ''Hail''—Mt. 26:49; Lu. 1:28. ''All hail''—Mt. 28:9. See SALUTATIONS in the EPISTLES.

SALVATION.—IN THE OLD TESTAMENT:

NATIONAL SALVATION FROM ENEMIES.—Deut. 21:8; 32:15; 33:29; I Sam. 2:1; 10:19; II Sam. 3:18; 7:23; 22:28, 36; II Ki. 14:27; I Chr. 16:23, 35; Neh. 1:10; 9:19–31; Ps. 14:7; 17:7; 18:27; 20:5–9; 33:2; 44:7; 60:5; 67:2; 68:19, 20; 69:35; 70:4; 72:4; 74:12; 77:15; 78:22; 80:3; 98:1–3; 106:4; 107:2, 13; 136:24; Is. 12:2, 3; 17:10; 25:9; 43:1, 9–12; 44:24; 45:8, 17, 20, 22; 46:13; 49:25; 59:1, 11; 62:11, 12; Jer. 3:23; Hos. 7:13; 13:4, 10; Mic. 6:4; Lu. 1:71.

Deliverance from captivity.—Ps. 106: 42–47; Jer. 8:20; 15:20; 23:1–4; 29: 12–14; 30:10, 11; 31:4–12; 42:11, 12; 46:27, 28; Ez. 36:21–38; 39:23–29; Hos. 1:7; Mic. 4:10; Zeph. 3:17–20; Zech. 8:7, 8, 13–15.

Deliverance from bondage in Egypt.—Ex. 6:6–8; 14:13, 30; 15:4–19; Deut. 7:8; 9:26; 13:5; 15:15; 24:18; I Sam. 10:18; II Sam. 7:23; I Chr. 17:21; Ps. 80:8–19; 106:7–11, 21, 22; Neh. 9:9–15; Mic. 6:4; Jude 5.

Salvation in time of war.—Num. 10:9; Deut. 20:4; II Ki. 19:32–34; Neh. 9: 24, 27–31; Ps. 44:7; Is. 37:35. Instances of—Gideon—Ju. 6:12–24, 36–40; 7:1–25; By Samuel—From the Philistines—I Sam. 7:4–11; 9:16; From the Ammonites—I Sam. 11:13; Jonathan's victory over the Philistines at Michmash—I Sam. 14:6–23, 39, 45, 46; David and Goliath—I Sam. 17:32, 53; 19:5; David at Pasdammim—I Chr. 11:14; By Jehoshaphat from Moab and Ammon—II Chr. 20:17–23.

PERSONAL SALVATION FROM ENEMIES.—Ps. 37:39, 40; 40:16; 71:1–5, 15, 23; 72:13, 14; 91:16; 109:31; 119:81, 123; 121:1–8; Pr. 20:22; Jer. 17:14; Mic. 7:7. For David—II Sam. 4:9; 22:3, 4, 36, 46–49; I Ki. 1:29; Ps. 3:8; 7:10; 9:14; 13:5; 18:2, 3, 35, 46; 21:5; 25:5; 27:1, 9; 28:8; 34:6; 35:3, 9; 38:22; 62:1, 2, 7; 69:13, 18, 29; 86: 13, 16; 103:4; 109:26; 138:7; 140:7; 144:10.

EQUIVALENT TO PERSONAL RIGHTEOUSNESS.—II Chr. 6:41; Ps. 132:9, 16; 149:4; Is. 61:10.

Salvation conditional.—Ex. 15:26; Lev. 26:3–8, 14–20; Deut. 7:12–26; 11:13–15; 28:1–68; I Ki. 3:14; 15:1–6; Ps. 106:7–47; 145:20; Is. 59:115; Jer. 3: 23–25; Ez. 3:17–21; 18:19–32; 33:1–19; 39:23, 24.

God the Author.—I Sam. 2:9; II Sam. 14:14; I Chr. 16:35; Ps. 3:7, 8; 28:8, 9; 31:5, 16, 23; 33:18–22; 37:1–40; 41: 1–4; 68:18–20; 71:23, 24; 74:12; 76:8, 9; 85:9–12; 97:10; 107:2–7; 118:14; 121:7, 8; 145:20; 149:4; Pr. 2:8; Jer. 29:14; 31:4–12; Ez. 39:23–29; Jonah 2:9; Hab. 3:8.

Delivers from Egypt—Ex. 3:7–17; 6: 2–8; 15:2–19; Is. 19:20.

God called a Redeemer—II Sam. 4:9; I Ki. 1:29; Job 19:25; Ps. 19:14; 78: 35; Pr. 23:11; Is. 41:14; 44:6, 24; 47: 4; 54:5, 8; 60:16; Jer. 50:34.

God called a Savior—II Sam. 22:3; Ps. 106:21; Is. 43:3–21; 45:15, 21, 22; 60: 16; 63:8, 9; Jer. 14:8; Hos. 13:4.

SALVATION FROM SIN; OR, THE CONSEQUENCES OF SIN: Under the Jewish dispensation—Gen. 49:18; Job 13:16; Ps. 24:5; 34:18; 50:23; 51:12, 14; 65:5; 85:4, 7, 9; 86:2; 91: 16; 95:1; 96:2; 107:9; 116:13; 118:14, 15, 20–25; 119:41, 155, 166, 174; 145: 19; Is. 1:18; 26:1; 35:4; 50:2; 52:7– 10; 59:16, 17; 63:1–5, 8, 9; 64:1–8; Lam. 3:22; Mic. 7:7.

Prophecies concerning salvation through Christ—Is. 35:8; 45:17; 47:12, 13; 49: 6–11; 51:5, 6; 52:7–10, 13–15; 55:1–7; 59:16, 17; 60:18; 62:1, 2, 11, 12; 63:4, 8, 9; Zech. 9:9; Mal. 4:2.

In the New Testament prior to the death of Jesus—Mt. 1:21; 9:12, 13; 18:11–14; Mk. 2:17; Lu. 1:69, 77; 2: 30–32, 38; 3:6; 5:30–32; 7:36–48; 8:12; 15:1–10; 19:9, 10; John 3:16, 17; 4:22; 5:34; 12:47.

After the death of Jesus—Acts 2:47; 4:10–12; 5:31; 10:43; 13:23, 26, 38, 39, 47; 16:17; Rom. 5:8; 10:9, 10; 11:11– 26; I Cor. 3:15; II Cor. 2:15; Eph. 1: 13; I Tim. 1:15; Heb. 5:9; I Pet. 1:8– 12; 3:5; 4:14; Jude 3; Rev. 5:9; 7:10; 14:3, 4; 19:1.

Salvation for all men.—Lam. 3:31–38; Ez. 18:1–32; 33:10–20; Joel 2:32; Mt. 18:12–14; Lu. 2:10, 31; John 1:7, 9; 3:16, 17; 4:14; 7:37; 10:16; 12:47; Acts 10:34, 35; Rom. 5:15–20; 10:11– 15; II Cor. 5:14, 15; Eph. 3:9; I Tim. 2:3, 4; 4:9, 10; Tit. 2:11; II Pet. 3:9; I John 2:2; Rev. 22:17.

Blessing to all men through seed of Abraham—Gen. 12:3; 18:18; 22:18; 26:4; Rom. 4:16–25; 9:6–33. Blessing through Christ—Ps. 72:17; Acts 3:25, 26; Gal. 3:8, 14, 27–29.

Prophecies concerning a world-wide gospel—Ps. 2:8; 22:27; 98:2, 3; Is. 52: 10. Jesus a light to the Gentiles—Is. 42:6; 49:6; 60:1–3. See Lu. 2:32; Acts 13:47.

The gospel to be preached to all men— Mt. 28:19, 20; Mk. 16:15, 16; Lu. 24: 47; Acts 1:8; Col. 1:5, 6, 23.

To the Jew first.—Mt. 10:5, 6; 15:24; John 4:22; Acts 3:25, 26; 10:34–37; 13:26, 32, 33; Rom. 1:16; 2:9–11; 3: 1, 2; 9:3–33; 15:8, 9.

Beginning at Jerusalem—Is. 2:3; Mic. 4:2; Mt. 23:37; Lu. 13:34; 24:47; Acts 1:8.

Salvation through Jesus rejected by the Jews.—Mt. 11:20–24; 13:57, 58; 23: 37; Mk. 6:3–6; Lu. 13:34; 19:14; John 1:11; 5:15, 16, 36–47; 8:37–59; Acts 7:51–54; 13:26–29, 46; 18:5, 6; 28:24– 28; Rom. 11:11; I Thess. 2:14, 16.

Jesus a stone of stumbling to those who reject Him—Is. 8:14; Lu. 2:34, 35; 20: 17, 18; Rom. 9:31–33; I Cor. 1:22, 23; I Pet. 2:6–8.

Parables concerning the rejection of Jesus by the Jews:
The Vineyard—Mt. 21:33–46; Mk. 12:1–10; Lu. 20:9–19. The Marriage Supper—Mt. 22:1–10; Lu. 14:16–24. The Prodigal Son—Lu. 15:11–32. The Rich Man and Lazarus—Lu. 16:19–31.

The Gospel sent to the Gentiles.—John 10:16; Acts 28:28; Rom. 2:9–11; 3:29, 30; 10:12; 11:17–25; 15:6–29; I Cor. 1:22–24; Eph. 2:11–17; I Thess. 2:16.

Gentiles are Abraham's seed—Rom. 4: 16–25; 9:6–9, 30–33; Gal. 3:1, 8, 14, 27– 29.

Gospel sent to the Samaritans—Acts 8: 1–25. To the Ethiopian eunuch—Acts 8:26–40. To Cornelius—10:1–48; 11: 1–18.

Paul an apostle to the Gentiles—Acts 9:15; 13:42, 46–49; 14:27; 18:5, 6; 22: 17–21; 26:16–18, 20, 23; Rom. 1:13–16; Gal. 1:15, 16, 22–24; Eph. 3:6–8; Col. 1:21–27; I Thess. 2:14–16; I Tim. 2:4– 7; II Tim. 4:17.

Conferences in Jerusalem — Acts 11:1– 18; 15:1–31; 21:17–26; Gal. 2:1–16.

Prophecies concerning—Is. 9:1, 2 (Mt. 4:14–16); Is. 11:1, 10 (Rom. 15:12); Ps. 118:22; Is. 28:16 (Mt. 21:41–44); Is. 42:1–7 (Mt. 12:14–21); Is. 49:6, 22 (Lu. 2:30–32); Is. 54:3; 55:8 (John 10:16); Is. 61:9; 62:2; 65:1; Hos. 1: 10; 2:23 (9:24–26); Amos 9:11, 12. See Acts 15:16, 17; Rom. 10:20; I Pet. 2:10.

Salvation conditional: In the Old Testament.—Ps. 34:14–19; 50:23; 85:9; 86: 2; 145:19; Lam. 3:25; Joel 2:32.

For the righteous only—Ps. 118:15; 119: 155; Is. 55:6, 7; 64:5–7; Jer. 3:19–25; Ez. 18:1–32; 33:10–20.

In the New Testament: Before the death of Jesus.—Mt. 7:13, 14; 18:3; 23:37; 25:31–46; John 5:40; 7:34; 8:12; 10:9.

Man must hear, believe, repent, and obey —Deut. 18:19; Mt. 10:32–39; 13:15; Lu. 6:46–49; 8:12; John 1:12; 3:3–19; 5:24; 6:28, 29, 40, 44, 45, 47; 20:30, 31.

Must practise self-denial, be unselfish, bear the cross—Mt. 19:23–30; 25:31– 46; Mk. 10:23–31; Lu. 9:23–26; 14: 26, 27; 16:10–17; 18:24–30.

The rich young ruler — Mt. 19:16–22; Mk. 10:17–25; Lu. 18:17–24.

Instances of conditional salvation.—*The Paralytic*—Mt. 9:1–7; Mk. 2:1–12; *The sinful woman in the Pharisee's house* —Lu. 7:36–50; *Zacchæus the Publican* —Lu. 19:1–10; *The Woman taken in adultery*—John 8:1–11.

Parables concerning conditional salvation.—The Sower—Mt. 13:1–23; Mk. 4:1–20; Lu. 8:4–15; The Tares—Mt. 13:24–30, 36–43; The Net—Mt. 13:47– 50; The Laborers in the Vineyard— Mt. 20:1–16; The Two Sons—Mt. 21: 28–32; The Wedding Supper—Mt. 22: 1–14; The Lost Sheep, the Lost Coin, and the Lost Boy—Lu. 15:1–31; The Rich Man and Lazarus—Lu. 16:19–31; The Pharisee and the Publican—Lu. 18:9–14; The Pounds—Lu. 19:12–27; Ten Virgins—Mt. 25:1–13; The Talents—Mt. 25:14–30.

After the death of Jesus.—Acts 2:37, 38; 3:19; 9:6; 10:33, 48; 11:14; 16:30– 33; 22:10, 16; Rom. 10:9, 10; Heb. 2: 2, 3; 12:24, 25; 13:4; I Pet. 3:21.

The wicked shall not inherit the kingdom of heaven—I Cor. 6:9, 10; Eph. 5:3–6; Col. 3:5–10; Jas. 5:1–6; I Pet. 4:1–16. See MAN MUST BELIEVE, CONFESS, REPENT, AND OBEY.

The judgment—Mt. 8:11, 12; 10:11–15; 12:36, 37; 16:24–27; 25:31–46; Mk. 6: 10, 11; 8:34–38; Lu. 10:10–12, 16; John 5:24–30; 12:47–50; Rom. 2:6–16; I Cor. 3:8; II Cor. 5:10; Heb. 10:28– 31; Rev. 2:23; 22:10–15.

God the Author. — Ps. 3:8; 34:16–22; 37:1–40; 76:8, 9; 103:2–4; 111:9; 118: 14; 132:16; 145:20; Pr. 2:6–20; Is. 46: 13; 52:10; Jer. 3:23; Mt. 10:28; Lu. 1:68; 3:6; John 6:44, 45, 63–65; Jas. 4:12; Rev. 7:10; 19:1; Called Saviour—Is. 45:15, 21, 22; Lu. 1:47; I Tim. 1:1; 2:3; 4:10; Titus 1:3; 2:10; 3:4; Jude 25; Sends His Son to redeem men—Lu. 2:30–32; John 3:27– 36; 17:4; Acts 4:26; II Cor. 5:18–21; Gal. 4:1–7; II Tim. 1:8–10; Heb. 6:17– 20; To do His will—Mt. 26:39, 42; John 4:34; 5:30; 6:38, 40; Heb. 5:5– 10; To die for mankind—Mt. 26:39, 42; John 3:14–17; 10:18; 14:28–31; 18:11; Rom. 3:24, 25; 8:3; Phil. 2:5– 11; I John 4:9–11.

God loves men.—Pr. 3:12; Jer. 32:18; Mt. 5:43–45; Lu. 6:35; 12:6, 7; Rom. 8:38, 39; 11:28, 29; II Cor. 13:11; Eph. 2:4–7; I Tim. 2:3, 4; Tit. 3:4–7; Heb. 12:6; II Pet. 3:9, 15.

God's love for Israel—Deut. 4:37; 7:8, 12, 13; 10:15; 23:5; Is. 63:7–9; Jer. 31:3; Mal. 1:1–5.

God so loved the world that He gave His only begotten Son—John 3:16, 17; Rom. 5:8; I John 3:1, 16; 4:7–16.

God is merciful.—Deut. 4:31; Ps. 69:13; 98:3; 107:1; 111:4; 116:5; 130:7, 8; 136:4, 8, 26; 145:8, 9; Is. 63:9; Lam. 3:22, 23; Dan. 9:4, 9; Lu. 1:50, 54, 68–72; Rom. 2:4; 15:9; I Cor. 7:25; II Cor. 4:1; Tit. 3:5; Jas. 5:11; I Pet. 1:3–5; 2:10; II Pet. 3:15.

God's mercy conditional—Ex. 20:6; 34: 6, 7; Num. 14:18, 19; Deut. 5:10; 7:9– 11; II Chr. 30:9; Ps. 62:12; 106:17, 18; Is. 55:7; Joel 2:12, 13.

God's mercy in spite of transgressions —Neh. 9:17–31; Ps. 78:38; 86:5, 15; 103:7–16; 106:6–46; Jer. 3:12; Lu. 6: 35–37; Rom. 11:30–32; I Tim. 1:13, 16; Heb. 8:12. *Parables concerning*—The Good Samaritan—Lu. 10:25–37; The Two Debtors—Lu. 7:36–47.

God plans man's salvation.—I Cor. 2:7– 9; Gal. 4:1–5.

The wicked husbandmen—Mt. 21:33–42.

Sends His Son to save—John 3:14–34; 4:34; 5:36; 6:38; 10:18; 17:4; 19:30; Acts 2:23; I John 4:7–14.

Prepares a place for His children—Mt. 20:23; Mk. 10:40; Heb. 11:16.

Plans before the foundation of the world
—Mt. 25:34; Rom. 16:25; Eph. 1:3–14;
3:1–11; II Thess. 2:13, 14; II Tim.
1:9, 10; Tit. 1:2, 3; II Pet. 1:10–12,
18–20; Rev. 13:6.

Foretells through His prophets—Is. 35:
1–10; 45:21; 46:10; 49:8 (II Cor. 6:2);
53:1–12; Dan. 9:20–27; Mt. 5:18; Lu.
24:25–27, 44–47; Acts 3:18, 21–26; 17:
2, 3; 18:28; 26:6, 22, 23; Rom. 3:21;
16:25, 26. *That the seed of David
should sit on his throne*—II Sam. 7:12,
13; Is. 9:6, 7 (Acts 2:25–30, 34, 35;
13:23; Rom. 1:1–3). *"Thou art my
Son, this day have I begotten Thee"*—
Ps. 2:7 (Acts 13:32, 33). *The stone that
the builders rejected*—Ps. 118:21–23;
Is. 28:16 (Mt. 21:42; Mk. 12:10, 11;
Lu. 20:17–19; Acts 4:11; Rom. 9:32,
33; Eph. 2:20; I Pet. 2:6–8). *A light
to lighten the Gentiles*—Is. 9:1, 2; 42:
6–9; 49:5–11 (Mt. 4:15, 16; Lu. 2:30–
32; Acts 13:47; 26:16–18, 23). *The
coming of John the Baptist*—Is. 40:3–
5; Mal. 3:1–3 (Mt. 3:3; 11:10; Mk.
1:2, 3; Lu. 3:4–6; 7:27; John 1:23).
The coming of Elias—Mal. 4:5 (Mt.
11:14; Mk. 9:11–13; Lu. 1:16, 17). See
Foreordination, Covenants, Prophets, inspiration of the, Prophecies
concerning Jesus. See *Mystery of
Godliness or God's Plan,* Foreordination, Calling, Election.

Man is saved through Jesus Christ.—
Mt. 1:21; Lu. 4:16–21; 24:44–47; John
3:14–17; 5:34–40; 12:47; Acts 3:26;
4:10–12; 10:43; 13:38, 39; 15:11; Rom.
5:15–21; 8:1–3, 10; 11:26, 27; I Cor.
6:11; Gal. 1:4; 2:20; 3:26–29; Eph.
5:2; I Thess. 1:10; 5:9; I Tim. 1:15;
3:16; II Tim. 2:10; 3:15; Heb. 2:1–3;
5:9, 10; II Pet. 2:20; I John 3:5; 4:
9, 10; 5:11, 12.

Christ came to save sinners—Mt. 9:13;
Mk. 2:17; Lu. 5:30–32; 19:10.

Jesus is called: The Author of salvation
—Heb. 2:10. The Bread—John 6:33–
56. The Door or Way—John 10:9; 14:
6; Heb. 10:20. Our High Priest—Zech.
6:13; Heb. 2:17; 4:14–16; 7:1–28; 8:1–
4; 10:21, 22. *Anointed and called of
God*—Heb. 3:1, 2; 5:4, 5. *After the
order of Melchizedek*—Ps. 110:4; Heb.
5:6, 10; 6:20; 7:15–17. *Offers Himself

as a sacrifice*—Heb. 7:27; 9:11–14, 23–
28. *Typified by Melchizedek*—Gen. 14:
18–20. *By Aaron*—Ex. 40:12–15. The
Lamb—John 1:29, 36; I Pet. 1:19;
Rev. 7:10, 17; 12:10, 11; 14:4; 21:23,
27. The Life—John 11:25, 26; 14:6;
Col. 3:4. The Light — Mt. 4:12–16;
John 1:4–12; 8:12; 9:5; 12:35, 36, 46;
Acts 13:47. The Mediator—Gal. 3:19,
20; I Tim. 2:5, 6; Heb. 8:6; 9:15, 24;
12:24. The Passover—I Cor. 5:7. The
Redeemer—See Rom. 8:34; Eph. 2:13;
3:11, 12; Heb. 7:24–27; 9:24. The
Resurrection — John 11:25. The Saviour—Lu. 2:11; John 4:42; Acts 5:
31; 13:23; Eph. 5:23; Phil. 3:20, 21;
I Tim. 2:3–6; Tit. 1:4; 2:13; 3:3–7;
II Pet. 1:1, 11; 2:20; 3:2, 18; I John
4:14. *Prophecies concerning Jesus as a
Saviour*—Is. 9:2; 42:6, 7; 49:6–12; 53:
4–6, 8–11; 59:20; 61:1–3, 10, 11; Dan.
9:26; Zech. 9:9. The Truth—John
14:6.

Reconciles man to God—Rom. 5:6–11;
II Cor. 5:17–21; Eph. 2:13–18; Col.
1:20–22; Heb. 2:9–18.

Man saved by the life of Jesus.—John
14:19; Rom. 5:10; 8:17; II Cor. 1:7;
4:10, 11; Phil. 3:10; Heb. 7:25–28; I
Pet. 5:1. By His Example—Mt. 11:29,
30; John 8:46; 13:15; Rom. 15:1–5;
Phil. 2:5–8; I Pet. 2:21; 4:13; I John
2:6.

Man saved by the death of Jesus.—Dan.
9:26; John 3:14–17; 10:15, 17, 18; 12:
31–34; Rom. 5:6–15; 8:34; 14:8, 9;
I Cor. 1:17, 18, 23, 24; 2:2; II Cor.
4:10, 11; 5:14, 15; 13:4; Gal. 1:4; 2:
20; 3:1; 6:14; Eph. 2:13–18; Phil. 2:
5–11; 3:10; II Tim. 2:11, 12.

In Fulfilment of the Scriptures—Lu.
24:25–27; Acts 3:18; 17:2, 3; 26:22,
23. Christ died to redeem Man—Is.
53:4–12; I Cor. 5:7; 6:20; 7:23; Gal.
4:4, 5; I Thess. 1:10; I Pet. 1:18–21;
II Pet. 2:1; I John 2:2; 3:16; 4:10;
Rev. 5:9; 13:8. See Sacrifices.

The life of Christ a ransom—Mt. 20:28;
Mk. 10:45; I Tim. 2:6. See Redemption.

Christ gave his life for mankind—John
6:51; 10:11, 15; 11:49–53; 15:13; Rom.
4:25; 5:6–9; 8:3, 32; 14:15; II Cor.
5:14–21; Gal. 3:1, 8, 13, 14; Eph. 5:2,
25; I Thess. 5:9, 10; Tit. 2:13, 14;

Heb. 2:9–18; 7:24–27; 9:11–17, 25–26; I Pet. 2:21–24; 3:18.

Christ's death for the remission of sins —Dan. 9:24; Lu. 24:44–47; Acts 5:30. 31; Rom. 4:25; 5:6–8; 6:3–11; I Cor. 15:1–3; Gal. 1:4; Heb. 1:3; 7:27; 9: 14, 26–28; 10:12; I Pet. 2:24; 3:18.

Man reconciled to God through the death of Jesus—Dan. 9:24; Rom. 5:10, 11; Eph. 2:13–23; Col. 1:20–22; 2:14. See FOREORDINATION.

Man saved by the blood of Jesus.— Christ's blood shed for the remission of sins—Mt. 26:28; Mk. 14:24; Rom. 3:25; Eph. 1:7; Col. 1:14; Heb. 9:11– 14; 13:12; I John 1:7; Rev. 1:5; 7:14, 15.

Redemption through His blood—Rom. 3: 24, 25; Eph. 1:7; Heb. 9:12–15; I Pet. 1:18–20.

Christ purchased with His blood—Acts 20:28; I Cor. 6:20; 7:23; II Pet. 2:21; Rev. 5:9.

Man reconciled through Christ's blood— Rom. 5:9, 10; Eph. 2:13; Col. 1:20– 22; Heb. 10:19–22. See RECONCILIA- TION.

Man saved by the resurrection of Christ. —Acts 3:26; Rom. 4:25; 10:9; 14:8, 9; I Cor. 15:12–19; I Thess. 4:14; I Pet. 1:21.

Salvation by the gospel.—Mk. 13:10, 11; 16:15, 16; John 5:34; 6:33–45; 20:31; Acts 2:22–42; 8:5, 12–14, 30–38; 9:15; 14:21–27; 16:14–17; 19:1–5; 26:15–23, 31; Rom. 1:15–17; 2:16; 15:16, 19–21; I Cor. 1:17–24; 15:1–4; Gal. 1:6–16; 3:8; Eph. 2:13–17; 3:6–8; Phil. 1:27– 29; I Thess. 2:2–16; II Thess. 2:10–15; I Tim. 2:4; II Tim. 1:10; 2:25; I Pet. 1:12, 25; II John 9.

Called Good Tidings—Is. 40:9–11; 52: 7; 61:1; Nah. 1:15; Mt. 11:5; Lu. 4: 18–19, 43; 8:1; Rom. 10:15; Heb. 4:2.

Words or sayings—Mt. 4:4; Mk. 8:31; Lu. 9:26; 24:44–48; John 8:31, 32, 37, 51; 12:48–50; 15:3; 17:6–8, 14, 17, 20; 20:31; Acts 4:4, 29–37; 6:4, 7; 8:4, 14, 25; 10:22, 36–44; 11:1, 14, 19; 12:24; 13:5–12, 15–49; 14:3, 4; 15:7; 16:6–14, 29–34; 17:11; 19:10, 18–20; 20:24, 32; Rom. 18:8–10, 14–17; I Cor. 2:4, 5, 13; II Cor. 4:1–5; 5:19; Eph. 1:13; 5:25, 26; Phil. 2:15, 16; Col. 1:5, 6, 23; I Thess. 1:5–8; II Thess. 3:1; Heb. 2:

2–4; 6:4–6; I John 2:5, 7, 14; Rev. 1:2, 9; 6:9; 20:4. A sword—Eph. 6:17; Heb. 4:12. Words of Life—John 6:63, 68; 12:48–50; Acts 5:20; Phil. 2:16. *Shall not pass away*—Mk. 13:31; Lu. 21:33.

Parable of the Sower—Mt. 13:3–9, 18– 23; Mk. 4:3–9, 14–20; Lu. 8:5–15.

Begotten of the gospel—I Cor. 4:15; I Thess. 2:11; Philemon 10; Jas. 1:18, 21; I Pet. 1:3, 33. See Lu. 8:11; John 3:3–8.

The gospel revealed to the apostles.— Mt. 11:25; 13:11; 16:17; 19:11; Gal. 1:11, 12, 15, 16. By the Holy Spirit— Mt. 10:19, 20; Mk. 13:11; Lu. 12:12; 21:15; 24:49; John 14:26; 16:13; Acts 2:2–4; 15:28; I Cor. 2:4, 5, 10–16; 14: 6; Eph. 1:16, 17; 3:1–6; I Tim. 4:1; I Pet. 1:12; II Pet. 1:20, 21; I John 2:20, 27.

The Holy Spirit directs the movements of the apostles in the preaching of the gospel.—Acts 8:29, 39; 10:19; 11:12; 13:2–4; 16:6–10.

The Holy Spirit confirms the preaching of the gospel with signs and wonders. —Acts 2:38, 43; I Cor. 12:4–11; Eph. 4:7, 8; Heb. 2:4. See HOLY SPIRIT, GIFTS OF.

The power of the Spirit promised—Mk. 16:17, 18; Lu. 24:49; Acts 1:8; 2:16–20.

Instances of: *The Lame Man*—Acts 3: 2–10. *In Solomon's porch*—Acts 4:30– 36; 5:12–16. *By Stephen*—Acts 6:8. *By Philip*—Acts 8:6. *By Paul*—Acts 19:11; Rom. 15:18, 19; I Cor. 2:4; II Cor. 12:12; I Thess. 1:5. *By Paul and Barnabas*—Acts 14:3; 15:12. See Gos- PEL; JESUS, DISCOURSES OF.

Man must believe.—Lu. 8:12, 13; John 1:7; Acts 13:38, 39; 15:7–9; 11:20; I Cor. 1:21; Gal. 3:8; Eph. 2:8; II Thess. 2:12, 13; I Tim. 4:10; Heb. 10:39; 11: 6; I Pet. 1:9; I John 3:23.

He that disbelieveth is condemned—Mk. 16:16; John 8:24.

He that believeth hath eternal life— John 5:24; 6:47; 11:25, 26; *On, or in, Jesus*—John 3:14–18, 36; 6:29, 40; Acts 10:43; 16:31; 19:4; Rom. 10:10– 17; Gal. 2:16–20; 3:22; Eph. 1:13; 3: 11, 12; Phil. 1:27–29; 3:9–11; I Tim. 1:13, 14; I John 5:10, 13; *In the name of Jesus*—John 1:12; I John 3:23; 5:

13; *That Jesus is the Christ*—John 20: 31. *That God hath raised Him from the dead*—Rom. 10:9; I Cor. 15:12–17. See FAITH.

The commandments of the gospel must be obeyed.—Acts 5:29–32; 6:7; Rom. 1:5; 2:8; 6:16–18; 16:19, 26; II Cor. 9:13; 10:5, 6; Gal. 5:7; II Thess. 1:7–10; Heb. 5:8, 9; Jas. 1:22–25; I Pet. 1:14, 22; 4:17; I John 2:5. The words of Jesus or the will of God—Mt. 7: 21–27; 12:50; Lu. 6:46–49; 8:21; John 8:51; 14:23, 24; 15:10, 14; Rev. 1:2, 9; 3:8. The gospel commandments—Mt. 28:19, 20; Mk. 16:15, 16; Lu. 24:26, 47; Acts 2:37–42; 8:12, 13, 36–38; 9:6, 18; 10:33–35, 47, 48; 16:14, 15, 30–33; 19: 1–5; 22:10, 16.

Obedience the test of love and faith— Mt. 7:16–27; Gal. 5:6; Heb. 11:1–40; Jas. 2:14–26. See OBEDIENCE.

Salvation by faith in Christ without the works of the Mosaic law.—Acts 13: 38, 39; Rom. 3:20, 21, 27–30; 4:1–25; 9:30–33; Gal. 2:16–21; 3:10–14, 19–29; Eph. 2:8–10; Phil. 3:8–10. Circumcision not necessary—Acts 15:1–21, 28; Rom. 2:25–29; 3:29, 30; 4:9–13; I Cor. 7:18, 19; Gal. 2:1–16; 5:1–6, 11–15; 6: 12–16; Phil. 3:2–7; Col. 3:11. See CIRCUMCISION.

Calling on the name of the Lord.—Joel 2:32; Acts 2:21; Rom. 10:13.

Confession of faith in Christ as the Son of God necessary.—Lu. 9:26; Rom. 10: 9, 10; II Cor. 9:13; Phil. 2:11; I Tim. 6:12; Heb. 3:1; 4:14; 10:23; I John 2:22, 23; 4:2, 3, 15; II John 7. See John 9:22; 12:42.

Christ will confess those who confess Him—Mt. 10:32, 33; Mk. 8:38; Lu. 12:8, 9; II Tim. 2:12.

Instances of: *Christ's confession*—Mt. 26:63, 64; 27:43; Mk. 14:61, 62; Lu. 22:67–70; I Tim. 6:13. *Confession of the angels*—Lu. 1:32–35; 2:11. *By John the Baptist*—John 1:29–34. *By the man with the unclean spirit*—Mk. 1:24; Lu. 4:34. *By the unclean spirits* —Mk. 3:11. *By the Gadarene demoniacs*—Mt. 8:29; Lu. 8:28. *By disciples in the boat*—Mt. 14:33. *By Nathaniel* —John 1:49. *By Peter*—Mt. 16:16; Lu. 5:8; 9:20; John 6:68–69. *By Martha* —John 11:27. *By the blind man*—

John 9:35–37. *By Thomas*—John 20: 28. *By the eunuch*—Acts 8:37 marginal. *By Paul*—Acts 9:20. See CONFESSION.

Repentance essential to salvation.— Taught by John the Baptist—Mt. 3:2, 3, 7–11; Mk. 1:4, 5; Lu. 3:3–14; Acts 13:24; 19:4.

By Jesus—Mt. 4:17; Mk. 1:15; Lu. 13: 3–5; 16:30; 24:47.

Jesus calls sinners to repentance—Mt. 11: 20–24; 12:41, 42; Lu. 10:11–15; 11:32. *Jesus compares ancient cities with the cities of His day, and condemns those of His time*—Mt. 21:28–32; Lu. 5:30–32; 15:3–32.

By the apostles—Mk. 6:12; Acts 2:38; 3:19; 5:31; 8:22; 11:18; 17:30; 20:21; 26:20; Rom. 2:4; II Cor. 7:9–11; 12: 21; II Tim. 2:25; Heb. 6:1; II Pet. 3:9; Rev. 9:20, 21; 16:9–11.

Repentance for, or unto, remission of sins.—Mk. 1:4, 5; Lu. 3:3; 24:47; Acts 2:38; 3:19. See REPENTANCE.

Baptism required.—Taught by John the Baptist—Mk. 1:8; 11:30–33; Lu. 7:29, 30; 20:4–8; John 1:26–28, 31, 33; Acts 3:23; 10:40; Acts 1:5, 22; 10:37; 11: 16; 18:25; 19:3, 4.

The baptism of Jesus—Mt. 3:13–17; Mk. 1:9–11; Lu. 3:21.

Unto repentance for the remission of sins—Mt. 3:6–11; Lu. 3:3, 7, 10–14.

By Jesus—Mt. 28:19; Mk. 16:16; John 3:22, 26; 4:1, 2.

By the disciples of Jesus after His death —Acts 2:38, 41; 8:12, 13, 36–38; 9:18; 16:14, 15, 33; 18:8; 19:3–5; Rom. 6:3–17; I Cor. 1:13–17; Eph. 4:5; Col. 2: 12; Heb. 10:22; I Pet. 3:21.

Into the name of Jesus—Acts 2:38; 8: 12; 19:3–5.

In water—Mt. 3:11; Mk. 1:5, 8, 9; John 1:26, 31, 33; Acts 8:36–38; 10:47; 19:5. See BAPTISM.

SALVATION OF SAINTS. Acts 15:11; Rom. 13:11; II Cor. 1:6; 6:2, 3; 7:10; Gal. 1:4; Eph. 4:30; 6:17; Phil. 1:19; 2:12; 3:8–14; I Thess. 5:9; II Thess. 2:13; II Tim. 3:15; Heb. 2:10; 5:9; 6:9; 9:28; Jas. 1:21; I Pet. 1:3–11; II Pet. 3:15; Jude 3; Rev. 7:10; 12:10.

Called eternal life—Mt. 25:46; Mk. 10: 17; John 5:24–30; 6:40, 44, 47, 51, 58, 68; 10:28, 29; 11:26; 17:2, 3; 20:30,

31; Rom. 5:21; 6:22, 23; II Tim. 1:10; Tit. 1:2; 3:7; I John 2:25; 3:14; 5:11, 13, 20. See LIFE, ETERNAL.

Called an inheritance—Mt. 25:34; Mk. 10:17; Acts 20:32; 26:18; Rom. 8:17; Gal. 3:29; 4:7; Eph. 1:11, 14, 18; 5:5; Phil. 3:11, 12; Col. 1:12; 3:24; I Thess. 2:12; II Tim. 2:12; Tit. 3:7; Heb. 1: 14; 6:12; 9:15; I Pet. 1:4; Rev. 21:7. See INHERITANCE.

Salvation conditional.—Mt. 7:13, 14, 21–27; 12:36, 37; 25:31–46; Lu. 6:46–49; 13:23–30; John 3:16–19, 36; 8:21, 24, 51; 11:25, 26; 20:30, 31; Rom. 2:6–16; 14:10–12; I Cor. 3:8, 15; 10:12; II Cor. 5:10, 19–24; 7:10; Gal. 5:4, 7; 6:7, 8; Phil. 2:12–16; 3:11–14; I Thess. 5:1–11 Heb. 2:2, 3; 4:1–10; 5:9; 6:9; 9:28; 10:25–29; I Pet. 1:17–23; 4:18; II Pet. 1:2–11; I John 1:7; 5:10–12; Rev. 2:23; 20:12? 21:27; 22:12–15.

Disciples must bear fruit—Mt. 7:16, 20; 12:31–35; Lu. 6:44; John 15:5–8.

Must endure—Mt. 10:22; 24:13; Mk. 13: 13; Rom. 11:22; I Cor. 9:24–27; 10:13; 15:2; Col. 1:23; II Tim. 2:12; Heb. 3:6, 14; 4:14; 10:35–39; Jas. 5:7–11.

Must practice self-denial—Mt. 5:29, 30; 10:39; 16:24–27; Mk. 8:34–38; 10:29, 30; Lu. 6:22, 23; 14:26, 33; 16:25; 18: 18–30; 22:28–30; John 12:25; I Cor. 9:24–27; Gal. 5:24; Col. 3:5–7; II Tim. 2:12, 13; Tit. 2:12. See SELF-DENIAL.

Must suffer tribulation—John 15:18, 20; 16:33; Acts 9:16; 14:22; Rom. 5:3; 8:17; Phil. 1:28, 29; I Thess. 3:3; II Tim. 2:11; 3:12; I Pet. 1:6–9; 2:21; Rev. 2:9–11: 7:14.

Must bear the cross—Mt. 10:38, 39; 16: 24–27; Mk. 8:34–37; Lu. 9:23–26; 14: 27–33.

Must not be conformed to this world—John 17:15, 16; Rom. 12:2; Eph. 4:7; Col. 3:2; 1 Pet. 4:3–6; I John 2:15–17; 4:5. See CONFORMATION AND TRANSFORMATION.

Parables concerning conditional salvation: *The Sower*—Mt. 13:18–23; Mk. 4:13–20; Lu. 8:11–15; *The Pounds*—Lu. 19:12–27; *The Ten Virgins*—Mt. 25:1–10; *The Talents*—Mt. 25:14–30; *The Rich Man and Lazarus*—Lu. 16: 19–31.

These shall not have a part in this inheritance:

The covetous — Mt. 6:19–24; 19:16–30; Mk. 10:17–27; Lu. 6:24–26; 16:13–31; 18:18–30; 19:12–27; Eph. 5:5; Col. 3: 5; I Tim. 6:9–11; Jas. 5:1–5; II Pet. 2:3.

The Drunkard—Lu. 21:34–36; Rom. 13: 13; I Cor. 6:9, 10; I Pet. 4:1–5.

The Lascivious—I Cor. 6:9, 10; Eph. 5:5; Col. 3:5–10; Heb. 13:4.

The Apostate—Lu. 9:61, 62; 11:24–26; Gal. 5:1–4; Eph. 4:14, 15; Col. 1:22, 23; I Tim. 1:19; Heb. 3:12, 13; 4:11–16; 6:4–6; 10:26–29; II Pet. 2:1–22; 3:13–17; I John 5:10–12.

Salvation illustrated by: A rock—Deut. 32:4, 15, 18, 30; Ps. 95:1; A horn—Ps. 18:2; Lu. 1:69; A helmet—Is. 59: 17; Eph. 6:17; A shield—II Sam. 22: 36; A lamp—Is. 62:1; Clothing—II Chr. 6:41; Ps. 132:16; 149:4; Is. 61: 10; Wells—Is. 12:3; Walls and bulwarks — Is. 26:1; 60:18; Chariots—Heb. 3:8; Victory—I Cor. 15:57; A crown—I Cor. 9:25; Rev. 2:10; 3:11.

SAMARIA, sa-mā'ri-a. From *Shamar*, to watch. A ''Lookout Mountain.'' When the traveller reaches the Vale of Shechem he finds himself at the true physical center of Palestine, from which the features of the whole country radiate and group themselves more clearly. Historical memories, too, burst about the paths of Samaria more lavishly than even those fountains, which render her such a contrast to Judæa. The altars at Shechem and Shiloh—Gen. 33:18–20; I Sam. 1:3. The fields round Dothan—Gen. 37:17. The palm tree of Deborah—Ju. 4:5. The winepress of Ophrah—Ju. 6:11. Carmel and Gilboa—I Sam. 28:4; I Ki. 18: 19–20. The vineyard of Naboth—I Ki. 21:1. The gates of Jezreel and Beth-shean—I Ki. 4:12; 18:45, 46. The fords of Jordan—Gen. 32:10; Ju. 3: 28. Elijah's apparitions—II Ki. 1:11. Elisha's passing to and fro—II Ki. 2:14. John baptizing at Ænon near to Salim—John 3:23. Ahab and the rain—I Ki. 18:44, 45. Gideon's campaign—Ju. 7:1. Jehu's furious driving —II Ki. 9:20. (G. A. Smith's *Hist. Geog. of Holy Land*.)

Origin of Samaria.—Omri, King of Israel, bought the hill Samaria (Heb.

Shomeron) from Shemer for two talents of silver and built the city on it—I Ki. 16:24. The date of building is about 880 B. C. It was made the capital of the kingdom of Israel, and was named after the owner of the hill. It lay 6 miles N.W. from Shechem and 23 miles east of the Mediterranean sea.

Characteristics of.—Its elevation and surrounding scenery not only made it a "thing of beauty." It was eminent as the site for a fortress, which Omri was not slow to utilize. It is surrounded with terraced hills, clad with fig and olive trees. The city depends on cisterns for its water.

Sieges and battles.—Shortly after its establishment as a city and fortress, Benhadad I, King of Syria, successfully attacked it, compelling Omri to grant him favorable trade facilities—I Ki. 20:34. Its strength, however, enabled it to withstand severe sieges by the Syrians—I Ki. Ch. 20; II Ki. Chs. 6-7. Benhadad II was compelled to reverse the terms his father had exacted—I Ki. 20:34. It finally fell before Shalmaneser and Sargon after a 3 years' siege—II Ki. 18:9-12. Its people were transported to Assyria—II Ki. 17:5, 6; and foreigners were established there—II Ki. 17:24. In B. C. 331 it was besieged again and conquered by Alexander and in B. C. 120 by John Hyrcanus.

Religious history.—This begins with Ahab, son of Omri, who built a Baal-temple there and set up the Asherah (I Ki. 16:32); and also built an ivory palace for the heathen Queen Jezebel —I Ki. 22:39; Amos 3:15. At a later day the Samaritans desired to unite with the Jews in building a temple at Jerusalem. Being refused, a temple was built on Mount Gerizim—John 4:21. The Samaritans gradually cast off their idols, adopting the Hebrew Pentateuch as their law. John Hyrcanus having destroyed the temple on Gerizim, they built another at Shechem. Stung by the actions of the Jews, they refused them passage through their country, even waylaying them—Josephus, Ant. 20:6. (Lu. 9:

51-53.) They were somewhat more tolerant in the days of Jesus—John 4:8. Although when the Jews would annoy Him, He was called a Samaritan—John 8:48. The enthusiasm of Jesus forbade his fear, as He sat by the well-side—John 4:6. He had a most remarkable reception—John 4: 28, 29, and a great conquest—John 4:39-42. Later on Philip preached to the Samaritans with large success—Acts 8:5-17.

Its present condition.—"Modern Sebaste (Samaria) is a squalid and fanatical Moslem village whose paths and fields are cluttered with a multitude of fallen columns. A few shafts still standing near the threshing-floor may mark the site of the temple which Herod erected to Augustus."—*The Standard Bible Dict.*

SAME. Lord—Rom. 10:12. Loveth little —Lu. 7:47. Mind, Of—Rom. 15:5; Phil. 2:2. Partook of—Heb. 2:14. Spirit—I Cor. 12:11. Things—Acts 15:27. Was in the beginning—John 1:2. Yesterday—Heb. 13:8.

SAMGAR-NEBO, săm′gar-nē′bo. **A prince of Babylon.**—Jer. 39:3.

SAMLAH, săm′lah. **King of Edom.**— Gen. 36:36, 37; I Chr. 1:47, 48.

SAMOS, sā′mos. **An island in the Aegean Sea.**—Acts 20:15.

SAMOTHRACE, săm′ŏ-thrāce. **Another island in the Ægean Sea.**—Acts 16:11.

SAMSON, săm′son. Heb. *Little sun*. Belongs to tribe of Dan. Son of Manoah, and a Nazirite — Ju. 13:1-5. Marries a Philistine woman of Timnah — Ju. 14:1-4. Samson displays great strength — Ju. 14:5-6. Propounds a riddle—Ju. 14:14. Smites 30 men—Ju. 14:19. Turns foxes into the Philistine grain—Ju. 15:4-5. Samson permits them to bind him, and he snaps the bands — Ju. 15:12-14. Slew a thousand with a jawbone—vs. 15-16. Carries away doors of the gates of Gaza — Ju. 16:3. Delilah tempts and betrays him—Ju. 16:4-20. After several attempts Philistines overcome him and put out his eyes—Ju. 16:18-21. He grinds in the prison—v. 21. Brought out to make sport, pulls down pillars of temple, and slays a multitude—Ju. 16:23-30. Death and burial —vs. 30, 31. Referred to—Heb. 11:32.

SAMUEL, săm'u-el. *Name of God.*—Interpreted "asked of God"—I Sam. 1:20. His mother was Hannah—I Sam. 1:20. Samuel pledged to God—I Sam. 1:11. Hannah's song of gratitude—I Sam. 2:1-10. Samuel's career began early—I Sam. 2:11. Appointed to a delicate mission—I Sam. 3:11-14. Feared to tell it—v. 15. Finally consented—v. 18. Anoints Saul—I Sam. 10:1. Samuel resigns his charge as Judge—I Sam. 12:1-5. Samuel reproves Saul for making the burnt-offering—I Sam. 13:11-15. Saul again reproved and rejected as king—I Sam. 15:1-23. He slays Agag—v. 33. Samuel anoints David as Saul's successor —I Sam. 16:12-13. David complains to Samuel of Saul's treatment—I Sam. 19:18.

As Judge, Samuel visits Bethel, Gilgal, Mizpah, and Ramah.—I Sam. 7:15, 16.

Home at Ramah.—I Sam. 7:17.

Makes his sons judges over Israel.—I Sam. 8:1-3.

Aids in organization of tabernacle service.—I Chr. 9:22; 26:28; II Chr. 35:18.

A prophet.—Acts 3:24; 13:20; compare —Ps. 99:6. Knew companies of prophets—I Sam. 10:5.

Death and burial.—I Sam. 25:1.

SANBALLAT, san-băl'lat. **An enemy who opposed the work of Nehemiah.**—Neh. 2:10, 19; 4:1, 7; 6:1-14; 13:28.

SANCTIFICATION. — Jehovah sanctified the Sabbath—Gen. 2:3. The tent and the altar—Ex. 29:43-44; 30:26-29. Aaron and sons—(same). Children of Israel—Ex. 31:13; Lev. 20:8; Ez. 37:28. Blemished Levites not to be sanctified—Lev. 21:15, 23; 22:9, 16. The temple—I Ki. 8:10-11; II Chr. 5:13; 7:3. The prophets—Jer. 1:5.

God sanctifies the Church through Christ. —I Cor. 1:2, 30; 6:11; Eph. 5:25-27; Heb. 2:11; 10:10, 14; 13:12. Through the Holy Spirit—Rom. 15:16; I Cor. 6:11; I Thess. 2:13; I Pet. 1:2. Through the atonement—Heb. 9:13-14; 13:12. Through the word—John 17:17; Eph. 5:26. Through obedience of faith—Acts 26:18.

The saints are the sanctified.—II Thess. 2:13; I Pet. 1:1-2. Have inheritance among—Acts 20:32. Church becomes glorious through sanctification—Eph. 5:25-27. Saints fit themselves for service by—II Tim. 2:21. Necessary in order to inheritance—I Cor. 6:9-11. Fruit of, is eternal life—Rom. 6:22.

The human side of sanctification.—The first-born—Ex. 13:2. Go and sanctify the people—Ex. 19:10. Let the priests sanctify themselves—Ex. 19:22. Sanctify the mount—Ex. 19:23. Anoint and sanctify Aaron and sons—Ex. 28:41; 29:33; 40:13; Lev. 8:12. The altar —Ex. 29:36-37; 40:10. The tabernacle and furniture—Ex. 30:29; 40:9-11; Lev. 8:11. Sanctify yourselves—Lev. 11:44; 20:7; Num. 11:18; Josh. 3:5; 7:13; I Sam. 16:5. Man shall sanctify his house—Lev. 27:14. Firstlings of herd—Deut. 15:19. Priests and Levites—I Chr. 15:12-14; II Chr. 29:34. Ye shall sanctify Jehovah— Is. 8:13; 29:33. An end to false sanctification—Is. 66:17.

New Testament references.—Husband sanctified by wife—I Cor. 7:14. Sanctified by purging oneself—II Tim. 2:21. Temple sanctifies gold—Mt. 23:17. Altar sanctifies gift—Mt. 23:19. See CONSECRATION, FIRST-BORN, HOLINESS, PURIFICATION.

SANCTUARY. Ex. 38:24; Lev. 10:17, 18; 14:13; Num. 4:20; Ps. 68:17; 77:13. Abhorred—Lam. 2:7. Bearing—Num. 10:21. Beauty of—Ps. 29:2; 96:6; Is. 60:13. Build—I Chr. 22:19. Charge of—Num. 3:28. Courts of my —Is. 62:9. Defile—Num. 19:20. Hands established—Ex. 15:17. Height of his —Ps. 102:19. Iniquity of—Num. 18:1. Judah became his—Ps. 114:2. King's —Amos 7:13. Make me a—Ex. 25:8. Minister in—Ez. 44:27. Profane— Lev. 21:12; Ps. 74:7; Is. 63:18; Lam. 2:20; Ez. 23:38; Dan. 9:26; 11:31; Zeph. 3:4. Purification of—II Chr. 30:19. Reverence my—Lev. 19:30. Service of—Ex. 36:1, 3. Shekel of— Ex. 30:13. Strength and beauty in Ps. 96:6. Toward—Ez. 21:2. Trodden down—Is. 63:18. Veil of—Lev. 4:6. Vessels of—Neh. 10:39. World, Of—

Heb. 9:1. Worship in—Ps. 63:2; 73:
17; 134:2; 150:1; Is. 16:12. See
HEAVEN, MOST HOLY PLACE, TABER-
NACLE, TEMPLE.

SAND: Upon the sea-shore.—Gen. 22:
17; Josh. 11:4; Ju. 7:12; I Sam. 13:5;
II Sam. 17:11; I Ki. 4:20, 29; Heb.
11:12.

Of the sea.—Gen. 32:12; 41:49; Job 6:3;
Ps. 78:27; Is. 10:22; Jer. 15:8; 33:22;
Hos. 1:10; Rom. 9:27; Rev. 13:1;
20:8.

Hid in.—Ex. 2:12; Deut. 33:19.

Weight of.—Pr. 27:3.

For bound of the sea.—Jer. 5:22.

Illustrative.—I shall multiply my days
as the—Job 29:18. More in number
than the—Ps. 139:18. As the sand of
the sea—Is. 10:22. As the—Is. 48:19;
Hab. 1:9; Rom. 9:27; Heb. 11:12.

Used in prophecy.—Glowing—Is. 35:7;
Hos. 1:10; Rev. 13:1.

In teachings of Jesus.—House upon the
—Mt. 7:26.

SANDALS. Song of Sol. 7:1; Mk. 6:9;
Acts 12:8. See SHOES.

SAND-LIZARD. Lev. 11:30.

SANG. Ex. 15:1. See SONGS, MUSIC.

SANHEDRIN. Gr. *Sanhedrion.* **The
Jews' supreme council at the time of
Jesus.**—Lu. 22:66. It consisted of 71
members, according to Jewish tradition, founded on the 70 elders appointed by Moses and including Moses
—Num. 11:16. But Moses' 70 were
merely temporary, no traces of them
being found in Deut. 17:8–11, nor under Joshua, the Judges, and the Kings.
The fact that Jehoshaphat called together a sort of supreme court favors
this—II Chr. 19:8. Elders are also
mentioned in Ezra 5:5; 6:7; 10:8; but
these, also, passed away. The earliest
mention of the Sanhedrin is found in
II Macc. 1:10; 4:44; 11:27. This puts
its origin under the Greek supremacy.
The Sanhedrin was composed of chief
priests, scribes, and elders, presided
over by an hereditary high priest—
Mt. 26:57; John 11:47–49. Although
but one head was recognized by the
Roman authorities the judgment of
the aged high priests was sought by the
Jewish officers—John 18:12–14. Their

power was recognized in all except
condemning to death—John 18:28–31.
They had lost their power shortly before the death of Jesus. It ranged
from minute contempt (Mt. 5:22) to
blasphemy of Jehovah—Mk. 14:61–
63. The Sanhedrin plotted the death
of Jesus—Mt. 26:14, 15; Mk. 14:10,
11; Lu. 22:3–5; John 11:47–53. They
caused the arrest of Jesus—John 18:2,
3. They tried Jesus in order to kill
Him, not to learn of His guilt or innocence—Mt. 26:59, 60; Mk. 14:55,
56. It was their insistence that caused
the death of Jesus—John 18:29, 30.
This council thrust itself between the
apostles and the people—Acts 4:15–
17. The Sadducees brought the apostles before the Sanhedrin—Acts 4:1–
7; 5:17, 18. Peter defies them—Acts
5:29–32. Had Stephen arrested and
tried—Acts 6:12, 13; 7:1. Saul acted
under the authority of the Sanhedrin
in his successful persecution of the
disciples—Acts 9:2, 14; 26:12. It was
a constant vexation to Paul—Acts
22:30; 23:1, 6, 15, 20, 28; 24:30; 25:
12. Finally forcing him to Rome—
Acts 25:9–12; for their power extended to Jews of foreign cities—Acts
9:2. Paul skilfully divided the Sanhedrin over his case—Acts 23:6–10.
With the destruction of Jerusalem the
Sanhedrin was abolished.

SANITATION. In primitive times no
note was taken directly of health as
such. Provisions for its preservation
and promotion were secured only indirectly. Disease was regarded as a
positive element, and health the absence of disease, and therefore a negative state. In general, disease was
viewed as a visitation of supernatural
beings.

Remnants of this view of health and
disease are to be found in the Bible
in the language used about them,
though the view itself had been probably left behind. A plague, for instance,
is a "stroke" (*nega'*, "blow"); a
fever holds and leaves a patient, and
is "rebuked"—Luke 4:39.

Sanitation is accordingly the subject
neither of teaching nor of legislation.
Yet it is held in view and is involved

in the ritual and other provisions of Old Testament law.

1. **Cleanliness.**—Provided for in laws regarding the disposal of the dead outside of the walls. Burial in the earth with or without coffin, construction of vaults and tombs for depositing embalmed bodies and embalming—Gen. 50:2–13, 26; 23:4–11; II Chr. 16:14; Mk. 15:46; 16:1. "Burnings" also are spoken of in the same connection—II Chr. 16:14; 21:19; Jer. 34:5; Amos 6:18.

Disposal of excrement.—Deut. 23:12–14.

Washing of hands before meals.—Mt. 15:2; Mk. 7:3. Sanitary aspect of this provision is seen clearly when it is borne in mind that the fingers were used instead of forks — Mt. 26:23; John 13:26.

Burial specifically intended to cleanse the land.—Ez. 39:12–16; a provision most effective for the prevention of pestilence from unburied bodies in war, famine, or earthquake.

2. **Treatment of infections.** — *General methods employed:* (1) Isolation (Quarantine)—Lev. 13:4, 26, 31. (2) Destruction of infected clothing, etc.—Lev. 13:52, 57, etc. (3) Purification—Equivalent to modern fumigation and exposure to open air and sunlight. *Special provisions:* Laws preventive of the spread of leprosy—Lev. Chs. 13 and 14. See LEPROSY.

Laws against cadaveric contamination.—Lev. 17:13–16; 21:1–3, 11; Num. 19:11–22. Absolutely necessary in a climate where decay sets in so quickly and infectious germs abound.

Diminution of risks from puerperal complications.—Lev. 12:1–8; from the menstrual function—Lev. 15:19–30; from the conjugal act—Lev. 15:8; from gonorrhœal discharges—Lev. 15:2–15; from spermatorrhœal discharges—Lev. 15:16 ff.

3. **Health-preserving conditions.**—Treatment of so-called "leprosy" of clothing (Lev. 13:47–59) and "leprosy" of house (Lev. 14:33–57) caused by minute fungous growth which predisposes to the entertainment of bacilli and results in epidemic contagions.

4. **Food laws.**—Prohibition of many unwholesome animals, and in particular of the swine's flesh—Lev. 11:1–24; Deut. 14:2–21. Prohibition of the flesh of unnaturally killed animals—Ex. 22:31; Lev. 11:11, 24 ff. "Strangled"—Acts 21:25; I Cor. 10:28. Prohibition of blood as an article of food—Lev. 7:26 f.; Deut. 12:16.

5. **Marriage laws.**—Prohibition of marriage within certain degrees of consanguinity; with the wife of a father—Deut. 22:30; 27:20; Lev. 18:8; 20:11; with a sister or step-sister—Lev. 18:9, 11; 20:17; with a mother-in-law—Deut. 27:23; with a niece—Lev. 18:10; with an aunt—Lev. 18:12 f.; 20:19; with a daughter-in-law—Lev. 18:15; 20:12; with a sister-in-law—Lev. 18:16; 20:21; with mother and daughter at the same time—Lev. 18:17; 20:14; with two sisters at the same time—Lev. 18:18.

SANK. I Sam. 17:49.

SANSANNAH, san-săn'nah. A city in Judah.—Josh. 15:31.

SAP. Ps. 92:14.

SAPH, săph. **An ancestor of the giants or Rephaim.**—II Sam. 21:18.

SAPPHIRA, sap-phī'ra. **Wife of Ananias who tried to deceive the church concerning his possessions.**—Acts 5:1–11.

SAPPHIRE. See PRECIOUS STONES.

SARAH, sā'rah. **Wife of Abraham.**—Gen. 11:29, 31. Is barren—Gen. 11:30; 16:1.

Also Abraham's half sister.—Gen. 12:13; 20:2, 5, 12. Goes out with others from Ur—Gen. 11:41. Dwells in Haran—Gen. 11:31. Sarai goes with husband into Egypt.—Gen. 12:10.

Is persuaded to pass as sister.—Gen. 12:15. Beholding her beauty, Pharaoh takes her as his wife—Gen. 12:15. Jehovah plagued Pharaoh and he releases Sarai—Gen. 12:17–20.

Sarai gives Hagar as a concubine to Abraham.—Gen. 16:1–3. Hagar despises Sarai—Gen. 16:4. Sarai drives her out—Gen. 16:6. Angel of Jehovah bids her return—Gen. 16:7–9. Ishmael is born to Hagar—Gen. 16:15.

Sarai's name changed to Sarah.—Gen. 17:15.

Sarah is promised a son.—Gen. 17:16–19; 18:10–15. Entertains messengers of God—Gen. 18:1–15.

Sarah visits Gerar with her husband and is taken into harem by Abimelech. —Gen. 20:2. God warns him concerning his act and Sarah is restored—Gen. 20:3–18.

Isaac is born.—Gen. 21:1–7.

Demands that Hagar be cast out.—Gen. 21:9–13; Gal. 4:23–30.

Sarah dies in Hebron at the age of 127 years.—Gen. 23:1, 2.

Buried in the cave of Machpelah.—Gen. 23:3–19.

The faith of Sarah.—Heb. 11:11.

Obeyed Abraham.—I Pet. 3:5, 6.

Justified in casting out Hagar.—Gal. 4:23–31. See ABRAHAM, ISAAC.

SARAPH, sā′raph. **A descendant of Judah.**—I Chr. 4:22.

SARDIS, sär′dis. **One of the seven churches.**—Rev. 1:11; 3:1–6.

SARDIUS. Ex. 28:17; Rev. 4:3; 21:20. See PRECIOUS STONES.

SARDONYX. Rev. 21:20.

SARGON, sär′gon. **King of Assyria whose reign was between Shalmanaeser and Sennacherib.**—Is. 20:1.

SARID, sā′rid. **A city.**—Josh. 19:10, 12.

SARSECHIM, sär′se-kim. **A prince of Babylon.**—Jer. 39:3.

SASHES. Is. 3:20.

SAT DOWN ON RIGHT HAND OF GOD. See JESUS, EXALTATION OF.

SATAN.—**Names:** Abaddon—Rev. 9:11. Accuser of Saints—Rev. 12:10. Adversary—Job Chs. 1, 2; Zech. 3:1; I Pet. 5:8. Angel of the Abyss—Rev. 9:11. Apollyon (Destroyer)—Rev. 9:11. Beelzebub—Mt. 12:24; Mk. 3:22; Lu. 11:15. Belial—II Cor. 6:5. Deceiver—Rev. 12:9; 20:3, 8, 10. Devil —Mt. 4:1. Thirty-five times only in the New Testament. Dragon—Rev. 12: 3, 7, 9. Enemy—Mt. 13:39. Evil One—Mt. 13:19, 38; I John 2:13, 14; 3:12; 5:18. Father of lies and liars— John 8:44. God of this world—II Cor. 4:4. Murderer—John 8:44. Prince of powers of air—Eph. 2:2. Prince of demons—Mt. 2:24; Mk. 3:22; Lu. 11: 15. Prince of this world—John 12:31; 14:30; 16:11. Satan—I Chr. 21:1. Serpent—II Cor. 11:3; Rev. 12:9; 20:2. Tempter—Mt. 4:3; I Thess. 3:5.

His nature and origin.—An angel—Job 1:6; 2:1; II Cor. 11:14. Fell from heaven—Lu. 10:18. Because of sin— II Pet. 2:4; Jude 6. Ruler of demons —Mt. 12:24, 26–28; Mk. 3:22, 23; Lu. 11:15, 18. Ruler of the unsaved—II Cor. 4:4; I John 5:19. Adversary of man—I Pet. 5:8.

His character.—Murderer—John 8:44. Liar and deceitful—John 8:44; II Thess. 2:9, 10; II Cor. 11:14. Sinner— I John 3:8. Tempter—Mt. 4:3; I Thess. 3:5. Enemy of righteousness— Acts 13:10. Cunning—II Cor. 2:11; Eph. 6:11, 12.

His works.—Author of all sin and suffering—Rom. 5:12; Rev. 12:9. Cause of sickness—Lu. 13:16; Acts 10:38. Has the power of death—Heb. 2:14. Tempts to evil: *David*—I Chr. 21:1. *Jesus*—Mt. 4:1, 11; Mk. 1:13; Lu. 4:2, 13. *Judas*—Lu. 22:3. *Peter*—Lu. 22: 31. *Ananias*—Acts 5:3. *Paul*—II Cor. 12:7. Adversary of Joshua—Zech. 3: 1, 2. Robs of the truth—Mt. 13:19; Mk. 4:15; Lu. 8:12; Mt. 13:17. Blinds to the glory of God—Mt. 13:17; John 8:54, 55; 9:39–41; 12:39, 40; II Cor. 4:4. Makes deaf—John 8:43, 45–47. Destroys the word of Christ—Mt. 13: 37–39; John 8:41–44. Hinders Christ's cause—Mt. 13:39; I Thess. 2:17, 18.

Overruled for good.—To prove the righteous—Mt. 4:10; Lu. 22:31, 32; I Tim. 3:6, 7. To check undue exaltation—II Cor. 12:7. To destroy the dominion of the flesh—I Cor. 5:7; II Cor. 2:5–11. To teach men not to blaspheme—I Tim. 1:20. To bring victory out of persecution—Rev. 2:10.

He counterfeits the spiritual universe.— False God—I Thess. 1:9; II Thess. 2: 3, 4, 9–12. False Christs—Mt. 24:24; Mk. 13:22. False angels—II Cor. 11: 14; Rev. 9:11; 12:7, 9. False prophets —Mt. 7:15; 24:11, 24; Lu. 6:26; Acts 13:6; II Pet. 2:1; I John 4:1; Rev. 16:13; 19:20; 20:10.

False teachers.—I Tim. 4:1, 2; 6:3–5; II Tim. 4:3, 4; Tit. 1:10; II Pet. 2:1. False apostles—II Cor. 11:13; Rev. 2:2.

False churches.—Rev. 2:9; 3:16; 18:4. Brethren—Acts 15:1, 24; II Cor. 11: 26; Gal. 2:4.

Our duty.—Watch and pray—Mt. 26:41; Mk. 14:38; Lu. 21:36; I Pet. 4:7; 5: 8, 9. Put on the whole armor of God— Eph. 6:11. Resist—Eph. 4:27; Jas. 4:7; I John 2:13, 14, 18.

His overthrow.—In fact, bound by the truth—John 8:31-36; Rom. 8:2; Rev. 20:1-3. To be destroyed—I John 3:8. Under man—Gen. 3:15; Rom. 16:20. Safety of the believer—Lu. 10:19; John 10:27-30. Reserved for eternal fire—Mt. 25:41; Rev. 20:10.

SATCHEL. Is. 3:22.

SATED. Lam. 3:15.

SATIATE. Jer. 31:14, 25; 46:10.

SATISFACTION. See RANSOM, SATISFY.

SATISFY. Ps. 59:15; Pr. 5:19; 6:30. Abide—Pr. 19:23. Awake, When I— Ps. 17:15. Bread, With—Ps. 105:40; 132:15; Pr. 20:13; Lam. 5:6. Children, With—Ps. 17:14. Company, With your—Rom. 15:24. Desire—Ex. 15:9; Ps. 103:5; 145:16. Eat and be —Deut. 6:11; 14:29; Job 31:31; Ps. 22:26; 36:8; 37:19; Pr. 20:13; Is. 44: 16; Joel 2:19, 26.

Not be.—Lev. 26:26; Job 27:14; Is. 9: 20; 55:2; Amos 4:8; Mic. 6:14. Favor, with—Deut. 35:23. Flesh of Job, With—Job 19:22. Good, With—Ps. 103:5; 104:28; Pr. 12:14. Good man— Pr. 14:14. Goodness, With—Ps. 65:4; Jer. 31:14. Honey, With—Ps. 81:16. Increase, With—Eccl. 5:10. Of his lips—Pr. 18:20. Jesus—Is. 53:11. Long life, With—Ps. 91:16. Manna, With—Ps. 105:40. Mercy, With thy— Ps. 90:14. Never—Ez. 16:28, 29; Hab. 2:5. Barren womb—Pr. 30:16. Earth with water—Pr. 30:16; Eccl. 1:8; 4:8. Sheol—Pr. 27:20; 30:16. Poor—Ps. 132:15. Riches, With—Eccl. 4:8. Silver, With—Eccl. 4:8. Soul—Ps. 63:5; 107:9; Pr. 13:25; Is. 58:10, 11; Jer. 50:19; Ez. 7:19. Spoil, With—Jer. 50: 10. Such and be—Is. 66:11. Waste and desolate ground—Job 38:27. See FILL.

SATRAPS. Ezra 8:36; Dan. 9:3.

SAUL. (1) **Son of Kish.**—I Sam. 9:2. Sent to find his father's asses—I Sam. 9:3-14, 20; 10:2, 14-16. Anointed—I

Sam. 9:15-27; 10:1. Among the prophets—I Sam. 10:2-13. Chosen as king —I Sam. 10:16-24. Saves Jabesh-gilead from Nahash the Ammonite— I Sam. 11:1-11, 13. Made king in Gilgal—I Sam. 11:14, 15. Offers sacrifice at Gilgal—I Sam. 13:1-13. Saul and Jonathan abide in Geba—I Sam. 13: 16-22. Saul in Gibeah—I Sam. 14:2, 16; 15:34; 23:19. Charges people with an oath—14:17-28. Threatens Jonathan, but the people save him—I Sam. 14:28-46. Wars and family—I Sam. 14:47-52. Disobedience concerning Amalek—I Sam. 15:1-35. Sends to Bethlehem for David to play the harp and soothe him—I Sam. 16:14-23. David slays Goliath the giant—I Sam. 17:1-58. Saul jealous of David—18: 1-9. Attempts to slay David—18:10-12. Gives his daughter Michal to David as his wife—I Sam. 18:17-28. Jonathan intercedes for David—I Sam. 19:1-7. Michal saves David—I Sam. 19:9-17. Pursues David to Ramah—I Sam. 19:18-24. Saul and his messengers prophesy—I Sam. 19:20-24. Saul attempts to slay Jonathan— I Sam. 20:24-33. Slays priests at Nob —I Sam. 22:11-22. Pursues David—I Sam. 23:7-13; 24:1-22. David spares Saul's life—I Sam. 24:1-7; 26:6-12. Visits witch of En-dor—I Sam. 28: 3-25. Death—I Sam. 31:1-13. Bones moved from Jabesh to Zela—II Sam. 21:12-14. See DAVID, JONATHAN.

(2) **Saul of Tarsus.**—See PAUL.

SAVE. I Ki. 3:18. Cross, In the—Gal. 6:14. In his own country—Mt. 13:51. Jesus only—Mk. 6:8. None good save one—Lu. 18:19. When the Son of man —Mk. 9:9.

SAVE, *v.* See SALVATION.

SAVIOR. See GOD, JESUS.

SAVOR. Gen. 8:21; Job 6:6. Death unto death—II Cor. 2:16. Salt hath lost its—Mt. 5:13. Sweet—Ex. 29: 18; Num. 28:13; Ez. 20:41; II Cor. 2:14, 15; Eph. 5:2. See OFFERING, SWEET.

SAVORY. Gen. 27:4. See FOOD.

SAWN. Asunder—Heb. 11:37.

SAYING. Job 22:20; Rev. 10:8. Dark —Ps. 49:4; John 16:25. Faithful is the—I Tim. 1:15. Hard—John 6:60.

Incline thine ear unto—Pr. 4:20. Kept in mind—Gen. 37:11. Memorable—Job 13:12. Receiveth not—John 12:48. This—Mt. 19:11. Voice of one—Is. 40:6.

SCAB. See LEPROSY.

SCALES. Fell from his eyes—Acts 9:18. Hath fins and—Lev. 11:9, 10, 12; Deut. 14:9, 10. Strong—Job 41:15. Weighed mountains in—Is. 40:12.

SCALP. Smite—Ps. 68:21. See HEAD.

SCANT. Measure—Mic. 6:10. See JUSTICE, WEIGHTS.

SCAPE GOAT. Lev. 16:8, 10, 26 (A.V.). See AZAZEL.

SCARCE. Gone out—Gen. 27:30. Restrained multitudes—Acts 14:18.

SCARCELY. For a righteous man—Rom. 5:7. Saved, Righteous—I Pet. 4:18.

SCARCENESS. Bread without—Deut. 8:9. See FAMINE.

SCAREST. Job 7:14. See FEAR, FRIGHTEN.

SCARLET. See COLORS.

SCATTER. Mt. 25:24. Abroad—Gen. 11:4; Acts 5:37; II Cor. 9:9. Among nations—Lev. 26:33. Destroy and—Jer. 23:1. Dust, As—Mt. 21:44; Lu. 20:18. Evil—Pr. 20:8. Flock—Jer. 3:2. He that gathereth not—Mt. 12:30; Lu. 11:23. Hoar frost—Ps. 147:16. Mountains—Hab. 3:6. Nest—Is. 16:2. Peoples—Ps. 68:30. Sheep, As—Mt. 9:36. Strife—Pr. 16:28. Stubble, As—Jer. 13:24. The proud—Lu. 1:51. With a whirlwind—Zech. 7:14. Wolf—John 10:12.

SCENT. Not changed — Jer. 48:11. Water, Of—Job 14:9. Wine of Lebanon, As—Hos. 14:7.

SCEPTRE: Of rulers.—Gen. 49:10; Is. 14:5; Ez. 19:14; Amos 1:5, 8; Zech. 10:11.

Golden sceptre.—Esth. 4:11. Used as a favor—Esth. 5:2; 8:4.

Sceptre shall not depart from Judah.—Gen. 49:10. Sceptre shall rise out of Israel—Num. 24:17.

Rod as a sceptre.—Is. 14:5.

Figurative.—Num. 24:17. Sceptre of iron—Ps. 2:9; Rev. 2:27; 12:5. Of God—Ps. 45:6. Of Israel—Ez. 19:14. Of uprightness—Heb. 1:8.

Prophecies.—Sceptre of Israel—Ez. 19:14.

SCHISM. In the body—I Cor. 12:25. See DIVISION, FACTION.

SCHOLAR. I Chr. 25:8. See INSTRUCTION.

SCHOOL. Of Tyrannus—Acts 19:9. See INSTRUCTION.

SCIENCE. Understanding—Dan. 1:4.

SCOFF, SCOFFER. Ps. 73:8; Lu. 16:14; 25:35. An abomination—Pr. 24:9. Be ye not—Is. 29:20. Correcteth a—Pr. 9:7. Delight in—Pr. 1:22. Drinketh—Job 34:7. Friends—Job 16:20. Hear word of Jehovah ye—Is. 28:14. Heareth not—Pr. 13:1. If thou—Pr. 9:12. Is his name—Pr. 21:24. Judgments are prepared for—Pr. 19:29. Kings, At—Hab. 1:10. Loveth not to be reproved—Pr. 15:12. Makest us—Ps. 44:13. Punished—Pr. 21:11. Reprove not a—Pr. 9:8. Scoffeth at—Pr. 3:34. Seat of—Ps. 1:1. Seeketh wisdom—Pr. 14:6. Set a city into flame—Pr. 29:8. Smite as a—Pr. 19:25. Soul is filled with—Ps. 123:4. Stretched out hand with—Hos. 7:5. We are become—Ps. 79:4. See SCORN, LAUGHTER.

SCORCH. Pr. 6:28; Mt. 13:6; Mk. 4:6; Rev. 16:8, 9. See FIRE, HEAT.

SCORN. Esth. 3:6; Job 39:7, 18; Ez. 16:31. Laugh to—II Ki. 19:21; II Chr. 30:10; Neh. 2:19; Job 22:19; Ps. 22:7; Is. 37:22; Ez. 23:32. See LAUGHTER, SCOFFER.

SCORPION. Deut. 8:15; Lu. 11:12; Rev. 9:5.

SCOURGE, *n.* Josh. 23:13; Job 9:23; Is. 10:26; 28:15, 18. Cords, Of—John 2:15. Tongue, Of the—Job 5:21. See PLAGUES.

SCOURGE, *v.* Job 30:8. Jesus—Mt. 20:19; 27:26; Mk. 10:34; 15:15; Lu. 18:33; Lu. 23:16; John 19:1. Roman, A—Acts 22:25. Son, Every—Heb. 12:6. Synagogues, In—Mt. 10:17; 23:34. See CHASTEN, PERSECUTION.

SCOURGING. Deut. 25:3; Acts 16:37, 38; 22:25. Jesus, Of—See SCOURGE. Paul, Of—Acts 16:23, 27; II Cor. 11:24.

SCRABBLE. I Sam. 21:13.

SCRAPE. Lev. 14:41.

SCREEN. Ex. 26:36; 40:3, 8, 28. See TABERNACLE.

SCRIBES: Originally writers, secretaries.—Ez. Ch. 9.

Writers.—I Chr. 24:6; Jer. 8:8; Ezra 4:8, 9, 17, 23; Esth. 3:12; Ez. 9:11.

Secretaries.—To kings—II Sam. 8:17; 20:25; I Ki. 4:3; II Ki. 12:10; 18:18; 19:2; I Chr. 18:16; 24:6; 27:32. To prophets—Jer. 36:27, 32.

Treasurers.—Neh. 13:13; II Ki. 12:10; II Chr. 24:11.

Families noted for furnishing scribes.— I Chr. 2:55; Ju. 5:14 (see marg. reading)—I Chr. 24:6; II Chr. 34:13.

Notaries.—In court—Jer. 32:11, 12; I Chr. 24:6.

Keepers of muster rolls.—Ju. 5:14; II Ki. 25:19; II Chr. 26:11; Jer. 52:25.

Teachers of the law.—II Chr. 34:18–21; Neh. 8:4–6; Ezra 7:6; Jer. 8:8; Mt. 23:2; 2:4; 17:10; 7:29; 13:52; Mk. 12:35.

Members of the council which opposed Jesus.—Mt. 2:4; 20:18; Lu. 22:66; Mt. 21:15; Mk. 8:31; 11:18; Lu. 19:47; 22:2; 23:10; John 8:3.

Charge Jesus with blasphemy.—Mt. 9:3; Mk. 2:6–7; Lu. 5:21.

Conspire against Jesus.—Mt. 26:3; 27: 41; Mk. 14:1; Lu. 22:6.

Reproved by Jesus.—Mt. 5:20; 15:1–9; 23:1–36; Mk. 2:16, 17; 3:22–30; Lu. 11:38–54; Lu. Ch. 20.

Persecuted disciples.—Acts 4:5, 18, 21; 6:12; 23:6–10.

Manner of teaching contrasted with that of Jesus.—Mt. 7:29; Mk. 1:22.

Characteristics of.—Garb and egotism —Mk. 12:38, 39. Various works—Mt. 23:1–7. Reputed wisdom—I Cor. 1:19, 20. Hypocrisy—Mt. 23:13–15.

SCRIPTURES. Searching of, commended—Deut. 17:19; Josh. 1:8; John 5:39. Cannot be broken—John 10:35. Given by inspiration from God—Acts 1:18; II Tim. 3:16; Heb. 1:1; 3:7; 10: 15; II Pet. 1:20, 21. Given through prophets—Lu. 16:31; Rom. 3:2; Heb. 1:1. Fulfilled in Christ—Mt. 5:17; Lu. 24:27; John 19:24; Acts 13:29. Expounded by Christ—Mt. 4:4; 26:54; Lu. 4:19–21; 24:26, 27, 32; John 7:42. By Peter—Acts 2:16–36; 3:17–24. By Stephen—Acts 7:51–53. By Philip— Acts 8:25–35. See WORD OF GOD, PROPHECY.

SCROLL. Is. 34:4; Rev. 6:14. See ROLL.

SCURVY. Deut. 28:27. See DISEASE.

SCYTHIAN, syth'i-an. A native of Scythia—Col. 3:11.

SEAS. The gathering together of the waters called seas—Gen. 1:10. The earth founded upon—Ps. 24:2. Bounds set to—Job 26:10; 38:8–11; Pr. 8:27– 29. Extent of—Job 11:9; Ps. 104:25. Replenished by rivers—Eccl. 1:7; Ez. 47:8. Wonders of God seen in—Gen. 1:20–21; Ps. 104:25–26; 107:24. Made to glorify God—Ps. 69:34; 148:7. To serve man, To sail on—I Ki. 9:26; Ps. 107:23. To build cities near—Gen. 49:13; Ez. 27:3; Nah. 3:8. To derive wealth from—Deut. 33:19; Mt. 4:18.

Seas mentioned in Scripture.—Adria, Sea of—Acts 27:27.

Dead Sea, or Arabah, called Vale of Siddim, or Salt Sea, Sea of Plains, Eastern Sea, Sea of Lot (40x8 miles). —Gen. 14:3, 10; Num. 34:12; Deut. 3:17; Josh. 3:16; 12:3; 15:2, 5; 18: 19. Eastern Sea—Zech. 14:8; Joel 2:20.

Galilee (12½ by 8 miles, 65 miles above Dead Sea and 680 feet below sea-level), or Tiberias, or Lake of Gennesaret or Chinnereth—Num. 34:11; Josh. 12:3; 13:27. Jesus by—Mt. 4: 18; 15:29; Mk. 1:16; 7:31; John 6:1; 21:1. Demons in—Mt. 8:32. Parable by side of—Mt. 13:34. Cities by the Sea of Galilee—Tiberias, Capernaum, Chorazin and Bethsaida.

Jazer.—Jer. 48:32.

Mediterranean, or Great, or Hinder, or Western, or Joppa, of Philistines (2200 by 1200 miles).—Num. 34:6, 7; Josh. 1:4; 9:1; 15:4, 12, 47; 23:4; I Chr. 2:16; Ezra 3:7; 47:10; Ez. 47:10, 15, 20; 48:28. Sea of Philistines—Ex. 23:31. The sea—Josh. 15:4, 46; Acts 17:14. Hinder sea—Deut. 11:24. Western sea—Zech. 14:8; Joel 2:20.

Merom, Waters of, or Lake of Senechon. —Josh. 11:5, 7.

Red, so-called from the hue of mountains (1400 by 150 miles).—Ex. 10:19; 13:18; 15:4–22; 23:31; Num. 14:25; 21:4; 33:10, 11; Deut. 1:40; 2:1; 11:4; Josh. 2:10; 4:23; 24:6; Ju. 11:16; I Ki. 9:26; Neh. 9:9; Ps. 106:7, 9, 22; 78:53; 136:13, 15; Jer. 49:21; Acts 7:36.

Brazen, or molten sea, made by Solomon for the temple.—I Ki. 7:23-40; II Chr. 4:2-6. It was 15 feet in diameter, stood in court 3000 baths—II Chr. 4:5; or 2000 baths, according to I Ki. 7:26. Probably bowls contained 2000 and foot basin 1000 more. Used for various ablutions of priests—II Chr. 4:6.

Christ's power over sea.—Mt. 8:26; Mk. 4:39; Lu. 8:24; John 6:19.

Sea to give up the dead.—Rev. 20:13. In redeemed earth no more sea—Rev. 21:1.

Figurative.—Of the wicked—Is. 57:20. Of afflictions—Is. 43:2. Of righteousness—Is. 48:18. Of devastating armies—Ez. 26:3. Of John's vision—Rev. 4:6. Unstable disciples—Jas. 1:6.

SEA-MONSTERS. God created them—Gen. 1:21. Job's comparison—Job 7:12. God's power displayed—Ps. 74:13; Is. 51:9-10; 27:1; Ez. 29:3. Praise enjoined upon—Ps. 148:7.

SEAL, *n.* John 3:33. Apostleship, Of——I Cor. 9:2. Clay under, As—Job 38. Close—Job 41:15. God, Of—John 6:27; II Cor. 1:22; Rev. 7:2; 9:4. God's foundation, Of—II Tim. 2:19. Heart, As a seal upon—Song of Sol. 8:6. Holy Spirit—Eph. 4:3. Righteousness, Of—Rom. 4:11. Royal—I Ki. 21:8. Seven—Rev. 5:1-9; 6:1-12; 8:1.

SEAL, *v.* Book—Is. 29:11; Dan. 12:4, 9. Covenant—Neh. 9:38; 10:1-27. See Covenants. Deed—Jer. 32:10, 11, 14, 44. Fountain—Song of Sol. 4:12. Trust—Rom. 15:28. Hand of every man—Job 37:7. Holy Spirit, With—Eph. 1:13; 4:30. See Holy Spirit. Instruction—Job 33:16. Kings ring, With—Esth. 8:8-10. Law—Is. 8:16. Letters—I Ki. 21:8. See Letters. Servants of our God—Eph. 4:30; Rev. 7:3. Son of man—John 6:27. Stars—Job 9:17. Stone—Mt. 27:66. Sum—Ez. 28:12. Transgression in a bag—Job 14:17. Treasures, Among—Deut. 32:34. Us—II Cor. 1:22. Vision and prophecy—Dan. 9:24.

SEAL-SKINS. See Skin.

SEARCH, *n.* Find out God, By—Job 11:7. Spirit maketh diligent—Ps. 77:6.

SEARCH, *v.* Job 11:18; 13:9; Ps. 139:1; Lam. 3:40. By wisdom—Eccl. 1:13. Diligently—I Pet. 1:10. Exactly—Mt. 2:8. Fathers have—Job 8:8. Glory—Ps. 25:27. Heart, With all—Deut. 4:29; Jer. 29:13. Hearts—Rom. 8:27. Innermost parts—Pr. 20:27. Jehovah, All hearts—I Chr. 28:9. Jehovah, The mind—Jer. 17:10. Jerusalem—Zeph. 1:12. Me, O God—Ps. 139:23. Out—Job 13:9; 29:16; Ps. 44:21; 139:3. Peril, After—Pr. 11:27. Reins—Rev. 2:23. Scriptures—John 5:39. Sheep, For—Ez. 34:11. Spirit, all things—I Cor. 2:10. Who is worthy—Mt. 10:11. With wine—Eccl. 2:3.

SEASONS. Job. 37:9; Pr. 26:1; Song of Sol. 2:11-13. Lights in the heavens for seasons—Gen. 1:14. Made permanent—Gen. 8:22. Rain given in its season—Deut. 28:12. Life likened to harvest—Job 5:26; Ps. 1:3. Stated season for feasts—Ex. 13:10; 23:14; Lev. Ch. 23; II Chr. 8:13; **Ez. 45:25,** Lu. 2:41. Moon appointed **for**—Ps. 104:19. For everything a season—Eccl. 3:1-8. Rains governed by—Jer. 5:24; Ez. 34:26. God changeth them—Dan. 2:21. Season of figs—Mk. 11:13. God continues them—Deut. 11:14; Job 38:22-32; Joel 2:23; Acts 14:17. Guilty husbandmen—Mt. 21:34-41; Lu. 20:10. Must ever watch—Luke 21:36. Spiritual refreshing—Acts 3:19. Times and seasons not revealed—Acts 1:7. Angel went down to pool—John 5:4. Always urgent—II Tim. 4:2. Felix dismisses Paul—Acts 24:25. Moses declines pleasure for a season—Heb. 11:25.

SEAT: Position of.—I Sam. 1:9; 4:13.

Of kings on thrones, and elders.—I Ki. 10:19; Rev. 11:16. David—I Sam. 20:18, 25. Solomon—I Ki. 2:19. Of honor—Esth. 3:1. High places—Pr. 9:14. Of scoffers—Ps. 1:1. Of Moses—Mt. 23:2. Fallen from—I Sam. 4:18. Chief seats in the synagogue—Mt. 23:6; Mk. 12:39; Lu. 11:43; 20:46. Overthrown, of them that sold the doves—Mt. 21:12; Mk. 11:15.

Of God.—Job 23:3; Ez. 28:2. Judgment seat—Mt. 27:19; John 19:13; Acts 18:12, 16, 17; 25:6, 10, 17; Rom. 14:10; Jas. 2:6.

Of Christ.—II Cor. 5:10.

Figurative.—Of image of jealousy—Ez. 8:3. Of violence—Amos 6:3.

SEBA, sē′ba. (1) **Grandson of Ham.**—Gen. 10:7; I Chr. 1:9.

(2) **Land of.**—Ps. 72; Is. 43:3.

SECACAH, sĕk′a-kah. **A city in Judah.**—Josh. 15:61.

SECOND. Admonition — Tit. 3:10. Brother was—II Chr. 31:12. Day—Acts 28:13. Epistle—II Pet. 3:1. Man —I Cor. 15:47. Sign—John 4:54. Time —I Sam. 18:21; Mk. 14:72. Watch —Lu. 12:38.

SECOND COMING. See JESUS, SECOND COMING OF.

SECOND DEATH. Rev. 2:11; 20:14; 21:8. See DEATH.

SECONDLY. I Cor. 12:23.

SECRET. Alms in—Mt. 6:4. Anything —Lu. 8:17. Bread eaten in—Pr. 9: 17. Concerning this—Dan. 2:18. Counsel of God—Job 15:8. Errand—Ju. 3:19. Gift in—Pr. 21:14. Heart, Of —Ps. 41:21. Hidden—Ez. 28:3. Keep me—Job 14:13. King demanded—Dan. 2:27. Learned—Phil. 4:12. Lurketh in—Ps. 10:9. Made—Mk. 4: 22. Men, Of—Rom. 2:16. Not spoken in—Is. 45:19. Not to be revealed—Pr. 11:13; 25:9; 26:20; Mt. 18:15. Places—I Sam. 19:2; Ps. 10:8; 64:4; 91:1; Jer. 49:10; Lam. 3:10; Ez. 7:22. Revealed unto Daniel—Dan. 2:19. Sins—Ps. 90:8. Smiteth neighbor in —Deut. 27:24. Talebearer revealeth—Pr. 11:13. Wisdom, Of—Job 11:6. See DEEP THINGS, MYSTERY, PRIVATELY.

SECRETLY. John 19:38. Brought—Job 4:12. Called Mary—John 11:28. Commune with David—I Sam. 18:22. Devour the poor—Hab. 3:14. Entice—Josh. 2:1; Job 31:27. Flee—Gen. 31: 27. Keep them—Ps. 31:20. King asked —Jer. 37:17. Show partiality—Job 13:10. Spies—Josh. 2:1.

SECRET THINGS. Belong unto Jehovah—Deut. 29:29. Come to light—Mk. 4:22. Doeth—John 7:4. Revealeth —Dan. 2:22. See DEEP THINGS, MYSTERY.

SECT. Acts 5:17; 15:5; 24:5, 14; 26:5; 28:22. See FACTIONS, HERODIANS, JUDAIZERS, PHARISEES, SADDUCEES.

SECU, se-cu. **A city in Benjamin.**—I Sam. 19:22.

SECUNDUS, se-cŭn′dus. **A disciple of Thessalonica.**—20:4.

SECURE, *adj.* Ju. 8:11; 18:10, 27; Job 11:18; 12:8; Ez. 34:27; Amos 6:1.

SECURE, *v.* Acts 27:16.

SECURELY. Dwell—Pr. 1:33; 3:29; Ez. 28:26. Pass by—Mic. 2:8. Walk—Pr. 3:29.

SECURITY. Dwell in—Ju. 18:7.

SEDITION. Ezra 4:15, 19. See INSURRECTION, REBELLION.

SEDUCTION, Leading astray.—Sexual seduction: Laws concerning—Ex. 22: 16–17; Deut. 22:23–29.

Instances of: Lot—Gen. 19:30–35. Dinah —Gen. 34:2. Bilhah by Reuben—Gen. 35:22; 49:3; Deut. 27:20; I Chr. 5:1, 2. Judah—Gen. 38:13–18. Attempted seduction of Joseph—Gen. 39:7–12. Bath-sheba—II Sam. 11:2–5. Warnings against—Pr. 6:23–35; 7:4–27; 9:13–18.

Political.—Israel—II Ki. 21:9–12; Ez. 13:10. Samson—Ju. 16:4–20. Egypt —Is. 19:13.

Spiritual.—Jer. 3:9; Mk. 13:22; I Tim. 4:1; II Tim. 3:13; I John 2:26; Rev. 2:20.

SEE. Ex. 25:40; Deut. 1:36; Num. 21: 8; Jer. 2:10; Acts 8:23; II Cor. 9:13. Aught—Mt. 8:23. Blood—Ex. 12:13. Clearly—Mt. 7:5. Come and—John 1:39. Death—John 8:51. Desire—Mic. 4:11. Eye to eye—Is. 52:8. Eyes shall —Mal. 1:5. Face, Not—Ex. 33:20. Faith—Mk. 2:5. God—Mt. 5:8; Gen. 16:13. He will never—Ps. 10:11. Him as he is—I John 3:2. Jesus—John 12:21. Lest they—Is. 6:10. Maid—Lu. 22:56. Man—Pr. 22:3; Acts 4:14. Many shall—Ps. 40:3. Not—Ps. 115: 5; Mt. 23:39; Heb. 2:8; I Pet. 1:8. Now I—John 9:25. Salvation—Ex. 14:13. Search and—John 7:52. Secret, In—Mt. 6:4. That Jehovah is good—Ps. 34:8. There is hope—Pr. 19:18. They are burned—Neh. 4:2. Thou art come—Pr. 6:3. Thou hold back—Pr. 24:11. Where he is—II Ki. 6:13. Ye despise not—Mt. 18:10. Ye seek a proof—II Cor. 13:3. See BLINDNESS.

SEED: Vegetable.—Development of—Gen. 1:11, 12, 29.

Seed time.—Gen. 8:22; Eccl. 7:6. Each kind has its own body—I Cor. 15:38. Must be put into ground and die—John 12:24. Not to be sown in Sabbatical year, nor Jubilee year—Lev. 25:4, 20; 25:11. Rechabites to sow nothing—Jer. 35:7, 9.

Law with regard to sowing.—Lev. 19:19; Deut. 22:9.

Seed in time of famine.—Gen. 47:19, 23, 24. Egyptian seed needs irrigation —Deut. 11:10. Seed like manna—Ex. 16:31; Num. 11:7. Place with no—Num. 20:5. Seed consumed by locusts —Deut. 28:38; Joel 1:4. Requires rain —Is. 55:10. Choked by thorns—Jer. 12:13; Mt. 13:7; Lu. 8:14. Seed rots under clods—Joel 1:17.

Parable of the Sower.—Mt. Ch. 13; Mk. Ch. 4; Lu. Ch. 8. Lessons from sowing of—Eccl. 11:6; Hos. 10:12; II Cor. 9:6, 10.

Signifying posterity.—Eve and the serpent—Gen. 3:15. Birth of Seth—Gen. 4:25. Noah and animals—Gen. 7:3; 9:9. Abraham's posterity—Gen. 12:7; 13:15, 16; 15:3, 13, 18; 16:10; 17:7–19; 21:12, 13; 22:17, 18; 24:7, 60; 28:4, 13, 14; 32:12; 35:12; Ex. 32:13; Deut. 1:8; 4:37; Lu. 1:55; John 8:33, 37; Rom. 4:13; 11:1; II Cor. 11:22; Gal. 3:29; Heb. 2:16; 11:18.

Seed of copulation.—Lev. 12:2; 15:16, 17, 18, 32. Seed passing through fire of Moloch—Lev. 18:21; 20:2, 3, 4. Aaronic seed must not be profaned or blemished—Lev. 21:14, 15, 17, 21; 22:3, 4. Destruction of royal—I Sam. 24:21; II Ki. 11:1; II Chr. 22:10. Mixture of holy—Ezra 9:2; Neh. 7:61. Jews in Esther's time, protect their—Esth. 9:27; 28:31. Raising up seed to brother—Mt. 22:24–28; Mk. 12:19–23.

Christ as seed.—Acts 13:23; Gal. 3:16, 19, 29; II Tim. 2:8.

Word of God, as seed.—Lu. 8:11; I Pet. 1:23.

Seed of righteous.—Never beg bread—Ps. 37:25–26. Shall come again bringing sheaves—Ps. 126:6. Shall be delivered—Pr. 11:21. Shall not labor in vain—Is. 65:23. Doth not commit sin—I John 3:9.

Seed of wicked.—Be cut off—Ps. 37:28; 106:27; Is. 1:4, 7; 57:3, 13; Jer. 22:28. Shall not prosper—Jer. 22:30. Shall cease from being a nation—Jer. 31:36. To be punished—Jer. 36:31.

SEEDTIME. See SOWING and REAPING.

SEEKING. God and His Christ seek men.—Sent messengers early—II Chr. 36:15, 16; Jer. 25:4. All day—Is. 65:2; Rom. 10:21. Seeks true worshippers —John 4:23. As a shepherd—Lu. 15:3–7; John 10:11, 15, 16. As a redeemer—Mt. 20:28; Mk. 10:45; Lu. 19:10.

Men sought to see Jesus.—Shepherds—Lu. 2:15, 16. Wise Men—Mt. 2:1, 2, 10, 11. John's disciples—John 1:37, 38, 41, 45. Nicodemus—John 3:1, 2. Galilæans—John 6:24. Zaccheus—Lu. 19:3. Greeks—John 12:20, 21.

Exhortations to seek God: Because—God requires it—Deut. 10:12, 13; Mic. 6:8; Acts 17:26, 27. He will punish—Deut. 11:16, 17; Josh. 24:19, 20, 23; I Sam. 12:14, 15; Amos 4:12; Zeph. 2:3; I Chr. 28:9; II Chr. 15:2; Jer. 29:13; Lam. 3:25, 26. He can be found—Deut. 4:29; Mt. 7:7, 8; Acts 17:27, 28. It glorifies His name—I Ki. 8:60, 61. Man always seeks a god—Is. 8:19, 20. Now is the time—Eccl. 12:1; Is. 55:3, 6, 7. God is good—Lam. 3:25, 26. Of what God has done—I Chr. 22:18, 19; Ps. 65:9–13; Ez. 34:26, 27; Acts 14:17. Of what God will do—Ezra 8:22; Ps. 1:3; 34:10; 37:4, 7, 9, 34; 69:32; 70:4; 105:4; 119:2; Heb. 6:11, 12, 17–20; 11:6.

Seeking knowledge of God is seeking God.—Pr. 2:3–5; John 17:3. It is blessed—Is. 30:18; Mt. 5:6. It is the step to strength—I Chr. 16:10, 11; Is. 40:29–31. It leads to honor—I Sam. 2:30; Is. 49:23; Rom. 2:7–10. It is the track to all things—Mt. 7:11; Rom. 8:16, 17, 28, 32. It is the path to mercy—Hos. 10:12; 12:6; Joel 2:12, 13.

It is the way of life.—Amos 5:4–9, 14. It is the road to heaven—Mt. 7:13; Lu. 10:42; 12:33; 13:24; John 6:27. It is the highway of holiness—Is. 35:8–10; II Pet. 3:14. It is the walk with God—Lu. 11:13; I Cor. 6:17, 19; Col. 3:1–3; I John 1:3.

An earthly good.—Israel—Ex. 17:3, 4–6; 1 s. 44:24–26. Samaritans—II Ki. 17: 26, 27. Palsied man—Mk. 2:3, 4. Bartimæus—Mk. 10:46–50.

Disciples in a storm.—Mt. 8:24–26. Paul—II Cor. 12:7, 8. Multitudes—Mk. 1:36, 37; John 6:25–27. Rebuked —Mt. 6:25–32; Lu. 12:22–30; John 6:26, 27.

A spiritual blessing.—Jacob at Peniel—Gen. 32:26. Job—Job 23:3, 4–6. The patriarchs—Heb. 11:10, 13, 14, 15, 25–27. David—I Ki. 3:6; 9:4; Ps. 42:1, 2, 10; 63:1, 2. Children of Israel—II Chr. 15:12–15. Jehoshaphat (partly) —II Chr. 19:3. Josiah—II Chr. 34:3. Ezra—Ezra 7:10. Daniel—Dan. 9:3, 4. Anna—Lu. 2:37. Zacchæus—Lu. 19:2, 3. Paul—Phil. 3:12–14. Christians—Heb. 13:14. Encouragement—Mt. 6:33; Lu. 12:31. Men traveled 600 miles to seek God—Ezra 6:21. Men pretended to be seekers of God—Ezra 4:2; Mt. 15:7–9. God is not sought in vain—Is. 45:19. Kings Uzziah and Hezekiah prospered as long as they sought Him—II Chr. 26:4, 5; 31:21.

SEEMLY. Behavior—I Pet. 2:12. For a fool—Pr. 19:10. That a woman pray —I Cor. 11:13.

SEER. Amos—Amos 7:12. Art thou not a—II Sam. 15:27. Asaph the—II Chr. 29:30. Covered—Is. 29:10. David's—II Sam. 24:11. Every—II Ki. 17:13. King's—I Chr. 25:5; II Chr. 29:25. Now called prophet—I Sam. 9:9. Put to shame—Mic. 3:7. Samuel the—I Chr. 9:22, 29. Words of—II Chr. 33:18. See PROPHETS.

SEGUB, se'gub. (1) Father of Jair.—I Chr. 2:21.

(2) Son of Hiel.—I Ki. 16:34.

SEIR, se'ir. (1) Gen. 36:20; I Chr. 1:38. (2) See EDOM.

MT. SEIR (a hilly region south of the Salt Sea and reaching to the Elanitic gulf).

Occupied in succession by Horites.—Gen. 14:6; 36:20–30; Deut. 2:12, 22. Edomites—Gen. 32:3; 33:14, 16; 26:8, 9; Num. 24:18; Deut. 2:4, 5.

Israel defeated in.—Deut. 1:44. Wanderings by—Deut. 1:2; 2:1. Blessing of Moses—Deut. 33:2. Predictions about

—Is. 21:11; Ez. 35:2, 3, 7, 15. Sons of Seir—I Chr. 1:38. Children of Mt. Seir—II Chr. 20:10, 22, 23. Smoke the Children of Seir—II Chr. 25:11. Gods of Children of Seir—II Chr. 25:14. When thou wentest out of Seir—Ju. 5:4. Went to Mt. Seir—I Chr. 4:42. See MOUNTAINS.

SEIZED. Darkness, Let—Job 3:6. Jesus—John 18:12. Passages—Jer. 51: 32. Trembling hath—Jer. 49:24. See FAKE.

SELA, se'la. (1) A hill.—I Sam. 23:28. (2) Capital of Edom.—II Ki. 14:7; Is. 16:6; 42:11.

SELAH. See MUSIC, PSALMS.

SELA-HAMMAHLEKOTH, se'la–hăm'-mah-le'koth. A mountain.—I Sam. 23: 28.

SELED, se'led. A man of Judah.—I Chr. 2:30.

SELEUCIA, se-leū'si-à. A seaport of Antioch.—Acts 13:4.

SELF. Lovers of—II Tim. 3:2. See SELFISHNESS.

SELF-CONTROL. See CHRISTIAN GRACES.

SELF-DENIAL: A Christian manner of conduct, result of love.—Practised by Christ—Mt. 4:8–10; 8:20; 20:22; Lu. 22:42; Rom. 15:3; II Cor. 5:14, 15; Phil. 2:4–8. The law of self-sacrifice—John 12:24–26.

Paul's teaching helpful.—Rom. 15:1, 2; I Cor. 6:12; 9:4–19; 10:23, 24; Phil. 3:7–9.

Resisting (avoiding) temptation.—Mt. 5:29, 30; 18:8, 9; Mk. 9:43; Rom. 6: 12, 13; 8:13; Gal. 5:24; Eph. 4:22; Col. 3:5; Heb. 11:24, 25; I Pet. 2:11; 4:2, 3.

Control of appetite.—Pr. 23:2, 3; Dan. 10:3; Rom. 14:15.

Avoiding entanglements.—II Cor. 6:3–5; II Tim. 2:4; Tit. 2:12.

Denial of self.—Gen. 13:9; Mt. 16:24; Mk. 8:34, 35; Lu. 9:23.

Losing and finding life.—Mt. 10:38, 39; 16:25; Mk. 8:35, 36; Lu. 9:24, 25.

Preferring others to Christ.—Mt. 8:21, 22; 10:35–37; Lu. 14:26, 27.

Ways to show self-denial.—Gen. 22:10–12; I Sam. 12:3–5; I Ki. 17:12–15; Dan. 1:8; Mt. 19:21, 22, 27; Mk. 1:16–20; Lu. 3:10, 11; 12:33; 18:22–24; 21: 2–4; Acts 2:45; 20:33–35; I Cor. 9:18;

Gal. 6:14. See CONVERSION, CHRISTIAN GRACES, JESUS, TEACHING OF.

SELF-EXAMINATION. Ps. 4:4; I Cor. 11:28, 31; II Cor. 13:5; Gal. 6:4; I John 3:20-22. See EXAMINE.

SELF, SELFISHNESS. Self-love is the root of egotism. Selfishness and self-righteousness. Unselfishness under the law—Lev. 17:18. More fully developed and taught by Christ and the apostles—Mt. 19:19; 22:39; Mk. 12: 31; Lu. 10:27; Rom. 13:9; 15:2; I Cor. 10:24, 33; 13:5; II Cor. 12:14; Gal. 5: 14. Royal law of unselfishness—Gal. 2:8. Lovers of self—II Tim. 3:2; Phil. 2:21. Abstain unselfishly, for sake of neighbor—Rom. 14:21; I Cor. 8:13. Giving no occasion for stumbling—Acts 24:16; I Cor. 10:32; II Cor. 6:3.

Examples of.—Cain—Gen. 4:9. Nabal—I Sam. 25:3, 11. Haman—Esth. 6:6. Priests—Is. 56:11. James and John—Mk. 10:37. See SELF-DENIAL.

SELF-RIGHTEOUSNESS. Pr. 30:12; Lu. 18:10-12. Church of Laodicea, Of—Rev. 3:17. Israel, Of—Rom. 10:3. Lawyer, Of—Lu. 10:25, 29. Pharisees, Of—Lu. 11:39; 18:11, 12; John 8:33; 9:28. Saul, Of—I Sam. 15:13. Young man, Of—Mt. 19:20. See BOASTING.

SELF-WILL. II Pet. 2:10. Bishop not —Tit. 1:7. In their—Gen. 49:6. See REBELLION, SELFISHNESS, STUBBORN, WILFUL, WILL.

SELL. Gen. 37:27. All—Mt. 13:44. Birthright—Gen. 25:31. Cloak—Lu. 22:36. Daughter—Ex. 21:7. Go to them that—Mt. 25:9. Land—Ez. 30: 12. Linen garments—Pr. 31:24. Nations—Nah. 3:4. Oil—II Ki. 4:7. Ox —Ex. 21:35. People for nought—Ps. 44:12. Sons—Joel 3:8. That which thou hast—Mt. 19:21. Truth, not—Pr. 23:23. See BUY, COMMERCE.

SELLER. Ez. 7:13. All kinds of wares, Of—Neh. 13:20. As with buyer so with—Is. 24:2. Mourn, not—Ez. 7:12. Purple, Of—Acts 16:14. See BUY, COMMERCE.

SEMACHIAH, sĕm′a-kī′ah. **A descendant of Obed-edom.**—I Chr. 26:7.

SEMEIN, sĕm′e-in. **An ancestor of Jesus.**—Lu. 3:36.

SENAAH, sē-nā′ah. **A city inhabited by returned exiles.**—Ezra 2:35; Neh. 7:38.

SEND. Is. 27:8. Angel before thee—Gen. 24:7. As lambs among wolves—Lu. 10:3. Captives—II Chr. 28:11. Forth—Job 37:3. Gentiles, Unto—Acts 26:17; 28:28. God did—Gen. 45: 5. Good speed—Gen. 24:12. Help—Ps. 20:2. Here am I—Is. 6:8. Him, whom thou didst—John 17:3. His own son—Rom. 8:3. Jesus—Acts 3:20. Laborers—Mt. 9:38. Light—Ps. 43:3. Lost sheep, Unto—Mt. 15:24. My messenger—Lu. 7:27. Peace—Mt. 10:34. Prosperity—Ps. 118:25. Salvation is —Acts 28:28. Servants—Mt. 21:34, 36. Sickle—Rev. 14:15. Soldier—Mk. 6:27. Sword—Ps. 107:20.

SENEH, sē′neh. **One of the crags in the pass of Michmash.**—I Sam. 14:4.

SENIR, sē′nir. **Amorite name for Hermon.**—Deut. 3:9; I Chr. 5:23; Song of Sol. 4:8.

SENNACHERIB, sen-năk′e-rĭb. **King of Assyria.**—II Ki. 18:13; 19:16, 20, 36; II Chr. 32:1, 2, 9, 10, 22; Is. 36: 1; 37:17, 21, 37.

SENSELESS. Hearts—Rom. 1:21. See PAST FEELING.

SENSES. Exercised—Heb. 5:14. Gave the—Neh. 8:8. See MIND.

SENSUAL. Jude 19. This wisdom is—Jas. 3:15. See LUST.

SENT. Ju. 6:14; John 8:29. But unto lost sheep—Mt. 15:24. Except they be—Rom. 10:15. Forth a raven—Gen. 8:7. From God—John 1:6. I am hath —Ex. 3:14. Me, to bind up—Is. 61:1. Receiveth him that—Mt. 10:40. Son—Mt. 21:37. You to reap—John 4:38. See GREAT COMMISSION.

SENTENCE: Sentence of judgment.—Deut. 17:9-11; Eccl. 8:11. See JUDGMENT.

Sentence of kings.—Ps. 17:2; Pr. 16:10. Of Pilate.—Lu. 23:24.

Dark sentences.—Dan. 5:12; 8:23.

Figurative.—Sentence of death—II Cor. 1:9.

SERORIM, se-ō′rim. **A priest.**—I Chr. 24:8.

SEPARATION. Gen. 13:9; Num. 6:12; Lu. 6:22. Aaron was—I Chr. 23:13.

Paul and Barnabas—Acts 13:2. Christ, From—Eph. 2:12. Friends—Pr. 16:28. Gospel, Unto—Rom. 1:1. Love, From—Rom. 8:35, 39. Make—Jude 19. Sheep from goats—Mt. 25:32. Sinners, From—Heb. 7:26. Wings—Ez. 1:11. See CONSECRATION, PURIFICATION, SANCTIFICATION.

SEPHAR, sē'phar. A place—Gen. 10:30.

SEPHARAD, sĕph'a-rad. An unknown locality.—Ob. 20.

SEPHARVAIM, sĕph'ar-vā'im. A city taken by Assyrians.—II Ki. 17:24, 31.

SEPULCHRE OF. Abraham is given choice of, to bury his dead—Gen. 23:6. Moses unknown—Deut. 34:6. Joash and Gideon—Ju. 8:32. Rachel—I Sam. 10:2. Zeruiah and Asahel—II Sam. 2:32. Kish—II Sam. 21:14. Jehoram—II Ki. 9:28. Elisha—II Ki. 13:21. Josiah—II Ki. 23:30. Asa—II Chr. 16:14. Sons of David—II Chr. 32:33. Prophets—Mt. 23:29.

Of our Lord.—Mary was sitting against—Mt. 27:61. Sepulchre made sure until third day—Mt. 27:64, 66. Mary and Mary Magdalene come to see—Mt. 28:1.

Kinds of.—Open—Ps. 5:9; Jer. 5:16; Rom. 3:13. Whited—Mt. 23:27.

Prepared during lifetime.—Hewed out here—Is. 22:16.

Places of.—Father's sepulchre—Neh. 2:3. Josiah buried in—II Chr. 35:24. Ahithophel in—II Sam. 17:23. Thy father's—I Ki. 13:22, 31. Prophet of Bethel—II Ki. 23:17.

Figurative.—Ps. 5:9; Is. 22:16; Jer. 5:16; Mt. 23:27; Rom. 3:13. See BURIAL PLACES, GRAVE.

SERAH, sē'rah. A daughter of Asher.—Gen. 46:17; Num. 26:46; I Chr. 7:30.

SERAIAH, se-rā'iah. (1) **A priest in the days of Zedekiah.**—II Ki. 25:18; I Chr. 6:14; Ezra 7:1; Jer. 52:24; I Chr. 6:14.

(2) **A scribe of David.**—II Sam. 8:17.

(3) **Brother of Othniel.**—I Chr. 4:13, 14.

(4) **A Simeonite.**—I Chr. 4:35.

(5) **Son of Tanhumeth.**—II Ki. 25:23; Jer. 40:8.

(6) **Son of Hilkiah.**—Neh. 11:11.

(7) **A priest who returned with Zerubbabel.**—Ezra 2:2; Neh. 10:2; 12:11, 12.

(8) **A man sent by Jehoiakim to take Jeremiah and Baruch.**—Jer. 36:26.

(9) **A prince of Judah.**—Jer. 51:59, 61.

SERAPHIM, sĕr'a-phim. Is. 6:2.

SERED. Son of Zebulun.—Gen. 46:14.

SERGIUS-PAULUS, sĕr'gi-us-pạu'lus. Proconsul of Cyprus.—Acts 13:7.

SERJEANTS. Magistrates sent.—Acts 16:35. Reported these words—Acts 16:38.

SERMON ON THE MOUNT. Mt. Chs. 5–7; Lu. 6:20–49.

SERPENT: As tempter.—Gen. 3:1, 14; II Cor. 11:3; Rev. 12:9; 20:2. Moses rod turned into—Ex. 4:3, 7, 9, 15. Brazen—Num. 21:9; II Ki. 18:4; John 3:14, 15. Fiery—Num. 21:6; Deut. 8:15; Is. 14:29; 30:6. Offspring of—Mt. 3:7; 12:34; 23:33; Lu. 3:7. Poisonous—Deut. 32:33; Job 20:16; Ps. 58:4; Eccl. 10:11; Mk. 16:18; Lu. 10:19; Acts 28:3. Will he give him a—Mt. 7:10; Lu. 11:11. Eating dust—Gen. 3:14; Is. 65:25; Mic. 7:17. Wise—Gen. 3:1; Eccl. 10:8; Amos 5:19; Mt. 10:6.

SERVANT: Early mention of.—Gen. 9:25–26.

Divided into: Male—Gen. 24:34. Female—Gen. 16:6. Bond—Gen. 43:18; Lev. 25:46. Hired—Mk. 1:20; Lu. 15:17. Called hirelings—John 10:12–13.

Servitude under the patriarchs.—Was of two kinds, born in the house, and bought with money—Gen. 17:13. Abraham formed an army out of his 318—Gen. 14:1–16. Those born in house had large privileges—Gen. 15:2–3; 24:2–9; 17:12–14. Jacob bought his wives with labor—Gen. 29:16–23. Joseph was sold into Egypt—Gen. 37:27–28.

Egyptian bondage.—Egyptians had servants—Ex. 8:21, 24; 9:14, 20, 21; 11:5. Israelites not distributed among Egyptians—Gen. 46:33–34; Ex. 8:21–24; 9:23. Service required of the males by taskmasters—Ex. 1:8–14; 5:4–21.

Servitude under Moses.—Laws of Moses concerning—Ex. 21:1–11, 20–32; Lev. 19:20–22; 25:6, 10, 44–54; Deut. 15:12–18.

Israelites were no men-stealers.—Ex. 21:16; Deut. 24:7. Service either voluntarily or judicially imposed—Lev. 25:

39, 47; Ex. 21:7; 22:3, 4; Deut. 20:14. Strangers, only, might be purchased—Lev. 25:44-46. Not to be oppressed—Deut. 24:14-15. Could change his master—Deut. 23:16. If abused he went free—Ex. 21:26-27. Term limited—Deut. 15:12.

Privileges of.—Admitted into covenant with God—Deut. 29:10, 13. Took part at festivals—Ex. 12:43, 44; Deut. 12: 18; 16:10-16.

Instructed in conduct of life.—Deut. 31: 10-13; Josh. 8:33-35; II Chr. 17:8-9; 34:30. Under same law as masters—Deut. 1:16, 17; 27:19; Lev. 19:15; 24:22. Rights the same—Num. 15:15, 16, 29. Intermarried with master's family—Gen. 16:1, 2, 6; 30:3, 9.

Hired.—Engaged by the day—Mt. 20:2. By the year—Lev. 25:53; Is. 16:14. To be paid when work is done—Lev. 19:13; Deut. 24:15. To be esteemed worthy of wages—Lu. 10:7. To partake of produce of land in Sabbatical year—Lev. 25:6. If foreigners, not allowed to partake of holy things—Ex. 12:45; Lev. 22:10.

Bondservants.—Bought and sold—Gen. 17:13, 27; 37:28, 36; 39:17; Lev. 22: 11; Deut. 28:68; Esth. 7:4; Ez. 27:13; Joel 3:6; Rev. 18:13. See BONDAGE.

Captives of war made slaves.—II Ki. 5: 2; II Chr. 28:8-10. Portion of captives given to priests and Levites—Num. 31:28-47.

Other classes made slaves.—Sojourners—Lev. 25:45. Belonging to foreign nations—Lev. 25:44. Unable to pay debts—II Ki. 4:1; Neh. 5:4-5; Mt. 18:25. Thieves unable to make restitution—Ex. 22:3.

Kindness enjoined.—Lev. 25:43; Eph. 6:9.

Shown by Job.—Job 31:13-14. By Boaz—Ruth 2:4. By Centurion—Mt. 8:8-13. In redeeming them—Neh. 5:8. Emancipation—II Chr. 36:23; Ezra 1: 1-4; Jer. 34:8-16; Acts 6:9; I Cor. 7:21.

New Testament principles. — Cannot serve two masters—Mt. 6:24; Lu. 16: 13. He that serves is greatest—Mt. 20:26-28; 23:11; Mk. 9:35; 10:43, 44. Advance from servants to friends—**John 15:15.** To serve one another—

Gal. 5:13. Render justice to servants—Col. 4:1. Must not be eye-servers—Col. 3:22. Obedience becomes servants—Eph. 6:5. Believing masters to be honored—I Tim. 6:1-2. Must not purloin from or gainsay—Tit. 2:9-10. Must treat believing servants as brothers and sisters—I Cor. 7:20-22. Philemon 16. See ''Teaching of Jesus concerning servants,'' FRATERNITY.

Term servant used by people to express courtesy.—Gen. 18:3; 32:5; 33:5; I Sam. 20:7; I Ki. 20:32.

Examples of good.—Eliezer—Gen. 24: 10. Jacob—Gen. 31:36-42. Joseph—Gen. 39:5; 41:39; Acts 7:10. Boaz—Ruth 2:4. Jonathan's—I Sam. 14:6-7. Abigail's—I Sam. 25:14-17. David's—II Sam. 12:18. Naaman's—II Ki. 5:2-13. Centurion's—Mt. 8:9. Cornelius—Acts 10:7. Phœbe—Rom. 16:1. Onesimus—Phil. 11.

Examples of bad: Hagar—Gen. 16:4. Of Abraham and Lot—Gen. 13:7. Of Abimelech—Gen. 21:25. Of Absalom—II Sam. 13:28-29; 14:30. Ziba—II Sam. 16:1-4. Zimri—I Ki. 16:9. Gehazi—II Ki. 5:20. Of Joash—II Ki. 12:19-21. Of Amon—II Ki. 21:23. See also Mt. 18:28; 25:14-30; Lu. 19: 12-26.

SERVICE. Acts 24:14. As deacons—I Tim. 3:10. Choose, whom ye will—Josh. 24:15. Cumbered about much—Lu. 10:40. God, Unto—Mal. 3:14; John 16:2. Grievous—II Chr. 10:4. Hard—Ex. 1:14. Most of heaven—Acts 7:42. King's—Esth. 8:10. Lord—Acts 20:19. Nations shall—Ps. 72: 11. One another—I Pet. 5:5. Perfect heart, With—I Chr. 28:9. Seed shall—Ps. 22:30. Spiritual—Rom. 12:1. Two masters—Mt. 6:24. War, In—I Chr. 7:40. Whom should I—II Sam. 16:19. See TABERNACLE, TEMPLE, CHURCH, WORSHIP.

SETH, sĕth. **Son of Adam.**—Gen. 4:25. Descendants of—Gen. 5:1-32.

SETHUR, sē'thur. **An Asherite spy.**—Num. 13:13.

SETTER. Forth of strange gods—Acts 17:18.

SETTINGS. Ex. 28:11. See JEWELS.

SETTLE. I Chr. 17:14; Is. 34:14; Acts 19:39.

SEVEN. Hebrew people had their favorite numbers to which they were constantly resorting. Seven and forty were conspicuous. Many modern writers think these numbers were sometimes used to express a group of things in an indefinite way. Some believe these numbers to be mystical.

I. **The number seven.**—Seven sabbaths shall be complete passover—Lev. 23: 15; Deut. 16:9–12. Build seven altars, prepare seven oxen, rams—Num. 23:1, 29. Rams and bullocks—Num. 29:32; I Chr. 15:26; II Chr. 29:21; Job 42:8; Ez. 45:23. Nations greater—Deut. 7: 1; Acts 13:19. Weeks thou shalt number—Deut. 16:9. Abraham offers seven ewe lambs to Abimelech—Gen. 21:28. Flee before thee seven ways—Deut. 28:7. Remained of Israel seven tribes —Josh. 18:2. Barren hath borne—I Sam. 2:5. In seven troubles no evil —Job 5:19. Abominations—Pr. 6:16– 19. Wisdom hath hewn seven pillars —Pr. 9:1. Portion to seven, also to eight—Eccl. 11:2. Women take hold of one man—Is. 4:1. Months to be burying—Ez. 39:12. Messiah, shall be seven weeks—Dan. 9:25. Lean and fat cattle—Gen. 41:2–4, 19, 20, 26–31. Good and thin ears of grain—Gen. 41:5–7, 26, 27. Upon one stone seven eyes—Zech. 3:9; 4:10. And seven men had her—Mk. 12:20–22; Lu. 20: 29, 31. John to seven churches—Rev. 1:4, 11, 20. When he cried, seven thunders—Rev. 10:3. Dragon having seven heads, etc.—Rev. 12:3. Plagues —Lev. 26:21, 24, 28; Rev. 15:1, 6. One of the seven angels—Rev. 15:1, 6, 7; 16:1; 17:1; 21:9. Better than seven sons—Ruth 4:15. Loaves and a few fishes—Mt. 15:34. Baskets left —Mt. 15:37. Men that can render a reason—Pr. 26:16.

II. **Seven days.**—The week—Gen. 2:3; Ex. 16:22–30; 20:8–11. Noah in Ark before the flood came—Gen. 7:4, 10; 8:10, 12. Dove sent out after seven days—Gen. 8:10, 12. Laban pursues Jacob—Gen. 31:23. Plague of bloody waters in Egypt—Ex. 7:20–25. Passover and unleavened bread—Ex. 12: 15; 23:15; 34:18; Deut. 16:3. Feast of Tabernacles—Lev. 23:34, 42; Deut.

16:13, 16. Israelites went round Jericho—Josh. 6:4; Heb. 11:30. Consecration of priests and altars—Ex. 29:30, 35–37; Lev. 8:33. Defilements lasted —Lev. 12:2; 13:4, 5; 15:19, 24, 28. Miriam shut up without the camp— Num. 12:15. Fasts—I Sam. 31:13. Wedding feast lasted seven days— Ju. 14:12–17. First-born of flocks before offering—Ex. 22:30. Feast of Ahasuerus—Esth. 1:5. Paul tarries at Troas—Acts 20:6; at Tyre—Acts 21: 4; at Puteoli—Acts 28:13, 14.

III. **Seven weeks.**—(See SEVEN.)

IV. **Seven months.**—Holy convocation—· Lev. 23:24–44; Num. 29:1–12; Ez. 45: 25. Ark rested in the seventh month —Gen. 8:4. Annual atonement in the seventh month—Lev. 16:29. The ark brought into the temple in the seventh month—I Ki. 8:1–6.

V. **Seven years.**—Jacob serves for Rachel and Leah—Gen. 29:15–20. Seven good kine are seven years— Gen. 41:26, 27. Plenty and famine in Egypt—Gen. 41:1–57. Famine in Canaan—II Ki. 8:1. Building of temple required seven years—I Ki. 6: 38. Insanity of Nebuchadrezzar— Dan. 4:32. Period of Jubilee, seven times seven—Lev. 25:8.

VI. **Miscellaneous.**—Clean beasts taken into ark—Gen. 7:2. Birds of the air taken into ark—Gen. 7:3. Rams and bullocks in sacrifices—Lev. 23:18. Seven steps in temple vision—Ez. 40: 22, 26. Heat of furnace—Dan. 3:19. Light of sun increased—Is. 30:26. Punishment of Israel—Lev. 26:18, 21, 24, 28. Purification of silver—Ps. 12: 6. Worshipping daily—Ps. 119:164. Seven chamberlains and princes at Ahasuerus' court—Esth. 1:10, 14. Seven deacons—Acts 6:3; 21:8. Seven shepherds sent against Assyria—Mic. 5:5, 6. Seven lamps and pipes—Zech. 4:2. Seven kings—Rev. 17:10. Seven seals—Rev. 5:1. Seven golden bowls —Rev. 15:7; 16:1. Samson is bound with seven green withes—Ju. 16:7, 8.

VII. **Spirits.**—Mt. 12:45; Lu. 11:26; Rev. 1:4; 3:1; 4:5; 5:6.

VIII. **Stars.**—Amos 5:8; Rev. 1:16, 20; 2:1; 3:1; 3:20.

IX. **Candlesticks.**—Ex. 25:31–37; 37:17–24; Zech. 4:2; Rev. 1:12, 20; 2:1.

X. **Angels.**—Rev. 8:2, 6–13; 9:1, 13; 11:15; 15:1, 6–8; 16:1; 21:9.

XI. **Gethsemane commands.**—Mt. 26:36, 38, 41, 45, 46, 52; John 18:8.

XII. **Easter promises of Jesus Christ.**—Mt. 28:10, 20; Mk. 16:16; 16:17; 16:18; Acts 1:5.

XIII. **Sevenfold Easter command.**—Mk. 16:15; Lu. 24:39, 49; John 20:22; 21:6, 10, 12, 15, 17. Last commands in v. 22.

XIV. **Last sentences of Jesus.**—Mt. 27:46; Mk. 15:34; Lu. 23:34, 43, 46; John 19:26–30.

XV. **Times.**—Jacob bowed before Esau—Gen. 33:3. Priests sprinkle blood—Lev. 4:6; 8:11; 14:7; 16:14; Num. 19:4. Sprinkle oil—Lev. 14:16. Sprinkle the house—Lev. 14:51. Forgive—Mt. 18:21; Lu. 17:4. Went around Jericho—Josh. 6:4. Elijah's servant looked for rain—I Ki. 18:43. Naaman washed in Jordan—II Ki. 5:10.

SEVENEH, sĕv′e-neh. **Tower of.**—Ez. 29:10.

SEVENTY SENT OUT. Appointed by the Lord—Lu. 10:1. Return of the seventy—Lu. 10:17. Indicating perhaps, prospectively, the broadening out of the commission, since the Jewish conception of mankind comprised 70 nations.

SEVENTY ELDERS. See ELDERS OF ISRAEL.

SEVER. Christ, From—Gal. 5:4. Wicked from—Mt. 13:49. See SEPARATE.

SEVERAL, SEVERALLY. Ability—Mt. 25:15. Building—Eph. 2:21. Dividing to every man—I Cor. 12:11. Love—Eph. 5:33. Members—Rom. 12:5; I Cor. 12:27. Speak—Heb. 9:5.

SEVERITY. God, Of—Rom. 11:22. Body, To the—Col. 2:23.

SEW. Fig-leaves—Gen. 3:7. Sackcloth under skin—Job 16:15. Pillows upon elbows—Ez. 13:18. Time—Eccl. 3:7. Undressed cloth—Mk. 2:21.

SHAALABBIN, shā′al-ăb′bin. **A city in Dan.**—Josh. 19:42; Ju. 1:35.

SHAALBIM, shā′al-bim. I Ki. 4:7. **Same as preceding.**

SHAALBONITE, sha-ăl′bo-nite. **Inhabitant of Shaalabbin.**—II Sam. 23:32.

SHAALIM, shā′al-im. Josh. 19:42; I Sam. 9:4.

SHAAPH, shā′aph. (1) **Son of Caleb son of Hezron.**—I Chr. 2:49.

(2) **Son of Jahdai son of Caleb.**—I Chr. 2:47.

SHAARAIM, shā′a-rā′im. **A city.**—Josh. 15:36; I Sam. 17:52; I Chr. 4:31.

SHAASHGAZ, sha-ăsh′găz. **One of the chamberlains of Ahasuerus.**—Esth. 2:14.

SHABBETHAI, shăb′be-thāi. (1) **A Levite in Jerusalem after the captivity.**—Neh. 11:16.

(2) **One who explained the law which Ezra read.**—Neh. 8:7.

(3) **Another Levite.**—Ezra 10:15.˙

SHACHIA, sha-kī′a. **A Benjamite.**—I Chr. 8:10.

SHACKLES. Jer. 29:26. See FETTERS.

SHADE. Heat, From—Is. 25:4. Jehovah is thy—Ps. 121:5. Rock, Of—Is. 32:2. Take refuge in—Ju. 9:15. See SHADOW.

SHADOW: Literal.—A protection or defence against heat. Of roof—Gen. 19:8. Forest—Ez. 31:3. Trees—Ju. 9:15; Job 40:22; Song of Sol. 2:3; Ez. 17:23; Hos. 4:13. Of Booth—Jonah 4:5. Gourd—Jonah 4:6. Mountains—Ju. 9:36. Pavilion for—Is. 4:6.

Other uses.—Cast by turning—Jas. 1:17. Shadow of Peter—Acts 5:15. On dial of Ahaz—II Ki. 20:9, 11; Is. 38:8.

Illustrative.—Of length of life. I Chr. 29:15; Job 8:9; 14:2; Ps. 102:11; 109:23; 144:4; Eccl. 6:12; 8:13. Time—Job 7:2; Song of Sol. 2:17; 4:6; Jer. 6:4. Rest—Is. 32:2. Goodness—Is. 25:4. Assyria's fate—Ez. 31:6, 12, 17. Jehovah's delight—Song of Sol. 2:3. Death—Job 3:5; 10:21, 22; 12:22; 16:16; 38:17; Ps. 23:4; 44:19; 107:10, 14; Is. 9:2; Jer. 2:6; 13:16; Amos 5:8; Mt. 4:16; Lu. 1:79.

Figurative.—Of the Almighty—Ps. 91:1; 121:5; Lam. 4:20; Hos. 14:7. Thy wings—Ps. 17:8; 36:7; 57:1; 63:7. His hand—Is. 49:2; 51:16. Vine—Ps. 80:10. Egypt—Is. 30:2, 3. Edom—Is. 34:15. Heshbon—Jer. 48:45. All members as—Job 17:7. The future—Col. 2:17. Heavenly things—Heb. 8:5; 10: 1.

Overshadowing. — Cherubim of glory overshadowing the mercy-seat—Heb. 9:5. See JESUS, TEACHING OF.

SHADRACH, shā'drak. Name given to one of Daniel's three companions.— Dan. 1:7; 2:49; 3:12–30.

SHAFT. Ex. 25:31; 37:17. Breaketh open—Job 38:4. Pointed—Job 41:26. Polished—Is. 49:2. Quiver, Of—Lam. 3:13. See ARCHERY, WEAPONS.

SHAGEE, shā'gee. Father of. one of David's mighty men.—I Chr. 11:34.

SHAHARAIM, shā'ha-rā'im. A Benjamite.—I Chr. 8:8.

SHAHAZUMAH, sha-hăz'u-mah. A city in Issachar.—Josh. 19:22.

SHAKE. Lu. 6:48. Bones—Job 4:14. Dust, Off—Mt. 10:14; Lu. 9:5. Earth shall be—Is. 13:13. Foundations—Ps. 82:5; Acts 16:26. Head—Jer. 18:16. Heavens and earth—Joel 3:16. Kingdom cannot be—Heb. 12:28. Lebanon, Like—Ps. 72:16. Mind, From—II Thess. 2:2. Mountains—Ps. 46:2. People—Job 34:20. Place—Acts 4:31. Together—Lu. 6:38. Wicked—Job 38: 13. Wind, With—Mt. 11:7; Lu. 7:24; Rev. 6:13. Yoke—Gen. 27:40.

SHALISHAH, shăl'i-shäh. A district in Ephraim.—I Sam. 9:4.

SHALLACHETH, shăl'le-kĕth. A gate of the first temple.—I Chr. 26:16.

SHALLUM, shăl'lum. (1) Husband of Huldah the prophetess.—II Ki. 22:14; II Chr. 34:22.

(2) A descendant of Jerahmeel.—I Chr. 2:40, 41.

(3) Son of Jabesh who slew Zechariah son of Jeroboam II.—II Ki. 15:10–15.

(4) Son of King Josiah.—I Chr. 3:15; Jer. 22:11.

(5) Grandson of Jacob.—I Chr. 7:13.

(6) Grandson of Simeon.—I Chr. 4:25.

(7) Father of Hilkiah the priest.—I Chr. 6:12, 13; Ezra 7:2.

(8) A Levite.—I Chr. 9:17, 19, 31; Ezra 2:42; Neh. 7:45.

(9) A gatekeeper who married a foreign wife.—Ezra 10:24.

(10) Father of Jehizkiah.—II Chr. 28: 12.

(11) One who, with his daughters, helped to repair the wall.—II Chr. 28:12.

(12) One of the family of Bani who married a foreign wife.—Ezra 10:42.

(13) Father of Hanameel uncle of Jeremiah the prophet.—Jer. 32:7.

(14) Father of Maaseiah.—Jer. 35:4.

SHALLUN, shăl'lun. One who repaired the fountain gate.—Neh. 3:15.

SHALMAN, shăl'man. Same as Shalmaneser, an Assyrian king, successor of Tiglath-pileser.—II Ki. 17:3, 6; 18: 11; Hos. 10:14.

SHALMANESER, shăl'man-ē'ser. Same as preceding.—II Ki. 17:3; 18:9.

SHAMA, shā'mà. One of David's mighty men.—I Chr. 11:44.

SHAME: Put to shame.—Gen. 38:23; Ju. 18:7; I Sam. 20:34; II Sam. 6:20; Ps. 69:6; Lu. 13:17; I Cor. 11:22. Christ put to open shame—Heb. 6:6; 12:2.

Proverbs concerning.—Pr. 3:35; 10:5; 11:2; 12:16; 13:5, 18; 14:35; 17:2; 18: 13; 19:26; 25:8; 29:15.

Result of sin.—Job 8:22; Ps. 35:4, 26; 40:14, 15; 44:7, 15; 53:5; 69:6, 7, 19; 70:3; 71:24; 83:17; 89:45; 109:29; 119:31; 132:18; Jer. 3:25; Ez. 16:52, 54, 63; 32:24, 30; 39:26; 44:13; Hos. 2:5; 4:7; Ob. 10; Mic. 1:11; 7:10; Nah. 3:5; Hab. 2:10, 16.

Consumed with.—Jer. 20:18.

Glory in.—Phil. 3:19. Of disgrace—II Sam. 13:13.

Of nations.—Ez. 34:29; 36:6, 7, 15. Egypt—Is. 20:4; 30:3, 5; Jer. 46:12. Babylon—Is. 47:3. Moab—Jer. 48:39. Face—II Sam. 19:5; II Chr. 32:21. Blush of—Ezra 9:6; Jer. 6:15; 8:12.

Prophecies concerning.—Is. 20:4; 22:18; 50:7; 54:4; 61:7; Jer. 13:26; 23:40; Ez. 34:29; 39:26; 44:13; Dan. 12:2. Hos. 4:7, 18, 19; 10:6; Zeph. 3:5, 19.

Not ashamed of the gospel.—Rom. 1:16.

Figurative.—Jude 13; Rev. 3:18; 16:15.

Miscellaneous.—Concerning women—I Cor. 11:6; I Tim. 2:9. Words spoken not to shame, but to admonish—I Cor. 4:14. To shame—I Cor. 6:5; 15:34.

Shameful things.—Jer. 11:13; Hos. 9: 10; I Cor. 14:35; II Cor. 4:2.

Shamefully treated.—I Thess. 2:2. See JESUS, TEACHING OF, REPROACH.

SHAMEFASTNESS. I Tim. 2:9. See HUMILITY.

SHAMEFUL. I Cor. 14:35. Speaking —Col. 3:8. Things—Deut. 22:14.

SHAMEFULLY. Handled—Mk. 12:4; Lu. 12:20. Hath done—Hos. 2:5. Treat —Mt. 22:6; Acts 14:5; I Thess. 2:2.

SHAMELESSLY. II Sam. 6:20.

SHAMGAR, shăm'gar. A judge of Israel.—Ju. 3:31; 5:6.

SHAMHUTH, shăm'huth. A captain under David.—I Chr. 27:8.

SHAMIR, shā'mir. (1) A city in Ephraim.—Ju. 10:1, 2.

(2) A city in Judah.—Josh. 15:48.

(3) A Levite.—I Chr. 24:24.

SHAMLAI, shăm'lāi. One who returned from exile.—Ezra 2:46.

SHAMMAH, shăm'mah. (1) Grandson of Esau.—Gen. 36:13, 17; I Chr. 1:37.

(2) Brother of David.—I Sam. 16:9; 17:13.

(3, 4, 5) Three of David's mighty men. —II Sam. 23:11, 25, 33.

SHAMMAI, shăm'māi. (1) A descendant of Caleb son of Hezron.—I Chr. 2:44, 45.

(2) Grandson of Jerahmeel.—I Chr. 2: 28, 32.

(3) I Chr. 4:17.

SHAMMOTH, shăm'moth. One of David's mighty men.—I Chr. 11:27.

SHAMMUA, sham-mū'á. (1) Son of David.—II Sam. 5:14; I Chr. 14:4. See SHIMEI.

(2) A Reubenite spy.—Num. 13:4.

(3) A Levite.—Neh. 11:17.

(4) A priest.—Neh. 12:18.

SHAMSHERAI, shăm'she-rāi. A Benjamite.—I Chr. 8:26.

SHAPE. Rev. 9:7. God, Of—John 5:37 (A.V.). Holy Spirit descended in bodily—Lu. 3:22 (A.V.). See FORM.

SHAPEN. In iniquity—Ps. 51:5 (A.V.).

SHAPHAM, shā'pham. A Gadite.—I Chr. 5:12.

SHAPHAN, shā'phan. (1) A scribe in the days of Josiah.—II Ki. 22:3–14; II Chr. 34:8–20; Jer. 36:10–12.

(2) Father of Elasah.—Jer. 29:3.

(3) Father of Ahikam, an officer under Josiah.—II Ki. 22:12; 25:22; II Chr. 34:20; Jer. 26:24; 39:14; 40:5, 9, 11; 41:2; 43:6.

(4) Father of Jaazaniah whom Ezekiel saw in a vision.—Ez. 8:11.

SHAPHAT, shā'phat. (1) Father of Elisha the prophet.—I Ki. 19:16, 19; II Ki. 3:11; 6:31.

(2) A Simeonite spy.—Num. 13:5.

(3) A Gadite.—I Chr. 5:12.

(4) Grandson of Shechaniah.—I Chr. 3:22.

(5) An overseer under David.—I Chr. 27:29.

SHARAI, shā'rai. One of the family of Bani who married a foreign wife.— Ezra 10:40.

SHARAR, shā'rar. One of David's mighty men.—II Sam. 23:33.

SHARE. Ill treatment—Heb. 11:25. Sharpen—I Sam. 13:20.

SHARERS. Heb. 2:14.

SHAREZER, sha-rē'zer. (1) Son of Sennacherib.—II Ki. 19:37; Is. 37:38.

(2) One sent to consult the priest and prophets in the temple.—Zech. 7:2.

SHARON, shā'ron. The western part of Ephraim and Manasseh noted for its rich soil.—Josh. 12:18; I Chr. 27: 29; 35:2; 65:10.

(2) A plain or city east of the Jordan. —I Chr. 5:16.

SHARP. Arrows—Ps. 45:5; Jer. 51:11. Eyes—Job 16:9. Iron—Pr. 27:17. Razor—Ps. 52:2. Sickle—Rev. 14:14, 17, 18. Sword—Pr. 5:4; Ez. 5:21; 21:9; Rev. 19:15. Tongue—Ps. 140:3.

SHARPER. Heb. 4:12.

SHARUHEN, sha-ru'hen. A city in Simeon.—Josh. 19:6.

SHASHAI, shā'shāi. One of the family of Bani who married a foreign wife.— Ezra 10:40.

SHASHAK, shā'shak. A Benjamite.—I Chr. 8:14, 25.

SHAUL, shā'ul. (1) Son of Simeon.— Gen. 46:10; Ex. 6:15; Num. 26:13; I Chr. 4:24.

(2) A king of Edom.—I Chr. 1:48, 49.

(3) Grandson of Levi.—I Chr. 6:24.

SHAULITES. Num. 26:13.

SHAVE. See HAIR, HEAD.

SHAVEH, shā'veh. A valley near Aenon.—Gen. 14:17.

SHAVEH-KIRIATHAIM, shā'veh-kir'-i-a-thā'im. A place in Reuben.—Gen. 14:5.

SHAVSHAH, shăv'shȧ. Same as SER-AIAH, SHEVA, SHISHA. David's scribe—I Chr. 18:16.

SHAWLS. Is. 3:22. See CLOTHING.

SHEAF, SHEAVES. Obeisance to—Gen. 37:7. Of first-fruits—Lev. 23:10. Wave of the sheaf-offering—Lev. 23: 11, 12, 15. Forgotten—Shall be for sojourner and fatherless—Deut. 24: 19. Sheaves for hungry—Job 24:10. Ruth gathers—Ruth 2:7, 15. Bringing in—Neh. 13:15. Bringing bound—Ps. 129:7.

Figurative.—Amos 2:13; Zech. 12:6.

Typical.—Ps. 126:6; Mic. 4:12; Mt. 13:30.

SHEAL, shē'al. One of the family of Bani who married a foreign wife.—Ezra 10:29.

SHEALTIEL, she-ăl'ti-el. Father of Zerubbabel.—Ezra 3:2, 8; 5:2; Neh. 12:1; Hag. 1:1, 12, 14; 2:2.

SHEAR. See SHEEP.

SHEARERS. Killed for my—I Sam. 25:11. Lamb before—Acts 8:32. Sheep before—Is. 53:7. Thou hast—I Sam. 25:7.

SHEARIAH, shē'a-rī'ah. A Benjamite. —I Chr. 8:38; 9:44.

SHEAR-JASHUB, shē'ar–jā'shub. A symbolic name given to a son of Isaiah.—Is. 7:3.

SHEATH. I Sam. 17:51; II Sam. 20:8; I Chr. 21:27; Ez. 21:3, 4, 5, 30; John 18:11. See SWORD.

SHEBA, shē'bȧ. (1) A descendant of Shem.—Gen. 10:28; I Chr. 1:22.

(2) Grandson of Abraham.—Gen. 25:3; I Chr. 1:32.

(3) A land in southwestern part of Arabia.—Job 6:19; Ps. 72:10; Is. 60: 6. Gold of—Ps. 72:15; Is. 60:6. Incense from—Jer. 6:20. Merchants of —Ez. 27:22, 23; 38:13. Queen of—I Ki. 10:1, 4, 10, 13; II Chr. 9:1, 3, 12.

(3) A city in Simeon.—Josh. 19:2.

(4) Son of Bichri who rebelled against David.—II Sam. 20:1–22.

(5) A Gadite.—I Chr. 5:13. See SEBA, BEER-SHEBA.

SHEBANIAH, shĕb'a-nī'ah. (1) A Levite.—Neh. 9:4, 5; 10:10.

(2) A priest who assisted in bringing up the ark.—I Chr. 15:24.

(3, 4) A priest and a Levite who assisted in sealing the covenant.—Neh. 10:4, 12; 12:14.

SHEBARIM, shĕb-a-rĭm. A place near Ai.—Josh. 7:5.

SHEBER, shē'ber. Son of Caleb son of Jephuneh.—I Chr. 2:48.

SHEBNA, shĕb-na. (1) Treasurer of the temple.—Is. 22:15.

(2) Secretary of Hezekiah.—II Ki. 18: 18, 26, 37; 19:2; Is. 36:3, 11, 22; 37:2.

SHEBUEL, shĕb'u-el. (1) Son of Haman, a singer in the sanctuary.—I Chr. 25:4.

(2) Grandson of Levi.—I Chr. 23:16; 26:24.

SHECANIAH, shĕk'a-nī'ah. (1) A priest under David.—I Chr. 24:11.

(2) A priest under Hezekiah.—II Chr. 31:15.

(3, 4) Ancestors of some who returned from exile.—Ezra 8:3, 5.

(5) I Chr. 3:21, 22.

(6) Son of Jehiel who married a foreign wife.—Ezra 10:2.

(7) Father-in-law of Tobiah who opposed Nehemiah.—Neh. 6:8.

(8) Father of Shemaiah who helped to repair the wall.—Neh. 3:29.

(9) A priest who returned with Zerubbabel.—Neh. 12:3.

SHECHEM, shē-kem. Heb. *Shoulder.* (1) Son of Hamor; seduces Jacob's daughter, Dinah; slain by Jacob's sons—Gen. Ch. 34; Josh. 24:32; Ju. 9:28.

(2) A city of refuge and district in Ephraim.—Josh. 17:7; 20:7; Ju. 21: 19. Jacob buys ground and erects an altar—Abraham comes to—Gen. 12:6. Jacob buys ground and erects altar—Gen. 33:18–20. Jacob hides idols and images under the oak by Shechem—Gen. 35:4. Joseph's brethren feed their flocks in—Gen. 37:12–14. Given to the Levites—Josh. 21:21; I Chr. 6:67; 7:28. Joshua gathers the tribes for his farewell address—Josh. 24:1–25. Bones of Joseph brought out of Egypt and buried there—Josh. 24: 32. Gideon's concubine in—Ju. 8:31. Abimelech made king at—Ju. 9:1-6, 16–18, 22. Jotham's fable—Ju. 9:7-21. Gaal's conspiracy against Abimelech—Ju. 9:23-45. Abimelech sets

fire to Shechem and destroys it—9:46–49, 57. Rehoboam goes to be made king—I Ki. 12:1; II Chr. 10:1. Jeroboam rebuilds—I Ki. 12:25. Prophecy concerning—Ps. 60:1; 108:7. Men came from Shechem with beards shaven and clothes rent—Jer. 41:5. Jesus talks to woman of Samaria—John 4:1–42. See SYCHAR.

(3) **A man of Manasseh.**—I Chr. 7:19.

(4) **Grandson of Manasseh.**—Num. 26:31; Josh. 17:2.

SHECHEMITES. Descendants of Shechem—Num. 26:31.

SHED. II Sam. 20:10. Blood—See BLOOD, MURDER. Blood shed for remission of sins—See REMISSION OF SINS, SALVATION THROUGH BLOOD OF JESUS. Love of God hath been—Rom. 5:5.

SHEDEUR, shĕd'e-ur. **A Reubenite.**—Num. 1:5; 2:10; 7:30, 35; 10:18.

SHEEP: The common sheep of Palestine was the fat-tailed.—Lev. 3:9; 7:3.

Places famous for feeding flocks.—Bashan—Deut. 32:14. Bethlehem—Lu. 2:8. Bozrah—Is. 34:6; Mic. 2:12. Carmel—I Sam. 25:2. Gedor—I Chr. 4:39. Haran—Gen. 29:7–10. Nebaioth—Is. 60:7. Tekoah—Amos 1:1.

Large numbers of.—Num. 31:32, 36, 43; I Sam. 14:32; I Chr. 5:21; II Chr. 14:15; 15:11; 30:24; II Ki. 3:4; Job 1:3; 42:12.

Flocks tended by sons.—Gen. 30:29; 37:12; I Sam. 16:11. By daughters—Gen. 29:6; Ex. 2:19.

Relation of shepherds to.—Gen. 31:38–41; 33:13; Num. 27:17; I Chr. 4:39–41; Ps. 23:1; 77:20; 78:71; 80:1; Is. 40:11; Jer. 23:1–2; Ez. 34:1–31; John 10:1–5, 10–13.

Shearing of.—Gen. 31:19; 38:12–13; Deut. 15:19; I Sam. 25:4; Is. 53:7.

Tribute paid in.—Num. 31:28, 37; I Sam. 8:17; II Ki. 3:4. Restoration of—Ex. 22:1, 4, 10, 12.

Uses of.—Skins: Clothing—Lev. 13:47; Deut. 22:11; Job 31:20; Pr. 31:13; Mt. 7:15; Heb. 11:37. For tabernacle—Ex. 25:5; 26:14; 35:7, 23; 39:34. Food—Lev. 11:3; I Sam. 25:18; I Ki. 1:19; 4:23; Ps. 44:11. Wool—Lev. 13:47–59; 19:19; Deut. 22:11; Ju. 6:37–40; II Ki. 3:4; Pr. 31:13; Is. 51:8; Ez.

27:18; 34:3; 44:17; Dan. 7:9; Hos. 2:5, 9; Heb. 9:19; Rev. 1:14. Horns, for trumpets—Josh. 6:4–13.

Sacrifice of.—Lambs of first year generally used—Ex. 29:38; Lev. 9:3; 12:6; Num. 28:9; I Sam. 7:9. No lamb under 8 days allowed to be killed—Lev. 22:27. Sheep for offering—Ex. 20:24; Lev. 1:10; 22:19, 27; 27:26; Num. 18:17; 22:40; Deut. 17:1; 18:3; I Sam. 14:32; 15:15; I Ki. 1:9; 8:5, 63; II Chr. 5:6; 29:33.

Illustrative of.—The Lord's people—Ps. 23; Is. 40:11; Lu. 15:4–6; John 10:8, 11, 27–29; 21:16–17; Heb. 13:20. (See also, RELATION OF SHEPHERD TO.) Care of his people—Ez. 34:4–16; I Pet. 5:2. Patience and submission of Jesus—Acts 8:32. See Is. 53:7. Jesus the Shepherd—John Ch. 10; Heb. 13:20; I Pet. 2:25. Man greater than a sheep—Mt. 12:11–12. Restoration of sinners—Mt. 10:6; 15:24; Lu. 15:5, 7. See SHEPHERD, LAMB.

Sheepcote.—I Sam. 24:3; II Sam. 7:8; I Chr. 17:7.

Sheepfold.—Num. 32:16, 24, 26; Ju. 5:16; Ps. 78:70; John 10:1.

SHEET. Acts 10:11; 11:5.

SHEHARIAH, shē'ha-rī'ah. **A Benjamite.**—I Chr. 8:26.

SHEKEL. Brass, Of—I Sam. 17:5. Find a—Mt. 17:27. Gold, Of—I Chr. 21:25. Half a—Gen. 24:22. Iron, Of—I Sam. 17:7. Sanctuary, Of—Ex. 38:24; Lev. 5:15; Num. 3:47; Ez. 45:12. Silver, Of—I Sam. 9:8. Sold for a—II Ki. 7:1. Value of—Ex. 30:13; Lev. 27:25. Weighed six hundred—I Sam. 17:7. See MONEY.

SHELAH, shē'lah. (1) **Son of Arphaxad.**—I Chr. 1:18, 24.

(2) **Son of Judah.**—Gen. 38:5, 11, 14, 26; 46:12; Num. 26:20; I Chr. 2:3; 4:2.

SHELEMIAH, shĕl-e-mī'ah. (1, 2) **Two of the family of Bani who married foreign wives.**—Ezra 10:39, 41.

(3) **A Levite gatekeeper.**—I Chr. 26:14.

(4) **A priest who had charge of the treasuries.**—Neh. 13:13.

(5) **Father of Hananiah who helped to repair the wall.**—Neh. 3:30.

(6) **Son of Abdiel, ordered to take Jeremiah and Baruch.**—Jer. 36:26.

(7) **Son of Cushi, sent to bring Baruch before the council.**—Jer. 36:14.

(8) **Father of Irijah who arrested Jeremiah as he was about to leave Jerusalem.**—Jer. 37:13.

(9) **Father of Jehucal who was sent to ask for the prayers of Jeremiah.**—Jer. 37:3; 38:1.

SHELEPH, shĕ'leph. **A descendant of Shem.**—Gen. 10:26; I Chr. 1:20.

SHELESH, shĕ'lesh. **Son of Helem.**—I Chr. 7:35.

SHELOMI, shĕl'o-mī. **An Asherite.**—Num. 34:27.

SHELOMITH, shĕl'o-mĭth. **Daughter of Dibri, mother of one who was stoned for blasphemy.**—Lev. 24:11.

(2) **A descendant of Gershon in the days of David.**—I Chr. 23:9.

(3) **Daughter of Zerubbabel.**—I Chr. 3:19.

(4) **A descendant of Eliezer son of Moses.**—I Chr. 26:25–28.

(5) **A Kohathite.**—I Chr. 23:18.

(6) **A child of Rehoboam's.**—II Chr. 11:20.

(7) **Ancestor of a family who returned with Ezra.**—Ezra 8:10.

SHELOMOTH, shĕl'o-mŏth. I Chr. 24:22.

SHELTER. Job 24:8; Ps. 55:8. See REFUGE.

SHELUMIEL, she-lū'mi-el. **A Simeonite appointed to help number the people.**—Num. 1:6; 2:12; 7:36, 41; 10:19.

SHEM. Signifies ''*name*.'' **From the order it seems he was Noah's first son.**—Gen. 5:32; 6:10; 7:13; 9:18; 10:1; I Chr. 1:4. Took a garment and covered his father—Gen. 9:23. Received blessing from father—Gen. 9:27. Noah's descendants.—Gen. 10:21–31. (His descendants dwelt chiefly in Western Asia, South of the Asiatic Japhethites in an unbroken line from the Mediterranean to the Mountains of Luristan and the Indian Ocean; Lydia, Palestine, Syria, Chaldea, Assyria, Persia, Northern and Central Arabia—Gen. 10:21; 11:10–29; I Chr. 1:17–54.)

Shem in lineage of Jesus.—Luke 3:36.

SHEMA, shĕ'ma. (1) **A Reubenite.**—I Chr. 5:8.

(2) **A city in Judah.**—Josh. 15:26.

(3) **Son of Hebron.**—I Chr. 2:43, 44.

(4) **One who stood with Ezra.**—Neh. 8:4.

(5) **A Benjamite.**—I Chr. 8:13.

SHEMAAH, she-mā'iah. (1) **Son of Shecaniah.**—I Chr. 3:22.

(2) **A prophet sent to prevent Rehoboam from waging war against Israel.**—I Ki. 12:22; II Chr. 11:2; 12:5, 7, 15.

(3) **A Reubenite.**—I Chr. 5:4.

(4) **A Simeonite.**—I Chr. 4:37.

(5) **A descendant of Merari.**—I Chr. 9:14; Neh. 11:15.

(6) **A Kohathite.**—I Chr. 15:8, 11.

(7, 8) **Two Levites.**—I Chr. 9:16; 24:6.

(9) **A Kohathite gatekeeper.**—I Chr. 26:4–7.

(10) **Son of Jeduthun.**—II Chr. 29:14.

(11, 12, 13) **Three more Levites.**—II Chr. 17:8; 31:15; 35:9.

(14) **A messenger to Iddo.**—Ezra 8:16.

(15) **Son of Adonikam who returned with Ezra.**—Ezra 8:13.

(16) **A priest who married a foreign wife.**—Ezra 10:21.

(17) **Another who married a foreign wife.**—Ezra 10:31.

(18) **A priest who sealed the covenant.**—Neh. 10:8; 12:6, 18, 34, 35.

(19) **One who attempted to intimidate Nehemiah.**—Neh. 6:10.

(20) **One who helped to repair the wall.**—Neh. 3:29.

(21) **One who assisted in the dedication of the wall.**—Neh. 12:42.

(22) **One who assisted in the purification of the wall.**—Neh. 12:36.

(23) **Father of Uriah who was slain by Jehoiakim.**—Jer. 26:20.

(24) **Father of Delaiah a prince of the Jews.**—Jer. 36:12.

(25) **One who wrote to the priests in Jerusalem to reprove Jeremiah.**—Jer. 29:24, 31, 32.

SHEMARIAH, shĕm'a-rī'ah. (1) **Son of Rehoboam.**—II Chr. 11:19.

(2) **A man who joined David at Ziklag.**—I Chr. 12:5.

(3, 4) **Two who married foreign wives.**—Ezra 10:32, 41.

SHEMEBER, shem-ē'ber. **King of Zeboiim.**—Gen. 14:2.

SHEMER, shĕ'mer. **Owner of hill on which Samaria was built.**—I Ki. 16: 24.

SHEMIDA, she-mĭ'dȧ. Grandson of Manasseh—Num. 26:32; Josh. 17:2; I Chr. 7:19.

SHEMINITH, shĕm'i-nĭth. **An octave.**—See MUSIC, PSALMS.

SHEMIRAMOTH, she-mĭr'a-mŏth. **Two Levites.**—I Chr. 15:18, 20; 16:5; 17:8.

SHEMUEL, shĕm'u-el. (1) **A man of Issachar.**—I Chr. 7:2.

(2) **A Simeonite.**—Num. 34:20.

SHEN, shĕn. **A place in Benjamin.**—I Sam. 7:12.

SHENAZZAR, she-naz'zär. **Son or grandson of Jeconiah.**—I Chr. 3:18.

SHEOL (Gr. *Hades*). **Described.**—Land of Darkness—Job 10:22; Lam. 3:6; Ps. 143:3. Place of silence—Ps. 31: 17. Work and wisdom absent—Eccl. 9:10. Cruel—Song of Sol. 8:6. Never satisfied—Pr. 27:20; 30:16; Hab. 2:5. Painful—Ps. 116:3. All beauty consumed by—Ps. 49:14. Sinner consumed by—Ps. 49:14. Memory gone—Ps. 6: 5. Praise and thanks unknown in—Is. 38:18; Ps. 6:5.

Death is the entrance to.—The Grave is the mouth of—Ps. 141:7. The Grave is the gate of—Is. 38:10. Sickness brings near to—Ps. 30:3; 88:3. Soul delivered from—Ps. 86:13. Figuratively—Jonah 2:2.

An underworld of departed persons.—Beneath—Pr. 15:24. Go down to—I Ki. 2:6, 9; Job. 7:9; 21:13; Ps. 55:15; Pr. 5:5; Is. 5:14; 14:15; Ez. 31:15, 16, 17; 32:27. Has depths—Deut. 32:22; Pr. 9:18; Ez. 32:21; Amos 9:2.

Visible to God.—His anger burns to lowest depth of—Deut. 32:22. Naked before God—Job 26:6.

Knowledge of God is deeper than.—Job 11:8.

Compared with heaven equally open.—Ps. 139:8; Amos 9:2. Before Jehovah—Pr. 15:11.

The wicked journey toward.—By sin—Pr. 7:27; Is. 14:11; Ps. 9:17; 49:14. Man cannot deliver from power of—Ps. 89:48.

The righteous to be delivered from.—Soul redeemed from power of—Ps. 49: 15. Soul not to be left in—Ps. 16:10.

By living wisely depart from—Pr. 15: 24.

Is evil.—Wicked make covenant with—Is. 28:15, 18. Wicked debase themselves unto—Is. 57:9.

God brings down to.—I Sam. 2:6.

God brings back from.—I Sam. 2:6; II Sam. 22:6, 7; Ps. 18:5, 6. See HADES, HELL.

SHEPHAM, shĕ'pham. **A place.**—Num. 34:10, 11.

SHEPHATHIAH, shĕph'a-thī'ah. (1, 2) **Two Benjamites.**—I Chr. 9:8; 12:5.

(3) **Son of David.**—II Sam. 3:4; I Chr. 3:3.

(4) **Son of King Jehoshaphat.**—II Chr. 21:2.

(5) **A prince of Simeon.**—I Chr. 27:16.

(6, 7, 8, 9) **Ancestors of some who returned from exile.**—Ezra 2:4, 57; 8:8; Neh. 7:9, 59; 11:4.

(10) **A prince of Judah.**—Jer. 38:1.

SHEPHERD. An abomination unto the Egyptians—Gen. 46:34. Shepherd stone of Israel—Gen. 49:24. Land of shepherds—Ex. 2:19; Zeph. 2:6. Shepherds of Nabal—I Sam. 25:5. A shepherd prophet—Amos 1:1. As sheep that have not—I Ki. 22:17; II Chr. 18:16; Mt. 9:36; 25:32.

Jesus the Good Shepherd.—John 10:11, 12, 14, 16; Heb. 13:20; I Pet. 2:25. Jesus Chief Shepherd of Jehovah—Mt. 26:31; Mk. 14:27; I Pet. 5:4.

Jehovah as Shepherd of Israel.—Num. 27:17; Ps. 23:1; 80:1; Eccl. 12:11; Is. 40:11; 44:28; Jer. 31:10; 49:19; Ez. 34:5, 8, 12; 37:24; Zech. 10:2; 11:16, 17.

Shepherds of: Judæa—Lu. 2:8, 15, 18, 20. Of Assyria—Nah. 3:18. Worthless shepherd—Zech. 11:17; II John 10:12, 13. Brothers of Joseph shepherds—Gen. 46:32; 47:3. Daughters of Midian delivered from shepherds—Ex. 2:17.

Prophecies concerning.—Is. 13:20; 31:4. Shepherds cannot understand—Is. 56: 11: Wail of—Jer. 25:34, 35, 36; 33: 12. Wail of pastures of shepherds—Amos 1:2. Shepherds from mountains—Jer. 50:6. Seven shepherds—Mic. 5: 5: Prophecies against—Ez. 34:2, 7; Zech. 10:3; 11:3, 5, 8. Shepherds pitch tents—Jer. 6:3.

"Shepherds" used figuratively.—Jer. 43:12; 51:23; Ez. 34:23; Amos 3:12. Nations separated as a shepherd separates his sheep—Mt. 25:32. Multitude as sheep without a shepherd—Mk. 6:34. He that entereth in by the door is the shepherd—John 10:2. Shepherd of souls—I Pet. 2:25.

SHEPHI, shē′phi. **Son of Shobal.**—I Chr. 1:40.

SHEPHO, shē′pho. **Same as preceding.** —Gen. 36:23.

SHEPHUPHAN, she-phū′phan. **Grandson of Benjamin.**—I Chr. 8:5.

SHEREBIAH, shĕr′e-bī′ah. (1) **A Levite.**—Neh. 10:12; 12:8, 24.

(2) **A priest.**—Ezra 8:18, 24; Neh. 8:7; 9:4, 5.

SHERESH, shē′resh. Son of Macher son of Manasseh—I Chr. 7:16.

SHESHACH, shē′shak̞. **A mystical name for Babylon.**—Jer. 25:26; 51:41.

SHESHAI, shē′shāi. **Son of Anak.**—Num. 13:22; Ju. 15:14; Ju. 1:10.

SHESHAN, shē′shan. **A descendant of Jerahmeel.**—I Chr. 2:31–35.

SHESHBAZZAR, shesh-băz′zar. **A governor of Judah.**—Ezra 1:8, 11; 5:14, 16.

SHETHAR, shē′thar. **A prince of Persia.**—Esth. 1:14.

SHETHAR-BOZENAI, shē′thar – bŏz′e-nāi. **An officer under the king of Persia.**—Ezra 5:3, 6; 6:6, 13.

SHEVA, shē′vȧ. (1) **A scribe of David.** —II Sam. 20:25. See SERAIAH.

(2) **Son of Maachah concubine of Caleb son of Jephuneh.**—I Chr. 2:49.

SHIBBOLETH, shĭb′bo-lĕth. **A word used to distinguish the Ephraimites from other Israelites.**—Ju. 12:6.

SHIELD. See ARMOR.

SHIGGAION, shĭg-gā′ion. Ps. 7 title. See MUSIC, PSALMS.

SHIGIONOTH, shĭg′i-ō′nŏth. Hab. 3:1. See MUSIC.

SHIHON. See SIHON.

SHIHOR, shī′hôr. I Chr. 13:5. See SIHOR.

SHIHOR-LIBNATH, shī′hôr–lĭb′nath. **A small river.**—Josh. 19:26.

SHILHI, shĭl′hi. **Father-in-law of Jehoshaphat.**—I Ki. 22:42; II Chr. 20:31.

SHILHIM, shĭl′him. **A town in Judah.** —Josh. 15:32.

SHILLEM, shĭl′lem. **Son of Naphtali.**— Gen. 46:24; Num. 26:49.

SHILLING. About seventeen cents—Mt. 18:28; 20:2; Mk. 6:37; 14:5; Lu. 7:41; 10:35; John 6:7; Rev. 6:6. See MONEY.

SHILOAH, shi-lō′ah. **A fountain.**—Is. 8:6.

SHILOH, shi′loh. **A city in Ephraim.**— Ju. 18:1, 8–10; 19:51; 21:2; 22:9, 12; Ju. 18:31; 21:12, 19, 21; I Sam. 1:3, 9, 24; 2:14; 3:21; 4:3, 4, 12; 14:3; I Ki. 2:27; 14:2, 4; Ps. 78:60; Jer. 7:12, 14; 26:6, 9; 41:5.

SHILONI, shi-lō′ni. **Father of Zechariah.**—Neh. 11:5.

SHILONITE, shi-lō′nite. **An inhabitant of Shiloh.**—I Ki. 11:29; 12:15; 15:29; I Chr. 9:5; II Chr. 9:29; 10:15.

SHILSHAH, shĭl′shah. **A man of Asher.** —I Chr. 7:37.

SHIMEA, shĭm′e-ȧ. (1) **Son of Jesse, brother of David.**—I Chr. 20:7.

(2) **Son of David.**—I Chr. 3:5.

(3, 4) **Two Levites.**—I Chr. 6:30, 39.

SHIMEAH, shĭm′e-ah. **A Benjamite.**— I Chr. 8:32.

SHIMEAM, shĭm′e-ăm. I Chr. 9:38. Same as Shimeah.

SHIMEATHITES, shĭm′e-ath-ites. **A Kenite family.**—I Chr. 2:25.

SHIMEI, shĭm′e-i. (1) **Grandson of Levi.**—Ex. 6:17; Num. 3:18; I Chr. 6:17, 42; 23:7, 10.

(2) **An officer of David.**—I Ki. 1:8.

(3) **A Benjamite who cursed David.**— II Sam. 16:5, 7; 16:13; 19:16–23; I Ki. 2:8, 38–44.

(4) **Grandson of Jeconiah.**—I Chr. 3:19.

(5) **Son of Elah.**—I Ki. 4:18.

(6) **A Reubenite.**—I Chr. 5:4.

(7) **A Benjamite.**—I Chr. 4:26, 27.

(8) **A man of Judah.**—I Chr. 8:21.

(9, 10) **Two Levites.**—I Chr. 23:9; 25:17

(11) **An overseer under David.**—I Chr 27:27.

(12) **A Merarite.**—I Chr. 6:29.

(13) **A descendant of Neman.**—II Chr 29:14.

(14) **A Levite in charge of offerings.**— —II Chr. 31:12, 13.

(15) **A Levite who married a foreign wife.**—Ezra 10:23.

(16, 17) Two who had married foreign wives.—Ezra 10:33, 38.

(18) Zech. 12:13.

(19) Grandfather of Mordecai.—Esth. 2:5.

SHIMEON, shĭm′e-on. Ezra 10:31.

SHIMON, shī′mon. **A descendant of Caleb son of Jephuneh.**—I Chr. 4:20.

SHIMRATH, shĭm′rath. **A descendant.** —I Chr. 8:21.

SHIMRI, shĭm′ri. **(1) One of David's mighty men.**—I Chr. 11:45.

(2) A Simeonite.—I Chr. 4:37.

(3) A Merarite.—I Chr. 26:10.

(4) A Levite.—II Chr. 29:13.

SHIMRITH, shĭm′rith. **A Moabitess.**— II Chr. 24:26.

SHIMRON, shĭm′ron. **(1) A city in Zebulun.**—Josh. 11:1; 19:15.

(2) Son of Issachar.—Gen. 46:13; Num. 26:24; I Chr. 7:1.

SHIMRONITES. Num. 24:24.

SHIMRON-MERON, shĭm′ron-mē′ron. **A Canaanite town.**—Josh. 12:20.

SHIMSHAI, shĭm′shāi. **A scribe who opposed the rebuilding of Jerusalem.** —Ezra 4:8, 9, 17, 23.

SHINAB, shī′năb. **King of Admah.**— Gen. 14:2.

SHINAR, shī′nar. **Probably Babylonia.** —Gen. 10:10; 11:2; 14:1, 9; Is. 11:11; Dan. 1:2; Zech. 5:11.

SHINE, SHINING. God is Light—Ps. 17:1; I Tim. 6:16; I John 1:5. See LIGHT. Christ, the Light ôf the World —Lu. 2:32; John 1:4; 3:19; 12:35; Rev. 21:23. Hence God is described as shining—Num. 6:26; Deut. 32:2; Ps. 31:16; 67:1; 80:1, 3; Dan. 9:17; Rev. 21:23. Shining of Moses' face—Ex. 34:29; II Cor. 3:7–18. Of Christ's face at transfiguration—Mt. 17:2; Lu. 9:19. John was a shining light—John 5:35. Believers are said to shine, reflecting the divine light—Pr. 4:18; Dan. 12:3. Exhorted to let the light shine—Mt. 5:16; Phil. 2:15; Is. 60:1. The gospel is said to shine—Is. 9:2. Miraculous shining—Acts 9:3; Mt. 17:2. See LIGHT.

SHIPS: Perhaps suggested by the ark. —Gen. 7:17, 18.

Antiquity of.—Mentioned by Jacob— Gen. 49:13. In Deborah's song—Ju. 5:17. In the Psalms—Ps. 104:26.

Various services.—Those of Kittim for war—Num. 24:24; Dan. 11:30. Of Tarshish for all sorts of traffic—I Ki. 22:48; Jonah 1:3; Is. 60:9. See TARSHISH. Of Adramyttium and of Alexandria for commerce—Acts 27:2, 6, 18, 38. Of Chaldea, for fugitives and captives—Is. 43:14. Of Tyre, for conveyance of building material—I Ki. 10:11; 9:26, 27.

Constructed of.—Gopher wood—Gen. 6:14. Papyrus—Is. 18:2.

Equipped with.—Tackling, masts, and sails—Is. 33:23; Ez. 27:5–9; Acts 27:17–19. Helm—Jas. 3:4. Rudder—Acts 27:40. Oars—Jonah 1:13.

BOATS. **Ferry boat.**—II Sam. 19:18.

Jesus and His disciples enter in.—John 6:22, 23.

Used in shipwreck.—Acts 27:16, 30, 32.

SHIPHI, shī′phī. **A Simeonite.**—I Chr. 4:37.

SHIPHMITE, shĭph′mite. I Chr. 27:27.

SHIPHRAH, shĭph′rah. **A midwife.**— Ex. 1:15.

SHIPHTAN, shĭph′tan. **An Ephraimite.** —Num. 34:24.

SHIPWRECK. II Cor. 11:25. See Acts 27:41–44. Faith, Of—I Tim. 1:19. See SHIP.

SHISHA, shi′sha. I Ki. 4:3.

SHISHAK, shī′shăk. **An Egyptian king.** —I Ki. 11:40; 14:25; II Chr. 12:2–9.

SHITRAI, shĭt′rāi. **An overseer under David.**—I Chr. 27:29.

SHITTIM, shĭt′tim. **A place in Moab.**— Num. 25:1; Josh. 2:1; 3:1; Joel 3:18; Mic. 6:5.

SHITTIM WOOD. Same as ACACIA.

SHIZA, shī′zä. **A Reubenite.**—I Chr. 11:42.

SHOA, shō′ä. **A tribe.**—Ez. 23:23.

SHOBAB, shō′băb. **(1) Son of Caleb son of Hezron.**—I Chr. 2:18.

(2) Son of David.—II Sam. 5:14; I Chr. 3:5; 14:4.

SHOBACH, shō′băk. **Captain under Hadarezer king of Zobah.**—II Sam. 10:16, 18.

SHOBAI, shō′bāi. **A gatekeeper of the tabernacle.**—Ezra 2:42; Neh. 7:45.

SHOBAL, shō′băl. **(1) Son of Caleb son of Hur.**—I Chr. 2:50, 52.

(2) Son of Seir.—Gen. 36:20, 23, 29; I Chr. 1:38, 40.

(3) **Son of Judah.**—I Chr. 4:1, 2.

SHOBEK, shō'bek. **Name of some who helped to seal the covenant.**—Neh. 10:24.

SHOBI, shō'bī. **Son of Nahash.**—II Sam. 17:27.

SHOCK. Ex. 22:6; Ju. 15:5; Job 5:26.

SHOD. II Chr. 28:15; Ez. 16:10; Mk. 6:9; Eph. 6:15. See FEET, SHOE.

SHOE *or* **SANDAL.** Mt. 3:11; Mk. 6:9; Acts 12:8.

Early use of.—Gen. 14:23.

Of women.—Of badger's skin—Ez. 16: 10. Ornamented—Song of Sol. 7:1.

When worn.—Put on before beginning a journey—Ex. 12:11. **Never.**—In mourning—II Sam. 15:30; Is. 20:2; Ez. 24:17, 23. In worship—Ex. 3:5; Josh. 5:15.

Worn out by a long journey.—Josh. 9:5, 13.

Preserved.—Deut. 29:5.

Latchet.—Not to be broken—Is. 5:27. Of whose shoes I am not worthy to unloose—Mt. 3:11; Mk. 1:7; John 1:27.

Customs connected with.—Loosing from the foot on refusing to marry a brother's widow—Deut. 25:9, 10; Ruth 4: 7, 8. Casting, a mark of conquest—Ps. 60:8; 108:9.

The apostles prohibited from taking for their journey more than the pair they had on.—Mt. 10:10; Mk. 6:9; Lu. 10:4.

Illustrative of.—Preparation of the gospel—Eph. 6:15. Beauty conferred on saints—Lu. 15:22. Having blood on, of being engaged in war and slaughter—I Ki. 2:5. Of something of little value—Amos 2:6; 8:6.

SHOHAM, shō'ham. **A Merarite.**—I Chr. 24:27.

SHOMER, shō'mer. (1) **A great-grandson of Asher.**—I Chr. 7:32.

(2) **A Moabitess.**—II Ki. 12:21.

SHOOK. Dust off feet—Acts 13:51. Earth—II Sam. 22:8; Ps. 18:7; 68:2; 77:18; Heb. 12:26. Raiment—Acts 18: 2. See SHAKE.

SHOOT. See SHOT; JESUS, TITLES OF.

SHOPHACH, shō'phak. **A captain under Hadarezer king of Zobah.**—I Chr. 19:16.

SHORE. Jer. 47:7; Mk. 6:53; Ex. 14: 30; Josh. 11:4. Red Sea, Of—I Ki. 9:26. Sand upon—Gen. 22:17; I Sam.

13:5; I Ki. 4:29; Heb. 11:12. See SEA.

SHORN. Song of Sol. 4:2; Acts 18:18; I Cor. 11:6. See HAIR.

SHORT. Bed—Is. 28:20. Cut—II Ki. 10:32; Rom. 9:28. Days made—Ps. 59: 45; 102:23; Mt. 24:22; Mk. 45:20. Glory of God, Of—Rom. 3:23; Heb. 4:1. Lime is—Ps. 89:47; I Tim. 2:17; Rev. 12:12. Triumph of wicked is—Job 20:5; Pr. 10:27. Upper chamber—Ez. 42:5.

SHORTLY. Bring to pass—Gen. 41:32; Jer. 27:16; Rev. 1:1. Come—I Cor. 4: 19; Phil. 2:19, 24; I Tim. 3:14; II Tim. 4:9. Forgive—II Cor. 2:7. Must be done—Rev. 22:6; Heb. 13:23; III John 14. Pour out fury—Ez. 7:8. Saved, Be—John 3:17.

SHOSHANNIM, sho-shăn'nim. Ps. 45 title. See MUSIC, PSALMS.

SHOSHANNIM-EDUTH, sho-shăn'nim-ē'duth. Ps. 80 title. See MUSIC, PSALMS.

SHOT. Forth: Blossoms—Gen. 40:10. Sprigs—Ez. 17:6, 7. Branches—Ez. 31:5.

Archers shot.—Gen. 49:23; Num. 21:30; II Chr. 35:23. Through—Ex. 19:13.

Shot with arrow.—I Sam. 20:20, 36, 37. See ARCHERY, SHOOT.

SHOULD. Be saved—John 3:17. Forgive—I Cor. 2:7. See BOUND, DUTY, OUGHT.

SHOULDER. Neh. 9:29; Job 31:26. Ark carried on—I Chr. 15:15. Carry in—Gen. 9:23; 21:14; 49:15; Ju. 9:48; 16: 3; II Chr. 35:3; Job 31:36; Ps. 81:6; Is. 10:27; 22:22; 46:7; 49:22; Ez. 12: 7, 12; Mt. 23:4; Lu. 15:5. Pitcher carried on—Gen. 24:15, 45. Ram, Of—Num. 6:19. Upward—I Sam. 9:2; 10: 23. Used in sacrifice—Num. 6:19; Deut. 18:3.

SHOUTING: Occasions for.—Appointing of king—I Sam. 10:24. Bringing of ark to camp—I Sam. 4:5, 6. To Jerusalem—II Sam. 6:15; I Chr. 15: 28. Fall of Jericho—Josh. 6:10, 16, 20. War—Ju. 15:14; I Sam. 17:20, 52; II Chr. 13:15; Job 30:25; Amos 1:14; 2:2.

Thanksgiving to Jehovah.—II Chr. 15: 14; Ps. 41:15; Pr. 11:10; Is. 12:6; 42: 11; 44:23 (fig.); Jer. 31:7; Zeph. 3:14;

Zech. 9:9. Joy—Ezra 3:11, 12, 13; Job 38:7; Ps. 6:11; 32:9, 16.
Because of wine.—Ps. 78:65. Oration of Herod—Acts 12:22. For mastery—Ex. 32:17, 18.
In prophecy.—Num. 23:21; Josh. 6:5; Jer. 20:16; 25:30; 48:33; 50:15; 51: 14; Ez. 21:22; Amos 1:14; 2:2; Zech. 4:7; I Thess. 4:16. See CRY, JOY.
SHOVEL. Ex. 27:3; 38:3; Is. 30:24; Num. 4:14; I Ki. 7:40, 45; II Ki. 25: 14; II Chr. 4:11, 16; Jer. 52:18. See TOOLS AND IMPLEMENTS.
SHOW. Ez. 35:11. Countenance—See COUNTENANCE. Faith — See FAITH. Fault—Mt. 18:15. Favor—See FAVOR. Fickleness—II Cor. 1:17. Interpretation—See INTERPRETATION. Kindness —See KINDNESS. Mercy—See MERCY. Righteousness — See RIGHTEOUSNESS. Sin—See SIN. Way—Gen. 46:28. Works—See WORKS. Yourselves men —Is. 46:8.
SHOWBREAD. See BREAD, OFFERINGS.
SHOWER. Blessing, Of—Ez. 34:26. Cometh—Lu. 12:54. Overflowing— Ez. 13:11, 13; 38:22. Rain, Of—Zech. 10:1. Wet with—Job 24:8. See RAIN.
SHRANK. Acts 20:27.
SHRINK. Heb. 10:38.
SHRUBS. See PLANTS.
SHUA, shu′å. (1) **An Asherite.**—I Chr. 7:32.
(2) **Mother-in-law.** — Of Judah — Gen. 38:2, 12; I Chr. 2:3.
(3) **Son of Keturah.**—Gen. 25:2.
SHUAL, shu′al. (1) **A descendant of Asher.**—I Chr. 7:36.
(2) **Land of.**—I Sam. 13:17.
SHUBAEL, shu′ba-el. I Chr. 24:20. See SHEBUEL.
SHUDDER. Jas. 2:19.
SHUHAH, shu′hah. Gen. 25:2; I Chr. 4:11.
SHUHAM, shu′ham. **Son of Dan.**— Num. 26:42. See HUSHIM.
SHUHITE, shu′hite. **A descendant of Shua.**—Job 8:1.
SHULAMMITE, shu′lam-mite. Song of Sol. 6:13.
SHUMATHITES, shu′math-ites. **A family of Kiriath-Jearim.**—I Chr. 2:53.
SHUN. Foolish questioning—Tit. 3:9. Profane babblings—II Tim. 2:16.

SHUNAMMITE, shu′nam-mite. (1) **Abishag, David's nurse.**—I Ki. 1:3.
(2) **A woman who showed kindness to Elisha.**—II Ki. 4:8–37; 8:1–6. Elisha restores her son to life—II Ki. 4:35.
SHUNEM, shu′nem. **A town assigned to Issachar.**—Josh. 19:18. Philistines encamp at—I Sam. 28:4. Home of the Shunammite woman who befriended Elisha—II Ki. 4:8.
SHUNI, shu′ni. **A Gadite.**—Gen. 46:16.
SHUPHAMITES, shu′pham-ites. **Descendants of Shephupham.**—Num. 26: 39.
SHUPPIM, shŭp′pim. I Chr. 7:42.
SHUR, shûr. **A wilderness.**—Gen. 16:7; 20:1; 25:18; Ex. 15:22; I Sam. 15:7; 27:8.
SHUSHAN, shu′shan. **A Persian City.** —Esth. 1:2; Neh. 1:1; Dan. Ch. 8.
SHUSHAN-EDUTH, shu′shan-ē′duth. Ps. 60 title. See MUSIC, PSALMS.
SHUT. Is. 60:11. Door was—Mt. 25:10. Eyes—Is. 6:10. Heaven—Lu. 4:25; Rev. 11:6. Jehovah — Gen. 7:16. Lions' mouths—Dan. 6:22. Lips—Pr. 17:28. None shall—Is. 22:22. Saints in prison—Acts 26:10. Unto disobedience—Rom. 11:32. Unto faith— Gal. 3:23. Up mercies—Ps. 77:9.
SHUTHELAH, shu′the-lah. **A son of Ephraim.**—I Chr. 7:20.
SHUTHELAHITES, shu′thel-ā′hites. **Descendants of Shuthelah.**—Num. 26: 35.
SHUTTLE. Weaver's—Job 7:6.
SIA, sī′å. **Head of a family of Nethinim.**—Ezra 2:44; Neh. 7:47.
SIBBECAI, sĭb′be-kaī. **An officer in David's army.**—II Sam. 21:18; I Chr. 11: 29; 20:4; 27:11.
SIBBOLETH, sĭb′bo-lĕth. Ju. 12:6. See SHIBBOLETH.
SIBMAH, sĭb′mah. **A city of Moab.**— Josh. 13:19; Is. 16:8, 9; Jer. 38:42.
SIBRAIM, sib-rā′im. **A city.**—Ez. 47: 16.
SICK. Mt. 14:35; Mk. 1:32; John 5:3. And ye visited me—Mt. 25:36. Father is—Gen. 48:1. Head is—Is. 1:5. Healed—Mt. 8:16; 10:8; Mk. 16:18; Lu. 7:10. Is any among you—Jas. 5: 14. Love, From—Song of Sol. 2:5. Maketh the heart—Pr. 13:12. Need of physician—Mt. 9:12. Prayer, shall

save—Jas. 5:15. See DISEASE, HEAL-
ING, TEACHING OF JESUS.

SICKLE. Cast into earth—Rev. 14:16,
19. Handleth—Jer. 50:16. Not move
—Deut. 23:25. Put forth—Mt. 4:29.
Put in—Joel 3:13. Put to grain—
Deut. 16:9. Send forth—Rev. 14:15.
Sharp—Rev. 14:14, 17, 18. See DIS-
EASE, HARVEST, HEALING.

SICKNESS. Deut. 29:22. Before me
continually—Jer. 6:7. Impurity of—
Lev. 12:2. Makest bed in—Ps. 41:3.
Recover of—II Ki. 1:2; 8:8. Sore—
Deut. 28:59. See DISEASE, HEALING.

SIDDIM, sĭd'dĭm. A place.—Gen. 14:3-
10.

SIDE. Ez. 41:12; Rev. 22:2. Between
two—I Ki. 18:21. Four—I Chr. 9:24.
Jehovah's—Ex. 32:26. Jordan, Of—
Josh. 22:11. Mountain—Mk. 5:11. My
—Ps. 118:6, 7. Passed by on the other
—Lu. 10:31. Pierced his—John 19:34.
Rock, Of—Ps. 141:6. Terror on every
—Jer. 46:5.

SIDE-CHAMBERS. I Ki. 6:8. See
CHAMBER.

SIDON. (1) Name of eldest son of
Canaan.—Gen. 10:15. Of city.—Gen.
10:19.

(2) Prophecies concerning.—Mt. 11:21,
22; Lu. 10:13. Jesus went into—Mt.
15:21; Mk. 3:8; 7:24, 31. Paul touched
Sidon on one of his journeys—Acts
27:3.

Land of.—Lu. 4:26; Acts 12:20.

Sea-coast of.—Mt. 15:21; Mk. 7:31; Lu.
6:17.

Inhabitants of Sidon mentioned.—Deut.
3:9; Josh. 13:4.

Prophecies concerning.—Josh. 13:6; I
Ki. 5:6. Left to prove Israel—Ju. 3:3.

SIEGES. Cities, Of. See CITIES. Forts
and mounds, Of—See WAR.

SIEGE WORKS. Is. 29:3.

SIEVE. See TOOLS AND IMPLEMENTS.

SIFT. Peter—Lu. 22:31. House of Israel—Amos 9:9. Nations—Is. 30:28.

SIGH. Ez. 21:6; Mk. 7:34. Children
of Israel—Ex. 2:23. Deeply—Mk. 8:
12. Flee away—Is. 35:10. Men that
—Ez. 9:4. Merryhearted—Is. 24:7.
Not aloud—Ez. 24:7, 17. People—Pr.
29:2. Prisoner, Of—Ps. 102:20.

SIGHT. Ex. 23:8; Ez. 6:9. Cyprus, Of
—Acts 21:3. Eyes, Of—Eccl. 6:9. Fa-

vor in thy—Ruth 2:10. God, Of—
Gen. 16:3; Ex. 3:7; Acts 4:19; 10:31;
II Cor. 2:17; 7:12; Gal. 3:11; I Thess.
1:3; I Tim. 6:13; I Pet. 3:4. Good in
thy—II Ki. 20:3. Jehovah, Of—I Ki.
16:25. Pleasant to the—Gen. 2:9. Receive—Lu. 18:42. Walk by faith, not
by—II Cor. 5:7. Well pleasing in thy
—Mt. 11:26. See BLINDNESS, EYES,
VISION.

SIGNAL. Jer. 6:1. See SIGNS AND WON-
DERS.

SIGNATURE. Job 31:35.

SIGNET: A seal.—Gen. 38:18, 25; Jer.
22:24; Hag. 2:23; Dan. 6:17.

Rings and armlets.—Ex. 35:22; Num.
31:50.

Engravings of.—Ex. 28:11, 21, 36; 39:6,
14, 30.

Worn.—By women—Ex. 35:22. By Men
—Gen. 35:22; 38:18, 26; Ex. 28:11;
35:22; Jer. 22:24; Lu. 15:22.

Kings.—Ring—Esth. 3:10; 8:2, 8, 10.
Pharaoh's—Gen. 41:42.

See JEWELS, SEAL.

SIGNIFICATION. I Cor. 14:10.

SIGNIFIED. Acts 23:22.

SIGNS AND WONDERS. Heb. Oth.;
Gr. Semeion, sign; Yeras, Wonder; Dunamis, Power.

A pledge of assurance.—Bow in cloud
—Gen. 9:13. The rite of circumcision
—Gen. 17:11; Rom. 4:11.

Indicative of divine will.—I Sam. 2:34;
14:10; Ez. 14:8.

Of divine co-operation.—Ju. 6:17; I
Sam. 10:7; Is. 8:17, 18; 38:7.

Of divine judgments.—Ex. 10:2; Num.
26:10; I Sam. 2:34; Is. 20:3, 4; Jer.
6:1; 44:29; Ez. 14:8; Lu. 21:25.

Given by Jesus.—John 2:11; 4:54; 6:26.

Pertaining to Jesus.—Mt. 24:30; Is. 7:
14; Lu. 2:12; John 3:2; 20:30.

Accompanying apostles and disciples.—
Mk. 16:17; Acts 4:16 (marg.); 6:8;
8:6, 13; 15:12; II Cor. 12:12.

Jews clamor, and Jesus censures their
greed for.—Mt. 12:38; 16:1; John 4:
48; I Cor. 1:22.

Those of false leaders.—Mt. 24:24; II
Thess. 2:9.

Unable to perform signs.—Mt. 17:14-16;
Mk. 9:17, 18; Lu. 9:38-40; John 10:41

Apocalyptic signs.—Rev. 12:1, 2; 13:13. See MIRACLES. See "Signs of the Heavens," under HEAVENS.

SIGNS OF THE HEAVENS. See HEAVEN.

SIHON, sī'hon. **An Amorite king.**— Num. 21:21-34; 32:33; Deut. 1:4; 2: 24-32; 3:2, 6; 4:46; 29:7; 31:4; Josh. 2:10; 9:10; 12:25; 13:10-27; Ju. 11: 19-21; I Ki. 4:19; Neh. 9:22; Ps. 135: 11; 136:19; Jer. 48:45.

SIHOR, sī'hôr. **A river.**—Josh. 13:3; I Chr. 13:5; Is. 23:3; Jer. 2:18.

SILAS, sī'las. **A disciple who was one of Paul's companions.**—Acts 15:22-40; 16:19-29; 17:4-15; 18:5.

SILENCE. Job 4:16; Rom. 16:25. Brought to—Jer. 49:26. Cast them forth with—Amos 8:3. Dumb with—Ps. 39:2. Folds are brought to—Jer. 25:37. Go into—Ps. 115:17. Heaven, In—Rev. 8:1. Ignorance to—I Pet. 2:15. Keep—Deut. 27:9; Ps. 94:17; Lam. 2:10; 3:28; I Cor. 14:30. Let the earth keep—Hab. 2:20. Made—Acts 21:40. Put in darkness—I Sam. 2:9. Put to—I Sam 2:9; Jer. 8:14; I Pet. 2:15. Soul dwelt in—Ps. 94:17. Women to keep—I Cor. 14:34.

SILENT. Be—Zech. 2:13. In Sheol—Ps. 31:17.

SILK. Covered thee with—Ez. 16:10. Merchandise of—Rev. 18:12. Raiment of—Ez. 16:13.

SILLA, sĭl'la. **A place near Jerusalem.** —II Ki. 12:20.

SILLY. Dove—Hos. 7:11. One—Job 5:2. See FOOLISHNESS, WOMAN.

SILOAM, si-lō'am. (1) **A pool near Jerusalem.**—John 9:7-11.

(2) **A tower.**—Ju. 13:4.

SILVANUS, sil-vā'nus. II Cor. 1:19. See SILAS.

SILVER. Early use: Cups of Joseph—Gen. 44:2. Abimelech's gift of pieces to Abraham—Gen. 20:16. Abraham buys field of Ephron—Gen. 23:15, 16. Abraham rich in—Gen. 13:2. Servant reports Isaac's wealth—Gen. 24:35. Midianites buy Joseph—Gen. 37:28.

Used in Tabernacle.—Given by Israelites—Ex. 25:3; 35:24. For sockets—Ex. 26:19; 36:24-30. For hooks—Ex. 27:17. Offerings of princes of Israel —Num. 7:13, 19, 25, 31, 37, 43, 49, 55,

61, 67, 73, 79. Total of princes' gifts —Num. 7:84, 85.

Used in temple.—Gifts of Toi to David —II Sam. 8:10; I Chr. 18:10. Payment to builders of—II Ki. 12:13-15. Turned over to Solomon by David—I Chr. 28:14-17; 29:2-5. Total given by princes—I Chr. 29:6, 7. Surplus money made into vessels—II Chr. 24:14. Given to those returning from Babylon for House of God—Ezra 1:4, 6. Silver vessels taken back from Babylon—Ezra 5:14; 6:5. Ezra turns silver over to the priests and Levites—Ezra 8:25-30. Belshazzar drinks out of Temple vessels—Dan. 5:2.

Solomon's silver becomes common.—I Ki. 10:22-27; II Chr. 1:14-17; 9:20; Eccl. 2:8.

In Israel and Judah.—Dan. 5:2. Israel is corrupted by the Eastern wealth— Is. 2:6-8. Philistines pay tribute to Jehoshaphat in silver—II Chr. 17:11. Governors of Judah exact tribute— Neh. 5:15.

Workers in.—Men of Tyre—II Chr. 2: 14. Men of Ephesus—Acts 19:24.

Refining.—Found with dross—Job 28:1; Is. 1:22; Pr. 25:4.

Purified by fire.—Num. 31:22, 23; I Chr. 29:4; Ps. 12:6; 66:10; Pr. 17:3; Mal. 3:3.

Made into: Cups—Gen. 44:2; II Ki. 12: 13. Platters—Num. 7:13, 84, 85. Bowls —Num. 7:13, 84. Trumpets—Num. 10:2; II Ki. 12:13. Chains—Is. 40:19. Idols—Ex. 20:23; Ps. 115:4; Is. 2:20; 30:22; Hos. 13:2. Shrines—Acts 19: 24. Candlesticks—I Chr. 28:15. Tables—I Chr. 28:16. Couches—Esth. 1:6. Studs—Song of Sol. 1:11.

References.—Apples of gold, etc.—Pr. 25:11. Tongue of righteous as—Pr. 10:20. Thy silver perish with thee— Acts 8:20. See MONEY, VESSELS.

SILVERSMITH. Demetrius—Acts 19: 24.

SIMEON, sĭm'e-on. (1) Jacob's second son by Leah—Gen. 29:33; 35:23. The slaughter of the Shechemites incurred Jacob's reproof—Gen. 34:25-30; 49: 5-7. Judah and Simeon joined together in the conquest of Canaan—Ju. 1:3-17. Joseph selects Simeon as a hostage for Benjamin's appearance—

Gen. 42:24, 36; 43:23. Simeon's sons
—Gen. 46:10; Ex. 6:15.

(2) **Tribe.** Descendants — Ex. 6:15;
Num. 26:12-14; I Chr. 4:24-43. Persons selected from, to number the
people—Num. 1:6. To spy out the
land—Num. 13:5. To divide the land
—Num. 34:20. Princes—Num. 2:12;
7:36; 10:19; 34:20. Encamped under
standard of Reuben — Num. 2:12.
Strength of, on leaving Egypt—59,300
—Num. 1:22-23. After 40 years—22,-
200—Num. 26:12-14. Plague on account of idolatry, etc., depletes the
tribe—Num. 25:9-14. Inheritance of
—Josh. 19:1-9. See ISRAEL.

(3) **A just man in Jerusalem who waited for the Messiah.**—Lu. 2:25, 34. See
SYMEON.

SIMILITUDES. See SYMBOLS AND SIMILITUDES.

SIMON, sī'mon. (1) **Peter.**—See PETER.

(2) **The "Canaanite."**—Mt. 10:4; Mk.
3:18. Called "the Zealot"—Lu. 6:
15; Acts 1:13.

(3) **One of the brothers of Jesus.**—Mt.
13:55; Mk. 6:3.

(4) **A leper in whose house Jesus was
anointed.**—Mt. 26:6; Mk. 14:3.

(5) **Cyrenian, who bore the cross after
Jesus.**—Mt. 27:32; Mk. 15:21; Lu. 23:
26.

(6) **A Pharisee in whose house the feet
of Jesus were washed and anointed.**—
Lu. 7:40, 43, 44.

(7) **Father of Judas Iscariot.**—John 6:
71; 13:2, 26.

(8) **A sorcerer.**—Acts 8:9, 13, 18, 24.

(9) **A tanner at Joppa.**—Acts 9:43; 10:
6, 17, 32.

SIMPLE. Backsliding of the—Pr. 1:32.
Believe—Pr. 14:15. Give understanding to the—Ps. 119:130; Pr. 8:5. Inherit folly—Pr. 14:18. Make—Ps.
19:7. Persons—Pr. 1:22; 7:7; 9:6, 13,
16. Presence the—Ps. 116:6. Prudence
of the—Pr. 1:4; 19:25; Ez. 45:20.
Punished—Pr. 22:3; 27:12. Wise, Become—Pr. 21:11. See FOOLS.

SIMPLICITY. II Sam. 15:11; Pr. 1:22;
Rom. 16:19; II Cor. 11:3.

SIN. Heb. *"Going astray";* Guilt,
Iniquity. *Gr.* Missing the mark; failure.

Kinds of: Transgression; *i. e.,* Going beyond—I Ki. 14:22-24; Rom. 2:12-24;
8:7; Heb. 10:26-29; Jas. 2:6-11; I
John 3:4.

Disobedience; *i. e.,* Falling short—I Sam.
15:6-9, 19-23.

Lawlessness.—I John 3:4.

Rebellion; *i. e.,* Antagonizing. Presumption—Deut. 9:7, 23; Josh. 1:18; II Chr.
24:19; Ps. 30:1.

Unrighteousness; *i. e.,* Yielding to temptation—I John 5:17.

Lust of the flesh.—Mt. 5:28; Rom. 7:13-
25; 8:3, 5-7; Gal. 5:16-21; Eph. 2:3;
II Pet. 2:18.

Evil thoughts.—Pr. 24:9; Is. 59:7; 65:
2; Jer. 7:24; I John 3:15; Acts 8:22.

Unbelief.—John 3:18; 15:22-24; Heb. 6:
4-6; 10:28, 29.

Omission.—Jas. 4:17.

Philosophy of.—Jas. 1:14, 15. Illustrated
—Gen. 3:6; Josh. 7:20, 21.

Whence it comes: From the devil—Mt.
13:24-43; John 8:44; Eph. 2:2; I John
3:8. From the heart—Jer. 44:20; Jer.
17:9, 10; Ez. 20:16; Mt. 12:33-35; 15:
11, 19; Mk. 7:21-23; Lu. 6:45. From
the tongue—Job 2:10; Ps. 39:1; 34:
13; Eccl. 5:6; Mt. 12:36; Jas. 3:5-12.
Through heredity—Gen. 2:17; 3:1-6;
Ps. 51:5; 58:3; Is. 48:8; Rom. 5:12-
19; Eph. 2:3, 5. Through environment
—Ps. 1:1; 140:1, 2; Pr. 1:10-19; 4:
14-16. Through knowledge of the law
—Lu. 12:47, 48; John 9:41; 15:22-24;
Rom. 1:21, 32; 3:20; 4:15; 5:13, 20; I
Cor. 15:56; Jas. 4:17; II Pet. 2:21.

Specifications of: Presumptuous—Ps.
19:13. Open and manifest—I Tim. 5:
24. Works of darkness—Eph. 5:11.
Dead works—Heb. 6:1; 9:14. Besetting—Heb. 12:1. Secret—Gen. 3:10;
Job 31:33; Ps. 64:2; 19:12; 90:8; Is.
29:15; Ez. 8:12; John 3:20; Eph. 5:
12. Deceitful—II Cor. 11:3; Eph. 4:
22; Heb. 3:13. Reproachful—Pr. 14:
34.—Not of faith—Rom. 14:23. An
abomination—Pr. 15:9; 16:12; Jer.
44:4. Evil imaginations—Gen. 6:5;
8:21.

Universality.—Gen. 5:3; I Ki. 8:46; Job
15:4; Ps. 14:3; 51:5; 130:3; 143:2;
Eccl. 7:20; Is. 53:6; 64:6; Rom. 3:10-
19, 23; 5:12; Gal. 3:22; I John 1:8.
Christ alone without sin—II Cor. 5:

21; Heb. 4:15. Paul conscious of his own sins—I Cor. 15:9; Eph. 3:8; I Tim. 1:15. Saints dead to sin—Rom. 6:2, 11. Made free from sin—Rom. 6: 18; I Pet. 4:1; I John 1:8, 10; 3:9; 5:18.

Characterized as: A disease—Job 20:11; Is. 1:4–6. Madness—Eccl. 9:3. Bitter thing—Deut. 29:18; Jer. 2:19; 3:18; Heb. 2:15. Selfishness—II Ki. 5:20–27; Jer. 45:3. Bondage—Pr. 5:22; Is. 49:9; John 8:24–36; Rom. 3:9; 6:6, 12, 15; 7:23, 24; 8:2, 21; II Pet. 2:19–22. Defiling—Pr. 30:12; Is. 1:15, 16; 59:3; Heb. 12:15.

Should be: Put away—Job 11:14; Ps. 34:14; II Tim. 2:19. Guarded against —Ps. 4:4; 39:1. Striven against— Heb. 12:4. Confessed—Mt. 3:5–6; I John 1:9. Avoided in appearance— I Thess. 5:22.

National: Bring down judgments—Mt. 23:35, 36; 27:25. Defile the land—Lev. 18:25; Num. 25:33, 34; Ps. 106:38; Ps. 24:5; Mic. 2:10. Sanctioned by rulers —I Ki. 12:26–33; 14:16; II Chr. 21: 11–13; Pr. 29:12. Rejected prayers— Is. 1:15; 59:2. Rejected worship—Is. 1:10–14; Jer. 6:19, 20. Prosperity induces—Deut. 32:15; Neh. 9:28; Jer. 48:11; Ez. 16:49. Privileges lost— Lam. 2:9; Amos 8:11.

Denunciations against.—Is. 1:24; 30:1; Jer. 5:9. Punishments—Is. 3:8; Jer. 12:17; 25:12; Ez. 28:7–10. Punishment averted—Ju. 10:15, 16; Ps. 106: 43–46; Jonah 3:10.

Individual, exemplified: Adam, Eve, Satan—Gen. 3; Moses—Num. 20:10–12; Saul—I Sam. 13:14, 15; 15:3–28; David—Ps. 50:1–5; II Sam. 12:7–15; Solomon—I Ki. 11:1–13; Jeroboam— I Ki. 11:26–33; 13:1–5, 33, 34; Gehazi —II Ki. 5:20–27; Peter—John 18:25–27; Judas—Mt. 26:14–16; Paul—I Tim. 1:15; Ananias and Sapphira— Acts 5:1–10.

National, exemplified: Sodomites—Gen. 18:20; Egyptians—Ex. Chs. 7–14; Israelites — Lev. 26:14–39; 15:30–36; Deut. 9:11–21; 32:30; Ju. 2:10–23; 3: 1–8; II Sam. 21:1; II Ki. 17:1–17; 24:3; II Chr. 36:21; Ezra 9:1–15; Neh. 9:36, 37; Ps. 78:8–78; Is. 1:21–23; 5: 5–9; Jer. 2:5; Ez. 2:7; 24:6–14; 28:18;

33:25–26; Hos. 4:11; 6:8–10; Amos 2: 1–16; 5:1–27; Judah—I Ki. 14:22–25; II Ki. 17:19; II Chr. 12:1–12.

Protection from.—Fear of God restrains —Ex. 20:20; Ps. 4:4; Pr. 16:6. Word of God keeps from—Ps. 17:4; 119:11. Being born of God—I John 3:9. An active conscience—II Cor. 1:12. Faith in Christ—I John 5:4–5.

Is against God.—Gen. 39:9; Ex. 16:7, 8; Job 21:14, 15; Ps. 10:4; 51:4; Jer. 3: 25; Lu. 15:21.

Abhorrent to God.—Gen. 6:6; Lev. 18: 24–30; Deut. 25:16; 32:19–21; II Sam. 11:27; I Ki. 14:22; Ps. 5:4; 10:3; 11: 5; 95:10; 106:40; Pr. 3:32; 6:16; 15:8; 21:27; Is. 43:24; Jer. 25:7; Heb. 1:13; Zech. 8:17; Lu. 16:15; Rev. 2:6, 15.

Separates from God.—Deut. 31:17; Josh. 7:12; II Chr. 24:20; Ps. 78:59; Is. 59:1, 2; 64:7; Ez. 23:18; Hos. 9:12; Mic. 3:4; Mt. 7:23; Lu. 13:27; Heb. 12:14.

Known to God.—Gen. 3:11; 4:10; Ex. 16:8, 9, 12; Num. 14:26, 27; Deut. 1: 34; 31:21; 32:34; Josh. 7:10–15; Job 11:11; 14:16, 17; 34:21–27; Ps. 44:20, 21; 69:5; 90:8; 94:11; Eccl. 5:8; Jer. 2:22; 16:17; 29:23; Hos. 5:3; 7:2; Amos 5:12; Mt. 10:26.

Repugnant to the righteous.—Gen. 39: 7–9; Deut. 7:26; Ps. 26:5, 9; 84:10; 101:3, 4, 7; 119:104, 113, 163; 139:19–22; Pr. 8:13; 29:27; Jer. 9:2; Rom. 7: 15, 19, 23, 24; II Pet. 2:7, 8; Jude 23; Rev. 2:2.

What sin leads to: Toil and sorrow— Gen. 3:16–19. Thorns and briers— Gen. 3:17, 18. Disquietude—Ps. 38:3; Is. 57:20–21; 59:8. Shame—Job 42:6; Is. 6:5; Ez. 6:9; 20:43; 36:31; Rom. 6:21. Hopelessness—Pr. 8:13; 11:7, 20; Eph. 2:12; I Thess. 4:13. Hardening of the heart—Rom. 1:32; Eph. 4. 18, 19; I Tim. 4:2; Tit. 1:15; Heb. 3:13. Death—Pr. 11:19; Rom. 6:21, 23; I Cor. 15:56. Exclusion from heaven—I Cor. 6:9–10; Gal. 5:19–21; Eph. 5:5; Rev. 21:27; 22:14.

Progressive.—Ps. 1:1; Is. 30:1; Jer. 16: 11, 12; Hos. 13:1, 2; II Tim. 3:13; Jas. 1:14, 15.

Reacts.—Job 4:8; Ps. 7:15, 16; 9:15, 16; 10:2; 94:23; 141:10; Pr. 1:31; 5:22,

23; 11:5, 6, 27, 29; 22:8; Is. 3:11; Jer.
6:19; Hos. 8:7; 10:13, 14; Gal. 6:7, 8.

Punishment for The children of Israel
and Judah.

Led into captivity because of—Deut.
28:47-52, 62-68; 29:25-28; 30:1-5; Ju.
3:7, 8; I Ki. 9:6-9; 14:1-16; II Ki.
17:18, 20, 23; 18:9-12; 23:27; 24:1-4;
II Chr. 7:20; Neh. 1:8, 9; 9:26-30; Ps.
106:34-47; Jer. 21:3-14; 22:1-30; 24:
1-10; 25:1-11; Ez. 39:23, 24.

The kingdom divided because of—I Ki.
2:1-4; 9:7-9; 11:9-13, 26-39; 12:19,
20; 14:6; II Ki. 17:21; I Chr. 28:6-9;
II Chr. 7:17-22; Ps. 89:29-33.

The soul that sins shall die—Gen. 2:17;
Pr. 8:36; Ez. 18:4; Rom. 7:13; Eph.
2:1; Heb. 10:26-28; Jas. 1:15.

Banishment—Mt. 24:51; 25:46; Rev.
22:15.

Cast into Sheol—Ps. 9:17; 49:10-14; Mt.
5:27-30.

Cast into lake of fire—Rev. 20:15; 21:8.
See WICKED, PUNISHMENT OF.

Children suffer for sins of parents.—
Ex. 20:5; 34:7; Lev. 26:39, 40; Num.
14:33; Deut. 5:9; I Ki. 14:9-10; Job
5:3-7; Ps. 21:10; 37:28; Is. 1:4; 13:
16; 14:20-22; Jer. 32:18; Lam. 5:7;
Mt. 23:32-36; John 9:2, 3, 34.

Children not punished for sins of parents.—Deut. 24:16; II Ki. 14:6; II Chr.
25:4; Jer. 31:29, 30; 32:18; Ez. 18:
2-4, 20; Mt. 19:13, 14; Mk. 10:13-15;
Lu. 18:15-17.

Cleansing from.—GOD AND MAN CO-
OPERATE.

Man must cleanse himself—Is. 1:16;
Acts 22:16; Jas. 4:8; I Pet. 1:22.

God cleanses us from—Job 9:30-31; Ps.
51:2, 7, 10; Pr. 20:9; Is. 1:18; Jer. 2:
22; John 15:3; 17:17; Eph. 5:26; I
John 1:9.

God opened a fountain—Zech. 13:1.

Christ's manifestation—John 1:29; I
John 3:5. *His blood sufficient*—Eph.
1:7; I John 1:7. *He died for our sins*—
I Cor. 15:4; II Cor. 5:17-21; Gal. 1:4;
Col. 1:4; Tit. 2:14; Heb. 1:3; 9:26-28;
I Pet. 2:24; 3:18. See ''Christ's death
and blood for remission of sins'' and
''Human and divine agency in redemp-
tion,'' under SALVATION; REMISSION
OF SINS.

Types of.—Uncleanness—Lev. 5:2-5;
Ez. 36:17, 29; Zech. 13:1; Mt. 23:27;
II Cor. 5:2-5; 6:17; Eph. 5:5; I Thess
2:3; 4:7; Heb. 9:13.

Unclean animals—Lev. 11:1-47; 20:25;
Deut. 14:3-20; Acts 10:14, 15.

LEPROSY—Lev. 13:1-59. Separated from
intercourse—Lev. 13:46; Num. 5:1-4;
12:14-15. Associate together—II Ki.
7:3; Lu. 17:12. Cut off from God's
house—II Chr. 26:21. Excluded from
priest's office—Lev. 22:2-4. Must cry
Unclean—Lev. 13:45; Lam. 4:13-16.

BLEMISHES—Ex. 12:5; Lev. 1:10; 3:1, 6;
22:18-20; Num. 28:3, 9, 11, 19, 31; I
Pet. 1:19.

Conviction of.—Deut. 28:67; Ps. 31:10;
51:2-9; 73:21, 22; Pr. 28:1; Is. 6:5;
Lu. 5:8.

BY THE HOLY SPIRIT—John 16:8, 9.

THROUGH THE GOSPEL—Acts 2:37; 24:25.

BY CONSCIENCE—Rom. 2:15.

Examples of: Adam and Eve—Gen. 3:
8-10; Cain—Gen. 4:13; Pharaoh's
butler—Gen. 41:9; Joseph's brethren—
Gen. 44:16; 45:3; Pharaoh—Ex. 9:27;
Balaam—Num. 22:34; Saul—I Sam.
15:24, 30; 24:16-20; David—II Sam.
12:13; 24:10, 17; I Chr. 21:17; Ps. 38:
1-4, 18; 40:12; 51:2-9; Job—Job 7:
20; 9:20; 42:5, 6; Isaiah—Is. 6:5;
Children of Israel—Num. 14:40; Deut.
1:41, 45; Ju. 10:10; Ezra 10:11-14;
Neh. 9:1-3; Is. 59:12-15; Jer. 3:21,
24, 25; 8:14; 14:20; Judas—Mt. 27:
3-5; Peter—Mt. 26:75; Lu. 5:8; The
Prodigal Son—Lu. 15:17-21; The publican—Lu. 18:13; Zacchæus the publican—Lu. 19:8; The Ephesians—Acts
19:18-20; The Scribes and Pharisees
—John 8:7-9; The Jews on the Day
of Pentecost—Acts 2:37; The Jailor
—Acts 16:29, 30; Paul—Acts 22:10; I
Cor. 15:9; I Tim. 1:15; Felix—Acts
24:25.

Confession of: ENJOINED.—To God—
Lev. 5:5-10; 16:21; Num. 5:6, 7; I Ki.
8:46-49; Pr. 28:13; Hos. 5:15; I John
1:8-10; To one another—Jas. 5:16.

Instances of: Adam and Eve—Gen. 3:
12, 13; Pharaoh's butler—Gen. 41:9;
Joseph's brethren—Gen. 44:16; Pharaoh—Ex. 9:27; 10:16, 17; Saul—I
Sam. 15:24, 30; David—II Sam. 12:
13; 24:10, 17; I Chr. 21:17; Ps. 32:5;

38:1-4, 18; 40:12; 41:4; 51:2-5; 69:5;
Job—Job 7:20; 9:20; 40:4; Isaiah—Is.
6:5; Daniel—Dan. 9:20; Judas—Mt. 27:
3-5; Peter—Lu. 5:8; The Prodigal Son
—Lu. 15:18-21; The Publican—Lu.
18:13; The Ephesians—Acts 19:18;
Paul—I Cor. 15:9; I Tim. 1:15; The
Children of Israel—Lev. 26:40; Num.
14:40; Deut. 1:41, 45; Ju. 10:10; I
Sam. 7:6; Ezra 10:11-14; Neh. 9:1-3,
16-18, 26-28, 34, 35; Ps. 64:5-7; Jer.
3:21, 24, 25; 8:14; 14:20; 31:18, 19;
Lam. 1:18, 20; 3:42; *At the baptism of
John*—Mt. 3:6; Mk. 1:5; *The sins of
the Israelites confessed by Aaron*—Lev.
16:21; *Hezekiah*—II Chr. 29:6, 7; *Ezra*
—Ezra 9:1-15; 10:1; *Isaiah*—Is. 64:
6, 7; *Jeremiah*—Jer. 14:20; Lam. 1:
18, 20; 3:42; *Daniel*—Dan. 9:4-16, 20.

Sin against man.—I Sam. 2:25; Mt. 18:
15, 21; Mk. 11:25; Lu. 11:4; 17:3, 4.
Oppression—Job 20:9-22; 27:13-23;
Pr. 14:31; Is. 30:12-14; Mic. 2:2; Mt.
18:23-35. Theft—Ex. 21:16; Lev. 6:
3-5; 19:11, 13; Deut. 24:7; Job 5:5;
Zech. 5:3, 4; Lu. 19:8; John 12:4-6.

False witness—Ex. 20:16; 23:1, 7. Murder—Gen. 4:8-15; I Sam. 19:1-3; 20:
30-34; Mt. 5:21, 22; I John 3:12.

Forgiveness of.—Acts 8:22; Rom. 4:7;
Col. 2:13; I John 1:9.

God is forgiving.—Ex. 34:6, 7; Num.
14:18-20; II Sam. 12:13; Ps. 85:2;
99:8; 130:4; Is. 1:18; 6:6; 43:25; 44:
21; 55:6; Jer. 31:34; 33:38; Dan. 9:9;
Heb. 8:12; 10:17; Jas. 5:15; I John
1:9.

**The sin and trespass offerings in order
to forgiveness.**—Lev. 4:1-35; 5:1-19;
6:1-7, 24-30; 7:1-10; 19:21-22.

Forgiveness conditional.—Man must repent—Ez. 18:21-32; 33:10-16. See
REPENTANCE.

Man must forgive his fellow man—Mt.
6:14, 15; 18:21, 22; Mk. 11:25; Lu.
11:4; 17:3, 4; Eph. 4:32.

Parable of the unmerciful servant—Mt.
18:23-35. Of the two debtors—Lu. 7:
41-50.

Forgiveness is in Christ.—Eph. 1:17;
Col. 1:14. Christ forgave the paralytic
—Mt. 9:2-6; Mk. 2:1-12; Lu. 5:18-25.
The woman in the Pharisee's house—
Lu. 7:36-50. Fallen woman—John 8:

1-11. **Apostolic forgiveness** — John
20:23. See REMISSION OF SINS.

The unpardonable sin.—Num. 15:30;
Mt. 12:31; Mk. 3:29; Lu. 12:10; Heb.
6:4, 6; 10:26-29; I John 5:16, 17.

The pleasures of sin.—Job 20:12-15; Lu.
8:14; Heb. 11:25. See HOLY SPIRIT,
THE SIN AGAINST THE; REMISSION OF
SINS, SALVATION FROM SIN, WICKED.

SIN OFFERING. See OFFERING.

SIN, WILDERNESS OF. Ex. 16:1; 17:
11; Num. 33:11, 12.

SIN. Eastern part of Egypt. Ez. 30:
15, 16.

SINAI. The name of this mountain varies. In the earlier portions of Scripture it is called Horeb—Ex. 3:1, 12;
4:27; 17:6; 18:5. Sinai is first mentioned after the battle of Rephidim—
Ex. 19:1, 2. This name is prominent until the breaking-up of the encampment
in the wilderness—Num. 10:12. In re-
stating the journey, Horeb is spoken
of as the point of departure—Deut.
1:2, 6, 19. See Ex. Ch. 20, and Deut.
Ch. 5.

Situation.—Nearly in the centre of the
peninsula which stretches between the
horns of the Red Sea, about 150 miles
from the crossing of the sea, including
the windings of the route. See Ex.
16:1; Deut. 1:2; Gal. 4:25.

Height.—Between 1500 and 2000 feet
above the plain, which reached almost
to the very cliff—Ex. 19:12.

Material of the mountain.—A wedge of
granite and porphyry rock in the
shape of a triangle.

Known as "The mount."—Ex. 19:12,
13, 14, 16, 17, 20; 24:17, 18; Deut. 9:15.

Moses sees burning bush.—Ex. 3:1-6.

Rock in Horeb smitten.—Ex. 17:6.

**The Children of Israel encamp at the
base of.**—Ex. 19:2. They meet Jehovah there—Ex. 19:11, 17; Ju. 5:5.
Moses called up to the top of the
mountain—Ex. 19:3, 14, 20, 24, 25; 24:
1, 2, 9-11, 12, 13, 15, 18; 32:15, 17; 34:
2. The Law received by Moses on Sinai—Ex. 20:1-17; 24:12-18; 32:15-16;
34:24; Lev. 7:37-38; 25:1; 26:46; 27:
34; Num. 3:1; Deut. 4:11-14; 5:4, 22,
26; 29:1; 33:2; Neh. 9:13; Ps. 68:8;
Mal. 4:4; Acts 7:38; Heb. 12:18-21.

Clouds, darkness, lightning, and thunder on.—Ex. 19:9, 16–19; 20:18; 24:15–17; Deut. 4:10–13, 33, 36; 5:4; 33:2; Ju. 5:5; Ps. 68:8, 17.

Sanctified.—Ex. 19:23.

Called "Mountain of God."—Ex. 3:1; 24:13.

Israelites worship golden calf.—Ex. 33: 6; Deut. 9:8.

Wilderness of.—Ex. 18:5; 19:1, 2; Num. 33:15.

Elijah journeyed toward this mountain when fleeing from Jezebel.—I Ki. 19:8.

Old Covenant called Sinai.—Gal. 4:24–31. See also LAW, MOUNTAIN.

SINCERITY. Phil. 1:10, 16. Bread of —I Cor. 5:8. God, of—II Cor. 1:12; 2:17. Love, of—II Cor. 8:8. Mind—II Pet. 3:6. Serve with—Josh. 24:14. Speak with—Job 33:3. See TRUTH.

SINEW. Job 10:11; 40:17; Ez. 37:6, 8. Iron, As—Is. 48:4. Shrank, That—Gen. 32:32.

SING. Idle songs—Amos 6:5. Jehovah, To—Ex. 15:21; Ps. 57:7; 87:7. Joy, For—Ps. 96:12. New song—Rev. 5:9. See MUSIC, POETRY, LYRIC.

SINGER. I Chr. 15:19; II Chr. 23:13; Ps. 68:25; Ez. 40:44. See MUSIC, POETRY, LYRIC.

SINGLE. Eyes—Mt. 6:22; Lu. 11:34. Heart—Acts 2:46; Eph. 6:5; Col. 3:22.

SINK. Babylon shall—Jer. 51:64. Ears, Down into—Lu. 9:44. Lead as—Ex. 15:10. Mire, In—Ps. 69:2, 14. Roof—Eccl. 10:18. Ship—Mt. 14:30; Lu. 5:7.

SINNER. John 9:16, 31; Rom. 5:8; Heb. 7:26. Betrayed into hands of—Mt. 26: 45. Consumed—Ps. 104:35; Eccl. 9:18. Entice righteous—Pr. 1:10. Evil pursueth—Pr. 13:21. Friends of—Mt. 11: 19. Instruct—Ps. 25:8. Joy over one that repenteth—Lu. 15:7. Law for—I Tim. 1:9. Mercy to—Lu. 18:13. Sane—I Tim. 1:15; Jas. 5:20. Stand in way of—Ps. 1:1. See SIN.

SION, sī'on. **Top of Mt. Hermon.**—Deut. 4:48. See ZION.

SIPHMOTH, sĭph'moth. **A city in Judah.**—I Sam. 30:28.

SIPPAI, sĭp'pāi. I Chr. 20:4. See SAPH.

SIRAH, sī'rah. **A well near Hebron.**—II Sam. 3:26.

SIRION, sĭr'i-ŏn. **Name given to Hermon by the Sidonians.**—Deut. 3:9; Ps. 29:6.

SISERA, sĭs'erá. **(1) Captain of Jabin king of Canaan, slain by Joel.**—Ju. 4:2–22; 5:20–30; I Sam. 12:9; Ps. 83:9.

(2) **Ancestor of some who returned with Zerubbabel.**—Ezra 2:53; Neh. 7:55.

SISTER: Mentioned.—Sister of Tubal-Cain—Gen. 4:22. Sarah pretends to be Abram's—Gen. 12:13, 19; 20:2, 5, 12. Rebekah, sister of Laban—Gen. 24:29, 30, 59, 60; 25:20; 29:13. Isaac pretends that Rebekah is his—Gen. 26:7, 9. Sister of Rachel—Gen. 30:1, 8. Dinah, sister to sons of Jacob—Gen. 34: 13, 14, 27, 31. Timna, sister of Lotan—Gen. 36:22; I Chr. 1:39. Miriam, sister of Moses and Aaron—Ex. 15:20; Num. 26:59. Cozbi, sister of the Midianites—Num. 25:18. Rahab asks that her sister be saved—Josh. 2:13. Sister to the wife of Samson—Ju. 15:2. Tamar, sister of Absalom and Amnon—II Sam. 13:1, 2, 4, 5, 6, 11, 20, 22, 32. Sister to sons of David—I Chr. 3:9. Hammolecheth, sister of Gilead—I Chr. 7:18. Sisters to sons of Job—Job 1:4. Sisters of Job—Job 42:11. Sisters of Jesus—Mt. 13-56; Mk. 6:3. Mary, the sister of Martha—Lu. 10: 39, 40; John 11:1, 5, 28. Sisters to Lazarus—John 11:3, 39. Mary, sister of Jesus' mother—John 19:25. Paul's sister—Acts 23:16. Sister to Nereus—Rom. 16:15. Phœbe, a servant of the Church, called sister—Rom. 16:1.

Laws concerning.—Lev. 18-9, 11, 12, 13, 18; 20:17, 19; 21:3; Num. 6:7; Deut. 27:22; Ez. 44:25. Sister humbled—Ez. 22:11. See JESUS, TEACHINGS OF.

Figurative.—Jer. 3:7, 8, 10; 22:18; Ez. 16:45, 46, 48, 49, 51, 52, 55, 56, 61; Ez. 23:4, 11, 18, 31, 32, 33; II John 13.

Illustrative.—Job 17:14; Pr. 7:4; Song of Sol. 4:9, 10, 12; 5:1, 2; 8:8; Hos. 2:1.

In teachings of Paul.—I Cor. 7:15; I Tim. 5:2.

Teaching of James.—Jas. 2:15.

SIT. Eat, And—Gen. 27:19; Mk. 6:39. Graves, Among—Ps. 65:4. Low place, In—Eccl. 10:6. Market places, In—Mt. 11:16. Oak, Under—I Ki. 13:14. Place of toll, At the—Mt. 9:9. Right

hand, At—Ps. 110:1; Mt. 26:64. Samaria, In—Amos 3:12. Teachers, In
the midst of—Lu. 2:46. Throne, Upon
—Ex. 11:5; Ps. 9:7. Wayside, By the
—Mt. 20:30. See JESUS, TEACHING OF.

SITHRI, sĭth'rī. **A Levite.**—Ex. 6:22.

SITNAH, sĭt'nah. **A well.**—Gen. 26:21.

SITUATION. II Ki. 2:19; Nah. 3:8.

SIVAN, sī'van. **Third Jewish month.**—
Esth. 8:9. See MONTHS.

SIX. Branches—Ex. 25:32–35; 37:18–21.
Days for work—Ex. 20:9, 11; 23:12;
31:15; 34:21; 35:2; Lev. 23:3; Deut.
5:13. Earth made in six days—Ex. 31:
17. Enchanter—Is. 3:3.

SKILFUL. Hunter—Gen. 25:27. Hands
—Ps. 78:72. Lamentation, In—Amos
5:16. Musician—I Chr. 15:22; I Sam.
16:16; Ps. 33:3. War, In—I Chr. 5:18;
Ez. 21:31. Wisdom, In—Dan. 1:4.
Worker—II Chr. 2:14. Works—Ex.
31:4.

SKILL. Ps. 137:5; Eccl. 9:11. Grave,
To—II Chr. 2:7; Hew, To—I Ki. 5:6;
II Chr. 2:8. Learning, In—Dan. 1:17.
Men, Of—Eccl. 9:11. Playing, In—II
Chr. 34:12. Weaving, In—Ex. 28:8.

SKIN. Made coats of—Gen. 3:21. Re-
becca put skins on hands of Isaac—
Gen. 27:16. His only covering—Ex.
22:27. Skin of bullock to burn—Ex.
29:14. See OFFERING. Skin of his face
shone—Ex. 34:29, 30, 35. Priest have
the skin of sacrifice—Lev. 7:8. Leprosy—Lev. 13:2, 4, 11, 56. Filthy skin
to be washed—Lev. 15:17. Skin for
skin, etc.—Job 2:4. After my skin is
destroyed—Job 19:26. Can Ethiopian
change skin?—Jer. 13:23. John had a
girdle of—Mk. 1:6. Wandered in
sheepskins—Heb. 11:37. See WINE.

SKIP. Ps. 29:6; 114:4; Song of Sol. 2:8.

SKIRT. Described—Ex. 28:33–34; 39:
25–26. Shall not uncover father's—
Deut. 22:30. Spread skirt over handmaid—Ruth 3:9. Saul laid hold of
Samuel's—I Sam. 15:27. David cut
off Saul's—I Sam. 24:4–5, 11. Oil
came down upon skirt of Aaron—Ps.
133:2. In thy skirts found blood of
innocent—Jer. 2:34. For iniquity,
skirts uncovered—Jer. 13:22, 26; Nah.
3:5. Filthiness in—Lam. 1:9. Bind
them in thy skirts—Ez. 5:3. See
CLOTHING.

SKULL. Ju. 9:53; II Ki. 9:35; Mt. 27:
33; Mk. 15:22; John 19:17. See HEAD.

SKY. II Sam. 22:12; Job 37:18. Ps. 18:
11; 77:17; Is. 45:8; Jer. 51:9; Mt.
16:3. See COSMOLOGY.

SLACK. Josh. 18:3. Hand—Josh. 10:6;
Pr. 10:4; Zeph. 3:16. Hate, To him
that—Deut. 7:10. Jehovah is not—II
Pet. 3:9. Law—Hab. 1:4. Pay, To—
Deut. 23:21.

SLANDER, SLANDERERS. See Gos-
SIP.

SLAUGHTER. Edomites, Of the—II
Chr. 25:14. First—I Sam. 14:14.
Great—Josh. 10:10, 20; Ju. 11:33; 15:
8; I Sam. 4:10, 17; 6:19; 14:30; 19:8;
23:5; II Sam. 18:7; I Ki. 20:21; II
Chr. 13:17; 28:5; Is. 30:25; 34:6.
Lamb to the, As—Is. 53:7; Ju. 51:40;
Acts 8:32. Ox goeth to, As—Pr. 7:22.
Sheep for the, As—Ps. 44:22. Valley
of—Jer. 19:6. See SACRIFICE.

SLAVE. See BONDAGE.

SLAY, SLAIN, SLAYER. II Ki. 11:15;
Ez. 21:11. Anger, In—Jer. 33:5.
Brother—Gen. 4:14; 27:41; 37:26.
Can—Gen. 4:8, 15. Children—Is. 57:5.
David—I Sam. 19:1. Jesus—Acts 5:
30. See JESUS, CRUCIFIXION OF. Lord
shall—Is. 66:16; II Thess. 2:8. Males,
All the—Gen. 34:25; Mt. 2:16. Man-
slayer—Num. 37:27. Neighbor—Deut.
22:26. Ready to—Pr. 24:11; Acts 23:
15. Saul, By—I Sam. 29:5. Silly—Job
5:2. Son—Ex. 4:23; I Ki. 17:20.
Streets, In the—Pr. 22:13. Wicked—
Ps. 34:21. Woman, By—Ju. 9:54. See
DEATH, MURDERER.

SLEEK—Deut. 32:15.

SLEEP: Gift of God.—Gen. 2:21; I
Sam. 26:12; Job 4:13; 33:15; Ps.
127:2.

Sloth.—Pr. 6:9–10; 10:5; 24:33; 19:15;
Is. 56:10; I Cor. 11:30; Eph. 5:14; I
Thess. 5:6–7.

Laboring Man.—Eccl. 5:12; Jer. 31:24–
26. Of weariness—Mt. 26:45; Mk. 14:
41; Lu. 9:32.

Vision.—Abraham's—Gen. 15:12–21. Jacob's—Gen. 28:10–17. Daniel's—Dan.
8:15–18. Zechariah's—Zech. 4:1. Of
Joseph—Mt. 1:20–24. The three apostles—Lu 9:32. Of Peter—Acts 10:10–
16.

Death.—Job 14:12; Jer. 51:39; Dan. 12: 2; Mt. 9:24; Mk. 5:39; Lu. 8:52; John 11:11–14; Acts 20:9; I Thess. 4:13–15. See "Death"—Rom. 5:12.

Jesus.—Mt. 8:24; Mk. 4:38; Lu. 8:23.

SLEIGHT. Eph. 4:14.

SLIDE. Back—Jer. 8:5. Foot shall—Deut. 32:35. Steps—Ps. 37:31.

SLIGHTLY. Jer. 6:14; 8:11.

SLIME. Daubed it with—Ex. 2:3. Mortar, For—Gen. 11:3. Pits—Gen. 14:10.

SLING. I Sam. 25:29. David—I Sam. 17:49. Hand, In—I Sam. 17:40. Stone in a—Pr. 26:8. Stones—Ju. 20:16; II Chr. 26:14. Job 41:28. See WEAPONS.

SLIP. I Sam. 19:10. Feet—Ps. 17:5. Foot—Ps. 38:16; 94:18; Job 12:5. Well nigh—Ps. 73:2. Strange—Is. 17: 10.

SLIPPERY. Dark and—Ps. 35:6. Places —Ps. 73:18; Jer. 23:12.

SLOPES. See HILLS.

SLOTHFUL. Be not—Ju. 18:9. Man—Pr. 12:27. Not—Rom. 12:11. Servant —Mt. 25:26. See SLUGGARD.

SLOTHFULNESS. By—Eccl. 10:18. Casteth into a deep sleep—Pr. 19:15. See SLUGGARD.

SLOW. Anger, To—Ex. 34:6; Num. 14: 18; Neh. 9:17; Ps. 86:15; Pr. 14:29; 19:11. Heart, Of—Lu. 24:25. Speak, To—Jas. 1:19. Speech, Of—Ex. 4:10.

SLUGGARD. Burieth his hand—Pr. 19: 24. Desireth—Pr. 13:4. Go to the ant —Pr. 6:6. How long wilt thou sleep? —Pr. 6:9. Is wiser—Pr. 26:16. Upon his bed—Pr. 24:14. Way of—Pr. 15: 19. Will not plow—Pr. 20:4. See SLOTHFUL.

SLUGGISH. Heb. 6:12.

SLUMBER, *n.* A little—Pr. 6:10; 24: 33. Give, to eyelids—Ps. 132:4; Pr. 6:4. See SLEEP.

SLUMBER, *v.* Destruction—II Pet. 2:3. He will not—Ps. 121:3. Loving to—Is. 56:10. None shall—Is. 5:27. They all—Mt. 25:5. See SLEEP.

SMALL. Among nations—Jer. 49:15. Are consolations too—Job 15:11. Beginning—Job 8:7. Be not—Jer. 30:19. Dust—Ex. 9:9; Is. 40:15. Fire—Jas. 3:5. Fishes—Mt. 15:34. He is—Amos 7:2. Island—Acts 27:16. Made thee — Ob. 2. Matters — I Cor. 6:2. Petition—I Ki. 2:20. Rain—Deut. 32:

2. Remnant—Is. 1:9; 16:14. Rudder Jas. 3:4. Strength—Pr. 24:10. Thing —Ex. 16:14; Num. 16:9; Is. 7:13; Zech. 4:10; I Cor. 4:3. Voice, Still—I Ki. 19:12. Whisper—Job 26:14. See LITTLE.

SMART. Pr. 11:15; 13:20.

SMELLING. Sense of—I Cor. 12:17 Of raiment—Gen. 27:27; Ps. 45:8; Song of Sol. 4:11. Substitute—Incense —Ex. 30:38. Sweet savor—Gen. 8:21 Lebanon—Song of Sol. 4:11. Sweet odors—Lev. 26:31; Phil. 4:18. Breath —Song of Sol. 7:8. Idols incapable of —Deut. 4:28; Ps. 115:6. Fire—Dan 3:27. Battle—Job 39:25.

Fragrance of.—Spikenard—Song of Sol 1:12. Vines—Song of Sol. 2:13. Oils—Song of Sol. 4:10. Mandrakes—Song of Sol. 7:13.

Figurative.—Of Israel—Hos. 14:6.

SMITE. Gen. 4:15; 34:30; II Sam. 2: 22. Again—Gen. 8:31. Anvil—Is 41:7. Cheek, On—Mt. 5:39. Earth—Mal. 4:6; Rev. 11:6. Race, On—II Cor. 11:20. Fellow—Ex. 2:13. Fist of wickedness, With—Is. 58:4. God shall—Acts 23:3. Head, Through—Ps. 68:21. Jehovah, To—Ez. 7:9 Knees, together—Nah. 2:10. Let the righteous—Ps. 141:5. Mortally—Deut 19:6. People—II Ki. 6:18. Scoffer—Pr. 19:25. Seven times—Lev. 26:24 Shepherd—Zech. 13:7. Sun shall not—Ps. 121:6. Though he—Is. 10:24 Tongue, With—Jer. 18:18. Uriah—II Sam. 12:9.

SMITER. Is. 50:6.

SMITH. Jer. 24:1; 29:2. Created the —Is. 54:16. Departed from Jerusalem —Jer. 29:2. Found, No—I Sam. 13:19 Jehovah showed me—Zech. 1:20. Maketh an axe—Is. 44:12. See TRADES AND ARTS.

SMITTEN. Is. 5:25. Cheek, Upon—Job 16:10. Contrary to law—Acts 23:3 Down—II Cor. 4:9. Enemies—Ps. 3:7 God, Of—Is. 53:4. Heart is—Ps. 102: 4. Life—Ps. 143:3. River—Ex. 7:25 Three times—Num. 22:28. See SMITE SMOTE.

SMOKE: Accompanies manifestation of God.—Gen. 15:17; Ex. 19:18; 20:18.

Pillars of.—Joel 2:30; Acts 2:19. Jehovah's jealousy will smoke—Deut. 29:

20. God's anger—Ps. 74:1. God touches the mountains and they—Ps. 104:32; 144:5. Sign to warriors—Ju. 20:38, 40. Of a burning city.—Gen. 19:28; Josh. 8:20, 21.

From nostrils.—II Sam. 22:9; Job 41: 20; Ps. 18:8; Is. 65:5.

Nineveh's chariots burned in.—Nah. 2:13.

Smoking firebrand.—Is. 7:4.

Figurative.—Consume as—Ps. 37:20; 102:3. Enemies driven as—Ps. 68:2. Heavens vanish as—Is. 51:6. Out of chimneys—Hos. 13:3. Compared to: As smoke to eyes, so sluggard—Pr. 10:26. Come up from wilderness like pillar of—Song of Sol. 3:6. Cometh a —Is. 14:31. The land smokes night and day—Is. 34:10. Like a wineskin in the—Ps. 119:83. Smoke of incense —Rev. 8:4. Of furnace—Rev. 9:2, 3. Out of horse's mouth—Rev. 9:17, 18. Of torment—Rev. 14:11. Temple filled with—Is. 6:4; Rev. 15:8. Smoke of Babylon—Rev. 18:9, 18. Smoke of the harlot—Rev. 19:3.

SMOOTH. Butter, As—Ps. 55:21. Make rough places—Is. 45:2. Man—Gen. 27:11. Nation—Is. 18:2. Oil, Than— Pr. 5:3. Speech—See FLATTERY. Stone — See STONES. Things — Is. 32:10. Ways, Rough—Lu. 3:5.

SMOOTHLY. Goeth down—Pr. 23:31; Song of Sol. 7:9.

SMOTE. First-born—Ex. 12:29. Many nations—Ps. 135:10. People—Ex. 32: 35. Peter—Acts 12:7. Rephaim—Gen. 14:5. Rock—Num. 20:11. Waters—II Ki. 2:8. See SMITE, SMITTEN.

SMYRNA, smyr'nà. Church at.—Rev. 2:8–11.

SNATCH. Is. 9:20; Mt. 13:19. Fire, Out of—Jude. 23. Hand, Out of— John 10:28. Wolf, By—John 10:12.

SNEEZE. II Ki. 4:35; Job 41:18.

SNORT. Job 39:20; Jer. 8:16. See HORSE.

SNOUT. Pr. 11:22.

SNOW. See METEOROLOGY.

SNUFF DISHES. Ex. 25:38; 37:23; Num. 4:9. See VESSELS.

SNUFFED. Mal. 1:13; Jer. 2:24.

SNUFFERS. Ex. 37:23; I Ki. 7:50; II Ki. 12:13; 25:14; II Chr. 4:22; Jer. 52:18. See VESSELS.

SO. Ethiopian king of Egypt.—II Ki. 17:4.

SOAKED. Lev. 6:21.

SOAP. Mal. 3:2.

SOARED. Job 39:26; Ps. 18:10.

SOBRIETY. Awake to—I Cor. 15:34. Commanded—I Thess. 5:6, 8; II Tim. 4:5; I Pet. 1:13; 5:8. Dress with—I Tim. 2:9. Life, Of—Tit. 2:12. Mind, Of—Rom. 12:3; II Cor. 5:13; I Tim. 3:2; Tit. 1:8; 2:4, 5, 6, 12. Prayer, Of —I Pet. 4:7. Sanctification with—I Tim. 2:15.

SOCHO, sō'ko. (1) Son of Heber.—I Chr. 4:18.

(2) A city in Judah.—II Chr. 11:7; 28: 18.

SOCKET. Eyes, Of—Zech. 14:12. Gold, Of—Song of Sol. 5:15. Silver, Of— Ex. 20:19. Talent for a—Ex. 38:27. See TABERNACLE.

SOCO, SOCOH, sō'ko. A city in Judah. —II Sam. 17:1; I Ki. 4:10.

(2) Another city in Judah.—Josh. 15: 48.

SODA. Pr. 25:20.

SODDEN. Lev. 6:28. Children—Lam. 4:10. Flesh—Num. 6:19; I Sam. 2:15. Water, With—Ex. 12:9. See DRUNK-ENNESS.

SODI, sō'dī. A man of Zebulun, sent to spy out the land.—Num. 13:10.

SODOM, sŏd'om. A city in the plain of Jordan—Gen. 13:10. In the vale of Siddim—Gen. 14:1–3. Chief of five cities—Gen. 10:19. Well watered, like the Garden of Jehovah—Gen. 13:10. The vicinity full of slime pits—Gen. 14:10.

Four kings make a raid.—Gen. Ch. 14: The kings of five cities in the valley meet them in battle—Gen. 14:2–3. Chedorlaomer overcomes the five kings and enslaves them for twelve years— Gen. 14:4. In the thirteenth year they rebel and are again attacked—Gen. 14:5–9. The kings of Sodom and Gomorrah are overcome in the slime pits—v. 10. Sodom and Gomorrah are sacked—v. 11. Lot and his goods captured—v. 12. Lot and family continue to reside in Sodom—Gen. 19:1. Abraham, hearing this, pursues the four kings with 318 trained men— Gen. 14:14. He divides his forces, smites them, and recaptures Lot, all the people, and all the goods—Gen. 14:15-16. Abraham is met and blessed by Melchizedek, king of Salem—Gen. 14:18-20. Abraham gives this priest of God, one-tenth of all—v. 20. The king of Sodom offers Abraham all the recaptured goods, which Abraham refuses—vs. 21-24.

Lot's residence in Sodom.—His grasping nature—Gen. 13:9-11. He pitched his tent towards Sodom—v. 12. Permitted his daughters to intermarry with sons of Sodom—Gen. 19:12. His sons-in-law depraved—vs. 12-14. Lot was vexed at the conduct of Sodom—II Pet. 1:7-8.

The cup of iniquity full to the brim.—Jehovah sends the three angels of destruction—Gen. 18:1, 2. Abraham intercedes for Sodom—Gen. 18:22-33. Not enough righteous people to save it—vs. 32-33. The angels arrive in Sodom at even—Gen. 19:1. Lot entertains them—Gen. 19:2-3. Men of Sodom demand the angels, but are struck blind—Gen. 19:4-11. Lot and family ordered out of Sodom—vs. 12-15. Lot lingering, the angels take Lot, the wife, and two daughters by the hand—v. 16. Lot sent to Zoar—v. 21. Sodom and Gomorrah destroyed—vs. 23-35; Lu. 17:29. Lot's wife, looking back, becomes encrusted with salt—v. 26; Lu. 17:32. Nothing remains but smoke and ruins—v. 28.

Reasons for the city's destruction: Lewdness—Gen. 19:5-7; Jer. 23:14; Ez. 16:50; Jude 7. Pride—Ez. 16:49-50; Zeph. 2:9-11.

Destruction of Sodom and Gomorrah used as typical.—Of children of Israel —Deut. 29:23. Of Judah—Is. 3:9. Of prophets of Jerusalem—Jer. 23:14. Of Jerusalem—Is. 1:9-10; Ez. 16:46-59; Rom. 9:29. Of Babylon—Is. 13:19; Jer. 50:40.

Threats of similar punishment.—Edom —Jer. 49:18. Moab—Zeph. 2:9-11. Cities rejecting apostles—Mt. 10:15; Lu. 17:29.

A warning to others.—Mt. 10:15; 11:23, 24; Lu. 17:28, 29; II Pet. 2:4-9; Jude 7.

SODOMITE. This word describes those who practised as a religious rite the unnatural vice of the people of Sodom and Gomorrah—Deut. 23:17; I Ki. 14: 24; 15:12; 22:46; II Ki. 23:7; Job 36:14 (*margin*). Women were also consecrated to this lewd religious rite —Gen. 38:21-23 (also *margin*); Deut. 23:17; Hos. 4:14; I Ki. 22:38.

SOFT. Answer—Pr. 15:1. Clothing— Mt. 11:8; Lu. 7:25. Showers, With— Ps. 65:10. Tongue—Pr. 25:15. Words —Job 41:3; Ps. 55:21.

SOFTLY. Blow—Acts 27:13. Lead— Gen. 33:14. Move—Ju. 4:21; Ruth 3:7; I Ki. 21:27; Is. 8:6; 38:15.

SOIL. Ez. 17:5, 8.

SOJOURNER. The term is used at times of class distinctions within Israel as priestly *vs.* non-priestly—Ex. 29:33; Lev. 22:10, 12. Applied to foreigners —Is. 1:7. Hostile to Israel—Ez. 11:9.

Israelites spoken of as.—Gen. 15:13; 17:4; 23:4; Ex. 18:3; 22:21; Deut. 10:19; 23:7; Is. 52:4.

Others mentioned.—Abram—Gen. 12:10. In Sodom—Gen. 19:9. Isaac—Gen. 26:3. Joseph's brothers—Gen. 47:4. In Ephraim—Ju. 17:8, 9. Elimelech— Ruth 1:1. Elijah—I Ki. 17:20. The Shunammite—II Ki. 8:1. In Meshech —Ps. 120:5. In Egypt—Jer. 42:15. In Gerar—Gen. 20:1; 21:23, 34; 26:3. With Laban—Gen. 32:4. Jacob—Gen. 35:27. Ham—Ps. 105:23. In Land of Promise—Heb. 11:9. Moses in Midian —I Pet. 1:1. Inheritance of—Gen. 28: 4; 37:1. Of Israel—Ez. 14:7. In fear —I Pet. 1:17.

Laws concerning.—One law to homeborn and sojourners—Ex. 12:49; Num. 15:15, 16, 26, 29. Treatment of—Ex. 20:10; 22:21; 23:9, 12; 30:33; Lev. 17: 8, 10, 13, 15; 19:10, 33, 34; 20:2; 25: 45, 47; Num. 15:15, 26; Deut. 14:21, 29; 16:11; 26:11-13. In connection with Passover—Ex. 12:19, 48; Num. 9:14. Sabbath unto Jehovah—Lev. 25:6; Deut. 5:14. Redemption of servants—Lev. 25:47. Blood shall not be eaten—Lev. 17:10, 12, 15. Shall not eat flesh—Lev. 16:29; 22:10, 13; Num. 15:29. In burnt-offerings—Lev. 17:8; 22:18; Num. 15:14, 16; 16:40. Cities of refuge for—Num. 35:15; Josh. 20:9. Exaction of usury from—Deut. 15:13; 23:20. Could not be king—Deut. 17:

15. Annual atonement—Lev. 16:29. Impurities forbidden — Lev. 18:26. Purification of the unclean—Num. 19: 10. Wives—Ezra 10:2; Neh. 13:26. Warning about—Pr. 2:16; 5:3, 20; 7:5. Sojourner left—Ezra 1:4. Marriage—Lev. 22:12; Deut. 25:5. Food for—Lev. 25:6. Children of—Lev. 25: 45. Surety for—Pr. 11:15; 20:16. Praise from—Pr. 11:15; 20:16; 27:2, 13; Lu. 17:18. Love for—Jer. 2:25. Hospitality to—I Tim. 5:10; Heb. 13: 2. Strangers, Tribute of—Mt. 17:25, 26. Judgment—Mt. 25:35, 38, 43, 44. In parable of sheepfolds—John 10:5.

Prophecies concerning.—Lev. 20:2; Is. 61:5. Shall serve—Jer. 5:19; 30:8; Ez. 7:21; 11:9; 14:7; 28:7; 30:12. Of Egypt—Jer. 42:15, 17; 43:2; 44:12, 14, 25. Misery of described—Lam. 4:15. Israelites—Ez. 20:38.

Figurative.—Lev. 25:35. Palace of—Is. 25:2, 5. A city—Is. 23:7.

Miscellaneous.—Did not sojourn—Lam. 4:15. Shall sojourn—In Egypt—Jer. 43:2; 44:12, 14. I beseech you as sojourners—I Pet. 2:11. No strangers—I Ki. 3:18. But fellow-citizens—Eph. 2:19. Enemies of David—Ps. 54:3. Doth not intermeddle—Pr. 14:10.

STRANGERS or SOJOURNERS. Mentioned: Abraham in Heth—Gen. 23:4. Before Jehovah—I Chr. 29:15; Ps. 93:12. To brethren—Ps. 69:8; III John 5. Ephraim—Hos. 7:9; 8:7. In Athens—Acts 17:21. From covenants of promise—Eph. 2:12. Inheritance of—Lev. 25:23; Lam. 5:2; Ez. 47:22, 23.

Burial place of.—Potter's field—Mt. 27:7.

Punishment by.—Zion destroyed by—Is. 1:7. Assyria—Ez. 31:12.

Punishment of.—Num. 1:51; 3:10, 38; 18:4, 7; Ps. 109:11; Pr. 6:1.

ALIENS. Mentioned: Job—Job 19:15. To brethren—Ps. 69:8. To the commonwealth of Israel—Eph. 2:12.

Inheritance of.—Lam. 5:2. Vanity of—Eccl. 6:2.

House of.—Pr. 5:10, 20. Armies of—Heb. 11:34.

Foreigners.—Mentioned: Rachel and Leah—Gen. 31:15. Ruth—Ruth 2:10. Gittite—II Sam. 15:19.

Laws concerning.—Deut. 14:21. Usury exacted—Deut. 23:20. Cities of—Ju. 19:12. Warning against—Pr. 2:16. Children of—Is. 2:6. Sanctuary—Ez. 44:7, 9.

Prophecies concerning.—Deut. 29:22; II Sam. 22:45, 46; I Ki. 8:41, 43; II Chr. 6:32, 33; Ps. 18:44, 45; Is. 60:10; 62:8; Ob. 11.

SOLACE. Pr. 7:18. See CONSOLATION.

SOLD. Birthright — See BIRTHRIGHT. Land—See LAND. Self—See BONDAGE. Shambles, Into—I Cor. 10:25. Sin, Under—Rom. 7:14. See BONDAGE, SELL, JESUS, TEACHING OF.

SOLDIER: Enrolment.—In the wilderness—Num. 1:1-46. Before Balak—Num. 26:1-50. At Mizpah—Ju. 20:14-18. In David's time—I Chr. Chs. 7 and 8. In Amaziah's time—II Chr. 25:5.

Order of Battle.—I Sam. 17:2-3, 21; I Ki. 20:14, 15; II Chr. 13:2, 3; 25:6-13. Exempt from service—Deut. 20:5-9; 24:5.

Relentless in battle.—Gen. 14:8-12; II Chr. 25:11-13; II Sam. 11:23, 24. Adopt an ambush—Josh. 8:12-23.

Means of protection.—Ez. 8:22; Acts 12: 4-6; 21:31-35; 23:10, 23, 31; 27:31-32.

Recklessness of.—Mt. 27:27, 31; Mk. 15: 16-20; Lu. 23:36; John 19:2-3.

Appropriation of spoils.—Deut. 2:35; Num. 31:9-12, 53, 54; Josh. 7:19-21; 11:14; 22:28; Ju. 5:30; I Sam. 15:19-21; II Chr. 14:13; John 19:23-25.

Assist at crucifixion.—John 19:32-34.

Bribery of.—Mt. 28:12.

Possessed of fear.—Deut. 20:1-9; Ju. 7:3; I Sam. 15:15; II Sam. 19:3; Ps. 68:12; Mt. 27:54; 28:4; Acts 12:18, 19.

Authority of.—Mt. 8:9; 27:27; Mk. 15: 16; Lu. 7:8.

Religious enquirers.—Lu. 3:14; Acts 10: 1-8. Type of Christian—II Tim. 2:3, 4. Bad counsellors—Acts 27:42-43. See WAR.

SOLE. Gen. 8:9; Deut. 28:35, 56, 65; Josh. 1:3; II Sam. 14:25; I Ki. 5:3; II Ki. 19:24; Job 2:7; 13:27; Is. 1:6; 37:25; 60:14; Ez. 1:7; 43:7; Mal. 4:3. See FEET.

SOLEMN. Assembly—Lev. 23:36; Num. 29:35; Deut. 16:8; II Ki. 10:20; II

Chr. 7:9; Neh. 8:18; Joel 1:14; 2:15; Amos 5:21; Zeph. 3:18. Day—Lam. 2:22; Hos. 9:5. Feast day—See FEASTS. Meeting—Is. 1:13. Protest—Gen. 43:3; I Sam. 8:9. Sound—Ps. 92:3.

SOLEMNITY. City of—Is. 33:20. Meat offering, In—Ez. 46:11.

SOLID. Heb. 5:12.

SOLITARY. Is. 49:21. City—Lam. 1:1. Dwell—Ps. 68:6; Mic. 7:14. Places—Is. 35:1.

SOLOMON: Son of David and Bathsheba.—II Sam. 12:24. Called also Jedidiah (Beloved of Jehovah)—II Sam. 12:25.

Anointed and proclaimed king.—According to Jehovah's purpose—I Chr. 22: 8–11; 28:5–7. On account of Adonijah's treachery—I Ki. 1:5–53; I Chr. 23:1. Promises Adonijah mercy if he cease from evil designs—I Ki. 1:51–53. Comes to throne at death of father —I Ki. 2:12; I Chr. 29:22–25.

David's charges to Solomon.—I Ki. 2:1–9; I Chr. 22:6–16; 28:8–21.

His choice of wisdom.—I Ki. 3:4–28; II Chr. 1:7–13.

Punishment of Adonijah and others.—I Ki. 2:12–46.

Preparations for building the temple.—David's—I Chr. 29:1–9. Hiram's—I Ki. 5:2–12; II Chr. 2:1–18. Solomon's —I Ki. 5:13–18; II Chr. 2:1–18. Began to build 480 years after leaving Egypt —I Ki. 6:1. Finished building—II Chr. 7:11.

Construction of temple, courts, and furniture.—I Ki. 6:1–38; 7:13–51; II Chr. 3:1–17; 4:1–22; 5:1.

Its dedication by Solomon.—I Ki. 8:22–53; II Chr. 6:12–42. Sacrifices and Praise—I Ki. 8:54–66; II Chr. 7:1–10.

Building of palace and structures connected.—I Ki. 7:1–12; 9:24–25; II Chr. 8:11.

Cities built by Solomon.—I Ki. 9:11–19; II Chr. 8:1–6.

Marries Pharaoh's daughter and brings her to city of David.—I Ki. 3:1; 9:24. Transfers her to palace when completed—II Chr. 8:11.

His officials.—Administrative—I Ki. 4: 1–19; II Chr. 8:9–10. Military—I Ki. 4:5; 9:22; II Chr. 8:9, 18. Ecclesiastic

—I Ki. 4:2–4; II Chr. 8:14–15. Builds a navy—I Ki. 9:26, 27; II Chr. 8:18.

His retinue.—Horsemen—I Ki. 10:26; II Chr. 1:14. Chariots and horses—I Ki. 4:26; 10:28, 29; II Chr. 1:14–17; 9:28. Hewers, builders and workmen—I Ki. 5:13–18; II Chr. 8:7, 8. Provision for king's court—I Ki. 4: 22, 23, 27. Provision for horses—I Ki. 4:28; II Chr. 9:25.

Solomon's revenues.—I Ki. 9:28; 10:11, 14, 15, 22, 25; II Chr. 1:15; 8:18; 9:10, 13, 14, 27.

Magnificence of court.—Targets, shields, bucklers, throne, etc.—I Ki. 10:16–21; II Chr. 9:15–22.

His wisdom.—Spake proverbs—I Ki. 4: 29–34; Pr. 1:1–6. Judgments pronounced—I Ki. 3:16–28. Visit of Queen of Sheba—I Ki. 10:1–10; II Chr. 9:1–9.

Wide extent of his reign.—I Ki. 4:20–25; II Chr. 9:26.

Failure of Solomon.—Many wives—I Ki. 11:1–4. Went after strange gods —I Ki. 11:5–8. Multiplied horses—I Ki. 4:26; 10:28, 29; II Chr. 1:16, 17. Multiplied silver and gold—I Ki. 10: 27; II Chr. 1:15.

Adversaries of Solomon raised up by Jehovah.—Hadad, the Edomite—I Ki. 11:14–22. Rezon of Damascus—I Ki. 11:23–25. Jeroboam the Ephraimite—I Ki. 11:26–40.

Reigned 40 years.—Death and burial—II Chr. 9:30, 31.

New Testament references.—Jesus compares Himself with—Lu. 11:31. Solomon and the lilies—Mt. 6:28, 29.

SON.—Heb. *"ben,"* a Son, in O. T. Aram. Equivalent, *"bar"* in N. T. Used frequently in composition with names of persons.

Used for descendant.—Num. 23:18; Ju. 5:12; I Sam. 10:11; 16:18; 20:27, 31; 22:7, 9, 12; 25:10, 17; I Ki. 12:16; I Chr. 12:18; II Chr. 10:16; Mt. 1:1, 20; 9:27; 12:23; 15:22; 20:30; 22:42, 45; Mk. 10:48; Lu. 18:38; 19:9.

Son of God.—Applied to Jesus some 40 times. Son of the Gods—Dan. 3:25. Son of the Most High God—Lu. 1:32.

Son of man.—Applied by Jesus to Himself 65 times. See "Son of Man" under DIVINITY OF JESUS. Applied by

others to Jesus 3 times (Stephen)—
Acts 7:56; (John) Rev. 1:13; 14:14.
(Possibly, also, in Dan. 7:13.) Applied
by Jehovah to Ezekiel some 90 times.
Applied generally to all descendants
of Adam—Num. 23:19; Job 25:6; Ps.
8:4; 80:17; 144:3; 146:3; Is. 51:12;
56:2; Jer. 49:18, 33; 50:40.

Sons of Israel.—Ex. 4:22; Hos. 11:1;
(Children of) Mt. 27:9; Lu. 1:16; Acts
5:21.

Sons of the prophets.—I Ki. 20:35; II
Ki. 2:3, 5, 7, 15.

Sons of the kingdom.—Mt. 8:12; 13:38.
Of the Bridechamber—Mt. 9:15.

Sons of the resurrection.—Lu. 20:36.

Sons of this world.—Lu. 16:8.

Sons of Anak.—Gen. 6:4; Num. 13:33.

Sons of disobedience.—Eph. 2:2; 5:6.

Son of perdition.—John 17:12; II Thess.
2:3.

A term of endearment.—I Sam. 3:6, 16;
Heb. 12:5–6; I Pet. 5:13.

A title of address.—Pr. 1:8, 10, 15; 2:1;
3:1, 11, 21; 4:1, 10, 20; 5:1, 7; 6:1, 20;
7:1, 24; 8:32.

Denoting character or quality.—Sons of
thunder—Mk. 3:17. Son of peace—
Lu. 10:6. Sons of light—Lu. 16:8;
John 12:36; I Thess. 5:5. Son of exhortation—Acts 4:36. Son of oil—Is.
5:1 (*marg.*). Lucifer, Son of morning
—Is. 14:12.

A wise son.—Pr. 3:12; 10:1, 5; 13:1; 15:
20; 28:7; Is. 19:11.

A foolish son.—Pr. 17:25; 19:13; Hos.
13:13; Mic. 7:6.

Son not responsible for sins of father.—
Ez. Chap. 18. See CHILDREN.

SOMEWHERE. Heb. 4:4.

SONS OF GOD. Saw and married daughters of men—Gen. 6:2, 4. Came to
present themselves before Jehovah—
Job 1:6. Shouted for joy—Job 38:7.
Ye are the sons of the living God—
Hos. 1:10; Rom. 9:26. As many as are
led by the spirit of God are sons of
God—Rom. 8:14–17. Power to become
children (Sons, A. V.) of God—John 1:
12. Children (Sons, A. V.) of God without blemish—Phil. 2:15. Waiting for
revealing of sons of God—Rom. 8:19.
We should be called children (sons,
A. V.) of God—I John 3:1. Now are
we children (sons, A. V.) of God—I

John 3:2. Adoption—Gal. 4:6–7.
Peacemakers called sons of God—Mt.
6:9. Ye shall be sons and daughters
of God—II Cor. 6:18. Sons of God,
through faith, in Christ Jesus—Gal.
3:26. See CHILDREN.

SONG. See MUSIC, POETRY, LYRIC.

SOOTHSAYER. See MAGIC.

SOP. After the—John 13:27. Dip—
John 13:26. Received—John 13:30.
See LORD'S SUPPER.

SOPATER, sŏp'a·ter. **A disciple from
Berea who accompanied Paul.**—Acts
20:4.

SORCERER. See MAGIC.

SORE. Afraid—Mk. 9:6. See FEAR.
Displeasure—Ps. 2:5. Distressed—
Ju. 2:15; 10:9. Famine—Gen. 12:10;
45:56; I Ki. 18:2; II Ki. 25:3. See
FAMINE. Pained—Ps. 55:4; Zech. 9:5.
See PAIN. Troubled—Mt. 26:37. Wept
—Acts 20:37. See TRIBULATION.

SOREK, sō'rek. **A valley or stream be-
twéen Ashkelon and Gaza.**—Ju. 16:4.

SORREL. See COLORS.

SORROW: Earthly.—Gen. 27:34; 42:38;
44:29, 31; I Chr. 4:9; Neh. 2:2; Job
17:7; Ps. 13:2; 38:17; 39:2; 69:29;
90:10; 107:39; 116:3; Pr. 10:22; 15:
13; 17:21; Eccl. 2:23; 7:3; Jer. 20:18;
Lam. 1:12, 18; Dan. 10:16.

Turned to gladness.—Esth. 9:22.

Jehovah's sorrow for His people.—Jer.
8:18.

Result of sin.—Gen. 3:16, 17; Ps. 16:4;
32:10; 38:18; Pr. 10:10; 23:29, 30; Is.
50:11; Jer. 45:3; I Tim. 6:10. Wicked
rich men—Jas. 5:1–6.

Influence of Godly.—II Cor. 7:9–11.

Mention of.—Egyptians—Ex. 3:7. Hannah—I Sam. 1:15. Joseph and Mary
sought Jesus sorrowing—Lu. 2:48.
Rich young man—Mt. 19:22; Lu. 18:
23. Of Herod—Mt. 14:9; Mk. 6:26.
Disciples—Mt. 17:23; 26:22; Mk. 14:
19; Lu. 22:45; John 14:1, 27; 16:6, 20–
22. Peter—Mt. 26:75; Mk. 14:72; Lu.
22:62. For Lazarus—John 11:19–35.
Jesus—Mt. 26:37–39; Mk. 14:34. For
Jesus—Lu. 23:27, 28; John 20:11–15.
Paul's—Rom. 9:2; Phil. 2:27, 28. For
Paul—Acts 20:38. Sorrowful letter
to the Corinthians—II Cor. 2:2–7; 7:8.
Sorrowful remorse of Judas—Mt. 27:
3. Of Esau—Heb. 12:17.

Concerning Christian dead.—I Thess. 4: 13.

Prophecies concerning.—Is. 13:8; 14:3; 17:11; 35:10; 51:11, 19; 53:3, 4; 65: 14; Jer. 13:21; 31:12, 13, 25; 49:23, 24; Ez. 23:33; Hos. 13:13; Zeph. 3: 18; Zech. 9:5; Rev. 21:4.

Miscellaneous.—No sorrow for Saul—I Sam. 22:8. Compared to laughter— Eccl. 7:3. Sorrowful yet rejoicing— Pr. 14:13; II Cor. 6:10. In knowledge —Eccl. 1:18. No sorrow in heaven— Rev. 21:4. See TEACHING OF JESUS, MOURNING, AFFLICTION, CONSOLATION.

SORT. Every—Gen. 6:19. Godly—II Cor. 7:9, 11. See CHRISTIAN GRACES. People, Of—II Ki. 24:14. Wine, Of— Neh. 5:18. Work, Of—I Cor. 3:13.

SOSIPATER, so-sĭp′a-ter. A kinsman of Paul to whom he sends a salutation.— Rom. 16:21.

SOSTHENES, sŏs′the-nēs. (1) An early disciple, a companion of Paul.—I Cor. 1:1.

(2) Ruler of the synagogue at Corinth. —Acts 18:17.

SOTAI, sō′tāi. Ancestor of some who returned with Zerubbabel.—Ezra 2: 55; Neh. 7:57.

SOTTISH. Jer. 4:22. See DRUNKENNESS.

SOUGHT. See SEEKING.

SOUL. *Heb.* Nephesh, Neshamah, Ruahh. Breath of life; Animating principle; Person.

Gr. Psyche, Pneuma—The vital breath; human soul as distinguished from body. Differs from spirit which denotes the higher faculties.

Paul differentiates:—"May your spirit and soul and body."—I Thess. 5:23.

The whole person.—Gen. 12:5; 17:14; 46:15, 18, 22, 25, 26, 27; Ex. 1:5; 12: 4, 15, 19; 31:14; Lev. 7:18, 20, 21, 25, 27; 17:10, 12, 15; 18:29; 19:8; 20:6; 22:3, 11; 23:29, 30; Num. 5:6; 9:13; 15:28, 30, 31; 19:13, 20, 22; 31:28; Josh. 10:28, 30, 32, 35, 37, 39; 11:11; Job 16:4; Ps. 142:4, 7; Pr. 11:25; 19: 15; Acts 2:41, 43; 3:23; 7:14; 27:37; Rom. 13:1; I Pet. 3:20.

Used as equivalent to personal pronoun or "self."—Gen. 27:4, 19, 25, 31; Lev. 26:15; Deut. 4:9; I Sam. 18:1, 3; 20: 17; Job 16:4; Ps. 3:2; 6:3, 4; 7:2, 5;

10:3; 11:1, 5; 13:2; 16:10; 22:29; 23: 3; 24:4; 25:1, 13, 20; 26:9; 30:3; 49: 18; 54:4; 63:8; 66:9, 16; 94:17; 109: 20; 120:6; Is. 51:23; Lam. 3:17, 24. O, my soul—Gen. 49:6; Ju. 5:21; Ps. 103:1, 2, 22; 104:1, 35; Jer. 4:19.

Animal life.—Gen. 12:13; 19:20; 35:18; Lev. 26:16; I Sam. 18:1, 3; 20:17; 25: 29; II Sam. 4:9; I Ki. 1:29; Job 27:8; Ps. 7:2, 5; 17:13; 22:20; 33:19; 40:14; 54:3; 56:6, 13; 59:3; 63:9; 70:2; 71: 10, 13; 72:13, 14; 74:19; 78:50; 86:2, 14; 94:21; 97:10; 116:4; 119:109, 175; 124:7; Pr. 6:32; 10:3; 16:17; 19:16; 22:5; Is. 53:10, 12; Jer. 2:34; 20:13; 38:16, 17, 20; Ez. 3:19, 21; 13:18, 19, 20; 14:14, 20; 18:27; 22:25, 27; 33:5, 7; Lu. 12:19, 20; 21:19; I Cor. 15:45; Rev. 16:3.

The soul of all living things, including animals.—Gen. 2:7; Num. 31:28; Job 12:10; Rev. 16:3.

Spiritual man.—Gen. 2:7; Ex. 30:12, 15, 16; Lev. 17:11; 20:25; 26:43; Num. 5:6; Deut. 13:6; I Ki. 17:21, 22; Ps. 16:10; 19:7; 31:9; 33:20; 34:2; 35:3, 9; 41:4; 49:18; 62:1, 5; 88:14; 109: 31; 119:167; 120:6; 121:7; 130:5, 6; 141:8; 143:3; Pr. 6:32; 8:36; 11:17, 30; 14:25; 15:32; 16:17, 24; 18:7; 19: 2, 8; 21:10, 23; 22:5, 25; 24:12, 14; 29:24; Eccl. 7:28; Is. 3:9; 10:18; 51: 23; 55:3; Jer. 6:16; 26:19; 42:20; 44: 7; Lam. 3:24, 25, 58; Ez. 4:14; 18:4, 27; Hab. 2:4, 10; Mt. 10:28; 11:29; Acts 2:27; 14:22; 15:24; Rom. 2:9; I Cor. 15:45; II Cor. 1:23; I Thess. 2:8; 5:23; Heb. 4:12; 6:19; 10:38, 39; 13:17; Jas. 1:21; 5:20; I Pet. 1:9, 22; 2:11, 25; 4:19; II Pet. 2:8, 14; III John 2; Rev. 6:9; 20:4.

The seat of emotion—mind—appetite.— Gen. 34:38; 42:21; Lev. 26:11, 15, 16, 30, 43; Num. 11:6; 21:4, 5; Deut. 4:9; 12:15, 20, 21; 14:26; 18:6; Ju. 16:16; I Sam. 1:10, 15; 2:16; 20:4; 23:20; 30:6; II Sam. 3:21; 5:8; I Ki. 11:37; II Ki. 4:27; Job 3:20; 6:7; 7:11, 15; 10:1; 13:2; 14:22; 19:2; 21:25; 23:13; 24:12; 27:2; 30:16, 25; 33:20; Ps. 35: 3, 9; 42:5, 6; 43:5; 44:25; 57:1, 4, 6; 69:1; 77:2; 84:2; 86:4; 94:14; 107:5, 9, 18; 119:20, 25, 28, 81, 129; 123:4; 124:4, 5; 131:2; 138:3; 139:14; Pr. 2:10; 3:22; 13:2, 4, 19, 25; 25:13; 27:

7; 31:6; Eccl. 2:24; 4:8; 6:2, 3; Song of Sol. 1:7; 3:1–4; 5:6; 6:12; Is. 15:4; 29:8; 53:11; 66:3; Jer. 4:31; 12:7; 13:7; 14:19; Lam. 2:12; 3:20, 51; Ez. 7:19; 24:21; 25:15; Jonah 2:5, 7; Mic. 7:1; Mt. 26:38; 27:31; Mk. 14:34; Lu. 1:46; 2:35; John 12:27; Phil. 1:27; Heb. 12:3; Rev. 18:14.

Used in speaking of God.—Lev. 26:11, 30; Ju. 10:16; Ps. 11:5; Is. 1:14; 42: 1; Jer. 5:9, 29; 6:8; 9:9; 14:19; 32:41; Zech. 11:8; Heb. 10:38.

Heart and.—I Chr. 22:19; Acts 4:32. In heart and soul—Deut. 13:18; Josh. 23: 14. With heart and soul—Deut. 4:29; 6:5; 10:12; 11:13; 13:3; 26:16; 30:2, 6, 10; Josh. 22:5; I Ki. 2:4; 8:48; II Ki. 23:3, 25; II Chr. 6:38; 15:12; 34: 31; Mt. 22:37; Mk. 12:30; Lu. 10:27.

Hunger of.—Ps. 42:1, 2; 63:1, 5; 106: 15; 107:9; 143:6; Pr. 10:3; 25:25; 27: 7; Is. 26:8, 9; 29:8; 32:6; 55:2; 58:11; Jer. 31:12, 14, 25; 50:19; Lam. 1:11; 16:19; Mic. 7:1.

As thy soul liveth.—I Sam. 1:26; 17:55; 20:3; 25:26; II Sam. 11:11; 14:19; II Ki. 2, 4, 6; 4:30.

Deliverance of.—Gen. 19:20; II Sam. 4: 9; 6:4; 17:13; 22:20; 23:3; 25:20; 30: 3; 33:19; 35:17; 56:13; 86:2, 13; 97: 10; 116:4, 8; 120:2; 142:4–7; 143:11; Pr. 14:25; Is. 38:17; 44:20; Jer. 20: 13; Ez. 3:19; 14:19, 20; 33:5, 9.

Redemption of.—I Ki. 1:29; Ps. 34:22; 49:15; 65:18; 69:18; 71:23; 72:13, 14.

Atonement for.—Ex. 30:12, 15, 16; Lev. 17:11; Num. 31:50.

Binding the soul with a vow.—Num. 30: 2, 4–10, 12, 13.

Afflicted.—Lev. 16:29, 31; 23:27, 32; Num. 29:7; Ps. 6:3; 31:7; 35:12, 13; 69:10; 77:2; 88:3; 107:26; 143:12; Is. 58:3, 5, 10.

Bitterness of.—Job 3:20; 7:11; 21:25; 24:12; Pr. 27:7; 31:6; Lam. 2:12; II Pet. 2:8.

Conversion of.—Ps. 19:7; Is. 55:3; Heb. 10:39; Jas. 5:20.

Destruction of.—I Sam. 24:11; Job 30: 15; Pr. 22:3; Mt. 10:28; I Pet. 2:11; Rev. 16:3.

SOUND, *adj.* Zech. 11:16. Brass—I Cor. 13:1. Counsels—Pr. 1:5. See COUN-SEL, WISDOM. Doctrine—I Tim. 1:10; II Tim. 4:3; Tit. 1:9; 2:1. See Doc-

TRINE. Faith, In—Tit. 1:13; 2:2. Mind —I Pet. 4:7. See MIND. Safe and— Lu. 15:27. Speech—Tit. 2:8. See SPEECH. Wisdom—Pr. 2:7; 3:21; 8: 14. Words—I Tim. 6:3; II Tim. 1:13.

SOUND, *n.* Job 37:2; Jer. 46:22. Abundance of rain, Of—I Ki. 18:41. Battle, Of—Jer. 50:22. Bells, Of—Ex. 28:35. Cornet, Of—I Chr. 15:28; Ps. 98:6; Dan. 3:5, 7, 10, 15. See MUSIC. Cry, Of—Jer. 48:3; 51:54; Ez. 27:28. See CRY. Cymbals, Of—Ps. 150:5. See MUSIC. Distinction of—I Cor. 14:7, 8. Fall, Of a—Ez. 26:15; 31:16. See DE-STRUCTION. Feet, Of—I Ki. 14:6. Grinding, Of—Eccl. 12:4. Harp, Of the—See HARP. Joyful—Ps. 89:15. See JOY. Leaf, Of a—Lev. 26:36. Marching, Of—II Sam. 5:24; I Chr. 14:15. Neighing, Of—Jer. 8:16. Pipes, Of—I Ki. 1:40; Job 21:12. See PIPES. Skies, Of—Ps. 77:17. Solemn—Ps. 92: 3. Terrors, Of—Job 15:21. Trumpet, Of—See TRUMPET. Viol, Of—Amos 6:5. See MUSIC. Waters, Voice of many—Rev. 1:15. Went out into all the earth—Rom. 10:18. Wind, Of— John 3:8; Acts 2:2–6. See VOICE.

SOUND, *v.* Alarm—See TRUMPETS. Brass —I Cor. 13:1.

Father.—I Sam. 20:12. Heart—Is. 16: 11; Jer. 48:36. Music—See MUSIC. Trumpets—See TRUMPETS. Water— Acts 27:28. Words of the Lord—I Thess. 1:8.

SOUNDNESS. Is. 1:6; Acts 3:16. Flesh, In—Ps. 38:3, 7.

SOUR. Drink—Hos. 4:18. Grapes—Jer. 31:29, 30; Ez. 18:2. See TASTE.

SOUTH, *the South country.* Creation— Ps. 89:12. Abram journeyed toward —Gen. 12:9; 20:1. Jacob—Gen. 28:14. Place toward—I Sam. 20:41. Stretch-eth her wings toward—Job 39:26. Into South: Abram with Lot and wife— Gen. 13:1. Dwelt in—*Isaac*—Gen. 24: 62. *Amalekites*—Num. 13:29. *Canaan-ite*—Num. 21:1; 33:40; Ju. 1:9. *Achsah* —Josh. 15:19; Ju. 1:15. Commands pertaining to: *Go in the*—Deut. 1:7. *Possess the*—Deut. 33:23. *Philip is told to go toward South*—Acts 8:26. Moses views—Deut. 34:3. When they were inhabited—Zech. 7:7.

SOVEREIGNTY OF GOD. See GOD.

SOWING AND REAPING: Clean seed required. — Lev. 11:37, 38; 19:19; Deut. 22:9.

Seeding corrupted by mixture.—Is. 1:4; 5:1-7; 13:24-28, 37, 38.

Laws of.—Reaping determined by sowing—Lev. 26:1-12, 14-20; Job 4:8; Ps. 126:5, 6; Pr. 11:18; 22:8; Ez. 18: 2-4, 10-13; Mt. 7:16-20; 25:34-46; Lu. 6:43-45; II Cor. 9:6; Gal. 6:7, 8; Jas. 3:11-13; Mt. 7:16-20; 25:34-46; Lu. 6:43-45; II Cor. 9:6; Gal. 6:7, 8; Jas. 3:11-13; Rev. 14:14-19.

Reaping more than sowing.—Jer. 12:13; Hos. 8:7; 10:13; Mt. 13:24-28; 25:37-40; II Cor. 9:8-12; Jas. 2:8-10; Rev. 22:11 (marg.).

Reaping proportionate to labor.—Eccl. 11:6; Mt. 13:23; Lu. 8:15; John 4:35-38; II Cor. 9:6; Gal. 6:10.

The crop controls the land.—Is. 5:1-7; Mic. 6:15, 16; Mt. 12:35; 13:7, 22, 28-30; 15:18-20; Lu. 8:7, 14; Eph. 4:22-25; 5:3-12.

Sowing here what shall be reaped there. —Job 21:29, 30; Ps. 9:17; Is. 13:9-13; Mt. 5:29, 30; 13:28-30, 49; 25:41-46; Rev. 3:8-12.

Figurative use (in Old Testament).—A crop of trouble—Job 4:8; 31:7, 8; Pr. 6:14, 19; 22:8; Is. 32:9-13; Jer. 4:3; 12:13; Hos. 8:7; Hag. 1:6. A crop of joy—Ps. 97:11; 126:5; Pr. 11:18; Is. 28:23-29; 32:20; 55:10, 11; 61:11; Jer. 31:27, 28; Hos. 2:21-23; 10:12; Amos 9:13; Zech. 10:9.

In New Testament.—God's care—Mt. 6:26; Lu. 12:24. Establishment of truth — John 4:36-38. Reward of apostle—I Cor. 9:11; Gal. 6:9. Resurrection—I Cor. 15:36-44. Liberal giving—II Cor. 9:6-10. Sowing to flesh and spirit—Gal. 6:8, 9. Peace-sowing —Jas. 3:18.

Parabolic.—The righteous—Mt. 13:8, 23; Mk. 4:8, 20; Lu. 8:8, 15. The deluded—Mt. 13:4-7, 19-22; 25:24-26; Mk. 4:4-7, 15-18; Lu. 8:5-7, 12-14. Growth of kingdom—Mk. 4:26-29. See JESUS, PARABLES OF, WICKED, SIN.

SPAIN. Paul desires to visit—Rom. 15: 24, 28.

SPAKE. As a child—I Cor. 13:1. Boldly —Acts 13:46. God—Deut. 10:9. Je-

hovah—Deut. 5:4. Never man so— John 7:46. Thou art my son—Heb. 5:5. See SPEAK, SPEECH.

SPARE. Is. 58:1. Angels, Not—II Pet. 2:4. Branches, Not—Rom. 11:21. Bread enough and to—Lu. 15:17. Life —Job 2:6. Own son, Not—Rom. 8:32. Place, Not—Gen. 18:24. Rod—Pr. 13: 24. Soul—Ps. 78:50. Words—Pr. 17: 27.

SPARING. Flock—Acts 20:29. Soweth —II Cor. 9:6.

SPARKS. Fire, Of—Job 49:19. See FIRE. Fly upward—Job 5:7.

SPARROW. Fall—Mt. 10:29. Like a— Ps. 102:7. Of more value than many —Mt. 10:31. Sold for a penny—Mt. 10:29. Wandering, In—Pr. 26:2.

SPAT. See SPITTING.

SPEAK. A time to—Eccl. 3:7. Evil of father or mother—Mt. 15:4. Evil of no man—Tit. 3:2. Idle word—Mt. 12: 36. In you, Your Father—Mt. 10:20. In the sight of God—II Cor. 12:19. I that—John 4:26. Not in hearing of a fool—Pr. 23:9. Scripture, in vain— Jas. 4:5. Slow to—Jas. 1:19. Soft words—Job 41:3. Truth—Zech. 8:6; Eph. 4:15. With the tongues—I Cor. 13:1. Word, My—Jer. 23:28.

SPEAR. See WEAPONS.

SPECKLED. Gen. 30:32-39; 31:8, 10, 12; Jer. 12:9.

SPECTACLE. I Cor. 4:9.

SPEECHES. Primitive speech was poetical—Gen. 4:23, 24. Song a—Deut. 32:2. Prayer a — Ps. 17:6. Public opinion a—II Sam. 19:11. Solomon's choice was a—I Ki. 3:10. A sentence also—Jer. 31:23.

Fulness of words issues in.—Eliphaz— Job 4:2. Job—Job 13:17; 21:2. Elihu —Job 33:1. It is refreshing—Job 32:20.

Speeches may be worthless.—Job 15:3; 24:25; II Cor. 10:10. Fruitless—Job 32:14. Desperate—Job 6:26. Fair but deceitful—Pr. 7:21; Rom. 16:18.

Sound speech is like distilled dew.—Job 29:22. Cannot be condemned—Tit. 2:8.

Speech not understood.—Because too deep—Is. 33:19. Strange, i. e., Foreign —Ez. 3:5. Dark—not easily inter-

preted—Num. 12:8. Hardness of heart
—John 8:43; *cf.* Mt. 13:15.

Miscellaneous.—Acts 20:11. Two sea-
sonings for Christian—Col. 4:6. Polished speech avoided—I Cor. 2:1; II
Cor. 10:10; 11:6. Speechlessness, Result of having no excuse—Mt. 22:12.

Instances of strong.—Judah—Gen. 44:
18–34. Moses—Deut. 1:9–40; 32:1–43.
Joshua—Josh. 24:1–15. Jephthah—
Ju. 11:14–28; Ruth—Ruth 1:16, 17.
Samuel—I Sam. 12:1–17. Solomon—I
Ki. 8:12–61. Isaiah—1:2–31; Jeremiah
—Jer. 2:1–37. Daniel—Dan. 5:17–28.
Amos—Amos 1:2–2:15. Peter—Acts
2:14–36; 3:12–26; 4:8–12. Stephen—
Acts 7:2–53. Paul—Acts 13:16–41;
14:14, 17; 17:22–31; 22:1–21; 26:1–23.
See JESUS, DISCOURSES OF, TONGUES,
WORDS, LANGUAGE.

SPEECHLESS. Mt. 22:12; Acts 9:7.

SPELT. Ex. 9:32; Is. 28:25; Ez. 4:9.

SPEND. Lu. 10:35; Jas. 4:3. Arrows—
Deut. 32:23. Days in prosperity—Job
21:13; 36:11. Life, as a shadow—
Eccl. 6:12. Money—Is. 55:2. Time—
Acts 20:16.

SPENT. All—Lu. 15:14. All that she
had—Mk. 5:26; Lu. 8:43. Bread—I
Sam. 9:7; Jer. 37:21. Day far—Ju.
19:11; Mk. 6:35; Lu. 24:29. Living
—Lu. 8:43. Money—Gen. 47:15. Night
far—Rom. 13:12. Strength—Is. 49:4.
Water was—Gen. 21:15. Without
hope—Job 7:6. With sorrow—Ps.
31:10.

SPICES: Kinds of.—Song of Sol. 4:13–
16. Chief—Ex. 30:23; Song of Sol.
4:4, 16. Sweet—Ex. 30:34; 37:29. Different—II Chr. 16:14. Chief of all—
Ez. 27:22. Cassia—Ex. 30:24; Ps. 45:
8; Ez. 27:19. Cinnamon—Ex. 30:23;
Pr. 7:17; Rev. 18:13. Aloes—Pr. 7:17;
Song of Sol. 4:14. Myrrh—Esth. 2:12;
Ps. 45:8; Pr. 7:17; Song of Sol. 3:6;
Mt. 2:11; Mk. 15:23; John 19:39. Saffron—Song of Sol. 4:14. Spikenard
—Song of Sol. 4:14; Mk. 14:3; John
12:3. Calamus—Song of Sol. 4:14.
Frankincense—Ex. 30:34; Lev. 2:1,
16; 5:11; 6:15; 24:7; Num. 5:15; Neh.
13:9; Is. 43:23; 60:6; 66:3; Jer. 6:20.
Stacte—Ex. 30:34. Onycha—Ex. 30:
34. Galbanum—Ex. 30:34.

Where found.—Gilead—Gen. 37:25. Palestine—Gen. 43:11. Sheba—I Ki. 10:
2–10; II Chr. 9:1; Ez. 27:22. Gardens
—Song of Sol. 4:13–16. Mountains—
Song of Sol. 8:14.

Treasures for.—II Chr. 32:27.

Uses of.—Sacred oil—Ex. 25:6; 35:8;
II Ki. 20:13; I Chr. 9:29. Anointing
—Ex. 35:8; Esth. 2:12; Mk. 16:1; Lu.
23:56; 24:1; John 19:40. Burial—II
Chr. 16:14; Lu. 23:56; 24:1; John 19:
39, 40. Incense—Ex. 30:34; 37:29.
Fragrance of—Song of Sol. 4:10.

Figurative.—Bed of—Song of Sol. 5:13;
6:2.

SPIDER. See Job 8:14; Is. 59:5.

SPIES. Gen. 42:9, 11, 14, 16, 30, 31, 34.
Sent into Canaan by Moses—Num.
13:3, 21; 14:36. Sent to Jericho by
Joshua—Josh. 2:1; 6:23. Sent by Da-
vid—I Sam. 26:4. Sent by Absalom
—II Sam. 15:10. Sent by Levites and
chief priests—Lu. 20:20. Received—
Heb. 11:31.

SPIKENARD. Plants—Song of Sol. 4:
13. Sent forth fragrance—Song of
Sol. 1:12. See SPICES.

SPILLED. Gen. 38:9. Water—II Sam.
14:14. Wine—Mt. 9:17; Lu. 5:37.

SPIN. Hands, With—Ex. 35:25. Lilies,
not—Mt. 6:28; Lu. 12:27.

SPIRIT. *Heb.* Neshamah; *Gr.* Pneuma.
Used in reference to God.—Gen. 41:38;
Ex. 31:3; 35:31; Num. 24:2; Job 26:
13; 27:3; 33:4; Ps. 104:30; 139:7; 143:
10; Is. 30:1; 34:16; 40:13; 48:16; 63:
14; Ez. 36:27; 37:14; Mic. 2:7; 3:8;
Hag. 2:5; Zech. 4:6; John 4:24; II
Cor. 3:17, 18. See HOLY SPIRIT. Spirit
of the Gods—Dan. 4:8, 9, 18; 5:11, 14.

An entity (real being).—Job 10:12;
14:10; 32:8, 18; 34:14; Pr. 20:27; Is.
38:16; 42:5; 57:16; Zech. 12:1; Mt.
27:50; Lu. 24:37; Acts 23:8, 9; I Cor.
2:11–15; 14:14–16, 32; Heb. 12:23;
Jas. 4:5. See Ez. 1:12, 20; 10:17; Mt.
14:26; Mk. 6:49.

Came forth from God—Job 26:4; I Cor.
2:12.

Returns to God—Ps. 31:5; Eccl. 12:7;
Lu. 23:46; Acts 7:59. Spirit came
again (*seems to mean* animation)—
Ju. 15:19. Lu. 8:55.

Contrast between flesh and spirit.—Is.
31:3; Lu. 24:39; John 3:6; I Cor. 5:3–

5; 7:34; 15:44, 45; II Cor. 5:1–8; 7:1; Col. 2:5; I Thess. 5:23; Jas. 2:26; I Pet. 3:18; 4:6.

Spirits of all flesh—Num. 16:22; 27:16.

Soul and spirit—I Thess. 5:23; Heb. 4:12.

Equivalent to person.—Gen. 41:8; Job 10:12; Ps. 77:3, 6; 106:33; Gal. 6:18; II Tim. 4:22; I John 4:1, 3.

Seat of emotion—Intellect—Heart.— Gen. 41:8; 45:27; Num. 14:24; Deut. 2:30; Josh. 5:1; I Ki. 21:5; I Chr. 5: 25, 26; II Chr. 9:4; 21:16; Ezra 1:1, 5; Job 6:4; 15:13; 17:1; 20:3; 34:14; Ps. 32:2; 76:12; 77:3, 6; 78:8; 142:3; 143: 4, 7; Pr. 14:29; 16:2, 32; 25:28; Eccl. 7:9; 10:4; Is. 29:9; Jer. 51:11; Ez. 13:3; Hag. 1:14; Zech. 6:8; Mal. 2:15, 16; Lu. 1:47; Rom. 1:9; II Cor. 2:13; 7:1, 13; 16:18; II Thess. 2:2.

Anguish of—Ex. 6:9; Job 7:11. Bound in—Acts 20:22; Broken—Ps. 51:17; Pr. 15:4, 13; 17:22; 18:14. Contrite— Ps. 34:18; 57:15; Is. 66:2. Cool—Pr. 17:27. Excellent—Dan. 5:12; 6:3. Fainting—Ez. 21:7. Fearfulness—II Tim. 1:7. Fervent in—Acts 18:25; Rom. 12:1. Gentle—I Cor. 4:21; Gal. 6:1. Grieved in—Is. 54:6; Dan. 7:15. Groaned in—John 11:33. Haughty— Pr. 16:18. Humble—Is. 57:15. Meek —I Pet. 3:4. New—Ez. 11:19; 18:31; 36:26; Rom. 7:6; Eph. 4:23. Patient —Eccl. 7:8. Poor in—Mt. 5:3. Proud —Eccl. 7:8. Provoked in—Acts 17: 16. Purposed in—Acts 19:16. Quiet —I Pet. 3:4. Sighed in His—Mk. 8:12. Sorrowful—I Sam. 1:15; I Ki. 21:5. Strong in—Lu. 1:80. Troubled in— Dan. 2:1, 3; John 13:21. Willing—Ps. 51:12. *Offerings for tabernacle*—Ex. 35:21–29. *Disciples of Jesus*—Mt. 26: 41; Mk. 14:38. *Paul*—Rom. 7:14–25.

Evil spirits.—Acts 19:15, 16; Eph. 2:2. Sent from God—Ju. 9:23; I Sam. 16: 14–16, 23; 18:10; 19:9; I Ki. 22:21–24; II Chr. 18:20–23.

Error, Of—Is. 29:24; I John 4:6.

Falsehood—Mic. 2:11.

Familiar—Lev. 19:31; 20:27; Is. 29:4. *The necromancer of En-dor*—I Sam. 28: 7–9. *Saul punished for consulting*—I Chr. 10:13. *Manasseh punished for associating with*—II Chr. 33:6–13.

Greed—Pr. 28:25.

Hasty—Pr. 14:29; Eccl. 7:9.

Jealousy—Num. 5:30.

Lying—I Ki. 22:22.

Perverse—Is. 19:14.

Seducing—I Tim. 4:1.

Unclean—Zech. 13:2; Mt. 8:16; 12:43–45; Mk. 1:23–27; 3:11, 12, 20; 5:2–16; 6:7; 7:25–30; 9:17–27; Lu. 4:33–36; 6: 18; 7:21; 8:26–36; 9:38–43; 11:24–26; Acts 5:16; 8:7; 19:13–16; Rev. 16:13, 14. See DEMONS, POSSESSION OF.

Whoredom, Of—Hos. 4:12; 5:4.

Miscellaneous uses of the word "spirit": Adoption, Of—Rom. 8:15. Antichrist, Of—I John 4:3. Bondage, Of—Rom. 8:15. Burning, Of—Is. 4:4. Different—II Cor. 11:4; I John 4:1, 3. Divination, Of—Acts 16:16–18. Egypt, Of—Is. 19:3. Excellent—Dan. 5:12; 6:3. Faith, Of—Pr. 11:13; II Cor. 4: 13. Grace, Of—Zech. 12:10. Holiness, Of—Rom. 1:4. Infirmity, Of—Lu. 13: 11. Just men, Of—Heb. 12:23. Justice, Of—Is. 4:4; 28:6. Letter and spirit—Rom. 2:2. Life giving—John 6:63; I Cor. 15:45; II Cor. 3:6. See Is. 38:16; Rom. 8:2–11; Gal. 6:8; I Pet. 3:18; 4:6. Ministering—Heb. 1: 14. Prophecy, Of—Rev. 19:10. Prophets, Of—I Cor. 14:32. Seven spirits of God—Rev. 1:4; 3:1; 4:5; 5:6. Sleep, Of—Is. 29:10. Stupor, Of—Rom. 11:8. Supplication, Of—Zech. 12:10. Truth, Of—John 14:17; 15:26; 16:13; I John 4:6. *In spirit and in truth*—John 4: 23. Unity of—Eph. 4:1–6; Phil. 1:27. See Acts 4:32; I Cor. 1:10–13; 6:17; II Cor. 12:18. Vexation of—Is. 65:14. Walking in—II Cor. 12:18. Wisdom, Of—Pr. 1:23. *Workmen under Moses*— Ex. 28:3. Joshua—Deut. 34:9. See Num. 27:18, 23. *Jesus*—Is. 11:2. *Ephesians*—Eph. 1:17. World, Of the—I Cor. 2:12.

SPIRITUAL. I Cor. 2:15; 3:1; 14:37; Gal. 6:1. See Rev. 11:8.

Blessings—Eph. 1:3. See BLESSINGS. Blindness—See BLINDNESS, SPIRITUAL. Body—I Cor. 15:44, 46. Drink—I Cor. 10:4. Food—I Cor. 10:3. Gifts—Rom. 1:11; I Cor. 12:1–11; 14:1–12. See HOLY SPIRIT, GIFTS OF. House—I Pet. 2:5. Judged, Spiritually—I Cor. 2:14. Law spiritual—Rom. 7:14. Sacrifices

—I Pet. 2:5. Songs—Eph. 5:19; Col. 3:16. Things—Rom. 15:27; I Cor. 2:13; 9:11. Wickedness—Eph. 6:12. Wisdom—Col. 1:9. Words—John 6:63; I Cor. 2:13.

SPITE. Ps. 10:14. See MALICE.

SPITTING. Upon in scorn—Lev. 15:8; Num. 12:14; Deut. 25:9; Job 30:10.

Jesus spat upon in scorn.—Mt. 26:27; 27:30; Mk. 10:34; 14:65; 15:19; Lu. 18:32.

Spittle.—Fell upon beard—I Sam. 21:13. Swallowed—Job 7:19. In face—Num. 12:14; Deut. 25:9; Job 30:10; Is. 50:6.

Used in miracles of Jesus.—Curing the deaf—Mk. 7:33. The blind—Mk. 8:33; John 9:6.

SPLENDOR. Job 37:22. See GLORY.

SPOIL: To the victor belonged all.—Soldiers, citizens, cities, and contents—Gen. 14:11, 12; 34:28, 29; Num. 31:7, 9–12; Josh. 6:2, 17. See BAN.

Spoil mentioned.—I Sam. 14:30; 17:53; II Sam. 3:22; 8:8; 23:10; II Ki. 7:8; I Chr. 5:21; II Chr. 14:14, 15; 20:25; 28:8, 14, 15.

Not to be taken.—Josh. 6:18; I Sam. 15:3, 9, 19.

Refused.—Gen. 14:21–24; Esth. 8:11; 9:10, 15, 16.

Recovered.—Gen. 14:16; I Sam. 30:18, 19.

Anticipated, never gained.—Ex. 15:9; Ju. 5:30; I Sam. 14:36; II Ki. 3:23; Esth. 3:13; Ez. 38:11–13.

Money indemnity or yearly tribute.—II Ki. 3:4; 18:14; Is. 33:18.

Portion dedicated to Jehovah.—Num. 31:37–41, 54; II Sam. 8:10, 11; I Chr. 26:27. Sacrificed—II Chr. 15:11.

Trophies hung up in temples.—I Sam. 21:9; 31:10; II Ki. 11:10.

Despoiled camps and cities.—Sodom—Gen. 14:11, 12. Hamor—Gen. 34:27. Ziklag—I Sam. 30:1–20. Syrians—II Ki. 7:16. Ethiopians—II Chr. 14:13. Moab, Ammon, and Seir—II Chr. 20:25. Judah—II Chr. 24:23; 25:13; 28:8, 14, 15; Rabbah—I Chr. 20:2.

Division.—Num. 31:32–47, 53; Josh. 22:8; Ju. 14:19; I Sam. 14:32. Leader's special share—Num. 31:52–54; Ju. 8:24–26; I Sam. 30:20, 26–31. Camp guards shared equally with warriors—Num. 31:27; I Sam. 30:24.

Prophecies.—Babylon—Jer. 50:10; 51:48, 53–56. Benjamin—Gen. 49:27. Chaldea—Jer. 50:10; Hab. 2:7, 8. Damascus and Samaria—Is. 8:4. Egypt—Ez. 29:18–20. Enemies of Israel—Is. 33:23; Jer. 30:10; 48:8. Ephraim—Hos. 13:15. Gog—Ez. 38:12, 13; 39:10. Israel—Ez. 7:21; Mic. 2:4. Jerusalem—Is. 10:5, 6, 12; 17:14; Jer. 20:5; Zeph. 1:13; Zech. 14:1. Judah—II Ki. 21:14; Jer. 17:3; 20:5. King of the North—Dan. 11:24; Jer. 48:8; Zeph. 2:8, 9. Moab, Ammon, Edom—Is. 11:14; Zech. 2:8, 9. Nineveh—Nah. 2:9. Tyre—Ez. 26:5.

Figurative.—Christ's victory over Satan—Mk. 3:27; Eph. 4:8. Satan's victory over Israel—Is. 42:22–24. Princes despoiled the people—Ez. 45:9. Of robbers—Pr. 1:13; Mic. 2:8. Humility excels—Pr. 16:19. The gospel gives equal joy—Ps. 119:162; Is. 9:3; 53:12.

SPOKESMAN. Ex. 4:16.

SPONGE. John 19:29.

SPOON. See VESSELS.

SPORT. Gen. 26:8. Am I not in—Pr. 26:19. Fool, To a—Pr. 10:23. Samson made—Ju. 16:25–27. See PLAY, REVELLING.

SPOT. Deut. 32:5 (A. V.); Job 31:17; II Pet. 2:13; Jude 12 (A. V.). Garment spotted by the flesh—Jude 23. Goats—Gen. 30:32–39. Leopard change his—Jer. 13:23. Leprosy, Of—Lev. 13:2–56. Without—Num. 19:2; Job 11:15; Song of Sol. 4:5; Eph. 5:27; I Tim. 6:14; Heb. 9:14 (A. V.); I Pet. 1:19; II Pet. 3:14. See BLEMISH.

SPOUSE. See BRIDE, WIFE.

SPOUT. Zech. 4:12.

SPRANG. Mk. 10:30; Acts 14:19; 28:13. See SPRING.

SPREAD. Abroad—Gen. 10:18; 28:14; Num. 11:32; I Sam. 30:16; II Sam. 22:23; II Chr. 26:8; Job 37:11; Is. 42:5; 44:24; Zech. 2:6; Mt. 9:31; Mk. 1:28, 45; Acts 13:49; I Thess. 1:8. See Acts 4:17. Battle—II Sam. 18:8. Bones—Jer. 8:2. Cloth—Num. 4:6–13; Deut. 22:17. Cloud—Job 26:9; 36:29; 37:11; Ps. 105:39. Couch—Pr. 7:16. See COUCH. Covering—II Sam. 17:18; II Ki. 8:15. Dawn—Joel 2:2. Dung—

Mal. 2:3. Earth—Is. 42:5; 44:24. See
EARTH. Garments—Ju. 8:25; Mt. 21:
8; Mk. 11:8; Lu. 19:36. Gold—I Ki.
6:32; Is. 40:19. Green tree, Like—
Ps. 37:35. Hands—See HAND. Heavens
—Is. 48:13. Jehovah, Before—II Ki.
19:14. Leprosy—Lev. 13:5–39; 14:48.
Letter—II Ki. 19:14; Jer. 37:14. Light
—Job 36:30. See LIGHT. Name—II
Chr. 26:8. Net—See NET. Philistines
—Ju. 15:9; II Sam. 15:18, 22; I Chr.
14:9, 13. Praise—II Cor. 8:18. Roll
of book—Ez. 2:10. Root—Job 29:19;
Jer. 17:8. Royal pavilion—Jer. 43:10.
Sackcloth and ashes—II Sam. 21:10;
Is. 58:5. Sail—Is. 33:23. Skirt—Ruth
3:9; Ez. 16:8. Sky—Job 37:18. Tent
—Gen. 33:19; II Sam. 16:22. See
TENT. Threshing-wain—Job 41:30.
Valley, As—Num. 24:6. Veil—Is. 25:
7. Vine—Ez. 17:6. See VINE. Wicked
—Ps. 37:35. See WICKED. Wings—
Ex. 37:9; Deut. 32:11; I Ki. 8:7; I
Chr. 28:18; II Chr. 3:13; 5:8; Jer.
48:40; 44:22. Word—Acts 13:49. See
WORD OF GOD. Worm—Is. 14:11.

SPRIGS. Cut off—Is. 18:5. Shot forth
—Ez. 17:6. See PLANTS.

SPRING, v. Num. 21:17. Cause right-
eousness to—Is. 45:8. Day began to
—Ju. 19:25. Earth, Out of—Job 8:19.
Forth—Is. 43:19. Judgment—Hos. 10:
4. Light—Mt. 4:16. Seed should—
Mk. 4:27. Truth—Ps. 85:11. Wall,
Out of—I Ki. 4:33. Water—John 4:
14. Wicked as grass—Ps. 92:7.

SPRINGING. Leaves—Ez. 17:9. Root
of bitterness—Heb. 12:15. Unto eternal life—John 4:14. Water—Gen. 26:
19.

SPRINGS. Hot springs.—Gen. 36:24.

Springs of water.—12 springs of water
—Ex. 15:27; Num. 33:9; Deut. 8:7.

Guided by.—Is. 49:10.

Thirsty ground shall become.—Is. 35:7;
41:18.

Achsah's request for.—Ju. 1:15.

Upper and nether springs.—Given to
Achsah—Josh. 15:19; Ju. 1:15.

Springs threatened.—Jer. 51:36; Hos.
13:15; II Pet. 2:17.

Springs in valleys.—Ps. 104:10. **Place
of spring.**—Ps. 84:5.

Figurative.—Spring of sea—Job 38:16.
Springs dispersed—Pr. 5:16. As a
corrupted spring—Pr. 25:26. Like a
spring of water—Is. 58:11.

SPRINKLING: Blood.—Ex. 24:6, 8;
29:16, 20, 21; Lev. 1:5, 11; 3:2, 8, 13;
4:6, 17; 5:9; 6:27; 7:2, 14; 8:11, 19,
30; 9:12, 18; 14:7, 51; 16:14, 15, 19;
17:6; Num. 18:17; 19:4; II Ki. 16:13,
15; II Chr. 29:22; 30:16; Ez. 43:18;
Heb. 9:19, 21; 10:22; 11:28; 12:24;
I Pet. 1:12. Of Jezebel's blood—II
Ki. 9:33. Of the wicked—Is. 63:3.

Water.—Ez. 36:25; Num. 8:7; 19:17–19;
Heb. 9:13, 14.

Ashes and water.—Num. 19:13, 18, 20,
21.

Ashes.—Ex. 9:8, 10; Heb. 9:13.

Oil.—Lev. 14:16, 27, 51.

Dust.—Job 2:12.

Nations (*marg.,* startle)—Is. 52:15.

Things or persons sprinkled with blood.
—The altar—Ex. 24:6; 29:16, 20; Lev.
1:5, 11; 3:2, 8, 13; 5:9; 7:2, 14; 8:11,
19; 9:12, 18; 16:19; 17:6; Num. 18:
17; II Ki. 16:13, 15; II Chr. 29:22; Ez.
43:18. The people—Ex. 24:8; Heb.
9:19; 12:24; I Pet. 1:2. The leper—
Lev. 14:7. Aaron and sons—Ex. 29:21.
Garments of priests—Ex. 29:21; Lev.
6:27; 8:30. Other garments—Is. 63:3.
The Holy Place—Lev. 4:6, 17; II Chr.
30:16; 35:11; Heb. 9:21. The house—
Lev. 14:51. The Book—Heb. 9:19. The
mercy-seat—Lev. 16:14, 15. In front
of the tent of meeting—Num. 19:4.
The door-posts—Ex. 12:7, 22; Heb.
11:28. Vessels of tabernacle—Heb. 9:
21.

**Things or persons sprinkled with ashes
and water.**—Levites—Num. 8:7. Unclean persons—Num. 19:13, 18, 20, 21.
Tent—Num. 19:18. Vessels—Num.
19:18. The slain—Num. 19:18. The
grave—Num. 19:18.

Things or persons sprinkled with ashes.
—The air—Ex. 9:8, 10. Persons—Heb.
9:13.

Things sprinkled with blood and water.
—The house—Lev. 14:51.

Sprinkling with oil.—Before Jehovah—
Lev. 14:16, 27.

Water of cleansing sprinkled on Israel.
—Ez. 36:25.

**Blood of Jezebel sprinkled on wall and
horses.**—II Ki. 9:33.

Dust sprinkled on heads.—Job 2:12.

Figurative.—Sprinkling of the blood of Christ cleanses our hearts—Heb. 9: 13, 14; 10:22. Calls for mercy—Heb. 12:24. Redeems—I Pet. 1:2, 18, 19.

SPROUT. John 14:7.

SPRUNG. Gen. 4:6. See SPRING, *v.*

STABILITY. Is. 33:6. See STEDFASTNESS.

STACHYS, stā'chys. **A disciple in Rome, one of Paul's friends.**—Rom. 16:9.

STACTE. Ex. 30:34.

STAFF. See TOOLS AND IMPLEMENTS.

STAGGER. Is. 19:14. But not with strong drink—Is. 29:9. Cup of—Is. 51:17. Earth shall—Is. 24:20. Like a drunken man—Job 12:25; Ps. 107: 27. Maketh them to—Job 12:25. Wine of—Ps. 60:3. See DRUNKENNESS, DESTRUCTION.

STAIN. Blood, With—Hos. 6:8. My raiment—Is. 63:3. Pride of all glory —Is. 23:9. See BLEMISH.

STAIRS. Neh. 3:15. Came upon—Acts 21:35. City of David, Of—Neh. 12: 37. Paul standing on—Acts 21:40. Stood up upon—Neh. 9:4. Top of— II Ki. 9:13. Winding—I Ki. 6:8.

STAKES. Never be plucked up—Is. 33: 20. Strengthen thy—Is. 54:2.

STALK. Flax, Of—Josh. 2:6. Seven ears on one—Gen. 41:5, 22. See PLANTS.

STALL. Calves of—Amos 6:4; Mal. 4: 2. Horses, Of—I Ki. 4:26. Loose ox from—Lu. 13:15.

STAMMERERS. Is. 32:4.

STAMP. Deut. 9:21. Feet, With—Ez. 25:6; Dan. 7:7, 19.

STANCHED. Issue of blood—Lu. 8:44.

STAND, *n.* Mt. 5:15; Mk. 4:21; Lu. 8: 16.

STAND, *v.* Able to—Rev. 6:17. Afar off—Ps. 10:1. Aloof—Job 30:10. Arrogant shall not—Ps. 5:5. Back—Gen. 19:9. Before jealousy—Ps. 27:4. Before judgment seat—Rom. 14:10. Before kings—Pr. 22:29. Cross, By— John 19:25. Door, At—Rev. 3:20. Fast in one spirit—Phil. 1:27. Fast in the Lord—Phil. 4:1. Good—I Tim. 3:13. Grace wherein we—Rom. 5:2. House divided—Mt. 12:25. House of righteous—Pr. 12:7. Fast, In faith— II Cor. 1:24. Having done all to— Eph. 6:13. Having girded loins—Eph.

6:14. Idle—Mt. 20:3. In awe—Ps. 4: 4. In way of sinners—Ps. 1:1. Jesus, on right hand of God—Acts 7:55. Let him that thinketh he—I Cor. 10:12. Life, For—Esth. 8:11. Perfect—Col. 4:12. Rock, Upon—Ex. 33:21. Son of God, Before—Lu. 21:36. Still—Josh. 10:12; I Sam. 12:16. Stedfast—I Cor. 7:37. Strong—Ps. 30:7. Testifying— Acts 26:22. Thou there—Deut. 5:31. Throne, Before—Rev. 20:12. Truth, In—John 8:44. Waters—Ps. 78:13. Wicked shall not—Ps. 1:5. Wisdom, In—I Cor. 2:5. Word of our God— Is. 40:8. See STEDFASTNESS, WITHSTAND.

STANDARD. Num. 1:32; 2:2-34; 10: 14, 18, 22, 25; 21:8; Is. 10:18; 49:22; 59:18; Jer. 4:6, 21; 50:2; 51:12, 27.

STANDING. I Sam. 22:6. Angel—Num. 22:23, 31. Grain—Ex. 22:6; Deut. 23: 25; Ju. 15:5. Lord, The—Amos 9:1. Before the—Zech. 6:5. Mire, In—Ps. 69:2. Tabernacle was yet.

STARS. Created—Gen. 1:16; Ps. 8:3; 148:5. Infinite in number—Gen. 15: 5; Jer. 33:22. Differ in degree of power—I Cor. 15:41. Stars bow down to—Gen. 37:9. Stars fought against Sisera—Ju. 5:20. Stars not pure in His sight—Job 25:5. God counts and names them—Ps. 147:4. Must praise Him—Ps. 148:3. Worship of, forbidden—Deut. 4:19. Are worshipped— II Ki. 17:16; 21:3; 23:5; Jer. 19:13; Amos 5:26; Zeph. 1:5; Acts 7:42, 43. Cometh forth a star out of Jacob— Num. 24:17. The morning stars—Job 38:7; Rev. 2:28; 22:16. Casting down of—Dan. 8:10; Mt. 24:29; Mk. 13:25; Rev. 6:13. Saw his star in east—Mt. 2:2. Seven stars of seven churches— Rev. 1:16-20. Crown of twelve stars —Rev. 12:1. Wandering stars—Jude 13. See ASTRONOMY, COSMOLOGY.

STALE. II Chr. 24:13; Pr. 28:2. Flocks —Pr. 27:23. Hear of, May—Phil. 1: 27. Know—Phil. 2:19. Last—Mt. 12: 45; II Pet. 2:20. Whatsoever—Phil. 4:11. See ESTATE, STATION.

STATELY. Bed—Ez. 23:41. Three things—Pr. 30:29.

STATION. Is. 22:19. See CAMP.

STATURE. I Sam. 16:7; Is. 45:15; Ez. 13:18; 19:11; 31:5, 10, 14. Add one cubit to—Mt. 6:27 (A. V.); Lu. 12:25 (A. V.). Fulness of Christ, Of—Eph. 4:13. Great—Num. 13:32; II Sam. 21:20; I Chr. 11:33; 20:6; Is. 10:33; Ez. 31:3. Little—Lu. 19:3. Palm tree, Like a—Song of Sol. 7:7. Vine of low—Ez. 17:6. Wisdom and—Lu. 2: 52.

STATUTES. He made a statute and ordinance—Ex. 15:25. Priest's office for perpetual—Ex. 29:9. A perpetual —Lev. 3:17; 16:34; 24:9; Num. 19: 21. Shall be for a—Num. 27:11; 35: 29. He set a statute in Shechem— Josh. 24:25. This was a statute for Israel—Ps. 81:4. Consulted to establish a statute—Dan. 6:7, 15. Make them know—Ex. 18:26. Teach Israel all the—Lev. 10:11. These are the statutes which the Lord commands— Num. 30:16. Which shall hear the— Deut. 4:6. Lord commands to do the —Deut. 6:24. Shall observe and do— Deut. 16:12. May learn to keep these —Deut. 17:19. Walking in statute of David—I Ki. 3:3. Walked in statute of nations—II Ki. 17:8, 19. Neither do they after—II Ki. 17:34. Take heed to do the—II Chr. 33:8. Commanded them—Neh. 9:14. Statutes of Lord are right—Ps. 19:8. I gave them statutes which were not good—Ez. 20:25. If wicked walk in statutes of life—Ez. 33:15. For statutes of Omri are kept—Mic. 6:16.

His statutes.—Thou wilt keep his—Ex. 15:26; Deut. 6:17; 10:13; 11:1. Thou shalt do his—Deut. 27:10. His statutes I did not depart from—II Sam. 22: 23. Perfect to walk in his—I Ki. 8: 61. They rejected his—II Ki. 17:15. Made a covenant to keep—II Ki. 23: 3; II Chr. 34:31. Ezra a scribe of his —Ezra 7:11. Did not put away his— Ps. 18:22; 105:45. In his law nor in his—Jer. 44:23.

My statutes.—Gen. 26:5; Lev. 18:5; 19: 19; 25:18; 26:3, 15, 43; I Ki. 3:14; 11:34; II Ki. 17:13; II Chr. 7:19; Ps. 50:16; 89:31; Jer. 44:10; Ez. 5:6, 7; 11:20; Zech. 1:6.

Thy statutes.—I Chr. 29:19; Ps. 119:12, 16, 23, 26, 33, 48, 54, 64, 68, 71, 80, 83, 112, 117, 118, 124, 135, 155, 171.

Statute forever.—Ex. 27:21; 28:43; 29: 28; Lev. 6:18; 7:34; 10:9; 16:31; 23: 21; Num. 18:23; 19:10.

STAVE. See TOOLS AND IMPLEMENTS.

STAY, n. I Ki. 7:35, 36. At a—Lev. 13: 5, 37. Jehovah my—II Sam. 22:19; Ps. 18:18. Water, Of—Is. 3:1.

STAY, v. Behind—I Sam. 30:10. Hand —II Sam. 24:16; Dan. 4:35. Madness of the prophet—II Pet. 2:16. Mind is —Is. 26:3. Moon—Josh. 10:13. Oil— II Ki. 4:6. Plague was—Num. 16:48. Proud waves—Job 38:11. Purpose, From—Acts 27:43. Waters—Ez. 31: 15.

STEAD. I Chr. 5:22; Job 34:24; Pr. 11:8. Christ's, In—II Cor. 5:20 (A. V.). God's, In—Gen. 30:2. Son, Of—Gen. 22:13. Soul's, In—Job 16:4. See BEHALF.

STEADY. Ex. 17:12.

STEALING: The law for.—Ex. 20:15; Lev. 19:11; Deut. 5:19; Mt. 19:18; Mk. 10:19; Rom. 13:9.

Ranked with other crimes.—Mt. 15:19; Mk. 7:22.

Punishment for.—Ex. 22:3; Zech. 5:3.

Restitution for.—Ex. 22:1-4; Pr. 6:30; 30:9; Lu. 19:8.

Thieves at work.—Mt. 6:19-20; John 10:10. Unrepentant thieves—Rev. 9: 21.

The Lord's House a den of robbers.— Jer. 7:9-11; Mt. 21:13; Mk. 11:17. Stealing God's words—Jer. 23:30.

Men-stealers.—Ex. 21:16; I Tim. 1:10. Stealing the Lord's body—Mt. 27:64.

Tempest stealing bodies.—Job 27:20.

Search yourself.—Rom. 2:21. Stop it— Eph. 4:28.

Stealing away from.—Gen. 31:27; 44:8; II Sam. 19:3. See COMMANDMENTS.

STEALTH. II Sam. 19:3.

STEDFAST. Job 11:15; Dan. 6:26; I Cor. 15:58. Faith—I Pet. 5:9. Grounded and—Col. 1:23. Hope—II Cor. 1:7; Heb. 6:19. Spirit was not— Ps. 78:2. Standeth—I Cor. 7:37. Word —Heb. 2:2. See FAITHFULNESS, STAND.

STEDFASTLY. II Ki. 8:11. Look— Acts 1:10; 7:55; II Cor. 3:3, 7, 13. Minded—Ruth 1:18. Prayer, In— Rom. 12:12. Set his face—Lu. 9:51.

STEDFASTNESS. II Pet. 3:17. Faith, Of—Col. 2:5. Tribulation worketh—Rom. 5:3. See FAITHFULNESS.

STEED. I Ki. 4:28; Esth. 8:14; Mic. 1:13. See HORSE.

STEEL. Nah. 2:3. See IRON.

STEEP. Song of Sol. 2:14; Mic. 1:4; Mt. 8:32.

STEERSMAN. Jas. 3:8.

STENCH. Joel 2:20; Amos 4:10. See SMALL.

STEPHANAS, stĕph'a-nas. A disciple in Achaia.—I Cor. 1:16; 16:15.

STEPHEN, stē'phen: Character of.—Faithful and powerful—Acts 6:5, 8. Chosen as one of the seven to serve tables—Acts 6:2-5. Confutes the Jews—Acts 6:9, 10. Accused of attacking Mosaic customs of the people—Acts 6:11-14. Arraigned before Sanhedrin on charge brought against the Jews—Acts 6:12, 13. His defence—Acts 7:59. Martyrdom—Acts 7:59, 60; 22:20. Presence of Saul—Acts 7:58; 8:1. Burial—Acts 8:2. Persecution of Christians as result of his death—Acts 11:19.

STEPS. Compassed us in our—Ps. 17:11. Declined—Ps. 44:18. Direct—Jer. 10:23. Directeth—Pr. 16:9. Enlarged my—II Sam. 22:37. Faith, Of—Rom. 4:12. Follow his—I Pet. 2:21. Go forward ten—II Ki. 20:9. Go up by—Ex. 20:26. Held fast—Job 23:11; Ps. 17:5. Mark my—Ps. 56:6. Needy, Of—Is. 26:6. Numberest my—Job 14:16. Same, In—II Cor. 12:18. Spreadeth a net for—Pr. 29:5. Straitened, Not—Pr. 4:12. Thrust aside my—Ps. 140:4. Washed—Job 29:6.

STERN. Asleep in—Mk. 4:38. Began to break up—Acts 27:41. Let go four anchors from the—Acts 27:29.

STEWARD. Gen. 43:16; Gal. 4:2. Daniel to—Dan. 1:11. Faithful—Lu. 12:42. Good—I Pet. 4:10. God's—Tit. 1:7. Joseph's house, Of—Gen. 43:19. Mysteries of God, Of—I Cor. 4:1. Rich man, had a—Lu. 16:1. Unrighteous—Lu. 16:8.

STEWARDSHIP. Account of thy—Lu. 16:2. Intrusted to me—I Cor. 9:17. Put out of—Lu. 16:4. Taketh away—Lu. 16:3.

STICK. Bone, out—Job 33:21. Closer than a brother—Pr. 18:24. Fast in me—Ps. 38:2. Unto thy scales—Ez. 29:4.

STICKS. Gather—Num. 15:32; I Ki. 17:10; Acts 23:3.

STIFF. See STIFFNECKED.

STIFFHEARTED. Ez. 2:4. See HEART.

STIFFNECKED. Ex. 32:9; Deut. 10:16; 31:27; II Chr. 30:8; 36:13; Jer. 77:23; Acts 7:51. See NECK.

STILL, *adj.* Gen. 12:9; Ju. 18:9; Ps. 4:4; 46:10; Is. 18:4. As a stone—Ex. 15:16. Do unrighteous—Rev. 22:11. Earth—Job 37:17; Ps. 76:8. Hold fast thine integrity—Job 2:9. Peace be—Mk. 4:39. Praising—Ps. 84:4. Sinned—Ps. 78:32. Small voice—I Ki. 19:12. Waters—Ps. 23:2. Waves are—Ps. 107:29. See QUIETNESS.

STILL, *v.* Pr. 29:11. People—Num. 13:30; Neh. 8:11. Roaring of the seas—Ps. 65:7. Waves—Ps. 89:5.

STING. Rev. 9:10. Like an adder—Pr. 23:32. O Death where is thy—I Cor. 15:55. Of death is sin—I Cor. 15:56.

STIR. Deut. 32:11; Ps. 35:23. City—Mt. 21:10. Contention—Pr. 15:18. Enemies—Is. 9:11. Gift of God—II Tim. 1:6. Grievous word—Pr. 15:1. Heart—Ex. 35:21. Might—Ps. 80:2. Mighty men—Joel 3:9. People—Lu. 23:5. Sea—Job 26:12. Sorrow—Ps. 39:2. Souls—Acts 14:2. Spirit—Ezra 1:5. Strifes, Hatred—Pr. 10:12. Zeal—II Cor. 9:2.

STOCK. Is. 40:24; Gen. 2:27; 10:8. Abraham, Of—Acts 13:26. Die—Job 14:8. Implement of punishment—See PUNISHMENT. Israel, Of—Phil. 3:5. Jesse, Of—Is. 11:1. Stranger, Of—Lev. 25:47. Tree, Of—Is. 6:13; 44:19. Vine, Of—Ps. 80:15. See CATTLE.

STOIC. Acts 17:18.

STOLE. See STEAL.

STOMACH. I Tim. 5:23.

STONES: Used in giving the law.—Ex. 24:12; 31:18; 34:1-4; Deut. 4:13; 5:22; 9:9-11; 10:1-3; II Cor. 3:7.

Used as a witness.—Gen. 28:18-22; 31:45-48; Deut. 27:4; Josh. 4:6, 20-24; 7:26; 8:29; 10:27; 24:26; I Sam. 7:12.

Used as memorials.—Ex. 28:16-21; 39:7-14; Deut. 27:2, 4, 5, 6, 8; Josh. 4:3-9, 20, 21.

Used as landmarks.—I Sam. 6:18; 20: 19; I Ki. 1:9.

Used for building: Houses—I Ki. 15:22; II Chr. 3:6; Is. 9:10; Amos 5:11. Walls —Neh. 4:3. Temple—I Ki. 5:17–18; 6:7; 7:9–12; 10:2, 10, 11, 27; Mt. 24: 2; Mk. 13:1; Lu. 19:44; 21:5–6; I Chr. 22:2; 29:2; II Chr. 3:6; Ezra 5:8; 6:4.

Used in altar building.—Ex. 20:25; I Ki. 18:31, 38; Is. 27:9.

Sepulchres hewn out of.—Mt. 27:60; Mk. 15:46; 16:3. Closed with a stone— Mt. 27:60; Mk. 15:46; 16:3.

Idols made of stone.—Num. 33:52; Deut. 4:28; 28:36, 64; 29:17; II Ki. 19:18; Is. 37:19; Ez. 20:32.

A man shall be stoned to death.—Lev. 20:2, 27; 24:23; Num. 14:10; 15:35, 36; Deut. 13:10; 17:5; 21:21; 22:21, 24; Josh. 7:25, 26; 8:29–32; I Ki. 12: 18; 21:13; II Chr. 10:18; 24:21; Ez. 16:40; 23:47. Stones of iron—Deut. 8:9; Is. 60:17.

Used as a weapon.—Ju. 20:16; I Sam. 17:40; II Sam. 16:6, 13; I Chr. 12:2; II Chr. 26:14, 15; Jer. 43:9, 10; Zech. 9:15, 16; John 8:59; 10:31, 32.

Knives made of.—Ex. 4:25; Josh. 5:2, 3.

Cast down from heaven.—Josh. 10:11, 18.

Pavement of.—II Ki. 16:17.

Cave closed with.—Josh. 10:27.

Absalom's monument.—II Sam. 18:17.

Mar good land with.—II Ki. 3:19, 25.

Hewers of.—Eccl. 10:9.

Special references.—Flints used in circumcision—Ex. 4:25; Josh. 5:2, 3. Lest thou dash thy foot—Ps. 91:12; Mt. 4:6. Stones of Ramah carried away— I Ki. 15:22; II Chr. 16:6. Revive the stones out of heap—Neh. 4:2. In league with the stones of field—Job 5:23. Place of stones—Job 8:17. Waters wear stone—Job 14:9. Our daughters as corner-stones—Ps. 144: 12. A time to gather and cast away —Eccl. 3:5; Is. 62:10. Hewn—Is. 9: 10; Amos 5:11. Cutting himself with —Mk. 5:5. Smooth—Is. 57:6. Stones of fire—Ez. 28:14, 16. Stones consumed —Zech. 5:4. Of stones to raise children unto Abraham—Mt. 3:9; Lu. 3:8. One stone upon another—Mk. 13:1. Not to be left here one—Mt. 24:2. Sealed the—Mt. 27:66. Roll away the—Mt.

28:2. Command that this stone be made bread—Mt. 4:3; Lu. 4:3. Stones will cry out—Lu. 19:40. First cast a stone—John 8:7. Godhead is not like —Acts 17:29. As living stone—I Pet. 2:5. A white—Rev. 2:17. For which do ye stone me—John 10:32.

The stone which the builders rejected.— Ps. 118:22 (Mt. 21:42; Mk. 12:10, 11; Lu. 20:17; Acts 4:11; Eph. 2:20; I Pet. 2:7, 8).

Christ the Corner-stone.—Mk. 12:10; Lu. 20:17; Acts 4:11; I Pet. 2:6. See PRECIOUS STONES.

STOOP. Lu. 24:12; John 20:5, 11. Down together—Is. 46:2. Heart causeth— Pr. 12:25. Jesus—John 8:6, 8. Proud —Job 9:13. Worthy to, Not—Mk. 1:7.

STOP. Boasting—II Cor. 11:10. Breaches—Neh. 4:7. Ears—Ps. 58:4, 3; Pr. 21:13; Is. 35:15; Zech. 7:11; Acts 7:57. Lies—Ps. 63:11. Mouth— Job 5:16; Ps. 107:42; Rom. 3:19; Tit. 1:11; Heb. 11:33. Moses—Ez. 39:11. Philistines—Gen. 26:15, 18. Rain—I Ki. 18:44. Water—II Ki. 3:19, 25; II Chr. 32:3, 4, 30. Windows of heaven —Gen. 8:2. Way—Ps. 35:3.

STORE. All manner of—Ps. 144:13. Food, Of—Gen. 4:36; Neh. 5:18. Glory, Of—Nah. 2:9. Hidden—Jer. 4:8. Lay up—Deut. 32:34; II Ki. 20: 17; Is. 39:6; I Cor. 16:2; I Tim. 6:19; II Pet. 3:7. Old—Lu. 25:22; 26:10. Violence and robbery—Amos 3:10.

STORECHAMBER. Lu. 12:24.

STORE CITIES. See CITIES.

STORE HOUSE. I Chr. 26:15; II Chr. 32:28; Ps. 33:7; Ju. 50:26. Egypt, Of —Gen. 41:56. Watch at—Neh. 12:25. See TREASURY.

STORK. Lev. 11:19, 20; Deut. 14:8; Ps. 104:17; Jer. 8:7; Zech. 5:9.

STORM. Afraid—Ps. 83:15; Pr. 1:27. Calm, made—Ps. 107:29. Carries— Job 21:18. Destruction, By—Is. 28:2. Dissolve in—Job 30:22. Driven by— II Pet. 2:17. Labored with—Acts 27: 18. Protection from—Is. 4:6. Whirlwind and—Is. 17:13; Nah. 1:3. Wind —Ps. 107:25; Mk. 4:37; Lu. 8:23. See WIND.

STORY. Second—Gen. 6:16. Third— Gen. 6:16; Ez. 42:3; Acts 20:9.

STOUT. Ps. 76:5; Is. 46:12; Dan. 7:20. Heart—Is. 9:9; 10:12. Words—Mal. 3:13.

STRAIGHT. Before—Josh. 6:5, 20. Course—Acts 16:11; 26:1. Crooked made—Eccl. 1:15; Is. 40:4; 42:16; Lu. 3:5. Feet—Ez. 1:7. Paths—Mt. 3:3; Mk. 1:3; Lu. 3:4. Street—Acts 9:11; Heb. 12:13. Way—I Sam. 6:12; Ezra 8:21; Ps. 5:8; Eccl. 1:15; Is. 40:3, 4; 45:13; Jer. 31:9; John 1:23.

STRAIGHTWAY. Arose—Mk. 5:42; Lu. 8:55. Baptized—Acts 16:33. Called them—Mk. 1:20. Cometh Satan—Mk. 4:15. Constrained His disciples—Mt. 14:22; Mk. 6:45. Fell—I Sam. 28:20. Find him—I Sam. 9:13; Mt. 21:2. Forgetteth—Jas. 1:24. Fountain of blood dried up—Mk. 5:29. Goeth after her—Pr. 7:22. Jesus spake—Mt. 14: 27. Lift their nets—Mt. 4:22; Mk. 1:18. Ran—Mt. 27:48. Send—Mt. 21: 3. Stumbleth—Mt. 13:21. Took counsel against him—Mk. 3:6. Took his journey—Mt. 25:15. Water out of—Mt. 3:16; Mk. 1:10. See IMMEDIATELY.

STRAIN. Gnat, Out a—Mt. 23:24. Jacob's thigh—Gen. 32:35.

STRAIT. I Sam. 13:6; II Sam. 24:14; II Ki. 6:1; I Chr. 21:13; Is. 49:20; Phil. 1:23. Gate—Mt. 7:13, 14; Lu. 13:24.

STRAITEN. II Cor. 4:8; 6:12. Breadth of waters—Job 37:10. Lives—Jer. 19: 9 (A.V.). Spirit of Jehovah—Mic. 2:7. Steps—Job 18:7; Pr. 4:12. Way—Mt. 7:14. Jesus—Lu. 12:50.

STRAITEST. Sect—Acts 26:5.

STRAITLY. Gen. 43:7.

STRAITNESS. Job 36:16.

STRANGE. Gen. 42:7. Children—Ps. 144:7; Hos. 5:7. Doctrine—Heb. 13: 9. Fire—Num. 3:4; 26:61. Gods—Gen. 35:2, 4; Deut. 32:12, 16; Josh. 24:20, 23; Ju. 10:20, 23; I Sam. 7:3; II Chr. 14:3; 33:15; Ps. 44:20; 81:9; Is. 43:12; Jer. 5:19; Dan. 11:39; Mal. 2:11; Acts 17:18. Incense—Ex. 30:9. Land—Ps. 137:4; Acts 7:6; Heb. 11: 9. Language—Ps. 114:1. Lips—Is. 28: 11. Nahon—Ex. 21:8. Speech—Ez. 3: 5, 6. Tongue—Is. 33:19. Waters—II Ki. 19:24. Wives—I Ki. 11:8; Ezra 10:2, 10, 11, 14, 17, 18, 24; Neh. 13: 27; Job 19:17. See MARRIAGE. Women

—I Ki. 11:1; Pr. 2:16; 5:3, 20; 6:24; 7:5; 20:16; 22:14; 23:27, 33; 27:13. Work—Is. 28:21. See HARLOT.

STRANGER. See SOJOURNER.

STRANGLED. Meat—Acts 15:20. See FOOD, UNCLEAN.

STRAW. Used for animals—Gen. 24:25, 32; Ju. 19:19; I Ki. 4:28; Is. 11:7; 65: 25. Trodden down—Is. 25:10. Used for making brick—Ex. 5:7, 10, 11, 12, 13, 16, 18.

Figurative.—Job 41:27.

STREAKS. Gen. 30:37.

STREAM. Gen. 32:23; Pr. 5:16. Blood, Streams turned into—Ps. 78:44. Dry place, In—Is. 32:2; 44:3. Foundation poured out as—Job 22:16. Honey and butter—Job 20:17. Oil, Of—Job 29:6. Planted by—Ps. 1:3. Righteousness as a mighty—Amos 5:24. Rushing, As—Is. 59:19. Soul, Had gone over—Ps. 124:4. Tears—Ps. 119:136. Whereof make glad—Ps. 46:4. See BROOKS, RIVERS.

STREET: Old Testament.—Will abide in the street all night—Gen. 19:2. Publish not in street of Askelon—II Sam. 1:20. Wisdom crieth aloud in —Pr. 1:20. Sluggard says, "Shall be slain in"—Pr. 22:13; 26:13. Now she is in the—Pr. 7:12.

New Testament.—Do not sound trumpet in—Mt. 6:2. Pray standing in—Mt. 6:5. Found a colt tied in—Mk. 11:4. If they receive you not go out into—Lu. 10:10. Thou hast taught in our —Lu. 13:26. Go out into streets and compel them—Lu. 14:21. Go into street called Straight—Acts 9:11. Angel leads Peter through streets—Acts 12:10. Dead bodies shall lie in—Rev. 11:8. Street of gold in heavenly city —Rev. 21:21. River in the midst of —Rev. 22:2. See CITIES.

STRENGTH. Deut. 33:25; I Pet. 4:11. All thy—Mk. 12:30. Established—Ps. 8:2. Filled with thy—Pr. 5:10. Full—Nah. 1:12. Girded with—II Sam. 22: 40. God is our—Ps. 46:1. Jehovah is —Ex. 15:2; Ps. 28:8. Israel, Of—I Sam. 15:29. Life, Of—Ps. 27:1. Mighty —Job 41:12. Pillars of—Ez. 26:11. Put on—Is. 51:9. Quickening of—Is. 57: 10. Salvation, Of—Ps. 140:7. Wisdom

is better than—Eccl. 9:16. Without
—Jer. 48:45; Lam. 1:6. See STRONG.

STRENGTHEN. Phil. 4:13. Churches
were—Acts 16:5. David, himself—I
Sam. 30:6. Grace, In—II Tim. 2:1.
Hands—Ju. 9:24; Is. 35:3. Millo—II
Chr. 32:5. Power, With—Eph. 3:16.
See STRONG.

STRETCH. Arm — See ARM OUT-
STRETCHED. Curtains—Is. 54:2. Forth
heavens—Is. 42:5. Forward—Phil. 3:
13. Hand—See HAND OUTSTRETCHED.
Rod, Out—Ex. 8:16. Shadows of evening—Jer. 6:4. Themselves upon their
couches—Amos 6:4.

STREWED. Grain—II Sam. 17:19.
Graves, Upon—II Chr. 34:4. Water,
Upon—Ex. 32:20.

STRICKEN. Is. 1:5. Esteem him—Is.
53:4. Hands—Pr. 6:1. Through—Lam.
4:9. Utterly—Is. 16:7. Years, In—
Lu. 1:7, 18.

STRICT. Acts 22:3.

STRICTLY. Mt. 9:30.

STRIFE: Born of evil.—Hatred—Pr.
10:12; 30:33. Pride—Pr. 13:10. Sin—
Pr. 17:19. Carnal men—I Cor. 3:1–3;
II Cor. 12:20; Gal. 5:19, 20. Conceit—
I Tim. 6:4, 5; 20:21. Foolish and ig-
norant questions—II Tim. 2:14, 23.
Earthly and demonical feeling—Jas.
3:14–17; 4:1.

Those who stir up.—Hating others—Pr.
10:12. Proud—Pr. 13:10. Perverse—
Pr. 16:28. Foolish—Pr. 18:6. Scoffers
—Pr. 22:10. Drunken—Pr. 23:29.
Whisperers—Pr. 26:20. Contentious
—Pr. 26:21. Greedy—Pr. 28:25. An-
gry—Pr. 29:22.

It leads to: Separation—Gen. 13:8–11;
26:20–22; Acts 15:39. Rejection of
Moses—Ex. 2;13, 14. Violence—Ex.
21:18, 22. Punishment—Ex. 21:19, 20,
22. Civil war—II Sam. 19:41–43; I
Ki. 14:30; 15:6. Destruction—Ps. 55:
9. Embittering—Pr. 17:1. Injury—
Pr. 26:17. Injustice—Hab. 1:3, 4. Bad
preaching—Phil. 1:15, 17.

STRIKE. Arrow through liver—Pr. 7:
23. Hands—Is. 2:6. Lintel—Ex. 12:
22. Man—Rev. 9:5. Mark—Job 36:
32. Through—Job 20:24. See SMITE.

STRIKER. I Tim. 3:3; Tit. 1:7.

STRING. Arrow upon—Ps. 11:2. Bow-
string—Ps. 21:12. Brake as a—Ju.
16:9. Jewels, Of—Song of Sol. 1:10.

STRINGED INSTRUMENT. Ps. 4:54;
55:61.

STRIP. Pr. 7:16; Is. 32:11; Mt. 27:28.
Aaron of his garment—Num. 20:26.
Forests—Ps. 29:9. Garment, Of—Job
41:13. Glory, Of—Job 19:9. Joseph
of his coat—Gen. 37:23. Robe—I Sam.
18:4; Mic. 2:8. Robbers—Lu. 10:30.

STRIPES: Used in punishment.—For
disobedience of Mosaic law—Ex. 21:
25; Ps. 89:32. Of Levirate law—Deut.
25:3.

Chastened with.—II Sam. 7:14.

For fools.—Pr. 17:30; 19:29.

Paul and Silas beaten with.—Acts 16:
23, 33.

Christians endure.—II Cor. 6:5; 11:
23, 24.

Used in parables.—Faithful and unfaithful servants—Lu. 12:47, 48.

Of Jehovah.—Is. 53:5.

Of Christ.—I Pet. 2:24.

Figurative.—That wound—Pr. 20:30.

STRIPLING. I Sam. 17:56.

STRIVE, STRIVING. See STRIFE

STROKE. Ez. 24:16. Between—Deut.
17:8. Continual—Is. 14:6. Healeth—
Is. 30:26. Heavier—Job 23:2. Remove—Ps. 39:10. Sword, Of—Esth.
9:5. See STRIKE.

STROLLING. Acts 19:13.

STRONG. As death—Song of Sol. 8:6.
Battle, to the—Eccl. 9:11. Be—I Sam.
4:9; Ps. 27:14; 31:24. Belt of—Job
12:21. Bones—Is. 58:11. Forest—
Zech. 11:2. Grown—Jer. 9:3. Inter-
dict—Dan. 6:7. Let hands be—II Sam.
2:7. Man—Ps. 19:5; Mt. 12:29. Ones
—Jer. 46:15. Out of the—Ju. 14:11.
Redeemer is—Pr. 23:11. Things—I
Cor. 1:27. To apprehend—Eph. 3:18.
Weighty and—II Cor. 10:10. See
STRENGTH.

STRONGHOLD. Job 39:28. Children
of Israel, To—Joel 3:16. In the—I
Chr. 11:7; Jer. 51:30. Jehovah my—
Pr. 10:29; Jer. 16:19. My—Ps. 31:4.
Poor, To—Is. 25:4. Set on fire—Ju.
9:49. Way of Jehovah is—Pr. 10:29.
Zion, Of—II Chr. 11:5. See FORTIFICA-
TIONS.

STROVE. See STRIFE.

STRUCK. Ju. 5:26. Child –II Sam. 12: 15. Ear off—Mt. 26:51, 68; Mk. 14:47. Him not—II Sam. 20:10. Jesus—John 18:22. Pan, Into—I Sam. 2:14. See SMOTE, STRICKEN, STRIKE.

STRUGGLE. Gen. 25:22. See STRIFE.

STUBBLE. Consumed as—Ex. 15:7. Fire devoureth, As—Is. 5:24; Joel 2: 5; Nah. 1:10. Gather—Ex. 5:12. Wicked shall be as—Mal. 4:1. Wind, As before—Job 21:18; Ps. 83:13. See GRASS.

STUBBORN. Deut. 9:27. Condemned— I Sam. 15:23; II Chr. 30:8; Ps. 32:9; 75:5. Generation—Ps. 78:8. Heart— Ex. 7:14; Deut. 29:19; Ps. 81:12; Ju. 23:17. Heifer, Like a—Hos. 4:16. Punishment of—Deut. 21:18; Pr. 1: 24–26; 29:1. See HARDNESS OF HEART, WILL.

STUCK. I Sam. 26:7.

STUD. Esth. 8:10; Song of Sol. 1:11. See HORSE.

STUDY. Destruction—Pr. 24:2. Quiet, To be—I Thess. 4:11. Righteous—Pr. 15:28; Eccl. 12:12. Show thyself approved—II Tim. 2:15 (A. V.). Weariness, Is—Eccl. 12:12. See INSTRUCTION.

STUFF. Gen. 31:37; 45:20. Mingled— Deut. 22:11. Sufficient—Ex. 36:7. See GOODS, POSSESSIONS.

STUMBLE. Pr. 3:23; 4:12, 19; Is. 5:27; 8:15; 59:10. Brother—Rom. 14:21; I Cor. 8:13. Cause—Mt. 5:29; 13:41; 18:7; John 6:61. Guard from—Jude 24. Judgment, In—Is. 28:7. Law, At —Mal. 2:8. Mountain, Upon—Jer. 13: 16. Oxen—I Chr. 13:9. Persecutors shall—Jer. 20:11. Proud shall—Jer. 50:32. Ways, In—Ju. 18:15. Word, At—I Pet. 2:8. See OFFENSE.

STUMBLING-BLOCK: Laws concerning.—Lev. 19:14.

Before Israel.—Ez. 44:12; Rev. 2:14.

Used in prophecy.—Is. 57:14; Ez. 3:20; 7:19; 14:3, 4, 7; Jer. 5:21; 18:15; Zeph. 1:3; Mal. 2:8.

In teachings of Paul.—Rom. 11:9; 14: 13; I Cor. 1:23. Warning—I Cor. 8:9. Self-denial for others—Rom. 14:21. Stumbling-block of the cross—Gal. 5: 11. Stone of offence—Rom. 9:32. See STONE, JESUS, TEACHING OF.

STUMP. I Sam. 5:4; Dan. 4:15, 23, 26.

STUPOR. Rom. 11:8.

SUAH, sū'ah. **An Asherite.**—I Chr. 7: 36.

SUBDUE. All things—Dan. 2:40. Ammonites—Ju. 11:33. Canaanites— Neh. 9:24. See ISRAEL. Earth, The— Gen. 1:28. Enemies—II Sam. 22:40; I Chr. 17:10; Ps. 18:39; 81:14. Jabin king of Canaan—Ju. 4:23. Kingdoms —Heb. 11:33. Lord—Num. 32:22, 29; Josh. 18:1; I Chr. 22:18. Midian—Ju. 8:28. Moab—Ju. 3:30. Nations—II Sam. 8:11; Is. 45:1. Peoples—Ps. 18: 47; 47:3; 144:2. Philistines—I Sam. 7:13; 8:1; I Chr. 18:1. See DOMINION, CONQUER.

SUBJECT. All things—Phil. 3:21. Church—Eph. 5:24. Devils are—Lu. 10:17, 20. God, To—Jas. 4:7. Him— Heb. 2:8; I Pet. 3:22. Law, To—Rom. 8:7. Ordinance, To—Col. 2:20; I Pet. 2:13. Parents, Unto—Lu. 2:51. Prophets, To—I Cor. 14:32. Son—I Cor. 15:28. Taskwork, To—Is. 31:8. Vanity, To—8:20.

SUBJECTION. I Cor. 14:34; Gal. 2:5. All things in—I Cor. 15:27; Heb. 2:8. Brought into—Ps. 106:42; Jer. 34:11, 16. Children, In—I Tim. 3:4. Father, Unto—Heb. 12:9. Masters, To—I Pet. 2:18. Must needs be in—Rom. 13:5. Wines, Of—Eph. 5:22; Tit. 2:5; I Pet. 3:1, 5. Women, Of—I Tim. 2:11.

SUBMISSION TO GOD. See OBEDIENCE.

SUBMIT. Gen. 16:9; Jer. 50:15; Heb. 13:17. Enemies shall—Deut. 33:29; Ps. 66:3. Solomon, To—I Chr. 29:24. Strangers shall—II Sam. 22:45; Ps. 18:44.

SUBORNED. Acts 6:11. See PERJURY.

SUBSTANCE. Gen. 31:18. Bless—Deut. 33:11. Carry away—Ob. 11, 13. Honor Jehovah with—Pr. 3:9; Mic. 4:13. Image, Of—Heb. 1:3. Love, Give for —Song of Sol. 8:7. Wasted—Lu. 15: 12, 13. See GOODS, POSSESSION, WEALTH.

SUBTLETY. Dead—I Sam. 23:22; Ps. 105:25. Man—II Sam. 13:3. Serpent —Gen. 3:1. Take him with—Mk. 14:1.

SUBURBS. Cities, Of—Lev. 25:34; Num. 35:4. Fields of—II Chr. 31:19. Levites left—II Chr. 11:14. Sharon, Of—I Chr. 6:15.

SUBVERTED. Job 19:6. A man in his cause—Lam. 3:36. Souls—Acts 15:24. Way—Pr. 19:3.

SUCATHITES, sū'păth-ītes. **A family of scribes.**—I Chr. 2:55.

SUCCEED. Acts 24:27; Deut. 2:21; 19:1. Children of Esau—Deut. 2:12, 22. In the name of brother—Deut. 25:6.

SUCCESS. Good—Josh. 1:7, 8.

SUCCOR. II Sam. 21:17. Able to—Heb. 2:18. Hadadezer—II Sam. 8:5. Ready to—II Sam. 18:3. See AID.

SUCCOTH, sŭk'koth. (1) **An encampment of Israel.**—Ex. 12:37; 13:20; Num. 33:5, 6. See CAMP, ISRAEL.

(2) **A place near Gad.**—Josh. 13:27; Ju. 8:5–16.

(3) **A place east of the Jordan.**—Gen. 33:17.

(4) **A city in Ephraim.**—I Ki. 7:46; II Chr. 4:17; Ps. 60:6; 108:7.

SUCCOTH-BENOTH, sŭk'koth-bē'noth. —A Babylonian idol—II Ki. 17:30.

SUCK. Honey out of rock—Deut. 32:13. Milk—Is. 60:16. Poison—Job 20:16.

SUCKLING. Out of the mouths of babes and—Ps. 8:2; Mt. 21:16.

SUFFER, SUFFERING. Jas. 5:3. Affliction—Ps. 9:13. Christ—See JESUS, SUFFERING OF. Conflict of—Heb. 10:32. Hardship—II Tim. 1:8; 2:3; 4:5. Holy one to see corruption—Ps. 16:10. Innocent blood, Not—Deut. 21:8. Little children—Mt. 19:14. Long—II Cor. 6:6. Loss—II Cor. 7:9. Love, long—I Cor. 13:4. Perfect through—Heb. 2:10. Same—I Pet. 5:9. Soul of righteous to famish, Not—Pr. 10:3. Well doing, For—I Pet. 3:17. Wrong—II Pet. 2:13. See ADVERSITY, AFFLICTION, JESUS, SUFFERING OF, SORROW.

SUFFICE. Deut. 3:26; I Ki. 20:10; I Pet. 4:3. Abominations—Ez. 44:6. Corn—Ruth 2:14, 18. Heads to—Num. 11:22. Israel—Ez. 45:9.

SUFFICIENCY. All things, in—II Cor. 9:8. Fulness of—Job 20:22. God, Of —II Cor. 3:5.

SUFFICIENT. II Cor. 2:16; 3:5. Burn, To—Is. 40:16. Day, Unto the—Mt. 6:24. Eat—Pr. 25:16; Is. 23:18; John 6:7. Grace—II Cor. 12:9. Lend—Deut. 15:8. Ministers—II Cor. 3:6.

Punishment—II Cor. 2:6. Stuff—Ex. 36:7.

SUIT. II Sam. 15:2; Job. 11:19; Acts 25:24. Clothing, Of—Ju. 17:10. See CASE.

SULTRY. Jonah 4:8.

SUM. Num. 1:49; 4:2, 22; Rom. 13:9. Children, Of—Ex. 30:12. Congregation, Of—Num. 1:2; 26:2, 4; II Sam. 24:2, 9; I Chr. 21:5. Men of war, Of —Num. 31:49. Money, Of—Esth. 4:7; Acts 22:28. Prey, Of—Num. 31:26. Silver, Of—II Ki. 22:4. Tabernacle, Of—Ex. 38:21.

SUMMER: Summer and winter.—Gen. 8:22. Turned into drought of—Ps. 32:4. Thou hast made—Ps. 74;17. Provided meat in—Pr. 6:8; 30:25. He that gathereth in summer is wise—Pr. 10:5. Snow in—Pr. 26:1. As hasty fruit before—Is. 28:4. Harvest past, summer is ended—Jer. 8:20. Chaff of summer threshing-floor— Dan. 2:35. In summer and winter— Zech. 14:8. Ye know that summer is nigh—Mt. 24:32; Mk. 13:28; Lu. 21:20.

Summer chamber.—Covers his feet in summer chamber—Ju. 3:24.

Summer fruit.—II Sam. 16:2; 17:1; Is. 16:9; Jer. 40:10; 48:32; Amos 8:1; Mic. 7:1.

Summer house.—Ju. 3:20; Amos 3:15.

SUMPTUOUS. Lu. 16:19; Rev. 18:14.

SUN. Created—Gen. 1:14–18; Ps. 74:16. A covenant made when sun went down—Gen. 15:17. Sun risen when Lot entered Zoar—Gen. 19:23. Sun made obeisance to Joseph—Gen. 37:9. When sun waxed hot, manna—Ex. 16:21. Must not worship—Deut. 4:19; 17:3. Sun, stand thou still—Josh. 10:12, 13; Hab. 3:11. In them hath he set tabernacle—Ps. 19:4. Thou hast prepared the light and the—Ps. 74:16. Jehovah is a Sun and Shield—Ps. 84:11. Sun shall not smite thee by day— Ps. 121:6. Praise ye him—Ps. 148:3. No new thing under the—Eccl. 1:9. Fair as the moon, clear as—Song of Sol. 6:10. Sun returned ten steps on dial—Is. 38:8. Sun and moon are darkened—Joel 2:10; 3:15; Mt. 24:29; Mk. 13:24; Lu. 23:45. To you who fear my name, sun shall arise—

Mal. 4:2. Maketh his sun to rise—
Mt. 5:45. Righteous shall shine as—
Mt. 13:43. His face did shine—Mt.
17:2; Rev. 1:16; 10:1. They brought
sick at setting of—Mk. 1:32; Lu. 4:
40. The sun into darkness—Acts 2:20.
Not seeing sun for a season—Acts 13:
11. Light above brightness of—Acts
26:13. One glory of the—I Cor. 15:41.
Let not sun go down on your wrath—
Eph. 4:26. Sun is no sooner risen—
Jas. 1:11. Appeared a woman arrayed
with—Rev. 12:1. Saw angel standing
in—Rev. 19:17. City had no need of
—Rev. 21:23. See ASTRONOMY, COSMOL-
OGY.

SUNDER. Beaten in—Is. 27:9. Break
bonds—Ps. 107:14; Nah. 1:13. Cut in
—Ps. 46:9; 107:16; Is. 45:2. Divided
in—Ps. 136:13. See DIVIDE, SEPARATE.

SUN-IMAGES. See IMAGES.

SUNG. Is. 26:1; Mt. 26:30; Mk. 14:26.
See MUSIC, POETRY, LYRIC.

SUNK. II Ki. 9:24; Lam. 2:9. Mire—
Jer. 38:22. Pit, Into—Ps. 9:15, 24.
Sea, Into—Ex. 15:4; Mt. 18:6. See
SINK, SANK.

SUP. See LORD'S SUPPER.

SUPERFLUITY. Mk. 12:44. See
ABUNDANCE.

SUPERFLUOUS. Lev. 21:18; 22:23; II
Cor. 9:1.

SUPERSCRIPTION. Mt. 22:20; Mk.
12:16; 15:26; Lu. 20:24; 23:38. See
WRITING.

SUPPER. Herod's—Mk. 6:21. Lord's
—See LORD'S SUPPER. Marriage—Mt.
22:2-14; Lu. 14:12-24; Rev. 19:9. See
MEALS.

SUPPLANT. Gen. 27:36; Jer. 9:4. See
JACOB.

SUPPLIANTS. Zeph. 3:10. See PRAYER.

SUPPLICATION. Jas. 5:16. Continueth
in—I Tim. 5:6. Hearken to—I Ki. 8:
30; Ps. 6:9; 28:2. Helping by—II Cor.
1:11. Make—II Chr. 6:37; Dan. 6:11;
Phil. 1:4. Thanksgiving, With—Phil.
4:6. See PRAYER.

SUPPLY. I Cor. 16:17. Body—Col. 2:
19. Entrance into the eternal kingdom
—II Pet. 1:11. Faith, In your—II
Pet. 1:5. God supplies—Phil. 4:19; I
Pet. 4:11. Joint—Eph. 4:16. Lack of
service—Phil. 2:30. Need, Every—
Phil. 4:19. Seed—II Cor. 9:10. Spirit

—Gal. 3:15; Phil. 1:19. Want—II
Cor. 9:12; 11:9. See ABUNDANCE, FILL.

SUPPORT. Ps. 41:3.

SUPPOSE. Mk. 6:49; Lu. 2:42; John
20:15; Acts 13:25; 14:19; 16:27; 21:
29.

SUPREME. I Pet. 2:13.

SUR, sûr. **A gate of Jerusalem.**—II Ki.
11:6.

SURE. Mt. 27:65. Anchor—Heb. 6:19.
Calling, and election—II Pet. 1:19.
Covenant—II Sam. 23:5. See COVE-
NANTS. Foundation—Is. 28:16; II Tim.
2:19. See STONE. House—I Sam. 2:
35; 25:28. Interpretation—Dan. 2:45.
Kingdom—Dan. 4:26. Mercies of David—Is. 55:3; Acts 13:34. Place—Is.
22:23, 25. Precepts—Ps. 111:7.
Promise—Rom. 4:16. Reward—Pr.
11:18. Testimony of the Lord—Ps.
19:7. Waters—Is. 33:16. Word of
prophecy—II Pet. 1:19.

SURETY. Judah—Gen. 43:9. Servant
—Gen. 44:32. In presence of friends
—Pr. 17:18.

Surety for.—Job 17:3. Good—Ps. 119:
122. Neighbor—Pr. 6:1.

Laws concerning.—For foreigners—Pr.
20:16; 27:13.

Warnings against.—Being surety for a
stranger—Pr. 11:15. For debts—Pr.
22:26. Jesus made a surety of a better
covenant—Heb. 7:22.

SURFEITING. Lu. 21:34. See DRUNKEN-
NESS.

SURGE. Of the sea—Jas. 1:6.

SURMISED. Acts 27:27; I Tim. 6:4.

SURNAME. Is. 44:5; 45:4; Mt. 10:3;
Mk. 3:16, 17; Acts 1:23; 4:36; 10:5,
18, 32; 11:13; 12:12, 25; 15:22, 37.

SURPASS. II Cor. 3:10.

SUSANNA, su-săn'na. **A female disciple,
wife of Herod's steward.**—Lu. 8:3.

SUSI, su'si. **A spy.**—Num. 13:11.

SUSPENSE. John 10:24.

SUSTAIN. Gen. 27:37; II Sam. 19:33;
I Ki. 17:9; Neh. 9:21; Ps. 3:5; 55:22;
Pr. 18:14; Is. 59:16. See MAINTAIN,
SUPPORT.

SUSTENANCE. Ju. 6:4; II Sam. 19:32;
Acts 7:11. See FOOD, MAINTENANCE.

SWALLOW. Pr. 21:20. Alive—Ps. 124:
3. Aaron's rod—Ex. 7:12. Camel—
Mt. 23:24. Death forever—Is. 25:8.
Death, in victory—I Cor. 15:54. Ears

—Gen. 41:7. Earth—Num. 16:32.
Egyptians were—Heb. 11:29. Life, Of
—II Cor. 5:4. Inheritance—II Sam.
20:19. Riches—Job 20:15. Wicked—
Hab. 1:13. Wicked, iniquity—Pr.
19:28.

SWALLOW. A bird.—Ps. 84:3; Pr. 26:
2; 38:14; Jer. 8:7.

SWARM. Bees, Of—Ju. 14:8. Flies, Of
—Ex. 8:24; Ps. 18:45. Frogs, Of—
Ex. 8:3; Ps. 105:30. See PLAGUES.
Grasshoppers—Ex. 8:24. Swarms of
living creatures—Gen. 1:20.

SWARTHY. Song of Sol. 1:6. See DARK,
COLORS.

SWEAR. See OATH, PERJURY, VOW.

SWEAT. Ez. 44:18. Blood—Lu. 22:44.
Face, Of thy—Gen. 3:19.

SWEEP. Destruction, With—Is. 14:23.
House—Lu. 15:8. Refuge of lies, Away
—Is. 28:17.

SWEET. Bitter for—Is. 5:20. Bitter
thing, Every—Pr. 27:7. Bread of deceit—Pr. 20:17. Calamus—Ex. 30:23.
Cane—Is. 43:24; Jer. 6:20. Cinnamon
—Ex. 30:23. Clods of the valley—Job
21:33. Counsel—Ps. 55:14. Desire accomplished—Pr. 13:19. Fruit—Song of
Sol. 2:3. Herbs—Song of Sol. 5:13.
Honey—Ju. 14:18; Ps. 19:10; 119:103;
Pr. 16:24; 24:13; Ez. 3:3; Rev. 10:9,
10. Incense—Ex. 25:6; 35:8, 15, 28;
39:38; Lev. 4:7; 16:12; Num. 4:16;
II Chr. 13:11. Light—Eccl. 11:7. Meditation—Ps. 104:34. Melody—Is. 23:
16. See MUSIC. Mouth—Song of Sol.
5:16. Odors—Lev. 26:31; II Chr. 16:
14; Dan. 2:46. Psalmist—II Sam. 23:1.
Savor—Gen. 8:21; Ex. 29:18, 25, 41;
Lev. 1:9, 13, 17; 2:2, 9, 12; 3:5, 16;
4:31; 6:15, 21; 8:21, 28; 17:6; 23:13,
18; Num. 15:3, 7, 10, 13, 14, 24; 18:17;
28:2, 8, 13, 24, 27; 29:2, 6, 8, 13, 36;
Ezra 6:10; Ex. 6:13; 16:19; 20:28, 41.
Sleep—Pr. 3:24; Jer. 31:26. Of laboring man—Eccl. 5:12. Smell—Eph. 5:
2; Phil. 4:18. Spices—Ex. 30:7, 34;
31:11; 37:29; 40:29; II Chr. 2:4; Is.
3:24. Voice—Song of Sol. 2:14. Waters
—Ex. 15:25. Salt — Jas. 3:11, 12.
Stolen—Pr. 9:17. Wickedness—Job
20:12. Wine—Is. 49:26; Joel 1:5;
Amos 9:13. Words—Ps. 119:103; 141:
6; Pr. 23:8. Pleasant—Pr. 16:24.

SWEETLY. Job 24:20.

SWEETNESS. Ju. 9:11. Friendship, Of
—Pr. 27:9. Lips, Of—Pr. 16:21.
Strong came forth, Out of—Ju. 14:
14. See SAMSON, TASTE.

SWELL. Body shall—Num. 5:21, 22, 27.
Foot—Deut. 8:4. Jordan—Job 40:23.

SWELLING. II Cor. 12:20. Breach—
Is. 30:13. Mountains tremble with—
Ps. 46:3. Words—II Pet. 2:18; Jude
16.

SWERVED. Law, From—Ps. 119:51.
Testimonies, From—Ps. 119:157.

SWIFT. Cloud—Is. 19:1. Destruction—
II Pet. 2:1. Foot, Of—Amos 2:15.
Hear, To—Jas. 1:19. In running to
mischief—Pr. 6:18. Messengers—Is.
18:2. Race is not to—Eccl. 9:11.
Righteousness, To do—Is. 16:5. Roes,
As—I Chr. 12:8. Serpent—Job 26:13;
Is. 27:1. Steed—Mic. 1:13. To shed
blood—Rom. 3:15. Witness—Mal. 3:5.
See RACE, RUN.

SWIFTER. Eagles, Than—II Sam. 1:
23; Jer. 4:13; Lam. 4:19. Leopards,
Than—Hab. 1:8. Post, Than—Job 9:
25. Weaver's shuttle, Than—Job 7:6.

SWIFTLY. Cometh—II Pet. 1:14. Fly
—Dan. 9:21. Return recompense—
Joel 3:4. Word runneth—Ps. 147:15.

SWIM. Bed—Ps. 6:6. Iron—II Ki. 6:6.
Land wherein thou—Ez. 32:6. Out
and escape—Acts 27:42. Spreadeth
forth hands to—Is. 25:11. They who
could—Acts 27:43. Waters to—Ez.
47:5.

SWINE: Forbidden as food.—Lev. 11:7;
Deut. 14:8.

Law against eating, violated.—Is. 65:4;
66:17.

Repudiated sacrifice.—Is. 66:3.

Feeding of.—Mt. 8:30-33; Mk. 5:11-14;
Lu. 8:32-34. Jewish degradation—
Lu. 15:15-16.

Habitations of demons.—Mt. 8:31-32;
Mk. 5:12-13; Lu. 8:32-33.

Turning back from truth.—II Pet. 2:
21-22.

Ornaments out of place.—Pr. 11:22; Mt.
7:6.

Gerasines punished by loss of.—Mt. 8:
32-34; Mk. 5:13, 14, 17; Lu. 8:33, 37.

Illustrative of.—The ravage of God's
people—Ps. 80:13. Want of judgment
in presenting truth—Mt. 7:6. Joy over
the redeemed—Mt. 18:12-13; Lu. 15:

4-6. False teachers—Mt. 7:15; John 10:1, 5, 8, 10, 12-13. Persecution of disciples—Mt. 10:16; 26:31; Mk. 14: 27; Rom. 8:36. Separation of, from sinners—Mt. 25:32-33.

SWING. Job 28:4.

SWOON. Children—Lam. 2:11. Wounded, As—Lam. 2:12. See FAINT.

SWOOPETH. Job 9:26.

SWORD. Esau lived by—Gen. 27:40. Joshua used sword in battle—Ex. 17: 13; Num. 14:3, 43; Deut. 13:15; Josh. 8:24; 10:11; 11:11; 13:22; 19:47; Ju. 1:25; 7:22; I Chr. 5:18; Neh. 4:13; Jer. 50:35-37; Ez. 24:21; 38:4. No sword in land—Lev. 26:6, 7. Making of—I Sam. 13:19; Joel 3:10; Mic. 4:3. David tries on—I Sam. 17:39; 21:9. Joab's girdle and—II Sam. 20:8. Multitude with—Mt. 26:47, 55; Mk. 14:43, 48; Lu. 22:52. Jesus tells disciples to buy—Lu. 22:36, 38. Gideon's watchword, "By the sword of the Lord and Gideon"—Ju. 7:20.

Illustrative.—Deut. 32:41; Ps. 17:13; 57:4; Zech. 13:7; Lu. 2:35.

Symbolical.—Gen. 3:24; Josh. 5:13.

The Word the sword of the Spirit.—Eph. 6:17.

SWORN. Josh. 9:18; Neh. 9:15; Ps. 119:106. See OATHS, SWEAR, VOWS.

SYCAMINE. Tree—Lu. 17:6.

SYCAMORE. Tree—I Ki 10:27; I Chr. 27:28; II Chr. 1:15; 9:27; Ps. 78:47; Is. 9:10. Amos a dresser of—Amos 7:14. Zacchæus climbed into—Lu. 19:4.

SYCHAR, sȳ'kar. A city near which Jesus talked with the woman of Samaria.—John 4:5. See SHECHEM.

SYMBOLS AND SIMILITUDES.—Sign of an idea, resemblance, comparison—Hos. 12:10. Similitude of the Lord—Num. 12:8; Deut. 4:12, 15, 16. Of oxen—II Chr. 4:3; Ps. 106:20. Of a palace, refers to polished daughters—Ps. 144: 12. Of sons of men—Dan. 10:16. Of Adam's transgression—Rom. 5:14. Of Melchizedek—Heb. 7:15. Of God—Jas. 3:9.

Symbols.—Tree of knowledge and of life—Gen. 2:9, 17; 3:3, 24; Rev. 22:2. Rainbow—Gen. 9:12-13. Circumcision—Gen. 17:11; Col. 2:11; Rom. 2:29. Passover—Ex. 12:23-24; I Cor. 5:7. Pillar of cloud—Ex. 19:9; Deut. 31:

15; Num. 12:5. Smitten rock—I Cor. 10:4. Blood of animals—Heb. 9:13-14. Canaan—Heb. 3:11-12; 4:9. Fire—Mt. 3:11-12; Mal. 3:2. Wind—Hos. 8:7; Mt. 11:7; John 3:8; Jas. 1:6. Wine—Is. 55:1; Jer. 25:15-17. Oil—Is. 61:3; Heb. 1:9. Vine—Is. 5:1-7; Ez. 15:2; John 15:1-8. Bread—Is. 55: 2; John 6:31-51. Salt—Mt. 5:13; Col. 4:6. Light—Is. 9:2; Hab. 3:4; Mt. 5:14; John 5:35. Water—Is. 12:3; John 4:10-15; Rev. 22:17.

(N. B.—Almost all descriptions of heaven and hell are symbolic, since these must be in earthly figures to be understood by us. For example—Rev., Chs. 11, 12, 14, 19, 20, 21, 22. Herein are the profoundest realities.) See TYPES.

SYMPATHY. See COMPASSION, CONSOLATION.

SYNAGOGUE (*a gathering together*). Congregation—Neh. 8:1-8.

Early references to.—Ps. 74:8. Places where Jews assembled for worship—Acts 13:5, 14, 43. Jesus taught in—Mt. 4:23; 9:35; 13:54; Mk. 1:39; Lu. 4:16; 13:10. Paul preaches in—Acts 13:5, 14; 14:1; 18:4.

Used as a court of justice.—Lu. 12:11. Scourged in—Mt. 10:17; 23:34; Mk. 13:9; Lu. 21:12; Acts 22:19; 26:11. Excommunicated—John 9:22, 34, 35; 12: 42; 16:2. Letters of condemnation—Acts 9:2.

Hypocrisies of.—In granting alms—Mt. 6:2. In prayers—Mt. 6:5. In ostentation—Mt. 23:5-7; Mk. 12:38-40; Lu. 11:43; 20:45-47.

Order of worship.—Synagogues in strict sense are not mentioned until after the desecration of temple by Antiochus Epiphanes. But Jews met and sat before prophets to be taught the law—Ez. 8:1; 11:15, 16; 14:1; 20:1; Ezra 8:15; Neh. 8:2; 9:1; Zech. 7:5. The synagogue required no priest—Anyone competent might take the roll and read therefrom—Lu. 4:16; Acts 15:21. They had a college of elders and a chief ruler—Acts 18:8, 17. Sometimes a wealthy Jew or proselyte built the synagogue—Lu. 7:5. If too poor to build, they built an oratory by a stream—Acts 16:13.

SYNTYCHE, sȳn'tȳ-ke. **An early disciple.**—Phil. 4:2.

SYRACUSE, sȳr'a-kuse. **A city in Sicily.** —Acts 28:12.

SYRIA (sȳr'ĭ-à), Aram. *"Mount-up."*— The wall of mountains north of Palestine, extending from the Mediterranean to the Euphrates, with Damascus as its capital—Num. 23:7; II Sam. 8: 5–6; Is. 7:8. Originally it was much more spacious, including Mesopotamia —Gen. 24:10; 25:20; 28:5.

Divided into provinces. — Zobah and Rehoh, Geshur, Hamath, Damascus— I Sam. 14:47; II Sam. 8:3, 5, 6, 9, 10; 10:6–8; 15:8; I Ki. 11:23; I Chr. 18:5, 9; 19:6; Jer. 39:5.

Famous rivers.—Abana and Pharpar— II Ki. 5:12. Orontes, Antioch, on this river.

Chief towns: Antioch, Damascus, Palmyra, Laodicea, Hamath, Hierapolis, Baalbec, Aleppo. **Mountain.**—Hermon —Deut. 4:48; Josh. 11:17; 12:1; I Chr. 5:23.

Occupants.—The Hamites, first; then a Shemite (Semitic) element entered from the southeast, *i. e.,* Abraham, Chedolaomer, Amraphel.

Conquest by David.—After the days of Abraham, Syria first appears in Scripture as a confederate against David, with Hadadezer, king of Zobah—II Sam. 8:3. Syria submits to David— II Sam. 8:4–5. David puts garrisons throughout the land—(II Sam. 8:6). In the days of Solomon, Syria revolted under Rezon of Zobah, and Damascus was recaptured—II Ki. 1:23–25.

Further strife of the kings.—Benhadad. This was the name of three kings of Damascus: (1) Benhadad I was the son of Tabrimmon and grandson of Hezion—I Ki. 15:18. He entered into an alliance with Asa, king of Judah, against Israel—I Ki. 15:18–20. Elisha anoints Hazael to be king and deplores his future development—I Ki. 19:15. (2) Benhadad II—This king had many wars with Israel, but was eventually defeated—I Ki. 20:29–32. His prestige shown in the three vassal kings who accompanied him to the siege of Samaria—I Ki. 20:1. In second siege of Samaria a famine resulted, and during a providential panic the Syrians fled in confusion—II Ki. 7:1–7. The king becoming ill, Hazael smothers him and seizes the throne—II Ki. 8: 7–15. The new king greatly oppressed Israel, but relief came through his death —II Ki. 13:22–24. (3) Benhadad III— This king was Hazael's son. He was unsuccessful, Jehoash recapturing the cities which were previously lost—II Ki. 13:25. Jeroboam II followed up this advantage, and in a subsequent reign the Syrian kingdom, under Rezin, makes an alliance with Israel against Ahaz, king of Judah—Is. 7:17.

The following references added to the above give the whole Syrian history: II Ki. 5:1–5; 6:8, 11, 23, 24; 9:14, 15; 12:17, 18; 13:3, 4, 7, 17, 19, 22; 15:37; 16:5–7; I Chr. 18:5, 6; 19:10–19; II Chr. 1:17; 16:2–7; 18:10, 30; 20:2; 22: 5–6; 24:23; 28:5, 23; Is. 7:1–8; 9:12; 17:3; Jer. 35:11; Amos 9:7.

Syria as a commercial country.—Traded with Tyre—Ez. 27:16. Was idolatrous —Ju. 10:6. Lewd—Ez. 16:57.

Story of Naaman, the leper.—II Ki. Ch. 5.

New Testament references.—Report of Jesus—Mt. 4:24. Enrollment under Quirinius—Lu. 2:2. Disciples first called Christians at Antioch—Acts 11:26. Starting-point for Paul's journeys—Acts 13:1–4; 15:35–41; 18:22– 23. Sails into Syria—Acts 21:3. Paul came into region of Syria—Gal. 1:21. Syrophœnician woman appeals to Jesus —Mk. 7:26–30. Barnabas preached in Antioch—Acts 15:35. Paul resisted Peter at Antioch—Gal. 2:11. See MESOPOTAMIA.

SYROPHŒNICIAN, sȳ'ro-phœ-ni'cian. **A woman whose daughter was healed.** —Mk. 7:24–30.

TAANACH, tā'a-năk. **A royal Canaanitish city. A Levitical city**—Josh. 21: 25. Inhabitants of, not driven out— Ju. 1:27. Conquered by Joshua—Josh. 12:21. Given to Manasseh out of Issachar—Josh. 17:11; I Ki. 4:12; I Chr. 7:29. Victory of Barak near—Ju. 5: 19.

TAANATH-SHILOH, tā'a-nath-shī'loh. **A city.**—Josh. 16:6.

TABBAOTH, tăb′ba-ŏth. **Ancestor of some who returned with Zerubbabel.** —Ezra 2:43; Neh. 7:46.

TABBATH, tăb′bath. **A city.**—Ju. 7:22.

TABEEL, tā′be-el. (1) **Persian governor of Samaria.**—Ezra 4:7.

(2) **Father of one whom Syria and Ephraim attempted to set up as king in place of Ahaz.**—Is. 7:6.

TABERAH, tăb′e-rah. **A stopping-place of Israel.**—Num. 1:3; Deut. 9:22.

TABERNACLE: Construction of.—Ex. Chs. 25–27, 36–39; Heb. 9:1–6. To be made after a divine pattern—Ex. 25: 9; 26:30; Heb. 8:5. Made of the free-will offerings—Ex. 25:1–8; 35:4–5, 21–29.

Called: Tabernacle of Jehovah—Josh. 22:19; I Ki. 2:28; I Chr. 16:39. Tabernacle of testimony—Ex. 38:21; Num. 1:50; Acts 7:44. Tent of testimony—Num. 17:7, 8; II Chr. 24:6. Tent of meeting—Ex. 27:21; 33:7; 40:22–35. See TENT. Tabernacle of Shiloh—Ps. 78:60. Tent of Joseph—Ps. 78:67. Temple of Jehovah—I Sam. 1:9; 3:3. House of Jehovah—Josh. 6:24; I Sam. 1:7, 24.

Manifestation of God's presence.—Ex. 25:8; 29:42–46.

Divided into: Court round about it—Ex. 27:9–17; 38:9–18; 40:8. The Holy Place —Ex. 26:31–37; 40:22–26; Heb. 9:2–8. The Most Holy Place—Ex. 26:33–35; 40:21; Heb. 9:3–8.

Furniture of: Court, brazen altar, laver of brass—Ex. 40:29–30. Holy Place, table of shewbread, golden candlestick, altar of incense—Ex. 26:35; 40:22–26; Heb. 9:2. See HOLY OF HOLIES. Ark and mercy seat—Ex. 26:33–34; 40:20– 21; Heb. 9:4.

For service of.—See PRIEST.

Vessels of the tabernacle: Basin.—Gold and brass—Ex. 12:22; 24:6; 27:3; 38: 3; Num. 4:14. Firepans—Ex. 27:3; 38:3. Flagons—Ex. 25:29. Flesh-hooks —Ex. 27:3; 38:3; Num. 4:14. Pots for ashes—Ex. 27:3. Shovels—Ex. 27:3; 38:3; Num. 4:14. Spoons—Ex. 25:29; Num. 4:7. Snuffers—Ex. 26:38. Snuff-dishes—Ex. 25:38. See VESSELS.

Finished.—Ex. 39:32. Anointed and sanctified—Ex. 29:43; 40:9–16; Num. 7:1. With holy oil—Ex. 30:25–26; Lev.

8:10. Sprinkled with blood—Lev. 16: 15–20; Heb. 9:21–23. Filled with glory of Jehovah—Ex. 40:34–35.

Prepared for removal.—Num. 1:51; 4: 5–15. By whom—Num. 4:5–33; 7:6–9.

Tribes camped about it.—Num. 2:1–32. Strangers forbidden to enter—Num. 1:51.

Defilement punished.—Lev. 15:31; Num. 19:13. Journeys regulated by cloud above—Ex. 40:36–37. See CLOUD OF GLORY.

Offerings brought to.—Lev. 17:4; Num. 31:54. Freewill offerings made at rearing and dedication—Num. 7:1–9; 7: 10–87.

Was set up.—At Sinai—Ex. 40:17–20; Num. 10:11–12. At Shiloh—Josh. 18: 1; 19:51; Ju. 18:31; 21:19; I Sam. 2: 14; 4:3–4; Jer. 7:12–14. At Gibeon— I Chr. 16:39; 21:29; II Chr. 1:3. David pitches a tent—II Chr. 1:3. Solomon offers sacrifice at—II Chr. 1:3–6.

Males required to appear before, three times annually.—Ex. 23:17. Required to pay a tax—Ex. 30:11–16.

Illustrative of: The Church—Heb. 8:2; Rev. 21:2–3. The Christ—Heb. 9:11– 14; 10:20. The body—II Cor. 5:1; II Pet. 1:13. Heaven—Heb. 6:19–20; 9: 12–24; 10:19. See PRIEST, ALTAR, OFFERING, TEMPLE, TENTS, VESSELS.

TABITHA, tăb′i-thả. **A woman in Joppa whom Peter restored to life.**—Acts 9:36, 40. See DORCAS.

TABLE: Kinds of, Tablet.—Stone, given to Moses—Ex. 31:18. Broken—Ex. 32:19. Restored — Ex. 34:1, 4; Deut. 10:1–5; II Cor. 3:3. Ten commandments written on — Ex. 34:28, 29; Deut. 4:13; 5:22; 9:9, 10, 11, 15, 17. In the Ark—I Ki. 8:9; II Chr. 5:10. Testimony—Ex. 31:18; 32:15, 16.

Furniture:—King's—Song of Sol. 1:12. Purity — Lev. 24:6; II Chr. 13:11. Rich Man — Lu. 16:21. Covenant— Heb. 9:4. Gold—I Ki. 7:48; I Chr. 28: 16. Home—Ps. 128:3; Mt. 15:27; Mk. 7:28. Money-changers — Mt. 21:12; Mk. 11:15; John 2:15. Jehovah—Mal. 1:7, 12. Unclean—Is. 28:8.

Lord's Table.—Lu. 22:21, 30; John 13: 28; I Cor. 10:21. Men chosen to wait on—Acts 6:2.

For offerings.—Burnt, Sin, Trespass—Ez. 40:39–43.

Table of Showbread.—Made of acacia wood — Ex. 25:23–28; Ex. 37:10–15. Set in Holy Place on north side—Ex. 26:35; 40:22, Heb. 9:2. Covered with blue cloth—Num. 4:7; Ex. 25:29, 30. Things to be set on—Ex. 37:16; Lev. 24:5–8. Who have charge of—Num. 3:31; 4:7. Table of showbread in temple built by Solomon—I Chr. 28:16; II Chr. 4:8, 19; Ez. 41:22; 44:16.

Told lies at.—Dan. 11:27.

Hospitality of.—Ju. 1:7. Of Kings—I Sam. 20:29, 34. Of David—II Sam. 9:7, 10, 11, 13; I Ki. 2:7. Solomon—I Ki. 4:27; II Chr. 9:4. Nehemiah—Neh. 5:17. Of God—Ez. 39:20.

Table prepared.—Ps. 23:5; Is. 21:5; 65:11; Ez. 23:41.

Figurative.—Job 36:16; Ps. 23:5; 78:19; Rom. 11:9. See MEALS, TABLET.

TABLET. Great—Is. 8:1. Heart, Of the —Pr. 3:3. Writing—Lu. 1:63. See TABLE.

TABOR, a Levitical city of Zebulun.—I Chr. 6:77. Tabor, a Plain in Benjamin—I Sam. 10:3.

MT. TABOR (Mountain Height). Position of.—Josh. 19:22; Jer. 46:18.

Scene of battle.—Barak's army assembled at—Ju. 4:6, 12, 14. Battle between Gideon and Zebah—Ju. 8:18.

Prophecy.—Hos. 5:1.

TABRET. Gen. 31:27: Is. 5:12. Adorned with—Jer. 31:4. Mirth of—Is. 24:8. Workmanship of—Ez. 28:13. See MUSIC.

TABRIMMON, tăb′rim-mŏn. Father of Ben-hadad, king of Syria.—I Ki. 15:18.

TACKLING. Cast out of ship—Acts 27:19. Loosed, Are—Is. 33:23.

TAHAN, tā′han. (1) Son of Ephraim. Num. 26:35.

(2) Descendant of Ephraim.—I Chr. 7:35.

TAHATH, tā′hath. (1) A Kohathite.—I Chr. 6:24, 37.

(2) Great-grandson of Ephraim—I Chr. 7:20.

(3) An encampment of Israel.—Num. 33:26, 27. See CAMP, ISRAEL.

(4) Grandson of (2).—I Chr. 7:20.

TACHEMONITE. Patronymic of one of David's mighty men—II Sam. 23:8. See HACHMONITE.

TAHPANES, tah-păn′es. A city in Egypt on the Nile.—Jer. 2:16; 43:7–9; 44:1; 46:14.

TAHPENES, tah-pē′nēs. Queen of Egypt in the days of Solomon—I Ki. 11:19, 20.

TAHREA, tah-rē′a. Grandson of Jonathan, son of Saul.—I Chr. 9:41.

TAHTIM-HODSHI, täh-tim-hŏd′shi. A district of Bashan.—II Sam. 24:6.

TAIL. Because of these two—Is. 7:4. Fat—Ex. 29:22. Foxes turned—Ju. 15:4. Month—Job 40:17. Scorpions, Like—Rev. 9:10.

TAKE. Job 36:8. Alive—II Ki. 7:12. Captive—Jer. 13:17. See CAPTIVITY. Counsel — Ju. 19:30. See COUNSEL. Crown—Rev. 3:11. False report—Ex. 23:1. See FALSE WITNESS. Form of a servant—Phil. 2:7. Hand—Gen. 13:9; Lu. 8:54. Heart, To—II Sam. 13:20. Hold—Jer. 13:21. Holy Spirit from me, Not—Ps. 51:11. Inheritance, For thine—Ex. 34:9. Jesus—Mt. 26:57. Leave—Acts 18:21. Life—Gen. 37:21; Jer. 40:14. See MURDERER. My yoke —Mt. 11:29. No more money—II Ki. 12:7. Reproach, Away — Ps. 119:22. Spoil — II Chr. 20:25. See SPOIL. Thought—Rom. 12:17. Up his cross—Mt. 16:24. Up thy bed—John 5:10. See BEAR, CARRY, LAY HOLD, JESUS, TEACHING OF.

TAKE HEED. And be quiet—Is. 7:4. Behold I have told you—Mk. 13:23. Beware of leaven of Pharisees—Mt. 16:6; Mk. 8:15. Do not your righteousness—Mt. 6:1. Every one of his neighbor—Jer. 9:4. How ye hear—Lu. 8:18. Keep yourselves from covetousness—Lu. 12:15. Lest this liberty become a stumbling - block — I Cor. 8:9. Lest haply there be in any one of you an evil heart — Heb. 3:12. Regard not iniquity—Job 36:21. Spirit, To your —Mal. 2:15. That no man lead you astray—Mk. 13:5; Lu. 21:5. To yourselves—Acts 20:28. See HEAR, JESUS, TEACHING OF.

TALEBEARER. See GOSSIP.

TALENT. Gold — Ex. 25:39. Lead—Zech. 5:7. Offering was twenty and nine—Ex. 38:24. Silver — Ex. 38:25, 27. Talents, Parables of—Mt. 18:24; 25:15. See MONEY.

TALITHA-CUMI. Mk. 5:41.

TALK. Ez. 33:20. Angel—Zech. 1:9, 13, 19; 2:3; 4:1–5; 5:5, 10; 6:4. Cain and Abel—Gen. 4:8. Commandments, About —Deut. 6:7. Daniel—I Sam. 17:23; I Ki. 1:14, 22. Deceitfully—Job. 13:7. Elijah and Elisha—II Ki. 2:11. Elisha —II Ki. 6:33. Full of—Job 11:2. Gehazi, With—II Ki. 8:4. God—See GOD, ANTHROPOMORPHISMS. Haman and family—Esth. 6:14. Joseph and his brethren—Gen. 45:15. Mischief, Of— Pr. 24:2. Moses and Elijah on Mount of Transfiguration—Mt. 17:3; Mk. 9: 4; Lu. 9:30. Paul—Acts 20:11. Peter and Cornelius—Acts 10:27. Power, Of thy—Ps. 145:11. Proudly—I Sam. 2: 3. See SPAKE, SPEAK, SPEECH, WORDS.

TALKER. Ez. 36:3. Vain—Tit. 1:10. See GOSSIP.

TALKING. I Ki. 18:27 (A.V.). Foolish —Eph. 5:4. Refrained from—Job. 29: 9. Vain — I Tim. 1:6. See VANITY. See SPAKE, SPEAK, SPEECH, WORDS.

TALL. Cedars—II Ki. 19:23. Nation— Is. 18:2. People—Deut. 2:10, 21. See HIGH.

TALMAI, tăl′mãi. (1) **King of Geshur, father-in-law of David.**—II Sam. 3:3; 13:37; I Chr. 3:2.
(2) **Son of Anak.**—Num. 13:22; Josh. 15:14; Ju. 1:10.

TALMON, tăl′mon. **A Levite.**—I Chr. 9:17; Ezra 2:42; Neh. 7:45; 11:19; 12:25.

TAMAR, tā′mar. (1) **Daughter of David, ravished by her brother Ammon.** —II Sam. 13:1–32; I Chr. 3:9.
(2) **Wife of Er, son of Judah.**—Gen. 38:6–24; Ruth 4:12; I Chr. 2:4.
(3) **A city in Judah.**—Ez. 47:19; 48:28.
(4) **A daughter of Absalom.**—I Sam. 14: 27.

TAMMUZ, tăm′muz. **A Syrian idol.**— Ez. 8:14.

TANACH, tā′năk. Josh. 21:25. See TAANACH.

TANHUMETH, tăn′hu-mĕth. **Father of** Seraiah the captain—II Ki. 25:23; Jer. 40:8.

TANNER. Simon a—Acts 9:43; 10:6, 32.

TAPESTRY. Carpets of—Pr. 7:16; 31: 22.

TAPHATH, tā′phath. **A daughter of** Solomon.—I Ki. 4:11.

TAPPUAH, tăp′pu-ah. (1) **A city.**— Josh. 16:8; 17:8.
(2) **A city in Judah.**—Josh. 12:17; 15: 34.
(3) **Son of Hebron.**—I Chr. 2:43.

TARALAH, tär′a-lah. **A city in Benjamin.**—Josh. 18:7.

TARE. Grievously—Mk. 9:20; Lu. 9:42. Lads—II Ki. 2:24. See FEAR.

TAREA, ta-rē′a. **Great-grandson of Jonathan, son of Saul**—I Chr. 8:35.

TARES. Parable of — Mt. 13:25–30. Meaning of parable—Mt. 13:36–40.

TARGET. See WEAPONS.

TARPELITES, tär′pel-ites. **An Assyrian tribe brought to Samaria by Shalmaneser.**—Ezra 4:6.

TARRY. All night. Ps. 59:15. At Ephesus—I Tim. 1:3. Jesus—Lu. 2:43. Long at the wine — Pr. 23:30. My Lord—Mt. 24:48. Night, For the— Ps. 30:5. No little time—Acts 14:28. Salvation shall not—Is. 46:13. Shall not—Heb. 10:37. Till I come—John 21:22. See JESUS, TEACHING OF, WAIT.

TARSHISH, tär′shish. (1) **Grandson of** Noah.—Gen. 10:4: I Chr. 1:7.
(2) **Great-grandson of Benjamin.** — I Chr. 7:10.
(3) **Ships of.**—I Ki. 10:22; 22:48; II Chr. 9:21; Ps. 48:7; Is. 2:16; 23:1, 14; 60:9; Ez. 27:25.
(4) **A prince of Persia.**—Esth. 1:14.
(5) **A city.**—II Chr. 9:21; 20:36, 37; Ps. 72:10; Is. 23:6, 10; 66:19; Jer. 10:9; Ez. 27:12; 38:13; Jonah 1:3; 3:3; 4:2.

TARSUS, tär′sus. **Capital of Cilicia and birthplace of Paul.**—Acts 9:11, 30; 11: 25; 21:39; 22:3.

TARTAK, tär′tăk. **An idol of the Avites.**—II Ki. 17:31.

TARTAN, tär′tan. **An Assyrian officer sent to Hezekiah.**—II Ki. 18:17; Is. 20:1.

TASK. Daily—Ex. 5:14, 19. Fulfilled— Ex. 14:13, 14. Giveth—Pr. 31:15. See LABOR.

TASKMASTER. Commanded the—Ex. 5:6. Cry by reason of—Ex. 3:7. Set over them—Ex. 1:11. Voice of—Job 3:18. See BONDAGE, LABOR.

TASKWORK. Became subject to—Ju. 1:30. Servants to do—Josh. 16:10. Servant under—Gen. 49:15. Slothful shall be put under—Pr. 12:24. See BONDAGE, LABOR.

TASTE: Physical.—The organ of—Job 12:11; 34:3. Of manna—Ex. 16:31; Num. 11:8. White of egg—Job 6:6. Honey—Pr. 24:13. Tasted by Jonathan—I Sam. 14:29, 43. Wine tasted by Belshazzar—Dan. 5:2. At marriage feast—John 2:9. Jesus tasted wine and gall—Mt. 27:34. Bread not tasted by David—II Sam. 3:35.

Proclamation against.—I Sam. 14:24; Jonah 3:7.

Warnings against taste of earthly things.—Col. 2:21-23.

Illustrative.—Song of Sol. 2:3.

Figurative.—Of Barzillai—II Sam. 19: 35. Mischievous things—Job 6:30. Moab—Jer. 48:11.

Spiritual taste.—Of the Lord—Ps. 34:8; 119:103. Death—Heb. 2:9. See JESUS, TEACHING OF. Heavenly gifts—Heb. 6:4, 5; I Pet. 2:3.

TATTENAI, tăt'te-nāi. **A Persian governor.**—Ezra 5:3; 6:13.

TAUGHT. See INSTRUCTION.

TAUNT. Ju. 8:15; Jer. 24:9; Ez. 5:15; Hab. 2:6. See MOCKING.

TAVERNS. Acts 28:15. See HOSPITALITY, INN.

TEACH, TEACHER, TEACHING. See INSTRUCTION.

TEAR. Ps. 35:15; Ez. 23:34. Anger did—Amos 1:11. Arm—Deut. 33:20. Flesh—Ju. 8:7. Pieces, In—Ps. 50: 22; Mic. 5:8. Soul—Ps. 7:2. Thyself —Job 18:4. Wild beast shall—Hos. 13:8.

TEARS: Of distress.—Hezekiah's—II Ki. 20:5; Is. 38:5. Esther's—Esth. 8:3. Job's—Job 16:20. David's— Ps. 6:6; 39:12; 56:8; 116:8. Of oppressed—Eccl. 4:1. Paul's—II Cor. 2:4. Timothy's—II Tim. 1:4. Christ's —Heb. 5:7. Esau's—Heb. 12:17.

Prophecies concerning.—Is. 25:8; Ez. 24:16; Rev. 7:17; 21:4.

Jesus' feet washed in.—Lu. 7:38, 44.

Serving the Lord with.—Acts 20:19, 31.

Figurative.—Ps. 42:3; 80:5. Sow with tears—Ps. 126:5. For oppressed—Is. 16:9; Jer. 9:1, 18; 13:17; 14:17; 31: 16. Of Zion—Lam. 1:2; 2:11, 18. Cover altar of Jehovah with—Mal. 2:13. See MOURNING, WAILING, WEEP.

TEBAH, tē'bah. **Son of Nahor brother of Abraham.**—Gen. 22:24.

TEBALIAH, tĕb'a-lī'ah. **A Merarite.**— I Chr. 26:11.

TEBETH, tē'beth. **Tenth Jewish month.** —Esth. 2:16. See MONTHS.

TEDIOUS. Acts 24:4.

TEEMETH. Lev. 20:25.

TEETH: Law concerning.—Ex. 21:24; Lev. 24:20; Deut. 19:21.

Old Jewish law made void.—Mt. 5:38.

Kinds of. — Man-servant — Ex. 21:27. Maid-servant—Ex. 21:27. Lions'— John 4:10; Ps. 58:6. Animals'—Dan. 7:5. Of bride—Song of Sol. 4:2; 6:6. Of an epileptic—Mk. 9:18. Broken— I Sam. 3:16. Iron teeth—Dan. 7:7, 19. Of instruments: Flesh-hook—I Sam. 2:13.

Use of.—Num. 11:33; Dan. 7:5.

Prophecies concerning. — Gen. 49:12; Deut. 32:24; Ps. 112:10. Shall not be set on edge—Jer. 31:29, 30; Ez. 18:2. Israel—Amos 4:6. In judgment—Mt. 8:12; 13:42, 50; 22:13; 24:51; 25:30; Lu. 13:28.

Figurative.—Pr. 25:19; Job 13:14; 16:9; 19:20; 29:17; Mic. 3:5. Of terror— 41:14. Of wicked—Ps. 3:7; Pr. 10:26. Of enemies—Ps. 35:16; 57:4; Pr. 30: 14. Escaped out of—Ps. 24:6. Of threshing instrument—Is. 41:15. Of lion—Joel 1:6; Rev. 9:8.

Miscellaneous.—At stoning of Stephen —Acts 7:54.

TEHAPHNEHES, te-hăph'ne-hēs. Ez. 30:18. See TAHPANHES.

TEHINNAH, te-hĭn'nah. **A descendant of Judah.**—I Chr. 4:12.

TEKEL, tē'kel. **A part of the writing on the wall at the Feast of Belshazzar.**—Dan. 5:25.

TEKOA, te-kō'a. (1) I Chr. 2:24; 4:5. (2) **A city in Judah.**—II Sam. 14:2-9; II Chr. 11:6; 20:20; Jer. 6:1; Amos 1:1.

TEKOHITE. A native of Tekoa.—II Sam. 23:26; I Chr. 11:28; 27:9; Neh. 3:5, 27.

TEL-ABIB, tĕl'ȧ'bib. A place on the river Chebar where Ezekiel spent a week.—Ez. 3:15.

TELAH, tē'lah. A descendant of Ephraim.—I Cor. 7:25.

TELAIM, te-lā'im. A place in Judah.—I Sam. 15:4.

TELASSAR, te-lăs'sar. An Assyrian province.—Is. 37:12.

TELEM, tē'lem. (1) A gatekeeper of the sanctuary.—Ezra 10:24.

(2) A city in Judah.—Josh. 15:24.

TEL-HARSHA, tel-här'shȧ. A place on the river Chebar.—Ezra 2:59; 7:61.

TEL-MELAH, tĕl-mē'lah. A place on the river Chebar.—Ezra 2:59.

TEMA, tē'ma. (1) A city or district in Arabia.—Job 6:19; Is. 21:14; Jer. 25:23.

(2) Son of Ishmael and his descendants.—Gen. 25:15; I Chr. 1:30.

TEMAN, tē'man. (1) A duke of Edom.—Gen. 36:42; I Chr. 1:53.

(2) Grandson of Esau.—Gen. 36:11, 15; I Chr. 1:36.

(3) A people and district.—Gen. 36:34; Jer. 49:7, 20; Ez. 25:13; Amos 1:12; Ob. 9; Hab. 3:3.

TEMANITES. Inhabitants of Teman.—I Chr. 1:45; Job 2:11; 4:1; 15:1; 22:1; 42:7, 9.

TEMENI, tē'men-i. A descendant of Caleb son of Hur.—I Chr. 4:6.

TEMPER. I Cor. 12:24.

TEMPERANCE. Bishop—I Tim. 3:2. Men be—Tit. 2:2. Women—I Tim. 3:11. See Abstinence, Drunkenness, Self-control.

TEMPEST. Breaketh me with—Job 9:17. Covert from—Is. 32:2. Great—Mt. 8:24. Mighty waters, Of—Is. 28:2. Pursue with—Ps. 83:15. Stealeth him away—Job 27:20. Stormy wind and—Ps. 55:8. Tossed with—Is. 54:11. Waters, Of—Hab. 3:10. Whirling—Jer. 23:19. See Storm, Wind.

TEMPESTUOUS. Ps. 50:3; Jonah 1:13. Sea—Jonah 1:11. Wind—Acts 27:14.

TEMPLE, Heb. *Hekhal.* "A large public building." "House of Jehovah." Temples, as places where the gods were worshipped, were common among the Semitic and other ancient people—*e. g.* Assyria, Babylon, Phœnicia, Egypt. Temples for the Hebrews are

of a later date. After the tabernacle days there must have been a permanent structure at Shiloh (see I Sam. 1:9; 3:3). The word temple, however, as applying to the Hebrews, designates three structures: those of Solomon, Zerubbabel, and Herod. Besides these we have also Ezekiel's ideal temple. The word *Hekhal* is used also of the dwelling place of God in heaven.

Solomon's temple.—Built on Mount Moriah, the Eastern hill, on the former site of the threshing-floor of Araunah, the Jebusite—II Sam. 24:18-25; I Chr. 21:18-26; II Chr. 3:1. David first conceived the idea—II Sam. 7:1-3. But God did not approve of this, preferring his Son—II Sam. 7:5-13. David then prepared the material—I Chr. 22:1-5; 29:1-5; Ps. 132:2-5; Acts 7:45, 46. He charged his son to build the temple—I Chr. 22:6-16. He prays for Solomon's success—I Chr. 29:18, 19. Solomon determines to build it—I Ki. 5:1-5; II Chr. 2:1.

Solomon prepares the material.—Employs Hiram, king of Tyre, David's friend—I Ki. 5:2-6; II Chr. 2:3. Calls on Hiram for a superintendent—II Chr. 2:7, 13. Contracts with Hiram for material and labor—I Ki. 5:8-11; II Chr. 2:8-10. Solomon and Hiram work together—I Ki. 5:18.

Form and dimensions of.—The temple was a rectangle, 60 cubits long and 20 broad—I Ki. 6:2. Its height was 30 cubits—I Ki. 6:2. There was a porch in front, facing eastward, of the same width as the building, and 10 cubits in depth. It is supposed that these are inner measurements. Ezekiel, in his vision of the temple, gives 6 cubits as the thickness of the walls—Ez. 41:5.

Inner chambers.—The temple was divided into two parts: the Holy Place and the Holy of Holies—I Ki. 8:6-11; II Chr. 3:5-8. The Holy Place was 40 cubits long and 20 wide; the Holy of Holies, 20 by 20. It was all 20 cubits high—I Ki. 6:16-20; II Chr. 3:3-8.

Surroundings.—Surrounded on all sides except the front, which contained the porch. The temple was surrounded by a lateral building of three stories, the whole 15 cubits high. Each story contained a number of small rooms for storage purposes and treasury. There were also windows of latticework—I Ki. 6:4–6.

The approaches.—This was through several gates. The upper gate, built by Jotham—II Ki. 15:35; II Chr. 27:3. The king's gate—II Ki. 16:18; I Chr. 9:18. The gate of the guard—II Ki. 11:19. The new gate—Jer. 26:10; 36:10. Benjamin's gate—Jer. 20:2.

Construction of exterior.—The solid part of the house was of stone hewn in the quarry; that is, the foundation and walls—I Ki. 5:17; 6:7. Not a tool heard in the building of them—I Ki. 6:7. In front were two pillars, each 18 cubits high, called Jachin and Boaz —I Ki. 7:15–22; II Chr. 3:15–17.

Interior.—Cypress wood. The folding-doors made of this, overlaid with gold —I Ki. 6:34–35. Floor was of stone covered with cypress wood—I Ki. 6:15. The walls were built within of cedar (I Ki. 6:18), the entrance doors of olive wood, and the covering of cedar—I Ki. 6:31. The whole house was overlaid, within, of gold (I Ki. 6:20–22) and carvings.

Furniture of the outer court.—As there is a duplication of the tabernacle measurements elsewhere, we may estimate the dimensions of the outer court as 100 cubits north and south and 200 east and west, the wall probably being 10 cubits in height.

Altar of burnt-offering.—This was before the porch, and was reached by an ascending platform—II Chr. 15:8. It was 32 cubits square and 15 high (Talmud, Middoth III, I).

Molten sea.—This was 10 cubits across and 5 high with capacity of 2000 baths. It stood on 12 oxen, 3 looking north, 3 south, 3 east, and 3 west. It was on the right side of the house, eastward, toward the south—I Ki. 7:39; II Chr. 4:2–10.

Ten lavers of brass.—Each contained 40 baths, 5 were on right side of house and 5 on left side—I Ki. 7:38, 39; II Chr. 4:6.

Furniture of holy place.—Tables of shewbread said to be 10, made in the form of an altar—I Ki. 7:48; II Chr. 4:8; 29:18. These made of gold and of silver—I Chr. 28:16; II Chr. 4:19. Candlesticks of gold and silver, 5 on each side of Holy Place, before the Holy of Holies—I Ki. 7:49; I Chr. 28:15; II Chr. 4:7, 20. Altar of incense— I Ki. 6:20; 7:48–50; I Chr. 28:17, 18; II Chr. 4:19, 22.

Holy of Holies.—Ark of the covenant. Hidden from view by a wall of cedar wood that separated the two sanctuaries—I Ki. 6:16. There was also a linen veil—II Chr. 3:14. The ark was overshadowed by cherubim 10 cubits high, whose wings met in the centre and stretched out to each wall—I Ki. 6:27. The ark and cherubim were overlaid with gold—I Ki. 6:22, 28. Within the ark were the two stone tables of the law—I Ki. 8:9.

Minor pieces of furniture.—Basins—I Ki. 7:40, 45; I Chr. 28:17; II Chr. 4:8, 11, 22; Neh. 7:70; Jer. 52:19. Bowls— II Ki. 25:15; I Chr. 28:17; Jer. 52:19. Cups—I Ki. 7:50; Jer. 52:19. Firepans I Ki. 7:50; Jer. 52:19. Shovels—I Ki. 7:45. Snuffers—I Ki. 7:50; II Chr. 4: 22; Jer. 52:18. Spoons—I Ki. 7:50; II Ki. 25:14; II Chr. 4:22; Jer. 52:18.

Further facts concerning Solomon's temple.—Began building in fourth year in month Ziv—I Ki. 6:37. Finished in eleventh year in month Bul—I Ki. 6:38. Thus, occupied 7 years and 6 months. It stood 3½ centuries and was burned to ground by soldiers of Nebuchadrezzar, in 587=6 B.C. Dedicated by Solomon—I Ki. Ch. 8; II Chr. 5:6–7. Sacred fire sent down through prayer—II Chr. 7:3. Used by king to rally his people—II Chr. 6:12. Pillaged by Shishak, king of Egypt—I Ki. 14:25, 26; II Chr. 12:9. Pillaged by Jehoash, king of Israel—II Ki. 14:13, 14. Ahaz, king of Judah, makes changes in structure—II Ki. 16:17, 18. He sacrifices to false gods, seeking to propitiate Tiglath-pileser—II Chr. 28:16–25. Repaired by Josiah—II Ki. Ch. 22. Temple purified and worship restored under Hezekiah—II Chr. 29:3–35. Treasures sacrificed by Jehoash —II Ki. 12:17, 18. By Hezekiah—II Ki. 18:13–16. By Asa—I Ki. 15:18.

Temple polluted by Manasseh—II Ki. 21:4–7. Burned by Nebuchadrezzar— II Ki. Chs. 24 and 25; II Chr. Ch. 36. **Appointed for.**—A house of sacrifice— —II Chr. 7:12. A dwelling-place for Jehovah—I Ki. 8:10–13; 6:12, 13. A house of prayer—I Ki. 8:27–30; II Chr. 30:27; Is. 56:7; Mt. 21:13. A depository for ark of covenant—I Ki. 8: 1–9; II Chr. 5:2–10. For dedicated things—II Chr. 5:1. For an armory— II Ki. 11:10; II Chr. 23:9, 10. As a refuge—I Ki. 1:50; 2:28.

The second temple.—This was built at the instigation of the prophets Haggai and Zechariah, under the leadership of Zerubbabel. Cyrus had already issued a building decree (Ezra 1:1–4), as predicted by Isaiah (Is. 44:28), and the Jews began to gather material for it (Ezra 3:7). Its dimensions are indicated in Ezra 6:3–5, and according to Haggai (Ezra 2:18), the foundation was laid in the second year of Darius, B.C. 520 (Prof. A. R. S. Kennedy). Those remaining in Babylon were required to contribute to this (Ezra 1:4–6). The vessels of the first temple were returned (Ezra 1:7–11; 6:5). The work was suspended because of false statements (Ezra 4:1–16). Darius searched into the matter, and justifying the Jews, they were authorized to continue the work (Ezra 6:1–14). The Samaritans offered to assist in building, but were not permitted (Ezra 4:1–3). The temple was finished and dedicated B.C. 516.

Differences between first and second temple.—The ground plan of the former temple, consecrated by centuries of worship, was followed as nearly as possible (G. A. Smith). In the main, the changes were with respect to the furniture. Instead of one court, as in the days of Solomon, there were two, an outer and an inner. An altar of unhewn stone took the place of the great brazen altar. In the holy place there was but one candlestick, and one table of shewbread where before there were ten. In a signal respect the glory of the first temple had departed; they had no ark of the covenant in the Holy of Holies. But it was the com-

parative poverty of the second temple as contrasted with the magnificence of Solomon's that so disconcerted the older exiles on their return to Jerusalem.

Desecration and renewal of second temple.—In B.C. 168, Antiochus Epiphanes spoiled and desecrated the temple, sacrilegiously setting up a small altar to Zeus Olympus, on which he offered up parts of a sow, smearng the furniture with the liquid in which the sow was cooked. Three years later Judas, the Maccabean, after recapturing Jerusalem, made new sacred furniture throughout, removing the polluted parts.

The temple of Herod.—In the 18th year of his reign, Herod the Great obtained permission of his Jewish subjects to rebuild the temple of Zerubbabel. In his heart he wished a new one, but feared to make the attempt. So he devised the reconstruction in such a way that it seemed, in its different stages, to be merely a repairing of the old temple. The temple proper was rebuilt by 1,000 specially trained priests, within the space of eighteen months. The rest of the buildings took years to finish, and when done it was a magnificent but different structure in many particulars (Mk. 13:1; Lu. 21:5). It was begun 19 B.C. and finished c. 27 A.D. It was said to have been 46 years in building (John 2:20). The temple area was enlarged so as to cover the whole surface of Mount Moriah. The tower, built as a fortress by John Hyrcanus II, was enlarged and beautiful, being transformed into a palace by Herod, and named Antonia, after Mark Anthony. A covered colonnade, called the Porch (Mk. 14:68), ran around the inner portion of the wall. The south division of this was known as the royal porch. It consisted of 162 gigantic columns arranged in four rows somewhere along the eastern portico. Overlooking the Kidron Valley was a section known as Solomon's porch (John 10:23; Acts 3:11). The outer court (of the Gentiles) was 900 feet square, and was approached by a series of gates and bridge. Warnings were posted forbidding foreigners, on the pain of death, from entering the inner court. This was divided into two parts—the court of men (or Israel), and the court of the women. Within the court of the women was the treasury (Mk. 12:41-44; Lu. 21: 1-3). Between the two courts was a flight of 15 steps, semi-circular in form, leading to the great gate, which was 40 cubits wide and 50 high—possibly the Beautiful Gate (Acts 3:2). Within the court of the men was a series of chambers for storage purposes. The rest of the temple was little different from the former one, except that there was no wall between the Holy Place and the Holy of Holies. The division was made by a veil consisting of parallel curtains of rich material (Mt. 27:51; Mk. 15:38; Lu. 23:45).

Ezekiel's temple.—In Ez., Chs. 40, 41, 42, 43, may be found a vision. An ideal temple is there described which doubtless had much to do with suggesting ideas to the builders of the restored Jerusalem. This temple is largely patterned after that of Solomon. One of its characteristic features was the emphasis on its sacredness. The whole area of the temple and its courts must have nothing to do with secularity. It was to be erected on a site 500 cubits square and was to be walled (Ez. 40:5-27). It was to have three gates, so arranged as to have lodges or guard chambers. Each gateway was to have arches (Ez. 40:16). The rest of the structure was patterned after the temple of Solomon.

Relation of Jesus to.—Presented in— Lu. 2:22-32. Carried to the pinnacle —Mt. 4:5; Lu. 4:9. Taught in—Mt. 26:55; Mk. 11:27-33; 12:35-44; John 5:14-47; 10:23-28; 14:49. Purified it —Mt. 21:12-13; Mk. 11:15-17; Lu. 19: 45, 46; John 2:15-17. Predicted its destruction—Mt. 24:2; Mk. 13:2; Lu. 21:6. Veil rent at crucifixion—Mt. 27:51.

Relation of Jews to.—Separation from Gentiles alluded to—Eph. 2:14. Exclusively for Jews—Acts 21:27-30. Jews prayed outside while priest of-

fered incense—Lu. 1:10. Thought it blasphemy to speak against it—Mt. 26:61; Acts 6:13; 21:28. Polluted it by selling oxen, etc., in—John 2:14. Desecration foretold—Dan. 9:27; 11: 31; Mt. 24:15. Ezekiel's vision of— Ez. 37:26-28; Chs. 40-48. Prophecies of restoration—Is. 44:28; Hag. 1:2; Zech. 1:16; 4:8-10; 6:12-15; 8:9-15.

Figurative.—Of body of Jesus—John 2: 19-22; Mt. 26:61; 27:40. Of Church of Christ—I Cor. 3:16; II Cor. 6:16; Eph. 2:20-22; 4:11-16. Individual bodies—I Cor. 6:13-20. Man of sin— II Thess. 2:4. Conquering Christians —Rev. 3:12. John's vision—Rev. 15: 5-8; 16:1-17.

Idolatrous temples.—House of Dagon— I Sam. 5:2. Jeroboam's act—I Ki. 12:31. House of Rimmon—II Ki. 5: 18. House of Baal—II Ki. 10:21-27. Temple at Babylon—II Chr. 36:7; Dan. 1:2. Temple of Diana—Acts 19:27. SEE TABERNACLE, KINGDOM OF JUDAH, PRIEST, OFFERING.

TEMPORAL. II Cor. 4:18. See COVENANT.

TEMPTATION. Enticing to evil; seduction; sometimes testing.

How it originates.—Jas. 1:14. God provides for it—I Cor. 10:13; II Pet. 2:9. Reward to the approved—Ps. 66:10-12; Is. 33:15, 16; Jas. 1:12.

Jesus succors.—Heb. 2:18; 4:15; Rev. 3:10.

Satan an enticer.—I Chr. 21:1. See II Sam. 21:1. Devil as an enticer—Mt. 4:1; Mk. 1:13; Lu. 4:2; John 13:2. God uses Satan to test Job—Job 1:8, 12. Other Satanic work—Mt. 13:19, 39; Lu. 8:12; 22:31; John 8:44; 13:2, 27; Acts 5:3; 26:18; Rom. 16:20; I Cor. 5:5; II Cor. 12:7; I Thess. 2:18; 3:5; I Tim. 1:20; Eph. 6:16; Rev. 2:10.

Pharisees tempt Jesus.—Mt. 16:1; 19:3; 22:35; Mk. 8:11; 10:2; John 8:6.

Duty of avoidance.—Is. 8:12, 13; Jer. 1:8; Mt. 18:6; Mk. 9:42; Lu. 17:1; Rom. 14:13, 15, 21; I Cor. 7:5; 8:9, 13; Gal. 6:1.

Duty of resistance.—Deut. 7:25; Pr. 1: 10-16; 4:14-16; 5:3-14; Mt. 26:41; Mk. 14:37, 38; Rom. 12:21; I Cor. 16: 13; Eph. 6:11-16; Heb. 12:4; Jas. 4:7; I Pet. 5:8, 9; II Pet. 3:17; Rev. 3:2, 3.

Some who failed.—Adam and Eve—Gen. Ch. 3. Cain—Gen. Ch. 4. Noah—Gen. 9:20. Abraham—Gen. 12:19. Lot's wife—Gen. 19:17, 26. Esau—Gen. 25:34. Jacob—Gen. 27:11–14. Aaron—Gen. 32:1–2. Moses—Num. 20:10–12. Achan—Josh. 7:21. Saul—I Sam. 15:1–3, 9. David—II Sam. Ch. 11. Solomon—I Ki. 11:4. Judas—John 13:30. Peter—Mt. 26:69, 70. Ananias—Acts Ch. 5.

Some who resisted.—Joseph—Gen. 39:7–12. Caleb and Joshua—Num. 14:6–9; Neh. 4:8, 9; Job Ch. 31; Dan. 1:8. Jesus—See SATAN AN ENTICER.

Benefits of.—Rom. 8:35–39; II Cor. 4:8–10, 17; Jas. 1:2–4; I Pet. 1:6, 7; 3:14; 4:12, 13. See AFFLICTIONS.

TEN — Commandments. — See COMMANDMENTS. Days — Dan. 1:12–20; Acts 25:6; Rev. 2:10; 12:3. Degrees—II Ki. 20:10, 11; Is. 38:8. Horns—Dan. 7:7–24; Rev. 12:3; 13:1; 17:3–16. Lepers—Lu. 17:12–17. Pieces of silver—Lu. 15:8. Pounds—Lu. 19:13–25. Reproached ten times—Job 19:3. Stringed instruments—See MUSIC. Talents—II Ki. 5:5; Mt. 25:28. Tribes —See ISRAEL. Virgins—Mt. 25:1. Wisdom strengtheneth more than—Eccl. 7:19. See TABERNACLE, TEMPLE.

TEN THOUSAND. Afraid of, Not—Ps. 3:6. Cast down—Dan. 11:12. Chief among—Song of Sol. 5:10. David has slain his—I Sam. 18:7, 8; 21:11; 29:5. Instructors—I Cor. 4:15. Put to flight —Lev. 26:8; Deut. 32:30; 33:2, 17. Ten thousand times—Dan. 7:10. Words—I Cor. 14:19.

TEND. Flock of God—I Pet. 5:2. Life, To—Pr. 10:16. Penury, To—Pr. 14:23. Plenteousness, To—Pr. 21:5. Sheep—John 21:16. See SHEPHERD.

TENDER. Pr. 4:3. Branch—Job 14:7. Calf—Gen. 18:7. Called—Is. 47:1. Eyes—Gen. 29:17. Grass—Deut. 32:2. Heart—II Ki. 22:10. Mercy—Lu. 1:78. Plant—Is. 53:2. See GENTLENESS.

TENDERLY. Affectioned—Rom. 12:10.

TENOR. Law, Of—Deut. 17:11. Words, Of—Gen. 43:7; 34:27. See MUSIC.

TENTS. Persons mentioned as dwelling in: Patriarchs—Noah—Gen. 9:21, 27. Abraham—Gen. 13:3, 5, 18; 14:18; 18:6, 9; 24:67. Lot—Gen. 13:5, 12. Isaac

—Gen. 26:25. Jacob—Gen. 31:25, 33, 34; 33:19; 35:21; Moses—Ex. 18:7. Achan—Josh. 7:21, 22. Heber and Jael—Ju. 4:11, 17, 18, 20.

Tent-pin. Ju. 4:21, 22.

David's tent.—I Sam. 17:54. Arabian tents—Is. 13:20.

Dream of.—Ju. 7:13.

Every man at his.—Ex. 33:8; Ju. 7:8; 20:8; I Sam. 4:10; 13:2; II Sam. 18:17; 19:8; 20:22; II Chr. 25:22; Jer. 37:10.

Tabernacle is called.—Ex. 26:7, 9, 11, 12, 13, 36; 33:8, 11; 35:11; 36:18, 19; 39:32, 33, 40; 40:2, 6, 7, 19, 22, 24, 26, 29, 30, 32, 34, 35; Num. 3:25; 9:15; II Sam. 7:6; I Chr. 17:5; II Chr. 1:3, 6; Ps. 78:60.

Tent over tabernacle.—Ex. 36:14.

Tent for the Ark.—I Chr. 15:1; 16:1; II Chr. 1:4.

A shepherd's.—Is. 38:12.

Lepers dwell outside of.—Lev. 14:8; II Ki. 7:8.

Cleansing of.—Num. 19:14, 18.

Pavilion.—Num. 25:8.

Door of.—Ex. 33:8, 10; Num. 11:10; 16:27; Ju. 4:20. Jehovah appears at—Gen. 18:1, 2, 10; 26:25; Deut. 31:15.

Of the tent of meeting.—Ex. 26:36; 29:4, 10, 11, 32, 42; 33:9, 10; 36:37; 38:8, 30; 39:38; 40:6, 12, 28, 29; Lev. 1:3, 5; 3:2; 4:4, 7, 18; 8:3, 4, 31, 33, 35; 10:7; 12:6; 14:11, 23; 15:14, 29; 16:7; 17:4, 5, 6, 9; 19:21; Num. 3:25, 26; 4:25; 6:10, 13, 18; 10:3; 16:18, 19, 50; 20:6; 25:6; 27:2; Josh. 19:57; I Sam. 2:22; I Chr. 9:21.

Figurative.—Enlarge thy tent—Is. 40:22; 54:2; Jer. 10:20.

TENT CORD. See CORD, TENT.

TENTH. Gen. 14:20; 28:22; Lev. 27:32. Month—Gen. 8:5; II Ki. 25:1; I Chr. 27:13; Ezra 10:16; Esth. 12:6; Jer. 39:1; Ez. 24:1; 29:1. See TITHE.

TENTMAKER. Acts 18:3.

TENT-PIN. Ju. 4:21.

TERAH, tē′rah. (1) **Father of Abraham.**—Gen. 11:24–32; Josh. 24:2; I Chr. 1:26; Lu. 3:34.

TERAPHIM. Gen. 31:19; Ju. 17:5; 18:14–20; I Sam. 15:23; 19:13; Hos. 3:4; Zech. 10:2. See IDOLATRY, IMAGES.

TEREBINTH. Is. 6:13. See IDOLATRY, IMAGES.

TERESH, tē′resh. **A chamberlain under Ahasuerus.**—Esth. 2:21.

TERRACE. II Chr. 9:11.

TERRESTRIAL. I Cor. 15:40.

TERRIBLE. Job 39:20; Ps. 10:18; Song of Sol. 6:4. Acts—Ps. 145:6. Crystal —Ez. 1:22. End—Zeph. 1:18. God— Deut. 7:21; Neh. 1:5; 4:14; 9:32; Ps. 47:2; 68:35; 76:12; Joel 2:11; Mal. 4:5. Hand of the—Jer. 15:21. Haughtiness of the—Is. 13:11. Majesty— Job 37:22. Name—Ps. 99:3. Things— Ex. 34:10; Deut. 10:21; Ps. 45:4; Is. 64:3. Wilderness—Deut. 1:19. Works —Ps. 66:30. See AFFRIGHT, FEAR, FRIGHTENED, HORRIBLE.

TERRIFY. Job 3:5; 31:34; Ps. 83:15; Zech. 1:21; Lu. 21:9; 24:37; Acts 24: 25; II Cor. 10:9.

TERROR. Job 13:21; 18:11; 41:14, 22; Ps. 78:33; Eccl. 12:5; Is. 17:14; 28: 19; 54:14; Ju. 17:17; 20:4; Lu. 21:11; I Pet. 3:6. Chamber of—Deut. 32:25. Consumed with—Ps. 73:19. Darkness, Of—Job 24:17; Ps. 91:5. Death, Of— Ps. 55:4. God, Of—Gen. 35:5; Ex. 23:27; Lev. 26:16; Job 9:34; 31:23; 33:1; Is. 3:10, 19, 21; 33:18. King, Of —Pr. 20:2; Rom. 13:3. Moab, Of— Jer. 48:39. Overtake—Job 27:20. People, Of—Hos. 10:5. Surrounded by— Jer. 46:5. See AFFRIGHT, FEAR, FRIGHTENED, HORROR, TERRIFY.

TERTIUS, tĕr′ti-us. **Paul's secretary.**— Rom. 16:22.

TERTULLUS, ter-tŭl′lus. **A Roman advocate.**—Acts 24:1.

TESTAMENT. Lu. 22:20; I Cor. 11:25; Heb. 7:22; 9:16. See COVENANTS.

TESTAMENT, NEW. See OUTLINE STUDIES IN THE BOOKS.

TESTAMENT, OLD. See OUTLINE STUDIES IN THE BOOKS.

TESTAMENT, OLD. Incidents referred to and quotations found in New Testament—See OUTLINE STUDIES IN THE BOOKS.

TESTATOR. Heb. 9:16, 17 (A.V.).

TESTIFY. Jer. 49:12; John 7:7; Acts 2:40. Against—Num. 35:30; Job 15: 6; Mic. 6:3. Gospel—Acts 20:24. Jehovah hath—Ruth 1:21. Pride of Israel doth—Hos. 7:10. Speak and— Jer. 6:10. Unto them—Lu. 16:28. Unto you—Acts 20:26. See WITNESS.

TESTIMONY. Ex. 31:18; 32:15; Ps. 25:10; Mt. 10:18. Apostles, Of—Acts 22:18; II Thess. 1:10; II Tim. 1:8. Bind up—Is. 8:16. Cleave unto—Ps. 119:31. Conscience, Of—II Cor. 1:12. Consider thy—Ps. 119:95. Delight, My—Ps. 119:24. Good—I Tim. 3:7. God, Of—I Cor. 2:1. Jesus, Of—Rev. 1:2; 19:10. Love thy—Ps. 119:119. Nations, Unto—Mt. 24:14. Our Lord, Of—II Tim. 1:8. Shake off dust for a —Mk. 6:11. Sure—Ps. 93:5. Wonderful—Ps. 119:129. See COMMANDMENT, WITNESS.

TETRARCH: Herod the.—Mt. 14:1. Of Galilee—Lu. 3:1, 19; Acts 13:1.

Philip the, of Ituræa—Lu. 3:1.

Lysanias the, of Abilene—Lu. 3:1.

THADDÆUS, thăd′dæ-us. One of the twelve, as given in Mt. 10:3; Mk. 3:18. He is probably to be identified with the Judas ("The Son of James") in Luke's lists—Lu. 6:16; Acts 1:13. In all four lists, Thaddæus, or Judas, comes next to Simon the Zealot, by which it seems he was either a brother or friend. Nothing is recorded of him except the question asked by him of Jesus, where it is said, "Not Iscariot" —John 14:22.

THANKSGIVING: Offered to God.— Ps. 69:30; 95:2; 100:4.

Occasion for.—II Cor. 4:15; 9:11, 12; Col. 2:7.

Through Christ.—Rom. 1:8; Col. 3:17. In the name of—Eph. 5:20; Heb. 13: 15.

Reasons for.—Gifts from God—I Tim. 4:3, 4. God's nearness—Ps. 75:1, 9. Supply of bodily needs—John 6:11; Acts 27:35; Rom. 14:6, 7; I Tim. 2:1. Conversion—Rom. 6:17. Victory over death—I Cor. 15:57. Divine guidance —II Cor. 2:14. Under all circumstances—Phil. 4:6.

Forms of.—Sacrifices—Lev. 7:12, 13, 15; 22:29; Ps. 50:14; 107:22; 116:17; Amos 4:5. Prayer—Neh. 11:17; Phil. 4:6; Col. 4:2. See PRAYER. Song— Neh. 12:8, 46; Ps. 147:7. See SONGS. Ministers appointed to lead in—I Chr. 16:4, 7; 23:30; II Chr. 31:2.

Occasions for.—Feasts—See FEASTS. In worship—Ps. 35:18; Dan. 6:10. Dedication—Neh. 12:27.

Prophecies concerning.—Is. 51:3; Jer. 30:19.

Christ sets example of.—Mt. 11:25; 26: 27–29; Mk. 14:22; Lu. 22:19; John 6: 11; 11:41.

THEATER. Adventure into—Acts 19: 31. Rushed into—Acts 19:29.

THEBEZ, thē'bez. A city near Shechem where Abimelech was slain.—Ju. 9: 50; II Sam. 11:21.

THEFT. Mk. 7:21. Sold for his—Ex. 22:3. Repented not of—Rev. 9:21. See STEALING.

THEOPHILUS, the-ŏph'i-lŭs. Name of the person to whom Luke addresses his Gospel and the Book of Acts.— Lu. 1:3; Acts 1:1.

THESSALONICA, thĕs'sa-lo-nī'ka. Capital of Macedonia.—Acts 17:1. See I and II THESSALONIANS in OUTLINE STUDIES IN THE BOOKS.

THEUDAS, theū'das. Name of a rebel. —Acts 5:36.

THICKET. Gen. 22:13; Ps. 74:5; Is. 10:34; Jer. 4:29.

THIEF. Deut. 24:7; Job 24:14; Ps. 50:18; Mt. 24:43. Ashamed—Jer. 2: 26. Cometh—Mt. 24:43; John 10:10; I Thess. 5:2. Day of the Lord cometh as—I Thess. 5:2. Despise a—Pr. 6:30. Night, In the—Mt. 24:43; Lu. 12:39; I Thess. 5:2; I Pet. 3:10; Rev. 3:2. See ROBBER, STEALING.

THIGH. Ex. 28:42; Song of Sol. 7:1; Ez. 24:4; Dan. 2:32; Rev. 19:16. Gird sword on—Ps. 45:3; Song of Sol. 3:8. Hand under—Gen. 24:2, 9; 47:29. Hollow of—Gen. 32:25, 31, 32. Make to rot—Num. 5:21, 22, 27. Smote upon —Ju. 3:16, 21; 15:8; Jer. 31:19; Ez. 21:12.

THIN. Ears—Gen. 41:6, 7, 23, 24. Glory —Is. 17:4. Hair—Lev. 13:30. Plates —Ex. 39:3.

THINK. Pr. 23:7; Jonah 1:6; Mt. 26: 36; Lu. 8:18; 10:36; 12:51; John 5: 39; 11:56. Above all that we ask or —Eph. 3:20. Affliction, To raise up— Phil. 1:17. Christ, Of—Mt. 22:42. Eternal life, Ye have—John 5:39. Evil, No—I Cor. 13:5. Heart, In his —Pr. 23:7. Highly, Not of himself more—Rom. 12:3. Himself—Prophet, To be a—I Cor. 14:37. Kill, To—Ex. 2:14. Not—Mt. 24:41. Rom. 12:3.

Prophet, Himself to be a—I Cor. 14: 37. Religious, To be—Jas. 1:26. Reprove—Job 6:26. Soberly—Rom. 12:3. Something, To be—Gal. 6:3. Spirit, I have—I Cor. 7:40. Standeth, That he—I Cor. 10:12. These things, On— Phil. 4:8. Wise, That he is—I Cor. 3:18. See MIND, THOUGHT.

THIRD DAY: Third day in creation.— Gen. 1:13.

Events occurring on.—Moses meets Jehovah in the mount—Ex. 19:11, 15, 16, 20. Abraham to sacrifice Isaac on— Gen. 22:4. Laban told, on third day, of Jacob's departure — Gen. 31:22. Third day after circumcision—Gen. 34:25. Pharaoh's feast on—Gen. 40: 20. Joseph interviews his brethren on —Gen. 42:18. Third day after childbirth—I Ki. 3:18. Interview between Jeroboam and Rehoboam—I Ki. 12: 12; II Chr. 10:12. Hezekiah goes to the house of Jehovah—II Ki. 20:5, 8. Esther appears before the king—Esth. 5:1. Temple finished on third day of the month—Ezra 6:15. Marriage in Cana on—John 2:1. David hides till —I Sam. 20:5. Offerings on—Lev. 7:17, 18; 19:6, 7; Num. 7:24; 29:20. Purification completed on third day—Num. 19:12, 19; 31:19. Israelites came unto their cities—Josh. 9:17. Battles on— Ju. 20:30; I Sam. 30:1; II Sam. 1:2.

Prophecies concerning Christ's resurrection on.—Hos. 6:2; Mt. 16:21; 17:23; 20:19; Mk. 9:31; 10:34; Lu. 9:22; 13: 32; 18:33; 24:46.

Prophecies fulfilled. — Lu. 24:7, 21, 46; Acts 10:40; I Cor. 15:4. Sepulchre of Christ guarded until the third day— Mt. 27:64.

Third day of Paul's voyage to Crete.— Acts 27:19. See THREE.

THIRST: Physical.—Children and cattle—Ex. 17:3. Of cattle—Ps. 104:11. Of Samson—Ju. 15:18. Of Israel—II Chr. 32:11; Neh. 9:15, 20; Is. 48:21. Of wounded—Job 24:11. Of Sisera— Ju. 4:19. In wilderness—II Sam. 17: 29; Ps. 107:5. Apostles—I Cor. 4:11; II Cor. 11:27. Jesus—John 19:28. I was thirsty and ye gave me drink— Mt. 25:35, 37, 42–44.

Laws concerning.—If he thirst give him to drink—Pr. 25:21; Rom. 12:20.

Figurative.—Picture of distress—Ps. 69:
21. Thirsty land—Ez. 19:13. As cold
water to a thirsty soul—Pr. 25:25.
Prophecies concerning.—Is. 21:14; 29:8;
32:6, 7. Shall thirst again—John 4:13.
Thirst as a punishment.—Deut. 28:48;
Is. 5:13; 41:17; 49:10; 50:2; Jer. 2:25;
Hos. 2:3; Amos 8:11, 13. Down from
thy glory and sit in thirst—Jer. 48:18.
Cleaveth to the roof of his mouth for
thirst—Lam. 4:4.
Spiritual thirst.—My soul thirsteth for
God—Ps. 42:2; 63:1; 143:6. Ho, every
one that thirsteth—Is. 55:1. In teach-
ings of Jesus: Thirst after righteous-
ness—Mt. 5:6. If any man thirst let
him come unto me—John 7:37. Proph-
ecies concerning: Shall never thirst—
John 4:14, 15; 6:35. See HUNGER,
LONG.
THISTLES: Prophecies concerning.—
Hos. 10:8.
Existence on earth punishment for sin.
—Gen. 3:18; Job 31:40.
In parables.—II Ki. 14:9; II Chr. 25:18;
Mt. 7:16. See JESUS, TEACHING OF.
THOMAS. Known as the doubter. His
character is greatly misunderstood.
He was querulous and gloomy; generally disposed to look on the dark side.
But though he fell into the depth of
despair on account of our Lord's
death, when he obtained the evidence
he demanded, he leaped to the very
summit of faith—John 20:24-28. The
trial of his faith made it harder to
endure, and Luke promotes him above
Bartholomew and Matthew—Acts 1:
13. Three incidents throw strong light
upon his character: (1) Ready to follow Jesus to death—John 11:16. (2)
Searching after the true way—John
14:5. (3) Reliance on sense rather
than on faith—John 20:24-29. He
was one of the seven who journeyed
north to Galilee to meet the Risen
Lord—John 21:2. Then again he was
among the apostles, awaiting the
power from on high—Acts 1:13. As it
is with some of the other apostles,
nothing is said in detail of his separate labors in the gospel.
THONGS. Acts 22:25.
**THORNS: Existence on earth punish-
ment for sin.**—Gen. 3:18; Ju. 8:7; Pr.

22:5; 24:31; Is. 32:13; Hos. 2:6; 9:6.
Consumed by fire.—Ex. 22:6; Is. 9:18;
10:17.
Warning against.—Jer. 4:3.
Prophecies concerning.—Is. 5:6; 7:23-
25; 34:13; 55:13.
Illustrative.—Ps. 58:9; 118:12; Pr. 15:
19; 26:9; Eccl. 7:6; Song of Sol. 2:2;
Is. 10:17; 33:12; Mic. 7:4; Nah. 1:10;
Heb. 6:8.
Figurative.—Num. 33:55; Josh. 23:13;
Job. 5:5; Is. 27:4; Jer. 12:13; Ez. 2:6;
28:24.
Crown of.—Mk. 15:17; John 19:2, 5. See
JESUS, TEACHING OF.
THOROUGHLY. Amend — Jer. 7:5.
Break—II Ki. 11:18. Healed—Ex. 21:
19. Purge—Is. 1:25. Wash—Ps. 51:2.
THOUGHT. Ps. 10:4; 73:16; II Cor. 10:
5. As a child—I Cor. 13:11. Diligent,
Of—Pr. 21:5. Evil—Mt. 15:19; Mk.
7:21. Foolishness, Of—Pr. 24:9. Fruit
of—Jer. 6:19. Guard your—Phil. 4:7.
Heart, Of—Acts 8:22. Jehovah knoweth—Ps. 94:11. Life, For your—Mt.
6:25; Lu. 12:22. Morrow, For the—
Mt. 6:34 (A.V.). Peace, Of—Jer. 29:
11. Peoples, Of—Ps. 33:10. Righteous, Of—Pr. 12:5. Troubled me—
Dan. 7:28. See MIND, THINK.
THOUSANDS. Ascribed but—I Sam.
18:8. Judah, Of—I Sam. 23:23. Ministered unto him—Dan. 7:10. Mother
of—Gen. 24:60. Showing lovingkindness unto—Deut. 33:2. Upon thousands—Ps. 68:17. See TEN.
THREAD. Abram said, "I will not
take a thread that is thine"—Gen. 14:
23. Scarlet thread, bound upon his
hand—Gen. 38:28, 30. Bind this in the
window—Josh. 2:18.
Figurative.—Samson breaks them like a
thread—Ju. 16:12. Like a thread of
scarlet—Song of Sol. 4:3.
THREATEN. Acts 4:17, 21; I Pet. 2:23.
THREATENING. Acts 4:29; 9:1. Forbear—Eph. 6:9. Heareth no—Pr. 13:8.
THREE. Apostles at transfiguration—
Mt. 17:1-8; Mk. 9:28; Lu. 9:28-36. In
Gethsemane—Mt. 26:36, 37; Mk. 5:37.
Days, In—Mt. 26:61. Jonah in whale's
belly—Mt. 12:40. Loaves—Lu. 11:5.
Measures of meal, Hid in—Mt. 13:33;
Lu. 13:21. Moses was hid—Heb. 11:
23. Now abideth faith, hope, love,

these—I Cor. 13:13. Son of man in heart of earth—Mt. 12:40. Tabernacles, Make—Mt. 17:4; Mk. 9:5; Lu. 9:33. Where two or—Mt. 18:20. Who bear witness—I John 5:8. See THIRD DAY.

THREE FOLD. Cord—Eccl. 4:12.

THRESH. Arise and—Mic. 4:13. Gilead —Amos 1:3. Mountains—Is. 41:15. Nations—Hab. 3:12. Sharp instrument, With—Is. 28:27. Wheat—I Chr. 21:20.

THRESHING-FLOOR. Jacob's death lamented at Atad—Gen. 50:10. Heave it as heave-offering of—Num. 15:20; 18:27. Gideon put fleece on—Ju. 6:37. Boaz winnows barley on—Ruth 3:2. Uzzah touches ark at Nacon's—II Sam. 6:6; I Chr. 13:9. David buys of Araunah—II Sam. 24:18-21. Place of temple—II Chr. 3:1. Image became like chaff of—Dan. 2:35. Purge his floor—Mt. 3:12; Lu. 3:17.

THRESHING-WAIN. Job 41:30.

THRESHING-WHEEL. Pr. 20:26.

THRESHOLD. Ez. 9:3. Dagon, Of—I Sam. 5:5. Desolation in—Zeph. 2:14. Gate, Of—Ez. 40:6, 7. Hands upon—Ju. 19:27. House, Of—Ez. 9:3; 10:4. Leap over—Zeph. 1:9. Shake—Amos 9:1. Shook—Is. 6:4. Water issued out from under—Ez. 47:1. Wood, Of —Ez. 41:25.

THRICE. Besought the Lord—II Cor. 12:8. I suffered shipwreck—II Cor. 11:25. Thou shalt deny me—Mt. 26: 34, 75; Mk. 14:30, 72; Lu. 22:34, 61. See THIRD day, THREE.

THRILL. Heart—Is. 60:5.

THROAT. Ps. 5:9; 115:7; Rom. 3:13. Catch by—Mt. 18:28. Dry—Ps. 69:3; Jer. 2:25. Knife in—Pr. 23:2.

THROB. Ps. 38:10.

THRONE: Temporal.—Establishment of —Col. 1:16.

Of kings.—Pharaoh—Gen. 41:40; Ex. 11:5; 12:29. Israel—I Ki. 2:4; 8:20, 25; 10:9; II Ki. 10:30; 15:12; II Chr. 6:10, 16. David—II Sam. 3:10; 7:13, 16; 14:9; I Ki. 1:13, 17, 20, 24, 27, 30, 35, 37; 2:12, 24, 33, 45; 3:6; 5:5; I Chr. 17:12, 14; 22:10; Ps. 89:4, 29, 36, 44; 122:5; Is. 9:7; Jer. 13:13. Solomon—I Ki. 1:37, 46-48; 2:19; 7:

7; 9:5; 10:18, 19; I Chr. 28:5; II Chr. 7:18.

Of ivory.—II Chr. 9:17, 18. Zimri—I Ki. 16:11. Jehoash—II Ki. 11:19; II Chr. 23:20. Jehoshaphat—I Ki. 22:10; II Chr. 18:9. Ahab—II Ki. 10:3. Jeroboam—II Ki. 13:13. Jehoiachin— II Ki. 25:28; Jer. 52:32. Ahasuerus— Esth. 1:2; 5:1. Nebuchadrezzar—Dan. 5:20. Nineveh—Jonah 3:6. Herod— Acts 12:21.

Spiritual.—Of Jehovah—I Ki. 22:19; I Chr. 29:23; II Chr. 9:8; 18:18; Job 26:9; Ps. 9:4, 7; 11:4; 45:6; 47:8; 89: 14; 93:2; 97:2; 103:19; Is. 6:1; 66:1; Jer. 3:17; 14:21; 17:12; 49:38; Lam. 5:19; Ez. 43:7; Zech. 6:13; Mt. 5:34; 23:22; Acts 7:49; Heb. 1:8; 8:1; 12:2. Of glory—I Sam. 2:8; Mt. 19:28; 25: 31. Of grace—Heb. 4:16. Revelation of—Rev. 1:4; 3:21; 4:2-10; 5:1, 6, 7, 11, 13; 6:16; 7:9, 10, 11, 15, 17; 8:3; 12:5; 14:3; 16:17; 19:4, 5; 20:4, 11; 21:5; 22:1, 3.

Prophecies concerning. — Governor — Neh. 3:7. Thrones of Nations—Is. 14: 9; 16:5; Jer. 1:15. Babylon—Is. 47:1; Jer. 43:10. Israel—Jer. 33:17. Princes —Ez. 26:16. David—Is. 22:23; Jer. 17:25; 22:2, 4, 30; 29:16; Lu. 1:32; Acts 2:30. Twelve—Lu. 22:30.

Proverbs concerning.—Pr. 16:12; 20:8, 28; 25:5; 29:14.

Visions of.—Ez. 1:26; 10:1; Dan. 7:9.

Figurative.—Wicked—Ps. 94:20; Is. 14: 13.

Illustrative.—Job 36:7.

THRONG. Ps. 42:4; 55:14; Mk. 3:9; 5:31. See MULTITUDE, JESUS, POPULARITY OF.

THROW. II Ki. 9:33; Mal. 1:4; Lu. 4: 29. Idols, Down—Ju. 6:25; See IDOLATRY. Overboard—Acts 27:18. Strongholds, Down—Mic. 5:11. Vaulted places, Down—Ez. 16:39. Wall, Down —II Sam. 20:15.

THROWN. II Sam. 20:21; Jer. 31:40. Altars, Down—I Ki. 19:10, 14. Another that shall not be—Mt. 24:2; Mk. 13:2; Lu. 21:6. Devil, By—Lu. 4:35. Mountains, Down—Ez. 38:20. Sea, Into—Ex. 15:1, 21. Walls, Down —Jer. 50:15. Wilderness, Into—Ez. 29:5. Wrath, In—Lam. 2:2, 17.

THRUST. Aside—Job 30:12; Ps. 140:4. Away—II Sam. 23:6; II Ki. 4:27; Acts 7:27, 39. Down—Ps. 36:12; 62: 4; Pr. 14:32. Office, From—Is. 22:19. Out—Ex. 11:1; 12:39; Ps. 5:10; Acts 7:45. Sword, With—II Sam. 11:2; 18: 14; I Chr. 10:4; Is. 13:15; Jer. 51:4; Zech. 13:3. See CAST.

THUMB. Ex. 29:20; Lev. 8:23, 24; 14: 14, 25, 28; Ju. 1:6, 7. See HAND.

THUMMIM. thum-mim. See URIM AND THUMMIM.

THUNDER. See METEOROLOGY.

THYATIRA. thy-a-ti-ra. A city in Asia Minor. Lydia comes from—Acts 16: 34. One of the seven churches—Rev. 1:11; 2:18.

TIBERIAS, ti-bē'ri-as. (1) **A city.—** John 6:23. Sea of—See GALILEE.

TIBERIUS CÆSAR, ti-bē'ri-us sē'sar. See CÆSAR.

TIBHATH, tĭb'hath. **A Syrian town.—** I Chr. 18:8. See TEBAH.

TIBNI, tĭb'ni. **Omri's rival for the throne of Israel.—**I Ki. 6:21.

TIDAL, ti'dal. **King of Gorim.—**Gen. 14:1.

TIDINGS: Good tidings.—Of Jacob to Laban—Gen. 29:13. Jonathan, Bearer of—I Ki. 1:42. Told by the four lepers —II Ki. 7:9. Glad tidings—Jer. 20: 15. From Gabriel to Zacharias—Lu. 1:19. By angel to the shepherds— Lu. 2:10. Of promise—Acts 13:32. The gospel as good tidings—Lu. 8:1; Rom. 10:15, 16; I Thess. 3:6. See GOSPEL.

Evil tidings.—Ex. 33:4; I Sam. 4:19; 11:4, 5; 27:9–11; II Sam. 13:30; Ps. 112:7. Of Saul's death—II Sam. 4:4, 10. Absalom's death—II Sam. 18:19. Brought to Joab—I Ki. 2:28. From Ahijah to Jeroboam—I Ki. 14:6. To chief captain—Acts 21:31. Of Pharaoh's army to Chaldeans—Jer. 37:5.

Taken to idols.—I Chr. 10:9.

Prophecies concerning.—Good tidings— Is. 40:9; 41:27; 52:7; Nah. 1:15. Of the east and the north—Dan. 11:44. Evil tidings—Jer. 49:23; Ez. 21:7. See GOSPEL.

TIE. II Ki. 7:10; Pr. 6:21; Mt. 21:2; Acts 22:25.

TIGLATH-PILESER, tĭg'lath-pil-ē'ser. **An Assyrian king.—**Conquers Pekah king of Israel—II Ki. 15:29. Forms alliance with Ahaz king of Judah— II Ki. 16:7, 10; II Chr. 28:20. Takes part of Israel captive—I Chr. 5:6, 26.

TIKVAH, tĭk'vah. (1) **Father of Jahaziah.—**Ezra 10:15.

(2) **Father-in-law of Huldah the prophetess.—**II Ki. 22:14.

TILE. Ez. 4:1; Lu. 5:19. See BRICK.

TILL, v. Ground—Gen. 2:5, 7; 3:19, 23; II Sam. 9:10; Pr. 12:11; Is. 30:24; Heb. 6:7. See AGRICULTURE.

TILLER. Gen. 4:2; Zech. 13:5.

TILON, ti'lon. **A man of Judah.—**I Chr. 4:20.

TIMÆUS, ti-mæ'us. **Father of Bartimæus the blind beggar.—**Mk. 10:46.

TIMBER. Lev. 14:45; I Ki. 5:6, 10; Hab. 2:11.

TIMBREL. Ex. 15:20; Ju. 11:34; I Sam. 18:6; II Sam. 6:5; Ps. 149:3; 150:4. See MUSIC.

TIME. Acceptable—Ps. 69:13; II Cor. 6:2. All—Job 27:10; Ps. 10:5. Appointed—Dan. 8:19. Drew near—Gen. 47:29. Eternal—Rom. 16:25; I Tim. 1:9. Every purpose, For—Eccl. 3:1. Evil, Of—Ps. 37:19. For a little— Jas. 4:14; Rev. 6:11. From this, forth —Is. 125:2. Is at hand—Mt. 26:18; Rev. 1:3. Is not yet come—John 7:6. Judge nothing before—I Cor. 4:5. Love, Of—Ez. 16:8. Past—II Sam. 15:34; Is. 16:13; Col. 1:21. Promise, Of—Acts 7:17. Redeeming the—Eph. 5:16. Set—Ps. 75:2. Short—Ps. 89: 47. Shortened, Is—I Cor. 7:29. That she should repent—Rev. 2:21. To seek Jehovah—Hos. 10:12. See SEEKING, DAY, HOUR, MEASURE, MONTH, YEAR.

TIMNA, tĭm'na. (1) **Daughter of Seir.** —Gen. 36:22; I Chr. 1:59.

(2) **Concubine of Eliphaz son of Esau.** —Gen. 36:12.

(3) **Grandson of Esau.—**I Chr. 1:36.

(4) **Duke of Edom.—**Gen. 36:40; I Chr. 1:51.

TIMNAH, tĭm'nah. (1) **A city in Judah.** —Gen. 38:12–14; Josh. 15:10, 17; II Chr. 28:18.

(2) **A city in Dan.—**Ju. 14:1-5.

TIMNATH-HERES, tĭm'nath-hē'rēs. **Place where Joshua was buried.—**Ju. 2:9.

TIMNATH-SERAH, tĭm-nath–sē′rah. Josh. 19:50; 24:30. Same as preceding.

TIMNITE, tĭm′nite. **A man of Timnah.** —Ju. 15:6.

TIMON, tī′mon. **One of the seven deacons**—Acts 6:5.

TIMOTHY. See OUTLINE STUDIES IN THE BOOKS.

TIMOTHY. Epistles to—See OUTLINE STUDIES IN THE BOOKS.

TIN. Is. 1:25; Ez. 22:18; 27:12. See METALS.

TINGLE. Ears—I Sam. 3:11; II Ki. 21:12; Jer. 19:3.

TIP. Ear, Of—Ex. 29:20; Lev. 8:23, 24; 14:14, 17, 25, 28. Finger, Of—Lu. 16: 24.

TIPHSAH, tĭph′sah. (1) **A city in Judah.**—II Ki. 15:16.

(2) **A city on the river Euphrates.**—I Ki. 4:24.

TIRAS, tī′răs. **Son of Japheth.**—Gen. 10:2; I Chr. 1:5.

TIRATHITES, tī′rath-ites. I Chr. 2:55.

TIRES. Ez. 44:18. See HEAD.

TIRHAKAH, tĭr′ha-kah. **King of Ethiopia.**—II Ki. 19:9; Is. 37:9.

TIRHANAH, tĭr′ha-nah. **Son of Caleb.** —I Chr. 2:48.

TIRIAH, tĭr′i-a. **A descendant of Judah.** —I Chr. 4:16.

TIRZAH, tĭr′zah. (1) **A city in Ephraim.** —Josh. 12:24; I Ki. 14:17; 15:21, 33; 16:6–23; II Ki. 15:14, 16; Song of Sol. 6:4.

(2) **Daughter of Zelophehad.**—Num. 26: 33; 27:1; 36:11; Josh. 17:3.

TISHBITE. Elijah the—I Ki. 17:1; II Ki. 1:3, 8; 9:36.

TITHES. Tenths of produce, property, or spoils, dedicated to sacred use—I Sam. 8:15, 17.

First mention of: Abraham presents to Melchizedek—Gen. 14:18–20; Heb. 7: 1–10. Jacob, conditionally, devotes one tenth to God—Gen. 28:20–22.

The usage of consecrated tithes existed among the Greeks, Romans and others. —See I Macc. 11:35; Herodotus 1:89; 4:152; 5:77; 7:132; 9:81; Cicero, vss. 2:3, 6, 7; Diod. Sic. 5:42; 11:33; 20: 44.

The Mosaic Law with regard to.—Lev. 27:30–32.

The Levites were the recipients.—Num. 18:21–24; Deut. 12:5–19; 14:22–27; Heb. 7:5–9.

Levites required to give a tithe of tithe to Jehovah.—(Num. 18:25–32; Neh. 10:38.) For the use of the priests.

If anything is redeemed a fifth part of value is added.—Lev. 27:31.

At the end of every three years all tithes brought for good of Levite, sojourner, poor, etc.—Deut. 14:28–29; 26:12–14.

Law to prevent covetous from changing the tithe.—Lev. 27:33.

Jews reproved for neglecting and abusing.—Neh. 13:10; Mal. 3:8.

Nehemiah adopts rigorous measures and restores.—Neh. 10:35–39; 12:44; 13: 5, 11–12.

Hezekiah restores the.—II Chr. 31:4–12. Must bring into store-house—Mal. 3: 10; Amos 4:4.

Rulers appointed to secure honest distribution.—II Chr. 31:12–20; Neh. 13: 13.

In the Jubilee year there was no.—Lev. 27:17–18.

Pharisees scrupulous about paying.— —Mt. 23:23; Lu. 11:42; 18:12.

New Testament teaching not limited to. —I Cor. 16:2; II Cor. 9:7–12. See GIFT, GIVING, LIBERALITY.

TITLE. Pilate wrote a—John 19:19, 20. See JESUS, NAMES AND TITLES.

TITTLE. Law, Of the—Mt. 5:18; Lu. 16:17.

TITUS, tī′tus. See OUTLINE STUDIES IN THE BOOKS.

TIZITE, tī′zīte. **One of David's mighty men.**—I Chr. 11:45.

TOAH, tō′ah. **A Levite**—I Chr. 6:34.

TOB, tŏb. **A district in Syria.**—Ju. 11: 3, 5.

TOB-ADONIJAH, tŏb-ăd′o-nī′jah. **A Levite.**—II Chr. 17:8.

TOBIAH, to-bī′ah. (1) **Ancestor of some who had lost their genealogies.**—Ezra 2:60; Neh. 7:62.

(2) **A Levite.**—II Chr. 17:8.

(3) **Ancestor of some who returned from exile.**—Zech. 6:10, 14.

(4) **An Ammonite who opposed Nehemiah.**—Neh. 2:10, 19; 4:3, 7; 6:1, 12–19; 13:4–8.

TOBIJAH, to-bī′jah. See TOBIAH (3).

TOCHEN, tō'ken. **A city in Simeon.**—I Chr. 4:32.

TODAY. Delivered into hand—I Sam. 24:10. Deny Jesus—Mk. 14:30. Salvation is come—Lu. 19:9. Seen things —Lu. 5:26. Thou shalt be one with me—Lu. 23:43. Work—Ex. 14:13; Ruth 2:19. See DAY.

TOES. Great—Ex. 29:20; Lev. 8:23, 24; 14:14, 17, 25, 28; Ju. 1:6, 7. Part of iron, part of clay—Dan. 2:41. Six— II Sam. 21:20; I Chr. 20:6. See FEET.

TOGARMAH, to-gär-mah. **Grandson of Japheth.**—Gen. 10:3; I Chr. 1:6; Ez. 27:14; 38:6.

TOGETHER. Acts 2:1; I Thess. 4:17. Assemble—I Sam. 14:20; Pr. 22:2; Acts 11:26; 16:13; 25:17. See CONGREGATION. Cry out—Lu. 23:18. Fashioned—Job 10:8. Gathered—See CONGREGATION, GATHER. Joined—Mk. 10:9. Praise—Ps. 34:3. Reason—Is. 1:18; Mk. 12:28; Lu. 24:15. See MIND, REASON. Run—Mk. 6:33. Set down—Lu. 22:55. Strive—See STRIVE. Take counsel—See COUNSEL. Walk—Amos 3:3. Work—Rom. 8:28. See FELLOWSHIP, GATHER, PARTAKE.

TOHU, tō'hu. **Ancestor of Samuel.**—I Sam. 1:1.

TOI, tō'ī. **King of Hamath in David's time.**—II Sam. 8:9, 16; I Chr. 18:9, 10.

TOIL. Gen. 5:29; 41:51; Deut. 26:7; Josh. 7:3; I Cor. 4:12. All night—Lu. 5:5. Bread of—Ps. 127:2. Eat in— Gen. 3:17. Not neither do they spin— Mt. 6:28; Lu. 12:27. Walketh upon —Job 18:8. See LABOR.

TOKEN. Of covenant—Gen. 9:12, 13, 17; 17:11; Ex. 3:12. Creates fear— Ps. 65:8. Blood as token—Ex. 12:13. Consecration of first-born—Ex. 13:16. Aaron's rod used as—Num. 17:10. Of virginity—Deut. 22:15, 17, 20. Asked for—Josh. 2:12; Ps. 86:17. Sent to Egypt—Ps. 135:9. Judas's kiss token of betrayal—Mk. 14:44. Paul's token —II Thess. 3:17. Of perdition—Phil. 1:28. Of righteous judgment of God— II Thess. 1:5.

TOLA, tō'lä. **(1) Son of Issachar.**—Gen. 46:13; Num. 26:23; I Chr. 7:1, 2.

(2) A judge of Israel.—Ju. 10:1.

TOLAD, tō'läd. **A city in Simeon.**—I Chr. 4:29.

TOLAITES. Descendants of Tola.— Num. 26:23.

TOLD. Beforehand—Mk. 13:23. Cain— Gen. 4:8. Esther, the king—Esth. 2: 22. Of these—Acts 3:24. See TELL.

TOLERABLE. Lu. 10:12.

TOLERANCE. See INTOLERANCE.

TOLL. Place of—Mt. 9:9. Receive— Mt. 17:25. See TAXES.

TOMB. Lu. 11:44. Coming forth out of —Mt. 8:28. Going unto—John 11:30. Had been in—John 11:17. Keep watch over—Job 21:32. Laid in—Mk. 6:29. New—Mt. 27:60. Opened—Mt. 27:52. Prophets, Of—Lu. 11:47. Stone at door of—Mt. 27:60. See BURIAL, BURIAL PLACE, SEPULCHRE.

TONE. Change my—Gal. 4:20.

TONGUES.

TONGUE (in the sense of speech).—Ex. 4:10; Josh. 10:21; II Sam. 23:2; Job 27:4; 33:2; Ps. 39:3; 51:14; 66:17; 71: 24; 139:4; Pr. 16:1. Speech hindered —Ps. 22:15; 137:6; Ez. 3:26.

Kinds of.—Wicked—Job 20:12; Ps. 10: 7; 31:20; 34:13; 39:1; 52:2, 4; 64:3, 8; Jer. 18:18. Deceitful—Ps. 50:19; 52: 4; 109:2; 120:2, 3; Jer. 9:8; Mic. 6:12; Zeph. 3:13; Rom. 3:13. Lying—Pr. 6: 36; Pr. 6:17; 12:19; 17:4, 7; 21:6; 26: 28; Jer. 9:3, 5; 23:31–32; Col. 3:9. Unjust—Job 6:30. Perverse—Pr. 10:31; 17:20. Crafty—Job 15:5. Flattering —Ps. 5:9; 12:3, 4; Pr. 6:24; 28:23. Mischievous—Pr. 17:4. Slanderous— Ps. 15:3. Soft—Pr. 25:15. Backbiting —Pr. 25:23. Against Jehovah—Is. 3:8. Gentle—Pr. 15:4.

Tongues mentioned.—Of the wise—Pr. 12:18; 15:2. Nobles—Job 29:10. Righteous—Ps. 37:30; Pr. 10:20. Learned —Is. 50:4. Child—Lam. 4:4. Men—I Cor. 13:1, 8; 14:5, 6, 18. Worthy woman—Pr. 31:26. Deaf-mute cured —Mk. 7:33, 35. Zacharias—Lu. 1:64. Rich man. See TEACHING OF JESUS. Viper — Job 20:16. Leviathan — Job 41:1. Dogs—Ju. 7:5; Ps. 68:23.

Prophecies concerning.—Stammerer—Is. 32:4. Dumb—Is. 35:6; 41:17. Wicked —Is. 54:17; 57:4. Rage of—Hos. 7:16. Destruction of—Zech. 14:12. Every tongue shall confess God—Is. 45:23; Rom. 14:11; confess Jesus—Phil. 2:11.

Figurative use of.—Ex. 11:7; Ps. 45:1; 57:4; 73:9; 140:3; Song of Sol. 4:11; Is. 11:15; 30:27.

Illustrative.—Is. 5:24; Acts 2:3; Rev. 16:10.

Miscellaneous.—Silence of—Pr. 21:23. Scourge of—Job 5:21. In songs of praise—Ps. 51:14; 119:172; 126:2; Acts 2:26. Power of—Pr. 18:21.

Control of.—Jas. 1:26; 3:5, 6, 8; I Pet. 3:10; I John 3:18.

TONGUES (or LANGUAGE). A particular language—Gen. 10:5, 20, 31; Deut. 28:49. All tongues—Rev. 7:9; 10:11; 11:9; 13:7; 17:15. Strange tongues—Ps. 55:9; I Cor. 13:1, 8; 14: 2, 4, 9, 13, 14, 19, 21, 26, 27; Rev. 5:9; 14:6. Syrian—Ezra 4:7. Chaldeans—Dan. 1:4. Greek—Rev. 9:11.

Prophecies concerning.—Strange tongues—Is. 28:11; 33:19. Of nations—Is. 66:18.

Gift of tongues at Pentecost.—Acts 2:3, 4, 11; 10:46; 19:6. Spiritual gift of—I Cor. 12:10, 28. For a sign—I Cor. 14: 22, 23, 39. See LANGUAGE, TONGUE.

TOOLS: First mentioned.—Gen. 4:22.

Uses of.—Is. 44:12–14. Aaron, in making calf—Ex. 32:4. David's disposition of captives—II Sam. 12:31; I Chr. 20:3. For plowing and harrowing—Is. 28:24–28; Lu. 9:62. Smiting with hammers—Ju. 4:21; 5:26; Is. 44:12; Jer. 50:23.

Sharpening of tools.—I Sam. 13:19–21.

Forbidden in erection of altars.—Ex. 20:25; Deut. 27:5.

Not used in erection of temple.—I Ki. 6:7.

Preparation of temple material.—Stones sawed out—I Ki. 7:9. Masons, woodmen, and ironmen employed—I Ki. 5:15–18; I Chr. 22:1–3; II Ki. 12: 11–12.

Tools and implements used.—Anvil—Is. 41:7. Awl—Ex. 21:6; Deut. 15:17. Axe—Deut. 19:5; 20:19; Ju. 9:48; I Sam. 13:20, 21; II Sam. 12:31; I Ki. 6:7; II Ki. 6:5, 6; I Chr. 20:3; Ps. 74: 5, 6; Is. 10:15; 44:12; Jer. 10:3; 46:22; Mt. 3:10; Lu. 3:9. *Axe-head*—II Ki. 6:5. *Axe-helve*—Deut. 19:5. *Battle axe* —Jer. 51:20; Ez. 26:9. Balances or scales—Lev. 19:36; Job 6:2; 31:6; Pr. 11:1; 16:11; 20:23; Is. 40:12, 15; 46:6;

Jer. 32:10; Ez. 5:1; 45:10; Dan. 5:27; Hos. 12:7; Amos 8:5; Mic. 6:11; Rev. 6:5. Bellows—Num. 7:13–85; Jer. 6:9. Besom—Is. 14:23. Buckets—Num. 24: 7; Is. 40:15. Coulter—I Sam. 13:20, 21. Distaff—Pr. 31:19. File—I Sam. 13:21. Firepans—Ex. 27:3; 38:3; Num. 16:6; I Ki. 7:50; II Ki. 25:15; Jer. 52: 19. Flesh-hooks—*Brazen forks with three prongs*—Ex. 27:3; 38:3, 28; Num. 4:14; I Sam. 2:13, 14. Fork—Ex. 27: 3; I Sam. 13:21. Goad—Ju. 3:31; I Sam. 13:21; Eccl. 12:11. Graving tool —Ex. 32:4. Hammer—Ju. 4:21; 5:26; I Ki. 6:7; Ps. 74:6; Is. 41:7; 44:12; Jer. 10:4; 23:29; 50:23. Harrow—II Sam. 12:31; I Chr. 20:3; Job 39:10; Is. 28:24. Hatchet—Ps. 74:6. Hoe—Is. 5:6. Hooks—Ex. 38:28. Knife—Gen. 22:6, 10; Ju. 5:23; 19:29; I Ki. 18:28; Pr. 23:2; 30:14; Ezra 1:9. Penknife—Jer. 36:23. Mattock—I Sam. 13:20, 21; Is. 7:25. Maul—Pr. 25:18. Mill—Ex. 11:5; Num. 11:8; Deut. 24: 6; Mt. 24:41; Rev. 18:22. Millstone—Deut. 24:6; Ju. 9:53; II Sam. 11:21; Job 41:24; Is. 47:2; Jer. 25:10; Mt. 18:6; Mk. 9:42; Lu. 17:2; Rev. 18:21. Mortar—Gen. 11:3; Num. 11:8; Pr. 27:22; Is. 41:25; Nah. 3:14; Nail—I Chr. 22:3; II Chr. 3:9; Is. 41:7; Jer. 10:4; John 20:25; Col. 2:14. *Figurative*—Ezra 9:8; Is. 22:23, 25; Zech. 10:4; Eccl. 12:11. Pen—Job 19:24; Ps. 45:1; Is. 8:1; Jer. 8:8; 17:1; III John 13. Penknife—See KNIFE. Plane —Is. 44:13. Plow—Deut. 22:10; Ju. 14:18; I Ki. 19:19; Job 1:14; Ps. 129: 3; Pr. 20:4; Is. 28:24; Jer. 26:18; Hos. 10:13; Amos 6:12; Mic. 3:12; Lu. 17: 7; 9:62; I Cor. 9:10. Plowshares—Is. 2:4; Joel 3:10; Mic. 4:3. Plummet—II Ki. 21:13; Is. 28:17; Zech. 4:10. Plumb-line—Amos 7:7, 8. Pruning hooks or knives—Lev. 25:3, 4; Is. 2:4; 5:6; 18:5; Joel 3:10; Mic. 4:3. Razor —Num. 6:5; Ju. 13:5; 16:17; I Sam. 1:11; Ps. 52:2; Is. 7:20; Ez. 5:1. Rod —Gen. 30:37, 39, 41; Ex. 7:12; Num. 17:2, 6, 7, 9; Is. 28:27; Jer. 48:17; Ez. 19:11, 12; II Cor. 11:25. Ropes—Ju. 16:11, 12; II Sam. 17:13; I Ki. 20:31, 32; Is. 5:18; Acts 27:32. Saw—II Sam. 12:31; I Ki. 7:9; I Chr. 20:3; Is. 10:15. Shovel—Ex. 27:3; 38:3;

Num. 4:14; I Ki. 7:45; II Ki. 25:14; Jer. 52:18. Sickle—Deut. 16:9; 23:25; Jer. 50:16; Joel 3:13; Mk. 4:29; Rev. 14:14–19. Sieve—Is. 30:28; Amos 9:9; Lu. 22:31. Snuffer—Ex. 37:23; Num. 4:9; I Ki. 7:50; II Ki. 12:13; 25:14; II Chr. 4:22; Jer. 52:18. Spindle—Pr. 31:19. Spoons—Ex. 25:29; Num. 4:7; 7:14–86; I Ki. 7:50; II Ki. 25:14; II Chr. 4:22; Jer. 52:18. Staff—Gen. 32: 10; 38:18, 25; Ex. 12:11; 21:19; Num. 13:23; 22:27; Ju. 6:21; I Sam. 17:7, 40; II Sam. 3:29; 21:19; 23:7, 21; II Ki. 4:29, 31; 18:21; I Chr. 11:23; 20:5; Ps. 23:4; Is. 9:4; 10:5, 15, 24; 14:5; 28:17; 30:32; 36:6; Jer. 48:17; Ex. 29:6; Hos. 4:12; Zech. 8:4; 11:10, 14; Mk. 6:8; Heb. 11:21. Threshing instrument—II Sam. 24:22; I Chr. 21: 23; Is. 28:27; 41:15; Amos 1:3. Tongs —I Ki. 7:49; II Chr. 4:21; Is. 6:6. Weaver's beam—Ju. 16:14; I Sam. 17: 7; II Sam. 21:19; I Chr. 11:23; 20:5. Weaver's shuttle—Job 7:6. Winepress. See WINE. Yoke—See YOKE, WAR, VESSEL.

TOOTH. See TEETH.

TOP. Ex. 26:24; Ez. 17:3. May reach unto heaven—Gen. 11:4. Mountain— Is. 17:9. Mulberry trees, Of—II Sam. 5:24. Pillars—Zech. 4:7. Staff, Of— Heb. 11:21. Woven from the—John 19:23.

TOPAZ. Rev. 21:20. A row of—Ex. 28: 17. Ethiopia, Of — Job 28:19. Thy covering—Ez. 28:13. See PRECIOUS STONES.

TOPHEL, tō'phel. A place in the wilderness of Sinai—Deut. 1:1.

TOPHETH, tō'pheth. A place in the valley of Hinnom—II Ki. 23:10. Events connected with.—Defiled by Josiah—II Ki. 23:10. Children were burned by Jews at—Jer. 7:31, 32; 32: 35. By Ahaz—II Chr. 28:3. By Manasseh at—II Chr. 33:6. Place of punishment.—Is. 30:33. Prophecies concerning.—Jer. 7:31, 32; 19:6, 11, 13. Jeremiah sent there to prophesy—Jer. 19:14.

TOPMOST. Ez. 17:4.

TORCH. Flaming torch—Gen. 15:17; Zech. 12:6. Chariots like—Nah. 2:4. Torches—John 18:3. Star burning as —Rev. 8:10. Torches in pitchers—

Ju. 7:16, 20. Burning torches—Job 41:19. Appearance of—Ez. 1:13. See LAMP.

TORMAH, tôr'mah. Ju. 9:31 (marg.).

TORMENT. Day and night—Rev. 20: 10. Diseases and—Mt. 4:24. Fear of —Rev. 18:15. Fire and brimstone, With—Rev. 14:10. Scorpion, Of— Rev. 9:5. Us—Mt. 8:29. See HELL, JUDGMENT, PAIN, PUNISHMENT, TORTURE.

TORN. Hos. 1:6; Mk. 9:26. Joseph— Gen. 37:33. In pieces—Gen. 44:28; Acts 23:10. Wrath, In—Job 16:9. See TARE, TEAR.

TORTURED. Heb. 11:35. See PUNISHMENT, TORMENT.

TOSS. To and fro—II Chr. 29:8; Eph. 4:14. Tempest, With—Is. 54:11. Up and down—Ps. 109:23. Waves—Jer. 5:22.

TOTTERING. Ps. 62:3.

TOU, tō'u. I Chr. 18:9. See TOI.

TOUCH. Gen. 3:3; Lu. 8:46; Col. 2:21. Apple of his eye—Zech. 2:8. Bone— Job 2:5. Burdens, Not—Lu. 11:46. East wind—Ez. 17:10. Evil, No—Job 5:19. Hearts, God had—I Sam. 10:26. Hope—Acts 23:6. Me not—John 20: 17. With feeling of our infirmities— Heb. 4:15.

TOUCHING. As—Acts 19:40. *Conscience, The*—Heb. 9:9. *Gentiles that have believed*—Acts 21:25. *Gospel, The*—Rom. 11:28. Law—Phil. 3:5. *Ministering to saints*—II Cor. 9:1. *Resurrection of dead* — Acts 24:21. *Those, once enlightened*—Heb. 6:4. Zeal—Phil. 3:6. Garment—Mt. 9:20, 21; 14:36; Mk. 5:28; 6:56; Lu. 6:19; 8:44. Jesus—Bier—Lu. 7:14. Disciples —Mt. 17:7. Ear—Lu. 22:51. Eyes— Mt. 9:29; 20:34. Hand—Mt. 8:15. Leper—Mt. 8:2, 3; Mk. 1:41; Lu. 5:12, 13. Tongue—Mk. 7:33.

TOW. Ju. 16:9; Is. 1:31; 43:17.

TOWEL. John 13:4.

TOWER. Tower of Babel—Gen. 11:4, 5. Eder—Gen. 35:21. Of Penuel—Ju. 8: 9, 17. Of David—Song of Sol. 4:4. Of the flock—Mic. 4:8. Of the furnaces —Neh. 3:11; 12:38. Of Hananel— Neh. 3:1; 12:39; Jer. 31:38; Zech. 14: 10. Of Hammeah—Neh. 3:1; 12:39. Of Lebanon—Song of Sol. 7:4. Of

Shechem—Ju. 9:46, 47, 49. Of Syene—Ez. 29:10; 30:6. Of Siloam—Lu. 13:4. Of Zion—Ps. 48:12. Of watchmen—II Ki. 17:9; 18:8. A strong tower—Ju. 9:50–52. In the Land of Chaldeans—Is. 23:13. In Jezreel—II Ki. 9:17. In Judah—II Chr. 14:7. In Jerusalem—II Chr. 26:9, 15; 32:5; Neh. 3:25–27. In wilderness—II Chr. 26:10. In forests—II Chr. 27:4. Valorous men in—Ez. 27:11. Lofty tower —Is. 2:15.

Destruction of.—Is. 30:25; 32:14; 33:18; Ez. 26:4, 9. Habakkuk upon—Hab. 2:1. Parable of householder—Mt. 21: 33; Mk. 12:1. Count the cost of— Lu. 14:28.

Figurative.—The Lord as—Ps. 61:3; Pr. 18:10. Nose like—Song of Sol. 7:4. Neck like—Song of Sol. 4:4. Breasts like—Song of Sol. 8:10. Built a tower —Is. 5:2; Mt. 21:33. High tower— II Sam. 22:3; Ps. 144:2.

TOWNCLERK. Acts 19:35.

TOWNS. Num. 21:25; Josh. 13:30; 15: 45, 47; 17:11; Ju. 11:26; I Ki. 4:13; I Chr. 2:23; 7:28; 8:12; II Chr. 13:19; Mk. 1:38. Buildeth with blood—Hab. 2:12. Evil against—Jer. 19:15. Unwalled—Deut. 3:5; Esth. 9:19. Walled —I Sam. 23:7. See CITIES, VILLAGES.

TRACED. Lu. 1:3; Rom. 11:33.

TRACHONITIS, trăk-ŏ-nī'tĭs. **Tetrarchy of Philip.**—Lu. 3:1.

TRADE, *n.* Acts 18:3. See ARTS and TRADES.

TRADE, *v.* Gen. 34:10, 21; Ez. 27:12– 17. Gain by—Lu. 19:15; Jas. 4:13. Pounds, with ten—Lu. 19:13. Talents, With—Mt. 25:16. See COMMERCE.

TRADERS. I Ki. 10:15; II Chr. 9:14. See COMMERCE, MERCHANTS.

TRADITION. II Thess. 3:6. Elders, Of the—Mt. 15:2–6; Mk. 7:3–13. See ELDERS OF ISRAEL. Fathers, Of—Gal. 1:14. Hold fast—I Cor. 11:2; II Thess. 2:15. Men, Of—Col. 2:8. See DOCTRINE.

TRAFFIC. Gen. 42:34; I Ki. 10:15; Job 41:6; Is. 23:8; Ez. 17:4; 28:5, 18. See COMMERCE.

TRAFFICKER. Is. 23:8; Ez. 27:20.

TRAIN, *n.* I Ki. 10:2; Job 38:32; Is. 6:1; 47:2.

TRAIN, *v.* Child—Pr. 22:6. Men—Gen. 14:14; I Chr. 12:8. See SOLDIERS, WAR. Young women—Tit. 2:4. See INSTRUCTION.

TRAITOR. II Tim. 3:4. Judas—Lu. 6: 16. See TREASON.

TRAMPLE. Job 39:15; Ps. 68:30; Is. 1:12; 63:3; Dan. 8:7. Pearls—Mt. 7: 6. Serpent—Ps. 91:13. See Gen. 3:15.

TRANCE. Num. 24:4; Acts 10:10; 11:5; 22:17.

TRANQUILLITY. Pr. 14:30; Dan. 4:27; I Tim. 2:2. See CHRISTIAN GRACES, QUIETNESS, PEACE.

TRANSFER. II Sam. 3:10; I Cor. 4:6.

TRANSFIGURATION OF JESUS. Mt. 17:1–8; Mk. 9:2–8; Lu. 9:28–36; John 1:14; II Pet. 1:16.

TRANSFORM. See CONFORMATION AND TRANSFORMATION.

TRANSGRESS, TRANSGRESSION. Num. 14:41; Ps. 59:3; 107:17; Is. 58: 1; Pr. 18:2; II Pet. 2:16. Adam's— Rom. 5:14. Added because of, Law— Gal. 3:19. Blot out—Is. 43:25. See FORGIVENESS. Commandments — See COMMANDMENTS. Confess—Ps. 32:5. See CONFESSION. Covereth—Pr. 10: 12; 17:9. Delivered from—Ps. 39:8. Into hand of—Job 8:4. Evil man, Of —Pr. 29:6. Forgive—Gen. 50:17; Ps. 32:1; 65:3. See FORGIVENESS. Jacob, Of—Mic. 1:5. Know—Job 13:23; Ps. 51:3. Law added because of—Gal. 3: 19. No transgression where there is no law—Rom. 4:15. Love covereth all—Pr. 10:12. Mouth—Pr. 16:10. See WORDS. Shall not—Ps. 17:3. No man —I Thess. 4:6. Pardon—Ex. 23:21; Job 7:21. See FORGIVENESS. Pass over —Pr. 19:11. Recompense of reward, Receive—Heb. 2:2. See JUDGMENT, PUNISHMENT. Redemption—Heb. 9: 15. See REDEMPTION, SALVATION. Rulers—Jer. 2:8. Sealed—Job 14:17. Traditions—Mt. 15:2. See TRADITIONS. Two—Hos. 10:10. Visit—Ps. 89:32. See JUDGMENT. Without—Job 33:9; 34:6; Ps. 19:13. See SIN.

TRANSGRESSOR. Is. 48:8. Law, Of the—Rom. 2:27. Numbered with—Is. 53:12; Lu. 22:37. Wicked—Ps. 59:5. See SIN, SINNER, WICKED.

TRANSLATION. Enoch, Of—Gen. 5: 24; Heb. 11:5. Elijah, Of—II Ki. 2:

11. Kingdom of the Son of His love —Col. 1:13.

TRANSPARENT. Rev. 21:21.

TRAP: Trap set.—Jer. 5:26.

Kinds of.—Nations as—Josh. 23:13. Table—Ps. 69:22; Rom. 11:9.

Uses of.—For wicked—Ps. 69:22; Rom. 11:9. For men—Jer. 5:26.

TRAPPINGS. Ps. 32:9. See HARNESS.

TRAVAIL: Of women.—Gen. 3:16; Is. 54:1; Jer. 31:8; John 16:21. Of Rebekah—Gen. 25:22–26. Rachel—Gen. 35:16–19. Of Tamar—Gen. 38:27, 28. Wife of Phinehas—I Sam. 4:19. Of Elisabeth—Lu. 1:57. In vision—Rev. 12:2.

Nation.—Israel—Ex. 18:8.

Saints.—Gal. 4:19; I Thess. 2:9; II Thess. 3:8.

Soul.—Is. 53:11.

In punishment.—Gen. 3:16; Job 15:20; Is. 13:8. To sinners—Eccl. 2:26; 3:10.

Illustrative.—Of pain or anguish—Ps. 48:6; Eccl. 1:13; Is. 21:3; Jer. 4:31; 6:24; 13:21; 22:23; 30:6; 49:24; Mic. 4:10; Gal. 4:19. Of grief—Eccl. 2:23. Of pang—Is. 42:14; Jer. 50:43; Mic. 4:9. Of sorrow—Hos. 13:13; I Thess. 5:3.

Figurative.—Of sea—Is. 23:4. Of Zion —Is. 66:7, 8; Mic. 5:3. With iniquity —Ps. 7:14. Of all creation—Rom. 8: 22. ''Thou that travailest not''—Gal. 4:27.

TRAVELLER: Travellers mentioned.— II Sam. 12:4. Stephen—Acts 11:14. Paul and companions—Acts 19:29; II Cor. 8:19. See PAUL.

Way of.—Ju. 5:6.

Hospitality to.—Job 31:32.

Prophecy concerning.—Is. 63:1. See JESUS, TEACHING OF—Lu. 2:21. See JOURNEY.

TRAVERSING. Jer. 2:23.

TREACHERY: Men dealing treacherously.—Ju. 9:23; Is. 21:2; 24:16; 33: 1; 48:8; Jer. 3:20; 9:2; 12:1, 6; Hos. 5:7; 6:7; Hab. 1:13; Mal. 2:10, 11, 14, 15, 16. Treacherous city—Jer. 3:8, 10, 11, 20; 5:11. Treacherous people —Zeph. 3:4. Treacherous friends— Lam. 1:2. Treachery of: Ehud—Ju. 3:17–26. Jael—Ju. 4:18. Joab—II Sam. 20:9. Jehu—II Ki. 9:23. Psalm-

ist's friend—Ps. 41:9. Ishmael—Jer. 41:1, 2. Judas—Mt. 26:49; Mk. 14: 10; Lu. 22:47; John 18:3.

TREAD. Adversaries—Ps. 60:12. Corn —Deut. 25:14; I Cor. 9:9; I Tim. 5: 18. Enemies—Zech. 10:5. Grapes— Jer. 23:30. High places—Mic. 1:3. Iniquities under foot—Mic. 7:19. Life down—Ps. 7:5. Lion—Ps. 91:13. Sea —Hab. 3:15. Serpents, Upon—Lu. 10:19. Waves, Upon—Job 9:8. Wicked—Job 40:12. Winepress—Rev. 19: 15. Winevat, In—Is. 63:2.

TREADER. Is. 16:10. Grapes, Of— Amos 9:13.

TREASON: Instances of.—Absalom— II Sam. 15:10–12. Ahithophel—II Sam. 17:1–4. Sheba—II Sam. 20:1, 2. Hadad and Jeroboam—I Ki. 11:14–26. Baasha —I Ki. 15:27. Zimri—I Ki. 16:9, 16, 20. Athaliah—II Ki. Ch. 11; II Chr. 22: 10–12. Servants of Joash—II Ki. 12: 19–21; 14:5. Amaziah—II Ki. 14:19– 21. Shallum—II Ki. 15:10. Menahem —II Ki. 15:14. Pekah—II Ki. 15:25. Hoshea—II Ki. 15:30. Adrammelech and Sharezer—II Ki. 19:37. Amon's servants—II Ki. 21:23. Bigthan and Teresh—Esth. 2:21. Ishmael—Jer. 40: 14–16; Ch. 41. Barabbas—Mk. 15:7. Egyptian—Acts 21:38. Cry of—II Ki. 11:14; II Chr. 23:13.

TREASURE. Of Moses—Deut. 32:24. Of House of Jehovah—Deut. 28:12; I Ki. 14:26; 15:18; II Ki. 12:18; 14:14. Carried out—II Ki. 24:13. Charge over—I Chr. 26:20, 22, 24; Neh. 12:44. Given to—I Chr. 29:8; II Chr. 5:1. Taken—II Chr. 12:9. Sent from—II Chr. 16:2. Taken to Babylon—II Chr. 36:18. Brought to—II Chr. 5:1. Tithes given—Neh. 10:38. Of King's house —I Ki. 14:26; 15:18; II Ki. 12:18; 14:14; 16:8; 18:15. Carried out—II Ki. 24:13. Taken—II Chr. 12:9; 25: 24. To Babylon—II Chr. 36:18. Treasure-house of King of Judah— Dan. 1:2. Of South—Is. 30:6. Hezekiah—II Ki. 20:13; Is. 39:4. Among treasures—II Ki. 20:15. Great treasure—Pr. 15:16; Is. 2:7. Precious— Pr. 21:20; Heb. 11:26. Getting of— Pr. 21:6. By wisdom and understanding—Ez. 28:4.

Where found.—Fields—I Chr. 27:25. Cities—I Chr. 27:25. Villages—I Chr. 27:25. Castles—I Chr. 27:25.

Law concerning.—II Chr. 8:15. Tithes given to House of God—Neh. 10:38. Promise of—Is. 45:3. Treasures of no avail—Jer. 48:7; 49:4.

Prophecies concerning.—Jer. 15:13; 17: 3; 20:5; 50:37; 51:13, 16; Hosea 13:15.

Figurative.—Of wickedness—Pr. 10:2; Mic. 6:10. The fear of Jehovah is thy treasure—Is. 33:6. In earthen vessels—II Cor. 4:7. Where thy treasure is, there will thy heart be—Mt. 6:21. Good treasure of his heart —Mt. 12:35; Lu. 6:45. Evil treasure of his heart—Mt. 12:35; Lu. 6:45. Laid up for self—Lu. 12:21; Jas. 5:3. Treasure hidden—Mt. 13:44. Of wisdom—Col. 2:3. In heaven—Mt. 19: 21; Mk. 10:21; Lu. 18:22. Bringeth forth out of, things new and old— Mt. 13:52. See GOODS, RICHES, WEALTH.

TREASURER. All the—Ezra 7:21. City, Of—Rom. 16:23. Mithredath the— Ezra 1:8. Treasuries, Over—Neh. 13: 13.

TREASURY: Of Jehovah.—Josh. 6:19, 24; I Ki. 7:51; II Ki. 12:18; I Chr. 9:26; 28:12; Neh. 13:12, 13; Mal. 3: 10; Mt. 27:6; Mk. 12:41, 43; Lu. 21:1; John 8:20. Pattern of—I Chr. 28:11.

Of Hezekiah.—II Ki. 20:13; II Chr. 32: 27.

Of king.—I Chr. 27:25, 27, 28; Ezra 5: 17; 6:1; Esth. 3:9; 4:7; Jer. 38:11.

Of idol temples.—Dan. 1:2.

Figurative.—Ps. 135:7.

TREAT. Kindly—Acts 27:3. Shamefully—Acts 14:5; I Thess. 2:2.

TREATIES. Made by joining hands— See DIPLOMACY, HAND.

TREATISE. Acts 1:1.

TREATMENT. Ill—Heb. 11:25. See PERSECUTION.

TREES: The tree of knowledge of good and evil.—Gen. 2:9, 17.

Illustrative of people of power.—Ps. 37: 35; Is. 2:13; 10:34; Ez. 31:7–10; Dan. 4:10–26; Zech. 11:1, 2.

Tree of life.—Gen. 2:9; 3:22; Pr. 3:18; 11:30; 13:12; 15:4; Rev. 2:7; 22:2, 14, 19.

Wisdom as.—Pr. 3:18.

Of righteousness.—Is. 61:3. Saints— Num. 24:6; Ps. 1:3; Jer. 17:8.

Good and bad.—Mt. 7:17, 18.

Dry.—Is. 56:3; Lu. 23:31.

Days of people as.—Is. 65:22.

Remnant left.—Is. 6:13.

Grafted.—Rom. 11:24. See PLANTS.

TREMBLE. Gen. 42:28; Ex. 15:14; Deut. 2:25; Job 43:23; Heb. 12:26. Before him—I Chr. 16:30; Ps. 96:9. Come to meet David—I Sam. 21:1. Children—Hos. 11:10. Deceased—Job 26:5. Earth—Ps. 68:8; 104:32; Pr. 30:21; Is. 14:16; Jer. 10:10. Fear, For —See FEAR. Good, For—Jer. 33:9. Heart—Job 37:1. Keepers of the house—Eccl. 12:3. Land to—Ps. 60: 2; Amos 8:8. Moses—Acts 7:32. Nations—Is. 64:2. Not—II Pet. 2:10. Peoples—Ps. 99:1. Pillars—Job 9:6. Turned into—Is. 21:4. Word, At his —Is. 66:5. See FEAR, HORROR, TERROR.

TRENCH. About the altar—I Ki. 18: 32. Filled with water—I Ki. 18:35. Valley full of—II Ki. 3:16.

TRESPASS. I Chr. 5:25; Ezra 10:6; Neh. 1:8; Ez. 17:20. Achan—Josh. 7:1–26; 22:20. Dead through—Eph. 2:1; Col. 2:13. Forgive—Mt. 6:14; Mk. 11:25; Col. 2:13. Not as the— Rom. 5:15. Offering—See OFFERINGS. Overtaken in—Gal. 6:1. Saul's—I Sam. 13:13, 14; 15:23; I Chr. 10:13. See TRANSGRESS, SIN.

TRESSES. Song of Sol. 7:5. See HAIR.

TRIAL. Deut. 4:34; Ez. 21:13. Affliction, Of—II Cor. 8:2 (A. V.). Faith— See FAITH, TESTING OF. Fiery—I Pet. 4:12. See PERSECUTION. God, Of—I Cor. 10:9. Hour of—Rev. 3:10. Innocent, Of the—Job 9:23. Jesus—Mt. 4: 7; 22:18. See JESUS, SUFFERING OF. Manifold, In—I Pet. 1:6. Mockings —Heb. 11:36. Paul's—Acts 20:19. See ADVERSITY, AFFLICTION, CONSOLATION, DISTRESS, PERSECUTION, TEMPTATON, TRIBULATION, TRY.

TRIBES. ''A tribe was a close corporation constituting a perfect social unit.'' The interest of each member was the same.

Tribes of Israel.—Number of, twelve— Gen. 49:28; Jas. 1:1.

Descent.—From Jacob's twelve sons—Gen. 35:22-26. Ephraim and Manasseh numbered among the twelve instead of Joseph and Levi—Gen. 48:5; Josh. 14:3-4.

Genealogies of.—Gen. 35:23-26; 46:8-25; Ex. 6:14-24; Num. 3:17-20; 26: 59-60; I Chr. 2:1-11; 4:1-37; 5:11-17; 6:16-30; 7:1-40; 8:1-28.

History of twelve tribes foreshadowed. —Gen. 49:3-27; Deut. 33:6-35.

Total strength of, on leaving Egypt.— Ex. 12:37; Num. 1:44-46; 2:32.

Census taken in the wilderness.—Num. 1:1-46; 26:5-65.

Organization of.—Each tribe had a prince or chief—Num. 1:4-16; Josh. 3:12. The tribes were in four divisions while in wilderness—Num. 10: 14-28. They encamped by divisions, and by their standards round the tabernacle—Num. 2:2-31. Prepared for war—Num. 31:4-5. Concerning landed property—Num. 36:1-9.

Total strength on entering Canaan.— Num. 26:51.

Canaan divided according to size of families.—Num. 33:54.

Tribes required to drive out inhabitants or take punishment.—Num. 33:55-56.

Two and a half tribes settle east of the Jordan.—Deut. 3:12-17; Josh. 13:23-32.

Must first assist in subduing Canaan.— Num. 32:6-32; Deut. 3:18-20.

Situation and bounds of nine and one-half tribes.—Josh. Chs. 15-17.

Names of tribes engraved on breastplate of high priest.—Ex. 28:21; 39: 14.

Division of tribes occasioned by folly of Rehoboam.—I Ki. 12:16-20. See ISRAEL.

TRIBULATION. Deut. 4:30. Anguish, And—Rom. 2:9. Come out of—Rev. 7:14. Deliver you up—I Sam. 26:24; Mt. 24:9. Faint at—Eph. 3:13. Flesh, In—I Cor. 7:28. Great—Mt. 24:21, 29; Mk. 13:24; 7:14; Rev. 2:22. Know thy—Rev. 2:9. Many—Acts 14:22. Partaker in—Rev. 2:10. Patient in—Rom. 12:12. Rejoice in—Rom. 5:3. Separate us from Christ—Rom. 8:35. Stedfastness, Worketh — Rom. 5:3. Stephen, About—Acts 11:19. Suffer—

I Thess. 3:4. Ten days—Rev. 2:10. Word, Because of—Mt. 13:21; Mk. 4:17. World, In the—John 15:33. See ADVERSITY, AFFLICTION, CONSOLATION, PERSECUTION, TRIAL, TRIED.

TRIBUTARY. Deut. 20:11; Lam. 1:1.

TRIBUTE: Exacted by kings.—I Sam. 8:10-17.

Unto Jehovah.—Num. 31:28, 37-40.

Exacted from all conquered nations.— Josh. 16:10; Ju. 1:30, 33, 35; II Ki. 23:33, 35.

How to give.—Deut. 16:10. Moses gives —Num. 31:41.

Often exacted in: Labor—Gen. 49:15; Josh. 17:13; Ju. 1:28; I Ki. 9:15, 21. Produce of land—I Sam. 8:15; I Ki. 4:7. Gold and silver—II Ki. 23:33, 35.

The Jews required to pay half a shekel. —Ex. 30:12-16. Found in fish's mouth (miracle)—Mt. 17:24-27.

Kings: Of Israel, forbidden to levy oppressive—Deut. 17:16, 17. Set officers over—II Sam. 20:24; I Ki. 4:6, 7. Often oppressed the people with—I Ki. 12:4, 11. Which led to rebellion— I Ki. 12:14-20. Priests and Levites exempted from—Ezra 7:24.

Roman periodical census.—The feast under Quirinius as Governor—Lu. 2: 1, 2. The second also under Quirinius —Acts 5:37. Persons enrolled in the native place of tribe—Lu. 2:3-5. Roman tribute, Collectors of—Lu. 3: 12, 13; 5:27. Resisted by Galileans— Lu. 31:1; Acts 5:37. Our Lord falsely accused of forbidding to pay—Lu. 23: 2. Jesus' instructions concerning payment of—Mt. 22:15-22; Mk. 12:13-17. All Saints exhorted to pay—Rom. 13: 6, 7.

TRICKLE. Job 28:1. See POUR.

TRIED. Abraham—Heb. 11:17. Gold— Zech. 13:9. Hearts—Ps. 7:9; Jer. 12: 3; Job 34:36. See ''Job'' in OUTLINE STUDIES IN THE BOOKS. Silver—Ps. 12: 6; 66:10. Stone—Is. 28:16. See STONE. Word of God—II Sam. 22:31; Pr. 30: 5. See ENDURE, REFINE, TEST, TRIAL, TRY.

TRIMMED. Beard—II Sam. 19:24. Lamps—Mt. 25:7. Way—Jer. 2:33.

TRIUMPH. Because of Me—Ps. 60:8. Christ, In—II Cor. 2:14. Enemies, Not —Ps. 25:2. Gloriously—Ex. 15:1.

Praise, In thy—I Chr. 16:35; Ps. 106: 47. Righteous, The—Pr. 28:12. Voice of—Ps. 47:1. Wicked—Job 20:5; Ps. 94:3. Works, In—Ps. 92:4. See JESUS, EXALTATION OF, VICTORY.

TROAS, trō'as. **A seaport of Phrygia.** —Acts 16:8, 11; 20:5, 6; II Cor. 2:12; II Tim. 4:13.

TROD. Anger, In—Is. 63:3. Foot, Under —II Ki. 9:33. Gate, In the—II Ki. 7:17. Grapes—Ju. 9:27. One upon another—Lu. 12:1. Thistle—II Ki. 14:9. See FEET, TREAD.

TRODDEN. Jer. 51:33. Down as the mire—Mic. 7:10. Foot, Under—Mt. 5: 13; Heb. 10:29. Jerusalem shall be— Lu. 21:24. Wicked men have—Job 22: 15. Winepress—Is. 63:3; Rev. 14:20. See FEET, TREAD.

TROGYLLIUM, tro-gyl'li-um. **A city in Asia Minor.**—Acts 20:15 (mar. A.V.).

TROOP. Captain ›over—I Ki. 11:24. Men, Of—Is. 21:9. Run upon a—Ps. 18:29. Posted—Is. 29:3. See SOLDIERS, WAR.

TROPHIMUS, trŏph'i-mus. **A disciple in Ephesus.**—Acts 20:4; II Tim. 4:20.

TROUBLE, n. Ps. 107:39. Born unto— Job 5:7. Bring my soul out of—Ps. 143:11. Cometh, When—Job 27:9. Cried unto Jehovah in—Day of—Ps. 50:15. Delivered out of—Ps. 54:7. Full of—Job 14:1. Hid—Job 3:10. Present help in—Ps. 46:1. Rest from —Is. 14:3. Righteous shall come out of—Pr. 12:13. Sore—Mt. 26:37. Sow —Job 4:8. See ADVERSITY, AFFLICTION, CONSOLATION, PERSECUTION, TRIAL, TRIBULATION.

TROUBLE, v. Job 21:6; Lu. 7:6; 11:7; John 11:33. Bones are—Ps. 6:2. Greatly—Lu. 1:29. Let not your heart be—John 14:1, 27. Not the teacher— Lu. 8:49. Sore—Acts 4:2. Soul—John 12:27. Spirit was—Gen. 41:8. Unclean spirits, With—Lu. 6:18. Waters— John 5:7. Wicked cease from—Job 3:17. Woman, The—Mt. 26:10. See ADVERSITY, AFFLICTION, CONSOLATION, PERSECUTION, TRIAL, TRIBULATION.

TROUBLOUS. Dan. 9:25.

TROUGH. Emptied pitcher into—Gen. 24:20. Filled the—Ex. 2:16. Kneading—See BREAD. Watering—Gen. 30: 38.

TRUE. Deut. 7:4. Bread—John 6:32. Faithful and—Rev. 19:11. God—John 3:33; Rom. 3:4. Heart—Heb. 10:22. Light—John 1:9. Men—Gen. 42:11. Riches—Lu. 16:11. Saying—John 4: 37. Thou art—Mt. 22:16; Mk. 12:14. Vine—John 15:1. Witness—John 8: 14. See TRUTH.

TRULY. Eccl. 11:7; John 8:31. Care— Phil. 2:20. Deal—Gen. 24:49. See TRUTH.

TRUMPETS: Memorial of blowing.— Lev. 23:24.
Silver.—Num. 10:1-10.
Priests blew.—Josh. 6:4, 6, 8, 9, 16, 20; II Chr. 13:14; 29:26, 27. Feast of— Lev. 23:24; Num. 29:1.
Alarm sounded with.—Num. 10:9; 31:6; II Chr. 13:12.
Blowing of.—Num. 29:1; Ju. 7:8, 18, 19, 20, 22; II Ki. 9:13; 11:14.
Sounding of.—Job 39:25.
Given to angels.—Rev. 8:2, 8.
In the temple.—I Chr. 13:8; II Chr. 5: 12; Ps. 98:6.
Psalms of thanksgiving.—I Chr. 13:8; 15:24, 28; 16:6, 42; II Chr. 5:12, 13; 7:6; 20:28; 23:13; Ezra 3:10; Neh. 12:35, 41; Ps. 98:6.
Sware to Jehovah with.—II Chr. 15:14. See Music—I Chr. 6:31.

TRUST. Job 39:11. Brother, In any— Jer. 9:4. Jehovah, In—Ps. 4:5; 22:9; Jer. 17:7; Mt. 27:43; I Tim. 4:10; 5:5; Heb. 3:13; I Pet. 3:5. Jesus, In—Mt. 12:21; Rom. 15:12; Phil. 2:19. Lying words—Jer. 7:4. Moses, In—John 5: 45. Name, In His—Mt. 12:21. Princes, In—Ps. 146:3. Riches—Mt. 10:24; Mk. 10:24; I Tim. 6:17. Tent, In—Job 18:14. Themselves, In—Lu. 18:9. True riches—Lu. 16:11. Wife, In—Pr. 31: 11. See FAITH, FAITHFULNESS, PARABLES OF POUNDS AND TALENTS.

TRUSTWORTHY. I Cor. 7:25. See FAITHFULNESS.

TRUSTY. Job 12:20.

TRUTH. In Old Testament usually means faithfulness, permanence, fidelity, sincerity, trustworthiness, honesty, justice, and reality.
God's faithfulness to covenant promises. —His stability and sincerity—Gen. 24:27; 32:10; Ex. 34:6; II Sam. 2:6; Ps. 25:5, 10; 30:9; 31:5; 40:10, 11;

43:3; 57:3, 10; 69:13; 71:22; 86:11, 15; 89:14; 91:4; 96:13; 108:4; 111:7, 8; 115:1; 117:2; 132:11; 138:2; 146:6; Is. 25:1; 38:19; 61:8; 65:16; Dan. 4: 37. See Rev. 15:3.

Trustworthiness in man.—I Ki. 17:24; Pr. 8:7; I Cor. 13:6; Eph. 4:14, 15; III John 3. Honesty—Gen. 42:16; Pr. 12: 17; Eph. 4:15, 25; John 8:44; I Tim. 2:7; II John 3. Justice—Ex. 18:21; Pr. 20:28; Rom. 2:2; Rev. 16:7. See Rev. 15:3. Justice of Messianic king —Ps. 45:4; Is. 16:5; 42:3.

God requires truth in character.—Ps. 51:6; Jer. 4:2; Zech. 8:16, 19; Eph. 4:15, 25; 6:14; I John 3:18.

Collective system of statements which conform to reality.—Law is truth— Ps. 119:142, 151, 160; Dan. 9:13; Mal. 2:6–8; Rom. 2:20. Words of truth— Pr. 22:19–21. Word of truth—Ps. 119: 43; Eph. 1:13; Col. 1:5; II Tim. 2:15; Jas. 1:18.

Gospel such a collective system.—John 8:31, 32; Rom. 1:18; II Cor. 13:6; Gal. 2:5; I Tim. 2:7; II Tim. 4:4; Tit. 11: 14; Jas. 3:14; II Pet. 1:12; 2:2; I John 3:19; II John 2; III John 3, 4, 8, 12. Knowledge of the truth—Col. 1:5; I Tim. 2:4; 4:3; II Tim. 2:15, 25; 3:7; Tit. 1:1; I John 2:21. Heard—Col. 1: 5, 6. Believed—II Thess. 2:10, 12, 13; I Tim. 4:3. Obeyed—Gal. 5:7; I Pet. 1:22.

Truth disregarded.—Is. 59:4, 14, 15; Jer. 7:28; 9:3, 5; I Tim. 6:5.

Man must serve God in truth (= Sincerity).—Josh. 24:14; I Sam. 12:24; I Ki. 2:4; 3:6; II Ki. 20:3; Ps. 15:2; 26:3; 86:11; 145:18; Is. 38:3; John 4:23; II John 4.

Exhortation to truth.—Pr. 3:3; 22:21; 23:23; I Cor. 5:8; 13:6; I John 3:18.

Reality.—Deut. 13:14; Ju. 9:15; Pr. 12: 17; Is. 43:9; Dan. 7:16; Mk. 5:33; John 8:40, 45, 46; 16:7; Acts 26:25; Rom. 9:1; Gal. 4:16; Eph. 4:15, 25; Phil. 4:8; I Thess. 2:13; I Tim. 2:7; I John 2:21, 27; 3:18, 19; II John 1, 3.

Welfare.—State of society in which justice and honesty prevail—II Ki. 20: 19; Esth. 9:30; Ps. 85:10; Zech. 8:16, 19.

Jesus the expression of the divine life. The highest expression of truth.—

John 1:14; 8:31–36; 14:6; 18:37, 38; Eph. 4:15, 21.

Spirit of truth.—John 14:17; 15:26; I John 4:16.

Witness unto the truth.—John 5:33; 18: 37; III John 12. See WITNESS.

Church a pillar and ground of truth.— I Tim. 3:15.

Of a truth.—I Sam. 21:5; II Ki. 19:17; Job 9:2; Is. 37:18; Jer. 26:15; Dan. 2: 47; Mt. 14:33; Lu. 4:25; 9:27; 12:44; 21:3; 22:59; John 7:40; Acts 4:27; 10:34. See WITNESS, FALSEHOOD, DECEPTION, JUSTICE, GOSPEL.

TRY. Ju. 7:4; Job 7:18; II Chr. 32:31; Ps. 66:10; 105:19; Jer. 9:7; Lam. 3: 40; Zech. 13:9; II Cor. 13:5; Rev. 2:2, 10; 3:10. Children of men—Ps. 11:4. David—Ps. 7:2; 26:2; 139:23. Fire, By—I Cor. 3:13 (A.V.); I Pet. 1:7 (A.V.). Heart—I Chr. 29:17; Ps. 7:9; Pr. 17:3; 26:2; Jer. 11:20; 12:3; 17: 10. Holy Spirit—Acts 5:9. Job—Job 23:10. Righteous, The—Ps. 11:5; Jer. 20:12. Spirits, The—I John 4:1 (A.V.). Way—Jer. 6:27; Lam. 3:40. Words— Job 12:11; 34:3. Work, Every man's —I Cor. 3:13 (A.V.). See PROVE, TEST, TRIAL, TRIED.

TRYPHÆNA, trȳ-phæ′na. **A woman in Rome whom Paul salutes.**—Rom. 16: 12.

TRYPHOSA, trȳ-phō′sa. **Another woman in Rome whom Paul salutes.**—Rom. 16:12.

TUBAL, tū′bal. (1) **Son of Japheth.**— Gen. 10:2; I Chr. 1:5.
(2) **A people.**—Is. 66:19; Ez. 27:13; 32: 26; 38:2, 3; 39:1.

TUBAL-CAIN, tū′bal-kāin. **Son of Lamech.**—Gen. 4:22.

TUBES. Brass—Job 40:18.

TUMBLED. Ju. 7:13.

TUMORS. I Sam. 5:9.

TUMULT. Arise—Mt. 26:5; 27:24. Be a—Mk. 14:2. City, Of—Job 39:7. Make—Mt. 9:23; Mk. 5:39. Noise, Of —I Sam. 4:14; Is. 13:4. Peoples, Of— Ps. 65:7. Sons of—Num. 24:17. Wars and—Lu. 21:9. Workers of iniquity, Of—Ps. 64:2. See RIOT.

TUMULTUOUS. City—Is. 22:2. Ones —Jer. 48:43. See TEMPESTUOUS.

TURBANS. Is. 3:23.

TURBULENT. Ez. 5:7.

TURN. Lam. 5:21; Is. 21:12. About—Josh. 15:3; Eccl. 1:6. See CONVERSION, REPENTANCE. Again—II Chr. 6:24; Is. 6:10; Mt. 3:15; Lu. 22:32; Acts 3:19. Aside—Num. 22:33; Deut. 17:11; II Chr. 34:2; Job 23:11; 38:16; I Tim. 5: 15. See SIN. Away—John 1:1, 8. Back —Job 39:22; Ps. 6:10; 9:17; 80:14; 89:43; 114:5; Is. 28:6. See APOSTASY. Battle, In—Ju. 20:39. Darkness, From —Acts 26:18. Evil, From—I Pet. 3: 11. Except ye—Mt. 18:3. Faces upward—Is. 8:21. Jesus—Mt. 9:22. Iniquities, From—Acts 3:36. Not into the way—Job 28:18. Precepts, From —Dan. 9:5. Profane, From—I Tim. 6:20. Shadow, cast by—Jas. 1:17. Shadow of death into the morning—Amos 5:8. Soft answer, Wrath—Pr. 15:1. To him the other also—Mt. 5: 39. Truth, From—Tit. 1:14. Upside down—Ju. 7:13. See CONVERSION, REPENTANCE.

TURRET. Song of Sol. 8:9.

TURTLE-DOVE. See DOVE.

TUTOR. I Cor. 4:15; Gal. 3:25. See COVENANT, INSTRUCTION.

TWAIN. II Ki. 4:33; Is. 6:2; Jer. 34: 18; Ez. 21:19. Go with—Mt. 5:41 (A.V.). One flesh, Be—Mt. 19:5, 6 (A.V.); Mk. 10:8 (A.V.). Veil of temple rent in—Mt. 27:31 (A.V.); Mk. 15:38 (A.V.). See TWO.

TWELVE. Angels—Rev. 21:12. See ANGELS. Apostles — See APOSTLES. Baskets of broken pieces—Mt. 14:20; Mk. 6:43; Lu. 9:17; John 6:13. Cakes —Lev. 24:5. Concubine divided into twelve pieces—Ju. 19:19. Fruit, Manner of—Rev. 22:2. Gates—Rev. 21:12. See GATES. Hours in the day—John 11:9. Jesus twelve years old when He went to the Feast in Jerusalem—Lu. 2:42. Legions—Mt. 26:53. Months—See MONTHS. Oxen in temple—See TEMPLE—II Ki. 7:25, 44. Pearls—Rev. 21:21. Pillars—Ex. 15: 27; 24:4. See PILLARS. Rode—Num. 17:6. Sons of Jacob—Gen. 35:22; 42: 13, 32. See JACOB. Springs—Num. 33: 9. Stars—Rev. 12:1. Stones—On priest's breastplate—Ex. 28:21; 39: 14. See PRIEST. *Memorial stones taken out of the Jordan*—Josh. 4:8, 9, 20. *Elijah built altar with*—I Ki. 18:31, 32.

Tribes—Gen. 49:28; Mt. 19:28; Acts 26:7; Jas. 1:1. See TRIBES.

TWENTY. Fathoms—Acts 27:28. Found there—Gen. 18:31. Gerahs, Shekel is —Ex. 30:13. Pieces of silver—Gen. 37:28. Shekels—Lev. 27:5.

TWICE. As much bread—Gen. 16:22. Before cock crow—Mk. 14:30, 72. Dead—Jude 12. Fast, I—Lu. 18:12. Have I heard this—Ps. 62:11. Smote the rock—Num. 20:11.

TWILIGHT. Adulterer waiteth for—Job 24:15. David smote them from—I Sam. 30:17. Fled in—II Ki. 7:7. In the—Pr. 7:9. Star of—Job 3:9. Went in the—Is. 21:4.

TWIN BROTHERS. Acts 28:11.

TWO. Gen. 6:19; Eccl. 4:12. Better than one—Eccl. 4:9. Divide living child in—I Ki. 3:25. Eyes, Avenged for my—Ju. 16:28. Go with him—Mt. 5:41. Men in the field—Mt. 24:40. Mites—Mk. 12:42. One new man, Of —Eph. 2:15. Shall become one flesh —Mt. 19:5. Strait betwixt—Phil. 1: 23. Veil of temple rent in—Mt. 27: 51. Walk together—Amos 3:3. Which of the—Mt. 27:21. See TWAIN.

TWO-EDGED. Sword—Pr. 5:4; Heb. 4: 12; Rev. 1:16; 2:12.

TYCHICUS, tўk'i-kŭs. **A disciple in Asia Minor who went with Paul to Jerusalem.** Sent by Paul to Ephesus and Colossæ—Acts 20:4; Eph. 6:21; Col. 4:7; II Tim. 4:12; Tit. 3:12.

TYPES. Form, Figure, Image, Character. *Gr.* Mark of a blow; impression made.

Type of sin.—Uncleanness—Lev. 5:2-5; II Cor. 6:17; Eph. 5:5; Heb. 9:13. Leprosy—Lev. 13:18-23. Separated from intercourse—Num. 5:2; 12:14, 15. Associate together—II Ki. 7:3; Lu. 17:12. Cut off from God's house —II Chr. 26:21. Excluded from priest's office—Lev. 22:2-4. Must cry "unclean"—Lev. 13:45. Leaven—Lev. 23:17; Mt. 16:6. Blemish—Lev. 14:10; I Pet. 1:19. See LEPROSY.

Types of Christ.—Scapegoat—Lev. 16: 7-10. Brazen serpent—Num. 21:9; John 3:14, 15. Tabernacle—Heb. 9:7-15; 10:1-10. Priesthood—Ps. 110:4; Heb. 5:6-11. Branch—Zech. 6:12, 13.

Sacrifices—Heb. 9:13, 14; I Cor. 5:7. See JESUS.

Possible types of Christ.—(Some features of Aaronic priesthood, though must not antagonize Melchizedekian.) Adam—I Cor. 15:45. Abel—Heb. 12: 24. David—Rev. 5:5. Moses—Deut. 18:15.

Type of baptism.—I Pet. 3:20, 21; I Cor. 10:1–2.

Church.—Bride—Rev. 21:2. Candlestick —Rev. 1:20. Tabernacle—Heb. Ch. 9. Temple—Rev. 3:12.

Eternal life.—Gen. 3:22; Rev. 22:14.

Deliverance from sin.—See DELIVERANCE FROM BONDAGE.

New and living way.—The veil—Heb. 10:20; II Cor. 3:13, 14.

TYPES OF CHRIST. See JESUS, TYPES OF.

TYRANNUS, tȳ-răn'nus. A person in Ephesus in whose school Paul taught for two years.—Acts 19:9.

TYRANNY. See OPPRESSION.

TYRE, tȳre. A fortress.—Josh. 19:29; Ez. 26:17; Zech. 9:3. Assigned to Asher; not conquered—II Sam. 24:7. Called: Ancient; Mart of nations; Stronghold of the sea; Joyous; Bestower of crowns; Daughter of Sidon; Daughter of Tarshish; Pride of all glory—Is. 23:3–10. Renowned; Merchant of the peoples; Very glorious— Ez. 26:17; 27:3, 25. Noted: *For army* —Ez. 27:10, 11. *For beauty*—Ez. 27:3, 4. Builders—II Chr. 2:7, 13. Commerce—I Chr. 22:4; Ezra 3:7; Ez. Ch. 27. Navy—I Ki. 9:27; II Chr. 8: 18. Wealth—Is. 23:3, 8; Ez. 27:33; 28:4, 5. Hiram, King of—II Sam. 5: 11; I Ki. 5:1; 7:13; 9:11, 12; II Chr. 14:1; II Chr. 2:3, 11, 12, 13. Helped Solomon build the temple—I Ki. 5:1– 10; II Chr. 2:3–16. Dependent on Galilee for food—Acts 12:20.

Wickedness.—See JESUS, TEACHINGS OF.

Prophecies against.—Is. 23:1, 5–9, 12, 15–18; Jer. 27:2–7; Ez. Ch. 26; 28:1– 10; Amos 1:9, 10. Against the king— Ez. 28:11–19. Nebuchadrezzar fulfilled, and received Egypt for pay— Ez. 29:18–20. Jesus visited—Mt. 15: 21; Mk. 7:24, 31. Disciples from—Mk. 3:8· Lu. 6:17; Acts 21:3, 4.

UCAL, ū'kal. Pr. 30:1.

UEL, ū'el. A son of Bani who married a foreign wife.—Ezra 10:34.

ULAI, ū'lāi. A river flowing into the Euphrates.—Dan. 8:2.

ULAM, ū'lam. (1) A Benjamite.—I Chr. 8:39, 40.

(2) Great-grandson of Manasseh. — I Chr. 7:16, 17.

ULLA, ŭl'lȧ. A man of Asher.—I Chr. 7:39.

UMMAH, ŭm'mah. A city in Asher.— Josh. 9:33.

UMPIRE. Job 9:33.

UNADVISEDLY. Ps. 106:33.

UNAPPROACHABLE. I Tim. 6:16.

UNAWARES. Came—Gen. 34:25. Destruction come—Ps. 35:8. Entertained angels—Heb. 13:2. Killeth neighbor—Deut. 19:4. See MURDERER. Stole away—Gen. 31:20.

UNBELIEF. Because of their—Mt. 13: 58; Mk. 6:6; Heb. 3:19. Heart of— Heb. 3:12. Help thou mine—Mk. 9: 24. I did it ignorantly in—I Tim. 1: 13. Upbraided them with their—Mk. 16:14. Wavered not through—Rom. 4:20. See DOUBT, FAITH.

UNBELIEVER. Before—I Cor. 6:6. Believer with—II Cor. 6:15. Worse than an—I Tim. 5:8. Yoked with— II Cor. 6:14. See DOUBT, FAITH.

UNBELIEVING. I Cor. 14:22; Tit. 1: 15. Fearful and—Rev. 21:8. Husband —I Cor. 7:14. Unlearned or—I Cor. 14:23. Wife—I Cor. 7:12. See DOUBT, FAITH, LACK OF.

UNBLAMEABLE. I Thess. 2:10; 3:13. See BLAMELESS, BLEMISH.

UNCEASING. Rom. 4:2; II Tim. 1:3. See CEASE.

UNCERTAIN. I Cor. 9:26; 14:8.

UNCERTAINTY. Riches, Of—I Tim. 6:17. See WEALTH.

UNCHANGEABLE. Priesthood—Heb. 7:24.

UNCIRCUMCISED. Gen. 17:14; Ex. 12:48; I Sam. 31:4; II Sam. 1:20; Acts 11:3; I Cor. 7:18. Heart, In—Acts 7:51. See CIRCUMCISION, GENTILES.

UNCIRCUMCISION. Lev. 19:23; Jer. 9:25; Rom. 2:26; 4:11; I Cor. 7:19; Col. 3:11. Gospel of—Gal. 2:7. See CIRCUMCISION, GENTILES.

UNCLE. Lev. 25:49; I Chr. 27:32; Esth. 2:7; Amos 6:10.

UNCLEAN. Job 14:4; 18:3; 36:14; Ez. 7:20; 44:23; Rom. 14:14; Rev. 17:4; 21:27. Bread—Ez. 4:13. Common or unclean—Acts 10:13, 28; 11:8. Demon —Lu. 4:33. See DEMON, POSSESSION. Land—Amos 7:17. Leper—Lev. 13: 46. See LEPROSY. Lips—Is. 6:5. See LIPS. Spirits—Mk. 9:25; Rev. 18:2. See DEMONS, POSSESSION OF, CEREMONIAL CLEANSING, PURIFICATION.

UNCLEANNESS. Mt. 23:27; Eph. 5:3. Called us not, God—I Thess. 4:7. Fountain for—Zech. 13:1. Land, Of— Ezra 9:11. Peoples, Of—Ezra 9:11. See CEREMONIAL CLEANSING, PURIFICATION, SIN.

UNCLOTHED. II Cor. 5:4. See LIFE, ETERNAL, SOUL, SPIRIT.

UNCOMELY. I Cor. 12:23. See UNSEEMLY.

UNCONDEMNED. Acts 16:37; 22:25. See CONDEMNATION, JUDGMENT.

UNCOVER. Deut. 22:30; Ruth 3:4; Is. 20:4. Arm—Ez. 4:7. David—II Sam. 6:20. Deep things—Job 12:22. See DEEP THINGS, REVELATION. Head—I Cor. 11:5, 13 (A. V.). Leg—Is. 47:2. Nakedness—Lev. 18:6–19; 20:11–21; Is. 47:3; Hab. 2:16. Noah—Gen. 9: 21. Roof—Mk. 2:14. Secret places— Jer. 49:10. Shield—Is. 22:6. Sins— Lam. 4:22.

UNDEFILED. Inheritance—I Pet. 1:4. See INHERITANCE. Religion—Jas. 1:27. Separate from sinners—See PURIFICATION, SALVATION, SANCTIFICATION.

UNDERSTAND. Deut. 32:29; Jer. 23: 20. Aged that—Job 32:9. Concerning the loaves, Not—Mk. 6:52. Hear and —Mt. 13:14; 15:10. Here after—John 13:7. Know and—John 10:38. Let him that readeth—Mt. 24:15. None that—Rom. 13:11. Not these things —John 3:10. Readest, What thou— Acts 8:30, 31. Sought to—Dan. 8:15. Speech, My—John 8:43. That I am he—Jer. 43:10. Worlds have been framed, That—Heb. 11:3. See KNOWLEDGE, MIND, WISDOM.

UNDERSTANDING. I Ki. 7:14; Job 12:3, 12; 26:12; Pr. 7:4; Is. 10:13; Jer. 10:12; Mt. 11:25; Col. 1:9; Jas. 3:13; I John 5:20. Almighty giveth

—Job 32:8. Amazed at—Lu. 2:47. Apply heart to—Pr. 2:2. Bribe destroyeth—Eccl. 7:7. Darkened in— Eph. 4:18. Faileth—Eccl. 10:3. Full assurance of—Col. 2:2. Give me—Ps. 119:34. Given, to the mind—Job 38: 36. Hath no—Pr. 17:16; 27:9. Hid heart from—Job 17:4. Infinite—Ps. 147:5. Lean not upon thine own— Pr. 3–5. Lord shall give—II Tim. 2:7. Made heavens, By—Ps. 136:5. Manifold in—Job 11:6. No delight in— Pr. 18:2. Passeth all—Phil. 4:7. People of no—Is. 27:11. Perceive my —Eph. 3:4. Place of—Job 28:12. Returned—Dan. 4:36. Searching of—Is. 40:28. Sing praises with—Ps. 47:7. Strength of—Job 36:5. Take away— Hos. 4:11. Times, Of the—I Chr. 12: 32. Unfruitful—I Cor. 14:14. Void of—Job 11:12; Rom. 10:19. Wellspring, Is a—Pr. 16:22. Without— Jer. 5:21; II Cor. 10:12. See KNOWLEDGE, MIND, WISDOM.

UNDO. Is. 58:6.

UNDONE. Num. 17:12; 21:29; Is. 6:5; Mt. 23:23; Lu. 11:42. Nothing—Josh. 11:15.

UNDRESSED. Lev. 25:5, 11; Mt. 9:16.

UNEQUAL. Ez. 18:25. Yoked—II Cor. 6:14.

UNFAITHFUL. Lu. 12:46; Pr. 25:19. See FAITHFUL.

UNFEIGNED. Faith—I Tim. 1:5; II Tim. 1:5. Love—II Cor. 6:6; I Pet. 1:22.

UNFORMED. Ps. 139:16.

UNFRUITFUL. Tit. 3:14; II Pet. 1:8. Become—Mt. 13:22; Mk. 4:19. Understanding—I Cor. 14:14. Works—Eph. 5:11. See FRUIT.

UNGIRDED. Gen. 24:32.

UNGODLINESS. Jer. 23:15; II Tim. 2:16; Tit. 2:12. Men, Of—II Sam. 22:5; Ps. 18:4. Revealed against— Rom. 1:18. Turn away from—Rom. 11:26. See CHRISTIAN GRACES, SIN.

UNGODLY. Jude 15, 18. Christ died for —Rom. 5:6; I Tim. 1:9. Delivered to —Job 16:11. Justification of—Rom. 4:5. Line—II Pet. 2:6. Men—Jude 4, 15. Punishment of—II Pet. 3:7. Where shall—I Pet. 4:18. World of the—II Pet. 2:5. See CHRISTIAN GRACES, SIN.

UNHOLY. I Tim. 1:9; II Tim. 3:2; Heb. 10:29. See HOLINESS, HOLY.

UNITY. Gr. *Henotes.* Oneness.

God.—Deut. 4:35, 39; 6:4, 5; Is. 43:10–13; 44:6–8; Rev. 1:8; 15:3, 4.

Christ with God.—Mt. 22:41–45; Lu. 24:37–40; John 1:1, 2, 14; 20:25–28; Heb. 12:2; Rev. 22:13.

Of the spirit.—I Cor. 12:4–13; Eph. 4:3.

Christ, the center of.—(Unity in Christ) —Gal. 3:28; Eph. 1:9, 10; 2:6, 7, 10, 13, 20; 3:6, 11; Col. 2:6. Desire for— John 17:20, 21.

Man.—Gen. 1:26, 27; 5:1, 2; Acts 17:26; Gal. 3:26–28; Phil. 3:20; I Thess. 5:23; Heb. 2:11–14.

The Saints (Church—Local and general).—Ps. 133:1–3; John 15:5; 17:22–26; Acts 2:42–47; Rom. 12:4, 5; I Cor. 1:10–13; 10:16, 17; 12:12; II Cor. 13:11; Eph. 2:19–22; 4:13; 5:25–27; I Pet. 2:4–6; 3:8.

In diversity.—Rom. 12:4–8; I Cor. 12:14–23.

Action.—Ezra 1:3, 4; Neh. 4:6; Acts 2:1–4, 44, 45; 11:29, 30; I Cor. 3:12, 13; 12:21.

The faith.—Acts 11:23; Eph. 4:4, 5, 13; Phil. 1:27; Jude 3.

Sufferings.—Rom. 8:17, 35–39; I Cor. 12:26; Phil. 3:10; II Tim. 2:12.

Burden-bearing.—Num. 11:11–16; Ex. 17:11, 12; Josh. 1:12–15; Mt. 20:12; Rom. 15:1–3; Gal. 6:2. See FELLOWSHIP, LOVE.

UNJUST. Mt. 5:45. Judgment—Ps. 82:2. Just and—Acts 24:15. Know no shame—Zeph. 3:5. Man—Ps. 43:1; Pr. 29:27; Lu. 18:11. See JUSTICE.

UNKNOWN. II Cor. 6:9. Face—Gal. 1:22. God—Acts 17:23. See KNOWLEDGE.

UNLADE. Ship—Acts 21:3. See BURDEN.

UNLAWFUL. Acts 10:28. See LAW.

UNLEARNED. I Cor. 14:16, 23, 24. Men —Acts 4:13. See INSTRUCTION.

UNLEAVENED. See BREAD.

UNLOOSE. Worthy to, Not—Mk. 1:7; Lu. 3:16; John 1:27. See LOOSE.

UNMARRIED. Women—I Cor. 7:8, 11, 32, 34. See MARRIAGE.

UNMERCIFUL. Rom. 1:31. See MERCY.

UNMINDFUL. Deut. 32:18. See MIND.

UNMIXED. Rev. 14:10.

UNMOVEABLE. Acts 27:41. Christians should be—I Cor. 15:58. See MOVEABLE.

UNNI, ŭn′ni. Levites.—I Chr. 15:18, 20; Neh. 12:9.

UNPERFECT. Ps. 139:16. See PERFECT.

UNPREPARED. II Cor. 9:4. See PREPARE.

UNPROFITABLE. Tit. 3:9; Philemon 11; Heb. 7:18; 13:17. Become—Rom. 3:12. Servant—Mt. 25:30; Lu. 17:10. Talk—Job 15:3.

UNPUNISHED. Pr. 16:5; 17:5; 28:20; Jer. 25:29; 30:11; 46:28; 49:12. Evil shall not be—Pr. 11:21. False witness shall not be—Pr. 19:5. See PUNISHMENT.

UNQUENCHABLE. Mt. 3:12; 9:43; Lu. 3:17. See FIRE.

UNREASONABLE. Acts 25:27; II Thess. 3:2. See REASON.

UNREPROVABLE. Col. 1:8, 22. See REPROOF.

UNRIGHTEOUSNESS. Brake jaws of —Job 27:17. Broken, Shall be—Job 24:20. Cleanse us from—I John 1:9. Depart from—II Tim. 2:19. Dwellings of—Job 18:21. God is not—Heb. 6:10. He that is—Rev. 22:11. Hand of— Ps. 71:4. Judge—Lu. 18:6. Is God— Rom. 3:5. Kingdom, Shall not inherit—I Cor. 6:9. Law before the— I Cor. 6:1. Let him be—Rev. 22:11. Mammon—Lu. 16:11. Men, Of—Rom. 1:18. No, in him—John 7:18. Pleasure in—II Thess. 2:12. Punishment, Under—II Pet. 2:9. Put away—Job 22:23. Rejoiceth not in—I Cor. 13:6. Speak, Shall not—Job 27:4. Steward —Lu. 16:8. Will ye speak—Job 13:7. Witness—Deut. 19:16; Ps. 35:11. Work—Ps. 37:1. Wrought, Thou hast —Job 36:23. See RIGHTEOUSNESS, SIN, WICKEDNESS.

UNRIPE. Job 15:33.

UNRULY. Lawless and—I Tim. 1:9. Men—Tit. 1:10. See REBELLION.

UNSEARCHABLE. Greatness is—Ps. 145:3. Heart of kings—Pr. 25:3. Judgments—Rom. 11:33. Riches of Christ—Eph. 3:8. Things—Job 5:9.

UNSEEMLINESS. Rom. 1:27.

UNSEEMLY. I Cor. 7:36. Behave—I Cor. 13:5. Thing—Deut. 24:1.

UNSPEAKABLE. Gift—II Cor. 9:15. Joy—I Pet. 1:8. Words—II Cor. 12:4.

UNSPOTTED. Jas. 1:27. See SPOTTED, RIGHTEOUS.

UNSTABLE. Jas. 1:8. Ways—Pr. 5:6.

UNSTEDFAST. II Pet. 2:14. See STED-FASTNESS.

UNSTOPPED. Ears—Is. 35:5.

UNTEMPERED. Mortar—Ez. 13:10, 11, 14, 15; 22:28.

UNTHANKFUL. Kind toward the—Lu. 6:35. See THANKSGIVING.

UNTIMELY. Birth—Ps. 58:8. Born—I Cor. 15:8.

UNVEILED. I Cor. 11:5; II Cor. 3:18. See VEIL.

UNWALLED. Towns—Deut. 3:5; Esth. 9:19. See WALL.

UNWASHEN. Hands—Mt. 15:20; Lu. 7:2. See ABLUTIONS, PURIFICATION.

UNWEIGHED. I Ki. 7:47.

UNWISE. Eph. 5:15. People—Deut. 32:6. Son—Hos. 13:13. See WISDOM.

UNWITTINGLY. Eat of holy things—Lev. 22:14. Done—Num. 15:24. Sin—Lev. 4:2. Unawares, And—Josh. 20: 3. See IGNORANCE.

UNWORTHY. I Cor. 6:2. Judge—Acts 13:46. Manner—I Cor. 11:27.

UPBRAID. Cities—Mt. 11:20. Not—Jas. 1:5. Them with unbelief—Mk. 16:14. See REPROACH.

UPHARSIN, u-phär'sin. Part of the writing on the wall at the Feast of Belshazzar.—Dan. 5:25.

UPHAZ, ü'phäz. A place in Arabia.—Dan. 10:5.

UPHEAVE. Nah. 1:5.

UPHELD. Righteousness—Is. 59:16. Wrath—Is. 63:5.

UPHOLD. Lev. 25:35; Pr. 51:12; Is. 41:10; 42:1; 63:5. Egypt—Ez. 30:6. Evil-doers—Job 8:20. Fatherless—Ps. 146:9. Jehovah, By—Ps. 37:24; 145: 14. Meek—Ps. 147:6. Righteous—Ps. 37:17. Soul—Ps. 54:4. Word—Ps. 119:116; Job 4:4; Heb. 1:3.

UPPER. Chamber—Ju. 3:24; II Chr. 3: 9; Ez. 42:5; II Ki. 23:12; I Chr. 28: 11; Acts 9:37, 39; 20:8. Coasts—Acts 19:1. Gate—II Ki. 15:35; II Chr. 23:20. Lip—Lev. 13:45. Millstone—Deut. 24:6; II Sam. 11:21; I Chr. 7: 24. Pool—II Ki. 18:17; Is. 7:3; 36:2. Room—Mk. 14:15; Lu. 22:12; Acts 1:

13. Springs—Josh. 15:19; Ju. 1:15. Water-course—II Chr. 32:30.

UPPERMOST. Basket—Gen. 40:17. Boughs—Is. 17:6.

UPRIGHT. I Sam. 29:6; Job 1:1; Ps. 19:13; 112:4; Mic. 7:4. Cut off—Job 4:7. Friendship of—Pr. 3:32. Good will of—Pr. 14:9. Jehovah is—Ps. 25:8. Man made—Eccl. 7:29. Might reason—Job 23:7. Path of—Pr. 15: 19. Praise for—Ps. 33:1. Prayer of—Pr. 15:8. Soul—Hab. 2:4. Wisdom for—Pr. 2:7. See RIGHTEOUSNESS.

UPRIGHTLY. Deal—Ju. 9:16. Walk—Gal. 2:14. Written—Eccl. 12:10. See RIGHTEOUSNESS.

UPRIGHTNESS. Pr. 17:26. Heart—I Ki. 3:6. Land of—Ps. 143:10. Path—Pr. 2:13; 4:11. Peace and—Mal. 2:6. Pleasure in—I Chr. 29:17. Preserve—Ps. 25:21. Sceptre of—Heb. 1:8. Walk in—Is. 57:2. Way of just is—Is. 26:7. Words of—Job 6:25. See RIGHTEOUS-NESS.

UPRISING. Ps. 139:2.

UPROAR. Acts 20:1. City in—I Ki. 1: 41; Acts 17:5. See TUMULT.

UPSIDE. Down—Is. 24:1; 29:16. Turn—II Ki. 21:13; Ps. 146:9. World, Down—Acts 17:6.

UR, ûr. (1) Of the Chaldees—A city or district in Mesopotamia, the birth-place of Abraham.—Gen. 11:28, 31; 13:7; Neh. 9:7.

(2) Father of one of David's mighty men.—I Chr. 11:35.

URBANUS, ur-bä'nus. A disciple in Rome whom Paul salutes.—Rom. 16:9.

URI, ü'rī. (1) Father of Geber.—I Ki. 4:19.

(2) Son of Hur.—Ex. 31:2; 35:30; 38: 22; I Chr. 2:20; II Chr. 1:5.

(3) One who married a foreign wife.—Ezra 10:24.

URIAH, u-rī'ah. (1) Husband of Bath-sheba who afterwards became the wife of David.—II Sam. 11:3–26; 12: 10, 15; I Ki. 15:5; I Chr. 11:41.

(2) A priest who helped to rebuild the wall.—Ezra 8:33; Neh. 3:4, 21.

(3) Another priest who acted as a wit-ness for Isaiah.—Is. 8:2.

(4) One who stood up with Ezra when he read the law.—Neh. 8:4.

URIEL, u-rī'ĕl. (1) **Father-in-law of Rehoboam.**—II Chr. 13:2.

(2) **A Kohathite.**—I Chr. 6:24.

URIJAH, u-rī'jäh. (1) **A high priest in Jerusalem.**—II Ki. 16:10–16.

(2) **A prophet.**—Jer. 26:20–23.

URIM AND THUMMIN. Placed in the breastplate of the high priest—Ex. 28:30; Lev. 8:8.

God to be consulted by.—Num. 27:21.

No answer from, on account of sin.—I Sam. 28:6.

Were wanting in the second temple.—Ezra 2:63; Neh. 7:65.

USE. I Cor. 9:12. Baal, For—Hos. 2:8. See BAAL, IDOLATRY. Fruit—Deut. 20: 6; 28:30. Gold—Ex. 38:24. Hospitality—I Pet. 4:9. King, By—Esth. 6:8. Profanity—Pr. 30:9. Vain repetitions —Mt. 6:7. World—I Cor. 7:31.

USEFUL. II Tim. 4:11.

USURY: The lending of money or other property for increase.—Lev. 25:37; Neh. 5:6, 7; Ez. 22:12.

Not taken.—By faithful Israelites—Ps. 15:5; Ez. 18:8, 9.

Laws concerning.—Year of release— Deut. 15:2. Forbidden to take from brethren, especially when poor—Ex. 22:25; 23:19, 20; Lev. 25:35–37; Deut. 23:19, 20.

Exacted from foreigners.—Deut. 23:20.

Unlawful.—Judgment against taking or giving—Is. 24:12; Jer. 15:10; Ez. 18: 13; 22:12.

Prophecy concerning.—He that hath not taken—Ez. 18:17.

Illustrative of.—Improvement of talents —Mt. 25:27; Lu. 19:23.

Lend.—Blessing at Gerizim—Shall lend, but not borrow—Deut. 28:12. Laws concerning—Ex. 22:25; Deut. 15:6, 8; 24:10, 11. Lending on interest— Deut. 23:19, 20. Lending to sojourner —Deut. 28:44. Year of release—Deut. 15:2. Servant of lender—Pr. 22:7. Prosperity of the man who lendeth— Ps. 112:5. Miscellaneous: He lendeth —Ps. 37:26. Lendeth unto Jehovah— Pr. 19:17.

Borrow.—Articles borrowed: Israelites borrowed of the Egyptians: Jewels and raiment—Ex. 3:22; 11:2. Vessels —II Ki. 4:3. Money on land—Neh. 5:4. Not borrow—In blessing at Gerizim, shall lend, but not borrow— Deut. 15:6; 28:12. Laws concerning: Restitution of borrowed things—Ex. 22:14. In year of release—Deut. 15:2– 6.

Miscellaneous.—The borrower is servant to the lender—Pr. 22:7. Wicked borroweth and payeth not again—Ps. 37: 21. In Teaching of Jesus concerning: From him that would borrow, turn not away—Mt. 5:42.

US-WARD. Ps. 40:5; Rom. 6:18; Eph. 1:19.

UTHAI, ū'thāi. (1) **One who returned with Ezra.**—Ezra 8:14.

(2) **A descendant of Judah.**—I Chr. 9: 4.

UTTER. Dark sayings—Ps. 78:2. Error —Is. 32:6. Hastily—Eccl. 5:2. Jesus —See JESUS. Knowledge—Pr. 15:2. Lies—Pr. 14:5. Memory—Ps. 145:7. Most high—Ps. 18:13; 68:33. Nothing —Pr. 29:24. Perverse things—See PERVERSE THINGS. Praise—Ps. 119: 171. Rashly—Lev. 5:4. Waste—Ez. 29:10. Works of Jehovah—Ps. 106:2.

UTTERANCE. Acts 2:4; I Cor. 1:5; II Cor. 8:7; Eph. 6:19.

UTTERMOST. Heb. 7:25. Cities—Josh. 15:21. Part of heaven—Neh. 1:9; Is. 13:5; Mt. 13:27. Parts—I Ki. 6:24. Camp, Of—Num. 11:1. Country, Of— I Sam. 14:2. Earth, Of—Ps. 2:8; 65:8; Mt. 13:27; Acts 1:8; 13:47. Egypt, Of—Is. 7:18. Sea, Of—Ps. 139:9. Wrath—I Thess. 2:16.

UZ, ŭz. (1) **Son of Dishon.**—Gen. 36:28; I Chr. 1:42.

(2) **A region south of Edom, home of Job.**—Job 1:1; Jer. 25:20; Lam. 4:21.

(3) **Grandson of Shem.**—Gen. 10:23; I Chr. 1:17.

UZAI, ū'zāi. **Father of Palal who helped to repair the wall.**—Neh. 3:25.

UZAL, ū'zal. **A descendant of Shem.**— Gen. 10:27; I Chr. 1:21.

UZZA, ŭz'zá. (1) **Son of Abinadab.**—He was slain for touching the ark—II Sam. 6:3–8; I Chr. 13:7.

(2) **A Benjamite.**—I Chr. 8:7.

(3) **Owner of a garden where Manasseh and Amon were buried.**—II Ki. 21: 18, 26.

(4) **A Merarite.**—I Chr. 6:29.

(5) **Ancestor of a family who returned with Zerubbabel.**—Ezra 2:49; Neh. 7: 51.

UZZEN-SHUREERAH,üz'zen–shē'e-rah. **A city in Ephraim.**—I Chr. 7:24.

UZZI, üz'zi. (1) **Grandson of Issachar.**— I Chr. 7:2, 3.

(2) **A descendant of Phinehas son of Aaron.**—I Chr. 6:5, 6, 51; Ezra 7:4.

(3) **A Benjamite.**—I Chr. 9:8.

(4) **Grandson of Benjamin.**—I Chr. 7:7.

(5) **A priest.**—Neh. 12:19, 42.

(6) **An overseer of the Levites.**—Neh. 11:22.

UZZIA, uz-zī'à. **One of David's mighty men.**—I Chr. 11:44.

UZZIAH, uz-zī'ah. (1) **King of Judah.** —II Ki. 15:13–34; II Chr. 26:1–23; 27:2; Is. 1:1; 6:1; 7:1; Hos. 1:1; Amos 1:1; Zech. 14:5. See AZARIAH.

(2) **A priest who married a foreign wife.**—Ezra 10:21.

(3) **A Kohathite.**—I Chr. 6:24.

(4) **Father of one of David's officers.**— I Chr. 27:25.

(5) Neh. 11:4.

UZZIEL, uz-zī'el. (1) **A Simeonite.**—I Chr. 4:42.

(2) **Grandson of Levi.**—Ex. 6:18, 22; Lev. 10:4; Num. 3:19, 30; I Chr. 6:2, 18; 15:10; 23:12, 20; 24:24.

UZZIELITES, uz-zī'el-ites. **Descendants of Uzziel.**—Num. 3:27.

VAGABONDS. Ps. 109:10.

VAIN. See VANITY.

VAINGLORIOUS. Gal. 5:26. See GLORYING, PRIDE, VANITY.

VAINGLORY. Phil. 2:3. See GLORYING, PRIDE.

VAIZATHA, va-ïz'a-thà. **Haman's son.** —Esth. 9:9.

VALE. Elah, Of—I Sam. 17:19. Kings —Gen. 14:17. See VALLEY.

VALIANT. Be thou—I Sam. 18:17. Men—I Chr. 5:18; II Chr. 28:6. Ones cry—Is. 33:7. See COURAGE.

VALIANTLY. Did—I Sam. 14:48. Israel doeth—Num. 24:18. Right hand of Jehovah doeth—Ps. 118:15. Through God we shall do—Ps. 60:12; 108:13.

VALLEY, *Tract of land between mountains.*—I Sam. 17:3. Called vales and dales.

Mentioned in Scripture.—Vale of Siddim—Gen. 14:3, 8. Shaveh, or King's

Vale—Gen. 14:17; II Sam. 18:18. Gerar—Gen. 26:17. Eshcol—Num. 32: 9; Deut. 1:24. Zared—Num. 21:12. Moab—Deut. 34:6. Jericho—Deut. 34: 3. Achor—Josh. 7:24; Is. 65:10; Hos. 2:15. Aijalon—Josh. 10:12. Hinnom or Tophet—Josh. 18:16; II Ki. 23:10; II Chr. 28:3; Jer. 7:32. Iphtahel— Josh. 19:14, 27. Lebanon—Josh. 11:17. Rephaim or Giant's—Josh. 15:8; 18: 6; II Sam. 5:18; Is. 17:5. Bochim— Ju. 2:5. Sorek—Ju. 16:4. Zeboim—I Sam. 13:18. Vale of Elah—I Sam. 17: 2; 21:9. Gad—I Sam. 24:5. Salt—II Sam. 8:13. Zephathah—II Chr. 14:10. Megiddo—II Chr. 35:22; Zech. 12:11. Beracah—II Chr. 20:26. Succoth—Ps. 60:6. Gibeon—Is. 28:21. Hamon-gog —Ez. 39:11. Jezreel—Hos. 1:5. Shittim—Joel 3:18. Of vision—Is. 22:1. Of the shadow of death—Ps. 23:4. Rough Valley—Deut. 21:4; Job 30:6; Is. 57:5.

Fat valley (when it is fruitful).—I Sam. 6:13; Ps. 65:13; Is. 28:1, 4.

Abounds with springs and fountains.— Deut. 8:7; 11:11; Ps. 104:10; Is. 41:18.

Trees of valley.—I Ki. 10:27.

A lily of the valley.—Song of Sol. 2:1. Ravens of—Pr. 30:17. Doves of— Ez. 7:16.

To be filled with hostile chariots.—Is. 22:7.

Miracles connected with.—Moon made to stand still over Aijalon—Josh. 10: 12. Ditches filled with water—II Ki. 3:16, 17. Water made to appear to Moabites like blood—II Ki. 3:22, 23.

Inhabitants of.—Jer. 21:13.

Illustrative of.—The tents of Israel— Num. 24:6. Affliction and death—Ps. 23:4. Removing obstructions to the gospel—Is. 40:4; Lu. 3:5. Church of Christ—Song of Sol. 6:11.

VALOR. See COURAGE.

VALOROUS. Ez. 27:11.

VALUE. Mt. 6:26; Lu. 12:24; Col. 2:23. Gold, With—Job 28:16, 19. Man, Of a—See MAN. More, than sheep—Mt. 12:12. More, than sparrows—Mt. 10: 31; Lu. 12:7. Physicians of no—Job 13:4. Priest shall—Lev. 27:8, 12. See WORTH.

VANIAH, va-nī'ah. **A son of Bani who married a foreign wife.**—Ezra 10:36.

VANISH. Away—Heb. 8:13; Jas. 4:14. Cloud—Job 7:9. Heavens—Is. 51:6. Is their wisdom—Jer. 49:7. Out of their sight—Lu. 24:31. See DISAPPEAR.

VANITY: Creation subject to.—Rom. 8:20.

All is.—Eccl. 2:1, 11, 15, 17, 19, 21, 23, 26; 3:19; 4:4; 6:4, 11; 7:15; 8:10; 11:8. Vanity of vanities—Eccl. 2:14.

All under the sun is vain.—Eccl. 4:7.

Riches.—Eccl. 4:8; 6:2.

Desire.—Eccl. 6:9. Laughter of fool is —Eccl. 7:6.

Abundance of increase is.—Eccl. 5:10; 12:8.

Vanity of dreams and words.—Eccl. 5:7. Of words—Job 16:3; 35:16.

Beauty is.—Pr. 31:30.

Vanity of life.—Job 7:16; Ps. 39:5, 11; Eccl. 9:9; 11:10.

Manner of life is.—I Pet. 1:18.

Applied to nations.—Is. 40:17; 59:4; Jer. 10:3; 14:22; Hab. 2:13; Acts 4:25. Vanity of Gentiles—Rom. 1:21. Of Gentiles' mind—Eph. 4:17. Of men —Ju. 9:4; 11:3; II Sam. 7:20; Job 11:12; 15:2; Ps. 62:9; Jas. 2:20. Of the godless—Job 27:2; Ps. 39:6; 89:47; Eccl. 6:12. Of wise—I Cor. 3:20. Of judges of the earth—Is. 40:23. Fathers inherited—Jer. 16:19. People meditate on vain things—Ps. 2:1. Vanity of women—Is. 4:3 (*fig.*). Thoughts of men are vain—Ps. 94:11.

Applied to idolatry.—II Ki. 17:15; Is. 44:9; Jer. 9:19; 10:15; Zech. 10:2; Acts 14:15. Oblation of vanity—Is. 1:13.

Warnings against.—I Sam. 12:21; Ps. 62:10. Deceitfulness of—Job 15:31; Ps. 31:6; Jonah 2:8. Wealth gotten by—Pr. 13:11. Reproof for—Ps. 4:2. Vain persons—Pr. 12:11; 28:19; Mt. 6:7. Vainglory—Gal. 5:26; Phil. 2:3. Vain deceit—Col. 2:8. Vain talking— I Tim. 1:6; Tit. 1:10. Vain religion —Jas. 1:26. False prophets—Jer. 23:16. False teachers—II Pet. 2:18. Unrighteousness of—Jer. 2:5. Jehovah angered with—Deut. 32:21; I Ki. 16:13, 26. Vanity as punishment — Ps. 78:33.

Prayer against.—Ps. 119:137.

Prophecy.—Israel's—Is. 49:4; Jer. 2:5, 30.

VANQUISH. Job 32:13. See CONQUER, TRIUMPH.

VAPOR. Causeth, to ascend—Ps. 136:7; Jer. 10:3; 51:16. Getting of treasures, is—Pr. 21:6. Rain from his—Job 36:27. Smoke, Of—Acts 2:19. Snow and —Ps. 148:8. Ye are a—Jas. 4:14. See CLOUDS.

VARIABLENESS. Jas. 1:17. See CHANGE.

VARIANCE. Man at—Mt. 10:35. Without—Jas. 3:17. See STRIFE.

VARIATION. Jas. 1:17.

VASHTI, văsh'ti. Queen of Ahasuerus whom he rejected.—Esth. 1:9–19; 2:1, 4, 17.

VATS. Pr. 3:10; Joel 2:24.

VAULT. Ez. 16:24; Amos 9:6.

VAUNT. Ju. 7:2; I Cor. 13:4.

VAUNTINGS. Jas. 4:16.

VEHEMENTLY. Lu. 23:10.

VEIL: of tabernacle.—See TABERNACLE.

Of temple.—See TEMPLE.

On Moses' countenance.—Ex. 34:33–35; II Cor. 3:13.

On heart of Israel.—II Cor. 3:14. Not on Christian's heart—II Cor. 3:16–18.

A garment worn by women.—Gen. 38:14; Is. 3:23. Symbolic of modesty— Gen. 24:65; 38:14; I Cor. 11:5–7.

Illustrative of spiritual blindness.—Is. 25:7; II Cor. 3:15, 16.

VENGEANCE. Cain in danger—Gen. 4:14–15. Forbidden—Lev. 19:18. Executing the vengeance of the covenant—Lev. 26:25. Belongs to God— Deut. 32:35, 41–43; Ps. 94:1; Rom. 12:19; Heb. 10:30. Widow seeks vengeance—Lu. 18:2–8. Jehovah takes vengeance on Ammon—Ju. 11:36. Upon Israel—Ps. 99:8. Sons of Jacob, on Shechem — Gen. 34:20–31. Jehovah hath a day of—Is. 34:8; 63:4. Will come with—Is. 35:4. Put on garments of — Is. 59:17. Vengeance on Babylon—Jer. 50:15, 28. On rebellious House of Israel—Ez. 24:8. On nations who hear not Jehovah — Mic. 5:15. Days of vengeance—Lu. 21:22. Concerning Paul's hand—Acts 28:4. On evil-doers—I Pet. 2:14. God not unrighteous—Rom. 3:5–6. On those that obey not—II Thess. 1:8–9. See JUDGMENT, PUNISHMENT FOR SIN, COMMANDMENTS.

VENISON. Eat of—Gen. 25:28; 27:19, 25, 31. Bring me—Gen. 27:7. Hunt for—Gen. 27:5. Taken—Gen. 27:33.

VENOM. Addest thy—Hab. 2:15. Asps, Of—Deut. 32:33. See MALICE, POISON.

VENOMOUS. Creature—Acts 28:4.

VENTURE. Drew bow at a—I Ki. 22: 34; II Chr. 18:33.

VERIFIED. Word—Gen. 42:20; I Ki. 8:26; II Chr. 6:17. See WITNESS.

VERMILLION. Painted with—Jer. 22: 14. Portrayed with—Ez. 23:14. See COLOR.

VESSELS. Used in the preparation of food: Basin—*Gold and Brass*—Ex. 12: 22; 24:6; 27:3; 38:3; Num. 4:14; II Sam. 17:28; I Ki. 7:40, 45, 51; I Chr. 28:17; II Chr. 4:8, 11, 22; Neh. 7:70; Jer. 52:19.

Baskets for bread—Ex. 29:3, 23; Lev. 8: 2, 26, 31; Mt. 15:37; Mk. 6:43. See BASKET. For figs—II Ki. 10:7; Ps. 81: 6; Jer. 24:2. For first fruits—Deut. 26:2, 4. For fruit—Amos 8:1, 2. For grapes—Jer. 6:9.

Bellows—Num. 7:13-85.

Bowls—*Gold and silver*—Ju. 6:38; I Chr. 28:17; Jer. 52:19; Amos 6:6; Rev. 5:8; 21:9. See BOWLS.

Bottles—Jer. 19:1, 10. For holding milk —Ju. 4:19. For holding water—Gen. 21:14, 15, 19. For wine—Josh. 9:4, 13; I Sam. 1:24; 10:3; 16:20; Jer. 13:12; Hab. 2:15. Of skin—Mt. 9:17 *marg.*; Mk. 2:22 *marg.*; Lu. 5:37, 38 *marg.* See BOTTLES.

Caldron—*Heb.* Sir—A large pot, often of brass—Jer. 1:13; Ez. 11:3, 7, 11; 24:3, 6. Called "Flesh-pots"—Ex. 16: 3. Called "Pots"—Ex. 27:3; I Ki. 7: 45; II Ki. 4:38; Jer. 52:18, 19; Zech. 14:20, 21. Called "Wash - pot"—Ps. 60:8.

Caldron—*Heb.* Dud—II Chr. 35:13.

Caldron—*Heb.* Kallachath—earthen—I Sam. 2:14; Mic. 3:3.

Coffer—I Sam. 6:8, 11.

Cruse—I Sam. 26:11; I Ki. 14:3; 17:12; II Ki. 2:20; Mt. 26:7; Mk. 14:3; Lu. 7:37.

Cups—Gen. 40:11; I Ki. 7:50; Pr. 23:31; Jer. 35:5; 52:19. Drinking cup—Mt. 10:42; 20:22, 23; 23:26; 26:27, 39, 42; Mk. 7:4, 8; 9:41; 10:38, 39; 14:23, 36; Lu. 11:39; 22:17, 20; I Cor. 10:16, 21;

11:26–28; Rev. 14:10; 16:19; 17:4; 18:6.

Dish—Ex. 25:20; II Ki. 21:13; Pr. 19: 24; 26:15; Mt. 26:23; Mk. 14:20.

Firepans—Ex. 27:3; 38:3; Num. 16:6; I Ki. 7:50; II Ki. 25:5; Jer. 52:19.

Flesh-hooks — *Brazen forks with three prongs*—Ex. 27:3; 38:3; Num. 4:14; I Sam. 2:13, 14.

Forks—I Sam. 13:21.

Jar—I Ki. 17:12, 14, 16; 18:33.

Kettle—I Sam. 2:14.

Mill or mortar for grinding meal—Gen. 18:6; Ex. 11:5; Num. 11:8; Deut. 24: 6; Is. 47:2; Jer. 25:10; Mt. 18:6; Lu. 17:2.

Oven—Ex. 8:3; Lev. 2:4; 7:9; 11:35; 26:26.

Pan—I Sam. 2:14; I Ki. 7:38; II Chr. 4:6; 35:13. Zech. 12:6. *Baking-pan*— Lev. 2:3; 6:21; 7:9. *Frying-pan*—Lev. 2:7; 7:9.

Pitcher—Gen. 21:14; 24:15, 20, 43–46; Ju. 7:10–20; Mk. 14:13; Lu. 22:10. Of *earth*—Lam. 4:2.

Platter—Mt. 23:25. *Silver*—Num. 7:13- 85. *Gold*—Ezra 1:9. *Wooden*—Mt. 14: 8, 11; Mk. 6:25, 28.

Pot—*Heb.* Parur—Ex. 16:33; Num. 11: 8; Ju. 6:19. See "Caldron."

Sieve—Amos 9:9.

Skin, Wine—See BOTTLE.

Shovel—Ex. 27:3; 38:3; Num. 4:14; I Ki. 7:45; II Ki. 25:4; II Chr. 4:22; Jer. 52:18.

Snuffer—I Ki. 7:50; II Chr. 4:22.

Spoon—Ex. 25:29; Num. 4:7; 7:14-86; I Ki. 7:50; II Ki. 25:14; II Chr. 4:22; Jer. 52:18.

See MEAL, SERVING OF; TABERNACLE, VESSELS OF THE.

VESTMENTS. II Ki. 10:22. See GARMENTS.

VESTURE. Ps. 104:6. Cast lots upon— Ps. 22:18. Change, As a—Ps. 102:26. Linen, Of fine—Gen. 41:42. Washed his—Gen. 49:11. Vesture, Casting lots for Christ's—Mt. 27:35; Mk. 15:24; Lu. 23:24; John 19:24. See GARMENTS.

VEXATION. Demon, With—Mt. 15:22. Fool's—Pr. 12:16. God did—II Chr. 15:6. Hearts of many—Ez. 32:9. Judah—Is. 11:13. Killeth the foolish man—Job 5:2. Soul—Job 19:2; II Pet. 2:8. Spirit, Of—Eccl. 1:14, 17 (A.V.);

Is. 65:14. See VANITY. Weighed—Job 6:2.

VIAL. Oil, Of—I Sam. 10:1; II Ki. 9:1. See VESSELS.

VICTORY. I Sam. 19:5; II Sam. 8:6; 19:2; I Chr. 11:14; 29:11; Ps. 98:1; Pr. 21:31; Rev. 15:2. Death, Over—Rom. 8:37, 38; I Cor. 15:54-57; Rev. 15:2. See LIFE, SALVATION. Judgment, Unto—Mt. 12:20. Overcome the world, That hath—I John 5:4. See BATTLE, WAR, TRIUMPH.

VICTUAL. I Ki. 20:27. See FOOD.

VIEW. Josh. 2:1; 7:2; Neh. 2:13, 15. See SEE.

VILE. Job 34:18; Jer. 15:19; Nah. 3:6. Clothing—Jas. 2:2. Deeds—Jas. 3:16. Passions—Rom. 1:26. See LUST, LASCIVIOUSNESS, SIN, PURIFICATION.

VILLAGES, *Chatzer.*—Properly an enclosure, as of buildings enclosing a court (Josh. 13:23, 28); the encampment of nomads (Gen. 26:16; Deut. 2:23) and of hamlets near towns (Lev. 25:31, 34; Josh. 15:32; I Chr. 4:33; Neh. 11:25). *Kopher.*—A village as protected by walls. Neither a hamlet nor a city, but between, as to size and character—I Sam. 6:18; I Chr. 27:25; Song of Sol. 7:11; Mt. 21:2; Mk. 8:22, 26; Lu. 8:1; 10:38; John 11:1; 7:42.

Cities were surrounded by villages.—Mk. 8:27.

Conditions prescribed for a city different from those of a village.—Lev. 25:29-31.

Villages by conquest.—Num. 32:42; Ez. 38:11-12; Hab. 3:14 (see *margin*).

Deborah arouses the villages.—Ju. 5:7, 11 (*margin*).

Villages of Philistines returning trespass offering.—I Sam. 6:18.

Villages as an inheritance.—Of Reuben —Josh. 13:23, 28. Of Judah—Josh. 15:32-62; Neh. 11:25-30. Of Ephraim —Josh. 16:9. Of Benjamin—Josh. 18: 24, 28. Of Simeon—Josh. 19:6. Of Zebulun—Josh. 19:15-16. Of Issachar —Josh. 19:22. Of Asher—Josh. 19:30, 31. Of Naphtali—Josh. 19:38-39. Of Dan—Josh. 19:48. Given to Caleb for —Josh. 21:12; Jᵀ Chr. 5:56.

The habitations of.—Simeon—I Chr. 4: 32-33. Of the Levites—I Chr. 9:14-16,

22, 25. Of the temple singers—Neh. 12:28-29.

Miscellaneous facts concerning.—Oversight of king's treasuries in—I Chr. 27:25. Nehemiah invited to meet Sanballat in—Neh. 6:2. Lodging place of lovers—Song of Sol. 7:11. Jews of Esther's day rejoice at their conquest —Esth. 9:19. Called on to give glory to Jehovah—Is. 42:11. The haunts of the murderer—Ps. 10:8.

Miscellaneous facts concerning Jesus and the disciples.—Jesus preaches in —Mt. 9:35; Mk. 6:6; Lu. 8:1; 13:22. He heals in—Mk. 6:56; Lu. 17:12. He abides in—Lu. 9:56; 10:38. Is refused hospitality in—Lu. 9:52-53. Sends crowd away to buy food—Mt. 14:15; Mk. 6:36. Sends disciples for a colt—Mt. 21:2; Mk. 11:2; Lu. 19:30. Meets two disciples near Emmaus—Lu. 24:13-15, 28. Apostles preach in Samaritan villages—Acts 8:25.

VINE: Often found wild.—II Ki. 4:39; Hos. 9:10.

Places where cultivated.—In vineyards —Gen. 9:20. On sides of hills—Jer. 31:5. In the valleys—Song of Sol. 6: 11. By the walls of houses—Ps. 128:3. Canaan abounded in—Deut. 6:11; 8:8.

How cultivated.—Pruned to increase fruitfulness—Lev. 25:3; II Chr. 26: 10; Is. 18:5.

Places celebrated for.—Eshcol—Num. 13:23, 24. Sibmah—Is. 16:8, 9; Jer. 48:32. Lebanon—Hos. 14:7.

Animals destructive to.—Foxes—Song of Sol. 2:15. Wild boar—Ps. 80:13.

Kinds of.—Dwarf and spreading vine—Ez. 17:6. Fruitful—Is. 32:12. Of Sodom unfit for use—Deut. 32:22. Choicest—Is. 5:2. Degenerate—Jer. 2:21. Wild—II Ki. 4:39. Luxuriant—Hos. 10:1.

Injured by hail and frost.—Ps. 78:47; 105:32, 33.

Sometimes cast its fruit before it came to perfection.—Job 15:33; Mal. 3:11.

Fruits of.—Lu. 22:18. Grapes—Gen. 40: 10. Sour when unripe—Jer. 31:30. Eaten fresh—Deut. 23:24. Clusters—Rev. 14:18, 19. Eaten dried—I Sam. 25:18; 30:12. Sold in markets—Neh. 13:15. Made into wine—Deut. 32:14; Mt. 26:29; Mk. 14:25.

Uses of.—Wood of, only fit for burning
—Ez. 15:2-5. Young cattle fed on its
leaves and shoots—Gen. 49:11. Produced fruit—Num. 13:20. Perfumes
the air with fragrance of its flowers—
Song of Sol. 2:13; Hos. 14:7. God
made fruitful to his people when obedient—Joel 2:22; Zech. 8:12. Unfruitful to disobedient—Is. 24:7; Jer. 8:13;
Hos. 2:12; Joel 1:7, 12; Nah. 2:2; Hag.
2:19. In fable—Ju. 9:9, 12.

Commandments concerning.— Nazirites
forbidden to eat any part of—Num.
6:3, 4. Manoah's wife forbidden to eat
fruit of—Ju. 13:14. Assyrians told
Jews to eat of their own—II Ki. 18:
31; Is. 36:16.

Prophecies concerning.—Is. 7:23; 34:4;
Hab. 3:17.

Proverbial allusions to.—Jer. 31:29, 30;
Ez. 18:2.

Figurative.—Christ the vine—John 15:
1, 2. Of Israel—Ps. 80:8; Is. 5:2-7;
Jer. 6:9. Saints (fruitful branches)—
John 15:5. Mere professors—Unfruitful branches—John 15:2, 6. Quick
growth—Hos. 14:7. Rich clusters—
Song of Sol. 7:8. Vine yields figs—
Jas. 3:12. Pruning of (God purifying
his people by afflictions)—John 15:2.
Worthlessness of wood (wicked)—Ez.
15:6, 7. Unfruitful (wicked)—Hos. 10:
1. Sitting under one's own—I Ki. 4:25;
Mic. 4:4; Zech. 3:10.

VINEDRESSER. II Ki. 25:12; Is. 61:5;
Jer. 52:16; Joel 1:11; Lu. 13:7.

VINEGAR. As, to the teeth—Pr. 10:26.
Dip thy morsel in—Ruth 2:14. Drink,
To—Ps. 69:21. Wine, Of—Num. 6:3.
Vinegar offered to Jesus—Mt. 27:34, 48;
Mk. 15:36; Lu. 23:36; John 19:29, 30.
See Ps. 69:21. See Food.

VINEYARD.   Ancient   husbandry. —
Gen. 9:20.

Valuable property given as inheritance.
—Num. 16:14; Deut. 6:11; Josh. 24:
13; I Sam. 22:7; II Ki. 5:26; 18:32;
Neh. 9:25; Is. 36:17; Jer. 32:15; 39:
10; Hos. 2:15.

Ownership of.—Deut. 20:6; Song of Sol.
8:12. Authority over—I Chr. 27:27;
Mt. 20:1, 2, 15; 21:40, 41. Keeper of—
Song of Sol. 1:6; 8:11; Is. 27:2.

Letting out of.—Mt. 21:33; Mk. 12:1;
Lu. 20:9. Mortgaging of—Neh. 5:
3-11.

Depriving owner of.—I Sam. 8:15; I Ki.
21:1-18.

Trespassing in.—Ex. 22:5; Num. 20:17;
21:22; Is. 3:14.

**Gleaned by poor at harvest and in sev-
enth year.**—Ex. 23:11; Lev. 19:10; 25:
5; Deut. 24:21. Permission to eat
grapes in—Deut. 23:24.

Planting and cultivation of.—Deut. 22:
9; II Ki. 19:29; Ps. 80:14, 15; 107:37;
Pr. 31:16; Eccl. 2:4; Is. 65:21; Jer.
2:21; Ez. 28:26; Amos 9:14; Mk. 12:
1; Lu. 13:6-9; John 15:1-6; I Cor. 9:7.

Styles of cultivation.—(1) Planting in
rows 8 or 10 feet apart each way.
Stock grows up large, 6 or 8 feet,
fastened to a strong stake, shoots allowed to extend from stake to stake.
(2) Planted on the side of a terraced
hill, stock trailing on the ground, while
fruit-bearing branches are propped up
with forked sticks.

Pruning.—Lev. 25:3, 4; John 15:2. Neglect of—Pr. 24:30; Is. 5:6.

Laboring in.—Is. 5:4; Mt. 20:1-14; 21:
28-31; Lu. 20:9, 10.

How protected.—Walls of stone—Num.
22:24; Pr. 24:31. Hedge—Mt. 21:33.
Walls and hedge combined—Ps. 80:12,
13; Is. 5:5.

Vineyards as places of concealment.—
Ju. 14:5; 21:20, 21; Job 24:18. Of
visitation—Song of Sol. 7:12. Lodges
in—Is. 1:8; 5:2; Mt. 21:33.

Vintage season.—People live there—Ju.
9:27; Is. 16:10. Gathering the crop—
Jer. 6:9. Shout with joy—Jer. 25:30.
Vintage withheld for punishment—
Deut. 28:30, 39; Is. 16:10; Amos 4:9;
5:11; Zeph. 1:13. Rechabites forbidden to maintain for sobriety—Jer. 35:
6, 7.

Satisfaction of destroyed.—Song of Sol.
2:15; Is. 16:10; Jer. 12:10; Amos 4:9;
5:11; Zeph. 1:13.

Emblems of peacefulness.—I Ki. 4:25;
Mic. 4:4; Zech. 3:10.

Parables of vineyard.—Is. 5:1-7; Mt.
20:1-14; 21:28-31; Mk. 12:1-9; Lu.
13:6-9; 20:9-16; John 15:1-6.

VINTAGE. Lev. 26:5; Num. 18:12; Job 24:6; Is. 16:10; 24:13; Mic. 6:15; Rev. 14:19. See GRAPES, VINE, VINEYARD.

VIOLENCE. Weapons of—Gen. 49:5. See WAR. Of waves—Acts 27:41. Acts of—Is. 59:6. In persecuting of Paul—Acts 21:35. Earth filled with—Gen. 6:11, 13. In city—Ps. 55:9. See CITIES. Without violence—Acts 5:26.

Warnings against.—Jer. 22:3, 17. Punishment for—Ps. 11:5; Jer. 51:35; Ez. 7:11, 23; 8:17, 18; 12:19; Joel 3:19; Amos 3:10; 6:3; Mic. 6:12, 13; Hab. 2:8, 17; Zeph. 1:9; 3:4, 5; Mal. 2:16.

Prophecies concerning.—Is. 60:18; Jer. 6:7; 51:46; Ez. 28:16; 45:9; Jonah 3:8; Hab. 1:9. No violence—Is. 53:9.

Figurative.—Ps. 73:6; Pr. 4:17; 10:6; 13:2. Kingdom of heaven suffereth violence—Mt. 11:12. See HANDS, VIOLENT.

VIPER. Came out—Acts 28:3. Offspring of—Mt. 3:7; 12:34; 23:33; Lu. 3:7. Tongue—Job 20:16. See SERPENT.

VIRGIN, Heb. *Bethulah.*—Separated, Unmarried woman. Gr. *Parthenos*—a virgin. Personification of city or state: Israel—Jer. 18:13; 31:4, 13, 21; Ez. 23:3, 8; Amos 5:2; 8:13. Zion—II Ki. 19:21; Is. 37:22; 62:5; Jer. 14:17; Lam. 1:4, 18; 2:10, 13, 21; Joel 1:8. Judah—Lam. 1:15; Ez. 23:3, 8. Babylon—Is. 47:1. Egypt—Jer. 46:11. Sidon—Is. 23:4, 12. Of the Church—II Cor. 11:2.

Laws for protecting.—Deut. 22:23–29. Tokens of virginity—Deut. 22:13–21. Abuse of virginity—II Sam. 13:1–14. Dowry of—Ex. 22:17. As respects marriage—I Cor. 7:28, 34, 36, 37. Fate befalling rebellious—Deut. 32:25.

Priests permitted to marry virgins only. —Lev. 21:13, 14. May handle their own dead—Lev. 21:3.

Occupied in watering stock.—Gen. 24: 14, 19, 43, 46. In carrying water—Gen. 24:14, 19, 43, 46.

Virgins sought for king's wife.—Esth. 2:2, 3, 17, 19. For Tribe of Benjamin —Ju. 21:12. For David's decline—I Ki. 1:2. Companions of king's daughter—Ps. 45:14. Love of—Song of Sol. 1:3. Praise of—Song of Sol. 6:8. Apparel of—II Sam. 13:18. Men so called

—Rev. 14:4. Prophetesses—Lu. 2:36; Acts 21:9.

Jephthah's daughter.—Ju. 11:37–38.

Parable of.—Mt. 25:1, 7, 11. See WOMEN.

VIRTUE. See CHRISTIAN GRACES.

VISAGE. Blacker than coal—Lam. 4:8. Changed—Dan. 3:19. Marred—Is. 52:14. See FACE.

VISIBLE. Col. 1:16.

VISIONS: Of.—Abraham—Gen. 15:1–17. Jacob—46:2–5. Moses—Ex. 3:3, 4; 33:11, 18–23. Aaron and Miriam—Num. 12:6; Balaam—Num. 24:6, 16. Samuel—I Sam. 3:10–15. Nathan—II Sam. 7:4–17; I Chr. 17:3–15. Micaiah —I Ki. 22:19–22; II Chr. 18:18–21. Iddo—II Chr. 9:29. Eliphaz—Job 4:12–17. Isaiah—II Chr. 32:32; Is. 1:1; 2:1; 6:1–8; 21:2; 22:1–5. Jeremiah—Jer. 1:11–13; 23:16; 24:1–8. Ezekiel—Ez. 1:1; 2:8–10; 8:4–18; 11:24; Chs. 40, 41, 42, 43. Nebuchadrezzar—Dan. Ch. 4. Belshazzar—Dan. 5:5. Daniel —Dan. 1:17; 2:19; 7:1, 7, 13, 15; 8:1, 2; 13:17, 26, 27; 9:21–24; 10:1, 7, 8, 14, 16. Hosea—Hos. 12:10. Obadiah—Ob. 1; Mic. 3:6, 7; Nah. 1:1. Habakkuk—1:1; 2:2, 3. Zechariah—Zech. 1:7, 8; Chs. 2–6. Zacharias—Lu. 1:11–22. Christ—Mt. 17:2–7. Peter—Mt. 17:2; Acts 10:10–17; 11:5–10; 12:7–11. James—Mt. 17:2. John—Mt. 17:2; Rev. 1:4–22. Stephen—Acts 7:55, 56. Ananias—Acts 9:10. Cornelius—Acts 10:3–6. Paul—Acts 9:3; 16:9, 10; 18:9; 22:6; 23:11; 26:13–19; 27:23; II Cor. 12:1–4; Ps. 89:19. Of God—Gen. 12:7; 17:1; 18:1; 26:2, 24; 35:9; Num. 24:4; Job 7:14, 15; Is. 1:1; Acts 2:17; II Cor. 12:1. No vision of Jehovah—I Sam. 3:1; Pr. 29:18; Lam. 2:9; Ez. 7:26; Mic. 3:6.

As a book that is sealed.—Is. 29:11.

False.—Ez. 12:24; 13:7, 23; Lam. 2:14.

Lying.—Jer. 14:14; 23:16; 29:8–9.

Their own.—Jer. 23:16.

Ashamed of.—Zech. 13:4; Mic. 3:7.

Fulfilment of.—Ez. 12:22, 23, 24, 27, 28. Young men shall see visions—Joel 2:28; Acts 2:17.

For multitude.—Ez. 7:13.

Of peace.—Ez. 13:16. Grievous—Is. 21:2.

Of night.—Job 4:13; 20:8; Is. 29:7.

Heavenly.—Acts 26:19.

Figurative.—Job 7:14; 20:8; 33:15; Is. 22:1; 29:7. Err in—Is. 28:7. **Valley of.**—Is. 22:1, 5. Saw horses in—Rev. 9:17. See DREAMS, APPEARANCES, OF GOD.

VISIT. Gen. 50:24; Job 7:18; 31:14; Jer. 5:9; Lu. 1:78. Anger, In—Job 35:15. Cephas—Gal. 1:18. Earth—Ps. 65:9. Fatherless—Jas. 1:27. See FRATERNITY, ORPHAN'S. Gentiles — Acts 15:14. See GENTILES, SALVATION. Iniquity—Ex. 20:5; Lev. 18:25; Num. 14:18; Deut. 5:9; Amos 5:2. Man—Ps. 8:4. Nations, All—Ps. 59:5. Sick —Mt. 25:36. See FRATERNITY, SEEK. Sin—Ex. 32:34. See FRATERNITY, JUDGMENT, PUNISHMENT.

VISITATION. Num. 16:29. Day of—Is. 10:3; Hos. 9:7; Mic. 7:4; I Pet. 2:12. Time of—Jer. 8:12; 10:15; 46: 21; 50:27; 51:8. Year of—Jer. 11:23; 23:12; 48:44. See JUDGMENT, PUNISHMENT, SIN.

VOICE: Of God.—Gen. 3:8, 10; Deut. 5: 25, 26; 18:16; II Sam. 22:14; Ps. 29:3– 9; 46:6; 81:11; 95:7; 106:25. Delegating Moses — Ex. 3:4. Giving the law—Ex. 19:19; 20:1, 18; Num. 7:89; Deut. 4:12, 33, 36; 5:24–26. To Ezekiel—Ez. 1:24; 10:5. His majesty—Job 37:4; Ps. 18:13; 29:4; 68:33; Jer. 25:30; Joel 2:11. Heard at baptism of Jesus—Mt. 3:17; Mk. 1:11; Lu. 3: 22. Disciples thought it thundered—John 12:28. Transfiguration—Mt. 17: 5; Mk. 9:7; Lu. 9:35; II Pet. 1:17, 18. Hearken to the voice of God—Ex. 5:2; 15:26; 23:21, 22; Num. 14:22; Deut. 8:20; 9:23; 13:18; 15:5; 26:14, 17; 28:1, 2, 15, 45, 62; Josh. 5:6; 22:2; 24:24; Ju. 2:2, 20; 6:10; I Sam. 12:14, 15. Obey the voice of God—Gen. 22: 18; 26:5; Deut. 13:4; 27:10; 30:2, 8,10, 20; I Sam. 15:19, 20, 22; 28:18; II Ki. 18:12; Jer. 3:13, 25. **Voices of Men.**—Gen. 3:17; 16:2; 21:12, 16, 17; 27:22; 30:6; Ex. 3:18; 4:1, 8, 9; 18:19, 24; 23: 21; 24:3; Num. 20:16; 21:3; Deut. 1:45; 21:18, 20; 26:7; 33:7; Josh. 10:14; Ju. 13:9; 18:3, 25; 20:13; I Sam. 1:13; 2:25; 8:7, 9, 19, 22; 12:1; 15:24; 19:6; 24:16; 25:35; 26:17; 28:21, 23; II Sam. 12:18; 13:14; 22:7; I Ki. 17:22; II Ki. 4:31; 7:10; 10:6; 19:22; Job 3:7, 18; 4:16; 9:16; 38:34; Ps. 3:4; 5:2, 3;

18:6; 44:16; 58:5; 74:23; 77:1; 116:1; 119:149; 130:2; 141:1; 142:1; Pr. 5: 13; Eccl. 5:6; Song of Sol. 2:8; 5:2; 8:13; John 3:8; 10:4; 12:30; Acts 9: 7; 22:14; I Cor. 14:8; I Thess. 4:16; II Pet. 2:16. Of adjuration—Lev. 5:1. Birds—Eccl. 12:4; Song of Sol. 2:12, 14. Charmers—Ps. 58:5. Cities—Is. 42:11. Floods—Ps. 93:3. Fools—Eccl. 5:3; Pr. 10:10, 14; 14:16; 18:6, 7; 29:11. Groaning—Ps. 102:5. Joy—Job 3:7; Ps. 42:4; 118:15. Lion — Job 4:10; Is. 31:4. Melody—Ps. 98:5; Is. 51:3. Praise—Ps. 42:4; 66:8. Prayer—Ps. 66:19. Singing—Ex. 32:18; II Sam. 19:35; I Chr. 15:16; II Chr. 5:13. Supplication —Ps. 28:2, 6; 31:22; 86:6; 130:2; 142: 1. Thanksgiving—Ps. 26:7. Thunder —Job 37:4, 5; 40:9; Ps. 18:13; 77:18; 104:7. Triumph—Ps. 47:1. Tumult—Is. 66:6. Weeping—II Sam. 15:23; 19: 4; Job 2:12; 30:31. See Ju. 2:4; Ruth 1:9. Wilderness—Is. 42:11. One crying in the wilderness—Is. 40:3, 6; Mt. 3:3; Mk. 1:3; Lu. 3:4; John 1:23. Wisdom—Pr. 1:20; 8:1, 4, 32; 5:13. Words, Of — Deut. 1:34; 5:28; I Sam. 15:1; Job 33:8; 34:16; Ps. 103:20.

Lifting up the voice.—Gen. 29:11; 39: 15, 18; Num. 14:1; Ju. 2:4; 9:7; Ruth 1:9, 14; I Sam. 30:4; II Sam. 3:32; 13: 36; I Chr. 15:16; II Chr. 5:13; Job 2: 12; Pr. 2:3; Is. 24:14; 40:9; 42:2; 52: 8; 58:1.

Loud voice.—Gen. 39:14; Deut. 27:14; I Sam. 28:12; II Sam. 19:4; I Ki. 8:55; II Ki. 18:28; Ezra 3:12; 10:12; Neh. 9:4; Pr. 27:14; Is. 36:13. See CRY, SHOUTING.

VOID. Gen. 1:2; Nah. 2:10. Counsel, Of—Deut. 32:28. Days—Num. 6:12. Faith — Rom. 4:14. Grace of God, Make— Gal. 2:21. Law—Ps. 119:126. Lest cross be made—I Cor. 1:17. Makketh it—Gal. 3:15. Offence, Of—Phil. 1:10. Return unto me, Not—Is. 55:11. Understanding, Of — Pr. 6:32; 9:4. Vow—Num. 30:8. Wisdom, Of — Pr. 11:12; 15:21. Word of God—Mt. 15:6.

VOLUNTARY. Col. 2:18.

VOMIT. Job 20:15; Pr. 23:8; 25:16. Dog to his, As a—Pr. 26:11; II Pet. 2:22. Drunken man, As a—Is. 19:14. Land—Lev. 18:25. Moab shall wallow in his—Jer. 48:26. Tables full of, All —Is. 28:8.

VOPHSI, vŏph'si. Father of one of the spies—Num. 13:14.

VOTE. Acts 26:10.

VOUCHETH. Job 16:19.

VOUCHSAFED. Acts 7:17.

VOW. A promise to God to do His pleasure on condition of receiving a blessing from Him.—Gen. 28:20; Num. 21:2; Ps. 65:1; Is. 19:21.

Two kinds of vows: The ordinary or lesser vow—Num. 30:2 ff.; the Nazirite or greater vow—Num. 6:2 ff.

Law regulating (governing) vows. — Num. 30:2–13. No compulsion to take vows—Deut. 23:22; Eccl. 5:5. But must be fulfilled if taken—Deut. 23: 21; Eccl. 5:4; Num. 30:2; John 2:9. Women's vows, to be approved by father or husband—Num. 30:3, 6–16. But widows and divorced women may vow for themselves—Num. 30:9. Sacrifice as vow offering—Lev. 7:16; 22: 21, 23; Num. 16:3, 8; Deut. 12:11.

Nazirite vow.—Num. 6:2–21. Prohibitions pertaining to strong drink— Num. 6:3. Shaving hair—Num. 6:5. Touching dead bodies — Num. 6:6. Sacrifice for the redemption of—Num. 6:10 ff. Ceremonial of redemption— Num. 6:13–21.

Notable vows in history. — Jacob's— Gen. 28:20; 31:13. Jephthah's—Ju. 11:30, 39. Hannah's—I Sam. 1:11, 21. Absalom's—II Sam. 15:7, 8. Paul's— Acts 18:18. Of the four whom he took into the temple with him—Acts 21: 23.

VOYAGE. Acts 21:7; 27:9, 10.

VULTURE. Lev. 11:14. See GIER-EAGLE.

WAFER. Honey, Made with—Ex. 16: 31. Unleavened—Ex. 29:23; I Chr. 23:29. Anointed with oil—Ex. 29:2; Lev. 2:4; 7:12; 8:26; Num. 6:15, 19. See BREAD, OFFERINGS.

WAG. Hand.—Zeph. 2:15. Head—Ps. 64:8; Jer. 48:27; Mt. 27:39; Mk. 15: 29. See DERISION, HAND, HEAD.

WAGES. Earning of wages. What shall thy wages be?—Gen. 29:15. Jacob's wages changed—Gen. 31:7, 41. Given to Moses' nurse—Ex. 2:9. Looketh for—Job 7:2. Nebuchadrezzar receives no wages—Ez. 29:18. To put'

in bag—Hag. 1:6. Is worthy of—Lu. 10:7. Of reaper—John 4:36. Rate of, mentioned only in—Mt. 20:1–14. Paid in money—Mt. 20:1–14. In portion of flock—Gen. 29:20; 30:32; 31:8. Babylonian spoils—Ez. 29:19.

Laws concerning. — To be punctually paid—Lev. 19:13; Deut. 24:15; Jas. 5:4. Wages of harlots and dogs an abomination — Deut. 23:18. Punishment for using service without wages —Jer. 22:13. Oppression in—Mal. 3:5. Contentment of—Lu. 3:14.

Wages of sin is death.—Rom. 6:23; II Pet. 2:15.

WAGON. Gen. 45:19–27; 46:5; Num. 7:3–8. I Sam. 17:20; Ez. 23:24.

WAIL. Esth. 4:3; Is. 13:6; 15:8; Jer. 9:10, 18, 20; Ez. 32:18; Amos 5:16, 17; Mic. 1:8; Mt. 13:42, 50 (A.V.); Mk. 5:38; Lu. 7:32; Rev. 1:7; 18:15, 19. Bitter—Ez. 27:31, 32. See MOURNING, WEEPING.

WAIST. Song of Sol. 7:2.

WAIT. Job 6:11, 19; 14:14; 17:13; 29:23; 32:4; 35:14; Ps. 39:7; 119:95; Jer. 9:8; Dan. 12:12. Altar, At the— I Cor. 9:13. Consolation of Israel, For—Lu. 2:25. Cornelius—Acts 10: 24. Fowlers lie in wait — Jer. 5:26. Fruit, For—Jas. 5:7. Gates of wisdom, At—Pr. 8:34. God—Is. 30:18. **For God.**—II Ki. 6:33; Ps. 25:3, 5, 21; 27:14; 33:20; 37:7, 9, 34; 40:1; 62:1, 5; 65:1; 69:36; 104:27; 106:13; 130: 5; 145:15; Pr. 20:22; Is. 8:17; 25:9; 26:8; 33:2; 40:31; 49:23; 51:5; 60: 9; 64:4; Jer. 14:22; Lam. 3:25; Hos. 12:6; Mic. 7:7; Zeph. 3:8. *Longsuffering of.*—I Pet. 3:20. Hope of righteousness, For the—Gal. 5:5. Israel— Ez. 19:5. Jesus, For—Lu. 2:25; 8:40; I Cor. 1:7; Phil. 3:20; I Thess. 1:10; II Thess. 3:5; Heb. 9:28. King, On the—II Chr. 17:19. Kingdom, For the —Mk. 15:43; Lu. 23:51. Law of God, For the—Is. 42:4. Lie in wait—See AMBUSH. LIERS-IN-WAIT. One for another—I Cor. 11:33. Patience, With— Ps. 37:7; 40:1; Rom. 8:25. Paul— Acts 17:16. Priests, On—I Chr. 23:28. Promise, For the—Acts 1:7. Revealing of sons of God—Rom. 8:19–25. Robbers for a man—Hos. 6:9. Service, Upon the—Num. 3:10; 4:23; 8:24, 25;

I Chr. 6:32, 35; Neh. 12:44; I Cor.
9:13. Soldier of Cornelius, Devout—
Acts 10:7. Sons of men, For—Mic. 5:
7. Soul, For my—Ps. 56:6. Sword,
For, of the—Job 15:22. Twilight, For
—Job 24:15. Vision, For—Hab. 2:3.
Words, For—Job 32:11, 16. See GIVE
HEED, LIERS-IN-WAIT, TARRY.

WAKE. Heart—Song of Sol. 5:2. Morning by morning—Is. 50:4. Sleep, and
not—Jer. 51:39. Sleep, Out of—Zech.
2:13; 4:1. Watchman—Ps. 127:1. See
SLEEP.

WALKING: With or before God.—I
Sam. 2:35; II Ki. 23:3. In fear of
God—Neh. 5:9. In laws—Neh. 10:29;
Acts 21:24. In statutes—Ez. 20:19. In
ways—Zech. 3:7; Mal. 2:6. In com-
mandments—II John 4, 6. After the
Spirit—Rom. 8:4. As called—I Cor.
7:17. Not deceitfully—II Cor. 4:2.
In good works—Eph. 2:10; 4:1. In
Christ—Col. 2:6. Worthily—Phil. 1:
27; 3:16; I Thess. 2:12; 4:1, 12. In
Truth—III John 3, 4.

Contrary to God.—Ju. 2:17; II Ki. 8:27;
10:31; 16:3; 17:8; 21:22; II Chr. 21:6,
13; 28:2; Ps. 12:8; 39:6; 82:5; Is. 8:
11; Ez. 20:18; I Cor. 3:3; II Cor. 10:2,
3; Gal. 2:14; Eph. 2:2; Col. 3:7; II
Thess. 3:6, 11; I Pet. 4:3; II Pet. 2:10;
3:3; I John 1:6; 2:11; Jude 16, 18.

Examples of.—Enoch — Gen. 5:22, 24.
Noah—Gen. 6:9. Abraham—Gen. 17:
1; 24:40. Isaac—Gen. 48:15. Hezekiah—II Ki. 20:3; Is. 38:3. David—
II Chr. 6:16; Ps. 26:3; 101:2; 116:9;
119:45. Zacharias and Elisabeth—Lu.
1:6. The Church—Acts 9:31; Phil.
3:17.

God's promise to walk with.—Lev. 26:
12; Deut. 23:14; II Cor. 6:16.

Exhorted to walk with God.—Deut. 8:6;
10:12; 11:22, 23; 13:4, 5; 19:9; 26:17;
30:16; Josh. 2:5; I Ki. 2:3, 4; 3:14;
6:12; 8:25, 36, 58, 61; 9:4; II Chr. 6:
27, 31; Eph. 4:17; 5:2, 8, 15.

How to walk.—Humbly—Mic. 6:8. In
the Spirit—Gal. 5:16, 25. With lowliness and meekness—Eph. 4:1, 2. In
newness of life—Rom. 6:4. In love—
Rom. 14:15; Eph. 5:2. By faith—II
Cor. 5:7. As children of light—Eph.
5:8. "As ye have received Christ Jesus, so walk"—Col. 2:6. In wisdom

—Col. 4:5. Walk as Christ walked—
I John 2:6. Walking in the light—
John 8:12; Eph. 5:8.

**Warnings against not walking with
God.**—Ps. 89:30, 31; Jer. 26:4.

Prophecies concerning. — Hab. 3:19;
Zech. 3:7; 10:12; Rev. 3:4; 21:24.

WALLET. Mt. 10:10. See PURSE.

WALLOW. Mk. 9:20. Ashes, In—Jer.
6:26; Ez. 27:30. Blood, In—II Sam.
20:12. Mire, In—II Pet. 2:22. See
MIRE.

WANDER. Abroad—Job 15:23. Bird,
from nest—Pr. 27:8. Blind men, As
—Lam. 4:14. Cities—Amos 4:8. Com-
mandments, From — Ps. 119:10, 21.
Far off—Ps. 55:7. For lack of food
—Job 38:41. God caused me to—
Gen. 20:13. Love to—Jer. 14:10.
Maketh the blind to — Deut. 27:18.
Sea to sea, From—Amos 8:12. Up and
down — Ps. 59:15. Wilderness, In—
Gen. 21:14; Job 12:24. See JOURNEY,
TRAVELLER.

WANDERER. Gen. 4:12; Is. 5:17.
Among nations—Hos. 9:17. Children
shall be—Num. 14:33. See JOURNEY,
TRAVELLER.

WANDERING. Deserts, In—Heb. 11:
38. Desire, Of—Eccl. 6:9. Field, In
—Gen. 37:15. Numberest my—Ps. 56:
8. Sparrow in, As—Pr. 26:2. Stars
—Jude 13. See JOURNEY, TRAVELLER.

WANT, n. Ps. 34:9; Mk. 12:44. Any
good things—Ps. 34:10. All things,
Of—Deut. 28:48. Bread, Of — Amos
4:6. Clothing, Of—Job 31:19. Come,
Shall—Pr. 28:22. Fruits, Of—Lam. 4:
9. Gaunt with—Job 30:3. In respect
of—Phil. 4:11. Lie upon me—Ju. 19:
20. Measure of—II Cor. 9:12; 11:9.
Place where there is no—Ju. 18:10.
She of her—Mk. 12:44; Lu. 21:4. Shelter, Of—Job 24:8. Supply, for—II
Cor. 8:14. Tendeth only to—Pr. 11:
24. To be in—Lu. 15:14; Phil. 4:12.
See DESIRE, POOR.

WANT, v. All things—Jer. 44:18. I
shall not—Ps. 23:1. Mate, Her—Is.
34:16. Transgression, Not—Pr. 10:19.
Wine is not—Song of Sol. 7:2. See
DESIRE.

WANTON. Against Christ—I Tim. 5:11.
Eyes—Is. 3:16. Heifer, As a—Jer.

50:11. Waxed—Rev. 18:7. See LUST, SIN.

WANTONNESS. Power of her—Rev. 18:3. Walk not in—Rom. 13:13. See LUST, SIN.

WAR: Jehovah orders it.—Ex. 17:16; Num. 31:1, 2; Deut. 7:1, 2; I Sam. 15: 1-3.

Jehovah gives the victory.—Num. 21:3; Deut. 2:33; 3:3; 4:34; 20:10-15; 21: 10; II Sam. 23:10; Pr. 21:31.

Jehovah uses war as a judgment.—Lev. 26:17, 31-33; Deut. 28:25; 32:30; Ju. 2:14-15; II Ki. 15:37; I Chr. 5:22-26; 14:10-15; II Chr. 12:1-12; Is. 5:25- 30; Ez. 23:22-29; Amos 4:10; Mt. 24: 6-8; Mk. 13:7-8; Lu. 21:9.

Enumeration of soldiery.—Num. 1:2-3, 20-43; 26:1-51; 31:1-6.

Spies sent to investigate.—Num. 13:17; Josh. 2:1; Ju. 7:10; I Sam. 26:4.

Consult the Urim and Thummin.—Ju. 1: 1; 20:27-28; I Sam. 14:37; 23:2; 28:6; 30:8. Consult the Prophets—I Ki. 22: 6; II Chr. 18:5. Divination—Ez. 21:21.

Took ark of covenant with them.—I Sam. 4:4-18; 14:18; II Sam. 11:11.

Challenges sent. — Ju. 11:12-27; I Ki. 20:2; II Ki. 14:8.

Formation of ranks.—Num. Ch. 2; Ex. 13:18; I Chr. 12:38. Must be united —Num. 32:6-7, 20-27; Deut. 1:41; Josh. 4:12-14.

Conduct of battle.—Ps. 110:3; II Chr. 20:21. Battle Signal—Num. 10:9; 31: 6. Response by host—I Sam. 17:20, 52; Is. 42:13; Ez. 21:22; Amos 1:14. See BATTLEFIELDS.

Ambush.—Josh. 8:12; Ju. 20:38.

War of extermination.—Num. 31:7-17; Deut. 2:33-34; 3:6; 20:13-18; Josh. 6:21,.24; 8:24-25; 10:2-40; 11:11-23; I Sam. 15:3-9; 27:8-11.

Sieges.—Deut. 20:19; 28:52-53; II Sam. 20:15; I Ki. 15:27; Is. 29:3; Mic. 5:1. Line of circumvallation — Ez. 4:2; Zech. 12:2. Mound—II Sam. 20:15; II Ki. 19:32; 25:1; Is. 37:33; Ez. 4:2. Forts—II Ki. 25:1; Is. 29:3; 32:14; Jer. 52:4; Ez. 17:17; 33:27. Protecting forts—II Sam. 11:21-24; Ju. 9:53; II Chr. 26:15. Battering ram—II Sam. 20:15; Ez. 4:2; 21:22. The slingers— II Ki. 3:25; I Sam. 25:29. Other

weapons—II Chr. 26:15. See FORTIFICATION.

Treatment of conquered.—Num. 31:26; Deut. 20:14; Ju. 1:6; 7:25; 9:45; I Sam. 11:2; 17:51; 31:8; II Sam. 12:31; II Chr. 25:12; II Ki. 8:12; 15:16; Is. 13:16-18; Hos. 10:14; 13:16; Amos 1: 13; Nah. 3:10; Mt. 24:15-22.

Booty fell to soldiers.—Ju. 8:24; I Sam. 30:26.

Victories celebrated by.—Monumental stones—I Sam. 7:12; II Sam. 8:13. Trophies—I Sam. 21:9; 31:10; II Ki. 11:10. By song and dance—Ex. 15:1- 21; Ju. 5:1-31; I Sam. 18:6-8; II Sam. 22:1-51.

Instances of war.—With Amalek—Ex. 17:8-16. With Midian—Num. 31:1-12. With Amorites—Deut. 1:41-44. With Philistines—II Sam. 21:15. Between Israel and Judah—II Sam. 3:1, 6; I Ki. 15:6. With Syria—II Ki. 16:5.

Evils of.—Ps. 79:1-3; Is. 3:25-26; 6:11- 12; 13:15-16; 15:1-9; Jer. 4:19-31; 5:15-17.

Weapons of war.—Sword—Ex. 17:13; Lev. 26:6-7; Num. 14:3, 43; Deut. 13: 15; I Sam. 13:19; 17:39; II Sam. 20:8; Josh. 8:24; 10:11; 11:11; 13:22; 19: 47; Ju. 1:25; 7:20-22; I Chr. 5:18; Neh. 4:13; Jer. 50:35-37; Ez. 24:21; 38:4; Joel 3:10; Mt. 26:47; Mk. 14:43; Lu. 22:38, 52. Bow and arrow—II Ki. 13:15; I Chr. 5:18; II Chr. 17:17; 18: 33; 26:14; Ps. 11:2; Is. 37:33; Jer. 6: 23; 46:9; Neh. 4:13. See ARCHERY. Spear—I Sam. 13:19; II Ki. 11:10; II Chr. 11:12; 23:9; 26:14; Neh. 4:13; Ps. 57:4; Joel 3:10; Acts 23:23. Sling— Ju. 20:16; I Sam. 17:40, 50; 25:29; Pr. 26:8; Jer. 10:18; Zech. 9:15. Slingers —II Ki. 3:25; II Chr. 26:14. Shield— II Ki. 11:10; II Chr. 11:12; 23:9; 26: 14; Is. 37:33; Jer. 46:9; Ez. 38:4; Eph. 6:16.

WARD. Public, In—Acts 5:18. Put into—Gen. 40:34; 42:17; Acts 4:3. Watch tower—Is. 21:8. See PRISON.

WARES. Bring—Neh. 10:31. Gather up thy—Jer. 10:17. Ship, In the— Jonah 1:5. Traded for—Ez. 27:16. See GOODS.

WARFARE. Accomplished, Is—Is. 40: 2. Changes and—Job 10:17. Great—

Dan. 10:1. Not a—Job 7:1. Weapons of—II Cor. 10:4. See WAR.

WARM. Be ye—Jas. 2:16. Coal to—Is. 47:14. Garments—Job 37:17. How can one be?—Eccl. 4:11. I am—Is. 44:16. See HEAT.

WARMING. Himself—Mk. 15:54. Themselves—John 18:18.

WARMTH. Eccl. 4:11.

WARNING. II Ki. 6:10. Earth, On—Heb. 12:25. Flee from the wrath, To—Mt. 3:7. Give—Ez. 3:17, 18, 20; 33:7. God, Of—Mt. 2:12, 22; Acts 10:22; Heb. 11:7. Heaven, From—Heb. 12:25. Moses is—Heb. 8:5. People—Ez. 33:3. Servant—Ps. 19:11. Taketh not—Ez. 33:4. Wicked—Ez. 3:18; 33:8, 9. See ALARM.

WARP. Lev. 13:48, 49, 51, 52, 53, 56, 57, 58, 59.

WARRIORS. Chosen men—I Ki. 12:21; II Chr. 11:1. Head of his—Hab. 3:14. See SOLDIERS, WAR.

WASH. Is. 1:16; Ez. 23:40; I Cor. 6:11; II Pet. 2:22. Away thy sins—Acts 22:16. Face—Mt. 6:17. Filthiness, From—Pr. 30:12. Hands—Ps. 26:6; Mk. 7:3. Heart—Jer. 4:14. Lye, With—Jer. 2:22. Milk, With—Song of Sol. 5:12. Pool of Siloam, In—John 9:7. Pure water, With—Heb. 10:22. Robes—Rev. 7:14. Steps were, My—Job 29:6. Thoroughly—Ps. 51:2. See ABLUTIONS, CEREMONIAL CLEANSING, FEET.

WASHING. Cups—Mk. 7:4. Divers—Heb. 9:10. Regeneration, Of—Tit. 3:5. **Washing feet.**—See FEET.

WASTE, *adj.* Altars—Ez. 6:6. Cities—Is. 37:26; 61:4; Jer. 4:7; Ez. 19:7. Countries—Jer. 37:18. Earth—Gen. 1:2; Is. 24:1. Egypt—Ez. 29:9, 10. Howling wilderness—Deut. 32:10. Jerusalem—Ez. 26:2. Lay—Nah. 3:7; Acts 3:8. Mountains—Is. 42:15. Nineveh—Nah. 3:7. Pasture—Jer. 25:36. Places—Is. 51:3; 52:9; 58:12; Ez. 13:4. Streets—Zeph. 3:6. Stronghold—Is. 23:14. See DESERT, WILDERNESS.

WASTE, *n.* Build the old—Is. 61:4. Go up into the—Job 6:18. Not a—Is. 45:18. Perpetual—Jer. 49:13. To what purpose is this—Mt. 26:8. Wander in—Ps. 107:40. See DESERT, WILDERNESS.

WASTE, *v.* Away—Ps. 88:9. Cities—Is. 6:11. Desolate—Ez. 36:4. Destruction that—Ps. 91:6. Goods—Lu. 16:1. Jar of meal—I Ki. 17:16. Kain shall be—Num. 24:22. Nations—Is. 60:12. River—Job 14:11. Substance—Lu. 15:13.

WATCH, *n.* Job 7:12; 40:24; Jer. 51:12. Keep—II Ki. 11:6, 7; II Chr. 23:6; Ps. 15:3; Pr. 15:3; Lu. 2:8. Set a—Ps. 141:3; Mt. 27:65, 66. Tomb—Job 21:32.

Time of.—Morning—Ex. 14:24; I Sam. 11:11. Night—Ps. 63:6; 90:4; 119:148. Fourth—Mt. 14:25; Mk. 6:48. Middle—Ju. 7:19. Second—Lu. 12:38.

WATCH, *v.* Ps. 102:7; Jer. 5:28; 20:10; Hos. 13:7; Mt. 24:42; Mk. 13:33; I Cor. 16:13; I Thess. 5:6; Heb. 13:17. Discretion—Pr. 2:11. Eyes—Ps. 77:4. Gethsemane, In—Mt. 26:38-41; Mk. 14:34-38. God watches—Gen. 31:49; Job 14:16; 29:2; Jer. 1:12. Iniquity, For—Is. 29:20. Law of God—Pr. 6:22. Righteous, The—Ps. 37:32. Sin—Job 14:16. Soul, For my—Ps. 71:10. Wicked—Ps. 37:32. Word, Over my—Jer. 1:12. See WATCHFULNESS, WATCHMEN.

WATCHERS. Ju. 1:24; Mt. 28:4.

WATCHFULNESS. Pr. 8:34; Mt. 24:42-51; 25:13; Mk. 13:35; Lu. 12:35-48; Acts 20:31; I Cor. 10:12; Eph. 6:18; Col. 4:2; I Thess. 5:6; I Pet. 5:8; Rev. 3:2; 16:15. See CHRISTIAN GRACES.

WATCHING. Pr. 8:34; II Cor. 6:5; 11:27.

WATCHMEN: Tower of.—II Ki. 17:9; 18:8.

On watch-towers.—Of Saul—I Sam. 14:16. Standing on the tower in Jezreel, watchman spies the company of Jehu—II Ki. 9:17. Tells of the messenger's failure to return—II Ki. 9:18, 20.

On city walls.—II Sam. 13:34; 18:24-27; Is. 62:6; Jer. 51:12. **About the city**—Song of Sol. 3:3; 5:7.

With God.—Hos. 9:8.

Voice of.—Is. 52:8.

Set watchmen over Jerusalem.—Is. 62:6; Jer. 6:17. Unto house of Israel—Ez. 3:17; 33:7; Mic. 7:4.

Command to set a watchman.—Is. 21:6.
Law concerning.—Ez. 33:2, 6.
"Watchman, what of the night?"—Is.
21:11. Said, "The morning cometh"
—Is. 21:12. Waketh but in vain—
Ps. 127:1.
Figurative.—Are blind—Is. 56:10.
WATCH-TOWER. II Chr. 20:24; Is.
21:5; 32:14.
WATER. Creation of—Gen. 1:1, 2; Ps.
95:5; 148:4-6. Divided by the firmament—Gen. 1:6, 7. Gathered into one
place—Gen. 1:9, 10. Stocked with
animals—Gen. 1:20-22. Contention
over—Gen. 26:19-22.
Uses of.—Supply of city—II Ki. 20:20;
II Chr. 32:30; Ez. 47:1-5. Ceremo-
nial cleansing: Aaron and sons—Ex.
29:4; 30:20; 40:12; Lev. 6:16; 4:24.
Jealous woman—Num. 5:17-27. Ves-
sels—Lev. 6:8; 15:12; 11:32. Of sepa-
ration—Num. 19:2-22. For irrigation
—Deut. 11:10; Eccl. 2:6; Is. 58:11.
Necessary to plant growth—Gen. 2:5,
6; Job 8:11; 14:9; Is. 1:30. Necessary
for the comfort of man—Is. 41:17, 18;
Zech. 9:11.
Collected in.—Springs—Josh. 15:19; Ju.
1:15. Pools—I Ki. 22:38; Neh. 2:14.
Ponds—Ex. 7:19; Is. 19:10. Foun-
tains—I Ki. 18:5; II Chr. 32:3. Wells
—Gen. 21:19; 25:30; 26:15; John 4:6.
Brooks—II Sam. 17:20; I Ki. 18:5.
Streams—Ps. 78:16; Is. 35:6. Rivers
—Is. 8:7; Jer. 2:18. Seas—Gen. 1:9,
10; Is. 11:9. Clouds—Job 26:8.
Supplied by miracle.—To Israel—Ex.
17:1-6; Num. 20:7-11. To Samson—
Ju. 15:19. To Jehoshaphat's army—
II Ki. 3:16-20.
Changed by miracle.—Into blood—Ex.
7:17, 20. Into wine—John 2:7-9.
Involved with miracle.—Consumed by
fire from heaven—I Ki. 18:38. Divided into heaps—Ex. 14:21, 22; Josh.
3:16. Trenches filled with—II Ki. 3:
17-22. Iron swims in—II Ki. 6:5, 6.
Walking on—Mt. 14:26, 29. Healing
power placed in—John 5:4; 9:7.
Special Old Testament references.—Beside still waters—Ps. 23:2. Weary
land where no—Ps. 63:1. Stolen waters sweet—Pr. 9:17. As cold water
to thirsty soul—Pr. 25:25. Face an-
swereth face in—Pr. 27:19. Cast thy

bread upon—Eccl. 11:1. Come ye to
the—Is. 55:1. Like a spring whose
waters fail not—Is. 58:11. Forsaken
me, the fountain of—Jer. 2:13. I will
sprinkle clean water—Ez. 36:25.
New Testament references.—Give cup
of—Mt. 10:42. Pilate took water and
washed his hands—Mt. 27:24. Jesus
coming up out of the—Mk. 1:10. A
man bearing a pitcher of—Mk. 14:13.
Boat was filling with—Lu. 8:23. Became wine—John 2:9. Born of—John
3:5. The water of life—John 4:10-15;
7:37-39. Came forth blood and—John
19:34. Can any man forbid—Acts 10:
47. Cleansed by washing of—Eph. 5:
26. Eight souls saved by—I Pet. 3:20.
Forget the earth overflowed by—II
Pet. 3:5, 6. This is he who came by—
I John 5:6. Clouds without—Jude 12.
Take water of life freely—Rev. 21:6;
22:17. See ABLUTIONS, BAPTISM,
BROOKS, CEREMONIAL CLEANSING, PURI-
FICATION, RIVERS, SEA, SPRINGS,
STREAMS.
WATERCOURSES. Ju. 5:15; II Sam.
5:8; Pr. 21:1; Is. 44:4; Ez. 35:8. See
BROOKS, RIVERS, SPRINGS, STREAMS.
WATERFALLS. Ps. 42:7.
WATERFLOOD. Job 38:25; Ps. 69:15.
See FLOOD.
WATERING-TROUGH. Gen. 30:38. See
TROUGH.
WATERLESS. Mt. 12:43. See DROUGHT,
DRY.
WATERPOT. John 2:6; 4:28. See VES-
SELS.
WATERSPRINGS. Ps. 107:33. See
SPRINGS.
WAVE. Hand—II Ki. 5:11; Is. 13:2.
Sheaf before Jehovah—Lev. 23:11. To
and fro—Ju. 9:9.
Wave-offering.—See OFFERING.
WAVER. Not—Heb. 10:23. Not through
unbelief—Rom. 4:20. Trusted, with-
out—Ps. 26:1. See CHANGE, FICKLE.
WAVES. Ps. 42:7; Jer. 5:22. Afflicted
me with—Ps. 88:7. Beat—Mk. 4:37.
Covered with—Mt. 8:24. Death, Of—
II Sam. 22:5. Distressed by—Mt. 14:
24. Floods lift up—Ps. 93:3. Proud—
Job 38:11. Roaring of—Ps. 65:7.
Smite—Zech. 10:11. Violence of—
Acts 27:41. Wild—Jude 13. Wind
lifteth up—Ps. 107:25. See SEA.

WAX, *n.* Before the fire, As—Mic. 1:4. Heart is like—Ps. 22:14. Mountains melted like—Ps. 97:5.

WAX, *v.* Cold, Love—Mt. 24:12. Corrupt—Eph. 4:22. Dim—I Sam. 3:2. Faint—II Sam. 21:15. Fat—Deut. 32:15. Feeble—Jer. 6:24. Great—Gen. 26:13. Gross—Acts 28:27. Hot —Ex. 22:24; 32:10, 11, 22. Lean—Is. 17:4. Louder—Ex. 19:19. Mighty—Ex. I:7, 20. Old—Deut. 29:5; Ps. 102: 26; Lu. 12:33. Pale—Is. 29:22. Rich —Lev. 25:47, 49; Rev. 18:3. Short—Num. 11:23. Strong in spirit—Lu. 1: 80. Stronger and stronger—II Sam. 3:1. Wanton—I Tim. 5:11. Warm—Job 6:17. Worse—II Tim. 3:13. See GROW.

WAY. I Ki. 8:44; II Ki. 7:15; Job 38: 19; 49:13; 77:19; Pr. 21:8; Is. 55:8; Mk. 8:3; Lu. 12:58; Acts 16:4, 9, 23; II Cor. 11:6. Commit thy—Ps. 37:5. Corrupted—Gen. 6:12. Delight to know my—Is. 58:2. Eagle, Of—Pr. 30:19. Earth, Of—Josh. 23:14. Escape, Of—I Cor. 10:13. Everlasting—Ps. 139: 24. Faithfulness, Of—Ps. 119:30. False—Ps. 119:104. Fool, Of—Pr. 12:15. God, Of—Mt. 22:16. God understandeth the—Job 28:23. Good—II Chr. 6:27; Jer. 6:16. Guide thy heart in—Pr. 23:19. He knoweth the —Job 22:15. Hid—Job 3:23. Holiness, Of—Is. 35:8. How know we the? —John 14:5. In all thy—Pr. 3:6. Jehovah hath—Nah. 1:3. Just, Of—Is. 26:7. Knowledge concerning—Acts 24:22. Leadeth unto life, That—Mt. 7:14. Life, Of—Pr. 6:23; Jer. 21:8. Made—II Ki. 11:16; II Chr. 23:15. Man, Of—Pr. 5:21. New and living, Christ the—See JESUS. Not good—Ps. 36:4; Pr. 16:29. Old—Job 22:15. Ordereth his—Ps. 50:23. Past tracing out—Rom. 11:33. Peace, Of—Is. 59:8. Perfect—II Sam. 22:31; Ps. 101:2. Perish in the—Ps. 2:12. Perverse—Num. 22:32. Prospered—Gen. 24:56. Return from his—Ez. 18:23. Right—I Sam. 12:23. Righteous and true—Rev. 15:3. Saints, Of—Pr. 2:8. Salvation, Of—Acts 16:17. Seen Lord in the—Acts 9:27. See—Job 31:4. Sheol, To—Pr. 7:27. Seemeth right—Pr. 14:12. Show the—Gen. 46:28.

Take heed to—Pr. 39:1. Teach—Ps. 25:9. Train up a child in—Pr. 22:6. Transgressor, Of—Pr. 13:15. Upright in the—Ps. 37:14. Violent, Of—Ps. 17:4. Walk in—Deut. 8:6; Ps. 85:13. Walled up—Job 19:8. Whence I shall not return—Job 16:22. Wicked, Of—Ps. 4:19. Wind, Of—Eccl. 11:5. See COVENANT, JESUS, SALVATION.

WAYFARING MEN. Ju. 19:17; Is. 33: 8; Jer. 9:2; 14:8. Fools, Yes—Is. 35:8. See JOURNEY, TRAVELLER.

WAYMARK. Jer. 31:21.

WAYSIDE. Gen. 38:21; I Sam. 4:13; Ps. 140:5; Mt. 13:4; 21:19; Mk. 10:46; Lu. 18:35.

WAYWARD. Pr. 2:15. Heart—Pr. 17: 20. Mouth—Pr. 4:24. See FROWARD, PERVERSE, SIN.

WE. Acts 16:10–17; 20:5–15; 21:1–18; 27:1; 28:16.

WEAK, *adj.* Num. 13:18; Ju. 16:7, 17; Is. 14:10, 12. Conscience—I Cor. 8: 7–12. See CONSCIENCE. David—II Sam. 3:39; 17:2. See DAVID. Faith, In—Rom. 4:19; 14:1, 2; I Thess. 5:14; Heb. 12:12. See FAITH; JESUS, TEACHING ON APOSTOLIC FAITH. Flesh—Mt. 26:41; Mk. 14:38; Rom. 8:3. Hands —II Sam. 17:2; II Chr. 15:7; Neh. 6: 19; Job 4:3; Is. 35:3. See HANDS. Heart—Ez. 16:30. Knees—Ps. 109: 24; Ez. 7:17; 21:7. See KNEES. Many are—I Cor. 11:30. Perish—I Cor. 8:11. Rudiments—Gal. 4:9. Strength made —Ps. 102:23. Water, As—Ez. 7:17. Strong, When I am—II Cor. 12:30. We—Rom. 5:6; I Cor. 4:10; II Cor. 11:21; 13:4, 9. Who is weak and I am not—II Cor. 11:29. Yet—Rom. 5:6.

WEAK, *n.* Joel 3:10; I Cor. 9:22. Gain the—I Cor. 9:22. Infirmities of the, Bear—Acts 20:35; Rom. 15:1; I Thess. 5:14.

WEAKER. II Sam. 3:1. Vessel, Wife is—I Pet. 3:7.

WEAKNESS. I Cor. 2:3; Heb. 7:18. God, Of—I Cor. 1:25. Jesus crucified through—II Cor. 13:3. Power made perfect in—II Cor. 12:9. Sown in—I Cor. 15:43. Strong, Out of weakness made—Heb. 11:34. Take pleasure in —II Cor. 12:10.

WEALTH, Heb. *Nekhaṣim.*—''Possessions''—II Chr. 1:11; Eccl. 5:19; 6:2.

Resources of Palestine.—Ex. 3:8; Deut. 8:7–9; Is. 2:7.

Power and social standing because of. —Job 31:25; Pr. 10:15; 18:11; 19:4; Acts 19:25. Given to turn back king of Assyria—II Ki. 15:20. Solomon exceeds in riches—I Ki. 10:23; II Chr. 1:11–12; 9:22.

Desirableness of.—I Sam. 2:32; Ezra 9: 12; Job 21:13; Pr. 10:15.

Comfort and luxury of.—Ps. 66:12; Pr. 24:4; Eccl. 5:19–20; Jer. 49:31.

Profitable for this life, with godliness. —II Chr. 1:11–12; Ps. 37:3–4, 9, 16, 18; 112:1–3; Pr. 13:22; Mt. 6:33; Mk. 10:30; I Tim. 4:8.

A gift of God.—I Sam. 2:7; I Chr. 29: 12; Eccl. 5:9.

Riches of: Kings—Ez. 27:33; Dan. 11:2. Nations—Is. 8:4; 10:14; 60:5, 11; 61: 6. Gentiles—Rom. 11:12. World—Ps. 104:24; Rom. 11:12. Secret places—Is. 45:3.

Transitory in character. — Gen. 34:28, 29; I Sam. 2:7; Job 21:13; Ps. 39:6; 49:6–20; Pr. 13:11; 23:5; Eccl. 5:13–17; Is. 39:5–6; Jer. 12:14–17; Mt. 6: 19–21; Jas. 5:1–5; Rev. 18:15–18.

Miscellaneous references. — Deceitfulness of, They that trust in riches— Ps. 49:6; 52:7; 62:10; Pr. 11:28; Mt. 13:22; Mk. 4:19. Profit not in day of wrath—Pr. 11:4. As ransom for man's life—Pr. 13:8. Uncertain riches—I Tim. 6:9–10, 17–19. How hardly shall they that have riches enter into the kingdom of God—Mk. 10:17–22; Lu. 18:24. Swallowed riches—Job 20:15. Are choked with riches — Lu. 8:14. Kinds of—Ez. 27:12, 18. Unsatisfied with—Eccl. 4:8. Riches carried—Is. 30:6. Taken away — Gen. 31:16. He that giveth to riches—Pr. 22:16. Spoil of—Ez. 26:12. Made desolate—Rev. 18:17. Great riches—Josh. 22:8; I Sam. 17:25. Poor, yet hath great riches—Pr. 13:7. A good name is rather to be chosen than great riches —Pr. 22:1.

Helpless when in trouble.—Ps. 49:6–12, 16–19; Ez. 7:19; Zeph. 1:18.

Wealth abused.—Deut. 6:10–12; 8:11–17; 31:20; 32:13–15; Pr. 30:8–9; Is.

2:7–9; 5:7, 8–12; Mic. 2:2, 11; Zech. 14:14.

Covetous never satisfied.—Ps. 62:10; Pr. 23:4; 28:20, 22; Eccl. 5:10–12; 6:2; Lu. 12:15.

Getting it dishonestly.—Pr. 11:16; 21: 6; 10:2; Jer. 17:11.

Envious of the wealthy. — Ps. 73:3–7, 10–12. Preferring the rich—Jas. 2: 1–8.

Wealthy sometimes need humbling.— Deut. 8:16–18; I Sam. 2:32–33; Ps. 44:12–13; Jer. 5:7–9; Hos. 12:8–9.

Spiritual danger of.—Mt. 13:22; 19:16–22; Mk. 4:19; 10:17–22; I Tim. 6:9–10, 17–19; Jas. 1:10, 11; 5:1–5; Rev. 3:17.

The conception Jesus has of it.—Mt. 7: 14; Mk. 10:21; Lu. 12:15, 20–21; 16: 19–25. Men only stewards of—Mt. 25: 14–30; Lu. 16:9–13; 19:12–27. See TEACHING OF JESUS CONCERNING RICHES.

Disciples distributed possessions.—Acts 2:44, 45; 4:34–35.

Noted examples.—Abraham — Gen. 24: 35. Lot—Gen. 13:5; 24:35. Isaac— Gen. 26:13–14. Jacob—Gen. 32:5, 10. Reuben and Gad—Num. 32:1. Joseph —Gen. 45:8, 13. Boaz—Ruth 2:1. Barzillai—II Sam. 19:32. David—I Chr. 29:28. Solomon—I Ki. 9:16–28; 10: 14–23; II Chr. 1:12; 9:1–28. Jehoshaphat—II Chr. 17:5. Hezekiah — II Chr. 32:27–29; Job 1:3; 42:12. Joseph of Arimathea—Mt. 27:57. Zacchæus— Lu. 19:2.

Figurative use: Riches of.—Wisdom— Pr. 3:16; 8:11, 18; 14:24; Eccl. 9:11; Ez. 28:4, 5. Liberality—II Cor. 8:2. Of Christ—Eph. 3:8; Heb. 11:26. Of full assurance—Col. 2:2. Of the glory of His inheritance—Rom. 9:23; Eph. 1:18; 3:16; Phil. 4:19; Col. 1:27. Of grace—Rom. 2:4; Eph. 1:7; 2:7. See RICHES, TEACHING OF JESUS CONCERNING.

WEAN. Ps. 131:2; Is. 11:2. See CHILDREN.

WEAPONS. See WAR.

WEAR. Away—Ex. 18:18; 9:12. Clothing—Deut. 22:11; Esth. 6:8; Is. 4:1. Fine—Jas. 2:3. Soft—Mt. 11:8; Zech. 13:1. Ephod—I Sam. 2:28; 14:3; 22: 18. Out—Dan. 7:25; Lu. 18:5; Rev. 13:7. Stones—Job 14:19.

WEARINESS. Of life—Job 10:1. Of men—Deut. 25:18; Ju. 8:15; II Sam. 16:14; 17:2, 29; Jonah 4:3, 8. Of the flesh—Eccl. 12:12. Weary soul—Jer. 31:25. Weary land—Is. 32:2. Weary beast—Is. 46:1. Jehovah gives rest to the weary—Job 3:17; Is. 28:12; 50:4. In prophecy—Is. 5:27.

WEATHER. Cold—Pr. 25:20. Fair—Mt. 16:2. Foul—Mt. 16:3.

WEAVE. Ex. 28:39. Locks of my head —Ju. 16:13. Spider's web—Is. 59:5. White cloth—Is. 19:9.

WEAVER. Ex. 35:35. Beam—1 Sam. 17: 7; I Chr. 11:23; 20:5. Rolled up, like a—Is. 38:12. Shuttle, Swifter than—Job 7:6.

WEB. Become garments, Shall not—Is. 59:6. Locks with the—Ju. 16:13. Plucked pin out of—Ju. 16:14. Spiders —Job 8:14; Is. 59:5.

WEDGE. Of gold—Josh. 7:21, 24.

WEEK. Appointed—Jer. 5:24. Fast twice in—Lu. 18:12. First day of—Mt. 28:1; Mk. 16:2; Lu. 24:1; John 20:1, 19; Acts 20:7; I Cor. 16:2. Fulfill—Gen. 29:27, 29. Seven—Deut. 16: 9; Dan. 9:25. Seventy—Dan. 9:25. Unclean two—Lev. 12:5.

Weeks, Feasts of—See FEASTS, SABBATH, SEVEN.

WEEPING. Gen. 43:30; Job 30:25; 31: 38; Ps. 126:6; Joel 1:5; Mk. 5:39; Lu. 23:28. Absalom, For—II Sam. 19:1. All were—Lu. 8:52. Ambassadors—Is. 33:7. At his feet—Lu. 7:38. Babe, The—Ex. 2:6. Bitterly—Is. 22:4; Mt. 26:75. Blessed are ye that—Lu. 6:21. Day and night—Jer. 9:1. Egyptians—Gen. 50:3. I will—Is. 16:9. Jazer, Of —Jer. 48:32. Jesus—Lu. 19:41; John —John 11:35. Loud voice, With—Ezra 3:12. Man of God—II Ki. 8:11. Mary, at the tomb—John 20:11. Many—Mk. 5:38. Mingled my drink with—Ps. 102:9. Mourn not nor—Neh. 8:9. No more power to—I Sam. 30:4. Noise of—Ezra 3:13. Not for the dead—Jer. 22:10. People—Num. 11:10. Rachel—Jer. 31:15. Secret, In—Jer. 13:17. Sore—Lam. 1:2. Tarry for the night—Ps. 30:5. There shall be—Mt. 8:12. Time to—Eccl. 3:4. When Jesus saw her—John 11:33. Why—I Sam. 1:8. Widows stood by

him—Acts 9:39. With them that—Rom. 12:15. Woman, why—John 20: 13. When we remembered Zion—Ps. 137:1. See MOURNING.

WEIGH. Ezra 8:29; Zech. 11:12. Actions—I Sam. 2:3. Balance, In—Job 31:6; Ez. 5:1; Lam. 5:27. Down—II Cor. 1:8. Hair—II Sam. 14:25. Hearts —Pr. 21:2; 24:12. Money—II Chr. 20:2; Jer. 32:9, 10. Mountain—Is. 40:12. Silver—Gen. 23:16; Ezra 8: 25, 26; Job 28:15; Is. 46:6. Spirits—Pr. 16:2. Vessels—Ezra 8:33. Vexations—Job 6:2. Violence—Ps. 58:2.

WEIGHT. Divers—Pr. 20:10, 23. Full —Gen. 43:21. Glory, Of—II Cor. 4:17. Just — Lev. 19:35; Deut. 25:13; Pr. 11:1; 16:11; 20:10, 23; Ez. 45:10; Hos. 12:7; Amos 8:5; Mic. 6:10. Minds, Of—Job 28:25. See MEASURES.

WEIGHTIER. Matters—Mt. 23:23.

WEIGHTY. Pr. 27:3; II Cor. 10:10.

WELCOME. Lu. 8:40; 9:11; III John 8.

WELFARE. Job 30:15. Ask of—Gen. 43:27; Ex. 18:7. Children of Israel, Of—Neh. 2:10. People, Of—Jer. 38:4.

WELL, *adj.* Lu. 17:2; Gal. 5:7. Done—Mt. 25:21; Mk. 7:37; Lu. 19:17; Acts 10:33; Phil. 4:14. Known—I Cor. 6: 9. Look—Pr. 14:15. Reported—Acts 16:2; 22:12; I Tim. 5:10. Speak—Lu. 6:26. With him—Gen. 29:6; 43:28; II. Sam. 18:29; 20:9; II Ki. 4:26. With them that fear God—Eccl. 8:12.

WELLS, *n.* The value of Abraham's—Gen. 21:25, 30. Isaac's—Gen. 26:15-22. Rarity of water in Sinaitic region explains rejoicing—Num. 21:16-18; Ju. 5:11. To destroy wells denoted conquest—Gen. 21:30; 26:15-33; Num. 20:17-19; II Ki. 3:19; Pr. 5:15. Contention for first right—Ex. 2:16-20. Fouling with feet of cattle, the reason —Ez. 34:17-19. Kept covered—Gen. 29:1-10. David longs for water out of well of Bethlehem—II Sam. 23:15, 16. Hagar gives name to first well mentioned in Scripture—Gen. 16:14. Beersheba, Rehoboth, and Jacob's well at Shechem—John 4:6. Cisterns hewn out—Deut. 6:11.

Figurative.—Valley of Baca—Ps. 84: 6. Wells of salvation—Is. 12:3. To woman of Samaria—John 4:14

WELL-BELOVED. Is. 5:1.

WELL-DOING. Eccl. 11:1; Is. 1:17; Rom. 2:7; Gal. 6:9

WELL-NIGH. Pr. 5:14; Acts 7:23.

WELL-PLEASING. Jehovah to—Lev. 10:19; Mt. 11:26; Rom. 14:18; II Cor. 5:9; Eph. 5:10; Phil. 4:18; Col. 3:20; Heb. 11:5, 6; 12:28; 13:21. See PLEASE.

WELLSPRING. Life, Of—Pr. 16:22. Wisdom, Of—Pr. 18:4.

WELTERING. Ez. 16:6.

WEN. Lev. 22:22.

WEST, WESTERN. Gen. 28:14; Mt. 24: 27. Border—Num. 34:6; Josh. 15:12; Ez. 45:7. Cloud rising in—Lu. 12:54. Countries—Zech. 8:7. East is from— Ps. 103:12. From the—Ps. 107:3; Is. 45:6; 49:12; 59:19; Mt. 8:11; Lu. 13; 29; Gather from—Is. 43:5. Quarter— Josh. 18:14. Sea—Joel 2:20; Zech. 14: 8. Toward the—I Ki. 7:25; I Chr. 9: 24; 12:15; II Chr. 4:4; Ez. 48:21; Zech. 14:4; Acts 27:12. Wind—Ex. 10:19.

WET. Dew of heaven—Dan. 4:15, 23, 25, 33; 5:21. Feet—Lu. 7:44. Showers, With—Job 24:8. See SPRINKLE, WATER.

WHALE. Mt. 12:40. See FISH.

WHEAT. II Sam. 4:6; 17:28. Finest of —Ps. 81:16. Article of food—Deut. 32:14; I Ki. 5:11. Bread made of—Ex. 29:2; Ps. 81:16; Ez. 4:9. Cakes made of—Ex. 29:2. Field of—Ex. 9:32; Deut. 8:8; Ju. 6:11; Jer. 41:8. Flour made of—Ex. 29:2. Growth, Curse on —Job. 31:40; Jer. 12:13. Harvest— Gen. 30:14; Ju. 15:1; Ruth 2:23; I Sam. 6:13; 12:17; I Chr. 21:20; Joel 1:11. Minnith, Of—Ez. 27:17. Miscellaneous—Song of Sol. 7:2; Is. 28: 25; Jer. 12:13; 23:28. Offerings used: Meal-offering—I Chr. 21:23; Burnt-offering—Ezra 6:9; Ez. 45:13. Parables—John 12:24; Mt. 13:25, 29, 30; Lu. 16:7. Payment, Used in—II Chr. 2:10, 15; 27:5; Ez. 7:22; Joel 2:24. Sale of — Amos 8:5, 6. Thrown into sea—Acts 27:38. See GRAIN, HARVEST.

WHEEL. Ez. 1:16. Broken—Eccl. 12:6. Whirling—Ez. 10:13. See TOOLS AND IMPLEMENTS.

WHELP. Ez. 19:2, 3, 5. Bear's—II Sam. 17:8; Pr. 17:12; Hos. 13:8. Lion's— Gen. 49:9; Deut. 33:22; Job 4:11; Jer. 51:38; Nah. 2:11, 12.

WHIP. I Ki. 12:11, 14; II Chr. 10:11, 14; Pr. 26:3; Nah. 3:2.

WHIRLING. Ps. 83:13; Eccl. 1:6; Is. 17:13.

WHIRLWINDS. See WIND.

WHISPER. See GOSSIP.

WHIT. Deut. 13:16; I Sam. 3:18; John 7:23; II Cor. 11:5.

WHITE. See COLORS, CLOTHING.

WHOLE. Armor of God—Eph. 6:11. Burnt-offering—I Sam. 7:9. See OFFERING. Duty of man—Eccl. 12:13. Habitation—Is. 4:5. Law—Mt. 22:40; Jas. 2:10. Made—Jer. 19:11; Mt. 9: 21; 12:13; 14:36; Mk. 3:5; 5:23; Lu. 6:10; 8:36; 18:42; Acts 14:9. See HEALING. Nation—John 11:50. Physician, Need not a—Mt. 9:12; Mk. 2: 17; Lu. 5:31. Vessel cannot be made —Jer. 19:11. World, Gain the whole —Mt. 16:26.

WHOLLY. Cut off—Josh. 3:16. Estranged—Job 19:13. Full of light— Lu. 11:36. Give thyself—I Tim. 4:15.

WHOM. Do men say that I am?—Mt. 16:13–15; Mk. 8:27–29; Lu. 9:18–20. Go, To whom shall we—John 6:68. Seek ye—Acts 8:34. Serve, Ye will— Josh. 24:15. Speaketh the prophet this, Of whom—Acts 8:34.

WHORE. See HARLOT, FORNICATION.

WHOREDOM. See ADULTERY, SPIRITUAL, HARLOT, FORNICATION.

WICKED: Source of wickedness in the heart.—Set to do evil—Eccl. 8:11; 9: 3. Wash thy heart—Jer. 4:14; Jas. 4:8. Soul of wicked desireth—Ps. 36: 4; 52:3; Pr. 2:14; 10:23; 15:21; 21:10; Hos. 4:18. Out of the heart proceeds evil—Mt. 12:34, 35; 15:18, 19; Mk. 7: 21–23; Lu. 6:45. Loving darkness rather than light—John 3:19. Evil heart of unbelief—Ps. 34:14; Heb. 3: 12.

God's attitude toward.—Will not justify them—Ex. 23:7; Deut. 10:17. See Is. 5:23. Withdraws Spirit—Gen. 6:3; Hos. 4:17; Rom. 1:24, 26, 28. Angry with them—Ps. 7:11; 11:5, 6; 78:49-51; Is. 13:9; 62:10; Jer. 4:4; 5:9; 21: 5; Ez. 5:13; Rom. 2:5; Col. 3:6; Rev. 21:8; 22:18. Shall be turned back to Sheol—Ps. 9:17; 49:14. He shall judge them—Ps. 75:2-4; Eccl. 3:17. See JUDGMENT. Will punish the wicked

—Ps. 50:22; 68:2; 119:119; 129:4; 146:9; 147:6; Pr. 3:33; 10:3; 11:8; Is. 1:20; 5:24; 13:11; 14:5; 24:6; 26: 21; 47:14; 50:11; Jer. 8:12; 12:3; 30: 14; Ez. 3:19; 21:32; Amos 1:3–15; 2: 1–16; Mic. 6:3. See PUNISHMENT. Punishment for sin—Gen. 3:6. Hell— Mk. 9:43. See HELL. The Judgment— II Pet. 2:4. Their light put out—Job 18:5; 21:17; Pr. 13:9; 20:20; 24:20; Is. 8:22. Their seed cut off—Ps. 21: 10; 37:9, 28; Pr. 2:22; 10:30. Stripped and banished—Ps. 92:7; 104:35; Ez. 22:15; Mt. 25:26–30. See COMMAND-MENTS, CHILDREN OF ISRAEL LED INTO CAPTIVITY BECAUSE OF VIOLATION OF. Shall be condemned—Ps. 91:8; 145: 20; Pr. 12:2; 16:4; Eccl. 8:13; Is. 28: 21, 22; Jer. 14:12; Ez. 18:4. Given over to reprobate mind—Rom. 1:24–28. Have part in lake of fire—Mt. 5: 22, 29, 30; 13:42, 50; Rev. 19:20; 21: 8. See HELL, TEACHING OF JESUS CON-CERNING HELL.

Description of.—Children in whom there is no faithfulness—Deut. 32:20. Children of transgression—Is. 57:4. Children of disobedience—Eph. 2:2; 5:6; Col. 3:6. Children of the devil—Mt. 13:38; John 8:44; Acts 13:10; I John 3:10. Children of the flesh—Rom. 9:8. Children who will not hear the law of the Lord—Is. 30:9. Rebellious children—Is. 1:2; 30:1. See Is. 65:2. Lying children—Is. 30:9. Servants of sin—John 8:34; Rom. 6:20. Servants of corruption—II Pet. 2:19. Unprofitable servants—Mt. 25:30. Seed of falsehood—Is. 57:4. Seed of the wicked—Ps. 37:28; Mt. 13:38. Seed of evil-doers—Is. 1:4; 14:20. Lovers of darkness—John 3:19–20. Despisers of God—Job 21:14. Dead in trespasses and sins—Eph. 2:1–3.

Results of wickedness.—Reap as they sow—Job 4:8; Pr. 22:8; Hos. 10:13; Gal. 6:7–8. Eat fruit of their deeds —Pr. 1:31; Jer. 6:19. Fall by their own wickedness—Pr. 5:22, 23; 11:5, 19. Wrath responds to expectation— Pr. 11:23. Overthrown by wickedness —Ps. 27:2; Pr. 13:6, 21. Driven out of power—Ez. 31:11. No peace—Is. 57:20, 21. Indignation and wrath their lot—Rom. 2:8. Wages of sin is

death—Rom. 6:23. Disinherited—I Cor. 6:9, 10; Gal. 5:19–21; Eph. 5:5. Everlasting destruction—II Thess. 1: 9. Brings many sorrows—Ps. 16:4; 32:10; Is. 47:11. Chaff—Job 21:18; Ps. 1:4; Mt. 3:12. Tares—Mt. 13:38–41. Autumn trees without fruit— Jude 12. Clouds without water—II Pet. 2:17. Springs without water—II Pet. 2:17. Fools building on sand— Mt. 7:26, 27; Lu. 6:49. Whited sepulchres—Mt. 23:27. Raging waves of the sea—Jude 13. Wandering stars —Jude 13. Goats—Mt. 25:32–33. Swine—Mt. 7:6; II Pet. 2:22. Blind —Zeph. 1:17; Mt. 15:14; 23:16–24. Bad fish—Mt. 13:48. Corrupt trees— Mt. 7:17, 18; Lu. 6:43. See TEACHING OF JESUS CONCERNING THE CHARACTER OF THE WICKED, HELL, AND THE JUDGMENT. SIN, COMMANDMENTS. PUNISHMENT, JUDGMENT, HELL.

WICKEDNESS. Job 34:10; 35:8; Ps. 26:10; 141:5; Pr. 8:7. According to— Deut. 25:2. Bread of—Pr. 4:17. Brought to pass—Ju. 20:3. Cut off in —Ps. 94:23. Devise—Ps. 52:2. Dwell in—Ps. 55:15; 84:10. Fall by own— Pr. 11:5. Great—Gen. 39:9; Job 22: 5. Men, Of—Ju. 9:57. Shall not rest —Ps. 125:3. Throne of—Ps. 94:20. Treasures of—Pr. 10:2. Utter—Is. 59:3. Work—Ps. 58:2. See SIN.

WIDE. Neh. 7:4. Gates open—Nah. 3: 13; Mt. 7:13. House—Pr. 21:9; 25: 24; Jer. 22:14. Land—I Chr. 4:40. Open mouth—Job 29:23; Ps. 35:21; 81:10; Pr. 13:3; Is. 57:4. Sea—Ps. 104:25.

WIDOW. Under God's protection— Deut. 10:18; Ps. 68:5; 146:9; Pr. 15: 25; Jer. 49:11. Laws relating to marriage—Deut. 25:5; Lev. 21:14; Ez. 44:22; Mk. 12:19. See also I Cor. 7:8.

Laws respecting: Not to be oppressed— Ex. 22:22; Deut. 27:19; Is. 1:17, 23; 10:2; Jer. 22:3; Zech. 7:10; Mal. 3:5. Creditors not to take raiment—Deut. 24:17. Bound to perform their vows— Num. 30:9. To be allowed to glean in fields—Deut. 24:19. To have a share of triennial tithe—Deut. 14:28–29; 26:12–13. To share in public rejoicings —Deut. 16:11–14.

When childless, to be married to husband's nearest kin.—Deut. 25:8-10; Ruth 3:10-13; 4:4-5; Mt. 22:24-26.

Widows to be cared for by church.—Acts 6:1; I Tim. 5:3-5, 9-16; Jas. 1: 27.

WIFE: Laws concerning.—Ex. 20:17; 21:3-5; 22:16; Lev. 18:8, 11, 14-16, 18, 20; 20:10, 11, 14, 21; 21:7, 13, 14; Num. 5:11-31; 30:16; 36:8; Deut. 5: 21; 13:6; 20:7; 21:11-14; 22:13, 30; 24:5. Divorce—Deut. 24:1, 3, 4; Mt. 5:31, 32; 19:3-10; Mk. 10:2-12; Lu. 16:18; I Cor. 7:32-40.

Proverbs concerning.—Pr. 12:4; 18:22; 31:10.

Duties of.—Gen. 3:16; Rom. 7:2; I Cor. 7:2-4, 10, 11, 13, 14, 16; Eph. 5:22, 24, 33; Col. 3:18; Tit. 2:4, 5; I Pet. 3:1. Honoring husbands—Esth. 1:20.

Illustrative.—Jer. 3:1, 20; Ez. 16:32; Eph. 5:25-27, 29, 33; Rev. 19:7; 21:9. See HUSBAND.

WILD. Ass—See ASSES. Beasts—See BEASTS. Goats—See GOATS. Grapes—Is. 5:2, 4. Honey—Mk. 1:6. Olive—Neh. 8:15; Rom. 11:17, 24. Ox—Job 39:9. See CATTLE, Ox. Roe—II Sam. 2: 18. Vine—II Ki. 4:93.

WILDERNESS. Arabah, a dry, desolate tract of land. Midbar, to drive, as cattle, to a scant pasture land

Place where wild animals roam.—Job 24:5; Ps. 102:6; Jer. 2:24; Lam. 4:3; Mal. 1:3. Whither Israel went to worship Jehovah—Ex. 3:18; 5:1; 7:16; 8:27, 28. Where Aaron met Moses—Ex. 4:27.

Of Shur, Just beyond East border of Egypt.—Hagar's flight into—Gen. 16: 7. Abraham resided near—Gen. 20:1. Place of Ishmael's posterity—Gen. 25:18; I Sam. 15:7; 27:8. First landing of Israel after crossing the Red Sea—Ex. 15:22. Called also wilderness of Etham—Ex. 13:20; 14:3, 11, 12; 15:22; Num. 33:8.

Of sin.—The Plain of El Markha—Ex. 16:1; Num. 33:11, 12. A desolate expanse of flints, gravel, and sand, needing aid from heaven in the gift of manna and quails—Ex. 16:11-22. Jethro meets Moses here, together with Moses' wife and sons—Ex. 18:

1-7. Judges appointed to aid Moses —Ex. 18:24-27.

Of Sinai.—In third month, Israel came into—Ex. 19:1, 2; Lev. 7:38. Law given—Ex. Ch. 20. Tabernacle built—Ex. Chs. 26-27. Priests appointed—Ex. Ch. 28. Moses commanded to number Israel—Num. 1:1-19. Also the Levites—Num. 3:15-16. Nadab and Abihu offered strange fire in the wilderness—Num. 3:4. Goat sent away alive into—Lev. 16:10. Israel keeps passover in—Num. 9:5. Children of Israel set forth out of—Num. 10: 12.

Of Paran.—The directing cloud rested in Paran—Num. 10:12. This desert extended from near Sinai to beyond Hazeroth and up to Kadesh-barnea—Num. 12:16; 13:3, 26. Called Mount Paran—Deut. 33:2; Hab. 3:3. Included wilderness of Zin—Num. 13: 21; 20:1; 27:14; 33:36. Spies sent into Canaan from there—Num. 13:3, 21. Israel murmured against Moses and Aaron there—Num. 14:2. Jehovah threatens their lives for it—Num. 14:20-35. The threat fulfilled—Num. 26:63-65; 27:3; 32:13-15; Josh. 5:4-6; Ez. 20:10-26.

Record of journeys in.—Num. Ch. 33; Deut. 1:19-40; 2:1-15; 8:2, 15-16; 29: 5-8; 32:10; Ju. 11:15-22; Neh. 9:12-25; Ps. 68:7; 78:15-33, 40, 41, 52.

David, as an outlaw, dwells in the Wilderness of Maon.—I Sam. 23:14-24. Saul pursues him thither—I Sam. 23:25-28. Of Engedi—I Sam. 24:1-7. He goes to the Wilderness of Paran—I Sam. 25:1. Meets Nabal there and protects his flock—I Sam. 25:21. Saul seeks David in Wilderness of Ziph—I Sam. 26:1-3. David's warriors pursue Abner to Wilderness of Gibeon—II Sam. 2:24. David flees from Absalom toward the—II Sam. 15:23. Is succored in wilderness by Ziba—II Sam. 16:1-2. Is warned not to lodge at fords of—II Sam. 17:16. Is again succored by friends—II Sam. 17:27-29. Warriors who rallied about David in the—I Chr. Ch. 12. David fled thither after Samuel's death—I Sam. 25:1.

Jehoshaphat makes battle in Wilderness of Jeruel.—II Chr. 20:14–26.

Natural history of.—Dry and parched—Deut. 8:15; 32:10; II Sam. 16:2; 17:29; Ps. 78:15; 102:6; Is. 35:6; 41:18; Jer. 9:12; 12:10; 17:6; 23:10; 51:43; Joel 1:19; 2:3; Zeph. 2:13. Winds—Is. 21:1; Jer. 4:11. Sands—Deut. 28:24; Jer. 4:12, 13.

Transformation of.—Ps. 65:11–13; 68:7–10; 78:15–29; Is. 32:15–16; 35:1; Ez. 19:10, 13; Joel 2:22.

New Testament references.—The preaching of John—Mt. 3:3; Mk. 1:34; Lu. 3:2–4; John 1:23. Jesus led into, by the Spirit—Mt. 4:1; Mk. 1:12; Lu. 4:1. There 40 days—Mt. 4:2; Mk. 1:13; Lu. 4:2. Jesus withdraws into—Lu. 5:16. What went ye out to see?—Mt. 11:7; Lu. 7:24. Miraculous bread furnished in—Mt. 15:33; Mk. 8:4; John 6:49. Lifted up serpent in—John 3:14. Leave 99 in—Lu. 15:4. Israel in—Acts 7:30, 36, 38, 42, 44; 13:18; I Cor. 10:5; Heb. 3:8, 17. Was Paul that Egyptian?—Acts 21:38. The woman in Revelations—Rev. 12:6, 14; 17:3.

Wilderness mentioned in Scripture.—Arabian — Ex. 23:31. Beth-aven — Josh. 18:12. Beer-sheba—Gen. 21:14; I Ki. 19:3, 4. Damascus—I Ki. 19:15. Edom—II Ki. 3:8. Engedi—I Sam. 24:1. Gibeon—II Sam. 2:24. Judæa—Mt. 3:1. Jeruel—II Chr. 20:16. Kedemoth—Deut. 2:26. Kadesh—Ps. 29:8. Maon—I Sam. 23:24, 25. Paran—Gen. 21:21; Num. 10:12. Shur—Gen. 16:7; Ex. 15:22. Sin—Ex. 16:1. Sinai—Ex. 19:1, 2; Num. 33:16. Ziph—I Sam. 23:14, 15. Zin—Num. 20:1; 27:14. Of the Red Sea—Ex. 13:18. Near Gaza—Acts 8:26.

Dangers of. — Trackless — Is. 43:19. Waste and howling—Deut. 32:10. Perils in—Ex. 14:3; II Cor. 11:26. Guides needed—Num. 10:31.

Robbers frequent.—Jer. 3:2; Lam. 4:19. Wild beasts—Is. 13:21; Mk. 1:13. Serpents—Num. 21:6; Deut. 8:15.

Jehovah's mercies in.—Ex. 15:13; Deut. 8:2; 11:5; Ps. 77:20; 78:52; 136:16; Jer. 31:2; Ez. 20:17, 34–36; Hosea 2:14–15; Amos 2:10; Acts 13:18.

WILES. Devil, Of—Eph. 6:11. Error, Of—Eph. 4:14. Vex with—Num. 25:18.

WILFULLY. Heb. 10:26.

WILILY. Josh. 9:4.

WILL. I Cor. 7:37; Jas. 3:4. Adversaries, Of—Ps. 27:12. Apollos, Of—I Cor. 16:12. Be done—Mt. 6:10; 26:42; Lu. 22:42. Counsel of—Eph. 1:11. Delivered up to their—Lu. 23:25. Do—Dan. 8:4; 11:3, 16, 36; Mt. 7:21; 21:31; Heb. 10:7–10. Enemies, Of—Ps. 41:2. Father, Of—Mt. 12:50; 18:14. Flesh, Of—John 1:13. Tree, Of—Philemon 14. God, Of—Dan. 4:17, 35; Ezra 7:18; Mk. 3:35; 40:8; 143:10; John 1:13; 7:17; 9:31; Acts 13:22; Rom. 9:19; 12:2; I Cor. 1:1; II Cor. 1:1; 8:5; Eph. 6:6; Col. 4:12; I Thess. 4:3; II Tim. 1:1; Heb. 10:36; 13:21; Jas. 1:18; I Pet. 2:15; 3:17; 4:2, 19; I John 2:17; 5:14. Good—Pr. 14:9. He that—Rev. 22:17. Him that sent me, Of—John 5:30; 6:38. Know—Acts 22:14. Knowledge of—Col. 1:9. Lord's—Lu. 12:47; Acts 21:14; Eph. 5:17. Man, Of—II Pet. 1:21. My meat is to—John 4:34. Mystery of—Eph. 1:9. Not as I—Mt. 2:39. See MAN, MIND.

WILLING. Absent, To be—II Cor. 5:8. Heart—Ex. 35:5; II Chr. 29:31. Mind—I Chr. 28:9. Receive, To—John 6:21. Rejoice, To—John 5:35. Spirit—Ps. 51:12; Mt. 26:41; Mk. 14:38. Wrath, To show—Rom. 9:22. See MAN, MIND, LIBERALITY.

WILLINGLY. Not of constraint, but—I Pet. 5:2. Offered—Ju. 5:2; I Chr. 29:5; Ezra 2:68. See MAN, MIND, LIBERALITY.

WILL-WORSHIP. Col. 2:23.

WILLOW. Brook, Of—Lev. 23:40; Job 40:22; Is. 15:7; 44:4. Hang on—Ps. 137:2. Tree—Ez. 17:5. See TREES.

WILY. Pr. 7:10.

WIN. II Chr. 32:1. Soul—Pr. 11:30; Lu. 21:19.

WIND. Amos 4:13. Bring forth, out of his treasuries—Ps. 135:7; Jer. 10:13; 51:16. Causeth the wind to blow—Ps. 147:18. Gathers in His hand—Pr. 30:4. Voice of—John 3:8.

Variable nature of.—Eccl. 1:6; 11:5.

Drying nature.—Gen. 8:1. Bringing of rain—I Ki. 18:44, 45. Clearing of—Job 37:21. Not cleansing—Jer. 4:11. Blighting—Ps. 103:16. Movement of the trees—Is. 7:2. Of the sea—Jas. 1:6. Reed shaken with—Mt. 11:7; Lu. 7:24.

Four winds of the earth.—Rev. 7:1. East—Gen. 41:6, 23, 27; Ex. 10:13; Job 15:2; 27:21; 38:24; Ps. 48:7; 78:26; Is. 27:8; Jer. 18:17; Ez. 17:10; 19:12; 27:26; Hos. 13:15; Jonah 4:8. West—Ex. 10:19. South—Job 37:17; Ps. 78:26; Song of Sol. 4:16; Lu. 12:55; Acts 27:13; 28:13. North—Pr. 25:23; Song of Sol. 4:16. Stormy—I Ki. 19:11; Job 1:19; 8:2; 30:15, 22; 107:25; 148:8; Mk. 4:37; Lu. 8:23; John 6:18; Acts 27:7, 15. Scorching—Is. 11:15. Contrary—Mt. 14:24, 30; Mk. 6:48. Mighty—Acts 2:2. Called Euraquilo—Acts 27:14. Great—Rev. 6:13. Calmed by Christ—Mt. 14:32; Mk. 4:39, 41; 6:51; Lu. 8:24.

Miracles connected with.— Locusts brought and removed by—Ex. 10:13, 19. Dividing of the Red Sea—Ex. 14:21; 15:10. Quails brought by—Num. 11:31. Raised because of Jonah —Jonah 1:4. Calmed by casting him out—Jonah 1:15. Elisha's prophecy—II Ki. 3:17.

Miscellaneous.—That snuffeth up the—Jer. 2:24. Hoisting foresail to the—Acts 27:40. Laboreth for—Eccl. 5:16. Observation of—Eccl. 11:4. Hiding-place from—Is. 32:2.

Illustrative.—Job 6:26; 8:2; Ps. 78:39; Pr. 25:14; Ez. 37:9. Of wicked: As stubble or dust before the—Job 21:18; Ps. 1:4; 18:42; 35:5; 83:13; Is. 17:13; Jer. 13:24; Dan. 2:35. Of sin —Is. 64:6. Shall inherit the—Pr. 11:29. Of false doctrines—Eph. 4:14.

Figurative.—Pr. 27:16; Is. 26:18; 41:29; Jer. 5:13; Hos. 8:7; 12:1. Wings of—II Sam. 22:11; Ps. 18:10; 104:3; Hos. 4:19.

WHIRLWIND. Called whirling dust—Is. 17:13. Whirling tempest—Jer. 23:19.

Usually came from the South.—Is. 21:1; Zech. 9:14.

Destructive nature of.—Hab. 3:14.

Events connected with.—Elijah taken to heaven in—II Ki. 2:1, 11. Jehovah answers Job from—Job 38:1; 40:6.

Illustrative.—Of wicked—Hos. 13:3. Of destruction of the wicked—Ps. 58:9; Pr. 1:27; 10:25; Is. 40:24; 41:16; 66:15; Amos 1:14; Nah. 1:3; Zech. 7:14. Fruit of sin—Hos. 8:7. Velocity of chariots—Is. 5:28; Jer. 4:13; Dan. 11:40. See METEOROLOGY.

WINDOWS. Of heaven—Gen. 7:11; 8:2; II Ki. 7:2, 19; Is. 24:18; Mal. 3:10. Of ark—Gen. 8:6. Of doves—Is. 60:8. Windows built — Jer. 22:14. In the temple—I Ki. 6:4. Closed windows—Ez. 40:16, 22, 25, 29, 33, 36; 41:16, 26. In Solomon's house—I Ki. 7:4, 5. They that look out of, Shall be darkened—Eccl. 12:3. Death in—Jer. 9:21. In the window—Josh. 2:18, 21; Song of Sol. 2:9; Zeph. 2:14. Fell from—Acts 20:9. Entered at—Joel 2:9. Out at —Gen. 26:8; II Ki. 9:30; II Sam. 6:16; I Chr. 15:29; Pr. 7:6. Through—Josh. 2:15; Ju. 5:28; I Sam. 19:12; II Cor. 11:33. To window—II Ki. 9:32. Open windows—II Ki. 13:17; Dan. 6:10.

WINE: Making of.—Gen. 9:20–21; Is. 16:10; 24:7; 27:2; Mt. 21:33; Mk. 12:1.

Token of prosperity.—Gen. 27:28, 37; 49:11–12; Deut. 7:13; 11:14; 16:13; 18:4; 33:28; II Ki. 18:32.

Mark of desolation.—Deut. 28:39, 51; 32:32, 33, 38.

Used in offerings.—Ex. 29:40; Lev. 23:13; Num. 15:5, 7, 10; 28:14; I Chr. 9:29; Ezra 6:9.

Denied to high priests.—Lev. 10:9; Ez. 44:21. Allotted to priests among first-fruits—Num. 18:12.

Forbidden in Nazirite vow.—Num. 6:3, 4, 20; Ju. 13:4, 7, 14; Amos 2:12; Lu. 1:15. Forbidden to Rechabites—Jer. 35:6, 7.

Used as a drink.—Gen. 27:25; I Sam. 1:24; 10:3; 16:20; 25:18; Pr. 9:5; Eccl. 9:7; Song of Sol. 8:2; Is. 24:9; Amos 9:14; I Tim. 5:23.

Vicious use of.—Gen. 19:32–35; I Sam. 1:14–15; 25:37; II Sam. 13:28; Esth. 1:10; 7:2, 7, 8; Ps. 78:65; Pr. 4:17; 20:1; 21:17; 23:30–31; 31:4–7; Eccl. 2:3; 10:19; Is. 5:11, 12, 22; 28:1, 7;

Hos. 4:11; Joel 1:5; Hab. 2:5, 15;
Rom. 14:21; Eph. 5:18; I Tim. 3:3, 8;
I Pet. 4:3.

Various uses.—As a tithe—Deut. 12:17;
14:23-26; Neh. 10:37; 13:5, 12, 15. In
trickery—Josh. 9:4, 13. In hospitality
—Ju. 19:19; Lu. 10:34. In king's
courts—I Chr. 27:27; Dan. 5:1-4. As
an exchange—II Chr. 2:10. For military supply—II Chr. 11:11. For taxes
—Neh. 5:11. Symbol of God's gracious gifts—Is. 55:1. As a false
charge—Acts 2:13. In a fable—Ju.
9:13.

New wine in old bottles.—Mt. 9:17; Mk.
2:22; Lu. 5:37.

Miracle.—John 2:3-10; 4:46.

For communion and blessing.—Gen. 14:
18-20; Mt. 26:26-29; Mk. 14:22-25;
Lu. 22:15-20; I Cor. 11:20-27.

Used figuratively.—Job 32:19; Ps. 60:
3; 75:8; Song of Sol. 1:2-4; 4:10; Rev.
14:8, 10; 16:19; 17:2; 18:3.

Winebibbers.—Pr. 23:30; Mt. 11:19;
Lu. 7:34.

Wine cellar.—I Chr. 27:27.

Wine cup.—See CUP.

Wine-offering.—See OFFERING.

Winepress.—Is. 5:1-2; Mt. 21:33; Mk.
12:1. See GRAPE, DRUNKENNESS.

WINE SKINS. Josh. 9:4; Ps. 119:83;
Mt. 9:17; Mk. 2:22; Lu. 5:37.

WINEVAT. Hag. 2:16.

WING. Creation of winged birds—Gen.
1:21. Birds of every wing—Ez. 17:23.

Mention of.—Bird—Deut. 4:17. Dove—
Ps. 55:6; 68:13. Eagle—Ex. 19:4;
Deut. 32:11; Is. 40:31; Ez. 17:3, 7.
Rev. 12:14. Hawk—Job 39:26. Os-
trich—Job 39:13; Dan. 7:4, 6. Stork
—Zech. 5:9.

Figurative.—Of Cherubim—Ex. 25:20;
37:9; I Ki. 6:24, 27; 8:6, 7; II Chr.
3:11, 12, 13; 5:7, 8; Ez. 1:6, 8, 9, 11,
23, 24, 25; 3:13; 10:8, 12, 16, 19, 21;
11:22. Of Jehovah—Ruth 2:12; Ps. 17:
8; 36:7; 57:1; 61:4; 63:7; 91:4; Jer.
48:40; 49:22. Morning—Ps. 139:9. Of
riches—Pr. 23:5. Of seraphim—Is 5:2.
Of wind—II Sam. 22:11; Ps. 18:10;
104:3; Hos. 4:19. Used in offering—
Lev. 1:17.

In prophecy.—Is. 8:8; 10:14; 18:1; Jer.
48:5; Mal. 4:2.

In vision.—Rev. 4:8.

Teaching of Jesus concerning.—Mt. 23:
37; Lu. 13:34.

WINK. Eyes—Job 15:12; Ps. 35:19;
Pr. 6:13; 10:10.

WINNOW. Is. 30:24; 41:16; Jer. 15:7.
Barley—Ruth 3:2. Wicked—Pr. 20:26.

WINTER. Summer and—Gen. 8:22.
Thou hast made—Ps. 74:17. The winter is past—Song of Sol. 2:11. By reason of the—Pr. 20:4. The beasts shall
winter upon them—Is. 18:6. I will
smite the winter house—Zech. 14:8. In
winter shall it be—Zech. 14:8. That
your flight may not be in—Mt. 24:20;
Mk. 13:18. Feast of Dedication was in
—John 10:22. Haven not commodious
to winter in—Acts 27:12. To Phenice,
and there to—Acts 27:12. I will abide
and winter with you—I Cor. 16:6.
Give diligence to come before—II
Tim. 4:21. Paul winters at Nicopolis
—Tit. 3:12.

Coldness and inclemency of.—Pr. 20:4;
John 10:22.

Ships laid up in port during.—Acts 27:
12; 28:11.

Unsuited for journeying.—Mt. 24:20;
Acts 27:9, 12; 28:11.

Winter houses.—King sat in winter
house—Jer. 36:22; Amos 3:15.

WIPE. Lu. 10:11; John 13:5. Feet—
Lu. 7:44; John 11:2; 12:3; 13:5. Good
deeds, out—Neh. 13:14. Jerusalem—
II Ki. 21:13. Mouth—Pr. 30:20. Re-
proach, Away—Pr. 6:33. Tears, Away
—Is. 25:8; Rev. 7:17; 21:4.

WIRES. Ex. 39:3.

WISDOM. God fills with the spirit of
—Ex. 28:3; 31:3; 35:31-35. God
shows the secrets of—Job 11:6; Ps.
51:6; Pr. 2:3-7; Eph. 1:7-10; Jas. 3:
17. Its value hard to estimate—Job
28:12-19; Pr. 3:13-18; 16:16. Fear of
the Lord is—Deut. 4:5, 6; Job 28:28;
Ps. 111:10; Pr. 1:7. Conceit defeats—
Shall die with you—Job 12:2. Rages
against it—Pr. 18:1-2. Cease from
thine own—Pr. 23:4; 28:11; Rom. 11:
25. Too high for the fool—Pr. 24:7.

Wisdom of this world: Foolishness.—
Is. 29:14; I Cor. 1:20; 3:19.

The wisdom of Solomon.—I Ki. 4:29-34;
5:12; 10:4-8, 23, 24; 11:41; II Chr.
1:10, 12; 9:1-8, 22, 23. Came from far

to hear Solomon—Mt. 12:42; Lu. 11: 31.

Vanity of worldly.—Eccl. 1:16–18; 2: 21; 9:15, 16.

Wisdom as related to Jesus.—Filled with—Lu. 2:40. Increased in—Lu. 2: 52. Whence hath this man this—Mt. 13:54. Christ the wisdom of God—I Cor. 1:24.

Wisdom to be sought and used.—Ps. 90: 12; Rom. 16:19; Eph. 5:15; Col. 1:9; 3:16; 4:5; Rev. 13:18; 17:9–14.

Special references.—No wisdom in the grave—Eccl. 9:10. Youths skilful in—Dan. 1:4; 2:20–24. Give you a mouth and—Lu. 21:15. Look out seven men full of—Acts 6:3, 10. God gave Joseph —Acts 7:10, 22. Greeks seek after—I Cor. 1:22. Not with words of man's —I Cor. 2:4, 5, 6, 7. If any lack, let him ask of God—Jas. 1:5. According to wisdom given me—II Pet. 3:15.

WISE. Old Testament: A tree to make one wise—Gen. 3:6. Making wise the simple—Ps. 19:7. Be not wise in thine own eyes—Pr. 3:7. Wise son maketh —Pr. 10:1. He that gathereth in summer is—Pr. 10:5. He that winneth souls is—Pr. 11:30. Wise son hears instruction—Pr. 13:1. Four things that are—Pr. 30:24. Woe to them that are—Is. 5:21. New Testament: Be ye wise as serpents—Mt. 10:16. Thou didst hide these things from—Mt. 11:25; Lu. 10:21. Who is that wise servant—Mt. 24:45. Five virgins were—Mt. 25:2. Who is that wise steward—Lu. 12:42. Am debtor to the—Rom. 1:14. Professing themselves wise, became fools—Rom. 1:22. Be not wise in—Rom. 12:16. To the only wise God—Rom. 16:27. Bear with foolish, being wise—II Cor. 11: 19. Scripture able to make wise—II Tim. 3:15. See SOLOMON, WISDOM LITERATURE IN OUTLINE STUDIES IN THE BOOKS.

WISH. Rom. 9:3; II Pet. 3:9. Day, For—Acts 27:29. Heart, Of—Ps. 73:7. Present, To be—Gal. 4:20.

WIST. Not—Ex. 16:15; 34:29; Josh. 2: 4; 8:14; Ju. 16:20; John 5:13; Acts 12:9; 23:5. What to say, Not—Mk. 9: 6; 14:40. Ye not—Lu. 2:49.

WITCH, WITCH CRAFT. See MAGIC.
WITHDRAW. Mt. 2:22; Acts 26:31. Anger—Job 9:13. Day—Ez. 30:18. Eyes—Job 36:7. Hand—I Sam. 14:19; Job 13:21; Eccl. 7:18; Lam. 2:8; Ez. 18:8; 20:22. Jesus did—Mt. 12:15; Mk. 3:7; Lu. 5:16. Light—Zech. 14: 6. Moon—Is. 60:20. Purpose—Job 33: 17. Self—Song of Sol. 5:6; Hosea 5:6. Shoulder—Neh. 9:29. Stars—Joel 2: 10; 3:15. Yourselves—II Thess. 3:6.

WITHER. Away—Ps. 6:2. Ears—Gen. 4:23. Fig tree—Mt. 21:20; Mk. 11: 20. Fruit—Ez. 17:9. Grass—See GRASS. Hand—See HAND. Heart—Ps. 102:4. Joy—Joel 1:12. Leaf—Ps. 1:3; 37:2; Is. 19:6; 40:7; Ez. 47:12; Jas. 1:11. Vine—Joel 1:12.

WITHHOLD. Bread—Job 22:7. Corn Pr. 11:24, 26. Correction—Pr. 23:13. Food—Jer. 2:25. Fruit—Gen. 30:2. Good—Ps. 84:11; Pr. 3:27; Jer. 5:25. Hand—Eccl. 11:6. Heart—Eccl. 2:10. Joy, From—Eccl. 2:10. Manna—Neh. 9:20. Mercy—Ps. 40:11. Offering—Joel 1:13. Poor, From—Job 31:16. Ram—Job 12:15; Amos 4:7. Requests —Ps. 21:2. Showers—Jer. 3:3; Amos 4:7. Sin, From—Gen. 20:6; Jer. 5:25. Son—Gen. 22:13, 16. Speaking, From —Job 4:2. Water—Job 12:15.

WITHSTAND. Lu. 21:15. Enemy—II Chr. 20:6; 26:18; Esth. 9:2; Eccl. 4:12. Evil—Eph. 6:13. Faith, In—I Pet. 5: 9. God—Acts 11:17; Rom. 13:2. Gospel—Acts 13:8; II Tim. 3:8; 4:15. Kingdom of the Lord—II Chr. 13: 7, 8. Persia—Dan. 10:13; 11:15. Wisdom—Acts 6:10. See STAND.

WITNESS: Kinds of. False—Lev. 19: 11; I Ki. 21:10, 13; Ps. 27:12; 35:11; Pr. 6:19; 12:17; 14:5; 19:5, 9; 21:28; 25:18; Jer. 7:9; Mt. 15:19; 26:16, 59, 60; Mk. 14:55–57; Acts 6:13. *Jesus accused of being*—John 8:13. Worthless—Pr. 19:28. Faithful—Pr. 14:5; Is. 8:2. True—Pr. 14:25.

Witnesses of Jehovah.—Is. 43:10, 12; 44:8.

Eye witness.—To Job—Job 29:11. John, to crucifixion of Jesus—John 19:35. Paul, to death of Stephen—Acts 7: 58. To confession—I Tim. 6:12.

Legal witness.—To marriage—Ruth 4: 10. Business transactions—Ruth 4:1-

9; Jer. 32:10-12, 25, 44. Laws concerning—Ex. 20:16; 22:13; 23:1; Lev. 5:1; Num. 5:13; Deut. 5:20; 19:16-18; Pr. 24:28; Mt. 19:18; Mk. 10:19; Lu. 18:20.

Two or three required.—Num. 35:30; Deut. 17:6, 7; 19:15; Mt. 18:16; John 8:17; II Cor. 13:1; I Tim. 5:19; Heb. 10:28; Rev. 11:3.

Memorial as.—Covenant between Laban and Jacob witnessed by a heap of stones—Gen. 31:44, 48, 50-52. Song as—Deut. 31:19, 21. Stone as—Josh. 24:27. Book of Law—Deut. 31:26. Altar—Josh. 22:26, 27, 28, 34. Lamb —Gen. 21:30.

Witnesses to Christ.—People of Nazareth—Lu. 4:22. Officer—John 18:23. Stephen — Acts 22:20. Prophets — Acts 10:43. Apostles—Lu. 24:48; Acts 1:8, 2:32; 5:32; 10:39, 41; 13:31. Paul—Acts 22:15; 23:11; 26:16; I Cor. 9:1. Peter—I Pet. 5:1.

Works of Christ bear witness to Him. —John 10:25; Acts 14:17.

Witness to Christ not by Himself.— John 5:31. See ''Teachings of Jesus.''

Disciples as.—Lu. 1:2; John 1:7, 8, 15; 3:26; 15:27; 21:24; I John 1:2; Rev. 1:2.

Jehovah as a witness.—Gen. 31:50; Ju. 11:10; I Sam. 12:5; Jer. 29:23; 42:5; Mic. 1:2; Mal. 2:14; 3:5; Acts 15:8; Rom. 1:9; II Cor. 1:23; I Thess. 2:5, 10; Phil. 1:8; Heb. 2:4; 11:4; I John 5:9. To Christ—Mt. 3:16, 17; John 5:34, 36, 37; 12:28; Heb. 2:4; I John 5:9; Rev. 3:14.

Holy Spirit witness to Christ.—Lu. 3: 22; John 1:33; 15:26; Acts 2:2-4; 5:32; Heb. 10:15; I John 5:7, 8, 11.

Christ a witness.—John 18:37; Acts 14: 3; Rev. 1:5.

Witness against Jesus.—Mt. 26:65; Mk. 14:63; Lu. 22:71.

Witness to resurrection.—Acts 1:22; 4: 33. Of Eternal Life—Rom. 8:16; I John 1:2.

Witnesses to faith.—Martyrs—Rev. 2: 13; 17:6.

Testimony.—Against rich—Jas. 5:3. Of Paul to small and great—Acts 26:22. Holy Spirit testifies unto Paul—Acts 20:23. People witness to Paul—II Tim. 2:2. High Priest a witness to

Paul—Acts 22:5. Paul—Witness to the power of the churches—II Cor. 8:3.

Given to saints.—Heb. 11:39; I John 5: 10; III John 12.

Prophecies concerning.—Is. 19:20; 44: 9; 55:4.

Figurative.—Heaven and earth—Deut. 4:26; 30:19. Leanness—Job 16:8. Cloud of mountain—Heb. 12:1. Conscience—Rom. 2:15; 9:1.

WIZARDS. See MAGIC.

WOE. City, To—Ez. 24:6, 9; Nah. 3:1; Rev. 18:10. Foolish Prophets, To— Ez. 13:3. Unbelief, To—Mt. 23:13; Lu. 10:13. Wickedness, To—Is. 10:1; 31:1; 45:9; Jer. 22:13; Amos 6:1; Mic. 2:1; Hab. 2:6; Zech. 11:17; Mt. 26: 24; Lu. 6:24; Jude 11; Rev. 8:13; 9: 12.

WOLVES. Gen. 49:27; Is. 13:22; 34: 14; Jer. 5:6; 50:39; Ez. 22:27; Hab. 1:8; Zeph. 3:8; Mt. 7:15; John 10:12; Acts 20:29; Lamb, Dwell with—Is. 11:6; 65:25. Sheep in midst of—Mt. 10:16; Lu. 10:3.

WOMAN, *i. e.,* **Taken out of man.**—Gen. 2:23. Created—Gen. 1:27; 2:21, 22. Blessed of God—Gen. 1:28. The function of—Gen. 1:28. A helpmeet to man—Gen. 2:18. Led astray by Satan —Gen. 3:1-7; II Cor. 11:3; I Tim. 2:14. Curse pronounced on—Gen. 3: 16.

Had separate dwelling.—Gen. 24:67; 31:33. Esth. 2:9, 11.

Had a court in the tabernacle assigned to them.—Ex. 38:8; I Sam. 2:22.

Dress.—II Sam. 13:18; Is. 3:16-23; I Tim. 2:9; I Pet. 3:3-5. May not wear man's clothing—Deut. 22:5. Wore a veil—Gen. 24:65; 38:14; I Cor. 11:5-7, 13. Often went unveiled—Gen. 12: 14; 24:16, 21. Wore long hair—I Cor. 11:5, 6, 14, 15. Wore hair plaited and adorned with gold and pearls—Is. 3: 24; I Tim. 2:9; I Pet. 3:3. Had head covered—I Cor. 11:5-7, 13. Wore Ornaments—Is. 3:16-23; I Tim. 2:9. Earrings—Gen. 24:47; 35:4; Ez. 16: 12. Nose jewels—Is. 3:21. Bracelets —Gen. 24:47; Ex. 35:22; Is. 3:9; Ez. 6:11. Armlets—Is. 3:18. Signet rings —Ex. 35:22. Anklets—Is. 3:18. Amulets—Is. 3:20.

Abiding as virgins.—I Cor. 7:25–38. Spared in war—Num. 31:18, 35; Deut. 21:14. Wives for the tribe of Benjamin—Ju. 21:12–14. Apparel of king's daughters—II Sam. 13:18. Nurtured for kings' wives—Esth. 2:8–13. No marriage without father's consent—Gen. 34:6–8; Ex. 22:17. Non-marriage a calamity—Ju. 11:37; Ps. 78:63. Punishment for corrupting betrothed—Deut. 22:23, 24. When not betrothed—Ex. 22:16, 17; Deut. 22:28, 29. Kingdom of heaven likened to—Mt. 25:1–12. Typify saints in heaven—Rev. 14:4.

Duties of women.—Subject to husband—Gen. 3:16; I Cor. 7:39; 11:8, 9; Eph. 5:22–24; Col. 3:18; Tit. 1:5; I Pet. 3:1–6. Helper of husband—Pr. 31:11–29. Housekeeping—Gen. 18:6; Pr. 31:15–21, 27. Spinning—Ex. 35:25, 26; Pr. 31:19. Tending flocks and herds—Gen. 29:9; Ex. 2:16. Gleaning—Ruth 2:7, 8, 15–23. Drawing and carrying water—Gen. 24:11–16; I Sam. 9:11; John 4:7. Work in fields—Is. 27:11; Ez. 26:6, 8. Grinding corn—Mt. 24:41; Lu. 17:35.

Social status of.—Esth. 1:10–22; Dan. 5:1, 2, 10–12; Acts 8:27; 24:24; 25:13, 23. Take part in public affairs—Ex. 15:20, 21; Ju. 4:4–22; 9:50–54; 11:24; I Sam. 18:6, 7; II Sam. 20:14–22; I Ki. 1:15–21; 10:1–13; 21:7–15; II Ki. 11:1–3; II Chr. 9:1–9; 21:6; 22:3; Ps. 68:25; Dan. 5:9–13.

In business.—I Chr. 7:24; Pr. 31:14, 16; Acts 16:14.

Required to attend the reading of the law.—Deut. 31:12; Josh. 8:35.

Celebrants of victories.—Ex. 15:20–21; I Sam. 18:6–7.

Mourners at funerals.—Jer. 9:17, 20.

Property rights.—Num. 27:1–9; Josh. 17:3–6; Ruth 4:3–9; Job 42:15. Wife sold for husband's debts—Mt. 18:25. Aid to widows—Deut. 14:29; II Ki. 4:1–7; Ps. 146:9; Acts 6:1; I Tim. 5:3, 16.

Characteristics. — Fair and graceful — Gen. 12:11; 24:16; Song of Sol. 1:8. Haughty—Is. 3:16. Ambitious—Mt. 20:20, 21. Wise—II Sam. 14:2; Pr. 31:26. Weaker than man—I Pet. 3:7. Timid—Is. 19:16; Jer. 51:30; Nah. 3:

13. Silly and easily led into error—II Tim. 3:6. Loving and affectionate—II Sam. 1:26. Clings to her children—Is. 49:15. Virtuous—Ruth 3:11. Fond of dress and ornaments—Is. 3:17–21; I Tim. 2:9. Mirthful—Ju. 11:34; 21:21; Jer. 31:13. Patriotic—Ex. 15:20–21; Ju. 4:4–22; 5:24–27; 9:53, 54; I Sam. 18:6; II Sam. 20:16–22; Esth.5:1–8; 7:1–4; Prophetic: *Deborah*—Ju. 4:4. *Hannah*—I Sam. 2:1–10. *Huldah*—II Ki. 22:14–20. *Elizabeth*—Lu. 1:41–43. *Philip's daughters*—Acts 21:9.

Woman's vows.—Num. 30:3–16.

Woman, charged with adultery, to be tried.—Num. 5:12–31.

Taken captive.—Num. 31:9, 15, 17, 18, 35; Deut. 28:32, 41; Ju. 5:30; Lam. 1:18; Ez. 30:18.

Treated with cruelty in war.—Is. 13:16; Lam. 5:11. Zech. 14:2.

Purification of.—Lev. Ch. 12; 15:19–33; II Sam. 11:4; Lu. 2:22–24.

Punishment of.—Ex. 22:16, 17; Deut. 22:23–27, 28, 29.

Religious privileges in N. T.—Lu. 2:36–38; Acts 1:14; 12:12–17; 21:9; I Cor. 11:5; 14:34, 35; Gal. 3:28; Phil. 4:3; I Tim. 2:12; 5:2–11; Tit. 2:3–5.

Church workers.—Phil. 4:3. Lydia—Acts 16:14–15. Dorcas—Acts 9:36. Priscilla—Acts 18:26. Phebe—Rom. 16:1, 2. Julia—Rom. 16:5. Mary—Rom. 16:6.

Paul's teaching concerning.—I Cor. 11:5–15; Eph. 5:22–24; Col. 3:18; I Tim. 3:11; 5:2–16; Tit. 2:3–5. Concerning public speaking—I Cor. 11:13; 14:34, 35; Gal. 3:28; I Tim. 2:12, 13. Paul welcomes women as church workers—Acts 16:13–15; 18:2, 3; Rom. 16:1–16.

First at the sepulchre.—Mk. 15: 46, 47; 16:1–6; Lu. 23:55, 56; 24:1–10; John 20:1.

Christ appears to the.—Mt. 28:8, 10; Mk. 16:8, 10; Lu. 24:9, 10, 22; John 20:2, 18. To Mary Magdalene—Mk. 16:9; John 20:14–17.

Precepts concerning: Seduction—Pr. 2:16, 19; 5:3–11; 6:25–29; 7:4–27; 23:27. Housekeeping—Pr. 14:1; 18:22; 31:10–31; Lu. 10:38–42. Keepers at home, sober—Tit. 2:1–5; Virtue—Pr. 12:4;

31:10–31. Contentiousness—Pr. 19:13; 21:9, 19; 25:24; 27:15, 16; I Cor. 14: 34. Prudence—Pr. 19:14. Idlers and tattlers—I Tim. 5:13. Examples to the younger—Tit. 2:3–5. Modesty— I Cor. 11:5, 6; 14:34, 35.

Two remarkable conversions.—Samaritan woman—John 4:7–39. Lydia— Acts 16:13–15.

Noted women—Good: Deborah—Ju. 4: 5–16; 5:1–31; Mother of Samson—Ju. 13:23; Naomi—Ruth 1:1–22; 2:1–3, 18–22; 3:1; 4:14–17. Ruth—Ruth 1: 4–22; Chs. 2–4. Hannah, the mother of Samuel—I Sam. 1:2–28; Abigail— I Sam. 25:14–37. Widow of Zarephath, who fed Elijah—I Ki. 17:8–24. The Shunammite woman—II Ki. 4:8–38. Vashti—Esth. 1:9–22; 2:1–4. Esther— Esth. 2:5–23; 4:4–17; 5:1–14; 7:1–10; 8:1–17. Mary, mother of Jesus—Mt. 1:18–25; 2:11–15; 12:46, 47; Mk. 3: 31; Lu. 1:26–56; 2:4–7, 16–19, 34, 35; 8:19; John 2:3–5; 19:25–27; Acts 1: 14. Mary Magdalene—Mt. 27:56, 61; 28:1–10; Mk. 15:40, 47; 16:1–9; Lu. 8: 2, 3; 23:55, 56; 24:1–7; John 19:25; 20:1, 11–18. Mary, sister of Lazarus —Mt. 26:7–13; Mk. 14:3–9; Lu. 10: 38–42; John 11:1, 2, 5, 29; 12:3. Mary, wife of Clopas—Mt. 27:55; Mk. 15: 47; John 19:25. Mother of John Mark —Acts 12:12. Elizabeth—Lu. 1:6, 41– 45. Anna—Lu. 2:37, 38; Widow with two mites—Mk. 12:41–44; Lu. 21:2–4. Joanna and Susanna—Lu. 8:3. Martha —Lu. 10:38–42; John 11:1–5, 17–40. Pilate's wife—Mt. 27:19. Dorcas— Acts 9:36–39. Lydia—Acts 16:14, 15. Priscilla—Acts 18:26; Rom. 16:3, 4. Phebe—Rom. 16:1, 2. Julia—Rom. 16: 15. Lois and Eunice—II Tim. 1:5.

Wicked women: Eve—Gen. 3:6; I Tim. 2:14. Lot's wife—Gen. 19:26; Lu. 17: 32. The daughters of Lot—Gen. 19: 31–38. Tamar—Gen. 38:14–24. Potiphar's wife—Gen. 39:7–21. Samson's wife—Ju. 14:15–19. Delilah—Ju. 16: 4–22. Michal—II Sam. 6:16–23. Jezebel—I Ki. 18:4; 19:1, 2; 21:1–29; II Ki. 9:30; Rev. 2:20. Athaliah—II Ki. 11:1–16. Herodias and her daughter— Mt. 14:3–11; Mk. 6:17–28; Lu. 3:19, 20. The woman of Samaria—John 4: 7–29. Woman taken in adultery—

John 8:1–11. The woman who was a sinner—Lu. 7:36–49. Sapphira—Acts 5:2–10. See MARRIAGE, WICKED, WIFE, WIDOW, MOTHER, DAUGHTER.

WOMB. Barren—Pr. 30:16; Lu. 23:29; Rom. 4:19. Formed from—Job 31:15; Is. 44:2, 24; 49:5. Fruit of—Gen. 30: 2; Is. 13:18; Hos. 9:16. Jesus concerned in—Lu. 1:31, 41, 42, 44; 2:21, 23. Lame from—Mt. 19:12; Acts 3:2; 14:8. Miscarrying—Hos. 9:14. Nazirite from—Ju. 13:5, 7; 10:17. Open— Gen. 29:31; 30:22; Ex. 13:2; Num. 8: 16; Ez. 20:26; Lu. 2:23. Second time in—John 3:4. Shut—Gen. 20:18; I Sam. 1:5, 6; Is. 66:9. Sons in—Ruth 1:11. Two nations in—Gen. 25:23, 24; 38:27.

WONDER. See SIGNS AND WONDERS.

WONDERFUL. Josh. 13:18. Counsel, In—Is. 28:29. Great and—II Chr. 2: 9. Knowledge—Ps. 139:6. Love—II Sam. 1:26. Name shall be called—Is. 9:6. Plagues—Deut. 28:39. Testimonies—Ps. 119:129. Things too wonderful—Job 42:3; Ps. 131:1; 139:6. Works of God—Ps. 40:5; 78:4; 40:5; 78:4; 107:8, 15, 21, 31; 111:4; 139:14. See SIGNS AND WONDERS.

WONDERFULLY. Destroy—Dan. 8:24. Made—Ps. 139:14.

WOOD: In building Noah's ark.—Gen. 6:14.

For instruments.—II Sam. 6:5; I Chr. 21:23; Is. 60:17; Jer. 28:13. Pulpit— Neh. 8:4.

Weapons.—Num. 35:18; Is. 10:15. Accidental strokes—Deut. 19:5; Eccl. 10:9.

Vessels of.—Ex. 7:19; Lev. 11:32; II Tim. 2:20; Rev. 18:12.

Used in uncleanness.—Lev. 11:32; 14:4, 6, 49–52; 15:12; Num. 19:6; 31:20.

For fuel.—I Sam. 6:14; II Sam. 24:22; I Chr. 21:23; Neh. 10:34; 13:31; Pr. 26:20–21; Is. 30:33; Jer. 5:14; 7:18; Lam. 5:4; Ez. 15:1–7; 24:10; Zech. 12:6.

Used in burnt-offerings.—Gen. 22:3–9; Lev. 1:7–17; 3:5; 4:12; 6:12; I Ki. 18:23, 33, 38; Neh. 10:34; 13:31.

In building tabernacle.—Ex. 26:15, 26, 32; 27:1, 6; 30:1, 5; 35:7, 24, 33; 36: 20, 31, 36.

Furniture of tabernacle.—Ark—Ex. 25: 5, 10, 13, 23, 28; 37:1, 4, 10, 15, 25, 28;

Deut. 10:1, 3. Altar of burnt-offering —Ex. 27:1, 6; 30:1, 5; 38:1, 6; Ju. 6: 26. Elijah's altar—I Ki. 18:23, 33, 38.

In building temple.—I Ki. 5:6, 8, 10, 18; 6:9, 15–20, 23, 31, 33, 36; I Chr. 22:4; 29:2. Ezekiel's temple—Ez. 41:16–22. Latter temple—Hag. 1:8. The church —I Cor. 3:12.

Used for idols.—Deut. 4:28; 28:36, 64; 29:17; II Ki. 19:18; Is. 37:19; 45:20; Ez. 20:32; Dan. 5:4, 23; Hab. 2:19; Rev. 9:20. Destruction of—Ju. 6:26; II Ki. 19:18; Is. 37:19; 45:20.

Pulpit of.—Neh. 8:4.

Wood-offering.—Neh. 10:34; 13:31.

Woods of Canaan.—Num. 13:20; Josh. 17:15, 18.

Woods or forest.—I Sam. 14:25–26; 23: 15–19; II Sam. 18:6, 8, 17; II Ki. 2: 24; 6:4; I Chr. 16:33; II Chr. 2:16; Ps. 80:13; 83:14; 96:12; 132:6; Eccl. 2:6; 10:9; Song of Sol. 2:3; 3:9; Is. 7:2; Ez. 34:25; 39:10; Mic. 7:14. David hides in—I Sam. 23:15–19.

Workmen in wood.—Deut. 19:5; 29:11; Josh. 9:21–23, 27; Jer. 46:22–23.

WOOL. See SHEEP.

WORDS. Words are the incarnation of: (1) Thought, (2) Purpose, and (3) Feeling, thus revealing the person.

Good words are: Upright and forcible— Job 6:25; 33:3. A sure guide—Pr. 22:21. End of debate—Job 29:22. Unanswerable—Job 32:12; Is. 41:28. Unspeakable—I Cor. 12:4. True wisdom and knowledge—Pr. 1:2, 3, 21; 2:1, 2; 17:27; I Cor. 1:17, 18; II Thess. 2:15. Strength to the weary—Job 4:4; Is. 50:4. Heavy on the wrong-doer— Amos 7:10. Not discerned by a fool —Pr. 23:9; Acts 26:24, 25. Good reasoning—Acts 2:14, 22, 40; 15:32; Heb. 13:22. Show life—Acts 5:20. Save— Acts 10:22; 11:14. Ideas not mere sound—I Cor. 14:19. Hunted out and set in order—Job 18:2; 33:5. Able to bring results—Rom. 15:18; Col. 3: 17. Messages: Rebekah to Laban— Gen. 24:28, 30. Jacob sending Joseph to his brothers—Gen. 37:14. Joseph sending for Jacob—Gen. 45:27. David to Nabal—I Sam. 25:9. Shaphan to Josiah—II Ki. 22:9. Esther to Mordecai—Esth. 4:12. Mordecai to Jews— Esth. 9:26.

Reports.—Spies' minority report—Num. 13:30; Josh. 14:7. Balaam to envoys —Num. 22:7. From Reuben and Gad —Josh. 22:32. To Queen of Sheba—I Ki. 10:7; II Chr. 9:5, 6. Ahab to Benhadad—I Ki. 20:9.

Business proposition.—Elders of Gilead to Jephthah—Ju. 11:10. David to the army—I Sam. 17:31. Memucan to Ahasuerus—Esth. 1:21.

The emotions.—Words reveal the heart —Job 8:10; 33:3.

Miscellaneous: Good words.—The ancients knew them—Gen. 49:21; I Ki. 12:7; Pr. 12:25; 15:23. Strong feeling compels speech—Job 32:18. Are righteous—Pr. 8:8. Pleasant, pure in peace and truth—Deut. 2:26; Josh. 22: 30; II Sam. 20:17; Esth. 9:30; Pr. 15:26. Sweet, like honeycomb, Healthgiving—Ps. 141:6; Pr. 16:24. Soft— Pr. 15:1. Express sorrow and reproach —Ju. 2:4; I Sam. 24:16; II Ki. 6:30; 22:11; Dan. 6:14. Triumph and joy— Deut. 32:1; I Ki. 5:7. Give comfort —II Sam. 14:17; I Thess. 4:18. Often a prayer—Num. 14:20; I Ki. 8:59; II Ki. 6:18; Ps. 5:1, 2; 54:2; 141:1. Or a petition—Gen. 44:18; Ju. 16:16; I Sam. 25:24; II Sam. 14:12. A vow —Ju. 11:11.

Bad words.—Wearied the Lord—Mal. 2:17. Without knowledge—Job 34:35; 38:2; Pr. 19:27. Counsel—Pr. 5:7. Are weak and vain—Job 8:2; 11:2; 16:3; Mt. 12:36; Lu. 24:11; Acts 18:14, 15; I Cor. 4:20; II Cor. 10:11; Eph. 5:6; I Thess. 1:5; I Tim. 6:4; Jas. 1:22, 23; I John 3:18. Held to account for idle words—Mt. 12:36 f. Ensnare the surety—Pr. 6:2. Of wisdom—I Cor. 2:4. Lost a kingdom—I Ki. 12:7; II Chr. 10:7. Lost an army—II Ki. 18:20. Conflict with facts—Gen. 34:18; I Sam. 24:9. Even of a king are abominable—I Chr. 21:6. Break a man to pieces—Job 19:2. Turn men away from God—Jer. 44:15–30. Poor reasoning—Ex. 14:12.

Messages.—Servants to David—I Sam. 18:23, 26. Elijah to Ahaziah—II Ki. 1:7. Tidings from Jerusalem—Neh. 1: 4.

Reports.—Spies' majority report—Num. 13:26, 32; Deut. 1:22, 25. People to

Samuel—I Sam. 8:21. Joab's word to Solomon—I Ki. 2:30. Sons to a prophet—I Ki. 18:37. Sanballat to Nehemiah—Neh. 6:6, 7, 19. Officers to Hezekiah—II Ki. 18:37. Mordecai to Esther—Esth. 4:9, 12.

Business proposition.—Balak to Balaam—Num. 22:7. Abimelech to men of Shechem—Ju. 9:3. A challenge: Goliath—I Sam. 17:23. Rabshakeh—II Ki. 19:4, 16. A petition dictated by Joab—II Sam. 14:3, 19.

Words of the will.—Good-will shown by good words. Acceptable to God—Ps. 19:14. Obeyed—Pr. 7:24. Correspond with fact and deed—Gen. 30:34; 43:7; Josh. 2:21; Ex. 8:10, 13, 31. Instances: Joseph made ruler—Gen. 41:40. Joseph—Gen. 44:2, 24. Of Moses—Ex. 12:35; 32:28; Lev. 10:7. Last of David's—I Chr. 23:27. Haman's sentence—Esth. 7:8. Of command—Lu. 5:5. Slay the wrong-doer—Hos. 6:5; II Thess. 2:8. Caused the death of the innocent—I Ki. 21:4. Restrained from evil—I Sam. 24:7. Declare law—Heb. 2:2. Elijah's—I Ki. 17:1. An oath to Ezra's—Ezra 10:5.

An evil purpose shown in will by bad words.—Against God—Job 15:13; 34:37; Dan. 7:25. Against man—Job 16:4; 32:14. Deceive and destroy—Gen. 39:17, 19, 20; Is. 32:7; II Pet. 2:3. Lying words not to be regarded—Ex. 5:9.

Miscellaneous.—Bad words: Anxious, Sisera's mother—Ju. 5:28. Envious, Laban's sons—Gen. 31:1. Saul and army—I Sam. 17:11. Saul—I Sam. 28:20. Ishbosheth—II Sam. 3:11. Fierce, Judah—II Sam. 19:43. Rash by affliction—Job 6:3. Troublesome—Acts 15:24; II Thess. 2:2; Jas. 3:2. Lying words called good, flatter, lure to destruction—I Ki. 22:13; Pr. 2:16; 7:5; Jer. 12:6; Dan. 2:9; I Thess. 2:5; II Tim. 2:17, 18. Words express blasphemy—Acts 6:11, 12. Mentioned: Words are verified and tried—Gen. 42:16, 20; Job 12:11.

A word sometimes means many words.—Ex. 14:2; Acts 28:25. The word of an angel is not to be doubted—Lu. 1:20. Your words will justify or condemn—Mt. 12:37. Words are received

or rejected—Acts 2:41; 4:4; 13:42, 45, 46; I Tim. 4:15; Jas. 1:21; cf. Lu. 8:15 John 8:47; 18:37.

Words became a pattern.—I Tim. 4:12. "Not a" under fear and cowardice—I Ki. 18:21. Answered not a—II Sam. 19:10; II Ki. 18:36; Mt. 15:23. Tact enjoined silence—Josh. 6:10; Job 2:13.

A king's word is mighty.—Moses—Deut. 33:5; Acts 7:22. David—II Sam. 24:4; I Chr. 21:4. Hezekiah—II Chr. 32:8. Artaxerxes—Neh. 2:18. King of the little horn—Dan. 7:8. To change a king's word means death—Ezra 6:11.

WORD OF GOD. Any expression of God's mind or will.

Names of.—Oracles of God—Rom. 3:2. Word of faith—Rom. 10:8. Word of the gospel—Acts 15:7. Word of Reconciliation—II Cor. 5:19. Word of truth—Eph. 1:13. See TRUTH.

Word of Life.—Phil. 2:16. Word of Christ—Mk. 10:24; Lu. 24:8, 44; Rom. 10:17; Col. 3:16; I Thess. 4:15. In prayer—Mk. 14:39. In temple—John 8:20. Sword of Spirit—Eph. 6:17. Word of promise—Rom. 9:6-9; I Tim. 4:5. Hearing of word—Lu. 11:28; Jas. 1:22. The word—Acts 10:36. Hence "Word" is a name of Christ—John 1:1; I John 1:1; Rev. 19:13. Jesus, the full self-expression of the God-head, is the Living Word—John 1:1-5, 14.

Character of.—Everlasting—Ps. 119:89, Is. 40:8; Mt. 24:35; Mk. 13:31; Lu. 21:33; I Pet. 1:23, 25. Not bound—II Tim. 2:9. Good—Is. 39:8. Pure—Pr. 30:5. John 15:3. Worlds framed—Heb. 11:3; II Pet. 3:5. Powerful—Jer. 23:29; Lu. 4:32; Acts 20:32; Heb. 4:12; Jas. 1:21. Source of strength—I John 2:14. Commanding—II Chr. 30:12; 35:6; Neh. 1:8. Wise—II Tim. 3:15.

Supreme authority of.—Deut. 4:1-10; 12:32; Josh. 1:8; Ps. 33:6; Pr. 30:5, 6; Mk. 4:24; Lu. 8:12; John 12:48-50; Heb. 1:1-3; 2:1-4; Rev. 1:1-3; 20:12; 22:18, 19.

Direct words of.—Alpha and Omega—Is. 44:6; 48:12; Rev. 1:8; 21:6. Word of—II Chr. 11:4; Jer. 30:4. To angel

—I Ki. 13:18. Man of Judah—I Ki. 13:1.

Functions of word of God.—Give life—John 6:63; I Pet. 1:23. Sanctifies—John 17:17. Gives hope—Ps. 119:74, 81, 114, 116; 130:5. Comforts—Ps. 119:82, 105.

Word of Jehovah is tried.—II Sam. 22: 31; Ps. 18:30; Pr. 30:5. Despised—Num. 15:31; Is. 5:24. Rejected—Ex. 9:21; I Sam. 15:26; II Chr. 34:21; Ps. 119:158; Jer. 8:9. Feared—Ex. 9:20; Ps. 119:161; Is. 66:5. Loved—Num. 22:18; I Sam. 3:1; Job 23:12; Ps. 119: 140. Received—Acts 2:41; 11:1; I Thess. 3:13. Obeyed—Ps. 119:67, 134; Acts 20:35; II Cor. 4:2; Tit. 2:5. Praised—Ps. 56:4, 10; 119:162. To be studied—Ps. 119:148; II Tim. 2:15.

Word revealed.—To Abraham—Gen. 15: 1, 4; Jacob—I Ki. 18:31; Ps. 147:19; Is. 9:8. Joseph—Ps. 105:19. To judges—*Joshua*—Josh. 3:9; *Samuel*—I Sam. 8:10; 9:27; 15:1, 10. To kings—*David*—I Chr. 22:8; II Chr. 6:17; *Solomon*—I Ki. 6:11; *Jehu*—I Ki. 16:1, 7, 12; II Ki. 15:12; *Jehoiakim*—Jer. 26: 1. To the people of Israel through the prophets—Is. 1:10; 28:14; 39:5; 66:5; Jer. 2:4, 31; 7:2; 9:20; 10:1; 17:20; 19:3; 21:11; 22:29; 29:20, 30; 31:10; 34:4. To prophets—I Ki. 13:20, 26, 32; Ezra 9:4; Zech. 7:7, 12. *Amos*—Amos 3:1; 7:16; 8:11. *Elijah*—I Ki. 17:2, 8; 18:1; 19:9; 21:17, 28. *Elisha*—II Ki. 3:12; 7:1. *Ezekiel*—Ez. 1:3; 3:16; 7:1; 11:14; 12:1, 8, 17, 26; 13:1, 2; 14:2, 12; 15:1; 16:1, 35; 17:1, 11; 18: 1; 20:2, 45, 47; 21:1, 8, 18; 22:1, 17, 23; 23:1; 24:1, 15, 20; 25:1, 3; 26:1; 27:1; 28:1, 11, 20; 29:1, 17; 30:1, 20; 31:1; 32:1, 17; 33:1, 23; 34:1, 7, 9; 35:1; 36:1, 4, 16; 37:4, 15; 38:1. *Gad*—II Sam. 24:11. *Haggai*—Hag. 1:1, 3; 2:1, 5, 10, 20. *Hosea*—Hos. 1:1, 2; 4:1. *Isaiah*—II Ki. 20:4, 16, 19; Is. 16:13; 24:3; 37:22; 38:4. *Jeremiah*—Jer. 1:2, 4, 11, 13; 2:1; 13:1, 3, 8; 14:1; 16:1; 18:1; 24:4; 25:3; 27:1; 28:12; 32:6, 26; 33:1, 19, 23; 34:12; 35:12; 36:4, 6, 8, 27; 37:6, 17; 38:21; 39:15; 42:7, 15; 43:8; 44:24, 26; 46:1, 13; 47:1; 49:34; 50:1; Dan. 9:2. *Joel*—Joel 1:1. *Jonah*—Jonah 1:1; 3:1, 3. *Malachi*—Mal. 1:1. *Micah*—Mic. 1:1; 4:2. *Mi-*

caiah—I Ki. 22:19, 22; II Chr. 18:18. *Moses*—Ex. 4:28, 30; 10:1; 19:7; 24:3, 4; 35:1; Num. 11:24; 36:5; Deut. 5:5; 34:5; Neh. 1:8. *Nathan*—I Chr. 17:3. *Shemaiah*—I Ki. 12:22, 24. *Zechariah*—Zech. 1:1, 7; 4:6; 6:9; 7:1, 4, 8; 8:1, 18; 9:1; 11:11; 12:1. To priests—*Zacharias*—Lu. 1:20. To apostles—*John*—Lu. 3:2. See HOLY SPIRIT, VISION.

Fulfilment of.—I Ki. 2:27; 13:2, 5, 9, 17; 14:18; 16:12, 34; 17:5, 16; 22:38; II Ki. 1:17; 4:44; 7:16; 9:25, 26, 36; 10: 10; 14:25; 15:12; 23:16; 24:2; I Chr. 10:13; 11:3, 10; 12:23; 15:15; II Chr. 36:21, 22; Ezra 1:1; Ps. 103:20; 119: 65, 76, 107, 154, 169, 170; 148:8; Jer. 13:2; 32:8; Lam. 2:17; Mt. 26:75; Mk. 14:72; Lu. 22:6; Col. 1:25; I John 2: 22; Rev. 17:17. Commands—Num. 3: 16, 51.

Spreading of.—Ps. 147:15, 18. Of gospel—Acts 6:7; 11:19; 12:24; 13:5, 7, 44, 46, 48, 49; 14:3, 25; 15:7, 35, 36; 16:6, 32; 17:11, 13; 18:11; 19:10, 20; 20:32; 22:22; Rom. 9:6; 10:17; I Cor. 14:36; I Thess. 1:8.

Ministry of the word of God.—Acts 4: 29, 31; 8:4, 25; II Cor. 2:17; I Thess. 4:15; II Thess. 3:1; Heb. 13:7. Eternal life—Mt. 4:4.

Martyrs for.—Rev. 6:9; 20:4.

Word of God sought for.—I Ki. 22:5; II Chr. 18:4; Jer. 17:15.

Followers of.—Num. 24:4, 16; I Chr. 25:5; II Chr. 29:15; Acts 4:4; 6:2; 8:14; I John 2:14.

Judgments for all despising the word of God.—Lev. 26:14-40; Deut. 28:15-68; II Ki. 22:13; II Chr. 36:15, 16; Pr. 1:24-32; Is. 55:11, 12; 56:4; Rom. 3: 11, 12, 16; II Thess. 1:7-9.

Prophecies concerning.—Is. 2:3; 28:13; 40:8; Jer. 6:10; Amos 8:11, 12; Mic. 4:2; Zech. 4:6, 8.

WORK. Neh. 13:30; John 10:25; Rom. 9:1; Eph. 2:9; Jas. 2:22. Abide—I Cor. 3:14. Accomplished—John 17:4. After their—Mt. 23:3. Beaten—Num. 10:2. Broidered—Ps. 45:14. Commit thy—Pr. 16:3. Darkness, Of—Rom. 13:12; Eph. 5:11. Destroy—Eccl. 5:6. Devil, Of—I John 3:8. Diversities of—I Cor. 12:6. Do no manner of—Num. 29:7. See FEASTS, SABBATH.

Done in faithfulness—Ps. 33:4. See FAITHFULNESS. Earth, Of—II Pet. 3: 10. Establish thou the—Ps. 90:17. See ESTABLISH. Evangelist, Of—II Tim. 4:5. See MINISTER. Evil—See EVIL. Faith apart from—Rom. 3:28; Jas. 2: 26. See OBEDIENCE. Fathers, Of—Lu. 11:48. Fingers, Of—See FINGER. Follow—Rev. 14:13. Fruit from—Phil. 1:22. Go forth to—Job 24:5. God, Of —See WORKS OF GOD. Good—Eph. 2: 10; II Thess. 2:17; Tit. 1:16. Greater —John 14:12. See CONVERSION, SALVATION. Grievous—Eccl. 2:17. Hands, Of—II Ki. 19:18; Job 1:10; Ps. 9:16; 90:17; Is. 2:8; Hag. 2:17. See HAND. House, Of—Ezra 6:7. Jesus, Of—Acts 13:41; John 14:12. See MIRACLES. Know—Is. 66:18; Rev. 2:2. Law, Of— See CIRCUMCISION. Manner of, By what—Rom. 3:27. Measure—Is. 65:7. Men, Of—Acts 5:38; Gal. 6:4. Mighty in—Jer. 32:19; Mk. 6:5; II Cor. 12:12. Ministering, Of—Eph. 4:12. See MINISTER. Miracles, Of—I Cor. 12:10. See MIRACLES. One—John 7:21. Paul, Of— I Cor. 9:1. See LABOR. Perfect—Jas. 1:4. Perfected—Rev. 3:2. Praise, Let her—Pr. 31:31. Prove man's—I Cor. 3:13. Pure, Whether his—Pr. 20:11. Repented not of—Rev. 16:11. Sake —I Thess. 5:13. Skillful—Eccl. 4:4. Spark, As a—Is. 1:31. Strange—Is. 28:21. Trusted in thy—Jer. 48:7. Ungodliness, Of—Jude 1. Wrought—Is. 26:12.

WORK, *v.* Is. 43:13; 64:4; Hab. 1:5; Hag. 2:4; John 6:30; Phil. 2:13. Arrogance of pride, In—Pr. 21:24. Death, in us—II Cor. 4:12. Deceit— Ps. 101:7. Doer that—Jas. 1:25. Evil —Mic. 2:1. See EVIL. God—See WORKS OF GOD. Good—Gal. 6:10. Hands, With —I Thess. 4:11. See HAND. Hire, For —Is. 19:10. If any will not—II Thess. 3:10. Jesus—John 9:4. See MIRACLES. Knowledge, With—Pr. 13:16. Night and day—I Thess. 2:9; II Thess. 3:8. Night cometh, When no man can— John 9:4. Not at all—II Thess. 3:11. Not for the food which perisheth— John 6:27. Power that—Eph. 3:20. Righteousness — Acts 10:35. See RIGHTEOUSNESS. Salvation, Out your own—Phil. 2:12. See SALVATION. Spir-

it that now—Eph. 2:2. Stedfastness —Rom. 5:3. See STEDFASTNESS. Thanksgiving—II Cor. 9:11. Together for good — Rom. 8:28. See FRATERNITY. Vineyard, In—Mt. 21:28. Wickedness —Ps. 58:2. Mal. 4:1. See WICKEDNESS. Wrath—Rom. 4:15. See JUDGMENT, LABOR.

WORKER. Deceitful — II Cor. 11:13. Evil, Of—Phil. 3:2. Home, At—Tit. 2:5. Iniquity, Of—Job 31:3; 34:8, 22; Ps. 5:5; 6:8; 14:4; 28:3; 36:12; 37:1; 53:4; 59:2; 64:2; 92:7, 9; 94:4, 16; 101:8; 125:5; 141:9; Pr. 10:29; 21:15; Lu. 13:27. Miracles, Of—I Cor. 6:1. Stone, Of—I Chr. 22:15. Timber, Of —I Chr. 22:15. See LABORER, WORKMAN.

WORKMAN. II Chr. 24:13; 34:10; Is. 44:11; Hos. 8:6; Acts 19:25. Abundance, In—I Chr. 22:15. Cunning— Ex. 35:35; 38:23; Song of Sol. 7:1; Is. 40:20. Hands of the—Jer. 10:3; II Chr. 34:17. House of God, In—Ezra 3:9. Make images—Is. 40:19. Overseer of—II Chr. 34:10. That needeth not to be ashamed—II Tim. 2:15. See LABORER.

WORKMANSHIP. Ez. 28:13. According to—II Ki. 16:10. All manner of —Ex. 31:3, 5; 35:31. We are his— Eph. 2:10.

WORLD. Belongs to God—Ps. 50:12. Christ prayed not for—John 17:9. Created by God—Job 34:13. Curses upon—Mt. 18:7. Established—Ps. 93: 1; Jer. 10:12. Evil—Gal. 1:4. Field is the—Mt. 13:38. See SALVATION FOR ALL MEN. Gain the whole world—Mt. 16:26. Hateth you—John 7:7; 15:18. Judgment of — Ps. 9:8; John 12:31. Rom. 3:19. Kingdoms of the—Mt. 4:8. Knew not Jesus—John 1:10, 29; 14:17. Light of—Mt. 5:14; John 8:12. Love of—II Tim. 4:10; I John 2:15. Love of God for—John 3:16. Prince of— John 14:30. Reconciliation of — II Cor. 5:19. Rich in this—I Tim. 6:17. Rudiments of—Col. 2:8. Saviour of —John 4:42; 6:33. Sin of—John 1:29; II Pet. 2:20. Sorrow of—II Cor. 7:10. Turned upside down — Acts 17:6. Without God in—Eph. 2:12. World to come—Lu. 20:35. See LIFE, ETERNAL.

Christians not fashioned like.—John 15:
19; 16:33; 17:15, 16; Rom. 12:2; Gal.
6:14; Jas. 1:17; 2:5; 4:4; I John 2:14.

Enquiry concerning when. — Mt. 24:3;
II Pet. 3:1–13.

Extent of starry message (*spatial*).—Ps.
19:4.

Extent of message of salvation (*spatial*).
—Is. 62:11; Rom. 10:18.

Compass of remembrance.—Ps. 22:27.

The final trial.—Rev. 3:10.

World and its lust pass.—I John 2:17.

Harvest of humanity.—Mt. 13:39, 40,
49.

Continual fellowship of Christ.—Mt. 28:
20.

End of.—Gr. *Kosmos*, "Orderly arrangement," by implication, "The World."

Time of end not known.—Mt. 24:36;
Mk. 13:22; II Pet. 3:1–13; Rev. 6:
16 f.; 10:7; 14:18 f.; 20:11–15. See
TEACHINGS OF JESUS on "Judgment"—
Lu. 2:21; "Judgment"—II Pet. 2:4.

WORLD-RULERS. Eph. 6:12.

WORMS: Used as punishment.—Job
24:20.

Where the worm dieth not.—Is. 66:24;
Mk. 9:48.

Eaten of worms.—Is. 51:8; Acts 12:23.

A destruction to food. — Manna — Ex.
16:20, 24. To gourd—Jonah 4:7. To
vineyard—Deut. 28:39.

Figurative use of worms.—Babylon covered with worms—Is. 14:11. Manna
worm—Job 7:5; 17:4; 21:26; 25:6; Ps.
22:6; Is. 41:14.

WORSE. I Cor. 8:8. Deal—Gen. 19:9.
Fathers, Than—Jer. 7:26. First, Than
the—Mt. 12:45; II Pet. 2:20. Grew—
Mk. 5:26. Last error will be—Mt. 27:
64. Nations—Ez. 7:24. Not for the
better but—I Cor. 11:17. Other, Than
—II Sam. 13:16. Put to the—II Sam.
10:15. Thing befall thee—John 5:14.
Thorn hedge, Than—Mic. 7:4. Unbeliever, Than an—I Tim. 5:8. Wax—
II Tim. 3:13. Wine—John 2:10.

WORSHIP: Of Jehovah.—Ex. 20:3; I
Chr. 29:30; II Chr. 7:3; Neh. 8:6; 9:3;
Job 1:20; Is. 27:13; John 12:20; Acts
24:11; I Cor. 14:25; Heb. 1:6; Rev.
Ch. 4.

Of Jesus.—Mt. 2:2, 8, 11; 8:2; 9:18;
14:33; 15:25; 28:9, 17; Mk. 5:6; Lu.
24:52; John 9:38; Rev. 7:9, 10.

With an offering.—Gen. 22:5; Ex. 24:1,
5; Deut. 26:10. Before one altar—II
Chr. 32:12; Ps. 95:6; 99:5; 132:7; Jer.
7:2; 26:2.

Toward the temple.—Ps. 5:7; 138:2; Ez.
46:2, 3.

In the beauty of holiness.—I Chr. 16:
29; Ps. 27:4; 29:2; 96:9.

With song and music.—Ps. 66:4; 100:1–
4; II Chr. 5:12–14; 29:27–30; Ezra 3:
10, 11; Is. 30:29; Rev. 5:8–14; 15:2–4.

In spirit.—John 4:23, 24; Phil. 3:3.

Universal.—Ps. 22:27–29; 86:9; Is. 49:
7; 66:23; John 4:20–24; Phil. 2:10, 11.
From the gods—Ps. 97:7.

Works of men's hands.—Ps. 115:4–8;
Is. 2:8, 20; 44:15; 46:6; Jer. 44:15–
19; Mic. 5:13; Acts 19:24–27; Rev.
9:20.

Vain.—Mt. 15:9; Mk. 7:7; Col. 2:18.

Ignorant.—John 4:22; Acts 17:23–25.

Of calves and images.—Ex. 32:8; I Ki.
12:28, 29; Dan. 3:5, 10, 15, 18; Acts
7:41.

Host of heaven.—II Ki. 21:3; II Chr.
33:3; Ez. 8:16; Zeph. 1:4, 5; Acts
7:42.

Of men.—Acts 10:25; 14:12–18.

Of the beast.—Rev. 13:1–8; 16:2; 19:20;
20:4.

Other gods.—Deut. 17:3; 29:26; I Ki.
9:9; 11:33; II Ki. 19:37; 21:21; II
Chr. 7:22; Jer. 1:16; 8:2; 16:11; 22:9.
Goddesses: Diana—Acts 19:24–28. Diana of the Ephesians—not the Greek
Diana. Both are named Artemis, but
the other was the maiden-goddess—a
huntress—the moon goddess, sister of
Apollo, the sun-god. She represented
perpetual virginity, while Diana of
the Ephesians was a Great Asiatic
nursing-mother, the patroness of the
sexual instinct, and the mother and
nurse of gods, men, animals, and plants.
Unchaste in character, the worship of
her was shameful. Such worship forbidden—Ex. 20:3–6; 34:12–15; Deut.
4:19; 8:19; 11:16; 30:17, 18; Ps. 81:
9; Jer. 13:10; 25:6; Mt. 4:10; Lu. 4:8.
Fate of false worshippers—I Ki. 11:
30–33; II Ki. 10:18, 28; Zeph. 1:4–6.
See PRAISE, PSALMS.

WORTHY, WORTHILY. Gen. 32:10;
Mt. 8:8; 22:8; Rev. 3:4. All accepta-
tion, Of—I Tim. 1:15. Attain the

world, To—Lu. 20:35. Beaten, To be —Deut. 25:2. Book, To open—Rev. 5: 3. Calling, Of—Eph. 4:1. Compared, To be—Rom. 8:18. Death, Of — Mt. 26:66; Mk. 14:64. Die, To—I Sam. 26:16. Done—Pr. 31:29. God, Of— III John 6. Gospel, Of—Phil. 1:27. Hire, Of—Lu. 10:7. Jesus, Of—Mt. 10:37. Journey—III John 6. Laborer, Of food—Mt. 10:10. Lord, Of—Col. 1:10. Man—I Ki. 1:42. Praised, To be —II Sam. 22:4. Repentance, Of—Mt. 3:8; Lu. 3:8; Acts 26:20. Saints, Of— Rom. 16:2. Shoes, To bear—Mt. 3:11. Shoes, To unloose—Mk. 1:7; Lu. 3:16. Son, To be called—Lu. 15:19. Stripes, Of—Lu. 12:48. Walk—Eph. 4:1; Col. 1:10. Woman—Ruth 3:11; Pr. 12:4; 31:10.

Worthless. Man—Pr. 16:27. Men—II Chr. 13:7. Person—Pr. 6:12. Shepherd—Zech. 11:17. Witness—Pr. 19: 28.

WOUNDS. Complaint of—Job 9:17.

In battle.—I Ki. 22:35.

Healed.—II Ki. 8:29; 9:15; II Chr. 22: 6; Ps. 147:3; Is. 30:26; Jer. 30:17.

Incurable—Job 34:6; Jer. 15:18; 30:12; Mic. 1:9.

In Parable of Good Samaritan.—Lu. 10: 34. **In Parable of Husbandmen.**— Mk. 12:4; Lu. 20:12.

As punishment.—Job 5:18; Pr. 6:33; Hos. 5:13; Nah. 3:19; Ps. 38:5; Pr. 23: 29; Hab. 3:13.

Of enemy.—Jer. 30:14.

Of a friend.—Pr. 27:6.

Wound, v. Deut. 32:39; Pr. 20:30.

Wounded.—Of Philistines—I Sam. 17: 52. Of prophet—I Ki. 20:37. Of heart —Ps. 109:22. In war—Ju. 9:40; I Ki. 22:34; II Ki. 8:28; II Chr. 18:33; 35: 23; Song of Sol. 5:7. Soul, of—Job 24:12.

Wounding of conscience.—I Cor. 8:12.

Laws concerning.—Deut. 23:1.

Punishment.—Ps. 64:7; 69:26; Jer. 30: 14; Lam. 2:12; Ez. 26:15.

Prophecies concerning.—Is. 1:6; 53:5; Jer. 6:7; 30:17; 37:10; 51:52; Ez. 28: 23; 30:24; Zech. 13:6.

WRANGLING. I Tim. 6:5.

WRAP. Ps. 119:61; Hos. 4:19. About my head—Jonah 2:5. Closely—Is. 22: 17. Cloth, In—1 Sam. 21:9. Face in

his mantle—I Ki. 19:13. Linen cloth, In—Mt. 27:59. Mantle together—II Ki. 2:8. Roots are—Job 8:17. Swaddling clothes—Lu. 2:7, 12. See BOUND.

WRATH. See ANGER.

WREATHEN. Chains—Ex. 28:14, 24, 25; 39:17, 18. Work—Ex. 28:22; 39: 15.

WREATHS. I Ki. 7:29.

WREST. Justice—Ex. 23:2; Deut. 24: 17. Unstedfast—11 Pet. 3:16. Words —Ps. 56:5.

WRESTLING. Eph. 6:12. Mighty— Gen. 30:8.

WRITING: As an art—Materials used in. Writing tablets—Is. 8:1; Hab. 2: 2; Lu. 1:63. Pens and Ink—Ps. 45: 1; Jer. 8:8; 36:18; II John 12; III John 13. Iron pen—Jer. 17:1. Paper —II John 12. Inkhorn—Ez. 9:2, 3.

Manner of. Written in scrolls or rolls —Jer. 36:23, 28; Rev. 6:14.

Written like engravings.—Ex. 39:30. In different languages.—*In Syriac*—Ez. 4:7. *Chaldean tongue*—Dan. 1:4. *Hebrew (Aramaic)*—Lu. 23:38; John 19: 13, 17, 20.

Unknown tongues.—Greek—Lu. 23:38; John 19:20; Rev. 9:11. Latin—Lu. 23: 38; John 19:20. Superscription in Latin, Greek, and Hebrew (Aramaic) —John 19:19-21. Writing by dictation—Jer. 36:17; Rom. 16:22.

Writers.—God—Ex. 24:12; 32:16; I Chr. 28:19. Finger of God—Ex. 31:18; Deut. 9:10. Writing on the wall as a warning—Dan. 5:7-25.

Written laws.—I Ki. 2:3; I Chr. 16:40; II Chr. 23:18; 31:3; Ezra 3:2, 4; Neh. 8:14, 15; 10:34, 36; John 1:45.

Writings.—Tablets of stone, Commandments written on—Ex. 32:15; 34:1, 27; Deut. 10:4; 27:3, 8. On door-posts— Deut. 6:9; 11:20. Bill of divorcement—Deut. 24:1; Mt. 5:31; Mk. 10:4. Written covenant—Neh. 9:38. Written bonds—Lu. 16:6, 7. Judgment written—Ps. 149:9. Name written— I Chr. 4:41. On rods—Num. 17:2, 3. On sticks—Ez. 37:16-21.

Act of writing.—Name of day—Ez. 24: 2. Jesus wrote on the ground—John 8:6, 8. Of history—II Chr. 26:22. In commentary—II Chr. 13:22. In place of speech—Of Zacharias—Lu. 1:63.

Writings of importance.—Of Moses—John 5:46, 47. Song written for children of Israel—Deut. 31:19. Written plans for house—Ez. 43:11. Of excellent things—Pr. 22:20; Eccl. 12:10. Perverse writings—Job 13:26; Is. 10:1. Tenderness in—II Cor. 2:3. Writing of a child—Is. 10:19.

Of prophecy.—Jer. 22:30.

Concerning visions.—Rev. 1:19; 3:12; 10:4; 14:13; 21:5.

Figurative.—Pr. 3:3; 7:3; Jer. 31:33; Heb. 8:10; 10:16. See WORD OF GOD, SCRIPTURES, BOOKS, LETTERS, PAUL'S EPISTLES.

WRONG. Col. 3:25. Brother—I Thess. 4:6. Cry out of—Job 19:7. Do no—Jer. 22:3; Mt. 20:13; Gal. 4:12. Done unto me—II Sam. 16:12. Forgive me this—II Cor. 12:13. Great—II Sam. 13:16. Jehovah, thou hast seen—Lam. 3:59. Neighbor—Acts 7:27. No man—II Cor. 7:2. Soul, His own—Pr. 8:36. Suffering—II Pet. 2:13. Take—I Cor. 6:7. Why do ye—Acts 7:26. See HARM, SIN.

WRONG-DOER. Acts 25:11.

WRONGFULLY. Ps. 119:78. Accuse any one—Lu. 3:14. Enemies—Ps. 69:4. Exacted—Lu. 19:8. Hate me—Ps. 38:19. Oppressed—Ez. 22:29. Persecute—Ps. 119:86. Rejoice—I Pet. 2:19.

WROTH. See ANGER.

YARN. Pr. 7:16.

YEAR: Governed by sun and moon.—Gen. 1:14.

Divide into months.—Gen. 7:11; Ex. 12:2; 40:17; Num. 10:10; 28:11; I Chr. 27:1.

Divided into seasons.—Gen. 8:22.

Into weeks.—Dan. 9:27; Lu. 18:12.

Into days.—Gen. 7:11–12; 25:7; Esth. 9:27–28.

New beginning after exodus.—Ex. 12:2.

Special years.—Sabbatical—Lev. 25:4. Jubilee year—Lev. Ch. 25; 27:17–24; Deut. 15:9, 12, 20.

Days reckoned prophetically as years.—Dan. 12:11–12.

Land to rest one year in seven.—Lev. 25:5.

Redemption of houses limited to one year.—Lev. 25:29–30.

Special references.—The days of the years of my life—Gen. 47:9. Atonement once in—Ex. 30:10; Lev. 16:34. Yearly sacrifice—Heb. 10:13. Years should teach wisdom—Job 32:7. Crownest year with goodness—Ps. 65:11. A thousand years in thy sight—Ps. 90:4. We bring our years to an end—Ps. 90:9. Go softly all my—Is. 38:15. The year of my redeemed—Is. 63:4. Revive work in midst of—Hab. 3:2. Let it alone this—Lu. 13:8. Year by year with blood—Heb. 9:25. A remembrance of sin—Heb. 10:3. Bound him 1,000 years—Rev. 20:2. Year of release—Deut. 31:10; Ez. 46:17. Year of recompense—Is. 34:8. Bring tribute to Solomon once a—I Ki. 10:25; II Chr. 9:13, 24. Bring tribute to king of Assyria once a—II Ki. 17:4, 6. Seven years of plenty, and seven years of famine—Gen. 41:53, 54. Third year of famine—I Ki. 18:1. Year of drought—Jer. 17:8. Dates after coming out of Egypt—Num. 1:1; 9:1, 22; 10:11; 14:34; 33:38; Deut. 1:3; I Ki. 6:1. No more manna after that—Josh. 5:12. Fourth year fruits given to Jehovah—Lev. 19:24. Fourth year house of Jehovah laid—I Ki. 6:37, 38. Feast of Jehovah—Ju. 21:19. Hannah takes coat—I Sam. 2:19. Appears before Jehovah once a—Ex. 34:23, 24; Zech. 14:16; Lu. 2:4. Three times a year appears before Jehovah—Deut. 16:16; I Ki. 9:25; II Chr. 8:13. Lambs a year old used in sacrifice—Ex. 29:38; Lev. 9:3; 12:6; 14:10; 23:12, 18, 19; Num. 6:12, 14; 7:15–88; 15:27; 28:3, 9, 11, 14, 19, 27; Ch. 29; Ez. 46:13. Samuel as circuit judge year by—I Sam. 7:16. Tithes year by—Deut. 14:22; 26:12. Man exempt from service for one year after marriage—Deut. 20:7; 24:5. Acceptable year of the Lord—Lu. 4:19. For a whole year the church was gathered—Acts 11:26. For a whole year Achaia was prepared—II Cor. 9:2. For a year and six months, Paul teaching—Acts 18:11.

YEARNING. Heart—Gen. 43:30; I Ki. 3:26; Is. 63:15. See HUNGER, LONG, THIRST.

YIELD. Causeth him to—Pr. 7:21. Fruit—Mt. 13:8; Heb. 12:11. See FRUIT. Increase—Lev. 19:25; Ps. 67:6. See

INCREASE. Olives—Jas. 3:12. Seed—Gen. 1:29. See SEED. Spirit—Mt. 27: 50. Strength—Gen. 4:12; Joel 2:22. Yourselves unto Jehovah—II Cor. 30: 8. See BEAR.

YOKE: Yoke of oxen.—I Sam. 11:7; I Ki. 19:19, 21; Job 1:3; 42:12; Jer. 51:23.

Uses of.—On animals—Num. 19:2; Deut. 21:3; I Sam. 6:7.

Figurative.—Gen. 27:40; Lev. 26:13; I Ki. 12:4, 9, 11, 14; II Chr. 10:4, 9, 11, 14; Is. 58:6, 9; Jer. 2:20; 5:5; 30:8; Ez. 34:27; Nah. 1:13.

Symbol of punishment.—Deut. 28:48; Is. 47:6.

Yoke of burden.—Is. 9:4; 10:27; 14:25. Of Egypt—Ez. 30:18. Of oppression—Jer. 27:8, 11, 12; 28:2, 4, 11, 14. Of transgression—Lam. 1:14. Of youth—Lam. 3:27. See JESUS, TEACHING OF—Lu. 2:21.

In teachings of Peter.—Acts 15:10.

Of Paul.—Gal. 5:1; I Tim. 6:1; II Cor. 6:14.

YOKE FELLOW. Phil. 4:3. See FELLOWSHIP.

YOUNG. II Chr. 34:3. Bullocks—Ex. 29:1; Lev. 4:3; 16:3; 23:18; Num. 7:15, 81; 8:8; 5:24; 28:11, 19, 27; 29: 2, 8, 13, 17. See SACRIFICES. Calf—Lev. 9:2. Eagles—Pr. 30:17. Flocks and herds have—Gen. 33:13. Fluttereth over—Deut. 32:11. Hart—Song of Sol. 2:9; 8:14. I have been—Ps. 37: 25. Lay her—Ps. 84:3. Lead those that have—Is. 40:11. Lion—Ju. 14:5; Job 4:10; Ps. 58:6; 91:13; 104:21; Is. 5:29; 11:6; 31:4; Jer. 2:15. Man—See YOUNG MEN. Pigeon—Gen. 15:9; Lev. 1:14; 5:7, 11; 12:6, 8; 14:22, 30; 15:14, 29; Num. 6:10. Ravens—Ps. 147:9. Twigs—Ez. 17:4. Virgins—Ju. 21:12; I Ki. 1:2; Esth. 2:2, 3; Lam. 2:21; Amos—8:13. When thou wast—John 21:18. Women—Ru. 4:12; Ps. 148:12; Ez. 9:6; Tit. 2:4.

YOUNG MEN: Ideals for.—Should follow after wisdom—Pr. 1:1-6, 20-33; 2:1-10; 3:13-18; 4:5-9; 8:1-12.

Must avoid evil companions.—Pr. 2:12-15; 4:14-19; 24:1.

Wise and foolish sons.—Pr. 10:1, 5, 8, 13, 14, 23; 13:1, 16, 20; 17:24-28.

Counsels to.—Obey parents—Pr. 1:8, 9; 6:20-23; 13:1. Consent not to sinners—Pr. 1:1-19. Avoid idleness—Pr. 6:6-11; 13:4. Avoid wine—Pr. 20:1; 23:20, 21, 29-35. Avoid strange women—Pr. 5:3-23; 6:24-35; 7:4-27; 23:27, 28. Avoid going surety—Pr. 6:1-5.

Possessed of vision.—Joseph—Gen. 37: 5-11. Daniel—Dan. 2:19, 28-35. Young men—Joel 2:28; Acts 2:17. The backward look—Job 29:2-4; Ps. 37:25; Eccl. 12:1.

Lacking in vision.—Elisha's servants—II Ki. 6:14-17. Prodigal son—Lu. 15:13-17.

Some mistakes made by.—Gave unwise counsel—I Ki. 12:8-11. Cling to possessions—Mk. 10:21, 22. Aided in slaughter—II Sam. 1:6-10; Acts 7: 58. Young man Mark drew back at Perga—Acts 13:13. Young man who fled at the arrest of Jesus—Mk. 14: 51, 52.

Ambitious.—David—I Sam. 17:32-37. Solomon—I Ki. 10:14-29. Absalom—II Sam. 15:4-6. Saul of Tarsus—Acts 9:1, 2.

Young men for war.—Abraham's—Gen. 14:23, 24. Jonathan—I Sam. 14:6-15. David—I Sam. 17:32-58. Ahab's—I Ki. 20:13-21.

Services rendered by.—Reapers—Ruth 2:9, 15, 21. Priestly service—Ex. 24: 5; Lu. 17:7-13; I Sam. 2:12-17. Spies—Josh. 6:23; I Sam. 30:13-15. King's servants—I Sam. 8:16. Foragers—I Sam. 25:4-12. Armorbearers—I Sam. 14:6; 26:22. Courtiers to king—Dan. 1:3-5. Rulers—Mk. 10:21, 22.

Worthy characters.—Abel—Gen. 4:4. Joseph—Gen. 39:7-12. Samuel—I Sam. 3:1-19. David—I Sam. 16:11-13. Solomon—I Ki. 3:5-9. Josiah—II Ki. Ch. 22. Daniel—Dan. 1:3-6.

Subjects of exhortations.—Tit. 2:6; I John 2:13, 14. Need fostering—John 21:15-17.

Youth not to be despised.—I Tim. 4:12. Young ruler beloved of Jesus—Mt. 19:16-30; Mk. 10:20, 21; Lu. 18:18-30. The beloved disciple (John 13:23), like all the apostles, was a young man.

YOUTH. Job 20:11; Ps. 71:5; Eccl. 11: 9, 10; Jer. 48:11; 51:22; Dan. 1:4; I Tim. 4:12. Afflicted from—Ps. 129:1.

Days of—Job 33:25; Ps. 89:45; Eccl. 12:1; Ez. 16:22. Dew of—Ps. 110:3. Die in—Job 36:14; Ps. 88:15. Evil from—Gen. 8:21; II Sam. 19:7; Jer. 32:30. Fear Jehovah from—I Ki. 18: 12. Friends of—Pr. 2:17. Grow in— Ps. 144:12. Guide of—Jer. 3:4. Iniquities of—Job 13:26; Ps. 25:7. Kindness of—Jer. 2:2. Labored from—Is. 47:12. Renewed—Ps. 103:5. Reproach of—Jer. 31:19. Shame of—Is. 54:4. See YOUNG MEN.

YOU-WARD. II Pet. 3:9.

ZAANAN, zā'ă-năn. A town.—Mic. 1:11.

ZAANANNIM, zā'a-năn'nim. Place where Joel slays Sisera—Josh. 19:33; Ju. 4:11.

ZAAVAN, zā'a-văn. Grandson of Seir the Horite.—Gen. 36:27; I Chr. 1:42.

ZABAD, zā'băd. (1) An Ephraimite.—I Chr. 7:21.

(2) A man of Judah.—I Chr. 2:36, 37.

(3) Son of Shimeath who assisted in staying Joash king of Judah.—II Chr. 24:26.

(4) One of David's mighty men.—I Chr. 11:41.

(5, 6, 7) Men who married foreign wives. —Ezra 10:27, 33, 43.

ZABBAI, zăb'baī. (1) One who helped to repair the wall.—Neh. 3:20.

(2) One who married a foreign wife.— Ezra 10:28.

ZABBUD, zăb'bud. One who returned from exile.—Ezra 8:14.

ZABDI, zăb'di. (1) A Benjamite.—I Chr. 8:19.

(2) Grandfather of Achan.—Josh. 7:1, 17, 18.

(3) A Levite.—Neh. 11:17.

(4) One of David's storekeepers.—I Chr. 27:27.

ZABDIEL, zăb'di-el. (1) An overseer of priests.—Neh. 11:14.

(2) Father of one of David's mighty men.—I Chr. 27:2.

ZABUD, zā'bud. Son of Nathan, an officer under Solomon.—I Ki. 4:5. See ZABBUD.

ZACCAI, zăk'kaī. Ancestor of some who returned from exile.—Ezra 2:9; Neh. 7:14.

ZACCHAEUS, zăk-kæ'us. A publican whom Jesus honored with a visit.— Lu. 19:2-8.

ZACCHUR, zăk'kur. (1) A Simeonite. —I Chr. 4:26.

(2) A Merarite.—I Chr. 24:27.

(3) A Reubenite spy.—Num. 13:4.

(4) Son of Asaph.—I Chr. 25:2, 10; Neh. 12:35.

(5) One who helped to rebuild the wall. —Neh. 3:2.

(6) Father of Hanan.—Neh. 13:13.

(7) A Levite.—Neh. 10:12.

ZACHARIAH, zăk'a-rī'ah. (1) Father-in-law of Ahaz, grandfather of Hezekiah.—II Ki. 18:2; II Chr. 29:1.

(2) Son of Jeroboam.—II Ki. 14:29; 15: 8, 11.

ZACHARIAS, zăk'a-rī-as. (1) Son of Barachias who was stoned for rebuking the Jews.—Mt. 23:35; Lu. 11:51.

(2) Father of John the Baptist.—Lu. 1:5-67; 3:2.

(3) Name given to John the Baptist by some.—Lu. 1:59.

ZADOK. (1) Priest; a descendant of Aaron.—I Chr. 6:4-50, 53; 24:6. Priest under David—II Sam. 8:17. Brought the ark in David's exile—II Sam. 15: 24-29. Loyal to Solomon and promoted—I Ki. 1:8, 26, 32, 34, 38, 39. Founder of clan of priests—Ez. 40:46; 43:19; 44:15; 48:11.

(2) A warrior.—I Chr. 12:28. Grandfather of Jotham—II Ki. 15:33; II Chr. 27:1.

(3, 4) Foremen under Nehemiah.—Neh. 3:4, 29.

(5) A Scribe appointed Treasurer.—Neh. 13:13.

(6) A prince of Israel.—Neh. 10:21.

(7) A high priest.—I Chr. 6:12; Ezra. 7:2.

(8) Ancestor of Joseph.—Mt. 1:14.

(9) Neh. 11:11.

ZAHAM, zā'hăm. Son of Rehoboam.— II Chr. 11:19.

ZAIR, zā'ir. II Ki. 8:21.

ZALAPH, zā'laph. Father of Hanum who helped to repair the wall.—Neh. 3:30.

ZALMON, zăl'mon. (1) One of David's mighty men.—II Sam. 23:28.

(2) A hill—Ju. 9:48; Ps. 68:14.

ZALMONAH, zal-mō'nah. An encampment of Israel.—Num. 33:41, 42. See CAMP, ISRAEL.

ZALMUNNA, zal-mŭn'nȧ. **A Midianite king.**—Ju. 8:5–21; Ps. 83:11.

ZAMZUMMIM, zam-zŭm'mim. **A tribe of the Rephaim.**—Deut. 2:20. See AMMONITES.

ZANOAH, za-nō'ah. (1) **A city of Judah.**—Josh. 15:56.

(2) **Another city of Judah.**—Josh. 15: 34; Neh. 3:13; 11:30.

(3) **A descendant of Caleb son of Jephunneh.**—I Chr. 4:18.

ZAPHENATH-PANEAH, zăph-ē'nath-pa-nē'ah. **Pharaoh's name for Joseph.** —Gen. 41:45.

ZAPHON, zā'phon. **A city in Gad.**— Josh. 13:27.

ZAREPHATH, zăr'e-phăth. **A city of the Phœnicians.**—I Ki. 17:9, 10. Elijah restores the widow's son—I Ki. 17:22. See Lu. 4:26.

ZARETHAN, zăr'e-thăn. **Place where Israelites crossed the Jordan.**—Josh. 3:16; I Ki. 4:12; 7:46.

ZATTU, zăt'tu. (1) **One who assisted in sealing the covenant.**—Neh. 10:14.

(2) **Ancestor of some who returned with Zerubbabel.**—Ezra 2:8; 10:27; Neh. 7:13.

ZAZA, zā'zȧ. **A descendant of Judah.**— I Chr. 2:33.

ZEAL, ZEALOUS. Ps. 119:139; Is. 63: 15; Gal. 2:10; Rev. 3:19. Clad with— Is. 59:17. Corinthian church, Of— II Cor. 7:11; 9:2. Good of that which is—I Pet. 31:13. Good works, Of— Tit. 2:14. House, Of thy—Ps. 69:9; John 2:17. Israel, For—II Sam. 21:2. Jehovah, For—II Ki. 10:16. Of Jehovah—II Ki. 19:31; Is. 9:7; 26:11; 37: 32; Ez. 5:13; Acts 22:3. Knowledge, Not according to—Rom. 10:2. Law, For the—Acts 21:20. Paul's—Phil. 3:6. Sick—Gal. 4:17, 18. Spiritual things, Of—I Cor. 14:12. Traditions of the fathers, Of—Gal. 1:14.

ZEALOT. Simon—Lu. 6:15.

ZEBA, zē'bȧ. **A Midianite king.**—Ju. 8: 4–28.

ZEBADIAH, zĕb'a-dī'ah. (1) **Son of Elpael.**—I Chr. 8:17.

(2) **A Benjamite.**—I Chr. 8:15.

(3) **A Kohathite.**—I Chr. 26:2.

(4) **One who joined David at Ziklag.**— I Chr. 12:7.

(5) **A Levite.**—II Chr. 17:8.

(6) **One who returned with Ezra.**—Ezra 8:8.

(7) **Ruler of house of Judah under Jehoshaphat.**—II Chr. 19:11.

(8) **A priest who married a foreign wife.** —Ezra 10:20.

ZEBEDEE, zĕb'e-dee. **Father of James and John the apostles, husband of Salome.**—Mt. 4:21; 10:2; 20:20; 26: 37; 27:56; Mk. 1:19, 20; 3:17; 10:35; Lu. 5:10; John 21:2.

ZEBIDAH, ze-bī'dah. **Wife of Josiah.**— II Ki. 23:36.

ZEBINAH, ze-bī'nah. **One who married a foreign wife.**—Ezra 10:43.

ZEBOIIM, ze-bōi'im. (1) **One of five cities in the valley of Siddim, destroyed with Sodom and Gomorrah.**— Gen. 10:19; 14:2, 8; Deut. 29:23; Hos. 11:8.

(2) **A town inhabited after the captivity.**—Neh. 11:34.

ZEBOIM, ze-bō'im. **A valley in Benjamin.**—I Sam. 13:18.

ZEBUL, zē'bul. **Governor of Shechem.** —Ju. 5:28–41.

ZEBULUN. (1) **Tenth of Jacob's sons; sixth and last of Leah's sons**—Gen. 30:20; 35:23; 46:14. (2) **Tribe.** Territory reached from Lake of Tiberias to Mount Carmel, and so nearly to Mediterranean Sea. Jacob's prophecy concerning dwelling place—Gen. 49: 13. Princes—Ps. 68:27. Zebulun possessed the fisheries of the Lake of Tiberias. Courageous—Ju. 5:18. Prediction concerning—Deut. 33:18–19, where it is said "they shall suck the abundance of the seas." Loyalty of the tribe in resisting the enemies of Israel, with Barak against Sisera— Ju. 4:6–10; 5:14. Also with Gideon against the Midianites—Ju. 6:34–35. Inheritance—Josh. 19:10–16; 21:7, 34; I Chr. 6:63, 77. Did not drive out Canaanites—Ju. 1:30. Number when leaving Egypt, 57,400—Num. 1:30, 31. After 40 years, 60,000—Num. 26:26, 27. Aided in David's coronation—I Chr. 12:33–40. Carried into captivity by Tiglath-pileser—II Ki. 15:29; Is. 9:1. Jesus dwelt in the land of Zebulun—Mt. 4:15. See ISRAEL.

ZECHARIAH, zĕk'a-rī'ah. (1) **A Levite.** I Chr. 9:21; 26:2, 14.

(2) A Reubenite whose genealogy was lost.—I Chr. 5:7.

(3) Another Levite.—I Chr. 15:18, 20; 16:5.

(4) A Benjamite.—I Chr. 9:37.

(5) A Kohathite.—I Chr. 24:25.

(6) A Merarite.—I Chr. 26:11.

(7) A priest.—I Chr. 15:24.

(8) A prince under Jehoshaphat.—II Chr. 17:7.

(9) Father of Iddo.—I Chr. 27:21.

(10) Son of Jehoshaphat.—II Chr. 21:2.

(11, 12) II Chr. 20:14; 29:13.

(13) Son of Jehoiada the priest.—II Chr. 24:20.

(14) One who was able to interpret visions.—II Chr. 26:5.

(15) A prince of Judah.—II Chr. 35:8.

(16) A Kohathite overseer.—II Chr. 34:12.

(17, 18) Two who returned with Ezra.—Ezra 8:3, 11, 16.

(19) One who married a foreign wife.—Ezra 10:26.

(20) A prince who stood up with Ezra.—Neh. 8:4.

(21, 22, 23) Ancestors of some who dwelt in Jerusalem.—Neh. 11:4, 5, 12.

(24, 25) Two priests.—Neh. 12:16, 35, 41.

(26) A witness for Isaiah.—Is. 8:2.

(27) One of the minor prophets. See OUTLINE STUDIES IN THE BOOKS.

ZECHER, ze'ker. A Benjamite.—I Chr. 8:31.

ZEDAD, ze'dad. A place in Palestine.—Num. 34:8; Ez. 47:15.

ZEDEKIAH, zed'e-ki'ah. (1) Son of Chenaanah.—I Ki. 22:11, 24; II Chr. 18:10, 23.

(2) Son of Josiah.—I Chr. 3:15; Jer. 1:3; 37:1. Name changed—II Ki. 24:17. King of Judah—II Ki. 24:18; II Chr. 36:10, 11; Jer. 21:1, 3, 7; 24:8; 27:3, 12; 28:1; 29:3; 32:1, 3, 4; 37:3, 17, 18, 21; Jer. 49:34; 52:1. Events of reign: Rebelled against Babylon—II Ki. 24:20; Jer. 52:3. Jerusalem destroyed—II Ki. 25:2; Jer. 39:1–10. Taken captive—Jer. 44:30; 51:59; 52:4–30. Imprisons Jeremiah—Jer. 32:2, 3; 37:15–21; 38:5–28. Sons killed—II Ki. 25:7. Prophecy concerning—Jer. 32:5; 34:2, 4, 6, 8, 21. Death of—Jer. 52:11.

(3) Grandson of Jehoiakim.—I Chr. 3: 16.

(4) False prophet, son of Maaseiah.—Jer. 29:21–23.

(5) Prince of Judah, son of Hananiah.—Jer. 36:12.

ZEEB, ze'eb. A Midianite prince.—Ju. 7:25; 8:3; Ps. 83:11.

ZELA, ze'la. A town in Benjamin where Saul and Jonathan were buried.—Josh. 18:28; II Sam. 21:14.

ZELEK, ze'lek. An Ammonite, one of David's mighty men.—II Sam. 23:37; I Chr. 11:39.

ZELOPHEHAD, ze-lo'phe-had. Grandson of Gilead.—Num. 26:33; 27:1, 7; 36:2–11; Josh. 17:3; I Chr. 7:15.

ZELOTES, ze-lo'tes. Surname of Simon.—Lu. 6:15 (A.V.); Acts 1:13 (A.V.).

ZELZAH, zel'zah. A city in Benjamin.—I Sam. 10:2.

ZEMARAIM, zem'a-ra'im. (1) Part of Ephraim.—II Chr. 13:4.

(2) A city of Benjamin.—Josh. 18:22.

ZEMARITE, zem'a-rite. A Canaanite tribe.—Gen. 10:18; I Chr. 1:16.

ZEMIRAH, ze-mi'rah. Grandson of Benjamin.—I Chr. 7:8.

ZENAN, ze'nan. A city in Judah.—Josh. 15:37.

ZENAS, ze'nas. A disciple who was learned in the law of Moses.—Tit. 3:13.

ZEPHANIAH, zeph'a-ni'ah. (1) A Kohathite.—I Chr. 6:36.

(2) Father of Josiah the priest.—Zech. 6:10, 14.

(3) A priest put to death by the king of Babylon.—II Ki. 25:18; Jer. 21:1; 29: 25, 29; 37:3; 52:4.

(4) One of the minor prophets. See OUTLINE STUDIES IN THE BOOKS.

ZEPHATH, ze'phath. A Simeonite city.—Ju. 1:17.

ZEPHATHAH, zeph'a-thah. A valley in Judah.—II Chr. 14:10.

ZEPHI, ZEPHO, ze'phi, ze'pho. Grandson of Esau.—Gen. 36:11, 15; I Chr. 1:36.

ZEPHON, ze'phon. A Gadite.—Num. 26:15.

ZER, zer. A city in Naphtali.—Josh. 19:35.

ZERAH, zē'rah. (1) **Father of Jobab king of Edom.**—Gen. 36:33; I Chr. 1:44.

(2) **Grandson of Esau.**—Gen. 36:13, 17; I Chr. 1:37.

(3) **Son of Judah.**—Gen. 38:30; Num. 26:20; Ju. 7:1, 18, 24; 22:20; I Chr. 2:4-6; Neh. 11:24.

(4) **A Levite.**—I Chr. 6:41.

(5) **Son of Simeon.**—Num. 26:13; I Chr. 4:24.

(6) **A Gershonite.**—I Chr. 6:21.

(7) **An Ethiopian king.**—II Chr. 14:9.

ZERAHIAH, zĕr'a-hī'ah. (1) **A descendant of Pahath-moab.**—Ezra 8:4.

(2) **An ancestor of Ezra.**—I Chr. 6:6, 51; Ezra 7:4.

ZERAHITES, zē'rah-ītes. **Descendants of Zerah.**—Num. 26:13.

ZERED, zē'red. **A brook.**—Num. 21:12; Deut. 2:13, 14.

ZEREDAH, zĕr'e-dah. **A city or district.** —I Ki. 11:26; II Chr. 4:17.

ZERERAH, zĕr'e-rah. **A district in Manasseh.**—Ju. 7:22.

ZERESH, zē'resh. **Wife of Haman.**— Esth. 5:10, 14; 6:13.

ZERETH, zē'reth. **A descendant of Judah.**—I Chr. 4:7.

ZERI, zē'ri. **Son of Jeduthun.**—I Chr. 25:5.

ZEROR, zē'rôr. **A Benjamite.**—I Sam. 9:1.

ZERUAH, ze-ru'ah. **Mother of Jeroboam king of Israel.**—I Ki. 11:26.

ZERUBBABEL, ze-rub'ba-bel. **Parentage.**—Ezra 3:2; I Chr. 3:19; Mt. 1:12; Lu. 3:27.

Leader of colony returning from captivity, 536 B.C.—Ezra 2:2; Neh. 7:7; 12:1, 47.

Builds altar, temple, etc.—Ezra 3:2-8; 4:2-3; 5:2, 14-16; Hag. 1:12-14; 2:2.

Sons of.—I Chr. 3:19.

Prophecies concerning.—Hag. 2:20-23; Zech. 4:6-14.

ZERUIAH, zĕr'u-ī'ah. **A sister of David, who had three sons, Joab, Abishai, and Asahel, in David's army.**—I Sam. 26:6; II Sam. 2:13, 18; 3:39; 8:16; 14:1; 16:9, 10; 17:25; 18:2; 19:21, 27; 21:17; 23:18, 37; I Ki. 1:7; 2:5, 22; I Chr. 2:16; 11:6, 39; 18:12, 15; 26:28; 27:24.

ZETHAM, zē'tham. I Chr. 23:8; 26:22.

ZETHAN, zē'than. **A Benjamite.**—I Chr. 7:10.

ZETHAR, zē'thar. **One of the chamberlains of Ahasuerus.**—Esth. 1:10.

ZIA, zī'à. **A Gadite.**—I Chr. 5:13.

ZIBA, zī'bà. **A servant of Saul and Mephibosheth.**—I Sam. 9:2-12; 16:1-4; 19:17, 29.

ZIBEON, zĭb'e-on. (1) **Son of Seir the Horite.**—Gen. 36:20-29; I Chr. 1:38, 40.

(2) **Grandfather of Adah wife of Esau.** —Gen. 36:2, 14.

ZIBIA, zĭb'i-à. (1) **A Benjamite.**—I Chr. 8:9.

(2) **Wife of Ahaziah, mother of Joash.** —II Ki. 12:1; II Chr. 24:1.

ZICHRI, zĭk'ri. (1) **Great-grandson of Levi.**—Ex. 6:21.

(2, 3, 4) **Benjamites.**—I Chr. 8:19, 23-27.

(5) **A descendant of Eliezer son of Moses.**—I Chr. 26:25.

(6) **Son of Asaph.**—I Chr. 9:15.

(7) **A Reubenite.**—I Chr. 27:16.

(8) **Father of Amaziah, a captain under Jehoshaphat.**—II Chr. 17:16.

(9) **An Ephraimite.**—II Chr. 28:7.

(10) **Father of Elishaphat.**—II Chr. 23:1.

(11) **Father of a Benjamite overseer.**— Neh. 11:9.

(12) **A priest.**—Neh. 12:17.

ZIDDIM, zĭd'dim. **A city in Naphtali.** —Josh. 19:35.

ZIDON. See SIDON.

ZIF. See MONTHS.

ZIHA, zī'hà. **Two Nethinim.**—Ezra 2: 43; Neh. 7:46; 11:21.

ZIKLAG, zĭk'lăg. **A city in the South of Judah**—Josh. 15:31. Given to Simeon—Josh. 19:5. Given to David for a residence—I Sam. 27:6. Burnt by Amalekites—I Sam. 30:1, 14. Spoil of, sent to elders of Judah—I Sam. 30:26. Rebuilt after the captivity— Neh. 11:28. David abode two days in —II Sam. 1:1. David slays messenger in—II Sam. 4:10. David's friends in —I Chr. 12:1.

ZILLAH, zĭl'lah. **Wife of Lamech.**— Gen. 4:19, 22, 23.

ZILLETHAI, zĭl-lē'thaī. (1) **A Benjamite.**—I Chr. 8:20.

(2) **A captain who joined David at Ziklag.**—I Chr. 12:20.

ZILPAH, zĭl'pah. (1) **Handmaid of Leah wife of Jacob.**—Gen. 29:24; 30: 9-12; 35:26; 37:2; 46:18.

(2) **Son of Johath.**—I Chr. 6:20.

ZIMMAH, zĭm'mah. (1, 2) **Two Gershonites.**—I Chr. 6:42; II Chr. 29:1, 2.

ZIMRON, zĭm'ron. **Son of Abraham and Keturah.**—Gen. 25:2.

ZIMRI, zĭm'ri. (1) **A Simeonite.**—Num. 25:14.

(2) **A Benjamite.**—I Chr. 8:36; 9:42.

(3) **A captain who slew Elah.**—I Ki. 16: 9-20; II Ki. 9:31.

(4) **Grandson of Judah.**—I Chr. 2:6.

(5) **An unknown place.**—Jer. 25:25.

ZIN, zĭn. **Wilderness of.**—Num. 13:21; 20:1; 27:14; 33:36; 34:3, 4; Deut. 32: 51; Josh. 15:1, 3.

ZINA, zī'na. **Son of Shimei.**—I Chr. 23:10.

ZION, zī'on. **Called.**—City of David— II Sam. 5:7-9; I Ki. 8:1; I Chr. 11:5, 7; II Chr. 5:2. Holy Hill—Ps. 2:6; 78:68. Mountain of Jehovah—Mic. 4:2. Zion, of the Holy One of Israel— Is. 60:14. Mountains of—Ps. 133:3.

Description of.—Beauty—Ps. 48:2; 50:2. Glory—Ps. 48:11. Towers of—Ps. 48: 12. Gates of—Ps. 87:2. Palaces of— Ps. 48:3, 13.

Chosen by Jehovah.—Ps. 132:13; Is. 51:16.

Ark brought from.—II Chr. 5:2.

Prayer for.—Ps. 51:18.

Dwelling of Jehovah.—Ps. 9:11; 65:1; 74:2; 76:2; 84:7; 99:2; 128:5; 134:3; 135:21; Is. 8:18; 24:23; 31:9; Joel 3: 16, 17, 21; Zech. 2:10.

Source of strength.—Ps. 20:2; 110:2; Is. 52:1.

Songs of.—Ps. 137:3.

Lament over.—Ps. 14:7; 53:6; Is. 10:24; 49:14; Lam. 1:4, 17; 2:6; 4:2, 11, 22; 5:11, 18.

Seat of worship.—Ps. 102:21; Jer. 51:10.

Captives return.—Ps. 126:1.

Zion's praise to Jehovah.—Ps. 146:10; 147:12; 149:2; Is. 12:6.

Prophecies concerning.—II Ki. 19:21, 31; Ps. 69:35; 87:5; 102:13; Is. 2:3; 3:17; 4:3, 4; 10:12, 32; 18:7; 24:23; 28:16; Mic. 3:10, 12; 4:7, 8, 11, 13;

Zech. 9:13. Entreated to repent—Jer. 3:14. Desolation of—Is. 64:10; Jer. 9:19; 14:19; 26:18; Joel 2:1, 15; Amos 1:2; 6:1. Redemption of—Is. 1:27; 30:19; 33:5; 37:22; 40:9; 41:27; 51: 11; 52:8; 59:20; 62:11; Jer. 30:17; 31:6, 12; 50:5; Joel 2:23, 32; Ob. 17, 21; Zeph. 3:14, 16; Zech. 1:14, 17; 2:7, 10; 8:2, 3; 9:9. People of Zion—Is. 10:24. Enemies of—Is. 29:8. Peace in —Is. 31:4; 33:14; 52:7. Sinners in— Is. 33:14. Zion avenged—Jer. 50:28; 51:24, 35. Exalted—Is. 34:8; 35:10; 46:13; 61:3, 6; 62:1.

Illustrative.—Ps. 125:1.

Figurative.—Joy of Zion—Ps. 97:8. Fire in—Is. 31:9. Children of—Is. 66:8. Daughter of Zion—Ps. 9:14; Song of Sol. 3:11; Is. 1:8; 3:17; 4:4; 10:32; 16:1; 37:22; 52:2; Jer. 4:31; 6:2, 23; 8:19; Lam. 1:6; 2:1, 4, 8, 10, 13; Mic. 1:13; 4:8, 10, 11, 13; Zeph. 3:14; Zech. 2:10; Is. 14:32; 51:3. Built by Jehovah—Ps. 102: 16; Is. 14:32; 51:3.

ZIOR, zī'or. **A city in Judah.**—Josh. 15:54.

ZIPH, zĭph. (1) **A city in Judah.**—Josh. 15:24; 23:14-24; 26:2; II Chr. 11:8.

(2) **Another city in Judah.**—Josh. 15: 55.

(3) I Chr. 4:16.

(4) **Grandson of Caleb son of Hezron.**— I Chr. 2:42.

ZIPHAH, zī'phah. **A descendant of Judah.**—I Chr. 4:16.

ZIPHION, zĭph'i-on. **Son of Gad.**—Gen. 46:16.

ZIPHITES, zĭph'ites. **Inhabitants of Ziph.**—I Sam. 23:19; 26:1; Ps. 54 (title).

ZIPHRON, zĭph'ron. **A place in Palestine.**—Num. 34:9.

ZIPPOR, zĭp'por. **Father of Balak king of Moab.**—Num. 22:2, 16; 23:18; Josh. 24:9; Ju. 11:25.

ZIPPORAH, zĭp-pō'rah. **Wife of Moses.** —Ex. 2:21; 4:25; 18:2. See MOSES.

ZIV. See ZIF, MONTHS.

ZIZ, ziz. **A place in Judah.**—II Chr. 20:16.

ZIZA, zī'za. (1) **Son of Rehoboam.**—II Chr. 11:20.

(2) **A Simeonite.**—I Chr. 4:37.

ZIZAH, zī'zah. **A Levite.**—I Chr. 23:11.

ZOAN, zō'an. **Capital of Egypt.**—Num. 13:22; Ps. 78:12, 43; Is. 19:11, 13; 30:4; Ez. 30:14.

ZOAR, zō'ar. A city in the Plain of Jordan—Gen. 13:10; Deut. 34:3. Sometimes called Bela—Gen. 14:2, 8. Saved by Lot's prayer—Gen. 19:22–30. A possession of the Moabites—Is. 15:5; Jer. 48:34.

ZOBAH, zō'bah. **A district and kingdom in Syria.**—I Sam. 14:47; II Sam. 8:3, 5, 12; 10:6, 8; 23:36; I Ki. 11:23; I Chr. 18:3, 5, 9; 19:6; II Chr. 8:3; Ps. 60 (title).

ZOBEBAH, zo-bē'bah. **A descendant of Judah.**—I Chr. 4:8.

ZOHAR, zō'har. (1) **Son of Simeon.**—Gen. 46:10; Ex. 6:15.

(2) **Father of Ephron the Hittite who sold Abraham the cave of Machpelah.**—Gen. 23:8, 9.·

ZOHELETH, zō'he-lĕth. **Name of a stone.**—I Ki. 1:9.

ZOHETH, zō'heth. **A descendant of Judah.**—I Chr. 4:20.

ZOPHAH, zō'phah. **An Asherite.**—I Chr. 7:35, 36.

ZOPHAI, zō'phaī. **Son of Elkanah father of Samuel.**—I Chr. 6:26.

ZOPHAR, zō'phar. **One of Job's friends.**—Job 2:11; 11:1; 20:1; 42:9.

ZOPHIM, zō'phim. **A place on Pisgah where Balak took Balaam.**—Num. 23: 14.

ZORAH, zō'rah. **Town of Dan**—Josh. 19:41. Birthplace of Samson—Ju. 13: 3, 24, 25. Burial-place of Samson—Ju. 16:31. Men sent by the Danites to seek an inheritance—Ju. Ch. 18.

ZORATHITES, zō'rath-ītes. **Inhabitants of Zorah.**—I Chr. 4:2.

ZORITES, zō'rites. **A family of Judah.**—I Chr. 2:54. See ZORATHITES.

ZUAR, zū'ar. **Father of a prince of Issachar.**—Num. 1:8; 2:5; 7:18, 23; 10:15.

ZUPH, zŭph. (1) **A district near Jerusalem.**—I Sam. 9:5.

(2) **An ancestor of Samuel.**—I Sam. 1:1; I Chr. 6:35.

ZUR, zûr. (1) **A Benjamite.**—I Chr. 8: 30; 9:36.

(2) **A Midianite prince.**—Num. 25:15; 31:8; Josh. 13:21.

ZURIEL, zū'ri-ĕl. **A Merarite.**—Num. 3:25.

ZURISHADDAI, zū'ri-shăd'daī. **Father of a prince of Simeon.**—Num. 1:6; 2:12; 7:36, 41; 10:19.

ZUZIM, zū'zim. **A primitive race.**—Gen. 14:5.